To Duncan and Christine,
with all best wishes,

Colin and Sue,

3 October 1987.

THE OXFORD
COMPANION TO
MUSIC

THE OXFORD COMPANION TO MUSIC

BY

PERCY A. SCHOLES

TENTH EDITION
REVISED AND RESET
EDITED BY
JOHN OWEN WARD

OXFORD   NEW YORK
OXFORD UNIVERSITY PRESS

Oxford University Press, Walton Street, Oxford OX2 6DP

Oxford New York Toronto
Delhi Bombay Calcutta Madras Karachi
Petaling Jaya Singapore Hong Kong Tokyo
Nairobi Dar es Salaam Cape Town
Melbourne Auckland

and associated companies in
Beirut Berlin Ibadan Nicosia

Oxford is a trade mark of Oxford University Press

Published in the United States
by Oxford University Press, New York

First edition 1938
Ninth edition (reset) 1955
Tenth edition (reset) 1970
Reprinted 1970, 1972, 1974, 1975,
1977, 1978, 1983, 1984, 1985, 1986

ISBN 0–19–311306–6

Printed in Great Britain
at the University Printing House
by David Stanford
Printer to the University

CONTENTS

It is suggested that the owner of this book should, before beginning to use it, read at least as much of the preliminary explanatory matter as is to be found in the Preface to the first edition (p. ix)

PREFACE TO THE TENTH EDITION

THE present edition of this book is the first to be completely reset since the death of the author in 1958. The first edition, which appeared in 1938, was the product of six years and more of work on the part of one superman and a varying number of paid and unpaid clerical helpers who at various times included W. McNaught, W. R. Anderson, the future wife of Emmanuel Litvinoff, Dr. Scholes's own wife, his mother-in-law, and numerous others. These assistants clipped and sorted and filed and typed and retyped articles for the fourth and fifth time, but the actual work of writing this encyclopedia, rather longer than the Bible, was Dr. Scholes's own. The only articles farmed out were those on tonic sol-fa, which he could never quite manage to his own satisfaction, and the plots of the operas, which he found too boring to engage his attention. The result of this solo performance was a book which has been called 'strongly personal, limited in range, but endlessly fascinating' and 'in some ways an ideal . . . the browser book par excellence'.

For the present revision it was considered quite inappropriate to change radically the characteristic rich anecdotal quality of Dr. Scholes's style. Nevertheless revisions do have to be made and, as there can be no clear way of differentiating Dr. Scholes's work from that of his successor, there follows a brief note of what has been attempted:

The following entries are wholly new:

Addison	Crosse	International
American Symphony	Dart	Musicological
Orchestra League	Davies, P. M.	Society
Apel	Floyd	Jahn
ApIvor	Gesamtausgabe	Jeunesses Musicales
Babbitt	Glanville-Hicks	Joubert
Bennett, R. R.	Goehr	Kerman
Berger, A.	Gray	Kirchner
Berio	Haieff	Lai
Blomdahl	Hamilton	Liebermann
Blume	Harrison, L.	Lincoln Center
Boulez	Hartmann	Linear Counterpoint
Boyden	Hemiola	Ludford
Bukofzer	Hoddinott	Lutosławski
Carner	Hovhaness	Maderna
Carter	Howard, J. T.	Martinon
Chrysander	Imbrie	Maw
Clemens	International Folk	Mellers
Cooper, M.	Music Council	Meyerowitz

Milner
Mitchell
Musgrave
Muzak
Mysliviček
National Federation
  of Music Clubs
Nono
Orr, C. W.
Orr, R.
Patrick, Millar
Peeters
Pincherle
Rainier

Redlich
Reese, G.
Reizenstein
Riego, T. del
Rochberg
Rosa, C.
Rosa, S.
Royal Music Associa-
  tion
Rubens
Sachs
Sanzogno
Scholes
Schonberg

School Music Associa-
  tion
Schuller
Shebalin
Skalkottas
Society for the Promo-
  tion of New Music
Stevens, H.
Stockhausen
Toye, F.
Toye, G.
Virelai
Wedge
Young, P. M.

A number of the articles have been revised, more particularly in later sections, with some consequent modifications of attitude, most notably 'Broadcasting', 'Germany', 'History', 'Jazz', 'Ragtime', 'Russia, 8'. Similarly, articles on a number of twentieth-century composers such as Berg, Schönberg, and Webern, who received somewhat cavalier or un-sympathetic treatment, have been revised and are now more 'objectively' treated, though certainly less entertainingly.

The patchwork correction of minor detail, involving countless excisions, additions, or changes of words or phrases, is unnecessary and indeed impossible to particularize, and has been done where possible without too much violence to the original. To take a popular analogy from architecture, we have under-restored rather than over-restored in our attempt to pre-serve the distinctive character of a firmly established institution.

J.O.W.

PREFACE TO THE FIRST EDITION

EXPLAINING ITS PURPOSE AND METHOD

THE first musical dictionary was published over four hundred and fifty years ago. How many such works have since appeared it is impossible to say—certainly a great number.

That earliest book of its kind was a mere collection of Latin musical terms with Latin definitions—Tinctoris, *Terminorum musicae diffinitorium* (probably printed at Treviso about 1495); some of its successors have also confined themselves to terminology, others to biography, others to histori-cal or theoretical information or to information concerning some specific branch of music, whilst still others have offered (as does the present volume) a combined treatment of all branches of musical knowledge.

Tinctoris and over fifty of the best of its successors in various languages, some of them in one thin volume and some of them in a dozen stout ones, stand upon the present author's library shelves, and to all of them, as his work has proceeded, he has in varying measure had recourse. It will, how-ever, he hopes, be recognized that he has attempted something beyond a mere compilation, and that the five or six years of very unremitting labour necessarily represented by these thousand pages, with their million words, have been partly occupied in the effort to see from a fresh view-point what is already known and recorded, and partly in original research.

Thousands of sheets of music have been played through or read through in order to get down afresh to the facts of music instead of taking them second-hand from existing books (one minor result of this procedure being that the number of performing directions translated and explained is per-haps greater than that in any previous publication), and thousands of pages of concert and radio programmes, gramophone record catalogues, etc., have been scrutinized in order to realize what are the matters on which the normal intelligent music-lover is likely to find himself in need of informa-tion; moreover, old literature and long-bygone musical journals, British and foreign, of which the author is happy to possess a considerable store, have been searched in the endeavour to obtain light upon details of musical life which are ordinarily ignored by the historians and encyclopedists of music. It is hoped, then, that it will be realized that in the measure in which a work of this sort can and ought to be original this one is so.

All this preliminary labour accomplished, the task of writing the volume was sectionalized, the author's attention being concentrated for a period on the preparation of all the articles concerned with some one particular aspect of the subject. Thus there gradually grew into existence a little library of fifty-five volumes, each devoted to one branch of musical knowledge, and only when these had been submitted to and discussed with specialists in the various branches were they broken up and their contents redistributed into the present alphabetical order.

SCOPE AND STYLE OF THE BOOK

A wide range of readers has throughout been kept in mind. The experienced and well-instructed professional musician, whatever many-volumed works of reference he may possess, has need also of a one-volume encyclopedia to which he can turn with the assurance that he will there be able to read a concise survey of some subject that interests him or find *quickly* some fact, name, or date of which he is at the moment in need, whilst the younger musician, the concert-goer, the gramophonist, or the radio-listener, has equally need of one which will neither be beyond the scope of his pocket nor embarrass him by a manner of expression so technical as to add new puzzles to the puzzle which sent him to the book.

As concerns this last practical point, it may be frankly admitted that in writing of music it is no more possible wholly to avoid technical terminology than it is in writing of any other art or science, but it is believed that in no article of the book can a technical term be met with of which an explanation is not speedily available by turning to that term in its own alphabetical position. It is obviously not the business of a work of reference to raise difficulties, but to solve them, and with memories of his own early days in mind (and sometimes his later ones, for not all life's puzzles vanish with youth) the author has tried to produce a series of articles which shall be at once exact and accurate and yet within the understanding of the attentive and intelligent general reader.

SELF-INDEXING AND CROSS-REFERENCING

Ease of reference is a quality that has been diligently sought after in the present work. It is hoped that any required fact or statement, even though it be buried in the middle of an article of many pages, can be readily disinterred. For the longer articles are divided into numbered sections and their separate facts are scrupulously indexed, by name of article and section number, in their alphabetical positions throughout the volume. The later editions of the *Encyclopaedia Britannica* and the first two editions (not, unfortunately, the subsequent ones) of Grove's *Dictionary of Music* are the only works of reference known to the author of which the contents have been so completely put at the immediate disposition of their readers; those two works possess their separate index Volumes; the present work is of a size to permit articles and index to be interspersed in one alphabetical order, and that is what is meant by the title-page's description of it as 'self-indexed'.

Another feature of this work is its very comprehensive system of cross-referencing. Abundant cross-references are given in the body of almost every considerable article and also of many a smaller one, and frequently at the end of an article will be found a list of further allusions, elsewhere in the book, to the subject of that article. The system will be at once understood if the reader of this preface will kindly turn to the end of the article on (say) Bach, Beethoven, Organ, England, or United States of America.

It must be known to any habitual user of the previously existing reference books on music that they have often contained a great deal more material than the reader has been able easily to lay hands on at the moment he wanted it, and it is hoped that in the present work, with its thorough system of indexing and cross-referencing, this very definite loss of efficiency has been avoided. A work of this kind, when fully indexed and carefully cross-referenced, must surely have many times the practical value it would have had without these advantages.

RELATIVE LENGTH OF ARTICLES

This leads to a passing comment upon a criticism which reviewers sometimes make when there comes into their hands any new work of reference. They are apt to assume (and not unnaturally) that the relative lengths of the articles upon various subjects may be taken as an indication of the author's views as to the relative importance of those subjects. This is by no means wholly so. In the present work the references at the end of an article to passages elsewhere in the book must be taken into account: thus the articles on Bach and Beethoven alluded to above, whilst complete in themselves and sufficient for the reader who wishes a brief conspectus of the life and work of these men, would have had to be very much lengthened had it not been possible to offer the reader who wishes to go more deeply into the subject a means of amplifying the main treatment. And, on the other hand, there are a number of articles which are considerably longer than they would have been because they, in themselves, include all or nearly all the book contains upon their subjects, and in some instances because those particular subjects are difficult to treat clearly in brief space, or because information on them previously available to the public has been insufficient or even misleading, so making a somewhat ample treatment now desirable.

BIOGRAPHICAL ARTICLES

A problem that must puzzle the writer or compiler of any musical work of reference with a biographical side to it is that of which composers to take in and which to leave out. No absolutely reliable criterion is, of course, available, and the difficulty of choice is very pronounced in regard to the large number of younger lights at any moment appearing above the horizon, of which it cannot be laid down with certainty by the most clairvoyant prophet which of them will rise higher and illuminate the

world and which will quickly pale away to extinction. The number of
biographies, longer or shorter, in the present work is about fifteen hundred,[1]
and in explanation of the choice made it may at least be said that counsel
has been taken with leading critics in the various countries and their advice
very largely followed.

Several persons who have read the proofs have remarked on a tiny
detail of most of the biographies that has struck them as unusual—the
statement after the date of death of the number of years the musician in
question lived. The explanation of this is that, in the author's opinion
the information thus prominently brought before the reader's attention is
of importance. There are in this volume the biographies of a number of
musicians who died when little past the age of twenty, and of a certain
number who lived four or even five times as long (one of them actually
attaining the age of 112 years).[2] The extent and value of the contribution
an artist has been able to make must always have depended greatly upon
the span of life allotted to him; it is a factor to which the intelligent reader
will give attention and there seems no reason why every user of the book
should be left to make his own calculation (not always quickly done when
the turn of a century intervenes, as it so often does, between birth and
death), since it is easy for the author to supply the figures once for all.

Whilst it is thought that the book includes all the chief composers of the
past and present, no attempt has been made to include the biographies of
large numbers of performers. Many such have also been composers and
thus become the subject of entries; many others are, necessarily, mentioned
in such articles as those on Singing, Pianoforte Playing, Violin Family, or
Conducting, and these too have been given short separate entries—on the
principle that a book of reference should not create a desire for information
about a person and then leave it unsatisfied. In these ways many performers have secured a place in the volume, but there has been no systematic
attempt to cover this very large field.

BRITISH AND AMERICAN TERMINOLOGY

As this book is to be published simultaneously on both sides of the
Atlantic, a slight difficulty has had to be met concerning a few little diver-
gencies in musical terminology that have unfortunately come to exist.
If readers will initially run through the quite short article on American
Musical Terminology, that difficulty will at once vanish.

GERMAN AND RUSSIAN SPELLINGS

There are also certain perplexities that confront the author of any book
of reference containing words and names of varying European national

---

[1] [In the present (tenth) edition this number is considerably exceeded.]

[2] As one or two curious readers have complained that they cannot find the entry in
question the reference is now given—see *Hempson*.

origin, and it may be well to state that in the alphabetization of the key words of the entries the fact that the German 'ö' is the equivalent of 'oe' has been ignored, 'ö' being positionally treated simply as 'o'. This is the most practical method when providing for readers in the so-called Anglo-Saxon countries and has respectable precedent in some German works, as, for instance, the great Muret-Sanders, *Enzyklopädisches Wörterbuch*; however, in cases where it seemed desirable a cross-reference has been inserted in the 'oe' position. As for the many varying transliterations of certain Russian names, the difficulty has been met by choosing for the main entry what seemed to be the most prevalent transliteration and freely cross-referencing from all others that are known to be in use. Thus, to take one instance of many, *Stcherbatchef* appears in three places, under 'Stch', 'Stsch', and 'Schtsch' (as for his final 'f', 'v', or 'w', that, happily, does not disturb his position alphabetically).

THE PRONOUNCING GLOSSARY

It will be noticed that at the close of the volume is given a very comprehensive Pronouncing Glossary of words and names that appear in the body of the book. The international character of musical literature and musical programmes seemed to make this desirable, particularly in the interests of younger readers.

THE ILLUSTRATIONS

The pictorial illustrations of this volume, as will be seen, are unusually abundant. For the most part, they are of the character that may be described as 'authentic'; that is, they are reproductions of photographs, of contemporary pictures, and so forth. But interspersed with these is a series of portraits which might be called 'imaginative' or 'synthetic'—neither adjective, however, quite accurately representing their nature. They are a speciality of the artist Oswald Barrett ('Batt' of the *Radio Times*), and represent years of research, study, and profound thought on his part. He is an ardent music-lover and a deep student of the great masters, and his process has been to assemble (often by very prolonged correspondence with authorities in different parts of Europe) all the existing pictorial documents concerning those composers at different periods of their lives. This done, he has essayed the double task of producing a portrait that shall penetrate to the mind of the character represented and express his personality, and that shall also, by its circumstantial details (as to which, also, he has carried out a great deal of research), recall to us both the operative influences of his surroundings and the manner in which those surroundings represented his own nature. It is the conviction of all connected with this book that nothing of this sort previously seen has been so successful in achievement, and they gratefully record the fact that the frontispiece, a reproduction of an oil painting specially executed for the purpose, which they regard as the most revealing portrait of its subject in existence, is the artist's personal gift to the volume and testifies to his deep interest in it.

THE ATTEMPT AT ACCURACY

An allusion has been ventured above to the attempt at a high degree of accuracy by the consultation with specialists in the various branches. But 'accuracy' is, alas, 'a relative term'. Dr. Johnson on the completion of his dictionary, after eight years of work on it, admitted candidly that to attain perfection 'would have delayed too much', and he might have gone farther and admitted frankly that 'perfection' in a work of reference is, in fact, unattainable. Such a work as the present, crammed as it is with definite statements as to facts, names, and dates, whatever the care taken in its preparation, must sometimes err. Indeed, it is well known to all authors and compilers of works of reference that a certain proportion of errors corrected during the day creep back during the night. And not only do some printed errors thus distress every author of such a book, but omissions also. The present author does not believe himself to be guilty of many unintended omissions, but to cover such wide ground is very difficult and he will be grateful if either errors or omissions noticed may be signalled to him with a view to rectification in any future edition.

Following this preface will be found the long list of the many who have tried to save the author from, at least, the faults of his own ignorance or inadvertence,[1] but should the reader chance to discover that the author is anywhere insufficiently saved he should not take it that the blame necessarily falls on those enumerated in the list. Boswell, in the preface to his *Account of Corsica*, tackled this question very boldly and honestly, and the present author would wish to do the same.

'I would however have it understood, that although I received the corrections of my friends with deference, I have not always agreed with them. An authour should be glad to hear every candid remark. But I look upon a man as unworthy to write, who has not force of mind to determine for himself. I mention this that the judgement of the friends I have named may not be considered as connected with every passage in this book.'

P. A. S.

Chamby Sur Montreux, Switzerland
September 1938

[1 In the present edition this long list, with its many additional names from the intervening editions, has been merely summarized.]

ACKNOWLEDGEMENTS

IN each of the preceding editions of this book there has appeared a list of the various authorities who, prior to its first publication, assisted the author by carefully reading through the whole of it in typescript or proof and communicating to him the results of their scrutiny. Amongst these may be recalled the late ERNEST WALKER, of Oxford, W. R. ANDERSON, and FREDERICK PAGE of the Oxford University Press.

Further editions profited by similar complete readings, voluntarily undertaken, by the late SIR HUGH P. ALLEN, the late EGERTON LOWE, VICTOR HODGSON, and the late JAMES RODGER.

But in this connection must, above all, be mentioned the late ALFRED EINSTEIN, who set himself the task of steadily working through this *Companion* from A to Z, closely scrutinizing every article.

So far what has been related has concerned scrutiny of the book as a whole. In addition to the persons already mentioned the book's first edition supplied a list of about one hundred specialist authorities of very many nationalities (British, American, Italian, French, German, Swiss, Dutch, Russian, etc.) on whom the author had called for an examination of what he had written concerning their particular countries or subjects.

Then, as the succeeding editions appeared, acknowledgement was gratefully admitted to about one hundred and forty readers who had spontaneously supplied information on points connected with their special interest or such as had come to their notice during their normal use of the book.

The following should be particularly mentioned as having given valuable assistance by their close inspection of articles submitted to them—articles as to which they were able to speak with special (and sometimes unique) authority:

The late H. K. ANDREWS of New College, Oxford; Miss M. E. BARBER, Assistant Secretary of the Society of Authors; CYRIL BEAUMONT; JOHN CLAPHAM, the late EDGAR T. COOK; ROBERT DONINGTON; the late F. GREEN, Director of the Curwen Memorial College; W. GRICE, Secretary of the Performing Right Society, London; R. F. NEWTON; A. HYATT KING, in charge of Printed Music at the British Museum; LL. S. LLOYD; H. LOWERY; MORGAN NICOLAS; The Revd. ERNEST A. PAYNE; E. G. RICHARDSON; ALEC ROBERTSON and his colleagues of the British Broadcasting Corporation; the late Revd. T. W. SCHOLES; CARLTON SPRAGUE SMITH; J. RAYMOND TOBIN; and EGON WELLESZ.

And in addition to all these NICOLAS SLONIMSKY kindly offered to check all the dates of the book—and on the chronology of the subject of music nobody in the world is so great an authority as he. In addition he has spent further months in drafting suggestions as to treatment of American personalities and in collecting valuable information concerning musical affairs in the United States and dozens of effective photographs of composers of that country.

Finally there must be added more than a word of gratitude to my Wife, DORA WINGATE SCHOLES.

P. A. S.

The present editor acknowledges for his part the welcome contribution of ERIC CROZIER, whose reading of the proofs of the tenth edition has prompted numerous corrections and improvements.

POSTSCRIPT

A REMARK may perhaps be permitted as to a matter of petty detail which has always given special trouble in the revision of the *Companion* for its successive editions. It concerns the article *Degrees and Diplomas* and is intended for the notice of British readers only—all others being requested tactfully to overlook it.

The British public that uses this book is entitled to expect to find in it an up-to-date explanation of the significance of the various alphabetical symbols that have attached themselves to the names of members of the musical profession in this country, and that seem to be always changing. How many such decorative appendages are now in daily use? Well, the British musical profession, in its infatuation for alphabetical decorations, goes so far that we may compassionately consider it as being (in one little matter alone) just a little mad, for it has provided itself with no fewer than fifty such adornments to choose from—indeed more than that are to be seen, for alterations in the syllabuses of the examining bodies frequently bring into existence new ones, and when these supplant older ones, these latter necessarily remain in some use until their holders in time die out. Slices of the alphabet at present obtainable by British organists, music teachers, etc., actually include all the following: B.Mus.; M.Mus.; D. Mus.; F.R.A.M.; Hon. F.R.A.M.; Hon. R.A.M.; A.R.A.M.; L.R.A.M.; F.R.C.M.; Hon. F.R.C.M.; Hon. R.C.M.; A.R.C.M.; Hon. A.R.C.M.; G.R.S.M.; A.R.C.O.; A.R.C.O.-CHM.; F.R.C.O.; F.R.C.O.-CHM.; A.D.C.M.; G.T.C.L.; F.T.C.L.; Hon. F.T.C.L.; L.T.C.L.; A.T.C.L.; Hon. T.C.L.; A.Mus. TCL.; L.Mus. TCL.; A.G.S.M.; L.G.S.M.; F.G.S.M.; G.G.S.M.; Hon. G.S.M.; A.R.M.C.M.; F.R.M.C.M.; A.B.S.M.; A.B.S.M. (T.T.D.); F.B.S.M.; G.B.S.M.; Dip. R.S.A.M.; Dip. Mus. Ed. R.S.A.M.; A.T.S.C.; L.T.S.C.; F.T.S.C.; Hon. F.T.S.C.; M.R.S.T.; p.s.m.; B.B.C.M.; A.B.C.M.; L.B.C.M.; A.L.C.M.; L.L.C.M.; L.L.C.M. (T.D.); F.L.C.M.; A.Mus. L.C.M.; L.Mus. L.C.M.

How *can* the British general public possibly learn to comprehend the significance, and assess the relative value of its country's musical degrees and diplomas when they are so many? No other country in the world practises so lavish an exploitation of the alphabet. May it be suggested that the good sense of the managers of British musical educational institutions, so evident in other matters, must some day bring home to them the desirability of forming a joint examining board and merging their tests and awards? (This will, of course, mean some financial sacrifice, but we are talking of *educational* bodies, not *commercial*.) It has only to be added here that in the meantime the somewhat baffling complexity of the article just alluded to has been brought up to date by correspondence with courteous officials of the various examining bodies and that it is believed to give a reliable statement of the position as it is at the moment of writing.

LIST OF PLATES

A READER'S SYNOPSIS
OF THE
OXFORD COMPANION TO MUSIC

*Showing how, in addition to
the use of the volume as a book of reference,
the dispersed articles upon various branches
of the subject may, if desired,
be read as a series of*

CONCISE COMPREHENSIVE SURVEYS
OF THE DIFFERENT ASPECTS
OF THE ART

A READER'S SYNOPSIS OF
THE CONTENTS

(The more important articles are indicated by the use of capitals)

1. THE SCIENTIFIC SIDE OF MUSIC

(a) THE PHYSICS OF MUSIC

ACOUSTICS; Partials; Timbre.

PITCH; TEMPERAMENT; Resonoscope.

CONCERT HALLS AND OTHER HALLS FOR MUSIC.

(b) THE PHYSIOLOGY AND PSYCHOLOGY OF MUSIC

EAR AND HEARING; VOICE.

Tests and Measurements for Musical Capacity; Absolute Pitch; Memory in Music.

(See also, for their psychological references and implications, *Scales*; *Melody*; *Harmony*; *Form*; *Composition*; *Improvisation*.)

2. THE STRUCTURE OF MUSIC

(a) RHYTHM

RHYTHM.

Measure (see also Table 10); Duplet; Triplet (see also Table 11); Syncopation; Agogic; RUBATO (or TEMPO RUBATO).

Phrase and Sentence; Phrasing; Phrase Marks.

Tempo; Metronome.

Proportion; Ars Nova.

PERCUSSION (for the Rhythm Instruments): Jazz; Scotch Snap.

Jaques-Dalcroze; Rhythm Band.

(b) SCALE, INTERVAL, MELODY

MODES; Key (see also Table 8); Tonality; SCALES; Modulation.

Intervals; Enharmonic Intervals; Microtones.

MELODY; Phrase and Sentence; Sequence; Fioritura.

Figure; Motif; Idée Fixe; Motto Theme; Metamorphosis of Themes.

(c) HARMONY

HARMONY; Counterpoint; Polyphony; Motion; Faburden; Descant.

Dominant Seventh; Diminished Seventh; Chromatic Chords; Neapolitan Sixth.

CADENCE or CLOSE; Tierce de Picardie.

Sequence; Point d'Orgue; Alberti Bass.

Figured Bass; Vamping.

(d) FORM

Phrase and Sentence.

Thematic Materials; Subject; Subsidiary or Subsidiary Theme; Figure; Motif; Leading Motif; Motto Themes; Idée Fixe; Metamorphosis of Themes; Sequence; Passage Work; Alberti Bass. (See also the sections 7 and 9 of the article *Composition*.)

FORM (including a general discussion, with section on Simple Binary, Ternary, Compound Binary, Rondo, Air with Variations, Fugue, Vocal. Forms, etc.); Development; Coda.

Movement; Cyclic Form; SUITE (see also *Galanterien*; *Partita*); SONATA (see also *Minuet and Trio*; *Scherzo*); SYMPHONY; CONCERTO (see also *Cadenza*; *Point d'Orgue*); OVERTURE; Symphonic Poem. (At the end of the main article *Form* will be found a list of over 160 short articles describing particular types of composition.)

Counterpoint: Polyphony; Canon; Invention. (For Fugue see the article *Form*.)

3. THE NOTATION OF MUSIC

NOTATION AND NOMENCLATURE (together with Tables 1–11; 18–26); Score; Orchestra 6 (section on 'The Reading of Orchestral Scores').

Tie or Bind; Dot, Dotted Note; Duplet; Triplet.

ORNAMENTS AND GRACES (together with Tables 12–16); Mordent; Shake or Trill.

Tablature; Ligature; Musica Ficta; Gamut.

EXPRESSION (with Table 17).

4. MUSICAL INSTRUMENTS AND INSTRUMENTAL PERFORMANCE

Obsolete instruments, and instruments revived in modern times, will be found later, under (f).

(a) THE PIANOFORTE

Keyboard; Klavier or Clavier; TEMPERAMENT; PIANOFORTE; PIANOFORTE PLAYING AND PIANOFORTE TEACHING; FINGERING; Virgil Practice Clavier; Pedalier; Mechanical Reproduction of Music (Pianola, etc.).

Phrase and Sentence; Phrasing; Phrase Marks; EXPRESSION (with Table 17); Interpretation; Tempo; Rubato (or Tempo Rubato); Accompaniment.

ORNAMENTS AND GRACES (together with Tables 12–16); Mordent; Shake or Trill.

Virtuoso; Recital.

Invention; Suite (see also *Partita*); SONATA; CONCERTO; Concertstuck; Prelude; Étude; Impromptu; Nocturne; Ballade; Moment Musical; Mazurka; Song without Words; Novelette. (At the end of the article *Form* will be found a list of about 160 short articles on the various types of piece adopted for pianoforte composition, as for other composition. The articles *Nicknamed Compositions* and *Misattributed Compositions* include information respecting a certain amount of music for pianoforte.)

(b) THE ORGAN

ORGAN (including a descriptive list of 150 organ stops, an account of the Unit Organ, etc.); Timbre; Acoustics (for 'Acoustic Bass', etc.); Fonds d'Orgue; Foundation; Keyboard; TEMPERAMENT; Electric Musical Instruments (for the Hammond Organ and other 'electrophonic' instruments).

Reed-Organ Family.

Plainsong (for its Accompaniment); Hymns and Hymn Tunes (for Accompaniment); Gathering Note.

Cathedral Music; Anglican Parish Church Music (these two for points in the history of the organ).

Voluntary; Choral Prelude; Toccata; Improvision; Verset; Sonata. (For Fugue see the article *Form*.)

Profession of Music 10 (for Royal College of Organists, American Guild of Organists, etc.); Degrees and Diplomas; Incorporated Association of Organists.

See under *Organ* 16 for a further list of references to the instrument throughout this volume.

(c) THE BOWED INSTRUMENTS

VIOLIN FAMILY; G String; Wolf; Stroh Violin, Viola, Cello, etc.; Contra-violin; Viola Alta; Viole-ténor; Violinda; Mechanical Reproduction of Music (Automaton Violinists).

SONATA (with historical list of sonatas for Bowed Instruments, etc.); CHAMBER MUSIC (with its history, lists of composers and their work for Bowed Instruments, etc.); ORCHESTRA; String Band and String Orchestra; CONCERTO; Conducting (for references to the former position and duties of the Leading Violin).

The technical terms and directions found in music for bowed instruments are scattered throughout the volume in their alphabetical positions and are too numerous to be listed here.

(d) THE WIND INSTRUMENTS

FLUTE FAMILY; Giorgi Flute; Boehm System.

Reed; OBOE FAMILY; CLARINET FAMILY; SAXOPHONE FAMILY.

BRASS; Whole-tube and Half-tube Instruments; Cylinder; Piston; Duplex Instruments; Embouchure; Cuivré; CORNET; TRUMPET FAMILY; HORN FAMILY; TROMBONE FAMILY; SAXHORN AND FLÜGELHORN FAMILIES; TUBA GROUP.

Transposing Instruments; Speaker Key; Tonguing; Aerophor.

BAGPIPE FAMILY; Alphorn; Bamboo Pipe; Bugle, Signal Horn; Bersag Horn.

ORCHESTRA; Military Band; Brass Band; Tattoo.

(e) THE PERCUSSION INSTRUMENTS

PERCUSSION FAMILY; Effects. (For some of the more recent and less seriously recognized percussion instruments see under 16 b.)

5. OPERA AND COGNATE SUBJECTS

6. THE DANCE

DANCE; BALLET; JAZZ; Ridotto; Seises; Allemande; Courante; Sarabande; Gigue; Minuet; Gavotte, Bourrée; Waltz; Danse Macabre. (In addition there are about 100 short entries treating of particular dances of different countries.)

7. CHAMBER MUSIC

CHAMBER MUSIC; SONATA; Consort; In Nomine; Fancy; Phantasy. (In addition the article *Nicknamed Compositions* contains references to particular pieces of chamber music.)

8. THE ORCHESTRA AND CONDUCTING

ORCHESTRA; CONDUCTING; Chapel; Ripieno; Additional Accompaniments. For the various groups of instruments making up the modern orchestra see under 4 (*c*), (*d*), (*e*), above.

9. VOCAL MUSIC

VOICE; Alto Voice; Falsetto; Jodel; Evirato.

SINGING; Messa di Voce; Filar la Voce; Coloratura; Fioritura; Melisma.

SIGHT-SINGING; TONIC SOL-FA; Lancashire Sol-fa; Vocalize; Solfeggio, Solfège; Solmization.

SONG; Recitative; Aria; Cantata; Lied; Cabaletta; Cavatina; Chanson; Patter Song; Song Cycle.

FOLK SONG; BALLAD; Shanty or Chanty; Volkslied.

Prima Donna; Recital.

10. CHORAL MUSIC

Choir or Chorus; Equal Voices; Liedertafel; Festival; Competitions in Music.

HARMONY (for the early history of choral composition); Canti Carnascialeschi; Frottola; Laudi Spirituali; MADRIGAL; GLEE; PART SONG; Round; Catch.

ORATORIO; MASS; Cantata; Choral Symphony. (See also under *Church Music*.)

11. CHURCH MUSIC

CHURCH MUSIC (general introduction to the subject); LITURGY; Office; Divine Office.

Matins; Lauds; Prime; Terce; Sext; None; Vespers; Compline.

MASS; Requiem; Caeremoniale Episcoporum; Gradual; Rituale; Antiphonal; Vesperal; Ferial; Festal; Litany; Litanae Laurentanae.

COMMON PRAYER; Matins; Evensong.

Canticle; Benedicite; Benedictus; Cantate Domino; Deus Misereatur; Jubilate; Magnificat; Nunc Dimittis; Te Deum; Venite.

Accentus; Preces; Versicles; Respond; Responses; Antiphon; Psalm; De Profundis.

Farcing or Farsing; Trope; Sequence; Victimae Paschali; Stabat Mater Dolorosa; Trisagion or Trishagion; Alleluia; Hallelujah; Doxology; Tract; Invitatory; Introit; Kyrie; Elevatio, Elevation; Offertory; Amen.

O Salutaris Hostia; Pange Lingua; Tantum Ergo; Veni Creator Spiritus; Veni Sancte Spiritus; Lauda Sion; Dies Irae.

Improperia; Tenebrae; Seven Last Words.

PLAINSONG; Gregorian Tones; Evovae or Euouae; MODES; Intonation; Inflexion; Melisma; Pneuma; Musica figurata.

HYMNS AND HYMN TUNES; Office Hymn; Chorale (or Choral); Chorale Prelude; Reports or Rapports; Gathering Note;

Gathering Psalm; Pope and Turk Tune; Old Hundredth; Tallis's Canon; Stilt; Emperor's Hymn.

MYSTERIES, MIRACLE PLAYS, AND MORALITIES; ORATORIO; PASSION; Motet; Hallelujah Chorus; Carols.

ROMAN CATHOLIC CHURCH MUSIC IN BRITAIN; Motu Proprio; Cecilia Movement.

GREEK CHURCH AND MUSIC.

ANGLICAN PARISH CHURCH MUSIC; CATHEDRAL MUSIC IN BRITAIN; CHAPEL ROYAL; Service; Anthem; Verse; ANGLICAN CHANT; Parish Clerk; Precentor; Vicar choral.

PURITANS AND MUSIC; PRESBYTERIAN CHURCH MUSIC; CONGREGATIONAL CHURCH AND MUSIC; BAPTIST CHURCH AND MUSIC; METHODISM AND MUSIC; Quakers and Music.

Bohemia (for Huss and Zinzendorf); Luther; Calvin; Wesley Family.

ORGAN; Mechanical Reproduction (section on the once-common Church Barrel Organ); Voluntary; Verset.

The chief composers of church music in various countries will, of course, be found briefly treated under their own names.

12. THE FOLK ELEMENT IN MUSIC

FOLK SONG; BALLAD; DANCE; Scotland; Ireland; Wales; O'Carolan; Petrie; Moore; Stevenson; Gow; Kennedy-Fraser; Sharp.

See also reference to Folk Song in the articles

on the various countries other than those mentioned here—of which a list is given below under *History of Music*. For the various national dances, briefly described under their own names, see list at the end of the article *Form*.

13. THE HISTORY OF MUSIC

HISTORY OF MUSIC.

MODES; SCALES; Key; Hexachord; Tablature; Notation and Nomenclature; Musica Ficta.

PLAINSONG; HARMONY; Counterpoint; Diaphony; Faburden; Gymel; Hocket; Figured Bass.

FORM (Section on 'The History of Forms'); SUITE; SONATA; SYMPHONY; OVERTURE; CONCERTO; Cadenza; PROGRAMME MUSIC; Symphonic Poem.

Church Music; Liturgy; MASS; Motet; PASSION MUSIC; ORATORIO; Choral or Chorale; HYMNS AND HYMN TUNES; CATHEDRAL MUSIC; Chapel Royal; ANGLICAN PARISH CHURCH MUSIC.

Ars Nova; Sumer is icumen in; Madrigal; Glee; Part Song.

OPERA; Dance; Ballet.

HARPSICHORD FAMILY; CLAVICHORD; PIANOFORTE; Pianoforte

Playing; ORGAN; VIOL FAMILY; VIOLIN FAMILY; Brass (and the articles on separate families listed at the end of this article); Flute Family; Oboe Family; Clarinet Family; Percussion Family.

Classical; Romantic; Nationalism; Impressionism; Expressionism; New Music; Zopf; Barocco; Gebrauchsmusik.

ENGLAND; SCOTLAND; IRELAND, WALES (for British Music see also under 14); BELGIUM; Brabançonne; HOLLAND; ITALY; FRANCE; Carmagnole; Ça ira; Malbrouck; Partant pour la Syrie; Rouget de Lisle (for Marseillaise); SPAIN; GERMANY AND AUSTRIA; Deutschland über Alles; O Deutschland; Watch on the Rhine; Emperor's Hymn; Horst Wessel Song; Wir fahren gegen Engelland; Pope and Turk Tune; BOHEMIA; HUNGARY; Rákóczy March; RUMANIA; POLAND; RUSSIA; SCANDINAVIA; UNITED STATES; Oriental Music. (At the end of each of these articles will be found a list of those composers of the country in question who are separately treated in this volume.)

14. BRITISH MUSIC

ENGLAND; SCOTLAND; IRELAND; WALES.

At the end of each of these articles will be found a list of further articles throughout the book treating of details in the musical life of the country in question, as also a list of the composers of that country who have been made the subject of separate entries. In addition the following national songs, etc., are treated under their own heads:

England. God save the Queen; Adeste Fideles; Arethusa; Bay of Biscay; Black-eyed Susan; Britannia, the Pride of the Ocean; British Grenadiers; Calino Casturame; Carman's Whistle; Dargason; Down among the Dead Men; Drink to me only with thine eyes; Dulce Domum; Farewell, Manchester; Girl I left behind me; Greensleeves; Heart of Oak; Home, Sweet Home; Jerusalem; Keel Row; Keep the Home Fires Burning; Lass of Richmond Hill; Lilliburlero; We won't go home till morning (see *Malbrouck*); Pack up your Troubles; Passing by; Red Flag; Rogue's March; Rule, Britannia; Sir Roger de Coverley; Sumer is icumen in; Tallis's Canon; Three Blind Mice; Tipperary; Vicar of Bray; When the King enjoys his own again; Ye Mariners of England; You Gentlemen of England.

Scotland. Annie Laurie; Auld Land Syne; Auld Robin Gray; Blue Bells of Scotland; Blue Bonnets over the Border; Bonnie Dundee; Caller Herrin'; Campbells are Coming; Flowers of the Forest; Jessie, the Flower of Dunblane; John Anderson, my Jo; Land o' the Leal; Lass o' Gowrie; Lass o' Paties Mill; Lochaber no more; Loch Lomond; O gin I were fairly shut of her (see under *Barley Shot*); Robin Adair; Scots wha hae; Skye Boat Song; There's nae luck; Will ye no come back again; Within a mile of Edinburgh town; Ye Banks and Braes.

Ireland. Eileen Aroon; Father O'Flynn; First of August; Kathleen Mavourneen; Last Rose of Summer; Londonderry Air; No Surrender; Rory O'More; Saint Patrick's Day; Wearing of the Green.

Wales. All through the Night (Ar Hyd y Nos); Barley Shot; Bells of Aberdovey; Brenhines Dido; Dafydd y Garreg Wen; God bless the Prince of Wales; Land of my Fathers; Rising of the Lark; Sibyl.

Canada. Canadian Boat Song; Maple Leaf; O Canada!

15. AMERICAN MUSIC

UNITED STATES OF AMERICA.

American Musical Terminology. At the end of the article *United States of America* will be found a list of further articles throughout the book treating of details in American musical life, as also a list of the numerous American composers who have been made the subject of separate entries.

16. THE MUSIC OF TODAY AND TOMORROW

(a) SERIOUS MUSIC

HARMONY (Sections on Empirical Systems, Chordal Streams, Polytonality, Atonality, The Harmony of the Future); MICROTONES; NOTE-ROW.

ELECTRIC MUSICAL INSTRUMENTS (for Ether Wave Instruments, Electric Bowed and Plucked Instruments, Electric Pianos and Organs, and instruments using the Photo-electric Cell).

History (Sections 8 and 9).

(b) POPULAR MUSIC

JAZZ (including Ragtime, Bebop, etc.); Syncopation; Plugging; Signature Tune; Musical Switch; Theme Song; Torch Song; Crooning; Tipica Orchestra.

SAXOPHONE FAMILY; Effects; Banjo; Banjolin; Bongos; Chinese Crash Cymbal; Chinese Temple Block; Chinese Wood Block; Choke Cymbals; Claves; Cow Bell; Crash Cymbal; Korean Temple Block; Maracas; Marimba; Rumba Bongos; Singing Saw; Sizzle Cymbal; Thunder Stick; Ukelele; Vibraphone; Victalle; Washboard.

17. THE SOCIAL HISTORY OF MUSIC

FOLK SONG; DANCE; Wait or Wayte; Inns and Taverns as Places for Music-making; Clubs for Music-making; Cecilia, Saint (for St. Cecilia societies and celebrations); Catch; Glee (for Glee Clubs); Fairs and their Music; Barber's Shop Music; Mealtime Music; Street Music; Patronage; Monopolies.

CONCERT; Recital; Virtuoso; Annotated Programme; Applause; Encore; Criticism of Music; National Federation of Musical Societies.

Opera (and articles listed at the end of that one); Sadler's Wells; Victoria Hall, Royal.

Community Singing; Competitions in Music;

BROADCASTING OF MUSIC; Festival; Hollywood Bowl; Negro Minstrels.

Copyists; Printing of Music; Publishing of Music.

See under *Church Music* for that side of the Social influence of music.

18. THE MUSICAL PROFESSION—ITS HISTORY AND PRESENT POSITION

PROFESSION OF MUSIC; Minstrels, Troubadours. Trouvères, Minnesingers, Mastersingers; Wait or Wayte.

Patronage; Knighthood and other Honours; Degrees and Diplomas.

Pianoforte Playing and Teaching; Concert; Virtuoso; Recital.

Incorporated Association of Organists; Music Teachers' Association; United States (especially sections 4, 5, 8).

Criticism of Music (see also *Quality of Music*).

Other articles will be found under *The Educational Aspects of Music*, following.

19. THE EDUCATIONAL ASPECTS OF MUSIC

EDUCATION AND MUSIC.

Schools of Music; Schola Cantorum.

Mendelssohn Scholarship; Prix de Rome; DEGREES AND DIPLOMAS; Choragus; Gresham Professorship; Musicology.

Sight-Singing; TONIC SOL-FA; Lancashire Sol-fa; PIANOFORTE PLAYING AND TEACHING; APPRECIATION OF MUSIC; Tests and Measurements for Musical Capacity.

Rural Music Schools; Competitions in Music.

PROFESSION OF MUSIC; Music Teachers' Association; Incorporated Society of Musicians.

UNITED STATES OF AMERICA (for Music Settlements; Music Weeks; Music Teachers' National Association, &c.).

JOURNALS DEVOTED TO MUSIC.

The chief books of reference on almost all these subjects will be found listed on pages 292–5, under the heading *Dictionaries of Music*.

TABLES OF NOTATION
AND NOMENCLATURE

TABLES OF NOTATION AND NOMENCLATURE

TABLE 1. VALUES OF NOTES

1 Semibreve equals		1 Whole-note equals
2 Minims or		2 Half-notes or
4 Crotchets or		4 Quarter-notes or
8 Quavers or		8 Eighth-notes or
16 Semi-quavers or		16 Sixteenth-notes or
32 Demisemi-quavers		32 Thirty-second notes

After this follow Hemidemisemiquavers (sixty-fourth notes, ♪) and, occasionally, Semi-hemidemisemiquavers (notes of 128 to the semibreve, ♪).

A dot after a note increases its value by half; thus $\textrm{♩·} = \textrm{♩♪}$ (but see exception mentioned in article *Dot, Dotted Note*). A double dot after a note increases its value by a half plus a quarter; thus $\textrm{♩··} = \textrm{♩♪♪}$ A third dot has very occasionally been used; thus $\textrm{♩···} = \textrm{♩♪♪♪}$

For the rarely used Breve (the value of 2 semibreves) see Table 3.

TABLE 2. VALUES OF RESTS
(Compare Table 1 above)

The ♩ rest hangs down; the ♩ rest remains on the surface. (Imagine the rest of greater value is the heavier.)

The ♩ rest (՟) turns to the right (Mnemonic: cRotchet—Right; or quaRter Note—Right; the ♪ rest (՚) turns to the left.

In addition to the above there is the Breve or Double Whole-note rest, occupying the width of the space between two lines: ▆.

Also, the Semibreve or Whole-note rest is used as a whole-bar rest, irrespective of the actual time-value of the bar.

A silence of several bars is often indicated thus (or in some similar way):

13

Rests can be dotted and doubly dotted, as notes are, and with the same effect; this, however, is less commonly done.

TABLE 3. NAMES OF THE NOTES AND REST VALUES

ENGLISH, ITALIAN, FRENCH, GERMAN, AND AMERICAN

	ENGLISH	ITALIAN	FRENCH	GERMAN	AMERICAN
	breve	breve	carrée (square) or breve	Doppeltakt-note (double measure note)	double whole-note
	semibreve	semibreve	ronde (round)	Ganze Taktnote (whole measure note)	whole-note
	minim	minima or bianca (white)	blanche (white)	Halbe (half) or Halbenote or Halbe Taktnote	half-note
	crotchet	semiminima or nera (black)	noire (black)	Viertel (quarter)	quarter-note.
	quaver	croma	croche (hook)	Achtel (eighth)	eighth-note
	semi-quaver	semi-croma	double-croche (double-hook)	Sechzehntel (sixteenth)	sixteenth-note
	demisemi-quaver	biscroma	triple-croche (triple-hook)	Zweiund-dreissigstel (thirty-second)	thirty-second note
	hemidemi-semi-quaver	semi-biscroma	quadruple-croche (quadruple-hook)	Vierundsech-zigstel (sixty-fourth)	sixty-fourth note

(The word 'Rest' is in Italian *Pausa*; in French *Silence* or *Pause*; in German *Pause*.)

The *English* names of the longer notes are based upon the old Latin names of the early Middle Ages.

The earlier *Italian* names are similar.

The *French* names stand alone as being purely descriptive of the appearances.

The German names are arithmetical and the American practically a translation of them. It must be admitted that the American and German names require no remembering, being logically descriptive of time-values. They are, then, undoubtedly the best, and the American names are now largely adopted in the British Empire.

TABLE 4. THE CLEFS

G or TREBLE CLEF On 2nd line up, fixing that as Treble G	F or BASS CLEF On 2nd line down, fixing that as Bass F	C(SOPRANO)CLEF On 1st line, fixing that as middle C	C (ALTO) CLEF On 3rd line, fixing that as middle C	C (TENOR) CLEF On 4th line, fixing that as middle C

The above shows the one note, middle C, represented in five different ways. For further particulars see article *Notation*, section 4, also *Great Staff*.

TABLE 5. PITCH NAMES OF THE NOTES

IN ENGLISH, GERMAN, FRENCH, AND ITALIAN

	C	D	E	F	G	A	B
English	C	D	E	F	G	A	B
German	„	„	„	„	„	„	H¹
French	ut or do	ré	mi	fa	sol	la	si
Italian	do	re	„	„	„	„	„

¹ Note that B flat in English is B in German, and that B in English is H in German. (See reference to this in the article *Notation and Nomenclature*.)

TABLE 6. INFLECTION OF NOTES

SHARP	DOUBLE SHARP	FLAT	DOUBLE FLAT
Raising the note a half-step or semitone	Raising the note a full step or tone	Lowering the note a half-step or semitone	Lowering the note a full step or tone
♯	✕	♭	♭♭

After a Sharp or Flat the Natural Sign ♮ restores the note to its normal pitch.

After a Double Sharp or Double Flat the Sign ♯ or ♭ (or ♮♯ or ♮♭) changes the pitch of the note to that of a single Sharp or Flat.

After a Double Sharp or Double Flat the Sign ♮ (rarely given ♮♮) restores the note to its normal pitch.

Any of these various signs is understood to affect not only the note before which it immediately occurs, but also, unless contradicted, any other notes on that same line or space of the staff throughout the measure (bar); and if the last note of the measure is thus inflected and is tied to the same note at the opening of the next measure, that latter also is understood to be included in the inflection. (See, however, the article *Note-row*.)

TABLE 7. NAMES OF INFLECTIONS OF NOTES

Additions are made to the names of the notes as shown below:

	♯	×	♭	♭♭	♮
English	sharp	double-sharp	flat	double-flat	natural
German	Cis Dis Eis Fis Gis Ais *His (The sign is called *Kreuz*)	Cisis Disis Eisis Fisis Gisis Aisis *Hisis (The sign is called *Doppel-kreuz*)	Ces Des Es Fes Ges As *B (The sign is called *Be*)	Ceses Deses Eses Feses Geses Ases *Bes (The sign is called *Doppel-Be*)	The sign is called *Quad-rat* or *Auflösungs-zeichen* ('release-sign')
French	dièse	double-dièse	bémol	double-bémol	bécarre
Italian	diesis	doppio diesis	bemolle	doppio bemolle	bequadro

On account of one or two little irregularities in the German names it has been thought best to set these out in full.

Notice particularly the names marked * (explained in the article *Notation and Nomenclature*, section 1).

TABLE 8. MAJOR AND MINOR KEY-SIGNATURES

(Seldom used)

The white note in each case represents the major key, the black note the minor key with the same signature (called 'Relative Minor').

It will be observed that, starting from C, the keynotes of the Sharp Keys rise five notes (a Perfect 5th) each remove, and that the keynotes of the Flat Keys fall five notes (a Perfect 5th) each remove.

It will also be observed that in the Sharp Major Keys the keynote is immediately above the last Sharp.

And that in the Flat Major Keys, the keynote is four notes below the last flat (i.e. is at the pitch of the last flat but one in the signature).

And that three notes down any Major Scale we come to the keynote of its Relative minor, or, to state it the other way, three notes up any Minor Scale we come to the keynote of its Relative Major.

Note that keys with six sharps (F♯ major and D♯ minor) are (on keyboard instruments) equivalents of the keys with six flats (G♭ major and E♭ minor) and that keys with seven sharps (C♯ major and A♯ minor) are the equivalents of the keys with five flats (D♭ major and B♭ minor). Thus composers use either one of the other of these signatures.

The order of the sharps in the signatures is by rising fifths, and the order of the flats is by falling fifths.

Sharps = F C G D A E B = *Flats*

That is, the one order is the other reversed.

TABLE 9. MAJOR AND MINOR IN FRENCH, GERMAN, AND ITALIAN

(IN SPEAKING OF KEYS AND SCALES)

ENGLISH	FRENCH	ITALIAN	GERMAN
major	majeur	maggiore	dur (i.e. 'hard')
minor	mineur	minore	moll (i.e. 'soft')

The above adjectives are used also of intervals, except for the German language, in which a major interval is called *gross* (i.e. big) and a minor one *klein* (i.e. small).

TABLE 10. TIME-SIGNATURES

Simple Duple	2/2 or ₵	2/4	2/8
Compound Duple	6/4	6/8	6/16
Simple Triple	3/2	3/4	3/8
Compound Triple	9/4	9/8	9/16
Simple Quadruple	4/2	4/4 or C	4/8
Compound Quadruple	12/4	12/8	12/16

Each Simple time has a corresponding Compound time. The beat in the Simple times is of the value of a plain note; in the Compound times of the value of a dotted note.

In other words, the beat-note value in the Simple times is divisible into halves, quarters, etc., and that in the Compound times into thirds, sixths, etc. The grouping of notes in a measure (bar) by means of the hooks of their tails (when they have such) should accord with these divisions, as shown above.

If the time-signature be regarded as a fraction it is to be understood in terms of Whole-notes, i.e. Semibreves; e.g. 3/2 = three halves of ○; 6/4 = six quarters of ○, and so on.

But note the difference between 3/2 and 6/4 (which are obviously of the same total time-duration per measure, yet differ in grouping and hence in rhythmic effect). And so with 3/4 and 6/8, and 3/8 and 6/16. On the other hand, between 2/2 and 4/4, 2/4 and 4/8, etc., there is little difference.

Occasional signatures other than those shown are to be met with, e.g. 8/8 in one of Bach's Partitas (in effect each bar can be considered two bars of 4/4).

Mixed bars of 2/4 + 3/4 or 3/4 + 2/4 (Quintuple Time) nowadays occur and are shown as 5/4; mixed bars of 4/4 + 3/4 or 3/4 + 4/4, shown as 7/4, and so on. There is, indeed, nothing to prevent a composer inventing any time-signature that he feels will help him to express the rhythm of any passage of his music, provided he keeps the denominator in powers of 2 (4, 8, 16, etc.).

TABLE 11. IRREGULAR RHYTHMIC GROUPINGS

(DUPLETS, TRIPLETS, QUADRUPLETS, ETC.)

Duplet or Couplet	Two in the time of three:
Triplet (see also under 'Sextolet' below)	Three in the time of two:
Quadruplet	Four in the time of three:
Quintuplet	Five in the time of four—or of three:
Sextolet or Sextuplet (and Double Triplet)	Six in the time of four: / If a grouping of 3+3 is desired it should be written as below: (really a triplet it will be seen) / (really a double triplet)
Septolet, or Septuplet, or Septimole	Seven in the time of four—or of six:

Various other combinations are possible, and it is hardly possible to list them or to lay down rules. When an irregular combination occurs the performer should observe the other notes of the measure, and he will quickly realize into what fraction of the measure the irregular grouping is to be fitted. In modern music such irregular groupings are often expressed as 4:5 (four in the time of five) especially when the basic unit is unusual.

NOTE ON TABLES 12–16

These tables are concerned with the interpretation of the most usual signs for Ornaments or Graces. It must be understood, however, that such signs have carried different significances in the usage of different periods, countries, and individual composers. Nothing less than a large book can cover the whole subject, so that the information given here must be accepted as merely a useful generalization.

For the general subject see the article *Ornaments or Graces*, and note especially section 5.

TABLE 12. ACCIACCATURA AND MORDENT

(a) The Acciaccatura.

The principal note retains its accent and practically all its time-value. The auxiliary note is theoretically timeless; it is just squeezed in as quickly as possible before the principal note is heard. Some pianists of high repute even play the two notes simultaneously, immediately releasing the Acciaccatura and retaining the principal note (*Acciaccatura* is Italian for a 'crushing in'); this is the correct classical technique prescribed by C. P. E. Bach. Compare the Appoggiatura (Table 13)—a totally different thing. (For the use of the Acciaccatura sign before a shake see Table 16.)

Sometimes two or more small notes are shown before the principal notes, and then they generally approximate to *Acciaccature* (being in most cases performed on the timeless and accentless principle), although they have no strokes through their tails, and although the name *Double Appoggiatura* or *Triple Appoggiatura* is often given them (as by C. P. E. Bach).

 etc.

Note a combination of Acciaccatura with spread chord (for spread chords see Table 18):

performed as though notated—

Although, as above stated, the Acciaccatura is theoretically timeless, it nevertheless must take a tiny fragment of time from somewhere. In the cases shown above (which we may look upon as the normal ones) it takes it from the note which follows (i.e. the ornament falls not before but *on* the beat). In two other cases, however, it takes it from the note which pre-cedes: (1) when, harmonically, and by considerations that common sense must determine, it clearly attaches to that note and not the following one; (2) when, in piano music, it appears in the bass followed by a chord in the left hand or in both hands—the composer's intention being to get the advantage of a richer harmony by sounding the bass note in a lower octave and then holding it by the pedal whilst the chord is played; in this case the chord (as a whole) is to be heard on the beat, the Acciaccatura slightly preceding it.

(b) The Lower and Upper Mordents.

Lower Mordent   Lower Mordent with
(or merely 'Mordent')   inflected note

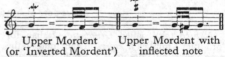

Upper Mordent   Upper Mordent with
(or 'Inverted Mordent')   inflected note

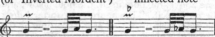

Mordent comes from the Italian *mordere*, 'to bite'. The term indicates the sharpness with which its notes are 'crushed in'. The accent falls on the ornament.

In the case of the standard or *Lower Mordent* these 'crushed in' notes are the main note itself and the note below; if the note below is to be inflected the relevant sign (♯, ♭, ♮, ×, ♭♭) generally appears, below the mordent sign.

In the case of the inverted or *Upper Mordent* the 'crushed in' notes are the main note itself and the note above; if the latter is to be inflected the relevant sign generally appears, above the mordent sign.

Some modern authorities call the Lower Mordent 'Inverted' and the Upper Mordent 'Standard'; but the correct classical usage is that given here. The one way of avoiding all misunderstanding is always to use the words 'Upper' and 'Lower'.

In music written between the early seventeenth and mid-eighteenth centuries, the Lower Mordent is the rule, the Upper Mordent the exception, whatever sign (if any) appears.

(See also the entry *Mordent* in the body of the book.)

TABLE 13. THE APPOGGIATURA

(See note at head of previous page, also entry under *Appoggiatura*)

(a) With Ordinary and Dotted Notes.

(b) With Tied Notes.

The Appoggiatura (Italian, from *appoggiare*, 'to lean') is not a timeless 'crushed in' note like the Acciaccatura (see Table 12); it is as important both melodically and harmonically as the note on which it 'leans', from which it takes normally half the time-value—or if the note on which it leans is dotted, two-thirds the time-value. Its *exact* interpretation varies greatly in different periods and contexts; but (with exceptions too untypical to lie within the scope of this book) it *always* steals the emphasis from its main note, which follows softly, like the resolution of a discord (as indeed it very often is).

When the Appoggiatura 'leans upon' two tied notes, it normally takes the whole of the time-value of the first of these to itself (see reservation in previous column).

(c) With a Chord.

As the Appoggiatura leans only upon one note of the chord the other notes are unaffected.

TABLE 14. THE TURN

(See note at head of previous page)

A turn (also called *Gruppetto*—Italian for 'grouplet') implies a figure of four notes—the note above, the note itself, the note below, and the note itself. This figure is performed *after* the note itself or *instead of it*, according as the turn sign is placed *after* the note itself or *over* it.

The inflection of the upper or lower note of the turn (in either form) may be shown by the placing of a sharp, flat, natural (etc.) sign above or below.

When the turn occurs after the note there is a good deal left to the taste of the performer as regards the division of the time available. The general principle seems to be that the turn is to be performed pretty quickly. To bring this about, the first example just given (if occurring in a slow tempo) might be treated thus:

Largo.

whilst in a very quick tempo it might be treated as follows (indeed there might be no time to treat it in any other way):

Prestissimo.

The number of different examples given in different textbooks is very large, and no two textbooks quite agree, but the above statement gives the chief general principles accepted by all.

TABLE 15. THE INVERTED TURN

(WITH THREE ALTERNATIVE SIGNS FOR IT)

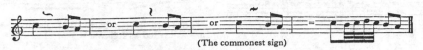

(The commonest sign)

The principles laid down as to the Turn (Table 14) apply, of course, to the Inverted Turn, which begins with the *lower* auxiliary note, instead of the upper one.

TABLE 16. THE SHAKE OR TRILL

(See note preceding Table 12 and also the entry *Shake* in the body of the book)

Essentially the Shake is an alternation of the note written and the note above.

But there is a diversity to be found in (*a*) its beginning, (*b*) its ending, and (*c*) the number of intervening alternations of the two notes.

(*a*) The Beginning of the Shake.

We may consider that nowadays the above beginning (i.e. on the written note itself) is the normal one.

But in the earlier music (up to and including Beethoven) it is normally intended that the shake shall begin on the upper of the two notes:

And, also, in music of any date, when the principal note is preceded by the same note the shake begins on the upper note, the principal note having already been sufficiently emphasized.

But nowadays if in any circumstances a composer wishes the shake to begin on the upper note he usually precedes it with an *Acciaccatura* sign, so as to leave no doubt.

It should be noted that the question whether a Shake begins on the upper or the lower note is much more than that way of stating the question seems to imply. The question which of the two notes is to be accentuated is involved, and the whole colour of the shake depends on this.

The upper-note trill (which was standard from say 1580 to 1830) actually to the ear (though not on paper) alters the harmony; the lower-note (modern) trill does not. Hence the importance of accenting the first (upper) note of the upper-note trill; in addition to which this first note is usually to be prolonged to some extent and frequently to the extent of a full normal appoggiatura (see Table 13), with very similar results so far as the alteration in the harmony goes. The first (lower) note of the modern (lower-note) trill is neither prolonged nor specially accented unless so shown, however.

Occasionally composers indicate that they intend a turn or inverted turn to precede the shake, the following being the best way of showing this intention:

(*b*) The Ending of the Shake.

All sorts of treatment may be demanded by the context, but one almost invariable rule is that the shake shall end on the written note itself.

Sometimes a turn precedes this, normally involving a triplet (or quintuplet), in order to fit the notes in, e.g.:

Sometimes, to make sure of the insertion of the turn, modern writers insert in their notation the two extra notes at the end.

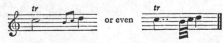

Observe the following formulae implying a shake, and (with others very similar) common in the earlier music, including that of Bach and Handel:

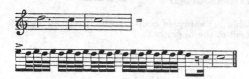

(c) The 'Body' of the Shake.

The number of alternations of the written note and the note above is left to the taste of the performer. He will naturally insert many more when the written note is a long one in a slow tempo than when it is a short one in a quick tempo.

Sometimes, in the latter case, the shake ceases to be such, nothing being left but the turn:

—or even less than that in cases where a turn is not felt to be suitable:

Inflected notes (sharps, flats, naturals, etc.) are indicated as follows:

Often a wavy line follows the sign 'tr':

Note. As with other 'ornaments' that of the shake differs in the details of performance in the music of different periods and different composers. The above gives a fairly safe generalization as to the practice of today, and in modern editions of old works where there is needed any departure from the rules here laid down a good editor can reasonably be expected to call attention to this.

TABLE 17. SIGNS OF RELATIVE INTENSITY

pp pianissimo or very soft	*p* piano or soft	*mf* mezzo forte or moderately loud	*f* forte or loud	*ff* fortissimo or very loud

Some composers have also used *mp, ppp, pppp, fff,* and *ffff*—the meaning being obvious.

crescendo, i.e. increasing gradually in power.

decrescendo, or *diminuendo,* i.e. decreasing or diminishing gradually in power.

See, in addition, the Signs of Accentuation, Table 24.

TABLE 18. PIANOFORTE SIGNS FOR 'SPREADING' OF CHORDS

('Arpeggioed', i.e. harp-fashion)

Instead of attacking the notes of the chord simultaneously, play them from the bottom upwards, holding each as struck. (Occasionally in old music the notes are to be played from the top downwards or in an irregular manner, and the question as to what is intended is sometimes a difficult one.) The best general rule is to bring in *last* the note from which the *melody* continues, whether this note is the top note, the bottom note, or even a middle note of the harmony.

Sometimes the wavy line is not continuous between the two staves, and then it is to be understood that the composer intends the arpeggio effect to go on in the two hands simultaneously.

It is to be noted that all spread chords should be so played as not to destroy the rhythm of the passage.

For the combination of spread chord with Acciaccature see Table 12 (*a*).

TABLE 19. PIANOFORTE RIGHT-HAND AND LEFT-HAND SIGNS

LEFT			RIGHT	
L.H. Left Hand Linke Hand (German)	M.S. Mano sinistra (Italian)	M.G. Main gauche (French)	R.H. Right Hand Rechte Hand (German)	M.D. Mano destra (Italian) or Main droite (French)

TABLE 20. REPEAT MARKS (FOR PASSAGES)

:‖ means return to ‖: or, if that does not occur, to the beginning of the composition.	D.C. or *Da Capo*, literally 'From the head', i.e. return to the beginning.	D.S. or *Dal Segno*, i.e. from the sign, meaning return to the mark '𝄋.	A.S. (rare) or *Al Segno*, i.e. to the sign. Usually the expression is *D.C. al Segno e poi la Coda*, i.e. 'From the beginning to the '𝄋 and then the Coda'.	*Bis* means perform the passage twice.

To avoid needless writing or engraving (especially in orchestral music) the repetition of a short passage is often indicated as below:

Sometimes when a section is marked to be repeated it ends in a way suitable for the return to the beginning, and, having been repeated, ends in a way suitable to proceed to the next section (or to close the whole composition if nothing more follows). The two endings are then shown thus:

etc.

Or instead of the '1', there may be used the expression '1*ma* Volta', or 'Prima Volta', or '1st Time'.

And instead of the '2', there may be used the expression '2*da* Volta', or 'Seconda Volta', or '2nd Time'.

When a return to the opening of the piece, or of some section of it, is indicated but only a part is to be repeated and then the piece brought to an end, the word *Fine* ('end') shows where to stop.

For instance, a Minuet is often followed by another Minuet called 'Trio' (see *Trio*), after which the first Minuet is to be repeated and then an end to be made. In this case the word *Fine* is placed at the end of the first Minuet to indicate that this is the place to conclude when performing the repetition. (Sometimes a pause sign ⌢ is used instead of the word *Fine*.)

TABLE 21. REPEAT MARKS (FOR NOTES)

There is a 'catch' in (*c*) and (*d*), the convention not being quite logical. In (*c*) (three examples are given) the time-value to be filled is that of *one* of the notes shown (in this case minim or half-note); in the first example of (*d*) the time-value to be filled is that of *both* of the notes shown (in this case quavers or eighth notes).

Note. If *Tremolo* (or *Trem.*) is added to any of the above or similar signs the notes concerned should be repeated very rapidly and without any attention to the exact number of repetitions attained during the time-value available.

TABLE 22. THE VARIOUS USES OF THE CURVED LINE

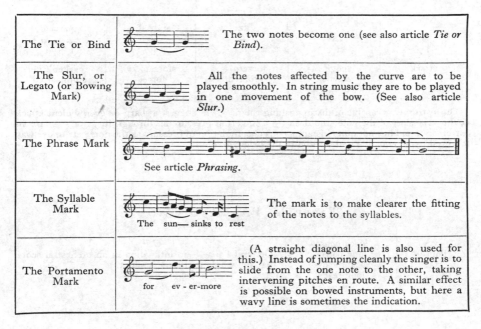

The Tie or Bind		The two notes become one (see also article *Tie or Bind*).
The Slur, or Legato (or Bowing Mark)		All the notes affected by the curve are to be played smoothly. In string music they are to be played in one movement of the bow. (See also article *Slur*.)
The Phrase Mark		See article *Phrasing*.
The Syllable Mark	The sun— sinks to rest	The mark is to make clearer the fitting of the notes to the syllables.
The Portamento Mark	for ev - er-more	(A straight diagonal line is also used for this.) Instead of jumping cleanly the singer is to slide from the one note to the other, taking intervening pitches en route. A similar effect is possible on bowed instruments, but here a wavy line is sometimes the indication.

See also *Staccato Marks*, below.

TABLE 23. STACCATO MARKS

This table gives a rough and generally accurate interpretation of the various marks, but is not to be taken too literally or mathematically.

	Mezzo-Staccato (shorten the notes by about ¼)	Staccato (shorten the notes by about ½)	Staccatissimo (shorten the notes by about ¾)
Written	*(musical notation)* or *(musical notation)*	*(musical notation)*	*(musical notation)*
Played (Approximately)	*(musical notation)*	*(musical notation)*	*(musical notation)*

The sign 𝆏𝆏𝆏 (i.e. a combination of accent marks and staccato marks) indicates a combination of pressure with a slight detachment.

Table 24. SIGNS OF ACCENTUATION

attack	agogic accent (see *Agogic*)	fz forzato = 'forced'	sf or sfz sforzato = 'forced'	marcato 'marked', i.e. emphasized

On instruments capable of distinguishing them, > will suggest a sharp or even violent attack at the very start of the note; the dash (–) a lingering pressure all through it; *fz* or *sf* or *sfz* an extremely rapid but not quite instantaneous accumulation of pressure as the note gets under way followed by an equally rapid decline to the original volume.

Table 25. PAUSE SIGNS

Pause	*lunga pausa* long pause (also means 'long rest')	*G.P.* 'General Pause'—an intimation in an orchestral score that the whole orchestra is silent.

Table 26. OCTAVE SIGNS

8va or *8* 'Ottava', i.e. perform an 8ve higher than written.	*8va bassa* or *8va sotto* Perform an 8ve lower than written ('sotto' = under).	*loco* 'Place', i.e. (after playing an 8ve higher or lower) resume the playing as written.	*con 8* Play the passage not in single notes, as marked, but in octaves.[1]

[1] The added line of 8ves will be *above* if the passage is in the treble of a pianoforte piece, and *below* if it is in the bass.

A

A (It.), **À** (Fr.). 'At', 'by', 'for', 'with', 'in', 'to', 'in the manner of', etc. A large number of expressions beginning with *A* or *À* will be found scattered through this book, generally alphabetically placed according to their principal word.

'A 2' has two opposite meanings, according to the musical context. If applied to two instruments that normally play separate parts (e.g. the two oboes of the ordinary orchestral score) it means they are now temporarily to play in unison. On the other hand, if applied to a set of instruments that normally plays in unison (e.g. the first violins) it means that they are now temporarily to divide into two bodies playing from the two parts provided for them.

'A = 435' and similar formulae. See *Pitch* 8.

A.A.G.O. See *Degrees and Diplomas* 4.

AB (Ger.). 'Off': e.g. in organ music, applied to a stop no longer required.

ABACO.

(1) EVARISTO FELICE DALL'. Born at Verona in 1675 and died at Munich in 1742, on his sixty-seventh birthday. He spent much of his life in Munich as a musician (cellist) of the court, and also in Brussels during the exile there of the Prince Elector. His music is much on the lines of that of Corelli and is by some thought to equal or even surpass that in value.

(2) GIUSEPPE CLEMENS FERDINAND DALL'. Born at Brussels in 1709 and died at Verona in 1805, aged ninety-six. He was son of the preceding, and a fine cellist and composer of string music, including 29 cello sonatas.

ABANDONNÉ (Fr.). 'Relaxed' (in such an expression as *Un rhythme un peu abandonné*).

ABBANDONO (It.). 'Abandon', i.e. free, impassioned style. So the adverb, *Abbandonatamente*, etc.

ABBASSARE (It.). To lower, e.g. to tune down a string of an instrument of the violin family, so as to obtain a note normally out of the compass.

ABBELLIMENTI (It.). Literally 'embellishments'. See *Ornaments and Graces*; also Tables 12–16.

ABBOT, GEORGE (1562–1633). Archbishop of Canterbury. See reference under *Church Music* 4.

A.B.C.M. See *Degrees and Diplomas* 2.

ABDÄMPFEN (Ger.). 'To damp off', i.e. to mute.

ABDOMINAL BREATHING. See *Voice* 3, 21.

ABDUCTION FROM THE SERAGLIO

(Mozart). Produced at Vienna in 1782. Libretto by Stephanie, adapted from Bretzner's *Belmont and Constance*.[1]

ACT I
SCENE: *The Garden of Selim's Palace*

We are to know that Constance, a Spanish lady, has been carried off, with her lively English maid, Blonda,[2] to the palace of a Turkish Pasha, Selim, who hopes the lady may come to love him. She, however, loves Belmont, whose servant, Pedrillo, loves Blonda. The two men are seeking their opportunity to run off with the ladies.

Belmont (*Tenor*) sings of his love. He cautiously tries Selim's overseer, Osmin (*Bass*), but gets little out of the suspicious guardian of the palace. Pedrillo (*Tenor*) in turn is introduced. He has obtained a post under the Pasha, and proposes to get Belmont into the palace under pretence of his being an architect.

Now Selim (*speaking part*) brings in Constance (*Soprano*), asking why she is sad. Belmont is introduced, and Selim welcomes him, but Osmin is doubtful.

ACT II
SCENE: *The Garden*

The maid Blonda (*Soprano*) is wooed, but is not to be won, by Osmin. When they have gone out, the Pasha, becoming impatient, threatens Constance with torture if she will not marry him. Once more the stage is clear, and Pedrillo whispers to Blonda of a midnight rescue. After several airs have been sung, Pedrillo proceeds to make Osmin drunk, and packs him off to bed, leaving the stage for the two pairs of lovers, who join in a quartet.

ACT III
SCENE 1: *An Open Space before the Palace, with a View of the Sea. Night*

Belmont and Pedrillo appear, ready for the escape. As Constance is about to flee with Blonda, Osmin, who has been warned by a Negro mute, intercepts them, and, in a scene of excitement, guards arrest the two pairs of lovers. Osmin sings a song of triumph.

[1] Original language of the opera is German—*Die Entführung aus dem Serail*.
[2] Or 'Blondina' in some translations (in original, 'Blöndchen').

SCENE 2: *The Pasha's Apartment*

The would-be escapers are brought before the Pasha, who, finding that Belmont is the son of his bitter enemy, sentences him to torture. The lovers' grief, however, moves him to relent. He magnanimously declares that he will not treat an enemy of his as he was treated by Belmont's father; and so he sets the four free. In the finale the lovers sing the Pasha's praises, while Osmin grumbles at his clemency.

See also *Arrangements*; *Copyists*.

ABEL, KARL FRIEDRICH (p. 1073, pl. 178. 6). Born at Cöthen in 1723 and died in London in 1787, aged sixty-three. After a boyhood under Bach in the Thomas School, Leipzig, and some years at Dresden in the opera orchestra of Hasse, he brought to London the high musicianship thus acquired, with an unusual skill as a player of the gamba, and there remained, associating much with Bach's son, John Christian (q.v.), and taking part in all the very active musical life of the court and capital at this brilliant period. He wrote chamber-music and symphonies, and, especially, much music for his own special instrument, of which he was the last great player. J. S. Bach was godfather to one of his children.

See *Concert* 8; *Pianoforte* 5; *Gainsborough*; *Saltbox*.

ABEND (Ger.). 'Evening.'

ABENDLIED (Ger.). 'Evening Song.'

ABENDMUSIKEN. See *Concert* 13.

ABER (Ger.). 'But.'

ABERDEEN. See *Scotland* 4, 6, 8; *Presbyterian* 4.

ABERDEEN CANTUS. See *Scotland* 8.

ABGESTOSSEN (Ger.). See *Abstossen*.

ABILITÀ, ARIA D'. See *Aria* 5.

ABINGDON, HENRY. See *Abyngdon*.

AB INITIO (Lat.). 'From the beginning.'

ABLÖSEN (Ger.). 'To loosen from one another', etc. There are various applications, e.g. to separate the notes (i.e. play staccato), to take the finger off.

ABNEHMEND (Ger.). 'Off-taking' (of tone), i.e. diminuendo.

ABRAHAM, GERALD ERNEST HEAL. Born at Newport, Isle of Wight, in 1904. He is chiefly self-taught in music. From 1935 to 1947 and from 1962 to 1967 he served in various capacities on the staff of the British Broadcasting Corporation and its journals, in the interim serving as the first Professor of Music in the University of Liverpool. He has written or edited a large number of books, covering a wide range of subjects but especially on Russian composers.

ABRUPT CADENCE. See *Cadence*.

ABRUZZESE (It.). A song or dance in the style of the Abruzzi district, to the east of Rome.

ABSCHIEDSSYMPHONIE (Haydn). See *Nick-named Compositions* 11.

ABSENT-MINDED MAN SYMPHONY (Haydn). See *Nicknamed Compositions* 11 (60).

ABSETZEN (Ger.). Same sense as *Ablösen* (q.v.).

ABSIL, JEAN. Born at Péruwelz, in Hainault, Belgium, in 1893. He was trained at the Conservatory of Brussels, and later (1923–58) was head of that of Etterbeck, a suburb of Brussels. He is a prolific composer of the atonal school and exploits unusual rhythmic devices such as the use of varying bars of two-and-three-quarter beats, five-and-a-half beats, etc. His list of works includes much chamber music, orchestral music, etc., and also choral music and songs.

A.B.S.M.; A.B.S.M. (T.T.D.). See *Degrees and Diplomas* 2.

ABSOLUTE MUSIC. This term exists as the antithesis to 'Programme Music' (q.v.), i.e. as a label for all that large class of music which has been composed *simply as music*, without any attempt to represent the sounds of nature or of human life, or to follow out a scheme of emotions dictated by a poem, a picture, etc. Thus the most part of the world's music comes under the description of 'Absolute'.

See also *Programme Music* 2; *Composition* 5.

ABSOLUTE PITCH, SENSE OF. By this is meant the faculty which many people possess of immediately singing any note asked for, or of immediately recognizing any note heard. It is really a form of memory; the possessor of the faculty retains in his mind (consciously or unconsciously) the pitch of some instrument to which he is, or has been in earlier life, accustomed, and instinctively relates to that every musical sound he hears. But it is a peculiar form of memory, because it is so multiple. To remember any one note, say A or C, might not be thought difficult (many violinists, from constantly tuning to A, come to remember that note at the pitch which they are accustomed to use); but to be able to sound, without reflection, any note within the compass of the voice, or to identify any note within the compass of the ear, is a striking example of the perfection to which human memory can attain —the more so as the perfection is often attained in very early years.

Mozart at the age of seven possessed this sense:

'He had, on a certain occasion, played the violin of his friend Schachtner, which was so great a favourite with him on account of its soft, smooth tone, that his usual name for it was "the butter fiddle". Some days after, Schachtner, on entering the house, found the boy amusing himself with his own little violin. "What have you done with your butter fiddle?" said he, and continued to play, but on a sudden he stopped, pondered awhile, and then added, "If you have not altered the tuning of your violin since I last played upon it, it is a half a quarter of a tone flatter than mine here". At this unusual exactitude of ear and memory there was at first a laugh, but the father thought proper to have the violin sent for and examined, and the result proved that the boy was perfectly correct.'

There are obvious reasons to distrust the exactitude of the details of this well-known incident as they have come down to us: to mention only one, not a single string on Schachtner's violin could be depended upon to stand for 'some days' accurate to so small an interval as an eighth of a tone, and any difference of temperature would affect it slightly. The main value of the anecdote lies, then, in the fact that in the highly professional musical circle around the Mozart family it was evidently recognized that the child did possess an absolute-pitch ear sensitive to very small differences.

Ouseley (q.v.) was all his life remarkable for his sense of absolute pitch. At five he was able to remark, 'Only think, papa blows his nose on G'. He would say that it thundered in G or that the wind was whistling in D, or that the clock (with a two-note chime) struck in B minor, and when the assertion was tested it would invariably be found correct. At eight, at a Philharmonic Concert he contended that Mozart's Symphony in G minor was really in A flat minor, and on inquiring it was found that, the great heat having sharpened the wind-instruments, the strings had been told to tune up a semitone. In later life, being asked the number of a house, he replied that he could not remember, but gave the pitch of the door-scraper as a means of recognizing it. At his college of St. Michael's, Tenbury, the organ breaking down during a service and a harmonium having to be brought in, he continued his intoning whilst it was being brought, imperceptibly changing the pitch to what he remembered to be that of the harmonium, and on this at last joining in he proved to be perfectly accurate.

Leslie, conductor of the once famous Leslie's Choir, of London, had an assistant, J. C. Ward, to whom he would say, at the end of the rehearsal of an unaccompanied piece, 'They have dropped in pitch; please give them the note'. Ward would then sing the note, perhaps a third of a tone higher, and this without an instrument.

It appears as though birds have something approaching the sense of absolute pitch. At all events, the pitch of their calls varies little; it may be that they are guided by muscular feeling—the tension of their vocal cords— though in that case it seems odd that human beings do not seem to be able to make use of such guidance. Sir James Swinburne, F.R.S., tested with a tuning-fork a parrot that had been taught a number of scraps of themes from Beethoven and found that it always whistled each tune at approximately its proper pitch, until one day, put out in the sun, it burst out into a riot of pieces from its repertory at all sorts of pitches. (See *Bird Music*.)

Sir Herbert Oakeley, Professor of Music at Edinburgh University, possessed the sense of absolute pitch. On the respectable testimony of a bishop, the following may be quoted: 'When he was staying with us at High Wych

the pig squeaked. He at once cried "G sharp". Some one ran to the piano—and G sharp it was.' (There are, however, probably thousands of living musicians who could emulate this feat.) Broadwood's pianos, in Oakeley's child-hood, were tuned to A = 432; 'He used to say that his ear retained that pitch throughout life, and that compositions early known to him always sounded unlike themselves when ren-dered at the higher pitch used in England from 1840 to 1890.'

This last statement illustrates the occasional disadvantage of what is otherwise a very desir-able possession. A vocalist endowed with the sense of absolute pitch can obviously read at first sight any music whatever, with complete accuracy as to pitch—provided that the pitch of the instrument to which he is to sing it is the one to which he is accustomed; otherwise (unless he possesses a power of adjustment, which many do not) he has consciously to transpose every note he sings. Instrumentalists sometimes suffer in the same way. Of the great Belgian violinist, César Thomson, it was com-plained in 1900, by one of his English pupils, that he had never yet been heard at his best in London, as he was 'so much embarrassed by our English pitch' (the effect of the high pitch on the instrument may, however, have been one factor here). MacDowell, a most able pianist, playing on one occasion the so-called 'Moon-light' Sonata (which 'every schoolgirl plays'), got through it with the greatest difficulty; the piano being at a pitch to which he was not accustomed, he experienced the distress of playing the piece in one key and hearing it in another, which, he said, 'nearly knocked me out'. Sir Walter Parratt, whose ear and musical memory were remarkable, was in similar diffi-culties when accompanying on a low-pitched spinet a Corelli violin sonata (relatively a very simple piece to play); here the difficulty was, probably, the conflict between what the eye saw and hands performed, and what the ear received.

A curious faculty is reported by certain string players or persons especially interested in string playing. On hearing for the first time a piece for (say) violin alone, they will be able to recognize the ostensible key of the piece and yet, at the same time, to remark that the tuning of the instrument is such that, in effect, it is not being *heard* in that key. For example, the remark may be, 'I don't know that piece he's playing, but it's in A flat and he's playing it in A'. The fact seems to be that the open notes of a stringed instrument are, by sensitive ears, unconsciously recognized as such. Thus the re-cognition in question is a double one; the obser-ver first subconsciously realizes that the open notes are below or above the pitch he regards as normal, that the instrument is therefore mistuned, and then, recognizing the key of the music as played, allows for the mistuning.

Something similar has been observed occa-sionally as regards pianoforte playing: the explanation here is possibly that a few keen-eared persons have unconsciously acquired the knack of observing slight dynamic variations of certain notes in the various keys, owing to the differing action of the fingers on the long (white) and short (black) finger-keys. (It does not appear that the organ lends itself to this sort of observation, the dynamics of performance on that instrument being unaffected by finger action. However, further investigation should be made.)

The possession of the sense of absolute pitch by no means invariably accompanies general high musical capacity; Schumann and Wagner, for example, lacked it. Whilst it may probably be taken that any one possessing it is potentially a good musician, there are, on the other hand, many good musicians who either do not possess it or who have only gradually come to possess it, or who, curiously, find that they possess it in a measure on one day yet not on another.

It is common now in children's singing-classes to try to give the pupils at least an A or a C, as a memorized standard of pitch, and this can often be achieved by constantly sounding the note. Just as any one can learn to know the time (within, say, ten minutes) by the habit of never looking at his watch before first making a guess at the time, and then checking the guess, so one can probably pretty well acquire 'absolute pitch' for at least an A or a C by never passing one's piano without singing what one imagines to be that note and then checking it.

It may be observed that the term 'absolute pitch' is, strictly speaking, a misnomer. The possessor of the faculty relates what he hears to an arbitrary standard, using a conventional series of alphabetical descriptions. The only truly 'absolute' pitch designation possible is by mention of the number of vibrations per second. An 'A' or 'C' designation means nothing definite until we are told to what vibrational number the person speaking is accustomed to attach that designation.

But the term 'absolute pitch' is quite reasonably used in the sense in which it has been used in this article; the term is used in that sense in antithesis to 'relative pitch', by which we ordinarily mean the pitch of a note in relation to the keynote of the key in use at the moment. Thus the absolute pitch of a note sounded may be A, B, or C, etc., and if other notes of a diatonic scale are then sounded, so as to establish a key, the note in question acquires also 'relative' pitch as the tonic or dominant (doh or soh), etc. of that key.

This is the ordinary sense of the terms 'absolute pitch' and 'relative pitch' amongst musicians—as distinct from physicists, to whom 'absolute pitch' means what it literally implies, i.e. the pitch of a sound without consideration of any standards such as instruments, the tuning of which has varied widely at different epochs and even today varies with different individual specimens (see *Pitch* and consult also the article *Colour and Music*, especially sections 4 and 5.)

It is curious to reflect that there is a sense in which every one who can tell one vowel from another possesses a form of absolute pitch—in the physicists' meaning of the term (see *Voice* 7).

ABSTOSSEN (Ger.). 'To detach notes from one another', i.e. to play staccato. (*Abgestossen* is the past participle.) Also, in organ playing, to cease to use a stop.

ABSTRACT MUSIC. Same as *Absolute Music* (q.v.). But as German writers use the term (*Abstrakte Musik*) it has a different meaning—music lacking in sensitiveness, 'dry' music, 'academic' music, or, at all events, music which has no connexion with feeling.

ABT, FRANZ WILHELM. Born near Leipzig in 1819 and died at Wiesbaden in 1885, aged sixty-five. He was a choral and operatic conductor, who wrote 'When the swallows homeward fly', and some hundreds of other songs and part-songs—not deep, but gracefully flowing.

See references under *Ear and Hearing* 4.

ABWECHSELN, ABZUWECHSELN (Ger.; various terminations according to person, case, etc.). 'To exchange.' Used of one instrument alternating with another in the hands of the same player, etc.

ABYNGDON (Abingdon, Habyngton, etc.), HENRY (*c.* 1420–97). He was a singer and organist and a composer—none of whose works have been preserved. Amongst a number of positions he held were those of Precentor of Wells Cathedral and Master of the Children of the Chapel Royal. He was the first person known to have taken a degree in music at Cambridge—or indeed anywhere (B.Mus. 1464). Sir Thomas More wrote in praise of him.

ACADEMY. See *Concert* 2. Also for Academy of Ancient Music and Academy of Vocal Music, *Concert* 6; for Academy of Floral Games, *Minstrels* 6. (See, too, *Schools*.)

A CAPELLA, A CAPPELLA. See *Cappella*.

ACCADEMIA. See *Concerts* 2.

ACCAREZZEVOLE, ACCAREZZEVOL-MENTE (It.). 'Caressing', 'caressingly'.

ACCELERANDO, ACCELERATO (It.). 'Accelerating', 'accelerated', i.e. getting gradually quicker. See reference under *Rubato* 1.

ACCENT. (1) For discussion of the subject in its commoner sense see *Rhythm*. It may be added that the Dynamic Accent is an important element in expression. But it feels natural, in addition to marking the periodic accent (to which in music from the seventeenth century onwards the position of the bar-lines is a guide), slightly to accentuate anything irregular (on the principle of 'grasping the nettle'); thus syncopated notes and strong discords are generally accented (see *Agogic*). It would obviously be impossible for a composer to mark all the notes that should receive such a stress, and even if he did this he could not show the *degree* of stress he desired. In this and similar matters Beethoven puts himself into the hands of the player much as Shakespeare puts himself into the hands of the actor, but we have the useful general information, derived from some of Beethoven's associates, that it was his custom to accent suspensions (see *Harmony* 24 k) particularly strongly, especially the pungent one of the minor ninth—'more emphatically than any player I ever heard', says Schindler, who adds, 'This gave his playing a great pregnancy'.

(2) The term 'Accent' is also applied to the simplest forms of plainsong tones, such as those used for the Epistle, Prophecy, and Gospel: they are very slightly inflected monotones.

ACCENTO (It.). 'Accent' (see *Accent* 1 above). So *Accentato*, 'accented'.

ACCENTUÉ (Fr.). 'Accented.'

ACCENTUS. The part of the Roman Catholic liturgy which is chanted only by the priest or his representative, as distinct from the *Concentus*, which is chanted by the congregation or choir.

See *Gradual* 1; *Chorale*.

ACCIACCATO (It.). 'Broken down', 'crushed' (e.g. of a hat), hence the notes of a chord sounded not quite simultaneously, but from the bottom to top. ('Vehement', 'violent', 'forcible', are translations given in some musical works of reference, but there does not seem warrant for this.)

ACCIACCATURA. See Table 12.

ACCIAIO, ISTRUMENTO D'. 'Instrument of steel.' Mozart's name for his Glockenspiel in *The Magic Flute*.

See *Percussion Family* 4 e, 5 c.

ACCIDENTAL. The sign indicating a departure from the key-signature, by the momentary raising or lowering of a note by means of sharp, flat, double-sharp, double-flat, or natural. The sign holds good for that note (in that octave) throughout the measure in which it occurs, unless expressly contradicted by another sign—though some composers, doubtful of the performer's memory, reinsert it in brackets in particular passages.

A.C.C.O. 'Associate of the Canadian College of Organists.'

ACCOMPAGNATO (It.). 'Accompanied.'

ACCOMPANIED CANON. See *Canon*.

ACCOMPANIED FUGUE. See *Form* 12 g.

ACCOMPANIMENT. The term as colloquially used today implies the presence of some principal performer (vocalist, violinist, etc.), more or less subserviently supplied with a background by some other performer or performers (pianist, orchestra, etc.).

This is not the original use of the word, an illustration of which we see in Samuel Wesley's speaking of Bach's '*Six Sonatas for harpsichord with an obbligato violin accompaniment*', which would be more likely to be described today by a reversal of the terms, i.e. 'for *violin with harpsichord accompaniment*', or (much better) by a suggestion of equality, 'for *violin and harpsichord*'. The title-pages of the music of the eighteenth and early nineteenth centuries largely conform to Wesley's usage, no subservience being then implied by the word 'accompaniment'.

It is clear that during the nineteenth century the word 'accompaniment' shifted in significance: this was probably due to the growth of importance of the instrumental virtuoso. Yet, paradoxically, the same period saw an enormous growth of importance in the piano parts of songs (Schubert, Schumann, Brahms, Wolf, etc.), which came to demand, in many cases, as great technical and artistic ability on the part of the pianist as on that of the vocalist.

Many famous vocalists are very remiss in their treatment of their accompanists, demanding an undue artistic deference, a too limited body of piano tone, and so forth. Undoubtedly there exist very many songs in which the role of the pianist is relatively unimportant (whence the common nineteenth-century idea of less gifted young ladies learning the piano 'sufficiently to play accompaniments'), but in other cases the pianist should insist on his right, or, more tactfully put, the vocalist should insist on giving him his rights, i.e. his name should appear prominently on the programme, he should take it for granted that he is included in any applause of the audience and act accordingly, and so forth. (As to fees, here economic principles enter; there are far more good accompanists than good vocalists, and the market for an overstocked article never shows such high prices as that for an understocked one.)

The false idea of the general public as to song-accompaniment during the first quarter of the twentieth century was strikingly brought home to the present writer when for some years he served as the first Music Critic to the British Broadcasting Corporation. It was his constant complaint that he could barely hear the piano accompaniments of broadcast songs (possibly from a bad position of the microphone in those experimental years), yet he weekly received many letters from listeners complaining that all the accompanists played too loudly; it would appear that at that period (and the fact is perhaps worth putting on historical record) there were thousands of listeners who, if they became consciously aware of the existence of the accompanist, instead of merely subconsciously accepting that existence, at once felt uncomfortable; this may have sprung from the inability of a naïve new public to listen to two things at one time, so that, if both were heard, one became registered as a distraction from attention to the other, or it may illustrate some more deeply rooted feeling.

The principles of accompanimental playing need hardly be discussed here. They are, essentially, no different from those of ensemble-playing in general. In all ensemble-playing

C

some one player is, at given moments, more important than the other or others, and thus, during those moments, legitimately takes more of the limelight; and this is so in song accompaniment, where, however, the fact that the voice is the sole carrier of the words, which are intended to be heard by the audience, constitutes, admittedly, a demand for a slightly larger share of the limelight, and this usually somewhat more continuously, than (say) a violinist can claim in a violin and piano sonata.

For Hymn Accompaniment see *Hymns and Hymn Tunes* 9.
For Plainsong Accompaniment see *Plainsong* 5.
For what are called 'Additional Accompaniments' see article under that head.

ACCOPPIARE (It.). 'To couple' (organ). Hence *Accoppiato*, 'coupled'; *Accoppiamento*, 'coupling' (the noun).

ACCORD (Fr.). (1) 'Chord'; (2) 'tuning'.

ACCORDARE (It.). 'To tune' (see below for past participle).

ACCORDATO, ACCORDATI (It., masc. sing., plur.); **ACCORDATA, ACCORDATE** (It., fem. sing., plur.). 'Tuned.' (The word is sometimes seen as a part of some expression indicating that a particular tuning is required, e.g. of the kettle-drums.)

ACCORDATURA (It.). 'Tuning.'

ACCORDEON. See *Reed-Organ Family* 4.

ACCORDER (Fr.). 'To tune.' Hence *Accordé*, 'tuned'.

ACCORDION. See *Reed-Organ Family* 4.

ACCORDO (It.). 'Chord.'

ACCOUPLER (Fr.). 'To couple' (organ). So *Accouplé*, 'coupled'; *Accouplement*, 'coupling' (noun), 'coupler'; *Accouplez*, 'couple' (imperative).

ACCUSÉ, ACCUSÉE (Fr., masc., fem.). Used with a musical significance, this means 'emphasized'.

ACHRON (Akhron, etc.).
(1) JOSEPH. Born at Lozdzieje, Lithuania, in 1886 and died in Los Angeles in 1943, aged fifty-six. He was a youthful prodigy of the violin and in early manhood continued his success as a performer, meantime composing and also interesting himself in the folk-music of the Jewish race to which he belonged. Approaching the age of forty, he settled in New York, and later he moved to Hollywood.

He composed orchestral, choral, chamber, and stage music, often with a Hebrew literary background or influenced by the idioms of Hebrew melody.

See *Concerto* 6 c (1886).

(2) ISIDOR. Born at Warsaw in 1892 and died in New York in 1948, aged fifty-five. Brother of the above. He was a pianist and composer. He settled in the United States in 1922.

ACHT (Ger.). 'Eight.' Also 'care'.

ACHTEL or **ACHTELNOTE.** German for 'eighth' or eighth-note, i.e. Quaver (Table 3); so *Achtelpause* for the corresponding rest. *Achtstimmig*, in eight voices or parts.

ACOUSTIC BASS ON ORGAN. See *Acoustics* 10.

ACOUSTICS

(See illustrations, p. 16, plate **1**.)

The following article has been kept as non-technical as is possible with such a complicated subject, and some of the simplifications may not be acceptable to all modern specialists. Scientific definitions of the terms used will be found, with many others, in the pamphlets on Standard Acoustical Terminology issued by the British and American Standards Associations.

1. Introductory. The word 'acoustics' properly means anything pertaining to the sense of hearing, but is used in two chief ways: first, as signifying the corpus of fact and theory concerning the properties, production, and transmission of sound, and, second, as signifying the suitability of a building for the hearing of speech or music. Thus we speak of 'the science of acoustics' and likewise of 'the acoustics of' such and such a concert-hall.

The latter aspect is merely incidentally considered in the following article and is more fully treated in the article *Concert Halls and other Buildings for Music*.

2. The Nature of Sound. The popular conception of sound as a *thing* is hardly correct. It is true that sound can be considered objectively, but for the purposes of such an article as the present the subjective aspect is the truer. From this aspect sound is a sensation. Some object is by some agency thrown into a state of vibration; it communicates its vibrations to the surrounding air; the vibrations impinge upon the ear-drum of a human or other animal and set up a nervous disturbance there which we call 'sound'. From this point of view, then, there is 'sound' only where there is an ear; a brass band of stone-deaf players (if the imagination can fly so high), in a deaf and dumb asylum where only the patients were present, would produce no 'sound'.

Looked at in this way, sound is created in the brain; and brains, of course, differ greatly in their ability to experience the sensation, or, as we more popularly say, to 'perceive' sound in its varying pitches, intensities, and qualities. Amongst any considerable group of people walking in the country on an evening when the crickets are chirping will generally be found one who cannot hear them, his ear not being able to receive such 'high' sounds; for him, the cricket is a silent creature. Sir Francis Galton constructed a dog-whistle the sound of which was inaudible to human beings, though dogs heard it perfectly and obeyed it. Objectively considered, sound existed; subjectively considered, sound existed in the dog world but not in the world of humans. (Cf. *Ear and Hearing* 4.)

The fact that sound is the effect of vibration is demonstrable by all manner of phenomena. The vibration of a tuning-fork can be felt by the finger, and even seen. The explosion of a powder-magazine produces air-waves which not only cause a loud sound but smash the windows of every house for miles around, and may so damage human ears as to cause temporary or permanent deafness. Some Alpine guides, passing under a dangerously poised mass of snow, will avoid speech or confine it to the softest whisper lest they should set up vibrations that would detach it. A booming organ-pipe may shake the church windows;[1] a shrill violin tone has been known to break a glass; vocalists have been known to possess destructive powers, e.g. D. G. Morhof published at Kiel in 1672 (several editions in later years) a book on an Amsterdam tavern-keeper who could vocally shatter twenty-five glasses in thirty minutes, and other writers then produced books discussing the subject. (See also 20.)

3. The Pitch of Sound is determined by the frequency of the vibrations of the original sound-producing body and, hence, of the transmitting air. Slowly-succeeding vibrations cause what we call 'low' sounds; rapidly-succeeding ones what we call 'high' sounds.

The fact that frequency of vibration conditions pitch is demonstrable in many simple ways. The writer is at the moment of compiling this article sitting at a desk of oak, a wood the surface of which is marked by a perceptible and regular 'grain'. Running his thumb-nail slowly over this wood, he produces less frequent vibration, running it quickly, more frequent vibration: in the first instance he finds he produces a low-pitched sound, in the second instance a high-pitched one. The same experiment can be conveniently carried out by running the nail over a piece of ribbed cloth or ribbon. An increase of speed in the turntable of a gramophone necessarily leads to a greater frequency of the vibrations communicated by the grooves on the surface of the disk waggling the needle; consequently, pitch is raised.

Any particular body capable of being set in vibration has its own natural 'frequency' of vibration, depending on such factors as size, density and tension. A violin-string, if long, or thick, or heavy in proportion to the pull on it, will vibrate more slowly than one which is short, or thin, or light in proportion to the pull on it; hence the first string will give a lower sound than the second.

Length is the first factor that occurs to the mind as determining pitch, but these other factors are equally influential. If piano-wires were all of the same diameter, density, and tension the lowest note of some instruments would require a wire of about 30 feet long; to avoid this inconvenience, the wires of the bass notes are thicker than those of the treble, and are loaded with a coiled surrounding wire; thus a short wire is made to do the work of a long one.

4. The Intensity of Sound. Where the vibrations of the generating agent of a note are extensive, we get an intense sound; where the vibrations of the generating agent of that same note are small, we get a slight one. Whereas *frequency* of vibration determines pitch, *amplitude* of vibration is the principal factor which determines loudness. Pluck a violin-string gently and you see it vibrate (say) one-sixteenth of an inch on each side of its normal straight line, pluck it more violently and you see it vibrate (say) one-eighth of an inch on each side of that line. In the first instance the sound is softer, in the second instance louder; the pitch, however, remains the same.

Here a passing explanation may be added, to remove a possible confusion in the mind of a young reader. The string has its own rate of vibration (dependent, as already explained, upon its length, thickness, density, and tension) and this rate is not affected by the varying extent or 'amplitude' of the vibrations. If you pluck it slightly it will make a certain number of slight vibrations per second; if you pluck it violently it will make *the same number* of vibrations per second, but the vibrations will be wider.

Similarly (within limits) a pendulum or a swing will make the same number of backward and forward movements per given unit of time, whether the extent of the displacement be great or small. Try the experiment with a garden swing; with a good push you send it high, with a lesser push you send it not so high. On the first occasion it travels quickly, on the second it travels slowly; consequently the time occupied by a complete forth-and-back motion is the same on both occasions, only the 'amplitude' varying. If a garden swing were rapid enough in its motion to produce an

[1] *Lincoln Cathedral*. On account of the precarious condition of the East window, and indeed of the whole of that part of the building, vibration of any sort must be reduced to the minimum. Messrs. Henry Willis have therefore been instructed to put out of action the two 32-ft. stops. The organ will hence lose the majestic effect of these fine stops until the East end has been restored' (*Musical Times*, July 1936).

audible note, that note would be always the same for a given swing, and if the swing were given a good initial impulse and then left to itself it would sound a loud note that would then progressively die away until the swing came to a state of rest, the pitch of the note sounded, however, remaining the same.

So with the string, reed, tube, or stretched membrane of a stringed, wind, or percussion instrument: so long as these various vibrating agents remain of the same vibrating size and tension the note remains constant, but, by greater or less force in setting them in vibration, greater or less tone is obtained. On the violin, to raise the pitch of a note we increase the tension of the string by turning the peg, or we shorten the string by the pressure of a finger. To alter the pitch of a trombone we lengthen or shorten its working length by pulling out or pushing in its sliding tube. To alter the pitch of a kettledrum we tighten or loosen the membrane. But we do not alter the pitch by bowing the violin-string a little more violently, or by banging the drum harder.

Pitch and loudness, then, are distinct, the former dependent on the speed, or 'frequency', of the vibrations, the latter on the extent of the vibrations. Pitch cannot be controlled without changing the *condition* of the sounding-agent itself; intensity can be controlled at will by applying more or less force of bow, breath, or bang, and so changing its *movement*.

5. The Vibrating Agencies of Various Instruments. These are as follows:

(a) Strings, in such instruments as the piano, violin, guitar, etc.

(b) Reeds acted on by air, as in harmonium, concertina, oboe, clarinet, reed pipes of organs, etc.

(c) Elastic membranes acted on by air, as in the human voice and in such instruments as the horn and trumpet, where the lips applied to a mouthpiece are the original vibrating agent, but communicate their vibrations to a column of air in a tube which produces the actual sounds and determines their pitch.

(d) Air columns set in vibration by a puff impinging on a sharp edge, as in the flute and also the flue stops of the organ.

In the flute, etc., the column of air in the tube is set in vibration by an 'edge-tone' formed at the mouth-hole by the player's breath striking the edge of the hole, and the fingers applied to side-holes affect the working length of this, so controlling pitch.

In the oboe, etc., the pressure of the breath sets in vibration the reed, which is the sounding-agent; the column of air in the tube then acts as a mere resonator (see 20 a). In both cases the fingers applied to holes affect the working length of this, which then, on its part, 'works back', setting up a control of the speed of vibration of the reed and so determining the pitch.

The principle of the 'resonator-control' of reed instruments has, however, some limits. A reed may be so designed as to be masterful or obedient. An oboe or clarinet reed is obedient; its rate of vibrations is controlled by the resonance of the tube. An organ reed (made of metal) is more masterful and hence can be tuned, within limits, by the use of a tuning-wire that shortens or lengthens its vibratory length (beyond these limits, however, the resonating tube will not give its consent and the pipe ceases to speak). One could also tune within wide limits (if the method were practicable) by altering the resonating length of the tube, and within those limits the reed would be obedient to the tube. Thus in the case of an organ reed pipe there is 'give and take' or 'mixed control'.

6. The Quality of Sound. Almost all vibrations are compound. Imagine a vibrating string: it is vibrating as a whole, and this is what catches the eye, but its two halves are vibrating independently, and so are other portions of its length. The conception may be a little difficult to the reader, but if he will recall an often-seen phenomenon in water-waves it will become easier—a series of big, rolling waves, each in its turn a sub-series of ripples (not a perfect analogy, but serving the present purpose).

Thus a string in motion produces, from its whole-length vibrations, a sound which we call the 'fundamental note' of the string, and this is what the ear most strongly seizes upon; but, at the same time, from the various portions of the length it produces a considerable number of higher sounds, a few of which can be detected by an attentive and trained ear. And so also with the column of air in a wind instrument, which constitutes *its* chief vibrating agent.

It is the presence or absence of (or greater or lesser strength of) particular individuals amongst these higher sounds (called 'harmonics', 'overtones', or 'upper partials') that determines the character, 'quality', or 'timbre' of a sound. This is, at any rate, the old and still commonly accepted theory. It may be called a 'relative pitch theory' of timbre, that is to say, according to it, if an instrument produces a number of notes, all of the same timbre, the harmonics responsible are always *numerically the same in relation to whatever note is in question* (see music-type in diagram section 8). There is also, however, an 'absolute pitch theory' according to which the group of harmonics responsible for any particular timbre (this group being called the 'formant'), consists unvaryingly of *all those within a certain fixed range of pitch, whatever the note in question*. (This latter theory somewhat resembles that explaining the production of vowel-sounds in speech and song, as laid down under *Voice*.) It seems probable that both theories are correct but neither complete in itself—that relative-pitch harmonics and absolute-pitch harmonics combine in the determination of timbre.

For a further treatment of harmonics see 8 below, and for what may be called the modern synthetic production of the harmonics needed for the achievement of any desired timbre see *Electric Musical Instruments*, passim.

It may be pointed out that in discussing pitch, intensity, and quality we have discussed every one of the factors by which single sounds can differ from one another, so that at this point we reach the end of a distinct division in the discussion of our subject.

7. Transient Tones. These are the short-lived sounds which precede and follow the 'steady-state' note of a musical instrument. (In the voice, consonants are transient sounds, while the vowels represent 'steady-state'.) Of late years it has been recognized that the duration and type of transient sounds, particularly at the onset of vibration, are very important for the recognition of musical instruments. Thus in a certain part of their range the steady sounds of the violin and the oboe are practically indistinguishable, but they have different 'starting noises', due to the action of the bow and the reed respectively. On some instruments, e.g. the reed organ pipe, the quality of the transient is the same as that of the steady note and it is only the intensity that changes; on others, e.g. the flue pipe, analysis shows that the timbre is different, e.g. the octave may appear before the fundamental and, perhaps, die out later as the final timbre is reached.

The absence of transients in the timbre of certain electrophonic organs, the manner in which the notes come 'on speech' with a 'plop', is a source of criticism by organists accustomed to the pipe organ. This can be met by adding circuits which produce a transient build-up of timbre, as, among others, Midgley has done in the Midgley–Walker organ.

See also *Electric Musical Instruments* 4.

8. Harmonics, Overtones, Upper Partials. Any note, as produced by any of the instruments, is accompanied by a varying number of attendant notes, called 'harmonics', 'overtones', or 'upper partials' (these words, though often used as synonyms, are not quite strictly so—see *Partials*). Thus the note C may be accompanied by the C next above, the G above that, the C above that, the E above that, and so on, the intervals between the notes getting smaller as the series ascends to infinity, and the sounds themselves getting fainter until they fade into silence. Taking the note G as the 'fundamental note' of a tube or string, the *Harmonic Series* (carried to a reasonable height) would be:

Not all of these are perfectly in tune, however, according to any scale in actual use.

It will be noted that the numbers of the recurrences of the fundamental note (also called the 'First Harmonic') are 1, 2, 4, 8, 16, etc., i.e. the initial number doubling itself continually up the series; this is so with any other notes (e.g. the D's run, 3, 6, 12, etc.), nature being very mathematical.

It should be understood that although the various harmonics are here shown successively they are heard simultaneously.

The untrained ear does not usually detect any of these overtones or harmonics, though when a bell is heard some of them can readily be seized, and if it is a bad bell a confused jangle of incompatible overtones is heard (the overtones of a bell are, in any case, not altogether normal). When a bell is 'rung' in a peal the overtones are much more prominent than the prime tone or 'hum note'. In any case, they have their effect in colouring the tone, according to the principles explained under 6. (For 'hum notes' see *Bell* 1.)

Whilst the harmonics are normally heard merely as constituents of what the ear accepts as a single tone, they can also be separately produced. By a certain method of blowing, a brass tube which ordinarily produces a certain C can be made to produce, instead, the octave of that C or a note an octave-plus-fifth above that C, as desired. And so with the other harmonics.

Similarly, by lightly touching a stretched string in its centre, or at a third of its length, the octave above, or a note an octave-plus-fifth above, can be obtained; the touch of the finger prevents the vibration of the whole but permits the vibration of the parts, and so the fundamental tone is in abeyance whilst the harmonics remain obtainable.

The above general principle is that by which all **Brass Instruments** produce their different notes (see *Brass*). Formerly a horn or a trumpet was a simple tube (for a very early example see *Scandinavia* 2) and the only notes that could be obtained from it were its natural harmonics—necessarily with large gaps in the lower stretches (i.e. the region near the fundamental tone) and smaller gaps in the higher stretches (this is exactly the position of the common military bugle and the coaching-horn today, the limitation of whose 'tunes' will be readily recalled). Then different **Crooks** or **Shanks**[1] were provided which the player could insert in his instrument, so lengthening his tube and providing him with another fundamental tone and, consequently, another series of harmonics. But crooks and shanks could not be quickly changed, and it will be found by a glance at the scores of Haydn and Mozart (for instance) that in their days, with 'natural' trumpets and horns, composers could not write for them a varied 'tune', but were much restricted to loud passages where the one or two chief chords of the composition were in use, which chords consist mostly of

[1] *Crook*, a curved piece of tube; *Shank*, a straight one. No difference of function.

the lower notes of the harmonic series. (For the freer brass passages of the Bach period see *Trumpet Family* 2 e, 3.) By the introduction of the modern system of **Valves** the fundamental note can be changed by mere pressure on a piston which opens the entrance into what we may call a permanent crook, and so different fundamentals, with their differing harmonic series, are instantaneously available, and even the most chromatic passages become possible.

The trombone (a very ancient instrument) has always had at command many fundamentals (with their attendant series of harmonics) by the simple device of sliding its tubes into one another, so lengthening and shortening the total length at will. The slide trumpet is on the same principle.

The harmonics of **Stringed Instruments**, obtained by lightly touching the string as already explained, have a special value on account of their peculiar silvery quality (the French and Germans call them 'Flageolet Tones'). They are often indicated by composers, the sign being 'o' over the note.

It should be observed that string harmonics are obtainable not only from the open string but also from the stopped string. This stopping of the string is the converse of the process of the adding of a crook to a brass instrument; the one shortens the vibrating body and provides a higher fundamental, and consequent higher series of harmonics, the other lengthens the vibrating body and provides a lower fundamental, and consequent lower series of harmonics. The harmonics obtained from a stringed instrument by touching the open string are called **Natural Harmonics**; those obtained by touching the stopped strings are called **Artificial Harmonics**; this is a distinction without a difference, physically considered, but there is some difference in quality.

On the **Harp** the harmonic an octave higher than the fundamental note can be obtained by touching a string lightly in the middle with the lower part of the hand whilst plucking it with a finger of the same hand.

Many **Organs** include a stop called 'Harmonic Flute'. This has pipes pierced with a small hole in their side at half-length, and then overblown (i.e. blown with extra pressure), so causing each pipe to sound an octave above its fundamental. The tone thus obtained is peculiarly smooth and sweet.

There are also organ-stops of which the pipes are overblown to sound their octave without the help of a half-way hole.

There are certain interesting and beautiful effects possible on the **Pianoforte** by players who understand the principles of harmonics, and modern composers fairly often avail themselves of these, using chords held down but not struck, and evoking sound 'sympathetically' from the strings thus left undamped by striking chords elsewhere on the instrument.

For some remarks on the general question of harmonics in pianoforte tone see *Pianoforte* 12.

For the influence of harmonics on tone quality see above (6. 'The Quality of Sound'), and also the separate entry *Timbre*.

See also the article *Aeolian Harp.*

9. 'Musical' and 'Unmusical' Sounds. When vibrations are more regular in their frequency, they give greater pleasure to the ear; when less regular, less pleasure. A piece of rough metal rudely struck gives out a number of vibrations at different frequencies, or of changing frequencies, which conflict with one another, producing what we call noise; a properly smoothed plate of metal, carefully struck, gives out vibrations that reinforce one another, producing what we call a musical sound.

The disorderliness of the vibrations that lie behind 'noise' is of two kinds. To begin with, the *successive* main vibrations are varying from moment to moment, and thus the frequency is ever changing so that no continuous fundamental note is heard—nothing for the ear to seize upon. Then, further, the *simultaneous*, or overtone, vibrations are in themselves probably out of proper relation to one another, since they arise from varying fundamentals. This latter detail establishes an obvious connexion between the subject of *noise versus musical tone* and that of *quality* (or timbre) discussed above.

It is of interest to notice that even sounds that are in themselves mere 'noises' can, if quickly and regularly repeated, amount in the aggregate to musical tone. In the days of horse-drawn vehicles, metal-tyred wheels, and cobbled roads, it was observable, on a quiet evening in London streets, that a vehicle travelling fast enough mounted up its 'noisy' wheel-impacts on the stones into a note; the same effect can be heard nowadays from the pattern of a new cycle tyre running over an asphalt road. The humming of a saw-mill is of a similar nature: each impact of a tooth of the saw on the wood is mere noise, but when such impacts are rapidly and regularly repeated they produce a note and vary in pitch according to the varying speed of the saw, i.e. the varying rate of vibration.

The effect of noise on the human nervous system has been much studied during the twentieth century, as a result of the large increase in town noises due to changed methods of locomotion, etc., and exhaustive reports have been issued by commissions appointed by the Health Departments of larger cities. In Switzerland the maximum noise level allowed for a motor-car is 80 decibels.

It may be pointed out that noise is allowed a small but not unimportant part in the modern orchestra. The sounds of the bass drum, for instance, are 'disorderly' in quality and cannot be assigned to any fixed note. Other noise-members are the cymbals, triangle, and tambourine. None of these produces a true note, and hence they can be used with any harmonies that happen to be going on at the moment they are required, whereas the kettledrums, which do possess a definite musical quality and pitch, have (unless some special effect be desired) to be used with reference to the chord with which they are to be heard.

10. Resultant Tones. When two loud notes are heard together, they give rise to a third and a fourth sound, the one of which (*Difference Tone*) is a low one tallying with the difference between the two vibration numbers, and the other of which (*Summation Tone*) is a high one, but a very much fainter one, tallying with their sum. There are other similar tones possible in certain circumstances. The generic term *Resultant Tone* (or *Combination Tone*) is given to these. There is not space here to go into the theory of the process but it may be said that Tartini (q.v.) discovered Difference Tones (which he called *Terzi tuoni*, or 'third tones'), and, finding that in all simple cases the differential is in good harmony with the two notes that give rise to it, insisted (as did Joachim and Wilhelmj later) that violin students should learn to listen for it as a check on the tuning of double stops (see *Double Stopping*).—'If you do not hear the bass your 3rd and 6th are not in tune.'

Another practical application of the difference tone is found in some large but cheap organs. In order to save the very great expense of the enormous register (i.e. the one with a 32-foot pipe for its lowest C and the other pipes in proportion), organ designers sometimes provide a 10⅔-foot, or 'Quint', stop (much smaller and hence cheaper pipes), to be used with the 16-foot stop. The difference tone of the C produced by a 16-foot pipe and the G produced by a 10⅔-foot pipe is C equivalent to that of a 32-foot stop, and similarly with the rest of the pipes right up the scale; thus the effect of the deep-toned stop (not very realistic, however) is suggested, without the expense (cf. p. 16, pl. **1.** 8).

Technical terms applied to this device are *Acoustic Bass*, *Resultant Bass*, and *Harmonic Bass* (the last not a good term in view of the different employment of 'Harmonic' in 'Harmonic Flute').

For the use of Resultant Tones in the curious trick of the production of Horn Chords see *Horn Family* 1, end. For their use in the electrical production of sounds of desired pitch see *Electric Musical Instruments*, 1 b.

See also section 16, on 'Beats'.

11. The Transmission of Sound. The consideration of the phenomena of sound really falls under three main heads, Origin, Transmission, Reception—involving a discussion of what occurs in the instrument, in the air, and in the ear. We now come to the second.

We have seen strings, membranes, and columns of air in tubes vibrating both as wholes (producing their fundamental notes) and as parts (producing their harmonics). Necessarily, they communicate their vibrations to the surrounding air. Every forward swing of a violin-string, for instance, creates an air-compression; every backward swing an attenuation of the air. The effect is most marked when the string is moving most rapidly, as it passes through its straight position. All this brings about alternate condensations and rarefactions of the air. The air as a whole does not move, for the violin-string, obviously, does not create a *wind* which continues until it meets the ear of the listener. The particles of air, however, swing forward and backward, alternately pressing together and separating. Thus, energy is communicated without continuous forward motion, just as when, six billiard balls being placed in a line and an end one given a sharp blow with the cue, the one at the other end moves away, showing that energy has been communicated through the other five, which, though they have momentarily swayed, are found to be still in the same place. Another analogy would be the conveyance of messages between two towns a hundred miles apart, not by a runner traversing the hundred miles, but by a hundred runners spaced at mile distances, each running one mile and then running back for the next message.

It has to be remembered, however, that sound is communicated not in one straight line but simultaneously in an infinite number of concentric spheres. The travelling of sound through the air is really the commotion of spheres of vibration around the vibrating object, the spheres being of the nature of alternate increases and decreases of the density of the air, i.e. alternate condensations and rarefactions. As the spheres widen, the condensation naturally diminishes, just as the ripple from a stone dropped in a pond diminishes in height as the wave expands. This amounts to a diminution of amplitude, and so the sound gradually diminishes to nothing. This is the explanation of distant sounds being fainter than near ones. A suitable mind-picture of what occurs is that of a series of concentric black, grey, and white circles around the sound-projecting agent—black circles shading into grey and passing into white, then into grey and black again, and so on, with the black and grey becoming fainter as the circles widen, until at last (all energy finally dissipated) nothing but white remains.

12. What is a 'Sound Wave'? Many less scientifically instructed readers (and the present article is solely for such) have been confused by reading of the propagation of sound by *waves* and by the examination of elaborate diagrams showing the waves as curves. Such use of the word 'wave' is a figure of speech, and such diagrams are in no sense pictures of anything that happens, but merely graphs of a kind very convenient to the physicist and hence universally accepted. And where in books on acoustics we see a certain kind of 'Photographs of Sound Waves', they are nothing of the kind, but merely photographs, greatly enlarged, of marks made by some recording instrument in which (generally) a membrane receives the varying impacts of the air-vibrations caused by sound and, by means of an attached needle, scratches a wavy line on a regularly travelling plate of smoked glass or something of the kind (cf. *Gramophone*).

Perhaps the confusion is the more pronounced since, in the case of sounding solid bodies, the origin of the sound happens to be in an actual wave, the movements of a vibrating string, for instance, taking the wave *shape*; the wave-motioning string does not, however, communicate to any one particle of the air a motion in wave shape, but merely communicates to and withdraws pressure from such particles along all its length.

It may be added that the unit wave in diagrammatic representation of sound-transmission is a compound curve; it extends from normal level up to a maximum, down through normal level to minimum, and back to normal. This corresponds to starting from grey (in the other kind of diagram just imagined), passing on to black, passing through grey again to white, and then on to grey. Think of the violin-string that originates vibration of the air; it passes from a straight shape to a bulge on one side, from that through a straight shape to a bulge on the other side, and then back to straight again. This, and nothing less, constitutes one *complete* vibration, and the above form of diagram recognizes the fact.

To some readers the whole of the above explanations will seem to be unnecessary, but it is believed that others will welcome them. They can be applied to light and electricity just as much as to sound.

13. Superposition of Vibrations. A somewhat difficult conception for the student is that of the superposition of vibrations. Obviously, as we can hear more than one note at a time, something of the sort must occur. Nay, even a 'single note', being in reality a multiple of harmonics, must send out not a simple vibration but a large number of stronger or weaker vibrations simultaneously affecting the same body of air. The analogy with water-waves was drawn on, under the heading 'Quality' (section 6), to explain how a string could vibrate simultaneously as a whole and in fractions, and the reader who has grasped the conception of the transformation of a *simple* string-wave to an impulse in the air should have little difficulty in grasping the rather more complex conception of the similar transformation of a *compound* string-wave: every point of a curve in the string-wave which is moving forward helps to produce a compression in the air; every point which is moving backwards helps to produce an attenuation; every point which is changing its direction of motion stops for an instant and then produces neither. The changes of pressure in the air in our ears may be pictured as the total result of all these effects.

The mental picture of the series of concentric circles may now be drawn upon again, only, instead of the white merging straight into grey and that straight into black, and so on, we now see intermediate temporary darkenings and lightenings—ripples on the water-waves, to recur to a recent figure. It is as though a very regular-living financier had recurrent periods of affluence and insolvency, with, however, occasional small losses and gains during his periods of affluence and occasional small gains and losses during his periods of insolvency.

Admittedly, however, it is difficult or impossible to *picture* what goes on in the air when a cord is struck. The mind is staggered at the thought of the thousands of superposed vibrations (or 'waves') in the air space in a concert-room when an orchestra is playing. Every note of every instrument is supplying a longer wave as its fundamental, with a number of shorter waves for the harmonics, these varying according to the 'timbre' of the instrument, and in addition there are being formed other vibrations for what have already been described in section 10 as 'Difference Tones' and 'Summation Tones', and these vibrations are brought into existence by every two notes heard, whether fundamental or harmonic notes —and so on! Some of these vibrations are inaudible: many of them simply duplicate one another; some of the harmonics merely doubling some of the fundamentals or some of the other harmonics simultaneously heard. Nevertheless, one's respect for the laws of nature is strengthened when one realizes for how much simultaneous yet unconflicting action they provide. ('Interference' is the rather misleading technical term for this phenomenon. Cf. 16.)

Throughout this section of the discussion, air has been usually spoken of as the transmitting medium. So it is, in general, but other substances may be substituted. An alarm clock placed under a bell jar from which all air is pumped (creating a vacuum) will still be heard if it rests on a wooden base in contact with the table, but if it be insulated by being placed on a non-sound-conducting substance, then it will cease to be heard, because there is nothing to convey the vibrations.

14. The Speed of Sound. Sound vibrations travelling through air move almost infinitely slowly as compared with the vibrations of light. The exact speed depends on the temperature, which affects the density of the air: normally it is about 1,120 feet per second, or about $12\frac{1}{2}$ miles a minute, whereas the speed of light in space is over 11,000,000 miles per minute. When what have begun as sound-vibrations are communicated by radio, they travel at the same rate as light vibrations. Thus of two listeners, one at the back of a concert-hall and the other hearing by means of his radio set a thousand miles away, the latter gets the music first. (See *Broadcasting* 1 c.)

Everybody has observed the widely different speeds of light and sound by noticing that a thunder-clap is heard long after the flash that originated simultaneously with it. When watching a street-mender or other person engaged in noisy action at a quite small distance, it is found that the motion is observed before the noise it occasions. This wide difference between the speed of light and sound is a disturbing factor in the effort to get simultaneous sounds out of a really large force of musicians; in a big choir the front row of ladies and the back row of men see the conductor's directing motions practically simultaneously, and in response to them utter their sounds simultaneously, but the audience does not receive those sounds together. A practical limit is thus clearly imposed upon the size of musical forces if finished performance is desired (see *Colour and Music* 10, at end).

The fact that sound travels comparatively slowly may enable man to enjoy curious phenomena in the near future. Roughly it travels at ten times the speed of the fastest express train, and though express trains now travel rather faster than they did in the middle of the nineteenth century they will presumably never catch up with the speed of sound. But many planes now travel faster than sound, and thus it should be possible for a flying man, after receiving a compliment from the Mayor of New York on having just broken the Atlantic record, to jump into his plane, outdistance the compliment, and hear it again in the middle of New Jersey—provided that the mayor was using a powerful enough megaphone.

A man shot may not hear the crack of the rifle, the bullet reaching him before the sound.

15. Vibration Numbers and Wavelengths. It has been said above that pitch depends upon frequency of vibration of the sounding-agent. Obviously the vibrations in the air will be of the same frequency as those of the agent, and, like it, they will differ for every note of the scale. A short string will vibrate more quickly than a long string of the same thickness, density, and tension. Every octave rise in pitch of the string means that there has occurred a doubling of the speed of its vibrations and those of the surrounding air.

The following gives the number of vibrations per second for a series of C's (at what is known as 'philosophical pitch', the numbers involved being all powers of 2 and easy to calculate):

C, the lowest note to be heard from most complete large organs ('32-foot C', its pipe being of about that length)	16
The next C higher ('16-foot C', or the lowest C on the piano)	32
The next ('8-foot C')	64
The next ('4-foot C')	128
The next ('2-foot C', **middle C** on the piano or stave)	256
The next ('1-foot C')	512
The next ('6-inch C', the one notated on the second leger line above the treble stave)	1,024
The next ('3-inch C')	2,048
The next ('1½-inch C'—the highest note on many pianos)	4,096

The vibration numbers of the harmonics in relation to the fundamental and to one another (as may have been deduced from the above) are orderly. E.g. a string 3 feet long gives off the harmonic of the octave by division into two lengths of 18 inches, and the harmonic of the fifth higher by division into three lengths of a foot. The vibration number of these harmonics arising from the third of the string is three times that of the vibration number of the fundamental, arising from the string's whole length. The harmonic derived from the division of the string into five portions (i.e. the note of two octaves and a third above the fundamental) has a vibration number of five times the fundamental. And so on.

The harmonics as shown in musical notation above (section 8) bear consecutive numbers, and the number each bears is not merely its place in the harmonic series, but is also the number of sections into which the whole length of the string is divided in order to produce that harmonic.

Thus the harmonic No. 13 arises from a division of the string into thirteen separately vibrating portions, and the number of vibrations per second is thirteen times that of the fundamental. And so on.

It is important to every student of music to memorize the first sixteen or so of the harmonics from the musical notation as above given, since, as has already been seen, the harmonic series has a considerable bearing on the study of the technique of several instruments (especially brass) and also on the general principles of harmony (q.v.).

The vibration lengths (or 'wave-lengths') of sound transmission through the air naturally differ with the rapidity of the motions of the initial vibrating agent. The speed of sound through air being constant for all pitches, yet the vibration number varying for different pitches, this must, of course, be so.

The speed of sound in air is, as already stated, at normal temperature 1,120 feet per second. The number of vibrations per second to produce the lowest C just mentioned being 16, its wave-length is necessarily $\frac{1120}{16} = 70$ feet. The number of vibrations per second to produce the highest C mentioned being 4,096, its wave-length is $\frac{1120}{4096}$, or something under 3 inches. (Cf. p. 16, pl. **1.** 1, 2.)

16. Beats. The phenomenon of the beat or throb (a form of 'Interference', see section 13 above) occurs when two notes close to each other in frequency are heard together. Its occurrence is due to reinforcement when the vibrations coincide, as they must and do at certain regular intervals. Imagine two pendulums swinging side by side, No. 1 at the rate of 100 (double) swings per minute and No. 2 at the rate of 103, i.e. in the first swing they coincide, and in every 100th of the one and 103rd of the other respectively, likewise. Obviously, in order that No. 2 may finish in time, it has to overtake No. 1 three times, i.e. on three occasions within the minute the two will arrive together at some point of their swing. Turned into terms of vibrations of the air this, as already stated, means three re-inforcements (each double swing correspond-ing to one complete vibration in the air).

The effect can be heard very plainly by striking and holding simultaneously two of the lowest notes on the piano (or better still the harmonium). Organists, in playing such a piece as Handel's Dead March in *Saul*, some-times produce a fair imitation of a kettledrum's rattle by putting the left foot upon the lowest two pedal notes; these notes are so low in pitch that many ears can hardly distinguish the difference between them when successively played, but when simultaneously played the 'beat' is easily perceptible by nearly everybody and somewhat resembles the impact of a drum-stick on the parchment of the drum. Renatus Harris, in building an organ for Salisbury Cathedral (1710—that is, at a period when pedal boards were not yet in use in England), provided a single 'drum pedal', with two pipes tuned to produce this effect. Some continental organs have a 'Storm Effects' stop (*Effets d'orage*) of the same nature.

Such beats as these are acceptable because they are not rapid. Slow beats offend the ear less than quick ones; near C in the treble clef the maximum harshness is produced by two notes one of which is vibrating about thirty times per second faster than the other, so pro-ducing beats of that frequency. With beats of more than a thirty-per-second frequency the harshness gradually diminishes: the beating tones, if loud enough, form an audible note of their own (i.e. a 'difference tone'—see 10, above). Organ designers use the phenomenon of beat in the Voix Céleste stop. Here two sets of very soft-toned pipes are used right up the scale, one set slightly out of tune with the other. The effect is ethereal and, in strict moderation, acceptable.

Every piano and organ tuner makes use of this phenomenon. In tuning two of the unison strings of the piano, for instance, at the outset eight beats (say) per second may be heard (not that he counts or times them, of course!); then the peg of one of the strings is turned a little and seven beats, six beats, or five beats are heard, and so on until the beating disappears.

When one 'tunes in' a radio receiving set to a broadcasting station one is performing virtually the same operation between the (variable) fre-quency of oscillation of the set and the ether waves sent out by the broadcasting station.

It is the greater intensity or lesser intensity of the mental impression of beats that consti-tutes the difference between dissonance and consonance (see *Harmony* 21, 24 h). There is no such thing as absolute consonance or disso-nance for an interval between the unison and octave; it is all a matter of degree.

17. Pitch-limits of Audibility. Ears (as already mentioned) differ greatly in their ability to 'pick up' extreme sounds.

The lowest C above mentioned, arising from sixteen vibrations per second, is as low as most

people can go; many would hear the separate vibrations without being able mentally to con-nect them into a definite musical tone, and probably very few indeed would be able to dis-tinguish this note from the D two semitones above it, or, indeed, to hear any difference between the two notes when consecutively per-formed. Even 16-foot C, with thirty-two vibrations per second, may be out of tune on the pedal bourdon of a church organ without any member of the congregation finding his devotions gravely disturbed thereby.

The highest C shown above (section 15) is by no means the highest note audible. Some people can hear sounds more than two octaves above that, and early investigators claimed to have heard painful sounds with vibrations as high as 38,000 per second; but such high notes do not occur in music, except as un-noticed harmonics. The normal ear probably takes in no sound higher than that of about 18,000 to 20,000 vibrations per second; if, then, the piano's range were extended by rather over two octaves at the top, few people would be able to hear any sound from its highest notes, and if it were extended still another octave nobody would hear them.

The highest sounds actually produced as fundamentals from any musical instrument are probably those of the tiniest pipes (less than ¼ inch long) of a Mixture stop on a big organ, but such pipes are not heard sounding alone (see *Organ* 2 c). The highest sound heard from any orchestral instrument is at the summit of the piccolo's range, with about 5,000 vibrations per second, being just about as high as the piano's highest note. The lowest sound of the orchestra comes from the double bassoon at about thirty-three vibrations, being very near the lowest note of the piano. Roughly, then, the pitch extremes of the orchestra are the same as those of the piano.

18. Reflection of Sound. Sound vibra-tions are capable of being returned from a reflecting surface, just as are those of light. This is the explanation of the phenomenon of echo. It is possible for a curved surface to reflect the same sound from several parts of the surface in such a way that the lines of vibra-tion of the reflection converge to a focus, and when this happens what is heard at that focus (being the sum of many echoes) may be louder than the original. (See *Concert Halls* 6.)

The author, at a concert in a London concert-hall, once sat in such a position that every note of the harp was heard magnified grotesquely beyond the tone of the other instruments: in this instance, it must have hap-pened that the hearer was at the exact focus of several reflecting surfaces in relation to that particular instrument, and possibly some other listeners elsewhere in the hall experienced the same distressing phenomenon in connexion with some other instrument.

Apses and much-rounded walls behind a platform are dangerous to music. An otherwise unresonant and 'dead' hall may be improved by the placing of a flat sounding-board behind the platform; this must, however, be near enough to the speaker or musicians for the echo it produces to merge with the original sound, so amplifying it and not being perceived as an echo; the right position must be experimentally found.

The explanation of 'whispering galleries', such as those of St. Paul's Cathedral, London, the Capitol, Washington, and a number of dome-shaped buildings in India, lies in reflection. The whisper is reflected and re-reflected from segment to segment of the curve. (Cf. p. 16, pl. **1. 7**.)

The use of hangings on the walls of halls, and of stretched wires, to prevent excessive reflection, is alluded to below under *Concert Halls* 2, 3.

Further remarks on reflection of sound will be found under 20 *d*. It will be understood that what is said above concerning walls applies also to ceilings.

19. Sound Shadows. Similarly, sound may be shaded as light is, but it needs a fairly large object to cast an appreciable sound-shadow, since sound waves (being long) tend to work *round* an object, as light waves (being short) do not; further, for sound waves to be checked the obstructing material must be non-vibratory, since sound waves are communicable through many solids, while light waves are not. The discovery of a cheap and not bulky material that will stop the course of sound is much to be desired in these days of thin-walled, small apartments.

20. Resonance. This word is used precisely by physicists and loosely in ordinary speech.

(*a*) In strict scientific parlance a resonator is an object so designed as to respond to a specific note (cf. *Wolf* 1). The commonest form is that of a hollow body with a small opening to the air, as, for instance, the resonators designed by Helmholtz for the analysis of sounds (see *Voice* 6, and p. 16, pl. **1**. 3) and those used in such instruments as the Kaffir piano and marimba (q.v.). When an object in a room is found to give out a note every time that particular note is sounded on the piano, that object is a true resonator. If two tuning-forks of the same pitch be placed in position for sounding and one of them be set in vibration, the other will take up the vibrations sympathetically; the first fork is then a generator of sound and the second a resonator. Similarly, if on the violin D be played on the G string, the D string will vibrate also, by resonance. Thus certain instruments have been provided with 'sympathetic strings' (q.v.), such as the viola d'amore (see *Viol Family* 4 f), i.e. with additional strings, 'resonating strings' as we may call them, vibrating in unison with the true or sound-generating strings of the instrument; such strings cannot, of course, resonate *as wholes* for every note played, but

only for those notes with which they are in tune; however, they can also respond harmonically (see 8) for other notes.

An instance of true resonance is found in the well-known power of certain singers to break a drinking-glass by loudly singing into it the note to which it happens to be attuned (see also 2–end). The French acoustician, Gariel, has called attention to the following very curious passages in the Talmud (the compilation of Jewish civil and religious law completed A.D. 500):

'When a cock shall stretch forth its neck into the hollow of a glass vessel and sing therein in such a way as to break it, the full loss shall be paid.'

'When a horse neighs or an ass brays and so breaks a glass vessel, the half of the loss shall be paid.'

This is, of course, academic legalism. We can hardly imagine such incidents occurring. Yet the provision made against them shows knowledge of theoretical possibilities.

(For the question of resonance in vocal tone-production see *Voice* 6, 7; for its relation to pedalling on the piano see *Pianoforte* 12).

By ordinary dictionary definition, the word 'resonance' is applied to several types of sympathetic awakening of tone other than the one just mentioned, and mention of these will now be made.

(*b*) If an instrument be played in close proximity to a flat surface of thin wood, a stretched sheet of parchment, etc., sympathetic duplication will take place *not of one particular note merely, but of any succession or combination of notes*, the wood or parchment adapting itself (within wide limits) to any frequency of vibration, and vibrating in sympathy. Colloquially, this, too, is 'resonance', and indeed it would seem to be on all fours with the resonance described under (*a*), except that the (*a*) type of resonator is, from the shape adopted, rigidly selective, while the (*b*) type is adaptive.

A sea shell (perhaps because it has many chambers of different sizes) is of the adaptive variety; its resonance is so great that it picks up many sounds inevitably constantly going on (yet so soft as to elude the unaided ear) and gives them forth as a perceptible murmur. (However, the sea-shell's procedure is difficult to grasp and does not seem to have been explained by physicists.)

(*c*) The third kind of sympathetic awakening of tone to be described is more doubtfully 'resonance', though the musician, as opposed to the physicist, always thinks of it as such. It is exemplified by the belly and back of the violin, the sound-board of the piano, and the sound-box of the (non-electric) gramophone. All these vibrate, not by mere 'sympathy', but by actual contact.

The violin string emits a very feeble sound, but being in contact with the back and belly (by means of the bridge and sound-post) it sets these vibrating too, and they then serve as true sound producers, the sound emitted by the string itself being swamped by the greater volume emitted by these larger vibrating surfaces.

So, too, in the piano, the actual sound emitted by the strings is small, but these are in contact, at the one end of their vibrating portions, with the sound-board, and this itself, set in vibration by them, emits sounds in which the original feeble sounds are lost. A familiar example of the same principle is the tuning-fork, which makes a feeble sound until its foot is placed on the table, when the table becomes a musical instrument and emits a much louder sound than the fork itself.

For a further example see *Gramophone* 3.

In all these cases there is a fresh *origination* of sound by the surface in question, which, being adaptive, is not a resonator in the strictest sense of the term.

(*d*) The meaning of the word 'resonance' is sometimes so greatly widened as to take in the duplication of sound by mere reflection (see 18). It is clear that if a long-drawn sound is produced in a room whose walls create echo, such echo may be heard before the original sound ceases, thus reinforcing it. This is much noticed in many cathedrals, which are commonly spoken of as 'very resonant'.

The walls, ceiling, and floor of a room, can, indeed, create so much of this kind of 'resonance' that the sounds of notes sung, played, or used in speech are prolonged into one another confusedly and the harmonics of those notes are modified and mingled into huge, vague clouds of tone.

An acoustical authority to whom this article has been submitted adds the following comment on certain of our architects:

'Why should music be muddled up with echo? A military band sounds perfectly clear in an open field with no echo. So does the orchestra at the Stadium concerts in New York, or the open-air opera at Ravinia near Chicago. The architects ask singers, conductors, and executants. They all like a room that echoes so that they can produce a good noise with little effort. The London errand-boy regards the Tube station as a good room for whistling, for the same reason. The musician who wants really to hear the music is not considered. The confusion of a choir and large organ in a cathedral is not properly music at all.

'Against this, many musicians seem to like a background of muddle, and it may be admitted that it does not seem to do as much harm as one might expect. I sometimes play an organ with a solo department up aloft, and the choir department at the usual level. If you play a scale with the coupler, you get a scale of discordant seconds at the console. Somehow *that* does not worry one!'

(As a comment upon the whole of this section of the article, it may be admitted that there are some points concerning resonance that do not seem yet to be clearly understood by physicists. In any case, the subject is an exceedingly difficult one to explain in short space. Certain of the statements concerning resonance found in books explaining musical instruments do not seem to bear close examination.)

21. Reception and Recognition of Sound. The chief phenomena of the origination and transmission of sound vibrations having now been set forth, it remains to consider their reception by the listener. This part of the subject is separately treated in the article *Ear and Hearing*.

ACTA MUSICOLOGICA. See *Journals*.

ACTION occurs in one or two musical connexions such as the French *Pas d'action*, a ballet dance with a dramatic basis, and the English *Action Song*, a children's song with some measure of dramatic movement on the part of the singers. Also, the mechanism of a piano or organ, or other musical instrument: e.g. in piano, 'Schwander' or 'Herrburger' actions; in organ, 'electro-pneumatic' or 'tracker' actions; in flute, 'Boehm' action.

ACT MUSIC (in English Universities). At Oxford and Cambridge an Act was a thesis maintained by a candidate for a degree, or an argument between graduates, publicly conducted. At Act time (at Oxford in early July) there was an 'Act Sermon' on 'Act Sunday'. 'Act Music' was the name for a public concert at Act Time and (concerts being rare) this was long looked upon as an important annual event. The last Act (after long interruption) was in 1733.

ACT TUNE (or Curtain Tune, or Curtain Music). Music between the acts of a play, whilst the curtain was down, was so called in England in the seventeenth and early eighteenth centuries. Such music often came to have an independent existence by separate publication, just as does some 'Entr'acte' music today.

ADAGE. See *Ballet* 8.

ADAGIETTO (It.). Slow, but less so than *Adagio*. Or a short adagio composition.

ADAGIO (It.). Literally, 'at ease', i.e. slow (not so slow as 'Largo', however). A slow movement is often called 'an Adagio' (cf. *Improvisation* 1). *Adagissimo*, extremely slow.

ADAM, ADOLPHE CHARLES. Born in Paris in 1803 and died there in 1856, aged fifty-two. He was an active composer of operas, ballets, etc. (especially successful in the type of opéra comique), his stage works numbering over fifty, of which the ballet *Giselle* must be the best known. He also composed quantities of popular easy piano transcriptions, songs, choruses for men's voices, and church music (including a Christmas vocal piece, *Minuit, Chrétiens*, which for a century had immense favour but in the 1930's began to find itself excluded from the churches by one French bishop after another, on the ground of its 'lack of musical taste and total absence of the spirit of religion'). He was, further, an opera-house proprietor, a music critic, and a

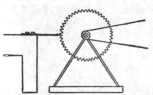

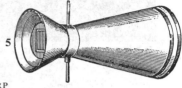

3. HELMHOLTZ RESONATOR (See *Acoustics* 20 a; *Voice* 6)

1, 2. INSTRUMENTS FOR MEASURING PITCH—*Savart's Toothed Wheel* and the *Siren*. The one sets in vibration a strip of metal, the other receives air from a tube at its side, its perforations producing a series of puffs. A required pitch being thus produced, it is easy to reckon the number of cogs or holes per minute, and this gives the vibration number

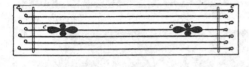

4, 5. AEOLIAN HARP —18th century and 20th century. See *Aeolian Harp*

4

6, 7. REFLECTION OF SOUND—two 17th-century illustrations of the phenomenon. See *Acoustics* 18

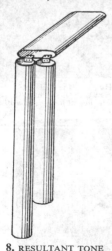

8. RESULTANT TONE WHISTLE See *Acoustics* 10

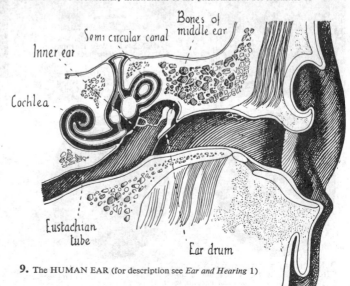

Semi circular canal

Bones of middle ear

Inner ear

Cochlea

Eustachian tube

Ear drum

9. The HUMAN EAR (for description see *Ear and Hearing* 1)

PLATE 2 ANGLICAN PARISH CHURCH MUSIC

1, 2. ENGLISH VILLAGE CHURCH (Winterborne Tomson, Dorset, in its 18th-cent. condition). See *Anglican Parish Church* 4

3. A VILLAGE CHOIR AND ORCHESTRA OF THE 1840's—Bow Brickhill Church, Bucks. (By Thos. Webster, R.A.)

5. VILLAGE CHURCH INSTRUMENTS (West Tarring, Sussex)—with choir-book and Pitch Pipe

4. SHEFFIELD PARISH CHURCH in 1854—looking East (the chancel is cut off and lies behind the organ. Clerk, Vicar, Curate, and Choir are seen)

6. CHURCH BARREL ORGAN, SHELLAND, SUFFOLK
See *Mechanical Reproduction* 10

7, 8. 'CHARITY CHILDREN' (in a town church) and their new rivals, the CHOIRBOYS. By Henry Barraud, 1849. (For the 'Charity Children' see *Anglican Parish Church Music* 5)

9. LATER 19TH-CENTURY SENTIMENTALIZATION OF CHURCH MUSIC (1890)

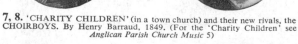

See also Plate 35 (page 172)

professor of composition at the Conservatory, and he left two interesting series of memoirs.

ADAM DE LA HALLE (or 'de la Hale'). He seems to have been born about 1237, and apparently in Arras. He was nicknamed 'Le Bossu d'Arras'—The Hunchback of Arras (though he himself records that he was no hunchback). He died in Naples about 1287.

He was a famous trouvère (see *Minstrels* 4, 5), and his works, in great measure, survive. They were published by Coussemaker in 1872 (not always quite correctly), and the most famous of them, *The Play of Robin and Marion* ('Le Jeu de Robin et de Marion') has had several subsequent editions, sometimes arranged for modern performance. It is a pastoral consisting of dialogue broken by songs (in the original unaccompanied) set to what were probably popular tunes of the day, and is sometimes spoken of as the precursor of opéra comique.

Other works of this composer are chansons, and also rondeaux (see *Form* 9) and three-part motets of the crude, early type (see *Motet*).

ADAM KEYBOARD. See *Keyboard* 4.

ADAM LE BOSSU. See *Adam de la Halle.*

ADAMS.
(1) THOMAS (1785–1858). A London organist with a high reputation for technical skill, extemporization, and composition for his instrument. See reference under *Organ* 13.

(2) JEAN (1710–65). See *There's nae luck.*

ADAM'S APPLE. See *Voice* 2, 21.

AD CANONES. See *Mass* 5.

A.D.C.M. See *Degrees and Diplomas* 2.

ADDED SIXTH. The Chord of the Added Sixth is the subdominant chord plus the sixth from the bass, for instance, in key C it is this: F–A–C–D. It is in common enough use. There occur some similar chords on other degrees than the subdominant to which the name might also be (but is not usually) given; this, however, is the commonest. It is now usually spoken of as (and more logically) as the 'First Inversion of the Chord of the Supertonic 7th' (of the diatonic chord of the Supertonic 7th, that is—not the one mentioned in the article *Chromatic Chords*). Another description of it is as the 'Third Inversion of the Dominant 11th, with the lowest two notes of the original chord omitted'.

An Added Sixth on the tonic, plus the **Added Ninth**, is commonly met with as the final chord in jazz cadences and tends to be adopted by serious American composers.

ADDINSELL, RICHARD. Born in Oxford in 1904 and died in 1977. He studied at Oxford and for a short time at the Royal College of Music and in Berlin and Vienna, and became known as a writer of incidental music for plays and then of music for films. His *Warsaw Concerto* (so-called—not a normal piano concerto, nor a work for which he claims the highest

value) was composed for the film *Dangerous Moonlight* (1941); it became very popular.

ADDISON, JOHN. Born at West Chobham in 1920. His studies at the Royal College of Music (where he later taught, 1950–7) were interrupted by six years of war service, after which he became known as a composer of skilful, nimble-witted music of immediate appeal. He is much in demand for film scores, of which he has provided many well-known examples.

ADDISON, JOSEPH (1672–1719). See *Community Singing* 3; *Ballad* 5; *Divisions*; *Voluntary.*

ADDITIONAL ACCOMPANIMENTS. When an oratorio, opera, or the like, of the seventeenth or eighteenth century, is performed today, it is often impossible to reproduce with perfect exactitude the instrumental intentions of the composer, since some of the instruments no longer exist and others have changed greatly in tone quality and tone quantity and even in compass. Hence a certain amount of adaptation becomes necessary. This should, of course, be carried out with scrupulous conservatism, and with the desire to attain as nearly as possible to the original effect.

Amongst changes in the constitution of the orchestral force and the practices of musical performance that have come about since (for example) the days of Bach and Handel, are the following:

1. We no longer commonly employ a keyboard instrument (harpsichord or organ) as a background to the orchestral tone. With us, no keyboard instrument is a normal feature of the orchestra.

2. Our balance of choral and orchestral forces is different. Bach and Handel usually had more performers in the orchestra than in the chorus, and we often have three times as many in the chorus as in the orchestra.

3. The oboe and bassoon have become greatly refined in tone and, also, are no longer used in mass. Handel's usual proportion was one hautboy (oboe) to every three violins, with one bassoon to each cello and double bass (oboes and bassoons are not always shown in the score because they often merely doubled the stringed instruments in loud passages).

4. Our trumpets and our trumpet technique are different, and except by special training or with a special instrument our trumpeters cannot play the high-flying florid trumpet passages of Bach and Handel. (See *Trumpet Family* 2 e, 3.)

5. We have the clarinet, which Bach and Handel had not—and so with other instruments.

6. But a host of instruments they had have almost or quite disappeared—special kinds of flutes, of oboes, and the like.

And so on—the above being merely a few of the most obvious changes that have come about (see also *Orchestra and Orchestration* 2).

Now a scrupulous conductor can undoubtedly adjust present-day forces so as to approach fairly near to the composer's intention, but the effort is by no means easy and so is not always made. Handel's *Messiah* is often performed with very elaborate additions to the score made by Mozart ('stucco ornaments on a marble temple', Hauptmann rudely called them), who prepared it for a certain occasion when there was no organ available for the performance of the figured bass (q.v.)—his 'Additional Accompaniments' being freely used today even where an organ is available and is brought into service. So familiar have his additions become to audiences that many people would feel aggrieved if they heard certain passages without them. But even the Mozart edition is rarely heard intact, as still further changes have been made by later editors, such as Costa, Franz, and Prout, whilst Sir Henry Wood completely rescored both *Messiah* and *Israel in Egypt* for the special conditions of the monster performances (3,000 voices and a mammoth orchestra) of the Handel Festival in the Crystal Palace, London.

Mendelssohn's alterations of some of Handel's scores are rather drastic, and he lived to express regret that they had ever been published, but the biggest and boldest 'additional accompanist' of history is Robert Franz (q.v.), who bestowed his attentions on Bach's *St. Matthew Passion*, *Magnificat*, Church Cantatas, etc., Handel's *Messiah*, numerous separate opera arias, and other things. He wrote a book (1871) explaining his principles in this kind of work.

The ethics of additional accompaniment are not easy to define. They cannot be laid down in any code or Ten Commandments, but are covered by a 'Golden Rule'—to attain as near as possible to the effect the composer himself imagined when he penned the score. Up to the present this rule has been much more conscientiously observed in respect of Bach than of Handel—probably because Handel remained popular throughout the rough-and-ready days of the eighteenth and nineteenth centuries, and amongst the masses, whereas Bach did not emerge until the period when musical scholarship was gaining ground, and then was for some time popular only amongst the *élite*.

For a cognate subject see *Arrangements*.

ADDOLCENDO (It.). 'Becoming *dolce*' (q.v.).

ADDOLORATO (It.). 'Grieved', i.e. sadly.

ADEL (Ger.). 'Nobility.'

ADELAIDE, South Australia. See *Schools of Music*.

'ADELAIDE CONCERTO.' See *Misattributed Compositions* s.v. 'Mozart'.

ADELOPHONE. See *Reed-Organ Family* 6.

ADESTE FIDELES ('O come, all ye faithful!'). The Latin hymn dates from only the seventeenth or eighteenth century: it seems to be of French or German origin, probably the former. The popular English translation is by Canon Frederick Oakeley, of Margaret Street Chapel, London (1841), but in an altered version as it appeared in Murray's *Hymnal* (1852).

The music seems to be of British origin. It exists in a manuscript of 1746 at Clongowes College, Ireland, and in manuscripts of a little later in Roman Catholic institutions in England. Its first appearance in print attached to these words is in *An Essay on the Plain Chant* (1782). It has been ascribed to John Reading (q.v.), composer of 'Dulce Domum', or to some other (and later) musician of this same name, but the ascription has, in either case, little to support it.

The same tune was heard in a Paris Vaudeville, *Acajou*, in 1744, and it was then described as 'Air anglais'. The first part of the air reproduces the first part of the tune almost exactly as sung today; the second part differs until the last few notes, which are like the last few of the present tune. G. E. P. Arkwright, in *The Musical Antiquary*, April 1910, pointed out that elements of the second part of the tune as we today know it seem to have been derived from a passage in Handel's air 'Pensa ad amare', in his opera of *Ottone* (1723). This air was exceedingly well known in England, Burney specially naming it (*History* IV, 287) as one of those which were 'favourites with all the performers on the German flute in the kingdom'. Arkwright concludes:

'This adaptation, by which a really fine tune was compounded out of rather incongruous materials, may have been made by some choirmaster (probably between 1740 and 1750), for the use of a Roman Catholic choir.'

The relevant passages from *Acajou* and *Ottone* are reproduced by Arkwright in the article quoted.

In 1947 a pamphlet by Dom John Stéphan, O.S.B., of Buckfast Abbey, Devon, discussed a newly discovered manuscript of the *Adeste Fideles* tune in the handwriting of John Francis Wade, a Latin teacher and music copyist of Douay who died in 1786. This he thinks to be 'the first and original version', dating it between 1740 and 1743, and giving reasons for considering both the original (Latin) words and the music of the hymn to be the work of Wade himself. In this case the surmise of Arkwright would seem to be remarkably near the truth.

The description 'Portuguese Hymn' is sometimes to be found attached to this tune in hymn-tune books, but that comes only from its use, in the late eighteenth century, in the Portuguese Chapel, London (see *Roman Catholic Church Music in Britain*).

À DEUX CORDES (Fr.). 'On two strings.'

AD FUGAM. See *Mass* 5.

ADIAPHONON. An early tuning-fork piano of the class of dulcitone (see *Percussion Family* 2 e).

ADIRATO (It.). 'Angered' (irate).

ADJUNCT (1). A term applied to notes inessential

to the harmony, such as passing notes (unaccented or accented: see *Harmony* 3). (2) But the word may also be used in the sense of 'related' (keys, etc.).

ADLER.

(1) GUIDO. Born in Moravia in 1855 and died in Vienna in 1941, aged eighty-five. He was a distinguished musicologist, author of learned works, and editor of an important History of Music. He was from 1885 a professor at the University of Prague and from 1898 of that of Vienna. Schönberg, Webern, and Wellesz were pupils of his.

(2) LARRY. Born at Baltimore in 1914. He early became a virtuoso of the twelve-hole chromatic harmonica (English 'Mouth Organ'; cf. *Reed Organ Family* 3). From 1934 he was, for four or five years, in Britain, then touring South Africa and Australia and returning to the United States. He plays on his instrument arrangements of some classical violin concertos, and also pieces by Bloch, Ravel, Debussy, etc. Milhaud, Roussel, and Vaughan Williams have composed for him.

AD LIBITUM (Latin), or *Ad lib*. 'At will.' This gives the performer liberty:

(1) To vary from the strict rhythm, tempo, etc., if so inclined.

(2) To include or omit the part of some voice or instrument so marked.

(3) To include or omit some passage so marked (possibly a cadenza), according to his preference.

(4) If he wants a cadenza at the place so marked, to make his own according to his fancy.

The context will show which of these liberties is in question.

ADLUNG, See *Clavichord* 3.

ADRIANA LECOUVREUR. See *Cilèa*.

A DUE CORDE (It.). 'On two strings.'

AEHNLICH or **ÄHNLICH** (Ger.). 'Similar', 'like'.

AELODICON. See *Reed-Organ Family* 6.

AELOPHONE. See *Reed-Organ Family* 6.

AENGSTLICH or **ÄNGSTLICH** (Ger.). 'Anxious.'

AEOLIAN COMPANY. See *Mechanical Reproduction* 13.

AEOLIAN HALL, LONDON. See *Concert* 8.

AEOLIAN HARP. (From Aeolus, the fabled keeper of the winds.) An instrument, introduced in its present form, apparently, at the end of the sixteenth century or beginning of the seventeenth, for the production of a vague, wayward outdoor music.

It consists of a number of gut strings (of different thicknesses but tuned in unison) on a wooden resonance box about 3 feet long, which can be attached to a tree or a building or (as frequently) fitted along the length of a window-ledge. The blowing of the wind sets the strings in vibration in such a way that their

harmonics (see *Acoustics* 8) are heard, rather than merely their 'fundamental' note, and this gives a chordal impression—the harmonics produced varying with the thickness of the strings and the velocity of the wind. The effect, then, is similar to that often heard from telegraph wires, but with the added resonance of a hollow sounding-board, and the added complexity of a distinct chordal suggestion.

The English shoemaker-poet, Robert Bloomfield, was, in the earliest years of the nineteenth century, making and selling Aeolian harps in London, and they seem to have been very popular in those days of romantic landscape gardening with its rustic summer-houses and sham ruins (p. 16, pl. **1**. 4, 5).

German names for this instrument are *Äolsharfe*, *Windharfe* ('Wind Harp'), *Wetterharfe* ('Weather Harp' or 'Atmosphere Harp'), and *Geisterharfe* ('Spirit Harp').

AEOLIAN MODE. See *Modes* 6, 7, 8.

AEOLINA. Organ stop; see *Organ* 14 III.

AEOLINE. See *Reed-Organ Family* 6; *Organ* 14 III.

AEOLOMELODICON. See below.

AEOLOPANTALEON. An instrument introduced in Poland in 1825. It consisted of a kind of combination of pianoforte and aeolomelodicon (another apparently Polish invention—a sort of harmonium). The young Chopin gave some recitals on it.

AEOLSHARFE. See *Aeolian Harp*.

AEQUAL (Ger.). Old organ term for '8-foot'.

AEROFORO (It.). Aerophor (q.v.).

AEROPHON. See *Aerophor*, below.

AEROPHONE. See *Reed-Organ Family* 6.

AEROPHOR. A device patented in 1912 to help wind-instrument players. A small bellows, worked by one foot, communicates by means of a tube with a corner of the mouth of the player, leaving him free to carry on his normal breathing processes through his nose whilst his mouth is supplied with the air required for his instrument by means of the bellows.

The inventor was Bernhard Samuels. Strauss has in his *Alpine Symphony* and *Festal Prelude* written passages actually requiring the use of this adjunct. In the former he calls it, however, *Aerophon*.

AETERNE REX ALTISSIME. See *O salutaris Hostia*.

AEUSSERST (Ger.). Same as *Äusserst*, i.e. 'extremely'.

AEVIA. This 'word' consists of the vowels of 'Alleluia' (q.v.). It is used as an indication in somewhat the same way as *Evovae* (q.v.).

AFFABILE (It.). 'Affable', i.e. in a gentle, pleasing manner.

AFFAIBLISSANT (Fr.). 'Weakening', diminuendo.

AFFANNATO (It.). 'Panting', i.e. in a distressful manner.

AFFANNOSO, AFFANNOSAMENTE (It.). 'Distressed', 'distressingly'.

AFFEKT (Ger.). 'Fervour.' So *Affektvoll*, 'full of fervour'.

AFFETTO (It.). 'Affection.'

AFFETTUOSO, AFFETTUOSA (It., masc., fem.). 'Affectionate', i.e. with tenderness, warmth. *Affettuosamente*, 'affectionately'.

AFFEZIONE (It.). 'Affection.'

AFFLITTO (It.). 'Afflicted.' So *Afflizione*, 'affliction'.

AFFRETTARE (It.). 'To hurry.' Hence *Affrettando*, 'hurrying'; *Affrettato, Affrettoso* (or *Affrettuoso*), 'hurried'; *Affrettatamente*, 'in a hurrying manner'.

AFRICAN MUSIC SOCIETY. This Society exists to encourage research into African music and 'its allied arts'. Its headquarters are at Johannesburg and it has representation in the different regions of South and Central Africa. It undertakes publication of research material and the issue of gramophone recordings of native music. Its founder and first Hon. Secretary was Hugh Tracey.

AGESILAUS AND THE NIGHTINGALE. See *Programme Music* 4.

AGEVOLE (It.). 'Comfortable', i.e. lightly and easily—not laboured. So *Agevolezza*, 'ease'.

AGGIUNTA, ARIA. See *Aria* 15.

AGGIUSTAMENTE (It.). 'Adjusting'—i.e. exact in point of rhythm. So also *Aggiustatamente*.

AGGRADEVOLE (It.). 'Agreeable.'

AGIATAMENTE (It.). 'Comfortably', 'Freely' (with suitable liberty as to speed, etc.). Not to be confused with *Agitatamente*, 'Agitatedly'.

AGILEMENT (Fr.). 'In an agile manner.'

AGILITÀ (It.), **AGILITÉ** (Fr.). 'Agility', implying speed and nimble execution. (For *Aria d'agilità* see *Aria* 5.)

AGILMENTE (It.). 'In an agile manner.'

AGINCOURT, FRANÇOIS D' (Dagincour, Dagincourt). He was born at Rouen about 1680 and died at Paris in 1758, aged about seventy-eight. He had wide celebrity as an organist and left organ music and a set of interesting harpsichord pieces. (See *Bird Music*.)

AGINCOURT SONG. A famous song commemorating the English victory of Agincourt (1415), and probably contemporary or nearly so. It is for two voices, with a chorus of three. The melody is exceedingly bold and dignified. The earliest existing copy is in the library of Trinity College, Cambridge. In some modern hymn-books the tune has been brought into use for congregational singing, as in the *English Hymnal* (where it is called 'Deo Gracias') and the *American Protestant Episcopal Church Hymnal* (attached to Kipling's 'Recessional').

AGITATO, AGITATAMENTE (It.). 'Agitated', 'agitatedly'. (Not to be confused with *Agiatamente*, q.v.)·

AGITAZIONE, AGITAMENTO (It.). 'Agitation.'

AGITÉ (Fr.). 'Agitated.'

AGITIRT, AGITIERT (Ger.). 'Agitated.'

AGNEW, ROY E. Born at Sydney, N.S.W., in 1893 and there died in 1944, aged fifty-one. He was a pianist and wrote for his instrument many sonatas and shorter pieces (these latter often with descriptive titles), as well as chamber and orchestral music and songs.

AGNUS DEI. See *Mass* 2 e, 3 e; *Requiem*.

A.G.O. See *American Guild of Organists*; *Degrees and Diplomas* 4.

AGOGIC. This term (first introduced by Riemann in his book *Musikalische Dynamik und Agogik*, 1884) is applied to that kind of accent which belongs to the nature of the phrase, as distinct from the regular pulsation of the so-many-beats-in-a-measure, and which is produced rather by dwelling on a note than by giving it additional force. The first note of a phrase often suggests the desirability of a slight lingering, which constitutes an agogic accent. So does a note longer than, or higher or lower than, those that have preceded it. So does a pungent discord about to proceed to its resolution (see *Harmony* 24 i). The agogic accent forms a notable element in rubato (q.v.).

Observe the distinction between the two possible forms of accent implied by the title of Riemann's book above mentioned—'dynamic' (i.e. of force) and 'agogic' (i.e. of movement).

It is obviously by the use of the agogic accent that a good organist makes his rhythm intelligible. Without this, a measure of eighth-notes (quavers) might, on his instrument, sound the same whether the signature were 6/8 or 3/4.

In the wider sense, 'Agogic' covers everything connected with expression by means of modification of rate of movement—rallentando, accelerando, the pause, accent of the kind above described, etc.

Cf. *Atempause*.

AGOULT, COUNTESS OF. See *Liszt*.

AGRÉMENS or **AGRÉMENTS** (Fr.). Grace-notes. See *Ornaments or Graces*, especially 3; *Singing* 8; also Tables 12–16.

AGRESTE (Fr.). 'Rural.'

AGRICOLA.

(1) ALEXANDER. Born in 1446 and died in Spain in 1506. A Netherlands composer of motets, masses, etc.

(2) MARTIN (original name 'Sore'). Born in Brandenburg in 1486 and died at Magdeburg in 1556. He was cantor at Magdeburg and an influential writer on all subjects of musical theory.

(3–4) JOHANN FRIEDRICH (1720–74) and BENEDETTA EMILIA (1722–*c*. 1780). Husband and wife. The former (a pupil of Bach) an organist, composer, and writer on music; the latter (of Italian birth) a soprano singer of wonderful powers. Both were employed at the court of Frederick the Great (q.v.).

(*Note*: Several other musicians of this name will be found in one or two very comprehensive works of reference, though the above are all that are likely to come the way of the ordinary reader.)

A.G.S.M. See *Degrees and Diplomas* 2.

AGUJARI. See *Voice* 17; *Prima Donna*.

ÄHNLICH or **AEHNLICH** (Ger.). 'Similar', 'like'.

AI (It.). 'At the', 'to the', etc.

AIDA (Verdi). Produced at Cairo, 1871 (a commission from the Khedive of Egypt for the inauguration of the new Opera House there). Story suggested by the Egyptologist, Mariette Bey. Libretto, in French, by C. du Locle, translated into Italian by A. Ghislanzoni.

ACT I

SCENE 1: *A Hall in the Palace of the Pharaoh at Memphis*

The High Priest **Ramfis** (*Bass*) tells General **Rhadames** (*Tenor*) that the defeated Ethiopians are again menacing Egypt. Rhadames hopes that he will be chosen leader against the invaders. Thus he may again lay before 'Heavenly Aida' his triumphs, and ask for her hand, although she is but a slave to **Amneris** (*Contralto*), the king's daughter, who now enters. Amneris is jealous, but pretends affection for **Aida** (*Soprano*).

The court assembles to hear the decision of the gods. It is that Rhadames shall lead the armies.

SCENE 2: *The Interior of the Temple of Vulcan at Memphis*

Chants and sacred dances, whilst Rhadames is invested with consecrated armour.

ACT II

SCENE 1: *A Hall in the Apartments of Amneris*

The jealous Amneris finds out that Aida loves Rhadames, by telling her first, falsely, that the hero is dead, and then that he lives. Aida's grief and then rapture reveal her secret. She fears her powerful rival's hate.

SCENE 2: *Entrance Gate, Thebes*

Triumphal return of Rhadames. In his captive train is **Amonasro**, the Ethiopian king (*Baritone*). Aida recognizes him as her father. He begs her not to let his identity be known, and lies to the Egyptians, telling them that the king is dead and asking for freedom for his followers. Rhadames claims that freedom as his boon, and the Pharaoh consents. Aida, with her father, is to be held at ransom. Rhadames is to wed Amneris, as his reward.

ACT III

SCENE: *The Banks of the Nile. Night*

Amonasro tells his daughter how she can defeat her rival and gain her home again. She must make Rhadames tell her by what path the Egyptian hosts will march. Then the Ethiopians will ambush and destroy them. For love of her people she consents. Amonasro hides.

When Rhadames comes to meet her, she tricks him into giving her the information she seeks. Amonasro reveals himself, and Amneris comes on the scene, denouncing Rhadames as a traitor. He is arrested, whilst Aida and her father flee.

ACT IV

SCENE 1: *A Hall in Pharaoh's Palace*

Amneris would save Rhadames, if he will renounce Aida, but he refuses and goes to his fate. His judges condemn him to be buried alive.

SCENE 2: *The Temple; below it is seen the Dungeon*

Aida has hidden in the dungeon, and now the two prepare to die together, whilst, in the temple above, hymns and sacred dances go on, and Amneris, in mourning, prays for the soul of him whom unavailingly she loves.

See *Grand Opera*.

AIGU, AIGUË (Fr., masc., fem.). 'Shrill', 'high in pitch'. In organ music *Octaves aiguës* means 'Super-octave Coupler'.

AIKIN, DR. W. See *Voice* 7.

AINSWORTH, HENRY (1571–*c.* 1622). See *Hymns and Hymn Tunes* 11.

AIR. Melody in the sense of a flowing, tuneful, uppermost part to a composition, or a composition itself of a melodious character.

For the more elaborate vocal development of the style see *Aria, Arioso, Arietta, Madrigal* 3, 6.

AIR DE CARACTÈRE. See *Ballet* 8.

AIRD'S 'SELECTION'. See *Yankee Doodle*.

AIR ON G STRING (Bach). See *G String*.

AIR WITH VARIATIONS. See *Form* 11; *Symphony* 6.

AIS (Ger.). The note A sharp (see Table 7).

AISE (Fr.). 'Ease.' So *À l'aise*, 'at ease', unhurried.

AISIS (Ger.). The note A double sharp (see Table 7).

AJOUTER (Fr.). 'To add.' So the imperative *Ajoutez*.

AKHRON. See *Achron*.

AKIMENKO (**Akimyenko**, etc.), FEODOR. Born at Kharkof in 1876 and died in Paris in 1945, aged sixty-eight. He was a pupil of

Balakiref, and later of Rimsky-Korsakof, and composed chamber and piano music, an opera (*The Snow Queen*, on a libretto by M. D. Calvocoressi), a ballet, etc.

AKKORD (Ger.). 'Chord.' *Akkordieren*, 'to tune'.

'A.L.'—Amelia Lehmann. See under *Lehmann*.

AL (It.). 'At the', 'to the', 'in the', etc., i.e. the same as *A* (q.v.), with the article added.

À LA, À L' (Fr.). 'To the', 'at the', 'on the', 'with the'. Also 'in the manner of'. (See *Mesure*.)

ALABIEF (Alabiev, Alabiew, Aliabiev), ALEXANDER. Born in Tobolsk in 1787 and died in Moscow in 1851, aged sixty-three. He was one of the Russian composers who preceded Glinka and the true national school (see *Russia* 4). He wrote songs and one opera. One of the songs ('The Nightingale') became widely known through prima donnas importing it into Rossini's *Barber of Seville*—in the Lesson Scene.

À LA CORDE (Fr.). Literally 'at the string', i.e. the bow kept on the string, producing a legato.

ALALÁ. A plainsong-like type of Spanish folk song, in four-line verses, much decorated in its melody at the taste of the singer.

ALALEONA, DOMENICO. Born at Montegiorgio in 1881 and there died in 1928, aged forty-seven. He was trained at the St. Cecilia Academy of Rome, afterwards occupying a place on its staff. He became known as a choral and orchestral conductor and the composer of choral and chamber works, etc., and as a writer of articles of musical research.

See reference under *Scales* 12.

À LA POINTE D'ARCHET (Fr.). 'With the point of the bow.'

ALARD, JEAN DELPHIN. Born at Bayonne in 1815 and died in Paris in 1888, aged seventy-two. He was a great violinist and teacher of violin, a diligent composer and editor of violin music, and the author of a famous *Violin School*.

ALBÉNIZ.

(1) PEDRO (I). Born at Biscay, in the north of Spain, about 1755, and died at San Sebastian in 1821, aged about sixty-six. He was a monk and in charge of the music of the Cathedral of San Sebastian. He composed church music.

(2) PEDRO (II). Born at Logroño, in Castile, in 1795, and died at Madrid in 1855, aged sixty. He was, like his namesake above, at one time in charge of the music at the Cathedral of San Sebastian, and later was court organist at Madrid. He was trained as a pianist in Paris under Herz and Kalkbrenner, became the founder of the modern art of piano playing in Spain, and wrote many piano compositions (not of high value) and a piano method.

(3) ISAAC (p. 977, pl. **164**. 5). Born at Camprodon, Catalonia, in 1860, and died at Cambo les Bains in the French Pyrenees in 1909, aged forty-eight. He was famous as pianist and as one of the first Spanish composers of importance to turn to account in developed composition the native rhythms and melodic phraseology.

His life was in the highest degree adventurous. He appeared as pianist at the age of four, and three years later applied for admission to the Conservatory of Paris, being, however, refused on the grounds of youth. He then studied at the Conservatory of Madrid. At nine he ran away, gave recitals all over Spain, and then hid himself on a vessel leaving for Porto Rico, giving performances to pay for his passage. Quite alone he undertook a recital tour which extended from Cuba in the east to San Francisco in the west. He came back to Europe at thirteen, played in Liverpool and London, and studied for a year at Leipzig. He returned penniless to Spain and was accorded a royal grant enabling him to study at Brussels and again at Leipzig. At twenty he toured in Cuba, Mexico, and the Argentine. On return he served for a time as conductor of a company playing zarzuelas (see *Opera* 15).

After a time he dropped public piano playing in favour of composition, and at thirty he was studying at Paris with d'Indy and Dukas; he came under the influence of Debussy also. He composed lavishly for the piano (e.g. his *Iberia* Suite of twelve movements reminiscent of different parts of Spain): some of his music is needlessly difficult to play, but all of it is of that happy kind that pleases both the greater and smaller musical publics. He wrote a number of successful operas, some to English libretti. For many years, until his death, he was in receipt of an income from the librettist of his opera *Henry Clifford* (i.e. Francis Money-Coutts, an English millionaire).

Liszt and Rubinstein approved him as pianist and did much to help him. He was notable as a performer of the classics.

See *Spain* 7 (for the 19th-cent. Spanish School); *Ornaments* 6; *Jota*; *Seguidilla*; *Bretón*; *Folk Song* 5; *Granados, Enrique*; *History* 7; *Nationalism*; *Percussion* 4 d; *Rhythm* 10.

ALBERT (Prince Consort to Queen Victoria). Born at Rosenau, Germany, in 1819, married in 1840, and died at Windsor in 1861, aged forty-two. He received a good musical training, played the organ, sang, and composed (though not, it has been hinted, without assistance). Some of his music was published in his lifetime, and a complete edition was brought out in the 1880s. A Morning Service is to be seen in some cathedral choir libraries; anthems by him were sung in Westminster Abbey on the occasions of Queen Victoria's two Jubilees. The Royal Albert Hall (see *Concert* 8) was dedicated to his memory.

See references under *Chapel Royal*; *Concert* 6.

ALBERT, D'. See *D'Albert*.

ALBERT HALL, LONDON. See *Concert* 8; *Albert (Prince Consort)*.

ALBERTI BASS. That form of accompaniment to a melody that consists of 'broken chords', i.e. a mere arpeggio treatment of a series of chords, e.g.:

It is the simplest sort of moving accompaniment possible. It is most commonly found in keyboard music, where the right-hand plays the melody and the left supplies a harmony and a sense of something going on.

It takes his name from the Italian composer Domenico Alberti (*c.* 1710–40), in whose popular harpsichord sonatas it is frequent. The keyboard sonata was then beginning to be developed, and during that century C. P. E. Bach, Haydn, Mozart, and every other sonata composer made more or less use of the formula. In the hands of second-rate composers it becomes extremely commonplace.

See references to Alberti under *Sonata* 10 d.

ALBERT PALACE, BATTERSEA. See *Concert* 8.

ALBICASTRO, HENRICO (italianized form of his real name, Heinz Weissenburg). He was a late seventeenth-century and early eighteenth-century Swiss mercenary soldier, a captain of horse in the wars of the Spanish succession. He was also a fine violinist and the able composer of a quantity of string music of all the types then current.

ALBIGENSES. See *Minstrels*, etc. 4.

ALBINONI, TOMASO. Born in Venice in 1671 and there died in 1750, aged seventy-eight. He was a violinist and a vocalist and the composer of over forty operas as well as many orchestral works, sonatas for various instruments, cantatas, etc. Bach evidently knew and respected his work, since he composed fugues on themes of his.

ALBORADA (Sp.). An 'aubade' (q.v.), or morning song. The word has come to be applied to a type of instrumental music (sometimes played on bagpipes and small drum). Composers have made use of the type, e.g. Rimsky-Korsakof in his orchestral *Spanish Capriccio*, and Ravel in no. 4 of his *Miroirs* for piano. A tendency to freedom of rhythm is a characteristic of the genuine and unsophisticated Alborada.

ALBRECHTSBERGER, JOHANN GEORG. Born near Vienna in 1736 and died in that city in 1809, aged seventy-three. He held various important positions as organist, including that of the Court of Vienna, where also he was given charge of the music in St. Stephen's Cathedral. He exercised some activity as composer, but is remembered today more as a teacher of composition and author of a once-important textbook on the subject—of which an English translation remained for many years in print. Amongst his many pupils was Beethoven (q.v.).

See *Chamber Music*, Period III (1736); *Mozart*.

ALBUMBLATT (Ger.; plural, *Albumblätter*), **ALBUM LEAF.** A fairly frequent title for a brief and not very important instrumental composition, such as, in the days when the autograph album was one of the fashionable nuisances of life, a complaisant composer might write for a lady friend.

There are some particularly beautiful specimens in Schumann's *Bunte Blätter* ('Gay-coloured Leaves'), op. 99 (nos. 4 to 8). These might all have been put into good-sized autograph albums.

A.L.C.M. See *Degrees and Diplomas* 2.

ALCOCK.

(1) JOHN (I). Born in London in 1715 and died at Lichfield in 1806, aged ninety. Beginning his musical life as a choir-boy of St. Paul's Cathedral, he passed through a series of parish church organistships to that of Lichfield Cathedral, then resigning it and becoming again organist of parish churches. (The reason for his abandonment of his cathedral position may perhaps be surmised from the extract from his writings given under *Cathedral Music* 7.)

He left church music, glees, and instrumental music, a novel called *The Life of Miss Fanny Brown*, and a son (see below).

(2) JOHN (II). Born, probably at Plymouth, in 1740, and died at Walsall in 1791, aged fifty-one. He was son of John (I), above. He was a parish church organist, like his father, with whom he collaborated in the publication of a set of anthems, also publishing church music independently. He, and not his father, is the composer of the well-known Double Chant in E flat.

(3) WALTER GALPIN. He was born at Edenbridge, Kent, in 1861 and died in 1947, aged eighty-five. After twenty years as assistant organist at Westminster Abbey (from 1896), with also the organistship of the Chapels Royal (1902), he became in 1916 organist of Salisbury Cathedral. He had a high reputation as player (see passing reference under *Improvisation* 2), and some of his church music is much in use. He had a close association under five sovereigns with the music of royal ceremonies, including the Coronation of George VI.

He was knighted in 1933.

ALCUIN (*c.* 735–804). A native of York, the friend and counsellor of Charlemagne at his court at Aix-la-Chapelle, and Abbot of Tours, where he died. Amongst his extensive and varied works is the treatise *De Musica*.

ALCUNO, ALCUNA, ALCUN' (It., masc., fem.). 'Some.' The plurals are *Alcuni, Alcune*.

ALDRICH.
(1) HENRY. Born in London in 1647 and died at Oxford in 1710, aged sixty-three. All but the earliest part of his life was spent at Christ Church, Oxford, as undergraduate, tutor, canon, and dean; there he is buried, and there is to be found his valuable collection of music. He also twice served as Vice-Chancellor of the University.

He was a classical scholar, theologian, heraldist, architect and writer on architecture, musical theorist, and composer. Some humorous catches and solid church music are still performed.

See passing references under *Cathedral Music* 7; *Anthem*, Period II; *Catch*.

(2) RICHARD (1863–1937). See reference under *Criticism of Music* 5.

ALEATORY MUSIC. Aleatory = Depending on chance (literally on the throw of dice).

See *History of Music* 9.

ALECSANDRI, VASILE (1821–90). See *Rumania*.

ALEMBERT, JEAN LE ROND D' (1717–83). See *France* 8; *Criticism* 3; *Bouffons*.

ALENTEJO (Portugal) and Organum. See *Harmony* 4.

ALESSANDRESCU, ALFRED. Born at Bucharest, Rumania, in 1893 and died there in 1959, aged sixty-six. He studied in Bucharest and then with d'Indy in Paris. In 1920 there was performed there his symphonic poem *Actaeon*. He shows in some of his orchestral and chamber music, songs, etc., a leaning to the styles and methods of Debussy and Dukas. His orchestration is extremely effective.

As opera conductor and music director of radio he occupied a leading position in Bucharest.

ALEXANDER, ARTHUR (1891–1969). Pianist and composer; teacher at the Matthay School and the Royal College of Music. See *Swain, F. M.*

ALEXANDRA PALACE. A North London centre of pleasure and popular culture (founded 1875), with a large concert hall and organ, etc. (similar to the Crystal Palace in South London —see *Concert* 7); the early home of British television.

ALEXANDRE, JACOB (1804–76). See *Reed-Organ Family* 6, 7, 8.

ALEXANDRI, VASILE (1821–90). See *Rumania*.

ALEXANDROF (Alexandrov, Alexandrow), ANATOL. Born in Moscow in 1888. He was a pupil of Taneief at the Conservatory of Moscow, and has written a number of songs, piano sonatas, orchestral works, etc.

ALFANO, FRANCO. Born at Posilippo, near Naples, in 1876 and died at San Remo in 1954, aged seventy-eight. After study in Italy and Germany, he devoted himself to opera composition. Amongst his works are *Resurrection*

(1904), *The Shade of Don Juan* (performed 1914), *Sakuntala* (1922), *Madonna Imperia* (1926), *The Last Lord* (1930), and *Cyrano di Bergerac* (1936). There are also ballets, orchestral works, songs, chamber music, etc. He completed Puccini's posthumous work, *Turandot*. In 1919 he became director of the Conservatory of Bologna, in 1924 of that of Turin, and in 1947 of that of Pesaro.

ALFONSO, MASTER. See *Ferrabosco* 1.

ALFONSO X, of León and Castile. See *Spain* 3.

ALFVÉN, HUGO. Born at Stockholm in 1872 and died at Falún, Sweden, in 1960, aged eighty-eight. A violinist, he was from 1910 to 1939 director of music at the University of Uppsala. His compositions, in the late romantic tradition and often founded on folk melodies, include five symphonies, symphonic poems, piano works, violin works, songs, etc. His one universally popular piece is *Midsommarvaka* ('Midsummer Vigil', 1904), the first of three Swedish Rhapsodies.

ALGAROTTI, FRANCESCO. Born in Venice in 1712 and died at Pisa in 1764, aged fifty-one. He was a man of high culture and wide learning and a musical amateur who in 1755 wrote an important book on the opera as presented in his period: *Saggio sopra l'opera in musica*. Translations of this into German, French, and English have appeared. Frederick the Great invited him to Berlin and made him a count.

ALIABIEV. See *Alabiev*.

ALIQUOT SCALING. See *Pianoforte* 16.

ALISON or **ALLISON**, RICHARD. At the end of the sixteenth century and the beginning of the seventeenth he composed madrigals, songs, and the like. For his famous book of settings of the metrical psalms, see *Hymns* 17 e, xi, *Anglican Chant* 5, and *Lute Family* 4.

ALKAN (real name Morhange), CHARLES HENRY VALENTIN. Born in Paris in 1813 and died there in 1888, aged seventy-four. From his sixth year (in which he entered the Conservatory of Paris) he was recognized as a remarkable pianist. He composed much music for his instrument, including small genre pieces as well as Études of high difficulty and often of very descriptive character (wind, the sea, etc.), in which his skilful invention added materially to the permanent technical resources of piano composition. (Also many pieces for pedal piano.)

See also *Pianoforte* 21.

ALL', **ALLA** (It.). 'To the', 'at the', 'on the', 'with the'; also 'in the manner of'.

ALLA BREVE. See *Breve*.

ALLA BREVE FUGUE (Bach). See *Nicknamed Compositions* 1.

ALLA DANZA TEDESCA. See *Allemande* 2.

ALL AMONG THE BARLEY. See *Stirling*.

ALLAN, MAUD. See *Bloch*.

ALLANT (Fr.). 'Going.' Sometimes also 'getting', e.g. Debussy's *Allant grandissant*, 'getting growing', i.e. becoming all the time louder. *Un peu plus allant* means 'with a little more "go"'.

ALLARD. See *Ballet* 9.

ALLARGANDO (It.). 'Enlarging', i.e. getting slower and slower, and fuller in tone.

ALLE (Ger.). 'All.' Thus if one violin has been playing alone all are now to enter. *Alle Ersten* means all the first violins and *Alle Zweiten* (sometimes 'Zwoten') all the second.

ALLE (It.). 'To the' (fem. plur.).

ALLEGRAMENTE (It.). **ALLÉGREMENT** (Fr.) 'Brightly', 'gaily'.

ALLEGRETTO (It.). Pretty lively (not so much so as allegro).

ALLEGREZZA (It.). 'Mirth', 'cheerfulness'.

ALLEGRI, GREGORIO (p. 516, pl. **93.** 5.) Born in Rome in 1582 and died there in 1652, aged seventy. He was a priest, a tenor singer, and a composer. About the last quarter-century of his life was spent in the musical service of the Pope, and a certain *Miserere* he wrote for quartet of soloists and five-part choir, sung annually in the Sistine Chapel during Holy Week, was intended to be the exclusive possession of that chapel, excommunication being at one time the punishment for infringement of the monopoly.

See *Miserere*; *Faburden* 2; *Memory* 3; *Chamber Music* 6 I.

ALLEGRO (It.). 'Merry', i.e. quick, lively, bright. Often used also as the title of a composition or movement in that style. The superlative is *Allegrissimo*.

ALLEIN (Ger.). 'Alone', e.g. *Eine Violine allein*, 'one violin alone'.

ALLEIN GOTT IN DER HÖH' SEI EHR. See *Chorale*.

ALLELUIA. This Latin form of Hebrew exclamation, meaning 'Praise Jehovah' (see *Hallelujah*), was added to certain of the responds (q.v.) of the Roman Catholic Church, suitably joyful music for it being grafted on to the traditional plainsong and, in time, itself becoming traditional; such a passage ends with the word 'Jubilate'. The Alleluia is omitted from Septuagesima to Easter Day, in Requiem Masses, etc., and a Tract (q.v.) takes its place.

Cf. *Aevia* and *Pneuma*.

'ALLELUIA' SYMPHONY (Haydn). See *Nicknamed Compositions* 11.

ALLEMAND (Fr.). 'German.'

ALLEMANDE (Fr.). Literally, 'German'. Sometimes the word appears as 'Alman' or 'Almand', 'Almayne' or 'Almain', etc. It is the name of two distinct types of composition,

quite unrelated to one another except that apparently both have been looked upon as of German origin, so that both have had the name applied.

(1) The allemande of real importance is that which has been made use of by many writers of the classical suite (see *Suite* 3), e.g. Purcell, Couperin, Bach, Handel. It is in a time of four beats to the measure (or it may be that two long beats are designated by the time-signature). It falls into two more or less equal halves (i.e. Binary Form, q.v.), and a feature is that each of these opens with a short note at the end of a bar, often the same as the note that opens the following bar—a sort of double knock. Sometimes, of course, other than the opening phrases of the two parts begin in this way. Occasionally three short notes take the place of the one.

The general character of the allemande, as found in suites, is serious but not heavy. The speed is generally moderate. Its melody is usually much decorated with curving groups of short notes, and it is probably really not of German but French or Netherlandish origin. In the sixteenth century it was already regarded as very old.

A ballroom association grew up between the slower allemande and the quicker courante (as earlier between the pavan and galliard, q.v.), and this association was continued when they survived as instrumental movements in the suite.

The traditional place of the allemande in the suite is at the opening, i.e. it is the first movement of all, unless a prelude precede it. (The Elizabethan composers wrote many 'Almans' as separate pieces.)

This sort of allemande appears to have developed from a certain old German dance in four-in-a-measure time (p. 273, pl. **49.** 3).

(2) The allemande still danced today amongst the peasants of parts of Germany and Switzerland is a different thing; like the Ländler, it is prophetic of the waltz, being in three-beats-in-a-measure and lively. This also appears amongst the classical composers occasionally, as, for instance, in Mozart's *Deutsche Tänze* (often called simply *Deutsche*) and in Beethoven's early book of twelve German Dances (1795) and String Quartet, op. 130 (where it is called *Alla danza tedesca*, i.e. 'in the German dance style').

ALLEN.

(1) HUGH PERCY (p. 289, pl. **51.** 7). Born at Reading in 1869 and died, as the result of a street accident, at Oxford in 1946, aged seventy-six. He became organ scholar of Christ's College, Cambridge (1892), and, later, organist of the cathedrals of St. Asaph (1897) and Ely (1898), and of New College, Oxford (1901–18). At this last place he had a very active career as choral and orchestral conductor. From 1918 he was both Professor of Music at Oxford (to his death) and Director of the Royal

College of Music (to 1937). He was conductor of the Oxford and London Bach Choirs (and in many other ways contributed to the Bach revival in England) and one of the conductors of the Leeds Festival.

He held doctorates from various universities and was knighted in 1920.

(2) A. E. See *Electric Musical Instruments* 2 b, 4.

(3) W. E. See *United States* 6.

ALLENDE, HUMBERTO. Born at Santiago, Chile, in 1885. He is a violinist and composer, trained at the conservatory of his native place. He is a close student of Chilean folk tune and the titles and idioms of his numerous orchestral and other compositions reflect his interest in this.

ALLENTAMENTO, ALLENTANDO (It.). 'Slowing' (noun), 'slowed'.

ALLGEMEINER DEUTSCHER CAECILIENVEREIN. See *Cecilian Movement*.

ALL IN THE DOWNS. See *Leveridge, Richard*.

ALLISON. See *Alison*.

ALLMÄHLICH, ALLMÄHLIG, ALLMÄLIG (Ger.). 'Gradually.'

ALLO. Short for allegro (q.v.).

ALLON, (1) REVD. HENRY; (2) HENRY ERSKINE. See *Congregational Church Music* 5.

ALLONGER (Fr.). 'To lengthen', i.e. to slacken in speed.

ALLORA (It.). 'Then.'

ALL' OTTAVA (It.). An octave higher (*All' ottava alta*), or lower (*All' ottava bassa*).

ALLT, WILFRID GREENHOUSE. Born in Wolverhampton in 1889 and died in London in 1969, aged eighty. After five years as assistant organist of Norwich Cathedral he settled in 1915 in Edinburgh, holding from 1923 the position of organist of St. Giles's Cathedral and becoming known as a choral conductor. He studied meanwhile at the University there, under Tovey, and for many years conducted the University Music Society. From 1944 to 1965 he was Principal of Trinity College of Music, London.

ALL THROUGH THE NIGHT. The tune usually known outside Wales by this title is that of the Welsh folk song *Ar hyd y nos*. An English setting to which it was formerly heard was 'Here beneath a willow weepeth poor Mary Ann'—words by the novelist, Mrs. Amelia Opie (1769–1853). The tune itself, with an analysis of its structure, will be found under *Melody* 3.

ALLURE (Fr.). 'Gait', 'manner'.

ALMAIN, ALMAN, ALMAND. See *Allemande*.

ALMA REDEMPTORIS MATER. See *Antiphons of the Blessed Virgin Mary*.

ALMAYNE. See *Allemande*.

ALPHORN, ALPENHORN (Ger.), **COR DES ALPES** (Fr.) (p. 545, pl. 100. 3). This, being made with a straight (or rather slightly curved) tube, is, in consequence (so far as appearance goes), one of the longest instruments in existence, being in some cantons of Switzerland commonly as much as 7 feet long, whilst specimens occur of 10 to 12 feet. It is made of wood but has a mouthpiece similar to that of the cornet and, on the principle of such an instrument, plays only the harmonics (see *Acoustics* 8) of its tube. It is not quite in tune with our accepted scale.

The Swiss peasants use it for calling the cattle (see *Ranz des vaches*) and for amusement, and in summer make a little money by stationing themselves where tourists pass and displaying their technique, usually with an echo as colleague.

A player of the alphorn, questioned and tested for the purposes of the present description, could not obtain either the first harmonic (i.e. the fundamental tone of the instrument) or the next two. After that, he could play all the harmonics for about two octaves, so that in his higher ranges he had available a number of contiguous notes—but, he said, so great a range as this was feasible only in the morning, not in the afternoon when his lips were tired from much playing to tourists. He had a large funnel-shaped bell which could be placed on the end of the instrument, but he showed that the quality of the tone was better without it. He was also a player of brass instruments in a village band, but began on the alphorn. Most alphorn players, he said, do not play any other instrument.

See also mention under *Rumania*; *Lur* 2.

AL ROVESCIO. See *Rovescio*.

ALS (Ger.). 'As', 'like', 'when', 'than'.

ALSAGER, THOMAS MASSA (1779–1846). An enthusiastic amateur musician who carried on a musical society at his house in London, where were performed, for the first time in Britain, Beethoven's great Mass and other works. A Beethoven Quartet Society was a part of the scheme. He was manager of *The Times*.

See *Criticism* 4.

AL SEGNO (It.). 'To the sign', meaning go to the mark 𝄋. This may mean '*Go back* to the sign' (the same, in that sense, as *Dal segno*, q.v.), or it may mean '*Continue* until you reach the sign' (see remarks under *Da capo*; also Table 20).

ALSO (Ger.). 'Thus.'

ALT (1) meaning 'high', is used of the note G above the treble stave and of all notes to the F above that, the expression being 'G in alt' and so forth. The superlative, *Altissimo*, is applied to the notes of the next octave, 'G in altissimo', etc. These are vocal terms. There is some variety in their application (see *Pitch*

7 i) but the above limits are those most generally accepted.

(2) In German, Alt has a different meaning —the alto voice. As a prefix, in the names of instruments in German ('Althorn', etc.), the word signifies an alto-pitched instrument of the family in question, i.e. one of which the compass lies about five notes lower than that of the treble member of the family.

(3) Another German meaning is 'old' (in which sense it has various terminations according to gender, number, case).

ALTA (It., fem.; for masc. see *Alto*). 'High', e.g. *Ottava alta*, 'high octave', i.e. one octave higher.

ALTENBURG, JOHANN CASPAR (1688–1761) and **JOHANN ERNST** (1734–1801), father and son, both celebrated trumpet players. The son, who was also an organist, in 1795 wrote a very important book on trumpet and kettledrum playing (see reference under *Inventionshorn, Inventionstrompete*—note).

ALTERNATIVO. In early eighteenth-century dance music the word often appears over the contrasting middle section, later usually called 'Trio' (see *Trio* 2). Sometimes it is found applied to the whole dance piece, apparently implying that the two contrasting sections can be alternated indifferently at the will of the performer. Later than the eighteenth century the word is little met with, but Schumann uses it.

ALTEZZA or **ALTEZZA SONORA.** See *Pitch* 8.

ALTFLÖTE. See *Flute Family* 5 c.

ALTFLÜGELHORN. See *Saxhorn and Flügelhorn Families* 3 c; *Tuba Group* 5.

ALTGEIGE (Ger.). Literally 'alto fiddle', i.e. the viola, but it has had a special meaning also attached to it (see *Viola alta*).

ALTHOBOE. See *Oboe Family* 5 b.

ALTHORN. See *Saxhorn and Flügelhorn Families* 2 c d; *Tuba Group* 5.

ALTISSIMO. See *Alt*; *Pitch* 7 i.

ALTISTE (Fr.).
  (1) A player of the 'alto', i.e. of the viola (see *Violin Family* 2 b, 7).
  (2) An alto singer (see *Alto Voice*).

ALTKLARINETTE. See *Clarinet Family* 5.

ALTKORNETT. See *Saxhorn and Flügelhorn Families* 2 c.

ALTO. Properly the word means 'high'. It is still applied to the highest (adult) male voice (see article following), and to instruments roughly corresponding in pitch with this, and in such expressions as *Horn in B flat alto* it implies a pitch an octave higher than some corresponding instrument (there is similarly 'Horn in B flat basso'). The following are the most important occurrences of the word:

1. **ALTO** (Fr.). The viola (see *Violin Family* 2 b, 7).
2. **ALTO** (BUGLE). See *Saxhorn* 2 c.
3. **ALTO CLARINET.** See *Clarinet Family* 4 e, 5.
4. **ALTO CLEF.** See *Notation* 4; also Table 4.
5. **ALTO FLÜGELHORN.** See *Saxhorn and Flügelhorn Families* 3 b, c; *Tuba Group* 5.
6. **ALTO FLUTE.** See *Flute Family* 3 c.
7. **ALTO MODERNE.** See *Viole-ténor*.
8. **ALTO SAXHORN.** See *Saxhorn and Flügelhorn Families* 2 b, c.
9. **ALTO STAFF.** See *Great Staff*.

ALTO-TENOR VOICE. This is a term that has been in common use since the late nineteenth century amongst school musicians in the United States, and is there to be seen in catalogues of school music and school music literature.

It describes the adolescent boy's gradually lowering voice at a late stage, when it is still alto but can be used also in the tenor range. Its extent can be put at an octave—G near top of bass clef to G near bottom of treble clef (see *Voice* 5 as to the use of the boy's voice at this stage).

ALTO TROMBONE. See *Trombone Family* 2 b, 3, 5.

ALTO VOICE. See *Voice* 5, 17. This male voice has always been most cultivated in Britain, where the older church music definitely implies its use, as does a special form of secular music (see *Glee* 2). Little solo music exists for it apart from that incidental to the seventeenth-century royal odes and the older anthems (e.g. Purcell), etc., and none is now written. Mendelssohn gave the corresponding women's voice (contralto) prominence by writing solos for Madame Sainton Dolby in *Elijah* (1847), and since then solos for that voice have been a recognized feature in oratorio composition, the alto voice falling more and more into the background, even in chorus work.

In the great Westminster Abbey Handel Commemoration of 1784, there were in the chorus forty-five altos (then called 'Countertenors'), with not a single contralto (not from any objection to the appearance of women in the cathedral, since there were such amongst the sopranos).

A hundred years later (1883) the Leeds Festival chorus still included forty-two altos as against seventeen contraltos.

Apparently there was at this period a definite movement set on foot in favour of contraltos as against altos, for in June 1884 a protesting letter in the *Musical Times* insists that 'it is a great mistake to do away with Altos and substitute Contraltos in oratorio music at all events'. And in the next Leeds Festival (1886) we find only sixteen altos as against fifty-seven contraltos, and in the Norwich Festival of forty years later (1924) seventy-one contraltos and not a single alto (even the altos of the cathedral not being brought into use).

Thus in 140 years we have a swing over from oratorio choirs with not a single contralto to oratorio choirs with not a single alto. The real alto being now so rare, it is becoming common to speak of contraltos as altos, and in publishers' catalogues 'S.A.T.B.' (Soprano, Alto, Tenor, Bass) is a commoner indication that 'S.C.T.B.'.

One point against the alto voice is that it does not last so well as the other male voices, often deteriorating rather seriously after the age of fifty or so. Peterborough Cathedral long (c. 1880–1920) used no adult altos—only boys.

ALTPOSAUNE (Ger.). Alto trombone. See *Trombone Family* 2 b.

ALTRA, ALTRE. See *Altro.*

ALTRA VOLTA. See *Encore.*

ALTRO, ALTRI (It., masc., sing., plur.). 'Another', 'others' (*Altra, Altre* are the fem.).

ALTUS. See *Voice* 17.

ALUMINOPHONE. See *Percussion Family* 2 f.

ALWYN, WILLIAM. Born at Northampton in 1905. He was trained at the Royal Academy of Music, where from 1926 to 1956 he was a Professor of Composition. For a time he was an orchestral flautist. His compositions include four symphonies, violin, piano, and oboe concertos, chamber music, piano music, as well as much successful film music, etc.

ALZATO, ALZATI (It., masc., sing., plur.). 'Raised', lifted off (of a mute or mutes, etc.). The fem. (sing., plur.) is *Alzata, Alzate.*

AM (Ger.). 'At the', 'on the', 'to the', 'by the', 'near the'. See *Frosch*; *Griffbrett*; *Steg.*

AMABILE (It.). 'Lovable', so *Amabilità,* 'lovableness'.

AMADINO. See *Publishing* 1.

AMAR, AMAR QUARTET. See *Hindemith.*

AMAREVOLE, AMAREZZA (It.). 'Bitterly', 'bitterness'.

AMATI. See *Violin Family* 4; *Italy* 6.

AMBOSS (Ger.). 'Anvil.' See *Percussion Family* 3 s, 4 c, 5 s.

AMBROS, AUGUST WILHELM (1816–76). He was a highly placed legal official, first at Prague, then at Vienna, who devoted the leisure of his life to musical research. His great *History of Music* (4 vols., 1862–78; unfinished) is of high value.

See a reference under *White, Robert.*

AMBROSE, SAINT (c. 340–97). See below. Also *Hymns and Hymn Tunes* 2.

AMBROSIAN CHANT. See *Plainsong* 3.

AMBROSIAN HYMN. The *Te Deum* (q.v.).

AMBROSIAN MODES. See *Modes* 2, 4, 6.

AMBROSIAN RITE. See *Liturgy.*

ÂME (Fr.). Literally, 'soul'—the sound-post (q.v.) of the violin, etc. The fanciful French name doubtless comes from its importance to the whole tone of the instrument, which depends much on its correct position. The Italians say *Anima,* which likewise means 'soul'.

AMEN. 'So be it'—in agreement to a remark made by someone else. The (Hebrew) terminal word of prayer in Jewish, Christian, and Mohammedan worship. It has been extended by composers, innumerable times, into a long composition, as, for instance, the 'Amen Chorus' of Handel's *Messiah.* For liturgical use shorter settings have been made, such as Stainer's Sevenfold Amen. The **Dresden Amen** comes from the threefold Amen of the Royal Chapel of Dresden (common also throughout Saxony); Wagner has introduced it in *Parsifal,* and it also appears in Mendelssohn's 'Reformation' Symphony, Stanford's Service in B flat, and elsewhere. Its composer was J. G. Naumann (q.v.).

AMEN CADENCE. See *Cadence.*

AMERICA. See *United States.* The following is a list of some detailed points treated in various articles:

1. **AMERICAN ACADEMY, ROME.** See *United States* 5 f; *Patronage* 7.
2. **AMERICAN GUILD OF ORGANISTS.** See article below and *Degrees and Diplomas* 4.
3. **AMERICAN INDIANS.** See *United States* 7; *Dance* 4.
4. **AMERICAN MUSICAL JOURNALS.** See *Journals.*
5. **AMERICAN MUSICAL TERMINOLOGY.** See article below.
6. **AMERICAN MUSICOLOGICAL SOCIETY.** See *Musicology.*
7. **AMERICAN NATIONAL ASSOCIATION OF ORGANISTS.** See *Profession of Music* 10.
8. **AMERICAN ORGAN.** See *Reed-Organ Family* 7, 9; *American Musical Terminology* 7.
9. **AMERICAN REFORMED PRESBYTERIAN CHURCH.** See *Presbyterian Church Music* 6.
10. **AMERICAN SCHOOL, FONTAINEBLEAU.** See *United States of America* 5 f.
11. **AMERICAN SPEECH.** See *Voice* 10, 12.
12. **AMERICA THE BEAUTIFUL.** See article below.

The table of contents at the head of the article *United States* should also be consulted. American composers treated in this work will, of course, be found under their own names, and references to the achievements of America in any branch of activity will be found under the appropriate heads.

'AMERICA' (the tune). See *God Save the Queen* 14.

AMERICAN GUILD OF ORGANISTS. This was founded in 1896 with 145 members and in 1966 had reached a membership of 15,000 (with 280 Chapters, every state being represented). It publishes a monthly magazine. It has been chartered by the Board of Regents of the University of the State of New York as an examining body and is active as such (see *Degrees and Diplomas* 4), but its functions cover a much larger field than that might suggest.

AMERICAN INSTITUTE OF MUSICOLOGY. See *Carapetyan*.

AMERICAN MUSICAL TERMINOLOGY. A certain number of technical terms differ amongst the musical communities on the two sides of the Atlantic. As these communities to a considerable extent share a musical literature (the publication of many valuable books being indeed economically possible only by this circumstance) the divergence is unfortunate. It seems to date from the activities of an American musical 'Committee on Terminology Reform' which sat from 1906 onwards, and it may be suggested that any such committee in the future should work in association with a corresponding British committee, reforms being introduced by common agreement. Moreover, in view of the large amount of musical literature already in existence, changes (however satisfying to a strict logical sense) should not be introduced without really pressing reason.

Before the following list of some of the chief divergences is read it should be stated that in the interests of the present book an extensive inquiry has been made in different cities of the United States, from which it has been established that some items of musical terminology are surprisingly local in their currency, being apparently in common use in one part of the country and almost unknown in another part.

1. The worst confusion arises from the different usage as concerns the words **Note** and **Tone**. Such expressions as 'three tones lower' or 'the scale of five tones' have quite different meanings to the American and the British reader. A British reader, finding these expressions in an American book or journal, must be careful to understand them as meaning merely, 'three notes lower' and 'scale of five notes', and an American reader finding such expressions in a British book must be careful to translate them into American as, precisely, 'three whole-steps lower' or 'a scale of five whole-steps'.

How serious is the divergence will be seen from that second example, the 'scale of five tones', which has been taken at random from a work on certain American Indian melodies. Read as every unwarned British musician would read it, it definitely implies a scale on the lines of the highly artificial modern scale commonly associated with Debussy; read as it is intended by the American author, it implies one of the simple primitive scales such as that of 'Auld Lang Syne' and similar Scottish melodies (see *Scales* 9 and 10 respectively).

The American contention as concerns 'Note' is that to use it for a *sound* is wrong because it 'names a *notation* element'. This is to defy more than five centuries of English usage and to accuse Chaucer, Shakespeare, Milton, and Tennyson (as also Morley, Simpson, Purcell, and the other English theorists) of ignorance

of their own language—and, further, to accuse all French and Italian writers (general and technical) of a similar ignorance. It is also to ignore earlier American usage, e.g. 'In learning the 8 notes get the assistance of some person well acquainted with the Tones and Semitones' (Lyon's *Urania*, 1761).

The suggestion that 'note' should be reserved for the sign and 'tone' used for the sound seems to have been first made by the Englishman John Curwen; it may still be found in some British tonic sol-fa literature, but has never been generally adopted in Britain for the reason that the word 'tone' has already too many accepted meanings ('tone-colour', 'Gregorian tone', etc.). Apart from such confusion as has been mentioned above, the change that has been introduced is particularly unfortunate, since, as a leading American musical lexicographer (Pratt) remarks, 'in many connexions the distinction is impossible to carry out'. (However, in the term 'Resultant Tone'—see *Acoustics* 10—it must be admitted that British scientific men side with the Americans.) The current American usage as regards the words 'note' and 'tone' derives from the German usage—*die Note* for the written or printed note and *der Ton* for the sounded one.

2. The frequent substitution of **Measure** for **Bar**, in the sense of a rhythmic period, leaving 'bar' as the name for the sign (another Curwen suggestion), though logical, does not seem to be very necessary. It does not, however, introduce any confusion, and has attained a good deal of currency in Britain, and it has therefore been adopted throughout the present work.

It may be added that recent American usage seems to tend to the use of 'bar' for the rhythmic period and of 'bar-line' for the sign, as in the common British usage.

3. The ancient names of the notes and rests, **'Semibreve'**, **'Minim'**, etc., have (again from German influences) been generally abandoned in America in favour of the nowadays more descriptive **'Whole-note'**, **'Half-note'**, etc. In the interests of the thousands of children learning music, to whom the arithmetical proportions are much more immediately significant than such terms as 'semidemisemiquaver', it is to be desired that the German–American system, though not perfect, should supersede the British–French–Italian system (see Table 3).

4. The substitution in some parts of the country of **Cancel** for **Natural** (after a sharp or flat) is sometimes seen, and is certainly logical.

5. For the term **Natural Notes** (of the brass instruments; cf. Ger. *Naturtöne*) some American writers substitute **Primary Tones.**

6. For the expressions 'to flatten' and 'to sharpen' they often say '*to lower*' and '*to raise*'.

7. The word **Organ** has a larger connotation in American usage than in British, since it often covers both the centuries-old traditional application of the word and also an application to the small reed organs long popular in hundreds

of American villages (see *Reed-Organ Family* 7). To prevent confusion, American writers often use **Pipe Organ** for the larger instrument and for many years they used **Cabinet Organ** for the smaller one—known by British writers as **American Organ**. Nowadays **Console** or **Console Organ** is used for this latter.

8. Phonograph and Gramophone. The American term is the earlier one, introduced by Edison in 1877; the English term dates from 1888. 'Victrola' (from the trade name of the Victor Co.) was also a good deal used in America. 'Record' is used in both countries, and 'Disc', or 'Disk', appears in 'Disk Jockey' —the broadcaster who puts on the records and comments on them.

9. Applied Music is an American term which has often puzzled British musicians. 'Applied Music' simply means 'Music', i.e. performed music as distinct from all the theoretical trimmings of the art. Thus some American universities include in their curricula 'Courses in Applied Music' (instruction in piano, violin, singing, etc.), and others do not, confining themselves, as do nearly all European universities, to the historical, theoretical, and appreciational sides of music.

There is some analogy here with the English term 'Applied Science' but less with the term 'Applied Art'.

10. The term **Folk Song** is more loosely used in America; a term of British origin, it has been allowed to drift into a wide meaning that deprives it of any real significance. For an explanation see *Folk Song* 1, and for the correct use of the often misused term **Folk Lore** see the same place.

11. For the common American terms **Concertmaster** and **Leader** see *Conducting* 4; *Leader*.

12. For **Glee Club** see *Glee* 3.

13. Voice-leading (an importation from Germany—*Stimmführung*) means simply 'part-writing', which is surely a far better term.

14. The term **Symphony** is in the United States often used for 'Symphony Orchestra'.

AMERICAN QUARTET. See s.v. *Nicknamed Compositions* 9.

AMERICAN SOCIETY OF COMPOSERS, AUTHORS, AND PUBLISHERS. See *Copyright and Performing Right* 2.

AMERICAN SYMPHONY ORCHESTRA LEAGUE. Founded in 1942, primarily to assist in the organization and development of smaller orchestras, and 'to stimulate interest in symphony orchestras, to further the welfare of the orchestras through interchange of ideas and problems, to make possible more opportunities for the American conductor, composer, and artist'.

AMERICA THE BEAUTIFUL. Few patriotic songs breathe such broad, humane idealism as this. The poem is the work of Katharine Lee Bates (1859–1929), Professor of English Literature at Wellesley College, Mass. It was written in 1893 (the opening lines on the summit of Pike's Peak, Colorado, with the 'sea-like expanse of fertile country spreading away under the ample skies'), but re-written in 1904, so as to be 'less literary and ornate'. Unfortunately, of the sixty tunes that have been provided for it by various composers, none has attained such a point of popularity as to establish a universal and indestructible association with the poem. The two tunes most used are those of Will C. Macfarlane and S. A. Ward.

AMORE (It.), **AMOUR** (Fr.). 'Love.' So *Amorevole, Amoroso,* 'loving'; *Amorevolmente, Amorosamente,* 'lovingly'. See also below.

AMORE, AMOUR (see also above). The qualification *d'Amore* (It.) or *d'Amour* (Fr.) is frequently found in the names of instruments of the seventeenth, eighteenth, and early nineteenth century. It seems to indicate, in every case, the claim to a sweeter tone than that of the corresponding instrument whose name was without the affix, and in some cases a rather lower pitch. In the bowed instruments, it usually implies, apparently, the possession of sympathetic strings (q.v.).

1. **FLAUTO d'AMORE** (Flûte d'amour). See *Flute Family* 3 d, 5.
2. **OBOE d'AMORE** (Hautbois d'amour). See *Oboe Family* 4 f, 5 f, 6.
3. **VIOLA d'AMORE** (of different sizes). See *Viol Family* 4 d, f.
4. **CLARINETTO d'AMORE.** See *Clarinet Family* 4 f.

There have also existed a **Guitare d'Amour** (see *Arpeggione*) and a **Cembalo d'Amore**— the latter invented by Silbermann in 1722 and not properly a cembalo (q.v.) but a sort of clavichord (q.v.).

AMORE DEI TRE RE. See *Montemezzi.*

AMOROSO, AMOROSAMENTE (It.). 'Loving', 'lovingly'. *Amorevolmente,* 'lovingly'.

AMOUR. See *Amore.*

AMPHIBRACH, AMPHIBRACHIC. See *Metre.*

AMPICO. See *Mechanical Reproduction* 13.

AMPLEUR (Fr.). 'Breadth.'

AMPLIFIERS. See *Concert Halls* 10; *Auxetophone; Bullphone.*

AMPLITUDE OF SOUND VIBRATIONS. See *Acoustics* 4, 11.

A.Mus.L.C.M. See *Degrees and Diplomas* 2.

A.Mus.T.C.L. See *Degrees and Diplomas* 2.

AN (Ger.). 'On', 'by', 'to', 'at'. In organ music it signifies that the stop in question is to be drawn.

ANACREON IN HEAVEN. See *Star-spangled Banner.*

ANACREONTIC SOCIETIES. See *Clubs for Music-Making; Star-spangled Banner; Flute Family* 4.

ANACRUSIS. An unstressed syllable at the beginning of a line of poetry or an unstressed note or group of notes at the beginning of a phrase of music. Plural, *Anacruses*.

This word was coined by G. Hermann (1772–1848) and first used in his *Elementa doctrinae metricae* (Leipzig, 1816).

ANALYTICAL PROGRAMME. See *Annotated Programme*.

ANAPAEST, ANAPAESTIC. See *Metre*.

ANBLASEN (Ger.). 'To blow.'

ANCHE (It.). 'Also.'

ANCHE (Fr.), **ANCIA** (It.). 'Reed.'

ANCIENT CYMBALS. See *Percussion Family* 3 o.

ANCIENT MUSIC, CONCERTS OF. See *Concert* 6.

AN COMUNN GÀIDHEALACH. See *Scotland* 1.

ANCORA (It.). 'Still', 'yet', e.g. *Ancora forte* = 'still loud'; *Ancora più forte* = 'still more loud'. The word is also used for 'Again', i.e. repeat. (In all these senses, compare the French word *Encore*.)

ANDACHT (Ger.). 'Devotion.' So *Andächtig* (or *Andaechtig*), 'devotional'.

ANDALUZ, ANDALUZA (Sp.), or **ANDA-LOUSE** (Fr.). A rather vague term sometimes applied to several types of Spanish dance common in Andalusia, as the fandango (q.v.), the malagueña (q.v.), and the polo (q.v.).

ANDAMENTO. A fugue subject of greater than ordinary length and development (from Italian *andare*, 'to go', perhaps because such subjects are usually of a running character). Compare *Attacco*.

ANDANTE (It.). From *andare*, 'to go'. It means 'moving along', 'flowing'; slowish but not slow. The word is often used as a title for a composition.

ANDANTINO (It.). A diminution of *andante* (see above). Unfortunately, some composers use it meaning a little slower than *andante*, and others as meaning a little quicker. (If a performer, use your own judgement; if a composer, avoid the ambiguous term.)

ANDAUERND (Ger.). 'Lasting', i.e. continuing.

ANDER, ANDERE, etc. (Ger.). 'Other' (various terminations according to gender, number, case).

ANDERSON, WILLIAM ROBERT. Born at Blackburn, Lancs., in 1891 (B.Mus. Durham, etc.). He is a well-known musical journalist and author, an adjudicator and critic, and Examiner for Trinity College of Music, London.

ANDERSSON, OLAF. Swedish musicologist, See *Scandinavia* 4 (end).

ANDNO. Short for *Andantino* (q.v.).

ANDRÉ. See *Publishing* 8.

ANDREAE, VOLKMAR. Born at Berne in 1879 and died in Zürich in 1962, aged nearly eighty-three. He was conductor of the orchestra of Zürich from 1906 to 1949 and was director of the Conservatory there from 1914 to 1939. He composed operas, orchestral music, chamber music, etc.

ANDREWS.

(1) HERBERT KENNEDY. Born at Comber, Co. Down, in 1904, and died at Oxford in 1965, aged sixty-one.Organist of Beverley Minster 1934, and of New College, Oxford, 1938–56; Lecturer in the Faculty of Music. Author of books on Palestrina and Byrd. See *Chromatic Chords*.

(2) HILDA. See *Lady Nevell's Book*.

ANDRICO, MICHAL. Born at Bucharest, Rumania, in 1894. He is a pupil of Castaldi, the well-known teacher of a whole generation of Rumanian composers. He began life as a violinist, and many of his compositions are for strings; he is director of chamber music at the Conservatory of Bucharest. His orchestral works have had much favour in that city; they are intensely national in spirit and for the most part based on folk music themes.

ANDRIESSEN.

(1) WILLEM. Born at Haarlem in 1887 and died in Amsterdam in 1964, aged seventy-six. He was a pianist, composer of a mass and other works, and professor of piano at the Conservatories of The Hague (1910) and Rotterdam. He directed the Amsterdam Conservatory from 1937, and in 1949 succeeded Sem Dresden at The Hague. Brother and teacher of (2).

(2) HENDRIK. Born at Haarlem in 1892. He is the brother of (1) above, and a composer of choral works, symphonies, sonatas, organ music, and so on. From 1937 to 1949 he was director of the Conservatory at Utrecht.

See *Opera* 24 f (1950).

ANERIO (The Brothers). Both were prominent in the Italian musical life of the Palestrina period and both composers of the unaccompanied choral music of the Palestrina school. **Felice** (c. 1560–1614) succeeded Palestrina as composer to the Papal Chapel and **Giovanni Francesco** (1567–1630), in later life a priest, was musical director to the King of Poland and afterwards held positions in Rome.

See references s.v. *Miserere*; *Plainsong* 3; *Faburden* 2.

ANFANG (Ger.). 'Beginning.' *Anfangs*, 'at the beginning'. *Wie anfänglich*, 'as at the beginning'.

ANGELICA (or in French *Angélique*). An instrument of the lute type with about sixteen strings tuned to the diatonic scale, of which only the highest was used for the melody, the others always being struck 'open'. A certain amount of music for it exists around 1700.

For Vox Angelica see *Organ* 14 I.

ANGEMESSEN (Ger.). 'Suitable to.'

ANGENEHM (Ger.). 'Agreeable.'

ANGIOLINI. See *Dance* 10.

ANGLAIS, ANGLAISE (Fr., masc., fem.). 'English' (see also below).

ANGLAISE. A vague term of very variable meaning, sometimes used by eighteenth-century composers. It may be found as the title of a hornpipe or of a country dance type of piece, or of anything else which the composer fancies is of an English character. Bach's third French Suite has an Anglaise of a very lively character in four-in-a-measure time.

ANGLEBERT, D' (Father and Son).

(1) JEAN HENRI (I). Born in Paris about 1628, and died there in 1691, aged about sixty-two. He was a pupil of Chambonnières (q.v.) and his successor as harpsichordist to the court. He published brilliant and effective music for harpsichord and organ (see *Folía*).

(2) JEAN BAPTISTE HENRI (II). Born in Paris in 1661, and died there in 1747, aged eighty-six. He was son of the above and his successor in his post at court, being in turn (1717) succeeded by Couperin.

ANGLICAN CHANT

1. Definition.
2. Not an Exclusively English Form.
3. The Early English Development.
4. The Introduction of Original Chants.
5. Double, Triple, and Quadruple Chants, etc.
6. The Introduction of 'Pointing'.

1. Definition. This is a simple type of harmonized melody used in the Anglican Church (and nowadays often in other English-speaking Protestant churches) for singing unmetrical texts, principally the Psalms and the Canticles (when these latter are not sung in a more elaborate setting).

The main principle is that of the traditional Gregorian tones (q.v.), i.e. a short melody is repeated to each verse of the text (sometimes to two or more verses; see 5 below), the varying numbers of syllables in the different lines of the words being accommodated by the flexible device of a **Reciting Note** at the opening of each line—this being treated as timeless and so capable of serving as the vehicle for many or few syllables, whilst the succeeding notes are sung in time and (normally) take one syllable each.

The resemblance of the Anglican chant to the Gregorian tone will be made clear by the following example of a popular Anglican chant which happens to have been fashioned out of such a tone (see 4).

GREGORIAN TONE.

Recitation.

Intonation.   Mediation.

ANGLICAN CHANT.

Glory be to the Father, and to   the   Son,

Recitation.

Final Cadence.

and   to   the   Ho - ly   Ghost.

It will be seen, then, that the principle of the Gregorian and the Anglican is the same, but that the intonation of the Gregorian, used in the opening verse of the psalm (see *Plainsong* 2), is altogether omitted in the Anglican. The frequent greater brevity of the Mediation as compared with the Final Cadence is, of course, reflected in the Anglican chant and results in its rather curious seven-bar structure. (Cf. *Faburden* 3.)

2. Not an Exclusively English Form. Although now considered to be, and often spoken of as, an exclusively English product, this form of chant may be said to have had very near relatives in other countries. Harmonized treatment of the plainsong, such as the following by Josquin des Prés (*c.* 1440–1521), obviously comes extremely near it.

Reciting Note.   Reciting Note.

Plainsong.

(Here the melody, the 8th Gregorian Psalm Tone, is in the tenor—as in most such settings of the period and for long after.)

At a later epoch, and in another part of Europe, we find such examples as the following, in which Bach sets a piece of prose to a piece of plainsong in quite the Anglican chant style, not excluding the accents on articles, conjunctions, and prepositions which are so distressing

1. NÄGELI of Zürich, who in 1826 published the first 'Appreciation' textbook. See p. 47

3. DR. FRANCES CLARK, American pioneer of Musical Appreciation. See p. 48

LA MUSIQUE

MISE A LA PORTÉE

DE TOUT LE MONDE,

EXPOSÉ SUCCINCT DE TOUT CE QUI EST NÉCESSAIRE
POUR JUGER DE CET ART,
ET POUR EN PARLER SANS L'AVOIR ÉTUDIÉ.

PAR M. FÉTIS,
DIRECTEUR DE LA REVUE MUSICALE.

PARIS.

ALEXANDRE MESNIER, LIBRAIRE,
PLACE DE LA BOURSE.

1830.

4. STEWART MACPHERSON British pioneer of Musical Appreciation. See p. 48

2. MUSICAL APPRECIATION. One of the earliest textbooks. It appeared in many languages. See p. 48

ENGLAND'S MOST DILIGENT EDITOR OF HER OLD MUSIC
Edmund Horace Fellowes, 1870–1951. See page 348

PLATE 4 CECILIA—PATRON SAINT OF MUSIC

See the Article on pages 166–7

1. AS ORGANIST
(By Raphael, 1483–1520)

2. AS ORGANIST
(By Lawrence, 1769–1830)

3. AS COMPOSER
(By Domenichino, 1581–1641)

4. AS VIOLINIST
(By Domenichino)

5. AS BASS-VIOLIST
(By Domenichino)

6. AS SINGER
Mrs. Billington (By Reynolds,
1723–92)

7. MADERNO'S ST. CECILIA (end of 16th century). In the church of
St. Cecilia in Trastevere, Rome, in the rebuilding of which her body was found
'uncorrupt in her tomb in the very same posture', as the sculptor relates

8. THE ASCENT TO HEAVEN

a characteristic of bad Anglican chanting and which he here determinedly and perversely makes unavoidable by his singers. The text Bach has set calls for three repetitions of the plainsong chosen (the *Tonus Peregrinus*), and he has therefore harmonized it three times differently. The first harmonization is given here.

It will be remarked that Bach has made use of an intonation to both strains of the chant. During the two centuries that lie between the Josquin des Prés example and that of Bach a large mass of similar music was provided. The **Falsobordone** of Italy was of the same general character (see *Faburden* 2 for a description). That continental protestantism, despite occasional approximations to the Anglican chant, never brought any form of the kind into regular and permanent use may be sufficiently accounted for by the fact that its custom was to turn into a metrical version almost any passage of Scripture it was desired to sing. Scotland did the same; and her national church, though devoted to the psalms, made no use of Anglican chants; England, on the other hand, so far as the national church was concerned, whilst admitting metrical psalms to a small place in worship, using them much as hymns are used now, retained (but in the vernacular) the use of the prose psalter and the prose canticle, and so was led to develop a form of song, which, whilst unmetrical, nevertheless was simple and capable of being indefinitely repeated musically unchanged.

3. The Early English Development. In England, very many examples of the falsobordone type were produced by all the leading composers of the Elizabethan period (Tallis, Morley, Byrd, Gibbons, and their contemporaries) in their settings of the prose psalms. The same principle was, curiously, applied to the setting of metrical psalmody in the first published book of the complete versified psalms, that of Crowley (1549), who supplied a single tune to be used to the whole series. This was a piece of plainsong (the 7th Gregorian Tone) harmonized in four parts with the plainsong in the tenor.

This, it will be seen, is to all intents and purposes what we nowadays call a Double Anglican Chant, the slight differences of detail being merely (*a*) that the division of the reciting note is shown in the notation; (*b*) some slight difference in rhythmic arrangement; (*c*) the tune in the tenor. (The application of the general principles of Anglican chanting to metrical words crops up occasionally in modern hymn-tune books: the nineteenth-century tune 'Troyte No. 1', to 'My God and Father, while I stray', to be found in many such books, is an example.)

Enough has now been said to show that the commonly supposed clear distinction between plainchant and Anglican chant is, in principle, non-existent—that Anglican chant is an offshoot of the harmonized plainchant which was very common throughout Christendom during the sixteenth and seventeenth centuries.

4. The Introduction of Original Chants.
Almost immediately after the Restoration, when the reinstatement of choirs and organs in the cathedrals called for the publication of works explaining the character of the cathedral service, of which the traditions had been weakened by the interruption of the Commonwealth, we find a few plainsong harmonizations appearing in print, set out in the way of our present single Anglican chant. Works with such are Lowe's *Short Directions for the Performance of the Cathedral Service* (1661): Clifford's *The Divine Services and Anthems usually sung in the Cathedrals and Collegiate Churches of the Church of England* (1664), and the Restoration editions of Playford's *Introduction to the Skill of Music*.

'Christ Church Tune', as set out by Clifford, is just that anglicanization of a Gregorian tone which is given as the first musical example of the present article, but with the melody in the tenor. It is one of three such adaptations that he supplies—which have all kept their place as popular Anglican chants.

Up to this date, it will be realized, English composers had no thought of 'composing' chants; all they did was to harmonize the existing traditional Gregorian tones. But it was a small step to the composition of original chants —a step, we may say, similar to that taken by the Italian and other composers who, from the arrangement of plainsong as falsobordoni, passed easily to the composition of original falsobordoni, of which they produced quantities.

The number of chants composed since the end of the seventeenth century is very great, and the quality very variable. During the eighteenth century there was a strong tendency to the provision of chants of a florid and sometimes flippant character; during the nineteenth to the provision of chants of a sentimentally chromatic type. The twentieth century has seen a strong movement towards dignity in church music and weaker specimens of the Anglican chant have increasingly tended to fall out of use, largely through the general adoption of several new 'Psalters' edited by musicians of more severe taste than some of their predecessors.

The greatest composer of chants is probably James Turle (q.v.), prolific in this branch though scanty in his output otherwise.

The chant repertory includes a certain number of curiosities, such as the effective (single) 'Grand Chant' of Pelham Humfrey (q.v.), the melody of which consists of merely two notes, a clever double chant of Crotch (q.v.), of which the second half is, note for note and chord for chord, the same as the first half but reversed, and two chants by Goss arranged from themes in Beethoven's 'Pathetic' Sonata and Seventh Symphony.

5. Double, Triple, and Quadruple Chants, etc. Confident statements as to the introduction of Double Chants (accommodating two verses of the text instead of one) have been made as follows. (*a*) They came into existence as a result of the suggestion of an accidental performance of two chants in succession by a pupil of Hine, who was organist of Gloucester Cathedral 1710–30; (*b*) they began with Flintoft's (d. 1727) composition of the still well-known one in G minor, which appeared in his collection of 'the most favourite chants' (said to be the first real chant collection ever issued); (*c*) they began with a chant by John Robinson, of which a manuscript copy exists at St. Paul's Cathedral, marked '1706'.

The date is, however, pushed back behind all those above mentioned by the appearance in Alison's Psalter of 1599 of a form of the chant now known as Flintoft's, and, as the reader will recall (see 3), by a specimen of the same kind of thing (the application of the Double Anglican Chant principle to metrical verses) in Crowley's Psalter, half a century before that. An approximation to the double chant form is also found in Byrd.

Triple Chants have in recent times been composed for use with two or three psalms whose verse arrangement seems to call for them. A few Quadruple Chants also exist, but in use they become very tiresome.

There exist also a certain number of 'Changeable Chants'—changeable in the matter of their mode, for they can be sung in either the major or minor according as different sections of the psalm or canticle call for joyful or more sober treatment.

Single chants with five measures (2+3) have been tried, in place of those with seven, and double chants with ten instead of fourteen. These (the device of L. L. Dix, of Dublin) offer the advantage of throwing more of the words into the reciting note section and, by thus reducing the number of first-beat accents, of facilitating the fitting of the words to the music. Obviously the seven-measure form is but a convention (see reference to its origin under 1) and there is no reason why variations from it should not be introduced. Five-measured chants can be used with any existing pointed psalter by ignoring the first bar-line in each half-verse.

6. The Introduction of 'Pointing'. Up to the Oxford Movement of the nineteenth century the Anglican chant was in very little use except in cathedrals and other collegiate churches. Dr. Burney says (1805) in Rees's *Cyclopaedia*, under 'Choral Service', 'The difference between cathedral or choral service and parochial consists in the choirs of the cathedrals chanting the psalms, accompanied by the organ, in 4 parts, antiphonally, instead of the minister and the clerk and congregation, as in parish churches, reading them verse by verse without music'. (These differing practices in the two places applied in general then also in the canticles, but from the early eighteenth century onwards there were some parish churches where these were chanted.)

Presumably, so long as the chanting was confined practically to trained choirs, singing together daily and going through the whole psalter twelve times a year, the method of dividing between the reciting note and the more regularly rhythmic part of the chant the varying number of syllables in the different verses could be picked up by experience—though the results cannot have been extremely or uniformly good. With the Oxford Movement of the early and mid-nineteenth century, however, the desire for a 'fully choral' service was extended, until (after much opposition, and sometimes even grave disorder) it gradually reached almost every village church. The old terms 'reading psalms' and 'singing psalms', for the prose psalms taken regularly in course, on the one hand, and the metrical version on the other (latterly Tate and Brady; see *Hymns and Hymn Tunes* 5), from which some item was congregationally sung as a hymn, became out of date because the prose psalms were now almost universally sung.

Some method of indicating to ordinary choirs the portion of the verse to be recited and the portion to be inflected became necessary. J. C. Beckwith (q.v.), organist of Norwich Cathedral, says in 1808:

'Suppose the organist and choir were to meet every morning and afternoon for one month, and agree on the proper place in each verse of the psalms, where the reciting should end in both the first and last parts of the chant, and under that particular word or syllable place a conspicuous *red* mark: if one book were thus marked, the others might be rendered similar to it. The benefit would be, all the members of the choir might recite as one person, and all come together to that word which they are previously sure is the most proper to end the recital.'

About thirty years later (1837) appeared the first attempt to present in printed form a method of 'pointing'. Its author was Robert Janes, organist of Ely Cathedral (and said to be the composer of what is known as the 'Ely Confession'). It was lavishly entitled: *The Psalter or Psalms of David, Carefully marked and Pointed to enable the Voices of a Choir to keep exactly together by singing the same Syllables to the same Note; and the accents as far as possible made to agree with the accents in the Chant; and also to remove the difficulty which individuals generally find who are not accustomed to the Chanting of the Psalms.*

Up to the 1850s and early 1860s, however, it was still very usual for a choir to prefer the pointing of the psalms that had become traditional with it, and to employ a copyist who wrote this into the prayer-books; the introduction of local festivals of combined choirs is said to have been a strong influence in bringing about a desire for printed books of fully pointed psalms and canticles.

Since that period almost innumerable pointed versions of the Psalms and Canticles have appeared, with a considerable variety of methods of indicating the allocation of the syllables to the notes. Of these *The Cathedral Psalter* (1875), edited by Stainer and others, long held the most prominent position, and it is still in wide use.

In some pointed versions gross distortions of the natural prose rhythms occur, and the late nineteenth and early twentieth century saw many attempts to provide more intelligently pointed editions.

A pamphlet by Robert Bridges (published by the Church Music Society in 1912) had great influence in promoting the spirit of reform. Then appeared (*a*) *The English Psalter*, edited by E. C. Bairstow, P. C. Buck, and C. Macpherson, which disregarded to a large extent the parallelism of Hebrew poetry in favour of emphasis on the sense of the words; (*b*) *The Psalter Newly Pointed*, issued by the Society for Promoting Christian Knowledge, the work of many minds but finally edited by Revd. A. Ramsbotham, which was felt by some to err in an excess of marks for the guidance of the singers; (*c*) *The Oxford Psalter*, edited by H. G. Ley, E. S. Roper, and C. Hylton Stewart, which may be looked upon as a compromise between the last two; (*d*) *The Parish Psalter*, edited by Sydney Nicholson, being a much simplified treatment with more modest aims; and (*e*) *The St. Paul's Cathedral Psalter* (free-speech-rhythm), by Maurice F. Foxell and Stanley Marchant. These represent the research and experiment inspired by Bridges's pamphlet.

The tendency of choirs and congregations is to gabble the recitation and dawdle over the rest of the music, and this has to be guarded against, an even pace throughout being insisted upon. The nearer the chanting approaches to good reading the better it is. An Anglican chant is, after all, merely a vehicle for sacred and poetic words.

Violent attacks have sometimes been made on the Anglican chant, as in 1920 by a well-known Anglican musician, Dr. Charles Pearce, who called for 'the complete abolition of an abuse which has disfigured the choral service of the Anglican Church for two centuries and more'. Probably, however, the average opinion of musicians agrees with that of Sir Richard Terry, who (though not himself, as the then Musical Director of a Roman Catholic Cathedral, using such music and naturally preferring the Gregorian Tones, q.v.) summed up as follows: 'The Anglican chant can be made very effective in the hands of a good choir. . . . Its rendering on the part of a bad choir must be horrible.'

Dom Anselm Hughes, O.S.B., Prior of Nashdom Abbey and long Hon. Sec. of the Plainsong and Mediaeval Musical Society, comments on these opinions as follows:

'After thirty years of "working" Plainsong I have come slowly but surely to believe that *good* Anglican chanting, as one hears it to-day in most Cathedrals, some Parish Churches, and a few Village Churches, is a perfect musical expression of the English Psalter. Plainsong psalms, for a similar degree of perfection, *must* have their antiphons, or they are like a body which has no skin.'

ANGLICAN PARISH CHURCH MUSIC

A great part of the general subject of Anglican Church Music is treated under a number of separate heads as follows: *Common Prayer, Psalm, Plainsong* (4), *Anglican Chant, Service, Anthem, Cathedral Music, Precentor, Vicar Choral, Chapel Royal, Parish Clerk, Hymns and Hymn Tunes,* and (smaller articles) *Preces, Responses, Litany, Magnificat, Nunc Dimittis, Use of Sarum,* etc. It remains to sketch briefly the conduct and development of music in the worship of the ordinary parish churches—a subject which has been a good deal neglected by historians.

(For illustrations see p. 17, pl. 2; 172, 35.)

1. The Parish Church after the Reformation.

At the Reformation, as may be gathered from the article *Common Prayer*, the Roman Catholic liturgy and customs were taken over into the new Church of England services, with the use of the vernacular but otherwise a minimum of change—therein differing greatly from those churches of the Continent that followed the lead of Calvin, though less from those that followed the lead of Luther.

There must have been up to this date a clear distinction of musical custom between the many monastery and cathedral churches and the ordinary town and village parish churches. The cathedrals and larger monasteries had possessed the equipment of large choirs and organs; hundreds of monasteries were now destroyed or, in a few cases, their churches were retained as cathedrals, and in this latter case the elaborate type of service was, *mutatis mutandis,* continued.

When the Reformation came few parish churches, it would appear, possessed anything of the nature of a choir, but, to judge from indications that remain, a surprising number (though probably very far from a majority) possessed organs; one is occasionally surprised to find early mention of an organ in some comparatively small village. The nature of the organ in those days, and the kind of work it was then supposed to do, must be remembered. The organs were usually small instruments (see *Organ*) and, by modern standards, exceedingly clumsy in manipulation. The cathedral 'service music' of the day (see *Service*), and the anthems, did not call for their use: they may in some instances have been employed to double the voices, but there were no independent 'organ parts' in such music (i.e. it was 'A Cappella', q.v.) and there was no repertory of organ music. Often there was no organist in the sense in which we use the word today; i.e. some member of the choir would be expected to do what little organ playing was called for. Most probably the organ served to accompany the plainsong (unisonally), where such accompaniment was desirable, and, as above suggested, it may have supported the voices in some choral compositions. This was in the greater monastery churches and the cathedrals. In the parish churches, where the music was so much simpler, it can have had little function beyond helping the priest and congregation in the performance of the plainsong.

As at the Reformation a very considerable party in the Church of England desired thorough reform, on the Calvinistic lines, a good many parish church organs were probably removed or allowed to decay; indeed there is evidence of this. The 'clerks' (lay or in minor orders) who had formerly, in the chancel, assisted the priest in the responsive parts of the service, now (perhaps in some places gradually) became reduced to one 'parish clerk' (q.v.), upon whom devolved the leading of the people's verses of the 'read' prose psalms and the responses, which latter may in some places have been chanted to the new adaptation of the old plainsong (see *Plainsong* 4) and in others merely uttered in a speaking voice. A metrical psalm (see *Hymns and Hymn Tunes* 5) was often also included in the service, as what we would today call a hymn, and this was announced, read, and led by the parish clerk, sitting at his desk.

There was an official reversion to Roman Catholicism during the short reign of Mary (1553–8), but with the ascent to the throne of her sister, Elizabeth, the churches returned to the use of Common Prayer.

The degree of ritual in churches varied very greatly, as did the degree of faithfulness in adherence to the official Prayer Book. The Puritan element in the Church was strong, and individual bishops and archbishops, from period to period, differed in their views as to the propriety of enforcing the Prayer Book's full provisions. Many very unsuitable persons were appointed to country livings, some being almost illiterate and quite incapable of preaching. A common practice was to appoint, as an additional member of the staff of a town or country parish, a 'Lecturer', i.e. a clergyman whose function was to give sermons on stated days. The general standard of church life was in many parishes too poor for us to suppose that anyone troubled if the musical part of the service was on a low level—or, indeed, if no musical part existed.

With Laud's appointment as Archbishop of Canterbury (1633) not merely did the High Church attitude find its expression in worship but seemliness in the conduct of services probably became more general. His execution, after twelve years of office, marked, amongst other things, the strong feeling his 'Romanizing' tendencies had aroused. The pendulum which he had tried to propel in one direction now swung right over to the other; services naturally tended to become less formal again and perhaps were less carefully carried out.

2. The Parish Church during the Commonwealth. In 1644, whilst Laud was in prison, came the parliamentary decree that all church organs should be silenced and church music reduced to its simplest. The parish church became in some places Independent and in others Presbyterian, and no music was now heard beyond metrical psalms sung by the congregation. Some few organs were left in position in cathedrals and college chapels (and apparently occasionally played, but not for service purposes—unless possibly for voluntaries after service), but it may be guessed that those remaining in parish churches now entirely disappeared. A century before, in the earliest days of the Reformation (1536), the Lower House of Convocation had declared organ playing to be amongst the '84 Faults and Abuses of Religion', and now this view was acted upon.

3. Post-Restoration Conditions. With the restoration of the monarchy in 1660 the Church of England became officially episcopal again, the Common Prayer was resumed, organs and choirs were again heard in the cathedrals and college chapels, and a great body of the clergy was expelled. Independency and Presbyterianism now suffered frequent severe persecution.

It does not appear that organs were quickly replaced in the parish churches in general—possibly through financial difficulty and possibly largely through lack of serious appreciation of their usefulness. The music in most churches was still confined to the congregational metrical psalms led by the parish clerk (probably usually only one psalm, or part of a psalm, in a service), so that the amount and character of the music during the Commonwealth and after the Restoration must in most churches have been just the same—a fact not usually realized.

Very many complaints as to the character of the singing are scattered through eighteenth- and early nineteenth-century English literature. Dr. Burney at the end of the eighteenth century is most violent in the expression of the view that from the untrained singers of a congregation nothing but a noise can ever be expected. Isaac D'Israeli, in 1793 (and as a member of the race that provided the psalms he has a right to be heard), inveighs against 'a mixed assembly roaring out confused tones, nasal, guttural and sibilant'. De Quincey, as late as 1840, complains, 'There is accumulated in London more musical science than in any capital in the world', and yet 'the psalmody in most parish churches is a *howling wilderness*'.

4. The Introduction of the Church Choir and Orchestra. Perhaps partly as a result of the lack of organs there grew up during the later eighteenth century a remarkably widespread custom of employing small orchestras in church. Many a village that would today certainly be incapable of supplying a body of instrumentalists had one then. Such an orchestra, with a small choir, occupied the west gallery; together they led the metrical psalms or hymns and performed occasional simple anthems. The exercises of these village musicians were, from accounts that remain, often what we should today consider hardly decorous, but the church, in hundreds of places, through them became the centre of a genuine musical life (p. 17, pl. **2**. 3).

An inquiry into the existence of church orchestras in the county of Sussex was made by a clergyman who happened to be also a competent musician (Rev. Canon K. H. MacDermott, A.R.C.M.). This is a county now reckoned unmusical and one that has been described by antiquarians who have studied its written and printed records as having always been so. Yet the investigator just mentioned, pursuing his researches in the twentieth century, when oblivion has largely passed over the musical doings of England's village orchestral age, was able to collect particulars of orchestras in 111 churches—haphazard little groups of flutes, clarinets, bassoons, trombones, serpents, violins, and cellos, twenty-four kinds of instrument in all (including nine bassoons simultaneously at work in one of the orchestras, for the bass instruments were always considered the most supporting to the singing; this was so elsewhere than in English villages, many continental cathedrals using serpents; cf. *Methodism and Music* 7).

Sheffield parish church, to take an instance of a town, remained organless for over a century and a half (1650–1805). There was, as an account of about 1770 informs us, 'no solemn loud pealing organ, but before the west window, high over the gallery, was a kind of immense box hung in chains, into which, by the aid of a ladder, musicians and singers, male and female, contrived to scramble, and with the aid of bumbasses, hautboys, fiddles, and various other instruments, accompanying shrill and stentorian voices, they contrived to make as loud a noise as heart would wish'.

Another Yorkshire town parish church, that of Huddersfield, had no organ until 1812. To avoid any difficulty with the citizens who paid the church rates a voluntary subscription was raised to endow the organistship; it is possible that in the question of church rates (paid by non-church-goers and dissenters equally with church-goers) we see one of the explanations of the tardiness with which church organs made their reappearance after the restoration of the episcopacy in 1660.

A Suffolk clergyman in 1764 described the arrangements in his part of England as follows:

'The Performers are placed in a Single Seat, sometimes a raised seat like a stage. Here they form themselves into a round Ring, with their Faces to each other and their Backs to ye Congregation.

Here they murder anthems, chuse improper Psalms, leave off in ye middle of a sentence, sing Psalms of all kinds to new, jiggish tunes. If ye Minister offers to direct them, "He may mind his Text; he may sing himself, they will sing as they list or not at all." They frequently leave their own Parish Church, and go in a Body to display their Talents in other Churches. I have known them stroll six or seven miles for this purpose, sometimes with a young female singer or two in their train.'

Porteus, Bishop of London, in a charge to the clergy in 1790, complains of the monopolizing of the psalmody in the country parishes by 'a select band of singers who have been taught by some itinerant master to sing in the worst manner a most wretched set of psalm tunes in three or four parts, so complex, so difficult, so totally devoid of true harmony, that it is impossible for any of the congregation to take part with them; who, therefore, sit absorbed in silent admiration, or total inattention, without considering themselves in any degree concerned in what is going forward'.

5. The 'Charity Children' as Choir. In the towns at this period the presence of an organ was more common than in the villages, and the singing was most often led by the 'charity children' of the parish—i.e. either the children of the various free (weekday) schools for the poor or, as the term is sometimes used in the later eighteenth and earlier nineteenth centuries, the Sunday School children, who were once a week receiving free instruction in reading, writing, the Catechism, and the Bible, and were marched to church to join in the service. The many thousands of charity children of London, gathered once a year in St. Paul's Cathedral, formed a choir that greatly impressed Haydn in 1792 and Berlioz in 1851. The Bishop of London just quoted was less appreciative of the innocent efforts of the infant choristers. 'In London and a great part of Westminster' it is the charity children who serve as choir and there is 'a contest between them and the organ which shall be the loudest and give most pain to the ear'. (For some similar strictures by another Bishop of London, earlier in the century, see *Hymns and Hymn Tunes* 5.) As late as 1840 a writer in the *Musical World* stated that not one church in London possessed 'anything like a full choir' (p. 17, pl. **2**. 7, 8).

6. The Coming of the Barrel Organ and Harmonium. The disappearance of the church orchestra is due in the first instance to the introduction of the barrel organ and then to that of the harmonium. The barrel organ (see *Mechanical Reproduction of Music* 10) appeared in church in the late eighteenth century and quickly overspread the country (p. 17, pl. **2**. 6); the harmonium (see *Reed-Organ Family* 6) was introduced from France in the 1840s and was followed by the American organ (see *Reed-Organ Family* 7). The well-known picture of the period of transition given in Thomas Hardy's *Under the Greenwood Tree*, though it has slips in detail, is a lifelike

one. The blow to village music-making was forceful and with enhanced decorum came diminished musical interest and variety.

7. The Surpliced Choir (p. 17, pl. **2**. 8, 9). The Oxford Movement of the early nineteenth century accentuated this desire for decorum and introduced a fashion for male choirs, surpliced and sitting no longer in the west gallery (a normal position in continental Roman Catholic churches today and arguably the best; see remark later), but in the chancel; and for the chanting of the responses and the psalms (see *Anglican Chant* 6). In fact it was attempted to transplant what had always previously been considered the cathedral and college chapel type of service to the town and village parish church. Inevitably a good deal too much was often expected of the modest choral resources available, so that the change was by no means all gain. (For an allusion by Burney to the degree of skill sometimes found amongst the organists of London churches see *Figured Bass*.)

The old type of service lingered, however, in a good many churches until nearly the end of the nineteenth century. *Church Music in the Metropolis*, by Charles Box (1884—note the late date!), reports on visits to London churches in 1882–3. In many he found the new quasi-cathedral type of service installed, in others 'a goodly array of charity children who surrounded the organ', or 'a few children in charity attire placed beside the organ', or 'board school boys', or 'six very young women —great girls in fact', or 'eight youths', or 'no choir except six youths stationed in a gallery near the organ', or 'no choir unless seven poor boys may be regarded as such', or 'no choir' (a good many), or a set of boys who 'rushed out of St. Olave just as the text was announced to get a good view of the raree show' (the Lord Mayor going in state to another church).

In reading the report just mentioned one notes that even where there is 'no choir', or where there remains the common eighteenth- and early nineteenth-century arrangement of drawing on the charity children to lead the singing, every church has an organ, all use the Anglican chant (for at least the canticles and if not for the prose psalms for at least the Glorias to them), and the metrical psalter has in every instance given way to a hymn-book (see *Hymns and Hymn Tunes* 6). Service settings of the canticles are comparatively rare and so are anthems. The congregation usually, though not always, represents so small a proportion of the population of the parish (in each case the number is given) as to show a generally low state of church life ('nineteen adults and seven children', 'six elderly male adults and four female', 'seven adult females and two males', or even 'the congregation consisted of one old lady and the writer himself'). The whole report is interesting and worth analysis by any Anglican musican interested in the history of his Church and its music, since it shows the transition period.

We may suppose that country places usually lagged behind London and that the change to present-day conditions took longer to accomplish. A stimulus to the development of music in the greater parish churches was given when Hook, vicar of Leeds from 1837 to 1857 (later Dean of Chichester), instituted a professional choir performing full daily (evening) cathedral services. This church had apparently been without an organ for over half a century after the Restoration, and then (1714) had one 'with two convenient galleries on each side of the Organ for the Charity Children'. The two sets of conditions, before and after Hook, mark a striking change of spirit.

To some extent it may be said that ambition has now over-reached itself, and there are many influential voices heard: (a) emphasizing the difference between a parish church, where the congregation has decided rights of participation in the whole of the musical part of the service, and the cathedral, where the choir can quite legitimately perform the whole service except the one or two hymns; and (b) urging the smaller churches not to attempt music beyond a reasonable measure of difficulty.

The foundation of the Royal College of Organists in 1864 has done much for the improvement of music in the Anglican Church, as has also that of the Church Music Society (1906); that of the School of English Church Music (1927; since 1945, Royal School of Church Music, q.v.) is now accomplishing much also. Diocesan organization (with inspection, visiting choir-trainers, conferences, festivals of service music by combined choirs) now exercises a very considerable influence both on the choice of music and on the standard of performance.

The development of musical conditions in the Anglican Church in other parts of the Commonwealth than England has, roughly speaking, followed that of the mother country, period by period, and the same may almost be said of the Protestant Episcopal Church of the United States.

ANGORE (It.). 'Pain', 'anxious wish'.

ANGOSCIA (It.). 'Anguish.' So *Angoscioso*, *Angosciosamente*, 'with anguished feeling'.

ANGREIFEN (Ger.). 'To seize hold', i.e. to attack.

ANGST (Ger.). 'Anguish', 'anxiety', 'fear'.

ÄNGSTLICH or **AENGSTLICH** (Ger.). 'Anxious', 'uneasy'.

ANHALTEN (Ger.). 'To hold on.' So *Anhaltend*, 'holding on'.

ANHANG (Ger.). Literally, something that hangs on to the end of something else ('appendix', 'supplement', etc.; in music a coda, q.v.).

ANIMA (It.). 'Soul.' Thus, fancifully, the sound-post of a violin, etc. Cf. *Âme* and *Sound-post*.

ANIMANDO (It.). 'Animating.' So *Animandosi*, 'becoming animated'; *Animato*, 'animated'.

ANIMÉ (Fr.). 'Animated.'

ANIMO, ANIMOSO (It.). 'Spirit', 'spirited'. So the adverb, *Animosamente*.

ANLAUFEN (Ger.). To increase the sound (i.e. *Crescendo*).

ANMUT or **ANMUTH** (Ger.). 'Grace.' So *Anmutig*, 'graceful'.

ANNIE LAURIE. The poem is by William Douglas of Fingland (c. 1800), but it has been a good deal altered by various people, especially by Lady John Douglas Scott (1810–1900), who also wrote the air. The date of first publication is 1838. The song had an immense popularity amongst the British troops during the Crimean War.

The heroine of the song was a real person and Douglas was in love with her. She married another, however. She died at the age of eighty-three (in 1864) and is buried in Glencairn churchyard, Dumfriesshire, close to the 'bonnie braes' of Maxwelton of which the poet speaks. She and her rejected lover appear in James Grant's novel *The Scottish Cavalier* (1850).

ANNOTATED PROGRAMMES

1. Arne's Innovation, 1768.
2. German Examples from 1783.
3. An American Example of 1787.
4. Scottish and English Examples from 1801.
5. Grove's Crystal Palace Programmes.
6. The Decline of the Annotated Programme.

1. Arne's Innovation, 1768. The beginning of the practice of providing elucidations of music in the programme of a concert cannot be positively dated. Possibly the earliest example is the programme of a Concert of Catches and Glees, given by Arne at Drury Lane Theatre in 1768. It has a preface explaining the nature of the catch and the glee, and the various items are provided with historical and critical notes. (For a printed opera synopsis as early as 1647, see *Opera* 11 a.)

2. German Examples from 1783. Fifteen years later (1783) Frederick the Great's Kapellmeister, J. F. Reichardt, a busy literary man as well as a fine musician, founded in Potsdam a regular Tuesday performance (*Concert spirituel*—obviously named after the famous Paris series) and provided in his programmes both the words of the songs and historical and aesthetic explanations enabling the audience to gain a more immediate understanding and thus enabling him to attain his end more easily'. The 'end' alluded to was the widening of the taste of the public, for Reichardt introduced a great deal of music previously unheard in that part of Germany.

Seven years after this (1790) the device is found in regular application at Biberach, in Swabia, where, in his capacity of an orchestral conductor, J. H. Knecht introduced it. Fétis and, after him, Grove say that he had been a professor of literature, in which case his view of music was likely to be a somewhat wider one that that of many conductors of the time; their statement seems open to doubt, as it is not mentioned in *Allgemeine Deutsche Biographie*, but Knecht was certainly a man of general and musical learning and very active and enterprising.

The same general intention as that of an annotated programme is seen in the advance articles that Weber during his opera conductorships at Prague (1813) and Dresden (1817) used to contribute to the local papers. Wagner at Dresden (1846) inserted a valuable treatise on Beethoven's Ninth Symphony.

3. An American Example of 1787. It is of interest to note that one of the earliest annotated programmes known is of American origin. It is that of the 'First Uranian Concert', given in Philadelphia on 12 April 1787. In the treatment of Handel's 'Hallelujah Chorus' (q.v.) a very practical double-column layout is adopted, the following being an extract:

'And he shall reign for ever, etc.	A beautiful fugue.
King of kings, and Lord of lords:	By the Treble and Counter in long notes; whilst the Tenor and Bass repeat "for ever and ever, Hal." in quick notes with intervals.
King of kings, and Lord of lords:	Two or three times in very low notes; by the Treble: whilst the Counter, Tenor and Bass are repeating "for ever and ever, Hal." often, in quick notes with intervals: *The effect is wonderful*.'

4. Scottish and English Examples from 1801. In Covent Garden Theatre, during Lent 1801, was given the first British performance of Mozart's *Requiem*. The director of the performance, the well-known John Ashley, provided a book of words with more than three pages of biographical and historical information.

In the London *Musical World* of 2 December 1836 appeared a letter written by a wellknown London musician of the day, C. H. Purday (q.v.), which is worth quotation as it exactly expresses the object presumed to be aimed at by the compilers of annotated programmes today:

'The public are not to be blamed for taking little interest in that which they do not understand. Although they know that the composition which has just been performed is the effusion of some such extraordinary mind as that of a Mozart, a Haydn or a Beethoven, with whose names they are familiar, from the circumstances of having their works so often brought before their notice—they are as ignorant (generally speaking) of the true character, design, and end of those stupendous efforts of genius, as are the Hottentots of their existence: consequently, the performance of them, if listened to at all, is heard with indifference. To effect the object which gave rise to this letter, I would propose that a prologue, if I may use the term, should preface every performance of the works of the great masters, giving a brief and pithy analysis of the composition to be performed, showing its relative character to the mind of the musician, the feelings by which he was actuated in the production of his work, and the circumstances (where known) under which it was brought out: this would, by the novelty, in the first place, attract attention, and by frequent repetition, keep that attention alive and lead us in tracing the mind of the author through the productions of his pen; and the design of his work would thus be made clear to the understanding of the amateur, and infuse in him the desire to become more intimately acquainted with the classical compositions of the great masters.'

Unknown to Purday the very thing he wanted had been brought into existence that same year (or possibly earlier) by John Thomson, in the programmes he provided for the concerts of the Professional Society of Edinburgh. In 1839 Thomson became Reid Professor of Music in the University of Edinburgh, and during the few months remaining before his early death provided similar programmes for the University concerts.

John Ella, long prominent in London musical life as the director of a chamber music organization, the Musical Union (1845–80), is often spoken of in Britain as the introducer of annotated programmes. It will be seen that he had been anticipated, but it was probably the utility of his analytical notes over so long a period that formally established the practice, and thenceforward it became a common one.

A very practical and ample annotated programme was provided in the 1840s to 1870s 'for the acceptance of the gentlemen visiting Evans's Supper and Music Rooms in Covent Garden'. This place of nightly entertainment took music seriously, and its booklets give the words of the glees and madrigals performed and instructive and sometimes learned notes on the composer (half a column on Orlando Gibbons, extracts from Weber's letters, quotations from Burney, Warton, and others concerning 'Sumer is icumen in', and so on); they also instruct the patrons in the handling of some of the more material attractions of the place, e.g. how to manipulate the celebrated Evans baked potato, so as to enjoy its qualities to the full (see further reference under *Music Hall* 2).

5. Grove's Crystal Palace Programmes. The most important series of annotated programmes ever issued in Britain is that supplied for forty years (1856–96) by Sir George Grove (with help as to the more modern works) for

August Manns's famous Saturday orchestral concerts at the Crystal Palace. These were admirably adapted for their purpose and were stored up by many regular attendants at the concerts, so that sets of them occasionally come into the market today; they offer an exposition of the best musical thought and knowledge of their period applied to performances that were representative of every type of serious orchestral music then current. The articles on the Beethoven symphonies were afterwards expanded into a book, which remains the standard one on its subject and which perfectly illustrates that combination of a persevering search for every kind of useful information with keen enthusiasm for the music itself which was characteristic of its author.

6. The Decline of the Annotated Programme. Since those days the annotated programme has in Britain tended to decline in practical value. Though sometimes admirably carried out, its compilation has been at other times entrusted to highbrow musicians who, losing sight of their audience and with the composer's score before them on their study table, produce a minutely detailed analysis such as cannot be followed in listening unless by a trained musician so much in love with detective work as to be willing to put aside artistic pleasure in its favour.

The standard in the United States is, on the whole, possibly higher, and the audiences of the best series of orchestral concerts are supplied with much helpful guidance; indeed, at one time they were supplied with it in advance, the programmes being sent to concert subscribers by mail without charge, whereas in Britain they are usually only obtainable in the concert hall and at a substantial cost. The late Philip Hale's annotations on the programmes of the concerts of the Boston Symphony Orchestra, from 1901 to 1934, won high admiration for their encyclopaedic completeness. They represent one type of such annotations—that which supplies historical, biographical, and bibliographical information rather than analysis.

It is much to be wished that writers of analytical programmes would answer in their mind, before beginning each task, a few obviously fundamental questions, such as whether they are writing for professional musicians or for the general public, whether they mean their notes to be read before the performance begins or during its course, and so on. If they intend the notes to be read by the general public and whilst the performance is in progress, these notes should be very concise and simple and such 'pointers' as to musical themes should be provided as can readily be identified by the ear.

Paris brought into existence in 1911 a weekly journal, *Guide du concert*, giving programme notes, with musical examples, of works to be performed during the following week.

The writing of annotations for programmes is clearly a branch of the work of Musical Appreciation, upon which an article will be found in this volume. (See *Appreciation*.)

ANREISSEN (Ger.). 'To tear at' (used of a very forceful pizzicato).

ANSATZ. See *Embouchure*.

ANSCHLAG (Ger.). (1) What is sometimes called a 'Double Appoggiatura' (see Table 12), but consisting of the notes immediately below and above the principal note. (2) Touch on (or of) a keyboard instrument. (3) 'Attack', etc.

ANSCHMIEGEND (Ger.). 'Bent to', 'shaped to', hence 'compliant'.

ANSCHWELLEND (Ger.). 'Swelling', i.e. crescendo.

ANSIA (It.). 'Anxiety.'

ANSON, HUGO. Born at Wellington, New Zealand, in 1894 and died in London in 1958, aged sixty-three. He was educated at Cambridge University and the Royal College of Music and from 1939 was Registrar of the latter. He published chamber music, piano music, etc.

ANSTATT (Ger.). 'Instead of.'

ANSTIMMEN (Ger.). 'To tune.'

ANSTRICH (Ger.). 'Stroke' (of bow). Cf. *Strich*.

ANSWER in Fugue. See *Form* 12 b.

ANTECEDENT. See *Canon*.

ANTES, JOHN. Born at Frederickstown, Pa., in 1740 and died at Bristol, England, in 1811, aged seventy-one. He was a minister of the Moravian body (cf. *United States* 3) and a composer of anthems, etc., which are to be seen in the archives of Bethlehem, Pa. From his twenty-fifth year he lived in England.

ANTHEIL, GEORGE (p. 1068, pl. **175. 6**). Born at Trenton, New Jersey, in 1900 and died in New York in 1959, aged fifty-eight. He came of Polish parents. For some years he lived chiefly in Paris, where he brought before the public a series of works of revolutionary character, such as his *Ballet mécanique* (1927), scored for anvils, aeroplane propellers, two octaves of electric bells, motor horns, sixteen player-pianos (controlled from a single switchboard), and pieces of tin and steel. Later he held less firmly to his position as 'Bad Boy of Music' (the title of his autobiography) and by 1936 was established as a successful writer of film music. Amongst his many and varied compositions are a number of symphonies and four operas.

See *Jazz* 5.

ANTHEM. (See first the article *Antiphon*.) The anthem may be considered as the English-speaking Protestant Churches' equivalent of the Latin motet (q.v.), from which it has sprung. It is an Anglican creation. In the liturgy of the Church of England there is a place provided for it (see *Common Prayer*), and churches other than that have given it an equivalent place, somewhere after the middle or towards the end of the service. It constitutes in ordinary churches the one occasion of the service when the choir alone undertakes the duty of song, and when an elaboration impossible and unsuitable in other parts of the service becomes proper and effective. (In a cathedral or large church, when a 'service', in the technical sense, is sung there are, of course, other opportunities.)

It is usually accompanied by organ, so differing from the motet (in the strict application of the latter term): it has frequently passages for solo voices, individually or in combination.

The anthems of the English Tudor composers often differed from motets in little but the use of the English language, and the development of solo passages (recitatives, arias, duets, quartets, etc.—see *Verse*) largely took place after the Restoration and in the Chapel Royal, where Charles II demanded a brighter music such as he had heard when in exile at the court of Louis XIV—including accompaniments for strings. The anthems of Purcell are some of them in the old serious motet style and others in this new style. When, a little later, Handel came to England he wrote large-scale and fine works of this class—the 'Chandos Anthems'. Such compositions tend towards the type of the Church Cantatas of Bach and other German composers of the period.

The English anthem repertory is large and varied, and includes many noble works, as well as a great deal that is trivial. From the middle of the nineteenth century onwards new anthems have been provided on principles of 'mass production', with a consequent loss of standard.

Certain general remarks made under *Church Music* 2 and *Hymns and Hymn Tunes* 15 may be applied to the anthem: there is no doubt that many organists and their clergy tolerate as 'churchly' (to use a convenient American term) settings of sacred words that they would find insipid if the words were secular and the place of performance the concert-room.

The principal styles of anthem composition might be set forth in 'periods' somewhat like the following:

I. The Period of Contrapuntal Unaccompanied Anthems (the motet, but with English words, as one might say). This lasted from the time of the Reformation until (roughly) the end of the great English choral school, say 1550 to 1625 (i.e. the late Tudor and early Stuart period). Some great names here are Robert White, William Mundy, Tallis, Tye, Farrant, Byrd, Gibbons, and Weelkes. Some of these composers introduced solos and in-dependent instrumental accompaniments, so leading the way to the next style. (Even the music of this period which we speak of as 'unaccompanied' seems often, in practice, to have been supported by organ and viols doubling the voices.)

II. The Earlier Period of the Accompanied Anthem, using recitative and solo voices and sometimes stringed and other orchestral instruments (a period on the whole of less gravity). This covered the period from the Restoration of the monarchy to the death of George I. Child, Blow, Humfrey, Purcell, Rogers, Aldrich, Croft, Wise, Turner, Tudway.

III. The Period of the Handelian Anthem (with a certain eighteenth-century solidity and dignity)—say 1730 to 1800. Handel, Greene, Boyce, Battishill, William Hayes, Kent, Nares, B. Cooke, Arnold.

IV. The Early Nineteenth-Century Anthem (with a more modern tinge)—say 1800 to 1875. Crotch, Attwood, Ouseley, Walmisley, S. S. Wesley, Goss, Elvey.

V. The Later Victorian Anthem (with an added grace and tunefulness but sometimes a tendency towards prettiness and sentimentality). Garrett, Stainer, Barnby, Sullivan, Stanford, Parry, Charles Wood, and a host of others.

Living composers of anthems (British and American) are extremely numerous, far too much so, since (with a number of noteworthy exceptions, of course) they are turning out a great deal of commonplace, conventional, and necessarily ephemeral music.

It is to be remembered that the anthem and 'service' (q.v.) repertory of the English church constitutes a possession that, however much it may be a source of national pride, must, from its nature, ever remain almost entirely unknown to other nations (apart from some of the Tudor and early Stuart anthems, which would be capable of translation into other languages and of use as motets).

The word 'Anthem' is often loosely used, as, for instance, in 'National Anthem'. The 'Easter Anthems' of the Prayer Book are a collection of Biblical passages of relevant character, nowadays usually sung to an Anglican chant.

For 'Verse Anthem' and 'Full Anthem' see *Verse*.
For anthems amongst bodies other than the Church of England see *Congregational Churches*; *Methodism* 6. And for 'the Father of the Anthem' see *Tye*.

ANTI-BOUFFONISTES. See *Bouffons, Guerre des*.

ANTICIPATION. See *Harmony* 24 m.

ANTICO, ANTICA (It., masc., fem.). 'Antique', 'ancient'. The plurals are *Antichi, Antiche*.

ANTILL, JOHN. Born at Sydney in 1904. He held a scholarship at the New South Wales Conservatory and then engaged in operatic enterprises—as a member of the orchestra, as chorus-master, and as conductor, afterwards becoming Senior Music Presentation Officer of the Australian Broadcasting Commission. His ballet suite, *Corroboree* (based on the dances of Australian aborigines), first introduced his name to British audiences and for its first British performance, in 1946, he was sent over by public subscription of Sydney citizens.

ANTIMASQUE. See *Masque.*

ANTIPHON.

(1) In the Roman Catholic Church it is a short extract consisting of a verse of a psalm and/or other traditional passage intoned or sung during the recitation of Divine Office (i.e. Matins, Lauds, Prime, Terce, Sept, None, Vespers, and Compline) before and after the psalm or canticle, which is itself responsively sung by the singers divided into two bodies. The antiphon may serve to enforce the meaning of the psalm, or to introduce a Christian application of the original Jewish text. It is attached very particularly also to the canticles Benedictus and Magnificat, where it gives the keynote of the Feast, and Nunc dimittis, where it emphasizes the intention of the service of Compline. It is sung in complete form only at the greater feasts. The plainsong tune of the antiphon, though not the same as the 'tone' of the psalm (see *Plainsong* 2), is in keeping with it as to mode, etc. (See remark under *Anglican Chant*, end.)

(2) Many antiphons now exist without psalms, and they are sometimes sung to settings by composers instead of to the original plainsong—hence the English word 'anthem', derived from 'antiphona', for an independent piece of choral music not an essential part of the service.

See also the various entries immediately following.

ANTIPHONAL, ANTIPHONARY, or ANTIPHONER. Properly the Roman Catholic Church's collection of traditional plainsong antiphons (see *Antiphon*), but the use of the word has become more comprehensive and it now generally means the book containing all the traditional plainsong for the Divine office, in distinction from the Gradual (q.v.), which contains all the plainsong for the Mass.

ANTIPHONAL SINGING. See *Service.*

ANTIPHONARY, ANTIPHONER. Same as Antiphonal (q.v.).

ANTIPHONS OF THE BLESSED VIRGIN MARY. There are four, each with its season: (1) during Advent and until the Purification of the Virgin Mary, *Alma redemptoris mater*; (2) thence until Wednesday in Holy Week, *Ave regina coelorum*; (3) thence until Whitsun, *Regina coeli laetare*; (4) from the Octave of Whitsun until Advent, *Salve regina, mater misericordiae.*

ANTWERP. See *Belgium* 2, 8, 9; *Holland* 2; *Publishing* 3; *Bull, John.*

ANVIL. See *Percussion Family* 3 s, 4 c, 5 a.

ANVIL BONE. See *Ear and Hearing* 1.

ANWACHSEND (Ger.). 'Growing', i.e. swelling out in tone.

ANZUBLASEN (Ger.). 'To be blown.'

ÄOLSHARFE. See *Aeolian Harp.*

APAISÉ (Fr.). 'Pacified', rendered more peaceful.

À PEINE (Fr.). 'Hardly', 'barely'. So *À peine entendu*, 'barely audible'.

APEL, WILLI. Born at Konitz in 1893. He studied at various German universities (D.Phil., Berlin) and in 1935 settled in the U.S.A., teaching at Harvard (1938) and Bloomington, Indiana (1950). He is the author of several valuable scholarly books on early music.

See also *Dictionaries* 2.

APERTO (It.). 'Open', i.e. (*a*) clear, distinct; (*b*) broad in style.

AP IVOR, DENIS. Born at Collinstown, Eire, in 1916. He was trained at the choir schools of Christ Church (Oxford) and Hereford, and under Hadley and Rawsthorne. His numerous compositions include ballets, concertos, chamber music, and many songs.

APOLLONICON. (1) Sort of harmonium; see *Reed-Organ Family* 6. (2) Mechanical organ; see *Mechanical Reproduction* 11.

APOSTLES' CREED. See *Creed.*

APPALACHIAN MUSIC. See *Folk Song* 3; *Ballad* 3; *Dance* 7.

APPASSIONATO, APPASSIONATA (It., masc., fem.). 'Impassioned'; so *Appassionatamente*, 'passionately'; *Appassionamento*, 'passion'. For the 'Sonata Appassionata' (Beethoven) see *Nicknamed Compositions* 5.

APPENA (It.). 'Hardly', 'scarcely', 'slightly' (like the Fr. *À peine*).

APPENATO (It.). 'Pained', i.e. tormented.

APPLAUSE

1. The Psychological Basis of Applause. The custom of showing one's pleasure at beautiful music by immediately following it with an ugly noise is perhaps as old as the art of music itself. Partly it springs from the unconscious desire of an excited audience to express its excitement rather than keep it pent, and it must have been often noticed by every observant concert-goer that the volume of tone in the last quarter-minute of a performance largely governs the volume of applause that follows, a very loud ending usually 'bringing the house down' whatever the merits or demerits of the composition or performance as a whole (a high note at the end of a vocal piece sometimes has the same effect).

After the performance of vocal compositions there is a strong tendency on the part of 'popular' audiences to applaud as soon as the last vocal note is heard, so drowning the composer's further thoughts—which may sometimes be merely conventional but are at other times a highly important part of his expressive scheme.

Audiences also often applaud during the course of a piano composition if the pianist, at a rest, is so incautious as to take his hands from the keyboard, so giving them the impression that he has finished—and this regardless of the finality or non-finality of the chord after which the rest occurs.

Certain cases occur where composers have 'asked for trouble'; it is rare to hear Weber's *Invitation to the Dance* performed (either in its original piano form or as arranged for orchestra) without premature applause.

2. Applause between Movements or during their Course.

Applause between the 'movements' of a symphony, string quartet, or sonata is now practically extinct. Applause between the movements of a concerto is still conventionally allowed and in concertos for bowed instruments, where in any case there would be an interruption for tuning, is perhaps not very objectionable; indeed, in concertos for other instruments the momentary rest is probably appreciated by many artists.

The restraint of applause can, of course, go too far. Visiting performers at the necessarily 'high-brow' Oxford Musical Club and Union in the 1930s were sometimes visibly embarrassed by the lack of applause between the items of a group of (often quite unconnected) songs or piano pieces.

There was a time when applause was considered no serious interruption, even during the course of a movement. The twenty-two-year-old Mozart, in Paris, wrote home from Paris of the first performance at the Concert Spirituel of a symphony of his own (the 'Paris' Symphony, K. 297).

'I began this with the violins alone, *piano* for eight bars. This was at once followed by a *forte*. The audience, as I expected, hushed down every noise during the *piano* and then, of course, as soon as the *forte* came began to clap their hands.'

Haydn and Mozart were delighted to have a movement encored: even at the first performance of Beethoven's late and difficult quartet op. 130, two movements had to be repeated (see *Encore*).

The practice of interrupting a concerto by clapping the cadenza (see *Concerto* 4; *Cadenza*)

is alluded to by Mendelssohn in a letter to a friend. In composing one of his concertos 'since, of course, the people would applaud the cadenza', a *tutti* had to be inserted after it, so that the following solo passage should not be disturbed by the applause. The famous soprano Clara Novello, after singing a duet with the contralto Brambilla in Milan in 1840, reported 'Our duet was applauded after each phrase, by claps sharp as the report of a cannon —not to prevent the next phrase being heard'. This practice of applauding during a vocal performance continues in the Near East. A correspondent writes: 'I witnessed in Cairo that the public accompanied a famous singer with cries of *Allah, Allah*, so that the song could scarcely be heard.' (Cf. the approving murmurs of *olé, olé* during a performance of *cante flamenco.*)

3. Applause at the Opera.

When the great Farinelli came to London in 1737 he sang a song by his brother in which the interruption of applause began after the very first note—which 'was taken with such delicacy, swelled by minute degrees to such an amazing volume and afterwards diminished to a mere point, that it was applauded for full five minutes' (Burney, q.v.).

At the opera (if the work is of the pre-Wagner type and therefore divisible into arias, etc.) the dramatic thread is often roughly snapped by applause, the sense of drama being apparently less well developed in the public than its sensuous enjoyment of vocal tone or its honest desire to applaud merit before it forgets.

President de Brosses (q.v.), visiting Milan in 1739, complained bitterly of the applause at the opera there. After a successful song there would be not merely a communal roaring at the top of the voice, but a striking of the benches with sticks brought for the purpose by men in the pit, whilst at this signal their friends in the gallery threw down thousands of printed leaflets with sonnets in praise of the singer.

Grétry, who was in Rome during the 1760s, says that it was a common thing during an opera performance to interject praise for players of the orchestra—*Brava la viola*, or *Bravo il fagotto*, or *Bravo l'oboe*, and Berlioz tells us how he in youthful days in Paris, seventy years later, would applaud 'a fine bass part, a happy modulation, a telling note of the oboe'.

Audiences nowadays do not go so far as that Dublin one which attended the performance of Weber's *Oberon* in 1868; on this occasion after Tietjens had sung 'Ocean, thou mighty monster', she was applauded for fifteen minutes and the applause only subsided when it was promised that she should sing 'The Last Rose of Summer'. As the orchestra had not got the music for this it was necessary to bring a piano on the stage (Oberon himself brought it, helped by five demons from the coming scene). All this accomplished, the opera was resumed.

4. Composers on Applause. Composers sometimes affect to despise applause. Berlioz said of one of his compositions, 'It brought enormous applause at a first hearing and therefore must be shallow and comparatively worthless—and I had thought so well of it!' Verdi hearing that a first performance of a new opera of his had evoked frantic applause exclaimed, 'Heavens! What is the matter with it?'

5. The Right to express Disapproval. The question has often been raised as to whether, since an audience assumes the right to express approval, it should not, in logic, assume also that to express disappointment. In Latin countries hissing is not unknown, but elsewhere the usual understanding is that the case is governed by that ordinary rule of social intercourse which prescribes that as compliments are pleasant to give and receive they may be indulged in but as complaints destroy the social atmosphere they shall be avoided. In England booing is rare enough to cause considerable newspaper comment.

Audiences occasionally pass beyond mere noisy protest. For instance, after Marinetti's futurist programmes (see *Italy* 7) in the early 1920s crockery and a large variety of fruit and vegetables were thrown at the performers, and when Kurt Weill's opera *The Rise and Fall of the City Mahagonny* was performed at Frankfort in 1930, stink-bombs were thrown, and a man was killed by a beer-mug during the discussion that followed.

The throwing of oranges seems to have been a more or less recognized means of expressing disappointment in the eighteenth century. Pergolese was once hit full in the face with one at the first performance of one of his operas, and there was a great stir in London in 1704 because the singer Mme Tofts was alleged to have sent her servant to the theatre to throw oranges at her rival. Even in the twentieth century the practice was not everywhere extinct. A close relative of the present author writes, 'I have seen at a Spanish music-hall a girl going round with a basket of rotten oranges, which she sold expressly for the audience to throw at performers when the latter did badly'.

Grétry says that the Rome opera audiences of the mid-eighteenth century made a practice of recognizing plagiarisms by calling out the name of the composer who suffered by it. Thus during the performance of a not very original opera one would hear cries of '*Bravo Sacchini! Bravo Cimarosa! Bravo Paesiello!*' Parma has the reputation of being particularly hard to please; singers of the greatest repute have been booed there unmercifully.

6. Applause in Sacred Places and during Sacred Music. Dr. Burney, in the 1770s, says that at the musical performances in the Italian churches, since clapping was prohibited, 'they cough, hem and blow their noses to express admiration'. This recalls the 'humming' of which we often read in the seventeenth century as common amongst English church congregations who wished to express approval of some passage in a sermon.

It is not always considered improper to applaud in sacred places in Italy, for the present writer, in the 1920s, saw the great organist Bossi loudly clapped after every item of his recital in a Florentine church and come on to the altar steps after every item to bow.

The refraining from applause in English churches seems to date only from the Oxford Movement. We can scarcely be surprised to learn that musical performers were applauded when we read that on the Duke of Wellington's appearance at the Grantham Musical Festival, in the parish church in 1834, 'the crowded audience on his *entrée* into the interior of the church arose, as with one accord, and testified their grateful admiration of the hero of a hundred battles by repeated and enthusiastic plaudits, Mr. Dixon the organist, with excellent discrimination, playing, *con spirito*, "See the Conquering Hero comes"', or that in Westminster Abbey, at Queen Victoria's coronation, 'The Duke of Wellington was more applauded than any other Peer'.

It is often considered unsuitable to applaud the performance of oratorio, but concert-room performances of Handel's *Messiah* in England until fairly recently still occasionally had their solemnity mitigated by applause and bowing after the solos—even after 'He was despised', than which no greater demonstration of impenetrability to the spirit of a piece of music can be imagined.

7. Applause as a Business. This brief treatment of the subject would not be reasonably complete if mention were not made of what may be called 'subsidized applause'. The 'claque', or group of hired applauders, is a regular part of musical and theatrical organization in many countries. The claques of Vienna and La Scala are considered to be particularly well organized.

This sort of thing was at one time common in London. *The Times* of 2 August 1828 contains the following paragraph:

'A pale-faced coxcomb with dirty linen is incessantly placing himself in the boxes at the little Haymarket Theatre, annoying the audience by his ridiculous and ill-timed plaudits. If this gentleman is paid to support the performances of certain individuals, he should do it with more judgement, and not render his venality and folly so conspicuous.'

And the following letter, thought to date from the 1860s, is extant:

'11, Canon-place, Mile End. E.
'Dear Sir—I beg to inform you that I have acted as leader of the claque for upwards of 20 years for nearly all the principle artists of the Royal Italian and english Opera Company's, and should you require any one to *serve you* for that purpose I should be most happy to do so for a small remuneration for my services.—Yours most truly.
N. Phillips.'

The following were the customary professional fees of the Italian claqueurs in 1919, as reported by an Italian correspondent of the London *Musical Times*:

For applause on entrance, if a gentleman . . . . . 25 lire.
For applause on entrance, if a lady . 15 ,,
Ordinary applause during performance, each . . . . 10 ,,
Insistent applause during performance, each . . . 15 ,,
Still more insistent applause . . 17 ,,
For interruptions with 'Bene!' or 'Bravo!' . . . . 5 ,,
For a 'Bis' *at any cost* . . . 50 ,,
Wild enthusiasm—A special sum to be arranged

Walter Damrosch, in 1923, in his *My Musical Life*, complained that at that time in the Metropolitan Opera House, New York, some singers and conductors, 'in rivalry with each other', foolishly spent their money 'on the hiring of twenty to fifty husky men, under a well-trained leader', who stood 'at the side of the balconies and family circle' and clapped 'with the machine-like regularity of a steel hammer in an iron foundry, so as to produce so and so many recalls after an act'. From time to time the administration decreed that no paid applause would in future be tolerated, often by limiting the number of standing-room occupants, but in the 1960's the Metropolitan claque was as active as ever, a small one of six or eight costing some $25 to $100 (the higher rates applying, logically enough, at Saturday matinees, which are broadcast).

(For applause reserved as a royal prerogative see *Concert* 6—the allusion to the Concerts of Ancient Music.)

APPLIED MUSIC. See *American Musical Terminology* 9.

APPOGGIANDO, APPOGGIATO (It.). 'Leaning', 'leaned', i.e. each note passing very smoothly to the succeeding one (i.e. *Portamento*, q.v.). It may also mean 'stressed'.

APPOGGIATURA. See Table 13. Less important varieties include the comparatively rare 'short appoggiatura' (what its name suggests, and sometimes accented, sometimes not), the still rarer 'passing appoggiatura' (*unaccented* and *before* the beat—i.e. everything the normal appoggiatura is *not*) and the 'double appoggiatura' and 'triple appoggiatura' (which may mean either those mentioned in Table 12 (a) or two or three normal appoggiaturas going on at the same time in different parts of the harmony).

The normal appoggiatura introduces (while disguising so far as paper appearance goes) what at the period of its emergence was a harmonic boldness, the so-called 'unprepared suspension' (see *Harmony* 12, 13). It is thus of no less importance harmonically than melodically, and for both reasons it is essential to perform it with proper length, weight, and conviction.

APPRECIATION OF MUSIC (p. 32, pl. 3). The words 'Musical Appreciation', taken together, have come to be accepted as the most usual time-table and textbook name for a form of educational training designed to cultivate in the pupil an ability to listen to seriously conceived music without bewilderment, and to hear with pleasure music of different periods and schools and varying degrees of complexity.

It must be obvious to anyone with a slight knowledge of the course of evolution of the art of music that its texture has become progressively elaborate.

To any music-lover, in any part of the world, born within the period between the birth of mankind and about A.D. 850–900, the ability to appreciate music implied (given the capacity for any emotional response to tone) merely the ability to give attention to and 'follow' a single line of notes. From the latter date it began increasingly to imply the ability to follow (more or less consciously and with more or less completeness) two or more simultaneous lines, the rhythms of which might be the same or different. The combination of lines brought a coincidence of notes, forming chords or harmonies, with the gradual conventionalizing of harmonic progressions and the ordering of them in something like patterns recognized by those sensitive to harmony as a sort of 'colouring'.

From about the year 1600 onwards (see *Harmony* 9; *Opera*; *Recitative*; *Figured Bass*), the codification of harmonic progression became more and more settled and this element in the appreciation of the art would, hence, have demanded less and less effort (through increased familiarity) but for the incessant introduction of more pungent combinations, which, until they reach the stage of familiarity, always constitute a difficulty to the normal listener.

The evolution of instruments had been all the time proceeding, so that in addition to harmonic colourings there came to exist a great variety of instrumental colourings, and, when the modern orchestra came into being (which may conveniently be put at the beginning of the Haydn–Mozart–Beethoven symphonic period—the latter half of the eighteenth century) the requirement that the listener's ear should be able to disentangle combined instrumental lines and should note the colour of each became urgent.

Meantime (spread over the whole period) a certain variety of forms (see *Form*), some of them of considerable length and complexity, had evolved, and without some ability to follow, *consciously or unconsciously*, the formal arrangement of musical material the listener was apt to feel himself in the presence of incoherence.

Further developments of the art are proceeding, and with them new kinds of demands upon the listener's perception. Lines are now combined which seem to be in no perceptible harmonic relationship, so that possibly a higher degree of the knack of 'disentangling' is required than in the height of the two great 'contrapuntal' periods, the second half of the sixteenth and the first half of the eighteenth century (e.g. Palestrina and Bach). There is a corresponding change in orchestral combinations, with an implication that since instrumental colours no longer merge they are meaningless if not identified individually. And there is at least the threat of an extensive use of smaller intervals (see *Microtones*), with, necessarily, a totally new harmonic system for which nothing in the older music has at all adequately prepared the ear.

Further to all the above-mentioned elements there is the undeniable fact that music, like the other arts, is in a considerable degree a personal and social reflection, so that for its full 'understanding' a knowledge of biography and history (in the sense of sympathetic acquaintance with the lives of composers and manners and feelings of different communities, nationalities, and periods) is also demanded.

A reading of the above summary by anyone with no initial musical experience whatever might well intimidate him, especially as these requirements, though similar to those imposed upon students of the other arts, take on an enhanced importance in the case of music from the fact that this art so often dissociates itself from the expression of 'ideas' and, like a man who has cast his clothing, leaves nothing but itself of which to catch hold.

As a matter of experience, however, it is found that by dint of mere hearing of sufficient music of different types and dates, a degree of 'knack' is unconsciously acquired. Most people find themselves susceptible of some measure of enjoyment from some kinds of music, but the degree can be enlarged and the kinds multiplied by well-directed training, and it is this fact which constitutes the argument for the adoption of 'Musical Appreciation' as a school and college subject, as which it has taken an ever-increasing place since about the beginning of the twentieth century.

The importance of accustoming youth to the better kinds of music and weaning it from the worse is a part of the appreciationist's programme, and the broad principle underlying this aim is recognized in Plato's *Republic* (*c.* 360 B.C.). The recreative use of instrumental and vocal music is recommended by Milton, in his *Tractate of Education* (1644)— 'either while the skilful Organist plies his grave and fancied descant, in lofty fugues, or the whole symphony with artful and unimaginable touches adorn and grace the well-studied chords of some choice composer', and so on. All this, however, is rather a use of music in education than the application of educational method to music, and by 'musical appreciation' is usually meant something more like what the

young Mendelssohn did for the old Goethe when, in what the poet called his daily 'music lesson', he played to him music of various schools, explaining it to him and calling his attention to its salient features—'from the Bach period downwards he has brought Haydn, Mozart, Gluck to life for me, and has given me clear ideas of the great modern masters.' This, in effect, is what any competent teacher of appreciation, from the elementary school to the university, tries to do, naturally varying his music and his methods according to the age and previous musical experiences of his pupils.

Apart from direct teaching of this sort, anything which cultivates a sensitiveness to tone and rhythm is, of course, of high value. Hence the *foundation* of musical appreciation work in school may be said to lie in the singing class, the eurhythmics class, piano lessons, the school orchestra, and similar activities. But it is an error to suppose, as some still do, that any full appreciation *necessarily* comes by 'doing', in the sense of performing. A very great deal of such 'doing' often takes place without seeming to arouse any strong impulse towards that other type of activity (really as much 'doing', in its own way), the keen listening to music.

The capacity for enjoyment of music is with children always in advance of the capacity to perform. Many a child-pianist who can play nothing beyond one of Beethoven's sonatinas is capable, when properly stimulated and led, of thoroughly enjoying his Fifth Symphony. It is, to say the least, unpractical to restrict children's opportunities for enjoyment to what they themselves can perform (a repertory limited by difficulty and restricted in quantity, and, in any case, somewhat worn by unavoidable over-repetition in the practice hours).

The enlightened music teacher strives to get out of his pupil all he can in the way of *both* performance and listening, and to have *both* these activities carried out with the utmost possible keenness and concentration of thought. He recognizes in music not one art but three— that of the composer, that of the performer, and that of the listener. These three individuals are essential to one another's existence; not one of them can do without the other two and, indeed, without the other two his art can hardly be said to exist.

There is a special technique to all three arts and all three can be taught and yet *cannot* be taught, being like other subjects in the curriculum in that there must exist both capacity and properly directed practice, in which latter the learner and not the teacher is the active agent (the teacher's functions, indeed, are merely inspiration and guidance; these supplied, it rests with the pupil to do the work).

The fact of the existence of an *art of listening* seems to have been first prominently acknowledged by the Zürich musician, Nägeli (q.v.), who lectured to amateurs and in 1826 published a book for their use, and then by the great musicologist Fétis, who in 1829 came to

London to give a series of lectures on *La Musique mise à la portée de tout le monde*; he gave only one of these lectures, but in 1830 he published a book with the same title, which was translated into several languages (nineteen editions known to the present writer, e.g. Paris, 1830, 1834, 1847; Berlin, 1830; Brussels, 1839 and 1849; Liège; Turin, 1858; Barcelona, 1840; St. Petersburg, 1831 and 1844; London, 1831 and 1844; Boston, 1842). In his preface he says, 'To supply sufficiently those ideas that are necessary to the increase of the enjoyment of music—that is my aim.' He speaks of having had several predecessors in Germany, but these are unknown to the writer of the present article (Quantz's so-called Flute Tutor of 1752 has a large amount of appreciation material, however), and probably for all effective purposes Fétis stands as the pioneer.

Definite experimentation with this sort of teaching, on any large scale and in class, began only towards the very end of the nineteenth century, and it seems to have begun more or less simultaneously in America and Britain. Landmarks are the publication, in America, of W. S. B. Matthews's *How to Understand Music* (1888), and, in Britain, of Oliveria Ann Prescott's *About Music and what it is made of* (the early 90s). In 1910 the appreciation publications of Stewart Macpherson (q.v.) began, and he became the first notable British exponent of the subject (p. 32, pl. **3**. 4), whilst in 1911 the appointment of Mrs. Frances Clark (p. 32, pl. **3**. 3) as head of a newly formed educational department of the Victor Phonograph Company, in America, gave her the opportunity for a nation-wide exercise of influence she had for some time been exerting in a more local way. British gramophone companies some years afterwards organized similar departments.

The terms 'Appreciate' and 'Appreciation', in a musical application, first came into use in the United States. In 1906 appeared *How to Appreciate Music*, by Gustav Kobbé, and in 1907 *The Appreciation of Music*, by T. W. Surette and D. G. Mason (extended gradually to six volumes of text and examples). It will be seen that these works slightly precede those of Stewart Macpherson, which were the earliest to introduce the term into British musical education. Macpherson's first knowledge of the new American Musical Appreciation movement came from an article on the subject by a Miss A. Langdale, who had just returned from the United States, published in a British periodical called *The Crucible* (March 1908), and within two months of seeing it, when founding the Music Teachers' Association, he included in that Association's aims—(*a*) the pressing 'upon Heads of Schools . . . a recognition of the important and often overlooked fact that music is a literature and should be studied and taught from that point of view'; (*b*) the insistence upon 'systematic ear-training from early childhood' as 'a preparation for the "art of listening"'; and (*c*) the supplementing of training in performance by the bringing of children 'into touch with good music, well played, and simply commented on by the teacher'.

The Music Memory Contest, a device for inducing close attention to, and the memorizing of, the main themes of a great listening repertory, began in New Jersey in 1916 (Mabel Bray) and was quickly taken up all over the United States; it has, up to the present, never been adopted in Britain. Special **Concerts for Children** became common in both countries, the example of the conductor Walter Damrosch in New York inspiring a music-loving London business man, Mr. (later Sir Robert) Mayer, to organize such concerts (which had formerly been only an occasional or local feature in musical life) all over Britain. From the late 1920s Damrosch did his work largely by means of the radio.

It is not possible in such an article as this to list even the most prominent of the many workers in the cause of musical appreciation, or even the most widely circulated of the books on the subject, which are now very abundant.

The term 'Musical Appreciation' has often been adversely criticized, partly on account of its ambiguity, the word 'appreciation' having come to mean, variously 'appraisal', 'approval', 'understanding', and 'enjoyment'. It is, of course, especially in the latter two senses that the musical educationist employs it. To his doing so an objection is sometimes made which could be expressed by the proverb, 'You can take a horse to the water but you cannot make him drink'—which is true but cannot be extended to include the corollary, 'Therefore it is no good ever taking horses to the water'.

There are, it is true, failures in musical appreciation teaching, but so there are in the teaching of every subject in the curriculum (certainly in that of sight-singing), and the case against it is precisely the same as the case that could be (but never is) made out against the teaching of English literature.

The 'appreciative' idea has gained ground in many other countries than Britain and the United States, largely stimulated by the facilities offered by radio and recordings. In the *Instructions du 2 septembre 1925 relatives à l'application des programmes de l'enseignement secondaire dans les lycées et collèges* the French Ministry of Education outlined a course to which in America or Britain teachers would give the name 'Musical Appreciation'; this is but one example out of many that might be mentioned.

See reference to Musical Appreciation under *Herschel, William*; *Ear Training*; *Jeunesses musicales*.

APPRENTICESHIP TO MUSIC. See *Minstrels*, etc., 3.

APPUYÉ, APPUYÉE (Fr., masc., fem.). 'Supported', emphasized.

APRÈS (Fr.). 'After.'

APSE (its effect on sound). See *Concert Halls* 6; *Acoustics* 18.

THOMAS AUGUSTINE ARNE (1710–78)
(Engraving by W. Humphrey)

ARNE AS A YOUNG MAN
(Attributed to Gainsborough)

ARNE AT THE ORGAN
(From a caricature by Bartolozzi)

1. BACH'S BIRTHPLACE AT EISENACH

2. THE ST. THOMAS CHURCH AND SCHOOL, LEIPZIG,
in 1723

3. A PERFORMANCE AT THE ST. THOMAS
CHURCH, 1710

4. BACH'S ELDEST SON
Friedemann

5. BACH'S GREATEST SON
Emanuel

6. BACH'S YOUNGEST SON
Christian—by his friend, Gainsborough

AP THOMAS or **APTOMAS** (i.e. Son of Thomas). See *Thomas Thomas*.

A PUNTA D'ARCO (It.). Literally 'with the point of the bow'.

ÄQUAL, AEQUAL (Ger.). Old organ term for '8-foot'.

AQUARELLE (Fr.). 'Water-colour'; sometimes musically applied to a piece of delicate texture.

AQUIN. See *Daquin*.

AQUINAS, SAINT THOMAS (1226–74). See references under *Lauda Sion, Pange Lingua, Tantum Ergo*.

ARABESQUE (Fr., Eng.), **ARABESKE** (Ger.). A florid melodic figure, or piece based on such (like Arabic style in architectural decoration, etc.).

ARABIC MUSIC. See *Spain* 1–3 (in a very general way the article *Oriental Music* also treats of this subject).

A.R.A.D. Associate of the Royal Academy of Dancing (founded 1927; chartered 1936).

ARADA (lit. 'ploughed land'). A type of folk song associated with ploughing in parts of Spain.

ARAGONESA (Sp.), **ARAGONAISE** (Fr.). A Spanish dance deriving from Aragon in Spain.

ARAJA. See *Opera* 17 a.

A.R.A.M. See *Degrees and Diplomas* 2.

ARBEAU, THOINOT. See *Dance* 6 (a) and passing references under *Morris*; *Romanesca*; *God save the Queen* 2, 4; *March*; *Tonic Sol-fa* 9.

ARBITRARY MINOR SCALE. Same as 'Melodic' Minor Scale. See *Scales* 6.

ARBLAY, MME D'. See *Burney*.

ARCADELT, JAKOB. Apparently of Netherlands descent. Born *c.* 1514 and died in Paris in 1568. His career was largely in Italy, and chiefly at Rome in the service of the Pope, but in 1555 he moved to Paris, where he entered the service of Cardinal the Duke of Guise. He enjoyed and retains high fame as a composer of madrigals and also of church music.

> See references to himself and his times under *Belgium* 1; *Italy* 4; *Misattributed Compositions*.

ARCATA (It.). Stroke of bow (violin, etc.): the words *in giù* (meaning 'down') or *in su* (meaning 'up') often follow. **ARCATO** (It.). 'Bowed' (after a passage of pizzicato).

ARCHANGELSKY (Archangelski), **ALEXANDER.** Born in the government of Penza in 1846 and died in Prague in 1924, aged seventy-eight. He gave his life to the music of the church in Russia, directing choirs and composing music. He was the first to introduce women's voices into choirs of the Orthodox church.

> For a general discussion of nineteenth-century developments in the music of the Orthodox church see *Greek Church* 5.

ARCHBISHOP OF CANTERBURY'S DIPLOMA. See *Degrees and Diplomas* 1.

ARCHDRUID. See *Wales* 7.

'ARCHDUKE' TRIO (Beethoven). See *Nicknamed Compositions* 4.

ARCHED VIALL. See *Clubs for Music-Making*.

ARCHET (Fr.). 'Bow' (violin, etc.). **ARCHI** (It.). 'Bows' (violin, etc.); the singular is *Arco*.

ARCHITECTURE. (1) General comparison with Music; see *History of Music* 1. (2) French Gothic architecture and the contemporary French music; see *France* 3. (3) Italian Renaissance architecture and the 'New Music'; see *Opera* 1. (4) Baroque architecture and the corresponding music; see *Baroque*; *Zopf*; *Ornaments* 3. (5) Fluctuations of taste in architecture and music; see *Quality* 8. (6) Architecture and Religion; see *Church Music* 1.

ARCHIVES INTERNATIONALES DE LA DANSE. See *Dance* (end).

ARCHIVIOLA. See *Arciviola*.

ARCHLUTE, ARCILIUTO. See *Lute* 5.

ARCIVIOLA, ARCIVIOLA DA GAMBA. Same as lira da gamba (see *Lyra* 3). The spelling 'archi-viola' is not correct, resulting apparently from a sixteenth-century misprint.

A.R.C.M. See *Degrees and Diplomas* 2.

ARCO (It.). 'Bow.' Used alone or in *Coll' arco* ('with the bow'), after a passage marked 'pizzicato' ('plucked'). The plural is *Archi*.

A.R.C.O. See *Degrees and Diplomas* 2.

ARDEMMENT (Fr.). 'Ardently.'

ARDENTE (It.). 'Ardent.'

ARDITI, LUIGI. Born in Piedmont in 1822 and died at Brighton in 1903, aged eighty. He travelled the old and new worlds as a conductor of operas, and composed a few of them, as also a waltz-song that has had universal circulation —*Il Bacio* ('The Kiss').

> See *Concert* 7; *Waltz*.

ARDITO (It.). 'Bold.' So *Arditamente*, 'boldly'.

ARDORE (It.). 'Ardour.'

ARENSKY (Arenski), **ANTONY** (p. 912, pl. 155. 3). Born at Novgorod in 1861 and died in Finland in 1906, aged forty-five. He was the son of talented amateur musicians, and himself showed early gifts for music. He studied at the Conservatory of St. Petersburg and became a professor of composition at that of Moscow. Later he was director of music in the Imperial Chapel at St. Petersburg.

His compositions brought him the heartiest admiration of Tchaikovsky, who had in common with him, so far as the choice of his musical material is concerned, a cosmopolitan rather than a narrowly nationalistic tendency (cf. *Russia* 6). Amongst his works are three operas, a ballet, two symphonies, chamber music, piano music, and songs.

ARETHUSA, THE. The poem closely describes a naval engagement that took place in the English Channel in June 1778. It is a newspaper report in verse. The tune, generally attributed to Shield (q.v.), was merely harmonized by him. It is a country dance tune once popular as *The Princess Royal*, which can be found under that name in Walsh's *Complete Country Dancing Master* (1730) and other collections of that period.

ARETINO, GUIDO. See *Guido d'Arezzo.*

AREZZO. See *Guido d'Arezzo.*

ARGYLL ROOMS, LONDON. See *Concert* 8.

AR HYD Y NOS. See *All through the Night; Melody* 3.

ARIA. This word, literally meaning 'air', has commonly (from the eighteenth century onward) a more definite implication—that of a lengthy and developed vocal piece, in three sections, of which the last repeats the first, the middle one offering variety of subject-matter, of key, of general mood, etc. It is not strophic, except in the sense that, from its form, it can readily be applied to the musical setting of a poem of two or three verses: the former is the more usual, the words, as well as the music, of the last section being almost always the same as those of the first.

As explained under *Opera* 1 and *Oratorio* 2, the solo vocal parts of those forms of musical composition were originally entirely, or almost entirely, in recitative (q.v.): that the desire to add to the attractions of dramatic declamation those of more regularly organized tune was the origin of the aria is explained under *Opera* 2. As early as Monteverdi's *Arianna* (1608) something that may be described as in principle an aria existed. As finally elaborated and, so to speak, codified under the Italian composers of the end of the seventeenth and beginning of the eighteenth century (especially A. Scarlatti, q.v.) the usual form of the aria was:

Instrumental Introduction.
First vocal section, beginning and ending in the main key to the piece.
Short Instrumental Postlude.
Second vocal section, in a contrasted key and often more modulatory than the first.
Third vocal section, merely repeating the first, but often without its instrumental introduction.

The third section was most often not written out but merely indicated by the words *Da Capo* ('from the beginning') or some other expression directing the performer to repeat the first section. It was usual, in doing this, to give variety by introducing impromptu decorations, often of an elaborate character.

The codification of the aria in its palmy days (the first half of the eighteenth century—A. Scarlatti, Handel, and the other composers of the Italian and Italianate school) was extraordinarily minute. Arias have been rather elaborately classified as follows:

1. The **Aria cantabile,** slow, smooth, pathetic, with opportunities for the singer to embellish his or her part by the addition of decorative passages.

2. The **Aria di portamento,** in long notes; dignified, with few opportunities for embellishment, to be sung with very smooth progression from one note to the next and a swelling and fading on each note (see *Portamento; Messa di voce*).

3. The **Aria di mezzo carattere,** more passionate and with an orchestral accompaniment that might become elaborate.

4. The **Aria parlante,** declamatory. 'Comfort ye', in Handel's **Messiah** (which he calls 'recitative'), may be considered an example of this intermediate type.

5. The **Aria di bravura,** or **Aria d'agilità,** or **Aria d'abilità** (i.e. 'of boldness', 'of agility', or 'of skill'). Handel's 'Rejoice greatly' in *Messiah* and the Queen of Night's Arias in Mozart's *The Magic Flute* are well-known examples.

6. The **Aria all'unisono,** with the accompaniment in unison or octaves with the voice part. Handel's 'The people that walked in darkness', in the authentic version of *Messiah* (i.e. without Mozart's or anybody else's additions), is a well-known example of this.

7. The **Aria d'imitazione,** a descriptive aria treating of birds, hunting horns, or anything else that has a musical effect capable of being imitated.

8. The **Aria concertata,** the 'concerted aria' with very elaborate accompaniment.

9. The **Aria senza accompagnamento**— 'without accompaniment', and naturally rare.

10. The **Aria da chiesa,** a 'church aria' with orchestral accompaniment.

11. The **Aria d'entrata,** perhaps hardly a special type, the term being applied to the aria with which any operatic performer made his or her first appearance in the score.

12. The **Aria fugata,** with a fugal accompaniment. 'But haste', in Handel's *Semele*, is an instance.

13. The **Aria tedesca** is simply an aria in the German style—a bit less showy and more solid than the Italian kind.

14. The **Aria buffa** was a comic aria (intentionally comic, that is).

15. By **Aria aggiunta** ('added aria') is merely meant one not in the original score and imported into the performance to please the singer or the audience.

As will be realized, the divisions between these numerous classes could not be absolute: many an aria might be qualified to be included in two of them, or might be on the border-line of the two. But the names meant something to the opera composers, performers, and audiences of the eighteenth century. There are other sorts of aria besides these, and indeed to make an absolutely complete list would be difficult.

The employment of the aria in an opera was governed by pretty strict rules: these are given under *Opera* 4.

The development of the aria is closely bound up with the growth of the Italian school of singing. Many arias were show pieces, pure and simple, and more instrumental than vocal in their essential character, the throat being treated as a human flute (see *Singing* 4).

In the middle of the eighteenth century the work of Gluck (see *Opera* 5; *Gluck*) showed the dramatic value of a closer attention to the details of the text. In principle he made a return to something like the ideals of those Florentines who originated the opera a century and a half earlier, as Wagner, a century later, also did, and as Debussy, later still again, did (see remarks under *Recitative*). In song there is no such thing as a permanent balance between manner and matter, between design and expression; the scales are always being tipped on one side or the other, and then some reformer, in the effort to balance them, tips them back.

As a definite form the aria is now dead, that is to say, composers do not now lay out their songs on its artificial three-section plan. The length of the regular three-section aria is, of course, against its holding its place in restless modern times. Hence in performances of the oratorios of Handel and the Passions and cantatas of Bach the *reprise* (i.e. the third section) is often omitted. Balance is thus destroyed but the audience gets home earlier.

The word aria is occasionally found applied to instrumental music, as for instance the bold 'Aria of the Athletes' in Gluck's *Paris and Helen* and occasional movements in suites of the Bach–Handel period.

See also *Arietta*; *Arioso*; *Cadenza*; *Cantata*.

ARIADNE AUF NAXOS (Richard Strauss). Produced at Stuttgart in 1912. Libretto by Hofmannsthal. One-Act opera, originally intended as a divertissement to follow a performance of Molière's *Le bourgeois gentilhomme*, for which play Strauss had written incidental music. Later revised and preceded by a prologue omitting any reference to the Molière play.

In the second version (which is the one usually given, and which has the practical advantage of avoiding the expense of a duplicate cast of speaking characters) the scene is laid in the music room of a wealthy Viennese. An opera on the subject of Ariadne is to be followed by a harlequinade given by the characters of the Italian impromptu comedy.

The wealthy patron decrees that owing to pressure of time the two entertainments are to be played simultaneously. What follows is a burlesque of seventeenth-century opera, in which the solitary laments of **Ariadne** (*Soprano*), abandoned by her lover Theseus on the desert isle of Naxos, are interrupted by the arrival of the sprightly **Zerbinetta** (*Coloratura Soprano*) with her motley following of farcical characters. Zerbinetta (her motto is 'off with the old love, on with the new') encourages Ariadne, who is later wooed and won by the god **Bacchus** (*Tenor*), amid general rejoicing.

ARIETTA (It.), **ARIETTE** (Fr.). A shorter and simpler aria. Usually it lacks the middle section which is normally so characteristic a feature of the aria proper (see *Aria* and compare *Cavatina* 1). The term is occasionally applied to instrumental music, as (rather unexpectedly) to the variations movement of Beethoven's Piano Sonata, op. 111.

ARIOSO. The word has several meanings.

(1) Recitative (q.v.) of the more melodious kind, midway between true recitative and the aria (q.v.). 'Aria-like' might be the best rendering in English here. This use of the word is common up to and including Bach.

(2) The kind of singing suitable for the greater arias, i.e. a sustained, developed, dignified singing; this is a definition given by Rousseau in his *Dictionary of Music* (1767), and the word is still used in something like this sense as a synonym for cantabile (q.v.).

(3) A melodic passage at the beginning or end of a Recitative—short and undeveloped, 'aria-like', but not 'aria'.

(4) Any short air in an opera, oratorio, etc. Mendelssohn occasionally uses the term in this sense in his oratorios, e.g. 'Woe unto them' in *Elijah*.

ARIOSTI, ATTILIO. Born at Bologna in 1666 and died, possibly in Spain, about 1740, aged about seventy-four. He was a monk who obtained a dispensation from his order and devoted himself to music, occupying important positions in German and Austrian courts and visiting London, where for a time he shared with Handel and Bononcini the directorship of the opera enterprise known as the Royal Academy of Music. He wrote numerous operas and oratorios and some instrumental works, including a volume of solos for the viola d'amore (an instrument on which he was a fine performer), dedicated to George II.

ARIZONA COWBOY SONGS. See *Folk Song* 4.

ARKANSAS TRAVELLER. See *Guion*.

ARKWRIGHT, GODFREY EDWARD PELLEN. Born in Norwich in 1864 and died near Reading in 1944, aged eighty. He was a distinguished musicologist who edited a comprehensive 'Old English Edition' (1889 and following years) and the quarterly journal, *The Musical Antiquary* (1909–13), etc.

See also *Adeste Fideles*.

ARLECCHINESCO (It.). Music in the spirit of a Harlequinade (see *Harlequin*).

ARMAILLIS DES COLOMBETTES. See *Ranz des Vaches*.

A.R.M.C.M. See *Degrees and Diplomas* 2.

ARMONIA (It.). 'Harmony'; also 'Wind Band'.

ARMONICA. See *Harmonica* 1, 5 c. *Armonica Meteorologica*, see *Harmonica* 5 c.

ARMONIOSO, ARMONIOSAMENTE (It.). 'Harmonious', 'harmoniously'.

ARMSTRONG.

(1) THOMAS HENRY WAIT. He was born at Peterborough in 1898. After choristership in the Chapel Royal and the sub-organistship of Peterborough Cathedral he became organ scholar of Keble College, Oxford, and has held organ posts in Manchester and London, Exeter Cathedral (1928), and (1933–55) Christ Church Cathedral, Oxford. From 1955 to 1968 he was head of the R.A.M. He was knighted in 1957. His compositions include choral and chamber music, church music, etc.

(2) (DANIEL) LOUIS—otherwise 'Satchmo' (Satchelmouth). Born in New Orleans in 1900 and died in New York in 1971, aged seventy-one. His career as trumpeter, singer, and band leader covered more than fifty-five years, and as 'the Einstein of Jazz' he is generally credited with the role of primary shaper of the art. See *Jazz* 3, 7.

ARNAMAGNAÄN MANUSCRIPT. See *Scandinavia* 5.

ARNE.

(1) THOMAS AUGUSTINE (p. 48, pl. 5). Born in London in 1710, and died there in 1778, aged nearly sixty-eight. He was D.Mus. (Oxon). At Eton he made himself a musician by practising on a 'miserable cracked common flute'; on leaving there, he used to enjoy opera by borrowing a footman's livery and spending the evening in the gallery provided for servants waiting for their masters. He practised the harpsichord against his father's wishes by putting a handkerchief over the strings to muffle the sound, and took violin lessons furtively. His sister became a professional singer, so he wrote an opera called *Rosamond*, in which she took the leading part, and this had some public success; then he wrote another, called *Tom Thumb*, so that his young brother might take the part of the hero.

Theatre managers now began to give him commissions; he wrote incidental music and operas and, at thirty, for a garden party of the Prince of Wales, that masque called *Alfred* from which come the still-living strains of 'Rule, Britannia'. Whether or not the whole English character can be expressed in eight notes, as Wagner said of the opening strain of this last, a great deal of it (or of what an Englishman would like people to think such) might be found in eight notes of any of Arne's songs, which are plain-dealing and direct and seem to have been composed in the open air.

It is chiefly by these songs that he is remembered today, and especially by certain Shakespearian ones, such as 'Where the bee sucks', 'Under the greenwood tree', 'Blow, blow, thou winter wind', and 'When daisies pied' (all these from his incidental music for the theatre).

Of his oratorios, one, *Judith* (1761), is remarkable as having offered the occasion for the first appearance of women singers in the choruses of such a work, at all events in Britain.

One of his operas, *Artaxerxes*, was a favourite of Haydn's. Some of the instrumental works well repay revival; see remark under *Sonata* 10 c. He married the vocalist Cecilia Young.

For references to T. A. Arne elsewhere in this work (some of them slight and others of more importance), see *England* 6; *Ireland* 6; *Harmony* 11; *Sonata* 10 c d; *Oratorio* 7 (1761); *Opera* 21 b, 24 c; *Ballad Opera*; *Masque*; *Pantomime*; *Glee* 4; *God save the Queen* 7, 15; *Rule, Britannia!*; *Miller of the Dee*; *Annotated Programmes* 1. Also p. 704, pl. **117**. 4.

(2) MICHAEL. Born in London in 1740, and died there in 1786, aged forty-six. He was the (natural) son of the above. He was unsuccessful as an opera singer, ruined himself in attempting to find the Philosopher's Stone, conducted the first performance of Handel's *Messiah* ever heard in Germany (Hamburg, 1772—thirty years after its composition!), and composed music for the stage—some of it whilst in prison for debt.

The song 'The Lass with a delicate air' (not 'the delicate air') is Michael Arne's, not (as often stated on programmes) his father's.

ARNELL, RICHARD ANTHONY SAYER.
Born in London in 1917. He was trained at the Royal College of Music and later joined the staff of Trinity College of Music as a teacher of composition. From 1943 to 1945 he was BBC Music Consultant in New York. He has composed five symphonies, concertos, a symphonic poem (*Lord Byron*), an opera, chamber music, etc.

ARNOLD.

(1) JOHN. He was born at Great Warley, Essex, in 1720, and died in 1792, aged about seventy-two. His name is very frequently met with in connexion with his publication of popular collections of psalm tunes, one of which (*The Compleat Psalmodist*) went into seven editions. (See *Hymns and Hymn Tunes* 11). He also published songs, catches, etc.

(2) SAMUEL. Born in London in 1740, and died there in 1802, aged sixty-two. He was a prolific and popular composer of operas, pantomimes, oratorios, services, anthems, etc., and at various times composer to Covent Garden Theatre, proprietor of Marylebone Gardens (see *Concert* 12), organist of the Chapel Royal and of Westminster Abbey, conductor of the Academy of Ancient Music, etc. He was one of the founders of the Glee Club (see *Glee* 3) and the editor of Handel's works in thirty-six volumes, and he published, in four volumes, a continuation of Boyce's *Cathedral Music* (see *Boyce*). He was responsible for a collection of psalm tunes which should not be confused with those of his namesake above.

See references under *Oratorio* 5; *Cathedral Music* 10; *Anthem*, Period 3; *Opera* 21 b; *Ballad Opera*; *Graduate's Meeting*.

(3) JOHN HENRY. Born in London in 1887 and died in Stanmore, Middlesex, in 1956, aged sixty-nine. He was a London Anglican organist who attained a high position as a

specialist authority on plainsong, producing practical treatises and collections.

(4) MALCOLM HENRY. Born at Northampton in 1921 (on his mother's side a descendant of William Hawes, q.v.). After boyhood study of the violin and trumpet he won a scholarship at the Royal College of Music and then joined the London Philharmonic Orchestra as a trumpet player. In 1943 his overture *Beckus the Dandiprat* called attention to his gifts as a composer: it was followed by a Horn Concerto (1945), a Symphony for Strings (1946), a Clarinet Concerto (1948), and other things. In that last year he was awarded the Mendelssohn Scholarship (q.v.) and was enabled to spend a year in Italy. The first of his six symphonies was composed in 1950 and closely followed by a Concerto for Piano Duet and Orchestra.

See *Concerto* 6 c (1921).

(5) MATTHEW (1822–88). See reference under *Education and Music* 2.

(6) FRANK THOMAS (1861–1940). See references under *Notation* 5; *Figured Bass*.

ARPA (It.). 'Harp.'

ARPÈGE (Fr.). 'Arpeggio.' So *Arpéger*, 'to spread a chord'; *Arpègement*, 'the spreading of a chord'.

ARPEGGIARE (It.). To play harpwise, i.e. (on the piano, etc.) to spread the notes of a chord, from the bottom up. So the present and past participles, *Arpeggiando* and *Arpeggiato*, and the noun *Arpeggio* (plur. *Arpeggi*) for any spreading (up or down). See Table 18.

ARPEGGIONE. A sort of guitar-shaped violoncello (six strings, fretted fingerboard, played with bow), invented by G. Staufer of Vienna in 1823. Its one exponent was a Vincent Schuster, and the one composition for it now known is a sonata which Schubert wrote for him in 1824 and which is now occasionally played on the violoncello or the viola da gamba, or (converted about 1930 by Gaspar Cassadó) as a concerto for violoncello and orchestra. This instrument may almost be considered a revived form of the lyra viol (see *Viol Family*, 4 c). Another name for it was **Guitare d'amour.**

ARPICORDO. An earlier Italian name for harpsichord.

ARRACHÉ (Fr.). 'Torn' (used for an extreme form of pizzicato).

ARRANGEMENT or TRANSCRIPTION. By 'arrangement' in music is meant the adaptation to one musical medium of music originally composed for another—the recasting of a song as a piano piece, of an orchestral overture as an organ piece, and so on.

Such a process, if seriously undertaken, commonly involves much more than the transferring from the one medium to the other of passages as they stand, since many passages that are effective on one instrument would sound ludicrous, or at any rate much less effective, on another. It is necessary, then, that the arranger should consider, not so much how nearly he can reproduce a given passage in the new medium, as, rather, how the composer would have written it had that medium been the original one.

In the early days of instrumental music, the differentiation of styles according to the special powers of different types of medium was not well understood, and indeed hardly existed, and so in the late sixteenth and early seventeenth century we find madrigals issued by their composers as 'apt for voyces or viols', and the Fitzwilliam Virginal Book (q.v.) has a certain quantity of choral music by foreign composers transcribed for keyboard with some added instrumental figuration, as was natural. Later in the seventeenth century, we find Purcell occasionally transcribing for the keyboard the voice part and accompaniment of a piece of his solo vocal music. Couperin, in his various books of harpsichord compositions, not infrequently appends a footnote suggesting that a piece is equally or more effective when played by some specified group of wind or string instruments. The fact that later composers did not always object to properly made arrangements of their work is illustrated by a programme now before the present writer—that of Chopin's London recital of 7 July 1848, where his own performances of his piano works were interspersed with vocal items by Madame Viardot Garcia and Mademoiselle de Mendi, including *Mazourkas de Chopin, arrangées par Madame Viardot Garcia* (p. 192, pl. 38. 4). These, it is clear, were considered unobjectionable, but it is very doubtful if the composer would have sanctioned the twentieth-century orchestral arrangements of his piano works for the purposes of the famous Russian ballet, which members of the audience who had ears, and not merely eyes, always found detestable, firstly because Chopin's essentially pianistic idiom does not arrange effectively for orchestra, and secondly because the tempo rubato (q.v.) which it demands is impossible when it is used for ballet purposes. Many crimes of arrangement have, indeed, been perpetrated in the interests of the ballet.

Bach was one of the greatest arrangers in the history of music. He arranged sixteen violin concertos of Vivaldi (for instance) for harpsichord, and three for organ, and did it with a freedom that would hardly be considered permissible today (but then we lack a Bach!). Occasionally Bach did more than doubtful deeds in arrangement, and so we find his most loving biographer and critic, Schweitzer, writing of the C minor Concerto for two violins and orchestra, 'How Bach could venture to transfer the two cantabile violin parts of the slow movement to the harpsichord, with its abrupt tone, must be left to himself to answer. Had he not done it himself we should be protesting in his name today against so un-Bach-like a transcription. This is not the only case in which he makes it hard for his prophets to go forth in his name against the evil transcribers.'

From time to time arrangers turn one or other of Bach's organ preludes and fugues into orchestral pieces (Esser, Elgar, Schönberg, etc.); these are then often played in some concert-room in which a fine organ meantime stands unused. Bach's famous Chaconne for violin alone has been arranged for piano by several, including Brahms (left-hand) and Busoni, and for orchestra, by Casella.

Liszt was another great 'arranger'. He was extremely free in his work, being influenced by his desire to produce astonishing keyboard display for his own use. He arranged for piano not only Bach organ fugues but Schubert songs (these latter rather travestied than arranged, perhaps) and all manner of things (cf. *Tausig*). The tendency nowadays is to much more conservatism in arrangement, and it is not usually considered 'correct' for an arranger to interpolate his own ideas as Liszt often did. He is looked upon, indeed, as the translator of a book, whose business it is to reproduce with as great an exactitude as respect for the natural idiom of the other language permits.

Many composers, besides Bach, have arranged their own works, as, for instance, Beethoven, who published his Violin Concerto turned into a Piano Concerto.

A point callously disregarded by commercial arrangers is that of the associations attaching to fine music in the minds of those in whose life it has been an important influence. To such people, the setting of the slow melody from the middle of Chopin's Fantaisie-Impromptu to a cheap set of verses is a desecration, and they do not even like the idea of '*The Moscow Waltz founded on Rachmaninof's Famous Prelude: Delightful to Dance! Easy to Play!! Charming to Listen to!!!*'. Nor do purists approve of the making of sentimental musical plays on the lives of composers, with the music drawn from their works and often most grievously deranged.

At one period during the jazz craze of the second and third decades of the twentieth century hardly any popular composition of Chopin, Schubert, Beethoven, etc., was respected by the world-famous jazz composers and arrangers of the day—not even Beethoven's noble tune to Schiller's 'Ode to Joy', in the Ninth Symphony. Gounod's addition of sentimental vocal and violin parts to Bach's first Prelude from the '48' (which is thus treated as a mere accompaniment) is a reprehensible example of a rarer type.

In the early nineteenth century Mozart's *Figaro* was performed as 'translated, altered, and arranged by Henry R. Bishop' (q.v.). It included two songs and six dances by the 'arranger'. Rossini's *Barber* was performed with the part of Figaro spoken. These are merely examples of a fairly common practice of the day.

Returning to the enormities of Chopin 'arrangements' it may be mentioned that Panigel's *L'Œuvre de Frédéric Chopin* (1949) devotes six pages to an historical list of gramophone records of the E flat pianoforte Nocturne, in which three-quarters are transcriptions, e.g. for four pianos, for mandoline, and for saxophone with guitar accompaniment. Six pages devoted to the Study in E major from op. 10 show a similar proportion, and include this piece as a trombone solo with jazz-band accompaniment and also 'arranged' (1933) for singing saw (q.v.) with accompaniment for violins and chorus (*Music and Letters*, October 1950).

But the ineptitude and callousness of arrangers have no end. Handel's 'Dead March' in *Saul* was in the early years of the nineteenth century published as a four-part glee, the trio of Chopin's Funeral March, a century later, as a comic song about Li Hung Chang. What is called Locke's *Macbeth* music (see *Misattributed Compositions*) was in the early nineteenth century in circulation as a 'Sacred Cantata, Praise God on High, by E. J. Westrop'. (The words of the fourth witch, 'Speak, sister, speak, is the deed done?' were replaced by 'Praise God on high; praise his great name!'; 'And nimbly dance we still' appeared as 'And in that day the dead shall wake'; 'My little merry, airy spirit, see, sits in a foggy cloud and waits for me' became 'The cherubim and seraphim continually do cry Holy! Holy!') Reversing this process of turning the secular to sacred uses, we find at about the same period a set of quadrilles on themes from *Messiah*. And we find the most sublime chorus from that work treated as follows:

Opening of the Hallelujah Chorus arranged as a duet for two flutes (published by G. Walker, London; he was in business at the end of the eighteenth century and beginning of the nineteenth).

The same arranged for concertina by W. H. Birch (1826–88).

Conclusion of an arrangement of the same composition for harp or pianoforte (with *ad lib.* parts for flute and violoncello), by J. F. Burrowes (1787–1852).

(It may safely be said that every country and every period has had its 'Tin Pan Alley'.)

Opera has always offered an attractive field for the arranger, on account of the wide public that becomes acquainted with its melodies and desires to domesticate them, or, at any rate, to hear them outside the opera-house. It will be remembered that Wagner, in Paris in 1839, supported himself by arranging the popular opera melodies of the day for cornet. The publication of arrangements was once one of the opera composer's chief sources of income, and it was a point with him to get out arrangements for harpsichord (or, later, piano) and for wind band before some unauthorized arranger stole his market. So we find Mozart writing to his father after the publication of *The Abduction from the Seraglio*, in 1782, 'I have now no slight task to get my opera arranged for wind band by Sunday week, lest somebody else should get in before me and reap the profit'.

An annoying kind of arrangement is that of an opera or similar work, for different voices, with a changed plot, and any other alteration that the arranger has thought to be of commercial significance.

A somewhat curious type of arrangement is that represented by Weingartner's transformation of Beethoven's opus 106, 'Hammerklavier' Sonata, into a symphony (1930), which he justifies by claiming that Beethoven in the original was aiming at more than the piano could express. (Then why did he not write it for orchestra?)

As will have been realized, certain compositions are nowadays heard more in arrangement than in the original, and many music-sellers could tell of the amateur vocalist customer who has lately heard and wishes to buy 'Schubert's *Ave Maria* arranged as a song'.

In our own days there is a general tendency amongst musicians sweepingly to condemn all arrangements, and it is, of course, almost always preferable that the original version shall be heard when the original resources are available. But it would be folly to condemn such utilities as the many arrangements of the classical symphonies for piano solo and especially duet, which, before the days of cheap gramophone records, enabled thousands to make an intimate acquaintance with their

beauties, and, likewise, it would be harsh to forbid the smaller cafés and restaurants to perform any music written for full orchestra because they do not possess that costly machine, or even to insist upon the recital organist remaining rigidly within the repertory (decidedly limited as concerns certain periods) left for him by the great musicians (see *Organ* 13). The wind bands of the world would be in a state of great poverty if they were restricted to the good music that has been specially composed for them: they are, indeed, *compelled* to draw upon the orchestral repertory. One absolutely necessary type of arrangement is that of operas, oratorios, and the like as 'vocal scores' (i.e. with the vocal parts plus a piano arrangement of the orchestral parts); all opera and oratorio composers have either provided or authorized this kind of arrangement.

No Ten Commandments can be graven on tables of stone for the guidance of the arranger, but he can be asked to observe the Golden Rule of doing to others as he would wish them to do to him. And we have a right to ask executants to make a thorough acquaintance with the 'legitimate' repertory of their instrument before drawing on the store of arrangements. It is absurd that even today there are world-famous pianists who never play in public any of Bach's clavichord-harpsichord fugues (every note of which can be performed on their instrument without change) and yet habitually play Liszt's and other arrangers' versions of Bach's organ fugues.

A subject cognate to that of arrangement is that of *Additional Accompaniment*, upon which an article will be found in this volume. For organ arrangements see *Organ* 13. For popular café arrangements, etc., see *Tavan*.

ARRIAGA. See *Spain* 7.

ARRIGO IL TEDESCO. See *Isaac, Heinrich*.

ARS ANTIQUA. See *Ars nova*.

ARSIN ET THESIN, PER. See *Canon*.

ARSIS (Gr.). 'Up-stroke' (in conducting), for the weak beat of the bar. (This reverses the sense of the word as applied to English poetical scansion.) Cf. *Thesis*.

ARS NOVA. The terms *Ars antiqua* and *Ars nova* (the 'Old Art' and the 'New Art') came into use at the beginning of the fourteenth century, to mark a change that at that period took place in music. 'Ars nova' represents a general freeing of style from the old influences of organum (see *Harmony* 4, 5), and conductus (q.v.). A greater variety of rhythm, more shapely melodic curves, and more independently moving voice parts were the marks of the new style. Probably the work of troubadours and trouvères (see the article *Minstrels*) had prepared the way for this more complex and sophisticated music.

The 'Ars antiqua' is particularly associated with the school of Paris (see *France* 2), and the 'Ars nova' in its inception with that of Florence. The 'Ars nova' may be looked upon as the beginning of a development that came to full flower in the Italian madrigal (see *Madrigal* 1).

See also references under *France* 3; *Landino*; *Tunsted*.

ARTARIA. See *Publishing* 8.

ARTEAGA, ESTEBAN (= Stefano). Born in Segovia in 1747 and died in Paris in 1799, aged fifty-one. He was a Jesuit. He lived in various Italian cities and then in Paris. His importance derives from his work, *Le Rivoluzioni del teatro musicale italiano dalla sua origine fino al presente* (1783: German translation 1789).

ARTEMOVSKY. See *Hulak-Artemovsky*.

ARTHUR, FANNY. See *Robinson, Joseph*.

ARTICOLATO (It.). [Well]-'articulated'; so *Articolazione*, [good] 'articulation'.

ARTICULÉ (Fr.). [Well]-'articulated'.

ARTIFICIAL HARMONICS. See *Acoustics* 8.

ARTIG (Ger.). 'Well-behaved', 'agreeable'. So the adverb *Artiglich*, and the noun *Artigkeit*. Note that *-artig* often appears as a suffix in the sense of 'like'. So *Marschartig*, 'march-like'.

ARTIKULIERT (Ger.). [Well]-'articulated'.

ART OF FUGUE ('Die Kunst der Fuge'). This is an unfinished work of Bach, apparently designed to exhibit the possibilities of one single, simple 'subject' in the various types of fugal and canonic writing. It was published by Bach's son, C. P. E. Bach, after its composer's death. Questions much discussed have been (*a*) whether the nineteen movements of this great work were intended for actual performance or only as a paper display of skill, and (*b*) in the former case, what medium was intended.

In 1924 a young Swiss, Wolfgang Graeser (1906–28), prepared a version in which the canons and fugues are set for various groups of instruments and a good many other versions have since been brought to performance—some for string quartet, some for two pianos, etc.

Tovey (q.v.) in 1932 published an edition in open score and also for keyboard, with the incomplete last movement worked out to an end (Nottebohm, Riemann, and Busoni having previously produced workings of this); and also, as a climax to the whole, a complete four-part 'mirror' fugue on the plan which Bach is reported to have intended to adopt as a technical grand finale. He argued plausibly that the keyboard medium was intended, since the work lies quite well under the hands.

ARTS COUNCIL OF GREAT BRITAIN. This was founded at the end of 1939 as the Council for the Encouragement of Music and the Arts (abbreviated to 'C.E.M.A.' and called 'Seema') and received a royal charter in 1946 under its new name. It is an independent body but under the old constitution it received, in a measure, the oversight of the Ministry of Education and under the new it still has a loose connexion with that Ministry and with the Treasury, from which it receives an annual grant of some twelve million pounds (1971). It consists of twenty persons selected by the Chancellor of the Exchequer in consultation with the Minister of Education, plus a small professional staff, including the Music Director.

So far as music is concerned its policy is to encourage and support independent orchestral and operatic organizations, music clubs, etc., rather than to set up concert and operatic enterprises of its own. In some cases the support takes the form of a guarantee against loss, in others of a definite grant. The executive body receives the advice of an influential Music Panel (cf. *National Federation*).

ARUNDELL, DENNIS DREW. Born in London in 1898. He graduated at Cambridge University, where he became a lecturer in music and on English drama. He has engaged in a large number of musical and dramatic enterprises, composed incidental music to plays, etc., and written books on Purcell, on opera criticism, etc.

ARYTENOID CARTILAGE. See *Voice* 21.

AS (Ger.). The note A flat.

A.S. See Table 20.

ASAF, GEORGE. See *Pack up your troubles*.

ASAPH, SONS OF. See *Jewish Music* 1.

ASAS or **ASES** (Ger.). The note A double-flat.

ASCAP. See *Copyright and Performing Right* 2.

ASHKENAZIC JEWS. See *Jewish Music* 3.

ASHLEY.

(1 and 2) J. (d. 1805) and his son C. J. (1773–1843). See references under *Oratorio* 5; *Annotated Programmes* 4.

(3) JOHN or JOSIAH (d. 1830). A bassoon player at Bath and a writer of popular songs. See reference under *God save the Queen* 19.

ASHTON, ALGERNON BENNET LANGTON. Born at Durham in 1859 and died in London in 1937, aged seventy-seven. An able and active composer, pianist, and teacher, and a yet more able and active writer of letters to the press upon every subject under the sun, with an especial attention to the neglected tombstones of great men of all walks of life, and to the errors of writers on all subjects. In the preface to two reprints of his letters in volume form, he claimed a world championship: 'I do not believe that any single individual has previously succeeded in getting 656 different letters published in the Press within the space of twenty-five months.' In 1932 he wrote to report the completion of 'twenty-four elaborate string quartets in all the major and minor keys . . . without the slightest hope or prospect of having one of them performed, let alone published'.

See *Toy Symphony*.

ASHWORTH, CALEB (and other members of his family). See *Baptist* 4; *Congregational* 3.

ASKAULOS. See *Bagpipe Family* 9.

A SOLIS ORTUS CARDINE. See *Hymns and Hymn Tunes* 2.

ASPIRATAMENTE (It.). 'Aspiringly.'

ASPIRATE. See *Voice* 13.

ASPRO, ASPRA (It., masc., fem.). 'Rough', 'harsh'. So the adverb *Aspramente* and the noun *Asprezza* ('asperity').

ASSAI (It.). 'Very', 'extremely' (formerly this word was synonymous with the French 'assez'—'enough', 'rather'—but the meanings have drifted somewhat). In its musical application the meaning of the word is often doubtful; with Beethoven it often seems to mean 'rather'.

ASSEZ (Fr.). 'Enough', but the usual and best translation is 'fairly', e.g. *Assez vite*, 'fairly quick'.

ASSIEME (It.). 'Together.'

ASSOCIATED BOARD of the Royal Academy of Music, the Royal College of Music, the Royal Manchester College of Music, and the Royal Scottish Academy of Music (founded in 1889, partly to combat the effect of numerous spurious examining bodies, with the first two of these institutions only, the others joining it in 1946). It is a purely examining institution. For its diploma examinations see *Degrees and Diplomas* 2. Its series of examinations of pupil grades (conducted all over the British Dominions) cover the whole period of pupil life.

ASSOLUTA. See *Prima Donna*.

ASSUMPTA EST MARIA. See *Mass* 5.

ASTON, HUGH. An English musician of the late fifteenth and early sixteenth centuries (d. 1522). He was a composer of church and virginal music, and is especially important as a pioneer of true instrumental style (as distinct from a mere transference to instruments of the then well-developed contrapuntal choral style; it is claimed that he was the first to introduce the variations form (see reference under *Spain* 8, also *Harpsichord* 9).

ASTORGA, BARON D' (Emanuele Gioacchino Cesare Rincón). Born in Sicily in 1680 and died in Spain or Portugal about 1757, aged about seventy-six. An amateur singer, harpsichordist, and composer of high artistic rank, who wrote (especially) chamber cantatas (*Cantate da camera*), operas, and a still-famous *Stabat Mater* (about 1707).

ASTURIANO, ASTURIANA (Sp., masc., fem.). Pertaining to Asturias (province of Spain in the Bay of Biscay, now Oviedo).

A.T.C.L. See *Degrees and Diplomas* 2.

ATEMPAUSE (German, 'breath pause'). This is an infinitesimal pause on a weak beat, made in order to give greater effect to the following strong beat. Viennese waltz conductors use it effectively, and it has a legitimate application also in more serious music (cf. *Agogic*).

ATHANASIAN CREED. See *Creed*.

ATHOLL, DUKE OF. See *Bagpipe Family* 4.

ATKINS, IVOR ALGERNON. Born at Cardiff in 1869 and died at Worcester in 1953, aged nearly eighty-four. After experience as assistant organist of various cathedrals, he was for over half a century (1897–1950) organist of that of Worcester, and thus one of the conductors of the Three Choirs Festival (see *Festival* 1, 3). He composed songs, church music, service settings, anthems, etc. With Elgar, he prepared an edition of Bach's *St. Matthew Passion*. He was knighted in 1921.

ATLANTIC CITY. See *Organ* 5 (end).

ATONAL, ATONALITY. See *Harmony* 18; *Hauer*.

A.T.S.C. See *Degrees and Diplomas* 2.

ATTACCA (It.). From the verb *attaccare*, 'to fasten together' (see *Attacco*). The word is used when the end of one movement is followed, without a break, by the beginning of the next.

ATTACCO. A very short *motif* (q.v.), say of three or four notes, used as material for *imitation* (see *Counterpoint*, end) or as a fugue subject. The term comes from the Italian verb *attaccare*, 'to attach', 'to fasten together'; the idea seems to be that short points of imitation are often used as connective tissue in a composition.

Compare *Andamento*.

ATTACK. The prompt and decisive beginning of a note or passage by either vocal or instrumental performers.

The principal first violin of an orchestra (in America 'concert-master') is in France called *chef d'attaque*, which is, after all, much the same as 'leader', the term often used in England.

Good 'attack' is a vital element in sound rhythm.

ATTAIGNANT (Attaingnant, etc.). See *Printing* 1; *Publishing* 2; *Dance* 10; *Verset*.

ATTAQUE (Fr.). See *Attack* above.

ATTENDANT KEYS. See *Modulation*.

ATTERBERG, KURT. Born at Göteborg in 1887, and died in Stockholm in 1974. He was by profession an engineer. In 1928, the centenary year of Schubert's death, he was awarded by a board of eleven well-known musicians a £2,000 prize offered by the Columbia Graphophone Company for a symphony dedicated to the memory of Schubert. The critics almost unanimously dissented.

Other compositions are a violin concerto, a cello concerto, string quartets, and operas. In 1934 he became one of the original members of the 'Permanent Council' referred to under *Germany and Austria* 9.

ATTEY, JOHN. Active in the early part of the seventeenth century. In 1622, a decade after the English lute songs had ceased to be published, he put forth work of this kind—the last to appear.

ATTWOOD, THOMAS (p. 165, pl. **34**. 4). Born in London in 1765 and died there in 1838, aged seventy-two. He was the son of a trumpet-playing coal merchant, sang as a boy chorister in the Chapel Royal, taught music to members of the British royal family, and became organist of St. Paul's Cathedral. As a composer he had a very successful early career in providing for the stage, and an equally successful later one in providing for the Church.

In youth he was Mozart's pupil in Vienna (his corrected studies survive); in old age Mendelssohn's host and friend in London.

See references under *Anthem*, Period IV; *Rule, Britannia!*

AU (Fr.). 'To the', 'at the', etc.

AUBADE (Fr., from *aube*, 'dawn'). As a serenade (q.v.) is evening music, so an aubade is early morning music. The troubadours (see the article *Minstrels*) had forms of song called *Aube* and *Serena*. Both imply the entertainment, from outside the house, of one (perhaps usually some fair lady) who is in bed. On certain official occasions aubades used to be played to the French sovereigns by military bands, and so also in provincial towns to municipal officials, or as a celebration of their election. The writer has stayed in a Swiss town during a musical festival week when the inhabitants of every street were cheered every morning at six by wind bands—'Waking Music', it was called.

In Spanish the corresponding word is *Alborada* and in Spain music of this kind was formerly usually played by bagpipes and drums.

Composers have used both terms as titles for instrumental music, e.g. Lalo's *Aubade* for five wind instruments and five string instruments, and the Alborada that opens Rimsky-Korsakof's *Spanish Caprice*.

AUBER, DANIEL FRANÇOIS ESPRIT (p. 368, pl. **61**. 9). Born at Caen in 1782 and died in Paris in 1871, aged eighty-nine. He came to London in early life and whilst earning his living in a business house took an active part in all musical pursuits.

At twenty-two he was back in Paris, where he quickly became known as a composer, at first of instrumental music. In his early thirties his operas began to be heard, and he now formed with the dramatist Scribe an alliance as close and essential as the later one between Gilbert and Sullivan. He felt the influence of Rossini and adapted Rossini's style to the French taste.

In all, he wrote about forty operas, of which *The Dumb Girl of Portici* (otherwise known as *Masaniello*), *Fra Diavolo, The Bronze Horse, The Crown Diamonds*, and others, are well known by name to the frequenters of popular concerts and cafés by the separate performance of portions or of the overtures. It was at a Brussels performance of *Masaniello*, with its revolutionary libretto, that there broke out the rebellion that resulted in the freedom of Belgium (1830), until then bound to Holland. It is a curious circumstance that Auber never attended performances of his own works.

He was a great melodist, an easy harmonist, and an effective orchestrator. His works offered no difficulty to the hearer. For the most part they belong to the genre of 'opéra comique' (or opera with spoken dialogue) but *Masaniello* is an example of 'French Grand Opera'—the first model of the type.

In 1842 he became head of the Paris Conservatory and in 1857 musical director to Napoleon III.

See passing references under *France* 9; *Opera* 21 g; *Comic Opera; Grand Opera; Overture* 5; *Criticism* 6; *Cornett and Key Bugle Families* 3 d; *Percussion Family* 4 c (allusion to Anvil).

AUBERT.

(1) JACQUES (*c.* 1689–1753). He was a famous Parisian violinist and composer of music for his instrument, as also of dramatic music, etc.

See reference under *Bagpipe Family* 6.

(2) LOUIS (full Christian names Louis François Marie). Born at Paramé in Brittany, in 1877 and died in Paris in 1968, aged ninety. He was a choir-boy at the Madeleine and a brilliant student of the Paris Conservatory under Fauré (q.v.). For a time he was before the public as a pianist.

He wrote songs, piano music, the fairy-tale opera *The Blue Forest* ('La Forêt bleue', first performed at Boston, U.S.A., in 1913), the symphonic poem *Habanera*, and other things.

AUCH (Ger.). 'Also', 'but'.

AUDACE (Fr.). 'Audacity.' (It.). 'Audacious.'

AU DESSOUS (Fr.). (*a*) 'Beneath'; (*b*) 'less than'.

AUDIBILITY, PITCH LIMITS OF. See *Acoustics* 17.

AUDRAN, EDMOND. Born at Lyons in 1840 and died at Tierceville near Paris in 1901, aged sixty-one. He was the son of a famous operatic tenor who was later head of the Conservatory of Marseilles. He himself occupied a position as church organist in that city and composed church music, but then turned to the stage, making a great reputation as a composer of comic operas.

AUER, LEOPOLD (1845–1930). Great Hungarian Jewish violinist and violin teacher.

AUF (Ger.). 'On', e.g. *Auf der G*, like the Italian *Sul G*, means 'on the G' (string).

'AUF DEM ANSTAND' SYMPHONY (Haydn). See *Nicknamed Compositions* 11.

AUFFÜHREN (Ger.). 'To perform.' So *Aufführung*, 'performance' (also 'development'); *Aufführungsrecht*, 'performing right' (often followed by the word *vorbehalten*, i.e. 'reserved').

AUFGEREGT (Ger.). 'Excited.'

AUFGEWECKT (Ger.). 'Wakened up', i.e. lively.

AUFHALTEN (Ger.). To 'hold up', i.e. to retard.

AUFLAGE (Ger.). 'Edition.'

AUFLÖSEN (Ger.). 'To loose', 'untie'. Thus, to resolve a discord, or (in harp playing) lower again a string which has been raised in pitch. So the noun *Auflösung*. But *Auflösungszeichen* means the natural sign.

AUFSCHLAG (Ger.). 'Up-beat' ('down-beat' being *Niederschlag*).

AUFSCHNITT (Ger.). 'Slit.' So, a portion omitted; a 'cut'.

AUFSCHWUNG (Ger.). 'Up-soaring', 'flight', e.g. *Mit Aufschwung*, 'in a lofty (i.e. impassioned) spirit'.

AUFSTRICH (Ger.). 'Up-stroke' of bow ('down-stroke' being *Niederstrich*).

AUFTAKT (Ger.). 'Up-beat' ('down-beat' being *Niederschlag*).

AUFZUG (Ger.). Literally 'up-pull' (i.e. of curtain), hence 'act'.

AUGENER. See *Printing of Music* 4; *Publishing of Music* 7.

AUGENGLÄSER. Beethoven's duet (*c.* 1796) for viola and violoncello 'with two Augengläsern obbligato' provides a puzzle for many readers, who naturally imagine that there must have been a musical instrument called the 'Augenglas'. This is one of Beethoven's little jokes. He wrote the piece, it appears, for two players who both wore eyeglasses, most probably himself and his close friend Zmeskall, an excellent cellist.

AUGMENTATION AND DIMINUTION, in melodic parts, are, respectively, the lengthening and shortening of the time-values of the notes of those parts. Thus (to take one instance), in a fugue the subject may (especially towards the end) appear in longer notes, the device adding dignity and impressiveness.

AUGMENTATION, CANON BY. See *Canon*.

AUGMENTED FOURTH. See *Tritone*.

AUGMENTED INTERVALS. See *Interval*.

AUGMENTED SIXTH. The chords of the Augmented Sixth are chromatic chords, i.e. they include elements borrowed from outside the key. There are three forms, to which apparently rather pointless names have been given as follows (taking key C as our example):

1. *Italian Sixth*, A flat–C–F sharp.
2. *French Sixth*, A flat–C–D–F sharp.
3. *German Sixth*, A flat–C–E flat–F sharp.

It will be seen that the basis of the chords above is the flattened submediant with the sharpened subdominant, these two notes forming the interval from which the chord takes its name of augmented sixth.

The chords can all be taken also on the flattened supertonic (e.g. D flat–F–A flat–B).

The 'German' form is the commonest; it admits of several resolutions and by enharmonic change (e.g. A flat–C–E flat–G flat) can become a dominant seventh (or chromatic tonic or chromatic supertonic seventh) in another key.

It will be realized that a considerable range of modulations becomes possible by means of a chord which can be taken or quitted as either on the submediant or the supertonic or, under one of its *aliases*, as a dominant, tonic, or supertonic seventh.

AUGMENTED TRIAD. See *Harmony* 24 d.

AUGUSTINE, SAINT. See *Hymns and Hymn Tunes* 1; *Te Deum*; *Plainsong* 4.

AULD LANG SYNE. The poem is a recasting by Robert Burns of a popular song (probably in origin a folk song) then current in various versions; this song may be the same as the one mentioned in 1677 in letters in the Duke of Argyll's manuscripts. In 1791 Burns wrote to George Thomson, his publisher, 'The air is but mediocre, but the following song, the old song of the older times, which has never been in print nor even in manuscript until I took it down from an old man singing, is enough to recommend any air'. The poem in its final form, as we have it today, was published in 1794.

The 'mediocre air' mentioned is not the one now known. The tune we now have is sometimes stated to be by Shield (q.v.): something like it certainly appeared in his opera *Rosina*, as a part of the Overture (Covent Garden, 1783), where it is used in imitation of Scottish bagpipe music, the oboe taking the tune itself and the bassoons the drone (the composer has written above their part, 'to imitate the bagpipes'). This origin, which gives the credit for the tune to England, has been disputed by certain Scots authorities, who point out that tunes bearing a very close similarity are to be found in certain Scottish publications at about the same period, under various names. One of these, 'Sir Alexr. Don's Strathspey' (issued possibly a year later than the performance of Shield's opera), seems to have a very good claim to be the original; it may have been already current and have become known to Shield, who was brought up at Durham, i.e. not very far from the Scottish border. In any case it is pertinent to remark that Shield's overture contains three other tunes that had enjoyed a previous existence.

There is, of course, a strong resemblance between the tunes of 'Auld Lang Syne' and 'Comin' thro' the rye' (q.v.). There is also another tune 'O can ye labour lea, young man', with a still closer resemblance. Still another, 'Roger's Farewell', seems to be a near relation.

The air is in the Pentatonic Scale (see *Scales* 10), like many Scottish tunes.

'Auld Lang Syne' has become the ritual song of parting—amongst the English almost as much as the Scots. All stand in a circle, and at the last verse take hands (with arms crossed, i.e. the left hand grasping the right hand of the neighbour on the right and the right hand grasping the left hand of the neighbour on the left); the whole circle of hands is then raised and dropped repeatedly and rhythmically to the music.

A correspondent of the *Manchester Guardian*, in January 1939, announced the curious fact that the tune is in religious use in Corsica. He had recently heard it sung on the occasion of an ecclesiastical street procession in honour of St. Lucy, and was told that it was 'a very old Corsican tune'.

AULD ROBIN GRAY. The words of this song were written in 1771 by Lady Anne Barnard (*née* Lindsay). The tune to which we now sing it is not the original one but was composed by a Somerset clergyman, the Rev. William Leeves, in 1772. The original tune was a traditional Scottish air, 'The bridegroom grat when the sun went down'.

The popularity of the song led to the composition of others, in which Auld Robin Gray appeared in the title and in which the adventures of the personages of the song were continued—with a view to a 'happy ending'.

AULIN, TOR. Born at Stockholm in 1866 and there died in 1914, aged forty-seven. He was virtuoso violinist, leader of a fine string quartet, orchestral conductor, and composer of violin concertos, orchestral works, etc.

AURA (It.). Jew's harp (q.v.).

AURAL CULTURE. See *Ear Training*.

AURIC, GEORGES (p. 388, pl. **65.** 3). Born at Lodève, Hérault, in 1899. He studied at the Paris Conservatory and under d'Indy at the Schola Cantorum. His compositions began to appear from his fifteenth year: later he became attached to the group called 'Les Six' (see *France* 11). He has written piano music, songs, orchestral music, ballets, etc. (to some extent showing the influence of Stravinsky), and also musical criticism, and he is France's most successful composer of film music. Since 1954 he has been president of the French performing right society (SACEM); from 1962 to 1968 he was general administrator of the Opéra and Opéra-comique in Paris.

AURRESKU. A sort of Basque folk dance. The zortziko (q.v.) forms a part of it.

AUS (Ger.). 'Out of', 'from', etc.

AUSDRUCK (Ger.). 'Expression.' So *Ausdrucksvoll*, 'expressively'.

AUSFÜLLGEIGER (Ger.). 'Filling-out-fiddler', i.e. *ripieno* (q.v.).

AUSGABE (Ger.). 'Edition.'

AUSGEHALTEN (Ger.). 'Held out', i.e. sustained.

AUSHALTEN (Ger.). 'To hold out', hence to sustain; so *Aushaltungszeichen*, 'holding-out sign', i.e. pause.

AUSSCHLAGEN (Ger.). 'To beat out', i.e. to beat time.

AUSSER (Ger.). 'Outer', 'out of', 'in addition to'.

ÄUSSERST (Ger.). 'Extremely.'

AUSSI (Fr.). Either (1) 'also', or (2) 'as', in the sense of 'as much', or (3) at beginning of a sentence may mean 'therefore'.

AUS TIEFER NOTH. See *Chorale*.

AUSTIN. (The Brothers.)

(1) FREDERIC, born in London in 1872 and died there in 1952, aged eighty. He had a varied and active career as baritone singer, composer, opera director, and arranger of music for the revival of Gay's *The Beggar's Opera* (q.v.) and its sequel *Polly* (1920 and 1922).

(2) ERNEST, born in London in 1874 and died at Wallington in 1947, aged seventy-two. At first a business man, he took to composition and became known by a mammoth 'Narrative Poem' for organ, in twelve sections (*The Pilgrim's Progress*), also producing many works of more normal dimensions.

AUSTRALIA. See *Benjamin*; *Glanville-Hicks*; *Broadcasting* 3; *Schools of Music*; *Voice* 6.

AUSTRIA. See *Germany and Austria*.

AUSTRIA (Hymn Tune). Same as *Emperor's Hymn* (q.v.).

AUSZUG (Ger.). 'Extract', 'arrangement' (q.v.).

AUTHENTIC CADENCE. See *Cadence*.

AUTHENTIC MODES. See *Modes* 5, 6, 9.

AUTOHARP. A type of zither (q.v.). It has no special melody strings, the melody notes being picked out by applying more force. Chords are played on it by depressing keys which damp all the strings except those required. The fingers or a plectrum can be used. The instrument is easily learnt and played and is necessarily capable of merely simple effects.

AUTOMATIC INSTRUMENTS. See *Mechanical Reproduction of Music* 9.

AUTO-SUGGESTION. See *Singing* 12.

AUTRE, AUTRES (Fr.). 'Other', 'others'.

AUXETOPHONE. A pneumatic sound amplifier, the principle of which was first suggested by Edison. It was later devised and patented by Horace Short and then improved by Sir Charles A. Parsons. The amplification was so great that a normal gramophone record could be heard all over a village half a mile away (but cf. *Bullphone*); in a more moderate degree it was for a time applied by Sir Henry Wood, in the Queen's Hall, London, to the amplification of the tone of the stringed double-bass. (For a brief description see *Musical News*, 27 Oct. 1906.)

AUXILIARY NOTE. This may be described as a variety of Passing Note (see *Harmony* 3), which, instead of passing *on* to another note, passes *back* to the note it has just left. Such a note may (as many a Passing Note) be either diatonic or chromatic. (Shakes, Mordents, and Turns offer examples of the Auxiliary Note applied decoratively.)

AVANT (Fr.). **AVANTI, AVANTE** (It.). 'Before', 'preceding'; also 'forward'.

AVEC (Fr.). 'With.'

AVE MARIA ('Hail Mary!'). A prayer used in the Roman Catholic Church consisting partly of the salutations of the Archangel Gabriel and of Elizabeth and partly of matter added in the fifteenth century. It has often been made the subject of a musical composition. See *Mass* 5.

AVE MARIS STELLA. See *Hymns and Hymn Tunes* 2.

AVE REGINA COELORUM. See *Antiphons of the Virgin Mary.*

AVE VERUM CORPUS ('Hail, true body!'). A hymn (anonymous and of unknown date) which possesses its own plainsong and has also been frequently set by composers (Josquin des Prés, Mozart, Cherubini, S. Wesley, Gounod, Elgar, etc.). Such motet settings are frequently sung in the Roman office of Benediction. Translations sometimes begin *Jesu, Word of God Incarnate*; *Jesu, Blessed Word of God Incarnate*; or *Word of God Incarnate.*

AVIDOM, MENAHEM. See *Jewish Music* 3.

AVIGNON. See *Singing* 3; *Italy* 4; *Belgium* 2.

AVISON, CHARLES. Born at Newcastle-on-Tyne about 1710 and died there in 1770, aged about sixty. He was a pupil of Geminiani in London, and the organist of the great church of his native town. He published fifty concertos, one or two of which have been republished in recent times, and many sonatas, and by *An Essay on Musical Expression* roused a lively controversy.

A certain 'Grand March' of his for harpsichord brought him the glory of resurrection a century after his death, as one of the heroes of Browning's *Parleyings with certain People of Importance in their Day.*

See *Criticism of Music* 4; also mention under *Shield.*

AVOIDED CADENCE. See *Cadence.*

AWAKE, MY SOUL. See *Hymns and Hymn Tunes* 7.

AYRE. See *Madrigal* 3 b.

AZIONE (It.). 'Action', 'drama'.

B

B. rve that in German this means B *flat*, B natural being called H (so 'B♭' in German is our B♭♭). For some explanation of the anomaly see *Notation and Nomenclature* 1. See also *Clarinet Family* 3 a.

BABBAGE, CHARLES (1792–1871). See *Street Music* 7.

BABBITT, MILTON BYRON. Born in Philadelphia in 1916. He is a graduate of New York and Princeton Universities and a pupil of Roger Sessions. A trained mathematician, his compositions are highly organized, some of them being pioneering attempts at 'total serialization' (see *Note-row*), extending serial principles into all aspects of a composition, including rhythm, dynamics, and the choice of instruments. His later works experiment imaginatively with electronic means. See *Harpsichord* 9.

BABCOCK, ALPHEUS. See *Pianoforte* 9.

BABELL, WILLIAM. Born about 1690 and died in London in 1723, aged about thirty-three. He was a celebrated player of harpsichord and violin, and his compositions for these and other instruments are still occasionally to be heard.

See reference under *Sonata* 10 c.

BABY GRAND. See *Pianoforte* 16.

BACCHANALIA. Riotous dancing or singing in honour of Bacchus, the god of wine.

BACCHETTA (It.). 'Stick', hence drumstick, baton. The plural is 'Bacchette'—e.g. *Bacchette di legno*, wooden drumsticks; *Bacchette di spugna*, sponge-headed drumsticks. See *Percussion Family* 2 a.

BACE DANCE. Basse Danse (q.v.).

BACH (The Family). The family of Johann Sebastian Bach was actively musical for seven generations, of which his was the fifth, and 'of some sixty Bachs known by name and profession all but seven were organists, cantors, or town musicians, many of them of eminence in their profession'.

It would be unsuitable, in a work of the scope of the present, to list these numerous Bachs. Thirty-eight of them receive separate treatment in the late Professor C. Sanford Terry's careful account in Grove's *Dictionary of Music* (see also the opening chapter of his *Bach, a Biography* and his *The Origin of the Family of Bach Musicians*). Of the great majority of these no music survives, and of many of the others only two or three compositions are available in print. The plan adopted

in the present article, then, has been to treat (*a*) Johann Sebastian and (*b*) those four of his sons whose position in the history of music is important and whose music (or a good deal of it) is available, adding at the end (*c*) a notice of one earlier member of the family, Johann Christoph (1642–1703).

(1) JOHANN SEBASTIAN. Born at Eisenach, in Thuringia, in 1685 and died at Leipzig in 1750, aged sixty-five (p. 49, pl. 6).

He lived in Protestant north Germany in the days when music there made an important part of the splendour of courts, of municipal dignity, of religious observance, and of the daily happiness of the people, and he occupied successively the posts of choir-boy, violinist in the orchestra of a prince, organist of town churches, chief musician in a court, and cantor of a municipal school with charge of the music in its associated churches.

This last position was at Leipzig, with the St. Thomas Church and School of which city (p. 49, pl. 6. 2, 3) his name is chiefly connected, since he remained there for almost the last thirty years of his life, at first composing much of the vast output of church music which, though apparently the product of a short period, gives him the distorted reputation of being primarily a 'religious composer'; then producing monuments of his art such as the *Goldberg Variations*, the *Musical Offering*, and the *Art of Fugue*; and finally collecting his works for future preservation. He returned from court life to the life of a church musician with some reluctance, and he experienced a good deal of that tribulation that often comes from contact between the clerical outlook and the artistic temperament.

He played many instruments, and as clavichordist, harpsichordist, and organist was supreme in his day.

He was twice married and the parent of twenty children, of whom several attained a high position in his own profession. Towards the end of his life his eyesight failed and his last months were spent in total darkness.

He was an indefatigable student of his art, eagerly learning from whatever he could procure of the production of other nations. His work closes a 'school', that of the later contrapuntal style, of which the fugue is the most definite expression, and (more narrowly considered) that of north German Protestantism, to which the chorale (q.v.) was an element of inspiration. He represents, too, the period when the suite (as distinct from the sonata) reached its highest point.

PLATE 7

THE ORGANIST BACH

By Batt

THOUGH for nearly a century after his death Bach's mighty genius as a composer was little recognized, yet during his lifetime his unique powers as an organist won for him a great reputation. 'Our Bach', said an obituary notice, 'was the greatest organ and clavier player that ever lived.'

As might be expected this reputation brought him many invitations to test new organs or advise on new ones. If the instrument pleased him he would extemporize at length on a theme, ending with an elaborate fugue, and thus show off the full resources of the instrument.

This picture, we may suppose, shows him eagerly scanning a newly issued organ composition by one of his many able contemporaries—for he was always eager to study the technique and idiom of other men.

After his death the trend of musical interest was in such a direction as temporarily left his works on one side. Their revival is due to enthusiasts of eighty to a hundred years later, amongst whom Mendelssohn in Germany and Samuel Wesley in England stand in honourable prominence; after another eighty to a hundred years the whole musical world rallied to the movement these men inaugurated, and the works of Bach have become as much a part of the world's accustomed musical enjoyment as they were of that of the citizens of Leipzig towards the middle of the eighteenth century.

His production may be divided roughly into three chronological periods: (1) that of organ composition; (2) that of composition for other instruments, including the orchestra of his day; and (3) that of church composition. A correspondence is observable between these departments of activity and the nature of the various official posts above mentioned.

The Brandenburg Concertos. Bach's set of

6 'Concerti Grossi' (see *Concerto*) for various combinations were commissioned by Christian Ludwig, Margrave of Brandenburg (1721). They are as follows:

(1) F MAJOR. 2 Horns, 3 Oboes, and Bassoon, Strings (including 'Violino Piccolo', i.e. small violin), Harpsichord.

(2)* F MAJOR. In 2 groups, plus Continuo— (a) *Concertino*: Trumpet, Recorder, Oboe, Violin; (b) *Ripieno*: Strings; (c) Harpsichord.

(3) G MAJOR. 3 groups of Strings (each Violin, Viola, Violoncello), Double-bass, and Harpsichord.

(4)* G MAJOR. In 2 groups, plus Continuo— (a) *Concertino*: Violin and 2 Recorders; (b) *Ripieno*: Strings; (c) Harpsichord.

(5)* D MAJOR. In 2 groups, plus Continuo— (a) *Concertino*: Harpsichord, Flute, Violin; (b) *Ripieno*: Strings (no 2nd Violins); (c) Harpsichord for the Continuo.

(6) B FLAT MAJOR. (No violins.) 2 Violas, 2 Viole da Gamba, Violoncello, Harpsichord.

It will be seen that the three marked * are true Concerti Grossi in the traditional style of contrasting groups (see *Concerto*).

A good many references to detailed points concerning Bach's life and work are necessarily dispersed through this volume. They can be found by means of the following list:

1. GENERAL REFERENCE TO HIS POSITION IN MUSICAL ART, etc. *Barocco; France* 5 (influence of Couperin); *Germany* 1, 3, 4, 8; *Handel; History* 5; *Italy* 8, 9; *Quality* 8.

2. QUESTIONS OF PITCH, SCALE, etc. *Keyboard* 3, 5; *Modes* 1, 10; *Modulation; Pitch* 3, 4; *Suite* 4; *Temperament* 5, 6, 7.

3. METHODS AND DETAILS OF COMPOSITION, etc. *Cadence; Canon; Composition* 4, 5, 10, 12, 15; *Figure; Figured Bass; Form* 4, 5, 6, 7, 9, 12 (the last discussing Fugue); *Harmony* 3, 6, 8, 10, 13, 17, 20, 23; *Melody* 4, 5; *Mordent; Ornaments* 1, 2, 3; *Programme Music* 5 c.

4. VOCAL AND CHORAL WORKS, etc. *Additional Accompaniments; Anglican Chant* 2; *Aria; Arioso; Beethoven; Cantata; Chorale; Chorale Prelude; Church Music* 1, 3; *Divisions; Franz; History* 5; *Hymns and Hymn Tunes* 3; *Magnificat;*

Mass 3, 4, 5; *Melisma; Motet; Old Hundredth; Oratorio* 3 5, 7; *Passion Music* 4, 5, 6; *Psalm; Quodlibet; Reay; Recitative; Rhythm* 6 (for *Chorale*); *Singing* 10; *Vocalize*.

5. INSTRUMENTAL FORMS AND STYLES. *Allemande; Anglaise; Art of Fugue; Badinage; Burla; Capriccio; Chaconne and Passacaglia; Chamber Music* 6, *Period* II; *Concerto* 2, 4, 5, 6 a; *Courante; Entrée; Fantasia; Folia; Forlana; Gavotte; Gigue; Ground; Improvisation* 1, 2; *Invention* (for Fugue see *Form* 12); *Loure; Minuet; Overture* 7; *Passepied; Pastoral; Pedalier* (for Trio Sonatas); *Polonaise; Prelude* 1; *Ricercare; Sarabande; Sonata* 3, 6, 10 b d e f; *Suite* 3, 4, 5; *Symphony* 1, 2; *Toccata*.

6. KEYBOARD MUSIC AND PLAYING, etc. *Best; Bird Music; Boëly; Buxtehude; Cathedral Music; Clavichord* 3, 5, 6; *Fingering* 2; *Goldberg; Grigny; Harpsichord Family* 5, 6, 7; *Klavier; Modes* 10; *Nicknamed Compositions* 1; *Organ* 2, 8, 13; *Pianoforte* 4, 18, 19, 20, 21, 22; *Reincken; Rhythm; Temperament* 5, 6; also p. 768, pl. **129**. 1.

7. INSTRUMENTS (OTHER THAN KEYBOARD). *Accompaniment* 7, 8; *Bagpipe Family; Bell* 4, 6; *Brass; Flute Family* 4, 6; *Horn Family* 3, 4; *Inventionshorn; Lute Family* 4; *Oboe Family* 2, 4 e f, 6; *Orchestra* 2, 4; *Percussion Family* 4 a e; *Recorder Family* 1, 2; *Trombone Family* 2 a, 3; *Trumpet Family* 2 b d e, 3; *Viol Family* 4 f, 6; *Violin Family* 2, 5.

8. VARIOUS. *Abel; Albinoni; Arrangement; Böhm, G.; Boughton; Bourgault-Ducoudray; Cathedral Music* 8; *Competitions* 1; *Concert* 13; *Concert Halls* 14; *Conducting* 2; *Congregational* 4; *Criticism* 6; *Expression* 5; *Festival* 2; *Gesamtausgabe; Gramophone* 6 (reference to 'Ave Maria'); *Franck, C.; Frederick the Great; Forkel; G String; Holland* 3; *Horn, K. F.; Improvisation* 1, 2, 5; *Khandoshkin; Krebs; Kuhnau; Luther; Misattributed; Nägeli; Nicknamed; Notation* 5; *Pachelbel; Patronage* 2, 7 (end), 8; *Poland; Presbyterian* 1; *Printing* 3; *Puritans* 3; *Schütz; Schweitzer; Street Music* 5; *Tempo; Terry, C. S.; Veni Creator; Wagner; Wait; Wesley, S.; Whittaker, W. G.; Zelter*.

---

(2) WILHELM FRIEDEMANN (commonly known as Friedemann). Born at Weimar in 1710 and died in Berlin in 1784, aged seventy-three. He was the second child and eldest son of Johann Sebastian, some of whose keyboard compositions were written for his instruction. He had the reputation of being a learned and able musician and held many important positions, but his life was marred by instability and he died poor and embittered. A novel has been written on his life by Brachvogel (1858; very many editions).

See *Form* 12; *Symphony* 8; *Sonata* 10 d (1760); *Polonaise; Mechanical* 5; *Misattributed*. Also p. 49, pl. **6**. 4.

(3) KARL (or CARL) PHILIPP EMANUEL (commonly known as Emanuel). Born at Wei-

mar in 1714 and died at Hamburg in 1788, aged seventy-four (p. 49, pl. **6**. 5).

He was the fifth child and third son of Johann Sebastian Bach. For a number of years he held a musical position at the court of Frederick the Great (q.v.). He was a notable keyboard performer and a prolific composer and enjoys a high importance in the history of music as one of the originators of the sonata-symphony form and style—as compared with the styles of the fugue and suite in which his father was pre-eminent. Mozart said of him, 'He is the parent and we are the children'. (Cf. *Haydn*.)

He wrote a highly important book, *The True Manner of Keyboard Performance*.

The last twenty-one years of his life were spent in Hamburg in direction of the music in the five leading churches. He seems to have died in some obscurity, since Haydn visited that city eight years later hoping to meet a pioneer to whom his own art owed the direction it had followed. His keyboard music is obtainable in modern editions.

See *Sonata* 6, 10 c, 10 d (1760); *Composition* 12, 14; *Oratorio* 3, 7; *Passion Music* 6; *Suite* 4; *Symphony* 4; *Folia*; *Alberti Bass*; *Clavichord* 5; *Fingering* 3; *Mordent*; *Pianoforte Playing* 2; *Rubato* 2; *Ornaments* 2; *Mechanical* 5; *Form* 7; *Misattributed*; *Nicknamed* 2 (Art of Fugue); *Fasch, C. F. C.*; *Art of Fugue*.

(4) JOHANN CHRISTOPH FRIEDRICH. Born at Leipzig in 1732 and died at Bückeburg in 1795, aged sixty-three.

He was Johann Sebastian's sixteenth child and ninth son. He held various musical posts and composed chamber music, keyboard sonatas and concertos, symphonies, etc. A fair amount of his music exists in modern editions.

See a reference under *Pianoforte* 18.

(5) JOHANN CHRISTIAN. Born at Leipzig in 1735 and died in London in 1782, aged forty-six (p. 49, pl. **6**. 6).

He was the Benjamin of the Bach household, the eighteenth child and eleventh son of Johann Sebastian. He is generally known as 'the English Bach' from the fact that (after a period as organist of Milan Cathedral and in other north Italian positions) he settled in London, where he spent nearly the last quarter-century of his life as an opera and concert director and as music master to the family of George III. His friend Gainsborough painted his portrait and he lies in the burial ground of St. Pancras.

He wrote operas, symphonies, and compositions for the harpsichord 'such as ladies can execute with little trouble' (Burney). Mozart as a child of eight played with him in London a sonata in which the two performers took alternate measures so perfectly that no interruption of the current of the music could be detected. Mozart always maintained a high opinion of Johann Christian Bach, and when he heard of his death, eighteen years after this meeting, wrote to his father, 'You have probably heard that the English Bach is dead. What a loss to the musical world!'

In Johann Christian Bach the family ability was maintained, but (perhaps owing to or perhaps accounting for Italian residence) there was manifested in him an easier attitude towards the art. Some of his harpsichord music has been republished and is quite worth playing.

See *Pianoforte* 5, 17; *Sonata* 10 d (1760); *Symphony* 8; *Concert* 8; *Misattributed*; *Abel*; *Opus*.

(6) JOHANN CHRISTOPH. Born at Arnstadt in 1642 and died at Eisenach in 1703, aged sixty. He belonged to the generation of J. S. Bach's father, who was his cousin; he was, then, J. S. Bach's cousin once removed. He was a bold and effective composer. J. S. Bach performed some of his music at Leipzig and C. P. E. Bach valued it. A good deal of his music is extant; it is mostly in manuscript, but a little keyboard and choral music is in print,

including the motet published by Novello under the title *I Wrestle and Pray*.

BACH, OTTO (1833–93). A Vienna-born conductor and composer (no relative of the J. S. Bach family). See *Tuba Group* 1.

BACH (French vocalist). See *Madelon, La.*

BACHE family.

(1) FRANCIS EDWARD (born at Birmingham in 1833 and died there in 1858, aged nearly twenty-five) was a fine pianist and prolific composer, a pupil of Sterndale Bennett and of several great continental teachers, whose opinion of him warrants the reflection that his early death was a loss to his country and to his art.

(2) His brother WALTER (born at Birmingham in 1842 and died in London in 1888, aged forty-five), was a pupil of Liszt and that master's doughtiest champion in Britain.

(3) Their sister CONSTANCE (born at Birmingham in 1846 and died at Montreux, Switzerland, in 1903, aged fifty-seven), led an active literary life, translating songs and libretti and promoting by lectures an appreciation of the Russian composers of the nineteenth century.

BACHGESELLSCHAFT. See *Gesamtausgabe.*

BACH TRUMPET. See *Trumpet Family* 2 e. Cf. *Brass* (near end).

BACKER-GRÖNDAHL. (Mother and son.)

(1) AGATHA URSULA. Born at Holmestrand in Norway in 1847 and died near Oslo (then Christiania) in 1907, aged fifty-nine. She was a pianist (a pupil of von Bülow), and a popular writer of songs and piano music. She became completely deaf in her later years. Her husband, Olavus Andreas Gröndahl, was a choral conductor in Christiania.

(2) FRITJOF, born at Oslo (then Christiania) in 1885 and died there in 1959, aged seventy-three. He was a pianist and composer for the piano who toured as recitalist. From 1920 to 1930 he lived in London.

BACK TURN = *Inverted Turn*. See Table 15.

BACON, ERNST. Born in Chicago in 1898. He was winner of the Pulitzer Prize in 1932 and of a Guggenheim Fellowship in 1939. He is an opera conductor, pianist, and teacher, a musical journalist, and the composer of symphonies, theatre music, songs, etc.

BACON AND GREENS. See *Saint Patrick's Day.*

'BAD' AND 'GOOD' IN MUSIC. See *Quality in Music.*

BADARZEWSKA, THEKLA. Born in Warsaw in 1834 and died there in 1861, aged twenty-seven. In this brief lifetime she accomplished, perhaps, more than any composer who ever lived, for she provided the piano of abso-

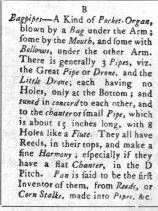

2. ENGLISH PIPES OF 14TH CENTURY (Finchingfield Church, Essex)
See *Bagpipe Family* 3

1. IRISH WAR PIPES, 1581
See *Bagpipe Family* 5

3. CHAUCER'S MILLER (14th-cent. drawing
See *Bagpipe Family* 3

4.
AN 18TH-CENTURY DESCRIPTION
(Tans'ur's *Dictionary of Music*, 1772. See *Dictionaries* 2)

B
Bagpipes—A Kind of *Pocket-Organ*, blown by a *Bag* under the Arm; some by the *Mouth*, and some with *Bellows*, under the other Arm. There is generally 3 *Pipes*, viz. the Great *Pipe* or *Drone*, and the *Little Drone*; each having no Holes, only at the Bottom; and *tuned* in *concord* to each other, and to the *chanter* or small *Pipe*, which is about 15 inches long, with 8 Holes like a *Flute*. They all have Reeds, in their tops, and make a fine *Harmony*; especially if they have a flat *Chanter*, in the D Pitch. *Pan* is said to be the first Inventor of them, from *Reeds*, or *Corn Stalks*, made into *Pipes*. &c.

5. FRENCH MUSETTE OF 18TH CENTURY (Ivory pipes and silken bag)
See *Bagpipe Family* 6

1514

6. 'THE BAGPIPE BOY' by Cibber (1630–1700)

7. GERMAN PIPER OF EARLY 16TH CENTURY (Dürer). See *Bagpipe Family* 7

See also the pictures on the other side of this plate

PLATE 9   THE BAGPIPE IN SOME NATIONAL VARIETIES

1. LOWLAND SCOTS PIPER
See *Bagpipe Family* 4

2. HIGHLAND PIPER IN THE
PENINSULAR WAR, 1810
See *Bagpipe Family* 4

3. GALWAY PIPES, 1840
See *Bagpipe Family* 5

6. POLISH PIPES, 1930

4. NORTHUMBRIAN PIPES, 18th century
See *Bagpipe Family* 3

5. CHRISTMAS PIPING IN ITALY
1830
See *Bagpipe Family* 7

7. MEMORIAL CAIRN TO THE MACRIMMONS OF SKYE
The inauguration in 1933. See *Bagpipe Family* 4

8. BRITTANY BINIOU, *c.* 1910
(Chanter and drone separate). See *Bagpipe Family* 6

See also the pictures on the other side of this plate

lutely every tasteless sentimental person in the so-called civilized world with a piece of music which that person, however unaccomplished in a dull technical sense, could play. It is probable that if the market stalls and back-street music shops of Britain were to be searched *The Maiden's Prayer* would be found to be still selling, and as for the world at large, Messrs. Allan of Melbourne reported in 1924, sixty years after the death of the composer, that their house alone was still disposing of 10,000 copies a year. (Cf. *Pianoforte* 22.)

BADCHONIM. See *Jewish Music* 7.

BADINAGE, BADINERIE (Fr.). 'Playfulness', 'trifling'. As examples of compositions so entitled may be mentioned Bach's *Badinerie* in his Overture for flute and strings in B minor and Godowsky's *Badinage*, which is a combination of Chopin's two studies in G flat.

BADINGS, HENK (HENDRIK HERMAN). Born in 1907 in Java. He began his life as an engineer, but having, as a boy, studied music with Pijper, continued to work at it, and in his thirtieth year abandoned his first profession to join the teaching staff of the Rotterdam school of music. He has composed orchestral, choral, and chamber works, as also music for pianoforte, for organ, and for violin. Though far from being a 'modernist', he has worked very much with electronic means.

BAGATELLE (Fr., Ger.). 'Trifle.' So, a short and unpretentious instrumental composition. The plural in Fr. is *Bagatelles* and in Ger. *Bagatellen*. Beethoven composed three sets of 'Bagatellen' for piano.

BAGENAL, HOPE. See *Concert Halls* 14.

BAGPIPE FAMILY

(For illustrations see opposite, pls. 8 and 9.)

1. Introductory. The bagpipe is one of the most ancient instruments that remain in use by mankind. It is said that a number of references to musical instruments in the Old Testament (however rendered by the translators) concern one or other form of bagpipe, and there are in existence Hittite carvings that definitely prove its use a thousand years before Christ. It was, as Procopius tells us, used in the Roman army, and it has been suggested, on the strength of a bronze figure found at Richborough (the Roman Rutupiae), that it reached Britain by that agency.

The literatures of all European countries testify to the bagpipe's universality from the Middle Ages onward. It is mentioned by Dante in the thirteenth century; by Chaucer, Froissart, and Boccaccio in the fourteenth; by Rabelais, Ronsard, Cervantes, Spenser, and Shakespeare in the sixteenth; by Drayton, Milton, Butler, and Pepys in the seventeenth; by Beaumarchais and a host of his countrymen in the eighteenth; and in the nineteenth by George Sand, who based her delightful novel *Les Maîtres sonneurs* on its contemporary practice in a rural part of France, and by Victor Hugo, who, in *Les Travailleurs de la mer*, wishing to display his knowledge of the English language, speaks of it as the 'bug-pipe'.

This instrument has had little attention from those whom we call 'the great composers', but it has played a large part in the social life of court and camp and cottage—in all of which its practitioners are, in some measure, still active. And in early times it found in church a sphere of usefulness it has now lost.

2. General Description. The essentials of the bagpipe are only two:

(a) It is a reed-pipe wind instrument.

(b) Interposed between the medium supplying the wind and the reed pipe is a bag-reservoir serving the same purpose as the wind chest of an organ, i.e. to provide a continuous supply of wind to the pipe, instead of leaving it dependent upon the necessarily intermittent supply of the original source of the wind.

Those two characteristics are invariable, the most important variable characteristics (from the point of view of construction) being as follows:

(c) The original source of the wind supply of the bag may either be the mouth of the player applied to a valved tube (a blow-pipe), or it may be a small bellows held under the arm of the player and expanded and contracted by the motion of the arm.

(d) The reed pipe (or *Chanter*) from which, by means of holes, and sometimes keys, the tune is obtained, may or may not be reinforced by one or more other reed pipes, confined each to a single note (and called *Drones*): these are tuned to the tonic of the key of the instrument or to the tonic and dominant (i.e. the doh and soh—cf. 'Pedal', under *Form* 12 d; *Harmony* 14, 24 p).

(e) The reed may be either single, like that of the clarinet, or double, like that of the oboe (see *Reed*); in practice the chanter reeds are usually (perhaps always) double, whilst the drone reeds vary in different types of the instrument.

It should be noted that the chanter is exposed to a limitation as compared with the other wood-wind instruments; these obtain their second octave by overblowing, which in the case of the bagpipe, as the mouth is not in direct contact with the reed-pipe, is not possible. (See section 5 for an exception.) The compass of the various bagpipes is, then, in most cases, a short one.

In some types of pipe the chanter is a cylindrical tube, like that of the clarinet, in others a conical one, like those of the oboe and flute.

3. **The Bagpipe in England** (p. 64, pl. **8.** 2, 3). The bagpipe seems to have been in favour in England before it reached Scotland. It figures in many English ecclesiastical carvings, especially of the fourteenth and fifteenth centuries (as for instance, at Boston, Great Yarmouth, York, Ripon, Hull, Beverley, Cirencester, and Exeter, and in Henry VII's Chapel at Westminster), and also in many illuminated manuscripts. There is definite record of bagpipers attached to the courts of many of the English monarchs for the three centuries between the accession of Edward II (1307) and the death of Elizabeth I (1603), and the collection of instruments left by Henry VIII included five bagpipes. The abundant references to the instrument in English literature from Chaucer onwards have already been alluded to.

The earliest bagpipe (called *Chorus*) had apparently no drones. This is so with the Roman example represented at Richborough and it is so with the English ones that followed. Drones seem to have been added during the thirteenth and fourteenth centuries. (They are still lacking in some parts of Europe today.)

We find special counties of England associated with the bagpipes, as though they possessed either an unusual reputation for bagpipe playing or, perhaps, cultivated a local type of the instrument. Thus Shakespeare (1 *Henry IV*, I. ii) alludes to 'the drone of a Lincolnshire bagpipe', and other writers also allude to the Lincolnshire instrument. Worcestershire, Nottinghamshire, and Lancashire are also sometimes specifically mentioned, as (to take a late instance) when Thoresby, in 1702, being in Preston at the time of the guild pageantry, 'got little rest, the music and Lancashire bagpipes having continued the whole night'; the newspapers of 1732 record 'a very merry wedding at Preston in Lancashire' with 'seven bagpipers'.

The English region that today retains a special association with the bagpipe is **Northumbria**. It may be said that the instrument, once so common everywhere in England, and (especially) so universal a feature of rural life, is extinct in the south of England, the midlands and, indeed, everywhere except the extreme northern counties, and it will be very interesting if some day a diligent and alert historian can discover to us the reason for this. As early as 1633 we find bagpipers in a London masque described as 'Northern Musick', and the Londoner, Pepys, who loved all other instruments and played most of them, alludes to a certain bagpipe performance in London as quite exotic; it was remarkably able, for what it was,

he says, but adds 'At the best it is mighty barbarous music'. In the early eighteenth century, as we have seen, the instrument was still cultivated in Lancashire, and there is perhaps point in the fact that later in the century (1776–9) Captain Cook, a Yorkshireman, took a bagpiper with him on his last voyage, but soon after this even Lancashire and Yorkshire dropped their piping and only the counties still further north maintained it. Lord Chief Justice North (see *North, Francis*) in 1676, entertained by the town of Newcastle, was taken down the river to Tynemouth Castle in the town barge. 'The equipment of the vessel was very stately; for, a-head, there sat a four or five drone bagpipe, *the north country organ*, and a trumpeter astern, and so we rowed merrily along.' A century later the 'north country organ' could be found nowhere out of the northernmost part of the country, and if today a bagpipe is heard elsewhere in England, it is in the hands of some kilted Scot seeking to entice reward from the pockets of his brethren in exile, or else at the head of some Scottish regiment of the British Army.

The Northumbrian pipe (p. 65, pl. **9.** 4) is a very interesting instrument. Its chanter has a straight bore, not a conical one. Unlike the Highland pipe to be described under 4, it is designed primarily for indoor entertainment, its tone being gentle and sweet—something between that of an oboe and that of a clarinet. Unlike the Highland instrument, again, it is bellows-filled, not mouth-filled. Its normal key is G major, and it has usually four drones tuned to G and D. All its pipes are end-stopped; thus when the performer closes all the finger-holes at once no sound can emerge. This complete stopping is often carried out by an adroit performer between every two notes of a passage and a crisp staccato thus becomes a characteristic feature of the effect.

The development of this instrument has not yet ceased, and some examples today have seventeen or eighteen keys and a chromatic range from G at the top of the bass staff to B above the treble staff, with *bead holes* to the drones enabling these to be tuned, and so making possible the playing in four or five different keys. Brass reeds, instead of cane ones, are now occasionally used. All these refinements probably now make the Northumbrian bagpipe the most sensitive in the world.

The instrument just described is the *Small Pipes*. Other forms of the instrument were formerly in use—as, for instance, the *Half-long*, or *Gathering Pipes* (a more martial instrument), attempts to revive which for outdoor use have latterly been made.

The Northumbrian pipe tunes have a light and lilting character, in keeping with the nature of the instrument, and the Northumbrian folk music in general shows the influence of the pipe. A number of collections of pipe tunes were published during the eighteenth and nineteenth centuries. An interesting detail of the present-day use of the instrument is the keeping up by the Duke of Northumberland, at his castle of Alnwick, of the tradition by which great houses maintained a family piper. There are humbler families that for generations have always enjoyed domestic performances from one of their own members; the Clough family, for instance, has been actively piping for many generations.

4. The Bagpipe in Scotland (p. 65, pl. 9. 1, 2, 7). The Northumbrian pipe just described has a relative over the border in the **Lowland Scottish Pipe** which, like it, is bellows-filled, but in other respects differs, much resembling the pipe now to be described.

The **Highland Pipe**, or **Great Pipe**, is the one known almost the world over; certainly when an English-speaking person (outside Northumbria) mentions the bagpipe this is the one he means, and as a rule he knows no other. As an instrument it possesses strongly characteristic features, as does its music also. It exists in three sizes—'great', 'half-size', and 'small'. The chanters of the two larger sizes are of conical bore, whilst that of the small size is of straight bore. It is mouth-filled. Its key (so far as this word can be used) is that of A major with a natural G (a bit sharp) and with the C and the F something between the sharp and the natural—a unique scale (see *Scales* 11), but one with some similarities to certain scales of the Near East, which has suggested to one or two authorities an importation at the time of the Crusades. (However, the late date of the instrument's coming into use in Scotland does not seem to support this.) The range is only one octave plus a note (G–A), i.e. only nine notes are possible.

There were until the eighteenth century two drones there are now three, generally tuned to two A's and a D, but sometimes to two D's and an A, or two high A's and a low A.

The drones are thrown over the left shoulder, the bag held under the arm, the blow pipe placed to the lips, and the chanter held in the fingers. The piper walks to and fro a good deal while playing. The tone of both chanter and drones is penetrating and suited to the open air. As they are open at both ends (not closed like those of the Northumbrian pipe) legato playing is the only kind possible and a longer or shorter wail on beginning to play and on ending is inevitable.

The music is at first sometimes baffling to those not accustomed to it, not only from the unusual intervals of the scale and the forceful tone, but also from the lavish graces introduced, which, until they are recognized as decorations, disguise the tune; the oldest tunes proceed almost entirely by leap, but the gaps are filled in by strings of rapid notes known as *warblers*. One function of the graces is to give an effect of articulation to the otherwise continuous flow of tone.

The technique of this instrument is certainly more difficult to acquire in perfection than that of any other instrument of so small a range of notes. The famous MacCrimmons of Skye, who during almost three centuries (1500–1795) were hereditary pipers to the MacLeods, and maintained what Dr. Johnson, in his *Tour of the Hebrides*, calls 'a college of pipers', kept their pupils under tuition for seven years. Caves are shown which served as practice rooms for the pupils, and there they would spend the first six months acquiring skill in the fingering of a mere motif of three or four notes, afterwards progressing by similar minute stages. There were other schools of piping besides those of the MacCrimmons. The Mac-Arthurs had one in the Island of Mull. Falkirk was a great centre of bagpipe culture.

The repertory of the instrument falls into three distinct classes: the *Ceòl beag* ('little music'), comprising marches, strathspeys, and reels; the *Ceòl meadhonach* (or 'middle music'), comprising old Highland folk songs, lullabies, laments, croons, and slow marches (some of which things may have derived originally from the *clàrsach* (q.v.), or Gaelic harp); and the *Ceòl mór* ('big music'), comprising salutes, gatherings, and laments, as also tunes composed in memory of some historical happening. This last class of music is also called *Piobaireachd* (or, in the anglicized form of the word dating from the early eighteenth century and popularized by Sir Walter Scott, *Pibroch*, q.v.); the form of this music is that of an air with variations of a peculiar type.

A curious ancient notation exists for the bagpipe—the Canntaireachd, in which syllables stand for recognized musical motifs (i.e. groups of notes). At present the staff notation is employed—without key-signature, the notes being of course, invariable.

As stated above (3), the bagpipe was popular in England some centuries earlier than in Scotland. It begins to be mentioned and pictured in the latter country only from the early fifteenth century. James I of Scotland (lived 1394–1437) was a performer of reputation, and one may surmise that his example had something to do with the vogue the instrument quickly obtained. There are carvings showing bagpipes at Melrose Abbey and Roslin Chapel: the latter (1446) shows a performer playing from book—presumably using the ancient notation just mentioned. Apparently some superiority in English playing was even after this period admitted, for in 1489 and 1491 the accounts of the Lord High Treasurer show payments to 'Inglis' players at the court.

Since the epoch in question the popularity of the bagpipe in Scotland has never diminished, and it has now long been looked upon as a national instrument and become an object of patriotic pride.

When in 1651 Charles II, a fugitive from England, was crowned at Scone, he was accompanied by a band of eighty bagpipes (which, we may hope, argues the adoption of a reliable conventional pitch); at the Battle of Worcester, in 1651, a piper he had brought with him was taken prisoner.

Many towns in Scotland have possessed their municipal pipers. The family of Hastie supplied such to the town of Jedburgh for 300 years, dying out at the beginning of the nineteenth century (this reminds one of the Bach family who so long supplied the musicians to certain places in north Germany); some towns possessed a field allotted to the sustenance of the players—a piper's croft. Perth had a town bagpiper until 1800.

The use of the Highland pipes in war has for centuries been very important. The 21st Royal Scots Fusiliers is known to have had them in 1624: in 1689 two drums and a piper were allotted to every infantry regiment. The pipes played an important part in heartening the Highland troops at the Battle of Waterloo. In an Edinburgh newspaper in 1702 is an advertisement for a piper willing to take service on a British man-of-war. In 1795 H.M.S. *Colossus*, with part of a Highland regiment on board, was engaged by the French and the piper was sent to the main topsail stays and told to play there until the battle ended, which he did, continuing his performance for three hours. More pipers were certainly employed in the Great War of 1914–18 than in any preceding war. Not only Scottish but Canadian, Australian, and New Zealand regiments brought their pipe bands, and, according to an old traditional custom, the keeping in memory of many heroic experiences was entrusted to the pipers of the future by those of the present—in such compositions as *The Highland Brigade at Mons* and *The Battle of the Somme*.

It was the complaint of the Duke of Atholl in the 1920s that the greatly increased cultivation of the pipes in bands, civil and military, had tended to reduce the level of individual artistic achievement.

In 1935 it was reported that the then Prince of Wales (later King Edward VIII and then Duke of Windsor) had been taking lessons on the instrument, and shortly afterwards a bagpipe march by him was printed and also issued as a gramophone record.

Throughout the nineteenth century the most famous makers of Highland bagpipes were Glens of Edinburgh. But it was stated in 1931 that the greater number of regimental pipes were at that date imported from England.

Competitions in pipe playing form an important feature in Highland social and musical life. It appears that the first of these was held at Falkirk in 1781.

See also information given under *Scotland* 3.

5. **The Bagpipe in Ireland** (p. 64, pl. 8. 1). Ireland has at different periods possessed two forms of bagpipe, roughly corresponding to the two forms extant in Scotland today—one (the war pipes) mouth-filled and loud, and the other bellows-filled and gentler.

The mouth-filled form of the instrument is the older one. It was the war pipes that accompanied the Irish contingent to Crécy in 1346. Galilei, the musician (father of the great astronomer), in his *Dialogue* published at Florence in 1581, says: 'The bagpipe is much used by the Irish. To its sound this unconquered, fierce, and warlike people march their armies and encourage one another to feats of valour. With it, also, they accompany their dead to the grave, making such mournful sounds as almost to force the bystanders to weep.'

This, presumably, is the pipe that was heard at the Battle of the Boyne, in 1690, when the bagpipes in the hands of Irish and Scottish players encouraged both the opposing forces, and that was heard also at Fontenoy in 1745. The somewhat surprising fact is recorded that in 1778 Lord Rawdon as Adjutant-General of the British forces in America was able to raise in Philadelphia a corps of 'Volunteers of Ireland' with a band of Irish war pipes.

This type of Irish bagpipe fell almost or entirely out of use but was revived in the early twentieth century. Meantime, apparently, the gentler bellows-blown instrument was making headway for domestic use. It received improvement at the beginning of the eighteenth century and gradually became very popular, until in the famine time of the mid-nineteenth century the westward tide of emigration carried away many of its exponents. There have been attempts to revive interest in it.

As now played, the instrument has a chanter with a soft, sweet reed, and three drones sounding the note C in three octaves. These drones are combined in one stock and the bore of the longest one traverses the length of the tube more than once, like that of a bassoon. A special feature lies in certain metal keys that, operated by pressure of the wrist, produce three-note chords (of the tonic and dominant) from these drones, so supplying a crude but not ineffective chordal bass to the melody of the chanter; these chords are not carried on continuously but interjected here and there in suitable places. The scale of the chanter is a nearly complete chromatic one from D below the treble stave to D three spaces above it, i.e. two octaves, the second octave being obtained by giving the bag a sharp squeeze and pumping the bellows a little faster, which results in overblowing (cf. section 2, near end).

The player sits to play, with the bag under his left arm and the bellows under his right and tied to it and to his body: the drones rest on the leg and the end of the chanter on a pad of leather on the knee, so facilitating the process known as *tipping*, connected with the clear articulation of the notes, a process that resembles in effect that mentioned in describing the Northumbrian instrument (section 3).

6. **The Bagpipe in France.** Like Scotland and Ireland, France has possessed the two forms of the instrument, the mouth-filled and the bellows-filled. The mouth-filled instrument is known as the **Cornemuse.** The nor-

1. AN ELIZABETHAN BALLAD SELLER
Detail from a drawing by Inigo Jones
See *Ballad* 1

2. AN 18TH-CENTURY BALLAD SELLER

Ein schön news

Lied, Von der Schlacht
voz Pauia geschehen: Gedicht vnd
erstlich gesungen/durch hansen von
Würtzburg/In eim newen
Thon zusingen.

3. GERMAN BALLAD OF 16TH CENTURY. The Battle of Pavia, 'to be sung to a new tune'

4. BALLAD SELLING AT A FRENCH FAIR, 1772. Note the sheet of pictures, the fiddle bow, the pocket stuffed with ballads, the singing of vendor and audience. The present writer saw Ballad selling like this in France in the early 20th century

See also the other side of this plate

PLATE 11 THE POPULAR BALLAD, II

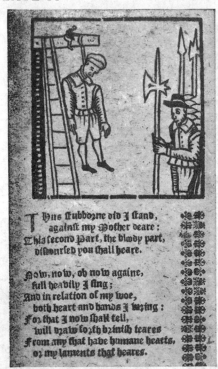

3. BALLADS IN AN 18TH-CENTURY LONDON WORKROOM.
Hogarth's 'Idle and Industrious Apprentices': the one with *Moll Flanders*
behind him, the other with *Valiant Apprentice* and *Turn again Whittington*

1, 2. LONDON
BALLADS of
the 17th and
18th centuries
—the first of
Murder and its
punishment and
the second of
War (Cumber-
land's campaign
in Scotland,
1745–6)

4. LONDON BALLAD-SELLING in the late 18th century
(note the woman's basket of ballads)

Two favorite SONGS,

made on the Evacuation of the Town of BOSTON,

by the *British Troops*, on the 17th of March, 1776.

IN seventeen hundred and seventy six,
  On March the eleventh, the time was prefix'd,
Our forces march'd on upon Dorchester-neck,
Made fortifications against an attack.
  The morning next following, as Howe did espy,
The banks we cast up, were so copious and high,
Said he in three months, all my men with their might,
Cou'd not make two such Forts as they've made in a night.
  Now we hear that their Admiral was very wroth,
And drawing his sword, he bids Howe to go forth,
And drive off the YANKEES from Dorchester hill ;
Or he'd leave the harbour and him to their will.
  Howe rallies his forces upon the next day,

IT was'nt our will that Bunker Hill
  From us should e'er be taken ;
We thought 'twould never be retook,
  But u.. find we are Mistaken.

The soldiers bid the hill farewell,
  Two images left senteit,
This they had done all out of fun
  To the American Yankees.

A flag of truce was sent thereon,
  To see if the hill was clear,
No living soul was found thereon,
  But these images stood there.

5. THE BALLAD IN NEW ENGLAND, 1776

See also the other side of this plate

mal cornemuse of old times had two drones tuned an octave apart. The players of Poitou were renowned.

A form of this instrument still in regular use in Brittany today is called the *Biniou*. Its player is often supported by a fellow musician who marches or sits beside him playing the melody an octave lower on a bagless (and so droneless) instrument, the *Bombarde* (p. 65, pl. **9. 8**; cf. *Bombard*).

The bellows-filled type, the **Musette**, originally a folk instrument, came into high popularity in court circles during and after the reign of Louis XIV (1645–1715), when there was a rage for rusticity and the mock-pastoral (cf. the popularity of the hurdy-gurdy, also a rustic drone-bass instrument). Ladies practised the musette, the Pompadour herself included. Many composers of standing attached themselves to the cult, such as Jacques Hoteterre (d. 1761), Jacques Aubert (*c.* 1683–1753), Henri Baton (born *c.* 1710), Michel Corrette, and the brothers Chédeville (q.v.). Lully introduced the instrument into operas, and the Paris Opéra had a player in its orchestra as late as 1758. An avocat and legal author of high standing, Charles Emmanuel Borjon (1633–91), a fine performer on the instrument, contributed to its culture by providing a *Traité de la musette* (1672); Jacques Hoteterre provided another instruction book (1737).

The musette (of which many examples are today to be seen in museums, with their bags often elaborately decorated with fine needlework and ribbons) had sometimes what may be called Siamese-Twin-Chanters, i.e. two chanters fixed side by side (one for the higher notes and the other for the lower). There were usually four or five drones, all enclosed in one cylinder; their reeds, like those of the chanter, were double. The scale was a more or less chromatic one.

There is a variety of musette in use in Auvergne today, the cabrette (compare the early French name, *chevrette*).

7. The Bagpipe in other Countries (p. 64, pl. **8.** and p. 65, pl. **9.**). Some of the **Italian** peasantry possess the bagpipe. It is (or was not long since) common in Sicily and it lingers in the mountainous region of the Abruzzi (to the north-east of Rome), where it is often accompanied by one or more separate droneless pipes (cf. the Brittany usage above). The type of music played by these *pifferari* (i.e. players on the *piffero*) and bagpipers is preserved in Handel's 'Pastoral Symphony' in his *Messiah*, he having, it is supposed, heard them in 1709 in Rome; for nearly two centuries after that they were to be heard in the streets there every Christmas time. They were also right into the early twentieth century to be found wandering about England and Scotland, wearing sheepskins and high conical hats. Spohr in his autobiography gives a tune which he heard played all over Rome at Christmas 1816 by these Neapolitan pipers, and in general

style it resembles Handel's. From his description there were three drones.

The *Zampogna* of Calabria much resembles the instrument just described, being mouth-filled and consisting of a chanter and a bag with four drones; but as two of its drones possess some finger-holes (cf. 5) it would appear that it is capable of varying to some extent the notes which accompany the melody.

In **Spain** there is the bagpipe of Galicia (*Gaita gallega*), a bellows-filled instrument with chanter and two drones; **Portugal** also has its form of the instrument (*Gaita de fole*).

Germany formerly made very much use of the bagpipe—the *Dudelsack* alluded to in the rhymes of Bach's Peasant Cantata. 'Duda' (plural 'Dudy') is Polish for bagpipe and it seems likely that the instrument alluded to was not the old German one but the smaller Polish type (however, see reference to 'Dudelsack' under 9). Bach's contemporary, Telemann, speaks of the popularity of the 'Polish' instrument in Prussia: 'I have heard as many as thirty-six bagpipes and eight violins together; it is unbelievable what extraordinary musical fancies the bagpipe and violin players introduced when they were playing whilst the dancers rested: any composer who might care to note them down would in a week have enough ideas to keep him supplied for the rest of his life. . . . All this proved later of service to me in many serious compositions.' Dittersdorf at a later date (in the 1760s) also associates Poland with the bagpipes: in the countryside near Vienna he seems to have found bagpipes in every village; they were in two sizes an octave apart, and the larger was called the 'Polnischer Bock' ('Polish goat'). Quartets of bagpipes of different sizes, playing in parts, were at one time (occasionally at any rate) heard in Germany.

Leopold Mozart (the greater Mozart's father) wrote a *Peasant's Wedding* for Strings, 2 Oboes, Bassoon, 2 Horns, Hurdy-Gurdy, and Bagpipe.

Norway has a form of the bagpipe, the *Penbrock*. **Russia** and **Finland** have the instrument also.

In the **Balkan Countries**, and in **Greece** also, the bagpipe is in use. The Scottish troops engaged in Macedonia during the Great War reported (not always with enthusiasm) having heard Serbian, Bulgarian, and Greek regimental pipers—the last-named playing a droneless instrument.

In **Persia** and **China** the bagpipe is native, as in **India**, where there are records of its use from very early times. In the British army in India there were pipe bands in Sikh, Gurkha, Pathan, and Dogra regiments, but these used the Scottish Highland instruments and had Scottish instructors—which seems anomalous.

8. Bagpipe Influence in Composition. Although, with slight exceptions, only at one period and in one country (France during the late seventeenth and early eighteenth centuries;

see 6) have serious composers set themselves to the task of adding to the bagpipe's repertory, they have been willing to borrow effects from the peasant instrument (and especially its drone effect) for use in music written for other instruments. Thus we find Byrd in *Mr. Bird's Battel* providing a short movement called 'The Bagpipe and Drum'. Couperin, in his harpsichord music, has several pieces that imitate the bagpipe and are indicated by him as doing so. The frequent *Musettes* and *Loures* in the domestic keyboard music of Bach and his contemporaries are all frank imitations of the bagpipe. Handel's 'Pastoral Symphony' in *Messiah* has already been mentioned; Beethoven's 'Pastoral' Symphony (in the other sense of 'Symphony') also has perhaps just a touch of the bagpipe—in the Shepherd's Song at the beginning of the Finale. Chopin's posthumous Mazurka in F (op. 68, no. 3), in its 'poco più vivo' section, also recalls the bagpipe, as, in a less marked manner, do passages in the Mazurkas op. 7, no. 1 and op. 56, no. 2. Berlioz has a bagpipe imitation in the third movement of his *Harold in Italy*. But the main and most definite contribution of the bagpipe to sophisticated music is in the Musette movement, named after it, which is associated with so many of the eighteenth-century gavottes (see *Gavotte*), appearing as a middle section to these (gavotte, musette, gavotte repeated). The possible influence of the bagpipe in the harmonic device of 'Pedal' is alluded to under *Harmony* 24 p.

9. Nomenclature.

FRENCH. *Cornemuse* (this is mouth-filled); *Musette* (this is bellows-filled); *Cabrette* (Auvergne—bellows-filled); *Biniou* (Brittany—mouth-filled and divided between two players); *Loure* (Normandy).

ITALIAN. *Cornamusa, Zampogna, Piva, Piffero.*

SPANISH. *Zampoña.*

GERMAN. *Sackpfeife* (literally 'bag-pipe'); *Dudelsack* (familiar name—'dudeln' is to tootle; however, the derivation may, as suggested under 7, be from the Polish 'Dudy').

EARLY ENGLISH. *Chorus* (but this name was also sometimes applied to the crwth, q.v.).

LATIN *Tibia utricularis* ('skin-flute'; 'utricularius' is a bagpiper).

GREEK. *Askaulos* (ancient); *Zampouna* (modern).

In most of these languages there were many other names at different periods and for different varieties. Note that the use of the word 'pibroch' as a name for the instrument is a complete error; the real meaning of this word is given in section 4 of the above article. The English language uses indifferently the singular or plural, in speaking of the instrument—'bagpipe' or 'bagpipes'.

BAGUETTE (Fr.). Drumstick (also sometimes used for 'baton', and as the name for the stick of a fiddle bow). *Baguettes de bois*, wooden drumsticks; *Baguettes d'éponge*, sponge-headed drumsticks. See *Percussion Family* 2 a.

BAHR, HERMANN (1863–1934). See *Expressionism.*

BAÏF, JEAN ANTOINE DE (1532–89). See *Concert* 2.

BAILE, BAYLE (Sp.). A ballet or dance; the word is really a generic name for Spanish dances of Moorish origin. The seventeenth-century bailes, which formed a part of the plays of such dramatists as Calderón, had singing and even speech (cf. English *Jig*). One type of baile used to be danced between the acts of operas.

BAILEY, LILIAN. See *Henschel.*

BAILLOT, PIERRE (in full, Pierre Marie François de Sales) (p. 1096, pl. 181. 6). Born near Paris in 1771 and died there in 1842, aged nearly seventy-one. His life was varied, comprising a period of violin study in Italy, a private secretaryship to a wealthy man, a position in the civil service and later in the private band of Bonaparte, some army experience, a professorship at the Paris Conservatory, leadership of the orchestra at the Paris Opéra, leadership of an excellent string quartet, wide travelling as a violin virtuoso, and some critical writing. He had a special reputation as a chamber music player. Mendelssohn in a letter (1838) lauds him for his splendid tone.

He composed nine concertos and many other things for his instrument, but is now chiefly remembered by his much translated and many times republished *Violin School.*

BAINES, WILLIAM. Born at Horbury, Yorkshire, in 1899 and died at York in 1922, aged twenty-three. He wrote a certain amount of music, especially for the piano, but died before he had fully developed or had won the suffrages of more than an enthusiastic few.

BAINTON, EDGAR LESLIE. Born in London in 1880 and died in Sydney in 1956, aged seventy-six. He was trained at the Royal College of Music. He worked as pianist and teacher in Newcastle-on-Tyne until he went to Australia as Director of the State Conservatorium of Music at Sydney (1933–47). His compositions, in many forms, have had wide performance, especially at the musical festivals of his native country.

BAIRD.

(1) JOHN L. (1886–1948). Inventor. See *Broadcasting* 6.

(2) TADEUSZ (b. 1928). See *Poland* (end).

BAIRSTOW, EDWARD CUTHBERT. Born at Huddersfield in 1874 and died at

York in 1946, aged seventy-one. After serving his articles to Sir Frederick Bridge (q.v.) at Westminster Abbey he occupied various organ positions, at length becoming organist of York Minster (1913). He was Professor of Music at Durham University from 1929, and was knighted in 1932. He published songs, part-songs, organ music, and church choral music.

See reference under *Anglican Chant* 6.

BAISSER (Fr.). 'To lower' (e.g. a string of the violin, etc.).

BAKFARK, VALENTINE. See *Hungary.*

BAKST, LEON (1866–1924). See *Ballet* 5.

BALAKIREF (Balakirev, Balakirew, etc.), MILY (p. 897, pl. **154.** 4). Born at Nijni-Novgorod in 1837 and died in St. Petersburg in 1910, aged seventy-three. Like Glinka and Dargomijsky he was of 'good birth', and like them he had the advantage of an early intimacy with peasant music—with, in his case, the further one of being able to make his personal experiments in orchestration. This last advantage he enjoyed through his friend Oulibichef (1795–1858), country gentleman and authority on Mozart, and owner of a private orchestra; through this friend, too, he became intimate with the standard classics of music. From an acquaintance with Glinka came the inspiration to nationalism. Glinka saw in him the Elisha to his Elijah; his style, however, may sometimes be called rather 'Oriental' or 'Caucasian' than 'Russian', and a good deal of his piano music (he was a fine pianist) shows the influence of Liszt.

He started in St. Petersburg an institution which was to do much to spread the doctrine of nationalism—the Free School of Music. He collected and edited native folk tunes. He was the founder of the group called 'The Five' (see *Russia* 5). His symphonic poem *Thamar* (dedicated to Liszt) and his oriental piano fantasy *Islamey* (played by Liszt) did much to establish his fame. He wrote two symphonies. He also wrote an overture and incidental music for Shakespeare's *King Lear*—but no opera.

Half-way through his life some spiritual change took place, which led to long periods of inactivity.

See references under *Russia* 5; *Spain* 10; *Rhythm* 10; *Composition* 13; *Greek Church* 5; *Jota*; *Folk Song* 5; *Akimenko*; *Mussorgsky.*

BALALAIKA (p. 449, pl. **77.** 5). The balalaika may be called the Russian guitar (see *Guitar*). Its body is usually triangular in shape. The fingerboard has frets (q.v.). The normal number of strings is three. The instrument exists in various sizes, the largest resting on the ground like the bowed double-bass.

Balalaika orchestras are to be heard not only in Russia but sometimes also in Britain, the United States, and other countries. Their development is largely due to Andreyev at the end of the nineteenth century. He had between forty and fifty players and toured extensively. A Russian composer, Privalof, wrote an opera, *Dreams on the Volga*, which was entirely accompanied by such an orchestra, and it had considerable success in Russia.

Associated with the balalaika, in its bands, is the *Domra*, a somewhat similar instrument.

It would appear that plucked string instruments have always made a special appeal to the Russian mind and continue to do so.

BALANCHINE, GEORGE. See *Ballet* 5.

BALDWIN. See *Electric Musical Instruments* 4.

BALFE, MICHAEL WILLIAM (p. 705, pl. **118.** 2). Born at Dublin in 1808 and died on his estate in Hertfordshire in 1870, aged sixty-two. His working life was spent in the theatre. As a youth he played the violin in the orchestra at Drury Lane; as a young man he sang in opera, being chosen by Rossini as his Figaro for the Paris performances of *The Barber of Seville*. In his thirties he was manager of the Lyceum Theatre in London, opening with an opera of his own, with his wife as leading lady. Then he lived for a time in Paris and Berlin, producing his operas in those cities, and visited St. Petersburg with the same object. At fifty-six, having won a comfortable competency, he retired to the English countryside and gave himself up to the pleasures of sowing and reaping and of rearing sheep and oxen.

His instinct for easy-flowing melody, unembarrassed by any subtleties of harmony or orchestration, is seen in his opera, *The Bohemian Girl*, which survived for many years on the smaller English stages, and was even taken off the shelf for a few performances at Covent Garden in 1951.

See *Ireland* 7; *Opera* 13 d e, 21 g h, 24 d (1843), 25; *Roman Catholic Church Music in Britain*; *Cornet* 2; *Concert* 7.

BALFOUR, Earl (1848–1930). See *Reed Organ* 5.

BALLABILE (It.). 'In a dance style.'

BALLAD

1. Definition.
2. The Ballad Metre.
3. The Nine Centuries of Ballad Making.

4. Theory of Communal Composition.
5. Literary Value of the Poems.

6. The so-called 'Drawing-Room Ballad'.

(For illustrations see pp. 68, 69, pls. **10** and **11**.)

1. Definition. Properly a ballad is, evidently, something danced (late Latin, *ballare*, to dance; cf. the word 'ballet', etc.), and dancing and singing at one time went much together. But the word soon lost that sense and in the sixteenth century we find a form of it used as a description for Bible poetry—*Salomon's Balettes called Cantica Canticorum* (title of the 'Song of Solomon' in Miles Coverdale's English Bible, 1535).

Apparently in the sixteenth century the word could be used for anything singable, if simple-minded and for solo voice. Shakespeare, in the pleasant variety entertainment he introduced in *The Winter's Tale* (Act IV, Scene iv) for the delectation of his music-loving Elizabethan audience, called in one of the pedlar ballad-singers of the day: 'He sings several tunes faster than you'll tell money; he utters them as he had eaten ballads, and all men's ears grew to his tunes.' The songs that are then performed are delightful, but they are hardly true ballads in the most usual sense, and that to which scholars today restrict the word. The true ballads are those mentioned in this scene but not there sung ('Here's another ballad, of a fish that appeared upon the coast on Wednesday the fourscore of April, forty thousand fathom above water, and sung this ballad against the hard hearts of maids'), i.e. the true ballad is a narrative poem, concerned with the marvellous, the historical, the heroic, the sentimental, or what you will, but always narrative. Its other essential characteristics are a verse-repeating form (with or without refrain) and an unsophisticated simplicity and unself-consciousness.

The Shakespeare ballad-seller, selling his (or her) broadsides or broadsheets, remained very popular in England up to the eighteenth century, as can be seen from several of Hogarth's pictures, and the present writer has listened to eye-witness accounts of the famous Mattha Doo and his family (sons and sons-in-law), who in the nineteenth century were, in west Cumberland, always to be seen at markets, fairs, public sales, wrestling matches, horse shows, races, and elections. There would be two of them on the ground at once, each standing on a little stool and singing his wares: at election time the two would take different sides and sing new ballads fashioned accordingly. Any murder, accident, or other tragedy was made the subject of a ballad, usually opening:

> Come all ye tender-hearted Christians
> And listen unto me.

Mr. Iolo A. Williams in his *English Folk-Song and Dance* (1935) records hearing in the market-place of Cambridge during the Crippen trial (in 1910 Crippen, who practised as an American doctor in London, was found to have murdered his wife, and he made history as the first criminal captured in mid-ocean by means of radio) a man hawking ballads with 'Here you are! The latest songs! All about the Dirty Doctor!' And during the financial crisis of the 1930s a poem on *The Suffering Unemployed* was hawked in the London streets.

It is very frequently stated (and often by writers of good standing) that the Puritans (q.v.), out of antipathy to music, put down ballad selling and singing during the brief period when they were in control of the country. There were, in fact, ordinances against the selling of ballads in 1643, 1647, 1648, and 1649, but not out of any antipathy to music (which antipathy did not exist) and purely for political reasons. The attempt to suppress ballad selling was repeatedly made in previous periods of English history and by governments that had nothing in common with the Puritans, as for instance by those of Henry VIII, Edward VI, and Mary. Such ordinances have had their near parallel, in the twentieth century, in the suppression of the free press in such countries as Russia, Germany, and Italy. Despite the ordinances a fair number of ballads appeared and were officially registered at Stationers' Hall (e.g. one hundred and sixty-five in 1656, when Cromwell's government was in full power); it may be surmised, then, that the law was not put in force when ballads were duly submitted to authority before publication and were found to possess nothing of an inflammatory or indecent character.

Ballad singers were long required to possess a licence to practise their calling, as were other itinerant performers; and the monopoly of licensing (a source of profit) belonged to the Master of the King's Revels. Thus we see in the *London Gazette* for 13 April 1682 the following:

'Whereas Mr. John Clarke, of London, bookseller, did rent of Charles Killegrew Esq. (the Master of the Revels) the licensing of all ballad singers for five years; which time is expired at Lady Day next: These are, therefore, to give notice to all ballad singers, that they take out licenses at the Office of the Revels, at Whitehall, for singing and selling of ballads and small books, according to an ancient custom. . . .'

2. The Ballad Metre. The most usual ballad metre of the great age of the English ballad was that of a four-lined stanza, with a two-in-a-measure rhythm, the first and third lines having four measures and the second and fourth having three measures and being rhymed together.

> In somer, when the shawes be sheyne,
>   And leves be large and long,
> Hit is mery in feyre foreste
>   To hear the fowlys song.

This is the same as the 'Common Metre' of the hymn-tune books, which probably derived from it.

3. The Nine Centuries of Ballad Making. The age of the ballads is, in most individual cases, impossible to determine. The beginnings of the form of them go back no further than the eleventh century, but the subjects are often older than that. In that century occurs a literary 'fault' (to use geological language)—a break in the continuity of literature which is not fully explicable. Early and later Medievalism there meet, and it may be that the same poetic and musical impulse which about then brought into existence the troubadours, trouvères, and minnesingers, with their new forms of song (see the article *Minstrels*), also stimulated the people at large to a new musical-poetical expression. From that day to this the making of ballads has never quite ceased. Sicily, which remains comparatively primitive in thought, was until recently in the full ballad-producing stage of civilization (7,000 have been collected there). The cowboy period of the middle western parts of the United States has turned out ballads in abundance, built much on the original British ballad lines and showing by their form and style, perhaps, their British ancestry—and certainly the old widespread European impulse that seems to assert itself wherever people are thrown together without organized means of entertainment.

As I walked out in the streets of Laredo,
　As I walked out in Laredo one day,
I spied a poor cowboy wrapped up in white linen,
　Wrapped up in white linen and cold as the clay.

This is to be found in Carl Sandburg's *The American Songbag* (1927); the tragedies in the ballads of this collection often end up with a 'rubber-tired hearse', and there are plenty of other indications of recent origin, yet their spirit is that of five hundred years earlier.

The cowboy is no longer the hero of American folk song (see the end of this section). Nor is the bank-robber, who has followed the old English greenwood outlaw into the retirement of the library shelves. ('There is something very interesting in the reproduction here on this new continent of essentially the conditions of ballad-growth which obtained in medieval England; including, by the way, sympathy for the outlaw, Jesse James taking the place of Robin Hood.'—Theodore Roosevelt, 1910, in a letter to John A. Lomax, compiler of *Cowboy Songs*.) It is, incidentally, noticeable that the less peaceful countries or portions of a country produce the greatest number of, and the most vigorous, ballads: thus Scotland and the north of England have more valuable relics of the ballad age to show than the south of England.

The Southern Appalachian region of North America, being still primitive in life and feeling, yielded many ballads to Olive Dame Campbell and Cecil J. Sharp when they collected folk music there in 1916, and these were largely (as to both words and tunes) of English and Lowland Scots origin, though they had, naturally, pursued their own course of evolution when cut off from their source.

In the report of the Division of Music of the Library of Congress for 1937–8, the account of Field Trips in the Southern Appalachians, taken with the object of enriching the 'Archive of American Folk-Song', records that 'the wives of the Holiness ministers (cf. *Dance*) sometimes act as song leaders' and that some of their productions are:

'composed in the heat of the service, and often the minister's wife picks the guitar and sings churchly ballads of her own composition. One such singer

in Cumberland, Ky., told us that all of her songs—ballads about floods, accidents and premature deaths that had sent the unconverted to Hell—were communicated to her in her dreams.'

There is also in this region a certain 'use of traditional tunes by union-conscious mountaineers in the composition of strike songs and ballads'.

'In Hazard, county seat of Perry County, two blue-jacketed miners walked into our hotel room one afternoon and asked if we weren't "the fellers who were catching mountain music", and then sang two narrative songs that they had made up about the union. In Harlan, Clay, Bell, and Johnson counties yet other union songs native to the region were heard.'

These 'songs of social protest' became in the fifties and sixties the theme of a whole new school of successful 'professional folk singers' (if this is not a contradiction in terms).

4. Theory of Communal Composition.

All ballads exhibit variants when collected in different periods or districts, and this tendency to change seems the true reading of the much discussed theory of communal composition, i.e. that they have not at the outset been fashioned by the people at large, but that some (possibly crude) composition of an individual has been passed from mouth to mouth, transforming itself, as a piece of gossip transforms itself when thus communicated, and producing variants, of which, by the law of the survival of the fittest, the most telling have survived, perhaps in time to deteriorate again in a period of decline of taste. Probably no two singers ever sing a ballad quite alike, either in words or tune, so that, as Vaughan Williams said, speaking of any folk song, 'It would appear to be a series of variations on a common theme'. The way in which this occurs is aptly illustrated by the experience of a writer given in the *Times Literary Supplement* (7 May 1931):

'I wrote a rhymed story of a man and maid meeting in a Hertfordshire lane, with the refrain—

　If you want the wife for a country life
　To Pencombe you must go.

This ministered to local patriotism and was very popular at village concerts. Twenty years later I heard it sung over mugs of beer by carters resting at a wayside inn, who assured me it was "an old ancient song". There was a "literary" epithet in one of the stanzas: "her cheek was touched with a vermeil stain". "Vermeil" had become "vermin", and, asking for an explanation, I was told that it referred to the old hunting custom of rubbing the bleeding brush on the cheek of a youngster newly entered.'

Nothing is said in this about the tune; it may plausibly be assumed that the poem was written to an existing and accepted tune, as poems of 'local patriotism' often are. (The same folk tune is often found to serve for several different sets of words.)

Another interesting personal account of the first floating of a ballad poem that after successive repetitions would probably take on the character of a communal composition, varying in different localities in words and tune (for a tune would probably later become attached to it), is the following by Evelyn Sharp (*The Listener*, 19 August 1931):

'I once heard what may have been the beginning of a folk-song. It was in a very remote part of Ireland. The evening before, some of us who had gone on an expedition in a jaunting car got lost, far out on the bog, and the driver threw down his reins and said it was no use driving any farther before the morning because the fairies had bewitched us and we should only drive round and round in a circle. We did manage to get home that night in spite of the fairies; and the next evening there was a dance in the barn, and, in one of the intervals between the reels and the country dances we were dancing, our driver suddenly stood up and began to recite a ballad in a sing-song sort of voice. Though I could not understand what he was saying, because it was in Irish, when it was translated to me afterwards I found it was an account—rather an imaginative account perhaps, but still, an account—of the way we were all bewitched in the bog. By this time I have no doubt that ballad has become a folk-song like any other you might find being sung in Ireland. Anyhow, it is a very good example of one of the ways our own English folk-songs may have been composed, ever so long ago.'

No printed ballads (except those collected since scientific folk-song study began) reach us quite in the form in which 'the people' gradually fashioned them. The printers of 'broadsides' (or 'broadsheets') and similar publications have always touched up the grammar a little and substituted somewhere a word of town English for some older word remaining current only in country places.

Of course stock phrases abound in both the poems and music of ballads and other types of folk song; so they do, for that matter, in composed song, as a glance through any collection of hymns and hymn tunes will show.

5. Literary Value of the Poems. In many ages men of the most refined literary taste have taken pleasure in the crude yet natural simplicities of ballad literature, as a practised and skilful gardener can take pleasure in wild flowers. Addison in the *Spectator* (no. 85, 1711) greatly praises this kind of composition and mentions that Dryden had a 'numerous Collection . . . and took a particular Pleasure in the Reading of them'. The musical Pepys (1633–1703) gathered all the ballads he could and left them to his old college of Magdalene at Cambridge, where they still are. During the eighteenth century ballads were somewhat forgotten and were despised by men of learning, but Bishop Percy, in 1765, rescued a manuscript collection of them from the hands of a servant who was lighting the fire and published it (with other similar folk material), to the contempt of his friend Dr. Johnson.

This collection, *Reliques of Ancient Poetry*, was eagerly táken up by certain German poets (especially Bürger), who were thus led to start the German romantic literary movement, which inspired the British romantic movement (Wordsworth, Coleridge, Scott), and led to the musical romantic movement associated with the names of Weber, Schumann, Wagner, etc. Loewe set very fine German translations of a number of Scottish ballads. Loewe's and Schubert's settings of 'The Erl King', and many other of the great songs of which the words are a German imitation of the British ballad style, would, apparently, never have been written but for Bishop Percy.

The greatest and most scholarly collection of English and Scottish ballads ever published is that of Professor Child of Harvard (definitive edition, 1882–98); this collection seems to be absolutely inclusive of the poems of the old ballads. The musical side of the form is explored in Bronson's *Traditional Tunes of the Child Ballads* (1959–   ). As the tunes did not so often get into print as the words, it offers more difficulty.

Imitations of the ballad form have often been attempted by poets (see allusion above to the German imitations), and it is noticeable that most often when they have received musical settings (at all events by British composers) it has been as cantatas. This is so, for instance, with Coleridge's *Ancient Mariner*, Browning's *Hervé Riel* (Walford Davies), Tennyson's *The Revenge* (Stanford's fine setting), and some of the humorous *Ingoldsby Legends* of Barham.

6. The so-called 'Drawing-Room Ballad'. A very degenerate descendant of the old English ballad was the Victorian 'ballad', a sentimental solo song, of verse-repeating form, generally with a refrain. It is curious today to recall that Sullivan, in the 1860s, held the post of 'Professor of Pianoforte *and Ballad Singing*' at the Crystal Palace School of Art, appointed to it by the serious-minded George Grove. During the latter part of the nineteenth century and the beginning of the twentieth, 'ballads' ('Drawing Room Ballads' or 'Shop Ballads') were being published by the hundred, and special 'Ballad Concerts' were, from 1867, held in London. Some of the principal publishers pushed the lucrative sale amongst tasteless amateurs by paying a fixed sum (or 'royalty') to professional vocalists for every inclusion of a particular ballad in a public programme, or by paying very eminent vocalists a royalty for a term of years on the complete sales of ballads which they undertook to introduce to the public. This form of publicity was so general that 'ballads' of this period were often spoken of as 'Royalty Ballads'.

See also *Ballade*, below; *Street Music* 6.

BALLADE. That the English ballad became a source of inspiration to composers, and helped to bring into existence the Romantic School of Music, has been hinted at in the above article (*Ballad*). The name 'ballade' seems first to have come into music with a member of this school, Chopin, though whether he attached the name to the compositions in question from the English idea of a ballad or the French of a ballade is not to be settled.

The French ballade was a smaller and non-narrative form of three stanzas and an *envoi* —which is against the theory that Chopin had it in mind, for his Ballades are long and dramatic. It continued the style of the troubadours (see *Minstrels*, etc.), came to a glorious end with Villon in the fifteenth century, and was revived by Théodore de Banville towards the end of the nineteenth century (i.e. after Chopin's lifetime).

The Chopin Ballades (for piano), wherever their name originated, are supposed to have taken their very strong Polish national inspiration from the epic poems of Mickiewicz (1798–1855), but they have certainly exactly the quality of some of the old heroic English ballads to which Sir Philip Sidney alluded in the sixteenth century, when he said 'I have never heard the olde songe of Percy and Douglas that I found not my heart mooved more than with a Trumpet'. They give us Chopin at his highest.

Since Chopin's day Brahms, Liszt, Grieg, and others, have adopted the title for piano works. Brahms's First Ballade, op. 10, no. 1, is definitely based on the emotions and thought of the Scottish ballad-poem 'Edward', and his Intermezzo, op. 117, no. 1, is similarly based on the Scottish ballad 'Lady Ann Bothwell's Lament', both of which ballads came to him from Percy's *Reliques*, via Herder's German translations.

No particular one form is associated with the instrumental ballade. That of Grieg is a series of masterly variations: the heroic old ballad spirit is in it.

BALLADENMÄSSIG (Ger.). 'In ballad style.'

BALLAD-HORN. See *Saxhorn and Flügelhorn Families* 2 c (footnote).

BALLAD OPERA (p. 101, pl. 18) is an English form of independent origin, though it closely resembles the French *Vaudeville* (q.v.) of the end of the seventeenth century and beginning of the eighteenth. It also resembles the German *Singspiel* (q.v.), upon which it had an influence.

It consists of spoken dialogue with frequent excursions into song, these latter being of the nature of poems in the simple ballad style set to well-known airs of the day. It began (as had French vaudeville a little earlier) as a sort of parody of opera proper, *The Beggar's Opera* (q.v.) being the first example and serving as the model.[1] People liked the simplicity of the form. Such works had words they could follow, because, unlike those of the Handel operas of the day, they were in plain English;

[1] Twenty-two years before *The Beggar's Opera* (i.e. in 1706) D'Urfey's *Wonders in the Sun* had been performed in London, and this had (as Burney relates) songs set to 'ballad tunes of true English growth'. These tunes, however (with words 'furnished by the most eminent wits of its age'), were interspersed amongst more elaborate music by G. B. Draghi, so that this was not a true 'Ballad Opera'.

subjects they could understand, since they were not, like those of the Handel operas, from remote mythology or medieval romance, but from the everyday life around; and a pace of action that kept their interest alive, since there were no tripartite arias (see *Aria*), with long roulades.

Of so rapid a growth was the popularity of this kind of entertainment that it seems as though Gay and Pepusch, with their *Beggar's Opera*, had just touched a button and set a waiting current flowing. *The Beggar's Opera* appeared in 1728. By the end of 1729 fifteen such ballad operas had been performed in London; in 1730 there were thirteen more; in 1731 ten; in 1732 eleven; in 1733 (the 'peak' year) twenty-two. During this period the competition of ballad opera created a real business difficulty for Handel and his rival Bononcini, with their Italian operas: Handel complained that ballad opera pelted Italian opera off the stage with Lumps of Pudding (the name of the last tune in *The Beggar's Opera*).

Then there was a sudden drop in 1734 to five; 1735 nine; 1736 seven; and this year marks the end of the real popularity of the type, for in 1737 there were only two and in 1738 there was one. Examples still appeared for a time, but from 1743 to 1749 there were none, in 1749 and 1753 there were only single instances, and thereafter the type is practically extinct. It may be said to have had a life of about twenty years, of which roughly the first ten were fat years and the second ten lean years. Probably many musicians, when they talk of the popularity of the eighteenth-century ballad opera, do not realize how evanescent that popularity was, for they are misled by knowledge of the frequent revivals of *The Beggar's Opera*, which began the vogue and is the only example today surviving.

A slight qualification is perhaps necessary to these references to *The Beggar's Opera* as the begetter of the race of ballad opera. Three years earlier (1725) Scotland had published an isolated example of its own, the Edinburgh wig-maker, bookseller, poet Allan Ramsay's *The Gentle Shepherd*: it is in verse throughout and in the Scots dialect, and the songs are set to Scots tunes. It was, however, not performed until the year after *The Beggar's Opera*, when it was heard at Haddington (an amateur performance); the following year an adaptation of it was given in London, and thenceforward there were numerous performances of it at Drury Lane almost to the end of the century (see *Ramsay, Allan*).

After the decline of ballad opera in the middle of the eighteenth century there is a gap of ten years or more when opera in English was no longer heard. Then, from 1760 onwards, there appear works in English like Arne's *Thomas and Sally* and *Love in a Village* and works of Dibdin, Arnold, Shield, Jackson of Exeter, Hook, and others. These are sometimes called 'Ballad Operas', but as most of the tunes are original they represent a different type and no purpose is served by confusing them with their predecessors. The same applies to Vaughan Williams's *Hugh the Drover*, of which the title page bears the description 'A Ballad Opera'.

The technical term **English Opera**, however, covers both types. It implies the use of the vernacular and that of spoken dialogue. Thus an opera can be English without being, in the technical sense, 'English Opera'. This type did not originate with ballad opera: nearly all Purcell's theatrical work belongs to it. (The Gilbert and Sullivan series offers us modern examples.)

The best account of the English ballad operas (the early type, accurately so described) is in the appendix to Schultz's *Gay's Beggar's Opera; its Content, History and Influence* (Yale University Press, 1923). It gives a complete list.

In America the popularity of ballad opera of the true type began with the importation of an English work *Flora, or Hob in the Well*, which was given at Charleston in 1735. The first American performance of *The Beggar's Opera* itself took place in New York in 1750 (but see *Opera* 21). Thereafter all the most popular English operas of both this and the later type were quickly imported, and, indeed, they for long formed the sole operatic entertainment, since Italian and French opera did not reach America until the 1790s (see *Opera* 21a), and no serious attempt to acclimatize Italian opera was made until 1825.

See also passing references under *Folk Song* 3; *Fair and their Music*; *England* 6; *Ireland* 6.

For the participation of the audience in ballad opera see *Community Singing*.

BALLARD. See *Publishing* 2; *Printing* 2.

BALLATA. See *Italy* 3. 'Ballatella' is the diminutive.

BALLERINA, BALLERINO. See *Ballet* 8.

BALLET

1. Introductory.
2. The Ballet in Seventeenth- and Eighteenth-century France.
3. Noverre and his Contemporaries.
4. The Early Nineteenth-century Innovations.
5. The Later Nineteenth Century, and the Twentieth.
6. Loans from Ballet to Concert Repertory and vice versa.
7. Ballet in Opera.
8. Some Common Technical Terms.
9. Short Historical List of Famous Ballet Artists.

(For illustrations see opposite, pl. **12.**

1. Introductory. The general subject of the dance and the history of social dancing are discussed under *Dance*, and the present article is devoted to the sub-subject of the Dance as Spectacle. For a proper background the article mentioned and also that on the *Masque* should be read. To complete the subject read after the present article that on *Pantomime*.

2. The Ballet in Seventeenth- and Eighteenth-century France (pl. **12.** 1). Spectacular dancing has existed amongst all races and in all periods. Some instances are mentioned incidentally in the article *Dance*. The ballet, as we understand the word today, may perhaps be said to have largely developed in France in the seventeenth and early eighteenth centuries and, more precisely, at the court of Louis XIV (reigned 1643–1715). It is difficult to fix, with exactitude, a time and place, since the line between masque and ballet is hardly a rigid one. Spectacles in which dancing played a part were before this period popular at the courts of Europe and especially those of Italy and of France. One which is, indeed, sometimes spoken of as the first important ballet, was the *Balet comique de la royne*, given in Paris in 1581 to celebrate the marriage of Margaret of Lorraine, sister of Henry III, to the Duc de Joyeuse. This was a most sumptuous entertainment; three and a half million francs were spent on it and its fame echoed through Europe. The influence of Catherine de' Medici was enormous during the whole of this reign and the two previous ones (i.e. the reigns of her sons, Francis II, Charles IX, and Henry III, cover-ing the period 1559–89), and it is she who is sometimes credited with the introduction into France of this type of entertainment, to which she had been accustomed during her brief Italian childhood. (The Medici were noted providers of lavish theatre festivals as early as 1539.) During the twenty-one years' reign of the next monarch, Henry IV (1589–1610), no fewer than eighty ballets were given at court. Under Louis XIII (1610–43) ballets were characterized by a decadent tendency towards the fantastic and the grotesque.

Louis XIV, then, though we may call him the patron-creator of the Ballet Spectacle, inherited a tradition. The presence about his court of two supreme masters respectively of the dance and of music, Beauchamp (see *Dance* 6 b) and Lully (q.v.), with his own personal interest in both arts, enabled the King to make Paris the capital of the dance, giving dancing law to the world. (As mentioned under *Dance*, it is worthy of note that, just as our standard terminology of musical performance is Italian, that of dancing is French.)

The King founded a Royal Academy of Dancing in 1661, which was followed by the establishment of a Royal Academy of Music in 1669. Three years later a school of dancing was added to the latter; this was the origin of the state ballet. The King himself was a great dancer and frequently appeared in court ballets, sometimes with Lully dancing beside him. At first ballets were given only at court, but after a time they were seen also in the public theatre.

1. A 17TH-CENTURY BALLET AT THE COURT OF LOUIS XIV (Lully's *La Princesse d'Élide*)

3. THE PRACTICE SCHOOL AT THE PARIS OPÉRA
(late 19th century). By Degas

2. CAMARGO, by Lancret (early 18th century)
See *Ballet* 2

4. A MID-20TH-CENTURY BALLET—'Pineapple Poll' (Sadler's Wells Theatre)

1. THE BIRTHPLACE OF BEETHOVEN
In the Bonngasse; now dedicated for ever as
a Beethoven museum

2. THE BIRTH-ROOM OF BEETHOVEN

3. BEETHOVEN'S EARLIEST
PORTRAIT

4. BEETHOVEN AT 21

5. BEETHOVEN AS SEEN IN
THE STREETS OF VIENNA
(sketched by Lyser about 1823)

6. THE HEILIGENSTADT MONUMENT, VIENNA

The ballet *Pomone*, in 1671 (book by Perrin, music by Cambert, dances by Beauchamp), ran, with crowded houses, for eight months. This was a sort of opera-ballet, since, as in other ballets of the period, there was some singing (it was called a 'Pastorale' and is sometimes spoken of as the first French opera).

The dances in the ballets of Lully and his contemporaries are gavottes, menuets (then a novelty), chaconnes, bourrées, gigues, canaries, and the like. The ladies of the court danced in the ballets there, but no woman appeared as a dancer on the public stage until 1681. The ballets of the period were very formal; there were heavy dresses, 'paniers' (projections on each side of the dress just below the waist) and wigs, helmets, high heels, and the other trappings of high life. The personages represented might come from Greek or Roman mythology or history, but they had to be dressed in the costume of the day—according to the universal theatrical custom of the time, which, of course, persisted in all countries well into the eighteenth century. In 1734 Sallé created a stir in London by an innovation she would never have dared to introduce in Paris; as Pygmalion she appeared in a mere muslin dress and without a head-dress. Nature was now bursting through. This stimulated interest in ballet, although programmes of dances and small ballets given by English dancers or distinguished dancers engaged from France had been a feature of the London stage since the beginning of the century.

A great ballerina of this period was Camargo, whose public career ran from 1726 to 1751. She introduced shorter skirts (but they still fell below the knees) and 'excelled in gavottes, tambourins, marches, and loures'. She set the fashions for dress, on and off the stage, and her shoemaker made a fortune. Lancret's very famous and often reproduced picture of her romantically dancing in a woodland glade (to the accompaniment of fiddles, hautboy, and bassoon, with pipe and tabor; p. 881, pl. **148.** 2) is in the Wallace Collection, London. When in 1934 a society for the revival of the best traditions of stage dancing was founded in London it was called the Camargo Society. The popularity of woman dancers in the eighteenth century was unbounded. When Guimard broke an arm prayers for its safe healing were said in Notre Dame.

The ballet of the French court ceased at the death of Louis XIV in 1715, but the Paris Opéra remained the ballet centre of the world, though Milan later became very important—when Blasis went there (see *Blasis*; *Dance* 10).

3. Noverre and his Contemporaries. Noverre (1727–1810) was the first great reformer of the ballet. He left an important treatise on the ballet, which will be found mentioned at the end of the article *Dance*. In it he states his ideals: 'To break hideous masks, to burn ridiculous perukes, to suppress clumsy panniers, to do away with still more inconvenient hip-pads, to substitute taste for routine, to indicate a dress more noble, more accurate, and more picturesque, to demand action and expression in dancing, to demonstrate the immense distance which lies between mere mechanical technique and the genius which places dancing beside the imitative arts.' He developed miming so as to make it a part of the ballet and thus made himself the founder of the Dramatic Ballet or *ballet d'action*. He was friendly with Garrick, who called him 'The Shakespeare of the Dance' and had much influence on him. It was partly on Garrick's advice that he established the ballet as a five-act entertainment in its own right. He collaborated with Gluck in the ballets of *Iphigenia in Tauris* (1779), and with Mozart, who for him and to his scenario wrote the ballet *Les Petits Riens* (1778).

Other important choreographers of this period were Dauberval (1742–1806) and Maximilien Gardel (1741–87). Distinguished dancers of this period were Louis Dupré (1697–1774), David Dumoulin, Gaetano Vestris (1729–1808), Charles Le Picq, and Auguste Vestris (1760–1842). Gaetano Vestris was the founder of a notable family of dancers—three generations; the famous singer, Mme Vestris, was wife of one of the old man's grandsons. At this time a great deal of the music used for ballets was not original but borrowed from the operatic, lyric, or symphonic repertory.

4. The Early Nineteenth-century Innovations. By the end of the eighteenth century the ballet might be said to have shaken off the last of the stately court influences and to have developed a gymnastic virtuosity; some conventionality, however, still remained, because the movement was confined too exclusively to the feet and legs.

Dancing on the *pointe* (that is, on the tips of the toes) came in at an undetermined date generally thought to be about 1820, though there are indications of its occasional use up to fifty years earlier. It calls for arduous practice and carries a danger of dislocation; it is executed in special shoes and (except in a few cases for certain effects) by women only. Taglioni (whose career was from 1822 to 1847) was its first notable exponent. The Romantic movement in literature, drama, painting, and music (see *Romantic*) was now in being, and this brought an attempt at ethereal informality into the ballet; dancers were expected to look and move like sylphs or phantoms. The chivalrous idealization of woman that constituted a feature of romanticism was perhaps a factor in the decline of interest in male dancers as compared with female.

The dancing costume now got shorter and the 'maillot' (named from its inventor, a Paris costumier), or skin-tight, was introduced. If one looks at a series of the numerous pictures of ballet favourites down to and including Taglioni one is surprised to realize how comparatively modern an innovation is the generally accepted ballet costume.

5. The Later Nineteenth Century, and the Twentieth. From the middle of the nineteenth century to its end great spectacular ballets, of a realistic and topical character and employing big forces, were in favour. Much effective ballet music was at this time and later written by French composers. The appearance of Delibes's *Coppélia* (1870) marks an epoch. A reaction from this spirit of display, megalomania, and realism is seen in the work of the American woman dancer, Isadora Duncan (1878–1927), who took her attitudes and costumes from Greek vases and mingled with classical motions some learned from the birds and the waves and other natural exponents of grace in action. She spent some time in Russia and taught there, and so, to some extent at any rate, influenced the dancer Fokine, and inspired the future impresario Diaghilef. St. Petersburg and Moscow had long had their Imperial schools of dancing, and had cultivated technique to a condition of the highest polish. These men introduced the classical and naturalistic ideals, added nationalistic traits and a good deal of their own thought, and so burst into western Europe (Paris 1909 and London 1911) like a refreshing breeze.

To a large extent the Russian ballet troupe rejected toe-dancing (at all events as the principal element), the two-feet-turned-out-in-a-straight-line stance, tight-lacing, and the other conventions. And they brought back into the European limelight the male dancer, who had receded into the background. They gave a number of ballets more or less on the old lines, generally adapted to music of Chopin or Schumann or the less modern-minded Russian composers, but they gave also a good many in which the dramatic emphasis was strong, so that one had the interest of a genuine plot. Diaghilef commissioned composers, and especially Stravinsky, whose *Firebird* and *Petrouchka* long remained to many people as memories of (one may say) the highest phase of ballet as a combination of the arts, whilst others dwelt with pleasure on the recollection of more 'advanced' works such as *The Rite of Spring* ('Sacre du Printemps') and *The Nightingale* (an opera turned into a ballet by its composer) or of later and even more startlingly novel works (see *Stravinsky*).

Diaghilef managed to collect around him a most able and enthusiastic group of dancers—Pavlova (for two seasons), Karsavina, Lopokova, amongst the women; Nijinsky, Massine (both of whom acted as ballet-masters at different periods) amongst the men. Fokine was largely responsible for the general design of the ballets, and amongst a wonderful series of painter-artists (Benois, Golovin, Roerich, Picasso, Derain, etc.) Bakst stood out as the master of all. Bold colour contrasts were a frequent feature of the stage scene. Crude realism was as ruthlessly cast aside as smooth conventionality; one spent one's evening in the realm of dream or fantasy.

In addition to Stravinsky, Ravel (*Daphnis and Chloë*), Falla (*The Three-Cornered Hat*), Milhaud, Poulenc, and others, composed to Diaghilef's commission. (See also references under *Lambert, Constant*; *Nabokof*; *Beecham*; *Programme Music* 3.)

A twentieth-century German ballet innovator was Rudolf von Laban, who led a movement which lays more emphasis on an intellectual basis. Amongst his disciples were Mary Wigman and Kurt Jooss. In the United States Martha Graham was the creator of a school of modern dance expressive of the most complex hidden emotions.

During the second quarter of this century, it is important to note the revival of ballet at the Paris Opéra, due to the influence of Serge Lifar, who produced many ballets there, danced in several of them, and much improved the technical efficiency of the company and the standard of training in the ballet school attached to the theatre.

England saw the birth of English ballet, springing from two root causes: (1) The work of Marie Rambert and her Ballet Club (later the 'Ballet Rambert') which produced many distinguished dancers and choreographers, and (2) The dynamic energy of Ninette de Valois, who established the Sadler's Wells Ballet (since the second World War attached to the Royal Opera House, Covent Garden, and rechristened the 'Royal Ballet'), which has produced ballets on the grand scale and has achieved a high standard of performance, arousing the greatest admiration when it has toured abroad.

In America, ballet also became very popular, owing largely to the efforts of two companies: the New York City Ballet, with George Balanchine for its artistic director and principal choreographer, Lincoln Kirstein as general director, and a considerable repertory of ballets, mainly of an abstract kind; and the American Ballet Theatre (from 1962 in Washington, D.C.) directed by Lucia Chase and Oliver Smith; this company's productions have a tendency towards Americana, and are more emotional in character.

In Russia, the great companies (often touring abroad) remain the Bolshoi (Moscow) and Kirov (Leningrad). Jugoslavia has developed national ballet at the State Theatre, Belgrade, and elsewhere, and in 1947 Turkey established at Istanbul its first school of ballet.

Amongst twentieth-century ballet compositions are Bartók's *The Wooden Prince* ('Der holzgeschnitzte Prinz'), Bliss's *Miracle in the Gorbals*, Falla's *The Three-Cornered Hat* ('Le tricorne'), Hindemith's *Nobilissima Visione* and *The Demon*, Lambert's *Horoscope*, Prokofief's *Romeo and Juliet*, *The Prodigal Son*, and *Cinderella*, Sauguet's *La nuit*, *Les forains*, and *Les mirages*, Stravinsky's *Card Party* ('Jeu de cartes'), *Orpheus*, and numerous later works (a number of these written for George Balanchine), Vaughan Williams's *Job*, and a number of works by such American composers as Copland (*Appalachian Spring*; *Billy the Kid*), Bernstein (*Fancy Free*), and Schuman (*Undertow*).

The Paris ballet dancers of the late nineteenth century have their record (and a very ample and perfect one) in the graceful and masterly paintings of Degas (1834–1917).

6. Loans from Ballet to Concert Repertory and vice versa. It should, perhaps, be added that a good deal of music written for ballet has come to have separate performance, so enriching the orchestral repertory. A few examples are: *The Nutcracker* ('Casse-noisette') of Tchaikovsky (somewhat rearranged by him as a concert suite); *Daphnis and Chloë* (1909) of Ravel; *The Spider's Feast* ('Le Festin de l'araignée', 1912) of Roussel; many of the ballets of Stravinsky; *Krazy Kat* (1922) and *Skyscrapers* (1926) of John Alden Carpenter; and numerous works of Leonard Bernstein and Aaron Copland.

On the other hand, a great deal of music intended by its composers purely as concert music has been used for the ballet, as, for instance, *The Afternoon of a Faun* of Debussy and the *Scheherazade* of Rimsky-Korsakof (a piece of definite and fairly detailed 'programme music' ruthlessly lashed on to an entirely different ballet programme). Indeed whole symphonies have been 'balletized', e.g. Beethoven's Seventh and Brahms's Fourth.

The use of Chopin's music for ballet purposes seems to be inartistic. It is essentially piano music and does not orchestrate well; and moreover its effectiveness depends largely on a delicate tempo rubato which becomes impossible when elaborate steps are fitted to it.

7. Ballet in Opera. Dancing was a frequent ingredient of opera almost from the first, as it had been of the entertainments that preceded opera, from which this was partly derived (for instance the masque). By the late seventeenth century it had become an important ingredient. Lully in France and Purcell in England, and their librettists, provided for it pretty lavishly. As examples, Lully's *Cadmus and Hermione* (1673) has dances of Nymphs and Shepherds, of the Winds, of Rustics bearing Oak Branches, of Gods of the Countryside, and the like; Purcell's *Dido and Aeneas* (c. 1688) ends its first scene with a 'Triumphing Dance' and its second with an 'Echo Dance of Furies', whilst later it has a 'Sailors' Dance' and a 'Dance of Witches and Sailors'. The dances of the opera composers of that period are more or less adroitly worked into the tissue of the dramatic scheme, but the object is plainly not so much to help towards the effectiveness of that scheme as to give the audience a varied and delightful entertainment. This has continued to be pretty much the position of ballet as a part of opera; librettists often try to justify its inclusion by making use of any opportunity that offers for personages to do a little communal rejoicing (or even sorrowing), and composers are glad to collaborate with their librettists in this, but the excuse is sometimes rather slender. Of course many operas have been written without ballets, but many others have had ballets thrust into them almost without any dramatic justification. Rousseau, in his *Dictionary of Music* (1767), grumbles much at the irrelevance of opera ballets in his time, and the complaint has been renewed at intervals by other writers ever since.

It is Rousseau's Paris public, as a matter of fact, which has the most firmly insisted on the provision in its opera of this sort of light relief. Gluck, during Rousseau's lifetime, had to please the Paris taste by providing ballets, but tried to make them part of the action. Nearly seventy years later the same exigence prevailed, and we find Berlioz called on to orchestrate Weber's *Invitation to the Dance* so that it might be used as a ballet interpolation in that composer's *Freischütz* on the occasion of its 1841 performance in Paris.

French and Italian opera of the earlier nineteenth century usually made great play with ballet. Meyerbeer's operas, written for the Paris stage of the 1830s to 1860s, are good examples. Scribe was his chief librettist, and between the two of them the public was always provided with something gaudily spectacular—in *Robert the Devil* (1831), a brisk ballet of perjured nuns raised from their graves; in *The Huguenots* (1836), one by the joint retinues of Marguérite de Valois and the Duc de Nevers, supported both by the orchestra and by a military band on the stage; in *The Prophet*, one by John of Leyden's friends rejoicing over his approaching wedding; in *The African*, one in celebration of an oriental coronation, and so on. 'Where there's a will there's a way' and, given the choice of suitable subjects and ingenuity in treating them, the delights of pageantry and the dance can generally be worked into the tissue of the entertainment.

Wagner, as has often been told, suffered painfully from the Parisian penchant for ballets, so cleverly satisfied at that time by Meyerbeer and others. When, sixteen years after the first production of *Tannhäuser*, it at last reached the Paris stage, he was urged to insert a ballet in the second act, according to Paris operatic custom. Instead of this he re-wrote and developed the Venusberg orgies of the first act, the only real opportunity that the subject of the opera logically offered for the introduction of a ballet. This was an offence to the ladies of the *corps de ballet*, who wished to be seen and applauded by the late diners; they worked up feeling amongst their gentlemen friends, the Jockey Club's gilded youth was mobilized, and hissing and whistling killed the performance. The provision of ballet for the sake of ballet was, of course, quite opposed to Wagner's principles (see *Wagner*); he was glad, no doubt, when in *The Mastersingers* his apprentices were seized with the impulse to have a dance among themselves, and when in the generally austere *Parsifal* the Flower Maidens decided to disport themselves in their garden, but he was emphatically not one of those opera-makers who can interrupt their characters in the midst of their action and insist on their relieving the public with a little light refreshment.

Wagner's view of the matter is the one since generally accepted by serious composers: if the subject calls for, or naturally admits of, dancing they will gladly provide for it, but they will not reject every subject that is incapable of making a place for dancing, nor will they distort a subject by thrusting dancing into it willy-nilly. Opera is one thing and ballet another, and it is not to be expected that these two can always be brought together.

This attitude has probably been good for ballet by encouraging its cultivation as a separate art and a free and self-sufficing entertainment, and so, perhaps, tending to its higher development in certain ways. It is an attitude that did not begin with Wagner. Mozart's dramatis personae indulge in a dance when the plot allows, but they never shoulder the plot out of the way to make room for it. Hence in *Figaro* we have the quite natural introduction of the wedding festival; as the action is in Spain there is dancing to a fandango, and, with a sudden desire for authenticity, Mozart chooses a genuine Spanish fandango tune (which Gluck, by the way, had used before him in his ballet of *Don Juan*). And in *Don Giovanni* we have the famous passage of the three simultaneous dances dovetailed, three orchestras playing respectively a minuet, a contredanse, and a waltz (in 3/4, 2/4, and 3/8 times, ingeniously contrived to fit), and three sets of characters of the opera dancing to their music.

The position of ballet in the Russian opera is important, since many of the subjects chosen readily admit of dancing and pageantry. The Dance of the Seven Veils in Strauss's *Salome* offers a perfect example of dance as an essential element in an opera scheme: it is, of course, a solo dance.

8. Some Common Technical Terms (such as are not explained in the body of the article).

Adage. A dance designed to enable a *danseuse*, generally assisted by a male partner, to display her grace, sense of line, and perfect balance; the first movement of the traditional four-part duet or pas de deux.

Air de caractère. In the *ballet de cour* most of the music was that of the various dance forms, but there were certain 'characteristic pieces' (e.g. for an entry of warriors or anything like that) and to these this name was attached.

Ballerina. A female dancer, but frequently used to imply the leading female dancer in a ballet company.

Ballerino. A male dancer.

Ballet de cour. The court ballet of the seventeenth century.

Chassé. The 'chasing' of one foot from its place by a touch from the other.

Choreography or **Choregraphy.** The art of dance-composition. The choreographer or choregrapher of a ballet-troupe is the designer of its dances.

Corps de ballet. The whole body of dancers attached to a particular theatre, but more generally applied to the rank and file of a ballet company.

Coupé. Like the chassé (see above), but the displaced foot goes into the air.

Enchaînement. A sequence of two or more steps.

Entrechat. A vertical jump into the air, during which the feet are repeatedly crossed.

Fouetté (literally, 'whipped'). A 'swing with a snap at the finish'—one leg swung out horizontally, a grand pirouette (see 'Pirouette' below), and the foot of the swung leg brought sharply in again. (This is one kind.)

Pas de basque. An alternating step, with one foot on the floor all the time—a little step used for contrast with bigger ones and as a connecting link.

Pas glissé. A simple gliding step.

Pirouette. A complete revolution made whilst balanced on the half point, quarter point, or full point of one leg. This was at first a man's evolution. The Grande Pirouette is the same thing with the other leg held out at right angles ('second position en l'air').

Rond de jambe. The tracing of a semicircle with one foot, on the ground or in the air, using the other foot as an axis.

Tour en l'air. A complete revolution made while leaping vertically upwards into the air.

Numerous attempts have been made to invent a notation for dance movements, and of all these Labanotation, invented by Rudolf von Laban (see 5) in the 1930s, is perhaps the best known.

9. Short Historical List of Famous Ballet Artists. Sallé, Marie (1707–56). Camargo, Marie Anne de Cupis de (1710–70). Noverre, Jean Georges (1727–1810). Vestris, Gaetano (1729–1808). Gardel, Maximilien (1741–87). Dauberval, Jean (1742–1806). Allard, Marie (1742–1802). Guimard, Madeleine (1743–1816). Heinel, Anna Friederike (1752–1808). Gardel, Pierre (1758–1840). Vestris, Auguste (1760–1842). Taglioni, Marie (1804–84). Elssler, Fanny (1810–84). Grisi, Carlotta (1821–99). Grahn, Lucille (1821–1907). Cerrito, Fanny (1817–1909). Perrot, Jules (1810–92). Petipa, Marius (1822–1910). Cecchetti, Enrico (1850–1928). Mauri, Rosita (1856–1923). Preobajenska, Olga (1870–1962). Trefilova, Vera (1875–1943). Geltzer, Catherine (1876–1952). Genée, Adeline (1878–1970). Fokine, Michel (1880–1942). Pavlova, Anna (1881–1931). Bolm, Adolf (1884–1951). Karsavina, Tamara (b. 1885). Kyasht, Lydia (1885–1959). Nijinsky, Vaslav (1890–1950). Lopokova, Lydia (b. 1891). Massine, Leonide (b. 1894). Idzikovsky, Stanislas (1894–1977). Spessivtzeva, Olga (b. 1895). Woizikovski, Leon (1897–1975). Ashton, Frederick (b. 1904). Balanchine, George (b. 1904). Dolin, Anton (b. 1904). Lifar, Serge (b. 1905). Limon, Jose (1908–72). Tudor, Antony (b. 1908). Helpmann, Robert (b. 1909). de Mille, Agnes (b. 1909). Markova, Alicia (born 1910). Ulanova, Galina (b. 1910). Youskevitch, Igor (b. 1912). Chauviré, Yvette

(b. 1917). Eglevsky, André (b. 1917). Robbins, Jerome (b. 1918). Fonteyn, Margot (b. 1919). Babilée, Jean (b. 1923). Béjart, Maurice (b. 1924). Bruhn, Erik (b. 1928). Joffrey, Robert (b. 1930). Fracci, Carla (b. 1936). Nureyev, Rudolf (b. 1938). Baryshnikov, Mikhail (b. 1948).

For a list of the most important of the older books on the ballet see *Dance* 10.

BALLETT (English) or **BALLETTO** (It.). See *Madrigal* 3 c.

BALLIOL COLLEGE, OXFORD. See *Farmer, J.* (II); *Carol*.

BALLO (It.). 'Ball', 'dance'; so *Tempo di ballo*, which can mean (*a*) at a dancing speed, or (*b*) a dance-style movement.

BALLO FURLANO. See *Forlana*.

BAMBERG, KARL. See *Trombone Family* 4.

BAMBOO PIPE. This is a simple instrument of the type of recorder (see *Recorder Family*), which from about the 1920s in the United States and from the 1930s in Britain it became common to teach schoolchildren to make and play. The founder of the movement in Britain was Miss Margaret James, and she induced some British composers of eminence to write music specially for the instrument.

BAMBOULA. (1) A primitive Negro tambourine, formerly in use in Louisiana and still in use in the West Indies. (2) A dance to which this instrument is the accompaniment. There is an orchestral piece by the Negro composer, Coleridge-Taylor (q.v.), so entitled.

BANATANKA. A sort of Serbian dance.

BANCHIERI, ADRIANO. Born at Bologna in 1568 and died there in 1634, aged about sixty-six. As organist, composer, and theorist he enjoyed great renown—and he was also a poet and playwright. He published a good deal of music and also many theoretical treatises.

See reference under *Concerto* 1.

BAND. In general this word is nowadays used musically to designate a body of wind-instrument players as distinct from an orchestra, the distinction (a useful one) being more strictly observed in the United States than in Britain. At one time the word was also often used for a company of chorus singers, and this last use continued in Scotland until at least the mid-nineteenth century.

See *Brass Band*; *Military Band*.

BAND, BÄNDE (Ger.). 'Volume', 'volumes'.

BANDA TURCA. See *Percussion Family* 4 b.

BANDONEON. See *Reed-Organ Family* 4.

BANDORE. See under *Cittern*.

BANDURRÍA. See mention under *Cittern*.

BANGOR CATHEDRAL. See *Cathedral Music* 2, 7; *Monks' March*.

BANGOR USE. See *Common Prayer*; *Use of Sarum*.

BANISTER, JOHN (p. 225, pl. **43.** 1). Born in London in 1630 and died there in 1679, aged forty-eight or forty-nine. He was a violinist (and as such a leader of the band of Charles II), a composer, and a musical *entrepreneur*.

For his public concerts (the first ever to be given in London) see *Concert* 3, 4; *Music Hall* 2.

BANJO. This instrument is of the same general type as the guitar (q.v.), but the resonating body is of parchment strained over a metal hoop and it has an open back. There are from four to nine strings (usually five or six), passing over a low bridge, and 'stopped' against a finger-board—often, but not always, without 'frets' (q.v.); one of them is played by the thumb, as a '*melody string*' (*thumb string* or *chanterelle*), the others providing simple accompaniment chords. Some types of banjo have gut strings, played with the finger-tips, and others wire strings, played with a plectrum.

The banjo is supposed to be of African origin, and was in use amongst the slaves on the plantations of the Southern States (see *United States* 6 for Negro Music), whence it became the accepted instrument of the 'minstrels' of the nineteenth century, and in the next century had its uses (and abuses) in jazz bands (see the article *Jazz*). The instrument is capable of remarkable virtuosic effects, but the dryness of its tone and the small variety of chords available limit its services for the most part pretty narrowly to amusement-music. An exception is a Duet-Sonata for Saxophone and Banjo by Jemnitz.

A *Tenor Banjo* has been used in jazz bands; it differs in some ways from the banjo proper, its tuning resembling that of the violin family, and it is said to have been introduced in the United States in the early days of jazz so that violinists and cellists could add to their earning power.

The *Zither Banjo* is a small size of banjo with wire strings.

BANJOLIN. A modern instrument of the family of the banjo (q.v.), but with a short fretted neck like that of the mandoline. It has four single strings or four pairs of strings, played with a plectrum.

BANJULELE. See under *Ukelele*.

BANKS, RALPH (1762–1841). See *Cathedral Music* 7.

BANKS AND BRAES. See *Ye Banks and Braes*.

BANTOCK, GRANVILLE (p. 336, pl. **53.** 4). Born in London in 1868 and died in 1946, aged seventy-eight. He was trained at the Royal Academy of Music, then started a journal called *The New Quarterly Musical Review*, toured the world as conductor to a theatrical company, married a poetess (Helen von Schweitzer, d.

1961, who supplied him with much excellent material for the exercise of his art), became director of music at New Brighton, near Liverpool, and at last came to rest (not in the sense of 'repose', however) as Principal of the School of Music at Birmingham and Professor of Music at the University there, remaining in these last positions until 1934, when he became chairman of the Corporation of Trinity College of Music, London.

He wrote a quantity of fine songs and part-songs, orchestral music, and, especially, choral music on a very large scale, including choral symphonies (without orchestra). Some of his compositions show his interest in Eastern thought (e.g. *Omar Khayyám*, for solos, chorus, and orchestra) and others in the spirit of the Gael (e.g. the 'Hebridean' Symphony for orchestra). He was knighted in 1930.

See passing references under *Symphony* 8 (1868); *Choral Symphony*; *Suite* 8; *Competitions in Music* 2, 3; *Flute Family* 4; *Bell* 4; *Pibroch*; *Degrees and Diplomas* 2 (Bandsmen's College of Music).

BANTU MUSIC. See *Harmony* 4.

BAPTIST CHURCHES AND MUSIC

1. Introductory.
2. The Dispute as to Congregational Singing.
3. The Introduction of Hymns.
4. Choirs and Orchestras.
5. Conditions in the 20th Century.
6. The Churches in the United States.

1. Introductory. The Baptists in Britain have always been of two divisions—that of the General Baptists, dating from 1611 (when it was formed in Holland, amongst the exiled Independents; see *Congregational Churches and Music* 1), and that of the Particular Baptists, dating from 1633. The common ground between them has always been the conviction that the Church, according to New Testament teaching, consists of persons who, being of age to make a decision, have done so; and the dividing line is that between the Arminian view that salvation is open to all believers ('General Redemption') and what is generally called the Calvinistic view, that it is open only to the elect ('Particular Redemption'). The two bodies joined in 1891 in the Baptist Union of Great Britain and Ireland (the 'Strict Baptists' and some smaller bodies retaining their independence). Seventy-five years later they were found to have rather over 300,000 enrolled members.

Roger Williams, in 1638, founded the first Baptist Church in America. The various Baptist denominations of the United States had in 1965 some twenty-two million enrolled members—about a third of all Protestants in that country; of Negroes enrolled as church members, 66 per cent. are Baptists. The Baptists of other countries are very numerous, and next to the Methodists the Baptists constitute the largest Protestant denomination of the world.

As the Baptist system of church organization is in principle Independent (cf. *Congregational Churches* 1), and as each church is thus free to organize its own type of service, and even to lay down its own creed, it will be understood that no general system of the use of music in worship has been possible, and that individual churches have always differed greatly, and still differ, in the degree of importance they attach to the cultivation of the art as an aid to devotion.

2. The Dispute as to Congregational Singing. At the time of the foundation of the Baptist denomination in Britain the music in practically all churches, except the Anglican cathedrals and some of the chapels of the colleges at Oxford and Cambridge, consisted merely of metrical versions of the psalms (see *Hymns and Hymn Tunes* 5; *Anglican Parish Church Music* 1, 3; *Congregational Churches and Music* 2). The extreme views of the founder of the English Baptists, John Smith or Smyth, led him to impose restrictions on the practice of congregational singing: 'We hold that, seeing a psalm is a part of spiritual worship, it is unlawful to have the book before the eye in singing a psalm.' That sort of extreme scrupulosity was typical of Baptist thought for many generations. There were always churches that sang, and always churches that opposed congregational singing on such grounds as (a) the risk of the impropriety of unbelievers taking part in the public praise of God; (b) the danger that singing other men's words might open 'a gap for set forms of prayer'; or (c) the danger that the 'singing by art of pleasant tunes' might bring back instruments into public worship—and then 'farewell to all solemnity!'

These objections (1678) are here quoted from Thomas Grantham, a leader of the General Baptists; they are offered merely as typical. In 1689 the General Baptist Assembly discussed the whole question. It found that the book most used was that of William Barton (q.v.; apparently his book of Psalms is meant, not one of his books of hymns), which had, like most metrical psalm books of the period, 'rules for singing these Psalms *secundum artem*, viz., as the musicians do sing according to their gamut, *sol*, *fa*, *la*, *my*, *ray*, etc.; all of which appeared so strangely foreign to the evangelical worship that it was not conceived anywise safe for the churches to admit such carnal formalities'.

Amongst the Particular Baptists a similar view was taken by many. It weakened greatly as the result of a pamphlet war in 1691, centring about the views and practice of Benjamin Keach, pastor of Horsleydown, on the south side of London (see 3). He had suffered the pillory and other punishments and had often been endangered by this practice of singing, which drew attention to his meetings, as when, in the days of penal laws against nonconformity (which ended with the Toleration Act of 1689), administering the Lord's Supper to his congregation at 'Widow Cope's house', and 'singing a hymn, the officers of the parish soon attended them, but having the conveniency of a back door, they all escaped except one'.

A practice in Keach's church and in some other churches where singing was a part of the service was to place it either at the beginning of the service, so that those whose consciences were against it could remain in the vestry until it was over, or at the end, so that such members of the congregation could leave before it began. Up to the middle of the eighteenth century this friendly and reasonable accommodation was to be found in practice here and there, and throughout that period there appeared learned works such as (1737) David Rees's *Reasons for and against the Singing of Psalms in Private and Public Worship, Inscribed to the Baptist Congregations in Great Britain and Ireland, wherein the Ground of that Controversial Practice is impartially laid down.*

Amongst those who approved of singing, as such, there were also, from time to time, discussions as to the propriety of restricting it to the metrical psalms or extending it to hymns (cf. *Presbyterian Churches and Music* 3); as to the propriety of admitting instruments; as to the propriety of allowing women to join in the singing; as to the propriety of abandoning 'lining-out' (see *Hymns and Hymn Tunes* 8); in fact, strict propriety was then a good deal considered, and definite scriptural warrant was required for pretty well everything in worship or church government—with the inconvenience that necessarily arises from varying individual interpretations of scripture.

John Bunyan was pastor of a Baptist congregation and it is of interest to consider his attitude towards music. He probably represents the Baptist community in general in seeing no objection to music as such. *Pilgrim's Progress* and his other works abound in references to music and dancing, of a sort that shows that he approved of both. There are still in existence his violin of metal (probably made by himself, for he was brought up to metal-working, and bearing his name engraved upon it), and a flute traditionally attributed to him (p. 865, pl. 146. 5, 6). Yet there was no singing in Bunyan's own church at Bedford during his lifetime; two years after his death (i.e. in 1690) a church meeting discussed the subject and gravely decided, by a majority of eighteen to two, 'That Publick Singing of Psalms be practised by the Church with a caushion that non others perform it but such as can sing with grace in their Hearts According to the Command of Christ'. It is not, of course, to be necessarily inferred that Bunyan himself was against public singing but it is rather surprising to find it excluded from the services of a church possessing so definitely music-loving a pastor.

3. The Introduction of Hymns. The debate upon the use of hymns, as distinct from metrical psalms, was, with the Baptists as with other denominations, often bitter. Keach's congregation (see 2) suffered a fission when in 1691 he issued a collection of original hymns —his being the first Baptist church to sing hymns as distinct from psalm versions.

The Methodist movement (see *Methodism and Music*) had a great influence upon the Baptist denomination, which was, in many places, inspired to new activity. Towards the end of the eighteenth century the General Baptists (although some were still opposed to all congregational singing and the embers of controversy were from time to time blown into fresh flame) published a good many collections of hymns. The Particular Baptists were issuing such collections right through the century, and as it drew to its close were especially prolific. The hymn books were, however, at first considered to be supplementary to the books of metrical psalms which were still in use. The Revd. Dr. John Rippon issued in 1787 a book of hymns intended to accompany Watts's psalm versions (see *Congregational Churches and Music* 3) and in 1791 a *Selection of Psalms and Hymn Tunes from the Best Authors*. New editions appeared up to well after the middle of the nineteenth century, the *Comprehensive Rippon* of 1844 (containing over 1,100 hymns in 100 different metres) being a book well known to all hymnologists today. In 1858 *Psalms and Hymns* (issued by the Particular Baptists) appeared and had a large influence. In 1866 Spurgeon issued *Our Own Hymn Book*. In 1879 appeared *The Baptist Hymnary*, which largely superseded all previous books. It was replaced in 1900 by the *Baptist Church Hymnal* (revised edition 1956).

4. Choirs and Orchestras. The impression of austerity that, on the whole, the story of Baptist music has, up to this point, no doubt presented, may be a little relieved by an allusion to activities in the north of England. Here, at least, instrumental music found an entrance comparatively early. An example is seen in the valley of Rossendale in Lancashire, where for nearly two centuries a group of instrumental and vocal musicians flourished, to whom was given the familiar name of 'The Deign Layrocks', i.e. the Larks of Dean (one of the villages of the valley). About 1720 this group went over to the Baptist Church, and with their orchestral playing and their specially written tunes they maintained the services of the valley on a high musical level. The names of many of their tunes are quaint—*Sparking Roger, Lark Tune, Happy Simeon, Sweet Harmony, Marvellous, Novelty, Grim Death.*

The families of Nuttall, Hargreaves, and Ashworth supplied many members of the group. Caleb Ashworth (1722–75), a carpenter, who seceded to Independency and became a minister, a D.D., and head of a theological college, published not merely a Hebrew grammar, a treatise on trigonometry, and a number of sermons, but also *A Collection of Tunes* (1760; three editions during the next six years; see *Congregational Churches and Music* 3) and an *Introduction to the Art of Singing* (London, 1770). The group greatly cultivated Handel and contributed singers to the Westminster Abbey Handel Festival of 1784 (see *Festival*). There is a tradition in the valley that the arrival of the first printed copy of *Messiah* was greeted with selections from that work (evidently already known from manuscript) as the carrier's cart entered the village. The community possessed several craftsmen capable of supplying it with stringed instruments. Its activities died out in the middle of the nineteenth century, apparently as the result of the installation of organs (e.g. Cloughfield 1852; Lumb 1858).

There were other places in the north of England and the midlands where Baptist church services were enlivened with instrumental and choral music. Indeed, the Baptist musicians in general came at last to play their full part in that eighteenth- and early nineteenth-century activity amongst simple-minded musical people which made the choir pew, both in the Establishment and in Nonconformity, a centre of orchestral and choral culture (cf. *Anglican Parish Church Music* 4; *Methodism* 5, 6, 7). An example of the type of man who was prominent in such work is Thomas Jarman, of Clipstone, Northamptonshire, who, from 1800 onwards, published over 600 hymn tunes and many anthems and settings of the Canticles, and who in 1837, at Naseby, organized a village choir festival that was long remembered. Another was Henry Dennis, of Tickenhill, Derbyshire, a fiddler and singer who published many hymn tunes. The spirit of the old country musicians is seen in the incident of the village players, on the news of the death of Dennis, coming and playing outside the house his tune *Euphony* (published in 1850 and still sung all over the world); part of this tune and a violin are carved on his gravestone.

5. Conditions in the Twentieth Century. Dr. W. T. Whitley, Secretary of the Baptist Historical Society, made in 1933 the following rather surprising statement:

'Some Baptist churches may still be found in isolated places which cling to the methods of that age [the early nineteenth century]. In the pews may be seen old-fashioned tune-books printed from copper plates, vocal scores with ancient clefs. A precentor blows a pitch-pipe, calculates the keynote, which he hums to a few neighbours and then, with the second or third note the whole congregation joins in. Such little Bethels still exhibit to the Christian a type of severe and genuine piety, to the musician a specimen of fine unaccompanied part-singing.'

The town Baptist churches of today are, however, equipped with organs, and their services differ musically in no general way from those of other Nonconformist bodies. The Anglican Chant (q.v.), the Anthem, and the simpler 'Service' settings of the Canticles (see *Service*) are in use.

6. The Churches in the United States. In the American colonies emigrants early established Baptist churches. The sojourn in Pennsylvania, in the seventeenth century, of Elias Keach (son of Benjamin, see 2, 3), and his foundation of churches there, probably led to the practice of hymn-singing. The opposition to organs seems to have lasted rather longer in some parts of the United States than in England.

As one of the most numerous, wealthy, and influential religious bodies of the United States the Baptists now possess many large (sometimes almost cathedral-like) churches and their music is on a commensurate scale.

For some particulars of the very interesting musical activities of the German Baptist Brethren at Ephrata Cloister, Pennsylvania, in the eighteenth century, see *United States* 3.

BAR, BAR LINE. See *Measure*; *Notation* 4; *Rhythm* 3; *History of Music* 5.

BARBARIE, ORGUE DE. See *Mechanical Reproduction of Music* 6.

BARBARY BELL. See *Saint Patrick's Day*.

BARBER, SAMUEL. Born at West Chester, Pennsylvania, in 1910. He studied at the Curtis Institute, Philadelphia. At twenty-five he won the American Rome Prize (see *Prix de Rome* 3), and two years running (the first to achieve this) the Pulitzer Prize (see *Patronage* 7). He has composed chiefly orchestral and chamber music in an individual style, neither highly experimental nor dully conservative, but lyrical and expressive, and some of it has had much performance; especially, perhaps, his early *Adagio for Strings* and his overture, *The School for Scandal*. His opera *Vanessa*, with libretto by his friend Menotti, won the 1958 Pulitzer Prize, and his *Anthony and Cleopatra* inaugurated the new Metropolitan Opera House (1966). He is the nephew of Louise Homer, the opera singer (see reference under *Homer, Sidney*).

See *Concerto* 6 c (1910); *History* 9; *Opera* 24 f (1958); *Symphony* 8; also p. 1068, pl. **175.** 9.

BARBER OF SEVILLE, THE (Rossini). Produced in Rome in 1816. Libretto by Sterbini, founded on the comedy by Beaumarchais. (Cf. *Marriage of Figaro*.) Italian title, *Il Barbiere di Siviglia* (originally *Almaviva*).

ACT I

SCENE 1: *A Street in Seville, by the House of Dr. Bartolo. Time, seventeenth century*

Count **Almaviva** (*Tenor*), attended by his servant **Fiorello** (*Tenor*), is serenading Rosina, the rich ward of Dr. Bartolo, whom the doctor intends to marry. **Figaro** (*Baritone*), the popular barber, comes along, and, being well known as a clever fellow who understands all the city's intrigues, is engaged by the count to further his amour. The lover is to be disguised as a tipsy soldier who is billeted on the doctor, and so to gain admittance to his house.

SCENE 2: *A Room in Dr. Bartolo's House*

Rosina (*Soprano*) has fallen in love with her serenader, whom she knows as 'Lindor'. Here occurs the famous aria 'Una voce poco fa'. She writes to 'Lindor', and a trusty messenger happens to turn up—the ubiquitous Figaro, who hides in the room, whilst her guardian **Dr. Bartolo** (*Bass*) and **Don Basilio** (*Bass*), a singing master, discuss the former's suspicions of the count. Basilio suggests starting a scandal about the unwanted lover. Bartolo thinks the best thing is to draw up a contract of his marriage to his ward. ('When once her husband, I'll know how to rule her!')

Figaro has overheard the plot, and he and Rosina discuss the next move. Bartolo comes back and questions Rosina, but she manages to deceive him.

Now the count plays his drunken-soldier masquerade, and contrives to tell Rosina that he is Lindor; but he is arrested, and only set free on proving himself, to the officer of the guard, to be a nobleman. The doctor and Basilio are still in the dark.

ACT II

SCENE: *Dr. Bartolo's House, as before*

The count's next attempt is to disguise himself as a music teacher, come to give Rosina her lesson in the place of Basilio, who, he says, is ill. He shows Bartolo the letter Rosina wrote, and pretends that he can persuade Rosina that he got it from one of the count's mistresses. He begins Rosina's music lesson, but is interrupted by Figaro, come to shave Bartolo. Bartolo leaves them, and the count and Rosina plot to run away.

Basilio enters, and seems likely to spoil the plan, but is bribed to be 'ill' (as had been alleged) and to clear out of the way. When Bartolo returns, to be shaved, he overhears the arrangement for flight, and decides to wed Rosina at once.

At midnight the count and Figaro carry off Rosina. Just then Basilio comes with a notary ready to witness the marriage of the doctor, not yet arrived. Threat and bribe quickly convince Basilio where his interest lies, and the lovers are made man and wife. Bartolo is satisfactorily consoled with Rosina's dowry, instead of her hand.

See also *Opera* 21 c d; *Opera Buffa*; *Conducting* 2; *Arrangement*; *Patter Song*.

BARBER SHOP MUSIC. One of the regular haunts of music in the sixteenth, seventeenth, and early eighteenth centuries was the barber's shop. Here customers awaiting their turn for shaving, hair-cutting, blood-letting, or tooth-drawing found some simple instrument (apparently almost always the *Cittern*, q.v.) on which they could strum. The barbers themselves, in their waiting time between cus-

tomers, took up the instrument and thus came to possess some repute as performers.

Cervantes in *Don Quixote* (1604) says: 'Of the priest I will say nothing; but I will venture a wager he has the point and collar of a poet, and that Master Nicholas, the barber, has them too, I make no doubt; for most or all of that faculty are players on the guitar and song makers' (Jarvis's translation, ch. cxix).

Morley, in his *Plain and Easy Introduction to Practical Music* (1597), reflects on the standard of the barbers' performance, making one of the characters in his dialogue say: 'You keep not time in your proportions; you sing them false . . . nay, you sing you know not what, it shoulde seeme you came lately from a Barber's shop.'

Ben Jonson, in his *Silent Woman* (1609), has a man take a wife on the barber's recommendation, to find that she is always talking. He says, 'That cursed barber! I have married his cittern' (i.e. an instrument that, in the hands of one waiting customer or another, was always sounding).

Hawkins, in his *History of Music*, gives some particulars of the late seventeenth-century musician John Est, who, as a barber, became proficient on the cittern and then passed on to fame as a performer on the more important and difficult lyra-viol (see *Viol Family* 4 c). The following is an extract from a contemporary poem on Est:

Each barber writes himself in strictest rules,
Master or bachelor i' th' musick schools,
How they the mere musitians do out-go,
These one, but they have two strings to their bow.

The musical proclivities of barbers ceased in England in the earlier part of the eighteenth century. Dr. William King (*Works*, vol. ii, 1760) says that they took to periwig-making (i.e. added an occupation that filled their vacant time) and forgot their music.

Apparently the tradition was maintained longer in America. Steinert, the great Boston musical instrument dealer, speaks of a man with whom he lodged in Georgia about 1860, 'As once upon a time he had been a barber he knew how to play the guitar'. The impresario Hammerstein in 1908 cancelled his promise to put on a certain Spanish opera because the score called for a large number of guitar players —'More than I could get together readily; I should have been obliged to engage all the barbers in New York' (reported by van Vechten in *The Music of Spain*).

The expressions 'Barber-shop music' and 'Barber-shop harmony' are still current in the United States. Apparently few who use them can give any account of their origin. They are generally applied to the rough-and-ready choral harmonization of popular tunes by any convivial party. In 1931 we find the Neosho, Mo., *Miner and Mechanic* lamenting that the 'barber-shop quartet' (i.e. vocal quartet) is a thing of the past, but in 1948 it was reported that a 'Society for the Preservation and Encouragement of Barber Shop Singing' existed (founded 1938 at Tulsa, Oklahoma), which boasted 23,000 members—including a branch allegedly made up of U.S. Senators. In that year the Manhattan branch of the Society announced a contest to be held in Carnegie Hall, New York. An organization of female barber shop quartets, the Sweet Adelines, Inc., claimed in 1959 over 8,000 members.

The allusion of the above American expressions may originally have been either to the vamping type of simple harmonic accompaniment on a guitar or to the beguilement of song in the days when a small-town barber's shop was a centre of social gathering for the men of the place. Possibly, however, these terms are a mere survival of an English expression now obsolete in the land of its origin—'Barber's Music'—for any kind of extemporized noisy tune-making; so we find that Pepys, on board the ship that went to fetch Charles II from his exile, at the suggestion of the admiral and with the help of the lieutenant's cittern and two candlesticks with money in them as cymbals, 'made barber's music, with which my Lord was well pleased'.

The barbers are rarely or never mentioned in books of musical reference. They are included in the present one (as are the equally neglected parish clerks) because they really played a part in musical life and for a pretty extended period—and, as the Cervantes extract shows, not only in Britain. The allusions in late sixteenth- and early seventeenth-century plays to barbers as musicians are innumerable.

BARBIERE DI SIVIGLIA (Rossini). See *Barber of Seville*.

BARBIERI. See *Spain* 6; also *Mechanical Reproduction* 6.

BARCAROLLE. A type of boat song (actually vocal or in instrumental imitation), supposed to be derived from the songs of the Venetian gondoliers (see *Gondola Song*). Chopin's piano Barcarolle is well known.

BARD. See *Wales* 4.

BARDI, GIOVANNI, Count of Vernio. He was a Florentine nobleman and an active member of the artistic and literary society of his city. In his house, about the year 1600, were held the first performances of the newly devised opera. (See *Opera* 1, 2.)

BÄRENREITER. See *Publishing* 8.

BARGIEL, WOLDEMAR. Born in Berlin in 1828 and died there in 1897, aged sixty-nine. He was a stepbrother of Clara Schumann, a disciple of her husband, and a composer of some repute.

BARING-GOULD, REVD. SABINE (1834–1924). Hymn-writer, folk-song collector, etc. (See *Folk Song* 3.) His hymn tune *Eudoxia* is very popular.

BARIOLAGE (Fr., 'motley colouring'). In violin playing, a quickly repeated shifting from a stopped string to an open string.

BARITON, BARYTON. See *Viol Family* 4 d.

BARITONE or **BARYTONE.** See *Voice* 17.

BARITONE OBOE. See *Oboe Family* 5 i.

BARITONE (SAXHORN). See *Saxhorn and Flügelhorn Families* 2 d.

BARKAROLE (Ger.). Barcarolle (q.v.).

BARLESS. See *Pianoforte* 16.

BARLEY, WILLIAM. Music printer. He held an assignment of monopoly from Morley and after Morley's death had the monopoly in his own name. (See *Morley*; *Monopolies*; *Hymns and Hymn Tunes* 17 e xi.)

BARLEY SHOT. This 'Welsh folk tune' is a Scotch air, *O gin I were fairly shut of her* (in the English language, 'O if only I were rid of her'). The title became abbreviated in some collections to 'Fairly shut', and then corrupted, presumably through somebody citing it and being misheard, into 'Barley shot'. The facts will be found in an article by the great authority on British song, Frank Kidson, in the *Musical Times*, February 1911.

BÄRMANN, HEINRICH JOSEPH (1784–1847). Great clarinettist (Weber's clarinet works were written for him). See *Clarinet Family* 6. His son Karl (1811–85) was also a famous clarinettist and composed much for his instrument.

BARNARD.

(1) REVD. JOHN. See *Cathedral Music* 4.
(2) LADY ANNE. See *Auld Robin Gray*.
(3) MRS. See *Come back to Erin*.

BARNARD'S COLLECTION. See *Scotland* 5.

BARNBY, JOSEPH. Born at York in 1838 and died in London in 1896, aged fifty-seven. He was a great choral conductor, and successively director of music at Eton College and principal of the Guildhall School of Music. He was knighted in 1892. His compositions include oratorios and part-songs and church music, formerly much sung.

See *Anthem* (Period V).

BARN DANCE. This rural American dance perhaps originated in the festivals customary on the building of a new barn—the consecration of it by jollity, so to speak. The practice may have its roots far back in pagan European practices and be akin to the old ritual dances connected with sowing and harvest, though it is, perhaps, hardly necessary to find an ancestral religious motive when the mere existence of a new large room, momentarily unoccupied, or perhaps the wish to reward neighbours who have helped with the building, will sufficiently account for the practice.

The music of the barn dance is in four-in-a-measure time.

During the late 1940s a considerable interest in this dance became observable in England.

BARNEA, AVIASAF. See *Jewish Music* 9.

BARNETT.

(1) JOHN. He was born at Bedford in 1802 and died near Cheltenham in 1890, aged nearly

eighty-eight. He was of foreign descent, the original name of his father, a German, being 'Beer' (as that of Meyerbeer, a relation), and his mother being a Hungarian. As a boy vocalist he appeared regularly on the London opera stage and all his life he was active as a composer of stage music, his most valued work being the opera *The Mountain Sylph* (1834). He also composed quantities of vocal solos and duets. During his last fifty years his residence was at Cheltenham, where he practised as a singing-master.

(2) JOHN FRANCIS. He was born in London in 1837 (the son of a well-known singing-teacher, Joseph Alfred Barnett and nephew of John Barnett, above), and there died in 1916, aged seventy-nine. He was trained at the Royal Academy of Music (of which he was later to be a professor) and the Leipzig Conservatory, and won a high reputation as a pianist and piano-teacher, and also as a composer of choral, orchestral, chamber, and piano music. Perhaps his most successful work was the cantata *The Ancient Mariner* (Birmingham Festival, 1867).

BAROCCO (It.), **BAROCK** (Ger.), **BAROQUE** (Fr.). 'Bizarre.' In architecture this has been applied since about 1867 to the highly decorated style (full of curves) of the seventeenth and eighteenth centuries in Germany and Austria. By association it has come to be applied (from about 1918 in Germany, and thence from 1939 in the U.S.A.) to the music of Bach's time, and sometimes also to that of a somewhat earlier period (from Monteverdi) and a somewhat later one; though a protest is possible on account of the long-standing use of the word in a more or less depreciatory sense.

The term 'baroque organ' is used in speaking of the few organs that remain in the state in which they were in Bach's day (e.g. the Silbermann organ at Rötha on which Bach himself is known to have played) and to modern imitations of these (such as the one at the University of Freiburg im Breisgau and the one in the Germanic Museum at Harvard University). Such expressions as 'a Sesquialtera of Baroque type' are now met with. Fortunately the rather better term 'classical organ' is used in some quarters.

The adjective 'baroque' seems most in place as used by President de Brosses in 1739 to describe Italian vocal composition of that high period of *Coloratura* (q.v.). Burney in his German Tour (1773), after using the term, gives its equivalents as 'coarse and uncouth'— much as writers then often used the word 'Gothic'. So does Rousseau in his *Dictionary of Music* (1767). This sense is now discarded.

Edward Holmes (q.v.), in his *Ramble among the Musicians of Germany* (1828), speaking of Boïeldieu's *La Dame blanche*, says that 'Noise, violent changes of key, and that species of modulation which may be termed *baroque*, are its characteristics'.

Cf. *Zopf*; *Ornaments* 3; *Rococo*.

BAROQUE ARCHITECTURE AND MUSIC. See *Barocco*; *Zopf*; *Ornaments* 3.

BARRAUD, HENRY. Born at Bordeaux in 1900. After a period in his family's wine business he entered the Paris Conservatory at the age of twenty-six. In 1945 he became musical director of the Paris Radio. He has written radio and film music, orchestral works, chamber music, etc.

BARRE. See *Capotasto*.

BARREL ORGAN. See *Mechanical Reproduction of Music* 10.

BARRÈRE, GEORGE. See p. 173, pl. **36. 3.**

BARRETT, THOMAS A. See *Stuart, Leslie*.

BARRIOS, ANGEL. Born at Granada in 1882. He is a violinist and the composer of orchestral works and operas, as also of guitar music much used by Segovia (q.v.).

BARTH, HANS (1897–1956). See *Microtones*; *Concerto* 6 c (1896); also p. 356, pl. **57. 5.**

BARTHÉLEMON, FRANÇOIS HIPPOLYTE. Born at Bordeaux in 1741 and died in London in 1808, aged sixty-six. He was a violinist and composer who in his early twenties settled in London and wrote operas and other stage music, violin music, etc. His tune to Ken's Morning Hymn is found in all English hymn collections.

BARTHOLOMEW FAIR. See *Fairs*.

BARTLET or **BARTLETT, JOHN.** End of sixteenth and beginning of seventeenth centuries. He was a lute player and composer of songs of the ayre type (see *Madrigal* 3 b). His life-history is obscure.

BARTLEY, WILLIAM. See *Electric* 2 b.

BARTÓK, BÉLA (p. 480, pl. **83. 5**). Born in 1881 at a small place then in Hungary but now in Rumania and died in 1945 in New York, aged sixty-four. His mother was his first music teacher, and, as his father died young, she had to support her family as a schoolmistress. In order to give him the advantages of a large town she managed to move to Pressburg, where more advanced music teaching was available and concerts and operas could be attended. His early life in country places had aroused in him an interest in folk music.

His first style as a composer was much influenced by the music of Brahms and by that of the Brahms-minded Dohnányi, on whose advice he moved to Budapest to study at the Conservatory, there remaining until he was twenty-two.

At the time he was an ardent student of Liszt and Wagner and for two years he relinquished his own composition, coming to be regarded as a brilliant pianist. At twenty-one he heard Strauss's tone-poem, *Thus spake Zoroaster* ('Also sprach Zarathustra'), which then horrified the middle-aged and entranced the young; he re-commenced composition, now in a Straussian manner.

F

The Strauss enthusiasm quickly waned, and a renewed period of Liszt study followed. The folk-music interest continued, but with a change—he came to realize that the songs usually known as Hungarian folk songs were of but superficial value, whilst all the time, quite unknown to musicians, amongst the genuine peasantry there existed a repertory of much older, finer, and more significant music. In the collection of this music he had a devoted collaborator in the person of a newly made friend, Zoltán Kodály (q.v.). To the study of Magyar tune was added that of Slovak and Rumanian tune. Few of the melodies collected were in the conventional major and minor scales. The ancient scales, in their variety, though abandoned in serious composition, were, then, still alive, and Bartók resolved to use them. Naturally, in doing so, he found himself bringing into existence new harmonies, and this, in time, led to his gradual abandonment of the existing diatonic system and of the chromatic system based upon it, and to the gradual taking up of a new style in which the twelve notes of the chromatic scale were considered as independent entities, ready to submit to all sorts of unheard-of combinations.

At twenty-six Bartók was appointed a professor at the Budapest Conservatory. His compositions met with great opposition in that city. He persevered in the task he had set himself, however, and continued the energetic collection of the peasant material that had inspired him. Straitened financial resources and the circumstances of the first World War were an impediment to the wider travels he had in mind, but he got as far as Biskra and made some study of Arab music. At the end of the war the public of Budapest became less hostile to the national composer in their midst. The pantomime ballet, *The Wooden Prince*, was heard (1922) and so was the earlier one-act opera, *Bluebeard's Castle*.

In 1940 Bartók left Europe for the United States. Here he found a temporary post at Columbia University (which conferred on him its doctorate of music) and also lectured for a time at Harvard. His health deteriorated, however, and on 26 September 1945, after a year in hospital, he passed away in his sleep.

Bartók's compositions are fairly numerous. They include, in addition to the stage works just mentioned, orchestral music, some choral music (e.g. *Cantata Profana*), six string quartets, violin sonatas, a large number of piano compositions (including three concertos), a violin concerto, and a good many volumes of arrangements of folk songs. There are also a great number of collections of folk music scientifically displayed (altogether Bartók collected about 7,000 tunes; see *Hungary* for his conclusions), and *Mikrokosmos* (153 piano pieces progressively arranged from very easy to very difficult); also student editions of classical works.

See references under *History* 8; *Romantic*; *Harmony* 21; *Pianoforte Playing* 10; *Pantomime*; *Hungary*; *Rumania*; *Russia* 8; *Stevens, H.*; *Ballet* 5; *Opera* 24 f (1918); *Concerto* 6 c (1881); *Jazz* 7.

BARTON.

(1) WILLIAM. He was an early seventeenth-century clergyman whose metrical version of the Psalms passed through very many editions (1644 and into the next century). He was also one of the earliest writers of English hymns, as distinct from psalm versions.

See *Baptist Churches and Music* 2.

(2) ANDREW. See *Opera* 21 b.

BARYTON. See *Viol Family* 4 d. **BARYTON (TUBA).** See *Tuba Group* 3 a.

BARYTONE. See *Voice* 17.

BASE. See *Bass*.

BASIL, LITURGY OF SAINT. See *Greek Church and Music* 1.

BASILAR MEMBRANE. See *Ear* 1.

BASKISCHE TÄNZE. 'Basque Dances'; generally the *Pordon Dantza, Zortzico,* and *Ezcudantza* (see under these heads).

BASKISCHE TROMMEL (Ger.). Tambourine; see *Percussion Family* 3 m, 4 c, 5 m.

BASQUES (Fr.). Same as *Baskische Tänze* (above). *Pas de Basque* is sometimes a general term, also, or it may indicate a particularly ancient dance of the Basque peasantry, with very varied rhythms.

BASS. The spelling *Bass* and *Base* have both been in use; only 'Bass' remains, but both pronunciations are to be heard, 'Base' being the more common. The word is applied to the lowest part of the harmony, whether vocal or instrumental. This part is, in a certain sense, the most important and the foundation of what lies above it, chords being reckoned from (and described by means of) their bass note. The harmonics (see *Acoustics* 8) set up by this lowest note are especially prominent and so exercise a predominant influence on the 'flavour' of the chord as a whole. As an adjective the word is applied to voices (see *Voice* 17, 19) and the various types of instrument, to indicate the lowest in range.

In Ger. the word is *Bass*, in Fr. *Basse*, and in It. *Basso*.

See also compound terms beginning with these words in their alphabetical positions below.

For Acoustic Bass, Harmonic Bass, Resultant Bass, see *Acoustics* 10.

BASS, MICHAEL T. (1799–1884). See *Street Music* 7.

BASSA (It.). Feminine form of *Basso*, 'low' or 'bass'. E.g. *Ottava bassa* means 'perform the passage an octave lower than the notation gives it'.

BASSANI (or **Bassano**, or **Bassiani**).

(1) GIOVANNI. A Venetian instrumental and vocal composer of the later sixteenth and earlier seventeenth centuries.

See *Ornaments* 1.

(2) GIOVANNI BATTISTA. Born at Padua about 1657 and died at Bergamo in 1716, aged

about fifty-nine. He was a fine violinist and a highly popular composer for his instrument. Corelli is thought by some to have been his pupil. His works include operas, masses, and solo cantatas. James Kent (q.v.) boldly borrowed from him passages and whole movements for his own anthems.

BASS-BAR. The strip of wood glued on the inside of the belly of a viol, violin, etc., along the line of the lowest string. It supports the left foot of the bridge. (In occasional examples, chiefly early, the bass-bar is carved out of the wood of the belly itself, i.e. the two are in one piece.)

BASS CLARINET. See *Clarinet Family* 2, 3 b, 5.

BASS CLEF. See *Notation* 4.

BASS DRUM. See *Percussion Family* 3 k, 4, 5 k.

BASSE (Fr.). Bass (q.v.).

BASSE CHANTANTE (Fr.). *Basso cantante* (see *Voice* 19).

BASSE CHIFFRÉE, BASSE CONTINUE (Fr.). Figured Bass (q.v.) and *basso continuo* (q.v.).

BASSE DANSE. An early dance type, which became almost extinct during the sixteenth century, but which has historical importance as the probable ancestor of other dances which survived it (see *Branle*) and in some cases developed into important instrumental forms and were taken into the classical suite.

It was a serious sort of dance, and the feet were often glided, not lifted (from this the name is supposed to have arisen—the feet were kept 'low'; however, this has been contested and it has been claimed that the name merely indicates lowly origin). There are generally two beats in a measure, but apparently the early form of the dance had three, and some examples are found in which these two rhythms are mixed.

The basse danse of one period fell into three sections called respectively *Basse Danse, Return of Basse Danse,* and *Tordion.*

See *Dance* 10—near opening.

BASSE DE FLANDRES. See *Bumbass.*

BASSE DE VIOLE D'AMOUR. See *Viol Family* 4 d.

BASSE D'HARMONIE (Fr.). Ophicleide; see *Cornett and Key Bugle Families* 2 g, 3 g, 4 g.

BASSET HORN. See *Clarinet Family* 2, 4 e f, 5, 6.

BASSET OBOE. See *Oboe Family* 5 i.

BASSETTFLÖTE. (Ger.). A seventeenth- and eighteenth-century name for a Recorder (see *Recorder Family*) of low pitch. Sometimes it was called *Bassflöte.*

BASSFLICORNO. See *Tuba Group* 5.

BASSFLÖTE. See *Bassettflöte.*

BASSFLÜGELHORN. See *Saxhorn and Flügelhorn Families* 2 d.

BASS FLUTE. See *Flute Family* 3 c d, 5 c; *Organ* 14 II.

BASS HORN. See *Cornett and Key Bugle Families* 2 e, 3 e f, 4 e.

BASSI (It.). Plural of *Basso*, 'low', 'bass'.

BASSIANI. See *Bassani.*

BASSO (It.). 'Low' or 'bass' (q.v.).

BASS OBOE. See *Oboe Family* 4 i.

BASSO CANTANTE. See *Voice* 19.

BASSO CONTINUO (It.). Literally, 'continuous bass'. The term belongs to the seventeenth and eighteenth centuries, when, whatever instruments or voices were or were not for the moment in action, the keyboard performer kept the forces together and supplied a harmonic background by extemporizing chords, etc., above the bass part of the music which was before his eyes, and to which the composer had usually added figures defining the harmonies required. For practical purposes, then, *basso continuo* is 'figured bass', though the term can be applied to any bass part written or printed for the purpose described, even though it may not have had the figures added.

See *Figured Bass.*

BASSON. (Fr.). Bassoon. See *Oboe Family* 5 c.

BASSON QUINTE. See *Oboe Family* 4 h.

BASSON RUSSE (Fr.). Russian bassoon, so called; see *Cornett and Key Bugle Families* 2 f, 3 f, 4 f.

BASSOON. See *Oboe Family* 2, 3 c, 5 c, *Organ* 14 VI.

BASSOON, DOUBLE. See *Oboe Family* 3 d, 5 d.

BASSOON, RUSSIAN. See *Cornett and Key Bugle Families* 2 f, 3 f, 4 f.

BASSO OSTINATO (It.). 'Obstinate bass', i.e. ground bass (q.v.).

BASSO PROFONDO. See *Voice* 19.

BASSPOSAUNE (Ger.). Bass trombone. See *Trombone Family* 2 d, 3, 5.

BASS RECORDER. See *Recorder Family* 2.

BASS-SAITE (Ger.). 'Bass string', i.e. the lowest on any (bowed or plucked) instrument.

BASS STAFF. See *Great Staff.*

BASS TROMBONE. See *Trombone Family* 2 d, 3, 5.

BASSTROMPETE. Bass trumpet. See *Trumpet Family* 2 f, 5.

BASS TRUMPET. See *Trumpet Family* 2 f, 5.

BASS TUBA. See *Tuba Group* 2 b, 3.

BASSUS. See *Voice* 17.

BASS VIOL. See *Viol Family* 3.

BASS VOICE. See *Voice* 17, 19.

BASTARDA, VIOLA. See *Viol Family* 4 c d.

BATE, STANLEY. Born at Plymouth in 1913 and died in London in 1959, aged forty-six. He began as a pianist, won a scholarship for composition at the Royal College of Music, where he studied under Vaughan Williams, and then, with a travelling scholarship, went abroad, taking further lessons from Nadia Boulanger and others.

His varied output includes 4 symphonies, concertos, incidental music, chamber music, and songs. From 1946 to 1950 he was resident in the United States.

BATES, KATHARINE LEE. See *America the Beautiful*; *National Anthems*.

BATESON, THOMAS. Born about 1570 and died in Dublin in 1630, aged about sixty. He was organist of Chester Cathedral and then of Christ Church Cathedral, Dublin, and a fine composer of madrigals. So far as is known he was the first graduate in music of Trinity College, Dublin (B.Mus., 1615).

BATH. See *Linley Family*; *Herschel, F. W.*; *Street Music* 3; *Clubs*; *Turk*.

BATH, HUBERT. Born at Barnstaple in 1883 and died at Uxbridge in 1945, aged sixty-one. He wrote stage and other music, chiefly of the somewhat lighter kind, and served as musical adviser to the London County Council, directing the organization of its park bands.

BATISTE, ANTOINE ÉDOUARD. Born in Paris in 1820 and died there in 1876, aged fifty-six. He held various important organ posts in Paris and was a great practitioner of Solfeggio, which he taught at the Conservatory and on which he wrote textbooks. His organ compositions keep his name faintly alive in the English-speaking world; within recent memory some of them were enormously popular, in particular a certain Andante in the form of an insipid air with florid variations, very easy to play and grateful to the less musically adult members of the congregation.

See *Melody* 7.

BATON.

(1) HENRI (born *c.* 1710). See *Bagpipe Family* 6.

(2) CHARLES (d. 1758). Brother of the above and a famous Parisian virtuoso and composer for the hurdy-gurdy (q.v.).

(3) RENÉ. See *Rhené-Baton*.

BATON. See *Conducting*.

BATTEN, ADRIAN. Born about 1585–90 and died in London in 1637. He was an organist of St. Paul's Cathedral, London, and a prolific composer of music for the Anglican Church.

See mention under *Cathedral Music* 10.

BATTERIE (Fr.). The noisier percussion instruments (see *Percussion Family* 4 b). Sometimes, too, the term is used for the whole body of percussion instruments, and sometimes, further, for any rhythmic formulae such as those used in the army for signalling. The word is also an old French name for *arpeggio*.

BATTISHILL, JONATHAN (p. 165, pl. **34**. 2). Born in London in 1738 and died there in 1801, aged sixty-three. He was one of the most eminent London musical practitioners of his time—organist and theatre musician and

composer for church, stage, and glee club. Some of his church compositions (e.g. his very fine anthem, *O Lord, look down*) and glees are still in favour.

He married an actress who then eloped with an actor, whereupon his flow of composition seemed stopped at the source and he gave himself to classical study.

He lies buried in St. Paul's Cathedral.

See references under *Anthem*, Period III; *Methodism* 2.

BATTLE CRY OF FREEDOM ('We'll rally round the flag, boys!'). Words and music are by George Frederick Root (1820–95). Written at the time of the American Civil War, it became a marching song of the Northern troops.

BATTLE OF PRAGUE. See *Kotzwara*.

BATTRE (Fr.). 'To beat.' So *Battre à deux temps*, 'to beat 2 in a bar'.

BATTUTA, BATTUTE (It.). 'Beat', 'beats'. So *a battuta* means 'to the beat', i.e. return to strict time again after some deviation from it, as, for instance, an *accelerando* or a *rallentando* or an *a piacere*, a strain of recitative, a cadenza, and so forth.

But, dating back to some pre-conducting period when a time-beater indicated merely the beginnings of the measures (bars), *Battuta* has, in addition to the general meaning above given, a precise one of 'measure' or 'bar' (indeed *misura* and *battuta* are synonyms). Thus *ritmo di tre battute* (as found, for instance, in Beethoven) does not mean 'three-beat rhythm', but 'three-measure rhythm' (i.e. three measures in each phrase, instead of the more normal four; cf. *Rhythm* 5).

BAUDRIER, YVES. Born at Paris in 1906. From law study he turned to music and has written orchestral works, etc. (See *Jeune France*).

BAUER.

(1) MARION. Born at Walla Walla, Wash., in 1887 and died at South Hadley, Mass., in 1955, aged sixty-seven. After study in Europe she became eminent as a teacher, lecturer, and writer with special sympathy for contemporary music and the problems of the composer. Her own compositions are numerous.

(2) LUDWIG. See *O Deutschland*.

BAUERNLEIER, BAWREN LEYER (Ger.) Hurdy-gurdy (q.v.).

BAX, ARNOLD EDWARD TREVOR (p. 352, pl. **55**. 3). Born in London in 1883 and died at Cork in 1953, aged nearly seventy. He was trained at the Royal Academy of Music, where his principal teachers were Corder and Matthay.

In his early phase as a composer he was a good deal influenced by the poetry of W. B. Yeats, and by the folk music of Ireland, where he travelled widely. Though not of Irish descent, he felt deep sympathy for things Celtic, and wrote short stories and poems under the pseudonym of 'Dermot O'Byrne'.

Amongst his plentiful output are to be found

a number of songs, some effective choral music (e.g. *Mater Ora Filium* for double choir, 1921), shorter pianoforte pieces, chamber music employing rather unusual instrumental combinations, and, especially, large-scale orchestral works, including symphonic poems (*November Woods, The Garden of Fand, Tintagel*, etc.), seven symphonies, a violin concerto, a viola concerto and a cello concerto, and ballets.

His orchestration is varied and able. He expressed himself as not interested in sound for its own sake but rather in sound as an expression of emotional states: he had little sympathy with those of his contemporaries who were exploring new ground. Of the nature of his artistic mind a good deal may be learned from his brief autobiographical volume, *Farewell, my Youth* (1943).

In 1937 he was knighted and in 1942 he became Master of the King's Musick (his first and only official appointment of any kind).

He was brother of the poet, playwright, and novelist, Clifford Bax.

See *Harp* 4; *Oboe Family* 6; *Clarinet Family* 6; *Concerto* 6 c (1883); *Impressionism*; *Programme Music* 5 e; *Chapel Royal*; *Pianoforte* 21.

BAXTER, RICHARD (1615–91). Presbyterian divine and author of *The Saint's Everlasting Rest*, etc. See *Presbyterian* 6.

BAYLE (Sp.). See *Baile*.

BAYLIS, LILIAN (1874–1937). See *Victoria Hall*; *Sadler's Wells*.

BAYNE, ALEXANDER, See *Mechanical* 13.

BAY OF BISCAY. This bold song comes from an opera *Spanish Dollars* (Covent Garden, 1805), by John Davy (q.v.); he is said to have taken the melody from some Negro sailors whom he heard singing it in London. The words are by Andrew Cherry, an actor and playwright, of Irish birth and London fame.

BAY PSALM BOOK. See *Hymns and Hymn Tunes* 5, 11, 17 f; *Lancashire Sol-fa*.

BAYREUTH. See *Wagner*; *Festival* 3; *Liszt*; *Wilhelmj*.

BAZZINI, ANTONIO. He was born at Brescia in 1818 and died at Milan in 1897, aged seventy-eight. As a violinist he had great international success, but abandoned solo work in favour of chamber music playing, which was at that time neglected in Italy. In 1882 he became head of the Milan Conservatory. Of his very varied compositions the best known is the violin solo *La Ronde des lutins* ('The Dance of the Elves').

BBC. British Broadcasting Corporation.

B.B.C.M. See *Degrees and Diplomas* 2.

B DUR (Ger.). The key of B flat major (not B major: see *B*).

BE (Ger.). The sign ♭ (Table 7).

BEACH, AMY MARCY (Mrs. H. H. A. Beach, *née* Cheney, p. 1056, pl. **171**. 2). Born in New Hampshire in 1867 and died in New York in 1944, aged seventy-seven. Phenomenally gifted as a child, she soon acquired a reputation as a piano virtuoso, but this was later superseded by a recognition of her accomplishments as a composer. She was the first composer in America to write a symphony of importance ('Gaelic' Symphony—Boston Symphony Orchestra, 1896). Her songs and chamber music have often been heard.

See general remarks under *United States* 8.

BEAK FLUTE. See *Recorder Family* 2.

BEALE.

(1) WILLIAM. Born in Cornwall in 1784 and died in London in 1854, aged seventy. He was successively choir-boy in Westminster Abbey, midshipman in the navy, Gentleman of the Chapel Royal, and organist of Trinity College, Cambridge, and of London suburban churches. He wrote glees and (two centuries after their period) madrigals, some still popular.

(2) FREDERICK; (3) THOMAS WILLERT (1828–94; wrote under the pseudonym 'Walter Maynard').

For both of these see *Recital*.

BEARBEITEN (Ger.). Literally 'to be-work', 'to work over', i.e. 'to arrange'. So *Bearbeitet*, 'arranged'; *Bearbeitung*, 'arrangement' (q.v.).

'BEAR' SYMPHONY (Haydn). See *Nicknamed Compositions* 11.

BEAT. See *Rhythm*. (But for 'Beat' in its scientific sense see *Acoustics* 16; *Harmony* 21.)

BEATING REED. See *Reed*.

BEAUCHAMP (Eighteenth-century French ballet-master, etc.). See *Dance* 6 b; *Ballet* 2; *Minuet*.

BEAUCOUP (Fr.). 'Much.'

BEAUMARCHAIS, CARON DE (1732–99). See *Barber of Seville*; *Marriage of Figaro*; *Vaudeville*.

BEAUMONT.

(1) FRANCIS (1584–1616). Dramatist. See mention under *Masque*.

(2) JOHN (1761–1822). See *Methodism and Music* 6.

(3) CYRIL WILLIAM (1891–1976). See *Dance* 6.

BEBOP. See *Jazz* 7.

BEBEND (Ger.). 'Trembling', i.e. tremolo.

BEBUNG (Ger.). 'Trembling.' This is the equivalent of *Tremolo* (q.v.), but the term is generally reserved for a special effect obtainable on the *Clavichord* (q.v.) and for the vibrato of stringed instrument players obtained by a similar means (rocking the finger).

Cf. *Bebend*, above.

BÉCARRE (Fr.). The sign ♮ (Table 7).

BECHSTEIN. Piano-making firm founded in Berlin in 1853. See reference under *Electric Musical Instruments* 3 a.

BECK. Short for *Becken* (see below).

BECK, CONRAD. Born at Schaffhausen,

Switzerland, in 1901. He studied under Andreae in Zürich, then in Berlin, and finally under Honegger in Paris. He has written chamber music, symphonies, a concerto for string quartet and orchestra, a piano concerto, etc. Despite his place of final study his style is rather German than French. It is austere in tone and contrapuntal in texture. In the 1930s he settled in Basle and in 1939 he became musical director of its radio station.

BECKEN (Ger.). 'Cymbals.' See *Percussion Family* 3 o, 4 b, 5 o.

BECKER. See *Hymns and Hymn Tunes* 4.

BECKER, JOHN J. Born at Henderson, Kentucky, in 1886 and died at Wilmette, Ill., in 1961, aged nearly seventy-five. He was engaged in various musical activities in St. Paul, Mo., was director of the Federal Music Project for Minnesota, and composed seven symphonies, half a dozen concertos, choral works, etc. His style was aggressively pioneering, and few of his works were widely heard.

See *Concerto* 6 c.

BECKET, THOMAS À. See *Britannia*.

BECKWITH, JOHN CHRISTMAS. Born at Norwich in 1750 and died there in 1809, aged fifty-eight. He was organist of St. Peter Mancroft's Church, Norwich, and also, during his last year or two, of the Cathedral. As an organist he was described as 'brilliancy itself', and he extemporized fugues with the greatest ease. He left anthems, etc.

See reference under *Anglican Chant* 6; *Improvisation* 2.

BÉCOURT (late eighteenth-century Parisian violinist). See *Ça ira*.

BEDÄCHTIG (Ger.). 'Careful', 'thoughtful', 'steady and unhurried'.

BEDARFSFALL (Ger.). Literally 'need-case'. So *Im Bedarfsfalle*, 'in case of need'.

BEDEUTEND (Ger.). 'Important', i.e. considerably.

BEDFORD, HERBERT. Born in London in 1867 and died in 1945, aged seventy-eight. He exhibited as a miniature painter, wrote operas, orchestral music, music for military band, and chamber music, and made himself the champion of a new type of unaccompanied solo song. His first wife was Liza Lehmann (q.v.).

See reference under *Song* 6.

BÉDOS DE CELLES, DOM FRANCIS, sometimes called merely Dom Bédos (1709–79). A French Benedictine, famous as an organ-builder. See *Mechanical Reproduction* 6.

BEDROHLICH (Ger.). 'Menacing.'

BEECHAM (Father and Son). Sir Joseph, proprietor of a patent medicine and so enabled to become a munificent patron of music (see *Opera* 17 d), was the first baronet. His son, Sir Thomas (1879–1961), was the second. From 1905 onwards, he took an ever more important position as orchestral conductor, at home and abroad, and from 1909 to 1920 he was active as impresario of opera and ballet (introduction to London of the Russian Ballet, 1911). From 1910 he carried on continuous propaganda for the music of Delius; in 1929 he organized a festival of his music.

See p. 133, pl. **25.** 5.

'BEE'S WEDDING' (Mendelssohn). See *Nicknamed Compositions* 14.

BEETHOVEN, LUDWIG VAN (front.; p. 77, pl. **13**; pl. **14**, opposite). Born at Bonn in 1770, and died in Vienna in 1827, aged fifty-six.

More than any other composer he deserves to be called the Shakespeare of music, for he reaches to the heights and plumbs the depths of the human spirit as no other composer has done, and it was his own ambition to be called 'Tone-Poet'. In him were combined, in a measure that remains (and may for ever remain) unique, the power to feel both passionately and tenderly and the mastery of musical resources necessary to express his feelings in the most direct and vivid way.

The technical equipment that made possible this expression consisted in (1) a command of pregnant melodic phraseology and of a varied, original, and sometimes daring harmonic idiom, with (2) such a sense of the innate principles of form as went far beyond a mere successful adherence to the conventions of balance and variety of material and key, and (3) an ability to imagine his melodies and harmonies in garbs of glowing instrumental colour, whether this be drawn from the more restricted prismatic scale of the pianoforte or string quartet or from the wider ranging one of the full orchestra.

His work may, on one side of it, be regarded as the continuation of that of Haydn and Mozart and, on another, as the inspiration of that of Wagner. Such a placing in succession of four great names does not, however, hint at degrees of perfection, but only at that process of development from simplicity to complexity which, in harmony, form, and instrumental treatment, went on consistently from about the middle of the eighteenth century to near the end of the nineteenth—and for that matter is in certain ways still in progress.

Looked at in this manner, and with an eye to the type of feeling he expressed, Beethoven may be considered as the last of the classical and the first of the modern composers, or as the last of the classical and the first of the romantic composers (see the definitions of 'classical' and 'romantic' elsewhere in this book), with the proviso that all these adjectives are relative and hence applicable in some sort of way to certain composers of every period.

Beethoven was born into a poor but musical family, that of a tenor singer in the service of the Elector of Cologne at Bonn, whose father, a sound old musician, was also in this service. His first teacher was his own father, but others of the court musicians gave him instruction, notably the able and kindly Neefe, the chief

PLATE 14

BEETHOVEN NEARS THE END

By Batt

HE is seen in his workroom in the old Schwarzspanierhaus. Behind him stands his Graf piano, wrecked by his frantic efforts to hear his own playing. Odd coins lie scattered among the litter on the table. There are his ear-trumpets, his conversation books—in which any visitor would have to write what he wished to say—with a carpenter's pencil, letters, quill pens, a broken coffee cup, remnants of food and his candlestick.

The squalid disorder meant nothing to him in those days. He had finished with the world. Since 1824 the medium of the string quartet had absorbed his mind to the exclusion of all else and now, stone-deaf, very ill but still indomitable, he rose to heights which even he had never reached before. His stormy life closed with a revelation which, in the last five quartets, was the crowning glory of his achievement.   B.

musician of the court, to whom the boy, at thirteen, became unpaid assistant in the capacity of orchestral harpsichordist, a responsible position implying some of the duties of conductor. (See *Conducting* 3.) He also played the violin, in which he had been well grounded.

At seventeen he was sent by his Elector on a visit to Vienna, where he remained for three months and received a little teaching from Mozart, who fully recognized his genius. In his twenty-second year he settled in that city permanently, taking lessons at first from Haydn and Albrechtsberger. His life henceforward was one of varied monotony; that is, whilst rarely quitting the immediate district or stepping outside his regular circle of intimacies, he yet incessantly changed from apartment to apartment and street to street, made friends and quarrelled and made friends again, so adding an ever-changing seasoning to the standing dish of life.

Music (apart from the simplicities of popular performance and the ritual of the church) was then one of the recognized luxuries of wealth and position. Every (or nearly every) great composer up to this time had been dependent upon the regular emoluments of musical service at some one of the courts of Europe (of which those of Germany were very numerous). On leaving Bonn Beethoven quitted such a service, and he never entered another. Nevertheless, in the absence, as yet, of any organized system of public concerts, the scarcity of music printing, and the lack of a copyright law, he could not throw himself with confidence upon the suffrages of any wide public, but remained dependent upon the support of that body of aristocratic amateurs who on his first coming to Vienna had recognized his high ability as pianist and had later found it even surpassed by his genius as composer.

The comforts of a home were ever denied to Beethoven, for, more than once disappointed in love, he never married. When he was about thirty the first signs of deafness appeared; thence onward the malady was progressive, until at last the loss of hearing was total (see reference to Maelzel, under *Mechanical Reproduction* 8). This, however, though it exposed him to many chagrins, did not terminate, or even diminish, his musical production. The ill behaviour of a nephew who had been made his ward was another element in what we may without exaggeration call his 'tragedy'. As the gloomy background to all these misfortunes stood the suffering from frequent, and at last continuous, ill health.

In character Beethoven was upright and conscientious. By turns he was cheerful and gloomy, affectionate and irritable, trusting and suspicious. He had a good deal of humour—of that boisterous kind that is musically reproduced in several of his Scherzos. Fundamentally his was a fine nature, and such faults as he had are of the kind that so frequently cry for pardon under the disarming plea that they are ebullitions of the 'artistic temperament'.

As an artist he stands supreme in several departments. It may fairly be said that the world's finest symphonies and overtures are amongst the nine of each that he wrote, its finest pianoforte sonatas amongst his thirty-two, and its finest string quartets amongst his seventeen; and his Mass in D is strong and purposeful, and of so individual a character, that, of all choral-orchestral settings of the text, only the Mass in B minor of Bach can be said to stand on equal terms beside it. He wrote only one opera, *Fidelio*, yet in that he can be credited with having made a contribution to the permanent repertory of the theatre.

Beethoven composed slowly and with much erasure. His processes can be minutely studied by means of such of his 'sketch books' as remain. The impression, as the material for any particular composition is there examined, is that of a powerful individuality with difficulty finding its adequate means of expression, and at last, after efforts that possibly surpass those of any other composer who ever lived, forcing its way into the light of day.

Beethoven's Symphonies are as follows: No. 1, in C (op. 21, 1st perf. 1800). No. 2, in D (op. 36, 1st perf. 1803). No. 3, in E flat (the *Eroica*, op. 55, composed 1804). No. 4, in B flat (op. 60, composed 1806). No. 5, in C minor (op. 67, 1st perf. 1808). No. 6, in F (op. 68, 1st perf. 1808). No. 7, in A (op. 92, composed 1812). No. 8, in F (op. 93, composed 1812). No. 9, in D minor (op. 125, composed 1823).

Beethoven's Concertos are as follows: PIANOFORTE. No. 1, C (op. 15. Really no. 2). No. 2, B flat (op. 19, composed before 1795. Really no. 1). No. 3, C minor (op. 37, composed 1800). No. 4, G (op. 58, composed about 1805). No. 5, E flat (op. 73, nicknamed 'Emperor', composed 1809). There are also the following: Early Concerto in D (one movement only, about 1790). Rondo in B flat (incomplete; finished by Czerny). Conzertstück (either never finished or latter part lost; 2 completions, by Joseph Hellmesberger in the 1870s and by Juan Manén more recently). Violin Concerto (see below) arranged for piano by the composer himself. VIOLIN. Concerto in D (op. 61, composed 1806). PIANOFORTE, VIOLIN, AND VIOLONCELLO. Triple Concerto in C (op. 56, composed about 1804).

Beethoven's Pianoforte Sonatas number 32, ranging from op. 2 (publ. 1796) to op. 111 (composed 1822).

Beethoven's String Quartets (17 in number) are as follows: Op. 18, nos. 1–6, in F, G, D, C minor, A, and B flat (composed about 1798–1800). Op. 59, nos. 1–3, in F, E minor, and C (nicknamed the *Rasoumoffsky Quartets*, because dedicated to the Count of that name, Russian Ambassador at Vienna, and a keen quartet player; composed before 1807). Op. 74 in E flat (nicknamed the *Harp Quartet* from the pizzicato arpeggios in the first movement; composed 1809). Op. 95 in F minor (composed 1810). Op. 127 in E flat (composed 1824). Op. 130 in B flat (composed 1825; finale 1826 to replace the original finale, the 'Great Fugue'; see below). Op. 131 in C sharp minor (composed 1826). Op. 132 in A minor (composed 1825). Op. 133 (*Grosse Fuge*, 'Great Fugue', originally composed as finale of op. 130). Op. 135 in F (composed 1826).

There are naturally many detailed references to Beethoven's life and work scattered about this volume, and they can be found by means of the following list:

1. GENERAL. *Belgium* 9; *Germany* 1, 5, 6, 8; *History* 6, 7; *Romantic*; *Rousseau*.

2. DETAILS OF COMPOSITION. *Arrangement*; *Canon*; *Coda*; *Composition* 5, 7, 8, 9, 11, 12; *Development*; *Form* 2, 6, 7, 9, 10; *Harmony* 12, 17, 20; *Melody* 3, 4, 5, 8; *Modes* 10; *Modulation*; *Recitative*; *Rhythm* 5, 9; *Scales* 7; *Scherzo*; *Subsidiary*; *Temperament* 9; *Tempo*; *Trio* 2.

3. INSTRUMENTAL FORMS. etc. *Ariette*; *Bagatalle*; *Cadenza*; *Cavatina*; *Chamber Music* 6, Period III (1770); *Characteristic Piece*; *Choral Symphony*; *Concertante* 1; *Concerto* 3, 6; *Equale*; *Fantasia*; *Fidelio* (for the *Leonora* and *Fidelio* overtures); *Kreutzer*; *Nicknamed Compositions*; *Overture* 3, 6; *Pasticcio*; *Pastoral*; *Programme Music* 5 d; *Septet*; *Sketch*; *Sonata* 6, 7, 8, 9, 10 c d

(1796); *Song without words*; *Suite* 7; *Symphony* 5, 6, 8; *Veränderungen*.

4. DANCE STYLES, etc. *Allemande*; *Chaconne and Passacaglia*; *Dance* 9; *Écossaise*; *Galop*; *Hungary*; *Ländler*; *Minuet*; *Polonaise*; *Ridotto*; *Tedesca*; *Waltz*.

5. KEYBOARD MATTERS, etc. *Accent* 1; *Arrangements*; *Clavichord* 6; *Diabelli*; *Fingering* 3, 4; *Harpsichord* 7; *Misattributed*; *Nicknamed*; *Organ* 12, 13; *Ornaments* 6; *Pianoforte* 6, 13, 18, 19, 20, 22; *Pianoforte Playing* 2, 3, 5, 10.

6. ORCHESTRA, etc. *Bagpipe Family* 8; *Brass*; *Clarinet Family* 4 f, 6; *Conducting* 3, 5; *Flute* 6; *Harmonica* 1; *Harp* 3; *Horn Family* 3, 4; *Military Band*; *Oboe Family* 3 d, 6; *Orchestra* 3, 4; *Percussion Family* 3 r, 4 a b; *Trombone Family* 3, 4; *Trumpet Family* 2 b, 3; *Wachtel*.

7. VOCAL AND THEATRICAL MUSIC, etc. *Cantata*; *Fidelio*; *Grand Opera*; *Incidental Music*; *Melodrama*; *Opera* 7, 9 c g, 21 g, 24; *Singspiel*; *Song Cycle*.

8. SACRED MUSIC. *Church Music* 1; *Doxology*; *Mass* 3, 4; *Oratorio* 3, 7; *Roman Catholic Church Music in Britain*.

9. FOLK SONG, etc. *Folk Song* 3, 5; *God save the Queen* 16; *Last Rose of Summer*; *Ranz des Vaches*; *Rule, Britannia!*; *Russia* 1.

10. VARIOUS. *Albrechtsberger*; *Alsager*; *Anglican Chant* 4; *Annotated Programmes* 2, 5; *Applause* 3; *Augengläser*; *Ballet* 6; *Belgium* 6; *Bird Music*; *Cinematograph*; *Clementi*; *Colour and Music* 4; *Competitions* 1; *Concert* 6, 14; *Criticism* 6, 7; *Ear* 4; *Fasch*; *Franck, César*; *Gesamtausgabe*; *Gramophone* 6; *Habeneck*; *Handel*; *Hummel*; *Huttenbrenner*; *Improvisation* 2, 3, 5; *Liszt*; *Mandoline*; *Marx, A. B.*; *Mechanical Reproduction* 5, 8; *Misattributed*; *Nägeli*; *Nicknamed* 10; *Notation*; *Nottebohm*; *Oboussier*; *Opus*; *Patronage* 6, 7 (end), 8; *Pitch* 4; *Potter*; *Profession* 8; *Quality* 2, 3; *Ries, F. A.*; *Rode*; *Rolland*; *Schubert*; *Smart, Sir George*; *Spohr*; *United States* 4; *Wölfl*; also p. 796, pl. **135**, 7; p. 768, pl. **129**. 2; p. 893, pl. **152**. 4.

BEGEISTERT (Ger.). 'Inspired, enthused'; *Begeisterung*, 'inspiration, exaltation'.

BEGGAR'S OPERA, THE (p. 101, pl. **18**). *The Beggar's Opera* is so called because it opens with an introduction in dialogue between a beggar in rags (professing to be its author) and a player. The beggar explains 'that it was originally writ for the celebrating the Marriage of James Chanter and Moll Lay, two most excellent Ballad-Singers'. He pokes sly fun at the fashionable opera of the period (of which the piece is, in some degree, a parody), and then withdraws and does not appear further until the closing scene.

The date of the first performance of *The Beggar's Opera* was 1728, and its place the Lincoln's Inn Fields Theatre, London. As explained under *Ballad Opera* (q.v.), its success and that of the many imitations of it that immediately arose was a serious blow to the Italian opera in London, of which Handel was then (and for years before and after) the principal exponent. Its nature is that of a spoken play of low life (indeed, of the lowest life—that of thieves and harlots), with songs interspersed, set to the popular tunes of the day—English and Scottish folk-song and folk-dance tunes, London street tunes, a few French airs, and a touch of Purcell and Handel. The author of the dialogue and song-lyrics was the poet Gay (1685–1732) and the selector and arranger of the music Dr. Pepusch (q.v.).

The piece is not merely a parody of Italian opera; it is also a political satire, hitting at the Prime Minister, Sir Robert Walpole, and his satellites, a picture of the political corruption of the period being presented in the guise of a picture of the life of highwaymen, pickpockets, and the equally criminal servants of the law. The public performance of a sequel, or second part of the opera, called *Polly*, was forbidden by the Lord Chamberlain at the time, and this

did not reach the stage until nearly half a century later (1777), though it was published, and, in book form, damaged the government and made a large sum for its author, Gay (p. 101, pl. **18**. 2).

It is generally considered that *The Beggar's Opera* had a prototype in the Scotsman Allan Ramsay's pastoral play, *The Gentle Shepherd*, published (but not performed) three years earlier (see *Ramsay*; *Ballad Opera*). This play is thought to have been in Swift's mind when (according to Pope) he said to Gay that 'A Newgate Pastoral might make an odd pretty sort of thing', which chance remark was the origin of the opera. Newgate was the chief prison of London for criminal prisoners awaiting trial, and some of the scenes of the opera are placed in it. The age was one of callous indifference to poverty and suffering, when men, women, and children were transported or hanged for very trifling thefts, without the prevalence of crime being in the least checked thereby, and in the pages of this opera and the pictures of the contemporary Hogarth (1697–1764) one has a vivid representation of the reckless, dissolute, and predatory spirit of a large section of the city population of England before the work of the Wesleys, Whitefield, Howard, and other religious and social reformers.

All the music of *The Beggar's Opera* is charming, and its subject-matter, piquant at the date it was written (as bringing on to the opera stage phases of life not before represented there), has become still more so after those phases have passed away; hence the piece has been capable of frequent revival during the eighteenth, nineteenth, and twentieth centuries. It is like the operas of Gilbert and Sullivan in retaining an interest for the public after the full significance of its topical allusions has ceased to reach their minds. The 1920 revival at the Lyric Theatre, Hammersmith, London, by Nigel Playfair, with scenery and dresses designed by Lovat Fraser and the music reharmonized and reorchestrated by Frederic Austin, was particularly notable: on the first occasion of the performance of the opera it broke all records by running for sixty-three nights; on the occasion of this revival it was performed nightly for two and a half years, and then toured. *Polly* was similarly revived in 1922.

The Beggar's Opera reached Paris in 1750 (as *L'Opéra des gueux*). It reached New York the same year, and thenceforward, and for long after, every theatrical company that visited America performed it: in America, so far from competing with Italian opera, it preceded it by over forty years (see *Opera* 21 a; *Oratorio* 1).

The moral effect of the popularity of this opera has been often discussed (p. 101, pl. 18. 6). Burke bitterly condemned it. Sir John Hawkins, in his *History of Music* (1776), says, 'Rapine and violence have been gradually increasing ever since its first representation', and Hawkins was a lawyer by profession and chairman of the Middlesex board of magistrates. Hawkins's friend, Dr. Johnson, on one occasion, took a different view: 'I am of opinion that more influence has been ascribed to *The Beggar's Opera* than it in reality ever had; for I do not believe that any man was ever made a rogue by being present at its representation', on another occasion, however, admitting that there was in the work 'such a labefactation of all principles as might be injurious to morality'.

For an instance of a modern German revival of the opera in a very distorted form see under *Weill, Kurt* and *Jazz* 1; for a new British version see *Britten*.

A reference to the colloquial use of the term *Beggar's Opera* will be found under *Pasticcio*.

Note also references under *England* 6; *Fairs and their Music*; *Bonnie Dundee*; *Opera* 21 a; *Oratorio* 1.

BEGLEITEN (Ger.). 'To accompany.' Hence *Begleitung*, 'accompaniment'; *Begleitend*, 'accompanying'.

BEHAGLICH (Ger.). 'Agreeably.'

BEHEND (Ger.). 'Nimble.' So *Behendig*, 'nimbly'; *Behendigkeit*, 'nimbleness'.

BEHERZT (Ger.). 'Courageous.'

BEHRENS-SENEGALDENS. See *Microtones*.

BEHRENT. See *Pianoforte* 5, 17.

BEIDE (Ger.). 'Both.'

BEINAHE (Ger.). 'Almost.'

BEIREIS. See *Mechanical Reproduction* 9.

BEISPIEL (Ger.). 'Example.'

BEISSEL, J. C. See *United States* 3.

BEISSER (Ger.). 'Biter', i.e. mordent. See Table 12.

BEKLEMMT, BEKLOMMEN (Ger.). 'Oppressed.'

BELAIEF (Belaiev, Belaiew, Byelyayeff, etc.), MITROFAN (p. 897, pl. **154.** 5). Born in St. Petersburg in 1836 and died there in 1904, aged sixty-seven. He was a well-to-do timber merchant who loved and practised music, who associated himself heartily with the national movement (see *Russia* 5), and who organized concerts and, inspired by hearing Glazunof's first symphony, founded a publishing-house to bring out the works of Russian composers. Russia not being a signatory to the Berne Copyright Convention, the headquarters of the publishing-house had to be in Germany so that the rights of the composers might not be lost. The name 'Belaief' is frequently seen upon copies of Russian music, and a string quartet is sometimes heard, written jointly by Rimsky-Korsakof, Borodin, Liadof, and Glazunof upon a theme based on the 'musical' letters of the name, 'B', 'La', and 'F'. (See also *Scriabin*.)

BEL CANTO (It.). 'Beautiful song.' This comprehensive term covers the vocal qualities of the great singers of the seventeenth and eighteenth centuries—the palmy days of Italian singing (see *Opera* 2–4). It is especially used to enforce a distinction between the lyrical style of song, in which beauty of tone made all its effect, and the more declamatory style of the nineteenth century, in which dramatic force was looked for.

The term is nowadays in use in the announcements of a large number of singing masters, each of whom (and he alone) possesses the secrets of the great Italian teachers.

See *Singing* 4–7; *Melisma*; *Divisions*; *Fioritura*; *Coloratura*.

BELCKE, F. A. See *Trombone Family* 4.

BELEBEND, BELEBT (Ger.). 'Animating', 'animated'; *Belebter*, 'more animated'.

BELFAST. See *Ireland* 5; *Clubs*.

BELGIUM

INCLUDING FLANDERS, BRABANT, AND PART OF NORTHERN FRANCE

1. The Great Days of the Fifteenth and Sixteenth Centuries.	4. The Belgian Opera Composers of the Eighteenth Century.	7. Musical Education.
2. Political, Ecclesiastical, and Commercial Factors.	5. The Nineteenth-century Belgian Violinists.	8. Instrument Manufacture.
3. The Vacant Seventeenth Century.	6. Fleming v. Walloon.	9. Relations with Foreign Countries.
		10. List of Articles amplifying the above.

(For illustrations see pp. 96, 97, pls. **15, 16.**)

The present article is designed to offer merely a brief conspectus of the history of music in Belgium, further information on almost every branch of the subject mentioned, as on the individual composers, being given under the appropriate heads scattered throughout this volume. A list of some of the chief of these heads appears at the end of the article. The article *Holland* should also be read, as in the earlier period no separation can be made between the two territories.

1. The Great Days of the Fifteenth and Sixteenth Centuries. The territory which, since 1830, has enjoyed separate existence under this name, with a part of northern France geographically and temperamentally associated with it and not detachable in such a sketch as the present, and with Holland, has played a very notable part in the development of the art of music. The fifteenth and sixteenth centuries were a period when its musicianship won the highest recognition and prepared a national heritage more precious than is perhaps even now generally realized.

The centuries just named constitute the period when, in Italy, England, Spain, and elsewhere, the art of unaccompanied choral counterpoint was moving towards its zenith. At the beginning of the period England, with Dunstable, was leading, the *Ars nova* (q.v.) with him reaching the beginning of its great flowering period. Then the Low Countries took up the race, their greatest early protagonist being **Dufay** (born before 1400; died 1474).

It has been usual to say that Netherlands music then degenerated into a scholastic art, with a cultivation of crabbed canonic writing (see *Canon*), ingenious but not expressive, and the name of **Ockeghem** (*c.* 1430–*c.* 1495) has been linked with this charge. Recent publication of Ockeghem's music largely frees him from any such stigma; there were ingenious 'puzzle canons' written by him and by his contemporaries, but there was likewise much beautiful music.

Ockeghem's pupil, **Josquin des Prés** (d. 1521), represents the point of climax in Netherlands music, in the sense that, after surpassing that of other countries for a period of (say) forty years, its composers were after him not without equals in England, Italy, and Spain. Nevertheless the Netherlanders continued in high repute abroad; they occupied important posts, especially in Italy, where for about two centuries the Papal Choir in Rome was largely recruited from the Netherlands (see remarks under *Dufay*; *Scandinavia* 2).

Both Dufay and Josquin, in the course of their careers in various countries, served in this choir, and a succession of Netherlands musicians of high artistic rank was employed at St. Mark's, Venice, amongst them being **Willaert** (1480–1562), **Arcadelt** (*c.* 1514–*c.* 1570), and **Cipriano de Rore** (1516–65). These men left behind them a store of church music of the finest quality, and (many of them) wonderful examples of the newly developing Italian art of the madrigal.

The long series may be considered to have come to its end with the two great composers, **Filippo di Monte** (*c.* 1521–1603), who left over a thousand madrigals and a quantity of fine church music, and **Lassus** (*c.* 1530–94), whose extraordinary professional career took him to widely separated parts of Europe and won him both wealth and the highest honours.

In great part the work of the period just described remains in manuscript, and largely in Italy, whither during the early 1930s Dr. A. Smijers, Professor of the History and Theory of Music at the University of Utrecht, was sent by the Dutch government to catalogue all the compositions of Netherlands musicians. In about twenty libraries he found nearly 4,000 unpublished compositions by the composers mentioned above and their contemporary compatriots.

In the earlier part of the period just discussed the Flemish composer **Tinctoris** published at Treviso (about 1495) the earliest known dictionary of music (see *Dictionaries*). He left also a large quantity of other valuable theoretical writing.

2. Political, Ecclesiastical, and Commercial Factors. The introduction of music printing and publishing, at the beginning of the sixteenth century, greatly helped in the dissemination and popularity of the music of these composers. The great publishers of Venice and Paris issued their works, and so, in their own country, did those of Antwerp and Louvain.

In noting the wide area of Europe over which the Netherlands composers of this period spread their activities, various historical happenings should be taken into account. The coming into prominence of the papal (or Sistine) Chapel as the chief centre of European musical life closely followed the return of the papacy from Avignon to Rome in 1376, and the determination to maintain the highest possible standards there led to the importation of singers, chiefly from Liège during the period of about 1390 to 1410, and after that from Cambrai, both of these places having attained a high reputation for choralism by means of well-directed song-schools. Thus was established the tradition of Netherlands primacy in this branch of the art. Then, also, the accession of a Netherlands prince, Charles V, to the kingdom of Spain, and his election as Emperor, gave Netherlands musicians easy access to positions in his courts at Madrid, Naples, Vienna, Prague, etc.

The period was, too, one of general prosperity in the Low Countries. Despite the cruelties of the Spanish rule there during the reigns of Charles V and his son Philip II of Spain (100,000 estimated to have been killed by the Inquisition), commerce flourished and cities, such as Bruges and Ghent, greatly developed. Money was available for the cultivation of music in the church and elsewhere.

None of these factors, nor the whole of them in combination, would, however, have operated without the existence of musical genius, which enters a country and departs from it in an unaccountable manner.

3. The Vacant Seventeenth Century. Musical genius now left Belgium, and the genius for painting took up her abode there, the seventeenth century being that of Matsys,

See the various Articles on the individuals pictured and also the Article *Holland*, pages 481–3

1. DUFAY (*c.* 1400–1474) with BINCHOIS (*c.* 1400–1460)

2. OCKEGHEM (*c.* 1430–*c.* 1495) and his choir in the Royal Chapel of Charles VII (from a contemporary manuscript)

3. JOSQUIN DES PRÉS (*c.* 1440–1521)

4. WILLAERT (*c.* 1480–1562)

5. FILIPPO DI MONTE (*c.* 1521–1603)

6. SWEELINCK (1562–1621)

7. LASSUS (*c.* 1532–1594)

PLATE 16

SOME COMPOSERS OF BELGIUM AND HOLLAND

See the various Articles on the individuals pictured

1. GOSSEC (1734–1829)

2. GRÉTRY (1741–1813)

3. LEKEU (1870–94)

4. CÉSAR FRANCK (1822–90)

5. PIJPER (1894–1947)

A COLLEGIUM MUSICUM

See the Article *Concert* 13 (page 231)

A 17TH-CENTURY SWISS 'COLLEGIUM MUSICUM' (St. Gallen, 1694)

Rubens, van Dyck, Franz Hals, and Teniers, all working in Flanders (whilst not far away in Holland were Ruisdael, Hobbema, and Rembrandt). Italy became the leading musical country, with some competition from Germany, France, and England. In a brief sketch such as the present it is not necessary to name a single Belgian composer of the seventeenth century.

4. The Belgian Opera Composers of the Eighteenth Century. The eighteenth century was one of more successful activity. Opera composers arose, and **Grétry** (1741–1813) became famous in Paris, where he produced fifty operas; his works were freely performed in almost all parts of the world—including North America. **Gresnick** (1755–99) had operatic success both in London and Paris. **Gossec** (1734–1829) took an important place in Paris musical life of the Revolutionary and post-Revolutionary period. The impossibility of making any incontestably just list of Belgian musicians is illustrated in the case of **Méhul** (1763–1817), who was born at Givet in the Ardennes, politically in France yet within a mile or two of the Belgian frontier, and with that frontier running around it everywhere except in the south; like Gossec he was a prominent figure in musical Paris of the Revolutionary and Napoleonic period. It will be observed that the emigration which was such a habit of the fifteenth- and sixteenth-century musicians was likewise a feature of their successors of the eighteenth century. Belgium, a small country, seems never to have offered a quite sufficient career to her musical children, and has, in consequence, been steadily drained of its talent.

5. The Nineteenth-century Belgian Violinists. Belgium, and particularly that part about Liège, has long cultivated the violin, all classes of society in the district mentioned being ardently devoted to it. In the nineteenth century there appeared a number of virtuoso players and composers—Vieuxtemps (1820–81), Marsick (1848–1924), Musin (1854–1929), César Thomson (1857–1931). Ysaÿe (1858–1931). With them must be classed the cellist Gerardy (1877–1929). All these were born in Liège or its immediate vicinity, except two who were born about twenty miles away—a remarkable phenomenon, to be accounted for only on the ground of the general love of string playing in the district and the influence of the Liège Conservatory. At the beginning of the twentieth century a quite disproportionate number of the string players in the Paris orchestras were of Walloon birth and training.

At Liège, also, was born **César Franck** (1822–90), and at its Conservatory he received his first training. He is, undoubtedly, the greatest figure amongst Belgian-born musicians of modern times. **Peter Benoît** (1834–1901), **Blockx** (1851–1912), **Tinel** (1854–1912), **Gilson** (1865–1942), **Lekeu** (1870–94), are also important names; the early death of the last-named possibly robbed the world of another really great composer of Belgian birth.

6. Fleming v. Walloon. At the end of the eighteenth century Flanders was incorporated in France. Then in 1815 Belgium (including most of Flanders and the Walloon districts) and Holland were united. Revolution brought freedom in 1830, and with it an accession of national feeling, that, despite the traditional antipathy between the population of Flanders (speaking Flemish—allied to Dutch) and of the Walloon provinces (speaking a French dialect), led to an increase of national organization. Subsequently there was some reaction on the part of the Flemings, who form some sixty per cent of the population, and their attempts during the later nineteenth and the twentieth centuries to preserve their language and their identity have at times taken on a somewhat truculent manner, of which the university dispute has offered an example. This desire to preserve intact the Flemish soul and not to allow it to merge into a general Belgian one has had its exemplification in music: a Flemish conservatory of music and a Flemish opera at Antwerp are instances.

The first strong protagonist of the Flemish movement in music was **Peter Benoît**, the founder and first director of the conservatory just mentioned (1867): he wrote many large-scale settings of patriotic texts in the Flemish language. His successor in the direction of the conservatory (1902) was his pupil **Blockx**, who founded the opera-house; he, also, set Flemish texts. This movement still continues.

An attempt to classify the Belgian musicians mentioned in this volume as Flemish or Walloon is interesting. In the main it seems that the composers of the great age of choral music (roughly 1400–1600) were Flemish, that the operatic and instrumental composers of the eighteenth century were Walloon, that the important nineteenth-century group of string players and composers was also Walloon, and that, apart from these, the Walloons and Flemings have been pretty equally active and successful during the nineteenth and twentieth centuries.

The Flemings, as their language suggests, are closely akin to the Dutch; in view of their pre-eminence as composers during the great choral age (the fifteenth and sixteenth centuries) it is a little curious to note that the Dutch during this period showed no remarkable aptitude for choral composition. The Walloons, on the other hand, are akin to the French, and their affinity has been patent during the whole of that later period (from the eighteenth century onwards) during which they have shown excellence in musical performance and production.

A special dance form of the Walloon parts of Belgium is the **Cramignon**, which, like the Cornish Furry Dance and the Provençal Farandole, is danced by great numbers of people, progressing through the streets of a town. The Liège composer Hamal (1709–78) has made use of Cramignon melodies in his Walloon opera *The Voyage to Chaudefontaine*.

It will be remembered that Beethoven was, on one side, of Flemish descent.

7. Musical Education. Belgium has numerous good conservatories of music founded and subsidized by the government, and others maintained by the municipalities. That of Brussels maintains a famous library and collection of instruments.

A Prix de Rome for composition is awarded to Belgian composers on much the same conditions as those of the French Prix de Rome (q.v.).

8. Instrument Manufacture. In the activity of instrument-making Belgium has won some distinction.

The great Ruckers firm of harpsichord makers was busy at Antwerp from about 1580 to about 1760. Hans Ruckers introduced many improvements, and the beauty of tone of the instruments of this family had great repute in many parts of Europe until, with the coming into general use of the pianoforte at the end of the eighteenth century; harpsichords disappeared into attics and museums.

C. J. and A. J. Sax (father and son) were Belgians, first working in Brussels, where the saxophone was invented about 1840, the saxhorn following later in Paris. Belgium (or the Flemish part of it) is of course, the home of the carillon (see *Bell* 4).

9. Relations with Foreign Countries. To an English reader there may be interest in recalling the threads of connexion between musical England and musical Belgium in the early seventeenth century. At this time English musicians travelled almost as Belgian ones had

done a little earlier. John Bull was one of the organists of the Royal Chapel at Brussels, 1613–17, and then of Antwerp Cathedral until his death in 1628. Peter Philips was one of the organists of the chapel at Brussels from 1611 to his death about the same year as Bull. Deering was organist of the English Convent at Brussels in 1617. Daniel Norcome was a member of the orchestra of the Royal Chapel at Brussels. Some of Dowland's lute songs were published at Antwerp. It seems evident that the English instrumentalists were appreciated abroad at this period as the Netherlands choralists had been previously, and that Belgium gave a welcome to some of the best of the English composers at the moment when her own skill in composition was dwindling.

It has been mentioned above that there is a well-attested Belgian claim to a share in the glory of Beethoven, his ancestors on his father's side having lived in the neighbourhood of Louvain and then in Malines, of which latter place his grandfather was a native.

As will already have been gathered by the reader, French music has gained a good deal by the Belgian loan of such personalities as Grétry and Franck, and many countries have profited by the visits or residence of Belgian instrumental virtuosi.

At the end of the eighteenth century was born **Fétis** (1784–1871), who was theoretician, historian, and critic, and as such has won the gratitude of the musicians of every country; his great musical dictionary remains one of the foundation stones of international biographical and bibliographical learning.

10. List of Articles amplifying the above. In order to amplify the information given above the following articles on cognate subjects should be consulted:

BELIEBEN (Ger.). 'Pleasure', 'will'. So *Nach Belieben* = *Ad libitum* (q.v.) and *Beliebig* = 'Optional'.

BELL

(For illustrations see p. 100, pl. **17**.)

1. Technical Description. The uses of this ancient and universally known instrument range all the way from summoning the fire brigade to playing beautiful and elaborate music in several parts for the artistic delectation of a whole city. The weight of the instru-

ment varies from a fraction of an ounce to 180 tons, which latter is the weight of the Great Bell of Moscow, which was cast in 1733 but broken before it was brought into use; the largest bell in actual use of later years was another in Moscow of 128 tons. There is one in a Burmese temple of 80 tons. The largest in Britain is the great one in St. Paul's Cathedral, London, weighing nearly 17 tons. (These are, of course, wide variations.)

The best and most usual **Bell Metal** is a bronze of thirteen parts of copper to four parts of tin. The **Shape and Properties** are the result of very intricate calculations based upon continuous experience; there are two factors to be considered, tone and tuning, and the latter involves subtle management on account of the several notes which any vibrating body produces simultaneously (see *Acoustics* 8) and which are more clearly heard from a bell than from any other musical instrument.

The note assigned to a bell in a carillon or a peal is called the **Strike Note**: it is accompanied by numerous overtones. A deeper tone persists after these have died out, and is called the **Hum Note**. It should be an octave below the strike note, and the securing of perfect tuning for this and for the chief of the various overtones is a tricky part of the bell-founder's business. The best bell-founders, as the result of careful study, can now tune the strike note, hum note, and chief three overtones with the most perfect accuracy.

So far as concerns Britain, the present perfection in tuning bells is due to the rediscovery in the latter half of the nineteenth century, by Canon Arthur S. Simpson (then Rector of Fittleworth, Sussex), of the principles of the old tuning of bells as practised in Holland three hundred years before. Canon Simpson's theories were put to practical test by English bell founders and, as a result of his writings and his continual appeals, the practice of the old tuning was successfully mastered. Messrs. Taylor of Loughborough first used the improved methods of tuning, on a peal at Werrington in Cornwall in 1896, and Messrs. Gillet and Johnston of Croydon, near London, on a set of bells at a school in Elstree in 1906.

The oldest existing bell foundry is that of Messrs. Mears & Stainbank, Whitechapel, London (see pl. **17.** 2), which dates from 1570; at the end of the first World War it was called upon to rehang bells in Westminster Abbey that it had supplied over three centuries earlier. The largest bell ever cast in England is the bourdon in the New Riverside Church, New York, cast at Croydon: it weighs 18½ tons. A window in York Minster, made in the earliest years of the fourteenth century, shows all the processes of bell founding—essentially much as they are today.

2. Change Ringing (see pl. **17.** 3). A 'Ring'[1] of church bells may consist of anything from five to twelve or more. With five bells, 120 **Changes** or variations of order are possible; with twelve, the number of changes mounts to the astonishing figure of nearly

[1] The correct name for a set of bells is a *Ring*; the sound made when they are rung is the *Peal*. This distinction is not, however, invariably observed in everyday speech.

480 millions. It is computed that to ring all the possible changes on the twelve-bell 'ring' of St. Paul's Cathedral, London, would occupy thirty years of unceasing ringing. Hawkins, in his *History of Music* (1776), says: 'According to the computation of ringers, the time required to ring all the possible changes on twelve bells is seventy-five years, ten months, one week and three days.' If the St. Paul's calculation is true then Hawkins's imaginary ringers slept at night and took occasional holidays—to which they were well entitled!

The complete accomplishment of a set of changes on a smaller ring may take many hours and becomes a considerable athletic feat. It is not unusual to find in English belfries a painted notice to the effect that on such and such a date such and such a set of changes was rung in so many hours. Perhaps the greatest feat to date has been the ringing of 21,000 changes in twelve hours. Change ringing is a great hobby with many men, and some ringing societies have long traditions. The oldest in England is the Society of College Youths, London, founded in 1637. To make a good ringer takes years of practice; there is usually a lack of trained ringers. Eighty of London's best ringers were killed in the first World War, and in 1919 it was stated that there were barely enough skilled men left for twenty-five or thirty of London's one hundred rings. Nevertheless it was reported forty years later that there were well over 40,000 bellringers, of whom about a quarter were women.

Visitors to London should walk through the city on Sunday, when there is little traffic noise, and hear the bells.

Changes have been given various names, Grandsire Triples, Bob Major, Oxford Treble Bob, and the like, according to the number of bells rung and the manner of ringing. The great protagonist of change-ringing was Fabian Stedman, of Cambridge (published *Tintinnalogia*, 1668). His art may be said to be not so much a branch of music as mathematics athletically applied to the making of a merry noise.

The ringers of England are sufficiently numerous to maintain a journal of their own, *The Ringing World*. Dorothy Sayers's novel, *The Nine Tailors*, gives an admirable description of English bell-ringing.

3. Method of Sounding. There are two main ways of sounding ordinary church bells, (1) the gentler method of **Chiming** (for announcing the hour of day), in which the bell is usually struck either by an external hammer or by a mechanical movement of the clapper, and (2) the more vigorous method of **Ringing**, in which the bell is swung round full circle. There is a third method, less used, of agitating the clapper of the bell by means of a string ('clocking'); this is the way of a lazy sexton with a single bell, and sooner or later he cracks it.

In ringing, the bell starts from an upside-down position, i.e. with its mouth upwards.

4. Carillons (p. 100, pl. **17**. 4, 5). On the continent of Europe rings such as those described are unknown, but the **Carillon** is an ancient tradition (especially in Belgium and Holland), and carillons have lately begun to become common in Britain and the United States, and also in the British Commonwealth.

These are played by skilful artists from a manual and pedal keyboard, similar in principle to that of an organ, but much more cumbrous, the whole hand (gloved in leather) being required to depress a manual key. Instead of mere changes, actual tunes are given out, often with simple accompanying harmonies. At the hours and their halves and quarters the carillon is mechanically played by means of clockwork and a barrel like that of a musical box; but at stated times during the week this will be thrown out of action and the municipal carillonneur will perform a recital programme. The best carillons and carillonneurs used to be those of Belgium, Bruges, with the earliest known keyboard carillon (1532), being especially famous for its carillon music (see Longfellow's poem). Most of the best carillons (as many of those in the United States and in Holland) are now, however, made in England. The 'action' (or system of mechanical connexions) of a carillon resembles that of an organ: the method is that of moving the clapper, not the bell (but with proper safeguards against the accidents mentioned in the description above of the third of the three means of sounding a bell.) Rapid passages, crescendos, and diminuendos, and even long-held chords (produced by a sort of tremolo motion), are possible; the simpler fugues and sonatas written for piano or organ can be played. Bach wrote some tunes for the carillon of one of his employers, the Prince of Anhalt-Coethen (published in Berlin, 1898).

The largest carillons have seventy bells. There are schools of carillon-playing at Malines, and at the Curtis Institute, Philadelphia (in connexion with Mr. Edward Bok's gift, the Mountain-Lake Singing Tower in Florida). The science and art of the carillonneur, and of bell-making and playing generally, bear the name of **Campanology**. Birmingham University, England, has held a course in this subject as an optional part of the preparation for the honours Mus.B. degree. Granville Bantock, long Professor of Music in the University, in 1924 wrote a setting of Tennyson's *Ring out, wild bells*, for male-voice choir and the Bournville carillon—the choir standing at the foot of the tower. (Cf. *Benoît, P. L. L.*)

5. Bells in History. Bells have played a great part in history. They gave the signal for the Sicilian Vespers in 1282 and for the Massacre of St. Bartholomew in 1571. They supplied Henry VIII with money at the time of the dissolution of the monasteries and Napoleon with cannon when he was fighting all Europe —whereby whole districts of France have to-day no old bells. The great 'Kaiser Bell' in

Cologne Cathedral, made from cannon taken in the war with France in 1870, was melted down for war purposes in the war of 1914–18: it was over 14 feet high and weighed more than 20 tons. The German invasion of Belgium in 1914 brought about the destruction of the carillons of Dixmude, Nieuport, Thorout, Louvain, Termonde, Ypres, and Dinant. That of Arras, over the French border, was also destroyed. Apart from war and accident, the bell is the most durable of all musical instruments: the earliest in the British Isles actually bearing a date is one in Lancashire, dated 1296, but there are several thought to be older.

The uses of the bell are innumerable. Besides calling men to church, it is used in Roman Catholic churches at the Elevation of the Host. The 'passing bell' used to be rung as a parishioner lay dying, to ask the prayers of his fellows; now a bell is in many places rung after a death, and on that of a national figure the bells of all the churches of a country are solemnly tolled. Victories are celebrated with bells: when Trafalgar was won and Nelson died the mingled joy and sorrow were represented in Chester by a merry peal from the cathedral tower, interspersed with single strokes from a muffled bell (muffling is done by putting a leather cap on the clapper). The curfew bell which William the Conqueror ordered for putting out the fires at eight o'clock is still maintained in some English cities, although the law enforcing it has been revoked for more than eight hundred years. Some Chinese pagodas are hung round with numbers of little bells, as Aaron's robe used to be. In some Roman Catholic countries bells are christened with the full ritual, as human babies are, and have sponsors assigned. The bell counts for a good deal in the Greek Orthodox Church, and bell effects have thus become popular with Russian composers. A few bells of English churches are accommodated in special towers separate from the churches, and the campanili or bell towers of certain Italian cities, as Florence and Venice, are famous. Most religions have used bells, but the Mohammedan religion has rejected them and reminds worshippers of their duty by the muezzin's cry. The Roman practice of hanging bells around the necks of cattle survives fully in Switzerland, where the high pastures in summer resound with their tinkling. This list of bell uses might be continued much further but had better stop before it is in danger of descending through ships' bells to mark the time, bell buoys, sleigh bells, striking and chiming clocks, to the shop bell and the dinner bell—which last is by some considered of all instruments to supply the sweetest music. Enough has been said to show that the bell is the most universal of all musical instruments, as until the advent of radio it was the one with the largest audience.

6. Treatment by Composers. The adoption of **Bell Effects by Composers** has been

1. FOURTEENTH-CENTURY BELL-PLAYING

2. A LONDON BELL-FOUNDRY dating from 1570. See *Bell* 1

3. BELL-RINGERS AT ST. PAUL'S CATHEDRAL, LONDON. See *Bell* 2

4. EARLY BELGIAN CARILLON. See *Bell* 4

5. THE CARILLON AT BOURNVILLE,
Birmingham. England. See *Bell* 4

PLATE 18

THE BEGGAR'S OPERA

See the Article on pages 94–9

1. ONE OF THE SCENES AS PICTURED BY HOGARTH

2. THE AUTHOR
John Gay (1685–1732)

3. THE ARRANGER OF THE MUSIC
Dr. Pepusch (1667–1752)

4. THE ORIGINAL POLLY
Hannah Norsa

5. ANOTHER SCENE PICTURED BY HOGARTH

DRAMATIC REVIEW

DRURY LANE THEATRE.

The Beggar's Opera.

If there be any one thing more disgraceful to the English stage than another, it is this opera. The subject, the ideas, the language, are all equally and horribly disgusting. The author has raked together the very offal of society; he is like the carrion crow, that leaves the wholesome fruits of the earth to batten upon carcases.

"Two boys, under nineteen years of age, children of worthy and respectable parents, fled from their friends, and pursued courses that threatened an ignominious termination to their lives. *After much search, they were found engaged in midnight depredations, and in each of their pockets was the* Beggar's Opera."

"A boy of seventeen, some years since tried at the Old Bailey for what there was every reason to think his first offence, acknowledged himself so *delighted with the spirited and heroic character of Macheath, that on quitting the theatre, he laid out his last guinea in the purchase of a pair of pistols, and stopped a gentleman on the highway*."

6. THE BEGGAR'S OPERA CONDEMNED
(below 1794; above 1815)

mentioned under 4. Wagner's use in *Parsifal* is notable: he provided a problem, however, that proved difficult to solve, for such deep tones as he requires call for very heavy and large bells, the hum notes and harmonics of which would clash disturbingly with the rest of the orchestra; at one time Bayreuth used very long thick piano wires stretched on a resonator and musically supported by gongs and the bass tuba. (See *Percussion* 4 e, and for a recent attempt to solve the problem see *Electric Musical Instruments* 1 c.)

Elgar, in his war-time setting of Cammaerts's *Carillon* (a spoken poem with an orchestral background), made thrilling use of a four-note bell theme treated on the principle of the 'ground bass' (q.v.). For the opening of the carillon at Loughborough (a great bell-making town) he wrote a special composition.

Handel used a large set of small bells in *Saul*, and Bach in his cantata *Schlage doch* has made awe-inspiring use of two bells. Mozart (German Dances) used sleigh bells. In Purcell's so-called 'Bell Anthem' he, perhaps unconsciously, uses a delightful bell theme (the nickname 'Bell Anthem' was given to it in his own days, as is shown by some of the manuscript copies—but possibly not by him).

Byrd has a long and highly ingenious fantasia for virginals called *The Bells*. (Late-sixteenth- and seventeenth-century composers often used bell effects in instrumental music.) Debussy's system of harmony was partly the result of his listening to bell overtones, and Ravel has a highly effective pianoforte piece, *The Valley of Bells*. Grieg, too, has a pianoforte *Bells*, and Liszt has *La Campanella* (an arrangement of a piece of Paganini's) and *Les Cloches de Genève*. Sibelius has a part-song, *Carillon for the Church of Berghäll* (op. 65)

and a very effective piano piece of the same name (op. 65 b).

7. Tubular Bells are now often placed in church towers. They are played by hammers (like the tubular bells of the orchestra) and these are operated electrically from a keyboard like that of a small piano—possibly by the vicar's wife sitting in her drawing-room. This system was of American invention and is greatly used in American churches. The carillon (or Glockenspiel) stop now present in many organs is somewhat similar.

8. Electrophonic 'Bells'. In 1937 there were put on the market Electrophonic Carillons. For the general principle of these compare what is said as to Electrophonic Organs under *Electric Musical Instruments* 4.

9. Handbells are small bells of varying sizes, with handles; they are ranged in pitch order on a table, and played by several performers, to each of whom are allotted two or three of the bells. The whole chromatic scale is available, and music in several parts is performed. The hobby of handbell ringing is popular in some places, and, in addition, such ringing is used as practice by English groups of change-ringers. Lancashire has (or had) a special reputation for handbell ringing, and in 1848 a body of Lancashire ringers performed before the Court in Paris and then passed on to Spain, where they enjoyed great success. (See p. 357, pl. **58**. 4.) There is an 'American Guild of English Handbell-ringers', with (1965) over five hundred members, and a periodical, *Overtones*.

For particulars of bells and bell-like instruments in the orchestra see *Percussion Family* 2 b c, 4 e, 5 b c. Also *Cowbell*, *Solo Bells*.

BELL, WILLIAM HENRY. Born at St. Albans in 1873 and died in Cape Town in 1946, aged seventy-two. After a period as professor at the Royal Academy of Music, he emigrated to South Africa as principal of the South African College of Music at Cape Town, later becoming Professor of Music at the university there (till 1934). He composed much orchestral and other music. By his foundation and direction of the Cape Town Little Theatre he did much to arouse interest in the drama and in ballet.

'BELL' ANTHEM. See *Bell* 6; *Nicknamed* 16.

BELLE VUE GARDENS, MANCHESTER. See *Competitions in Music* 3.

BELL GAMBA. See *Organ* 14 III.

BELL HARP (p. 449, pl. **77**. 4). This was a sort of psaltery (q.v.), invented in the early eighteenth century by John Simcock of Bath. It resembled in appearance (very roughly) a zither or dulcimer, consisting of eight or more strings stretched over a sounding-board. The player swung it in the air (like players on the English concertina today), holding it with the

fingers and plucking its strings meanwhile with plectra attached to both thumbs. Four different reasons are given for the name by different authorities: (*a*) its swinging was reminiscent of that of a bell; (*b*) its shape was much that of a section through a bell; (*c*) its inventor wished to honour an army officer called Bell; (*d*) it produced 'the effect of a peal of bells borne on the wind'. Never, then, was an instrument named with more adequate appropriateness.

BELLICOSO (It.). 'Warlike.' So, too, the adverb, *Bellicosamente*.

BELLINI, VINCENZO (p. 524, pl. **95**. 3). Born at Catania in Sicily in 1801 and died near Paris in 1835, aged nearly thirty-four. He was a celebrated contributor to Italian opera in the days when singers sang (cf. *Donizetti*; *Bel Canto*). He wrote flowing, expressive melody which his friend Chopin greatly admired, and gave the human voice every opportunity to display both its natural charm and its acquired technique. He had enormous popularity in Paris and elsewhere. The twentieth century saw a long period of near-eclipse in most countries except his own, where he remained a national idol. A successful revival gathered momentum in the 1950s and 1960s.

See *Opera* 6, 21 i, 24 d (1831–2); *Chopin*; *Hexameron*.

BELL-LYRA. A portable form of the Glockenspiel (see *Percussion Family* 2 c, 4 e, 5 c) for band use. It is mounted on a rod to be held perpendicularly in the left hand of the player whilst his right hand holds the beater.

BELL MACHINE. See *Percussion Family* 4 e.

BELLMANN, CARL MIKAEL. Born in Stockholm in 1740 and died there in 1795. He was a Swedish poet who set his popular lyrics to French folk and similar melodies or to melodies of his own composition.

BELLOWS AND TONGS (p. 512, pl. **91**.8). One of the burlesque means of music making, common in the eighteenth century (and possibly also earlier and later). Presumably the sound evoked was merely that of adroit rhythmic tapping.

BELL QUARTET (Haydn). See *Nicknamed* 12 (76).

BELLS OF ABERDOVEY. This is not a Welsh folk song, as claimed in very many books of such songs, but appears to be the composition of Charles Dibdin (q.v.). Dibdin published it as his in 1785 and it appeared many times subsequently in volumes of his songs, not figuring in any of the numerous Welsh collections before 1844, when Miss M. J. Williams included it in hers with the words 'the origin of this air is unknown'.

The false attribution probably springs from the fact that the song was first heard in Dibdin's Drury Lane opera, *Liberty Hall*, from the mouth of a comic Welsh character. The nature of the words doubtless led to its being taken up in Wales, until it acquired the reputation of being a native folk song. (All the facts are to be found in an article by the authority on British songs, Frank Kidson (q.v.), in the *Musical Times* for February and May 1911.)

BELLY. The upper surface of a stringed instrument, over which the strings are stretched. It is also called the 'Table'.

BELMONT, JOHN. See *Pianoforte* 5.

BELUSTIGEND (Ger.). 'Amusing', 'gay'.

BEMBERG, HERMANN-EMMANUEL (also known as HENRI), was born in 1859 in Paris (of French or Argentine parentage, according to the account to which credence is given) and died at Berne, Switzerland, in 1931, aged seventy-two. His operas and graceful songs in the lighter French style have had success.

BÉMOL (Fr.), **BEMOLLE** (It.). 'Flat.'

BEN, BENE (It.). 'Well' or 'much'.

BENDA, GEORG (or JIRI) ANTONIN (1722–95). He was a member of a remarkable Bohemian family of musicians, of whom seven or eight appear in the larger books of reference. Above all his brothers and sons, however, he

stands out by reason of the works mentioned under *Melodrama*.

BENDEL, FRANZ. Born in northern Bohemia in 1833 and died in Berlin in 1874, aged forty-one. Pianist and composer. Pupil of Liszt. Best remembered through an album of tuneful piano pieces prompted by sights around the eastern end of Lake Geneva—*Am genfer See*.

BENDIX, VICTOR EMANUEL. Born at Copenhagen in 1851 and died in 1926, aged seventy-four. He was a pupil of Gade who became a successful choral and orchestral conductor and composed several symphonies (of which one is called 'Summer Sounds in South Russia') and other orchestral works, choral works, chamber music, piano music, songs, etc.

BENE (It.). 'Well' or 'much'.

BENEDICITE. The *Song of the Three Holy Children*, i.e. Shadrach, Meschach, and Abednego, whilst in Nebuchadnezzar's fiery furnace. It is not in the Hebrew version of the Book of Daniel, but comes from the Septuagint (or early Greek translation of the Old Testament). In the Roman Catholic Church it is sung at Lauds on Sundays and festivals. It is one of the canticles of the Anglican service and often replaces the *Te Deum* during Lent, Advent, or Septuagesima. It invites all the works of the Lord to praise Him. From its form it offers somewhat of a problem for musical setting. As, like the Psalms, it is a Jewish hymn, and so has no mention of the Trinity, the *Gloria Patri* (or, in the Roman Catholic service books, its own Doxology) is sung after it.

BENEDICT.

(1) JULIUS. Born at Stuttgart in 1804 and died in London in 1885, aged eighty.

He was the son of a Jewish banker and the favourite pupil (and later the biographer) of Weber. He became conductor successively of the Kärnthnerthor Theatre in Vienna, of the San Carlo in Naples, and in London of the Lyceum, Drury Lane, and Her Majesty's.

He settled permanently in England, won recognition as one of the great opera and oratorio conductors of the day, appeared at all the festivals, and was thrice knighted, by the sovereigns of Britain, Austria, and Württemberg, being decorated in minor ways by six or seven other monarchs. He toured America as accompanist and director for Jenny Lind. He not merely conducted operas and oratorios and cantatas, but composed them freely, though of all his output one item only now remains in public remembrance, the opera *The Lily of Killarney* (1863).

See references under *Opera* 13 d; *Cruiskin Lawn*; *God save the Queen* 18; *Oratorio* 7 (1870).

(2) SAINT. See under *Singing* 3.

(3) BISCOP. See under *Plainsong* 4.

BENEDICTION. Properly speaking this means any blessing, as that with which a service often ends, but it is applied specifically to an informal rite in the Roman Catholic

Church, closing the office; of this the essential act is the blessing of the congregation with the host (see *Tantum ergo* and *O salutaris hostia*). As the rite is extra-liturgical its details are variable; it became general only in the nineteenth century, though in the seventeenth century in France it was important, being made the occasion of much elaborate music (French name, *Salut*).

BENEDICTUS. As a single word this has two distinct applications:

(1) In the Roman Catholic Mass it means the *Benedictus qui venit*, i.e. simply the words 'Blessed is he that cometh in the name of the Lord', which follow the *Sanctus*, of which section they form a part (see *Mass* 3 d). It is separated from the *Sanctus* by a ceremonial pause during the Consecration and Elevation of the Host, but is treated by composers (following Gregorian and medieval tradition) as one unit with the earlier part.

(2) The name is also applied to the song of Zacharias (Luke i. 68 et seq.), 'Blessed be the Lord God of Israel', which is sung daily at Lauds in Roman Catholic· churches (best known from its use at Lauds in Holy Week, forming part of the popular service of *Tenebrae*, q.v.) and in the English Prayer Book occurs in the Order for Morning Prayer (see *Common Prayer*).

BENEPLACITO, BENEPLACIMENTO (It.). 'Good pleasure.' Preceded by the words *A suo* ('at one's') this has the same sense as *Ad libitum* (q.v.).

BENET. See *Bennet*.

BEN-HAIM, PAUL. See *Jewish Music* 9; *Harpsichord* 9.

BENJAMIN, ARTHUR L. Born at Sydney, New South Wales, in 1893 and died in London in 1960, aged sixty-six. He studied at the Royal College of Music and after a period in his native place as professor of the pianoforte at the Conservatory, returned to the Royal College as a member of its staff. He wrote much music in many forms, including four operas, orchestral works, a violin concerto, and a piano concertino. In later years he wrote much music for films. (See p. 352, pl. **55. 7.**)

BENJAMIN COSYN'S VIRGINAL BOOK. This is a manuscript collection of music, chiefly for virginals, made by Benjamin Cosyn, who was organist of Dulwich College and then of the Charterhouse during the years 1622–43. It belongs to the Queen and is in the Royal Library of the British Museum; it was published in 1923 under the editorship of Fuller Maitland and Barclay Squire.

See *Harpsichord* 3, and compare *Fitzwilliam Virginal Book*, *Will Forster's Virginal Book*, and *Parthenia*.

BENNET (or Benet), JOHN. Late sixteenth and early seventeenth century. Nothing whatever is known of his life, but of his art his own age thought highly and the best connoisseurs of madrigals today amply endoise the judge-

ment. From the mood of his most successful compositions he may be guessed to have been of cheerful temperament.

BENNETT.

(1) WILLIAM STERNDALE (p. 336, pl. **53.** 1). Born at Sheffield in 1816 and died in London in 1875, aged fifty-eight. His grandfather and father were professional musicians and he himself started on a professional career at the age of eight as a choir-boy at King's College, Cambridge. At ten he was studying at the Royal Academy of Music, and there at seventeen he was found by Mendelssohn, who, on hearing him play a concerto of his own, invited him to Germany, 'not as my pupil but as my friend' (p. 289, pl. **51.** 5). Accepting this invitation, he was made much of at Leipzig by the Mendelssohn–Schumann circle.

The later life of Bennett did not fulfil his early promise. He was never a voluminous composer and from about his thirtieth year he became a Pegasus in harness, drawing the heavy loads with which an extensive teaching connexion, the professorship of Music at Cambridge (1856), the principalship of the Royal Academy of Music (1866), and the conductorship of the Philharmonic Society of London, had charged him. He gave himself heart and soul to such tasks, but the gain to his own generation became the loss of posterity. The work of his that has been the most performed is probably the oratorio, *The Woman of Samaria* (1867).

He was knighted in 1871 and is buried in Westminster Abbey.

See *Composition* 7; *Sonata* 10 d—towards the end of the section; *Pianoforte* 22; *Pianoforte Playing* 7; *Concerto* 6 b (1816); *Slur*; *Holland*, 6, 7; *Memory* 7; *Degrees* 1; *Bache, F. E.*; *England* 7.

(2) JOSEPH (music critic; 1831–1911). See passing reference under *Melodrama*.

(3) ROBERT RUSSELL. Born at Kansas City, Mo., 1894. Beginning as a music copyist he gained a very high reputation as a skilful arranger and orchestrator of theatre music and the like. Amongst his own works are operas and a symphony, *Abraham Lincoln* (1931). He inclines to the use of the jazz idiom.

(4) RICHARD RODNEY. Born at Broadstairs in 1936. He studied at the Royal Academy of Music, and in Paris under Boulez. He has composed operas, orchestral works, chamber music, and much music for films and radio, generally making use of note-row techniques, and often showing his interest in modern jazz.

See *Opera* 24 f (1961).

BENOIST, FRANÇOIS. Born at Nantes in 1794 and died in Paris in 1878, aged eighty-three. He was a student at the Paris Conservatory, and in 1815 the winner of the Rome Prize (see *Prix de Rome*) and later professor of the organ there. He wrote much organ music and several operas, and also a good many magazine articles on musical subjects.

BENOÎT, PETER LÉOPOLD LÉONARD.
Born at Harlebeke in Flanders in 1834 and
died at Antwerp in 1901, aged sixty-seven.
He was a protégé of Fétis and a student
under him at the Brussels Conservatory. He
had an early success as a composer of church
music. After some travel and the short tenure
of a position as opera conductor in Paris he
returned home with the ambition of founding
a genuine Flemish school of composition,
making Antwerp his headquarters, receiving
municipal and governmental support, and
writing many propagandist pamphlets and
articles. A society still exists in Antwerp to
propagate his works.

He composed many cantatas and other
choral works on national subjects, often to texts
in the Flemish language by the contemporary
poet Emmanuel Hiel; some of these called for
huge resources, as, for instance, the *Rubens
Cantata* (1877), which used an immense choir,
brass, the carillon of Antwerp Cathedral, etc.
Amongst his works is a *Children's Oratorio*, in
which he makes effective use of a children's
choir.

See *Belgium* 6; *Oratorio* 4, 7 (1866); *Blockx*.

BENTHAM, FREDERICK. See *Colour and
Music* 10.

BENTZON, JØGEN (1871–1951) and NIELS
VIGGO (born 1919). See *Scandinavia* 2.

BEQUADRO (It.). The natural sign (Table 7).

BEQUEM (Ger.). 'Comfortable' = Comodo (q.v.)

BÉRARD, CAROL. See *Colour and Music* 10.

BERCEMENT (Fr. substantive). 'Rocking',
'lulling', 'swaying'.

BERCEUSE. A lullaby or cradle song ('ber-
cer', in French, is to rock to sleep). The term
is applied not only to actual songs, but also to
quiet instrumental compositions, generally in
a six-in-a-measure rhythm and always of a
lullaby character. Chopin's *Berceuse* for piano
is one of the most famous.

BEREITE VOR (Ger.). 'Make ready', 'prepare'
(such and such organ stop).

BEREITS (Ger.). 'Already', 'previously'.

BEREZOVSKY (Beresowsky, etc.).

(1) MAXIM. Born in the Ukraine in 1745 and
died in St. Petersburg in 1777, aged thirty-one
or thirty-two. As he had a fine voice Catharine
the Great sent him to study in Italy (cf. *Bortniansky*; *Greek Church* 5), where he worked
under Padre Martini. When he returned he
tried to gain a position whence he could reform
the music in the church, and, failing or not
sufficiently persevering, killed himself in a fit
of madness.

He wrote operas in the current Italian style,
one of which, *Demofoonte*, was performed at
Leghorn. He also wrote church music and
songs which are said to have value.

(2) NICOLAI. Born in St. Petersburg in 1900,
and died in New York in 1953, aged fifty-three.
He was a violinist, who after holding orchestral

and other positions in Russia, left it for the
United States in 1922, there carrying out additional study at the Juilliard School. In 1948 he
was awarded a Guggenheim Fellowship. He was
active as a conductor and wrote symphonies,
concertos, chamber music, an opera, and other
things.

See *Harp* 3.

BERG.

(1) ALBAN (p. 416, pl. **71**. 3). Born in Vienna
in 1885 and died there in 1935, aged fifty. He
was an associate and disciple of Schönberg (see
Note-row), and a notable composer of his
school. He wrote chamber music, some orchestral music, etc., but the opera *Wozzeck* (q.v.;
see also *Opera* 9 f), constituted one of his
highest claims to attention. Symphonic extracts from the opera *Lulu* were produced in
1934; at his death two acts had been completed
and were performed in Zürich in 1937; the
third existed in short score but remained unpublished. His Chamber Concerto for violin,
piano, and thirteen wind instruments and his
Lyric Suite for string orchestra are important
amongst his productions. A posthumous violin
concerto appeared in 1936. It has been said
(by René Leibowitz) that it was the function of
Webern to relate Schönberg's discoveries to
the future, of Berg to relate them to the past.

See *Clarinet Family* 6; *Vibraphone*; *Germany* 9 b.

(2) NATANAEL. Born at Stockholm in 1879
and died there in 1957, aged seventy-eight.
He was a singer and composer, for long
President of the Society of Swedish Composers.
His works include a considerable number of
operas (e.g. *Engelbrekt*, 1929) and ballets,
orchestral and choral compositions, etc. By
profession he was an army veterinary surgeon.

BERGAMASQUE (Fr.), **BERGAMASCA** (It.).
See *Bergomask*.

BERGER.

(1) FRANCESCO. Born in London in 1834
and there died in 1933, aged ninety-eight. He
had a long career as a London piano teacher
(on the staff of the Royal Academy of Music,
etc.) and as an active spirit in the life of the
musical profession (nearly thirty years secretary of the Philharmonic Society). Almost to
the last weeks of his life he was publishing
articles (reminiscences, etc.) in the periodical
press. Some of his piano pieces and songs had
great popularity.

See *Programme Music* 3.

(2) V. PETERSON (1867–1942). See *Scandinavia* 4.

(3) ARTHUR. Born in New York in 1912.
A composer and writer on music, he is a pupil
of Piston, Nadia Boulanger, and Milhaud.
After some years as teacher and musical
journalist in New York he joined the staff of
Brandeis University. He has written chamber
music, songs, and other things, as well as a
book on Copland and many critical pieces.

See *Harpsichord* 9; *Jewish Music* 9.

BERGERETTE (Fr.). A shepherd's song (from *berger*, 'shepherd'), or a composition in the simple style of such.

BERGOMASK (Engl.), **BERGAMASQUE** (Fr.), or **BERGAMASCA** (It.). This was originally a peasant dance from the district around Bergamo in north Italy. It was usually in two-in-a-measure time. Unlike so many rural dances it was never adopted into the repertory of the aristocratic ballroom; but it had some popularity in the form of instrumental compositions for lute, viols, etc.

Piatti (q.v.) published a bergamasca for cello and piano which was in six-in-a-measure: he was himself a native of Bergamo and this, apparently, was the kind of dance he had come across in his youth; it is really more a kind of tarantella (q.v.) than a true bergamasca.

Today the word bergomask would be little known but for Bottom, in *A Midsummer Night's Dream*, having asked the Duke, 'Will it please you to see the epilogue, or to hear a bergomask dance between two of our company?' So that something called by that name may still be 'heard' in our theatre, but the composer responsible has usually not bothered much about historic accuracy, and any bright dance style suits (this includes Mendelssohn). In Debussy's *Suite Bergamasque* for piano it is difficult to see that the title has any significance.[1]

BERGSMA, WILLIAM (p. 1069, pl. **176.** 7). Born at Oakland, California, in 1921. He received his musical training at the University of Southern California, at Stanford University, and at the Eastman School, Rochester, N.Y., then for some time occupying a position on the staff of this last. Later he taught at the Juilliard School, and in 1963 became head of the school of music in Seattle, Washington. His compositions are mostly in a lyrical, contrapuntal, somewhat unassertive style, and include orchestral works, chamber music, and an opera, *The Wife of Martin Guerre* (1955).

See *Symphony* 8 (1921); *Opera* 24 f (1956).

BERINGER, OSCAR. Born near Baden, Germany, in 1844 and died in London in 1922, aged seventy-seven. He was a member of the staff of the Royal Academy of Music and also conducted a piano school of his own.

See *Pianoforte* 22; *Pianoforte Playing* 6; *Memory* 7; also p. 800, pl. **137.** 8.

BERIO, LUCIANO. Born at Oneglia in 1925. A pupil of Ghedini and Dallapiccola, his orchestral and chamber music works, of the most advanced school, have aroused heated dis-

[1] Mr. Nicolas Slonimsky remarks, 'The suggestion that the reason why Debussy used this word as the title of his Suite is not apparent, seems not quite just. Debussy's *Suite Bergamasque* is a fairly good approximation of the classical suite, comprising as it does a Prelude, a Minuet, and a Passepied. *Clair de lune* replaces here the slow movement. The word *Bergamasque* conjures up the characters of the Italian commedia dell'arte with its symbolic masks. Debussy takes a direct lead from Verlaine's *Clair de lune* with the specific allusion to the lines:

". . . que vont charmant masques et bergamasques
Jouant du luth et dansant et quasi
Tristes sous leurs déguisements fantasques".'

cussion. They include *Nones* (1953), *Variations* for chamber orchestra (1953), and *Circles* (1960). His position in Italian radio enabled him to organize radio and other concerts of contemporary music; he has special interest in electrophonic techniques. He joined the Juilliard faculty in 1965.

See *Italy* 8.

BÉRIOT.

(1) **CHARLES AUGUSTE DE** (p. 1097, pl. **182.** 2). Born at Louvain, in Brabant, in 1802 and died at Brussels in 1870, aged sixty-eight. He was one of the most famous travelling violin virtuosi of his period and second of the two husbands of the great contralto Malibran (see *Garcia Family*), who was the first of his two wives. For some time he was a professor of the Brussels Conservatory. In addition to his musical activities he was also a good mechanic, a violin maker, a landscape painter, a poet, and a sculptor. After Malibran's death he designed a tomb upon which she appeared in the character of St. Cecilia, and also a bust of her which enjoyed great fame.

His last twelve years were spent in total blindness, and in the sadness of inactivity as a performer, owing to paralysis of his left arm. He wrote seven concertos, as also variations, and other compositions for his instrument, and some valuable duets for two violins. His *Violin School* had a wide circulation. For his son see below.

(2) **CHARLES WILFRID DE.** Born in Paris in 1833 and died in London in 1914, aged eighty-one. He was son of the above, a fine pianist, and, as professor of piano at the Paris Conservatory, the teacher of many famous musicians (Granados, Ravel, etc.). He wrote concertos and other works for his instrument.

BERKELEY, LENNOX (p. 353, pl. **56.** 5.). Born near Oxford in 1903. He is partly of French descent and, though his general education was completed at Oxford, his musical education was completed in Paris—his musical sympathies being largely Parisian or, at any rate, continental. A good deal of piano music, chamber music, and orchestral music of his has been heard, as also the operas *Nelson*, *A Dinner Engagement*, and *Ruth*.

He was on the staff of the BBC 1942–5 and is a professor of composition at the Royal Academy of Music. He was knighted in 1974.

BERKSHIRE (MASS.) FESTIVAL. See *Festival* 2.

BERLIN. See *Schools of Music*.

BERLIN, IRVING. See *Jazz* 1; *Jewish* 9.

BERLINER. See *Gramophone* 2, 3, 8; p. 432, pl. **73.** 2.

BERLIOZ, (LOUIS) HECTOR (p. 369, pl. **62.** 1). Born at Côte St. André, near Grenoble, in the Dauphiné, in 1803, and died in Paris in 1869, aged sixty-five. He is the greatest musical figure in the French Romantic movement. A native of southern France, he early became a Parisian of the Paris of the growing Romantic movement, and the romantic writers, Hugo, Dumas, Gautier, Balzac, etc., were his friends, as were the romantic painters, with Delacroix at their head, and the romantic musicians, Chopin and Liszt. Gautier, looking back to the Paris intellectual and artistic life of his early days, long after they had become a memory, picked out the types of French romanticism in the words 'Hector Berlioz seems to me to form with Hugo and Delacroix the Trinity of Romantic Art'.

The romanticism of Berlioz was innate. His romantic sensibility showed itself in childhood when he would weep at a touching phrase of Virgil, and it expressed itself all through his life in a series of love affairs, varied and numerous even for his nationality and his period. At fourteen he was in love with a local charmer with pink shoes. Then in young manhood, in Paris, he was carried away by admiration for the Irish Shakespearian actress Harriet Smithson whose indifference nearly drove him mad.

He then devoted himself to the fine pianist afterwards well known as Madame Pleyel, and on her taking this name set off on a journey from Rome (where he held the 'Prix de Rome', q.v.), with the intent to murder her and then commit suicide. Thinking better of this, he went back to Rome, and when his study period there was elapsed, in Paris found Miss Smithson again, broke down her resistance, and married her. He now fell in love with a Mademoiselle Recio, a second-rate vocalist with whom he toured Europe, and when his legal wife died, incomprehensibly heart-broken at the loss of one he had neglected, he married the woman for whom he had neglected her. When death overtook his second wife, heart-broken once more he found his thoughts turning again to the lady with pink slippers, sought her out, travelled from Paris to Geneva to see her, and endeavoured to persuade her (now a widow) to marry him; the most she ever accorded him, however, was the privilege of standing godfather to one of her grandchildren.

These romances (enclosed within one another parenthetically, as it were), and some minor ones which cannot be entered into here, may seem irrelevant in a discussion of his position as a composer, but really are directly to the point, as life and art were one with him and such incidents show him as true to one principle of the extremist romantic theory—*not Rule but direct reaction to Feeling*.

Another romantic characteristic of his (shared by some other French composers of the period) was the love of immensity. His Requiem (1837), written for the soldiers killed in the Algerian campaign, calls for over two hundred voices (with a preference for seven or eight hundred), an enormous orchestra, sixteen kettledrums, and four brass bands.

Another (and very marked) characteristic is

the literary influence, his works often being the musical re-expression of the romantic poets—Shakespeare, Scott, Moore, Byron, Goethe, and others. This literary leaning had another side in his activities as a newspaper music critic and author of lively books upon music.

Still another romantic characteristic is the emphasis laid on colour. As an orchestrator he not only demanded giant forces (his ideal included 240 string instruments, 30 grand pianos, 30 harps, and wind and percussion to scale) but also exhibited the most delicate sensibility, studying tiny nuances of tint as nobody before him. In this way he exercised a great influence on all his successors, of whatever nationality.

Finally may be mentioned the romantic characteristic of 'programme' in instrumental music, i.e. a scheme embodying in tone emotions aroused by a series of events or of visible scenes. Thus the five sections of his 'Fantastic' Symphony (with its sub-title 'Episodes in the Life of an Artist') are respectively headed: (1) 'Reveries—Passions'; (2) 'A Ball'; (3) 'Scene in the Country'; (4) 'March to the Scaffold'; and (5) 'Dreams of a Witches' Sabbath'. The whole is bound together by the use of a 'fixed idea' (*idée fixe*), a recurring theme common to all the movements but varied in shape and treatment according to the fluctuating demands of the dramatic scheme. This resembles the devices of two of his friends and contemporaries, the 'metamorphosis of themes' of Liszt and the 'leading motif' of Wagner.

The actual value of the work of Berlioz is the subject of continual debate. There are those who point to a certain naïve childishness in some of his musical themes and his treatment of them, and others who maintain that, interpreted with understanding, passages condemned as commonplace are found to be simple but direct expressions of sincere emotion. Probably he is little likely to be appreciated (even when well interpreted) by those who know nothing of his life and of the literary and artistic school to which he was attached—the school that on enormous canvases or in three-volume novels depicted scenes of horror, glory, or passion.

Amongst his works are the overtures *Waverley*, *Les Francs Juges*, *King Lear*, *The Corsair*, *Rob Roy*, and *The Roman Carnival*; the *Fantastic Symphony*, the symphony with viola obbligato entitled *Harold in Italy*, and the dramatic symphony *Romeo and Juliet*; the Requiem (or *Grande Messe des Morts*) and the *Te Deum*; the charming oratorio *The Childhood of Christ*, and the operas *Benvenuto Cellini*, *Beatrice and Benedict*, and (in two sections) *The Trojans*. There are also certain songs that show him as an effective miniaturist.

His life facts have been partly indicated above. He was the son of a doctor and was sent to Paris to study medicine, but studied music instead, first privately and then (a somewhat rebellious student) at the Conservatory.

The glory and advantage of the Prix de Rome came to him only after five attempts. For a quarter of a century he was music critic of the *Journal des Débats*. He travelled much as conductor of his own music and that of others, and in 1848, 1852, and 1855, was engaged for seasons in London. He had a son whom he dearly loved and sadly lost. His last days were somewhat empty and solitary. The epitaph he suggested for himself came from his admired Shakespeare—the lines which describe life as 'a tale told by an idiot, full of sound and fury, signifying nothing'.

References of greater or lesser importance will be found as follows: *Anglican Parish Church Music* 5; *Applause* 3, 4; *Bagpipe Family* 8; *Ballet* 7; *Cinematograph*; *Clapison*; *Clarinet Family* 4 c; *Colour* 3; *Composition* 5, 12; *Cornet* 1, 2; *Cornett and Keyed Bugle* 2 f, 3 d g; *Criticism* 3, 4, 5, 6; *Dies Irae*; *Expression* 5; *France* 10; *Gesamtausgabe*; *Guitar*; *Harmonica* 2; *Harp* 3; *Harty*; *History* 7; *Leading Motif*; *Lesueur*; *Liszt*; *Mute*; *Octo-basse*; *Opera* 11 d, 12, 24 e; *Opus*; *Oratorio* 1, 4, 7; *Organ* 2, 13; *Osborne*; *Pantomime*; *Percussion Family* 3 o, 4 a b c; *Rákóczy March*; *Ranz des vaches*; *Reed Organ* 9; *Reyer*; *Romantic*; *Rubato* 2; *Symphony* 7; *Tempo*; *Saxophone*; *Scales* 9; *Singing* 7; *Te Deum*; *Temperament* 8; *Trombone Family* 1, 3 (towards end), 4; *Tuba Group* 1; *Waltz*. See also p. 257, pl. **47**. 5.

BERNARD, VALÈRE. See *Colour and Music* 10.

BERNERS, GERALD HUGH TYR-WHITT-WILSON (Lord Berners). Born at Bridgnorth in 1883 and died in London in 1950, aged sixty-six. He entered the diplomatic service (meanwhile composing under his name of 'Gerald Tyrwhitt'), and succeeded to the barony of Berners in 1918. Many of his works were prompted by a sense of irony and some are of the nature of parody. He was for some short period a pupil of Stravinsky and of Casella.

Amongst his musical works are the opera *Le Carosse du Saint Sacrement* (Paris, 1923), and a number of ballets. He had a considerable literary production, including work of an autobiographical nature, and held in London exhibitions of his oil paintings. He was a wealthy man, leaving an estate of nearly a quarter of a million pounds.

BERNIER, RENÉ. See *Synthétistes*.

BERNSTEIN, LEONARD (p. 1069, pl. **176**.6). Born at Lawrence, Mass., in 1918. He studied at Harvard and at the Curtis Institute, Philadelphia. He is a pianist, an orchestral conductor of great popularity (New York Philharmonic 1958–69), and a skilful composer of lively ballets (*Fancy Free*, 1944) and musical comedies (*On the Town*, 1944; *Candide*, 1957; *West Side Story*, 1958), as well as symphonies (*Jeremiah*, 1944; *The Age of Anxiety*, 1949; *Kaddish*, 1963) and other serious works.

See *Clarinet* 6; *Jazz* 5; *Jewish Music* 9; *Oriental* (end); p. 1069, pl. **176**.

BERSAG HORN (Bersaglieri Bugle) (p. 113, pl. **22**. 12). A brass bugle furnished with a single valve lowering the pitch a fourth. It is made in different sizes, all standing in the key of B flat. Being easier to play than a three-valved instrument and giving more variety than the ordinary military bugle, it became popular with bugle bands during the war of 1914–18.

BERTINI, HENRI JÉRÔME. Born in London in 1798 and died near Grenoble in 1876, aged nearly seventy-eight. He was a prolific composer of works for piano solo, chamber music with piano as one of its constituents, and (especially) piano studies. These last are still in use and in good repute, having both technical and musical value (see *Étude*).

BERTRAND, RENÉ. See *Electric Musical Instruments* 1 i.

BERUHIGEN (Ger.). 'To make restful.' So *Beruhigt*, 'restful'; *Beruhigter*, 'more restful'; *Beruhigend*, 'becoming restful'; *Beruhigt*, 'become restful' (past participle); *Beruhigung*, the act of calming.

BERWALD, FRANZ ADOLF. Born at Stockholm in 1796 and died there in 1868, aged seventy-one. He wrote a number of symphonies as well as an opera, several quartets, and numerous other works, and is said by some good judges to show an originality that would have justified a larger impression on the contemporary mind and a more general remembrance of his claims by concert-givers today.

BES (Ger.). B double-flat (see Table 7).

BESCHLEUNIGEN (Ger.). 'To speed up.' Hence the adjective *Beschleunigt*, etc.

BESEELT (Ger.). 'Animated.'

BESSY BELL AND MARY GRAY. See *Vicar of Bray*.

BEST, WILLIAM THOMAS (p. 784, pl. **131**. 5). Born at Carlisle in 1826 and died at Liverpool in 1897, aged seventy. He was recognized as far and away the greatest concert organist of his period, his chief scene of activity being the St. George's Hall, Liverpool, of which he was organist for about forty years (1855 to 1894). He may, indeed, be said to have been the first distinctively concert organist England ever possessed; his repertory was enormous and included not only all the classics of the organ but also quantities of orchestral and other music arranged by him (see *Organ* 13), much of which he published. In addition to this he left some original organ music, church music, and other things, and an edition of Handel's organ works, and another of Bach's.

He was a man of great independence of character and of caustic utterance, and anecdotes illustrative of these traits abound.

See references under *Temperament* 6; *Chorale Prelude*; *Recital*; *Organ* 13.

BESTIMMT (Ger.). 'Decided' in style; also applied to a particular line in the score which is to be made prominent.

BETEND (Ger.). 'Praying.'

BETHLEHEM (Pa.). See *Bohemia*; *United States* 3; *Festival* 2; *Concert* 15; *Clarinet Family* 2.

BETONT (Ger.). 'Stressed', 'emphasized.' *Betonung*, 'accentuation'.

BETRÜBNIS (Ger.). 'Sorrow.'

BETRÜBT (Ger.). 'Saddened.'

BETTERTON, THOMAS (actor, *c.* 1635–1710). See p. 689, pl. **116**. 3.

BEVERLEY. See *Minstrels*, etc. 3.

BEVIN, ELWAY. End of sixteenth and beginning of seventeenth century. He was organist of Bristol Cathedral, wrote a noted book on theory, and composed church music that may still be heard in English cathedrals.

BEWEGLICH (Ger.). 'Agile.'

BEWEGT (Ger.). 'Moved'—either in the sense of motion or of emotion. *Bewegter*, 'quicker'; *Beweglichkeit*, 'agility'.

BEWEGUNG (Ger.). (*a*) 'Rate of motion, speed', or (*b*) 'emotion', or (*c*) 'commotion'.

BÉZA.

(1) THEODORE (1519–1605). Genevan reformer, friend and successor of Calvin. See *Hymns and Hymn Tunes* 4, 17 d; *Old Hundredth*.

(2) MARCU. See *Rumania*.

BG. Short for *Bogen*, i.e. 'Bow'.

BIANCA (It., 'white'). The minim or half-note (Table 3).

BIBELORGEL, BIBELREGAL (Ger.). Bible Regal. See *Reed-Organ Family* 2, 10 a.

BIBER, HEINRICH JOHAN (or Ignaz) FRANZ von (1644–1704). A great violin player and a considerable violin composer. His *Biblical* (or 'Mystery') *Sonatas* offer an early and interesting instance of the use of 'Scordatura' (q.v.).

See references under *Sonata* 10 b; *Bohemia*; *Violin Family* 6.

BIBLE AND MUSIC. See *Jewish* 1; *Psalms*; *Dance* 7.

BIBLE REGAL. See *Reed-Organ Family* 2, 10 a.

BICHORD. Having two strings tuned in unison.

BIEN (Fr.). 'Well', 'very'.

BIGOPHONE or **BIGOTPHONE.** A sort of improved mirliton (q.v.) introduced by one Bigot, a Frenchman, in the 1880s. It seems to be or to have been widely popular, for in 1910 gatherings of 'bigophonists' took place in Paris. It was often made up to resemble in appearance the various brass instruments.

BIHARI, JÁNOS. See *Rákóczy March*.

BILLINGS, WILLIAM. See *United States* 3; *Hymns* 11, 17 f; *Concert* 15 ; *Pitch* 6 a; p. 496, pl. **89**. 2.

BIN. See p. 465, pl. **82**. 3.

BINARY FORM ('Simple' and 'Compound'). See *Form* 4, 5, 7, 8, 13, 14.

BINCHOIS, GILLES. Born about 1400 and died at Soignies in 1460.

He was a soldier who turned musician. He became a chaplain to Philip the Good, composing church music and chansons (q.v.).

See reference under *Passion Music* 1.

BIND. See *Tie or Bind*. Also Table 22.

BINET, JEAN. Born at Geneva in 1893 and died at Trélex-sur-Nyon in 1960, aged sixty-six. He was a well-known Swiss composer (pupil of Jaques-Dalcroze and Ernest Bloch) of choral, orchestral, and chamber works. Periods of his life were spent in the United States and in Belgium, but he later returned to his native country.

BINGHAM, SETH. Born at Bloomfield, N.J., in 1882, and died in New York in 1972. A prominent organist (pupil of Widor and Guilmant), he taught composition and organ on the Columbia University staff, and was the composer of choral, orchestral, and chamber works, etc.

BINIOU. See *Bagpipe Family* 6.

BINNEY, REVD. DR. THOMAS (1798–1874). See *Congregational* 5.

BIRD.

(1) NAPOLEON. See *Memory* 7.

(2) WILLIAM. See *Byrd*.

BIRD MUSIC. But for the humans, birds are perhaps Nature's only musicians.

Bird music is very varied and sometimes quite elaborate. It is an error to suppose that love is, as commonly believed, the one impulse that inspires birds to sing—'Song with birds is in each generation an expression of the whole joy of life at its climax of achievement and well-being. One of its conditions undoubtedly is leisure. It begins with the melting of the snows when winter lifts its hand, and wanes when the duties of family life tax energy to the utmost' (Garstang, *Songs of the Birds*, 1935).

A degree of isolation is another condition for bird music. The social sparrows, jackdaws, and rooks, do not sing, but only chatter, and starlings in flocks do the same, but solitary starlings may often be heard to break out into song—generally of a character closely imitative of some genuine song-bird. There are exceptions from the above general statement as to solitariness as a condition of song. Singing in chorus occurs. It has been recorded of the following amongst American birds—the rice troupial, the red-winged starling, and the goldfinch. The swallows sometimes organize community singing, perched upon telegraph wires, and Witchell (*The Evolution of Bird Song*, 1896) records two instances when he has observed a group of English starlings to be led by a sort of precentor who began a phrase which they completed in chorus. W. H. Hudson (*Birds of La Plata*, 1920) records observing, scattered about a plain, a number of flocks of the crested screamer which sang in turn, each group singing for three or four minutes, until the new song had circulated round the whole area and the turn came back to the first group again—and so on.

It may be observed that the bigger varieties of bird are songless: this may be connected with the fact that one important function of bird song is to advertise as loudly and persistently as possible the singer's identity and his presence on his private territory, thus avoiding unnecessary physical encounters with invaders.

1. HUSS GOING TO THE STAKE, 1415

2. A HUSSITE WAR HYMN, c. 1419

3. COUNT ZINZENDORF (1700–60)

4. AT HERRNHUT IN THE 20TH CENTURY

5. DUSSEK (1760–1812)

6. SMETANA (1824–84)

7. FIBICH (1850–1900)

See also the other side of this plate

1. JANÁČEK (1854–1928)

2. DVOŘÁK (1841–1904)

3. J. B. FOERSTER (1859–1951)

4. SUK (1874–1935)

5. NOVÁK (1870–1949)

6. MARTINU (1890–1959)

7. HÁBA (1893–1973)

8. WEINBERGER (1896–1967)

See also the other side of this plate

Biologically primitive types of birds (says Garstang) have primitive types of song, and the biologically most advanced and modern types show the greatest complexity and variety. This agrees with human musical conditions.

Highest of all in rank comes the blackbird, whom Garstang calls 'The Beethoven of the Birds'. He has long abandoned the mere short cries of his ancestors and freely invents continuous and developed tunes, quite comparable with some of those that our human composers have taken as the subject-matter of their sonatas and symphonies. The blackbird, thrush, and some others of the artistic aristocracy of the bird community, show, as many must have noticed, an appreciation of the octave and the common chord (doh-me-soh) and introduce these into many of their tunes. There is a great variety in blackbird song, and it appears as though an individual will fashion a little tune that pleases him and then somewhat extend it from year to year.

Birds can sometimes be observed engaged at something that looks like definite 'practice'. The fine vocalist, Ffrangcon Davies (*The Singing of the Future*, 1905), describes an instance of an American robin which he noticed to be so engaged, day after day, in Central Park, New York. The bird gradually acquired the power to utter clearly the notes at which he was striving, and then it was easy for the observer to record his song in musical notation, as dozens of bird songs have been recorded.

Keen observers report that young unfledged birds in the nest can be heard quietly trying their throats and accustoming them to vocal utterance: lapwings have been noticed to make sounds whilst still in the egg.

Birds learn their song, in the first instance, from their parents.[1] A bird reared in captivity and in isolation from its species will not sing the natural song of its race. All birds are very imitative, and though gifted individuals, like those amongst the blackbirds, may be said to compose, for the most part the bird community expresses itself through what we may call 'folk song' handed down the generations. This 'folk song' will, like human 'folk song', vary somewhat in different districts, though the same tune is obviously in mind.

Good songsters are rarely gay-coloured. It is the sober nightingales, larks, linnets, blackbirds, and thrushes that sing best. (There are exceptions from this, as the American bluebird and the British goldfinch.)

The demeanour of birds in song varies according to their temperament. The nightingale is lost in ecstasy; the pigeon utters its song lazily, like a cat purring. Many birds accompany their songs with some invariable characteristic gesture.

Certain birds are definitely mimics, as the American mocking bird (which has a fine song of its own also) and the catbird. Mozart, who,

[1] The cuckoo appears to be an inexplicable exception: it does not adopt the song of its foster-parents but that of its real parents, whom it has never known.

like some other musicians, managed to keep a ledger for a few weeks, records in it the expenditure of 34 Kreutzer (approximately 7*d.*) on a trained starling. He enters in the ledger, in musical notation, the song it had been taught to sing and adds the words 'Das war schön' ("That was beautiful'). Various instruments have been sold for teaching birds to sing tunes (see *Mechanical Reproduction* 6), and the British Museum has a manuscript (*c.* 1700) on the subject by John Hamersley, with a series of simple little tunes (*A Description of all the Musical Birds in the Kingdom . . . also several New Tunes made for Birds, and may be taught them by the Cantillo or Small Flageolet*).

The question has been raised as to the system on which birds sing. Is it by fixed pitch or relative pitch? Are they 'Fixed-dohists' or 'Movable-dohists'? Sir James Swinburne, Bt., F.R.S. ('Mental Processes in Music', in *Proceedings of the Musical Association*, 1918–19), recorded observation of a grey parrot that had been taught to whistle bits of Beethoven. When the words 'Pastoral Sonata' were uttered he would whistle a fragment of it and so forth. 'I kept a sheet of paper and whenever the parrot whistled a tune I noted the tune and the pitch. For about a week he whistled each tune approximately at its own pitch. One day, put out in the sun, he seemed to run melodious riot. He whistled most of the tunes, repeating them over and over again, and at all sorts of pitches. It is clear, therefore, that a parrot does not work on the absolute pitch principle; but I cannot penetrate further into its mental processes.' (See *Absolute Pitch.*)

Most people think that only cock birds sing. This is not quite true: some hens have a sort of whispered song, noted only by keen observers. The European bullfinch is an example.

The best British song-birds are said to be the nightingale, blackbird, blackcap, and skylark, which the naturalist Sir William Beach Thomas has cleverly likened, from their style and the temperament it seems to express, to Shakespeare, Milton, Chaucer, and Wordsworth. To these the thrush (? Tennyson) must surely be added.

Amongst North American birds with definite tunes as songs, and these of considerable length (20–30 notes) and an attractive rhythm, are the rose-breasted grosbeak, the scarlet tanager, the warbling vireo, and the ruby-crowned kinglet (see a very detailed article by W. B. Olds in the *Musical Quarterly*, April 1922). The song of the canary has been carefully developed by breeders, so that a good bird, such as is entered for one of the singing competitions held all over the world, should have as many as fourteen different 'tours' or phrases (the 'glucke', the 'shuckle', the 'roll', etc.), and such a bird may sell for £50. Daines Barrington, the eighteenth-century naturalist and littérateur, conducted a sort of singing competition of his own, of another sort, in which he entered all the chief British birds: he devised a detailed marking-sheet, with 20 marks each for such points as mellowness of tone, compass, etc.: the nightingale comes out top with 90 marks and the 'red sparrow' bottom with 10. (Article in *Harmonicon*, 1825.)

A little instrumental music is to be observed amongst birds. Certain species beat with the wing and drum with the beak, etc. There is also some dancing. The South American cock-of-the-rock (*Rupicolina*) gathers for dancing displays and competitions, several individuals dancing in turn whilst the others look on.

Garstang emphasizes the view that we are not to regard birds as automatic musical-boxes, but as sound-lovers who cultivate the pursuit of sound-combination as an art as truly as we have cultivated our arts of a similar aesthetic character. To many of the birds 'art has become a real object in life—no less real than the pursuit of food or the maintenance of a family'. It is a mistake to think that the sole object of bird song is the attracting of a mate. Whether birds find what we would call aesthetic pleasure in their own or each other's song is much discussed. For those who hold that aesthetic appreciation has a biological foundation, it is reasonable to assume its presence in some degree among animals. Three British birds sing regularly in autumn: the thrush, blackbird, and robin (quite different from the American bird called by the same name). The blackbird's songs are much softer and more restrained in autumn than in spring; the thrush's and robin's are little changed.

The human composers who have recalled or imitated their bird colleagues are very numerous. In the sixteenth century we have two very famous choral pieces, Jannequin's *Song of the Birds* and Gombert's piece of the same title, and a three-part string fancy by John Baldwin, based on the cuckoo's cry. The eighteenth-century French harpsichord composers, such as Couperin, Daquin, Dagincourt, and Rameau, abound in compositions of which the titles and the character of the music remind us of the songs and calls of nightingales, linnets, cuckoos, and turtle-doves. J. J. Walther (b. 1650) imitates bird sounds in his chamber music. Handel often introduces imitations of bird notes, as, for instance, in his 'Cuckoo and Nightingale' Organ Concerto, his 'Nightingale Chorus' in *Solomon*, and his 'Hush, ye pretty warbling choir' in *Acis*. In the opera *Rinaldo* the description before Act I, Scene vi, is 'a delightful place with fountains, an avenue, and an aviary in which birds are flying and singing': here he makes play with two flutes and a flageolet and at the opera's first performance (in London, 1711) quantities of sparrows were let loose on the stage (Addison in the *Spectator* made great fun of the circumstances—'Instead of perching on the trees and performing their parts, these young actors either get into the Galleries or put out the Candles'). Handel's contemporaries (e.g. Telemann) wrote innumerable 'Nightingale Arias'. Bach wrote a fugue with a cock-crow as subject (*Tema all' imitatio gallina cucca*); it seems as though it

may have been suggested by Poglietti's fugue on the song of the nightingale (1683). Haydn's 41st String Quartet (in C) is sometimes called 'The Bird Quartet'; the nightingale and other birds are alleged to be represented in the first movement and the cuckoo in the last. Haydn had, of course, to make a place for the birds in his *Creation* and his *Seasons*, and Leopold Mozart's 'Toy' Symphony (like others later) brings them in by means of imitative toys. Boccherini has a string quintet, *L'uccelliera* ('The Aviary'). Beethoven's bird music in the 'Pastoral' Symphony, and Wagner's in *Siegfried*, are known to everybody. Saint-Saëns's *Animals' Carnival* and Granados's piano pieces, *Goyescas*, have bird music. Vaughan Williams's *The Lark Ascending* is based on Meredith's poem. In the prologue of Rimsky-Korsakof's opera, *The Snow Maiden* (which prologue is intended to suggest the coming of spring), are many imitations of bird music. Respighi published a suite, *The Birds* ('Gli Uccelli'), which is an orchestral recasting of bird pieces by various old composers, and in his orchestral *The Pines of Rome* he introduced a gramophone recording of the actual song of the nightingale. These are just a few examples.

The cuckoo (i.e. the bird of that name in the eastern hemisphere, not the American one, which is silent) has quite a literature of its own. In addition to the compositions above mentioned we find it in several English madrigals of the early seventeenth century, in keyboard music such as Frescobaldi's *Capriccio sopra il Cucho* (1624), Kerll's *Capriccio Kuku* (1679), and Pasquini's *Toccata con lo Scherzo del Cuccó* (1698), in Purcell's *Fairy Queen* (1692), and so on, down to the cheap 'Storm Pieces' played by old-time organists, in which, when the weather takes up, the cuckoo tells the world (some early organs actually had a special cuckoo stop). Vivaldi (*c.* 1675–1741) has amongst his twelve string concertos a 'Cuckoo' Concerto illustrative of the changing year. Delius's orchestral composition *On Hearing the First Cuckoo in Spring* is a well-known modern instance.

The American composer, Wallingford Riegger, made a hobby of collecting bird songs, of which he notated some hundreds. Messiaen has studied the subject in great depth and a number of his works show this.

The well-known gramophone recordings of bird songs, by Dr. Ludwig Koch (1881–1974), are important as a means of studying the subject. Processes of transcribing bird-song are fully discussed by M. E. W. North in *The Ibis*, 92 (1950).

BIRD QUARTET. See above and *Nicknamed Compositions* 12.

BIRGE, EDWARD BAILEY. See *Education* 3.

BIRMINGHAM (England). See *Festival* 1; *Jew's Harp* (end).

BIRMINGHAM SCHOOL OF MUSIC. See *Degrees and Diplomas* 2.

BIS (Fr.). 'Twice.' (So used in French when English use 'Encore'; also used in a score to indicate that a passage is to be repeated.)

BIS (Ger.). 'Until.'

BISBIGLIATO (It.). 'Whispered.'

BISCROMA (It.). Demisemiquaver or thirty-second note (see Table 3).

BISHOP.

(1) HENRY ROWLEY (p. 705, pl. **118**. 1). Born in London in 1786 and died there in 1855, aged sixty-eight. He was a famous London opera conductor and composer, and Professor of Music successively at the Universities of Edinburgh and Oxford. One song from an opera of his is universally known, 'Home, sweet home' (q.v.), as are a few of his many glees and part-songs. Queen Victoria, in 1842, dubbed him knight, this being the first occasion upon which a British monarch had so honoured any musician. (For earlier instances due to Lieutenant-Governors of Ireland see *Ireland* 6.)

Allusions to Bishop will be found under *Opera* 13 d, 21 c, 25, 26; *Arrangement*; *Theme Song*; *Knighthood*; *Flute Family* 4; *Bochsa.*

(2) BAINBRIDGE. See *Colour and Music* 10.

BITTEND (Ger.). 'Entreating.'

BITTNER, JULIUS. Born in Vienna in 1874 and there died in 1939, aged sixty-five. After an early and successful career in the law he turned to music. He is known as the composer of a number of successful operas and other stage works (a ballet, etc.), as also of songs, chamber music, etc.

BIZET, GEORGES (really Alexandre César Léopold) (p. 369, pl. **62**. 8). Born in Paris in 1838 and died near there in 1875, aged thirty-seven. At the Paris Conservatory he won the Prix de Rome, and he married the daughter of his composition professor, Halévy.

His efforts to win recognition as an opera composer were slow in fruition. Three works still occasionally to be heard are *The Pearl Fishers* (1863), *The Fair Maid of Perth* (1867), and *Djamileh* (1872). They seem today thin-blooded and conventional.

A hit was made with an overture to Sardou's *Patrie*, and this is still frequently seen in concert programmes. The incidental music to Daudet's *L'Arlésienne* is most of it charming, and is known to concert audiences in its form of two suites for orchestra. Two other suites are *Rome* (intended as a symphony and sometimes so called) and *Children's Games*. In addition there exist a youthful Symphony in C (first performed only in 1935) and two movements of another symphony.

The now universally popular *Carmen* (q.v.) was a setting of a libretto taken from the story of the same name by Mérimée. It is a Spanish gipsy opera. Its success was not immediate and the composer died three months after its first performance, 1875. The tunefulness and delicate, piquant orchestration of Bizet are very attractive, and in this work, at any rate, he shows dramatic power.

When Nietzsche burned his idol, Wagner, whom he had long faithfully worshipped, he set up Bizet in his place—'With *Carmen* we take leave of the damp north, of all the mists of the Wagnerian ideal. This music possesses the limpid, dry atmosphere of warmer climes.' All the same, the inhabitants of the 'warmer climes' the opera purports to represent have never cared for it; one does not hear a Spaniard praise *Carmen*. But that is on the ground of its alleged lack of fidelity as a reproduction of Spanish life and Spanish musical style, and the setting up of *Carmen* as a model specimen of what Nietzsche called 'Mediterraneanism' in musical art has nevertheless a good deal to recommend it.

See *Opera* 12, 21 k, 24 e, 25; *Opéra Comique*; *Carmen*; *Incidental Music*; *Melodrama*; *Suite* 7; *Spain* 10; *Habanera*; *Farandole*; *Polo*; *Seguidilla*; *Horn Family* 3; *Cornet* 2; *Saxophone*; *Percussion* 4 c; *Lacombe, Paul*; *Chaminade*; *Halévy.*

BIZZARO (It.). 'Bizarre', 'whimsical'.

BJÖRNSON. See references under *Grieg*; *Kjerulf*; *Halling.*

BKl. Short for *Bassklarinette*, i.e. bass clarinet.

BLACHER, BORIS. Born in Newchwang, China (of Russian-German parents) in 1903 and died in Berlin in 1975. He taught at the Berlin Hochschule from 1948 (director from 1953), and composed in a closely organized 'mathematical' style with an instinct for theatrical effect. He composed operas (e.g. *Die Flut*, 1946; *Romeo und Julia*, 1950), ballets, an oratorio, orchestral music and piano music, etc.

BLACK BOTTOM. A form of foxtrot (q.v.) which had a short career in American and European ballrooms during the 1920s.

BLACK-EYED SUSAN. The words of this song were by Gay (about 1720). There have been a number of different tunes to it, the one now known being by Leveridge (q.v.).

BLACK PUDDING. Serpent. See *Cornett and Key Bugle Families* 2 d, 3 d, 4 d.

BLACKSMITH. See *Greensleeves.*

BLADDER AND STRING. One of the burlesque means of music-making common in the eighteenth century (and possibly earlier and later). Hogarth's print of *The Beggar's Opera Burlesqued* (p. 512, pl. **91**. 6) will make clear the manner of performance (cf. *Bumbass*).

For other instruments of this class see: *Bellows and Tongs*; *Tongs and Bones*; *Marrow Bones and Cleaver*; *Saltbox.*

BLAHOSLAV, JOHN (d. 1571). See *Bohemia.*

BLAKE, WILLIAM. See *Jerusalem.*

BLANC, GIUSEPPE (1886–1969). See *Giovinezza.*

BLANCHE (Fr. for 'white'). The minim or half-note (Table 3).

BLANDFORD, W. T. H. See *Clarinet Family* 4 f (note); *Mechanical Reproduction* 9; *Inventionshorn.*

BLASEND, STARK. See *Horn Family* 5.

G

BLASINSTRUMENTE (Ger.). 'Blow-instruments', i.e. wind instruments.

BLASIS, CARLO. Great early nineteenth-century ballet master, whose academy at Milan (with a very severe eight years' course) became the leading dancing-school in Europe. He spent some time in England.

See *Dance* 10.

BLASMUSIK (Ger.). 'Blow-music', i.e. music of wind instruments.

BLECH (Ger.). 'Sheet metal'; so the Brass.

BLECHMUSIK (Ger.). 'Brass music', i.e. brass band.

BLEIBEN (Ger.). 'To remain.' So *Bleibt*, 'remains', in organ music, means that the stop in question remains in use.

BLENDING THE REGISTERS. The act, in vocal practice, of so controlling the voice that the break between one register and another (see *Voice* 4) is little perceptible.

BLIND HARRY. See *Scotland* 6.

BLIND TOM (Born in Georgia in 1849 and died in New York in 1908). He was a Negro musician (born a slave and an idiot) with an amazing musical memory.

See *Memory* 7.

BLISS, ARTHUR (p. 352, pl. 55. 4). Born in London in 1891 and died there in 1975, aged eighty-three. He studied at Cambridge University under Charles Wood, and at the Royal College of Music under Stanford and Vaughan Williams, the first World War interrupting the latter course of study. He lived for a time in California. A symphony of his in 1922 aroused discussion from the fact that, each movement being initially inspired by a colour impression, he gave it the title 'Colour' Symphony. (See *Colour and Music* 11). The large-scale choral-orchestral *Morning Heroes* dates from 1930. He supplied the music for H. G. Wells's *Things to Come* and other films. In 1937 his ballet *Checkmate* had its first performance—in Paris by an English company. A piano concerto dates from 1939. In 1944 a remarkable tragedy-ballet, *Miracle in the Gorbals*, was introduced and, from the sensational nature of its subject, much discussed. Another ballet is *Adam Zero*. In 1949 an opera, *The Olympians* (libretto by J. B. Priestley), was introduced at Covent Garden.

Bliss was Musical Director of the BBC 1941–4.

He was knighted in 1950 (K.C.V.O. 1969) and in 1953 became Master of the Queen's Musick.

See references under *Composition* (near end); *Melodrama*; *Competition* 3; *Oboe Family* 6; *Clarinet Family* 6; *Concerto* 6 c (1891); *Opera* 24 f (1949); *Ballet* 5.

BLITHEMAN, WILLIAM. Died 1591. He was a famous organist of Queen Elizabeth's Chapel Royal and composed church music and also virginal music, this latter of great originality and important for its influence on the work of his pupil, colleague, and successor in the organistship, John Bull (q.v.).

BLITZSTEIN, MARC. Born in Philadelphia in 1905 of a Russian Jewish family; killed in an affray in Martinique in 1964, aged fifty-eight. He began public life as an accomplished solo pianist and then studied composition with Nadia Boulanger, Schönberg, and others. His compositions, though at first in line with contemporary feeling, were never experimental in idiom. His acute social consciousness (he was a member of the Communist party, 1938–49) showed itself in his choice of subjects, as in his notable musical play, *The Cradle will Rock* (1937). He also translated and adapted the Brecht–Weill *Dreigroschenoper* ('Threepenny Opera') and at the time of his death was at work on an opera commissioned by the Metropolitan, *Sacco and Vanzetti*. His *Regina* (1949) was also successful, and he wrote incidental music for numerous plays and films. His concert music is less often heard.

See *Concerto* 6 c, 1905; also p. 1068, pl. **175.** 7.

BLOCH, ERNEST (p. 1057, pl. **172.** 5). Born at Geneva in 1880 and died at Portland, Ore., in 1959, aged seventy-eight. He was a Jew, trained in Switzerland and in Belgium, Germany, and France.

When his varied musical education was completed he returned to his native place and entered the family business, composing in his spare time. When he was thirty his opera *Macbeth*, written many years before, was performed in Paris, where it made a stir as the work of an overturner of the good old musical customs. About the same time he directed in Switzerland concerts of some of his orchestral works, and so began to come further into notice.

Five years later he went to the United States as the conductor for the dancer, Maud Allan, and there he remained, occupying for a time various educational positions. Many of his works were first performed in the United States. He often chose Jewish themes, and showed in much of his work an oriental and rhapsodic exuberance. Yet there are certain pieces of his in a more atmospheric, evocative, or impressionistic style, and his Concerto Grosso (1925) for string orchestra and piano shows decided neo-classic tendencies.

In his later life his work (symphonies, symphonic poems, a violin concerto, chamber music, a 'Sacred Service', songs, etc.) gained steadily in reputation, and in 1937 a society was formed in London to secure its performance.

See *Concerto* 6 c (1880); *Microtones*.

BLOCKFLÖTE, BLOCK FLUTE. See *Recorder Family* 2; *Organ* 14 II.

BLOCKX, JAN. Born at Antwerp in 1851 and died there in 1912, aged sixty-one. He was a pupil of Peter Benoît in the Royal Conservatory of Antwerp, of which he later joined the staff, rising to be its principal. He also received training at the Conservatories of Brussels and of Leipzig.

Like Benoît, he was a strong propagandist of

See the Article *Brass* on pages 126–7

1. ROMAN TRUMPETS—Tuba (straight) and Buccina (circular). From Trajan's Column, Rome—1st century A.D.

2. REBEC and CORNETT
In the 12th-century crypt of Canterbury Cathedral

AN 18TH-CENTURY BRASS INSTRUMENT WORKSHOP
(From the *Dictionnaire des Arts*, vol. xx)

FIG. 1. A bar ('mandrin', *a*, *b*) is fixed to the wall and is partly covered with a thin piece of copper to which the workman is giving its first form

FIG. 2. The different pieces of which a Horn or Trumpet is made are being soldered together

FIG. 3. Melted lead is being poured into a Horn in order that it may be possible to bend it into shape without it losing its roundness

FIG. 4. The Horn is being shaped, after which it will be heated to melt the lead so that this may be poured out

FIG. 5. Anvil for the shaping of the bell of an instrument

For further pictures see other side and page 140

1–9. CORNETT AND KEY BUGLE FAMILIES.
(1) Small Treble Cornett, 1518. (2) Treble Cornett, *c.* 1600. (3) Great Cornett, *c.* 1600. (4) Mute Cornett, 17th cent. (5) Straight Cornett. (6) Serpent, late 18th cent. (7) Bass Horn, *c.* 1800, (8) Ophicleide, early 19th cent. (9) Key Bugle, *c.* 1820. See pp. 256–8

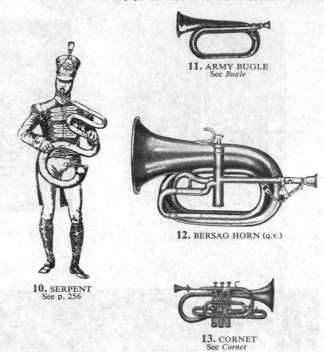

10. SERPENT
See p. 256

11. ARMY BUGLE
See *Bugle*

12. BERSAG HORN (q.v.)

13. CORNET
See *Cornet*

14, 15. FRENCH MILITARY BUGLE AND TRUMPET OF THE 1870's. See *Bugle* and *Trumpet Family*

16. TUBA. See *Tuba Group*

17. TROMBONE. See *Trombone Family*

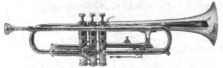

18. TRUMPET OF TODAY. See *Trumpet Family*

For other pictures illustrating the Brass see other side and page 140

the national Flemish movement (cf. *Belgium* 6). He wrote cantatas and operas, often to Flemish texts, and also some instrumental music. His death came suddenly, from apoplexy.

BLOM, ERIC WALTER. Born in Berne in 1888 and died in London in 1959, aged seventy. He was of partly Danish and Swiss descent but British nationality. He was an active musical journalist (critic of the *Birmingham Post* 1931–46, and later of the London *Observer*) and author of many biographical and critical books on music and of *Everyman's Dictionary of Music* (1947); editor of Dent's *Master Musicians* series and the fifth edition of Grove's *Dictionary of Music and Musicians*; editor of *Music and Letters* 1937–50 and from 1954 (cf. *Fox Strangways*; *Capell*).

BLOMDAHL, KARL-BIRGER. Born at Växjö in 1916 and died at Kungsängen, near Stockholm in 1968, aged fifty-one. He was a pupil of Hilding Rosenberg. His works include symphonies, concertos, chamber music, and a successful opera, *Aniara* (1959).

BLOOMFIELD, ROBERT. See *Aeolian Harp*.

BLOSS (Ger.). 'Mere', 'merely'.

BLOW, JOHN (p. 164, pl. **33.** 6). Born near Newark in 1649 (not 1648) and died at Westminster in 1708, aged fifty-nine. When, after the Commonwealth, organ and choir were again admitted to the service of the English Church, he was one of the first choir-boys of the Chapel Royal, of which place he was appointed organist in later life, as also of Westminster Abbey. His songs and harpsichord compositions are worthy of being kept in remembrance, and he was a voluminous and dignified and, indeed, really valuable writer for the services of the church.

He is thought to have been one of the masters of Henry Purcell, some of whose idioms apparently derive from him, as do those of other composers of the Purcell period.

See references under *Anthem* (Period II); *Masque*; *Cecilia*; *Degrees and Diplomas*; *Publishing of Music* 5; *Cooke, Henry*; *Wise*; *Turner*.

BLUE BELLS OF SCOTLAND (properly 'Bell' and not 'Bells'). This song first appears at the very end of the eighteenth or the beginning of the nineteenth century, as one sung by the famous London actress, Mrs. Jordan (an Irishwoman), at Drury Lane Theatre. The origin of the words and tune are not known—the conjectures of various writers not appearing to possess much substance.

BLUE BONNETS OVER THE BORDER. The poem is by Sir Walter Scott, the tune an old Scottish one.

BLUE DANUBE WALTZ. See *Gramophone* 6; *Waltz*.

BLUE LAWS. See *United States of America* 2.

BLUEMEL or **BLUEHMEL.** See *Trumpet Family* 3.

BLUES. As heard since about 1920, the Blues takes the form of a sort of bitter-sweet jazz song or dance-song. It is written in quadruple time, and generally moves at slow speed and in more or less flowing style over an unvarying twelve-bar bass. Stanzas are of three lines, each covering four bars of music. The third and seventh of the key are often prominent, being played somewhere between the major and minor form of the interval, and are known as 'blue notes'.

The earlier history of the Blues belongs almost entirely to the Negro. It can be traced by oral tradition as far back as the 1860s; the conventional harmonic foundation is largely a European contribution. Researchers have suggested the pedigree: India—Arabia—Spain—Africa—Caribbean—New Orleans. As with other forms of jazz, there are various developments for mass consumption. These include 'Rhythm and Blues', 'Rock and Roll', and the like.

BLUME, FRIEDRICH (1893–1975). He studied medicine, philosophy, and music at Eisenach, Munich, Berlin, and Leipzig, and then embarked on a distinguished career as editor of old music and writer of scholarly studies on a wide variety of subjects. Beginning in 1943, he directed the preparation of the monumental work *Die Musik in Geschichte und Gegenwart* (see *Dictionaries* 1).

BLÜMEL or **BLÜHMEL.** See *Trumpet Family* 3.

BLUMENFELD, FELIX. Born in the district of Kherson, Russia, in 1863 and died in Moscow in 1931, aged sixty-eight. He studied at the Conservatory of St. Petersburg, became a fine pianist, and joined its staff as a teacher of piano. Later he became one of the conductors of the State Opera House. His piano music is popular, and he also wrote chamber music and songs.

BLUMENTHAL, JACOB. Born at Hamburg in 1829 and died in London in 1908, aged seventy-eight. He was pianist to Queen Victoria and teacher to the ladies of the London aristocracy, and for the drawing-rooms of the British Isles, in all their thousands, provided much tuneful vocal and instrumental recreation.

BLÜTHNER. Piano-making firm founded at Leipzig in 1853. See *Pianoforte* 16.

BLYTHE (Salem, Mass.). See *Harpsichord Family* 4.

B.M. 'Bandmaster' (but see also *Degrees* 3).

BMI. See *Copyright* 2.

B MOLL (Ger.). The key of B flat minor (*not* B minor: see *B*).

B.MUS. See *Degrees and Diplomas* 1.

BOAR'S HEAD CAROL. See *Carols*.

BOAS, F. S. See *God save the Queen* 19.

BOATSWAIN'S MATE, THE. See *Smyth*.

BOBILLIER. See *Brenet*.

BOBS (change ringing). See *Bells* 2.

BOCCA CHIUSA (It.). 'Closed mouth'—the

term used (in occasional choral music) to indicate a wordless humming.

BOCCHERINI, LUIGI. Born at Lucca in 1743 and died at Madrid in 1805, aged sixty-two. He was a fine cellist and a writer of instrumental music, especially of chamber music, of which he wrote enormous quantities (nearly fifty string trios and over one hundred each of string quartets and quintets—and so on), much influencing the new school.

His life period was much the same as that of Haydn (1732–1809), and his ideals, methods, and spirit were much the same.

See under *Symphony* 8; *Spain* 10; *Misattributed*; *Concerto* 6 b (1743); *Chamber Music* 6, Period III (1743); *Bird Music*.

BOCETO (Sp.). A 'sketch'. Granados and other Spanish composers use the word.

BOCHSA, NICOLAS (in full, Robert Nicolas Charles). Born at Montmédy, in Lorraine, France, in 1787 and died at Sydney, New South Wales, in 1856, aged sixty-eight. He was the official harpist both to Bonaparte and to Louis XVIII, and the inventor, or perfecter, of modern harp technique. He wrote a famous Harp Method, composed harp music (see *Harp* 4) and operas, left his country for his country's good on being detected in large-scale forgeries to the tune of £30,000 in the names of his Parisian colleagues Boïeldieu and Méhul, and of the Duke of Wellington, was condemned in absence to twelve years' imprisonment, and so, instead of returning, conducted oratorios in London, there committed bigamy, and, in addition, ran away with the wife of his brother opera composer, Sir Henry Bishop, toured the Old World and the New as a harp virtuoso, and wrote an oratorio called *The Flood*, and, when death approached, a solemn Requiem which was duly performed at his funeral—let us hope with effect!

BODLEIAN LIBRARY, OXFORD. See *Libraries*; *Modes* 10.

BOECK, AUGUSTE DE. Born at Merchtem, Belgium, in 1865 and there died in 1937, aged seventy-two. He held a number of important educational positions and wrote a symphony, operas, and ballets.

BOEHM.

(1) GEORG. See under *Böhm*.
(2) THEOBALD. See *Boehm System*; *Flute Family* 2; *Clarinet Family* 2.

BOEHM FLUTE. See *Boehm System*; *Flute Family* 2.

BOEHM SYSTEM. This takes its name from a Munich flute-player, Theobald Boehm (1793–1881), who applied inventive talent to his instrument, so as to replace its system of holes in compromise positions by a system of keys enabling all holes to be cut in the ideal acoustical positions and yet to be under the easy control of the fingers (see *Flute Family* 2). The convenience gained for chromatic passages was so great that despite some incidental loss of tone quality the system is now almost uni-

versally adopted in flute-making. It has also been applied, though less successfully, to the oboe (and more rarely to the bassoon) and also to the clarinet (see *Clarinet Family* 2).

(From advertisements in English musical journals of 1840 it is clear that this was the date when the Boehm flute was becoming known in England.)

BOËLLMANN, LÉON. Born at Ensisheim, in Upper Alsace, in 1862 and died in Paris in 1897, aged thirty-five. He had his musical training at the Niedermeyer School of Church Music in Paris, where his master was Gigout, under whom he acquired high ability as an organist. He became organist of the church of St. Vincent de Paul and wrote good organ music (including an often-heard *Gothic Suite*) and also music for other instruments (including the well-known Symphonic Variations for cello and orchestra).

BOËLY, ALEXANDRE PIERRE FRANÇOIS. Born at Versailles in 1785 and died in Paris in 1858, aged seventy-three. He was organist of St. Germain l'Auxerrois, in Paris, and was one of the first French organists to appreciate Bach and to play him. He composed chiefly for the keyboard instruments, and influenced César Franck and others of those who in the nineteenth century were working towards the worthier development of French music, especially in the neglected instrumental field. (Cf. *Pianoforte* 15 (end).)

BOEMO, PADRE. See *Bohemia*.

BOESSET (or Boësset, or Boisset), ANTOINE. He was born about 1585 and died in Paris in 1643, aged about fifty-eight. He was a favourite of Louis XIII and director of music at his court, and the son-in-law of Guédron (q.v.). He had an outstanding melodic gift, and his fame in his own days was high, but his music, which lacked dramatic strength, was superseded by that of Lully (q.v.).

BOETHIUS and **BOETHIAN NOTATION.** See *Notation* 1; *Education and Music* 1.

BOG. Short for *Bogen* (see below).

BOGEN (Ger.). (1) 'Bow'; so *Bogenstrich*, 'bow stroke'. (2) Short for *Krummbogen* (q.v.).

BOHÈME, LA (Puccini). Produced at Turin in 1896. Libretto (Italian) by Giacosa and Illica, founded on Murger's novel *La Vie de Bohème*.

ACT I

SCENE: *A Garret in Paris. Time, about 1830. Christmas Eve*

Marcello (*Baritone*), a painter, and Rodolfo (*Tenor*), a poet, are hard up, like their friends Colline (*Bass*), a philosopher, and Schaunard (*Baritone*), a musician. A tiny windfall produces a feast. Benoit (*Bass*), the landlord, comes in for the rent, and, being plied with wine, forgets about it, so the money is saved for an evening out.

When Rodolfo is alone **Mimi** (*Soprano*), his neighbour, knocks at the door. Her candle has gone out, and she asks for a light. She loses her key, which Rodolfo, finding, privily pockets. In feeling for it on the floor, their fingers meet, and he sings 'Your tiny hand is frozen'. They exchange confidences, fall in love, and then go out together to join Rodolfo's friends at the café.

Act II

Scene: *A Street in the Latin Quarter*

A lively crowd is abroad this Christmas Eve. Along comes **Musetta** (*Soprano*), an old flame of Marcello's, who has taken up with a new, though older, lover, **Alcindoro** (*Bass*). Marcello can still be attracted, she finds, and by a trick Alcindoro is left to pay for everybody's supper, while the former lovers pair off again.

Act III

Scene: *One of the City Gates (the 'barrière d'enfer'). February*

Mimi enters. She is ill of consumption. Rodolfo, she tells Marcello, is jealous. She hides when Rodolfo appears and tells Marcello that he wants a separation from her. Her coughing reveals her presence. Rodolfo is repentant at seeing her so ill. Meanwhile Marcello and his Musetta, in their turn, have a quarrel: so those who were together part, and those who parted come together again, singing 'Our time for parting is when the roses blow'.

Act IV

Scene: *The Garret*

The four friends are working. The two lovers, Marcello and Rodolfo, have again lost their fickle partners. The jokes of the careless Bohemians are silenced when Musetta brings home Mimi, who dies in Rodolfo's arms.

BOHEMIA (with references also to Moravia). The activity of Bohemia in the art of music has been very great, and its contribution to the development and repertory of the art merits recognition. To discuss in a short article this activity and this contribution is difficult. The Bohemians proper are of that Slav race that (extending a term beyond its strict limits) we call Czech. But not only has the race expanded (for instance, into the neighbouring Moravia), but many of its members have carried through their life work in Austria and Germany; and, on the other hand, from the fourteenth century there has been a great deal of German colonization in Bohemia, so that, at the present time, Bohemia (forming since 1918 the western province of the republic of Czechoslovakia) has 2½ million persons of German race and language mingled with its 4½ million Czechs—or had up to the close of the Second World War, since when precise information is difficult to obtain.

Christianity was introduced into this territory in the ninth century. Of musical relics of the pre-Christian era none is certainly known to exist, but the great musicologist O. Hostinsky (1847–1910) was of the opinion that certain Christmas begging songs, still to be heard in his time, had come down from that era.

The branch of Christianity represented by the missionaries who undertook the conversion of Bohemia being the Roman one, the Gregorian chant quickly overspread the country. The cathedral of St. Vitus, at Prague (founded by 'Good King Wenceslas'), has always been a great centre of religious musical culture. In 1254 the records speak of a 'new' organ, showing that the use of the instrument goes back behind this period. Five years later there is mention of the choir being reconstituted on ampler lines, and in 1343 of a still wider development in the choral resources of the church, bringing the total personnel, on the greater occasions, up to one hundred, organized, apparently, in several separate bodies, responsible for different features of the services.

The religious and nationalist movement initiated by John Huss (1373–1415), a precursor of the general Protestant movement of northern Europe of the sixteenth century, had a considerable influence on church music. The Hussites in Bohemia (like the Calvinists a century and a half later in other countries) insisted on the use of the vernacular in the singing of the church, and (in many places) disapproved of the church use of the organ and other instruments. Like their successors in the other countries, both Calvinist and Lutheran, they greatly favoured congregational singing and brought into religious use both secular airs adapted to new words and new melodies specially composed.

A division of the Hussites into several different sects soon took place. The members of the Utraquist section (moderate in views) ultimately became reabsorbed in the Roman Catholic body, or joined the Lutherans, whilst the Taborite section (more extreme) became socially and politically very important and then was almost crushed out of existence at the beginning of the Thirty Years War, after the Battle of the White Mountain (1620). In the early eighteenth century the remnant (largely German by race, and many of them in Moravia rather than Bohemia itself) fled from persecution into Saxony, where they settled on the estate of Count Zinzendorf, founded the town of Herrnhut (whence the name sometimes given to their sect, 'Herrnhuter'), and then, on again being subjected to persecution, migrated to other parts of Germany, to England, and to America. In this way were brought into existence such settlements as those at Bethlehem, Pennsylvania (1742), of which the musical traditions are still maintained (see *United States* 3; *Concert* 15; *Festival* 2; *Clarinet Family* 2), and at Fulneck, near Bradford, Yorkshire (1748—named after Fulnek in Moravia), which was at once equipped with an organ by Snetzler, and forthwith began its musical activities. It is clear from these examples that the early Hussite dislike of instrumental music was not transmitted to the Moravian Church, which (perhaps from the effect of its later German associations) took the Lutheran view (p. 108, pl. **19.** 1–4). It is worthy of mention that John Wesley's consorting with the Moravians of London not only led to his conversion but probably also strengthened his view of the importance of congregational singing (see *Methodism and Music* 3), and, of course, the Methodists' practice in time influenced the Anglican and other churches.

There may, perhaps, be a little interest for some readers in thus tracing (however sketchily) the influence of the Bohemian, John Huss, martyred at Constance in 1415, in the musical activities of British and American religious life today. It would not be difficult to deduce some influence upon Luther and a consequent impulse to the development of the German chorale, and it would even be possible to show that, stimulated to competition, the Roman Catholic Church in all countries has also benefited (in Bohemia itself, for instance, a large and important book of Catholic religious song, largely in the Czech language, appeared in 1601).

The oldest hymn book of the Hussite body (or, for that matter, of any body) dates from the beginning of the sixteenth century (see *Hymns and Hymn Tunes* 3, 17 a). Some of its successors contained remarkably large numbers of tunes (often of French provenance—e.g. those of Goudimel). Thus a Czech book of 1561 has nearly 750 tunes and one in German of 1566 has over 450. The book of 1561 was due to the efforts of **John Blahoslav** (died 1571), later a bishop of the Hussite Church, and the fact of his being also the author of the first theoretical treatise in the Czech language (*Musica*, published at Olmütz in 1558; modern edition by Hostinsky in 1896) is sufficient confirmation of the implication of the above sketch of Hussite activities—the implication that the Hussite Reformation was favourable to general musical development in Bohemia. However, the temporary (partial) ban on instrumental music in church, at the opening of the movement in the fifteenth century, and, still more, the abolition of the ancient Latin liturgy, had necessarily some limiting effect: the latter, indeed, cut Bohemia off from participation in the developments that were then occurring through the innovations and improvements of the Flemish school, which at the period sent its practitioners to Italy and other countries (see *Belgium* 1; *Italy* 4; *Scandinavia* 2), leading in a few years to great native developments in those countries.

It is true that the court of Rudolph II, at Prague, in the late sixteenth and early seventeenth centuries, welcomed foreign musicians. Rudolph was, however, king not merely of Bohemia but of Hungary, and was, in addition, Holy Roman Emperor, and his court was not national but cosmopolitan. Cultivating all the arts and sciences, he invited to Prague such celebrities as Gallus (or Handl), Leo Hassler,

and Filippo di Monte, but they had little direct influence on Czech general musical culture, though perhaps they contributed somewhat to a movement which established domestic bands of musicians in the castles and town houses of many of the nobility, where some of them remained through the eighteenth century, as witness, for instance, the memoirs of the Vienna-born composer Dittersdorf.

Burney travelled through Bohemia in 1772 and remarks as follows upon the matter just mentioned:

'It has been said by travellers that the Bohemian nobility keep musicians, in their houses; but, in keeping servants, it is impossible to do otherwise, as all the children of the peasants and tradespeople, in every town and village throughout the kingdom of Bohemia, are taught music at the common reading schools, except in Prague, where, indeed, it is no part of school learning, the musicians being brought thither from the country.'

He speaks of his own visits to several country schools. One of these 'was full of little children of both sexes, from six to ten or eleven years old, who were reading, writing, playing on violins, hautboys, bassoons, and other instruments'. The village schoolmaster, he says, 'had in a small room of his house four clavichords, with little boys practising on them all; his son of nine years old was a very good performer'. The village church was visited, where the schoolmaster 'played an extempore fugue, upon a new and pleasing subject, in a very masterly manner'.

As a result of the school teaching, Burney declares, 'the Bohemians are remarkably expert in the use of wind instruments in general', those on the Saxon side of the kingdom being in special repute for the hautboy and those on the Moravian side for 'the tube or clarion'.

Prague had a 'Collegium Musicum' (see *Concert* 13) from 1616.

The social practice of choral music seems to have been very widespread in Bohemia from early times, attaining its greatest height of popularity in the great choral-singing age, the sixteenth and early seventeenth centuries. Despite the troubles of war during the seventeenth century, and the ban upon all but Roman Catholic singing societies that followed the defeat of the Hussites at the Battle of the White Mountain in 1620, there were a hundred of these societies still in existence near the end of the eighteenth century, and one continued to the period of the first World War. It seems impossible to recall any other country where social singing societies were so common at such an early period or existed for so long.

Amongst Bohemian composers of importance during the seventeenth century are **Andreas Hammerschmidt** (1611–75), a great organist and a Bohemian representative of the new style of composition which originated in Italy with Peri, Caccini, and Monteverdi, and **Biber** (1644–1704), the violin virtuoso and early composer of string sonatas and the like. A composer whose fame was great but most of whose works have perished in a fire was the Minorite friar **Bohuslav Černohorský** (1684–1742), teacher of Gluck at Prague (Gluck, though not a Bohemian, was born near the frontier) and of Tartini at Assisi (for Černohorský spent much of his earlier life in Italy, where he was known as 'Padre Boemo', the 'Bohemian Father').

In the early eighteenth century an Italian opera troupe was established at Prague, where were now performed works of Hasse and Gluck and also of such native composers as **J. A. Kozeluch** (1738–1814) and his nephew **Leopold Kozeluch** (1752–1818). The Italian opera-house thenceforward existed in Prague until 1807. A 'national' theatre was founded towards the end of the eighteenth century, and here operas were given in German.

The success of some of Mozart's works at these two theatres led to the invitation of the composer to appear in person, and to *Don Giovanni* here receiving its initial performance (1787).

Mozart had, much earlier than this, learnt something of the musical aptitude of the Bohemians, for he had admired at Mannheim the work of one of them in the person of the great orchestral director, **J. Stamitz** (1717–57), who receives notice elsewhere in this volume, as do also **J. L. Dussek** (properly 'Dusík': 1760–1812), the piano composer; **G. A. Benda** (1722–95), the composer of melodramas; **J. W. Tomaschek** (1774–1850), the composer and pianist; and **A. Reicha** (1770–1836), the Parisian composer and theorist. Other well-known names are those of **J. Krumpholz** (1745–90), the harpist; **F. Benda** (1709–86), the violin virtuoso and composer; **J. B. Vanhal** (or Wanhall, 1739–1813), the much fêted composer of 100 symphonies and other things in proportion; **Johann W. Stich** (746–1803), otherwise known as 'Punto', the greatest horn virtuoso of the eighteenth century, the chief developer of the horn as an artistic instrument, and a composer of horn music; **A. Gyrowetz** (1763–1850), the composer of innumerable operas, ballets, masses, symphonies, sonatas, etc., very famous in their time—which time, however, was not even as long as the composer's own life; and **F. L. Gassmann** (1729–74), the Viennese conductor and composer.

It will be realized from this list that the later eighteenth century was a flowering period for Bohemian musicality, and that Bohemian musicians at this period were of good standing in the courts and capitals of Europe.

At the opening of the nineteenth century (1811) was founded the Conservatory of Prague, of which the earliest director was **Friederich Dionys Weber** (1766–1842), prominent composer and theorist. This institution has sent into the world a long series of well-equipped musicians, especially players of bowed instruments, including the great violin-pedagogue Ottokar Ševčik (1852–1934); the violinist Franz Ondříček (1859–1922); the violoncellist and violoncello composer and teacher, David Popper (1843–1913); and the violinist Jan Kubelik (1880–1940).

A German opera-house (as distinct from the mere inclusion of German opera in the performances at a theatre) was founded in Prague in 1807, and from 1813 to 1816 its musical director was a great German, Carl Maria von Weber.

The growth of the Romantic movement in music (with which Weber is connected), and of that movement in all the arts, had the same effect in Bohemia as in, for instance, some of the Scandinavian countries (see *Scandinavia*); it stimulated an interest in the native folk music (see *Romantic*; *Nationalism*), and this the growing agitation for independence from Austria naturally reinforced. From the 1820s onwards many collections of Czech folk songs were published, and in 1823 opera performances in the Czech language began. Soon the operas of Méhul, Mozart, and Weber were being performed in that language. The first operas to be actually written in Czech were those of **Franz Škroup** (Škraup or Schkraup; 1801–62). From the 1860s onwards (the opening of an actual Czech theatre in 1862 gave a great fillip) many such works have appeared, of which those of **Smetana** (1824–84) are, of course, the most famous.

It is with Smetana and with **Dvořák** (1841–1904) that the Bohemia of the nineteenth century really shines out on the map of musical Europe as a patch with a colour of its own. The age was one that welcomed national expression, expression of the 'folk soul', and in their works it got this. It should be added that Smetana's contribution was not merely that of a composer; as a conductor, a teacher, and a writer on music he made himself the central figure of a great national musical movement.

A host of fine musicians was contemporary with or has followed these two, of whom **Zdeněk Fibich** (1850–1900), **Leoš Janáček** (1854–1928), **Joseph Bohuslav Foerster** (1859–1951), **Gustav Mahler** (1860–1911), **Vitězslav Novák** (1870–1949), **Josef Suk** (1874–1935), **Oscar Nědbal** (1874–1930), **Ottokar Ostrčil** (1879–1935), **Ladislav Vycpálek** (born 1882), **Bohuslav Martinů** (1890–1959), **Karel B. Jirák** (1891–1972), **Aloys Hába** (1893–1973), and his brother **Karel**, **Erwin Schulhoff** (1894–1942), and **J. Weinberger** (1896–1967) receive attention elsewhere in this volume.

The critic **Eduard Hanslick** (1825–1904) is also noticed separately. So is the famous historian of music, **A. W. Ambros** (1816–76).

Up to the close of the Second World War the musical institutions of Prague existed in duplicate. In addition to the Conservatory there was a State-aided German Academy of Music, and there were fully organized departments of music at the Czech University and the German University. The National Theatre and the German Theatre both gave opera performances. There were Czech and German choral societies, chamber music societies, etc.

(In Cobbett's *Cyclopedic Survey of Chamber Music* will be found articles on the considerable Bohemian contribution to chamber music, both in composition and performance.) The double current of cultural activity, Czech and German, has now ceased.

Prague is, of course, by no means the only great cultural centre of Bohemia, and in the adjoining Moravian section of Czechoslovakia the capital Brno (Brünn) is active in all types of musical enterprise.

A word or two must be said about the Bohemian dances. Dancing has always been a very popular amusement, and the native dance tunes have great vitality. Brief entries will be found under *Furiant, Redowa, Rejdováčka*. For Dvořák's use of a dance type not strictly Bohemian see *Dumka*. For a dance which originated in Bohemia in the early nineteenth century and overspread the world, see *Polka*.

See also pp. 108, 109, pls. **19, 20**.

BOHÉMIEN, BOHÉMIENNE (Fr., masc., fem.). 'Gipsy' (based on an old idea that the gipsies came from Bohemia).

BOHM, CARL (1844–1920.) A German composer, of great fecundity and the highest saleability—songs (such as 'Still as the Night'), light piano music, etc. He occupied an important position in the musical commonwealth inasmuch as his publisher, Simrock, declared that the profits on his compositions provided the capital for the publication of those of Brahms.

BÖHM.

(1) GEORG (1661–1733). A sort of minor J. S. Bach—a north German composer writing suites, Passions, preludes and fugues, choral preludes, etc., like his great contemporary, upon whom he probably exercised a good deal of influence when they were both at Lüneburg.

(2) THEOBALD. See *Boehm System*.

BÖHME, OSCKA. See *Trombone Family* 4.

BOHNENBLUST, GOTTFRIED. Born at Berne in 1883. He is Professor of the History of German Literature at the Universities of Geneva and Lausanne, a poet and general author, and the composer of many songs, choral works (especially some cleverly contrived canons), and other things.

BOÏELDIEU, FRANÇOIS ADRIEN (p. 368, pl. **61**. 8). Born at Rouen in 1775 and died at Jarcy, near Paris, in 1834, aged fifty-eight. He studied under the organist of Rouen Cathedral and at eighteen had an opera performed.

He then began an operatic career in Paris, winning fame at twenty-five with *The Caliph of Bagdad*. It is said that after a performance of this work Cherubini, his superior at the Paris Conservatory (where he now held a post as piano professor), in leaving the theatre exclaimed 'Aren't you ashamed of such ill-deserved success?', that the reply was a humble request for instruction, and that this was gladly given and perseveringly pursued.

From his twenty-eighth to his thirty-sixth year he was director of the Royal Opera at St. Petersburg; then he took up the Paris career again with *La Dame blanche* and other works. Under both Charles X and Louis-Philippe he enjoyed a pension.

See passing references under *Opera* 21 e, 24 d (1800); *Overture*; *France* 9; *Roman Catholic Church Music in Britain*; *Criticism* 6; *Barocco*.

BOIS (Fr.). 'Wood', e.g. *Avec le bois d'archet* = 'Col legno', i.e. playing with the wood of the bow instead of with the hair. *Les bois*, 'the wood-wind'. *Baguette de bois*, 'wooden-headed drumstick' (see *Percussion Family* 2 a).

BOISSET. See *Boesset*.

BOÎTE (Fr.). 'Box' (e.g. swell-box of organ).

BOITO, ARRIGO (p. 524, pl. **95**. 5). Born at Padua in 1842 and died at Milan in 1918, aged seventy-six. He enjoyed a double fame, as librettist and composer. In the former capacity he not only wrote libretti for himself but also supplied Verdi with the excellent books of *Othello* (q.v.) and *Falstaff* (q.v.). In the latter capacity he is most spoken of in connexion with his *Mephistopheles*, first performed in 1868, and his scenically and musically elaborate *Nero*, first performed over half a century later (Milan, 1924).

BOLERO. A Spanish three-beats-in-a-measure dance, almost identical with the *Cachucha*, but danced by a couple or several couples. It is performed to the accompaniment of the performers' own voices and of castanets (see *Percussion Family* 3 q, 4 c, 5 q), and the movements of the arms are an important feature.

It is not of folk-origin, having been invented in 1780 by the dancer, Sebastian Cerezo (or Zerezo), or more likely refashioned by him out of some older dance.

The bolero has made its appearance in artistic music. Chopin wrote one for piano (op. 19), and in 1928 Ravel brought out one that quickly won a popularity by the hypnotic effect of its incessantly repeated slow, rhythmic melody, and its quarter-of-an-hour crescendo, continuing from the first measure to the last: this bolero was, on its first appearance, danced by Ida Rubinstein (to whom it is dedicated), and then took its place in the concert repertory.

Naturally, the dance has also appeared sometimes in opera—in situations where national 'colour' called for it.

Note that the *Seguidilla Boleras* has no connexion with the Bolero.

BOLM, ADOLF. See *Ballet* 9.

BOLOGNA. See *Italy* 4; *Street Music* 4.

BOMBARD, BOMBARDA, BOMBARDE. (1) See *Oboe Family* 2, where the *Bombard* is described as one of the bass sizes of the ancient shawms. In France, apparently, the name was applied to shawms of all the sizes, of which the treble is still in use as the regular companion of the Brittany bagpipe or Biniou (see *Bagpipe* 6);

during the War of 1914–18 the Breton regiments marched to the music of these two instruments. Apparently these older forms of the oboe family have had some slight local survival in Germany also, since in September 1934 the Nazi authorities debarred the firemen of Hesse from using their shawm (probably as a street warning of their approach, the instruments of this class being possibly the loudest instruments that have ever existed).

(2) The name *Bombardon* is, however, today given to a brass instrument (see *Tuba Group* 1, 3 b c), and the euphonium (*Tuba Group* 3 a) is in Italy sometimes called *Bombarda*.

(3) A certain reed stop on some organs. See *Organ* 14 VI, 15.

BOMBARDON. See reference under *Bombard*.

BONDEVILLE, EMMANUEL. Born at Rouen in 1898. He has been active both as conductor (musical director of Eiffel Tower Radio, etc.) and as a composer of symphonic poems, stage works, etc.

See reference under *France* 11.

BONES. The nineteenth-century American and British Negro Minstrels' equivalent of the Spanish castanets. It consists of two pieces of a rib bone of an animal held between the fingers and rhythmically clacked. Every minstrel troupe had a 'Mr. Bones'.

BONGOS. Small Cuban drums—bucket-shaped vessels cut out of the solid wood, bound with brass, and having strong vellum heads. Two of them are fixed together by a bar of metal. They are played with sticks, or with the thumb and fingers. A tunable variety of the instrument is also manufactured.

BONNET.

(1) JACQUES (1644–1724). French historian of music and the dance. See *Dance* 10.

(2) JOSEPH ÉLIE GEORGES MARIE. Born at Bordeaux in 1884 and died near Quebec in 1944, aged sixty. He was a pupil of Guilmant, and at twenty-two became organist of the church of St. Eustache (Paris). As a virtuoso organist he toured widely, and some of his organ music enjoys considerable popularity.

BONNIE ANNIE. See *John Peel*.

BONNIE BANKS OF LOCH LOMOND. See *Loch Lomond*.

BONNIE DUNDEE. The poem is by Sir Walter Scott, and was written for his play *The Doom of Devorgoil* (1830); it refers not to the town but to Viscount Dundee. The tune is the old one of *The Jockey's Deliverance*, which Scott seems to have had in mind, as it is a perfect fit.

There was a 'Bonnie Dundee' song current before Scott's, with different metre and melody; he took a part of his refrain from this. The tune was incorporated in *The Beggar's Opera* as 'The Charge is Prepared'.

BONNO, GIUSEPPE (1710–88). See reference under *Wellesz*.

BONONCINI or **BUONONCINI FAMILY** (father and sons).

(1) GIOVANNI MARIA (*c*. 1642–78) held important positions in Modena and was an active composer, as also author of a treatise on practical music (1673).

(2) GIOVANNI BATTISTA (born at Modena in 1670; died in Vienna in 1747). He had fame as a composer in Italy, Vienna (Court Composer for eleven years), and London. In this last-named place he enjoyed high success, proving (for a time) a formidable operatic rival to Handel.

See *Pasticcio*; *Ballad Opera*; *Ariosti*.

(3) MARC ANTONIO—properly Antonió Maria (1677–1726) was, especially, an opera composer, popular in Italy and England.

BONPORTI, FRANCESCO ANTONIO. Born at Trent in 1672 and died at Padua in 1749, aged seventy-seven. He studied in Rome under Corelli, then taking holy orders and settling in Trent. He paid for the printing of his compositions and sent them round Europe, so that his name became well known. He wrote in a personal style with occasional surprising turns of harmony.

See reference under *Invention*.

BOOGIE-WOOGIE. See *Jazz* 7.

BOOK OF THE HOWLAT. See *Scotland* 3.

BOOSEY. See *Publishing* 7.

BOOTH, WILLIAM. 'General Booth' (1829–1912). See references under *Church Music* 2; *Hymns and Hymn Tunes* 12; *Luther*.

BOP. See *Jazz* 7.

BORDES, CHARLES. Born at Vouvray, in the Department of Indre et Loire, France, in 1863, and died at Toulon in 1909, aged forty-six. He was a pupil of César Franck in Paris and became organist of the church of St. Gervais, where he founded a choral body for the performance of the earlier church music, under the name of 'Les Chanteurs de St. Gervais', which has become independent of its church associations and is still active. He also, with Guilmant and d'Indy, founded the Schola Cantorum, for the study of church music (1894), and later established branches of this at Avignon and Montpellier. He collected and published old church music and Basque folk tunes, and wrote music for piano, orchestra, etc.

BORDONI, FAUSTINA. See under *Hasse*.

BORE. See *Brass*; *Trumpet Family*; *Horn Family*; *Cornet*; *Saxhorn and Flügelhorn Families*; *Trombone Family*; *Tuba Group*; *Bugle*. ('For 'Bore', the dance, see *Bourrée*.)

BORIS GODUNOF (Mussorgsky). Produced at St. Petersburg in 1874. Libretto from a drama by Pushkin.

The version of the opera here given is that most often presented, and is the result of the well-intentioned revisions of Rimsky-Korsakof. Of late years, however, successful attempts have been made to revive the original form of the work as left by Mussorgsky. This involves some changes in the sequence of the action, including the reversal of the order of the last two scenes.

Boris, a councillor of the Tsar Ivan the Terrible, has caused the assassination of the ruler's brother, who would have succeeded to the throne; and, on the death of the Tsar, he seeks supreme power.

The opera shows the working in him of remorse.

PROLOGUE

SCENE 1: *Courtyard of the Monastery of Novo-dievich, near Moscow. Time,* 1598

Police are urging the crowd to demand that Boris shall take up the government. The people are apathetic and have little hope of redress for their troubles.

SCENE 2: *The Courtyard in the Kremlin at Moscow*

Boris (*Baritone*) is hailed as Tsar, and moves, in a grand procession, to the cathedral for his coronation. On the threshold a presentiment of evil oppresses him.

ACT I

SCENE 1 : *A Cell in the Monastery*

The monk **Pimen** (*Bass*) is recording the history of his country. A young monk, **Gregory** (*Tenor*), describes a dream in which he, upon a tower, faced a mocking crowd, and then awoke as he was falling from the height. Pimen tells him that he has arrived, in his recording of history, at the point of Boris's crime, and narrates the story of the slaughter of the late Tsar's son Dimitri—who had he lived would have been Gregory's age. Upon this Gregory ponders.

SCENE 2: *An Inn on the Lithuanian Frontier* (In some performances this scene is placed in Act II.)

Varlaam (*Bass*) and **Missail** (*Tenor*) are two vagabond monks, in the company of Gregory, who, now calling himself 'Dimitri', seeks the overthrow of Boris, and power for himself. After being welcomed by the **Hostess** (*Mezzo-Soprano*), the three are questioned by soldiers who are searching for Gregory. After a while they recognize him, but he escapes.

ACT II

SCENE: *The Interior of the Tsar's Apartments in the Kremlin*

The **Princess Xenia** (*Soprano*), whose husband is dead, and her little brother **Feodor** (*Mezzo-Soprano*) are with their old **Nurse** (*Contralto*). Boris comes to see them. He has attained to power, but in the six years of his reign remorse has not left him. **Prince Shuisky** (*Tenor*), whom he suspects of treason, comes to tell him that a pretender has arisen in Poland and is being strongly sup-

ported. He is said to be Dimitri, who was supposed to be (and indeed was) murdered. In reality he is Gregory. Boris, in terror, has a vision of the murdered child.

ACT III

SCENE 1: *The Room of Marina Mnishek, at Sandomir, in Poland*

(This is sometimes omitted.)

Marina (*Mezzo-Soprano*), the daughter of the governor of Sandomir, loves 'Dimitri', through whom, as his consort, she hopes to attain power. To her comes **Rangoni** (*Bass*), a Jesuit in disguise, who tells her that she must strive to captivate 'Dimitri' and then use her power to make him advance the Roman Catholic cause against the Russian Orthodox Church.

SCENE 2: *A Garden of the Castle of Mnishek, at Sandomir*

To the false 'Dimitri' comes Rangoni, telling him of Marina's longing for him and the malicious gossip that surrounds her name. 'Dimitri' resolves to wed her. A love scene between the two follows.

ACT IV

SCENE 1: *In the Forest of Kromy*

The people have risen to support 'Dimitri'. They mock one of Boris's generals. An **Idiot Youth** (*Tenor*) is introduced, and Missail and Varlaam exhort the people to welcome their lawful ruler, 'Dimitri'. Two **Jesuits** (*Basses*) are roughly handled. 'Dimitri' is hailed as the people's saviour-to-be. Only the idiot is left, prophesying woe.

SCENE 2: *The Granovitaya Palace in the Kremlin*

The nobles are debating about the revolt, and what shall be the Pretender's fate. Boris, haggard and distracted, appears. The old monk, Pimen, comes to tell how an aged man had been cured of blindness by praying at Dimitri's tomb. Boris is overcome. His fears and remorse have brought him to his end. He calls for his son Feodor, tells him he is dying, and gives him counsel for the hard future when he must rule. Then, praying for forgiveness, he embraces his son for the last time, and dies.

See *Opera* 17 d.

BORJON, C. E. (1633–91). See *Bagpipe* 6.

BORLAND, JOHN ERNEST (1866–1937). Valuable worker for musical education, etc. See reference under *God save the Queen* 19.

BORODIN (Borodine), ALEXANDER (p. 897, pl. **154**. 3). Born in St. Petersburg in 1833 (not 1834, as often stated), and died there in 1887, aged fifty-three. He was a medical man and a professor of chemistry, holding many official posts. He founded a School of Medicine for Women.

Always keenly musical, his artistic activity took a leap forward when, in his late twenties, he met Balakiref and became a member of the group known as 'The Five' (see *Russia* 5). He wrote two symphonies and an unfinished third, the 'symphonic sketch' *In the Steppes of Central Asia*, three string quartets, songs, piano music and the opera, *Prince Igor* (q.v.), left unfinished but brought to completion by his friends Rimsky-Korsakof and Glazunof. He was not so dramatically Russian as some of his fellows, and he loved melody and bold outlines.

His work, admirable as it was, was done amidst the distraction of a busy professional life—generally, as he said, in the little leisure given him by a bad cold in the head. The complete list of his works runs to only twenty-one.

Liszt appreciated and encouraged him, as he did others of the Russian national group (cf. *Balakiref*). His death was sudden; he dropped dead at a party.

See *Chopsticks*; *Belaief*; *Chamber Music* 6, Period III (1833); *Nationalism*. (For opera in Russia see *Opera* 17, 21 m, and *Ballet* 7, near end.)

BOROWSKI, FELIX. Born at Burton, Westmorland, England, in 1872 and died in Chicago in 1956, aged eighty-four. He was of mixed Polish and British descent, but a naturalized citizen of the United States. After a career as violinist and teacher of violin he settled in Chicago. For nine years (1916–25) he was president of the Chicago Musical College, and later he was Professor of Musicology at Northwestern University. He composed for orchestra, organ, chamber combinations, voice, etc. From 1908 for many years he compiled the admirable programme notes of the Chicago Symphony Orchestra.

See reference under *Ballet* 6.

BORRE, BORREE. Old English spellings of 'Bourrée' (q.v.).

BORTNIANSKY, DIMITRI. Born in Ukraine in 1751 and died in St. Petersburg in 1825, aged about seventy-four. As a boy he had a fine voice, and Catharine the Great had him trained, first under Galuppi, at her capital, and then in Italy (cf. *Berezovsky*), where some of his operas were performed.

On return, in 1779, he was put in charge of the choir which some years later became the 'Imperial Chapel'; this he brought to a state of excellence, setting a tradition that lasted until the revolution of the twentieth century.

He composed much church music (unaccompanied, according to the tradition of the Greek Church; see *Greek Church* 5), and this was, long after his death, published in ten volumes under the direction of Tchaikovsky. He also wrote some instrumental music.

BOSANQUET, R. See *Colour and Music* 3; *Keyboard* 3; *Temperament* 3.

BOSSI.
(1) MARCO ENRICO. Born near Lake Garda in 1861, and died on the Atlantic in 1925, aged sixty-three. He was a noted organist and composer, in the latter capacity best known by his works for his own instrument, He died at sea when returning from an American recital tour.

See reference under *Applause* 6; *Malipiero*.

(2) His son, RENZO (1883–1965), was known as a composer and teacher of composition (Milan).

BOSTON (Mass.). See *United States* 2, 4, 5; *Harpsichord Family* 4; *Organ* 9; *Concert* 15; *Festival* 2; *Annotated Programmes* 6; *Cecilia*; *Journals*; *Publishing* 9; *Education and Music* 3; *Schools of Music*.

BOSWELL, JAMES (1740–95). See quotation under *Ranz des Vaches*.

BOTE AND BOCK. See *Publishing* 8.

BOTTESINI, GIOVANNI (p. 1088, pl. **179.** 7). Born in Lombardy in 1821 and died at Parma in 1889, aged sixty-seven. At the age of eleven he applied for admission to the Conservatory of Milan. It was full except for one place for a double-bass student. He therefore took up this instrument, passed the examination, and started on that career which made him perhaps the champion double-bass player of history. (See *Violin Family* 9.) He composed for his instrument. (Cf. *Carnival of Venice*.)

He was also a successful opera conductor in Paris, Barcelona, Cairo, and London, and composed operas and (for the Norwich Festival of 1887) an oratorio, *The Garden of Olivet*.

See also *Concerto* 6 b (1821).

BOUCHE FERMÉE (Fr.). 'Closed mouth' singing, i.e. humming.

BOUCHÉS, SONS (Fr.). Stopped notes in horn playing. See *Horn Family* 2 b c, 3, 5; also *Gestopft* and *Schmetternd*.

BOUFFE, BOUFFES PARISIENS. See *Opera buffa*.

BOUFFONISTES. See *Bouffons, Guerre des*.

BOUFFONS (or *Mattachins*, or *Matassins*). 'An old sword dance of men in armour of gilded cardboard' says Arbeau, the great sixteenth-century authority mentioned under *Dance* 6; he describes it in detail, gives many pictures, and sets out the traditional air. The spelling 'Buffens' occurs in England. (Cf. *Dance* 2.)

BOUFFONS, GUERRE DES. The 'War of the Comedians'. This was a mighty Parisian quarrel which first broke out in 1752 over an opera of Destouches and led to the invitation to Paris of a troupe of Italian comedians, who made a great stir with the performance of their countryman Pergolese's comic opera, *The Servant as Mistress* ('La Serva Padrona': see articles *Intermezzo*; *Opera buffa*; *Opéra-comique*; *Pergolese*).

The Bouffons performed in Paris from 1752 to 1754. Pergolese's twenty-year-old opera had been given in Paris six years before and had then aroused some interest but now aroused much more; it was followed by comic operas of other Italian composers.

The musical and literary world of Paris promptly divided itself into two camps—that favouring Italian opera and that favouring French. The gods of the national party were Lully, dead sixty-five years before, and, especially, Rameau (q.v.), now nearing seventy; this was the more numerous party, and (according to Rousseau, who opposed it) included especially 'the wealthy, the highly placed, and the ladies', whereas (also according to him) the other side numbered amongst its adherents 'the true connoisseurs and the intelligent people'.

In the theatre the national party took to sitting under the King's box, and the Italian party under the Queen's, and so they became known as the 'King's Corner' party and the 'Queen's Corner' party. The association of the Queen with the anti-nationalists (as of the King with the nationalists) is explained by the fact that Madame de Pompadour was a nationalist.

The Queen's Corner, or Italian party, numbered, in addition to Rousseau, such men of distinction in letters as d'Alembert, Grimm, Diderot, and Holbach (the Encyclopedists, in fact; see *France* 8). Naturally, the war soon became one of pamphlets. Rousseau says that the fighting was as hot as though it were over some question of politics or religion.

Rousseau was so anti-nationalist as to write 'there is neither measure nor melody in French music, because the language itself is not susceptible of either; French song is nothing but a continual bark, insupportable by any unprepared ear; the harmony is crude, without expression and not suggestive of anything beyond a pupil's work; French airs are no airs at all, and French recitatives no recitatives. From all of which I conclude that the French have no music, and never can have any, or, if they ever have, so much the worse for them' (*Letter on French Music*, 1753).

Yet at the very time he himself produced a French opera, *The Village Soothsayer* ('Le Devin du village'), and one that was to remain in the Paris repertory for seventy-five years.

Largely the dispute was one on the merits or demerits of simplicity. The Italian music was supposed to be less complex than the French. Rousseau hated counterpoint, as 'a relic of barbarism and of bad taste, that only survives, like the doorways of our Gothic churches, to perpetuate the shame of those who had the patience to make it'. And the Italians, he said, more musically civilized than the French, had more completely shaken off the influences of the crabbed contrapuntal period.

An ingenious fraud was perpetrated in 1753 by Monnet, director of the Opéra-comique. He had an opera written which he announced as by an Italian composer living in Vienna. It was warmly approved by the anti-national (Bouffonist, Queen's Corner) party, and then Monnet announced that it was by the Paris poet, Vadé, and the Paris composer, Dauvergne.

This work, *Les Trocqueurs*, is considered to mark an era. It was one of the first French comic operas to have recitative throughout, instead of spoken dialogue, and it has been called 'the first French comic opera of which the libretto is the work of a poet and the score that of a composer'.

So the attacks of the anti-nationalists had acted as a tonic to the nationalist school!

BOUGHTON, RUTLAND (p. 337, pl. **54**. 6). Born at Aylesbury in 1878 and died in London in 1960, aged nearly eighty-two. He was a student, at the Royal College of Music, London, of Stanford and Walford Davies. For seven years he was on the staff of the Birmingham School of Music under Bantock.

As a composer he allied himself with the poet, Reginald Buckley, in the project of producing a cycle of music dramas, on Wagnerian scale and of nationalist import, *Arthur of Britain*. In 1914 he chose Glastonbury as his British Bayreuth, carrying on in its town hall annual festivals, preparatory to building a festival theatre; these were later abandoned.

His opera setting of 'Fiona Macleod's' (William Sharp's) *The Immortal Hour* (1916) had remarkable success, and some other operas (e.g. *Alkestis*; *The Queen of Cornwall*; *The Ever Young*) had a hearing, as did *Bethlehem*, a choral drama based on the old Coventry Christmas Play (see *Mysteries*).

He wrote a book on Bach and many articles on Wagner and on subjects connected with his interest in the relation between social problems and the arts. In 1938 he was awarded a Civil List pension.

See also *Flute Family*; *Oboe Family* 6; *Opera* 24 f (1914, 1916 twice, 1919, 1922, 1924).

BOUHY, JACQUES JOSEPH ANDRÉ (born in Belgium in 1848 and died in Paris in 1929). See references under *Voice* 17.

BOULANGER.

(1) NADIA. Born in Paris in 1887. She won the second Prix de Rome (q.v.) at twenty-one and has composed orchestral music, songs, etc. She holds a high place as a teacher of composition, pupils coming to her from distant parts of the world. She is the sister of (2).

(2) LILI. Born in Paris in 1893 and died there in 1918, aged twenty-four. She was the sister of (1) and was the first woman to win the Grand Prix de Rome (see *Prix de Rome*). At her early death she left two symphonic poems, various choral works, and other things.

BOULEZ, PIERRE (p. 388, pl. **65**. 6). Born at Montbrison in 1925. He studied under Messiaen at the Paris Conservatoire, where he won the *Premier prix* in 1946, and later under Leibowitz. He supports himself as a conductor of exceptional gifts (New York Philharmonic 1969–77; also BBC Symphony Orchestra 1971) and like many of his colleagues he is a writer and lecturer. From 1945 he was writing music, mostly for piano or small groups, in a style influenced by Messiaen. A later more 'constructional' phase ensued, during which he produced his *Le Marteau sans maître* (1955) for singer and six instruments, based on poems by René Char about a 'neurotic navvy'. This work, described variously as 'Webern sounding like Debussy', a 'totally serial lollipop', and 'an inexpert gamelan orchestra', has come nearer to being accepted by the general public than any other of the works called 'advanced'. He gives his compositions long and meticulous preparation, and sometimes withdraws them before or after their long-delayed first performances. In 1977 he became Director of the Institut de recherche et coordination acoustique et musique (IRCAM). See *History* 9.

BOULT, ADRIAN CEDRIC. Born at Chester in 1889. He was educated at Westminster School, Christ Church, Oxford, and Leipzig Conservatory. Orchestral conductor. From 1924 he was in charge of the Birmingham City Orchestra; from 1930, Musical Director of the B.B.C., and from 1941 its Conductor in Chief (cf. *Bliss*), on reaching retiring age for this last appointment (1950) becoming conductor for the next seven years of the London Philharmonic Orchestra. He was knighted in 1937 and made C.H. in 1969. See *Broadcasting* 4; *Conducting* 8; *International Music Association*.

BOULTON, SIR HAROLD EDWIN, Baronet (1859–1935). Editor of several collections of songs and author of song poems. See *Skye Boat Song*.

BOUQUIN, CORNET A. See *Cornett and Key Bugle Families* 4.

BOURDON.

(1) The French name given to the drone strings in the hurdy-gurdy (q.v.) and the drone pipes in the bagpipe (q.v.).

(2) The lowest string of the lute and violin used to be called the bourdon, as is still the lowest bell in a ring of bells.

See also *Organ* 3, 14 I.

BOURGAULT-DUCOUDRAY, LOUIS ALBERT. Born at Nantes in 1840 and died at Auteuil, near Paris, in 1910, aged seventy. He was a student at the Paris Conservatory under Ambroise Thomas, and then made a name as conductor of a choral society which revived the works of Palestrina, Handel, Bach, Rameau, and others, and as a composer of choral works and operas, orchestral music, etc. He became Professor of the History of Music at the Conservatory and enjoyed a special reputation as a collector of the folk music of Greece and of his native Brittany.

BOURGEOIS, LOYS. See *France* 4; *Hymns and Hymn Tunes* 4, 17 d.

BOURGUIGNON, F. DE. See *Synthétistes*.

BOURNEMOUTH MUSIC LIBRARY. See *Libraries*.

BOURRÉE, or BORRY, or BORE—a good many other spellings also are to be met with. A dance form of French origin, very like the gavotte (q.v.), except that its phrases begin at the last quarter of the measure, not at the halfway (see *Rhythm* 9). It was taken into fashionable French social life at much the same time as the gavotte, and its subsequent history is in every way similar. Like the gavotte, it came to have an optional place in the classical suite (see *Suite*), in which, just as the gavotte was often followed by a similar dance, the musette, after which the gavotte was played again, so the

bourrée would be followed by another bourrée, after which the first one would be played again. Thus, as a whole, the form became ternary.

In Auvergne a dance called bourrée is still popular but it seems to have little in common with that mentioned above, as it is in three-in-a-measure time. It is danced to the music of the instrument, the musette (see *Bagpipe Family* 6), or to that of the hurdy-gurdy (q.v.) and the dancers sing words of a pastoral or amorous character.

BOUT (Fr.). 'End', e.g. *Avec le bout de l'archet*, 'with the end (point) of the bow'. The curve at the waist of a stringed instrument is also called a 'Bout'.

BOUTADE. An improvised dance or other composition. The word in French means (amongst other things) a *jeu d'esprit*. Rousseau in his *Dictionary of Music* (1767) gives it both as a little ballet executed extemporaneously (or appearing to be so executed) and as an instrumental capriccio (q.v.) or fantasia.

BOUTON. See *Reed-Organ Family* 4.

BOW. See *Violin Family* 5 and *Viol Family* 2 i; *Heel*.

BOWED HARP. A name recently (and misleadingly) applied to the Crwth (q.v.).

BOWEN.

(1) YORK (EDWIN), Born in London in 1884 and died there in 1961, aged seventy-seven. He studied at the Royal Academy of Music and became known as a fine pianist and a fertile minor composer in many forms.

See references s.v. *Oboe Family* 6; *Concerto* 6 c (1884); *Pianoforte* 21; *Horn* 4.

(2) EDWARD. See *Farmer, John* (II).

BOWER, JOHN DYKES. Born at Gloucester in 1905. After a Cambridge career he became organist successively of Truro Cathedral (1926), New College, Oxford (1930), Durham Cathedral (1933), and St. Paul's Cathedral, London (1936–67). C.V.O. (1953). Knighted 1968.

BOWING (of a stringed instrument).

(1) The general technique of the use of the bow.

(2) The way in which notes are grouped in one movement of the bow, as an element of phrasing (q.v.).

Bowing is, in this sense, an important part of expression, and it is interesting to note that Bach, though he did not usually trouble to insert bowing marks in his scores, was often extremely scrupulous in adding them to the 'parts' of the separate players. In much music, however, the responsibility for a good deal of the bowing rests with the player. Even if the composer has marked every detail of the bowing, his ideas, if he is not himself a string player, may need modification.

BOWLES, PAUL FREDERIC. Born in New York in 1910. He is a collector of folk music, in search of which he has travelled extensively in North Africa, Central and South America, Spain, and elsewhere. He has

BOX   124   BRAHMS

composed much music for the theatre, as also some orchestral, chamber, and choral music, and has published some fiction.

BOX, CHARLES. See *Anglican Church Music* 7.

BOYAU (Fr.). 'Catgut.'

BOYCE, WILLIAM (p. 165, pl. **34.** 1). Born in London in 1710 and died there in 1779, aged sixty-nine. He was a notable London organist and composer of music for stage and church, and master of the orchestra of George III. On being overtaken by deafness, he gave the remainder of his life to the completion of a great collection of the finest compositions of the English church composers (begun by his friend Greene, q.v.), under the title of *Cathedral Music*, his work upon which (though not always quite satisfactory by modern standards) has been recognized as the erection of a national monument and the execution of a public service. He lies buried under the dome of St. Paul's. (Cf. *Arnold, Samuel*.)

See also under *Cathedral Music* 10; *Anthem* (Period III); *Sonata* 10 c; *Heart of Oak*; *Lambert, C.*; *Misattributed* (Locke's 'Macbeth').

BOYDEN, DAVID DODGE. Born at Westport, Conn., in 1910. Violinist and musical scholar, trained at Harvard and at Hartt College, Conn. He is on the staff of the University of California, Berkeley, and is the author of several books, including an exhaustive history of violin playing.

BOYS' VOICES. See *Voice* 5; *Singing* 3.

BR. Short for *Bratschen*, i.e. violas.

BRABANCONNE, LA. The Belgian national anthem. It was written and composed at the time of the 1830 demonstration in Brussels which led to the separation of Belgium from Holland (see also *Auber*). The author of the words was a French actor then in Brussels, named Jenneval, and the composer of the music was Campenhout (q.v.). The name comes from Brabant and the spirit breathed is that of the famous Brabançons—in the twelfth century the best fighters in Europe.

BRACCIO and GAMBA. Since the publication of Burney's *History of Music*, at the end of the eighteenth century, a mistake concerning these terms (arising largely from a diagram in that work) has been repeated over and over again—and a similar mistake has crept into continental publications.

The two terms originally distinguished the violin family (q.v.) from the viol family (q.v.).

The whole of the members of the viol family (little and big) were held downwards, resting between the knees or legs, according to their size. To them, then, was given the name *Viole da Gamba*, or 'leg viols'. The chief soloist and latest survivor of this family was the bass viol, and the sole inheritance in this name therefore fell to it, so that today when we speak of a viola da gamba we mean the bass viol (not the double-bass one, of course). The tendency so

to use the term existed even in the seventeenth century.

Having called all the downward-held instruments 'leg viols', it was natural enough to call all the upward-held ones (violin, viola) 'arm viols' or *Viole da Braccio*; they are, at least, held at arm level as the others are at leg level (p. 1073, pl. **178.** 3, 7; p. 1097, pl. **182.** 1) And not only those but all the members of the violin family came to be included under the name, even the cello and double-bass. Later, the term became restricted to the alto violin (sometimes also called tenor), and in German today this is called *Bratsche*.

For the *Lira da braccio* and *Lira da gamba* see under *Lyra*.

BRACE. The perpendicular line combined with a bracket that joins the two staves in pianoforte music and performs a similar function in music for other media.

BRACHVOGEL, ALBERT (1824–78). German poet, dramatist, and novelist. See *Bach, Wilhelm Friedemann*.

BRADBURN, SAMUEL (1751–1816). See *Methodism and Music* 5.

BRADBURY, W. B. See *Hymns and Hymn Tunes* 12.

BRADE, WILLIAM. Born in England about 1560 and died at Hamburg in 1630. He was an English viol player and composer who held important continental royal and municipal positions in Copenhagen, Berlin, Hamburg, Gottorp, and Halle. He published a good deal of music in Germany (pavans and galliards for groups of viols, etc.), some of which has now been reprinted.

BRADFORD, JOHN (of Charleston, S.C.). See *Pianoforte* 5.

BRADSTREET, ANN. See *United States* 2.

BRADY, NICHOLAS (1659–1726). Anglican divine and minor poet; collaborator with Tate in the famous metrical version of the psalms. See *Hymns and Hymn Tunes* 5; *Old Hundredth*.

BRAHAM (properly 'Abraham'), **JOHN**. Born in London in 1774 and died there in 1856, aged nearly eighty-two. He was a tenor vocalist of European renown who sang in the first performance of Weber's *Oberon*, and also the composer of operas and widely popular English songs, of which 'The Death of Nelson' was at one time known to every patriotic Briton. He made a fortune as a musician and lost it as a theatre manager.

See mention under *Robin Adair*.

BRAHE, MAY HANNA. See *Melody* 7.

BRAHMS, JOHANNES (see opposite). Born at Hamburg in 1833 and died in Vienna in 1897, aged sixty-three. His work, whilst largely couched in classical forms, is romantic in temper (see *Classical* and *Romantic*) and, indeed, of the most pronounced type of nineteenth-century German romanticism. He avoided the symphonic poem (q.v.), preferring the accepted classical form of the symphony; he was in no degree drawn to the reproduction

PLATE 23

BRAHMS BEGINS THE DAY

By Batt

He was a confirmed bachelor, very simple in his habits and frugal in his tastes. When in later years he became affluent he did not change his mode of life, but remained, as he began, a lodger in furnished rooms.

He is seen above in his bedroom in the Carlgasse, Vienna, having brewed his early morning coffee, which daily rite took place at about 5 a.m. He always prepared his own brew, as nobody else would make it strong enough. The coffee-machine and cup are the actual ones he used. With his strong coffee he would smoke an equally strong cigar, to be followed by many others throughout the day.

B.

in terms of tone of the emotions of a series of events or physical facts or definite psychological happenings (see *Programme Music*); he wrote music *as* music and not as a branch of literary or pictorial art. Yet, despite their sheer musical beauty, his compositions are strongly charged with what may be called an extra-musical emotion; hence the classification of their composer as a romantic, though, in view of all the facts, the term 'classic-romantic' is perhaps more exact.

There is an obvious similarity of thought and feeling between his works and those of his first herald, Schumann, but in Schumann the literary and pictorial element is often predominant and the instinct for form and proportion is not so marked.

Nineteenth-century criticism had the habit of placing Brahms and Wagner in strong antithesis, and so indeed they stand, for the mind and the methods of the one are lyric and those of the other essentially dramatic. Not content with such distinction, the critics and their followers, especially in Germany and in Britain, divided themselves into two camps, and their oppositions generated a bitterness that, however, did not greatly touch their respective divinities themselves (Brahms, at any rate, large-minded, remained aloof from the fight, expressing profound admiration for the mature Wagner). Both Wagner and Brahms were continuators of Beethoven, the one developing upon the stage the romantic suggestions of his master and the other doing so in the concert-room. There need be no conflict when frontiers are so clearly defined.

Brahms was the son of a humble double-bass player in the theatres of Hamburg. At the hands of a local teacher he received a thorough training, meantime supporting himself by playing in cafés and dancing-halls. At twenty he toured with a Jew-Hungarian violinist, Reményi (q.v.), and came to the notice of Joachim and of Liszt, who helped him forward. For a time both Joachim and Brahms were enrolled in the ranks of the 'New German' part of Liszt, but in 1860, when Brahms was twenty-seven, they definitely seceded.

It was the enthusiasm of Schumann and an article he wrote, 'New Paths' (1853), that brought Brahms into wide notice, and the friendship of Schumann and that of his wife were the most precious that ever entered the younger composer's life.

For four years Brahms held a position at a German court; then he lived for a year or two in Switzerland, finally settling in Vienna, where the last thirty-five years of his life were passed.

In character he was honest and sincere, and in manners plain-spoken and often rough. He never married, and to him Art was Life.

Amongst the works of Brahms are the following:

Four **Symphonies:** No. 1, in C minor (op. 68, 1876); No. 2, in D (op. 73, 1877); No. 3, in F (op. 90, 1883); No. 4, in E minor (op. 98, 1885).

Two **Piano Concertos** (op. 15, in D minor, 1861; op. 83, in B flat, 1882).

A **Violin Concerto** (op. 77, in D, 1879), and a **Double Concerto** for violin and cello (op. 102, in A minor, 1888).

A quantity of fine chamber music and piano music and a great number of songs and choral and choral–orchestral compositions, the German Requiem being prominent amongst the last.

References, mostly on small points of detail, will be found as follows: *Accompaniment*; *Arrangement*; *Ballade*; *Ballet* 6; *Bartók*; *Bohm*; *Bruckner*; *Bülow*; *Cadenza*; *Chaconne and Passacaglia*; *Chamber Music*, Period III (1833); *Chorale Prelude*; *Clarinet Family* 6; *Coenen*; *Colour and Music* 3; *Concerto* 3, 6 b; *Criticism* 2, 6; *Dvořák*; *Enesco*; *Form* 11; *Germany* 6; *God save the Queen* 16; *Gramophone* 6; *Ground*; *Hanslick*; *Harp* 3; *History* 7; *Hoffmann, E. T. A.*; *Horn Family* 4; *Hungary*; *Improvisation* 1; *Intermezzo* 6; *Mahler*; *Medtner*; *Memory* 6, 7; *Metronome*; *Nicknamed Compositions* 7; *Oratorio* 7 (1867); *Organ* 13; *Overture* 8; *Paganini*; *Percussion* 4 b (Triangle); *Pianoforte* 21; *Requiem*; *Rhapsody*; *Sonata* 9, 10 c d; *Stanford*; *Suite* 7; *Symphony* 5, 8; *Trombone Family* 2 d; *Waltz*.

BRANDENBURG CONCERTOS. See *Nicknamed* 2; *Bach, J. S.*

BRANDIN, PROFESSOR L. M. See *Voice* 9.

BRANLE, BRANSLE, BRAWL, BRAUL (various other spellings). A dance type of French origin—a round dance originally carried out to the singing of the dancers. Of rustic provenance, it was taken into aristocratic use (p. 273, pl. **49.** 2) and was (like the gavotte and bourrée) popular in the court of Louis XIV. It travelled to England early in the sixteenth century and there became even more common than in France; apparently its French origin was for a time kept in mind, for Shakespeare (*Love's Labour's Lost*, III) says, 'Master, will you win your love with a French Brawl?' It remained in favour for some time after Shakespeare. Pepys, in 1662, speaks of seeing the King (Charles II) and others dance 'the Brantle', and four years later he records seeing the King and Queen and 'about fourteen more couples' dance 'the Bransles'.

The music was (as a rule) two-in-a-measure and not unlike that of the gavotte (q.v.). The word comes from the French 'branler', to sway, and refers to one of the characteristic motions of the dance. The basse danse (q.v.) is supposed to be nearly related, perhaps as ancestor; and so, too, with the passepied (q.v.). It is thought by some that the minuet (q.v.) may derive from the branle, though others prefer to consider that it derives from the galliard.

Different countries and provinces seem to have had their different types of branle. That of Poitou was in three-in-a-measure rhythm.

Dance collections of the sixteenth century sometimes have long strings of branles with variations.

Cf. *Pavan and Galliard*. For the *Double Branle* see *Dance* 6 b.

BRANSCOMBE, GENA. Born at Picton, Ontario, in 1881. She is a pupil of Fielitz and Humperdinck. Amongst her compositions are over seventy songs, some song-cycles, and violin and piano pieces. She is resident in the United States.

BRANSLE, BRANTLE. See *Branle*.

BRAS (Fr.). 'Arm.'

BRASS. The term 'brass', as technically applied, covers all the wind instruments formerly made of that metal though now sometimes made of other metals. It does not include instruments formerly made of wood but now made of metal (as, for instance, the flutes sometimes are), nor does it include metal instruments with reed mouthpieces (e.g. saxophone and sarrusophone). For the method of tone production in the brass see *Acoustics* 5 c.

The brass in the symphonic orchestra in the period of Haydn, Mozart, and the earlier Beethoven included usually merely two horns and two trumpets.

In later Beethoven and music of the same period we find either two or, more commonly, three trombones sometimes added; sometimes also four horns are used (occasionally three) instead of two.

In Wagner we find three trumpets (instead of two) and a bass trumpet also; four horns (or even eight), three trombones, and a contrabass trombone, and tubas (sometimes four, plus a contrabass tuba).

Some account of all these instruments (as also of the saxhorns) will be seen under their own names in this volume. The principle of them all is the same. They make use of the Harmonic Series (see *Acoustics* 8). The horns and trumpets implied in Haydn and Mozart scores were the 'natural' instruments, i.e. they were simple tubes and played merely the notes of the harmonic series—the 'natural notes'. By the addition of a **crook** (a curved additional length of tubing) or a **shank** (a straight additional length), the fundamental note could be altered, and the harmonic series obtained at a different pitch. The higher notes of the series were difficult to obtain, so that the composer was restricted more or less to the notes of the common chord of the keynote (for the crook chosen was naturally usually that of the keynote). Thus any real melodies were almost impossible (unless some highly skilful player was available, as certain works of the period show us he sometimes was) and in general in scores of that period the brass came into action only at the loud tonic-dominant passages which constituted the climaxes of the composition.

The introduction of **valves**, in the early years of the nineteenth century, removed the physical drawbacks and gave the horns and trumpets an enormously increased utility. Roughly speaking, valves can be explained in this way: the various crooks now formed *a permanent part of the mechanism* and could be *brought into use or thrown out of use by finger pressure on one or more pistons*. All notes were, then, quickly available, and the brass instruments became capable of melody—*any* melody within their compass and suitable to their genius.

The trombones form a case apart. The pitch of their fundamental note (and consequently of their Harmonic Series) could always be quickly changed by altering the tube-length. Two parallel sections of the tubing are constructed each with an inner and outer tube, the latter sliding over the former to lengthen the instrument or return it to its original length.

The **mouthpiece** of a brass instrument is of the nature of a cup or funnel pressed against the player's lips, which vibrate within it somewhat like the double reed (see *Reed*) of the oboe family (q.v.), or like the double vocal cords of the human throat (there is, then, a sense in which all wind instruments, save the flutes, are reed instruments).

The shape of the mouthpiece affects the quality of the tone. That of the French horn is deep (funnel-shaped), and has a good deal to do with the smoothness of horn tone; that of the trumpet is hemispherical (cup-shaped), and has a good deal to do with the brilliance of trumpet tone; the trombone mouthpiece is something between the two.

The **bore** of the tube also affects the tone; that of the horn is conical; that of the trumpet, for the greater part of its length, cylindrical. A wide bore like that of the tubas makes it easier to obtain the lower harmonics; a narrow bore makes it harder. The **bell** also has an effect on tone; that of the horn is much broader than that of the trumpet and, with the other factors already mentioned, plays its part in producing the smooth, agreeable timbre characteristic of the instrument.

A curious circumstance in the history of orchestras is that the **melodic use** of the trumpet and horn, which came in largely with Wagner and his contemporaries (who profited by the introduction of the valve system), had been anticipated in, and even before, the time of Bach and Handel (who were confined to the 'natural' system), and that it was, after them, largely dropped. But the melodies of the earlier period all lay high, i.e. they were limited to the upper part of the Harmonic Series, where the notes obtainable are near together, and involved a technique for the obtaining of high notes which afterwards became comparatively rare. It will be realized that Bach and his contemporaries, writing contrapuntally, could have made little use of instruments which could not move melodically, and that the change in the time of Haydn and Mozart to composition in a more harmonic style is reflected in the general decline in the brass players' technique which evidently occurred. (See *Trumpet Family* 3; *Horn Family* 2 c.)

In addition to their orchestral use the brass instruments are very important in wind bands of the two types—*Military Bands* (q.v.), i.e. bands using both brass and wood-wind, and *Brass Bands* (q.v.), i.e. bands using entirely or mainly actual brass instruments.

With this article should be read the following: *Acoustics* 8; *Horn Family*; *Trumpet Family*; *Trombone Family*; *Saxhorn and Flügelhorn Families*; *Tuba Group*; *Cornet*; *Duplex Instruments*—as also (for an abandoned principle in the making of brass instruments) *Cornett Family*, and (for a very early example of a brass instrument) *Scandinavia* 2. See also pp. 112, 113, pls. **21, 22**; p. 140, pl. **26.**

BRASS BAND. The brass band is a type of instrumental combination particularly suitable for open-air performance and allowing of amateur cultivation. It is found all over Europe and in countries settled by Europeans, but its greatest popularity is in the north of England, where an extremely high standard of performance is common. The brass band movement began there shortly before the middle of the nineteenth century, and by the beginning of the twentieth it was reported (see, for instance, Dunstan's *Cyclopaedic Dictionary of Music*) that in Lancashire and Yorkshire alone between 4,000 and 5,000 bands existed, with 40,000 in the whole country (the present writer, however, considers these figures were much exaggerated; 5,000 in the whole of England, Scotland, and Wales, exclusive of the Salvation Army, may be nearer the mark). Many of these bands were attached to particular factories or collieries, and this affiliation still continues in some cases.

It is difficult to lay down the constituents of a brass band (cf. *Military Band*), as these differ considerably. Usually they consist of members of the cornet and saxhorn families plus trombones. What may be looked upon as the normal British band is that of twenty-four players (plus percussion). Its constitution as suggested for the National Contests (see *Competitions in Music* 3) is as follows:

1 cornet in E flat, called 'soprano', and 6 in B flat. (See *Cornet.*)

3 Flügelhorns in B flat; 3 alto saxhorns in E flat, often called simply 'horns'; 2 tenor saxhorns in B flat, called 'baritones'. (See *Saxhorn and Flügelhorn Families.*)

2 tenor trombones and 1 bass trombone. (See *Trombone Family.*)

2 tenor tubas in B flat, called 'euphoniums'; 2 bass tubas in E flat, called 'E flat bombardons' or simply 'basses in E flat'; 2 bass tubas in B flat, called basses in B flat or 'BB flat bombardons'. (See *Tuba Group* 4, 5.)

Snare drums, bass drums, and cymbals must be added. Saxophones may also appear, in which case (these being reed instruments) the term 'Brass Band' is not strictly applicable, but it is nevertheless used.[1]

Another typical constitution is as follows: 1 soprano cornet in E flat; 4 solo cornets in B flat; 1 Flügelhorn in B flat; 1 'Repiano' (i.e. *ripieno*) cornet in B flat; 2 second cornets in B flat; 2 third cornets in B flat; 3 saxhorns (called solo first and second); 2 baritones in B flat (first and second); 3 trombones (2 B flat and 1 G); 2 euphoniums; 2 bombardons in E flat; 2 bombardons in B flat.

It might be supposed that it would be comparatively easy to read a score which, though

[1] Foden's Band, which won the championship in 1936, was made up according to the following scheme, which is said to be very usual—1 cornet in E flat and 8 in B flat; 1 Flügelhorn in B flat; 3 tenor horns in E flat; 2 baritones in B flat; 2 tenor trombones (B flat) and 1 bass trombone; 2 euphoniums in B flat; 2 bombardons in E flat and 2 in B flat, and 2 percussion players. This, like the scheme above, allows for 24 players plus percussion.

entirely made up of 'Transposing Instruments' (q.v.), includes such in only two keys, and were the parts for these instruments notated as are those for an orchestra this would certainly be so. Unfortunately, a complication occurs. From a desire, apparently, to notate all the instruments in the band alike, and so to facilitate class teaching of them and the transference of a player from one instrument to another if need arise, all the music (with the exception of that for the bass trombone and the drums) is notated in the treble clef.

Evidently if the note C is found in the score it will produce B flat on all the B flat instruments and E flat on all the E flat ones. But that same note C will produce B flats and E flats in different octaves according to the instrument in question:

E flat soprano sounds E flat a 3rd above.
B flat cornet ,, B ,, 2nd below.
B flat Flügel ,, B ,, 2nd ,,
E flat horn ,, E ,, 6th ,,
B flat baritone ,, B ,, 9th ,,
B flat trombone sounds B flat a 9th below.
Bass trombone sounds as written.
B flat euphonium sounds B flat a 9th below.
E flat bass sounds E flat an 8ve+a 6th below.
B flat bass sounds B flat two 8ves+a 2nd below.

It will be observed that the practice as to the notation of some of these instruments is different in orchestral music and band music: it is most different of all in the case of the B flat (i.e. tenor) trombone, which in orchestral music is treated as a non-transposing instrument.

It will be understood that the parts for all the B flat instruments in a brass band bear the key-signature of the key a major 2nd above (i.e. the one with two flats less or two sharps more) and that all the E flat instruments bear the key-signature of a major 6th above (i.e. the one with three flats less or three sharps more). The actual key of the composition can be seen by a glance at the part of the only brass instrument which receives notation at the true pitch, i.e. the bass trombone.

Not all keys are equally convenient (acoustically and as to playing convenience) for treatment by these instruments. The best keys (actual pitch) are those, major or minor, with no flats or sharps, or with 1, 2, 3, 4, or 5 flats. It is significant that a favourite key for brass band writing is that with 5 flats, which means that the B flat instruments are shown in the key of 3 flats, and the E flat ones shown in the key of 2 flats. (They have sections in other keys but never go very far to the sharp side.)

The repertory of the brass band was long an impoverished affair consisting of arrangements, or original music of poor quality (cf. *Military Band*, near the end of the article, for a similar situation). In more recent times matters have improved somewhat, with contributions from prominent composers such as Elgar, Ireland, Howells, Rubbra, and Vaughan Williams.

For Brass Band Contests see *Competitions in Music* 3.

BRASSED NOTES ON HORN. See *Horn Family* 2 c, 5.

BRATSCHE (Ger.). 'Viola' (see *Braccio and Gamba*). So 'Bratschist' means *Viola Player*.

BRAUL, BRAULE. Same as *Branle* (q.v.).

BRAUNFELS, WALTER. Born at Frankfurt-on-Main in 1882 and died at Cologne in 1954, aged seventy-one. He was a piano pupil of Leschetizky and a notable performer; from 1925 to 1933 he was a co-director of the Cologne Conservatory (with Abendroth). His activities as a composer in neo-romantic style were extremely varied, including piano music, songs, church music, orchestral music, operas (e.g. *The Birds*), and other things.

BRAUTLIED (Ger.). 'Bridal song.'

BRAVOURE (Fr.). 'Bravery', 'gallantry'; or used in the same sense as the following Italian word—

BRAVURA (It.). 'Skill', e.g. *Aria di bravura*, a brilliant aria making great demands on the singer.

BRAWL, BRAWLE. Old English name for *Branle* (q.v.).

BRAZIL. See *Broadcasting* 3.

BREAK. (1) A sort of brief cadenza (q.v.) used in jazz. The band suspends its activities and a soloist extemporizes perhaps two measures (see *Jazz* 3). (2) Change of vocal register (see *Breaking of Voice*). (3) A momentary silence after a phrase (often shown by a comma above the staff). No loss of time must occur, the break being made by slightly shortening the last note of the phrase.

BREAKING OF VOICE. This can mean either of two things—the place in the scale where occurs the change from one vocal 'register' to another, generally called 'the break' (see *Voice* 4); or the permanent change in character that comes over the voice (especially the male voice) at puberty (see *Voice* 5).

BREATHING. See *Voice* 3.

'BREATHY' SINGING. See *Voice* 4.

BREAZUL, PROFESSOR. See *Rumania*.

BRECHT, BERT. See *Gebrauchsmusik*; *Weill*.

BREIT (Ger.; various terminations according to gender, case, etc.). 'Broad', i.e. (often) *Largo*. Sometimes it is applied to style of bowing, e.g. *Breit gestrichen*, 'broadly bowed'.

BREITKOPF AND HÄRTEL. See *Publishing* 8; *Printing* 5; *Copyists*.

BREMNER, ROBERT (1720–89). See *Publishing of Music* 6; *Presbyterian Church Music* 4; *Sibyl*; *Metronome*.

BRENET, MICHEL (1858–1918). Pen-name of Marie Bobillier, eminent French musicologist and author of a long series of valuable books of musical historical research.

See references under *Mechanical Reproduction* 10; *Country Dance*; *Whistling*; *Dictionaries* 2.

BRENHINES DIDO. This 'Welsh air' first appeared as such, and with its Welsh title, in a publication of 'Blind' Parry, 1781. It is an adaptation of an English song, Dr. John Wilson's 'Queen Dido', which appears in his *Cheerful Ayres* (Oxford, 1659). The facts can be seen in an article by the great authority on British songs, Frank Kidson, in the *Musical Times*, February 1911.

BRENT, JOHN. See *Pianoforte* 5.

BRENTA, GASTON. See *Synthétistes*.

BRESLAU. See *Organ* 5.

BRETÓN, TOMÁS. Born at Salamanca in 1850 and died in Madrid in 1923, aged nearly seventy-three. He had early struggles as a café violinist, but rose to the position of conductor of the Royal Opera and the Philharmonic Society's Orchestra of Madrid and Director of the Conservatory of Music there.

Like Albeniz (who helped him and brought him to London as a conductor), he fought for the cause of musical nationalism, his particular contribution being the artistic treatment of the operatic form of the Zarzuela (see *Opera* 15), in which he wrote prolifically and with high popular success. He also wrote symphonic poems, a suite, a violin concerto, chamber music, and choral music.

BRÉVAL, JEAN BAPTISTE (1756–1825). He was a Paris violoncellist who had a reputation as a composer of orchestral and chamber music, etc. (See *Chamber Music* 6, Period III.)

BREVE (𝄺). Formerly, as its name reminds us, the *short* note of musical notation, but the longer ones have all fallen into disuse and shorter ones been devised, so that the breve is now the longest that exists (twice the length, of course, of the semibreve or whole note) and even so, rather rarely appears. (The change mentioned does not necessarily imply any change in the speed of the music, but merely a different convention in recording it.) See *Notation* 3, 4.

The expression **Alla Breve,** of which the origin is disputed, usually means 'Make your speed twice as fast as you would have done'. The same effect is indicated by the use of the sign ₵ instead of C, or $\frac{2}{2}$ instead of $\frac{4}{4}$.

Sometimes the term *alla breve* indicates merely $\frac{2}{2}$ time. Anyhow, it always means 'Take the Minim (or Half Note) as the unit, not the Crotchet (or Quarter Note) as you might otherwise do'. (Towards the end of Bach's St. John Passion he has an aria in $\frac{3}{4}$ time so marked; this is quite exceptional.)

Cf. *Cappella* 2; and for Bach's organ fugue called 'The Alla Breve Fugue', see *Nicknamed Compositions* 1.

BREVIARY. See *Liturgy*; *Common Prayer*.

BRÉVILLE, PIERRE ONFROY DE (p. 385, pl. 64. 1). Born at Bar-le-Duc, in the northeast of France, in 1861 and died in Paris in 1949, aged eighty-eight. He was a pupil of Dubois at the Conservatory of Paris, and then of Franck, of whose group (cf. *d'Indy*) he was a devoted member. He also joined the staff of the Schola Cantorum (cf. *Bordes*), attached himself to that National Musical Society which has worked for the regeneration of French music, and served as music critic on the staff of the *Mercure de France*.

His compositions are numerous and varied, and include masses, cantatas, orchestral and chamber works, an opera, songs, and piano and organ pieces. His style is one of fastidious refinement.

BREWER, ALFRED HERBERT. Born at Gloucester in 1865 and there died in 1928, aged sixty-two. He was organist for a short term of Bristol Cathedral and then (in 1897) of Gloucester Cathedral—which last position carried with it the conductorship, in his turn, of the Three Choirs Festival. He was a fairly active minor composer. In 1926 he was knighted.

See reference *Oratorio* 7 (1901–4).

BRIAN, HAVERGAL. Born in Staffordshire in 1876, and died in Shoreham in 1972. He was the self-taught composer of thirty-two symphonies, five operas, and various choral works, all on a very large scale, and mostly unperformed.

BRIDEGROOM GRAT. See *Auld Robin Gray*.

BRIDEL. See *Ranz des vaches*.

BRIDGE. (1) That piece of wood on a stringed instrument which supports the strings and communicates their vibrations to the belly (q.v.). The sounding length of the strings begins at the bridge and extends to the nut (q.v.) of the finger-board (q.v.) or to that point on the finger-board at which they are 'stopped' (see *Stopping*).

See *Viol Family* 2 g; *Violin Family* 4.

(2) For Bridge in composition see *Form* 7.

BRIDGE.

(1) (JOHN) FREDERICK, i.e. Sir Frederick Bridge. Born near Birmingham in 1844 and died in London in 1924, aged seventy-nine.

He was well known as organist of Westminster Abbey for over forty years (1875–1918; see allusion under *Cathedral Music* 7), and occupied very many posts as conductor and professor (Royal College of Music, 1883–1924, London University, Gresham College, etc.). He was knighted in 1897, and later received other official honours. He took a large part in professional organization and in musical antiquarian research, and was indeed active in almost every way open to the most general practitioner. He wrote many oratorios, cantatas, anthems, textbooks, etc.

See references under *Oratorio* 7 (1890–4); *Gresham Professorship*.

(2) JOSEPH COX (1853–1929), long organist of Chester Cathedral, Professor of Music at Durham University, and finally Chairman of the Board of Management of Trinity College, London, was brother of the above.

(3) FRANK (p. 352, pl. **55.** 1). Born at Brighton in 1879 and died in Eastbourne in 1941, aged nearly sixty-two. In composition he was a pupil of Stanford at the Royal College of Music. He had high repute as a viola player, as a chamber music coach, as a conductor, and

as a composer for orchestra, for chamber combinations, and for the voice. He was not related to (1) and (2) above.

BRIDGE PASSAGE. See *Form* 7.

BRIDGES.

(1) ROBERT (1844–1930). Poet Laureate. See *Anglican Chant* 6; *Hymns and Hymn Tunes* 14.

(2) HENRY. Inventor. See *Mechanical* 10.

BRIDGETOWER, GEORGE AUGUSTUS POLGREEN (1780–1860). Violinist. See *United States of America* 6 (end); also p. 1096, pl. **181.** 8.

BRIGHTON CAMP. See *Girl I left behind me*.

BRIGGS, H. B. See *Plainsong* 4.

BRILLANT, BRILLANTE (Fr., masc., fem.),

BRILLANTE (It.). 'Brilliant.'

BRINDISI (Italian for a 'toast'). The term is applied to a jovial song to which a 'health' is (actually or in imagination) drunk. Such songs sometimes occur in operas, e.g. the air *Libiamo* ('Let's drink') in Verdi's *La Traviata*.

BRIO (It.). 'Vigour', spirit, fire. So the adj. *Brioso*.

BRISÉ (Fr.). 'Broken'—used of a chord played arpeggio fashion, or of string music played with short, detached bow movements.

BRISTOL CATHEDRAL. See *Cathedral Music* 2. Organists who receive notice in this volume are (with their periods of office)—*Bevin* (c. 1589–1637); *P. C. Buck* (1899–1901).

BRISTOL MADRIGAL SOCIETY. See *Madrigal* 5.

BRISTOW, G. F. See *Opera* 21 j.

BRITAIN. See *England*; *Scotland*; *Ireland*; *Wales*; *Oratorio* 5, 7; *Opera* 13, 14.

BRITANNIA, THE PRIDE OF THE OCEAN. The words were written in 1842 by an Irish journalist, Stephen Joseph Meany (d. 1890), the tune at the same period by Thomas E. Williams, of London (d. 1854)—the composer of a duet still perhaps occasionally heard, 'The Larboard Watch', and of several songs popular during the mid-nineteenth century.

An American version of the words, 'Columbia, the Gem of the Ocean', was provided by one Thomas à Becket, who in 1876 put forward a claim to be both author and composer of this song. There is, however, no doubt that à Becket did nothing but adapt a British production, and the American writer, L. C. Elson, in his *The National Music of America* (1900), admits that 'gem of the ocean' is a 'very odd metaphor to apply to a continent over 3,000 miles broad, and bounded by land on two of its sides', whereas it is evident that it is 'a very apt appellation to bestow upon an island kingdom such as Great Britain'.

BRITISH AND AMERICAN SPEECH. See *Voice* 10, 12.

BRITISH BROADCASTING CORPORATION. See *Broadcasting of Music* 3; *Monopolies*; *Scotland* 1; *Accompaniment*; *Bliss*; *Boult*.

BRITISH COUNCIL, THE. This was founded in 1935 with the object of maintaining and enlarging cultural relations with foreign countries. It possesses a Music Department, which organizes practical activities such as sending on foreign tours British musicians (including choirs and orchestras), enabling foreign musicians and journalists to attend performances in Britain, circulating British orchestral music abroad, and maintaining in foreign countries libraries of British music and collections of gramophone records.

BRITISH FEDERATION OF MUSICAL FESTIVALS. See *Competitions in Music* 2.

BRITISH GRENADIERS. The words date from the very end of the seventeenth century, as proved by their allusion to practices concerning hand grenades which were only in operation from 1678 to about the end of the century. (However, a later version is sometimes now sung—one with allusion to Waterloo.)

The origin of the tune is unknown, but it has strong resemblances to other tunes—the Dutch *William of Nassau* (1581) and the French *O la folle entreprise du Prince de Condé* (1568). The earliest copy of the song as we know it, so far as it could be traced by the great authority on British songs, Frank Kidson (q.v.), dated from 1735 or 1740.

BRITISH INSTITUTE OF RECORDED SOUND. See *Gramophone* 7.

BRITISH MUSEUM. See *Libraries*.

BRITISH MUSIC. See *England*; *Scotland*; *Ireland*; *Wales*; *Oratorio* 5, 7; *Opera* 13, 14.

BRITISH SOUND RECORDING ASSOCIATION. This was formed, in 1936, by a number of engineers and amateur enthusiasts 'with the primary purpose of uniting in one organization all persons, in England and abroad, whether professionals or amateurs, engaged or interested in the art and science of sound recording'. It conducts experiments and encourages research, arranges lectures and demonstrations, etc.

BRITTEN, (EDWARD) BENJAMIN (p. 353, pl. **56**. 9). Born at Lowestoft in 1913 and died at Aldeburgh in 1976, aged sixty-three. He began composition at the age of five and during the following five years wrote six string quartets and ten piano sonatas. Whilst still at school he worked at the piano with Harold Samuel and at composition with Frank Bridge. Then he won a scholarship at the Royal College of Music, where his composition teacher was John Ireland and his piano teacher Arthur Benjamin. Amongst his early publications were many choral works and solo songs. The string *Variations on a theme by Frank Bridge* was one of the early works which brought him into serious public notice (1937) and from the same period he began a considerable activity as a composer of music for over twenty documentary films, also providing incidental music for several stage plays.

In 1940 appeared his *Sinfonia da Requiem* and his *Seven Sonnets of Michelangelo* (tenor and piano; much sung by Peter Pears, his friend and frequent interpreter).

Operatic activity became prominent from 1945, in which year his *Peter Grimes* was produced; it was followed by *The Rape of Lucretia* (1946) the comic opera *Albert Herring* (1947), a freely treated version of *The Beggar's Opera* (1948), *Let's make an Opera* (for children) (1949), *Billy Budd* (1951), *Gloriana* (1953), *The Turn of the Screw* (1954), *Midsummer Night's Dream* (1960), *Owen Wingrave* (1970), and *Death in Venice* (1973).

Important later works include the *War Requiem* (1961) and a *Cello Symphony* (1964). *Curlew River* (1964), a combination of medieval music drama and Japanese Noh play, *The Burning Fiery Furnace* (1966) and *The Prodigal Son* (1968), were seen by some as the beginning of a new stage in his creative life. In England the work of the English Opera Group and the annual festival at Aldeburgh in his native Suffolk helped materially to widen interest in his music.

He received numerous prizes, notably the $30,000 Aspen Award in 1964. In 1953 he was made a Companion of Honour, in 1965 he was named a member of the Order of Merit and in 1976 was granted a life peerage.

See *Oboe Family* 6; *Cinematograph*; *Concerto* 6 c (1913); *Opera* 21 f, 24 f; *Peter Grimes*; *Pianoforte* 21; *Requiem*; *History* 9; *Ghedini*.

BRITTON, T. (1644–1714). See *Concert* 4; also p. 225, pl. **43**. 2, 3.

BROADCASTING OF MUSIC

1. The Scientific Basis of Broadcasting.
2. The History of Broadcasting.
3. The Administration of Broadcasting.
4. How True is Radio Reproduction?
5. The Effect of Broadcasting on Public Taste, etc.
6. Television.
7. Wired Broadcasting.
8. Broadcasting as Nuisance.

(For illustrations see pp. 132–3, pls. **24, 25**.)

1. The Scientific Basis of Broadcasting. It is assumed that the reader has acquainted himself with the main facts concerning the nature, production, and propagation of sound in general and of musical sounds in particular, as set forth in the article *Acoustics*.

Radio broadcasting is a means of rapid transmission of human thought—one of three such means now in daily operation; its process will be more easily understood if the processes of the other two are first considered. They are all electrical. The nature of electricity as such cannot be treated here, but it may be said briefly that, like heat, light, and sound, for our present purposes it may be considered to be a form of vibratory motion. (We use the word 'current' merely for convenience, and so with the word 'flow'; they are metaphors.)

(*a*) The **Electric Telegraph** (which dates from 1837) is essentially nothing more than the controlling at place *A* of a current flowing along a wire to place *B*, where it works a galvanometer or detector. By the alternate turning on and off of the current at *A*, the detector at *B* can be made to emit sounds, to make marks on paper slips, or to control a printing machine. The apparatus, then, consists of a *Transmitter*, a *Conductor* (the wire), and a *Receiver*—the last-named with some means attached to it of conveying to the ear or eye a series of sounds or signs.

(*b*) The **Telephone** (which dates from 1876) is, essentially, the telegraph with one very important modification—the interruption and resumption of the current at place *A* (or the variation of its strength) is controlled by means of a *microphone* (this is the modern system). The diaphragm of the microphone is vibrated by the voice; a mass of carbon granules lies behind, which are, by the inward and outward expansion of the diaphragm, pressed together and allowed to separate again, the resistance to the current being thus varied in accordance with the frequency of the vibrations, answering to the fluctuations of pitch of the sounds emitted (and the element of pitch, as may be seen under *Voice* 7, covers, amongst other things, the distinctions between the various speech sounds), of the amplitude of the vibrations according to the sounds' loudness (see *Acoustics* 4), and so forth.

The current passes through a transformer which changes these variations into an alternating current passing along a wire connected to the receiving telephone, where it acts (by a polarized electric magnet) upon a disk, which is made to reproduce the original vibrations and consequently the original sounds of the voice. (It is nowadays forgotten that as early as 1881 arrangements were made by which the Leeds Musical Festival could be heard by telephone—the press of the day not, however, reporting very favourably on the result. Five years earlier than that the then famous English poet, Martin Tupper, visiting New York, writes home of his intention of attending a 'Telephone Concert' in the Steinway Hall, New York: 'Tunes played in Philadelphia and heard here on a wire. *What a world we live in!*')

(*c*) **Wireless Telephony** may be explained as follows (and the nature of wireless telegraphy may be sufficiently inferred from it):

A small electrical apparatus is arranged to give a minute alternating current of high frequency (i.e. the vibrations are very rapid—up to some millions of them per second). This is amplified (made more powerful), over and over again, till several horse-power is applied to the masts carrying the aerial that

is radiating it. These send out what is known as a continuous wave of electrical vibrations which have the same speed as light, i.e. for the distances that are in question the transmission may be called instantaneous (see *Acoustics* 14).

A microphone (see *b* above) is arranged to control the original minute alternating current, automatically weakening or strengthening it according to the nature of the sounds that impinge on the diaphragm.

Thus if the frequency of the minute alternating current mentioned were a million vibrations per second, and a musical note having a frequency of a thousand vibrations per second (roughly the C above the treble staff) were sounded before the microphone, it would increase and diminish the high-frequency current a thousand times a second; if a lower note of five hundred vibrations (roughly the C in the middle of the treble staff) were sounded, it would do this five hundred times a second, and so forth.

The sound of a frequency of a thousand, it will be clear, does not affect the rapidity of the current's own vibrations, which continue as before. It merely increases, so many times per second, what we may call the volume of the current, reinforcing one vibration in every so many and leaving the others unaffected.

At the other end, which can be anywhere in the world where anyone cares to set up a receiving set, that set is so constructed as to cancel out the high-frequency vibrations, handing on only the rises and falls of the high-frequency current; thus the frequency of the vibrations passed to the earphones or loud-speaker corresponds again to the frequency of the original vibrations given to the microphone.

The receiving apparatus works a telephone (headphone) or loud-speaker, and a sound whose vibrations at the transmitting end were one thousand per second therefore reappears at the receiving end as one thousand per second, i.e. the original sound is reproduced.

The above makes clear, it is hoped, the general method of radio transmission of pitch. As for timbre, that too, being purely a matter of notes of various pitches associated with the main pitch (see *Acoustics* 6), is covered by the explanation just given. And as for the loudness of the sound, that, of course, is a matter of the amplitude of the vibrations, as at (*b*) above.

The communication of music or speech in this way is called, from the nature of its apparatus, *Wireless*; or, from the resemblance of the giving-off of its vibrations to the radiation of light or heat, *Radio*; or, from the throwing out of its gift to the world as a sower throws out seed, *Broadcasting*.

The speeds of communication (i) by ordinary sound-waves (e.g. music in a concert room), (ii) by electric waves (e.g. music conveyed by the old electrophone, q.v., which was merely an improved telephone), and (iii) by radio transmission, differ widely, being as follows:

(i) through the **Air** (music in concert

rooms, etc.), about one-fifth of a mile per second.

(ii) by **Wire** (Telephone, Electrophone, etc.), a fraction of a second per mile, depending on the electrical properties of the wire and apparatus.

(iii) by **Radio**, the same speed as light, i.e. 186,330 miles per second.

From this it follows that every note of a performance broadcast from a concert room may be heard at the other side of the world before it has been heard by many persons in the room itself (compare *Acoustics* 13).

The explanation that has just been given is probably clear, even to the reader without any scientific training, so far as it concerns a *single pure note*. Its extension to the conception of the transmission of a *note with a definite timbre*, and to the larger conception of the simultaneous transmission of a *number of notes each with its distinctive timbre*, will be easily made after a reading of *Acoustics* 12.

To summarize what happens when a musical note is broadcast:

(i) Its **Pitch**, being the result of a certain fixed number of vibrations per second, is communicated to the diaphragm as that number of pressures and pressure-releases per second, thus creating vibrations, or 'waves' of fixed length, that are superimposed on the electric vibrations or 'waves'.

(ii) Its **Force**, being the result of the amplitude of sound 'waves', is communicated to the diaphragm as that same amplitude and then accepted as the amplitude of the new 'waves' superimposed on the electric 'waves'.

(iii) Its **Timbre**, being a result of a number of subsidiary sounds of varying force, is communicated in the manner mentioned under (*a*) and (*b*).

Thus the whole of the characteristics possible to a musical note are transmitted.

2. The History of Broadcasting. The chief landmarks in the history of the development of radio transmission are as follows:

1830. 'Wireless telegraphy may quite rightly trace its development back to the days of Michael Faraday, for it was through his discovery, in 1830, that it was not necessary for two electrical circuits to be in actual physical contact for electric energy to pass between them that he directed attention to the medium separating the two electric circuits which plays such a great part in wireless communication.' (Article by Marconi in London *Times*, 21 Sept. 1931.)

1863. The Scotsman, James Clerk Maxwell, demonstrated mathematically the existence of electro-magnetic 'waves'.

1888. The German, Heinrich Hertz, produced such 'waves'.

1894. The Englishman, Oliver Lodge, showed that signals could be transmitted without wires by means of the 'Hertzian Waves'.

1895. The Italian, Guglielmo Marconi (opposite, pl. **24**. 4), evolved a method of propagating and receiving these 'waves', and in the following year the British Post Office gave him opportunities for displaying and developing his system. Russians attribute the invention to Alexander Popov, who demonstrated an apparatus in April of that year.

1899. The first wireless telegraphic messages passed between England and France, and soon after this ships began to be equipped with wireless apparatus. In 1898 messages had been communicated over a distance of 12 miles; by 1901 they were communicated by Marconi over a distance of 1,800 miles.

Armies of experimenters and inventors were now at work in many countries, and many discoveries were made and new types or details of apparatus brought into existence, the present telegraphic news service to ships at sea being inaugurated in 1904. In the same year Thaddeus Cahill proposed a system of broadcasting by telephone and patented it under the name 'Telharmonium'. (See Busoni's *New Aesthetic of Music*.) In 1907 passengers on a train travelling from Salt Lake City, Utah, to Ely, Nevada, were able to make calls to both terminal points. Marie Corelli 'opened' such a system for the London, Brighton, and South Coast Railway in 1911.

1914. Marconi succeeded in telephoning between Italian warships at a distance of 50 miles, and next year America made a great advance by telephoning from Washington to Honolulu and to Paris. Wireless telephony arrived, then, just in time to be used during the first World War.

At this point justice requires the insertion of a guarding statement. The above dates and names are those accepted almost everywhere, but a music-teacher turned scientist, the Londoner, David Edmund Hughes (for a time Professor of Music, and then of Natural Philosophy, in an institution at Bardstown, Kentucky, 1850–4), recognized as the inventor of the telegraph type-printing instrument, deserves recognition, it is claimed, also as the predecessor of several other 'discoverers' or 'inventors'. See the *Electrical Review* for 2 June 1899: 'Hughes discovered the "Hertzian Waves" before Hertz . . . and the wireless telegraph before Lodge, Marconi, and others' (opposite, pl. **24**. 3).

1917. Captain D. de A. Donisthorpe and colleagues of the Royal Engineers Wireless Training Centre at Worcester sent out a regular evening programme of talks and music for the benefit of other wireless training units. This may have been the world's first series of broadcast programmes.

1919. Broadcasting began in America by amateur experimenters giving entertainments to one another.

1920 (February). The first public British broadcasting station was opened by the Marconi Company at Writtle, near Chelmsford,

1. AN EARLY ANTICIPATION OF BROADCASTING
(From Johann David's *Veridicus Christianus*, 1601)

2. A LATE 19TH-CENTURY FRENCH PROPHECY
(Note the battery and loud-speakers)

3. DAVID HUGHES'S FIRST WIRELESS SET, 1879. This Kentucky Professor of Music and then of Natural Philosophy is said by some to 'have discovered the Hertzian waves before Hertz and the Wireless Telegraph before Lodge, Marconi, and others'. See *Broadcasting* 2

4. MARCONI WITH HIS EARLIEST APPARATUS. From *The Illustrated London News*, 31 July 1897. The heading is 'Signor Gugliemo Marconi with his newly-invented Electric Telegraph without a wire conductor'. He was then 22 and was profiting by experiments he had made on Salisbury Plain, with the help of the British Director-General of Telegraphs, W. H. Preece. See *Broadcasting* 2

5. SIR AMBROSE FLEMING (1849–1945). He was Professor of Electrical Engineering at University College, London, and a pioneer in the development of Electric Light, the Telephone, and Radio

1. THE EARLY DAYS—Transmitting a duet (London, 1921)

2. MAIN CONTROL DESK, Radio City, New York, 1936

3. EARLY TELEVISION IN LONDON (1936)

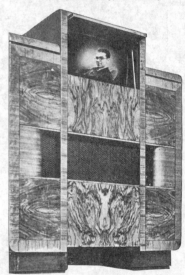

4. BRITISH TELEVISION SET IN 1937

5. SIR THOMAS BEECHAM IN A LONDON TELEVISION STUDIO, 1952

and (June) Melba broadcast from a high-power experimental station at Chelmsford itself.

1920 (December). The first public American station was opened at East Pittsburgh, Pa. (later known as KDKA). Within less than two years after that there were 500 stations. East Pittsburgh is regarded as the world's pioneer amongst fully organized stations.

1922. The British Broadcasting Company was formed by four of the chief electrical manufacturers. France established two stations in this year and Holland one.

1923 (8 January). *The Magic Flute*, performed by the British National Opera Company, was broadcast from Covent Garden; this is believed to be the world's first opera-broadcast.[1]

1925. The Daventry high-power station was opened, disseminating programmes from the London stations.

1927. The British Broadcasting Company became the British Broadcasting Corporation under government control, licences being issued by the Post Office at 10 shillings per annum. Later this was increased to £1. 5s. (sound), £6 (sound and black-and-white television), £11 (same plus colour). (The number of such licences in force early in that year was 2¼ millions, by 1937, 8¼ millions, and by 1969, 16·6 millions.

In 1927, also, the United States Government brought into existence the Federal Radio Commission (later the Federal Communications Commission) to control the licensing of broadcasting organizations, etc. (Five—later seven—members appointed by the President and answerable to Congress.)

1928. Experimental BBC television broadcasts took place.

1930. The total number of radio sets in the United States was reported as 13 millions (in rather over 12 million homes). By 1960 there were over 100 millions in 48 million homes.

1936. The BBC instituted a regular television service from Alexandra Palace, resumed after the interruption of the second World War.

1950s. In the US, and later in the UK, the use of the Frequency Modulation ('FM'—see 4) system of sound broadcasting spread rapidly.

3. The Administration of Broadcasting. For obvious reasons, broadcasting has in every country of the world been brought under some degree of public control. Great Britain (with which is linked Northern Ireland) offers an example of the stricter form of control, the United States of America of the looser.

In Great Britain the whole of the broadcasting activities were at first entrusted to one non-profit-making Corporation, functioning under charter from the Government. The original charter was dated 1927, and was renewed in 1937, 1947, 1952, and 1963. These periodical renewals involved periodic exhaustive inquiries by independent committees,

[1] Note the development. In 1968 the BBC broadcast 138 complete different operas, many of them more than once.

a procedure apparently welcomed by the BBC itself. In 1954 the BBC television monopoly was ended when the Independent Television Authority (ITA) was set up by the government to provide additional programmes at no cost to viewers, the revenue being provided by advertisers. ITA built transmitters, which were then leased to fifteen programme companies, which produce programmes and sell spot announcements (an average of six minutes per hour) to advertisers. ITA retains the right to veto programmes or advertisements. There is no sponsorship of programmes by advertisers. An exhaustive report (the Pilkington Report) in 1962 recommended that in future ITA should itself plan the programmes and sell advertising time, the programme companies producing programmes and selling them to the ITA.

BBC finances are provided for the most part by the above-mentioned system of licensing of radio-receiving apparatus. A small fraction of each licence fee went until 1961 to the Post Office, and a larger fraction to the Exchequer, as, in effect, a tax on broadcasting. The statement frequently made in the United States that British broadcasting was 'subsidized' by the government was, then, the reverse of the truth, the fact being rather that the British government was 'subsidized' by broadcasting. In 1961, however, the BBC began to keep 100 per cent. of the licence revenue. The statement that it is administered by the government is almost equally untrue, for it is administered by an independent organization of large but defined powers, which, within the limit of those powers, is a free agent. The BBC does not consider itself in any sense a government agency, but a public corporation established by Parliament and explicitly independent of the government. Its governors are nine 'trustees in the national interest'.

The British early realized some of the wider implications of the development of radio and planned accordingly, so there are some grounds for considering British broadcasting a standard to which other systems can be compared. A weekly paper, the *Listener*, reprints many of the best talks as well as acting as one of the few outlets for new poetry.

In the United States the Government exercises little control over broadcasting beyond licensing the private individuals and companies that set up stations, and allotting them wavelengths, etc., in order to avoid the chaotic 'interferences' that would otherwise result. For the most part the broadcasting organizations exist for commercial purposes. In the U.S.A. there are no receiving licences: stations are supported by the revenue from broadcast advertisements ('commercials').

The 1927 Radio Act set up the Federal Radio Commission (later the Federal Communications Commission—F.C.C.) as the 'traffic cop of broadcasting'. The F.C.C. licenses stations which serve 'public interest, convenience, or necessity'. It may, but very seldom does, revoke a licence.

The National Broadcasting Corporation (N.B.C.) was formed in 1926, and the Columbia Broadcasting Service (C.B.S.) in the following year. Forty years later these two giant organizations, each with a network of semi-independent subsidiary stations, still dominated the scene.

It is maintained by critics of the U.S.-type system that the payment by an advertising firm of large sums for the right to use a broadcasting station naturally leads it to draft such programmes as will constitute immediate attractions to the largest possible number of listeners, with the result of a very natural tendency repeatedly to employ the same few performers (those who are already 'stars'), and to broadcast the same compositions (those that are already 'popular'). In other words, the contention is that the American system (by no means approved by all Americans) places obstacles in the way of the considered planning of programmes with a view to the gradual widening of the tastes of the community. (It must be remembered, however, that the American stations do not, and cannot, sell *all* their time, and that in what are called 'sustaining' programmes they are somewhat freer than in what are called 'sponsored' programmes.)

The 'free-for-all' American system is linked in the minds of its apologists with an essential freedom: the freedom of the press, or the right of everyone to publish—to communicate his ideas and proposals to his fellow citizens, if necessary from a soap-box. But radio has not yet reached the point where every citizen can own a radio or television transmitting station, so some regulation of the licensees who do own stations is essential. Also, even in a newspaper there are parts that are for sale, and others that are not: a balance between editorial and advertising content. Big sponsors are often 'imperfectly competitive', so that the existence of several broadcasting outlets in one area does not necessarily mean that a wide range of tastes and interests will be served.

It is impossible here to describe the systems in all European countries. The French system somewhat approximated to the American until 1935, when it was reorganized on lines that brought it nearer the British system, though with rather more direct government control. The German system, at first comparable to the British, after the advent of the Nazi government in 1933 became one of the most rigid control, with political aims, and was directed by the Minister of Propaganda. After the second World War there was a period of Allied control until 1948, when the reins were gradually handed back to the various German organizations. The Russian system is similarly government-controlled, largely in the interests of the creation of political sentiment. The Moscow station is the most powerful in Europe.

The total number of short and medium wave broadcasting stations in Britain in 1952 was 56; in the United States 4,510. Until the outbreak of the second World War a 'Union internationale de radiodiffusion', with its seat at Geneva, acted as a liaison between the broadcasting organizations of the various countries, its particular concern being to avoid the chaos of overlapping wave-lengths. Its post-war successor is U.E.R. (Union européenne de radiodiffusion) for Western countries; O.I.R. (Organisation internationale de radiodiffusion), in Prague, includes the East European countries.

Canada (Canadian Broadcasting Commission —CBC) combines features of Great Britain and the U.S.A. CBC was set up in 1936 on much the same lines as the BBC. Some stations are owned by CBC, others are privately owned but may on occasion transmit CBC programmes. In 1957, of 189 radio stations 22 were CBC, 167 private.

Australia, where the Australian Broadcasting Commission (ABC) was set up in 1932, has a similar system. It may be that countries like Australia and Canada, with this kind of 'mixed' commercial and public service, have the best of both worlds. The South African Broadcasting Corporation dates from 1936; its commercial branch (Springbok Radio) was established in 1950. In New Zealand, with a Broadcasting Board (later Service) dating from 1936, there are also commercial stations.

Details of the U.S.S.R. are not easy to obtain on a systematic basis, but in 1962 Moscow Radio transmitted from 5 a.m. until 2 a.m. daily, with six or seven hours of television over two channels.

In 1961 Japan, where television began in 1953, was reported to have 6 million television sets.

Radio and television audiences were in 1963 estimated to be: U.S.A. 220 million; U.S.S.R. 78 million; China 15 million; Great Britain 17 million; Japan 20 million; Brazil 4½ million; and so on to the Solomon Islands, with 226.

4. How True is Radio Reproduction?

Varying views are often expressed as to the fidelity with which music is reproduced by radio.

Undoubtedly under good atmospheric conditions (freedom from electric discharges from one cloud to another, etc.) many performances as heard in the home are practically identical with the same performances as heard in the studio in which they originated. The string quartet has from the first transmitted well. The piano at first transmitted badly but now does so far better, indeed, often almost perfectly. The organ does not reproduce quite so successfully; still less do large choral bodies, whose wide dispersion causes an aural effect which cannot be satisfactorily reproduced from a single loudspeaker.

By no means all receiving sets are competent to accept all that is offered them. Some will not reproduce the longest sound-waves and so they cut out the lowest notes (a universal fault in the earliest days of broadcasting). Others will not accept the shortest sound-waves, and though few actual notes may exist in musical notation higher than their reproductive range, yet they omit a multitude of high harmonics arising from the notes within that range and so modify the original timbre (see *Acoustics* 6, 8).

As shown elsewhere (*Acoustics* 15), the actual vibration-per-second range required by music, if only the notes printed are taken into account, is from about 16 to about 5,000 per second. This latter figure represents the upper limit of most receivers at present, yet a 'frequency' of about 15,000 per second is required if the harmonics (upon which depends the timbre of the instruments, etc.) are to receive complete justice. And very few transmitters in the world at present go beyond a frequency of 9,000.

However, an improved system of broadcasting increasingly employed may suitably receive mention at this point. As explained in 1 above, in the standard method of transmission a 'carrier wave' of fixed frequency is varied in power 1,000 times a second in order to transmit a musical note of 1,000 vibrations a second; in the method now under discussion it is the frequency of the carrier wave itself which will vary up and down 1,000 times a second—to an extent depending on the loudness of the note. The advantages claimed for this system ('Frequency Modulation'—FM) are the reduction of outside 'interference' and the ease with which the full range of musical frequencies up to at least 15,000 vibrations a second can be transmitted without serious distortion even in louder passages. Because of the very short wave-length employed (about 3 metres), the effective radius of transmitters using this system is normally limited to less than 100 miles.

With the FM system of transmission, there is far less interference from other stations or from electrical appliances, and there is generally greater fidelity of reproduction. The 1950s saw in the U.S.A. a tremendous growth in the number of independent or network FM stations, often deriving their revenue from the free-will offerings of their listeners. Their programmes included virtually the entire range of recorded music, as well as talks and discussions often drawing on recordings of BBC programmes.

So much for the closely associated factors of pitch and timbre.

As regards intensity, there enters the vexed question of the 'Control Room', at present a necessary evil. The range of intensities produced by a large orchestra (or by a singer with particularly telling top notes) is so great that the loudest sounds given out would be unbearable in an ordinary living room if reproduced faithfully. The aim of the 'Control Room' is to reproduce the excitement of a *crescendo* passage by beginning a *pianissimo* at a very low level, so that without further alteration of the controls the whole passage can be transmitted untouched, including the final *fortissimo*. But in the case of string quartets or the symphonies of Mozart and Haydn, for example, there is in general no intervention on the part of the 'Control Room'.

It is important, of course, if the loss in effect is to be reduced to a minimum, that the 'Control Man' shall be a highly skilled musician, with the score before him, carefully marked at rehearsals. In the best-equipped stations this is now the case. In 1924 or 1925 a friendly dispute arose at the London station of the BBC between the engineering staff and the musical staff, the one holding that 'control' was best left in the hands of a member of their scientific body and the other that it imperatively called for a trained musician. To settle the dispute a special programme was given to a board of adjudicators consisting of the then Musical Director, the heads of the Royal Academy and Royal College of Music, and the present writer. Three pieces were performed, *The Mastersingers* overture being one. The concert was transmitted by wire to a room in which the board met, but not broadcast to the public. Each item was given twice, once 'controlled' by an electrical expert and once by a skilled musician, the board not being informed which was which. One performance of a piece immediately followed the other and each member of the board made his private marking. The marks were compared at the end, when it was found that in the case of every item the higher mark of every member of the board had been given to the musician-controlled transmission —a conclusive result!

At the same time the fact remains that the dual conductorship (for so it is in effect) of (*a*) the musician in charge of the orchestra and (*b*) the musician in charge of the control apparatus must sometimes result in details being either exaggerated or lost.

A characteristic of normal broadcast transmission is that an effect which might perhaps be called (for want of a better term) 'auditory perspective' is lost when for the two receiving ears of the listener in the concert-room the one receiving ear of a microphone is substituted. This question is discussed in *Concert Halls* 12. 'Stereophonic transmissions' over two frequencies, one corresponding to each 'ear' of the listener, are in much use in the U.S.A., and have been experimentally employed by the BBC. The placing of the microphone or microphones is, in any case, a very delicate business. One very experienced musician, Kostelanetz, as early as the 1930s conducting light music at a New York station, shifted his men about a great deal during a performance, so varying the position of particular instruments in relation to the microphone according to their momentary importance in the score.

At various times there has been put forward the suggestion that broadcasting, as a special medium, requires compositions conceived *ad hoc* and taking account of its strong and weak points, and in 1932 E. A. Sarnette, appointed 'Professor of the Microphone' at the École Supérieure de Musique in Paris under the auspices of the Conservatory and the Ministry of Instruction and Fine Arts, developed a scheme 'to teach composers to write for the microphone as they already do for the piano, violin and other instruments', the pupils 'having their exercises played before the microphone, so that they may hear the effects by wireless'.

In this connexion may be mentioned the 'Italia Prize', a sum of money awarded annually since 1949 by an international jury for one or more works (musical and literary–dramatic in alternate years) written in such a form that they can best be presented through the medium of radio.

5. The Effect of Broadcasting on Public Taste. Broadcasting's influence upon the public love and understanding of music has undoubtedly been enormous. In the earlier days of radio, for thousands of potential music-lovers Bach, Beethoven, and Wagner were born only when these persons bought their first radio set. The complete change in listening opportunity offered by the advent first of the gramophone and then of broadcasting may be realized from the statement of the very eminent professor of music at one of the chief British universities; he stated that at the date when he took his musical degree he had never heard a Beethoven symphony.

The weekly journal of the BBC (the *Radio Times*) was something that the most ardent and sanguine worker for music of the beginning of the century never expected to live to see. The journal referred to, by printing every week the complete programmes for the stations of the country and drawing attention to special features, at least made it possible for an enormous public to plan its listening and to listen more attentively and intelligently. By 1960 the weekly circulation of the *Radio Times* (for the printing of which a special London factory had been built) had reached the enormous total of nine million, being the largest circulation of any periodical in the world.

One welcome result of broadcasting is the gradual re-emergence of composers, works, and instruments that had been neglected and almost totally forgotten; the exigencies of daily musical programmes lasting (with some intervals of speech) for many hours inevitably tend to a widening of the public musical repertory. Similarly, broadcasting has served to offer the contemporary composer a chance to become more quickly appreciated.

The Third Programme. The idea of a programme aimed at a relatively highly educated minority seems to have been conceived during the second World War, perhaps in 1943. A budget of £1 million was set, and the first transmissions were made in September 1946. On the musical side, the opportunity was taken to present in full works, notably operas, whose length made them unsuitable for frequent inclusion in a service made up of programmes seldom exceeding an hour to an hour and a half

in length. As a result of extensive research, music of the less accessible periods, formerly available only to scholars in printed or manuscript form, was revived and brought to performance. Generous programme-space was allotted to performances of new works by young composers who had yet to make their way. In this manner the BBC can be said to have taken over to a large extent the role formerly filled by the wealthy private individual (see *Patronage* 7). Similar developments followed shortly in West Germany, Italy, and Belgium.

In 1957 there was a degree of reorganization, the daily hours being cut from five or six to three; the 'Home' programme was to some extent combined with the 'Light', and the number of light background programmes was increased. In 1964 was launched the 'Music Programme', bringing, as do many U.S.A. programmes, a continuous stream of music to be listened to, either intensively or as a background.

6. Television. In the broadcasting of sight, the photo-electric cell plays the part of the microphone in the broadcasting of sound, electric impulses from the receiver being controlled by the varying degrees of luminosity of the different parts of the object viewed, which are very rapidly exposed in turn to the receiving apparatus by a process called 'scanning'. Thus light is made to affect the continuous wave of high frequency in the same sort of way as sound (see 1 *c* above). The whole scene must be 'scanned' in a period of about one-twentieth of a second and then, by an optical illusion, the separate elements appear to the observer to come before him simultaneously on a fluorescent screen. (In this respect there is a reliance upon the same slowness of action of the optic nerve that enables the cinematograph to produce an effect of continuity by means of the rapid supersession of one image by another.)

The idea of television, as a practical device, dates from 1884, when Nipkov patented the present scanning device. It waited for appreciation, however, until the development of the telephone and of the broadcasting of sound had brought means of 'amplifying' the waves. In fact, television makes use ingeniously of a number of inventions made over a long period of years, among which may be mentioned: the electric telegraph (1832); photography (1839); the 'copying telegraph' (a scanning device, 1847); fluorescence 1852); the photo-electric cell (1873).

The American C. F. Jenkins and the Scotsman J. L. Baird were notable experimenters from about 1925, and Baird succeeded in transmitting in colour across the Atlantic in 1928. In Britain public broadcasting of sight began tentatively late in 1932, and was more definitely taken up by the British Broadcasting Corporation early in 1936 (p. 133, pl. **25.** 1). It was dropped during the second World War and later resumed, rapidly gaining a large public. In the United States the popularity of this new device grew quickly. In 1949–50 there were just over three million television sets in use in that country; in the following year nearly ten millions, and television rapidly displaced sound broadcasting as the major medium. In 1965 it was estimated that, taking the world as a whole, two million new 'TV homes' were added to the total each month. By 1972 there were 250 million television sets in the world.

The first opera performance to be televised anywhere in the world was the third act of Gounod's *Faust*, by the BBC in June 1937. In the United States Leoncavallo's *Pagliacci* was televised in March 1940; the opera *Amahl and the Night Visitors* by Menotti (q.v.) was specially written for television performance on Christmas Eve 1951.

The 'Early Bird' relay satellite (May 1965) opened up the possibility of a world-wide live television system.

7. Wired Broadcasting (Radio and Television). The problems created by the limited number of radio wave-lengths and television channels may be overcome by cable transmission. A single cable can carry 10 programmes, and twenty are considered possible. The cost of adapting a set to such a system is about £10, and the running costs can be paid for by a licence fee, by advertising, or by a 'pay as you view' arrangement ('Pay TV'). This last system is current in Canada and the U.S., and in Britain several companies have been set up. There are some 40,000 relay stations in the Soviet Union, where the system was introduced in 1924.

8. Broadcasting as Nuisance. The invention of the tiny 'transistor' as a substitute for the vacuum tube ('valve') led to progressively smaller radios, which could easily be carried in a breast pocket and turned on full blast while their owners went about their daily business. The Noise Abatement Act of 1960 forbade the operation of loud-speakers in the streets between 9 p.m. and 8 a.m. This prohibition does not extend to car radios.

The common law on noise treats sound vibrations as if they were a visible phenomenon such as smoke, and enables the occupier of land to claim against anyone who causes an unreasonable amount of noise. The amount of noise which can be called reasonable becomes ever harder to define, however, and in any case this aspect of the law does not protect the visitor to a beach or to the countryside, for he is not occupying his own property.

For the effect of the introduction of broadcasting upon the popularity of the pianoforte see *Pianoforte* 19; for its influence on concert life see *Concert* 16. For two means of magnifying tone see *Auxetophone* and *Bullphone*. See also *Gramophone* 4.

BROADCAST MUSIC INC. See *Copyright* 2.

BROADSIDES or **BROADSHEETS.** See *Carol*; *Ballad* 1, 4.

BROADWOOD.

(1) JOHN (I) (and piano-making firm bearing his name). See *Pianoforte* 5, 11, 12, 13, 16, 17; *Pianoforte Playing* 2; *Temperament* 5.

(2, 3) JOHN (II) and his niece LUCY (1858–1929). See *Folk Song* 3.

BROCKES. See *Passion Music* 4.

BROKEN CADENCE. See *Cadence*.

BROKEN CHORDS. See *Alberti Bass*; *Dominant Seventh*.

BROKEN CONSORT or **BROKEN MUSIC.** See *Consort*.

BROKEN OCTAVE. See under *Short Octave*.

BROMAN, K. NATANAEL. Born at Kolsva, in Sweden, in 1887. He is a pianist and composer who has written symphonic poems, chamber music, piano pieces, etc.

BROMPTON ORATORY. See *Hymns* 6.

BROOKS, MRS. GORHAM. See *Festival* 2.

BROSSARD, SÉBASTIEN DE (1655–1730). Canon of Meaux, minor composer and writer of books on music. See *Organ* 8; *Grassineau*; *Dictionaries* 2.

BROSSES, CHARLES DE (1709–77). He was a French geographer, historian, philologist, and lawyer, and President of the Parliament of Burgundy (hence generally known as 'Président de Brosses'). His letters on his travels in Italy are of importance to musicians from the information they contain on eighteenth-century musical conditions there.

See *Opera* 3; *Schools of Music*; *Applause* 3.

BROWN, JOHN HULLAH (b. 1875). See *Violinda*.

BROWNE, ROBERT (*c*. 1550–*c*. 1633). Founder of Independency or Congregationalism (see *Puritans* 8).

BROWNING, ROBERT. The poet. Born in London in 1812 and died in Venice in 1889, aged seventy-seven. From early life he showed strong musical interests: a number of songs which he then composed were afterwards destroyed, but his continued love of the art was shown in many of his poems.

See references s.v. *Vogler*; *Slug-horn*; *Avison*; *Ballad* 5; *Galuppi*; *Improvisation* 2; *Program*.

BROWNISTS. See *Puritans* 8.

BRUCH, MAX (p. 401, pl. **70**. 3.) Born at Cologne in 1838 and died at Friedenau in 1920, aged eighty-two. He enjoyed a long life of activity as conductor of various musical bodies, including for three years (1880–3) the Liverpool Philharmonic Society. As a composer his greatest achievements lie, say some, in his choral works, and, say others (including the great public), in his works for violin (or cello) with orchestra, of which the G minor Violin Concerto is the most famous.

BRUCKEN-FOCK, GERARD VAN. Born

H

at Middelburg, Holland, in 1859, and died in 1935. He wrote orchestral and choral music, songs, and very able piano works.

BRUCKNER, ANTON (p. 400, pl. **69.** 9). Born in Upper Austria in 1824 and died in Vienna in 1896, aged seventy-two. Like Brahms, he is classic-romantic, and, like Beethoven, he wrote nine symphonies. Unlike Brahms, he had absorbed some Wagner into his system, and hence the pro-Brahms-anti-Wagner Viennese school of criticism of his day (see *Criticism* 2) bitterly opposed him. He has now a considerable reputation in Germany and Austria, and not much elsewhere, though some have long said the advent of a general Bruckner cult is to be expected.

His life was at first that of a devoted church musician and highly successful organist, giving recitals in Paris, in London, and elsewhere. This, however, was but a passing phase. In his forties he went to Vienna, devoted himself more and more to composition, was encouraged by the Emperor Francis Joseph, and became the enigmatic figure that, despite all the discussion, he still remains.

There is a certain naïvety in his work, and a lack of adroitness in contrivance (particularly an amount of repetition of phrases perhaps beyond that of any other composer whatever), but some partisans brush aside criticism on such grounds, and point to what they maintain to be more than counterbalancing elements of musical beauty and of emotional content. They speak of a resemblance between his mind and that of Schubert.

A German writer has said that he was half a Caesar and half a village schoolmaster; such men are, in art or life, difficult to place.

Bruckner's Symphonies are as follows: No. 1, in C minor (1866, revised 1891); No. 2, in C minor (1872, revised 1876 and again 1877); No. 3, in D minor (1873, revised 1877 and again 1888); No. 4, in E flat, the *Romantic* (1874, revised 1880); No. 5, in B flat (1877, revised 1878); No. 6, in A (1881); No. 7, in E (1883); No. 8, in C minor, the *Apocalyptic* (1887, revised 1890); No. 9, in D minor (1896; the finale remained incomplete). For some time shortened and 'improved' versions of these works, by various hands, had currency.

There are also early Symphonies in F minor (1863) and D minor (1864, revised 1869).

See references s.v. *Horn, Camillo; Te Deum.*

BRUCKNER SOCIETY OF AMERICA. This was founded in 1931, its headquarters being in New York. It has published literature on Bruckner and Mahler, etc. (including, from 1932, a journal, *Chord and Discord*), and awards medals to distinguished conductors who have performed the works whose merits it exists to proclaim.

BRUHN (or Bruhns), NIKOLAUS. Born in Schleswig-Holstein, *c.* 1665, and there died in 1697. He was a pupil of Buxtehude, and like him a great organist and a composer of organ music, as also of motets and cantatas. If we are to believe the sober and generally reliable Fétis (who presumably had some contemporary account as the basis for his assertion), Bruhn 'had made himself so able a player of the violin that he could perform on it pieces in three or four parts, sometimes, moreover, accompanying himself on the organ pedals!'

BRÜLL, IGNAZ. Born at Prossnitz in Moravia, in 1846, and died in Vienna in 1907, aged sixty. He toured as a pianist and composed a large number of operas, orchestral pieces, and chamber works. Vienna was his chief centre and there he was a prominent member of the Brahms entourage.

See *Concerto* 6 b (1846).

BRUME (Fr.). 'Mist.'

BRUMMEISEN (Ger.). Jew's harp (q.v.).

BRUMMSCHEIT (Ger.). See *Tromba Marina.*

BRUNEAU, ALFRED (in full, Louis Charles Bonaventure Alfred; p. 384, pl. **63.** 7). Born in Paris in 1857 and there died in 1934, aged seventy-seven. He was, as a student, the best cellist at the Paris Conservatory, and studied composition there under Massenet. He made his name as an opera composer with *Le Rêve*, based on Zola's novel; this was performed within the same year (1891) and by the same cast at both the Opéra-Comique, Paris, and Covent Garden, London; it was then regarded as very 'advanced'. His later operas were either based on novels by Émile Zola or had libretti specially written for them by that author. *L'Attaque du moulin* is one of the best known. The association with Zola led to disadvantages at the time of the Dreyfus trouble, when both took the side of the oppressed.

In addition to operas, he wrote a Requiem, songs, and other things, and he was known as a newspaper critic and an author of books on music. He was a member of the Institute.

BRUNNER, ULRIC. See *Competitions* (end).

BRUSCAMENTE (It.). 'Brusquely.'

BRUSH, WIRE. See *Percussion Family* 4 d.

BRUSSELS. See *Belgium* 9; *Bull, John; Philips, Peter; Brabançonne; Schools of Music.*

BRUSTWERK (Ger.). 'Choir Organ.'

BRUYÈRE. See *Mechanical Reproduction* 9.

BRYCESON (Organ Builders). See *Mechanical Reproduction* 10.

Btb. Short for *Basstuba.*

BUCCOLICO (It.). 'Bucolic', rustic.

BÜCHNER. See *Opera* 9 f; *Einem, G. von; Wozzeck.*

BUCK.

(1) **PERCY CARTER.** Born at West Ham in 1871 and died in 1947, aged seventy-six. He studied at the Royal College of Music and then at Worcester College, Oxford. He was organist of the Cathedrals of Wells and Bristol, director of music at Harrow School (1901–27), Professor of Music in the University of Dublin (1910), and (1925–37) at London University. He was knighted in 1935. His thoughtful books on

organ playing, etc., as also his work in connexion with the *Oxford History of Music*, are a valuable contribution, and so are his various organ and choral compositions, etc.

See references s.v. *Anglican Chant* 6; *Organ* 2 c.

(2) DUDLEY (I). Born at Hartford, Conn., in 1839 and died at Orange, N.J., in 1909, aged seventy. He studied at Leipzig Conservatory and in Paris, and then, returning to America, became organist successively in Hartford, Chicago, Boston, and Brooklyn, serving also as orchestral conductor in the capacity of assistant to Theodore Thomas.

He composed much church and other choral music, operas, cantatas, etc., and wrote some books on musical subjects.

(3) DUDLEY (II). Born at Hartford, Conn., in 1869, and died at Fairfield, Conn., in 1941, aged seventy-one. He was son of the above and after a career as vocalist became a well-known singing-master.

(4) ZECHARIAH. Born at Norwich in 1798 and died at Newport, Essex, in 1879, aged nearly eighty-one. Almost the whole of his life was passed in connexion with the cathedral of his native place, of which he was a chorister and later organist, continuing in the latter position until his eightieth year approached. His fame, which long endured, attached solely to the one capacity in which he was pre-eminent, that of training choir-boys—by ingenious and sometimes harsh methods that have garnished his memory with much piquant anecdote.

See a reference s.v. *Mann, Arthur Henry*.

BUCKWHEAT NOTATION. See *Lancashire Sol-fa* (end).

BUDAPEST. See *Hungary*; *Bartók*; *Dohnányi*; *Hubay*; *Kodály*.

BUECHNER. See *Opera* 9 f; *Einem*; *Wozzeck*.

BUÉE (Fr.). 'Mist.' So Debussy's *Comme une buée irisée*, 'like an iridescent mist'.

BUFFA (It.). 'Comic' (see *Opera buffa*).

BUFFENS. See *Bouffons*.

BUFFET D'ORGUE. See *Organ* 15.

BUFFO, BUFFA (It., masc., fem.). 'Comic.'

BUFFONESCO (It.). 'Buffoon-like', droll; so the adverb *Buffonescamente*.

BÜGELHORN. See *Saxhorn and Flügelhorn* 5.

BUGLE (Eng.), **CLAIRON** (Fr.), **SIGNAL-HORN** (Ger.), **CORNETTA SEGNALE** (It.). A brass or copper instrument, of treble pitch, with wide tube of conical bore, moderate-sized bell, and cup-shaped mouthpiece (p. 113, pl. 22. 11, 14). By the shape of its tube it is related to the horn, and by the shape of its mouthpiece and size of its bell to the trumpet. It is a mere means of military or other signalling, except that bands of Bugles (necessarily limited to a few notes of the harmonic series; see *Acoustics* 8) are sometimes used for marching. It has occasionally been introduced into

artistic music (e.g. in Stanford's *The Last Post* and Ethel Smyth's *The Prison*, both choral works, in which it is called on to perform the military call of farewell to the dead), but musically its importance lies rather in its progeny than in any great value of its own. See *Last Post*.

BUGLE À CLEFS. Key Bugle. See *Cornett and Key Bugle Families* 2 h, 3 h, 4 h.

BUGLE À PISTONS. See *Saxhorn and Flügelhorn Families* 5.

GRAND BUGLE, PETIT BUGLE. See *Saxhorn and Flügelhorn Families* 3 a and note 2.

KENT BUGLE, ROYAL KENT BUGLE. See *Cornett and Key Bugle Families* 2 h, 3 h, 4 h.

KEY BUGLE. See *Cornett and Key Bugle Families*.

BUHAIU. See *Rumania*.

BÜHNENFESTSPIEL and **BÜHNENWEIH-FESTSPIEL.** See *Festspiel*; *Festival* 3.

BUKOFZER, MANFRED F. Born at Oldenburg, Germany, in 1910, and died at Oakland, Calif., in 1955, aged forty-five. He was trained at the universities of Heidelberg, Berlin, and Basle, and under Hindemith, later joining the staff of the University of California. He became an authority on the music of the earlier periods, his best-known work being *Music in the Baroque Era*.

BULL.

(1) JOHN (p. 289, pl. **51. 2**). Born in England about 1562 and died at Antwerp in 1628, aged about sixty-six. He was a choir-boy in the Chapel Royal of Queen Elizabeth I, of which (after a period as organist of Hereford Cathedral) he became organist. He took the doctorate of music in the universities of Cambridge and Oxford and was appointed the first Professor of Music in the newly founded Gresham College, London. (See *Gresham Professorship*.) As a player on the keyboard instruments he had the highest reputation, and, falling into some trouble at the English court and hence leaving England, he was welcomed first in Brussels as one of the organists in the royal chapel, and then at Antwerp, where for the last eleven years of his life he served as organist of the cathedral.

His high importance in the history of music is as a composer for the virginals, and by the ingenuity with which he profited from the special powers of a keyboard instrument (see *Pianoforte* 20) he ranks as one of the founders of the keyboard repertory. It is worthy of mention that he was on terms of friendship with his contemporary Sweelinck (q.v.), the founder of the great Dutch and North German school of organ-playing, who included a canon by him in his book on composition (as Bull wrote a fantasia on a fugue of Sweelinck), that Sweelinck, through his pupil Scheidemann, passed on the tradition to Reinken, and that Reinken greatly influenced Bach. Bull, in fact, stands, with Sweelinck, at the beginning of that great period of the development of contrapuntal keyboard music which culminated with Bach.

For various references see *Hexachord*; *Temperament* 5; *History* 3; *Parthenia*; *Belgium* 9; *Germany* 4; *God save the Queen* 4, 5, 9; *Organ* 13; *Blitheman*.

(2) OLE BORNEMAN (p. 1097, pl. **182**. 3). Born at Bergen in Norway in 1810 and died near there in 1880, aged seventy. He was a Norwegian patriot violinist, who, inspired equally by love of his country and admiration of the playing of Paganini, set himself to acquire high technique, and then toured the world, playing Scandinavian melodies. (Cf. *Scandinavia* 3.) He thus earned large sums for the putting into effect of grandiose schemes such as the foundation of a Norwegian colony in the United States and a conservatory of music in the capital of his own country—all of which schemes, however, proved abortive.

The music he played in public was of his own composition or arrangement. Little of it has been published, its value being, presumably, largely personal. (See *Grieg*; *Concerto* 6 f, 1810.)

BULLOCK, ERNEST. Born at Wigan in 1890. He has been organist of St. Michael's College, Tenbury (1919), Exeter Cathedral (1919), and Westminster Abbey (1928). In 1941 he became head of the Scottish National (later Royal Scottish) Academy of Music and Professor of Music in Glasgow University, and was from 1953 to 1960 Director of the Royal College of Music. His published compositions include songs, part-songs, organ music, and church choral music. In 1951 he was knighted.

BULLPHONE. This loud-speaker invented in the United States in the late 1930s gloried in a range of 25 miles. Cf. *Auxetophone*.

BULL ROARER. See *Thunder Stick*.

BÜLOW, HANS GUIDO VON (p. 401, pl. **70**. 1). Born at Dresden in 1830 and died at Cairo in 1894, aged sixty-four. He was the son of a noted man of letters whose interests and intimacies were with the romantic writers of the early nineteenth century: in this respect his domestic background somewhat recalls that of Schumann, and the association is reinforced by the fact that his first piano teaching was received from Wieck (Schumann's teacher and the father and teacher of Schumann's wife). His chief teacher of composition was Hauptmann.

Whilst engaged in the study of law at the universities of Leipzig and Berlin, he began to take an interest in the 'New Music' movement of Liszt and Wagner, and soon definitely abandoned law for music and placed himself under the guidance of these two masters, the former for piano and the latter for conductorship. He quickly became known as a pianist and travelled extensively as such, and was also active in journalism as a propagandist of the movement with which he had identified himself. In 1857 he married Liszt's daughter, Cosima, who after

twelve years left him for Wagner. When this happened he held the position of conductor of the royal opera at Munich, which he had made a notable centre of Wagner performance, *Tristan* being produced there in 1865 and *The Mastersingers* in 1868.

He now visited Britain as a conductor and toured extensively in the United States.

In 1878 he became conductor at Hanover, in 1880 at Meiningen, and in 1886 at Hamburg and Berlin.

His magnificent gifts of orchestral directorship and interpretation were shown at their highest in Meiningen, with its fine orchestral tradition. He exhibited similar gifts as pianist, and embodied in valuable editions of the classics much of the careful thought that lay behind the perfection of his personal performance. He was responsible for the official piano arrangement of *Tristan*. His own compositions were chiefly orchestral.

His fame rests almost equally on his piano playing, his conducting, and his advocacy of Wagner and Brahms, and is tinged by memories of a forceful and independent personality and a power of significant, ready, and often tart speech that has become almost legendary.

See references as follows: *Conducting* 6; *Expression* 5; *Memory* 6, 7; *Pianoforte Playing and Teaching* 6, 8; *Fingering* 5 c; *Clavichord* 6; *Scotland* 10; *Mastersingers* (Wagner).

BUMBASS or **BASSE DE FLANDRES.** An ancient, simple, rustic, one-stringed, bowed instrument—much the same as Bladder and String (q.v.).

BUNDFREI. See *Clavichord* 3.

BUNTE BLÄTTER. See under *Albumblatt*.

BUNTING, EDWARD. Born in Armagh in 1773 and died in Dublin in 1843, aged seventy. He was an organist in Belfast who attended the final meeting of Irish harpers in 1792, recorded their music as played, and then travelled, adding to his collection. He published volumes of music in 1796, 1809, and 1841. Their supreme value lies in their supplying the actual harpers' tunes and not vocal, violin, or pipe versions, often corrupted—in which he goes beyond Petrie (q.v.) and Joyce. He died in obscurity but is now famous for the service he rendered to his nation.

See *Ireland* 5.

BUNYAN, JOHN (1628–88). See *Puritans* 5; *Baptist* 2; also p. 865, pl. **146**. 5, 6.

BUONONCINI. See *Bononcini*.

BURANELLO. See *Galuppi*.

BURDEN or **BURTHEN.** A recurring line of sense or nonsense after the verses of a ballad, etc. ('I would sing my song without a burden', Shakespeare, *As You Like It*, II. vii). The choral form known as the ballet (see *Madrigal* 3 c) has a *fa-la* burden.

BÜRGER, GOTTFRIED AUGUST (1748–95). See *Ballad* 5.

BURGMÜLLER.

(1) JOHANN FRIEDRICH. Born at Ratisbon in 1806 and died at Beaulieu in France in

2. THE 'NATURAL' HORN, with Crooks

1. THE HUNTING HORN

3. THE MODERN HORN

4. 'LET THE BRIGHT SERAPHIM.' Clara Novello (q.v.) and the celebrated trumpeter of the first half of the 19th century, Thos. Harper

5. THE TOWN HORN OF RIPON, YORKSHIRE
See *Horn Family* 3

6

7

8

6, 7, 8. SAXOPHONE, FLÜGELHORN, ALTO SAXHORN (not photographed to scale)

For other pictures illustrating the Brass see pages 112–13

1. CHRISTMAS EVE CAROL SINGING IN THE HOME OF MARTIN LUTHER (*c.* 1535)

2. CHRISTMAS CAROLS IN RUSSIA IN THE LATE 19TH CENTURY

3 Wise Men.

Christ tempted.

Christ brought before
Pilate.

Taken down from
the Cross.

3. CAROL BROADSIDE ILLUSTRATIONS—as seen on sale in London streets as late as 1820

1874, aged sixty-seven. He was a composer of light piano music, studies, and music for the young.

(2) NORBERT (brother of the above). He was born at Düsseldorf in 1810 and died at Aachen in 1836, aged twenty-six. He was a gifted composer of the German romantic type of the period and was greatly admired by Schumann.

BURKHARD, WILLY. Born near Bienne, Switzerland, in 1900, and died at Zürich in 1955, aged fifty-five. He studied at the Conservatories of Berne, Leipzig, and Munich, and then became a teacher of piano and composition in Berne. His compositions are largely choral, and they include an austere oratorio, *The Vision of Isaiah* (1936), which has received considerable recognition.

See *Concerto* 6 c; *Harpsichord* 9; *Opera* 24 f (1949).

BURLA (It.). 'Jest.' So *Burlando*, 'jestingly'; *Burlesco*, *Burlesca*, 'burlesque'; *Burlescamente*, 'in a burlesque manner'; *Burletta*, a musical farce. Bach has a 'Burlesca' in one of his keyboard partitas, and one of the twenty pieces in Schumann's book of piano 'Album Leaves' is called 'Burla'.

BURLEIGH.

(1) HENRY THACKER. Born at Erie, Penn., in 1866, and died at Stamford, Conn., in 1949, aged eighty-two. He was a composer of songs and arranger of Negro melodies. He had been a church singer, and in former years student and teacher successively (under Dvořák) at the National Conservatory, New York. In 1917 he received a prize in recognition of conspicuous achievements as a representative of the Negro race.

For a general treatment of Negro music and musicians see *United States* 6.

(2) CECIL. Born at the town of Wyoming, New York State, in 1885. He has had a successful career as violinist, teacher of violinists, and composer, largely for the violin, but also for the orchestra. His violin concerto won the prize for a concerto by an American in Chicago in 1916.

BURLESCO, BURLESCA (It., masc., fem.). 'Burlesque', 'jocular'. So the adverb *Burlescamente*. See also under *Burla*.

BURLESQUE, SYMPHONIE. See *Toy Symphony*.

BURLETTA. (It., 'jest' or 'farce'). In eighteenth-century Britain the word was applied to a light type of musical entertainment, something of the type of the Ballad Opera (q.v.).

BURNAND. See *Strelezki*.

BURNEY, DR. CHARLES (p. 389, pl. **66**. 6). Born at Shrewsbury in 1726 and died in London in 1814, aged eighty-eight. He was an organist, a very minor composer, a keen amateur astronomer, something of a poet, a connoisseur of painting, a man of considerable general learning, and a genial companion, the

friend of Johnson and Garrick, Reynolds, Burke, and of many of the leaders in the politics, science, art, and literature of his time. In the ardent pursuit of musical knowledge he travelled France, Italy, Germany, and the Low Countries, describing his tours themselves in three volumes octavo and embodying the information thus acquired in four volumes quarto—his great *History of Music* (see also *Hawkins*). Almost every member of his family achieved some distinction, and his second daughter was the famous novelist, Fanny Burney (Madame d'Arblay). She wrote his life with considerable fullness, the most genteel elegance, and very marked emphasis on the doings of his second daughter.

He was a D.Mus. of Oxford University and a Fellow of the Royal Society. In 1806, when Britain and France were at war, he nevertheless was accorded the honour of election as a Corresponding Member of the Institute of France (Classe des Beaux Arts).

The quotations from and references to Burney throughout the present volume are necessarily numerous, and some are important. See as follows:

Anglican Chant 6; *Anglican Parish Church Music* 3; *Annotated Programmes* 4; *Applause* 3, 6; *Barocco*; *Bohemia*; *Braccio and Gamba*; *Cadenza* 2 a; *Capotasto*; *Catch*; *Chamber Music* 1; *Clavichord* 5; *Clubs*; *Concert* 8, 14; *Conducting* 6; *Copyists*; *Criticism* 4, 6; *Descant*; *Dictionaries*; *Fairs* (near end); *Festival* 1; *Figured Bass*; *Fioritura*; *Folk Song* 3; *God save the Queen* 7, 15; *Gondola Song*; *Graduates' Meeting*; *Harpsichord* 7; *Hawkins, John*; *Horn Family* 3; *Hungary*; *Improperia*; *Improvisation* 1, 2; *Improvisatore*; *Josquin des Prés*; *Libretto*; *Linley, Thomas* (Junior); *Mechanical Reproduction of Music* 10, 11; *Melody* 10; *Messa di Voce*; *Opera* 9 c; *Organ* 3, 8; *Percussion Family* 4 a; *Pianoforte* 5, 21; *Pianoforte Playing* 1; *Profession of Music* 9; *Rees*; *Ricercare*; *Round*; *Rousseau*; *Rule of the Octave*; *Saltbox*; *Schools of Music*; *Sequence* (in musical construction); *Shake*; *Singing* 6, 7, 9; *Street Music* 4, 5; *Toccatina*; *Trombone Family* 2 f, 3; *Voluntary* 2, 5; *Waltz*; *White, Robert*; *Whythorne*.

BURNS, ROBERT (1759–96). See *Auld Lang Syne*; *Ye Banks and Braes*; *There's nae luck*; *John Anderson*; *Comin' through the Rye*; *Scots wha hae*; *Folk Song* 3.

BURRELL, MARY (1850–98). Daughter of Sir John Banks, K.C.B., Regius Professor of Medicine in Trinity College, Dublin. Wife of Hon. Willoughby Burrell (after her death, Lord Gwydyr).

By persistent and carefully directed effort she amassed an enormous collection of Wagner manuscripts, correspondence, and documents of every kind. She planned a complete *Life of Wagner* based on these documents. Of this only the first volume appeared, being issued privately (100 copies) in the year of her death as an elephant folio 2½ feet high, covering the first 21 years of the composer's life. The collection was ultimately bought in 1929 by Mrs. Curtis Bok of Philadelphia. *The Truth about Wagner* by Hurn and Root (1930) professes to be based upon this material but is untrustworthy. The major part of the collection was published in 1950 as *Letters of Richard Wagner* (edited and annotated by John N. Burk).

BURTHEN. See *Burden*.

BUSBY, THOMAS (1755–1838). Active minor composer, writer on music, etc., D.Mus. Cantab. Author of a *History of Music* (1819), *Anecdotes of Music* (1825). See *Dictionaries* 2; also quotations from him under *Ridotto; Mechanical Reproduction* 11, 13.

BUSCH. The Brothers, FRITZ (1890–1951), orchestral conductor in many important centres; ADOLF (1891–1952), violinist, leader of a string quartet and composer of symphonies, concertos, etc.; and HERMANN 1897–1975), violoncellist. Born and trained in Germany, all assumed Swiss nationality when the Nazis came to power.

BUSCHMANN. See *Reed-Organ Family* 4; *Terpodion.*

BUSH, ALAN DUDLEY (p. 353, pl. **56**. 1). Born in London in 1900. He was a pupil of John Ireland at the Royal Academy of Music, later joining its staff. His *Dialectic* for String Quartet was heard at the Prague International Festival in 1935 and his *Dance Overture* in London in the same year. His Marxist views find expression in his operas (*Wat Tyler*, 1950; *Men of Blackmoor*, 1956) and in many of his activities. He has written three symphonies, a piano concerto (with voices, 1938), as well as choral music.

BUSNOIS, ANTOINE. Died at Bruges in 1492. He was a pupil of Ockeghem, and, like him, a leading light in that early Netherlands school which exercised so much influence on the development of music.

See *Homme armé.*

BUSONI, FERRUCCIO BENVENUTO (p. 524, pl. **95**. 9; p. 801, pl. **138**. 2, 8). Born at Empoli in 1866 and died in Berlin in 1924, aged fifty-eight. He was of half-Italian and half-Austrian parentage.

He won world fame as a pianist, combining an amazingly easy agility with a quite extraordinary sense of 'colour', a perfection of phrasing, and a sense of proportion that unerringly put part in the proper relation to part and to the whole. He was, in the fullest sense, both pianist and musician.

As a composer he wrote four operas (including *Turandot*, 1917) and orchestral, chamber, and piano music, and a number of songs. In his later works he must be classed with the 'anti-romantics'; these, like his writings upon musical subjects, show him to have been a man of high intellectual interests and powers. There are those who take his compositions very seriously indeed and allege that the rest of the world underrates them.

See references under *Dent; Pianoforte Playing* 9; *Harpsichord* 9; *Concerto* 6 c (1866); *Sonata* 10 d; *Sonatina; Opera* 24 f; *Opus; Clarinet Family* 6; *Pfitzner; Arrangement; Art of Fugue; Chorale Prelude; Jarnach; Electric* 1; *Scales* 12.

BUTE, THIRD EARL OF (1713–92). See *Mechanical Reproduction of Music* 10.

BUTLER, REVD. C. (1559–1647). See *Lancashire Sol-fa.*

BUTLER, SAMUEL. Born at Langar, Notts.,
in 1835 and died in London in 1902, aged sixty-six. After a period as a painter he was a sheep farmer in New Zealand and, returning to England, gradually won a selected public, and then a wider one, as author of philosophical, scientific, satirical, and ironic works, including fiction. He had strong musical interests of very narrow range, expressing contempt for Bach and Wagner and unqualified admiration for Handel, in whose general style and idiom (but at an immense distance), he himself composed, publishing, with his friend and companion Festing Jones (presumably at the composers' own expense), a dramatic cantata, *Narcissus* (Weekes), and a book of *Gavottes, Minuets, Fugues, and other Short Pieces for the Piano* (Novello).

BUTT, CLARA (1873–1936). See *Encore; Knighthood.*

BUTTERFLIES' WINGS (Chopin). See *Nicknamed Compositions* 8.

BUTTERWORTH, GEORGE SAINTON KAYE. Born in London in 1885 and killed in action on the Somme in 1916, aged thirty-one (Military Cross). After Eton, Oxford, and the Royal College of Music, he became active in the movement for the revival of English folk song and dance and wrote some delicate music in which this element usually shows its influence, though not always directly. The songs from *A Shropshire Lad* and the orchestral idyll *The Banks of Green Willow* may be mentioned as examples.

BUTTON. The pin at the end of a violin, etc., which bears the pull of the strings.

BUXTEHUDE, DIETRICH. Of Danish origin and born at Oldesloe, Holstein (then a Danish possession, now in Germany), in 1637; died at Lübeck in 1707, aged sixty-nine or seventy. He is one of the fathers of the arts of composing for the organ and playing it. His performance of sacred music, instrumental and vocal, made Lübeck a place of pilgrimage for musicians anxious to advance in their art, and the great Sebastian Bach himself, when a young man, tramped two hundred miles to hear them and to sit at the feet of the Master.

His compositions are of high intrinsic value, apart from their historic importance. Some of the Church Cantatas and organ compositions are heard today, and a society founded at Lübeck in 1932 is still occupied in preparing a complete edition of his work.

See passing references under *Scandinavia* 4; *Organ* 13; *Chaconne and Passacaglia; Chorale Prelude; Cantata; Concert* 13.

BUYSINE. See *Trumpet Family* 3.

BY CELIA'S ARBOUR. See *Horsley.*

BYELYAYEFF. See *Belaief.*

BYLINI. See *Russia* 1.

BYRD, or BYRDE, WILLIAM (pl. **28**, opposite). Born probably at Lincoln in 1542 or 1543, and died probably on his estate at Stondon, Essex, in 1623, describing himself in his

PLATE 28

BYRD EAGERLY SCANS HIS PROOF

By Batt

IT must have been an exciting moment when the three collaborators, Byrd, Bull, and Gibbons, learnt that the proofs of England's first printed virginal music, *Parthenia*, were at last off the press. And when the music was finally on sale the news of that must have given delight to the many performers of the day, professional and amateur—formerly dependent on any manuscripts with which they had been able to meet and which they had been able to borrow in order to make their own manuscript copies.

That moment was a great one in English musical life, for (as is now everywhere recognized) it was the English composers who led Europe in the considered development of a true keyboard style. So within two years the flow of reprints began.

will, made a little previously, as 'nowe in the eightieth year of myne age'.

He studied, it is said, under Tallis (q.v.) and at twenty or twenty-one was organist of Lincoln Cathedral, as later (jointly with his master) of Queen Elizabeth's Chapel Royal (see *Chapel Royal*).

He wrote church music, music for viols, keyboard music, and secular choral music all of the finest quality, in some examples (especially of his sacred choral music) reaching sublimity. He was one of the founders of the English Madrigal School and one of the most active and able of those English writers of keyboard music whose bold and well-considered experiments laid the very foundations for all future building in this domain of art.

'Byrd is a pastoral poet who loves misty distances, graduated tints, softly undulating landscapes . . . a rustic whose rural lyricism decks itself in the most exquisite graces that an artistic temperament at once simple and refined can imagine' (Van den Borren, *Les Origines de la Musique de Clavier*, 1912).

'An attentive reading of the choral works of William Byrd shows that he was one of the greatest musicians of the sixteenth century, and that he is the inferior of no Italian or Belgian master of his time. . . . One may say without exaggeration that Byrd was the Palestrina and the Orlandus Lassus of England.' (Fétis, *Biographie Universelle des Musiciens*, 2nd edn., 1867.)

For incidental references to Byrd, his life and his work, see the following entries:

CHORAL WRITING. *History of Music* 2; *Composition* 12; *Harmony* 8; *Mass* 2, 4; *Service*; *Motet*; *Anthem*, *Period* I; *Passion Music* 2; *Anglican Chant* 3, 5; *Non Nobis*; *Madrigal* 8 c; *Cecilia*; *Whittaker*.

KEYBOARD WORKS. *History of Music* 3, 5; *Hexachord* (end); *Programme Music* 5 a; *Bell* 6; *Carman's Whistle*; *Pianoforte* 20; *Bagpipe Family* 8; *Scotland* 7; *Parthenia*; *Lady Nevell's Booke*.

VARIOUS. *England* 3; *Printing of Music* 1; *Publishing of Music* 4; *Patronage* 8; *Tallis*; *Profession* 9; *Counterpoint*; *Modes*; *Morley*; *Spain* 5; *Chamber Music* 6, *Period* I; *Holst*.

BYRON, LORD (1788–1824). See *Berlioz*; *Symphonic Poem*.

BYZANTINE MUSIC. See *Greek Church*; *Tillyard*; *Wellesz*.

C

C.A. 'Coll' arco' (q.v.).

CABALETTA or **CABBALETTA.** (1) This title is sometimes given to a short aria (q.v.) of simple and much reiterated rhythm, generally with repeats. Rossini has many in his operas; his instructions (reported by the famous singer Clara Novello as given to her) were: 'The repeat is made expressly so that each singer may vary it, so as best to display her (or his) peculiar capacities; therefore the first time the composer's music should be exactly given.'

(2) The name is also given to a sort of song in rondo form, sometimes with variations, or to a recurring passage in a song, which at first appears simply and afterwards varied; several authorities make a triplet accompaniment, suggesting the gallop of a horse (Italian 'cavallo') to be a characteristic.

(3) During the nineteenth century the word came to be applied to the final section of an elaborate operatic duet or aria (e.g. in Verdi's operas).

CABEZÓN. See *History* 3; *Spain* 8.

CABINET ORGAN. See *Reed-Organ Family* 7; *American Musical Terminology* 7.

CABINET PIANO. See *Pianoforte* 16.

CABRETTE. See *Bagpipe Family* 6 (end).

CACCIA (It.). 'Chase', 'hunt', e.g. *Alla caccia*, 'in hunting style'. For *Oboe da caccia* see *Oboe Family* 4 e, 5 e, 6; for *Corno da caccia* see *Horn Family* 5.

CACCINI, GIULIO. Born in Rome about 1550 and died in Florence in 1610, aged about sixty. From 1564 he was at the court of the Medici in Florence, where he was one of the most important of the early operatic experimenters, and his book of songs called *Nuove Musiche* (literally 'New Musics', 1602) is the typical early example of the 'monodic style'; the preface to this collection is the manifesto of the new school.

See *Opera* 1, 2, 7, 8, 11 a; *Singing* 3, 4; *Composition* 12; *History* 4; *Poland*; *Leading Motif*; *Orchestra* 1.

CACHUCHA. A graceful Spanish dance in three-in-a-measure time, danced by a single performer. It originated in Cadiz at the time of the French siege, between 1810 and 1812. Its music is not unlike that of the bolero, q.v. (The well-known piece of this name in Sullivan's *The Gondoliers* is apparently not typical, or at any rate, represents only one type of the dance.)

CÄCILIENVEREIN. See *Cecilian Movement*.

CADENCE or **CLOSE.** The word 'cadence' comes from the Latin *cadere*, to fall (Shake-speare: 'That strain again; it had a dying fall.') In speaking, it is natural to drop the pitch of the voice on the last syllable of a sentence; the ancient plainsong melodies drop at their close to the chief note ('final') of the mode, from the note above, and if any book of folk-song melodies, hymn-tunes, and the like be examined it will be found that a considerable majority of them end by the corresponding downward step—from the 'ray' to the 'doh', the supertonic of the key to the tonic. There is, then, a general tendency to close by a fall, and this doubtless accounts for the word 'cadence'. The word 'cadenza' (q.v.) is the equivalent in Italian, though it has come, in musical terminology, to possess a special meaning.

Nowadays any melodic or harmonic figure which has come to have a conventional association with the ending of a composition, a section, or a phrase is called a cadence, whether there is or is not a fall in the melody or upper-most part of the harmony.

In the post-modal harmony, i.e. that of the major and minor scales that began to sweep away the modes in the sixteenth century (see *Modes*) and reigned supreme up to the end of the nineteenth (Monteverdi, Scarlatti, Corelli, Bach, Handel, Haydn, Mozart, Beethoven, Mendelssohn, Chopin, Schumann, etc.), the distinctive characteristics of cadences were harmonic.

Almost every composition at this period ended with the **Perfect Cadence** or **Full Close**, i.e. the succession of the two chords dominant–tonic (soh–doh).

To this might be added, as a sort of 'clincher', a **Plagal Cadence**, i.e. the progression of the two chords, subdominant–tonic (fah–doh)—often used today as the 'Amen' of a hymn-tune.

Midway through a composition, or at the end of some phrase during its course, there might be a perfect cadence in some related key, or, instead of this, the **Imperfect Cadence** or **Half Close**, tonic or other chord–dominant (doh or other chord–soh), or the **Interrupted Cadence**, dominant–submediant or other chord, but not the tonic (soh–lah or other chord, but not doh).

To any of the dominant chords mentioned above the seventh might be added, and any of the cadences could have their chords inverted (see *Harmony* 24 f), but if this latter were done in the case of the perfect cadence it lost finality, ceased to be 'perfect', and became unsuitable for the actual ending of a composition.

Any of these cadences could be decorated in various ways, and in the chromatic system

See the Article *Carols* on pages 156–8 and Plate 27, facing page 141

1. IN THE VILLAGE CHURCH, December 1863. From the *Illustrated London News* of that date

2. IN THE CRYPT OF CANTERBURY CATHEDRAL, 1941

1. 'SUMER IS ICUMEN IN'. The original manuscript (*c.* 1226). See Article on p. 996

2. A CATCH CLUB (from *Essex Harmony*, 1764)

3. AN 18TH-CENTURY ANACREONTIC SOCIETY, by Gillray. See references under *Anacreontic*, p. 30

4. SAMUEL WEBBE, senr. See p. 1111

5. THE MEDAL OF THE CATCH CLUB (See *Glee* 3 and *Clubs for Music-Making*), with Stephen Paxton, who won it in 1784 for 'the best serious glee'—'Blest Power'

6. COMMONWEALTH CATCHES (1652)

7. THE CANTERBURY CATCH CLUB with its Organ and Orchestra See *Clubs*, p. 198

of Wagner and his followers so they often are. Other notes are added, but the basis is felt to be the same.

A cadence sometimes found in Bach's harmonizations of choral melodies is one in which in a major key the piece is brought to an end on the dominant chord of the relative minor, e.g. in a piece in C major the final chord would be that of E (E, G♯, B). It is difficult to explain why this very beautiful ending gives so satisfactory an effect—not exactly an effect of full finality but yet one of sufficient finality with a sense of something left unsaid, as when an author, after dismissing some subject, ends with a significant 'but . . .' or 'yet . . .'. This is called the **Phrygian Cadence**. It appears to derive from a practice in plainsong accompaniment whereby in the Phrygian Mode (on a keyboard the 'white notes' E–E), the last chord was given the major third, G♯ (cf. *Tierce de Picardie*). Since to modern, un-modal ears a piece in the Phrygian Mode might be heard as in the key of C major, this final chord (E, G♯, B) might be heard as the dominant chord of the relative minor (A minor). Possibly it was the practice just mentioned which accustomed composers' ears to this effect and, in the post-modal period (Corelli, Handel, Bach, etc.) led to the use of the cadence in question.[1]

For a form of perfect cadence in a minor key, ending on the major chord of the tonic instead of the minor, see *Tierce de Picardie*.

Usually the final chord of a cadence falls on an accented beat; sometimes, however, the effect of the cadence is softened by bringing its final chord on an unaccented beat, and the cadence is then spoken of as a **Feminine Cadence** ('Feminine Perfect Cadence', 'Feminine Interrupted Cadence', and so forth).

In the music of today, from much of which the major and minor scale system has entirely disappeared (in our polytonality, atonality, microtonality—see *Harmony* 17–19), it is hard to say what constitutes a cadence. Composers naturally need and secure cadential effect, but it would be difficult to classify the very various processes in the way in which have been classified above the processes adopted during the diatonic (i.e. major and minor) era of musical composition.

As for the more traditional cadences, some further names to be found in use are as follows:[2]

[1] There appear to be varying applications of the term 'Phrygian Cadence'. For instance, in A. F. C. Kollman's *Practical Guide to Thorough Bass* (1801) the term seems to be applied to any sort of Imperfect Cadence (Half Close) in the minor mode. A century later C. W. Pearce, in his *Text Book of Musical Knowledge* (Intermediate Grade) says: 'The Phrygian Cadence is but another form of the Half Close, or Imperfect Cadence in the minor, being in fact a Mixed Cadence, with the subdominant chord inverted (IVb to V, instead of IV to V).'
There seems, however, to be no purpose in applying another name to any variety of the Imperfect Cadence.
[2] The terminology used in harmony textbooks and musical works of reference in the U.S.A. sometimes differs from any British usage. A large number of such books have been consulted, and they have been found to vary considerably in their application of the terms. Most (not all) of them, however, agree in one particular: the

Abrupt Cadence = Interrupted Cadence.

Amen Cadence = Plagal Cadence.

Authentic Cadence = Perfect Cadence (Full Close).

Avoided Cadence = Interrupted Cadence.

Broken Cadence = Interrupted Cadence.

Church Cadence = Plagal Cadence.

Complete Cadence = Perfect Cadence (Full Close).

Deceptive Cadence = Interrupted Cadence.

Demi-Cadence = Imperfect Cadence (Half Close).

Dominant Cadence = Imperfect Cadence (Half Close).

Evaded Cadence = Interrupted Cadence.

False Close = Interrupted Cadence.

Greek Cadence = Plagal Cadence.

Half Cadence = Half Close.

Inverted Cadence = A Perfect or Imperfect Cadence (Full Close or Half Close) with its latter chord inverted. (Some confine the name to the Perfect Cadence thus changed; others extend it to all cadences having either chord, or both, inverted.)

Irregular Cadence = Interrupted Cadence.

Mixed Cadence. The term is used in two ways (both of them superfluous).
The first way implies a 'mixing' of the Plagal and Imperfect Cadences, consisting of subdominant–dominant (this is merely the Imperfect Cadence in one of its commonest forms).
The second way implies a mixing of the Plagal and Perfect Cadences, consisting of the Perfect Cadence preceded by the subdominant—making three chords, instead of the usual two. This is merely the Perfect Cadence led up to in one of its commonest manners and should not require any special name.

Radical Cadence = any cadence of which the chords are in root position, i.e. the roots of the chords in the bass.

Semi-perfect Cadence = Perfect Cadence with the 3rd or 5th of the tonic in the highest part.

Surprise Cadence = Interrupted Cadence.

Suspended Cadence = A hold-up before the final cadence of a piece, as that in a concerto (or, in former times, an aria) for the solo performer to work in his cadenza (see below). The chord upon which the hold-up occurs is usually the second inversion of the tonic chord, and the chord on which the resumption occurs the dominant chord (i.e. there is a $^{6-5}_{4-3}$ on the dominant bass, followed by the tonic chord, with the soloist's peregrina-

term *Perfect Cadence* being reserved for that form of *Authentic Cadence* (tonic chord–dominant chord) in which the last melody note is a duplication of the bass note, i.e. is the tonic and not the third or fifth of the tonic chord.

tion interpolated after the first of these three chords. (The use of the words 'final cadence', above, does not preclude the possibility of a subsequent Coda passage.)

All the above are taken from various British theoretical works and books of reference now current and it will be seen that there are in use far too many names for the various members of the little group of simple 'punctuation marks' of music.

CADENZA. This is simply the Italian word for cadence (q.v.), but as an English technical term means a flourish before the cadence. A cadenza, in the palmy days of such things, was an interpolation in the final cadence of a vocal aria (or in one of the sections of such), or in that of an instrumental movement. The conventional cadence at such a point consists of three chords—the second inversion of the tonic chord, and the original position of the dominant chord, and the original position of the tonic chord ($\frac{6}{4}$–$\frac{5}{3}$ on the dominant bass followed by $\frac{5}{3}$ on the tonic bass). The interpolated cadenza began after the first of these chords and was expected to end with a long trill and in such a way that the orchestra could join in with the second of the chords. But flourishes or extended passages in the cadenza style could, of course, be introduced into compositions at other than the points mentioned, and came to be so introduced.

The custom dates from the days of 'Bel Canto', i.e. the eighteenth century, when the ability to invent and execute some elaborately decorative passage was one of the marks of an able singer. The motive has been shrewdly expressed by Sir Hubert Parry: 'so that, the piece coming to an end immediately afterwards, the audience might have the impression of astonishment fresh in their minds to urge them to applause.'

(From Haböck's *Farinelli*.)

The aria form of the day (see *Aria*) conveniently admitted of three cadenzas, one at the end of each of its three sections; the last was, naturally, the most startlingly brilliant, all the singer's cleverest 'stunts' being reserved for this.

The term *Melisma* (q.v.) has also been applied to the vocal cadenza.

The period of 'Bel Canto' was likewise the period when the instrumental concerto (see *Concerto* 3) took on the colour of a solo display piece and the cadenza passed into that, with the same root motif, though this motif could be redeemed by the skilful use of the device for various artistic purposes. Again, the cadenza was a test of invention and execution. It was based upon the musical themes of the preceding movement, but the treatment was supposed to be improvised, and the successful practice of the art of the cadenza gave the subconscious impression that the solo performer, worked up to an artistic frenzy, had burst away from his companions to indulge himself in the unrestrained expression of his enthusiasm.

Doubtless many of these spur-of-the-moment impromptu flights were carefully thought out and oft repeated, and from the time of Mozart, who prepared a certain number of cadenzas to his piano concertos (apparently for the use of his pupils), and of Beethoven, who issued a book of cadenzas to his piano concertos (very little used, by the way), many composers have felt that if anyone was to prepare beforehand such material for insertion in their music it might as well be themselves. Indeed, the late nineteenth- and the twentieth-century concerto composer does not leave the performer free to rhapsodize in his own way; what the performer has to play at any one point in the composition is as precisely prescribed as what he has to play at any other point. Perhaps the most recent instance of a composer leaving the cadenza to the performer to supply is that of Brahms in his Violin Concerto (1879); but his friend Joachim immediately composed a fine cadenza for the work, and this has been almost invariably associated with it ever since. (The cadenza frequently played with the Beethoven Violin Concerto is also his.)

Clementi published a collection of 'points d'orgue composés dans le style de Haydn, Mozart, Kozeluch, Sterkel, Vanhall, et Clementi' (see *Point d'Orgue*). Reinecke (q.v.) was another prolific contributor to the cadenza repertory. Indeed, many good composers have published cadenzas for the eighteenth- and early nineteenth-century classics, so that nowadays the invention of the cadenza by the performer is in some danger of becoming a lost art. Often the performer has a considerable choice of published cadenzas to a particular concerto, and it is much to be wished that his programme might indicate the author of the one played, as this is a legitimate object of intelligent curiosity.

Latterly, an occasional accompanied cadenza (a thing impossible under conditions of extemporization) has been provided. Beethoven provides accompaniment to part of the cadenza in his so-called 'Emperor' Piano Concerto, and a most beautiful and effective accompanied cadenza is to be heard in Elgar's Violin Concerto.

The usual place of the cadenza in a concerto is towards the end of the last or first movement, or both of these.

Of special renown were the improvised cadenzas of Handel when playing his own organ concertos (but he extemporized much of the solo part—not merely the cadenzas). His public chaff of a famous violinist of the period who extemporized too long and wandering a cadenza in the accompaniment of a song is well remembered to this day.

'One night, while Handel was in Dublin, Dubourg having a solo part in a song, and a close to make *ad libitum*, he wandered about in different keys a great while, and seemed indeed a little bewildered, and uncertain of his original key; but at length, coming to the shake which was to terminate this long close, Handel, to the great delight of the audience, and augmentation of applause, cried out, loud enough to be heard in the most remote parts of the Theatre, "You are welcome home, Mr. Dubourg."' (Burney's *Commemoration of Handel*).

The following extract from a letter of Mendelssohn would seem to indicate that in his time (as, apparently in Handel's and Dubourg's time) audiences sometimes applauded a cadenza without waiting for the conclusion of the movement. He is recounting 'a first trial of my Double Concerto in E in Clementi's piano manufactury', with Moscheles as his fellow-player—a private trial at which only one or two friends were present.

'When it was over, all said it was a pity that we had made no cadenza; so I at once hit upon a passage in the first part of the last *tutti* where the orchestra has a pause, and Moscheles had *nolens volens* to comply and compose a grand cadenza. We now deliberated, amid a thousand jokes, whether the small last solo should remain in its place, since of course the people would applaud the cadenza. "We must have a bit of *tutti* between the cadenza and the solo," said I. "How long are they to clap their hands?" asked Moscheles. "Ten minutes, I dare say," said I. Moscheles beat me down to five. I promised to supply a *tutti*; and we so took the measure, embroidered, turned, and padded, put in sleeves *à la* Mameluke, and at last with our mutual tailoring produced a brilliant concerto. We shall have another rehearsal today; it will be quite a picnic, for Moscheles brings the cadenza, and I the *tutti*.'

The word 'capriccio' was at one time used for 'cadenza' (see Dittersdorf's *Autobiography*, ch. vii).

CADENZATO (It.). 'Cadenced', i.e. rhythmic.

CADMAN, CHARLES WAKEFIELD (p. 1057, pl. **172**. 7). Born at Johnstown, Pennsylvania, in 1881 and died in Los Angeles in 1946, aged sixty-five. He made extensive employment of American Indian themes in his compositions. Lillian Nordica first made him known and popular by performing his song-cycle, *The Land of Sky Blue Water*. His opera *Shanewis* (on an American Indian theme) was performed by the Metropolitan Opera House in 1918.

He adapted American Indian musical material to the more conventional standards of the day, rather than attempted to meet the Indian aesthetically on his own ground, and his compositions found a wide public.

For American Indian music see *United States* 7.

CAECILIENVEREIN. See *Cecilian Movement*.

CAEREMONIALE EPISCOPORUM. In the Roman Catholic Church the book which contains instructions completing the Rubrics in the Pontifical and Missal (see *Liturgy*). It is of special importance to the choirmaster and organist on account of the laws it lays down.

CAFFARELLI (real name Gaetano Majorano; 1703–83). A castrato singer, famous in all the chief capitals of Europe. He earned an enormous fortune and bought an Italian dukedom. (Cf. *Singing* 5.)

CAGE, JOHN. Born at Los Angeles in 1912. He was a pupil of Cowell and Schönberg. A feature of some of his compositions is their inclusion of a variety of percussive and other novel sound-effects—including those produced by a 'prepared piano' of his invention:

'The changement is achieved by the addition of divers objects to the strings at varying distances from the damper point. Screws, bolts (with careful specification as to type and size), rubber bands, bamboo slats, hairpins, and a miscellany of objects of quite humble origin are pressed into service. . . . The "Prepared" sound, however, may not only bear no relationship in timbre to its unprepared piano counterpart, but its tonality, pitch, and whole position in the piano range territory may be totally unexpected. The sound may jump up three octaves, down one, up a second, down a ninth, all while the fingers are playing notes adjacent to each other in a simple scale passage.' (P. Glanville-Hicks, in the *Musical Courier*, Sept. 1948.)

He may be considered a notable member of the romantic avant-garde, whose work is more talked of than thought about. Some aspects of his art, such as his interest in 'randomness', the relation between noise and music, and the place of silence, are said to derive from Oriental philosophy. See *History* 9 for accounts of some of his feats.

CAHIER (Fr.). 'Part' of a book, i.e. the equivalent of volume but on a smaller scale. *Cahier I*, *Cahier II*, etc. = 'Part I', 'Part II', etc.

CAHILL, THADDEUS (1867–1934). See *Electric Musical Instruments* (near opening); *Electrophone*; *Broadcasting* 2.

CAHUSAC. See *Dance* 10 (1785).

ÇA IRA! (French for 'that will go', i.e. 'it will succeed'). This expression, many times repeated, made up about half the words of a revolutionary song which is said to have originated on that October night in 1789 when the mob marched to Versailles to bring the King and royal family to Paris, and which became the musical accompaniment to almost every incident of the Terror. The words by a popular singer of the day, Ladré (some say Poirier), give the impression of having been more or less extemporized for the occasion, and they varied from period to period with the varying phases of the Revolution. The tune adopted was that of a popular contredanse, called *Carillon National*, by a theatre violinist of the day, Bécourt.

This song was regarded as the official song of the Revolution. Crabb Robinson, from Frankfurt-on-Main, in July 1800, when the French entered it, wrote home to England, 'With colours flying and in great order they invested the gates, struck up the *Ça ira!* and demanded admission.'

In Britain the tune became popular in various arrangements as a piano piece and also as an item in piano tutors. It became the regimental march of the West Yorkshire Regiment (Prince of Wales's Own), as the result of an incident in the campaign in the north of France in 1794. The French, inspired by this tune played by their band, were winning, when the Yorkshire colonel called to his own band to strike up the same tune, and crying, 'Come on, lads, we'll beat them to their own damned tune', led his men in a victorious charge.

(It may be added that the traditional date for the origin of the song above given is contested by C. B. Rogers in *The Spirit of Revolution in 1789: a Study of Public Opinion as revealed in Popular Songs . . . 1949*. He would put the date earlier.)

Cf. *Carmagnole.*

CAISSE (Fr.). 'Box', hence 'Drum'.

CAISSE CLAIRE ('claire' = 'clear', 'distinct'). Snare drum, otherwise side drum. See *Percussion Family* 3 i, 4 b, 5 i.

CAISSE, GROSSE ('grosse' = 'large'). Bass drum. See *Percussion Family* 3 k, 4 b, 5 k.

CAISSE PLATE. See *Percussion Family* 5 i.

CAISSE ROULANTE ('roulante' = 'rolling'). Tenor drum. See *Percussion Family* 3 j, 4 b, 5 j.

CAISSE SOURDE ('sourde' = 'dull', as opposed to 'claire', above). Tenor drum. See *Percussion Family* 3 j, 4 b, 5 j.

CAIX D'HERVELOIS, LOUIS DE. Born in Paris about 1670 and died there about 1760, aged about ninety. He was a great performer on the viola da gamba, and his works are still frequently performed by cellists.

CALANDO (It.). 'Lowering.' It implies diminuendo, with also rallentando.

CALATHUMPIAN CONCERT (or Calathumpian Serenade). See *Charivari.*

CALCANDO (It.). 'Trampling.' It implies much the same as accelerando, i.e. quickening gradually.

CALCUTTA. See *Clubs.*

CALDARA, ANTONIO. Born in Venice about 1670, and died in Vienna in 1736, aged about sixty-six. He spent his life in Venice, Rome, Madrid, and Vienna, in which last place he was second in charge (under Fux) of

the music in the Imperial Chapel. He wrote over seventy operas and over thirty oratorios, many motets and masses and much instrumental music (especially string sonatas in the Corelli style).

CALDERÓN DE LA BARCA (1600–81). See references under *Zarzuela*; *Baile*; *Tono.*

CALEDONIAN HUNT'S DELIGHT. See *Ye Banks and Braes.*

CALINDA (or **Calenda**). A South American Negro dance, for both sexes, and with gestures of sexual suggestiveness. Drums and other percussion instruments are much used in its accompaniment. Delius has introduced a piece based on it in his opera, *Koanga.*

CALINO CASTURAME (or **Calen o custure me**). This is the tune alluded to by Shakespeare in *Henry V* IV. iv. It is to be found in the Fitzwilliam Virginal Book (q.v.). In *A Handefull of Pleasant Delites*, 1584, the words 'Caleno Custureme' are interpolated as a refrain between every two lines of the poem 'When as I view your comly grace'. They seem to be a perversion of the Irish 'Cailín, ó coist suire, mé (I am a girl from the banks of the river Suir)'.

CALKIN. The musical members of this family are here listed somewhat fully.

(1) JAMES. Born in London in 1786 and there died in 1862, aged about seventy-five. He was a pianist and a composer of orchestral, chamber, and pianoforte music.

(2) JAMES JOSEPH. Born in 1813 and died in London in 1868, aged fifty-five. He was a son of James, and a violinist.

(3) JOSEPH. Born in 1816 and died in London in 1874, aged fifty-eight. He is stated (in spite of the partial duplication of names) to be a brother of (2) above. He was a well-known tenor vocalist, singing teacher, and song composer (known as 'Tenielli Calkin', his mother being a Tenniel, relative of the artist).

(4) JOHN BAPTISTE. Born in London in 1827 and died there in 1905, aged seventy-eight. He also was a son of (1) above. He held organ posts in Ireland and then in London, where he was also a professor at Trinity College of Music and the Guildhall School of Music. He wrote services, anthems, glees and part-songs, solo songs, organ and pianoforte music, chamber music, etc. All this had considerable popularity, and a little of the church and organ music is still heard.

(5) GEORGE. Born in London in 1829 (date of death unknown). He also was a son of (1) above. He was a well-known violoncellist, organist, and choral conductor, a composer of popular organ voluntaries, etc., and an arranger for the organ of much of Mendelssohn's music.

(6) JOSEPH. Born in London in 1781 and there died in 1846. Probably a brother of (1) above. He was an orchestral violinist and also a bookseller ('Calkin & Budd, Booksellers to the King'). His son (7) JOSEPH GEORGE

succeeded him in the business, and also taught the violin.

CALLCOTT. At the end of the eighteenth century and during the earlier part of the nineteenth there were a number of well-known English musicians of this name (apparently of two distinct families). The following are the more noteworthy:

(1) JOHN WALL. Born in London in 1766 and died there in 1821, aged fifty-four. He was one of the most prominent London musical practitioners of his time, and especially famous as a composer of glees and catches (see *Glee* 3; and also *Catch* for some interesting details of his work in this branch). This is the often-alluded-to Dr. Callcott.

See references under *Horsley, William* and *O'Neill.*

(2) WILLIAM HUTCHINS. Born in London in 1807 and died there in 1882, aged seventy-four. Like his father (see above) he composed glees, etc. He also published many piano arrangements of orchestral and other music.

CALLER HERRIN'. The poem is by Lady Nairne (q.v.), the music is by Nathaniel Gow (q.v.), who wrote it about 1798 as a harpsichord piece, incorporating the traditional fishwives' cry of Edinburgh with the bells of St. Andrew's Church—and thus, a quarter of a century later, prompting Lady Nairne's muse.

CALLITHUMPIAN (or Calthumpian) **CONCERT** (or Serenade). See *Charivari.*

CALMATO, CALMANDO (It.). 'Calmed', 'calming'.

CALME (Fr.). 'Calm.'

CALORE (It.). 'Heat'; hence 'passion'. So the adjective *Caloroso.*

CALTHUMPIAN CONCERT (or Serenade). See *Charivari.*

CALVIN, JOHN (p. 484, pl. **85.** 1). Born at Noyon, in Picardy, in 1509 and died at Geneva in 1564, aged fifty-four. He was a great scholar, theologian, and religious reformer, making Geneva 'the Protestant Rome'. It is commonly stated that he objected to recreation and the arts, including secular music, but there is no truth in this—beyond the fact that he protested against abuses of these things, which he looked on as good in themselves.

Like the English and the Scottish Puritans, however, who owed many of their ideas, ideals, and principles to him, he banished instrumental music and the elaborations of choral music from the services of the church, in which he believed them to be out of place.

Indirectly he exerted a great influence on popular musical activity in certain countries (including England and Scotland) through the development of the metrical psalm and thus of congregational and domestic singing.

See *Presbyterian* 1, 3; *Puritans* 2, 3; *Hymns and Hymn Tunes* 4, 5, 17 d; *France* 4; *United States* 2; *Rhythm* 6; *Pitch* 6 a.

CALYPSO. A kind of patter-song (often improvised and abounding in satirical and topical references) sung by the natives of Trinidad. The infectious rhythm and the characteristic trick of cramming in polysyllabic words without regard for the metre assisted the spread of its popularity to Britain and the United States in the late 1940s.

CALZABIGI, RANIERO DE (1714–95). He was Gluck's librettist and to a large extent his inspirer in the reform of the opera (see *Libretto*).

CAMARGO. See *Ballet* 2, 9.

CAMBERT, ROBERT. Born in Paris about 1628 and died in London in 1677, aged about forty-nine. He was a harpsichordist and organist who became director of music in the household of the Queen Mother and Regent, Anne of Austria, and later, when the librettist, Pierre Perrin, obtained a grant of monopoly for the performance of musical stage works in the French language, attached himself to him. Under the privilege of this monopoly was performed (1671) his opera, *Pomone*, the first French opera. This, largely, constitutes his historical importance.

Lully (q.v.) bought Perrin's monopoly and Cambert went to England. It is said that he was murdered by his valet.

Some passing references will be found under *Opera* 24 b; *Pastoral*; *Ballet* 2; *Rhythm* 5.

CAMBERWELL GREEN (Mendelssohn). See *Nicknamed Compositions* 14.

CAMBIARE (It.). 'To change'; *Cambiamento* means the act of changing. (For *Nota Cambiata* see *Changing Note.*)

CAMBRAI. See *Belgium* 2.

CAMBRENSIS. See under *Giraldus.*

CAMBRIDGE (England). See *Fairs*; *Inns*; *Clubs*; *Puritans* 4; *Degrees and Diplomas*; *Temperament* 6; *Agincourt Song*; *Abyngdon*; *Act Music*; *Dictionaries* 11.

University Professors of Music who receive notice in this volume are (with their periods of office): M. Greene (1730–55); Clarke-Whitfeld (1821–36); Walmisley (1836–56); W. Sterndale Bennett (1856–75); G. A. Macfarren (1875–87); Stanford (1887–1924); C. Wood (1924–6); Dent (1926–41); Hadley (1946–63); Dart (1963–4); Orr (1965).

Other Cambridge musicians who receive notice are W. Beale; Crotch; Garrett; Gibbons Family; Gray; J. Hilton, senior; Kent; Mace; Rootham.

CAMBRIDGE (Mass.). See *Hymns and Hymn Tunes* 11.

CAMERA (It.). 'Chamber'—as opposed to hall, opera-house, etc. *Cantata da Camera*, see *Cantata. Concerto da Camera*, see *Concerto* 2. *Sonata da Camera*, see *Sonata* 2; *Suite* 1.

CAMIDGE FAMILY. This remarkable family supplied the organists of York Minster for a century. The members were (1) JOHN I (1735–1803), in office 1756–1803; he had been a pupil in London of Dr. Greene and of Handel. (2) John's son MATTHEW (1758–1844), in office 1799–1842. (3) Matthew's son JOHN II (1790–1850), in office 1842–59; he was a Cambridge and Lambeth D.Mus.

In addition there are (4) the last named's

son, THOMAS SIMPSON (1828–1912); he deputized for his father (who was paralytic for the last ten years of his life) and then held various other posts; and finally, (5) Thomas's son JOHN III (1853–1939), organist of Beverley Minster for fifty-seven years (1875–1933).

(Music by all the above five formed part of the farewell service in York Minster for Bishop E. Camidge in 1887, on his leaving for his See of Bathurst, New South Wales.)

CAMMERTON or **KAMMERTON** (Ger.). See *Pitch* 3, 8.

CAMMINANDO (It.). 'Walking', 'proceeding', used in a sense of 'covering the ground', 'pushing on'.

CAMPANA, CAMPANE (It.). 'Bell', 'bells', e.g. those used in the orchestra. See *Percussion Family* 2 b, 4 e, 5 b; *Bells* 6.

CAMPANELLA. Italian for 'Little Bell' (the 'Glöckchen' of Strauss). *Campanelle* (plur.) is sometimes used for the Glockenspiel. Liszt's piano composition *La Campanella* (an arrangement of one of Paganini's solo violin Caprices) is a glorification of 'The Little Bell', in various manifestations.

See *Percussion Family* 2 b, 4 e, 5 b; *Bell* 6.

CAMPANETTA (It.). Glockenspiel. See *Percussion Family* 2 c, 4 e, 5 c.

CAMPANOLOGY. See *Bell* 4 (near end).

CAMPBELL, OLIVE DAME. See *Ballad* 3.

CAMPBELLS ARE COMING, THE. This popular Scottish tune first appeared in print in 1745, at which time it was used as a country dance under the title 'Hob or Nob', but about the same period it is also found with its present title. There are many contradictory statements as to its origin. The folk-song authority Frank Kidson (q.v.), thought that there might be truth in the story that it was used as 'the gathering tune of the clan Campbell during the Scots rebellion of 1715'. Another story connects it with the imprisonment of Mary Queen of Scots, and still another ascribes its origin to Ireland.

CAMPENHOUT, FRANÇOIS VAN. Born at Brussels in 1779 and died there in 1848, aged sixty-nine. He was a well-known tenor singer, who composed operas, and is now remembered by *La Brabançonne*, the Belgian National Anthem. (See *Brabançonne*.)

CAMPIAN or **CAMPION**, THOMAS. Born in London in 1567 and died there in 1620, aged fifty-three. By profession a medical man, he is by after-reputation one of the most charming poets of the Elizabethan age and one of its most delicate writers of vocal music with the lute accompaniment usual at the period. He also left treatises upon prosody and counterpoint—and an estate of twenty pounds.

See *Rosseter*; *Masque*; *Lancashire Sol-fa*.

CAMP MEETING. See *Hymns and Hymn Tunes* 12; *Presbyterian Church Music* 6.

CAMPO, CONRADO DEL (in full, Conrado del Campo y Zabaleta; 1879–1953). He was a professor of harmony at the Conservatory of Madrid who composed symphonic poems, operas, chamber music, and choral music.

CAMPRA, ANDRÉ. Born at Aix en Provence in 1660 and died at Versailles in 1744, aged eighty-three. After directing the music in several provincial cathedrals, he was placed in charge of that in Notre Dame, Paris, to which crowds flocked to hear his work. About the age of forty he turned to the stage. Lully had been ten years dead, and Rameau was not to produce his first opera for thirty more; Campra filled his gap, and in so doing won great renown—especially by opera-ballets, of which *L'Europe galante* and *Fêtes vénitiennes* had quite triumphant success.

CANADA. See *Broadcasting* 3, 6; *Dictionaries* 4 c.

CANADIAN BOAT SONG. (1) The tune is a French-Canadian folk song (*Dans mon chemin*); the poem is by Thomas Moore, who heard the tune when visiting Canada in 1804 and then wrote his poem.

(2) But there is another production, often called 'Canadian Boat Song', the authorship of which is extremely obscure, the question cropping up periodically in the press and never being settled (as, for instance, in the London *Times* of February and March 1934). This is the song of which the very beautiful stanza is so often quoted:

From the lone shieling of the misty island
  Mountains divide us, and the waste of seas—
Yet still the blood is strong, the heart is Highland,
  And we in dreams behold the Hebrides.

Amongst persons to whom the lines are often attributed are the novelist John Galt (but he disliked the Highlands), the twelfth Earl of Eglinton (1739–1819), Lockhart (who possibly wrote two verses), John Wilson (whose claim disappears under scrutiny), and David Macbeth Moir, otherwise 'Delta'. Edward McCurdy's *A Literary Enigma* (1936) was responsible for the theory that Moir wrote the first three verses and Lockhart the last two. Professor G. H. Needler, of Toronto University, a few years later, in his *The Lone Shieling*, sees the hand of Moir in the whole poem, basing his belief on a careful prosodical study.

The poem apparently first appeared in *Blackwood's Magazine* in 1829, and it is found set to music in a posthumous publication *A Selection of Songs and Marches, etc.*, composed *by Hugh, late Earl of Eglinton*. This nobleman, though a composer, is not known to have written poetry; it has been suggested that he was the translator of the verses, which are described in the book as 'from the Gaelic' (but this theory is now discredited).

Scott is accepted by some as the author.

CANARIES, or **CANARIE**, or **CANARY.** An old dance in three-in-a-measure or six-in-a-measure time, something like the gigue (q.v.). The rhythm is distinctive; the phrases all begin on the first of the measure, with a note of a beat-and-a-half length. This dance type entered somewhat into independent instrumental music, examples being found in seventeenth- and eighteenth-century composers such as Purcell, Lully, and Couperin.

Apparently the hay (q.v.) or hey was danced to similar music; indeed, some Elizabethan pieces are marked as for use with either dance.

The name 'Canaries' presumably refers to an origin in the Canary Islands, and the recorded fact that it was considered in England to be an old Spanish dance and was believed to be danced in Spain with castanets supports this.

Shakespeare several times mentions the dance: '. . . make you dance Canary with sprightly fire and motion' (*All's Well that Ends Well*, II. i).

CAN-CAN (or Chahut). A boisterous and latterly indecorous dance, of the quadrille order and including much high kicking, dating from about 1840 and then exploited in Paris for the benefit of such British and American visitors as were willing to pay well to be well shocked.

CANCEL. See *American Musical Terminology* 4.

CANCIÓN (Sp.). 'Song.' There are diminutives—*Cancioncica, Cancioncilla, Cancioncita*. The *Canción Danza* is a Spanish dance-song.

CANCIONERO MUSICAL. See *Spain* 4.

CANCRIZANS. See *Canon*.

CANNABICH, CHRISTIAN (1731–98). See *Conducting* 6; *Symphony* 8 (1731).

CANNTAIREACHD. See *Bagpipe Family* 4.

CANON (Fr., Canon; It., Canone; Ger., Kanon). The word means 'rule' and in music is applied to that sort of counterpoint (q.v.) in which rule is most strictly followed—a rule that the voice (or, it may be, melodic instrumental part) that begins the canonic passage shall be closely imitated, note for note, by some other voice (or part), beginning later and overlapping the first one. If the canon is in more than two voices (or parts) then the overlapping is manifold. Necessarily such writing as this makes great demands on the technical skill of the writer, and the composition of canon may be regarded as the most difficult practice in composition.

For the enlightenment of any uninstructed reader who has not easily grasped the above definition, it may be said that the *catch* and *round* (e.g. the universally familiar Elizabethan 'Three Blind Mice') are forms of canon. There is a well-known hymn tune called (in most hymn books) *Tallis's Canon*; in it the tenor exactly follows the treble at a distance of four beats. This happens to be a **Canon in the Octave** (below). Canons can, however, exist at any interval, and those at the fifth and fourth (above or below) are very commonly met with. There are also canons at the unison, and rounds and catches are examples of this; they further illustrate the principle of the **Perpetual Canon**—or **Infinite Canon**, i.e.

the canon in which each part, having come to the end, merely begins again and so on until, the canon having been sung the prearranged number of times, an end of it is made. The converse of this is the **Finite Canon**.

A canon for two voices is called a **Canon Two in One** (meaning that one line of melody suffices for two voices), and so, too, we have canons 'three in one', 'four in one', etc. Sometimes two canons are carried on simultaneously (e.g. soprano and tenor in one canon and alto and bass in another). Such canons are called **Four in Two**.

There are canons in which the imitative voice gives out the melody in longer notes; such a canon as this is called a **Canon by Augmentation**. Likewise there are canons in which it gives out the melody in shorter notes —**Canon by Diminution**.

There is also a highly artificial form in which the imitating voice gives out the melody backwards (the two voices usually beginning together, and so departing from the usual idea of canon). From a defective knowledge of natural history this has been called the **Canon Cancrizans** ('Crab-Canon'—but crabs move *sideways*; in German this is called **Krebskanon**—cf. *Krebsgang*: other names for it are **Canon Recte et Retro** or **Rectus et Inversus** (indicating a simultaneous forward and backward motion); **Retrograde Canon** is still another name. This type of canon, however much it may contribute to the pride of its contriver, is necessarily artistically futile, since no listener can possibly discover what is going on, a melody sung backwards being in effect a new melody, and not being (by the ear) recognizably related to its original self.

Canons are **Strict** or **Free** according as the intervals are or are not exactly imitated. All canons in the octave are necessarily strict, but as soon as the octave is left it is evident that the slice of scale substituted for the previous one has its tones and semitones in new positions, and that to adjust these so that the original melody may be strictly reproduced is to introduce accidentals that may create modulation, with consequent hardship on the original voice, which, probably, cannot easily be adjusted to such modulations without itself modulating, so creating still further difficulties when *its* modulatory notes come, in their turn, to be imitated. Hence free canon is commoner than strict.

Canon necessarily occurs in the 'Stretto' of a fugue (see *Form* 12), i.e. if the stretto is a true one—if each voice entering with the subject continues with it after the next voice enters.

The voice first entering with the melody in a canon is called **Dux** ('leader') or **Antecedent**, and any imitating voice is called **Comes** ('companion') or **Consequent**.

There exists **Canon by Inversion**, in which any upward interval of the Dux becomes a downward interval in the Comes, and vice versa; **Canon per Arsin et Thesin** is another name for this, but unfortunately the same term is used to denominate canon in which the notes on strong beats in the Dux become notes on weak beats in the Comes.

In early times the word 'fugue' was used for canon; now that term has a separate and distinct meaning.

One of the earliest genuinely musical (i.e. enjoyable) canons known is the English *Sumer is icumen in* (q.v.); this dates from near the beginning of the thirteenth century. In the century after this composers (especially amongst the Flemings) carried the practice of canon to an absurd point, rejoicing in ingenuity at the expense of music. In the sixteenth-century church music and madrigals canon is effectively used (often merely fragmentarily, of course) for truly musical purposes.

There is an intellectual pleasure to the listener in observing the imitation of one voice or part by another, and this is the aesthetic justification of a discreet use of canon. Bach uses much canon in his writing—but always with a really artistic aim. Beethoven (and all the great composers) have enjoyed canonical writing, both as a mental exercise (comparable to chess problems and crosswords) and as a musical device.

The great contrapuntist Fux (1660–1741) wrote a very wonderful *Missa Canonica*, a Mass including canon of every possible variety; despite its apparent artificiality it is said to create a thoroughly devotional impression in performance. Some of the English Elizabethan musicians were untiring composers of canon; John Farmer in 1591 published a series of forty accompaniments in canon to the plainsong *Miserere*, and George Waterhouse (d. 1601) wrote 1,163 more of these (still in manuscript at Cambridge).

Sometimes a choral canon may have freely moving instrumental parts. This is **Accompanied Canon**; it is fairly common in eighteenth- and nineteenth-century oratorio.

In addition to actual canon there is a great deal of very free canonic writing in music, and to this is given the wide-embracing name of **Imitation**.

For particulars of a very early English canon see *Sumer is icumen in*; for a later popular canon see *Non nobis*; for discussion of a Bach canon see *Harmony* 17; and for a canon by Haydn see *Turk*.

CANONICAL HOURS. See *Divine Office*.

CANONIC IMITATION. See *Canon* (end).

CANORUM. See *Methodism and Music* 2.

CANTAB. Indicates a Cambridge degree.

CANTABILE (It.). 'Singable' or 'singingly'; hence with the melody smoothly performed and well brought out.

CANTANDO (It.). 'Singing.' Same as *Cantabile*.

CANTANTE, BASSO. See *Voice* 19.

CANTATA (It. 'sung'; fem. of 'Cantato'). The most usual use of this word today is as a description for a sacred or secular work with solos, choruses, and orchestral accompaniment in much the style either of an opera meant to

be performed without scenery and action, or of a short oratorio.

The cantata began in the earliest years of the seventeenth century as what may be called a miniature concert form of the opera (though there were no *public* concerts in those days). The first operas were entirely in recitative (see *Opera*) and so were the first cantatas; most of the music in an opera was for solo voices, and so, too, that of the cantata (usually for only one voice).

As the aria (q.v.) crept into being and became important in opera and oratorio, so it came at the same time into the cantata.

In fact right through its history the cantata has maintained much the position it still holds —that defined in the first paragraph of this article, of an unacted opera or a briefer oratorio (in early days often very brief).

A secular piece of this kind in the seventeenth and eighteenth centuries was a *Cantata da Camera* ('Chamber Cantata'); a sacred piece was a *Cantata da Chiesa* ('Church Cantata'). The introducer of the latter type was Carissimi (q.v.; cf. also *Oratorio* 2).

Note that the word *Cantata* ('sung') had its counterpart, *Sonata* ('sounded', or 'played'), and that just as there was a *Cantata da Camera* and a *Cantata da Chiesa*, so there was a *Sonata da Camera* and a *Sonata da Chiesa* (cf. *Canzona*; *Sonata* 1, 2).

In the earlier eighteenth century the solo cantata continued to be popular. The two Scarlattis, Pergolese, Handel, and others, wrote many (Alessandro Scarlatti, the father, composed over 500). A common form at this time was that of three recitatives alternating with as many arias.

The solo cantata tended after the middle of this century to give place to the operatic *Scena*, i.e. actual extracts from operas were used in concert performance instead of the cantata composed as such. Rousseau in his *Dictionary of Music* (1767) reports this change as pretty well accomplished in Paris. The purely concert scena of a later period (e.g. Beethoven's 'Ah, perfido!' or Mendelssohn's 'Infelice') is really nothing but a cantata in the old sense; it is a long vocal solo cast into several movements, with both recitatives and arias, with orchestral accompaniment; practically, then, it is the seventeenth- and eighteenth-century cantata in more modern idiom.

Early specimens of the cantata in the present-day sense of the term (i.e. with vocal solos for different voices, choruses, and orchestral accompaniment) are Handel's *Acis and Galatea* (which in its own day was called a 'masque', a 'serenata', or a 'pastoral opera') and *Alexander's Feast*, and Bach's *Coffee Cantata*, *Peasant Cantata*, and *The Strife betwixt Phoebus and Pan*. The concert cantata of today is just this type in modern idiom.

The seventeenth- and eighteenth-century *Cantata da Chiesa* or *Church Cantata* has been mentioned above. German Protestantism of the seventeenth and eighteenth century developed this on its own lines. Schütz, Buxtehude, and Bach, were composers of such works, the period of popularity of which lasted nearly fifty years and ended with Bach. Bach composed five complete series for the ecclesiastical year. About 200 of these remain: they vary greatly in scope and length (from about 10 to 35 minutes), but may in general be described as developed motets or anthems, using both scriptural prose and devotional verse. Some make little use of the chorus; others great use of it. The Chorale (q.v.) is an important feature. All have the accompaniment of a greater or smaller orchestra. Their place in the Lutheran service was before the sermon. Bach's *Christmas Oratorio* is really a series of cantatas for separate performance on six days of the season.

It will be realized that, like the opera and oratorio, the cantata is an Italian form accepted by other nations (cf. *Clérambault*) and developed by them in their own ways. The British development has, naturally, been greatly influenced by the British love of choral singing.

It will also be realized that, though at first there seems to be so great a difference between the seventeenth-century solo cantata and the cantata as the choral society member understands it today that the same name is hardly with propriety applicable, yet both are essentially the same thing—or rather one is a development of the other.

The British choral society and choral festival cantata was during the Victorian period turned out by the hundred.

Cf. *Canzona*. For 'Missa Cantata' see *Mass* 1.

CANTATE (Fr., Ger.). 'Cantata.'

CANTATE DOMINO. The 98th Psalm, 'O sing unto the Lord a new song' (see *Common Prayer*). In the Prayer Book of the American Episcopal Church part of the *Cantate Domino* is joined to part of the *Venite*.

CANTATRICE. Italian for a female singer.

CANTE FLAMENCO. A type of melody, probably of Arab origin, popular in Andalusia (see *Spain* 3), and used both in song and dance. The significance of the word *Flamenco* ('Flemish') is much disputed; it may be a corruption of the Arabic *pelagmengu*. The term is especially applied to gipsy music, but it seems to have acquired a very comprehensive meaning nowadays and to take in almost anything. Cante Flamenco is a lighter version of Cante Hondo (q.v.).

See *Applause* 2.

CANTE HONDO (or Cante Jondo: *hondo* means 'deep' and *jondo* is a form of the same word). A type of popular Spanish song, with a good deal of repetition of the note, much melodic decoration, and the use of some intervals that do not occur in the accepted European scales. The Phrygian cadence (see *Cadence*) is much used. In 1922 Falla organized a Festival of Cante Hondo at Granada.

See *Spain* 3; *Cante Flamenco*.

CANTEMIR, PRINCE DEMETRIUS (1673–1723). See *Rumania*.

CANTERBURY (England). See *Plainsong* 4; *Cathedral Music* 2; *Palmer*; *Organ* 8; *Minstrels* 3; *Clubs*; *O. Gibbons*; *Marson*; *Degrees and Diplomas* 1. Also p. 144, pl. **29**. 2; p. 145, pl. **30**. 7.

CANTI CARNASCIALESCHI ('Carnival Songs'; singular, *Canto carnascialesco*). Gay processional madrigals of an early, simple sort, with several verses to the same music—something on the lines of the English Ayre (see *Madrigal* 3 b), but with the tune in the tenor, in the old fashion, and often with improper words. They formed a part of the social life of Florence in the fifteenth and sixteenth centuries and were opposed by the religious leader, Savonarola (burnt 1498), who wrote his *Laudi Spirituali* (q.v.) to take their place. There was a tendency latterly to cast them into series and to give them dramatic qualities, and thus they rank amongst the precursors of opera.

CANTICLE. A Bible hymn (other than a psalm) as used in the liturgy of the Christian Church. The Common Prayer of the Church of England uses the term only for the *Benedicite*, but usage applies it also to the *Benedictus*, the *Magnificat*, and the *Nunc Dimittis*—not properly to the *Venite*, the *Jubilate*, the *Cantate Domino*, or *Deus Misereatur*, which are psalms. The *Te Deum*, which is not from the Bible, is generally also looked on as one of the Canticles.

In the Roman Catholic Church the Canticles drawn from the New Testament are called the Evangelical Canticles, or the Major Canticles in distinction from those in the Old Testament called the Minor Canticles.

(*Canticles* is the alternative name to the book in the Bible, *The Song of Solomon*.)

CANTIGA. A Spanish or Portuguese folk-song; also a type of religious song (see *Spain* 3, end).

CANTILENA. (1) The term nowadays usually indicates smooth, melodious, and not rapid vocal writing, or performance in that style.

(2) It means, literally, a small song, and has in the past been used in this sense, or even for song generally.

(3) It was also at one period sometimes applied to the uppermost part of a piece of choral music, or to the part with the main tune (then equivalent to 'Canto Fermo', q.v.).

(4) It has also been used for a type of solfeggio (q.v.) in which were introduced all the intervals of the scale.

CANTILENAS VULGARES. See *Spain* 4.

CANTILÈNE (Fr.). Same as Cantilena (q.v.).

CANTILLATION. Chanting in free rhythm, in a plainsong style. The term is most used in connexion with the Jewish liturgical music.

See *Jewish Music* 3.

CANTIONES SACRAE. See *Motet*.

CANTO (It.). 'Song', 'melody'. So *Col canto*, 'with

the song', i.e. the accompanist to take his time throughout from the performer of the melody.

CANTO FERMO (It.). See *Mass* 5; *Conductus*; *Gymel*; *Harmony* 6, 7; *Counterpoint*. In eighteenth-century literature it often means 'plainsong'.

CANTOR. In modern Anglican and Roman Catholic usage the Cantor is the singer who is charged, for the occasion, with the duty of intoning the first words of psalms, antiphons, and hymns. Cantors, especially on feast days, often work in pairs at the desk in the middle of the choir.

For the Jewish Cantor (or Chazzan) see *Jewish Music* 3, 4, 6.

CANTORIS. See *Precentor*; *Service*.

CANTUAR. See *Degrees and Diplomas* 1.

CANTUS (Lat.). 'Song', 'melody'. In the later fifteenth and sixteenth centuries applied to the uppermost part of madrigals, church music, viol consorts, etc. (see *Voice* 17). For the collection of songs and madrigals known as 'Forbes' Cantus' or the 'Aberdeen Cantus' see *Scotland* 8.

CANTUS CHORALIS. See *Chorale*.

CANTUS FICTUS. Same as *Musica ficta* (q.v.).

CANTUS FIGURATUS. See *Plainsong* 1.

CANTUS FIRMUS (Lat.). See *Canto fermo*.

CANTUS MENSURATUS. See *Plainsong* 1.

CANTUS PLANUS. See *Plainsong* 1.

CANU PENILLION (Welsh). 'Penillion singing.' See *Wales* 5.

CANZONA or **CANZONE**; plural **CANZONI** (It.). The word originated as the name of a type of poem of the troubadour period—in several stanzas, the last one being short. From this the word came to be applied to musical settings of such poems (solo or choral —see *Napolitana*) and hence, in a rather vague sort of way, to short compositions (generally loosely fugal and resembling the severer sort of madrigal) for lute, for organ, etc.

In more modern use the word is found as meaning an instrumental piece with marked melody, i.e. in the Song without Words style. This revives a sixteenth- to seventeenth-century use of the word for purely instrumental music. There was the *Canzona Cantata* and an imitation of it, the *Canzona Sonata*, i.e. the 'Sung' Canzona and the 'Sounded' (played) Canzona—whence, by abbreviation, the terms 'Cantata' (q.v.) and 'Sonata' (see *Sonata* 1) used as nouns. The early canzona cantata was sometimes in several sections or movements, and in the imitation of this is (partly) to be found the origin of the several-movement sonata.

CANZONET or **CANZONETTA** (It.). The word is the diminutive of *Canzona* (q.v.). Its most important application is to certain madrigals, e.g. Morley's *Canzonets, or Little Short Songs to Three Voyces* (1593), etc. Later the word came to be applied to a light, flowing kind of solo song, e.g. Haydn's *Six Original Canzonets* (London, 1796), of which 'My

mother bids me bind my hair' is an example. (See *Madrigal* 6).

CAOINE. Irish funeral song, with wailing (the English spelling is 'keen').

CAPELL, RICHARD. Born at Northampton in 1885 and died in London in 1954, aged sixty-nine. After music study on the continent of Europe and a journalistic apprenticeship he became music critic of the London *Daily Mail* and then (1933) of the *Daily Telegraph*. He published a study of *Schubert's Songs* (1928). From 1950 he owned and edited the valuable quarterly *Music and Letters* (cf. *Fox Strangways*; *Blom*).

CAPELLA. See *Cappella*.

CAPELLE, CAPELLMEISTER, CAPELLMEISTERMUSIK. See under *Chapel*.

CAPE TOWN. See *Schools of Music*.

CAPLET, ANDRÉ. Born at Le Havre in 1878 and died near Paris in 1925, aged forty-six. He studied at the Paris Conservatory, won the Grand Prix de Rome, and was early known as an able conductor and as the composer of delicate and poetical songs, choral and orchestral pieces, and chamber music. He was a close friend of Debussy and the first conductor of some of his works. From 1910 to 1914 he conducted at Boston, U.S.A. His death came as a result of injuries sustained during the first World War.

CAPO. See *Da Capo*.

CAPOTASTO, CAPO D'ASTRO, CAPODASTRO (It.); **CAPODASTÈRE** (Fr.); **CAPODASTER** (Ger.). Literally 'head (of the) touch', or 'head (of the) feel', i.e. the 'nut' or raised projection at the top of the fingerboard (It., *Tasto* or *Tastiera*) of a stringed instrument, over which the strings pass and which defines their sounding length at that end.

A movable capotasto has sometimes been used, which can be placed at any point lower down the finger-board, as, for instance, at such a distance as to raise the pitch of all the strings by a semitone. In cello playing the left thumb, by its pressure, serves as a capotasto, and Burney seems to have understood the term in this sense.

Another name is *Barre* (Fr.).

CAPPELLA, CAPELLA (It.). 'Chapel' (for origin of the word see *Chapel*). So the expression *A Cappella*, *A Capella* (or *Alla Cappella*, *Alla Capella*), 'in the church style'. (The spelling with the double 'p' is the correct one, the word *Capella* meaning 'she-goat').

(1) The usual application of this is to choral music composed to be sung unaccompanied (or, at any rate, if accompanied, this by the instrument merely doubling the voice parts). It may be that the origin of this use of the term is in the custom of the Sistine Chapel, in the Vatican, where no instrumentalists have ever been engaged. (2) A rarer application of the

term makes it a synonym for *Alla Breve* in either of its two senses (see *Breve*).

CAPRICCIO (It.) or **CAPRICE** (Eng. and Fr.). The term is of early introduction, being applied to some of the sixteenth-century Italian madrigals. Frescobaldi uses it for organ pieces (1624). Sometimes in the seventeenth century we find it applied to a kind of free fugue for keyboard. Handel, Scarlatti, and Bach have also used the word, as have very many later composers.

A capriccio is almost always in quick tempo (though Haydn has in one of his 'Salomon' Symphonies a capriccio marked 'largo', but there is no essential quality except the general one indicated by the name. Rousseau, in his *Dictionary of Music* (1767) says, 'A kind of free music, in which the composer, without subjecting himself to any theme, gives loose rein to his genius and submits himself to the fire of composition'. This fairly describes most capriccios, with the provision that the words 'without subjecting himself', etc., are rarely true, for most capriccios do work to a particular musical theme or themes. Often the term 'fantasia' might be substituted.

In the early eighteenth century the word 'capriccio' seems to have been used for cadenza (q.v.).

As a performing direction, *a capriccio* means according to the 'caprice' or fancy of the performer.

CAPRICCIOSO (It.), **CAPRICIEUX** (Fr.). 'Capricious', hence in a lively, informal, whimsical style. So the adverb *Capricciosamente*.

CARCELERA. A sort of *Saeta* (q.v.)—supposedly a prisoner's song.

CARAPETYAN, ARMEN. Born in Persia of Armenian parents, 1908. He was educated at Teheran and then the Sorbonne and Harvard and also studied the violin under Capet and composition under Malipiero. In 1944 he founded the Institute of Renaissance and Baroque Music, which was later superseded by the American Institute of Musicology, of which he is director. Its headquarters are at Rome. It publishes a journal, *Musica Disciplina*.

CARDUS, NEVILLE. Born at Manchester in 1889 and died in London in 1975. In 1917 he joined the staff of the *Manchester Guardian* and in 1927 succeeded Samuel Langford as its chief music critic, serving also as its cricket expert. From 1941 to 1947 he was in Australia attached to the *Sydney Morning Herald*. He wrote books on his two subjects and an autobiography. C.B.E., 1964. Knighted 1967.

CARESSANT (Fr.). 'Caressing.'

CAREY, HENRY. Born about 1688 and died (by suicide) in London in 1743, aged about fifty-six. He wrote much music for the theatre, including the ballad-opera *A Wonder, or The Honest Yorkshireman*.

See references to him under *God save the Queen* 10, 15; *Sally in our Alley*; also p. 817, p. **140.** 4.

CAREZZANDO, CAREZZEVOLE (It.). 'Caressing', 'caressingly'.

CARILLO. Common misspelling of *Carrillo* (q.v.).

CARILLON. See *Bell* 4 (pictures, p. 100, pl. **17**); *Percussion Family* 5 c; *Mechanical* 2; also *Organ* 14 V.

CARILLON NATIONAL. See *Ça ira!*

CARISSIMI, GIACOMO. Born near Rome in 1605 and died there in 1674, aged sixty-eight. From 1630 until his death he directed the choir of the Jesuit church of S. Apollinare. He belongs to the second group of writers in the style of monody or the 'new music' (see *Opera* 1, 2) and enjoys fame as having both brought the recitative to perfection and introduced more instrumental variety into the cantata and oratorio. He was a pioneer in the expressive use of the solo voice in cantatas and oratorios, of which his *Jephte* (1650) is a famous example (see *Oratorio* 2).

See a reference under *Homme Armé*.

CARLISLE HOUSE, LONDON. See *Concert* 8.

CARLTON.

(1) **RICHARD.** Born about 1558 and died about 1638, aged about eighty. He was a Norfolk vicar and a notable writer of madrigals (see *Madrigal*) with a peculiarly individual harmonic style.

(2) **NICHOLAS** (virginal writer). See brief reference under *Pianoforte* 21.

CARLYLE, THOMAS. See *Program*; *Programme Music* 4; *Street Music* 7.

CARMAGNOLE. Originally this is the name of a sort of short coat, worn in the north Italian district of Carmagnola, and brought into France by workmen from that district. The insurgents of Marseilles in 1792 (cf. *Rouget de Lisle*) introduced it to Paris, where it became identified with the Revolution. A round dance of the time was given the name and a song with the refrain, 'Dansons la Carmagnole, vive le son du canon', to a very catchy air, became identified with revolutionary festivities such as executions.

The authorship of both words and music is unknown.

Cf. *Ça ira!*

CARMAN'S WHISTLE. This is a tune to be found, with variations by Byrd, in the Fitzwilliam Virginal Book (q.v.). It is that of a ballad which was published in 1592, mentioned in Chappell's *Old English Popular Music* as 'not suitable for publication in this work'. There are in the literature of the sixteenth and seventeenth centuries innumerable references to the whistling of carmen, i.e. carters (as, for instance, in Shakespeare's *Henry IV*, Part 2, Act III).

CARMEN (Latin). (1) Tune, song, strain, poem. (2) In fourteenth- and fifteenth-century parlance, either the voice part of a composition that has also instrumental parts or the uppermost part of a composition for several voices.

CARMEN (Bizet). Produced in Paris in 1875. Libretto by Meilhac and Halévy, founded on the novel by Mérimée.

ACT I

SCENE: *A Square in Seville. Time, about 1820*

A soldiers' guard is being relieved: **Morales** (*Bass*) and **Zuniga** (*Bass*) are officers. **Micaela** (*Soprano*), a peasant girl, comes to seek **Don José** (*Tenor*), a sergeant. As he is not yet here, she goes away. At noon the cigarette-factory girls come out. Among them is **Carmen** (*Mezzo-Soprano*), an alluring, fickle gipsy girl, who seeks to fascinate José. When the girls have gone back to work, Micaela brings José a message from his mother. Now there is a commotion in the factory. Carmen, in a quarrel, has stabbed a fellow worker. Zuniga arrests her, but by using her fascinations upon José she makes him forget his duty and help her to escape.

ACT II

SCENE: *A Tavern*

Carmen has found her gipsy friends at a tavern where smugglers gather. **Escamillo** (*Baritone*) sings the famous 'Toreador's Song'. He attracts Carmen, but her immediate purpose is to meet José, who for his lapse from duty has been imprisoned. Now he ought to return to duty, but Carmen tries, though not with complete success, to beguile him from it again. Zuniga enters, and orders José out. Jealousy springs up, and José draws his sword upon his superior officer. The smugglers rush in and part the two. Now José's only path is to flee. He resolves to take to the mountains with Carmen.

ACT III

SCENE: *The Smugglers' Hiding-place in the Hills*

José is homesick. Carmen taunts him. She is thinking of the handsome Escamillo, and wondering what he is like. Together with her gipsy friends **Frasquita** (*Soprano*) and **Mercedes** (*Mezzo-Soprano*), Carmen reads the cards to find in them the message of fate—that first she and then José will soon end their lives.

When the others have gone, Escamillo comes seeking Carmen. He and José fight, only to be separated by the smugglers, alarmed at the commotion. Escamillo goes away, but he has seen Carmen's look, and knows that he has won. José knows too.

Micaela brings José the news that his mother is dying. With the warning to Carmen that he will meet her again, he goes to his home.

ACT IV

SCENE: *A Street outside the Bull Ring at Seville*

Carmen promises Escamillo that if he is successful in his combats she will be his. When the people have gone in to see the bull-fight José approaches her and impassionedly begs her to love him. She refuses, and he stabs her. As the victorious Escamillo comes from the bull-ring José gives himself up to justice.

See also *Habanera*; *Nietzsche*; *Percussion* 4 c; *Seguidilla*; *Spain* 10.

CARNAVAL DE VENISE. See *Carnival of Venice.*

CARNEGIE, CARNEGIE FUND, CARNEGIE UNITED KINGDOM TRUST. See *Patronage* 6, 7; *Scotland* 11; *Presbyterian* 2.

CARNER (orig. Cohen), MOSCO. Born in Vienna in 1904. After studying at the Conservatory and University of his native city he became known as a conductor and critic. He settled in England in 1933 and has written an admirable life of Puccini.

CARNICER. See *Spain* 6.

CARNIE, WILLIAM (1824–1908). See *Presbyterian Church Music* 4.

CARNIVAL OF VENICE. This is the name of various once highly popular compositions by various hands—by Paganini and others for violin, Shulhoff and Herz for piano, Bottesini for double-bass, and so forth. They are all more or less of the nature of an air and variations. The air is a popular tune which Paganini heard in Venice at the beginning of the nineteenth century and made known everywhere by his own playing of an arrangement of it; the settings by other composers quickly followed.

Massé's opera, *La Reine Topaze* (1856), introduced it as a vocal air with variations, and the next year Ambroise Thomas wrote an opera *Le Carnaval de Venise*, basing the overture upon the tune. A song setting of the tune was well known in England. In fact for some years this melody haunted the opera stage, the concert platform, and the drawing-room, and it is not yet extinct, various arrangements of it being still on sale.

See also *Ernst.*

CAROLAN. See *O'Carolan.*

CAROL-BÉRARD. See *Colour and Music* 10.

CAROLS (p. 141, pl. 27; p. 144, pl. 29). It is difficult to frame a satisfactory definition of 'Carol'. One which would include most of what we call by the name would be 'a religious seasonal song, of joyful character, in the vernacular and sung by the common people'.

Amongst the suggestions that cluster round the word are that of *dancing* (for the early carols were danced as well as sung and many of their tunes have a dance lilt, certain of the words retain hints of the original purpose, and the very name 'carol' is thought to imply dancing); that of the *open air*, for carols always were and still are a good deal sung in the open; that of *Christmas*, since the carols for that season have, of all carols, the most vigorously survived; that of *simplicity* and *crudity*, for true carols are always simple in thought, indeed they are often crude both in thought and expression; and that of *age*, for the best carols have served many generations of men. A refrain after the verses is of rather frequent occurrence in carols.

Obviously, a mere Christmas or Easter hymn is not, *ipso facto*, a carol, though such a hymn, if it is marked by the qualities of simplicity of thought and diction, of sincerity and of rhythmic brightness, may be allowed the name.

All Christian nations, Western and Eastern, have carols, some of them evidently of pagan origin (like Christmas holly and candles and cake) and taken over and adapted in the early days of Christianity, as the Church took over the pagan seasons and, under other names and with new associations, put them into its calendar.

The nature of the carol varies: it may be dramatic, narrative, or lyrical.

The Christmas carols of France are called Noëls (Noël = Christmas), and, through the Norman, the word has survived in Britain as 'Nowell', sometimes found as the refrain of a carol. Those of Germany are called 'Weihnachtslieder', i.e. Christmas Eve Songs.

Many of the Christmas carols of the various nations owe their origin to the practice (said to have been initiated by St. Francis of Assisi; *c.* 1182–1226), of installing a 'crib' in church during the Christmas season, a group of figures in a stable, representing the Babe and His parents, the oxen and so forth, which is still to be seen in almost every Roman Catholic church and many Anglican churches. Singing around the crib was apparently common (probably dancing also in some places). There are no carols of this type and date remaining, but in later times the crib certainly served as an inspiration.

Others obviously survive from some Miracle Play or Mystery; the fifteenth century was the period when these primitive dramatic activities were at their height (see *Mysteries, Miracle Plays, and Moralities*), and that is the period of the earliest carols we possess—in English, at any rate.

The best source we have for the words of early carols is an old commonplace book found behind a bookcase about 1850 and now in the library at Balliol College, Oxford. In this book Richard Hill, grocer of London, recorded from about the year 1500 to 1536 all manner of things that he did not wish to forget—tables of weights, dates of fairs, medical prescriptions, cookery recipes, dates of his children's births, notes on the breaking of horses and the brewing of beer, and the like, with riddles, puzzles, poems in English, French, and Latin, and a number of carols. Many other carols have been kept alive by the broadsheets, or broadsides (sheets of paper, crudely printed on one side with some ballad or the like, and hawked through the country—compare Shakespeare's Autolycus). Still others have been handed down orally for generations and at last recorded by some folk-song collector.

The pastoral element enters into some, perhaps especially in France, and it may be re-called that the association of shepherd life with the event of Christmas was long kept up in certain places, as in Naples, where shepherds from the hills descended at Christmas and played in the streets, before the various figures of the Virgin and Child, bagpipe music of the type that Handel has preserved in his 'Pastoral Symphony' in *Messiah*—his original score admitting the source of this tune (p. 65, pl. **9. 5**).

The song of the angels comes into many carols in one way or another, for the first Christmas carol was sung from the sky and its inspiring words (though not, alas! its tune) have been preserved.

Other Christmas carols enshrine pleasant superstitions and quaintly charming ideas that are anything but Biblical.

The oldest printed Christmas carols are those in the collection of Wynkyn de Worde (Caxton's apprentice and successor), published in 1521. One of these is the *Boar's Head Carol*, still sung as the traditional dish is carried in on Christmas Day at Queen's College, Oxford. This is but one aristocratic member of a large group of carols that are associated with good cheer as an element in Christmas joy.

As the English and Scottish Puritans of the seventeenth century disapproved of keeping religious feasts they, of course, discouraged Christmas celebrations of every kind, including carols. At the Restoration in 1660 the Christmas celebrations were revived in England, but in Presbyterian Scotland they have never fully come back, the Scottish New Year's Day corresponding to the English Christmas Day as a day of feasting and merriment. The strongest attachment to domestic Christmas celebrations exists in Teutonic countries, and the German Christmas Eve festivities tend to keep up carol singing (p. 141, pl. **27. 1**).

During the later nineteenth century the singing of carols in England, which had long become a matter of door-to-door visitation, often of a very picturesque nature (see Thomas Hardy's *Under the Greenwood Tree*), tended to be degraded into a petty beggary: in every district little children in groups paraded from door-step to door-step, from the end of November onwards, building up a Christmas fund by the extortion of what may very fairly be called 'hush money'.

At the same period what may be described as the 'Ancient and Modern' movement (see *Hymns and Hymn Tunes* 6) brought into popularity a poorish type of newly composed music of very Victorian idiom, and also somewhat weakly harmonized versions of the old carol tunes: these were the musical counterpart of the imitative Gothic church architecture of the period.

Towards the beginning of the twentieth century a movement for better Christmas music made itself felt, and especially one for the revival of the genuine traditional carols. This movement, which had a natural connexion with that for the collection and presentation of folk song and folk dance (see *Folk Song*; *Dance* 5), has been stimulated by the publication of several large and carefully edited collections.

The Pilgrim Fathers, holding the Puritan view as to observance of the Church's seasons, naturally took no carols to America, and carol singing there is a comparatively modern activity. Sometimes it is carried out on a large scale, on the lines of community singing. In *We Three Kings of Orient are* (written and composed by the Revd. Dr. J. H. Hopkins, of Williamsport, Pa., about 1857) the New World made a contribution to the Old of a modern carol in the true carol tradition.

CAROSO, FABRITIO. See *Dance* 10.

CARPENTER, JOHN ALDEN (p. 1057, pl. **172.** 2). Born at Park Ridge, Illinois, in 1876 and died in Chicago in 1951, aged seventy-five. He inherited affluence, with family traditions and duties which compelled him to give much of his time in early years to business. His teacher of theory was John Knowles Paine. He profited by contact with Sir Edward Elgar in 1906. Later he pursued his work with Bernhard Ziehn in Chicago.

He was a composer of exceptional sincerity and technical brilliancy, and though possessed of eclecticism, nevertheless expressed in ways suggestive of the American tempo and environment certain phases of the life of his place and time.

Amongst his most important works are the orchestral *Adventures in a Perambulator* (1915), a symphony, and a concertino for piano and orchestra, an orchestral work, *Sea Drift* (1935), two ballets (*The Birthday of the Infanta* and *Skyscrapers*, 1926), some fine songs, piano pieces, a string quartet, and a jazz pantomime, *Krazy Kat* (see *Jazz* 5).

See reference under *Ballet* 6.

CARR, BENJAMIN (1769–1831). See *Opera* 21 b; *Publishing* 9; *Yankee Doodle*.

CARRÉE (Fr.). 'Square.' The breve (Table 3).

CARRILLO, JULIAN. Born at San Luis Potosí, Mexico, in 1875 and died in Mexico City in 1965, aged ninety. He studied at the Mexican National Conservatory and in 1899 won a scholarship to Leipzig. He transcribed Bach fugues and Beethoven sonatas in quarter-tones. As a violinist he played in the Leipzig Gewandhaus Orchestra under Nikisch, and his first symphony and other works were produced by the orchestra of the Leipzig Conservatory. He held a number of important positions in Mexico and then settled in New York. For the greater part of his life he was engaged in formulating and propagating a system of microtonal composition (see *Microtones*) which divides the octave into ninety-six parts; his works written on this system have had some performance, and some were recorded under his direction. His compositions include symphonies, operas, masses, chamber music, etc., and he was author of books on harmony, counterpoint, fugue, instrumentation, etc.

CARROLL, WALTER (1869–1955). He was occupied in church music and in teaching at the University of Manchester and the Royal Manchester College of Music, but his greatest contribution was as Musical Adviser to the Education Committee of his city, in which capacity he did pioneer work in remodelling the system and methods of musical instruction in elementary and secondary schools and in organizing children's concerts (retired 1934). His pianoforte compositions for children have had a very great success.

CARSE, ADAM (VON AHN). Born at Newcastle-on-Tyne in 1878 and died at Great Missenden, Bucks., in 1958, aged eighty. He was musically educated at the Royal Academy of Music. From 1909 to 1922 he was on the staff of Winchester College and later on that of the Royal Academy of Music. He had a good deal of music of various types performed and published and was known as an authority and author on the history of instruments and the orchestra, etc., and as a disinterrer and editor of long-neglected musical classics (see *Symphony* 8, under 'Schwindl').

See also *Jullien*.

CARTAN, JEAN. Born at Nancy in 1906 and died in Paris in 1932, aged twenty-six. He studied at the Paris Conservatory under Widor and Dukas. He then appeared as a composer, with chamber works, piano music, songs, orchestral works, and a cantata, *Pater Noster*. In the six years of active composition that were accorded him he showed promise such as caused his early death to be deeply regretted.

CARTE, R. D'OYLY (Impresario, 1844–1901). See p. 705, pl. **118.** 7.

CARTER, ELLIOTT COOK. Born in New York in 1908. He studied at Harvard under E. B. Hill and Walter Piston and in Paris under Nadia Boulanger. He has taught at Peabody Conservatory (1947), Columbia University (1948), and Yale University (1960). His compositions are few and difficult to play and show little concern with fashionable technical fads. He has been awarded two Guggenheim fellowships; his second quartet won the Pulitzer Prize in 1960. He has written ballets, orchestral music, choral pieces, and a concerto for piano and harpsichord.

CARTIER, J. B. (1765–1841). French violinist. See *Misattributed Compositions*.

CARUSO, ENRICO. Born at Naples in 1873 and died there in 1921, aged forty-eight. The most famous tenor of his period. See *Gramophone* 6; *Cinematograph*.

CARVER, ROBERT (16th cent.). See *Scotland* 5.

CASADESUS, MARIUS R. M. (born 1892). See a reference under *Misattributed Compositions*, s.v. 'Handel's Viola Concerto' and 'Mozart's "Adelaide Concerto"'.

CASALS, PAU—formerly Pablo, Pau being later adopted as the Catalan form (p. 1088, pl. **179.** 6). Born at Vendrell, in Catalonia, in

1876 and died at Rio Piedras, Puerto Rico, in 1973. He was a very highly honoured violoncello virtuoso, a chamber music player (with the pianist Cortot and the violinist Thibaud), conductor (1920–36) of the Barcelona orchestra he himself founded, and a composer of symphonic, choral, and chamber music.

From 1940 his lack of sympathy for the Spanish Government led him to make his home in Prades, near the Spanish border, where from 1950 he organized and directed a remarkable annual festival, to which a large audience was drawn, from both sides of the Atlantic. In 1956 he moved to San Juan, Puerto Rico. His large-scale oratorio *El Pessebre* ('The Manger') was widely heard in the 1960s.

See references under *Festival* 2; *Germany* 9; *Garreta*.

CASAVANT, the brothers. They started the famous Quebec firm of organ builders in the latter part of the nineteenth century. See *Organ* 9 (end).

CASELLA.

(1) PIETRO. Died before 1300. See *Madrigal* 1.

(2) ALFREDO (p. 525, pl. **96.** 4). Born at Turin in 1883 and died in Rome in 1947, aged sixty-three. He studied at the Paris Conservatory under Fauré, and then enjoyed much success as pianist and conductor. In his compositions he may be classed as an anti-romantic (see *Romantic*), and he wished to see Italy forsake the type of music which shows a 'predominance of vocal melodramatic melody' and regain that sense of 'true music' which she had long lost.

See references under *Italy* 7; *Composition* 9; *Concerto* 6 c (1883–1947); *Mechanical* 13; *Opera* 24 f (1937); *Arrangement*; *Berners*.

CASSA (It.). 'Box', hence 'drum' (but applied only to the larger kinds. See below).

CASSA GRANDE, or **GRAN CASSA.** Bass drum. See *Percussion Family* 3 k, 4 b, 5 k. (The word 'Cassa', used alone, generally means this one.)

CASSANEA. See *Mondonville*.

CASSA RULLANTE ('rullante' = 'rolling'). Tenor drum. See *Percussion Family*, 3 j, 4 b, 5 j.

CASSATION, CASSAZIONE. See *Suite* 7.

CASSON (organ builder). See *Organ* 6, 8 (note).

CASTAGNETTE (It.), **CASTAGNETTES** (Fr.). Castanets. See *Percussion Family* 3 q, 4 c, 5 q.

CASTALDI. See reference under *Andrico*.

CASTANETS. See *Percussion Family* 3 q, 4 c, 5 q.

CASTEL. See *Colour and Music* 6.

CASTELIONE. See *Toccata*.

CASTELNUOVO - TEDESCO, MARIO (p. 525, pl. **96.** 5). Born at Florence in 1895 and died in Hollywood, Cal., in 1968, aged seventy-two. A pupil of Pizzetti, he wrote songs, choral music, piano pieces, and five operas, and attained reputation for a delicate refinement. A special interest of his is shown in his having written overtures to seven plays of

Shakespeare and also settings of all the Shakespeare songs. In 1939 he went to the United States.

See *Harpsichord* 9; *Oratorio* 7 (1947); *Concerto* 6 c (1895).

CASTILLANE. A dance of the province of Castile in Spain.

CASTILLON, ALEXIS DE (Vicomte de Saint-Victor). Born at Chartres in 1838 and died in Paris in 1873, aged thirty-four. At first a soldier (a cadet at St. Cyr), he later turned to music, working under Franck. He was one of the band of ardent spirits who immediately after the Franco-German War founded the Société Nationale de Musique, and himself composed chamber music (especially) and orchestral music, songs, etc., of fine quality. His early death was much deplored.

CASTLE, V. and I. See *One-step*.

CASTLE CONCERTS (Castle Society). See *Concert* 6.

CASTLE HYDE. See *Last Rose of Summer*.

CASTRATO. See *Singing* 3; *Voice* 5; *Opera* 3.

CASTRO, THE BROTHERS. Argentinian composers:

(1) JOSÉ MARIA. Born in Avelleneda in 1892 and died in Buenos Aires in 1964, aged seventy-two. He was a cellist, conductor, and composer of works for orchestra, for piano, etc.

(2) JUAN JOSÉ. Born in Buenos Aires in 1895 and died there in 1968, aged seventy-three. Composer and conductor. He studied in Paris with d'Indy and composed ballets, symphonies, chamber music, etc.

(3) WASHINGTON. Born in Buenos Aires in 1909. He is a cellist and composer, partly trained in Paris. His works are largely of the nature of chamber music.

CASWALL, EDWARD (1814–78). See *Hymns and Hymn Tunes* 6 (end of section); *Veni Sancte Spiritus*; *Pange Lingua*.

CATALÁN (Sp.), **CATALANE** (Fr.). A Spanish dance type deriving from Catalonia.

CATALANI, ALFREDO. Born at Lucca in 1854 and died at Milan in 1893, aged thirty-nine. His operas, especially *La Wally*, have had popularity.

CATALANI, ANGELICA (1780–1845). Soprano. See *Chopin*.

CATCH (p. 145, pl. 30). This is a variety of the distinctively English musical form, the *Round* (q.v.), and everything that is found under that head applies here also with (as the term is today generally used) one addition—that the words and their treatment are so contrived as to introduce some point of humour (often a pun). As examples may be mentioned, 'Ah, how, Sophia, can you leave your lover?' of J. W. Callcott (q.v.), which, in singing, suggests 'Our house afire', the later words 'Go fetch the Indian's borrowed plume, yet richer far than that you bloom', suggesting 'Go fetch the engines'. Another well-known sample by the same composer makes mirth out of the appearance in the same year (1776) of both Hawkins's and Burney's Histories of Music, the words 'Have you Sir John Hawkins's History? Some folks think it's quite a mystery', being followed by 'Burney's history I like best', with the effect that as the voices are singing together one comes in with 'Sir John Hawkins' and another immediately retorts 'burn 'is history'.

These are discreet late specimens of the catch. Many (especially in the later Stuart times, such as some of those of Purcell) were less respectable; as the popular late eighteenth-century William Jackson of Exeter remarks: 'The reign of Charles II carried every sort of vulgar debauchery to its height, the proper aera for the birth of such pieces as, when quartered, have ever three parts obscenity and one part music. . . . I will confess there are catches upon other subjects (drunkenness is a favourite one) . . . but these are not sufficient to contradict a general rule.' It has been said that the only catches of the Restoration period that can be sung without change of words at the present day are Aldrich's *Christ Church Bells*, and *Smoking Catch*—which is perhaps a slight exaggeration.

It should be noted that, though in general the word 'catch' is now restricted to rounds with some verbal humorous device, at an earlier period it was applied to *any* round or short choral composition of that character. The idea that the word 'catch' refers to the nature or treatment of the words is, then, erroneous: it alludes to the necessity for each singer to 'catch up' his part when the moment arrives, or is, perhaps, derived from the Italian *caccia* (q.v.). It is probably from the false etymology referred to that has come about the present-day restriction of the term to the one particular type of round.

For Catch Clubs see *Clubs for Music-Making*.

CATHEDRAL MUSIC AND MUSICIANS IN BRITAIN

(For illustrations see pp. 160, 161, pls. 31, 32; 164, 165, 33, 34; 144, 29. 2)

1. The Place of the Cathedral in British Musical Life. The present article is concerned with cathedral music in Britain from the date when this became a distinctively British thing, i.e. from the Reformation.

For the music of a country to flourish and develop, a number of centres of activity are necessary. Where Germany, divided into many separate states (in the seventeenth century about 300), found these centres in the multitude of great or petty courts, many of them with their full equipment for opera, instrumental music, and church music, England, apart from the Chapel Royal (q.v.), had only the monasteries and cathedrals, and the monasteries ceased to exist in the reign of Henry VIII, while the Chapel Royal declined in importance after the death of his daughter, Elizabeth. Thus Britain's development became very one-sided. To 'get on' in music meant generally to secure a post as cathedral organist. In the days before professional schools of music (i.e. up to the nineteenth century) it was the cathedrals that gave a clever youth his musical training—first through a choristership and then through apprenticeship (or 'articles') to the organist. It was doubtless partly this one-sided (if practical) training, and this limited environment, that for long made British musicianship so insular. The average British musician, even the good one, was not much in touch with the developments of orchestral music or opera; he lived in an organ loft and a choir room. So far as organ music was concerned his repertory was limited by the fact that his organ (until about the beginning of the nineteenth century) had no pedals, had a compass different from that of most continental organs, and was, moreover, not tuned to equal temperament (see *Temperament*). For want of pedals he could not play Bach, if he had known of him, nor could he play any of the organ music of Bach's countrymen. As for the choral music, after the Reformation that was devised to meet the needs of a special liturgy (see *Common Prayer*) in use in no other country in Europe, so that, practically speaking, the works of only native composers were available.

From the Reformation onwards (say, in round figures, from 1530 to 1830), then, British music had a very isolated existence, and, to understand musical conditions in Britain during that period, one thing we must do is to turn our backs upon the rest of Europe and pry into the life of the small bodies of people engaged in making music in the twenty-seven cathedrals of England, Wales, and Ireland, that existed from the date of Henry VIII's suppression of the monasteries onwards.

2. Old and New Foundations. What we know as the cathedrals of the 'Old Foundation' are Bangor, Chichester, Exeter, Hereford, Lichfield, Lincoln, Llandaff, St. Asaph, St. David's, St. Paul's (London), Salisbury, Wells, and York (opposite, pl. 31)—thirteen in all. These were already cathedrals, and cathedrals only, at the suppression of the monasteries under Henry VIII in 1536–9.

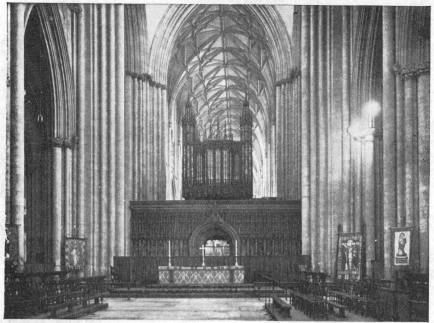

1. YORK MINSTER. The Nave, with the Organ Loft

3. BANGOR CATHEDRAL
in the early 19th century. See p. 162

4. A CATHEDRAL PRACTICE-
ROOM IN THE 18TH CENTURY
(Contemporary caricature)

2. YORK MINSTER. West Front

See also the three plates immediately following

PLATE 32   THE ENGLISH CATHEDRAL AND ITS MUSIC, II

1. BARNARD'S 'SELECTED CHURCH MUSIC', 1641. See *Cathedral Music* 4

2. LOWE'S 'DIRECTIONS', 1661. See *Cathedral Music* 6

3. CLIFFORD'S 'DIVINE SERVICES AND ANTHEMS', 1664. See *Cathedral Music* 6

4. MARIA HACKETT, 1783–1874. See *Cathedral Music* 7, 8

ANTHEM XXXII.
Hosanna to the Son of David, &c.
These words are taken out of the 9th verse of the 21 Chapter of the Gospel written by S. *Matthew.*

HOsanna to the Son of David, Blessed be he that cometh in the name of the Lord. ii Blessed be the King that cometh in the name of the Lord. ii Peace in heaven and glory in the highest places, ii Hosanna in the highest heavens. ii
Orlando Gibbons.

5. S. S. WESLEY

6. He replies to a request for the music lists of his Cathedral

See also plates at pages 160 and 164–5

What are known as the 'New Foundation, cathedrals are (*a*) Canterbury, Carlisle, Christ Church at Dublin (the position of St. Patrick's Cathedral in the same city is peculiar and cannot be gone into here), Durham, Ely, Norwich, Rochester, Winchester, and Worcester, and (*b*) Bristol, Chester, Gloucester, Oxford, and Peterborough—fourteen in all. Of these, those marked (*a*) had previously been both monasteries and cathedrals and now became merely the latter, whilst those marked (*b*) became cathedrals for the first time, new sees being set up. (Over 500 monasteries and nunneries, all more or less centres of musical activity, went completely out of existence during these three years 1536–9. Thousands of volumes of music were destroyed or shipped abroad as parchment for bookbinding, etc. In fact, a great musical loss was sustained.)

Distinction between Old and New Foundations is frequently made in discussions on cathedral music, and it has its point, for the musicians on the staffs are in somewhat different positions in the one and in the other. In the Old Foundation cathedrals the precentor (q.v.) is a 'dignitary' (as in the cathedrals of the Continent); generally he ranks next to the Dean. In cathedrals of the New Foundation the precentor is usually merely a minor canon (q.v.). The Old Foundation cathedrals, whose statutes all dated from a time when organs were primitive and organists had little importance, barely recognized the organist as a special official, but in drafting the statutes of the New Foundation cathedrals he was generally taken into account (the exceptions are Winchester and Ely). In four or five cathedrals at the present time the organist is *officially* one of the vicars choral (see *Vicar Choral*). In the Old Foundation cathedrals the office of Master of the Choristers was often a separate one; in those of the New Foundation this was rare.

The office of **Succentor** exists in the cathedrals of the Old Foundation. The cleric holding this office serves as deputy to the precentor.

In addition to the cathedrals, certain other churches, similarly equipped, functioned as centres of musical activity, such as Westminster Abbey, St. George's Chapel in Windsor Castle, and the larger colleges of Oxford and Cambridge Universities. It can be taken that what follows applies to them, as to the cathedrals. The Chapel Royal is discussed, under its own name, elsewhere in this volume.

A large number of new cathedrals have come into existence as the result of the nineteenth- and twentieth-century desire for more efficient organization; they are usually old parish churches converted to diocesan use, but some are new buildings (Truro, Liverpool). They have none of them been sufficiently lavishly financed to undertake the traditional full daily cathedral programme. There are also a certain number of cathedrals of the Anglican communion in Ireland, in addition to the two mentioned above, and in Scotland, in which latter, however, the old buildings (e.g. Glasgow Cathedral) were deprived of cathedral status on the completion of the Reformation under Knox, and, where still in existence, are in use as Presbyterian churches.

For brief references to the Scottish and Irish cathedrals see *Scotland* 5, 8; *Ireland* 3.

3. Reformation Objections to Cathedral Music. At the time of the Reformation, and for a century afterwards, there were two currents of religious thought contending for the control of the service of the Church. One school would much reduce or even abolish choirs and organs and the other would retain them. In 1552 the organ in St. Paul's Cathedral was silenced, but the accession of the Roman Catholic Queen Mary the following year set it sounding again. In Queen Elizabeth's reign (1558–1603) there were strong efforts to abolish organs and 'curious' singing, and on one occasion these were saved in Convocation by a majority of only one. From Cranmer's time composers were urged to write syllabically (that is a note to a syllable) and with plain chordal progressions rather than counterpoint. These limitations, though prompted by the good motive of enabling the congregation to hear the words, tended somewhat to restrict the interest of the music, and have led to the rather marked differentiation of what we call the 'Anglican style' from the style of Church music in pre-Reformation days and in other countries.

4. The Early Stuart Period. The Tudor monarchs were musical. Henry VIII (q.v.), for instance, played various instruments and composed, and Elizabeth was also a performer and is said to have done a little composition. Under the Tudors, then, cathedral music was fostered. Under the early Stuarts it somewhat declined. A contemporary anonymous memorial in the British Museum says that 'few prebendaries and canons which now are do think it other than only a tolerable convenient ornament for a Cathedral church to have', and speaks of their 'turning of singing men out of the Quire' so that the funds might be applied to the advantage of the clergy. This is a complaint that is heard henceforth, from time to time, down to the nineteenth century, and, alas! even the twentieth. Nevertheless, up to the beginning of the Civil War cathedral music flourished considerably and produced a body of composition of which any country might be proud (though admittedly the Chapel Royal must have the credit for much of this).

A very important collection of cathedral music was printed in 1641, that of Barnard, a minor canon of St. Paul's (opposite, pl. **32. 1.**) It was in ten separate books for the different voices, and no one absolutely complete set of the printed books exists, though at Christ Church, Oxford, there is a set now made up by manuscript additions. This collection is a 'source' for many fine compositions.

5. The Civil War and Commonwealth. In the same year, 1641, a House of Lords Committee advised 'That the Music used in cathedral and collegiate churches be framed with less curiosity', i.e. with less elaboration— the old cry. In that year, too, a Puritan mob tried to get into St. Paul's to pull down the organ.

The following year civil war broke out and the Puritan soldiery destroyed some cathedral organs and music books. In 1644 an Act was passed for the removal of 'superstitious monuments', and this included organs. A few organs remained, including those at York, St. Paul's, Durham, and Lincoln (and some of the Oxford and Cambridge colleges), but it is to be assumed that they were not used during services. The statement that orders were given for the destruction of music books is incorrect. However, church music during this period (i.e. until the Restoration in 1660) was in England, Wales, and Ireland reduced to the unaccompanied congregational singing of metrical psalms.

For a general treatment of the musical condition of the period see the article *Puritans and Music.*

6. The Restoration Period. When King and Church came to power again in 1660, a great era of organ building began. Three or four builders remained from pre-Commonwealth days and now began work again (Dallam, Thamar, Preston). Schmidt (henceforth 'Smith') came from Germany, and Harris returned from France. There was a dearth of singers, especially boys, whose line of music was for a little time, in some cathedrals, supplied by men singing falsetto or by wind instruments.

In order to re-establish the tradition, Edward Lowe (formerly organist of Christ Church Cathedral, Oxford) brought out his *Short Direction for the Performance of Cathedral Service* (1661; reprinted with additions 1664; see p. 161, pl. **32.** 2). The Revd. James Clifford's collection of anthem words as used at St. Paul's and other cathedrals (1663; reprinted 1664; see p. 161, pl. **32.** 3) shows about 400 anthems as in use—a considerable repertory to have reinstated in such a short time! It also gives the earliest Anglican chants ever printed: the use of such chants was long confined to the cathedrals (see *Anglican Chant*).

7. The Epoch of Neglect. Thence onward there has been no break in the continuity of cathedral services, but there have been periods of the grossest neglect on the part of those charged with their conduct. John Alcock (q.v.), organist of Lichfield Cathedral, grumbles (1771, in the preface to a collection of his anthems, etc.), 'All the time I was organist, which was upwards of ten years, there was not a book in the organ loft fit for use, but what I bought or wrote myself (for which I was never paid one halfpenny)', and goes on: 'It is not greatly to be wondered at that there are no more subscribers to these Anthems considering how much the Cathedral service is at present disregarded. . . . I have received letters from several organists which mention that their *Choir Music* was never of so low an ebb.'

Banks, organist of Rochester Cathedral, wrote: 'When I came from Durham to this Cathedral in 1790, only one Lay Clerk attended during each week. The daily service was chanted. Two services (Aldrich in G and Rogers in D) and seven Anthems had been in rotation on Sundays for twelve years.' (He wrote this in one of the manuscript music books provided for use in the organ loft.)

During the early part of the nineteenth century great abuses remained. The boy choristers were often very ill educated, and ill cared for. A wealthy and enthusiastic lady, Miss Maria Hackett, 'the choir-boys' friend', (p. 161, pl. **32.** 4), took up this subject, and once in three years visited every cathedral in the country to inquire and stimulate. Goss, later organist of St. Paul's, was as a boy a chorister at the Chapel Royal; he says, 'We had a writing master from half-past twelve to two on Wednesdays and Saturdays, if my memory does not deceive me, and no other instruction in reading, writing, and arithmetic and a little English Grammar than we could get out of the time' (this would be from 1811 to about 1815). Miss Hackett, about the same date, was pleading for an arrangement whereby the boys of St. Paul's should have at least an hour's general schooling per day. There were then eight boys; they received only £40 a year amongst them, with no board and lodging, and the service hours prevented their parents sending them to school.

There is a rather comical account of the installation of a Bishop at Llandaff Cathedral as late as 1850: 'On the opening of the door to the bishop's summons . . . the National Schoolmaster,[1] heading the procession, gave out a Psalm, which was sung by about a dozen of his scholars, a bass viol being the only instrument then in possession of the Cathedral. In this way the bishop was conducted to his throne.' (This bishop, however, later made it his business to reinstate the choral service after a silence of 170 years—an exceptional case, of course, doubtless due partly to lack of funds and partly to lack of any sufficient population immediately around the cathedral.)

Bangor Cathedral (p. 160, pl. **31.** 3), when De Quincey visited it in 1802, no longer possessed a choir, and this evidently not through any severe poverty of the diocese, since the stipend of the bishop was £6,000 per annum. The famous anthem of Samuel Sebastian Wesley (q.v.), *Blessed be the God and Father*, was originally written at the Dean of Hereford's request for performance in his cathedral on Easter Day 1833, when the choir was to consist of boys with no altos or tenors and only one bass—the dean's butler.[2]

[1] Master of the 'National School' i.e. a school of the National Society for Educating the Children of the Poor in the Principles of the Established Church. (This was a bit of that Education!)
[2] There are in existence three manuscript services for the same combination (two trebles and a bass), by Wesley's predecessor in the organistship of this cathedral, Clarke-Whitfeld (q.v.). The explanation is that the men of the choir, all minor canons, held livings

At this period the men in the choir of St. Paul's Cathedral, Westminster Abbey, and the Chapel Royal were practically the same body; they did their double or triple duty by means partly of employing deputies at a small fee and partly by leaving one service as soon as the anthem was over in order to hurry to another.

When Bridge went to be organist of Westminster Abbey in 1875 there was no such thing as a full rehearsal. The boys rehearsed daily, but the men did not consider rehearsal to be part of their duties. Herbert Oakeley (afterwards Professor of Music at Edinburgh University), when an undergraduate at Christ Church, Oxford, in 1850, begged the senior censor for permission to absent himself from the cathedral (which also serves as the equivalent of a college chapel) on Sunday afternoons 'when the noise is at its height'. The censor readily gave permission in the now historic phrase, 'Well, to a musical man the singing *must* be 'orrid'.

S. S. Wesley's agitation all through his varied cathedral life is well known (p. 161, pl. **32.** 5). He was successively organist of Hereford Cathedral (1832), Exeter Cathedral (1835), Leeds Parish Church, with a daily choral service (1842), Winchester Cathedral (1849), and Gloucester Cathedral (1865), and he said in a pamphlet (1849): 'Painful and dangerous is the position of a young musician who, after acquiring great knowledge of his art in the Metropolis, joins a country Cathedral. At first he can hardly believe that the mass of error and inferiority in which he has to participate is irremediable. . . . If he gives trouble in his attempts at improvement, he would be, by some Chapters, at once voted a person with whom they "cannot go on smoothly", and "a bore".' We can readily believe that some such expressions as these would have been used by the Revd. Charles Almeric Belli, Precentor of St. Paul's Cathedral for more than half a century in Victorian times; it is recorded of him that he so rarely put in an appearance at the cathedral that when he presented himself at the door on the occasion of the funeral of the Duke of Wellington the vergers did not know him and refused him admittance. This precentor, when Miss Hackett threatened legal proceedings, asserted that he had been given the position 'as a perfect sinecure'. Even the Dean, Miss Hackett had complained in 1813, was not averaging attendance in the cathedral one day per month (he was simultaneously bishop of a see three hundred miles away).

Right through the nineteenth century correspondence in the British musical press is found complaining of the parsimony of wealthy cathedral chapters in their dealings with those responsible for the musical parts of the service. As late as the end of the century we find many definite instances adduced of cathedrals where canons received £700–£1,000 per annum for three months' attendance at the two daily services, with one sermon per week during this period (still drawing their stipends from their own parishes and with the power to retain both positions indefinitely after they had grown too infirm to perform any duty), whilst choirmen, in attendance at the two services throughout the whole year, received £50–£80, with dismissal at three months' notice on a breakdown of health or a loss of voice (and no pension). 'In some instances', writes, in 1885, a precentor who has held office in three cathedrals, 'the stipend of one Canon is equal to the aggregate salaries of all the Lay Clerks, and it is frequently four or five times that of a Minor Canon or Organist, and this in opposition to the provision of the ancient statutes and of any modern sense of justice.' There is no doubt that at this period to hold office as a member of the musical staff of a cathedral must have called for an effort in spiritual gymnastics in order to retain one's own Christianity—and in the charity that suffereth all things and is kind, to believe in that of one's ecclesiastical superiors. Even in the twentieth century there must be a considerable strain on patience in some quarters. In 1931 attention was publicly called to three cathedrals of which the aggregate stipends of deans and canons amounted to £13,640 (at which, it was agreed, they were not greatly overpaid), whilst those of organists and lay-clerks (which must have meant at least twenty-four persons) amounted to £2,780. The average cathedral organist's salary, it was mentioned, had now risen to £250–£300, but usually without house or pension. Today the average salary is perhaps about £1,000, with house—not a great increase when the depreciated value of money is taken into account.

8. The Renascence of Cathedral Music. Partly, perhaps, as a result of Wesley's heroic battlings and those of Miss Hackett, the Revd. Mr. Whiston of Rochester, and others, and partly, certainly, as a result of the Oxford Movement, the conditions of cathedral music began greatly to improve after the middle of the nineteenth century. Narrow ideas gradually disappeared and a higher standard was expected by the clergy and attained by the musicians. There is one trifling matter that may be mentioned here as showing the interest of the clergy and public in cathedral music—the practice, very rarely followed on the Continent but universal in England, of the publication on the church doors and in the public press of the list of music to be performed day by day during the coming week. However, even during the present century these lists have not always given complete satisfaction. Stanford complained to the Church Congress at the beginning of the century that, having obtained the complete service lists of fifty-one cathedral and collegiate churches, he found their repertory to be very defective.

in the city and its neighbourhood. They attended a Sunday cathedral service at 8 a.m. and another in the evening, but at the time of the eleven o'clock morning service (the one which everywhere nowadays attracts the largest congregation) they were serving in their own parish churches.

'Purcell's "Evening Service" in G Minor, one of the very finest works we possess, appears only in eight lists; on the other hand, a modern service of wonderful vapidity, which shall be nameless, appears in thirty-four. Gibbons' magnificent anthem, "O Thou, the central orb", appears only in three; S. S. Wesley's finest work, "Let us lift up our hearts", in four; Walmisley's best anthem, "If the Lord Himself", in ten; while a vulgar modern anthem of foreign origin is given in thirty-one places. I have observed also the relative value given to foreign composers. Palestrina receives but forty performances of seventeen works, and is recognized only in eighteen cathedrals; Sebastian Bach, the greatest of all, and the most in sympathy with our tastes and traditions, received but ninety-nine performances in twenty-six cathedrals of his innumerable masterpieces. While, on the other hand, a modern foreign composer, alien to our style, and representing all that is most empty, showy, and superficial in religious music, gets two hundred and thirty-one performances of thirty-three anthems in no less than forty-four of our cathedrals.'

He put this down to 'the trammelled position of the man who is responsible for the performance of the music and who is, perhaps, in many cathedral bodies the only representative of thoroughly trained knowledge of the subject—the organist'. 'In most cases', he complained, 'the responsibility for the choice of the music is not centred in him, the expert, but either altogether in the hands of one of the clergy or divided between a precentor and the organist.'

Genuine difficulties came in the years following the 1914 War, when the funds available would in some places no longer suffice; in some cathedrals, instead of two choral services daily only one was given, and other severe economies were undertaken. Organists and singers, as already mentioned, were still (now almost unavoidably) underpaid, and efforts to do them greater justice were largely unavailing. In one respect little cause for complaint remains. The boy choristers are now well cared for; the Elementary Education Act of 1870 ensured their receiving a good training in the most foundational subjects, but improvement has been carried far beyond that, and boys at cathedral schools now share in the general educational system of the country.

Another innovation that must receive comment is the increasing and now great use of the cathedrals for performance of the finest large-scale music by amateur choirs, forming a sort of auxiliary to the smaller professional bodies. It may, then, be fairly claimed that the English cathedral is once again an influential centre of national musical activity.

In one respect the English cathedrals, taking them as a whole, undoubtedly lead Europe—they maintain a tradition for vocal performance unequalled elsewhere. This tradition is either more recent than is often thought, or it was for a time much weakened. The American musician Lowell Mason (q.v.), who visited many English cathedrals in the mid-nineteenth century, reports, on the whole, unfavourably of their choral standard, and is particularly severe on 'the terrible roughness of the boys' voices' (*Musical Letters from Abroad*, 1854). The chanting of the psalms at this period was, according to him, usually slovenly in the extreme. But this was the epoch of neglect discussed under 7 above, and it is possible that at an earlier period the standard was as high as it is at present. The musical activities of Anglican cathedrals outside the British Isles are necessarily usually on a relatively restricted scale. Daily musical services are rare. Melbourne has had such, however, since the cathedral was consecrated in 1890. Christchurch, New Zealand, had them for many years, but has now abandoned them.

9. Chronological List of Composers of Cathedral Music (all of whom receive notice in this *Companion* under their own names):

Tye (d. 1572); R. White (d. 1574); Farrant (d. 1580); Merbecke (d. about 1585); Tallis (d. 1585); W. Mundy (d. end of 16th century); Morley (d. 1603 or 1604); Bevin (d. earlier part of 17th century); W. White (17th century); Byrd (d. 1623); Weelkes (d. 1623); O. Gibbons (d. 1625); Philips (d. about 1628); Deering (d. 1630); Giles (d. 1633); Ravenscroft (d. 1633); Batten (d. 1637); Milton (d. 1647); M. Este (d. 1648); Tomkins (d. 1656); Hilton (d. 1657); H. Cooke (d. 1672); Humphrey (d. 1674); Locke (d. 1677); Wise (d. 1687); Purcell (d. 1695); Child (d. 1697); Rogers (d. 1698); Clarke (d. 1707); Blow (d. 1708); Croft (d. 1727); Hine (d. 1730); Creyghton (d. 1734); Weldon (d. 1736); Turner (d. 1740); Kelway (d. 1749); Greene (d. 1755); Kent (d. 1776); Boyce (d. 1779); Mornington (d. 1781); Nares (d. 1783); B. Cooke (d. 1793); Battishill (d. 1801); W. Jackson (d. 1803); Beckwith (d. 1809); Ebdon (d. 1811); Clarke-Whitfeld (d. 1836); S. Wesley (d. 1837); Attwood (d. 1838); Crotch (d. 1847); Walmisley (d. 1856); S. S. Wesley (d. 1876); Dykes (d. 1876); G. Smart (d. 1879); Goss (d. 1880); Turle (d. 1882); Ouseley (d. 1889); W. H. Monk (d. 1889); Elvey (d. 1893); Barnby (d. 1896); Tours (d. 1897); Garrett (d. 1897); Sullivan (d. 1900); E. G. Monk (d. 1900); Hopkins (d. 1901); Stainer (d. 1901); Rea (d. 1903); Oakeley (d. 1903); Reay (d. 1905); Martin (d. 1916); Lloyd (d. 1919); Stanford (d. 1924); Charles Wood (d. 1926); C. Macpherson (d. 1927); Davies (d. 1941); Bairstow (d. 1946); Harwood (d. 1948); Noble (d. 1953).

See also *Dictionaries* 6 c, 7.

10. Collections of Cathedral Music. Barnard's seventeenth-century collection of cathedral music has already been referred to (4). Two valuable publications of the later eighteenth century should be mentioned: Boyce's *Cathedral Music* came out 1760–78 (new editions, 1788, 1841, 1848, and 1849): it was the first collection of anthems and services to be printed in score instead of in separate part books, and its contents covered nearly 300 years of English cathedral composition. Arnold's collection followed, as a supplement to Boyce, in 1790 (republished 1847); so low was the musical interest of cathedral chapters and other church authorities at that time that the list of subscribers accounts for only 150 copies in the whole kingdom. The era of cheap music, of services and anthems printed in

1. TAVERNER (*c.* 1495–1545). Five out of the six part-books of his Mass *Gloria Tibi Trinitas* have decorative initials, varying in design but all including the same portrait, which is evidently that of the composer

2. TALLIS (*c.* 1505–85). The signature is from a volume from his library, now in the British Museum

3. PETER PHILIPS (1561–1628). From a contemporary picture of a royal funeral procession at Brussels in 1623

4. ORLANDO GIBBONS (1583–1625)

5. CROFT (1678–1727)

6. BLOW (1649–1708)

8. GREENE (*c.* 1695–1755)

7. WELDON (1676–1736)

See also plates at pages 160–1 and 165

PLATE 34   THE ENGLISH CATHEDRAL AND ITS MUSIC, IV

1. BOYCE
(1710–79)

2. JONATHAN BATTISHILL
(1738–1801)

3. BENJAMIN COOKE
(1734–93)

4. ATTWOOD
(1765–1838)

5. SIR JOHN GOSS
(1800–80)

6. TURLE
(1802–82)

7. T. A. WALMISLEY
(1814-56)

8. SIR GEORGE ELVEY
(1816–93)

9. SIR FREDERICK OUSELEY
(1825–89)

See also plates at pages 160–1 and 164

score, in handy size, and sold for a few pence, dates from the middle of the nineteenth century and is much associated with the name 'Novello' (see *Publishing of Music* 7).

CATHEDRAL PSALTER. See *Anglican Chant and Chanting* 6.

CATHERINE DE' MEDICI (1519–89). See *Ballet* 2.

CATOIRE (Katuar, etc.**), GEORGE.** Born and died in Moscow (1861–1926). Whilst studying mathematics at the University of Berlin he studied music also. On returning, he continued his study under Liadof in St. Petersburg. He won the approval of Tchaikovsky and gradually his compositions spread abroad. They include orchestral pieces, chamber music, pianoforte music, and songs.

He was partly of French descent, and, apparently, of cosmopolitan sympathies; his music, like that of some others of the Moscow group, hardly ranks amongst that of the Russian nationalists.

CAT'S FUGUE (D. Scarlatti); **CAT'S VALSE** (Chopin). See *Nicknamed Compositions* 8, 17.

CATURLA, ALEJANDRO GARCÍA. Born in Remedios, Cuba, in 1906, and there murdered in 1940. He studied in Havana and Paris. Some of his works show his interest in Afro-Cuban folk-music.

CAT VALSE. See *Nicknamed Compositions* 8.

CAUDELLA, EDWARD. See *Rumania.*

CAULDRON OF ANWYN. See *Holbrooke.*

CAURROY, FRANÇOIS EUSTACHE DU. Born near Beauvais in 1549 and died in Paris in 1609, aged sixty. He was canon of the Sainte Chapelle in Paris, prior of a monastery sixty miles away, and 'Superintendent of the King's Music' to Henri IV of France. He enjoyed high fame as a composer of both choral and instrumental music, some of which has been reprinted of recent years.

CAUS, SALOMON DE. See *Mechanical Reproduction* 4 (end).

CAUSTUN (or Causton or **Cawston**), THOMAS. Died in London in 1569. He was a gentleman of the Chapel Royal under Mary and Elizabeth, who composed psalm tunes, services, and anthems, some of which are still sung.

CAVAILLÉ-COL, ARISTIDE (1811–99). Parisian organ builder, greatest member of a family that had practised the craft from the early eighteenth century. See *Organ* 8 (end).

CAVALIERI, EMILIO DI. Born about 1550 and died in Rome in 1602. He lived most of his life at Florence in the service of the Medici Court, and there he was a member of the little group who towards the end of his life (or possibly just after its end) brought into existence the opera (see *Opera* 1). He himself is credited with the composition of several musical dramas and of the first oratorio (see

Batten's Organ Book (see *Batten*), a quarto of nearly five hundred pages, has preserved for us, in his handwriting, in organ score, a quantity of important church music.

Oratorio 2); he was also one of the earliest composers to use figured bass (q.v.)

CAVALLERIA RUSTICANA, i.e. RUSTIC CHIVALRY (Mascagni). Produced in Rome, 1890. Libretto by Targioni-Tozzetti and Menasci, after the story by Giovanni Verga, the Sicilian novelist, author of exciting tales of a 'realist' type.

SCENE: *Before the Church, in a Village Square in Sicily, on Easter Day*

Turiddu (*Tenor*), a young soldier, is heard, behind the curtain, singing the praises of Lola. When the curtain rises, **Santuzza** (*Soprano*), a girl of the village, is asking Lucia (*Contralto*), Turiddu's mother, where her son is. Santuzza suspects that the soldier is losing his love for her, and giving it again to Lola (who, before her marriage to Alfio, the wagoner, had been attracted by Turiddu).

Alfio (*Baritone*) comes on. He is not yet worried about his wife's old flame.

Santuzza wants a reckoning with Turiddu. He plays on her fear for his life by hinting that, if Alfio knew of his visits to Lola, the wagoner might kill him.

After the famous 'Intermezzo', played whilst the villagers are in church, the climax comes quickly. Turiddu and **Lola** (*Mezzo-Soprano*) drink together. Alfio, whom Santuzza has persuaded of Turiddu's treachery, challenges the soldier to fight. Swearing that Lola was not to blame, he accepts. They go off, and the fight is heard outside. Santuzza rushes in and falls fainting, amid cries of 'Turiddu is killed!'

CAVALLI, PIETRO FRANCESCO. Born at Crema, in Lombardy, in 1602, and died at Venice in 1676, aged nearly seventy-four. A composer who, like Carissimi and Cesti, belongs to the second generation of the 'new music' or 'monodic' style (see *Opera* 1, 2). He wrote forty-two operas, church music, etc.

See references under *Opera* 11 a, b; *Requiem*; *Lully.*

CAVATINA. (1) Practically the same as arietta (q.v.), i.e. a short aria in only one section instead of the aria's three. Mozart uses the term. Rossini's 'Una voce poco fa' in *The Barber of Seville* is so entitled. In the eighteenth-century opera a cavatina may often be found interpolated as a relief in a long stretch of 'recitativo stromentato', i.e. orchestrally accompanied recitative (see *Recitative*).

(2) A piece of instrumental music, generally slowish and shortish (e.g. in Beethoven's String Quartet in B flat, op. 130, the 'adagio molto espressivo' is so described, and a certain highly popular sentimental piece for violin and piano is known everywhere as 'Raff's Celebrated Cavatina').

CAVENDISH, MICHAEL. Born about 1565 and died in 1628, aged about sixty-three. He was a composer of ayres with lute accompaniment, and of madrigals.

CAVOS. See *Opera* 17 b.

CAWSTON. See *Caustun*.

CAXTON, WILLIAM (c. 1422-91). See *Printing* 1.

CAZALIS, HENRI (1840-1909), French poet and general man of letters. See reference under *Danse Macabre*.

CB. Short for *Contrabassi*, i.e. double basses.

C.B.E. See *Knighthood and other Honours*.

CC, CCC, etc. See *Pitch* 7 f.

C CLEF. See Table 4.

CEBELL. An English type of gavotte (q.v.), rather quicker than the ordinary. Purcell and one or two other English composers of his period occasionally adopt the type as a basis for harpsichord compositions, and the violin and lute composers of the time use it also. Wide range (suggestive of a lute origin), in the way of contrasting high passages and low, seems to have been a feature. The best-known example is the one in Purcell's harpsichord works, and this shows that feature. So does the one for lute (also arranged for two lutes) in Mace's *Musick's Monument* (1676), which he wrote in honour of his wife—called *My Mistress*, and 'most of my scholars since call it Mrs. Mace to this day'. The latter is, says its composer, 'lively, ayrey, neat, curious and sweet', and 'uniform, comely, substantial, grave and lovely', and 'spruce, amiable, pleasant, obliging and innocent'—all, he says, 'like my mistress'. From this it will be gathered that Master Mace was a lucky dog, and that the absence of the cebell in the works of the composers of the two and a half centuries that have since passed is perhaps due to lack of matrimonial inspiration.

CECCHETTI. See *Ballet* 9.

CECILIA, SAINT. The patron saint of music. She was martyred in Sicily about the year 176, under Marcus Aurelius (230 as the year and Rome as the place were long quoted but were later disproved by the researches of the great authority on early Christian archaeology, de Rossi). The Church of St. Cecilia, Rome (i.e. St. Cecilia in Trastevere, for there are several churches in Rome with this dedication), was built in the fourth century, ostensibly over the house in which she lived and was put to death. Her remains were placed in it in the ninth century. The present church largely dates from 1599. The remains were examined at the time of the rebuilding and the famous statue by Stefano Maderno, under the high altar (p. 33, pl. 4. 7), shows the body lying on its side in the curious position in which it was then found. Maderno's inscription says: 'Behold the body of the most holy virgin, Cecilia, whom I myself saw lying uncorrupt in her tomb. I have in this marble expressed for thee

the same saint in the very same posture and body.'

The connexion of St. Cecilia with music is obscure. There are vague legends of her attracting an angel to earth by her singing, and of her singing under martyrdom and so forth, but they are not found before the twelfth century. As late as the fourteenth century we find Chaucer, in his Second Nun's Tale, giving a fairly full account of the saint, yet with no reference to music (beyond a passing allusion to organs playing at her wedding, and without any personal application of this detail). His account is almost entirely drawn from the thirteenth-century 'Golden Legend', which also does not mention the musical attributes of the saint.

It seems that traditions of Cecilia as patron saint of music go back no further than the fifteenth century, and that even at the end of the sixteenth century there were some of her ardent devotees who knew nothing of her musicianship, for in 1594 a long poem published at Florence in her honour does not mention it, though this is strange, as by this time she was sometimes appearing in Italian painting, with harp, organ, and other musical instruments. It is probably the painters who are responsible for the dissemination of the belief that St. Cecilia was a musician, and their introduction of musical instruments into their pictures of her begins about the opening of the fifteenth century. She even came to be spoken of as the inventor of the organ. For a suggestion that the association of music with St. Cecilia arose out of a misunderstanding of the wording of an antiphon for her day see Dom Gregory Murray's paper in *Music and Liturgy*, Jan. 1938.

The first musical festival in honour of St. Cecilia of which any record has been found is one at Évreux, in Normandy, about 1570. It was called a 'Puy de Musique' (see *Minstrels* 6; *Competitions* 1). Part of the celebration took the shape of a competition in composition, and amongst those who won prizes in 1575 and 1583 was Orlandus Lassus.

The date when British celebrations of St. Cecilia's Day (22 November) began is not known. The first of which definite record exists was in London in 1683, but they had been annual for some time before. From that year the programme was a church service followed by an entertainment of which an important part was an ode, written and composed for the occasion. Purcell's *Te Deum* and *Jubilate* in D were written for the celebration of 1694, and he composed two odes (for the one of 1683 and for that of nine years later, in 1692). Dryden was the poet in 1687 and 1697.

After being kept up pretty regularly for twenty years, these London celebrations became merely occasional until 1905, when a revival took place under the auspices of the ancient Musicians' Company. The services were held in St. Paul's Cathedral, to which a stained glass window in honour of this doubtfully musical saint was in 1907 presented. The Club of the Company brought about performances of much of the music originally composed in the saint's honour, including the motet by Orlandus Lassus with which he won the prize above mentioned. The Musicians' Benevolent Fund now carries on these celebrations.

In the late seventeenth and the eighteenth centuries the musicians of several English provincial cities (Wells, Oxford, Salisbury, Winchester, Devizes—all these in the west, curiously) had celebrations of St. Cecilia's Day. Dublin also celebrated the day (from 1726). So did Edinburgh, from 1695, when what appears to be the first public concert that city had known took place, with an orchestra of thirty (nineteen gentlemen of rank and fashion, with eleven professionals); they played works by Corelli, Torelli, and Bassani, with an opening piece called *Clerk's Overture*.

Musical celebrations have also taken place annually, for longer or shorter periods, in many cities of the continent of Europe, for example, in France, Spain, and Germany. In Brazil, Rio de Janeiro has had annual celebrations from 1919 or before.

A history of celebrations, British and continental, was published by W. H. Husk in 1857.

Many musical societies, from the early sixteenth century onwards, have taken the name of music's patron saint. Palestrina founded one in Rome: in 1847 Pius IX turned this into an academy for the furtherance of church music, and it still exists and is of great importance. In 1867 a 'Cecilia Society for German-speaking Countries' was founded; three years later it received papal patronage (see *Cecilian Movement*).

Charleston, South Carolina, had a St. Cecilia Society for a century and a half (1762–1912 ; see *Concert* 15). New York had one in 1791. Cincinnati, Boston, and other cities of the United States have had Cecilia choral societies.

The long-famous (and still existing) concert hall of Edinburgh, the St. Cecilia Hall, was built in 1762.

See also p. 33, pl. 4.

CECILIAN MOVEMENT. This was a movement for the reform of Roman Catholic church music. It was inspired, in the first instance, by the labours of Dr. Karl Proske (1794–1861), canon and choirmaster of Ratisbon Cathedral, and of the brothers Mettenleiter, his collaborators. By publication and active propaganda these workers succeeded in reviving interest in the church music of the period of Palestrina, which they desired should replace the unliturgical and often meretricious music that had come into use during the late eighteenth and early nineteenth century (cf. *Mass* 3; *Roman Catholic Church Music in Britain*). This stimulated the priest, Dr. Franz Xaver Witt (1834–88), a pupil of Proske and of one of the Mettenleiters, to the foundation of the Allgemeiner Deutscher Caecilien-

verein (General German Society of St. Cecilia), which received the formal sanction of the Holy See. Ten thousand musicians quickly joined it, a huge catalogue of compositions (old and original) was brought into existence, and twenty-four periodicals devoted to the reforms advocated were issued in different countries.

The principles of the society may be briefly laid down as follows: (1) The Gregorian Chant is basically the true music of the Church. (2) The Italian music of the late sixteenth century is the best of all harmonized church music that has appeared. (3) The Viennese school of church music (the Masses of Haydn, Mozart, etc.) is quite unecclesiastical and should be disused. (4) Modern music may and should be composed for church use, but it should respect the tradition and spirit of 'the ages of faith'.

Unfortunately, after the death of Witt, when the society came under the direction of Dr. Franz Xaver Haberl (1840–1910), a great deal of dull amateurish music was published, and, moreover, commercial motives entered into the work of the publishing organization.

Inaccurate editions of the polyphonic music were issued and an edition of plainsong based on the spurious sixteenth-century 'Medicean' text (see *Plainsong* 3), for which edition papal authority was given in 1870, and indeed a monopoly granted for a term of years (not renewed in 1903, cf. *Motu Proprio*).

CECILIAN SOCIETIES, ACADEMIES, CONCERT HALLS, etc. See under *Cecilia, Saint.*

CÉDEZ (Fr.). 'Give way', i.e. diminish the speed. The present and past participles are *cédant, cédé.*

CÉILIDH. See *Scotland* 1; p. 945, pl. **160.** 1.

CEILING, effect on sound. See *Concert Halls* 2.

CELERE (It.). 'Quick', 'speedy'. Hence *Celeritá* 'speed'; *Celeramente,* 'with speed'.

CELESTA or **CÉLESTE,** or **CÉLESTE MUSTEL.** *Percussion Family* 2 d, 4 e, 5 d; *Harmonica* 1 (note), 3. For **VOIX CÉLESTE** see *Organ* 3.

CÉLESTE (Fr.). A sort of soft pedal on some pianos. It interposes a strip of cloth between the hammers and the strings.

CELLARIUS. See *Waltz.*

CELLES. See *Bédos de Celles.*

CELLIER, ALFRED. Born in London in 1844 and died there in 1891, aged forty-seven. He was active and successful as a composer of light opera—*Dorothy* being his best-known work. He spent some time in Australia and in the United States.

See *Concert* 7, n. 1.

CELLO. Short for 'Violoncello'. See *Violin Family* 2, 8.

CELTIC HARP. See *Clàrsach.*

C.E.M.A. See under *Arts Council of Great Britain.*

CEMBALIST. A harpsichord player. See *Cembalo.*

CEMBALO. Italian for 'Dulcimer'; and hence 'Clavicembalo' ('keyed-dulcimer'—not a good description) came to be used for 'harpsichord', and then, shortened, became 'cembalo' again, which word thus became ambiguous. The word is common in eighteenth-century scores, as indicating the figured bass (q.v.) part; occasionally it is used in old organ music as indicating the manual part (as distinct from that of the pedal). In old Italian it often means cymbal. Beethoven, in one of his four 'Hammerklavier Sonatas' (see *Nicknamed Compositions* 5; the one in question is that in A major, op. 101), oddly reverted to the idea of the harpsichord. After a long 'Una Corda' passage (see *Pianoforte* 12; explanation of the Soft Pedal) instead of using one of the terms 'Due Corde' (see *Due*), 'Tre Corde', or 'Tutte le Corde' (q.v.), he adopted the term *Tutto il cembalo*, i.e. 'The whole harpsichord'.

CEMBALO D'AMORE. See *Amore*.

CENTO, CENTON, CENTONE. See *Pasticcio*.

CENTRAL MUSIC LIBRARY. London. See *Libraries*.

CEÒL BEAG, CEÒL MEADHONACH, CEÒL MÓR. See *Bagpipe Family* 4.

CÉ QU' É LAINÔ. See *God save the Queen* 2.

CEREZO. See *Bolero*.

ČERNOHORSKY, BOHUSLAV (1684–1742). See *Bohemia*.

CERONE. See *Spain* 9.

CERRITO. See *Ballet* 9; *Pas de Quatre*.

CERTON, PIERRE. Died 1572. He was a pupil of Josquin des Prés and master of the boys at the Sainte Chapelle, Paris. His compositions are numerous and important—masses, motets, and many chansons (see *Chanson*).

CERVANTES (1547–1616). See references under *Spain* 5; *Dance* 7; *Masque*; *Barber Shop Music*; *Bagpipe Family* 1.

CERVELAS. See *Rackett*.

CES. C flat (see Table 7).

CESES. C double flat—if this note is anywhere to be found (see Table 7).

CESTI, MARCANTONIO (really Pietro Antonio). Born at Arezzo, Tuscany, in 1623, and died in Florence in 1669, aged forty-six. He was a Franciscan monk who, after study under Carissimi, served in turn as musical director at the Medici Court at Florence, as a member of the papal choir in Rome, and as assistant musical director at the Imperial Court at Vienna. He wrote operas, solo cantatas, canzonets, etc. His most famous work is *Il Pomo d'oro* (1667), which inaugurated a new style in court opera.

His special importance is as a contributor to the progress of the music of the Italian stage, and in this he stands beside his somewhat senior contemporary Cavalli—both of them being important members of opera composition's second generation.

CETERA. See under *Cittern*.

C.H. See *Knighthood and other Honours*.

CHABRIER, EMMANUEL—in full, Alexis Emmanuel (p. 384, pl. **63.** 1). Born at Ambert,

Puy-de-Dôme, in 1841, and died in Paris in 1894, aged fifty-three. At fifteen he came to Paris and here he entered the Civil Service, at the same time associating with the Symbolist poets and the Impressionist painters, and, likewise, the Franck group of musicians. He enjoyed amongst these people the reputation of a brilliant pianist.

In his mid-thirties he successfully produced a comic opera, resigned his government position, and became assistant to the great conductor Lamoureux and helped him in the early Paris performances of Wagner (cf. *d'Indy*), to whose music he was greatly devoted.

He had a triumph with his orchestral rhapsody, *España*. The Paris Opera refused, as 'Wagnerian', his opera *Gwendoline*, but accepted his *Le Roi malgré lui* ('King despite himself'), which is still performed.

Then, in mid-career, temperamental excitability increased to the point of disease; paralysis followed, and death.

Despite a melodic vulgarity, he may, on the score of his harmonic and orchestral experiments, be looked on as a precursor of Debussy and Ravel.

See *Habanera*; *Quadrille*; *Ravel*; *Spain* 10.

CHACONNE and PASSACAGLIA. These two forms of music soon became practically indistinguishable and are hence here treated together. Both originated in dances, the chaconne in one that seems to have come from Spain (where it was considered of native South American origin), and the passacaglia in one that came either from Spain or from Italy. Both were slow dances of three-beats-in-a-measure, and their music apparently usually shared the characteristic peculiarity of being framed upon a ground bass (q.v.).

The passacaglia was danced in France as late as the early eighteenth century. The two dance rhythms and forms were before this taken into music as a basis of instrumental composition, and the names were apparently applied almost indifferently by composers. Wellnigh every work of musical reference distinguishes between the two, but hardly any two such works of reference agree as to what are the distinguishing marks, and an examination of any considerable number of chaconnes and passacaglias will show that any clear distinction can be sustained only by basing it on selected examples.

Sometimes the two terms are applied to the very same piece, as with the 'Chiacone' of Gluck's opera *Paris and Helen*, which reappears in *Iphigenia in Aulis* under the name 'Passecaille'.

Individual compositions will be found to differ widely from one another (for instance, in some the 'ground bass' may be transferred here and there to an upper part, and perhaps this is more common under the title 'Passacaglia' than under that of 'Chaconne'), but composers have not used the names systematically and it would seem that almost any instrumental composition based on a ground can be called a passacaglia or a chaconne, whilst some not so based, but planned in short sections similar to those resulting from a ground bass, are yet so called. Whether there be the recurring bass or not, the composition, indeed, always falls into a number of short sections of 4 to 8 measures, and this is one of its genuine distinguishing marks.

The keyboard composers of the seventeenth and early eighteenth centuries made great use of this form (in the sense of an elaborate ground-bass piece in three-in-a-measure), and fine examples will be found in Frescobaldi, Buxtehude (who also has a cantata in chaconne form—*Quemadmodum desiderat cervus*), Couperin, Handel, Bach, and others.

Lully and then Rameau often ended their operas with a piece in this form, and so did other composers of the late seventeenth and early eighteenth century and even later. Gluck's *Orpheus*, 1762, ends with a fine one, and so also his *Alceste* and his *Iphigenia in Aulis*. These opera-finale chaconnes are not always on ground basses. They are mostly strings of brief passages, of which the first and principal one frequently recurs: the French called these separate passages or sections 'couplets'. Lully will sometimes have as many as sixty to seventy four-bar sections of this sort.

The names chaconne and passacaglia are rarely found in British music, but many examples of ground (q.v.) and divisions (q.v.) are much the same thing.

Very occasionally a chaconne in two-in-a-measure is to be found. Couperin, for instance, has such amongst his harpsichord music. Purcell also does not confine himself to three-in-a-measure, and he prefers the title 'ground'.

Perhaps the most famous example of the use of the word 'chaconne' is in connexion with the last movement of Bach's D minor Suite (otherwise called '2nd Partita') for unaccompanied violin, and the most famous example of the use of the word 'passacaglia' in connexion with his Passacaglia and Fugue in C minor—considered one of his greatest organ works but originally written for a two-manual-and-pedal harpsichord: the magnificent 'Goldberg' Variations for double-manual harpsichord, though not called by either name, are something of the same kind—at any rate, in so far as they are based on a ground. The Thirty-two Variations in C minor for piano by

Beethoven and the Finale of the Brahms Fourth Symphony can be considered more modern instances of the same form. It will, then, be realized that some of the grandest compositions the world has yet had have been based upon the principle of the chaconne-passacaglia type of variation.

Italian *Ciaccona* and French *Passecaille* are forms of the words sometimes seen. The words *Hahnentrapp* and *Gassenhauer* are given in some musical dictionaries as German equivalents, but they are probably mere attempts at translation based on two different doubtful etymologies. An occasional English spelling is *Passingala*.

See also *Folia*; *Jazz* 7.

CHACONY. Old English for *Chaconne*.

CHADWICK, GEORGE WHITEFIELD (p. 1041, pl. **170.** 5). Born at Lowell, Massachusetts, in 1854 and died in Boston in 1931, aged seventy-six. His principal teachers in Europe were Reinecke, Jadassohn, and Rheinberger. He was organist and teacher in Boston from 1880; for fifty years he served on the staff of the New England Conservatory of Music, and for thirty-three of them as its Director.

He composed three symphonies, many choral works and songs, and in the later years symphonic suites and tone-poems with a more modern accent than his earlier pieces; also five string quartets, a piano quintet, a comic opera and an operetta, and a 'lyric drama' for the concert stage, *Judith* (1901).

His style was distinguished by melodic line, a sure and brilliant technique, sentiment, and native humour.

He was for many years before his death the doyen of American composers.

CHAHUT. See *Can-can*.

CHAIKOVSKI. See *Tchaikovsky*.

CHAINS, IRON (as musical instrument). See *Percussion Family* 4 d.

CHAIR EISTEDDFOD. See *Wales* 7.

CHAIRING OF BARDS. See *Wales* 7.

CHAKMAKJIAN. See *Hovhaness*.

CHALEUR (Fr.). 'Warmth.' So *Chaleureux, Chaleureusement*, 'with warmth'.

CHALIAPIN, FEODOR. See *Russia* 8 (end); *Virtuoso*.

CHALUMEAU. See *Clarinet Family* 2, 5.

CHAMBER CONCERT. See *Chamber Music*.

CHAMBER MUSIC

(For illustrations see p. 173, pl. 36.)

1. Definition. Before public concert-giving began (in the late seventeenth century; see *Concert* 3) set musical performances fell into three classes, those of the church, those of the theatre, and those of the halls of royalty and

the aristocracy. Those of the last class, whether vocal or instrumental, were 'Chamber Music'. We find the adjective also in the terms *Sonata da Camera*, or 'chamber sonata', as distinguished from the *Sonata da Chiesa*, or 'church sonata' (see *Sonata* 2), and *Cantata da Camera* as distinguished from *Cantata da Chiesa*.

A definition of chamber music at the very beginning of the nineteenth century, when the concert had long been a public thing, is that by Dr. Burney in Rees's *Cyclopædia* (*c.* 1805): 'Chamber Music—compositions for a small concert room, a small band, and a small audience; opposed to music for the church, the theatre, or a public concert room.' Similarly, in his *History* Burney spoke of chamber music comprehensively as 'cantatas, single songs, solos and trios, quartets, concertos and symphonies of few parts'.

The term 'chamber music', as now used, has a narrower sense than it had in the seventeenth, eighteenth, and early nineteenth centuries. It excludes (quite logically) music for orchestra, chorus, and other large combinations, but it also (more arbitrarily) excludes all vocal music and all instrumental music for one instrument (e.g. piano sonatas). It includes all seriously intended instrumental music for two or more instruments played with one instrument to a 'part'—and it includes nothing else. A concert of music of this sort is a 'Chamber Concert'.

2. Chief Combinations. The chief combinations within the term as now used are the following:

1. The Duet Sonata for Violin and Piano.
   The Duet Sonata for Cello and Piano.
2. The String Trio (i.e. violin, viola, and cello).
   The Piano Trio (i.e. violin, cello, and piano).
3. The String Quartet (i.e. 2 violins, viola, and cello).
   The Piano Quartet (i.e. violin, viola, cello, and piano).
4. The String Quintet (i.e. the string quartet plus sometimes another viola and sometimes another cello).
   The Piano Quintet (i.e. the string quartet plus piano).
   So, too, Clarinet Quintet and the like.
5. The String Sextet (2 each of violin, viola, and cello).

Of these the string quartet is far and away the most important, both as to the size of its repertory and the value of this. Of course there are many other combinations besides the above. Groupings of wind and strings are important, and a good deal of chamber music for wind instruments alone exists, as also for combinations with piano (sonatas for clarinet and piano, horn and piano, etc.). There are, too, a good many compositions for 'Chamber Orchestra', i.e. some comparatively large combinations with only one instrument to a 'part'. (But this definition is not always accepted. There are organizations calling themselves 'Chamber Orchestras' that are merely small ordinary orchestras. The term is a new one and has not yet settled down to precise meaning.)

Note that, short of the chamber orchestra, the string double-bass has comparatively rarely a place in chamber music—partly from its lack of agility, which disables it from taking part on quite equal terms with the other strings, partly from its thickness of tone, and partly from the fact that the cello already supplies a sufficient bass to the music.

It should be noted that it is of the essence of true chamber music that an equality of importance, as between the different instruments, shall be recognized. In this it resembles the madrigal music of the sixteenth century (also properly performed 'one to a part'). The methods of the full orchestra are out of place. There is an intimacy about the best chamber music that comes from the impression of a conversation amongst the participants. A poetic definition of it is 'The Music of Friends'.

3. The Older Conception. The modern conception of chamber music may be said to date only from Haydn and the mid-eighteenth century. It would have been impossible for such a conception to become current during the period of a century and a half preceding this, which, from its greatest figure, we may call the Corelli period. During that period the harpsichord (nearly always played from a figured bass, q.v.) was used as an invariable background for music (vocal music, sonatas, orchestral music, etc.) and the principle of, say, two violins and cello (a very common combination) drawing lines upon a background of harpsichord tone (often thickened by the use of 4-feet and 16-feet registers, three octaves in all—see *Harpsichord Family* 5) is opposed to the conversational ideal just mentioned. This principle, indeed, may be said to savour more of that of the concerto, in which one or more solo instruments, as one entity, are heard, with the main body of the orchestra (here represented by the figured bass) as another entity. It might be thought that the piano quartet and piano quintet would fall into this same quasi-concerto class, but this is not necessarily so, for the tone of the piano, in the opinion of many listeners, blends with that of stringed instruments in a way that the tone of the harpsichord does not, and, moreover, the piano has no octave-below and octave-above doubling devices to give an orchestral thickness of effect. Further, the piano part is written out in full, the composer thus being able exactly to define its role. And (most important of all) it *has* a role; it is a member of the party on equal terms with the others, not a mere background to them. However, only a comparatively small number of piano quartets and quintets have been written, and perhaps this indicates that composers have felt some degree of difficulty in the matter.

Going further than the harpsichord-background period, there was in the sixteenth century music for viols (see *Viol Family*) that approximated much more closely to the present-day general chamber music ideal, but, even where it was not originally composed for voices and then transferred by the performers to these instruments, it was much in a choral style, the idioms of instrumental composition not having yet been differentiated from those of choral composition. Michael Este, in a publication of 1638, distinguished between compositions that could be both sung and played and compositions that, though of much the same character, could (from the compass of their parts, etc.) *only* be played—'Ayerie Fancies [see *Fancy*] that may be as well sung as plaied' and others 'so made as they must be plaied and not sung'.

4. The More Modern Conception. Chamber music, as we are accustomed to use the term today, may then be fairly said to date from Haydn, and he, Mozart, Beethoven, and Schubert are the greatest creators of it up to the end of the first quarter of the nineteenth century, when Beethoven and Schubert died. For the most part, it has been of the nature of the sonata (q.v.), a piece of chamber music being, usually, so far as form is concerned, merely a sonata or symphony for a small group of instruments—understanding 'sonata' and 'symphony' in the more modern sense.

The Romantics, Schumann and Mendelssohn (hardly Chopin, who wrote very little chamber music), handed the torch on to Brahms, and most of the serious composers of the nineteenth and twentieth centuries (omitting Wagner) took it in turn.

All the varying emotional and intellectual tendencies, or 'isms', have been reflected in chamber music—Romanticism (see *Romantic*), Impressionism (q.v.), Expressionism (q.v.), etc., and all the technical experiments, or 'itys' —Polytonality, Atonality, and Microtonality (see *Harmony* 17, 18, 19). One type of activity it has, however, almost completely shunned— that of 'Programme Music' (q.v.), for which its austerity of resource has been generally felt to unfit it. Curiously, few chamber works of significance have come from Russia.

Chamber music is not the entertainment of crowds. It is not heard to effect in very big halls, nor does it usually draw big audiences. It is the delight of the performing amateur and of the listening connoisseur, who find in its very restraint, due to its limitations of tonal variety and volume, something which appeals to them differently from (and perhaps beyond) any other musical experience. Indeed, it is an accepted commonplace that the string quartet is the one perfect medium for musical expression—a claim inferentially endorsed by the great masters. The public performance of chamber music was rare until in 1831 the famous Müller Brothers String Quartet left their service at the court of the Duke of Brunswick and began touring Europe with a fine classical repertory.

5. The History Summarized. Summing up the historical side of the subject, there are three clear periods in the composition of chamber music, and they are distinct in the sense that the principles are different and that it can hardly be said that the chamber music of one period very directly develops out of that of the previous one:

I. The sixteenth century—the period of choral influence, the period of music published as 'Apt for Viols and Voyces' (see *Madrigals* 3 c), with chamber music not yet fully on its own feet.

II. The seventeenth century and first half of the eighteenth century—the extemporized 'Harpsichord-basis' principle, with a figured bass as a part of the score.

III. The second half of the eighteenth century onwards—the 'Equal-terms' principle (more nearly related to the principle of Period I than to that of Period II).

From about 1750 it might be said that the true chamber music principle had been found (worked out experimentally by Haydn), and thenceforward the changes in chamber music merely reflected the changing styles and idioms of the music of the times.

It is interesting to remember that the *implements* of string chamber music during this third period have remained unchanged. Domestic keyboard music has passed from the harpsichord and clavichord to the early piano and then to the present-day piano, which is almost as different from the earlier one as that is from the harpsichord or clavichord. The orchestra has undergone enormous changes. But the string quartet of the twentieth century is the same thing as the string quartet of the eighteenth century, and the quartet composer of today has just the same medium at his disposal as had Haydn.

6. List of the Chief Composers.

PERIOD I. THE PERIOD OF CHORAL INFLUENCE. In addition to the following, who all composed chamber music expressly for instruments (though chorally influenced), we might include all the Italian, English, and other madrigal composers, since any madrigal was liable to be used as a piece of instrumental chamber music.

A. Gabrieli (c. 1510–86). Byrd (1543–1623). G. Gabrieli (1557–1612). Brade (1560–1630). Cifra (1584–1629). G. Allegri (1582–1652); a string quartet of his is believed to be the earliest composed (i.e. the earliest piece expressly made for four stringed instruments without any harpsichord). O. Gibbons (1583–1625); many Fantasy Trios for strings, madrigals 'apt for viols and voyces', etc.

PERIOD II. THE 'FIGURED BASS' OR HARPSICHORD-BACKGROUND PERIOD.

J. H. Schein (1586–1630). J. Jenkins (1592–1678). W. Lawes (1602–1645); music for viols. Rosenmüller (c. 1620–84). Reinken (1623–1722). William Young (died 1672); an Englishman who published chamber music at Innsbruck in 1653. Locke (1630–77); consorts for viols. Biber (1644–1704). Stradella (c. 1645–82). Muffat (c. 1645–1704). J. J. Walther (born 1650); a gay spark who imitated various birds, etc., in his chamber music. Corelli (1653–1713); sonatas and trios. Marais (1656–1728). Bassani (c. 1657–1716). G. B. Vitali (died 1692); a great variety of works. Purcell (1658–95). Torelli (1658–1709). A. Scarlatti (1660–1725); wrote little chamber music, but it includes four actual string quartets expressly marked 'without harpsichord' (about 1715); these are very early examples, if not the first since the primitive 'period of choral influence', as it has been called above. Pepusch (1667–1752). Couperin (1668–1733). Vivaldi (c. 1675–1741). Loeillet (1680–1730). Astorga (1680–1736). Telemann (1681–1767); a most prolific composer of music for very varied combinations. Rameau (1683–1764). J. S. Bach (1685–1750); he wrote comparatively little chamber music—twenty-one works only (not all with mere figured bass), the six sonatas for violin and keyboard being the most important. Handel (1685–1759); especially sonatas for two treble instruments (oboes, flutes, violins), and cello, with figured bass; also for one instrument and figured bass. Marcello (1686–1739). Porpora (1686–1767). Babell (c. 1690–1723). F. M. Veracini (1690–1750). Tartini (1692–1770); a great pioneer in the art of violin playing and string composing. Locatelli (1695–1764). Leclair (1697–1764). Quantz (1697–1773); chamber music with flute. G. B. Sammartini (1698–1775); one of the earliest writers of the new kind of chamber music, often said to have strongly influenced Haydn—who denied it. J. Gibbs (1699–1788). C. H. Graun (1701–59). Henry Eccles (died c. 1742). Pergolese (1710–36). Arne (1710–78). W. F. Bach (1710–84). Boyce (1710–79). Frederick the Great (1712–86); chamber music with flute. Gluck (1714–87); string trios on a harpsichord basis. C. P. E. Bach (1714–88). G. C. Wagenseil (1715–77); of great importance in his day. Giardini (1716–96); eighteen string quartets, etc. J. W. A. Stamitz (1717–57); an original mind in the realm of chamber music as in that of orchestral music; he helped towards the coming of the new style. Schobert (c. 1720–67). Abel (1723–87); one of the last great viola da gamba players and composers. Filtz (c. 1730–60). Pugnani (1731–98).

PERIOD III. ALL INSTRUMENTS ON EQUAL TERMS, WITHOUT KEYBOARD BACKGROUND. Note an overlap here. Towards the end of what has been called Period II, some chamber music is composed without figured bass, and in what has been called Period III some chamber music with figured bass is still composed. It would be impossible to disentangle the two types in lists such as these—and indeed in some case the same composer wrote music of both kinds. For convenience either Sammartini (in 'Period II') or Haydn (in 'Period III') can be taken as representing the beginning of the new style.

Sacchini (1730–86). Joseph Haydn (1732–1809); over eighty string quartets, forty-five piano trios, etc. J. C. Bach (1735–82). Albrechtsberger (1736–1809); much, including forty-four 'fugal quartets' for strings. Michael Haydn (1737–1806, brother of Joseph Haydn). Dittersdorf (1739–99). Rust (1739–96). Vanhall (1739–1813); a hundred string quartets and other things—once of great repute. Paesiello (1741–1816). Boccherini (1743–1805); has an amazing list of works, including over a hundred each of string quartets and string quintets; he was a contemporary of Haydn and exercised great influence on the new school of chamber

music. Carl Stamitz (1745–1801). Vogler (1749–1814). Clementi (1752–1832). Anton Stamitz (1754–c. 1809). Viotti (1755–1824); twenty-seven quartets of different kinds, thirty-four trios, and other things. Bréval (1756–1825); thirty string quartets, etc. W. A. Mozart (1756–91); a string trio, twenty-seven string quartets, seven string quintets, seven piano trios, two piano quartets, about forty sonatas for violin and piano, seventeen divertimenti for different combinations of strings and wind, or wind alone, etc. Wranitzky (1756–1808). Pleyel (1757–1831); sixty-six quartets and much other chamber music. Krommer (1760–1831); ninety-six quartets, etc. Cherubini (1760–1842). Dussek (1760–1812); an enormous amount of chamber music, including eighty sonatas for violin and piano. Gyrowetz (1763–1850); sixty string quartets, etc. Kreutzer (1766–1831). A. Romberg (1767–1821); twenty-eight string quartets and many other things. B. Romberg (1767–1841). Reicha (1770–1836); a prolific composer for very varied chamber combinations. Beethoven (1770–1827); five string quintets, seventeen string quartets, five string trios, eight piano trios, ten sonatas for piano and violin, five for piano and cello, one septet for strings and wind, two wind octets, etc. Tomaschek (1774–1850). Hummel (1778–1837). Mazas (1782–1849). Paganini (1782–1840); wrote a number of pieces of chamber music with a part for guitar, as well as other things. Onslow (1784–1853). Spohr (1784–1859); thirty-four string quartets and any number of other things, including octets in the form of responsive double quartets. F. Ries (1784–1838). Kalkbrenner (1785–1849). Kuhlau (1786–1832); especially wrote chamber music for combinations including flute, and many trios for flutes alone. Weber (1786–1826); not a great deal of chamber music; a clarinet quintet is prominent. Aloys Schmitt (1788–1866). Mayseder (1789–1863). Rossini (1792–1868); twenty quartets for different combinations. Hauptmann (1792–1868); eighty chamber works, all including the flute. Moscheles (1794–1870). Marschner (1795–1861). Schubert (1797–1828); twenty string quartets, string quintet, two piano trios, the 'Trout' piano quintet (with double bass), octet, etc. Reissiger (1798–1859); twenty-three piano trios and many other things. Kalliwoda (1801–66). Ellerton (1801–73); forty-four string quartets, etc., once very popular with amateurs. Molique (1802–69). F. Lachner (1803–90). I. Lachner (1807–95). Mendelssohn (1809–47); string octet, two quintets, and seven quartets, piano sextet, three quartets, and two trios, etc. Robert Schumann (1810–56); three string quartets, one piano quartet, and one piano quintet, three piano trios, and four 'Fantasy Pieces' for that combination, etc. Félicien David (1810–76); twenty-four string quintets in four sets called 'The Four Seasons'. Wilhelm Taubert (1811–91). V. Lachner (1811–93). Hiller (1811–85). Verdi (1813–1901); one string quartet. Wagner (1813–83); his place in this list is justified by his Siegfried Idyll, written practically as a chamber work (1 flute, 1 oboe, 2 clarinets, 1 bassoon, 2 horns, 1 trumpet, first violin, second violin, viola, cello, double-bass —13 instruments, but at the first performance the first and second violins and viola were doubled, making 16 in all); the only other chamber work of this composer is an early clarinet quintet movement. Volkmann (1815–83). Sterndale Bennett (1816–75). Verhulst (1816–91). Gade (1817–90). E. Franck (1817–93); a German composer of sixty chamber works, much praised. Litolff (1818–91). Vieuxtemps (1820–81). Gurlitt (1820–1901). Raff (1822–82). César Franck (1822–90); one string quartet, one piano quintet, four piano trios, one sonata for

See the Article *Parish Clerk* on pages 759–60 and Plate 2, facing page 17

1. PARSON AND PARISH CLERK about 1730. (Hogarth's *Sleeping Congregation*)

2. OLD ORGAN IN THE HALL OF THE WORSHIPFUL COMPANY OF PARISH CLERKS, LONDON

3. ARMS OF THE WORSHIPFUL COMPANY OF PARISH CLERKS

THE CHAPEL ROYAL, ST. JAMES'S

4. IN THE 16TH CENTURY

6. IN THE 19TH CENTURY

5. IN THE 18TH CENTURY

1. ELLA'S MUSICAL UNION QUARTET (Vieuxtemps, Deloffre, Hill, and Piatti). Ella is seated at the table with the score in his hands (see *Concert* 7; *Annotated Programmes* 4; *Criticism* 8

2. THE JOACHIM QUARTET. Founded in 1869 it occupied, for over thirty years, the premier position all over Europe. The members as here shown (1903) were Joachim, Halir, Wirth, and Hausmann (See *Joachim*)

3. THE BARRÈRE ENSEMBLE (founded in New York, in 1910, by George Barrère, flautist)

piano and violin. Lalo (1823–92). Smetana (1824–84). Reinecke (1824–1910). Bargiel (1828–97). A. Rubinstein (1829–94); wrote a considerable number of quartets, quintets, sextets. K. Goldmark (1830–1915). Brahms (1833–97); three sonatas for piano and violin, two for piano and cello, and two for piano and clarinet, five piano trios, three string quartets, three piano quartets, two string quintets, one piano quintet, one quintet for clarinet and strings, two string sextets, etc. Borodin (1833–87); three string quartets. Scholz (1835–1916). Cui (1835–1918). Saint-Saëns (1835–1921). P. Lacombe (1837–1927). Rheinberger (1839–1901). Napravnik (1839–1916). Tchaikovsky (1840–93); one string sextet, three string quartets, and one piano trio. Goetz (1840–76). Svendsen (1840–1911). Dvořák (1841–1904); eight string quartets, two string quintets (one with double-bass) and a string sextet, four piano trios, two piano quartets, and a piano quintet. Sgambati (1841–1914). G. Jensen (1843–95). Herzogenberg (1843–1900). Grieg (1843–1907); two string quartets (one being incomplete), three sonatas for violin and piano, and one for cello and piano. Rimsky-Korsakof (1844–1908); one string sextet, one string quartet and some single movements, one piano quintet. Widor (1844–1937). Fauré (1845–1925). P. Scharwenka (1847–1917). Parry (1848–1918). Godard (1849–95). Bretón (1850–1923). Scontrino (1850–1922). X. Scharwenka (1850–1924). Fibich (1850–1900); Bohemian ranking after Smetana and Dvořák. D'Indy (1851–1931). Huber (1852–1921); a very prolific Swiss composer. Stanford (1852–1924). Janáček (1854–1928). Chadwick (1854–1931). Prince Heinrich XXIV of Reuss-Köstrich (1855–1910). Chausson (1855–99). Taneief (1856–1915). Templeton Strong (1856–1948). Schütt (1856–1933). Sinding (1856–1941). Martucci (1856–1909). Stillman Kelley (1857–1944). Kienzl (1857–1941). Elgar (1857–1934). Ethel Smyth (1858–1944). Ippolitof-Ivanof (1859–1935). Algernon Ashton (1859–1937). Wolf (1860–1903); only two works—both for string quartet. Rezniček (1860–1945). Bossi (1861–1925). Arensky (1861–1906). Loeffler (1861–1935). Bréville (1861–1949). Delius (1862–1934). Debussy (1862–1918); one string quartet and three sonatas for various combinations. Pierné (1863–1937). Weingartner (1863–1942). Strauss (1864–1949); a few youthful works. Ropartz (1864–1955). Gretchaninof (1864–1956). D'Albert (1864–1932); two string quartets. Sibelius (1865–1957); a string quartet and one or two other things. Magnard (1865–1914). Glazunof (1865–1936); much chamber music. Charles Wood (1866–1926). Rebikof (1866–1920). O. Nováček (1866–1900). Busoni (1866–1924). Koechlin (1867–1950). Mrs. H. H. A. Beach (1867–1944). McEwen (1868–1948); fourteen string quartets and some other things. Roussel (1869–1937). Pfitzner (1869–1949). Ernest Walker (1870–1948). Vierne (1870–1937). Florent Schmitt (1870–1958). Novák (1870–1949). Lekeu (1870–94). Converse (1871–1940). Vaughan Williams (1872–1958); two string quartets, one phantasy quintet for strings, song cycle with piano quintet, etc. Zemlinsky (1872–1942). Walthew (1872–1951). Juon (1872–1940). R. Goldmark (1872–1936). N. Tcherepnin (1873–1945); his chamber music includes six quintets for horns only. Reger (1873–1916). Rachmaninof (1873–1943). D. G. Mason (1873–1953). Jongen (1873–1953). Roger-Ducasse (1873–1954). Suk (1874–1935). Schönberg (1874–1951); atonal harmony and very novel schemes, with some use of

the voice. Coleridge-Taylor (1875–1912). Ravel (1875–1937); one string quartet, one piano trio, one sonata for violin and cello only, and one for violin and piano, Introduction and Allegro for harp, flute, clarinet, and string quartet, etc. Glière (1875–1956). J. A. Carpenter (1876–1951). Wolf-Ferrari (1876–1948). Falla (1876–1946); a concerto for harpsichord, flute, oboe, violin, and cello. David Stanley Smith (1877–1949); three string quartets, piano quartet, etc. Samazeuilh (born 1877). Huré (1877–1930). Dohnányi (1877–1960). Karg-Elert (1877–1933). Dupont (1878–1914); a remarkable Poème for piano quintet. Holbrooke (1878–1958). R. Jullien (born 1878). Tommasini (1878–1950). Frank Bridge (1879–1941). Ireland (1879–1962); piano trios, sonatas for violin and piano, and cello and piano, etc. Medtner (1879–1951). Respighi (1879–1936). Cyril Scott (1879–1970). Arthur Shepherd (1880–1958). Pratella (1880–1955). Pizzetti (1880–1968). Inghelbrecht (1880–1965). Bloch (1880–1959). Roslavets (1881–1930). Bartók (1881–1945). Dresden (1881–1957). Turina (1882–1949). Stravinsky (1882–1971); in addition to some music for string quartet he wrote compositions for various combinations including wind instruments and voice. John Powell (1882–1963). Pick-Mangiagalli (1882–1949). J. Marx (1882–1964). Malipiero (1882–1973). Kodály (1882–1967). Saminsky (1882–1959). Szymanowski (1883–1937). Steinberg (1883–1946). Hauer (1883–1959); atonal chamber music. Gniessin (1883–1957). Casella (1883–1947). Webern (1883–1945); a Schönberg disciple—an 'expressionist'. Bax (1883–1953); various quartets, quintets, trios, sonatas, etc. Bowen (1884–1961). Gruenberg (1884–1964). Van Dieren (1884–1936). Wellesz (1885–1974). Dale (1885–1943). Berg (1885–1935); atonal music. Varèse (1885–1965). Paray (born 1886). Toch (1887–1964). Villa-Lobos (1887–1959). Durey (born 1888). Gál (born 1890). Prokofief (1891–1953). Jirák (1891–1972). Jacobi (1891–1952). Bliss (1891–1975). Tailleferre (born 1892). Rowley (1892–1958); specialized in chamber music for children. Jarnach (born 1892). Honegger (1892–1955). Milhaud (1892–1974). Howells (born 1892). Hába (1893–1973); quarter-tone string quartet. Pisk (born 1893). Goossens (1893–1962); a considerable and varied output. B. Wagenaar (1894–1971). Piston (born 1894). Moeran (1894–1950). Pijper (1894–1947). Erwin Schulhoff (1894–1942). Rudhyar (born 1895). Ornstein (born 1895). Hindemith (1895–1963); string quartets (some atonal), sonatas for violin and piano, cello and piano, wind chamber music, etc. H. Hanson (born 1896). R. Sessions (born 1896). Virgil Thomson (born 1896). Cowell (1897–1965); including music for chamber orchestra. Porter (1897–1966). Korngold (1897–1957). Tansman (born 1897). Rieti (born 1898). Roy Harris (born 1898). A. N. Tcherepnin (born 1899). Poulenc (1899–1963). Antheil (1900–1959). N. T. Berezowsky (1900–1953). Křenek (born 1900). Copland (born 1900). Rubbra (born 1901). Walton (born 1902). Blacher (1903–75). Alwyn (born 1905). Rawsthorne (1905–71). Tippett (born 1905). Shostakovich (1906–75). Frankel 1906–75). Fortner (born 1907). Messiaen (born 1908). Carter (born 1908). Schuman (born 1910). Françaix (born 1912). Britten (1913–76). Persichetti (born 1915). Berio (born 1925). Fricker (born 1926). Henze (born 1926). Stockhausen (born 1928).

See also *Dictionaries* 9.

CHAMBER ORCHESTRA. See *Chamber Music* 2.

CHAMBER PITCH. See *Pitch* 3, 8.

CHAMBONNIÈRES, JACQUES CHAMPION DE (properly Jacques Champion). Born in 1602 and died in Paris about 1672, aged about seventy. He came of a musical stock, his father being harpsichordist to Louis XIII, as he himself became later to Louis XIV, who appointed him Maître d'Hôtel and ennobled him. His harpsichord compositions are important; he is, in fact, regarded as the father of the French school of harpsichord composers.

Chambonnières was the name of the estate of his mother's family, in Brie.

See *Harpsichord Family* 2; *France* 5; *Anglebert* 1.

CHAMINADE, CÉCILE. Born in Paris in 1857 and died at Monte Carlo in 1944, aged eighty-six. When she was eight Bizet heard some of her compositions and prophesied a brilliant career; when she was eighteen Ambroise Thomas did so and exclaimed, 'This is not a woman composer, but a composer-woman'. Her skill as a pianist helped to bring her work before the public, and in that capacity she toured widely, for a period regularly visiting Britain. She wrote orchestral music, ballets, and songs, but is known to most people as the writer of tuneful and graceful short piano compositions, with no intricacy of texture, no elaboration of form, and no depth of feeling, but pleasant to hear and to play, and so tasteful in conception and execution as to disarm the highbrow critic.

See *Flute Family* 6.

CHAMPÊTRE (Fr.). 'Rural', 'rustic'. A *Danse champêtre* is any peasant dance in the open air.

CHAMPION. See *Chambonnières*.

CHANDOS, DUKE OF (James Brydges, 1673–1744). See *Oratorio* 5; *Mealtime Music*.

CHANDOS ANTHEMS. See *Anthem*.

CHANG. See p. 465, pl. 82. 5.

CHANGEABLE CHANT. See *Anglican Chant and Chanting* 5.

CHANGE RINGING. See *Bell* 2.

CHANGEZ (Fr.). 'Change' (imperative).

CHANGING NOTE (It., *nota cambiata*). An idiomatic melodic formula whose salient characteristic is the leap of a third away from an unessential note. The earliest form (in the polyphonic age) was a 3-note figure, as in (*a*) in the example below. This was soon joined and eventually superseded by a 4-note idiom, (*b*). In the harmonic age of counterpoint (from Bach and Handel onwards) a variety of other changing-note figures appear, (*c*), (*d*), (*e*).

In the U.S.A. the term *Cambiata* is commonly used for 'Changing Note'. Also when the leap of a third is in the direction opposite to that of the step-wise movement the term *Échappé*, or *Escape Tone*, is sometimes used, and, where the movement is back to the original note, the term *Returning Tone* (for these see examples (*c*) and (*d*) above.)

CHANNON, THOMAS. Psalmody teacher. See *Presbyterian Church Music* 4.

CHANSON in ordinary French parlance is merely any sort of simple verse-repeating song. Rousseau's definition in his *Dictionary of Music* (1767) is: 'A sort of very short lyric poem, generally upon some pleasant subject, to which an air is added so that it can be sung on intimate occasions, as at table, with one's friends, with one's sweetheart, or even when one is alone, in order for a few moments to drive away boredom if one is rich, and to help one to bear misery and labour if one is poor.'

The more technical application of the word is to the type of song in several parts or voices, or for one voice with accompaniment for instrument, that grew up in France and northern Italy in the fourteenth century and flourished until near the end of the sixteenth or somewhat later. It arose out of the art of the troubadours (see *Minstrels, Troubadours, Trouvères*). This type was really a sort of early madrigal, generally of the 'Ayre' kind (see *Madrigal* 3) and with the tune in the tenor. It flourished in France, the Netherlands, and northern Italy. Its tune was sometimes a folk melody. Josquin des Prés is considered one of its greatest exponents; his dates are 1440-1521. Jannequin, a little later, was another famous writer of chansons: some of his are of a very descriptive character, 'The Battle', 'The Song of the Birds', and the like (see *Madrigal* 8 d and *Jannequin*). Orlandus Lassus (q.v.), 1532–94, was also a very great composer of French chansons.

But the word 'chanson' covers a territory of very wide extent and has its varying meanings from early times to the present. (For the Chansons de Geste, about 1050–1350, see an allusion under *Minstrels* 1.)

CHANSON SANS PAROLES (Fr.). 'Song without words' (q.v.).

CHANSONS DE GESTE. See *Minstrels* 1. Cf. *Spain* 4.

CHANT. See *Anglican Chant*, and for 'Gregorian Chant' see *Plainsong* 1, 3.

CHANTANT (Fr.). 'Singing', i.e. in a singing style. This is the present participle; sometimes the past participle is used, *chanté*, 'sung'.

CHANTER. See *Bagpipe Family* 2.

CHANTERELLE (Fr.). The highest (E) string of the violin—or the highest string of any such instrument.

CHANTEURS DE ST. GERVAIS. See *Bordes*.

CHANTY. See *Shanty*.

CHAPEAU CHINOIS (literally, 'Chinese Hat'). See *Turkish Crescent*.

CHAPEL. St. Martin's famous cloak (in Latin *cappa*, or diminutive *capella*), which he divided with the beggar, was preserved in a sanctuary, which hence came to bear the name *capella* (or in Italian *cappella*). Thus any smallish church building, such as that of a royal palace or of the Pope, came to have the name, and the German *Kapelle* (or *Capelle*) is the same word.

The whole staff of priests, musicians, and other functionaries then came to be called the 'King's Chapel', the 'Pope's Chapel', etc. Later the term came to be, in common usage, restricted to the musicians and the German term *Kapellmeister* (or *Capellmeister*), the French *maître de chapelle*, etc., were applied to the musical director.

From this any musical director (even in a theatre) came to be called *Kapellmeister*. And as many such officials were men of routine, especially in their compositions, a derogatory term *Kapellmeistermusik* came into use as a description of the well-constructed but uninspired. And nowadays Kapelle is the normal term applied to an orchestral body, from symphony orchestra to dance orchestra, e.g. *Sachsische Staatskapelle* (Saxon State Orchestra), *Jack Hyltons Kapelle* (Jack Hylton's Band).

And thus the charitable Bishop of Tours is found to have divided his cloak amongst more beggars than he ever guessed.

Cf. *Cappella*.

CHAPEL ROYAL (p. 172, pl. **35.**). No one institution has been more useful in fostering English musicianship and promoting the development of English music than the Chapel Royal—by which must be properly understood not a building but a body of clergy and musicians (like German 'Kapelle'; see article *Chapel*).

Existing records of the Chapel go back to 1135. In 1200 it visited York with King John. During the French campaigns of which Agincourt formed a part Henry V sent, in 1418, for his Chapel to help him worthily to celebrate Easter in Bayeux. (It has been established that this monarch was himself something of a composer.)

During the reign of Edward IV (1461–83) the Chapel consisted of twenty-six chaplains and clerks, thirteen minstrels (a very wide term), eight choir-boys and their master, and a 'Wayte', or musical watchman, sounding three times nightly (see a reference to Edward IV's Chapel under *Psalm*).

At this time, or earlier, there grew up the custom of members of the musical staff of the Chapel performing plays (or 'Interludes') before royalty—a custom which in time had a good deal to do with the establishment of the English drama and perhaps (from the songs interspersed) the English lyric; Shakespeare, in *Hamlet*, alludes to the choir-boy players in his own day.

Under Richard III (1483–5) a press-gang system was authorized (though the practice of pressing seems to have existed earlier); this remained in operation for about a couple of centuries. Representatives of the Chapel were now definitely entitled to travel about the country listening to all the best cathedral choirs, and robbing them of any boys whose voices marked them out as fit to sing before the King (St. Paul's Cathedral exercised a like privilege).

Under Henry VIII (q.v.), a luxury-loving monarch, one fond of display, and, moreover, a practical musician, the musical staff of the Chapel rose to seventy-nine. When the King travelled he took with him some of these musicians, including a little choir of six boys and six men to sing mass daily. Henry VIII's Chapel attended him to the Field of the Cloth of Gold (1520): they were part of that amazing retinue that helped him to consume 2,000 sheep in one month—with, of course, other provisions. They were a necessary part of his state.

Edward VI had a chapel of one hundred and fourteen, and Mary the same.

Under Elizabeth (1558–1603) the Chapel reached its greatest glory, for its personnel was of high distinction. Such servants as Tye, Tallis, Byrd, Gibbons, Morley, Tomkins, and Bull would do honour to any monarch in any age. These brought church music to a point not exceeded even by the musicians of the Sistine Chapel at Rome; they developed the English madrigal, and they are prominent amongst those who laid the very foundations of artistic keyboard music. Some of them were still in the service of the Chapel during the reign of James I. Then came that of Charles I, and with the fall of his head in 1649 the Chapel ceased. Cromwell was a great lover of music and kept up a small body of domestic musicians, but he did not maintain a princely state, and, of course, he did not approve of choirs as an instrument of public worship (see *Puritans*).

In 1660 came back a King, and the Chapel was recalled to help him in his devotions. Charles II, after lively music from Lully at the court of Louis XIV, wanted lively music at the English court. A talented choir-boy, Pelham Humfrey, was sent abroad to learn foreign styles; a younger boy, Purcell, without going abroad, was very apt to learn, and these youths and others, largely trained by Captain Henry Cooke (q.v.), were quickly able as they matured to put to good use the new resources (such as the band of twenty-four fiddlers in church) with which the King had provided himself. From 1677 to his death in 1695 Purcell was 'Composer in Ordinary' to the Chapel. Looking at his church music, we see two distinct styles, the one in grave and solemn counterpoint, that looks back to the Elizabethans, and the other in brighter style, with many short movements and long instrumental interludes, looking to nothing so much as the immediate pleasure of a very rhythmically-minded royal master. It is, perhaps, not too fanciful to consider that Purcell's two positions, as organist of Westminster Abbey and of the Chapel Royal, conditioned his two styles.

Under William and Mary, Anne, and the Georges, we hear less of the Chapel. George III was a keen music-lover, but, like these other monarchs, he had musicians in his employ beyond those of his Chapel; he spent little time in London, and when at Windsor had no need of his Chapel Royal, in the technical sense, since the Chapel of St. George, in Windsor Castle, had its own distinct staff, as it still has.

The great days, then, were over, but a line of organists continued, the name of almost every one of whom is well known to the student of English musical history. Today the Chapel Royal consists of a body of clergy, choirmen and boys ('Priests in Ordinary', 'Gentlemen', and 'Children'), and the organist charged with the conduct of the Sunday services. Their place of duty is chiefly the chapel of St. James's Palace, and there the brilliant scarlet uniforms of the boys and the efficient singing of a cathedral service attract many visitors— for a portion of the chapel is open to the public, a fact not known to every musical visitor to London. But they have other places of duty, at Buckingham Palace and Marlborough House.

The chapel building of St. James's Palace dates from 1532; its ceiling decorations are by Holbein. It was out of use during the reigns of the later Stuarts, as their court was at Whitehall, so the chapel which heard the music of Purcell was that of Whitehall Palace, which chapel was destroyed by fire in 1698, soon after which a return was made to the old (and present) chapel in St. James's Palace. (Inigo Jones's banqueting hall, built in the early part of the seventeenth century, is practically the only part of Whitehall Palace which now remains; it, too, has been used for a certain period, ending 1891, as a Chapel Royal, supplementary to that of St. James's Palace.)

Distinct from the Chapel Royal is the Private Band of the monarch, presided over since the days of Charles I by the 'Master of the King's (or Queen's) Musick', the band in Charles II's reign being reconstituted, so that its string section should be capable of separate performance, on the lines of the 'Vingt-quatre Violons du Roi' of the court of Louis XIV, where Charles's years of exile had been spent. The band used to play to the monarch at meals and at state ceremonies and to combine with the gentlemen and children of the Chapel Royal for the performance of King's Birthday Odes and New Year's Day Odes, and its string section used to take part in the service of the Chapel Royal. It accompanied the monarch wherever he went. At Queen Victoria's accession the band had come to be merely a small body of wind-instrument players, but the music-loving Prince Consort reorganized it (in 1840) as an orchestra. Edward VII abandoned the custom of giving State Concerts and

though the position of 'Master' still exists there is now no band. Masters since the reign of Charles I include: Nicholas Lanier (1626); Louis Grabu (1666); Nicholas Staggins (1674); John Eccles (1700); Maurice Greene (1735); William Boyce (1755); John Stanley (1779); William Parsons (1786); William Shield (1817); C. Kramer (1829); F. Cramer (1834); G. F. Anderson (1848); W. G. Cusins (1870); Walter Parratt (1893); Elgar (1924); Walford Davies (1934); Bax (1941); Bliss (1953); Malcolm Williamson (1976).

See also *Anthem*; *Composition* 10.

For references to the Scottish Chapel Royal at different periods of history see *Scotland* 6.

Musicians connected with the English Chapel Royal and the subject of entries in this volume include: W. G. Alcock, S. Arnold, Attwood, Blow, Boyce, Bull, Byrd, R. Clark, H. Cooke, Croft, Dupuis, Fairfax, O. and C. Gibbons, Goss, M. Greene, Humfrey, H. and W. Lawes, Morley, Mundy, Nares, R. Parsons, Purcell, Roper, J. S. Smith, G. T. Smart, Tallis, Tomkins, Travers, Tye, Weldon.

CHAPI. See *Spain* 6; *Opera* 15.

CHAPMAN, GEORGE (c. 1559–1634). Poet and dramatist. See mention under *Masque*.

CHAPPELL.

(1) WILLIAM (1809–88). Musical antiquarian. See mentions under *God save the Queen* 5; *Carman's Whistle*; *Nicknamed Compositions* 10.

(2) Publishing and piano-making firm, Chappell & Co. See mention under *Publishing of Music* 7.

CHAPUIS, AUGUSTE PAUL JEAN BAPTISTE. Born at Dampierre-sur-Salon in 1868 and died in Paris in 1933, aged seventy-five. He was a pupil of Massenet, Franck, and Dubois at the Paris Conservatory, and composed operas, choral music, songs, chamber music, etc.

CHAQUE (Fr.). 'Each', 'every'.

CHARACTERISTIC PIECE. A rather vague term occasionally applied by composers to their shorter pieces (especially for piano). Some one motif or mood is generally in evidence throughout, and perhaps in most cases what the composer means by the title is much the same as what a German composer means by the title 'Stimmungsbild' (see under *Stimme*), though the word 'Charakterstück' is also used in Germany, e.g. Schumann's *Davidsbündlertänze* have as sub-title '18 Charakterstücke'.

An earlier use of the word 'characteristic' in a musical connexion is that of Beethoven's 'No. 1' *Leonora* Overture. On the first-violin part of this he called it 'Characteristic Overture'. Here the intention was, apparently, to suggest the expression of dramatic feeling.

CHARACTER NOTATION. Same as Buckwheat Notation (see *Lancashire Sol-fa*).

CHARAKTERSTÜCK. See *Characteristic Piece*.

CHARGER, SE (Fr.). 'To take upon oneself.' (*Ils*) *se chargent*, '(they) take upon themselves', undertake.

CHARITY CHILDREN AS CHOIRS. See *Anglican Parish Church Music* 5, 7; *Oratorio* 4.

CHARIVARI. This is a French word, of unknown origin, signifying extemporized music of the most violent kind, performed with any household utensils capable of making a noise, before the house of some person of whom it is thought proper to express communal disapprobation (e.g. in Le Sage's *Le Diable boiteux*, when a woman of sixty married a youth of seventeen). The engaging practice here mentioned has, apparently, obtained in almost all ages and all countries, for most languages have a term for it. The English say *Rough Music*; the Italians *Chiasso* (i.e. 'uproar') or *Scampanata* (i.e. a 'bell-ringing'); the Germans, *Katzenmusik* (or 'cat-music'). The American terms are *Shivaree* (a corruption of 'charivari') and *Calthumpian* (or 'Callithumpian', or 'Calathumpian') *Concert* (or *Serenade*).

For a less 'rough' extemporized orchestra see *Marrowbones and Cleaver*; *Saltbox*.

CHARLEMAGNE (743–814). See *Plainsong* 3; *Schola Cantorum*; *Italy* 4; *Alcuin*.

CHARLES I of England (b. 1600; came to throne 1625; executed 1649). See references under *Chapel Royal*; *Scotland* 6; *Minstrels* 3; *Monopolies*; *Wilson, John*; *Dowland*.

CHARLES II of England (b. 1630; came to throne 1660; d. 1685). See references under *Chapel Royal*; *Anthem*; *Parish Clerk*; *Scotland* 9; *England* 5; *Monopolies*; *Bagpipe Family* 4; *Wilson, John*; *Wise*; *Locke*.

CHARLES V. Holy Roman Emperor and King of Spain (b. 1500; d. 1558). See *Belgium* 2; *Holland* 2; *Spain* 5.

CHARLES V of France. See *France* 3.

CHARLES VI of France. See *France* 3.

CHARLES THE GREAT. See references under *Charlemagne*, above.

CHARLESTON (S.C.). See *Concert* 15; *Opera* 21 a; *Cecilia*; and see below.

CHARLESTON (see also above). A variety of fox-trot (q.v.), long popular amongst the Negroes of the Southern States. It had a short career in American and European ball-rooms from about 1925, and about 1950 had a period of revival. Its rhythmic characteristic is that its bars, of four crotchets (quarter-notes) each, are divided into two unequal parts of respectively three and five quavers (eighth-notes)

$| \; \flat \; . \; \flat \flat \; |$

CHARLIE IS MY DARLING. The poem is by Lady Nairne (q.v.), though there seems to have been an earlier Jacobite ballad of the same name; the tune is old Scottish traditional.

CHARPENTIER.

(1) **MARC ANTOINE.** Born in Paris about 1636 and died there in 1704, aged about sixty-eight. He went to Rome to study painting, but, hearing the music of Carissimi, became that composer's pupil, and on return to Paris associated himself with the dramatist Molière in the performances of his theatre. He earned a high reputation as a composer, especially for his oratorios in the style of Carissimi (see *Oratorio* 4, 7 (1690)). His compositions include operas and masses.

(2) **GUSTAVE** (p. 384, pl. **63.** 9). Born at Dieuze, in Lorraine, in 1860 and died in Paris in 1956, aged ninety-five. He received his training first at the Conservatory of Lille and then at that of Paris, at which latter he was a pupil of Massenet and won the Prix de Rome (q.v.). His *Impressions of Italy*, composed during his tenure of that distinction, are still heard and always please by their naïvety and noise. Amongst all his output there is one work that won him real fame, and this is the opera *Louise* (1900), which reveals not only skill in composition in a style that may be called successful commonplace, but also the dramatic instinct and the social sympathies of the composer-librettist. The heroine of *Louise* belongs to a class her creator understood and with which he sympathized, that of the Parisian work girl, for whom he founded an institution in Paris which was to provide both theatrical entertainment and the chance to learn to sing, to dance, and to act.

See passing references under *Opera* 11 d; *Street Music* 2; For plot of *Louise* see under that heading.

CHASINS, ABRAM. Born in New York in 1903, of Russian parents. He is a pianist and teacher, and has done much work as musical director for radio. He is a sensitive and varied composer, especially of piano music.

See *Concerto* 6 c (1903).

CHASSE, COR DE (Fr.). 'Hunting horn.' See *Horn Family* 2 a, 3, 5.

CHASSÉ. See *Ballet* 8.

CHASSE, LA. Symphony by Haydn (see *Nicknamed* 11(73)). Quartets by Haydn (see *Nicknamed* 12.1) and Mozart (see *Nicknamed* 15, K. 458).

CHÂTEAUMINORS, ALPHONSE. See *Percussion Family* 4 c (under 'Tabor').

CHAUCER, GEOFFREY (c. 1340–1400). See references under *Inns and Taverns*; *Minstrels* 5; *Cecilia*; *Bagpipe Family* 1.

CHAUSSON, ERNEST (p. 384, pl. **63.** 6). Born in Paris in 1855 and died near Mantes-sur-Seine in 1899, aged forty-four. He studied at the Paris Conservatory under Massenet and then transferred himself to the circle and influence of Franck (q.v.). He was a man of good education, trained for the law, and also a man of wealth. He was killed in a bicycle accident on his own estate.

His music (chamber, orchestral, operatic, etc.) shows the influence of Franck and sometimes of Wagner or of Brahms, but at the time of his death he appeared to be moving towards the ideals of Debussy. His songs are very fine.

Cf. *Concerto* 6 c (1855).

CHÁVEZ, CARLOS (p. 209, pl. **41.** 7). Born near Mexico City, Mexico, in 1899. He is looked upon by many as the most eminent living Mexican musician. He founded the Symphony Orchestra of Mexico (1928: conducted by him till 1949) and has been head of both the National Conservatory of Music and the Government Department of Fine Arts. His symphonies (the sixth appeared in 1964) and other compositions (often showing the influence of the native Indian melody) have met with favour in his own country, in the United States, and elsewhere. He is the author of a book, *Towards a New Music*.

See *Concerto* 6 c (1899).

CHAYKOVSKY. See *Tchaikovsky*.

CHAZZAN. See *Jewish Music* 3, 6.

CHE (It.). 'Who', 'which'.

CHÉDEVILLE, the brothers PIERRE (1694–1725), ESPRIT PHILIPPE (1696–1762), and NICHOLAS (1705–82). They were celebrated Parisian players of, and composers for, the musette (see *Bagpipe* 6) and the vielle or hurdy-gurdy (see *Hurdy-gurdy*).

CHEER, BOYS, CHEER. See *Russell, Henry*.

CHEETHAM'S PSALMODY. See *Hymns and Hymn Tunes* 17 e, where, however, there is used the correct spelling 'Chetham's'—that of all the editions for which the compiler was himself responsible.

CHEF D'ATTAQUE (Fr.). 'Leader of the attack', i.e. orchestral leading violin (American, 'concert-master').

CHENG. See *Reed-Organ Family* 1, 6.

CHERRY, ANDREW. See *Bay of Biscay*.

CHERRY RIPE. The poem is by Herrick (published in *Hesperides*, 1648), the music by C. E. Horn (q.v.).

CHERUBINI, MARIA LUIGI CARLO ZENOBIO SALVATORE (p. 517, pl. **94.** 7). Born at Florence in 1760 and died in Paris in 1842, aged eighty-one. Almost all his life was spent in Paris, where he was for over forty years connected with the Conservatory, for the greater part of the time as its director. He was a learned contrapuntist and writer on counterpoint, and a voluminous and successful composer of operas, church music, etc. His long activities as official and composer brought him into contact with many musicians.

Beethoven greatly esteemed his music, and so did Mendelssohn.

See *Mass* 4; *Requiem*; *Opera* 24 d (1800); *Pianoforte Playing* 3; *Criticism* 6; *Folia*; *Percussion* 4 c; *Boïeldieu*; *Mechanical Reproduction* 5; *Ave Verum*; *Sarti*; *Vidal*.

CHERYEPNIN. See *Tcherepnin*.

CHESHIRE ROUND. See *Round* 2.

CHESTER. See *Minstrels*, etc. 2; *Mysteries*, etc.; *Waits*; *Scotland* 8; *Recorder Family* 2; *Cathedral Music* 2. Organists of the Cathedral who receive notice are (with their periods of office): R. *White* (c. 1535–74); *Bateson* (1602–9); J. C. *Bridge* (1877–1925); C. *Hylton Stewart* (1930–2).

CHESTER, Messrs. J. and W., Ltd. See *Publishing of Music* 7.

CHESTERFIELD, LORD (1694–1773). See quotation under *Minuet*.

CHESTER WAITS TUNE. See *Waits*.

CHEST OF VIOLS. See *Viol Family* 3.

CHEST VOICE or **CHEST REGISTER.** See *Voice* 4, 14.

CHETHAM'S PSALMODY. See *Cheetham's Psalmody* above, and *Hymns and Hymn Tunes* 17 e.

CHEVALET (Fr.). 'Trestle', i.e. the bridge (q.v.) of instruments of the violin family, etc.

CHEVÉ, ÉMILE JOSEPH MAURICE (1804–64). See *Sight-Singing* 2; *Tonic Sol-fa* 9.

CHEVILLE (Fr.). 'Peg', e.g. of a stringed instrument.

CHEVRETTE. See *Bagpipe Family* 6 (end).

CHEZY, WILHELMINA VON. See *Libretto*.

CHIARO, CHIARA (It., masc., fem.). 'Clear', unconfused. Hence *Chiaramente*, 'clearly', 'distinctly'; *Chiarezza*, 'clarity', 'distinctness'.

CHIASSO. See *Charivari*.

CHIAVE (It.). Clef. See *Notation* 4.

CHICA (Sp.). An earlier form of the Fandango (q.v.).

CHICAGO. See *Concert* 15; *Opera* 21 i; *Organ* 5; *Patronage* 7; *Applause* 7; *Schools of Music*.

CHICHESTER CATHEDRAL. See *Cathedral Music* 2. Organists who receive notice in this volume are (with their periods of office): *Weelkes* (c. 1602–23); T. *Kelway* (1726–47); *Grace* (1931–8).

CHICKERING. See *Pianoforte* 9.

CHIESA (It.). 'Church.' 'Aria da Chiesa', see *Aria*. 'Cantata da Chiesa', see *Cantata*. 'Concerto da Chiesa', see *Concerto* 2. 'Sonata da Chiesa', see *Suite* 1; *Sonata* 2.

CHIFONIE (Fr.). An early name for the hurdy-gurdy (q.v.).

CHILD.

(1) WILLIAM. Born at Bristol in 1606 and died at Windsor in 1697, aged about ninety-one. He was, before the Commonwealth, one of the organists of Charles I, and after it of Charles II. He left much church music (see reference under *Anthem*, Period II), and a marble pavement in the choir of St. George's Chapel, Windsor, this latter the result of his losing a sort of bet with the canons as to whether he would ever receive the arrears of salary owed him by the King.

Cf. *Windsor*.

(2) FRANCIS J. (1825–96). A reference will be found under *Ballad* 5.

CHILDREN OF THE REVELS. See *Jones, Robert*.

CHILMEAD, EDMUND (1610–54). See *Clubs for Music-Making*.

CHIMING of bells. See *Bells* 3.

CHINA. See *Oriental*; *Broadcasting* 3.

CHINESE CRASH CYMBAL. This differs in shape from the normal cymbal (see *Percussion Family* 3 o, 4 b, 5 o). The cup is much shallower and its edge turns up. It is made of a special alloy peculiar to the Chinese, and when struck with a drum-stick gives a brilliant crash, 'of oriental atmosphere'; its home is the dance band.

CHINESE CRESCENT. Same as *Turkish Crescent* (q.v.).

CHINESE LANGUAGE and Intonation. See *Melody* 2.

CHINESE TEMPLE BLOCK. See *Korean Temple Block.*

CHINESE WOOD BLOCK. An oblong block of wood, 7 or 8 inches long, with slots cut in it. It exists in various sizes, and consequently at various pitches. Struck with the stick of a snare drum it gives a hard, hollow tone, but various types of mallet are available. Other names are *Clog Box* and *Tap Box.* The jazz movement (p. 789, pl. **134.** 9) seems to have brought this instrument into use.

CHIPP, EDMUND THOMAS. Born in London in 1823 and died at Nice in 1886, aged nearly sixty-three. He held important organ posts in London and Belfast, and then became organist of Ely Cathedral (q.v.). Some of his organ music is still heard.

CHIROPLAST. A hand-rest for piano practice, which formed a part of the once popular Logier system (see *Logier*).

CHISHOLM, ERIK (p. 289, pl. **51.** 8). Born in Glasgow in 1904 and died at Rondebosch, South Africa, in 1965, aged sixty-one. He held various Scottish organistships, spent some time in Canada, and, returning in 1928, studied at the University of Edinburgh (D.Mus. 1934). He was active in Glasgow musical activities. For a time he was one of the conductors of the Carl Rosa Opera Company, and he toured Italy and the Far East. In 1946 he settled in Cape Town as Professor of Music in the University and Director of the South African College of Music. His numerous and varied compositions fall mainly into two classes—works written in Scotland and nationalistic in character, technique and style, and works influenced by his residence in the Far East. He composed several operas.

CHITARRONE or **CHITTARONE.** See *Lute* 5.

CHIUSO, CHIUSA (It., masc., fem.). 'Closed.' See *Horn Family* 5.

CHLADNI. See *Clavicylinder.*

CHM. See *Degrees and Diplomas* 2, 4.

CHŒUR (Fr.). 'Chorus', 'choir'. (But *Grand Chœur*, besides meaning 'Full Chorus', 'Big Choir', means 'Full Organ', or a loud composition for such.)

CHOIR or **CHORUS.** (1) A *Mixed Voice Choir* or *Chorus* is one of both women and men. (2) A *Male Voice Choir* or *Chorus* is (*a*) one of men only (this is the more usual use of the term), or (*b*) one of boys and men. (3) A *Double Choir* or *Chorus* is a choir arranged in two equal and complete bodies, with a view to the singing of music not merely in double the usual number of parts (i.e. generally eight) but of a kind which, by its responsive effects or in other ways, makes use of the quasi-independent character of the two bodies.

Architecturally a choir is that part of a cathedral which, in a church other than a cathedral, is called the chancel.

CHOIR BOYS AND PRESS GANG, etc. See *Chapel Royal.*

CHOIR BOYS, neglect of them in early nineteenth century. See *Cathedral Music* 7.

CHOIR ORGAN. See *Organ* 2 d.

CHOIR PITCH. See *Pitch* 3, 8.

CHOIR, THE (periodical). See *Methodism and Music* 10.

CHOKE CYMBALS. These are two ordinary cymbals (see *Percussion Family* 3 o, 4 b, 5 o), fixed face to face on a rod, with a device by which their pressure, one on the other, can be adjusted according to the tone-quality desired. They are played with a drum-stick, giving a short sharp crash. The jazz movement seems to be responsible for their coming into use.

CHOPIN, FRÉDÉRIC FRANÇOIS (p. 192, pl. **38**). Born at Zelazowa Wola, about thirty miles from Warsaw, Poland, in 1810, and died in Paris in 1849, aged thirty-nine. He was the poet of the piano—a lyric poet, for the most part, but sometimes a dramatic and sometimes also an epic poet. What music he wrote for other media than his own instrument is negligible, and when he associated other instruments with that one they submissively played the part of humble attendants. The piano was to him as much a means of natural self-expression as if it were a part of him. He expressed through it thoughts and feelings that had not previously found expression in music and that could not have been expressed through any other instrument or any combination of instruments. He is in turn tender, gay, and bold, but whatever his mood it is not merely a mood turned into tone by a composer; it is a mood of Chopin expressed through the piano, Chopin's other self.

By parentage he was half Polish and half French—by residence also, spending about half his life in Warsaw and half in Paris. Strong sympathies with the country of his birth in the darkest period of her oppression moved him often to proud and defiant musical utterance, and the grace of the country of his partial origin and of his adoption also constantly made itself felt.

His father was first a book-keeper and then a teacher in Warsaw. The boy showed early genius. At nine he played in public; at ten the great singer Catalani, amazed and admiring, gave him a watch with a complimentary inscription. He had for teacher of piano Zywny, a Bohemian, and for teacher of composition Elsner, a Silesian, and to them he ever remained grateful, yet in a large measure he was self-taught, and Elsner's wise saying was, 'Leave him alone; his is an uncommon way, because his gifts are uncommon'.

He had a social instinct. He loved company and company loved him. He loved the peasantry for their music, and he loved men and women of higher station for the stimulus of their thought and for the pleasure of cultured companionship. He was not a great reader, in this differing from his fellow-members of the great triad of the Romantic school that the wonderful two years 1809 and 1810 brought into the world; his music was infinitely less literary than Schumann's, and he was little drawn to the musical setting of graceful or noble words, as both Schumann and Mendelssohn were. Yet he loved intellectual company, and all his life moved in it.

His twenty-first year found him in Paris (p. 192, pl. **38.** 2; p. 192, pl. **38.** 3). Here the novelist George Sand was his intimate companion, and he lived much in her literary and artistic circle. He was the friend of the Hungarian Liszt (q.v.), as of the Italian Bellini (q.v.), from whose graceful vocal writing he learnt a good deal of his knack of making the piano sing, as he did also from the study of the Irishman Field (q.v.), upon whose nocturnes his own are closely modelled.

Ill health came early upon him. A sad incident in his life is the expedition (with George Sand and her children) to Majorca, where the health he sought was denied him by the intolerable discomfort of living amongst a half-civilized peasantry in a phenomenally inclement season.

The revolution that was to lead to the Second Empire drove him from Paris to London (p. 192, pl. **38.** 4), and to Manchester, Glasgow, and Edinburgh. He was much fêted —too much for his strength. At last he became so weak that when he was to play at some great house they had to carry him upstairs. Hysterically, at last, he hurried back to Paris.

He was now dying. A generous Scottish friend, Miss Stirling, sent him a thousand pounds (of which he consented to retain only a portion). One of his sisters hastened from Poland to care for him. A countrywoman of his, the Countess Potocka, visited him; he begged her to sing; a piano was brought to the door of the bedroom and she sang airs of Stradella and Marcello, two of his Preludes (Nos. 4 and 6), being also performed. As she ended it was thought he was passing, and all dropped on their knees to pray. He rallied and lived two days more. Then, kissing the hand of his favourite pupil, Gutmann, in appreciation and gratitude, he passed away.

There was a service at the Church of the Madeleine, where the choir and orchestra of the Paris Conservatory performed Mozart's *Requiem* before a congregation of four thousand. He was buried in the spot he had chosen —in Père-Lachaise, next to his friend Bellini. As they lowered him into his last resting-place there was opened the silver box of Polish earth, given him nearly twenty years before, on the day he left Poland never to return, and at the words 'earth to earth' it was sprinkled on his coffin.

The legacy he left the world included many shorter or longer single-movement compositions—twenty-seven études, twenty-five preludes, nineteen nocturnes, fifty-two mazurkas, four impromptus, a barcarolle, a berceuse, and so on. It also included three sonatas and two concertos. Some of these remain today the most played and the most popular of all recital items.

See references under: *Aeolopantaleon*; *Arrangement*; *Badinage*; *Bagpipe Family* 8; *Ballade*; *Ballet* 5, 6; *Barcarolle*; *Berlioz* ; *Bolero*; *Cinematograph*; *Colour and Music* 2; *Composition* 9 (his method of composing); *Concerto* 6 b (1810); *Cracovienne*; *Criticism* 2 (Schumann's championship), 5 (Dwight's championship in the U.S.A.); *Dance* 9; *Écossaise*; *Étude*; *Expression* 2; *Fingering* 5; *Form* 6; *Franchomme*; *Gesamtausgabe*; *Harmony* 22 (use of 'consecutives'); *Hexameron*; *Holland* 6; *Kalkbrenner*; *Klindworth*; *Mazurka*; *Measure* (wrong barring); *Mendelssohn*; *Misattributed*; *Nationalism*; *Nicknamed Compositions* 8; *Osborne*; *Pianoforte* 13, 18, 22; *Pianoforte Playing* 5 (his use of pedal), 7, 10; *Polonaise*; *Prelude* 2; *Romantic*; *Rubato* 2; *Scherzo*; *Scriabin*; *Sonata* 9, 10 c; *Szymanowski*; *Waltz*.

CHOPSTICKS. This is a quick waltz tune for the piano, four hands, performed by schoolgirls, as an amusement, in a traditional manner —the flat hand being held perpendicularly and the notes struck with its side (i.e. with the side of the little finger), with a touch of glissando intercalated and a dominant–tonic vamping bass part. Obviously the name has no reference to the Chinese table tool but rather to the operation of cutting firewood; in some countries there has been adopted a French name which suggests another kind of chopping, *Côtelettes* (in German *Koteletten Walzer*).

A famous collection of compositions based on a version of the chopsticks tune is the joint work of Borodin, Cui, Liadof, Rimsky-Korsakof, and Liszt. It consists of twenty-four variations plus fourteen little pieces; it is published under the title 'Paraphrases'.

CHORAGUS. An official peculiar to the University of Oxford. When the Lecturership or Professorship in Music was founded and endowed by William Heyther in 1626, he laid it down that the professor was to be concerned with the teaching of theory and that a subordinate official, called Choragus, was to conduct practices of music twice a week. The office still exists (but not with that duty), and it is still remunerated by the same annual sum as in 1626—£13. 6s. 8d. For a time, during the late nineteenth century, there was also an assistant official called Coryphaeus.

CHORALE (in Ger., **CHORAL**). See *Hymns and Hymn Tunes* 3 and *Germany* 3 for a discussion of the subject. The following remarks may, however, be added here.

Whilst, in general speech, when we mention 'Chorales' we refer to the hymn tunes, Protestant in origin, treated of in the articles alluded to above, this is not the strict meaning of the German word 'Choral'. Originally it is a word belonging to the unreformed Church and means the ecclesiastical *Plainsong* (q.v.), the *Cantus choralis*: it is worthy of note that the long article 'Choral' in Mendel's great *Musiklexikon* (Berlin, 1872) is, rather curiously perhaps, entirely devoted to an explanation of plainsong, what we call 'Chorale' being treated under other headings.

Properly, the 'Choral' in the German Roman Catholic Church is that part of the plainsong

PLATE 37

CHOPIN LEAVES HIS LAST CONCERT

By Batt

ON November 16 1848, a Polish ball and concert were given at the Guildhall, London. Chopin, who had recently fled from Paris on account of the Revolution, volunteered his services for the occasion. It was destined to be his last appearance in public.

The occasion was a melancholy one from every point of view. He had an intense dislike for playing in public at any time, but now he was very ill and, moreover, the hot, excited dancers were in no mood to listen to his playing.

To crown the disaster, the London Press next day ignored his presence at the function.

As he stepped into his cab that night after the Guildhall concert he must have been more than usually disconsolate: there was an element of tragedy which was characteristic of his whole life, and it hangs like a pall of gloom over the close of his career.

B.

sung by more than one voice (the 'Concentus' as distinguished from the 'Accentus'), but this distinction of terminology is not always observed. A good deal of metrical Latin hymnody had come to have a place in the service, and Luther drew largely upon this in translation; the plainsong melodies, in some cases, were taken into the Protestant service, a number of what we now call 'chorales' (in the limited sense) being, indeed, such melodies adapted and harmonized for four voices. The congregation had no recognized part in the music of the pre-Reformation Church, and one of Luther's most striking innovations was in the provision of hymns and tunes for their singing. Those hymns largely took the place of the plainsong of the choir in the unreformed Church, and it was natural that the same name 'Choral' should be employed.

The first Lutheran chorales had not the regular rhythms that they later took on. They had often a mixture of two-in-a-measure and three-in-a-measure, and, indeed, a good deal of the free rhythm of plainsong. The steady procession of even notes came gradually into use, and by Bach's day (a century and a half or so after Luther's death) it was invariable—often by no means with advantage to the original melodies, Bach being sometimes an offender here. During the late nineteenth century there was a movement to restore the old 'Rhythmic Chorale', as its defenders called it.

With the Lutheran chorales, as with the Genevan and English and Scottish hymn tunes, the melody was at first in the tenor. During the seventeenth century it gradually became usual to place it in the treble, as today.

The repertory of the German chorale may be said to have been completed in Bach's day. He himself composed only about thirty—writing, however, 400 reharmonizations of existing chorale melodies (see remark under *Melody* 5 and examples under *Harmony* 3; also *Passion Music* 5; *Cantata*). Since then few have been composed, and, whilst in England the manufacture of hymn tunes is still a fairly flourishing musical industry, in Germany it may be said to have stopped; there every hymn has its traditional tune (though sometimes several have the same tune), and nobody thinks of disjoining the two.

Seven chorales are of particular importance in the Lutheran service—the versified Commandments (*Dies sind die heil'gen zehn Gebot*), the versified Creed (*Wir glauben all' an einen Gott*), the versified Lord's Prayer (*Vater unser im Himmelreich*), the hymn to the Trinity (*Allein Gott in der Höh sei Ehr*), the hymn for Baptism (*Christ unser Herr zum Jordan kam*), the hymn of Confession (*Aus tiefer Noth*), and the hymn for Communion (*Jesus Christus unser Heiland*).

The words of all these but one (*Allein Gott in der Höh sei Ehr*) are by Luther.

It has always been the custom that the congregational singing of chorales should be in unison. It was usual to precede the singing of

MIT FRIED UND FREUD

Free version of 'Nunc dimittis' by Luther; melody also possibly by Luther; harmonization by Bach, *c.* 1740.

Mit Fried und Freud ich fahr da - hin In
In peace and joy I now de - part, As

Got - tes Wil - le; Ge -
God would have . . me. At

- trost ist mir mein Herz . . . und
rest and still are mind . . . and

Sinn, Sanft und stil - le.
heart, He doth save . me.

Wie Gott mir ver - heis - sen hat: Der
As my God hath pro - mised me, Death

Tod ist mein Schlaf wor - den.
is be - come my slum - ber.

a chorale by the playing of an organ prelude (see *Chorale Prelude*) and to interpolate short interludes between every two lines (see Mendelssohn's arrangements of chorales in *St. Paul*). Chorale singing has often been incredibly slow. J. S. Curwen, when in Germany in the 1880s, timed some of the singing and found one verse of an eight-lines long metre (see *Hymns and Hymn Singing* 13) took 2¾ minutes.

For the old custom of playing chorales from church towers see *Trumpet* 2 d; *Trombone Family* 3.

An allusion to Coverdale's attempt to introduce the German chorale into England in 1539 will be seen under *Hymns and Hymn Tunes* 17 e.

For the Hussite precursor of the Lutheran chorale see *Bohemia*. For a secular tune adopted as a chorale see *Church Music* 3.

CHORALE PARTITA. See *Chorale Prelude*.

CHORALE PRELUDE (Ger., *Choral Vorspiel*). In addition to what appears above, some account of the traditional German hymn-tunes ('Chorales') is given in the article *Hymn*, and the statement is there made that they have provided a source of high inspiration to German composers.

Out of the custom of playing organ preludes and interludes to the chorale grew up the technique of two special forms of composition, one based upon a treatment of the chorale melody, often taken line by line and surrounded by other melodic parts woven together into elaborate counterpoint, and the other not reproducing the chorale intact but suggesting it to the minds of the hearers by taking its first few notes as the theme to be elaborated. To a North German congregation, to whom the melodies were all known from childhood, such a piece of organ music had great interest and significance.

Amongst the composers who helped to develop this form were Sweelinck (1562–1621), Scheidt (1587–1654), Pachelbel (1653–1706), Buxtehude (1637–1707), Reinken (1623–1722), and Böhm (1661–1733). Such of Bach's forebears as were organists also naturally took their part in the working out of the form, and he himself crowned the labours of all his predecessors and contemporaries by presenting the form in perfection.

This perfection is twofold. The technical devices employed are masterly and the motifs used in building up the scheme and the treatment of them associate themselves in a wonderful symbolic or mystical way with the thought and feeling of the hymn upon whose melody the chorale is founded.

Busoni and others have arranged many of the Bach Chorale Preludes for piano.

In addition to the Chorale Preludes of Bach, there are certain early works which he called **Chorale Partitas,** the word Partita here, as with certain other composers, having not the usual sense of a suite (q.v.) but that of an air with variations. The number of variations corresponds to the number of the verses of the hymns. Each variation seems to be designed to re-express the thought of the corresponding verse. It has been suggested, on the one hand,

that the several variations were intended to be interpolated between the verses as sung by the congregation, and, on the other, that they were intended to be played, continuously, as a complete set to a congregation that would certainly be well acquainted with the words of the hymn thus illustrated and thus able to interpret the 'programme' of each variation as played.

Since Bach, many other German composers have written chorale preludes, e.g. Brahms (11), Reger (over 80), Karg-Elert (who seems to prefer the description 'Chorale Improvisations'—he has about 90 of these). Certain lesser writers have been very prolific, as Paul Cloussnitzer, who wrote 100, and Carl Piutti (German; 1846–1902), who wrote 200.

To some extent the same form has been cultivated in England. Purcell has a Voluntary on the *Old Hundredth* that, in its primitive way, is quite on the lines of the Bach Chorale Prelude. In the late nineteenth century and early twentieth there was a revival of interest in this form amongst British composers, and many examples were written by Parry, Stanford, Charles Wood, Vaughan Williams, C. C. Palmer, H. Coleman, Alan Gray, Tertius Noble, Harvey Grace, and others. (The famous organist W. T. Best, 1826–97, had led the way towards their revival with a considerable group of compositions of the kind.)

An interesting light on the British growth of interest in Bach's Chorale Preludes is seen by comparing the closing words of the article 'Voluntary' in the various editions of Grove's *Dictionary of Music*. In the 1889 edition (article by Parratt) we read:

'Some day we may hope to hear the best of all— John Sebastian Bach's wonderful settings of all the Chorales.'

In the 1910 edition (article also by Parratt) this becomes:

'It is even possible occasionally to hear John Sebastian Bach's wonderful settings of the Chorales.'

In the edition of 1928 no mention of the chorale prelude occurs in this connexion, the need for propaganda-suggestion being apparently considered no longer to exist.

CHORAL SINGING AND EQUAL TEMPERAMENT. See *Temperament* 10.

CHORAL SOCIETIES. See *Madrigal* 2, 5; *Clubs for Music Making; Oratorio* 5; *Publishing* 7; *United States* 3, 4; *Liedertafel*; *Orphéon*.

CHORAL SYMPHONY. The term may mean several things. Beethoven's Ninth Symphony (1824; generally understood to be the first use of the term) adds vocal soloists and choir in its last movement, the emotion of the previous part of the work here becoming articulate in an enthusiastic declamation of stanzas from Schiller's *Ode to Joy*. Liszt's *Dante Symphony* (1856) has a choral ending and his *Faust Symphony* has one which is optional. Holst's 'First Choral Symphony' (1925) is a four-movement setting for soprano solo, choir, and orchestra of four poems of

Keats. Bantock's two choral symphonies, *Atalanta in Calydon* and *Vanity of Vanities*, are in several movements and for twenty and twelve voice-parts respectively (no instruments). There are also examples by Mahler, Britten, and others.

CHORAL VORSPIEL. See *Chorale Prelude.*

CHORD. See *Harmony* passim, and for descriptions of particular types of chord see, in especial, *Harmony* 24 d–m and also *Augmented Sixth*; *Diminished Seventh*; *Dominant Seventh*; *Leading Seventh*; *Neapolitan Sixth.*

CHORDAL STREAMS. See *Harmony* 16.

'CHORD AND DISCORD.' See *Bruckner Society of America.*

CHORDING. This is a term used by choir-trainers and adjudicators of the choral classes at competition festivals. 'Bad chording' is a form of out-of-tune singing—not that form which results in the close of the piece being at a higher or lower pitch than the opening, but that form which (sometimes in a quite simple passage and sometimes in one of recondite harmonies) results in the notes of the chords not sounding quite true to one another. 'Good chording' is, of course, the absence of this fault.

CHOREGRAPHY, CHOREOGRAPHY. See *Ballet* 8.

CHOREOGRAPHIC POEM. A symphonic poem (q.v.) developing dance rhythms and expressing the dance spirit.

CHORLEY, HENRY FOTHERGILL (1808–72). See references under *Criticism* 4; p. 257, pl. 47. 3.

CHORMÄSSIGE STIMMUNG, CHORSTIMMUNG. See *Pitch* 8.

CHÔROS. See *Villa-Lobos.*

CHORTON. See *Pitch* 3.

CHORUS. See *Choir or Chorus*. Some instrumental uses of the word are as follows: (*a*) Bagpipe. See *Bagpipe Family* 3, 9. (*b*) An old stringed instrument. This use of the word probably generally implies the crwth (q.v.). (*c*) Chorus Reed Stops. See *Organ* 3.

CHOR ZINCK. See *Cornett and Key Bugle Family* 4.

CHOSTAKOVICH. See *Shostakovich.*

CHRISTCHURCH (New Zealand). See *Cathedral Music* 8.

CHRIST CHURCH (Oxford). See *Harwood*; *Armstrong, T. H. W.*; *Cathedral* 4; *Concert Hall* 4.

CHRIST CHURCH TUNE. See *Anglican Chant and Chanting* 4.

CHRISTE ELEISON. These words are in the Mass of the Roman Catholic Church associated with the 'Kyrie Eleison'; see *Kyrie*; *Mass* 3 a.

CHRISTIANS, AWAKE! See *Wainwright, John.*

CHRISTIE (1) JOHN (1882–1962). See *Glyndebourne*. (2) WINIFRED. See *Moór.*

CHRISTIE UNIT ORGAN. See *Electric Musical Instruments* 2 c.

'CHRISTMAS' SYMPHONY (Haydn). See *Nicknamed Compositions* 8.

CHRIST UNSER HERR. See *Chorale.*

CHRISTY. See *Negro Minstrels.*

CHROMATIC. For a general explanation of the term see *Diatonic and Chromatic.*

CHROMATIC CHORDS. Chords containing one or more notes foreign to the prevailing diatonic key. They may be used as mere incidents in harmonic progressions without upsetting the existing tonal centre, or as pivot chords in the process of modulating to some other key. The Augmented Sixths (q.v.), the Neapolitan Sixth (q.v.), and the Supertonic Chromatic Chords (q.v.), are examples. (For a full list consult especially the *Oxford Harmony*, vol. ii, by Dr. H. K. Andrews, which is devoted solely to such chords.)

CHROMATIC DRUMS. See *Percussion Family* 2 a, 5 a.

CHROMATIC HARP. See *Harp* 1.

CHROMATIC SCALE. See *Scale* 7.

CHROMATIQUE (Fr.). 'Chromatic.' For *Cor chromatique* see *Horn Family* 5 c.

CHROMOPHONIE. See *Colour and Music* 10.

CHROTTA. Sometimes used for crwth (q.v.).

CHRYSANDER, KARL FRANZ FRIEDRICH (1826–1901). Authority on Handel, the editor of his complete works for the German Handel Society, and the author of a biography (uncompleted). He worked also on other subjects, editing the works of Palestrina, Schütz, Corelli, Couperin, and Bach.

CHRYSANTHUS. See *Greek Church* 3.

CHRYSOSTOM, LITURGY OF SAINT. See *Greek Church and Music* 1.

CHURCH, (1) JOHN. Born in 1675 and died in 1741, aged sixty-six. He was a Gentleman of the Chapel Royal and Choirmaster of Westminster Abbey (1704 to death). He wrote an *Introduction to Psalmody* (1723), church music, and some fine songs in much the Purcell style.

(2) JOHN. See *Publishing* 9.

CHURCH CADENCE. See *Cadence.*

CHURCH CANTATA. See *Cantata.*

CHURCH MODES. See *Modes.*

CHURCH MUSIC

1. Its Place and Purposes.
2. The Question of Good Taste.
3. What Constitutes Church Music?
4. The History of Music in the Christian Church.
5. A Present-day Difficulty.
6. A Plea from the Scaffold on behalf of better Church Music.

1. Its Place and Purposes. There is no art which has not been used in worship.

Art comes from the co-operation, in varying proportions, of the sense of beauty and the need for self-expression. Every religious cult provides its devotees with some opportunity of self-expression and it is a human instinct, when expressing the high things of human thought and feeling, to do so with all the beauty of which humanity is capable.

Architecture is in a sense the most important of the arts as used in religion, both because a building for worship is almost a necessity and because fine performance in architecture has a permanency beyond that of performance in any other art whatever. But music is, in another sense, the most important, for, being (unlike architecture) *un-material*, (unlike painting) *unconcerned with representation of physical objects*, and (unlike poetry) *independent of ideas*, it is able to fly, unburdened, into regions beyond their utmost reach. When, abandoning this independence, it takes upon itself the pious duty of carrying with it thought and such emotion as can be expressed in words, thought and emotion are the gainers, something having been added to them.

The flame of emotion that is kindled by the thought of holiness is caught up and carried aloft into the regions of the sublime in the *Sanctus* of Palestrina's *Missa Papae Marcelli*, or of Bach's Mass in B minor, or of Beethoven's Mass in D. And the attainment of the realization of an escape from the world (that is, of sublimity) is one of the supreme objects of religious exercise.

It is some such trend of thought as the above which provides the strongest motive for the demand for the use in public worship of the finest music and the most expressive performance. The 'sacrificial' character of religious musical expression strengthens the motive; indeed, many would put this first, for they would say that, in their minds, music in worship is first of all an offering to the Being worshipped, and that as such it must be of the highest. The relation of these two views as to the chief purpose of fine music in public worship is very close, and it is perhaps unimportant whether those concerned in the ministry of music look upon the music as their offering or whether they look upon it as exalting the mood of the worshipper into a more intense devotion, and so making that mood a more acceptable offering.

But it must be remembered that there are in the musical exercises of religion other purposes than the helping of the worshipper to experience those moments of mystical communion or of making an 'offering'. In music lies the one effective means of communal expression. The largest bodies of worshippers may join in expressing their faith, their hope, or their charity in song whose necessary simplicity seems to detract nothing from its emotional strength when it is sung with unanimity and fervour. The duty here imposed upon those charged with the ordering of music in the service of religion is the provision of a large and varied body of religious poetry and accompanying music, dignified yet simple.

Moreover, in a missionary religion such as Christianity it is impossible altogether to overlook a third purpose, less noble in itself, perhaps, but of high importance from practical considerations—and it is part of the teaching of Christianity that religion should be practical. The outer world is to be evangelized, and those who do not belong to the outer world but whose devotional enthusiasm is, in itself, insufficient to draw them to the gatherings of the faithful are to be brought in. Music, then, is to 'go into the highways and hedges and compel them to come in'.

2. The Question of Good Taste. There are those who maintain that the importance of this last great purpose justifies the use of any kind of music. To the musician this sounds very like the false doctrine of 'doing evil that good may come'. As one of Shakespeare's characters puts it, 'To do a great right do a little wrong'; as the proverbial expression goes, 'The end justifies the means'.

It is very difficult to argue with those who support the use of bad music to lead men into good ways, since usually they are, from some natural incapacity, or through lack of early musical environment, incapable of feeling the difference between good and bad in music, and, sometimes, even of realizing that 'bad' exists. The argument from analogy may be ventured. There is good and bad in everything else, so it is reasonable to suppose that there is good and bad in music. Association with the 'bad' in any department of life has, to say the least, a 'cheapening' effect on the mind, whereas association with the 'good' raises it. Hence if two pieces of music, good and bad, have equally strong attractive qualities the ultimate end in view will be better attained by the use of the good.

And 'good' yet highly 'attractive' music does exist and has powerfully aided religious movements from the beginning of Christianity to the present day. The *Laudi Spirituali* (q.v.) sung by bodies of pious believers about the streets of Florence and other Italian cities, from the fourteenth to the eighteenth centuries, were the expression of a great popular movement, and (at the outset, at any rate) seem to have been of high musical and poetical quality. Luther, a musician of culture, found in good music one of his greatest weapons of offence and defence, and the melodies his followers sang are amongst those most treasured by musicians today. John Wesley (see *Methodism and Music*), who, though he came of a family that in the next two generations showed itself to be intensely musical yet had himself no musical knowledge or practical musical ability, in his many hymn-books supplied music at least as good as that in general congregational use in the Anglican worship at the period; that is, he did not find it necessary to descend. (For his views on the words of hymns see *Hymns and Hymn Tunes* 15.) And had such evangelistic leaders as General Booth and Messrs. Moody and Sankey enjoyed the advantage of possessing literary and musical taste they would have gained and held just as many ardent converts by means of wholesome, simple, popular song as they did by the simple reiteration of some elementary religious thought set to a 'catchy' rhythm. There is, however, at least as much to be said for the jigging rhythms, facile melodies, and commonplace harmonies of the music of street and mission-hall evangelism as there is for the use of cheap sentimentalities in the more 'respectable' places of Christian activity. And any casual but scrupulously open-minded examination of a few of the hymn-books of various denominations, or of a chance bundle of anthems issued by almost any publisher, will show that mere sentimentality is in the church music of the nineteenth and twentieth centuries very often allowed to masquerade as high devotional feeling. As this is so often undetected, it would appear that the first duty of any church musician is the acquisition of a standard of musical taste—which means the thoughtful acquaintance with a large and varied body of all that music which time, the only infallible critic, has endorsed. It should be emphasized that simplicity and elaboration are not the same thing as bad and good. The decision as to simple or elaborate music in a church is one to be made on purely practical grounds, the decision as to bad or good being, on the other hand, essentially a moral question. Much of the simplest music in use is perfectly strong and good, and much of the most elaborate is extremely weak and poor—the converse being likewise true. The effort to improve the music in any particular church has too often taken the line of adding to its elaboration instead of that of raising its quality.

'Elaborate service-music may claim to be considered seriously as an embellishment on the same footing as fine carving, pictures, or architecture only when it is fine music. Too often its decorative analogy would be a fretwork lectern, or a poker-work pulpit, or a screen of deal painted with red, white, and blue stripes and festooned with artificial flowers. In view of the quality of at least a third of the most popular services and anthems, the less their advocates insist on the decorative value of such music the better' (Harvey Grace).

3. What Constitutes Church Music? If it be asked 'What is Church Music?' the answer is that no precise definition is possible. It cannot be claimed that there has in any age been any distinguishing mark between a piece of music expressing serious emotions of a religious order and one expressing serious emotions of a non-religious order. A motet and a serious madrigal, in the sixteenth century, were musically the same, and so later were many of Bach's sacred and secular settings. David dancing before the ark probably danced in just the same way as on any other occasion when he wished to express rejoicing, and the music of some of the graver court dances of the seventeenth and eighteenth centuries (sarabandes and the like) would not offend any religious purist if, unaware of its provenance, he

heard it as a Lenten cathedral voluntary. Bach arranged a graceful courante as a hymn-tune. Conventions establish certain styles of music as 'churchly', as they do certain styles of architecture (to use a convenient American word), but they are mere conventions, and even *they* do not control the choice of music with any definiteness, for an idiom that in church is felt to be 'churchly' will be found to be in use out of church without any such connotation. Good music *is* good music, in church or out of it, and sincerity is equally felt wherever music is heard. If music heard in church is good and sincere, and suitable to and expressive of the words or thoughts to which it is allied, then the association of time and place will convert it into 'church music'.

LIEBSTER IMMANUEL, HERZOG DER FROMMEN

Melody (1679) an adaptation of a courante; harmonized by Bach, c. 1740 (Cantata 123).

Finally, a word may be added about the standard of performance. This, it need not be said, should be the highest possible. A frequent cause of a low standard lies in small churches with small resources trying to give the same kind of music as large churches with large resources. Simplicity, beautifully achieved, is a high quality.

4. The History of Music in the Christian Church. It is impossible here to trace the development of musical activities in the various religions of the world, or even to trace it in the Jewish religion and the Christian religion which flowed out of that and took so many different channels. That the Jewish religion gave a large place to musical expression is evident from the records (see *Jewish Music*). The very existence of the Book of Psalms (see *Psalm*) is, indeed, itself sufficient evidence. The Books of Samuel and Chronicles tell us that 'David played before the Lord on all manner of instruments made of fir wood, even on harps, and on psalteries, and on timbrels, and on cornets, and on cymbals'. In the temple of Solomon, at the outset, 'four thousand praised the Lord with instruments' and 'the number of them ... that were instructed in the songs of the Lord were two hundred fourscore and eight'. Before the last of the Temples of Jerusalem was destroyed, after twelve hundred years of musical service, the system of synagogues had spread, and with it a liturgical service making large use of song (but no longer of instruments—see *Jewish Music* 2).

When Christianity came there was at first no break with the Jewish Church; Christians still attended the Temple in Jerusalem and their synagogues (as Christ had done), and in the separate Christian meetings they carried on the musical tradition. It is somewhat surprising, however, that in the accounts of the preaching journey of Christ with his disciples there is no record of communal song—except at the last solemn meeting of the Master and his companions before the Crucifixion (Matt. xxvi. 30: 'When they had sung an hymn, they went out into the Mount of Olives.' The hymn sung is taken by Biblical authorities to have been certainly the 'Hallel', or Psalm 113 or 114, sung by the Jews at the Passover celebration).

The organization of Christianity into a distinct society brought much use of song—in such times and places as meetings were not compelled to be held secretly, and even in these, when conditions made it safe, there was singing. We find Paul exhorting the Ephesians and Colossians to use psalms, hymns, and spiritual songs (Eph. v. 19; Col. iii. 16); he is speaking, apparently, of both their private devotions and their public.

The younger Pliny, writing to the Emperor Trajan (A.D. 61–113), and asking for instructions as to the degree of rigour with which he was to carry out the prosecution of the Christians in his province of Bithynia, describes them as blameless in life but the devotees of a superstition, whose practice was to gather on stated days before sunrise and to repeat antiphonally 'a hymn to Christ as God'. The singing of Paul and Silas at night, in prison, nearly a century earlier (Acts xvi. 25) will be recalled; most probably they sang Psalms antiphonally.

Hebrew and Greek elements probably blended in the worship music which grew into a traditional corpus during the first three centuries of Christianity and was further codified from time to time. It appears as though the accompaniment of instruments was not favoured; despite their long use in the Temple they had perhaps acquired theatrical and other undesirable associations (possibly the objection applied only to certain instruments). In the late fourth or early fifth century St. Jerome wrote that a Christian maiden ought not even to know what a lyre or a flute is like or to what use it is put. It is said that the introduction of the organ (q.v.) into Christian worship was due to Pope Vitalian in the seventh century. The process of systematization and of development of the Church's song may be traced in other articles in this volume (especially *Liturgy, Plainsong, Mass, Schola Cantorum, Harmony*).

Throughout the ages there have been in the Christian Church alternating processes of the accumulation of undesirable musical practices and of reform. As the preface of the Common Prayer of the Church of England says, 'There was never any thing by the wit of man so well devised, or so sure established, which in continuance of time hath not been corrupted'. In the case of church music the 'corruption' has usually come from a tendency to overemphasize the purely musical attractiveness of the church's song in the interests either of the professional performers or of the congregation. Against this tendency authority has repeatedly thundered, and presumably (humanity being what it is) will often have cause to thunder again. Thus John XXII, in the early fourteenth century, forbade the use of secular melodies as a basis for the harmonized settings of portions of the Mass, and, indeed, tried to put down harmony altogether. Thus the Council of Trent (1545–63) recommended bishops to exclude 'music in which anything impious or lascivious finds a part'; Pius IV soon after appointed a committee of cardinals to see that the council's recommendation was carried out, and there seems to have been again some danger at this time of harmonized music being forbidden, largely on the ground of the inaudibility of the words, owing to the interweaving of the voices. The edicts of two recent Popes are mentioned under *Motu Proprio*.

The Reformed Churches also have had their complaints and their struggles. Some reference to the musical views of the English reformers will be found under *Common Prayer*. Archbishop Abbot (in the early days of the seventeenth century) was against choirs and organs. When, with the Commonwealth (1649–60), first Presbyterian and then Independent influence became apparent, organs and choirs were removed from the churches (see *Puritans and Music*). In Scotland (see *Presbyterian Church Music* 2) organs were considered sinful until the nineteenth century, after the middle of which they gradually crept back. The Greek Church still forbids all instruments (see *Greek Church* 2; *Russia* 2). The general position in England today is that the Anglican Church, having endowments, a liturgy that calls for a good deal of music, musical traditions, beautiful ancient buildings, and the relics of a social status which tends to make it the chief spiritual home of the more cultured classes, is, generally speaking, much in advance of the Nonconformist churches in its musical provision. The larger Roman Catholic churches give a great deal of attention to their music. In the United States of America, where traditions count for less and old endowments do not exist, there is little distinction except such as comes from the fact that the Protestant Episcopalians and the Roman Catholics have liturgies which more definitely call for highly organized musical resources.

See also *Cathedral Music*; *Anglican Parish Church Music*; *Roman Catholic Church Music*.

5. A Present-day Difficulty. A special difficulty of the composer of church music at the present day may be referred to. The very boldly experimental mood of the age has brought into existence new idioms that are as yet not accepted by the public in general, and the composer who finds in one of these his natural means of expression is debarred from the composition of church music, since no choirmaster could for a moment think of exposing a congregation to the shock of a plunge into the entirely unfamiliar. The older members of any congregation tend to cling to familiar hymn-tunes and service settings which to their juniors are 'not a spiritual consolation but a soporific'. We may go further than this and state that the accepted idioms of currently composed church music are in general several generations behind those of serious secular music: a casual examination of a year's output of any church music publisher will reveal the fact that it might largely have been written in the days of Mendelssohn, or, at any rate, of Brahms. History (at least for the last two or three centuries) seems to indicate that it is a permanent condition now imposed on the composer of church music that his expression shall flow in channels already prepared; it would seem that secular composition must lead the way, and that only when the average congregation has come in some measure to accept the harmonic novelties that every age produces (i.e. when they are no longer novelties) can they be put into the mouths of the church choir or under the hands of the organist. Whether the application of this principle has been carried a little too far owing to the timidity of those responsible for the general conduct of the churches' services and those responsible for the ministry of music is an interesting subject of debate. There have been indications of a somewhat bolder spirit latterly, and even hymn-tune books, since about 1925, have included occasional examples of harmonies that could not have been found there twenty years earlier.

6. A Plea from the Scaffold on behalf of better Church Music. It is Switzerland that offers us what must surely be the only case of a plea for church music uttered from the scaffold. In 1723 the rash but heroic Major Daniel Abraham Davel set on foot in Lausanne an insurrection to liberate the Pays de Vaud from the control of the Bernese Republic. His attempt was abortive and he was condemned to be beheaded. With calmness he took his place in the procession out of the town to the spot where the sentence was to be carried out, and, mounting the scaffold, made a long and thoughtful dying speech. In childhood he had studied music with the precentor of the cathedral (i.e. the leader of the psalm-singing in the simple Calvinistic services), and he attached great importance to the practice of this art in connexion with the work of the church. In his address from the scaffold, enumerating some of the evils of the life of the times, he touched first on the spirit of litigation then prevalent, which caused much distress amongst the peasantry, passed on to the negligence of some of the pastors in the lack of adequate preparation of their sermons, and then dwelt upon the disorder common in the church service, saying:

'As it concerns the praise of God, in what manner is it sung? Is there any sense of orderliness, any real music, anything whatever calculated to excite and sustain the devotion? Yet this part of divine service is one of the most considerable and the one by which is the most effectively demonstrated the lifting up of our hearts to God. . . . Such being the importance of this part of Christian worship, I cannot too much emphasize my exhortation to you to give it a new and serious attention, in order to correct the faults of which you are at present guilty in connexion with it.'

He passed to the question of improper expenditure of funds destined for the upkeep of the church building and the education of the young, and then turned to the students of divinity, telling them that many of them showed by the conduct of their lives that they had no vocation for the high office to which they aspired, and pressing them to apply themselves more seriously to their studies:

'You neglect your studies for worldly pleasure. You take no pains to learn music, which is so necessary for the singing of God's praises. The songs of the church form an essential part of divine worship, and have an infinite value in helping us to lift our hearts to God. I pray you, then, to apply yourselves with all possible zeal to your preparation for the holy ministry.'

After touching on other subjects, he declared himself ready for death ('C'est ici le plus beau jour de ma vie'), listened to a long and moving address from one of the pastors of the city, said good-bye to all the weeping pastors who stood

K

beside him on the scaffold, took off his coat, and laid his head on the block.

So far as the present writer knows, no reference to this remarkable incident has previously been made in any work on music, and he takes pleasure in bringing it to the notice of church musicians—and divinity students.

See *Dictionaries* 7.

CHURCH MUSIC SOCIETY. See *Hymns and Hymn Tunes* 14; *Anglican Parish Church Music* 7.

CHURCH OF ENGLAND. See *Common Prayer*; *Church Music* 4; *Cathedral Music*; *Anglican Parish Church Music*; *Parish Clerk*; *Anthem*; *Hymns and Hymn Tunes* 5–9, 11; *Psalm*.

CHURCH OF SCOTLAND. See *Presbyterian Church Music* 3.

CIACCONA. See *Chaconne and Passacaglia.*

CIAMPI. See *Misattributed* (Pergolese).

CIBBER.

(1) COLLEY (1671–1757). Actor and dramatist. See quotation under *Community Singing* 4.

(2) MRS. Vocalist. See *Shore Family.*

CIFRA, ANTONIO (1584–1619). He held many positions in church music in Italy and had a high reputation as a composer of church music, of madrigals, of chamber music, and of organ music. A good deal of his music was published during his own lifetime.

See references under *Scherzo*; *Opus.*

CIGÁNY (Hungarian). 'Gipsy.' What are called *Cigány Bands* (e.g. in Vienna radio programmes) seem to consist of strings, clarinet, and dulcimer.

CILÉA, FRANCESCO. Born in Calabria in 1866 and died in 1950, aged eighty-four. He was trained at the Conservatory of Naples (of which he was half a century later to become Director), and at twenty-three produced his first opera. The most popular of his several works in this form was *Adriana Lecouvreur* (Milan 1902; London 1904; New York 1907). In addition he composed orchestral and chamber works, etc.

CILINDRO, CILINDRI. See *Cylinder.*

CIMAROSA, DOMENICO (p. 517, pl. **94. 5**). Born near Naples in 1749 and died in Venice in 1801, aged fifty-one. His life as an opera composer was triumphant. When in Vienna in 1792 he performed his *The Secret Marriage*, the Emperor ordered supper to be served to the performers and then told them to go through it all again.

Of revolutionary views, he helped to welcome the French republican troops into Naples in 1799, and on the return of the Bourbon monarchy was arrested and for a short time imprisoned. He died soon after.

His special gift was for light-hearted comedy, and as to style he might be called 'the Italian Mozart'.

See reference under *Intermezzo* 2; *Opera* 24 c (1792).

CIMBAL, CIMBALOM, CIMBALON, CIMBELOM. The dulcimer (q.v.); also spelt *Czimbalum, Cymbalom.*

CINCINNATI. See *Concert* 15; *Cecilia*; *Festival* 2; *Schools of Music.*

CINELLI (It.). 'Cymbals'. See *Percussion Family* 3 o, 4 b, 5 o.

CINEMATOGRAPH AND MUSIC. Musical accompaniment to the films was at first supplied by small groups of instrumentalists or by an inferior type of organ (see *Organ* 6), or by the gramophone; however, the idea of specially composed incidental music emerged very early. One of the first such scores was written by Saint-Saëns for *L'Assassinat du Duc de Guise* (1907). With the advent of synchronized sound films in the later 1920s, the artistic use of music in the cinema quickly took a great extension, and the provision of scores for recording on films became an important and remunerative feature of the work of composers. Amongst those who became active in such provision were (to take but a few examples) Richard Addinsell, John Addison, William Alwyn, Georges Auric, Hubert Bath, Arthur Benjamin, Richard Rodney Bennett, Arthur Bliss, Benjamin Britten (his work including an educational film, *Instruments of the Orchestra*, 1946), Anthony Collins, Aaron Copland, Arthur Honegger, Gordon Jacob, Walter Leigh, Darius Milhaud, Serge Prokofief, Dmitri Shostakovich, Ralph Vaughan Williams, and William Walton. Schönberg nearly became one of the company: he turned down an offer of $50,000 to write a score for Pearl Buck's *The Good Earth.* Amongst conductors and solo performers who have engaged in the work of recording have been Walter Goehr, Myra Hess, Ernest Irving, Yehudi Menuhin, Ignace Paderewski, Sir Malcolm Sargent, and Sir Henry J. Wood.

An objectionable feature of film activities in the 1940s and early 1950s has been alluded to by Nicolas Slonimsky as follows:

'In recent years, the Hollywood magnates found it profitable to make cinematic biographies of great musicians. Of course, they had to adapt the known facts in musicians' lives to the Hollywood formula "from poverty to riches". In the movie on Gershwin's life, *Rhapsody in Blue*, he is pictured as a poor boy who never has enough to eat. As a matter of fact, Gershwin's father owned six restaurants in Brooklyn, and Gershwin could have six dinners a day if he could digest the food. "Love interest" is the absolute prerequisite of all biographical movies. When a picture on Tchaikovsky's life was made, Mme. von Meck, Tchaikovsky's rich benefactress whom he never met, is represented on the movie as a young niece of the Czar. Together, she and Tchaikovsky take an underwater swim and emerge on the surface in a soul-filling kiss! The most successful of recent Hollywood films on musical subjects was *The Great Caruso*. Mario Lanza, the latest idol of the screen, sings *Ridi, Pagliaccio*, and *Sobre las Olas*. In the picture, Caruso-Lanza dies on the stage of the Metropolitan Opera House. In reality, he died in Naples, of prosaic appendicitis.'

There have been films on the lives of, among others, Beethoven, Chopin, Schumann, Liszt, Berlioz, Paganini, Wagner, and Glinka.

A discussion of the technique and history of

film music composition and recording, with a list of British films and a bibliography of the subject, will be found in John Huntley's *British Film Music* (1947). Earlier works are Sabaneef's *Music for the Films* (1935) and Kurt London's *Film Music* (1936).

See also *Organ* 6; *Metamorphosis*; *Gramophone* 4; *Electric Musical Instruments* 5 c; *Music Hall* 5.

CINQ (Fr.). 'Five'; hence *cinquième*, 'fifth'.

CINQUE (It.). 'Five.'

CINQUE-PACE, also CINQUE-PAS, and CINQUE-PASSI. See *Pavan and Galliard*.

CINQUIÈME POSITION (Fr.). Fifth position —of the hand in playing stringed instruments. See *Position*.

CIOÈ (It.). 'That is', 'i.e.'.

CIPHER, CIPHERING. The continued sounding of a note on the organ, due to some mechanical defect.

CIS (Ger.). C sharp (see Table 7).

CISIS (Ger.). C double-sharp (see Table 7).

CISTER, CISTRE. See under *Cittern*.

CITHAREN. See *Cittern*.

CITHER. Same as 'Cittern' (q.v.); not to be confused with the zither (q.v.), though there may exist relationship in origin.

CITHERN, CITHREN. See *Cittern*.

CITOLE. See *Cittern*.

CITTERN (p. 449, pl. **77. 8**). A wire-stringed instrument of great antiquity, played with a plectrum until the end of the sixteenth century, when English writers, for improved tone, encouraged the use of the finger. Seen from the front it was much like a lute (more circular in outline, however), but its back was flat like that of a guitar (q.v.); indeed, the eighteenth-century form of it in England went by the name of the *English Guitar* (a misnomer; see *Guitar*). In Shakespeare's time it was exceedingly popular with all classes and was to be found in barbers' shops for the use of waiting customers (see *Barber Shop Music*; also note allusion to Chaucer's mention of it under *Inns and Taverns*); but it must not be deduced from this latter circumstance that it was capable of only simple music, for much serious and complex music was produced for it at this very period.

Other spellings and names (for the same or slightly differing instruments, and in various places and periods) were *Cither*, *Cithern*, *Cithren*, *Citharen*, *Citole*, *Sitole*, *Sittron*; *Cistre* (Fr.); *Cister*; *Cetera* (It.); *Zither* (Ger.; this language appears to have only one name for two instruments).

The **Orpharion** or **Orpheoreon**, **Bandore** (or **Bandora**), **Pandore**, and certain other instruments, inferior to the cittern in their capabilities, are yet of the same general type—in different sizes (the bandore being a bass instrument). The distinctions are sometimes small, and it is not proposed to attempt a detailed description of all these instruments in a book of this scope.

Note that the **Gittern** was a different instrument (e.g. Playford's *Booke of Newe Lessons for the Cithern and Gittern*, 1652); one dissimilarity was in its use of gut strings, the cittern having metal ones. The gittern is best looked upon as an early guitar, and after about 1600 the words 'gittern' and 'guitar' seem to be synonymous.

The **Bandurría** and **Laud**, popular in Spain today as forming a trio with the guitar, may be considered to be forms of cittern (originally 'Laud' was Spanish for the true 'lute', and the sixteenth-century bandurría, a gut-string instrument, was not the same as the present-day one).

'Pandore' above must not be confused with 'Pandora', which is the same as *Tambora*—an Eastern plucked-string instrument of high antiquity and wide dissemination ('Bandore' and 'Bandora', however, appear to be true synonyms).

CIVETTERIA (It.). 'Coquetry', 'flirtatiousness'. So *civettando*, 'coquetting'; *civettescamente*, 'coquettishly'.

CL. Short for *Clarinet*.

CLAGGET, CHARLES (1740–c. 1795). Ingenious inventor of many improved instruments. See *Horn Family* 3; *Trumpet Family* 3.

CLAIRE, CAISSE (Fr.). Side drum. See *Percussion Family* 3 i, 4 b, 5 i.

CLAIRON (Fr.). 'Bugle' (q.v.). Also, on French organs, a 4-foot trumpet stop.

CLAPHAM SECT. See *Puritans* 9; *Dance* 7.

CLAPISSON, ANTOINE LOUIS. Born at Naples in 1808 and died in Paris in 1866, aged fifty-seven. He studied at the Conservatory of Paris (where in later life he was appointed a professor of harmony and keeper of the museum), held a position as violinist at the Opéra, was elected a member of the Institute of France (in preference to Berlioz), amassed a great collection of musical instruments, and wrote a score of operettas and a couple of hundred songs.

See reference under *Street Music* 2.

CLAQUE. See *Applause* 7.

CLAQUEBOIS. French for xylophone. See *Percussion Family* 2 f, 4 e, 5 f.

CLARABEL, CLARABELLA, CLARIBEL FLUTE. See *Organ* 14 II.

CLARIBEL (really Mrs. Barnard). Born in 1830 and died at Dover in 1869, aged thirty-eight. In the last decade of her life she published large numbers of gentle songs. Her poems and melodies strongly moved the susceptible hearts of the Victorians, but were slighted by their children and forgotten by their grandchildren, so that 'Come back to Erin' is perhaps the one example now generally familiar.

CLARIBEL FLUTE. See *Claribel* above.

CLARICEMBALO, CLARICHORD. Same as *Clavicembalo* (i.e. harpsichord), and *Clavichord*.

The 'r' for 'v' has probably originated in some copyist's mis-spelling.

CLARINA. See *Clarinet Family* 4 h.

CLARINET, AUTOMATIC. See *Mechanical Reproduction* 8, 9.

CLARINET FAMILY

1. Construction, etc.
2. History.
3. Chief Members of the Family.
4. Other Members of the Family.
5. Nomenclature.
6. The Family's Repertory.

(For illustrations see p. 672, pl. **113.** 2, 3, 5, 10, 11.)

1. Construction, etc. The clarinet consists of a cylindrical tube with a single reed—a 'beating' reed (see *Reed*), the members of its family differing from the oboe family in all these three particulars (and in their consequently smoother and, in general, more 'creamy' tone). The cylindrical bore is an important feature, as it largely eliminates the even-numbered harmonics from the tone-colour (see *Acoustics* 6, 8). As the reed at one end of the tube serves to close it at that end, the pipe acts as a 'stopped' one, sounding an octave lower than it would do if open; this explains why the pitches of the flute and clarinet differ markedly, the one instrument being acoustically an 'open pipe' and the other a 'stopped pipe'.

Like other cylindrical tubes, that of the clarinet overblows at the interval of an octave-plus-a-fifth (compare the flute and oboe, which overblow at the interval of an octave). The notes of its first octave are obtained in the usual way, and the gap of the fifth that occurs before the overblowing begins has then to be filled by certain means which are not entirely satisfactory, inasmuch as the tone is weaker here than elsewhere in the range of the instrument, and the fingering somewhat awkward. The best parts of the range are the parts above this gap, and the lowest few notes of the instrument. The complete (notational) range of what may be called the normal clarinet (i.e. the treble instrument, the one in A or B flat, as mentioned below) is of three-octaves-plus-a-sixth from E in the bass stave upwards; all the instruments of the clarinet family now in use are, however, 'transposing instruments' (q.v.), so that their actual range differs by a few notes from their notational one.

The power of pianissimo and of crescendo and diminuendo is greater in the clarinets than in any other wind instruments. Several varieties of single-tonguing (see *Tonguing*) are possible, giving different degrees of staccato. Double-tonguing and triple-tonguing are also possible, but much more difficult. Flutter-tonguing, too, is possible.

2. History. The clarinet family, the youngest to gain a footing in the orchestra, is often (but not altogether conclusively) stated to be the successor to a family of instruments on the same principles but of simpler character, the family of **Chalumeau**—a family of at least four instruments of various sizes, from treble to bass. It is not known whether the chalumeau was ever anything but a popular instrument, i.e. whether it ever found a place in artistic music-making. Its improvement into the clarinet is attributed to Denner of Nuremberg, about 1690–1700; thereafter the word 'chalumeau' is sometimes found in scores (Gluck uses it as late as *Alceste*, 1767), but most probably is simply the older name transferred to the newer instrument. The word 'chalumeau' is still retained in use to define the lowest part of the compass of the clarinet. It should be noted that Denner's chief improvement had been the addition of the 'speaker-key' enabling the upper range of the instrument to be used. Another Denner, possibly a son, introduced further improvements twenty years later; more and more keys were gradually added, and the instrument became increasingly capable of artistic use. Considerable improvements are due to Iwan Müller, in 1810, and these almost form the basis of the instrument as we know it. Klosé, in 1842, applied the Boehm System (q.v.), which is largely, but not exclusively, used today, German, Austrian, and Hungarian clarinettists, for instance, still preferring the old type of instrument.

The first mention of the clarinet in any score is in 1720, in a mass by J. A. J. Faber, an Antwerp organist; this is, however, an isolated instance. As the facts relating to the introduction of the clarinet are often imperfectly or incorrectly stated, the following ascertained dates are here recorded:

In 1739 the orchestra of Kremsmünster, Austria, had two clarinets, and a Frankfort paper bore an advertisement of the arrival of two good clarinet-tists and invited the public to go to their inn to hear them.

There exists a MS. Handel Overture in D (Fitzwilliam Museum, Cambridge) for two clarinets in C and Corno di Caccia. A song in Handel's opera *Tamerlano* appears (in one version) to be scored for violins and two clarinets. In 1742, when Handel was in Dublin, he may have heard a 'Mr. Charles, the Hungarian', who played the clarinet at a public concert.

The last-named player appears in the local news reports of *Barrow's Worcester Journal* in 1748: 'Mr. Charles, senior and junior, from Vauxhall, performed on the French horn and two foreign instruments, the shallamo [chalumeau: see above] and clarinet.'

In 1749 the instrument was used in an oratorio performance at Frankfort.

In the same year Rameau, in Paris (see *France* 7), used it in an opera.

In 1751 a clarinet concerto figures in the programme of 'a grand concert of vocal and instrumental music by gentlemen' in the New Theatre in the Haymarket. In the same year we find it mentioned in the famous French Encyclopedia, which, however, calls it 'a sort of hautboy'; in 1753 the Concert Spirituel of Paris (see *Concert* 14) was using it in symphonies of J. W. A. Stamitz and others; as the scores do not show the instrument, it probably doubled or replaced the oboe parts. Soon after this Gossec introduced it into the Paris Opera Orchestra; he did much to popularize it in France.

In 1754 mention of it is found in London, and in 1756 it was in use in oratorio performance in the Haymarket Theatre. In 1755 it is found in Edinburgh.

If we are to trust Benjamin Franklin's memory (thirty years after the event he records), he heard clarinets in the orchestra at Bethlehem, Pa., in 1756—'Good musick, the organ accompanied with violins, hautboys, flutes, clarinets, etc.' (see *United States of America* 3).

In 1758 the famous Mannheim Orchestra had two clarinets. Thenceforward it gradually appeared in the various German and Austrian orchestras, and it is noteworthy that in several places we find it first in a military band (see *Military Band* for examples), and a year or two later in the orchestra.

In view of some of those early dates it is a little curious to find that great traveller in musical Europe, the young Mozart, writing to his father from Mannheim as late as 1778, 'Oh, if only *we* had clarinets; you can't guess the lordly effect of a symphony with flutes, oboes and clarinets.' In the same year he used clarinets in his 'Paris' Symphony.

Some important orchestras do not seem to have had clarinets until the late 1780s or 1790s (Vienna Court Orchestra, 1787; Leipzig Gewandhaus, 1792; Dresden, 1794), and it is to Mozart's love of the instrument that we owe the first really notably artistic treatment of it; he developed its capacities to a very high point (e.g. in his Quintet in A for clarinet and strings, K. 581; his set of Divertimenti for two clarinets and bassoon, K. 229, or 439 b according to the revised Köchel list; the Clarinet Concerto, K. 622, etc.). Haydn used the clarinet much less than Mozart.

After that period two clarinets of the normal size became an indispensable feature of every orchestra. Weber showed great love for the instrument.

From Wagner three normal clarinets plus the bass clarinet (which was in some use from the end of the eighteenth century) and sometimes the small (E flat) clarinet, are to be found in scores. The Russian composers, especially Rimsky-Korsakof, have shown a great fondness for the clarinet. In *Elektra* and *Salome* Strauss uses pretty well the whole family of clarinets— one E flat, two B flats, two A's, one bass clarinet, and two basset horns. (See 3 b, 4 f.)

The clarinet family has become of the highest importance in military bands (the Honourable Artillery Company, of London, had clarinets from 1762), the upper members now taking the place occupied in the orchestra by the violins. In Switzerland, the Tyrol, and elsewhere in central Europe the clarinet is now almost a peasant instrument, being much used in village dance combinations. In the hundreds of church orchestras that existed in England during the late eighteenth and early nineteenth centuries the clarinet was one of the commonest instruments.

For the enormous popularity of the clarinet in the English country-side during the early nineteenth century see a remark under *Oboe Family* 2.

3. Chief Members of the Family.

(*a*) **Clarinet in C, B flat, or A** (p. 672, pl. **113.** 5, 10). This is the normal treble instrument of which the range has been mentioned above (1). It formerly existed in the three pitches here mentioned in order to facilitate performance of music in various keys, the composer indicating that pitch of the instrument which would give the player the fewest flats or sharps to negotiate (cf. *Transposing Instruments*).

The C pitch instrument, indicated in various scores of all the 'classical' composers, has now definitely been abandoned on account of inferior tone, leaving only the B flat (which diminishes the number of flats by two when the music is in a flat key) and the A (which diminishes the number of sharps by three when the music is in a sharp key). The music for the B flat instrument is, of course, written a tone higher than it is to sound, and that for the A instrument a minor third higher.

Many players, however, owing to mechanical improvements and improvements in technique, now think it needless to possess more than the B flat instrument, transposing as they play any music they have put before them that bears the indication 'Clarinets in C' or 'Clarinets in A'. (This is, perhaps, particularly so in the United States.) The use of only one clarinet during (say) the movements of a symphony, in their different keys, has the advantage of avoiding change to an instrument that has not been 'warmed up' (with consequent rise of pitch).

It is to be noted that the B flat instrument is often loosely spoken of as the 'B Clarinet'— probably from German usage, what the English language calls 'B flat' being 'B' in German (see *Notation and Nomenclature* 1).

(*b*) **Bass Clarinet** (p. 672, pl. **113.** 11). The range of this lies an octave below that of the one just described (generally the B flat, but often with an extra note, making it correspond to that of the A). It differs somewhat in shape as, to avoid an unwieldy length, the lower end of the tube is curved upwards (ending in a bell) whilst the upper end is continued by a tube bent downwards, so bringing the reed within reach of the player's mouth.

There are two methods, in orchestral music, of notating music for this instrument—the French, which uses the treble clef and writes a ninth above the sounding-pitch, and the German, which uses the bass clef and writes a second above the sounding-pitch. In some military band music, however, the instrument is not notated as a transposing instrument at all, the real sounds being shown. The usage of some Russian composers is to mingle the German and French methods. In British military band music the French orchestral practice is usually followed. Sometimes, however, the player merely uses the bassoon part.

4. Other Members of the Family.

(c) **High E flat Clarinet.** This is pitched a perfect fourth above the B flat instrument. It is demanded by some orchestral scores (e.g. Berlioz, Strauss, Mahler, and Schönberg; it is possible that Berlioz's use of it in the last movement of the 'Fantastic' Symphony, in 1830, was its first appearance in orchestral music), and is an invariable constituent of the military band. Its tone is harder than that of the lower-pitched members of the family. When 'E flat Clarinet' is spoken of, it is this one that is intended, and not the one described under (e). Its music is written a minor third lower than it is to sound.

(d) **High D Clarinet.** This serves the same purpose as the E flat, but is much rarer, though it is found indicated in a few scores from Gluck to Strauss. Its music is written a tone lower than it is to sound.

(e) **Alto Clarinet (in E flat and F).** The E flat instrument (practically a military band instrument, but, even as such, now rare—being replaced by the alto saxophone) is a sixth below the now abandoned C clarinet; the F a fifth below. The treble clef is used, with the music written respectively a sixth or fifth higher than it is to sound. The E flat is used in Britain, the F (generally) elsewhere, though it appears in a few British scores. The F is practically the basset horn (see below) modernized. 'Tenor Clarinet' might be a better description than 'Alto'.

(f) **Basset-Horn.** This in appearance resembles the bass clarinet but is really a tenor instrument. Its pitch is a fifth below that of the now abandoned C clarinet, and its notation (in the treble clef) is thus a fifth above the actual pitch of the sounds desired. The tone is somewhat less sensitive than that of the clarinet proper.

The name of this instrument often gives rise to conjecture. Why 'Horn'? Then 'Basset hound', 'Basset-horn'—what is the connexion? Or has it to do with the card-game or the geological term?

The word 'Basset', in the musical sense, is merely a diminutive of 'Bass' (cf. the German 'Bassettoboe', 'Bassettflöte', etc.). The combination 'Bassetthorn' is said to have been introduced by a German instrument-maker in 1770. His own name was Horn and the order of words is as in such expressions as 'Pêche Melba' or 'Hotel Astoria' (cf. 5).[1]

It will be seen that the instrument appeared in time for Mozart to use it—which he did largely (*Magic Flute, Requiem,* etc.). Beethoven used it only once. Mendelssohn wrote two Concert Pieces for it, clarinet and pianoforte.

An obsolete sort of basset horn at a slightly higher pitch was the clarinetto d'amore.

(g) **Pedal Clarinet** or **Contrabass Clarinet** or **Double-bass Clarinet.** This is a clumsy, large instrument, pitched an octave below the bass clarinet in B flat and related to it much as the double-bassoon to the ordinary bassoon or the stringed double-bass to the violoncello. It is really a military band instrument, but appears in just a few modern orchestral scores (d'Indy's *Fervaal*; Strauss's *Legend of Joseph*; Weingartner's opera *Orestes*).

Its notes are written a ninth higher than their sound.

The word 'pedal' does not apply to any part of the mechanism but (presumably) alludes either to the fact that it stands to the other members of the family much as the normal-pitched pedal stops of an organ stand to the normal-pitched manual stops, or else to its usefulness in holding on to a harmonic pedal (see *Harmony* 24 p).

(h) There are three rather obscure modern instruments, related to the clarinet family by their possession of a single reed, but not in other ways, and all invented with a special narrow purpose—the playing of the shepherd-youth music in *Tristan*. They are the **Clarina, Heckelclarina** or **Heckelklarinette** (invented by Heckel),[2] the **Holztrompete** (literally 'wooden trumpet'), invented by Wagner, and an instrument resembling, but not, as sometimes stated, identical with the Holztrompete, the **Tarogato** (invented by W. T. Schunda somewhat on the basis of a still-used Hungarian peasant instrument of the name, which, however, is a double-reed instrument). None of these is much used, the air in question being almost invariably entrusted to the cor anglais. However, at Covent Garden a custom, from the 1930s and perhaps earlier, has been to employ the Tarogato for the very excited bit of piping when the shepherd-boy at last sees the ship actually approaching. It was Nikisch who introduced this practice. The instrument is played from the wings.

A whole family of Tarogatos (four, of different sizes) has been made.

[1] Bessaraboff, in his *Ancient European Musical Instruments* (Boston, Mass., 1941), says that this instrument 'appears to have been invented about 1770 by Mayrhofer of Passau'—*not* (in that same year) by a maker of the name of 'Horn'. He gives as his authority an article by W. Altenburg in the *Zeitschrift für Instrumentenbau,* xxviii. 555.
The late Mr. W. T. H. Blandford, the authority on wind instruments, discouragingly also deprecated the neat derivation of the second word of the name 'Basset Horn', as given above and in Forsyth's *Orchestration* and other works. He pointed out that Sachs in his *Reallexikon der Musikinstrumente* (1914) does not mention this derivation and that he considers the first maker of the instrument to have been not Horn but Mayrhofer—about 1770, in Passau. (Lavoix, in his *Histoire de l'Instrumentation,* 1878, mentions a 'Horn', also in Passau, in 1777, but does not state his authority.)
[2] It may be as well to state categorically that no such instrument as *Heckelclarind* exists. This word first appeared, by a mere misprint for *Heckelclarina,* in an English book of reference in 1907. It was then copied into one of the leading British–American works on orchestration and so given wider currency.

1. CHOPIN AT WORK
A drawing by 'George Sand'

2. THE FAMOUS NOVELIST GEORGE SAND
(1804–76)—Chopin's close friend

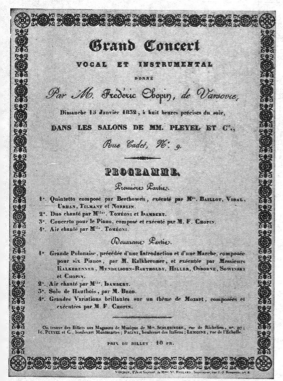

3. CHOPIN'S FIRST PARIS CONCERT, 1832.
(Note the composition by Kalkbrenner performed by Chopin and
five eminent contemporaries)

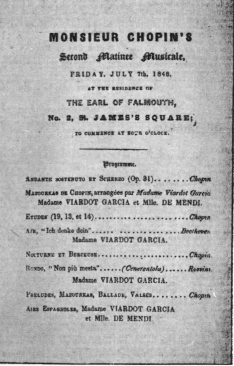

4. PROGRAMME OF ONE OF CHOPIN'S LONDON
RECITALS OF 1848
(Note the vocal arrangement of some of the Mazurkas)

See also the portrait of Chopin at page 180

1. CLAVICHORD (one of the oldest representations of the instrument—Weimar, mid-15th century)

2. CLAVICHORD (from Virdung's *Musica Getutscht*, 1511)

3. VIRGINALS. By W. Hollar (1635)

5. ENGLAND'S FIRST VIRGINAL PUBLICATION. See *Parthenia*

4. FROM THE FITZWILLIAM VIRGINAL BOOK (q.v.)

Harpsichord — A Wire Instrument, with Keys, like an Organ, under whose small Strings the Belly is made thicker than under the Great Strings, to give the finer Tone, &c. — Some *Harpsichords* may be fixed over the Strikers of the Pallets of an *Organ* to play both the *Organ* and the Harpsichord together with *one Set* of Keys; or either to be play'd alone, by moving the Keys forwards, or more back; a Hole being under to drop over the Sticker when the *Harpsichord* plays alone: which when pull'd out of the Hole, forward, they both are play'd together, &c.

6. THE HARPSICHORD. A description from Tans'ur's *New Musical Dictionary* (1766) —singularly incomplete yet giving some interesting information as to a use forgotten today

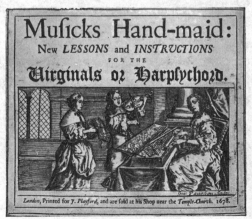

7. FINGERING ON THE VIRGINALS. See *Fingering*

5. Nomenclature.

Chalumeau, meaning merely 'reed' (Lat. *calamus*), has no logical restriction to the single reed instruments, and was sometimes, probably, used in a general sense, including the double reed. (The same is true of the related words 'schalmey' and 'shawm'. See *Oboe Family* 2.)

Clarinet, Clarionet. *Clarinette* (Fr.); *Clarino* (which at one time meant 'trumpet') or *Clarinetto* (It.); *Klarinette* (Ger.). 'Clarionet' is generally regarded as a misspelling, suggesting a false derivation from 'clarion'.

Bass Clarinet. *Clarinette basse* (Fr.); *Clarinetto basso* or *Clarone* (It.), but note that in Italian the latter name sometimes indicates the basset horn.

Alto Clarinet. *Clarinette alto* (Fr.); *Clarinetto alto* (It.); *Altklarinette* (Ger.).

Basset Horn (or Bassett Horn). The French and Italian terms are (see 4 f)—*Cor de basset* (Fr.) and *Corno di bassetto* (It.).

Pedal Clarinet. *Clarinette contrebasse* (Fr.); *Clarino contrabasso, Clarinetto contrabasso* (It.); *Kontrabassklarinette* (Ger.).

The ambiguous and misleading term *Sub-Tone Clarinet* was introduced in connexion with popular music of the 1930s. It indicates the ordinary treble B flat clarinet or the alto clarinet 'breathed into instead of blown'.

6. The Family's Repertory.

Clarinet literature necessarily begins late in date; we do not know what Bach might have done with this instrument. As for Handel's very slight use of it see 2. But once Mozart leads the way other composers follow, providing a repertory of such variety and quality as no other wind instrument can boast.

J. W. A. Stamitz (see 2) left a concerto that must be the first.

Mozart's important contribution includes a fine concerto and a good deal of chamber music—twelve Duos for clarinet and basset horn; six Trios for two clarinets and bassoon, and one for clarinet, viola, and pianoforte; an Adagio for two clarinets and three basset horns, and another (in canon) for two basset horns and bassoon; a Quintet for clarinet and strings, and another for clarinet, oboe, horn, bassoon, and pianoforte.

Beethoven left three Duets for clarinet and bassoon; a Trio for clarinet, violoncello, and pianoforte (and another which he arranged from the Septet); and a Quintet for clarinet, oboe, horn, bassoon, and pianoforte.

Of **Spohr** we possess two Concertos. **Weber,** a very great exponent of the art of writing effectively for this instrument, left two Concertos and a Concertino, a Grand Duo Concertante for clarinet and pianoforte (the greatest 'show piece' in the whole repertory of the clarinet), and a Quintet for clarinet and strings. **Schubert** wrote a song, 'Der Hirt auf dem Felsen', with a notable clarinet obbligato; his Octet also includes the instrument.

Schumann wrote three Phantasy Pieces for clarinet and pianoforte and four Fairy Tales for clarinet, viola, and pianoforte. **Mendelssohn** wrote two Concert Pieces for clarinet, basset horn, and pianoforte.

Brahms is the third really great exponent of the instrument (Mozart–Weber–Brahms). He wrote two Sonatas for clarinet and pianoforte; a Trio for clarinet, violoncello, and pianoforte, and a Quintet for clarinet and strings.

Reger left three Sonatas for clarinet and pianoforte (of which one, op. 107, ranks next to the Brahms works).

It is to be noted that several of the above composers have been incited to activity by contact with some great clarinet virtuoso, as, for instance, Mozart by Anton Stadler, Weber by H. J. Bärmann (1784–1847), and Brahms by Richard Mühlfeld (1856–1907).

Amongst other items in the clarinet's repertory are the following:

Strauss, Duet-Concertino for clarinet, bassoon, strings, and harp; **Glinka,** a *Pathetic Trio* for clarinet, bassoon, and piano; **Saint-Saëns,** Sonata for clarinet and piano: **d'Indy,** Trio for clarinet, cello, and piano; **Debussy,** Rhapsody for clarinet and orchestra, and a 'Little Piece' for clarinet and piano; **Karg-Elert,** Sonata for clarinet and piano; **Poulenc,** Sonata for two clarinets, and another for clarinet and bassoon; **Honegger,** Sonata (atonal) for clarinet and piano; **Busoni,** Concertino for clarinet and small orchestra and Elegy for clarinet and piano; **Berg,** Four pieces for clarinet and piano; **Mihalovici,** Sonata for three clarinets; **Hindemith,** Quintet for clarinet and strings, Sonata for clarinet and piano; **Villa-Lobos,** *Chôros* for flute and clarinet; **Dubensky,** Variations for eight clarinets; **Prokofief,** Overture on Jewish themes for clarinet, string quartet and piano; **Stravinsky,** 'Ebony Concerto' and Three Pieces for clarinet solo; **Křenek,** Sonatina for flute and clarinet.

Amongst British composers who have provided works are **Stanford,** with a Concerto, a Sonata, and three Intermezzi for clarinet and pianoforte; **Coleridge-Taylor, Herbert Howells,** and **Bliss,** each with a Quintet for clarinet and strings; **Tovey** and **Bax,** each with a Sonata for clarinet and pianoforte; **Herbert Murrill,** with a Prelude, Cadenza, and Fugue for clarinet and piano; **Alan Frank,** with a Suite for two clarinets alone; **Phyllis Tate,** with a Sonata for clarinet and violoncello; **Gerald Finzi,** with a Concerto and some smaller pieces; **Howard Ferguson,** with Five Pieces for clarinet and piano, and **Alun Hoddinott,** with a Concerto for clarinet and strings.

Amongst American composers, **E. Burlingame Hill** has written a Sonatina for clarinet and pianoforte; **Daniel Gregory Mason** a Sonata for clarinet and pianoforte, and a Trio for clarinet, violin, and pianoforte; **Roy Harris** a Sextet for clarinet, string quartet, and piano; and **Bernstein** a Sonata for clarinet and piano.

With the advent of the Schönberg, Berg, and Webern school of composition the bass clarinet was featured in a good deal of chamber music.

CLARINET FLUTE STOP. See *Organ* 14 II.

CLARINET QUINTET. See *Quintet*.

CLARINET STOP. See *Organ* 3, 14 VI.

CLARINETTE ALTO, CLARINETTE BASSE, CLARINETTE CONTRABASSE (Fr.). See *Clarinet Family* 5.

CLARINETTO, CLARINETTO ALTO, CLARINETTO BASSO, CLARINETTO CONTRABASSO (It.). See *Clarinet Family* 5.

CLARINO. See *Clarinet Family* 5; *Trumpet Family* 5.

CLARINO CONTRABASSO. See *Clarinet Family* 5.

CLARION. See *Trumpet Family* 3; *Organ* 14 VI.

CLARIONET. See *Clarinet Family* 5.

CLARK.

(1) **RICHARD.** Born at Buckingham in 1780 and died in 1856, aged seventy-six. He was a singer in the choirs of Westminster Abbey, St. Paul's Cathedral, and the Chapel Royal, and a zealous antiquary of Pickwickian acumen, so that to him the world owes one or two of its most romantic delusions as to musical origins.

See references under *God save the Queen* 19; *Nicknamed Compositions* (Handel).

(2) **FREDERICK SCOTSON.** Born in London in 1840 and died there in 1883, aged forty-two. He was, in turn, organist, principal of a secondary school, clergyman, and founder of a London school of organ playing. He enjoyed enormous popularity as a performer on and composer for his instrument, and his gay march strains possibly still temper the solemnity of some country churches.

(3) **FRANCES ELLIOTT** (1860–1958). See *Appreciation*; p. 32, pl. **3**. 3.

CLARKE.

(1) **JEREMIAH.** Born probably about 1670 and died in 1707. He was successively Organist (1692) of Winchester College; Master of the Children (1693) and Organist (1695) of St. Paul's; and composer at the Theatre Royal (1700). He wrote theatre music, songs, harpsichord music, and church music which long kept a place on the music lists of English cathedrals.

He fell in love, was refused, and shot himself in the house in St. Paul's Churchyard which he occupied in virtue of his position.

See references under *Form* 9; *Winchester College*; *Misattributed* (Purcell's Trumpet Voluntary).

(2) **ADAM** (Methodist preacher, 1762–1832). See *Methodism and Music* 5.

(3) **STEPHEN.** Born at Durham and died at Edinburgh in 1797. Music editor of Johnson's *Scots Musical Museum* (6 vols., 1787–1803), which has 600 airs, has many contributions by Burns, and remains the great repository of Scottish national song.

See *Ye. Banks and Braes*.

(4) **REBECCA.** Born at Harrow in 1886. She was trained at the Royal College of Music and is a viola player and composer. In 1919 she won the second Coolidge Prize for a sonata for viola and piano. She was married to James Friskin, and is resident in New York.

(5) **DOUGLAS.** Born in Reading in 1893 and died at Warwick in 1962, aged sixty-nine. He graduated and went in 1927 to Winnipeg as a a conductor, later becoming in turn principal of the McGill Conservatory in Montreal and Dean of the Faculty of Music at McGill University, retiring in 1955, and returning to England in 1958. He composed orchestral and other works.

CLARKE-WHITFELD, JOHN. Born at Gloucester in 1770 and died near Hereford in 1836, aged sixty-five. He was organist at different times of four Irish and English cathedrals and two Cambridge colleges, a Doctor of Music of three universities, and Professor of Music at that of Cambridge. His church music had wide vogue and some of it is still heard. In one of his most popular anthems ('Behold how good and joyful') he graphically represents, by a long descending solo bass passage, 'the precious ointment upon the head, that ran down upon the beard, even Aaron's beard: that went down to the skirts of his garments'. Such happy entertainment is all too rare in the sober repertory of the English Church.

See references under *Cathedral Music* 7 (footnote); *Cambridge*; *Hereford*.

CLARO. See *Trumpet Family* 3.

CLARONE. See *Clarinet Family* 5.

CLÀRSACH (p. 452, pl. **78**. 2, 4, 9). The ancient small Celtic harp, revived during the twentieth century in Scotland. It is probably of Irish origin, but the new interest in it is due to the collection, publication, and performance of the Hebridean folk songs by Mrs. Kennedy-Fraser, whose daughter Patuffa found in this instrument the ideal means of self-accompaniment for her singing. Certain English and Scottish firms began to make the harp on the ancient Caledonian model, and some music has been published for it. Contests in playing it were from the late 1920s included in certain Mods, or competition festivals, and a Comunn na Clàrsaich, or Clàrsach Society, was founded on the occasion of the National Mod at Dingwall in 1931.

A small harp corresponding to the clàrsach existed in other than Celtic countries, and such a harp was made by Dolmetsch (q.v.)—in two forms, a smaller one, wire-strung, and a slightly larger one, gut-strung; these are used for playing medieval music (see *Wales* 4). Compare p. 481, pl. **84**. 1, 2).

CLASHPANS. Old name for cymbals. See *Percussion Family* 3 o, 4 b, 5 o.

CLASSICAL. In connexion with music the word is unfortunately used in several ways.

1. It is used as a distinguishing adjective for all that large class of music (roughly from the end of the sixteenth century to the end of the eighteenth century) in which a more or less

consciously accepted formalistic scheme of design is evident, with an emphasis on elements of proportion and of beauty as such—as distinguished from that class in which the main object appears to be the expression of emotion, or even the representation in tone of ideas which usually receive, not a musical, but rather a literary or pictorial expression. The antithesis here is 'Romantic' (see *Romantic*; *Programme Music*; *History* 7).

Protests have sometimes been uttered against this application of the word 'Classical', and not without cogent argument, but it is very generally accepted, and such use (i.e. its use as antithetical to 'Romantic') dates back at least as far as 1820, when the Romantic movement in the arts was in full swing. It is probably the sense in which today nine musicians out of ten use the word. It seems impossible to displace this use, and if it were displaced no accepted general term would be found to exist to describe the music prior to the advent of the Romantic school. On practical grounds, then, it seems that the dichotomy Classical–Romantic should continue to be allowed.

2. It is frequently used as a label to distinguish what is obviously of more or less established and permanent value from what is ephemeral. (This is the sense in which it is perhaps most often used in connexion with literature and the other arts, and from that point of view the most desirable sense.) The antithesis here is 'Modern'. Riemann's definition conforms to this idea: '*Classical—a term applied to a work of art against which the destroying hand of time has proved powerless. Since only in the course of time a work can be shown to possess the power of resistance, there can be no living classics.*'

3. Amongst less educated people 'Classical' is used in antithesis to 'Popular' ('Do you like classical music?' 'No, I like something with a *tune* to it!')

CLASSICAL PITCH. See *Pitch* 5.

CLASSICAL SUITE. See *Suite* 3.

CLAUDIN (or CLAUDE LE JEUNE). Born at Valenciennes in 1528 and died in Paris in 1600, aged seventy-two. He was a priest and musician of the Sainte Chapelle at Paris and of the royal private chapel. He is important and famous as a composer of chansons (q.v.), masses, motets, madrigals, and (being of Huguenot sympathies) metrical psalms (Genevan Psalter, in four and five voices, published posthumously in 1613 and used in the Reformed churches of France, Holland, and Germany).

See references s.v. *Publishing* 2.

CLAUSULA. A cadence (q.v.). *Clausula vera*, perfect cadence; *Clausula falsa*, interrupted cadence; *Clausula plagalis*, plagal cadence ; and so on. These terms belong really to medieval music.

CLAVECIN (Fr.). 'Harpsichord' (q.v.); *not* 'Clavichord' (q.v.).

CLAVECIN OCULAIRE. See *Colour and Music* 6.

CLAVES. These are round sticks of hard wood 7 or 8 inches long. The player (in Cuban dance bands, etc.) holds one over the upturned finger-nails of his left fist and beats it with the other held lightly in the right hand.

CLAVICEMBALO (literally 'Keyed Dulcimer'). Italian for harpsichord (q.v.). See also *Cembalo*.

CLAVICHORD

(For illustrations see p. 193, pl. 39. 1, 2.)

1. General Appearance. This is, in appearance when opened, like a small rectangular piano—usually a sort of box that can be placed upon a table for playing, though sometimes it has legs. A long side of the rectangle faces the player and the strings run more or less parallel with that side.

2. Method of Tone Production. Its speciality, differentiating it strongly from the harpsichord (q.v.), is its method of tone-production; for, whereas in the harpsichord the strings are plucked from below by quills put in action by a mechanism operated from the finger-board, in the clavichord the strings are subjected to a sort of pressure-stroke from below, by small pieces of metal similarly put in action. These pieces of metal are called **Tangents**.

3. The Stopping of the Strings. Another peculiarity which decisively separates the instrument from those of the harpsichord class is that the vibrating agent (i.e. the tangent) is at the same time a 'stopping' agent—in the sense in which the fingers of the violinist's left hand 'stop' a string to adjust its length to the pitch of the note required. In hitting the string, the tangent necessarily divides it into two lengths: one end of the string being permanently 'damped' by the presence of a piece of felt, only the length from the tangent to the other end is free to vibrate, and thus the note is both 'pitched' and produced at one and the same time.

In all the earlier clavichords (up to as late, say, as 1720–30) there was an economy of strings, since the tangents operated by two or more adjacent keys of the keyboard impacted on the same string, meeting it at the different points necessary to produce the different lengths required for their respective pitches. Hence, if a clavichordist had wished to play these notes together, he could not have done so.

The term **fretted** is applied to clavichords

which embody this ancient device of obtaining more than one note from a string; it would seem to have some connexion by analogy with the same word as applied to viols and lutes (q.v.); in German the term is **gebunden**, or 'bound', and a fret on a viol or lute is a 'Bund'—evidently alluding to the fact that such frets usually consisted of strings tied round the neck of the instrument at the appropriate places. Clavichords on the later pattern, i.e. with a sounding string for each note, are called **unfretted**, or in German **bundfrei**.

The choice of those notes which were to be (as one might say) 'string-fellows' on a 'gebunden' clavichord was, in a good instrument, adroitly made, so that when playing in all the commoner keys they offered little or no impediment, i.e. the two notes educed from the same string were little likely to be required together. If Bach's *Well-tempered Clavier* be searched, very few instances of possible embarrassment will be found; though the unfretted clavichords came into use in his day and it seems certain he would possess one (Adlung, who died twelve years after Bach, speaks in *Musica Mechanica Organœdi* of the advantages of the unfretted keyboard as having been 'discovered long ago').

The principle of obtaining several notes from one string was that of the monochord (q.v.), and hence the earlier clavichords were often spoke of as monochords (see 7). It is, of course, also that of the hurdy-gurdy (q.v.), and all the members of the lute, viol, and violin families, etc.

4. Tone Quality and Expression. The tone of the clavichord is soft and ethereal, so that the instrument is constitutionally unfitted for any public room but the smallest; it is ideal for domestic solo use and unsuitable for concerted music.

It should be noted that the clavichord, unlike the harpsichord, offers virtually unlimited opportunity of modifying the tone by means of the touch. Thus, in a fugue, the subject, though in an inner part, can (as on the piano) be 'brought out', which on the harpsichord is only possible when the instrument is one with two keyboards and the composer had so laid out his score that one hand is free to play the part in question on another keyboard than that of the accompanying parts.

There is also possible with the clavichord a sort of vibrato prolongation of the note (called in German '**Bebung**')—obtained by a rocking motion of the finger; this particular technique is out of the question both on the harpsichord and on the piano.

5. The Bachs and the Clavichord. A dispute has arisen concerning Bach's use of the clavichord. Some say that the definite statement of his first biographer, Forkel, as to his fondness for the instrument is discredited by the fact that his will mentions his possession of six instruments of the harpsichord class, but

no clavichord; others contest the value of this evidence.

Carl Philipp Emanuel Bach (q.v.), the great man's greatest son, was a notable clavichordist: Burney (q.v.), who visited him at Hamburg in 1772, records:

'After dinner, which was elegantly served, and chearfully eaten, I prevailed upon him to sit down to a clavichord and he played, with little intermission, till near eleven o'clock at night. During this time, he grew so animated and *possessed*, that he not only played, but looked like one inspired. His eyes were fixed, his under lip fell, and drops of effervescence distilled from his countenance. He said if he were to be set to work frequently in this manner, he should grow young again.'

6. Period of Popularity. The period of popularity of the clavichord was an extended one—from at least the fourteenth century to the beginning of the nineteenth. It seems to have exhausted its popularity much earlier in Britain (where its vogue was never very great) than in Germany, losing ground to the spinet (see *Harpsichord Family* 4). It should be noted that in Germany the clavichord and harpsichord types existed side by side for four centuries, and that they were displaced by the pianoforte. Beethoven reputedly thought that 'among keyboard instruments the clavichord was that on which one could best control tone and expression', yet such keyboard virtuosi as von Bülow, Hallé, Madame Schumann, and Rubinstein had never heard a clavichord until it was, in the 1880s, introduced to their notice by the English authority on old instruments, A. J. Hipkins.

Like the harpsichord, the clavichord is today again being made and is a good deal used amongst connoisseurs who like to play old music upon the instruments for which it was written. Such a piece as the first prelude of Bach's '48' is a different thing when played on a clavichord from what it is when played on a piano or a harpsichord.

7. 'Manichord', 'Monochord', 'Pair of Clavichords'. The term 'pair of clavichords' was sometimes used (for the single instrument); for a suggested explanation cf. *Harpsichord Family* 3 ('Pair of virginals'). In ancient times the terms 'Manicord' and 'Monochord' (q.v.) are found attached to this instrument. In the development of keyboard instruments the clavichord obviously historically connects the monochord (q.v.) with the pianoforte, attaching itself to the former by its production of several notes from one string, and to the latter by the use of a form of hammer.

For the out-of-order arrangement of the lowest notes of the clavichord see article *Short Octave and Broken Octave*.

CLAVICYLINDER. A keyboard instrument invented by the great acoustician, Chladni (1756–1827). The principle was that of a glass cylinder in revolution, acting by friction on metal or wooden rods of graduated sizes controlled by depressing the keys.

See also *Terpodion*.

CLAVICYMBAL. English form of the Italian 'clavicembalo', i.e. 'keyed dulcimer', i.e. the harpsichord (q.v.).

CLAVICYTHERIUM. A spinet or harpsichord, but upright (foreshadowing the upright piano of today), instead of flat (like the grand piano of today). See *Harpsichord Family* 4.

CLAVIER. A keyboard—whether for hands or feet; see *Klavier*.

CLAVIER DE RÉCIT. See *Organ* 15.

CLAVIER DES BOMBARDES. See *Organ* 15.

CLAVIER HANS. See *Keyboard* 4.

CLAVILUX. See *Colour and Music* 9.

CLAVIOLINE. See *Electric* 4.

CLAY.

(1) CHARLES (early eighteenth century). see *Mechanical Reproduction* 5.

(2) FREDERICK EMES. Born in Paris in 1838 and died at Great Marlow in Buckinghamshire in 1889, aged fifty-one. He abandoned the Civil Service for music and achieved much nineteenth-century fame (the echoes of which have not yet died away) as the provider of stage music and such vocal pleasantnesses as 'I'll sing thee songs of Araby', 'The Sands of Dee', and 'She wandered down the mountain side'.

CLEAR FLUTE. See *Organ* 14 II.

CLEF. Table 4; see *Notation* 4; *Orchestra* 6.

CLEF UNIQUE. See *Notation* 7.

CLEMENS NON PAPA (JACOBUS—JACQUES—CLEMENT). Born probably *c.* 1510, and died *c.* 1556-8. A Netherlands composer of whom little is known otherwise than by inference. His family may have come from Valenciennes, and he seems to have been active in Bruges or Leyden. The 'non Papa' appears on a publication of 1546 and may refer, not to the Pope, but to the poet Jacobus Papa. His output included masses, motets, and chansons.

CLÉMENT. See *Dance* 10.

CLEMENTI, MUZIO (p. 797, pl. **136.** 1). Born in Rome in 1752, and died at Evesham in Worcestershire in 1832, aged eighty.

He was a many-sided man. At fourteen, as a prodigy pianist, he was taken to England by an English gentleman and there given every opportunity of general and musical education. He quickly won a European reputation. Approaching the age of sixty, he abandoned public performance and successfully took to piano manufacture in London.

He was one of the most famous teachers of his day; amongst his pupils were Field, Kalkbrenner, and J. B. Cramer (see the entries under these names). His long-famous *Gradus ad Parnassum* (a collection of piano studies) is today by no means forgotten.

Beethoven thought highly of him as a composer of piano sonatas, learnt much from them as a composer, and as a teacher prescribed his works in this form for the daily practice of his

nephew. Mozart's allusions to him, both as player and as composer, are uniformly scornful.

He may be looked upon as the first genuine composer for the pianoforte, with its special characteristics, as distinct from composers who in writing for that instrument showed the influence of the harpsichord.

See references under *Pianoforte* 17, 18, 22 (towards end); *Pianoforte Playing* 2, 4; *Fingering* 4; *Sonata* 8, 10 d (1773); *Symphony* 8 (1752); *Cadenza*; *Improvisation* 3; *Competitions*; *Composition* 14; *Percussion* 4 c; also p. 517, pl. 94. 6.

CLEMENTI, COLLARD & CO. See *Mechanical Reproduction* 13.

CLEMM, JOHN. See *Organ* 9.

CLÉRAMBAULT, LOUIS NICHOLAS (p. 368, pl. **61.** 5). Born in Paris in 1676 and died there in 1749, aged seventy-two. He was a noted Paris organist, and composer for organ and harpsichord, as also for voice—a minor but by no means insignificant contemporary of Bach, Couperin, and Scarlatti. His French cantatas (four books of them) are the best of their period. His organ works have been republished under the editorship of Guilmant.

CLEVELAND (Ohio) Orchestra. See *Concert* 15.

CLIFFORD, JAMES (1622-98). See *Cathedral Music* 6; *Anglican Chant* 4.

CLOAK, THE (Puccini). See *Trittico*.

CLOCHES (Fr.). 'Bells', e.g. those used in the orchestra. See *Bell*, also *Percussion Family* 2 b, 4 e, 5 b.

CLOCHETTE. Small bell. The 'Glöckchen' of Strauss.

CLOCK CHIMES, MUSICAL CLOCKS, AND CLOCKWORK INSTRUMENTS. See *Mechanical Reproduction of Music*.

CLOCK SYMPHONY (Haydn). See *Nicknamed Compositions*.

CLOG BOX. See *Chinese Wood Block*.

CLOG DANCING. See *Tap-dancing*.

CLOSE. The same as *Cadence* (q.v.).

CLOSE HARMONY (or Harmony in **CLOSE POSITION**). See *Harmony* 24 b.

CLOUGH. See *Bagpipe Family* 3 (end).

CLOUSSNITZER, PAUL. See *Chorale Prelude*.

CLOWES. See *Printing* 5.

CLUBS FOR MUSIC-MAKING. The musical club apparently played a considerable part in the development of musical culture during the seventeenth century in England, and probably also did so in other European countries.

One of the first glimpses we get of such an organization is in the dedication of the first book of madrigals published in England—the *Musica Transalpina* issued from London by **Nicholas Yonge** (q.v.), or Young, in 1588. In this he states (see *Madrigal* 2) that a body of substantial merchants and gentlemen was accustomed to gather at his house in the parish of St. Michael, Cornhill, 'for the exercise of musicke daily'. It is clear that madrigal singing must have made an important part of their activities, but there is no reason to think that their 'exercise of musicke' was restricted to that.

Yonge is thought to have been a choirman of St. Paul's Cathedral, and from time to time in the century that follows we get glimpses of other professional musicians adding to their income by conducting musical clubs—generally, however, meeting merely weekly.

It may be suggested that the existence of a musical club is indicated by the following incident related by Roger l'Estrange (see *Puritans and Music* 4) in his pamphlet *Truth and Loyalty Vindicated* (1662):

'Being in St. *James* his *Parke*, I heard an *Organ* Touched in a little low Room of one Mr. Hinckson's. I went in, and found a Private Company of some five or six Persons. They desired me to take up a Viole, and bear a *Part*. I did so. . . . By and by (without the least colour of a *Design* or *Expectation*) in comes *Cromwell*; He found us Playing and (as I remember) so he left us.'

The Hinckson (or **Hingston**; see *Puritans and Music* 4) mentioned was the chief of Cromwell's little band of musicians. It is quite likely that he carried on a musical club, as there seem to have been many of them during the period of the Commonwealth.

Another professional musician who carried on a club at this period was **Ellis**, the former organist of St. John's College, Oxford. Like Hingston, he had a chamber organ in his dwelling; here there gathered every week various members of the University (violists, violinists, lutenists, virginalists, vocalists). Anthony Wood, from whose diary our information comes, pathetically tells us that 'if he had missed the weekly meetings in the house of William Ellis, he could not well enjoy himself all the week after'—which is the true club spirit!

Wood mentions three other such **Oxford** clubs (or 'Musick Meetings', as they were usually called), one in Exeter College, another in Magdalen College, and one in various colleges by turns. He also tells us of a club carried on in London by an Oxford man, Chilmead, who, as a Royalist and Anglican, had got into trouble in those republican and Puritan times:

'Being ejected by the Parliamentary Visitors in 1648, he was forced, such were the then times, to obtain a living by that, which before was only a diversion to him, I mean by a weekly Musick-meeting, which he set up at the Black Horse, Aldersgatestreet, London.'

There was smoking at the clubs Wood attended and (as the record of his weekly expenditure of twopences and sixpences shows) liquid refreshment.

It is more than likely that **Cambridge** had similar clubs during the Commonwealth, as we have evidence of the presence there of a good many active musicians, but as that university, unlike Oxford, had at the period no music-loving diarist, actual information is lacking. We know that Christ's College, from 1710, had a musical club meeting weekly.

Pepys, in 1664, twice mentions going to a **'Musique Meeting'** at the **Post Office** (i.e. the Black Swan in Bishopsgate). On the first occasion he heard instrumental music performed. On the second occasion the Royal Society attended to hear a performance on a new instrument called the 'Arched Viall', but it proved to be a disappointment.

Henry Playford, the music publisher (son of John Playford; see *Publishing* 5), seems to have been active in promoting a national movement for Catch Clubs. In the preface to his *Musical Companion* (1701) he says:

'And that he (the publisher) may be beneficial to the publick in forwarding a commendable society, as well as the sale of his book, he has prevailed with his acquaintance and others in this city to enter into several clubs weekly, at taverns of convenient distance from each other, having each a particular master of musick belonging to the society established in it, who may instruct those, if desir'd, who shall be unskilled, in bearing a part in the several catches contained in this book, as well as others; and shall perfect those who have already had some insight in things of this nature, that they shall be capable of entertaining the societies they belong to abroad. In order to this he has provided several articles to be drawn, printed, and put in handsome frames, to be put up in each respective room the societies shall meet in, and be observed as so many standing rules, which each respective society is to go by; and he questions not but the several cities, towns, corporations, etc. in the kingdom of Great Britain and Ireland, as well as foreign plantations, will follow the example of the well-wishers to vocal and instrumental musick in this famous city, by establishing such weekly meetings as may render his undertaking as generally received as it is useful. And if any body or bodies of gentlemen are willing to enter into or compose such societies, they may send to him, where they may be furnished with books and articles.'

Whether as the result of this propaganda or otherwise, Catch Clubs and Glee Clubs became very common during the eighteenth century (p. 145, pl. **30.** 2). At these clubs the tradition of the older 'Musique Meetings', in the way of smoking and liquid refreshments, was maintained, and, in addition, there was often supper. The **Canterbury Catch Club** (p. 145, pl. **30.** 7), which began in a tavern in 1779 and later built its own hall, the 'Apollonian Hall', is seen in an early nineteenth-century picture to favour the churchwarden pipe, and its last survivor told the present writer that its refreshments consisted of 'gin punch and mutton pies'; this club progressed beyond the choral region into the instrumental and, whilst never abandoning its catches and glees, came to possess an organ and an orchestra. It met weekly. Bath, Belfast, Dublin, and other cities possessed such clubs.

The London Club, **Concentores Sodales,** was founded in 1798; all the members were composers and the performance of their choral compositions (canons, glees, etc.) provided the staple of the evening's activity. This club ceased to exist in 1812, was revived in 1817, and was still alive in 1864 or later.

The **Anacreontic Society,** founded in 1766, lasted until 1794. It was an aristocratic club of musical amateurs, admitting a certain number of professional musicians so as to have their aid in the performances. Songs, catches, glees, and supper made up the entertainment. Haydn once paid the club a visit. (See *Star-spangled Banner* for the club's song, performed at every meeting.) Belfast also had a club of this name, but later (1814 to the 1860s), and for instrumental practice (p. 145, pl. 30. 3).

One London eighteenth-century club, the **Noblemen and Gentlemen's Catch Club** (see *Glee* 3), founded in 1761, still meets every month. Its minute books go back to 1767, and we find that at that period every member had to sing a song at every meeting. If anyone sang out of tune he was to drink a glass of wine (though it is difficult to see how this would improve matters). One bottle of sherry was provided to every three members, and one bottle of Madeira to every seven, and nobody was to bring to the table 'coffee, tea, or such heterogeneous beverages—on any account!' It was wisely provided that no politics or religion was to be talked.

On the model of this club was founded the **Catch Club of Calcutta,** which met weekly at 10 p.m. and continued its session until sunrise, with an interval for 'a kettle of burnt champagne as soon as the clock struck two'.

In addition to the Noblemen and Gentlemen's Catch Club there are one or two similar but less ancient clubs still existing in London, e.g. the **Round, Catch and Canon Club** (dating from 1843), and the **City Glee Club** (see *Glee* 3). The **Adelphi Glee Club** of London (1833) is no longer in existence.

For a London club for madrigal singing (in principle a revival of Yonge's), founded in 1741 and still meeting regularly, see *Madrigal* 5.

The **Edinburgh Harmonists' Club,** dating from 1822, was absorbed by the Edinburgh Society of Musicians in 1951. But there were similar clubs in Edinburgh more than a century before that (see Allan Ramsay's poems, *The City of Edinburgh's Address to the Country,* 1716, and *To the Music Club,* 1721).

It is interesting to note that one still-existing English Choral Society of high repute, the **Huddersfield Choral Society** (Yorkshire), was, at its inception in 1836 and for some years, run on club lines. There were monthly practices, on a night near full moon (for the sake of members walking from a distance). Male members paid half a crown each half-year, female members nothing, both being allowed at every meeting 'three gills of ale and bread and cheese'. the object of the Society was enjoyable practice, not public performance, and members in rotation had 'the privilege of selecting the Oratorio to be performed at the next meeting, provided that a majority of the members think that copies can be procured'. At each of the monthly meetings 'the band' played 'not more than four instrumental pieces'. Any member was 'allowed to give his opinion after the performance of any piece of music', provided he did so 'in a respectable, friendly, and becoming manner'.

The **Oxford University Musical Club,** for the intimate performance of chamber music (a revival of the clubs described by Anthony Wood, as we might say), was founded in 1872. It was in 1915 combined with a similar body, the Oxford Musical Union, founded in 1884 (see a reference s.v. *Applause* 2).

The Cambridge University Musical Society began in 1843 as a club (the 'Peterhouse Musical Society') for the performance of instrumental music. It is now conducted on lines too broad to qualify it for description in this article, but the **Cambridge University Musical Club,** which holds weekly meetings for chamber performance by its members (supported very valuably by an ensemble-playing class under skilled professional direction), continues the tradition of the seventeenth-century musical clubs.

For some treatment of cognate subjects see parts of the articles on *Concert, Music Hall, Barber Shop Music*; the articles *Liedertafel, Orphéon,* and *Graduates' Meeting.*

CLUTSAM KEYBOARD. Plate **101** (p. 560) has a figure of this keyboard, the general character of which will be evident from the figure and the description that accompanies it. It was introduced near the end of the nineteenth century, but the Department of Folk Culture and Industries of the National Museum of Wales, Cardiff, reported to the present author, in 1940 (apropos of the illustration in question), 'We have recently acquired an upright grand pianoforte by D. C. Hewitt, about 1840–50 in style, which appears to have this type of keyboard'. The maker in question is presumably the Daniel Hewitt mentioned in the text of the present book, under *Pianoforte* 15.

In another 'Clutsam Keyboard' (*c.* 1915) the improvement lay in a more scientific weighting of the keys.

COACH-HORN. See under *Posthorn.*

COATES.

(1) JOHN (1865–1941). Admirable English operatic and concert tenor of high repute.

See reference under *Voice* 18.

(2) ALBERT. Born in St. Petersburg in 1882, his father being a Yorkshireman and his mother Russian, and died at Cape Town in 1953, aged seventy-one. He studied violoncello, piano, and conducting (this last under Nikisch) at Leipzig Conservatory and then held various conductorships in Germany and St. Petersburg, travelling much and conducting in London, New York, and elsewhere. In 1946 he took up residence in South Africa. His compositions include the operas *Samuel Pepys* (1929), performed in several continental opera houses, *Pickwick* (London, 1936), and *Tafelberg se Kleed* ('Table Mountain in Cloud'; South Africa, 1952).

(3) ERIC. Born at Hucknall in Nottinghamshire in 1886 and died at Chichester in 1957, aged seventy-one. He became known first as a leading viola player, and then as a talented composer of songs and orchestral and other music, usually of the somewhat lighter type.

Cf. *Saxophone Family*.

COBBETT, WALTER WILLSON (1847–1937). English amateur violinist and keen enthusiast for chamber music, who devoted himself to the encouragement of its culture. Editor of *Cyclopedic Survey of Chamber Music* (1929; 2nd edn. 1963). See under *Phantasy*.

COBBOLD, WILLIAM. Born at Norwich in 1560 and died at Beccles, in Suffolk, in 1639, aged seventy-nine. He was for a time organist of Norwich Cathedral (cf. *Norwich*), and is remembered today as the composer of one or two madrigals.

COCHLEA. See *Ear and Hearing* 1.

COCKBURN, ALICIA or ALISON (c. 1712–94). See *Flowers of the Forest*.

COCKRAM. See *Passing By*.

COCLICO. See *Musica Reservata*.

COCTEAU. See *Poulenc*; p. 388, pl. 65. 4.

CODA (Italian for 'tail') is the term applied to any passage, long or short, added at the end of a composition or of a section of a composition in order to give a greater sense of finality. For instance, in compound binary form (also known as 'Sonata Form' and 'First Movement Form'—see *Form* 7) there is commonly a coda at the end of the exposition, and another, of greater length and importance, at the end of the whole movement. These were of little importance in the earlier classical sonatas, but Mozart and (above all) Beethoven greatly developed them, the final coda with Beethoven sometimes becoming of great interest and artistic value.

The coda at the end of the exposition is sometimes, for distinction, called the *Codetta*. However, 'codetta' may also mean, as the diminutive ending of that word implies, simply a short coda. (For the distinct meaning of the word 'codetta' in fugue see *Form* 12.)

In the period preceding that of the classical sonata, i.e. that of the suite (q.v.), almost every movement was in simple binary form, i.e. there were two sections, the first usually ending in the key of the dominant (i.e. fifth of the scale), and the second in the original key of the piece: in almost every case the composer marked each section to be repeated, and it is noticeable that whereas Bach, Handel, and many others allowed the second part to be repeated without any addition, Couperin (q.v.), in France, usually tacked on a little coda for use after the repetition, so that the piece as a whole should end with some addition to what a mere section of the piece had ended with. His codas are, however, very perfunctory as compared with those which a later period was to introduce.

The feeling that a coda was required in order to round off a piece of music seems to have come in strongly only with the period of the classical sonata, and Beethoven, as above mentioned, is largely responsible for it.

CODETTA. See *Coda*. (For 'codetta' in fugue see *Form* 12.)

CODIAD YR EHEDYDD. See *Rising of the Lark*.

COENEN, WILLEM. Born at Rotterdam in 1837 and died in Italy in 1918, aged eighty. He settled in Dutch Guiana, travelled as pianist in North and South America, and spent nearly half a century in London—amongst other activities there holding series of chamber concerts at which the concerted music of Brahms had its first London hearing. Some of his songs (which once enjoyed huge popularity) are still sung.

See *Pianoforte* 21.

COERNE, LOUIS ADOLPHE. Born at Newark, New Jersey, in 1870, and died at Boston, Massachusetts, in 1922, aged fifty-two. He was responsible for over 500 compositions in various forms. His opera, *Zenobia*, performed at Bremen in 1905, is believed to be the first grand opera by a native-born American produced in Europe. He was given the degree of Ph.D. by Harvard University in 1908, his book *The Evolution of Modern Orchestration* and the opera score being accepted jointly as a thesis—the first instance of the university conferring such a degree for music.

COFFEY, CHARLES (d. 1745). See *Singspiel*; *Ireland* 6; *Fairs and their Music*.

COGHLAN (music printer). See *Printing of Music* 1.

COGLI, COI (It.). 'With the' (plural).

COL, COLL', COLLA, COLLE (It.). 'With the', e.g. *Col basso*, 'with the bass'; *Colla voce*, 'with the voice' (indication to accompanist to be subservient, i.e. as to time details).

COLASCIONE. An instrument of Eastern origin chiefly associated with southern Europe, but used also in Germany. It was a kind of lute, with a small circular body with rounded back and a very long neck, usually fitted with three strings, but sometimes with more.

COLD AND RAW. This is a song of D'Urfey (q.v.), published in his *Comes Amoris* (1688). The air, which is to be found in Playford's *The Dancing Master* (1650, etc.) and elsewhere, was, until D'Urfey took it in hand, known as *Stingo*, or *Oil of Barley*. There is an anecdote in Hawkins's *History of Music*, of Purcell, summoned to play the harpsichord to Queen Mary, sitting 'unemployed and not a little nettled at the Queen's preference of a vulgar ballad to his music'—for Mrs. Arabella Hunt, the famous singer and lutenist, had also been summoned, and the Queen had commanded her to sing this song to her lute. This was three years after D'Urfey's song appeared, and it was doubtless popular at the time. In the next Birthday Ode to the Queen, Purcell delicately (and perhaps slyly) recalled the incident by using the tune as the bass of the song 'May her blest example'.

See also *Lilliburlero*.

COLEMAN.

(1) CHARLES. See *Opera* 13.

(2) (RICHARD) HENRY (PINWILL) (1888–1965). Organist of Peterborough Cathedral and author of church music and books on choir training, etc.

COLERIDGE, SAMUEL TAYLOR. See *Ballad* 5; *Romantic*.

COLERIDGE-TAYLOR, SAMUEL (p. 337, pl. **54**. 5). Born in London in 1875 and died at Croydon, Surrey, in 1912, aged thirty-seven.

His mother was an English girl, his father a West African Negro doctor practising in London, who, unsuccessful, returned to Africa, leaving his wife and child.

He first appeared in public at the age of about eight as a violinist at a surburban concert; a benefactor sent him to the Royal College of Music, where, very poor and 'with a large circular patch on his trousers', he studied under Stanford.

His first substantial recognition as a composer came when Elgar, unable to accept a request to write for the Gloucester Festival, recommended him to the committee, which led to the composition and performance of his orchestral Ballad in A minor.

Soon after this (in 1898) his choral–orchestral *Hiawatha's Wedding Feast* was given.

Thenceforward, though there were struggles to make a sufficient income, his reputation was assured. He followed up *Hiawatha's Wedding Feast* by *The Death of Minnehaha* (1899) and *Hiawatha's Departure* (1900), thus elaborating the work into a trilogy, and he wrote other cantatas, such as *A Tale of Old Japan* (1911), as well as works for orchestra, for chamber combinations, for violin, piano, voices, etc., and a good deal of incidental music for plays.

He died before attaining full development. Nevertheless, he had provided choral societies with material of distinction—and of a new 'flavour' that came as a welcome relief from existing conventions.

See *Clarinet Family* 6; *Oratorio* 7 (1903); *Bamboula*.

COLINDA. A type of Rumanian Christmas song, being part of the folk-lore of the country. Béla Bartók (q.v.) made a collection and a special study of these songs.

COLL', COLLA. See *Col*.

COLLABORATION IN COMPOSITION. Literary collaboration has been fairly frequent (Beaumont and Fletcher, 'Erckmann–Chatrian' etc.). Musical collaboration has been rarer but cases have existed. F. Rebel (q.v.) and F. Francoeur jointly produced two books of violin sonatas, ten or eleven operas, and some ballets. Boïeldieu wrote opera in collaboration with nine different composers—in one instance with three at one time (Isouard, Kreutzer, and Méhul). Honegger and Ibert jointly produced the operas *L'Aiglon* and *La Famille Cardinal*. For the life-long collaboration of two brothers see *Hillemacher, P. L.*

Some attempts at collaboration have not 'come off'. In 1868, on the death of Rossini, Verdi suggested that the thirteen sections of a Requiem in his memory should be undertaken by thirteen composers, but the results showed such a clash of idiom and style that the idea of joint performance or publication was dropped. (Five years later, on the death of Manzoni, Verdi composed his complete Requiem, incorporating his contribution to the former work, i.e. the *Libera me*.)

For a piece in which there collaborated four Russian composers plus Liszt see *Chopsticks*. For another instance of Liszt as a member of a band of collaborators see *Hexameron*. For the oratorio *Genesis*, whose composers included Schönberg, Stravinsky, and four others, see *Oratorio* 7 (1947).

COLLA PUNTA DELL' ARCO (It.). 'With the point of the bow.'

COLL' ARCO. 'With the bow'; i.e. after a passage marked 'pizzicato'. (Sometimes shortened to *c.a.*)

COLLARD FELLOWSHIP. See under *Minstrels, etc.* 3.

COLLECTIONS OF OLD MUSIC. The following English manuscript collections receive notice in this book under their respective heads: *Benjamin Cosyn's Virginal Book*; *Eton College Choirbook*; *Fitzwilliam Virginal Book*; *Lady Nevell's Book*; *Mulliner Manuscript*; *Old Hall Manuscript*; *Will Forster's Virginal Book*.

COLLEGE OF ST. NICHOLAS. See *Royal School of Church Music*.

COLLEGIUM MUSICUM. See *Concert* 13, 15; *Fasch, Johann Friedrich*; p. 97, pl. **16**.

COL LEGNO (It.). 'With the wood', i.e. striking the strings with the stick of the bow, instead of playing on them with the hair.

COLLES, HENRY COPE. Born at Bridgnorth in 1879 and died in London in 1943, aged sixty-three. He was educated at the Royal College of Music (of whose staff he became a member) and Worcester College, Oxford (M.A., Hon. D.Mus.), and was from 1906 attached to the London *Times*, first as assistant Music Critic and then (1911) as chief Music Critic. He wrote a number of books on music and was the editor of the third and fourth editions of Grove's *Dictionary of Music*.

See *Form* 14.

COLLETT, JOHN. Mid-eighteenth-century composer. See *Sonata* 10 c.

COLLINGWOOD, LAWRANCE ARTHUR. Born in London in 1887. After serving as a choir-boy in the choir of Westminster Abbey, he studied at Oxford, at the Guildhall School of Music, and at the Conservatory of St. Petersburg. He served as an opera conductor, particularly at Sadler's Wells (Musical Director 1931–46), then becoming Musical Adviser to the Gramophone Company. His compositions include the opera *Macbeth* (heard in 1934) and a good deal of music for orchestra, chamber combinations, piano, etc.

In 1948 he was created C.B.E.

COLLINS.

(1) ANTHONY. He was born at Hastings in 1892. He studied at the Royal College of Music under Holst, Boult, and others. His first career was as a viola player. He has later made another career as conductor and composer (film music, chamber music, etc.), and spent some time in the United States.

(2) LOTTIE. See *Music Hall* 4.

COLMONELL. See *Use of Colmonell*.

COLOFONIA (It.). 'Colophony', or bow resin.

COLOGNE. See *France* 2 (for Franco of Cologne); *Schools of Music*.

COLONNA, GIOVANNI PABLO (*c.* 1640–95). See *Oratorio* 7 (1670).

COLONNE, ÉDOUARD (real 'Christian' name Judas). Born at Bordeaux in 1838 and died in Paris in 1910, aged seventy-one. He was for many years leading violin of the Paris Opéra and then (1873) founded the orchestra which bore his name, which he so long conducted, and which came to enjoy great fame.

See *Enesco*.

COLOPHONY (Fr., *Colophane*, It., *Colofonia*, Ger., *Kolophon*). Resin for the bow of the violin family.

COLORATURA. An Italian word meaning 'coloured' music, and applied to the (extemporary or other) decoration of a vocal melody by the division of longer notes into shorter ones, in the shape of runs, roulades, and cadenzas of all kinds. Another word for the same thing was *figurato* (masc.) or *figurata* (fem.), 'figured' ('musica colorata', or 'musica figurata'; 'canto figurato'. Cf. *Musica figurata*).

We speak of a *Coloratura Soprano*, meaning one with a light flexible voice equal to the demands of, say, Mozart in his 'Queen of the Night' part in *The Magic Flute* (see *Voice* 19).

For incidental light on coloratura see *Singing* 4, 6, 7, 8; *Melisma*; *Fioritura*.

COLOUR AND MUSIC

1. The Faculty of Synaesthesia and some Forms it takes.
2. Association of Particular Composers or Compositions with Particular Colours.
3. Association of Timbres with Colours.
4. Association of Keys with Colours.
5. Physical and Mental Associations of Definite Pitches with Definite Colours.
6. Early Attempts at Combining Music and Colour on Scientific Principles.
7. The Rimington Colour Organ.
8. The Fallacy of 'Translation' from Sound into Sight.
9. The Clavilux.
10. Other Attempts to Produce a 'Colour-Music'.
11. Use of Colour Concomitants by Composers.
12. The Approach through Occultism.
13. Educational Use of Colour with Music.

(For illustrations see p. 208, pl. **40**.)

1. The Faculty of Synaesthesia and some Forms it takes. The theory of a relationship between sound and colour is natural, the tendency to create an association between these two orders of phenomena being extremely common. All languages register such an association. In discussing painting, we speak of 'tones' ('quiet' or 'loud', or 'low' or 'high'); in the parlance of music. we make use of 'chromatic' and 'coloratura' (both of them implying the introduction of tints—the former by the addition of notes extra to the diatonic scale, the latter by the addition of decorative passages to a simple melody). Whistler borrowed from music as titles for some of his paintings such words as 'Nocturne' and 'Symphony'. Many other examples of this kind of indication of affinities between the processes and objects of sight and hearing could, of course, be added.

More than this, actual detailed examples are common of *Synaesthesia* ('the production from a sense-impression of one kind of an associated mental image of a sense-impression of another kind'). Thus psychologists are familiar with the phenomenon of a colour-impression attaching to words or letters. Even children often regard figures, or the names of persons or of the days of the week, as each possessing its distinctive colour. The French Symbolist poet Rimbaud wrote a sonnet, *Les Voyelles*, in which he attached to each vowel the colour in which it appeared to him ('A black, E white, I red, O blue, U green'), and another French poet has done the same thing—with a totally different set of colour correspondences, such associations as all those just mentioned being entirely subjective and largely personal.

Galton's *Inquiries into Human Faculty* (1883) has interesting remarks on the nature and value of associations such as those discussed in this article.

The first attempt to show an analogy between colours and tones is very ancient; such an attempt was made by Ptolemy, the famous Alexandrian scientist of the second century.

2. Association of Particular Composers or Compositions with Particular Colours. A form of synaesthesia that would appear to be entirely subjective is the association of particular compositions or even the whole output of particular composers with one or another colour.

Wagenseil, in his book on the Mastersingers (1697), speaks of their knowing certain tunes as the 'Evening Red Tune', the 'Blue Corn Flower Tune', the 'Black Amber Tune', the 'Yellow Lion Skin Tune', etc.

Cases have been reported where a whole opera has possessed, for a particular person, an association of this kind (*Aida* and *Tannhäuser* blue; *The Flying Dutchman* a misty green—this last possibly from some suggestion of the sea).

Persons have also been found who looked upon Mozart's music as blue, Chopin's as green, and Wagner's as 'luminous, with changing colours'—this last probably derived from general effects of shifting harmonies and orchestrations. The psychologist Flournoy speaks of the music of Gounod as evoking a sensation of violet in one individual and of blue in another, whilst Beethoven aroused the sensation of black in a third. If in such cases as these the persons concerned can be shown to be acquainted with any considerable and varied portion of the output of the composer mentioned (i.e. if they are not influenced by acquaintance merely with one or two compositions of the composer that happen to be in more or less agreement emotionally) they must surely be looked upon as merely the victims of fanciful obsessions.

In 1923 an experiment was carried out at Wellesley College, Mass. (a women's college), by the late Professor Clarence G. Hamilton. He played to a group of students Schubert's Impromptu, op. 142, no. 3, which consists of a theme and five variations, asking them to write down any colour-suggestions that came into their minds. It is significant that there was general agreement as to whether any particular variation suggested vivid shades or fainter pastel shades, i.e. as to the degree of luminosity, but not as to particular colours evoked.

3. Association of Timbres with Colours. Amongst musicians, the most general example of synaesthesia is that which connects particular colours with the timbres of particular instruments. There is probably more tendency to agreement amongst persons possessing these associations than amongst persons possessing any others.

At a meeting of the Musical Association in 1876 Mr. R. H. M. Bosanquet, a distinguished scientist and researcher on the scientific side of music, suggested that, in order to make the reading of orchestral scores easier, different colours should be used in printing the staves devoted to the various families of instruments. 'Upon the point of colours he had found a remarkable agreement amongst musicians, and he suggested black for strings and voices, red for brass and drums, and blue for wood.' Probably most musicians today would agree as to the propriety of these associations, whereas very few would agree as to there being any associative suitability in printing (say) the strings in red and the brass in black or blue.

The principle here is probably not one of direct association; analysed, it seems to be somewhat as follows: In music, strings are (relatively) emotionally sober, brass thrilling; in colours, black is emotionally sober, red thrilling. The vague general emotion aroused equally by a sound and a sight thus serves to link them. The link is probably often overlooked, but it is there nevertheless. Some link of this kind probably underlies Zola's remark to Daudet (which most of us would admit to embody a genuine correspondence between a timbre and a feeling) that 'the clarinet repre-

sents sensual love, whilst the flute at most represents platonic love'.

The conductor Sir Dan Godfrey, in his *Memories and Music* (1924), set out a tabular description of each of the instruments of the orchestra, in one column of which he attached to each a colour: to him the flute was blue and the clarinet 'rose-pink to blush red'.

Few books on orchestration exist which do not make at least occasional use of colour suggestions. Sir Henry Wood's article on orchestration in the *Dictionary of Modern Music and Musicians* (1924) is entitled 'Orchestral Colours and Values'; Prout's *Orchestration* (1897) has a section on 'The Analogy of Orchestration and Painting'. Widor's *Technique of the Modern Orchestra* (1904) opens with the statement that 'Within the last fifty years . . . the orchestral palette has been enriched with a variety of tone-colour formerly unknown'. Berlioz's *Treatise of Instrumentation* (1843) speaks of the art of instrumentation as 'the application of the various sonorous elements for colouring the melody, harmony, and rhythm', and so on.

The German word for timbre is *Klangfarbe* (or 'sound-colour') and an English synonym is 'tone-colour'.

One writer on the subject, Sabaneef, gives a list of composers in whom the association between colour and sound is known to have been weak (e.g. Schumann and Brahms), and another list of those in whom it is known to have been strong (e.g. Berlioz, Wagner, Debussy). He says (and his examples in general support him) that those who are organically deficient in orchestral 'colouring' are usually found to lack the 'colour ear', whereas those who are strong in this element are usually found to possess it. (Sabaneef's estimate of Brahms as an orchestrator may, however, have aroused protest in the minds of some readers.)

4. Association of Keys with Colours. Many musicians possess key–colour associations. If these associations are as constant with them as they seem to imply, it is difficult to trace any intermediate link of emotion aroused on the one hand by the colour and on the other by the musical effect, as was possible in the case of timbre. Beethoven is said on one occasion to have spoken of B minor as 'black'. He often said things on impulse, and we need not attach much importance to chance remarks made by him, which he might perhaps contradict next day; but supposing he did intend this association of his to be taken seriously, one would wish to know whether he meant it to apply to music at all speeds and in all rhythms and styles, and in all orchestrations, and on receiving an affirmative reply would be able to turn over the pages of his own works and call attention to such variety of emotional content amongst pieces in that key as would seem to exclude any colour-description common to all, unless colour be divorced entirely from emotional suggestion, which, as just suggested, may sometimes be the case.

Then there is, of course, the question of pitch, for what is B minor on one instrument may be B flat minor or A minor or C minor or C sharp minor on another.

This last point may, however, be met by supposing that the mind of a person possessing this particular type of colour-association somehow takes account of the relative rather than the absolute pitch-position of keys. Beethoven, on this assumption, would have in his mind a sort of unconscious image of the whole circle of keys of his pianoforte, an image in which the position of B minor would be marked by an effect of darkness. If, in the house of a friend, he played or heard a piano of different pitch from his own, he would, on noting the key and pitch of the first piece played, instinctively adjust his whole colour scale, pushing it bodily, as it were, a little to the right or left.

And so with MacDowell, to whom one key was blue, another red, etc. And the sober savant, Riemann, who in his book on Bach's '48' suddenly surprises us by alluding to E major as the 'key of the deep green of fully developed spring', and Hoffmann, the fanciful composer-novelist, who speaks of his hero Johannes Kreisler as 'the little man in a coat the colour of C sharp minor with an E major coloured collar' (which presumably means something definite to him), and the composer Grétry, who in his *Essays on Music* attaches colours to the various keys—and the dozens of others who have claimed to possess such an association.

The following are the colours evoked by the major scales in the minds of two Russian composers: they are interesting as showing both one or two correspondences and some very wide divergences.

It is interesting to note a point that these lists, being arranged in the 'circle of fifths' order, throw into relief. The general scheme in both lists is: sharp keys, bright colours; flat keys, sober colours. It may be suggested that the very *words* 'sharp' and 'flat' have tended to create in the minds of most of us an emotional association.

The relativity of all these key-colour associations was illustrated during a debate on the whole subject organized in London in 1886 by the journal *Musical Opinion*. That section of the audience that maintained the definite existence of 'key colour' by which it could aurally identify a key was submitted to a test, a well-known piece being played in both G and A flat, to which they applied and defended their usual

G and A flat associations, maintaining that the transposition had totally changed the key-colour. The meeting broke up in recrimination and disorder on its being revealed that the piano possessed a mechanical transposing device, so that whilst those present had *seen* the performer playing in A flat major they had *heard* her playing in G major as before (presumably they had been adroitly given an interval of time to forget the pitch of the first performance).

It would appear that in such a case as this the association is one of relation to the whole circle of keys, and that to such people as these A flat major is A flat major, whatever the pitch of the instrument, because they unconsciously hear it in contrast with an imagined series of relatively 'darker' keys and another series of relatively 'lighter' keys. In the first performance they were *thinking* of the key as one up on the sharp side of C, and in the second of it as four down on the flat side of C.

It has been suggested that in such cases certain differences of fingering as between keys may account for difference of effect. Thus one person present on the above occasion argued: 'Nearly all the sharp keys have as their third a black projecting key, which may cause the third to be played more loudly; and as the third is the interval that gives brightness, possibly this accounts for the difference. The reverse is, of course, the case with the flat keys.'

Similarly, it is often pointed out that the greater or less use of open strings on bowed instruments, according as they are in one key or in another, may influence key-colour.

The difficulties in the way of the acceptance of any such hypothesis are many. The hypothesis conveniently frees key-colours from dependence on the actual pitch of the instrument, but as the open strings on a bowed instrument do not correspond either to the white or the black keys on a keyboard instrument it would imply differing sets of colours for the keys according as one or the other type of instrument is used, and it is the usual contention of 'key-colourists' that their associations are independent of the particular instrument. Further, organ music would, presumably, on this theory, be free of key-colour associations, since finger-force does not have any dynamic effect on organ playing as it has on the playing of the pianoforte. Moreover, there is the difficulty offered by those keys which, whilst exactly the same on keyboard instruments, possess two manners of notational statement, e.g. D flat and C sharp,

Key	Rimsky-Korsakof	Scriabin.
C major.	White.	Red.
G major.	Brownish-gold, bright.	Orange-rose.
D major.	Yellow, sunny.	Yellow, brilliant.
A major.	Rosy, clear.	Green.
E major.	Blue, sapphire, sparkling.	Bluish-white.
B major.	Sombre, dark blue shot with steel.	Same as above.
F sharp major.	Greyish-green.	Bright blue.
D flat major.	Dusky, warm.	Violet.
A flat major.	Greyish-violet.	Purple-violet.
E flat major.	Dark, gloomy, bluish-grey.	Steel-colour with a metallic lustre.
B flat major.	—	Same as above.
F major.	Green.	Red.

which to most or all key-colourists suggest widely different colour effects.

On the whole, it would seem that 'key-colour' is an entirely subjective experience, dependent partly (probably largely) on the emotional suggestions of the words 'flat' and 'sharp', partly on the subject's theoretical knowledge of the series of sharp keys (rising by fifths) and the series of flat keys (falling by fifths) and, probably, also, on the unconscious recollection of particular pieces met with in early life—pieces in which the composer has been influenced in his choice of key by the convention that flats are, on the whole, solemn, and sharps brilliant.

At the base of this last convention is the fact that the lowering or raising of the pitch *of a particular piece* does tend to give it more solemnity or more brilliance, as the case may be. Thus a composer who imagines the opening phrase of a new piece, rhythmically and harmonically of solemn character, at about the A pitch or the D pitch, is likely instinctively to put it in A flat or D flat rather than in A natural or D natural, because he is mentally (consciously or subconsciously) comparing the two keys. Beethoven's Funeral March in his 'Eroica' Symphony is in C minor (3 flats); the one in his Pianoforte Sonata (op. 26) is in A flat minor (7 flats; it would sound exactly the same in G sharp minor, 5 sharps!). On the other hand, Mendelssohn's, in his *Songs without Words*, is in E minor (one sharp), which would seem to show that Mendelssohn was less under the flat-solemn obsession than Beethoven.[1] Yet even Beethoven was not always under its influence, as is shown by some of his compositions, and also by his description of B minor (2 sharps) as a 'black' key.

The conclusion, then, of all the foregoing seems to be that key-colour associations are in part conventional (general tendency to attach darker colours to keys with flats in their signature and brighter to those with sharps) and partly arbitrary and personal—for probably no two musicians have yet agreed on the same series of associations. However, the permutations on the twelve major or the twelve minor keys alone are 479,001,600, and those on the twenty-four major and minor ascend to figures far beyond what are necessary to provide all the inhabitants of the world with their own individual tables of key-colour associations. The scope for variety of association may then be looked upon as unlimited, and perhaps all that we could legitimately expect would be some degree of general agreement as to the approximate colour suggestions of a few of the most used keys. Beyond the tendency amongst musicians to accept the sharp–bright, flat–sad convention, this moderate measure of agreement does not, however, appear to exist.

How entirely subjective the whole associa-

tion is we may note from the following remarks of Riemann on a certain edition of the third prelude and fugue of the '48':

'Kroll has written this number in the key of D flat in place of C sharp, and might plead by way of justification that Bach, had he lived at the present day, would certainly have done the same; for without doubt D flat is a key more familiar to us than C sharp, but in his day, the reverse was the case. The C sharp prelude, however, affords convincing proof that his powers of feeling and of invention were definitely influenced by the key; this ardent midsummer mood, this flashing, glimmering and glistening ("Blitzen, Flirren und Flimmern") were evolved from the spirit of the C sharp major key; the veiled, soft key of D flat would have suggested treatment of a totally different kind.'

5. Physical and Mental Associations of Definite Pitches with Definite Colours.

We here approach a type of association as to which the claim has long been made that its basis is not subjective but capable of justification by the mathematical statement of physical fact. This general idea effectively began with Newton in his *Opticks* (1704; collecting papers dating from 1672 to 1675).

White light is a blending of all the colours, and, analysing it spectroscopically, Newton laid out a scheme of seven chief colours (red, orange, yellow, green, blue, indigo, violet) and remarked on analogies that he found between these and the seven different notes of the diatonic scale. These analogies were based on the breadth of the seven colour-bands in the spectrum and the seven string lengths required to produce the scale.

Later speculations and experiments have proceeded from the recognition that sounds we hear and colours we see are, alike, sensory responses to vibrations. There is, however, a stupendous difference of rapidity, sound vibrations perceptible to the human ear ranging from about 16 to about 20,000 per second (individuals varying somewhat in the range of their aural perception; the second figure just given is that for the squeak of a bat, which some people cannot hear) and colour vibrations from about 451,000,000,000,000 to 780,000,000,000,000 per second—covering the complete range of the spectrum from red to violet. It has been surmised from the proportions of the vibration figures of the spectrum that if we could perceive the effect of higher light vibrations we should find the red of one end of the spectrum repeating at the other, with a figure double that of its previous figure, the two reds thus corresponding to an octave in music, of which the vibration figure of the higher note is always double that of the lower note. It is, also, pointed out that the proportions of the vibration figures for the intermediate colours correspond very nearly to those of the vibration figures for the various notes within the octave (these notes, as stated by Newton, not being the complete major or minor diatonic scale, however, but a scale on this pattern—C, D, E flat, F, G, A, B flat, which amounts to a major scale without its bottom note).

[1] As stated in the article, *Nicknamed Compositions*, Mendelssohn did not himself apply the title 'Funeral March' in the published copies. Neverthess it has always been accepted as a Funeral March, could, indeed, hardly be anything else, and was played as such at the composer's own funeral.

Against this, Helmholtz and others have pointed out that the colour-scale relied upon is arbitrary, the colour-bands shading imperceptibly into one another and Newton's original division having itself been influenced by analogy with the musical scale. For example, Newton recognized indigo (between blue and violet) as a definite colour; but he might just as logically have recognized yellow–orange (between yellow and orange) and, equally, yellow–green (between yellow and green) and blue–green (between blue and green). Specific points in the spectrum have been fixed upon by Newton and others in order to facilitate nomenclature, but they are not real entities. Later scientists have adopted nomenclatures that differ from that of Newton and recognize more than his seven 'colours'.

Moreover, the behaviour of sounds in combination is completely different from the behaviour of colours in combination, so pointing to a radical difference in nature. If we combine two notes we get an effect of combination in which the ear can still clearly distinguish the two elements. The two notes remain what they were before, i.e. retain their two positions in the scale. But if we combine two colours they both of them disappear, and in place there appears a single colour from another portion of the spectrum (i.e. the colour scale); e.g. red and green, when combined, go out of existence altogether, and yellow replaces them. Consider the difference between re-combining all the colours of the spectrum, which gives pure white light, and of simultaneously sounding all the notes of the octave (with, to make the analogy complete, all the innumerable pitches in between them)!

The sole genuine correspondence between sound and colour is, indeed, that both are the effect of vibrations. As long ago as 1810 Goethe in his *Zur Farbenlehre* ('Towards a Knowledge of Colour'; 1810) expressed the following view:

'The error which writers have fallen into in trying to establish this analogy we would thus define— Colour and sound do not admit of being compared together in any way, but both are referable to a higher formula; both are derivable, though each for itself, from a higher law. They are like two rivers that have their source in one and the same mountain, but subsequently pursue their way, under totally different conditions, in two totally different regions, so that throughout the whole course of both no two points can be compared.'

(Scientists today would not approve the reference to 'higher law'.)

Such statements as the following, taken from a description in an American musical journal of a system called Marcotone (the invention of Edward Maryon), express the other view.

'Sound is color, made audible, and color is sound, made visible. . . .

'By correlating sensations that come to the ear with those that come to the eye, it is possible to think the tone "C", as it is possible to think the color "red" or any other notes, or colors, in the scale. This correlation makes absolute pitch a fact for everyone. . . . This condition is accomplished by "placing, in the sub-conscious mind, the abso-lute pitch, as tone-color of the chromatic scale, and by so doing becoming attuned to Universal Laws governing vibration and motion".'

There is this much to be admitted, on the basis of careful experiments made with 250 persons by Sabaneef (recorded in *Music and Letters*, July 1929)—'Persons with a poor idea of pitch usually appear to be almost or altogether wanting in colour-vision.'

However, Sabaneef's investigations do not support the idea of a correspondence between the musical scale and the spectrum. He found a certain approach to unanimity (varying from 70 to 87 per cent.) respecting the colours associated with just a few notes, but when these are put in scale order the colours do not at all follow spectrum order: D yellow; E bluish; F red; G greyish or brownish; B bluish (like E).

It would appear from all this that such associations as exist between either relative pitches and colours or absolute pitches and colours are (like the associations between keys and colours already discussed) purely subjective and individual.

Moreover, they are shifting. Save with persons possessing the sense of absolute pitch, Sabaneef (cf. 3) found that the same individuals reacted differently to a note when they were told its name from what they did when they were not told this, showing that when they were told the name intellectual associations entered. A person told to listen to a chord of F sharp would attach a colour to it, and if given the identical chord under the name of G flat would attach quite another.

He says that 'a great deal of the evidence was confused and was entirely altered upon a repetition of the experiment'.

6. Early Attempts at Combining Music and Colour on Scientific Principles. The Jesuit priest and professor of mathematics and physics, **Athanasius Kircher** (1602–80), called music 'the ape of light' and said that everything visible could be made audible and vice versa. He was, then, rather before Newton, under the empire of a false analogy, and pushed it to the extremest point.

In the next century his ideas and those of Newton inspired another Jesuit priest-professor. **Louis Bertrand Castel** (1688–1757) published a book, *La Musique en Couleurs* (1720), and, going further, constructed a 'Clavecin Oculaire', or 'harpsichord for the eyes', which had an arrangement of coloured tapes (one for each finger-key), through which light passed. Telemann, in Germany, published a translation of Castel's description of this instrument (1739), and an English adaptation of the work also appeared (Castel had scientific standing in England, having been elected a Fellow of the Royal Society).

The inventor was clearly unfortunate in living before the days of the application of electricity, and never made a success of his instrument, but it was much discussed and stands in history as the first attempt in its direction. The colours attached to the different notes were arranged according to the widths of the colour-bands of the spectrum (Newton's idea, though Castel did not adopt Newton's details of pitch and colour equivalences), not on vibration ratios, the vibratory explanation of light dating only from the nineteenth century.

The scientist–poet, **Erasmus Darwin**, in 1789 made similar proposals to those of Castel, suggesting the use of the newly invented Argand oil-lamps to send strong light through 'coloured glasses' on to 'movable blinds' communicating with the keys of a harpsichord, and so producing 'visible music'. He took for granted the Newtonian proportions for notes and colours.

7. The Rimington Colour Organ (p. 208, pl. **40.** 1). From the latter part of the nineteenth century onwards there has been a greatly increased activity in the attempt to combine colour and music, due to the researches of Clerk Maxwell into the nature of light and colour, and the practical application of electricity to mechanism and lighting, which have enormously facilitated the attempt.

One of the most important efforts was that of the artist and Professor of Fine Arts at Queen's College, London, **A. Wallace Rimington** (1854–1918), whose Colour Organ was first demonstrated in London and elsewhere in 1895. This organ did not produce music, but accompanied with a play of colour on a screen performances on piano or orchestra (Chopin, Wagner, etc.). In 1911 Professor Rimington published *Colour Music—the Art of Mobile Colour*. He 'does not propose to prove that certain waves of light have their exact parallel in certain waves of sound', nevertheless he sets out a colour scale above the musical scale, with twelve 'semitones' in each. As the spectrum includes only colours corresponding to the different notes of one octave, Rimington accounted for further octaves by repeating the same colours with increased luminosity. He adopted, to some extent, the fallacy of *translating* music into colours by playing a musical score on his colour keyboard, but the organ had an attachment by which the single spectrum could be spread over the whole extent of the keyboard, and then it was no longer possible to play actual musical compositions, because the (imagined) colour correspondence had disappeared. The inventor was evidently also willing to abandon on occasion any correspondence with the notes of the musical scale in favour of an association between timbre and colour, for he imagines 'Wagnerian trumpet blasts' to a screen flooded by an intense orange, the same passage then being repeated as a faint echo on the violin, while the screen pulsates in pale lemon and saffron hardly discernible—and so forth.

Rimington is, it will be seen, not too straitly tied to the idea of vibrational analogies, and he states plainly his conviction that correspondences between music and colour are as much a question of psychology as of physics. Yet he did indulge in *translation*.

8. The Fallacy of 'Translation' from Sound into Sight. At this point may be interpolated a remark upon the entire and obvious futility of the attempts made and still from time to time being made to *translate* existing music into a new colour music. Not only (as explained under 5 above) do the imagined vibrational correspondences not exist, but music, as we know it, is based upon an apparatus of harmonies and counterpoints, of concords and discords of varying pungency, of shifting dynamics and timbres, which exercise their influence on our emotions as the result of a long evolution in human perceptions applied to the phenomena of sound. We have all been brought up on this complex art, and suddenly to produce a new art in which the equivalents (if such were possible) were presented visually to human eyes which had not acquired any corresponding perceptions would be to present that vision with a mere bewilderment.

Then there is no reason to suppose that the time-periods which are proper for the appreciation of harmonic effects must necessarily be proper for the appreciation of colour effect, the eye and ear differing in their powers (it was a complaint when the Rimington organ was first exhibited that 'when the keys are played at all rapidly the effect is blinding': *Musical Times*, 1895).

There is thus no proof, or even probability, that the emotional effects of a musical passage (depending, as they do, on an elaborate system, partly physical and partly conventional) would find their correspondence in a mechanical 'translation' into a colour passage.

And so forth—there are a hundred reasons against the assumptions underlying this idea of 'translation' from the terms of sound to the terms of light.

9. The Clavilux (p. 208, pl. **40.** 2, 3). This is the invention of a Danish-born singer and scientist working in the United States, Thomas Wilfrid. He first exhibited it in New York in 1922, soon afterwards visiting London and other European cities. He abandoned entirely the misleading analogy between the vibrational proportions of sound and colour, and with him the term 'Colour-Music' means an art of colour which resembles music in that it includes the factors of time, rhythm, and ever-shifting combination. His keyboard does not at all closely resemble that of a musical instrument. He introduced form, showing upon a screen fantastic figures which move rhythmically and incessantly change their shapes and colours. His instrument has, on the whole, had a favourable reception, partly, probably, because his compositions or extemporizations, being freed from the false control of attachment to another and differently functioning art, have tended to develop according to the principles governing the powers of the particular bodily organ to which they address themselves.

Mr. Wilfrid, then, looked on his use of colour as a sort of music *in itself*; indeed, to apply the word 'music' to what he produces is really to use a metaphor. He borrowed to some extent the terminology of music for his programmes, in which are found such items as 'Op. 42, Sketch', 'Op. 39, Triangular Étude', 'Op. 30, A Fairy Tale of the Orient'.

There is, of course, nothing to prevent the use of the clavilux in conjunction with music, but in such a use the moving colours would, so to speak, *run in an emotional parallel* with the course of the music, not attempt to 'translate' in any way its mere notes. An early attempt at such a parallel was the collaboration in 1926 of the Philadelphia Orchestra, under Stokowski, with Wilfrid and his clavilux, in a performance of Rimsky-Korsakof's *Sheherazade*. Such a treatment is, to say the least, quite as legitimate as that by which the music has been 'interpreted' in dance by the Russian Ballet—an entertainment that is subject to the criticism that it introduces a definitely detailed drama where the composer provides little more than a fluid series of emotions.

Mr. Wilfrid's machine is on permanent exhibition at the Museum of Modern Art, New York.

It would seem, surely, that in the power to present beauty and emotion free of literary and pictorial detail the art of music and the new art of colour find one of their closest resemblances, and that therein lies one of the most defensible justifications of the term 'Colour-Music'.

10. Other Attempts to Produce a 'Colour-Music'. It is not possible to list here all the attempts that have been made to introduce instruments for the production of a play of colour.

D. D. Jameson, as early as 1844, wrote on Colour-Music and exhibited an instrument to produce it.

Bainbridge Bishop, an American, in 1877 combined a colour-projection instrument with a chamber organ, so that he could play music and produce a blend of colours simultaneously.

Alexander Burnett Hector demonstrated the use of his Colour Organ in Australia in 1912. More than his English contemporary Rimington, he appears to have been dominated by the idea of a vibrational correspondence between pitches and colours ('The striking of a note must mean the striking of its own colour equivalent, and that colour or colour shade only').

Mrs. Mary Hallock Greenwalt, an American pianist, first publicly exhibited her Colour Organ in New York in 1919. She accompanied music with colour, but without basing anything whatever on the unfortunate pseudo-scientific analogies of some other workers, and states that, in her art, variation in luminosity is the indispensable factor ('The breaking up of light into its component rays or colors supplies only an added element of beauty').

George Lawrence Hall, of Boston, U.S.A., was, in the 1930s, working on lines that appeared to be similar, i.e. he based nothing on false analogies between sound and colour, but used his *Musichrome* (a type of Colour Organ) purely as a 'color accompanying device', attempting 'to create a color accompaniment which co-ordinates with the music and helps to enhance the mood and spirit of the composition'.

Alexander László is the inventor of a Colour Piano which projects colour on to a screen. This was first introduced at the German Music Art Festival at Kiel in 1925, when compositions composed for it by László himself were performed. He uses a special colour notation which he prints above the music lines in his piano scores. He published in the same year an extensive theoretical work, *Die Farblicht-musik* ('Colour-light music').

Vladimir Stcherbatchef (q.v.) wrote a 'Nonet' for piano, harp, string quartet, violin, dance, and light.

The French composer, **Carol-Bérard** (1881–1942; a pupil of Albéniz), introduced the term *Chromophonie* to designate a new art for which he longed, and inspired a painter-scientist, Valère Bernard, to the invention of an instrument for the purposes of this art. He projected colours on to a revolving, faceted globe. He was bound hand and foot by the false-analogy principle ('It is easy to state precisely the correspondence between the different nuances of a colour and the sound. It is only a question of arithmetic'). But he did not attempt to accompany music by a parallel performance of its every note on his instrument ('It is not a question, as one can easily understand, of a translation of each note of a polyphonic work, but only a translation of the essential part of the chain of chords, of the essence of the work'). Carol-Bérard explained his ideas in *La Revue musicale* in 1922.

Frederick Bentham from 1934 made considerable experiments with a 'Light Console', giving recitals in London (Palladium, etc.) and in Lisbon. His experience suggested to him that (*a*) too much emphasis must not be placed on the perception of colour, which should be merely accessory to the perception of form; (*b*) lighting must glide from one change to another, flashing and violent effects being generally avoided. He agreed that no analogy with the musical scale exists ('the link between what you see and what you hear must be emotional'). In 1951 Mr. Bentham supervised the installation of a colour organ in the Royal Festival Hall, London—primarily for ballet; this is believed to be the first such (permanent) installation (see opposite, pl. **40.** 6).

Walt Disney's film *Fantasia* and the Seine fountains at the 1937 Paris Exhibition offer examples of attempts to apply the combination of colour and music, as also the use of a Light Console playing colour duets with a Compton Electrophonic Organ upon an 80-foot tower at the 1939 Earl's Court Exhibition and the later demonstration of *Son et lumière* in Paris and elsewhere.

The English colour expert, Major **Adrian**

2. THOMAS WILFRID AND HIS CLAVILUX of 1925
See *Colour and Music* 9

1. RIMINGTON AND HIS COLOUR ORGAN,
1893. See *Colour and Music* 7

4

3. THOMAS WILFRID preparing a composition
From Klein's *Colour Music*

5

4, 5. KLEIN COLOUR PROJECTOR of 1921
See *Colour and Music* 10

6. COLOUR CONSOLE ('Strand Light Console', invented by
Frederick Bentham), ROYAL FESTIVAL HALL, London
See *Colour and Music* 10

PLATE 41

If Punchions, or Pipes, of Flattery, could either have fattened, or enriched a Man Sir John Falstaff had been a very Shrimp; and King Croesus a mere Beggar, in Comparison of

Wesley

1.

August 19 1828

2.

THREE COMPOSERS OF EASTERN EUROPE

See the Articles under the respective names

3. TANSMAN (Polish; b. 1897)

4. SZYMANOWSKI
(Polish; 1882–1937)

5. ENESCO (Rumanian; 1881–1955)

TWO COMPOSERS OF SOUTHERN AND CENTRAL AMERICA

See the Articles under the respective names

6. VILLA-LOBOS (Brazilian; 1887–1959)

7. CHAVEZ (Mexican; b. 1899)

Bernard Klein, son of Herman Klein the teacher and critic, made a close study of the subject (*Colour Music—The Art of Light*, 1926; revised 1937), bringing to it a combination of cool scientific spirit and artistic enthusiasm. He was in early life a painter, and his interest in the subject was aroused by study of the later works of Turner. He first came before the public in 1913 with an exhibition in London of 'Composition in Colour-Music, and Studies in Line and Shape' (his ideas then, apparently, somewhat resembling those of the Russian Expressionist painter, Kandinsky, whose *Art of Spiritual Harmony* greatly influenced both the painting and the music of Schönberg; p. 356, pl. 57. 1, 2). In 1921 Klein introduced an elaborate Colour Projector (p. 208, pl. 40. 4, 5) primarily designed for spectacular stage-lighting. In his speculations as to an art of colour-music he totally abandons the pseudo-scientific analogies based on the vibration-frequencies of sound and light. His projector has, nevertheless, as its operating mechanism a two-octave keyboard with white and black keys arranged exactly like those of a pianoforte. He says:

'A sequence of tones arranged in logarithmic order decreasing in intensity is extraordinarily beautiful to witness, and it has probably been impossible to obtain such measured relationships with any Light Projector previously constructed. Whether it be increasing increments of white light added to pure colour, or increasing or decreasing intensity of a given mixture, or alteration of hue step by step, all these changes may be effected in predetermined measure, order, and degree. The significant beauty of these orders will eventually constitute the main support of the claim of a language of light to be raised to the dignity of a fine art.'

In 1932 Major Klein exhibited in London a Colour Organ, accompanying with it compositions played upon a normal organ.

The above are only a few of the most prominent of the many workers in this field: it is interesting to notice that some of those who enter it (e.g. Castel) enter it in the first instance from the scientific side; others (e.g. Rimington, Klein) from the side of the painter's art; and still others (Greenwalt, Wilfrid) from the side of music.

11. Use of Colour Concomitants by Composers. The occasional practice of colour-suggestions in the title of compositions (Ireland, *Scarlet Ceremonies*, and the like) was carried a stage further by Bliss in his 'Colour' Symphony (1922), in which he labelled the movements 'I, Purple', 'II, Red', 'III, Blue', and 'IV, Green'. There is a sub-title to each movement in which the suggestion is rather that of the symbolism of colour than of colour itself, e.g. green is described as 'The colour of Emeralds, Hope, Joy, Youth, Spring, and Victory'. But the composer states that when composing he always experiences a play of colour sensation, and that such a play was especially vivid in his mind when working on this symphony.

A more advanced stage is reached in Scriabin's *Prometheus* (or 'Poem of Fire'), and Schönberg's *Die glückliche Hand*, both of which have a line throughout the score in which are notated the details of an actual play of colours to be projected on to a screen during the performances of the musical work. (Schönberg, it will be recalled, was himself a painter.)

The *Tastiera per luce* ('Light-keyboard') prescribed by Scriabin for his work was one of twelve notes, colour-tuned (if one may coin the word) to a colour-scale of his own, said to have been based on the musical cycle of fifths—though in what way is not clear, and the score does not, unfortunately and strangely, give the colour equivalents of the twelve notes of the keyboard. The play of light is indicated by ordinary musical notation on the top stave of the score. It is not elaborate, never using more than two colours in combination, and often using only one. The colour changes are very slow as compared with the speed of the music, the same colour often accompanying many bars together. The changes do not appear to be made arbitrarily or as a mere interpretation or enhancement of the emotional changes of the music, since the part of the *Tastiera per luce* often coincides with some note or notes in the musical score, and occasionally faithfully follows the bass. The colour association in the composer's mind is, then, one based on pitch, and the 'Luce' line of the score resembles in general suggestion that of a line for two horns in which a composer has tried to use those instruments as a binding harmonic element against the quicker motion of the other parts.

The work was performed in Moscow in 1911 without attempting to introduce a colour apparatus. In 1915 it was given in New York with an apparatus that apparently 'worked', but the general impression seems to have been that the music gained nothing from the use of the colour effects. The score contains an indication by the composer that it may be performed without the colour effects, and this is how it has usually been performed.

The composer planned a great *Mystery*, in which not only a play of colours but also gestures and a play of perfume would be included; but death intervened. (For an instance of an actual concert of music, colours, and odours see *Odour and Music*.)

12. The Approach through Occultism. As to interest in the subject, and study of it, there exists still another gate of entry, mentioned here for the sake of completeness—the occult. This sometimes combines with the musical approach, as in the case of Scriabin (see 11) and Cyril Scott. The following from Scott's *Philosophy of Modernism* (1917) is quoted with all reserve—some of the terms used conveying no meaning whatever to the present writer.

'Every musical composition produces a thought-and-colour-form in the astral space, and according to that form and colour is to be gauged the spiritual value of the composition under review. If the preponderating colours be lilac, violet, blue, pink, yellow, and apple-green, combined with a form of lofty structure and vastness, then the work is one of intrinsic spiritual value; if, however, the preponderating colours be muddy browns, greys, cloudy-reds, etc., then the work may be recognized at once to be one of a lower order. This method of gauging the spiritual value of art, however, is only possible to him who has awakened the latent faculties of the pineal gland and pituitary body.'

(Scott explains that the 'trained psychic' can awaken 'the latent faculties of the two glands in the brain, known as the pineal gland and the pituitary body, the two physical organs of psychic perception'.)

13. Educational Use of Colour with

Music. As hinted in section 5 above, attempts have sometimes been made to employ colour associations to assist vocal sight-reading, etc., and occasionally the pseudo-analogy between the musical octave and the spectrum is used to justify such methods. From what has been said above it will be clear that there is no justification in physical science for a linking of colour effects and the degrees of the scale, so that the only practical justification is that of expediency from a purely instructional point of view. On this side there seems to be little to be said for the practice, which, apparently, is merely an illus-tration of the way in which ingenious and kindly teachers often complicate comparatively simple subjects by inserting unnecessary steps.

COLOUR ORGAN. See *Colour and Music* 7, 8, 9.

COLPO (It.). 'Stroke', e.g. *Colpo d'arco*, a stroke of the bow.

COLUMBIA BROADCASTING SYSTEM. See *Broadcasting of Music* 3.

COLUMBIA GRAPHOPHONE CO. See *Gramophone* 6.

COLUMBIA, THE GEM OF THE OCEAN. See *Britannia, the Pride of the Ocean.*

COMBINATION PEDALS. See *Organ* 2 f.

COMBINATION TONE. See *Acoustics* 10.

COMBINED COUNTERPOINT. See *Counter-point.*

COMB INSTRUMENTS. See *Mechanical Re-production of Music* 7.

COME (It.). 'As', 'like', 'as if'; *come prima*, 'as at first'; *come stà*, 'as it stands'; *come sopra*, 'as above'.

COME BACK TO ERIN. Words and music are by 'Claribel' (Mrs. Barnard; 1830–69). The song is, hence, of purely English provenance.

COMES, JUAN BAUTISTA (1568–1643). See *Spain* 5.

COMES. See *Form* 12 b; *Canon.*

COMIC OPERA. The term explains itself, and the history, so far as Italy and France are concerned, can be gathered from the articles *Intermezzo*; *Opera buffa*; *Bouffons, Guerre des*; and *Vaudeville*; whilst the article *Opéra co-mique* guards against a common misconception.

Usually a comic opera has spoken dialogue, like the Gilbert and Sullivan and most of the English and French examples. But it may be entirely set to music, like Verdi's *Falstaff* and most of the Italian examples. (This general national difference is traditional; it dates from the seventeenth century.)

Rossini's *Barber of Seville* (1816), Nicolai's *Merry Wives of Windsor* (1848), the hundred or more works of Offenbach (1819–80), the works of Herold, Auber, Lecocq, Suppé, Johann Strauss, and innumerable later light composers come under the head of comic opera.

Very often the term *Operetta* is used, though strictly that should mean merely a short opera. Mozart's *Così fan tutte* ('That's what

women are!'), *The Marriage of Figaro*, *The Magic Flute* (for the most part), and even *Don Giovanni*, are comic operas (the last becomes intolerable when the conductor and performers do not realize this).

COMIN' THRO' THE RYE. It is not cer-tain whether this is a genuine Scottish song or merely one of the London imitations (see reference to these under *Scotland* 1). A song opening with similar lines, which may have been adapted from a Scottish original, appears in a pantomime, *Harlequin Mariner* (1795). The tune gives the impression of being an adapta-tion from a genuine Scottish strathspey. The poem of Burns is only in part the same as that sung, and is probably an adaptation of an older Scottish original.

There is a considerable resemblance between the tunes of 'Comin' thro the Rye' and 'Auld Lang Syne' (q.v.).

COMIQUE (Fr.) 'Comic.' But see *Opéra comique.*

COMMA. Any very minute interval resulting in some such way as that described under, *Tempera-ment* 3.

COMME (Fr.). 'As', 'as if', 'like', etc.

COMMEDIA DELL' ARTE. See *Pantomime.*

COMMÈRE (Fr.). See under *Compère.*

COMMIATO. See *Giovinezza.*

COMMITTEE FOR ADVANCEMENT OF MUSICK. See *Minstrels, etc.* 3.

COMMODO. See *Comodo.*

COMMON, as applied to a portion of the liturgy, means that it is a part of the regular and invariable service of the kind in question, and not special to a particular day of the Church's year, which latter is distinguished by the word 'Proper'. Thus the 'Common' of the dedica-tion of a church as opposed to the 'Proper' of St. ——'s Day.

Cf. *Mass* 2.

COMMON CHORD. See *Harmony* 24 d.

COMMON FLUTE. See *Recorder Family* 2.

COMMON METRE. See *Hymns and Hymn Tunes* 13.

COMMON PRAYER, BOOK OF. This is the complete service book of the Anglican Church, containing everything authorized for use in the services except the Lessons and the Anthems and Hymns (both alluded to later in this article). It fulfils the same purposes, then, as the Missal, Breviary, Manual, and Pontifical of the Roman Catholic Church (see *Liturgy*).

The Anglican liturgy is, in the main, a translation and recasting of the Roman; from the time of St. Augustine (see *Plainsong* 4) the Roman Rite had gradually superseded the British Rite, which is usually supposed to have been a form of the Gallican; in Norman times the Roman Rite as used in Britain had certain Gallican features grafted on to it, and considerable differences of detail were to be found in the 'Uses' of Sarum, York, Hereford, Bangor, etc. (see *Use of Sarum, etc.*). One of the declared objects of the compilers of the Prayer Book, as stated in the Preface which still appears in every copy printed, was to secure uniformity by the abolition of conflicting 'Uses'. The dates of the various English Prayer Books which have followed one another are: First Prayer Book of Edward VI, 1549; Second Prayer Book of Edward VI, 1552 (never actually introduced into use); Prayer Book of Elizabeth, 1559. These differed only in detail. Various small revisions have taken place since (especially one in 1662), but essentially it is Queen Elizabeth's book that is now in use. A revision was put forward by the Church Assembly in 1927 and was accepted by the House of Lords, but was rejected by the House of Commons (see *Psalm*). The Episcopal Church of Scotland, the Church of Ireland, the American Episcopal Church, etc., have their own Prayer Books, closely based, however, upon that in use in England. The first separate Prayer Book of the American Church dates from 1789.

From the musician's point of view, the main difference between the Roman Breviary and Missal and the order of Morning and Evening Prayer and Communion as set forth in the English Prayer Book lies in the greater simplicity of the latter in both the part for the minister and that for the people.

The choir has, properly, no standing, save that in both Morning and Evening Prayer there is a place where occurs the indication 'In Quires and Places where they sing, here followeth the Anthem'.

In practice, however, certain portions, or even the whole of the people's part, is in larger churches and cathedrals reserved for the choir as the people's representative: one or two metrical hymns constitute in these places the only opportunity of the people's vocally joining in the service (see *Anglican Parish Church Music* 7). These last were allowed by the 'Injunctions' of 1539 but are not mentioned in the Prayer Book except as concerns the services for Ordination and Confirmation, for each of which a hymn is provided.

The Anglican Use makes provision for the reading or singing of the whole of the Psalms in rotation, the complete book being gone through in a month of daily morning and evening services (see *Psalm*); during the twentieth century, however, the observance of this rule has tended to weaken. In the Morning Prayer the 95th Psalm (*Venite*) is normally sung before the Psalms for the day.

The Canticles (cf., however, the article *Canticle* for a more restricted definition of the word) are as follows: At Morning Prayer, the *Te Deum* (or at certain seasons the *Benedicite*) and the *Benedictus* (or, on one or two occasions, the *Jubilate*); at Evening Prayer, the *Magnificat* (or, rarely, the 97th Psalm, *Cantate Domino*) and the *Nunc Dimittis* (or, rarely again, the 67th Psalm, *Deus Misereatur*).

It may be noted that there are many traces of the fact that the English Morning Prayer has, as base, a combination of elements from the Latin Matins (q.v.), Lauds (q.v.), and Prime (q.v.), and that the Evening Prayer similarly bears evidence of compilation from the offices for Vespers (q.v.) and Compline (q.v.). In the morning the Canticles come as follows: the *Te Deum* from Matins and the *Benedictus* from Lauds; in the evening they come as follows: the *Magnificat* from Vespers and the *Nunc Dimittis* from Compline. And so on.

In the order for Holy Communion (which is translated, with alterations, from the Sarum Use) occur four of the five great passages from the Ordinary of the Mass which are commonly set chorally (see *Mass* 2): *Kyrie, Gloria in excelsis, Credo,* and *Sanctus,* the last, however, without its *Benedictus qui venit* section. The *Agnus Dei* does not occur in the Prayer Book (except in the Litany), but a custom has grown up of setting both this and the *Benedictus* in composed 'services' (they were declared lawful by the Lincoln judgement of 1892); thus translated adaptations of Roman Mass settings have become available.

In speaking of 'A Communion Service' a musician today usually means a complete setting of the above passages, but earlier composers frequently set only some of them. In speaking of a 'Morning Service' or 'Evening Service' he means a setting of the Canticles just spoken of as prescribed for Morning and Evening Prayer.

The remainder of the Order for the three services consists of prayers spoken or chanted by the minister; Preces and Versicles (see *Versicles*) spoken, monotoned, or sung by him to a simple note-for-syllable adaptation of the ancient plainchant, with Responses by the People or Choir, similarly treated (see *Responses*), and Lessons read. When the portions of the Communion Service above mentioned are not chorally set, they are either spoken or monotoned like the rest of the prayers, etc. It has become a common practice to accompany the monotoned Creed by varied harmonies on the organ, enabling the choir and people to maintain the pitch. The Psalms (including the *Venite*) are either spoken or sung to Anglican chants (q.v.) or the Gregorian Tones (q.v.), and when the Canticles are not 'set' they are treated in the same way.

The Litany (q.v.) 'to be sung or said after Morning Prayer upon Sundays, Wednesdays, and Fridays' is, if sung, generally set to plainsong, either in unison or with descant.

The first adaptation of the traditional plainsong to the new English words (including the Psalms) was made by Merbecke (q.v.), in the year following the appearance of the First Prayer Book (i.e. 1550), in his *The Booke of Common Praier Noted* (p. 816, pl. **139**. 5, 6). A good deal of what he did is perhaps rather to be described as in the style of plainsong than as the older plainsong adapted. He strove, following the wishes of Archbishop Cranmer and others of the ecclesiastical reformers, to achieve a one-note-to-a-syllable setting, and to respect the natural accentuation of the English language. Various rearrangements of Merbecke's settings soon appeared, with two objects: firstly, adaptation to the later Prayer Book, and secondly, the provision of harmonies. Tallis's arrangements (in four and five parts—two settings the relation of which has been much discussed) were those generally adopted: so far as Merbecke's melodies were applicable they were placed in the tenor.

The English Prayer Book is occasionally made the basis of worship amongst individual congregations of some of the English Nonconformist churches. John Wesley, himself a clergyman of the Church of England, adapted it for use in the Methodist communities, and some Methodist churches still base their Sunday morning services upon his adaptation. John Knox drafted a Prayer Book for the Presbyterian Church, and it was in use from 1560 to 1645. In 1637 Archbishop Laud attempted to force on Scotland a book based on the English Book of Common Prayer, but Jenny Geddes flung her stool at the head of the Bishop in St. Giles's Cathedral, Edinburgh, and set agoing an opposition that abolished the innovation. The Directory drawn up at the Westminster Assembly of 1643 superseded it; the Act of Parliament recognizing this was annulled after the Commonwealth, but it still largely guides Scottish Presbyterian practice.

COMMON TIME. Another name for $\frac{4}{4}$ time. See Table 10. (The 'C' sometimes used instead of $\frac{4}{4}$ does not stand for 'Common'; it dates from a period when Triple Time, considered, from some fanciful analogy with the Trinity, to be 'perfect time', was indicated by a full circle and Duple or Quadruple Time, considered to be 'imperfect time', was indicated by a broken circle.)

COMMONWEALTH. See *Profession of Music* 9; *Puritans.*

COMMUNAL COMPOSITION. See *Folk Song 2.*

COMMUNION (in the Mass). See *Mass* 2.

COMMUNION (as a title to an organ composition). This is sometimes seen attached to a soft, slow piece for church use—having no precise implication beyond the emotional suggestion.

COMMUNION SERVICE (Anglican). See *Common Prayer.*

COMMUNITY SINGING
(or COMMUNITY MUSIC)

1. Definition. A rough definition of 'Community Singing' would be 'the audience as its own vocal performer'. This, looked on by many as a recent activity, is in reality a very ancient one; its origin probably lies somewhere hidden in the mists of prehistory.

2. The Sixteenth Century in England. Obviously any sort of hymn sung by a congregation is an example of community singing, and as an early instance of English community singing on a large scale may be mentioned the singing of metrical psalms outside St. Paul's Cathedral, London, in the first flush of enthusiasm after the Reformation. Stow (1559) says, 'You may now see at Paul's Cross, after the service, six thousand people, young and old, of both sexes, singing together.' Bishop Jewel says the same thing the following year (p. 492, pl. **87**. 1)[1]

3. The Eighteenth Century in France. Addison in the *Spectator* (1711) tells us that community singing was common in the French opera of his day:

'The Musick of the French is indeed very properly adapted to their pronunciation and accent, as their whole opera wonderfully favours the genius of such a gay, airy people. The chorus in which that opera abounds, gives the parterre frequent opportunities of joining in consort with the stage. This inclination of the audience to sing along with the actors so prevails with them, that I have sometimes known a performer on the stage do no more in a celebrated song than the clerk of a parish church, who serves only to raise the Psalm, and is afterwards drown'd in the musick of the congregation.'

The great authority on early stage matters, W. J. Lawrence, commenting on the above (*Musical Quarterly*, January 1915), says:

'Not long after Addison embalmed his impressions curious advantage was taken in Paris of the

---

[1] In 1935 an effort was made to organize New Year's Eve singing from the steps of the cathedral, so replacing the sporadic efforts of the crowd that always assembles to 'see the New Year in' by something more orderly and effective. This was clearly a revival rather than an innovation. It was abandoned the following year, on police representations, as having attracted so great a crowd as to create serious traffic difficulties.

French predilection for chorussing. With the view of suppressing the comedians who played in booths at the great annual fairs of Saint Germain and Saint Laurent, the Royal Academy of Music, otherwise the controllers of the Opera, exercised their prerogative and forbade the comedians from favouring their patrons with any singing. Highly ingenious was the method whereby the harried players evaded the issue. When a juncture came in the performance when one of the characters should have sung a song, a large scroll descended from the sky-borders on which was inscribed in bold letters the words of the ditty. Then the orchestra proceeded to play the air and the audience, having caught its rhythms, sang the song. Meanwhile the silenced actor went on with the dumb show of his part. All the world and his wife were attracted by this novelty. So far from injuring the mummers, the Royal Academy of Music had done them service.'

It has, however, been claimed that the practice above alluded to was Italian in its origin.

4. The Eighteenth Century in Britain. A somewhat similar practice shortly sprang up in England and Ireland. Thus Colley Cibber's ballad-opera, *Love in a riddle* (Drury Lane, London, 1729), included an invitation to the audience issued by the mouth of the chief comedian:

> Since songs to plays are nowadays,
>   Like to your meals a salad;
> Permit us then, kind gentlemen,
>   To try our skill by ballad:
> While you, to grace our native lays,
>   As France has done before us,
> Belle, beau and cit from box and pit,
>   All join the jolly chorus.

Chorus:

> Then, freeborn boys, all make a noise,
>   As France has done before us;
> With English hearts all bear your parts,
>   And join the jolly chorus.

This, of course, suggests a practice that has been not uncommon in the British 'Free and Easy' (public-house concert) and music-hall (q.v.). In Dublin it is said to have been very popular, especially at Freemasons' gatherings. In 1728 at Drury Lane, London, a performance of Shakespeare's *Henry IV, Part 2*, was bespoken by the Freemasons, who had a scene in it altered to allow of the introduction of *The Freemasons' Apprentice Song* sung by all 'the Freemasons in the pit and boxes'.

5. Modern Community Singing. The modern expression 'Community Singing' apparently originated in the United States, where the practice was definitely organized in camps during the first World War, official 'Song Leaders' being appointed. A similar practice already obtained in the British army. In 1925 a London newspaper (Lord Beaverbrook's *Daily Express*) took up the movement as a journalistic 'stunt' and organized meetings for community singing in the Royal Albert Hall (holding 10,000) and elsewhere.

But in Britain at any rate, community singing remained sporadic rather than regular and organized.

Wherever a regiment on the march, or a crowd at a football or baseball game, or the audience at a Welsh Eisteddfod (see *Wales* 7) bursts into song, or a street crowd, on the news of a national success, strikes up the National Anthem (i.e. whenever the audience is its own performer), there is 'community singing'. In certain manufacturing districts of the north of England ordinary audiences can pretty effectively join a choir in the singing of the four voice-parts of Handel's 'Hallelujah Chorus', and that is, perhaps, community singing at the point of greatest cultivation attainable.

The social effect of community song is marked; it diffuses a spirit of friendliness, the common effort tending to sink temperamental differences and class distinctions. At any time when unity of spirit is particularly essential (especially in the United States, where so many racial origins have to be welded into one national consciousness) community singing is found to be of enormous public value.

In 1935 Mascagni was commissioned to compile a national song book for the Italian army.

COMMUNN GÀIDHEALACH. See *Scotland*.

COMODO (It.). 'Convenient', i.e. without any suspicion of strain, e.g. *Tempo comodo*, at a comfortable, moderate speed. So the adverb, *Comodamente*.

COMPAGNIA DEL GONFALONE. See *Passion Music* 1.

COMPASS. The range of pitch obtainable from an instrument or voice. See *Voice* 17; *Keyboard* 5; *Pianoforte* 13, 21; and the various bowed and wind instruments.

COMPÈRE (Fr.). Literally 'godfather'; applied to the announcer in a light entertainment. The feminine, *Commère*, is also occasionally seen.

COMPÈRE, LOYSET. Died at St. Quentin in 1518. He was a pupil of Ockeghem and became canon and chancellor of the Cathedral of St. Quentin and a church music composer of importance. One of his motets, familiarly known as the 'Singers' Prayer', asks for protection for a long list of Netherland musicians, beginning with Dufay and ending 'last of all for me, Loyset Compère'.

COMPETITIONS IN MUSIC

1. Introductory. The competition movement in music may be described in a general way as an effort to harness man's love of sport to the interest of his cultivation of art. It took a large expansion in Britain and the British Empire generally in the closing years of the nineteenth century and the opening years of the twentieth century, and since about the time of the close of the first World War has experienced a very considerable growth in the United States.

It may be pointed out that the introduction of the competition element into music is no new thing. There are the respectable precedents of the musical battle between Phoebus and Pan; the Pythian Games of the sixth century B.C. (for these were especially musical contests); the thirteenth-century Song Contest of the Minnesingers at the Wartburg, kept in popular memory today by Wagner's opera *Tannhäuser*; the Eisteddfod (see *Wales* 7), or meeting of the Bards, alleged to date back to the seventh century; and so on. The 'Puys' of the Middle Ages held literary and musical competitions, the winner being crowned 'king' (see *Minstrels* 6); Orlandus Lassus was king of the Puy of Évreux in 1575 and 1583.

There is a record of Merulo and A. Gabrieli engaging in a 'duel of two organs' in St. Mark's, Venice, at the end of the sixteenth century. In 1708 Handel and Domenico Scarlatti competed together in Rome under the auspices of the famous Cardinal Ottoboni; in 1717 Bach and Marchand were to do so at Dresden, under the auspices of the King of Poland (accounts differ as to whether some part of this competition had been held before Marchand fled); in 1781 Mozart and Clementi did so in Vienna under the auspices of the Emperor Joseph II; about twenty years later there were many competitive meetings between Beethoven and Wölfl at the castle of Baron Raymond von Wetzler. All these meetings had a good result; in the 1708 Rome Competition Festival two great players were drawn into warm and lasting mutual admiration and friendship; in the 1717 Dresden event a pretentious performer was exposed to a humiliation that must have done him some moral good; in the Vienna event of 1781 one of the performers (Clementi) learnt, as he afterwards admitted, a life's lesson as to the greater worth of solid musical structure as compared with showy brilliance. These instances, then (and others could be offered), all form good precedents for what is attempted today.

Singing and band competitions have been popular on the continent of Europe since the beginning of the railway era made travel easy. In 1851 Schumann was one of the adjudicators at a competition held in Brussels by the Belgian Men's Singing Society: many competitions have since been held, including a curious international one at Ostend in the early 1920s, at which the effort to achieve complete fairness in adjudication curiously threw the responsibility on the shoulders of chance—'75,000 francs in Prizes, besides many Cups, are drawn by Lottery amongst all Bands and Choral Societies competing'.

Germany has had some developments of the choral competition. Lowell Mason, in his *Musical Letters from Abroad*, gives an interesting account of a competition he attended at Düsseldorf in 1852, for Men's Choirs. As at Brussels, Schumann was one of the adjudicators. Before the first World War there was held every four or five years an Imperial Choral Contest, the highest award being the Kaiser's gold chain. In 1903 the Kaiser and Kaiserin sat out four days of singing at this contest.

2. Competitions in Britain and the Commonwealth. The date at which musical competitions began in Britain is difficult to ascertain. Probably the Welsh Eisteddfodau were the first. (See *Wales* 7.)

In the eighteenth century we see the English love of choral song and of sport exploited by rural publicans in the organization of competitions.

'*To all lovers of Music.* At Mr. William Kirkham's, at the sign of the Horse and the Jockey on Warley Common near Brentwood, Essex, on Thursday, Whitsun Week, 1773, will be given gratis a Punch Bowl, etc., to be sung for by any company of Singers in this County. Each Company to sing 3 songs in 2 parts, and 3 catches in 3 parts, the catches to be sung out of Mr. Arnold's Catch Club Harmony.

Singing to begin at 2, and to be decided by 3 proper judges of music, after which there will be a Concert of Vocal and Instrumental Music.'

'*Singing on Monday, November 10th., at Coward Fricker's, the Bell Inn, Corsham,* by three or more companies of Singers; each Company to sing two three-voice Songs, two two-voice songs, and two catches; the best singers to have two guineas, the second-best to have one guinea, and the third half-a-guinea. Proper umpires to be chosen by the companies. The music to be delivered to the umpires before singing. To dine precisely at one o'clock. Ordinary 1s. 6d. No company to sing unless they dine.' (*The Bath Chronicle*, 30 Oct. 1783.)

The first English competitions on modern lines were probably those held in one or two places where there were colonies of Welsh people who organized replicas of their own Eisteddfodau, carrying them out in their own language and purely as a national expression, the English community not being concerned in them. The next were Wind Band Competitions (see 3), of which it is said the earliest was one at Burton Constable, Yorkshire, in 1845.

A few early vocal competitions have come to the notice of the present author:

1855, **Manchester**: Belle Vue Gardens. 'Prize Glee-singing.' 1864, **Bradford**: Temperance Hall. 'Prize Singing' (solo vocalists and glee parties). 1872, and following years, **Crystal Palace**: Choral Competitions, organized by Thomas Willert Beale, with £1,000 as the chief prize (solo vocal and other classes also). 1874, **Manchester**: Royal Pomona Palace. Madrigal singing and choral sight-singing competitions, etc. 1874, **Liverpool**: St. George's Hall. Competitions for solo vocalists and choirs. 1881, **Sheffield**: Competitions for solo vocalists, vocal quartets, choirs, etc. (with also some instrumental classes). 1881, **Brighton**: Competition of French 'Orphéons' (i.e. male-voice choral societies). 1882, **London**: Royal Victoria Hall ('Old

Vic.'). Competition for choral societies of the London district.

In addition there were in the 1870s a number of what were called 'Bees'. These were nothing but small local competitions for instrumental, solo vocal, and choral performers. (Cf. the 'Spelling Bees' of that period.)

The part that the Curwens (see *Curwen*) took in the movement was, of course, important. It can be summarized as follows:

In 1860–1–2 John Curwen, the founder of the tonic sol-fa movement, organized competitions for choirs at the Crystal Palace and Exeter Hall, London. In 1882 his son, John Spencer Curwen, who had recently served as an adjudicator at the Welsh National Eisteddfod, was inspired by his experiences there to found at Stratford, London, a competition on the modern lines, with classes for solo and combined vocal performance and instrumental performance. He not very correctly described it, in a preliminary circular, as an attempt to naturalize in England the musical department of the Welsh Eisteddfod. In the same year village choirs were called together at Oswestry to compete and to sing together in a festival concert, Mr. Curwen being one of the adjudicators; this, however, was a purely choral enterprise.

Three years later, in 1885, Miss A. N. Wakefield, a notable singer of professional status though a woman of some means, introduced competitions for vocal quartets at a village flower show in Kendal, Westmorland. From this beginning she developed. Her example was very widely taken up in villages and small towns. In 1905 the Association of Competition Festivals was formed, largely on the initiative of Miss Wakefield and those associated with her, and in 1921 this was succeeded by the present British Federation of Musical Festivals, in which are associated some 275 festivals in all parts of the Commonwealth—except Wales, the mother of the movement, who has always gone her own way, with ideas and ideals somewhat different from those most generally accepted by her children. In addition to these competitions which have joined the Federation there are a few others still unattached.

Pains have been taken to set out these chronological details with exactitude here, as they are often mis-stated and hence tend, unnecessarily, to become matters of dispute.

The Irish national musical competition, the Feis Čeoil, was founded in 1897: it has usually been held at Dublin.

One quite definite result of the competition festival movement in Britain was a raising of the standard of choral technique. In the early years of the twentieth century, Elgar, Bantock, and others were writing choral music that could not have been performed twenty years previously. At the same period a large amount of competition music was written *ad hoc* by secondary composers; it bristled with difficul-

ties, served its immediate purpose, and was then forgotten.

During the twentieth century the competition movement took a large extension in parts of the Commonwealth outside Great Britain. In Canada it was thoroughly organized, and musicians from the British Isles adjudicated at the principal festivals each year. There are very large and important competitions in various parts of Australia. New Zealand has developed the system. South Africa has a very active organization. Jamaica has competitions. Most of these countries have joined the British Federation of Musical Festivals already mentioned, an institution which has done extremely useful work by means of its annual conference, its annual handbook, and its permanent London office, which forms a centre of standardization and encouragement.

3. Wind Band Contests. Contests of wind bands (which stand rather apart from all other musical competitions) are very popular in Britain. The industrial and colliery districts of the north of England have long made a special cultivation of brass and 'military' band music, and in 1853 were begun the famous contests of the Belle Vue Gardens, Manchester. Forty-five years later (1898) J. Henry Iles attended one of these contests and was so much impressed that he brought some of the prize bands to London to give a concert at the Albert Hall. Sir Arthur Sullivan, who took part as conductor on this occasion, suggested an annual competition festival, and Iles organized this at the Crystal Palace in 1900, when about twenty bands took part—a number that by 1930 had grown to nearly 200. Special contest compositions have been written by many of the leading British musicians (Elgar, Bantock, Holst, Ireland, Howells, Bliss, etc.). The promoter of this movement towards a worthier repertory was Herbert Whiteley, who published the works mentioned in a band journal of which he was editor.

A peculiarity of wind band contests is the rigid control of the adjudicators—a control entirely foreign to the spirit in which other British musical competitions (see 6) are conducted:

'The system of adjudication adopted at all these contests is, first to elect a supervision committee by ballot, secondly for this committee to install the Judges in a tent or room and to see that a policeman is on duty at the entrance, who is instructed by them that no person must be permitted to communicate with the Judges, thirdly that representatives from each band draw for the order in which their band is to play, fourthly, as each band plays they are known to the Judges only by their number in order of playing. Notes are taken of their merits and demerits, the Judges' awards being arrived at by the total number of marks resulting from each performance. Fifthly, after the last band has played the supervision committee releases the Judges, who then announce their awards or hand them in writing to the Officer in charge to announce. The Judges' notes are subsequently available for the contestants, having an educational value to them.'

Another feature entirely absent from every other part of the musical competition field is indicated by the following extract from the *British Bandsman* of 25 September 1920:

'It is said that in the Colliery districts there is considerable betting on the Crystal Palace result, and that a good deal of money will change hands this week-end—especially in South Wales and Durham.'

The technique displayed at these contests is amazing, and there is no doubt that they have had a highly stimulating effect upon the arts of performance, conducting, and composition, so far as these concern wind bands.

4. Competitions in the United States. In America the first musical competition may have been that of Dorchester, Mass., in 1790. The Stoughton Musical Society had been founded in 1786 (it was the first singing society ever founded in America); the church music at Stoughton had been much praised, and the singers of the Dorchester First Parish challenged the Stoughton singers to a contest. It took place in a hall in Dorchester and attracted an audience from Boston and other places in the vicinity.

'The Dorchester choristers were male and female, and had the assistance of a bass viol. The Stoughton party consisted of twenty selected male voices, without instruments, led by the president of Stoughton Musical Society, Elijah Dunbar, a man of dignified presence and of excellent voice. The Dorchester singers began with a new anthem. The Stoughtonians commenced with Jacob French's *Heavenly Vision*, the author of which was their fellow townsman. When they finally sang, without books, Handel's *Hallelujah Chorus*, the Dorchestrians gave up the contest and gracefully acknowledged defeat.' (Elson's *History of American Music*, 1915.)

The musical competition movement in the United States is to a great extent a high-school activity, carried out in larger or smaller areas, from the single city to the state. It greatly expanded during the 1920s. In 1924 school band contests were held in five states, thirty bands entering; in 1931 all but five states held such contests, and 1,100 bands entered, whilst in the same year about 700 orchestras competed. A national school band contest was first held in 1926, and a national orchestral contest in 1929. When the long distances to be travelled by many bands and orchestras in order to attend a state contest are remembered, and the immensely longer distances to attend a national contest, this development must be regarded as a sign of tremendous activity and enthusiasm, and to any thoughtful European musician the question presents itself whether some day a similar extension may not take place in Europe —one of an international character.

In 1914 an inter-collegiate singing contest was organized in which four Eastern colleges took part: before long such contests were held all over the country, and the 'glee club' remained an important feature of university life.

5. Objections to Competitions. The thought underlying the word 'competition'

being found objectionable by some musicians, efforts to modify the associations of the word have often been made. A more definite festival element is often brought into British competition meetings in the way of massed singing, etc. Sometimes there is a choral work, such as a Bach cantata, prepared by all choirs for this purpose (it has often been found that a number of poor choirs combined under efficient conductorship becomes a comparatively good one), but in any case the word 'festival' is in the British Commonwealth usually preferred to that of 'competition' (without suffix) or 'contest', and in one way or another some attempt is made to suggest the spirit of communal pleasure.

In this preference for an avoidance of over-stress of the idea of rivalry there is perhaps seen a more or less subconscious recognition of one of the objections to the movement sometimes made. Those who oppose the objection point out that a great amount of sport is carried on in the greatest amity, the match or game taking its proper place as offering a stimulus and a standard. A chance expression thrown out by a prominent British adjudicator, Sir Walford Davies, has been widely adopted as a motto by competition festival committees and is often seen printed on programmes: '*Our object is not to gain a prize or to defeat a rival, but to pace one another on the road to excellence.*' (Prizes, it may be remarked, are rapidly disappearing from British competition festivals.) A frequent saying of another great adjudicator of a somewhat earlier period, Dr. W. G. McNaught (1849–1918), may be recalled: '*We're out to win—a Lesson.*' The following motto is sometimes seen: '*Do thy best and rejoice with them that do better*'—sometimes varied as '*Do thy best and rejoice when thy neighbour shows thee how to do better.*'

There is a certain small body of opinion in Britain which regards all solo classes as objectionable. These have even been called 'Personal Pride Classes'. The element of personal pride, though it cannot (and perhaps should not) be utterly abolished from any successful human undertaking, can, by tact on the part of adjudicators and others, be reduced to proper proportions.

6. Practical Questions that arise. It may fairly be said that the best minds in the movement regard it not merely as a means of raising the national musical standard but also as a means of teaching sportsmanship. With this object, general practice has, as a result of experience, been greatly reformed in various ways. The old custom of allowing the adjudicator to know the candidates only by number has practically disappeared, the names now being freely put before him and openly mentioned by him in his adjudications. The adjudication is, in Britain, invariably entirely public. Competitors are expected not to be thin-skinned, and in general they live up to the expectation. It is recognized that the presence of candidates throughout the performance of their fellow candidates, and the free and open statement by the adjudicators of both virtues and faults constitute a unique lesson to young musicians; such free and open statement also tends most valuably to train the audience in discrimination.

The practice of keeping joint adjudicators apart, taking their markings separately, and combining the figures to arrive at the result is probably quite unknown in Britain (except in wind band competitions; see 3) and may be expected soon to die out elsewhere. If this were proposed to British adjudicators they would take it as an insult and would probably refuse to act; moreover, they would point out that the award of two or more adjudicators who have discussed performers individually as each finished his performance, or collectively at the end of the class, is something more than the sum of average of a series of figures; mind plays upon mind, and two or more adjudicators in conference invariably feel that each has gained by hearing the other's views, so that, we may say $1 + 1 = 3$. A serious difference of opinion *after conference* is, in practice, almost unknown amongst adjudicators.

The question of the audience's applause is variously treated. An audience which graduates its applause according to its views of excellence or the degree of local popularity of one or another candidate is working against the best spirit of the festival. A friendly word from the adjudicator will generally adjust this; he may feel inclined to suggest that applause is a cheering thing and that, given to each candidate equally *on appearance*, it may be taken as a recognition of pluck in entering the competition and an expression of good wishes.

Some faults of the less experienced adjudicators are a caustic or sarcastic manner (sometimes necessarily reflecting upon the teacher behind the candidate—which reflection, however, is in any case often difficult to avoid); a timidity as to the use of plain speech concerning defects, or an incapacity to combine with this (as can almost always be done) the recognition of virtues; a tendency too readily to accept the standard (of vocal tone for instance) they find to be current in the district, and so to cast away their opportunity of raising the standard; a rambling method of speech that wastes valuable time and fails to hold the attention of the audience; a lack of humour; a cheap jocosity; an inability to make themselves heard by the backmost man at the top of the balcony—and so on through the wide-ranging gamut of human imperfections.

Systems of markings are a frequent source of debate. A usual division in Great Britain is that of 50 marks for technique, tone, etc., and 50 for interpretation and effect: the former figure is commonly split up into detailed heads with 10 marks under each, but there is a tendency to use the detailed heads (often with many still more detailed sub-heads) merely for underlining and doubly underlining as an indication of weakness, and to allot the marks for this

department as a lump sum. (For the question of the liberty of interpretation allowed to competitors see *Expression* 3.)

Competition festivals organized by political or religious bodies are, on the whole, perhaps, to be deprecated. The ideal festival is one which unites the community, not emphasizes its divisions.

7. Some Points for Competition Committees. Some points to be remembered by committees are: To try to encourage every kind of ensemble music, as this tends to be neglected; to choose the music for competition with the greatest care as to its high artistic standard, its suitability for the purpose of differentiation between candidates in various branches of technique and interpretation, and its interest for the audience; to avoid so overcrowding the time-table as to embarrass the adjudicators; in school singing competitions to avoid as far as possible giving encouragement to the practice of picking a select party to compete (to the neglect of the rest of the school section concerned) and the practice of putting aside the normal school musical course in favour of intensive study of the competition pieces; to avoid regulations that lead to one-sided study (for instance, every competitor in every class should have a sight-reading test with a fair number of marks allocated to it)—and so on!

Occasionally competition festivals have been devoted to some special composer or period, as Bach Festivals, Festivals of British Music, or the series of Elizabethan Festivals held for some years in London. These have sometimes been powerful means of awakening interest in a more or less neglected phase of musical composition, and, as occasional tonics, may be conducive to musical health. Competition has sometimes been used as a means of reviving, stimulating, or sustaining interest in some local speciality. The 'Contentions of Bards' in Ireland in the eighteenth century were valuable as checking the decay in the cultivation of the Irish harp, and the same means has been used to encourage the use of the Northumbrian bagpipe. Is it not possible that committees might do more than they do at present in the way of arousing interest in neglected composers or types of composition, or of giving new life to flagging local interest in some special branch of musical activity?

During the late 1920s and early 1930s there grew up in Britain a movement supplementary to the Competition Festival movement—aiming at the promotion of festivals of a similar popular kind, and with the same object of stimulating local musical endeavour, but without the actual competitive element.

These Non-Competitive Festivals, deriving from the work of Ulric Brunner, of Bridgnorth, Shropshire, found considerable support all over England.

For Competitions for Composers see remarks under *Patronage* 7; *Prix de Rome*.

COMPIACEVOLE (It.). 'Pleasing.' So *Compiacevolmente*, 'pleasingly'; *Compiacimento*, 'pleasure'.

COMPLETE CADENCE. See *Cadence*.

COMPLINE. Meaning 'completion'; the eighth and last of the daily services of the Roman Catholic Church (cf. *Matins*, *Lauds*, *Prime*, *Terce*, *Sext*, *None*, and *Vespers*).

COMPONIERT (Ger.). 'Composed.'

COMPONIUM. See *Composition* 14.

COMPOSÉ (Fr.). 'Composed' or 'compound'.

COMPOSERS. See *Profession of Music* 8; *Composition*.

COMPOSER'S COUNTERPOINT. See *Counterpoint*.

COMPOSERS' GUILD OF GREAT BRITAIN. Founded 1945, to protect the business interests of composers and affiliated with the much older Society of Authors (founded 1884). Vaughan Williams was the first President.

COMPOSITION

1. Introductory. Composition, etymologically and practically, is merely the 'putting-together' of materials—words to make a poem, an essay, or a novel; notes to make a waltz or a symphony.

For all but the most recent and relatively tiny fraction of the world's history, musical composition has been entirely melodic and probably has been far more instinctive than reasoned.

Melody is a 'putting-together' of notes in succession; harmony a 'putting-together' of notes simultaneously. The first notions of harmony date apparently only from the ninth century. Those two aspects of composition are, in this volume, treated under the headings *Melody* and *Harmony* (the growth of the harmonic sense during a period of a thousand years being briefly demonstrated in a series of musical examples); similarly, that view of composition which regards harmony as resulting from the 'putting-together' of melodies, and studies the texture thus brought into existence, is treated under the head of *Counterpoint*.

Further, the aspect of composition which is called *Form*, i.e. the 'putting-together' of 'phrases' into 'sentences', and so forth, up to the 'putting-together' of 'themes' and of long sections into 'movements' of various types, and the 'putting-together' of 'movements' into such 'cyclic' forms as suites, sonatas, and symphonies, is treated elsewhere in this volume (see *Phrase and Sentence*, *Form*, *Sonata*, *Symphony*, etc.).

The 'putting-together' of 'timbres' may also be held to constitute a part of composition and is briefly discussed under *Orchestra and Orchestration*. By a 'putting-together' of the above-mentioned articles themselves, then, the reader may obtain a view of the art of composition in its melodic, harmonic, contrapuntal, formal, and orchestral aspects, and it remains, in the present article, to consider briefly some questions concerning the philosophy and practice of the art of composition.

2. The Object of the Composer may be formulated in several ways. He has the desire to express himself. If he were a poet he would do so in words, if a painter he would do so in line and colour, and so forth. As he is a musician, he uses sounds. In all these instances the artist has a dual aim; his work must embody his emotion and also satisfy his sense of design.

The necessity for design is in itself dual; it is a condition of beauty and is also a requirement for the holding of the attention of the auditory (the latter part of the necessity is discussed at the opening of the article *Form*).

3. 'Rules.' There are, in a sense, no rules in composition. The only really valid questions one can ask about a composition are not as to its observance of rule, but are such as the following: (*a*) Has the composer succeeded in expressing his emotion and his sense of beauty? and (*b*) has he done so in such a way that he can gain and hold the attention of a reasonable proportion of an audience reasonably accustomed to the particular type of treatment he has adopted?

Rules of composition have certainly been laid down by theorists, but (when good) they merely codify the results of experience, i.e. it is in general found that when they are violated the link between the composer and his audience is in some degree weakened. If, however, the composer can maintain that link at full strength, and on repeated occasions, whilst nevertheless infringing what is generally accepted as a 'rule', he is at full liberty to do so. Every great composer has carried into effect in his work this principle of freedom, there being no rule whatever in any of the textbooks that cannot be shown to be repeatedly violated in the world's repertory of fine music.

James VI of Scotland (later James I of England), 'the wisest fool in Christendom', talking of rules in his *Essayes of a Prentise in the Divine Art of Poesie*, hit the right nail full on the head in his enunciation of this general principle:

'Gif Nature be nocht the cheif worke in this airt,

Reulis wilbe bot a bond to Nature . . . quhair as, gif Nature be cheif and bent to it, Reulis wilbe ane help and staff to Nature.'

Rules are, indeed, mainly 'safety-first' devices for students—and many have high value as such. In the days when composition was a very wholesale process (see 10) they had a further utility: by establishing a routine they enabled composers to turn out with speed the quantities of music that were expected of them, and to do so with a guarantee that they would, at least, not shock their audience by either incompetence or the too unexpected.

See some remarks on Rule under *Harmony* 21.

4. Inspiration. Very many composers have, at various times, been asked to describe their mental processes, and, apparently, almost all agree in admitting the existence of something that can be called 'inspiration', whilst all (without exception) admit also the necessity for labour if the inspiration is to be turned to account.

The nature of the 'inspiration' (that is to say, the *thing given* to the composer, as distinct from the making of a work of art out of it) seems to vary. As may be expected, and as above hinted, some composers are able to state that the 'thing given' to them is a musical motif, or theme, upon which they then proceed to work—a seed which under their horticultural care grows into a plant, with leaves, buds, and blossoms.

Surprisingly many, however, affirm that the 'thing given' is merely a strong and definite mood which possesses them and which they thereupon, under a feeling of compulsion, proceed to express in music. In such cases, apparently, the 'thing given' would be the same if the recipient were an artist not in tones but in words, lines, and colours, masses, or any other medium, and it is merely the accident of his being a musician that results in its expression not in a poem, drama, novel, picture, or piece of statuary, but in a symphony, fugue, or nocturne.

Certain composers declare that the 'thing given' (the starting-point of a composition) is more often a mood in the case of such a work as an opera or a piece of programme music (q.v.), and more often a specifically musical idea in the case of a composition in the realm of 'absolute music' (q.v.).

It is remarkable that even in the case of 'absolute music' the 'thing given' can sometimes be not a musical motif or 'theme' but something much less tangible. Apparently some composers are able to conceive the musical idea of a composition without its being clothed in melodic shapes, harmonies, and the like, and to plan out its treatment, in the first instance, without yet knowing the material with which they will so clothe it. Thus Franck would, on occasion, conceive and then mentally elaborate a composition as a mere scheme of modulations, and Ravel stated that long before he had conceived any of the musical motifs or themes for his Violin Sonata (1923–7) he had

clearly framed it in his mind as to form and instrumental texture, and as to the *character* of the themes (but not as to the themes themselves). Dukas defined the 'thing given' to him as a *ton d'ensemble* (general character), to which the musical themes and their treatment must then be made to conform.

Nothing above stated is to be understood as meaning that inspiration is always and necessarily the mere *starting-point* of a composition (then ceasing and leaving the composer entirely to his skill as a technician): the processes of composition may be spread over days, weeks, and months, and, at many a point, further inspirational enlightenment may come to the composer. But, says Arthur Bliss, 'moments of inspiration are so intermittent and irretrievable that with most of us they only suffice for a few bars' thought, a turn of a phrase, a few strokes of the brush, an instant modelling of a muscle' (cf. 9).

The value of inspiration was reduced to that of perspiration in a saying of Bach, 'Work as well as I do and you will do as well as I do'— probably the biggest lie ever told by a Christian man.

5. Stimuli to Inspiration. Composers possess, in many cases, means of stimulating inspiration. Franck found it in pounding out on the piano some work of Wagner or Bach: as he did this the mood (and perhaps even, strange as it may seem, the principal musical motifs of a composition) would come to him (see also 7).

Haydn would frequently court inspiration by extemporizing at the piano. He said, 'I sit down and extemporize, sadly or joyously, gravely or playfully, as I happen to be feeling, until I lay hold of an idea.' And the idea having come, he probably turned from his instrument to his desk to elaborate it.

Actual composition at the instrument is very rare, and the village church near London which exhibits 'the organ upon which Handel composed his *Esther*' is a place of pious deception. Berlioz held the opinion, apparently, that only second-rate composers used the piano when at work, for he expressed gratitude that his father had never allowed him to learn to play:

'Sometimes I regret my ignorance, yet, when I think of the ghastly heap of platitudes for which that unfortunate instrument is every day made responsible (tasteless productions, that would be impossible if those who perpetrated them had to rely, as they should do, on pencil and paper), then I thank the fates for having compelled me to compose in silence, for having saved me from the tyranny of finger work—the grave of all originality.'

As most musicians make a very clear distinction between 'absolute music' and 'programme music' (q.v.), it is of importance to realize that the border-line is less precisely drawn than is often supposed, since very much music that is supposed to be 'absolute' is based upon an unrevealed 'programme' which has supplied the composer with the required stimulus to 'inspiration'. Thus Beethoven declared 'I always have a picture in my mind when composing'. His friends and pupils, Ries and Czerny, agree that his works were very frequently 'inspired' by visions and pictures, the product of his reading and imagination. It is known that one of the unrealized projects of his later years was the preparation of a new edition of his piano sonatas, in which would be indicated the poetic ideas on which many of them were based, his object being to facilitate the understanding of them and make clear the proper interpretation.

Haydn often worked to a narrative programme. Many of his symphonies which offer no indication of an underlying story were, apparently, written to such—God speaking to a hardened sinner and begging him to mend his ways, but in vain; the emigration of a poor man to America, his voyage, his success, his return (was this, perhaps, suggested by the exploits at this time of the German, Jacob Astor?), and so on. In most cases Haydn has left no clue as to the story he had in mind (the above two symphonies have not been identified); in others he has given the symphony a name as a clue. Schumann, of course, very frequently worked under a literary stimulus, and indicated this by his titles.

A good example of the admission of inspiration derived from a literary source is that of Mendelssohn, who said of his youthful *Midsummer Night's Dream* Overture: 'I call it great luck to have had such a subject to inspire me. . . . What I could do as a composer I could do before writing the overture, but I had not yet before my imagination such a subject as that. That was indeed an inspiration, and I was very fortunate in it' (conversation repeated by Lobe: cf. *Programme Music* 2 on this whole general subject).

A stimulus acknowledged by some composers, and occasionally actually sought by them, is that of pressure of time. Rossini advised a young opera composer never to write his overture until the evening before the first performance:

'Nothing excites inspiration as necessity does; the presence of an anxious copyist and a despairing manager tearing out handfuls of his hair is a great help. In Italy in my days all the managers were bald at thirty. I wrote the overture to *Otello* in a small room where the fiercest of managers had imprisoned me with nothing but a dish of macaroni and the threat that I should not leave the place alive until I had written the last note. The overture to the *Gazza Ladra* I wrote on the actual day of the first performance of that opera, under the guard of four scene-shifters who had orders to throw my manuscript out of the window sheet by sheet as I wrote it, to the waiting copyist—and if I didn't supply the manuscript then they were to throw me out myself.'

This sounds humorous, but most journalists would understand it; there is many a newspaper task for which ideas will not come until the time-pressure offers an excitant (and much of Rossini's music was musical journalism). Mozart, it has often been said, wrote the overture to *Don Giovanni* during the night before the first performance, with his wife beside him

telling him fairy tales to keep him from dropping asleep. (The story rests on very slight foundation, and even if true this may not have been actual composition, but only transcription of what was already thoroughly planned in the composer's mind. Elgar worked in this latter way. Many of his compositions were quickly written down, but they had already been mentally composed in practically all their detail—surely a wonderful example of concentration and memory.)

6. Three Examples of Composers' Methods—Schubert, Wolf, and Sullivan. Schubert is the classic example of 'inspiration' as the novelists picture it. A poem that appealed to him would at once suggest its own musical setting. Thus, on his opening a volume of Shakespeare at a restaurant, his 'Hark, hark, the lark' at once occurred to him and was written in a few minutes on the back of a menu card, and it is believed that he wrote later in the same day 'Sylvia' and the drinking song from *Antony and Cleopatra*. He could so completely forget a song he had composed that a few weeks later he did not recognize it as his. (The same thing once happened with Sir Walter Scott and one of his poems.) When asked how he composed, he replied simply, 'I compose every morning, and when one piece is finished I begin another'.

Lachner remembered a morning when Schubert wrote six of the *Winter Journey* songs (sold for about one shilling each). The very sight of a poem produced 'inspiration' in Schubert. We must assume that he is an extreme instance of a speeding up of the normal processes: it has been suggested that a genius is but an ordinary man whose brain 'works quicker and better', and in that sense Schubert is one of the greatest geniuses that ever lived.

In some of Schubert's instrumental music there are to be noticed a considerable lack of balance and other faults, and we may suppose these to be due to his applying to long instrumental movements a method of immediate and unreflective writing that served him wonderfully for brief lyrical compositions. Revision was sometimes undertaken, but often not enough. It is hard to see how any composer can be fully 'inspired' with the plan of the 'development' portion of a symphonic movement (see *Development*). Brain-work and revision and re-revision seem almost essential here—whether performed on paper or mentally. A curious point about Schubert (and one possibly unique) is the fact that his forgetfulness of his own compositions could be so complete that he could be 're-inspired' with an old theme in a slightly different shape—e.g. the slow movement of the A minor Quartet, the B flat Piano Impromptu, and the B flat Entr'acte in the *Rosamunde* music; or the Finale of the A major Piano Sonata (the one without opus number) and the middle movement of the Op. 164 Sonata (there are other instances). It seems impossible that in such cases he was consciously quoting and doing so inaccurately, and of course the fact already mentioned, that items of his own music could, on occasion, be put before him without his recognizing them, is well attested.

With Wolf as a song-writer there was a very deliberate excitation of inspiration, his process being to examine in the greatest detail the poem he intended to set and to saturate himself in it, 'living its life for the moment, to the exclusion of every other influence'. He always conjured up before his mind's eye a realistic picture of the scene. He

'neglected nothing, in fact, that could help him to concentrate his whole faculties upon the little picture to be painted or the drama to be acted, so that his hypnotic possession of it might be complete. He would go to sleep, and in the morning the song would be already made by some mysterious alchemy—so fully formed that in noting it down his pen could hardly keep pace with his brain, while scarcely a note or rest of it required to be altered afterwards. The poems literally set themselves. Wolf was only the expressive medium through which all the deeper significances that were latent in the poem were made visible and audible.' (Ernest Newman, *Hugo Wolf*.)

This composing in one's sleep is merely the equivalent of what many a wise business man does with his problems—thinks them out and then leaves them to his subconscious during that part of the twenty-four hours when its too intrusive partner, the conscious, is out of the way.

Sullivan, whose operatic melodies often seem so spontaneous, arrived at them not by any such process as that just mentioned, but by a very systematic effort of another kind. His first step was to write out the possible rhythms (it might be seven or eight) for the lyric to be set. Having chosen the best one, he proceeded to develop a melody upon this.

'As for the inspiration theory,' he said, 'although I admit that sometimes a happy phrase will occur to one quite unexpectedly, rather than as the result of any definite reasoning process, musical composition, like everything else, is the outcome of hard work, and there is really nothing speculative or spasmodic about it. Moreover, the happy thoughts which seem to come to one only occur after hard work and steady persistence. . . . The miner does not sit at the top of the shaft waiting for the coal to come bubbling up to the surface. One must go deep down, and work out every vein carefully.' (Conversation reported in Lawrence's *Life of Sullivan*: see further conversation under 7 below.)

7. Musical Themes. It will be sufficiently evident from the article *Form* (as also from the article *Melody*, sections 3, 4) that every composition, short or long, is an outgrowth of a small number of brief themes or tunes, and that each of these themes itself, if analysed, is found to be the outgrowth of one or more tiny motifs. The actual material of a composition, then, is much slighter in quantity than uninstructed listeners realize.

The germ motifs of a composer's themes apparently come to him as a part of his 'inspiration', as do sometimes the themes themselves. Mozart said:

'When I am completely myself, entirely alone, and of good cheer—say, travelling in a carriage, or walking after a good meal, or during the night when I cannot sleep—it is on such occasions that my ideas flow best and most abundantly. *Whence* and *how* they come I know not; nor can I force them. Those ideas that please me I retain in my memory, and am accustomed to hum them to myself. If I continue in this way it soon occurs to me how I may turn this or that morsel to account so as to make a good dish of it—that is to say, agreeably to the rules of counterpoint, to the peculiarities of the various instruments, etc.'

Beethoven, as is well known, kept 'sketch books', in which the musical ideas that came to him were recorded for future use. But apparently what we now see in these books (such of them as remain) is not his thematic material in its first state, for he said, 'I carry my ideas about with me a long time (often a very long time) before I write them down'. (It is, however, somewhat difficult to reconcile this with Beethoven's habit, of which his friends have told us, of carrying his sketch book always with him, and of stopping in the street, it might be, to notate a musical idea.)

Other composers have had the sketch book habit. Of Sullivan it has been told:

'In a crowded drawing-room he would laugh and joke with the rest, then, unobserved, draw apart and, producing the note-book, jot down a few bars of a melody that had stolen in vagrant fashion across his mind during the conversation. From these pencilled notes were built up some of the most beautiful numbers in his operas.' (*Life of Sullivan*, by H. Sullivan and Sir Newman Flower.)

Thus he salved the 'happy phrase' (see 6) 'that will occur to one unexpectedly'.

The spontaneous generation, so to speak, of musical motifs may well be given the name of 'inspiration'. They often come unsought and even when the recipient is otherwise engaged than in composition. Franck, a most absorbed and conscientious teacher, would often, when giving a lesson, jump up suddenly, go to his desk, and write down a measure or two that had come to him, and then resume his teaching. (This agrees with what was said in 5 as to the performance of the works of other composers often 'inspiring' him with ideas for his own.)

The finding of musical ideas does not seem to be usually the most difficult part of a composer's task. The sifting and selecting of them is more important. Sterndale Bennett said: 'My life has been spent in rejecting ideas'; probably he became too exacting, as his output almost ceased after middle life (though this has often been put down to his absorption in the routine of teaching, etc.).

This reminds one of what Bernard Shaw says of literary ideas:

' I have not to find ideas; they come and have to be rejected mostly, as not bearing examination. Good writing represents the survival of about two per cent. of the notions that present themselves.

It often takes much longer to revise a page than to write it.'

Prosaic as it may seem, very many composers keep what we may call a 'stock pot', into which go the musical motifs and themes that come to them. This, of course, has its counterpart in the literary life; the de Goncourts, Arnold Bennett, Charles Dickens, and Samuel Butler are just a few out of dozens of instances that could be given of writers much of the material of whose books was selected from a repertory brought together methodically over a term of years.

8. Technique and Invention. It follows from the above that a composer's acquirement of technique is nothing more than the acquirement of the ability to achieve the effects he wants to achieve in the various branches mentioned—melody, harmony, counterpoint, form, instrumentation.

Like an athlete, he has to train himself in his technique to the point where it becomes largely subconscious. It is very difficult, as one studies the process of composers, to realize where the dividing line is to be drawn between the purely inventive (or 'inspirational') part of composition and the technical. Often passages that we should have imagined to have sprung into their minds whole and perfect are found, when we turn over the composer's rough sketches, to have been slowly and painfully put together, altered, and re-altered. On the other hand, there are composers whose first thoughts and whose last show little divergence.

The problem is somewhat simplified by remembering the role of the subconscious mind and supposing that the difference between composers in this matter is one of the greater or lesser amount of work that their brains carry out above or below the level that separates the conscious from the subconscious. As examples of the two extremes we may take Beethoven and Schubert. But not even of Schubert, whose music often seemed to well up in him of its own pressure, can it quite always be said, as it was of Shakespeare by the editors of the first collected edition of his plays, that 'what he thought he uttered with that easiness that we have scarce received from him a blot [i.e. an erasure] in his papers', or, as Shakespeare's players told Ben Jonson, 'whatsoever he penned he never blotted a line'. (As for Beethoven, his slow and painful method of working is somewhat exemplified under *Melody* 8.)

9. The Manipulation of Thematic Material. Though the genesis of themes is so often spontaneous, the after-treatment of them is usually anything but so. At this stage very heavy labour has often to be undertaken.

Schumann once printed in the musical journal he edited a letter containing what he called 'golden words' that, as a youth of eighteen, he had received from an older composer; it distinguishes clearly between the processes of 'inspiration' and reflective revision:

'During the moment of divine consecration we should abandon ourselves mercilessly to the first inspiration; but afterwards calm searching reason must have its due and with its bear's paws scratch out mercilessly any human imperfections that have crept in. What is wild may grow up wild; nobler fruits demand care; the vine needs not only most diligent cultivation but pruning as well.'

(In later life Schumann reported that his processes had become much quicker and surer, so that little revision was now necessary.)

The last surviving pupil of Chopin gave an account of his methods of composition as follows:

'As to Chopin's methods of composition they were, contrary to popular opinion, most laborious. He had the habit of first writing down his ideas, then trying over at the piano what he had written, and correcting it over and over again until hardly a note of the original remained.'

George Sand, who had perfect opportunities for observation of Chopin's processes, writes:

'His creation was spontaneous and miraculous. He found it without seeking it, without foreseeing it. It came on his piano suddenly, complete, sublime, or it sang in his head during a walk, and he was impatient to play it to himself. But then began the most heart-rending labour I ever saw. It was a series of efforts, of irresolutions, and of frettings to seize again certain details of the theme he had heard; what he had conceived as a whole he analysed too much when wishing to write it, and his regret at not finding it again, in his opinion, clearly defined, threw him into a kind of despair. He shut himself up in his room for whole days, weeping, walking, breaking his pens, repeating and altering a bar a hundred times, writing and effacing it as many times, and recommencing the next day with a minute and desperate perseverance. He spent six weeks over a single page—to write it at last as he had noted it down at the very first.'

Even Mendelssohn, whose works seem to run their course so unobstructedly, suffered agonies when composing his bright and easily flowing 'Italian' Symphony (he said it had given him 'the bitterest moments he ever endured'). He altered his D minor Piano Trio up to the last moment, so that some plates already engraved had to be destroyed, and so changed his *Hymn of Praise* after his first hearing of it that the whole had to be re-engraved. He sometimes called attention to the difficulties that Beethoven found in composing by exhibiting a manuscript of his which had had thirteen different slips of paper, embodying as many attempts at improvement, pasted over one passage: Mendelssohn had removed them all, and the last one was found to reproduce the first state of the passage. Beethoven's state of mind when trying to reduce to order his ideas was often one of extremest excitement. His friend Schindler describes him at work on the Credo of his great Mass, 'shut up in his room, singing, shouting, stamping, as if in actual conflict of life and death . . . wild, dishevelled, faint with toil and twenty-four hours' fasting'.

In general, it may be said that the passages that are apparently most spontaneous are in reality the most truly the product of labour, doubt, and revision. Not one in ten thousand who hears Haydn's 'Emperor's Hymn' (the tune *Austria* of many hymn-books) has any idea that in its present easy flow and balance it is but the last of a series of versions in which the composer sought and at last attained perfection (see '*Emperor's Hymn*').

It must not be assumed, however, that the painful labour of manipulation of themes is with all composers carried out in a state of excitement. There are composers who are naturally cool at this stage or have schooled themselves to 'keep their heads'. Richard Strauss, whose music is so often strenuous and emotional, laid stress upon the necessity of keeping one's head when composing:

'I work very coolly, without agitation, without emotion, even. One has to be thoroughly master of oneself to regulate that changing, moving, flowing, chess-board, orchestration. The head that composed *Tristan* must have been cold as marble.'

Casella said:

'I may affirm that emotion has never been present during the creation of those pages which are generally looked upon as the least imperfect of my production. Without any doubt the most favourable state for artistic creation (that state which the uninitiated look upon as a more or less divine fever) is simply an extremely lucid phase of cerebral activity.'

10. Quantity and Length in Composition. It is to be noted that composers, from the nineteenth century onwards, take their function more seriously than those of any previous age—and have it so taken by the public. A new symphony or sonata was in the eighteenth century nothing to make a fuss about. Indeed, it was against the custom to issue a mere single composition of this kind. In the later seventeenth and the eighteenth centuries the set of twelve, ten, or six was the usual thing. Purcell issued two books respectively of twelve and ten sonatas for two violins, cello, and harpsichord; Corelli's works were issued in books of twelve; Bach's 'English', 'German', and 'French' keyboard suites are all in sets of six; so are his organ sonatas, his violin sonatas and partitas (three of each in the album), and other things. Haydn was commissioned to come to England to compose six symphonies there, and then to come again and compose another six; in the lively autobiography of Haydn's contemporary, Dittersdorf, we meet with expressions such as 'We set to work on [practising] the 6 new quartets by Richter', or 'He ordered me to write 6 new symphonies', or 'If you want to earn a little money write me 6 new symphonies and 2 concertos for my oboe player', or 'It had occurred to me to take some of Ovid's *Metamorphoses* as subjects for characteristic symphonies, and by the time of my arrival in Vienna I had finished 12 of them', or 'During that month I made preparation for my journey to Berlin and composed 6 new symphonies.'

A factor in this high productivity was that the composer looked upon himself more as a craftsman doing daily work and less as an inspired poet, that he composed to order or for occasions, and that he made little more fuss about waiting for inspiration than does a baker ordered to produce a batch of loaves. In fact, the art of composition in general was less on the level of literature than of journalism; yet the survival average of compositions was probably quite as high then as since.

Kuhnau, Bach's predecessor at Leipzig, writing of a set of seven sonatas that are still considered as of value, says: 'I experienced such eagerness that without neglecting my other occupations I wrote one every day, so that this work, which I began on a Monday, was finished on the Monday of the following week.'

Handel wrote *Israel in Egypt* in twenty-nine days and *Messiah* in twenty-two. Bach wrote five complete sets of cantatas for every Sunday and feast-day in the church's year (and his contemporary Telemann wrote twelve such sets!). Metastasio wrote the libretto of an opera, Hasse set it to music, and it was rehearsed and performed, all within eighteen days. Mozart's greatest three symphonies all date from the same period of two months. One of the prize-winners of all time for quantity (and hence, almost necessarily, for speed in composition) was the sixteenth-century Flemish composer, Filippo di Monte, who left over 1,000 madrigals and 300 motets.

Archbishop Trench used to maintain that nearly all the great poets of the first excellence were as remarkable for the quantity as for the quality of their productions—'Witness the 70 dramas of Aeschylus, and the more than 90 of Euripides and the 113 of Sophocles' (and Lope de Vega wrote 2,200!). There have been composers of the nineteenth century who have shown something of this fecundity of earlier periods, but they have been comparatively rare. Schubert wrote over 600 songs and a great quantity of instrumental music; Wolf wrote over 500 songs, Reger 200 and an incredible quantity of other things. But in general the days of mass production may be said to have ended with the eighteenth century.

Partly, of course, this is due to the greater length of compositions. It is unusual for a sixteenth-century composition (even a cyclic one such as the rudimentary suites of the day) to play for more than eight minutes and most compositions of that period are much shorter than that. In the next century, Purcell's 'Golden' Sonata takes only about ten minutes. Compare these figures with the progressively higher ones of the eighteenth and nineteenth centuries given later under *Form 2*.

Up to the end of the eighteenth century, a large amount of composition was 'occasional'. Composers were attached either to courts, churches, or opera-houses; it was taken for granted that music should be composed as a part of the regular work of the officials to whom the duty fell. At the British court, the organist of St. James's Palace is still 'Organist *and Composer* to H.M. Chapels Royal'.

11. Emotional 'Time-Periods' in Composition. A very notable phenomenon in the art of musical composition, as compared with that of poetry, drama, or fiction, is the frequent and rapid change of emotional states. To take a simple instance, an ordinary sixteen measures of Mozart (e.g. the middle portion of the Andante of the String Quartet in D minor, K. 421) passes through so many different phases of emotional expression that only an actor declaiming the meditations of a very unstable character in a moment of high excitement could equal it. This quality is especially marked in and since Beethoven, and is much in evidence in his 'development' sections. Clearly music is the most flexible of the arts and hence the most capable of expressing a rapid play of changing emotion.

12. Originality in Composition. There seem to be two distinct qualities passing under this title: (*a*) actual novelty in melody, harmony, form, orchestration, etc., and (*b*) a strong expression of personality allied to a high degree of craftsmanship.

Original in the first sense of the word were: the first man to employ Organum (see *Harmony* 4); Dunstable (q.v.), in the early fifteenth century, in his introduction of new contrapuntal devices; Peri and Caccini at the opening of the seventeenth century, in their introduction of the recitative style; Carl Philipp Emanuel Bach in the mid-eighteenth century, in his introduction of the sonata style; Field in the early nineteenth, in his introduction of the piano nocturne; Berlioz, in his development of orchestral resources; Wagner in the mid-nineteenth, in his use of the 'leading motif' (q.v.), his great enlargement of the scope of chromatic harmony, and half a dozen other things; Debussy in the early twentieth, in his introduction of 'impressionist' harmony and orchestration (see *Impressionism*); and the experimenters who a little later attempted the application of microtones (see *Harmony* 19).

Original in the second sense were Byrd and Palestrina and Victoria and a number of their contemporaries, who in the late sixteenth century used the then existing unaccompanied choral style to better purpose than their predecessors; J. S. Bach, who did the same with the early eighteenth-century contrapuntal style; Haydn and Mozart, who exploited the sonata style of C. P. E. Bach; and so on.

Such a dichotomy as the above must not, however, be pushed too far. Many composers (perhaps all 'great' composers) show in lesser or greater measure originality of both kinds. Of this Beethoven is an outstanding example: even in many of his earlier works, which introduce few innovations upon Haydn and Mozart, there are felt that impress of a strong personality and that high degree of craftsmanship that we all of us recognize as the product of one side of an

original mind, whilst progressively, to the end of his output, we see the search for new harmonies, innovations in form and orchestration, and the like, which are the product of another side of it.

It may be observed that this other side is rarely very evident in the earliest compositions of any composer. So far as technique is concerned, every composer necessarily begins by adopting the processes he finds already in existence. An 'originality' that ignored these would, indeed, put him back in the Stone Age for his beginnings, with a hopeless chance of ever reaching the point of attracting the slightest attention of his contemporaries, and the man who is, like Beethoven, highly original in both senses of the word is the one who has most quickly absorbed the style of his day and then taken complete liberty to make that the base for his pioneering.

If we were to ignore the existence of the second type of originality (the combination of strong personality with complete craftsmanship) we should have to class C. P. E. Bach as a more original composer than his father, which in playing the works of the two we do not feel to be a justifiable distinction. J. S. Bach could write a fugue which we recognize as highly 'original' whilst using as its chief musical theme a scrap of melody that had been used over and over again before him, and following out the methods of fugue as accepted and codified by the composers of his day. C. P. E. Bach, in attempting that task, would fail to convince us of originality, but in his work in another style shows so much ingenuity and enterprise as to win himself the title of 'Father of the Symphony'.

Comparable with the music of J. S. Bach is the drama of Shakespeare, who used stock plots and the dramatic technique of his day and yet produced work that the world has admitted to be highly original. As Ruskin has said:

'Originality in expression does not depend [here we might insert 'necessarily'] on invention of new words; nor originality in poetry on invention of new measures; nor in painting on new modes of using them. . . . Originality depends on nothing of the kind. A man who has the gift will take up any style that is going, the style of his day, and will work in that, and be great in that, and make everything that he does in it look as fresh as if every thought of it had just come down from heaven.'

Elsewhere he says (truly, but again one-sidedly taking account of our second kind of originality only), 'Originality is not newness but genuineness'.

The question of what is original in music has often been fought in courts of law. Nobody takes a symphony into court, but a light opera (involving large cash interests) sometimes finds its way there. The defence is always that the defendant's music is *not* a copy of the plaintiff's, and expert witnesses are called to substantiate this. A better plea might be that the plaintiff's music is in itself a copy. It seems to be possible to take almost any musical composition and

1. PEPYS'S 'MUSARITHMICA MIRIFICA' (c. 1670). A number of drawer-slats, with figures inscribed on them (now preserved in Pepys's old college (Magdalene) at Cambridge)

2. MOZART'S (SPURIOUS) INSTRUCTIONS FOR COMPOSING BY DICE. Published posthumously (1793). A similar work by Haydn appeared about 1790

3. A MORE MODERN MUSICAL DICE-GAME. The dice are marked with letter-names, intervals, chords, modulations, &c., and there are ivory men whose purpose is difficult to fathom

PLATE 43   CONCERTS AND CONCERT HALLS, I

See the Articles *Concert* on pages 227–33, and *Concert Halls* on pages 234–6, as also Plates 45 and 46, facing pages 241 and 256

1. THE WORLD'S EARLIEST
CONCERT-GIVER—BANISTER
See *Concert* 3

2. BRITTON—THE MUSICAL
SMALL-COAL MAN. See *Concert* 4

3. LONDON
SMALL-COAL
MAN OF 1709—
possibly Britton

4. VAUXHALL GARDENS, with its Musicians' Gallery
By Rowlandson. See *Concert* 12

5. MARYLEBONE GARDENS, with Musicians' Gallery on
right. For all these London Gardens see *Concert* 12

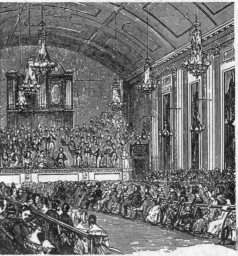

6. THE ROTUNDA OF RANELAGH, with Musicians' Gallery on right
See *Concert* 12

7. HANOVER SQUARE ROOMS (1775–1874). See *Concert* 8

trace its musical themes and processes, one by one, to previous compositions, yet in sum the composition may be highly original.

DONIZETTI, *La Favorita* (1840).

LISZT, *Les Préludes* (1850).

WAGNER, *Dusk of the Gods* (1876).

The extracts printed above are but three examples of what certainly looks like the same theme used by various composers, taken from a long series of such examples of the repeated use of this same theme, extending from Donizetti to Debussy, given by Mr. Henri du Saurrine in the *Revue Musicale* for August 1921. (Cf. *Melody* 7.)

13. The Teaching of Composition. There is a sense in which it may be said that composing cannot be taught—but only learnt. Any one who will trouble to turn over the earlier pages of the biographies of the world's great composers will find a marked similarity in the methods there employed in learning their craft. Invariably we find them, once they have made their necessary exercises in harmony and counterpoint, studying minutely the works of their predecessors and contemporaries. Thus Bach as a youth was always copying other people's music—German, French, Italian—and so gaining an insight into their methods. Mozart, whom it is usual to regard as one of the most instinctive composers (one who 'lisped in numbers, for the numbers came'), said that it was a great mistake

to imagine that his art had been easy to him. He claimed that hardly any one had worked as he had, and said: 'You could scarcely mention any famous composer whose writings I have not diligently and repeatedly studied from their earliest to their latest.' Wagner, under his teacher Weinlig, would take a piece of Mozart and, after attentively examining the length and balance of its sections, the character of its musical themes, its modulations, and so on, would attempt a piece closely modelled upon it—the work of his teacher then being to criticize it in patient detail. The greater nineteenth-century Russian school were enormously indebted to their leader, Balakiref, who directed their studies. Mussorgsky, under his guidance, made an exhaustive analysis of the chief works of the Classical and Romantic schools: he played them in four-hand arrangement with his mentor, who made critical running comments.

It is sometimes suggested, however, that the intensive study of earlier and contemporary work, whilst essential in the pupil stage, should not be too long continued, lest originality be quenched. It is commonly (though not invariably) found that the compositions of conductors and virtuoso pianists, men engaged in the constant interpretation of the work of others, fail to attain the highest level in anything but a technical sense.

A notable and saddening phenomenon is the general drying-up of originality in early manhood. Schools of music are filled with promising composers of whom only a low percentage fulfil their promise and the music critics often hail with approval young composers who in a few years fall completely out of their ken, having transformed themselves into teachers. This is partly due, no doubt, to economic pressure, and if any case of the other professions be considered a similar phenomenon will probably be noticed. The world has certainly not room for all the young composers listed in books on contemporary music, any more than it would have for all the oak trees if every acorn germinated and developed to maturity.

14. Composition Systems and Mechanisms. From time to time methods of composing without effort appear; indeed, they are one of the recurring curiosities of musical life. Kircher, in his *Musurgia Universalis* (Rome, 1650), describes a composing machine, and apparently Pepys in London, a little later, had an apparatus for the same purpose (now to be seen in the Pepysian Museum at Magdalene College, Cambridge (p. 224, pl. 42. 1)).

In the late eighteenth century the London music publisher, Welcker, issued a *Tabular System whereby any person, without the least knowledge of music, may compose ten thousand minuets in the most pleasing and correct manner.*

In 1824 a machine called the 'Componium', invented by a Dutchman, Winkel, was exhibited in Paris and reported on by the celebrated theorist of the day, Catel, and the equally celebrated scientist, Biot, representing respectively the Academy of Sciences and the Academy of Fine Arts. They said:

'When this instrument has received a varied theme, which the inventor has had time to fix by a process of his own (pins in barrels) it decomposes the variations of itself, and reproduces their parts in all the orders of possible permutation, the same as the most capricious imagination might do; it forms succession of sounds so diversified, and produced by a principle so arbitrary, that even the person the best acquainted with the mechanical construction of the instrument is unable to see at any given moment the chords[1] that are about to be produced. . . . None of the airs which it varies lasts above a minute; could it be supposed that but one of these airs was played without interruption, yet through the principle of variability which it possesses, it might, without ever resuming precisely the same combination, continue to play not only during years and ages, but during so immense a series of ages that though figures might be brought to express them common language could not.'

A similar machine was then devised by Baron Giuliani and exhibited in Vienna. The English musical journal the *Harmonicon* (1824) says that Winkel's invention was 'bought by some speculating merchants' and expresses the hope that the unhappy race of unoriginal composers, 'gnawing their pens for whole days together' in the efforts to discover original ideas, and then in despair stealing them from the works of other composers, might in future be relieved and 'their amazing industry dispensed with'.

There is a pamphlet that occasionally appears at a high price in second-hand booksellers' catalogues showing (in English, French, German, and Italian) how to compose 'as many German waltzes as one pleases', all 'without the least knowledge of music', by throwing dice. Its title-page ascribes it to Mozart (p. 224, pl. **42.** 2) though it is considered spurious. We do have, however, in Mozart's hand a sheet of paper on which he sketched the possible permutations in the musical motifs of a minuet and trio (K. Anh. 294d)—a popular pastime of the period.

There existed in the late eighteenth century many such methods of composing dance music of various types by means of dice (or sometimes a teetotum). Amongst musicians to whom these are credited are Kirnberger, C. P. E. Bach, Haydn, and Clementi. Attached to the British Museum's copy of the 'Haydn' production is a mathematical calculation showing that 'the astounding number of nearly forty-six thousands of millions of different melodies' may be composed by its means.

In 1822-3 *The Euterpiad*, of Boston, Mass., carried an advertisement of *Kaleidacousticon*—a set of cards by means of which upwards of 214 million waltzes might be composed, and as late as 1865 there was advertised *The Quadrille Melodist, composed and invented by J. Clinton, Professor in the Royal Academy of Music* which, by means of a set of cards, enabled a pianist at a quadrille party to keep the evening's pleasure going by means of a modest provision of

428,000,000 quadrilles. A work entitled the 'Melographicon' enabled 'Young People who have a taste for poetry' to produce 'an interminable number of Melodies' and thus to 'set their verses to music for the Voice and Pianoforte without the necessity of a Scientific Knowledge of the Art'. (See also p. 224, pl. **42.** 3.)

The development of the electronic computer has made possible a more sophisticated kind of mechanical composition. A trained 'programmer' can feed a computer with instructions based on a text-book analysis of form and style and receive in return an acceptable piece of classroom composition. A good deal of the drudgery implicit in working out the permutations used in some note-row techniques may certainly be eliminated in this way, particularly in some varieties of 'totally organized' music where the various elements such as pitch, rhythm, dynamics, and orchestration are determined by an unvarying sequence of numbers (see *History* 9).

In 1955 a series of experiments with ILLIAC, a high-speed digital computer, produced at first two-voice counterpoint said to be reminiscent of Palestrina. The experimenters considered that with a suitable programme the machine could produce a Mozart Symphony (No. 42), which would be 'a representative but almost certainly undistinguished work'.

15. The Nature of 'Progress' in the Art of Composition. Popular books upon the history of music often leave the impression that each great composer goes beyond the achievements of his predecessors, so that the art of composition undergoes a process of progressive improvement.

It is common for more instructed writers to scoff at this, to represent that the music of any age represents that age and is not better or worse than what precedes or follows it, but only different.

The truth seems to lie between these two extremes. There are periods when the resources of a new style are being gradually exploited, and during such a period improvement does undoubtedly go on until at last that style attains completeness and is exemplified by masters whose works supersede those of their predecessors and often cast them into comparative or even complete obscurity. There is progress here of much the same character as that which we find in almost any individual composer, whose earliest works are commonly superseded by his later and whose latest are often markedly the most mature.

But it cannot be said that the great masters of the culmination of one period show an advance upon the great masters of the culmination of another. Palestrina and Bach may be looked upon as the greatest composers of their periods, but nobody can say that Bach is greater than, or has 'improved upon', Palestrina.

[1] 'Chords' must be an error. Read 'combinations'. The machine apparently tackled only melodic composition.

The best things of the best periods of any art may be looked upon as equal. But there are periods of experiment in the technique of a style and periods of the perfection of that technique, and in that sense 'progress' does occur.

ARTICLES ON COGNATE SUBJECTS.

History of Music; England; Scotland; Ireland; Wales; Belgium; Italy; Spain; France; Germany and Austria; Russia; United States; Nationalism in Music; Romantic; Classical.

Key; Note; Scales.

Melody; Harmony; Counterpoint.

Rhythm; Phrase and Sentence; Figure; Motif; Idée Fixe; Metamorphosis of Themes; Sequence; Point

d'Orgue; Cadence; Movement; Development; Coda.

Form (including sections on Simple and Compound Binary, Ternary, Rondo, Air and Variations, Fugue, Vocal Forms, History of Form; see at the end a full list of the various instrumental forms treated under their separate heads in this volume).

Madrigal; Glee; Part Song; Round; Catch; Canzona; Chanson; Villan-

cico; Villanella; Canti Carnascialeschi; Cantata.

Church Music; Mass; Motet; Anthem; Hymns and Hymn Tunes; Chorale; Anglican Chant; Laudi Spirituali; Oratorio; Passion Music; Seven Last Words.

Opera.

Chamber Music.

Improvisation.

Collaboration.

COMPOSITION PEDALS. See *Organ* 2 f.

COMPOUND BINARY FORM. See *Form* 4, 7, 8.

COMPOUND INTERVALS. See *Intervals.*

COMPOUND TIME (Duple, Triple, Quadruple). See Table 10.

COMPRIMARIO (It.). In opera, a role of secondary importance; a singer taking such a part.

COMPTER (Fr.). 'To count.' *Comptent*, 'count' (plur.), as an indication in an orchestral score that the instruments in question have fallen out for the moment and are merely 'counting their bars'— 'marking time'.

COMPTON (organ-builder). See *Organ* 6, 7; *Electric* 4.

COMPUTERS and music. See *Composition* 14.

COMUNN NA CLÀRSAICH. See *Clàrsach.*

CON (It.). 'With.'

CONCENTORES SODALES. See *Clubs.*

CONCENTUS. See *Accentus; Chorale.*

CONCERT

(For illustrations see p. 225, pl. **43**; 240, 241, **44, 45**; 256, **46**; 739, 752, **122, 123**.)

1. The Word 'Concert'. The word 'Concert' (of which the word 'Concerto' is the Italian form) means a performing *together*, and was long used solely in that sense. It is, therefore, not etymologically applicable to a performance by one person, and is not so used as a rule in the English language—though it is in other languages (French, 'Concert d'orgue', etc., see *Recital*). Nor is it properly applicable to a programme of solo performances by different performers, though in this sense modern English usage does admit it.

In reading older musical literature we have always to take into account the fact that 'concert' does not mean an *event in musical performance but a combination of performers*. As late as 1776 we find Hawkins in his *History of Music*, using the word in this way: 'Of vocal concerts . . . a judgement may be formed from the madrigals of that time. . . . Concerts of instruments alone seem to be of later invention, at least there is no clear evidence of the form in which they existed other than treatises and compositions for concerts of viols called Fantasias.'

The present article is concerned, of course, with 'Concert' in the modern sense.

2. The 'Academies', Musical Clubs, and University 'Music Acts'. Music performance for long took place either privately, in the homes of the middle or upper classes or in the courts of princes, or else in churches and opera-houses (which, however, are excluded from the purview of this article).

An extension of organization took the direction of the founding of 'Academies' for music, in the sense not of schools but of societies on the lines of those academies of general and scientific learning which arose in Italy from the fifteenth century onwards as a result of the Renaissance. The name 'Accademia' is nowadays given in Italy, not merely to a musical society, but also often to a single concert: it thus reminds us of the origin of concerts in that country. In the eighteenth century, London had its Royal Academy of Music (simply an operatic enterprise and not related in any way to the institution of the same name today) and, later, its Academy of Ancient Music (a concert enterprise, see 6).

The poet de Baïf and the musician Thibaut de Courville founded in Paris in 1570 an 'Academy of Poetry and Music'; here the seven poets of the 'Pléiade' (Ronsard, de Baïf, etc.)

heard, performed by the most able performers of Paris, the verses that they had written and that had been set to music, and gave their friends the opportunity of admiring them.

Somewhat akin to the academies were the musical clubs, to which a special article is devoted (see *Clubs for Music*). These were apparently very common in England at the end of the seventeenth century.

The '**Music Acts**' at Oxford and Cambridge must also be remembered. Under *Degrees and Diplomas* 1 will be found mention of those 'Acts'. They consisted in the performance of a degree composition (now called 'Exercise'); the word 'Act' was used in faculties other than that of music for a thesis publicly maintained, and the public performance of a musical exercise was considered to be equivalent to this. It would appear that occasional musical performances were given by the university independently of the conferring of degrees, and that these, too, by analogy, took the name 'Act'. Thus during the Commonwealth there was a 'Music Act' at Cambridge (1659), and the Restoration was celebrated at Oxford by a Music Act with stringed instruments and voices, after which 'some of the performers retired to the Crown tavern, where they drank a health to the King'.

None of these, however, were 'concerts' in the modern sense, as defined below.

3. The First Public Concerts. The early history of the Concert in Britain has been closely investigated by D. G. T. Harris, who scrutinized the whole newspaper press, from its beginnings, and pursued other lines of research. He found that the origin of public concerts in London appears to have been in the theatres, which were accustomed to provide a programme of music before the play began. One such concert is recorded as taking place at Blackfriars as early as 1602 (see a reference in Sir E. K. Chambers's *The Elizabethan Stage*, ii. 557).

The first actual concerts, organized as such and *open to the general public for a payment at the door*, were (as seems to be admitted by the historians of music in all countries) those which a London violinist, **John Banister** (p. 225, pl. **43**. 1), started in his house in Whitefriars, in 1672, though some London taverns had used musical performances as an attraction earlier and even installed organs for the purpose (see *Music Hall* 1). He gathered around him a little body of performers and gave a programme daily at four.

An account of these concerts is given in Roger North's *Memoires of Music* (written in 1728; see *North, Roger*). It will be seen that something of the tavern atmosphere was retained:

'. . . He procured a large room in Whitefryars, neer the Temple back gate, and made a large raised box for the musitians, whose modesty required curtaines. The room was rounded with seats and small tables, alehous fashion. One shilling was the price, and call for what you pleased; there was very good musick, for Banister found means to procure the best hands in towne, and some voices to come and performe there, and there wanted no variety of humour, for Banister himself (*inter alia*) did wonders upon a flageolett to a thro' Base, and the severall masters had their solos.'

These concerts continued for six years, with various changes of building. In one of his advertisements Banister used a capital synonym for 'concerted music'—'*a Parley of Instruments,* composed by Mr. John Banister, and performed by eminent masters, at six o'clock and to continue nightly'.

These, then, are the first genuinely *public* concerts of the world, and it will be noted that they followed the opening of public operahouses by a good many years, London having had its first such house sixteen years before, Paris three years before, and Venice (the first) thirty-five years before (see *Opera* 23).

4. Britton's Concert Series, etc. The next series of concerts in London (and possibly in the world) was that of **Thomas Britton** (p. 225, pl. **43**. 2, 3); the gatherings took place weekly for thirty-six years, beginning in the year Banister's ceased (i.e. 1678). Britton was a man of humble origin and occupation, a self-taught musician and scholar who enjoyed the friendship of a number of the most cultured people of the London of his day, including many of the nobility. His business was that of hawking charcoal, which he carried about the streets in a sack on his back. Over his coalhouse in Clerkenwell he had a loft which he converted into a music-room, complete with the necessary musical apparatus, including a tiny organ of five stops, on which Handel was wont to play for him, and a Ruckers virginal, thought by some to be the best in Europe, at which often sat the great Dr. Pepusch. At first admission was free, but afterwards Britton imposed a subscription price of ten shillings a year; he supplied coffee at one penny a cup. The loft was small, and the contemporary humorist, Ned Ward, reports that 'anybody that is willing to take a hearty Sweat may have the Pleasure of hearing many notable performers in the charming Science of Musick'.

Concerts now became extremely common and many are announced in the London press of the period. The neighbourhood of Covent Garden was the centre of London concert life at this time, and a concert hall in Charles Street, 'newly built for that purpose', is spoken of in the *London Gazette* in 1690. It enjoyed royal patronage and gave concerts 'every Thursday by Command'.

5. Hickford's Room, etc. About the time that Britton's series had come to an end with his death (1714) a custom began of giving occasional concerts in what was called Hickford's Room, in James Street, Piccadilly. Hickford was a dancing-master, and this was his school; unlike the private premises of Banister and Britton, it was of considerable size, and the many foreign singers and players who then visited or resided in London made great use of it for 'benefit concerts' on their own behalf. In 1738 or 1739 Hickford removed to Brewer Street, near Golden Square; his room there existed until 1937, but its use as a public concert hall seems to have ended in 1779.

A series of concerts that began in 1710, a little before those of Hickford's Room, was that of J. Loeillet, the flute player and harpsichordist, who had settled in London as a member of the orchestra at the King's Theatre in the Haymarket and gave weekly programmes at his house—chiefly of Italian music.

It is interesting to see the famous **Norwich Waits** taking part in this early eighteenth-century concert-giving. In 1714 new by-laws were laid down for them by the 'Mayor, Sheriffs, Citizens, and Comminalty of the said city', and these included a provision that the Waits should 'hold and keep upon the first Monday in every month a Musick meeting for the Accommodation and diversion of the lovers of Musick in this City at which meeting none shall be admitted (unless he shall play his part in the said performance) under the summ of One Shilling'.

6. The Eighteenth Century and Early Nineteenth Century.

During the eighteenth century there was an enormous increase of public and semi-public concert-giving. An important early (and long-lived) society was the **Academy of Ancient Music**, which is said by Hawkins (q.v.) to have begun operations in 1710 and continued till 1792. At the outset it was, as its name implied, definitely anti-modern, and this for some years meant, very largely, anti-Handel. It met for a long time at the Crown and Anchor Tavern in the Strand—a favourite place for concerts.[1]

The **Castle Society** ('Castle Concerts') began as such in 1724, taking its name from its place of meeting, the Castle Tavern in Paternoster Row; it grew out of earlier meetings at other places: later it moved to other premises, but always keeping its old name.

The **Concerts of Ancient Music** (not to be confused with the 'Academy of Ancient Music' mentioned above) began in 1776 and continued until 1848; they were also known as the King's Concerts (because attended regularly from 1785 by George III and later sovereigns—the royal box was the only part of the hall from which applause or encores might proceed). The intention expressed in the title had its embodiment in a rule that no music less than twenty years old was to be performed; largely the concerts were an opportunity for Handel-worship, with the King (George III and George IV were great Handelians) as the chief

worshipper. The directors, of whom George III was one and, toward the end, Prince Albert another, chose the programmes in turn. There were twelve concerts a year, plus a performance of *Messiah*. The last programme ever given was chosen by the great Duke of Wellington (in his youth an amateur violinist).

The **Professional Concerts** ran from 1783 to 1793 and did good work in introducing Haydn's and Mozart's symphonies, etc. They ceased through the competition of the famous **Salomon Concerts**, for which Haydn twice visited England and for which he wrote his greatest twelve symphonies.

The **Philharmonic Society** (now Royal Philharmonic Society) began in 1813 for the encouragement especially of instrumental music; it has always been the professional musicians' society, i.e. 'membership' and 'associateship' are open only to professionals, though there is provision for the general musical public to join it as 'Fellows', and any seats not subscribed for are open for box-office purchase, concert by concert. For many years the programmes of this Society were such as would now be thought 'heavy'—regularly two symphonies, two overtures, a concerto, and other things.[2]

The many works commissioned by the Society include such famous pieces as Mendelssohn's Italian Symphony, Dvořák's in D minor, the Tchaikovsky B♭ minor Piano Concerto, and Beethoven's Ninth Symphony. From 1871 the Gold Medal of the Society has been one of the most prized awards to eminent artists.

The **Sacred Harmonic Society** had a half-century (1832–89) of oratorio performances.

7. The Later Nineteenth Century.

A new era in London concert-giving began with the **Crystal Palace Concerts** held every Saturday afternoon in the winter season from 1855 to 1901, with August Manns (p. 289, pl. **51**. 4) as conductor throughout; altogether (with Saturday concerts and less important ones twice daily) he directed quite 20,000 programmes, and more than any other single individual he taught the British people to love the orchestral classics and not to be too timid in making acquaintance with the orchestral novelties (see mention under *Annotated Programmes*; also p. 241, pl. **45**. 5).

The famous **'Popular Concerts'**, or Monday and Saturday 'Pops', provided for many years London's chief opportunity to hear chamber music. They took place at the St. James's Hall; Joachim was much associated with them. These partially overlapped Ella's **Musical Union** (1845–80; see mention under *Annotated Programmes* and p. 173, pl. **36**. 1). The Monday Popular Concerts began in 1858 experimentally, and in 1859 definitely, whilst

[1] The history of the Academy of Ancient Music is strangely obscure. Our main information comes from Hawkins's *History of Music* and a pamphlet of his on the Academy. His date 1710 is probably too early. There is a possibility that this body was identical with the Academy of Vocal Music, which began its operations in 1726 (see Davey's *History of English Music*).

[2] The name 'Philharmonic Society' was not a new one. Hawkins, in his *History of Music*, mentions a society of that name, consisting of 'noblemen and gentlemen performers', which met weekly during the winter season at the Crown and Anchor tavern already mentioned. Festing, who died in 1752, was the leading violin.

the Saturday Popular Concerts did not begin until 1865. Both series came to an end in 1898.

The **Queen's Hall Promenade Concerts** began in 1895 and carried on the same kind of propaganda as that of the Crystal Palace series. The names that will ever be associated with them are those of their promoter and manager for the first thirty years, Robert Newman, and conductor from the opening to his death in 1944, Sir Henry Wood.[1]

The Queen's Hall was destroyed by enemy action from the air in 1941. The Promenade Concerts continued without interruption, transferring their headquarters to the Royal Albert Hall. After the war ended in 1945 there was a movement to rebuild the Queen's Hall, a fund being opened for the purpose; but eventually it was decided that the new Royal Festival Hall (see 8), together with the already existing halls, sufficed for the needs of the metropolis.

The **South Place Concerts, London** (chamber music at 'popular' prices—a piece of musical missionary work of high value), began in 1878, by 1927 had reached their thousandth programme, and are 'still running'.

These are just a few of the more important of the London concert societies and series that have followed the activities of Banister and Britton. Many more have been left unmentioned on grounds of space.

8. Some London Concert Halls from the Eighteenth Century to the Present Day.

Carlisle House, Soho Square, under the proprietorship of the vocalist, Mrs. Cornelys, was famous as a place of music-making from about 1760 to about 1780.

The **Pantheon** in Oxford Street (of which the façade remained until 1937 as that of Messrs. Gilbey's premises—the building on the south side of the street near Tottenham Court Road with a pillared portico extending over the pavement) was opened in 1772. It was employed at various times for masquerades and concerts, as a theatre, and as an opera-house. Its musical purposes ended in 1814. It figures largely in Burney's writings and those of his daughter Fanny.

The famous **Hanover Square Rooms** (p. 225, pl. **43.** 7; p. 752, pl. **123.** 4) opened in 1775, when J. C. Bach (youngest son of J. S. Bach), joined with the famous viola da gamba player, Abel, to give concerts there. Haydn made his first British appearance here in 1791 at one of Salomon's concerts. The solo instrumental performers here always wore a sword; it was kept hung over the chimney-piece in the artists' room, and an official 'sword-bearer' girt it about each performer before he went on the platform. When the Argyll Rooms were burnt down (see

below) the Philharmonic Society used these rooms, and it continued to do so until 1869. Liszt, Rubinstein, Wagner, Clara Schumann, Joachim (aged 13), and indeed all, or nearly all, the great musicians of the period appeared in these rooms, which were closed in 1874.

The favourite London concert hall of the early nineteenth century was the **Argyll Rooms** in Regent Street (p. 241, pl. **45.** 1). Here, in 1812, Domenico Corri offered, as one evening's entertainment, the contrasting attractions of Pergolese's *Stabat Mater* and a Ball. The Philharmonic Society used these rooms from its foundation until their destruction by fire in 1830. Spohr, Moscheles, Liszt (aged 12), Mendelssohn, and, indeed, all the leading musicians of the period, appeared here.

Exeter Hall (p. 752, pl. **123.** 5) was opened in 1831 for religious purposes and became a centre for oratorio performances—especially those of the Sacred Harmonic Society. Mendelssohn heard his own *St. Paul* there in 1837 and received a silver snuff-box from the Society as a memento. In 1847 he conducted four performances of *Elijah* in this hall. The hall was in 1880 bought by the Y.M.C.A. and closed for all musical purposes except organ recitals. That body (in those days very severe) objected to the performances of 'oratorios for amusement' and also feared that the lives of some of the singers might not always reflect the sentiments they uttered, so making their singing insincere.

The ancient **Crosby Hall** in Bishopsgate Street was a regular place of concert-giving from 1842 (towards the end of the century it was pulled down and re-erected in Chelsea and used for other purposes).

St. James's Hall, Regent Street (p. 241, pl. **45.** 3), was opened in 1858 and closed in 1905. Its acoustics were excellent and for nearly half a century it was London's principal concert hall.

The **Albert Hall** (1871), in Kensington, was built with part of the profits from the Great Exhibition. Its huge size made it acoustically precarious, but it is much used for large choral concerts and for concerts (such as the BBC Promenade Concerts) aimed at a large popular public.

The **Royal Festival Hall,** on the South Bank of the Thames, near Waterloo Bridge, was opened in 1951 as one of the buildings of the Exhibition held on that site during the Festival of Britain then taking place, and was extensively renovated in 1963–4. It is a scientifically designed structure with exceptionally clear acoustics. The main hall holds nearly 3,500 persons and has an up-to-date organ; there are also smaller halls (Queen Elizabeth Hall and Purcell Room) for recitals, a large restaurant, and ample foyer space. (See *Concert Halls* 10.)

The following is a list of some of the other chief London concert halls from the later eighteenth century to the present day:

[1] Promenade Concerts in London before the opening of Queen's Hall have included series (beginning about 1838) at all the chief theatres, the Crown and Anchor, the Royal Adelaide Gallery, etc., under such conductors as Eliason, Willy, Musard, Jullien, Balfe, Mellon, Rivière, Arditi, Sullivan, Cellier, Crowe, and Cowen (for particulars of these see the present author's *The Mirror of Music*, i. 192 et seq.).

1765–1890	Willis's Rooms.
1855–61	Surrey Gardens.
1871	Royal Albert Hall (p. 241, pl. **45**. 4).
1873	Alexandra Palace.
1875–c. 1939	Steinway Hall (from 1925 known as Grotrian Hall).
1876–1903	Royal Westminster Aquarium.
1885–c. 1887	Albert Palace, Battersea.
1893–1941	Queen's Hall.
1901	Wigmore Hall (for some time Bechstein Hall).
1904–41	Æolian Hall (after 1941 used by the BBC as a broadcasting studio).

9. Concerts in Oxford. Oxford has always been a centre of musical enterprise. In the mid-seventeenth century there were weekly private gatherings for music. Pepusch (q.v.) caused offence by some public concerts he gave in 1713. Being admitted to the degree of Doctor of Music, and hence under the necessity of publicly performing his 'Exercise', he took theatre performers from London and profited by the opportunity to give 'concerts in the city for his own benefit, which was censured as a very unacademical practice and unwarranted by any precedent', says Hawkins.

Public concerts were usually given in the chief public building of the University, the Sheldonian Theatre, where Handel gave five in 1733; fifty-eight years later Haydn there directed his 'Oxford' Symphony (see *Conducting* 4). The oldest music-room remaining in Europe is that in Holywell, Oxford (p. 241, pl. **45**. 2), opened in 1748; innumerable are the performances that have taken place in this room and the great musicians who have appeared there. It is now in use as a part of the headquarters of the University's Faculty of Music and is also a centre of Oxford chamber music activities, etc. (Cf. *Clubs for Music-Making*.)

10. Lancashire Concert Life. The Liverpool Philharmonic Society ('Royal' from 1957) has been active from 1840 to the present day. Its first hall was opened in 1849 and burnt down in 1933; it was considered to be remarkable for its acoustical perfection. The present hall was opened in 1939.

Manchester had a series of subscription concerts from 1744. The Gentlemen's Concerts began thirty years later; they ceased in 1920, after nearly a century and a half of usefulness. (See a reference under *Flute Family* 4.) The Hallé Orchestra, Choir, and Concert Series, still existing, owe their inception to the pianist and conductor, Charles Hallé (q.v.), and date from 1857.

Some further information as to the growth of concert activities in England can be gleaned from the article *Oratorio*.

11. The Edinburgh Music Room. Scotland has a very old music-room in the St. Cecilia's Hall in the Niddry Wynd, Edinburgh,

opened in 1762 as the headquarters of a concert-giving society that was then over thirty years old and was to survive for another forty (1728–1801).

12. The London 'Gardens'. The above is the merest sketch of a subject that would become very congested did one attempt to list all the more or less public concert-giving organizations of importance in the eighteenth and nineteenth centuries. Those mentioned may be taken as typical. It will be noted that during the eighteenth century concert-giving was largely in the hands of more or less aristocratic or 'society' groups—the audiences often consisting of definitely enrolled subscribers or elected members. One type of eighteenth-century concert activity requires to be added in order that this impression of exclusiveness may not remain too pronounced—the music of the 'Gardens' and similar resorts, especially **Vauxhall** (see *Tyers*) (p. 225, pl. **43**. 4), 1660 to 1859, but musically particularly active from 1730; **Ranelagh** (p. 225, p. **43**. 6), 1742 to 1803; **Marylebone** (p. 225, pl. **43**. 5), about 1650 to 1776. Very good music was given in these places, often to immense audiences, and the best musicians of the day took part. But the prices of admission were often high, and the wide popularization of concert-going did not take place until the nineteenth century, and then, for a long time, 'concert', to a great part of the music-loving public, meant 'Oratorio' (q.v.). The 'Garden' fashion was taken up in other cities than London. Norwich at one time had both a Vauxhall and a Ranelagh. (See also *Sadler's Wells*.) For Continental and American imitations see 13 and 15 below; and for a reference to one type of entertainment at such places, in London and elsewhere, see *Ridotto*. For the Crystal Palace (which, with its extensive grounds, varied amusements, and regular orchestra, may be looked upon as the last descendant of the old London 'Gardens') see 7.

13. Germany, Switzerland, Austria, Holland, etc. In Germany the institution of the Collegium Musicum (p. 97, pl. **16**) had a large influence in the bringing into existence of concert organizations. This was a private gathering, something like the clubs of Oxford (see *Clubs for Music-making*). The same title for a similar activity is found in **Switzerland** (e.g. Zürich, 1613; Wintherthur, 1629), **Sweden**, **Bohemia** (Prague, 1616), etc. These institutions tended to widen out, and the famous *Gewandhaus Concerts* of Leipzig, dating from 1743, but located in the *Gewandhaus*, or Cloth Hall, only since 1781 (this hall then being rebuilt in 1884, and destroyed during the second World War) were the continuation of a Collegium that was active in Bach's day (see *Fasch, Johann Friedrich*). The name 'Collegium Musicum', revived by Riemann when Professor of Music at Leipzig, came to be used in universities for series of historical concerts given by their music departments.

Buxtehude's *Abendmusiken* (Evening Music Makings) at Lübeck, for some weeks before Christmas, began in 1673 and were famous. Bach travelled 200 miles to attend them. They were carried on until the early nineteenth century.

The very important **Austrian** society, the *Tonkünstlersocietät* ('Musical Artists' Society') of Vienna, was founded in 1772; it is now (since 1862) called the *Haydnverein*. The *Gesellschaft der Musikfreunde* ('Company of Friends of Music') has been active since 1813 (the same year as the London Philharmonic Society—and the names are nearly identical).

The concert societies of Germany and Austria are, of course, very numerous, and to mention those of even the large cities would be impossible. Garden concerts have been an important feature in musical life in Continental countries, as in Britain, and the names 'Vauxhall' and 'Ranelagh' were often applied to them in imitation. (There is a spot called Ranelagh in Paris to this day.)[1]

In 1782 Mozart entered into a speculation with one Martin to hold concerts in the gardens and squares of Vienna, with an orchestra of amateur strings and professional wind.

Holland had a famous and valuable society, the *Felix Meritis* of Amsterdam, from 1777 to 1889; music was, however, only one of its activities. The celebrated *Concertgebouw* ('Concert-building') organization of Amsterdam dates from 1883.

14. Italy and France. In Italy the private or semi-public *Accademia*, or musical gathering, was very common during the eighteenth century, often meeting weekly. Burney, in his travels, mentions many instances. Opera (q.v.) began out of an Accademia (see 2) in Florence, and during the seventeenth and eighteenth centuries every town in Italy had such an organization. The girls' orphanages of Venice and the boys' conservatories of Naples were recognized concert-giving institutions (see *Schools of Music*).

The real beginning of public concert-giving in **France** (see reference under 2 to Academies) was with the *Concert spirituel*, founded in Paris by A. D. Philidor in 1725 (see *France* 7; *Oratorio* 4; *Clarinet Family* 2; *Applause* 2; also, for a German imitation, *Annotated Programmes* 2). This provided a model which was followed in many parts of Europe. A licence was obtained to give concerts during the period before and just after Easter (cf. Handel's English scheme a little later; see *Oratorio* 5) and on certain other days when the Opéra was closed, and to avoid competition with the Opéra a condition for some time existed that no French music and no extracts from opera should be included in the programmes. The 'Concert Spirituel' continued until the time

[1] In the Russian language a word pronounced and transliterated 'Vokzal' (i.e. 'Vauxhall') actually came to be used as meaning 'concert hall'—later being extended to include the public hall of a railway station and lastly to mean, as it now does, the station itself.

of the Revolution, and another series under the same name was established in 1805. Its place of performance was a hall in the Tuileries.

The *Concerts du Conservatoire* were started by Habeneck (q.v.) in 1828 and still continue; they have done much to introduce orchestral music (e.g. Beethoven) to the French public (see also *Pasdeloup*.) From the late nineteenth century (1881) the series of orchestral concerts founded (and carried on until his death in 1899) by the great conductor Lamoureux have been very important.

15. The United States. Concert-giving in the United States has an interesting history. The earliest allusion to a public concert in the American Colonies that Sonneck was able to find (see his *Early Concert Life in America*) refers to one in Boston in 1731, and he found another to one in Charleston, S.C., in the same year. Apparently the early concerts in the American Colonies were closed with a ball. He believed that in 1732 a series of subscription concerts began in **Charleston**. There is thereafter a dearth of announcements of such events in the press until the 1750s, but he did not believe that this meant that concerts were not given. In 1765 a 'Concert of Vocal and Instrumental Music' was given in the Orange Garden, Charleston, *'by Gentlemen of the place, for the entertainment of all lovers of harmony; Concerto on the French Horn and Bassoon by Mr. Pike. . . . N.B. It is hoped that no person will be so indiscreet as to attempt climbing over the fence to the annoyance of subscribers, as I give the public notice that I will prosecute any person so offending, to the utmost rigour of the Law. Thomas Pike.'* It would certainly have been a pity to have had Mr. Pike's programme disturbed by the necessity of chasing intruders, for it was of a serious nature, including no fewer than eight concertos—two for bassoon, one for harpsichord, three for horn, and two for instruments unnamed (probably concerti grossi; see *Concerto* 1), an overture (*Scipio*—probably Handel's), and other things. The only composers named are Stanley and Hasse.

It appears that Charleston had a concert-giving society at this time, the St. Cecilia Society, founded in 1762. This lasted for a hundred and fifty years (to 1912). It was a rather expensive society, with an annual subscription of £25 (but the member could bring *'as many ladies as he thinks fit'*), four dinners a year at £1 per head, and heavy fines for delinquencies. One rule says, *'No boys are on any account to be admitted'*. In 1772 we find the society (which maintained a good orchestra) engaging *'one who is said to blow the finest horn in the world'* at *'fifty guineas for the season'*, and *'a Frenchman just arrived'* as first violin at 500 guineas a year—surely a very large sum for those days.

About the same time (1767) Charleston started a 'New Vauxhall' on the London model; its music, too, was on that model.

The first known mention of a concert in

Philadelphia is in 1757, but there must have been concerts before this. A Mr. John Palmer was giving concerts there at that date, and George Washington's ledger shows he was buying tickets for them. Francis Hopkinson, the composer of the first piece of secular music in America (see *Hopkinson*), and later to be a signer of the Declaration of Independence, carried on a series of subscription concerts at which he played the harpsichord. The 'Pennsylvania Tea Gardens', too, supplied programmes of good music.

The Moravians at **Bethlehem,** Pennsylvania (see *Bohemia*), were, from their arrival in 1741, very active musically. We find the name *Collegium Musicum* (see 13) in use there from the beginning. The musical activities of Bethlehem have continued to the present day (notably in the famous Bach festivals).

New York's first recorded concert took place in 1736, Boston's, as already mentioned, in 1731. Such programmes as remain of these American concerts in Colonial days give the impression that the standard of taste was about as good as that in the old country and that the music current in London pretty quickly found its way to the cities of North America. A fact thoroughly well brought out by Sonneck is that secular music did not, as sometimes supposed, suffer greatly from religious repression, nor instrumental music from the competition of choral. After the separation from Britain the character of the immigrants declined and concert life for a time declined with it, the growth of interest in opera (see *Opera* 21) tending to increase the declension.

The oldest North American concert-giving society still existing is the Musical Society of **Stoughton,** Massachusetts, founded by Billings (see *United States* 3; *Competitions* 4) in 1786.

A feature of concert life in the United States today is the presence of fine orchestras in the great centres of population. Much valuable work is done for local orchestras by committees of energetic and public-spirited women. Some dates are: 1837, Academy of Music Orchestra, Boston; 1842, Philharmonic Society, New York; 1848, Germania Orchestra, New York (refugees in this revolutionary year); 1850, Chicago Philharmonic Society; 1868, Thomas's Symphony Orchestra, New York; 1873, a Germania Orchestra at Pittsburgh; 1878, Leopold Damrosch's Symphonic Society, New York; 1881, Boston Symphony Orchestra; 1886, Chicago Symphony Orchestra (Hans Balatka); 1891, Chicago Symphony Orchestra (Thomas); 1895, San Francisco Symphony Orchestra; 1895, Cincinnati Orchestral Association (van der Stucken); 1896, Los Angeles Symphony Orchestra; 1899–1910, Pittsburgh Symphony Orchestra (Frederic Archer); 1900, Philadelphia Orchestra; 1918, Cleveland Orchestra. (For pictures of halls in Boston and Chicago, see p. 256, pl. **46.** 1, 2).

New York is one of the great concert cities of the world, and the music critic's life there is even more taxing than that of his brother in London; on a single evening there may be fifteen public musical events taking place. Every travelling virtuoso looks to the United States as one of his best fields for remunerative work.

See *American Symphony Orchestra League*; *Lincoln Center*.

16. The Future of the Concert ...? The development of the concert having now been briefly sketched, it may be asked, What of the future? At the moment this is quite uncertain. When the earlier editions of this book appeared it was suggested that radio broadcasting might conceivably utterly destroy the concert. That fear has declined or disappeared, but another threat has taken its place in the greatly increased expense of orchestral concert-giving, due to the rising cost of living and the consequent increase in the remuneration of performers, and indeed, everyone employed in any capacity. There is no longer money to be made from orchestral concert-giving. Except when there is a very large hall subsidies seem to have become a necessity. This applies on both sides of the Atlantic.

CONCERTANTE. (1) The word is adjectival, meaning 'of a concerto nature', or something like that. Beethoven described his Kreutzer Sonata for violin and piano (1805) on the title-page as 'scritto in uno stilo molto concertante, quasi come d'un concerto' ('written in a very concertante style, almost that of a concerto').

Generally, however, the suggestion is of the older type of concerto (q.v.), the 'concerto grosso', in which a group of solo instruments, detached from the general force of the orchestra for the purpose, co-operated with their fellows, passages by the one body and the other alternating, or the two sometimes combining. Thus a 'concertante symphony' is a work of the classical symphony period, i.e. the period following that of the 'concerto grosso', yet on thes ame general lines as the concerto grosso so far as the interplay of two sets of forces is concerned. In fact a 'concertante symphony' is much the same as a double or triple concerto, etc. So, too, the occasional term applied to a string quartet, a 'concertante quartet', seems to imply an individuality on the part of the first violin's music which tends to divide the participants into two parties, 1 + 3. In the historical list at the end of the article *Concerto* will be found mention of several works with the title, from the eighteenth century to the twentieth.

(2) The instruments taking this more prominent solo service as their province are sometimes called the 'concertante instruments', as distinct from the 'ripieno instruments' (see *Ripieno*; also *Concertino*).

CONCERTATA, ARIA. See *Aria*.

CONCERTATO. See *Concerto* 2.

CONCERT D'ORGUE. See *Concert* 1.

CONCERT FLUTE. See *Flute Family* 3 a; *Organ* 14 II.

CONCERTGEBOUW SOCIETY. See *Concert* 13; *Holland* 9; *Mengelberg.*

CONCERT GRAND. See *Pianoforte* 16.

CONCERT HALLS AND OTHER BUILDINGS FOR MUSIC

1. Size of Room.
2. Effect of the Ceiling.
3. Absorbent Materials.
4. Effect of Vaulting.
5. Effect of a Dome.
6. Effect of an Apse.

7. Interruptions in the Path of Sound.
8. Outside Noises.
9. General Furnishings.
10. Use of Amplifiers, etc.

11. The Position of an Organ.
12. Stereophonic Reproduction.
13. Sound Diffusion.
14. Need of Definite Planning for Good Acoustics.

(For illustrations see p. 241, pl. **45**; 256, **46**.)

Certain facts concerning the phenomena of sound as affected by the conditions of concert halls have been mentioned incidentally in the article *Acoustics* (sections 18 and 20), under the headings of 'Reflection' and 'Resonance'. The following further remarks may here be added:

1. Size of Room. A large size of room is inimical to good hearing in two ways: the original vibrations from the platform lose much of their power before they reach distant auditors, and the time taken by echoes to return from the distant confining surfaces is so long that the echoed vibrations of one sound are simultaneous with the original vibrations of the next, producing a confusion. Practised public speakers, in a large hall, often fall unconsciously into the knack of discarding their conventional variety of tones and keeping much to one continuing pitch, which is helpful, for a reason to be explained later (section 5). Probably when the inconvenience is excessive there should be added the precaution of a slow *detached* utterance. Speakers should understand that a large room always requires slow utterance, since without killing all resonance (and so rendering the room 'dead') it is impossible to do away with all echo, and in a large room the 'time-lag' on the echoes cannot be avoided.

Music will stand more reverberation than speech, especially, perhaps, organ and orchestral music, where a number of notes and timbres are usually heard together and the 'time-lag' echoes are more or less covered up by what follows (see section 5). For the differences of speed required when performing the same composition in different halls see the remarks under *Tempo*.

2. Effect of the Ceiling. The ceiling calls for special consideration. If it be high, it, also, will produce echoes with a distressing 'time-lag', unless this has been provided against by the architect's having broken its surface by division into deep-set panels (i.e. coffering) or in some other way, or by his having covered it with some effectively absorbent material. The stretching of wires near a ceiling 'to break the sound-waves' is now recognized as practically useless, the interference they create being infinitesimal.

3. Absorbent Materials. The proper position of absorbent materials is distant from the platform, whether upwards or forwards; echoes near the platform assist hearing by merging with the original sound and increasing its volume; it is the slow-returning echoes that call for treatment.

4. Effect of Vaulting. Gothic vaulting often has a very prolonging effect on sound. The Houses of Parliament in London, built in the early days of the Gothic revival (1840–52), have certain vaulted private dining-rooms in which a party of twenty dining together produce an acoustic Bedlam. A hall of the University of Pennsylvania which is well-nigh impossible for hearing was also designed under the influence of the English Gothic revival. The staircase of Christ Church, Oxford, is famous for its power of turning a sung arpeggio into a sustained chord; the Baptistry at Pisa has the same quality: these two places would be most unsuitable for public speech.

It is to be noted in passing that some authorities have suggested the reverberations of Gothic vaulting as the source of the original idea of harmony (i.e. of the simultaneous performance of different sounds); this is probably fantastic, for though it may be admitted that the practice of harmony first sprang up in the very period (the late Romanesque and early Gothic period) when groined vaulting, with its numerous reflecting and re-reflecting curved surfaces, was first developed, yet there are African tribes, possessing no architecture more advanced than wattle huts, that have arrived at a harmony very like that of the Europe of the eleventh century.

5. Effect of a Dome. The large domes of the period following the decline of the Gothic style may have a very disastrous effect on hearing. That of St. Paul's Cathedral, London, produces so much reverberation that before a microphone system was installed a listener just outside it might hear the speech of a clergyman under it as one continuous sound devoid of speech characteristics. The practice of intoning (which is, of course, largely monotoning) probably grew up partly as an attempt to minimize such difficulties when speaking in large and reverberant spaces; where speech is confined to one note it avoids, at any rate, the extreme confusion of the prolongation by echo of persistently shifting and clashing chords made up of fundamental sounds and their harmonics.

As already implied (section 1), no room is equally satisfying for both speech and music: an uncritical congregation will wallow pleasantly in the sensuous booming reverberations of an organ voluntary, yet become restless when they lose the words of a preacher.

6. Effect of an Apse. As mentioned in the article on *Acoustics* (section 18), curved vaults or alcoves may be dangerous because, by the principle of focus, they produce freakish intensification in particular parts of the auditorium. In fact it may be said that curved surfaces anywhere in an auditorium are a possible source of acoustical difficulty and should not be introduced if they can be avoided. A curved surface behind a speaker or singer may be useful, firstly, as adding to the general sound-intensity, like a mirror, and, secondly, if the source of sound is at the focus of the mirror, in directing a 'beam' of sound into the auditorium. This device is not possible, however, with a large orchestra.

7. Interruptions in the Path of Sound. Direct interruptions to the course of sound, such as columns and alcoves and members of the audience seated on the level of those behind them, should as much as possible be avoided. If the floor surface be great, the only way to prevent the members themselves serving as interruptions is to rake the floor. Roughly speaking, if a member of the audience cannot see the platform he cannot adequately hear what comes from it.

8. Outside Noises. The distraction of sounds from outside a concert-room should be guarded against in certain obvious ways. Usually little sound passes through the walls, but the audience often has to choose between the evils of suffocation and noise through open windows. Ventilation should be provided for by abundant openings that do not communicate immediately with the open air but with some ventilating space in the building at a little distance from the auditorium itself. Windows, even if closed, often admit the passage of a good deal of sound and should therefore be double. A surface of small leaded panes admits less outside noise than a single sheet of glass because it yields somewhat to the vibrations instead of passing them all on.

9. General Furnishings. The nature of the furnishings of a hall and the size of the audience are considerable influences in the degree of perfection of audibility. Architects cannot altogether allow for such variable factors, but, generally speaking, if they allow for the minimum of absorbent hangings, carpetings, and dresses, the effect will be reasonably good at the maximum, too little echo and resonance being not so bad as too much. When the first Anglo-American Music Education Conference was held in 1929 at Lausanne, Switzerland, the Hall of the University, used for the chief gatherings, was found to be well-nigh impracticable as a place of hearing. On inquiry it was found that when built no such inconvenience had existed, and that the reduction in the length of ladies' skirts (which in the year mentioned reached the highest point ever attained to that date) had, by allowing an excessive resonance and echo from the wooden floor, set up all the trouble.

10. Use of Amplifiers, etc. The application of some of the apparatus used in radio transmission to the solution of acoustical difficulties is now receiving general attention. It is possible that in the near future architects may find it to be the best policy to use such constructional materials (or such wall and ceiling coverings) as to reduce both echo and resonance to a minimum, then experimentally deciding on the best distribution of the sound by means of the judicious placing of microphones and loudspeakers. The Festival Hall in London (see *Concert* 8) makes use of amplifiers to achieve 'assisted resonance', prolonging the reverberation of certain of the weak lower frequencies.

If amplification is used, the loud-speakers should preferably be directive in their transmission, set above the heads of the audience, and directed downwards. The audience will then act as absorbers of the sound, which will not filter up into the vault, if any. Some people may be embarrassed to hear the sound coming to them from a direction not in a direct line from the source. This may be overome if to the directly transmitted sound from the loudspeaker there is artificially added an echo having a suitable time-lag. This (the so-called 'Haas effect') obliterates to the ear all appreciation of directivity in the sound-source.

Excessive amplification is an obvious embarrassment to a speaker and does not help his audience; the electric amplifiers which began to come into use from about 1925 onwards were often very inconsiderately adjusted in this respect (often, too, they turned the pleasantest human voice into a dull, booming sound).

11. The Position of an Organ. The placing of church organs is often very bad. Frequently they are in chambers so small that every part of the apparatus impedes the transmission of sound from some other part of it, and, moreover (in Europe much more than America), the organist is often placed in the worst position of any member of the auditory for hearing what he is doing. It is an obvious absurdity that an organist should have to get a friend to play to him so that he can test the actual effect of the various stops and combinations as heard in the church, and then, by guesswork, allow for this in his own playing. The writer on one occasion, sitting by a famous cathedral organist, failed to hear any organ tone whatever in the softest passages of the accompaniment of the psalms, yet the accompaniment was reported by those in the body of the church to have been perfect, so accustomed had the organist become to making the proper allowance where a less imaginative organist or a stranger to the instrument would have failed completely. Yet in such cases as these a detached console is evidently called for.

Some concise counsel as to provision for the placing of an organ may here be offered to those who have to do with the designing of a church. (i) An organ should not be crowded; it needs ample space around it and above it; (ii) As for the space above, it should amount to at least the speaking-length of the pipes—and that, in the smallest organ, means 16 feet; (iii) The organ chamber should not be partly masked by an arch; (iv) The common expression 'the organ chamber' in itself argues a wrong attitude of mind; an organ should have its back to a wall but should be open on the other three sides if at all possible; (v) The old position in the west gallery was much the best—particularly for leading congregational singing, and when it can be adopted today this will be found a great advantage.

12. Stereophonic Reproduction. By the use of our two ears we are able to judge the direction from which a sound reaches us in the same way as, using two eyes, we are able to judge visual direction. If we hold the head normally while listening there will be a difference of phase[1] and a different loudness of the sounds arriving at them from a source to one side. Experiment shows that we use both factors, phase difference and loudness difference, in arriving at our estimate of direction and if blindfolded cannot distinguish between a sound in front and one behind, if they have the same bearing.

In the application of the technique two or three microphones are ranged in front of the player(s) in the 'live' hall. They transmit the sounds they pick up *by separate cables or other channels* to a corresponding array of loud-speakers in the reproduction hall, or cinema, and the audience, ideally, should have the same stereophonic impression as in the live hall. The difficulties of realization seem to be mainly: (1) the acoustics of the concert-hall where the microphones are situated is overlaid by that in which the loud-speakers and audience are situated; (2) even if the live hall is made acoustically 'dead' only members of the audience sitting in certain directions and at certain distances from the loud-speaker in the second hall get the true stereophonic sensation.

For the application of the principle to gramophone recording, see *Gramophone* 3.

13. Sound Diffusion. This technique aims at the directly opposite impression (on a listener

[1] When a sound-'wave' impinges on the head from one side each ear will pick up a different portion of the 'wave' at any time, because of the longer path which the sound has to travel to reach the more distant ear. This difference (in the part of the 'wave' picked up) is called a 'phase difference'.

or a microphone) to that in stereophonic reproduction (see above), i.e. the sound is to come at him from all directions at once so that he loses all appreciation of the direction of the source. It is mostly employed in small broadcasting studios with a view to securing a completely indifferent location for the microphone, in place of the careful research for its best location, needful in the old style of studio.

The condition is secured by an irregular distribution of irregularly-sized pillars or convex cylinders mounted on the walls, the ceiling, and as much of the floor as it is feasible to cover with these 'diffusors'.

14. Need of Definite Planning for Good Acoustics. There is still a common impression that the good or bad acoustics of a hall or church is a matter of chance—that until the building is completed nobody can tell how it will turn out. This impression is naturally strengthened when (as in the case of several very important public buildings, in London and elsewhere, erected during the twentieth century) the purposes for which an erection is intended are found to be impossible of realization until large alteration has taken place. The principles of acoustic planning have, however, now been very completely worked out by such authorities as Sabine (*Acoustics in Architecture*) in the United States and Hope Bagenal in England (Bagenal and Wood, *Planning for Good Acoustics*); nevertheless such important post-war halls as the Royal Festival Hall in London, the Philharmonie in Berlin, and most spectacularly the Philharmonic Hall in New York, have all failed to solve the fundamental subjective problem: a satisfactory ratio of direct to reverberated sound. Such mishaps are as disconcerting to the architect as would be the collapse of the building immediately after completion.

Even before the principles were enunciated there were people who had grasped them experimentally or intuitively. Bach is an example. Forkel relates that when introduced to a room he took in its good and bad acoustic qualities at a glance. Thus, visiting Berlin and being taken into the new Opera House, he looked at the roof of the adjoining saloon and at once remarked 'the architect has produced a novel effect here, which probably neither he nor others expected': it appears that there was, in fact, in this room a marked 'whispering gallery' phenomenon.

It would, perhaps, be good if musicians could study the subject of building-acoustics more than they do, so as to be in a position to advise or warn building committees when plans are produced for new churches and concert halls. This ought to be unnecessary, but until all architects come to take the subject as seriously as the best of them already do musicians may fairly be looked upon as the natural guardians of the rights of sound.

Something of the history of concert halls will be found under the heading *Concert*.

CONCERTINA. See *Reed-Organ Family* 5; *Temperament* 8.

CONCERTINO. This may mean either of two things: (1) the solo instrumental group in the older form of concerto, 'Concerto Grosso' (see *Concerto* 2; cf. *Concertante*). This is the usual eighteenth-century meaning. (2) A shorter and lighter type of concerto. This is the usual later nineteenth- and twentieth-century meaning.

CONCERT MASTER, CONCERTMEISTER. See *Conducting* 4.

CONCERTO

1. The Original Application of the Term.
2. The Concerto from Corelli to Bach.
3. The Advent of the Virtuoso Concerto.
4. The Development of the Cadenza.
5. Less Common Applications of the Term 'Concerto'.
6. Short Historical List of Concertos.

1. The Original Application of the Term. The term 'Concerto' (Fr., *Concerto*; Ger., *Konzert*), as generally used in our own day, implies the solo display of an instrument (occasionally two or more—a 'Double Concerto', etc.) in combination with the orchestra.

This was not the original sense of the word, which properly means merely a composition in which several performers combine contrasted forces, make 'a concerted effort' to entertain the audience, play 'in concert' (see *Concert* 1).

In this sense the term was used as far back as the two Gabrielis (1587), Banchieri (1595), and Viadana (1602), whose motets for choir with organ were called 'concerti ecclesiastici'. The sense here is obvious; this was the high period of unaccompanied choral music, and the use of the term 'concerto' marked the departure from the normal. Schütz (1636) published *Kleine geistliche Concerten* ('Little Spiritual Concertos') which were simply motets with a figured bass for organ accompaniment.

2. The Concerto from Corelli to Bach. At the end of the seventeenth century the term was used by the violinists Corelli, Torelli, and others of the notable Italian violinist-composer school of the time, to describe a type of composition in which a small body of solo strings was heard in alternation with a large body of orchestral strings. Two bodies were combined and the word 'concerto' was applicable in this sense. The larger body in such an arrangement is called **Ripieno** (i.e. 'full'), the smaller **Soli**, or **Concertino**, or **Concertato**, or **Concertante**; thus we can speak of the 'concertino strings' and the 'ripieno strings'. The two groups might largely play separately in alternation, at other times being combined.

The form of the concerto at this period was that of the sonata of the period (see *Sonata*), i.e. it was in three or more contrasted movements; it was, in fact, a sonata with solo and orchestral contrast. As there were two types of sonata, the *Sonata da chiesa* (church sonata, with abstract movements) and *Sonata da camera* (chamber sonata, with dance-style movements), so there were two types of concerto, the **Concerto da chiesa** and **Concerto da camera**.

This kind of concerto was very definitely established in favour when Corelli wrote his famous Concerti Grossi (*c.* 1714). A **Concerto grosso** is really nothing more than what has just been described—a composition in which a group of solo instruments (string, wind, or keyboard, or any combination of these) is heard in alternation with the strings or with the orchestra as a whole. The antiphonal idea is inherent (the word *grosso*, 'big', refers to the solo element being represented by a group, not by an individual). Of this kind are many of the concertos of Bach and Handel.

The most famous concerti grossi ever written are the six Brandenburg Concertos of Bach, which employ six different combinations of instruments (see *Bach* 1).

Solo concertos at this period are on the same lines as the 'concerti grossi', and it is a pity that there exists no one inclusive term to take them in.

3. The Advent of the Virtuoso Concerto. When the modern sonata and symphony were born, immediately following Bach's time (see *Sonata* and *Symphony*), the concerto adopted the same general ground plan of a first serious movement in what is called 'first movement form' or 'sonata form', a middle slower movement of lyrical character, and a bright, rapid last movement generally in rondo form. The sonata and symphony came to have four movements; the concerto, however, remained a three-movement composition. The reason is not clear; perhaps the missing movement, the minuet (a pure dance form) was not felt to be suitable for the antiphonal treatment. Later concertos have very occasionally had the four movements (e.g. the Brahms Second Pianoforte Concerto).

At the same time the concerto lost its scheme of alternating solo group and orchestral group and took on the plan of alternating passages for, generally, (*a*) one solo instrument accompanied by the orchestra and (*b*) orchestra, as such, without the solo instrument. The solo writing now acquired the distinctly virtuoso character which it still retains; there had been precedents for this (e.g. in many works of Vivaldi and Bach), but it now assumed the character of a definite requirement.

The greatest concerto composer of this period (the end of the eighteenth century) was Mozart, who wrote between forty and fifty concertos for different instruments. Beethoven followed with five piano concertos, a famous violin concerto, etc.; he gave the orchestra a more seriously interesting part to play than had been common in Mozart's day; in fact, he deepened the concerto as he did the solo sonata, the string quartet, and the symphony.

For an allusion to the organ concerto see *Organ* 13.

4. The Development of the Cadenza. In the newer concerto just described (i.e. the concerto of the Mozart and post-Mozart period) the Cadenza (q.v.) was an important feature, offering the soloist a great opportunity of displaying his ability to invent and perform technical difficulties. The respectful silence of the orchestra at this point focuses the limelight on the soloist, and this stamps the late eighteenth- and nineteenth-century concerto as something essentially different in spirit from the early eighteenth-century concerto (the 'concerto grosso'). However high may be the cadenza's artistic value, there is always some flavour of virtuoso display.

The words *solo* and *tutti* (literally 'all') have, in the post-Bach concerto, taken the place of *concertino* and *ripieno* in the pre-Bach and Bach period concerto.

5. Less Common Applications of the Term 'Concerto'. Like other musical terms, that of 'Concerto' has been variously and often loosely applied. To the above statement, which outlines, it is hoped clearly, the history of the form, must be added, for completeness, the following:

(*a*) Like the word 'symphony' (literally 'sounding together'), the word has sometimes been used in the sense of a mere combination (without the added idea of contrast mentioned at the beginning of this article). Thus in 1553 the Spaniard Ortiz writes what he calls concertos of vihuelas (guitar-shaped lutes), and in the eighteenth century some concertos are found totally without the principle of contrasting forms, being, in fact, nothing but sonatas for bodies of strings.

(*b*) The word is, up to the mid-eighteenth century, sometimes used for any work of church cantata type; thus Bach sometimes uses it.

(*c*) The word has sometimes been applied even to a composition for a single instrument, as Bach applied it to his 'Italian' Concerto, his idea apparently being that he was in that composition, by means of tonal contrasts obtained from a two-manual harpsichord, attempting something of the scheme of contrasting passages that was typical of the true concerto.

From a glance over the latter end of the list which follows it will be gathered that in the twentieth century, whilst there has been no tendency to abandon the principle of the combination of a solo instrument with the orchestra, there has nevertheless been a distinct tendency to abandon the name, with its tradition of eighteenth- and early nineteenth-century formalism and solo display.

6. Short Historical List of Concertos.
(*a*) The Period of the 'Concerto Grosso' and the Solo Concerto on the Same Lines. The great period for this was the end of the seventeenth century and beginning of the eighteenth, when there was a high cultivation of string playing, especially in Italy. Amongst the chief composers are:

Italian: Corelli (1653–1713); Torelli (1658–1709); Vivaldi (*c.* 1675–1741); Geminiani (1687–1762); F. M. Veracini (1690–1750); Tartini (1692–1770); Locatelli (1695–1764). **German**: Telemann (1681–1767); J. S. Bach (1685–1750), who wrote them for a very great variety of instruments, including two Triple Concertos for three harpsichords and strings, and a Quadruple Concerto for four harpsichords and strings (arranged from one by Vivaldi for four violins and strings); Handel (1685–1759), whose organ concertos are important and who wrote also many for other instruments; Quantz (1697–1773), who wrote three hundred flute concertos for his master, Frederick the Great; Hasse (1699–1783); Johann W. A. Stamitz (1717–57). **French**: Leclair (1697–1764). **English**: Avison (*c.* 1710–70), who published fifty.

(*b*) **The Late Eighteenth and Nineteenth Century Display Concerto.**

Haydn (1732–1809), twenty piano (of which only two are ever heard); nine violin; six cello (not all published; see *Haydn*); one double-bass; others. **Dittersdorf** (1739–99), two double-bass. **Boccherini** (1743–1805), four cello and eight 'Concertante Symphonies'. **Viotti** (1755–1824), twenty-nine violin; ten piano. **Mozart** (1756–91), over twenty piano; six violin; four horn, and eighteen others. **Pleyel** (1757–1831), eight piano and five 'Concertante Symphonies'. **Dussek** (1760–1812), twelve or more for piano. **Steibelt** (1765–1823), many for piano. **Kreutzer** (1766–1831), nineteen violin and two for two violins. **B. Romberg** (1767–1841), nine cello. **Beethoven** (1770–1827), five piano (the so-called 'Emperor' is the 5th); one violin (which he also arranged as a piano concerto); a 'Triple Concerto' for violin, cello, and piano and orchestra. **J. B. Cramer** (1771–1858), seven piano. **Baillot** (1771–1842), nine violin and one 'Concertante Symphony' for two violins. **Rode** (1774–1830), thirteen violin. **Hummel** (1778–1837), seven piano. **Field** (1782–1837), seven piano—once very famous and still somewhat used as study pieces. **Paganini** (1782–1840), two violin. **F. Ries** (1784–1838), nine piano. **Spohr** (1784–1859), fifteen violin, a string quartet concerto (compare the old concerto grosso) and two clarinet concertos. **Weber** (1786–1826), two piano and a 'Concertstück' also; two concertos and a concertino for clarinet; one and a shorter piece for bassoon; also various shorter pieces for various instruments with orchestra. **Czerny** (1791–1857), many for piano. **Moscheles** (1794–1870), eight piano. **Hutschenruyter** (1796–1878), 'Concertstück' for eight kettledrums. **Schubert** (1797–1828), one violin. **De Bériot** (1802–70), seven violin. **Berlioz** (1803–69); his 'Harold in Italy' symphony has an obbligato viola part. **Mendelssohn** (1809–47), two piano and three smaller concerto-like pieces for piano; one violin. **Schumann** (1810–56), one piano and a 'Concert Allegro' and also an Introduction and Allegro for piano; one violin (first performed in 1937!); one cello; a Phantasie for violin; a 'Concertstück' for four horns and orchestra. **Ole Bull** (1810–80), two violin. **Chopin** (1810–49), two piano concertos and some other pieces for piano with orchestra. **Hiller** (1811–85), one for piano (F sharp minor) has had very great popularity. **Liszt** (1811–86), two piano concertos and one so-called concerto for two pianos without orchestra, and the 'Dance of Death' for piano and orchestra. **Henselt** (1814–89), one piano concerto. **Pieranzovini** (1814–85), one for kettledrums. **Sterndale Bennett** (1816–75), four piano. **Gade** (1817–90), one violin. **Vieuxtemps** (1820–81), six and some smaller works for violin. **Bottesini** (1821–89), several double-bass. **Raff** (1822–82), one piano; two violin; one cello, and several suites, etc., for solo instruments and orchestra. **Lalo** (1823–92), several concertos and concerted works for violin and for cello. **Goltermann** (1824–98), six cello. **Reinecke** (1824–1910), four piano; one violin; one cello; one harp. **Julius Tausch** (1827–95), one for kettledrum and a March and Polonaise for six kettledrums and orchestra. **Rubinstein** (1829–94), five and a 'Concertstück' for piano; two violin; two cello. **Goldmark** (1830–1915), one violin. **Joachim** (1831–1907), three and some other pieces for violin and orchestra. **Brahms** (1833–97), two piano; one violin; a double concerto for violin, cello, and orchestra. **Saint-Saëns** (1835–1921), five piano; three violin; two cello. **Wieniawski** (1835–80), two violin. **Bruch** (1838–1920), violin, three concertos and a 'Concertstück'. **Rheinberger** (1839–1901), two organ. **Tchaikovsky** (1840–93), three piano and a fantasia; one violin. **Svendsen** (1840–1911), violin, a concerto and a Romance; cello, a concerto. **Dvořák** (1841–1904), one piano; one violin; two cello (one unpublished). **Sgambati** (1841–1914), one piano. **Massenet** (1842–1912), piano; cello; two violins. **Grieg** (1843–1907), one piano. **Rimsky-Korsakof** (1844–1908), one piano. **Widor** (1844–1937), three piano; cello. **Fauré** (1845–1924), several shorter pieces for piano and orchestra. **Brüll** (1846–1907), piano, two concertos and a 'Concertstück'. **Mackenzie** (1847–1935), one piano ('Scottish'); two violin.

(c) The late Nineteenth and Twentieth Century Period of Freer Treatment.

Franck (1822–90), 'Variations Symphoniques' for piano. *The Djinns*, tone-poem for piano and orchestra. **Tchaikovsky** (1840–93), *Variations on a Rococo Theme* for cello and orchestra. **D'Indy** (1851–1931), works not in concerto form for orchestra with piano, for oboe, and for cello. **Stanford** (1852–1924), three piano; two violin; one cello; one clarinet; also a 'Concertino' for violin, cello, and orchestra. **Cowen** (1852–1935), one and a 'Concertstück' for piano. **Chausson** (1855–99), a 'Poème' for violin and orchestra. **Sinding** (1856–1941), one piano; two violin. **Elgar** (1857–1934), one violin; one cello. **Ethel Smyth** (1858–1944), double concerto for violin and horn. **Liapunof** (1859–1924), two piano. **Loeffler** (1861–1935), several orchestral works have solo parts for violin or some other instrument. **MacDowell** (1861–1908), two piano. **Debussy** (1862–1918), *Fantaisie* for piano and orchestra. **Delius** (1862–1934), one piano; one violin; one violin and cello; one cello. **R. Strauss** (1864–1949), oboe; violin; piano left hand; two horn. **D'Albert** (1864–1932), two piano; one cello. **Sibelius** (1865–1957), one violin. **Jaques-Dalcroze** (1865–1950), two violin. **Glazunof** (1865–1936), two piano; one violin; one saxophone. **Busoni** (1866–1924), concertos and smaller pieces for piano, violin, clarinet, etc. **Pfitzner** (1869–1949), cello (1940). **Walford Davies** (1869–1941), *Conversations* for piano and orchestra. **Roussel** (1869–1937), one piano (1927); cello concertino (1936). **Scriabin** (1872–1915), one piano. **Vaughan Williams** (1872–1958), two pieces for violin and orchestra (a Romance, *The Lark Ascending*, and a concerto); piano; oboe; suite for

viola and orchestra, **Joseph Jongen** (1873–1953), piano (1943). **Rachmaninof** (1873–1943), four piano. **Reger** (1873–1916), one piano; one violin, and two Romances for violin; one 'Concerto in the Olden Style'. **Holst** (1874–1934), one for two violins; Fugal Concerto for flute, oboe, and strings. **Schönberg** (1874–1951), violin; piano (1944). **Koussevitzky** (1874–1951), one double bass. **D. F. Tovey** (1875–1940), one piano; one cello. **Ravel** (1875–1937), two piano (one for left hand alone). **Carpenter** (1876–1951), a concertino for piano. **Falla** (1876–1946), harpsichord concerto and *Nights in the Gardens of Spain* for piano and orchestra. **Dohnányi** (1877–1960), one piano; *Variations on a Nursery Theme* for piano; one violin; a 'Concertstück' for cello. **Holbrooke** (1878–1958) violin; piano (*Song of Gwyn ap Nudd*); saxophone or bassoon. **Medtner** (1879–1951), three piano. **Cyril Scott** (1879–1970), one piano; one violin. **Ireland** (1879–1962), one piano. **Bloch** (1880–1959), one violin and a Rhapsody ('Schelomo') for cello. **Enesco** (1881–1955), 'Concertante Symphony' for cello, etc. **Miaskovsky** (1881–1950), one violin. **Bartók** (1881–1945), one violin (also several rhapsodies for violin and orchestra and piano and orchestra); viola (unfinished); four piano; also a 'concerto for orchestra'. **Stravinsky** (1882–1971), concerto for piano and wind instruments (1924); capriccio for piano (1929); *Ebony Concerto* for clarinet and swing band (1946). **Kodály** (1882–1967), viola (1947); string quartet (1947). **Malipiero** (1882–1973), one violin. **Bax** (1883–1953), Symphonic Variations for piano; Phantasy for violin; concerto for cello; concerto for violin; viola, harp, and string sextet (1936); piano, left hand. **Casella** (1883–1947), cello. **Dyson** (1883–1964), violin. **York Bowen** (1884–1961), three piano; one violin. **Gruenberg** (1884–1964), violin. **Salzédo** (1885–1961), harp with seven wind instruments. **Werner Josten** (1885–1963), a *Concerto Sacro* for string orchestra and piano. **Berg** (1885–1935), one violin. **J. J. Becker** (1886–1961), horn. **Achron** (1886–1943), one violin and a *Konzertanten Kapelle* for voice and orchestra. **Atterberg** (1887–1974), one each piano, violin, and cello. **Walter Kramer** (1890–1969), Rhapsody for violin. **Frank Martin** (1890–1974), piano; violin. **Harold Morris** (1890–1964), one piano. **Martinů** (1890–1959), two pianos; violin (1945); cello (1945). **Ibert** (1890–1962), cello with one wind instrument. **Bliss** (1891–1975), one for piano, tenor voice, and strings (1920), later re-written for two pianos and full orchestra; one for piano (1938); violin. **Prokofiev** (1892–1953), five for piano; two for violin; cello. **Milhaud** (1892–1974), piano; viola; cello, percussion instruments. **Honegger** (1892–1955), cello. **Sorabji** (born 1892), two for piano. **Goossens** (1893–1960), oboe. **Benjamin** (1893–1960), violin and viola. **B. Wagenaar** (1894–1971), flute, cello, and harp (1941). **Piston** (1894–1976), violin (1940). **Moeran** (1894–1950), violin; rhapsody for piano and orchestra; cello. **Hindemith** (1895–1963): in his Chamber Music ('Kammermusik') series are a concerto for piano and twelve instruments, another for cello and ten instruments, another for violin, and another called simply 'Concerto for Orchestra', and similar things; also a clarinet concerto. **Sowerby** (1895–1968), a Ballad for two solo pianos and orchestra. **Ornstein** (born 1895), one piano. **Castelnuovo-Tedesco** (1895–1968), guitar. **Gordon Jacob** (born 1895), viola. **Howard Hanson** (born 1896), one organ (several of his symphonic poems have obbligato parts for violin or piano). **Hans Barth** (1896–1956), two piano (one half-tone and the other quarter-tone). **Roger Sessions** (born 1896), violin. **Cowell** (1897–1965), one piano (using 'tone clusters', q.v.); one rhythmicon. **Quincy Porter** (1897–1966), one viola. **Gershwin** (1898–1937), one piano (his *Rhapsody in Blue* also has a piano solo part). **Dorothy Howell** (born 1898), one piano. **Roy Harris** (born 1898), accordion and chamber orchestra; piano; violin. **Poulenc** (1899–1963), *Concert champêtre* for harpsichord and orchestra; for piano a concertino and a concerto; concerto for two pianos; for organ, kettledrums, and strings. **Chávez** (born 1899), piano. **Antheil** (1900–1959), violin; piano. **Fuleihan** (1900–70), two pianos (1941). **Copland** (born 1900), piano; clarinet. **Burkhard** (1900–55), organ; viola. **Conrad Beck** (born 1901), violin and chamber orchestra (1941). **Finzi** (1901–56), cello; clarinet. **Walton** (born 1902), viola; violin; *Sinfonia concertante* for piano; cello. **Khatchaturian** (born 1903), piano; violin; cello. **Chasins** (born 1903), two for piano. **Dukelsky** (1903–1969), violin (1943); cello (1946). **Jolivet** (born 1905), harp. **Rawsthorne** (1905–71), two for piano; two for violin; oboe. **Blitzstein** (1905–1964), piano. **Lutyens** (born 1906), clarinet, saxophone, and strings; bassoon and strings; viola. **Creston** (born 1906), saxophone; concertino for marimba; Fantasia for trom-

bone. **Shostakovich** (1906–75), two for piano; violin; cello. **Fortner** (born 1907), cello. **Carter** (born 1908), piano and harpsichord. **Barber** (born 1910), violin; cello; piano. **Schuman** (born 1910), piano. **Menotti** (born 1911), piano. **Britten** (1913–76), piano; violin; *Diversions on a Theme* for piano left hand. **Leibowitz** (1913–72), viola; piano. **Diamond** (born 1915), cello (1942); violin (1948). **Ginastera** (born 1916), violin. **Malcolm Arnold** (born 1921), clarinet; horn; piano duet (believed to be the only one existing in this medium). **Lukas Foss** (born 1922), two for piano; clarinet; oboe; cello. **Mennin** (born 1923), piano; violin; cello.

It is, of course, impossible to make such a list as the above complete, but in the later period it has been thought of interest to record in a little special fullness examples by British and American composers. The division into three periods is, it is hoped, helpful, but it cannot, obviously, be in any way exact.

For a reference to harp concertos see *Harp* 3. For a concerto for mouth organ see *Reed-Organ Family* 3. And see *Concertstück* below.

CONCERT OVERTURE. See *Overture* 8.

CONCERT PITCH. See *Pitch* 5.

CONCERTS DU CONSERVATOIRE. See *Concert* 14.

CONCERT SPIRITUEL. See *Concert* 14.

CONCERTSTÜCK. This German word (or rather agglutination of two words) means, literally, 'Concert Piece'—but usually with the first word understood in the sense of 'in concert', or 'concerted', i.e. with some solo instrument or instruments operating against a background of, or in alternation with, full orchestra. A reference to the Historical List at the end of the article *Concerto* will show that from the beginning of the Romantic period (Weber wrote a very famous one) to the present day, composers who have written a briefer and less formal concerto, without breaks between sections, have often applied this description to it.

CONCITATO (It.). 'Roused up', 'stirred'. So *Concitamento, Concitazione*, 'agitation'.

CONCORD (or **CONSONANCE**). (1) Definition—*Harmony* 3, 24 h. (2) Concordant Intervals—*Intervals*. (3) Physical Nature of Concord—*Acoustics* 16; *Harmony* 21.

CONDITOR ALME SIDERUM. See *Hymns and Hymn Tunes* 2.

CONDUCTING

1. The Nature of Conducting.
2. The Early History of the Baton.
3. Conducting from the Harpsichord and Organ.
4. Conducting with Violin and Bow.
5. The Reintroduction of the Baton.
6. Influences leading to Refinement —Stamitz and von Bülow.
7. The Modern Conductorless Orchestra.
8. The Practice of Conducting.

(For illustrations see opposite, pl. **44**; 739, 752, **122, 123**; 753, 756, **124, 125**.)

1. The Nature of Conducting. Conducting is generalship on the battlefield of music. Forces, often large and very varied in their functions, have to be so controlled that they will combine together not only accurately but with unity of spirit. Such control implies the easy possession of a large body of traditional technique plus the same genius for the interpretation of a composer's mind that is to be felt underneath the playing of a great pianist or violinist. Orchestral or choral forces are nowadays, in effect, an instrument on which a virtuoso plays.

2. The Early History of the Baton (see illustrations). The history of the art of conducting has been somewhat obscured by general statements based upon the records of mere local or temporary practice. Naturally methods have varied with local conditions and individual preferences.

It is often declared or implied that conducting with a baton came in only with the nineteenth century, and then in the teeth of opposition. In reality the practice is very old —perhaps as old as the combination of large bodies of singers or players with artistic ends. To go back no further than the earliest period at which what we still look upon as an artistically valuable combination of separate vocal parts began to be developed, the fifteenth century, we find choirs directed by a leader who held a roll of paper (called a 'Sol-fa'; see *Tonic Sol-fa* 10), or a short stick. It is unlikely that such a 'conductor' would beat a regular two, three, or four, as later became invariable; written music in those days had no 'bar lines'; the phrase (see *Phrase and Sentence*) was the unit, and the

2. JOHANN STRAUSS THE YOUNGER (at an earlier age than in the preceding picture) conducting one of his waltzes in Vienna—with a violin bow and with his back to the orchestra. See *Conducting* 4

1. JOHANN STRAUSS THE YOUNGER in the 1860's. He has adopted the baton

3. EDUARD STRAUSS conducting one of his waltzes in London about 1885. (By 'Spy' in *Vanity Fair*. Cf. *Conducting* 4)

4. JULLIEN. At one of his London Promenade Concerts, 1838–59

5. VERDI conducting, 1879. Note the firm grasp of the 'Field Marshal's Baton'. (From *Vanity Fair*)

6. COSTA conducting in London, 1872, with a combination of baton and keyboard. (By 'Spy' in *Vanity Fair*)

7. WEBER CONDUCTING AT COVENT GARDEN in 1826. The occasion is a concert performance of portions of *Der Freischütz*. He is using a roll of paper. (Contemporary sketch by J. Hayter)

8. SIR HENRY WOOD London's leading conductor from 1904 to 1944

9. SAFONOF. (For his prophecy concerning the disuse of the baton see *Conducting* 5)

PLATE 45   CONCERTS AND CONCERT HALLS, II

See the Articles *Concert* on pages 227–33, and *Concert Halls* on pages 234–6, as also Plates 43 and 46, facing pages 225 and 256

1. ARGYLL ROOMS, LONDON
See *Concert* 8

2. EUROPE'S OLDEST CONCERT HALL, OXFORD
(1748; still in use). See *Concert* 9

3. ST. JAMES'S HALL, LONDON (1858–1905). See *Concert* 8

4. ROYAL ALBERT HALL, LONDON
(Built 1871)

5. QUEEN ELIZABETH HALL, LONDON
(Built 1967)

phrases of the various 'parts' or voices often overlapped in an intricate way; nevertheless, a 'pulse' or 'beat' was felt, and probably the main part of a conductor's duty was to set the right tempo at the outset, to restore a unanimous beat when the singers seemed in danger of parting company, and, from a knowledge of the composition as a whole, to bring in voices accurately and properly at their 'entries'. Yet where a crescendo is felt to be desirable it is natural for the beating arm to take a longer sweep, a rallentando at the final cadence must often have seemed suitable, with necessarily a slackening of the motions of the arm, and so it is evident that a conductor of five hundred years ago cannot have acted completely differently from one of today.

The practice of beating with a roll of paper or baton continued and, indeed, though other methods have also been used and for certain periods in certain places have superseded it, has at no time been universally abandoned. In a picture of the organ loft of Bach's church of St. Thomas, Leipzig, in 1710 (thirteen years before Bach came there), we see a gorgeously bewigged personage, probably Bach's predecessor, Kuhnau (q.v.), wielding a roll of paper before a varied force of bowed instrument players, a lute player, a horn player, a trumpeter, a kettledrummer, an organist, and some choralists. In Walther's *Musikalisches Lexikon* (1732) we see a similar group. Leigh Hunt, in 1822, found the roll of paper in use in Pisa Cathedral, noisily wielded by a conductor who 'did not seem much to rely upon his singers by the noise he made in beating time', since 'his vehement roll of paper sounded like the cracking of a whip'. Over seventy years later C. Abdy-Williams (*Musical Times*, October 1895) described a performance of Rossini's *Barber of Seville* which he heard in that same city:

'The conductor had to beat time on his desk so often in order to keep his forces together, that he had a small sheet of copper fastened on it to save wearing it out. . . . He struck this at the first beat of every bar in the opera.'

These obtrusive practices were apparently long common. Many conductors were wont to beat audibly upon a desk or with a long baton upon the floor. The great Lully (q.v.), in 1687 whilst conducting a *Te Deum* for the recovery from illness of Louis XIV, brought on an illness of his own from which he speedily died; he was thumping out the time on the floor with a long baton and struck his foot, which developed an abscess. Eighty years later Rousseau, in his *Dictionary of Music* (1767), in speaking despitefully of the musical performances of the opera in Paris as compared with those of the opera-houses in certain other European capitals, mentions as one of the faults of the conductor 'le bruit insupportable de son bâton qui couvre et amortit tout l'effet de la Symphonie' ('the unbearable noise of his baton [on a desk,] which covers up and deadens the whole effect of the

orchestra'). Three years later Beethoven was born.

For early eighteenth-century girl conductors in Venice see *Schools of Music*.

3. Conducting from the Harpsichord and Organ. And how did Beethoven conduct? In his younger days according to the manner that had become accepted in his country and elsewhere—at the harpsichord. The old system of a figured bass (q.v.), from which a performer on a keyed instrument played a background to all the music, was not yet extinct, and even when a figured bass was no longer provided a musician at the harpsichord, with the score before him, directed the orchestral activities. As a child of twelve Beethoven served as 'Cembalist im Orchester' (i.e. as orchestral harpsichordist) in the opera band of his patron, the Elector of Cologne. His master, Neefe, was official head of the opera and would presumably control rehearsals and undertake the general direction of performers on the stage and elsewhere, but to the boy would fall the duty of keeping the band together and helping to bring about the 'interpretation' of the music indicated by his superior at rehearsals. Or it may be that the common practice was followed of having two harpsichords—one for the figured bass player and the other for the conductor (in this case Neefe), who would play here and there when necessary, to dictate the tempi, etc. (For a conductor at the organ see allusion to Haydn at Oxford, below.)

4. Conducting with Violin and Bow (p. 240, pl. **44.** 2, 3). As the keyboard background to concerted music fell more out of usage the functions of direction were partially or completely handed over to the leading violinist, or, perhaps, in some cases, it would be more correct to say that the director now took up the violin and controlled his forces by playing the leading part or by beating with his bow, as passing circumstances demanded; usually the keyboard player was also retained, apparently as an additional means of 'pulling things together' when necessary. When Haydn appeared in London (1791 and 1794) he and his impresario, the fine violinist Salomon, jointly kept the orchestra together in this way—the composer at a piano. At Oxford Haydn conducted one of his symphonies from the organ.[1]

The German title of what the British call 'Leader', or 'First Violin', or 'Principal Violin', is 'Konzertmeister' (now generally adopted in

[1] In the very year when Haydn was first seen in London we find an allusion to time-beating in *The Present State of Music in London, 1791*, by William Jackson (q.v.):
'Instrumental music has been of late carried to so great perfection in London, by the consummate skill of the performers, that any attempt to beat the time would justly be considered as entirely needless. I am sorry to remark that the attention of the audience, at *one* concert, has been interrupted by the vulgarity of this exploded practice.'
(It may quite well be that the time-beating referred to in this passage was of the audible sort. See section 2 above.)

America as 'Concertmaster'), and is probably a relic of those days, as is also the general acceptance of the chief violinist's position as the representative of the orchestra in negotiations with conductor or management and his free access to the conductor's room—a comfort and honour not enjoyed by the other instrumentalists. As it is probably today realized by few musicians up to how recent a date the 'leader' or 'concertmaster' insisted upon exercising his function in the spirit of the full sense of those titles, it may be well to close this section of the article with a protest made just half a century before the first issue of the present work (by Dr. William Spark, organist of Leeds Town Hall, in his *Musical Memories*, 1888; this protest was probably prompted by Spark's own experiences of the Leeds Musical Festivals).

'I cannot but think that the purity of style of some of our best violinists has been impaired, while that of several of the old school has become barbarous, from the habit of strong bowing, grown habitual through the supposed necessity of making the fiddle growl, grumble, shout, scold, and admonish the arrant propensities of other instruments in the band. If it were not that the whole beauty of a performance is frequently marred by the intermittent playing of the leader, now executing a few bars pleasantly enough, anon giving a fortissimo plunge, with a rasp as musical as the sharpening of a saw, then revolving convulsively on his axis and waving his bow to beat time, or, to all appearance, to menace some unlucky wight with a rap on the knuckles, and again bowing away with a forty-fiddler power—if, I say, we were not conscious that all this is ruinous to the smooth and regular flow of harmony, we might regard it as a series of sportive feats, performed by the leader with a celerity that astonished the beholder.

'Such is the love of power, that, although the exchange of the position of leader for that of first violinist places the artist in a far better position for the exercise of his musical skill and taste, yet there is no doubt that many performances are marred in consequence of the reluctance of the gentleman who has *violino primo* to take the time and general reading of a composition from the conductor.'

5. The Reintroduction of the Baton

(p. 240, pl. **44.** 1, 7). By the time Beethoven had come to mature manhood direction from a keyboard instrument and direction by the chief violinist (both of them, as it were, direction from *within* the band) were, here and there at any rate, giving way to our modern system of direction by a god descended from on high with an all-compelling wand. We read that 'at a *pianissimo* Beethoven would crouch down so as to be hidden by his desk, and then as the *crescendo* grew would gradually rise, beating all the time, until at the *fortissimo* he would spring into the air as if wishing to float on the clouds'. This extravagance of personal display (which partakes somewhat of the nature of expressive ballet or of a sort of early Dalcroze exhibition) was natural and instinctive with Beethoven; he was lost in the music and oblivious of the audience—which probably cannot be so safely affirmed today of every conductor who indulges in something approaching a like excess of gesture.

After a period in which orchestras had been controlled by pianist and violinist (i.e. by two of the actual players themselves, whatever their superior authority) they did not take kindly to the control of a conductor at a desk; this was especially true, perhaps, of London players, but the repeated experiments of various conductors from 1820 to 1830 seem to have convinced them. When Spohr had to direct one of his symphonies for the London Philharmonic Society in 1820 he found that he was supposed to sit at the pianoforte, and, moreover, to share the responsibilities with the leading violinist; he insisted on conducting from the desk with a baton, and this seems to have been the first instance of such a proceeding at any orchestral concert in London.[1] Mendelssohn at a concert of this Society in 1829 conducted his C minor symphony with a baton: eighteen years later (1847) when he conducted with a baton the first London performance of *Elijah*, *The Times* critic complained, 'Mr Perry, the leader, was constantly beating time with his fiddlestick in such a manner as to obstruct the view of the Conductor and to confuse the attention of the instrumentalists.'

There is a rather curious apparent conflict between the statements concerning Mendelssohn's conducting of his C minor symphony in 1829. In a letter to his family next day he records that at the rehearsal he had conducted with a specially made 'white stick', yet in referring to the concert itself he says 'old John Cramer led me to the pianoforte like a young lady'. The *Morning Post* report says 'Mr. Mendelssohn conducted his Sinfonia with a baton'. Can it be that at the concert he sat at the pianoforte (conforming to the old custom) yet used a baton instead of the keyboard as had been usual? It will be noted from the paragraph below that he was not accustomed to beat time throughout a movement, so that he may have preferred to sit at the pianoforte rather than stand at a desk as Spohr had done (as also Weber in 1826: see p. 240, pl. **44.** 7).

In a symphony Mendelssohn is said to have beaten time merely for the first few bars of each movement, then listening and applauding with the audience; for a special effect (e.g. some crescendo or rallentando not shown in the music copies) he would momentarily resume the baton. He was, by the way, the first conductor of the famous Gewandhaus concerts at Leipzig to use a baton and to insist upon directing both the choral and orchestral forces, and he had trouble in abolishing an old understanding there whereby the conductor was responsible for the doings of the choir, and the leading violinist, with his bow, for those of the orchestra. In 1853 Schumann had opposi-

[1] This is Spohr's own statement in his autobiography (written nearly thirty years later). Doubt has been cast on its accuracy, and Mr. Arthur Jacobs (*Music and Letters*, Oct. 1950) shows reason for believing that the incident occurred merely at a rehearsal.

tion at Düsseldorf on the ostensible ground that in training a choir he would use a baton instead of sitting at the pianoforte (but he was a bad batonist and actually thought he had done a clever thing in attaching his baton to his wrist with a string so that he should not drop it). From these later instances it will be seen that even after the introduction of the baton the full recognition of its value was slow.

Old prints show that in the early days of baton conducting the conductor often (or usually) faced not the orchestra but the audience (see p. 240, pl. **44**, for some examples). Rimsky-Korsakof records that until, in 1865, Wagner went to Moscow and set an example this was the regular practice there.[1]

Tempo rubato (see *Rubato*) was, of course, practically impossible in orchestral performance until conductors began to face their forces and direct them in the present-day manner.

Certain conductors have latterly reintroduced the practice of conducting with the hands, without baton, which Cipriani Potter (q.v.) made familiar to London audiences in the mid-nineteenth century. Safonof was one of the first to do this, and in 1906 he said, 'Mark my words: in ten or fifteen years there will be no batons in orchestras'. That period has, however, elapsed and a great many batons remain, the advantage of having, as that great conductor put it, 'ten sticks instead of one' not having been widely admitted (p. 240, pl. **44**. 9). Stokowski (q.v.) is a notable example of a 'batonless conductor'.

6. Influences leading to Refinement—Stamitz and von Bülow (p. 401, pl. **70**. 1). Two German influences have been active in leading to the prevalence of the element of personal display on the part of the conductor—the Mannheim school of the eighteenth century and the example of von Bülow at Meiningen and elsewhere in the nineteenth.

Under Johann Stamitz (1717–57) the electoral band at Mannheim reached a hitherto unheard-of pitch of excellence, and the high reputation it won was maintained under later directors such as Cannabich (1731–98). The English musical historian, Burney, travelling in 1772, records the wonderful ability of the individual members of the orchestra ('an army of generals'), and both the delicacy and the force of the playing ('it was here that the *Crescendo* and *Diminuendo* had birth; and the *Piano*, which was chiefly used as an echo, with which it was generally synonymous, as well as the *Forte*, were found to be musical *colours* which had their shades as much as red or blue in painting'). It is evident that perfections

such as these could be introduced only by the compelling personality of one able man, and from this place and period probably dates the origin of the 'Virtuoso Conductor', in our own days become something of both a blessing and a curse.

Von Bülow's example was before the world in three important German centres (Munich, Hanover, Meiningen) from 1864 to 1885, and in his tours during this period and for a few years after. He set another new standard by his attention to detail and the fire of his performances, but (accepting Weingartner's opinion) 'with Bülow began musical sensationalism'. There has perhaps, in modern times, rarely been a quieter conductor than Weingartner. Strauss, in early years vehement, later came to declare 'conducting can be done quietly'.

7. The Modern Conductorless Orchestra. Rushing to another extreme, the attempt has been made to dispense entirely with a conductor. In 1922 the Moscow orchestra 'Persimfans' was formed, and for a few years it was recognized and subsidized by the Soviet Government. From the first it employed no conductor, the theory (probably partly the result of political views) being that the members of an orchestra have the right to the same degree of personal freedom and responsibility as those of a chamber-music combination. Members were expected to study the full orchestral score, rehearsals were abundant and prolonged (as they are in chamber music), and every member in turn was expected to put down his instrument and consider himself an audience. This way of preparing for performance seems to be more educational than economical. The experiment is said to have succeeded (at any rate up to a point), but it is alleged that the members of the orchestra were all experienced artists who had played the classics repeatedly under many conductors, and the task of forming an orchestra of young players on these methods would appear to be (to say the least) very difficult. Other orchestras were founded on this model, but after a few years they tended to diminish in numbers.

It may be pointed out that the Russian experiment originated from the same democratic feeling (much exaggerated) that largely led to the opposition to the introduction (or reintroduction) of the baton in the early nineteenth century.

In the late 1920s New York had for a short time a conductorless orchestra. So in 1928 had Budapest (see *Weiner*).

8. The Practice of Conducting. Like every art, that of conducting has two sides, the aesthetic and the technical.

On the aesthetic side, the requirements are the same as those in any other branch of musical performance—roughly speaking, the securing of a performance that would satisfy the composer, the ideal performance that re-expresses what he felt himself to be expressing

---

[1] In Britain conductors of the 'popular' seaside type continued the practice much later than that, e.g. Rivière at Colwyn Bay, a conductor named Delicat, at Margate, whom the present writer saw so conducting in 1901, and one Henton at Eastbourne, who in 1912 was the cause of a stormy meeting of the Town Council, it being complained 'Eastbourne spends nearly £4,000 a year on its music and is too big a place to allow of trifling in that way'. (*Observer*, Sept. 1912).

M

as he penned the work. This part of the subject is covered by the article *Interpretation* later.

On the technical side, there are the four requirements of knowing the score, knowing the performers, knowing the instruments, and knowing the use of the baton and of the hands. As for knowing the performers, this is largely a matter of human sympathy and of tact, which cannot be taught, though it can be practised. (Some of the best practitioners in the less exalted ranges of orchestral and choral conducting are experienced school teachers, who understand how to secure easy class discipline.) As for knowing the instruments, see list of the various articles on such in this *Companion*, given at the end of the article *Orchestra and Orchestration*. (The would-be conductor should if possible get some actual experience in orchestral playing and choral singing, however small.) As for knowing the use of the baton, it is useful carefully to watch the various motions of able conductors, especially at rehearsal, and also to practise assiduously before a mirror with a score and a gramophone.

Clarity and grace are equally necessary

qualities in a conductor; undue multiplication of signs makes muddled performance, and stiff, awkward gestures kill all 'flow'—and perhaps flow is the greatest foundational quality of good musical performance in any medium. Details cannot have too much care bestowed upon them, and yet they must remain subordinate to the 'all-through' impression. Sir Adrian Boult puts this well in his *Handbook on the Technique of Conducting* (1921): 'The audience should be made to feel that the whole score is laid out on two gigantic pages which can be seen at a glance without even the disturbance of turning over.'

In closing this article it may be of interest to recall to the reader's mind the immense change that has come over the whole conception of orchestral conducting by asking him to reflect for a moment on the implication of a statement (by the well-informed Sir George Grove) concerning a performance of Beethoven's Ninth Symphony—during Beethoven's lifetime:

'At Leipzig, on March 6, 1826, it was played from the parts alone, the conductor never having seen the score.'

CONDUCTUS. A type of sacred or secular choral composition of the twelfth and thirteenth centuries. Right through this period the art of composing was, in general, the art of adding voice-parts to an existing melody or canto fermo (see *Harmony* 4–7); this existing melody was usually a piece of plainsong, but in the 'Conductus' was either original or else a secular melody. Apparently the actual words sung were confined to the voice singing the canto fermo, the other voices (usually two in number) vocalizing—on the chief vowel of the words of the canto fermo.

All these terms of the early days of harmonized music seem to be used in somewhat different ways by different contemporary writers, but the above very general definition covers most cases of the use of this one.

CONFITEOR. See *Mass* 3 c.

CONFRÉRIE DE LA PASSION. See *Passion Music* 1.

CONFREY, ZEZ. See *Shimmy*.

CONFUTATIS. See *Requiem*.

CONGA. A modern Cuban dance with a good deal of syncopation interspersed. Cf. *Rumba*.

CONGREGATIONAL CHURCHES AND MUSIC

1. Introduction. If the conditions under which musical life has developed in the Congregational churches are to be understood, it is necessary that some slight historical sketch of the body should be given.

The definite laying down of the principles of Independency (or Congregationalism) in church economy can be most conveniently dated from the writings of Robert Browne between the years 1578 and 1586. By 1592 Sir Walter Raleigh declared in the House of Commons that there were 20,000 Brownists in England—possibly an exaggeration, but as it was considered credible we may assume that the figure does not give an utterly false impression. Severe persecution drove many abroad, and Holland offered the nearest asylum. In 1620 many of the refugees went

further and, as the *Mayflower* emigrants, founded their colony at Plymouth, New England. In 1628 Puritan members of the Church of England (not 'Brownists') founded the Massachusetts Bay Colony and, cut off from their original Church and in any case out of sympathy with its episcopal method of government and its liturgy and ritual, they also became in effect Independents. Indeed, it may be said that here Independency, fleeing from the principles of a state religion, became one itself.

With the Commonwealth, Independency in England passed from a condition of persecution to one of control jointly with Presbyterianism. With the Restoration it came again under persecution, which continued until the Toleration Act of 1689. (The civil and religious disabilities of Nonconformists were not finally removed until the nineteenth century.) During the eighteenth century a good many Independent churches became in doctrine Unitarian. But the Methodist movement influenced Independency, tending to communicate new life to it.

It is of the essence of Independency or Congregationalism that each church is free as to doctrine and form of service. That is indeed the meaning of both words; each *congregation* is *independent*. The local body of believers, organized as a church, is autonomous, and whatever collective arrangements may, for convenience, be made are a secondary matter. In 1965 there were some 200,000 members in England and Wales and 100,000 in the United States.

2. From the Elizabethan Period to the Commonwealth and Restoration. It will be understood that amongst a religious body purposely loosely organized, possessing no liturgy or imposed order of service and no written common creed, the development of a uniform system in the employment of music in worship is impossible. It will be understood, too, that the persecutions of the first century of this body's existence in England and the obscurity and social inferiority thrust upon it are also adverse factors. The earlier Independents were led by a group of university men; later, as Nonconformists unable to subscribe to the Articles of the Church of England they were excluded from the universities and had to organize their own 'Academies'—a condition of things which lasted into the nineteenth century. As Oxford and Cambridge were for long amongst the most active centres of musical life in England this deprivation had an adverse effect upon musical culture.

From the first and throughout, however, music of a simple character has been employed in the services of the Independent churches. That Robert Browne, already mentioned, who may, in a sense, be looked upon as the founder of Independency, was himself 'a singular good lutenist'; in his later life, when he had reverted to the Episcopalian ministry (though even then he seems to have maintained the meetings of a local 'Brownist' group in his rectory), he 'made his son Timothy bring his viol to church and play the bass to the psalms that were sung'. (Cf. *Anglican Parish Church Music* 4 for the common practice, for several centuries, of supplying or strengthening the bass by the use of instruments.)

The early Independent congregations in most cases made great use of the metrical psalms, as did all English-speaking Protestant bodies for two hundred years and more. They probably employed the psalm books current at the time amongst the Anglican and other bodies (see *Hymns and Hymn Tunes* 5) but frequently showed a desire to secure what they would consider a more faithful version. Hence Ainsworth, the refugee pastor at Leyden, produced his admirable book, which the Pilgrim Fathers took to America with them. It was doubtless from this book that they sang on that parting day when:

'They that stayed at Leyden feasted us that were to go, at our pastor's house, being large; where we refreshed ourselves, after tears, with singing of psalms, making joyful melody in our hearts, as well as with the voice, there being many of our congregation very expert in music; and indeed it was the sweetest melody that ever mine ears heard' (Winslow's *Brief Narration*).

Twenty years later the neighbours of the Pilgrims, the Massachusetts Bay Puritan party, still seeking the perfect version that so many (for two centuries and more) were seeking, produced their 'Bay Psalm Book' (for these two books see *Hymns and Hymn Tunes* 11). As the 'Bay' book had eighteen English editions it is probable that it came into large use in the English Independent congregations, amongst others; the very fact that Sternhold and Hopkins was the authorized book of the Church of England would perhaps be likely to suggest a preference for some other than that. In 1657 the record of the church at Beccles says: 'It was agreed that the New England translation of the Psalms be made use of by the Church at their times of breaking bread.'

Amongst prominent Independents who showed a great love for secular music during the mid-seventeenth century were Cromwell and Milton (for Milton may be considered an Independent). But the love of music was common amongst the Puritans (see *Puritans and Music*). John Owen, the great Independent divine, Vice-Chancellor of Oxford during the Commonwealth, who had in youth been a lutenist, appointed as Professor of Music in the University his former master, the famous lutenist Wilson (q.v.). Anthony Wood, a music-lover but a bitter anti-Puritan, says of the Independents and Presbyterians at Oxford at this period, 'They encouraged instrumental music and some there were that had musick meetings every week in their chambers'.

3. The Eighteenth Century and Hymns. After the Restoration we find hymns as well as metrical psalms in some use amongst the Independents, though for fear of the officers of the law singing had often to be omitted or restrained, as at Southwark in 1684, where 'we sang a psalm in a low voice'. Then, with the accession of William and Mary in 1689, came toleration, and the worshippers could at last sing out.

Isaac Watts (p. 485, pl. **86**. 5), at the age of twenty, and before he had obtained his first pastorate as an Independent minister, began the writing of hymns intended by superiority to supersede those then current, and of metrical psalm versions of a free kind, omitting the imprecatory passages and introducing New Testament thought. His book of hymns appeared in 1707 and his book of psalms in 1719: they were often reissued bound together. Such hymns as 'There is a land of pure delight', 'Jesus shall reign where'er the sun', 'When I survey the wondrous cross' (see *Hymns and Hymn Tunes* 7), and 'O God, our help in ages past' are now found in all Protestant hymn-books throughout the English-singing world. Watts also wrote the earliest children's hymn-book (1715); it averaged an edition every eighteen months or so for the next century and a half. As a result of Watts's publications there was established at the King's Weigh House Chapel in London a regular lecture on 'How to sing'.

Until 1784 Watts's hymns had almost a monopoly amongst the Independent congregations, but in that year George Burder issued a supplement to them chosen from various sources, and thence onwards various collections were used. Watts, however, is the virtual 'creator of the modern English hymn'.

The *Collection of Tunes* edited by Caleb Ashworth, an Independent, was issued in 1760 (see *Baptist Churches and Music* 4); Wainwright's still current tune to 'Christians, awake!' appeared for the first time in this. Henceforward new books of hymns and of tunes were pretty frequent and a certain number of the tunes most widely loved today appeared in these books issued by and for the Independents.

We have Wesley's evidence for the existence of a certain fault in the singing of the Independents, for they, with the Baptists and Presbyterians, must have been in his mind when in 1758 he included amongst the faults of 'Dissent' (he being a clergyman of the Church of England and his followers at that date a 'Society' and not a dissenting 'Church') the slow and drawling singing. From his brother, Charles Wesley, we learn that as regards approval of music as a secular recreation the spirit of the Dissenters (including presumably the Independents) had greatly changed; he mentions their adverse attitude when he is reassuring the mother of a musical child, who had had doubts raised in her mind by 'some good people's aversion to music' (see *Puritans and Music* 9). This aversion was a phase of eighteenth-century evangelical religion and lasted in some degree well into the nineteenth century.

4. The Introduction of Organs. We may suppose that there was no organ at this date in any Independent church building; there were as yet none in the Wesleys' own buildings and very few in the churches of the Establishment. Later, organs came gradually into use. That of Surrey Chapel, Blackfriars Road, London, where under the famous Rev. Rowland Hill (cf. *Rule, Britannia!*), Benjamin Jacob (p. 784, pl. **131.** 2) was organist from 1794 to 1823, may be considered to be the instrument by means of which Bach was first introduced to the British public, since it was upon it that Benjamin Jacob, Samual Wesley (q.v.), and Crotch (q.v.) gave their series of Bach organ performances in 1809 and the following years.

Wesley also played some of Bach's violin sonatas at the chapel. The programmes of these remarkable occasions are preserved at the Royal College of Music, and Wesley's correspondence with Jacob has been published. It is considered that what we now call the 'organ recital' had its British beginnings in these performances in an Independent place of worship. No recital audience nowadays, it is to be feared, would stay out such programmes —forty to fifty items lasting from three to four hours!

5. Nineteenth-Century Activities. The democratic development of music through the opportunity offered by Nonconformist choirs will be found illustrated under *Baptist Churches and Music* and *Methodism and Music*. Mrs. Gaskell, in her *Life of Charlotte Brontë*, shows that at times the democratic spirit flared up into rebellion against authority. She is speaking of West Yorkshire about 1830:

'A scene which took place at the Lower Chapel at Heckmondwike will give you some idea of the people at that time. When a newly-married couple made their appearance at chapel, it was the custom to sing the Wedding Anthem, just after the last prayer, and as the congregation was quitting the chapel. The band of singers who performed this ceremony expected to have money given them, and often passed the following night in drinking; at least, so said the minister of the place, and he determined to put an end to this custom. In this he was supported by many members of the chapel and congregation, but so strong was the democratic element, that he met with the most violent opposition, and was often insulted when he went into the street. A bride was expected to make her first appearance, and the minister told the singers not to perform the anthem. On their declaring they would, he had the large pew which they usually occupied locked; they broke it open; from the pulpit he told the congregation that instead of their singing a hymn, he would read a chapter. Hardly had he uttered the first word, before up rose the singers, headed by a tall, fierce-looking weaver, who gave out a hymn, and all sang it at the very top of their voices, aided by those of their friends who were in the chapel. Those who disapproved of the conduct of the singers, and sided with the minister, remained seated till the hymn was finished. Then he gave out the chapter again, read it, and preached. He was about to conclude with prayer, when up started the singers and screamed forth another hymn. These disgraceful scenes were continued for many weeks, and so violent was the feeling, that the different parties could hardly keep from blows as they came through the chapel yard. The minister, at last, left the place, and along with him went many of the most temperate and respectable part of the congregation, and the singers remained triumphant.'

The Independents of the nineteenth century were responsible for certain definite efforts to improve church music, and indeed to improve the general popular culture of music.

One of the pioneers was the Revd. John Waite, a blind minister who devoted himself to the promulgation of the idea that congregations could be taught to sing in parts. He brought out a series of tune books, called

Hallelujah, in staff notation with a numeral system added, and travelled to the large towns holding meetings of congregations and teaching them to sing.

The famous Dr. Thomas Binney, minister of the King's Weigh House Chapel, London, from 1829 to 1869, was one of the first to introduce into a Nonconformist church the chanting of the prose psalms.

Union Chapel, Islington, with a large organ and a series of eminent musicians as organists (Gauntlett, Prout, etc.), instituted a psalmody class which began about 1848 and was still active and successful in 1888, at which date between 200 and 300 members of the congregation were paying a fee to be taught to sing their part in the service. A somewhat surprising feature of the services here was the singing of anthems by the congregation. It was reported in 1888, 'The congregation now sing the anthems as generally, easily, and heartily as the hymn tunes'. According to reliable accounts, the singing of this congregation of a thousand people, many of whom had passed through a course of training, was very remarkable, if not unique. Every Christmas Day the congregation performed with great effect a portion of Handel's *Messiah*. An Anthem Book was issued in 1872 and led to congregational anthem singing becoming fairly common in other parts of the country—with generally indifferent advantage, since other congregations that introduced the book usually lacked the singing-class preparation which made the Union Chapel results possible.

In all this is to be seen the hand of the Revd. Henry Allon, D.D. (1818–92), who was connected with the church from 1844 to his death nearly half a century later. The many hymn-tune books, the chant book, and other such publications of which he was editor had a very large circulation and contributed to an upward trend in the music of Congregationalism and nonconformity generally. (His son, Henry Erskine Allon, 1864–97, was a fine musician whose promising career as a composer was brought to an end by an early death.)

The King's Weigh House Chapel, at about the same period (cf. reference under 3), also made rather remarkable experiments in the development of singing, organizing large psalmody classes, publishing music books, and encouraging the congregation (apparently with considerable success) to take part in music of a type that amongst most religious bodies, then and now, would be considered to require a trained choir. The intelligent use of the Anglican chant was a feature of the singing. Carr's Lane Church, Birmingham, was another Congregational church that exercised a wide musical influence by its example and its publications.

This assembly of a few of the facts concerning the popularizing musical activities of the Independents during the middle part of the nineteenth century is surely rather striking. But their greatest contribution was made through the instrumentality of one of their ministers, John Curwen (1816–80), who, desirous of improving congregational singing, introduced a more scientific and practical method of sight-singing than the world had yet seen, publishing a hymn-tune book (1852), a number of useful textbooks, and a great quantity of oratorios and other music in a simple notation accessible to all (see *Tonic Sol-fa*); to-day the hymn-tune books of practically every British religious body can be obtained in this notation.

At the present time music in Congregational churches in England is on a par with that of other Nonconformist bodies. Not possessing the liturgy, the financial endowments, or the long-standing musical tradition of the Church of England, or its cathedrals and their equipment, all such bodies must ever be at some disadvantage. Fine organs and good choirs are, however, common, and there is a general level of achievement that would satisfy the sixteenth- and seventeenth-century music-loving Puritan ancestors of the Congregationalists of to-day. They would approve the music, though they might think some of it out of place in church.

CONJUNCT MOTION. See *Motion.*

CONNSONATA. See *Electric* 4.

CONSECUTIVES. See *Harmony* 4, 16, 22.

CONSEQUENT. See *Canon.*

CONSERVATORIO (It.); **CONSERVATOIRE** (Fr.). See *Schools of Music.*

CONSERVER (Fr.). 'To preserve.' So *Conservant le rhythme*, 'preserving rhythm'.

CONSOLE. See *Organ* 1 (end), 4.

CONSOLE PIANO. A term used by American manufacturers for a type of miniature upright piano.

CONSONANCE. See references given under *Concord (or Consonance).*

CONSONANTS. See *Voice* 11; *Acoustics* 7.

CON SORDINO (It.). 'With mute' (see *Mute*).

CONSORT. This is the old English for the later word 'Concert' and bears the earlier sense of a body of performers in ensemble and the later one of a performance by several players or singers simultaneously (see *Concert* 1).

A *Consort of Viols* in the sixteenth and earlier seventeenth centuries meant a group playing on the various-sized instruments of the viol family (see reference to 'Chest of Viols' under *Viol Family* 3).

A *Whole Consort* was one in which all the instruments were of one kind, i.e. all wind or all strings, a *Broken Consort* one in which this was not so. Shakespeare mentions 'broken music' in *Henry V*, Act v, Scene ii, and elsewhere. Matthew Locke (q.v.) has a set of *Compositions for Broken and Whole Consorts of 2, 3, 4, 5, and 6 parts* (1672).

CONTE (Fr.). 'Tale.' Sometimes used as a 'fancy title' for a piece of instrumental music.

CONTEMPORARY MUSIC SOCIETY. See *Festival* 3.

CONTES D'HOFFMANN (Offenbach). See *Tales of Hoffmann*.

CONTEST. See *Competitions in Music*.

'CONTINENTAL' FINGERING. See *Fingering* 6.

CONTINUO. See *Figured Bass*.

CONTRABASS, CONTRABASSO. See *Violin Family* 2 d; *Organ* 14 III.

CONTRABASS CLARINET. See *Clarinet Family* 4 g.

CONTRABASSOON. See *Oboe Family* 5 d.

CONTRADANZA. See *Country Dance*.

CONTRAFAGOTTO. See *Oboe Family* 5 d.

CONTRALTIST. See *Voice* 5.

CONTRALTO (saxhorn). See *Saxhorn and Flügelhorn Families* 2 b.

CONTRALTO voice. See *Voice* 17; *Alto Voice*.

CONTRAPPUNTO ALLA MENTE. See *Descant* (near the end).

CONTRAPUNTAL. The adjective of 'Counterpoint' (q.v.).

CONTRARY MOTION. See *Motion*.

CONTRA-VIOLIN. A violin for the playing of second violin parts, introduced in 1917 by Herbert Newbould, of Jersey, Channel Islands. It is slightly bigger than the normal violin in width and depth, and has somewhat thicker strings, with the result that it acquires an individuality, i.e. it is not a mere 'second violin', but an instrument in its own right like the viola and violoncello. It is said that in the string quartet a great gain is perceptible, and it is argued that a similar gain would be observed in the orchestra were this instrument there adopted. (It is really an unconscious reinvention of an eighteenth-century slightly 'outsize' second violin.)

Cf. *Violin Family* 2 a.

CONTREBASSE (Fr.). Double-bass. See *Violin Family* 2 d, 9.

CONTREBASSON. See *Oboe Family* 5 d.

CONTREDANSE. See *Country Dance*.

CONTROL, CONTROL ROOM (in Radio Broadcasting). See *Broadcasting* 4.

CONUS, GEORGE. Born and died in Moscow, 1862–1933. He was a pupil under Serge Taneief of the Moscow Conservatory and later professor there. He composed orchestral music, songs, pianoforte music, etc., and had great repute as a profound and thoughtful theorist, being the author of a theory of the *Metrotectonical Structure of Musical Tissue*.

(The spellings 'Konyus', 'Konus', and Konius', sometimes seen, are misguided attempts at transliteration from the Russian, the original name being French and spelt as above.)

CONVERSE, FREDERICK SHEPHERD (p. 1056, pl. **171.** 5). Born at Newton, Mass., in 1871 and died near Boston, Mass., in 1940, aged sixty-nine.

His early traditions were those of Chadwick and Paine (his American teachers) and Rheinberger of Munich. Later he found a freer and more personal style. His *The Pipe of Desire* was the first American opera to be performed at the Metropolitan Opera House, New York (1910).

He also wrote symphonic works; chamber music; *Job*, a dramatic poem for soloists, chorus, and orchestra; piano pieces and songs; and an orchestral witticism (inspired by Honegger's *Pacific 231*) entitled *Flivver 10,000*.

See reference under *United States* 8.

COOKE.

(1) **HENRY** ('Captain Cooke'). Born probably about 1616 and died at Hampton Court in 1672, aged about fifty-six. He was a choir-boy in the Chapel Royal who, on the outbreak of the Civil War, joined the Royalist forces (hence his title of Captain), and at the Restoration returned to the Chapel Royal as Master of the Children. His boys, amongst whom were Pelham Humfrey (afterwards his son-in-law), John Blow, and Henry Purcell, became quickly famous not only as singers but also as prodigies in instrumental performance and in composition, whilst he himself was very favourably known as a composer of music for stage and church, and as actor and singer. He composed part of the music for Davenant's *Siege of Rhodes* (see *Opera* 13 a).

Both Pepys and Evelyn praise him.

See *Chapel Royal*; *Bagpipe* 3.

(2) **BENJAMIN.** Born in London in 1734 and died there in 1793, aged fifty-eight or fifty-nine. He was organist of Westminster Abbey and there lies buried, with one of the canonic contrivances for which he was famous graven on his monument. His church music and (particularly) his fine glees are still sung.

See references under *Anthem*, Period III; *Organ* 8; also p. 165, pl. **34.** 3.

(3) **THOMAS SIMPSON.** Born in Dublin in 1782 and died in London in 1848, aged sixty-five or sixty-six. He kept a music shop in Dublin and led a theatre orchestra there, and then, gaining success as a tenor vocalist, removed to London, where he was long attached to Drury Lane Theatre. He performed adequately on almost all string, wind, and keyboard instruments, had fame as a teacher of singers (amongst them Sims Reeves), composed and arranged much music for the stage, and left behind him glees that are still popular, notably 'Strike the Lyre'.

(4) **ARNOLD.** Born at Gomersal, Yorks., in 1906. He studied at Cambridge and under Hindemith at the Berlin Hochschule. For a short time he served as Director of Music at the Festival Theatre, Cambridge, and then

passed to Manchester, where he became Professor of Harmony and Counterpoint at its Royal College of Music (1933–8); after war service he settled in London, joining the staff of Trinity College of Music in the same capacity as at the Manchester institution above mentioned. His numerous compositions include many and varied chamber, orchestral, choral, and solo vocal works.

COOLIDGE, MRS. E. S. (1864–1953). See *United States* 5 2; *Festival* 2.

COON SONG. A type of pseudo-Negro song very popular in the early nineteenth century—usually sentimental.

COOPER, MARTIN DU PRÉ. Born at Winchester in 1910. He studied with Wellesz in Vienna and worked as critic of the *London Mercury* (1935), the *Daily Herald* and *Spectator* (1946), and the *Daily Telegraph*. He is the author of books on French music, on Bizet, etc. C.B.E. 1972.

COOPER, JOHN. See *Coperario*.

COPERARIO (or **COPRARIO**) JOHN. Born about 1570 and died in London in 1626, aged about fifty-six. His name, until a visit to Italy changed it, was plain John Cooper. He played the lute and viola da gamba and composed pieces for these instruments and for the organ, songs, music for masques, etc.

His chamber music for viols was especially popular and, according to contemporary accounts, he was a highly influential composer.

See *Masque*.

COPERTO. Italian for 'covered' (plural 'coperti'). Used, for instance, of drums muted by being covered with a cloth, i.e. 'muffled' (but this method is little used now). See *Percussion Family* 2 a, 5 a.

COPLA. A type of Spanish popular poem and song in short verses (see *Seguidilla*). Sometimes it was extemporized. The term is also applied to the solo movements in a *Villancico* (q.v.).

COPLAND, AARON (p. 1068, pl. **175.** 5). (The original family name was Kaplan, the change being due to a mistake by immigration officials at the reception of his family in New York.) He was born in Brooklyn in 1900 and spent his first twenty years there in, as he says, 'a street that can only be described as drab'. He had some early piano lessons and at about the age of fifteen was gradually seized with the idea of becoming a composer. At seventeen he began harmony lessons with Rubin Goldmark (q.v.). At twenty-one he was enabled to go to Paris where he studied with Paul Vidal and then with Nadia Boulanger (q.v.)—becoming the first of her very many American composition students.

In 1924 he returned to his native country and, whilst earning his living as an hotel pianist, composed, at Nadia Boulanger's request, an organ concerto for her to play during her American tour. The production of this work and the acceptance by the League of Composers of two Piano pieces (*The Cat and the Mouse* and a *Passacaglia*) made him known to a large and influential public and definitely established his position in American musical life. Shortly after this he was awarded the first scholarship of the Guggenheim Memorial Foundation, this being renewed for a second year.

A great variety of compositions quickly followed, amongst the earlier ones being a *Dance Symphony* and a *Symphonic Ode*. A new phase opened with the more austere *Piano Variations* (1930), the *Short Symphony* (1933), and the *Statements* (for orchestra, 1935). For a time he adopted a simpler style, calculated to make a wider appeal: amongst the works which belong to this phase are the orchestral *El Salón México* (based on Mexican tunes), the ballet *Billy the Kid* (based on cowboy tunes), and the film compositions, *The City*, *Of Mice and Men*, *Our Town*, and *The Red Pony*.

Then came the ballet, *Appalachian Spring* (commissioned by the Elizabeth Sprague Coolidge Foundation and in 1945 awarded the Pulitzer Prize), and the Third Symphony, first performed (in Boston) by Koussevitzky. Later works such as the Piano Quartet (1950), the *Piano Fantasy* (1960), and the *Connotations for Orchestra* (1962), return to a non-tonal or serial style.

In addition to his compositions Copland has written the books *What to Listen for in Music* and *Our New Music*, etc. He is active as an adviser and 'committee man' in the service of his profession.

See *Ballet* 5; *Concerto* 6 c (1900); *Symphony* 8 (1900); *Jazz* 5; *Opera* 24 f (1954); *History* 9; *Berger, A.*

COPLANDE. See *Dance* 10.

COPPEL (Ger.). 'Coupler' (organ).

COPRARIO. See *Coperario*.

COPRIFUOCO, COPRIFOCO (It.). 'Curfew'; an occasional 'fancy title' for an instrumental composition—sometimes with a bell effect.

COPYISTS. The duties of music copyist have long been, and still are, very important. At one time, of course, the copyist provided the only copies of music put into circulation. From the end of the fifteenth century onwards his functions began to become very gradually less essential to the performance of music, but even today he provides the 'parts' for chamber music and orchestral music where (as is very often the case) it would be too costly to produce them by engraving or similar means.

Many important musicians have held the honourable position of copyist. The young Purcell earned money on occasion by copying music for Westminster Abbey (see the article on this composer). Practically no church music was sung from printed copies in those days.

During the prolific eighteenth century, when symphonies and operas were being poured out at all the major German courts and in the chief

Italian states, the position of the copyist was lucrative. He enjoyed a valuable perquisite in the sale of copies to those who desired them, from which sale the composer received no benefit. Thus when Mozart and his father were in Milan for the performance of the boy's opera *Mithridate*, in 1770, the father wrote home after the first rehearsal, 'The copyist is well satisfied with the work and this promises well, since when the music succeeds he gets more money by the sale of the songs than the composer gets for the whole of the opera'.

In later life Mozart himself wrote from Vienna to the Prussian Ambassador, who had ordered a copy of *The Abduction from the Seraglio*, 'I am very grateful to the Baron for having ordered the copy from *me* and not from the copyist, from whom he could have got it at once by paying a certain sum down'.

Travellers in Italy, from the sixteenth century onwards, often employed music copyists wherever they went. The poet Milton in the early seventeenth century, and the poet Mason in the eighteenth, sent home collections of Italian music.

It is curious to note that after the publication of printed music had been going on for nearly three centuries there came a temporary decline in it and an increase in the activities of copyists. The music catalogue of Breitkopf of Leipzig, of 1755, has more manuscript copies than printed; although he had invented a new process of music printing, of which he was very proud, he yet retained a staff of copyists for the purpose of supplying current compositions that remained unprinted. Burney, writing in Rees's *Cyclopædia* about 1805, says (obviously exaggerating somewhat, at all events as concerns Germany):

'Thirty or forty years ago there was no music published in Italy or Germany; all was manuscript. By which employment so many copyists obtained a livelihood that it was thought a cruelty to shorten labour by the press, as in the first attempts at erecting silk and cotton mills. . . . Cheapness has not been eventually the consequence of musical typography or engraving, as printed music is now dearer than written was early in the last century.'

As late as 1836 Novello, in his list of printed voice and orchestral parts of oratorios, etc., in the advertisement pages of the *Musical World*, placed at the top of it 'In addition to the music here mentioned J. A. Novello has large collections of scores from which MS. parts can be obtained'.

In the middle of the nineteenth century very much English choral music was performed from manuscript. Dr. Joseph Summers, as a boy chorister of Wells Cathedral in the 1850s, had the duty of copying music and has recorded that he was constantly employed in making for visitors copies of the anthems and services they had heard and enjoyed. 'In 1851 it was not so easy to obtain printed music, and then only folio size, which was very expensive.'

Burney's acquaintance Rousseau (q.v.) long gained a large part of his living by music copying, an occupation he never despised, whatever fame might come to him as man of letters, philosopher, and composer. In his *Musical Dictionary* of 1767 he inserts on the subject an article that he admits to be disproportionately long, being perhaps somewhat carried away by his interest in the subject. He points out the difficulties of the use of music type and says that music engraving, though a little better than type-printing, is still subject to the inconvenience that one pulls off what turns out to be too many or too few copies, whereas the copyist works strictly to the orders received: moreover, as he adds, if you engrave the score people will demand parts, and if parts they will demand the score, whereas when copying you can give them just what they require. Further, printing processes of any kind, he says, can only be safely ventured upon with music that has already won popularity. He adds something which partly confirms the statement of Burney just quoted:

'In Italy, where they make the most music, they have long ago done away with the type-printing of music without replacing it by engraving, from which I judge that in the opinion of experts the custom of copying is the more convenient.'

He then goes on to point out the importance of *good* copying, i.e. not merely correct but well arranged for the performer: 'The cleverest copyist is the one whose music is performed with the most ease without the performer guessing why.'

He gives elaborate rules for copyists, beginning with the choice of a strong white paper that will not be pierced by the pen and an ink that is black but 'neither shiny nor gummy'. He insists on clear ruled lines not quite as black as the writing upon them, and condemns the makers of the manuscript music paper of that day. He discusses the best order of instruments in a full score—and so on.

And, being a bit of a composer himself, it occurs to him to say that if the copyist is a better composer than the man whose work he is copying he should nevertheless refrain from touching up his composition.

And to all these (and many other) rules he cautiously prefaces the admission, 'I know how much I may damage myself if anyone compares my work with my own rules'.

An advertisement of 1769 shows the profession of copyist in full activity in the American colonies. John Gualdo, 'the wine merchant from Italy but late from London', announces that he sells instruments and 'adapts and composes' music and 'keeps a servant boy who at a moment's notice copies any desired fashionable piece of music'.

For cognate subjects see the articles *Printing of Music*; *Publishing of Music*.
Cf. *Pergolese*.

COPYRIGHT AND PERFORMING RIGHT

1. Britain.   2. United States of America.   3. Reciprocity between Britain and other Countries.

1. Britain. Copyright means the sole right to produce or reproduce in any material form an original literary, dramatic, or musical work. So far as Britain is concerned no such right was enforceable until the passing of the first Copyright Act in 1709, and even then protection was extremely restricted, musical works being inadequately safeguarded and other artistic work receiving no protection at all until many years later. This Act has had many successors, the one of 1956 being that now in force. The scope of protection takes in such modern methods as, for instance, Mechanical Reproduction in the shape of gramophone records, films, and the like. It provides that an author's, artist's, or composer's work is his own property without any formality of registration. He and his heirs can control not only publication, but also public performance of a play or musical composition, etc., or can assign the right of control to a publisher or other person. The period of control is the life of the author, artist, or composer plus 50 years—with some conditional exceptions.

As regards the right to **Mechanical Reproduction,** once a composer or author has allowed this, other persons or bodies than the one to whom or to which he has allowed it may also reproduce, but a royalty payment (of 6¼ per cent. of the retail price in the case of works first published after 1 July 1912, with a minimum of ¾d.) has to be made for every copy of the reproduction (disk, roll, etc.) issued. Thus a composer can absolutely bar all reproductions of a work, but if he has once shown that he has no objection in principle to such he has thrown open the right to all who wish to reproduce it. There are, of course, certain conditions laid down.

Performing Right (i.e. the sole right to give a performance in public), which prior to the 1911 Act was a separate right, is now an integral part of copyright. It can be granted to another party only by licence or assignment from the composer, or from the person or body to whom or to which he has assigned his performing right. This assignment may either be entire or partial, i.e. the whole right may be ceded for the full term of copyright or a mere single performance or series of performances may be licensed. It is not necessary that any notice be printed on a piece of music to the effect that performing right is reserved; it is understood to be so reserved unless the holder of the performing right makes a statement to the contrary.

The Performing Right Society (1914) exists to license public performances and collect fees on behalf of composers, lyric authors, and music publishers in respect of all their musical works other than certain large choral works and those coming within the sphere of dramatic rights. (Dramatic rights comprise performances in their entirety of operas, musical plays, ballets, etc., or any substantial vocal excerpt therefrom.)[1]

It will readily be understood that the rights of Mechanical Reproduction and of Performance may turn out to be far more valuable than the right of Publication, and a composer should therefore beware of signing such a form of contract with his publisher as would confer upon the latter any rights other than that of Publication, unless these additional rights are adequately covered by stipulations as to payment.

Whenever possible, composers should avoid parting with the possession of any one of their three rights (Publication, Mechanical Reproduction, and Performance)—never 'assigning' them to a publisher, but only giving a licence in respect of them. It will be understood that by assigning his copyright to a publisher a composer parts with control, so that, for instance, altered, abridged, and simplified editions might be issued contrary to his wish. It should be noted, however, that the Performing Right Society, for the purpose of prompt action against infringers, requires its members' non-dramatic rights to be assigned to it for the period of their membership, but its Rules provide that the fees collected shall be divided between its composer, author, and publisher members, irrespective of whether the legal ownership of the right itself was assigned by one member to the other before being assigned to the Society.

The various self-governing countries of the British Commonwealth have their own Copyright Acts, as also has Eire; most of them are more or less closely based on the British Act of 1911, but the copyright law of Canada contains several objectionable provisions foreign to that Act.

2. United States of America. The beginning of copyright in the United States was with Acts passed by the States of Connecticut and Massachusetts in 1783, and based on the 1709 British Copyright Act. Other States quickly followed and at last, in 1891, Congress passed the first National Copyright Act. The Act was in force from 1909 up to 1977, modified by various subsequent Amendments. It was, in principle, very similar to the British Act. To composers are secured the rights of publication, performance, and mechanical reproduction—the last being subject to a proviso (similar to the one in the British Act) that, once the composer has allowed mechanical reproduction, the door is open for any further such reproduction, on payment of a fixed royalty of 2 cents per disk, roll, etc. It is no longer necessary that literary

[1] The French term *petits droits* ('little rights') may be met with in English usage. It covers all rights except those in stage performances and includes even those of a symphony or oratorio.

works by British authors be printed in the United States in order to obtain copyright protection there, as was the case until 1957. Under the Universal Copyright Convention, protection is guaranteed in the United States (except to U.S. citizens) without formalities provided each copy of a work bears the copyright symbol ©, the name of the copyright owner, and the year of publication. In 1895 it was held that musical scores need not be printed and published in the U.S.A. in order to secure protection there.

One main difference between the British Act and that of the United States is that the latter requires the author or composer (or owner of the copyright if it has been assigned) to register his title, to print the word 'Copyright' on his publication, and to fulfil certain other formalities. The term of copyright in the United States under the 1909 Act was 28 years from the first publication, subject, on application and approval, to an extension for another period of 28 years. In 1978 a new Copyright Act provided for a period consisting of the life of the author plus fifty years, as in Britain.

As for Performing Rights, in the United States these enjoy the protection of a powerful organization, the American Society of Composers, Authors, and Publishers ('ASCAP'). In addition there is a second performing rights collection agency, Broadcast Music Inc. ('BMI'). This was formed in 1938 by the broadcasting interests, following a dispute with ASCAP.

3. Reciprocity between Britain and other Countries. Britain is an adherent to the Berne Convention of 1886, and the subsequent International Conventions, by which practically all the civilized countries of the world, Russia being among the exceptions, bind themselves to give the owners of copyrights of other countries which have accepted the Convention equal rights with their own nationals. Thus a British author is automatically protected in France, Germany and Italy, Japan, and over twenty other countries (for a reference to Russia see *Belaief*). Other performing rights societies include the French *Société des auteurs, compositeurs et éditeurs de*

musique ('SACEM', 1851—the oldest such society); the German *Gesellschaft für musikalische Aufführungs- und mechanische Vervielfältigungsrechte* ('GEMA', 1915, successor to a society founded by Richard Strauss in 1903); and the Italian *Società italiana degli autori ed editori* ('SIAE', 1882). All of these, together with the British PRS and the American ASCAP and BMI, and the numerous other national societies, have reciprocal agreements which enable a composer to be paid in respect of performances of his music in any of the signatory countries.

The above article is merely a summary statement, and there are many dangers connected with publication, such as are likely to be hidden from any but the experienced legal mind. British composers should, then, obtain professional advice before signing any agreement. (There are a number of firms of solicitors with experience in this field.) *The Writers' and Artists' Year Book* (A. & C. Black) contains useful articles on copyright, with full text of the Copyright Act, lists of music publishers, etc.

As illustrating the serious need for composers to combine for the protection of their interests, owing to the existence of a considerable public ignorance of, and lack of sympathy with, the conditions of the exercise of their profession, it may be mentioned that, but for the efforts of the Societies mentioned in this article, there might have passed into British law, in 1930, a Bill which would have compelled every composer to accept for an unlimited number of performances of any work 'a fee not exceeding two pence' for each published copy used for such performances. The promoter and supporters of this Bill had not even the small amount of musical knowledge necessary to make a distinction between a two-minute song and a two-hour oratorio or three-hour opera (as George Bernard Shaw wrote at the time, 'Sir Edward Elgar may not charge more than two pence for a perpetual licence to perform *Gerontius*'). This Bill actually got so far as a second reading and had to be very strenuously opposed before it, happily, reached the rubbish bin of the Houses of Parliament.

See also *Libraries*; *Gramophone* 4.

'COQ D'OR, LE', i.e. *The Golden Cockerel* (Rimsky-Korsakof). Produced at Moscow in 1909. Libretto by Bielsky, based upon Pushkin's *Golden Cock*.

ACT I

SCENE: *The Council Chamber in the Palace of King Dodon*

The **Astrologer** (*High Tenor*) appears for a few moments before the curtain to tell us that though the story is a fable we can find a moral in it.

King Dodon (*Bass*) is worried. Lazy, greedy, and embroiled in wars, he knows not

what to do and consults his sons, **Princes Guidon** (*Tenor*) and **Afron** (*Baritone*), besides his counsellors and **General Polkan** (*Bass*). They disagree. The Astrologer appears, to suggest a happy solution: he will give the King a golden cockerel, which will crow whenever danger threatens. As a reward (though he asks none) the Astrologer is promised whatever he likes to command, at his own time.

The King, relieved of his cares, has his bed brought on and takes his ease and his gluttonous pleasure therein. **Amelfa**, his housekeeper (*Contralto*), translates for him the highly complimentary speeches of a green parrot. He falls asleep. The golden cockerel sounds the alarm and the King sends his sons off to do battle. Again the alarm, and Dodon, to his disgust, has to go himself.

Act II

SCENE: *A Rocky Gorge at Night*

Dodon finds his sons, dead. When dawn comes he sees a rich tent, from which comes the **Queen of Shemakha** (*Soprano*), who makes love to him, compels him to dance, enchants him by her singing, and promises to marry him.

Act III

SCENE: *A Street before the Council Hall*

In a gorgeous procession Dodon brings home his Queen, who is already tired of the foolish old man. The Astrologer appears and claims his reward—the Queen! Dodon in passion strikes the insolent fellow dead. Thunder is heard: the sky darkens. The Queen tells Dodon he is a fool. The cockerel again cries the alarm, but this time flies down and pecks at the King, who falls dead. More thunder and complete darkness, amid which is heard the laughter of the Queen. But when the light returns both she and the Astrologer have disappeared. The populace laments its loss.

In the **Epilogue** the Astrologer reminds us that it is all moonshine; but, 'Of the shadows passing by, Two were mortal, Queen and I', and with this cryptic hint he disappears.

In 1937 a ballet version of this opera was produced, the music adapted by Nicholas Tcherepnin (q.v.) and the choreography devised by Fokine.

COR (Fr.). Properly 'horn' (see *Horn Family*), though the term enters into the names of several instruments that are not truly horns.

COR ANGLAIS. See *Oboe Family* 3 a b, 4 e, 5 b, 6, and also *Organ* 14 VI.

CORANT or **CORANTO.** See *Courante*.

COR À PISTONS. 'Valve horn.' See *Horn Family* 2 c, 3, 5 c.

CORBETT, WILLIAM (d. 1748). He was a notable violinist and a composer of instrumental music. He spent much time in Italy, ostensibly engaged in musical activities (he was a great collector of Italian violins and music), but it was said really as a spy on the movements of the Old and Young Pretenders.

COR CHROMATIQUE. See *Horn Family* 5 c.

CORDA, CORDE (It.). 'String', 'strings'. So *una corda*, 'one string', i.e. use the 'soft' pedal, which causes the hammer (on a grand piano) to strike only one string instead of the usual two (nowadays two instead of three, except for the lower notes). This may be countermanded by *tutte le corde*, 'all the strings', or *tre corde*, 'three strings' (in older music by *due corde*, 'two strings').

Corda vuota (in violin music, etc.), 'empty string', i.e. 'open string'; *Corda soprana*, the highest string.

CORDE (Fr.). 'String.' (In Italian the same spelling means 'strings'—see *Corda*.)

CORDE À JOUR, CORDE À VIDE (Fr.). 'Open string' (q.v.).

COR DE BASSET. See *Clarinet Family* 5.

COR DE CHASSE. The simple 'hunting horn'. See *Horn family* 2 a, 3, 5 a.

COR DE NUIT. See *Organ* 14 I.

CORDER, FREDERICK (1852–1932). After a promising beginning as composer of opera, etc., he settled into the position of professor of composition at the Royal Academy of Music, London (where he had been a student), and there became responsible for the training of a long line of British composers. See, under *Improvisation* 5 and *Cornet* 1, two typically outspoken pronouncements.

COR DES ALPES. See *Alphorn*.

COR D'HARMONIE is the French horn with or without valves (see *Horn Family* 2 b c).

COREA (Sp.). A dance accompanied by song. Hence the adjective *Coreado*.

CORELLI, ARCANGELO (p. 1096, pl. **181.** 1). Born near Imola in 1653 and died in Rome in 1713, aged nearly sixty. In his day the violin was superseding the viol (see *Viol Family*), and he became one of the first great violinists, violin teachers, and violin composers, enjoying in all these capacities universal fame. Monarchs sought him out, pupils came from all countries, and his music was everywhere played. Most of his life was spent in Rome in the palace of Cardinal Pietro Ottoboni, whose concerts he directed. When he died he was found to have amassed a large fortune—in addition to a valuable collection of pictures.

He wrote five books of twelve sonatas each and also one of Concerti grossi. The list is as follows:

Op. 1. Sonatas 'in three parts' (2 violins, violone or archlute with bass for organ), 1681. These are Sonatas 'da chiesa' (see *Sonata* 2).

Op. 2. Sonatas 'in three parts' (2 violins and violone or harpsichord), 1685. These are Sonatas 'da camera'.

Op. 3. Sonatas 'in three parts' (2 violins, violone or archlute with bass for organ), 1689. These are Sonatas 'da chiesa'.

Op. 4. Sonatas 'in three parts' (2 violins and violone or harpsichord), 1694. These are Sonatas 'da camera'.

Op. 5. Sonatas for violin and violone or harpsichord, 1700. The first six of these are 'da chiesa', the next five 'da camera', and the last the famous set of variations on 'La Folía' (see *Folía*).

Op. 6. Concerti grossi, the concertino part consisting of 2 violins and violoncello and the ripieno part of the general body of strings. About 1714. The first eight of these are in the 'da chiesa' style and the other four in the 'da Camera' style.

Corelli's name ranks very high in the roll of those who laid the foundations of the present art of instrumental composition and performance, yet his works never range beyond his instrument's third position.

See references under *Italy* 6; *Violin Family* 5; *Chamber Music* 3; *Composition* 10; *Sonata* 3, 5, 10 b; *Suite* 3, 4, 5; *Concerto* 2; *Melody* 7; *Figured Bass*; *Folia*; *Publishing* 6; *Abaco, E. F. dall'*; *Bassani, G. B.*; *Cecilia*; *Geminiani*; *Malipiero*; *Opus*; *Italy* 6, 9; *History of Music* 5; *Misattributed* (Tartini); *Patronage* 8.

'CORELLI' FUGUE (Bach). See *Nicknamed* 1.

CORELLI, MARIE. See *Broadcasting* 2.

CORILLA. See *Improvisatore*.

CORISTA, CORISTA DI CORO, CORISTA DI CAMERA. See *Pitch* 8.

CORKINE, WILLIAM. End of sixteenth and beginning of seventeenth century. Nothing is known of him except that he composed and published some ayres (see *Madrigal* 3 b) and a little music for lute and viol.

COR MIXTE. See *Corno alto and Corno basso*.

CORNELIUS, PETER (p. 400, pl. **69**. 8).

Born at Mainz in 1824 and died there in 1874, aged nearly fifty. He was a member of the Weimar circle of the mid-nineteenth century, a friend of Wagner, and a colleague of his at Munich. Liszt at Weimar gave one performance of his opera *The Barber of Baghdad* (1858), and its failure caused his resignation; its success began only when its composer had been ten years dead.

Cornelius is favourably looked upon by cultured solo singers and intelligent members of capable choral societies for his very poetical songs and part-songs.

(He is not to be confused with Peter Cornelius, the popular Danish operatic tenor, 1865–1934.)

CORNELL UNIVERSITY. See *Musicology*.

CORNELYS, THERESA. Born in Venice in 1723 and died in London in 1797, aged seventy-four. See *Concert* 8.

CORNEMUSE. See *Bagpipe Family* 6.

CORNET (or CORNET À PISTONS)

(Not to be confused with the older Cornett. See *Cornett and Key Bugle Families*.)

1. Construction, Tone Quality, etc.   2. History.   3. Nomenclature.

(For illustration see p. 113, pl. **22**. 13.)

1. Construction, Tone Quality, etc. The cornet (in full *Cornet à Pistons*) is a metal instrument, of bore partly cylindrical (like that of the trumpet for the most part of that instrument's length) and partly conical (like that of the horn). It has, nowadays, a cup-shaped mouthpiece (like the trumpet's but deeper, not more or less funnel-shaped like the horn's; some players, indeed, prefer to use an actual trumpet mouthpiece).

Like both trumpet and horn (q.v.) it operates on the harmonic series (see *Acoustics* 8), filling in the gaps of that series by the use of three valves which lengthen the tube to the extent of a lowering of pitch by one, two, or three semitones respectively or, using combinations of valves, by four, five, or six semitones.

The range (nominally F sharp on bass staff to C above treble staff—but some players in the United States have greatly extended this) is about the same as that of the trumpet. The tone is something between that of the horn and that of the trumpet. Unlike those two instruments, it is easy to produce from it any note, and owing to its wide bore (wider than that of the trumpet) it has great flexibility, so that passages almost like those of a clarinet or flute in its most active runabout mood are within its powers. With the horn and trumpet the listener is sometimes made aware of a sense of effort on the part of the performer; with the cornet this is not so.

As with trumpet and horn, double and triple tonguing (see *Tonguing*) are possible and effective.

Like the trumpet now found in most British orchestras, the cornet exists in the two keys of B flat and A. The key is determined by the insertion of a straight shank of appropriate length between the body and the mouthpiece. In the most modern designs shanks are dispensed with; the instrument is constructed to play in B flat, but has, permanently 'built in', a short length of tubing which can be added to the wind-way by means of a 'Rotary Transposing Cylinder' to put it into A.

As the cornet is a chromatic instrument it should theoretically be able to play in any key, and there should exist no need whatever for any means of changing the key, but it happens that the extreme keys are less easy to play in, and with the B flat shank the player is, of course, eased of two of his flats before he starts to play, as with the A shank he is eased of three sharps.

In addition to the 'Cornet in B flat' and 'Cornet in A' (one instrument, with means to convert it from one to the other) there exists a 'Cornet in E flat'—a separate instrument almost exclusively for wind-band use.

The cornet is, it will be gathered, a transposing instrument (see *Transposing Instruments*), its music being written a tone or a minor third higher, or a minor third lower than it is to sound, according as the instrument is in B flat, A, or E flat.

Like the trumpet and horn it possesses a pear-shaped mute for insertion in the bell, and, in addition, some examples have an *Echo attachment*, enabling the player to perform at will at what sounds to be half a mile's distance from himself. (See *Duplex Instruments*.)

The tone of the cornet has been much discussed. Here follow some typical opinions of admitted authorities over a space of seventy years—at the beginning of which period the instrument was still 'coming in' and at the end of it 'going out'.

Berlioz (1843). 'Has neither the nobility of the horn nor the loftiness of the trumpet.' In melodic use must play only 'phrases of large construction and indisputable dignity'. 'Jocund melodies will always have to fear from this instrument the loss of a portion of their nobility, or, if they have none, an addition of triviality.'

Gevaert (1885). 'Vulgar accent, boorish origin.' 'It is only in Latin countries that the cornet has been admitted into the opera and concert orchestra ...; a deplorable abuse; it cannot take the place of the trumpet.'

Widor (1904). 'The timbre of the cornet and of the trumpet cannot for a moment be compared—the one being thick and vulgar, the other noble and brilliant.'

Prout (1897). 'The tone of the cornet is absolutely devoid of the nobility of tone of the trumpet, and, unless in the hands of a very good musician, readily becomes vulgar. . . . In light music it can sometimes be employed with advantage, and in dance music it is in its proper place.'

Corder (1895). 'The trumpet in the orchestra [he means the F trumpet then in vogue] is an almost unmitigated nuisance. . . . And—though I am aware that few agree with me on this point— I think the vaunted brilliancy of the trumpet its most serious drawback, because it simply kills all the other instruments. . . . I maintain that in competent hands it [the cornet] can play not only all existing trumpet parts more discreetly and bearably than the trumpet itself, but can furnish a far better upper part in the trombone harmony. A good cornet-player can do all that a trumpet-player can, and nearly as brilliantly.'

Forsyth (1914). 'Absurd prejudice against it, based . . . principally on ignorance.' 'We must not forget that the contempt which is usually bestowed on the cornet by those who have never heard it properly played is mainly a contempt because it cannot equal or beat the trumpet *in trumpet passages*.' 'Let us accept the fact that a cornet is a cornet, not a trumpet. Then we shall be able to see what can be done with it.'

On one point all these authorities would absolutely agree—the cornet is horrible when overblown.

2. History. The cornet à pistons was developed from the small coiled continental posthorn (q.v.) in the early nineteenth century (via an instrument called the 'Cornet Ordinaire'); its earliest appearance in the orchestra seems to have been in Paris, at the première of Rossini's *William Tell* in 1829 (not, as sometimes stated, in Balfe's *Maid of Artois* in 1836). At that time it possessed not three pistons but two, and

was called in France *Cornet d'harmonie* and in Britain *Cornopean* (there is an organ stop sometimes met with that perpetuates this latter name). In wind bands and dance bands (this was the palmy period of the quadrille) it soon superseded the key bugle (see *Cornett and Key Bugle Families*), and tended, in Latin countries at any rate, to supersede the trumpet in the orchestra.

It was in those early days played in a number of different keys, i.e. it was provided with a number of different crooks and shanks; Berlioz's *Orchestration* (1843) gives it as possessing nine. Obviously, as a chromatic instrument, it should have no need of so many, and as there disappeared the imperfection in construction that had caused valve notes (notes produced by the valves) to be not so good as open notes (the pure harmonics produced by the open tube), together with some faults of intonation, these crooks and shanks disappeared also, except the A and B flat shanks for orchestral use and the separate E flat instrument (with again the B flat) for wind-band use.

In Britain in the 1880s and earlier 1890s trumpets were rarely to be found in the orchestra. In 1892 Walter Morrow, the great British exponent of the trumpet, wrote of the cornet, 'It has dethroned the trumpet . . .: we rarely hear the latter now, even in our finest orchestras or military bands' (p. 756, pl. **125.** 3).

The French composers have been particularly partial to the cornet and it completely displaces the trumpet in many of their scores (e.g. Bizet's *Carmen*, 1875). Sometimes they have used two trumpets and two cornets (e.g. Berlioz's *Faust*, 1846). The introduction of the smaller, lighter-toned, and more agile trumpets in B flat and A (see *Trumpet Family* 2 c) has been one factor in driving the cornet into the orchestral background even in France, and it now tends to disappear also from the wind band, in which the trumpet and the flügelhorn (q.v.) threaten to take its place.

Stravinsky in *Petrushka*, *The Soldier's Tale*, etc., has found a characteristic use for the cornet.

3. Nomenclature. In France the cornet is still called in full, *Cornet à pistons*, or, more usually, simply *Piston*.

In Italy the B flat–A instrument is called *Cornetta* ('Cornetto' generally but not always seems to mean the old 'Cornett'—see *Cornett Family*). The E flat instrument is there known as *Sopranino*, *Cornettino*, or *Pistone*.

In Germany the cornet is *Kornett*, *Piston*, *Pistonkornett*, or *Ventilkornett* (i.e. 'valve cornet').

For the organ stop 'Cornet' see *Organ* 14 V; *Cornett* 3; *Voluntary*.

CORNET À BOUQUIN. See *Cornett and Key Bugle Families* 4.

CORNET D'HARMONIE. See *Cornet* 2.

CORNETTA (It.). 'Cornet' (q.v.). *Cornetta segnale*, 'signal cornet', means 'bugle' (the simple military one); *Cornetta a chiavi*, 'key bugle'.

CORNETT AND KEY BUGLE FAMILIES

This cornett family is not to be confused with that of the modern cornet. In the present work, as has now become usual, the very ancient spelling 'cornett' is revived for the older type of instrument and the somewhat more modern spelling 'cornet' is reserved for the newer type of instrument. Where

in the English Bible, Shakespeare, etc., 'cornet' is mentioned, it is the instrument here called 'cornett' that is intended. In fact, any mention of 'cornet' before the nineteenth century inevitably means this 'cornett'. For the modern cornet see a preceding article.

1. Principles and Shapes.
2. Members of the Families

3. History.
4. Nomenclature.

(For illustrations see p. 112, pl. **21**. 2; 113, **22**. 1-10.)

1. Principles and Shapes. These two families (formerly of high importance but now entirely superseded) have affinities with both the wood-wind and the brass.

The affinity with the wood lies in the method of varying the notes by the use of holes in the tube (not by devices for lengthening the tube, like the valves and slides of the brass).

The affinity with the brass lies in the fact that the sounding agent is the lips of the player applied (like that of a trumpet, for instance), and there to a hollow cup-shaped mouthpiece vibrating, 'reed' fashion.

The combination of these two features (finger-hole or finger-key system plus hollow mouthpiece) is a peculiarity of these two families alone and justifies their being treated together here, despite their marked differences of bore and timbre.

The difference between the two families is as follows: In the cornett family the first octave of notes is obtained by successively uncovering the holes, and the second octave by doing the same and overblowing (cf. *Recorder Family*—both cornetts and recorders have six finger-holes and a thumb-hole behind). On the other hand, in the key bugle family *each note* obtained by uncovering the holes gives rise to a series of notes (a section of the harmonic series, see *Acoustics* 8).

The cornett family for centuries consisted of a wooden tube, usually leather-covered (or sometimes an ivory tube), straight, or curved in the arc of a circle—or curved in two such arcs like a flattened-out S but reversed. Then an allied bass member (*d* below) was added, whose length (8 feet) prescribed another treatment, and for this a kind of zigzag shape was adopted.

Modification of the last took the form of a tube bent back on its length like that of a bassoon (*e*, *f*, below).

Of the straight cornetts a quiet kind was known as *Mute Cornett*.

2. Members of the Families. The instruments in use in different periods and places necessarily differed in detail, but the following is sufficiently accurate as a general statement. (It corresponds, as to the cornetts, with the pictures and details given by Praetorius in 1618.)

(*a*) **Small Cornett.** This was either straight or curved in the arc of a circle; its compass was

a fourth above that of the cornett proper (see below).

(*b*) The **Cornett** proper (i.e. the one which is intended wherever the word is used without qualification) was made either straight or curved in the arc of a circle. Its compass was from A two leger lines below the treble staff, or the G immediately below this, to (roughly) A one leger line above that staff. It was, then, a treble instrument.

(*c*) **Great Cornett.** This was bent in two curves, one of them the reverse of the other, i.e. the elongated S shape. Its pitch was from C on the bass staff, so that it may be regarded as a tenor-pitched instrument.

(*d*) **Serpent** (p. 113, pl. **22.** 10). The above instruments lacking any bass companion, a longer one was at last (in the sixteenth century) introduced. It was not strictly a cornett, either in bore or fingering, but provided a link between the cornett family proper and the key bugles. It was about 8 feet long and therefore required to be shaped in a whole series of sharp curves, so leading its contours to resemble those of a snake in progress over the ground and giving it its very descriptive name. Its lowest note, in theory, was the C or B flat below the bass staff and its compass a good three octaves. (But a fine player by relaxing his lip could 'force' his way down to notes several degrees lower than the fundamental—as some horn players can do.) In later specimens the instrument was provided with keys lifting round covers from the holes.

It was a 'transposing instrument' (q.v.); its natural scale being B flat, its part was written a tone higher than the effect intended.

In the York Festival orchestra of 1825 (with 248 performers) there were eight serpents and bass horns (see below).

[1](*e*) **Bass Horn.** Not a horn at all but a variant of the serpent (see above), in which the reptile, instead of proceeding in a series of waggles, merely doubles back on itself. It was introduced at the end of the eighteenth century and was not very long lived. *Keyed Horn* is another name. For a variety of the bass horn see below.

[1](*f*) **Russian Bassoon** (or Ophibaryton). A variety of the bass horn (see above). Whether it be Russian or not it is no bassoon, the resem-

[1] Authorities differ a good deal in their statements about the two instruments (*e* and *f*), but the information here given is believed to be correct.

See the Articles *Concert* on pages 227–33, and *Concert Hall* on pages 234–6, as also Plate 43, facing page 225

1. SYMPHONY HALL, BOSTON. Built 1900

2. ORCHESTRA HALL, CHICAGO. Built 1904

3. A MID-20TH-CENTURY CONCERT HALL INTERIOR—the Free Trade Hall, Manchester

1. WAGNER BEFORE HANSLICK'S JUDGEMENT SEAT
By Dr. Otto Bohler. See *Criticism* 2

2. HANSLICK LECTURING WAGNER while other anti-Wagnerians wait

3, 4. TWO FAMOUS LONDON CRITICS OF THE 19TH CENTURY—Chorley and Davison. See *Criticism* 4

3

4

5. BERLIOZ AND THE MUSIC CRITICS. *Above*, In his lifetime. *Below*, After his death. By a 19th-century Parisian caricaturist

blance to this being simply a slight one of appearance owing to the tube being bent back on itself. It is generally alluded to as a brass instrument, but Berlioz, who despised it, in his *Orchestration* (1843) speaks of it as of wood, so apparently both materials were used.

(*g*) **Ophicleide.** (We here pass to the family which we have called the key bugle family.)

The ophicleide existed in three sizes, alto, bass, and double-bass, but only the bass was found practically valuable, and so the others never came into much use. The bass tuba has now entirely superseded the bass ophicleide.

(*h*) **Key Bugle** or Keyed Bugle (Fr., *Bugle à clefs*). This was a treble instrument of the ophicleide type; indeed the key bugle came first and the ophicleide was an adaptation of it to bass uses, and the object in allowing the more recently introduced instrument to appear in the present list before the less recently introduced one is merely to bring it into association with the serpent, bass horn, and Russian bassoon, whose place in the orchestra and the wind band it usurped.

3. History. (*a–c*) The *Cornett* is mentioned in English writings as early as the tenth century. In Elizabethan and Stuart times it frequently crops up in literature (stage directions of Shakespeare's plays, etc.). The lists of the musical instruments and musical performers of the courts of the Tudor and Stuart monarchs constantly mention it. Monteverdi, in his opera *Orfeo* (Mantua, 1607), has two movements of great brilliance and technical difficulty for cornetts and trombones.

It was a regular member of the cathedral musical forces (e.g. Westminster Abbey, York, Durham). Louis XIII, in his chapel, replaced with cornetts two treble voices. After the Restoration in England, trained singing boys being at first lacking, cornetts took the place of them in the Chapel Royal. They blend particularly well with voices: Roger North (q.v.), in his life of Francis North, at the end of the seventeenth century, says, 'Nothing comes so near, or rather imitates so much, an excellent voice as a cornet pipe.' (For cornetts in the Scottish Chapel Royal see *Scotland* 6, near end.)

The tone was also considered to blend well with that of the seventeenth-century organ. In 1662 Evelyn, alluding to the King's introduction of a string band, says: 'Now we no more heard the cornet, which gave life to the organ, that instrument quite left off in which the English were so skilful.' The popular 'Cornet Voluntaries' of eighteenth-century England (voluntaries using the cornet stop of the organ) were probably intended to perpetuate this effect (see *Voluntary* 5).

Apparently the English had a special fondness for the cornett and cultivated performance upon it, for in 1604 the Duke of Lorraine sent his chief cornett player to enlist recruits in England.

Bach uses the cornett in eleven of his Church cantatas—in almost every case to support the voices in a chorale melody, the accompanying voices being supported by trombones.

It seems that the last notable use of the treble cornett was in the Vienna production of Gluck's *Orpheus* in 1762. It lingered apparently after this, as some time later Schubart, who died in 1791, in *Suggestions for an Aesthetic of Music* speaks as though a few players were still to be found (probably the town 'waits', called *Stadtpfeifer* or *Zinkenisten*). He agrees with other writers in saying that its playing made great demands on the player—apparently because, like the oboe, it used so little breath. D'Indy revived the cornett for use in his opera *Fervaal*, but gave it merely a two-note call to play.

(*d*) It has usually been stated that the *Serpent* was the invention of a French priest, about 1590, but earlier specimens are now said to have existed in Italy. However, the instrument seems always to have found its greatest popularity in France in the service of the church there. There were two kinds of serpents in use in France—not only the *Serpent d'église* ('church serpent'—a strange association of ideas) but also another form more convenient for marching purposes, the *Serpent militaire*. Berlioz, in his book on *Orchestration* (1843), is severe on the church use of the serpent, which was evidently in full swing in his day, saying that it 'would better have suited the sanguinary rites of the Druidical worship than those of the Catholic religion'. This confirms the judgement of Handel, who, hearing it in England a century earlier (apparently he had not come across it in Germany or Italy), exclaimed 'Vell, dat vos not de serpent dat tempted Eve'. Obviously a great deal depended on the way it was played; Mersenne, early in the seventeenth century, said that, though a mere boy playing on it could drown twenty robust voices, yet the sound could be attempered to the softness of the sweetest voice, and such modern experience of the instrument as has been obtained amply confirms this high praise.

There have been players of great agility on the serpent, as one Hurworth, of Richmond, Yorkshire, in the band of George III, who could play rapid flute variations on it with perfect accuracy.

The serpent has not long dropped out of common use in England and France. Stainer and Barrett's *Dictionary of Musical Terms* (1876), rather surprisingly for that date, says: 'It is frequently used in the orchestra to strengthen the bass part, but requires to be very skilfully blown. . . .' The Riemann *Musiklexikon*, in its 1929 edition, speaks of it as 'wohl ganz ausser Gebrauch gekommen' ('probably gone completely out of use'), but it is noticeable that the French editor of this work (1931), in translating, has slightly modified the statement, speaking of the instrument as—'*presque* complètement disparu de nos jours' ('*almost* completely disappeared nowadays').

Amongst composers who have used the serpent as a part of the orchestra are: Handel in his *Firework Music* (1749); Auber in his *Masaniello* (1828); Mendelssohn in *St. Paul* (1836); and Wagner in *Rienzi* (first performed 1842) and in *The Love Feast of the Apostles* (1843).

(*e, f*) The *Bass Horn* and *Russian Bassoon* had short careers at the end of the eighteenth century and beginning of the nineteenth.

(*g*) It was the *Ophicleide* that really took the place of the serpent, and it may be noted that Mendelssohn, who in 1836 scored for the serpent in *St. Paul*, in 1846 scored for the ophicleide in *Elijah*. This instrument was of French invention. It appears in the following, amongst other scores: Spontini's opera *Olympia* (1819); Mendelssohn's *Midsummer Night's Dream* Overture (1826); Wagner's *Rienzi* (1842); Berlioz's *Faust* (1846); Mendelssohn's *Elijah* (1846); Verdi's Requiem (1874). Nearly all the French composers of this period used it freely, but soon after the date of the last work mentioned it began to disappear. It lingered longest in wind bands.

(*h*) The *Key Bugle* was invented by an Irish bandmaster, Joseph Halliday, about 1810, and went out gradually after about 25 years' popularity, as the modern cornet (see *Cornet*) came in.

4. Nomenclature.

Cornett. *Cornet à bouquin* (Fr., 'bouquin', meaning 'goat' and alluding either to the original source of the instrument or to its shape); *Cornetto* (It.); *Zinke, Zink*, or *Kornett* (Ger.). These are the general terms applying to all sizes and shapes of the instrument except the serpent, but, in the absence of precise definition, to be understood as implying (*b*) in the list given under 2 above.

Any of the straight forms of the instrument is a *Cornetto diritto* (It.). Any of the curved forms is a *Cornetto curvo* or *Cornetto torto* (It.).

The **Mute Cornett** is also known as *Cornetto Muto* (It.), and *Stiller Zink* (Ger., 'quiet cornett').

Names for the three individual members of the family are:

(*a*) **Small Cornett.** *Cornettino* (It.; also used for the high-pitched E flat modern cornet; see *Cornet* 3). *Klein Discant Zink* (Ger. name given in Praetorius).

(*b*) **Cornett** proper. Simply *Cornetto* (It.), *Zinke* (Ger.), etc. Praetorius calls the curved form *Recht Chor Zinck* (i.e. 'true choir cornett') and the other form *Gerader Zinck* (i.e. 'straight cornett').

(*c*) **Great Cornett.** *Cornetto torto* (It., 'crooked cornett') generally implies this instrument. Also *Cornone, Corno torto*, or simply *Corno*.

(*d*) **Serpent.** *Serpent* or *Serpent d'église* (Fr.) or (a slightly different instrument) *Serpent militaire*; *Serpentone* (It.); *Serpent* or *Schlangenrohr* (Ger., literally 'snake-tube'). In the north of England there survive, apparently, memories of the serpent as the 'black pudding'.

(*e*) **Bass Horn.** *Keyed Horn*; *Basshorn* (Ger.).

(*f*) **Russian Bassoon.** *Basson russe* (Fr.).

(*g*) **Ophicleide** (the word is a concoction from Greek and means 'keyed serpent'—literally, however, a 'door-keyed' one!). *Serpentcleide* was an early bastard name also marking the relationship; properly the serpentcleide and the ophicleide are slightly different, but the names were practically interchangeable. *Basse d'harmonie* (Fr.—'harmonie' here apparently in the sense of a wind band); *Oficleide* (It.); *Ophikleide* (Ger.).

(*h*) **Key Bugle.** *Kent Bugle* or *Royal Kent Bugle* (from the Duke of Kent, Queen Victoria's father—apparently so named by the inventor after giving a performance of it before this personage); *Bugle à clefs* (Fr.); *Klappenhorn* (Ger.; it is sometimes stated that the Klappenhorn is the bass horn, but this seems to be an error); *Cornetta a chiavi* (It.).

For Cornett-Ton see *Pitch* 3.

CORNETTA SEGNALE. See *Bugle*.

CORNETTINO. See *Cornett and Key Bugle Families* 4 a.

CORNETTO (It.). Cornet (q.v.).

CORNETT-TON. See *Pitch* 3.

CORNET VOLUNTARY. See *Voluntary*; also *Cornett* 3.

CORNISH. See *Cornyshe*.

CORNO (It.). Properly, 'horn' (see *Horn Family*), though the word enters into the name of one or two instruments that are not horns. Also the great cornett (see *Cornett Family* 4 c).

CORNO ALTO and **CORNO BASSO.** These are names for the horn players who, anciently, specialized in the high and low registers. In Germany they were called *Primarius* and *Secundarius*. The terms did not imply superiority and inferiority, as '1st horn' and '2nd horn' do. At the beginning of the nineteenth century a third register, introduced by the famous French player Duvernoy, was that of *Cor mixte*, which avoided both very high and very low notes.

CORNO A MACCHINA (It.). Valve horn. See *Horn Family* 2 c, 3, 5.

CORNO A MANO (It.). 'Hand horn', i.e. the 'natural' French horn. See *Horn Family* 2 b, 3, 4, 5.

CORNO A PISTONI (It.). 'Valve horn.' See *Horn Family* 2 c, 3, 5 c.

CORNO BASSO. See *Corno Alto* above.

CORNO CROMATICO (It.). Valve horn. See *Horn Family* 2 c, 3, 5.

CORNO DA CACCIA (It.). 'Hunting horn'. See *Horn Family* 2 a, 3, 5.

CORNO DI BASSETTO. See *Clarinet Family* 5; Organ 14 VI.

CORNO DOLCE. See *Organ* 14 II.

CORNO INGLESE. See *Oboe Family* 5 b.

CORNONE (It.). Great cornett. See *Cornett Family* 4 c.

CORNOPEAN. See *Cornet* 2; *Organ* 14 VI.

CORNO TORTO (It.). Great cornett. See *Cornett Family* 4 c.

CORNO VENTILE (It.). Valve horn. See *Horn Family* 2 c, 3, 5.

CORNYSHE (or Cornish), WILLIAM. Born about 1468 and died in 1523. He was a noted composer, playwright, actor, and pageant master (and, curiously, on occasion, provider of guttering, paving, and even sanitary conveniences) about the court of Henry VIII. In some of these varied and useful capacities he served his master at the Field of the Cloth of Gold, to which he took ten choir-boys, being allowed twopence a day for their 'diette'.

Some of his sacred music, a little music for viols, and also some jovial secular choral compositions, survive.

CORO (It.). 'Choir', 'chorus'. *Gran coro*, 'great chorus', in organ music, means 'full organ'.

COR-OBOE. See *Organ* 14 I.

CORONACH. See *Corranach*.

CORONATION CONCERTO (Mozart). See *Nicknamed Compositions* 15.

CORONATION MASS (Mozart). See *Nicknamed Compositions* 15.

CORONATION OF POPPÆA. See *Monteverdi*.

CORPORATION OF MINSTRELS. See *Profession of Music* 3.

CORPORATION OF MUSICIANS. See *Minstrels*, etc. 3; *Puritans* 4.

CORPS DE RECHANGE (Fr.). 'Crook'—of a brass instrument (see, for instance, *Trumpet Family* and *Horn Family*).

CORRANACH. A funeral dirge in the Highlands of Scotland. It was in old times chanted by a bard to the harp. The Irish Celts had a similar custom.

Apparently the word was at one time also used for the persons who performed the dirge. Smollett, himself a Scot, in *Humphrey Clinker* (1771) speaks of a corpse being 'attended by the coronach, composed of a multitude of old hags, who tore their hair, beat their breasts, and howled most hideously'. At the grave 'the orator, or *senachie* [seanchaidh], pronounced the panegyric of the defunct, every period being confirmed by a yell of the coronach'.

CORRENTE. See *Courante*; *Suite* 3.

CORRETTE, MICHEL (1709–95). Paris organist, composer of music, and author of tutors for various instruments.

See references under *Folia*; *Bagpipe* 6.

CORRI, DOMENICO. Born in Rome in 1746 and died in London in 1825, aged seventy-eight. He became a prominent Edinburgh singing-master, impresario, author of textbooks of music, and music publisher, later settling in London.

See *Concert* 8; *Dussek*.

CORSICA. See *Auld Lang Syne*.

COR SIMPLE (Fr.). 'Natural' horn. See *Horn Family* 2 a b, 3, 5.

CORTÈGE (Fr.). 'Procession.'

CORTO, CORTA (It.) 'Short', hence *Cortamente*, 'shortly'. The plurals are *Corti*, *Corte*.

CORTOT, ALFRED (1877–1962). See *Mechanical Reproduction* 13; *Electric Musical Instruments* 1 f.

CORYPHÆUS. See under *Choragus*.

COSACCO, COSACCA (It., masc., fem.). 'In the Cossack style.'

COSAQUE (Fr.). 'Cossack'—sometimes applied to a Cossack dance, two-in-a-measure and with a continued *accelerando*.

COSÌ FAN TUTTE[1] (Mozart). Produced at Vienna in 1790. Libretto by da Ponte (attempts to improve it have been made and consequently several versions exist, the names of the personages sometimes being changed). The original language is Italian.

SCENE: *Naples*

ACT I

Two officers, **Ferrando** (*Tenor*) and **Guglielmo** (*Bass*), are in love respectively with two women, Fiordiligi and Dorabella. **Don Alfonso**, an old philosopher and cynic (*Baritone*), lays a wager that the women will not be faithful when their lovers are away.

Don Alfonso comes to the ladies (**Fiordiligi**, *Soprano*; **Dorabella**, *Mezzo-soprano*) in their garden to tell them that their lovers are ordered on active service. Farewells are tearfully made, and the men leave. In the next scene **Despina** (*Soprano*), the ladies' maid, is taken into the plot. The two officers are introduced, as foreigners, and make love to the ladies, but unsuccessfully. They pretend to be heart-broken, and to take poison. Despina, disguised as a doctor, restores them by mystic passes. The men determine to try the ladies once more.

ACT II

Guglielmo makes progress with his friend's betrothed Dorabella, who gives him her lover's portrait. Ferrando, too, succeeds with Fiordiligi, and Despina, impersonating a notary, prepares marriage contracts. Alfonso now raises an alarm that the women's lovers are returning. The pretended 'foreigners' make their escape, to re-enter a few moments later, rid of their disguises, and to confront their betrothed with the marriage contracts. Alfonso reveals the truth and all ends happily.

COSIN, JOHN (1594–1672). Bishop of Durham. See under *Veni Creator Spiritus*.

COSTA, MICHAEL ANDREW AGNUS (p. 240, pl. **44.** 6). Born in Naples in 1806 and died at Brighton in 1884, aged seventy-eight. After a short career in his native country as composer of oratorios, symphonies, and operas,

---

[1] There has always been a difficulty in translating this title, the English language lacking a means of indicating the gender of 'tutte'. 'Thus do all [women]' would be literal. 'That's what women are!' might do.

he came, at the age of twenty-one, to direct a certain composition of his compatriot Zingarelli at the Birmingham Festival, but (curiously) was refused permission to do this and made to sing the tenor part of the composition instead. He remained in the country and came to occupy a dominating position both as composer and as conductor of opera, oratorio, and orchestral works—in which last capacity his skill and authority helped to set a new standard.

His oratorios *Naaman* and *Eli* had great fame, and a march from the latter is perhaps, in its pianoforte and organ arrangements, still obscurely in use. Queen Victoria knighted him, and many other monarchs also conferred their honours upon him.

See references under *Additional Accompaniments*; *God save the Queen* 16; *Oratorio* 7 (1855, 1864); *Cowen*.

COSTAL BREATHING. See *Voice* 3, 21.

COSTELEY, WILLIAM. Born in Normandy (not, as some say, Ireland) in 1531, and died at Évreux, in Normandy, in 1606, aged seventy-four or seventy-five. He was organist and valet de chambre to Henry II and Charles IX of France, and a composer of secular choral music (of the chanson type) that has been reprinted by Henry Expert (q.v.).

COSYN, BENJAMIN. See *Benjamin Cosyn's Virginal Book.*

CÔTELETTES. See *Chopsticks.*

COTILLON (p. 273, pl. **49.** 4). An elaborate ballroom dance often used in the nineteenth century to close the evening's pleasure. The name appears to have been known in France at the beginning of the eighteenth century and in Germany somewhat later, but probably the dance then so called had little in common with the later one, though a German publication of 1769 speaks of it as a sort of country dance (q.v.), and so it seems to have remained.

In Victorian times in England, and probably at the same period in America, it was danced by any number, all imitating a leading couple, who chose their figures out of a very large number available. In the course of the dance almost every gentleman would dance with almost every lady.

The music was simply that of various waltzes, mazurkas, etc.

COTTAGE PIANO. See *Pianoforte* 16.

COTTON, JOHN (late eleventh or early twelfth century). The writer of an important treatise on music. He is thought to have been an Englishman.

COUCHED HARP. An old name for the spinet. See *Harpsichord* 4.

COULAMMENT (Fr.). 'Flowingly.'

COULÉ. (Fr., 'flowing'.) Slide, slur, legato.

COULISSE (Fr.). The slide of a trombone or slide trumpet. *Coulisse à accorder*, on the other hand, means the tuning-slide of a wind instrument.

Trombone à coulisse—see *Trombone Family*. *Trompette à coulisse*—see *Trumpet Family* 2 d, 5.

COUNCIL FOR ADVANCEMENT OF MUSIC. See *Puritans* 4.

COUNCIL FOR THE ENCOURAGEMENT OF MUSIC AND THE ARTS. See under *Arts Council of Great Britain.*

COUNCIL OF LAODICEA. See *Greek Church and Music* 2; *Singing* 3.

COUNCIL OF TRENT. See *Church Music* 4; *Sequence.*

COUNTER-EXPOSITION. See *Form* 12.

COUNTERPOINT. The word derives from the expression *punctus contra punctum*, i.e. 'point against point', or 'note against note', the word 'point' being in early times common for 'note' (the expression 'nota contra notam' is also to be found). This carries us back to the early days of written composition (see *Harmony* 4, 5, 6), when the only idea of the practice of the art was to write down an existing piece of plainsong melody (or *Canto Fermo*), and then against each of its notes to write another note for the accompanying voice, the two voices thus proceeding together at the same pace.

A single part or voice added to another is often still called 'a counterpoint' to the other, but usually the word is given the general meaning of '*the combination of simultaneous voice-parts, each independent, but all conducing to a result of uniform coherent texture*'—which is a terse definition given in the American *Webster's Dictionary*, quoting from W. H. Hadow. In this sense 'Counterpoint' has a synonym in 'Polyphony'. (The term 'voice-part' in the definition is intended to include instrumental strands as well as choral, the word 'voice' being commonly used by musicians in this comprehensive sense.)

The element of counterpoint is present in some measure in practically all music, though it is more important in that of some periods than in that of others (see again article *Harmony*). The sixteenth century was the high point of pure contrapuntal art, the period of Palestrina in Rome, the Belgian Lassus in Munich, Victoria in Madrid, and Byrd in London (see *History of Music* 2, 4), and consequently when, later, attempts were made to formulate rules for students of the art, they were based on the practice of the composers of that time. A comprehensive textbook that came into existence (in the form of a dialogue, in Latin, between master and pupil) was Fux's *Gradus ad Parnassum* (1725). It was translated into many languages and repeatedly republished, remaining the standard for two centuries and even today influencing the teaching of the subject. The general appearance of an exercise in Fux still bears a strong resemblance to that of an exercise in any modern treatise on what is called **Strict Counterpoint** or **Student's Counterpoint,** as distinct from **Free Counterpoint** or **Composer's Counterpoint.** (The distinction between those two types of counterpoint may be compared to that between the impersonal and abstract examples of an arithmetical textbook and the practical calculations actually carried out in commerce; the one being an academic preparation for the other.)

The system of strict counterpoint involves an analysis of the practice of composers of the period mentioned into five 'species', which are practised separately and then combined. Following out the old conception, a *Canto fermo* or 'fixed song' (C.F. is the common abbreviation) is set by the master, in long notes, one to a measure, and the student adds to it a part or several parts.

The species are as follows: *Species I*—'Note against note' (the canto fermo and the added voice or voices proceeding at an equal pace). *Species II*—the added voices have two (sometimes three) notes to the canto fermo's one. *Species III*—The added voices have four notes (sometimes six or eight) to the canto fermo's one. *Species IV*—The added voices, as in Species II, proceed two against one, but the second note of each bar is tied over into the following measure, so producing syncopation. *Species V*—Here the devices of the other species are all used from time to time, with a few others, so producing **Florid Counterpoint**.

By the term **Combined Counterpoint** is meant the practice of several species at one time—one in one voice and another in another. (It may be added that Strict Counterpoint, formerly an important element in the examination syllabuses of British universities, had by 1940 dropped out of most of them in favour of freer contrapuntal writing.)

Invertible Counterpoint means counterpoint of which upper and lower voices may change place, the effect still remaining good.

Double Counterpoint means two-part invertible counterpoint.

Triple Counterpoint means three-part invertible counterpoint; there are now five inversions possible, making six positions in all.

Quadruple and Quintuple Counterpoint, etc., are similarly explained; quadruple gives twenty-four possible positions and quintuple one-hundred-and-twenty.

Imitation is common in contrapuntal composition—one voice entering with a phrase more or less closely modelled on that of a previous voice. When imitation is perfectly strictly carried out it becomes *Canon* (q.v.).

COUNTERSUBJECT in fugue. See *Forms* 12 a.

COUNTER-TENOR. See *Alto Voice*.

COUNTRY DANCE (Eng.), **CONTRE-DANSE** (Fr.), **CONTRADANZA** (It.). These are all one thing, and they originate in England, where the name 'Country Dance' is found much earlier than any of the foreign names that have apparently been derived from it by plausible false etymology (e.g. *Contredanse*, one in which the performers stand 'counter', or opposite to one another, in distinction to a round-dance; there were at one time round country dances, but they died out and so

the mistake became possible). Despite the statements found in foreign dictionaries and elsewhere, the English origin not only of the dance (which is generally admitted), but also of its name, may be accepted.

The country dance was imported into France at the end of the seventeenth century and then into Germany, as a French thing. 'Michel Brenet', in her *Dictionnaire . . . de la Musique* (1926), says that two dancing-masters, Isaac and Lorine, returning at about the same time as one another from London, introduced the dances to the court of Louis XIV, and that a manuscript copy of the English airs and steps made for the King by Lorine still exists.

The term 'country dance' is a generic one. There is no such thing as 'the country dance'. A whole series of figure-dances (i.e. dances of set geometrical evolutions) deriving originally from the amusements of the English village green are entitled to the name. They penetrated to aristocratic circles and became popular at the court of Queen Elizabeth I, who loved them, and, at last, during the Commonwealth (1650), were systematically described; the work in which the results were given, Playford's *English Dancing Master*, remains the authority for both the steps and the tunes (over 100 tunes, with the directions for dancing attached to each—a great variety!). This book went through eighteen editions (some much enlarged) during the following eighty years, and its information was carefully studied and republished by Cecil Sharp in a series of practical guides to the dancing.

Sharp gives the characteristics of a country dance as 'simplicity and gaiety', and Rousseau in his *Dictionary of Music* (1767), discussing the tunes, shows us that in France those were the recognized qualities of the type. 'They should have marked rhythms and be brilliant and gay yet with much simplicity.' (It may be noted in passing that at this period in France the term sometimes had a special application to square dances for four couples.)

Two upstart rivals of the country dance ousted it from ball-rooms in the early years of the nineteenth century—the waltz and the quadrille.

Sir Roger de Coverley was until the early twentieth century the only country dance still known in England (see *Dance* 6 b), except in a few out-of-the-way villages, but the work of such pioneers as Mary Neal, Cecil J. Sharp, and the English Folk Dance Society brought many dances into active life again. The Scots have retained a number of their old country dances.

In old times country dances were used as refreshment at the end of the evening's series of the more stately minuets. This was English practice and, according to Rousseau, French also. Right through the eighteenth century nearly every British music publisher issued an annual collection of country-dance tunes, generally of twenty-four in a narrow oblong book suited for the dancing-master's pocket.

Mozart wrote country dances for the balls of

Salzburg and Vienna; some of them are, however, lost.

See a reference to the use of Irish tunes for English country dances under *Ireland* 1.

COUNTRY GARDEN. See *Vicar of Bray*.

COUP D'ARCHET (Fr.). Bow-stroke or bowing.

COUP DE GLOTTE. See *Voice* 3.

COUPÉ. See *Ballet* 8.

COUPERIN FAMILY. There were five generations of musicians in this notable family. They all practised in Paris; the earliest was born about 1626 and the latest died about 1850, so their activities, men and women, as organists, harpsichordists, violists and violinists, vocalists, and composers, extended over more than two centuries. At least nine of them were, at different periods, organists of the church of St. Gervais (see p. 768, pl. **129.** 3).

The one whose music is often heard today is that François (p. 368, pl. **61.** 3) who was born in Paris in 1668 and died there in 1733, aged sixty-four. To distinguish him from his relations he is often called Couperin the Great (Couperin le Grand). At twenty-five he was organist in the private chapel of Louis XIV at Versailles, and at twenty-eight he added the duties of organist of St. Gervais in Paris.

His special fame today rests on his well-shaped and ingenious harpsichord music; most of his pieces are miniatures, and many of them bear fanciful titles, as (picturing states of feeling) 'Regrets', 'Tender Languors', 'Happy Ideas'; or (portraits) 'Princess Marie', 'Sister Monica', 'The Enchantress', 'Tender Fanchon', 'The Lovable Theresa'; or (nature impressions) 'The Rose Bushes', 'The Blossoming Orchard', 'Daybreak', 'Bees', 'Butterflies', 'The Frightened Linnet', 'The Nightingale in Love'; or (imitative of sounds or motions) 'The Little Windmills', 'The Spinning Woman', 'The Bagpipe of Taverni', 'The Harp'. Some of the pieces are cast into sets, as, for instance, the *Annals of the Great and Ancient Minstrelsy* ('Fastes de la grande et ancienne ménestrandise'—celebrating a great dispute in the musical profession, settled in 1707), in five 'acts' or separate sections—I, 'The Minstrels', 'Notables and Jurymen'; II, 'The Hurdy-gurdy Players and Beggars'; III, 'The Jugglers', 'Tumblers and Mountebanks with their Bears and Monkeys'; IV, 'The Infirm, or those injured in the service of the Great Minstrelsy'; V, 'Rout of the whole Troupe, caused by the Drunkards, Bears, and Monkeys'.

Thus Couperin the Great was an early writer of 'Programme Music' (see *Programme Music* 5 c), and an excellent discussion of him in this light will be found in Niecks's *Programme Music in the last Four Centuries*. In addition to the harpsichord works Couperin left chamber music, religious choral music, some organ music, and songs. Couperin's didactic work on harpsichord playing, *L'art de toucher le clavecin*, is valuable and celebrated.

References will be found under: *Allemande*; *Anglebert*; *Arrangement*; *Bagpipe Family* 8; *Bird Music*; *Canaries*;

Chaconne; *Coda*; *Couplet*; *Courante*; *Expression*; *Form* France 5; *Germany* 4; *Harpsichord* 2; *Keyboard* 3; *Mellers*; *Misattributed*; *Notation* 5; *Ornaments* 2 *Phrasing*; *Pianoforte* 1, 20, 21; *Publishing* 2; *Suite* 3, 4.

COUPLER. See *Organ* 2 e.

COUPLET. (1) In the early French rondos (see *Form* 9) the episodes were often called 'Couplets'. The term is frequent in Couperin's work, for instance.

See also *Chaconne and Passacaglia*.

(2) Same as *Duplet* (see Table 11).

(3) The 'two-note slur', i.e. two notes of *equal* value slurred together (♩♪). In such cases, in pianoforte music especially, the second note must be slightly curtailed (♪ ♩ ♪), this being one of the most important rules in phrasing. Authorities differ as regards accenting but the rule sometimes found that, irrespective of position in the bar, the first note is *always* to be stressed is now recognized as a fallacy; the performer should be guided by his musical sense as to when cross-accent is applicable (see Matthay's booklet, *Slur or Couplet of Notes*).

COUPLEUX and **GIVELET.** See *Electric* 4.

COUPPEY. See *Le Couppey*.

COUPURE (Fr.). 'Cut', i.e. portion omitted.

COURANTE, or **CORRENTE,** or **CORANTO,** or **CORANT** (literally a 'running'). Like other old dance types, this has existed in a bewildering variety of rhythms and styles. As met with by performers and students today it falls into two classes.

(1) The Italian type, or *Corrente*, or *Coranto*. This is simply a rapid, running, three-in-a-measure dance type. Incessant motion and triple time are its chief marks. It consists of two balancing sections, i.e. is in simple binary form (see *Form* 5).

(2) The French type, or *Courante*. This was the great dance of the elegant world of the France of Louis XIV. It, also, is a three-in-a-measure type and in simple binary form, but instead of a more or less even flow of quick notes it often has a greater variety of rhythm. Each of its two balancing sections ends with a bar that departs from the simple triple time of the signature and substitutes compound duple time ($\frac{6}{4}$ instead of $\frac{3}{2}$); presumably this had its rise in some peculiarity of the final steps of each section of the dance. Frequently this rhythmic anomaly (see *Rhythm* 6) appears, also, earlier in the course of the music and there are even instances in Bach's keyboard music of the one kind of time in one hand simultaneously with the other kind in the other hand.

The courante (of one or the other type) was a standard constituent of the classical suite (q.v.). It followed the allemande and stood to it in the same relation as the galliard to the pavan in earlier usage (see *Pavan and Galliard*). All the seventeenth- and earlier eighteenth-century instrumental composers wrote courantes of one type or the other, or both—Purcell, Couperin, Bach, Handel, etc. Sometimes courantes are seen which do not conform very precisely to either of the two types. These are usually mere rapid three-in-a-measure pieces.

Occasionally the courante was followed by 'Doubles', i.e. variations (see *Ornaments* 3).

As a dance the courante seems to have been, in all countries, an aristocratic, not a folk type. There are many allusions to the coranto in Elizabethan literature (e.g. Shakespeare's in *Henry V*—'lavoltas high and swift corantos' and other references), and in Stuart literature (e.g. Pepys at a court ball—'The Corants grew tiresome'). The Elizabethan composers wrote many as virginal pieces.

COURCELL. See *Mechanical Reproduction of Music* 13.

COURROIE (Fr.). 'Strap.'

COURVILLE, THIBAUT DE. See *Concert* 2.

COURVOISIER, KARL. He was born at Basle in 1846 and died in Liverpool in 1908, aged sixty-one. He was a distinguished violinist and violin teacher (pupil and follower of Joachim), a conductor, and a composer. For the last twenty-three years of his life he lived in Liverpool, where (curiously) he specialized as a teacher of singing.

See *Temperament* 10.

COUSINEAU. See *Harp* 2 c.

COUVERT, COUVERTE (Fr., masc. and fem), 'Covered.'

COVENT GARDEN THEATRE. See *Opera* 23; *Hallelujah Chorus.*

COVENTRY. See *Mysteries*, etc.

COVERDALE, MILES (1488–1568). Translator of the Bible. See *Psalm* (near end); *Hymns and Hymn Tunes* 17 e i; *Ballad* 1.

COWARD, HENRY. Born at Liverpool in 1849 and died at Sheffield in 1944, aged ninety-four. Beginning life as an apprentice in a Sheffield cutlery works he became, in his early twenties, a school teacher and, in a short time, headmaster. He had studied music ardently under Tonic Sol-fa teachers and from Tonic Sol-fa books and when nearing forty adopted the musical profession. For nearly half a century he occupied the leading position in Britain as a trainer of choirs, from time to time taking choirs to various parts of the continents of Europe, America, and Africa, and to Australasia. He retired from active work at the age of 84.

His knighthood, in 1926, gave pleasure to all his musical countrymen.

COW-BELL. This instrument, nowadays to be found in dance bands, but also used by Strauss in his 'Alpine' Symphony, and perhaps by some other serious composers, consists of the ordinary cow-bell of the mountain districts of Central Europe, with the clapper removed. It is fixed to a drum and struck with the stick of a snare drum. See *Bell* 5.

COWBOY SONGS. See *Folk Song* 4.

COWELL, HENRY (p. 1061, pl. **174.** 8). Born at Menlo Park, California, in 1897 and died at Shady, N.Y., in 1965, aged sixty-eight. He was a violin prodigy until the age of eight, then a pianist who at fourteen invented 'tone clusters' (q.v.), played with the fists and forearm. As a composer he went his own way, experimenting with instrumental effects and seeking a common basis for Eastern and Western musical art. He composed over 900 works, including nineteen symphonies, many other orchestral works, and ten quartets and other chamber music, most of them distinguished by wit and skill rather than profundity. He was very active as lecturer, writer, and organizer.

See *Cage, J.*; *Symphony* 8 (1897); *Pianoforte Playing* 10; *Electric Musical Instruments* 5 a; *Thunder Stick*; *Chamber Music* 6 (Period III—1897); *Concerto* 6 c (1897); *History* 9; *Harpsichord* 9.

COWEN, FREDERICK HYMEN. Born in Jamaica in 1852 and died in London in 1935, aged eighty-three. He came to England in infancy, and when he was six a waltz and when he was eight an operetta of his were published.

He early made a name as pianist (playing a concerto of his own in London when seventeen), and studied at Leipzig and Berlin. He quickly became known as composer and conductor, in the latter capacity for a time helping Costa (q.v.) at His Majesty's Theatre and later succeeding Sullivan at the Philharmonic Society.

At thirty-six he went to Melbourne, conducting at the Exhibition there for a fee of over eight hundred pounds per month for six months. A few years later he was appointed conductor of the Hallé Orchestra in Manchester and, after that, of the Scottish Orchestra. He conducted at all the festivals and received all the possible official honours, including that of knighthood.

His music is variable in quality. He descended to the Victorian drawing-room level in a number of 'ballads', the 'sacred' ones marking perhaps his lowest point; but he wrote also songs of considerable artistic merit and orchestral music that is always, though light and fanciful, yet soundly designed. His operas, both grand and light, are dead and his oratorios dying; one or two of his cantatas still have vitality. Probably his best music is amongst that for orchestra—usually very ably scored.

For passing references see *England* 7; *Oratorio* 7 (1877, 1888, 1895, 1910); *Concerto* 6 c (1852); *Symphony* 8 (1852).

COWPER, WILLIAM (1731–1800). Poet and hymn-writer. See reference under *Hymns and Hymn Tunes* 6.

CRAB CANON (*Canon Cancrizans*). See *Canon.*

CRACOVIENNE (Fr.) or **KRAKOWIAK** (Polish). A lively Polish dance, presumably originating in the district of Cracow. It is sometimes described as a sort of simpler polonaise (q.v.), but is in two-in-a-measure time—with some syncopation. It is usually danced by a large party: there is a good deal of striking of the heels together and often extemporized stanzas are sung by performers. Sometimes it is danced by a mere couple, with dramatic actions (see a description in Niecks's *Chopin*, vol. ii, p. 233).

Chopin's neglected op. 14 is a krakowiak (Grand Concert Rondo for Piano with Orchestra); it is his only example. Paderewski published five.

CRADLE SONG. Same as *Berceuse* (q.v.).

CRAFTSMANSHIP IN MUSIC. See *Quality in Music* 4.

CRAMER FAMILY. The founder of this important musical family was Jacob Cramer, a violinist in the famous orchestra at Mannheim (for an allusion to which orchestra see *Stamitz Family*). It is impossible to list here all those of his sons and grandsons who made a name for themselves. The most prominent are the following:

(1) WILHELM. Born at Mannheim in 1745 and died in London in 1799, aged fifty-four. He came to London at the age of twenty-seven and soon attained a commanding position as solo violinist and as leader of all the chief orchestras and director of that of the King. His compositions are of slight importance.

(2) FRANZ, or François (1772–1848). Son of the above. He also was a London violinist and he also attained the position of director of the royal orchestra.

(3) JOHANN BAPTIST (p. 797, pl. **136**. 3). Born at Mannheim in 1771 and died in London in 1858, aged eighty-seven. He was a son of Wilhelm, and coming to London at the age of one year made that his chief place of residence henceforth. He studied piano under J. S. Schroeter (see description of his methods under *Pianoforte Playing* 1) and then under Clementi (q.v.), and appeared in public from the age of ten, at times touring a good deal on the Continent and sometimes living there for a year or two. He wrote quantities of pianoforte studies, which have not dropped out of use, and some of which are available in an edition, by J. S. Shedlock, reproducing a copy Beethoven (who thought very highly of his playing) prepared for the use of his own nephew. He also wrote over 100 sonatas and a good many concertos and other works, but these are now superseded.

Like his master Clementi, he founded an English business firm—that now known as Cramer & Co., at first devoted to publishing and afterwards also to piano-making.

See *Pianoforte Playing* 2, 5; *Étude*; *Publishing of Music* 7; *Recital*; *Rousseau's Dream*; *Nicknamed Compositions* 3 (allusion to Beethoven's 'Emperor' Concerto); *Concerto* 6 b (1771).

(4) CRAMER & CO. See under 3 above, and also under *Recital*; *Publishing of Music* 7.

CRAMIGNON. See *Belgium* 6 (end).

CRANMER, THOMAS (1489–1556). Archbishop of Canterbury. See references under *Common Prayer*; *Cathedral Music* 3; *Psalm* (near end).

CRANZ. See *Publishing* 8.

CRAS, JEAN. Born at Brest in 1879 and died in 1932, aged fifty-three. He was a Rear-Admiral in the French Navy and the successful composer of operas, orchestral music, chamber music, etc.

CRASH CYMBAL. See *Chinese Crash Cymbal*.

CRAWFORD, MRS. ·JULIA. See *Kathleen Mavourneen*.

CRAWFORD, RUTH PORTER. Born at East Liverpool, Ohio, in 1901 and died at Chevy Chase, Md., in 1953. She was a composer of chamber music, etc.

CRAXTON, HAROLD. Born in London in 1885 and died there in 1971, aged eighty-five. His early career was as an able accompanist. As a recitalist he specialized in sixteenth-, seventeenth-, and eighteenth-century English music, and he published editions of some of this, as well as original compositions. He was a Professor at the Royal Academy of Music from 1919 to 1960.

CREATION MASS (Haydn). See *Nicknamed Compositions* 13.

CRÉCELLE (Fr.). 'Rattle'. See *Percussion Family* 3 r, 5 r.

CREDO. See *Mass* 2 c, 3 c. For the versified Lutheran version see *Chorale*.

CREDO MASS (Mozart). See *Nicknamed Compositions* 15 (K. 257).

CREED. Three creeds are in use in both the Roman Catholic and Anglican Churches. The earliest in origin is probably the so-called *Apostles' Creed*. The *Nicene Creed* is a little later in date; it was framed to rebut the Arian heresy by the Council called together by Constantine the Great, at Nicaea in Bithynia, A.D. 325. The so-called *Athanasian Creed* ('Quicunque vult') is much later than Athanasius, dating from the fifth or sixth century. The Roman Catholic Church has also the *Creed of Pope Pius* (1564), or 'Professio Fidei Tridentina', arising out of the Decrees of the Council of Trent. The Greek Church has formally accepted only one of the above creeds, the Nicene, without, however, the clause which states that the Holy Spirit proceeds from the Father *and the Son* ('filioque'), which clause was not in the original creed but dates from the fifth or sixth century and has been a source of division between the Eastern and the Western Churches.

In the Anglican Church the Apostles' Creed is recited in Morning and Evening Prayer, the Nicene Creed in the Communion service (as in the Roman Mass), and the Athanasian Creed is appointed to replace the Apostles' Creed on certain mornings of festivals during the year. The Athanasian damnatory clauses are regarded by many as inconsistent with Christian charity and the Protestant Episcopal Church of the United States has deleted it from its Prayer Book. In defiance of the rubric, it is never heard in a number of English churches.

Some particulars as to the place of the Creed in the services of the Roman Catholic and Anglican churches, and of the music associated with it, will be found under *Mass* 2 c, 3 c, and *Common Prayer*.

CREED (inventor). See *Improvisation* 4.

CREIGHTON. See *Creyghton*.

CREMBALUM (med. Lat.). Jew's Harp (q.v.).

CREMONA. See *Italy* 6; *Violin Family* 4. Also (for organ stop) *Organ* 14 VI; *Krumhorn*.

CREOLE MUSIC. The name applied to the indigenous music of Latin America. Some of its rhythms are peculiar to it. The melodies are often accompanied by a short bass phrase (largely consisting of tonic, dominant, and subdominant) repeated over and over again with slight changes.

The castanets are a good deal used in the Spanish version and claves and maracas in the Cuban.

See also *Rumba*.

CRESCENDO (It.). 'Increasing' (in tone, i.e. getting gradually louder). (Cf. *Geminiani*.)

CRESCENDO PEDAL. An organ device which brings into action all the stops successively, according to their power. There is a similar device for throwing them out of action.

CRESTON, PAUL (original name Joseph Guttoveggio; p. 1068, pl. **175**. 8.). Born in New York in 1906. He comes of a family that was not able to afford him anything beyond an elementary general education and, though he had some piano and organ lessons, as a composer he is practically self-taught. In 1934 he became organist of a New York church. In 1938 he won a Guggenheim Fellowship. His works include many for piano, as well as five symphonies, twelve concertos, and choral compositions. He has made an intensive study of rhythmic problems, and has engaged in other musicological research.

See references under *Percussion* 2 g; *Concerto* 6c (1906).

CREYGHTON or **CREIGHTON,** RO-BERT. Born about 1639 and died at Wells, Somersetshire, in 1734, aged about ninety-five. He was the son of the Bishop of Bath and Wells, and was himself in orders and canon and precentor of Wells Cathedral. For a short time he was Professor of Greek at Cambridge. He composed church music that is still widely sung.

CREYGHTONIAN SEVENTH. In all diatonic compositions it is common for the final Perfect Cadence (see *Cadence*) to be preceded by the subdominant chord in root position and it was a mannerism with Creyghton (see above) to add to this chord the (diatonic) seventh.

CRICOID CARTILAGE. See *Voice* 21.

CRIES OF LONDON. See *Street Music* 2.

CRIES OF PARIS. See *Street Music* 2.

CRIPPEN. See *Ballad* 1.

CRISP, SAMUEL (d. 1783). See *Pianoforte* 17.

CRISTOFORI, BARTOLOMEO (1655–1731). See *Pianoforte* 2, 3, 10, 13.

CRITICISM OF MUSIC

1. The Beginnings of the Newspaper Press.
2. Musical Criticism in Germany and Austria.
3. Musical Criticism in France.
4. Musical Criticism in Britain.
5. Musical Criticism in the United States.
6. The Qualifications of a Critic.
7. Criticism is Opinion.
8. Anonymity.
9. The Duty of Attack.
10. Critics and the Law of Libel.
11. The Disabilities of Critics.
12. Neglected Events.
13. 'Every Man his own Critic.'

(For illustrations see p. 257, pl. **47**.)

The public criticism of music is an intellectual activity in which very many are now professionally engaged, and which is an unceasing subject of discussion amongst those interested in the art, so that, indeed, it may be said that nothing is more criticized than criticism. Some brief treatment of the subject should, then, appear in a musical work of reference.

1. The Beginnings of the Newspaper Press. Newspapers, as we now recognize them, may be said to have begun in the early seventeenth century, the dates generally accepted for the first in Germany, Britain, and France being respectively 1609, 1622, and 1631. The first American newspaper (the *Boston News Letter*) followed early in the next century —1704. Although some news notices of concert and opera performances occur in comparatively early times, there is little or nothing of what we should today call music criticism. The critical spirit was, it is true, very actively applied to music during the eighteenth century, but it found its place of expression rather in pamphlets and books than in the periodical press.

2. Musical Criticism in Germany and Austria. It is perhaps fair to say that the serious criticism of current musical activities began in Germany with the issue by the prolific Mattheson, of Hamburg, from 1722 to 1725, of his occasional essays, with news and criticism, in his sheet called *Critica Musica*. Mizler's *Bibliothek* (mostly monthly) ran from 1736 to 1754, and Scheibe's *Der critische Musikus* (weekly) from 1737 to 1740.

It will be seen later that these German critical publications (only a few of many which appeared during the eighteenth century) considerably antedated any in Britain, and such publications have, since the initial attempts, played an important role in German musical life. The idealistic, philosophical, and polemical tendencies of the German temperament, combined with its attachment to music, have always promoted a vigorous critical expression.

The name of E. T. A. Hoffmann (q.v.;

p. 397, pl. **68**. 6) can hardly be omitted, nor that of Thibaut (q.v.), who wrote a striking book *On Purity in Music* (frequently republished between 1825 and 1861 and translated into English in 1877)—'Read it often as you grow older,' said Schumann in his *Advice to Young Musicians*. Schumann's own *Neue Zeitschrift für Musik* (see *Schumann*), which began under his editorship in 1834 with a laudatory and prophetic article about Chopin, and in which he ceased writing in 1853 with a similar article on Brahms, exercised a most valuable, purifying, and progressive influence.

In the strategic centre of Vienna the greatest name has been that of Hanslick (q.v.), who was critic of various papers there from 1848 to 1895. He is famous for his support of Schumann and Brahms and notorious for his bitter opposition to Liszt and Wagner (p. 257, pl. **47**. 1). His book *On Musical Beauty* went through a dozen German editions during the sixty years that followed its appearance in 1854, and has been much translated.

3. Musical Criticism in France. Active musical criticism in France (which for this purpose means Paris) may be said to have begun with the pamphlet-fisticuffs of the 'Guerre des Bouffons', 1752–4 (see *Bouffons*), and to have received a fresh stimulus from the similar struggle between the Gluckists and Piccinists, 1776–9 (see *Piccini*).

The great names of the French Encyclopedia (1751–72) are great names also in the history of French musical discussion at the period— Diderot, d'Alembert, Rousseau, Grimm; there has never been another period or another country where the best intellects devoted themselves to the discussion of music as those in Paris did at this period. Later names of high importance are those of Fétis, who in 1826 founded his *Revue musicale* and who served as critic of the *Temps* and the *National*, and Berlioz, whose critical writing in the *Journal des débats* from 1835 to 1863 was very vigorous, much of it being still obtainable in book form. (For a caricature of Berlioz himself under criticism see p. 257, pl. **47**. 5.)

The first French periodical definitely devoted to music was the *Journal de musique française et italienne* (1764–8).

4. Musical Criticism in Britain. In the very thoughtful introductory chapter of the last volume of Burney's *History of Music* (1789) he says, 'Musical criticism has been so little cultivated in this country that its first elements are hardly known', and he goes on to credit the Newcastle organist Avison with being the 'first and almost the only writer, who attempted it'. The allusion is to Avison's famous *Essay on Musical Expression* (1752 and subsequent editions), which provoked much discussion and several public replies, at the time it appeared, by its frank treatment of Handel and others. It may, perhaps, as Burney suggests, be conveniently taken as marking the beginning of the free public critical discussion of music in

Britain. Of course there had been sporadic expression of opinion before this (as, for instance, of opera in the *Spectator*), but this was serious and systematic critical writing by an accomplished musician.

Burney's *History* itself, in its later chapters, abounds in candid expressions as to the composers and executants of his day (especially opera singers); and as these are brought down to the very musical season preceding the issue of the volume it may be said to approach the condition of criticism of current activities. His famous book on the great Handel Festival of 1784 includes a good deal of criticism of performers. One or two items of this (especially an encomium upon Fischer's oboe playing) are from the pen of George III, who asked to see the work before the stage of binding was reached, read it carefully, and made these additions, which the author felt it incumbent on him to accept, cancelling the existing sheets in question and printing others in their place. Here, then, we have a king as critic.

As there appears to have been a public for this sort of writing it seems a little curious that the ordinary newspapers did not make any real attempt to meet it. Mrs. Oliphant, in *The Victorian Age in English Literature*, states that the *Morning Post* (founded 1772, amalgamated with the *Daily Telegraph* 1937) was 'the first amongst newspapers to give systematic reports of plays and concerts', but the first to employ a professionally trained musician as critic is said to have been *The Times*, the step being taken through the influence of one of the managers of the paper, T. M. Alsager (q.v.), who was a keen enthusiast for music.

The great traditions of English musical criticism may be said to have been established by two men in particular, J. W. Davison (p. 257, pl. **47**. 4) 'who was music critic of *The Times* from 1846 to 1879, and H. F. Chorley (p. 257, pl. **47**. 3), who was music critic of the (weekly) *Athenaeum* from 1833 to 1868. These men were powerful, well-informed, and sincere writers with a conservative or 'classical' tendency, standing in the gate as adversaries of Schumann, Berlioz, and Wagner. Referring to the antagonism of *The Times* critic in 1855, Wagner, years afterwards, said, 'Just reflect how colossal and universal is the paper of which I am speaking'. At the period complained of Davison had comprehensively and emphatically stated, 'Robert Schumann has had his innings and then been bowled out like Richard Wagner'.

Complaints of the conservatism of British critics long persisted, and as late as 1895 we find Hadow, in the influential opening chapters of his *Studies in Modern Music*, where he lays down a theory of criticism, averring, 'Our guides are astray', and supporting his assertion with a sketch of the blunders of British music critics during the previous three-quarters of a century.

Coincident with the rise of musical criticism in the British general press was that of a musical periodical press (see *Journals devoted to Music*).

5. Musical Criticism in the United States. The first musical journal in the United States was *Dwight's Journal of Music* (1852–81) which fought the battle of Chopin, Mendelssohn, and Schumann, but only lukewarmly supported the more radical innovators, Berlioz, Wagner, and Liszt; in fact, Dwight's position was much that of Hanslick, already mentioned (2). It is to be noted that at the time this valuable organ was founded in Boston none of the newspapers of that city had a specialist writer on music. In later life Dwight himself served as critic of the *Boston Transcript*.

Critics of the daily press who did a great deal to inform and lead public opinion were Horace Howland and Frederick Schwab on the *New York Times*, and William Fry (q.v.) and John Rose Green Hassard (1836–88) on the *New York Tribune*. The last-named held a position of outstanding influence; he was one of the most discerning champions of Wagner and other contemporary composers.

From the closing years of the nineteenth century, musical criticism in the United States became very important, such names as those of Finck (1854–1926), Krehbiel (1854–1923), Hale (1854–1934), Henderson (1855–1937), Huneker (1860–1921), and Aldrich (1863–1937) being almost as familiar to and respected in the European music world as in the American.

The large amount of space given to music in American journals (and especially in their enormous Sunday editions, which are quite unlike anything known in Europe) has contributed towards the serious development of the art of criticism.

6. The Qualifications of a Critic. In discussing literary criticism with the novelist, Fanny Burney, Dr. Johnson said:

'There are three distinct kinds of judges upon all new authors and productions; the first are those that know no rules but pronounce entirely from their natural taste and feelings; the second are those that know and judge by rules; and the third are those who know but are above the rules. These last are those you should wish to satisfy. Next to them rate the natural judges; but ever despise those opinions that are formed by the rules.'

Had he been competent to discuss music with Fanny Burney's father he might have said just the same of that art.

By knowledge of 'rules' can be meant nothing more than a knowledge of precedents and a wise generalization therefrom, and indeed incessant and thoughtful reflection upon a wide previous experience, either of music or of its performance, is the best foundation for the music critic's work. It amounts to the same thing as the possession of general principles and a standard by which to judge.

The frequent but thoughtless demand that the critic should be able himself to do the action he criticizes was on another occasion quickly answered by Johnson:

'Why no, Sir; this is not just reasoning. You may abuse a tragedy, though you cannot write one. You may scold a carpenter who has made you a bad table, though you cannot make a table. *It is not your trade to make tables.*'

At the same time it may be admitted that the critic of tables who has himself made them is likely to offer more 'constructive' criticism than the one who has never done so. But to expect the music critic to be able to 'make' in all the varied arts of composer, conductor, pianist, violinist, vocalist, etc., and even librettist and ballet dancer, is obviously unreasonable. The indispensable qualification for good judgement on a table is, obviously, not the having made one or two but the having *seen and used* many.

It may even be that there is some disadvantage in the critic being himself a composer. John Drinkwater said that it is a mistake for a man to attempt to criticize the art he himself professes: 'the poet-critic, for instance, is bound to be attracted by the man whose habit in poetry resembles his own.' There have been many instances of composers' failure to recognize one another's virtues. Cherubini, Auber, and Boïeldieu could see nothing in Berlioz; Schumann and others did not appreciate Wagner; Weber at one time attacked Beethoven; Schubert did not care for Weber; Saint-Saëns admired the 'inexhaustible patience' of English audiences that were able to listen to Bach's 'fugues and interminable airs'; Tchaikovsky did not understand Brahms; and so on. Nevertheless, those composers who have exercised criticism professionally (one or two of whom are mentioned above) have not always been contemptible in their published judgements. Perhaps the best critic of composition is the widely read musician who has acquired the technique of composition and proved a good enough critic of himself to realize that he does not possess genius; he knows the game from the inside yet is probably not biased. The tart saying, 'He who can does and he who can't criticizes', is, then, not to be resented but to be accepted and welcomed.

But however much *knowledge* the critic may possess he must, as Dr. Johnson suggests, be largely guided by his instincts. The difference between the criticism of the general public and that of the expert is (or should be) that the general public likes or dislikes without knowing why and that the expert likes or dislikes and then checks his feelings by analytical examination—perhaps by this means bringing himself to an adjustment which he may find to be confirmed by fuller experience of the work or performance in question.

It must be recognized that sound judgement often depends upon the ability to recognize various qualities and then to strike a balance, and this is one respect in which the trained and experienced critic should naturally surpass the public.

7. Criticism is Opinion. When all is said as to the professional qualifications of the critic, it has to be recognized that criticism is but widely communicated personal opinion. The critic may make a show of passing judgement, but in point of fact he is only telling how he thinks judgement should be passed. Bernard Shaw, himself for some time (1888–94) music critic successively of the London *Star* and *World*, maintained that 'a critic should constantly keep his reader in mind of the fact that he is reading only one man's opinion and should take it for what it is worth'. And an admirable German critic has said that, after 'Courage, Love of Truth, and Discretion', the critic's greatest moral requirement is a 'Recognition of the subjectivity of all judgements even with the greatest striving after objectivity' (article in the Riemann–Einstein *Musiklexikon*, 1929 edition).

It may, indeed, be claimed that the best criticism is that which Gibbon, the historian of the Roman Empire, commended in the eighteenth century when discussing Longinus. There are, he says in effect, three kinds of criticism, the analytical, the merely explanatory, and the one he finds in the author mentioned—'He tells me his own feelings, and tells them with so much energy that he communicates them.' Gibbon is here speaking of that criticism which arises from admiration, but the principle is applicable to condemnatory criticism also. In certain instances any less personal sort of criticism becomes patently absurd; Beethoven's 'Grosse Fuge' for string quartet (op. 133) and the finale of his 'Choral' Symphony are examples of widely differing types of music about which competent critics have always differed and perhaps always will do, and the only helpful criticism of such things is the frankly subjective.

The assertion of a prominent British composer [Walford Davies] in 1921 (in a friendly letter to the present writer, who was at that time music critic of the London *Observer*): 'We stand in such great need at the moment of musical criticism with the weight of simple impersonal truth', means nothing more than 'We stand in such great need at the present moment of music critics who think as I do'. In the face of the notorious professional differences of opinion not only of critics of literature and painting, but also of eminent theological, medical, legal, and military authorities, it would be arrogant of any music critic to claim that he knows the way to 'simple impersonal truth'.

An official attempt to put into practice a system similar to that above mentioned was made in Nazi Germany in 1936, when Dr. Joseph Goebbels, Minister of Propaganda, decreed that in future critics of all forms of art should not be permitted to praise or blame but merely to describe.

8. Anonymity. As a corollary to the principle stated above that all criticism is opinion it may be suggested (without any claim that even this suggestion bears the stamp of 'simple, impersonal truth') that all criticism should be signed. Properly looked at, the most downright signed article is more modest than an expression of gentle opinion that bears no signature.

Roughly, the contents of a newspaper fall into three categories: news, leaders, and criticism. News is (or purports to be) mere fact, and as such requires no signature; the 'leading articles' represent the considered policy of the journal, and are thus proper matter for 'we', being, so to speak, signed by the controlling staff of the journal itself; literary, dramatic, art, and music criticism, on the other hand, is merely the opinion, in each case, of one individual, and as its value depends on his identity this should be known. This is of the more importance as almost every journal employs on occasion more than one critic in any branch of art; in some cases three or four critics are employed, and if neither signature nor initials be appended the public never comes to individualize these and to observe the special personal leanings of each. Cases have been known where a performer has been highly praised on one day by the 'we' of a paper and utterly condemned on another day of the same week, again by the anonymous 'we'.

It is quite unfair to composer and artist that their powers should be subjected to public dissection by individuals who conceal their identity. This is increasingly recognized in British journalism, but, on the whole, general American practice has, in this regard, longer been correct.

Ella, the great chamber-music impresario of London in the mid-nineteenth century, so strongly objected to anonymous criticism that he reproduced in each programme the various notices of the previous concert, appending what he believed to be the name of the writer of each. *The Times* objected; its critic, Davison, considered Ella's action an impertinence, and so *The Times* ceased to notice Ella's concerts. Present-day journalistic opinion would, usually, support Ella, but there still remains some difference of view on the point.

9. The Duty of Attack. It is sometimes said that condemnatory criticism is illegitimate and if a composition or a performer is bad the critic should ignore it, giving his space only to what he can praise. This overlooks what may be called 'the double duty of the gardener', whose cultivation of the flowers will not be successful if he does not remove weeds. Schumann said, 'The critic who dares not to attack what is bad is but a half-hearted supporter of what is good'. There is much composition and performance which every critic and every musician of experience knows to be vulgar and merely pretentious, and it is this which an idealist like Schumann would wish to see denounced for the public instruction.

It is true that in the past a good deal of attack upon novel types of composition or idiom has been later proved mistaken, but it has at least promoted healthy discussion when critical silence would have failed to do so.

At all events, a critic who is only expressing half his mind is only half a critic, and the constant repression of deeply felt opinion is bound in time to injure his critical faculty.

10. Critics and the Law of Libel. The statement is sometimes seen that British critics are, by the Law of Libel, unfairly restricted in the free expression of their opinions on a composition or a performance.

Any book upon the English Law of Libel would show that this view is mistaken. It has been said over and over again that criticism of an artist who exhibits himself to the public is never actionable, no matter how severe or mistaken; provided only that it is not a cloak for personal invective or based on matters not connected with the performance under discussion. The same sound principle naturally applies to the criticism of compositions, or anything offered for public exhibition. Music critics at a concert or opera performance are invariably there by the invitation of the concert-giver or opera manager, who has sent them tickets with the very purpose of securing their criticism, and who is then 'asking for it'— whether 'it' should turn out to be pleasing to him or the reverse.

It has been thought well to include this article in the present book in order to remove a somewhat common misconception, which, if it gained ground, would become a menace to the artistic standards of the country to which it applies.

There is unfortunately one group of performers almost immune from adverse criticism —those who have attained high public fame. In many cases these fall greatly from their own original standard, either from declining powers, or from the carelessness of security, or from a growing inability to hear their own performance, due to repeating the same limited repertory to an unlimited extent; yet (in Britain at any rate) editors are shocked at any plain speaking about public favourites such as would offend a public loyal to its favourites long after the claim to favour has gone. Some British critics are, then, in the position of being able to write with perfect freedom of every performer except a protected half a dozen—which is dishonest![1]

11. The Disabilities of Critics. The main complaint of the conscientious critic, however, is that he is overworked. If he exercises his craft in any but one of the few greatest centres of artistic activity he is expected to earn a good part of his living by teaching or in some other way; if he exercises it in one of those centres he

is compelled to hear so much music that he has little time or energy left for study, and, moreover, has the fine edge of his perception and his enthusiasm blunted by excessive listening.

When a complex new work is produced it is obvious that the critic who has carefully studied its score is at the first performance in the position for adequate appraisement that he would otherwise have occupied after two or three hearings. Real efficiency, then, demands such study, but the time and effort demanded are usually too great. Undoubtedly a proportion of the critical blunders that are made respecting new productions are due to the partial or complete bewilderment of the critic, expected to express a considered opinion after one hearing of a work to which the composer has perhaps devoted many months.

The British and American custom of going straight from the concert-room to the hasty drafting of a notice for the following day's issue is an aggravating factor, and the practice in most Continental countries of allowing the critic a day or two in which to reflect on his impressions and to shape a balanced expression of them has advantages.

The opportunity of reflection is further reduced when the critic has to attend several concerts on the same afternoon and evening. 'Criticism' so produced is obviously unfair to concert-givers.

From certain objectionable practices of the past, British critics have now, however, been delivered. There is practically nowhere in the newspaper world any connexion between advertisement and criticism, and attempted bribery may be said to be quite unknown.

12. Neglected Events. On the other hand, a vicious convention (perhaps a relic of the days when advertisement was supposed to give a right to notice) still remains in force. A programme of very slight interest given to a small audience in a public hall in the centre of the city will receive attention whilst a more interesting one in the suburbs will be entirely neglected. Organ recital activities are frequently overlooked, and the immense amount of music to which by means of radio great numbers of a newspaper's readers are listening in their own homes does not, as a rule, receive the advantage of public discussion.

13. 'Every Man his own Critic.' Finally, it may be laid down, without any suggestion derogatory to the value of the work of professional critics, that the true principle of music criticism is 'Every man his own critic'. In other words, the public should be encouraged, whilst carefully reading the views of experts, to form its own—and to be ready to change them on cause being shown. This is a necessary condition of a healthy artistic life, and the best service the professional critic can render is to stimulate the amateur to think for himself.

See also *Journals devoted to Music*; *Germany* 9 b.

[1] P. A. S. can safely be assumed to be thinking of an incident during his period with *The Observer*, when his outspoken criticism of Paderewski incurred much displeasure from the editor, J. L. Garvin.

CROCHE (Fr.). Literally, 'Hook', i.e. a quaver or eighth-note (*not* a crotchet, or quarter-note, which is 'Noire'; see Table 3).

CROFT, WILLIAM (p. 164, pl. **33.** 5). Born in Warwickshire in 1678 and died at Bath in 1727, aged forty-eight. He wrote dignified and effective church music that has always remained in use (including the setting of the Burial Service), harpsichord music that was republished in 1921 and well merits the attention of pianists, violin music, and other things.

Some of the finest English hymn tunes (including *St. Anne*) are his.

He was organist of St. Anne's, Soho (1700–11), and of the Chapel Royal under Anne and George I, as also of Westminster Abbey, in which latter place he lies buried.

See references under *Sonata* 10 c; *Anthem* II; *Hymns and Hymn Tunes* 6; *Westminster Abbey*; *Nicknamed Compositions* 1.

CROISER (Fr.). 'To cross' (*Croiser les mains*, 'to cross hands'). So *croisant*, *croisé*, 'crossing', 'crossed'.

CROIX SONORE. See *Electric Musical Instruments* 1 g.

CROLE, CROLEUS. See *Crowley*.

CROMA (It.). 'Quaver' or 'eighth-note' (see Table 3).

CROMATICO, CROMATICA (It.; masc., fem.). 'Chromatic'; the plurals are *cromatici*, *cromatiche*.

CROMATICO, CORNO. Valve horn; see *Horn Family* 2 c, 3, 5.

CROMATISCHE HARMONIKA. See *Harmonica* 6 b.

CROMORNE. On French organs it is a delicate type of clarinet. But see *Krumhorn*.

CROMWELL, OLIVER (1599–1658). See *Puritans* 4; *Chapel Royal*; *Minstrels* 3; *Waits*; *Clubs for Music-Making*; *Street Music* 3; *Dance* 7; *Rogers, Benjamin*; *Deering, Richard*; *Masque*; *Mealtime*.

CROOK (or Shank). See *Acoustics* 8; *Brass*; *Trumpet Family* 2 b, 3; *Horn Family* 2 b; *Cornet*.

CROONING. An excessively sentimental type of soft singing, introduced about 1928 by male radio entertainers in the United States. The first prominent exponent was Rudy Vallée (Hubert Prior Vallée, born in Vermont in 1900).

CROS, CHARLES. See *Gramophone* 1.

CROSBY HALL, LONDON. See *Concert* 8.

CROSS-ACCENT. Syncopation (q.v.).

CROSSE, GORDON. Born at Bury, Lancs., in 1937. He studied under Wellesz at Oxford and later under Petrassi in Italy, then rapidly came to the fore as the composer of orchestral, chamber, and choral pieces, sometimes with children in mind as participants.

CROSS-FINGERING. Devices in the playing of wood-wind instruments to produce notes otherwise unobtainable owing to the absence of keys for them.

CROSS FLUTE. See *Flute Family* 5.

CROSS-RHYTHM. See *Rhythm* 6; *Proportion*.

CROT. Sometimes used for 'crwth' (q.v.).

CROTALES. See *Percussion Family* 3 q.

CROTCH, WILLIAM. Born at Norwich in 1775 and died at Taunton in 1847, aged

seventy-two. He was the son of a carpenter who loved music and had built himself an organ, in which, when little more than eighteen months old, the child began to show an interest. When two years and three months old, he had taught himself to play *God save the King* on this instrument, supplying by ear a true bass (p. 784, pl. **131.** 4). At four years old he was giving daily organ recitals in London. At seven he was playing violin and piano. At eleven he was pupil-assistant to the organist of King's and Trinity Colleges, Cambridge, and at fourteen he had an oratorio of his performed in that city. At fifteen he was organist of Christ Church Cathedral, Oxford; at nineteen he took his Mus.Bac.; at twenty-two he was Professor of Music in the University, having in the meantime accumulated a number of academic musical positions that need not be mentioned here. At twenty-four he took his Mus.Doc. Later he became the first Principal of the Royal Academy of Music in London.

The promise was that he would become a second Mozart; he became instead a man of musical learning and the composer of works that, whilst popular in their day, did not rise so high above the level of contemporary production as to secure immortality. His oratorio *Palestine* (published 1812) had great vogue, and one number in it, 'Lo, Star-led Chiefs', appears with amazing frequency in early nineteenth-century English programmes and is still sung in English churches and cathedrals at Epiphanytide.

He was an able water-colour painter.

See references under *Anglican Chant* 4; *Anthem* Period IV; *Organ* 13; *Congregational Churches* 4; *Oxford*; *Schools of Music*.

CROTCHET. (♩) The 'quarter-note', i.e. a quarter the time-value of the whole-note or semibreve. (Avoid confusion with the French *Croche*, i.e. 'hook', which means quaver or eighth-note, *Noire*, i.e. 'black', being crotchet.) See Table 1.

CROTOLA. Same as 'Crotales'. See *Percussion Family* 3 q.

CROUCH, FREDERICK NICHOLLS. Born in London in 1808 and died at Portland, Maine, in 1896, aged eighty-eight. At nine he was playing in the orchestra of a London theatre. Later, from poverty, he served as a common seaman on coasting smacks plying between the Thames and the Forth. Then he played the cello in the orchestra of Drury Lane Theatre, sang in the choirs of Westminster Abbey and St. Paul's Cathedral, and studied at the Royal Academy of Music. He taught singing at Plymouth, invented the engraving process known as zincography, took his cello to New York and played it in orchestras there, practised the profession of music in Boston and elsewhere, and served through the American Civil War on the Confederate side.

He is remembered by one composition out of a great number once popular—the song 'Kathleen Mavourneen' (q.v.). His daughter Eliza achieved fame in another profession as 'Cora Pearl'.

CROUTH. Same as 'crwth' (q.v.).

CROWD. Same as 'crwth' (q.v.). Hence the old English word *Crowder* for 'fiddler'.

CROWLEY, ROBERT. Also known as **Crole** and **Croleus** (*c.* 1518–88). See *Hymns and Hymns Tunes* 17 e (ii); *Anglican Chant* 3.

CROWN AND ANCHOR TAVERN. See *Concert* 6.

'CROWN OF JESUS' MUSIC. See *Roman Catholic Church Music in Britain.*

CROWTH. Same as 'crwth' (q.v.).

CRUCIFIXUS. See *Mass* 3 c.

CRÜGER, JOHANN (1598–1662). See *Germany* 3.

CRUISKIN (or **CRUISKEEN**) **LAWN** ('Little Jug Filled'). A famous Irish drinking-song, of the origin of which nothing is known. Benedict (q.v.) introduces it in his opera *The Lily of Killarney.*

CRUIT. Same as 'crwth' (q.v.).

CRUSADES, INFLUENCE OF. See *Bagpipe Family* 4; *Percussion Family* 4 (Kettledrums).

CRWTH (p. 417, pl. **72.** 2, 3). An ancient plucked and bowed stringed instrument which had a more or less rectangular frame, the lower half of which was filled in as a sound-box, with flat (or occasionally vaulted) back, the upper half being left open on each side of the strings. The strings ran over a bridge—of a peculiar kind, since one of its feet passed through a hole in the belly and rested on the back, thus serving as a sound-post. Through one side of the upper half of the frame the left hand was pressed to stop the strings. In the later forms there was a finger-board over which four strings could be stopped, and beside it two strings not capable of being stopped and only used as open strings (possibly plucked by the thumbs).

In the sixth century, as a plucked instrument, it seems to have been considered specifically British, and it lingered longest in the ancient British fastness of Wales (see *Wales* 4), a specimen having been heard at Caernarvon as late as the opening of the nineteenth century. The English name is *Crowd*, the Irish *Crot* or *Cruit*, the Medieval Latin *Chorus*. Other forms of the word are *Croud*, *Crowth*, and *Crouth*. It is said that in remote parts of Wales a violin is still called a crwth as in England a fiddler was long called a crowder. Still another name is *Rote*, or *Rotte* (not 'Rota', which is a hurdy-gurdy). Latterly the misleading name of 'Bowed Harp' has been applied to the crwth.

CRYSTAL PALACE See *Concert* 7, 12; *Annotated Programmes* 5; *Festival* 1; *Competitions in Music* 2, 3; *Additional Accompaniments.*

CSÁRDÁS. See *Czardas.*

CTESIBIUS. See *Hydraulus.*

CUCKOO. A single small two-note wind instrument that imitates the two-note song of the cuckoo and is used in 'Toy Symphonies' (q.v.) such as those of L. Mozart and Romberg. Something similar is often embodied in 'Cuckoo Clocks' (p. 544, pl. **99.** 5).

CUCUZELES. See *Greek Church* 3.

CUI, CÉSAR (p. 897, pl. **154.** 7.) Born at Vilna in 1835 and died in Petrograd in 1918, aged eighty-three. His name indicates his French origin, his father having been left wounded in Russia at the time of Napoleon's retreat and having remained there. The son entered the Russian army, became an authority on fortification, and attained the rank of general. He was a member of the group of 'The Five' (see *Russia* 5), but although theoretically devoted to their nationalistic principle he hardly applied it in practice. He was active as a composer of operas, songs, piano music, etc., and also as a critical writer.

See allusions under *Chopsticks*; *Dargomijsky.*

CUIVRE (Fr.). 'Copper', 'brass'. So *Les Cuivres* are 'the brass' of the orchestra.

CUIVRÉ (Fr.). 'Coppered', 'coppery', 'brassy'. The term is found occasionally in music for brass instruments, especially the horn, and indicates that the tones are to be forced, with a harsh, ringing timbre. Same as (Ger.) 'Schmetternd' (q.v.); see *Horn Family* 5. (A verb *cuivrer*, with imperative *cuivrez*, is sometimes seen; the present participle is *cuivrant*.)

CULMELL. See *Nin-Culmell.*

CUMMINGS, WILLIAM HAYMAN (1831–1915). Tenor singer, then professor of singing at the Royal Academy of Music and Principal of the Guildhall School of Music (1896). Musical antiquarian.

See *Fingering* 6; *God save the Queen* 18; *Misattributed* (Locke's 'Macbeth').

CUMMUN GAIDHEALACH. See *Scotland* 1.

CUM SANCTO SPIRITU. See *Mass* 3 b.

CUNDELL, EDRIC. Born in London in 1893 and died there in 1961, aged sixty-eight. His professional life began in the capacity of horn player at Covent Garden. He held a Scholarship for piano at Trinity College of Music, London, and then joined the staff. He did much orchestral conducting and composed chamber music, orchestral music, songs, etc. He was Principal of the Guildhall School of Music (1938–59).

CUPO (It.). 'Dark', 'sombre'.

CURTAIN MUSIC or **CURTAIN TUNE.** Same as *Act Tune* (q.v.).

CURTALL and **DOUBLE CURTALL.** See *Oboe Family* 2, 5 c.

CURTIS INSTITUTE. See *United States of America* 5 f; *Patronage* 7; *Notation* 4; *Organ* 8.

CURTIS, NATALIE. See *United States* 7.

CURWEN.

(1) **JOHN** (1816–80). Congregational minister. Founder of the Tonic Sol-fa method of teaching sight-singing, as also of the firm mentioned below (4).

See *Tonic Sol-fa*; *Oratorio* 5; *Measure*; *Congregational Churches* 5; *American Terminology* 1; *Hullah*; *Tone*; *Notation* 6; *Education* 1; *Ear Training*; *Chorale*; p. 976, pl. **163.** 4.

(2) **JOHN SPENCER** (1847–1916). Son of

John. He carried on his father's principles in life and work, his propaganda, and his business. He wrote the useful *Studies in Worship Music* (two series) and edited *The Musical Herald*.

See *Competitions* 2.

(3) ANNIE JESSY (Mrs. J. S. Curwen, wife of the above, *née* Gregg; 1845–1932). She was a very practical teacher of piano, who accepted the educational principles of her father-in-law and applied them logically to her own instrument in a series called *The Child Pianist*. She also wrote an admirable book on *The Psychology of Music Teaching*.

(4) J. CURWEN & SONS LTD. Founded by John Curwen in 1863, to publish material for his work, it later took on a wider range. It published *The Musical Herald* (at first under the name *Tonic Sol-fa Reporter*) until 1927.

See *Publishing* 7.

CURWEN MEMORIAL COLLEGE. See *Tonic Sol-fa College.*

CUSHION DANCE. An old dance in which the participant chose a partner by dropping a cushion before her or him. Cf. *Trescone.*

CUTTING. See *Scandinavia* 2.

CUVELIER, MARCEL. See *Jeunesses musicales.*

C.V.O. See *Knighthood and other Honours.*

CYCLIC FORM, or CYCLICAL FORM. This term is used in two meanings, one more general and the other more particular.

In the more general sense it means simply any work in several movements (see *Movement*), as, for instance, a suite, sonata, string quartet, or symphony. For the beginnings of Cyclic Form in this sense see *Nachtanz.*

In the more particular sense it means any such work of which the movements are connected in thought by the use of some musical theme (or themes) common to all.

The more general use is certainly the more common in works on Form in the English language, but when a French writer (e.g. Vincent d'Indy in his *Cours de composition*, 1909) uses the term 'Forme Cyclique' he apparently usually implies the more particular use. For an early exemplification of Cyclic Form in this sense see *Pavan and Galliard.*

The term is doubtless borrowed from literary usage—'A series of poems or prose romances collected around a central event or epoch of mythic history and forming a continuous narrative, as "The Arthurian Cycle"' (*Shorter Oxford English Dictionary*). Both musical uses of the term could be justified by this analogy, but, of course, in the more particular use the analogy is most complete.

Throughout the present work where the term is used it is in conformity with the commoner English application, i.e. the more general sense is implied.

Cf. *Song Cycle.*

CYKLUS (Ger.). 'Cycle.' So *Liedercyklus*, 'Song Cycle' (q.v.).

CYLINDER (Rotary), CYLINDRE (Fr.), **CILINDRO** (It., plural *Cilindri*). A type of valve in brass instruments, used a good deal in some parts of the continent of Europe; also in Britain and the United States, but there for the French horn only. *Rotary Valve* is another name.

The word 'cylinder' (without the word 'rotary'), in any language, has occasionally been used to mean merely the ordinary type of valve. Thus the *Trombone a Cilindri* is the valve trombone (see *Trombone Family* 1, 5).

CYLINDER REPRODUCTION OF MUSIC. See *Mechanical Reproduction of Music.*

CYLINDRICHORD. See *Mechanical Reproduction of Music* 13.

CYMANFA GANU. See *Wales* 8.

CYMBALOM, CYMBALON. The dulcimer (q.v.); also spelt 'cymbalum', 'czimbalom', and 'zymbalum', etc. See reference under *Hungary* (near end).

CYMBALS (Eng.), **CYMBALES** (Fr.). See *Percussion Family* 3 o, 4 b, 5 o; also *Choke Cymbals*; *Sizzle Cymbal*; *Chinese Crash Cymbal*; *Sting Cymbal.*

CYMBALUM ORALE (medieval Latin). Jew's Harp (q.v.).

CYMBASSO. This term, found in some of Verdi's scores, apparently indicates the use of the Tuba.

CYMBEL. See *Organ* 14 V.

CZAKANE. See *Recorder Family* 3 b.

CZARDAS, or CSÁRDÁS, or TCHARDACHE. One of the national dances of Hungary. It has two parts, a slow and melancholy *Lassú* and a quick and fiery *Friss*, which are taken in frequent alternation. The word comes from 'Tcharda'—tavern.

Cf. *Verbunko*; *Palotache.*

CZECHOSLOVAKIA. See *Bohemia.*

CZERNY, CARL (p. 797, pl. **136**. 5). Born in Vienna in 1791 and died there in 1857, aged sixty-six. He was a great pianist–pedagogue, the pupil of Beethoven, the teacher of Liszt (see p. 797, pl. **136**. 8), and the world's champion as writer of popular pianoforte studies. Of these he wrote hundreds and they are perhaps the only remaining public relics of a varied production that ran to 'Op. 1,000'.

See references of more or less importance under *Pianoforte Playing and Teaching* 2, 3, 5; *Improvisation* 2; *Délié* (3); *Composition* 5; *Concerto* 6 b (1791); *Hexameron*; *Étude.*

CZERVENKA. See *Gramophone* 4.

CZIBULKA, ALPHONS. Born in Hungary in 1842 and died in Vienna in 1894, aged fifty-two. He was a bandmaster in the Austrian army and a composer of popular operettas and dance music, as also of salon music for the piano (e.g. the *Stéphanie Gavotte*, which had an enormous vogue).

CZIMBAL, CZIMBALOM, CZIMBALON. Same as 'Cymbalom' (q.v.).

See the Article on page 274, Plate 49 and the Plate, *Ballet*, facing page 76

1. THE MORRIS IN THE 17TH CENTURY. (From a painting by Vinckenboom)

2. SWORD DANCE—THE LOCK

3. COTSWOLD MORRIS DANCERS

4. ABBOTS BROMLEY HORN DANCE (1944)

5. A SOUTH AFRICAN TRIBAL DANCE

6. A MODERN JAVANESE DANCE

1. DANCING FIGURES in the Cloisters of Magdalen College, Oxford

2. BRANLE. From the 'Romance of Renaud de Montaubon'

3. AN 18TH-CENTURY ALLEMANDE

4. THE COTILLON. By J. Collet, 1771

5. THE WALTZ IN 1816. From Wilson's *Description of German and French Waltzing*

6. THE POLKA (*c.* 1840)

D

D' (Fr.). 'Of', 'from' (abbreviation of *De*).

DA (It.). 'Of', 'from'.

DA CAPO (It.). 'From the head'; in other words, go back to the beginning and start again. There is then some indication where to stop, either the word *Fine*, 'end', or the pause mark, ⌒.

Sometimes the expression used is *da capo al segno*, 'from the beginning to the sign', or *da capo al fine*, 'from the beginning to the end'.

Sometimes, also, to one of these expressions is added *poi segue la coda*, 'then follows the Coda', meaning that, once arrived at the point indicated, a jump is to be made to the final section of the piece, generally in such a case marked 'Coda'.

Instead of *da capo*, the abbreviation *D.C.* is sometimes used.

DACTYL, DACTYLIC. See *Metre*.

DAFYDD Y GARREG WEN, i.e. David of the White Rock, otherwise David Owen, 1720–49 (see under *Rising of the Lark*). The tune called by his name is supposed to have been composed by him on his death-bed, on awakening from a trance in which he believed himself to have heard it in heaven. Sir Walter Scott wrote words to it, 'The Dying Bard'.

DAGINCOUR, DAGINCOURT. See *Agincourt*.

DAILY EXPRESS. See *Community Singing* 5.

DALAYRAC, NICOLAS (1753–1809). A very popular French operatic composer, writing delicate music of high dramatic effectiveness. For a reference see *Opera* 21 a.

D'ALBERT, EUGENE FRANCIS CHARLES. Born in Glasgow in 1864 and died at Riga in 1932, aged nearly sixty-eight. His father (a piano pupil of Kalkbrenner and a composition pupil of Samuel Sebastian Wesley) took up the dance, held important London theatrical positions as ballet master, settled in Newcastle-on-Tyne as a teacher of dancing, and wrote popular quadrilles and polkas, with a book on *Ballroom Etiquette*. The son became a scholarship-holder at the National Training School of Music (the predecessor of the Royal College of Music), whilst still a student made a London reputation as a public pianist, and at seventeen won the Mendelssohn Scholarship, entitling him to a period of study abroad. This period he spent at Vienna, then passing on to further study under Liszt. His playing soon became familiar to the public in all parts of the world, and his operas (especially *Tiefland*, 1903) had much performance, particularly in Central Europe.

He wrote two piano concertos, a symphony, two string quartets, piano pieces, and other things, and produced editions of the piano classics. (Cf. *Pianoforte Playing* 8.)

Amongst his six (successive) wives were Carreño, the pianist, and Hermine Finck, the singer.

DALCROZE. See *Jaques-Dalcroze*.

DALE, BENJAMIN JAMES. Born in London in 1885 and there died in 1943, aged fifty-eight.

He studied at the Royal Academy of Music, London, winning many prizes, and of this institution he later became a professor and (in 1937) Warden.

His Piano Sonata in D minor, op. 1 (1905) attracted much attention when it appeared. He composed a good deal of music for the neglected viola, as well as other things, but his later work failed to fulfil his early promise.

His first wife was the writer, Kathleen Dale.

DALL' ABACO. See *Abaco*.

DALLAM. Family of organ builders active in the late sixteenth century and throughout the seventeenth century. See references under *Mechanical Reproduction of Music* 4; *Cathedral Music* 6.

DALLAPICCOLA, LUIGI (p. 525, pl. **96**.6). Born at Pisino, Istria (then in Austria), in 1904 and died in Florence in 1975, aged seventy-one. He had his musical training in the Conservatory of Florence, and later joined its staff. As a composer he distinguished himself, beginning with his opera *Volo di notte* ('Night Flight'), 1940, as the possessor of an idiom uniting the demands of note-row technique with an exceptionally lyrical and expressive vocal style. In 1956 he joined the staff of Queen's College, New York. His best-known work is the opera *Il prigioniero* ('The Prisoner', 1949), and most of his compositions are for chorus or solo voice.

DALLEY-SCARLETT, ROBERT. Born in Sydney in 1887 and died in Brisbane in 1959, aged seventy-two. He became active as organist and as conductor and organizer of musical societies successively in Sydney, Adelaide, and Brisbane. He was known as a composer and through his broadcasting and literary activities, and was a notable Handel enthusiast.

DAL SEGNO (It.). 'From the sign', i.e. return to the sign 𝄋: and repeat thence to the word *Fine* (= 'end') or to a double-bar with a pause-sign above it.

DALYELL, SIR JOHN GRAHAM (1776–1851). Scottish antiquary. See reference to a useful work of his under *Horn Family* 3.

DAMAN. See *Damon*.

DAME. See *Knighthood and other Honours*.

DAMIAN. See *Reed-Organ Family* 4.

DAMON (or **Daman**), WILLIAM. A foreign musician employed at the court of Queen Elizabeth I. Some of his anthems, lute pieces, etc., exist (mostly in manuscript), but he is chiefly known by his collection of metrical psalm tunes.

See *Hymns and Hymn Tunes* 17 e (ix).

DAMP. To check the vibrations of an instrument (e.g. the kettledrum), generally by touching it in some way. For damping in the *Pianoforte* see under that instrument. Cf. *Gedämpft*.

DAMPER PEDAL (of pianoforte). See *Pianoforte* 12; *Pianoforte Playing* 5.

DAMPERS. See *Pianoforte* 2, 3, 6, 12, 16, and *Harpsichord* 5.

DÄMPFER (Ger.). 'Mute.' *Mit Dämpfern*, 'with mutes'—in any of the applications mentioned under *Mute*. *Dämpfung*, 'muting', or (piano) 'soft-pedalling'.

DAMROSCH, WALTER JOHANNES (p. 1041, pl. **170.** 9). Born at Breslau, Prussia, in 1862 and died in New York in 1950. On the death of his father, Leopold Damrosch (see *United States* 4; *Concert* 15; *Opera* 21 k), he became a conductor of opera and oratorio, thereafter conductor of the New York Sym-

phony Society—from 1885 until that body became amalgamated with the New York Philharmonic Society in 1927.

In the course of a long, busy, and extremely successful career he gave first American performances to many of the greatest works of the symphonic and operatic repertoires. It was he who brought Tchaikovsky to America in 1891, who proposed to him the composition of the Sixth Symphony, and who first conducted in America the Fifth and Sixth Symphonies.

He was long active as conductor of radio symphony concerts and radio educational concerts.

His compositions include four operas; incidental music; a Manila *Te Deum* (1898), a violin sonata, and songs. It is principally, however, as conductor and educator that he is remembered.

See *Appreciation of Music*; *Jazz* 5; *Applause* 7; *Te Deum*; *Opera* 24 f (1942); and see p. 1040, pl. **169.** 9.

DANBY, JOHN. Born 1757, probably of a Yorkshire family, and died in London in 1798, aged forty or forty-one. He was organist to the chapel of the Spanish embassy in London, and published some of the best glees ever written, notably the ever-popular 'Awake, Aeolian Lyre' (see *Glee* 2).

He lost the use of his limbs through sleeping in a damp bed at an inn, and died on the very night of a concert organized to relieve the poverty that had thus come upon him.

DANCE

1. Introductory.
2. The Ancient Nations.
3. The Orient.
4. The American Indians.

5. English Folk Dances.
6. The Court Dances of Europe.
7. The Religious Attitude towards Dancing.

8. Dancing as a Spectacle.
9. Influence of Dance on Music.
10. Old Authorities on the Dance.

(For illustrations see pp. 272, 273, pls. **48, 49.**)

1. Introductory. The impulse to express one's feelings or to recreate oneself in the dance is instinctive and universal. Dancing can be either a solo or a group performance; it can be either almost merely ornamental or the expression of generalized emotion (like 'Absolute Music', q.v.), or its gamut of expression can range all the way from that of the most solemn religious feeling to that of obscenity or the impulse to cruelty; it can be sober, dignified, and controlled, or it can burst out into hysteria, as in the whirlings of the dancing dervishes of some Muslim countries, which continue until the participants fall into a cataleptic state, or the dance manias of medieval Europe, when large portions of communities, moved by religious excitement, fell to dancing in the streets, some individuals at last dashing out their brains against the walls (see also *Tarantella*).

2. The Ancient Nations. In Ancient Egypt dancing was left to the lower orders and to professionals—mostly women; the sculptors convey much information about the place of the dance in daily life. Pottery designs show the

dance to have been greatly developed in Phoeni cia. Etruscan paintings show much dancing.

The Greeks were one of the greatest dancing peoples and brought the art of dancing to the highest point it ever reached, for the Parthenon frieze shows dancers in attitudes which have never been surpassed for suppleness and grace and which remain a perpetual source of reference for those who, from time to time, try to bring back the art of dancing to the ideal of beauty. The Greeks made dancing a part of their religious rites; they had many dances to Demeter and Aphrodite, and had also wild and even obscene dances in honour of Dionysus. They had also gymnastic, mimetic, and social dances, and in drama a part of the expression of the chorus was through the dance; the Greek Pyrrhic dance was a kind of dramatic ballet representing attack and defence by helmeted warriors (cf. *Bouffons*); the Romans later adopted it. The Greeks held the dance in honour. Youths and maidens danced together, but in adult life the sexes danced separately. There were several chain dances, holding hands (cf. *Farandole*). In Greek mythology Terpsichore was the muse of the dance.

The Romans gave dancing a lower place; the peasants danced on days of festivity but the better class thought dancing inconsistent with their dignity. Dancing by priests was a part of public worship, and by professionals a part of social entertainment. Mimetic dancing, or Pantomime (q.v.), was wonderfully developed during the Imperial period. The Romans had a funeral dance—as later had also the Spaniards (see *Pavan and Galliard*).

3. The Orient. All over the East the dance is greatly cultivated. There is a practice of setting aside girls for the profession of dancing, as the Geishas of Japan and the Nautch girls of India. In the Nautch dance there is very little movement of the feet, but the body and arms are used very beautifully and expressively. There is much dancing in Hindu temples. Bells round the ankles (cf. 5, also *Morris*) are much used in India. The Devil Dances of India and Ceylon are a means of exorcism in cases of illness. India has nothing like the European ballroom dances, and Indians are shocked when they see the sexes dancing together. (For a Javanese dancer see p. 272, pl. **48.** 6.)

Dancing forms some part of the traditional Nō Drama of Japan, the entertainment of the aristocratic and warrior class in feudal times. There are religious dances in Japan. In Japanese dancing, generally, the fan is a very important accessory for dramatic and symbolic suggestion; indeed, it may almost be said that a kind of fan-language has been developed.

4. The American Indians. Amongst the American Indians (see *United States* 7) dancing is important. The dance is in use as a social entertainment and singing often accompanies it. The drum rhythms allotted to the different dances form an elaborate system. Dances sometimes last for many hours (twelve or more) and are renewed for several days. Dancing ceremonies are used when a death occurs. In some tribes Buffalo dances were formerly in use before hunting expeditions. Beautiful seasonal dances of many sorts (the Eagle Dance, the Rainbow Dance, the so-called Dance of the Sprouting Corn) are regularly performed by the Pueblo Indians and others in New Mexico and Arizona. The dances of the Mexican Indians are even more numerous.

5. English Folk Dances. All European nations have their folk dances, which show an infinite variety. Those of England may be taken as an example. They fall into three categories: Sword Dances, Morris Dances, and Country Dances (perhaps a fourth category might be added—Children's Singing Dances and Games).

The **Sword Dances** are for men. Each carries a wooden or blunt steel sword or a short flexible strip of steel with a handle at each end, called a 'rapper', and, with the other hand, grasps one end of that of his neighbour. The evolutions are those of an elaborate figure dance in which the performers jump over the swords, pass under them, etc. Finally the swords are brought together in such a way that they wedge one another into position in a 'knot', 'nut', or 'lock', so that they can be raised as one. Sometimes there is, at the climax, a ceremony symbolical of cutting off a head, the whole dance having a religious origin based on nature worship and sacrifice. Such dances exist all over Europe; they are often associated with a play in which occurs a theme of death and resurrection. They can be studied in the writings of Cecil Sharp (1859–1924) and the publications of the English Folk Dance Society. Like all the English folk dances, they have been revived (though in some districts they did not need this, having never died out). (See p. 272, pl. **48.** 2.)

The **Morris Dances** may possibly have been evolved from the sword dances, but sticks or handkerchiefs are often carried instead of swords. Bells are tied to the legs. Formerly the face of one of the characters was blacked, and this may be the origin of the word 'Morris' (i.e. 'Moorish'). In some districts the word 'Morris' is applied to a sword dance. (See also *Morris*.)

The **Country Dances** are for men and women. In the eighteenth and early nineteenth centuries they spread over Europe—in their more sophisticated 'court' forms (see 6 below, and *Country Dance*).

6. The Court Dances of Europe. Throughout modern history there has been a tendency for the European folk dances to pass from the village greens to the salons of the aristocracy and the courts of monarchs—and thence many of them passed, so far as their rhythms and musical idioms are concerned, into instrumental music, which gives the history of the dance a great importance for the student of the history of music. It is necessarily impossible in any section of this brief article to cover the ground suggested by the heading of that section, and under the present heading the following information may be sufficient; such information must be conveyed largely by means of lists, but every dance mentioned receives treatment in this volume in a brief separate article under its own name.

(*a*) In the **Sixteenth Century** the following dances were in most use in polite circles— *Basses danses* (they had already enjoyed about 150 years of popularity), the *Pavan* and *Galliard*, the *Volta* (or *Lavolta*), *Courante*, *Allemande*, *Gavotte*, *Bourrée*, *Passamezzo*, *Passepied*, *Canaries*, *Rigaudon*, *Chaconne*, *Sarabande*, *Passecaille*, *Bergomask*, *Branle*, *Cinquepace*, *Dump*, *Jig*, *Hey*. Many of these are familiarly alluded to in the literature of the time. Shakespeare (q.v.) makes incidental mention of most of the above and some others.

The music and the actual steps of a number of these dances are accurately known to us through the publication in 1589 of *Orchésographie*, by a canon of Langres, in eastern France; he gives his name on the title-page as

'Thoinot Arbeau', but this is an anagram of his true name, Jehan Tabourot. He has many quaint passages, as this (after speaking of good dancing as an invaluable means of winning the favour of a lady one wishes to marry):

'There is even more in it than this, for dancing is practised to make manifest whether lovers are in good health and sound in all their limbs, after which it is permitted to them to kiss their mistresses, whereby they may perceive if either has an unpleasant breath or exhales a disagreeable odour as that of bad meat: so that, in addition to divers other merits attendant on dancing, it has become essential for the well-being of society.'

In Tabourot's period, as in every period since, there were complaints of unseemly modern dancing:

'At the present time, dancers have none of these modest considerations in their *Voltes* and other similarly lascivious and wayward dances which have been brought into use, in the dancing of which the damsels are made to jump in such a manner they very often show their bare knees if they do not keep one hand on their dresses to prevent it.'

The Canon's general advice to dancers is sound:

'When you dance in company never look down to examine your steps and ascertain if you dance them correctly. Hold your head and body upright with a confident mien, and do not spit or blow your nose much. And if necessity obliges you to do so, turn your head away and use a fair white handkerchief. Converse pleasantly in a low and modest voice, let your arms fall by your sides neither in a lifeless nor in a restless manner, and be suitably and neatly dressed, your hose well drawn up and your shoes clean.'

This invaluable work appeared in 1925 in an English translation by Cyril W. Beaumont (from which the above extracts are taken).

(*b*) In the **Seventeenth Century** the Pavan and Galliard and many other dances gradually fell out of use. A *Branle* called the Double Branle, of a processional nature, was much used for the opening of balls, the *Minuet* was invented (in France), and the English *Country Dances* came to their greatest popularity and at the end of the century spread to France and from there to other countries. The influence of France at this period was great. Louis XIV was a great dancer and patron of the dance. For twenty years he took daily dancing lessons from his chief dancing master, Beauchamp. He founded a Royal Academy of Dancing (1662). It was at this period that Paris began to give dancing laws to the world and the convention of the use of the French language in dancing terminology dates thence.

(*c*) In the **Eighteenth Century** the *Minuet* was the great dance (see *Minuet*). The *Country Dances* were still popular. The *Cotillon* and *Écossaise* came in. The *Gavotte* was still in use, but the other old Court Dances declined. The popularity of the Minuet at this period is very important on account of its entry into full instrumental rights as a movement in the sonata, string quartet, and symphony.

(*d*) In the **Nineteenth Century** the popularity of the country dance at last declined, save that one example (*Sir Roger de Coverley*) was often used to close a ball. This was the century of the *Waltz*, the *Quadrille*, the *Polka*, the *Schottische*, the *Mazurka*, and (at the end of the century) the *Barn Dance*.

(*e*) The general nature of the **Twentieth Century** dances can be gathered from a perusal of the article *Jazz*. The period following the end of the first World War was one almost of dance mania. A similar phenomenon had marked the close of the Napoleonic wars a century earlier, when there were 1,800 dance saloons open every evening in Paris alone. What particularly marked the twentieth-century dance epidemic was the influence of America, North and South, for the United States, having imported dances for a century and a half, suddenly became the chief exporting nation of the world. Elderly European dancers criticized the new entertainment thus introduced on the grounds (amongst others) of its lack of motion. It was bluntly said to suggest 'a middle-aged workman, trudging home after a night shift, with a nail inside his boot'.

7. The Religious Attitude towards Dancing. In every land and in every age there have been abuses of dancing which have led to the denunciation of it by religious people. The Christian Church, in general, has not been against dancing as such. There is much dancing in the Old Testament—the dancing of Miriam the prophetess and her maidens (Exod. xv. 20) to celebrate the passing of the Red Sea; the dancing of Jephtha's daughter to greet her father's return; the dancing of the people crying, 'Saul has slain his thousands and David his ten thousands'; David at the return of the Ark, dancing 'before the Lord with all his might'; 'the Preacher' telling us that 'there is a time to mourn and a time to dance', and the Psalmist exclaiming, 'Thou hast turned for me my mourning into dancing'. And when the New Testament is reached we see Christ mentioning dancing without rebuke—the children in the market-place complaining, 'We have piped unto you and ye have not danced', and the prodigal son welcomed with 'music and dancing'.

In the early Christian Church there is found some ritual use of the dance. Tertullian (A.D. 155–222) says that the congregation danced to the singing of hymns: for this they had a precedent in the ancient Temple ritual (see Psalm cxlix. 3). Judging from the Apocryphal Acts of St. John (from which Holst took the text of the *Hymn of Jesus*), a mystical use of dancing formed a part of the worship of some of the Gnostic sects of the second and third centuries; this book actually represents Christ as dancing with his disciples. It is evident that, later, religious dancing was in use in the more orthodox branches of the church since in A.D. 744 Pope Zacharias felt called on to prohibit it;

it continued, however, in some places—in Notre-Dame, Paris (as a part of the Easter Day celebrations), up to the twelfth century, for instance, and in the Balearic Isles, Seville, Catalonia, the Basque country (in Spain and France), Canton Valais (Switzerland), and other places, until the present day (see *Seises*). It is said by some that the original Mozarabic Rite (see *Liturgy*) included provision for dancing to tambourines.

At Bailleul, in the north of France, a funeral dance in the church by young girls on the death of one of their number subsisted up to 1840 (cf. *Pavan and Galliard*). Funeral Jotas are still danced in Valencia. It seems probable that the custom of dancing before the dead, which survived in the Highlands of Scotland up to at least the opening of the nineteenth century, had a religious origin.

The painters of the best age of Christian art took dancing to be one of the natural expressions of religious joy by saints and angels (e.g. Fra Angelico and Botticelli—see the latter's 'Nativity' at the National Gallery, London, with angels dancing to celebrate the birth of Christ).

Particular dances have at different periods awakened the objection of moral and religious people. The older form of the sarabande of Spain at one time did so. Some authors ascribed its invention to the devil. Cervantes attacked it (second part of *Don Quixote*), and Father Mariana (1563–1623) spoke strongly against it in his *Treatise against Public Amusements* (see *Sarabande*).

It is on the ground of sexual provocativeness that the dance has often been attacked: the waltz came in for opposition on these very grounds, and the famous American preacher, T. de Witt Talmage, towards the end of the nineteenth century, in one of his sermons, put it squarely to parents whether they would allow their daughters to submit to such intimate bodily contact with young men anywhere but in the ballroom (cf. *Waltz*).

It is an error to say that in England 'dancing practically disappeared during the Puritan régime'. The first three editions of Playford's *The English Dancing Master* appeared during the Commonwealth and Protectorate period, so that there must have been a considerable dancing public. Cromwell himself danced at his daughter's wedding in 1657, on which occasion there was an orchestra of forty-eight with 'mixt dancing', and the 'mirth and frolics' were kept up until five in the morning (cf. article *Puritans and Music*). The American conscience about this time and later (at all events in the northern colonies) was somewhat straiter perhaps, but there is sufficient evidence that dancing was not (as often alleged) prohibited, but freely indulged in.

The English Evangelicals of the early nineteenth century (the 'Clapham Sect' and the like, the Wilberforces and such, and their opposite numbers in North America) undoubtedly discouraged their young people

from dancing, not only as being a 'worldly' amusement but as being one leading to late hours and promiscuous acquaintances, and, moreover, one with no intellectual basis; no doubt some parents of today would be glad if they could dare to take a similar stand on similar prudential grounds.

The Holiness sect, which flourishes in the primitive region of the Southern Appalachians, 'the keystone of its own doctrine being "Enjoy your religion"', frowns upon dancing outside its churches (as also upon secular singing) but makes use of sacred dancing within their walls (as it does of lively religious ballads; cf. *Ballad* 3).

For Christmas dancing in English churches in the sixteenth century see *Mysteries*, etc. (poem at end).

8. Dancing as a Spectacle. For the connexion between dancing and the drama, and the use of dancing in the theatre in general, see the articles *Masque* and *Ballet*.

9. Influence of Dance on Music. The influence of the dance on music has been great and is, indeed, incalculable. The transition from free rhythms, such as we find in plainsong and the early harmonized music (even down to the hymn tunes of the sixteenth century), to steady two-, three-, four-, or six-in-a-measure rhythms, is probably largely due to the dance, and so is the use of equal and balanced phrases, regularly recurring cadences, contrasting passages followed by repetition of what has preceded, and so on. As has been mentioned in several places above, the actual dance forms were widely taken up by composers in the early days of independent instrumental music (see *Pavan and Galliard, Sarabande, Allemande, Courante, Gigue*, etc., and also *Suite*), and one of them passed as a legacy from the suite to the classical sonata, string quartet, symphony, etc. (see *Minuet*). During the Romantic period of the nineteenth century innumerable single-movement compositions were based on particular dance forms: the works of Chopin offer an outstanding example of this. As Romanticism developed into Nationalism many more dance forms (e.g. Norwegian and Spanish) came into instrumental music.

A notable vocal influence of the dance was in that form of madrigal called ballett (see *Madrigal* 3 c). But apparently (to judge by the name) even the ballad (q.v.) had originally been a song and dance.

Modern composers have used modern dance forms and rhythms in suites and other instrumental pieces. There is, indeed, hardly a dance, old or new, of which the student or concert-goer does not need to be informed if he is to understand the titles of compositions and movements that at one time or another come before him in programmes. For that reason separate short articles on the various dances are more numerous in this book than in most works of musical reference.

The dance spirit is often to be discovered where there is no actual imitation of the rhythms and forms of particular dances: Wagner (in a rather extravagant mood, perhaps) called Beethoven's Seventh Symphony 'the Apotheosis of the Dance'.

10. Old Authorities on the Dance. The following are of historical importance:

1521. Coplande, *The Maner of dauncynge of Bace daunces after the use of fraunce* (a very valuable work, republished 1937).
1529–30. Attaignant,[1] Two important books of dance music.
1581. Fabritio Caroso, *Il Ballarino*.
1588. Arbeau, *Orchésographie* (described under 6).
1604. Negri, *Inventioni di Balli* (a collection of dance tunes).
1650. Playford,[1] *The English Dancing Master*.
1699. Feuillet (or Lefuillet), *Chorégraphie* (it went through eighteen editions, the last in 1728).
1712. Weaver, *An Essay towards a History of Dancing* (he published several other books also, including a translation of Feuillet—see above).
1723. Bonnet, *Histoire de la Danse sacrée et profane*.
1760. Noverre, *Lettre sur la Danse et sur les Ballets* (see information upon Noverre under *Ballet* 3).
1771. Clément, *Principes de Chorégraphie*.
    [1] Those so marked were music publishers.

1773. Angiolini, *Lettere al signor Noverre*, etc.
1785–1814. Cahusac,[1] *Annual Book of Country Dance Music*, published in London.
1828. Blasis, *Code of Terpsichore* (this work, published in English, promulgates a classical ideal—the influence of ancient Greece).

In 1934 there was founded in Paris an institution called 'Les Archives Internationales de la Danse'. It possesses a museum and a library of growing importance.

See also the following: *Allemande, Anglaise, Barn Dance, Basse Danse, Bergomask, Black Bottom, Blues, Bolero, Bourrée, Branle, Cachucha, Calinda, Canaries, Čebell, Chaconne and Passacaglia, Charleston, Conga, Cotillon, Country Dance, Courante, Cracovienne, Czardas, Danse Macabre, Drabant, Dump, Écossaise, Entrée, Fandango, Farandole, Fling, Folia, Forlana, Fox-trot, Furiant, Galop, Gangar, Gavotte, Gigue, Gopak, Granadina, Habanera, Halling, Hanacca, Haute Danse, Hay, Hornpipe, Jig, Jota, Kolomyika, Kozachok, Ländler, Loure, Malagueña, Manchega, March, Matelotte, Maxixe, Mazurka, Minuet, Moresca, Morris, Muiñeira, Murciana, Nachtanz, Obertas, Onestep, Paso Doble, Passamezzo, Passepied, Pastoral, Pavan and Galliard, Périgourdine, Polka, Polonaise, Polska, Quadrille, Redowa, Rejdováčka, Romanesca, Rondeña, Rueda, Rumba, Saltarello, Sarabande, Sardana, Schottische, Seguidilla, Sevillana, Shimmy, Siciliano, Springar, Springdans, Strathspey, Tambourin, Tango, Tarantella, Tedesca, Trepak, Volta, Waltz.*

DANCING DERVISHES. See *Dance* 1.

DANCLA, JEAN BAPTISTE CHARLES. Born in the French Pyrenees in 1817 and died at Tunis in 1907, aged nearly ninety. He was a prominent violinist of the old French school and a prolific composer for his instrument, his studies being useful and well known. He also wrote several books.

DANDRIEU, JEAN FRANÇOIS. Born in Paris in 1682 and died there in 1738, aged fifty-five. He was a Paris priest, who played and composed with skill and acceptance for the organ and harpsichord. Much of his harpsichord music has been republished in recent times and some of it is to be heard in piano programmes.

See references under *France* 5; *Pianoforte Playing* 10.

DANICAN. See *Philidor*.

DANIEL. See *Danyell*.

DANIELS, MABEL WHEELER. Born in 1878 in Swampscott, Mass. and died in Boston in 1971, aged ninety-two. She was a pupil in composition of Chadwick and then studied in Germany. She composed in a poetical, neo-romantic style, with some impressionistic touches. Her ably-written choral works are well known. (See *Harp* 4.)

DANISH MUSIC. See *Scandinavia* 2.

DANNREUTHER, EDWARD GEORGE. Born at Strasbourg in 1844 and died at Hastings in 1905, aged sixty. He was trained at the Leipzig Conservatory and then settled in London as a pianist and teacher, lecturer and writer. He was prominent as an active pioneer in Wagner propaganda. His long and

thorough book on Musical Ornamentation was for years the standard work.

DANNY BOY. See *Londonderry Air*.

DANSE (Fr.). 'Dance.'

DANSE MACABRE. The idea of Death as a dancer, or as a fiddling inciter to the dance, is very ancient. A dance of skeletons has been found pictured on an ancient Etruscan tomb, and pictures of Death fiddling whilst people of all sorts and conditions dance to his music were extremely common in many parts of Europe during the Middle Ages. In England there was an example in the fifteenth century when the cloisters of St. Paul's Cathedral were decorated with such pictures and the poet Lydgate was commissioned to write verses to be attached. 'Queen Elizabeth's Prayer Book' (published 1559) has the Dance of Death used as a border throughout the Psalms; Holbein's Basle designs, published as woodcuts in 1538, are well known, as are the ancient paintings of the subject that at every step admonish the tourist who crosses one of the covered bridges of Lucerne. The English painter, Rowlandson (1756–1827), has also a series but Holbein's are the best known and have been discussed in a vast literature, a single second-hand bookseller's catalogue before the present writer at the moment including twenty books on the subject in German, French, Italian, Dutch, and English.

Actual mimed representations of this symbolic dance were sometimes carried out in Germany and Flanders, France, and elsewhere, during the fifteenth century, and a children's dance of Germany today (*The Black Man*) is supposed to perpetuate the practice. Ballets based on the gruesome theme have sometimes been performed (e.g. Dessau 1905; Berlin 1925), and Saint-Saëns's symphonic poem (1874), based on an actual poem by Henri Cazalis, reproduces all imaginable details: it includes (perhaps with debatable taste) a parody of the traditional melody of the *Dies Irae* (q.v.). Liszt has provided a piano transcription of this (1877), as well as a Dance of Death of his own for piano and orchestra (c. 1855).

Glazunof's suite *The Middle Ages* has a scherzo representing the Dance of Death as in medieval times it was often performed in booths in the street as a part of the dramatic performances (see *Mysteries, Miracle Plays, and Moralities* for these).

DANTE (1265–1321). See *Italy* 2; *Minstrels*, etc. 5; *Bagpipe Family* 1.

DANTON'S DEATH, DANTONS TOD. See *Einem.*

DANYELL (Daniel), JOHN. Born in the 1560s and died in 1630. Little is recorded of his life, but it is known that, as lutenist, he was a member of Queen Elizabeth I's Chapel Royal and that he took his B.Mus. at Oxford in 1604. He published a book of music for voices and lute of which the sole remaining copy is in the British Museum; on its evidence he ranks high as a composer. In some pieces he carried chromaticism far—for the period.

DANZA (It.). 'Dance.'

DANZA ESPAÑOLA (Sp.). 'Spanish Dance' (in some parts of South America this name is applied to some particular type of dance, usually two-in-a-measure).

DANZA TEDESCA. See *Waltz.*

DANZON, DANZONETTA. See *Rumba.*

DA PONTE, LORENZO (1749–1838). See under *Opera* 21 f, 23; *Così fan tutte; Don Giovanni; Marriage of Figaro.*

DAQUIN (or d'Aquin), LOUIS CLAUDE. Born in Paris in 1694 and died there in 1772, aged nearly seventy-eight. He was a prodigy keyboard player who at six played the harpsichord before the King (Louis XIV) and at twelve was on occasion to be found carrying out the organist's duties at the Sainte-Chapelle. Thenceforward he held various organ posts, including that of the Chapel Royal.

His music is sometimes heard at harpsichord and piano recitals today, and the composition *The Cuckoo*, from the first book of harpsichord pieces, is familiar to thousands of concert-goers.

See reference under *France* 5.

D'ARBLAY. See *Burney.*

DARGASON. An English folk tune, used from the sixteenth century onwards for a country dance. It is also used for the folk song 'It was a maid of my country'.

DARGOMIJSKY (Dargomyzhsky, etc.), ALEXANDER (p. 897, pl. **154**. 2). Born in the government of Toula in 1813 and died in St. Petersburg in 1869, aged nearly fifty-six. Like his older contemporary, Glinka (q.v.), he was

brought up on a country estate. He early showed musical talent and was taught to play piano and violin, and to compose.

Engaged in St. Petersburg in the Civil Service (again like Glinka), he shone, as a composer and performer, in the drawing-rooms of the *élite*. Meeting Glinka, he was led to shake off the dilettante and to equip himself for more serious work. He wrote the opera *Esmeralda* (1839) on a theme from Hugo, but turned to the national poet, Pushkin, for the plots of his *Russalka* (1856) and *The Stone Guest* (1872). The last he left unfinished, charging two of his friends (Cui and Rimsky-Korsakof) to bring it to completion, which they did. His views upon opera resembled those of Gluck and Wagner (though the music of the latter was then unknown in Russia); he aimed at making his music reinforce the dramatic significance of the text, and to this end favoured the style of recitative rather than that of continuous and shapely melody. *The Stone Guest* became the Bible of the contemporary Russian school—one, however, the precepts of which, like those of other bibles, were not always strictly applied in practice.

He was a copious song-writer in many styles, including the comic.

For an account of the musical conditions of Dargomijsky's country and period see *Russia* 4. References to him will be found under *Opera* 17 c; *Ballet* 7; *Kozachok.*

DARKE, HAROLD EDWIN. Born in London in 1888 and died there in 1976, aged eighty-eight. He was trained at the Royal College of Music (whose staff he later joined) and at Oxford. By means of many choral performances, organ recitals and an annual festival he made the London church of St. Michael's, Cornhill, of which he was organist from 1916 until 1966, an outstanding centre of musical culture, and specialized in Bach. He was awarded the C.B.E. in 1966.

His numerous compositions are largely, but not exclusively, choral and organ works.

DART, (ROBERT) THURSTON. Born in London in 1921 and died there in 1971, aged forty-nine. Trained at the Royal College of Music, he became known as a harpsichordist and as a well-informed writer on the earlier music. He was professor of music first at Cambridge (1962) and then at London (1964) Universities.

DARUNTER (Ger.). 'There-under', 'there-amongst', etc.

DARWIN, ERASMUS (1731–1802). Medical man, botanist, and poet (grandfather of the great scientist). See reference to his proposed 'visible music' under *Colour and Music* 6.

DASSELBE (Ger.). 'The same.'

DAUBERVAL. See *Ballet* 3.

DAUDET, ALPHONSE. See *Farandole.*

DAUER (Ger.). 'Duration.'

DAUERND (Ger.). 'Enduring', in the sense of lasting, continuing.

DAUNEY, WILLIAM (1800–43). Scottish antiquary and musician. See reference to his chief work under *Scotland* 7.

DAUVERGNE, ANTOINE. Born at Moulins in 1713 and died at Lyons in 1797, aged eighty-three. He was a violinist and composer of music for the violin and for the orchestra, as also of stage music and church music. He held various posts under Louis XV, finally rising to that of Superintendent of the King's Music.

His long Paris career covered almost the whole of Rameau's Paris activities, the whole of those of Gluck, and the beginning of those of Méhul.

See reference under *Bouffons*.

DAVEL, MAJOR D. A. See *Church Music* 6.

DAVENANT, SIR WILLIAM (1606–68; p. 689, pl. 116. 1, 2). England's earliest opera manager. See *Opera* 13 a; *Locke*; *Misattributed* (Locke); *Cooke, Henry*; *England* 5.

DAVEY, HENRY (1853–1929). Writer on music, and especially notable for the research embodied in his *History of English Music* (1895, later edition 1921).

See reference under *Eton College Choirbook*.

DAVID.

(1) FÉLICIEN CÉSAR (p. 369, pl. 62. 2). Born at Cadenet, in the south of France, in 1810, and died at St. Germain-en-Laye, near Paris, in 1876, aged sixty-six. At twelve he had composed a string quartet. After some little time spent in a lawyer's office, as provincial theatre conductor, and as an organist, at twenty he reached the Paris Conservatory, where he stayed only about a year, during which period, however, he made much progress.

He then accepted the Christian-Socialist ideas of the Saint-Simonians, and, on the dispersal of the sect shortly after, travelled in the Holy Land and elsewhere, always carrying with him a piano. On his return he published a collection of *Oriental Melodies* for piano and occupied himself quietly in the composition of chamber and orchestral music, songs, and other things.

His public recognition came at the age of thirty-four, when his orientally-coloured symphonic ode, *The Desert*, was performed in Paris. Like almost all his works, this was picturesque and descriptive.

He ranks as a pioneer in the use of 'oriental idioms', and as such has had many followers in France and elsewhere.

See *Flute* 4; *Chamber Music* 6, period III (1810).

(2) FERDINAND (p. 1097, pl. 182. 4). Born at Hamburg in 1810 (the same year as his namesake above) and died in Switzerland in 1873, aged sixty-three. He early made a name as a violinist, appearing at the famous Gewandhaus Concerts at Leipzig when he was fifteen; in later life he was, under his friend Mendelssohn's conductorship, leader of the Gewandhaus Orchestra. He also taught, under Mendelssohn, in the Leipzig Conservatory and helped, by violinistic counsel, in the composition of Mendelssohn's Violin Concerto, of which he

was the first public performer. He himself wrote five violin concertos, as well as many other instrumental compositions, and was an assiduous reviver and editor of the older violin classics.

Himself the pupil of Spohr, he became the master of Joachim and Wilhelmj.

Brief references will be seen under *Fioritura*; *Trombone Family* 4.

(3) PAUL (in full, Julius Peter Paul; 1840–1932), for forty years music-master of Uppingham School under the great headmaster Thring, and, as such, one of the leaders in the development of school music activities in England, was son of Ferdinand.

(4) JOHANN NEPOMUK. See *Germany* (end).

DAVID OF THE WHITE ROCK. See *Dafydd y Garreg Wen*.

DAVIDSON.

(1) MALCOLM GORDON. Born at Harrow in 1891 and died in 1949, aged fifty-eight. He was educated at the Royal College of Music (later joining its staff) and at Cambridge University. His published compositions include songs, part-songs, and chamber music.

(2) HAROLD G. See *History* 9.

DAVIE, CEDRIC THORPE. Born in London in 1913—but of Scottish descent. He studied at the Royal College of Music and in Germany, joined the staff of the Royal Scottish Academy of Music and held a position as a Glasgow organist. In 1948 he became Professor of Music at the University of St. Andrews. Many of his compositions (choral, orchestral, etc.) have Scottish subjects.

DAVIES.

(1) HENRY WALFORD. Born at Oswestry in 1869 and died near Bristol in 1941, aged seventy-one. Of Welsh parentage, he was first a choir-boy at St. George's Chapel, Windsor, later a scholar of the Royal College of Music, and organist of various London churches, last of all in the Temple Church. Other positions he held were those of Professor of Counterpoint at the Royal College of Music, Conductor of the Bach Choir, London, Professor of Music at University College, Aberystwyth, organist of St. George's Chapel, Windsor Castle, and Master of the King's Musick. He had a great popularity as a broadcasting lecturer on music. He was knighted in 1922.

As a composer he won acceptance with his oratorios and some shorter pieces. His thought tended to mysticism and his style to delicacy. He was not without humour.

See *Wales* 9; *Chapel Royal*; *Ballad* 5; *Improvisation* 3; *Competitions* 5; *Concerto* 6 c; *Criticism* 7.

(2) EVAN THOMAS. Born at Merthyr Tydfil, S. Wales, in 1878 and died at Aberdare in 1969, aged ninety-one. He was Director of Music at University College, Bangor, 1920–43. His compositions, popular in Wales, are national

in feeling, and include songs, part-songs, and some chamber music.

(3) CLARA NOVELLO. See reference under *Keep the Home Fires Burning*.

(4) MARIANNE (1744–92). See reference under *Harmonica* 1.

(5) D. T. FFRANGCON (baritone vocalist; 1855–1918). See *Bird Music*; *Singing* 12.

(6) EDWARD HAROLD (1867–1947; elder brother of H. Walford Davies). See *Folk Song* 3 (near end).

(7) PETER MAXWELL. Born in Manchester in 1934. He studied at the Royal Manchester College of Music and later under Petrassi. He first came to public attention following his success, as a grammar-school music teacher, in training his pupils in the effective performance of his own and other 'progressive' music. His style, while often complex and pointillist, reflects also his interest in medieval tradition.

(8) JOHN H. See *Dictionaries* 15.

DAVISON, JAMES WILLIAM (1813–85). See *Criticism of Music* 4, 8; *Goddard, Arabella*; p. 257, pl. **47.** 4.

DAVRAINVILLE. See *Mechanical Reproduction* 6.

DAVY.

(1) RICHARD. End of fifteenth and beginning of sixteenth century. He was organist of Magdalen College, Oxford, and later a priest. A 'Passion' (see *Passion Music*) of his was, in 1921, revived by Sir Richard Terry at Westminster Cathedral, and the high quality of his work thus revealed.

(2) JOHN. Born near Exeter in 1763 and died in London in 1824, aged sixty. He was brought up by his uncle, a harmonious blacksmith, and his first musical performances were upon an instrument he himself constructed out of old horseshoes chosen according to the notes they gave out. The village parson gave him a harpsichord, on which he quickly learned to play. Later he was articled to the organist of Exeter Cathedral, William Jackson (q.v.). He then went to London and for many years was a prominent composer of the lighter kind of theatre music.

He published very many compositions, and some of his songs, notably 'The Bay of Biscay' (q.v.), have passed into the permanent popular national repertory.

He died of drink and was buried by two charitable London tradesmen.

DAWSON.

(1) WILLIAM LEVI. Born at Anniston, Alabama, in 1898. He is a trombonist and composer. For some years he occupied various positions in Chicago and he was appointed Director of Music at Tuskegee Institute (of which he had been a student) in 1931. He has composed a *Negro Folk Symphony* (Philadelphia Orchestra, 1934), etc.

(2) PETER (1882–1961). See *Gramophone* 5.

DAY.

(1) JOHN (1522–84; p. 849, pl. **144.** 1). See *Publishing* 4; *Hymns and Hymn Tunes* 5, 11, 17 e (vi), (viii).

(2) ALFRED (1810–49). He was a doctor of medicine who wrote a theoretical *Treatise of Harmony* (1845) in which he worked out a very logical system, derived partly from Rameau (q.v.) and tracing the origin of the chords then in use to a few basic combinations that had relation to the acoustical phenomenon of harmonics (see the references to this subject given under *Acoustics* 6, 8). This system, widely known as the 'Day System', or 'Day Theory', was adopted, in whole or in part, by many writers of textbooks, including Macfarren in his *Rudiments of Harmony* (1860) and his *Six Lectures on Harmony* (1867) and Prout in the earlier editions of his *Harmony, its Theory and Practice* (1889—abandoned in the 16th edition, 1901). The system no longer holds serious attention.

DAZU (Ger.). 'Thereto', i.e. (in organ playing) the stops mentioned are to be 'added to' the others.

D.B.E. See *Knighthood and other Honours*.

D.C. = Da Capo (q.v.).

DE, D' (Fr.). 'Of', 'from'.

DEACONING. See *Hymns and Hymn Tunes* 8.

DEAD CITY, THE. See *Korngold, E. W.*

DEAFNESS. See *Ear* 3.

DEAGANOMETER. See *Pitch* 6 b.

DEAN, WINTON. Born at Birkenhead in 1916. He was educated at Cambridge, and is the author of important books on Bizet and Handel, as well as numerous scholarly articles.

DEARMER, PERCY (1867–1936). Canon of Westminster. Copious author on artistic, theological, and liturgical subjects, active and unconventional editor of hymn-books and the like (especially *Songs of Praise* 1925; enlarged 1931).

DEAS, JAMES STEWART. Born at Edinburgh in 1903 and graduated at its University, then studying under Weingartner. He conducted the Edinburgh Opera Company 1921–3, as also various orchestras, and in 1948 became Professor of Music at Sheffield University.

'DEATH AND THE MAIDEN' QUARTET (Schubert). See *Nicknamed Compositions* 18.

DEATH OF NELSON. See *Braham*.

DEBAIN, ALEXANDRE FRANÇOIS (1809–77). See *Reed-Organ Family* 6, 7.

DE BÉRIOT. See *Bériot*.

DEBILE (It.), DÉBILE (Fr.). 'Weak.'

DE BOECK. See *Boeck*.

DEBOLE (It.). 'Weak.'

DEBUSSY, CLAUDE ACHILLE (pl. 385, pl. **64.** 2). Born at St. Germain-en-Laye, near Paris, in 1862 and died in Paris in 1918, aged fifty-five. He was the founder of what has been aptly called the Impressionist School in music—aptly, because, like the pictorial

Impressionists, the members of that school largely avoided the dramatic, the narrative, the formal, the conventional, and the involved, pre-occupying themselves with tone *qua* tone as the painters did with light *qua* light ('light is the chief personage in a picture', was one of the maxims of Monet, founder of pictorial Impressionism).

This school has also its relationship to the Symbolist procedure in poetry, the practitioners of which (Baudelaire, Verlaine, Mallarmé, and others), in reaction against the strong emotions of the French Romantic poets (e.g. Hugo), attempted the expression of a delicate, sensitive voluptuousness, suggesting their meaning rather than stating it. Mallarmé said, 'To name an object is to sacrifice three-quarters of that enjoyment of the poem which comes from the guessing bit by bit. To *suggest* it—that is our dream.' Debussy frequented the house of Mallarmé, and, significantly, re-expressed in orchestral tone the emotion of Mallarmé's vague, obscure, yet lovely poem, 'The Afternoon of a Faun', as well as setting to music, as songs, many poems of Verlaine, Baudelaire, and Mallarmé, and taking as the libretto of his only opera Maeterlinck's symbolist drama, *Pelléas and Mélisande* (q.v.).

The art of Debussy, then, represents, on the face of it, a revolt against both the Classics and the Romantics. Yet on careful analysis it will be found to possess the classic qualities of balance and restraint and of the skilful treatment of definite melodic themes; and, similarly, when its emotional content is closely observed it is realized that, essentially, Impressionism is not so much an expression of antagonism to Romanticism as a refinement of it. The devotion to form which we call classicism, and the expression of emotion which at its strongest we call romanticism, appear to be essential qualities of music, and it is only a question of degree when, as principles of composition, they are pushed into the background.

The 'vagueness' which in Debussy veiled the clear statement of the formal construction and softened the expression of the emotion that inspired the composition resulted in some measure from the frequent use of a scale without semitones, the 'Whole-tone Scale' (see *Scales* 9; *Harmony* 14), and also from the use of harmonies of a character then novel, derived from the 'overtones' or component parts of what we call a single note, studied by the composer in his early observations of bugles and of bells (see *Acoustics* 8; *Partials*; *Timbre*). These harmonies give a very 'atmospheric' effect. Harmonically the composer departed equally from the diatonic system (see *Harmony* 24 a) of Haydn, Mozart, and Beethoven, and from the warmer chromatic system (see *Harmony* 12, 13, 24 a) of Wagner and Strauss. His music was at once felt to be very individual and, despite the subsequent growth of an Impressionist 'school', remains so.

The career of Debussy can be quickly outlined. At twelve he was already a student at the Paris Conservatory. At twenty-two he won the Rome Prize (see *Prix de Rome*), which entitled him to three years' quiet work at the Villa Medici. Wagner was a temporary influence, Mussorgsky (q.v.) a more lasting one. For a short time the composer was in Russia.

At thirty-two (1894) he brought forward the tone-poem *Prelude to 'The Afternoon of a Faun'* already mentioned, and this provoked much discussion, as did also his one String Quartet. At forty (1902) he became the subject of still louder discussion as the composer of the opera *Pelléas and Mélisande* (q.v.), which, with its absence of set movements and of developed melody, struck some people as one long recitative. In 1911 he provided incidental music to d'Annunzio's *Martyrdom of St. Sebastian*.

In his fifties he was seized with a painful malady which he bore patiently and of which he prematurely died.

Debussy was a master of orchestration, economical, pointed, and forceful. His piano compositions, which are numerous, are finely conceived as expressions of the genius of the instrument; they make many of their effects by the skilful employment of the pedals. His many songs are neatly turned and delicate.

There is a strong 'programmatic' element in Debussy (see *Programme Music*), but it is treated with aristocratic refinement, not with the crudity that is sometimes found in Strauss. Such piano music as *The Submerged Cathedral* or *The Island of Joy* (originally 'L'Embarquement pour Cythère'—after Watteau), when examined minutely, will be found to be highly programmatic. So in a more general way are the nature impressions (for piano) *Gardens in Rain, Reflections in the Water, Goldfish, Mists, Dead Leaves*, and the like, and (for orchestra) *Clouds* and *The Sea* (3 pieces; 1903–5).

References to Debussy, of greater or lesser importance, will be found as follows: *Albéniz*; *Allant*; *Aria*; *Ballet* 6; *Bell* 6; *Bergomask*; *Caplet*; *Chabrier*; *Chamber Music* 6, Period III (1862); *Chausson*; *Clarinet Family* 6; *Colour and Music* 3; *Composition* 12; *Concerto* 6 c (1862); *d'Indy*; *Drame Lyrique*; *Étude*; *Falla*; *Fingering* 5 e; *Flute Family* 6; *France* 10; *Franck* (at end); *Gamelan*; *God save the Queen* 16; *Gradus ad Parnassum*; *Guiraud*; *Habanera*; *Harmony* 18 (note); *Harp* 3, 4; *Impressionism*; *Jazz* 5; *Lalo*; *Melody* 5; *Messager*; *Misattributed*; *Mouvement*; *Negro Minstrels*; *Opera* 11 e, 21 m; *Oriental*; *Passepied*; *Pianoforte Playing* 7; *Ravel*; *Recitative*; *Rhythm* 10; *Russia* 7; *Satie*; *Saxophone Family*; *Scales* 9; *Spain* 10; *Temperament* 9; *Trombone Family* 3.

DÉBUT (Fr.). 'Beginning', 'opening', e.g. first public appearance, i.e. beginning of a career.

DECANI. See *Precentor, Service*.

DECCA CO. See *Gramophone* 6.

DECEPTIVE CADENCE. See *Cadence*.

DÉCHANT (Fr.). *Descant* (q.v.).

DÉCIDÉ (Fr.). 'Decided', with decision.

DECIMETTE. A piece for ten instruments or voices.

DECISO (It.). 'Decided', with decision, firmly, not flabbily. So the superlative, *Decisissimo*.

DECLAMANDO, DECLAMATO (It.). 'Declaiming', 'declaimed', i.e. in a declamatory style.

DECORATION in Harmony. See *Harmony* 10.

DÉCOUPLER (Fr.). 'To uncouple.'

DECRESCENDO, DECRESCIUTO (It.). 'Decreasing', 'decreased' (i.e. in force; getting gradually softer).

DÉDÉ, EDMUND. See *United States* 6 (near end).

DEERING (or **Dering**), RICHARD (born about 1580 and died in London in 1630). He was born in England but certainly spent some of his earlier life in Italy. He later became organist to the convent of English nuns at Brussels (cf. *Belgium* 9). Later he was one of the musicians of Henrietta Maria, queen of Charles I.

He was one of those who wrote amusing choral pieces bringing in the cries of the various London street vendors (see *Street Music* 2), and he also composed music for viols, English anthems, and Latin motets—the last-named (not without artistic justification) the favourite music of Oliver Cromwell (see *Puritans and Music* 4).

DÉFAUT (Fr.). 'Fault' or 'lack'. So À *défaut de*, 'in the absence of'.

DEGEYTER, PIERRE (1849–1932). See *Internationale*.

DEGREES AND DIPLOMAS IN MUSIC

1. British Degrees.
2. British Diplomas.
3. American Degrees.
4. American Diplomas.

The statement has been made that the earliest instance of a university degree in music is the medieval one of 'Master of the Organ' at Salamanca (see Rashdall's *Universities of Europe in the Middle Ages*). Outside the English-speaking world university degrees in music are not now given, though, in the past, a few cases of honorary doctorates in music have occurred—e.g. Spontini and Franz (Halle), Romberg (Kiel), Liszt (Königsberg). For the German doctorate in Philosophy (Ph.D.) and the French and Swiss doctorate in Letters, a thesis on a musicological subject may be presented.

1. British Degrees. The degrees in music given by British and Irish universities are Bachelor ('B.Mus.' or 'Mus.B.') and Doctor 'D.Mus.' or 'Mus.D.'), music being like medicine in proceeding straight from the 'Bachelor' to 'Doctor' without the intermediate 'Master' (exceptions—Cambridge, since 1893, has all three degrees; Wales and Birmingham have also the three degrees).

The universities conferring musical degrees, with the dates from which they have been conferred, are as follows: Cambridge (1464, see *Abyngdon*), Oxford (c. 1499), Dublin (1615), London (1879), Durham (1892), Edinburgh (1893), Manchester (1894), University of Wales (1905), Birmingham (1905), National University of Ireland (1908), Sheffield (1931), Glasgow (1933); Leeds (1946); Nottingham (1948); Bristol (1951); Queen's University, Belfast (1953); York University (1964). It will be seen that some universities do not yet confer such degrees.

For 350 years after Oxford and Cambridge began to grant degrees in music the conditions were very vague. Apparently the degrees were sued for and refused or granted, the composition and performance before the University of an 'exercise' (at what was called an 'Act'; see *Concert* 2; *Act Music*) being expected—though apparently the Professor of Music had power to excuse this and occasionally did so. The exercise for the doctorate was, from the eighteenth century onwards, usually something of the nature of a psalm or oratorio set for solo voices, chorus, and orchestra (see *Concert* 2). The engagement of the performers was at the candidates' expense. Haydn, on being made Doctor of Music at Oxford, submitted merely an extremely ingenious three-voice canon, but he gave three grand concerts (probably looked upon as an 'Act') whilst he was in the city (cf. *Concert* 9).

Definite examinations were instituted during the professorship of Sterndale Bennett at Cambridge (in 1857) and that of Ouseley at Oxford (in 1862). The examinations at these universities have been the model for those at the others and, broadly generalizing, such examinations are usually something as follows:[1]

B.MUS.

(*a*) Some sort of Entrance Examination constituting a general educational test.

(*b*) A First Examination in Music—Four-part Harmony and Counterpoint.

(*c*) A Second Examination in Music—Five part Harmony and Counterpoint; Four-part Fugue; Orchestration; History of Music; Critical Knowledge of certain specified Scores, etc.

(*d*) An 'Exercise', being an extended work for chorus and orchestra, or other tests in actual composition.

(*c* and *d* are reversed in some universities.)

D.MUS.

(*a*) An 'Exercise' consisting of an extended work for eight-part chorus, vocal solos, etc., with orchestral overture and accompaniment, or several works, vocal and instrumental, of different characters.

(*b*) An Explanation in advanced Composition, Orchestration, History of Music, Form (sometimes Acoustics), etc.

At Oxford and Cambridge the B.A. can now be taken with honours in music, the B.Mus. then being added as the result of a further examination. At Durham and some other universities music can be taken for the B.A. (pass or honours).

[1] For precise information as to the conditions at any university application should be made to its Registrar.

As will be seen, British degrees in music are for the most part, evidence of the possession of the technique of composition, but in one or two universities some measure of instrumental performance is allowed to count towards a degree, and in one or two musicological research can also so count.

In many universities it is possible to obtain by research in musical subjects the degree of Litt.B., Litt.D., and Ph.D. or D.Phil. (Bachelor and Doctor of Letters and Doctor of Philosophy).

By an old custom dating from the thirteenth century, the Archbishop of Canterbury (by virtue of his former office of Legate of the Pope) has the power to grant degrees, and he not infrequently exercises this power by conferring a doctorate of music on some Anglican cathedral organist or other meritorious individual. These degrees are known as 'Canterbury Degrees' (D.Mus.Cantuar.) or (from the Archbishop's London palace, from which they are issued) 'Lambeth Degrees'. It appears that when the archbishopric is vacant the power of conferring degrees passes to the Dean and Chapter of Canterbury Cathedral; this principle is stated in the faculty by which Blow (q.v.) was created Doctor of Music in 1677, his doctorate being so conferred.

Various universities in the British Commonwealth confer musical degrees, their requirements being not so much standardized as those of the universities of the old country. As some of these universities possess conservatories of music and teach performance, that receives more recognition as a degree qualification.

Throughout the Commonwealth, degrees, whether in music or any other subject, can be granted only by a university (with the exception just mentioned and an almost unexercised right of the Royal College of Music, which can grant the degrees of B.Mus., M.Mus., and D.Mus.), and a university must possess a Royal Charter. The value of a degree in music is, then, fairly stable, and counts accordingly in public estimation. A Union of Graduates in Music was formed in 1893 to protect that value by excluding foreign bogus degrees (at one time a fairly considerable evil and still existing), and in other ways to promote the interests of graduates; it still functions.

'Residence' (i.e. actual study in the university) is now normally required for a degree in music. Exceptions are Dublin, London, and Durham, the latter two of which grant both residential and non-residential degrees.

2. British Diplomas. As will have been realized, the issue of degrees in music in Britain is well controlled. On the other hand, there is so large a number of genuine diplomas (there are no fewer than fifty; see p. xvii) that the public is bewildered by them, and added to these a (happily greatly diminished) number of bogus diplomas given by private groups of individuals posing as public bodies. It seems much to be desired that some increased co-operation should come about between the genuine diploma-giving institutions; they might agree to examine only jointly, and so reduce the number of alphabetical decorations in use.

The diploma-conferring bodies in the list now to be given are recognized as important public bodies. Their diplomas, it will be seen, are usually graded as follows:

(1) Associateship, (2) Licentiateship (not always present), (3) Fellowship. This is not quite invariable, however; for instance, the Royal Academy of Music confers Licentiateship upon external or internal candidates and Associateship (of at least equal grade) upon internal candidates. Fellowship is reserved by some institutions as a purely honorary distinction. (It is not possible within our present limits to be precise; the calendars and prospectuses of the various institutions must be consulted for complete information, particularly as changes are now fairly frequent.)

Royal Academy of Music (founded 1822). F.R.A.M. (limited to 150 distinguished past students); Hon. F.R.A.M. (non-professional musicians who have rendered service); Hon. R.A.M. (honorary members); A.R.A.M. (distinguished past students); L.R.A.M. (open to non-students and with the differentiation, 'teacher' or 'performer'); Special Diploma of the Teachers' Training Course.

Royal College of Music (founded 1883, succeeding the National Training College of Music, founded 1873). F.R.C.M. (honorary, limited to 50); Hon. R.C.M. (distinguished non-students); Hon. A.R.C.M. (distinguished past students); A.R.C.M. (by examination, open to non-residents—as Teachers or Performers); Teachers' Training Course certificate, awarded to students selected from certain colleges for a one year's course.

Associated Board. The R.A.M. and R.C.M. combine, under the title 'Royal Schools of Music, London', to confer in the Commonwealth the diploma, formerly known as 'L.A.B.' (Licentiate of the Associated Board), now entitled 'L.R.S.M., London'. This is the overseas equivalent of the L.R.A.M. and the A.R.C.M.

The teacher's diploma, G.R.S.M. (Graduate of the Royal Schools of Music), is open only to internal students at the R.A.M. and R.C.M. after three years' work, including Teaching Course. The Associated Board, from 1946, became a combination, for examination purposes, of the Royal College of Music, the Royal Academy of Music, the Royal Manchester College of Music, and the Royal Scottish Academy of Music. All four were henceforth combined in the (overseas) examining organization for the conferring of the L.R.S.M. diploma. In Australia there is co-operation between the Associated Board and the Australian Music Examinations Board (representing the Universities of Melbourne, Adelaide, Tasmania, Queensland, and Western Australia, and the State Conservatory of New South Wales) and the diploma conferred, although equivalent to the above-mentioned one, is designated 'L.Mus.'.

The combination in London for training and examining for the G.R.S.M. diploma remains one of purely the Royal Academy and Royal College of Music.

Royal College of Organists (founded 1864). A.R.C.O.; F.R.C.O.—with an additional (optional) diploma entitling the candidate to add the letters CHM. (i.e. 'Choirmaster') to either. In 1936 the Archbishop of Canterbury instituted a Diploma in Church Music to the examination for which he admits only F.R.C.O.s holding the CHM. diploma, who on passing his examination become A.D.C.M.s.

Trinity College of Music (founded 1872). *Internal*; G.T.C.L. (Graduate), F.T.C.L. (Research), L.T.C.L. (Trained Teacher's Diploma), and L.T.C.L. (Speech and Drama). *External*: A.T.C.L. and L.T.C.L. teacher or performer in all executive subjects including Speech; L.T.C.L. in Class Music Teaching and in Musicianship; A.Mus.T.C.L. and L.Mus.T.C.L. as teachers (theoretical subjects); F.T.C.L. in all executive subjects and in composition.

Guildhall School of Music and Drama (founded in 1880, under the control of the Corporation of the City of London). A.G.S.M. (internal students); L.G.S.M. (internal and external students); G.G.S.M. (internal students); F.G.S.M. and Hon. G.S.M. (both honorary—and each limited to 100).

The **London College of Music** (originally founded 1887, incorporated 1939). *Internal*: G.L.C.M. (Graduate), L.L.C.M. (School Music Diploma). *External*: A.L.C.M. and L.L.C.M. (Peformers), L.L.C.M. (T.D.) (Teacher's Diploma), A.Mus.L.C.M. and L.Mus.L.C.M. (Theoretical Diplomas), F.L.C.M. (Performers or Composers).

Royal Manchester College of Music (founded 1893). A.R.M.C.M. (after a three years' course and examination) and F.R.M.C.M. (honorary only).

Birmingham and Midland Institute (1854). The **Birmingham School of Music** (1887); A.B.S.M. as Teacher or Performer; A.B.S.M.(T.T.D.) Teacher's Training Diploma, approved by the Ministry of Education; F.B.S.M. (Honorary); B.S.M., Graduate Course, instituted 1948.

Royal Scottish Academy of Music (founded 1929, succeeding the Glasgow Athenaeum School of Music). Dip. R.S.A.M. and (in musical education) Dip. Mus. Ed. R.S.A.M. (both after a full course in the Academy and examination).

Incorporated London Academy of Music (founded 1861; now ceased). A.L.A.M.

The **Tonic Sol-fa College** (founded 1863; since the late 1940s known as the **Curwen Memorial College**). A.T.S.C.; L.T.S.C.; F.T.S.C.

Royal Military School of Music (Kneller Hall). All Bandmasters in the British Army must take the three years' course and graduate in this institution. There is a special advanced certificate available for appointment as Director of Music—p.s.m., meaning 'passed school of music'.

Bandsman's College of Music. This is an examining body (1931), not for profit and with unpaid officials and described as 'The National Institution of the Brass Band Movement'. Its President for some years was Sir Granville Bantock. It awards, after examination, three diplomas, B.B.C.M. ('Bandmaster'), A.B.C.M., and L.B.C.M.

Overseas Schools of Music. Some of the universities in different parts of the Commonwealth, having schools of music attached, grant a diploma.

The Canadian College of Organists grants diplomas of A.C.C.O. and F.C.C.O.

3. American Degrees. The earliest American degrees in music seem to be the honorary doctorates of Georgetown (now part of Washington, D.C.; its University dates from the end of the eighteenth century), 1849, and New York, 1855 (the latter conferred on Lowell Mason). The Baccalaureate was apparently first conferred by Boston in 1876.

The number of universities, colleges, schools of music, etc., conferring Mus.B. and Mus.D. is now very great, and owing to the varying laws of different states the standing of these institutions and the value of their degrees vary widely. Naturally the value of degrees at the more responsible institutions is as great as their value in any country. From about the year 1927 a movement tending towards standardization began. From time to time there have sprung into existence institutions of which nothing seems to be known in their own country but which tout for the sale (for such it is) of musical and other degrees in Britain (see reference under 1 to the British Union of Graduates in Music); these institutions have always adopted high-sounding titles.

Mus.B. (or B.Mus., or B.M.) generally signifies the successful carrying out of a four years' course of study, which may be largely execution (or, as it is called in the United States, 'Applied Music')—not, as in Britain, restricted to theory, composition, and the like.

More than in Britain, the study of music is allowed to count towards a degree in Arts, Science, or Philosophy, so that many musicians take the B.A., M.A., B.Sc., or Ph.D.

The degree of M.Mus. (or Mus.M., or M.M.) exists also. Some institutions confer a masters' degree in Sacred Music—M.S.M.

In general, and, indeed, practically exclusively in the United States, unlike Britain, the degree of Mus.D. is reserved as an honorary distinction.

4. American Diplomas. The United States fortunately does not possess the bewildering variety of diploma-conferring institutions of Britain, nor are alphabetical distinctions of any kind so much valued. The American Guild of Organists (q.v.) confers diplomas of Associate-

ship and Fellowship—A.A.G.O. and F.A.G.O.

When the examination as choirmaster is passed the letters Ch.M. may be added. (Those founders who are still alive are entitled to the distinction A.G.O.)

See *Dictionaries* 11.

DEGRIGNY. See *Grigny*.

DEHN, SIEGFRIED WILHELM (1799–1858). See references under *Russia* 4; *Glinka*.

DEHORS (Fr.). 'Outside.' So, also, 'prominent' (sometimes the expression is *en dehors*).

DEJONCKER, THEODORE. See *Synthétistes*.

DEKKER, THOMAS (c. 1570–1641). Dramatist and pamphleteer. See passing reference under *Masque*; *Incidental Music*.

DE KOVEN, HENRY LOUIS REGINALD. Born at Middletown, Conn., in 1859 (not 1861, as often stated) and died in Chicago in 1920, aged sixty. He was a facile melodist and the composer of one of the most successful of American comic operas, *Robin Hood* (1890). He composed nineteen works in this lighter vein and two grand operas, *The Canterbury Pilgrims* (Metropolitan Opera House, New York, 1917) and *Rip Van Winkle* (Chicago and New York, 1920). He was socially prominent, and also engaged in criticism.

DE LA (Fr.). 'Of the', 'from the' (fem. sing.).

DELANNOY, MARCEL. Born in 1898 at Ferté Alais and died in Paris in 1962, aged sixty-four. He composed four operas, the best-known being *Le Poirier de misère*, as well as other music for the stage, and songs, piano music, etc.

See *History* 9.

DELATRE, FATHER. See *Hydraulus*.

DE LATTRE, ROLAND. See *Lassus*.

DELIBES, (CLEMENT PHILIBERT) LÉO (p. 369, pl. **62**. 7). Born at St. Germain-du-Val, in the Department of Sarthe, France, in 1836, and died in Paris in 1891, aged nearly fifty-five. He studied at the Paris Conservatory and then at once appeared before the public as a composer of successful operettas, operas, and ballets. Of the ballets, *Coppélia* (see *Ballet* 5) and *Sylvia* are favourite specimens. Of the operas, *Lakmé* has been popular. In melody, harmony, and orchestration he had that graceful light-handed touch which is always welcomed by musicians and non-musicians alike.

Like Chabrier, but in a lesser degree, Delibes has influenced many composers of a very different temperament from his own.

See also *Percussion Family* 4 b; *Saxophone*; *Lesquercade*; *Raptak*.

DELICATO (It.). 'Delicate.' So *Delicatamente* 'delicately'; *Delicatissimo*, 'as delicately as possible'; *Delicatezza*, 'delicacy'.

DÉLIÉ (Fr.). 'Untied.' The expression can be used in several senses.

(1) The notes detached from one another, i.e. staccato.

(2) Unconstrainedly, lightly, easily.

(3) The infinitive of the same verb has been used by Czerny in the French title of a famous work—*L'Art de délier les doigts*; literally, 'The Art of untying the fingers', i.e. of making them supple and agile.

DELIRIO (It.). 'Frenzy.' So *Delirante*, 'frenzied'.

DELIUS, FREDERICK (p. 336, pl. **53**. 5). Born at Bradford in 1862 and died at Grez-sur-Loing, France, in 1934, aged seventy-two. Both his parents were German, his father being of remote Dutch descent.

He showed musical precocity, but was intended for a business career. After residence in Germany and visits to Norway and Sweden, ostensibly for business purposes but actually made use of for musical development, he went to Florida as an orange grower. There he met a Brooklyn organist who had been sent south for his health, and the intimacy was turned to educational advantage.

He now left his estate and set up as a pianoforte teacher and violinist in Danville, Virginia, whence he was recalled by his family, who had discovered his retreat. Permission to study at Leipzig was partly due to the tactful intercession of Grieg.

His first public appearance as a composer was with the suite, *Florida*, performed at Leipzig by Hans Sitt and an orchestra of sixty, the latter paid by the gift of a barrel of beer. This was in 1889, and next year, at the age of twenty-seven, the composer made his first London appearance with a complete programme of his own works conducted by Alfred Hertz. Audience and critics were equally puzzled at the unfamiliar idiom, and the effort seems to have had little result. The definite acceptance of Delius by British music-lovers came later, largely through the advocacy and loving interpretation of Beecham. Germany received him more readily: the operas *A Village Romeo and Juliet* and *Fennimore and Gerda* were first heard in Berlin (1907) and Frankfort-on-Main (1919) respectively, *Koanga* at Elberfeld (1904).

From his middle thirties he spent much of his time on a small property he had acquired near Fontainebleau, France. There he ended his life, crippled and blinded—apparently by the disease which somewhat similarly attacked his father years before. In 1929 Beecham and other admirers organized a great Delius Festival in London, at which everything of note was performed (other than works requiring stage performance, and suitable extracts even from these were included). The result was to reveal a greater Delius than had formerly been recognized. The composer, despite his affliction, was present.

Delius may be roughly classed as a Romantic of the Impressionist School (see *Impressionism*). He is very individual in his feeling, style, and idiom—especially in his harmonic idiom, which is characterized by a subtle chromaticism.

His works include operas, orchestral variations, rhapsodies, concertos for piano, for violin, for cello, and for violin and cello, choral orchestral pieces, a *Mass of Life*, a so-called *Requiem* (both these on words from Nietzsche), chamber music, and songs.

See references under *Incidental Music*; *Oboe Family* 4i; *Bird Music*; *Nietzsche*; *Heseltine, Philip*; *Calinda*; *Concerto* 6 c (1862); *Harpsichord* 9.

DELIZIOSO (It.). 'Delicious', 'sweet'. So the adverb, *Deliziosamente*.

DELLO JOIO (or **'Ioio'**), NORMAN, p. 1069, pl. **176. 4**. Born in New York in 1913. He began musical life as a pupil of his father and later worked under Hindemith. He took a position as a New York organist, made public appearances as a pianist, won a Fellowship at the Juilliard Graduate School (1939), and as a composer was twice awarded a Guggenheim Fellowship (1944–6). In 1972 he was appointed Dean of the Fine Arts School of Boston University. He has written a number of ballets, and a good deal of orchestral and chamber music, piano music, and choral music.

See *Opera* 24 f (1950); *Harp* 3.

DELONEY, THOMAS (c. 1543–c. 1607). Ballad writer, novelist, and pamphleteer. See quotations from him under *Inns and Taverns*; *Mealtime*.

DELVINCOURT, CLAUDE. Born in Paris in 1888; killed in a road accident in 1954, aged sixty-six. He studied at the Paris Conservatory, and in 1913 won the Rome Prize. In 1941 he was appointed director of the Conservatory at which he had received his training. (For his courageous activities during the second World War see *France* 12.) Amongst his compositions are *L'offrande à Sivà*, *Lucifer* (a lyric drama), chamber music, songs, etc.

DÉMANCHER (Fr.). The 'manche' of a stringed instrument is its neck. *Démancher* (literally, 'to un-neck') means to move the left hand along the neck, i.e. to shift. Strictly it means to shift the hand *away* from the neck and closer to the bridge. (The term can be found as long ago as the sixteenth century, in Rabelais.)

DEMI (Fr.). 'Half.'

DEMI-CADENCE. See *Cadence*.

DEMI-JEU (Fr.). 'Half-play', i.e. at half power (organ, harmonium, etc.).

DEMI-PAUSE (Fr.). 'Half-rest', i.e. minim rest.

DEMISEMIQUAVER (♬). The thirty-second note, i.e. having one thirty-second of the time-value of the Whole-note or Semibreve; see Table 1.

DEMI-TON (Fr.). 'Semitone.'

DEMI-VOIX (Fr.). 'Half voice', i.e. half the vocal power (= Ital. *Mezza voce*).

DEMUTH, NORMAN. Born in South Croydon in 1898, and died at Chichester in 1968, aged sixty-nine. He was on the teaching staff of the Royal Academy of Music. He wrote piano, violin, and other concertos, symphonies, choral music, chamber music, operas, ballets, incidental music to plays, etc., and also books on composers, on composition, and on the technique of warfare.

Cf. *Saxophone*; *Pianoforte* 21.

DEMÜTIG, DEMÜTHIG (Ger.). 'Meek.' So, too, *Demutsvoll*, *Demuthsvoll*. And the noun *Demut*, *Demuth*; *Demütigung*, *Demüthigung*.

DENCKE, JEREMIAH. Born in Silesia in 1725 and died at Bethlehem, Pa., in 1795, aged sixty-nine. He was a minister of the Moravian sect and an organist, first at Herrnhut (the Moravian headquarters in Europe) and then at Bethlehem, Pa. (the headquarters in America), at which latter place he did a good deal of composition.

DENMARK. See *Scandinavia* 2.

DENNER, JOHANN CHRISTOPHER. See *Clarinet Family* 2.

DENNIS, HENRY. See *Baptist Churches and Music* 4.

DENNOCH (Ger.). 'Nevertheless.'

DENNY, JAMES RUNCIMAN. Born at Kingston-on-Thames in 1908. After studying at the Royal College of Music and Christ's College, Cambridge (M.A., B.Mus.), he became Music Director of Bedford School, and later joined the staff of the BBC, in 1946 becoming Head of Music for the Midland Region. In 1950 he was appointed Professor of Music at Leeds University.

DENSMORE, FRANCES (1867–1957). See *Folk Song* 5; *United States* 7.

DENT, EDWARD JOSEPH. Born at Ribston Hall, Yorkshire, in 1876 and died in London in 1957, aged eighty-one. He was educated at Eton and King's College, Cambridge, where he was Professor of Music, 1926–41. He was President of the International Society for Contemporary Music from its foundation (1923–37 and from 1945), and President of the International Society for Musical Research. He was, indeed, in Continental circles far and away the best-known British musical scholar. His many books testify to an equal width of interest and of grasp. He prepared English performing translations of many Mozart and other operas, served as music critic of London journals, and composed.

DENZA, LUIGI. Born near Naples in 1846 and died in London in 1922, aged seventy-five. He wrote hundreds of songs of great popularity, including 'Funiculì Funiculà' (1880), which Strauss, under the impression that it was a Neapolitan folk song, used as a theme in his early suite, *Aus Italien*.

For the last quarter-century of his life Denza was a professor of singing in the Royal Academy of Music, London.

DEPPE, LUDWIG. Born at Lippe in 1828 and died at Pyrmont in 1890, aged sixty-one. He was a conductor (Court Kapellmeister in Berlin for a time) and a composer, but is chiefly remembered as a notable pianoforte teacher and as an author on pianoforte technique.

DE PROFUNDIS. *Out of the deep.* It is one of the seven Penitential Psalms and has a place in the Office of the Dead of the Roman Catholic Church, where, of course, it has its traditional plainsong. It has been set to more elaborate music many times, as by Orlandus Lassus, Lully, and others.

It is Psalm cxxix in the Vulgate (following the Septuagint and followed by all the Roman Catholic versions), but cxxx in the English Authorized and Revised Versions (following the Hebrew).

DE QUINCEY. See *Quincey, Thomas de.*

DER, DIE, DAS, DEM, DEN (Ger.). 'The' (according to gender, number, and case).

DERB (Ger.). 'Firm', 'solid', 'rough' (various terminations according to person, case).

DER FREISCHÜTZ. See *Freischütz.*

DERING. See *Deering.*

DER ROSENKAVALIER. See *Rosenkavalier.*

DERSELBE (Ger.). 'The same.'

DERVISHES. See *Dance* 1.

DES (Fr.). 'Of the' (plur.).

DES (Ger.). 'Of the' (masc. and neut. sing.); also the note D flat (see Table 7).

DESCANT. Like *Faburden* (q.v.), this is a puzzling term because of its application at different periods to somewhat different things; most musical works of reference leave difficulties in the mind of the careful reader, and an attempt will here be made to clear the subject of these.

Webster's *English Dictionary* gives a very fair summary of the various uses of the word:

1. Originally, melody or counterpoint sung above the plainsong of the tenor . . .
2. The art of composing or singing part-music; the early form of counterpoint; the music so composed or sung.
3. The upper voice in part-music; the soprano or treble.

A quotation then given from Tyndale (1492–1536) illustrates the first of these meanings—'*Twenty doctors expound one text twenty ways, as children make descant upon plainsong.*' (The 'children' are probably choir-boys, descanting on the plainsong of the men.)

Morley, in his *Introduction to Practical Musick* (1597), treats of the art of descant as 'singing extempore upon a plainsong', and it was a common practice in his days for two singers to amuse themselves with this sort of descant, one singing a song and the other improvising a free-running accompanying part to it.

With Simpson, seventy years later (*Compendium of Practical Musick*, 1667), the term seems to lose the implication of improvisation and takes the second of the meanings above given.

A part of his book is devoted to 'The Form of Figurate Descant', which he defines as follows: 'Figurate Descant is that wherein Discords are concerned as well as Concords, as distinct from 'Plain Descant', i.e. 'the use of the Concords'. In Figurate Descant, 'the Ornament or Rhetorical part of Musick . . ., are introduced all the varieties of Points, Fuges, Syncopes, or Bindings, Diversities of Measure, Intermixtures (Discording Sounds; or what else Art and Fancy can exhibit; which as different Flowers and Figures do set forth and adorn the Composition)'. He then goes on to treat of setting basses to melodies, writing fugues, etc., of song composition, the composition of instrumental music, etc. In fact, by this period 'descant' meant little less than 'composition'—mainly in its contrapuntal aspect. Playford, in 1683, published, as a part of the tenth edition of his *Introduction to the Skill of Musick*, 'A Brief Introduction to the Art of Descant or Composing Musick in Parts' (in later editions this appeared under the same title but revised by Purcell).

Rousseau, in his *Dictionary of Music* (1767), treats 'Descant' as a mere synonym for 'Counterpoint', which also conforms to the second definition above given.

Although the term had thus widened its meaning the practice of descant in the old sense of the term long continued. Thus Padre Martini, in his great work on counterpoint, says that in 1747 he heard very perfect extemporaneous singing in four parts in the church of St. John Lateran at Rome, and Dr. Burney in Rees's *Cyclopaedia* (c. 1805) affirms, 'There are musicians in the church so well versed in this kind of singing that they lead off, and even carry on, fugues extempore when the subject will allow it, without confounding or encroaching on the other parts or committing a single fault in the harmony'—which, despite the respectable authority of the writer, is scarcely credible to us today.

The term **Descant Viol** (see *Viol*) was sometimes used for the treble viol, and the term **Descant Clef** for the soprano clef (the C clef placed on the first line of the staff): this agrees with the third of the Webster definitions given above.

As the word is met with by readers nowadays, it usually means one of two things, both of them consistent with the literal meaning of the word—something that stands *off* from the main *song* (note French equivalent, *déchant*), and both of them conforming to the first of the definitions just given.

1. The practice, in the very early days of harmonization, of having the plainsong sung by one part of the choir whilst some individual member or some members extemporized a free accompanying part or parts in quicker notes. Wherever the free part was sounded at the same time as a note of the plainsong, it was expected to make with it a perfect interval (fourth, fifth, or octave—cf. *Harmony* 4, 5, 6), but in between it could move to other intervals

1. THE THEREMIN. See *Electric Musical Instruments* 1 d

2. THE MARTENOT. See *Electric Musical Instruments* 1 f

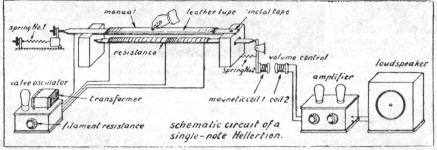

3. THE HELLERTION. See *Electric Musical Instruments* 1 k

4. PROFESSOR KARAPE-TOFF WITH HIS ELECTRIC 'CELLO. See *Electric Musical Instruments* 2 b

5. CLAVIOLINE. See *Electric Musical Instruments* 4

6, 7. THE NEO-BECHSTEIN PIANO. See *Electric Musical Instruments* 3 a

PLATE 51 · SOME PROMINENT FIGURES IN BRITISH MUSIC, I

See the Article *England* on pages 329–33, and Articles under the individual names, as also the Plates opposite pages 336–7 and 352–3

1. NICOLAS LANIER (1588–1666). Master of King's Musick under Charles I and then Charles II. Credited with introduction of Recitative into England

2. JOHN BULL (*c.* 1562–1628). Choirboy in Queen Elizabeth's Chapel Royal and later organist there; then organist in Brussels and Antwerp. Highly skilled virginalist and keyboard composer

3. VINCENT NOVELLO (1781–1861). Roman Catholic organist. Reviver and publisher of old English music, out of which activity grew the present firm

4. AUGUST MANNS (1825–1907). German military bandsman who settled in England. Founder of famous Crystal Palace orchestra and its conductor 1855–1901. See *Concert* 7

5. STERNDALE BENNETT (1816–75), in his uniform as one of the early students of the Royal Academy; later its Principal and also Professor of Music at Cambridge. Mendelssohn and Schumann greatly admired his gifts as composer

6. TOBIAS MATTHAY (1858–1945). Famous investigator of physical and artistic sides of piano playing

7. SIR HUGH P. ALLEN (1869–1946). Organist of various cathedrals and colleges. Oxford Professor and Director of Royal College of Music

8. ERIK CHISHOLM (1904–1965). Prominent Scottish composer and holder of important posts in many parts of the world

at the descanter's wide discretion. He had the plainsong before him on paper, as a guide, and hence this custom was known as *discantus supra librum* or *contrappunto alla mente*, i.e. an extemporization 'upon the book', or a 'mental counterpoint' (like 'mental arithmetic'). With successive modifications, following the evolution of harmonic practice, the custom lasted until at least the end of the sixteenth century, by which time it had become a popular recreation. (It is perhaps worth mentioning that it was not quite extinct in the later part of the nineteenth century; Lightwood, in *Music and Literature*, 1931, mentions two old ladies in the north of England who, perhaps sixty or seventy years earlier, had 'quite a reputation for improvising a high part above the melody' of hymn tunes).

2. A modern unextemporized imitation of the effect, applied to hymn-singing. The congregation and the bulk of the choir sing the normal melody and harmony of the tune, and, in a few verses of the hymn, for the sake of variety, a picked small body of trebles festoons the melody with a more or less florid accompanying melody that mostly rises above the melody itself. The term *Faburden* (q.v.), or *Fauxbourdon*, is also, but with rather less historical propriety, applied to this kind of singing. Books of standard hymn-tunes have been published arranged in this way.[1]

DESCANT RECORDER. See *Recorder Family* 2.

DESCANT SACKBUT. See *Trombone Family* 3.

DESCANT VIOL. See *Viol Family* 3.

DESES (Ger.). D double-flat (see Table 7).

DESIDERIO (It.). 'Desire'; hence *Con desiderio*, 'longingly'.

DESINVOLTO, DESINVOLTURA (It.). 'Ease.'

DÉSIR, LE ('Beethoven'). See *Nicknamed Compositions* 18 (under 'Mourning Waltz').

DES PRÉS. See under *Josquin Des Prés*.

DESSOUS (Fr.). 'Below', 'under'; or (as a noun) 'the lower part'.

DESSUS (Fr.). 'Above', 'over'; or (as a noun) 'the upper part'.

DESSUS DE VIOLE (Fr.). The treble viol; see *Viol Family* 3.

DESTO (It.). 'Wide-awake', i.e. in a buoyant, sprightly manner.

DESTOUCHES, ANDRÉ CARDINAL. Born in Paris in 1672 and died there in 1749, aged seventy-six. He was first a sailor, then a soldier, then a student of music under Campra (q.v.), and finally Superintendent of the King's Music and director of the Opera under Louis XV. He wrote ballets and operas, and

[1] The terms 'Descant' and 'Faburden', in their present-day application, tend towards the following distinction:
DESCANT. Two vocal lines, i.e. the melody, sung by the bulk of the choir, combined with an independent free treble part (sung by a few voices) and with instrumental accompaniment. Such treatment is now applied not merely to hymns but also to folk songs, etc.
FABURDEN. Four-part harmonization with the tune in the tenor, and with or without instrumental accompaniment.

some church music. Some of his works have been republished in recent times.

DESTRO, DESTRA (It.; masc., fem.). 'Right', e.g. *Mano destra*, 'right hand'. *Destro* also means 'dexterous'.

DE SUITE (Fr.). (*a*) 'One following the other'; (*b*) 'immediately'.

DÉTACHÉ (Fr.). 'Detached', i.e. more or less staccato (in the playing of the violin, etc.). *Grand détaché* means with the full bow for every note; *Petit détaché*, with the point of the bow for every note; and *Détaché sec* is the same as *martelé* (q.v.).

DETACHED CONSOLE. See *Organ* 4.

DETERMINATO (It.). 'Determined.'

DETT, ROBERT NATHANIEL. Born at Drummondville, Quebec, in 1882 and died at Battle Creek, Mich., in 1943, aged sixty. He was a Negro composer whose style was fluent and agreeable and whose piano pieces and songs had a measure of racial feeling. He was an honorary D.Mus. of Oberlin and of Harvard, and was head of the vocal department of Hampton Institute, Virginia.

DEUS MISEREATUR. The 67th Psalm, 'God be merciful unto us, and bless us'. In the Anglican Prayer Book (see *Common Prayer*) it is found as a part of the marriage service as an alternative to Ps. cxxviii, and in the evening service as an alternative to *Nunc Dimittis*.

DEUTEROMELIA (1609). See under *Ravenscroft; Round; Three Blind Mice.*

DEUTLICH (Ger.). 'Distinct.'

DEUTSCH (Ger.). 'German.'

DEUTSCH, OTTO ERICH. Born in Vienna in 1883 and died there in 1968, aged eighty-four. He was a high authority on musical bibliography, and the author of about fifty books on musical subjects, especially on Mozart, Handel, and Schubert—including, as to this last, a complete chronological thematic catalogue (1951). He came to Britain in 1939 and was naturalized in 1947. He resided in Cambridge until 1952, when he returned to Vienna.

See also *Nottebohm.*

DEUTSCHE, DEUTSCHER TANZ. See *Allemande* 2; *Waltz.*

DEUTSCHLAND ÜBER ALLES ('Germany beyond everything' or 'Germany before everything'), known also as the *Deutschlandlied* ('Germany Song'). This is a poem of aspiration for the unity of the German peoples. It was written, in the period which preceded the 1848 revolutionary disturbances, by August Heinrich Hoffmann, generally called Hoffmann von Fallersleben (1798–1874), a university professor who in the following year was deprived of his chair for the political trend of his poetry. There is in it nothing whatever of the ideal of world-conquering that a misunderstanding of the title has sometimes led foreigners to believe—a misunderstanding that has sometimes appeared to exist in Germany itself. It is innocent love of country that is expressed.

The tune to which this poem is sung is that which Haydn wrote as the Austrian national anthem, the *Emperor's Hymn* (q.v.), the 'Austria' of many hymn-tune books.

During the Austrian 'Anschluss' activities of the early 1930s (the movement for bringing Germany and Austria together) the song was taken up in Austria with a special significance.

After the second World War it was in Germany dropped for a time and then restored in May 1952—minus the stanza containing the ambiguous 'über alles'.

DEUX (Fr.). 'Two.' Hence *Deuxième*, 'second'. *À deux*, 'At two', usually means 'for two' voices or instruments, but occasionally is short for *À deux temps* (see *Deux temps*).

In orchestral music *À deux* has two (opposite) meanings: (*a*) Two normally separate instrumental parts are now merged in one line of notes; (*b*) One instrumental part is now divided into two, the players becoming two bodies.

DEUXIÈME (Fr.). 'Second.' So *Deuxième position*, second position—of the hand in playing stringed instruments (see *Position*).

DEUX TEMPS (Fr.). (1) in 2/2 time. (2) A *Valse à deux temps*, however, is a quick one in which there are only two steps to the three beats of each bar or measure. (3) There appears to be another use of the expression **Valse à deux temps.** 'Temps' is in common use as the word for 'beat', and the expression *Valse à deux temps*, in the application now under consideration, seems to mean, quite logically, 'Waltz in Two Values of Beat' (i.e. two 'simultaneous values'). The waltz in Gounod's *Faust* is an example. The under parts proceed in a regular three-in-a-measure, whilst the melody proceeds in a regular three-in-two-measures, i.e. in effect, one measure of the melody = two measures of the accompaniment. There are thus two simultaneous 'waltz rhythms' going on—one at half the speed of the other.

melody

accompaniment

DEVELOPMENT (Fr., *Développement*; Ger., *Durchführung*, literally, 'through-leading'; It., *Svolgimento*, literally, 'unfolding'). In examining the forms of music (see article *Form*) we shall often find three processes: (*a*) the statement of musical themes or subject, (*b*) the treatment of them by breaking them up into their constituent members, and making new passages out of these (often very modulatory), and (*c*) the repetition of them. Compound binary form (otherwise called 'Sonata Form' and 'First Movement Form'; see *Form* 7) is, indeed, nothing but a realization of this scheme exactly as above outlined; but in other forms too, the processes can be observed, on a greater or lesser scale.

The second of the two processes referred to is called development, and a section of a composition devoted to it is called a **Development Section**: the 'Development Section' in compound binary form is often called the **Free Fantasia**, because the composer has now left the realm of direct statement and allows his fancy to roam (see under *Fantasia*): **Working-out** is another name for it.

Sometimes (indeed often) a 'Subject' or 'Theme', placed under the microscope, so to speak, is found to be in itself a development of a motif or motifs (see *Motif*); of this the first subject of the opening movement of Beethoven's Fifth Symphony is an obvious example. Thus the process of development, though most obviously practised in the 'Development Section' of a sonata, etc., is by no means confined to it.

A frequent method of development is the following. A phrase is taken and repeated two or three times at different pitches or in different keys; the phrase is then disintegrated successively into halves, quarters, and so on, and these are treated in a similar way. The general effect of this is to build up a growing excitement, the period of reiteration becoming shorter and shorter as the passage proceeds. For examples see any of Beethoven's sonatas, symphonies, or chamber works.

In some development sections in a movement in compound binary form two subjects may be drawn into combination (perhaps in the right hand and the left in a piano sonata), and may then change places, the upper one becoming the lower and vice versa, perhaps so alternating several times.

The Episodes of a Fugue are frequently of the nature of brief developments of previous material (see *Form* 12).

In the great days of the classical sonata, string quartet, and symphony, Haydn, Mozart, and Beethoven stood out above all their contemporaries in the ease, ingenuity, and force with which they 'developed' their subject-matter, and this, in part, gave them their supremacy.

DEVIL. For a reference to this celebrated composer and performer see under *Tartini*. For Devil Dances see *Dance* 3.

DEVIZES. See *Cecilia*.

DEVOTO (It.). 'Devout', 'With devotion'.

DEVOZIONE (It.). 'Devotion.'

DI (It.). 'By', 'from', 'of', etc.

DIABELLI, ANTONIO (p. 517, pl. **94. 9**). Born near Salzburg in 1781 and died in Vienna in 1858, aged seventy-six. In Salzburg he was a pupil of Michael Haydn and in Vienna a friend of Michael's brother Joseph. He became a very popular composer and teacher and at length rose to the dignity of music publisher, in which capacity he was concerned with the issuing of works of Beethoven and Schubert. Beethoven's famous *Diabelli Variations* for pianoforte were composed on a waltz theme of his and for his publication (see *Pasticcio*).

Some of Diabelli's smaller works are still played by piano pupils, and his easy masses for country churches are popular in Austria.

DIABOLUS IN MUSICA ('The Devil in Music'). The Tritone (q.v.).

DIAGHILEF, SERGE (1872–1929). See *Ballet* 5; *Opera* 17 d; *Programme Music* 3.

DIAMOND, DAVID LEO (p. 1069, pl. **176.** 5). Born at Rochester, N.Y., in 1915. He won a Juilliard Publication Award in 1937 (*Psalm for Orchestra*), and a Guggenhcim Prize in 1938, etc., and is the composer of eight symphonies, concertos for various instruments, six string quartets, and other things. In 1965, after prolonged residence in Europe, he joined the staff of the Manhattan School of Music.

See *Jewish Music* 9; *Concerto* 6 c (1915).

DIAPASON. Poets and musicians have used this word in so many senses, clear and vague, that definition is difficult. The following includes all musicians' uses common today.

Its derivation is from the Greek and shows its original sense to be 'through all' (with the implication of 'notes' or 'strings' or some such word)—in other words, either (*a*) the octave, or (*b*) the entire compass of an instrument. So Dryden:

Through all the compass of the notes it ran,
The diapason closing full in man.

Apparently the use of the word as the name of certain (tonally basic) organ stops (see *Organ* 3, 14 I) originated in the fact that these extended to the whole compass of the instrument, as some others did not.

In French the word has come to mean 'Pitch Pipe' (*Diapason à bouche*) or 'Tuning Fork' (*Diapason à branches*), perhaps because this fixes the pitch of the whole series of notes to be employed (see *Pitch* 6). The note A at 435 vibrations per second (at a temperature of 15 degrees Centigrade or 59 degrees Fahrenheit), as fixed by the French Academy in 1859, is known as the *Diapason normal*.

For Diapason Phonon see *Organ* 14 I.

DIAPENTE (Greek). The interval of the perfect fifth.

DIAPHONE. See *Organ* 14 I.

DIAPHONY. The same as *Organum* (see *Harmony* 4, 5). Some define it as a freer form of organum, admitting a greater variety of intervals, i.e. not merely the perfect ones; others speak of it as a later form of organum, admitting of contrary motion between the parts engaged, crossing of parts, etc.

There is another sense, in which it was also used in ancient Greek and (sometimes) medieval treatises—'discord', as opposed to 'symphony,' which latter meant 'concord'.

But in ordinary reading it will be well to consider 'Diaphony' and 'Organum' as synonymous.

DIAPHRAGM and **DIAPHRAGMATIC BREATHING.** See *Voice* 3, 21.

DIATONIC AND CHROMATIC. The diatonic scales are the major and minor, made up of tones and semitones (in the case of the harmonic minor scale, also an augmented second), as distinct from the chromatic, made up entirely of semitones. The modes (see *Modes*) are diatonic in structure.

Diatonic Passages, Diatonic Intervals, and *Diatonic Chords* (or *Diatonic Harmonies*) are such as are constructed from the notes of the diatonic key prevailing at the moment, whilst *Chromatic Passages, Chromatic Intervals*, and *Chromatic Chords* (or *Chromatic Harmonies*) introduce notes not forming any part of that key. (See also *Harmony* 12, 13, 24 a, and *Chromatic Chords*.)

For Chromatic Drums see *Percussion Family* 2 a, 5 a.
For Chromatic Harp see *Harp* 1.
For Chromatic Scale see *Scales* 7.

DIBDIN.

(1) CHARLES (p. 817, pl. **140.** 5). Born at Southampton in 1745 and died in London in 1814, aged sixty-nine. He was a choir-boy at Winchester Cathedral, an assistant in a London music shop, an actor–singer, a very successful composer for the theatre (innumerable 'musical dramas'), a public entertainer, and the composer of songs which he himself sang into popularity. Twenty years after his death a 'Dibdinian Club' was formed in London for the regular performance of his musical works.

His lasting fame is as a writer of sea-songs; they had great popularity in their day and made the navy popular; some have lived and seem likely to continue to do so. 'Tom Bowling', the best known of them, is a portrait of the composer–poet's brother, Captain Thomas Dibdin; a stanza of it is carved on his own tombstone.

He also wrote musical textbooks, two novels, a 'Didactic Poem', two accounts of his *Musical Tours*, and his *Professional Life*, to which latter was appended a set of six hundred of his song poems (being about half of his output of such).

See references to him under *Pianoforte* 17; *Pantomime*; *Bells of Aberdovey*; *Rogue's March*; *Opera* 21 b; *Sadler's Wells*; *Recital*; *Ballad Opera*.

(2) CHARLES II (1768–1833). He was an illegitimate son of Charles Dibdin I and, like him, wrote plays, songs, etc.—these for performance at Sadler's Wells Theatre, of which he was proprietor.

(3) THOMAS JOHN (1771–1841). He, also, was an illegitimate son of Charles Dibdin I and like his brother (see above), wrote for Sadler's Wells Theatre—as he did, also, for Covent Garden, etc. It is said that his operas and plays numbered about two hundred and his songs over two thousand. He published his *Reminiscences* (1827).

(4) HENRY EDWARD (1813–66). He was a son of Charles Dibdin II and was a harpist in London and then an organist and music teacher in Edinburgh, where he published two books of hymn tunes. He was also a capable painter.

DICHTUNG (Ger.). 'Poem' (see *Symphonic Poem*).

DICK (Ger.). 'Thick.'

DICKENS, CHARLES. See *Hogarth, G.*; *Hullah*.

DICTION. Properly the word means verbal phrasing, or style in the choice of words (in 1930 the American Academy of Arts and Letters awarded a gold medal for Diction to a famous author), but singing-masters use it for 'enunciation'. The same word exists in the French language, in which it is freely used in both senses.

DICTIONARIES OF MUSIC

Man is the world's dictionary-making animal. In every country, like ants bringing together fragments of material to make their ant-hill, men are busy collecting tiny scraps of information and heaping them up into dictionaries. In London alone at the present time there are published fifteen hundred dictionaries and the same may probably be said of some other European capitals and of New York. There are dictionaries of all languages, ancient and modern, of mythology and religion, of all the arts, sciences, trades, and sports, of biography and bibliography, of synonyms and antonyms, of quotations, of slang, of abbreviations, and indeed of all the details of every branch of human thought and activity.

Almost as soon as Gutenberg had introduced to Europe the art of printing the stream of dictionaries began, and by the time that art had been in existence only about fifty years a musical work of this class was before the public. This was the Fleming Tinctor's work, in Latin, defining musical terms—*Terminorum musicae diffinitorium*, which was published in Treviso about 1495. It was long thought that all copies of it had disappeared, but when Burney, in the late eighteenth century, in preparation for the writing of his great *History of Music*, was labouring in the library of George III he found a copy, and since then two more have been unearthed and the valuable little work has been several times reprinted.

Tinctor stood alone in the field for over two centuries and then, at Prague, there appeared a work of somewhat similar aims, Janowka's *Clavis ad thesaurum magnae artis musicae* (1701).

Walther's *Musikalisches Lexikon* (Leipzig 1732) led the way into a wider field, for it added the personal side, whilst Mattheson's famous *Grundlage einer Ehren-Pforte* (Hamburg 1740) devoted itself to the personal side alone. Mattheson was rather limited in his scope. He devoted thirty-one pages to his own biography against fifteen to Telemann, eight to his friend Handel, and very much less to other men. Despite the fact that he was Secretary to the British Legation in Saxony he included only two Englishmen—Heather, the early seventeenth-century founder of the Oxford professorship of music, and Henry Symonds, an eighteenth-century London organist.

The terminology with which Tinctor had been concerned was that of what we may call 'Musical Theory'. In the seventeenth century another sort of terminology came into existence. So far as England is concerned we can date its use from the time of Purcell, who attached to some of his compositions a few terms of tempo and expression borrowed from the Italian composers. In the closing words of the preface to his *Sonnata's of III Parts* (1683) he said: 'It remains only that the English Practitioner be enform'd, that he will find a few terms of Art perhaps unusual to him, the chief of which are the following: Adagio and Grave, which import nothing but a very slow movement: Presto Largo, Poco Largo, or Largo by itself, a middle movement: Allegro, and Vivace, a very brisk, swift, or fast movement: Piano, soft.' The anonymous *Short Explication of such Foreign Words as are made use of in Musick Books* of half a century later (1730) represents probably the earliest organized assistance offered to musicians in this department.

In time musical dictionaries of all kinds abounded—Comprehensive, Biographical, Factual but Non-biographical, Terminological, Regional, etc.—including special works treating of Opera, Chamber Music, and other special branches.

The list that here follows has been carefully compiled and classified by categories. An attempt has been made to make it complete as to *pioneer works in each category* and thereafter to list the historically most important works and those that will today be found to be the most practically useful in the everyday work of the musician, even though defective in one department or another.

CONTENTS OF THE FOLLOWING LISTS

1. Comprehensive Dictionaries (covering the whole field).
2. General Non-biographical Dictionaries (covering the whole field other than the personal side).
3. Purely Biographical Dictionaries.
4. Regional Musical Dictionaries.
5. Terminological Dictionaries.
6. Dictionaries of Instruments, Instrumental Artists, and Instrument Makers:
   (a) General.
   (b) Pianoforte.
   (c) Organ and Organists.
   (d) Violin, Violinists, and Violin Makers.
7. Dictionaries of Church Music and Matters related thereto.
8. Dictionaries of Opera.
9. Dictionaries of Chamber Music.
10. A Sight-singing Dictionary.
11. Dictionaries of University Degrees in Music.
12. A Dictionary of the Dance.
13. Dictionaries of Gramophone (Phonograph) Records.
14. Dictionaries of Thematic Material.
15. Bibliographical Dictionaries.

1. **Comprehensive Dictionaries** (i.e. covering the whole field—including biography).

WALTHER: *Musikalisches Lexikon* (Leipzig 1732; 666 pp.; 86 pp. supplement of particulars of busts and statues of famous musicians, and lists of 'great and famous organists', and of instruments and their inventors. The first few pages, comprising letter A, had been previously published in 1728; facsimile reprint by Bärenreiter, Basle 1953).

FRAMÉRY and GINGUENÉ (and de Momigny): *Dictionnaire de musique* (2 vols., Paris, the 1st in 1791, the 2nd, by de Momigny, in 1818).

SCHILLING: *Encyclopädie der gesammten musikalischen Wissenschaften oder Universal-Lexicon der Tonkunst* (6 vols., Stuttgart 1835–8; supplementary vol. by Gassner, 1842).

ESCUDIER: *Dictionnaire de musique d'après les théoriciens, historiens, et critiques les plus célèbres* (2 vols., Paris 1844; 1854 as *Dictionnaire de musique théorique et historique*).

GASSNER: *Universallexikon der Tonkunst* (Stuttgart 1849; a resumé of Schilling, above).

MOORE: *Complete Encyclopedia of Music* (Boston, Mass., 1854; appendix 1875).

MENDEL (and REISSMANN): *Musikalisches Conversations-Lexikon* (12 vols., the last 5 being by Reissmann. Berlin, vols. 1–11, 1870–9; vol. 12, i.e. supplement, 1883).

GROVE: *Dictionary of Music and Musicians* (4 vols., plus index vol., London 1878–89; this first edn. limited to events after 1450, but with an appendix (by Fuller Maitland) including the earlier period; 2nd edn. by Fuller Maitland, 5 vols. 1900; 3rd edn. by Colles, 5 vols. 1927; 4th edn. by Colles, 5 vols. and supplementary vol., 1940. American supplement by Pratt and Boyd, New York 1900 and 1939; 5th edn. by Blom, 9 vols., 1954; supplementary vol. 1961).

MATHEWS: *Dictionary of Music and Musicians* (New York 1880).

RIEMANN: *Musik-Lexikon* (Berlin 1882; of later edns. 9th to 11th, 1929, ed. by Einstein. 12th edn. ed. by Gurlitt, 3 vols. 1958–61. A Nazi edn. was begun in 1939. English edn. by Shedlock, London c. 1893, and Philadelphia 1897. French edn. by Humbert and others, 1899, 1913, 1931. Also edns. in Danish and Russian, 1902).

CHAMPLIN and APTHORP: *Cyclopedia of Music and Musicians* (3 vols., New York 1888–90).

HUGHES: *Music Lover's Encyclopedia* (New York 1903; new edn. by Deems Taylor and Kerr, 1939).

DUNSTAN: *Cyclopedic Dictionary of Music* (London 1909, 1919, 1925).

PRATT: *New Encyclopedia of Music and Musicians* (New York 1924, 1929, 1947).

HULL: *Dictionary of Modern Music and Musicians* (London 1924; German edn. by Einstein).

ABERT: *Illustriertes Musik-Lexikon* (Stuttgart 1927).

DELLA CORTE and GATTI: *Dizionario di musica* (Turin 1925, 1930, 1952).

KELLER and KRUSEMANN: *Geillustreerd Musieklexicon* (The Hague 1932, appendix 1942).

MOSER: *Musiklexikon* (Berlin 1935, 1943; Hamburg 1951).

THOMPSON: *International Cyclopedia of Music and Musicians* (New York 1938; subsequent edns. by Slonimsky and R. Sabin).

SCHOLES: *Oxford Companion to Music* (London 1938; 9th edn. 1955, 10th edn. 1970).

BLOM: *Everyman's Dictionary of Music* (London 1946, 1954, etc.).

BLUME, FRIEDRICH (ed.): *Die Musik in Geschichte und Gegenwart* (15 vols., Kassel 1949–68).

SOHLMAN: *Musiklexikon* (Stockholm 1948–51).

SCHOLES: *Concise Oxford Dictionary of Music* (London 1952, 2nd edn. 1964).

——*Oxford Junior Companion to Music* (London 1954, etc.).

WESTRUP and HARRISON: *Collins Music Encyclopaedia* (London 1959: in U.S.A., *New College Encyclopedia of Music*).

DUFOURQ (ed.): *Larousse de la musique* (2 vols., Paris 1957–8).

2. **General Non-biographical Dictionaries** (covering the whole field other than the personal side).

JANOWKA: *Clavis ad thesaurum magnae artis musicae* (Prague 1701).

BROSSARD: *Dictionnaire de musique* (Amsterdam 1702; Paris 1703, 1705).

BARNICKEL: *Kurzgefasstes musikalisches Lexikon* (Chemnitz 1749).

GRASSINEAU: *Musical Dictionary* (London 1740, 1769, 1784, and possibly other edns. Based on Brossard).

TANS'UR: *New Musical Dictionary* (1766. See p. 1007).

ROUSSEAU: *Dictionnaire de musique* (Geneva 1767 and other edns. in Paris and elsewhere; English edn. by Waring, London 1770, 1779).

HOYLE: *Dictionarium musicae, being a complete Dictionary or Treasury of Music* (London 1770, 1790, 1791).

BUSBY: *Dictionary of Music* (London 1786 and many later edns.).

WOLF: *Kurzgefasstes musikalisches Lexikon* (Halle 1787, 1792, 1806).

KOCH: *Musikalisches Lexikon* (Frankfurt 1802; new edn. by Dommer, 1865).

CASTIL-BLAZE: *Dictionnaire de musique moderne* (2 vols., Paris 1821, 1825, 1828).

LICHTENTHAL: *Dizionario e bibliografia della musica* (4 vols., Milan 1826. The first two vols. come into the present category; for the other two see 15, *Bibliographical Dictionaries*. French edn. by Mondo, Paris, 2 vols., 1839).

STAINER and BARRETT: *Dictionary of Musical Terms* (London 1876, 1898; condensed version 1880). 'Musical Terms' is misleading as this is a general dictionary of everything in music except the personal side.

'BRENET' (Marie Bobillier): *Dictionnaire pratique et historique de la musique* (Paris 1926).

APEL: *Harvard Dictionary of Music* (Cambridge, Mass., 1944, 1969).

3. **Purely Biographical Dictionaries.**

MATTHESON: *Grundlage einer Ehren-Pforte voran der tüchtigsten Capellmeister, Componisten, Musikgelehrten, Tonkünstler, &c. Leben. Werke, Verdienste, &c. erscheinen sollen. Zum fernen Aufbau angegeben von Mattheson* (Hamburg 1740, also ed. Schneider, Berlin 1910).

GERBER: *Historisch-biografisches Lexicon der Tonkünstler* (2 vols., Leipzig 1790–2; supplemented by the work below).

—— *Neues historisch-biografisches . . . Lexicon* (4 vols., Leipzig 1812–14).

CHORON and FAYOLLE: *Dictionnaire historique des musiciens* (2 vols., Paris 1810–11; English edn. 1824).

ANON [John S. Sainsbury]: *Dictionary of Musicians from the Earliest Ages to the Present Time* (2 vols., London 1824–7. There is an informative research article on this work, by H. G. Farmer, in *Music and Lettters*, Oct. 1931).

FÉTIS: *Biographie universelle des musiciens* (8 vols., Paris 1835–44; 1860–5: supplement by Pougin, 2 vols., 1878).

EITNER: (1900–4). See under 15, *Bibliographical Dictionaries*.

SCHMIDL: *Dizionario universale dei musicisti* (2 vols., Milan 1936–7; supplement in 1938).

BAKER: *Biographical Dictionary of Musicians* (New York 1900; 3rd edn. by Remy, 1919; 4th edn. by Pisk and others, 1940; 5th edn. by Slonimsky, 1958; supp. 1965, 1971).

—— *Musikens Hvem, Hvad, Hvor* (3 vols., Copenhagen 1950).

International Who's Who of Music (New York 1918; Chicago 1951 etc.).

4. Regional Musical Dictionaries.

(a) Britain.

BROWN: *Biographical Dictionary of Musicians* (Paisley 1886).

—— and STRATTON: *British Musical Biography* (Birmingham 1897).

KIDSON: *British Music Publishers, Printers, and Engravers* (London [1900]).

HUMPHRIES and SMITH: *Music Publishing in the British Isles* (1954).

PULVER: *Dictionary of Old English Music and Musical Instruments* (London 1923).

—— *Biographical Dictionary of Old English Music* (London 1927).

Who's Who in Music (London; 1915–35–50–62).

(b) United States.

HUBBARD: *American History and Encyclopedia of Music* (New York 1910).

REIS: *Composers in America* (New York 1938).

—— *American Composers Today—a Catalogue* (New York 1930, 1947, etc.).

EWEN: *American Composers Today* (New York 1934, etc.).

(c) Canada.

KALLMANN: *Catalogue of Canadian Composers* (Toronto 1952).

(d) Germany.

MÜLLER: *Deutsches Musik-Lexikon* (Dresden 1928).

(e) Italy.

DE ANGELIS: *L'Italia musicale d'oggi: dizionario dei musicisti* (Rome 1922; 3rd edn. 1928).

(f) Belgium.

VANNES (completed by SOURIS): *Dictionnaire des musiciens: compositeurs* (Brussels 1947).

(g) Switzerland.

REFARDT: *Historisches-Biographisches Musiker-Lexikon der Schweiz* (Zürich 1928).

SCHUH and REFARDT: *Schweizer Musikbuch: Musikerlexikon* (Zürich 1939: biographies only).

(h) Russia.

VODARSKY–SHIREFF: *Russian Composers and Musicians* (New York 1940).

BOELZA (ed. BUSH): *Handbook of Soviet Musicians* (London 1943).

(i) Poland, etc.

SOWINSKY: *Les musiciens polonais et slaves* (Paris 1857).

(j) South American Countries.

SLONIMSKY: *Music of Latin America* (New York 1945).

MAYER–SERRA: *Música y Músicos de Latino-américa* (2 vols., Mexico City 1947).

There exist also regional dictionaries for the Baltic countries, Berlin, Czechoslovakia, Finland, Greece, Holland, Lübeck, Portugal, Schleswig, Spain, and Valencia. For particulars of many of these see the works of Duckles and Davies listed in section 15 of this article.

Note that Pratt's *New Encyclopedia of Music* (see 1 above) has a comprehensive section devoted to musical activities of all periods in the chief towns and cities of the world.

An Antisemitic *Lexicon der Juden in der Musik*, by P. Stengel and H. Gerigk, appeared in 1941 as a part of the activities of the Nazi 'Institut der N.S.D.A.P. zur Erforschung der Judenfrage'.

5. Terminological Dictionaries (brief definitions of words and expressions used in music).

TINCTORIS: *Terminorum musicae diffinitorium* (Treviso *c.* 1495. Also included in Forkel, *Allgemeine Literatur der Musik*, Leipzig 1792; Lichtenthal, *Dizionario e bibliografia della musica* vol. 3, Milan 1826; Adams, *Five Thousand Musical Terms*, London 1861; John Bishop's edn. of Hamilton's *Dictionary of Musical Terms*, and perhaps some other works).

ANON: *A Short Explication of such Foreign Words as are made use of in Musick Books* (London 1724).

KOCH: *Kurzgefasstes Handwörterbuch der Musik* (Leipzig 1802; abridged edn. 1807).

HILES: *Dictionary of 12,500 Musical Terms, Phrases, and Abbreviations* (London 1871, 1882).

WOTTON: *Dictionary of Foreign Musical Terms* (London 1907).

GREENISH: *Dictionary of Musical Terms* (London 1917).

VANNES: *Dictionnaire universel comprenant plus de 15,000 termes de musique en italien, espagnol, portugais, français, anglais, allemand, latin, et grec* (Paris 1925).

SCHOLES: *Radio Times Music Handbook* (1935; 4th edn. 1950).

6. Dictionaries of Instruments, Instrumental Artists, and Instrument Makers.

(a) General.

JACQUOT: *Dictionnaire . . . des instruments de musique* (Paris 1886).

SACHS: *Real-Lexicon der Musikinstrumente* (Berlin 1913).

WRIGHT: *Dictionnaire des instruments de musique* (London 1941).

BESSARABOFF: *Ancient European Musical Instruments* (Boston, Mass., 1941).

(b) Pianoforte.

PAUER: *Dictionary of Pianists and Composers for the Piano* (London 1895).

(c) Organ and Organists.

WEDGWOOD: *Comprehensive Dictionary of Organ Stops* (London 1905).

AUDSLEY: *Organ Stops and their Artistic Registration* (New York 1921).

LOCHER: *Die Orgel-Register und ihre Klangfarben* (Berne, 4th edn., 1912).

WEST: *Cathedral Organists Past and Present* (London 1899 and 1921).

STOCKS: *British Cathedral Organists* (32 pp., London 1950).

(d) Violin, Violinists, and Violin Makers.

PEARCE: *Violins and Violin Makers; a Biographical Dictionary* (London 1866).

CLARKE: *Dictionary of Fiddlers* (London 1895).

C. STAINER: *Dictionary of Violin Makers* (London 1896).

EMERY: *The Violinist's Dictionary* (London 1913).

VIDAL: *Les instruments à archet* (3 vols., Paris 1876).

See also list 15, s.v. *Heron-Allen*.

7. Dictionaries of Church Music and Matters related thereto.

D'ORTIGUE: *Dictionnaire liturgique, historique, et théorique de plain-chant et de musique d'église* (Paris 1854, 1860).

KUMMERLE: *Encyclopädie der evangelischen Kirchenmusik* (4 vols. 1888–95).

JULIAN: *Dictionary of Hymnology* (1750 pp.; London 1892 and 1907; see *Hymns and Hymn Tunes* 7).

HUGHES: *Dictionary of Liturgical Terms* (London 1941).

BUMPUS: *Dictionary of Ecclesiastical Terms* (London, c. 1900).

HOOK: *Church Dictionary* (London, 15th edn., 1896).

ADDIS and ARNOLD: *Catholic Dictionary* (London 1883; 10th edn. 1928).

STUBBINGS: *Dictionary of Church Music* (London 1949).

SLATER: *Salvation Army Dictionary of Music* (London 1908, 1909).

For Cathedral Organists see 6 c above.

8. Dictionaries of Opera.

CLÉMENT and LAROUSSE: *Dictionnaire des opéras* (Paris 1872; new edns. by Pougin 1897, 1905).

TOWERS: *Dictionary Catalogue of upwards of 28,000 Operas and Operettas which have been performed on the Public Stage from the Earliest Times to the Present* (Morgantown, U.S.A., 1910).

SONNECK: *Catalogue of Opera Librettos* [in the Library of Congress] *printed before 1800* (2 vols., Washington, D.C., 1914).

LOEWENBERG: *Annals of Opera—1597–1940* (Cambridge 1943; 2nd ed. Geneva 1955.) This completely supersedes all previous works of the kind.

ROSENTHAL and WARRACK: *Concise Dictionary of Opera* (London 1964).

9. Dictionaries of Chamber Music.

ALTMANN: *Chamber Music Literature; Catalogue of Chamber Music published since 1841* (Leipzig 1910, 3rd edn. 1923; other edns. in English, London and New York).

COBBETT: *Cyclopedic Survey of Chamber Music* (2 vols., London 1929; 3 vols., 1963).

10. A Sight-singing Dictionary.

PHILLIPS: *Dictionary of the Tonic Sol-fa System* (London, ? c. 1900).

11. Dictionaries of University Degrees in Music.

OELRICH: *Historische Nachrichten von den academischen Würden in der Musik* (chiefly English degrees and graduates; 1752).

WILLIAMS: *Degrees in Music at Oxford and Cambridge . . . from the year 1463* (London 1893).

12. A Dictionary of the Dance.

JUNK: *Handbuch des Tanzes* (Stuttgart 1930).

13. Dictionaries of Gramophone (Phonograph) Records.

Gramophone Shop Encyclopedia of Recorded Music (New York 1936, 1948, etc.).

CLOUGH and CUMING: *The World's Encyclopedia of Recorded Music* (London 1952; later supplements).

SACKVILLE-WEST and SHAWE-TAYLOR: *The Record Guide* (London 1951, etc.).

14. Dictionaries of Thematic Material.

BARLOW and MORGENSTERN: *A Dictionary of Musical Themes* (New York 1948).

—— —— *A Dictionary of Vocal Themes* (New York 1950).

These two dictionaries enable the user to establish the identity of almost any musical theme that he may find 'running in his head'.

15. Bibliographical Dictionaries and Works on Musical Bibliography (see 3, *Biographical Dictionaries*; many of these include bibliographies).

LICHTENTHAL: *Letteratura generale della musica* (Milan 1826); this comprises vols. 3 and 4 of the author's *Dizionario e bibliografia della musica*. See 2, *Non-biographical Dictionaries*).

EITNER: *Biographisch-bibliographisches Quellen-Lexikon der Musiker und Musikgelehrter . . . bis zur Mitte des neunzehnten Jahrhunderts* (10 vols., Leipzig 1900–4, continued by 10 brochures, *Miscellanea Musicae Bio-bibliographica*, by Springer, Schneider, and Wolffheim, 1912–14).

VILLANIS: *Piccola guida alla bibliografia musicale* (Turin 1906).

SONNECK: *Classification of Music and Books on Music in the Library of Congress* (Washington, D.C., 1917).

HERON-ALLEN: *De fidiculis bibliographia—being an attempt towards a bibliography of the violin*, etc. (2 vols., London 1890–4).

BLOM: *General Index to Modern Musical Literature in the English Language* (London 1927).

ABERT: *Handbuch der Musik-Literatur* (Leipzig 1922).

McCOLVIN and REEVES: *Music Libraries . . . with a Bibliography of Music and Musical Literature* (London 1937).

SCHOLES: *A List of Books about Music in the English Language* (1939; also issued as an appendix to the author's *Oxford Companion to Music*, 2nd edn.).

DUCKLES: *Music Reference and Research Materials* (London 1964).

DAVIES: *Musicalia; Sources of Information in Music* (London 1966).

In addition to the above there is a most valuable type of bibliographical material too extensive to be listed here—the published catalogues of music and of books on music of the great libraries—the British Museum, London; the Library of Congress, Washington; the Fitzwilliam Library, Cambridge; the Edward A. Fleisher collection in the Public Library of Philadelphia; the Berlin Stadtbibliothek; and the Basle University Library—to mention merely a few examples. And many auction catalogues and antiquarian booksellers' lists also afford useful information.

A word may be added here as to the innumerable 'Hidden Dictionaries of Music' (as they may be called). Of these Rousseau's articles on music scattered through the twenty-eight volumes of the famous *Encyclopédie* of d'Alembert and Diderot (1751–72) are a notable early example, as are, thirty years later, Burney's articles similarly dispersed through the pages of the forty-five volumes of Rees's *Cyclopædia*

(1802–20). Rousseau was led, by his lexicographical work on the *Encyclopédie* later, to compile and put together an actual Dictionary of Music (see section 2 in the above list).

D. F. Tovey's erudite musical articles in the *Encyclopædia Britannica* (14th ed.) have been reprinted (in alphabetical order) under the title *The Forms of Music* (London 1944).

DIDDLING. A Lowland Scottish practice similar to the Highland practice of *Port à Beul* (q.v.). Dance tunes are sung to nonsense syllables such as 'dee-diddle-di-dee'. In rural districts competitions are held.

DIDEROT, DENIS (1713–84). See references under *France* 8; *Criticism* 3; *Bouffons*; *Dictionaries* 15 (near end).

DIDO AND AENEAS (Purcell). Produced about 1689 at the boarding school for girls kept by Josias Priest at Chelsea. Revived, on the stage, in 1895. Libretto by Nahum Tate. It is Purcell's only true opera, and it is 'grand opera', in the sense that it has no use of the speaking voice.

ACT I

SCENE 1: *The Palace at Carthage*

Belinda (*Soprano*), lady in-waiting to **Dido**, Queen of Carthage (*Soprano*), bids her mistress shake off her care. Belinda knows that her mistress has been moved by pity for Aeneas, a Trojan Prince, who, on a voyage, has been driven by storms to the coast of Africa and has come to Dido's court; Belinda knows also that each loves the other.

Aeneas (*Tenor* or *Baritone*) enters. Dido fears some danger fated for their love, but the hero is confident.

SCENE 2: *A Sorceress's Cave*

A **Witch** (*Mezzo-soprano*) bids her attendants go as messengers to Aeneas, pretending that they are sent by Jove himself. They are to tell him that Jove commands him to depart at once from Carthage.

ACT II

SCENE: *A Grove*

Dido and Aeneas pursue the chase. When all but Aeneas have been driven back to the court by a storm that the Witch has raised, the Witch's spirit, appearing to Aeneas in the likeness of **Mercury** (*Soprano* or *Tenor*), the messenger god, gives the pretended message from Jove. Aeneas is to leave love's delights and sail for Troy, which he is to restore from its ruins. Aeneas, heavy-hearted, obeys, doubting how he shall pacify Dido.

ACT III

SCENE: *The Ships*

A **Sailor** (*Tenor*) instructs his mates how to take their leave of the damsels of Carthage—by vowing to return, 'though never intending to visit them more'. The Witch sings her triumph. Dido is broken-hearted at Aeneas's desertion and has caused her funeral pyre to be prepared. Though he is willing to risk Jove's displeasure by staying, she bitterly rejects his

offer, regarding him as faithless and herself as slighted.

He goes, and she, after singing the famous Lament (see *Ground*), stabs herself upon the pyre, which consumes her body.

DIECI (It.). 'Ten.'

DIEPENBROCK, ALPHONSE. Born in Amsterdam in 1862 and there died in 1921, aged fifty-eight. He was a schoolmaster, and as a musician was completely self-taught. He wrote large-scale church compositions, dramatic songs, etc., and also articles on the aesthetics of music. His activities count as one of the stimulating influences in Dutch music of this period.

See allusions under *Holland* 8.

DIEREN, BERNARD VAN. Born in Holland in 1884, his father being Dutch and his mother Irish, most of his own life, however, being spent in London, where he died in 1936, aged fifty-one.

He composed an enormous variety of works, in almost every form, and in a style of his own such as did not make an immediate appeal to large numbers of musical people but attracted around him a group of warm admirers. The versatility of his spirit and width of his interests also urged him to the writing of a book on the sculptor Epstein, as of a book of essays on various aspects of music, *Down among the Dead Men* (1935).

See references under *Violin Family* 10.

DIÈSE (Fr.). 'Sharp' (see Table 7).

DIESELBE (Ger.). 'The same.'

DIES IRAE. See *Requiem*. The poem is by Thomas of Celano (died *c.* 1250). The plainsong tune has occasionally been introduced into instrumental music, as in Berlioz's 'Fantastic' Symphony and Saint-Saëns's *Danse Macabre*.

DIESIS. (1) The quarter-tone in the ancient Greek system. (2) In modern acoustical terminology the theoretical difference between B sharp and C, C sharp and D flat, etc. (3) It. 'sharp' (see Table 7).

DIES SIND DIE HEIL'GEN ZEHN GEBOT. See *Chorale*.

DIETRO (It.). 'Behind.'

'DIE UHR' SYMPHONY (Haydn). See *Nicknamed Compositions* 11 (101).

DIFFERENTIAL TONES. See *Acoustics* 10, 13.

DIGITAL. Any one of the keys making up the keyboard of a piano or similar instrument.

DIGITORIUM. A five-keyed dumb keyboard, in use in the nineteenth century, the keys of which had a strong resistance. Practice on such an instrument would now be considered harmful, suppleness rather than muscular 'strength' being the aim, and rigidity such as this instrument tended to cause being shunned.

DILUENDO (It.). 'Dissolving', i.e. dying away.

DILUNGANDO (It.). 'Lengthening.'

DIMA, GEORGE. See *Rumania*.

DIMINISHED INTERVALS. See *Interval*.

DIMINISHED SEVENTH. As an interval (see *Intervals*) this chiefly occurs with the leading note as the lower note—e.g. in key C (major or minor) in the frequent chord B, D, F, A flat, which is hence called the *Chord of the Diminished Seventh* of that key.

The theoretical explanation of the chord is that it is a dominant minor ninth (G–B–D–F–A flat) with the root (G) absent.

The chord has a luscious effect, and if overused lessens the vigour of the harmony.

It plays a great part in modulation, chiefly by the device of enharmonic change. Notate the A flat as G sharp and we have the chord G sharp, B, D, F, i.e. the chord of the diminished seventh in key A (major or minor). In addition to that, notate the F as E sharp, and we have the chord E sharp, G sharp, B, D, i.e. the chord of the diminished seventh in F sharp (major and minor). And so with other changes —by means of which modulation can be effected in a very natural way.

The chord is indeed the most Protean in all harmony. In England the nickname has been given it of 'The Clapham Junction of Harmony' —from a railway station in London where so many lines join that once arrived there one can take a train for almost anywhere else.

DIMINISHED TRIAD. See *Harmony* 24 d.

DIMINUENDO (It.). 'Diminishing', i.e. gradually getting softer (cf. *Geminiani*).

DIMINUTION. See *Augmentation and Diminution*.

DIMINUTION, CANON BY. See *Canon*.

DI MOLTO (It.). 'Of much', i.e. very.

D'INDY, VINCENT (in full, Paul Marie Théodore Vincent, p. 384, pl. 63. 4). Born in Paris in 1851 and died there in 1931, aged eighty. He was the pupil, friend, helper, and biographer of César Franck (q.v.), and his whole life-work was evidence of a community of ideals with his master.

A formative influence in his life was his attendance in 1876 at the first performance of *The Ring* at Bayreuth. He returned an ardent Wagnerian and later became the right-hand man of the great Lamoureux in his laborious twelve months' preparation for the first Paris performances of *Lohengrin* (cf. *Chabrier*). Lamoureux was a conductor after d'Indy's own heart; he performed certain Handel and Bach works then little known in Paris, took the leadership of the Wagnerian movement in France, and in 1887 gave the *Lohengrin* performance just alluded to; he also helped the

younger French composers, including d'Indy himself, by performing their works.

D'Indy's own social–musical activities were not unlike those of Lamoureux. He gave the first Paris performances (or revivals after long neglect) of work by Monteverdi, Bach, Rameau, and others of the older composers, and offered many of his younger compatriots their chance. It is worth remembering that, whilst we class d'Indy as a Franckist, and hence look upon him as in the opposite camp to Debussy, he was one of those who defended *Pelléas and Mélisande* at a time when it was laughed at by many. Conducting once in Rome, he included in his programme Debussy's *Nuages* and *Fêtes*; at the close the audience shouted and whistled, whereupon d'Indy took up the baton again and repeated both pieces—with the result that they (or he for his boldness) won applause.

With the famous choral conductor, Bordes, and the equally famous organist, Guilmant, d'Indy founded in Paris the Schola Cantorum, a complete school of music, largely of religious aim, and of the highest artistic effort, which based its teaching upon a close study of plainsong and the classics. Its ideals were, we may say, those of Franck (it was founded six years after his death). D'Indy acted as Principal of this institution and also as its chief teacher of composition. He wrote an important three-volume *Treatise of Composition*, based upon his lessons there.

Amongst d'Indy's works are operas, symphonies, tone poems, chamber music, etc. Everything he wrote was of serious intention and most conscientious workmanship. Opinion as to the value of his music varies, but this much may be said—it is, from the constructive ability displayed, almost always genuinely interesting to the thoughtful musician.

D'Indy was a great nature-lover, and many of his works (e.g. *Summer Day in the Mountains*, etc.) testify to this.

See *France* 10, 13; *Opera* 24 e (1897) f (1920); *Oratorio* 4, 7 (1920); *Concerto* 6 c (1851); *Cyclic Form*; *Clarinet Family* 4 g, 6; *Trumpet Family* 4; *Trombone Family* 3; *Cornett Family* 3 a–c (end); *Percussion Family* 4 e; *Saxophone*; *Lalo*; *Albéniz, Isaac*; *Magnard*; *Oboe Family* 6.

DI NUOVO (It.). 'Anew.'

DIODORUS SICULUS. See *Wales* 1.

DIPHTHONGS. See *Voice* 9, 10, 20.

DIPLOMAS IN MUSIC. See *Degrees*.

DIP. R.S.A.M.; DIP. MUS. ED. R.S.A.M. See *Degrees and Diplomas* 2.

DIRECT. The sign occasionally used at the end of a page or line to give a warning of the next note that will be met with (p. 484, pl. 85. 2. 5).

DIRECT FLUTE. See *Recorder Family* 2.

DIRECTORIUM CHORI. In the Roman Catholic Church the book containing all the Tones to be used in the Mass (see *Gregorian Tone*).

DIS (Ger.). 'D sharp' (see Table 7).

DISCANT. Same as 'descant' (q.v.).

DISCANT SACKBUT (or Descant Sackbut). See *Trombone Family* 3.

DISCANTUS SUPRA LIBRUM. See *Descant*.

DISCANT ZINCK. See *Cornett and Key Bugle Families* 4.

DISCORD (or **DISSONANCE**). (1) Definition, see *Harmony* 24 h. (2) Discordant Intervals, see *Interval*. (3) Physical Nature of Discordance, see *Acoustics* 16, end; *Harmony* 21. (4) Examples and Treatment, see *Harmony* 3, 21. (5) 'Fundamental' and 'Un-fundamental' Discords, see *Harmony* 24 j k l m.

DISCRETO (It.). 'Discreet', 'reserved'.

DISCREZIONE, DISCRETEZZA (It.). 'Discretion', 'reserve'.

DISINVOLTO (It.). 'Self-possessed', hence easygoing in manner.

DISIS (Ger.). D double-sharp (see Table 7).

DISJUNCT MOTION. See *Motion*.

DISPERATO (It.). 'Desperate.' So, too, *Disperante*. *Disperazione* means 'despair'.

D'ISRAELI, ISAAC (1766–1845). Learned general author and father of the famous Prime Minister. See his views on congregational singing under *Anglican Parish Church Music* 3; *Hymns* 5.

DISSONANCE. See list of references under *Discord*.

DISSONANCES, LES; DISSONANZEN QUARTETT (Mozart). See *Nicknamed Compositions* 15.

DISTANZA (It.). 'Distance.'

DISTINTO (It.). 'Distinct', clear.

DISTRATTO SYMPHONY (Haydn). See *Nicknamed Compositions* 11.

DITAL HARP. This is an instrument invented in 1798 by Edward Light, 'lyrist to the Princess of Wales'. He was a teacher of the guitar, and his instrument was at first called *Harp Guitar*. By 'Dital' is meant a finger-key—by which a string can be raised in pitch a semitone (as opposed to 'Pedal'—see *Harp*); the word was in some use in connexion with lutes and guitars. In appearance the instrument somewhat resembled the body of a lute continued upwards by that of a small harp—hence one of its common names, *Harp Lute*.

Cf. *Harp* 2 f.

DITHYRAMB (Eng.), **DITHYRAMBE** (Fr., Ger.), **DITIRAMBO** (It.). A wild choral hymn in ancient Greece. Thus the word has occasionally been adopted as a fancy title for some composition of a passionate character.

DITSON. See *Publishing* 9.

DITTERSDORF, KARL DITTERS VON (p. 397, pl. **68.** 2). Born in Vienna in 1739 and died near Neuhaus in Bohemia in 1799, aged nearly sixty. He was a lesser contemporary of Haydn and Mozart, and his activities, like theirs, centred upon the princely houses of central Europe. His reputation as a violinist was very high and in this capacity he made in early life (in the company of Gluck) the tour of Italy.

As a composer he was voluminous and successful. A string quartet or symphony of his is still occasionally to be heard, and in his own part of Europe his opera *Doctor and Apothecary* is maintained in the repertory. Haydn was amongst his intimate friends and admirers.

His original surname was Ditters, and the addition to it comes from an ennoblement which testified to his striking success in his profession.

See some quotations from his autobiography under *Composition* 10 and brief reference under *Singspiel*; *Symphony* 8 (1739); *Bagpipe Family* 7; *Misattributed Compositions*; *Cadenza*; *Concerto* 6 b (1739); *Gluck*; *Storace*.

DIV. See *Divisi*.

DIVA. See *Prima Donna*.

DIVER, THE. See *Loder*.

DIVERSIONS. An occasional synonym for 'Variations' (see *Form* 11).

DIVERTIMENTO. See *Suite* 7. In addition to the use of the word given there it is sometimes used in the sense of a fantasia, in popular easy-going style, on airs from some opera, etc.

DIVERTISSEMENT. The term has three meanings:

(1) A meaning something like that sardonically given to it by Rousseau in his *Dictionary of Music* (1767): 'Certain collections of dances and songs which it is the rule in Paris to insert in each act of an opera, ballet or tragedy . . . to break the action at some interesting moment.'

(2) A fantasia (q.v.) in popular style.

(3) An entr'acte (q.v.).

DIVINA, LA (Symphony) see *Nicknamed* 6.

DIVINE OFFICE. The Canonical Hours. See *Matins, Lauds, Prime, Terce, Sext, None, Vespers*, and *Compline*. These are daily said by all Roman Catholic clergy, and in cathedrals and monastic churches are daily said or sung. In the Anglican Church it comprises the services of Matins and Evensong.

DIVISÉS (Fr.), **DIVISI** (It.). 'Divided' (used, for instance, where the first violin part shows double notes and the players, instead of attempting to play both, by double stopping, are to divide themselves into two groups to perform them). The abbreviation 'Div.' is often seen.

DIVISIONS.

(1) This old term (17th and 18th centuries) means the splitting up of the notes of a tune into shorter notes, so creating a variation. For the practice as in use amongst viol players see the quotation from Simpson's *The Division Violist* (1659), under *Ground* (and compare a reference to later practice under *Fioritura*). Other instruments than viols were used for division playing; there is an early eighteenth-century publication called *The Division Flute*.

(2) The long vocal runs in Bach, Handel, and other seventeenth- and eighteenth-century composers are called divisions, the idea apparently being that if these passages are closely regarded they will be seen to consist of a small number of essential notes that form a part of

the underlying harmonies, divided into smaller notes on a decorative principle.

The eighteenth-century fondness for vocal divisions was excessive and led to some absurdities. Addison says: 'I have known the word "and" pursued through the whole gamut, have been entertained with many a melodious "the", and have heard the most beautiful graces, quavers and divisions bestowed upon "then", "for", and "from", to the eternal honour of our English particles' (*Spectator*, 21 March 1710).

DIVISION VIOL. See *Viol Family* 4 b.

DIVOTO, DIVOTAMENTE (It.). 'Devout', 'devoutly'. So, too, *Divozione*, 'devoutness'.

DIX (Fr.). 'Ten'; hence *Dixième*, 'tenth'.

DIX, L. L. See *Anglican Chant* 5.

DIXIE. It is said that the original Dixie (or Dixye) was a large slave-holder in Manhattan Island in the seventeenth century who, on the growth of Abolition sentiment, thought it wise to get rid of his slaves, shipping them to one of the Southern States, where, as they suffered greater hardship, they looked back with regret to their old home. Thus 'Dixie's Land' meant Manhattan Island, or, more vaguely, the Northern States.

But, by a paradoxical change of usage, the term now means the Southern States—possibly through some confusion connected with the 'Mason and Dixon Line' that defined the division between the free and the slave states, or possibly from some other cause.

The song 'Dixie' is by Daniel Decatur Emmett (q.v.), one of the 'Negro minstrels' (q.v.) so popular during a great part of the nineteenth century. He wrote it in 1859 as a 'walk around' song. The Southern sentiment he expresses in it was purely histrionic, and when the war broke out it was a blow to him, as a Northerner, to find his song adopted as a marching song by the Southern troops and a rallying song for the Southern cause.

D.MUS. See *Degrees and Diplomas*.

DO and DOH. See *Ut*; *Tonic Sol-fa* 2.

DOBRZYNSKI, IGNACY F. (1807–67). See *Poland*.

DOCH (Ger.). 'Yet', 'still', 'nevertheless'.

DODD, WILLIAM (born 1729; hanged 1777). See under *Methodism* 2.

DODDRIDGE, PHILIP (1702–51). English Nonconformist divine (varying between Congregational and Presbyterian) and notable hymn-writer. See *Hymns and Hymn Tunes* 6.

DODECACHORDON (1547). See *Modes* 6.

DODECAPHONIC. See *Note-row*.

DODECUPLE. Another word for *Dodecaphonic*.

DOGLIA (It.). 'Sorrow.' So *Doglioso*, 'sorrowful'; *Dogliosamente*, 'sorrowfully'.

DOG VALSE (Chopin). See *Nicknamed Compositions* 8.

DOG WHISTLE, 'SILENT'. See *Ear and Hearing* 4; *Acoustics* 2.

DOH and DO. See *Ut*; *Tonic Sol-fa* 2.

DÖHLER, THEODOR VON (1814–56). A very popular pianist and piano composer—of Italian birth and largely of Italian residence.

See allusions under *Pianoforte* 22.

DOHNÁNYI, ERNÖ, formerly known as 'Ernst von Dohnányi' (p. 480, pl. **83.** 4). Born in 1877 in Pozsony (otherwise Pressburg and now called Bratislava—then in Hungary and now in Czechoslovakia) and died in New York in 1960, aged eighty-two. He studied at the Conservatory of Budapest, was recognized as a remarkable pianist, and toured Europe and the United States. For ten years he taught the piano in the Conservatory of Berlin, after which (1916–39) he settled in Budapest, where he was for a brief period (1919) director of the Conservatory, resuming that position in 1934. He also became (1931) Musical Director of the Hungarian Broadcasting Service. In 1949 he settled in Florida.

As a composer he was of the school of Brahms, i.e. a classic in form and a romantic in spirit. His works are numerous and include, of course, many for piano. His chamber music is of rather special importance, and some of his orchestral music is played, and there are songs and an opera or two.

Cf. *Hungary*; *Bartók*; *Concerto* 6 c (1877); *Rhapsody*.

DOIGT (Fr.). 'Finger.' So *Doigté*, 'fingering'.

DOIT, DOIVENT (Fr.). 'Must' (3rd person sing. and plural respectively).

DOLCAN. See *Organ* 14 I.

DOLCE (It.). 'Sweet' (with the implication of soft also). Hence *Dolcissimo*, 'very sweet'; *Dolcemente*, 'sweetly'; *Dolcezza*, 'sweetness'. See also *Organ* 14 I.

DOLENTE (It.). 'Doleful', 'sorrowful'. So the adverb *Dolentemente* and the superlative *Dolentissimo*.

DOLES, JOHANN FRIEDRICH (1715–97). One of Bach's pupils and one of his successors at Leipzig, and a voluminous composer of church music, songs, etc. His style was light and his sympathies quite un-Bachian.

See anecdote recorded under *Mass* 2.

DOLIN. See *Ballet* 9.

DOLMETSCH.

(1) ARNOLD (p. 1073, pl. **178.** 7). Born at Le Mans, France, in 1858 and died at Haslemere in 1940, aged eighty-two. His father and grandfather were, respectively, a piano-maker and an organ-builder, and in their workshops he acquired craftsmanship. He studied music in the Brussels Conservatory and the newly founded Royal College of Music, London. The musical collections of the British Museum aroused his interest and dictated his life-work.

Clavichord playing had never died out in his family, and he started making clavichords and harpsichords for firms in Boston and Paris. He later made and revived the playing of almost every instrument of the fifteenth to eighteenth centuries, as well as some earlier ones, training every member of his family to make and play them (p. 1073, pl. **178**. 7), establishing workshops (Haslemere, Surrey) and an annual festival (begun 1925), and publishing a valuable book on the interpretation of the old music. A 'Dolmetsch Foundation' (suggested by Bridges, the Poet Laureate) stood behind these activities and is continuing them. In 1937 he received a British Civil List pension and was decorated by the French government. His wife and children are listed below.

See *Notation* 5; *Harpsichord Family* 5; *Klavier*; *Pianoforte* 2; *Fingering* 1; *Violin Family* 4; *Recorder Family* 1; *Rubato* 2; *Clàrsach*; *Harp* 2.

(2) **MABEL** (Mrs. Arnold, 1874–1963) played the bass viol and other instruments and wrote a book of reminiscences of her husband.

(3) **RUDOLPH** (1906–42), a highly skilled harpsichordist and clavichordist, regrettably lost his life whilst serving in the British Navy during the second World War.

(4) **NATHALIE** plays the viol and other instruments. She is musical director of the Viola da Gamba Society.

(5) **CARL FREDERICK** (born at Fontenay sous Bois, France, 1911) is a highly skilled performer on the recorder and from 1940 he has directed the Society of Recorder Players. He is managing director of Arnold Dolmetsch, Ltd.—the organization which carries on the manufacture of the old instruments.

(6) **CÉCILE** is deputy musical director of the Viola da Gamba Society.

DOLORE (It.). 'Dolour', 'pain'. Hence *Doloroso*, 'dolorous', painful, and the adverb, *Dolorosamente*.

DOLZFLÖTE (Ger.). Same as *Flauto dolce* (It.). A soft flute-toned organ stop. See *Organ* 14 II.

DOMES. Effect on sound. See *Concert Halls* 5.

DOMINANT. (1) The fifth degree of the major or minor scale, and the most important in its functions except the tonic.

(2) For the Dominant of Modes see *Modes* 4.

DOMINANT CADENCE. See *Cadence*.

DOMINANT SEVENTH. One of the commonest chords in music. It consists of the dominant with its third, fifth, and seventh, e.g. in the key of C it is G–B–D–F.

It is (like all sevenths) a discord, one discordant element being the diminished fifth between the third and the seventh (B–F). In order to secure a satisfactory 'resolution' (see article *Harmony* 3, 24 i), the seventh should normally fall a note, the third rise (i.e. the F should fall to an E in the next chord and the B rise to a C). This leaves only two chords competent to undertake the resolution—that of the tonic (C–E–G) and that of the sub-mediant (A–C–E). A rarer resolution is that on the first inversion of the sub-dominant, the seventh remaining stationary.

In piano music the chord often occurs in 'broken' form, hence pianists practice the arpeggio of the dominant seventh in all keys.

DOMINE DEUS. See *Mass* 3 b.

DOMINE JESU. See *Requiem*.

DOMINICUS MASS (Mozart). See *Nicknamed Compositions* 15.

DOMRA. See *Balalaika*.

DONA EIS. See *Requiem*.

DONAJOWSKI. See *Eulenburg*.

DONA NOBIS. See *Mass* 3 e.

DONEMUS. See *Holland* 8.

DON GIOVANNI (Mozart). Produced at Prague, 1787. Libretto by da Ponte. Original language Italian; in some languages 'Giovanni' becomes 'Juan'.

ACT I[1]

SCENE 1: *A Courtyard in Seville, with the Commandant's Palace. Period, the seventeenth century*

Leporello (*Bass*), servant to the libertine **Don Giovanni** (*Baritone*), is assisting his master in one of his many intrigues. Pursuing **Donna Anna** (*Soprano*), daughter of the Commandant of the Knights of Malta, the roué is interrupted by the **Commandant** (*Bass*) and kills him. Anna's betrothed, **Don Ottavio** (*Tenor*), swears vengeance.

SCENE 2: *A Street*

Don Giovanni, meeting by chance his deserted love, **Donna Elvira** (*Soprano*), leaves her to Leporello, who reads her a list of his master's amours.

SCENE 3: *The Country near Don Giovanni's Palace*

Two peasants, **Zerlina** (*Soprano*) and **Masetto** (*Bass*), about to be married, appear with their friends. Giovanni, telling his servant to take the party to see the palace, is left with Zerlina, but Elvira appears to denounce him. He seeks to pooh-pooh her accusations, to Anna and Ottavio, as those of a madwoman.

SCENE 4: *Ballroom in the Palace*

Masked, the two wronged women and Don Ottavio gain admission to the festivities. From the room to which Don Giovanni has taken Zerlina are heard her cries for help. Giovanni rushes out, pretending that Leporello is the guilty one. Though menaced by the company, Giovanni makes his escape.

ACT II

SCENE 1: *Before Elvira's House*

Elvira is still infatuated. Giovanni changes cloaks with Leporello and lets the latter serenade her, while he seeks the favours of Elvira's maid. Masetto, attempting to beat the roué, gets drubbed himself. Zerlina consoles him.

[1] See an allusion to the overture under *Overture* 3.

SCENE 2: *Elvira's Room*

Ottavio and Anna reveal to Elvira that her former lover is a murderer. Ottavio renews his pledge to revenge the Commandant.

SCENE 3: *A Cemetery*

Upon the statue to the murdered Commandant Giovanni reads, 'Here I await Heaven's vengeance on him who slew me'. He invites the statue to sup with him, and hears the answer: 'Yes!'

SCENE 4: *Don Giovanni's Room*

Whilst Giovanni is getting ready for the feast, there enters Elvira, begging him to amend his ways. He is callous and refuses. As she goes away, she screams. Going to see what is the matter, he meets the statue, come to claim him, for he refuses to repent. So, brazen to the last, he meets his fitting end: demons appear and drag him down to hell.

There follows (or *should* follow, for it is often most improperly omitted) a brief finale in which the remaining characters moralize on the catastrophe that has just occurred.

See also references as follows: *Ballet* 7; *Bohemia*; *Composition* 5; *Expression* 5; *Holland* 6; *Kierkegaord*; *Opera* 9, 19, 21 d f; *Opera buffa*.

DONINGTON, ROBERT. Born at Leeds in 1907. He graduated at Oxford University and also worked under Dolmetsch (q.v.). He is a musicologist, specializing in old instruments and playing the viola da gamba and treble viol. He is author of comprehensive and authoritative books on musical instruments and interpretation, and on Wagner. He contributed to the accuracy of the present work by checking all the articles relevant to his special interest.

DONIZETTI, GAETANO (p. 524, pl. 95. 2). Born at Bergamo in 1797 and died there in 1848, aged fifty. He composed seventy-five operas, which were performed all over the world. His melodies were attractive, and they demanded capable singers in a period when opera was, above all, an exhibition of vocal tone and technique (cf. *Bellini*).

There is no truth in the story sometimes heard that he was of Scottish descent.

See references under *Opera* 6, 21 g, 24 d (1835–40–43); *Home, Sweet Home*; *Flute Family* 4; *Composition* 12.

DON JUAN (Mozart). See *Don Giovanni*.

DONKEY QUARTET (Haydn). See *Nicknamed Compositions* 12 (76).

DONOVAN, RICHARD FRANK. Born at New Haven, Conn., in 1891 and died there in 1970, aged seventy-eight. He studied at Yale University (on staff 1928–60) and elsewhere, and under Widor in Paris. He was active in New Haven and composed orchestral and choral works and chamber music.

DONT, JACOB. Born in Vienna in 1815 and died there in 1888, aged seventy-three. He was the son of a cellist of reputation and himself a fine violinist and a celebrated teacher in Vienna. His studies and other works for his instrument are well known.

DOO, MATTHA. See *Ballad* 1.

DOPO (It.). 'After.'

DOPPEL (Ger.). 'Double.'

DOPPEL B, DOPPEL-BE (Ger.). 'Double-flat' (Table 7).

DOPPELCHOR (Ger.). 'Double chorus.'

DOPPELFAGOTT. 'Double bassoon.'

DOPPELFLÖTE. See *Organ* 14 II.

DOPPELFUGE (Ger.). 'Double fugue.'

DOPPELHORN. See *Horn Family* 2 c.

DOPPELKREUZ (Ger.). 'Double-sharp' (Table 7).

DOPPELN (Ger.). 'To double.'

DOPPELSCHLAG (Ger.). 'Double stroke', i.e. a turn.

DOPPELTAKTNOTE (Ger.). 'Double-Measure note', or 'two-bar note', i.e. breve or double whole-note.

DOPPELT SO SCHNELL (Ger.). 'Double as fast.'

DOPPER. See *Holland* 8.

DOPPIO (It.). 'Double.' So *Doppio diesis, Doppio bemolle*, 'double sharp', 'double flat' (see Table 7); *Doppio movimento*, 'double speed' (i.e. double the preceding speed).

DORET, GUSTAVE (1866–1943). See p. 880, pl. **147**. 6.

DORIAN FUGUE. See *Nicknamed Compositions* (under 'Bach's Organ Fugues'); *Modes* 10.

DORIAN MODE. See *Modes* 6, 7, 9, 10.

DORIAN TETRACHORD. See *Scales* 5.

DORIC. Same as *Dorian* (q.v.).

DOT, DOTTED NOTE. A dot placed after a note makes it half as long again. Note, however, that in older music (up to and including Bach and Handel) the addition to the note was *approximately* half, and the exact rendering was left to a combination of tradition, taste, and common sense. Thus in [musical notation], the rendering would usually be [musical notation] and [musical notation]

in a very slow movement (especially) a [musical notation] might be rendered [musical notation] (the opening of the overture of Handel's *Messiah* is, according to Prout's edition, a case in point). To meet this last case Leopold Mozart, in 1769, introduced the use of the double dot, and his son is the first great composer in whose works it is to be found. He also very occasionally uses the triple dot.

As regards the above reference to Prout's

O

edition of *Messiah* it may be added that few conductors seem to agree with him, the general view being, apparently, that his interpretation of the dot leads to too jerky an effect. The whole involved question of the intentions of composers of various periods as to the treatment of passages with dotted notes is thoroughly discussed in such comprehensive books on the subject as those by Dannreuther and Donington (q.v.)

When more than one dot follows a note it is understood that each of them adds half the value of the preceding note or dot.

DOUBLE.

(1) The word 'Double' as applied to **instruments** usually indicates a low pitch. The origin of the word seems to lie in the sixteenth- and seventeenth-century practice of using double letters to indicate the notes below the regular gamut or normal range as expressed in the ancient hexachordal system (see *Gamut* and compare 'Double Regal' under *Reed-Organ Family* 2). Thus there was the 'Single Curtall' (a bassoon whose lowest note was within the range of the gamut) and the 'Double Curtall', whose range extended below it. And adopting the same general idea we have the 'Double Bass' (to which the 'single' is the violoncello), the 'Double Bassoon' (whose 'single' is the ordinary bassoon), and the organ stop the 'Double Diapason' (a 16-foot stop on the manuals or 32-foot on the pedals, whose 'single' is the 8-foot diapason on the manuals or 16-foot on the pedals).

It is observable that the sounding pitch of music played on most 'double' instruments lies an octave below what the notation indicates.

DOUBLE-BASS. See *Violin Family* 2 d, 9.

DOUBLE-BASS CLARINET. See *Clarinet Family* 4 g.

DOUBLE-BASS FLUTE. See *Flute Family* 3 c.

DOUBLE BASSOON. See *Oboe Family* 3 d, 5 d.

DOUBLE-BASS TROMBONE. See *Trombone Family* 2 f, 3.

DOUBLE-BASS TUBA. See *Tuba Family* 2 c.

DOUBLE-BASS VIOL. See *Viol Family* 4 a.

DOUBLE CURTALL. See *Oboe Family* 5 c.

DOUBLE DIAPASON. See *Organ* 14 I.

DOUBLE DRUMS. See *Percussion Family* 5 a.

DOUBLE ENGLISH HORN. See *Organ* 14 VI.

DOUBLE FLAGEOLET. See *Recorder Family* 3.

DOUBLE HARP. See *Harp* 2 b.

DOUBLE HORN. See *Horn Family* 2 c.

DOUBLE OPEN DIAPASON. See *Organ* 14 I.

Note that the old term **Double Organ** seems to have been variously used. Properly it indicates a keyboard descending to 8-foot C

or 12-foot G, but apparently it sometimes indicated the presence of two manuals; and in more recent times, in the United States, it has occasionally indicated an organ with a separate 'sanctuary' division.

A **Double Virginal** was one of which the keyboard descended to bass C, i.e. the C below the stave (like that of the Double Organ).

(2) Some **other instrumental uses** of the word 'Double' are the following:

DOUBLE ACTION. See *Harp* 1.

DOUBLE-HANDED. See *String Band* 1.

DOUBLE REED. See *Reed.*

DOUBLE TONGUING. See *Tonguing.*

DOUBLE TOUCH. See *Organ* 6.

DOUBLE STOPPING, in the playing of a bowed string instrument, means stopping (and, of course, also bowing) two strings at one time (see *Violin Family* 3 e; *Acoustics* 10). In common parlance the term is used also when one of the strings is open, or both of them so.

(3) **Notationally** the word occurs as follows (including some French terms):

DOUBLE BAR. That double perpendicular line at the end of a composition, or of some definite section thereof, which marks the end of the composition or the section. It is also used to mark the verse-lines of hymn tunes and for similar purposes. It may or may not coincide with one of the bar-lines which mark the rhythm of the music, having itself no rhythmic function.

DOUBLE BÉMOL (Fr.). 'Double flat.' (Table 7.)

DOUBLE C, etc. See *Pitch* 7.

DOUBLE-CROCHE (Fr.). 'Double hook.' The semi-quaver or sixteenth note (Table 3).

DOUBLE DIÈSE (Fr.). 'Double Sharp.' (Table 7.)

DOUBLE DOT. See *Dot.*

DOUBLE FLAT. The sign (♭♭) which, placed before a note, lowers it in pitch by a whole-step or tone (Table 6).

DOUBLE MORDENT. See *Mordent.*

DOUBLE SHARP. The sign (×) which, placed before a note, raises it in pitch by a whole-step or tone (Table 6); a curious case of two such signs before a note is to be found in at least one composition, Nicodé's Sonata in G for cello and piano, where it clearly means not a double-double sharp but a triple sharp.

DOUBLE WHOLE-NOTE (Amer.). The breve (Table 3).

(4) **Harmonically**, etc., there are:

DOUBLE COUNTERPOINT. See *Counterpoint.*

DOUBLE PEDAL. See *Harmony* 24 p.

DOUBLE SUSPENSION. See *Harmony* 24 k.

(5) In **Form**, etc., there are:

DOUBLE (Fr.) as an old term for 'Variation', e.g. *Air avec doubles.* See *Form* 11; *Ornaments* 3.

DOUBLE CHANT. See *Anglican Chant* 3, 5.

DOUBLE CHORUS OR CHOIR. See *Choir or Chorus.*

DOUBLE CONCERTO. A concerto (q.v.) with two principal instruments.

DOUBLE FUGUE. See *Form* 12 f.

DOUBLE QUARTET. See *Quartet.*

DOUBLETTE 2. On French organs the 'fifteenth'.

DOUCE (Fr.). 'Sweet.' (This is the fem.; the masc. is *Doux.*)

DOUGLAS.

(1) PATRICK. See *Scotland* 5.
(2) GAVIN. See *Scotland* 3.
(3) WILLIAM (of Fingland). See *Annie Laurie.*

DOULEUR (Fr.). 'Sadness.' So *Douloureux, Douloureuse* (masc., fem.), 'sad'; *Douloureusement,* 'sadly'.

DOUX, DOUCE (Fr.; masc., fem.). 'Sweet'; hence *Doucement,* 'sweetly', 'softly'.

DOWLAND.

(1) JOHN (p. 817, pl. **140.** 1). Born near Dublin in 1562 and died in London in 1626, aged sixty-three. He was the greatest lutenist of his age, holding at different times the position of Court Lutenist to the King of Denmark (at an enormous salary—equal to that of the Admiral of the Realm) and that of one of the six such officials employed by Charles I of Britain. His fame in his art took him far afield, and he boasted that works of his had been published in Paris, Antwerp, Cologne, Nuremberg, Frankfort, Leipzig, Hamburg, and Amsterdam. He is mentioned by many of the poets and dramatists of his day. With him money came and went freely; he was latterly neglected and he seems to have died somewhat poor and embittered.

His songs (mostly intended to be sung either in four parts or alternatively as solos with lute accompaniment) were the most celebrated of their day and, republished during the present century, have again become widely known.

For passing references see *Song* 3; *Hymns and Hymn Tunes* 17 e (x); *Ireland* 8; *Belgium* 9; *Ornithoparcus*; *Patronage* 8.

(2) ROBERT. Born in 1591 and died in 1641. He was the son of the above and succeeded him in his British royal office. He published a collection of lute music by various composers of different countries.

DOWN AMONG THE DEAD MEN. This bold drinking song (the 'dead men' being the empty bottles under the table) has been in print, words and music, since 1715, but is probably earlier. Its authorship is unknown. The words have existed in many forms, adapted to the political circumstances of different periods.

DOXOLOGIA, DOXOLOGY. Any liturgical formula of praise, as the *Gloria patri* ('Glory be to the Father', etc., i.e. the Lesser Doxology, or 'Doxologia parva', used at the end of the Psalms), or the *Gloria in excelsis Deo* (q.v.) 'Glory to God in the highest'—the 'Greater Doxology', or 'Doxologia magna').

The 'Greater Doxology' is a part of the Roman Mass (sung to differing plainsong according to the feast); properly it should be left to the priest until the words 'Et in terra pax', when the choir should enter, but composers such as Bach, Mozart, and Beethoven have ignored this. In its English wording the 'Greater Doxology' is a part of the Anglican Communion Service.

In the non-liturgical Protestant churches 'The Doxology' usually means a metrical form of the Lesser Doxology, generally that sung to the tune *Old Hundredth*—'Praise God from whom all blessings flow', etc., from Bishop Ken's (1637–1711) Morning and Evening Hymns, 'Awake, my soul' and 'Glory to Thee'. In the 1640s there was great strife in certain parts of Scotland over the abandonment of the 1595 Psalter's use of a doxology of this kind after the metrical psalms.

The word 'doxology' is from the Greek *doxa*, 'glory', and *logos*, 'discourse'.

DRABANT. A Polish dance ceremony popular in aristocratic circles during the eighteenth and early nineteenth centuries. It began with a solemn march and then changed to an Obertass (q.v.).

DRAGHI.

(1) ANTONIO (Italian Opera Composer in Vienna). See *Opera* 26.
(2) GIOVANNI BATTISTA. Harpsichordist-composer, in London 1667–1706. See *Ballad Opera* (note).

DRAGONETTI (p. 1088, pl. **179.** 9). See *Violin Family* 9.

DRAKE, SIR FRANCIS (c. 1540–96). See under *Mealtime Music.*

DRAMATIC SONATA (Beethoven). See *Nicknamed Compositions* 5.

DRAMATIC SOPRANO. See *Voice* 19.

DRAME LYRIQUE. Simply one of the French names for opera. Debussy calls his *Pelléas and Mélisande* a 'drame lyrique': in this work the music is very subtly adjusted to the libretto, and perhaps by the use of this term Debussy implies some fine shade of differentiation from ordinary opera or the (heavier) Wagner 'music drama'. Many French operas, however, bear this description without any special reason.

DRAMMA LIRICO (It.). Same as French *Drame lyrique* (q.v.).

DRAMMA PER MUSICA (It.). Literally 'drama by music', or 'drama through music'. Simply another name for opera. The term was a good deal used in Italy in the seventeenth and eighteenth centuries. Sometimes it meant rather 'libretto' than 'opera', the 'per' in this case having the force of 'for'. The early Florentine composers of opera (see *Opera* 1, 2) often used the term 'dramma per la musica' as describing their works.

DRAMMATICO (It.). 'Dramatic.'

DRÄNGEND (Ger.). 'Urging forward', hurrying.

DRAWING-ROOM BALLAD. See *Ballad* 6.

DRAW STOP. See *Organ* 1.

DRDLA, FRANZ. Born at Saar, in Moravia, in 1868 and died in Vienna in 1944, aged seventy-five. He wrote operas, but is best known for his violin compositions, of which a Serenata in A, *Souvenir,* and *Visions* are universally popular.

DREAM OF ST. JEROME. See *Misattributed Compositions,* s.v. 'Beethoven'.

'DREAM' QUARTET (Haydn). See *Nicknamed Compositions* 12.

DREHER. See *Waltz.*

DREHLEIER (Ger.). The hurdy-gurdy (q.v.).

DREI (Ger.). 'Three.'

DREIFACH (Ger.). 'Threefold.'

DREINFAHREN (Ger.). 'To talk roughly.'

DREITAKTIG. See *Takt.*

DRESDEN AMEN. See *Amen.*

DRESDEN, SEM. Born in Amsterdam in 1881 and died at The Hague in 1957, aged seventy-six, having been in turn principal of the conservatories of both cities. He composed chamber music, orchestral music, songs, etc., and wrote a book on Dutch musical life during the late nineteenth and early twentieth centuries.

See *Holland* 8; *Harp* 4.

DRIGO, RICCARDO. Born at Padua in 1846 and died there in 1930, aged eighty-four. He was a pianist and for many years director of the Imperial Theatre at St. Petersburg. He had a vein of taking melody and his ballets had a great success—especially *Harlequin's Millions,* of which the Serenade is everywhere known.

DRINGEND (Ger.). 'Urgent', 'pressing on'. So the comparative *Dringender.*

DRINK TO ME ONLY WITH THINE EYES. The poem is by Ben Jonson (1616), but is closely based on expressions in certain of the Letters of Philostratus (third century). The present fine tune cannot be traced back beyond about 1770, when it was published as a glee. The usual attribution to a Colonel Mellish seems to be unwarranted, as he is understood to have been born in 1777. There is no authority for the attribution to Arne. Grattan Flood asserted that he had seen an edition of the song dating from about 1803 with Henry Herrington of Bath (1727–1816) named as composer.

DRINKWATER, JOHN. See *Criticism* 6.

DRITTE (Ger., various grammatical terminations). 'Third.'

DRIVING NOTE. An old-fashioned term, rather variously applied to a Suspended Note (see *Harmony* 24 k), a Retarded Note (see *Harmony* 24 l), or any note causing syncopation (q.v.) by anticipating the succeeding accent.

DROHEND (Ger.). 'Threatening.'

DROIT, DROITE (Fr.). 'Right', so *Main droite,* 'right hand'. So also the noun *Droit,* 'right', in such an expression as *Droits d'exécution,* 'performing rights'.

DRONE, DRONE BASS. See *Bagpipe Family* 2 d, etc., and also references to 'Pedal' under *Harmony* 14, 24 p; *Form* 12 d.

DROUET. See *Partant pour la Syrie.*

DROZ, P. J. and H. U. J. See *Mechanical Reproduction* 9.

DRUIDS. See *Wales* 1, 7.

DRUM. See *Percussion Family.*

DRUM AND FIFE BAND. See some particulars under *Fife.* The drums used in such bands are of the side drum (snare drum) type (see *Percussion Family* 3 i).

DRUMSLADE. Old word for drummer—generally in the army.

DRURY LANE THEATRE. See *Annotated Programmes* 1.

DRYDEN, JOHN (1631–1700). Great English poet, playwright, essayist, opera librettist, and author of a famous essay on opera. See references under *Ballad* 5; *Publishing of Music* 5; *Cecilia.*

DU (Fr.). 'Of the' (masc. sing.).

DUB. Old name for tabor. See under *Pipe* 3.

DUBENSKY, ARCADY. Born at Viatka, Russia, in 1890, and died at Tenafly, N.J., in 1966, aged eighty-six. He was a violinist who became a New York orchestral player.

He composed a number of works in conservative idiom which were performed in the 1930s and 1940s.

Cf. *Violin Family* 10; *Clarinet Family* 6; *Flute Family* 6; *Oboe Family* 6.

DUBLIN. See *Ireland* 3, 5, 6; *Publishing* 6; *Scotland* 8; *Cecilia*; *Cathedral Music* 2; *Applause* 3.

Organists of Christ Church Cathedral who receive notice are (with their periods of office): *Farmer*; *Bateson* (c. 1608–31); *B. Rogers* (1639–41); *D. Roseingrave* (1698–1727); *R. Roseingrave* (1727–47); *John Robinson* (1841–4); *R. P. Stewart* (1844–94); *C. H. Kitson* (1913–20).

Organists of St. Patrick's Cathedral who receive notice are (with their periods of office): *Farmer*; *D. Roseingrave* (1698–1727); *R. Roseingrave* (1727–47); *John Robinson* (1829–43); *R. P. Stewart* (1852–61).

DUBOIS.

(1) **THÉODORE** (in full, François Clément Théodore). Born at Rosnay, in the Department of the Marne, France, in 1837 and died in Paris in 1924, aged eighty-six.

He had a brilliant career at the Paris Conservatory, ending with the winning of the Rome Prize. Returning from Italy, he took up the duties of organist, at forty succeeding Saint-Saëns at the Madeleine. For nine years he was head of the Conservatory (see allusion to his resignation under *Ravel*). He wrote for the stage, for the concert platform, the church, and the class-room—for the last, certain well-known theoretical treatises.

Cf. *Oratorio* 4, 7 (1878); *Bréville*; *Passion Music* 6.

(2) LÉON. Born in Brussels in 1859 and died there in 1935, aged seventy-six. He studied at the Conservatory of his native city, won its Rome Prize in 1885, and was its principal from 1912 to 1925. He composed operas and other works.

DUBOURG, MATTHEW (eminent violinist and minor composer; 1703–67). See *Ireland* 6; *Cadenza*.

DUCASSE. See *Roger-Ducasse*.

DUCAURROY. See *Caurroy*.

DUCKLES, VINCENT. See *Dictionaries* 15.

DUCOUDRAY. See *Bourgault-Ducoudray*.

DUDA (plural *Dudy*). See *Bagpipe Family* 7, 9.

DUDELSACK. See *Bagpipe Family* 7, 9.

DUE (It.). 'Two', e.g. *A due*, divided between two instruments or voices; or (the opposite) two instruments join in playing the same line of music (see *Divisi*). *Due corde*, 'two strings'—used in violin music where a passage that is playable on one string is directed to be played on two strings for the purpose of obtaining an undulating effect, and occasionally in piano music as countermanding *Una corda* (see *Corda*).

DUET (Fr., *Duo*; Ger., *Duett*; It., *Duo*, *Duetto*). Any combination of two performers (with or without accompaniment).

DUFAY, GUILLERMUS or GULIELMUS (p. 96, pl. **15.** 1). Born in the Low Countries (possibly Hainault) before 1400 and died at Cambrai in 1474. His most enduring association was with the city of Cambrai. There he began his musical life as a chorister in the cathedral, then went to Rome (and to some of the other cities in which the wandering Pope lived during this period), singing in the Papal Choir. He then took his degree of Master of Arts at the Sorbonne in Paris. He was appointed a canon both of Cambrai and of Bruges, as also later of Mons, and lived apparently for several years somewhere in Savoy, and for another period at the Court of Burgundy. He spent about his last thirty years in Cambrai, ranking (as he still does) as the greatest Netherlands composer of his time.

This career is typical of those of the leading musicians of the Netherlands School at the period. That School then dominated and was everywhere respected. Nearly all the singers in the Pope's service were Netherlanders; indeed, at one time there was only one Italian amongst them. Cambrai had, apparently, a quite special reputation, for there is extant a letter from Philip of Luxembourg in which he says that the singing in that Cathedral is the best in Europe; anyhow, Cambrai was especially drawn upon by the Pope when recruiting his choir, and from 1420 onwards most of his singers were drawn from there. The rewarding of the Pope's singers by ecclesiastical preferment was a common practice at that time, and, as will have been seen, Dufay got his share.

When the old musician made his will, a few months before his death, he expressed the wish that in his last hour, after he had received the sacraments, eight choristers of the cathedral should enter his room and sing very quietly the hymn *Magno salutis gaudio*, and then his own motet *Ave Regina coelorum*.

It must not be supposed that Dufay, Papal Singer and Canon, wrote only church music. He wrote many lively secular pieces.

For this composer and his period see also *History* 2; *Belgium* 1; *Mass* 4; *Singing* 3; *Faburden* 2; *Homme armé*; *Compère*.

DUFTIG (Ger.). 'Misty.'

DUKAS, PAUL (p. 385, pl. **64.** 5). Born in Paris in 1865 and died there in 1935, aged sixty-nine. Like practically every nineteenth- and twentieth-century French composer of importance, he studied at the Paris Conservatory (where he was later a professor of composition). The work of Lalo had some influence on him, as on others of his age. His vivid, descriptive symphonic scherzo, *The Sorcerer's Apprentice*, is known everywhere, his ballet, *The Peri*, has had much success, but his opera, *Ariadne and Bluebeard*, is considered his *chef-d'œuvre*. He was a great friend and adviser of Albéniz, and thus the modern Spanish school owes something to him.

He was also a conscientious editor of the works of Scarlatti and Rameau, and wrote a good deal of musical criticism.

A curious idiosyncrasy robbed the world of a great part of his creative work. In his early forties, whilst still composing, he stopped publishing and, before his death, he burnt the products of over a quarter of a century's labour.

See a reference under *Composition* 4; *Impressionism*; *Opera* 24 f (1907); *Lalo*; *Falla*.

DUKE.

(1) JOHN WOODS. Born at Cumberland, Maryland, in 1899. He is a pianist and composer, from 1923 on the music faculty of Smith College, Northampton, Mass. His works include chamber music and some orchestral music.

(2) VERNON. See *Dukelsky* below.

DUKELSKY, VLADIMIR. Born near Pskov, Russia, in 1903 and died at Los Angeles in 1969, aged sixty-five. He studied at the Kieff Conservatory but from the age of twenty-six was resident in the U.S.A. He was a prolific composer of ballets, operas and operettas, orchestral and chamber music, etc. For his lighter works he adopted the *nom de plume* of 'Vernon Duke'; from 1957 he abandoned his original name.

See *Concerto* 6 c (1903).

DULCE DOMUM. This is a Winchester College song. The composer is John Reading (q.v.). The original poem, by an unknown author, is in Latin. There have been various English translations; that generally used is one of several proposed by readers of the *Gentleman's Magazine*, in which correspondence on the subject appeared in March 1796. The tradition as to the occasion of the origin of the song is thus told in that journal:

'It is sung on the evening preceding the Whitsun holidays at St. Mary College, Winton; at which time the masters, scholars, and choristers, attended by a band of musick, walk in procession round the courts of the college singing the above verses; and which, tradition says, is in commemoration of a boy belonging to that school, who, for some misdemeanor, was confined to the college during the holidays, which lay so heavy on his mind, that after composing these verses he is said to have pined and died.'

The song is still sung before holidays at Winchester, though no longer in the precise manner above described.

DULCET. See *Organ* 14 I.

DULCIAN (in Ger. organ music). A soft reed stop (8 or 16 ft.); *not* the same as 'Dulciana'.

DULCIANA and **DULCIANA MIXTURE.** See *Organ* 14 I, V.

DULCIMER (p. 449, pl. **77.** 9, 10). This is a shallow closed box upon which are strung wires to be struck with small wooden hammers; in fact, it is a psaltery (q.v.) hammered instead of plucked, or, looked at in another way, it is a pianoforte minus mechanism.

The dulcimer is mentioned in English literature from the *Sqyre of High Degree* (c. 1400) onwards. Apparently by the late seventeenth century it had become rather rare (possibly owing to the competition of keyboard instruments). Pepys, at the age of nearly thirty (1662), records his first hearing of it, and he had always been interested in musical instruments. He heard it at a puppet show, and about eighty years later (1740) we find Grassineau in his *Musical Dictionary* saying, 'This instrument is not much heard except at puppet shows'. Since then it seems never to have quite dropped out of use in Britain, and it can still be heard occasionally in the London streets or entertaining the waiting queues at the doors of theatres. In a modified form it is now widely used in school percussion groups.

It is in eastern Europe, however, that the capacities of the dulcimer are today seriously appreciated. The dulcimer players of the gipsy bands of Hungary, Rumania, and Bohemia, using a developed form of the instrument, display an amazing execution. The Hungarian name is *Czimbalom* or *Cymbalon* (also *Cimbalom, Zimbalon, Zymbalum*). The Hungarian composer, Kodály (q.v.), has used this instrument in his orchestral suite *Háry János*. Early in the twentieth century Schunda of Budapest invented a system of dampers for the instrument.

In Kentucky an instrument in use, called a dulcimer, is in reality a form of psaltery or zither, as its strings (over a shallow box, like those of the true dulcimer) are plucked, not hammered.

The *Pantaleon* (q.v.) was an elaborated dulcimer.

Dulcimers made of natural stones, carefully chosen as graduated in size, have occasionally existed. Such was the 'Rock Harmonicon' with which, in the early years of the nineteenth century, the three Cumberland brothers Richardson performed in London for a season and then toured the United States (their gigantic instrument may now be seen in the museum of Keswick). Another, forty years later, was that of a father and two sons from the same district, the Tills. Still another North Country one was that of Neddy Dick, of Swaledale, Yorkshire. A French example was 'Baudré's Geological Piano'.

For the glass dulcimer see *Harmonica* 2, 5. For the Hungarian instrument see *Hungary*. And cf. p. 465, pl. **82.** 7.

DULCITONE. See *Percussion* 2 e, 4 e, 5 e.

DUMB KEYBOARD. See *Keyboard* 4.

DUMB ORGANIST. See *Mechanical Reproduction of Music* 10.

DUMB WAITER. See *Keel Row*.

DUMKA (plural **DUMKY**). A type of Slavonic folk-ballad, alternately elegiac and madly gay; often in the minor.

Dvořák has frequently used the type in instrumental music, and his Dumky Piano Trio (op. 90) is a string of six movements of this nature. Although used by a Bohemian composer, the Dumka is not Bohemian. The word and the form are from Little Russia and are plausibly related to the English 'Dump' (q.v.). The Poles have the Dumka.

DUMP, DUMPE. An old dance of which nobody now knows anything except that the word is generally used in a way that suggests a melancholy cast of expression. Shakespeare does so repeatedly ('doleful dumps' and 'merry dumps' are both mentioned in his *Romeo and Juliet*, IV. v, but the latter is thought to be one of his little jokes). There is a *Triste Dumpe* in the Fitzwilliam Virginal Book, and it is not particularly doleful—but then it is Irish.

DUMPF (Ger.). 'Dull', 'muted'.

DUNCAN, ISADORA. See *Ballet* 5.

DUNDEE (hymn tune). See *Tye*.

DUNELM. Indicates a degree of Durham University.

DUNHILL, THOMAS FREDERICK. Born in London in 1877 and died at Scunthorpe in 1946, aged sixty-nine. He wrote orchestral and piano music, songs (especially for children), chamber music, and a successful light opera, *Tantivy Towers* (1931), as well as books on chamber music and on Sullivan and Elgar.

See *Oboe* 6.

DUNI. See *Duny*.

DUNKEL (Ger.). 'Dark.' So *Dunkler*, 'darker'.

DUNKERS. See *United States of America* 3.

DUNSTABLE, JOHN. Born probably in Dunstable and died, probably in London, in 1453. At a period when music, having only six or seven centuries before emerged from the mainly unisonous stage, was laboriously attempting to find adequate expression in counterpoint (q.v.), his sensitive perception was applied to the new and difficult problems that had arisen. The enormous reputation he thus attained amongst his contemporaries all over Europe has been endorsed by scholars in recent times, who have profited by the discovery of collections of manuscripts of his music in Italy (see *Italy* 4).

See also references to the musical development of Dunstable's period under *Harmony* 7; *History of Music* 2; *England* 2; and cf. *Composition* 12; *Patronage* 3.

DUNSTER AND LYON. See *Hymns and Hymn Tunes* 11.

DUNY (or DUNI), EGIDIO ROMOALDO. Born near Naples in 1709 and died in Paris in 1775, aged sixty-six. He studied in Naples, and then, as an opera composer, had successes in various Italian cities, in London, and in Paris, in which last city he settled in his late thirties, there composing twenty operas and attaining great popularity.

He ranks, with his contemporaries Monsigny, Philidor, and Grétry, as one of the important members of the eighteenth-century group of writers of French comic opera (see *Opera buffa*).

DUO (It., Fr.). 'Duet' (q.v.).

DUO-ART. See *Mechanical Reproduction of Music* 13.

DUODECUPLE. Same as 'Dodecuple'. See *Scales* 7; *Temperament* 9.

DUODRAMA. Same as *Melodrama* (q.v.), with the restriction that it is for two speakers.

DUOLO (It.). 'Grief.'

DUPARC, HENRI (in full, Marie Eugène Henri Fouques). Born in Paris in 1848 and died in 1933, aged eighty-five. He was a very favourite pupil of César Franck, and, like d'Indy and some other French composers of the period, he was a good deal influenced by visits to Bayreuth in its early days. He was one of the Founders of the National Musical Society. Whilst he was still in his thirties his health broke down and composition practically ceased; the invalid lived another half-century—but in almost complete silence. His songs especially, few in number as they are (only a dozen), have made his a name of importance.

DUPIN, PAUL (p. 385, pl. **64**. 3). Also known as 'Louis Lothar'. He was born at Roubaix in 1865 and died in Paris in 1949, aged eighty-three. After a boyhood of which some years were, owing to an accident, spent in complete deafness, he regained his hearing and became a railway employee. He abandoned his career and threw himself into music. In 1908, by means of a eulogistic article by Romain Rolland (whose novel *Jean Christophe*

had inspired some of his compositions), he came to the notice of the musical world. His works (which include chamber music, an oratorio, an opera, 370 canons in from three to twelve voices, etc.) were greatly praised by several of the most competent critics and by a number of fellow composers of distinction, but the larger world persistently refused him recognition and his life in Paris was one of obscurity and relative poverty.

DUPLET. The reverse of triplet (q.v.). A triplet is a group of three notes (or the equal of this in notes plus rests), to be performed in the time which, in the composition in question, two would ordinarily take. A duplet is a group of two or its equivalent, to be performed in the time of three. The duplet occurs especially in compound time in positions where the normal group would be one of three, a '2' placed over the two notes being the indication.

See Table 11.

DUPLE TIME. See Table 10.

DUPLEX INSTRUMENTS (BRASS).

There are two types:

(*a*) To produce two qualities of tone without alteration of pitch. The instrument is provided with two bells of different bore, e.g. a wide euphonium bell and a narrow saxotromba or baritone bell, either of which can be connected with the wind-way by a special valve. Double euphoniums of this type are often used in the United States. Theoretically, the echo cornet is an instrument of this class.

(*b*) To play in two different keys, without change of tone quality. The only instrument generally recognized as of this class is the double horn in F and B flat. Each valve is furnished with tubing of the correct length for both keys, and a fourth valve brings the desired key into play by introducing the appropriate lengths of valve tubing.

Instruments with a quick-change action enabling them to play in two adjoining keys, such as B flat and A, but without any special arrangement for adjusting the valve slides accordingly, are not usually regarded as duplex instruments.

DUPLEX SCALING. See *Pianoforte* 16.

DUPONT.

(1) AUGUSTE. Born near Liège in 1827 and died in Brussels in 1890, aged sixty-three. He was a professor of piano at the Brussels Conservatory and the writer of a great deal of worthy music for his instrument in the romantic style of his period, some of which had much popularity. (His brother **Joseph** was a well-known opera conductor.)

(2) GABRIEL. Born at Caen in 1878 and died near Paris in 1914, aged thirty-six. He was a Parisian composer, a pupil of Widor, who wrote piano and orchestral music, operas, and other things, all the time facing the growing menace of consumption. The discouragement of the

composer is recorded in fourteen pieces called, collectively, *Hours of Sadness* ('Les heures dolentes'); of these he orchestrated some and they figure at times in orchestral programmes.

He had put his whole heart into the opera *Antar*, which reached rehearsal when, on one and the same day, war was proclaimed and he died. It reached performance seven years later and has been spoken of in very high terms by many of the best Paris critics.

DUPORT.

(1) JEAN PIERRE. Born in Paris in 1741 and died in Berlin in 1818, aged seventy-seven. He was a very famous violoncellist for whom Beethoven composed two sonatas (op. 5). He himself composed music for his instrument.

(2) JEAN LOUIS (p. 1088, pl. **179**. 2). Born in Paris in 1749 and there died in 1819, aged nearly seventy. He was an even greater violoncellist than his brother (above), and the present system of fingering the violoncello rests upon a foundation established by him. He also composed for his instrument.

DUPRÉ, MARCEL. Born at Rouen in 1886 and died near Paris in 1971, aged eighty-five. He was the son of a Rouen organist, who was his first teacher and from those hands he passed to those of Guilmant and Widor. He succeeded Widor as organist of Saint Sulpice and for some years was acting-organist of Notre-Dame. He wrote organ and choral works and had a reputation as an improviser.

DUPUIS, THOMAS SANDERS (1733–96). He was a London organist (latterly at the Chapel Royal) and a D.Mus. of Oxford. He composed for various instruments and combinations and a little of his organ and church choral music has been published in modern editions and is thus still in use.

Haydn, meeting him as he was leaving the Chapel Royal, publicly kissed him in appreciation of his extemporaneous fugues.

DUPUY, J. B. E. L. C. (otherwise Camille Dupuy). See *Scandinavia* 4.

DUR. German for 'major' in the sense of major key, e.g. *Dur Ton* or *Dur Tonart*, 'major key', *A dur*, 'A major'. Also French for 'hard'.

DURAMENTE (It.). 'With hardness', 'harshness', 'sternness'.

DURAND KEYBOARD. See *Keyboard* 4.

DURANTE, FRANCESCO. Born near Naples in 1684 and died in that city in 1755, aged seventy-one. The events of his life are but obscurely known, or rather, the confident statements concerning them by some authorities are considered suspect by others. He seems to have occupied official posts in connexion with several conservatories and to have enjoyed a well-merited celebrity as the composition teacher of a number of worthy pupils (Jommelli, Piccini, Paisiello, Pergolese, Traetta, etc.). His compositions are mainly for the church, and these, by their judicious mixture of the flowing melodic character of the Neapolitan school of the day with the contrapuntal characteristics of the Roman school, brought him respect that lasted long after his death.

See reference under *Sonata* 10 d (1684).

DURCH (Ger.). 'Through.'

DURCHAUS (Ger.). 'Throughout.'

DURCHDRINGEND (Ger.). 'Through-forcing', i.e. penetrating, shrill.

DURCHFÜHRUNG (Ger.). 'Through-leading', i.e. development (q.v.).

DURCHKOMPONIERT (Ger.). 'Through-composed'—applied to songs of which the music is different for every stanza, i.e. not a mere repeated tune.

DURCHWEG (Ger.). 'Throughout', 'on the whole', 'nearly always'.

DURETÉ (Fr.). 'Hardness', 'severity'.

DUREY, LOUIS (p. 388, pl. **65**. 4). Born in Paris in 1888. He studied music privately and fell under the anti-romantic influences of the French capital, and particularly those of Satie (q.v.) and of Stravinsky. He was one of the group known as 'Les Six' (see *France* 11), but definitely left it in 1921. His few works are restrained and 'aristocratic' in their appeal.

DUREZZA (It.). 'Hardness', 'severity'.

D'URFEY, THOMAS (1653–1723). Poet and dramatist, author of burlesque songs, etc. (especially *Wit and Mirth, or Pills to Purge Melancholy*, 6 vols., 1719–20). Purcell and others set his poems to music. (See references under *Ballad Opera*, note; *Cold and Raw*; *Folia*; *Within a Mile*.)

DURHAM CATHEDRAL. See *Cathedral Music* 2; *Cornett and Key Bugle Families* 3.

Organists who receive notice in this volume are (with their periods of office): *J. Heseltine* (1711–63); *Ebdon* (1763–1811); *Dykes Bower* (1933–6).

DURO (It.). 'Hard', 'firm'.

DURUFLÉ, MAURICE. Born at Louviers, in the north of France, in 1902. He is one of the most distinguished French organists and a respected though unprolific composer for his instrument, as also for other media. He has given recitals in England on various occasions.

DUSK OF THE GODS ('Twilight of the Gods'). See *Ring of the Nibelung*.

DUSSEK, JAN LADISLAV (p. 108, pl. **19**. 5). Born in Bohemia in 1760 and died near Paris in 1812, aged fifty-two. He was once of European fame as a public pianist and composer for his instrument. He came to London in 1790 and went into partnership as a music publisher with Domenico Corri (q.v.), whose daughter, Sophia, the vocalist, he married. Haydn praised him and Marie Antoinette tried in vain to retain his services, yet he is now remembered by little more than a few pleasant sonatas (out of his 53), and these used merely as teaching pieces.

His manner of death is a warning. He took too little exercise, became stout, found motion tiresome, spent his days in bed, felt bored, drank, and died.

See *Pianoforte Playing* 2; *Pianoforte* 22; *Recital*; *Harmonica* 1; *Chamber Music* 6, Period III (1760); *Concerto* 6 b (1766).

DÜSTER (Ger.). 'Sombre.'

DUTTILE, TROMBONE (It.). Slide trombone. See *Trombone Family* 5.

DUTTON Family of Cheshire. See reference under *Minstrels* 2.

DUVERNOY, FRÉDÉRIC (1765–1839). See allusions under *Corno alto and Corno basso.*

DUX. See *Form* 12 b; *Canon.*

DVOŘÁK, ANTONIN (p. 109, pl. **20.** 2). Born near Prague in 1841 and died in that city in 1904, aged sixty-two. His father was a village butcher and publican, and he himself began life as a butcher boy. His interest in music was aroused by his father's zither-playing and by what he heard in his village from travelling bands. He took to singing and to playing the violin, and later got some lessons on piano and organ.

In 1862, when he was twenty-one, a great national musical event occurred. Smetana returned from his post in Sweden to help to establish the soon famous National Theatre of Prague. Dvořák gained admission to the orchestra as a viola player. He spent a good deal of time in composition.

About ten years later he obtained a good position as church organist, gave up orchestral playing, and married. His orchestral works began to get a hearing, and an opera of his, *King and Collier*, was at last performed at the National Theatre. The Austrian Ministry of Fine Arts now gave him a small pension. Brahms, who was one of the inspectors appointed to examine his compositions, gave him great encouragement and helped him to a publisher. He now wrote the Slavonic Dances for Pianoforte Duet, the melody and spirit of which caught everybody's attention, so that his name became European.

The *Stabat Mater* made him known in England, and the various English musical festivals began to give performances of his music under his own conductorship, and sometimes to commission new works.

For three years (1892–5) he was in New York as head of the National Conservatory. He then returned to Prague, and a few years later became head of the Conservatory there.

A touch of Negro influence comes into three or four of Dvořák's works as a result of his stay in America. One such work is the popular 'New World' Symphony, where, although there are no actual Negro themes, there are a number of themes that suggest the Negro idiom.

After his first opera, *King and Collier*, mentioned above, Dvořák wrote eight other operas, including *The Water-Nymph* (*Rusalka*). Other important and sometimes extremely popular works of his not yet mentioned are the overtures *Carnival, My Home, Nature,* and *Othello*; a violin, a piano, and a cello concerto; a string

sextet, a piano quintet, eight notable string quartets, three piano trios, and Dumky (plural of Dumka) for piano trio; a sonata, a sonatina, a ballade, etc., for violin and piano; quite a number of piano solos and duets, which should be better known than they are; five or six biggish choral works (including a *Requiem*, a *Te Deum*, a *Stabat Mater*, and the immensely popular though gruesome *Spectre's Bride*); and many good songs and part-songs (the well-known 'Songs my Mother taught me' is one of his *Zigeunerlieder*, or 'Gipsy Songs'). Other works include nine symphonies. 'The' *Humoresque*, so often heard arranged for all possible combinations of instruments, is merely the seventh of eight he wrote for piano.

It should be noted that the numeration long used for the symphonies does not correspond with their order of composition. Owing to the first four being unpublished or posthumously published they were not included in the numeration. The facts are recorded in the following chronological list, it is believed correctly:

Real No. 1. C minor. 1865. No opus no. Bears name *Zlonitzer Glocken* ('Bells of Zlonice', in Bohemia, where the composer lived 1854–7).

   ,,   2. B flat. Likewise 1865. No opus no.

   ,,   3. E flat. 1873. No opus no. (originally 'Op. 10').

   ,,   4. D minor. 1874. No opus no. (originally 'Op. 13').

   ,,   5. F. 1875. Op. 76 (originally 'Op. 24' and also called 'Third').

   ,,   6. D. 1880. Op. 60 (sometimes called 'First').

   ,,   7. D minor. 1885. Op. 70 (sometimes called 'Second').

   ,,   8. G. 1889. Op. 88 (often called 'Fourth').

   ,,   9. E minor. 1893. Op. 95. 'From the New World' (called also 'Fifth').

Among Dvořák's particular gifts are a characteristic and often unexpected harmony, a remarkable, fresh, vital use of the orchestra, and a real genius for chamber music for strings. Apart from the positive value of his contribution to the repertory, he is of importance as one of the leaders in the great nationalist movement of the nineteenth century.

See *Romantic; Nationalism; Bohemia; Opera* 19, 20, 24 f (1901); *Oratorio* 3, 7 (1886); *Overture* 8; *Suite* 7; *Chamber Music* 6, Period III (1841); *Rhapsody; Dumka; United States* 8; *Quality* 4; *Folk Song* 5; *Reed-Organ Family* 9; *Harmony* 22; *Suk; Nicknamed* 9; *Te Deum; Sonata* 10 c; *Furiant.*

DVORSKY. See *Misattributed Compositions.*

DWIGHT'S JOURNAL OF MUSIC. See *Journals; Criticism of Music* 5.

DYER, LOUISE B. M. (Mrs. Louise B. M. Hanson Dyer; 1890–1962). See *Patronage* 7; *Greek Church* 4; *France* 13.

DYKEMA, PETER WILLIAM (1873–1951). See *Tests and Measurements*.

DYKES, JOHN BACCHUS (p. 485, pl. **86**. **6**). Born at Hull in 1823 and died in 1876, aged fifty-two, at (according to the register) 'Asylum, Ticehurst, Sussex'. He was minor canon and precentor of the cathedral of Durham and, later, vicar of a parish in that city. His career is closely bound up with the high church movement, of which, in defiance of his bishop, he was a strong partisan. To the typical hymn-book of the more moderate branch of the movement, *Hymns Ancient and Modern*, he contributed a large number of tunes, melodious and suavely harmonized and the most attractive of their kind—which kind savours perhaps a little too strongly of the Victorian part-song. These tunes are still in constant use in all English-speaking Protestant communions.

See references under *Hymns and Hymn Tunes* 6, 11.

DYNAMIC ACCENT. See references under *Agogic*; *Accent*; *Expression*.

DYNAMICS. That part of musical expression concerned with the varying degrees of intensity (loudness) of the sound produced. A list of the *Dynamic Marks* is given in Table 17. See also Table 24.

DYNAMOPHONE. See *Electric Musical Instruments* (near opening).

DYNAPHONE. See *Electric Musical Instruments* 1 i.

DYSON, GEORGE. Born at Halifax, Yorkshire, in 1883 and died in Winchester in 1964, aged eighty-one. He was educated at the Royal College of Music, London, won the Mendelssohn travelling scholarship, and spent some years in Italy and Germany. After thirty years as a school music-master he became (1937–52) Director of the Royal College of Music; in 1941 he was knighted, and he was made K.C.V.O. in 1953.

He wrote several books: *The New Music* (1924), *The Progress of Music* (1932), *Fiddling while Rome Burns* (1954). He was notable as the author of the official *Manual of Grenade Fighting* adopted by the War Office in World War 1.

His compositions, skilful, sometimes deeply felt, but never forward-looking in idiom, include several large-scale choral works, such as *The Canterbury Pilgrims* (1932), *Nebuchadnezzar* (1935), and *Quo Vadis?* (1949), and also a symphony (1937) and a violin concerto (1943).

DZERZHINSKY, IVAN. Born at Tambov, Russia, in 1909. He studied in Moscow and Leningrad. In 1935 there was produced his opera, *Quiet Flows the Don*, which has enjoyed phenomenal success (a Czech version was produced at Brno). He has composed other operas (see *Opera* 24 f), orchestral music, piano music, film music, etc.

E

EAR AND HEARING

1. General Description of the Ear (p. 16, pl. **1**. 9). For the purposes of a musical work of reference a 'diagrammatic' rather than a precisely anatomical description will be adequate, and few anatomical terms need be used.

The human ear consists of three portions, an outer one which collects the vibrations of the air, a middle one which conveys them, and an inner one which receives them and passes on its sensations to the brain—where what we call 'sound' thus originates (see *Acoustics* 2).

The **outer ear** consists of (*a*) the visible exterior auricle, or 'pinna', commonly called 'the ear' (which is a mere survival from remote ancestry and entirely useless, so that persons who have had it completely removed have not suffered in their hearing), and (*b*) a tube (the 'auditory meatus'). The tube ends with a membrane (*Membrana Tympani* or 'ear drum').

In the **middle ear** is a chain of three small bones, called from their shapes the *Hammer*, the *Anvil*, and the *Stirrup*. The hammer is attached to the inner side of the membrane just mentioned (i.e. to the ear-drum) and the stirrup to a membrane which covers an aperture in the wall of the inner ear; the anvil connects these two. The whole series of three bones is joined into one by elastic cartilages. One purpose in there being a series of three bones thus flexibly jointed, rather than one rigid bone, is obviously to soften the impact of the vibrations on the ear-drum, so that when excessive they may not be conveyed with dangerously violent force to the delicate inner ear.

The middle ear is in communication with the atmosphere through the *Eustachian Tube*, which emerges in the pharynx or upper part of the throat. An object of this is, by admitting air, to assimilate the pressure of the atmosphere on the inner side of the ear-drum to that on the outer side so that the drum may not be exposed to undue strain. There is also a wonderfully delicate mechanism to aid it to adjust its tension to varying pressures from without.

The structure of the **inner ear** (or *Labyrinth*) is very intricate and cannot be closely described here. The essential part, from a musician's point of view, is the **Basilar Membrane**, about an inch and one third long, which runs along the middle of a canal filled with liquid. The canal is in spiral form, reminding one of a snail shell, hence its name *Cochlea*. In the explanation of the function of the cochlea accepted by most physiologists and physicists the basilar membrane takes the most important part, since the sensation of pitch is believed to be localized in it. These pitch localities are described as *levels* of the basilar membrane.

2. The Action of the Inner Ear. The basilar membrane is in contact with a series of about 20,000 very fine long fibres or long hair-cells.

Vibrations which have entered the outer ear set the ear-drum vibrating; this in turn sets in motion the chain of three long levers (for so these may be called), and these in turn act upon the further membrane of the inner ear and by it are connected to the liquid of the canal which, through the membraneous walls, acts upon the fibres. The fibres are, by means of the auditory nerve, connected with the brain, and so arises the sensation we call sound. If there be some temporary disturbance or permanent defect in the fibres or the nerve of the brain we may get the effect of sound without any outside stimulus, and we then say we have 'a singing in our ears'.

One modern theory is that each region or level of the basilar membrane responds to the vibrations of a different pitch, just as the appropriate string of a piano (if the damper pedal be depressed and the strings thus left free) can be caused to vibrate, and so to sound, by singing a note into the instrument—the other strings remaining unaffected (see *Acoustics* 20). According to another theory, the faster the basilar membrane vibrates, the greater the number of nerve fibres affected, thus giving the sensation of pitch.

Loudness or intensity is recorded (as with our other senses) by the *number* of stimuli passing along a specified nerve fibre in one second.

It may be noted that 'sound' can be communicated to the inner ear without passing through the outer and middle ear. Place a watch between the teeth and this will be noticed. Here the vibrations are passed on to the inner ear by the intervening bony structure.

In addition to being the organ of hearing, the ear is also the organ of equilibration, by means of certain structures in the labyrinth. This function, however, lies beyond the scope of the present work.

3. Deafness. Deafness may result from a number of different causes.

(*a*) The walls of the outer ear-passage secrete wax, which serves to catch dust and small insects that might have penetrated to the ear-drum, and this wax may accumulate and harden, so causing a degree of deafness until it is removed.

(*b*) The Eustachian tube may be blocked by inflammation or catarrh. This interferes with the air communication of the middle ear and throws its delicate apparatus out of gear.

(*c*) The ear-drum may be ruptured, as, for instance, by a violent explosion (it can, however, heal again), or it may be unduly strained. 'Sportsmen' often become deaf on the side closer to the barrels of their guns.

(*d*) The delicate mechanism of the inner ear may be injured by similar means, and this is much more serious (see cases mentioned under 4).

(*e*) Where deafness runs in families it is generally due to chronic thickening of the membranes.

(*f*) There may be disease of the auditory nerve.

(*g*) There may be disease of the centre of hearing in the brain.

There is, thus, no such disease as 'deafness', this condition being merely a symptom of some one of a number of possible pathological states.

4. Some Phenomena of Pitch Perception. It is not uncommon for the hearing to suffer as regards high pitches whilst remaining normal for middle or low pitches. The writer, when living on a mountain-side where in summer the high-pitched cry of the cricket is continuous, found one summer that when sleeping on his right side he did not hear a sound, the left ear not responding to high pitch which the right ear accepted perfectly; the following summer he could hear the crickets again with both ears, some abnormality having apparently corrected itself. Many people cannot hear the cricket with either ear—nor the cry of the bat. Some animals can hear sounds of a pitch so high that they are inaudible to human beings. A 'Silent Dog Whistle' is on sale, advertised as 'the whistle you cannot hear' (cf. *Acoustics* 2).

It is to be noted that the sense of hearing does not gradually diminish as one ascends to the pitch where it ceases. Every one has a note beyond which his power of hearing *suddenly* disappears into total silence.

The sensitiveness of the ear for very high or very low notes (see *Acoustics* 17) varies with individuals and becomes less as we grow older.

The composer Franz Abt was deafened by a steam-engine: he recovered his hearing except for pitches above the C on the second leger line above the treble stave. The composer Robert Franz found his hearing gradually narrowing, both high and low pitches disappearing until he became totally deaf. The *Musical Times* of November 1927 published the letter of a reader who, at 74, found all notes above E (bottom of treble stave) a semitone or tone sharp, notes below E being heard at their true pitch.

A friend of the writer, once conductor of a famous European orchestra and head of an important continental conservatory, retained, as the after-result of illness, the inability to hear any sounds at their proper pitches. All music for him was an intolerable jangle, some notes sounding lower than they should, and some higher. His interest in music was as keen as ever, and he occupied himself with musical research—but was never again able to listen to music without acute distress. A less painful form of what is probably the same malady results in the sufferer hearing everything at the wrong pitch, e.g. a semitone too high or too low: thus music in key F may be heard in key E or vice versa.

Sir August Manns for a considerable period heard certain instruments a third too high, and, as a conductor, had to conceal the painful experience. Sir Hubert Parry, suffering from a cold, heard certain notes a tone and a half too high. Sir Alexander Mackenzie records in his autobiography that, conducting on one occasion in St. Paul's Cathedral, the brass 'sounded like nothing exactly, so that he could get through the piece only by automatically following the first violins and totally ignoring the blatant chaos produced by the orchestra'.

Cases have been known where, temporarily or permanently, one ear has come to hear all sounds at a slightly higher or lower pitch than the other. A doctor of medicine thus suffering, in an article in the *Musical Times* in February 1928, said: 'The sensation produced by two simultaneous performances of a Chopin Scherzo in keys a semitone apart may be imagined in some degree, but the performance must be heard for a full appreciation.'

An even more distressing malady is that of which the principal symptom is the imagined hearing of one continuous pitch (always the same one). Presumably some inflammation has excited a particular nerve or group of nerves communicating with the brain—or it may be that, by auto-suggestion, the patient merely imagines himself into the state mentioned, or after being in a state of physical disrepair continues it imaginatively by auto-suggestion. Schumann suffered from this malady, and the persistent high note in the last movement of Smetana's string quartet *From my Life* is his sad memorial of the similar symptom of the illness which was to bring his life to its end.

Many musicians have, of course, entirely lost their sense of hearing. Beethoven and Fauré are two well-known instances. In such cases musical activity does not cease; the victim can read a score' and can compose, the trained imagination being quite equal to enabling him mentally to 'hear' what he sees before him.

A curious case of a stone-deaf yet successful musical worker is that of Percy Wood (d. 1931), an English organist who, after taking his F.R.C.O. diploma, suffered an attack of meningitis and never afterwards heard a sound. Undaunted, he retired to the sea-side, prepared himself successively for the B.Mus. and D.Mus. of Oxford University, won these degrees (the examinations for which are almost entirely tests in various branches of composition), and then passed the remaining years of his life in preparing others for similar examinations—in all, a quarter of a century of intense, useful, and very successful non-hearing musical activity.

An apparent deterioration of voice may be the result of a defect in the ear, presumably because the singer's own power of criticism of his tone is reduced: the mere removal of impacted wax has in some cases restored the quality of the voice.

5. Two Warnings. It cannot be too widely known that no attempt should ever be made by any one but a medical man to remove foreign bodies from the ears of children or adults, as grave injury may be caused to the ear-drum.

The habit of blowing the nose with the nostrils pinched tight is very bad for the hearing, since it results in air being violently forced through the Eustachian tube into the middle ear. The nostrils should, then, always be left in some degree open. School music teachers might suitably make it a part of their duty to disseminate this information.

6. The Outer Ear as an Alleged Evidence of Musical Capacity (p. 16, pl. **1**. 9). It has been stated above that the visible cartilaginous outer part of the organ is of no value to the hearing. Nevertheless, it has been contended that its shape reflects in some way the degree of fineness of the inner and invisible portion of the ear upon which hearing depends. It is said (see Miriam A. Ellis, *The Human Ear: its Identification and Physiognomy*, 1900) that good musicians have greater than normal width in the hollow of the ear and especially in the orifice which connects this with the tube beyond.

'With this large, wide orifice a good power of hearing seems always to be owned by the possessor of the ear. Such persons seldom become in the least deaf until well over seventy or eighty. As ears are never exactly alike in a pair there is always one ear slightly less wide in the orifice or in the inlet . . . and it is sure to become the first to be "hard of hearing". Where the orifice, on the contrary, is narrow, slight deafness frequently begins even before middle life.'

These statements are not accepted by otological authorities.

EARDSLEY'S Patent Chromatic Pitchpipe. See *Pitch* 6 c.

EARLE, JOHN (*c.* 1601–65). Bishop of Salisbury. His *Microcosmographie* (1628) includes descriptions of certain types of musicians of the day. See quotation under *Inns and Taverns*.

EARLY BIRD. See *Broadcasting* 6.

EAR TRAINING or **AURAL CULTURE.** This is now an accepted branch of any course of musical education professing to base itself upon the fundamentals of the musical faculty and tests in it are included in almost all musical examinations in Britain.

The term 'Ear Training' may have originated with a paper read by Dr. Frederick G. Shinn in January 1899, which paper was followed by a book, *Elementary Ear Training*.

The term 'Aural Culture' (intended to suggest a wider implication) seems to have been introduced by Stewart Macpherson as a part of his campaign for musical appreciation (see *Appreciation*). With Ernest Read he issued, from 1912 onwards, the several volumes of a comprehensive work, *Aural Culture based upon Musical Appreciation*.

But the general idea, of course, goes behind these dates. It is implicit in all the teaching of John Curwen (q.v.) and explicit in the 'Ear Exercises' or 'Ear Tests' which formed an essential part of the practice of teachers of sight-singing upon his methods. And both in Britain and on the continent of Europe the useful exercise of 'Musical Dictation' has long been in use in the more enlightened institutions for serious musical study. F. L. Ritter's book with this title seems to have for some time stood alone amongst literature on this subject in the English language; it is not clear at what date it was first issued, but its author (head of the music department of Vassar College, New York State) died in 1891. Its full title was *Musical Dictation, A Practical Method for Instruction of Choral Classes*; in Britain it was included amongst the early numbers of 'Novello's Music Primers', and it presumably enjoyed some considerable British as well as American circulation.

Ear Training covers the recognition of the identity of the pitch (relative or absolute) of single notes, intervals, chords, and rhythmic units, and, in its completest form, goes on to that of instrumental colours and the following of the formal structure of a piece of music. It is clear that the recognition of the pitch of notes and their rhythmic arrangement is the converse of the processes employed in sight-singing, and that exercises in such recognition are, therefore, valuable to the vocalist. The same applies to brass instruments, to play which the performer must first mentally 'hear' the note. The recognition of rhythms is, of course, the converse of a process applied by all instrumentalists, and the recognition of *all* the items above mentioned is the converse of the processes of the composer.

As regards the training of the listener it would appear that the importance of the ability to attach names to (or to reproduce on paper) notes, rhythms, and harmonies, is not so definite as that of the ability to seize on subject-matter, to follow its treatment, and to note its recurrence, together with the ability to recognize single and combined orchestral colours. The distinction is necessary for teachers of musical appreciation, who should realize that their direct concern is not so much with single notes, intervals, or chords, as with what we may call the larger units—melodies, 'subjects', harmony as concerns its general character and emotional suggestion, etc.

In fact, though every kind of ear training is useful as a background to every type of musical activity, there is reason, if only owing to the importance of the time-factor in any curriculum, to differentiate the course according to the branch of activity to which the student wishes to apply his increased perception.

EAST, EASTE. See *Este*; *Publishing* 4.

EASTER ANTHEMS. See *Anthem* (end).

EASTMAN, GEORGE (1854–1932). American inventor and manufacturer of photographic apparatus ('Kodak') and benefactor of music; founder of the Eastman School of Music, Rochester, N.Y. See references under *Publishing of Music* 9; *Patronage* 7; *Hanson*; *Libraries*.

EBDON, THOMAS. Born at Durham in 1738 and died there in 1811, aged seventy-three. As his name has been carved with a pocket-knife on the choir screen of Durham Cathedral (cf. *Locke*) it is supposed, from a knowledge of the propensities of choir-boys, that he served as one there. He was later organist of the same cathedral (1763 to death). He is remembered today by some of his church music, particularly the evening portion of his Service in C.

EBENFALLS (Ger.). 'Likewise', 'in the same way'. **EBENSO.** 'Just as ' (followed by adjective).

ECCARD, JOHANN. Born in Mühlhausen in 1553 and died in Berlin in 1611, aged about fifty-eight. He was a pupil at Munich of Orlandus Lassus and a voluminous and able composer of sacred and secular vocal music. His work in the development of the German chorale (see *Chorale*) is important.

See reference to the German school of his day under *Germany* 2.

ECCLES family (the name sometimes appears as 'Eagles').

(1, 2) **SOLOMON** (I, II). Born in London in 1618 and died there in 1683, aged sixty-four or sixty-five. He was a composer and a teacher of virginals and viol. In middle life, becoming a Quaker, he publicly burned his instruments and music on Tower Hill and took to shoe-making. To show his contempt for 'steeple-houses' he for two Sundays running insisted on making shoes in the pulpit of a London church during service, and had to be removed

by the constable. During the plague of London he ran about the streets stripped to the waist and with a burning brazier on his head, warning men to repent. Later he accompanied George Fox, the founder of Quakerism, to the West Indies, and also went to New England. He wrote a wild book against music, *A Musick Lector*, which appeared in 1667. He is often confused with (2) that other Solomon Eccles (II) who is known to have been one of the musicians of James II and may have been his son.

(3) **JOHN.** Born in London about 1650 and died at Kingston-on-Thames in 1735, aged eighty-four or eighty-five. He was the eldest son and pupil of (2), and wrote much stage music. He also became Master of the King's Band. He wrote charming songs, and these and some of his keyboard music are occasionally to be heard.

(4) **HENRY.** Lived about 1652–1742. He was the second son of (2). He went to Paris and became a member of the band of Louis XIV Some of his violin music is still heard.

See *Sonata* 10 c; *Misattributed* (Locke's 'Macbeth').

(5) **THOMAS.** Youngest son of (2). He became a mere tavern fiddler.

(6) **HENRY.** Probably brother of (2). He was a violinist, etc., and in the King's Band.

ECCLESIASTICAL MODES. See *Modes* 11.

ÉCHAPPÉ. See *Changing Note*.

ÉCHARPE (Fr.). 'Scarf.' So *Pas des Écharpes*, a dance involving evolutions with waving scarfs.

ÉCHELETTE (Fr.). Xylophone; see *Percussion Family* 2 f, 4 e, 5 f.

ÉCHELLE (Fr.). 'Scale' (but *Gamme* is the more usual word for the musical scale).

ECHO. (The acoustical phenomenon.) See *Acoustics* 17.

ECHO ATTACHMENT. See *Cornet* 1.

ECHO CORNET. See *Cornet* 1; *Organ* 14 V.

ECHO GAMBA. See *Organ* 14 III.

ECHOKLAVIER. See *Organ* 15.

ECHO ORGAN. See *Organ* 2 d.

ÉCLATANT (Fr.). (a) 'Brilliant', 'gorgeous'; (b) 'piercing'.

ECLOGUE. A short pastoral poem, e.g. of Theocritus or Virgil or some of the English or French poets. The word is sometimes used as the title of a piece of music.

ECO (It.). 'Echo.' For 'Flauto d'eco' see *Recorder Family* 2.

ÉCOLE (Fr.). 'School.'

ÉCOSSAISE. There is some mystery about this dance and its name. The usual statement of dictionaries of music in various languages is that the dance is of Scottish origin and that it was originally in three-in-a-measure time but is now a sort of contredanse (see *Country Dance*) in two-in-a-measure. Occasionally there will be some reference to the bagpipes.

Cecil Sharp and A. P. Oppé (*The Dance*, 1924) state that, about 1780, écossaises were danced in England; they 'were very similar to the English Country Dances but executed more energetically, to a faster tempo, and often to Scottish tunes'.

An experienced Scottish musician, Sir Alexander Mackenzie, wrote: 'Though repeatedly stated, it is difficult to believe that the *Écossaise* is of Scottish origin, for it bears no resemblance either to the strathspey or to the reel . . . which solely represent the dance music of Scotland.'

The fact of a French name being used would seem to point to an origin in the ballrooms of Paris, or, if the origin were Scottish, to Paris being the first place on the route of the dance's travels. W. Barclay Squire, a careful investigator, said it was a country dance of Scottish

origin introduced into France towards the end of the eighteenth century. The Scottish melodic idiom seems to be absent from all the tunes to which the name is given. Beethoven, Chopin, and Schubert have left écossaises for piano, and there is nothing Scottish about any of them.

For the confusion between the Écossaise and the Schottische see *Schottische*.

ED (It.). 'And'—form of *E* (see above) as used before a vowel.

EDEL (Ger.). 'Noble.'

EDINBURGH. See *Scotland* 6, 9, 10; *Presbyterian* 4; *Printing* 1; *Publishing* 6; *Concert* 11; *Annotated Programmes* 4; *Wait*; *Cecilia*; *Caller Herrin'*; *Clubs*; *Festival* 1.

EDISON, THOMAS ALVA (1847–1931). See *Gramophone* 1, 2, 3, 8; *Improvisation* 4; *Megaphone*; *Auxetophone*; *H.M.V.* Also p. 432, pl. **73**. 1.

EDUCATION AND MUSIC

1. General History of Music in Education in Europe.
2. Music in British Education since the Sixteenth Century.
3. Music in Education in the United States of America.
4. Some General Principles.

(For illustrations see p. 961, pl. **162**.)

1. General History of Music in Education in Europe. From the earliest times of which we have any record of an educational system instruction in music has formed (intermittently, at any rate) a part of it.

In the great days of **Ancient Greece** all education was divided into two categories, 'Music' and 'Gymnastic'. These terms indicated a dichotomy between the culture of the mind and that of the body, and by 'Music' was meant every form of literary and artistic culture, including what we today call by that name. The important place which Plato gives to music (in our sense) in the scheme of education outlined in his *Republic* is well known. He regarded it as having a great influence upon character, and attached to each of the modes (q.v.) some special influence, relaxing or fortifying, such as dictated its use or non-use in education. It must be remembered that Plato's views were the expression of ideals; it may not, therefore, be safe to deduce from them a general recognition by his contemporaries of so high a value in music as he put upon it.

Less attention appears to have been given to education in the **Roman** civilization, and music seems not to have enjoyed any special prominence.

In **Early Christian Europe** education came into the hands of the Church, and as a subject of education music was considered chiefly from the point of view of the church service. It was important that the traditional plainsong (q.v.) should be passed on intact, and its singing doubtless formed a part of the curriculum in many schools. The university curriculum was modelled on a division of the Seven Liberal Arts into 'Trivium' and 'Quad-

rivium', the 'Trivium' consisting of Grammar, Dialectic, and Rhetoric, and the 'Quadrivium' of Geometry, Arithmetic, Music, and Astronomy. 'Grammar' included the study of literature; 'Dialectic' was mainly logic; 'Rhetoric' included both law and composition in prose and verse; 'Geometry' included geography and natural history, with the medieval qualities of herbs; 'Astronomy' was largely considered from an astrological standpoint; as for 'Music', it took in both the knowledge of plainsong and that of the acoustical theories of Boethius (A.D. 470–524), whose five books recorded the theory of the Greeks. Candidates for degrees were expected to be thoroughly grounded in these seven arts (the 'Trivium' for the bachelor's degree and the 'Quadrivium' for the master's), and consequently every man of learning possessed a theoretical knowledge of music.

Feudalism provided for the secular musical education of the knightly classes, since the arts of chivalry taught to the young included the making and singing of verses, the playing of the lute, and so forth.

The **Renaissance**, with its cultivation of Humanism and its new emphasis on the joy of life, brought a renewed and discriminating study of all forms of art; as the movement looked back to Greek civilization for its models, music necessarily received attention.

The religious **Reformation** which followed, especially on its Lutheran but also on its Calvinistic side, encouraged the use of music in education. Luther, who, as a schoolboy of Eisenach, had, with his fellows, sung in the streets, according to the old German custom, was also a lute player and, in some small measure, a composer, and was anxious that music should not be neglected in the schools of his new faith. Thus was established a tradition which lasted on in Germany, so that two centuries later we find Frederick the Great (reigned 1740–86) laying it down that the schools of his dominion should provide a singing lesson thrice weekly (see *Frederick the Great*).

The **Song Schools** of Europe played an important part in musical education for about a thousand years. The first of them were founded in the fourth century, for the teaching of the plainsong of the Church (see *Schola Cantorum*).

Some of the choristers' schools of English cathedrals are very ancient foundations, dating back to the early days of British Christianity. There were at one time hundreds of such schools scattered up and down the British Isles, and they functioned actively until the dissolution of the monasteries (1523–39), under Henry VIII, and of the chantries (1547), under Edward VI, brought most of them to an end. Some of the Scottish song schools survived the Reformation and had the duty allotted to them of leading the metrical psalms in Presbyterian worship. They were not quite extinct in the seventeenth century (see *Schola Cantorum*; *Presbyterian Church Music* 3).

Some allusion must be made to the eighteenth- and nineteenth-century French, Swiss, German, and Italian educational reformers. **Jean-Jacques Rousseau** (who in youth earned his living for a time as a very inefficient teacher of music in France and Switzerland, who attempted a reformed notation, compiled a dictionary of music, and all his life took an interest in the art) gives a thought-out scheme of musical training in his *Émile, ou de l'éducation* (1762). He demands that the songs used shall be simple and undramatic, their object being to secure flexibility, sonority, and equality of voice, and nothing more; he would even prefer wordless songs, but if not these, then songs specially written and very simple in their ideas. The reading of music should come later, when the love of music has been awakened; in his exposition of this principle there is some anticipation of the Curwen (q.v.) doctrine of 'the thing first and then the sign'. Rousseau shows himself very modern in advising that every child should be exercised in the composition of melodies, and he argues forcibly and rationally in favour of what we call the 'movable doh' rather than the 'fixed doh' (and of the 'lah' minor also). Rousseau, in fact, is amazingly up to date in his ideas—to arrive at which it took other musical educationists (in general completely ignorant of his writings) a full century.

The Swiss **Pestalozzi** (1746–1827) laid great stress on the value of the school use of national songs and fully recognized the cultivation of song as having a harmonizing influence on character. His one-time associate, the German **Froebel** (1782–1852), the initiator of the Kindergarten movement, strongly advocated the cultivation of singing (with painting and modelling) 'not with the aim of making some sort of an artist out of every pupil . . . but with the simple and explicit intention of securing for each pupil a complete development of his nature, that he may be conscious of its wealth of interest and energy, and, in particular, may be able to appreciate true art'. This is exactly the attitude of the most thoughtful educationists of today. We have not gone and cannot go beyond it, for it comprehends everything.

The treatment of music in the educational method of **Maria Montessori** was a complete disappointment to musicians. Many thought her general psychology defective (an over-dependence on mechanical apparatus is one example), and all were compelled to recognize that she knew too little of the art of music to realize the best way of incorporating it in her system. Moreover, the actual music recommended for the use of children and printed in *The Advanced Montessori Method* (English translation 1918) was for the most part of extremely low quality.

2. Music in British Education since the Sixteenth Century. English writers on education during the sixteenth and seventeenth centuries commonly considered music as a valuable part of the curriculum. **Sir Thomas Elyot**, in his *The Governour*, in 1531, urges that serious studies should be 'entrelased and mixte' with 'some pleasant lernynge and exercise, as playeng on instruments of musike'. **Mulcaster**, headmaster of Merchant Taylors' School (1561–86) and of St. Paul's School (1596–1608), says of music: 'For my own part I cannot forbear to place it among the most valuable means in the upbringing of the young', and then enlarges on this, discussing the musical curriculum—prick-song (i.e. sight-singing), harmony and composition, virginals and lute, etc. The allusion to music in **Milton's** *Tractate of Education* (1644) is referred to in the present work, under *Appreciation of Music*. **Locke** (1693) thinks less of music: 'A good hand upon some instruments is by many people mightily valued; but it wastes so much of a young man's time, to gain but a moderate skill in it, and engages often in such odd company. . . .' The Golden Age of British music was just ending and the dull eighteenth century beginning, a century during which music largely dropped out of the British curriculum, except as an 'accomplishment' for the young ladies of gentility, or of those who wished to be considered such.

And as 'accomplishments' have a limited value in the eyes of serious people, **Hannah More**, in 1799, was to point out the waste of time incurred in the music practice of one of her young friends 'now married to a man who dislikes music'; she calculates on the very considerable allowance of four hours a day ('Sundays excepted') devoted to music practice from the age of six to that of eighteen, 13 days allowed for travelling, making 300 days per annum and giving $(4 \times 300 \times 12)$ a grand total of 14,400 hours—all wasted, the husband being what he was!

With the growth of **Popular Education in England** music received a new recognition, and instruction in singing at sight became common (see *Hullah*; *Tonic Sol-fa*).

It is interesting to find a fine poet and prose-writer, in the person of Matthew Arnold, in his capacity of Inspector of Schools to the English Board of Education, giving in his official report of 1863 his experience that it was much easier 'to get entrance to the minds' of children and 'to awaken them' by music than by literature. The elementary schools, indeed, for some time gave music more systematic attention than did the **'Public Schools'** (in Britain this term means the big boarding-schools, some of them very ancient, for the boys of the upper classes), and hence the poorer had a privilege denied to the richer. Thring, headmaster of Uppingham School from 1853 to 1887, set an example by his recognition of the value of the arts; he himself had no appreciation of music but, by analogy with the other arts, he could realize its value. Since that period the musical resources of all the 'public schools' have been enormously enlarged and they are now doing a great work for the musical culture of the country.

Following this movement has come a corresponding one for the fuller recognition of music in the **Universities,** at which opportunities are now increasingly provided for the gaining of a taste for music as a recreation and also for serious training of a professional character, so far as 'paper work' of every kind is concerned. (British universities do not—with one or two recent exceptions—make provision for instrumental teaching as some American ones do, nor do their degrees usually take account of this. The Royal Academy of Music, Royal College of Music, etc., provide certificates of proficiency in this department, which are taken by professional musicians either as sufficient in themselves or as supplementary to a university degree. See *Degrees and Diplomas* 2.)

A feature of musical education throughout the British Commonwealth from the late 1870s onward has been a system of local examinations in piano, violin, theory, etc., conducted by the musical colleges at many hundreds of local centres. It has had the intended good effect of enormously raising the level of teaching by imposing a standard and revealing to teachers their shortcomings, and the unintended bad one of leading thousands of children and parents to look upon the passing of examinations almost as an end in itself. Moreover it led to the creation of what may be called a 'business' of examining, by quite unauthorized bodies, only nominally 'colleges', and concerned not primarily with the creation or maintenance of standards but with the earning of examination fees. These bodies have now greatly declined in number and in activity.

The local examination system does not obtain in any European country except Britain.

Nor does it obtain in the United States of America (with the exception that one British institution does some examining there—Trinity College of Music, from about 1930). It is common, however, throughout the British Commonwealth, examiners being sent out every year from the chief London institutions.

From about 1920 onwards a wonderful widening of musical activity came about in British schools—percussion bands (for the youngest children), pipe making and playing, class teaching of piano and of stringed instruments, school orchestras, melody composition by children, Dalcroze Eurhythmics (see *Jaques-Dalcroze*), opera performance, oratorio performance (the whole school taking some part—especially developed at Oundle School), the addition of instrumental and theoretical music (as an optional subject) to the syllabuses for the various School-Leaving Certificates, the general use of the gramophone in schools, the giving of lessons by radio, and special concerts for children. Not all these activities were first introduced at this period and not all of them were at once taken up equally widely, but the mere list (which is by no means complete) gives an idea of the new spirit that was now entering into school music.

A great extension of the practice of holding holiday courses for music teachers took place from about the same time, and the great schools of music now added to their curricula schemes of study in musical educational method as a part of professional training, as well as instituting diplomas in various branches of school music.

3. Music in Education in the United States of America. Although the British colonies in America were founded at a period when musical culture in England was at one of the highest levels it has ever attained, and although the Puritan class from which several of them were populated was, as a class, in no way antagonistic to or unappreciative of music (see article *Puritans and Music*), there seems to be no record that the art took any place in the curricula of the schools, the provision of which was so commendable a feature of the life of the early colonists. That curriculum was probably in general rather severely utilitarian (as was natural in a new country), religious, and (in the best schools) classical, and many of the teachers were probably not very widely equipped for their profession.

Instruction books in singing, with the aim of improvement of the psalmody of the churches, began to be issued early in the eighteenth century, and towards the middle of that century evening singing schools, with the same object, began to become common.

The work of **Lowell Mason** (q.v.), from about 1830 onwards, led to a great advance. He conducted musical conventions, founded the Boston Academy of Music (1832), published educational textbooks and collections of music, and (1838) succeeded in introducing music into the public schools of Boston (public schools in the wide American sense). In his wish to see music a part of popular education, and in his methods, he was a good deal influenced by Pestalozzi (see 1), through his disciple Nägeli (q.v.) of Zürich, whose methods he had studied during European tours, but he had previously been interested in it by William C. Woodridge (1795–1845), who had translated some of the Pestalozzi textbooks. The principles adopted will be found set forth in Edward Bailey Birge's *History of Public School Music in the United States* (1928) and, in the main, they are valid today. The example of Mason and of Boston soon spread. The steps by which the inclusion of music in the school curriculum at last became universal are so well told in the work just mentioned as to make it hardly necessary to give space to recording them here.

For a time, despite notable efforts, the United States lagged behind Britain, but during the early years of the twentieth century music, on its vocal, its instrumental, and its appreciative sides, became a very important subject in all schools—except some of the rural ones in sparsely populated districts, which remained for later special organization.

By 1933 the United States had gone ahead of all nations in the world in the provision of school orchestras and was rapidly developing a very high standard in *a cappella* choral singing (for a reference to the Appreciation of Music see the article devoted to that subject).

The large size of many American High Schools (far exceeding what is common in Europe), the lavish expenditure on education in a country that was during this period very wealthy, the adoption of the 'supervisor' system, by which the teaching of music and direction of musical activities in schools and groups of schools were brought under specialist control, and the elasticity of curriculum which allowed pupils to select and give adequate time to subjects that really appealed to them, were factors that encouraged this surprising development.

The foundation of the National Supervisors' Conference (now the Music Educators' National Conference—MENC) in 1907, with its growth during the next sixty years to an attending membership of nearly 50,000, was also a great encouragement to progress, as it brought isolated workers into touch with their fellows and made possible the adoption of the latest methods over wide areas. The Music Teachers' National Association, founded in 1876 and still admirably active, has also done fine work, but, its membership being somewhat restricted to the higher branches of educational activity, in addition to the private teachers, its influence upon the public schools has been perhaps less general.

There has been a readiness in the United States to adopt experimental methods in school music, and it has been a leader in such activities as piano teaching in class, the use of mechanical reproduction in Appreciation teaching, and the application of tests for natural musical ability, as a guide to pupil and teacher.

If anything, there is, perhaps, too great a readiness to discard old methods for new before it is quite certain that the old have failed through any defect in themselves (as distinct from a defect in the teaching), and it may perhaps not unfairly be said that, whilst in general the British teacher has been in the past too unready to consider the adoption of new methods, the American has been too ready to adopt them without full consideration.

Music takes, on the whole, a larger place in the American University than in the British. Many universities have schools of music attached to them, in which all branches of the art are taught. The preparation of teachers for musical work in the common schools is an important part of the programme in some of these music schools. It is not unusual to allow credit for musical study to count towards an arts degree, and this encourages the regarding of music as a cultural subject.

An outstanding feature of American university life is the provision of first-class series of concerts and recitals on campus. The 'resident composer', who occupies in the university a position not wholly different from that of the artist in the household of a great Renaissance patron, is a notable feature of the American scene, and represents an ingenious solution of the problem of patronage (q.v.) in a modern capitalist society.

The first chair in music in any university in the United States was occupied at Harvard by J. K. Paine (q.v.) from 1875 to 1905—a period that was very fruitful.

4. Some General Principles. Musical organization in the educational field has two aims, neither of which should be neglected—the cultivation of the ability to *do* and the cultivation of the ability to *enjoy*. For a long time almost the whole attention of teachers was given to the first. Sight-singing was stressed and Song-singing confined to a very tiny repertory. It is now recognized that the acquaintance with a wide area of song literature (not all, or even a majority, of the items of which need be practised to concert perfection) is a valuable foundation for musical sympathy and taste. Similarly in piano teaching the pupil often learnt only three or four 'pieces' in the course of the year (generally too difficult and hence laboriously learnt and gladly discarded), instead of being brought in contact with a great number of compositions of varied periods and styles. This was deadening and, obviously, no music teaching is worthy of the name if it does not awaken enthusiasm. An over-emphasis on technique may be a grave fault, whether it be the technique of vocal sight-reading or that of choral singing or that of instrumental performance. Obviously there should be a striving after the highest polish attainable, but not to the absorption of so much time that other aspects of musical study are perforce neglected.

Sight-reading, vocal and instrumental, is of great importance, as without it the pupils' progress in performance ends with his formal education. In general, vocal class teachers have inclined to give too great a proportion of the pupils' time to it and instrumental teachers too small a proportion.

The importance of the cultivation of the musical memory in instrumental teaching (a real *cultivation*—not a mere learning by heart of a limited repertory), is now, happily, increasingly recognized. The study of form should obviously go hand in hand, stage by stage, with instrumental teaching, and, the piano being a harmonic instrument, it is desirable that some keyboard treatment of harmony should be associated with its lessons. Ensemble work in instrumental practice has a valuable social influence, as well as encouraging alertness and confidence. A desirable ideal at which to aim is that no instrumental pupil should be without this in some form (piano-duet playing, piano and violin, etc.).

Whatever the medium of instruction, proficiency in that medium should be looked upon as insufficient (and recognized, indeed, as unattainable) unless the wider aim of *musicianship* is also present.

Listening should be looked upon as a form of 'doing'—active, not passive, and with its own technique to be gradually acquired by the habit of close attention (see *Appreciation of Music*).

Throughout the whole of the musical activities in school or college the students' future musical life should be kept in view. The teacher of mathematics can hardly expect that many of his pupils will carry to a more advanced point what they have learnt under his instruction, but the teacher of literature or music whose pupils' progress stops dead on the day they leave his classroom has failed.

Articles upon cognate subjects in this volume are: *Appreciation of Music*; *Sight-Singing*; *Tonic Sol-fa*; *Pianoforte Playing and Teaching*; *Degrees and Diplomas*; *Broadcasting*; *Memory*.

EDWARD IV (b. 1442; seized throne 1461; d. 1483). See under *Chapel Royal*; *Scotland* 6; *Minstrels* 2; *Psalm*.

EDWARD VI (b. 1537; came to throne 1547; d. 1553). See *Chapel Royal*; *Ballad* 1.

EDWARD VII (b. 1841; came to throne 1901; d. 1910). See *Chapel Royal*.

EDWARD VIII (b. 1894; came to throne 1936; abdicated 1936). See *Bagpipe Family* 4.

EDWARDS.

(1) RICHARD. Born in Somerset about 1523 and died in London in 1566, aged about forty-three. He was educated at Christ Church, Oxford, and became Master of the Children of the Chapel Royal. He wrote poems (one of which is quoted by Shakespeare in *Romeo and Juliet*—'When griping grief'), acted a play before Queen Elizabeth, who 'laughed heartily thereat and gave the author great thanks for his pains', and is reputed to have been the author of a book of 'comic short stories'—which is most unfortunately lost.

Besides all this, he was (it is thought), the composer of that lovely and still favourite madrigal (q.v.) 'In going to my naked bed'. This may be considered a very early madrigal; it is grave and sober, and in style indistinguishable from a piece of church music of the period.

See references under *Wales* 10; *Madrigal* 8c.

(2) ROBERT (of Angus). See *Scotland* 7.

(3) Performer on musical glasses. See *Harmonica* 1.

EFFECTS (p. 544, pl. **99**. 4, 5). A term used in dance-band parlance, etc., for imitative instruments such as various forms of whistle and anvil, baby cry, bantam rooster, bear growl, calf bawl, cow bawl, cuckoo, dog bark, duck quack, pig grunt, hen cackle, cock crow, drum call, glass crash, horse trot, lion roar, locomotive, nose blow, peacock, pop-gun, rain, siren, sleigh-bells, steam exhaust, surf and thunder, typewriter, whip crack, etc.

EFFETS D'ORAGE (Organ stop). See *Acoustics* 16.

EFFLEURER (Fr.). 'To touch very lightly.'

ÉGAL, ÉGALE (Fr.; masc., fem.). 'Equal.' So *Également*, 'equally'.

EGERTON MANUSCRIPT. See *Tregian, Francis*.

EGK, WERNER. Born near Augsburg, Bavaria, in 1901. Until 1953 he directed the Berlin Hochschule; he has been an active opera conductor, and is a composer with a talent for orchestral effect, and the creator of a musico-dramatic style in which rhythmical impulses from Stravinsky are blended with post-impressionistic harmonies. He has composed operas, ballets, works for broadcasting, music for the Olympic Games, etc.

See *Opera* 24 f (1938, 1948).

EGLINTON, Earl of (1739–1819). See *Canadian Boat Song*.

ÉGLOGUE (Fr.). 'Eclogue' (q.v.).

EGUALE (It.). 'Equal.' So *Egualità, Egualezza*, 'equality'; and *Egualmente*, 'equally'. *Voci eguali*, 'equal voices' (q.v.).

E. H. Short for *Englisches Horn*, i.e. *Cor Anglais*.

EIFER (Ger.). 'Zeal', heat.

EIFRIG (Ger.). 'Zealous', i.e. ardent in style.

EIGHT-FOOT. See *Organ* 2 b; *Pitch* 7.

EIGHTH-NOTE (Amer.). Quaver (Table 3).

EILE (Ger.). 'Haste.'

EILEEN AROON. See *Robin Adair*. Thomas Moore (q.v.), in his Irish Melodies, set to the original *Eileen Aroon* tune the lyric 'Erin, the tear and the smile'.

EILEN (Ger.). 'To hurry'; hence *Eilend*, 'hurrying' (i.e. *Accelerando*).

EILIG (Ger.). 'Speedy.'

EIN, EINE (Ger.; masc., fem.). 'One', 'A' (various terminations according to grammatical case—*em, en, er, es*).

EINEM, GOTTFRIED VON. Born in Berne (of Austrian parentage) in 1918. After various operatic activities in minor capacities (including Bayreuth) he came prominently into world notice with his opera *Danton's Death* (Salzburg Festival 1947), based on the famous play by Georg Büchner. He has composed orchestral music, songs, etc. He lives near Salzburg.

See *Opera* 24 f (1953).

EINFACH (Ger.). 'Simple', 'single'.

EIN' FESTE BURG. See *Hymns and Hymn Tunes* 3.

EINIGE (Ger., various terminations according to gender, number, case). 'Some.'

EINLENKEN (Ger.). 'To turn back'; a 'turning back'.

EINMAL (Ger.). 'Once.'

EINSTEIN, ALFRED. Born at Munich in 1880 and died at El Cerrito, Calif., in 1952, aged seventy-one. After musicological study at the University of Munich, under Sandberger, he took his Ph.D. with a thesis on the German repertory of the viola da gamba, and he then followed this with many other publications embodying the valuable results of careful research. He served as editor of the eleventh edition of Riemann's *Musiklexikon*. He was for many years music critic of the *Berliner Tageblatt* and editor of the *Zeitschrift für Musikwissenschaft*, but the Nazi régime in Germany necessitated his exile. In 1936 his *Short History of Music* was, in sympathy, translated by a group of sixteen British colleagues; his *Gluck* appeared in the same year. After periods of

waiting in Italy, England, and Switzerland, he was, in 1939, admitted to the United States and appointed Professor at Smith College, Northampton, Mass. (retired to California in 1950). He issued a revised edition of Köchel's catalogue of Mozart's works, and a very important history of the Italian madrigal, a book on Schubert, and many other valuable works.

Cf. *Germany* 9; *Köchel*; *Misattributed Compositions* ('Mozart's Adelaide Concerto'); Acknowledgements, p. xv.

EINSTIMMIG (Ger.). 'One-voiced', i.e. for one part.

EINTRITT (Ger.). 'Entrance', beginning.

EINZELN (Ger.). 'Single.'

EIRE. See *Ireland*.

EIS (Ger.). E sharp (see Table 7).

EISIS (Ger.). E double sharp—if that note exists anywhere (see Table 7).

EISLER, HANNS. Born at Leipzig in 1898 and died in Berlin in 1962, aged sixty-four. He was a pupil of Schönberg (see *Note-row*). He composed orchestral and chamber music, and other works, including 'musical cartoons' for singing at political gatherings. The Nazi government ordered the destruction of all his music, published or gramophonically recorded. He was from 1933 in the United States engaging in film activities at Hollywood, but was expelled in 1947 for Communist leanings, and later took up residence in Vienna.

EISTEDDFOD. See *Wales* 7.

EITNER, ROBERT (1832–1905). Distinguished musicologist.

See *Dictionaries* 3, 15.

ÉLAN (Fr.). 'Dash', in the sense of impetuosity.

ÉLARGIR (Fr.). 'To broaden', i.e. to take more slowly. So *Élargi*, 'broadened'; *Élargissant*, 'broadening'; *Élargissez*, 'broaden' (imperative).

ELECTRA. See *Elektra*.

ELECTRIC MUSICAL INSTRUMENTS

1. 'Ether Wave' Instruments.
2. Semi-Electric Bowed and Plucked Instruments.
3. Semi-Electric Pianos.
4. The Pipeless (Electrophonic, Electrotonic) Organ.
5. Instruments using the Photo-Electric Cell.

The present article is not concerned with instruments which use electricity merely as motive power, or as a substitute for a mechanical system (as it has long been used in organs, in partial or complete replacement of the former 'pneumatic' action), but with instruments in which the actual sound is brought into existence electrically or, at least, transmitted electrically (sound vibrations being made to induce electric vibrations which in their turn are made again to evoke sound vibrations).

Such instruments fall into two main classes, those that use electro magnetic energy transmitted independently of the atmosphere, or 'through the ether' in older terminology (Class 1 below), and those that merely use

electrical vibrations in materials in the instrument itself (Classes 2 and 3 below). These latter may be called 'Semi-Electric'.

What are commonly called radio instruments are not included in this article (being merely instruments for transmitting and reproducing music produced outside themselves), but are treated under *Broadcasting of Music*. And electric gramophones are also not included here (being merely instruments for repeating music produced elsewhere), but are treated under *Gramophone*.

The great pioneer of electric musical instrument invention (before the thermionic valve and loud-speaker became available, however) was the American scientist Dr. Thaddeus Cahill, whose 'Dynamophone' was alluded to with approval by Busoni, in 1907, in his *A New Aesthetic of Music*. This instrument, also called the Telharmonium, produced musical sounds ('Telharmony') in a telephone receiver from the rotation of suitable toothed wheels near the poles of electro-magnets, the pure sounds being combined to imitate the timbre of orchestral instruments.

1. 'Ether Wave' Instruments

(a) **Introduction.** The importance of instruments of this class is expressed in the following sanguine pronouncement of the conductor Stokowski in 1929 or 1930:

'It is only a few years before we shall have entirely new methods of tone production by electrical means. . . . Thus will begin a new era in music. . . . One wonderful feature of the new electric instruments is, or will be, the practical absence of technical difficulty in playing them. There will be no long hours of practice every day, for electricity will do all the mechanical part. The performer will give musicianship, interpretation, variety of tone-colour and tone-volume and all the non-material side of music.'

There are constant reports of new developments on these lines, though on account of the difficulties of incorporating the basic ideas in instruments suitable for use by practical musicians, few have reached the stage of commercial production.

(b) **General Principle.** The general principle of all these instruments is the employment of 'heterodyning' (otherwise 'oscillation'), i.e. the combining of two electric currents of which the vibrations differ in frequency. The rapidity of the vibration of any such current is far too great to produce the phenomenon we call 'sound', but the conflict or 'interference' of the two produces regularly recurring 'beats' of a lower rapidity (compare for a similar effect the production of 'differential tones', under *Acoustics* 10), and thus sound is created. For instance, if one series of vibrations had a rapidity of 1,000,000 per second and the other of 1,000,500, the difference would be 500, which would give a note roughly corresponding to the C in the middle of the treble stave.

The vibration speed of one or both of the currents is, then, adjusted so as to vary the difference between them, and in this way notes of any desired pitch are produced. The smaller the difference, of course, the slower the beats and the lower the note obtained.

All instruments embodying this principle include also a means of amplifying and radiating the vibrations on the lines of the loudspeaker of a radio set.

(c) **Mager's Inventions.** One of the earliest instruments of the kind was the **Spherophone** ('Sphärophon', also called 'Electrophone', but this name had been previously used for something quite different; see *Electrophone*), introduced by Jörg Mager (q.v.), and described in a pamphlet by him (1924) called *A New Epoch in Music through Radio*. One of Mager's objects was to provide a means of easily producing quarter-tones, etc., he being a believer in the

possibilities of microtonal music (see *Microtones*). All instruments of this sort (unless limited by being provided with keyboards, and these of the normal twelve notes to an octave) can produce the minutest differences of pitch required, and are thus capable of such an application. Mager's keyboard is of a highly developed type, and hence use is sometimes made of the misleading term 'Electric Organ'. By ingenious mechanism the 'overtones' or harmonics of the notes produced can be influenced (see *Acoustics* 8), so varying their timbre (see *Timbre*). In 1931 Mager was engaged at Bayreuth to produce the bell-tones of *Parsifal* (see *Bell* 6), which was perhaps the first artistic application of the type of instrument described in the present article, i.e. the first application on its own merits and altogether free of any idea of propaganda.

The spherophone is purely melodic.

In 1935 Mager introduced his **Partituro-phon**, a development of the spherophone, for the performance of any keyboard music.

(d) **Thérémin and Taubmann.** From 1927 onwards a Russian scientist of French descent, Professor Léon Thérémin (born 1896), demonstrated in the chief capitals of the world an apparatus of very modest appearance which was called the **Etherophone** but is now usually called the **Thérémin** (p. 288, pl. **50.** 1) or **Théréminovox**. In its simplest form, two electric circuits are represented by a perpendicular metal rod and a horizontal metal loop, attached to right and left of a desk plugged to the electric light main, and by moving the right hand nearer to or further from the rod the rate of oscillation of the valve circuit is controlled, so bringing into existence sounds of higher or lower pitch. Loudness is controlled by similar movements of the left hand over the loop, quality by the adjusting of a switch operating on an apparatus for 'filtering' the harmonics (see *Timbre*).

In 1929 the RCA Victor Co. placed a simple Thérémin on the market, as also a combined Thérémin and electric gramophone, with records providing the accompaniment of melodies to be played by the Thérémin operator and instruction records giving scale and arpeggio passages, etc., for imitation by the 'Théréminist'. (It will be understood that the Thérémin itself is necessarily purely melodic.) In the same year (1929) there appeared a pioneer composition for the Thérémin—the *First Airphonic Suite* of Joseph Schillinger (q.v.).

From 1928 to 1938 Professor Thérémin was in the United States; he then returned to Russia.

A fine ear is required of the 'Théréminist', as the notes required must be aurally preimagined and, when sounded, aurally checked: in this respect the conditions might be described by the terrifying conception of a violinist with the string in the air and with no neck or finger board to help him as to the placing of his fingers. (The difficulties are comparable to those encountered in playing the singing saw, q.v.). A piano-like and a cello-like form of the instrument have been devised, free from this uncomfortable condition, and hence more susceptible of orchestral exploitation (see *Riegger*).

In 1933 Taubmann introduced his **Electronde**, an instrument on much the same lines as the above.

(e) **Trautwein.** In 1930 Dr. F. Trautwein, professor of acoustics at Cologne, exhibited the **Trautonium**. It is somewhat on the lines of the Thérémin, but is played by depressing a steel wire on to a steel bar, so causing a short circuit at the point desired and thus altering the resistance of the wire. Timbres are changeable at will by the use of condensers affecting the upper partials (see *Timbre*), or, apparently, in a later form of the instrument, by the adding to the main circuit of a series of additional circuits of inferior power, corresponding in frequency to various groups of harmonics (see *Timbre*); these additional circuits are controlled by small press-buttons. The inventor had the help of Hindemith in his researches, and this composer both played the instrument and composed for it—including a Concerto for Solo Trautonium and String Orchestra (1931). The Trautonium is a melodic instrument.

(f) **Martenot** (p. 288, pl. **50.** 2). The instrument known as **Ondes Musicales** ('Musical Waves'), or the **Ondium Martenot**, or the **Martenot**, is the invention of the musician Maurice Martenot, of Paris (born 1898). It was first exhibited in 1928, when a *Poème Symphonique pour Solo d'Ondes Musicales et Orchestre*, by the Parisian Greek, Dimitri Levidis, was performed at a Pasdeloup Concert under Rhené-Baton, with the inventor in the solo part: this work makes use of quarter-tones and eighth-tones. In 1930 the Philadelphia Orchestra under Stokowski gave the same work, the inventor again being the soloist. During the following six years nearly thirty composers (Honegger, Milhaud, Koechlin, etc.) wrote works for, or including, this instrument, and the preface to the published 'Method' for it was written by Cortot. Gramophone records have been issued.

In this instrument the movements of the right hand control pitch, (a) much as in the Thérémin; or (b) in another form, by means of a graduated scale in the shape of a dummy keyboard against which the hand moves, so being assisted in precision; or (c) by means of an actual keyboard, of which (a new feature in keyboard instruments) the keys are capable of a secondary or lateral movement, microtonally influencing the pitch and allowing of effects of vibrato and *glissando*.

A great variety of timbres is possible, these being produced by a left-hand device introducing or removing 'filters' in the amplifier, which control the upper partials (see *Timbre*). The left hand also controls force.

The instrument is purely melodic.

(g) **Obouhof.** The **Croix Sonore** ('Sounding Cross') of Nicholas Obouhof, a Russian resident in Paris (see also *Scales* 13), was introduced in 1934—'a cross about 4 feet high surmounting a globe about 2 feet in diameter'. It appears to be essentially of the same nature as the instruments above described and is purely melodic.

(h) The **Mellertion**, exhibited in 1933, is built to a ten-division octave, instead of the usual twelve-division one. 'Altogether new types of melodies, far beyond the range of our present musical experience, emanate from this instrument.'

(i) **Bertrand.** The **Dynaphone**, invented by René Bertrand, can produce vibrations covering the whole audible range, and in addition to single notes it can produce fifths and octaves. Timbres can be controlled and created. Several of the instruments can be performed upon together. Amongst early compositions for the instrument are Fromaigeat's *Variations caractéristiques* and Honegger's ballet, *Roses en métal*.

(j) The **Emicon** is another melodic instrument; it possesses a keyboard of thirty-two notes. It was constructed in America about 1930 by Messrs. Langer and Halmagyi.

(k) The **Hellertion** (p. 288, pl. **50.** 3; the name results from a collision between the names of its inventors Helberger and Lertes) was introduced in 1936. There are four 'manuals', being leather bands with ridges across them corresponding to the semitones of a keyboard. When those ridges are pressed down upon their bed a current passes, the number of vibrations per second (and consequently the pitch produced) varying with the position of the ridge. By playing in the four 'manuals' simultaneously four-note chords can be played. There are devices for controlling tone quantity and quality.

An earlier form of the instrument (1931) consisted of one electrophone manual attached to an ordinary piano; the electrophonic powers of the instrument being then confined to melody.

(l) The **Wurlitzer 'Electronic' Piano** has two flexible metal strips or 'manuals' with ridges corresponding to the notes of a normal keyboard. The back one is played by the fingers and the front one by the thumbs. By playing between the ridges on a strip microtones are available, and by sliding a finger along the strip a *glissando* can be obtained. Tone quantity varies with the pressure applied. A row of twelve push-buttons, each bearing the name of an orchestral instrument, gives a command of timbre; if desired two of these may be used together.

2. Semi-Electric Bowed and Plucked Instruments

(a) The **Vierling Violin and Violoncello.** These instruments are played in the usual way, but instead of the tone of the strings being amplified acoustically by a sound-board, as in the normal instruments, the vibrations are picked up by electro-magnets (one for the fundamental tones and another for the harmonics; see *Acoustics* 8 and *Timbre*), conveyed to an amplifier similar to that of a radio set, and issued through a loud-speaker. By manipulation of the amplifier concerned with the harmonics the timbre can be varied; thus the violin can be made, for instance, to sound like an oboe.

(*b*) The **Allen Instruments,** etc. Mr. A. E. Allen and Mr. V. A. Pfeil (both of the Allencraft Laboratories, Orange, N.J.) have developed a complete set of stringed instruments (both bowed and plucked) much on the same general lines as the Vierling instruments (*a*). Professor V. Karapetoff, of Cornell University, has created a five-string violoncello with amplifier (p. 288, pl. **50. 4**). Marshall Moss, first violin of the National Symphony Orchestra of Washington, D.C., and William Bartley, an engineer, in 1938 introduced the **Electrofonic Violin,** with a belly but no back, the vibrations being microphonically received and then amplified.

(*c*) The **Radiotone.** This instrument, of French origin, introduced about 1931, has a keyboard of the piano kind operating on metal fingers, which are by its means depressed on to a single metal string tuned to the G of the lowest string of the normal violin and set in vibration by circular bows, one for each octave (the bows being differently designed as to their diameter and other details so as to accord as much as possible with the average frequency of the vibrations of the range of pitch with which each is concerned). The vibrations of the strings affect electro-magnets, and amplifiers and a loud-speaker of the type used in a radio set then come into operation. Condensers can be brought into action to influence the harmonics heard, and, thus, the tone colour (see *Timbre*); by this means other instruments can be imitated.

This instrument can, if desired, be built into an organ, as in the Christie Unit Organ of the Electric Theatre, Bournemouth (1931); it was played from one of the manuals and could be accompanied on another of the manuals.

(*d*) **Electric Guitars, Mandolins,** etc., were by 1936 on the market, and in a few years the electric guitar was ubiquitous.

3. Semi-Electric Pianos

The pioneer in this field was Dr. W. Nernst of Berlin, who won the Nobel Prize in Physics in 1920, and his principles are applied in various ways in the instruments mentioned below.

(*a*) The **Neo-Bechstein (or Siemens-Bechstein) Piano** (p. 288, pl. **50. 6, 7**). In this instrument, which was introduced in 1931, the strings are set in vibration by hammers, as in the older pianos, but with much less force. There is no sound-board and thus the tone *mechanically* produced is negligible. The vibrations of the strings are picked up by electro-magnets, amplified (on the lines of radio sets),

and, being turned into sound vibrations again, are given out from a loud-speaker cabinet which is attached by a cable and can be placed anywhere in the room.

The impact of the hammers on the strings produces little tone, the volume being controlled by a pedal acting on the amplifying part of the apparatus; the tone, even of a held chord or note, can be swelled or diminished at will. The sounding-period of notes and chords can be prolonged considerably beyond that of notes or chords on the normal piano.

The tone-colour of the instrument can be adjusted to the taste of the owner by reducing or increasing the strength of particular harmonics (see *Timbre*) by means of condensers. For practical purposes, or to produce a harpsichord-like effect, the electric part of the apparatus can be put out of action so that only the gentle percussive impact of the hammers on the strings is heard. Or the player can leave the electric apparatus in action but cut off the loud-speaker, wearing headphones instead, when only he, and not the neighbours, will hear his efforts.

Broadcasting and electric gramophone attachments can be built into the instrument, so making it serve three purposes. It is possible to use the gramophone and piano effects of the instrument simultaneously, so that the performer can, if he wishes, practise accompanying the great singers.

This instrument was developed by Siemens and Halske and produced under the direction of Professor Nernst. (See also *Pianoforte* 15.)

(*b*) The **Vierling Piano,** developed at the Heinrich Hertz Institute of Berlin, appears to be, in general principles and effects, somewhat similar to the Neo-Bechstein (*a*). See a further reference to Vierling under (*c*) below. It is claimed that the most worn-out, thin-toned piano, with the Vierling attachment added, can be made to sound like one of the finest 'grands', and indeed there is no reason why this should not be so, since the tone quality of the original sound-producing medium must be quite lost under the electric amplification.

(*c*) The **Electrochord,** built by Förster, but applying patents of Vierling (see (*b*)), is on somewhat similar lines to the Neo-Bechstein (see (*a*)), but uses separate sets of electro-magnets for the fundamental tones and the harmonics (see *Timbre*). It can, like the Neo-Bechstein, have a broadcasting set and gramophone built into it.

(*d*) The **Miessner Piano.** This is, in essentials, like the instruments above described. But definite changes of tone-colour can be produced by touching buttons and turning dials that control the amplification of particular sets of harmonics (see *Timbre*); unlimited experiments in tone-colour are thus possible.

4. The **Pipeless (Electrophonic, Electrotonic) Organ** (p. 769, pl. **130. 4, 5**). In 1930 it was announced that two French inventors, Messrs. **Coupleux and Givelet,** had

produced a pipeless organ. 'Pipes are replaced by radiophone lamps, which give all the sounds of an ordinary organ, with all the *timbres* of the various stops. For varying the intensity and qualities of sound this new organ is fitted with amplifiers. Such an organ will cost considerably less to construct than the ordinary pipe organ.' Since then, such organs have been put on the market and have become fairly common.

An American, Captain **Richard Ranger,** demonstrated in 1931, in New York, a pipeless organ of his invention involving the use of vibrations in combination with photo-electric cells. He used the term *Rangertone.*

In 1935 the **Hammond** Instrument Company of Chicago put on sale an electric organ without pipes or wind: it is very compact, all the mechanism being contained in the console, connected by a cable with a power-cabinet which can be placed in any convenient place. The whole is as portable as a small piano. A vast range of tone colours is at the disposal of the player through a system of direct control of the harmonics on which timbre depends. Technical details are as follows:

A small metallic plate, or 'tone-wheel', about an inch-and-a-quarter in diameter, is arranged so that it will rotate in close proximity to a permanent magnet. About the permanent magnet is wound a coil. The 'tone-wheel' is not circular but has a number of high points equally spaced around its periphery. As it rotates it does not touch the permanent magnet, but the high points pass close enough to disturb the magnetic field. Each time a high point passes the magnet it varies the magnetic field and induces a minute flow of current into the coil. Should the tone-wheel be rotated at such a speed, for instance, that 439 high points pass the magnet each second a minute alternating current of a frequency of 439 would be generated in the coil and flow in the circuit with which it is associated. Such a frequency of 439 when converted into sound would be the New Philharmonic Pitch 'A' (see *Pitch* 5).

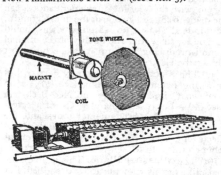

In the generator there are 91 such wheels, all permanently geared together and driven by a constant-speed synchronous motor. Their speeds of rotation and the number of high points on each are so calculated that each wheel produces one of the 91 frequencies necessary for the 91 pitches which are to be used in the fundamentals and harmonics. Ninety-one frequencies are thus continuously available at the generator. When a key is depressed it selects the proper frequency for the fundamental of the note it represents, together with the proper frequencies for eight harmonics of that note (as previously set up by the player according to the tone-colour he desires, by means of controls provided). These various frequencies are superimposed upon one another, and flow as a single complex electrical 'wave' to a pre-amplifier, also located in the console.

From here the wave (amplified somewhat) flows through the connecting cable to a power cabinet placed anywhere in the church, hall, or room. Here it is further amplified and caused to operate speaker-cones.

The operation is entirely electrical. No sound is created in the console—only electrical vibration combinations. What is played first becomes sound at the power cabinet. A 'Reverberation Unit' can be built into the power cabinet or attached to it, enabling the period of reverberation to be adjusted to the surroundings (larger or smaller stone church, carpeted drawing-room, etc.).

In 1935 the Everette Piano Co. of New Haven, Mich., put on sale an electric pipeless organ, called the **Orgatron,** invented by F. A. Hoschke, and Jörg Mager introduced his **Partiturophon.** (See 1 c above.)

For the interest of readers already possessed of some knowledge of the technical side of the subject, here are brief particulars of some other instruments based on similar principles:

The Everette Orgatron (now further developed and marketed by the Wurlitzer Company of New York and Chicago) uses vibrating reeds as electrostatic generators, the harmonic content being filtered electrically. The instrument employs a limited amount of 'extension' and is controlled by a normal organ console. Besides the Hammond and Wurlitzer organs, there are other electrophonic organs on the American market including the **Allen** (Allentown, Pa.), the **Baldwin** (Cincinnati), and the **Connsonata** (Elkhart, Ind.). In all these the sound is produced by oscillating valve circuits, each in its own distinctive way; thus, in the Baldwin instrument, twelve master oscillators give the top notes, those of lower pitch being derived from these by electrical frequency dividers. The Connsonata employs unit oscillators, each giving four semitones. Indeed there seems no limit to the versatility of oscillating radio circuits as a source of musical sounds.

Outstanding success has been achieved in England by the John Compton Organ Company with an electrostatic instrument, the **Compton Electrone,** generating sound by regular changes in capacitance of suitably engraved and contoured plate condensers in which one plate is fixed and the other rotated. The musical quality is greatly enhanced by the skill with which the harmonic synthesis of the various stops has been evolved, due care being taken with the development of the transients and formants (see *Acoustics* 7 for these terms). A standard organ console is provided. An outstanding installation is one of three manuals in the Royal Festival Hall, London (1951), in which two generators of complete tones (specially chosen for appropriate synthesis and 'extension' in ordinary pipe fashion) are used, one for the Great and half the Pedal, and the other for Choir, Swell, and the remainder of the Pedal, each generator consisting of twelve disk units, one per semitone of the musical scale. By deliberately delaying the rate of discharge of the condensers a time-lag in the die-away of the notes may be introduced, thereby simulating to any desired degree the reverberation period of an auditorium, thus overcoming defects due to unsatisfactory architectural acoustics. The same device may also be employed to produce the effect of orchestral percussion and bells.

The **Miller Organ Company** (Norwich) markets a valve organ invented by the Frenchman, Constant Martin. Individually tuned and voiced oscillators give up to thirty untempered harmonics for each note and a special harmonic selector unit is responsible for the various organ stops. An electro-mechanically derived carillon operated from a keyboard is also due to the same inventor.

Akin to oscillating valve organs is the **Novachord**, a domestic six-octave keyboard instrument giving fourteen different tonal qualities: piano, organ, strings, woodwind, etc. A valve instrument called the **Solovox** may be used as an adjunct to an ordinary piano. It consists of a subsidiary three-octave keyboard (having a pitch-range of five octaves) operated by special keys and a knee-controlled volume-variator. It enables orchestral effects to be readily associated with piano music. A similar development is the **Clavioline** (Selmer, licensed by Constant Martin; p. 288, pl. **50.** 5).

Advantages claimed for electrophonic organs include the following: (1) They require no tuning. (2) They are unaffected by atmospheric conditions. (3) Their small size compared with that of pipe organs allows them to be placed in an acoustically advantageous position. (4) They cost little to keep up. The initial outlay varies, naturally, according to the degree of musical quality and the extent of tonal resources required. The fact that the actual sounds produced are delivered via a loud-speaker sets a serious limitation to the musical effect.

Sales of these instruments reached their peak in the U.S.A. in 1959 (350,000) and then declined.

5. Instruments using the Photo-Electric Cell. Reference to the use of the photo-electric cell will be found under *Broadcasting of Music* 6, where is briefly described its use in television. The extension of the use of this cell for the creation of musical sounds began about the 1930s. The general principle is that a beam of light falling on a photo-electric cell is regularly interrupted by some form of rotating disk (see (*b*) below), or by the varying density of a cinematograph film (see (*c*) below) the consequent vibrations being transformed into musical sounds. Technical difficulties have retarded the development of the former type of instrument, but the following may be mentioned:

(*a*) The **Rhythmicon** is the joint invention of Thérémin (see 1 (*d*) above) and the American composer Henry Cowell. 'It produces overtones in rhythmic beats from one to sixteen times to a bar, the overtones being proportionately higher in faster rhythms. A special keyboard controls the rhythms; so long as the key remains depressed the note continues to be repeated. When several keys are held down a rhythmic harmony of overtones is heard; when single keys are depressed successively, a rhythmic melody results. The pitch and the tempo can be varied at will by an electric device.

(*b*) The **Photona**. This is an instrument introduced in 1935 by the WCAU Broadcasting Company of America, working on patents held by Mr. Ivan Eremeef. It is a keyboard instrument of two manuals, with stops like those of an organ to control the tone colours on the general principles of selection of harmonics (see *Timbre*), as mentioned in connexion with the Hammond organ (see 4). The tones are produced by rotating discs between a light source and a photo-electric cell, and are amplified on the lines of the instruments described above.

Spielman's **Super-piano** (1927) is another keyboard instrument using the photo-electric cell. So is the **Welte Photophone** (Berlin).

(*c*) The **Sound Film**. The general principle upon which are produced cinematograph films reproducing sound as well as sight can be grasped from the description of the photoelectric cell process under *Gramophone* 4.

By a close analysis of the photographic image of the 'sound-track' on a film, it is theoretically possible to reproduce musical sounds, and even speech, by drawing. In 1939 the sound film was, apparently for the first time, used for the public introduction of a new work, the fifth symphony of Shostakovich, recorded in Russia, being heard in London by this medium. The reproduction was reported to be 'unsatisfactory, except according to mechanical standards'.

ELECTROCHORD. See *Electric Musical Instruments* 3 c.

ELECTROFONIC VIOLIN. See *Electric Musical Instruments* 2 b.

ELECTRONDE. See *Electric Musical Instruments* 1 d.

ELECTRONE. A name applied by some organbuilders (e.g. Compton of London) to the type of instrument described under *Electric Musical Instruments* 4.

ELECTRONIC. See under *Electric*.

ELECTROPHONE. (1) A form of telephone service which, from the 1880s up to the advent of radio, had a considerable vogue in large cities. A number of theatres and concert halls (e.g. Queen's Hall, London) were supplied with sound-transmitting apparatus and wired to a central office. Subscribers to the system had a listening apparatus attached to the telephone in their houses and could ask to be switched on to any of these theatres or concert halls. The pioneer of this system in the

United States was Dr. Thaddeus Cahill (see *Electric Musical Instruments*, near opening).

(2) A musical instrument using electric bells, invented by the Dutch composer Daniel Ruyneman, who has written a part for it in some of his compositions.

(3) See *Electric Musical Instruments* 1 c.

ELECTROPHONIC (or **ELECTROTONIC**) **INSTRUMENTS.** See *Electric Musical Instruments*.

ELEGANTEMENTE (It.). 'Elegantly.'

ELEGIA, ELEGIACO (It.). 'Elegy', 'elegiac' (see below).

ÉLÉGIE (Fr.), **ELEGY.** A song of lament—or an instrumental composition with that suggestion.

ELEKTRA (Strauss). First produced at Dresden, 1909. Libretto by von Hofmannsthal, based on Sophocles.

SCENE: *The Inner Court of Clytemnestra's Palace in Mycenae*

Five Maid Servants (*Sopranos, Mezzo-Sopranos*, and a *Contralto*) and an **Overseer** (*Soprano*) are discussing **Elektra** (*Soprano*), whose father, Agamemnon, has been murdered by her mother, Clytemnestra. Elektra seeks vengeance, and, devoured by this passion, has become almost like a wild beast, solitary and half mad. Elektra's sister, **Chrysothemis** (*Soprano*), tells her that her mother and her mother's paramour Aegisthus intend to shut her up. Chrysothemis rails upon Elektra for having, by her wildness, frightened their mother so that she will let neither of them go; and Chrysothemis wants to be free to wed.

Clytemnestra (*Mezzo-Soprano*) is terrified by dreams, and in her lonely fear comes to seek sympathy even from Elektra, who tells her that she will cease to dream when 'beneath the axe the appointed victim bleeds'. She hints that the sacrificed one is to be a woman and the executioner a kinsman—her absent brother Orestes; but Chrysothemis tells her he is dead.

Elektra insists to the horrified Chrysothemis that they two must avenge their murdered father, and is digging up the axe with which the deed was done when she sees a stranger watching her. It is **Orestes** (*Baritone*), who first asserts aloud that her brother is dead (a report which he has given out to deceive the murderers) and then whispers to her the truth—that he stands before her, prepared to execute vengeance. He goes into the palace. Shrieks are heard. **Aegisthus** (*Tenor*) saunters in, unaware of what is going forward. He questions Elektra, who is beside herself with the lust for death. Orestes slays both his mother and Aegisthus, while Elektra dances herself madly to death in the joy of her fulfilled purpose.

ELEVATIO (Lat.), **ELEVATION.** Music to be performed during the Elevation of the Host in the Roman Catholic Church is known by this name. No liturgical text is prescribed by the missal, but sometimes a motet is sung and more commonly an organ composition or extemporization is played.

ELEVATO (It.). 'Elevated' in spirit.

ELEVAZIONE (It.). 'Elevation' (of spirit).

ÉLÈVE (Fr.). 'Pupil.'

ELEVENTH. See *Interval*.

ELFENREIGEN (Ger.). See *Reigen*.

ELGAR, EDWARD WILLIAM (pl. **52,** opposite). Born at Broadheath near Worcester in 1857 and died at Worcester in 1934, aged seventy-six. He was brought up in an atmosphere of music. His father was an organist and music-seller: 'A stream of music flowed through our house and the shop and I was all the time bathing in it.' His first real awakening to the power of the art came, however, when he caught sight of a copy of Beethoven's First Symphony, a glance at the Minuet of which electrified him, so that he ran off to study it in quiet, and experienced an immediate artistic enlightenment.

He graduated as a performer in ways he could hardly recall or explain, playing piano, violin, cello, and double-bass, bassoon and trombone, and in one or another of his capacities taking part in all the local music-makings. From his twenty-second to twenty-seventh years he was bandmaster of the staff of a mental home, and this gave him his first experience in conducting.

His staple trade as a professional musician was for long that of violin playing and teaching, and after local success he tried with this to effect a lodgement in London musical life, but, not succeeding, settled first in Malvern and then in Hereford. Gradually he came forward as a composer, the English festival system giving him his opportunity and the works by which he became known being of the choral–orchestral kind demanded by festival committees.

At forty-two his *Enigma Variations* for orchestra placed him at a bound in the very front rank. This masterly collection of musical portraits of his friends is still the most played of all his major works and is perhaps the only one that has been heard in every musical centre of the world—for, despite a certain welcome given him at one period in Germany, he inexplicably remains an 'English composer', known outside his own country more by name and fame than by intimacy with his art.[1]

His oratorio setting of Cardinal Newman's *The Dream of Gerontius*, in the year following the production of *Enigma*, revealed him as a distinctively Roman Catholic composer of a strongly mystical turn of mind. *The Apostles* and *The Kingdom* followed, with the brilliant concert overture *Cockaigne*, the elaborate tone-poem *Falstaff*, songs and chamber music, and

[1] Probably Elgar never knew that his *Enigma Variations* had a predecessor. In 1825 was published *The Enigma-Variations and Fantasia on a Favorite Irish Air for the Piano Forte, in the style of five Eminent Artists, composed and dedicated to the Originals by Cipriani Potter* (see *Potter*. The eminent artists were guessed to be Ries, Kalkbrenner, Cramer, Rossini, and Beethoven).

PLATE 52

ELGAR AT HIS WORK-TABLE

By Batt

HE has been at work on his last symphony—the one commissioned by the British Broadcasting Corporation and destined, alas! to remain unfinished. His period of old age was a sad one. The death of his wife left him without zest for work and he had the depressing feeling that public appreciation, which had for so long been widespread and keen, was now weakening. The B.B.C.'s commission must have cheered him, but he had sadly to recognize that his task was never to be completed. The work remains, then, a mere unfinished sketch.

the two symphonies (a third merely in sketch), a violin concerto, and a cello concerto. He wrote no important piano music and no opera.

An American musician (Daniel Gregory Mason, q.v.) wrote of Elgar's 'tenderness coupled with aspiration', and 'noble plainness'. These are some of the qualities that English musicians feel in Elgar. In 1904 he was knighted, in 1911 he received the Order of Merit, in 1924 he became Master of the King's Musick, and in 1931 he was created baronet.

See *Arrangement*; *Atkins*; *Ave Verum*; *Bell* 6; *Cadenza*; *Carpenter*; *Chapel Royal*; *Competitions*, 2, 3; *Composition* 5; *Concerto* 6 c (1857); *Copyright* 3; *England* 7; *Enigma Variations*; *Form* 2, 11; *God save the Queen* 16; *Ground*; *Improvisation* 5; *Knighthood*; *Leading Motif*; *March*; *Oratorio* 5, 7—giving dates and places of first performances; *Part Song*; *Percussion* 4 a (near end); *Programme Music* 5 e; *Romantic*; *Ronald*; *Sonata* 10 c; *Suite* 7; *Symphonic Poem*; *United States* 6; *Wolstenholme*.

ELIOT, REVD. JOHN (eighteenth-century New England divine). See *Hymns and Hymn Tunes* 11.

ELIZABETH I (b. 1533, came to throne 1558, d. 1603). See references, of lesser or greater importance, under *Anglican Parish Church Music* 1; *Chapel Royal*; *Cathedral Music* 3, 4; *Wales* 7; *Italy* 9; *Harpsichord Family* 3; *Fitzwilliam Virginal Book*; *Profession of Music* 9; *Street Music* 6; *Printing of Music* 1; *Mechanical Reproduction of Music* 4; *Country Dance*; *Volta*; *Morley, Thomas*; *Rosseter, Philip*; *Tye*; *Patronage* 5; *Edwards, R.*; *Byrd*.

ELLA, JOHN (1802–88). See references under *Concert* 7; *Annotated Programmes* 4; *Criticism* 8.

ELLING, CATHARINUS (1858–1942). See *Scandinavia* 3.

ELLINGTON, 'DUKE' (really Edward Kennedy Ellington; p. 1068, pl. **175**. 4). Born in Washington, D.C., in 1899 and died in New York in 1974, aged seventy-five. As a boy he was a member of rag-time bands. His later achievements as a jazz composer are described under *Jazz* 5.

ELLIOTT, JANE. See *Flowers of the Forest*.

ELLIS.

(1) WILLIAM. Seventeenth-century Oxford musician. See *Clubs for Music-Making*.

(2) MIRIAM A. See *Ear and Hearing* 6.

(3) T. E. See *Holbrooke*.

ÉLOIGNER (Fr.). 'To put further away.' So *s'éloignant*, 'getting further away'.

ELSNER, JOSEPH (1769–1854). See *Poland*; *Chopin*.

ELSON, L. C. (1848–1920). See reference under *Britannia, the Pride of the Ocean*.

ELSSLER, the sisters FANNY (real name Franziska) and THERESE (1810–84 and 1808–78). Famous ballet dancers of Austrian origin, Fanny being much the more important. See reference under *Ballet* 9.

ELVEY.

(1) GEORGE JOB (p. 165, pl. **34**. 8). Born at Canterbury in 1816 and died in Surrey in 1893, aged seventy-seven. He was organist at St. George's Chapel, Windsor Castle, for nearly half a century, first to William IV and then to Queen Victoria, who knighted him. His service-music and anthems keep his name alive in the English church.

See *Anthem*, Period IV; *Windsor*.

(2) STEPHEN. Born at Canterbury in 1805 and died at Oxford in 1860, aged fifty-five. He was brother of Sir George Elvey (see above), and like him an organist. Some of his church music is still heard.

ELWELL, HERBERT. Born at Minneapolis in 1898 and died at Cleveland in 1974. In composition he was a pupil of Bloch and (in Paris) of Nadia Boulanger. From 1932 he was music critic of the Cleveland *Plain Dealer*. His ballet *The Happy Hypocrite* (1925), after Max Beerbohm, has been a good deal performed, and in 1945 he was awarded the Paderewski Prize for his oratorio *Lincoln*.

ELWES, GERVASE (1866–1921). See reference under *Voice* 17.

ELY CATHEDRAL. See *Cathedral Music* 2. Organists who receive notice in this volume are (with their periods of office); *Tye* (1541–62); *Robert White* (1562–7); *J. Farrant* (1567–72); *J. Ferrabosco* (1662–82); *Chipp* (1867–86); *Harwood* (1887–92); *Noble* (1892–9); *Allen* (1898–1901).

ELY CONFESSION. See under *Anglican Chant* 6.

ELYOT, SIR THOMAS. See *Education and Music* 2.

EMBASSY CHAPELS IN LONDON. See *Roman Catholic Church Music in Britain*.

EMBELLISHMENTS. See *Ornaments or Graces*.

EMBOUCHURE. In the playing of brass instruments this means the mode of application of the lips, or their relation to the mouthpiece. The word is French and in that language it means also the mouthpiece itself—a double usage generally avoided in English. A colloquial English equivalent is 'lip' ('to have a good lip'). The German is *Ansatz*; however, this not only has the double meaning of the French 'embouchure' (more commonly in the English sense of that word), but is also used for a shank or crook.

See *Brass*.

EMER'S FAREWELL. See *Londonderry Air*.

EMICON. See *Electric Musical Instruments* 1 j.

EMMANUEL, MAURICE (in full Marie François Maurice). Born at Bar-sur-Aube, near Troyes, in 1862, and died in Paris in 1938, aged seventy-six. He was both an erudite musicologist and an active composer, whose work included operas, chamber music, two symphonies, etc.

EMMETT, DANIEL DECATUR (p. 1040, pl. **169**. 4). Born at Mount Vernon, Ohio, in 1815, and died there in 1904, aged eighty-eight. He is the composer of the singularly original and racy tune 'Dixie' (q.v.), which is one of the most popular and characteristic of American airs. Successively a printer's devil, soldier, and member of a circus troupe, Emmett formed the first of the troupes of black-face comedians, 'Negro Minstrels' (q.v.), who were for long the popular purveyors of clean humour, music, and the folk-lore of the country. It was on a Saturday night, when he was a member of Dan Bryant's minstrel troupe, that Emmett composed 'Dixie' as a new song for the 'walk-around' of the next Monday night's show. He also composed 'Old Dan Tucker' and other songs of lesser popularity.

EMOTION IN MUSIC. See *Quality in Music* 6.

EMOZIONE (It.). 'Emotion.'

'EMPEROR' CONCERTO (Beethoven). See *Nicknamed Compositions* 3.

'EMPEROR' QUARTET (Haydn). See *Nicknamed Compositions* 12; also the article below.

EMPEROR'S HYMN ('Gott erhalte Franz den Kaiser', i.e. 'God preserve the Emperor Francis'—the tune being found in many hymn-books under the name *Austria*). This was the national hymn of Austria from the time of the composition of the tune by Haydn (1797) to the setting up of the Republic in 1918, and after that the tune was officially retained, but other words adopted—those of Ottokar Kernstock, *Sei gesegnet ohne Ende* ('Thine be never-ending blessings')[1]

The original words were by Lorenz Leopold Haschka (1749–1827). Count von Saurau, Imperial High Chancellor, caused them to be written—'Regretting that we had not, like the British, a national song calculated to display to all the world the loyal devotion of our people to the king and upright ruler of our *Fatherland*, ... I caused that meritorious poet Haschka to write the words, and applied to our immortal countryman Haydn to set them to music, for I considered him alone capable of writing anything approaching in merit the English *God save the King*.' In a considerable degree the enterprise was intended as a counterblast to the influence of the French Revolution.

Haydn took one of the Croatian folk melodies of his childhood (p. 464, pl. **81**. 5), which probably suggested itself to him as fitting metrically and rhythmically the opening lines, and altered and extended its later part so that it might accommodate the whole of Haschka's stanza-lengths. He made a number of versions (still to be seen), improving it gradually here and there until he arrived at the version still current (see Hadow's *Haydn: a Croatian Composer*, 1897, or his *Collected Essays*, 1928).

Haydn afterwards used this tune as the basis of a set of variations in his string quartet in C, usually numbered as op. 76 no. 3 (hence called 'Kaiser' Quartet or 'Emperor' Quartet), and loved in old age to play the tune on the piano—especially in the year of his death, when the French were bombarding the city. It was, indeed, the last music he ever performed.

For the application of the tune in Germany see *Deutschland über Alles*. And note a reference under *Composition* 9.

[1] In 1946 the Austrian Cabinet decided to adopt a tune by Mozart for the national anthem, one of his pieces of Masonic music (K. 483). For this a new poem was specially written.

EMPFINDUNG (Ger.). 'Feeling', 'sentiment'; hence *Empfindungsvoll*, 'feelingly'.

EMPHASE (Fr., Ger.). 'Emphasis.'

EMPORTÉ (Fr.). 'Carried away', i.e. 'excitedly'.

EMPRESSÉ (Fr.). 'Eager.'

ÉMU (Fr.). 'Moved' (emotionally).

EN (Fr.). 'In', 'whilst', etc. Used in such expressions, for instance, as *En accélérant*, 'accelerating'; *En rondeau*, in rondo style, etc.

ENCHAÎNEMENT. See *Ballet* 8.

ENCHAÎNEZ (Fr.). Literally 'chain together', i.e. join up (next movement to be played without break).

ENCLUME (Fr.). 'Anvil.' See *Percussion Family* 3 s, 4 c, 5 s.

ENCORE in French means 'again', and in English has been adopted as the word of demand for the repetition of a performance (properly, perhaps, of the same piece, but it is often used of a mere return to the platform to give an additional performance, whether of the same or another piece). The verb 'to encore' has also come into use.

Although, as above stated, the word 'encore' is French, its entry into the English language was by corruption of the Italian *ancora* (with the same meaning), which word, from the early eighteenth century onwards, was in use amongst the audience of the Italian Opera in London (indifferently with the words *altra volta*, 'another time'; see *Spectator* for 29 Feb. 1712); in the press of those days the word was sometimes spelt 'ancore' or 'anchore'.

The word the French themselves use is *bis* (Latin, 'twice'), with the verb 'bisser'.

The practice of the 'encore' can become one of the trials of the concert-going life. Many performers are very ready to 'take encores', and thus a few determined individuals in an audience can detain the rest.

Encores in opera are, of course, destructive of dramatic quality. During the first London performance of *Lohengrin* (1875) the audience encored the chorus that is sung during the arrival of the swan. Gilbert and Sullivan operas are in Britain greatly damaged by encores.

In Latin countries, up to at least the 1930s, opera producers were compelled to be very tolerant of irrelevant interpolations. Fleta, the Spanish tenor, 'would respond to a *bis* with encore after encore of popular songs which had nothing to do with the opera', and Kiepura, the Polish tenor, 'would make sure that a piano was ready in the wings for accompanying him as he rushed out to take his encores—all, of course, irrelevant to the opera' (Gaisberg, *The Music Goes Round*, 1943).

At one time the progress of a symphony was frequently broken by the 'encoring' of a particular movement.

Haydn, in the note-book he kept of his 1792 visit to England, records an incident he witnessed at Covent Garden when the demand for the repetition of a duo was resisted: 'The controversy lasted nearly a quarter of an hour before parterre and boxes triumphed and the duo was repeated. The two performers stood in a fright on the stage, now retiring, then again coming to the front.' The practice of printing 'No Encores' on programmes is occasionally found and is much to be commended (p. 464, pl. **81**. 6). The writer recalls that at the Bristol Festival of 1912 large placards on all the walls of the concert-room displayed this prohibition, but that when Clara Butt was applauded for one of her songs the orchestra were found to have the 'parts' for an 'encore' song ready provided on their desks. In 1844 (as the *Musical Times* of June of that year records) the singing of Handel's *Sweet Bird* by a soloist at a concert of the York Choral Society 'elicited such immense applause that the performers could not proceed with the next piece and, it being a standing rule with the Committee to allow no encores, the concert broke up'. (Thus the demands of the audience resulted in their being given less, and not more!)

A perfectly inhuman demand is sometimes made upon the generosity and physical endurance of a soloist who has concluded a heavy concerto and is then expected to sit down again and play one or more solo pieces.

ENCYCLOPEDIA AND ENCYCLOPEDISTS (FRENCH). See *France 8*; *Bouffons, Guerre des*; *Criticism 3*.

ENERGIA (It.). 'Energy.' So *Energico*, 'energetic'.

ENESCO (orig. **ENESCU**), **GEORGES** (p. 209, pl. **41**. 5). Born at Dorohoiû, in Moldavia, Rumania, in 1881 and died in Paris in 1955, aged seventy-three. At seven he was studying and composing in Vienna. Later he became a violinist in an orchestra there. Then he went to Paris, and was eventually admitted to the Conservatory, where he studied violin under Marsick and composition under Fauré and Massenet. He took the first prize for violin playing at eighteen and entered upon a brilliant career as virtuoso. At sixteen he had given a concert of his own works in Paris and the next year his début as composer may be considered to have taken place, his *Rumanian Poem* being performed under Colonne. It

counts as his 'op. 1' and was followed by many orchestral and chamber works, an opera (*Oedipus*; libretto by Edmond Fleg), and other things.

His eventual style was personal but at the same time national, being based to some extent upon a loving study of the varied folk tunes of his native country (cf. *Nationalism*). He ranks as Rumania's greatest composer. He had a wide reputation as a conductor, and also as the chief master under whom Yehudi Menuhin studied. He lived latterly in Paris.

ENFANT PRODIGUE. See *Pantomime*.

ENFASI (It.). 'Emphasis.'

ENFATICO, ENFATICAMENTE (It.). 'Emphatic', 'emphatically'.

ENGEL.

(1) CARL (I). Born near Hanover in 1818 and died in London in 1882, aged sixty-four. He was a piano teacher who settled as a young man in England, wrote many works on piano playing and other musical subjects, and developed into an authority on ancient instruments, of which he got together a great number. He had much influence in the development of the musical side of the Victoria and Albert Museum, South Kensington, where many of his instruments now remain.

See reference under *Folk Song 3*.

(2) CARL (II) (unrelated to his elder namesake). Born in Paris in 1883 and died in New York in 1944, aged sixty. He studied at the Universities of Strasbourg and Munich, migrated to the United States in 1905, took part in the work of music-publishing firms (especially Schirmer of New York), and became editor of the *Musical Quarterly*, and later Chief of the Music Division of the Library of Congress, Washington (1921–35). He was especially active in national and international organizations for the prosecution of musicological research.

ENGELSTIMME (Ger.). Literally 'angel-voice', i.e. the *Vox Angelica* stop on the organ.

ENGER (Ger.). Literally 'narrower', i.e. 'drawn together', 'quicker'.

ENGLAND

(For illustrations see p. 289, pl. **51**; 336, **53, 54**; 352, **55, 56**.)

The present article is designed to offer merely a brief conspectus of the history of music in England, further information on almost every branch of the subject mentioned, as on the individual composers, being given under the appropriate heads scattered throughout this volume. A list of some of the chief of these heads appears at the end of the article.

Scotland, Wales, and Ireland are treated under their own names.

1. Folk Music. The roots of English music are, necessarily, to be looked for in its folk songs and folk-dance tunes, which, so far as they have been preserved and put on record, constitute a valuable national possession, possessing perhaps as much beauty and as much variety as those of any nation in the world, and often expressing intimately the instinctive national characteristics (see *Folk Song*).

2. Composers and Theorists, A.D. **1000–1500.** Anything that we can call 'composition' seems (so far as we can find out) to have begun, in Europe, only in the eleventh century. The earliest remaining English example to merit the serious attention of historians of music throughout the world is the thirteenth-century six-part choral piece, *Sumer is icumen in*, the precociously complex structure of which is discussed under its own name. But somewhat earlier than this Giraldus Cambrensis had written that in one northern part of England even the children sang entrancingly in two parts.

The songs of the Trouvères of northern France had exercised some influence in southern England in the twelfth and thirteenth centuries, and Richard Cœur de Lion (born 1157; died 1199) was, of course, a Troubadour (see *Minstrels*, 2, 3, 4, for some discussion of this general subject).

The fourteenth-century English friar, Simon Tunsted (q.v.), was of high fame as a theorist. In the early part of the fifteenth century England possessed in John Dunstable (q.v.) a composer of high contemporary European renown, to whose genius the art owes a great forward leap. After this, for a short time, the Flemish composers (see *Belgium* 1) outran the English. The English theorist, John Hothby (q.v.; d. 1487), had great influence in Italy and elsewhere.

3. The Sixteenth and Early Seventeenth Centuries. The sixteenth and early seventeenth centuries constituted throughout Europe a period of great achievement in **Unaccompanied Choral Music** for church and home. In this branch of the art (the Latin Mass and, after the Reformation, the vernacular 'Service', the Anthem, and the Madrigal in its various forms) England was the equal of any nation, whilst in another branch, that of **Music for the Keyboard Instruments** of the day, she actually led, the processes of the great Italian, German, and French schools of writers of keyboard music of the later seventeenth, the eighteenth, and the nineteenth centuries being largely based upon the successful experimentation of the English late sixteenth and early seventeenth centuries (for an example of its wide influence see *Hungary*). In this same fertile period, and the thirty years or so that followed, there was a high cultivation of chamber music, especially marked by the composition of the string **Fancy** (q.v.) in huge quantities; and the solo song with lute accompaniment had high importance. The greatest name of this period is that of Byrd, who was, however, surrounded by a group of companions many of them little less able than himself.

During the late sixteenth and early seventeenth centuries English musicians had great reputation in continental Europe, and very many of them held positions at the courts of princes (see *Scandinavia* 2) or were in the service of the municipalities of free cities. For their employment at the court of Scotland see *Scotland* 6. (English dancers and actors were likewise popular abroad at this time.)

The English were reckoned the best players of that important instrument, the Viola da Gamba (see *Viol Family* 3), and not only did English gamba players hold positions abroad and publish music there, but Continental players frequently came to England for instruction.

4. The Civil War and the Republican Period. During the Civil War and the republican period of Puritan control that followed, i.e. from about 1644 to the restoration of the monarchy in 1660, all church music was prohibited, except the unaccompanied singing of metrical versions of the Psalms, and, the theatres being closed by parliamentary ordinance, public performances of the simple music of the very rudimentary orchestras of the day, which seem to have been amongst their attractions, necessarily ceased. **Opera** in England began, however, during this very period (1656), and the domestic cultivation of both vocal and instrumental music was particularly active. The madrigal forms and style had now outworn their popularity throughout Europe, and in England their place was taken by the solo song and the musical dialogue. Dance music was published and was apparently in great use.

See also *Puritans and Music*; *Minstrels* 3; *Opera* 13 a.

5. The Restoration. The end of the Republican period (1660) brought with it some changes of musical taste, largely due to Continental influence brought into the country by Charles II on his return from the court of Louis XIV. The serious contrapuntal style of church music tended to disappear in favour of a more harmonic and rhythmically simple style, with much use of solo voices and (so far as the Royal Chapel was concerned) orchestral accompaniments and interludes, reinforcing the organ. Recitative, which had been heard in the opera (introduced in 1656 by Davenant; see *Opera* 13 a), now found its place in church music. The string Fancies drifted out of favour, as now seeming to be too dully contrapuntal. The violin, which had attained considerable popularity during the Republican period, now largely superseded the viol.

Two unfortunately short-lived geniuses, **Pelham Humfrey** (q.v.), whom the King sent abroad to study foreign methods, and his pupil **Henry Purcell** (q.v.), were notable figures, especially the latter, whose achievements in ecclesiastical and theatrical music, the song, keyboard music, and other branches have given him rank as one of the two or three greatest composers the country has ever brought forth. The work of Purcell is somewhat cut off from that of the period that preceded (the period whose greatest names were those of Palestrina in Italy, Victoria in Spain.

and Byrd in England), and classifies itself rather with that of the period just about to open (that of Bach, Handel, Couperin, and Scarlatti)—though its methods are necessarily more tentative.

6. The Eighteenth-century Decline. With the death of Purcell (1695) a period of decline set in. The English musical achievements of the eighteenth century are respectable but not outstanding, and the composers no longer rank with the greatest of the Continent. During the first half of that century a naturalized Englishman, Handel, occupied the centre of the stage, and the native-born composers were grouped somewhat humbly about him. However, in 1728 the production of **The Beggar's Opera** (q.v.), a deliberate manifesto against the Italianate opera of Handel and his foreign competitors in England, set a new fashion for Europe and not merely resulted in the composition of a number of native imitations (see *Ballad Opera*), but also gave the impulse to the introduction of the German Singspiel (see *Opera* 9 g). English influence abroad was, therefore, not yet extinct.

The leading English composer of this period was **Arne** (q.v.), who wrote chiefly for the theatre and showed a great gift for simple, flowing melody. Straightforward tune (obviously related to folk song), rather than any subtlety of design or of texture, characterizes the period. The **Glee** (q.v.), a definitely English form, was very popular and composers were lavish in their provision of it. Music for the services of the English Church in general manifested a boldness and simplicity of structure that contrasted strongly with that of the sixteenth and seventeenth centuries; it often expressed a sober dignity but rarely mysticism, and indeed closely reflected the general spirit of the church of the day, in which there was a marked tendency to rationalism.

There seems to have been during this century a serious decline in the domestic cultivation of music, which tended to be left to the female portion of the 'comfortable classes', and even so to be regarded as a mere 'accomplishment', an unhappy tradition being thus established that took long to destroy (cf. *Education and Music* 2). And with the worship of the foreign virtuoso (especially the Italian operatic vocalist), and an over-generous forgetfulness of their own past productiveness, the English became the great importing nation in music.

7. The Nineteenth Century. The early part of the nineteenth century was an undistinguished period in English music. The one notable British innovation was the piano style of **Field** (on which that of Chopin was partly based), and he was an Irishman. The two popular opera composers of the day, **Balfe** and **Wallace**, were also Irish.

Towards the middle of the century the orchestral works, piano works, and songs of **Sterndale Bennett** aroused great expectations, both in Britain and on the Continent,

being highly praised by Mendelssohn and others, but he sunk himself in the task of earning a living by teaching and ceased to be productive.

In the latter half of the nineteenth century and the earlier part of the twentieth the comic operas of **Sullivan** and the varied compositions of **Parry**, **Stanford** (Irish, however, though he worked in England), and **Mackenzie** (Scottish, working in England), gave great hopes of a renascence of British music, which came to full flower with the very individual and sincerely felt work of **Elgar**. The English 'Musical Festival' offered all these composers their greatest opportunity.

Amongst church musicians Barnby and Stainer held high rank, and they undoubtedly helped the movement towards a more serious standard, but, in the main, their work has come to be looked upon as somewhat tainted with effeminacy. S. S. Wesley's was stronger.

Cowen, Goring Thomas, and others wrote in a style that appealed to the later Victorians, but despite some fine qualities their output later lost its hold upon the attention of audiences. Cowen was, moreover, unfortunately much connected in the public mind with the deft production of a type of song of which he was only one of the exponents, the 'drawing-room ballad', felt by more serious music-lovers to constitute an article of commerce rather than a product of art; this type tended to disappear from the early years of the twentieth century onward, and with it a once highly popular institution, the 'Ballad Concert'.

A new standard in orchestral conducting dates from the advent of Richter (q.v.) in 1877.

8. The Twentieth Century. Towards the end of the nineteenth century and at the beginning of the twentieth composers somewhat younger than Elgar who came forward were (ranging them in order of birth): Ethel Smyth, William Wallace (Scottish by birth, however), Edward German, Delius, McEwen (Scottish by birth), Bantock, Vaughan Williams, Holst, Coleridge-Taylor, Ireland, Frank Bridge, Bax (Irish by sympathy). For the main characteristics of each of these reference should be made to the separate treatment under their names. It is difficult to make a synthesis of their styles and achievements—the more so because, unlike Continental composers, who are largely grouped into 'schools' (and, more than that, into cliques for mutual support and for defence and attack), these pursued their way individually. To a great extent, whilst not unaware of modern tendencies, they showed an indisposition to accept blindly the theories and influences of the extremer of their Continental contemporaries.

A phase of return to British folk tune (see *Folk Song*; *Nationalism*) was a source of inspiration and marked the first twenty years or so of the century. It was due to the admirable work done at this period by devoted collectors, in going into the highways and hedges and compelling the lost songs and dances of England to come back into their proper place in the national consciousness. Parallel with this there went on an important movement for the publication of the music of the English madrigal school and the noble church music of Tudor times, and all these things began to be known not only to the British public but, to some extent (by the performances of British performers), throughout the Commonwealth, on the continent of Europe, and in the United States of America.

The War of 1914–18 robbed England of a number of very promising younger composers and the War of 1939–45 added several names to the saddening list. Walton and Britten are pre-eminent among the composers born during the twentieth century who have achieved international stature; among the names in the list below are those of several members of the younger generation who, while rejecting what has been called 'common-market avant-gardism', have nevertheless taken what they needed from Schönberg and his followers.

The part which music in England has played in education, social life, the church, etc., can be studied on other pages of this book.

9. List of Articles amplifying the above. In order to amplify the information given above the following articles should be consulted:

a. *Folk Song*; *Ballad*; *Song*; *Opera* 13, 14.
b. *Church Music*; *Common Prayer*; *Cathedral Music*; *Precentor*; *Vicar Choral*; *Parish Clerk*; *Anthem*; *Hymns and Hymn Tunes*; *Anglican Chant*.
c. *Catch*; *Round*; *Madrigal*; *Glee*; *Part-Song*; *Sumer is icumen in*; *Oratorio*; *Opera*.
d. *Chapel Royal*; *Wait*; *Minstrels*, etc.; *Concerts*; *Festivals*; *Competitions in Music*; *Criticism*; *Education*; *Degrees and Diplomas*; *Profession of Music*; *Broadcasting of Music*.
e. *Parthenia*; *Printing of Music*; *Publishing* 4–7; *Puritans and Music*.
f. *Pianoforte*; *Organ*; *Viol Family*; *Violin Family*; *Fancy*.
g. *Wales*; *Scotland*; *Ireland*; *Spain* 5; *Italy* 4; *Hungary*.
h. COMPOSERS. The following list gives an idea of the representative English composers of the past 700 years. They are arranged in chronological sequence according to date of birth, so far as this is known. Entries on all of them will be found in the course of the book.

Amongst the composers listed are a few who were of Continental birth but who settled in England and became accepted there, so that their productions formed part of the national repertory of their period.

13th CENTURY: John of Fornsete.
15th CENTURY: Aston; Cornyshe; R. Davy; Dunstable; Fayrfax; Henry VIII; Ludford; Power; Taverner; Tye.
1500–49: Blitheman; Byrd; Edwards; Thos. Este; Farrant; Ferrabosco; Merbecke; Parsons; Patrick; Redford; Tallis; Thorne; Ward; Robt. White; Wm. White; Whythorne; Youll.
1550–99: Alison; Bartlet; Bateson; Batten; Bennet; Bevin; Brade; Bull; Campion; Carlton; Caustun; Cavendish; Coperario; Danyell; Deering; Dowland; Michael Este; Farmer; Farnaby; Ford; O. Gibbons; Giles; John Hilton (Senr.); John Hilton (Junr.); Holborne; John Holmes; Thos. Holmes; Hume; Jenkins; Edw. Johnson; Robt. Johnson; Robt. Jones; Kirbye; Henry Lawes; Lichfield; Marson; Thos. Morley; John Mundy; Wm. Mundy; Nicholson; Norcome; Peerson; Philips; Pilkington; Porter;

Ravenscroft; Rosseter; Tomkins; Vautor; Weelkes; Wilbye; Wilson.
1600–49: Aldrich; Alison; Banister; Blow; Child; H. Cooke; Creyghton; Eccles; Humfrey; Ives; King; Locke; Reading; Rogers; Simpson; Wise; Young.
1650–99: Babell; Carey; Clarke; Croft; J. Eccles; Flintoft; Galliard; Greene; Handel; Kelway; Leveridge; Purcell; Ramsay; D. Roseingrave; T. Roseingrave; Tudway; Turner; Weldon.
1700–49: John Alcock (Senr.); John Alcock (Junr.); T. A. Arne; M. Arne; J. Arnold; S. Arnold; Avison; Barthélemon; Battishill; Boyce; Burney; B. Cooke; W. Cramer; Dibdin; Dupuis; Ebdon; Festing; Garth; W. Hayes; P. Hayes; Herschel; J. Heseltine; Hook; Humphries; Jackson ('of Exeter'); Richard Jones; Kelly, Earl of; J. Kelway; Kent; Lampe; Lates; T. Linley (Senr.); Miller; Mornington; Mudge; Nares; Paxton; Shield; Theodore Smith; Stanley; Travers; T. Vincent; J. Wainwright; Wm. Walond (Senr.); S. Webbe (Senr.).
1750–99: Attwood; Beale; Beckwith; Bishop; Callcott; Clarke-Whitfield; T. S. Cooke; J. B. Cramer; Crotch; Danby; J. Davy; Dibdin; Field; Hawes; E. G. Horn; Horsley; T. Linley (Junr.); W. Linley; Mazzinghi; Novello; Onslow; Pearsall; Potter; Purday; Sir G. Smart; J. Stafford Smith; Spofforth; Storace; R. Wainwright; S. Webbe (Junr.); S. Wesley.
1800–9: Balfe; J. Barnett; Benedict; Crouch; Eliza Flower; Goss; Hatton; Jebb; Osborne; Turle.
1810–19: Prince Albert; Sterndale Bennett; Elvey; J. L. Hopkins; E. J. Hopkins; Hullah; Jackson; J. A. Lloyd; Loder; G. A. Macfarren; G. Monk; J. Orlando Parry; Pierson; H. Smart; Eliz. Stirling; W. Vincent Wallace; Walmisley; Wm. Walond (Junr.); S. S. Wesley.
1820–9: Best; Chipp; Dykes; W. C. Macfarren; W. H. Monk; Ouseley; J. Owen; Pinsuti; Rea; Reay; C. Steggall; Rev. Edw. Stephen; Stewart; Ap Thomas.
1830–9: F. E. Bache; Barnby;

J. F. Barnett; Butler; 'Claribel'; Clay; Garrett; Gaul; Oakley; Prout; Alice Mary Smith; Sydney Smith; Tours.
1840–9: J. Fredk. Bridge; Cellier; Scotson Clark; Jenkins; C. H. Lloyd; Mackenzie; G. Martin; Hubert Parry; Stainer; Sullivan.
1850–9: Cowen; Elgar; Gray; Hardelot; Harwood; Mann; Maunder; Ethel Smyth; Stanford; 'Strelezki'; Goring Thomas; M. V. White.
1860–9: W. G. Alcock; Bantock; Bedford; Brewer; D'Albert; Carroll; E. T. Davies; Walford Davies; Delius; Drysdale; German; S. Jones; Liza Lehmann; Lemare; McCunn; McEwen; Noble; Somervell; R. Steggall; Wm. Wallace; Wolstenholme; Chas. Wood.
1870–9: Fredk. Austin; Ernest Austin; Bairstow; Bell; Boughton; Brian; Frank Bridge; Carse; Coleridge-Taylor; Dunhill; Gardiner; Gatty; Harty; Holbrooke; Holst; Hurlstone; Ireland; Keel; Ketèlbey; Alick Maclean; O'Neill; Peel; Quilter; del Riego; Ronald; Rootham; Cyril Scott; Martin Shaw; Geoffrey Shaw; W. H. Squire; Tovey; Vaughan Williams; Walker; Walthew; Warner; Whittaker; H. J. Lane Wilson.
1880–9: Bainton; Bath; Bax; Berners; Bowen; Braithwaite; Butterworth; Rebecca Clarke; A. Coates; E. Coates; Collingwood; Craxton; Dale; Van Dieren; Dyson; Farrer; Foulds; Friskin; Gibbs; Greaves; Harris; Harrison; Ley; R. O. Morris; Peterkin; Swinstead; F. H. White; Haydn Wood.
1890–9: Arundell; Baines; Benjamin; Bliss; Bullock; D. Clarke; Cundell; Davidson; Demuth; Foss; Arnold Foster; E. Goossens; Gurney; Hadley; Heseltine; Howells; Jacob; Jacobson; Macmillan; Moeran; C. W. Orr; Rowley; Sorabji; Thos. Wood.
1900–9: Alwyn; Berkeley; Dykes Bower; Chisholm; A. Cooke; Denny; Ferguson; Finzi; Fogg; Frankel; Gundry; Head; Hely-Hutchinson; Imogen Holst; Hutchings; Lambert; Leigh; Lutyens; Maconchy; Milford; Murrill; Robin Orr; Elizabeth Poston; Rawsthorne; Rubbra; Freda Swain; Tippett; Walton; Wordsworth.

ENGLAND, GEORGE and GEORGE PIKE (father and son). London organ builders active from about 1740 to 1815.

ENGLISCHES HORN (Ger.). 'English horn', i.e. cor anglais (see *Oboe Family* 5 b).

ENGLISH. For expressions beginning with this adjective see as follows: **Action**, see *Pianoforte* 8. **Concertina**, see *Reed-Organ Family* 5. **Fingering** (for keyboard), see *Fingering* 6; (for Recorder), see *Recorder Family* 2. **Flute**, see *Flute Family* 4. **Folk Dance Society**, see *Country Dance*; *Folk Song* 3. **Guitar**, see *Cittern*. **Horn**, see *Oboe Family* 3 b, 5 b; *Organ* 14 VI. **Hymnal**, see *Hymns and Hymn Tunes* 6. **March**, see *March*. **Opera**, see *Opera* 13 d; *Ballad Opera*. **Psalter**, see *Anglican Chant* 6. **Singers**, see *Madrigal* 8 d. **Violet**, see *Viol Family* 4 f.

ENGLISH FOLK DANCE AND SONG SOCIETY. This represents an amalgamation of the Folk Song Society (founded 1898; cf. *Sharp, Cecil*) and the Folk Dance Society (founded 1911). Its headquarters are Cecil Sharp House, 2 Regent's Park Road, London, N.W.1. It has over ten thousand members and associates, organized into three hundred and and fifty-six Groups. It undertakes publications, training of teachers, festivals (including International Folk Dance Festivals in London), vacation courses, broadcasting, examinations, etc.

ENGLISH SINGERS. See *Madrigal* 8 (end).

ENGLISH SUITES (Bach). See *Nicknamed* 2.

ENGRAMELLE, M. D. J. See *Mechanical Reproduction* 6.

ENGRAVING OF MUSIC. See *Printing of Music* 3.

ENHARMONIC INTERVALS. The term derives from the name of an ancient Greek theoretical system which admitted the existence of smaller intervals than the semitone (see *Intervals*).

It is chiefly used today in speaking of such intervals as that from A sharp to B flat, C to B sharp, etc. There is a difference of pitch involved here; it cannot be represented in keyboard performance and is microscopic (even if and when achieved) in performance on stringed instruments (see *Temperament* 10) or by voices. Hence change of key is easily effected by approaching a note or combination of notes in one sense and quitting it in another. For instance, the note F sharp may be considered to have become the note G flat, and so to have taken us into another key. This method of changing key is called Enharmonic Modulation (see *Modulation*).

ENIGMATIC SCALE (*Scala Enigmatica*). See *Scales* 12.

ENIGMA VARIATIONS. See *Elgar*.

ENLEVEZ (Fr.). 'Take up', 'take off' (e.g. pedal or mute).

ENSALADA (literally 'salad'). A kind of Spanish comic choral Quodlibet (q.v.). Flecha (1530–1604) was one of the most famous composers of such things.

ENSEMBLE. French for 'together'. Any combination of two or more performers is an ensemble, but the term is in usage generally limited to one-to-a-part combinations, such as those of chamber music (q.v.). Such a combination produces a 'good ensemble' or 'bad ensemble' in so far as it secures both unanimity and balance of tone, or fails to do so. A 'good ensemble' necessarily implies the subordination of opportunities for individual display; in other words, a 'good ensemble' in music is the same as good 'team work' in games. (Cf. *Accompaniment*.)

A *Morceau d'ensemble* is one in which several of the leading performers (e.g. in an opera) combine.

ENTENDRE (Fr.). 'To hear.' So *Entendu*, *Entendue* (masc., fem.), 'heard'.

ENTFERNT (Ger.). 'Distant' (in reality or effect). So *Entfernung*, 'distance'.

ENTFÜHRUNG AUS DEM SERAIL, DIE. See *Abduction from the Seraglio*.

ENTR'ACTE (Fr.). An interval between the acts of a play, or a piece of music to be then performed.

ENTRADA. The Spanish equivalent of *Entrée* (q.v.).

ENTRAIN (Fr.). 'Vigour', 'dash', 'go'.

ENTRATA (It.). 'Entrance' or 'beginning', hence introduction or prelude. For *Aria d'entrata* see *Aria*. And cf. *Entrée* below.

ENTRECHAT. See *Ballet* 8.

ENTRÉE. This is a seventeenth- and eighteenth-century term, and Rousseau's definitions in his *Dictionary of Music* (1767) may well be accepted:

1. An instrumental piece before a ballet.
2. An act in one of those opera-ballets in which each act is self-contained and devoted to its own subject. (The word in this sense is a corruption of 'entremets', i.e. 'side dishes'—an old title for a sort of masque.)
3. The moment of the opening of any part of a work.

Bach's Suite in A for piano and violin has a movement called 'Entrée'—probably because it is of a march-like character and so resembles the music used before a ballet for the procession on to the stage of the performers.

ENTREMÉS (Spanish). A comic musical intermezzo in a play—from which the term came to be applied to a type of brief humorous independent play.

ENTRÜCKUNG (Ger.). The state of absence, hence of being rapt away—'rapture'.

ENTRY. See *Form* 12.

ENTSCHIEDEN (Ger.). 'Decided', 'resolute'. Or 'decidedly', i.e. considerably.

ENTSCHLOSSEN (Ger.). 'Determined' in style. So *Entschlossenheit*, 'determination'.

ENTUSIASMO (It.). 'Enthusiasm.' So *Entusiastico*, 'enthusiastic'.

ENUNCIATION. See *Form* 7.

ENZINA. See *Spain* 6.

EPHRATA CLOISTER. See *United States of America* 3.

EPIDIAPENTE (Greek). A term used in connexion with canon (q.v.)—'at the fifth'.

EPIGLOTTIS. See *Voice* 21.

ÉPINETTE. See *Harpsichord Family* 8.

EPISODE. See *Form* 9 (episode in rondo), 12 (episode in fugue).

EPISODICAL FORM. Another name for rondo form.

EPISTLE SONATA. See *Sonata* 2.

EPITHALAMIUM. A marriage song. Psalm xlv is one—thought by some to have been written for the marriage of Solomon and by others to have a purely mystical interpretation.

Occasionally the name is given by some composer of organ music to a piece intended for use at weddings.

ÉPONGE, BAGUETTE D' (Fr.). Sponge-headed drum-stick. See *Percussion Family* 2 a.

EQUABILE (It.). 'Equable.'

EQUAL. See *Equal Voices*, below. For Equal Temperament see *Temperament*.

EQUALE (It.; plural *Equali*; but in modern Italian it would be *Eguale, Eguali*). This word means 'equal' (see below), but came in the eighteenth or early nineteenth century to have a special connotation—the short pieces, usually for a quartet of trombones, played in Austria before, in the middle of, and after a funeral. Beethoven composed a set of three such pieces for use in the Cathedral of Linz on All Souls' Day, 1812, and they were played (two of them; and sung to words taken from the Miserere) at his own funeral fifteen years later. It is in connexion with these short works of Beethoven that the word is now generally met with. They have been introduced into Britain, being performed (in their instrumental form) at Gladstone's funeral in Westminster Abbey in 1898.

EQUAL TEMPERAMENT. See *Temperament*.

EQUAL VOICES (It., *Voci eguali*; Lat., *Voces aequales*; Ger., *Gleiche Stimmen*). A choral composition is said to be for 'equal voices' when it is for voices of the same kind, generally for two sopranos, or three sopranos (school music and music for ladies' choirs). In such music, in fairness to the voices of the performers, the parts are usually so arranged that sometimes one voice and sometimes another is at the top.

Occasionally the term is less correctly used as implying 'for children's voices' (unmixed with adults), or 'for women's voices' (unmixed with men's), or 'for men's voices' (unmixed with women's).

ÉQUIVAUT (Fr.). 'Is equivalent to.'

ERARD. See *Pianoforte* 8, 13; *Harp* 1, 2 d.

EREMEEF, IVAN. See *Electric Musical Instruments* 5 b.

ERGRIFFEN (Ger.). 'Gripped', or emotionally moved. So *Ergriffenheit*, 'emotion'.

ERHABEN (Ger.). 'Sublime'; hence *Erhabenheit*, 'sublimity'.

ERKEL, FERENC. See *Hungary*.

ERLANGER, FREDERIC D' (Baron). Born in Paris in 1868 and died in London in 1943. His father was German and his mother American, but he became a naturalized British subject. He composed operas and most other things. His early works appeared under the anagrammatic name 'Frédéric Regnal'.

ERLEICHTERUNG (Ger.). An 'easing', i.e. a simplified version.

ERLÖSCHEND (Ger.). 'Becoming weaker.'

ERMANGELUNG (Ger.). 'Default.'

ERMATTEND, ERMATTET (Ger.). [As if] 'becoming tired out', 'tired out'.

ERNIEDRIGEN (Ger.). 'To lower' (pitch).

ERNST, ERNSTHAFT (Ger.). 'Earnest', 'serious'.

ERNST, HEINRICH WILHELM. Born in Moravia in 1814 and died at Nice in 1865, aged fifty-one. As a young violinist he followed Paganini from town to town in the effort to capture his secret, and in later life he rivalled his idol in the scope and triumph of his virtuoso tours (see p. 797, pl. **136**. 8). He composed for his instrument, and some of his works are still in use by violin students and are occasionally heard in public. A famous *Carnival of Venice* is his; it is modelled on that of his idol, Paganini.

EROICA SYMPHONY (Beethoven). See *Nick-named Compositions* 3.

EROICO, EROICA (It.; masc., fem.). 'Heroic.'

EROTIKON (Greek). A 'love-song'.

ERSATZ (Ger.). 'Substitute' (noun).

ERSCHÜTTERT (Ger.). 'Shaken', i.e. agitated.

ERSKINE, JOHN. See under *United States* 5.

ERST, ERSTE (Ger.; masc., fem.). 'First' (with various terminations for grammatical cases—*em, en, er, es*).

ERSTERBEND (Ger.). 'Dying away.'

ERSTICKT (Ger.). 'Suffocated', 'stifled'.

ERWEITERT (Ger.). 'Widened', 'broadened' (i.e. slower and with steadiness).

ERZÄHLER. See *Organ* 14 III.

ERZÜRNT (Ger.). 'Irritated.'

ES. German for E flat (see Table 7). Also the pronoun 'it'.

ESALTATO (It.). 'Excited', 'exalted'.

ESATTO, ESATTA (It.; masc., fem.). 'Exact.' So *Esattezza*, 'exactness'.

ESCALADE. See *God save the Queen* 2.

ESCAPEMENT. See *Pianoforte* 2.

ESCAPE TONE. See *Changing Note*.

ESCHALLOT. See *Organ* 2 a.

ESECUZIONE (It.). 'Execution.'

ESERCIZIO, ESERCIZI (It.). 'Exercise', 'exercises'.

ESES. German for 'E double flat' (see Table 7).

ESIPOFF. See *Strelezki*.

ESLAVA, MIGUEL HILARION (1807–78). See *Spain* 7.

ESMERALDA. See *Thomas, A. G.*

ESOTICO, ESOTICA (It.; masc., fem.). 'Exotic.'

ESPAGNE (Fr.). 'Spain'; for *Folies d'Espagne* see *Folia*.

ESPAGNOL, ESPAGNOLE (Fr.; masc., fem.). 'Spanish.'

ESPAGNOLO or **ESPAGNUOLO, ESPAGNOLA** or **ESPAGNUOLA** (It.; masc., fem.). 'Spanish.'

ESPAÑOLA. See *Danza española*.

ESPIRANDO (It.). 'Expiring', 'dying away'.

ESPLA, OSCAR. Born at Alicante in 1886 and died in Madrid in 1976, aged ninety-six. His music shows the influence of his study of the native folk music of eastern Spain, and adopts, as tonal basis, a scale of his own fashioning (C, D flat, E flat and natural, F, G flat, A flat, B flat—and so at other pitches).

Amongst his compositions are an opera, *The Sleeping Beauty*, symphonic poems, an orchestral suite, chamber and piano music. He also wrote several books on musical subjects.

ESPOSITO, MICHELE (1855–1929). See *Ireland* 6.

ESPRESSIONE (It.). 'Expression.'

ESPRESSIVO (It.). 'Expressively.'

ESQUISSE (Fr.). 'Sketch' (q.v.).

ESSAY ON THE PLAIN CHANT (1782). See *Adeste Fideles*.

ESSENTIAL NOTE. An actual note of a chord, as distinct from a Passing Note, Suspension, Appoggiatura, etc. These latter are 'Unessential Notes'.

ESSER, HEINRICH (1818–72). Conductor of opera (Vienna) and composer. See reference under *Arrangement*.

ESSEX, CLIFFORD. See *Negro Minstrels*.

EST.

(1) THOMAS. See *Este*.

(2) MICHAEL. See *Este*.

(3) JOHN. See *Barber Shop Music*.

ESTAMPIE (Fr.) or **ESTAMPIDA** (Provençal). A type of tune for dancing (with or without words—more properly, perhaps, without). Each phrase (*punctum*) has a first ending (*ouvert*) and a second ending (*clos*). It belonged to the life of southern Europe in the thirteenth and fourteenth centuries, and was, apparently, one of the forms associated with the art of the Troubadours. Boccaccio calls it *stampita*.

ESTE, or **EASTE**, or **EAST**, or **EST**.

(1) THOMAS, born about 1540 and died in London about 1608, was one of the greatest music publishers who ever lived, issuing the works of nearly all the Elizabethan madrigal composers, as well as books of metrical psalm tunes and other lesser things (p. 849, pl. **144.** 2).

See *Hymns* 5, 17 e (x); *Publishing of Music* 4.

(2) MICHAEL, born about 1580 and died about 1648, aged about sixty-eight, is thought to have been the son of Thomas. He was organist of Lichfield Cathedral and composed madrigals, anthems, and fancies for viols.

See *Chamber Music* 3 (end).

ESTERHÁZY. See *Haydn*; *Hummel*; *Liszt*.

ESTEY ORGAN. See *Reed-Organ Family* 8.

ESTINGUENDO (It.). 'Extinguishing', i.e. 'dying away'.

ESTINTO (It.). 'Extinct', i.e. as soft as possible.

ESTOMPÉ (Fr.). 'Toned-down.'

ESTONIA. See reference under *Scandinavia* 6 (end).

ESTRANGE, ROGER L'. See *Puritanism* 4; *Clubs*.

ESTRAVAGANZA (It.). 'Extravagance'—i.e. a composition of an extremely erratic type. Cf. *Extravaganza*.

ESTREMAMENTE (It.). 'Extremely.'

ESTRIBILLO (Sp.). A choral movement appearing at the beginning and end of a *Villancico* (q.v.).

ESTUDIANTINO, ESTUDIANTINA (Sp., masc., fem.). 'In the spirit or style of a party of students.' The latter word is also a substantive, meaning either (*a*) a party of student instrumentalists, such as are accustomed to roam the streets, or (*b*) a piece of music such as they play.

ESULTAZIONE (It.). 'Exultation.'

ET (Fr., Lat.). 'And.'

ÉTEINDRE (Fr.). 'To extinguish.' So *Éteint*, 'extinguished'.

ÉTENDUE (Fr.). 'Extent', compass, range.

ETERNE REX ALTISSIME. See *O Salutaris Hostia* ('Eterne' is a medieval spelling now replaced by 'Aeterne'.)

ETHNOMUSICOLOGY. See *Musicology*.

ET INCARNATUS EST. See *Mass* 3 c.

ET IN SPIRITUM SANCTUM. See *Mass* 3 c.

ET IN UNUM DOMINUM. See *Mass* 3 c.

ETON. See *Eton College Choirbook*. Musicians connected with the college who receive notice are: *T. A. Arne*; *Barnby*; *Ley*; *C. H. Lloyd*; *C. D. Maclean*; *J. Mundy*; *C. H. H. Parry*; *B. Rogers*; *Weldon*.

ETON COLLEGE CHOIRBOOK (Eton MS. 178). Eton College (Windsor. One of the leading 'Public Schools' of England) was founded in 1440 by Henry VI. Its constitution included provision for a professional choir (ten men and sixteen boys) for the conduct of the daily chapel services. The Choirbook (a parchment volume large enough for the whole choir, standing round a desk, to read from it) dates from the time of Henry VII (reigned 1485–1509). Its index shows that it originally contained ninety-three works by twenty-six composers, but missing pages account for thirty-seven of these. Some of the music remaining is by composers otherwise unknown and much of it is extremely beautiful and of interest as illustrating the technique of the pre-Elizabethan period. It is still kept in the College. The contents were described by W. Barclay Squire (q.v.) in *Archaeologia* in 1898, it is fully described in Vol. 3 of the *New Oxford History of Music*, and it has been printed in the series *Musica Britannica* edited by Frank Ll. Harrison (1956–8).

Cf. *Old Hall Manuscript*.

ÉTOUFFER (Fr.). To 'damp', 'stifle' (with violin-mute, piano-pedal, etc.). The imperative is *Étouffez*, the past participle *Étouffé*. So *Étouffoir*, 'damper' (piano).

ET RESURREXIT. See *Mass* 3 c.

ÉTUDE (Fr., 'study'). (1) Any composition intended as a basis for the improvement of the performer may be so entitled. Under its Italian form *Studio* the word is, in this sense, found a few times in the harpsichord work of Domenico Scarlatti (1685–1757) and one or two of his contemporary countrymen. (The English word 'lesson', at the same period, suggests a similar purpose, but its actual meaning is different. See *Suite* 1.)

With the development of the new piano technique in the early nineteenth century, a great many books of études came into existence, though the term was by no means always applied to them by their composers, whatever later publishers may have done. The special mark of such a piece is the restriction of its thematic material to some one type of passage, or to some one *motif*, out of which the whole piece grows; thus a particular technical difficulty, in varying forms, is presented throughout, and a book of études, composed as a unit by some one composer, would pass various branches of technique in review—with a measure of completeness. Such books are extremely numerous (for piano, Czerny, Cramer, Bertini, Moscheles, etc., and for violin, Kreutzer, Rode, etc.).

This type of thing was carried into the realm of poetry by Chopin, in his op. 10 and op. 25 for piano, and so there came into existence what we may call the Concert Étude. (The title

Étude de concert is sometimes seen.) Debussy has written very beautiful études of this character.

The *Études d'exécution transcendante* of Liszt are Concert Etudes of immense difficulty and high romantic quality.

(2) See *Journals*.

ETWAS (Ger.). 'Some', 'something', 'somewhat'.

EUCHORICS. The name given in Britain (apparently from the early 1930s) to the art of verse-speaking in chorus, an art successfully practised in various countries.

EULENBURG. A firm of Leipzig music publishers founded in 1874 by the musician Ernst Eulenburg (1847–1926). In 1892 it took over from Albert Payne (q.v.) his catalogue of miniature scores of chamber music, and later Donajowski's catalogue of orchestral scores, both of which it greatly developed. By 1965 it included over 1,000 titles.

EULENSTEIN, CHARLES (1802–90). He was a great German virtuoso of the Jew's Harp and as such travelled extensively, living for many years in Scotland, London, and Bath. An interesting youthful biography of him was published in London in 1833.

See reference under *Jew's Harp*.

EUNUCH FLUTE (*Flûte eunuque*). See *Mirliton*.

EUPHONION (Ger.), **EUPHONIUM** (Eng.). See *Tuba Group* 3 a.

EURHYTHMICS. See *Jaques-Dalcroze*. Also *Eurhythmy* below.

EURHYTHMY (*Eu* = Greek 'good', 'well'). This is a branch of the activities of the followers of the German philosopher and apostle of 'Anthroposophy', Rudolf Steiner (1861–1925). It was spoken of as a 'new art' seeking to represent 'the inner movement of the spoken word (or of some piece of music) through the medium of the whole body', but did not appear to go essentially beyond what had previously been done in the modern manifestations of the ballet and in the more advanced stages of training in Dalcroze Eurhythmics (see *Jaques-Dalcroze*).

Such words as *Eurhythm*, *Eurhythmy*, *Eurhythmics* have also been applied to other systems aiming at a perfect harmonization of mental conception and bodily actions.

EUROPEAN ASSOCIATION OF MUSIC FESTIVALS. See *Festivals* 3.

'EURIDICE.' See *Harmony* 9.

EUSTACHIAN TUBE. See *Ear and Hearing* 1, 5; *Voice* 21.

EUTERPION. See *Mechanical Reproduction of Music* 11.

EVADED CADENCE. See *Cadence*.

EVANGELICAL MOVEMENT. See *Hymns and Hymn Tunes* 6; *Puritans* 9.

EVANS.

(1) DAVID. Born at Resolven, Glam., in 1874 and died at Rhos, Denbigh, in 1948. He was

See the entries under the individual names

1. SIR W. STERNDALE BENNETT (1816–75)
By Millais

2. SIR HUBERT PARRY (1848–1918). By Rothenstein

3. DAME ETHEL SMYTH (1858–1944)

4. SIR GRANVILLE BANTOCK (1868–1946)

5. FREDERICK DELIUS (1862–1934)

6. R. VAUGHAN WILLIAMS, O.M. (1872–1958)

See also Plate 51, facing page 289, as also the plates following the present one

1. ERNEST WALKER (1870–1949)

2. GUSTAV HOLST (1874–1934)

3. SIR DONALD TOVEY (1875–1940)

4. ROGER QUILTER (1877–1953)

5. COLERIDGE-TAYLOR
(1875–1912)

6. RUTLAND BOUGHTON
(1878–1960)

7. JOHN IRELAND (1879–1962)

educated at University College, Cardiff (of which he was Professor of Music 1908–39).

He was editor of the journal *Y Cerddor* ('The Musician') from 1916 to 1921 and musical editor of *The Revised Church Hymnary* and *Llyfr Emynau a Thonau* ('Book of Hymns and Tunes').

He wrote a number of Welsh works, including *Deffro! Mae'n ddydd* ('Wake! It is day'), and *Alcestis* for choir and string orchestra.

(2) DAVID EMLYN. Born at Newcastle Emlyn, Wales, in 1843 and died in London in 1913, aged sixty-nine. He was a composer of church and other choral music, and a great worker for the music of his native land, taking a leading part in various Eisteddfod activities, editing (with David Jenkins, q.v.) the periodical *Y Cerddor* ('The Musician'), compiling a biographical dictionary of Welsh musicians, and collecting and publishing a collection of Welsh folk tunes.

(3) EDWIN (1874–1945). Well-known London music critic, with a special interest and activity in everything concerning modern developments, and President of the International Society for Contemporary Music.

See brief quotations under *Melody* 7; *Libraries*.

EVANS'S SUPPER AND MUSIC ROOMS. See *Annotated Programmes* 4; *Music Hall* 2.

EVE, ALPHONSE D' (1662–1727). See *Misattributed* (Arne).

ÉVEILLÉ (Fr.) 'Awakened.'

EVELYN, JOHN (1620–1706). The diarist. See *Cornett and Key Bugle Families* 3; *Holland* 3; *Cooke, Henry*; *Matteis*; *Music Hall* 1.

EVENING HYMN. See *Tallis's Canon.*

EVENSONG. This is the name given in the First Prayer Book (see *Common Prayer*) to the Anglican service of Evening Prayer; its basis is the ancient Office of Vespers (q.v.) and Compline (q.v.). In the Roman Catholic Church the name was formerly a synonym for Vespers.

EVESHAM, WALTER DE. See *Odington.*

EVIRATO (It.). 'Unmanned', i.e. a vocalist castrato, singing (as the result of that surgical operation) soprano or alto, when otherwise he would be singing tenor or bass (see *Voice* 5).

EVOCACIÓN (Sp.). 'Evocation', 'invocation'.

EVOVAE or **EUOUAE.** This 'word' consists of the vowels of 'seculorum, Amen', being the last words of the Gloria Patri (see *Doxology*), and so it is used as a name for the cadential endings of the Gregorian Psalm tones. These letters are, indeed, often placed under the notes of the plainsong as an abbreviation of the words they represent.

Cf. *Aevia.*

EXACTEMENT (Fr.). 'Exactly.'

EXALTÉ (Fr.). 'Exalted', 'very excited'.

EXAMINATIONS. See *Education and Music* 2; *Degrees and Diplomas.*

EXERCISE. (1) An instrumental passage purely for technical practice and with little or no artistic interest. (2) In the eighteenth century, a keyboard suite. (3) For the word in its university sense see *Degrees and Diplomas* 1.

EXETER. See passing references under *Minstrels* 3; *Inns*; *Cathedral Music* 2; *Locke.*

Organists of the Cathedral who receive notice in this volume are (with their dates of office): *Edward Gibbons* (Priest-Vicar 1609–44, and probably, in part, organist); *W. Jackson* (1777–1803); *S. S. Wesley* (1835–42); *Bullock* (1919–28).

EXETER HALL, LONDON. See *Concert* 8.

EXIMENO Y PUJADER, ANTONIO (1729–1808). See *Spain* 9.

EXPERT, HENRY. Born at Bordeaux in 1863 and died in 1952, aged eighty-nine. He was a very eminent musicologist, untiring in deciphering, copying, publishing, and performing the music of the French composers of the sixteenth century.

EXPOSITION. See *Form* 7, 12.

EXPRESSIF (Fr.). 'Expressive.'

EXPRESSION

1. The Seventeenth-century Introduction of Terms of Expression.
2. The Modern Tendency to Excess of Marking.
3. Tempo, Phrasing, Accent, Rubato, Bowing, etc.
4. Some Broader Principles.
5. Was Old-time Performance 'Expressive'?
6. A Modern Reaction.

Expression in performance is, we might almost say, the name for that part of the music which the composer was not able to commit to writing and which the performer must therefore supply out of his own musical sense and his emotion.

1. The Seventeenth-century Introduction of Terms of Expression. At one time no composer thought it his duty to try to supply more than the mere notes. Then from the seventeenth century onwards the custom grew up of giving a little guidance towards the broad lines of performance by marking indications of speed and force. It was in Italy that this practice began (e.g. D. Mazzocchi, in 1638, published a book of madrigals using the signs *f*, *p*,

etc.), and as Italian music was then very widely circulated the Italian words and signs used became universally known and acquired the character of conventional technical indications. We find Purcell, in 1683, in an address to what he calls the 'Ingenuous Reader', prefixed to his sonatas for 2 violins, cello, and harpsichord, saying:

'It remains only that the English Practitioner be enform'd, that he will find a few terms of Art perhaps unusual to him, the chief of which are these following: *Adagio* and *Grave*, which import nothing but a very slow movement [i.e. speed]: *Presto Largo* [sic], *Poco Largo*, or *Largo* by itself, a middle movement: *Allegro*, and *Vivace*, a very brisk, swift or fast movement: *Piano*, soft.'

Geminiani (q.v.) is said to have been the

earliest to use the conventional wedge-shaped signs to indicate *crescendo* and *diminuendo* (*Prime Sonate*, 1739).

Handel and other eighteenth-century composers as a rule used terms and marks of expression only where a real doubt was possible as to their intentions. The contemporary Couperin, however, used a series of very significant adjectives in his native French; Telemann (1681–1767) introduced terms of expression in German and French, and other composers at times did the same.

expressive performance and before going further the reader of the present article should carefully read the separate articles devoted to these subjects, as also that under the heading *Agogic*.

4. Some Broader Principles. Some of the broader principles of expression are:

(*a*) Curves, not straight lines, i.e. in dynamics, have always some *crescendo* or *diminuendo* in progress, never a dead level, and in rhythm always some (slighter or greater) hastening or

(8) Quinta vox. (Soprano II). (6²)
CODA.
(6²)

Since Schumann, the practice of the composer using his own language has become very common. It springs partly from the modern wish (born of the Romantic Movement and the more 'dramatic' attitude of composers) to enter into greater detail than the mere use of the few accepted Italian terms would allow, but the result is that (to take an example) if one does not understand French pretty thoroughly one cannot understand just what Debussy wants one to do. Amongst recent composers Percy Grainger was singular in the colloquialism of his directions—such as 'louden lots', an expression that might puzzle a French or German pianist.

2. The Modern Tendency to Excess of Marking. Much modern music (and old music re-edited—see the extract here given from a Bach edition by Riemann) is over-marked, leaving the performer little latitude for the expression of the music as *he* feels it.

An excessive array of marks tends to defeat itself and is best looked on by the performer as a record of the composer's (or editor's) suggestions, offered to him with a reasonable measure of take-it-or-leave-it. (Some composers will, of course, object to this, e.g. Florent Schmitt, with his dictatorial and reiterated 'On observera rigoureusement les nuances indiquées'.) Strongly constructed, vital music will, indeed, bear several 'interpretations', and there have been many instances where a composer has thanked a performer or conductor for showing him a better way of bringing out his 'meaning' than he had himself discovered. Chopin's marks of expression are decidedly not sacred, for it is on record that when asked to repeat a piece he almost invariably did so with very marked changes of nuance.

3. Tempo, Phrasing, Accent, Rubato, Bowing, etc. are all important elements in

lingering, never a perfect clock-tick. (Naturally it takes musicianship to apply this precept, nothing being gained by *arbitrary* changes.)

(*b*) Always 'go somewhere', i.e. the sense of progression must be well felt in the performer's mind, and hence conveyed to that of the listener —moving towards a greater or lesser climax.

The observance of these two maxims alone (if such observance springs from feeling and is not a mere obedience to rule) will give 'life' to a performance.

5. Was Old-time Performance 'Expressive'? To any one who has studied the history of musical performance it is an interesting question how much 'expression' was possible or likely under the conditions at various periods.

When we consider the almost chance collection of vocalists and instrumentalists under Bach's direction at Leipzig it seems incredible that, whatever his inspiring power as director, he could on most occasions get much beyond the bare notes.

In reading Mozart's letters we find him sometimes performing a concerto or other elaborate composition (e.g. the Overture to *Don Giovanni*) without even a single rehearsal. It would seem as though up to the latter part of the eighteenth century musical conditions in the great centres of Europe were what some of us today have at one time known them in certain remote parts of Britain and America, where a keen appreciation of good music was linked with a lack of any demand for refinement in performance.

The very methods of conducting (q.v.), up to the beginning of the nineteenth century, must have been against any high degree of polish in concerted performance and any 'expression' must have been of a very general character. It was only gradually that the idea of crescendo and diminuendo in orchestral performance replaced the older idea of a mere 'echo' between loud and soft. The example of Johann Stamitz at Mannheim in the mid-eighteenth century, the teaching of Berlioz in the earlier nineteenth century, and the example of Wagner and von Bülow in the later nineteenth century are amongst a number of successive stimuli that have led to the present high standard.

It seems impossible to avoid the conclusion that there have until quite recent times been two standards—one for solo performance or performance by small groups, and another for performance by large groups. We know that Bach's preference for the clavichord (q.v.) over the harpsichord (q.v.) was due to a desire for complete control, and that the piano, when it had been brought to a degree of perfection, was valued by musicians as offering advantages similar to those of the clavichord—which shows a recognition of the beauty of delicate phrasing and graded crescendos and diminuendos, fine accentuation, and other expressive qualities. Bach's and Mozart's playing of keyboard instruments (even the clumsy organ of their days, which had no swell pedal) was reckoned to be movingly expressive, and we must therefore credit their playing with a perfection of phrasing and nuance far beyond that then attainable in orchestral performance.

Bach and Handel, on the one hand, and Haydn and Mozart, on the other, mark as composers the transition from music laid out on broad lines to the music of detail—the change, for instance, from simple binary form to the dramatic compound binary ('Sonata' or 'First Movement') form, from the type of composition which treated merely one theme and that which placed two themes in contrast, reached strong climax, and even attempted surprise (see *Form* 5 and 7).

In passing from one style to the other, music necessarily began to demand a new kind of expressiveness in interpretation. All the old expressive qualities of phrasing, accent, rubato, etc., were required, and, in addition, the

stronger rhetoric called for a greater and more 'quick-change' variety of tones of voice.

When, with the full tide of the Romantic Movement of the nineteenth century (see *Romantic*), to the free play of the most contrasted human emotions was added the emulation of the qualities of literature and painting in the attempt of Programme Music (q.v.) to tell a story or paint a picture, the demand for that more modern type of 'expression' in performance naturally became still more insistent.

Our idea of expression today is, then, somewhat fuller than that of our ancestors. It has been suggested that we now play Bach with an emotional type of expressiveness that would have been repugnant to him. Do we sing the madrigals of a century earlier than Bach in a style that their composers would have thought both sentimental and finicking? Who can say?

6. A Modern Reaction. Perhaps our whole idea of expression today is over-coloured by the influences of the Romantic period, and in reaction certain composers have written works that they have begged may not be performed 'expressively'. The curious incident is recorded of Stravinsky, present at the first London performance of his 'Symphonies of Wind Instruments', writing to a newspaper to complain that it had been played 'expressively', and of Koussevitzky, as the conductor of the occasion, writing in turn to say that, so far from playing expressively, his performers having received the parts only just before the concert, had all their work cut out to play the mere notes.

Putting together the complaint of the above composer and the statement of the conductor it would seem that nowadays so ingrained is the romantic type of 'expression' as a part of the orchestral performer's technique that adequate rehearsal is needed when one wishes to dispense with it.

For a treatment of cognate subjects see the following articles:
  (a) *Interpretation*; *Rhythm*; *Tempo*; *Rubato*; *Agogic*; *Atempause*; *Attack*; *Conducting*.
  (b) *Ornaments or 'Graces'*; *Mordent*; *Shake*.
  (c) *Singing*; *Tremolo and Vibrato*; *Messa di Voce*.
  (d) For 'Expression Stop' see *Reed-Organ Family* 6.

EXPRESSIONISM. This term, applied to the music of certain twentieth-century composers, is borrowed from the vocabulary of a group of painters who first began to come into notice about 1912. It implies an antithesis to 'Impressionism', but in doing so introduces an unfortunate confusion.

What the word 'Impressionism' is generally understood to mean is explained in the present book under its own head, but the sense in which it is implied here is much wider. In that sense 'Impressionism' in painting covers all that large class of picture which records any kind of impression received from without—every kind of 'Realism' (in the widest sense), or, better, of 'Representationism'. Expressionism in painting, on the other hand, is supposed to record merely the 'inner experiences' of the artist. Whether such 'inner experiences' can

be recorded in line and colour is a question beyond the scope of the present book; that is, at any rate, what expressionistic painting is supposed to do, and expressionistic sculpture, poetry, and music are supposed to do the same thing.

A notable exponent of Expressionism in painting was the Russian Kandinsky (1866–1944; see examples of his work at p. 356, pl. 57. 1, 2); another exponent in painting was his friend Schönberg (see examples on same plate), who was also the chief exponent of Expressionism in music. To quote the Brockhaus *Lexikon*:

'In music Expressionism is especially led by A. Schönberg, who in his composition and manner of instrumentation *casts off all rules, thereby to win a complete freedom for his musical expression*. Schreker and his school also follow this direction.'

The words italicized above seem to indicate that the 'casting off of rules' by the expressionistic composer is regarded as the equivalent of the abandonment of the representation of objects of any kind by the expressionistic painter. The parallel here is not very evident. The copying of the forms and colours of nature and the observance of musical conventions may both, it is true, be regarded as types of 'objectivity', yet the chief literary exponent of Expressionism, Hermann Bahr (1863–1934), has himself admitted 'I never feel quite comfortable when Expressionists begin to theorize; they are fond of speaking in a fog'—and perhaps they are doing so here.

Inasmuch as instrumental music has always been (and from its nature *must be*) an art in which emotion is 'delivered direct from the manufacturer to the consumer' (i.e. without the 'representation' of objects as in painting and sculpture, or of ideas, as in literature), instrumental music would seem to be necessarily an expressionistic art in the sense in which Kandinsky's painting is intended to be expressionistic—with the exception of the comparatively rare instances in which composers attempt to imitate the sounds of nature or of human life (see *Programme Music*). And if the casting aside of 'rules' be the criterion of expressionism in music we can hardly feel it to be met in some of the music of Schönberg—as, for instance, in that movement of his *Pierrot Lunaire* which runs to its middle point as a canon two-in-one (see *Canon*) and thence to the end simply reverses, until with its last chord it arrives again at its first one.

To the present writer (and this is a subject upon which opinions must be personal—even in a work of reference) Expressionism in music, judged by its products, is just an advanced phase of Romanticism in music (see *Romantic*). The art of Beethoven, for example, went beyond that of Mozart in laying weight rather on emotion than on beauty as such; the art of Wagner often went further still in this direction; and the art of some twentieth-century composers, casting aside all remaining reticences, carries the process to perhaps the furthest point attainable. In other words, the objective element and the subjective are at the opposite ends of a see-saw, and with these composers the subjective heavily outweighs the objective. The music of the composers who call themselves Expressionists is, then, looked at in this way, simply 'ultra-emotional'.

It does not cast off rules any more than does that of contemporary composers who are not regarded as Expressionist (e.g. Stravinsky).

And for some strange reason it does *not* seek the obvious parallel with Expressionism in painting in the abandonment of 'impressions of the outer world', since more than half of Schönberg's opus numbers consist of settings (or groups of settings) of poems or other literary matter.

All matters considered, then, the label 'Expressionists', as applied to musical composers, seems to be almost meaningless—and, indeed, perhaps a mere piece of self-delusion or affectation on the part of those making use of it.

EXPRESSION STOP. See *Reed-Organ Family* 6.

EXPRESSIVE INTONATION. See *Temperament* 10.

EXTEMPORIZATION. See *Improvisation*; *Jazz* 3; *Metamorphosis of Themes*.

EXTENDED MORDENT. See *Mordent*.

EXTENSION ORGAN. See *Organ* 6.

EXTRANEOUS MODULATION. See *Modulation*.

EXTRAVAGANZA. The term is often applied to musical works which embody the spirit of grotesquerie or caricature. Thus the Gilbert and Sullivan *Trial by Jury* bears the word on its title-page—as all the Gilbert and Sullivan operas could, except perhaps *The Yeomen of the Guard*. (Cf. *Estravaganza*.)

EXTRÊMEMENT (Fr.). 'Extremely.'

EZCUDANTZA. A Basque festival dance, for two performers with accompaniment of guitar or bandurría, and sometimes of voice.

F

FA. The fourth degree of any major scale according to the system of vocal syllables derived from Guido d'Arezzo (see *Guido*), and so used (spelt *Fah*) in Tonic Sol-fa (q.v.). Also in that system the sixth degree in the minor scale (see *Tonic Sol-fa* 8). In French and Italian usage, however, the name has (on 'fixed-doh' principles) become attached to the note F, in whatever scale or other association this may occur. (See Table 5.)

For still another use of 'Fa' see *Lancashire Sol-fa*.

FABER.

(1) J. A. J. See *Clarinet Family* 2.

(2) FREDERICK WILLIAM. See *Hymns and Hymn Tunes* 6; also p. 485, pl. 86. 7.

FABURDEN (Eng.), **FAUXBOURDON** (Fr.), **FALSOBORDONE** (It.). The word has several applications at different periods and is thus often a source of trouble to readers.

1. In the first use of the word it is nearly synonymous with one of the earlier senses of gymel (q.v.), i.e. it implies an easy-going sort of choral harmonization of a plainsong melody by accompanying it, in two parallel added parts, by rows of thirds and sixths (together)—a string of chords all in their 'first inversion'.

If, as is believed by some, this practice was introduced at a period (tenth and eleventh centuries) when the usual accompaniment was one of little more than bare fifths or fourths with octaves (see *Harmony* 4, 5), it marked a growth of the harmonic sense. The date of the beginning of the practice is, however, debatable; in manuscript it is found only at the end of the thirteenth century and beginning of the fourteenth.

The introduction of this style of composition is, by many of the highest continental authorities, credited to England, whilst, paradoxically, some of the highest British authorities contest this.

2. By a natural extension the term was, from about the time of Dufay (fifteenth century) onwards, applied to simple harmonization which (like the true faburden) moved note-for-note with the canto fermo. Apparently the term is restricted, however, to passages of such harmonization interpolated amongst unison singing of plainsong, as, often, in the psalms. It would seem to be in this sense that Pius X used the term in his famous *Motu Proprio* (q.v.) of 1903: 'It will be lawful on solemn occasions to alternate the Gregorian chant with the so-called *falso-bordoni*, or with verses similarly composed in a proper manner.'

Some writers seem to classify faburden of this type as 'strict' or 'free' according as it does or does not comprise the plainsong in one of its voice-parts. The faburden interpolation may then be musically the same every time it appears, or it may be quite different according to the changed sentiment of the words (Allegri's *Miserere* and Anerio's *Te Deum* are familiar examples of the latter type).

3. The name came to be given also to a sort of chanting in which the whole of a phrase was declaimed on one chord except that the cadences were harmonized, the music being the same for every verse of a psalm or other passage so treated (there is a clear resemblance here to the principle of the Anglican chant, q.v.).

4. The name was, further, sometimes applied to any sort of monotoning.

5. And to a drone bass, such as that of a bagpipe. (Allied with this is the use of the word 'bourdon' by the French as the name for the bumble-bee, and the use of the word 'fauxbourdon' for the idler-male which we call 'drone'.)

6. And in sixteenth- and seventeenth-century English usage, to the tenor part of a metrical psalm tune or the like, which part at that period commonly carried the melody.

7. And to any metrical psalm tune (as a whole) that was harmonized in the single-note-against-note style, i.e. the voices all moving at equal pace (cf. 2 above).

8. And to a refrain to the verses of a song.

9. And nowadays the word is in common use as describing means of giving interest to hymn-singing by supplying some of the choir sopranos with a freely-written part, which often soars above the hymn-tune as sung by the congregation (see also *Descant* 2; *Hymns and Hymn Tunes* 16); in the choir's copies the actual hymn tune may be given to the tenors—a manner of setting that was universal in the early days of metrical psalm tunes.

The above attempt to define all the meanings of faburden has not been made without trouble. Treatises and dictionaries in English, French, German, and Italian have been compared; they all give one or more of the above, but their common ground is not extensive; indeed, as concerns the earlier period (referred to in the paragraph numbered 1 above), the statements even of the best students of the music of the earlier faburden period are extremely contradictory, and, as they are, in essentials, supported by the quotation of equally contradictory musical examples of the fourteenth and fifteenth centuries (some showing the plainsong as normally in the bottom part, some as in the middle part, and some as in the top part—to give one illustration of the diversity), each seems very convincing until the next one is read. The wish in the present brief statement has been as far as possible to omit mention of inessential details upon which the authorities seriously differ and to supply a general description from which most of the authorities would not dissent.

Of the name in its various languages the French form 'Fauxbourdon' is supposed to be the earliest, the English being an anglicization of it and the Italian a translation. The explanation of the genesis of the early faburden (confidently offered by some and tentatively accepted or definitely scouted by others) is as follows:

In 1322 Pope John XXII (at Avignon), scandalized at the growing decorativeness of church music, issued a decree (for the actual text see the *Oxford History of Music*, 2nd edition, vol. i) reducing such music to the ancient unison but allowing ('especially upon Feast days', etc.) the use of some consonant intervals, for example the octave, fifth, and fourth. In other words he insisted on a return to the tenth- and eleventh-century parallel organum (see *Harmony* 4).

The plainchant was thereupon, by cunning choirmasters, written out in three parallel lines—the outer a fifth apart, with a harmless-looking middle line a third from each of the outer parts (which of these was the actual plainsong is one of the points of difference in the accounts). This pretty nearly conformed to regulations (anyhow, parallel fifths were present throughout), but high voices, presumably boys', being allotted to the lowest part, it was thus automatically transposed an octave.

The intervals now became (reckoning from the lowest part as heard) those of the third and sixth. Thus, though the subtleties of the part-writing (which had already become common throughout Europe but was now under condemnation) duly went by the board, the ears of the congregation were at least spared the bareness of the mere 'perfect' intervals, and the Pope's decree was largely circumvented.

The 'falsity' implied by the name is thus explained, since the bass or 'bourdon' was such only on paper. But another explanation is that the plainsong being (according to this theory) in the uppermost part instead of in the lowermost part, where it had formerly often been, the lowermost part was now false in the sense that it did not carry the expected tune.

ARTICLES ON COGNATE SUBJECTS. *History of Music*; *Harmony*; *Counterpoint*; *Descant*; *Gymel*; *Hocket*; *Musica Ficta*; *Anglican Chant* 2.

FACH (Ger.). 'Fold', as *Zweifach* or *2-fach*, 'two-fold'; *Dreifach* or *3-fach*, 'three-fold'; *Vierfach* or *4-fach*, 'four-fold'. The commonest use of these words is in indicating a division of (say) the first violins of an orchestra, but there is an organ application indicating the number of ranks in a mixture stop (see *Organ* 2 c, 14 V).

FACILE (Fr., It.). 'Easy.'

FACILEMENT (Fr.), **FACILMENTE** (It.).

'Easily', i.e. fluently and without an effect of striving.

FACILITÀ (It.). 'Facility', hence ease, fluency; or 'simplification'.

FACKELTANZ. German for torch dance, but really more often a torchlight procession to music. Such processions were from the early nineteenth century carried out at the court of Prussia on the occasion of royal weddings. Up to recent times this dance was restricted to certain of the higher social grades (and marriage between a royal person who belonged to such a grade and one who did not was impossible).

FADING or **FADDING.** An Irish dance mentioned in English literature of the sixteenth and seventeenth centuries.

FADINHO. Much the same as Fado (q.v.).

FADO. A type of popular Portuguese song and dance, with guitar accompaniment, which first (under this name, at all events) made its appearance about 1850. It is in four-in-a-measure time and may be either fast or slow. It is essentially café or tavern entertainment, and as such enjoyed for hours by the lower class of Portuguese—whilst a good deal looked down upon by the more educated classes.

FA FICTUM. The term belongs to the old system of the *Hexachords* (q.v.) and was applied to the note B when flattened, i.e. to the Fa in the 'Soft' Hexachord.

Cf. *Musica Ficta*.

F.A.G.O. See *Degrees and Diplomas* 4.

FAGOTT, FAGOTTO. See *Oboe Family* 5 c; *Organ* 14 VI.

FAH. See *Fa*.

FAHREN (Ger.). 'To go.' So *Fahren sogleich fort*, 'go on at once'.

FAIBLE (Fr.). 'Feeble', weak in tone.

FAIRE (Fr.). 'To do', 'to make'.

FAIRFAX. See *Fayrfax*.

FAIRS AND THEIR MUSIC. (For illustrations see p. 357, pl. 58.) Nowadays it is usually overlooked that the fairs of Europe have played a part in the encouragement of musical pleasure, and hence of musical development.

The fairs of England were for many centuries a most important commercial and social institution. St. Bartholomew Fair, London, was held on the same spot in Smithfield for over 700 years (1133–1855). It used to be opened by the Lord Mayor of London in state. Sturbridge (or Stourbridge) Fair, near Cambridge, had a similar extended existence. It began under a charter of King John in 1211 and came to an end only in 1934. In its palmy days merchants came from all over Europe to attend it and, as Defoe tells us in 1723, it did some hundreds of thousands of pounds of business in a week. It was opened in alternate years by the Mayor of Cambridge and the Vice-Chancellor of the University. Like all the big fairs, it possessed its own court of summary justice (its 'Pie Powder' court). These are examples of the larger fairs; the smaller ones, though more local in their interest, were yet important annual centres of business, social meeting, and amusement.

Music and drama, and sometimes the combination of them in opera, found their place in the fairs. Sturbridge Fair for a long period had a theatre for the legitimate drama (you could see *Hamlet* there, for instance), at which the university dons and the county families did not disdain to reserve places and at which they would occasionally commission performances of plays they wished to see.

Bartholomew Fair performed *The Beggar's Opera* (q.v.) in the very first year of its existence (1728); it was given by 'the Company of Comedians from the Haymarket' and included 'All the Songs and Dances set to Music, as performed at the Theatre in Lincoln's Inn Fields (N.B. There is a commodious passage for the Quality and Coaches through the Half-Moon Inn, and care will be taken that there shall be Lights and People to conduct them to their places)'. *The Beggar's Opera* was by no means the only opera given at this and other fairs, but so far as remaining evidence is available it would appear that opera of its type, i.e. ballad opera (q.v.), was the usual variety presented; for instance, we find Coffey's famous *The Devil to Pay* announced at Southwark Fair in 1731 (again the very year of the first appearance of the work).

The ballet was one of the attractions of the larger fairs. Thus at Bartholomew Fair in the eighteenth century you might see 'A dance between three Bullies and Three Quakers; the Wonder of the Sex, a Young Woman who dances on the Swords and the Ladder with that Variety that she challenges all her Sex to do the like; a Cripples' Dance by six Persons with Wooden Legs and Crutches in Imitation of a Jovial Crew; and a New Entertainment between a Scaramouch, Harlequin and a Punchinelle, in imitation of Bilking a Reckoning'. You could also be entertained at one of the 'Musick Booths' not only with 'a Glass of good Wine, Beer, Mum, Syder and all other sorts of Liquors', but also with 'good Musick, Singing and Dancing' including a 'Sarabande and a Jig and a Young-Woman that dances with Fourteen Glasses on the Backs and Palms of her Hands, and turns round with them above a Hundred Times, as fast as a Wind-mill turning'.

These 'Musick Booths' were a feature of Bartholomew Fair. They had their orchestras, with a considerable variety of stringed and wind instruments, and their singers, solo and choral. Ward (*The London Spy*, 1678 and 1703) tells us that on one side of Bartholomew Fair 'musick houses stood thick by one another'. When Ward went to a theatre booth in the fair he found that it, too, had its orchestra. At another London fair, May Fair, he found much music.

At Bartholomew Fair it was 'the thing' to eat sucking pig and roast pork (Ben Jonson's play named after this fair turns largely on this custom). And it was eaten to music. A broadsheet ballad of 1679 (well after Jonson's day) shows us this custom still maintained. It is called *Roger in Amaze; or the Countryman's Ramble through Bartholomew Fair* (to be sung 'To the tune of the Dutchman's Jig')—

> I thrust, I scrambled,
> Till further I rambled
> Into the Fair,
> Where Trumpets and Bagpipes, Kettledrums and
> Fiddlers all were at work,
> And the Cooks zung, 'Here's your delicate Pig
> and the Pork'.

The English fairs continued on exactly the old lines during the Commonwealth. Anthony Wood, the Oxford antiquarian, tells us how for a 'frolick' he and some other amateur string players in 1654 disguised themselves and played at Faringdon Fair. George Fox, the founder of the Quakers (see *Quakers and Music*), says in his Journal (1649) that he made a practice at this period of attending the fairs 'to preach against all sorts of musick'. The only Puritan suppression was that of the drama (the London theatres being closed), and even so puppet plays were allowed (*Patient Grisel, Fair Rosamund, The History of Susanna* at Bartholomew Fair, as described in a ballad of 1655).

One can get a pretty good idea of the dramatic and musical attractions of an earlier nineteenth-century fair from Dickens's description of Greenwich Fair in *Sketches by Boz*. English country dances (see *Dance* 5) to an orchestral accompaniment were one of the features, also a dozen bands and the famous Richardson's Melodrama which gave you 'three murders, a ghost, a pantomime with a comic song, an overture and some incidental music' all in twenty-five minutes.

It will be seen, then, that the fairs of England were considerable centres of popular musical enjoyment. And there is some evidence that it was the same in other countries. They were also centres for the sale of printed music—to judge from a remark of Burney's in Rees's *Cyclopædia*. Speaking of the activities of the important music publisher Johnson of Cheapside, in the middle of the eighteenth century, he says that he 'attended all the great fairs in the kingdom'.

FAITES (Fr.). 'Do', 'make' (imperative).

FA-LA. Same as ballett (see *Madrigal* 3 c), the refrain or burden being a setting of these syllables.

FALKNER (DONALD) KEITH. Born at Sawston, Cambs., in 1900. After a period in the Navy and training at the R.C.M. he had a distinguished career as a bass singer. From 1950 he was on the staff of Cornell University, and from 1960 to 1974 was director of the Royal College of Music. He was knighted in 1967.

FALL. 'Cadence', cf. Shakespeare: 'That strain again; it had a dying fall.' The word 'cadence' itself has, etymologically, the same idea of a drop.

FALL, FALLE, etc. (Ger.). 'Case', e.g. in the expression *Im Falle*, 'in case'.

FALL, LEO (1878-1925). A popular Austrian composer of operas and operettas. See *Waltz*.

FALLA, MANUEL DE (p. 977, pl. **164**. 8). Born in Cadiz in 1876 and died in Argentina in 1946, aged sixty-nine. He was a pupil of Pedrell (q.v.), the founder of the modern national Spanish school. He won the prize offered for the best national opera, with his *La Vida breve* ('Life is Short'—ironically, it waited eight years for its first performance). For seven or eight years he lived in Paris (as most of the modern Spanish composers have done), where he associated with Debussy, Ravel, and Dukas. The ballet *The Three-Cornered Hat*, performed by the Diaghilef Russian troupe in 1919, had much popularity. Another ballet, *Magician Love* ('El Amor Brujo'), has had success, as have the marionette-opera, *Master Peter's Puppet Show* ('El Retablo de Maese Pedro', a Don Quixote incident) and the three pieces for piano and orchestra, *Nights in the Gardens of Spain* (1916). There are also a Harpsichord Concerto, Four Spanish Pieces for piano, a guitar solo as a tribute to the memory of his friend Debussy (who, though he was never in Spain, had shown his love of its native idiom in several compositions), and some songs.

He was a keen student of native folk song and organized festivals to maintain its cultivation, and in that and in the literary subject-matter and musical idiom of his compositions stood forward as a strong representative of national musical aspiration.

He was not a prolific or fluent writer, and took the greatest care to refine and polish his products before they reached the public. In his Harpsichord Concerto and some other of his later works he used pungent and personal harmonies. His gift for the subtle use of orchestral colour was an outstanding quality.

(To write of 'de Falla', as is frequently done, is incorrect; unless the Christian name precedes, the surname should be given as simply 'Falla'; this is Spanish usage.)

See *Spain* (for general national background); *Opera* 15, 24 f (1961); *Folk Song* 5; *Harp* 4; *Rhythm* 10; *Jota*; *Cante Hondo*; *Impressionism*; *Ballet* 5; *Concerto* 6 c (1876); *Harpsichord* 9.

FALSE ACCENT. Syncopation (q.v.).

FALSE CLOSE. See *Cadence*.

FALSE RELATION. See *Harmony* 24 n.

FALSETTO (It., but now adopted into the English language). The head-voice in adults, an unnatural effect producible by practice (as distinct from the voice of a castrato produced by means of a surgical operation). The male alto sings falsetto. **Falsettist** is a falsetto singer.

See *Voice* 5; *Singing* 3; *Spain* 8 (end).

FALSE VOCAL CORDS. See *Voice* 3.

FALSOBORDONE (It.). Same as English faburden. See *Faburden*; *Anglican Chant* 2, 3, 4.

FALSTAFF (Verdi). Produced at Milan in 1893. Libretto by Boito, adapted from Shakespeare's *The Merry Wives of Windsor* and *Henry IV*.

ACT I

SCENE 1: *A Room at the Garter Inn. Time, the Fifteenth Century*

Sir John Falstaff (*Baritone*), with his disreputable followers **Bardolph** (*Tenor*) and **Pistol** (*Bass*), is accused by **Dr. Caius** (*Tenor*) of having broken into his house and beaten his servants. He gets no satisfaction, and goes off. Falstaff, who is pursuing Mistress Ford and Mistress Page, the Merry Wives, asks his men to take a letter to each of the ladies, but, as they have suddenly become delicately 'honourable', he abuses them and sends the letters by a page boy.

SCENE 2: *Master Ford's Garden*

The two **Ladies** (*Soprano* and *Mezzo-Soprano*), with their crony **Mistress Quickly** (*Mezzo-Soprano*), finding that their letters are identical, resolve to play a trick on Falstaff. The smarting braggarts, Bardolph and Pistol, have betrayed their master to Dr. Caius, to Mistress Ford's jealous **husband** (*Baritone*), and to **Fenton** (*Tenor*), who loves **Anne**, Ford's daughter (*Soprano*). A short love-scene between Anne and Fenton occurs amidst the plotting of Falstaff's downfall.

ACT II

SCENE 1: *The Inn, as in Act I*

Dame Quickly brings Falstaff Mistress Ford's invitation to visit her when her husband is absent.

Ford, under the name of Brook, asks Falstaff to aid him in overcoming Mistress Ford's coldness to lovers. If Falstaff can succeed, 'Brook' may. Falstaff tells him that he already has a rendezvous with the lady. Thus Ford's suspicious jealousy is fed.

SCENE 2: *A Room in Ford's House*

The ladies prepare to fool Falstaff. Anne's father, it appears, wants to marry her to Caius, but her mother is on her (and Fenton's) side. Falstaff comes, all agog for gallantry. He finds Mistress Ford alone (the others being hidden). Mistress Quickly, playing her part, agitatedly runs in to say that Mistress Page is coming: Falstaff must hide behind a screen. Complication!—here comes Ford with a whip. He rages about, tumbles the linen out of its basket, and rushes out to seek Falstaff elsewhere. The fat knight is now hidden in the basket, under the clothes. In comes Ford again, hears a kiss behind the screen, overturns it—and finds Anne with Fenton. This fans his anger. Away he goes again, and the women order their servants to empty the basket into the river.

ACT III

SCENE 1: *A Street outside the Inn. Sunset*

Dame Quickly prevails on Falstaff, now suspicious after his ducking, to come to another meeting with Mistress Ford—at midnight, at Herne's Oak in Windsor Forest, legendary trysting-place of gnomes. Ford, overhearing, with his wife, is now convinced he has no cause for jealousy. He privately whispers to Caius that when the party assembles at the oak, disguised as imps and sprites, he is to find Anne and come with her to Ford, who will bless them as bride and bridegroom.

SCENE 2: *At Herne's Oak. Midnight*

Mistress Ford, to outwit her husband's design for marrying Anne to Caius, tells Fenton to dress as a monk. The other plotters appear, affrightingly disguised, and hide. When Falstaff is enjoying a few moments with Mistress Ford, the revellers spring out and terrify him. Meanwhile Anne and Fenton seek cover. Bardolph has been given the Fairy Queen disguise that Anne was to have worn, and when Ford has ordained the nuptials of 'this rash young couple', the masks are removed; Ford, at first angry at the deception, soon grants forgiveness, and even Falstaff, sore from the elves' pinching, demands 'One rousing song, to end the frolic!'

See also *Form* 12; *Italy* 8; *Opera* 21 l.

FALTIN, F. R. (1835–1918). See *Scandinavia* 6.

FANCY. This is an English term corresponding to the Italian 'fantasia' and used in the late sixteenth century and the seventeenth by the many fine composers of music for groups of viols in England at that period (see *England* 3). The fancy is, then, one of the predecessors of the string trio, quartet, quintet, etc., but the name was restricted to single-movement compositions. There was an obvious relationship to the ricercare (q.v.). The vast repertory of the fancy remains almost entirely in manuscript. Purcell's Fantasias for strings (early works of his, written in 1680, when he was about twenty-two) may be looked upon as the last fancies to be composed.

The title was occasionally used in keyboard music, and also in music for other instruments, e.g. there is one by Hingston for two cornetts (see *Cornett Family*), sackbut, and organ.

Cf. *In Nomine*. For a particular kind of fancy employing both strings and voices see *Street Cries*; for a modern revival of the idea of the fancy in slightly different form see *Phantasy*.

FANDANGO. A lively Spanish dance for a single couple. It is believed by some to be of South American origin and is said to have become popular in the mother country only during the eighteenth century.

It is in three-in-a-measure or six-in-a-measure time. The speed increases as the dance proceeds. A feature is the sudden stop introduced in places, upon the occurrence of which the dancers remain motionless, in the attitude in which it found them, until the music resumes. The castanets are used. Like the seguidilla (q.v.), the fandango has strains sung by the performers; during these the dancing stops. The details differ a good deal in northern and southern Spain.

One of the movements of the *Goyescas* of Granados is in fandango style and rhythm. Mozart has introduced a fandango into *Figaro*. He took it apparently from Gluck's ballet of *Don Juan*; it is an actual Spanish folk-dance melody.

Cf. *Granadina*.

FANDANGUILLA. A sort of fandango.

FANELLI, ERNEST. Born in Paris in 1860 and died there in 1917, aged fifty-seven. He was a music copyist and kettledrummer who, quite unknown to serious circles of the musical world, was busily composing. At fifty-two he first began to hear his works performed (by the Colonne Orchestra), and they caused a sensation—for a time, at any rate.

FANFARE. (1) A flourish of trumpets. The word is so used in both English and French. In Italian the word is *Fanfara*, in German *Tusch*.

(2) In French the word also means a brass band (as distinct from a band of brass and wood, which is 'Harmonie', q.v.).

FANTAISIE (Fr.). A fanciful composition, one not strict as to form, etc. A fantasia (q.v.). See *Suite* 4.

FANTASIA. The word is Italian for 'fancy', and its musical application is to any kind of composition in which form takes second place in deference to the demands of imagination or even of mere wilfulness—or, indeed, to any kind of composition for which no other name happens to occur to the composer.

1. Often the suggestion of a piece so styled is that of extemporization rather than of ordered composition on settled lines: indeed, Rousseau, in his *Dictionary of Music* (1767), actually defines 'Fantaisie' as 'a piece of instrumental music that one performs as one composes it'. And he adds that a 'Fantaisie' can never be written, because 'as soon as it is written or repeated it ceases to be a Fantaisie, and becomes an ordinary piece'. Despite Rousseau, nearly all the great composers before and after his day have left us written fantasias, as, for instance, Bach (some of his organ preludes to fugues are of a very free-ranging character and are called fantasias, and he has, of course, a famous Chromatic Fantasia and Fugue for the domestic keyboard instrument). Mozart, Chopin, Schumann, Brahms, and others have applied the title to pieces in no way specially informal. Beethoven wrote a 'Choral Fantasia'.

2. The title sometimes descends to a lower level, being applied to strings of tunes out of an opera or the like—'Fantasia on *William Tell*', and so on.

3. There is still another use of the word. In sixteenth-century (and earlier) instrumental music it is applied to a composition of a very contrapuntal character—indeed, one of the immediate ancestors of the fugue (see *Form* 14, and compare *Fancy*).

4. The term '**Free Fantasia**' used sometimes to be given to the 'development' section of a movement in 'sonata form' (see *Develop-*

ment), the idea being that, whereas the section before was given to the careful statement of the two subjects of the piece, in keys more or less dictated by intelligent convention, and the section that follows is to be given to the recapitulation of these subjects, again in rather formal style, the middle or 'development' section roves freely through any keys, evolving itself out of fragments of one or both of the subjects, treated in a way somewhat like that of competent extemporization on a theme or themes.

For 'Fantasia Ricercata' see *Ricercare*.

FANTASIESTÜCK. See under *Phantasie*.

FANTASTICO (It.), **FANTASQUE** (Fr.), **FANTASTISCH** (Ger.). 'Fantastic', 'whimsical', 'capricious'.

FANTINI. See *Trumpet Family* 3.

FARADAY, MICHAEL (1791–1867). See *Broadcasting* 2.

FARANDOLE. A lively dance in six-in-a-measure time, in use in Auvergne, Provence, the Basque country, Catalonia, etc. It is a street dance like the annual Furry Dance of Helston, Cornwall. It allows of many participants, and holding hands they dance through the town to the accompaniment of the galoubet and tambourin (see *Recorder Family* 3 c). A description of the farandole of Provence will be found in the first chapter of Daudet's novel *Numa Roumestan*, and it enters into his play *L'Arlésienne*, to which Bizet supplied the music. Gounod has introduced a farandole into his opera *Mireille*, which is founded on a Provençal poem by Mistral.

A dance apparently identical with the farandole appears frequently on ancient Greek vases.

FARBE (Ger.). 'Colour', hence 'tone-colour'.

FARCING or **FARSING.** The practice of inserting tropes (q.v.) into the plainsong of the Roman Catholic Liturgy, or into polyphonic settings of it. So we speak of a 'farced Kyrie', etc. (The word comes from the Latin 'farcire', to stuff. 'Farce', in theatrical parlance, derives from the same word, from the practice of introducing comic interludes into the primitive miracle plays and the like.)

FAREWELL, MANCHESTER. The tune is the favourite 'Felton's Gavotte', a harpsichord piece by the Revd. William Felton (q.v.), of Hereford, about 1740. It has been stated that it was played in front of the army of the Young Pretender when they left Manchester—which implies that this army possessed some sort of a band. Several old sets of words have been sung to it—none of them, so far as has been traced, having any Manchester references.

'FAREWELL' SYMPHONY (Haydn). See *Nicknamed Compositions* 11.

FARINA, CARLO. Born at Mantua (date unknown), but lived largely at Dresden and Danzig. He was one of the earliest writers of virtuoso music for the violin (five books published 1626–8).

See *Sonata* 10 a.

FARINELLI.

(1) MICHEL (b. 1649). He was a French violinist and singing-master (real name Farinel), who travelled much and enjoyed a high reputation as a performer on his instrument. In English literature he sometimes appears as 'Faronell'.

See reference under *Folia*.

(2) JEAN BAPTISTE (Giovanni Baptista). He was brother of the above, was in the service of George I of England, and composed flute concertos and other things. But there seems to be some confusion of him with a 'Christian Farinelli'.

(3) (Real name Carlo Broschi; 1705–82.) He may have been nephew of the two above and possibly adopted their name because it was already favourably known in a musical connexion. He was the most famous castrato (see *Voice* 5) of his period (p. 688, pl. 115. 5).

See also *Spain* 6; *Messa di Voce*; *Applause* 2; *Cadenza*; *Ornaments* 1.

FARINGDON FAIR. See *Fairs and their Music*.

FARMER.

(1) JOHN (I). End of sixteenth and beginning of seventeenth century. He was, for a part of his life, organist of Christ Church Cathedral, Dublin, and lived in London for another part, but the facts of his career are rather obscure. His madrigals are charming.

See mention under *Ireland* 3; *Canon*; *Dublin*.

(2) JOHN (II). Born at Nottingham in 1836 and died at Oxford in 1901, aged sixty-four. He will long be remembered for the songs he made for Harrow School, to the words of his colleague Edward Bowen; of this place he was musical director for nearly a quarter of a century, and he then exerted influence upon the cultivation of music in the universities as chief musician of Balliol College, under the famous Jowett. (Cf. *Walker, Ernest*.)

(3) HENRY GEORGE. Born at Birr, Ireland, in 1882 and died at Law, Lanarkshire, in 1966, aged eighty-three. He was educated at the University of Glasgow and, while conducting a theatre orchestra, became an authority on Arab music. He wrote also on music in Scotland and on military music, etc. (See *Hydraulus*.)

FARNABY (Father and Son).

(1) GILES. Born in Truro *c*. 1560 and died in London in 1640, aged about eighty. Only a few trifling facts of his life-history are known, but he will be ever remembered by the discerning for his charming pieces for the domestic keyboard instruments (there are over fifty of them in the Fitzwilliam Virginal Book, q.v.), and, too, for his madrigals. Important manuscripts of his music, formerly in the possession of Francis Hopkinson (q.v.), are preserved in Philadelphia.

Allusions will be found under *History* 3; *Harmony* 8; *Hymns and Hymn Tunes* 17 e x; *Pianoforte* 21; *Under the Spreading Chestnut Tree*.

(2) RICHARD (dates unknown). He was the son of (1), and beyond that all that is known of him is that he left a little keyboard music.

FARNON, ROBERT J. (JOSEPH). Born in Toronto in 1917. He was a trumpeter in the orchestra of the Canadian Broadcasting Commission from 1936 to 1942; from 1943 to 1946 he was conductor of the Canadian army orchestra, subsequently making his home in Britain. He has composed much lighter music for films and radio, as well as more serious works.

FARONELL. See *Farinelli* 1; *Follia*.

FARRANT, JOHN. See below.

FARRANT, RICHARD. Died at Windsor in 1580 or 1581. He was organist to Queen Elizabeth I at St. George's Chapel, Windsor, and is nowadays remembered by a few anthems and a Service in A minor. (The simple but touching anthem, *Lord, for Thy Tender Mercies' Sake*, long attributed to him, is now said by some to have been written by John Hilton the elder—or perhaps Tye. The service 'Farrant in D minor' is by John Farrant, organist of Ely Cathedral from 1567 to 1572.)

See *Windsor*; *Anthem*, Period I.

FARRUCA. An Andalusian dance of gipsy origin. There is one in Falla's *The Three-Cornered Hat*.

FARWELL, ARTHUR (p. 1056, p. **171.** 7). Born at St. Paul in 1872 and died in New York in 1952, aged seventy-nine. He made a long and close study of the American Indians and many of his compositions are influenced thereby. He also took a public-spirited interest in American musical life in general, and engaged in a number of activities designed to further it.

See reference under *Publishing* 9.

FASCH.

(1) JOHANN FRIEDRICH. Born near Weimar in 1688 and died at Zerbst, in Anhalt, in 1758, aged seventy. He was a pupil, at the Leipzig Thomas-School, of Kuhnau (Bach's predecessor there), and afterward active in establishing a 'Collegium Musicum' (see *Concert* 13) which later developed into the celebrated Gewandhaus concert organization. After holding various positions in other places, he settled, in his thirties, in Zerbst, as Court Capellmeister. Bach greatly valued his compositions, which included operas, French overtures (for the Collegium above mentioned), motets, church cantatas, etc.

(2) CARL FRIEDRICH CHRISTIAN. Born at Zerbst in 1736 and died in Berlin in 1800, aged sixty-three. He was son of the above and became colleague to C. P. E. Bach as accompanist to the flute-playing Frederick the Great (q.v.). He later founded a Berlin choral organization which became the basis of the famous Singakademie. He was a composer of great skill and high reputation, and a great teacher of composers. Beethoven valued him and visited him. Six volumes of his works have been published, but when he felt himself to be dying he had many of his manuscripts burnt before his eyes by Zelter.

FASOLA. See *Lancashire Sol-fa* (end).

FASSUNG (Ger.). 'Drafting', etc. Hence *Neue Fassung*, 'new version'.

FAST (Ger.). 'Almost.'

FASTOSO (It.). 'Pompous.' So *Fastosamente*, 'pompously'.

FATHER O'FLYNN. The words are by A. P. Graves; the music is an Irish folk song collected by him in County Kerry—'I had often danced the jig to this tune, and one morning found myself whistling it as I crossed the London parks to my work as a young clerk in the Home Office. As I whistled, recollections of Father Michael Walsh, the old parish priest of Kilcrohane, rose to my mind, so that when I reached Whitehall they had woven themselves into my song of *Father O'Flynn*.'

FAURÉ, GABRIEL URBAIN (p. 384, pl. **63.** 3). Born at Pamiers in 1845 and died in Paris in 1924, aged seventy-nine. For thirty years he held a series of positions connected with church music, culminating with the organistship of the Madeleine at the age of fifty-one. At the time he took up his work at that church he also became a professor of composition at the Paris Conservatory, of which institution he was, from the age of sixty to that of seventy-five, director.

His compositions are very numerous. His songs are important, and so are his opera *Penelope* and his chamber music. His style is a logical and balanced one; his music flows easily, yet he attains 'finish'. These are usually to be considered 'classical' qualities, and so in themselves they are, but the general bent of Fauré's mind was romantic.

For a long period in the later part of his life he was looked up to with veneration by almost the whole body of his juniors amongst French composers, very many of whom (Ravel, Florent Schmitt, Roger-Ducasse, etc.) were his pupils.

See references under *France* 10, 13; *Ear and Hearing* 4; *Pavan and Galliard*; *Concerto* 6 b (1845); *Requiem*.

FAURE, JEAN BAPTISTE. Born at Moulins (Allier) in 1830 and died in Paris in 1914, aged eighty-four. He was an enormously famous operatic baritone. He published books on singing, and some songs, of which one, *Les Rameaux*, is universally known.

FAUSSET (Fr.). 'Falsetto' (q.v.).

FAUST (Gounod). First produced in Paris in 1859. Libretto, based on Goethe's drama (much altered), by Barbier and Carré.

Act I

Scene: *Faust's Study, at Night. Time, Sixteenth Century*

Weary at his failure to uncover creation's secrets, **Faust** (*Tenor*) is about to end his life. Voices of happy peasants, without, tantalize him, and he calls on the powers of evil to justify life. **Mephistopheles** (*Bass*) appears, and promises to restore Faust's youth at the price of his soul hereafter. The bargain is sealed when the devil shows Faust a vision of the lovely Marguerite.

ACT II
SCENE: *A Fair at the City Gate*

Amid the merry-making, **Valentine** (*Baritone*) appears. He, Marguerite's brother, is going off to war, and his friend **Siebel** (played by a woman—*Soprano*) promises to look after Marguerite.

Mephistopheles enters. Telling fortunes, he predicts that every flower that Siebel touches shall wither. Valentine, hearing his sister's name lightly taken by the stranger, challenges him, but finds his sword powerless in the magic circle drawn by the Evil One, who, however, retreats before the sign of the cross. Now the rejuvenated Faust first meets **Marguerite** (*Soprano*), who declines his escort.

ACT III
SCENE: *Marguerite's Garden*

Siebel, gathering flowers, finds Mephistopheles's prophecy true. The Devil brings Faust to Marguerite's house, giving him a casket of jewels wherewith to tempt her. Her attendant **Martha** (*Contralto*) is diverted by Mephistopheles's flattery, while Faust makes love to, and wins, Marguerite, with whom he remains.

ACT IV

There is some diversity in the presentation of this Act: the first Scene, in some versions, showing Marguerite, betrayed by Faust, hoping that he will come back, whilst in another version (the one to be followed here) the Scene is a street, with the soldiers, Valentine among them, returning from war. Mephistopheles watches, with Faust. The Devil insults Marguerite's name, and, on being challenged by her brother, orders Faust to fight him. He does so, and kills Valentine, who, as his sister bends over him, curses her, dying.

The second Scene of the Act (sometimes played first) is in a church. Marguerite, repentant, is tortured by the voice of the unseen Mephistopheles.

ACT V

Here again there are differing versions. The first Scene (now to be described) was interpolated to afford a further spectacle, taken from another part of Goethe's work. Mephistopheles carries Faust to the Brocken for the Walpurgis Night revels, and shows him many women lovers of former times. At the end there is a vision of Marguerite to whom Faust commands the Devil to transport him.

FINAL SCENE: *A Prison*

Marguerite is about to die for killing her child. Her mind is clouded, and she cannot respond to Faust's loving urgence to escape. She repulses him, and, as Satan enters to claim the despairing Faust's soul, there is a vision of her apotheosis and salvation.

FAUXBOURDON (Fr.). Same as English fauburden (q.v.).

FAVART, CHARLES SIMON. Born in Paris in 1710 and there died in 1792, aged eighty-one. He was a playwright and theatre manager of the highest importance for his influence on the development of the stage in France (especially that of opéra comique), and also as one of the librettists of Gluck, Grétry, and many others of the operatic composers of the period; altogether he supplied 150 libretti.

FAWCETT, John (1789–1867). See *Lancashire Sol-fa*.

FAYRFAX, ROBERT. Born at Deeping Gate, Lincs., 1464 and died at St. Albans in 1521, aged fifty-seven. He attended Henry VIII at the Field of the Cloth of Gold, amongst the singing men. He appears to have been organist of the abbey of St. Albans, and was there interred. He was in his day 'in great renown and accounted the prime musitian of the nation' (Anthony Wood). The quater-centenary of his death brought the revival of some of his church music after long neglect due, doubtless, to its period preceding that of the full development of the sixteenth-century choral style.

He was D.Mus. of Cambridge (1502) and the earliest recorded as taking this degree at Oxford (1511).

F.B.S.M. See *Degrees and Diplomas* 2.

F.C.C. See *Broadcasting* 3.

F.C.C.O. See *Degrees and Diplomas* 2.

F CLEF. See *Table* 4.

FEDERAL COMMUNICATIONS COMMISSION. See *Broadcasting* 3.

FEDERATION OF MUSIC FESTIVALS. See *Competitions in Music* 2.

FEDERATION OF MUSIC SOCIETIES. See *National Federation of Music Societies.*

FEDERATION OF RURAL MUSIC SCHOOLS. See *Rural Music School Movement.*

FEELING IN MUSIC. See *Quality of Music* 6.

FEIERLICH (Ger.). This has a double meaning —in the mood of 'Holy Day' (solemn) or in that of 'Holiday' (rejoicing), for 'Feier' is a public celebration of the one kind or the other. (Cf. *Ferial.*)

FEIS CEOIL. See *Competitions in Music* 2.

FELDPARTITA (Ger.). A composition for wind-band, of the type of partita (q.v.) or of divertimento (see *Suite* 7).

FELICE (It.). 'Happy.'

FELIX MERITIS. See *Concert* 13; *Holland* 9.

FELLOWES, EDMUND HORACE (p. 32, pl. 3). Born in London in 1870 and died at Windsor in 1951, aged eighty-one. In his Oxford days known as an able violinist, he was from 1900 a minor canon of St. George's Chapel, Windsor (for three years director of the choir there), meantime editing the complete series of English madrigal and lute-song music (68 volumes in all), the complete works of Byrd (20 volumes), as also a great deal of the Tudor church music, and writing a large number of books on cognate subjects, on which subjects he also lectured a great deal (repeatedly undertaking American tours for this purpose). With such as Dent and C. S. Terry he belonged to the pioneering generation of modern English musical scholarship. Though details of his work are justly criticized by his younger successors, the artistic and national service he performed cannot be questioned.

He is not correctly designated 'Canon' Fellowes.

See references under *Madrigal* 3; *Pitch* 2; *Tomkins, Thomas*; *Viola Family* 3 h.

FELTON, WILLIAM. Born in 1715 and died in 1769. He was a clergyman and a minor canon of Hereford Cathedral who was well known as an organist, harpsichordist, and composer of concertos for his instruments.

For 'Felton's Gavotte' see under *Farewell Manchester*.

FEMININE CADENCE. See *Cadence*.

FENBY (inventor). See *Improvisation* 4.

FERGUSON, HOWARD. Born at Belfast in 1908. He was heard as pianist at a competition festival there by Harold Samuel, who suggested his coming to London and with whom he then lived until Samuel's death, studying with him and with R. O. Morris and at the Royal College of Music, where he held a scholarship for composition. He has written piano music, chamber music, and songs, and some orchestral music.

See *Clarinet* 6.

FERIAL. The word comes from the Latin *feria*, a feast-day. The early church apparently applied the term 'Feria' to Sunday and then adopted a plan of naming the days of the week Monday to Friday, as 'second feria', i.e. 'second [after the] feria' to 'sixth feria' (Sunday itself, the original Feria, not now coming into this reckoning but being called 'Dominica'), and then of speaking of the 'office' (q.v.) of such week-days as the 'ferial office'. Thus 'ferial' has, by etymological perversity, come to be, ecclesiastically, the opposite of 'Festival' (an ordinary day, as distinguished from a feast), and the term now takes in Sundays as well, provided they are not feasts: hence the application of the expression 'Ferial Use' to liturgy and music. (For the Ferial and Festival Responses see *Responses*.)

The confusion in the use of this word is indeed extreme (cf. *Feierlich*). In French law and business the 'Ferial Days' are Easter Sunday and Monday, Ascension, Whit Sunday and Monday, Assumption, All Saints, Christmas, and the Fête Nationale on 14 July; so for these official and secular purposes 'ferial' retains its original sense of 'feast'.

FERMAMENTE (It.). 'Firmly.'

FERMATA (It.), **FERMATE** (Ger.). 'A pause' ⌢ Sometimes the use is a special one—the pause mark in a concerto which indicates the point where the cadenza begins (see *Cadenza*).

FERME (Fr.). 'Firm.'

FERMER (Fr.). 'To close.' So *Fermé*, 'closed'. In French organ works these terms may have application to the Swell Box, or they may mean that a stop in use is now to be put out of action.

FERMEZZA (It.). 'Firmness.'

FERMO (It.). 'Firm', in style of performance. For 'Canto Fermo' see *Harmony* 6, 7; *Counterpoint*.

FERNANDEZ, OSCAR LORENZO. Born in Rio de Janeiro in 1897 and died there in 1948. He composed the opera *Malazarte*, orchestral works, piano music, etc. all strongly imbued with the spirit of Brazilian folk music.

FERNE (Ger.). 'Distance', e.g. *Wie aus der Ferne*, 'as if out of the distance'.

FERNFLÖTE. See *Organ* 14 II.

FERNWERK (Ger.). Echo manual of organ.

FEROCE (It.). 'Ferocious.' So *Ferocità*, 'ferocity'.

FERRABOSCO (The family). Active first in Italy, and then in England from about 1560 to about 1680.

(1) ALFONSO (I). Born in Bologna in 1543 and there died in 1588. He was the son of a singer in the papal chapel in Rome—a composer of motets and madrigals. From about 1560 to 1578 he lived in England, where he was in the service of Queen Elizabeth and was highly celebrated, especially for his madrigals and music for viols. This is the musician known in the cultured England of those days as 'Master Alfonso'.

(2) ALFONSO (II). Born at Greenwich about 1575 and died there in 1628. He was the son of the above. He spent his whole life in England—being in the service of James I and Charles I. He composed much instrumental music (his viol consorts are really important) and many songs.

See reference under *Masque*.

(3, 4, 5) ALFONSO (III), HENRY, and JOHN, all, apparently, sons of Alfonso II, were, like their father and grandfather, in the royal service. John (1626–82; B.Mus. Cambridge 1671) became organist of Ely Cathedral, where much church music of his remains.

FERROUD, PIERRE OCTAVE. Born near Lyons in 1900. Killed in a motoring accident in Hungary in 1936, aged thirty-six. He was a pupil of Florent Schmitt; he served as a Paris music critic and composed piano music, chamber music, orchestral music, ballet music, a comic opera, and other things. His talent for orchestration was especially notable.

FERTIG (Ger.). 'Ready', dexterous, finished in style. So *Fingerfertigkeit*, fluent finger technique.

FERVENTE (It.). 'Fervent.'

FERVIDO, FERVIDAMENTE (It.). 'Fervid', 'fervidly'. **FERVORE** (It.). 'Fervour.'

FES (Ger.). F flat. See Table 7.

FESES (Ger.). F double flat—if this note is anywhere to be found. See Table 7.

FEST (Ger.). 'Festival.' Also 'firm', 'strict'.

FESTA (It.). 'Festival.' So *Festevole*, 'merry'; *Festevolmente*, 'merrily'.

FESTA, COSTANZO. Born about 1490 near Turin and died in 1545, aged about fifty-five. At a time when the Flemings occupied all the commanding positions in church music, he, as musical director of the Vatican, was the only Italian in such a position in Italy. His church music is still sung in Rome, and of his madrigals one (called in English *Down in a flowery vale*) is everywhere known.

FESTAL. Applied in the distinction of ecclesiastical feast days from ordinary or Ferial days (see *Ferial* and *Responses*).

FESTING. The brothers.

(1) MICHAEL CHRISTIAN. Died in London in 1752. He was a violinist, orchestral leader, opera director and composer, very prominent in London during the period of Handel's activities there. He left works for his instrument, songs, choral works, etc., and deserves remembrance as one of the founders of the Royal Society of Musicians (see *Profession* 10; *Festival* 1), and its first Secretary. *Cf. Concert.* 6 (note).

(2) JOHN. Died 1772. A prominent hautboy player, and said to be the original of the one caricatured in Hogarth's *The Enraged Musician* (see p. 992, pl. 165. 2).

FESTIVAL

1. The Festival in Britain.
2. The Festival in the United States.

3. The Festival on the Continent of Europe.

1. The Festival in Britain. In musical usage this generally means a performance or series of performances on a larger scale than ordinarily (as to number of performers or number of performances) held, periodically or to celebrate some special occasion. The word, now adopted into several languages, is English, apparently coming into use with the Festival of the **Sons of the Clergy.**

This began as an annual charity sermon in 1655 (i.e. during the Commonwealth, when all church music but the simplest was prohibited), and at the Restoration or soon after took on a musical complexion, with the employment of an orchestra from 1698; this benevolent celebration continues annually; it is, however, a mere musical service on grand lines. A history of it, by the Revd. E. H. Pearce, was published in 1904.

The next English festival in order of foundation is that of the **Three Choirs**, held annually at the three West Country cathedral cities of Gloucester, Worcester, and Hereford, in rotation; it dates from 1724 in its form as a means of raising money for charity, but in its primitive form it dates from 1715. It lasts for several days. Its charitable purpose is similar to that of the above named. It combines the choral forces of the three cities.

The Festival of **Birmingham** began in 1768 and lasted until 1912, being held at irregular intervals (for a period triennially). It was for the benefit of local hospitals.

The **Norwich** Festival has been held at irregular intervals since 1770 (since 1824 for a period triennially). It is for the benefit of the local hospitals. (Cf. *Alto Voice*.)

In 1784–5–6–7 and 1791 were held monster **Handel Commemorations** in Westminster Abbey, warmly supported by that great Handelian, George III. Of the first of these an 'Account' was written by Dr. Burney (with hints from the King). Burney was anxious to have an attestation of his belief that this occa-

sion had witnessed the greatest aggregation of vocal and instrumental performers the world had ever seen, and, since if any rival for this primacy existed it was likely to have been in musical Italy, he consulted a musical Italian nobleman then in London, who admitted 'it is only your great and very respectable nation that is capable of planning and executing such enterprises as carry us back to heroic times by their grandeur and sublimity. . . . Indeed, I am persuaded that it requires near a million inhabitants, and as great a passion for music as there is at present in London, to furnish upwards of five hundred professional musicians.'

This event raised a large sum of money for the philanthropic Society of Musicians, henceforward the Royal Society of Musicians, the charter being granted on this occasion. (See p. 753, pl. 124.) There was another Abbey festival in 1834.

The Crystal Palace **Handel Festivals** began in 1857 and were held at first irregularly and then triennially until 1926.

Manchester had great festivals in 1777, 1786, 1828, and 1836—at the last of which Malibran died (see *Garcia Family* 3).

The **Leeds** Festival is a mid-nineteenth-century creation (1858, 1874, and thence onward to the present day triennially except in war periods); it is for the benefit of the city's medical charities.

In addition to these there have been a great many sporadic festivals, some in celebration of some special event. And a number of festivals intended to become permanent enterprises have continued for some years and then died out.

It will be gathered from the above list that charity has been the motive (or the excuse) for most of the English festival activity. This circumstance has been the subject of frequent adverse criticism, for it has been felt by some that music is in itself a good enough motive for making music, and that where another motive takes its place musical standards may suffer.

A further criticism of festivals calls attention to the fact that concentration of local effort upon a periodical great musical event temporarily exhausts the musical energies of the locality and tends to paralyse its normal and continuous musical activities.

The English festivals have been the occasion of bringing into existence an enormous number of specially composed works—a statement which may be illustrated by a glance over the chronological list at the end of the article *Oratorio*. Choral singing has always been a special feature of the English festivals. In York Minster in 1851 there was a choir of 2,700 trained singers.

Many annual diocesan festivals are held for the performance of church music, choirs of the diocese combining in its cathedral.

A festival of contemporary British music at **Cheltenham** is well established. **Aldeburgh, Bath,** and the **City of London** may also be mentioned.

Festivals have for some years been a conspicuous feature of the musical life of Wales. The oldest is that of **Harlech,** held in the Castle annually since 1867: about twenty choirs take part, making 1,800 or 2,000 singers. (For the more ancient Eisteddfodau see *Wales* 7.)

Since 1947 a very important and successful annual series of international summer festivals has attracted large audiences at **Edinburgh.**

In Ireland, Cork, Wexford, and Dublin have all been the scene of festivals.

See also *Oratorio* 5; *Glyndebourne*; *Hatton, J. L.*; *Kuhe*; *Cornett and Key Bugle Families* 2 d; *Pianoforte* 22; *Voice* 17.

2. The Festival in the United States. In the United States festival activities began in the middle of the nineteenth century (Boston and Worcester, 1858; Cincinnati, 1871, etc.). The Bach Festivals at Bethlehem, Pennsylvania, began in 1900 and have, with intervals, gone on annually since. The Berkshire Festivals of Pittsfield, Massachusetts (for chamber music), held under Mrs. E. S. Coolidge's aegis, were in 1931 transferred to the Library of Congress, Washington. In 1937 Mrs. Gorham Brooks gave an estate, 'Tanglewood', in Berkshire (Stockbridge Bowl), to the Boston Symphony Orchestra as a permanent summer festival home.

There are said now to exist over 120 permanent festival organizations in the United States, some of the best known being at Aspen, Colo.; Carmel, Calif. (Bach); Chautauqua, N.Y.; Newport, R.I. (jazz); and Nashville, Tenn. ('rock and roll'). The presence of Pablo Casals has stimulated the festival of Puerto Rico. Summer concerts in New York's Lewisohn Stadium were begun in 1918, originally as entertainment for the military, and continued to 1966. There are similar open-air series at the Hollywood Bowl, Robin Hood Dell (Philadelphia), and other sites. These, though often called festivals, are perhaps not strictly such. But many are of high importance, and the U.S.A. would seem now, in some ways, to rank first amongst festival-giving countries.

3. The Festival on the Continent of Europe. France is not a festival-giving country—though the name is sometimes applied to single concerts in which unusually large resources are employed. An exception is the annual festival at Aix-en-Provence. **Italy** was in somewhat similar case, but of recent years, with government encouragement, there have been organized annually at Florence a Maggio Musicale ('Musical May'), a festival of concerts and opera, and festivals of contemporary music at Venice, Palermo, Spoleto (see *Menotti*), etc. Wind-band Festivals are held regularly in **Switzerland** and other countries—generally with the element of competition. **Germany** has a number of important festivals, of which the Lower Rhine Festival (dating from 1817) is the most important; this resembles the English 'Three Choirs' Festival, in that it is held annually in turn in Cologne, Düsseldorf, and Aachen (Aix-la-Chapelle). Darmstadt and Donaueschingen are centres for the latest developments in contemporary music. In **Poland,** Warsaw (1956) is regarded as a safety-valve for the iron curtain avant-garde.

Many special festivals in celebration of German composers have taken place in the cities of their birth. The Bayreuth Wagner performances have always borne the name of 'Bühnenfestspiel' or 'stage-festival-play'. After the first World War German festivals and Austrian (e.g. Salzburg) were organized as attractions to holiday tourists.

The success of the Salzburg festival led to a multitude of festivals which were little more than a commercial device for attracting tourists; the word is misleadingly applied quite indiscriminately to any short season of standard concert fare. The European Association of Music Festivals, with headquarters in Geneva, represents twenty-odd of the more clearly defined and better established festivals in some dozen countries.

An important festival in which composers and performers of many nations participate and at which the audience is cosmopolitan is that of the **International Society for Contemporary Music,** dating from 1923, at which (exaggerating slightly) no work composed more than five minutes before the festival opens is allowed to be heard. It has been held at Salzburg for two years, and then at Siena, Venice, Geneva, Oxford, New York, San Francisco, and many other centres, and has accomplished a good deal of valuable service in enabling modern-minded musicians to become acquainted with one another and with one another's work, and in giving an opportunity to young composers. The Society has national committees in over thirty countries.

For a different type of activity to which the word 'Festival' is increasingly applied see *Competitions in Music.* And for Harp Festivals see *Ireland* 5.

FESTIVAL HALL. See *Colour* 10; *Concert* 8; *Concert Hall* 10, 14; *Electric* 4.

FESTIVO (It.). 'Festive'; so *Festivamente*, 'festively'.

FESTLICH (Ger.). 'Festive', 'solemn', 'splendid'.

FESTOSO (It.). 'Festive.' So the superlative *Festosissimo.*

FESTSPIEL. German for 'Festival Play', and as such applied to certain musical stage works or works in which music takes a place. Thus the poet Kotzebue's play, *The Ruins of Athens*, was called a 'Festspiel', and Beethoven wrote the music for it. Wagner, recalling that amongst the ancient Greeks all stage performances were festival performances, attached the title to his *Ring* tetralogy, calling it a 'Bühnenfestspiel' (Stage Festival Play), whilst his *Parsifal* he, with solemn grandiloquence, called a 'Bühnenweihfestspiel' (Stage-consecration Festival Play).

FÉTIS, FRANÇOIS-JOSEPH (1784–1871). See *Belgium* 9; *Criticism* 3; *Appreciation*; *Benoît*; *Dictionaries* 3. Also p. 389, pl. **66. 7.**

FEUDAL SYSTEM. See *Song* 2; *Education* 1.

FEUER (Ger.). 'Fire.' So *Feurig*, 'fiery'. For Haydn's *Feuersymphonie* see *Nicknamed* 11.

FEUILLE D'ALBUM (Fr.). 'Album leaf' (q.v.).

FEUILLET, RAOUL AUGER. See *Dance* 10.

FEURIG. See *Feuer.*

FF, FFF, etc. = *Fortissimo*, i.e. very loud.

FFRANGCON-DAVIES, DAVID THOMAS (1855–1918). See references under *Bird Music*; *Singing* 12.

Fg. Short for *Fagott*, i.e. bassoon.

F.G.S.M. See *Degrees and Diplomas* 2.

F HOLES. The sound holes in the belly of some viols and the various members of the violin family —roughly in the shape of an *f*.

FIACCO (It.). 'Weak', as though tired out. So the adverb *Fiaccamente* and the noun *Fiacchezza.*

FIATA, FIATE (It.). 'Time', 'times', in the sense of 'once' (*Una fiata*), 'twice' (*Due fiate*), etc.

FIATO (It.). 'Breath.' Hence wind instruments are *Stromenti a fiato.*

FIBICH, ZDENĚK (p. 108, pl. **19. 7**). Born in 1850 at Všeborice (or Šebořice), near Časlav (or Chaslaw), Bohemia (at that time Austrian territory), and died at Prague in 1900, aged forty-nine. He studied at Leipzig, Paris, and elsewhere, and then, after a few years at Vilna, in Poland, settled in his native place and devoted himself to composition. At first he was greatly influenced by the German romantics, especially Schumann and Wagner, and to the end he showed little of the national feeling of his elder contemporaries, Smetana and Dvořák. Despite his comparatively short life, his works are very numerous; they include orchestral and chamber music, operas, and a number of melodramas—plays performed to a background of musical accompaniment, a form much cultivated in Bohemia. See *Melodrama.*

FIDDLE. A colloquial term for any kind of bowed string instrument, especially the violin.

'FIDDLE' FUGUE (Bach). See *Nicknamed Compositions* 1.

FIDDLE G. See *Pitch* 7.

FIDELIO, or MARRIED LOVE (Beethoven). Produced at Vienna, 1805; with changes, 1806; in present form, 1814. The composer made four attempts at the Overture (see *Overture* 3), in the following order, employing the accepted but incorrect enumerations: *Leonora* No. 2 (1805), *Leonora* No. 3 (1806), *Leonora* No. 1 (1807), *Fidelio* (1814): the last is the one now always used with the opera, but *Leonora* No. 3 (the most developed and finest) is sometimes interpolated between the acts.[1] The libretto is by Sonnleithner, after the French play by Bouilly, *Léonore, ou l'amour conjugal.*

The Spanish nobleman Florestan, having incurred the hatred of Pizarro, has been secretly lodged in the prison of which his enemy is the governor. Pizarro has given it out that Florestan is dead, but the nobleman's devoted wife, Leonora, suspects the truth, and, disguising herself as a boy and calling herself 'Fidelio', she gets employment in the prison as assistant to the chief jailer, Rocco.

The only other solo characters during the greater part of the opera are Rocco's daughter, Marcellina, and her assistant-jailer lover, Jaquino.

Act I

SCENE: *The Prison Yard. Time, Eighteenth century*

Jaquino (*Tenor*) urges his suit, but **Marcellina** (*Soprano*), encouraged by **Rocco** (*Bass*), favours the new-comer, ' **Fidelio** ' (*Soprano*). 'Fidelio' discovers that her husband lies in a deep dungeon.

The tyrant **Pizarro** (*Bass*) hears that the Minister, Don Fernando, suspecting some mischief, is going to inspect the prison. He determines to murder Florestan. A watchman is to blow a warning trumpet when the Minister's cavalcade is seen. Pizarro tries to bribe Rocco to do the murder. Rocco, refusing, is sent to dig a grave. Pizarro himself will make an end of his enemy.

Act II

SCENE 1: *Florestan's Dungeon*

Rocco and 'Fidelio' come to dig the grave. Pizarro enters, and is about to stab Florestan, when 'Fidelio' draws a pistol and reveals herself as the prisoner's wife. At that instant the trumpet rings out, Pizarro hastens to meet the Minister, and husband and wife are left together.

[1] It is right to add that Josef Braunstein, in *Beethovens Leonore-Ouvertüren, eine historisch-stilkritische Untersuchung* (1927), supported by Romain Rolland in *Beethoven: les grandes époques créatrices* (1928), maintains that the numbers attached to these overtures are, after all, correct. The dates he gives are *Leonora* No. 1, 1805; No. 2, 1805; No. 3, 1806; *Fidelio*, 1814.

See the Articles under the individual names

1. FRANK BRIDGE (1879–1941)

2. CYRIL SCOTT (1879–1970)

3. SIR ARNOLD BAX (1883–1953)

4. SIR ARTHUR BLISS (1891–1975)

5. HERBERT HOWELLS (b. 1892)

6. SIR EUGENE GOOSSENS (1893–1962)

7. ARTHUR BENJAMIN (1893–1960)

8. E. J. MOERAN (1894–1950)

9. GORDON JACOB (b. 1895)

1. ALAN BUSH (b. 1900)

2. EDMUND RUBBRA (b. 1901)

3. SIR WILLIAM WALTON, O.M.
(b. 1902)

4. ROBIN MILFORD (1903–59)

5. SIR LENNOX BERKELEY (b. 1903)

6. CONSTANT LAMBERT (1905–51)

7. ALAN RAWSTHORNE (1905–71)

8. MICHAEL TIPPETT (b. 1905)

9. BENJAMIN BRITTEN, O.M.
(1913–76)

SCENE 2: *A Courtyard in the Castle*

Don Fernando (*Bass*) recognizes Florestan as his friend, whom he had thought dead. Pizarro's punishment is decreed, and Leonora removes her husband's chains, amid rejoicings at the reward of her devotion.

Cf. *Opera* 21 g.

FIDLA. See *Scandinavia* 5.

FIELD, JOHN (p. 481, pl. **84**. 5). Born in Dublin in 1782 and died in Moscow in 1837, aged fifty-four. His grandfather was a Dublin organist and pianist and his father a violinist in a theatre orchestra. The two of them, who lived together, tried to whip music into him, and either they magnificently succeeded or it was there to begin with.

Giordani, then in Dublin, gave him lessons, and at nine he appeared in public as 'the much admired Master Field, a youth of eight years of age'.

When he was eleven his father settled in London and he became pupil to Clementi (q.v.), and at twelve, 'aged ten', appeared before a London audience that included Haydn, who predicted a great future for him. Clementi used him to display the pianos in his warehouse, and when he went abroad, giving recitals and selling his instruments, took him with him. At St. Petersburg, when the master left the pupil remained, and, taken up by 'society', had many aristocratic pupils (Glinka had three or four lessons from him), becoming very spoiled. He travelled Europe as a virtuoso pianist, playing in a simple, unaffected, but very finished style.

As a composer for the piano he had high fame. His concertos were everywhere to be heard and were in later years greatly praised by Schumann. The style and name of the pianoforte Nocturne (q.v.) were of his devising, and Chopin owes these to him; Liszt published an edition of his nocturnes preceded by a panegyric.

Latterly he lived at Moscow. Intemperance and carelessness had some part in his comparatively early death.

See *England* 7; *Ireland* 7; *Pianoforte Playing* 2, 5; *Sonata* 10 d; *Song without Words*; *Opera* 17 b; *Concerto* 6 b (1782).

FIER, FIÈRE (Fr.; masc., fem.). 'Proud.' So *Fierté*, 'pride'; *Fièrement*, 'proudly'. (But in painting this word is sometimes used for 'boldness of touch', and it may be that it should sometimes be so interpreted in music.)

FIEREZZA (It.). 'Fierceness.' (In painting used in same sense as Fr. *fierté*, so that remark above may apply.)

FIERO (It.). (*a*) 'Fierce', 'fiery', (*b*) 'haughty'. So the adverb *Fieramente*, with the same implications, and *Fierezza* (see above).

FIFE (p. 365, pl. **60**. 5). A small, high-pitched instrument of the side-blown flute class (see *Flute Family*). Properly it is a small cylinder-bore, side-blown flute with six finger-holes and no keys, but nowadays the name is applied to a small flute of the normal modern type. It seems to have been introduced into England

for military purposes, in the sixteenth century, and from the country from which it came was then known as the *Swiss Pipe*. It remained a British army instrument until the 1680s, when drum and fife bands largely gave way to bands of hautboys, etc. (see *Oboe Family* 2); it came back into some army use in 1748 (see Hogarth's picture, *The March to Finchley*, etc.), and has remained in use ever since. Handel brought such a band on to the stage in *Almira* (1704), and Meyerbeer in *The Star of the North* (1854).

The chief instrument now used in a *Drum and Fife Band* is the B flat piccolo, others being the E flat piccolo, the F flute, the B flat bass flute, and occasionally the F bass flute, the E flat flute, and the E flat bass flute. As will be seen, some of these depart from the original idea of the fife as a *small, high-pitched* flute (see *Flute Family* 3 b).

The German word for fife is *Trommelflöte* ('drum-flute').

Cf. also *Whiffle*.

FIFTEENTH. See *Organ* 14 I.

FIFTH. See *Interval*.

FIFTH, PERFECT (as a part of most scales) See *Scales* 4.

FIFTH FLUTE. See *Recorder Family* 2.

'FIFTHS' QUARTET (Haydn). See *Nicknamed Compositions* 12.

FIFTHS, WHISTLING IN. See *Scales* 4.

FIGARO (Mozart). See *Marriage of Figaro*.

FIGURAL, FIGURED (Eng.); **FIGURÉ** (Fr.); **FIGURATO** (It.); **FIGURIERT** (Ger.). 'Figured' much in the sense in which a figured satin or muslin is one with a pattern on it. So, for instance, a *Figured Chorale* is a chorale, embellished with accompanimental parts in quicker notes, etc. Often the word 'florid' is a good equivalent. (Cf. *Musica figurata*.)

FIGURATO, FIGURATA. See above; also *Coloratura*.

FIGURE (1), in **Musical construction**, is the same as *motif* (q.v.) in its principal meaning —i.e. it is tune reduced to its lowest terms, the smallest unit. Often a figure is a succession of only two notes, but these two notes, if there is anything characteristic about their interval or rhythm, will be capable of being 'worked up', by presentation at varying pitches, etc., and thus organized into phrases, sentences (see *Phrase and Sentence*), and long passages of development (see *Development*).

Certain compositions are entirely constructed out of one longer or shorter figure, as, for instance, the first Prelude of Bach's '48'.

We often speak of a **Figure of Accompaniment**, meaning the germ out of which (by continual repetition at different pitch-levels and with different harmonies) a certain type of song accompaniment, etc., is evolved.

(2) Figure in **Dancing** is a set of evolutions of the dancers as a body, making a distinct

division of the dance as a whole. A *Figure Dance* is one of which the carrying out of figures is an essential part, as distinguished from a *Step Dance*, in which the element of figure is largely or entirely absent and the whole duty of the dancer consists in making the proper motions with his own feet.

FIGURED BASS (or *Thorough-Bass* or *Continuo*) is the shorthand of harmony that came into use at the opening of the seventeenth century, when the vogue of unaccompanied choral music in elaborately woven pattern (see *Counterpoint*; *Harmony* 9) was declining and that of solo vocal recitative (q.v.) accompanied by plain chords was beginning.

Such music as this latter often had as its accompaniment a mere line of bass notes with a certain number of figures under or over them, from which more or less complete indications the player of harpsichord or organ (or, alternatively, of a large lute) could tell what chords the composer intended to be used, and could construct his own accompaniment—with a good deal of scope for his own invention and artistry in the arrangement of his part. Whilst he was doing this the actual bass (without the chords) was duplicated by the players of the cellos and double-basses, so providing a firm foundation. A knowledge of harmony, it will be realized, was an absolute necessity to a keyboard accompanist right through the seventeenth and eighteenth centuries. Burney tells an anecdote of the famous singer Frasi (his own pupil) and Handel—'When Frasi told him she was going to learn Thorough-bass, in order to accompany herself, Handel, who well knew her want of diligence, said "Oh! vaat may ve not expect?"'

Bach, in the book of music for his wife's study ('Anna Magdalena's Book'), provided her with four pages of rules for playing from figured bass.

Mozart wrote a concise treatise of figured bass for a lady pupil, and it was published and republished after his death (in Germany and in England).

The following types of work, still frequently performed, originally had figured basses, so that in printed editions of today some editor has had to supply the fully written-out part that the modern keyboard-player requires:

(*a*) The sonatas for one or two violins, so common during the seventeenth and early eighteenth century (including Purcell, Corelli, Handel, etc.).

(*b*) The oratorios, passions, etc., down to the time of Bach and Handel (all these require a keyboard player as a part of the orchestra throughout, and it is his part that is indicated in the figured bass and now has to be supplied).

(*c*) Bach's Brandenburg Concertos and similar works (though conductors sometimes, improperly, omit the keyboard background provided for by the composer).

(*d*) The *recitativo secco* in seventeenth-, eighteenth-, and even early nineteenth-century operas—such as those of Gluck, Mozart, and Rossini.

(*e*) The organ part in the older church music (to near the end of the eighteenth century).

As concerns (*e*), it may be said that the cathedral organists were in England the last branch of the musical profession to keep in exercise the art of playing from figured bass, no fully worked-out organ part existing for much of the church music repertory until the era of modern reprints (Vincent Novello, in 1811, issued a volume of church music with the organ part in full, and this was the first in Britain to be so published; it brought violent protests!). There are few organists now who could emulate the eighteenth-century London organist of whom Burney in his *History* speaks so slightingly—'The harpsichord at Covent Garden was played by old Short, organist of St. Sepulchre's Church, who was only able to drum thorough-bass' (for the last expression see below).

The great textbook of figured bass used by English musicians in the latter part of the eighteenth century was that of the Edinburgh violinist Pasquali (published 1757); some, however, preferred the book (1768) of J. C. Heck, a German settled in London. So good a property was a standard book on the subject in those days that the publishers of that of Pasquali (the brothers Thompson of St. Paul's Churchyard) said it was the foundation of their fortune.

In 1931 F. T. Arnold published, as the result of thirty years' work, a volume called *The Art of Accompaniment from a Thorough-Bass*, which set out 'to give information concerning the way in which the accompaniment founded on a *Basso Continuo*, or Thorough-Bass, was actually treated during [its] period'. The ancient tradition of playing from a figured bass in this book completely restored, for the student who will master its contents in a musicianly manner.

The custom of the composer providing a figured bass may be said to have endured for almost two centuries—from about 1600 to nearly 1800.

The working of figured basses on paper still remains one of the means of instruction in harmony and, up to the 1920s or 1930s, was a not uncommon examination test—a very imperfect means of acquiring harmonic ability, let it be said, and a very delusive means of proving its possession, since figured basses can be admirably worked on paper by almost purely mechanical methods and without any real mental hearing of the harmonies.

Synonyms for figured bass are *Thorough-Bass* (really 'through bass') and *Basso Continuo*, i.e. a bass which 'continues' or goes 'through' the whole composition. And so, indeed, it does; in a piece of the seventeenth or earlier eighteenth century, whatever other instruments may momentarily drop out or come into the score, the figured bass goes on, and so the harpsichord has to provide an unbroken background to the music. (But see *Basso Continuo*.)

The German term is *General-Bass*, the French, *Basse chiffrée* (*Chiffre* = 'figure') or *Basse continue*. The Italian term is the already mentioned *Basso continuo*, and from this the musicians of all countries often take the second word as an alternative to the term in their own language, speaking of 'playing the continuo', and so forth.

The word *Cembalo* (properly 'dulcimer', but used as short for 'Clavicembalo', i.e. harpsichord) is often attached in a score to the figured bass part.

Curiously enough, in the period when harpsichord accompaniments to songs were invariably supplied as mere figured basses, lute accompaniments were invariably (or almost so) written in full.

Articles in this volume with a bearing on the above subject are *Opera*; *Oratorio*; *Chamber Music*; *Sonata*; *Orchestra* (all of them in their earlier parts, in which they treat of the works of the seventeenth and eighteenth centuries). See also *Cavalieri*; *Viadana*; *Additional Accompaniments*; *Franz*.

FIGURIERT (Ger.). See *Figural*.

FILAR LA VOCE (It.), **FILER LA VOIX, FILER LE SON** (Fr.). Literally, 'to draw out the voice' (like 'wire-drawing'), i.e. to sustain a note for a long time, gradually swelling it and then letting it die away, and all with one breath. This effect is also called *Messa di voce* (q.v.), and as a singing exercise the old Italian school of singing masters used it enormously. Very confusingly some modern books define this term variously as (1) to sustain a note without *crescendo* and *diminuendo*; or else (2) to sustain it 'with or without' that effect (sometimes adding 'avoiding any *tremolo*'); or even (3) 'to draw the tone out to a mere thread of sound'.

FILTZ, ANTON. Born (possibly in Bohemia) about 1730 and died at Mannheim in 1760, aged about thirty. He was leading violoncellist in the orchestra of J. Stamitz at Mannheim,

and his pupil. He composed over forty symphonies, as also cello and flute concertos, chamber music, etc., but although these have value he died before he had completely fulfilled his promise.

FIN (Fr.). 'End.'

FIN (It.). Same as *Fino* (q.v.).

FINAL (of Modes). See *Modes* 4, 5.

FINALE. Obviously anything which brings to an end anything else can be so called. The main musical uses of the word are for the last movement of a cyclic work (sonata, symphony, concerto, etc.), and the closing passages of an act of an opera. An opera finale should combine continuous and high musical interest with dramatic culmination, and this duality of effect is most successfully achieved by Mozart. With him the more or less broken character of the act (broken by spoken dialogues or by *recitativo secco* with a mere harpsichord accompaniment) ceases, many personages are brought in together and many musical resources employed, and the whole works up to a great climax.

FINCK, H. T. See reference under *Criticism* 5.

FINE (It.). 'End.'

FINE, IRVING. Born at Boston, Mass., in 1914 and died there in 1962, aged forty-seven. He taught at Harvard and from 1950 was Chairman of the School of Creative Arts at Brandeis University. He was a choral conductor and the composer of orchestral and chamber music, etc., at first under the influence of Stravinsky's neo-classic manner, but latterly in the Note-row system.

See *Symphony* 8; *History* 9.

FINGER BOARD. That long strip of hard wood in a stringed instrument above which the strings are stretched.

FINGERED TREMOLO. See *Tremolo*.

FINGERFERTIGKEIT. See under *Fertig*.

FINGERING OF KEYBOARD INSTRUMENTS

1. Early History of Fingering.
2. J. S. Bach's Innovations.
3. C. P. E. Bach and Mozart.
4. The Coming of the Pianoforte—Clementi.
5. The Nineteenth and Twentieth Centuries.
6. 'English' and 'Continental' Systems of Marking.
7. Organ Fingering.

1. Early History of Fingering. The accepted methods of applying the fingers to keyboards have varied at different periods in different countries, and have only since the latter part of the eighteenth century become standardized on something like the modern principles.

A pianist of today, looking at some keyboard composition of the later sixteenth, seventeenth, or earlier eighteenth century which happens to bear contemporary fingering marks feels completely bewildered; it may, in some instances, seem to him, on first glance, as though the fingering had been deliberately and maliciously designed to obstruct the performer—and as

though the composition could never have been got through (at anything like its proper speed) if the fingering attached were really adhered to.

There is invariably during this long period (a period of about two centuries of very high cultivation of domestic keyboard performance) a great deal of passing of fingers over one another—a process almost entirely avoided today as being the extreme of unpractical clumsiness. The thumb and often the little finger are in this earlier period used so sparingly that, but for the necessity of bringing them into play for the wider intervals and chords, it looks almost as though they might as well not exist. For the most part, a sixteenth- or seventeenth-century performer on the virginals, spinet, harpsichord, clavichord, or organ was a six-finger practitioner (p. 193, pl. **39.** 5), but it is, of course, an exaggeration to say, as it sometimes is said, that the thumb and little finger were *never* used.

The explanation of the ease with which the earlier keyboard players evidently passed one finger over another lies partly in the small 'fall' of the finger-keys of the instruments of the day (perhaps, in general, about half that of the finger-keys of the modern pianoforte) and partly in the quite different motions of the fingers, which on the clavichord and harpsichord alike are held flatter and withdrawn more horizontally than on the modern pianoforte (cf. 2). The three fingers used were placed at an angle upon the keys, and the thumb and little finger hung down in front of the keyboard. Necessarily there was somewhat more twisting of the hand, and a very supple wrist must have been a requirement for the rapid playing required for some of the difficult passage work of (say) Elizabethan virginal music.

It strikes one as curious, in looking at the fingering of a scale in any one of the old books, that there was so little attempt at equal treatment of the two hands. One frequently finds the right hand instructed to play up and down the scale with a mere alternation of two fingers, whilst the left hand is, more generously, allowed to employ three or even four.

Nature's insistence on symmetry in the planning of our hands is, of course, unfortunate for the keyboard player. With both thumbs on the same side (i.e. with either two right hands or two left) how much easier would be our scale and arpeggio practice! Nature not having foreseen this type of manual activity, a rather more rational planning of the keyboard would have been helpful. But it is too late to introduce that now (see *Keyboard* 4 for one attempt). The early players do not seem to us today to have solved very cleverly the problem of how to reduce to a minimum the difficulties put in their way by nature and the keyboard, and though it may be conceded that their fingering system seems to have 'worked' (given their instruments and their music), yet it is hard to believe that our present system would not have 'worked' much more effectively.

In performing the old music, however, there is, claimed Mr. Dolmetsch, a great advantage in being accustomed to the usual fingering of the particular period and composer in question; which, he maintained, conduces to the phrasing intended by the composer. No doubt this is in some measure true, the composer of those days, like one of today, accepting 'playability' as one of the conditions imposed upon him, and shaping his passages accordingly to the methods of playing with which he was acquainted. Unfortunately, however, to accustom oneself nowadays to the various methods of fingering of the various periods is the work of a specialist.

2. J. S. Bach's Innovations. The various systems of fingering up to the early part of the eighteenth century were, then, irrational. The introduction of a more considered method of fingering is, like several other musical reforms, to be credited largely to J. S. Bach, though Couperin, Rameau, and other contemporaries made their contribution. Bach told his son, Emanuel (who told Forkel, Bach's biographer), that when he was young the great players used the thumb for big stretches only. He himself, however, used it freely, bringing it out of its hanging position and permanently to the surface of the keyboard by adopting a curved instead of a somewhat flat position for the fingers. He depressed the keys and in due time allowed them to rise, of course, rather by drawing the fingers towards him than by lifting them (see 1). A moment's reflection will show that the bending inward of a finger causes its tip to describe the segment of a circle, so that when it is placed on a key this motion will effect the result desired. Quantz, the great flautist, Frederick the Great's chief musician, in his well-known work on flute playing (which takes a much larger range that its title would lead one to expect) has this passage:

'In the performance of running passages the fingers should not be immediately raised; their tips should rather be slid up to the front of the keyboard and thus withdrawn. In this way will runs be most clearly performed. My advice here is based upon the example of one of the greatest keyboard players, who both followed this method himself and taught it.'

The reference to this paragraph in Quantz's index shows that it is Bach to whom he alludes.

It will be remembered that what is said here about fingering and about finger movement applies to a gentle *tangent* instrument (clavichord, q.v.) or a *plectrum* instrument (virginals, spinet, harpsichord—see *Harpsichord Family*), or to a *wind* instrument (organ)—not to a instrument in which hammers are thrown at strings (pianoforte), in which a different principle is necessary if what we may call the scale of forces, from very soft to very loud, is to be obtained. Nevertheless, in adopting the curved position of the fingers and the free use of the thumb and little finger, Bach had unconsciously taken a step on the road towards the coming pianoforte technique. The previous system had been based on a distinction between 'good' and 'bad' fingers (though, curiously, the views as to which were 'good' and which 'bad' varied in different countries). 'Good fingers' were to be placed on 'good notes' (i.e. accented ones) and 'bad fingers' on 'bad notes' (i.e. unaccented ones). Bach's idea was that all fingers should, by due practice, be brought to the 'good' condition and equally employed—with the general proviso that the thumb and little finger, being nearer to the edge of the keyboard, should not be used on the short keys (what we call black keys, though in those days the colour was often reversed). Forkel says that Bach made the thumb the principal finger, yet it does not

See the Article *Expressionism* on pages 339–40

EXPRESSIONISM. **1.** *Weisse Zickzack* ('White Zigzag'), by Kandinsky, 1922   **2.** *Kleine Freuden* ('Little Joys') by Kandinsky

3, 4. *Visions,* by Schönberg

MICROTONES

See the Article, pages 636–7

5. HANS BARTH AT THE QUARTER-TONE PIANO, 1929. See *Microtones* and *Concerto* 6 c

6. GROTRIAN-STEINWEG QUARTER-TONE PIANO, with extra notes intercalated throughout the keyboard. For such pianos see *Microtones*

7. VYSCHNEGRADSKY'S QUARTER-TONE NOTATION. See *Microtones*

PLATE 58

MUSIC IN THE ENGLISH FAIRS

See the Article on pages 342–3

1. BARTHOLOMEW FAIR, LONDON

'Where Trumpets and Bagpipes, Kettledrums and Fiddlers all were at work'. This fair had a run of over seven centuries (1133–1855). It used to be opened by the Lord Mayor in state. In the 18th century opera performances were one of its attractions

At *LEE* and *HARPER*'s Great Theatrical Booth,

BEHIND the *Marshalsea-Gate*, leading to the *Bowling-Green*, during the Time of *Southwark-Fair*, will be presented, A new Opera, never perform'd here before, call'd,

The DEVIL *to* PAY: Or, *The* WIVES Metamorphos'd Intermix'd with above Thirty New Songs, made to old Ballad Tunes, and Country Dances.

The Part of Sir John Loverule, by Mr. Mullart.

Ranger, by Mr Taylor; Doctor, Mr. Ayres; Butle, Mr. Rosco; Cook, Mr. Eaton. Lady Loverule, Mrs. Mullart; Noll Jobson, Miss Tollet; Lettice, Mrs. Coker; Lucy, Mrs. Hulett: And the Part of Jobson, the Cobler, by Mr. Halett.

And the better to entertain the Gentry, Mrs. Lee has engag'd a Company of Tumblers, lately arrived in London, who perform several surprizing Tricks; particularly, one throws himself off a Scaffold twelve Foot high; another throws himself over 12 Mens Heads; He likewise leaps over 6 Boys, sitting on 12 Men's Shoulders; another tumbles over 16 Swords, as high as Men can hold them; and several other diverting Things too tedious to mention

With Variety of Singing and Dancing by the best Masters.

The Cloaths and Scenes are all entirely New.

We shall continue Playing from Ten in the Morning, 'till Nine at Night.

N. B. The right Book of the Droll is Sold in the Booth, and is Printed and Sold by *G. LEE*, in *Blue-Maid Alley*, *Southwark*; and all others (not Printed by him) are false.

2. AT BARTHOLOMEW FAIR in the early 18th century

3. AN OPERA ANNOUNCEMENT— Southwark Fair

4. A BELL VIRTUOSO at Bartholomew Fair (1760)

appear that he gave it the pivotal position it later held: the idea of proceeding up a right-hand or down a left-hand scale by passing the thumb under fingers, or in the reverse direction passing fingers over the thumb, does not seem to have occurred to him. Bach thus still had a good deal of passing of finger over finger, even making the little finger pass over the ring finger occasionally. In any extended passage on a chordal basis he used the thumb freely, and indeed adopted a mode of fingering hardly distinguishable from that of today, which aims at the minimum of change of hand position.

The equalizing of the fingers, however, went so far with him that he could perform a shake with his ring-finger and little finger just as easily as with any other pair, and meanwhile occupy the rest of the fingers of the same hand in playing some independent melody—which few players would care to attempt on the heavy pianoforte action.

3. C. P. E. Bach and Mozart. Bach's ablest son, Carl Philipp Emanuel, worked out his father's principles a little nearer to a logical conclusion; he ranks, indeed, as one of the founders of modern practice. The only finger-crossing he retained was that of the middle finger over the index finger—a long over a short, and hence not so unreasonable.

To some extent the reforms of both father and son may be due to their preference for the clavichord over the harpsichord. With the clavichord, something like a real 'singing' style (a true legato) was possible if a perfectly smooth passage from finger to finger was secured. And this singing style (or cantabile) was very important to their eyes. Mozart seems to have built on C. P. E. Bach's foundation. He, too, sought cantabile. He asked for a 'quiet, steady hand', and expected that running passages should 'flow like warm oil'.

It is worthy of note that nearly half a century after C. P. E. Bach had published his famous book, *Attempt at the True Manner of Keyboard Performance* (1st part 1753, 2nd part 1762), Beethoven was making his pupils buy and study it, and that, moreover, he was particularly insistent on their learning how to use the thumb. (Related by his pupil Czerny.)

4. The Coming of the Pianoforte—Clementi. We have now reached the period of the pianoforte, which had been played on rare occasions by J. S. Bach, and no doubt more frequently by his sons, but now began to assume the front rank amongst the domestic and concert keyboard instruments, so that Mozart is known to have played it frequently and to have composed his later keyboard works aware that they would be performed upon it.

The pianoforte killed finger-crossing because it demanded an actual blow—though, properly, a blow by pressure, yet a blow, one sufficient to *throw* the hammer at the strings, yet so exactly controlled in force as to throw it with either a piano or a forte result, or a pianissimo or a fortissimo.

The physical differences between clavichord, harpsichord, and pianoforte have just been hinted at and can be grasped more fully by reading the articles devoted to those instruments. Clementi (1752–1832) is looked upon as the founder of a true pianoforte style in composition. He composed, definitely and from the outset, for the pianoforte, whereas his predecessors had at any rate begun by composing for clavichord and harpsichord. He went well beyond C. P. E. Bach. In his fingering-marking will be found no finger-passing in scale passages (except of course in scales in double notes, when it is inevitable). His use of the thumb is the modern one (except that it is not used by him on the short keys, as is sometimes done today). Beethoven, eighteen years Clementi's junior, thought most highly of his compositions, and was much influenced by them and by his technical methods.

For an account of Beethoven's own methods, by his pupil Czerny, see *Pianoforte Playing and Teaching* 3.

5. The Nineteenth and Twentieth Centuries. Later developments in fingering followed, *pari passu*, the developments in keyboard composition. The wide-spreading left-hand chords of Chopin, and his singing right-hand melodies adorned with arabesques, had their influence, of course, as had the greater use of the sustaining pedal that he introduced. The works of Liszt exploited the power of the human hand to the last degree—as it then seemed, though a few degrees later-than-the-last have since been exploited. Fingers had to be prepared to get anywhere and to do anything at a moment's notice, and they learnt to do it (Liszt once played Beethoven's E flat Concerto without the third finger of his right hand, which he had cut on the day of the concert); yet, in fact, the powers of the hand were very closely considered by the composer and types of passage invented accordingly.

Some accepted present-day main principles of fingering are as follows:

(*a*) All fingering looks forward; in planning the fingering of a passage, then, it is well to work backwards.

(*b*) The normal major or minor scale is considered to consist of two groups of three and four notes respectively, representing two hand positions, which are joined by a lateral movement of the thumb under the fingers or the fingers over the thumb. This join is best effected at a point where a long key and a short one happen to lie contiguous in such a way that the thumb can take the long one and the finger immediately concerned the short one. The little finger is not used in scale passages except for the one highest note in the right hand and the one lowest in the left.

(*c*) Though it is preferred, in principle, to follow nature's hint and keep the thumb for the long keys, yet in most sequential passages (longer passages made up of some shorter passage repeated at a higher or lower pitch) this is usually better sacrificed in the interests of

Q

uniformity of fingering throughout. In order to gain freedom, pupils sufficiently advanced are now told to practise all their scales with the C major fingering. Plaidy (1810–74) in his famous book of technical studies directed that every one of them should be practised in every key with the same fingering, and thus finally established the idea, which von Bülow (edition of Cramer's studies), Klindworth, Tovey, and others have strongly supported.

(d) Arpeggio passages are fingered on the basis of an octave span between thumb and little finger, and the choice of the intermediate fingers according to the spaces involved and the natural lie of the fingers in an extended hand.

(e) It is recognized that there exists no one 'right' fingering for a passage. The size and shape of the individual hand have often to be taken into account. Debussy has a piquant introduction to his *Twelve Studies* (1915), in explanation of the lack of fingering-marks. The differences between individual hands is his main reason, but he concludes: 'The absence of fingering marks offers the player an excellent exercise, evading the spirit of contradictoriness which impels us to prefer *not* to put our fingers where the composer has told us, and confirming the eternal principle—"Self-help is the best help".'

This 'eternal principle' was at one time greatly overlooked by pedagogues and the editors of 'instructive editions'. The great player Charles Hallé edited (from 1873 onwards) a *Pianoforte School* and a *Musical Library*, consisting of hundreds of classical compositions, from very easy to very difficult, every note of every one of which had its fingering-mark attached. These publications were for many years in the hands of British pianoforte pupils and, with the numerous 'Scale and Arpeggio Manuals' which also fingered every note, must have trained thousands of young pianists to neglect that 'eternal principle' mentioned with such respect by Debussy. In any case, the fingering of 'every note' is both useless and confusing; nothing is usually necessary beyond the marking of that 'key finger' (as it may be called) which puts the hand in the right position for its next group of notes.

Although, as admitted above, there is no one complete method of fingering good for all hands, every player, if he is to enjoy facility, must have his own more or less fixed method for every type of passage. The thoughtful devising of this is of high importance.

A word or two may be added on the modern device (recommended by Leschetizky and now in common use) of settling the fingering of a passage by the method of 'physical groups'. In this method the unit is considered to be not the single finger but the group of fingers. The grouping is decided experimentally by placing the hand over portions of the passage (as though each portion were a chord), the aim being to discover the means of reducing the fingering of the passage to the smallest possible numbers of groups.

Beethoven, Adagio of Sonata in C minor, No. 5.

3 3 4 5 5
2 2 3 3 3
1 1 2 1 2 etc.

6. 'English' and 'Continental' Systems of Marking. Various methods of indicating fingering have been adopted at different periods in different countries and by different composers. Uniformity has now been very nearly secured, the code being the same as that found by the late Dr. Cummings in use in an English manuscript virginal book in his possession, dated 1599: namely, the numbering of the thumb as 'one' and of the other fingers accordingly. This plan continued in Britain (with occasional fluctuations) until about 1760 and was then gradually abandoned in favour of the German system, which, like the violinist's numeration, called the index finger '1' (using a cross for the thumb). By some strange process, the two systems, British and German, then became reversed, the British calling the index finger 'one' and the German attaching this figure to the thumb. The difficulty thus created in players' simultaneous use of both British and Continental printed music has now caused the almost total abandonment of the so-called 'English' fingering, and the fingers are, for keyboard purposes, now everywhere numbered 1–5, beginning with the thumb—but an illogicality now exists, of course, from the point of view of the pianist who is also a player of some stringed instrument.

7. Organ Fingering. Organ fingering follows the same principles as pianoforte fingering, with an added feature to meet a special characteristic of the instrument.

With the organ, a note ceases sounding the moment the finger is raised from the key (there being no 'sustaining pedal' to prolong the sound), and, further, the note sounds with the same intensity until the finger is raised, so that its cessation is very much more marked than with the pianoforte. Hence, to produce a legato effect a very close joining of notes is needed and a great deal of 'substitution' of fingers is practised, the finger with which a note has been played being replaced (the finger-key still depressed) by another which places the hand in a more suitable position for the notes that are to follow. There is a good deal of this substitution in good pianoforte playing (more than some pupils are taught, perhaps), but not so much as in organ playing.

FINGER ORGAN. See *Mechanical Reproduction of Music* 10.

FINGERSATZ (Ger.). 'Fingering.'

FINITE CANON. See *Canon*.

FINLAND. See *Scandinavia* 6.

FINO (It.). 'As far as', e.g. *Fino al segno*, 'as far as the sign (𝄋)'.

FINZI, GERALD. Born in London in 1901 and died at Oxford in 1956, aged fifty-five. He studied under Bairstow at York and R. O. Morris in London and then devoted himself to composition, producing song cycles; a 'Cantata for Soprano or Tenor and String Orchestra', *Dies Natalis*; *Ode for St. Cecilia's Day* (1947); *Intimations of Immortality* (1950); a *Requiem da Camera*, a clarinet concerto (1949), a violoncello concerto, and other things.

FIOCCO, Father and Son.

(1) PIETRO ANTONIO. Born at Venice in 1650 and died in Brussels in 1714, aged about sixty-four. He held several church and other posts at Brussels and directed the royal orchestra. He left church music, etc.

(2) GIOSEFFO HECTORE. Born at Brussels in 1703 and died there in 1741, aged thirty-eight. He became choirmaster of the cathedral of Antwerp and then of that of Brussels. He had a reputation as harpsichordist and left music for his instrument, as well as motets, etc.

FIORILLO.

(1) FEDERIGO (1755–1823 or later). Violinist-composer (his *36 Caprices or Études* much used) who travelled widely, spending six years in London.

(2) DANTE (born 1905). Prolific American composer; self-taught, but the winner of various (e.g. Guggenheim and Pulitzer) awards.

FIORITURA (It., 'flowering'; plural *Fioriture*). The term is applied to that type of decoration of a melody which was especially common in the eighteenth-century operatic aria (see *Opera* 4); such decorations were often extemporized, and the ability of a singer was largely judged by the ability to introduce *fioriture* that were thought by the audience to be appropriate, skilfully fitted to their place in the melody, and (especially) well designed to show the quality of the voice and the vocal agility of its owner.

The practice of interpolating such embellishments as these was not confined to vocalists. Violinists indulged themselves in the same way, and as late as the 1830s we find the great violinist Ferdinand David, when playing the first violin part in Haydn's string quartets, introducing elaborations of the subject-matter when it reappeared in the recapitulation portion of a movement (see also *Ornaments* 4). It is quite probable that some of (say) the slow movements of Mozart's piano concertos were intended to be embellished in this way. Burney, about 1805 (Rees's *Cyclopædia* s.v. *Adagio*), discussing 'adagios, vocal and instrumental', says: 'An adagio in a song or solo is generally little more than an outline left to the per-

former's abilities to colour. . . . If not highly embellished they soon excite languor and disgust in the hearers.'

Melisma (q.v.) and *Coloratura* (q.v.) are cognate terms. See also *Ornaments or 'Graces'*; *Spain* 1.

FIPPLE FLUTE. See *Recorder Family* 1.

'FIRE' SYMPHONY (Haydn). See *Nicknamed Compositions* 11.

FIRST INVERSION of a Chord. See *Harmony* 24 f.

FIRST MOVEMENT FORM. See *Form* 4, 7, 8.

FIRST OF AUGUST. This tune, claimed as a Welsh folk tune, first came into notice in Britain at the opening of the eighteenth century when a party of Swedish dancers used it: it was then called *The New Swedish Dance*. Later it was attached to a song in praise of the Hanoverian succession, called *The Glorious First of August* (George I came to the throne on 1 August 1714). The name was ingeniously accounted for in Welsh collections, from 1802 onwards, by a reference to the payment of Welsh tithes and the observance of Lammas Day (i.e. 1 August). The history of the whole confusion will be found in articles by the great authority on British songs, Frank Kidson, in the *Musical Times* of September 1895 and February 1911.

FIRST POST. See *Tattoo*.

FIRST VIOLIN. See *Violin Family* 2 a; *Conducting* 4.

FIS (Ger.). F sharp (see Table 7).

FISCHER, CARL. See *Publishing* 9.

FISIS (Ger.). F double sharp (see Table 7).

FISK UNIVERSITY. See *United States of America* 6.

FITZWILLIAM LIBRARY. See *Libraries*.

FITZWILLIAM VIRGINAL BOOK (p. 193, pl. **39.** 4). This is so called because it forms an item in the valuable collection of books, music, paintings, etc., left to Cambridge University by Viscount Fitzwilliam in 1816. It used to be known as 'Queen Elizabeth's Virginal Book', but it is now realized that it can never have belonged to her, and that title is abandoned.

It is the manuscript repertory of an early seventeenth-century amateur virginal player, and constitutes the largest and most valuable treasury of early English keyboard music. The handwriting establishes the fact that the compiler was a Cornish amateur, Francis Tregian (q.v.). It has been published by Breitkopf & Härtel, under the editorship of Fuller Maitland and Barclay Squire, and a book upon it, giving a critical description of its contents, was supplied by Dr. E. W. Naylor (1896).

See references under *Calino Casturame*; *Farnaby*; *Harpsichord* 3; *Folk Song* 5; *Dump*; *In Nomine*; *Carman's Whistle*; *Hexachord*; *Suite* 2; *Mundy, John*; *God save the Queen* 4; *Patronage* 5; *Pianoforte* 21; also compare *Benjamin Cosyn's Virginal Book*; *Will Forster's Virginal Book*; *Parthenia*. For a description of the type of music found in such a collection see *History of Music* 3.

FIVE, THE. See *Russia* 5, 6, 7.

FIVE-THREE CHORD. See *Harmony* 24 e.

FIXED-DOH. See *Tonic Sol-fa* 1.

Fl. Short for 'Flute'.

FLAGEOLET. See *Recorder Family* 3; *Flute Family* 4; *Organ* 14 II.

FLAGEOLET NOTES, FLAGEOLET TONES. The harmonics of the violin, etc., this being the French name for them. See *Acoustics* 8.

FLAGEOLETT, FLAGEOLETTÖNE (Ger.). Flageolet (q.v.), flageolet notes (see above).

FLAMENCO. See *Cante Flamenco*.

FLAT (♭). The sign which, placed before a note, lowers it in pitch by a half-step or semitone. See Table 6. (There is a slight difference of usage in the language of Britain and the United States—in the former 'to flatten' and 'flattened'; in the latter 'to flat' and 'flatted'.) As an adjective applied to a performance 'flat' means inexact intonation on the under side.

FLATTER (Fr.). 'To caress', e.g. *Flatter la corde* 'to caress the string', to bow delicately.

FLATTERZUNGE. See *Tonguing*.

FLAT TWENTY-FIRST. See *Organ* 14 IV.

FLAUTANDO, FLAUTATO (It.). Literally, 'fluting' and 'fluted'—referring to the producing of flute-like tones from the violin, etc., either by (a) bowing near the finger-board with the point of the bow, or (b) using harmonics (see *Acoustics* 8).

FLAUTENDO. A Debussy term, apparently a mis-spelling of *Flautando* (q.v.).

FLAUTI (It.). Flutes (the singular is *Flauto*).

FLAUTINA. See *Organ* 14 II.

FLAUTO (It.). 'Flute'; (the plur. is *Flauti*). See *Flute Family*; *Recorder Family*; *Organ*.

FLAUTO A BECCO. See *Recorder Family* 2.

FLAUTO AMABILE. See *Organ* 14 II.

FLAUTO D'AMORE. See *Flute Family* 5 c.

FLAUTO D'ECO (It.). See *Recorder Family* 2.

FLAUTO DIRITTO. See *Recorder Family* 2.

FLAUTO DOLCE. See *Organ* 14 II.

FLAUTONE. See *Flute Family* 5 c.

FLAUTO PICCOLO. See *Flute Family* 5 b; *Recorder Family* 2.

FLAUTO TRAVERSO. See *Flute Family* 5 a; *Recorder Family* 2; *Organ* 14 II.

F.L.C.M. See *Degrees and Diplomas* 2.

FLEBILE, FLEBILMENTE (It.). 'Mournful', 'mournfully'.

FLECHA, MATEO. Born in Catalonia c. 1520 and there died in 1604, aged eighty-four. He was a churchman and a composer attached for some time to the imperial court at Prague, and composed madrigals and church music. (Cf. *Spain* 5.)

FLECHTENMACHER, ADOLF. See *Rumania*.

FLEET, THOMAS. See *Mother Goose Songs*.

FLEHEND (Ger.). 'Entreating.'

FLEISCHER, OSKAR (1856–1933). See *Greek Church* 4.

FLEMING, SIR AMBROSE. See p. 132, pl. **24. 5.**

FLEMISH SCHOOL. See *Belgium*.

FLESSIBILE, FLESSIBILITÀ (It.). 'Flexible', 'flexibility'.

FLETA, MIGUEL. See *Encore*.

FLETCHER.

(1) JOHN (1579–1625). Dramatist. See reference under *Masque*.

(2) ALICE CUNNINGHAM (1838–1923). See reference under *United States* 7.

FLEURY, LOUIS. See *Flute Family* 4.

FLICORNO, FLICORNI. See *Saxhorn and Flügelhorn Families* 4; *Tuba Group* 5.

FLIEGENDE HOLLÄNDER, DER. See *Flying Dutchman*.

FLIES, BERNHARD. See *Misattributed* (Mozart's 'Wiegenlied').

FLIESSEND (Ger.). 'Flowing.' So *Fliessender*, 'more flowing'.

FLIGHT AND ROBSON, organ-builders, in business about 1800–35. See *Mechanical Reproduction of Music* 10, 11.

FLING. A Scottish dance type, a specially vigorous kind of Reel (q.v.) popular in the Highlands.

FLINTOFT, LUKE. Born (probably at Worcester) on a date unknown, and died in London in 1727. He was a Gentleman of the Chapel Royal, and, being in orders, a minor canon of Westminster Abbey. His importance lies in the claim made for him as the originator of the double-chant, the popular specimen in G minor usually attributed to him being one of the earliest known (see *Anglican Chant* 5).

FLONZALEY QUARTET. See *United States of America* 4.

FLOOD, WILLIAM HENRY GRATTAN (1859–1928). He was organist of several Irish (Roman Catholic) cathedrals, a composer of church music, and an ardent and untiring (but not very cautious or balanced) researcher into the history of British and (especially) Irish music.

See allusions to some of his theories under *Ireland* 8; *Drink to me only*.

FLORA, FLORAL DANCE. See *Furry Dance*.

FLORENCE. See *Italy* 3, 4; *Opera* 1; *Concert* 14; *Ars nova*; *Canti carnascialeschi*; *Street Music* 4; *Isaac, Heinrich*; *Landino*.

FLORID COUNTERPOINT. See *Counterpoint*.

FLÖTE (Ger.; the plur. is *Flöten*). See *Flute Family* 5 a; *Recorder Family*; (for *Stimmflöte* see *Stimme*).

FLÖTENUHR. See *Mechanical Reproduction of Music* 5.

FLOTOW, FRIEDRICH VON (p. 400, pl. **69.** 3). Born in Mecklenburg in 1812 and died at Darmstadt in 1883, aged seventy. He was born a nobleman and educated for the diplomatic service, but discovered in himself a gift for music and gave his life to the theatre. The easy-flowing *Martha*, first heard at Vienna in 1847, is the one of his nearly twenty operas by which he is chiefly remembered today.

See allusions under *Last Rose of Summer*; *Opera* 21 j.

FLOTTANT (Fr.). 'Floating.'

FLOTTER (Fr.). 'To float' (referring to an undulating movement of the bow in violin playing, etc.).

FLOURISH. A trumpet call of the fanfare type. Shakespeare and other Elizabethan dramatists often use the word in this sense in their stage directions. In a more general sense the word has come to mean any florid instrumental passage.

FLOWER, ELIZA. Born at Harlow, Essex, in 1803 and died at Hurstpierpoint in 1846, aged forty-three. She was the daughter of the political writer, Benjamin Flower. She wrote anthems and hymns for the congregation of South Place Chapel, London, and the once familiar chorus 'Now pray we for our Country'. Her sister, Mrs. Sarah Flower Adams, wrote the hymn 'Nearer, my God, to Thee', and she herself wrote the original tune for it—not one of the tunes now usually sung.

See reference under *National Anthems*.

FLOWERS OF THE FOREST. The melody is an old Scottish one. The original words are lost, all but a few lines which were incorporated by Jane Elliott in her version in the middle of the eighteenth century. The words now usually sung are by Mrs. Cockburn and were written a little later (about 1765). Miss Elliott's poem begins, 'I've heard the lilting at our ewe milking'; Mrs. Cockburn's, 'I've seen the smiling of fortune beguiling'. Mrs. Cockburn's version properly has its own tune but is now generally sung to the same one as Jane Elliott's.

The Forest is a district of Selkirk and Peebles; the 'Flowers' are its young men.

FLOYD, CARLISLE. Born at Latta, South Carolina, in 1926. A composer and pianist, on the staff of Florida State University from 1947, he came to notice after the appearance of his successful opera, *Susannah* (1955).

FLÜCHTIG (Ger.). 'Fleet', 'agile'. The comparative is *Flüchtiger* and the noun *Flüchtigkeit*.

FLUE STOPS, FLUE PIPES. See *Organ* 2 a, 14 I-V.

FLÜGEL (Ger.). Grand piano (literally 'wing', alluding to the shape); before the days of the piano the name was applied to the harpsichord. Cf. *Kielflügel*; *Pedalflügel*.

FLÜGELHORN. See *Saxhorn and Flügelhorn Families* for the upper Flügelhorns and *Tuba Group* for the lower ones.

FLUIDO (It.). 'Fluid.' So *Fluidità*, *Fluidezza*, 'fluidity'.

FLÜSSIG (Ger.). 'Fluid', flowing. So *Flüssiger*, 'more fluid', more flowing.

FLÛTE (Fr.). Flute. See *Flute Family* (below); *Recorder Family*; *Organ*.

FLÛTÉ (Fr.). Same as *Flautando* (q.v.).

FLÛTE À BEC. See *Recorder Family* 2.

FLÛTE À CHEMINÉE. See *Organ* 14 II.

FLÛTE ALTO. See *Flute Family* 5 c.

FLÛTE À PAVILLON. See *Organ* 14 II.

FLÛTE D'AMOUR. See *Flute Family* 3 d, 5 c; *Organ* 14 II.

FLÛTE D'ANGLETERRE. See *Recorder Family* 2.

FLÛTE DOUCE. See *Recorder Family* 2.

FLUTE FAMILY

1. Introductory.
2. Structure, Tone Quality, etc.
3. Members of the Family.
4. The Earlier Orchestral and Solo Use.
5. Various Names of the Flute.
6. The Repertory.

(For illustrations see p. 365, p. 60; 465, 82. 4; 865, 146. 6)

1. Introductory. The very ancient race of flutes has long existed in two branches which are in this book, for convenience treated separately, all end-blown flutes being (rather loosely) classed under the heading *Recorder Family*, and all side-blown flutes ('transverse flutes') under the present heading of *Flute Family*. To forestall cavilling it may be noted that this distinction has a certain degree of ancient warrant in the English language: much of our knowledge of instruments in early days comes from the documents concerning the royal household musicians, and these documents use the two terms distinctively; thus in 1543, we find Princess Mary making a New Year's gift of ten shillings to the flute players and another gift of the same amount to the recorder players, and a century and a half later we find the great Purcell occupying amongst other positions that of 'keeper, maker, mender and tuner of . . .

flutes, recorders and all other kinds of wind instruments'.

Only the side-blown flute-proper type is in general orchestral use today.

2. Structure, Tone Quality, etc. The flute as we have it today is a cylindrical tube, but with a more or less conical (parabolic) head, stopped at one end. The player blows across a mouth-hole in the head, and his breath, impinging on the edge of the hole, sets in vibration the column of air inside the tube. Acoustically the tube acts as an 'open' one, the mouth-hole serving to prevent it acting as 'stopped' (for open and stopped pipes see *Organ* 3). The lowest octave of the scale is produced by altering the effective length of the tube by the use of keys covering finger-holes; the next octave is produced in the same way but with increased wind-pressure, and the third octave is produced in a more complicated way by 'cross-fingerings' that are impossible of description here. Thus there is a three-octave range.

The tone of the flute is comparatively weak in the upper partials which make for colourfulness (see *Acoustics* 6). Hence its limpid quality. The lowest octave, particularly when softly blown, is the nearest orchestral approach to a pure tone devoid of upper partials—so that it has a neutral and not very penetrating tone and is sometimes mistaken for the clarinet, which has a hollow sound on its lower notes from their lack of even-numbered partials. The second octave of the flute, being richer in upper partials, sounds smooth and clear; the third octave, being richer again, sounds bright and penetrating. Another well-recognized quality of the flute is its extreme agility—a quality that has sometimes been abused by composers to the point of vulgarity. Shakes and some tremolos are easy, and so are rapid reiterations of notes by the processes called 'double-tonguing' and 'triple-tonguing', and also 'flutter-tonguing' (see *Tonguing*).

The flute, though officially and from its nature a member of the wood-wind section of the orchestra, is now frequently made of silver. A few wealthy amateurs have had flutes of gold.

The flute as we have it today is largely due to Theobald Boehm (*c.* 1793–1881), who greatly modified its structure and mechanism. He invented the modern cylinder-bore flute (with parabolic head), enlarged the finger-holes to increase its power and range of expression, fitted more of them with keys, and invented the system of fingering that bears his name and that has revolutionized flute playing.

See *Boehm System*, and for some further attempts at improvement see *Giorgi Flute*.

3. Members of the Family. The members of the family in use today are as follows:

(*a*) The **Concert Flute** or **Flute in D** (p. 365, pl. **60.** 2). This is the particular member of the family we nowadays mean when we speak simply of 'a flute'. The explanation of the designation 'in D' is that this used to be (in pre-Boehm days) the normal scale of the instrument (corresponding to what we call the 'natural scale' of C on the pianoforte). The range was, however, extended down to C (sometimes to B) by means of keys, and thus the term 'Flute in C' was (and is) occasionally used. The term 'Flute in D' does not imply that the notation used classes it amongst the 'transposing instruments' (q.v.), as does such a similar designation as 'Clarinet in B flat' or 'Horn in F'.

In the normal orchestra of the Haydn–Beethoven period two flutes are usual; from Wagner onwards three are often found.

(*b*) The **Piccolo** or **Octave Flute** (p. 365, pl. **60.** 3). The pitch of this, as used in the orchestra, is an octave above that of the concert flute, but its music is written an octave lower than it sounds. (It is not on this account considered to be a 'transposing instrument', the transposition being merely one of pitch, not

one of key.) It is one of the smallest instruments of the orchestra, yet the brightest, and its shrill tone can, if required, be made to ring out above all the others. It gives the highest notes the orchestra possesses. It is frequently in use in orchestral and military band and drum and fife band music (in the latter in other keys). When it is stated, as above, that the range of the piccolo is an octave above that of the flute, one small qualification should be added—that it lacks the extra notes at the bottom mentioned under 3 *a* above.

The old word **Fife** now usually implies the B flat piccolo—the chief instrument of the drum and fife band (see *Fife*).

In the orchestra the piccolo is usually not provided with a player *ad hoc*, but is taken up as called for by the player of the second flute (or third flute, if there is one).

(*c*) The so-called **Bass Flute**, which ought to be called (as it is in some languages) **Alto Flute**. Its range is the same as that of the concert flute, but a fourth lower. But it is one of the 'transposing instruments' (q.v.), the notation showing its range the same as that of the concert flute; in other words, the composer writes his passages a fourth higher than he intends them to sound. Its tone quality is rich and smooth—comparing with that of the concert flute much as that of the viola does with that of the violin. This instrument is comparatively little used by composers. For a name sometimes given it see (*d*) below.

There is a special *Bass Flute in B flat* used in drum and fife bands, and a **Double Bass Flute** (an octave below the concert flute) now also exists. For other flutes used in drum and fife bands see under *Fife*.

(*d*) **Flûte d'amour.** This now obsolete flute, found in some old scores, had a pitch a third below that of the flute in D, than which it has a more mellow tone. But the bass flute (see above) has sometimes been called by this name.

4. The Earlier Orchestral and Solo Use. In the scores of Purcell, though the side-blown flute, as we have seen, existed, the recorder type of instrument is implied. So it is also in many of the scores of Lully, but in France in his time improvements were effected in the side-blown flute, and he was probably the first to introduce it into the orchestra. Bach and Handel use sometimes one form and sometimes the other, indicating which they wish and so recognizing the essential difference of tone quality. From Haydn onwards it can be taken that the side-blown instrument is intended, though Mozart (in *The Abduction from the Seraglio*) has used the flageolet, and so has Gluck.

The side-blown flute had an enormous popularity during the eighteenth and earlier nineteenth centuries, and vast quantities of music were composed for it. This form of flute seems to have been popular in Germany earlier than in England (though it was in some use there from the early sixteenth century) and to have really 'come in', in England, with the Hanoverian succession (but cf. *Loeillet, Jean*); hence its common name *German Flute* (and the corresponding name for the end-blown instrument, *English Flute*). Once the instrument 'caught on' in England it became an enormous social success (p. 365, pl. **60**. 7), so that if any collection of eighteenth- or early nineteenth-century family portraits be examined one or two male members of the family of that period are likely to be found pictured with a flute in their hands (the corresponding lady's interest, in fashionable society, was the harp). Whole operas and oratorios were 'arranged' (cf. *Arrangement*) for flute solo. The 'Gentlemen's Concerts' (see *Concert* 10) were founded in Manchester in 1774, as a band of twenty-six flutes. Macfarren, visiting the Isle of Man in 1837, found an orchestra consisting of a few violins, one violoncello, one clarinet, and sixteen flutes. Stanford relates that in Dublin in his youth (the 1850s and 1860s) the 'Anacreontic Society' passed a rule that their orchestra should henceforward never include more than twenty flutes.

The use of the flute as an 'obbligato' instrument with the voice was at one time common. Bach used it in this way a good many times. Handel's 'Sweet Bird' (*Il Penseroso*) is another example. Three or four elderly *chevaux de bataille* are still occasionally ridden into action —Bishop's 'Lo, here the gentle lark', the Mad Scene in Donizetti's *Lucia* (1835), and the air of Mysoli in Félicien David's *Perle du Brésil* (1851). In more recent music the flute is used in a much less showy but not less effective way (e.g. Ravel's 'La Flûte enchantée', from *Schéhérazade*) and some works of Bantock for flute and voice (unaccompanied). The late nineteenth and early twentieth centuries produced some very fine expressive players, such as the Frenchman Louis Fleury (1878–1925) and the British-naturalized Dutchman, A. L. Fransella (1865–1935).

5. Various Names of the Flute. (*a*) The normal side-blown flute (see 3 a) is or has been known by these various names:

German Flute.
Cross Flute, Transverse Flute, Flauto traverso, Traverso, Traversa (It., Handel often uses this form of the word); *Flûte traversière* (Fr.); *Traversflöte, Querflöte* (Ger.).
Concert Flute; Flute in D; Flute in C.
Grande Flûte (Fr.); *Grosse Flöte* (Ger.).

The French 'Flûte', the Italian 'Flauto', and the German 'Flöte', without prefix or suffix (in music later than Bach) also imply this type.

(*b*) The **Piccolo** (see 3 b) is also known as *Octave flute*; *Petite flûte, Petite flûte Octave* (Fr.); *Kleine flöte* or *Pickelflöte* (Ger.); and *Flauto piccolo* or *Ottavino* (It.).

(*c*) The **Bass Flute** (see 3 c) is also known as *Flûte Alto* (Fr.); *Altflöte* (Ger.); *Flautone* (It.).

The **Flûte d'amour** (Fr., see 3 d) is also known as *Flauto d'amore* (It.) and *Lieblichflöte* (Ger.).

For the various names of the end-blown flutes see *Recorder Family.*

6. The Repertory. The following list is a mere sketch, but it serves to give an idea of the character of the repertory.

Quantz was the great flute performer and composer of the eighteenth century; his association with that keen flautist **Frederick the Great** (q.v.) led to the composition of 300 flute concertos and 200 sonatas and other works by the professional and a great quantity of music also by the amateur, a good deal of which is still available.

Bach and **Handel** each left half a dozen Sonatas for flute and harpsichord. Bach's Overture (i.e. Suite) in B minor is for flute and strings; his son Emanuel wrote a fine Sonata for unaccompanied flute.

Haydn left one Sonata for flute and harpsichord, three Trios for flute, cello, and piano, two Trios for two flutes and cello, a number of Trios for flute, violin, and cello, and a few other compositions of this character.

Mozart provided two Concertos and a Double Concerto for flute and harp, and also three Quartets for flute and strings.

Beethoven wrote a Serenade for flute, violin, and viola, and a Trio for flute, bassoon, and piano. His friend **Kuhlau,** in the early nineteenth century, is the friend also of all flautists, for from him they have received a plentiful provision of material of good quality and of deeper emotion than had previously been common, so that he has been called 'The Beethoven of the Flute'; some of his music is for two, three, or four flutes alone. **Schubert** wrote a set of variations for Flute and Piano.

Karg-Elert wrote a *Sonata Appassionata* for flute alone.

Reger left two Trios (Serenades) for flute, violin, and viola, and other composers have also used this combination.

A Suite by **Benjamin Godard** and a Concertina by **Chaminade** are popular.

Of recent years **Koechlin** and one or two others have revived a type that was very popular during the eighteenth century—the composition for two flutes alone: **Hindemith** has a Canonic Sonatina for this combination.

Tovey composed Variations on a Theme of Gluck for flute and string quartet. **Dubensky** has written a Caprice for piccolo.

Boughton wrote a concerto for flute and strings; **Ibert** one for flute and orchestra.

Debussy's short *Syrinx* is for a single unaccompanied flute. He has also a Sonata for flute, viola, and harp.

Philippe Gaubert (q.v.) was one of the finest composers for flute of recent times.

For Flute Stops see *Organ* 14 II. For Mechanical Flute see *Mechanical Reproduction* 9.

FLÛTE HARMONIQUE (Fr.). Mouth organ. See *Reed-Organ Family* 3, 10 b.

FLÛTE PETITE. See *Flute Family* 5 b.
FLUTTER-TONGUING. See *Tonguing.*

FLYING DUTCHMAN, THE (*Der Flie-gende Holländer*, Wagner), Produced at Dresden in 1843. Libretto by the composer.

ACT I

SCENE: *A Rocky Shore, with Daland's Ship*[1]

Daland (*Bass*), a Norwegian sea-captain, meets the **Flying Dutchman** (*Baritone*) in his ghostly vessel. The latter, having sworn an oath to sail round the Cape of Good Hope, was taken at his word by the Devil and condemned to range the seas eternally, unless, in coming on land once in every seven years, he should find a woman whose faithful love should redeem him.

He longs for a home, and offers Daland his treasures if he will receive him, even for a night. Finding that Daland has a daughter, he wonders if she is to be his redeeming angel.

ACT II

SCENE: *A Room in Daland's House*

Senta (*Soprano*) is spinning and singing with her maidens: singing about the legendary Dutchman, of whom she has a picture. She longs to be his means of salvation.

Erik (*Tenor*), a young huntsman, loves her. He has dreamed that the Dutchman carried her off. The latter, brought in by her father, pleads his cause, and she agrees to marry him.

ACT III

SCENE: *The Bay, and Daland's House*

Daland's sailors and village maidens at first invite the Dutchman's crew to join their cheer, but soon become frightened by these ghostly sailors. Erik, pleading with Senta not to desert him, is overheard by the Dutchman, who, believing that he has lost, with her, his only hope, rushes aboard his ship, revealing to the horrified villagers his name and nature. Senta casts herself into the sea, the Dutchman's ship vanishes, and he, redeemed at last, is seen ascending with her in apotheosis.

See *Opera* 21 k.

FOCO. Older form of *Fuoco* (It.), 'fire'.

FOCOSO. 'Fiery'; *Focosamente*, 'in a fiery way'; *Focosissimo*, 'very fiery'.

FOERSTER, JOSEF BOHUSLAV (p. 109, pl. **20**. 3). Born at Dětenice, Bohemia (at that time Austrian territory), in 1859 and died at Nový Vesteč in 1951, aged ninety-one. He was the son of another Josef, also a musician. Before the 1914 War he worked (as teacher and critic) for ten years in Hamburg and for fifteen years in Vienna, in which cities his wife, the singer Berta Lauterer, was engaged in the opera. After the War he returned and settled in Prague, where he occupied a position of importance.

His compositions, which are numerous and include operas and symphonies, are very subjective in character. If they are to be considered

[1] See allusion to the Overture under *Overture* 4.

as nationalistic it is in the sense that through them a Czech speaks, rather than that in them the idioms of Czech folk music appear. They are remarkable as the expression of a highly ideal conception of life.

FOGG, ERIC (in full, Charles William Eric). Born in Manchester in 1903 and died in London in 1939, aged thirty-six. He aroused attention by fluent composition at an early age, and produced a considerable list of works in different forms to his credit. He was attached to the British Broadcasting Corporation.

FOIRE DES ENFANTS. See 'Toy' Symphony.

FOIS (Fr.). 'Time', e.g. *Première fois*, 'first time'; *Deux fois*, 'twice'.

FOKINE. See *Ballet* 5, 9; *Coq d'or*.

FOLGE (Ger.). 'Succession', 'series', 'continuation'.

FOLGEN (Ger.). 'To follow'; so the various parts of the verb, as *Folgt*, 'follows'.

FOLÍA or **FOLLÍA** (accent on the 'i'). The story of the Folía is one of the most curious in the history of music. The name is originally that of a wild Portuguese dance having many of the elements of the English Morris dance, and like it connected with fertility rites. Various melodies used for this dance are extant, but a particular one of these came to have an enormous vogue that endured for at least three and a half centuries, and this tune is still extremely familiar to concert audiences all over the world, owing to one famous composer's treatment of it. (See *Melody* 7.)

etc.

(Cf. *Melody* 7 for the above tune in full, and for a somewhat similar obsession of composers with a very simple melody over a long period—but in this case little more than a century and then only in one country—see *In Nomine*.)

During that long period composer after composer has used this melody as a basis for some more or less elaborate piece of music (almost always in the shape of an Air and Variations; cf. *Romanesca* for a similar case). This becomes more striking when we notice its simplicity (its compass, as generally found, is no more than a perfect fifth) and the fact that in a great many cases the composers use the same bass as one another—one that has somehow become traditional. Corelli, for instance, uses this melody and bass in his twelfth Sonata for violin and harpsichord (figured bass), which sonata is nothing but a sort of combined Variation and Ground (q.v.) on this melody and bass, and is the still popular piece alluded to above.

The following is an attempt at a chronological list of composers known to have used this Folía tune. It is thought to be, at any rate,

1. FRANK KIDSON
See the Article on p. 553

2. MARJORY KENNEDY-FRASER
See the Article on p. 550

3. CECIL SHARP
See the Article on p. 947

4. REBECCA HOLLAND
One of Sharp's sources

5. JOHN SHORT
Another of Sharp's sources

6. SHARP AND HIS ASSISTANT, MAUD KARPELES
IN AN ENGLISH-SETTLED MOUNTAIN DISTRICT
OF THE APPALACHIANS

7. ANOTHER OF SHARP'S
APPALACHIAN SOURCES
Mrs. Wheeler and family

1. ELEVENTH-CENTURY FLUTE. The discovery of this wall-painting in the cathedral of Kieff, South-west Russia, shows the antiquity of the transverse form of the instrument to be far greater than had before been suspected. (For an account see paper by John Finn read at the Exhibition of the Worshipful Company of Musicians, 1904)

2. CONCERT FLUTE—English make

3. PICCOLO—Boehm system. See the Article on p. 114

4. FLUTE PLAYER, by the Netherlands painter O. Vorsterman (engraved by L. Vorsterman, 1595–1676)

5. A YOUNG FIFER in the 18th century (from Hogarth's *March to Finchley*, 1750). See Article *Fife*

6. AN OLD FIFER IN THE 19TH CENTURY IN RETIREMENT (Chelsea Military Hospital, 1882)

7. SOLEMN CULTURE OF THE FLUTE amongst English gentlemen of the 19th century (from *Punch* 1870, where examples of the amazing popularity of the instrument at that date and for a century before make for us today entertaining reading). Cf. *Flute Family* 4

8. A ROYAL FLAUTIST. See the Article *Frederick the Great*

more complete than any list that has heretofore appeared, but it is certain that dozens of examples have been overlooked.

Juan Ponce, apparently for guitar, *c.* 1500; **Giovanni Stefanini,** song with lute accompaniment, 1622; **Carlo Milanuzzi,** lute piece, 1623; **Ambrosio Colonna,** cittern piece, 1627; **Enrico Schmelzer,** a movement in his music for an equestrian ballet; **Frescobaldi,** keyboard setting, 1630; **Christopher Simpson,** in *The Division Violist,* 1685 (at this period the air and bass were recognized and customary material for the art of playing 'Divisions', i.e. extemporary variations, on the viol); **Gaspar Sanz,** for guitar, *c.* 1670; **d'Anglebert,** harpsichord piece, 1689; **J. P. Förtsch,** in opera, *Die grossmüthige Thalestris,* 1690; **Marais,** for viols, 1692; song of poet, Neumeister, *Du strenge Flavia,* set to this melody, *c.* 1697; **G. Grimm,** harpsichord variations in *Tablaturbuch,* 1698; **Pasquini** (1637–1710), *Partite diverse di Follia,* for the harpsichord; **Corelli,** Sonata XII, 1700; Copenhagen MS. (Tablature Book of Charlotte Trollens), *Le Voli de Spang,* 1702; (D'Urfey poet), verses 'The King's Health set to Farinel's Ground', *c.* 1718; **Keiser,** in a Singspiel, *Der lächerliche Prinz Jodelet,* 1726; *Book of Cantiques of Diocese of Alais,* 1735, has Passion of Christ set to this air, which at this period was commonly used for such purposes; **Vivaldi,** as a sonata for two violins and cello, 1737; **A. Scarlatti,** in *Toccate per Cembalo,* and also in *Varie Introduttioni per sonare;* **D. Scarlatti,** *Variazioni sulla Follia di Spagna;* **Bach,** in the *Peasant Cantata,* 1742; **Corrette,** in a harpsichord piece for beginners, 1753, and in *Les Amusements de Parnasse* for harpsichord, *c.* 1775; **Grétry,** in the opera, *L'Amant jaloux,* 1778; **C. P. E. Bach,** twelve variations for harpsichord or pianoforte; **Cherubini,** in the opera *L'Hôtellerie portugaise,* 1798; **J. F. Reichardt,** song in his *Liederspiele,* 1804; **Liszt,** Spanish Rhapsody for piano, 1863; **Rachmaninof,** Variations on a Theme by Corelli (*sic*).

A name often given to the tune connects it with Michel Farinelli (q.v.). Thus Simpson in his *Division Violist* (1685) gives 'Faronell's Division on a Ground'. But the commonest name connects the tune with Spain, as *Les Folies d'Espagne;* probably, whilst the dance is in origin a Portuguese one, either it or this particular tune for it passed into general European currency through Spain.

Occasionally we find the fact of the existence of the ground-bass principle in so many settings of the tune leading to the use of the term 'Folía' as almost the equivalent of the general term Chaconne or Passacaglia (see *Chaconne and Passacaglia*).

Referring to the allusion above to Corelli's *La Follía,* or Sonata XII, it is necessary to state that elaborations of it, bearing his name but going far beyond the violin technique of Corelli's time, and exhibiting a spirit very foreign to the original, are often heard in the concert-room, sometimes with orchestra—and often with no note in the programme as to the unauthenticity of the version.

A word may be added on the general character of both the particular folía air used by Corelli and so many of his predecessors and successors and on the general folía style as exemplified in other airs bearing the name. Usually the style is that of a dignified saraband (q.v.). Then where does the wild 'folly' or 'madness' of the original dance come in? (But the stately saraband itself was at one time denounced as 'lascivious'; see *Sarabande*.)

FOLIES D'ESPAGNE. See *Folia.*

FOLK DANCE. See *Dance; Form* 14.

FOLK DANCE SOCIETY. See *English Folk Dance and Song Society; Country Dance.*

FOLK MASS. See *Mass* 5.

FOLK SONG

(For some portraits see p. 364, p. 59.)

1. Origin and Meaning of the Term. The expressions 'Folk Music', 'Folk Song', and 'Folk Dance' are comparatively recent. They are extensions of the term 'Folk Lore' which was coined in 1846 by W. J. Thoms, a famous English antiquary (editor of *Notes and Queries*), to cover the idea of the traditions, customs, and superstitions of the uncultured classes: his term is now understood to include arts and crafts, and as investigation has proceeded and the branches of the subject have become more individually important, various sectional terms have come into use, even to 'Folk Cookery' (exhibition in London, 1931).

The term 'Folk Lore' seems to have fixed itself in usage amongst some continental European nations as securely as 'football' or 'five o'clock tea', but such nations do not as a rule use the words 'Folk Music', 'Folk Song', and 'Folk Dance', the one term 'Folk Lore' covering all. The Germans, however, have the word 'Volkslied' for Folk Song (see further mention below).

A large part of the modern interest in folk poetry and folk music comes from the work of Bishop Percy in the middle of the eighteenth century (see *Ballad* 5): this it was that first aroused a largely town-living world, that was beginning to lose touch with its own countryside, to the fact that something valuable had, in the migration, been left behind. Percy was concerned only with the poetry, but the interest in the music has been a natural consequence.

The British Folk Music has now been, perhaps, as diligently collected and as thoughtfully studied as any in Europe—and possibly more so than any other. A clear distinction is made between Folk Song (no composer traceable and no single composer to be postulated) and mere Popular Song. This distinction corresponds to that of the German *Volkslied* and *Volkstümliches Lied* (mere national or popular song)—but the Germans do not sufficiently maintain this valuable, and indeed necessary, distinction. Nor do American musicians at present always preserve the original significance of the term 'Folk Song', tending to apply it indiscriminately both to the genuine product of the folk mind and to any songs that have become widely accepted, as, for instance, those of Stephen Foster (see *American Musical Terminology* 10).

2. Nature of Folk Song. There are two opposing theories as to the origin of folk song. One is that mentioned under *Ballad* 4: it is a communal composition—which does not preclude the fact that any individual specimen (or the germ of it) must necessarily have been originally launched into use by some individual. According to this theory folk music is the composition of the race that produces it; it commonly expresses racial characteristics in a very definite way. The difference between English and Irish folk song is just one obvious example; the English is tuneful and rhythmic, but much less mystical in feeling than the Irish (cf. *Ballad* 1). The other theory sees folk music as no more than art music changed and probably debased by the successive guardians of an oral tradition.

Folk-song tunes are always verse-repeating; they are often in the old modes (see *Modes* 6), the Dorian and Mixolydian being common in England; some, especially in Scotland, are in the pentatonic scale (see *Scales* 10). The rhythms are often free, so that when they are notated measures of unequal value have to some extent to be employed: in both these respects there is an obvious resemblance to plainsong. (Many experts, however, consider the metrical irregularities carefully notated by collectors to be no more than an expression of that vagueness as to rhythm often encountered among singers.) Further, as in plainsong so in folk music, the tunes are purely melodic: there is little evidence of the existence of any folk harmony. (But see references to Iceland, Portugal, and South Africa under *Harmony* 4; also to Russia under *Russia* 1). Practically all folk music (using the term in the strictest sense) has come into existence as the accompaniment of song or dance. It may almost be said that primitive music meant simply for instrumental performance does not exist.

A provisional definition of folk music adopted by the International Folk Music Council (q.v.) in 1955 runs as follows: 'Folk Music is music that has been submitted to the process of oral transmission. It is the product of evolution and is dependent on the circumstances of continuity, variation, and selection. ... The term can therefore be applied to music that has been evolved from rudimentary beginnings by a community uninfluenced by art music; and it can also be applied to music which has originated with an individual composer and has subsequently been absorbed into the unwritten, living tradition of a community. But the term does not cover a song, dance, or tune that has been taken over ready-made and remains unchanged. It is the fashioning and re-fashioning of the music by the community that give it its folk character.'

3. History of the Folk Music Movement. The business of taking down folk song from the lips of the people, and similarly of taking down folk-dance tunes and steps from their fiddles and their legs, was very actively pursued in Britain towards the end of the nineteenth century and at the beginning of the twentieth (probably only just in time to save a great mass of beautiful material). Some of the leaders in the movement were the Revd. Sabine Baring-Gould (English), Revd. John Broadwood, Miss Lucy Broadwood (English), Frank Kidson (chiefly English), Mary Neal (English), Mrs. Milligan Fox (Irish), Mrs. Kennedy-Fraser (Hebridean, p. 364, pl. **59.** 2; also p. 945, pl. **160.** 4), Vaughan Williams (English), and, especially, Cecil Sharp (1859–1924; p. 364, pl. **59.** 3). Sharp's publications are many and valuable; they include a book of about 500 songs collected in the Southern Appalachians of the United States (with Olive Dame Campbell), very many of these being variants (as to words and music) of songs still or lately current in the British countryside.

British folk music societies have been established as follows: English Folk Song Society, 1898; Irish Folk Song Society, 1904; Welsh Folk Song Society, 1908; English Folk Dance Society, 1911 (combined with the English Folk Song Society, 1932). All these societies publish journals, in which newly collected examples are given permanent record. Largely as a result of the work of these societies both folk songs and folk dances have come much into school use, and thus the fear that these two branches of national traditional art may become extinct has been removed. (It was the admirable policy of Sir Arthur Somervell, during his tenure of office as chief inspector of music in the schools of England and Scotland, to emphasize the value of the heritage of national tune and the right of the child to the enjoyment of this heritage, but the pure folk-songists criticized him for not sufficiently distinguishing between national composed song and true folk song.) There has been a corresponding effort in the United States to enable the children to express themselves in the songs of the different European races from which they come.

It is to be noted that Scotland and Ireland were greatly helped in the preservation of their folk tunes by the work of Burns (1759–96) and Moore (1779–1852), who wrote new and lovely poems to the old tunes. Burns was in close touch with George Thomson (p. 945, pl. **160.** 3), who for half a century was Secretary to the Board for the Encouragement of Arts and Manufactures in Scotland, and thus in touch with all parts of the country. He was a musical enthusiast who set to work to collect the old songs of Scotland and Ireland and the harpers' airs of Wales. He engaged the foremost composers of the time, including Haydn, Beethoven, and Weber, to write accompaniments; he even tried to persuade Beethoven to write sonatas and chamber music with the airs as subject-matter. This was an unscientific yet, for its period, highly commendable attempt to conserve a national possession. (See *Scotland* 1; *Ireland* 1.)

It is to be noted that English folk tune does not enter into Thomson's scheme; and indeed none was then believed to exist, so far had the musicians and the educated classes become separated from the 'folk'. About 1805 Burney (Rees's *Cyclopædia*, s.v. 'Simplicity in Music') wrote: 'Though the natives of Scotland, Ireland and Wales can boast of national tunes, both plaintive and spirited, that are characteristic, pleasing and distinct from each other, the English have not a melody which they can call their own except the hornpipe and the Cheshire round' (see *Round* 2). In 1878 we find Carl Engel, the then authority on national music, who had at that time been over thirty years living in England, writing with but half-conviction: 'Some musical enquirers have expressed the opinion that the country people of England are not in the habit of singing, but this opinion would probably be found to be only partially correct if search were made in the proper places.' In Grove's *Dictionary of Music*, 1st edition (1878 and following years), there appeared articles on Scottish, Irish, and Welsh national music, but none on English, because, as the 2nd edition tells us (1910), 'it was the settled conviction of musicians that English folk music worth speaking about did not exist'. And even in this 2nd edition the English Folk Music article got in, apparently, by the skin of its teeth, for it is placed in the Appendix to the last volume.

Over 5,000 English folk tunes and variants have now been collected; it is curious that the non-existence of English folk tunes should ever have been suggested, in view of the fact that since the early eighteenth century (1728) many operas have been made out of very little else (see *Beggar's Opera* and *Ballad Opera*). The large number of English ballad operas (apparently forgotten by Burney) would today offer an invaluable treasury of folk tune but for the fact that the eighteenth-century arrangers greatly 'civilized' the tunes—turning the modes into modern keys, ironing out the rhythms, etc.

The decline in the popularity of the English folk song began, according to old singers, with the greater spread of means of transport and the increased migration to the towns about 1860, so that the collecting movement began too late to save all that should have been saved. A very large body of British folk music has been collected in various parts of the United States (see reference above to Sharp and Campbell; also *Ballad* 3), and its publication there is frequent. Obviously a great proportion of the corpus of the folk music of Europe could have been collected there if no immigrant had been allowed to leave Ellis Island until he had been stripped of all he possessed of it. (See 4, below, for the 'dogie songs' that have developed in Arizona.)

Eastern Canada forms one of the best collecting grounds for French folk song. A unique opportunity for the study of music in its most primitive forms was taken by the late Professor Harold Davies, of the University of Adelaide, who phonographically recorded some of the tunes of the aboriginals. He stated that they possess no musical instruments whatever—in which they are probably unique.

The phonograph and tape recorder have been of the greatest service in the collection of folk music everywhere (see *Gramophone* 7); they can, of course, record any interval and any rhythm—which no notation can.

4. The Words of Folk Songs. Returning to the re-writing of the poems of folk songs, it may be observed that, although many lovely and sensitive folk poems exist, yet as a body the tunes are finer than their words, education being more of a factor in the production of a poem than of a tune. Frequently the words of a folk song have become so corrupted by successive singers as to contain lines that make strange sense or no longer make any sense at all (cf. *Ballad* 4). Obsolete expressions are preserved in some songs, as, for instance, old numerals in some children's singing games. The poems of some folk songs have a religious significance that is now lost, except to the archaeologist and anthropologist, and the motions of many folk dances point to pagan rites. The words of folk songs undergo much mutation, and the same tune can be found in different parts of the country set to different words. A proportion of songs in every country has to do with particular occupations, to which they form an accompaniment: examples of widely different character are the songs used in the processes of domestic cloth manufacture in the Hebrides and some of the cowboy songs of the states of Texas, New Mexico, and Arizona, where a folk-song growth was still until recently in process. Professor John A. Lomax, in his *Cowboy Songs* (1927), says:

'Not only were sharp, rhythmic yells (sometimes beaten into verse) employed to stir up lagging cattle, but also during the long watches the night-guards, as they rode round and round the herd, improvised cattle lullabies which quieted the animals and soothed them to sleep. Some of the best of the so-called 'dogie songs' seem to have been created for the purpose of preventing cattle stampedes—such songs coming straight from the heart of the cowboy, speaking familiarly to his herd in the stillness of the night.'

This quotation is given here to emphasize the fact that folk song is not necessarily archaic, and that its making still goes on in less sophisticated communities where the conditions of life call for self-entertainment: there are probably many parts of Europe where the origination and evolution of folk poems, folk tunes, and folk dances are still in full activity.

5. Composers' Use of Folk Tune. The outburst of national feeling all over Europe during the middle of the nineteenth century (and especially about 1848) gave a great impetus to the cult of folk tune; the desire of composers to express their nationality in their music thrust them into the activity of collecting and studying their national melodies. Previous to this, folk tune had often been used by composers. A glance through the mere titles of the three hundred compositions in the Fitzwilliam Virginal Book (an amateur performer's manuscript collection made in the early years of the seventeenth century) will show how often the English Elizabethan and early Stuart composers evolved their music from folk tune themes. The indebtedness of Haydn to Croat folk tune has been demonstrated by Kuhač (1880) and Hadow (1897); it has been argued that folk themes enter occasionally into Beethoven's symphonies, piano sonatas, and string quartets. The nationalist movement in music brought a much more frequent, definite, and open use of folk themes or themes in folk idiom: Grieg (Norwegian) and Dvořák (Bohemian) are two names that will occur to every reader. The nineteenth-century Bohemian School (Smetana, Dvořák, etc.) and nineteenth-and early twentieth-century Spanish school (Albéniz, Granados, Falla, Turina, etc.) have made much use of the national folk-tune idiom; the French, Italian, and German schools hardly any; some of the British school a great deal (Stanford, Vaughan Williams, etc.; see also *Grainger*); the music of the Russian school of the nineteenth century was very much based on folk study, in which study Balakiref and Rimsky-Korsakof were pioneers; Hungary, from Liszt to Béla Bartók, has made use of folk material. Roughly speaking, it would seem that it was the nations that were just asserting themselves (or, after a period of eclipse, reasserting themselves) that sought the means of national expression in the use of the national melodic and rhythmic idioms. It will be remembered that Dvořák's stay in America (1892–5) gave him the idea that an American inspiration for truly national music might be derived from the Negro melodies or Indian chants, and that his 'New World' Symphony actually embodies Negro elements. This idea (probably a false one, since the tunes in question are alien to the white races) has never been seriously and systematically followed up, but the American Indian melodies have been carefully collected under Government auspices by Frances Densmore and others and have formed the basis for a certain amount of composition, and the Negro music has likewise been collected and studied by Krehbiel, Professors Odum and Johnson, and others, and (especially in the form of 'spirituals') has become widely known, whilst Negro dance-rhythms and orchestral effects have found their way into every dance hall (see *United States*; *Jazz*).

6. Folk Music the Basis of all Music. It is self-evident that the germ of all music lies in folk music. Music existed for thousands of years before the coming of the professional and academically-trained composer, and has continued to develop since, quite apart from his activities (until comparatively recently in ways barely recognized by him). Every form of vocal and instrumental music we possess has developed out of folk song or dance, and it is no more possible to make a balanced and comprehensive study of the history of music without an examination of the treasures of folk tune than it is to make a similar study of literature without an examination of folk poems and folk tales.

The simplest way of asserting this truth, perhaps, is to put it that folk music represents the culture of the countryside and art music the culture of the city, and that no complete understanding of life is possible to a man who knows it only in its city complexities.

For folk dance see general article *Dance*. The chief dances of all races are briefly described in articles under the names of those dances. There are also references in the articles bearing the names of various races and countries (e.g. *Scotland* 1; *Spain* 3; *Jewish Music* 7; *United States* 6, 7).

For more on folk song see the articles *Song*, *Ballad*, *Street Music*, *Shanty*. There are also references under the names of the various races and countries, as also under the names of composers mentioned in the present article, and under *Form* 14.

'FOLK SONG' (Mendelssohn's, for piano). See *Nicknamed Compositions* 14.

FOLK SONG SOCIETY. See *English Folk Dance and Song Society*.

FOLLÍA. See *Folia*.

FOMIN, YEVSTIGNEY. See *Opera* 17 b.

FONDS D'ORGUE (Fr.). The 'Foundation Stops' of the organ, or the 'Foundation Tone' —for the term is, unfortunately, like the corresponding English word, used in two senses (see *Foundation*). *Jeux de fonds* definitely means the Foundation Stops (i.e. all the stops except the Mutation Stops).

FOOT. See *Metre*.

FOOTE, ARTHUR WILLIAM (p. 1041, pl. 170. 3). Born at Salem, Massachusetts, in 1853 and died at Boston in 1937, aged eighty-four. He was the only important American composer of his generation to have been educated entirely in his own country. Amongst his works are orchestral overtures, an orchestral suite, a serenade, and a suite for strings; a string quartet, choral works, some excellent songs, and many piano pieces. (Cf. *United States* 8.)

FORBES, JOHN. Seventeenth-century Aberdeen music printer. See *Scotland* 8.

See the Articles under the individual names

1. LULLY (1632–87)

2. J. F. REBEL (1661–1747)

3. COUPERIN (1668–1733)

4. RAMEAU (1683–1764). By J. Allasseur

5. CLÉRAMBAULT (1676–1749)

6. MÉHUL (1763–1817)

7. HABENECK (1781–1849)

8. BOÏELDIEU (1775–1834)

9. AUBER (1782–1871)

See also plates at pages 369, 384–5, and 388

1. BERLIOZ (1803–69). The most striking example of 19th-century French Romanticism—*Not Rule but direct reaction to Feeling*

2. FÉLICIEN DAVID (1810–76) in his costume as a Saint-Simonian (1832)

3. OFFENBACH (1819–80)—as a contemporary caricaturist saw him

5. LALO (1823–92)

6. SAINT-SAËNS (1835–1921)

4. GOUNOD (1818–93)

7. DELIBES (1836–91)

8. BIZET (1838–75)

See also the plates at pages 384–5 and 388

FORD.

(1) THOMAS. Born about 1580; died in London in 1648, aged about sixty-eight. He was a lutenist and author of *Musick of Sundrie Kindes*, including some beautiful ayres with lute accompaniment.

(2) JOHN (early seventeenth-century dramatist). See reference under *Masque*.

(3) MRS. L. G. See *Keep the Home Fires Burning*.

FORD FOUNDATION. See *Jeunesses musicales; Opera* 21 m.

FOR HE'S A JOLLY GOOD FELLOW. See *Malbrouk*.

FORKEL, JOHANN NIKOLAUS (1749–1818). He was a German organist and director of music at the University of Göttingen who wrote many useful books on music, including one of the earliest histories of the art, and, in particular, the first biography of Bach.

See passing references under *Clavichord* 5; *Jewish Music* 8; *God save the Queen* 16; *Fingering* 2.

FORLANA or **FURLANO**(It.); **FORLANE** (Fr.). A popular old Italian dance, six-in-a-measure—a sort of sarabande or gigue (q.v.). Bach has one in his orchestral suite in C, Ravel one in *Le Tombeau de Couperin*. (The name 'Ballo Furlano' is found in the sixteenth century attached to four-in-a-measure compositions, something like Allemandes.)

FORM

1. The Psychological Necessity of Form.
2. Requirements on the Part of Composer and of Audience.
3. The Main Principle.
4. The Six Existing Forms.
5. Simple *Binary* Form.
6. Ternary Form.
7. Compound *Binary* Form.
8. A Summary of Preceding Points.
9. Rondo Form.
10. An Elaboration of the Rondo.
11. The Air with Variations.
12. Fugue Form.
13. Vocal Forms.
14. The History of Forms.
15. List of Further Material in this Volume.

1. The Psychological Necessity of Form. The principles of form in music will be most easily grasped by recognizing form, at its outset, as a psychological necessity.

To put it very bluntly (and to ignore for the moment many fine and true poetic ideas about music), form is one of the composer's chief means of averting the boredom of his audience. If he possess the power of spinning out shapely melody, as a spider spins out thread, he has one such means, and perhaps the most fundamental of all. To this may be added the gift of rhythmic subtlety, enabling him to add significance to his melody, and that of harmonic aptness, enabling him to colour it beautifully—both of which increase his chances of commanding and retaining attention. But the application of all these gifts must be according to some principle of form, or his audience will soon be yawning.

To imagine an extreme case—few of us could sit out with smiling face a fifteen minutes' composition in which something new was being uttered all the time. The psychological explanation of our distress is the fatigue of sustained effort (conscious and subconscious) to take in the 'something new', and behind this mental fatigue lies almost certainly some physical exhaustion, for the phenomena of psychology have most probably all a physiological explanation, though it may not, in the present state of knowledge, be easily traced. Physical man is simply not made in such a way as to be capable of absorbing unlimited new ideas, as the conscientious person found who tried to read the dictionary through but had to give up because 'it changed the subject too often'.

Textbooks on form and critical discussions of particular compositions often talk of 'symmetry' and 'balance'. Such terms as these, though handy, are borrowed from the criticism of other arts—space-arts—and music is a time-art. They are of the nature, then, of useful metaphor, enabling one to take hold of ideas, and when metaphor is put aside in favour of plain speech we are driven to the statement of time-consideration—'This composition failed because its composer set out to hold the interest of his audience for ten minutes and held it for only five' (after which we may proceed to discuss why it did this).

Reference has been made above to an imagined extreme case of a 'composition' which was all novelty, and which, though at the outset it might be entrancing, necessarily failed on this time-test. Another such extreme case may be imagined—that of a 'composition' of some length made up of the mere reiteration of the same little scrap of tune, which we may postulate as a very beautiful scrap and hence in itself entirely acceptable. Obviously that extreme, too, would fail, and, equally obviously, between these two extremes which bring failure must be a mean which will bring success. It is the different devices for the achievement of that mean which constitute the apparatus of musical form in its several varieties.

2. Requirements on the Part of Composer and of Audience. The attainment of success in the achievement of the mean obviously rests upon two linked factors: (*a*) the composer's skill, in relation to (*b*) the audience's degree of musical receptivity, due to a combination of temperament and previous experience.

It is significant that in the early days of musical composition works were very short and that they have (consistently, though with temporary setbacks) tended to become longer. As late as the sixteenth century very few instrumental compositions (i.e. single 'movements') lasted as long as five minutes. In the eighteenth century a Haydn or Mozart symphony movement might last longer, but rarely or never more than eight or ten. In the nineteenth, the first movement of Beethoven's Third Symphony lasts about seventeen minutes, the first movement of Brahms's Second Symphony about eighteen. At the opening of the twentieth the first movement of Elgar's First Symphony lasts about nineteen.

The average length of the symphonies (as wholes) of the maturity of Haydn and Mozart is twenty-four minutes; of Beethoven's (excluding, for obvious reasons, the 'Choral' Symphony), thirty-seven; of Brahms's forty, and of Elgar's fifty-one. These figures reflect, in some measure, the increasing variety of harmonic and orchestral resources, with the enhanced power of obtaining striking contrasts, of holding the attention of the audience by the attraction of these two means of 'colour'; but they also reflect the cumulative growth of skill of composers in handling their musical material (i.e. of applying devices of musical 'form'), and of audiences in grasping and recalling the musical material (i.e. of appreciating the application of these devices).

All this points to the importance of an understanding of the principles and devices of form by the three participants in every musical performance—the Composer, who 'creates', the Performer, who 'interprets', and the Listener, who 'receives'. The Composer's need of mastery of Form is evident from what has been said above. The Performer's is little less important, as without an understanding of Form he will in some passages fail to notice the Composer's intentions and hence may stultify them. The Listener's need of an understanding of Form is not so generally recognized, and, admittedly, it does not require to be so complete, but experience shows that where he possesses it his bewilderment when confronted with any new and involved composition is diminished, whilst to the full enjoyment of certain types of composition it is almost essential.

3. The Main Principle. The main principle of form is obvious, from the above suggestion as to the 'extremes' and the 'mean'. The extremes are perpetual change and perpetual repetition: the mean is a degree of change plus a degree of repetition. Thus the mind, after the effort of taking in something new, is rested by the reversion to something it has already experienced; and after this reversion it enjoys again the adventure of taking in something new.

The 'something' (new or already experienced) is twofold, or perhaps threefold: (a) thematic material, or, if the word be preferred, 'tunes', and (b) keys—to which may be added, (c) manner of treatment of the thematic material. (The factor of key has, of course, been available only since about the end of the sixteenth century; see *Modes* and *Scales*.)

4. The Six Existing Forms. It might be imagined that these three factors could be combined into an almost unlimited variety of forms,

but as a matter of fact only about six really distinct forms have ever been in use, though in detail these can, indeed, vary endlessly. The six forms in question are:

(a) A two-section form, '*Simple Binary*'.
(b) A three-section form, '*Simple Ternary*'.
(c) A form derived from the first, '*Compound Binary*' (also called '*First Movement Form*' and '*Sonata Form*')—really a variety of *Ternary*.
(d) An elaboration of the second, the *Rondo*.
(e) The *Air with Variations*.
(f) The *Fugue*.

Combinations of these are possible. For example, in the three-section form each section may, in itself, be in the two-section form; in the compound binary form a part of the material may be fugal—and so on.

Perhaps, for completeness, it should be added that there are a certain number of short pieces running on perfectly continuously, without any divisions that would enable us to define the form (e.g. the first prelude of Bach's '48'): probably *Unitary* would be the best adjective to use in describing these.

5. Simple Binary Form. There is no strong contrast, and the main principle is a contrast of key. The piece falls into two sections, of which the first begins in the tonic key (or main key of the whole piece) and modulates to the dominant (i.e. the original fifth note or soh becomes the new key note or doh). The second section then starts in the new key and works back to the old one. There are two distinct cadences, the first in the dominant and the second in the tonic. In a piece in the key of C the first section would move from key C to key G and the second from key G to key C (of course, other keys might be passed through incidentally between these points).

If the piece is in the minor the first section sometimes ends in the relative major (e.g. if in A minor it will end in C major); then the second section modulates back to the original key (key A minor to key C major; key C major to key A minor).

The principle of simple binary form is: drive out to a related key; rest there a moment and drive home again (and of course on the way out and home other related keys may be driven through).

This form, though it attained fairly considerable dimensions in the mid-eighteenth century, is not suitable for very long pieces on account of the lack of contrast in the musical material employed. Nearly all the dance movements (allemandes, sarabandes, courantes, gigues, gavottes, bourrées, minuets, etc.) adopted into the seventeenth- and eighteenth-century suite (q.v.) were written in this form, which is seen at its finest in Bach and Handel. In the binary form of those composers and their contemporaries the material is often treated very contrapuntally (see *Counterpoint*), and this enables them to write at somewhat greater length without losing the interest of the listeners.

After the middle of the eighteenth century this form practically ceased to be used except for hymn tunes, occasional tiny piano pieces (e.g. some by Schumann and Mendelssohn), and the like—and for some of the 'subjects' out of which longer pieces were made.

A simple example of the form in miniature is the following Minuet from Purcell's First Harpsichord Suite. It will be noticed that nearly the whole grows out of the little motif propounded in the first two measures—used at different levels and either in its original upward-working shape or in an inversion of this.

Usually, as in this instance, each half of the piece is played twice.

6. Ternary Form. This is one of the most commonly used forms for single, short compositions. It consists of (i) a tune or passage, more or less self-contained and complete; (ii) another one, almost always in a new key, normally one closely related to that of the first one (dominant, or relative major or minor); and (iii) the first one repeated.

Note these usual differences between the simple binary and ternary forms: that in the binary the first section leads on to the key in which the second section opens, and that in the ternary it often closes in its own key; and that, whereas in the binary the material of both sections is the same, in the ternary it is most frequently different (and sometimes, indeed, strongly contrasted).

There is a real difference of *style* between the two forms, the binary being commonly much more unified than the ternary. The binary form, though in two sections, with a cadential moment of repose in the middle, is felt to be *one thing*, whereas the ternary is quite openly three things (of which the first and the last are the same, or nearly so).

The ternary form is so obviously effective that it is to be expected that we should find early examples of it. It is foreshadowed in some folk songs, in some of the songs of the Minnesingers (twelfth century), in some of the German chorales (sixteenth century), and so forth. It is much found from the late seventeenth century onwards, but especially in the eighteenth century.

In the seventeenth and early eighteenth centuries (the period of Purcell, Bach, Handel, etc.) it is chiefly a vocal form—the stereotyped form of the normal operatic aria (see *Aria*).

In the next period, that of Haydn, Mozart, etc., and into Beethoven's time, it is also the form of the minuet and trio found as one movement of sonata, symphony, string quartet, and such 'cyclic' works. The plan then is (a) Minuet; (b) another Minuet, called Trio (see *Trio*); and (c) original Minuet repeated intact (the Minuet, *in itself*, may be either binary or ternary, and so with the Trio).

A little later, in the days of Chopin, Mendelssohn, etc., the ternary form becomes the form for most short piano pieces, such as nocturnes, songs without words, and the like—somewhat modified in detail, on occasion, of course. (Cf. *Song Form.*)

The following miniature example is a Musette of Bach, in the book of music he wrote for his wife's use:

Da Capo.

It is perhaps desirable to close this discussion of Ternary Form with a word of warning, for an examination of the works of various theorists shows a difference of opinion as to classification.

The view taken by the present writer is that, music being the art of the ear, the ear is the officially appointed judge as to music's categories. Thus a piece of music which is *heard* as a first section, a second section, and then the first section repeated, is ternary. Such a question as to whether the first section is self-complete, in the sense of beginning and ending in the same key, is not, in his opinion, relevant to the decision. Nor is the question whether the second section consists of entirely new material or, instead of this, is merely a treatment of material already heard in the first section.

The simple principle here adopted is, then, that what is heard as threefold *is* threefold. Examination candidates may, however, be warned that this common-sense principle is not universally accepted, and, moreover, that the theorists who do not accept it are at variance among themselves as to the exceptions upon which they insist. The safe plan, then, where a piece of music is not ternary in the very simplest and the very fullest sense, is to give alternative descriptions of it, with the reasons for each, and to leave the examiner to make his choice. If he is a person of intelligence it is a recognition of musical facts for which he is looking, and not a conformity to any particular system of nomenclature.

Cf. *Song Form.*

7. Compound Binary Form (= 'Sonata Form', or 'First Movement Form'). This is binary historically, i.e. it derives from simple binary, but as it falls into three parts it is in a sense ternary. Neither term exactly fits it, and the term 'Sonata Form' is bad, because, logically, that would indicate a whole sonata, whilst the term 'First Movement Form' is defective both because a fair number of first movements (of sonatas, etc.) are not in this form and also because the form is frequently used for middle and final movements, as well as for independent compositions (overtures, etc.).

What the form is like can be quickest illustrated by the use of a very tiny and very early example of its main principle. The following is a hymn-tune by Tallis, composed about 1567:

This is obviously an example of binary form: it falls into two sections, of which the first modulates to the dominant and the second takes us back to the tonic.

But it has this peculiarity: Each section falls into two distinct strains (each with its own individuality), arranged as follows:

1st Section: Strain I in tonic key: Strain II in dominant;

2nd Section: Strain I in tonic key; Strain II also in tonic.

That is the form of the normal first movement of a Beethoven sonata, string quartet, or symphony, put in a nutshell. With Beethoven we should find the two strains greatly extended (into what we call **Subjects,** q.v.) and strongly differentiated so as to secure contrast; we should also find them not cheek by jowl, but connected by a long and elaborate passage effecting the modulation from the key of the first to the key of the second. (This is called a **Bridge Passage.**) At the end of each section of the piece we should find a closing passage (or **Coda,** q.v.). And, most important, between these two sections (called respectively **Exposition,** or **Enunciation,** and **Recapitulation**) we should find a new section interpolated, not a section of new material, but a **Development** (q.v.) of material from the two subjects—a free treatment of such material, of a very modulatory character. (Other names for 'Development' are **Working-out** and **Free Fantasia**.)

To print here an example of such a movement as this would take too much space, but the early anticipation of the form given above will serve as a model to keep in mind. It shows us real essentials (less the 'development' section).

A tendency towards this compound binary form can be seen in a few of J. S. Bach's works, but its real exploitation is associated with the name of his greatest son, Karl Philipp Emanuel Bach (q.v.), and with a host of other late-eighteenth-century names, of which the most prominent are Haydn and Mozart. The form is still in frequent use, though from the mid-nineteenth century onwards there is seen a growing desire to modify it in detail.

8. A Summary of Preceding Points. For the sake of perfect clarity, certain facts already alluded to in passing may be separately stated and put into other words:

(*a*) Properly, any composition in which the ear seizes two clear divisions is binary, and any in which it seizes three is ternary.

(*b*) In simple binary form neither of the two divisions is complete in itself, inasmuch as the first ends out of the chief and original key and the second begins out of it.

(*c*) In simple ternary, in the great majority of cases, each of the divisions is complete in itself, the first beginning and ending in the chief key of the piece, the second beginning and ending in some other key, and the third reproducing the first.

(*d*) 'Sonata Form', or 'First Movement Form', is historically an elaboration of simple binary, and resembles it in that its first division ends out of the original key and its second begins out of it and then works back to it.

(*e*) But the ear certainly detects three clear divisions ('Exposition, Development, Recapitulation') and in this sense it is ternary.

(*f*) Because of the facts stated in paragraph (*d*) above, most textbooks speak of this form as 'Compound Binary'.

(*g*) Because of the facts stated in paragraph (*e*) above, certain textbooks (beginning probably with Hadow's *Sonata Form*, 1896) speak of it as 'Ternary'.

(*h*) There is an additional argument for the 'Compound Binary' designation—in simple binary form the same musical material is used throughout, and this (with slight exceptions) is so with 'Sonata Form', otherwise 'First Movement Form', in which the whole is made from the same two subjects first announced. In 'Simple Ternary Form' the middle division usually introduces new musical material, and this is (with slight exceptions) not so with 'Sonata' or 'First Movement' Form. Nevertheless the ear detects three sections, not two, and hence 'ternary' is probably the more logical description.

9. Rondo Form. This may be looked upon

as an extension of simple ternary form. Let the three parts of that form be called A–B–A. Then the formula for this one becomes A–B–A–C–A, or some further elaboration of this, such as A–B–A–C–A–D–A. An early and simple example is given below. It is a 'Rondeau' of Rameau (1683–1764). To save space we have not here repeated the first section but have merely indicated its reappearances.

Repeat First Section.

Repeat First Section.

There is an obvious resemblance between this musical form and the old French poetical form (revived at the end of the nineteenth century by Swinburne, Gosse, Austin Dobson, and others), the rondel. As an example is offered the following attempt at a free rendering of a rondel of Prince Charles d'Orléans (1391–1465).

> *The year has cast his garment old*
> *Of wind and frost and soaking rain,*
> And clothed himself in tints again,
> And shining sunbeams, clear and gold.
> Now bird on tree and lamb in fold
> Each of its joy sounds a refrain.
> *The year has cast his garment old*
> *Of wind and frost and soaking rain.*
> The streamlet strays through verdant wold,
> Its bosom decked with glist'ning chain
> Of sunlit ripples—all the train
> Of nature dressed in colours bold.
> *The year has cast his garment old*
> *Of wind and frost and soaking rain.*[1]

In examining the Rameau composition it will be noticed that the three different tunes, or subjects, are in the keys of A major, E major, and F sharp minor respectively (i.e. tonic, dominant, and relative minor). Often only the first (and most important) subject is called by that name, the intervening passages then being called **Episodes.**

This is the rondo reduced to its lowest terms; or rather it is the rondo not yet grown up. On these simple lines it can be found in the works of Rameau, Couperin, Bach, and their contemporaries, and also of Haydn, Mozart, and, often, Beethoven. It was one of the most favourite forms for popular drawing-room harpsichord and piano music in the last third of the eighteenth century and (especially) the first third of the nineteenth.

An old English name for it was *Round-o* (e.g. in Jeremiah Clarke's *Choice Lessons for the Harpsichord or Spinnet*, 1711).

The portions of the composition that intervene between the repetitions of the main tune

[1] *Le temps a laissié son manteau*
De vent, de froidure et de pluye,
Et s'est vestu de brouderie
De souleil luisant, cler et beau.
Il n'y a beste ne oyseau
Qu'en son jargon ne chante ou crie—
Le temps a laissié son manteau
De vent, de froidure et de pluye.
Rivière, fontaine et ruisseau
Portent, en livrée jolie,
Gouttes d'argent d'orfaverie;
Chascun s'abille de nouveau;
Le temps a laissié son manteau
De vent, de froidure et de pluye.

(i.e. the episodes) were, in the early French rondos, called 'Couplets'.

10. An Elaboration of the Rondo. Modifications of the pure rondo occur, of which a frequent one is the introduction of a 'development' (see 7—Compound Binary Form) for the third subject (the one called 'C' above) and especially the addition of an extra appearance of 'B' (*now in the main key of the piece*) near the end. The plan is then A–B–A, Development, A–B–Coda derived from A, or even A itself plus some coda matter, which is very like compound binary form. This is often called **Sonata-Rondo Form,** and, as will be seen, its outstanding divergence from sonata (= compound binary) form is the reappearance of A before the development begins. This type of sonata-rondo movement (with variants) is frequently used by Beethoven (sometimes, too, by Mozart; rarely by Haydn).

A word may be added as to the most important of the variants mentioned above. It consists in the replacement of the development by new matter, so that the formula runs, A–B–A–C–A–B–Coda as above.

This retains one of the two great resemblances to Sonata Form—the reappearance, near the end, of B, now in the main key of the movement.

As to other variants, they are relatively less important. A trouble is that textbook writers choose some particular variant as the normal type (almost ignoring the others) and also adopt differing terminology. Thus the textbook statements on Sonata-Rondo (or Rondo-Sonata) Form are more confusing to the student than musical textbook statements on any other subject.

Note that in all the varieties of Rondo-Sonata, 'B', by the added importance given it, becomes, in effect, not a mere Episode, but a true 'Second Subject'.

11. The Air with Variations. This, which is a dinner of one sort of fish served up in many courses with different cooking and sauce, is one of the very earliest instrumental forms. It has, from the sixteenth century onwards, been used by every great composer, is still popular, and seems likely to go on for ever. It has been the medium for some of the most trivial human expression and some of the deepest.

The formula mentioned as the basis of all musical form perhaps requires a little modification in speaking of the Air with Variations, since instead of the repetition and change appearing in alternation they appear in combination.

A tune, or 'subject', is given out in all its simplicity, and then repeated many times with changes such as do not conceal its identity—though in the more modern examples (as, for instance, in some of Brahms's, and still more in the *Enigma Variations* of Elgar) it is an identity of spirit rather than of body.

A well-known example of the simpler type is the first movement from the Piano Sonata in A of Mozart.

Var. VI. *Allegro.*

For another type of Variation see *Ground*; *Chaconne and Passacaglia*; *Folia*.

12. Fugue Form. In all the forms previously mentioned there might be much or little counterpoint (i.e. interweaving of melodies); but counterpoint is the very essence of the fugue.

A fugue is more or less strictly (generally quite strictly) in a fixed number of melodic strands—called **Voices**, the form being obviously in its origin a choral one.

These voices, at the outset, enter in turn with a scrap of melody called **Subject** (a different thing in nature from the subjects spoken of in connexion with the other forms), until at last all are singing—if we may use that term.

The word fugue, 'Fuga' in Italian or 'Fugue' in French, means 'flight' ('Il semble que M. — ait fait la fugue', we may read at the end of a French newspaper's account of an embezzling bank manager). The idea seems to be that the opening of a composition of this sort gives the idea of each 'voice' as it enters chasing the preceding one, which flies before it.

All the voices having thus made their appearance with the subject (the portion of the Fugue to this point being called its **Exposition**), they wander off to the discussion of something else, or (more likely) of some motif or motifs already heard. The passage in which this occurs is called an **Episode**, and one of its functions is to effect a modulation to some related key, in which again the voices (or some of them) enter with the subject.

At the end the piece veers round to the original key.

All that is a very general description which may now be amplified and modified as follows:

(*a*) At the outset the first voice to enter with the subject has, when the second voice enters with this, to find something else to sing; then the second voice has to find something whilst the third voice enters, and so on. If this 'something' is the same in all voices throughout these initial entries (and possibly elsewhere in the fugue) it obviously merits a distinctive name, and so it is called the **Countersubject** —the bit of melody which moves 'counter' (i.e. against) the subject.

(*b*) Imagine a choral fugue in which the soprano enters first, the alto next, the tenor next, and the bass last. Obviously the subject, as the soprano sings it, will be too high for the natural range of the alto. Then the tenor can sing just what the soprano sang, but an octave lower, but this will be too high for the bass. In the early days, when fugue was developing as a choral form, this difficulty was got over by transposing the subject for the alto and bass into the key of four notes lower, i.e. the dominant key. For instance, if the soprano and tenor sang it in key C, the alto and bass would sing it in key G, and so on—the principle being that contiguous voices do not sing the subject in the same key, but in the keys of tonic and dominant respectively. For distinction the dominant entries are not called 'Subject' but **Answer.** And so in a four-part fugue (vocal or instrumental) we get the opening entries in the order Subject –Answer–Subject–Answer (the subject and answer have also been called **Dux** and **Comes** —'leader' and 'companion').

See *Redundant Entry* and in the description below of a fugue by W. F. Bach note point ii—*Counter-Exposition.*

(*c*) Sometimes in later entries the composer feels he can introduce an added effect by drawing nearer to one another the appearances of the subject (or of subject and answer), so that one voice appears on the scene with that scrap of melody before the previous voice has finished with it. The overlapping that then occurs is called **Stretto** (an Italian word meaning 'squeezed together'). The term Stretto Maestrale (It., 'Masterly stretto') is sometimes applied to a stretto in strict canon (see *Canon*).

(*d*) Sometimes he will work up a feeling of climax by making the bass voice stand firm on one note (tonic or dominant) whilst the others move above it. From the fact that on the organ the bass note would be held by one of the feet, this device has come to be called **Pedal** (see *Harmony* 14, 24 p).

(*e*) The device of **Augmentation** is sometimes effectively used in fugue (see *Augmentation and Diminution*).

(*f*) Fugues exist with two subjects. There are two ways: (i) the two subjects appear in double harness from the beginning (really very like a subject and countersubject together from the very opening), or (ii) the first subject appears and is treated to a certain point, when the second subject enters and is likewise treated, after which there is a section in which the two subjects combine. Both these types go by the names **Double Fugue** or **Fugue on Two Subjects.** The same principles apply to **Triple** and **Quadruple Fugues.**

(*g*) In choral fugues there is often an independent instrumental part going on, and in oratorio especially the **Accompanied Fugue** is of some importance.

There are many details in connexion with fugue construction into which it would be out of place to enter here, as they would occupy much space, and they belong rather to an actual textbook of fugue. It may, however, perhaps be well briefly to allude to **Real and Tonal Answers**. The real answer is the one that has been implied above, in which the answer is an exact transposition of the subject. The tonal answer is a modification in transposition. As an example of cases where composers often prefer to make such a modification may be mentioned a subject opening with the drop, soh–doh (e.g. G–C), which, literally transposed, would become soh–doh (D–G) in the new key: in such a case there is a general preference that the soh–doh shall be answered fah–doh in the new key, i.e. G–C would be answered C–G, the interval of a fifth becoming the interval of a fourth. (In terms of the main key of the piece the subject has begun with Dominant–Tonic and the answer with Tonic–Dominant.) A quite obvious case of a need for a tonal answer is that where the subject modulates (as it not infrequently does) from the tonic key to the dominant key, and a literal transposition would carry the modulation farther, from the dominant to *its* dominant (e.g. subject modulating C to G and answer modulating G to D), with the result that we should have passed into an unrelated key and far away from the original key in which the subject ought now to return. The remedy here is that the modulation tonic–dominant should be answered by the modulation dominant–tonic (e.g. subject modulates from C to G and answer from G back to C). Elaborate rules covering all sorts of finicking modifications are to be found in textbooks, but they are very imperfectly observed by composers, who often succeed in making quite good fugues in defiance thereof. Bach is a notorious offender. He breaks all the commandments yet 'gets away with it'—which is the main point!

The following fugue, which might, from its restricted dimensions, more properly be called a **Fughetta,** has been chosen as an example on account of this brevity. It is by Bach's son W. Friedemann Bach. It does not illustrate all the points above mentioned. But few fugues do; for example, the first fugue in Bach's great collection of 48 has no episode but much stretto, whilst some others in that collection have important episodes and no stretti, and so on.

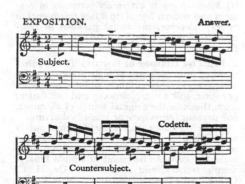

Subject.

Subject.

STRETTO.

Subject.

The following points will be noticed:

(i) The fugue is in three voices.

(ii) Its main scheme is (*a*) An *Exposition* with further entries in the same keys—which are called a **Counter-Exposition**; (*b*) a long *Episode*; and (*c*) some entries in the original key to close with, these beginning in *Stretto*. It is, then, somewhat abnormal in having no middle entries in new (related) keys.

(iii) The answer is *Tonal*.

(iv) There is a *Countersubject*, but it is by no means consistently used (for instance, at the third entry of the Exposition it never appears, and at the next entry it appears in altered form and only in the next entry after that does it appear authentically).

(v) The Episode is a long and modulatory one: it is largely made out of material from the subject, so maintaining the unity of the composition.

(vi) Into the first group of entries there is introduced an episodical passage (between the entries of the 2nd and the 3rd voice); such a passage is called a **Codetta**.

(vii) There is no *Pedal*.

It is quite a mistake to suppose that fugue is necessarily a very serious type of composition. There are all manner of fugues expressing all varieties of mood. To take contrasted examples from choral works, there is the pleading of the 'Libera me' in Verdi's *Requiem*, and the rollicking of the fugue that ends his gay opera *Falstaff*.

See also *Inversion of Melodies*.

13. Vocal Forms. Solo vocal and choral forms have not been touched on above (apart from a few passing allusions), because they follow the same patterns. It should be noticed, however, that it is possible for any setting of words to be less definite in its form than a purely instrumental composition, because the words being the *raison d'être* of the music, the mind follows these, which have their own logic, and so long as the music is felt to enhance the meaning and emotional content of the words the mind may feel satisfied. In some modern songs the vocal part seems to occupy itself completely in an interpretation of the poem and such form as the song possesses is largely contributed by some consistent use of a motif or motifs in the accompaniment.

Taking in order the various forms mentioned above, it may be said that (*a*) *Simple Binary Form* is common in short folk songs, hymn tunes, and the like, and less common in longer vocal compositions; (*b*) *Simple Ternary Form* is exceedingly common in solo vocal and choral compositions; (*c*) *Compound Binary Form* is rare, though not unknown; (*d*) *Rondo Form* is rarer, but by no means unknown (indeed its origin is by some supposed to be in musical settings of the medieval poetic form, the rondel); (*e*) the *Air with Variations* is rare, being obviously a form of instrumental intention; (*f*) *Fugue Form* is extremely common in oratorio and is even found (in a free treatment) in opera; however, incidental passages in fragmentary fugue style (**Fugato**) are even more common.

14. The History of Forms. The requirement of form (as a sort of logic in music) is instinctive and is seen in those rudimentary types of music, folk song, plainsong, and folk dance; from these, as the original source of all music, our present forms may be taken as deriving.

In the traditional plainsong (designed purely as a vehicle for words and hence not dependent on form to give it point and meaning) early adumbrations can be found of simple binary, simple ternary, and rondo form (Dr. H. C. Colles, in the Introduction to the article 'Form', in Grove's *Dictionary of Music*, gives a handy small list of examples to be found in the *English Hymnal*).

So, too, with folk song, which, as it was to be handed down by generations of unlettered people without musical training and with no knowledge of notation, needed, if it was to survive, to be more definite in form. (In other words, examples that were more definite in form benefited by the law of the 'survival of the fittest'.) Moreover, folk song was a setting of metrical verse, and it was, further, often influenced by folk dance, and these were influences making for definiteness of form.

The work of the *Troubadours* (see article *Minstrels, Troubadours*, etc.) had also its results; poetic metrical schemes were brought into existence by them which eventually affected both vocal and instrumental music. Later poetic forms (e.g., as already mentioned, the French form, the rondeau, stereotyped in the fifteenth century) also had influence.

The introduction of part-singing, from about the year A.D. 900 onwards, gradually brought into existence a contrapuntal style suitable for choral music. In the sixteenth century music in this style was (in the absence of sufficient purely instrumental music) often played, and pieces were in England actually published as 'Apt for voyces or vyols'. So arose the instrumental fantasia (see *Fantasia*), which in the late seventeenth and early eighteenth century grew into the more definite and pointed fugue.

The folk dance, in its almost infinite number of national and regional varieties, also provided a basis for instrumental music, and during the sixteenth century the linking of a couple of contrasted pieces in dance style (especially *Pavan and Galliard*, q.v.) opened the way to the development of the extended suite (q.v.)—a string of pieces based on dance rhythms and styles.

Rather later the sonata developed, and in one of its two main categories departed from the dance type, adopting a more 'abstract' style (see article *Sonata*).

The introduction of the opera in the seventeenth century led to the evolution of the *Overture* (q.v.), and this, in turn, to that of the *Symphony* (q.v.). It also led to a stereotyping of the ternary form in the *Aria* (q.v.); this form was, curiously, not greatly used at this period in instrumental music, in which it later became extremely common.

Wagner's use of a less sectional lay-out of opera (see *Wagner*) with the *Leading Motif* (q.v.) as the unifying element, had its effect in the loosening of ideas on instrumental form, and the application of the old formal principles in a less cast-iron way. So came the *Symphonic Poem* (q.v.).

In the twentieth century some composers have attempted composition in an almost or quite formless way, though few compositions have been brought forward that do not conform in some way and some degree to the dual principle of form, i.e. Unity plus Variety. What the future will bring is still unsure, but it may be surmised that this principle is a part of the mental make-up of the human mind and that its application can never be entirely discarded.

15. List of Further Material in this Volume.

(*a*) **Cyclic Forms.** The combination of several shorter compositions into one larger one is treated in this volume under such heads as *Suite, Sonata*, and *Symphony*.

(*b*) **Style-Pieces, etc.** The following so-called 'forms' have separate entries in this volume. They are mostly not really 'forms', but rather 'styles'—applications in various distinctive speeds, rhythms, and manners of some of the forms above discussed. They can even be found changing their form in different periods, yet retaining their style and so their individuality: for instance, a Purcell minuet in binary form has been given above; very many (most?) minuets, however, are in ternary form, yet a minuet is always recognizable by its rhythm and style, and that, and not the form, defines it.

Alalá, Alborada, Albumblatt, Allemande, Alternativo, Anglaise, Aubade, Badinage, Bagatelle, Ballade, Barcarolle, Barn Dance, Basse Danse, Berceuse, Bergomask, Black Bottom, Blues, Bolero, Bouffons, Bourrée, Branle, Burla or Burlesca, Cachucha, Canaries, Canzonet or Canzonetta, Capriccio, Cassation, Cavatina, Cebell, Chaconne and Passacaglia, Characteristic Piece, Charleston, Concerto, Concertstück, Copla, Corronach, Cotillon, Country Dance, Courante, Cracovienne, Czardas, Dithyramb, Divertimento, Divertissement, Drabant, Dumka, Dump, Écossaise, Eclogue, Élégie, Entrée, Étude, Fancy, Fandango, Fantasia, Farandole, Fling, Folia, Forlana, Fox-trot, Furiant, Galop, Gangar, Gavotte, Gigue, Gopak, Granadina, Ground, Habanera, Halling, Hanacca, Haute Danse, Hay, Horn-pipe, Humoresque, Idyll, Impromptu, Intermezzo, Invention, Jig, Jota, Kolomyika, Kosatchok, Lament, Ländler, Lesquercade, Loure, Lyric Piece, Malagueña, Manchega, March, Matelotte, Maxixe, Mazurka, Minuet, Moresca, Morris, Muiñeira, Murciana, Nachtanz, Nachtmusik, Nocturne, Novelette, Obertas, One-step, Overture, Partita, Paso Doble, Passamezzo, Passepied, Pastoral, Pavan and Galliard, Périgourdine, Perpetuum Mobile, Pes, Phantasy, Pibroch, Polka, Polonaise, Polska, Postlude, Pot-pourri, Prelude, Quadrille, Quartet, Quodlibet, Redowa, Reel, Rejdováčka, Rhapsody, Ricercare, Rigaudon, Romance, Romanesca, Rondeña, Round, Rueda, Rumba, Saeta, Saltarello, Sarabande, Sardana, Scherzo, Schottische, Seguidilla, Serenade, Sevillana, Shimmy, Siciliana, Sinfonietta, Sketch, Soled, Song without Words, Springar, Springdans, Strathspey, Suite, Symphonic Poem, Tambourin, Tango, Tarantella, Tedesca, Toccata, Toccatina, Tonadilla, Trepak, Trio, Villancico, Voluntary, Volta, Waltz, Wiegenlied.

(*c*) **Literature, Picture, and Drama in Music.** For the question of the adaptation of form to the instrumental representation of pictorial, literary, or dramatic ideas see under *Programme Music* and under *Wagner* ('Leading Motif'), *Liszt* ('Metamorphosis of Themes'), and *Berlioz* ('Idée Fixe').

(*d*) **The Smaller Units of Form.** For these see *Phrase and Sentence*; *Motif*.

(*e*) For the former practice of adding **ex-**

temporary decorations to a subject of a sonata, etc., on its return see *Ornaments* 4; *Fioritura*.

(*f*) For a general sketch of the development of form in its **Historical Perspective** see *History of Music*.

FORMANT. See *Acoustics* 6.

FORMAT DE POCHE (Fr.). 'Pocket-size' (score, etc.).

FORMBY, GEORGE. See p. 432, pl. **73**. 5.

FORNSETE. See *John of Fornsete*; *Sumer is icumen in*.

FORRAGE, STEPHEN. See *Harmonica* 1.

FÖRSTER. See *Electric Musical Instruments* 3 c. And see also *Foerster*.

FORSTER.

(1) GEORG (1514–68). See *Germany* 2.

(2) WILL. See *Will Forster's Virginal Book*.

FORSYTH, CECIL (1870–1941). Valuable author on musical subjects and authority on orchestration. See references under *Tuba Group* 1, 2; *Cornet* 1; *Clarinet Family* 4 f (note).

FORT (Ger.). (1) 'Forwards', 'continually'. (2) 'Away'—in organ music this means that the stop in question is now to be silenced.

FORTE (It.). 'Strong', i.e. loud (abbreviated, *f*). So *Fortissimo*, 'very strong' (abbreviated *ff*, or *fff*); *Fortemente*, 'strongly'.

FORTFAHREN (Ger.). 'To go forward.'

FORTISSIMO (It.). See *Forte*.

FORTNER, WOLFGANG. Born at Leipzig in 1907. He holds positions as teacher of composition and orchestral conductor in Heidelberg and is Director of its University's Collegium Musicum (cf. *Concert* 13). As an active composer (orchestral works—including concertos for organ and for viola—chamber music, choral compositions, and several operas) he has shown versatility, at first with a disposition to follow the lines of Hindemith, and later (from about 1948) in the Note-row system.

See *Opera* 24 f (1957).

FÖRTSCH, JOHANN PHILIP (1652–1732). German medical man and composer of church music and operas. See reference under *Folia*.

FORTSETZUNG (Ger.). 'Continuation.'

FORTUNATUS, VENANTIUS (A.D. 530–609). See *Pange lingua*.

'FORTY-EIGHT', THE. A common name for Bach's collection of Preludes and Fugues which he called *The Well-Tempered Clavier*. See *Temperament* 5; *Klavier*.

FORZA (It.). 'Force', 'vigour'. So *Forzando*, *Forzato*, 'forcing', 'forced'.

FOSS.

(1) HUBERT JAMES. Born at Croydon in 1899 and died in London in 1953, aged fifty-three. He served as music critic of various London journals and was the first head of the music department of the Oxford University Press; he was also a pianist and composer.

(2) LUKAS (p. 1069, pl. **176**. 8). Born in

Berlin in 1922. He had his early training there but since the age of fifteen has been resident in the United States, with a period of study in Paris and then at the Curtis Institute, Philadelphia, and under Hindemith at Yale. In 1950 he was awarded a scholarship to the American Academy at Rome (cf. *Prix de Rome*). He was on the staff of the University of California from 1953 and from 1963 to 1969 was conductor of the Buffalo Philharmonic. He has composed ballets and other orchestral music, solo vocal music (e.g. 'Solo Biblical Cantatas'), choral music, etc. A short opera, *The Jumping Frog* (after Mark Twain), has had many performances in the United States (see *Opera* 24 f, 1950). He considers himself a traditionalist, though he is versatile enough to make adroit use of avant-garde techniques, such as experiments in 'ensemble improvisation'.

See *Concerto* 6 c (1922).

FOSTER.

(1) ELIZABETH. See *Mother Goose Songs*.

(2) STEPHEN COLLINS (p. 1040, pl. **169**. 7, 8). Born near Pittsburgh in 1826 and died in New York in 1864, aged thirty-seven. A Southerner by descent, in the days before the Civil War he depicted musically, in humorous or sentimental fashion, the life of the South, leaving behind him over 175 songs and a few choral and instrumental compositions. He died in the last phase of the war that freed the slaves who had taught him so much by their singing.

His songs, 'My Old Kentucky Home' and 'Swanee Ribber' (or 'Old Folks at Home') have become, as it were, a part of the American popular tradition and a memorial building at Pittsburgh (opened 1937) commemorates his national contribution.

See references under *Negro Minstrels*.

(3) ARNOLD WILFRID ALLEN. Born at Sheffield in 1898 and died in London in 1963, aged sixty-four. He studied composition under Vaughan Williams, to whom he owed that strong interest both in English folk tune and in the English Tudor composers which showed itself in certain of his own compositions. He succeeded Holst at Morley College (1928–40), and was thirty-five years a master at Westminster School. In 1946 he launched the Arnold Foster Choir and Orchestra, doing much to promote out-of-the-way works.

FOUETTÉ. See *Ballet* 8.

FOUGUEUX, FOUGUEUSE (Fr., masc., fem.). 'Impetuous.'

FOULDS, JOHN HERBERT. Born in Manchester in 1880 and died in Calcutta in 1939, aged fifty-eight. He was the son of a member of the Hallé Orchestra, Manchester, and himself began professional life as a cellist in that orchestra. He composed much and varied music, including incidental music for plays and a *World Requiem* (1923) that calls for enormous forces, and experimented in the use of microtones (q.v.), as, for instance, in his *Dynamic Triptych*. His wife was the fine violinist and authority on Indian music, Maud MacCarthy (d. 1967; see reference under *Microtones*). In 1934 he published a book on *Music To-day*.

FOUNDATION. In organ parlance this word is, unfortunately, used in two senses: (*a*) *Foundation Tone* means the tone of the most dignified stops, i.e. diapasons, the more solid of the flutes, etc. (*b*) *Foundation Stops* means all stops except the mutation stops (see *Organ* 2 c).

Cf. *Fonds d'orgue.*

FOUNDLING HOSPITAL. See *Schools of Music*; p. 448, pl. 76. 7.

FOUR-FOOT C, etc. See *Pitch* 7.

FOUR-FOOT STOP. See *Organ* 2 b.

FOUR-IN-ONE, FOUR-IN-TWO. See *Canon.*

FOURNITURE. See *Organ* 14 V.

FOURTH. See *Interval.*

FOURTH FLUTE. See *Recorder Family* 2.

FOX.

(1) GEORGE (1624–91). Founder of the Society of Friends. See *Quakers and Music*; *Fairs and their Music.*

(2) MRS. MILLIGAN. See *Folk Song* 3.

FOXELL, REVD. MAURICE F. See *Anglican Chant* 6 e.

FOXE'S BOOK OF MARTYRS (1563). See *Merbecke.*

FOX STRANGWAYS, ARTHUR HENRY (1859–1948). Writer on music and founder (1920) and first editor of the quarterly *Music and Letters.*

See reference under *God save the Queen* 1.

FOX-TROT. An American dance of Negro ancestry, which became popular from about 1913 onwards and spread over the world. Its music is a sort of march-like ragtime—slow or quick. Variants arose, such as the Charleston and the Black Bottom, and 'Fox-Trot' tended to become a sort of generic term. The slow foxtrot resembles the 'Blues' (q.v.).

F.R.A.D. Fellow of the Royal Academy of Dancing (founded 1927; chartered 1936).

FRAIS, FRAÎCHE (Fr.; masc., fem.). 'Fresh.' So *Fraîcheur*, 'freshness'.

F.R.A.M. See *Degrees and Diplomas* 2.

FRANC (Fr.). 'Frank', open-hearted, bluff.

FRANC (or **Le Franc**), **GUILLAUME.** Born at Rouen; died at Lausanne in 1570. He was a Huguenot composer, who served as precentor (i.e. leader of the congregational singing) successively at the cathedrals of Geneva and Lausanne.

See reference to him and to the leading contemporary Protestant musicians under *France* 4.

FRANÇAIS, FRANÇAISE (Fr.; masc., fem.). 'French.'

FRANÇAISE. An old round dance in triple or compound duple time. It came into great popularity for a period in the 1830s.

FRANÇAIX, JEAN. Born at Le Mans, France, in 1912. He is son of the director of the Conservatory of his native place and a pupil in composition of Nadia Boulanger and in piano of Philipp. He came definitely before the public in 1932 at the Vienna festival of the International Society of Contemporary Music, with Eight Bagatelles for string quartet and piano. A few months later the performance of his first symphony in Paris provoked, by the novelty of its idiom, a demonstration of protest. Much instrumental music has followed, as also a number of ballets.

See *Harpsichord* 9; *Opera* 24 f (1950).

FRANCE

(Illustrations, p. 368, pls. **61, 62**; 384, **63, 64**; 388, **65**.)

The present article is designed merely to offer a brief conspectus of France as a musical country, further information on almost every branch of the subject mentioned, as on the personalities, being given under the appropriate heads, scattered throughout the book. A list of the chief of these heads appears at the end of the article.

1. Troubadours and Minstrels. In the study of early French musical life the **Troubadours** of the south and the **Trouvères** of the north are of high importance. The period of their activity was one of about two centuries, from the end of the eleventh century to the end of the thirteenth, and its developments outside France are briefly described in the special article *Minstrels, Troubadours, Trouvères*, etc.

Adam de la Halle (q.v.) is a very important figure in European music at this time—as a Trouvère, as a composer of choral music, and (especially) as the composer of the dialogue play *Le Jeu de Robin et de Marion* (c. 1280).

The **Jongleurs,** or more plebeian minstrel class, active at the same period and later, had their headquarters in Paris; their guild possessed powers of control which, under changed conditions, it was still exercising in the eighteenth century.

2. Early Harmonists and Theorists of Paris. In those developments of music which, from the tenth to the sixteenth century, turned it from a purely unilinear art to one of the utmost elaboration of interwoven lines, the musicians of France took their full part. The earliest treatise to codify the notation of fixed time-values (a necessity if the interwoven lines are to move in due pace with one another) was that of the thirteenth-century theorist, **Franco of Cologne.**[1]

Three successive chief musicians of Notre Dame of Paris (or of the church which preceded it on the same site) helped to push forward the art, the twelfth-century **Léonin,** reported to be *optimus organista* ('an outstanding composer of organa'), **Pérotin** (at Notre Dame about 1183–1236; some of his compositions are now published and performed), and **Robert de Sabilon** (presumed author of a treatise on music of about 1250–60).

It is interesting to note the argument of one French author, Gastoué (*Les Primitifs de la musique française*, 1922), that the advance in French music at this period may have been due to the presence in Paris of a large number of British students, such as Giraldus Cambrensis (who, when he came to write of his travels in Wales, Ireland, and northern England, showed an interest in, and apparent knowledge of, music), Walter de Odington (alias Walter of Evesham) and John of Salisbury (later Bishop of Chartres), both of whom wrote important treatises on music, John Garland, the very famous theoretician, and Stephen Langton (Archdeacon of Notre Dame and later Archbishop of Canterbury). It will be remembered that this period is the one which produced the remarkable English composition 'Sumer is icumen in' (q.v.), which is extremely effective and skilful for the date, and this may by some be thought to support Gastoué's theory.

However this may be, Paris was for a period evidently a very active centre of theoretical discussion and practical experiment. Writers of musical treatises in those days were usually mathematicians and astronomers as well as musicians, and their minds were clogged with a mass of erudition and a tendency to speculation of a very academic kind, but some of those just mentioned were practical working composers;

[1] The attribution to Franco of Cologne of the introduction of fixed time-values into musical notation (or of their codification) is based on the tradition of his authorship of the treatise *De musica mensurabili* (or *Ars cantus mensurabilis*), of which four manuscript copies of various dates exist.
The date of Franco of Cologne is nowadays accepted as being the later part of the thirteenth century. But a sound authority (Miss Sylvia Townsend Warner) in the fifth edition of Grove's Dictionary, s.v. *Franco, Magister*, discusses various possibilities and inclines to a far earlier date—in the eleventh century.

Walter de Odington, to take one instance, was able to illustrate his treatise by apt examples composed by himself.

3. The Ars Nova. The Ars Nova (q.v.), representing a freeing of style from the old rhythmic modes (introducing the use of binary as well as the traditional ternary rhythms) and from the stiffness of general technique, was especially cultivated in Italy (see *Landino*), but spread to France. The poet–bishop–composer, **Philippe de Vitry** (1291–1361), wrote treatises on the subject, and his principles were carried out extensively by **Machaut** (*c.* 1300–72). Machaut was the last of the French poets who composed his own music; a good many of his compositions (sacred and secular) remain.

An important theorist of the early fourteenth century is **Johannes de Muris** (whom some think to have been an Englishman by birth). He was famous all over Europe. He was a close friend of Philippe de Vitry, and a supporter of the Ars Nova.

The reign of the music-loving Charles V (1364–80) and part of that of Charles VI (1380–1422) made a very brilliant period in French music.

It may be said that from the twelfth century to the end of the fourteenth France was Europe's most important centre of musical culture, and it will be remembered that this coincides with the period of great intellectual development under the influence of the University of Paris and of the wonderful florescence of French Gothic architecture.

4. The Huguenot Repertory. As the high-watermark period of polyphonic music approached (the period represented in England by Byrd and his companions, in Italy by Palestrina, and in Spain by Victoria) France produced choral music of fine quality such as that of **Bourgeois** (*c.* 1523–1600) and **Goudimel** (born *c.* 1505; killed at Lyons in the Massacre of St. Bartholomew, 1572). These represent the strong Huguenot element in the French culture of the times. In addition to providing music of the more complex kind they contributed greatly to the popularity of the Huguenot and Calvinist practice of **Psalm Singing**, by the settings they provided; **Guillaume Franc** is a name also connected with this latter activity, as is **Claude Le Jeune.**

Bourgeois spent the period 1541 to 1557 at Geneva, the headquarters of Calvinism, and Franc was there for a few years, afterwards removing to Lausanne, where he remained until his death in 1570. It is worthy of note that the leaders of Calvinistic song were, like Calvin himself (q.v.), of French birth and upbringing, and that, via Switzerland, France greatly influenced the religious song of England and Scotland, as it did their theology.

Versions of some of the psalm books appeared for use in the Calvinistic churches of Germany, but their permanent influence was not so marked as that of the versions issued in England and Scotland.

Unison singing of the metrical psalms was the rule in the Huguenot and Calvinistic churches at this period, but the composers mentioned produced many full choral settings of psalms for domestic use, the practice of psalm singing being for a time universal amongst both Catholics and Protestants, though later forbidden to the Catholics.

Compare *Calvin, John.*

5. Early Keyboard Music. In the provision of a repertory of music generally adapted to instruments of the harpsichord class French composers of the seventeenth and earlier eighteenth century took a large part. The first French composer to produce harpsichord music clearly differentiated from that for the organ was **Chambonnières** (1602–*c.* 1672), who may be called the founder of the French Harpsichord School. Amongst his followers were **Dandrieu** (1682–1738) and **Daquin** (1694–1772), but especially **François Couperin** surnamed 'The Great' (1668–1733) and **Rameau** (1683–1764); all these, it will be noted, were contemporaries of Bach, and the influence of Couperin upon Bach's domestic keyboard music is marked.

6. Early Opera. In opera, France, unlike Germany and England, took from the first and throughout a line of its own, accepting inspiration and suggestion from Italy but at once developing a national school, of which the greatest masters were **Lully** (Italian born, however) in the late seventeenth century, and **Rameau** in the mid-eighteenth. The development and nature of early French Opera and Ballet are discussed under *Opera* 11 and *Ballet* 2. The determination of Louis XIV to make his court a centre of culture gave a great encouragement to the development of such activities. Lully was his principal musician, and the residence of the exiled Charles II at the court of Louis brought Lullyan influence into English music at the time of the Restoration (1660). Some reference to this will be seen under *Humfrey* and *Purcell.*

7. Eighteenth-century Orchestral Developments. A famous Paris concert series of the eighteenth century was that of the '*Concerts spirituels*' (1725–91), established by A. D. Philidor; it had a great influence upon the development of orchestral music in France in the middle of the eighteenth century and had a considerable repercussion abroad (see *Concert* 14). The clarinet was first heard in an orchestra in two operas of Rameau about 1750 and it quickly passed into the symphonic orchestra; Stamitz, who at Mannheim was showing the world what orchestral playing really meant, hearing this instrument so used, introduced it into his own works, and at Mannheim Mozart heard it and enthusiastically adopted it in some of his works, with the result that it quickly became a standard part of the orchestral equipment everywhere.

Through Stamitz the French orchestral repertory of the period came to be greatly enriched, for the performance of symphonies of

his, during his visit, stimulated **Gossec** (Belgian born, but domiciled in Paris), who is to be looked upon as 'The Father of the Symphony in France'; the earliest symphonies of Gossec slightly precede the earliest of Haydn; they are at present almost totally unheard, but have great historical importance.

8. Eighteenth-century Theorists and Composers. A notable feature of French musical life in the eighteenth century is the active part played in it by the group of *savants* known as the '**Encyclopedists**'. The great French Encyclopedia (1751–72), designed both to sum up existing human knowledge and to put forward the advanced philosophic and political ideas of its promoters, was directed by **Diderot** and **d'Alembert,** both of whom wrote works on music. The musical articles were the work of **Rousseau** (q.v.), and out of them he developed an independent Dictionary of Music (1767), which exercised important influence and remains a standard work of reference for those who make a study of eighteenth-century ideas upon the art.

Of the work of the composers of this century it will be best to leave the reader to gain a general idea by a glance through the articles upon them listed below, and also by references to the article *Opera.* Outstanding names are those of **Monsigny, Grétry** (Belgian born), **Lesueur,** and **Méhul,** which brings us to the date of the French Revolution and the opening of the Romantic Period in music.

The Paris Conservatory dates from 1784. The *Prix de Rome* (q.v.), which annually sends some talented young composer to work in the Villa Medici at government expense, dates from 1803; the list of its beneficiaries is a very distinguished one.

9. The Early Nineteenth Century. French composers of the early part of the nineteenth century may be studied in the same way, the principal names here being those of **Boïeldieu, Auber,** and **Halévy** (all opera composers, and all tending to place French opera on a lower level than that on which Rameau had left it, the example of Wagner being what later restored it to its position).

As this century opened certain **Violinists** were at work who gained for France a high reputation for enterprise in their department; the chief of these are **Kreutzer, Baillot,** and **Rode,** who were close colleagues and form a little 'school'.

10. The Later Nineteenth and Early Twentieth Centuries. The greatest name in French music in the middle part of the nineteenth century (a period when Paris became the centre of musical Europe, though in general more by a hospitable cosmopolitanism than by any strong expression of national interest) is that of **Berlioz,** who exhibited a most original mind of decidedly French cast (Berlioz was the first to give France, amongst other benefits, any great symphonic works), but the names of importance now become very numerous, including those of Félicien David, Ambrose Thomas, Gounod, Offenbach (German born), Lalo, Reyer, Lecocq, Delibes, Bizet, Chabrier, Massenet, Messager, Bruneau, and Charpentier (all prominent in opera and ballet), Alkan (novel pianoforte effects), Lefébure-Wély, Batiste, Gigout, Guilmant, Dubois, Widor (chiefly known for their organ works of varying merit but all showing a definite French mentality), de Bériot (violin works).

An outstanding name of this period is that of **César Franck** (Belgian born, but resident in Paris), who imported into French music, at that time somewhat inclined to the cultivation of the immediately effective, a seriousness and solidity together with a mystical religious feeling; the influences of Bach, Beethoven, and Wagner were to be felt in his work, which nevertheless expresses its composer's personality as fully as any music has ever done. Amongst his many notable pupils (of very varied temperaments) were Bruneau, Chabrier, and Boëllmann. His most devoted disciple, and the one most imbued with his spirit was **Vincent d'Indy** (1851–1931), and the Schola Cantorum, at Paris, founded by Bordes, Guilmant, and d'Indy in 1894 with the primary object of elevating church music in France, has, by its teaching, publications, and performances, had a powerful effect—not merely to that end, but also in reviving interest in old music of all the great schools and, further, in encouraging contemporary composers.

Amongst composers of the Franck–d'Indy group must be numbered Duparc, Dukas, Pierre de Bréville, Magnard, Ropartz, and Sévérac.

A contrasted group of French composers is that of those who either owe their inspiration to, or in some degree share the general sympathies of, **Debussy** (1862–1918). Amongst these are Ravel (who, however, developed independently), Florent Schmitt, and Roussel. For a further discussion of the characteristics of this group see under *Impressionism* and under their several names.

A complete eclectic, contemporary with these two groups but independent of both, is **Saint-Saëns** (1835–1921). **Fauré** (1845–1924) had likewise no very distinct affiliation to any group: he had great influence both by the example of his integrity and by his teaching, amongst his pupils being Ravel, Florent Schmitt, Koechlin, and Aubert. Quite alone stands the whimsical **Satie** (1866–1925).

11. After the first World War. A group which always maintained that it was to be considered rather as a band for mutual friendship and attack and defence than a school was made up of **Durey** (b. 1888), **Honegger** (Swiss by parentage; 1892–1955), **Milhaud** (1892–1974), **Germaine Tailleferre** (b. 1892), **Auric** (b. 1899), and **Poulenc** (1899–1963)—known as 'Les Six'.[1] Milhaud may be said to have led the

way in a reaction against the influence of Debussy, his style being very downright.

12. The second World War. During the German occupation of 1940–5 the Paris Opéra and Opéra-Comique were, of course, completely controlled, and a high proportion of German works was performed: at the Opéra French artists had to produce a new German opera and ballet five times a year. There was a similar control of radio musical activities, but their Musical Director, the composer Emmanuel Bondeville, boldly organized outside festival-programmes, each devoted to the work of some French composer (Berlioz, Lalo, Chabrier, Saint-Saëns, Fauré), and these drew large audiences. A new society in Paris, 'La Pléiade', organized and financed by the proprietors of the *Nouvelle revue française*, from early 1943 onwards gave private concerts of music by French composers. The Director of the National Conservatoire, Delvincourt (q.v.), secured an agreement that the students should be formed into an orchestra to play in prison camps in Germany, then interminably prolonged the process of training and rehearsal. The device was at last seen through and the students and Director went into hiding and there remained until the liberation of Paris —in which many of his students assisted, two being killed.

An underground National Committee of Musicians, under the chairmanship of the well-known conductor Roger Desormière, united many musicians in a movement against cooperation with the enemy. It secretly published and circulated literature and gave performances of banned works, including those of Jewish, British, and Russian composers.

In the years following the second World War the principal figures of international reputation were **René Leibowitz** (1913–72), an early pupil of Schönberg but standing somewhat alone, and the more influential **Olivier Messiaen** (born 1908), among whose pupils the best known is **Pierre Boulez** (born 1925). Not many other French composers of this generation are internationally known.

13. The 'Société Nationale'. Much of the achievement of French composers since the war of 1870 may be attributed to the activity of a society then founded, the **Société nationale de musique**, one of whose objects was to fight the prevailing obsession with operatic music. Its founders were themselves of varied affiliations (Franck, d'Indy, Saint-Saëns, Lalo, Fauré, etc.), and some of them themselves opera composers: the bond of union was the desire for national achievement in a national mode and style, these, however, not rigidly defined in any way. Perhaps it is easiest to

He drew a parallel between the two groups in the two countries, both of them determined to be national rather than cosmopolitan, and drew attention to the recent publication of an album containing a suite of six pieces —one by each of the six young French composers in which, he said, 'the six temperaments jostle without jarring'.

[1] The name 'Les Six' was initiated by an article by Henri Collet in *Comoedia* (Jan. 1920), of which the subtitle was *Les Cinq Russes, les Six Français et Erik Satie*.

See the Articles under the individual names

1. CHABRIER (1841–94)
By E. B. Detaille

2. MASSENET (1842–1912)

3. FAURÉ (1845–1924)

4. D'INDY (1851–1931)

5. MESSAGER (1853–1929)

6. CHAUSSON (1855–99)

7. BRUNEAU (1857–1934)

8. ROPARTZ (1864–1955)

9. CHARPENTIER (1860–1956)

See also plates at pages 368–9, 385, and 388

1. BRÉVILLE (1861–1949)

2. DEBUSSY (1862–1918)

3. DUPIN (1865–1949)

4. SATIE (1866–1925)
By Alfred Frueh

5. DUKAS (1865–1935) with his daughter

6. KOECHLIN (1867–1950)

7. ROUSSEL (1869–1937)

8. FLORENT SCHMITT (1870–1958)

9. RABAUD (1873–1949)

See also plates at pages 368–9, 384, and 388

define by negative: the Society rebelled against the pronounced German influence that had been at work in French composition during the later nineteenth century, as a little earlier Italian influence had been. It deplored equally the obsession with Rossini, Bellini, and Donizetti in the post-revolutionary period and the obsession with Wagner at the date when it began its operations.

14. Modern French Musical Scholarship. A field in which French musicians have done excellent work is that of historical scholarship. Many fine editions of French folk music and pre-classical and classical compositions have been published and a great deal of valuable research has been carried out. A Société Française de Musicologie (founded 1917) has published an important journal.

A brief mention of the notable work done in the re-establishment of a sound tradition of plainsong by the French Benedictines of Solesmes will be found under *Plainsong* 3.

15. French Influences Abroad. For the hospitality France (or, more properly, Paris) has shown to foreign composers, and the opportunity she has offered them of developing their gifts, see under Duny, Gluck, Piccini, Grétry, Chopin, Spontini, Meyerbeer, Offenbach, Albéniz, Stravinsky, etc. The modern Spanish composers (see *Spain*) have frequently gone to school in Paris and so have the Rumanians (a largely Latin race); both seem to have found it possible to acquire a technique there without any submerging of their own national temperament and idiom.

16. List of articles amplifying the above. In order to amplify the information given above the following articles on cognate subjects may be consulted:

a. Overture 1; *Suite*; *Opera* 11, 12, 21; *Bouffons*; *Opera buffa*; *Opéra comique*; *Recitative*; *Song* 10 b; *Vaudeville*.
b. Song; *Minstrels*, *Troubadours*, *Trouvères*, etc.; *Profession of Music* 2; *Chanson*; *Marseillaise*; *Malbrouk s'en va*.
c. Maîtrise; *Oratorio* 4; *Hymns and Hymn Tunes* 4; *Plainsong* 3.
d. Romantic; *Impressionism*.
e. Ballet; *Basse Danse*; *Bourrée*; *Bouffons* (or *Matassins*); *Branle*; *Cancan*; *Chaconne*; *Cotillon*; *Country Dance*; *Courante*; *Gavotte*; *Minuet*; *Passepied*; *Périgourdine*; *Quadrille*; *Rigaudon*; *Tambourin*; *Trihory*.
f. Organ 8 (Pedals); *Pianoforte* 3, 8; *Bagpipe Family* 6; *Sight-Singing* 2; *Schools of Music*.
g. Concert 14; *Broadcasting* 3; *Journals*.
h. Italy 4; *England* 2, 3, 5; *Spain* 7, 10.
i. CHRONOLOGICAL CONSPECTUS OF COMPOSERS—arranged according to century of birth.
12th CENTURY: Pérotin-le-Grand.
13th CENTURY: Adam de la Halle.
14th CENTURY: Machaut.
15th CENTURY: Claudin, Jannequin.

16th CENTURY: Boesset, Caurroy, the brothers Chédeville, Costeley, Franc, Goudimel, Guédron, Passereau, Titelouze, Verdelot.
17th CENTURY: Agincourt, Anglebert, Caix d'Hervelois, Cambert, Campra, M. A. Charpentier, Clérambault, Couperin, Dandrieu, Daquin, Destouches, Grigny, Lalande, Leclair, Lully, Marais, Montéclair, Moreau, Mouret, Rameau, J. F. Rebel, Senaillé.
18th CENTURY: Auber, Baillot, Barthélemon, Benoist, Bertini, Bochsa, Boïeldieu, Bréval, Dauvergne, Duny, Guillemain, Halévy, Hérold, Isouard, Kreutzer, Lesueur, L. A. Loulié, Mazas, Méhul, Mondonville, Monsigny, Panseron, F. A. Philidor, F. Rebel, Rode, Rouget de Lisle.
19th CENTURY: A. C. Adam, Alard, Alkan, Aubert, Audran, Batiste, Bemberg, de Bériot, Berlioz, Bizet, Boëllmann, Boëly, Bondeville, Bonnet, Bordes, Nadia and Lili Boulanger, Bréville, Caplet, Chabrier, Chaminade, G. Charpentier, Chausson, Clapisson, Dancla, David, Debussy,

Delannoy, Delibes, Delvincourt, d'Indy, L. and T. Dubois, Dukas, Duparc, Dupin, A. and G. Dupont, Dupré, Durey, Emmanuel, Fanelli, Fauré, Franchomme, Franck, Gaubert, Gigout, Godard, Gounod, Grovlez, Guilmant, Guiraud, Hahn, Hardelot, Hillemacher, Holmès, Huë, Huré, Ibert, Inghelbrecht, Jarnach, Koechlin, L. and P. Lacombe, Ladmirault, Lalo, Laparra, Lecocq, Lefébure-Wély, Lefebvre, Leroux, Luigini, Magnard, Maillart, Manziarly, Marteau, Marty, Massé, Massenet, Messager, Migot, Milhaud, Mulet, Niedermeyer, Offenbach, Paray, Pierné, Planquette, Poulenc, Rabaud, Ravel, Reyer, Rhené-Baton, Rivier, Roger-Ducasse, Ropartz, Roussel, Rudhyar, Saint-Saëns, Salomé, Samazeuilh, Satie, F. Schmitt, Sévérac, A. Thomas, Varèse, Vidal, Vierne, Weckerlin, Widor, Witkowski.
20th CENTURY: Baudrier, Barraud, Boulez, Cartan, Duruflé, Ferroud, Françaix, Jolivet, Lesur, Martinon, Messiaen, Sauguet, Tomasi.
See also *Six*; *Jeune France*.

FRANCHETTI (Baron), **ALBERTO**. Born at Turin in 1860 and died at Viareggio in 1942. He was a wealthy Italian who received his musical education at German conservatories and then, at twenty-eight, became known to the world by an opera, *Asrael*, this being followed by other operas (including *Germania*, 1902), and chamber and orchestral works.

FRANCHEZZA (It.), **FRANCHISE** (Fr.). 'Freedom of spirit', 'boldness'.

FRANCHOMME, **AUGUSTE JOSEPH**. Born at Lille in 1808 and died in Paris in 1884, aged seventy-five. He was a cellist of great distinction and one of the most intimate friends of Chopin, whom he aided in the composition of one or two works for his instrument. He himself wrote some chamber music, a cello concerto, and other things—in general of a rather trivial character.

FRANCK.

(1) CÉSAR AUGUSTE (p. 97, pl. **16**. 4). Born at Liège, Belgium, in 1822 and died in Paris in 1890, aged nearly sixty-eight. His father was engaged in banking but, as a keen lover of music, gave his two sons, Joseph and César, a good musical education, and, to complete it effectively, removed to Paris, placing them at the Conservatory there. Here César, at any rate, won several prizes, generally breaking the rules of the competition in some extraordinary manner to make the test more difficult, and so placing the judges in a quandary.

Joseph's after-career was that of an organist and teacher, a minor composer (chiefly of church music), and an author of textbooks; César's career was, as it appeared to many, little more glorious. After dallying a little with opera composition he took up the work of a church musician and, as a devout Christian, threw himself into it, heart and soul. For nearly forty years, and until his death, he occupied the organ loft of St. Clotilde, where he had a fine Cavaillé-Col (q.v.), his improvisations upon which were famous amongst the discerning.

At fifty he was appointed organ professor at the Conservatory, and here he was little understood by his colleagues and superiors. His compositions attracted little notice, and when at last he received government recognition his decorations were awarded to him in his capacity of teacher. Yet he had collected around him a group of pupils who revered him, d'Indy (q.v.) being one of the leading spirits of the group. What he felt to be his first real success as a composer came to him in his sixty-eighth year when his String Quartet was warmly applauded at a concert of the National Society for Music (see *France* 13). Next month, on his way to give a lesson, he was struck by the pole of a horse omnibus, and after lingering a few months he died.

The life of Franck was that of a saint—but a 'cheerful saint', as a friend records of him ('always crackling with wit and repartee'). He rose early, lived simply, and set aside a period every day for quiet meditation.

Some of his earlier works are trivial, but there is no mistaking the mastery of such things as the Symphony; the Prelude, Choral, and Fugue and the Prelude, Aria, and Finale for Piano; the Symphonic Variations for Piano and Orchestra; the Sonata for Violin and Piano, the String Quartet and (an earlier work) Piano Quintet, and the three sets of organ compositions. He wrote some programme music (q.v.), e.g. *The Djinns*, a tone poem for piano and orchestra, based on Hugo, and *The Accursed Hunter*, a tone poem based on Bürger. His *Beatitudes* is a setting for vocal solo, eight-part chorus, and orchestra.

The music of Franck is very personal in idiom, certain turns of melodic and harmonic expression indelibly stamping it as his. It is romantic in feeling, with a peculiar sort of mystical exaltation. The influence of Bach, Beethoven, and Liszt is felt in his work. He and his younger contemporary, Debussy (q.v.), stand as the leaders in two very different schools in nineteenth-century French musical art, the school of heavy romanticism and the school of light-handed impressionism. Yet Debussy, in his capacity of newspaper critic, felt able to write of Franck as 'one of the greatest' of the great musicians.

See references, of greater or lesser importance, under: *Belgium* 5; *Boëly*; *Bordes*; *Bréville*; *Castillon*; *Chabrier*; *Chamber Music* 6, Period III (1822); *Chausson*; *Composition* 4, 5, 7; *Concerto* 6 c (1822); *Duparc*; *France* 10, 13; *d'Indy*; *Mass* 4 V; *Oratorio* 4, 7; *Psalm*; *Reed-Organ Family* 9.

(2) JOSEPH (1820–1891). See under (1).

(3) EDUARD (1817–93). He was a professor of piano first at the Conservatory of Cologne, then at that of Berne, and, finally, at the Stern Conservatory, Berlin. He wrote a symphony, chamber music (see *Chamber Music* 6, Period III—1817), piano sonatas, etc., and his music has value. He was not related to César Franck.

FRANCŒUR, FRANÇOIS (1698–1787). French violinist and court musician. See *Misattributed Compositions*; *Collaboration*.

FRANCO OF COLOGNE. See *France* 2.

FRANK, ALAN CLIFFORD. Born in London in 1910. Composer, writer and Head of the Music Department of the Oxford University Press. He is author of many articles on contemporary music, and of a book on the playing of chamber music. (Cf. *Clarinet Family* 6.) His wife is the composer Phyllis Tate (q.v.).

FRANKEL, BENJAMIN: Born in London in 1906, and died there in 1973. After a period as a watchmaker's apprentice he studied music in Germany and at the Guildhall School of Music, where he was later a teacher. The profits from a career in light music (especially as a composer for the cinema) enabled him after some years to devote himself entirely to serious composition. Among his works are string quartets and other chamber music, as well as some orchestral pieces, including a violin concerto (1951) and a symphony (1960); some of these show the influence of his Jewish background.

FRANKLIN, BENJAMIN. Born at Boston, Mass., in 1706 and died at Philadelphia in 1790. American statesman, scientist, and writer. On his musical side it has to be recorded that he was the inventor of an improved form of musical glasses (see *Harmonica* 1), on which he himself performed, that he is said to have been also a performer on the harp, guitar, and violin, and that he was a lover of Scottish song. Moreover a quartet by him for three violins and violoncello was in 1940 discovered in the library of the Paris Conservatory; it is on novel lines—*scordatura* (q.v.) and only open strings used.

See also *United States* 3; *Clarinet Family* 2. Also p. 512, pl. **91. 4.**

FRANKLIN IS FLED AWAY. See *God save the Queen* 5.

FRANZ, ROBERT (p. 400, pl. **69. 4**). Born at Halle in 1815 and died there in 1892, aged seventy-seven. After a boyhood of furtive music study and a younger manhood of unemployment owing to the difficulty of finding a 'niche', he brought out, when nearing thirty, a book of songs that was hailed by Schumann in his musical journal as in 'the noble, new style', and as 'reflecting the poems with life-like profundity'. Mendelssohn, Liszt, and others took up the cry and he became famous. Certain musical and academic positions were offered to him and life became happier.

Hardly was success thus attained than there

set in a nervous malady, with deafness as one of its symptoms. He struggled on until, in his early fifties, he became too ill to work, when Liszt, Joachim, and others raised money to provide for his needs.

His songs are in forty-five sets, making about 350 in all. They are nearly all for the mezzo-soprano voice and are restrained in expression. They are all lyrical—never dramatic. They are simple in conception yet finished in execution; he was a minor poet of music but a good one.

He wrote also a little choral music, and he did a great deal of musical editorship, especially of the works of Bach and Handel, working out in full the 'figured bass' (q.v.) and supplying 'additional accompaniments' to make them effectively performable with the modern orchestra; most of these 'additional accompaniments', however, are today put aside, as not sufficiently in consonance with the composers' aims. His 'Open Letter' to the critic Hanslick (1871) explains his principles as an editor of the classics.

See references under *Germany* 6; *Additional Accompaniments*; *Ear* 4.

FRAPPER (Fr.). 'To strike.' So *Frappant*, *Frappé*, 'striking', 'struck'.

FRASER, MARJORY KENNEDY. See *Kennedy-Fraser*.

FRASI. See *Figured Bass*.

FRAUENCHOR (Ger.). 'Women's Choir.'

FRAUENLOB. See *Minstrels*, etc. 8; p. 640, pl. 110. 6.

F.R.C.M.; **F.R.C.O.** See *Degrees and Diplomas* 2.

FREDDO (It.). 'Cold.' So *Freddamente*, 'coldly'; *Freddezza*, 'coolness', indifference.

FREDERICK THE GREAT (p. 365, pl. 60. 8). Born in Berlin in 1712 and died near there in 1786, aged seventy-four. He not merely maintained at his court a musical establishment, as did other princes of central Europe in his day, but himself practised diligently upon the flute and composed lavishly for it. A considerable body of his work has been published in recent times; it is said, however, that only the flute part was written by himself, the rest being supplied by his court organist, Agricola (1720-74), a pupil of J. S. Bach.

One of this king's court musicians is said to have remarked, 'If you are under the impression that the King loves music you are wrong; he only loves the flute—and more than that the only flute he loves is his own.' And it is reported that when in his sixties he lost his teeth and could play no longer he took an actual aversion from music. (This, however, has been questioned.)

C. P. Emanuel Bach was for long his chief harpsichordist (see also *Fasch, Carl Friedrich Christian*) and Quantz his flute master, flute maker, and official flute composer (writing for him no fewer than three hundred flute concertos). J. S. Bach visited his court and the *Musical Offering*, in which he worked out a fugue subject given him by the King, was the result.

See references under *Flute Family* 6; *Pianoforte* 4; *Military Band*; *Annotated Programmes* 2; *Opera* 9 a; *Education and Music* 1; *Graun*; *Ricercare*; *Agricola*; *Reichardt*.

FREDONNER (Fr.). 'To hum.'

'FREE AND EASY.' See *Community Singing* 4.

FREE CANON. See *Canon*.

FREE CHURCH OF SCOTLAND. See *Presbyterian Church Music* 3.

FREE COUNTERPOINT. See *Counterpoint*.

FREE FANTASIA. See *Development*; *Fantasia*.

FREE REED. See *Reed*.

FREI, FREIE, etc. (Ger.; various terminations according to case, etc.). 'Free.'

FREIE KOMBINATION (Ger.). 'Free Combination', i.e. 'Independent Combination'—one of the facilities provided on an organ for preparing registration.

FREISCHÜTZ, DER ('The Marksman') (Weber). Produced at Berlin in 1821. Libretto by Friedrich Kind. (Some spoken dialogue.)

ACT I

SCENE: *At the Shooting Range in the Woods, near an Inn*

Max, a forester (*Tenor*), has been defeated in a shooting competition by a forester, **Kilian** (*Bass*). He feels humiliated. The peasants tease him. Max is anxious to win a match which will bring him not only the right, in due course, to become head forester, but the hand of Agatha, daughter of **Kuno** the present head forester (*Bass*).

Kaspar (*Bass*), another forester, seeks Max alone, with a strange proposal. He can show Max how to mould magic bullets that will make it impossible for him to miss any target. They are to meet at midnight in the Wolf's Glen. (Kaspar has sold his soul to the devil, and the forfeit is to be paid tomorrow, unless he can entice another victim into the Evil One's net.)

ACT II

SCENE 1: *Agatha's Room*

Agatha (*Soprano*) is sad, she knows not why. Her cousin, **Annette** (or **Aennchen**) (*Soprano*), tries in vain to cheer her. A hermit has told her that some danger will threaten, but her bridal wreath, prepared in expectation of Max's success, will protect her. Max arrives. She is horrified when he speaks of going to the Wolf's Glen, but he tells her that he must bring home from there a deer he has killed.

SCENE 2: *The Wolf's Glen. Midnight*

Zamiel (speaking part), the Black Ranger—otherwise the Devil—is engaged with Kaspar in the casting of magic bullets, six of which will speed where Max wills; the seventh (but Max does not know this) is under Zamiel's control. The spirit of Max's mother warns him to flee the evil, but Zamiel counters with a vision of Agatha committing suicide in her despair at the failure which, Max knows, awaits him unless he makes the devilish bargain. He agrees, though with horror.

ACT III

SCENE 1: *Agatha's Room*

Agatha puts on her bridal array, and the bridesmaids bring her a wreath of flowers; but it is a funeral wreath. In place of it Annette makes for her cousin a wreath of roses which the warning hermit gave her.

SCENE 2: *The Shooting Range*

Prince Ottakar (*Baritone*) is present to see the great contest. Max has already used six of the magic bullets. As the Prince selects the mark for the final test—a dove—Agatha appears with the Hermit (*Bass*). She cries to Max to hold his hand, but the shot has been fired. Zamiel guides it to her, but her bridal wreath protects her. Instead, Zamiel's victim is Kaspar, who dies cursing the Devil. The Prince hears the truth, and decrees but a light punishment for Max's dabbling with evil: a year's probation, at the end of which, we may be sure, he and Agatha will be united.

Cf. *Opera* 21 d.

FRENCH HARP. Mouth organ; see *Reed-Organ Family* 3, 10.

FRENCH HORN. See *Horn Family* 2 b c, 3, 4, 5 b c.

FRENCH OVERTURE. See *Overture* 1.

FRENCH PITCH. See *Pitch* 5.

FRENCH SIXTH. See *Augmented Sixth*.

FRENCH SUITES (Bach). See *Nicknamed* 2.

FRENCH TIME-NAMES. See *Tonic Sol-fa* 9.

FRENETICO, FRENETICA (It.; masc., fem.). 'Frenzied.'

FREQUENCY MODULATION. See *Broadcasting* 4.

FREQUENCY OF SOUND VIBRATION. See *Acoustics* 3.

FRERE, RIGHT REVD. WALTER HOWARD (1863–1938). Bishop of Truro. See *Plainsong* 4.

FRESCO (It.). 'Fresh', 'cool'. So the adverb *Frescamente*.

FRESCOBALDI, GIROLAMO (p. 516, pl. 93. 6). Born at Ferrara in 1583 and died in Rome in 1643, aged fifty-nine. He was an organist of such repute that when he was appointed to St. Peter's at Rome thirty thousand people were reported to have flocked to hear his first performance there. He was also a great composer of organ music, some of which, despite its belonging to the childhood of instrumental composition, is still played. He left also some vocal music (madrigals, etc.). Through his pupils (Froberger, etc.) he had much influence on German music.

See references under *History* 3; *Chaconne and Passacaglia*; *Folía*; *Bird Music*; *Organ* 13; *Notation* 4; *God save the Queen*; *Capriccio*; *Malipiero*.

FRETS in a stringed instrument are raised lines across the finger-board (or strings tied round it), occupying the positions where the pressure of the finger-tips should be applied in order to produce the various notes. See *Viol Family* 2 e; *Lute*; *Mandoline*; *Guitar*; *Banjo*; *Balalaika*.

It must not be assumed that the object of frets is merely to aid incompetent performers to find their notes; they exist on the viols and lutes in order to give the strings, when 'stopped', the resonance of open strings, i.e. to obviate the 'softening' effect of the finger-tips. The player can (and, to be finely in tune, must) control his exact intonation by slightly pushing or pulling on the string.

FRETTA (It.). 'Haste.' Hence *Frettevole, Frettoso, Frettoloso, Frettolosamente,* 'hurried'.

FRETTED. See *Frets*; also see *Clavichord* 3.

FREUDE (Ger.). 'Joy.' So *Freudig,* 'joyful'.

FREYLINGHAUSEN, JOHANN ANASTASIUS (1670–1739). German theologian and compiler of two important books of hymns and tunes. See reference under *Methodism* 3.

FRICKER, PETER RACINE. Born in London in 1920. He studied at the Royal College of Music and then under Mátyás Seiber. From 1950 his compositions began to be heard and aroused much interest. They include four symphonies, concertos for violin and for viola, an oratorio, *A Vision of Judgement,* chamber music, etc.

In 1952 he became Director of Music at Morley College, London. In 1965 he moved to California.

FRICTION DRUM. Several forms of this instrument exist and it appears to be both widespread and ancient in origin. The general principle is that of rubbing the parchment with the fingers or thumb (instead of beating with a drumstick) but in some forms a stick or a string is attached to the parchment, this being rubbed to produce the sound, and in others the instrument is attached to a string and whirled in the air.

FRID, GÉZA. Born in Hungary in 1904. He studied at the Conservatory of Budapest under Kodály and Bartók, and has composed chamber music and other things.

FRIENDS. See *Quakers and Music*.

FRISCH (Ger.). 'Fresh' (in the English, not the American sense), i.e. brisk and lively.

FRISKIN, JAMES. Born in Glasgow in 1886 and died in New York City in 1967, aged eighty-one. He studied composition and piano at the Royal College of Music and settled in the United States in 1914, joining the staff of the Juilliard School. He composed in various media, but especially for chamber combinations. He was married to Rebecca Clarke (q.v.).

FRISS, or FRISZKA. See *Czardas*.

F.R.M.C.M. See *Degrees and Diplomas* 2.

FROBERGER, JOHANN JACOB. Born at Stuttgart in 1616 and died at Héricourt, Haute-

1. RAVEL (1875–1937)

2. IBERT (1890–1962)

3. AURIC (b. 1899)

5. MESSIAEN (b. 1908)

4. *From left to right*: DUREY (b. 1888), MILHAUD (1892–1974) seated, POULENC (1899–1963), COCTEAU (1891–1963), and TAILLEFERRE (b. 1892). See *France* 11

6. BOULEZ (b. 1925)

See also plates at pages 368–9 and 384–5

1. MERSENNE (1588–1648)
Theologian, philosopher, mathematician, and musician. Author of the famous *Harmonie Universelle*

2. CHRISTOPHER SIMPSON (d. 1669)
Player of the viola da gamba, author of *The Division Violist* and *Principles of Practicall Musick*

3. THOMAS MACE (*c.* 1620–1710). Cambridge choirman and author of the quaint and valuable treatise, *Musick's Monument*

4. PADRE MARTINI (1706–84)
Franciscan friar and learned musical scholar, composer, and teacher

5. SIR JOHN HAWKINS (1719–89). Lawyer and magistrate; author of the very informative five-volume *History of Music* (5 vols., 1776)

6. DR. CHARLES BURNEY (1726–1814). By his friend Reynolds. He was organist, teacher, European traveller in search of musical information, and author of a valuable four-volume *History of Music* (1776–89)

7. FRANÇOIS-JOSEPH FÉTIS (1784–1871). Learned musicologist, composer, and author. His *Biographie Universelle des Musiciens* is still indispensable

8. SIR GEORGE GROVE (1820–1900).
Civil Engineer, then Director of the Royal College of Music, and first editor of the great *Dictionary of Music and Musicians* (1879–89)

9. SIR HENRY HADOW (1859–1937). Oxford don, head of two great provincial universities, author of the much admired *Studies in Modern Music* and first editor of the *Oxford History of Music*

Saône, France, in 1667, aged fifty. He became a choir-boy in Vienna and then held a subordinate organist's position at the court there. When twenty-one he went to Rome and studied for over three years with Frescobaldi (q.v.), afterwards returning to Vienna and then travelling to Brussels, Paris, and (it is said) London.

Froberger was an organist of high reputation and his works seem to be all for keyboard. They have great historical importance (see *Gigue*; *Suite* 3; *Frescobaldi*).

As to Froberger's alleged surprising adventures on the way to, and whilst in, London an extremely picturesque account is given in Mattheson's *Ehrenpforte* (1740, that is over seventy years after Froberger's death). As Mattheson gets the birth date wrong by nearly twenty years he cannot, in any case, be looked upon as a very well-informed relator. His story of the London visit has been repeated (often greatly extended and embellished) in nearly every musical book of reference since his time (Gerber, 1790; Fétis, 1869; Grove in various editions; Blom, 1947—to mention only a few), these accounts differing widely amongst themselves. That Froberger ever held the position of organ blower to the English Court (as the original account says) or to Westminster Abbey (as Grove and others have changed it) is in the highest degree improbable—and a search for his name in Lafontaine's exhaustive collection of the court register records, *The King's Musick* (1909), affords no confirmation of the constantly repeated statement that he was appointed as Court Organist.

FROEBEL. See *Education* 1.

'FROG' QUARTET (Haydn). See *Nicknamed Compositions* 12.

FRÖHLICH (Ger.). 'Happy.'

FROID (Fr.). 'Cold.' So *Froidement*, 'coldly'.

FROMAIGEAT. See *Electric Musical Instruments* 1 i.

FROSCH (Ger.). Literally 'frog'—the nut of the bow of the violin, etc.; so *Am Frosch*, 'at the nut'.

FROSCHQUARTETT (Haydn). See *Nicknamed Compositions* 12.

FROTTOLA, plural **FROTTOLE** (It.). A late fifteenth- and early sixteenth-century popular choral form, for singing unaccompanied, a sort of simpler madrigal treatment of humorous or sentimental words, somewhat preceding in period the madrigal proper (q.v.). The same music is repeated for several verses, in which respect there is a resemblance to the ayre type of madrigal (especially as the air is in the highest part, not in the tenor, as was still common at that date). It is the opinion of some authorities that only the uppermost part was to be sung, the others being played, as was often done with the English Ayre.

The celebrated Venetian music printer, Petrucci, in the opening years of the sixteenth century published eleven books of Frottole, of which ten books remain, containing over 500 compositions.

The frottola is related to the *Villanella* (q.v.).

F.R.S. This distinction occurs occasionally in the *Companion* and should, thus, have a line or two of explanation. It indicates 'Fellow of the Royal Society' (founded in 1645 and becoming 'Royal' by charter granted by Charles II in 1662). At one time the Society, now purely 'scientific', did not exclude music from its interests, and its *Philosophical Transactions*, during the first century or so, include papers of musical interest. Burney, as a man of high musical erudition, was in 1773 elected a member, but in more recent times any rare musicians elected have attained the honour (one of the highest available in the field of learning) on other grounds (cf. *Pole*). Its full title is 'Royal Society of London for Improving Natural Knowledge'.

FRÜHER (Ger.). 'Earlier', 'previous'.

FRÜHLINGSLIED (Ger.). 'Spring song.'

FRÜHLINGSSONATE (Beethoven). See *Nicknamed Compositions* 4.

FRY, WILLIAM HENRY (p. 1040, pl. **169.** 3). Born in Philadelphia in 1813, and died at Santa Cruz, West Indies, in 1864, aged fifty-one. He is remembered as the composer of the first notable American opera. This was *Leonora* (1845), a score of amateurish workmanship, after the Italian model of the early nineteenth century and performed in Italian because of the lack of trained American opera singers. The Jullien Orchestra of Paris played his overtures and his symphony, and Berlioz befriended him.

A second opera, *Notre Dame de Paris*, was produced in Philadelphia in 1864 under the leadership of Theodore Thomas. (Cf. *Opera* 21 h j.)

He was one of the pioneers of music criticism in America (see *Criticism* 5), being music reviewer and later European musical correspondent of the *New York Tribune*.

F.T.C.L.; **F.T.S.C.** See *Degrees and Diplomas* 2.

FUGA. See *Form* 12.

FUGA ALLA GIGA (Bach). See *Nicknamed Compositions* 1.

FUGARA. See *Organ* 14 III.

FUGATA. See *Aria*.

FUGATO. A passage in fugal style (see *Form* 12) introduced into a non-fugal composition; e.g. many operas, even comic operas, have fugato.

FUGHETTA. A short fugue. See *Form* 12.

FUGUE. See *Form* 12, 13.

FUGUING TUNES. See *Hymns and Hymn Tunes* 6.

FÜHREND (Ger.). 'Leading.'

FULEIHAN, ANIS. Born in Cyprus in 1900 and died in Stanford, Calif., in 1970, aged seventy. At fifteen he settled in the United States. He enjoyed success as pianist and composer. From 1953 to 1960 he directed the National Conservatory at Beirut. His orchestral and other works are numerous and include violin and pianoforte concertos, a *Symphonie Concertante* for string quartet and orchestra, chamber music, etc.

FULL, as applied to Anthems and other music in the church service. See *Verse*.

FULL CLOSE. See *Cadence*.

FULLER MAITLAND, JOHN ALEXAN-DER. Born in London in 1856 and died near Carnforth, Lancs., in 1936, aged nearly eighty. He was music critic of *The Times*, 1889–1911, and a good pianist and harpsichordist, published a number of books, and edited the second edition of Grove's *Dictionary of Music*. With *English County Songs* (1893; compiled in collaboration with Lucy Broadwood) he became one of the pioneers in the publication of English folk music, and in the editing of the Fitzwilliam Virginal Book (1899; in collaboration with W. Barclay Squire, q.v.), one of the pioneers in the re-publication of early English instrumental music. He was an honorary D.Litt. of Durham University.

See *Temperament* 10; *Benjamin Cosyn's Virginal Book*.

FÜLLFLÖTE (Ger.). A full-toned (i.e. loud) flute stop on the organ.

FÜLLIGSTIMMEN (Ger.). 'Full-toned voices', i.e. organ stops of loud tone.

FULL ORGAN. A term in organ music directing the player to use Great and Swell manuals coupled, with all their stops in operation.

FULL SCORE. See *Score*.

FÜLLSTIMME (Ger., literally 'filling-voice'). (1) An additional orchestral part (cf. *Ripieno*), etc. (2) The mixture stop of an organ.

FULL TRICHORD. See *Pianoforte* 16.

FUMAGALLI, ADOLFO. Born near Milan in 1828 and died at Florence in 1856, aged twenty-seven. He made a great reputation as pianist and composer of piano music of the lighter kind, some of which is still played.

FUNDAMENTAL BASS. See *Harmony* 24.

FUNDAMENTAL DISCORD. See *Harmony* 24.

FUNDAMENTAL NOTES. See *Acoustics* 6, 8.

FUNÈBRE (Fr.), **FUNEBRE** (It.). 'Funeral', etc. So *Marche funèbre*, 'funeral march'.

FUNERAL MARCH (Mendelssohn). See *Nicknamed Compositions* 14; *Colour and Music* 4.

FÜNF (Ger.). 'Five.' So *Fünfstimmig*, 'five-voiced', i.e. in five 'parts' or strands.

FUNICULÌ FUNICULÀ. See *Denza*.

FUOCO (It.). 'Fire', i.e. a combination of force and speed. So *Fuocoso*, 'fiery'. (Cf. *Foco*.)

FÜR (Ger.). 'For.'

FURIA (It.). 'Fury.' So *Furioso, Furibondo*, 'furious'; *Furiosamente*, 'furiously'.

FURIANT. A Bohemian dance type, rapid, of decided yet often-changing rhythm. Smetana (*The Bartered Bride*, etc.) and Dvořák (Piano Quintet, etc.) have used it, the latter very freely and with exhilarating effect.

FURIEUX, FURIEUSEMENT (Fr.). 'Furious', 'furiously'.

FURIOSO, FURIBONDO (It.). 'Furious'; *Furiosamente*, 'furiously'.

FURLANO. See *Forlana*.

FURNISHINGS, EFFECT ON MUSIC. See *Concert Halls* 9.

FURNITURE STOP. See *Organ* 14 V.

FURORE (It.). (*a*) 'Fury', or (*b*) 'enthusiasm'.

FURRY DANCE. An ancient processional dance celebrating the coming of spring, still kept up at Helston in Cornwall. It is sometimes called 'Floral Dance' or 'Flora'. In general type it resembles the farandole (q.v.).

FUSA. See *Notation* 4.

FUTURISM. See *Italy* 7.

FUX, JOHANN JOSEPH. Born near Graz in 1660 and died at Vienna in 1741, aged about eighty-one. He was choirmaster of St. Stephen's Cathedral, Vienna, and Court Composer and Capellmeister, and an industrious composer (fifty masses, nearly twenty operas, etc.). He is remembered today chiefly by his great treatise on counterpoint (*Gradus ad Parnassum*); this formulated rules which governed the teaching of the subject for many generations, and in the early twentieth century was still influential.

See references s.v. *Canon; Counterpoint; Gradus ad Parnassum; Caldara*.

FUYANT (Fr.). 'Fleeing.'

G

G. in French organ music means 'Grand Orgue', i.e. 'Great Organ'.

GABELKLAVIER. See *Percussion Family* 5 e.

GABRIELI (or **Gabrielli**), uncle and nephew.

(1) ANDREA (born at Venice about 1510 and died there in 1586, aged about seventy-six). He was a pupil of Willaert (q.v.) and served under that master at St. Mark's, Venice, as a singer, later becoming one of its organists. He wrote much for choir and for organ and was famous throughout Europe. Amongst his most important pupils was the great Dutch organist and composer Sweelinck.

See *Concerto* 1; *Sonata* 10 a; *Chamber Music* 6, Period I; *Hassler*; *Competitions* 1.

(2) GIOVANNI (born at Venice in 1557 and died there in 1612, aged fifty-four or fifty-five). His career was very like that of his uncle (above). He became one of the organists of St. Mark's and wrote much choral music (sacred and secular) and organ music, and developed the use of the orchestra in accompaniment. His fame was international and the great German composer Schütz was his pupil.

See *Concerto* 1; *Sonata* 10 a; *Passion Music* 3; *Trombone Family* 3; *Chamber Music* 6, Period I.

GADE, NIELS VILHELM (p. 896, pl. 153. 2). Born at Copenhagen in 1817 and died there in 1890, aged seventy-three. In the early days of the movement for national expression in music it looked as though his native Denmark would find in him her mouthpiece, but Leipzig training and the influence of the German school, especially Mendelssohn and Schumann, largely overpowered his nationality as it did also his individuality.

In the last years of Mendelssohn's life he assisted him in the capacity of second conductor at Leipzig, and after his death he succeeded him for a short time. Then he returned to Copenhagen as organist and conductor, and there henceforth resided. He more than once visited England to conduct his cantatas. One of them, *The Crusaders*, had a long popularity. His works include eight symphonies, a violin concerto, piano compositions, a few organ pieces, songs, etc. They are graceful and well proportioned.

See *Concerto* 6 b (1817); also *Scandinavia* 2 for the music of Denmark in Gade's period and the preceding one.

GAFORI, GAFORIO, GAFURI, etc. (1451–1522). Famous theoretical writer of Milan, whose *Practica Musicae* was published in 1496.

GAGLIANO.

(1) MARCO DA. Born at Gagliano, near Florence, about 1575 and died at Florence in 1642, aged about sixty-seven. He was a canon and musical director of San Lorenzo in Florence, musical director at the Medici court, founder of a famous musical society (the Accademia degl' Elevati), and in every way the leading musician of the city. He was one of the Florentine group of early opera composers (see also *Peri* and *Caccini*) who were inspired by what they believed to be the Greek dramatic ideal and practice; his *Daphne* was performed at Mantua in 1608. He also wrote madrigals and church music.

(2) Important Neapolitan family of violin makers—ALESSANDRO (active at the end of the seventeenth century and beginning of the eighteenth), two sons (GENNARO and NICOLO), and two grandsons (sons of Nicolo —FERDINANDO and GIUSEPPE), as well as a few less important later members of the family.

GAGLIARDA (It.). Galliard. See *Pavan and Galliard*.

GAGNEBIN, HENRI. Born in 1886 at Liège, but of Swiss parents. He became head of the Conservatory of Geneva in 1925, and is known as the composer of a good deal of orchestral music, chamber music, etc., as also of an oratorio, *St. Francis of Assisi* (1935).

GAI, GAIEMENT (Fr.). 'Gay', 'gaily'. So *Gaité*, 'gaiety'.

GAILLARD (Fr.). (1) 'Merry', 'lively'; (2) Galliard. (See *Pavan and Galliard*.)

GAINSBOROUGH, THOMAS (1727–88). The painter. A great musical enthusiast and an associate of Abel (q.v.), John Christian Bach (q.v.), Stanley (q.v.), and Jackson of Exeter (q.v.).

GAIO, GAIA (It.; masc., fem.). 'Gay.' So *Gaiamente*, 'gaily'.

GAISSER, (Dom) UGO ATANASIO, otherwise **Josef Anton** (1853–1920). See *Greek Church* 4.

GAITA. See *Bagpipe Family* 7; *Spain* 8 (near end).

GAJO (It.). Older spelling of 'Gaio' (q.v.).

GÁL, HANS. Born in 1890 at Brunn-am-Gebirge, Austria. He is a distinguished musicologist (taking his doctorate at Vienna in 1913 with a thesis on *The Style of the Young Beethoven*) and a well-known composer (operas, orchestral works, chamber music, songs, etc.).

In Edinburgh since 1938 (lecturer in the University).

GALANT, GALAMMENT (Fr.). 'Gallant', 'gallantly'. So, too, (It.) *Galante, Galantemente*. For *Style Galant* see under that head and also *Sonata* 6.

GALANTERIEN (Ger.), **GALANTERIES** (Fr.). In the classical suite (see *Suite* 3) of the early eighteenth century the Galanterien are those movements which are not essential to the scheme and may perhaps be looked upon as interpolations of light relief.

The essential movements of the normal German suite of this period (e.g. Bach) are the allemande, courante, sarabande, and gigue. The galanteries (inserted normally after the sarabande) are usually taken from the following: minuet, gavotte, bourrée, passepied, loure, polonaise, air.

Cf. *Style Galant*.

GALANTER STIL. See *Style Galant*; *Sonata* 6.

GALAXY MUSIC CORPORATION. See *Kramer, A. W.*; *Ward, R.*

GALILEI, VINCENZO (or Vincentino). Born at Florence about 1533 and died there in 1591, aged about fifty-eight. He was one of the celebrated group of Florentine musicians who took part in the researches and activities mentioned under *Opera* 1, 2, was a singer, violist, lutenist, composer, and writer upon music, and was father of the great astronomer, Galileo Galilei.

See *Bagpipe Family* 5; *Harp* 2; *Lute Family* 1.

GALIN, PIERRE (1786–1821) and **GALIN-PARIS-CHEVÉ**. See *Sight-Singing* 2; *Tonic Sol-fa* 9.

GALLEGADA. See *Muiñeira*.

GALLIARD. See *Pavan and Galliard*; *Form* 14; *Minuet*; *Suite* 2; *God save the Queen* 2.

GALLIARD, JOHN ERNEST. Born at Zell, in Hanover, in 1687 and died in London in 1749, aged about sixty-two. He was a notable oboist who at the age of twenty-eight settled in London, playing in theatre orchestras. His compositions were varied—anthems, operas, pantomime music, solos for violoncello, flute, etc., and a piece for twenty-four bassoons and four double-basses. The song *With Early Horn* (from one of his operas) enjoyed high popularity. He translated under the title of *Observations on the Florid Song* (1742) the famous work of Tosi (for whom see *Singing* 5; *Rubato* 2).

GALLICAN RITE. See *Common Prayer*; *Liturgy*.

GALLUS. See *Handl*.

GALOP, or **GALOPADE**. A quick, lively round dance, in two-in-a-measure time, with the characteristic of a change of step, or hop, at the end of every half-phrase of the music. Its original (German) names were *Hopser* ('hopper') and *Rutscher* ('slider'), alluding to the peculiarity above mentioned. From Germany it spread to England, France, and elsewhere in the middle of the nineteenth century. After a time it ceased to be danced independently, but became part of a set of the quadrille (q.v.).

In 1935 was discovered at Vienna a galop that Beethoven had appropriately provided (to the order of the Archduke Rudolph) for an exhibition of horsemanship. *Pferdemusik* ('Horse-music') the composer called it.

GALOUBET AND TAMBOURIN. See *Recorder Family* 3 c.

GALPIN, FRANCIS WILLIAM (1858–1945). English clergyman (Canon of Chelmsford), erudite antiquarian of high authority on the history of musical instruments. In 1946 was founded, in his memory, the Galpin Society, 'with the object of bringing together all those interested in research into the history of European instruments of music and associated subjects'.

See references under *Hydraulus*; *Horn Family* 5 (note); *Whiffle*.

GALT, JOHN (1779–1839). Scottish novelist and 'Empire builder'. See *Canadian Boat Song*.

GALTON, SIR FRANCIS (1822–1911). See *Colour and Music* 1; *Acoustics* 2.

GALUPPI, BALDASSARE. He was born in 1706 on the Venetian island of Burano (hence being nicknamed 'Il Buranello') and died at Venice itself in 1785, aged seventy-eight. His father, a barber and theatre fiddler, gave him some elementary musical instruction. By the excellence of his natural parts, and by careful study under Lotti, he rose to eminence as an opera composer, visiting London and St. Petersburg and composing for the theatres in these cities. He was placed in charge of the music in St. Mark's, Venice.

He is reported to have been an able harpsichordist; he certainly left some harpsichord music, and that, presumably, is why Browning wrote a poem on an imaginary *Toccata of Galuppi's*:

'Brave Galuppi! That was music! Good alike
    at grave and gay:
I can always leave off talking when I hear a
    master play.'

See references under *Opera* 17 a, 26; *Greek Church* 5; *Harmonica* 1; *Malipiero*.

GAMBA. See *Braccio and Gamba*; *Viol Family* 3, 5; *Organ* 3, 14 III.

GAMELAN. A type of orchestra common in the East Indies consisting primarily of an assortment of instruments of the marimba, xylophone, and gong type. Debussy made acquaintance with it at the Paris Exhibition of 1889 and it is said to have influenced him.

GAMME (Fr.). 'Scale.' (For the names by which the scales are known in French see Tables 5, 7, and 9.)

GAMUT (p. 960, p. **161**. 5). (1) Properly, i.e. primarily, this is the note G at the pitch indicated by the bottom line of the bass staff. This was the lowest note recognized in the old system of the hexachords (q.v.). The Greek letter, gamma, was used as its designation, and it was at the same time the *Ut* (or, as we now call it, *Doh*) of the lowest hexachord, hence the collision-word 'Gamut', a literal rendering of which, today, would be 'G–doh'. Organ builders still (tautologically) speak of 'Gamut G' for the note in question.

(2) By an extension the word came to be used for the whole series of hexachords as displayed in writing (like our Tonic Sol-fa Modulator) or by the 'Guidonian Hand' (see, again, *Hexachord*). Shakespeare in *The Taming of the Shrew* (III. i) shows knowledge of the gamut in this sense, indeed the scene turns very much on this. And he uses several expressions like 'to teach you Gamut'. Pepys records spending time 'Conning my Gamut', for, although the actual hexachord system no longer had importance in his day (end of seventeenth century) the hexachord names of the notes were still regularly used. Thomas Purcell at the same period uses the old names: in writing to a friend, a deep bass, for whom his son is composing something with the low F and E, he says, 'F faut and E lamy are preparing for you'. Any F was fa in the hexachord of C and Ut in its own hexachord (hence F–fa–ut), and any E likewise had two hexachordal functions, those of lah and mi (hence E–lah–mi). If Purcell had said 'F and E are preparing for you', it would have meant exactly the same, but apparently it was the custom of the time to use the needlessly elaborate names (actually the two notes he meant were not included in the old hexachord table, which reached down only to G, once considered, perhaps from the use of low pitch, as the lowest practicable vocal sound). Cf. *Notation* 1.

(3) By a slight further extension it came also to mean 'scale' in general (cf. French *gamme*).

(4) And it came also to mean the whole range of musical sounds from lowest to highest.

GAMUT G. See *Gamut*; *Pitch* 7.

GANGAR. A 'walking' dance of Norway.

GANZ (Ger.). 'Quite', 'whole', e.g. *Ganzer Bogen*, 'whole bow'; *Gänzlich*, 'completely'.

GANZE, GANZE NOTE. Same as 'Ganzetaktnote' (see below).

GANZE PAUSE. Semibreve rest.

GANZETAKTNOTE. 'Whole-measure note', or 'whole-bar note'. The whole note or semibreve (Table 3).

GAPPED SCALES. See *Scales* 10.

GARBO (It.). 'Manners' (in a good sense), bearing, grace. So *Garbato*, *Garbatamente*, 'elegantly', 'gracefully'; *Garbatissimo*, 'very graceful'; *Garbatino*, 'rather graceful'; *Garbatezza*, 'gracefulness'.

GARCÍA Family.

(1) MANUEL I (in full Manuel del Popolo Vicente). Born at Seville in 1775 and died in Paris in 1832, aged fifty-seven. He was a great operatic tenor, popular opera composer, and most successful singing-master, in high repute in Paris, London, New York, and elsewhere.

(2) MANUEL II (in full Manuel Patricio Rodriguez). Born, probably in Madrid, in 1805 and died in London in 1906, aged over one hundred and one. Son of Manuel I, he was a singing-master of immense reputation, and the inventor of the Laryngoscope. For nearly half a century (1848–95) he served on the staff of the Royal Academy of Music in London.

Cf. *Singing* 11, 12, Also p. 977, pl. 164. 2.

(3) MARIA FELICIA, known by her first married name of MALIBRAN. Born in Paris in 1808 and died in Manchester in 1836, aged twenty-eight. She was a daughter and pupil of Manuel I, and enjoyed unlimited admiration as an operatic contralto. Her second husband was de Bériot (q.v.).

Cf. *Festival* 1.

(4) PAULINE (in full Michelle Pauline)—known by her married name of VIARDOT, or as VIARDOT-GARCIA). Born in Paris in 1821 and died there in 1910, aged eighty-eight. She was a daughter and pupil of Manuel I, and a very celebrated operatic mezzo-soprano, of unusually extended compass. She had talent as a composer, and in this field had lessons from Liszt. (See *Arrangement*.)

(5) GUSTAVE. Born at Milan in 1837 and died in London in 1925, aged eighty-eight. He was the son of Manuel II, and had a successful career as an operatic baritone, and a teacher of singing (long on the staff of the Royal Academy and Royal College of Music, London).

(6) ALBERT. Born in London in 1875 and there died in 1946. He was son of Gustave, a baritone, and a teacher of singing on the staffs of the Royal College of Music, Trinity College, and the Guildhall School.

See references to the family under *Opera* 21 d; *Spain* 10; *Singing* 12.

GARDANO. See *Publishing* 1, 3.

GARDEL, MAXIMILIAN. See *Ballet* 3, 9.

GARDENS (Vauxhall and the like). See *Concert* 12, 13, 15.

GARDER (Fr.). 'To keep', 'to hold'.

GARDINER, HENRY BALFOUR. Born in London in 1877 and died at Salisbury in 1950, aged seventy-two. He was educated at Charterhouse and Oxford, and after study in Germany became for a time a music-master of Winchester College. He collected English folk songs and composed (in moderate quantity) attractive and very English music, and just before the first World War did great service by a series of orchestral concerts in London devoted to the popularization of the works of his British contemporaries. Latterly, however, he discontinued public musical activity, buying a farm on the Shaftesbury Downs and carrying out a programme of afforestation, later giving two areas of woodland to the nation—one of them now known as the 'Gardiner Forest'.

See *Knorr*.

GARDNER, JOHN LINTON. Born in Manchester in 1917. After studying at Oxford

University he served in the Royal Air Force. In 1946 he became répétiteur and assistant conductor at the Royal Opera House. He was appointed to Morley College in 1952, and to the staff of the Royal Academy of Music in 1956. His first symphony was performed with success in 1951. He has to his credit a considerable list of other works, instrumental and vocal, including an opera, *The Moon and Sixpence* (1957).

GARLAND, JOHN (Johannes de Garlandia). A learned English theologian and grammarian of the early thirteenth century, resident in Paris. He was a composer and theoretician, but only fragments of his works remain. Confusion has occurred between him and other writers of similar name, and the above particulars, though probably correct, are offered with reserve.

See references under *France* 2; *Voice* 14.

GARRETT, GEORGE MURSELL. Born at Winchester in 1834 and died at Cambridge in 1897, aged sixty-two. He was organist of St. John's College, Cambridge, and composed sound service music and anthems that remain in use in the English church.

See references under *Anthem*, Period V.

GARRICK, DAVID (1717–79). Famous actor. See *Heart of Oak*; *Burney*; *Ballet* 3.

GARTH, JOHN. Born at Durham in 1722 and died in 1810. He was an organist and composer whose chief work was to combine the psalm-settings of Marcello (q.v.) with the English version of the words. He also produced various organ and instrumental works, including a set of violoncello concertos with string accompaniment—early examples of their kind.

GARVIN, J. L. See *Criticism* 10.

GASSENHAUER. See *Chaconne and Passacaglia* (end). But 'Gassenhauer' means also a street song.

GASSMANN, F. L. (1729–74). See *Bohemia*.

GAST, PETER (1854–1918). See *Nietzsche*.

GASTEIN SYMPHONY (Schubert). See *Nicknamed* 18.

GASTOLDI, GIOVANNI GIACOMO. He was born about 1555 at Caravaggio and died in 1622, aged about sixty-seven, at Mantua, of whose ducal chapel he had previously for some years been choirmaster.

He was a productive and accomplished composer of church music and madrigals, of which he successfully published many books. His five-voiced Balletts, of 1591, 'to sing, play and dance', went through many editions and are thought to have served as models for Morley.

GASTOUÉ, AMÉDÉE (1873–1943). He was an eminent church music director, plainsong expert, authority on early French music, and general musicologist.

See *France* 2; *Greek Church* 4.

GATES, BERNARD (1685–1773). See *Oratorio* 5.

GATHERING NOTE. This term, which has to do with hymn tunes, is applied in two slightly different ways:

(*a*) To the single treble note (or sometimes pedal note) with which old organists used to precede the first or every verse of a hymn, as a signal, presumably, to the congregation to open their mouths and be ready. (At one time if the treble note was used, it was often given an ictus, or preliminary stress, by the use of the semitone below it as an acciaccatura.)

(*b*) To the note, longer than the succeeding notes, with which each line of some hymn tunes begins, probably put there by the composer with the same purpose.

This latter kind of gathering note was very usual in the four-lined common-metre English tunes (see *Hymns and Hymn Tunes* 13) from the last quarter of the sixteenth century to the last quarter of the seventeenth, and is sometimes found in tunes of the eighteenth century. The tunes of this whole long period were largely superseded as the eighteenth century went on by the more elaborate and often rococo tunes (see *Hymns and Hymn Tunes* 6) which with the Oxford Movement of the nineteenth century gave way again to the staider old tunes—but almost always printed without the original lengthening of the first note (logically, according to the iambic rhythm of the verse).

Steggall, Hullah, and one or two others in the 186os tried to reinstate the gathering notes, but without success. The *English Hymnal* of 1906 (see *Hymns and Hymn Tunes* 6) on grounds of rhythmic variety, repeated this attempt, even imposing the device on tunes in which it was not originally used. The principal objection to the practice seems to be that to the first and unaccented syllable of the words (often a mere article or preposition) is given an unsuitable importance. It has also been alleged by opponents that 'although it was the practice to print iambic Psalter tunes with a semibreve at the beginning and end of each line, it was not necessarily the *universal* custom so to sing them'.

GATHERING PIPES. See *Bagpipe Family* 3.

GATHERING PSALM. The first psalm in old Scottish Presbyterian worship. So called from the fact that at one time it was sung as the congregation was assembling—like the organ's opening voluntary today.

GATTI, GUIDO MARIA (1892–1973). Distinguished Italian critic, author, and journalist, editor of *La Rassegna musicale* and able organizer of musical congresses, etc.

See *Dictionaries* 1.

GATTY, NICHOLAS COMYN. Born near Sheffield in 1874 and died in London in 1946, aged seventy-two. He studied at Cambridge and the Royal College of Music, and practised as a music critic on various important London newspapers. As a composer he largely specialized in opera (*Greysteel*, *Prince Ferelon*, *The Tempest*, etc.). His style was direct and uninvolved, his melody pleasant, and his sense of the stage considerable.

Cf. *Opera* 24 f (1906–9–19–20).

GAUBERT, PHILIPPE. He was born at Cahors in 1879 and died in Paris in 1941, aged sixty-two. At the Paris Conservatory his first subject was the flute, of which in 1919 he was to become professor there. He conducted the orchestra of the Concert Society of the Conservatory and at the Opera.

As a composer he produced chamber music, orchestral works, songs, and operas.

See *Flute Family* 6.

GAUCHE (Fr.). 'Left.' *Main gauche,* 'left hand'.

GAUKLER. See *Minstrels, etc.* 1.

GAUL, ALFRED ROBERT. Born at Norwich in 1837 and died at King's Norton in 1913, aged seventy-six. He practised in Birmingham, and wrote sacred cantatas (*Ruth, The Holy City,* etc.) which during the last third of the nineteenth century had immense vogue in his own country, and some in America.

In the public museum at Rouen is to be seen the pencil he used in composing his cantata *Joan of Arc* (presented by himself)—likewise the indiarubber.

GAUNTLETT, H. J. (1805–76). See *Hymns and Hymn Tunes* 16; *Congregational* 5.

GAVAZZENI, GIANANDREA. Born at Bergamo in 1909 and resident in Milan. He is a pianist and conductor, and a composer whose works include operas, ballets, and orchestral music, the last named including three *Concerti di Cinquanda* (Cinquanda is a village near Bergamo). He has published books on Donizetti, Pizzetti (of whom he was a pupil), etc.

GAVEAU. The Paris piano-making firm of this name (with a branch in Brussels) was founded in 1847. It is owner of a famous Paris concert hall, the Salle Gaveau.

See reference under *Harpsichord* 5.

GAVOTTE (p. 881, pl. **148**. 4, 5). A dance form coming originally from the Pays de Gap, in France, where the inhabitants are called Gavots. It was taken up at the court of Louis XIV, where Lully composed many specimens, and where it became very popular, its court and Paris popularity lasting until the French Revolution. The ball-room custom grew up of following the minuet with a gavotte. Both were slow and stately dances, but the minuet was in three-in-a-measure time and the gavotte in two or four (really, perhaps, four, but the alla breve signature was often used); further, the feet were shuffled along the floor in the minuet, whereas in the gavotte they were lifted. In its first aristocratic use kissing was a part of the ritual of this dance, but this was superseded by the presentation of bouquets or chaplets.

From France the gavotte passed into England and other countries, and it became one of the optional members of the classical suite (q.v.), following (or sometimes preceding) the sarabande (see some of Bach's keyboard suites, for instance). Like the other dance forms of the suite the gavotte was in simple binary form (see *Form* 5), with each section usually repeated.

The rhythm was steady and the beats were not broken up into a multitude of short notes. Each section, and indeed, each phrase, opened at the half-measure, i.e. the third beat (cf. *Bourrée,* which is much the same except that its phrases open at the three-quarter-measure, i.e. the fourth beat: Gluck in *Orpheus,* however, has what he calls a gavotte with the phrases opening at the three-quarter-measure. See also *Rhythm* 9).

Just as a minuet was followed by another minuet, called 'Trio', the minuet then being repeated, so the gavotte was often followed by another gavotte, frequently a musette, i.e. it had a persistent bass note, imitating the drone bass of the instrument, the musette (see *Bagpipe Family* 6). Thus, as a whole, the form became ternary (cf. *Bourrée; Form* 6).

Some of Handel's opera and oratorio overtures end with a gavotte, just as others end with a minuet. There are many gavottes in the operas of Lully, Rameau, and Gluck.

In the nineteenth century a good many rather flimsy drawing-room pieces were written in this form and style, which was felt to be graceful, quaint, and 'old world' without being archaic (see *Pianoforte* 22).

An old English spelling is *Gavot.* The seventeenth-century *Cebell* (q.v.) was a variety.

See a reference under *Overture* 7.

GAY, JOHN (1685–1732; p. 101, pl. **18**. 2). The poet. See *Beggar's Opera; Black-eyed Susan.*

G.B.E. See *Knighthood and other Honours.*

G.B.S.M. See *Degrees and Diplomas* 2.

G CLEF. See Table 4.

G.C.V.O. See *Knighthood and other Honours.*

GEBET (Ger.). 'Prayer.'

GEBRAUCH (Ger.). 'Use', e.g. *Pedalgebrauch,* 'use of the pedal' (in piano playing).

GEBRAUCHSMUSIK, i.e. 'Music for Use', 'Utility Music'. The term was coined by the composer Hindemith (though later disowned by him) to describe the products of a movement with which were connected certain twentieth-century German composers, such as Hindemith himself and Kurt Weill (q.v.). This movement was the result of the preaching of the revolutionary poet Bert Brecht, who maintained the necessity for artists to preserve contact with the masses of the population and, in order to do so, to seek their inspiration in subjects of actuality and to use idioms in everyday use, especially with amateur performers in mind. Regarded in one way, this movement sternly opposed any lingering ideas of 'Art for Art's Sake'; it regarded Art, in fact, as a social expression and a social influence (which is not an entirely new idea) and was content if a good deal of what it produced should turn out to be, so to speak, journalism rather than literature.

Typical examples of works written according to the 'Gebrauchsmusik' theory are Kurt Weill's *Der Jasager* and Hindemith's *Wir bauen eine Stadt* (a children's musical play).

The advent of the Nazi government in 1933, which discountenanced the music of Hindemith and drove Weill out of the country, was, of course, a blow to this movement.

GEBUNDEN (Ger.). 'Bound', (1) in the sense either of 'tied' or 'slurred'. (2) See *Clavichord* 3.

GEDACT. See *Organ* 14, I, II.

GEDÄMPFT (Ger.). 'Damped', i.e. (stringed and brass instruments) muted; (drums) muffled; (piano) damped, soft pedalled. In a general way, 'muffled', 'deadened', by whatever means are available with the medium in use.

GEDECKT. See *Organ* 14 I.

GEDEHNT (Ger.). 'Stretched out', i.e. sustained. So *Gedehnter*, more sustained or prolonged.

GEDICHT (Ger.). 'Poem.'

GEDIKE. See *Goedicke.*

GEFALLEN (Ger.). 'Pleasure', in the phrase *Nach Gefallen*, 'at one's own pleasure' = *Ad libitum* (q.v.).

GEFÄLLIG (Ger.). 'Agreeable', in a pleasant sort of way; effortless and cheery.

GEFÜHL (Ger.). 'Feeling'; hence *Gefühlvoll*, 'full of feeling'.

GEGEN (Ger.). 'Towards', 'near', 'about', 'against', 'counter'.

GEHALTEN (Ger.). 'Held out', i.e. sustained; so *Gut gehalten*, 'well sustained'.

GEHAUCHT (Ger.). 'Whispered.'

GEHEIMNISVOLL (Ger.). 'Mysterious.'

GEHEND (Ger.). 'Going', i.e. andante (q.v.).

GEHÖRIG (Ger.). 'Proper', 'suitable'.

GEHOT, JEAN. See *Programme Music* 4.

GEIGE (Ger.). Originally any bowed instrument, now the violin (plur. *Geigen*).

GEIGEN, GEIGEN PRINCIPAL or GEIGEN-PRINZIPAL. See *Organ* 14 I, III.

GEIRINGER, KARL. Born at Vienna in 1899. He is an eminent musicologist—an authority especially on musical instruments, but also on Haydn, Brahms, and some other composers (especially those associated with his native city). He lived for some time in London, but in 1941 migrated to the United States, where he taught at the University of Boston and (from 1962) at Santa Barbara.

GEISHA. See *Dance* 3.

GEISHA, THE. See *Jones, Sidney.*

GEIST (Ger.—cf. Eng. 'Ghost'). 'Spirit', 'soul'.

GEISTERHARFE. See *Aeolian Harp.*

'GEISTER' TRIO (Beethoven). See *Nicknamed Compositions* 4.

GEISTLICH (Ger.—cf. *Geist* above). 'Spiritual.' So *Geistliches Lied, Geistliche Lieder,* 'spiritual song', 'spiritual songs'.

GEKNEIPT (Ger.). 'Plucked' (i.e. pizzicato).

GEKOPPELT (Ger.). 'Coupled.'

GELASSEN (Ger.). 'Quiet', 'calm'.

GELÄUFIG (Ger.). From *laufen,* to run, hence 'fluent', nimble. So *Geläufigkeit,* 'fluency'.

GELTZER. See *Ballet* 9.

GEMA. See *Copyright* 3.

GEMÄCHLICH (Ger.). 'Comfortable', i.e. unhurried. So *Gemächlicher,* 'more leisurely'.

GEMÄSSIGT (Ger.). 'Moderate', i.e. with regard to speed.

GEMENDO, GEMEBONDO (It.). 'Moaning.'

GEMESSEN (Ger.). 'Measured', i.e (a) precise (in time values), or (b) at a moderate speed, or (c) 'grave', heavy in style.

GEMINIANI, FRANCESCO (p. 517, pl. **94.** 2). Born at Lucca in 1687 and died in Dublin in 1762, aged seventy-four. He was a much-admired violinist and composer for stringed instruments, who spent a good deal of time in London, Dublin, and Paris, and handed on to his pupils in all those places the traditions of his master, Corelli. He also wrote an early violin 'Method', and is stated to have been the earliest composer to use the now conventional signs (< >) for *crescendo* and *diminuendo* (cf. *Mazzocchi; Expression* 1).

GEMSHORN. See *Organ* 14 II.

GEMÜT(H) (Ger.). 'Feeling.' So *Gemütvoll,* 'feelingly'. But *Gemütlich,* 'easy-going', 'comfortable'.

GENANNT (Ger.). 'Called', 'known as'.

GENAU (Ger.). 'Exact'; so *Genauigkeit,* 'exactitude'.

GENÉE. See *Ballet* 9.

GENERAL-BASS. See *Figured Bass.*

GENERAL CRESCENDO PEDAL. An organ device which brings into action all the stops successively, according to their power. There is a similar device for throwing them successively out of action.

GENERAL PAUSE. Rest or pause for all the executants.

GENEROSO (It.). 'Generous', lofty in style.

GENEVA. See *Hymns and Hymn Tunes* 4; *France* 4; *Presbyterian* 3; *Calvin; God save the Queen* 2.

GENOSSENSCHAFT ZUR VERWERTUNG MUSIKALISCHER AUFFÜHRUNGS-RECHTE. See *Copyright* 3.

GENRE, ORCHESTRE DE. See *Orchestre de Genre.*

GENTIL, GENTILLE (Fr.). 'Gentle', pleasant, pretty; so the adverb *Gentiment.*

GENTILE (It.). 'Gentle', delicate; so the adverb *Gentilmente* and the noun *Gentilezza.*

GENTLEMAN'S MAGAZINE. See *God save the Queen* 13.

GENTLEMEN'S CONCERTS, MANCHESTER. See *Concert* 10; *Flute Family* 4.

GENTLE SHEPHERD, THE. See *Ballad Opera; Beggar's Opera; Ramsay.*

GEOLOGICAL PIANO. See *Dulcimer.*

GEORGE II (b. 1683; came to throne 1727; d. 1760). See *Ariosti; Hallelujah Chorus.*

See the Article *Germany and Austria* on pages 397–401, and Articles under the individual names

1. HASSLER (1564–1612)

2. SCHÜTZ (1585–1672)

3. QUANTZ (1697–1773)

4. GRAUN (1704–59)

5. TELEMANN (1681–1767)

6. HASSE (1699–1783)

7. GLUCK (1714–87) AND HIS WIFE. A contemporary portrait

8. THE FATHER OF THE SINGSPIEL, J. A. HILLER (1728–1804). See the Article *Singspiel*

1. MICHAEL HAYDN (1737–1806)

2. DITTERSDORF (1739–99)

3. SALIERI (1750–1825)

4. PLEYEL (1757–1831)

5. SPOHR (1784–1859)

6. E. T. A. HOFFMANN (1776–1822)

7. FERDINAND RIES (1784–1838)

8. WEBER (1786–1826)

9. MEYERBEER (1791–1864)

GEORGE III (b. 1738; came to throne 1760; d. 1820). See references under *Chapel Royal*; *Concert* 6; *Festival* 1; *Cornett and Key Bugle Families* 3 d; *Criticism of Music* 4; *Stanley, John*; *Bach, J. C.*

GEORGE IV (b. 1762; came to throne 1820; d. 1830). See reference under *Glee* 3.

GEORGE V (b. 1865; came to throne 1910; d. 1936). See reference under *God save the Queen* 17.

GERADER ZINCK. See *Cornett and Key Bugle Families* 4 b.

GERALD OF WALES (Giraldus Cambrensis). See *Wales* 6; *England* 2; *Scotland* 3; *Ireland* 5; *France* 2; *Scandinavia* 1, 3, 5; *Russia* 1; *United States* 6.

GERARDY. See *Belgium* 5.

GERBER, ERNST LUDWIG (1746–1819) Author of two great German musical-biographical dictionaries. See reference under *Harmonica* 1; *Dictionaries* 3.

GERHARD, ROBERTO. Born at Vals, Catalonia, in 1896 and died in Cambridge in 1970, aged seventy-three. He was a pupil of Pedrell and Schönberg, and composed in many forms. In 1939 he settled in Cambridge, England.

His music, at first showing the influence of French Impressionism and the modern Spanish school, gradually adopted Note-row principles, though not in any doctrinaire way. His orchestral works show an exceptionally imaginative grasp of tone colour. They include four symphonies and concertos for piano and for violin; there are also a number of chamber works. C.B.E. 1967.

See *Opera* 24 f (1951).

GERMAN. A sort of *Cotillon* (q.v.).

GERMAN, EDWARD (p. 705, pl. **118.** 6). Born at Whitchurch, Shropshire, in 1862 and died in London in 1936, aged seventy-four. He taught himself the violin and organized a band in his town, studied at the Royal Academy of Music, London, and played in orchestras, quickly graduating, however, to the theatrical conductor's desk. His gift for charming melody and light orchestration, combined with his theatrical interests and experience, soon made him one of the leading London providers of 'incidental music', and his three dances written for Shakespeare's *Henry VIII* became known in every British place of entertainment and in almost every British home.

His light operas (perhaps, particularly, *Merrie England*) have had a great success. He also wrote symphonies, suites, and rhapsodies. He was knighted in 1928.

(His original name was Edward German Jones—the 'G' pronounced hard.)

GERMAN BANDS. See *Street Music* 7.

GERMAN CONCERTINA. See *Reed-Organ Family* 5.

GERMAN FINGERING. See *Fingering* 6.

GERMAN FLUTE. See *Flute Family* 4.

GERMANIA ORCHESTRAS. See *Concert* 15; *United States* 4.

GERMAN PEDALS. See *Organ* 8.

GERMAN SIXTH. See *Augmented Sixth*.

GERMAN SUITES (Bach). See *Nicknamed* 2.

GERMANY AND AUSTRIA

1. Introductory.
2. The Fifteenth and Sixteenth Centuries.
3. The Influence of the Reformation.
4. Early Instrumental Composers.
5. The Viennese Period.
6. The Lieder School and the Pianoforte.
7. Gluck—Wagner—Strauss.
8. The Twentieth Century.
9. The Nazi Régime and After.
10. List of articles amplifying the above.

(Illustrations: p. 396, pls. **67, 68**; 400, **69, 70**; 416, **71**.)

The present article is designed to offer merely a brief conspectus of the history of music in the part of Europe mentioned, further information on almost every branch of the subject, as on the individual composers, being scattered throughout this volume under the appropriate heads. A list of some of the chief of these heads appears at the end of the article. It will be noted that, in general, throughout this article the word 'Germany' is, for convenience, used as covering the activities of the two chief German-speaking countries, Germany and Austria.

1. Introductory. In the world at large no part of Europe possesses so settled a reputation for musical production as that central part which speaks the German language, because no part of Europe can show so large a list of names of composers whose works are still in the concert and domestic repertory. Putting aside the music of the present century, which, whatever

its value, has not yet had time to acquire the prestige that attaches to the 'classical', the great musical names of Britain are those of Byrd and his late sixteenth- and early seventeenth-century colleagues and that of the late seventeenth-century Purcell; the great name of Italy is that of Palestrina, contemporary with Byrd; the great names of France are those of the late seventeenth-century Lully and the early eighteenth-century Rameau (all this is, of course, a very rough generalization, but it is sufficiently accurate from the broad aspect). Compare with this the position of the Central European German-speaking countries, whose great names are those of the eighteenth and nineteenth centuries—Bach and Handel, Haydn and Mozart, Beethoven, Wagner, and Brahms. These composers worked in a past sufficiently recent for their musical idiom to remain fully intelligible to the ordinary audience of today. One would not dare to say that the music of Bach, Beethoven, and Wagner scales any heights or sounds any depths that were inaccessible to Palestrina or Byrd, but to the 'ordinary man' of the twentieth century it has 'meant' more. Thus the country of Bach, Beethoven, and Wagner has come to be regarded in wide circles as the musical country *par excellence*.

It is interesting to speculate on the part which political and social factors have played in enabling the musical Germany of the eighteenth and nineteenth centuries to race ahead of the other countries of Europe; and this has been briefly done in the article *Patronage*.

Up to the time of the Renaissance in the mid-fifteenth century, Germany, though busy everywhere with music, had attained no preeminence. The four great classes all had their music—the peasantry their folk songs and folk dances, the burghers their town bands; they and the clergy their church choirs and organists; and the nobility and royalty their courtly musical activities of various kinds. All this was for internal consumption. It is only with the eighteenth century that Germany is found to become what we may call an exporting country in music, and then music became, indeed, one of her most notable exports.

2. The Fifteenth and Sixteenth Centuries. The fifteenth and sixteenth centuries in Germany resemble musically the same period in Italy, in that out of an abundant and varied folk music grew up valuable art forms. Secular development in these countries is particularly marked, as compared with England. The madrigal school of the late sixteenth and the early seventeenth centuries in England was largely the product of long-developing skill in ecclesiastical choral music turned in another direction at a given movement by the example of Italy; as far as we can see, if a certain chairman of St. Paul's Cathedral, London, had not happened to meet with some Italian madrigals there might have been no English ones (see *Madrigal* 2). But Germany, apparently, from natural impulse and partly from the example of Italy, which lay just across the Alps, had by the mid-fifteenth century worked out a number of simple secular choral forms on the lines of the Italian villanella, frottola, and canzonetta (see separate entries under these heads).

The first half of the sixteenth century was a great flowering time in German song. The able and versatile **Heinrich Isaac** offers perhaps the representative name, and possibly we may add that of his pupil **Ludwig Senfl**. This first high season of German song may be considered to end in the middle of the century with the completion by **Georg Forster** of his great Nuremberg song collection (published 1539–56), which included choral arrangements and compositions by himself, Isaac, Senfl, and all the best composers of the time. **Eccard** (1553–1611) is important a little later. Towards the end of the sixteenth century a great name in German music is that of **Hassler** (1564–1612), whose madrigals and church music are of high value. But the most famous name of all is that of **Schütz** (1585–1672).

3. The Influence of the Reformation. The musical taste of **Luther** had led him to lay emphasis upon the value of song in Christian worship and in the Christian home, and many of the secular compositions of these composers were adapted—as, for instance, when Isaac's 'Innsbruck, I must forsake thee' became 'O world, I must forsake thee', known today in English-speaking countries as a much-loved hymn-tune. Some of them also composed directly for the Lutheran Church. **Crüger** (1598–1662) was a later composer of many chorales of sensitive melodic line yet much vigour.

The chorale, or Lutheran hymn, was a great source of inspiration. Not only were hundreds of examples either arranged from the old ecclesiastical plainsong or from secular melody, or specially composed, but these, in turn, became the basis of organ compositions and various forms of vocal church music. (It is of interest to note the neat arrangement of dates of birth of three great leaders in the German Protestant church musical movement: Luther, 1483; Schütz, 1585; Bach, 1685. During the whole period covering these lifetimes the chorale was a fructifying influence in German music.)

Hymns and Hymn Tunes 3, *Chorale, Motet, Passion,* etc. can be consulted for a fuller understanding of the part played by the Reformation in the encouragement of North German musical genius.

4. Early Instrumental Composers. Instrumental music of all kinds was successfully cultivated in Germany at this period and earlier. An important early worker was **Conrad Paumann** (*c.* 1410–73), who, born blind, nevertheless won wide fame as lutenist, flautist, and especially organist (compiled *Fundamentum organisandi*, 1452). In all the instrumental music a good deal of Italian influence is to be felt. Some English influence, also, is admitted by the best German authorities—entering by way of Flanders, where in the sixteenth century Bull and Philips lived and worked. (Bull, who excelled as a keyboard executant and composer, was in touch with Sweelinck, who founded the great Dutch and North German school of organ playing.) **Bach** shows a thorough acquaintance both with French technique (Couperin) and Italian (Vivaldi, etc.); his work for harpsichord and clavichord, organ, orchestra, and chorus, represents the highest development of the contrapuntal method: the fugue reaches its highest point with him. His contemporary, **Handel,** represents the same development, but his talent was (by early residence in Italy and later devotion to the composition of Italian opera) directed more consciously to the obtaining of immediate effect and the winning of the suffrages of a wide cosmopolitan public. Bach's son, **C. P. E. Bach,** is of great importance as one of the founders of the sonata (in the modern sense of this word).

The early developments of opera in Germany are treated under *Opera* 9, 10.

5. The Viennese Period. We now reach the period where Vienna becomes the most important centre, and one of astonishing productivity and high achievement, and with it are associated the great names of **Haydn, Mozart, Beethoven,** and **Schubert.** Their activities brought it about that the forms of the string quartet and the symphony were for a time almost looked upon as German possessions. This period is discussed under other heads (see list in section 10).

6. The Lieder School and the Pianoforte. German song under the inspiration of the German schools of romantic poetry is a typical native product of the late eighteenth and early nineteenth century. Zumsteeg is little known today, but he was the principal model of Schubert. The later school of Lieder composers, from about the 1830s to the end of the century, includes **Schumann, Franz, Brahms,** and **Wolf.** It is interesting to see in it a fresh blossoming of the German instinct for vocal melody and the expressive setting of poetry that, as we have seen, had its first great springtime in the fifteenth century.

The Italian invention of the pianoforte and the English, French, and German improvements of it were nowhere turned to such advantage as in the German lands, and this new flowering of song was bound up with a first realization of the high value of that instrument as the ideal medium of accompaniment (cf. *Song* 5).

The German romantic spirit showed itself very prominently in the pianoforte solo works of Beethoven, Schubert, Schumann, Mendelssohn, and Brahms.

7. Gluck—Wagner—Strauss. The more serious view of **Opera** (the one which sees it as a combination of arts rather than as an application of music to entertainment with the aid of drama and scenery) came from Germany. **Gluck,** in the eighteenth century, and **Wagner,** in the nineteenth, are the two great reformers of this branch of art. They were specialists in musical dramatic activities, leaving practically no music but that for the stage.

The Hungarian Liszt is associated with Wagner in the propaganda for the revolutionary methods nicknamed at the time 'The Music of the Future'.

To Wagner's flexible counterpoint, rich harmony, and glowing orchestration **Richard Strauss** fell heir, applying them with some added touches, personal and modern, not merely to opera but also to the symphonic poem.

8. The Twentieth Century. The twentieth century brought with it a marked effort, in Germany as elsewhere, to break away from the methods of the past. New harmony, a new ideal in orchestration, an abandonment of the old set forms—all these are but examples in the musical field of an impatience that was being manifested in the other fields of art and in that of politics.

Schönberg (1874–1951), followed by his pupils **Berg** and (especially) **Webern,** made himself, as composer, the centre of a great deal of activity on the part of a school that is best described perhaps (though it does not so describe itself) as Neo-Romantic. In the next generation, **Hindemith** (1895–1963) is important. He may, perhaps, be called (in distinction from the school just mentioned) a Neo-Classicist.

The aims of the most important contemporary German composers are tersely outlined under their own names, to the finding of which the list of composers (given under 10) offers guidance. See also *Gebrauchsmusik* for a brief account of a between-the-wars movement.

9. The Nazi Regime and After. In 1933 Germany became a dictatorship under what was called the 'National Socialist' regime (colloquially shortened to 'Nazi'). Some of the effects of this on musical life are mentioned below.

(*a*) Many musicians and writers on music who had enjoyed a position of high importance in Germany were reduced to silence or forced to settle abroad. In particular composers of Jewish or partly Jewish origin were silenced. Even the dead were deprived of their positions; the statue of Mendelssohn which stood in front of the Gewandhaus in Leipzig, for whose musical development he did so much, was removed.

The composer Schönberg, the conductors Bruno Walter and Otto Klemperer, and the pianist Schnabel, were compelled to seek opportunities abroad. The distinguished music critic and author Alfred Einstein was (like his cousin, the famous scientist) also forced to depart. Hundreds of composers, performers, conductors, and critics of lesser rank were deprived of all means of earning a living. Public protests were made by eminent non-German musicians such as Toscanini, Paderewski, and Casals, who refused to perform in Germany so long as such conditions continued to exist.

Necessarily hundreds of musicians lost their lives, in concentration camps, in the army, or otherwise, and those who remained had for years to live under conditions such as greatly limited their energy and their enthusiasm.

(*b*) A ban was imposed on both music of the past, if its composer had been wholly or partly of Jewish blood (e.g. Mendelssohn and Mahler), and that of the present if its composer were Jewish or if it displayed 'modernistic' tendencies. The German section of the International Society for Contemporary Music, dating from 1922, was, in 1935, compulsorily 'liquidated'.

In November 1936 all criticism of works of art, literature, music, and drama, was forbidden.

(*c*) Music was degraded by its use as an accompaniment to the most dreadful atrocities, as when at the notorious Belsen

Concentration Camp the S.S. men employed as guards formed an orchestra of prisoners of seven nations, amongst the occasions on which it had to play being those on which hundreds of women had to stand naked for hours whilst waiting for the selection of those to be gassed or burned alive.

(*d*) The destruction of centres of musical activity through allied bombing was enormous. The Leipzig Gewandhaus (see *Concert* 13) and Conservatory (see *Schools of Music*) were reduced to rubble. Very many opera houses completely disappeared. Not only large stocks of music but also, in many cases, the plates from which it could be reproduced were lost in the destruction by bombing of the premises of such publishers as Breitkopf & Härtel (see *Publishing* 8). As for musical manuscripts, these disappeared in wholesale fashion, and some have still not been recovered.

See also passing references to the Nazi régime under *Einstein, Eisler, Gebrauchsmusik, Hindemith, Kletzki, Profession of Music* 9, *Schreker, Weill*.

The adventurous experimentalism that had been brought to a grinding halt in 1933 was resumed in 1945. A new school of younger composers taking Webern rather than Berg as their point of departure followed with enthusiasm the possibilities opened up by the development of electronic means of manufacturing musical sounds. Perhaps the most important single influence in post-war German music is the strong element of big business observable in the performances of new music by the tax-subsidized radio stations. Such performances often take place late at night and are therefore heard by few, but nevertheless a substantial income accrues to composer and publisher. Generous publicity leads to performances on other stations in Germany and the rest of Europe. For the opera composer there are over forty German towns offering regular opera seasons which as a matter of course will include contemporary works.

Among the names prominent in this period are Wolfgang Fortner, Hans Werner Henze, Giselher Klebe, Karl Amadeus Hartmann, and the articulate and restlessly experimental Karlheinz Stockhausen. It has been observed that the adventurousness shown on the nocturnal airwaves can by no means be taken for granted in the programmes offered in the concert halls. Along with the iconoclasts, room is still found in German musical life for more traditionally-minded figures such as Johan Nepomuk David and Philipp Jarnach.

The most definite and distinctive contributions of the German lands to the development of the musical art seem to be (as the above brief sketch will have shown): (1) the application of counterpoint, in the most easy yet complex manner, in the work of Bach and Wagner; (2) the provision of a repertory of fine organ music —especially that of Bach; (3) the development of the sonata and symphony in the work of C. P. E. Bach, Haydn, and Beethoven; (4) the development of the *Lied*; (5) the application of a new ideal to opera in the work of Gluck and Wagner.

In addition, a great deal of theoretical investigation has been pursued and in the nineteenth century Germany became a centre of musical education, to which resorted the young musicians of all western countries. Thus by the dual means of the example of her composers and the precepts of her teachers she for a time dominated the whole of the musical world, provoking outside her borders in the mid-nineteenth century the revolt to which the name Nationalism is attached.

10. List of Articles amplifying the above. In order to amplify the information given above the following articles on cognate subjects should be consulted:

a. Hymns and Hymn Tunes 3, 17 b; *Chorale; Mass* 2, 4; *Motet; Plainsong* 3; *Cantata; Oratorio* 3, 7; *Passion Music; Luther; Street Music* 5.
b. Opera 9, 10; *Singspiel; Libretto; Metastasio.*
c. Suite 3–7; *Sonata* 2–4, 6, 7–10; *Overture* 2–4, 5–8; *Symphony* 2–6, 8; *Symphonic Poem; Programme Music* 2, 5; *Concerto* 2, 3, 5, 6; *Scherzo; Waltz; Chorale Prelude; Improvisation* 1–3, 5; *Tedesca; Allemande.*
d. Orchestra; *Pianoforte; Organ; Bagpipe Family* 7.
e. Minstrels, etc., 1, 7; *Profession* 4, 9; *Song* 10 f; *Song Cycle; Romantic; Zopf; Nationalism; Expressionism.*
f. Patronage 4–6, 8; *Printing* 3, 4; *Publishing* 3; *Journals; Criticism* 2; *Concert* 13; *Jeunesses musicales; Broadcasting* 3.
g. Deutschland über Alles; *Emperor's Hymn; Jewish* 5, 6.
h. CHRONOLOGICAL CONSPECTUS OF COMPOSERS. Arranged according to century of birth. (*Note:* This list includes the chief com-

posers born in German lands, or in such parts of central Europe as, in their lifetime, led to their ranking amongst the German or Austrian composers, or who composed in such a style as affiliated them to the German or Austrian school. The conditions governing the attempt to complete this list are such as would necessarily prevent any two authorities drawing it up in quite the same way; it must be taken, then, as suggestive rather than exact).

15th CENTURY: Agricola, Isaac.
16th CENTURY: Eccard, Hassler, Lechner, M. Praetorius, Scheidemann, Scheidt, Schein, Schütz.
17th CENTURY: J. C. Bach, J. S. Bach, Biber, Böhm, Bruhn, Buxtehude, Fasch, Förtsch, Froberger, Fux, Handel, Hasse, Keiser, Kerll, Kuhnau, Georg and Gottlieb Muffat, J. and W. H. Pachelbel, Petzold, Quantz, Telemann, Walther.
18th CENTURY: J. F. Agricola, Albrechtsberger, C. P. E. Bach,

J. C. Bach, J. C. F. Bach, W. F. Bach, Beethoven, Cramer, Czerny, Dittersdorf, Doles, Filtz, Frederick the Great, Gluck, Graun, Hassler, J. and M. Haydn, Himmel, Hoffmann, Hummel, Hüttenbrenner, Kalkbrenner, Kirnberger, A. Klengel, Knecht, Kraft, Krebs, Kuhlau, Lampe, Loewe, Lortzing, Marpurg, Marschner, Martini, A. B. Marx, J. Marx, Mayr, Mayseder, Meyerbeer, Monn, Moscheles, Mozart, Naumann, Neukomm, Pleyel, Reichardt, Reissiger, F. Ries, Rinck, Romberg, F. W. and W. K. Rust, Schobert, Schubert, Schwindl, Seyfried, Spohr, Stamitz family, Steibelt, Tausch, Türk, Vanhall, Vogler, G. C. Wagenseil, Weber, Wölfl, Wranitsky, Zelter, Zumsteeg.
19th CENTURY: Abt, Bargiel, Karl Bärmann, Bendel, Benedict, A. Berg, Bittner, Blumenthal, Bohm, Brahms, Braunfels, Bruch, Bruckner, Brüll, J. F. and N. Burgmüller, Cornelius, D'Albert, Deppe, Dont,

See the Articles under the individual names

1. LOEWE (1796–1869)

2. MENDELSSOHN (1809–47)

3. FLOTOW (1812–83)

4. FRANZ (1815–92)

5. SUPPÉ (1819–95)

6. RAFF (1822–82)

7. REINECKE (1824–1910)

8. CORNELIUS (1824–74)

9. BRUCKNER (1824–96)

1. VON BÜLOW (1830–94)

2. RHEINBERGER (1839–1901)

3. BRUCH (1838–1920)

4. HUMPERDINCK (1854–1921) with his Hänsel and Gretel. By Garvens

5. HUGO WOLF (1860–1903)

6. MAHLER (1860–1911)

7. PFITZNER (1869–1949)

8. RICHARD STRAUSS (1864–1949)

9. REGER (1873–1916)

Drdla, Eisler, Ernst, Flotow, E. Franck, Franz, Gál, Goetz, Goltermann, Gurlitt, Hauer, S. von Hausegger, G. and J. Hellmesberger, Henselt, Herzogenberg, Hindemith, Horn, Humperdinck, A. and G. Jensen, Joachim, Kaminski, Karg-Elert, Kienzl, Kirchner, J. and P. Klengel, Knorr, Köhler, Korngold, Kreisler, Kücken, Kullak, F. and I. Lachner, Lanner, Lehár, Levi, Loesch-

horn, Mahler, Mendelssohn, Merkel, Millöcker, Molique, Moszkowski, Nicolai, Nietzsche, Nowowiejski, Offenbach, Orff, Petersen, Pfitzner, Pisk, Raff, Rathaus, Reger, Reinecke, Reubke, Reutter, Rezniček, Rheinberger, H. Ries, E. Roeckel, L. P. and X. Scharwenka, Schillings, Schmidt, Schönberg, Schreker, Schulhoff, Schumann, Schütt, Sekles, Stein, O. Straus, Strauss family (dance

composers), R. Strauss, Suppé, Taubert, Tausch, Tausig, Thuille, Toch, Vogel, Volkmann, R. and S. Wagner, Wasielewsky, Webern, Weingartner, Wellesz, Wolf, Zemlinsky, Zilcher.
20th CENTURY: Blacher, Egk, Einem, Fortner, K. A. Hartmann, Henze, Jelinek, Kollreutter, Křenek, Reizenstein, Stockhausen, Wagner-Régeny, Weill.

GERSHWIN, GEORGE (p. 1068, pl. 175. 1). Born at Brooklyn in 1898 and died at Hollywood in 1937, aged thirty-eight. After a career as a jazz pianist and a successful popular composer, at twenty-five, by the intermediacy of the conductor Paul Whiteman, he came prominently before the public with his *Rhapsody in Blue* and was hailed by some as a link between the jazz camp and that of the intellectuals. He followed this up with numerous other compositions, some for the one camp and some for both—a Piano Concerto, the tone-poem *An American in Paris*, the musical comedy *Of thee I sing* (1931), the Negro 'folk-opera' *Porgy and Bess* (1935), songs such as *I got Rhythm* and *The Man I love*, etc. Since his death he has acquired a national fame somewhat akin to that of Stephen Foster (q.v.).

See references under *Jazz* 5; *Jewish* 9; *Grofé*; *Concerto* 6 c (1898); *Cinematograph*.

GERÜHRT (Ger.). 'Moved' (in the emotional sense).

GES (Ger.). G flat (see Table 7).

GESAMTAUSGABE. Literally 'collected edition', i.e. any publication of the complete works of one composer. More or less complete collections of the works of various composers appeared as early as the sixteenth century. Since the publication of the famous editions of Bach, Mozart, Beethoven, and many others during the nineteenth century, however, such an edition is generally understood to include not only a correct text, but also the accompanying scholarly apparatus of sources, variant readings, and the like, as in the scholarly edition of a standard literary figure. Larger dictionaries give lists of 80 or more such editions. A few landmarks are the editions of Bach, begun in 1851; Handel (1858); Beethoven, Palestrina (1862); Mozart (1876); Chopin, Purcell (1878); Schubert (1883); Schütz (1885); and Berlioz (1900).

GESANGVOLL (Ger.). 'Song-like.'

GESCHLAGEN (Ger.). 'Struck.'

GESCHLEIFT (Ger.). 'Slurred', i.e. legato.

GESCHLOSSEN (Ger.). 'Closed.'

GESCHMACK (Ger.). 'Taste'; hence *Geschmackvoll*, 'tastefully'.

GESCHWIND (Ger.). 'Quick.'

GESE. See *Gesius*.

GESELLSCHAFT DER MUSIKFREUNDE. See *Concert* 13.

GESELLSCHAFT ZUR ERFORSCHUNG

DER MUSIK DES ORIENTS. See *Oriental Music*.

GESES (Ger.). G double-flat (see Table 7).

GESIUS or **GESE** or **GOESS**, BARTHOLOMÄUS. Born at Müncheberg near Frankfurt-on-the-Oder *c.* 1555 and died probably in 1613. After studying theology he turned to music and spent the latter part of his life as cantor at Frankfurt-on-the-Oder. His compositions, which are numerous and important, include every type of church music of the day—passions, masses, motets, psalms, hymns, etc. He was also the author of a theoretical treatise, *Synopsis musicae praticae* (editions in 1609–15–18).

GESPROCHEN (Ger.). 'Spoken.'

GESTEIGERT (Ger.). 'Increased', i.e. crescendo or, it may be, sforzando.

GESTES. See *Minstrels*, etc. 1.

GESTOPFT (Ger.). 'Stopped' notes in horn playing, i.e. notes produced with the bell of the instrument more or less completely closed by the fist. Sometimes used as an equivalent for *Gedämpft* (q.v.). Cf. *Schmetternd*; *Horn Family* 2 b, 3, 5.

GESTOSSEN (Ger.). 'Detached', i.e. staccato.

GESUALDO, CARLO, Prince of Venosa (p. 516, pl. 93. 3). Born at Naples in 1560 and died there in 1613, aged fifty-two or fifty-three. He was a modernist madrigalist, using, for purposes of vivid expression, harmonies that went far beyond the most advanced then dreamed of by his contemporaries. His six books of madrigals were much reprinted in his own day. Musically he was like Melchizedek, 'without father and mother', and so, too, he was parent of no progeny; his very dramatic style stands as an isolated phenomenon—though it may just possibly be that some of the growing chromaticism of the English and other madrigals about the turn of the century owed a little to him.

In 1590 (not without provocation) he murdered his wife.

GETHEILT, **GETEILT** (Ger.). 'Divided', e.g. of violins—corresponding to 'Divisi' (q.v.). Sometimes abbreviated, *Geth*.

GETRAGEN (Ger.). 'Carried', i.e. sustained.

GEVAERT, FRANÇOIS AUGUSTE (1828–1908). He was the successor of Fétis in the direction of the Conservatory of Brussels, and, like him, author of a large number of valuable theoretical and musicological works. In addition, he composed many choral works, operas, etc.

See references under *Spain* 7; *Reed-Organ Family* 9; *Cornet* 1.

GEWANDHAUS CONCERTS, LEIPZIG. See *Concert* 13; *Fasch, Johann Friedrich*; *Conducting* 5.

GEWICHTIG (Ger.). 'Weightily' (either in a more literal or more figurative sense, the latter amounting to 'with dignity').

GEWIDMET (Ger.). 'Dedicated.'

GEW-JAW. See *Jew's Harp*.

GEWÖHNLICH (Ger.). 'Usual'—employed to countermand a previous indication that the instrument concerned was to play in an unusual way, e.g. the violin after it has been playing *Am Griffbrett* (near the fingerboard).

GÉZA, FRID. See *Frid*.

GEZOGEN (Ger.). 'Drawn', i.e. (1) drawn out, sustained; (2) same as portamento (q.v.).

G.G.S.M. See *Degrees and Diplomas* 2.

GHEDINI, GIORGIO FEDERICO. Born at Cuneo, Piedmont, in 1892 and died at Nervi in 1965, aged seventy-two. He studied at the Conservatories of Turin and Bologna, and joined the staff of that of Parma in 1938, then that of Milan in 1942. He was active as an instrumentalist and as a composer who, when he finally found his mature style, was much performed in his native country. His best-known work is the *Concerto dell'albatro* (1945).

See *Opera* 24 f (1949).

GHEESTELIJKE LIEDEKENS. See *Hymns and Hymn Tunes* 17 c.

GHIRIBIZZO (It.). 'Caprice.' So *Ghiribizzoso*, 'capricious'.

GIANNINI, VITTORIO. Born in Philadelphia in 1903 and died in New York in 1966, aged sixty-three. He won a scholarship at the Milan Conservatory and studied at the Juilliard School, New York (on its staff 1939–64). As a composer he first came into international recognition by the performance at Vienna in 1937 of his large-scale and dramatically conceived Requiem Mass. He also composed operas, choral and orchestral music, chamber music, etc., mostly in a traditionally romantic idiom.

GIANT FUGUE (Bach). See *Nicknamed Compositions* 1.

GIARDINI, FELICE DE. Born at Turin in 1716 and died in Moscow in 1796, aged eighty. He was a brilliant, widely-travelled violinist, fond of introducing long extempore cadenzas into the music he played, which once caused Jommelli, irritated by such an addition to one of his own works, to step forward and publicly box his ears. He had a great success in London as violinist and opera conductor and composed many operas, a dozen violin concertos, much chamber music, etc. The place of his death has doubtless suggested the usual name of that hymn-tune of his which is to be found in most collections and which the tone-deaf but rhyth-mically-hearing sometimes mistake for 'God save the Queen'.

See references under *Shield*; *Chamber Music* 6, Period II (1716).

GIBBON, EDWARD (1737–94). Historian of the Roman Empire. See quotation, *Criticism* 7.

GIBBONS Family.

(1) EDWARD. Born about 1570 and died about 1650, aged about eighty. He was a member of the choir of King's College, Cambridge, and then of Exeter Cathedral. A few pieces of church and other music of his survive.

(2) ELLIS. Born at Cambridge in 1573 and died in 1603, aged twenty-nine or thirty. He was brother of the above, and is known by two madrigals in *The Triumphs of Oriana*.

(3) ORLANDO (p. 164, pl. **33**. 4). Born, reputedly at Cambridge but really at Oxford, in 1583 and died at Canterbury in 1625, aged forty-one. He was brother of the two musicians above. He became a choir-boy at King's College, Cambridge, and, at twenty-one, organist of the Chapel Royal of James I. At forty he was also organist of Westminster Abbey. Commanded, with other members of the Chapel Royal corps of musicians, to attend Charles I on his journey to meet his bride, Henrietta Maria, who was to land at Dover and join her husband at Canterbury, he was seized with apoplexy at the latter place, died, and lies buried in the cathedral there.

He was a notable keyboard executant, ranking as the best in the country, and as a composer left much dignified church music, some beautiful madrigals, and music for viols and for virginals. His is one of the greatest names in the roll of musicians of the early seventeenth century.

See *Chapel Royal*; *History of Music* 3; *Hymns and Hymn Tunes* 17 e xv; *Anglican Chant* 3; *Service*; *Cathedral Music* 8; *Anthem*; *Parthenia*; *Printing* 3; *God save the Queen* 4; *Street Music* 2; *Chamber Music* 6, Period I; *Madrigal* 6; *Pianoforte* 20; *Wait*.

(4) CHRISTOPHER. Born in London in 1615 and died there in 1676, aged sixty-one. He was the son of Orlando, and like him organist of Westminster Abbey, and left anthems, string fantasias, etc.

See allusion under *Masque*.

GIBBS.

(1) RICHARD. He was organist of Norwich Cathedral in the early part of the seventeenth century and left a little church music.

(2) JOHN. A shadowy personage to whom part of the work generally credited to Richard is by some assigned.

(3) JOSEPH. Born in 1699 and died in 1788, aged eighty-nine. He was an organist at Ipswich and the composer of excellent string sonatas. See mention of the group of composers to which he belongs under *Sonata* 10 c; *Chamber Music* 6, Period II (1699).

(4) CECIL ARMSTRONG. Born near Chelmsford in Essex in 1889 and died there in 1960, aged 70. He studied at Cambridge and

the Royal College of Music (on the staff 1921–39), and wrote songs, chamber music, comic operas, and other things, all revealing a composer of modest but real talents.

GIBSON, EDMUND (1669–1748), Bishop of London. See quotation from him under *Hymns and Hymn Tunes* 5.

GIGA. See *Gigue*.

GIGG, GIGGE. Old English spellings of *Gigue* (q.v.).

GIGOUT, EUGÈNE. Born at Nancy in 1844 and died in Paris in 1925, aged eighty-one. He was a noted Paris organist, the pupil and son-in-law of Niedermeyer (q.v.), of the famous school of church music, a member of the staff of that school, the founder of another of his own, and a professor of organ at the Conservatory of Paris. As a composer he is, naturally, best known as a writer for his own instrument, in which capacity he won much praise.

See *Boëllmann*.

GIGUE, or **GIGA.** This is in origin a rustic English (or Scottish or Irish) dance type (see *Jig*). Its first appearance in artistic music is in the work of the English virginal and lute composers of the late sixteenth century, from which it was taken up by German, French, and Italian composers. (Its first appearance on the Continent is said to have been in compositions of Froberger (q.v.), the famous German keyboard performer and composer, in 1649.)

As the suite (q.v.) developed the gigue was taken into it as a suitably lively piece with which to end: nearly all of Bach's keyboard suites, for instance, end with gigues.

The rhythm of the gigue is normally some sort of combination of threes: it runs along with either three beats in a measure or some multiple of three—3, 6, 9, or 12. Often there is a long–short effect, a sort of merry limp throughout, but sometimes there is, instead of this, a continuous run of short notes, and sometimes the rhythmic figures are varied. Exceptionally, Bach has a (so-called) gigue or two in plain two- or four-in-a-measure time. Sometimes one melodic motif predominates throughout.

The form is simple binary (see *Form* 5), generally with each section repeated. It became a frequent custom to open the second section with the same melodic figure as the first. Sometimes this figure was inverted, as often in Bach; with this composer the opening of each half is frequently on the lines of a fugal exposition (see *Form* 12). A *Fuga alla Giga* of Bach, for organ, is a well-known and extremely cheerful feature in organ recital programmes (the title, however, appears to be a modern nickname; see *Nicknamed Compositions* 1).

GILBERT.

(1) SIR WILLIAM SCHWENK (1836–1911). See allusions under *Sullivan*; *Opera* 13 e; *Savoy Operas*; *Prima Donna* (quotation from *Gondoliers*); *Encore*; *Gondoliers*; *Iolanthe*; *Mikado*; *Patience*; *H.M.S. Pinafore*; *Princess Ida*; *Pirates of Penzance*; *Ruddigore*; *Yeomen of the Guard.* Also p. 705, pl. **118.** 5.

He was knighted in 1907.

(2) HENRY FRANKLIN BELKNAP (p. 1056, pl. **171.** 3). Born at Somerville, Mass., in 1868 and died at Cambridge, Mass., in 1928, aged fifty-nine. He was the first American composition pupil of Edward MacDowell, and the first composer of significance to recognize the possibilities for an American school of composition that lay in the use of native musical idioms.

In 1905, long before it was the fashion to write in 'rag-time' or 'jazz' style, he composed his *Comedy Overture on Negro Themes*. He also experimented successfully with other folk music—that of the Indians and various immigrated people on American soil.

See a reference s.v. *Ballet* 6.

GILBERT'S MUSICAL MAGAZINE. See *Journals*.

GILCHRIST, ANNE GEDDES. Born in Manchester in 1863 and died at Lancaster in 1954. She was well known amongst all who take an interest in British folk song from her lifelong activities as collector and editor. She was also an authority on the history of hymn tunes.

GILES or **GYLES**, NATHANIEL. Born, probably at Worcester, about 1558–60 and died at Windsor in 1633, aged about seventy-three or seventy-five. He was organist of Worcester Cathedral and then of St. George's Chapel, Windsor, and of the Chapel Royal (q.v.). He was a very learned musician and of great repute for the piety of his life and conversation; he left much church music.

GILLET & JOHNSTON, MESSRS. See *Bell* 1.

GILMAN, L. See *History* 9 (note).

GILMORE'S BAND. See *When Johnny comes marching home.*

GILSON, PAUL. Born at Brussels in 1865 and died there in 1942, aged seventy-six. He won the Rome Prize of the Brussels Conservatory at twenty-four, and later became a professor of that institution.

His compositions are numerous, including operas, ballets, orchestral music, chamber music, songs, etc. Some of the earlier ones show the influence of study of Wagner and of the Russian School, but in later days he declared himself a Flemish composer, his style taking a nationalistic tinge which endorsed the claim.

GIMEL. See *Gymel*.

GINASTERA, ALBERTO. Born in Buenos Aires in 1916 of Italian and Spanish parents. He studied at the National Conservatory of his native city. Earlier compositions such as the ballet *Estancia* sought a national style by reflecting the folk music of rural gaucho life. Following a Guggenheim Fellowship taken up in 1946 his ties to the U.S. became close. He assimilated other elements including serialism, and established himself among the leading composers of Latin America. He is active as an administrator and as a successful writer of film music. Well-known works include his *Variaciones concertantes* (1953), a violin concerto (1963), and the operas *Bomarzo* (1966) and *Don Rodrigo* (1968).

See *Harp* 4; *Opera* 24 f (1964); *History* 9.

GIOCO, GIUOCO (It.). 'Play', 'game'.

GIOCOLINO. See *Italy* 2; *Minstrels*, etc. 1.

GIOCONDO, GIOCONDOSO (It.). 'Jocund.' So the adverbs *Giocondevole* and *Giocondamente*, and the nouns *Giocondità, Giocondezza*.

GIOCOSO (It.). 'Jocose.' So the adverb *Giocosamente*.

GIOIA, GIOJA (It.). 'Joy'; hence *Gioiante, Gioioso, Giojoso, Gioiosamente*, 'joyfully'.

GIOIOSO, GIOJOSO, GIOJOSAMENTE, GIOIOSAMENTE (It.). 'Joyful', 'joyfully'.

GIORDANI FAMILY. This well-known family of Neapolitan musicians consisted of a father, two daughters, and three sons. The father, daughters, and two sons settled in Britain in 1753, and the other son came over some years later: here all six were at various dates active, especially in operatic and general theatrical enterprise. The father's Christian name was CARMINE (dates unknown); two of the sons are of some importance:

(1) TOMMASO. Born *c.* 1740 in Naples, died in 1806. In 1762 he appeared at the Haymarket Theatre as a vocalist; in 1779 he was organizing Italian opera in Dublin, where he settled as a music teacher, being known also as the composer of operas, cantatas, songs, and much chamber music and keyboard music.

(2) GIUSEPPE (popularly known as 'Giordanello'). Born at Naples *c.* 1753 and died at Fermo in 1798. He appears to have remained in Naples until 1772, in which year he joined the rest of the family in London. He was associated with his brother in the operatic enterprise in Dublin but returned to Italy in 1782, finally becoming choirmaster of the cathedral at Fermo. Like his brother he composed operas (thirty-five or more of them, much performed in Italy), religious music, and instrumental music. It is most probably he who has provided for the perpetuation of the memory of the family name by the composition of the favourite song, *Caro mio ben*.

GIORDANO, UMBERTO. Born at Foggia in 1867 and died at Milan in 1948, aged eighty-one. He was a popular opera composer somewhat of the Mascagni stamp. The opera of *Andrea Chenier* (1896) is his most popular work. His *Fedora* (1898) is noteworthy as bringing bicycles on to the stage.

GIORGI FLUTE. This is a form of concert flute introduced in 1896 by Carlo Tommaso Giorgi and claimed 'to do away at one blow [a very appropriate metaphor!] with many difficulties hitherto considered insuperable'. The basis is strictly acoustical. The bore is cylindrical (not, as in the normal flutes of today, parabolic in the head). The embouchure is placed at the end, i.e. the instrument is 'end-blown' (like a recorder but without the mouthpiece), so that the 'wrynecked' attitude of the player (Shakespeare's 'wrynecked fife') disappears. The holes are changed in position and all keys abolished. All trills, it is said, are equally easy; the tremolo is less difficult than on the normal flute, and the chromatic scale can be played with perfect facility. Admirable as all this appears, the instrument appears to have almost breathed its last.

GIOVIALE, GIOVIALITÀ (It.). 'Jovial', 'joviality'.

GIOVINEZZA ('Youth'). This was the official song of the Italian Fascist party. The tune, by Giuseppe Blanc (born 1886), began as that of *Commiato* ('Farewell'), of which the words were by Nino Oxilia (killed in battle, 1917).

Commiato was written in 1909. It was the song of Turin University. A *Canto degli Arditi* (later called *Canto dei Fascisti*), of which both words and music bore an obvious resemblance to those of *Commiato*, was published in 1918 as the work of Marcello Manni.

In 1926 Blanc, who was not only a composer but had taken a degree in law, found means of securing recognition of his paternity of this song, stopped its diffusion by Manni, and published a new edition, with words by Salvatore Gotta. It was now that the title *Giovinezza* first appeared.

The tune does not appear to be highly original since it is said to resemble a certain Italian popular song (*Il Cerchio*), as also a Swiss song, and a Croat song.

Blanc, a popular composer of songs, piano music, ballets, etc., seems to have become a specialist in Fascist hymnology since he was also the composer of the official song of the Balilla (the children's corps), of the official song of Italian Somaliland, and of the Imperial Hymn, *The Eagles of Rome*.

GIPSIES. See *Rumania*; *Hungary*.

GIRAFFE. See *Pianoforte* 16.

GIRALDUS CAMBRENSIS (or Giraldus de Barri). See *Wales* 6; *England* 2; *Scotland* 3; *Ireland* 6; *France* 2; *Scandinavia* 1, 3, 5; *Russia* 1; *United States* 6.

GIRL I LEFT BEHIND ME, THE. The words (anonymous) can be traced back to the end of the eighteenth century. The tune (also anonymous), sometimes alluded to as *Brighton Camp* (which camp was held in 1793–5), can be traced back to the same period. It is traditionally associated with the British Army, being played on occasions of departure.

GIRL'S VOICE. See *Voice* 5.

GIS (Ger.). G sharp (see Table 7).

GISIS (Ger.). G double-sharp (see Table 7).

GITANO, GITANA (Sp., masc., fem.). 'Gipsy.' For *Seguidillas Gitanas* see *Playera*.

GITTERN. For a brief description of this instrument see under *Cittern* (from which, however, as will be seen, it differed).

GIÙ (It.). 'Down', e.g. *Arcata in giù*, 'downbowed'.

GIUBILO, GIUBILIO (It.). 'Joy.' So *Giubiloso*, 'joyous'; *Giubilante*, 'jubilant'.

GIULIANI, MAURO. See *Guitar*.

GIULIVO (It.). 'Joyous.' So the superlative *Giulivissimo* and the adverb *Giulivamente*.

GIUOCO (It.). 'Play', 'game'.

GIUSTA. See *Giusto*.

GIUSTAMENTE (It.); 'With exactitude.'

GIUSTEZZA (It.). 'Exactitude', i.e. unvarying speed and rhythm.

GIUSTINI. See *Pianoforte* 18; *Temperament* 5.

GIUSTO, GIUSTA (It.; masc., fem.). 'Just.' This word is used in the two senses (*a*) exact, (*b*) appropriate (e.g. *Tempo giusto* puzzlingly means either 'strict time' or 'suitable time').

GLANVILLE-HICKS, PEGGY. Born in Melbourne, Australia, in 1912. She studied at the Melbourne Conservatory and at the Royal College of Music, and later under Nadia Boulanger and Wellesz. She has composed several operas, and orchestral, chamber, stage, and film music.

GLÄNZEND (Ger.). 'Brilliant.'

GLAREANUS. See *Modes* 6; p. 880, pl. **147.** 2.

GLASGOW. See *Scotland* 9, 10, 11; *Presbyterian* 3; *Schools of Music*.

GLASHARMONIKA. See *Harmonica* 5 b.

GLASSES, MUSICAL. See *Harmonica* 1.

GLASSPIEL. See *Harmonica* 1.

GLASSTABHARMONIKA. See *Harmonica* 5 b.

GLASTONBURY. See *Boughton*.

GLATT (Ger.). 'Smooth.' So *Glätte*, 'smoothness'.

GLAZUNOF (**Glazounow**, etc.), ALEXANDER (p. 912, pl. **155.** 5). Born in St. Petersburg in 1865 and died in Paris in 1936, aged seventy. As a youth he won the favour of the group of Russian musical nationalist pioneers (see *Russia* 5), especially Balakiref and Rimsky-Korsakof, the latter of whom gave him lessons. His first symphony was performed when he was only sixteen, under the conductorship of Balakiref. The wealthy amateur Belaief (q.v.) supported him loyally, publishing his works, which were quickly taken up.

In his thirties he joined the staff of the St. Petersburg Conservatory of Music, and later he became its director. The Soviet government later conferred on him the title of 'People's Artist of the Republic', but in 1928 he left for France and there remained.

He wrote eight symphonies, piano and violin concertos, ballets and incidental music, and many other works (no operas). His chamber music is important.

At the outset he had an attachment to the principles of 'The Five' (see *Russia* 5, 6), but he later shed this and took the position of a writer of music of a more absolute and cosmopolitan type.

He was made an Hon. D.Mus. (Cantab. and Oxon.) during one of his visits to England (1907).

See *Russia* 6; *Trumpet Family* 4; *Prince Igor* (Borodin); *Belaief*; *Concerto* 6 c (1865); *Danse Macabre*: *Miaskovsky*; *Percussion* 4 a; *Trombone* 4; *Oboe* 6.

GLEE

1. Description.
2. Period and Place.
3. Glee Clubs.
4. A Bird's-eye View of the Glee Composers.

1. Description. The word 'glee', in its musical application, has properly no necessary connotation of mirth, deriving from the Old English *gliw* or *gleo*, meaning 'music'. The word was in vague use for various choral types from the middle of the seventeenth century, but it was not until the middle of the eighteenth that it took on a definite meaning. That meaning implies the following characteristics:

1. An unaccompanied composition (there are 'accompanied glees', but these are glees only in name).
2. (Properly) for male solo voices.
3. Neither through-composed like the madrigal proper, nor verse-composed like the ballett and ayre, but in a number of short movements, each expressing the mood of the particular passage of the poetry and each self-contained and ending with a full close.
4. Moving in blocks of chords rather than in woven voice-parts, i.e. harmonic rather than contrapuntal.

It may be added that the poem set is usually a pretty good one; the glee, like its predecessor of two centuries earlier, the madrigal, had no use for doggerel.

2. Period and Place. The high period of glee composition, like the high period of madrigal composition, was only about eighty years in extent—say madrigals (q.v.) 1550–1630; glees 1750–1830. That is just a rough statement, but not misleading; glees were composed later than 1830, but by that time composers were paying much more attention to the part-song (q.v.).

The glee is a purely English form. No other nation has it; indeed, one of its characteristics is the fact that the highest part is written for adult male altos, singing in that falsetto which has never been much cultivated elsewhere than in Britain. And the glee is a national possession to be proud of, for such compositions as Webbe's *Glorious Apollo*, Danby's *Awake, Aeolian Lyre*, and Stevens's *From Oberon* are masterly.

3. Glee Clubs have played a notable part in musical life in England, the first club bearing that name being the important one in London which lived from 1783 to 1857. But societies with other names were singing glees before this, e.g. the famous Noblemen and Gentlemen's Catch Club (see *Clubs*), founded in 1761. Several personages of the royal family were members of this; the members took the chair by rotation, and George IV (as Prince of Wales and as King) did his part in this, as in choosing the glee in his turn and singing in it. Prizes were offered for the best new glees, and this stimulus was very successful in producing fine compositions. In 1787 a young man of twenty-one, J. W. Callcott (q.v.), having submitted nearly 100 glees in one of the competitions, it was decided that three should in future be the maximum to be received from any one competitor at any one competition (p. 145, pl. **30**. 5). This notable club is still alive. (The City Glee Club of London, sometimes spoken of as founded in 1669, is a reconstitution, in 1853, of the Civil Club, which, apparently, did not exist for specifically musical purposes.)

The older form of the catch and the newer of the glee appealed, from their nature and from their vocal requirements, to much the same constituency. Hence the double object of the many choral clubs of the late eighteenth and early nineteenth centuries.

For further information on clubs for glee singing see *Clubs for Music-Making*.

The name of 'Glee Club' has been much used in the universities of the United States. Such clubs have usually been merely male voice choral societies giving no special attention to glees; they tend now to become choral bodies singing the best music, but not particularly glees; the Harvard Glee Club was one of the leaders in reform.

4. A Bird's-eye View of the Glee Composers. The following have separate articles in this volume. They are arranged here in order of birth.

Arne (1710–78); Jackson, of Exeter (1730–1803); Benjamin Cooke (1734–93); Lord Mornington, father of the Duke of Wellington (1735–81); Stephen Paxton (1735–87); William Paxton (1737–81); Battishill (1738–1801); Arnold (1740–1802); Samuel Webbe, senior (1740–1816); Shield (1748–1829); John Stafford Smith (1750–1836); Danby (1757–98); Stevens (1757–1837); Richard Wainwright (1758–1825); Storace (1763–96); Attwood (1765–1838); Mazzinghi (1765–1844); J. W. Callcott (1766–1821); S. Wesley (1766–1837); Samuel Webbe, junior (*c.* 1770–1843); Spofforth (1770–1827); Horsley (1774–1858); Thomas Simpson Cooke (1782–1848); T. F. Walmisley (1783–1866); Beale (1784–1854); Hawes (1785–1846); Bishop (1786–1855); Goss (1800–80).

Not one of the composers of the high period of the glee, it will be noted, was born in the nineteenth century, though more than half of them lived to compose in it.

GLEEMEN. See *Minstrels*, etc. 1, 2.

GLEICH (Ger.). 'Like' (= similar); equal. So *Gleichsam*, 'as it were', 'as if', etc. *Gleichmässig*, 'equal'; *Gleichstark*, 'of equal strength'; *Gleiche Stimmen*, 'equal voices' (q.v.).

GLEISSNER, FRANZ (1760–*c.* 1820). See *Printing* 4.

GLEITEND (Ger.). 'Gliding' (= glissando, q.v.).

GLEN. See *Bagpipe Family* 4.

GLI (It.). 'The' (masc. plural).

GLIER, J. W. See *Reed-Organ Family* 3.

GLIÈRE, REINHOLD. Born at Kiev in 1875 and died in Moscow in 1956, aged eighty-one. He was a pupil, at the Moscow Conservatory, of Taneief and Ippolitof-Ivanof. Later he became a professor of that conservatory. He wrote symphonies and symphonic poems (showing a fine grasp of orchestral effect), a harp concerto, chamber music, operas, and ballets, etc.

See reference s.v. *Harp* 3.

GLINKA, MICHAEL (p. 897, pl. **154**. 1). Born in the government of Smolensk in 1804 and died in Berlin in 1857, aged fifty-two. He was brought up on his father's country estate, where he heard much folk music, as also the performances of a small private house-orchestra belonging to his uncle.

Going to St. Petersburg, he had a few piano lessons from the Irishman Field. He held a civil service position, but owing to bad health threw it up and went to Italy, where he made

the acquaintance of Bellini and Donizetti and, at Milan, heard Italian opera well performed.

When nearly thirty, having resolved to acquire the technique that would enable him to write a Russian opera, he went to Berlin and studied laboriously with the great teacher Dehn. Then he returned to his native country and, setting to work on a thoroughly national subject (that of the invasion of Russia by the Poles in 1613), he produced an opera that was to become famous, *A Life for the Czar* (1836). It is lyrical and to some extent, as we realize today, still Italian in style, but there is folk influence in it, and there are national Russian details of melodic phraseology and rhythm (measures of 5 beats, etc.); moreover, the Polish rhythms of the mazurka and polonaise are used appropriately in certain scenes.

His next opera, *Ruslan and Liudmila* (1842), is based on a fanciful poem of the Russian poet Pushkin. This opera may be looked upon as laying the foundations of a true Russian national style, and it is also the starting-point of the 'oriental' vein in Russian music.

He spent two years in Spain and based some orchestral music on the folk tunes of that country (see *Spain* 10).

He is recognized as the father of the Russian national school, and he counts, too, as one of the founders of the Romantic movement in music, and of the expression of national feeling through that art (see *Russia* 4).

For an account of music in Glinka's country and period see *Russia* 4. References to him will be found under *Balakiref*; *Ballet* 7; *Cinema*; *Clarinet* 6; *Dargomijsky*; *Field*; *Greek Church* 5; *Jewish* 5; *Jota*; *Mazurka*; *Mussorgsky*; *Nationalism*; *Opera* 17 c; *Russia* 7, 8; *Spain* 10; *Titof*.

GLI SCHERZI QUARTETS (Haydn). See *Nicknamed Compositions* 12 (37–42).

GLISSANDO (It.). This is a made word, not genuine Italian—an Italianization of the French word 'glisser', to slide. As applied to the piano, it means drawing the finger quickly down or up a series of adjacent notes (double glissandos, usually octaves, exist, as also, but much rarer, triple ones). Harp glissandos are common. With bowed instruments and voice not distinct notes are passed through, but an infinity of pitches (see, further, *Trombone* 1).

Glissando being the present participle of an imaginary verb *Glissare*, there is also a past participle, *Glissato*. And, quite unnecessarily, there is another imaginary infinitive, *Glissicare* (same meaning as *Glissare*), with present and past participles *Glissicando*, *Glissicato*.

GLISSER, GLISSANT (Fr.). 'To slide', 'sliding'. See above for explanation.

GLISSICARE, etc. See *Glissando* above.

GLOCK, WILLIAM. Born in London in 1908. He studied music in Cambridge and Berlin, and became active as a critic and lecturer. He was musical director of Dartington Hall from 1948 and from 1959 to 1972 Controller of Music of the BBC. C.B.E. 1964.

GLÖCKCHEN. Small bell (used by Strauss).

GLOCKE, GLOCKEN (Ger.). 'Bell', 'bells'; see *Bell*; *Percussion Family* 2 b.

GLOCKENSPIEL. See *Percussion Family* 2 c, 4 e, 5 c.

GLORIA IN EXCELSIS DEO. This, known as the 'Doxologia Magna' (see *Doxology*), occurs in the Mass of the Roman Catholic Church and in the Communion Service of the Anglican Church: it is not found in the liturgy of the Greek Church. It is an amplification of the hymn sung by the angels to announce the birth of Christ. Its place in the Roman Catholic Mass will be seen by reference to the article *Mass* 2 b, 3 b.

GLORIA PATRI. See *Doxology*.

GLORIOUS FIRST OF AUGUST. See *First of August*.

GLORY TO THEE. See *Tallis's Canon*.

GLOTTIS. See *Voice* 3, 4, 21.

GLOUCESTER CATHEDRAL. See *Cathedral Music* 2. Organists who receive notice in this volume are (with their periods of office): *D. Roseingrave* (1679–81); *Hine* (1710–30); *S. S. Wesley* (1865–76); *C. H. Lloyd* (1876–82); *C. L. Williams* (1882–97); *A. H. Brewer* (1897–1928).

GLOVER, SARAH ANN (1785–1867). See *Tonic Sol-fa* 1, also p. 976, pl. **163**. 2.

GLUCK, CHRISTOPH WILLIBALD VON (p. 396, pl. **67**. 7). Born in 1714 near Neumarkt in Bavaria and died in Vienna in 1787, aged seventy-three. (The 'von' in the name comes from a Papal knighthood. See under *Mozart*.) In his twenties he was composing operas in Italy and in his early thirties in London, in which latter place he also publicly performed upon certain musical glasses, claimed to be of his own invention (see *Harmonica* 1). Thereafter he is heard of in many European cities, incessantly travelling and producing new operas. We may, however, consider that his further life falls into three periods, in which he was resident and active in opera production mainly in Vienna (1749–73; age 35–59), Paris (1773–9; age 59–65), and Vienna again (1779–87; age 65 to death at 73—this last period being in the main one of illness and retirement).

His most famous opera of the first Vienna period is *Orpheus and Eurydice* (1762)—the only work of his still to be found in the normal repertory of European opera houses. Calzabigi was its librettist, as he was of *Alcestis* (1767), which is also of very high importance.

Of the Paris period the most celebrated productions are those of *Iphigenia in Aulis* (1774; librettist du Roullet) and *Iphigenia in Tauris* (1779; librettist Guillard).

The years in Paris were years of strife—of an intense pamphlet and newspaper war between the supporters of Piccini (q.v.), whose style was that of the melodious Italian operas of the day, and Gluck, whose aim was much more definitely dramatic. This aim had first been realized in *Orpheus*, the principles behind it being definitely set out in the preface to *Alcestis*. For a fairly full statement of these principles see *Opera* 5; they may be regarded as an attempt at a return to the general aims of those Italian composers who in the early seventeenth century first introduced opera, and they entitle Gluck to be considered as a forerunner of Wagner, a century later.

In addition to about forty-five operas and four ballets Gluck left nine 'symphonies' (really overtures), seven sonatas for two violins and bass, and a few vocal works.

See *Opera* 5, 9 b d, 19, 24 c; *Libretto*; *Calzabigi*; *Overture* 2; *Pantomime*; *Aria*; *Ballet* 3, 7; *Chaconne and Passacaglia*; *Figured Bass*; *Fandango*; *Gavotte*; *Passepied*; *Flute Family* 4; *Oboe Family* 3 b; *Clarinet Family* 2, 4 d; *Cornett and Key Bugle Family* 3; *Trombone Family* 3; *Percussion Family* 4 b (Bass Drum, Side Drum, and Cymbals; Triangle); *Harp* 3; *Harmonica* 1; *Scandinavia* 2; *Bohemia*; *Germany* 7, 8; *Chamber Music* 6, Period II (1714); *Singing* 8; *Knighthood*; *Méhul*; *Mozart*; *Sammartini*; *Wagner*. The plot of *Orpheus and Eurydice* will be found under that heading; its frontispiece at p. 704, pl. **117**. 2.

GLÜHEND (Ger.). 'Glowing.'

GLYNDEBOURNE FESTIVAL THEATRE. This was opened in 1934 on the private estate of John Christie, at Glyndebourne, near Lewes, Sussex. Opera performances of a very high standard were given (especially of Mozart) and were made accessible to the London public by a special train service. War and after-war difficulties interrupted activities but from 1950 Festivals were again held. In 1954 Mr. Christie announced his decision to ensure continuity by handing over the enterprise and property to a body to be called the 'Glyndebourne Arts Trust Limited'.

GMÜNDEN SYMPHONY (Schubert). See *Nicknamed* 18.

GNECCHI, VITTORIO. Born at Milan in 1876 and died there in 1954, aged seventy-seven. He composed a number of operas, including *Cassandra* (1905), about which a few years later a great dispute arose because of the similarity between its musical themes and those of Strauss's subsequent *Electra* (1909), and *La Rosiera* (written 1910; performed 1927); this latter is said to be the earliest opera in which quarter-tones (see *Microtones*) have been used.

GNIESSIN (Gniessine, Gnessin, Gnyesin, etc.), **MICHAEL.** Born in 1883 at Rostov and died in Moscow in 1957, aged seventy-four. He was the son of a Jewish rabbi. After working at composition at St. Petersburg under Rimsky-Korsakof, he became a zealous partisan of Jewish racialism in music, travelled in Palestine to study folk tune, made researches into ancient Hebrew music, and won recognition as one of the leading composers of the Jewish National School. He wrote an opera, *The Youth of Abraham*, songs, a symphonic prelude to Shelley's *Prometheus Unbound*, etc.

GNOMENREIGEN (Ger.). See *Reigen*.

GNYESIN. See *Gniessin*.

G.O. in French organ music means 'Grand Orgue', i.e. 'Great Organ'.

GODARD, BENJAMIN LOUIS PAUL. Born in Paris in 1849 and died at Cannes in 1895, aged forty-five. He was a violinist who studied at the Conservatory of Paris, and then had much success as a composer of chamber music, violin concertos, symphonies and operas, and many songs. These are now little known, but the composer's name is kept alive by a trifle, the Berceuse from his opera *Jocelyn* (1888).

Cf. *Flute Family* 6.

GOD BLESS THE PRINCE OF WALES. The words of this song were written in Welsh by Ceiriog Hughes and the music at the same time by Brinley Richards (see *Pianoforte* 22). They were published together in 1862. The tune has become the official tune of the British Royal Air Force—and has remained such even at periods when there is no Prince of Wales to receive the blessing.

GODDARD, ARABELLA (1836–1922). Celebrated pianist and wife of the music critic J. W. Davison. See *Pianoforte* 22; *Memory* 7.

GODFREY Family. Of this remarkable family of musicians, prominent from the opening of the nineteenth century, nine or ten are to be found mentioned in the larger books of reference—mostly military bandmasters. The best remembered is Daniel Eyers Godfrey (Sir Dan Godfrey, 1868–1939; knighted 1922), who from 1893 to 1935 was conductor of the municipal orchestra at Bournemouth, making of that town a centre for musical enjoyment and for the performance especially of the works of young English composers. (See quotation from him under *Colour and Music* 3.)

GODFREY OF STRASBOURG. See *Minstrels*, etc., 7.

GODOWSKY, LEOPOLD. Born near Vilna, Poland, in 1870 and died in New York in 1938. He was a world-famous pianist, a great piano-teacher, and a very considerable and much admired composer for his instrument. He was resident in the United States (of which he became a citizen) from 1891 to 1900 and 1918 onwards.

See *Badinage*; *Pianoforte* 21.

GOD PRESERVE THE EMPEROR. See *Emperor's Hymn*.

GOD SAVE GEORGE WASHINGTON. See *God save the Queen* 14.

GOD SAVE THE KING. See *God save the Queen*.

GOD SAVE THE PRESIDENT. See *God save the Queen* 14.

GOD SAVE THE QUEEN

1. A Plainsong Forerunner.
2. Galliard Resemblances.
3. A Christmas Carol (1611).
4. A Keyboard Piece of John Bull (1619).
5. A Song (1669).
6. Two Instrumental Pieces of Purcell (1683 and 1696).
7. A Catch of Purcell (1685).
8. The Present Song Appears in Print (1744).
9. Some Conclusions.
10. Various Untenable or Doubtful Claims.
11. The Words of the Song.
12. Attempts at Improvement of the Words.
13. The Tune in America.
14. The American Words.
15. An American Misattribution of the Tune.
16. Introduction of the Tune into Various Compositions.
17. Official British Government Regulations for Performance.
18. Finally . . .

This must be the best-known tune in the world, having long been familiarly sung or ceremonially played throughout the British Commonwealth under its own title, throughout the United States of America as 'My country, 'tis of thee', throughout the German Reich as 'Heil dir im Siegerkranz', and in many other countries under other names, often as an official or semi-official national hymn.

1. A Plainsong Forerunner. It has been pointed out that the plainsong antiphon for the Saturday before the Seventh Sunday after Pentecost could almost be called, so far as its series of notes is concerned, an early modal (see *Modes*), free-rhythm form of the tune as we know it. Moreover, the words of this antiphon are the Latin equivalent of parts of the Scriptural account of the coronation of Solomon

(1 Kings i. 38–40), which may be thought to have significance.

However, the way the main accents and natural divisions of verbal phrases fall in this plainsong is of such a character that few or none hearing it would be reminded of the present-day national tune, and in this connexion reference may be made to the remarks on the importance of rhythm as a factor in the recognition of tunes, under *Melody* 4 in the present volume, where, as it chances, 'God save the Queen' has been taken as an example.

Nevertheless, there is interest in the resemblance and it may be that there is some connexion.

2. Galliard Resemblances and a Geneva Song.

The tune, as we know it, is in rhythm and style a galliard (see *Pavan and Galliard*). The standard authority on the old dances is Arbeau's *Orchésographie*, 1589 (see under *Dance* 6 a). It gives amongst its music examples, as a typical galliard, a tune beginning thus (and built up on the same rhythm):

There is, Arbeau explains, a step to each beat, except on the second note of the second measure, at which moment the dancer is engaged in a leap in the air, the little note in the tune there being put in merely for smoothness, and the dancing significance of the phrase (as he sets this out in notation) is:

Now the rhythmic motif of this typical galliard tune is, obviously, the rhythmic motif of 'God save the Queen', which is, in fact, a true galliard and could be danced to by anyone who knows the galliard steps.

A tune of this galliard type of which some phrases are common to 'God save the Queen' is that of the patois song which forms a sort of national anthem of the canton of Geneva—'Cé qu'è lainô, le Maître de bataille' ('Celui qui est là en haut', 'He who is there on high, the Lord of Battle'). This celebrates the Escalade—the unsuccessful attempt of the Duke of Savoy to seize Geneva in 1602, and it is still sung at the great public celebration every year.

It seems more likely that the unknown author of the long narrative poem of this song wrote it to an existing popular tune than that the tune was composed specially for the poem. It may have been an actual dancing galliard. Note the slurred passages below:

3. A Christmas Carol (1611).

This galliard rhythm seems to have been found very attractive and is seen in a good many pieces of music during the seventeenth century; sometimes, as above, with it go melodic phrases that are also found in 'God save the Queen', and thus a piece of this kind is often claimed by some researcher to be that tune in its original form, or, at any rate, a source of the tune.

The earliest example to which attention has previously been called is a Christmas Carol printed in *Melismata*, 1611 (see under *Round*).

Re-mem-ber, O thou man, O thou man,

O thou man, Re-mem-ber, O thou man,

thy time is spent.   Re-mem-ber,

O thou man, how thou wast dead and gone,

and I did what I can; there-fore re-pent.

This, it will be realized, is nothing but a vocal galliard. The passages marked with slurs are very suggestive of the corresponding passages in 'God save the Queen', the fact that the present tune is in the minor being of small importance, as tunes are often found in both major and minor forms and change readily from one to the other without losing their identity. It will be seen that the whole tune falls into two sections of eight measures, whereas 'God save the Queen' has the abnormal division of 6+8.

4. A Keyboard Piece of John Bull (1619).

About the same time is found a manuscript copy of a keyboard piece of Dr. John Bull (q.v.):

S

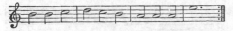

This is much more like the present tune, and, as it has the division 6+8, may perhaps be considered the original from which that tune derives. (It is not certain that the above is exact, in that a fraudulent hand in the nineteenth century added sharps before the G's and C's. Consequently we here wipe out *all* the sharps, yet one or two of the G's may well have been sharpened in the original or may have been intended to be supplied by the performer, on the principle of *Musica Ficta* (q.v.). The manuscript seems now to be lost, but a copy exists in the hand of Sir George Smart—see Cummings's *God save the King*, Novello, 1902.)

Regarding the division of a galliard into two sections of 6 measures plus 8 measures, it may be pointed out that a galliard by Bull in the Fitzwilliam Virginal Book, No. 185 (also in *Parthenia*, No. 15), has exactly this division: 8+8 was usual but not invariable (Gibbons, in *Parthenia*, No. 19, has one 7+9+8; Bull, in the Fitzwilliam Virginal Book, No. 137, has one 10+6+10). Arbeau's *Orchésographie*, amongst a great many galliard tunes that are in sections of 8 or 4 measures, has one that is 6+6. Frescobaldi has more than one with sections of 6 measures.

As (from a character in a satire of Dr. Arbuthnot's) 'John Bull' has since the beginning of the eighteenth century come to be the name for the typical Briton, there is a quaint appropriateness in the apparently most authentic provenance of the national tune.

5. A Song (1669). A song, 'Franklin is fled away', first printed just fifty years after the date of the Bull manuscript, has also been quoted as a possible source of 'God save the Queen' (it will be found in Chappell's *Old English Popular Music*, edition of 1893, vol. ii, p. 20). It is not so near the tune as we know it as Bull's composition, but is of interest as emphasizing the fact that some of the phrases of 'God save the Queen' were for long common to many tunes.

6. Two Instrumental Pieces of Purcell (1683 and 1696). The galliard rhythm, as above mentioned, remained popular, and there exist two instrumental pieces by Purcell in that rhythm which have been, on that slender ground, claimed by some as the original of 'God save the Queen'—the *Largo* from his Sixth Sonata for two violins and harpsichord (published 1683), where the resemblance is very slight, and a Minuet for harpsichord (posthumously published 1696), where it is rather more marked (the slurs added below again call attention to the points of resemblance).

In this we have 8+8 instead of 6+8, but we have the typical galliard rhythmic motif, and, in the second half, the melodic motif that at that point appears in 'God save the Queen', though on different degrees of the scale (cf. *Form* 5).

7. A Catch of Purcell (1685). So far there is no suggestion of the use of the tune to loyal words, but in another composition of Purcell's, a catch printed in 1685 'Upon the Duke's Return' (the Duke of York, afterwards James II), a curious association occurs. The words of the second verse of the poem set begin:

'Make room for the men that never deny'd
To *God save the King and Duke* they replied,'

and when the words 'God save the King' are arrived at, the voice which carries them is thrust up above the others and declaims them to these notes:

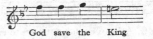

God save the King

which are, of course, the opening notes of the tune as we know it today. The suggestion is of an acknowledged connexion between these notes and words, which enabled Purcell to make a pointed quotation such as he could expect to be recognized. It is natural to connect with this the information in a letter of Burney (who got it from old Mrs. Arne, mother of the composer) that the words and tune were in popular use, 'not only in the Playhouse but in the street', in 1688-9, 'when the Prince of Orange was hovering over the coast'. Confirming this, Arne himself said that it was a received opinion that the song was written for the Catholic Chapel of James II. The end of the reign of Charles II (on the supposition that Purcell was quoting it in his catch), or that of the reign of James II (excluding that supposition but accepting Arne's 'received opinion') is the earliest period that can plausibly be given for the coming into use of the tune as we know it.

8. The Present Song Appears in Print (1744). Apart from this, the first definitely known association of the present tune and words (or something like them) is in the first printed version, in *Thesaurus Musicus* (1744—according to Chrysander in the *Jahrbuch für musikalische Wissenschaft* i. 384); here, by the way, it is curious to note that the opening phrase is not quite as in Purcell's quotation (if it is a quotation):

God save our Lord, the King, Long live our

no - ble King, God save the King.

Send him vic - to - ri-ous, Hap-py and glo - ri-ous,

Long to reign ov - er us, God save our King.

An early impression of this collection bears the title *Harmonia Anglicana*. Perhaps the slight differences from the Purcell quotation and other versions known today were recognized as an error, for in the second edition of *Thesaurus Musicus*, almost immediately after (1745), the third note is altered to the Purcell (and present) version—the fourth measure, too, being adjusted to the present form.

Great use was made of the song in 1745 (the year of the landing of the Young Pretender), and its high popularity dates from this period.

9. Some Conclusions. Any conclusion from the above facts can only be of the nature of surmise. Apparently 'God save the Queen' has no one composer. It is probably a late-seventeenth- to mid-eighteenth-century recasting of folk-tune and plainsong elements such as we see in the antiphon mentioned at the beginning of this article, in the old carol above given, and in the tune Bull arranged for virginals (for a great many of the virginal pieces were arrangements of popular airs of the day, and from the resemblance with the carol above this looks to be an example of the process, and such as come also into one or two pieces of Purcell and of other composers that there is not space to quote here. It seems as though there were certain phrases that drifted from tune to tune and found themselves a part of galliards during the sixteenth and early seventeenth centuries, of minuets during the later seventeenth century, of carols, and at last of a widely accepted patriotic song. If any attempt be made to trace the origin of the famous psalm tune called the *Old Hundredth*, its elements will be found similarly dispersed through French psalm tunes, German chorales, etc., a version at last coming into existence which by wide dissemination through the printing-press became definitive. The process is a common one.

10. Various Untenable or Doubtful Claims. Claims that have been made for the composition of this tune by Lully and Handel and others (or even for its final arrangement by them) are not worth entering into here, as under examination they have been found to be vitiated by gross errors of date, etc. The claim on behalf of Henry Carey is equally untenable; it

is dealt with below (15). The suggestion has been made that the first printed version, as given above, is the work of James Oswald (q.v.), who may have been the editor of *Thesaurus Musicus*; this cannot at present be proved or disproved.

11. The Words of the Song. As for the words: the phrase 'God save the King' is familiar enough to readers of the Authorized Version of the Old Testament, occurring in three well-known passages, 1 Samuel x. 24 (cry of the people when Samuel proclaimed Saul); 2 Samuel xvi. 16 (greeting of Hushai the Archite on meeting David's son, Absalom); 2 Kings xi. 12 (cry of the people at the coronation of Jehoash).

As an English phrase the words go behind the King James (Authorized) Version of 1611 to the Coverdale version of 1535, and as they are not an exact translation of the original Hebrew (which reads, rather, 'Let the King live'), it is suggested that they were adopted because they already had currency as the accepted way of expressing loyal sentiment. A watchword of the navy as early as 1545 was 'God save the King', and to this the countersign was 'Long to reign over us'. The prayer appointed to be read in churches on the anniversary of the Gunpowder Plot (5 Nov. 1605) contains lines which might be the origin of part of the second verse of the National Anthem, 'Scatter our enemies . . . assuage their malice and confound their devices'. Going further back, Udall's play *Ralph Roister Doister* (c. 1540; printed 1566) has 'The Lord strengthen her most excellent Majestie long to reign over us in all prosperitie'.

The present poem, which exists in both Latin and English versions (it not being sure which is the earlier), is apparently a cento of familiar loyal phrases, probably put together at a time of some national disturbance (as the second verse especially suggests), either the invasion of the Young Pretender or something in the post-Commonwealth Stuart Period (the allusion in the Purcell catch favouring the earlier date).

An attempt is sometimes made to connect the origin of the words of the song (substantially as they now stand) with the exile of James II, or of his son the 'Old Pretender', the basis of the argument being that the word 'send', in 'Send him victorious', necessarily implies the absence of the person prayed for. But 'send' does not always imply absence (cf. Shakespeare's 'God send him well', meaning merely 'God grant him welfare'—*All's Well that Ends Well*, I. i).

There exist early eighteenth-century Jacobite drinking glasses with some form of the 'God save the King' poem inscribed on them, and on some or all of these ambiguity of intention is removed by the use of the word 'soon', instead of 'long'—

> Send him victorious,
> Happy and glorious,
> Soon to reign over us:
> God save the King.

These glasses, some of which can be more or less accurately dated, were undoubtedly intended for drinking the health of the 'Old Pretender' ('James III' of England and 'James VIII' of Scotland) but they do not prove that the present English words (with 'long' instead of 'soon') were not in use at the same period and earlier.

We know from the verse quoted with its music in section 8 of the present article that in 1745 the general population (whose loyalty was strongly Hanoverian) accepted the song with the word 'send' in it, and if that word implied, to their mind, an absent king, we may be sure that they would have altered it to 'keep' or some such word. They could not have overlooked a glaring inconsistency.

The word 'send' in this passage is today understood by everyone who sings the song to mean 'keep', or 'grant that she may be', and it probably always has been so understood—except by the early eighteenth-century Jacobites, who naturally preferred its other and more literal meaning and apparently altered the next line but one to make the intention of their toasts definite.

12. Attempts at Improvement of the Words. Frequent attempts have been made by people of poetical sensibility or of Christian feeling to have the verse about the monarch's enemies deleted or toned down ('Confound their politicks, Frustrate their knavish tricks', etc.). There was even an official 'Peace Version' approved by the Privy Council in 1919. But no improvement is ever at all widely taken up; pious persons write to the papers defending the expressions of the old version by ingenious commentary and interpretation, such as bring them into line with the soundest ethics, the poetical deficiencies being at the same time defended on the grounds that what has long become traditional, however faulty, should be continued for ever.

However valuable a piece of loyal expression the poem may be, it is not in the wide sense a 'national anthem', there being many long-standing desiderata for which the country might well pray besides those that happen to be mentioned therein. But to float into circulation additional verses seems to be as difficult as to drop existing ones.

13. The Tune in America. The history of the tune's adoption in America does not seem as yet to have been quite fully explored. In the colonial days any piece of music popular in Britain quickly became known there (cf. *Opera* 21), and hence when, at the time of the Young Pretender's invasion, this tune was sung at the London theatres, printed in *Thesaurus Musicus* (1744 and 1745) and the *Gentleman's Magazine* (1745), and widely disseminated, it must almost certainly have won also some measure of colonial popularity. Sometimes it was set to a hymn, as in Lyon's *Urania* (1761).

14. The American Words. After the Declaration of Independence the tune seems to have remained current with many different sets of words—'God save America', 'God save George Washington', 'God save the Thirteen States', 'God save the President', and the like.

The present American words, 'My country, 'tis of thee', date from 1831, having been written by Revd. Samuel Francis Smith (then a student), for Lowell Mason (q.v.), probably in Andover, Mass., and sung at a children's celebration of Independence Day in Boston in that year (not 1832, as always stated). It is said that Smith found the tune in German and Danish books, which is quite likely, as by that date it had been adopted widely by Continental nations. But as remarked, it was already current in America, and it can only have been chance that Smith did not know it. The tune is usually known in the United States as *America*.

15. An American Misattribution of the Tune. The composer's name often attached to it in American song-books is that of Henry Carey, but Carey is not known to have claimed the song and never included it amongst his many publications. The first claim on Carey's behalf was made by his son, who wished to get a pension from the British Government on that score. This was in 1795; he stated that his father wrote the words in 1745 or 1746, and quoted a verse his father wrote as a part of the song, relating to the rebellion of 1745. But he had forgotten that his father died in 1743! It may be added that the younger Carey's claim was necessarily based on hearsay (at the best) or invention (at the worst), as he himself was not even born at the date of his father's death.

The great popularity of the tune did, however, begin in 1745, when it was sung at the London theatres. Dr. Arne made the arrangement for Drury Lane and his pupil Burney for Covent Garden. A letter of Burney dated 29 July 1806 is conclusive to the effect that neither Arne nor he knew anything of Carey being connected with the song (see also Burney's articles in Rees's *Cyclopædia*, on Carey and Young.) If any attribution is necessary in song-books, the word 'traditional' seems to be the only one possible, or, perhaps, '*Traditional; earliest known version by John Bull, 1562-1628*'.

16. Introduction of the Tune into Various Compositions. Many composers have admired the tune of 'God save the Queen'. Haydn was by it inspired to the composition of his *Emperor's Hymn*. Forkel (Bach's earliest biographer) once wrote a set of variations on it. So did Beethoven, saying 'I must show the English what a blessing they have in *God save the King*' (Diary, 1813); in addition to the variations, he arranged it for solo and chorus with piano accompaniment and also used it in the 'Battle' Symphony. Weber introduced it into his cantata *Battle and Victory* and his *Jubilee Overture*, and twice harmonized it for vocal quartet. Brahms used it in his *Triumphlied*. Debussy brought it into his *Pickwick*. The number of more commonplace treatments by lesser composers (especially in the form of piano variations, e.g. Thalberg's) is not to be counted.

Various musicians have made choral–orchestral arrangements for use on festival and ceremonial occasions, e.g. Costa and Elgar. About twenty nations have at different times adopted it as an official or semi-official national tune.

17. Official British Government Regulations for Performance. King George V, who for a quarter of a century heard the tune played more often than did any other person in the world (unless it were his Queen), showed an interest in its proper interpretation and on occasion remarked on the improper tempi sometimes adopted. In 1933 an Army Order laid down regulations for tempo, dynamics, and orchestration. The following is from a London *Times* summary of the order:

'The chief changes are in speed and dynamics: the opening section of six bars will be played quietly by the reed band with horns and basses in a single phrase. Cornets and side-drum are to be added at the little scale-passage leading into the second half of the tune, and the full brass enters for the last eight bars. Bass drum and cymbals will not be used, and their omission is an improvement that will make for greater dignity.

'For the quiet (*pianissimo*) opening the official *tempo* is M.M. ♩ = 60; the second part of the tune is to be played in two-bar phrases, *fortissimo*, in a broader manner, rather more slowly, at a metronome rate of ♩ = 52.

'This interpretation applies to occasions when the whole verse is played or when the National Anthem is sung (for singing the official key is F major). But when only the first six bars are required, as for saluting, they are to be played loud and at the quicker *tempo*, and by the full band.'

An official score of the music according to these instructions is published by Messrs. Boosey & Hawkes Ltd.

It is, of course, usual in Britain to play the tune whenever the monarch appears in public. But no longer is this rule applied in the rigid way in which, according to a report made by

an old musician, it was in the middle of the reign of Queen Victoria; for he asserts that he has known an opera performance at Covent Garden broken off when the Queen appeared, in order that the tune might be played. (See *Mechanical Reproduction* 7 for an anecdote concerning Queen Victoria.)

The tune (or the first part of it) is usually played in London at the close of theatrical performances, so perpetuating, it may be, the Elizabethan custom of the actors kneeling and praying for the Queen (see second part of Shakespeare's *Henry IV* for an example). It is also played at the close of the BBC's broadcasting day, and at the opening of such series of concerts as those of the Royal Philharmonic Society.

18. Finally . . . Long as this article may seem as a treatment of the history of a very short song, it is far from mentioning all the hypotheses that have been advanced as to the origin of the tune and words, or the evidence on which many of them have been overthrown.

In addition to the sources of reference already mentioned in this article and the author's *God save the King* the following (neither of them containing the latest information, but both having much of great value) may be consulted: W. H. Cummings, *God save the King, the Origin and History of the Music and Words* (London, 1902); F. S. Boas and J. E. Borland, *The National Anthem* (official publication of the Education Committee of the London County Council, 1916).

Richard Clark's (q.v.) elaborate *Account of the National Anthem* (London, 1822) is merely a notorious example of faked research and ingenious irrelevances—Clark being clearly as much a fool as a knave, and as much a knave as a fool. He was answered in his own day by John (or Josiah) Ashley in two pamphlets of 1827, and has been thoroughly exposed since.

Cf. the article on *National Anthems* and see also *Ireland* 8; *Giardini*.

GOD SAVE THE THIRTEEN STATES. See *God save the Queen* 14.

GOEBBELS. See *Criticism* 7.

GOEHR, ALEXANDER. Born in Berlin in 1932, son of the conductor Walter Goehr (1903–60). He studied at the Royal Manchester College of Music and under Messiaen, returning to London in 1956. One of the first of the generation of British composers growing up in the tradition of serialism rather than experiencing 'conversion', his works such as the cantata *The Deluge* (1959) and his *Little Symphony* (1963) are vigorous and direct in style.

GOESS. See *Gesius*.

GOETHE (1749–1832). See *Appreciation*; *Song* 5; *Melodrama*; *Colour and Music* 5; *Berlioz*; *Quality*

7; *Symphonic Poem*. (He composed a little—'in the style of Jommelli', according to his own description.)

GOETSCHIUS, PERCY. Born at Paterson, New Jersey, in 1853 and died in Manchester, New Hampshire, in 1943, aged ninety. He was composer of a symphony, two overtures, an orchestral suite, and works in smaller forms, but his reputation was principally that of a leading theorist and teacher of composition, his textbooks being greatly used. His musical leanings were conservative.

GOETZ, HERMANN. Born at Königsberg, East Prussia, in 1840 and died near Zürich in 1876, aged nearly thirty-six. His opera *The Taming of the Shrew* (1874) is famous. He wrote, also, many vocal and instrumental works, including an important symphony in F major.

GOLDBERG, JOHANN GOTTLIEB. Born in Danzig in 1727 and died in Dresden in 1756, aged twenty-nine. As a keyboard player he was one of the best pupils of Bach, who wrote the long and difficult *Goldberg Variations* for him, at the request of a count who required musical performance nightly to relieve his sleepless hours. The purposes of the commission to the composer and the engagement of the player surely made these hardly a compliment to either, but as the former was rewarded by the presentation of a golden goblet and one hundred golden louis, and the latter by a regular stipend, we may suppose that both master and pupil tolerantly overlooked any ambiguity.

GOLDEN COCKEREL. See *Coq d'or.*

GOLDEN SEQUENCE. See *Veni Sancte Spiritus.*

GOLDEN SONATA (Purcell). See *Nicknamed Compositions* 16.

GOLDMARK.

(1) KARL. Born in Hungary in 1830 and died in Vienna in 1915, aged eighty-four. He was the son of a poor Jewish cantor, who at fourteen was sent, by some who saw his promise, to study in Vienna, where in time he established himself as a piano teacher. As a composer he first became widely recognized by his *Sakuntala* Overture, and he later confirmed the expectations then formed of him by his opera *The Queen of Sheba*, which has been performed all over the world. He was a defender and, to some extent, a follower of Wagner.

See *Percussion Family* 4 c (Anvil); *Opera* 24 e (1875); *Concerto* 6 b (1830).

(2) RUBIN. Born in New York in 1872 and there died in 1936, aged sixty-three. He was a nephew of the above. He studied in his native city and in Vienna, and then took various positions in the United States. He composed, with much authority and technical resource, overtures, symphonic poems, church music, piano pieces, and songs, and by his teaching strongly influenced members of the rising generation (cf. *Copland*).

GOLDSMITH, OLIVER (1728–74). See references under *Mother Goose Songs*; *Harmonica* 1.

GOLESTAN, STAN. Born at Vaslui, Rumania, in 1872 and died in Paris in 1956, aged eighty-three. He studied with d'Indy and A. Roussel in Paris, and became a music critic on the journal *Figaro*. He wrote a widely performed *Rumanian Rhapsody*, and other orchestral works, with chamber music, etc.

GOLTERMANN, GEORG (EDUARD) (1824–98). Eminent German violoncellist and composer for his instrument. See *Concerto* 6 b (1824).

GOMBERT, NICHOLAS. He was a distinguished pupil of Josquin des Prés, who held church positions at Brussels and (1537) Madrid (at which latter he seems to have risen to be chief musician to Charles V).

See a reference under *Bird Music.*

GOMÓLKA, NICOLAS (*c.* 1539–1609). See *Poland.*

GONDELLIED. See *Gondola Song.*

GONDOLA SONG. A barcarolle (q.v.) supposed to be of the type sung by the Venetian gondoliers at their work. Burney (*Present State of Music in France and Italy*, 1771) speaks of 'The songs of the Gondolieri, or Watermen, which are so celebrated that every musical collector of taste in Europe is well furnished with them' (see *Street Music* 4).

The title 'Gondola Song' (or in German *Gondellied*) has sometimes been applied to instrumental compositions of a swaying rhythm (e.g. three of Mendelssohn's pianoforte *Songs Without Words*). Gondola songs are generally in six-in-a-measure time, or in other times in which the beat is subdivided into three (i.e. 'Compound Times').

GONDOLIERA. See *Siciliano.*

GONDOLIERS, THE, OR THE KING OF BARATARIA (Sullivan). Produced at the Savoy Theatre, London, in 1889. Libretto by W. S. Gilbert.

ACT I

SCENE: *The Piazzetta at Venice*

Giuseppe and **Marco Palmieri,** two gondoliers, come to choose, blindfold, their brides from a number of girls. Giuseppe catches **Tessa,** and Marco, **Gianetta.**

Now enters the haughty but hard-up **Duke of Plaza Toro,** a Spanish grandee, with the **Duchess,** their daughter **Casilda,** and their attendant **Luiz.** They have come to visit the Grand Inquisitor, Don Alhambra del Bolero. A secret must be revealed to Casilda: as a babe she was married by proxy to the infant son of the King of Barataria, whom they are now, after twenty years, seeking. The babe was stolen by the Grand Inquisitor.

As soon as the Duke and Duchess go off, Casilda and Luiz embrace. They are in love; but she is another's! What is to be done?

The **Inquisitor** arrives, and tells them that the young King is now a gondolier; but, as the old gondolier who reared him had a child of his own, got the two mixed, and is now dead, nobody knows which is the king and which the humbly-born lad. But their old nurse, now a brigand's wife, should be able to decide. It seems that the two children, now of course well grown, are none other than Giuseppe and Marco, the supposed brothers, who have just got married to the girls they chose by chance. As it is necessary that a king shall at once take office, the Inquisitor arranges that they shall reign jointly. They must, however, leave their wives behind; and they embark for their kingdom as the curtain falls.

ACT II

SCENE: *A Pavilion in the Court of Barataria*

The dual kings, republicans at heart, have given all their fellow gondoliers court office and do most of the palace work themselves. The Venetian girls enter: they have brought hither the wives to look after the kings. The Duke of Plaza Toro and his companions have also arrived. The Inquisitor explains to the kings that one of them is really Casilda's husband. Poor Tessa and Gianetta, their queenly hopes dashed, are disconsolate, and threaten dire things for Casilda, who, unknown to them, is hoping that when her 'husband' sees what a poor, pretentious family hers is he will repudiate the contract. She takes an opportunity of letting Marco and Giuseppe know this, and also that she is in love with someone else. So, they tell her, are they.

In the end **Inez**, the prince's foster-mother, arrives, and tells how, when traitors came to steal the royal babe, she substituted her own son, keeping the prince—and his name is Luiz! He now ascends the throne, and of course marries Casilda, while the two gondoliers and their wives are free to return to their simple life.

See *Cachucha*.

GONG. See *Percussion Family* 3 p, 4 c, 5 p.

'GOOD' AND 'BAD' IN MUSIC. See *Quality in Music*.

GOOFUS. An instrument of the 1920s or 1930s. It looks like a saxophone (p. 140, pl. **26.** 6), but has twenty-five finger-valves, each with its own reed (resembling in this respect the harmonium, concertina, etc.). Thus it can produce chords. It can be held to the mouth like a saxophone or laid on the table and blown through an india-rubber tube.

GOOGE, BARNABE (1540–94). Poet. See quotation under *Mysteries*.

GOOSSENS Family.

(1) EUGENE (I). Born at Bruges in 1845 and died in Liverpool in 1906, aged sixty-one. He studied at the Brussels Conservatory and became a successful opera conductor in Belgium, France, Italy, and England, in which last country he settled, directing the Carl Rosa Opera Company in its palmiest days. He then lived in Liverpool, organizing the famous 'Goossens Male Voice Choir' and serving as organist and choirmaster of a Roman Catholic Church. His wife was the dancer, Madame Sidonie.

(2) EUGENE (II). Born at Bordeaux in 1867 and died in London in 1958, aged ninety-one. Son of (1), he studied at the Brussels Conservatory and the Royal Academy of Music, London; served, like his father, with the Carl Rosa Opera Company and other operatic enterprises, and married a musician, the daughter of T. Aynsley Cook, an operatic bass of his day. (She died in 1946.)

(3) EUGENE (III) (p. 352, pl. **55.** 6). Born in London in 1893 and died in Hillingdon, Mdx., in 1962, aged sixty-nine. Grandson of (1) and a son of (2). He studied at the Bruges Conservatory, the Liverpool College of Music, and the Royal College of Music, London. He early made a name as violinist in both chamber and orchestral music, and a little later as conductor of orchestral concerts, opera, and ballet. Like his father and grandfather, he had some connexion with the Carl Rosa Opera Company, and he also served the Beecham companies, National Opera Company, Russian Ballet, and most of the British musical enterprises of his time and place. In 1923 he became conductor of the Symphony Orchestra at Rochester, N.Y., and a well-known guest conductor all over the United States, and in 1931 conductor of the orchestra at Cincinnati. From 1947 to 1956 he was in Sydney as conductor of its orchestra and director of the New South Wales Conservatorium. His compositions are mostly terse and direct. They are in almost all forms—piano, chamber, and orchestral music, opera, etc. The one-act opera *Judith* was heard in London in 1929, and *Don Juan* in 1937; the libretti of these are by Arnold Bennett. His oratorio, *Apocalypse*, was completed in 1951. He was knighted in 1955.

See *Concerto* 6 c (1893); *Symphony* 8 (1893); *Harp* 4; *Oboe Family* 2, 6; *Mechanical* 13.

(4) Other children of Eugene II are LEON, first oboist of Queen's Hall Orchestra at seventeen (see *Oboe Family* 6), and SIDONIE and MARIE, the gifted harpists. ADOLPHE, a fine horn player, died from wounds in 1916.

GOPAK (or Hopak). A lively dance of Little Russia. It is in a two-in-a-measure time. There is a well-known example by Mussorgsky. 'Hopak' is merely another transliteration of the same Russian word.

GOPSAL. See *Hymns and Hymn Tunes* 6.

GORCZYN, ALEXANDER. See *Poland*.

GORDON LUTE BOOK. See *Scotland* 7.

GORDON, ROBERT (seventeenth century). See reference under *Scotland* 7.

GORECKI, HENRYK (born 1933). See *Poland*.

GORGHEGGIO. This term (from the Italian *gorgheggiare*, to trill, or warble) is applied to any long, rapid passage in which one vowel takes many notes.

GORSEDD. See *Wales* 7.

GOSPEL HYMN (in American Colonies). See *Hymns and Hymn Tunes* 12.

GOSS, JOHN (p. 165, pl. **34.** 5). Born in Hampshire in 1800 and died in London in 1880, aged seventy-nine. He was a pupil of Attwood (q.v.) and hence a grand-pupil of Mozart; he succeeded his master as organist of St. Paul's Cathedral and wrote admirable church music. Queen Victoria knighted him.

See *Anthem*, Period IV; *Cathedral Music* 7; *Anglican Chant* 4.

GOSSEC, FRANÇOIS JOSEPH (p. 97, pl. **16.** 1). Born at Vergnies, near Beaumont, in what is now Belgium, in 1734 and died in Paris in 1829, aged ninety-five. He was a cowherd who showed musical ability and was accepted as a chorister of Antwerp Cathedral. When about seventeen he went to Paris, where Rameau took him up. He began to compose string quartets, symphonies, and other things, and showed invention in his treatment of these styles, then new, and afterwards, as an opera writer, had great fame. He was active as a conductor and concert manager, and when the Paris Conservatory was founded was attached to it as professor of composition. In fact, he was 'in' everything musical in Paris during the greater part of his nearly eighty years' residence in that city, including the various public occasions of the Revolution, for which he was usually called upon to provide music. His *Requiem* was long in use.

French music owes a good deal to his inspiration and example. He was the first symphony writer in France (see *Symphony* 3), and also the first musician in that country to apply to its orchestras modern ideas of efficiency.

See *France* 7; *Belgium* 4; *Symphony* 3, 8 (1734); *Oratorio* 4, 7 (1780–1); *Percussion* 4 c; *Requiem*; *Clarinet Family* 2.

GOTHIC ARCHITECTURE. See *France* 3; *Bouffons, Guerre des.*

GÖTTERDÄMMERUNG. See *Ring of the Nibelung.*

GOTT ERHALTE FRANZ DEN KAISER. See *Emperor's Hymn.*

GOTTFRIED VON STRASSBURG. Same as Godfrey of Strasbourg. See *Minstrels*, etc. 7.

GOTTSCHALK, LOUIS MOREAU (p. 800 pl. **137.** 5). Born at New Orleans in 1829 and died at Rio de Janeiro in 1869, aged forty. His father was an English Jew and his mother a French Creole. At fifteen he played in Paris and Chopin praised him. He toured as a virtuoso in Europe and in North and South America, and did a certain amount of conducting of a spectacular kind. His career was singularly romantic and adventurous.

His simple piano pieces, such as *The Last Hope, The Aeolian Harp*, and, above all, *The Dying Poet*, were for years very popular because of their sentimentality and pianistic charm. But they belong wholly to a past phase of musical taste.

See references under *Spain* 10; *Pianoforte* 22; *United States* 4.

GOUDIMEL, CLAUDE. Born at Besançon during the first decade of the sixteenth century and murdered at Lyons in 1572. He was a great church musician who wrote masses, motets, and psalm-tune settings of the metrical French versions of Marot and Béza, sung equally by Roman Catholics and Protestants until they were forbidden to the former by authority. In middle life he was living at Metz, definitely associated with the Huguenots. Thence, on the warning of trouble, many Huguenots flocked elsewhere and he returned to his native town, at last settling in Lyons. When the St. Bartholomew massacres spread from Paris to the provinces he perished with his brethren.

See references under *France* 4; *Hymns and Hymn Tunes* 4, 5, 17 d; *Bohemia.*

GOULD.

(1) BARING, REVD. S. See *Baring-Gould.*

(2) MORTON. Born at Richmond Hill, Long Island, N.Y., in 1913. He is a pianist and composer who was trained at the New York Institute of Musical Art. He has composed both serious music in the large forms, and music showing the influence of jazz. His works are often distinctively national in intention and style, e.g. several 'American Symphonettes' (the pavan from the second of which soon became extremely popular), an *American Concertette* for piano and orchestra, a *Cowboy Rhapsody, Foster Gallery* (composed of Stephen Foster's tunes), and a musical comedy, *Billion Dollar Baby.*

See *Jazz* 5; *Harp* 3; also p. 1069, pl. **176.** 3.

GOUNOD, CHARLES FRANÇOIS (p. 369, pl. **62.** 4). Born in Paris in 1818 and died near there in 1893, aged seventy-five. He inherited music from his mother, who was a fine pianist, worked at the Paris Conservatory, and won the Rome Prize. At Rome he studied church music with particular interest, and especially that of the finest period, the sixteenth century.

On return to Paris, he became an organist and studied with a view to the priesthood, which, however, he never entered. His Solemn Mass, which (or part of which) had its earliest performance in London, in 1851, first brought him the 'publicity' which every composer needs as much as every business man. He was then thirty-four.

A few months later the opera *Sappho* was produced in Paris. The work which was to bring him real fame was, of course, *Faust* (q.v.), which appeared eight years later (1859). It shows real stage-skill and flowing melody and these have made it one of the most popular operas ever written—but those who love Goethe do not love Gounod. Other operas were also written (*Romeo and Juliet* is well known—but those who love Shakespeare do not love Gounod), and a symphony or two had an ephemeral career. There were, further, a number of oratorios, many devout songs (and some less devout but better), and popular trifles such as the *Funeral March of a Marionette*, and the sentimental ('Ave-Maria') *Meditation* on Bach's Prelude in C (see *Arrangement*), which show no sign of dropping out of use.

The oratorios, especially, were popular in England, and there Gounod went at the time of the Franco-Prussian War, staying for five years—until 1875. (See *Weldon, Georgina.*)

With intervals, Gounod retained his devotion, and a Mass for Rheims Cathedral he intended, he said, to write kneeling on the stone on which Joan of Arc knelt at the Coronation of Charles VII.

He had a lyric gift, a dramatic gift, and a gift of very pleasant orchestration; in fact he had

See the Articles under the individual names

1. SCHÖNBERG (1874–1951)

2. MEDTNER (1880–1951)

3. ALBAN BERG (1885–1935)
A sketch by Dolbin

4. WEBERN (1883–1945)

5. HINDEMITH (1895–1963)

6. WEILL (1900–50)

7. KŘENEK (b. 1900)

8. STOCKHAUSEN (b. 1928)

1. INSTRUMENT-MAKING IN THE 18TH CENTURY. From the French *Encyclopédie*, 1767

2. CRWTH, 12th century
(Worcester Cathedral)

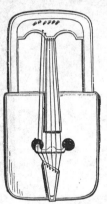

3. WELSH CRWTH
18th century

4. TROMBA MARINA

5. THE HURDY-GURDY IN FLAN-
DERS, depicted by the younger Teniers in
the early 17th century

6. EARLY HURDY-
GURDY (9th century)

7. BOWED HURDY-GURDY of Sweden

For other pictures of old or uncommon instruments see pages 449, 465, 512–13, and 544–5

all the 'popular' qualities, but he veered too much in the direction of the effeminate and sensuous.

A curious controversy concerning *Faust* may be just alluded to in closing. When first performed it was said by critics in general to be far in advance of Gounod's previous works and one critic, going so far as to doubt his ability to compose it, was challenged to a duel and forced to withdraw his allegation. Fifty years later the subject was revived, and certain old people who had known Gounod produced a story of his stealing the score from a young genius who died in a lunatic asylum. The question received discussion again in the Paris press in the late 1920s, the doubters of Gounod's authorship basing their case (surely rather precariously) on comparison of the style with that of other works of the composer.

References to Gounod, mostly slight, will be found as follows: *Opera* 11 d, 24 e (1859, 1867); *Oratorio* 4, 7 (1882, 1885); *Mass* 4; *Seven Words*; *Roman Catholic Church Music in Britain*; *Waltz*; *Farandole*; *Horn Family* 3; *Percussion Family* 4 b (Cymbals), c (Anvil); *Lesueur*; *Ave Verum*; *Arrangement*.

GOÛT DE CHANT. See *Singing* 8.

GOW. Famous family of Scottish musicians. The following are the most important members of the family:

(1) NIEL (I). Born near Dunkeld, Perthshire, in 1727 and died there in 1807, aged nearly eighty. He was a famous violinist, appearing at balls and assemblies, playing only the traditional music of his native country and adding to its published store many collections of reels and strathspeys. (He spelt his name as above, not 'Neil', as sometimes seen.)

See also references under *Scotland* 2, 3; *Ye Banks and Braes*; *Marshall, William*.

(2) DONALD. He was brother of Niel (I) and a notable performer on the violoncello.

(3) WILLIAM. He was born in 1751 and died in 1791, aged thirty-nine or forty. He was son of Niel (I) and a prominent Edinburgh violinist.

(4) NATHANIEL. Born at Inver (Ross and Cromarty) in 1763 and died in Edinburgh in 1831, aged sixty-seven. He was son of Niel (I) and almost equally famous as a violinist. He was also actively engaged as a publisher of Scottish dance music (see *Caller Herrin'*).

(5) NIEL (II). Born in Edinburgh in 1795 and died there in 1823, aged twenty-eight. He was son of Nathaniel and of fame as a composer of some songs still current, and a partner of his father in the publishing business.

GOYESCAS. See *Granados*? (1).

GOZZI, CARLO. See *Prokofief*; *Turandot*.

G.P. 'General Pause' (q.v.). Also 'Grand-Positif', i.e. Great and Choir Organs to be coupled.

G.P.R., in French organ music, means 'Grand-Positif-Récit', i.e. 'Great-Choir-Swell' coupled.

G.R. = 'Grand-Récit', i.e. Great and Swell organs coupled.

GRACE, HARVEY. Born at Romsey in 1874

and died at Bromley in 1944, aged seventy. He had a triple career: (1) as organist (from 1931 to 1938 at Chichester Cathedral), composer and editor of organ works; (2) as journalist (editor of the *Musical Times* from 1918) and author; and (3) as adjudicator at competitions. He showed an interest in every movement for the widening and deepening of British musical culture amongst all classes of the population.

See references under *Chorale Prelude*; *Church Music* 2.

GRACES, GRACE NOTES. See *Ornaments or 'Graces'*; *Notation* 5; Tables 12–16.

GRACIEUX, GRACIEUSE (Fr.; masc., fem.). 'Graceful.'

GRADATAMENTE (It.). 'Gradually.'

GRADENWITZ, PETER. See *Jewish Music* 8.

GRADEVOLE (It.). 'Pleasing'; so the adverb *Gradevolmente*.

GRADITO (It.). 'Pleasant'; so the adverb *Graditamente*.

GRADUAL. (1) The Respond sung in the service of the Mass between the Epistle and the Gospel (see *Respond*).

(2) The book containing the Concentus of the traditional plainsong music of the Mass (q.v.), i.e. it is the choir's (or congregation's) musical companion to the Missal, the only music in which is the Accentus (q.v.), or priest's parts.

These two meanings of the word are quite distinct, but the latter comes from the former, the Gradual *book* being the collection of Gradual music for the various occasions of the church's year, plus the other music for the Mass.

Cf. *Antiphonal*.

GRADUATE'S MEETING. This was a society founded in 1790 to bring together monthly (at dinner at one another's houses) all the holders of the degrees of B.Mus. or D.Mus. resident in or near London—then numbering less than a dozen. It lasted until at least October 1802, when the death of Dr. Samuel Arnold (q.v.) caused a temporary or permanent cessation of the gatherings. (Letter of Dr. Callcott to Dr. Burney in the British Museum.)

Haydn, as an Oxford D.Mus., was a member, and on one occasion took his turn at entertaining his fellow members—at a coffee house, since he had no house of his own.

GRADUELLEMENT (Fr.). 'Gradually.'

GRADUS AD PARNASSUM. A poetical title, meaning the steps up to the abode of Apollo and the Muses, given to dictionaries of Latin prosody (to help in making Latin verses), of Greek, etc., from the early eighteenth century onwards, and common in England in the nineteenth century.

The first recorded use is that by Father Aler for a Latin dictionary, in 1702, and thirteen years later Fux took the title for his celebrated treatise on Counterpoint (q.v.). A century after that Clementi borrowed it for his great collection of piano studies. Debussy has a humorous piano piece, *Dr. Gradus ad Parnassum*, in his 'Children's Corner' series.

GRAESER. See *Art of Fugue.*

GRAHAM, THOMAS. Seventeenth-century Baptist divine. See quotation under *Baptist Churches and Music* 2.

GRAHN. See *Ballet* 9; *Pas de quatre.*

GRAIL, in a liturgical and musical sense, is the same as Gradual (q.v.), i.e. the Respond sung in the Roman Catholic Mass between the Epistle and the Gospel. But by 'Holy Grail' is meant the vessel used by Christ at the Last Supper and then by Joseph of Arimathea to receive Christ's blood at the Crucifixion (see Wagner's *Parsifal*).

GRAINGER, PERCY ALDRIDGE (p. 1057, pl. **172.** 8). Born at Melbourne, Australia, in 1882 and died at White Plains, N.Y., in 1961, aged seventy-eight. From 1914 he lived largely in the United States, of which he became a citizen. He was educated at Frankfurt, and studied with Busoni. At eighteen he appeared as pianist in London. The influence of his friend Grieg led him to a keen interest in folk song, and he took an active part in the English folk-music revival, making English folk tune the basis of many of his compositions, which are mainly of the type of the brief and pithy.

What may be called the open-air influence appeared in all his work, whether as a pianist (heard frequently in every part of the world) or as a composer; indeed, no musician ever less suggested the atmosphere of either the salon or the study.

Everything he said, wrote, or did was different from what anyone had said, written, or done before—one example of this trait being his marriage to the Swedish poetess Ella Viola Ström, which took place in the Hollywood Bowl before an evening audience of over 20,000 people, for whose pleasure before and after the ceremony he conducted a Bridal Song composed by him for the occasion, and others of his works. In 1935 he applied the proceeds of an Australian tour to the founding of a Grainger Museum, of wide cultural scope, in the grounds of the University of Melbourne. His skeleton was bequeathed to the Museum 'for preservation and possible display'.

See *Reed-Organ Family* 5; *Hay*; *Expression* 1; *Percussion* 2 g.

GRAMOPHONE (or PHONOGRAPH)

1. The Edison Invention.
2. The Berliner Improvements.
3. The Application of Electricity.
4. Tape Recording.
5. Recording Conditions over Half a Century.
6. Records—Past, Present, and Future.
7. The Use of the Gramophone in Education and Research.
8. The Name of the Instrument.

(The scientific parts of this article will be better understood if the article *Acoustics* is read first and the article *Broadcasting of Music* afterwards. Some pictorial illustrations will be found at p. 432, pl. **73.**)

1. The Edison Invention. From the very beginning of the nineteenth century occasional attempts are found to record sound by attaching a needle to a membrane vibrating in sympathy with sounds made in front of it, and by allowing the needle's point to mark a plate travelling before it at a fixed speed, the object at first being to enrich the science of acoustics with a knowledge of the differences between the vibrations evoked by sounds of different pitches and timbres. Here is obviously included one of the germ ideas of the gramophone.

E. L. Scott, Irish by origin but of a family long resident in France, carried this idea to a very high point of realization in his *Phonautograph* of 1857. Practically all the elements of the gramophone are present so far as the recording is concerned, but there is no idea of reproduction by the instrument 'playing back' what has been performed to it.

The French poet and physicist, Charles Cros, in a communication to the Académie des Sciences in April 1877, added the idea of reversibility, i.e. of causing the disk or cylinder (he mentioned both) on which the record had been made by the membrane to act on the membrane in its turn and so to reproduce the original sounds. He called his projected apparatus the *Paléophone.*

Meantime, in the United States, Edison (p. 432, pl. **73.** 1) was actually constructing just such a machine as Cros was imagining. It seems to be usual in France to claim the priority for Cros and in America to claim it for Edison. It may fairly be considered that these two men were co-inventors, and the one essential of their invention lay in the principle of reversibility of the process of recording, i.e. the idea of 'performing back'.

Cros bore no ill will towards Edison. He said, 'Mr. Edison has been able *to construct* his machine. He is the first who has ever reproduced the human voice. He has accomplished something admirable.'

Edison's idea as to the utility of this particular one of his 1,200 patents was modest. The invention was a by-product of his experiments in recording Morse code on wax-coated paper disks, and was demonstrated in December 1877. He regarded the phonograph as a 'dictating-machine', and the letter-heads of the Edison firm at the time read '*The Phonograph —The Ideal Amanuensis*'.

But at this point Edison became wrapped up in the development of electric lighting, and for a decade little more was heard of the phonograph. An extract from the *Musical Times* of November 1887 (i.e. at the end of that decade) will show what then occurred:

'That modern miracle worker, Mr. Edison, is "at it again". Having got the electric light out of hand, his restless inventiveness has taken up once more with what most of us had come to regard as a discarded toy—the phonograph. A few years ago we were all talking about the phonograph. They had one, of course, at the Crystal Palace, and there eminent singers, and others, were wont to warble into it, afterwards grinding from the interior sounds supposed to be a reproduction of their most sweet voices. The instrument became a nine-days' wonder, and then was practically forgotten.'

The writer goes on to say that Edison is now developing the phonograph on its dictating-machine side, for use in business offices, and continues:

'But what of developments that may arise? Will singers and instrumentalists sing and play into the "receiver", and scatter examples of their skill over the globe to order? Will Rubinstein or little Hofmann make a tour of the world by phonogram, sitting quietly at home and preparing new specimens, while agents travel about displaying them? Shall we have shops for the sale of Albani, Patey, Lloyd, and Santley phonograms?'

By 'phonograms' are meant the wax cylinder records such as were later used in business offices in connexion with the 'Dictaphone'.

About three years after the appearance of the article above quoted there were to be found in certain European cities rooms, temptingly open to the streets, where one could go to hear music by means of rows of ear-phones. One chose one's pair of ear-phones according to the list of records available with it, put a coin into the appropriate slot, and then listened to the music.

The following extract from the 'Answers to Correspondents' columns of the *Musical Times* a decade later (November 1898) gives a good description of the Edison phonograph as it was at the end of the nineteenth century.

'In reply to your question as to the newest Edison phonograph, we can say from practical knowledge that it is a very wonderful instrument. The tone qualities of various musical instruments are reproduced with remarkable fidelity, though the various gradations of tone are, perhaps, not so marked a feature, though they are by no means absent. You ask, "Does it reproduce music (orchestral music, principally) in a manner that would satisfy a musical ear?" That question is a little difficult to answer. There is naturally a ventriloquistic character about the reproductions, but by no means sufficient to be offensive to the ear. There will probably be improvements in the construction of the instrument, whereby the most delicate effects will be absolutely reproducible, though it is almost too much to expect that the results obtained will be equal to the original sounds. But, as we have already said, it is a wonderful invention, and one whose use will give much pleasure and not a little amusement. The cost is six guineas; but a large metal bell, which amplifies the sound and effectively disperses it in a large room, would cost about fifty shillings more.'

2. The Berliner Improvements. About the time that Edison was again taking interest in his invention, another American, the German-born Emile Berliner, obtained patents for several marked improvements. He replaced the cylinder with a plate revolving on a turntable (p. 432, pl. **73.** 2), and the perpendicular 'dig' of the needle (making 'hill and dale' impressions) by a horizontal movement, making lateral impressions in the walls of a spiral track of even depth. After experiment, he fixed on a shellac mixture as the material of the records. The gramophone and its records as we know them may, then, be said to have been born in 1888. One advantage of the new record form was, of course, greater 'storability'.

As Edison (who, by the way, was partly deaf) had not at first known to what use to put his invention, so Berliner did not know what to do with his. It was thought that it might serve for 'talking dolls', and Berliner actually produced some of these.

The first record heard in Britain was of Sullivan's *The Lost Chord*, sung by Mrs. Ronalds, and its first audience consisted of about a hundred people in his drawing-room.

3. The Application of Electricity. Instruments such as those so far described came to be known as 'Acoustic', because the whole process, from the making of the records to the hearing of them, was directly the result of the action of sound vibrations. Vibration in the air, originating in a voice or instrument, impinged on a diaphragm in the recording machine, which diaphragm operated a needle, which needle cut a wax record; from this (soft) record was then made a (hard) 'master record', from which, by the use of a mould, any number of shellac-composition copies could be made.

In playing back, the process was reversed. The indentations in the grooves provoked corresponding vibrations in the needle which were in turn communicated to the diaphragm of the 'sound-box', which, with its large surface, reproduced them greatly amplified, then throwing them into the air through a horn, originally an external fitment, but at a later stage usually concealed in the cabinet.

In the electric record player the process is a little different. The needle communicates the vibration not to a 'sound-box' but to a 'pick-up' containing an electro-magnet (later a crystal), which is affected by the needle's vibrations and transmits corresponding *electric* vibrations (or 'waves') to the interior of the instrument. Here they are amplified by electric 'valves' or transistors (as in radio-receiving sets) and then passed to a device by which the electric vibrations provoke corresponding mechanical vibrations and communicate them to a 'loud-speaker' (answering to the diaphragm in the 'acoustic' instrument), from which they issue as sound vibrations.

But electricity is used not merely for the reproduction of sound from the 'consumer's' disk; it is also used for the recording of sound on the 'producer's' disk from which the 'consumer's' disk is made. The sound vibrations, received by a microphone (similar to that used in broadcasting), are made to provoke corresponding electrical vibrations, which cause mechanical vibrations in a needle travelling over the wax disk already spoken of.

The whole process, from electric recording to electric reproduction, will be better understood if *Broadcasting of Music* 1 b, on the Telephone, be read, for it is, essentially, the telephonic process with one difference: instead of the sound as originally uttered being heard at a distance within a fraction of a second and then done with for ever, it is, by the interposition of a recording process, stored to be heard later, whenever and wherever required. Thus an electric gramophone may be called a telephone with a storage device in the middle.

It will be understood that there is no difference between disks acoustically recorded and those electrically recorded except in quality (the latter being much better). The first electric recordings were introduced very quietly in 1926, and the process soon became universal.

In the early Edison and Berliner instruments the revolution of the record in reproduction was brought about by a handle turned by the operator. Later this was replaced in turn by clockwork and an electric motor.

The bugbear of short-playing records (whereby an extended composition had to be cut up into record sides lasting four or five minutes) was early recognized. In 1926 Edison produced a 'long-playing' record with 400 grooves to the inch, playing at 80 revolutions per minute. In 1931 the Victor Company announced a 'High Fidelity Electrola' playing at 33⅓ r.p.m., but it was not until 1948 that the (American) Columbia Company succeeded in solving all the problems inherent in trying to combine a narrower groove (300 to the inch) and slower speed (33⅓ r.p.m.) without sacrificing the satisfactory reproduction of a wide range of frequencies. In Great Britain the Decca company put 'LP' records on sale, with suitable reproducing apparatus, in 1950, and the Gramophone Company (EMI) followed suit in 1952. The last 78s were deleted from the EMI catalogue in March 1962.

In 1958 the industry announced the advent of 'stereo'. Stereophony is defined by the Magnetic Recording Industry Association as 'A technique of transmitting sound which employs two or more complete transmission channels for the purpose of creating in the listening environment the sense of auditory perspective inherent in the source environment. Each channel must include a separate microphone, amplifier, and loudspeaker.'

For a further explanation of the effect, see *Concert Halls* 12.

4. Tape Recording. Methods of recording by magnetizing wire or metal tape, or paper tape coated with metallic powder, instead of by scratching disks, have been heard of from as early as 1898, when Valdemar Poulsen, a Dane (inventor of the Poulsen Arcs), introduced such a device in his *Telegraphone*; this was later im-

proved by the German, Stille. Here sound vibrations received by a microphone cause variations in the current passed through an electro-magnet, and steel wire passing through the field at a uniform speed receives corresponding magnetization. The principle was much developed and improved by German industry during the second World War, and commercial machines were very widely distributed from 1945 onwards.

Tape made the initial recording process far simpler, and this, together with the immense demand for the new LP records, gave rise in the United States to a great number of adventurous but under-capitalized and short-lived companies during the early 1950s.

It must be pointed out in passing that the ease with which home tape recordings can be made from radio broadcasts should not obscure the fact that such recordings are often an infringement of copyright, and potential grounds for legal action. A machine for making television tape recordings in the home was shown in 1964 (price $500), and in the same year there were reports of a 'videodisc' reproducing vision as well as sound. At about the same time much was expected of the 'thermoplastic' system by which information is converted by an electronic beam into microscopic wrinkles in plastic material. With this and similar 'high density' techniques there were opened up prospects of the eventual elimination altogether of record or tape handling. It was already possible to record the whole of the *Encyclopædia Britannica* on a spool of tape the size of a watch. Such developments are delayed only by the difficulty of reducing complicated electrical circuits to an economically feasible mass-produced system.

Still another method of recording is that by the use of the photo-electric cell (cf. *Electric Musical Instruments* 5 c). In this case a record is made like the sound-track on a modern cinematograph film. A cylinder covered with photographically sensitive material is rotated whilst a fluctuating beam of light controlled by the microphone plays upon it. From the print thus obtained unlimited copies can be printed on ordinary paper, and this, wrapped again round a cylinder, can be made to reflect a fluctuating beam reproducing the original one, which falls in its turn on a photo-electric cell, so controlling the vibrations of an electric current. These can be amplified and made to work a loud-speaker, so reproducing the original sound vibrations. Apparatus employing this method was developed and put on sale in the later 1930s.

In the interests of accurate history it may be stated that attempts in the direction just mentioned date from at least the opening of the twentieth century, when the *Photophonograph* of the Prague engineer Czervenka provided the matter for a cause célèbre, whilst in 1908 Dr. C. V. Hartmann of Stockholm published details of an invention of his, the *Photographon, an Instrument that will replace the Gramophone*.

5. Recording Conditions over Half a Century. The early records were all 'master' records, i.e. all made direct, not reproduced by moulds. Peter Dawson, a bass-baritone very popular for over fifty years, recalled in his autobiography the hard work of his youth. He made his first records in 1904. He would sing a song to the horns of twelve machines, grouped before him in rows of four on three shelves; thus he produced a dozen records every time he sang the song. And he would continue to repeat the same song for six hours a day, five days a week.

Vocal and violin solos made the most successful records in the early days. The piano was hopeless. The orchestras used were necessarily tiny, for bigger ones could not have 'got into' the recording machine's horn. The instruments were quaintly dispersed, the trombone on a high platform, and the oboe on a low stool. The violins had a horn-like contraption fixed to them to amplify and direct the sound. (Cf. *Stroh Violin*.)

Nowadays, by use of the microphone and the magnetized tape process, recording can be done in any hall, cathedral, or theatre—as, for instance, in the Wagner theatre at Bayreuth. Thus normal public performances, not organized for recording, can be recorded.

6. Records—Past, Present, and Future. Musical people were slow to recognize the value of the gramophone, which, as has been seen, was at first regarded, even by its inventors, as little more than a toy, or at best, an apparatus capable of being usefully applied to business purposes. A change of view began to come about when some of the great singers allowed their voices to be recorded—Caruso in 1902, Santley in 1904, Melba in 1905. (Up to his death in 1921 Caruso had received £600,000 in royalties on his 154 records and many of these were later re-recorded, the voice part being taken from the old records and a new orchestral accompaniment being added.)

The first opera to be recorded was Verdi's *Ernani* (on forty single-side records, by the Italian branch of H.M.V.) in 1903. The first chamber music records were those of single movements of Schumann and Mendelssohn (H.M.V.) in 1905. The first complete symphony was Beethoven's Fifth by Nikisch and the Berlin Philharmonic Orchestra in 1909. Apparently no complete string quartet was recorded until Brahms's op. 51, no. 1, appeared in 1923. There was discovered (1935) a pianoforte record of a Brahms Hungarian Dance made by the composer (cylinder) shortly before his death in 1893; in view of the very poor recording at that date it is of doubtful documentary value.

Records were for long single-sided. Double-sided ones began to come in from 1905, the German Odeon Co. being, apparently, the pioneer.

There was a great deal of surface noise, i.e. noise from the scratch of the needle on the disk. This was announced as finally 'abolished' in 1923—yet obstinately remained (though greatly diminished) until the introduction of vinyl in 1948.

Nearly all chamber music and orchestral movements, as recorded, were more or less drastically 'cut' until 1920; thenceforward the practice began to disappear until before long practically all works were played complete.

Albums of the records of a whole symphony, string quartet, etc., were first introduced, by the Gramophone Co., in 1918 and soon became common. The institution in 1931, by the same company, of 'Societies' for the production of the works of particular composers, etc. (corresponding to publication by subscription of books for which there is but a limited demand), had greatly enriched the repertory. In 1928 a symphony was for the first time issued to the public in the form of records before it had been heard in the concert-room (see *Atterberg*), whilst in 1930 a government for the first time arranged to have some of the works of its leading composer recorded so that they might become more familiar to music-lovers everywhere (see *Sibelius*).

In Britain the British Council (q.v.) underwrites a certain number of records of British music by guaranteeing to purchase them in quantity for distribution abroad.

Duplication of recordings was long an annoyance to music-lovers who wished to see a big repertory established, and is still too frequent. In 1933 there were on sale in Britain thirty-seven records of 'Handel's Largo', forty-one of the 'Blue Danube' Waltz, and thirty of the Bach–Gounod 'Ave Maria'. Thirty years later the duplication had extended to the recordings of longer works. In Britain, catalogues listed over forty recordings of such works as Beethoven's Fifth Symphony and Tchaikovsky's First Piano Concerto, and a dozen or more of *Messiah* and Vivaldi's 'Four Seasons' Concertos.

It may be safely said that London leads in the production of gramophone records and that the names and trade-marks of the London firms are the best known all over the world.

In 1929 the sale of both instruments and records reached their 'peak' both in Europe and America, and they remained not far below in 1930; in one month of 1929 the (British) Columbia Co.'s factory turned out over four million records. Owing to a combination of circumstances a terrible drop occurred in 1931. The figures of the Gramophone Co.'s net profits for these three years, 1929–31, may be given as representative of those of all the companies: £1,700,000, £1,450,000, £160,000 (cf. *Pianoforte* 19). It was reported that while this 'slump' lasted the records of 'serious' music suffered very much less than those of 'popular' music, proving that by this date the value of the gramophone had been fully realized by the genuinely music-loving classes, and had, indeed, come to rank amongst them as a necessity. In the course of a few years the gramophone regained its full popularity and by 1950 it was reported that no fewer than five hundred new records (mostly of ephemeral music, however) were being issued every month, a figure maintained through the next decade. Many have a very short life, and the number of new recordings is in general balanced by the number of deletions from the catalogues. In 1959 the American industry was offering some 20,000 titles under the labels of over 300 different firms.

7. The Use of the Gramophone in Education and Research. As already mentioned, the gramophone did not for some time gain the approval of musicians. Vincent d'Indy once wrote of it as 'without a soul' and as worthy only of a 'majorité de snobs-idiots', and this represents a view long common. The period of gradual conversion is represented by that of the issue of the great French *Encyclopédie de la Musique*, of which the first volume appeared in 1914 and the last in 1929. The article on the gramophone is found only at the end of the very last volume, with the explanation, 'At the moment when the plan of this Encyclopedia was drafted the "talking machine" was merely a disagreeable toy from which musicians turned away in horror. Today all is changed!' Chambers's *Encyclopædia*, as late as the 1926 edition, spoke of it as employed for 'amusement purposes' and as 'an office adjunct', although at this time there already existed in England a serious journal, *The Gramophone* (1923), founded and edited by the novelist Sir Compton Mackenzie and his brother-in-law, Christopher Stone, and a 'National Gramophonic Society' (connected with that journal) issuing to its members sets of records of the masterpieces. This shows how long ignorance of the gramophone's musical powers persisted in some quarters.

In 1911 the Victor Talking Machine Co. (H.M.V.) of America founded an educational organization under Dr. Frances Clark, who conducted it until 1936, and this appears to be the pioneer organization of its kind.

In 1919 the Gramophone Co. Ltd. (H.M.V.) set up in London an educational department to carry out a propaganda for the use of the instrument in schools, and the Columbia Co., jointly with this company, subsequently maintained a similar department. Nowadays the use of the gramophone as a teaching tool is universal.

The use of gramophone records made by great performers as models for study by vocal and instrumental pupils is evident, as is that of the tape recorder for recording the pupil's own performance so that he may dispassionately and at leisure criticize himself.

In 1935 there was placed on the market a series of records (under the trade-name 'Tilophane') of string quartets with one part missing, to be supplied by the violinist, viola player, or violoncellist, as the case might be. They were made by a Viennese company, and similar records are on sale today.

The gramophone is now very much used in research into the folk music of European, Oriental, and other countries, and many countries now possess archives of records of their national music (see *Folk Song* 3). By 1950 such records existed in about fifty different languages. For an adverse influence of the gramophone on national song repertories see *Oriental*.

There is much use, also, of the gramophone in the teaching of foreign languages. (For a curious point as to the necessity of maintaining the exact speed of revolutions if the vowels are to be correctly heard see *Voice* 8.)

The value of the gramophone for illustrative purposes in lecturing on musical subjects has long been well established. The music departments of many universities in the United States possess very large collections of records for use in the appreciative and historical study of music, and such collections are becoming more common in British institutions also. In both Britain and the United States many public libraries possess collections of records.

The British Institute of Recorded Sound (29 Exhibition Road, London S.W.7.) was incorporated in 1951 with the object of acting as a central repository for the preservation of all kinds of recordings. In the U.S.A. the principal record companies voluntarily present copies of their new recordings to the Library of Congress, which has the largest collection in the world. Another very comprehensive library is that of the New York Public Library. The Phonothèque Nationale in Paris is a division of the Bibliothèque Nationale. Italy has the Discoteca di Stato (Rome, 1929). The Viennese collection, founded in 1899, is the oldest of all. Many broadcasting organizations have important collections, the largest being that of the BBC. A much discussed eventual goal is a 'union catalogue' listing the holdings of the great record libraries.

The factors affecting the condition of stored records have been closely studied. Ideally, all records should be stored vertically with no pressure from other records, at a steady temperature of about 70 F. (20 C.), free of the excess humidity which encourages the development of fungus. The vinyl of which modern records are made, though less breakable than the shellac previously used, is easily scratched and must be kept free of dirt and fingermarks.

8. The Name of the Instrument. The word 'phonograph' (from the Greek words for 'voice' and 'writer') was apparently first introduced by one Fenby, in 1863, but with reference to a different type of instrument (see *Improvisation* 4); the word then seems to have been dropped, and it was re-coined by Edison in 1877 as the name of his instrument; as already mentioned, he called his records 'Phonograms' ('voice-writings'). As he for long insisted on his exclusive rights in the name 'Phonograph', Berliner, in 1888, invented and used for his disk instrument the name 'Gramophone', which appears to be an inversion of 'Phonogram'. Later, apparently, the title to exclusive rights in these words has been dropped, since the instrument, of whatever make, is in the United States familiarly called 'Phonograph' and in Britain 'Gramophone'.

Particular firms have, of course, often given special names to their own makes of instrument, as, for instance, the Pathé firm, which used 'Pathéphone', the Columbia Co., which used 'Graphophone', and the Victor Company, which uses 'Victrola'—this last word being often loosely applied by the American public to any make of instrument.

See also *Libraries*; *Music Hall* 5; *Juke Boxes*; *Dictionaries* 13.

For a very full account of the genesis and development of the gramophone industry, on all its sides, consult the volume by one of its most active workers for a period of half a century—*The Music goes Round*, by the late F. W. Gaisberg (1943).

GRAMOPHONE CO. LTD. See *Gramophone* 7; *H.M.V.*

GRAN (It.). 'Great', 'big'.

GRANADINA. A kind of fandango (q.v.) of Granada, in southern Spain, with the same harmonic and vocal peculiarities as the malagueña (q.v.).

GRANADOS, Father and Son.

(1) ENRIQUE (p. 977, pl. **164**. 6). Born at Lérida, Catalonia, in 1867, and died in 1916, aged forty-eight. In composition he was a pupil of Pedrell (q.v.), the founder of the modern national Spanish school, in piano of several Spanish masters and then of de Bériot (son of the famous violinist) in Paris. He founded a school of music at Barcelona and directed it until the year of his death. His reputation as a pianist was very high, and his technical mastery of his instrument enabled him to write effectively for it. He was somewhat influenced by his fellow Catalan, Albéniz (q.v.), who was seven years his senior, but there is in his work a peculiar simplicity due equally to a comparative lack of both contrapuntal and harmonic complexity.

His set of piano pieces, *Goyescas*, is based on pictures and tapestries of the great Spanish painter Goya (1746–1828). Out of these pieces he fashioned an opera of the same name—a very unusual proceeding. It was to have had its first performance in Paris, but the War prevented this and the first performance took place at the Metropolitan Opera House, New York. The composer was present, and on his return voyage he and his wife lost their lives when the *Sussex* was torpedoed in the English Channel by a German submarine.

See *Spain* 7; *Nationalism*; *Pianoforte* 20; *Opera* 15, 24 f (1916); *Rhythm* 10; *Bird Music*; *Bériot, C. W. de*; *Ornaments* 6; *Folk Song* 5; *Fandango*.

(2) EDWARD. Born at Barcelona in 1894 and died in Madrid in 1928, aged thirty-four. For a few years after his father's death he took the direction of the school of music founded by him (see above). He was a conductor and composer, and in the latter capacity known as the author of several stage compositions in the typical Spanish form of the zarzuela (q.v.).

GRAN CASSA. 'Big box', i.e. bass drum (see *Percussion Family* 3 k, 4 b, 5 k).

GRAND, GRANDE (Fr.; masc., fem.). 'Great', 'big', etc.

GRAND BUGLE. See *Saxhorn and Flügelhorn Families* 3 b.

GRAND CHŒUR (Fr.). 'Full Choir' or Full Organ (sometimes abbrev. *Gd. Chœur* or *Gd. Ch.*). The expression is sometimes used as the title of a loud organ piece.

GRAND DÉTACHÉ (Fr.). See *Détaché*.

GRANDE (Fr., It.). 'Great', 'big', etc.

GRANDE FLÛTE (Fr.). See *Flute Family* 5.

GRANDEZZA (It.). 'Grandeur', dignity.

GRANDIOSO (It.). 'With grandiloquence.'

GRANDISONANTE (It.). 'Sonorous.'

GRAND JEU (Fr.). 'Full Organ' (or Harmonium, of which a combination stop is so named).

GRAND OPERA. This, properly, means opera of which the libretto is entirely set to music, i.e. with no spoken dialogue. It is a stupid term, since it rules out such works as Mozart's *Magic Flute* and Beethoven's *Fidelio* and yet admits a mass of work far less 'grand' than these.

The terms 'Grand Opera' and 'Comic Opera' are French in origin, and, in France, were strictly attached to the two classes of work historically associated with the two official Paris opera houses, the 'Grand Opéra' and 'Opéra-Comique', in the first of which everything was sung, and in the second of which spoken dialogue was allowed.

Hullah, in the article on 'Grand Opera' in the original edition of Grove's *Dictionary* (1879) adheres to the French usage, saying:

'The term—fast becoming obsolete—is French and purely conventional, and denotes a lyric drama in which spoken dialogue is excluded, and the business is carried on in melody or recitative throughout. It may contain any number of acts, any ballets or divertissements, but if spoken dialogue is introduced it becomes a "comic" opera.'

The term has, however, in the eighty-odd years that have elapsed since Hullah wrote, *not*, after all, 'become obsolete', but merely become so varied in its application that different classes of the community (judging by letters received by the present author) consider it to include:

(*a*) 'All opera that is not operetta or Gilbert and Sullivan.'

(*b*) 'Just Spontini, Meyerbeer, Auber, and similar large-scale composers of their general period, and nothing else.'

(*c*) 'Opera of *any* period on the large ("grand") scale, which brings together all the resources of the stage (scenery, "machines", ballet, etc.) and unites them to music. That implies that all words are set to music, but the exclusion of spoken dialogue does not make Grand Opera. It represents a certain ideal, which was that of Lully, but was not that of the Opera Seria (e.g. Handel). The French "grand" ideal is traceable through all the serious Parisian opera, whether written by French composers or by foreigners, to recent times. It may be said to have expired with Saint-Saëns (*Henry VIII*) and Massenet (*Thaïs*). Verdi adopted it when writing *Aida* for Cairo but scarcely elsewhere. It was never applicable to any German-produced opera.'

It will be seen that definitions (*b*) and (*c*) resemble one another. These latter two definitions come from historically minded music critics and the other from a member of the 'general public'. And none of the three agrees with the present writer, who prefers the simple and historically correct definition of Hullah.

Terms, whatever their origin, are, after all, *merely what they have come to mean*, and this one has evidently come to mean so many different things to different people that it is a pity that it cannot be dropped and a fresh start made with a new terminology of the playbill. As today's practice goes 'Grand Opera' is evidently not safely definable.

GRAND ORCHESTRE (Fr.). 'Full orchestra', 'large orchestra'.

GRAND ORGUE (Fr.). 'Full Organ', or 'Great Organ' (as distinct from 'Swell Organ', etc.), or simply 'Pipe Organ' (as distinct from 'Reed Organ', i.e. from 'American Organ' or 'Cabinet Organ').

GRAND PRIX DE ROME. See *Prix de Rome.*

GRANDSIRES (Change Ringing). See *Bell* 2.

GRAND STAFF OR STAVE. See *Great Staff.*

GRANER MASS. See *Mass* 4.

GRAN GUSTO (It.). 'Great taste.'

GRAN TAMBURO. Big drum, i.e. the bass drum (see *Percussion Family* 3 k, 4 b, 5 k).

GRAPHOPHONE. See *Gramophone* 8.

GRASSINEAU, JACQUES (1715–67). London musician, assistant to Pepusch (q.v.), and compiler of a *Musical Dictionary* (1740); largely translated from that of Brossard, 1703). See under *Folía*; *Toccatina*; *Organ* 8; *Dulcimer*; *Lute Family* 1.

GRATIAS. See *Mass* 3 b.

GRAUN, CARL HEINRICH (p. 396, pl. **67.** 4). Born in Saxony in 1704 and died in Berlin in 1759, aged fifty-five. He was for about twenty years musical director at Potsdam to the music-loving Frederick the Great. He was an able singer and wrote well for the voice, and his many operas had due success in their time and place. Latterly he composed much church music, and his Passion Cantata, *The Death of Jesus*, was very frequently to be heard in Germany and is still occasionally heard in England and elsewhere.

See some references under *Passion Music* 6; *Te Deum*; *Mechanical Reproduction* 5; *Opera* 9 a.

GRAVE (It., Fr.). As a term of expression its meaning is obvious; it implies slow speed and solemnity. As a term of pitch it means 'Low'. *Octaves graves*, in French organ music, means 'Sub-octave Coupler'.

GRAVEMENT (Fr.). **GRAVEMENTE** (It.). 'Gravely.'

GRAVE MIXTURE. See *Organ* 14 V.

GRAVES.

(1) RICHARD (1715–1804). Poet and novelist. See quotation under *Horn Family* 3.

(2) JOHN WOODCOCK. See *John Peel.*

(3) ALFRED PERCEVAL (1846–1931). He was an inspector of schools, a poet, and a leader in the revival of Irish letters, and collaborated with Stanford and with Charles Wood in the publication of books of Irish folk songs and ballads. See *Londonderry Air*; *Father O'Flynn*.

GRAVICEMBALO. An Italian name for the harpsichord. The word is supposed to be a corruption of 'clavicembalo' (q.v.).

GRAVITÀ (It.). 'Gravity', seriousness.

GRAY.

(1) ALAN. Born at York in 1855 and died at Cambridge in 1935, aged seventy-nine. He was educated at Cambridge, trained for the law, but turned to music, took the degree of Mus.D., and became first director of music, Wellington College, and then organist of Trinity College, Cambridge (1892–1930). A number of cantatas, etc., by him were heard at festivals and he composed also chamber music and solo vocal and choral works. But it is his church music and organ works that are the most important.

See references under *Chorale Prelude*; *Temperament* 6 (end).

(2) H. W. & Co. See *Publishing of Music* 9.

(3) CECIL (1895–1951). Composer; writer on Gesualdo, Sibelius, on his friend Peter Warlock, etc., and author of a somewhat speculative history of music.

GRAZIA, GRAZIOSO, GRAZIOSAMENTE (It.). 'Grace', 'graceful', 'gracefully'.

GRAZIÖS (Ger.). 'Gracious', graceful.

GREAT CORNETT. See *Cornett and Key Bugle Families* 2 c.

GREATER DOXOLOGY. See *Doxology.*

GREAT ORGAN. See *Organ* 2 d.

GREAT PIPE. See *Bagpipe Family* 4.

GREAT SERVICE. See *Service.*

GREAT STAFF, or GREAT STAVE (or Grand Staff or Stave). This is a fictional notational device rather unnecessarily introduced

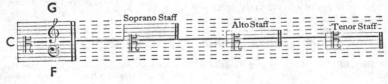

by musical pedagogues for the purpose of explaining the clefs 𝄞 𝄡 and 𝄢 or ‖𝄢‖.

The two staves in common use are brought near together. It suffices then to place between them one extra line for Middle C ('middle' in a double sense: in the middle of this diagram, as it is in the middle of the piano keyboard). The C Clef is placed on this line. The Treble (or G) Clef now comes two lines above and the Bass (or F Clef) two lines below.

The **Treble staff**, **Bass staff**, **Soprano staff** (in some choral use in Germany still), the **Alto staff** (in use in older choral music, in music for the viola, etc.), and the **Tenor staff** (in use in the older choral music, for the Trombone, etc.)—all these are seen as but sections of the one 'Great Staff', with Middle C as the connexion.

See also *Notation* 4.

GREAVES.

THOMAS. End of sixteenth and beginning of seventeenth century. He was a lutenist and wrote ayres and madrigals. In 1604 he published *Songs of Sundrie Kindes*.

GRECHANINOW, GRECHANINOV, etc. See *Gretchaninof*.

GREEK CADENCE. See *Cadence*.

GREEK CHURCH AND MUSIC

1. Introductory.
2. The General Nature of the Music.
3. The Systematization of the Plainsong.
4. Present-day Research into the Plainsong.
5. Special Developments in the Russian Church.
6. Developments in Greece.

1. Introductory. The 'Greek' or 'Orthodox' or 'Eastern' Church (in full, the 'Holy Oriental Orthodox Catholic Apostolic Church') includes all those Eastern Christian bodies which own their allegiance to or retain communion with the four ancient patriarchates of Jerusalem, Alexandria, Antioch, and Constantinople (now Istanbul). It includes the Hellenic Church, the Russian Church (so far as that can be said still to be allowed existence), the national churches of Yugoslavia, Rumania, Bulgaria, etc. A branch of the Greek Church has existed in London since the middle of the seventeenth century, and its first building (in Greek Street, Soho), still exists, though now in Anglican use; the magnificent church in Moscow Road, Bayswater, London, is now the chief one in Britain; there are others in Liverpool and Manchester. The United States has cities with a large Eastern population and a good many Greek churches exist there.

It is impossible to estimate at all precisely the number of adherents to the Greek Church (especially in view of altered conditions in Russia and Russian-controlled countries), but they must be something between 120 and 150 millions.

The Greek Church possessed anciently many liturgies, but now uses that of the patriarchate of Jerusalem (or of St. James in the East), which exists in a longer form called that of St. Basil (used only on certain days of the year), and a shorter form, called that of St. Chrysostom. This liturgy was originally in Greek, but the service is now conducted either in Greek or in Old Slavonic, or, in certain countries, in other languages. When the liturgy is sung in Greek the modern pronunciation is used.

2. The General Nature of the Music. A brief general sketch of the development of music in the Christian Church is given under *Church Music* 4. The treatment of music in the Greek Church is conditioned (*a*) by the decision of the Council of Laodicea (A.D. 367) that, in order to avoid corruption of the ancient Byzantine plainsong, the congregations should be deprived of all vocal part in the service, only trained choirs acquainted with the tradition being allowed to sing; and (*b*) by adherence to the early Christian prohibition of the use of instruments in worship. (Cf. *Russia* 2.)

A characteristic that at once strikes the Western visitor to a Greek Church where the plainsong is in use is the fact that throughout an entire piece of plainsong the tonic of the mode is hummed (preferably by a boy); the intention is to keep the singers of the plainsong in the key. A nasal quality of the voice-production and the force employed (legacies of Turkish times) fall strangely on Western ears. The singing is properly entirely in unison. (But see 5 and 6 below.)

3. The Systematization of the Plainsong. The systematic ritual arrangement of the ancient hymns is attributed to St. John of Damascus (A.D. 676–756), as is also the codification of the music of the service on a basis of eight Byzantine modes, four authentic and four plagal (cf. *Modes* 2). Little has been added to the hymns since the ninth century, but the music of the services in general has been developed, especially by the theorist and composer John Koukouzéles (or Cucuzeles) about the beginning of the twelfth century—or it may be as late as the fifteenth century, a remarkable vagueness as to his period existing, due to a conflict between tradition, which assigns the earlier date, and the notation attributed to him, which appears to belong to the later date.

An Oriental influence in the music of the Greek Church seems to have been active from the fourteenth century onwards.

Chrysanthus, Archimandrite of Constantinople, in the 1820s and 1830s put forward a new system of notation and a complete theory of Byzantine music, which forms the basis of all subsequent treatises.

4. Present-day Research into the Plainsong. A great deal of investigation of the

Byzantine musical system has been carried on during the twentieth century, previous to which the territory was unexplored by Western musicians. Some of the chief workers have been Professor Oskar Fleischer in Germany; the Augustine monk, J. B. Thibaut, and also Professor A. Gastoué in France; the Benedictine monk, U. A. Gaisser in Italy; Wellesz in Austria and Britain; Hoëg in Denmark; and H. J. W. Tillyard in Britain. A conference held in Copenhagen, in 1931, by invitation of the Danish Academy, found the chief authorities on the subject in general agreement, and, supported by the World's Union of Academies, put in hand a project of publication of texts—*Monumenta Musicae Byzantinae*, and of treatises.

Valuable collections of Byzantine music have also been issued by J. B. Petresco of Bucharest and Wellesz, the latter, published in Paris, being subsidized by the Australian musical benefactress, Mrs. Louise B. M. Hanson Dyer, through her Lyre Bird Press. A comprehensive work on the subject is that of Wellesz, *A History of Byzantine Music and Hymnography* (Oxford, 1949; 2nd edn. 1961).

5. Special Developments in the Russian Church. In Russia, from the fifteenth century, attempts have been made to create a purely Russian church music, and the ancient plainsong was, in some measure, departed from in favour of harmonized song. Already in the twelfth century a rough harmonization of the plainchant in fifths and fourths (cf. *Harmony* 4) began. Later a painful sort of polyphony arose fortuitously, when the desire to expedite the over-long services led to the participants often singing their several portions concurrently: this practice practically ceased, after strong official action, in the later seventeenth century, but some traces of it lingered until the twentieth. In the eighteenth century Russian church music received a strongly Italian cast from the influence of the Italian composers attached to the Russian court, especially Sarti and Galuppi. Bortniansky (1751–1825) and Berezovsky (1745–77), both trained in Italy, are examples of Russian church music composers thus, in some measure, influenced.

In the late nineteenth century Balakiref, as director of the music in the Court Chapel, issued, with the help of Rimsky-Korsakof, a great collection of plainsong harmonized according to its true modal character.

Amongst composers who have provided music for the Russian Church have been Turchaninof (1779–1856), Lvof (1798–1870), Archangelsky (1846–1924), Glinka, Balakiref, Rimsky-Korsakof, Gretchaninof, Tchaikovsky, Rachmaninof, Kalinnikof, Rebikof, and Kastalsky (all these appearing in this volume under their own names).

6. Developments in Greece. There has been a movement for giving the music of the Church in Greece a more European character, and in 1870 a type of elementary four-part singing was introduced at Athens—to be officially sanctioned and forbidden, by turns, on several occasions since.

GREEK DRAMA. See *Opera* 1. **GREEK EDUCATION.** See *Education and Music* 1. **GREEK MUSIC SYSTEM.** See *Notation* 1.

GREEN, SAMUEL (1740–86). Famous London organ-builder. See *Organ* 8.

GREENE.

(1) MAURICE. Born in London in 1695 and died there in 1755 'aged sixty' (as the parish register records). He was organist of St. Paul's Cathedral and of the Chapel Royal of George II, and was master of that king's band and Professor of Music at Cambridge University. Handel for a time haunted his organ (see *Organ* 8). He composed songs, theatre music, and much church music (see *Anthems*, Period III); also a series (Bodleian Library, Oxford) of anthems in all the old ecclesiastical modes (see *Modes*)—a very late example of this kind of music and presumably done as a sort of exercise of skill.

See reference s.v. *Boyce* and portrait on p. 164, pl. 33. 8.

(2) HARRY PLUNKET. Born in Ireland in 1865 and died in London in 1936, aged seventy-one. Bass singer of great artistic refinement. See references under *Song* 7, 8; *Londonderry Air*.

GREENSLEEVES. This is the tune twice mentioned by Shakespeare in *The Merry Wives of Windsor*: it is also mentioned by other writers of this period and later. It is first referred to in the Register of the Stationers' Company in 1580, where it is called 'a new Northern Dittye', but there is evidence that it is of somewhat earlier date. There seem to be many ballads to the tune, as also some examples of its being converted to pious uses, as, for instance (again in 1580), 'Green Sleeves moralised to the Scripture'—which recalls Shakespeare's Puritan in *The Winter's Tale* (IV. iii), who 'sings psalms to hornpipes', and his reference in *The Merry Wives of Windsor* to the disparity between the words and deeds of Falstaff—'they do no more adhere and keep pace together, than the Hundredth Psalm to the tune of Green Sleeves!'

During the Civil War of the seventeenth century 'Green Sleeves' was a party tune, the Cavaliers setting many political ballads to it. From this period the tune is sometimes known as 'The Blacksmith' and under that name Pepys alludes to it (23 April 1660).

GREENWALT, MRS. M. H. See *Colour and Music* 10.

GREENWICH FAIR. See *Fairs and their Music*.

GREENWOOD, JAMES. See *Lancashire Sol-fa*.

GREGORIAN. Connected with Saint Gregory (Pope 590–604). See below.

GREGORIAN CHANT. See *Plainsong* 1, 3.

GREGORIAN MODES. See *Modes* 2, 5.

GREGORIAN TONES. The eight plainsong melodies prescribed for the psalms in the Roman Catholic Church, one in each of the eight Modes (see *Plainsong* 3; *Modes*; *Anglican Chant* 1, 3). They have alternative endings (or 'inflexions') so as to connect properly with the varying antiphons which follow them (see *Antiphon*). The *Tonus Peregrinus* ('Alien Tone'; see *Anglican Chant* 2) is additional to the eight.

3ee also *Parisian Tones*.

GREGORY, SAINT (p. 816, pl. **139.** 1). See *Plainsong* 3; *Gregorian*; *Singing* 3; *Schola Cantorum*; *Modes* 2, 5, 6, 11; *Plainsong* 4.

GREGORY, SOCIETY OF ST. See *Society of St. Gregory*.

GRELOTS (Fr.). Little bells (sleigh bells, sometimes used in orchestra).

GRENADIERS' MARCH. See *March*.

GRENIÉ. See *Reed-Organ Family* 6.

GRESHAM PROFESSORSHIP OF MUSIC. Sir Thomas Gresham (*c.* 1519–79), founder of the Royal Exchange, London, bequeathed his house in Bishopsgate (now demolished) to the Corporation of the City of London and the Mercer's Company for the founding of a college with seven resident professors and gratuitous instruction in astronomy, geometry, music, law, medicine, and rhetoric. John Bull (q.v.) was the first Professor of Music (in office 1596–1607). After that, for a century and a half, the professorship was maladministered, the (nominal) professors being medical men, parsons, lawyers, etc.—a bad case of graft, apparently. From 1771 the administration has been better, the professors all being musicians (e.g. 1801, R. J. S. Stevens; 1890, Frederick Bridge; 1924, Walford Davies; 1946, Peter Latham). The provision made is merely a series of popular lectures.

When in late seventeenth-century literature (e.g. Pepys's *Diary*) Gresham College is mentioned, the reference is usually to the Royal Society, which met on these premises up to 1666.

GRESNICK (or **Gresnich**), ANTOINE FRÉDÉRIC. Born at Liège in 1755 and died in Paris in 1799, aged forty-four. He was educated in Rome and Naples and in his thirties lived for some years in London, where a number of his Italian operas were produced and where he became chief musician to the Prince of Wales. He then wrote French operas for Lyons and Paris—generally with high success, but at last one or two of his efforts failed to meet with approval, and, discouraged, he died.

See *Belgium* 4.

GRETCHANINOF (Gretchaninow, Grechaninov, etc.**), ALEXANDER** (p. 912 pl. **155.** 4). Born in Moscow in 1864 and died in New York City in 1956, aged ninety-one. He was a pupil of Rimsky-Korsakof, and gained especial repute as a composer of songs, children's music, and church music. His *Demestvennaya* is a kind of Mass, which, contrary to the traditions of the Russian church (see *Greek Church*), has accompaniments for orchestra and organ. He composed operas, symphonies, and other things.

He resided in New York from 1940 and became an American citizen. His book *My Life* (translated by Slonimsky) appeared in 1952.

See *Opera* 24 f (1950).

GRÉTRY, ANDRÉ ERNEST MODESTE (p. 97, pl. **16.** 2). Born at Liège in 1741 and died in 1813 at Montmorency, near Paris, aged seventy-two. He began his musical life as a choir-boy, but was turned away as lacking in ability. Then, under the care of a sympathetic teacher, and inspired by the performance of a visiting Italian opera company, he blossomed out and began to compose. One of the clergy of his native place supplied him with the money for travel to Rome, and there he went—on foot. For some years he studied at the college there maintained for the benefit of natives of his city. Then, *en route* for Paris, he spent a year at Geneva as a teacher of singing, meeting Voltaire, who gave him help and counsel and urged him on to the completion of his journey. He had had some little success as a stage composer in Rome and Geneva, and in Paris at once made a hit by a comical piece, *The Speaking Picture*.

Thenceforward his career was one of almost unbroken success. He produced fifty operas for Paris. Thin in texture and not very ably orchestrated, they yet charmed by their melody and by their faithful expression of the accent and sense of the words.

In addition to his writings for the stage he left some sacred compositions and some theoretical and critical treatises. The publication of his complete works, musical and literary, has been undertaken by the Belgian government.

See references under *Belgium* 4, 9; *Opera* 21 a, 24 c (1784); *Opera buffa*; *Folia*; *Colour and Music* 4; *Applause* 3, 5; *Mandoline*.

Gr. Fl. Short for *Grosse Flöte*, i.e. ordinary flute.

GRIEG, EDVARD HAGERUP (p. 896, pl. **153.** 5). Born at Bergen in Norway in 1843 and died there in 1907, aged sixty-four. In him Norwegian nationalism found its musical expression. He soaked himself in Norwegian folk tune and absorbed its idioms into his vocabulary. The titles of many of his compositions, such as 'Norwegian Peasant March', 'Norwegian Bridal Procession', and the like, in themselves frankly announce his sympathies, and the melodies and harmonies of many of the others shout them just as loudly. It should be noted that he was definitely Norwegian, not vaguely Scandinavian; 'the national characteristics of the Norwegians, Swedes, Danes are wholly different and their music differs just as much', he said, and 'I am *not* an exponent of Scandinavian music but of Norwegian'. In thus taking his stand upon the value of the peasant tune and the mentality of his own country, he fought not only its battles but those of other countries in which the desire to express national feeling (as being natural feeling) was at that time felt (see *Nationalism*).

Yet though thus sturdily Norwegian in spirit, he had a proportion of alien blood, and his name (originally 'Greig') is a reminder of the fact that his great-grandfather came from Scotland.

The music in him came from his mother, a Hagerup of Bergen, a fine pianist who became his first teacher. His ardour for music was always great, but he was listless in its practice until he met Ole Bull (q.v.), on whose advice he was sent to Leipzig (cf. *Gade*). His training there completed, he settled for a time in Copenhagen and then left the Danish capital for that of his own country. Here, at Christiania (now Oslo), he founded a musical society and conducted it for thirteen years. He associated much with the musicians Nordraak, Kjerulf, and Svendsen (see the entries under these heads), and with the national writers Björnson and Ibsen, for the *Peer Gynt* of which latter he provided incidental music, some of which was later to become popular in the form of two orchestral suites.

He married his cousin, Nina Hagerup, a fine singer, who did much to create a public love of his songs. She survived him by nearly thirty years, dying in 1935.

In his young manhood he was cheered by a spontaneous communication from the generous Liszt, who had seen his first Sonata for violin and piano and wrote to congratulate him. On the strength of this the Norwegian government made him a grant to visit Rome, where he met Liszt, who rejoiced to be shown the Piano Concerto, which remains today one of the most popular concertos of the world, as it is one of the most personal and national in expression of the whole concerto repertory.

His latter years were spent largely upon a small estate on the Norwegian coast, and then in a villa near his native Bergen. Though his courage was ever robust his constitution was frail, and when illness came upon him he quickly collapsed. His body rests high up in a wall of cliff which juts out into the fiord within sight of his home.

He wrote no symphony and no opera. In addition to works of the types already mentioned, there are one string quartet (and another unfinished and posthumously published) and a multitude of other things. Much of his piano music is simple and, indeed, to express *himself* and his *country*, yet to do so with small apparatus, was one of his gifts. 'It is surely no fault of mine', he said, 'that my music is heard in third-rate restaurants, and from school-girls.' It is indeed 'no fault', one of the world's most legitimate artistic demands being more and yet more music that both the learned and the unlearned can enjoy.

His harmonic originality has influenced later composers.

See *Harmony* 22 (end); *Suite* 7; *Sonata* 9, 10 c d; *Rigaudon*; *Bell* 6; *Springdans*; *Lyric Piece*; *Incidental Music*; *Nordraak*; *Pianoforte* 22; *Ballade*; *Chamber Music*, Period III (1843); *Programme Music* 5 d; *Humoresque*; *Halling*; *Nationalism*; *Grainger*; *Delius*; *Svendsen*; *Kjerulf*; *Halvorsen*.

GRIFF. German for 'grip' or anything 'gripped' or 'grasped'. Hence the knob on the handle of a drumstick.

GRIFFBRETT (Ger.). Literally 'grip board', i.e the fingerboard of the violin, etc. Thus *Am Griffbrett* = *Sul tasto* (It.), i.e. play on or near the fingerboard (see *Gewöhnlich*).

GRIFFES, CHARLES TOMLINSON (p. 1057, pl. **172.** 9). Born at Elmira, N.Y., in 1884 and died in New York in 1920, aged thirty-five. He had a distinctive and imaginative artistic personality and a rich sense of colour.

His largest orchestral work was *The Pleasure Dome of Kubla Khan*, after Coleridge. There are also two pieces for string quartet; a Poem for flute and orchestra; *Shojo*, a Japanese mime-play; a 'dance-drama' in two scenes, *The Kairn of Koridwen*; and piano pieces and songs.

GRIGNY, NICOLAS DE (Degrigny). Born at Rheims in 1671 and died there in 1703, aged thirty-two. He was a famous organist and his organ compositions, which are highly esteemed, were amongst the French music that Bach thought it worth his while to copy and to add to his personal collection.

GRIMM.

(1) C. See *Folia*.

(2) FRIEDRICH MELCHIOR VON (1723–1807). Man of letters. See *Bouffons*; *Criticism* 3.

GRIMMIG (Ger.). 'Grim', 'furious'.

GRISI, CARLOTTA. See *Ballet* 9; *Pas de quatre*.

GROANING STICK. Thunder stick (q.v.).

GROB (Ger.). 'Coarse', 'rough'.

GROFÉ, FERDE (correctly Ferdinand Rudolph von Grofe; p. 1060, pl. **173.** 7). Born in New York in 1892 and died at Santa Monica, Calif., in 1972, aged eighty. Pianist in Paul Whiteman's orchestra; later composed light music. His *Grand Canyon* Suite is well known; orchestrated Gershwin's *Rhapsody in Blue*.

See *Jazz* 5.

GROS, CHARLES. See *Pianoforte* 21.

GROS, GROSSE (Fr.; masc., fem.). 'Great', 'big' (in the case of an organ-stop this means of low pitch, e.g. 16 ft. instead of 8 ft.).

GROS-BOIS. See *Oboe Family* 2.

GROSS, GROSSE, etc. (Ger.). 'Great', 'large' (various terminations according to case, gender, and number). So *Grösser*, 'greater'.

GROSSE CAISSE (Fr.). 'Big box', i.e. bass drum. See *Percussion Family* 3 k, 4 b, 5 k.

GROSSE FLÖTE (Ger.). See *Flute Family* 5 a.

GROSSE ORGELMESSE (Haydn). See *Nick-named Compositions* 13.

GROSSE QUARTETTE (Haydn). See *Nick-named Compositions* 12.

GROSSES ORCHESTER (Ger.). Full orchestra.

GROSSE TROMMEL (Ger.). 'Great drum', i.e. bass drum. See *Percussion Family* 3 k, 4 b, 5 k.

GROSSFLÖTE (Ger.). See *Organ* 14 II. See also *Grosse Flöte* above.

GROSSO, GROSSI (It.). See *Concerto* 2, 6.

GROS TAMBOUR (Fr.). Great drum. Same as *Grosse caisse* (q.v.).

GROSZ, W. (Born 1894, died 1939.) See *Shimmy*.

GROTESK (Ger.). 'Grotesque.'

GROTRIAN HALL, LONDON. See *Concert* 8.

GROTTESCO (It.). 'Grotesque.'

GROUND or **GROUND BASS.** This is a variant of the Variation form, or, rather, it is perhaps, the first state of that form, for it came into use very early in the history of music. It consists of a short piece of bass repeated over and over again with changing upper parts.

A simple and well-known instance is Purcell's song from the opera *Dido and Aeneas*, 'When I am laid in earth'. Here the instrumental basses enter alone with a three-in-a-measure passage. This bass is then repeated six times with varied harmonies erected over it, and above these a vocal line both so free and so continuous that the limitation the composer has imposed upon himself is not in the least apparent. To the listener who is aware of the device, the persistence of the very poignant chromatically descending bass passage, which so vividly expresses the emotion of the song as a whole, has great artistic and dramatic value, but many a less instructed or less musically attentive listener must be touched by the solemnity of the music and its effective enhancement of the emotion of the words without observing the element of formality in its structure. Other composers of the Purcell–Bach–Handel period also used this particular bass for grounds. Bach has used almost the same bass as a 'ground' in the affecting 'Crucifixus' chorus of his Mass in B minor, and elsewhere.

A curious instance of a particular bass with an allied melody being taken as the material for varied treatment by a number of composers will be found mentioned under *Folia*.

These are two familiar examples of the application of the principle of a ground bass; such examples are very numerous, and they occur both in vocal and instrumental music.

The device of ground bass is ancient yet still in use. We see it in the early thirteenth-century part song *Sumer is icumen in* (q.v.), and we see it also in the last movement of Brahms's Fourth Symphony and the Finale of his *Variations on a Theme of Haydn*, and in Elgar's *Carillon*, where (as has been contrived sometimes by other composers) a short passage of bass is used which does not exactly coincide in length with any precise number of measures, so that its notes change their position in the measure at each repetition, and the incidence of the accents is likewise changed.

Two forms in music have the ground bass as their main distinguishing mark—the Chaconne and the Passacaglia. These are treated in a separate article.

The art of extemporizing upon a ground bass was much cultivated in the sixteenth and early seventeenth centuries—often duet extemporizing. The method is explained in Simpson's *Division Violist* (1659):

'A ground, subject, or bass, call it what you please, is pricked down in several papers; one for him who is to play the ground upon an organ, harpsichord, or whatever other instrument may be apt for that purpose; the other for him that plays upon the viol, who having the said ground before his eye as his theme or subject plays such variety of descant or division in concordance thereto as his skill and present invention do then suggest unto him. In this manner of play, which is the perfection of the viol or any other instrument, if it be exactly performed, a man may show the excellency both of his hand and invention, to the delight and admiration of those that hear him.'

GROVE, GEORGE (p. 389, pl. **66.** 8). Born at Clapham in 1820, and died at Sydenham in 1900, aged seventy-nine. He was a civil engineer, who erected lighthouses in the West Indies and became secretary successively to the Society of Arts (1850) and the Crystal Palace (1852), in which latter position he valuably seconded the influence of the conductor August Manns (see *Annotated Programmes* 5).

He helped to edit Smith's *Dictionary of the Bible* and to found the Palestine Exploration Fund, and wrote articles and books on a variety of subjects, including a *Primer of Geography*. For fifteen years he was editor of *Macmillan's Magazine*, until, in 1883, he became the first Director of the Royal College of Music, receiving at the same time the honour of knighthood.

His rightly famous *Dictionary of Music and Musicians* appeared in four volumes, 1879–89, and since his death has appeared in further and enlarged editions in 1904–10 (ed. J. A. Fuller Maitland), 1927–8 and 1940 (ed. H. C. Colles). A new edition, in nine volumes, by Eric Blom, appeared in 1954 (supplement 1961).

See *Conducting* 8; *Ballad* 6.

GROVES OF BLARNEY. See *Last Rose of Summer*.

GROVLEZ, GABRIEL. Born at Lille in 1879 and died in Paris in 1944, aged sixty-five. He studied at the Paris Conservatory and taught piano for many years at the Schola Cantorum in Paris, then taking up a career as an operatic conductor and in it attaining great success. His works include piano music, symphonic poems, ballets, comic operas, etc., and he edited old French music.

G.R.S.M. See *Degrees and Diplomas* 2.

Gr. Tr. Short for *Grosse Trommel*, i.e. big drum. See *Percussion Family* 3 k, 4 b, 5 k.

GRUENBERG, LOUIS (p. 1060, pl. **173.** 1). Born at Brest-Litovsk (then in Poland) in 1884 and died in Hollywood, California, in 1964, aged seventy-nine. He was brought to the United States at the age of two and spent his later life there. His career was at first that of a pianist (he studied with Busoni), but at twenty-nine he won a prize with a symphonic poem and he continued to compose orchestral music, a violin concerto, chamber music, and a number of operas (*The Emperor Jones*, New York, 1933—an operatic treatment of Eugene O'Neill's play). Some of his works attempted a synthesis of jazz and European elements, e.g. *The Daniel Jazz* (1925).

See references under *Jazz* 5; *Blues*.

GRUNDSTIMMEN (Ger.). 'Ground voices', i.e. foundation-stops of an organ.

GRUNDTHEMA. See *Leading Motif*.

GRUPPETTO. Italian name for 'Turn'. See Table 14.

GRÜTZMACHER, F. See *Misattributed* (Boccherini).

G.S.M. Guildhall School of Music (London). See *Schools of Music*; *Degrees and Diplomas* 2.

GSP. Short for *Glockenspiel*.

G STRING (violin). The lowest string, with a rich tone, so that composers occasionally direct that a passage shall be played on it alone. (Bach's 'Air on the G string' is really the second movement from that composer's third orchestral suite in D, rearranged as a violin solo in key C, the melody a ninth lower and with pianoforte accompaniment, by Wilhelmj in 1871.)

G.T.C.L. See *Degrees and Diplomas* 2.

GUAJIRA. A type of Cuban folk dance in alternating rhythms of ¾ and ⅜ and ending on the dominant.

GUARACHA, GUARRACHA. A type of Mexican folk dance in two sections, respectively in three-in-a-measure and two-in-a-measure.

GUARDS' MODEL (of side drum). See *Percussion Family* 5 i.

GUARNERI. See *Italy* 6; *Violin Family* 4.

GUARNIERI, CAMARGO. Born at Tiete, Brazil, in 1907. He studied at the Conservatory of São Paulo and then in Paris under Koechlin. His orchestral, chamber, piano, and vocal compositions, etc., express the Brazilian temperament and reflect the folk idiom. His style is polyphonic in character rather than harmonic.

GUARRACHA. See *Guaracha*.

GUÉDRON (or **Guesdron**), **PIERRE.** Born in Beauce, Normandy, in 1565, and died, probably in Paris, after 1620. He was a singer in the chapel of Henry IV of France, later composer to (and master of the children of) that chapel, and valet to the King, whose particular favourite he became, and, still later, musical director to Mary of Medici. He composed the music for many court ballets, in it showed rhythmic vigour and a sense of drama, and is thus looked upon as a precursor of Lully (q.v.).

His work tended in the same direction as that of Peri, Caccini, and others in Italy (see *Opera* 1). Boesset (q.v.) was his son-in-law.

GUERRE DES BOUFFONS. See *Bouffons*.

GUERRERO.

(1) PEDRO. He was a sixteenth-century Spanish composer of lute music, church music, etc.

(2) FRANCISCO. Born at Seville in 1527 and died there in 1599, aged seventy-two. He was brother and pupil of the above. He held a number of important positions in church music and composed a large amount of contrapuntal sacred music and some secular music. Much of his music was printed during his lifetime in Rome, Venice, Paris, and Louvain.

GUERRIERO, GUERRIERA (It., masc., fem.). 'Warlike.'

GUESDRON. See *Guédron*.

GUGGENHEIM FELLOWSHIP. See *Patronage* 7; *United States* 5 f.

GUI, VITTORIO (1885–1975). His career was that of orchestral conductor and of composer of songs, symphonic poems, etc. He also wrote critical articles.

GUIDE DU CONCERT. See *Annotated Programmes* 6.

GUIDO D'AREZZO, or Guido Aretino, or **Guido Arentinus** (p. 609, pl. **107.** 1). Born possibly in Paris about 995 and died at Avellano in 1050 (Arezzo was for some time his place of residence). He was a learned Benedictine of great fame as a theoretician, whose influence on music is not, to this day, exhausted.

See references under *Sight-Singing* 1, 2; *Hexachord*; *Ornaments* 1; *Pitch* 7 e; p. 960, pl. **161.**

GUIDONIAN HAND. See *Hexachord*.

GUILDHALL SCHOOL OF MUSIC (London). See *Schools of Music* and *Degrees and Diplomas* 2. In addition to the activities there mentioned the School conducts, in various parts of the country, a series of examinations covering the period of pupil-life.

GUILDS OF MINSTRELS. See *Minstrels*, etc. 3.

GUILFORD, LORD. See *North, Francis*.

GUILLEMAIN, GABRIEL. Born in Paris in 1705 and died (by his own hand) near there in 1770. He was a notable composer of music for stringed instruments, chamber music combinations, and harpsichord.

GUILMANT, FÉLIX ALEXANDRE (p. 784, pl. **131.** 3). Born at Boulogne-sur-Mer in 1837 and died near Paris in 1911, aged seventy-four. His father was an organist in Boulogne, and at sixteen he himself occupied a similar position. In his early twenties he took an intensive course of study with Lemmens in Brussels, and thenceforward held a great reputation as a recitalist. At thirty-four he removed to Paris as organist of the church of the Trinity, where he remained for thirty years. The Trocadéro organ was the instrument that for years brought his talent before the notice of a wide international public. He travelled widely, everywhere recognized as at the head of his art. He was on the staff of the Paris Conservatory and, with Bordes and d'Indy (q.v.), founded the Schola Cantorum. He was the teacher of many of the most famous organists of the succeeding generation. His effective organ compositions are much played, as are the many organ works of earlier composers revived and edited by him.

See references as follows: *Titelouze*; *Bonnet, Joseph*; *Sonata* 10 e; *Clérambault*.

GUIMARD. See *Ballet* 9.

GUIMBARDE (Fr.). Jew's harp (q.v.).

GUION (Guyon), DAVID WENDEL FENTRESS. Born at Ballinger, Texas, in 1895. His early musical training was in Texas. Later he studied the piano under Godowsky in Vienna. He has occupied many academic positions.

His witty and felicitous transcriptions of melodies popular and traditional in the United States earned him a special place in the esteem of his countrymen (*Turkey in the Straw, Arkansas Traveller*, etc.).

GUIRAUD, ERNEST. Born at New Orleans, U.S.A., in 1837 and died in Paris in 1892, aged fifty-four. He was the son of a French musician. His work as a composer was principally for the opera stage. He also wrote some orchestral music. He held an important position on the staff of the Conservatory (where he was the teacher of Debussy).

GUITAR. An instrument somewhat of the lute type (cf. *Mandoline*) with fretted finger-board like the lute, played, as the lute is, by plucking the strings with the fingers; unlike the lute, however, it has a flat (or, in some old guitars, slightly rounded) back and the surface of its resonance-chamber is curved inward on each side somewhat like that of the violin family. The normal modern guitar has six single strings; the early guitar was double-strung, like the lute (q.v.).

It is very widespread and of great antiquity. Its cultivation today is highest in Italy and Spain, especially the latter.

One Spanish form of the guitar (having affinities with the lute and entirely taking the place of this in Spain) is the **Vihuela** (q.v.); it enjoyed always aristocratic rather than general favour.

The guitar, after popularity in the seventeenth century, had a passing vogue of great intensity in Britain and America, beginning soon after the middle of the eighteenth century (first British guitar tutor published 1758) and lasting for perhaps ninety years or so. Possibly it was at its highest in the 1830s, when advertisements of music published show a great proportion of guitar compositions. (For the so-called English Guitar of the eighteenth century see under *Cittern*.)

Great figures in the history of the guitar are Robert de Visée (c. 1650–c. 1725; guitarist to the Dauphin), Mauro Giuliani (born c. 1780; famous Italian player, composer of three concertos for the guitar and of chamber music employing it); and, very especially, the Spaniard, Fernando Sors, or Sor (1778–1839), who developed an extraordinary technique as player and composed much music for the instrument. The learned Fétis styles Sors 'the Beethoven of the Guitar'. Francisco Tárrega, or Tárrega Eixea (1852–1909), another virtuoso and composer, has, on his part, been called 'the Chopin of the Guitar'. From the second decade of the twentieth century the instrument became widely known again by the travels of the virtuoso Andrés Segovia (born 1893), and largely as a result of his admirable playing music was composed for it by various Spanish, French, and other composers—Falla, Turina, Salazar, Rodolfo Halffter, Roussel, Samazeuilh, Tansman, Castelnuovo-Tedesco (a concerto), Ponce (a concerto), Villa-Lobos (a concerto), etc. It also became a very popular instrument for amateur music-makers and manufacturers put a number of different designs on the market.

Paganini for three years abandoned the violin and devoted himself to the guitar; he wrote much chamber music that included a part for it. Weber played it and wrote songs with its accompaniment. One of Schubert's friends, Umlauf, records that he used to visit him in the mornings before he got out of bed, and usually found him with a guitar in his hands— 'He generally sang to me newly composed songs to his guitar'. In 1926 there was published a newly found quartet said to be by Schubert for violin (or flute), viola, violoncello, and guitar; it is now established that Schubert only added a cello part to a trio by the Bohemian guitar-player Matiegka, who published his work in 1807. Berlioz played the guitar and treated it seriously in his *Treatise on Instrumentation*.

See *Spain* 8; *Oriental*; *United States* 6; *Stroh Violin*, etc.; compare also *Balalaika* and see references to the gittern under *Cittern*. For Hawaiian Guitar see *Ukelele*; for Electric Guitar see *Electric Musical Instruments* 2 d. Also p. 433, pl. **74**; p. 977, pl. **164**. 4.

GUITAR, ENGLISH. See *Cittern*.

GUITARE D'AMOUR. Same as Arpeggione (q.v.).

GULBRANSON, ELLEN. See *Scandinavia* 4.

GUNDRY, INGLIS. Born in London in 1905. He studied at Oxford and the Royal College of Music. During the second World War he served in the navy and whilst at sea began his opera *The Partisans* (performed in London 1946). Earlier dramatic works were *Naaman—the Leprosy of War* and *The Return of Odysseus*. Some orchestral pieces, songs, etc., are also amongst his compositions.

GUNG'L, JOSEPH. Born in Hungary in 1810 and died at Weimar in 1889, aged seventy-eight. He began life as a schoolmaster, became a military bandmaster, and composed enormous quantities of popular dances and marches.

See references under *Horn Family* 3; *Waltz*.

GURIDI, JESUS. Born at Vitoria, Spain, in 1886 and died in Madrid in 1961, aged seventy-five. He was of Basque birth, and both collected Basque folk song and used it as the basis of some of his compositions, which include vocal, organ, and orchestral works and operas. He was director of the Madrid Conservatory.

GURLITT.

(1) CORNELIUS. Born in Altona, Germany, in 1820 and died there in 1901, aged eighty-one. He rose to be the chief organist of his native town and one of the later nineteenth century's most liberal providers of well-graded and not uninteresting pianoforte music, often to be seen in the hands of the musical youth of all civilized nations. He also composed operas, etc.

(2) WILIBALD (1889–1963), grand-nephew of (1). Noted German musicologist. Organ expert and editor of Riemann's *Musiklexikon*.

GURNEY, IVOR. Born at Gloucester in 1890 and died at Dartford in 1937, aged forty-seven. He was a choir-boy and then assistant organist of Gloucester Cathedral; he won a scholarship to the Royal College of Music, served in the army 1914–18, was wounded and gassed, returned to the College and completed his studies, and then appeared before the public with a certain number of delicate songs, pianoforte works, and chamber music compositions and orchestral works, all of which exhibited great promise. The effects of his war service, however, unfortunately caused his retirement from the active practice of his profession and his art to the seclusion of a mental hospital.

GUSIKOF, MICHAEL JOSEPH (1806–37). See *Percussion Family* 4 e (Xylophone).

GUSLA, or **GUSLE,** or **GUZLA.** An ancient one-stringed bowed instrument still highly popular in Bulgaria.

Not to be confused with *Gusli* or *Guslee* (q.v.).

GUSLAR. A player on the *Gusli* (q.v.).

GUSLI or **GUSLEE.** A Russian instrument of the zither class (in the eighteenth century sometimes provided with a keyboard). Rimsky-Korsakof uses it in his opera *Sadko*, and the sound is imitated in Glinka's *Ruslan and Liudmila*.

Not to be confused with the *Gusla* (q.v.).

GUSTO (It.). 'Taste', i.e. sense of fitness as to speed, force, phrasing, etc. So *Gustoso*, 'tastefully'. The word is also used in the other sense of 'taste', e.g. Bach's *Concerto nach italienischem Gusto* ('Concerto in the Italian Taste').

GUT (Ger.). 'Good', 'well'.

GUTMANN, ADOLF. Born at Heidelberg in 1819 and died at Spezia in 1882, aged sixty-three. He was a pianist and a fluent composer for his instrument.

See *Chopin*.

GUYON. See *Guion*.

GUZLA. See *Gusla*.

GWINETH, GWYNEDD, GWYNETT, GUINNETH. A clergyman and composer who lived in the mid-sixteenth century. He studied at Oxford and became Doctor of Music there (1531). He held a London rectory and was known as a controversial writer on religion. Practically all his music has perished.

See *Wales* 10.

GYLES. See *Giles*.

GYMEL or **GIMEL.** The word comes from the Latin *gemellus* and has been used in music in three senses, all with the idea of twinship.

In the first sense it describes a style of singing alleged, but on small and doubtful evidence, to have been common in parts of Britain (but nowhere else in Europe) as early as the tenth or eleventh century. Whilst one body of singers took the tune of a song another body would extemporaneously add a part in thirds beneath it—what today English people call 'singing seconds', i.e. adding a second part. (Cf. *Faburden*.)

In the second sense it is applied to a type of composition found in the fourteenth and early fifteenth centuries in which, whilst the main tune or canto fermo (probably usually a bit of plainsong) was sung in a lower voice, two upper voices sang an accompaniment in which they moved independently of the other voice but in thirds with one another.

In a third sense we find the term used in sixteenth-century choral music. In the parts for any particular voice we may find the word 'gymel' meaning that the singers of that part are here divided—our *divisi*, in fact. The restoration of the status quo is then indicated by the word *Semel*.

GYROWETZ, ADALBERT. Born in Bohemia in 1763 and died in Vienna in 1850, aged eighty-seven. He had a highly successful career as a composer of symphonies (sixty in number), chamber music, operas, ballets, and masses—Vienna, Paris, and London in turn acclaiming him. He wrote, however, merely in the Haydn style, accomplishing nothing that was genuinely personal or original, and hence, unfortunately, he outlived his popularity and fell into neglect and poverty.

See references under *Nocturne*; *Chamber Music* 6 Period III (1763); *Symphony* 8 (1763); *Bohemia*.

See the Article on pages 418–23

1. EDISON SHOWS HIS FIRST PHONO-GRAPH TO A LATER GENERATION
See *Gramophone* 1

2. BERLINER GRAMOPHONE of 1888 (hand-driven). See *Gramophone* 2

3. BRITISH GRAMOPHONE AS SOLD IN THE 1900's

4. AN H.M.V. ('Victor') ADVERTISEMENT OF 1905

5. GEORGE FORMBY (SENIOR) MAKING A RECORD—with Tetrazzini as spectator. The horn is wrapped with tape to reduce resonance

PLATE 74 THE GUITAR IN THREE CENTURIES

1. A FLEMISH PEASANT PLAYER. By Teniers (1609–90)

2. PAGANINI'S GUITAR. (See p. 431.) It was afterwards owned by Berlioz

3. THE GUITAR-MAKER AT WORK

4. SEGOVIA. See p. 431

H

H. German for B, B flat being called B. Some explanation of this anomaly is offered under *Notation* 1.

HÁBA.

(1) ALOIS (p. 109, pl. **20**. 7). Born at Vyzovice (Wisowitz), Moravia (then in Austrian territory), in 1893, and died at Prague in 1973. He studied at the Conservatories of Prague, Vienna, and Berlin, and then settled in Prague. Inspired, it is said, by early acquaintance with the folk singers of his native country, and encouraged and guided by acoustical studies at the University of Berlin, he applied in his composition a system of microtones and included in the media he employed certain microtonal instruments; his microtonal opera *The Mother* has been heard in Munich (1931) and Florence (1964). He became, indeed, the most active and prominent champion of microtonic composition.

See references under *Microtones*; *Harmony* 19; *Temperament* 9; *Chamber Music* 6, Period III (1893); *Scales* 12.

(2) KAREL. Born at the same place as his brother (above) in 1898. He is a composer and supporter and practitioner of his brother's theories.

HABANERA. A slow Cuban dance (Habana = Havana) which came to have a large popularity in Spain. It is in two-in-a-measure time with a dotted rhythm (like that of the tango). Bizet has a Habanera in *Carmen* (borrowed by him from a song by the Spanish composer Sebastien Yradier, which appeared in 1840), and Debussy's *La Puerta del Vino*, *La Soirée dans Grenade*, and some other instrumental pieces of his, have the habanera as basis. Chabrier has an effective habanera for piano. Raoul Laparra has an opera *La Habanera*.

Cf. *Havanaise*; *Tango*.

HABENECK, FRANÇOIS ANTOINE (p. 368, pl. **61**. 7). Born at Mézières, Ardennes (France), in 1781 and died in Paris in 1849, aged sixty-eight. He was a violinist and also a violin teacher of great repute who was, further, very active as an operatic and orchestral conductor, and especially as founder and director of the Société des Concerts du Conservatoire; at these concerts he gave Beethoven's symphonies their earliest French performances. He composed music for the violin, etc.

HABERL, FRANZ XAVER (1840–1910). See under *Cecilian Movement*.

HABYNGTON, HENRY. See *Abyngdon*.

HACKBRETT (literally, 'chopping board'). German for 'dulcimer' (q.v.).

HACKETT, MARIA (1783–1874). See *Cathedral Music* 7, 8. Also p. 161, pl. **32**. 4.

HADLEY.

(1) HENRY KIMBALL (p. 1056, pl. **171**. 4). Born at Somerville, Mass., in 1871 and died in New York in 1937, aged sixty-five. As a composer he was a sure technician, somewhat after the Wagnerian model, and he composed in all forms. (Cf. *United States* 8.)

Among his works are four symphonies, two tone-poems, four operas, including *Cleopatra's Night* (Metropolitan, 1920), and *Safie* (Mainz, 1909), chamber music, and over one hundred songs. He conducted in Europe from 1904 to 1909 and then in America. A 'Henry Hadley Society' gives concerts of his music.

(2) PATRICK ARTHUR SHELDON: Born at Cambridge in 1899 and died at London in 1973. He studied at Cambridge University and the Royal College of Music. He composed chamber music and works for chorus and orchestra, including (1934) a four-movement 'symphonic ballad' based on the folk song 'The trees so high'. He was Professor of Music at Cambridge from 1946 to 1963.

HADOW, WILLIAM HENRY (Sir Henry Hadow, p. 389, pl. **66**. 9). Born at Ebrington, Gloucestershire, in 1859 and died in London in 1937, aged seventy-seven. He was scholar and then fellow, lecturer, and tutor of Worcester College, Oxford. Whilst holding a high position as a scholar in fields other than the musical, he lectured for some years for the Professor of Music at Oxford (Stainer), composed chamber music, songs, etc., and wrote a number of works which set a new standard in English musical literature. From 1901 he edited the *Oxford History of Music*.

In 1909 he became Principal of Armstrong College, Newcastle-on-Tyne (University of Durham), and in 1919 Vice-Chancellor of the University of Sheffield (to 1930). He was knighted in 1918.

See *Criticism* 4; *Quality* 1; *Folk Song* 5; *Oratorio* 3; *Roberts, J.* (1); *Form* 8; *Haydn*; *Emperor's Hymn*.

HAENDEL. See *Handel* (note at end).

'HAFFNER' SERENADE, 'HAFFNER' SYMPHONY (Mozart). See *Nicknamed Compositions* 15.

HAGEN, PETER VAN. See *Profession* 9; *Nail Fiddle*.

HAGENAUER. See *Nicknamed Compositions*, s.v. 'Mozart's Dominicus Mass'.

HAGGADAH. See *Jewish* 3 (end).

HAHN, REYNALDO. Born in Venezuela in

1875 and died in Paris in 1947, aged seventy-one. At the age of eleven he became a pupil of Massenet at the Paris Conservatory. He developed into a successful stage conductor and composer and a popular writer of songs. He did much careful study with a view to the better performance of Mozart's operas, for which he was an enthusiast. The winter musical season at Cannes became his chief official responsibility.

Cf. *Lesquercade*.

HAHNEBÜCHEN (Ger.). 'Coarse', heavy.

HAHNENTRAPP. See *Chaconne and Passacaglia* (end).

HAIEFF, ALEXEI. Born in Siberia in 1914. He went to the United States in 1932 and was trained at the Juilliard School and under Nadia Boulanger. He has composed orchestral music and chamber music in a spare, contrapuntal, 'neo-classic' style.

See *Harpsichord* 9.

HAIL, COLUMBIA! The history of this song is best told in the words of Joseph Hopkinson (who wrote the verses):

'*Hail, Columbia!* was written in the summer of 1798, when war with France was thought to be inevitable. Congress was then in session in Philadelphia, debating upon that important subject, and acts of hostility had actually taken place. The contest between England and France was raging, and the people of the United States were divided into parties for the one side or the other, some thinking that policy and duty required us to espouse the cause of "republican France", as she was called, while others were for connecting ourselves with England, under the belief that she was the great preservative power of good principles and safe government. The violation of our rights by both belligerents was forcing us from the just and wise policy of President Washington, which was to do equal justice to both but to take part with neither, and to preserve an honest and strict neutrality between them. The prospect of a rupture with France was exceedingly offensive to the portion of the people who espoused her cause, and the violence of the spirit of party has never risen higher, I think not so high, in our country, as it did at that time upon that question. The theatre was then open in our city. A young man belonging to it [Gilbert Fox], whose talent was high as a singer, was about to take a benefit. I had known him when he was at school. On this acquaintance he called on me one Saturday afternoon, his benefit being announced for the following Monday. His prospects were very disheartening; but he said that if he could get a patriotic song adapted to "the President's March" he did not doubt of a full house; that the poets of the theatrical corps had been trying to accomplish it, but had not succeeded. I told him I would try what I could do for him. The object of the author was to get up an American spirit which should be independent of, and above the interests, passion and policy of both belligerents, and look and feel exclusively for our honour and rights. No allusion is made to France or England, or the quarrel between them, or to the question which was most in fault in their treatment of us. Of course the song found favour with both parties, for both were American, at least neither could disown the sentiments and feelings it indicated. Such is the history of this song, which has

endured infinitely beyond the expectation of the author, as it is beyond any merit it can boast of except that of being truly and exclusively patriotic in its sentiment and spirit.'

'The President's March', which, as is above stated, supplies the music for the song, was in all probability composed by Philip Phile (or 'Pfyle', or 'Fayles', or 'Feyles', or 'Fyles', or 'Pfalz', or 'Pfalzes', or 'Pfeil', or 'Pfyles', or 'Philo', or 'Phyla', or 'Phyles', or 'Phyls', or 'Phylz', or 'Thyla'—but 'Phile' is the preferred form). He was a violinist and leader of a Philadelphia orchestra towards the end of the eighteenth century. The whole puzzling question of the genesis of the music and the identity of its composer was thrashed out by O. G. Sonneck in a *Report on 'The Star-Spangled Banner'*, *'Hail, Columbia!'*, *'America'*, *and 'Yankee Doodle'*, published by the Library of Congress in 1909.

Joseph Hopkinson (1770–1842) was a lawyer, legislator, and judge. His father was Francis Hopkinson (q.v.).

HAIL, SMILING MORN. See *Spofforth*.

HAKENHARFE. See under *Harp* 2 c.

HALB, HALBE (Ger.). 'Half.' (Various grammatical terminations.)

HALBE or **HALBENOTE** (Ger.). 'Half-note' or minim. (Table 3.)

HALBE-PAUSE (Ger.). 'Half-rest', i.e. minim rest. (Table 3.)

HALBETAKTNOTE (Ger.). 'Half-note', or minim. (Table 3.)

HALBPRINZIPAL (Ger.). 'Half-diapason', i.e. organ 4-foot Principal.

HALBSOPRAN (Ger.). 'Mezzo-soprano.'

HALBTENOR (Ger.). 'Baritone.'

HALE.

(1) Philip. See *Criticism* 5; *Annotated Programmes* 6.

(2) ADAM DE LA. See *Adam de la Halle*.

HALÉVY (original name Lévy), JACQUES FRANÇOIS FROMENTAL ÉLIE. Born in Paris in 1799 and died at Nice in 1862, aged sixty-two. He was of a Jewish family. He entered the Paris Conservatory, where he became a pupil of Cherubini and at twenty-one won the Rome Prize. On return from Italy he gradually made his way as an opera composer, his fame being at last established with the production of the 'grand' opera *La Juive* and the 'comic' opera *L'Éclair* in 1835. His predilections were for pageantry and grandeur, and the work of Meyerbeer influenced him. The list of his operas is a long one. He held many official positions, including that of professor at his old school, where amongst his pupils was his future son-in-law, Bizet.

Wagner, whose personal experiences of French musical life had perhaps embittered him, cuttingly said: 'Halévy was, like all the Paris composers of our time, only inspired with enthusiasm for his art so long as success was still to be won; once that was achieved and he was safely ranged with the lions of the world of composition, all he thought of further was to manufacture operas, and to pocket the money.'

References to this composer will be found under *France* 9; *Opera* 24 d (1835); *Trumpet Family* 3 (near end); *Percussion Family* 4 c.

HALF CLOSE. See *Cadence*.

HALFFTER.

(1) **ESCRICHE ERNESTO.** Born in Madrid in 1905. He is an orchestral conductor and composer of chamber music, orchestral music, songs, etc. During the 1940s he settled in Portugal.

(2) **RODOLFO.** Born in Madrid in 1900. He is brother of the above and has written piano music, string quartets, etc. After the defeat of the Spanish loyalist government, with which he was associated, he settled in Mexico.

HALF-LONG PIPES. See *Bagpipe Family* 3.

HALF-NOTE (Amer.). 'Minim.' (Table 3.)

HÄLFTE (Ger.). 'Half.'

HALL, GEORGE LAWRENCE. See *Colour and Music* 10.

HALLE. See *Adam de la Halle*.

HALLÉ, CHARLES (p. 800, pl. **137.** 4). Born in Westphalia in 1819 (original name, Karl Halle) and died in Manchester in 1895, aged seventy-six. He had a distinguished career as pianist, conductor, and educationist. He made his home in Manchester from 1848, founded his famous Manchester orchestra in 1857, was knighted in 1888, and became the first Principal of the Royal Manchester College of Music in 1893. His second wife (Mme Norman-Neruda) was a famous violinist.

See *Recital*; *Concert* 10; *Pianoforte* 22; *Fingering* 5 e; *Rubato* 2; *Memory* 7; *Clavichord* 6.

HALLÉ CHOIR AND ORCHESTRA. See *Concert* 10.

HALLELUJAH. It means 'Praise Jehovah', from Hebrew *Hallel*, 'praise' and *Jah*, Jehovah. 'Alleluia' (q.v.) is the Latin form. Hallelujah Choruses (perhaps usually prompted by Revelation xix. 1) are common in music (see below).

HALLELUJAH CHORUS. By this is usually meant one particular such chorus out of very many which exist—the chorus which so triumphantly closes Part II of Handel's *Messiah*. It is reported by Miss Laetitia Hawkins, daughter of the historian of music (on the authority of Dr. Allott, Dean of Raphoe) that Handel spoke of having composed it under the influence of great emotion—'I did think I did see all Heaven before me—and the great God himself!'

At the first London performance, in Covent Garden Theatre (23 March 1743), the whole assembly, with George II at its head, rose to its feet as this chorus opened, and remained standing to the end, thus establishing a tradition which is still maintained.

Many anthems of Purcell and his period end with Hallelujah Choruses (often of what now seems to us a distressingly perfunctory character). Handel himself has other such choruses, as in *Judas Maccabaeus*. In *Messiah*, then, he takes a common type and dignifies it to the point beyond which nothing greater of that type can be imagined.

As often with Handel, and all composers, the thematic material of this composition is not completely original. Consciously or (more likely) unconsciously, Handel has for the sections 'The kingdoms of this world' and 'And he shall reign for ever and ever' made use of melodic themes which closely resemble lines of a German chorale, with which he must have been very familiar in youth—one to be found in most English hymn-tune books today, *Wachet auf* ('Sleepers, wake! A voice is calling'). And the section 'For the Lord God Omnipotent reigneth' is a treatment of a phrase familiar as the opening of the canon *Non nobis Domine* (q.v.), and in other connexions—including several other choruses of Handel.

For a description of this chorus in an early American concert programme see *Annotated Programmes* 3. For Haydn's estimate of the chorus see under *Handel*. For curious versions of the chorus see *Arrangement*. For the 'Hallelujah' Organ Concerto see *Nicknamed* 10.

HALLEN (Ger.). 'To clang.'

HALLÉN, A. (1846–1925). See *Scandinavia* 4.

HALLIDAY, JOSEPH (early nineteenth-century Irish bandmaster). See *Cornett and Key Bugle Families* 3 h.

HALLING. A popular solo dance of Norway, taking its name from the Hallingdal district, where presumably it is supposed to have originated. Judging from the description of it in Björnson's *Arne* it is one of the most vigorous dances of the world, with a good deal of kicking of the rafters and many somersaults. It is in two-in-a-measure time. Examples will be found in Grieg, his op. 71, no. 5, being a fine specimen well illustrating Björnson's description.

Cf. *Reel*.

HALLSTRÖM, IVAR (1826–1901). See *Scandinavia* 4.

HALMAGYI. See *Electric Musical Instruments* 1 j.

HALSKE. See *Electric Musical Instruments* 3 a.

HALT (Ger.). 'Pause' ($\frown$).

HALTEN (Ger.). 'To hold', 'sustain'.

HALVORSEN, JOHAN. Born at Drammen in Norway in 1864 and died at Oslo in 1935, aged seventy-one. He studied at the Conservatory of Stockholm, at Leipzig, Berlin, and Liège.

He held a position as violinist at Aberdeen, travelled as a virtuoso player, and conducted the orchestra at Bergen. He married the niece of Grieg, and his music, which includes a violin concerto, violin and piano sonatas, orchestral pieces, and other things, reflects, in another way, his Griegian sympathies.

HAMAL, J. N. (1709–78). See *Belgium* 6.

HAMBURG. See *Opera* 9, 23; *Keiser*; *Publishing* 8; *Holland* 3; *Reinken*; *Criticism* 2.

HAMERIK, originally 'Hammerich'.

(1) ASGER. Born at Copenhagen in 1843 and died at Frederiksborg in 1923, aged eighty. He studied piano under von Bülow and then associated in Paris with Berlioz. He composed operas and other works, and from his late twenties to his early fifties lived in Baltimore as director of the musical department of the Peabody Institute, afterwards returning to Copenhagen. He composed six symphonies, five Scandinavian suites, cantatas, etc.

(2, 3) His brother ANGUL (1848–1931) was a notable musicologist and historian; whilst his (Asger's) son, EBBE (1898–1951) was an orchestral conductor and the composer of orchestral and chamber music and opera, etc.

HAMILTON.

(1) IAIN ELLIS. Born in Glasgow in 1922. At first an engineer, he entered the Royal Academy of Music in 1947 and has taught at Morley College (1952), London University (1955), Duke University, U.S.A. (1962), and City Univ., N.Y. (1971). He has composed a number of orchestral, choral, and chamber works, independently dissonant in idiom, and sometimes showing jazz influences. He is active in professional organizations (chairman of the Composers' Guild in 1958) and is in demand as a touring lecturer.

(2) CLARENCE G. (1865–1934). See *Colour and Music* 2.

HAMLET. See *Thomas, A.*

HAMMER BONE. See *Ear and Hearing* 1.

HAMMERICH. See *Hamerik*.

'HAMMERKLAVIER' SONATA (Beethoven). See *Nicknamed Compositions* 5.

HAMMERSCHMIDT, ANDREAS (1611–75). See *Bohemia*.

HAMMERSTEIN, OSCAR (1846–1919). See reference under *Barber Shop Music*.

HAMMOND, J. H. See *Pianoforte* 15.

HAMMOND ELECTRIC ORGAN. See *Electric* 4.

HAMPEL, ANTON JOSEPH (d. 1771). See *Horn Family* 3.

HANACCA or **HANAKISCH** (Ger.), **HANAISE** (Fr.). A Moravian dance, in three-in-a-measure time; a sort of quick polonaise.

HAND, HÄNDE (Ger.). 'Hand', 'hands'.

HANDBELLS. See *Bell* 9.

HANDEL, GEORGE FRIDERIC (p. 448, pl. 76). Born at Halle, in Saxony, in 1685, and died in London in 1759, aged seventy-four. Born in the same year as Bach and dying but nine years later, springing from similar North German middle-class stock and reared in the same North German Protestant environment, representing like him the climax of the later contrapuntal school, Handel's life and art nevertheless followed a very different course. In both domains Bach may be called intensive and Handel extensive. Where Bach moved but from one North German town to another and remained always a member of the lower-middle class in which he was born, Handel became the successful, much-travelled man of the world, consorting on familiar terms with the more intelligent of the idle aristocracy, and enjoying at the same time the reverent worship of the prosperous and sober middle classes. He was composing operas and oratorios for the largest audiences and with bachelor venturesomeness making and losing fortunes in his speculations in public entertainment at a time when Bach was carefully expending a small if regular income upon the rearing of a large if promising family.

Handel's art has not the concentration of Bach's; he is not so thorough. He has been called 'a magnificent opportunist'. Yet there is a nobility in his music, as there was in his presence, and though facile he is never trivial. Beethoven has said of Handel, 'Go and learn of him how to achieve great effects with simple means', and Haydn, hearing the 'Hallelujah Chorus' in Westminster Abbey, rose to his feet with the crowd, wept, and exclaimed, 'He is the master of us all'.

After a childhood in which music steadily asserted its claims in the teeth of parental displeasure, Handel became a violinist in the opera orchestra of Hamburg, and then, at twenty-one, went to Italy, a century earlier the birthplace (as it was still the favoured home) of opera. Here he acquired a high reputation as a performer on harpsichord and organ, and underwent that process of Italianization which affected all his later composition.

On his return he accepted the position of director of music to the Elector of Hanover, but soon left for England, of which a few years later his Elector, as it happened, became King. London operatic enterprises, first successful and then (through the excessive cost of performance and production, which is always the dangerous burden borne by this branch of art) a failure, were followed by the period of oratorio composition which produced what was for the next century and a half to prove that part of Handel's legacy capable of maintaining in splendour his golden reputation in the minds of crowds of music-lovers in Britain and other countries.

During the earlier years of the twentieth century considerable revival of the operas was seen, chiefly in German theatres (see list in Loewenberg's *Annals of Opera*); the oratorios had previously fallen away in popularity, with the exception of two or three, of which the greatest and most imperishable is *Messiah*. It is regrettable that the latter half of the nineteenth century, which saw the bringing within the lighted circle of public familiarity of more and more of Bach's work, should have seen the withdrawal into obscurity of more and more of Handel's.

PLATE 75

THE WAITING HANDEL

By Batt

THE blind old man is seen smoking as he awaits the arrival of his amanuensis. Behind him hangs the portrait of himself, painted for him in earlier days by Balthasar Denner. It now hangs in the National Portrait Gallery.

His harpsichord (to be seen in the Victoria and Albert Museum) stands open near at hand. His wig and stock, symbols of a world in which he is no longer much interested, are thrown off for his greater ease. His food is left untouched, for his immense appetite of former days is now gone.

Thus Handel must have waited many times for John Christopher Smith to come and commit his last music to paper.   B.

At sixty Handel's health began to fail; at sixty-eight his eyesight was completely lost after an operation by (it is believed) the same English travelling oculist who had been equally unsuccessful with his great contemporary; at seventy-four he died and was buried with high honours in Westminster Abbey, which on five occasions before the century ended was to be the scene of magnificent musical festivals in his honour. (See *Festival* 1.)

Handel's temper was quick, yet the essential basis of his character was benign. He used his art on many occasions during his lifetime for the assistance of charity, as it has been used on innumerable occasions since his death. Like Bach, he was a sincere Christian and (within the limits which human nature commonly attains) a consistent one.

(*Note.* In continental European countries the name is spelt *Händel* or *Haendel*. The family is known to have spelt its name in at least fifteen different ways. The composer himself used four forms at four periods, Händel, Haendel, Hendel, and Handel. He adopted the last form soon after settling in England, used it in the Act of Naturalization as a British subject in 1726, and adhered to it henceforth; in British and American literature, at any rate, it should, then, obviously be maintained.

The spelling of his second Christian name *Frideric* appears in his petition for British naturalization in 1726.)

A good many details of Handel's life and work are necessarily scattered through this volume, and they can be found by means of the following list:

1. HISTORICAL POSITION, etc. *Expression* 5; *Germany* 4; *History of Music* 5.

2. QUESTIONS OF PITCH, KEY, etc. *Keyboard* 3; *Modes* 1 c, 10; *Modulation*; *Pitch* 3, 4, 6 a b; *Temperament* 5.

3. MELODY, HARMONY, etc. *Figured Bass*; *Harmony* 1, 10; *Melody* 10.

4. VOCAL MATTERS. *Aria*; *Cadenza*; *Cantata*; *Division* 2; *Melisma*; *Notation* 5; *Ornaments* 1; *Recitative*; *Singing* 10; *Vocalize*; *Voice* 8, 9.

5. ORATORIOS, etc. *Additional Accompaniments*; *Amen*; *Annotated Programmes* 3; *Anthem*, Period III; *Arne, Michael* (ref. to *Messiah*); *Bagpipe Family* 7 (ref. to *Messiah*); *Carols* (ref. to *Messiah*); *Composition* 5, 10 (refs. to *Messiah* and *Israel in Egypt*); *Congregational* 5;

Hallelujah Chorus; *Hymns and Hymn Tunes* 6; *Ireland* 6 (ref. to *Messiah*); *Kerll*; *Methodism* 2, 8; *Nicknamed Compositions* 1 (reference under Bach's 'St. Anne's' Fugue); *Oratorio* 1, 5, 7 (1720, 1818); *Passion Music* 4; *Serenata*; *Symphony* 1; *Te Deum*; also p. 738, pl. **121.** 4, 6; p. 704. pl. **117.** 1; p. 753, pl. **124.**]

6. OPERAS. *Ariosti*; *Ballad Opera*; *Beggar's Opera*; *Bononcini, G. B.*; *England* 6; *Grand Opera*; *Opera* 9 a, 13 c, 24 c; *Pasticcio*; *Street Music* 2 (ref. to *Serse*).

7. FORMS AND STYLES. *Allemande*; *Capriccio*; *Chaconne and Passacaglia*; *Chamber Music*, Period II (1685); *Coda*; *Concerto* 6 a (1685); *Courante*; *Form* 5; *Gavotte*; *Hornpipe*; *March*; *Minuet*; *Overture* 1, 7; *Pavan and Galliard*; *Polonaise*; *Programme Music* 5 c; *Sarabande*; *Sonata* 10 b d; *Sonatina*; *Suite* 3, 4, 5.

8. KEYBOARD MUSIC AND PERFORMANCE. *Acoustics* 16; *Bird Music*; *Dot*; *Harpsichord Family* 7; *Improvisation* 1; *Kelway, Joseph*; *Nicknamed Compositions* 10; *Organ* 8; *Pianoforte* 18, 22; *Pianoforte Playing* 1; also p. 453, pl. **79.** 5.

9. INSTRUMENTS OTHER THAN KEYBOARD. *Bell* 6; *Brass*; *Cornett and Key Bugle Families* 3 d; *Fife*; *Flute Family* 4, 6; *Harp* 3; *Horn Family* 3, 4; *Mandoline*; *Mechanical Reproduction* 5, 10; *Misattributed Compositions*; *Oboe Family* 2, 3 d, 6; *Percussion Family* 2 a c, 4 a e (Kettledrum, Glockenspiel); *Recorder Family* 1, 2, 3; *Trombone Family* 3; *Trumpet Family* 3, 4, 5; *Viol Family* 4 f.

10. QUESTIONS OF PERFORMANCE. *Applause* 6 (ref. to *Messiah*); *Cecilia*; *Community Singing* 5; *Concert* 4, 6; *Criticism* 4; *Festival* 1.

11. VARIOUS. *Adeste Fideles*; *Arnold, Samuel*; *Arrangement*; *Baptist Churches* 4; *Bourgault-Ducoudray*; *Chrysander*; *Concert* 9; *Dictionaries*; *Expression* 1; *Franz*; *Gesamtausgabe*; *God save the Queen*, 10; *Gramophone* 6; *Mealtime Music*; *Nicknamed* 10; *Opus*; *Pastoral*; *Patronage* 8; *Philidor*; *Profession* 8, 10; *Publishing* 6, 7; *Purcell*; *Rule, Britannia!*; *Scarlatti, D.*; *Smart, Sir George*; *Stanley*.

HANDEL AND HAYDN SOCIETY. See *United States of America* 4.

HANDEL COMMEMORATION. See *Alto Voice*.

HANDEL SOCIETY. (*a*) Founded in London in 1843 for the publication of the composer's works; after a few volumes were published, however, it was dissolved. (*b*) Founded in 1882 for the performance of the composer's (and other) music, chiefly large choral works. It still exists.

HANDHARMONIKA. See *Harmonica* 6 b.

HAND HORN. The 'Natural' French Horn, when designed for playing with the hand in the bell. See *Horn Family* 2 b, 3.

HANDL, JACOB (otherwise known as Händl, Gallus, Jacob le Coq, etc.). Born in Carniola in 1550 and died at Prague in 1591, aged nearly forty-one. He held important court and church positions in Vienna, Olmütz, and Prague, and wrote masses, motets, etc., such as give him very high rank in the body of fine composers of various countries who were, in this high-water period of musical art, writing works of this kind.

See *Bohemia*.

HANDLO, ROBERT DE. An English writer on musical notation, of the early fourteenth century.

HAND ORGAN. See *Mechanical Reproduction of Music* 10.

HANDREGISTRIERUNG (Ger.). Manual piston (on organ).

HANDTROMMEL (Ger.). Tambourine. See *Percussion Family* 3 m, 5 m.

HANDY, WILLIAM CHRISTOPHER (p. 1056, pl. **171.** 9). Born in Florence, Alabama, in 1873 and died in New York in 1958, aged eighty-four. He was a Negro who early developed activities in various capacities connected with popular music. His numerous compositions are imbued with the Negro spirit and exploit the Negro musical idioms. As an author he is known by *Blues* (1926), *Negro Authors and Composers* (1936), *Father of the Blues* (an autobiography), etc.

'HANOVER.' See *Hymns and Hymn Tunes* 6.

HANOVER SQUARE ROOMS, LONDON. See *Concert* 8; p. 752, pl. **123.** 4.

HANS. See *Keyboard* 4; *Notation* 7.

HÄNSEL AND GRETEL (Humperdinck). Produced at Weimar in 1893. Libretto by Adelheid Wette (the composer's sister).

ACT I

SCENE: *A Poor Broom-maker's Home near a Forest*

The boy **Hänsel** (*Mezzo-Soprano*) and his sister **Gretel** (*Soprano*) are working away, very hungry, at broom-making and knitting respectively. Food is their chief thought; a jug of milk promises well—an unusual treat, rice pudding. A little play together helps to put on the time until their worried **Mother** (*Mezzo-Soprano*) comes back. Angry at their neglecting work, she looks about for a stick, and in her haste upsets the milk: so there will be no supper. The children are sent out into the woods to gather wild strawberries.

Now **Father** (*Bass*) comes home, having sold all his brooms and 'liquidated' some of the profit—happily, not before laying in a stock of provisions. On hearing that the children are alone in the wood he is aghast, for there lives an ogress who turns children to gingerbread in her oven and eats them! Father and Mother hurry away to seek the children.

ACT II

SCENE 1: *In the Forest*

Hänsel and Gretel have gathered a good basket of berries, but the boy has absent-mindedly eaten them all. Now they have lost their way, night comes down, and they are frightened.

The Sleep Fairy, the **Sandman** (*Soprano*), appears and sprinkles sand into their eyes. They say their prayers, and sleep.

SCENE 2: *A Vision of Angels*

This is known as the Dream Pantomime. Through the mist breaks a light. A staircase is seen, down which angels come to protect the children.

ACT III

SCENE: *The Witch's House*

The Dawn Fairy, the **Dewman** (*Soprano*), sprinkles the children with dew, and they awake to see the mist clearing away, revealing the **Ogress's** house, made of sweetmeats, with, outside, her oven and a cage. She (*Mezzo-Soprano*) casts a spell upon the children so that they cannot run away, and puts Hänsel into the cage, meaning to make Gretel fatten him up for the oven. But clever Gretel knows a spell too: with a branch of elder she disenchants Hänsel so that he can move again; and when the witch tells her to see if the gingerbread in the oven is ready she pretends not to know what to do. The witch shows her and opens the door to peer inside; the children give her a push and slam the door. An ogress is too much of a load for any oven, and this one bursts. The end of the witch has set free a number of children who had been turned into the semblance of ginger-bread. They crowd delightedly round Hänsel and his sister, and, the Father and Mother now appearing, all join in a dance and a song of thanksgiving for the happy escape.

HANSLICK, EDUARD (p. 257, pl. **47.** 1, 2). Born in Prague in 1825 and died near Vienna in 1904, aged seventy-eight. This great Viennese critic for long bestrode the world as its most confident musical censor. He was the central figure in many a hot fight, being one of Wagner's bitterest opponents and Brahms's warmest supporters. Wagner undoubtedly had him in mind (and a malicious twinkle in his eye) as he drew the figure of Beckmesser in *The Mastersingers* (indeed in two early sketches of this libretto the name 'Hans Lich' appears instead of 'Beckmesser').

See *Criticism* 2; *Franz.*

HANSON, HOWARD HAROLD (p. 1061, pl. **174.** 7). Born at Wahoo, Nebraska, in 1896. He has composed orchestral music in the form of symphonies and symphonic poems, chamber music and choral works, piano pieces and songs, and his compositions have been much performed.

He is active in all sorts of enterprises which encourage native composition, including the valuable series of concerts of manuscript compositions, of which the best are chosen and published under the auspices of the Eastman School of Music (Rochester, New York), of which school he was director from 1924 to 1964, following a three years' fellowship of the American Academy in Rome.

In 1934 was produced in New York his opera *Merry Mount* (unfortunate in its libretto, which grotesquely misrepresents the character of the Puritan founders of New England; see *United States* 2).

See references under *Programme Music* 5 e; *Symphony* 8 (1896); *Harp* 3; *Concerto* 6 c (1896).

HANSON-DYER. See *Dyer.*

'HAPPENINGS.' See *History* 9.

HARDANGERFELE, HARDANGER FIDDLE. See *Scandinavia* 3.

HARDELOT, GUY D' (really Mrs. Rhodes; maiden name Helen Guy). Born at the Château d'Hardelot, near Boulogne, in 1858 and died in London in 1936, aged about seventy-seven. Popular song composer, many of whose productions had wide currency through their inclusion in the repertories of Calvé and other famous vocalists.

HARD HEXACHORD. See *Hexachord.*

HARDI, HARDIMENT (Fr.). 'Bold', 'boldly'.

HARDY, THOMAS (1840–1928). English novelist and poet. See references under *Carols; Mysteries; Anglican Parish Church Music* 6.

HAREWOOD, SEVENTH EARL OF (George Henry Hubert Lascelles). Born in 1923; succeeded to the earldom in 1947. He has taken a leading place in musical affairs. He was a founding associate of the English Opera Group, and at various times has been on the Board of Covent Garden, editor of the illustrated monthly *Opera*, artistic director of the

Edinburgh Festival, and (1972) managing director of Sadler's Wells Opera.

HARFE (Ger.). 'Harp.'

HARGREAVES (Lancashire musical family). See *Baptist Churches and Music* 4.

HARK, MY SOUL. See *Hymns and Hymn Tunes* 6.

HARK THE GLAD SOUND. See *Hymns and Hymn Tunes* 6.

HARK! THE HERALD ANGELS SING. See *Hymns and Hymn Tunes* 7.

HARLECH. See *Festival* 1.

HARLEQUIN. A buffoon character in the old Italian comedies, transferred (as a mute actor) to the English pantomime; the part of the pantomime in which his greatest activity occurs is called the *Harlequinade*.

HARLEQUIN MARINER. See *Comin' thro' the Rye*.

HARLEQUIN'S INVASION. See *Heart of Oak*.

HARMONIA ANGLICANA. See *God save the Queen* 8.

HARMONIC. See references under *Harmonics*.

HARMONICA. This is a word of so many different applications in different countries and periods that precise definition becomes almost impossible. What is nowadays generally meant by the word is explained below, and then, under the heading 'Nomenclature', a number of variants of the word and of further applications of it are set out.

1. The Musical Glasses of Goldsmith's 'Shakespeare and the musical glasses'—topics of society conversation at the end of the eighteenth century. Goldsmith's novel was published in 1766, i.e. a year or two after Benjamin Franklin had introduced his improved form of the musical glasses. It will be well to describe here both the earlier and the later forms.

The invention of the earlier form was claimed by Gluck, but surely mistakenly or mendaciously, as it had been known for a century before he made his famous appearance with it in 1746, advertised in the London press as follows:

'A Concerto upon Twenty-six Drinking-Glasses, tuned with Spring-Water, accompanied with the whole Band, being a new instrument of his own Invention; upon which he performs whatever may be done on a Violin or Harpsichord, and thereby hopes to satisfy the Curious, as well as Lovers of Musick.'

As a matter of fact there must have been many readers of the advertisement who realized its lack of exactness, for an Irishman named Richard Pockrich or Puckeridge (1690–1759) had toured England with such an instrument two years earlier. The tone was obtained by friction of the wetted fingers on the rims of the glasses. (In other times small hammers, held in the hands, have occasionally been employed.) Gluck's assertion that he was able to perform harpsichord music on the glasses must have been a gross exaggeration.

Pockrich was still performing when Benjamin Franklin arrived in England in 1757, and his performance inspired Franklin to an attempt to mechanize the instrument. This he did by providing a number of glass basins of graded sizes (i.e. self-tuned, not, as in the former instrument, tuned by pouring into them less or more water). These basins (each with its convexity fitted into the concavity of the one to its left, but with its rim projecting) he attached to a horizontal spindle running the length of a trough of water in which their lower portions were submerged so that, as they revolved, they should be always wet and hence responsive to the friction of the fingers. The spindle was made to revolve by means of a pedal and the fingers were applied to particular basins according to the notes desired (p. 512, pl. **91**. 4). A good many museums contain specimens of this instrument.

The name 'Harmonica' was apparently introduced in connexion with this, the more developed form of the instrument, but since then the less developed form has often been referred to by the same name. The *Oxford English Dictionary* gives 1762 as the earliest use of the word in English—the date at which Franklin described his instrument in a letter to the Italian physicist, Beccaria. (The name of the earlier form of the instrument was, in German, *Glasspiel*.)

Franklin's own spelling of the name of his instrument was *Armonica*. In 1764 one Stephen Forrage gave a concert in Philadelphia (Franklin's city) at which he introduced 'the famous Armonica or Musical Glasses, so much admired for their great sweetness and delicacy of tone'. Numerous attempts were made to modify or improve Franklin's version, one being effected by Karl Leopold Röllig, of Hamburg, who added to it a keyboard. He published a short treatise on it in 1787.

In Gerber's music lexicon, in 1790, the author recounts with enthusiasm his hearing of a performance on a keyboard form of the instrument ('*Klaviaturharmonika*') by the composer J. L. Dussek (q.v.) five years earlier, at Cassel: its inventor was named Hessel.

Franklin's instrument (but, to judge by extant compositions, almost certainly in keyboard form) had for a time great vogue. A number of players rose to fame and travelled widely. The Englishwoman Marianne Davies introduced it to Vienna, and Mozart wrote a composition for another woman virtuoso in which the harmonica was combined with the flute, oboe, viola, and violoncello. Mozart himself played the harmonica at a garden concert in Vienna when he was seventeen; his father wished to buy him an instrument but could not afford it, and such a wish on the part of a violinist and violin teacher of high standing is significant of the high esteem this, the first American invention of importance in the realm of musical instrument making, had quickly attained. The Frankfurt journals of July 1792 notified the presence of Haydn in that city where, said they, he had played and approved of 'a newly invented instrument, the *Harmonica Celestina*'. We may take it that it is the Keyed Harmonica that is referred to and that the 'Solo for Harmonica' to be found in the lists of his works was composed for this instrument. Beethoven, too, composed something for the instrument. And lesser composers naturally did the same, including J. G. Naumann (who provided six sonatas), Padre Martini, Hasse, Galuppi, and Jommelli. To judge by Beethoven's composition (which is of the nature of melodrama —a combination of speech and instrumental music), simple three-part harmony was looked upon as the effective thing in harmonica performance.[1]

The earliest form of the Glass Harmonica (the kind Gluck used) has the distinction of having had attached to it the longest section of the Greek language ever attached to any musical instrument, for a reader of *The Times* wrote to that paper in 1932 to say that in his youth he had heard a performance the advertisement of which styled the instrument the *Hydrodaktulopsychicharmonica*. It will be seen that, despite the application of American inventive skill, the old-fashioned simple form of the instrument never quite went out, and indeed it is occasionally heard today. A high development of the simple form was that of one Edwards, who, in 1823, with two colleagues, gave performances in Scotland on a set of over 120 glasses, the largest of which held three gallons and the smallest of which was the size of a thimble, the whole providing a six-octave scale.

One Anne Ford (otherwise the Hon. Mrs. Thicknesse) published in 1762 a book of '*Instructions for Playing on the Musical Glasses . . . with such directions that any person, of a musical turn, may learn in a few days, if not in a few hours*'. (See caricature p. 512, pl. **91**. 1.)

2. A Sort of Glass Dulcimer—strips of glass struck by hammers and furnished with a keyboard. It was occasionally used in the orchestra and is described by Berlioz in his *Instrumentation*, but is now obsolete. (Obviously the celesta fulfils its function.)

3. The Mouth Organ. See *Reed-Organ Family* 3.

4. Nail Harmonica. See *Nail Fiddle*.

5. Nomenclature in Other Languages.
(*a*) **French.** *Harmonica*—either musical glasses (commonest use of word), mouth organ,

[1] Throughout this article the writer has more or less closely followed a number of what are considered to be very sound authorities. He cannot, however, repress a slight suspicion that the more developed of the compositions here mentioned may have been intended, not for the Franklin Harmonica, but for that very different type of instrument described under 2. He has heard the Mozart composition broadcast on the Continent, apparently played on this (though it may have been a celesta), and it seemed to suit it very well.

or the sort of dulcimer with strips of metal or other material. The mouth organ is, properly, *Harmonica à bouche*.

Harmonica de Franklin—the developed form of musical glasses. *Harmonica à clavier* is either the same in its keyboard form or the one described under 2 above.

Harmonica à lames de verre—the dulcimer with graduated strips of glass.

Harmonica à lames d'acier—the same with strips of steel (i.e. Glockenspiel).

Harmonica à lames de pierre—the same with strips of stone.

Harmonica de bois—xylophone (see *Percussion Family* 2 f, 4, 5 f).

Harmonica à bouche—mouth organ (see *Reed-Organ Family* 3).

(*b*) **German.** *Harmonika*—either musical glasses (commonest use of word), mouth organ, or the sort of dulcimer with strips of metal, etc. *Mundharmonika* (mouth harmonica) is used for either mouth organ or Jew's Harp, generally the former.

Glasharmonika—musical glasses of either form.

Klaviaturharmonika. The Franklin type of musical glasses supplied with a keyboard, or else the one described under 3 above.

Glasstabharmonika ('glass-stick-harmonica') —sort of dulcimer with strips of glass.

Stahlharmonika—the same with strips of steel (Glockenspiel).

Steinharmonika—the same with strips of stone.

Holzharmonika ('wood-h.')—xylophone (see *Percussion Family* 2 f, 4 e, 5 f).

Mundharmonika ('mouth-h.')—mouth organ or mouth harmonica (see *Reed-Organ Family* 3).

Handharmonika ('hand-h.')—accordion (see *Reed-Organ Family* 4).

Ziehharmonika ('draw-h.')—the same (see *Reed-Organ Family* 4).

Klavierharmonika—the same with keyboard (see *Reed-Organ Family* 4).

Chromatische Harmonika—the same with full chromatic scale (see *Reed-Organ Family* 4).

In addition, *Harmonika* may mean a kind of stop on the organ (see under *Harmonika*).

(*c*) The **Italian** language apparently customarily applies the word *Armonica* to the musical glasses and nothing else. But the name has formerly been applied to five or six other instruments, mostly short-lived (including the extraordinary *Armonica meteorologica* which the priest Giulio Cesare Gattoni, of Como, made in 1785 by stretching wires of varying thickness from his third floor to a tower 150 paces distant —apparently a sort of giant Aeolian Harp, q.v.).

(*d*) **Latin.** In addition to all the above the monochord (q.v.) was sometimes called the *Harmonica regula*.

HARMONIC BASS. See *Acoustics* 10.

HARMONIC FLUTE. See *Acoustics* 8; *Organ* 3, 14 II.

HARMONIC MINOR SCALE. See *Scales* 6.

HARMONICON. See *Journals*.

HARMONIC PICCOLO. See *Organ* 14 II.

HARMONICS. See *Acoustics* 6, 8, 10, 15; *Partials*; *Timbre*; *Pianoforte* 12; *Organ* 14 V; *Voice* 6.

HARMONIC SEQUENCE. See *Sequence*.

HARMONIC SERIES. See *Acoustics* 8; *Brass*; *Horn Family*; *Trumpet Family*; *Trombone Family*; *Cornet*.

HARMONIC TRUMPET. See *Organ* 14 VI.

HARMONICUM. See *Reed-Organ Family* 6.

HARMONIE. The French for harmony, but it has also a special application, *Harmonie* or *Musique d'harmonie* meaning a band of wood, brass, and percussion (as distinct from *Fanfare*, a band of brass and percussion), or sometimes the wind instruments of an orchestra.

HARMONIE, BASSE D'. Ophicleide. See *Cornett and Key Bugle Families* 2 g, 3 g, 4 g.

HARMONIE, COR D' (Fr.). French horn—when without valves. See *Horn Family*.

HARMONIE, CORNET D'. See *Cornet* 2.

HARMONIEMESSE (Haydn). See *Nicknamed Compositions* 13.

HARMONIEMUSIK (Ger.). A band of wood, brass, and percussion.

HARMONIE, TROMPETTE D' (Fr.). The ordinary trumpet of today. See *Trumpet Family*.

HARMONIKA (Ger.). See *Reed-Organ Family* 3, 10 *b*; *Harmonica* 5 *b*; also a German organ stop, a small-scaled, soft, open wood stop—sometimes, too, a mixture stop.

HARMONIKON. See *Reed-Organ Family* 6.

HARMONINE. See *Reed-Organ Family* 6.

HARMONIOUS BLACKSMITH (Handel). See *Nicknamed Compositions* 10.

HARMONIQUE (Fr.). 'Harmonic.'

HARMONISCHE TÖNE (Ger.). Harmonics. (See references under *Harmonics*.)

HARMONIUM. See *Reed-Organ Family* 6, 9; *Lefébure-Wély*.

HARMONY

1. Definition of the Word.
2. Shifting Ideas as to what is Good Harmony.
3. Some Bach Examples Analysed.
4. The History of Harmony: Phase I. Parallelism and Perfect Intervals.
5. Phase II. A Tincture of the Non-Parallel and the 'Imperfect'.
6. Phase III. Increased Freedom.
7. Phase IV. The New Mastery of the Resources.
8. Phase V. Polyphony in Perfection.
9. Phase VI. Harmony in a Dramatic Application.
10. Phase VII. Free Polyphony on a Harmonic Framework.
11. Phase VIII. Ease and Grace.
12. Phase IX. Emotional Intensity.
13. Phase X. 'Romantic' Harmony.
14. Phase XI. 'Impressionism' and the Whole-tone Scale.
15. Phase XII. Empirical Systems.
16. Phase XIII. Chordal Streams.
17. Phase XIV. Polytonality.
18. Phase XV. Atonality.
19. Phase XVI. Microtones.
20. The Teaching of Harmony.
21. 'Rules' in Harmony.
22. Consecutives.
23. The Harmony of the Future.
24. Some Definitions of Common Terms in Harmony.

1. Definition of the Word. Harmony may be described as the clothing of melody. It was so conceived from its introduction (see *History of Music*). At this period (ninth century) and for long afterwards traditional chants of the church, formerly sung by all the voices in unison, were given into the care of the singers of a middle voice (hence tenors, literally 'holders') whilst the other voices enwrapped them with accompanying melodic parts; and in ninety-nine pages of music out of a hundred today the composer, in 'harmonizing', still maintains, as one of the strands at any given moment, a melody which ranks in his mind as the principal one and which he intends the listener also to take as such, whilst any other melodies he may combine with it (however interesting, individual, and apparently independent they may be) he regards as decorative accessories.

This definition of harmony as 'the clothing of melody' is, however, strictly considered, rather too wide and calls for a little limitation. The 'voices' or 'parts' that accompany the chief one inevitably produce, amongst themselves and with it, a succession of **Chords**, and it is this chordal aspect of the combination of voices or parts which is properly described as the element of harmony.

With the printed page before us we may analyse the composer's combination in two ways, which we may call the horizontal and the perpendicular. If we apply our thoughts in one direction, we may see them as a series of layers or strata of tone, i.e. as several melodies superposed. A choral conductor, if handed a new part-song and told he would have to begin to train his choir in it five minutes hence, would be likely to do this: he would mentally run through the music, noting how the voice-parts weave in and out, one ceasing for a moment and another entering, one holding a long note while others are engaged with a number of shorter notes, and so forth. On the other hand, the pianist who was to accompany the choir would be likely to look at the music as a series of successive handfuls of notes, observing the nature of the groups of notes to be simultaneously sounded, the way in which these carried the music into new keys (or 'modulated'), and so forth. In other words, whilst the conductor was engaged in *contrapuntal* exploration the pianist would be engaged very largely in *harmonic* exploration, each so preparing for the foundational part of his coming task.

At different periods of history composers and audiences have given more attention sometimes to one and sometimes to the other of these two complementary aspects of music, but at all times almost every piece of music written has been capable of being considered in either one aspect or the other, at the will of the student. A normal piece of music possesses these two elements as a piece of fabric possesses a warp and a woof. There are, it is true, occasional passages for keyboard instruments which are merely chordal, no movement of parts being traceable; thus it is possible (though relatively rare) to have harmony without counterpoint. But it is not possible to have melodies in combination without these producing chords, and hence there exists no counterpoint without harmony. The following examples (from Handel's Fourth Harpsichord Fughetta) illustrate respectively harmony without counterpoint and counterpoint necessarily producing harmony:

2. Shifting Ideas as to what is Good Harmony.

The combinations, or chords, which the human ear (i.e. the European ear, for with small exceptions only European races have yet developed harmony) has respectively enjoyed, tolerated, and abhorred have varied greatly at different periods. For the most part the resources have widened. New combinations introduced by pioneer composers are at first condemned as ugly, then gradually accepted, and finally drafted into the common idiom. That is the usual process, though, of course, the reverse has taken place, combinations at one time considered amongst the accepted features or mere commonplaces of music gradually dropping into disuse until they come to sound archaic and are largely abandoned.

Before briefly sketching the history of harmony it may be well to study in some little detail some examples of what to most people's ears today seems to be the 'normal' period, i.e. the period of some two hundred and fifty years from about 1650 to about 1900. To the inexperienced listener a good deal of harmony dating from any period earlier than this is apt to sound strange and old-world-like, and a good deal dating from after this period subversive; but in listening to music whose date of composition falls within the limits mentioned he usually feels quite at home. A period of that length necessarily takes in many developments, and this one includes the very varied work of Purcell and Corelli, Bach and Handel, Haydn and Mozart, Beethoven and Schubert, Mendelssohn, Schumann, and Chopin, Berlioz, Liszt, and Wagner. Despite the tremendous range indicated here, these composers have something in common, and it is something which the ordinary listener of today (with little historical

curiosity and no wish for pioneering) demands —they all conform to the system of the major and minor keys (see *Key* and *Scales*) and they all accept the **Triad** (the chord consisting of a note with its third and fifth) as the basis of their systems. Harmony earlier than this is either framed on the old modes (q.v.) or at least shows their influence still lingering. Harmony later than this, if it comes from one of the more 'advanced' composers, may use the whole-tone scale (see *Scales* 9) or some scale devised by the particular composer. Moreover, these composers of the later period may completely abandon the triad and employ chords of what seem like notes taken at random.

3. Some Bach Examples Analysed.

As examples of the harmony of the 'normal period' we will take a chorale that Bach has harmonized, or 'clothed', in no fewer than eleven ways, and examine the first line of each of five of the harmonizations. The melody is that of a secular song adopted into the hymn-books of the Lutheran Church, and these harmonizations of it come from the *St. Matthew Passion*, the *Christmas Oratorio*, and certain cantatas.

V.

1   2   3   4   5   6   7   8

The first thought that springs to mind as one examines these examples is their wonderful diversity. The soprano part is precisely the same throughout, but no two alto parts, tenor parts, or bass parts resemble one another.

The point as to the harmony of the period being based upon the major and minor key system may now be taken. Example I begins, as we are inclined to feel, momentarily in the key of A minor, but, if so, by beat 3 it gives the suggestion of having shifted to C major; at beats 6 and 7 it seems just momentarily to touch on G major, and at beat 8 to be back in C major. (Some will prefer to consider the F sharp at 6 to be mere 'chromatic colour', not effecting any modulation; in fact, in all such examples different ears tend to recognize slightly differing effects, it may be admitted.)

Example III begins in A minor, immediately goes into C major, and at the close is in A minor again.

Example IV begins in A minor, but at beat 3 goes into D minor and stays in it.

Example V is throughout in C major.

Example II is interesting. Until its very last chord we cannot assign it definitely to any one key. The feeling is most like A minor, but there are those very prominent G naturals. The fact is that a little of the old modal influence lingers here. We have here the exception that (because we feel it to be such) 'proves the rule'.

We may now pass to the second point—that the harmony is based on the **Triad.**

Looking at Example I we find that the chords on its seven beats are all arrangements, in some dispersed order, of a note with its third and fifth. Reducing these chords to their simplest terms, we find them to be as follows:

1   2   3   4   5   6   7   8

The lowest note of a triad when so set forth is called its **Root.** If the root is taken from the bass and placed in an upper part (as at beat 3) we say that the chord is in **Inversion** (first or second inversion, according as the third or the fifth is left in the bass).

At beat 6 in the example we have a triad with an added note, a root with its third and fifth plus its seventh. All the mere triads gave a feeling of satisfaction in themselves: they were **Concords.** This 'chord of the seventh' gives a feeling of restlessness: the ear is dissatisfied until it has passed to the next chord and the seventh itself (C) has moved to the note below (B). This chord of the seventh, then, is a

Discord—not necessarily, observe, a chord of harsh effect, but a chord that demands following in a certain way, i.e. **'Resolution'.**

At beat 1 we see a connecting note inserted in the bass. This is not a part of the harmony, but is a mere **Passing Note.**

At beat 2 we see two such notes inserted in the middle voices, but here the feeling seems to be of the creation of a new chord B, D, F, A, a chord of the seventh—duly resolved at beat 3, the seventh falling, as in the other case.

At beat 4 we see a note inserted in the alto, but here also we feel that a new chord has been created, the triad D, F, A thus subtly changing to the triad B, D, F, so that the new alto note is not properly a passing note.

Turning now to Example II, we see, at beat 1, passing notes running parallel in the bass and alto. (They are true passing notes, i.e. they do not create the feeling of a new chord.)

At beat 2 the chord is changed at its second half and we get a chord of the seventh, duly resolved. It is not intended to analyse all these examples in detail, but attention may be called to beats 6 and 7, where the triad is D, F, A, and, in the tenor, the D and the A are connected by the passing notes C and B.

In Example III is an instance of another kind of discord. At beat 5 the chord is the triad C, E, G, but though there is a C in the bass this one in the alto is delayed a moment, the D being held over from the previous beat and then falling to the C. This is a **Suspension.**

Example IV begins with a chord of the seventh (E, G sharp, B, D) resolved on beat 2, and at beat 3 has another chord of the seventh (a particularly pungent variety, a diminished seventh), duly resolved at the following beat. (Compare this restless *discordant* opening of the phrase with the peaceful *concordant* opening of Example V, and note how harmony can become the servant of emotion.)

This examination of a mere melodic phrase of eight beats, as 'clothed' by a master of harmony in the early part of the eighteenth century, does not, of course, reveal to us more than a tiny fraction of his harmonic resources, and still less of the harmonic resources of the whole long period mentioned above as what the ordinary listener feels to be the 'normal-harmony' period. There are very many other types of discord used during that period (especially from Wagner's middle phase onwards). But we at least see the most general principles of the period—the recognition of key and the use of the triad as the basis, with the decoration of it by the use of connecting or passing notes and suspensions and the 'gingering' of it by the addition of an extra third on the top of it (the seventh) and sometimes another on top of that (the ninth), and so on.

Having now grasped what we may call the normal conception of harmony (that, shall we say, of the reader brought up on what is still the standard concert repertory), we can look before and after and trace its genesis and its transformation.

4. The History of Harmony: Phase I. Parallelism and Perfect Intervals. The earliest conception of harmony (if at this stage we can make use of that word) seems to have been that of a mere parallel doubling, tripling, or quadrupling of the traditional plainsong. The plainsong had necessarily always been doubled in octaves whenever boys or women had joined with men in singing it, and in the ninth and tenth centuries (perhaps earlier) it became common to double it at the interval of the fifth or fourth. It is clear that this practice (called **Organum**) was a vocal convenience; a melody that suits tenors being, when transposed a fourth or fifth below, comfortable for basses, and these two parts when transposed an octave higher being comfortable for sopranos and altos. Herein may, conceivably, have been one motive behind the innovation.

The following example (from the tenth-century treatise *Musica Enchiriadis*; see *New Oxford History of Music*, vol. ii) shows the plainsong entrusted to a high tenor as 'Vox principalis' and paralleled at the interval of the fifth below by a bass, as 'Vox organalis'. Another bass then doubles the 'Vox principalis' in the octave below and a higher voice doubles the 'Vox organalis' in the octave above. So we get four-part harmony.

10th century.

Vox principalis.

Vox organalis.

Instead of the 'Vox principalis' being the top but one it might have been the bottom but one, or there might have been only two voices or only one voice accompanying: the interval between the 'Vox principalis' and the 'Vox organalis' might have been a fourth instead of a fifth. And so on, many varieties being possible; those are details, the essential being that the accompanying voices should move in the open intervals of fourth, fifth, and octave which, from a study of acoustical theory (such study preceding the practice of harmony by centuries) had come to be looked upon as the 'perfect intervals'—as which they still appear in our textbooks of harmony (see *Acoustics* 8, 15; *Scales* 4, 5).

The warning may be given that it is not quite fair to judge of the value of the process illustrated above by its effect when reproduced on the piano. Performed by voices, in good tone and a flexible manner, and with the plainsong emphasized above the accompanying parts (which latter were, probably, always entrusted to a smaller body of singers), these strings of consecutives are, to most ears today, far from unpleasant.

It may be observed that the 'Mixture' stop, which has for centuries been a feature of the organ (see *Organ* 2 c), is contrived on this same general principle—that of enriching a main note with fainter reproductions of those other notes that acoustics has shown to be closely related to it (see *Acoustics* 8).

Because of the prohibition by harmony textbooks of consecutive fifths, fourths, and octaves (a prohibition based on their forming no part of the system of music during the long period of, say, 1400 to 1900; see 22) this early practice of organum is now often looked upon as unnatural and hence inexplicable. Yet there is something instinctive about it; the two sexes singing together naturally sing in octaves and men and women street-singers in London have occasionally been noticed to be singing in parallel fifths; the boy Mozart and his father, in Venice in 1771, heard 'a duet in pure fifths sung by a man and woman in the street without missing a note'. Sir John Stainer complained at a Church Congress in 1894 that he once had his worship disturbed by an individual singing at the top of his voice 'uniformly a perfect fifth below the trebles'. The present writer was charged, when a youth, with the habit of accompanying any music he heard out of doors by whistling 'out of tune', but it was then pointed out by a more acute observer that his practice was unconsciously to whistle at the interval of a fifth (or an octave plus a fifth) higher; it has since appeared, from correspondence in the musical press, that this practice is not uncommon.

It is interesting to note that Russia practised organum up to the twelfth century and that Iceland, much cut off from the general currents of European art, still does so, its folk songs being sung according to this method (see *Scandinavia* 5).

The province of Alentejo in Portugal is said to be another place where singing largely in fourths and fifths still obtains.

Professor Kirby, of Johannesburg, has gramophonically recorded and then reduced to notation songs of un-Europeanized South African tribes, in fifths and octaves, almost exactly like the early European example given above, with the exception that, the usual South African scales being pentatonic, the maintenance of parallelism brings in an occasional interval of the sixth (this will be understood at once if the black notes of the piano, which represent the normal pentatonic scale, be played in parallel, starting a perfect fifth apart).

The present author has, in Professor Kirby's company, heard this singing in consecutive fifths in one of the mine compounds of Johannesburg. Records of Shona (= Mashona) singing, showing the same characteristic, have been made by Mr. Hugh Tracey, of the African Music Society, and are issued by the Columbia Company in South Africa. It is reported that in West Africa certain tribes sing in parallel thirds and that in Central Africa there is singing to be heard in fourths, in fifths, and in thirds.

A further instance of a European survival of the practice of singing in consecutive fifths is the following. It appears that in Treia, in the Marches of Ancona, Italy, folk songs may be heard in three-part harmony of consecutive common chords in their root positions (see *Musica d'oggi*, Dec. 1939).

We may fairly say then that the Icelanders, the Alentejans, and the African Bantus, etc., have, from a European point of view, harmonically reached the ninth century.

The following, by Albert Wellek (*Musik-pflege*, August 1932), is perhaps worth inserting here as indirectly illustrating the principle involved in the above discussion. It refers to recognition of notes heard:

'Having ascertained that I could never go wrong by a semitone (the two notes seem to me far too different in quality), but might under certain conditions go wrong by a fourth or fifth, I discovered by experiments at Vienna and Prague a number of good musicians who would never, or hardly ever, confuse two notes separated by a semitone, but went wrong by a fourth or fifth often enough for such errors to constitute fifty or seventy-five per cent. of the total number of their errors.'

(For a passing reference to the supposed singing in thirds of people in Britain in the tenth century see *Gymel*. For another term for organum see *Diaphony*.)

5. Phase II. A Tincture of the Non-Parallel and the 'Imperfect'. From parallel organum it seems to us today a smaller step than it perhaps actually was to an organum that did not scrupulously maintain parallelism and, also, admitted some admixture of 'imperfect' intervals (such as thirds and sixths). The following comes from *Scholia Enchiriadis Musica*, somewhat later than the *Musica Enchiriadis* from which the previous example came, upon which work it is a commentary:

Late 10th century.

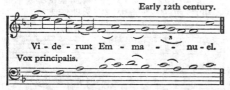

Vox principalis.

Vox organalis.

6. Phase III. Increased Freedom. What may be considered the next phase is that of **Descant** (q.v.), often carried out extemporaneously. Here one or more accompanying voices move in a free way against the steadier plainsong. The following is an example, in two parts, of the Paris school of the early twelfth century (example given by Gastoué; rhythm partially conjectural):

Early 12th century.

Vi - de - runt Em - ma - - - nu - el.
Vox principalis.

Naturally the introduction of freer rhythmic movement is important harmonically; it led in time to the coming into existence, largely by

what we call 'accident', of a variety of new combinations (remember the meeting of passing notes that formed chords in the Bach chorale examples)—a process that continued down to the days of Wagner and beyond.

A term which it is necessary to introduce here is **Canto Fermo** (It., 'fixed song')—applied to any piece of melody taken as the basis of a composition, other (and original) melodies being then woven into a fabric with it by the other voices (in 5 it is called 'Vox principalis').

7. Phase IV. The New Mastery of the Resources. The art of harmony is now obviously on the way to great expansion, and by the beginning of the fifteenth century we get such developed compositions as this of Dunstable. It is a secular song for tenor voice (from the Trent Codex) with a part for a bass voice and another for an instrument, perhaps a bowed one, and looks astonishingly modern (the bar lines, however, are an editorial addition). The composition may well be a harmonized treatment of a popular song—the song being given to an inner part to 'hold' just as the plainsong of the previous example was. But with Dunstable we find the occasional abandonment of the crutch of a *canto fermo*.

Early 15th century.

Puis-que m'a-mour m'a pris *(remainder of words not clear.)*
TENOR.

BASS.

8. Phase V. Polyphony in Perfection. We may now overleap a century or more of wonderful activity (in England, Flanders, Italy, Spain, and elsewhere) and take an example of the harmony of the high period of pure polyphony, with all the parts freely moving and the necessity of a *canto fermo* no longer recognized—the period of Palestrina, Lassus, Victoria, and Byrd. Here hundreds, if not thousands, of examples are today available in published form for actual performance by choirs, many of them showing the greatest skill in the management of the voice parts and the production of subtle and moving harmonic effects. The following example comes from the madrigal of Palestrina known in its English version as 'By flow'ry meadows'. We have here something that we can analyse on the same principles as we did our introductory Bach examples. It is not in a mode, but in the major key:

Late 16th century.

Lest the last two examples should lead the reader to suppose that composers had now, in gradually abandoning the modes, achieved at once a perfect command of the major and minor key system, the following passage, quaintly indeterminate in tonality, is added (from a virginal piece by Farnaby):

Late 16th century.

(We may find passages of wandering tonality a century and more later, in some of the ancient chorale tunes harmonized by Bach—tunes which, from their date of origin, unlike the chorale quoted at the opening of this article, were hardly susceptible of treatment according to the conventions of key.)

9. Phase VI. Harmony in a Dramatic Application. The following example of the same period (from the earliest existing opera, Peri's *Euridice*, 1600) is given to suggest the way in which the process of accompanying vocal recitative led composers to emphasize the emotional qualities of chords as such. The words here are a protest to 'cruel Death'. The accompaniment in the original is a mere line of notes plus figures, i.e. it is an example of the new *figured bass*—the technical device that showed a new attitude to harmony as a factor in itself, i.e. no longer as a by-product, however valuable, of the contrapuntal weaving of 'parts' (see articles *Opera*, *Recitative*, and *Figured Bass*).

Early 17th century.

Cru - da mor - te, ahi pur po - te - sti

10. Phase VII. Free Polyphony on a Harmonic Framework. This is the phase represented by the works of Handel, Bach, and their contemporaries. Bach's works are contrapuntally and harmonically much the most intricate of those of the greater composers of the period. With a clear, simple, and natural harmonic scheme in his mind, he sets to work

to 'decorate', and does this with such ease that until we analyse a given passage we do not realize that he was working to such a harmonic scheme. As an elementary example of the process the following (from his English Suite no. 5) may be given. The mental harmonic scheme is this:

The elaboration is this:

Early 18th century.

On this principle of contrapuntal elaboration Bach and Handel and their contemporaries construct whole movements, often of great length (a similar example from Handel was given at the opening of this article).

11. Phase VIII. Ease and Grace. The phase that followed was one of re-simplification. In the music of Bach's sons, Haydn, Mozart, the later eighteenth-century Italian opera composers, Arne, and others of that period, we do not find the complex polyphonic network of Bach and Handel. Indeed, such elaboration was now, for a time, and by many musicans, despised. Even Mozart, who greatly admired what he knew of the works of Bach, did not often emulate their depth and complexity. From his works, and from those of his elder contemporary Haydn (for example, from their string quartets) specimens of clever and effective counterpoint could be exhibited but (generalizing boldly) the typical quality of the period is grace, not profundity. Below is the introductory orchestral phrase to a soprano solo (the recitative 'Giunse alfin' il momento') in Mozart's *Figaro*. Here is a dainty bit of tune, very simply but not meagrely harmonized. This style was coming in during Bach's lifetime and was, perhaps, what he alluded to when, proposing to his son a visit to the neighbouring city, Dresden, to enjoy Italian opera,

Late 18th century.

Allegro vivace assai (very quick & vivacious).

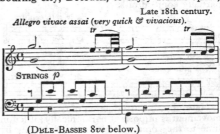

STRINGS *p*

(DBLE-BASSES *8ve* below.)

he would say 'Shall we go and hear pretty tunes?' (This is no denigration; if Bach went to hear music it was good enough—whatever its type.)

12. Phase IX. Emotional Intensity. We arrive now at the Beethoven–Schubert period (French Revolution, 'Sturm und Drang', and the passion and introspection of the *Werther* type of literature). The following is the opening of the air on which the well-known set of variations is based in Beethoven's Piano Sonata in A flat (op. 26);

Early 19th century.

Andante (at a steady, gentle pace).

There is here a typical richness of effect and emotional feeling. The tune at the top is simple and diatonic and the harmonization at first is peaceful. At the opening of the fifth measure the right-handful of notes includes (at the top) a strong example of what we have earlier in this article seen as a suspension, but here it has no 'preparation' (we call it an appoggiatura) and, moreover, the intruded D flat, which is to 're-solve' on to a C, is sounded simultaneously with a C in an inner part of the chord, so greatly intensifying the discordance. In the following measures (7, 8, and 9) the harmony includes several pungent discords of a 'chromatic' nature. Note that the final chord of the passage is the simple triad of E flat, G, B flat, but that the G and the B flat are momentarily withheld, being displaced by the notes a semitone below them (rising appoggiaturas, in fact). We shall see all this sort of chromatic work and intensification by temporary displacements greatly developed in the following phase.

13. Phase X. 'Romantic' Harmony. In the following typical passage from Wagner (*Parsifal*, Act I, where Gurnemanz leads Parsifal into the Hall of the Grail) we see a perfectly simple fundamental harmonic scheme profusely decorated in a very chromatic fashion: passing notes, appoggiaturas, and suspensions creep so naturally into the web of sound that it is difficult at first to realize that they are inessential to the harmonic framework.

Like Bach, Wagner has in mind a clear framework of harmonies, but, like him, he weaves his 'voices' so naturally as to give the impression that the counterpoint was his primary conception and that the harmonies are

(Slow and expressive.)   Late 19th century.

STRINGS *p*

The harmonic basis of the above.

D minor.

The harmonic basis of the above.

C minor.   B flat minor.

the mere outcome of the free movement of the melodies. Wagner is, in this sense, Bach reincarnate in a later age—the introducer of a new polyphony, a chromatic one in which the 'voices' creep about by semitones. It will be seen that we have as the harmonic basis shown merely a familiar progression in triads (some with the seventh added).

14. Phase XI. 'Impressionism' and the Whole-tone Scale. The vague, elusive harmonies of the French Impressionists and those who, in the latest years of the nineteenth century and the earliest of the twentieth, came under their influence, are illustrated in the following (from Debussy's *Island of Joy*, for piano):

1904.

Here we see a sustained 'pedal' C (see 24 p for explanation of 'pedal') and over it a passage constructed from the whole-tone scale of C. (Some may feel it to be, in effect, more an arpeggio than a scale.)

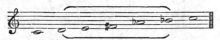

It will be observed that, although the preceding examples have covered a thousand years' activity, this is the first example yet given that gets clean away from the diatonic scale and the triad as the basis. Henceforth the rupture with the past is frequently to be almost complete.

15. Phase XII. Empirical Systems. Of the various attempts to secure new means of expression by the adoption of systems arbitrarily conceived we may take as our example that of Scriabin in his later works where he uses a synthetic scale C, D, E, F sharp, A, B flat, or, conceived rather as a chord of superposed fourths, C, F sharp, B flat, E, A, D. This scale or chord he uses, of course, at any pitch. Most people, when this scheme was first introduced, found it easier to enjoy its products in their soft and slow passages, finding loud and swifter ones rather brutal.

This group of notes offers, by selection, a very considerable variety of chord effects. The

following (a pianoforte passage from *Prometheus*) will illustrate its use: it is here taken at the pitch F sharp, G sharp, A sharp, B sharp, D sharp, E—or, regarded as a chord of superposed fourths, F sharp, B sharp, E, A sharp, D sharp, G sharp).

Very animated, scintillating.   1909.

The adoption of arbitrary systems has latterly taken an enormous extension. As an example see the entry *Note-row*.

16. Phase XIII. Chordal Streams. A frequent phenomenon in the harmony of the twentieth century is the use of consecutives quite in the old style of the organum of a thousand years before. The following example (from Vaughan Williams's 'Pastoral' Symphony) shows two-part counterpoint, each of the two strands being thickened in this way —as though two choirs of A.D. 1000 were performing in the same building:

Molto moderato (very moderate speed).   1922.

17. Phase XIV. Polytonality. Polytonality is not an absolutely new phenomenon of the twentieth century. Here is an example from Bach (extract from one of the four so-called 'Duetti' for clavichord or harpsichord; Peters edition, no. 208):

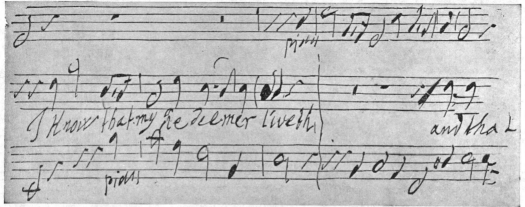

1. A HANDEL MANUSCRIPT—From his score of *Messiah*

2. CHARLES JENNENS, the Leicestershire squire who often entertained Handel at his country seat at Gopsal, and who compiled the libretti of *Messiah*, *Saul*, &c.

3. REV. THOMAS MORELL, D.D., who compiled the libretti of *Judas Maccabaeus*, *Theodora*, and others of Handel's oratorios

4. NEAL'S MUSIC HALL, DUBLIN, where *Messiah* was first performed. See *Ireland* 6

5. HANDEL'S SIGNATURE (*Frideric*, and not 'Frederick'; *Handel*, and not 'Händel' or 'Haendel')

6. HANDEL'S MEMORIAL IN WESTMINSTER ABBEY. It is by Roubiliac, and when it was erected in 1762 was said by those who had known the composer to present the best likeness of him extant

7. THE CHAPEL OF THE FOUNDLING HOSPITAL, London, of which Handel was a Governor. The organ was his gift and he himself eleven times directed performances of *Messiah* here, so raising the sum of £7,000 for the charity. (The hospital was in 1926 removed to the country and is now at Berkhamsted)

PLATE 77   INSTRUMENTS—ARCHAIC, EXOTIC, OR UNCOMMON, II

1. PSALTERY (13th century). See p. 838

3. OLD ZITHER (three in one —Treble, Tenor, and Bass) See p. 1127

4. 18TH-CENTURY 'BELL HARP'. See p. 101

2. PSALTERY (late 18th century)

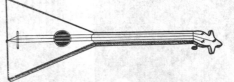

5. BALALAIKA. See p. 71

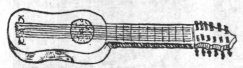

6. VIHUELA. See p. 1078

7. UKELELE. See p. 1059

8. CITTERN. See p. 189

9, 10. THE UNCHANGING DULCIMER. *Left*—15th-century carving in Manchester Cathedral. *Right*—as played by Moravian Gipsies in Czechoslovakia in the 1930's. See p. 306

For other pictures of old and uncommon instruments see pages 417, 465, 512–513, and 544–5

1739.

It will be seen that this is a canon (see *Canon*) at the fourth below; as it is a strict canon, all the intervals of the leading 'voice' are exactly imitated by the following 'voice', and since the key of the leading part is D minor modulating to G minor, that of the following part is necessarily A minor modulating to D minor. Here, then, we have a case of polytonality, but Bach has so adjusted his progressions (by the choice at the critical moment of notes common to two keys) that while the right hand is doubtless quite under the impression that the piece is in D minor, etc., and the left hand is in A minor, etc., the listener feels that the whole thing is homogeneous in key, though rather fluctuating from moment to moment. In other words, Bach is trying to make the best of both worlds—the homotonal one of his own day and (prophetically) the polytonal one of a couple of centuries later (it will be found that he 'gets away with it' better if his canon is played quickly).

The following example is from Ravel's Sonata for violin and cello. Here there is no pretence of 'give and take'; the two instruments go their own way 'regardless' (in both key and rhythm).

VIOLIN.   1922.
'CELLO.

It would seem that a new art of listening is required—one using the two ears independently (however, that would not serve for such works as Milhaud's Third Symphony for small orchestra, which has passages in which six different instruments carry six melodies simultaneously in six different keys).

Arguments in favour of polytonality (for what arguments may be worth in matters of art) are as follows:

A thousand years ago music passed from the stage of one line (unison) to the stage of several lines (polyphony); to an extent the modes then went by the board (for, whilst the plainsong upon which the composition was based observed its mode, it was not practicable to main-

tain all the accompanying parts in the same or any one mode, the limitations being too severe); thus a polymodal (or almost non-modal) type of composition may be said to have arisen. By and by the modes disappeared, replaced by our major and minor keys; for long every voice or strand of a composition was in the same key, but as history repeats itself we may feel that it was inevitable that in time there should come about independence of key in the various strands, as there had previously come independence of modal treatment.

A simpler similar argument is this: Since a thousand years ago we passed from homophony to polyphony, there is no reason why we should not now pass on from homotonality to polytonality.

Still another argument is based on the exhibition of a degree of something resembling polytonality in music for two centuries past in the form of chromatic appoggiaturas and the like. Look back at the Beethoven example (section 12). The A natural and F sharp in the last measure are coupled with an E flat that belongs to the normal key of the piece. They *may* be looked upon as a loan from some other key, in which case we are for a fraction of a second in two keys at one time, and if for a fraction of a second why not for five minutes?

Readers who have some harmonic experience will readily think of other arguments of this type.

Of course, a reply to all this is possible, and the following has been offered:

'The normal human ear cannot get into practically useful focus more than a limited number of lines of a score as (strictly) *simultaneously* realizable. The normal human ear realizes vertically; horizontal hearing of individual strands is a very limited affair. Unless we deceive ourselves by dodging rapidly about, the estimate that has been suggested of $1\frac{1}{2}$ strands as the utmost capable of receiving fixed attention is about right. (Of course, in music that we have heard before synthetic memory plays a large share, and in printed music there is the eye to help mental hearing.)

'The polytonalists appear to claim that the value of their work lies in the significance of the horizontal lines as such, and that the vertical element is quite disregardable. No such claim has been previously made in the history of music, even by the most advanced ultra-contrapuntalists. Is it not really asking the human ear to do more than it *can* do?'

18. Phase XV. Atonality. If polytonality be perpendicularly (instead of horizontally) considered, i.e. harmonically instead of contrapuntally, we already have atonality—the absence of key; for, looked at in this way, the keys brought into combination are mutually destructive, the chords they produce by their

1910.

p

impingement being, as such, referable to no key whatever. 'Ce n'est que le premier pas qui coûte', and it is but a small further step to abandon all pretence of key in any strand whatever. Schönberg does this as early as his Three Piano Pieces, op. 11.[1]

19. Phase XVI. Microtones (see separate article). For the sake of completeness an example of quarter-tone music is given (from Hába's String Quartet, op. 7, 1920). It cannot of course, be played on the piano, but probably some keen-eared readers may be able to 'feel' the effect. Two novel signs are used: the one with the projection turned to the right means that the note is to be sharpened a quarter tone, and the one with the projection turned to the left that it is to be flattened a quarter tone. As mentioned in the article *Microtone*, there were proposals for the use of quarter tones, with an appropriate notation, as early as the seventeenth century.

20. The Teaching of Harmony is essentially a branch of ear-training, yet in the past the subject has been taught almost as a branch of mathematics, and certainly students have passed examinations in it who had little idea of what their exercises sounded like. The instructions and treatises left by great composers of the eighteenth and early nineteenth centuries (e.g. by Bach, Mozart, Beethoven) seem to be no more pedagogically sound than those of the conscientious hack academics of the later nineteenth century, and in reading the treatises of somewhat earlier writers (e.g. Purcell—see reference under *Descant*) it is very difficult for us today to realize how the student was guided, by what he read, towards the production of actual music; such treatises often seem to be very haphazard collections of rules, sometimes stated in so broad a way as to be largely unworkable. Possibly in the past only students with some genuine gift attempted

[1] A friendly critic of this article writes:
'I believe atonalists repudiate atonality. "Key" may go but there is always a sense of tonal direction. I must say that in twelve-note music I always seem to hear the tonal direction clearly enough. I believe atonality does not, and cannot exist. Debussy thought (and so did his first hearers) that, with his whole-tone scale, he had destroyed tonality, but he had not! It may be really a matter of terminology but possibly also a result of some confusion of thought.'

composition, and they, we may suppose, learnt more by observation of the actual music of their predecessors and contemporaries than from textbooks (remember Bach's youthful incessant copying of music in order to learn thereby).

It must be remembered, however, that eighteenth-century textbooks are often rather treatises on the interpretation of figured bass, enabling the student to learn his duties as a keyboard accompanist, than treatises on composition, and that these treatises unfortunately set the method that was followed long after musicians had almost ceased to be called upon to accompany from anything but fully worked-out keyboard scores. The exercises in such books as Macfarren's (1860) and Stainer's (1878), which had an immense vogue in English-speaking countries, and E. F. E. Richter's (1876), which had such in German-speaking countries, have little musical suggestion, and study of them conferred, in effect, not much beyond an ability to draw four vocal parts out of the series of chords indicated by the figures attached to the given bass, duly resolving all discords that occurred: these exercises could be successfully worked by an intelligent and persevering student even if almost totally unmusical; such books were, therefore, fundamentally unsound (cf. some remarks on teaching in the article *Figured Bass*).

The later plan of using unfigured basses or melodies as the given materials of exercises makes a far more genuine call upon musical perception, but the first step should undoubtedly be the writing of exercises without even these materials (which are at once crutches and shackles), as, for instance, the filling in of mere rhythmic schemes supplied by the teacher or textbook, the student choosing his own chords from those he has, at any particular stage, been taught to recognize by ear.

Possibly Adolf Weidig of Chicago, though his views can certainly not be looked on as always balanced, was, at any rate, the pioneer in the provision of a textbook based neither on given basses nor melodies, and demanding original work throughout the course. The present writer, independently, produced a small elementary book of this sort in 1924.

It is a safe generalization that the student should never be called upon to write what he cannot mentally hear, and that thus the earliest lessons should give exercises in recognition of chords played on the piano—in fact, exercises in dictation.

The measure in which the contrapuntal and the harmonic sides should be combined in teaching is debatable, and may always remain so. There have been attempts to teach harmony through counterpoint, beginning with the writing of a single melodic line, following this by the writing of a combination of two melodic lines, passing on to the combination of three such lines, and so forth.

21. 'Rules' in Harmony. The foregoing historical sketch will have suggested to most readers the nature of the 'Rules of Harmony'. There is no such thing as a rule of eternal validity, just as there is no such rule in the grammar of language. Grammar grows out of language, not language out of grammar. Grammar is merely a codification of language practices at a particular date, and re-codification is needed as the practice changes. 'You was' used to be a perfectly grammatical expression, and up to the beginning of the twentieth century was still occasionally heard from older people in England, though already considered ungrammatical, so that younger people thought those survivors to have escaped a proper education, which was by no means always the case. There are many good old English expressions surviving in the United States that to an English ear sound wrong—and vice versa. On the other hand, the United States has introduced changes in the language that tend to be adopted in the original home of that language. The English language is in a perpetually fluid state, and so is music, and the grammars of both must therefore be fluid.

The above must not be misunderstood, however, as a suggestion that rules in harmony are a mere matter of fashion. Those rules (when they are not merely pedantic, as they sometimes are) are codifications of the practices which maintain the purity of a particular period-style. If formulated in a sufficiently complete fashion they may be said to constitute a definition of that particular style: write according to those rules, and you will at any rate keep pretty well within the style, however poor your music may otherwise be. Schumann said, 'Nothing is wrong that sounds right', and many other composers have said the same. Rules tell us what will and what will not sound right to normal unadvanced listeners of our own day; a student with abnormally strong observation and judgement could get on without them, but would lose time thereby. They are a short cut to the acquiring of a period technique, and little more.

There are psychological and even physical laws behind all valuable rules, and the more the pupil is encouraged to get behind the rules to the laws the better, because those laws are valid for all times and all styles, a rule being merely a means of bringing a law to bear on the requirements of a particular style. The rules are ephemeral, the laws eternal.

As an example, there are general laws governing the relation of discord and concord, but the rules prescribing the behaviour of any particular discord vary from century to century because as the public ear gets more and more used to a discord it becomes milder in effect, and no longer demands the same careful handling. The type of discord we call 'suspension' was once so pungent as to require 'preparation', whereas it later became so comparatively mild in effect that it was a commonplace to take it unprepared and call it an 'accented passing note'.

The rule here was that a particular form of discord must be prepared. The psychological law then, apparently, is the very general one that if discords are to have effect they must be preceded and followed by concord, and if they are to have intelligibility the way in which they come into existence and the way they go out of existence must be clear to the unconscious mind of the listener—or something like that. How this law (if it has been correctly stated) can be applied to the later compositions of Bartók or Stravinsky is not quite clear, but there is an application which will become plain at a later stage.

Referring to the physical law that lies behind the psychological law, it should be noted that discord and concord are relative terms. The science of acoustics (see *Acoustics* 16) shows that there is no line to be drawn between discord and concord. Chords are relatively more or less concordant or discordant. It is a matter of degree. There is only one complete consonance—the octave. All other intervals are in some measure dissonant, i.e. have some degree of harshness owing to the existence of a more or less perceptible throb or 'beat' set up by discrepancy in their vibration numbers. The degree of dissonance bearable differs according as the human ear is more or less accustomed to it. Thus a child musician born in 1900 heard around him, and became thoroughly accustomed by adult years to a degree of dissonance that would have shocked Palestrina. Hence such dissonances as did *not* shock Palestrina are consonances to the adult musician of today. It follows that we can none of us hear any of the older music as the people of the time heard it: we may conceivably love for its placid beauty music that when composed was loved for its bold vigour—to imagine an extreme case.

There is one gross anomaly about the rules of harmony today. In every other age the rules have been based more or less upon the music of the time. The *essentials* of music from Bach to Brahms were the same and hence the rules remained practically unchanged. We are still teaching on the basis of these rules (as every published harmony textbook shows—even Schönberg's). Yet not merely the *idiom* but the very principles of the art have changed. We are still teaching rules based on the major and minor key system and the triad to students who if they become composers will perhaps write atonally and take no account of the triad. We are compelled to this because the rules for the new period-style of music are not yet formulated—and perhaps not yet capable of formulation, the style itself being insufficiently settled (and, indeed, we are not yet quite sure that it ever will be settled).

For a further discussion of the idea of 'rules' in music see *Composition* 3.

22. Consecutives. The question of consecutives (already referred to in section 4) is often a puzzling one to the student. If the practice of harmony was originally nothing but performance in parallel perfect intervals, why is such parallelism (especially of fifths and octaves, of course) forbidden to the harmony pupil of today?

It will have been realized from what has just been said that as there is no fixed criterion of harmony, but merely a constant flux, it is impossible to teach the pupil harmony as such, and what he is really taught is 'period harmony', the period chosen being naturally that in which the largest portion of the present repertory was written—that long period that takes in all the 'classical' and 'romantic' composers from Bach to Chopin. During this period (and indeed for some time before and after it) consecutive perfect intervals were looked at askance for the practical reason that they weakened the part-writing. An octave duplication of a few notes of a melodic strand makes those few notes stand out unnaturally and, at the same time, practically reduces by one the number of strands; these effects are particularly felt in any type of composition in which a definite number of 'parts' or 'voices' is in use, as, for instance, a normal choral composition. If this effect be desired on any occasion as an artistic manœuvre the composer has a perfect right to his octaves, but if it occurs fortuitously it merely points to deficient craftsmanship, and hence the student must learn how to evade such parallelism when he wants to do so.

The effect of parallelism in the fifth is something the same as that of parallelism in the octave, but less marked, and that of the fourth is the same again, only a good deal less marked still (so that the rules about consecutive fourths are much less stringent). Parallelism in the third or sixth does not have this effect. Parallelism in the second or seventh is parallelism of strong discords, all of which, in the practice of the period mentioned, have a normal 'resolution' which is thus precluded.

It should be noted that 'consecutives' on various instruments and in the orchestra are much less observable than in pure choral writing in so many parts. We find Peacham, in his *Compleat Gentleman* (1634), praising Marenzio's madrigals for their 'delicious Aire and sweet Invention . . . though sometimes an oversight (which might be the Printers' fault) of two eights or fiftes escapt him'. Probably similar 'eights or fiftes' occurred in some of the lute music Peacham heard without his noticing them. It is quite certain that hundreds of consecutives must have occurred in harpsichord accompaniment of solo vocal, string, choral, and other music, in Peacham's day and right through the long period when such accompaniment was invariable yet the harpsichordist's copy merely a line of 'figured bass', so that he had no knowledge of the other parts written by the composer. Domenico Scarlatti (1685–1757), in a preface to his harpsichord compositions, apologized for his many consecutive fifths; such an apology was merely a way of informing pedantic purchasers that what they might otherwise have taken for composer's or printers' errors were intended effects. In the nineteenth century Chopin, Grieg, Dvořák, and other composers have occasional long passages in consecutive fifths. The seventeenth-century Italian composer Picchi (q.v.) uses them as a standing feature in his idiom.

23. The Harmony of the Future. It is impossible to forecast the harmonic procedure of fifty years hence. We are still passing through a highly experimental phase, and the experiments are going on in a good many directions at one time. One such is in the direction of quarter-tones, but will the ears of a human race whose solo vocalists have not yet learnt to sing its tones and semitones invariably in tune be able successfully to perform in quarter-tones, and will audiences be able to distinguish them, when heard, from mere out-of-tune performance?

Is there a limit to the 'size' of interval that the ear can perceive? And if the employment of quarter-tones be the next logical step forward, what can we imagine will be the steps after that? Eighth-tones? Sixteenths? Obviously progress in that direction has its limits (see *Microtones*).

24. Some Definitions of Common Terms in Harmony.

(a) **Diatonic Harmony** is harmony which confines itself to the major or minor keys in force at the moment, as distinct from **Chromatic Harmony**, which employs notes extraneous to that key; figuratively, then, we may say that diatonic harmony is plain food without condiments. Roughly speaking, chromatic harmony begins, with the Romantics, to be a basic part of the musical language, and it becomes almost the rule with Wagner; but earlier composers are often very chromatic, as Bach in certain compositions.

(b) **Open Harmony** is that in which the notes of the chords are spread widely, as distinct from **Close Harmony**, in which they lie near together. (Usually the bass is exempted from this requirement, i.e. if the upper parts lie near together the harmony is spoken of as 'close' or as in **Close Position**.)

(c) **Progression** means merely the motion of one note to another note, or one chord to another chord. Thus we may speak of 'an ineffective progression' when a chord, perfectly good in itself, passes to another also perfectly good in itself but awkward in conjunction with the first one.

(d) Any combination of notes simultaneously heard can be called a **Chord**, though usually incidental notes such as passing notes, appoggiaturas, and the like are not considered part of the chord. A three-note chord consisting of a note with its third and fifth is, as above explained, known as a **Triad**. A triad of which the fifth is a perfect one is a **Common Chord**. A common chord of which the third is major is a **Major Common Chord**, and one of which the third is minor is a **Minor Common Chord**. A Triad with an Augmented Fifth is called an **Augmented Triad** and one with a Diminished Fifth is called a **Diminished Triad**.

1. ASSYRIAN LYRES

2. CLÀRSACH—Tristan teaching Isolde
(Chertsey Tiles, British Museum)
See *Clàrsach*

3. WELSH HARPER (John Roberts), using the Triple Harp—chromatic without pedal
See *Harp* 2

4. CLÀRSACH—Henry VIII as performer (and his Court Fool as candid critic). From a manuscript in the British Museum

5. PLEYEL CHROMATIC HARP in the year of its introduction, 1897
See *Harp* 1

6. DOUBLE ACTION PEDAL HARP
See *Harp* 2 d

7. CLÀRSACH—Marjorie and Patuffa Kennedy-Fraser (1916)

PLATE 79 THE HARPSICHORD IN ITS THREE VARIETIES

See the Article on pages 457–60

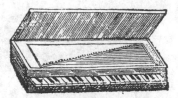

1. EARLY VIRGINALS (from Virdung's *Musica Getutscht*, the earliest printed work on musical instruments, Basel, 1511) See *Harpsichord Family* 3

2. VIRGINALS by Ruckers, Antwerp, 1610

3. VIRGINALS. Engraving by Goltzius, *c.* 1600 (note the manner of holding the hand; and cf. p. 193, pl. **39.** 5, 7)

4. THE LESSON ON THE VIRGINALS (unknown Dutch master of 17th century)

5. HANDEL'S SPINET. See *Harpsichord Family* 4

6. HARPSICHORD by Shudi and Broadwood, 1770 See *Harpsichord Family* 5

(*e*) The note from which a chord *originates* is called its **Root**; for instance, the root of the major common chord (or 'five–three' chord) C, E, G is C; the root of the chord of the seventh, G, B, D, F is G; and so on.

(*f*) When the root of a chord is in the bass the chord is in **Root position**; when it is not in the bass we have an **Inversion**. If the third is in the bass it is a **First Inversion** (also spoken of as 'chord of the 6th' or 'six–three' chord), if the fifth it is **Second Inversion** (also spoken of as 'six–four' chord); in a chord of the seventh, if the seventh is in the bass it is a **Third Inversion**—and so on.

(*g*) In addition to the actual bass of a passage, we can imagine a bass consisting of the roots of all the chords; that is what is meant by **Fundamental Bass**. This realization of the fact that the chord E, G, C (a 'six–three' chord) is essentially the same as the chord C, E, G (a 'five–three' chord), with the consequent theory of roots and of a fundamental bass, did not arise until the early eighteenth century (largely through Rameau).

(*h*) An interval or chord which, so to speak, enjoys a certain amount of self-satisfaction is a **Concord**, whilst one which restlessly tries to push on to something in front is a **Discord**: the words **Consonance** and **Dissonance** have similar meanings. (But see 21 for the purely relative application of these terms.)

Note that the word 'Discord' is sometimes more narrowly applied to the particular *note* of an interval or chord which is responsible for the onward urge—the irritant matter of the chord, so to speak.

(*i*) The progression of a discordant note or chord to its note or chord of satisfaction is called its **Resolution**.

(*j*) A **Fundamental Discord** is one (such as an ordinary chord of the seventh) existing as a chord with an entity of its own. (There are chords of the ninth, eleventh, and thirteenth also, and these, too, are 'Fundamental Discords'.) See (*k*) below.

(*k*) The distinction above is from discords that arise as the result of **Suspensions**—i.e. (properly) the holding over momentarily of a note from one chord into the next one, to which it does not belong, it then falling a degree to the note whose place it has taken. At one time suspensions all had **Preparation**; later, as they became familiar to the ear, it was found not essential always to prepare them, and thus we have (perhaps a contradiction in terms) **Unprepared Suspensions**. The commonest notes to be deferred by the interpolation of a suspension are the third and the octave from the root; both may be deferred together, and then we have a **Double Suspension**. Or, the bass moving, the rest of the chord may be held back, and then we have **Suspension of the Chord**.

(*l*) There exists the equivalent of a suspension but with the suspended note resolved upwards instead of downwards; the name for this is **Retardation**.

(*m*) Occasionally one or more notes of a chord are heard before their time, i.e. before the rest of the harmony is changed. The effect is called **Anticipation**. Or the whole chord, obviously expected by the ear on (say) the first of the measure, may appear just before it (i.e. at the end of the previous measure) and then be repeated at its proper moment: this also is called Anticipation.

(*n*) Occasionally the harmony proceeds in such a way that a B flat appears in one chord and a B natural in the next, an F natural in one and an F sharp in the next, and so on—the two notes of the same letter-name appearing not in the same 'voice' or 'part' (e.g. in a four-part choral composition one chord might have a C sharp in the tenor and the next a C natural in the soprano). This is called **False Relation**. The normal scholastic rule is that false relation should be avoided (as, for instance, in the above case, by following the C sharp in the tenor by C natural *also in the tenor*). But there are many cases where the effect of false relation is not bad, and the rule admits of many exceptions. In music of the sixteenth and early seventeenth centuries false relations are rather common, and it is clear that until a realization of the full sense of the major and minor key system had been attained they were little regarded.[1] In the music of certain composers of this period we may even find simultaneous false relations, as, for instance, a chord in which one 'voice' or 'part' has the major third from the root and another the minor third (almost a faint prophecy of polytonality).

(*o*) Consecutive octaves and fifths have been explained in the course of the discussion above (section 22). There are also progressions called **Hidden Octaves** and **Hidden Fifths**, formerly rather rigorously proscribed by the textbooks but now usually either tolerantly winked at or totally ignored. They occur when some interval proceeds to the octave or the fifth by similar motion (i.e. both notes of the first interval ascending to the said octave or fifth, or both descending to it). If a little thought be given it will be seen that in such a case it is possible for the purist to imagine that consecutive octaves or fifths, though not present to eye (or ear?), exist in hiding. It is especially when two 'voices' concerned are the outermost ones that this progression is supposed to be a fault. There is rarely ground for its condemnation.

(*p*) **Pedal** (cf. *Form* 12 d) is an ancient, often-used, and generally highly effective device in harmony—especially in the building up of a climax. Imagine an organist keeping his foot on one of the pedals and so producing a persistent bass note, whilst his hands move freely to chords of which that note does not form any constituent part. Or imgaine a kettledrummer sounding a long-continued roll on a note whilst the other instruments proceed to chords to which that note is a stranger—a very common

---

[1] The critic already quoted (who is a specialist in the older music) writes:
'For "little regarded" read "greatly admired". The effect, when well and deliberately used, is lovely.'

thing. The most usual notes thus to be used as pedals are the tonic and dominant (i.e. the keynote and the fifth note, the doh and the soh).

Inverted Pedal is the same device but with the persistent note in an upper part: a **Double Pedal** is the same device with two different persistent notes (usually tonic and dominant).

It is quite possible that the conception of harmony first began with the device of pedal, for early instruments have it (the hurdy-gurdy, q.v., and the bagpipes with their 'drones'); also it is today common amongst oriental races that otherwise use notes purely melodically.

ARTICLES ON COGNATE SUBJECTS: *Acoustics*; *Scales*; *Modes*; *Tritone*; *Musica Ficta*; *Melody* 5 (for harmonic basis of much melody); *Counterpoint*; *Faburden*; *Descant*; *Gymel*; *Motet*; *Ars Nova*; *Hocket*; *Sequence*; *Cadence*; *Tierce de Picardie*; *Figured Bass*; *Vamping*; *Rhythm* 7; *History of Music*. See also *Wales* 4, and for a suggestion that the idea of harmony originated (in Europe) in Gothic vaulting and its echoes see *Concert Halls* 4.

HARP

(For illustrations see p. 452, pl. **78**; 465, **82**. 6; 1104, **184**. 3.)

1. Construction. The principle of the harp is that of a series of strings stretched over an open frame and set in vibration by the fingers. Each string produces one note, as in the pianoforte.

Describing the modern orchestral instrument (p. 452, pl. **78**. 6), it may be said that (unlike the pianoforte) its series of strings is not chromatic (with the exception of a special form of the instrument to be mentioned shortly); they represent seven notes to the octave (not the pianoforte's twelve), the seven being those of the major scale of B, for convenience treated as that of C flat.

There are seven pedals, each affecting one note of that foundational scale; each pedal works to two notches, and by depressing it to its first and second notch respectively the vibrating length of the corresponding strings can be shortened by fractions representing a semitone and a tone.

Thus all keys are possible, and obviously by depressing all pedals simultaneously to one notch, the pitch of the whole instrument can be raised from C flat to C natural, or, by depressing them to two notches, to C sharp.

The fact that changes of pitch are obtained by mechanical means, and that these means alter not merely one note but several (i.e. that same note in all octaves), is an obvious limitation. To put it in another way, the instrument is closely tied to the seventeenth- and eighteenth-century diatonic system. Fundamentally its arrangements represent the diatonic scales which followed the 'modal' period (see *Modes*), and which preceded the nineteenth-century chromaticism of which Wagner is the first great representative. The player, by the use of his seven pedals, within their various possible positions, can set his instrument to all diatonic scales, and all manner of chords, 'common' and uncommon, and then sweep his hand over them. But the very word 'set' suggests restrictions.

This 'sweeping' method is the main method of producing chords on the harp and has given rise to the common term 'arpeggio' applied to any chord of which the notes are produced not simultaneously but in succession. Of course, in addition to this typical 'glissando' chord and scale technique, there is that of the plucking of strings as individuals, obviously of limited application. (See also *Acoustics* 8.)

The 'double-action' harp (that described above) is due to the invention of Sebastian Erard, about 1810 (cf. *Pianoforte* 8); its main advantages over the previous 'single-action' harp derive from the ability to raise the pitch either a tone or a semitone, instead of only a semitone; this is what is meant by 'double-action'.

To what has just been said a reservation must now be made. A *Chromatic Harp* does exist (p. 452, pl. **78**. 5). It needs no pedals, since it possesses a string for every semitone—so nearly doubling the number of strings. Against its admitted advantages are counterbalanced the facts that it involves the learning of a new technique and that the old diatonic *glissandos* are impossible, and the allegation that the tone is poor. This form of the instrument has been taken up less in Britain than in some other countries: that it will displace the diatonic harp is still considered doubtful; however, it has continued in existence since 1897, when Messrs. Pleyel, of Paris, introduced it.

2. History. The harp is ancient and universal; there is record of it, in some form, in every age of human history and in every place inhabited by men or spirits—except Hell. Paintings of it have been discovered in the necropolises of Thebes dating from the thirteenth century B.C., and remains of actual specimens in Egyptian tombs date from long before that. It was popular with the ancient Greeks and Romans. It appeared early in British history and remained longest in popular use in those parts of the British Islands where descendants of the ancient races were least disturbed and where the customs of 'civilization' advanced most slowly (Wales, Ireland, and the Scottish Highlands). In the British Museum are fragments of a harp found in the Anglo-Saxon ship-grave at Sutton Hoo, Suffolk: Arnold Dolmetsch (q.v.) made a reconstruction of this. Vincenzo Galilei, father of the great natural philosopher and one of the promoters of the new opera movement in Italy, writes in 1589 that the Italians derived their knowledge of the harp from the Irish, and the Italian harps which formed a frequent part of the orchestras of the earliest operas were, indeed, still much on the model of the Irish harp. (For some further particulars of the Irish harp and harpers see *Ireland* 5; *Clàrsach*; the latter makes some reference to the smaller forms of the harp which were long widespread and are now being revived. And see p. 452, pl. 78. 2, 4.)

The harp is possibly the only musical instrument adopted as a national symbol. During the Commonwealth it appeared in the British flag as representing Ireland, and at the present time the southern Irish always greet visitors to their shores with this suggestion of harmony somewhat incongruously displayed upon the caps of their customs officers.

The Welsh bards were famous harpists, and at one period the harp was the only possession that the laws of Wales did not allow to be seized for debt. Every noble home in Wales possessed its hereditary harp, handed down the generations for the use of the domestic bard. Up to near the end of the nineteenth century many villages in Wales boasted their harper or family of harpers: the last harp-maker in Wales was probably Abram Jeremiah of Llanover, who died some time during the 1880s. (For some further particulars of the Welsh harp and harpers see *Wales* 2, 4, 5.)

In the early Victorian days, when in every refined English family one of the gentlemen played the flute (see *Flute Family* 4), one of his sisters or daughters was usually capable of accompanying him upon the harp—which of all instruments most incites the performer to graceful action and particularly to the display of well-rounded arms. Messrs. Stainer and Barrett, in 1876, in the *Dictionary of Musical Terms*, deplore the weakening of this drawing-room cultivation of the instrument, consequent upon the ageing of the generation that had initiated it, and do so in terms that do more credit to their penetration than to their gallantry— 'As the fair performers grew old the charms of the harp decayed, and although the instrument is still played and taught, it is not cultivated to the extent that its merits might seem to warrant.'

Something has been said above about the introduction of certain definite improvements in the construction of the instrument, but it will be well to set these out here a little more definitely.

(*a*) The **Welsh Harp**, or **Telyn** (p. 452, pl. 78. 3), which we will take as one of the more advanced examples of the simple type of instrument, had three rows of strings, the two outer giving the diatonic scale and the inner one the intermediate semitones. The two outer rows might in different specimens be tuned either in unison with one another or in octaves. A simple

modulation could be effected by touching a string of the inner row. (See also *Wales* 4). It is said that the strings were of horse-hair (those of the English harp were of gut and those of the Irish harp of wire).

(*b*) The **Double Harp** had but two rows of strings, tuned diatonically. Any accidental could be played only by shortening the sounding-length of a string by the thumb whilst plucking it with the finger. It was, then, in that respect more primitive than the Welsh instrument. Praetorius, however, in the early seventeenth century, describes a double harp 'with all semitones'.

(*c*) The **Single-Action Pedal Harp** (said to have been invented by a Bavarian maker, Hochbrucker, of Donauworth, in 1720) represented an enormous step in advance, since by the use of the pedals any string could be immediately shortened in sounding-length and so altered in pitch by a semitone. The player was, however, embarrassed by many clumsinesses and imperfections in the mechanism, and these rendered some keys impracticable. A considerable improvement upon this form was effected by the Parisian harpist and instrument maker, Cousineau, in the 1780s and 1790s. Hochbrucker's Pedal Harp was an improvement on an instrument introduced by an unknown (Tyrolese?) maker some few years earlier—on much the same system but with the string-shortening apparatus actuated by the left hand, thus unsatisfactorily leaving the actual playing to the right hand. This was called, *Hakenharfe*, i.e. 'Hook Harp', or, in French, *Harpe à crochets*.

(*d*) The **Double-Action Pedal Harp** (p. 452, pl. 78. 6) introduced by Erard about 1810 has (as already explained) seven pedals so contrived that each can be depressed to a lesser or greater extent according as the string is to be shortened to the extent of a semitone or a tone's alteration in pitch. Many other improvements in the details of the building of the instrument add to its effectiveness. This is the form of the instrument the introduction of which led to such activity in the English drawing-rooms referred to above, and it is, essentially, the harp as it is generally heard today.

(*e*) The **Chromatic Harp** of Pleyel (p. 452, pl. 78. 5) has been sufficiently described above.

(*f*) As a by-way in the history of the instrument it may be added that in the late eighteenth century some small specimens were on sale with finger-keys added on the post. From surviving specimens they seem to have been quite effective (cf. *Dital Harp*).

3. Orchestral Use. As already stated, the harp was a frequent member of the orchestras employed in the performance of the first operas in Italy in the early years of the seventeenth century. Harpsichords, lutes, and harps here supplied that background of 'figured bass' (q.v.) which was a characteristic of all orchestral music in those days.

Later the harp almost disappeared from the orchestra. There is no single instance of its use by Bach. **Handel** used it a few times; and in *Esther* (1720) he provided parts for the Welsh harp in order to avail himself of the services of two Welsh players, the Powells.

Gluck used it in *Orpheus* (1762). At this period the instrument rarely appeared in a score except as 'local colour'.

Haydn and **Mozart** did not use the harp orchestrally except that the latter wrote one concerto for harp and flute, with orchestra. **Beethoven** provided a part for it in his *Prometheus* music.

The Romanticists were strongly individual in their attitude towards the instrument. Weber ignored it. **Berlioz** used it largely; in France he seems to have had no difficulty in getting his harp parts performed, but in Germany he complained of the great difficulty in finding players. Mendelssohn, Schumann, and Brahms used it very little; Liszt and Wagner much (in the Finale in *Rhinegold* six harps are heard, each performing its own independent scheme of arpeggios so that the Gods may enter Valhalla to heavenly music).

The Impressionist school initiated by Debussy (see *Impressionism*) found in the harp an admirable exponent of the misty and mystical, and nowadays two harpists are to be seen on the platform on most occasions when large-scale works of late-nineteenth- or of twentieth-century origin are to be heard.

The silvery tone of the harp is particularly pleasing. A mere touch of it in an orchestral composition may have an electrical effect, but with any excessive use the charm quickly wanes. The harp is, then, rarely able to contribute to the staple of the musical texture of a composition, but it provides a delightful embellishment. It was the complaint of Carlos Salzédo, that '*in general orchestral harp parts are a sort of compromise between the piano and an imaginary harp. . . . Richard Strauss's scores, for instance, are filled with such unharpistic parts.*'

Harp concertos are rather rare, as it is difficult for the instrument to sustain a solo interest in competition with the more melodic instruments of the orchestra. The celebrated Bohemian harpist, Johann Baptist Krumpholz (*c.* 1745–90) wrote six, Reinecke, in the late nineteenth century, one, and amongst more recent concertos, or quasi-concertos, are the following: 1927, Salzédo (harp and wind instruments); 1935, Wagenaar (triple concerto for flute, harp, cello, and orchestra); 1938, Glière; 1940, Hanson (Serenade for flute, harp, and strings); 1944, Nicolai Berezovsky; 1945, Morton Gould (*Harvest* for strings, harp, and vibraphone); 1947, Dello Joio; 1952, Křenek.

4. The Solo and Chamber Music Repertory. There is a lack of solo music for the harp, most of what is available having been produced in the days when the instrument was more one of fashion than of art.

Haydn wrote a Sonata for flute, harp, and double-bass, and **Spohr** left a few pieces.

The great harpist **Bochsa** (1789–1856) left music of no high artistic worth and his most eminent pupil, the Englishman **Parish-Alvars**, operatic fantasias and the like. These two were normal specimens of the producers of harp-fodder of their day, being more harpist-composers than composer-harpists.

Saint-Saëns always wrote well for the harp in his orchestral works, and he composed an effective Fantasia for violin and harp. The influence of **Debussy** has already been mentioned: his Sonata for flute, viola, and harp began a new vogue and set a new standard. The French composers pay the harp great attention, and some examples of their love and understanding of it are seen in **Ravel's** Septet for strings, flute, clarinet, and harp; **Roussel's** Serenade for flute, violin, viola, violoncello, and harp; **Inghelbrecht's** Sonatina for flute and harp, and Quintet for strings and harp; and **Florent Schmitt's** Quartet for strings and harp (which last is interesting as calling for the use of the chromatic harp above mentioned).

The Dutchman **Sem Dresden** has composed a Sonata for flute and harp.

Some British composers have given attention to the instrument, especially **Bax**, who wrote a Sextet for strings, harp, and cor anglais, a Sonata for viola and harp, and a Sonata for flute and harp. **Goossens** has written a Sonata for flute, violin, and harp.

Amongst American composers who have remembered the existence of the harp are **Daniel Gregory Mason** (Suite for flute, harp, and string quartet), and **Mabel Daniels** (*Songs of Elfland*, for soprano, women's chorus, flute, harp, strings, and percussion).

The popularity of the harp in the United States has been greatly increased by the activity of Salzédo (see *Concerto* 6 c; 1885), and additions to the repertory from this country are many.

Amongst composers who have provided songs with accompaniment in which the harp plays an important part are **Ethel Smyth**, **Falla**, and **Webern**.

Some Latin Americans are **Ginastera** (*Cantos del Tucuman*, soprano, flute, violin, harp, and two drums) and **Villa Lobos** (Nonet for wood-wind, harp, celesta, and choir).

In 1947 there were reports of an underwater performance on an Irish harp fitted with waterproof nylon strings.

For the twentieth-century revival of the Celtic harp and other small harps see under *Clàrsach*. For *Bell Harp*, *Dital Harp* (*Harp Lute*; *Harp Guitar*), *Aeolian Harp*, and the so-called *Jew's Harp* see under those heads.

For the so-called *French Harp* see *Reed-Organ Family* 10 b.

For Beethoven's so-called 'Harp Quartet' see *Nicknamed Compositions* 4.

HARPE À CROCHETS. See *Harp* 2 c.
HARP QUARTET (Beethoven). See *Nicknamed Compositions* 4.

HARPSICAL. Same as harpsichord (q.v.)—an eighteenth-century English corruption of this word, possibly to parallel 'virginal'.

HARPSICHORD FAMILY
(Virginals, Spinet, Harpsichord)

1. Introductory.
2. The Principle of Tone Production.
3. The Virginal or Virginals.
4. The Spinet.

5. The Harpsichord Proper.
6. A 'Bach' Specification.
7. The Decline of the Spinet and Harpsichord.

8. Varying Names for the Instrument.
9. Some Leading Composers.

(For illustrations see p. 193, pl. **39**; 453, **79**; 608, **106**. 3.)

1. Introductory. In its three forms of virginals, spinet, and harpsichord proper, the harpsichord was the favourite domestic keyboard instrument from the beginning of the sixteenth century to the end of the eighteenth. In its most developed form, that of the harpsichord proper, it also served (except when replaced by the organ) as the supporting basis of almost every instrumental combination during the period of the development of chamber music and the orchestra—roughly 1600 to 1800 (see *Chamber Music* 3; *Orchestra* 2; *Conducting* 3). An understanding of its nature and history is hence of high importance to an understanding of the history of music. The plan adopted in the present article is first briefly to explain the main principle of its construction and then to discuss severally the three forms in which it was found.

2. The Principle of Tone Production. Keyboard stringed instruments fall into two classes: (*a*) that of the clavichord (q.v.) and pianoforte (q.v.), in which the string is *struck*, and (*b*) that of the harpsichord, in which it is *plucked*. It will be realized, then, that whilst the clavichord and pianoforte are closely related to the dulcimer (q.v.), the harpsichord derives from the psaltery (q.v.).

In the harpsichord (in all its three forms) the strings lie horizontally, and on the finger-keys being depressed small pieces of wood called **Jacks**, provided with plectra, rise. The plectra are quills (or sometimes points of leather); they pass the strings, plucking them in passing; the jacks then fall back and the plectra, by means of an escapement, repass the strings without plucking them. The tone thus produced is a sort of agreeable twang. An unappreciative American humorist has described it as 'a scratch with a sound at the end of it', and a still more unappreciative English one as suggesting 'a performance on a bird-cage with a toasting-fork'; the authors of these libels, however, were undoubtedly biased by long familiarity with the modern domestic keyboard instrument; the harpsichord must be listened to as an instrument in its own right, with its own quality of tone and scale of resonance—not as an imperfect pianoforte, and then it is hardly likely that an instrument that gave pleasure to every musician from Byrd to Mozart will fail to give pleasure to us.

The amount of tone of the harpsichord can be substantially modified only by certain mechanical means available in the more developed instruments. In other words, the speed and pressure of the finger does not in any prominent degree affect the volume of sound. Slight accentuation is, however, possible and 'touch' evidently had some meaning, since the French player Chambonnières (1602–72) had a very special reputation for the quality of tone he drew from the strings, and Couperin, in his *Art de toucher le clavecin* (1717) drily inquired how it could be, if touch made no difference, that two players sitting down in turn at the same harpsichord made such profoundly different sounds.

For the difference between the harpsichord and the clavichord in this matter of expression through finger action see *Clavichord* 4.

3. The Virginal or Virginals (see plates) is the earliest and simplest form of harpsichord, with only one string to a note. It is oblong in shape, as a rule a mere box of varying size suitable to be placed on a table, though sometimes it stands upon a four-legged frame. The strings run from right to left of the player, i.e. parallel to the keyboard.

The origin of the name is disputed: it does not, as has often been stated, lie in the fact that the virgin queen, Elizabeth I of England, played the instrument, as the word was in use before she was born; perhaps it meant an instrument for young ladies, and as supporting this idea it seems worthy of note that the first music printed for the instrument in England was called *Parthenia* (q.v.), i.e. 'Maidens' Songs', and bore on the title-page a picture of a young lady playing (p. 193, pl. **39**. 5).

The term 'Pair of Virginals' was in use (so was 'Pair of Organs'; cf. the present French usage, 'les orgues'): the origin of this term also is unsettled; a likely derivation is that which finds an analogy in 'pair of steps' (meaning a flight of stairs, i.e. a gradation), or it may mean simply a *set* of keys in a keyboard (cf. Cornish usage a 'pair of miners', for a gang; or Chaucer, a 'pair of beads', for a rosary; recall also German 'ein paar', a few).

The period of the virginals was roughly that of the sixteenth and seventeenth centuries, but in the latter half of the seventeenth it was declining, being superseded by the spinet and the fully developed harpsichord proper.

The English virginal music is of the highest

importance in the history of music, as it shows the earliest considered development of the resources of a keyboard instrument. There is a large body of this music in the four chief contemporary manuscript collections remaining, the *Fitzwilliam Virginal Book* (published 1894–9), *My Ladye Nevell's Booke* (published 1926), *Will Forster's Virginal Book* (British Museum), and *Benjamin Cosyn's Virginal Book* (published 1923); in addition, there is the first volume of music printed for this instrument, *Parthenia* (1611; reprinted 1847 and since): all these collections will be found to have brief entries under their own names.

In loose usage, up to near the end of the seventeenth century, the word 'virginals' was often continued in Britain for *any* quilled instrument, including the spinet and the harpsichord. The names have never been so distinct as the instruments.

For some English virginal composers see *Mundy, John*; *Gibbons, Orlando*; *Byrd*; *Farnaby*; also *Pianoforte* 20. For four-handed virginal music see under *Pianoforte* 21. For the virginal in Scotland see *Scotland* 3. For the pitch at which the old English virginal music should properly be played see *Pitch* 2.

4. The Spinet (p. 453, pl. **79**. 5). This resembles the virginals in having only one string to a note, but differs from it in being not rectangular but wing-shaped (Pepys sometimes calls it the 'triangle virginal' or merely 'tris angle'); the shape, it will be realized, follows roughly the curves prescribed by the varying lengths of the strings, as does that of the modern grand pianoforte. And whereas in the virginals the strings ran from right to left of the player, i.e. parallel to the keyboard, in the spinet they ran out from the player at an angle of about 45 degrees to the keyboard. This shape permits proportionately longer bass strings, with a favourable influence on sonority. Another name for 'Spinet' was 'Couched Harp'; this, it will be seen, has reference to the shape of the instrument.

The spinet was in use from the later seventeenth century to the end of the eighteenth century. Spinets were made in America during the eighteenth century, the earliest known being apparently one by Hasslinch of Philadelphia, dated 1742. Harris of Boston (son of a London harpsichord and spinet maker) is reported to have made spinets from 1769; Blythe of Salem is known to have made them from at least 1789.

The origin of the name 'spinet' is not settled: the most plausible derivation is that which connects the quills with 'spine', but there are adherents for the derivation from the name of a Venetian inventor, Spinetti. Second-hand furniture dealers in England today incorrectly use the word 'Spinet' for the early oblong form of the pianoforte.

The **Clavicytherium** was a spinet with the strings perpendicular (like those of an upright piano).

5. The Harpsichord Proper (p. 453, pl. **79**. 6). This form of the instrument, representing the highest state of development reached by the family, had two or more strings to a note. It was, like the spinet, shaped, not rectangular, but its strings ran out directly in front of the player, i.e. at right angles to the keyboard. It was often of considerable size and, in fact, in general appearance much resembled the modern grand pianoforte. (The earliest instrument of this kind now known to exist is one in the Victoria and Albert Museum, London; it is dated 1521 and was made in Rome.)

The number of strings to a note could be varied by mechanical means. Stops resembling those of an organ, or pedals resembling those of a piano, threw the extra strings into or out of action and modified the quantity or quality of tone in other ways. An additional set of strings tuned an octave above or (rarely) below normal might thus be added; compare the use of the 4-foot and 16-foot organ manual stops: this added grandeur to the tone—an effect missing from the pianoforte. (But cf. the reference to the Moór pianoforte s.v. *Keyboard* 4.) Tschudi or Shudi of London, in 1769 (apparently following some slightly earlier Continental makers), applied the Venetian swell, on the principle of the Venetian blind, as a means of letting out or shutting in the sound, operating this by a pedal like the unbalanced swell pedal of an organ.

Often there were two keyboards, and very occasionally three; a pedal keyboard was also sometimes to be found. The double-keyboard (or two-manual) form of the instrument seems to have been more popular in Britain and Germany than in Italy, and the abundant and brilliant harpsichord works of Domenico Scarlatti, despite the strong *prima facie* evidence of their frequent crossing of the hands, are by some supposed to have been written for the single keyboard instrument.

With all these above-mentioned contrivances the power of expression of the harpsichord was not primarily *direct*; finger touch affected it little, and no mechanical means could compensate for this lack, especially as they did not admit of detailed accentuation.

It must, however, be clearly realized that while the influence of finger touch on tone and expression is limited the degree which *is* possible is of the very highest importance, and the ability to exploit it is the first requirement of a good harpsichordist.

It is often stated that the harpsichord had no power of sustaining tone, that the tone died away immediately the quill had plucked the string. There is considerable exaggeration in this. We find Voltaire, in discussion with an Italian correspondent, defending the final mute 'e' of French words like 'empire', 'couronne', 'diadème', etc., by likening them to the lingering sound of a harpsichord when the fingers have ceased to strike the keys (presumably he means the fingers still to remain on the keys, as otherwise the dampers would fall and check the sound—and, for that matter, the very presence of dampers shows the existence of a resonance needing to be controlled).

It is of interest to note that many of the harpsichords and spinets (also the clavichords) that we see in museums today were made by amateurs; schoolmasters, organists, cabinet makers, etc., often made their own instruments, and they followed out specifications of their own devising, whence much variety. Further, it was customary for players to tune their own instruments and to carry out small repairs, and so the instrument will often be found to include some small drawer for the tuning-hammer, for coils of wire for restringing, etc.

Bach, helped by an unusually quick ear and general high competence, is reputed to have been able to tune his harpsichord in a quarter of an hour. Very frequent tuning was necessary owing, amongst other things, to the thinness of the strings and their comparatively great length, and the cultivation of speed in tuning became important to every intelligent owner of an instrument. London gentry who employed a professional tuner had a contract for his weekly attendance. Re-quilling was frequent, and Francis Hopkinson (1737–91), of Philadelphia, not only wrote the first American secular song and helped to draft the Declaration of Independence, but also introduced new methods both of tuning and of quilling harpsichords. The trouble of such frequent attention to tuning and quilling was, doubtless, one of the subsidiary causes of the harpsichord's defeat by the pianoforte.

The Flemish harpsichord makers (e.g. the famous Ruckers firm, 1579–c. 1670) and others on the continent of Europe often decorated their harpsichords with elaborate and beautiful painting, especially inside the lid. The British makers apparently never did this.

Many modern instruments introduce mechanical advantages unknown in the older ones, and it would seem that tonal modifications (certainly a great deal more tonal variety) have also been achieved. In fact, the harpsichord is no longer a mere 'revival'; it has resumed life and growth.

6. A 'Bach' Specification.

There follows the specification of an early harpsichord of a well-developed kind, at one time considered to have been the property of J. S. Bach and fashioned according to his ideas, though evidence is lacking. The specification is copied in many modern instruments, but it should be noted that it is very unusual (possibly unique) among early instruments. Lower octave stops were rare, and in two-manual instruments the higher octave (4 ft) strings were almost invariably operated from the lower manual and not the upper. According to some authorities, there are signs that this instrument was altered some time after it was built; its original specification may have been very different.

2 Manuals.

4 Strings to every finger-key, 2 of the normal pitch, one of an octave higher, and one of an octave lower (what an organist would call of 8-foot, 4-foot, and 16-foot pitch).

One normal-pitched set of strings and the set of an octave higher are operated from the higher manual. One normal-pitched set and the set of an octave lower are operated from the lower manual. The manuals can be coupled so that in playing on one of them the whole 4 sets of strings will be in use.

Stops exist making it possible to use pairs of the normal-pitched strings alone, etc.

A 'Lute' stop ('harp-stop' or 'buff-stop') acts on the upper manual, bringing a piece of cloth in contact with the strings and so producing a tolerable imitation of lute-tone [in some instruments the lute stops, instead of the device of cloth, had their jacks nearer to the ends of the strings].

The lowest strings are wrapped with a coil of wire like those of a modern pianoforte.

The keyboard compass is 5 octaves, F to F (7 octaves of tone owing to the octave-lower and octave-higher stops).

7. The Decline of the Spinet and Harpsichord.

Spinet and harpsichord (the less and more costly forms of the instrument) existed side by side throughout the later seventeenth and the eighteenth centuries, and then, at the end of the eighteenth century, the gradually improving pianoforte began seriously to compete with them, and by the early nineteenth century reigned supreme.

Burney (in Rees's *Cyclopædia*) attributes much of the change of feeling in England to the pianist J. S. Schroeter, who settled in London in 1772. (The passage to be quoted dates from about 1805, when its writer was nearing eighty.)

'The piano-forte was a new instrument in this country: when he first arrived the hammer instruments of a large size were bad, and harpsichord players produced no great effects upon them; but Schroeter may be said to have been the first who brought into England the true art of treating that instrument. We were unwilling to give up the harpsichord, and thought the tone of the pianoforte spiritless and insipid, till experience and better instruments vanquished our prejudices; and the expression and chiaroscuro in performing music expressly composed for that instrument, made us amends for the want of brilliancy in the tone so much, that we soon found the scratching of the quill in the harpsichord intolerable, compared with the tone produced by the hammer.' (See also *Pianoforte Playing* 1.)

There is a tradition that Himmel, in Berlin, played the harpsichord publicly as late as 1805. If so, he was probably one of the very last to do so until the modern revival of the instrument. The last recorded occasion of its public use in Britain, until that revival, is that of the performance of the annual 'King's Birthday Ode' at St. James's Palace in 1795. In France the harpsichord remained in use for twenty years longer than in Britain.

Much of the music we often play upon the piano today was really composed for the harpsichord—the 'pianoforte' works of Handel, those of Bach, of Scarlatti, and others (where they were not written for the clavichord or for clavichord or harpsichord indifferently), the earliest of what we call the 'pianoforte' sonatas of Haydn and Mozart, and even the very earliest of the works of Beethoven. It strikes us today as very curious that what seem to us such essentially pianistic works as Beethoven's Sonatas in A flat and C sharp minor (popularly known as the 'Sonata with the Funeral March' and the 'Moonlight' Sonata) should have been announced on their original title-pages (1802) as 'For Harpsichord or Pianoforte'.

8. Varying Names for the Instrument.

Amongst the many names applied in different periods and countries to instruments of the various harpsichord types are:

In Italian *Arpicordo*, *Clavicembalo* (meaning keyed-dulcimer, which it is not, its strings not being struck but plucked), or *Claricembalo*, or *Gravicembalo*, or simply (for short) *Cembalo*.

The French name for harpsichord is *Clavecin*, and *Épinette* seems to be used indifferently for spinet and virginals.

The German name for virginals and spinet was *Tafelklavier* ('table-keyboard'); for harpsichord, *Flügel* ('wing'—though for that matter the spinet is wing-shaped); *Flügel* nowadays usually means 'Grand piano'.

The English name varies as above given— *Virginals*, *Spinet*, *Harpsichord*, with sometimes, instead of the last, *Harpsicon*, or *Harpsical*. Or we may meet with *Cymbel* (anglicization of 'Cembalo') or *Clavicymbal*. Occasionally, as already stated, we find *Triangle* for 'Spinet', from the shape of the instrument. The present article's distinction of the three forms of the instrument under the heads of 'Virginals', 'Spinet', and 'Harpsichord proper' is logical and follows the best usage, but it will be understood that all three terms were, in familiar parlance, often carelessly applied.

9. Some Leading Composers (for the three forms—virginals, spinet, and harpsichord proper).

ENGLISH. Hugh Aston (early sixteenth century—a great innovator and founder of a true keyboard style), Byrd (*c.* 1542–1623), Farnaby (*c.* 1560–1640), Bull (*c.* 1563–1628), Gibbons (1583–1625), Blow (*c.* 1649–1708), Purcell (*c.* 1658–95), Clarke (*c.* 1670–1707), Arne (1710–78).

Low COUNTRIES. Sweelinck (1562–1621).

GERMAN. Froberger (*c.* 1616–67), Kuhnau (1660–1722), Pachelbel (1653–1706), J. S. Bach (1685–1750), Handel (1685–1759), W. Friedemann Bach (1710–84), C. P. Emanuel Bach (1714–88), J. Christian Bach (1735–82), Haydn and Mozart in their earlier works.

ITALIAN. Frescobaldi (1583–1643), Picchi (early seventeenth century), Pasquini (1637–1710), Zipoli (1688–1726), D. Scarlatti (1685–1757).

FRENCH. Chambonnières (1602–72), d'Anglebert (born *c.* 1625), Marchand (1669–1732), Couperin (1668–1733), Clérambault (1676–1749), Rameau (1683–1764), Dandrieu (1682–1738), Daquin (1694–1772), Dieupart (died *c.* 1740).

In recent times composers have begun again, in a small way, to write for the harpsichord. Its peculiarities of expression fit the views of some of those who desire to avoid artificial inflexion and who seek merely tonal pattern on a level surface, so to speak. One of the most important efforts at the reintroduction of the instrument is Falla's Concerto for harpsichord and small orchestra. Among the 150 or so composers who have contributed to the modern repertory are Babbitt, Ben-Haim, Berger, Burkhard, Busoni, Carter, Castelnuovo-Tedesco, Cowell, Delius, Françaix, Haieff, Henze, Leibowitz, Milhaud, Orff, Petrassi, Piston, Poulenc, and Stravinsky.

For the out-of-order arrangements of the lowest notes of earlier instruments of the harpsichord type see *Short Octave and Broken Octave*. For mechanical virginals and harpsichord see *Mechanical Reproduction* 3, 9.

For old English Manuscript Collections of (or including) Virginal Music see *Benjamin Cosyn's Virginal Book*; *Fitzwilliam Virginal Book*; *My Ladye Nevell's Book*; *Mulliner Manuscript*; *Will Forster's Virginal Book*.

HARPSICON. Same as harpsichord (q.v.).

HARRIS.

(1) RENATUS. Born in France, *c.* 1652 and died at Salisbury in 1724, aged about seventy-two. He was one of the great English organ-builders of the Restoration period and following years. His father and grandfather and his two sons were also organ-builders. The grandfather and one of the sons also bore the name Renatus.

See under *Acoustics* 16; *Organ* 8; *Cathedral Music* 6.

(2) A Boston, Mass., instrument maker of early eighteenth century.

See *Harpsichord Family* 4.

(3) WILLIAM HENRY. Born in 1883, died 1973. He studied at the Royal College of Music (where he became a professor), was organist of New College, Oxford, and of Christ Church Cathedral there, and then organist of St. George's Chapel, Windsor Castle. Amongst his compositions are the choral–orchestral work *The Hound of Heaven* (Carnegie award 1919) and much choral and organ music.

(4) ROY ELLSWORTH (p. 1068, pl. **175**. 2). Born in Oklahoma in 1898. Up to early manhood he earned his living as a farmer, a truck driver, etc., studying music in his spare time. Taking up more serious study he received training at the hands of various teachers in America and then in Paris where, winning a Guggenheim Fellowship, he worked (1927–8) under Nadia Boulanger.

He has composed a long list of orchestral works (including twelve symphonies), and of chamber music works; these enjoy frequent performance. He is reported to have 'developed a system of modal semantics, in which psychological moods are ranged from optimistic to sad in proportion to the remoteness of the semitone from the keynote'.

He has occupied positions on the staffs of

Cornell University, Colorado College, and Los Angeles (UCLA).

See references as follows: *Clarinet Family* 6; *Chamber Music* 6, Period III (1898); *Concerto* 6 c (1898); *Reed-Organ Family* 4; *Symphony* 8 (1898); *When Johnny comes marching Home*; *History* 9.

(5) D.G.T. See *Concert* 3.

HARRISON.

(1) JULIUS. Born at Stourport in Worcestershire in 1885 and died in London in 1963, aged seventy-eight. He was educated at the Birmingham School of Music and had a successful career as orchestral and opera conductor until deafness forced his retirement in 1940; he also composed orchestral and other music, including a much admired Mass in C (1949).

(2) LOU. Born in Portland, Ore., in 1917. He is a composer and teacher, having been a pupil of Cowell and Schönberg; he has taught at Mills College, at the University of California, and elsewhere, and has worked as a music critic and as an animal doctor. He has composed operas, symphonic and chamber works, ballets, etc., in many styles, and has won numerous awards.

HARROW SCHOOL. See *Farmer, John (II)*; *Buck, Percy C.*

HARRY, BLIND. See *Scotland* 6.

HART, HARTE (Ger., various terminations according to case, etc.). 'Hard'; also 'major'.

HART, ANDRO. See *Hymns and Hymn Tunes* 17 e xii; *Stilt*.

HÄRTEL. See *Publishing* 8.

HARTMANN.

(1) and (2). J. P. E. (1805–1900) and EMIL (1836–98). See *Scandinavia* 2.

(3) C. V. See *Gramophone* 4.

(4) KARL AMADEUS. Born in Munich in 1905 and died there in 1963, aged fifty-eight. He was a pupil of Webern and a composer of the note-row school, though in a personal rather than a rigid way. His works include eight symphonies, concertos, an opera and other vocal works, and two string quartets. He founded Musica Viva, devoted to the performance of contemporary music.

HART'S PSALTER. See *Hymns and Hymn Tunes* 17 e, xii; *Stilt*.

HARTY, HERBERT HAMILTON. Born in County Down, Ireland, in 1879 and died at Brighton in 1941, aged sixty-one.

At the age of twelve he became a church organist. At twenty-one he was in London, rapidly becoming known as an admirable pianoforte accompanist and (later) orchestral conductor. He was appointed to the Hallé Orchestra, Manchester, in 1920, and, during the dozen and more years he retained the position, fully sustained the high reputation it had acquired. Later he conducted a good deal in the United States, as also in Australia. As a composer he produced choral and orchestral works at festivals, concertos, etc.

He was knighted in 1925.

HARWOOD.

(1) EDWARD (1707–87). Lancashire com-poser of hymns, anthems, and songs, at one time popular. See *Methodism and Music* 6.

(2) BASIL. Born in Gloucestershire in 1859 and died in London in 1949. His career was for the most part in Oxford, where he was organist of Christ Church Cathedral (retiring in 1909), and was active as a conductor. He wrote dignified and effective music for organ and for choir.

HASCHKA. See *Emperor's Hymn*.

HASLER. See *Hassler*.

HASSARD, J. R. G. See *Criticism* 5.

HASSE, JOHANN ADOLPH. (p. 396, pl. 67. 6) Born near Hamburg in 1699 and died in Venice in 1783, aged eighty-four. He was a highly celebrated composer of the Handelian times, resident for the most part in Dresden, Vienna, and Venice. He was amazingly prolific, his operas alone amounting to over a hundred, and his masses, oratorios, symphonies, sonatas, etc., being very numerous. His operatic style was Italianate and he had the gift of writing melodiously and with high effectiveness for the voice.

His wife was the famous Italian prima donna, Faustina Bordoni (1693–1781).

See references as follows: *Libretto*; *Opera* 9 a; *Harmonica* 1; *Composition* 10; *Concert* 15; *Abel*.

HASSLER (or Hasler), HANS LEO (p. 396, pl. 67. 1). Born at Nuremberg in 1564 and died at Frankfurt-on-Main in 1612, aged forty-seven. He was a member of a musical family of considerable distinction, his father (Isaac) and his two brothers (Kaspar and Jacob) being musicians of some standing.

After an early career as organist he was sent to Venice to study with Andrea Gabrieli, being the earliest of the German composers of importance thus to receive an Italian training. Returning to Germany, he held positions in Augsburg, Nuremberg, and elsewhere. His numerous compositions (madrigals, motets, chorale harmonizations, organ pieces, etc.) are of such a standard as to give him a high place in the annals of German music, and most of them have been reprinted in modern times.

The well-known Passion Chorale, *O Haupt voll Blut und Wunden* ('O sacred head, surrounded' is the usual English version), is an adaptation of a secular choral song of his.

See references under *Germany* 2; *Bohemia*; *Madrigal* 8 d; *Mechanical Reproduction* 4 (end).

HÄSSLER, JOHANN WILHELM. Born at Erfurt in 1747 and died in Moscow in 1822, aged seventy-five. He was an able organist and a pianist of international fame who composed much music for his instruments, as also vocal music. A Gigue in D minor for pianoforte is well known today. From 1794 he lived in Moscow, where he held a high musical position at court and was in much demand as a teacher.

HASSLINCH (Philadelphia). See *Harpsichord Family* 4.

HASTIE FAMILY. See *Bagpipe* 4.

HASTIG (Ger.). 'Hasty', impetuous.

HASTINGS, THOMAS (1787–1872). See *Hymns and Hymn Tunes* 11.

HATTON, JOHN LIPTROT (p. 817, pl. 140. 7). Born in Liverpool in 1809 and died at Margate in 1886, aged nearly seventy-seven. He was an active theatre conductor and composer in London, most of Charles Kean's productions including music composed by him.

In 1844 he went to Vienna to superintend the performance of an opera there, and (a many-sided artist!) obtained reputation as a pianist by playing Bach's Preludes and Fugues. At the Hereford Festival in 1846 he not only played a piano concerto of Mozart but appeared on the programme also as a vocalist. He toured more than once in the United States as solo pianist, accompanist, and vocalist. 'It was often uncertain whether the place allotted to him in the programme would be occupied by one of Bach's fugues or by a comic song of his own composition' (*Dict. Nat. Biog.*), and he tickled the American fancy by a song called 'The Sleigh-Ride', in which he had bells tied to his legs.

Many of his three hundred solo songs are admirable. Simon the Cellarer may some day, perhaps, succumb to the effect of his protracted potations, but Anthea will surely continue to live. Some of his part-songs still give pleasure—and to give pleasure (to himself and to others) seems to have been his object in life.

HAUER, JOSEF MATTHIAS. Born at Wiener-Neustadt in 1883 and died in Vienna in 1959, aged seventy-six. He wrote music for piano and harmonium, chamber and orchestral music, songs, an oratorio, etc. He claimed to have anticipated the Note-row (q.v.) principle of Schönberg and he published books on his system: *Lehrbuch* ('text-book') of twelve-note music; an *Einführung* ('Introduction') to twelve-note music (1925), and *Zwölftontechnik* ('twelve-note technique'; 1926). Schönberg seemed at one time to approve his activities but later took umbrage and gave a musically illustrated lecture (to which he invited Hauer), after which, as he claimed, 'Everyone recognized that my system was different from others.' It was probably in response to this that Hauer had a rubber stamp made—*Josef Matthias Hauer, der geistige Urheber und trotz vielen schlechten Nachahmern immer noch der einzige Kenner und Könner der Zwölftonmusik.* ('Josef Matthias Hauer, the spiritual begetter of twelve-note music, and, despite many bad imitators, still the only one who understands and knows how to use it.')

See *Chamber Music* 6, Period III (1883).

HAULTAIN. See *Printing* 1.

HAUPT (Ger.). 'Head.' Or as an adjective, 'principal', 'chief'.

HAUPTMANN, MORITZ (1792–1868). See *Temperament* 10; *Modes* 10; *Additional Accompaniments*; *Chamber Music* 6, Period III (1792).

HAUPTSATZ. See under *Satz*.

HAUPTSTIMME (Ger.). 'Principal voice' (or part).

HAUPTTHEMA (Ger.). Principal theme (i.e. principal musical subject) of a composition.

HAUPTWERK (Ger.). Great Organ; see *Organ* 15.

HAUSEGGER.

(1) FRIEDRICH VON. Born in Carinthia in 1837 and died at Graz in 1899, aged sixty-one. He was a lawyer turned musicologist who taught the history and theory of music at the University of Graz and wrote valuable books on the aesthetics of music, on Wagner, etc.

(2) SIEGMUND VON. Born at Graz in 1872 and died at Munich in 1948. He was son of the above and was active as composer, producing an opera, symphonic poems, choral works, and, especially, songs. He also did much work as conductor of organizations in various German cities, and was Director and (1923–34) President of the Academy of Music at Munich. His music has a Wagnerian trend. In his later years he produced little.

HAUT, HAUTE (Fr., masc., fem.). 'High.'

HAUTAIN. See *Printing* 1.

HAUTBOIS. See *Oboe Family* 2, 5 a.

HAUTBOIS D'AMOUR. See *Oboe Family* 5 f.

HAUTBOY. See *Oboe Family* 2, 6; *Organ* 14 VI.

HAUTE (Fr.). 'High.'

HAUTE DANSE. In a haute danse the feet were lifted; in a basse danse (q.v.) they were kept close to the ground.

HAUTEUR. See *Pitch* 8.

HAVANAISE (Fr.). 'Habanera' (q.v.)—the Cuban capital being 'Habana' in Spanish and 'Havane' in French.

HAWAIIAN GUITAR. See *Ukelele*.

HAWEIS, REVD. HUGH REGINALD. Born at Egham, Surrey, in 1838 and died in 1901. He was a Cambridge graduate who became incumbent of a London West End church and editor of *Cassell's Magazine*, a keen amateur violinist, and the author of two highly popular books—*Music and Morals* (1873 and sixteen or more further editions) and *My Musical Life* (1884).

HAWES, WILLIAM. Born in London in 1785 and died there in 1846, aged sixty. He was master of the choristers at both St. Paul's Cathedral and the Chapel Royal, a music publisher, director of opera at the Lyceum Theatre in London (in which capacity he gave the first British performance of Weber's *Der Freischütz*, in 1824), a considerable composer and adapter of stage music, conductor of the Madrigal Society, and an organist. He found time, withal, for the composition of glees, and by these he is now chiefly remembered.

HAWKINS.

(1) JOHN (p. 389, pl. **66**. 5). Born in London in 1719 and died there in 1789, aged nearly seventy. He was the son of a builder and became an attorney, married money and abandoned business, was made a justice of the peace

PLATE 80

HAYDN AND HIS SUMMER-HOUSE

By Batt

A SUMMER-HOUSE was provided for Haydn's use at the country estate of Eisenstadt, where the earlier part of his period of service with the Esterhazy family was spent, and it was in this that he spent much of his time and wrote many of his earlier works. He is seen here descending its flight of wooden steps.

Thus he would emerge to go to his rehearsals and performances, a genial good-humoured man, loved of all who came into contact with him.

B.

(becoming Chairman of the Middlesex Quarter Sessions), and achieved eminence by his public services, his activity winning him, in 1772, the honour of knighthood.

Throughout his career he devoted much attention to literature and music, associating with the writers of the age (e.g. Horace Walpole and Dr. Johnson—whose life he wrote and whose complete works he edited,) and compiling a great five-volume *History of Music*, published 1776, which remains a storehouse of valuable antiquarian information but which at the time suffered unfairly from the competition of that of Burney, of which the first volume appeared in the same year.

The present work necessarily contains a good many scattered references to and quotations from him. See *Concert* 1, 6, 9; *Beggar's Opera*; *Barber Shop Music*; *Catch*; *Stilt*; *Cold and Raw*; *Power, L.*; *Bell* 2; *Pitch* 6 b. A quotation from his literary daughter Laetitia's well-known book of anecdotes is given under *Hallelujah Chorus*.

(2) ISAAC (eighteenth-century Philadelphia piano-maker). See *Pianoforte* 6, 9.

HAWLEY, H. STANLEY (1867–1916). London pianist, editor of piano music (simplifying the notation by frequently adjusting the key signature and so abolishing hundreds of accidentals during the course of a piece), composer, and organizer of many kinds of useful musical activity.

See reference under *Melodrama*.

HAY, HAYE, or **HEY.** See *Canaries*. The dance was usually a round one, but there seem to have been several different dances all called by this name. Dr. Johnson in his dictionary (1755) suggested that the name came from the practice of 'dancing round a haycock'—ingenious if unconvincing! Shakespeare (*Love's Labour's Lost*, v. i) says, 'I will play on the Tabor to the Worthies, and let them dance the Hay.'

Percy Grainger (q.v.) wrote a lively piece called *Shepherd's Hey*.

HAYDN.

(1) JOSEPH (in full, FRANZ JOSEPH). See p. 464, pl. **81**). Born at Rohrau in 1732, and died in Vienna in 1809, aged seventy-seven. He was one of two musical brothers born in a wheelwright's cottage in a village in Lower Austria, who both, by dint of great natural gifts and painstaking development of them, climbed into European eminence—and he climbed the higher.

Some of his ancestors may have been of Slav descent, and the merry tunes of which so much of his music is compacted are, it has been claimed, often those of the Croatian peasants who had ages before settled in the district, or tunes modelled upon these. 'It is hardly too much to say that he stood to the folk music of Croatia as Burns to the peasant songs of Scotland' (Hadow). Both in music and in conversation he all his life cheered people by his happy touches of Croatian peasant humour or won their sympathy with his simple-minded Croatian religious feeling, and he had the Croatian love of what is called 'sport', so that on the princely estate where for many years his musical duties were performed the saying was proverbial, 'As good a shot and fisherman as Haydn.'

From the cottage he graduated at six to the choir school of the neighbouring town, and thence, at eight, to the cathedral of Vienna. When his voice broke he took an attic, found a few pupils, and, charmed with the sonatas and symphonies of Emanuel Bach, then in his early thirties but already a recognized pioneer, set himself to compose upon their model. At twenty-eight he married unwisely and began the proverbial leisurely repentance.

He had now become musical director to a nobleman of the neighbourhood; and later he entered the service, on the same footing, of that Hungarian family of Esterházy whose name has for four centuries been prominent in the political annals of central Europe. With orchestra, choir, and solo singers at command for the service of the chapel, the theatre, and the concert room of the palace, he had a never-failing incentive to compose and a standing opportunity for experiment.

Amongst his finest compositions, his 'Salomon Symphonies' (see *Salomon*) were written for performance in London, where he himself conducted them, sitting at the keyboard in the manner of the day. He was a great favourite in England, flattered, caressed, and honoured by all who took part in its artistic and social life, and the University of Oxford proudly adorned his somewhat dumpy figure with the white-figured silk and cherry-coloured satin of a doctorate in music.

In his old age he composed the oratorio *The Creation*. It is naïve but charming, and admirably reflects the simple devotion of its author—'Never was I so pious as when I was composing this work; I knelt down daily and prayed God to strengthen me for it.' When it was first performed (in Vienna in 1798), the whole audience was deeply impressed, but no one more so than its composer—'One moment I was as cold as ice, the next I was on fire. More than once I was afraid I should have a stroke.'

The still later work, *The Seasons* (1801), is an oratorio-like setting of a German translation of Thomson's poem—a fresh, youthful work for a man of his age, but one the composing of which tried him so that he said it gave him his 'finishing blow' (its composition was not, however, his last effort, as in the remaining few years he composed a certain number of smaller things).

His 'Emperor's Hymn' (q.v.), the favourite *Austria* of our hymn-books, was suggested by admiration of the British National Anthem. In 1809, Vienna being then in the occupation of Napoleon, Haydn, old, feeble, and ill, had himself carried to the piano, and solemnly played this tune. It was the last time he touched an instrument, and a few days later he died.

Haydn is called 'The Father of the Symphony', and this he is in the double sense that the classical symphonic form and the classical symphonic orchestration were both largely of his development—upon the basis of the more experimental work of the elder composer he had taken as his exemplar. His capacity and his opportunity made him, equally, the founder of the String Quartet and, indeed, of modern chamber music and instrumental music generally. For the relationship between his music, that of Mozart, and that of Beethoven, see the articles on these latter composers.

It is a remarkable and regrettable fact that only a portion of Haydn's output is today accessible in print; a complete and scholarly edition is, however, now in slow progress.

References will be found as follows:

1. GENERAL. *History* 6; *Germany* 1, 5, 8; *France* 7; *Hungary*.

2. HIS METHODS OF COMPOSITION, etc. *Alberti Bass*; *Composition* 5, 9, 10, 12, 14; *Development*; *Fioritura*; *Folk Song* 5; *Form* 2, 7, 9, 10; *Harmony* 11, 23; *Modulation*; *Ornaments* 6; *Romantic*; *Sonata* 6, 7, 8, 10 c d (1760-7); *Suite* 4, 5, 7; *Tremolo*.

3. VOCAL AND CHORAL WORKS. *Cecilian Movement*; *Folk Song* 3; *Mass* 2, 3; *Oratorio* 1, 3, 7 (1775-98); *Roman Catholic Church Music in Britain*; *Singspiel*.

4. INSTRUMENTAL FORMS, etc. *Canzonet*; *Capriccio*; *Chamber Music* 6, *Period* II (see *Sammartini* 1700), *Period* III (1732); *Concerto* 6 b; *Minuet*; *Nocturne*; *Overture* 4, 7; *Programme Music* 5 c; *Scherzo*; *Symphony* 1, 4, 5, 6, 8; *Trio* 2; *Waltz*.

5. INSTRUMENTS. *Brass*; *Clarinet Family* 2; *Expression* 5; *Flute Family* 4, 6; *Harp* 3, 4; *Harpsichord* 7; *Horn Family* 3, 4; *Mechanical Reproduction* 5; *Oboe Family* 2, 3 d, 6; *Organ* 13; *Percussion Family* 4 a b; *Pianoforte* 18, 20; *Pitch* 4; *Toy Symphony*; *Trumpet Family* 3, 4; *Viol Family* 4 d; *Wachtel*.

6. QUESTIONS OF PERFORMANCE, etc. *Conducting* 4; *Encore*.

7. INDIVIDUAL COMPOSITIONS. *Bird Music*; *Concert* 9; *Deutschland über Alles*; *Emperor's Hymn*; *God save the Queen* 16; *Kraft, A.*; *Mis-attributed Compositions*; *National Anthems*; *Nicknamed Compositions* 11-13; *Nightingale*; *Ridotto*; *Seven Last Words*; *Spain* 10; *Stabat Mater*; *Toy Symphony*.

8. PERSONS. *Arne, T. A.*; *Bach, C. P. E.*; *Beethoven*; *Boccherini*; *Diabelli*; *Dupuis*; *Handel*; *Hummel*; *Mozart*; *Neukomm*; *Pleyel*; *Porpora*; *Salomon*; *Scarlatti, A.*; *Shield*; *Storace*; *Turk*; *Wranitzky*.

9. VARIOUS. *Anglican Parish Church Music* 5; *Clubs* (Anacreontic Society); *Concert* 6, 8; *Degrees* 1; *Graduates' Meeting*; *Memory* 8; *Opus*; *Patronage* 6, 8. Also p. 608, pl. **106**. 2; p. 796, pl. **135**. 4.

(2) JOHANN MICHAEL (p. 464, pl. **81**. 4), generally called 'Michael Haydn'. Born at Rohrau, in Lower Austria, in 1737 and died at Salzburg in 1806, aged nearly sixty-nine. He was the younger brother of Joseph Haydn and the teacher of Weber. For over forty years he was musical director to the Archbishop of Salzburg at the time when the Mozarts were also active there. His fame is now overshadowed by that of his brother, to whom many of his works have been mistakenly attributed.

Probably there is a case to be made out for the revival of some of the works of a composer of whom Schubert, visiting his grave, could say, 'No man living reverences him more than I do. My eyes filled with tears as we came away.'

See *Mechanical Reproduction* 5; *Symphony* 8. Also p. 397, pl. **68**. 1.

HAYDNVEREIN. See *Concert* 13.

HAYE. See *Hay*.

HAYES (Father and Son).

(1) WILLIAM. Born at Gloucester in 1705 and died at Oxford in 1777, aged seventy-one. He was organist of Worcester Cathedral and then of Magdalen College, Oxford, of the university of which place he became Professor of Music. His glees, canons, and catches are not forgotten.

(2) PHILIP. Born in 1738 and died suddenly whilst on a visit to London in 1797, aged nearly fifty-nine. On his father's death he succeeded him in both his Oxford positions. His compositions were much on the lines of those of his father. As one of the worst-tempered men in England he was the legitimate object of wit; as one of the bulkiest he gave additional opportunity for it, 'Phil Hayes' becoming, popularly, 'Fill Chaise'. Some of his church music is still heard. (See reference under *Anthem, Period* III.)

(3) ROLAND (tenor singer). See reference under *United States* 6.

HAYMARKET THEATRE. See *Fairs and their Music*.

HAZZAN. See *Jewish Music* 3.

Hb. Short for *Hoboe*, i.e. oboe.

HEAD, MICHAEL. Born at Eastbourne in 1900 and died in Cape Town in 1976, aged seventy-six. Educated at the Royal Academy of Music, where he was a professor of piano (1925-75). He wrote deft and delicate songs, and gave recitals of them, accompanying himself at the piano. He travelled much as examiner, competition adjudicator, etc.

HEAD REGISTER or **HEAD VOICE.** See *Voice* 4, 14.

HEAD RESONANCE. See *Voice* 6, 14 (references to the frontal sinuses).

HEART OF OAK (*not* 'Hearts of Oak'). This bold patriotic song comes from a pantomime, *Harlequin's Invasion*, written by Garrick in 1759, the music being supplied by Boyce (q.v.). It is a topical song, alluding as it does to 'this wonderful year' (the victories of Minden, Quiberon Bay, and Quebec).

In 1768 an Americanized version was introduced, which, as 'The Liberty Song', had enormous popularity.

HEATHER, WILLIAM. Same as William Heyther (*c*. 1584-1627). See *Choragus*; *Dictionaries* (beginning of article).

HEAVENLY LENGTH SYMPHONY. See *Nicknamed* 18.

HEBENSTREIT, PANTALEON (1669-1750). See *Pantaleon*; *Pianoforte* 3.

1. A HAYDN MANUSCRIPT 'The Heavens are telling', from *The Creation* (1798). From the score in the British Museum. The composition of this work was suggested by Salomon (see below)

2. JOSEPH HAYDN. The London portrait, by Hardy

3. SALOMON—Haydn's London impresario

4. MICHAEL HAYDN—Younger brother of Joseph

Vju tro ra-no se ja sta-nem Ma-lo pred zo-rom Vju-tio ra-no se ja sta-nem Ma-lo pred zo rom

5. EMPEROR'S HYMN ('Austria'). The Croatian folk melody from which Haydn developed this famous tune

Nichts kann für Haydn schmeichelhafter seyn, als der Beyfall des Publikums. Den zu verdienen hat er sich stäts eifrigst bestrebt, und ihn bereits oft, und mehr, als er es sich versprechen durfte, zu erwerben das Glück gehabt. Nun hoffet er zwar für das hier angekündigte Werk diejenige Gesinnung, die er zu seinem innigen Troste und Danke bis jezt erfahren hat, ebenfalls zu finden; doch wünscht er noch, daß auf den Fall, wo zur Aeusserung des Beyfalls sich etwann die Gelegenheit ergäbe, ihm gestattet seyn möge, denselben wohl als ein höchstschäzbares Merkmahl der Zufriedenheit, nicht aber als einen Befehl zur Wiederholung irgend eines Stückes anzusehen, weil sonst die genaue Verbindung der einzelnen Theile, aus deren ununterbrochenen Folge die Wirkung des Ganzen entspringen soll, nothwendig zerstöret, und dadurch das Vergnügen, dessen Erwartung ein vielleicht zu günstiger Ruf bey dem Publikum erwecket hat, merklich vermindert werden müßte

6. ENCORES DEPRECATED, by Haydn on the announcement of the first public performance of *The Creation*, 1799. He says that nothing can be more flattering for him than the approval of the public but begs that in case he is so happy as to enjoy that approval on the present occasion it may not be expressed in the form of a demand for the repetition of any part of the work, which would destroy its continuity

1. INDIAN VINA of the late 18th century (7 strings and frets; two gourds to increase the sonority)

2. DRUMMER AT AMRITSAR
Different tone qualities are obtained by striking with the whole hand or with several fingers at different places

3. KASHMIRI BIN

4. ANCIENT EGYPTIAN FLUTE CONCERT. From a painting on a tomb—date before 2000 B.C.

5. CHINESE CHANG

6. TURKISH HARPIST
A sketch from life by Melchior Lorich in the 17th century (the harp has no fore-pillar)

7. PERSIAN SANTIR (Dulcimer)
From a painting at Teheran

For other pictures of old or uncommon instruments see pages 417, 449, 512–13, and 544–5

HECK, J. C. See *Figured Bass.*

HECKEL, WILHELM (1856–1909). For instruments invented by him see references below.

HECKELCLARINA, HECKELKLARI-NETTE. See *Clarinet Family* 4 h. (For the non-existent 'Heckelclarind' see note to 4 h.)

HECKELPHONE. See *Oboe Family* 4 i, 5 h.

HECTOR, A. B. See *Colour and Music* 10.

HEEL. That end of the bow of a string instrument at which it is held, as distinguished from the other end, which is called 'point'.

HEFTIG (Ger.). 'Violent', impetuous.

HEIL DIR IM SIEGERKRANZ. See *God save the Queen* (opening paragraph).

HEILIGMESSE (Haydn). See *Nicknamed Compositions* 13.

HEINE, HEINRICH (1797–1856). See *Song* 5.

HEINEL. See *Ballet* 9.

HEINRICH XXIV, PRINCE. See *Chamber Music* 6, Period III (1855).

HEISE, PETER ARNOLD. Born in Copenhagen in 1830 and died at Stockerup in 1879. He was a pupil of Gade and also studied at Leipzig. He composed operas, quantities of fine songs, etc.

HEISS (Ger.). 'Hot', 'ardent'.

HEITER (Ger.). (*a*) 'Merry'; (*b*) 'clear'.

HELBERGER. See *Electric Musical Instruments* 1 k.

HELDENTENOR (Ger.). Literally 'hero-tenor', i.e. *Tenore robusto*, a big-voiced tenor suitable for heavy operatic parts.

HELICON. See *Tuba Group* 3 b c.

HELL (Ger.). 'Clear', bright.

HELLENDAAL.

(1) PETER (Senior). Born at Rotterdam in 1721 and died at Cambridge in 1799, aged seventy-eight. He studied violin playing at Padua under Tartini (q.v.), and from about 1752 was active as violinist and organist in London, King's Lynn, and Cambridge. His published compositions were varied but largely for strings and he edited a collection of tunes for the metrical psalms.

(2) PETER (Junior). His activities and career were much the same as those of his father (above). He, also, was a resident of Cambridge.

HELLER, STEPHEN. Born at Budapest in 1813 and died in Paris in 1888, aged seventy-five. He wrote innumerable graceful short compositions, for the domestic instrument, upon which he was a refined and accomplished performer, and deserved well of the better-class amateur pianists of the mid-nineteenth century, to whose technique his style was grateful.

His youthful studies were pursued in Vienna, but in his late twenties he settled in Paris and there lived, a member of the romantic circle of those days—Chopin, Liszt, Berlioz, and others. Schumann formed high expectations of

Heller, a Romantic 'but not one of that vague nihilistic no-style, behind which many scribblers ape Romance . . . on the contrary he generally feels naturally and expresses himself clearly and cleverly'.

The comparative neglect of Heller today is probably due to his over-fluency and to an inferiority of matter as compared with manner.

See reference under *Pianoforte* 22.

HELLERTION. See *Electric Musical Instruments* 1 k.

HELLFLÖTE (Ger.). 'Clear flute' (an organ stop).

HELLMESBERGER Family.

(1) GEORGE (I). He was born at Vienna in 1800 and died near there in 1873. He enjoyed great fame as a teacher of the violin, and trained several violinists who attained celebrity (e.g. Joachim). He composed string music.

(2) JOSEF (I). He was born at Vienna in 1828 and there died in 1893. As a violinist he was a notable pupil of his father (above). He founded a celebrated string quartet and was principal of the Conservatory of Vienna. He composed violin studies, etc.

(3) GEORGE (II). He was born at Vienna in 1830 and died in Hanover in 1852. He was the son of (1) above, and a composer of operas, etc.

(4) JOSEF (II). He was born at Vienna in 1855 and there died in 1907. He was a member of the string quartet founded by his father (see no. 2 above) whom he later succeeded as leader, held important operatic posts, and composed many operettas and ballets.

HELMHOLTZ, HERMANN VON (1821–94). Eminent physiologist and physicist. Author of the standard work, of great originality, *Sensations of Tone* (1863 and very many subsequent editions in German and English). See *Acoustics* 20; *Temperament* 10; *Voice* 6, 7; *Colour* 5; *Ocarina*; *Organ* 2 c; *Pitch* 7 a.

HELY - HUTCHINSON, (CHRISTIAN) VICTOR. Born at Cape Town in 1901 and died in London in 1947. He was educated at Eton, Oxford, and the Royal College of Music, and later joined the staff of the British Broadcasting Corporation, to which in 1944 he returned as Music Director. He was Professor of Music in the University of Birmingham 1934–44.

He wrote some effective compositions, orchestral and other, usually in a cheerful vein. He was also a capable pianist.

HEMIDEMISEMIQUAVER (𝅘𝅥𝅲). The sixty-fourth note, i.e. of the value of one sixty-fourth of a semibreve. (Table 3.)

HEMIOLA or HEMIOLIA. The rhythmic device of superimposing two notes in the time of three, or three in the time of two, e.g.:

Cf. *Deux Temps.*

HEMPSON, DENNIS A. (p. 481, pl. **84**. 3). He was born in County Londonderry in 1695 and (living in three centuries) died at Magilligan in 1807, retaining his mental faculties to the end of his 112 years and playing the harp, on which he was a great performer, the day before his death. He had (and apparently deserved) great fame as an exponent of the old Irish harp technique, showing himself master of an astonishing variety of effects.

See reference to him under *Robin Adair*.

HENDERSON, WILLIAM JAMES (1855–1937). See references under *Criticism* 5; *Voice* 14.

HENRICI. See *Passion Music* 5.

HENRY I OF ENGLAND (b. 1068; came to throne 1100; d. 1135). See reference under *Minstrels* 2.

HENRY III OF ENGLAND (b. 1207; came to throne 1216; d. 1272). See reference under *Parish Clerk*.

HENRY V OF ENGLAND (b. 1388; came to throne 1413; d. 1422). Compositions of his are included in the Old Hall MS. (q.v.). See also reference under *Chapel Royal*.

HENRY VI OF ENGLAND (b. 1421; came to throne 1422; deposed 1461; d. 1471). He composed church music of value.

HENRY VII OF ENGLAND (b. 1456; came to throne 1485; d. 1509). See reference under *Trombone Family* 3.

HENRY VIII OF ENGLAND (p. 452, pl. **78**. 4). Born at Greenwich in 1491; came to the throne in 1509; and died in 1547, aged fifty-six. He played various instruments and composed masses, now lost. The anthem 'O Lord, the Maker of all thing', long attributed to him, is now generally attributed to W. Mundy or Shepherd; the three-part song, 'Passetyme with good companye', and some other compositions for voices and viols, are probably really his.

(See *Chapel Royal*; *Cathedral Music* 2; *Recorder Family* 2; *Trombone Family* 3; *Trumpet* 3; *Percussion Family* 4 a; *Bagpipe Family* 3; *Mechanical Reproduction of Music* 3; *Misattributed*; *Ballad* 1.)

HENRY IV OF FRANCE. See *Opera* 11 a.

HENRY OF MEISSEN. See *Minstrels*, etc. 8.

HENSCHEL, GEORGE (Isidor Georg). Of Polish (Jewish) descent but born at Breslau in 1850, British subject from 1890, and died in Scotland in 1934, aged eighty-four. He first appeared in public, as pianist, at the age of twelve. Four years later he was appearing in public again—as a basso-profondo. He studied at the Conservatory of Leipzig, was much approved in concert and oratorio (singing in Bach's *St. Matthew Passion* under Brahms), and in 1877 made his first appearance in Britain, which became his favoured home. He married the American singer Lillian Bailey, and their joint recitals had enormous success in Britain and the United States.

In 1881 he became conductor of the Boston Symphony Orchestra, a position he retained for three years, after which he settled in England, carrying on in London for eleven years an important series of symphony concerts. He served as the first conductor of the Scottish Orchestra (1893–5)—all the time maintaining his position as a public singer of the highest rank. His second wife was the American singer Amy Louis (died 1956).

George V knighted him in 1914. Fifty years after his first concert in Boston he accepted an invitation to conduct there a concert reproducing the same programme.

He several times retired from the platform, but ever returned to it, and on approaching his eightieth year became a favourite radio vocalist. He held an exhibition of his paintings in London when eighty-four.

His list of compositions is a long one; it includes, naturally, many works for vocal solo. His *Requiem Mass*, first performed at Boston in 1902, was revived in London in 1925. His daughter Helen Henschel (1882–1973) was likewise known as a vocalist who accompanied herself, as her father did.

See *Metronome*.

HENSELT, ADOLF VON (p. 800, pl. **137**. 2). Born in Bavaria in 1814 and died in Silesia in 1889, aged seventy-five. He was a virtuoso pianist and a keen student of the possibilities of his instrument, which he exploited with art in a large number of compositions, especially in twenty-four studies. Some of his graceful salon music is still to be heard.

See *Concerto* 6 b (1814); *Toccatina*.

'HEN' SYMPHONY (Haydn). See *Nicknamed Compositions* 11.

HEN WLAD FY NHADAU. See *Land of my Fathers*.

HENZE, HANS WERNER. Born at Gütersloh, Westphalia, in 1926. He studied under Fortner and Leibowitz and soon had to his credit a considerable list of compositions, including five symphonies, concertos for piano and for violin, cantatas, and ballet music. He is a successful non-doctrinaire member of the younger German school; his operas include *Boulevard Solitude* (1952), *König Hirsch* (1956), *Der Prinz von Homburg* (1960), *Elegy for Young Lovers* (1961), *The Young Lord* (1965), and *The Bassarids* (1966). Since 1953 he has lived in Italy.

See *Harpsichord* 9.

HEPTACHORD. See *Hexachord*.

HERABSTRICH (Ger.). 'Here-down-stroke', i.e. down-bow (cf. *Heraufstrich*).

HERAUFSTRICH (Ger.). 'Here-up-stroke', i.e. up-bow (cf. *Herabstrich*).).

HERBERT, VICTOR (p. 1041 pl. **170**. 6). Born in Dublin in 1859 and died in New York in 1924, aged sixty-five. He was a grandson, on his mother's side, of Samuel Lover, the novelist. His first musical activities were as cellist and composer for the cello, his next as conductor of military bands and orchestras. Turning to the composition of operettas, he won great applause from a wide public, to whom he presented between thirty and forty works in this form, as also some orchestral music. He composed, further, two grand operas, *Natoma* (1911) and *Madeleine* (1914). His numerous sentimental songs (e.g. *Kiss me again*) had a nation-wide popularity.

HERBSTLIED (Ger.). 'Autumn song.'

HERE BENEATH A WILLOW. See *All through the Night*.

HEREFORD CATHEDRAL. See *Cathedral Music* 2, 7; *Festival* 1.

Organists who receive notice in this volume are (with their periods of office): *J. Bull* (1582–?); *Clarke-Whitfield* (1820–32); *S. S. Wesley* (1832–5).

HEREFORD USE. See *Common Prayer*; *Use of Sarum*, etc.

HERE'S A HEALTH UNTO HIS MAJESTY. See *Savile*.

HERNACH (Ger.). 'Hereafter.'

HÉROÏQUE (Fr.), **HEROISCH** (Ger.). 'Heroic.'

HEROLD, LOUIS JOSEPH FERDINAND. Born in Paris in 1791 and died there in 1833, aged nearly forty-two. He was the son of a musician (a pupil of C. P. E. Bach). He studied at the Paris Conservatory under Méhul and others, and at twenty gained the Prix de Rome and went to that city for three years' study. He devoted himself to opera, his first success being in Naples. Returning to Paris he produced a long series of operas (including *Zampa* in 1831 and *Le Pré aux Clercs* in 1832), of ballets, and of pianoforte compositions. (Cf. *Comic Opera*.)

HERON-ALLEN, EDWARD (1861–1943). Lawyer and violin expert. See *Dictionaries* 15.

HERRICK, ROBERT (1591–1674). The delicate lyric poet, many of whose verses were set by contemporary composers such as Henry Lawes, Lanier, and Wilson (see references under *Lawes, Henry*; *Cherry Ripe*), and by later ones such as Hatton (*To Anthea*).

HERRINGTON, HENRY. See *Drink to me only*.

HERRMANN, BERNARD. Born in New York in 1911 and died in Hollywood, Calif., in 1976, aged sixty-four. Conductor and composer. His film scores (*Citizen Kane*, *The Magnificent Ambersons*, *Psycho*, *The Birds*, and many others) are well known. Amongst his other works are the dramatic cantata *Moby Dick* (1st perf. New York 1940), ballets, orchestral works, radio melodramas, etc.

HERRNHUTER. See *Bohemia*; p. 108, pl. **19. 4**.

HERSCHEL Family.

(1) FREDERICK WILLIAM (Sir William Herschel). Born at Hanover in 1738 and died at Slough, near Windsor, in 1822, aged eighty-three. Like his father and one of his brothers he was a hautboy player in the Hanoverian guard. Coming to England, he was engaged to train the band of a regiment of militia quartered at Richmond, Yorkshire, and was then invited to settle in Leeds, as director of concerts, afterwards becoming, for a brief period, organist at Halifax (see *Organ* 8) and a popular teacher.

He then went to Bath as organist to the Octagon Chapel, and there did much composition, principally of church music. The study of harmony led him to mathematics, and he passed on to astronomy, abandoning the professional practice of music and becoming, after his discovery of Uranus, Court Astronomer to George III. The king later gave him two thousand pounds to make the world's greatest telescope, and fifteen years after his death, before its dismantling, his family assembled in the tube and sang a Requiem of his composition.

Like the 'appreciation' teachers of today he saw that observation is an acquired art: 'Seeing is in some respects an art which must be learnt', he said, and compared the intelligent use of sight to 'playing one of Handel's fugues upon the organ'.

His published compositions include a symphony for orchestra, two concertos for military band, and an 'Echo' catch.

(2) JACOB, brother of William, also settled in England. He published sonatas for two violins and bass.

(3) CAROLINE, sister of William, was trained by him as a singer in the Bath days and had considerable success in Handel's oratorios under her brother's conductorship. (The method of training adopted was for her to sing the violin parts of concertos with a gag in the mouth.) It was with great reluctance that she dropped music to be trained as an assistant astronomer, yet she made discoveries—eight minor planets, one of them named after her. Retiring to Germany she lived to be nearly a hundred, never missing a concert as long as she was able to attend.

HERSTRICH (Ger.). Literally, 'hither-stroke' (the one towards the player), i.e. the down stroke on violoncello and double-bass (cf. *Hinstrich*).

HERTZ, HEINRICH RUDOLPH (1857–94). See *Broadcasting* 2.

HERUNTERSTIMMEN (Ger.). 'To tune down' a string to (*nach*) a specified note.

HERUNTERSTRICH (Ger.). Literally 'hereunder-stroke', i.e. the down-bow on violin and viola.

HERVORGEHOBEN (Ger.). 'Forth-heaved', i.e. a melody to be made to stand out.

HERVORRAGEND (Ger.). 'Forth-projecting', i.e. prominent (e.g. of a melody to be 'brought out'). So too, *Hervortretend*, literally 'forth-stepping'.

HERZ, HEINRICH or Henri (1803–88). See *Pianoforte* 18; *Pianoforte Playing and Teaching* 2; *Albéniz, Pedro II*; *Carnival of Venice*; *Hexameron*. Also p. 797, pl. **136. 7**.

HERZHAFT, **HERZLICH** (Ger.). 'Hearty'; 'very'.

HERZIG (Ger.). 'Tender', 'charming'.

HERZOGENBERG, HEINRICH VON (1843–1900). Conductor of the Bach Society at Leipzig and then chief professor of composition, etc., in the Hochschule at Berlin; minor composer. His correspondence exists in an English translation and there is much about him and his wife in Ethel Smyth's volumes of reminiscences.

HES (Ger.). B flat. In practice, however, the Germans call this note B (see *H* above).

HESELTINE.

(1) JAMES. Died at Durham in 1763. He was organist of Durham Cathedral and wrote anthems. Those of them that remain are still sung, the rest he destroyed when he quarrelled with his Dean and Chapter.

(2) PHILIP. Born in 1894 and died in London in 1930, aged thirty-six. Under his own name he edited the lute-songs of the Elizabethans and other old music, and wrote on *Delius, The English Ayre,* and other subjects. Under the name of 'Peter Warlock' he composed delicate songs, chamber music, etc.

He united the highest ideals in art with a cynical view of human life and died despairing —apparently by his own hand.

See *Saudades; Gray.*

HESSE, ADOLF FRIEDRICH. Born at Breslau in 1809 and died there in 1863, aged nearly fifty-four. He was the son of an organ-builder, and a great organist, and his compositions for his instrument are still played.

See *Lemmens.*

HEWITT.

(1) DANIEL C. See *Pianoforte* 15; *Clutsam Keyboard.*

(2) JAMES. See *Programme Music* 4; *Opera* 21 b.

HEWSON, GEORGE HENRY PHILLIPS. Born at Dublin in 1881. He has occupied posts as organist of Armagh Cathedral, St. Patrick's Cathedral, Dublin, the Chapel Royal, and also of Dublin University—of which in 1935 he became Professor of Music. He has composed church music, etc.

HEXACHORD (p. 960, pl. **161**). A group of six consecutive notes, regarded as a unit for purposes of singing at sight—somewhat as the octave is, in most systems, regarded today. Guido d'Arezzo introduced it (or possibly only perfected it) in the eleventh century. The method embodied the main principle of all present-day 'movable doh' systems in that, the whole compass of vocal sounds (the compass as then recognized) being divided into groups of like arrangement as to the position of tones and semitones, names were then given to the members of the group, which names remained constant for such members wherever in the vocal range the group occurred. It was, then, a 'relative pitch' system, not an 'absolute pitch' one.

The defining interval was the semitone. With us today the group is the octave and it includes two semitones. With Guido d'Arezzo and his six-note system only one semitone occurred in each group. This semitone was to be called 'mi-fa'. No semitone was ever to be called *anything but* 'mi-fa' and the notes on each side of a semitone, wherever in the vocal range it occurred, took names accordingly, the whole series running *Ut-re-mi-fa-sol-la,* as in the tonic sol-fa system of today the seven different notes of the octave run *Doh-ray-me-fah-soh-lah-te.*

In passing, it may be pointed out that our 'octave' is, in one sense, a misleading method of grouping, there being only seven, not eight, different notes in it. By analogy with 'tetrachord' (see *Scales* and *Modes*) and with 'hexachord', it should be 'heptachord' (from the Greek words for 'four', 'six', and 'seven').

Guido evidently possessed two of the most important qualifications of a teacher, the power of systematization and the knack of profiting by any favourable chance circumstance. The latter is seen in the names of the degrees of his hexachord as given above. They came from a Latin hymn for the Feasts of St. John the Baptist, of four centuries before, of which he noticed that each line happened to begin one note higher than the previous one.

There was a particular fitness in the application of this hymn to the helping of choir-boys:

UT que-ant la - xis RE-so-na-re fi - bris
MI - ra ge-sto-rum FA-mu-li tu-o-rum,
SOL - ve pol-lu-ti LA-bi-i re - a-tum,
San - cte Io - han - nes.   *(Vatican Edition, as restored by the monks of Solesmes.)*

His view was this: 'If an experienced singer shall so know the opening of each of these sections that he can, without hesitation, begin forthwith any one of them that he pleases, he will easily be able to utter, with absolute correctness, each of these six notes, wherever he may see them.'

It will be realized that the music of Guido's day was (to our minds) extremely simple. Not only had harmony (or the performance of several different notes simultaneously) barely begun, but the element of chromaticism was entirely absent, only one inflected note being in use (see *Musica Ficta*). Music was then in Modes (q.v.), drawn, as we should say, entirely from the key of C major, with an occasional B flat substituted for B natural where the latter interval was for some reason undesirable (perhaps as creating the 'tritone', q.v.). The letter names were already in use and Guido retained them as what we call the 'absolute' names for the notes, using his new syllables as 'relative' names, i.e. singable names relative to the hexachord in which the note occurred, which, as before explained, was governed by the position of the semitone. Similarly, today, in our tonic sol-fa system we use C, D, E, etc., as unchangeable names of the notes according to their absolute pitch and doh ray me, etc., as changeable names according to their pitch relation to the key (or heptachord group) in which we are at the moment working—treating the doh-ray-me names as those for the mouth and mind of the singer.

Guido began his hexachords on three different notes, making three different hexachords, which overlapped one another. One hexachord (called the *Natural Hexachord*) began on every C of the vocal compass. Another (called the *Hard* or 'Durum' *Hexachord*) began on every G, and still another (the *Soft* or 'Molle' *Hexachord*) began on every F; this last one had the B flat instead of B natural and was called into use whenever that note was required. In proceeding up the scale you would pass from one hexachord to another by a process called **mutation**, which has a close equivalent in the tonic sol-fa method of today. The process is illustrated in the following:

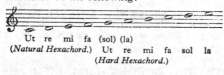

Ut re mi fa (sol) (la)
(*Natural Hexachord.*) Ut re mi fa sol la
(*Hard Hexachord.*)

La sol fa mi (re) (ut)
(*Hard Hexachord.*) La sol fa mi re ut
(*Natural Hexachord.*)

The brackets above indicate the names that would be discarded for the other names, on its being noticed by the singer, looking ahead, that the scale or other passage was going to proceed beyond the hexachord in which he was singing. If this process be applied, not to a change from the 'Natural' to the 'Hard' hexachord, as above, but from the 'Natural' or the 'Hard' to the 'Soft', or vice versa, then will be seen a 'Mutation' that is also, as *we* should say, a 'Modulation', and negotiated on very much the same lines as the tonic sol-fa method would prescribe today.

Our tonic sol-fa system of today bases itself upon the supremacy of the tonic or key-note and the 'mental effects' which the other notes take on when they are heard in relation to that tonic. There is no evidence that Guido did that or, indeed, had any grasp of the idea of 'key'. His mind was occupied with the practical use of the semitone as a valuable recurring landmark, and it will be observed that his hexachordal system had no relation whatever to the (heptachordal) modes, to one of which every piece of music in those days necessarily belonged. He was a practical teacher and choirmaster intent on finding a handy system of sight-singing. Modes concerned the make-up of the music, hexachords its performance. The modes, with their varying position of the semitone, possessed no fixed landmarks; he wanted *one device that would apply whatever the Mode*, and he found it in the hexachord.

As a mnemonic device he introduced what is sometimes called the **Guidonian Hand** (p. 960,

pl. **161.** 2, 3). This is a most elaborate plotting out of the chorister's hand as a sort of 'modulator'—as a modern tonic sol-faist would call it. The tips and joints of the fingers each have notes allotted to them, so that a conscientious chorister, having learnt the place of each note, could mentally exercise himself.

The whole apparatus looks rather unwieldy to a musician of today, but apparently it worked. One of Guido's treatises caused him to be turned out of his monastery, near Ravenna, but Pope John XIX restored him, Guido having, it is said, taught the Pope to sing at sight in a single lesson.

The system spread from monastery to monastery and cathedral to cathedral, and was soon dominant over Europe. It began to weaken its hold, after nearly six centuries of usefulness, as the old Modes began to weaken theirs; obviously the increasing introduction into music of accidentals other than B flat would in the end be fatal, since no provision had been made for them.

Various adaptations now appeared in different countries. The seventh note, *Si*, was added to the system of note names as being the initial letters of the two words 'Sancte Iohannes' (see last line of the hymn above). The syllable 'Doh' was substituted for the rather unsingable syllable 'Ut' in (perhaps) the sixteenth century: France still uses 'Ut'. In Latin countries generally, the Guidonian syllables were at last attached to the absolute pitch sounds (the Natural Hexachord being retained for the purpose, the other two Hexachords being dropped), instead of the old alphabetical names, which continued in use for absolute pitch purposes in other countries.

Relics of the hexachord may be found in composition. A reference to its use as a musical theme will be found under *Mass* 5 ('Missa super Voces Musicales'). In the *Fitzwilliam Virginal Book* (q.v.) are pieces by Sweelinck, Byrd, and Bull, called *Ut, re, mi, fa, sol, la*, and based on an ascending scale of six notes. Shakespeare understood the Guidonian system, the music lesson in *The Taming of the Shrew* being based upon it. (See *Gamut*.)

The words 'Solmization', 'Solfège', and 'Solfeggio' are derived from the hexachordal syllables.

HEXAMERON. This is a series of piano variations on the march from Bellini's opera *I Puritani*. The variations were contributed by six famous pianists—Liszt, Thalberg, Pixis, Herz, Czerny, and Chopin. At a charity concert in Paris in 1837 these notabilities sat at six pianos, each in turn playing his own variation, and Liszt contributing an Introduction, connecting links, and Finale. Later Liszt often performed the whole series at his recitals, with an orchestral accompaniment which he had added.

'HEXENMENUETT' (Haydn). See *Nicknamed Compositions* (under *Quintenquartett*).

HEXENTANZ (Ger.). 'Witches' Dance.'

HEY. See *Hay.*

HEYTHER, WILLIAM (*c.* 1584–1627). See *Choragus.*

HEY, TUTTI TATTI. See *Land of the Leal*; *Scots wha hae.*

HIBBERD, LLOYD. See *History* 9.

HIBERNIAN CATCH CLUB. See *Ireland* 6.

HICKFORD'S ROOM. See *Concert* 5.

HICKS, PEGGY GLANVILLE. See a reference under *Cage, John.*

HIDDEN FIFTHS. See *Harmony* 24 o.

HIDDEN OCTAVES. See *Harmony* 24 o.

HIER (Ger.). 'Here.'

HIERONYMUS OF MORAVIA. See *Ornaments* 1.

HIGDEN'S POLYCHRONICON (by Ranulf Higden, Benedictine of Chester, who died 1364). See *Printing of Music* 1.

HIGHLAND BAGPIPE. See *Bagpipe Family* 4.

HIGHLAND FLING. See *Reel.*

HIGHLAND MOD. See *Scotland* 1.

HILARY, BISHOP. See *Te Deum.*

HILL.

(1) **RICHARD.** See *Carols.*

(2) Violin makers. See *Violin Family* 4.

(3) **ROWLAND.** See *Rule, Britannia!*; *Congregational Churches* 4; *Luther.*

(4) **EDWARD BURLINGAME** (p. 1056, pl. 171. 6). Born at Cambridge, Massachusetts, in 1872 and died at Francestown, N.H., in 1960, aged eighty-seven. He composed piano pieces, songs, choral and orchestral music for two pantomimes, symphonic poems, and two symphonies. He was a musical impressionist (see *Impressionism*), painting musical colours with extreme subtlety.

In 1908 he became instructor and later professor in the music department of Harvard University, retiring in 1940. He was the author of a book, *Modern French Music.*

See reference under *Clarinet Family* 6.

HILL BILLY SONGS. The traditional songs (largely of European origin) of the primitive peoples of the mountain regions of the southeastern parts of the United States.

'HILLEMACHER, P. L.' This was the name adopted for a remarkable combination of two French brothers, posing and composing as one—Paul Joseph William Hillemacher (1852–93) and Lucien Joseph Édouard Hillemacher (1860–1909). Both were trained at the Paris Conservatory and both won the Grand Prix de Rome (see *Prix de Rome*)—the elder at twenty-four and the younger at twenty. They composed operas, oratorios, cantatas, piano music, etc., and published a life of Gounod.

Cf. *Collaboration in Composition*; also *Misattributed*, s.v. 'Debussy'.

HILLER.

(1) **JOHANN ADAM.** See *Singspiel*; p. 396, pl. **67. 8.**

(2) **FERDINAND.** Born at Frankfurt-on-Main in 1811 and died at Cologne in 1885, aged seventy-three. He was a pianist but was especially prominent as a conductor in various towns of Germany, particularly Cologne, and was a friend of Mendelssohn, Schumann, Chopin, Berlioz, Liszt, Meyerbeer, and the Romantics generally. He left a number of literary works throwing light upon the activities of this circle.

See *Improvisation* 2; *Concerto* 6 b (1811); *Chamber Music* 6, Period III (1811).

HILTON, the two Johns (probably Father and Son).

(1) **JOHN (Senior).** Born *c.* 1560, and died in 1608. He was organist of Trinity College, Cambridge. He wrote anthems, etc., but it is sometimes difficult to say whether a particular composition should be assigned to him or to—

(2) **JOHN (Junior).** Born in 1599 and died in 1657, aged fifty-seven or fifty-eight. He was organist of St. Margaret's, Westminster. He wrote anthems, madrigals, catches, music for viols, and other things.

See *Farrant.*

HIMMEL, FRIEDRICH HEINRICH. Born in Brandenburg in 1765 and died in Berlin in 1814, aged forty-eight. Once prominent as a composer of works of many types, especially operas, he is now chiefly remembered by the small piece of church music known in England as *Incline Thine Ear.*

See reference under *Harpsichord Family* 7.

HINCKSON. See *Hingston.*

HINDEMITH, PAUL (p. 416, pl. **71.** 5). Born at Hanau, near Frankfurt-on-Main, in 1895 and died at Frankfurt in 1963, aged sixty-eight. After studying in Frankfurt he came before the public first as a violin player and then as leader of the orchestra of the opera-house at that place. In 1922 he became for a time a member (viola) of the newly founded Amar String Quartet (taking its name from the leader, the Hungarian-born Turk, Licco Amar), which had its headquarters in Frankfurt, and which speedily established itself internationally by its interpretations of contemporary music; this organization his brother Rudolph (cello) also joined. Later he was attached, as teacher of composition, to the Berlin State Conservatory.

At the start of his career as a composer Hindemith was regarded in Germany as the destined successor of Richard Strauss, and he soon became a leading figure in European musical life. However, in the twenties he came to stand in the public mind for the extremest modernism. He was for some time influenced by the 'atonalist' movement (see *Harmony* 18), with a strong tendency to neoclassicism.

Much of his work took chamber music form (sonatas for violin alone, and for violin and piano; for viola alone and for viola and piano, for cello alone and for cello and piano, for string quartet, etc.) and was often written with amateurs in mind (see *Gebrauchsmusik*). Some was written for chamber orchestra (including concertos for piano, violin, viola, and cello). There are also some songs and a few piano compositions, some stage music, including several operas, an oratorio, *Das Unaufhörliche* ('The Unceasing'), and a *Requiem* ('for those we love'; a setting of poems of Whitman, 1946). His opera *Mathis der Maler* ('Mathis the painter', i.e. Matthias Grünewald of Colmar) supplied also the material for a three-movement symphony (1934) of the same name. Other operas were *Die Harmonie der Welt* (1957) and *The Long Christmas Dinner* (1962).

In 1938 he published his ballet *Nobilissima Visione* and in 1943 his *Ludus Tonalis*, a set of twelve fugues for pianoforte, connected by interludes in free lyric and dance forms and with a prelude and postlude. This latter is a work of uncompromising 'modernity' and a good deal of highly complex artifice. His output, always showing transcendental craftsmanship, was particularly large and strikingly varied in the resources employed; a buoyant spirit of adventure is everywhere strongly in evidence, and a sense of humour is another characteristic.

Performance of his works was forbidden in Germany during the Nazi régime (see *Germany and Austria* 9). In 1940 he settled in the U.S.A., later becoming an American citizen. In 1940 he became a Professor of Music at Yale University and in 1953 at the University of Zürich. In addition to the violin and viola, he also played the piano, the clarinet, and the saxophone (and in some degree all orchestral instruments), and he published *The Craft of Musical Composition* (2 vols.), *Traditional Harmony*, etc. His outspoken opposition to the Schönberg–Webern school made him a somewhat unfashionable figure in his later days.

See references under *Germany* 8, 9 (note); *History* 8;

Saxophone; *Suite* 8; *Viol Family* 4; *Violin Family* 7; *Chamber Music* 6, Period III (1895); *Opera* 24 f (1938, 1957, 1963); *Concerto* 6 c (1895); *Flute Family* 6; *Oboe Family* 4 i, 6; *Sonata* 10 e; *Clarinet* 6; *Horn Family* 4; *Mechanical* 13; *Ballet* 5; *Shimmy*; *Electric* 1 e; *Trombone* 4; *Trumpet* 4; *Military Band*; *History* 9; *Russia* 8.

HINDU SCALES. See *Scales* 8.

HINE, WILLIAM. Born in Oxfordshire in 1687 and died at Gloucester in 1730, aged forty-two or forty-three. He was organist of Gloucester Cathedral, on whose walls a mural tablet to his memory still records the notable fact that the Dean and Chapter once, without being asked, increased his annual stipend by twenty pounds. He left church music.

See a passing reference under *Anglican Chant* 5.

HINGSTON or **HINCKSON, JOHN** (d. 1683). See references under *Puritans* 4; *Clubs for Music-Making*; *Purcell, Henry*; *Fancy*.

HINSTERBEND (Ger.). Literally 'away-dying'.

HINSTRICH (Ger.). 'Away-stroke' (the one away from the player), i.e. the up-bow on violoncello and double-bass (cf. *Herstrich*).

HIPKINS, ALFRED JAMES (1826–1903). See *Clavichord* 6.

HIRSCH, PAUL ADOLF. Born at Frankfurt-on-Main in 1881 and died in Cambridge in 1951, aged seventy. He was a successful business man in Frankfurt until 1936, when, for political reasons, he settled in Cambridge. He had a very extensive and valuable library which was purchased in 1946 by the British Museum.

HIRT (Ger.). 'Herd.' So *Hirtenlied*, 'herdsman's song', and similar expressions.

HIS (Ger.). B sharp. *Hisis*, B double sharp (if this note is anywhere to be found). See Table 7 and for the reason of B being called H in German see *Notation* 1.

HISTORY OF MUSIC

The following article has been left much as it stood in the ninth edition, apart from the correction of an occasional detail and the rewriting of the last section. It is founded on an approach to the subject no longer fashionable, taking for granted as it does the idea of the 'evolution' of the art of music from primitive beginnings to a full flowering in the eighteenth–nineteenth centuries. But it will serve as well as any other as the peg on which future reading can be hung.

1. Introductory. The history of art in general is the history of man's efforts simultaneously to express his emotions and to achieve beauty by the arrangement of lines, colours, masses, words, and tones, the specific arts thus resulting being those of drawing and painting, sculpture and architecture, literature and music.

With all its sister arts music shows some analogies. The ordering of notes consecutively into *Melody* (q.v.) and the combination of melodies into *Counterpoint* (q.v.) resemble the art of drawing; the giving of depth to melodies by the addition to them of accompanying harmonies has something in common with the art of sculpture; the contrasting of different tone-qualities (as those of the strings, woodwind, brass, and percussion families) much suggests the art of painting; the placing of musical 'subject-matter' in contrast, and its effective alternation and repetition, has a parallel in the art of architecture; the metrical side of music (its scheme of balanced 'phrases' and 'sentences' —see *Phrase and Sentence*) has an obvious close connexion with poetry; and many musical compositions (even some that are purely instrumental) have a descriptive quality that also closely approximates to some branches of both poetry and prose.

These resemblances thus existing, it seems a little strange that music should have reached adequate artistic development so much later than did any of the other arts. The nations of what we loosely call 'antiquity' possessed noble buildings, beautiful sculpture, and moving poems and dramas, and showed skill and a sense of effect in the pictorial art, but their development of music (much as they valued it) seems to us, from what we can today learn of it, to have been crude. In this we may, of course, be misled, either by imperfect knowledge or by a lack of power to adapt our point of view to that of races with which we have little in common and civilizations now very remote, and in favour of this theory there is the fact that the music of oriental and 'savage' races today, when sympathetically studied with a view to a genuine understanding, is generally found to possess a purposefulness and attractive quality previously unrealized by us. But whether the term 'crude' can or cannot be justified as applied to the music of ancient times, the term 'simple' certainly can.

The most obvious instance of the simplicity of early music is the fact that it was entirely or almost entirely melodic. In that it resembles non-European music of the present time, for to this day almost all music but that of European origin (or music plainly influenced by such) is melodic, whereas amongst European peoples, though a mere melodic line may satisfy an individual singing or whistling to himself, such a simplicity is practically never brought forward in public—save in some of the plainsong of Christian worship, and even that (in the Western Church, at all events) is frequently accompanied by chords on the organ.

The addition of harmony to melody, it has been suggested above, has some analogy with the method of sculpture as compared with the method of drawing upon a plane surface. But there is a sculptural element even in drawing and painting, called perspective, and perhaps some interest may be felt in the reflection that this element was little understood by the ancients, whose painting was not much more than a silhouette, and that its natural principles were not fully worked out until the time of Paolo Uccello (1397–1475), that is to say, at the period when in music the corresponding element of harmony was emerging from the stage of mere experiment. Thus the earliest paintings that satisfy us as complete representations of nature, and the earliest compositions that today please us harmonically, belong to much the same period.

2. The Polyphonic Phase. The stages by which European music passed from mere unison to elaborate 'part-writing', with each part moving in apparent liberty yet the sum of the 'parts' amounting at any moment to such intervals, chords, and successions of chords as produce a natural and pleasant effect, are briefly detailed under *Harmony*. By the period just mentioned (the latter part of the fifteenth century) the principles of this kind of music had been discovered.

When in the tenth century the earliest glimmer of the idea of combination of voices entered people's minds it did so in the shape of a mere doubling of the traditional church melodies at the interval of a fourth or fifth (see example in *Harmony* 4). Later it assumed the aspect of the addition of more or less free-moving parts to a fixed one. In a church choir one voice or set of voices would carry the ancient plainsong, whilst other voices would weave in with this their own melodic lines, such as more or less fitted both with it and with each other. (See example in *Harmony* 6.)

From the eleventh century (when these first efforts towards the abandonment of mere parallelism began) to the fifteenth this was what composition meant—the addition of new melodic parts to an existing melody—of free songs, so to speak, to a fixed song (or 'Canto fermo').

Towards the end of this period commendable skill was attained in the use of such devices as (a) the preparation of the ear for the coming of a discordant interval, the actual impingement of that interval and the passing of it into smooth concord (or its 'resolution'); (b) the increase of the interest of singers and listeners by the occasional dropping into silence of a voice, so that it might re-enter with effect; (c) the taking up by one voice of some wisp of melody just uttered by another, i.e. the device we call 'imitation'; (d) the close and even exact melodic following of one voice after another—a more complete form of imitation, called 'canon'.

The development of such processes as these much occupied the minds of composers; sometimes they were, indeed, more intent upon mechanism of this kind than upon what we may call a truly musical effect, whilst at other times a suitable balance was secured between that contrivance which gives a desirable intellectual interest to listening and that contour of melodic line and expressiveness of harmonic combination and progression that in music of this type constitutes 'beauty'.

Note that up to this period, and, indeed, for more than a century later (say to nearly the year 1600), the attention of composers was largely concentrated upon choral writing; not much effective composition remains for a single voice with instrumental accompaniment, for chorus with independent instrumental accompaniment, or for instruments without voices. (But see *Minstrels*, etc., for the Troubadours and Trouvères; and also *Harpsichord* 9.)

As the sixteenth century came towards its close the phase of pure choral writing rose to its climax and the first group of composers in whose works real interest is felt today by lovers of church music or by concert audiences is that whose work was done during the thirty years or so on each side of that date, 1600. This was the great period of the *a cappella* Mass and motet, of the Anglican 'service' and anthem, and of the madrigal. The choral music then composed ranks as high in the classification of every discerning and experienced music-lover as the very finest of that of any later period. The solo song with lute accompaniment was also a product of the period.

It is aside from the purpose of this article to give any great number of dates and names, but a few are indispensable; and for this period of about 700 years, the following will be sufficient:

The Earlier Group of Great Polyphonic Composers

ENGLAND. Dunstable (d. 1453).
FLANDERS. Dufay (d. 1474); Josquin des Prés (d. 1521).

The Later Group of Great Polyphonic Composers

FLANDERS. Lassus (c. 1530–94).
ITALY. Palestrina (c. 1525–94).
SPAIN. Victoria (1549–1611).
ENGLAND. Byrd (1543–1623).

The contributions made by each of the countries above mentioned may be better grasped by consulting the separate articles upon those countries (for Flanders see under *Belgium*) and also upon the individual composers.

The emergence out of the large number of 'modes' (which had originated in the days of unisonal melody) of the major and minor scales (which have proved more suitable for harmonic writing) may be traced by consulting the appropriate articles in the list given at the end of the present article. It may be said that in the works of the latest of the composers just mentioned the modal system is seen in gradual decay, whilst the two scales just referred to are seen to be rising into prominence, so that shortly after the death of the last of these composers the modal period definitely closed.

3. The Beginnings of Artistic Instrumental Composition. At the time when this great effort towards the attainment of perfect freedom, beauty, and expressiveness in the pure choral style was reaching its culmination, an effort was simultaneously taking place in the devising of effective techniques for instrumental performance and instrumental composition. The viol and lute families were in their glory, as was the family of recorders (end-blown flutes); reed and brass instruments were somewhat rudimentary and pungent in tone, as was the organ; the domestic keyboard instruments of the clavichord and harpsichord classes had attained considerable development, and the simple, early form of the harpsichord then known, the virginals, was in much use. (For all these instruments see the articles devoted to them.)

The tendency had been to write for instruments much as for voices; indeed, a group of viol players would often take up a book of madrigals and, according to the respective size and compass of their instruments, divide amongst themselves the various vocal parts. Where special music was written for viols it was often in the 'fantasia' (q.v.) or 'fancy' (q.v.) style, which was often not very different from that of the madrigal. Much of the keyboard music was in the same style. It would greatly surprise us today to find a string quartet or a pianist performing an actual choral composition, yet the performance of a Handel chorus on the organ is not unknown. Moreover, whenever an organist, pianist, string quartet, or orchestra plays a fugal movement we are obliged to admit that, although the music may have been specially written for the instrument or instruments concerned, yet there is to be recognized in it a composing procedure essentially choral, so that such music may be looked upon as a relic of the late sixteenth-century and early seventeenth-century practice. Some English madrigals were actually printed as 'apt for voices or viols', and some Dutch choral pieces as 'om te singen of te spelen' ('to sing or to play'), and players of the domestic keyboard instrument occasionally copied choral works into the manuscript books that represented their repertory—the Fitzwilliam Virginal Book (q.v.) offering an example.

But a differentiation was then rapidly taking place. A distinction between the passages suitable for instruments as compared with those suitable for voices, and of passages suited for fingers on a keyboard as compared with those suitable to be played with the bow, was being increasingly admitted. The development of a true keyboard style (e.g. the use of rapid scales, arpeggio passages, and repeated chords) was a particular feature of the period, and the English composers especially distinguished themselves in this, as also in the bringing into existence of suitable forms of keyboard music.

Amongst such forms two were of outstanding importance. The first of these is the Variation. Some short tune (as, for instance, a folk tune or popular song of the day) was first given out in a simple harmonized style and then in a series of elaborated presentations, employing the harmonic, contrapuntal, and technical resources of the composer. The practice of this form was obviously of great value in sharpening the skill of composers in dealing with their thematic material, and so in contributing to the development of the art of composition in general. (See *Form 11* and compare *Chaconne and Passacaglia*; *Ground*; *Folia*.)

The other form was derived from dance styles of the day, consisting of a contrasted pair of dance-like movements (generally a duple-time pavan and a triple-time galliard), sometimes preceded by a prelude. This is one of the sources of the later cyclic forms, the Suite (q.v.), Sonata (q.v.), Symphony (q.v.), and classical String Quartet (see *Chamber Music*), etc.

The art of combining instruments was as yet but little systematized. There were used (as already mentioned) groups of viols of different sizes, and so, too, groups of recorders. Sometimes a group would be made up partly from one family of instruments and partly from another (Shakespeare's 'broken music'). Heterogeneous collections of instruments of all types might be brought together for a performance, but there was no standardized collection like our present-day orchestra. And as with the choral music, so with the instrumental, the modern major or minor scale system had not fully emerged from the older system of modes—and with the instrumental music of the next three centuries that system, with its opportunity of presenting contrasted thematic material in contrasting keys, was going to be very important, and indeed foundational. In fact, in every way the instrumental branch of the art, though actively pursued, was in a state of infancy, or perhaps we might more fairly say, of promising adolescence.

Of composers who produced notable and permanently valuable instrumental work in this experimental period it will be sufficient here to mention the following:

SPAIN. Cabezón (1510–66); a great blind organist and clavichordist and one of the earliest composers of keyboard music.

ENGLAND. Byrd (1543–1623). Bull (c. 1562–1628). Giles Farnaby (latter half of sixteenth century). Orlando Gibbons (1583–1625). These were great composers for the virginals, and Byrd and Gibbons also wrote fine music for bodies of viols.

HOLLAND. Sweelinck (1562–1621); a famous organist and organ composer. He did much to develop the more definite fugue out of the freer fantasia.

ITALY. Frescobaldi (1583–1643); the greatest Italian organist and organ composer of his day.

For further details see the articles upon these countries and composers.

4. The Dramatic Application of Music. The next phase in the development of music (and it is a very definitely novel phase) results from the application of music to the purposes of drama—either secular drama acted, or religious drama in which the acting was (after the opening period) merely imaginary. This phase is sufficiently described under the headings *Opera* and *Oratorio*, to which the reader should turn.

Not only were the social and cultural uses of music increased by the introduction of these forms, but the new style of solo-vocal writing (see *Recitative*, and also example under *Harmony* 9), with its simple accompaniment of mere supporting chords, gave an immediate and powerful impetus to the harmonic way of looking at music, i.e. it laid stress upon the consideration of music as a succession of simultaneously sounding groups of notes, as distinct from its consideration as a number of superposed layers of melody.

Taking a common hymn tune of today to illustrate the two aspects of music we might ask soprano, alto, tenor, and bass to sing off, in turn, their respective parts, and might then say, 'This piece of music consists of those four melodies proceeding together as a four-in-hand': or, instead of this we might, at the piano, play in a detached way, the chords of the tune, and say, 'This music consists of these handfuls of notes, succeeding one another'. Both descriptions would be correct but neither would be complete, for almost any piece of harmonized music has both aspects.

During the polyphonic phase of composition it was the first of these aspects (the horizontal one, as we may say) that had most dominated the minds of composers, but the necessities of the recitative style brought the second aspect (the perpendicular one) into prominence—so much so indeed that a great deal of keyboard accompaniment of solo-vocal music (which now became a leading variety) was henceforward, for nearly two centuries, expressed merely as a line of bass notes with figures attached (see *Figured Bass*), indicating the chords out of which the keyboard accompanist was to work out his part as he went along, according to the measure of his own skill and taste.

The solo voice now became of high importance (see *Bel Canto*), and until well into the nineteenth century no type of performer received such emoluments as the possessor of a fine voice who, by natural aptitude and well-directed training, had arrived at the possession of the ability to use it expressively and with agility.

The exigencies of the stage drama led to a study of instrumental resources and began to tend somewhat towards a standardization of them on the lines of the modern orchestra. As the basis of the combination there was always a harpsichord, at which a performer, playing from the figured bass provided by the composer, supplied an unceasing background of plucked-wire tone. Upon this somewhat neutral background the composer might superpose (say in the various movements of an opera or oratorio) the coloured line of a stringed instrument, or he might associate with it the full four-line design of the whole group of stringed instruments, or the melodic curves of some wind instrument or of a number of such instruments, or pretty well hide it under varying combinations of these and also of the percussion element (kettledrums).

In comparison with the previous phase something was now lost and something gained; the mystical purity of unaccompanied choral singing was gone, but there had been introduced the element of a shifting variety of instrumental tone colourings, and, above all, the power of forceful dramatic expression.

It was in Italy that this new movement began and that country, which during the previous period had become especially a place of high culture of the *a cappella* choral style, now became the leading place of culture of the solo voice (maintaining pre-eminence in this department of musical activity down to the middle of the nineteenth century).

The Italian vocal *Aria* (q.v.) became extremely important.

Flanders and England, which had been to the fore during the previous period, now fell into the rear.

The names which it seems most essential to mention in connexion with the early dramatic development of music are the following:

ITALY. Caccini (c. 1546–1618). Peri (1561–1633). Monteverdi (1567–1643). Cavalli (1602–76).

FRANCE. Lully (1632–87; Italian born).

GERMANY. Schütz (1585–1672).

For further details see the articles upon these countries and composers.

5. The New Balance of the Harmonic and the Polyphonic.

It is impossible to expel polyphony from music, and though the earliest operas and oratorios had very little it quickly crept back—especially into oratorio, with its well-developed chorus-work, for (to take two very familiar examples from the period of climax of the oratorio type) Handel's *Messiah* and Bach's *St. Matthew Passion* are full of the interweaving of melodic lines.

These two composers, whose composing life may be said to have begun a century after the opening of the new harmonic phase, are the typical figures of the phase that succeeded this —a phase in which polyphonic activity is again in full swing. Comparing any choral page of Bach or Handel with many a one of Palestrina or Byrd, and submitting both to close analysis, we find that from the point of view of the singer of any individual part they are very much alike. The singer has, throughout, something very melodious to occupy him; his part is never dull, for every strand in the choral texture is beautiful in itself. To the choral singer it does not much matter whether a Palestrina Mass or a Bach Passion is put before him, except that in the latter there is the added excitement of an instrumental accompaniment. But the listener feels a great difference and it springs chiefly from the following factors:

1. In the Palestrina composition the influence of the old modes may often be felt, whereas in every moment of the Bach music every phrase can be clearly assigned to either the major or the minor system—with well-defined modulations from one key to another, as from the key of C major to that of G major or that of A minor and eventually back again.

2. In the Palestrina composition there is often a freer rhythm, the voice-parts largely moving each in its own rhythmic way, in accordance with the stresses and 'quantities' of the words as uttered and with the requirements of effective expressional emphasis upon those words. Thus we can often hardly say 'This piece is in a four-in-a-measure rhythm', or 'in three-in-a-measure rhythm'. As a matter of fact such music was written and originally printed without bar lines, and when a modern editor inserts these he either bars each vocal part separately (not troubling about the co-incidence or lack of it in the bar-lines of the different voices, and varying the number of beats in the measures of

any voice-part from moment to moment), or else he bars the whole composition in the conventional modern way, and (if he is wise) adds a printed warning that his bar lines are a mere guide to the eye, devoid of the modern accentual significance so far as the individual parts are concerned, though, in the main, they may mark the general metre of the whole (cf. *Rhythm* 6). In a Bach composition the conditions are, of course, different: the composition as a whole (whatever the apparent freedom of each separate part) is felt to move with a steady two, three, four, or six beats in a measure.

3. If we try to reduce the Palestrina composition to a scheme of mere chords we may possibly, in some places, find ourselves in hesitation, because it has hardly been conceived as such; if we try to do the same with the Bach composition we shall find little trouble. In the one there is a polyphonic motion from which chords necessarily result; in the other there is a harmonic scheme out of which a polyphonic web has been drawn. (See example under *Harmony* 10.) This way of putting the distinction is, perhaps, a little too emphatic, but one cannot be clear without emphasis, and the general principle, at all events, is correctly stated. Up to and including the Palestrina period, then, harmony was a by-product of the counterpoint, whereas in the period now under consideration harmony and counterpoint were conceived of as on equal terms.

The instrumental music was on the same lines as the choral music, and there was a great development of it. The 'primitive' period of musical colour work (corresponding, say, to the fourteenth century in painting—the Giotto period) had been passed, and the earliest works we today regularly hear at instrumental concerts are some of this first period of really accomplished instrumental composition, the keyboard and orchestral suites of Bach, his keyboard preludes and fugues, and his compositions for violin and for violoncello.

These last two instruments were fast superseding the old treble viol and bass viol, indeed the whole viol family was in decline and the new violin family was ever rising into popularity. The orchestra (see *Orchestra* 1, 2) was still comparatively unstandardized, yet it was coming to be realized that the new violin family constituted its most effective basis. The ubiquity of the harpsichord has already been mentioned.

The position of Germany in musical production was now a very strong one.

The chief instrumental form of the period was binary (see *Form* 5). Almost every movement of a suite was laid out in this way.

Dance rhythms formed the usual basis, and it is amazing to see what a variety of interesting allemandes, courantes, sarabandes, minuets, gigues, and the like, Handel and Bach and their contemporaries constructed on these simple formal lines.

The chief solo vocal form of the period was ternary (see *Form* 6). Hundreds of arias (see *Aria*) were laid out in this way.

In addition to these, the fugue form (a development of the sixteenth- and early seventeenth-century fantasia; see 3) was very common in instrumental and choral music, and, indeed, in the hands of Bach now reached perfection (see *Form* 12).

The chief names and dates of the phase are as follows:

ITALY. Corelli (1653–1713); especially a composer for the violin and its family. A. Scarlatti (1660–1725), especially a composer of operas and hence of the aria. D. Scarlatti (1685–1757); son of the foregoing and especially a harpsichord player and composer.

ENGLAND. Purcell (1658–95).

FRANCE. Couperin (1668–1733); especially a harpsichord composer.

GERMANY. Bach (1685–1750). Handel (1685–1759).

For further details see the articles upon these countries and composers.

6. The Sonata and Symphony, the Piano, and the German 'Lied'. The next period (that which opened as Bach and Handel were passing away and closed about seventy years later, say 1760 to 1830) was that of the perfecting of the classical sonata (for one instrument or two), the string trio and quartet, and the symphony (all these being merely sonatas in other media).

The articles *Form, Sonata, Symphony,* and *Chamber Music* should be referred to for an explanation of this general type of composition and of its historical development.

Towards the end of the period a very forceful and dramatic quality was imported into such music by Beethoven. The orchestra was now fully standardized and its harpsichord background completely abandoned: there was a continual kaleidoscopic play of colour, wind instruments being greatly improved and the technique of composition for all instruments becoming much more subtly developed.

Toward the end of the period the *Pianoforte* (invented during the previous period but only slowly perfected) superseded the clavichord and harpsichord and lent itself readily to the strongly subjective expression of Beethoven (especially in his piano sonatas) and of Schubert (especially in a number of shorter poetical compositions—'impromptus' and the like). It also made it possible for Schubert and other composers of the period to give an adequate musical treatment to the romantic German lyrical poetry of the period in that very important and abundant type of solo song called the 'Lied' (see *Song* 5).

From the beginning of the history of artistic European music up to nearly the end of this period the art had been dependent upon the support of either the Church or royalty and aristocracy. It now began to appeal to a wider constituency and to seek economic freedom (see *Patronage*).

The principal names and dates of this period are:

GERMANY AND AUSTRIA. C. P. E. Bach (1714–88); a son of the greater Bach, and one of the principal founders of the Sonata and Symphony in the sense in which we generally use the terms nowadays. Haydn (1732–1809). Mozart (1756–91). Beethoven (1770–1827). Schubert (1797–1828).

For further details see the articles upon these countries and these composers.

7. The Romantic Period. From Beethoven onwards music expressed emotion in that direct, detailed, and powerful manner that marks all the painting and literature of the Romantic period (see example under *Harmony* 12). And so the musical Romantic period might very fairly be dated from Beethoven. It is commoner, however, to look upon Beethoven and Schubert, both of them great symphonists, as the culmination of the 'classical' period, and Weber, Berlioz, Wagner, Chopin, Schumann, and Mendelssohn as opening the 'romantic' period. Either classification is equally defensible, and the main reason for adopting the latter one is perhaps that the close connexion between the Haydn–Mozart symphony and the Beethoven symphony makes it a little difficult to thrust a dividing knife between them.

In the present article it is unnecessary to discuss the musical Romantic Movement at any length, as a special article upon the subject is given elsewhere in this volume (see *Romantic*).

Later developments of the Romantic Movement were the Nationalistic Movement associated with such names as those of Smetana, Dvořák, Grieg, Mussorgsky, and Albéniz (see *Nationalism in Music*), and Musical Impressionism, associated with the names of certain French composers, particularly Debussy (see *Impressionism*; also example under *Harmony* 14).

The present article was originally written in the early thirties of the twentieth century, and at that date the Romantic Movement in music had by no means exhausted itself, for not only were Strauss and Elgar (both then still alive) strongly romantic, but some of the then most modern-minded composers (especially the German and Austrian group clustered around Schönberg, q.v.) were, whatever they might think of themselves, extremely romantic—sometimes to the point of exaggeration.

The period of a century from the death of Beethoven (roughly 1830 to 1930) probably saw a greater change in the texture and forms of music than any similar period at any earlier stage in the history of the art. Beethoven's harmonies may be looked upon as those of his elder contemporaries, Haydn and Mozart, plus an added force and pungency, but Wagner's go far beyond these. The work of Wagner in the strengthening and (in a sense) rationalizing of the musical drama is discussed under his own name. His very free polyphony (see example under *Harmony* 13), and his introduction of new chromatic resources, brought into existence a harmony so distinctive that if one or two consecutive measures are played we can infallibly ascribe them to their author. Abandoning very early in his career the symphonic forms of composition and devoting himself solely to the dramatic, his desire to give immediate expression to every fleeting emotion and to bind a whole long dramatic setting into one led him to discard set divisions into recitative, aria, chorus, etc., and to weave a seamless web throughout a whole Act by the adroit handling and rehandling of short pithy musical motifs. With this he also added to both the variety of instruments in the orchestra and the number of players of each individual instrument, with the result that from his middle-period works onward to our own day orchestral music of every type is much more highly coloured than before. In all such matters Strauss was merely the follower and continuator of Wagner. Brahms, however, though in the nature of his thought a typical German Romantic, inclined in processes to the classical side, having 'taken off' directly from Beethoven, and deviated relatively little from his methods.

The application of the general Wagnerian system to orchestral music led to the introduction of the *Symphonic Poem* (q.v.), a mid-nineteenth-century application of that type of composition that has always in some measure existed, called *Programme Music* (q.v.).

Perhaps the principal figures in the Romantic phase are the following:

GERMANY AND AUSTRIA. Weber (1786–1826). Wagner (1813–83). Mendelssohn (1809–47). Schumann (1810–56). Brahms (1833–97). Strauss (1864–1949). Schönberg (1874–1951).

FRANCE. Berlioz (1803–69). Franck (1822–90; Belgian by birth). Debussy (1862–1918). Ravel (1875–1937).

POLAND. Chopin (1810–49).

HUNGARY. Liszt (1811–86).

BOHEMIA. Smetana (1824–84). Dvořák (1841–1904).

RUSSIA. Glinka (1804–57). Balakiref (1837–1910). Mussorgsky (1839–81). Rimsky-Korsakof (1844–1908). Tchaikovsky (1840–93). Scriabin (1872–1915).

ITALY. Verdi (1813–1901). Puccini (1858–1924). Malipiero (1882–1973). Casella (1883–1947).

SPAIN. Albéniz (1860–1909). Granados (1867–1916). Falla (1876–1946). Turina (1882–1949).

BRITAIN. Elgar (1857–1934). Vaughan Williams (1872–1958). Holst (1874–1934). Bax (1883–1953). Walton (born 1902). Britten (1913–76).

8. The Revolt against Romance. The musical texture of the latest of the Neo-Romantics, as we may call them, is, in places, almost totally different from anything that any composer had imagined possible thirty years before they began their work. The old distinc-tion between concord and discord seems to be abandoned, the old key system has gone, the old forms are perceptible only as underlying the composition in the most general sort of way, and, in an orchestral piece, the instruments are used in a manner that to the older Romantics would have seemed intolerably harsh. Yet one can sense in their works (though in some cases they do not themselves seem to realize this) the old romantic ideals, and, indeed, some of them seem to be even overcharged with emotional content.

We may take Schönberg (Austrian born: 1874–1951), already mentioned, as typical of this school—at any rate in his earlier and middle periods.

Contemporary with them was another school that not only deliberately attempted to eschew romanticism but to some extent succeeded in doing so. The members of this school decried the 'subjective', which seems to mean that their music is intended to be not an expression of human feeling but merely a pattern in sounds. A number of composers were associated with this anti-romantic or neo-classical ideal, but for the purposes of the present article it will be sufficient to name three whose position is admitted:

RUSSIA. Stravinsky (1882–1971) in his later phases.

HUNGARY. Bartók (1881–1945).

GERMANY. Hindemith (1895–1963).

As indicating the anti-romantic aims of these composers the reader may be reminded that Stravinsky has taken pains to secure that certain of his works shall be played entirely without 'expression', and that Bartók, as a pianist playing his own works, sought that hard percussive tone which in a pianist playing any of the older music would be looked upon by every listener as an affront to the composer and to himself.

There have been attempts from time to time to make use in composition of intervals smaller than have hitherto been used (see *Microtones*; *Harmony* 19), though there is little sign of their widespread adoption.

9. After the second World War. The later 1930s, followed by the second World War, brought a halt to the experimentalism of the previous period. While the United States, where Schönberg continued to live and teach, saw the development of note-row methods, European countries were cut off until 1946, when the opportunities opened up by centres such as Darmstadt gave young composers a chance at last to hear and study the works of Schönberg and (especially) Webern. In a very short time experimentalism had produced results that some traditionally minded musicians could not regard as music at all, their only response being a despairing 'What next'? —a question that has occurred to similarly minded lovers of painting, sculpture, and literature. There is a particular analogy with the successive phases passed through by painting during the first half of the twentieth century—with the 'schools' of various innovators, each school apparently convinced that a revolution was called for and then, in a very few years, giving place to another school just as sure. Many observers see the apparent confusion in the arts as a reflection of an unstable age of transition politically and sociologically. Most of the main trends in music: the note-row of Schönberg, Webern, and their followers; microtonal experiments; electronic music, and the like, have in common the fact that they are all reactions against the immediate past.

Music has been called 'a compromise between chaos and monotony', and much of the experimentation of modern composers seems to be a fluctuation between the two extremes of randomness and mechanical repetition. From about 1950 there was observable the phenomenon of 'total serialization', in which the composer resigned his free will to a predetermined system. In this 'totally organized' music not only the notes, but also the rhythms, dynamics, and other elements of a composition are organized according to set principles. At the other extreme there are composers who allow chance to take a hand to a varying degree in the end result of their labours; sometimes the choice between a number of alternatives may be made by the throw of dice, so that no two performances will ever be quite alike. Other composers, such as Stockhausen, have provided works with sections of varying length which can be played in any order. Sometimes a little window in one page may give the player a chance to introduce a few bars from another page, and so on. Taking a leaf from the jazz musician's book, room is often left for joint or separate improvisation. (There is precedent for this in some of the works of, for instance, Frescobaldi.) The notion of chance-governed art is met with elsewhere than in music. In 1962 there appeared in France the novel *Composition No. 1*, by Marc Saporta, consisting of separate pages intended to be shuffled like a pack of cards, giving endless variations in the sequence of episodes in the hero's life.

Once the point of complete freedom is reached, it is no longer possible to distinguish between bad art and non-art. The general music-lover and even the trained musician—not necessarily of the most conservative kind—is often at a loss to distinguish certainly between genuine creative talent and charlatanry.

Somewhere between the theatre and the plastic arts is the 'Happening', which has been defined as 'an assemblage of events which also includes people as part of the whole', in other words, an audience-participation affair owing much to Dadaist occurrences of the 1920s. During a performance of John Cage's *Theater Piece* in Rome in 1963 a packed house watched while 'the pianist made his entrance by throwing a dead fish into his instrument. . . . One musician was walking around the stage noisily dragging a chair while another, dressed in a nightgown, was handing out clammy pizzas to the audience'. The more advanced parlour-game manifestations have an unfortunate tendency to bring all advanced music into disrepute.

The German radio stations are able to place almost limitless resources at the disposal of a composer, who is then tempted to write works with little chance of a hearing in other circumstances. A performance of Stockhausen's *Gruppen*, written for three orchestras, makes impossible demands on some halls, and there are other works for five groups of players, or for four orchestras and four choruses. But see *Germany* 9 for the somewhat cartel-like situation attending the promotion of contemporary music in that country.

The term 'Third Stream' was coined by the American composer Gunther Schuller in about 1958 during a lecture; it describes the attempts being made at that time to fuse 'the improvisational spontaneity and rhythmic vitality of jazz with the compositional procedures acquired in Western music during 700 years of musical development', producing a kind of music separate from either ingredient.

Faced with the inability of conventionally trained musicians to perform his increasingly complex music, the contemporary composer frequently takes refuge in electronic music, where he has absolute control over the final result as it reaches the listener. *Musique concrète* is the term coined in 1949 by Pierre Schaeffer to describe music made of real sounds, tape-recorded and manipulated in various ways: played faster or slower or backwards, or as a montage of scraps, with overtones added or subtracted, and so on. Radiodiffusion Française set up a studio in 1950. Among the composers who first interested themselves in these developments were Boulez, Messiaen, Jolivet, Delannoy, Irving Fine, and John Cage. In Germany 'electronic music' pursued a somewhat different, and in the event more fruitful, path: the raw materials were not natural sounds, but combinations of tones themselves electronically produced (see *Electric Musical Instruments*). Studios for the development of these techniques were set up in Cologne, and later in New York, Milan, Tokyo, Darmstadt, Rome, and elsewhere. These studios have provided many composers with the means of training themselves in novel techniques which promise in time to become part of the common coin of their art.

In any period of experimentalism, much time has to be spent exploring blind alleys in order to make sure that they really are blind. To listeners with long memories, much of what is presented as 'new' seems no more than an identical recapitulation of yesterday's experiments. With the development of the avant-garde festivals there seems to have developed a paradoxical 'avant-garde tradition' forming a self-contained society with its own audience, fascinated by novelty as such to a degree that becomes ritualistic. Much of the music heard is presented by under-rehearsed and not always very enthusiastic orchestras, or by singers few of whom have the ear or rhythmic sense demanded in the performance of modern music. But the unaided ear can rarely if ever follow the thread of a serial work through its various rearrangements; wrong notes and general inaccuracy in performance are constantly accepted not merely by the public, but also by initiates. Verbal explanations are not always helpful. Those who undertake to spread the gospel of modern music by means of the written word often forget that the basis of any technical language must be clarity and precision. Composers (not always the clearest expounders of their own music) frequently freely borrow terms from logic and mathematics, though familiar with neither subject. As a result of this and other trials, the 'ordinary listener' may be forgiven if he does not bother to discover whether the music produced as a result of the latest of a succession of short-lived technical fads means anything worth understanding.

Much is made of what seems to be a complete cleavage between the ordinary music-lover and the doings of the avant-garde. Nevertheless, in spite of what is sometimes seen as a small group of advanced composers writing music for each other, something of the new styles and techniques does find its way into the main stream of music, particularly into television background music and commercial jingles; just as the influence of Mondriaan can be seen in the packages on the shelves of a supermarket.

During the fifties and sixties a number of established figures made their own efforts to come to terms with the new resources: Stravinsky with his *Canticum Sacrum* and *Threni*, Copland (*Piano Fantasy*), Ginastera, and many others.

Whether music has really reached the point beyond which no further development is possible must be doubted. Note-row methods do not preclude the appearance of composers with the lyrical expressiveness of Berg and Dallapic-

cola, and amid all the extremes of experimentation there are no doubt younger men who can take what they need for their own purposes.

The latter part of this article has necessarily dwelt in the first instance with the technical innovations of the twentieth century. However, the standard concert fare offered to the subscription audiences of the world's great orchestras does not reflect much of the result of these endeavours. And it is important to bear in mind that in the midst of all this experimentation many highly successful composers such as Walton, Britten, Hindemith, Barber, Menotti, Milhaud, and many others have continued to write traditional music in their own personal styles, apparently unaffected by what was going on around them. Whatever the future may hold, most certainly it is impossible to draw a line and say, 'beyond this there is no art'.

10. Conclusion. In concluding this article it may be pointed out that a brief well-balanced generalization of the history of any art is extremely difficult to achieve, and must always leave room at some point or another for the dissent of some student of the subject equally instructed, perhaps, with the framer of the generalization but temperamentally different. Nevertheless, it is felt that the rough classification in which the above rapid sketch presents the labours of the composers of over a thousand years would be accepted with little reservation by most authorities. The history of music may be thought of in terms of cycles. Each cycle has periods of growth, maturity, and decline; yet the cycles overlap, so that composers are experimenting with new styles while a previous style is at its point of maturity. The most debatable points are probably the drawing of a line after which the Romantic School may be said to have come into being, and the division of the more advanced composers of the twentieth century into Neo-Romantics and Anti-Romantics. The selection of names for mention is also, inevitably, debatable ground, but it is felt that the chief names have been included.

For further details see the articles upon some of these countries and upon the composers named.

ARTICLES ON COGNATE SUBJECTS:

Modes; Scales; Key; Hexachord; Musica Ficta; Notation and Nomenclature; Tablature; Melody; Harmony (and articles listed at the end of this); *Counterpoint; Figured Bass; Ornaments; Phrasing.*

Form (including section on 'History of Forms'); *Suite; Sonata; Symphony; Overture; Concerto; Cadenza; Symphonic Poem; Programme Music; Ground; Canon; Chorale Prelude; Voluntary; Chamber Music;*

Ars Nova; Cantata; Canzona; Chanson; Sumer is icumen in; Round; Catch; Frottola; Madrigal; Glee; Part Song.

Church Music; Liturgy; Common Prayer; Plainsong; Mass; Requiem; Passion Music; Oratorio; Motet; Psalms; Hymns and Hymn Tunes (including 'Metrical Psalms'); *Chorale; Cathedral Music in Britain; Chapel Royal; Opera* (and articles mentioned at end of that one); *Ballet.*

Harpsichord Family; Clavichord;

Pianoforte; Organ; Orchestra; Violin Family; Violin Family; Brass; Cornett Family; Cornet; Trumpet Family; Trombone Family; Horn Family; Tuba Family; Clarinet Family; Oboe Family; Percussion Family; Military Band.

Classical; Romantic.

Nationalism in Music; England; Scotland; Wales; Ireland; Italy; Spain; France; Germany and Austria; Belgium; Holland; United States; Jewish Music.

HITTITES. See *Bagpipe Family* 1.

HLZBL. (Ger.). Short for *Holzbläser*, 'wood-blowers', i.e. the wood-wind department.

H.M.S. PINAFORE, or THE LASS THAT LOVED A SAILOR (Sullivan). Produced at the Opéra Comique, London, in 1878. Libretto by W. S. Gilbert.

ACT I

SCENE: *The Quarterdeck of H.M.S. Pinafore, off Portsmouth. Noon*

The sailors at work are visited by **Little Buttercup**, the bumboat woman, with a miniature general store in her basket. She hints at an aching heart beneath her cheery manner, and **Dick Deadeye,** a saturnine, ugly seaman, agrees. At the name of **Ralph Rackstraw,** another seaman, but this time a melodious one, Buttercup murmurs: 'That name! Remorse! Remorse!' Ralph loves above his station—Josephine, the daughter of Captain Corcoran of the *Pinafore.*

The **Captain,** a regular nautical Turveydrop for deportment, confides in Buttercup that his daughter, sought in marriage by Sir Joseph Porter, First Lord of the Admiralty, will not accept him. **Josephine** now appears, and tells her father that her heart is already given to one of his sailors.

Now **Sir Joseph** comes on board, attended by 'his sisters, his cousins, and his aunts'. His democratic ideas encourage Ralph to approach Josephine, but she, too conscious of disparity in rank, haughtily rejects him, though secretly she loves him, and when she finds him about to take his life in lovelorn despair, she avows her real feelings. They determine to steal ashore that night and be married, though warned of their folly by Dick Deadeye.

ACT II

SCENE: *The Deck by Moonlight*

Buttercup finds the Captain in sentimental mood, and darkly hints that she has gipsy blood, and that she can foresee a change in store for him. She leaves the ship, and Sir Joseph Porter comes to complain to the Captain that Josephine will not have him. Taking her suitor's democratic opinions at their face value, she gets him to admit that disparity in rank should not impede a love-match. He imagines she is thinking of her position and his, but actually he is unwittingly justifying Ralph's cause.

Now comes Dick Deadeye to reveal that Ralph and Josephine plan to elope. The Captain springs out on the pair as they are about to go ashore. Ralph defies him, and he uses a swear-word, on which the shocked Sir Joseph, who has come on deck, orders him to his cabin. He is still more shocked when he finds that Josephine wants to marry Ralph, whom he puts in irons.

Buttercup now unburdens herself of her secret: as a baby-farmer in earlier days she mixed up two children, one of whom was Ralph, the other, the Captain! Things are put right: Ralph appears in Captain's uniform, and Corcoran in that of an A.B. Sir Joseph's democratic principles will not carry him as far as marrying the daughter of a common sailor, so Ralph gets his Josephine, and the former Captain pairs off with Buttercup.

HMV (His Master's Voice). An artist, Francis Barraud, had painted (about 1900) a picture of a fox-terrier intently listening to an Edison phonograph which was supposed to be reproducing the voice of the dog's owner. This was offered to Edison (see *Gramophone* 1), but as he refused it the cylinder instrument was painted out and a disk and horn instrument substituted. The changed picture was bought by its present proprietors, the Gramophone Co. Ltd. and their former associates in the USA, the RCA Victor Co., both of whom use it as a sort of trade mark.

HOB AND NOB. See *Campbells are coming.*

HOBERTUS. See *Obrecht.*

HOBOE (Ger.; plur. *Hoboen*). Oboe. See *Oboe* 5 a.

HOBRECHT. See *Obrecht.*

HOCHBRUCKER. See *Harp* 2 c.

HOCHDRUCKSTIMMEN (Ger.). 'High-pressure stops' (organ tubas).

HOCHKAMMERTON. See *Pitch* 3.

HÖCHST (Ger.). 'Highest', 'in the highest degree' (followed by some adjective or adverb).

HOCHZEITSMARSCH (Ger.). 'Wedding march.'

HOCHZEITSZUG (Ger.). 'Wedding procession.'

HOCKET (or **Hoquet,** or **Ochetto,** etc.). Literally, 'hiccough'. A device in early contrapuntal music (twelfth and thirteenth centuries) by which rests were introduced in two vocal parts (without any respect for the words), in such a way that a note in one would coincide with a rest in another, and so something would always be sounding. One would get an idea of the effect in its most extreme form by playing notes on a keyboard instrument alternately with one finger of the right hand and another in the left. At the period of the Hocket composers were eagerly experimenting with all sorts of new-invented devices and apparently this one greatly pleased their innocent developing minds.

HODDINOTT, ALUN. Born at Bargoed, Glam., in 1929. He gained his D.Mus. at the University College of South Wales and joined the staff in 1959; he has also studied under Arthur Benjamin. His works include five symphonies and concertos for viola, piano, clarinet, and harp. His style, though not discarding tonality, is advanced harmonically and often somewhat sombrely romantic and dramatic in character.

HODGES, EDWARD (1796–1867). See *Organ* 9.

HOËG. See *Greek Church* 4.

HOFFDING, FINN (born 1899). See *Scandinavia* 2.

HOFFMANN.

(1) E. T. A.—i.e. Ernst Theodor Amadeus (p. 397, pl. **68.** 6). Born at Königsberg in 1776 and died in Berlin in 1822, aged forty-six. He was a government official who loved drama and music and who developed a vein of whimsical authorship in novels and essays, which greatly attracted Weber and still more strongly Schumann, and at a somewhat later date Brahms (Schumann's *Kreisleriana* was based upon the fantastic novel about 'Johannes Kreisler, the Kapellmeister', this Johannes being of the nature of a self-portrait of the novelist).

See the Articles under the individual names

1. LIŚZT (1811–86)

2. HUBAY (1858–1937)

3. LEHÁR (1870–1948)

4. DOHNÁNYI (1877–1960)

5. BARTÓK (1881–1945)

6. KODÁLY (1882–1967)

7. HUNGARIAN MUSICIANS IN THE 18TH CENTURY
In the centre, a bagpipe player

8. A PLAYER OF THE TAROGATO
From an 18th-century print
See *Clarinet* 4 h

1. MINSTRELS AT AN IRISH FEAST
Wood engraving in Derricke's *Image of Irelande*, 1581

2. TURLOGH O'CAROLAN (1670–1738)
See *Ireland* 1, 5

3. HEMPSON, THE IRISH HARPER (1695–1807)

4. THOMAS MOORE (1779–1852)
By Sir Thomas Lawrence, P.R.A.

5. JOHN FIELD (1782–1837)
The inventor of the Nocturne

6. JOSEPH ROBINSON (1816–98)
By Goedecker

7. SIR ROBERT STEWART (1825–94)

8. SIR CHAS. STANFORD (1852–1924)
By 'Spy'

In this way Hoffmann, like Jean Paul Richter, was a literary force behind the Romantic movement in music (see *Romantic*). But he was also himself a composer, writing ten or eleven operas (including the romantic *Undine* beloved by Weber), chamber music, piano sonatas, choral works, and all manner of things.

He was, indeed, a very many-sided and able man, a far-seeing critic of contemporary music, theatre manager, conductor, novelist, poet, and competent civil servant. He was odd in manner, original in thought, and 'nobody's enemy but his own'. He represents a phase of German mentality and his memory is prized by his countrymen today as that of one who made a contribution to the nation's cultural traditions.

See references under *Criticism* 2; *Colour and Music* 4; *Tales of Hoffmann*; *Schumann*.

(2) A. H. ('of Fallersleben'). See *Deutschland über Alles*.

HOFMANN, JOSEF (CASIMIR) (1876–1957). Great pianist. See references under *Misattributed Compositions* ('Dvorsky'); *Gramophone* 1.

HOFMANNSTHAL, HUGO VON (1874–1929). See *Libretto*; *Ariadne*; *Elektra*; *Rosenkavalier*; *Strauss, Richard*.

HOGARTH.

(1) WILLIAM (1697–1764). The painter and engraver, many of whose productions chronicle the general and musical life of the time, as for instance, the series *Masquerades and Operas*, *The Beggar's Opera*, and various detached pieces. See references under *Street Music* 6; *Beggar's Opera*; *Festing, John*; *Ballad* 1; *Bladder and String*; *Fife*; also p. 101, pl. **18**. 1, 5; 992, **165**. 2.

(2) GEORGE (1783–1870). An Edinburgh lawyer who came to London and established himself firmly as a writer, especiall yon the drama and music, and as editor of song and hymn-tune books, etc. His father-in-law was George Thompson (q.v.) and his son-in-law Charles Dickens, under whose editorship of the *Daily News* he became music critic of that journal. For fourteen years he served as secretary to the Philharmonic Society.

HOHLFELD. See *Improvisation* 4.

HOHLFLÖTE. See *Organ* 14 II.

HOHNER. See *Reed-Organ Family* 3.

HO-HOANE. Corruption of the Irish lament 'Och-one'.

HOL, RICHARD. Born at Amsterdam in 1825 and died at Utrecht in 1904, aged seventy-eight. He was a piano teacher, organist, choral and orchestral conductor, and man of valuable general musical activity. He also composed symphonies, chamber music, operas, an oratorio, masses, many songs and other things, wrote a book on Sweelinck, and edited a journal called *The Organ*.

For a reference to the conditions of his time in Holland and his influence thereon see *Holland* 7.

HOLBACH, PAUL HEINRICH DIETRICH, BARON D' (1723–89). See *Bouffons, Guerre des*.

HOLBORNE.

(1) ANTHONY. Died in 1602. He was an Englishman who published (1597) a book of music for the cittern, etc.

(2) WILLIAM. He was the brother of the above, and contributed Ayres in three voices to the book above mentioned.

HOLBROOKE, JOSEPH CHARLES (sometimes signed 'Josef'). Born near London in 1878 and died there in 1958, aged eighty. He was a student of the Royal Academy of Music and led an early professional life of great activity and variety.

He wrote works of every kind, including an opera trilogy, *The Cauldron of Anwyn*; his patron, Lord Howard de Walden ('T. E. Ellis'), was the librettist.

He composed fluently and ably, but sometimes without sufficient self-criticism. He was a vigorous, even violent, controversialist in support of British music in general and his own in particular. In later life he was largely forgotten, and became embittered and eccentric.

See *Saxophone*.

HOLINESS SECT. See *Dance* 7.

HOLLAND

1. Before the Reformation. The musical history of Holland naturally attaches itself to that of the Flemish part of *Belgium* (q.v.), which by race, language, and history is closely associated with it. The great blossoming time of Flemish musical art was a period of two centuries, roughly from 1400 to 1600. Curiously, the part of the Netherlands which English-speaking people now call Holland did not share very largely in the activity of this period, its one really notable composer being **Obrecht** (1453–1505).

2. The Reformation. With the coming of protestantism, psalm singing became impor-

tant, as in France and Switzerland. A publication of note is that of *Souter Liedekens*, i.e. 'Psalter-songs', in 1540 (additional volumes later); this was published at Antwerp and in its many editions during the next sixty or seventy years helped to popularize the metrical psalms and also (being cleverly harmonized for three voices) to carry into modest homes the choral singing that had, under catholicism, been the glory of the greater churches (see also *Hymns and Hymn Tunes* 17 c). Like the German chorales, those of Dutch protestantism were partly popular tunes. The Emperor Charles V and his son, Philip II of Spain, in whose reigns the Inquisition was active in the Netherlands, both issued edicts against the use of this book. From the early years of the seventeenth century onwards it was superseded by other works of its kind.

It may be noted that at the end of the sixteenth century English actors and musicians were popular in the Netherlands, and that thus English tunes tended to creep into song and psalm books.

3. Organ Music. The organ does not appear to have been excluded from the Dutch churches but, owing to their generally Calvinistic leanings, though organ playing was cultivated it was in the sixteenth and earlier seventeenth centuries rarely used during services; in fact, the church, out of service time, was a sort of public promenade and organ music a recreation. The greatest Dutch organist of all history is **Sweelinck** (q.v.) of Amsterdam, who at the end of the sixteenth century and the beginning of the seventeenth enjoyed high fame and exercised wide influence, and whose compositions (now completely republished) form one of the firm foundations of the organ repertory (he also left much choral music). An important contemporary of his was **Schuyt** (d. 1616), organist at Leyden, who left instrumental music and madrigals. **Reinken**, at whose feet at Hamburg Bach was glad to sit, spent most of his early years in Holland, and for a time held a position as organist at Deventer. The English diarist Evelyn, travelling in Holland in 1641, records that 'generally all the churches in Holland are furnished with organs'—which was then far from being the case in Evelyn's own country. The traditional interest of the Dutch in organ playing continued, and the organs of Holland became renowned throughout the world, so that if the standard nineteenth-century English work on the organ (Hopkins and Rimbault, 1877) be examined, it will be found that the authors felt it necessary to include specifications of no fewer than ten Dutch organs, including, of course, the celebrated one of Haarlem (1735–8), long looked upon as one of the musical marvels of the world.

4. The Carillon. Another keyboard art, that of the Carillon (see *Bell* 4), began to attain important development about the beginning of the sixteenth century. There are now about twenty carillons of the first importance in Holland, and probably over a hundred altogether.

5. The Seventeenth-century Decline in Composition. After Sweelinck no Dutch composer of importance appears for a long time, the life suddenly evaporating out of the art, exactly as it did in the southern part of the same territory (see *Belgium*). Dutch artistic genius seemed to be fluid and to be led off into the channel of painting (Hals, b. 1581; Rembrandt, 1606; Steen, 1626; Ruysdael, 1628; Vermeer, 1632; Hobbema, 1638, etc.).

6. The German Influence. There seems to have been a new impulse in Dutch musical activity towards the end of the eighteenth century, but it was largely governed by German example. It is curious to note that Mozart's *Don Giovanni* was performed in Amsterdam in 1793, only six years after its first production, at Prague—and the more curious because operatic enterprise has never been typical of Holland, operatic institutions there always proving of a more or less ephemeral character.

During the first part of the nineteenth century all the northern countries were musically under the sway of Germany; most of the talented composers were sent to Leipzig for training, the German outlook and musical idiom prevailed, and, in Holland, at any rate, texts chosen for setting in solo or choral style were often German. The hint of a coming revival of independence in music in Holland may be seen in Schumann's musical journal for 1843, in which he published this suggestion:

'It really looks as if the nations bordering on Germany desired to emancipate themselves from the influence of German music. This might annoy a German nationalist, but could only appear natural and cheerful to the more profound thinker, if he understood human nature. So we see the French-Pole, Chopin, the Englishman Bennett, and Verhulst the Dutchman . . .'

7. Verhulst, Hol, Nicolai. Verhulst (1816–91), a gifted composer, though he set Dutch texts and worked hard and successfully to cultivate a more intense musical life in his native country, failed to fulfil the promise he showed, and to justify the companionship accorded him with Chopin, and even that with Bennett, another promise-breaker. Whilst he encouraged musical development in Holland, he in certain ways retarded it, for he was a conservative, opposed to Liszt, Wagner, Berlioz, and others of the more advanced school of the day. His contemporaries **Richard Hol** (1825–1904) and **Willem Nicolai** (1829–96) were not reactionaries, fortunately. The names of these three are usually uttered together as those of the men who helped to make a new musical Holland, in the sense of one in which music was taken seriously. And they definitely abolished the idea that the Dutch language was unsuitable for musical setting.

8. The Later Nineteenth-century Renascence and After. In the 1880s there came into prominence three other fine musicians, who as composers exercised, more evidently than any before them, the Dutch spirit— **Bernard Zweers** (1854–1924), **Alphons Diepenbrock** (1862–1921), and **Johan Wagenaar** (1862–1941). Zweers wrote, amongst other things, a symphony, 'To my Country'; Diepenbrock (whose works were, after his death, published by means of a subscription and a government subvention) wrote theatre music, church music, songs, etc. Wagenaar wrote, with a light and humorous touch, operas and orchestral works (serious works also). Zweers and Wagenaar had influence as teachers, and the composers of

Holland today owe a good deal to them. It is difficult in a short article like this to choose composers for mention, but of the older group perhaps the following should be added to those already mentioned—**Julius Röntgen** (1855–1934), who amongst other valuable activities issued editions of old Dutch songs and dances, and **Cornelis Dopper** (1870–1939), who wrote many symphonies including one entitled 'Rembrandt', another 'Amsterdam', and another 'Zuyder Zee'. Amongst the prominent later men are **Sem Dresden** (1881–1957), **Bernhard van den Sigtenhorst-Meyer** (born 1888), who, having visited the Dutch East Indies, shows the influence of the East in some compositions, and **Willem Pijper** (1894–1947). (Sigtenhorst-Meyer wrote a string quartet on a novel scheme—five movements, respectively entitled *The Adoration of the Magi, The Flight into Egypt*, and so on to *The Angels at the Empty Tomb*.) These not only became known abroad, but laboured to make contemporary foreign music known in their own land; they are, then, important links with the outside world. It may be remarked that, in general, the Dutch musical public leans to conservatism, and the Dutch music publishers equally, so that the work of the younger men has usually been published not at home but in France or England; though the subsidized organization 'Donemus' ('Documentation in the Netherlands for Music'), founded in 1947, publishes the scores of works by Dutch composers together with recordings.

9. Musical Organizations. There have been a number of valuable musical societies in Holland. The Felix Meritis, for letters, art, and science, was founded in 1777, and came to an end in 1889; it included orchestral concerts in its scheme. The Maatschappij tot Bevordering der Toonkunst (Association for the Furthering of Music) was founded in 1829, and has forty branches, with headquarters in Amsterdam; it encourages choral singing and other music-making and carries on seventeen schools of music. A branch of this last society is the Vereeniging voor Nederlandsche Muziekgeschiedenis (Society for the History of Dutch Music), which has published the music of Sweelinck and Obrecht and also that of the Fleming, Josquin des Prés (see *Belgium*). The Concertgebouw (Concert-hall) Society carries on the world-famous orchestra conducted first by Willem Kes (q.v.), from 1895 by Mengelberg (q.v.), and then, from 1947, by Van Beinum and Haitink; this orchestra gives every season eighty to ninety concerts in Amsterdam, with many more in other cities. At The Hague is the equally celebrated Residentie Orchestra, and Utrecht has a symphony orchestra. Altogether there are eleven subsidized orchestras and three radio orchestras, together with a great number of less prominent concert organizations of various kinds.

ARTICLES ON COGNATE SUBJECTS:

(*a*) *Belgium* 1–3; *Concert* 13; *Germany* 4.
(*b*) *Andriessen, W. and H.; Anrooy; Badings; Brucken-Fock; Dresden, Sem; Hellendaal; Hol; Hutschenruyter; Kes; Mengelberg; Obrecht; Pijper; Röntgen; Schäfer; Schwindl; Silas; Sweelinck; Van Dieren; Vermeulen; Wagenaar; Wert.*

HOLLINS, ALFRED. Born at Hull in 1865 and died in Edinburgh in 1942, aged seventy-six. Though born totally blind, he established a high reputation as a performer. In his youth he toured many countries as a pianist and as an organist. From his early thirties he was organist of West St. George's Church, Edinburgh. He was an admirable extemporizer. His organ compositions are numerous and much played. In 1936 he published his reminiscences.

Cf. *Macmillan.*

HOLLYWOOD BOWL. This is a natural amphitheatre near Los Angeles in California, where, since the 1920s, concerts, etc., have been given. The seating capacity is 25,000. A ten weeks' summer symphony concert season, directed by the most famous conductors of the world, and an annual prize of $1,000 for a symphonic poem have been features of the many and varied activities.

HOLMBOE, VAGN (born 1909). See *Scandinavia* 2.

HOLMES.
(1) JOHN. In the latter part of the sixteenth century and earlier part of the seventeenth he was organist successively of Winchester and Salisbury Cathedrals and a composer of church music and madrigals.

(2) THOMAS. Died at Salisbury in 1638, was son of the above, and is faintly remembered as a composer of catches.

(3) EDWARD (1797–1859). Pianist and the author of a well-known biography of Mozart, and of other things; friend of Leigh Hunt and the Novello family.

See *Barocco.*

HOLMÈS, AUGUSTA MAY ANNE. Born in Paris in 1847 and there died in 1903, aged fifty-five. She was a pianist and composer—as the latter a pupil of César Franck (q.v.). Her works included symphonies, operas, songs, etc. She was of partly Irish descent and her name had originally no accent on the 'e'. (She used also the *nom-de-plume* of 'Hermann Zenta'.)

HOLST.

(1) GUSTAV THEODORE (p. 337, pl. **54.** 2). Born at Cheltenham in 1874 and died near London in 1934, aged fifty-nine. He composed as soon as he could hold a pen and played various instruments as fast as they came his way. He began professional life as a village organist and conductor of village choral societies, and then at nineteen went to the Royal College of Music, where he spent five years, Stanford being his master for composition.

To earn his living he enlisted as a trombonist, at first in theatre orchestras and then in the Scottish Orchestra. Approaching thirty he laid down his trombone and engaged in various music masterships in schools in and around London. From 1906 he took direction of the music of St. Paul's Girls' School, to which, helped by an excellent staff, he was able to give exceptional importance. At about the same period he became connected with Morley College, a working-class institution in South London, where he developed many activities.

During the later part of the first World War, at the request of the present author, he readily agreed to go to Salonica and then to Constantinople to organize musical activities amongst the soldiers; he was successful in arousing enthusiasm, and sent home for large consignments of harmony textbooks, song-books, and copies of Byrd's three-part Mass—a special edition of which was printed for his use, several performances duly taking place. This is mentioned as typical of his power, from his village days, of communicating a love for the finest music to any body of men, women, or children with whom he might happen to meet.

His compositions all have an original cast— The Planets Suite (in the scheme of which astrological leanings exhibit themselves), The Hymn of Jesus (in which a Gnostic tendency is seen), The Perfect Fool, an opera of a particular type of humour all his own, At the Boar's Head, an opera in which he has aimed at making Falstaff move to genuine folk-tune strains, and so forth. Some of the later works, such as the Fugal Overture and the Fugal Concerto, resemble in formal aim the neo-classic (see History 8) works of Stravinsky (q.v.), which they slightly anticipate, and the change from the huge body of instruments of The Planets to the tiny group used in these later works recalls Stravinsky's similar drop to modest demands after the crushingly orchestrated Rite of Spring. He had an unusually strong interest in rhythmic problems.

In view of the occasional raising of the question of his origin, it may be added that his paternal great-grandfather, of Swedish descent, was born at Riga and thence came to England.

See *Choral Symphony*; *Dance* 7—for 'The Hymn of Jesus'; *Opera* 24 f (1916–23–25); *Concerto* 6 c (1874); *Competitions* 3; *Percussion* 4 a; *Oboe* 4 i.

(2) IMOGEN. Born in London in 1907. She studied under her father (see above) and at the Royal College of Music and became known as a pianist and composer. She was for some time attached to the Music School of Dartington Hall, Devon, and was later closely associated with the group surrounding Benjamin Britten. She has published a biography of her father and also a critical discussion of his works.

'HOLY' MASS (Haydn). See *Nicknamed Compositions* 13.

HOLYWELL MUSIC ROOM, OXFORD. See *Concert* 9.

HOLZ (Ger.). 'Wood.'

HOLZBLÄSER (Ger.). 'Wood-blowers', i.e. wood-wind players.

HOLZBLASINSTRUMENTE (Ger.). 'Wood-blow-instruments', i.e. the wood-wind.

HOLZFLÖTE (Ger.). 'Wooden flute' (organ stop).

HOLZHARMONIKA (Ger.). Xylophone; see *Percussion Family* 2 f, 4, 5 f.

HOLZSCHLÄGEL (Ger.). Wooden drumstick.

HOLZTROMPETE (Ger.). See *Clarinet Family* 4 h.

HOME FOR RETIRED MUSIC TEACHERS. See under *Patronage* 7.

HOMER, SIDNEY. Born at Boston, Massachusetts, in 1864 and died in Florida in 1953, aged eighty-eight. Certain of his songs have won wide popularity. In 1895 he married his pupil, Louise D. Beatty (Louise Homer, the opera singer—1871–1947). Cf. *Barber, Samuel*.

HOME, SWEET HOME. Before reading what follows see *Opera* 21 c. (The reference is to the opera *Clari*).

There is a story that the tune is of Sicilian origin, but Bishop, who composed *Clari*, successfully claimed the tune as entirely his own when it became the subject of litigation: he explained its previous appearance as a 'Sicilian Air' by the circumstance that he had been engaged to edit an album of national melodies, had lacked one from Sicily, had composed this, and had published it as 'Sicilian'. Thus in taking it into his opera he was adopting his own child—which must not be stolen from him by others. The court accepted this explanation, and gave the case against the publishers who had accepted as literal the attribution 'Sicilian' and had issued their own editions of it in rivalry with Bishop's own.

The song appears repeatedly throughout the opera, which has led to a suggestion in recent times that Bishop was the pioneer 'plugger' and the first exponent of the 'theme-song'. The original manuscript of the opera is in the possession of the University of Rochester, N.Y.

Donizetti uses a version of the tune in his opera *Anne Boleyn*, and this has sometimes led to the error of supposing him the composer.

When Adelina Patti was the world's 'Queen of Song' every audience demanded this of her as one of her encores.

The long-sustained magic of this song at last began to fade. The following is taken from a United States newspaper of October 1935:

'At Lawton, Oklahoma, John Brett, an attorney, sang *Home Sweet Home* to a jury so as to induce clemency for his client Lloyd Grable, a bank robber. The jury responded with a verdict of life imprisonment for Mr. Grable.'

HOMME ARMÉ, L'. See *Mass* 5. The earliest known masses based on this old French melody are those by Busnois (q.v.) and Dufay (q.v.) and their fifteenth-century contemporaries; the latest is by Carissimi (1605–74). Over thirty examples are known.

HOMOPHONE. Two strings (of harp) tuned to produce the same note.

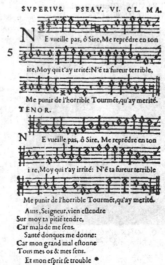

1. CALVIN

2. LUTHER'S 'EIN' FESTE BURG'—
Tenor part (i.e. melody) of his friend
Walther's four-part setting, in Walther's
handwriting, as presented by him to Luther
See p. 498

3. LUTHER. See pp. 498, 584–5

4, 5. MAROT'S METRICAL PSALMS,
set to four-part music by Goudimel,
1565. See pp. 599–600 and references
there given

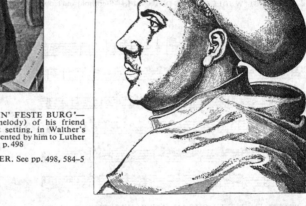

PLATE 86   THREE CENTURIES OF ENGLISH HYMN-SINGING

1, 2. THE FIRST 'WHOLE BOOKE' OF PSALMS—Sternhold and Hopkins, published by Day, 1562. See *Hymns and Hymn Tunes* 5

3. A PSALM TUNE WITH ORGAN INTERLUDE. (From Gresham's *Psalmody Improved, c.* 1780.) See *Hymns and Hymn Tunes* 9

4. DR. EDWARD MILLER, of Doncaster (*c.* 1730–1807)

5. ISAAC WATTS (1674–1748). See *Hymns and Hymn Tunes* 6, 7; *Baptists* 3

6. JOHN BACCHUS DYKES (1823–76)

7. FREDERICK WILLIAM FABER (1814–63). See *Hymns and Hymn Tunes* 6

HOMOPHONIC. See *Homophony* below.

HOMOPHONY is the term applied to music in which the parts or voices move in 'step' and without individual rhythmic interest. Its converse is *Polyphony* (q.v.).

See also *Monophonic*.

HONDO. See *Cante Hondo*.

HONEGGER, ARTHUR (p. 880, pl. **147.** 7). Of Swiss parentage, but born at Havre in 1892 and died in Paris in 1955, aged sixty-three. He studied at the Conservatories of Zürich and Paris, and towards the end of the first World War began to be known as a composer. He was a member of the temporary Paris group called 'Les Six' (see *France* 11).

He wrote chamber music, orchestral music, and a sort of oratorio with spoken connective tissue, called *King David*. The last was composed for the folk theatre of Mézières, near Lausanne, Switzerland, where it was performed (1921) as a play with music; the author was René Morax, one of the founders of the theatre. The work has been performed with success in Rome, Paris, New York, London, and elsewhere. It is curiously varied; the musical movements are all very brief and some of them are in a style reminiscent of the eighteenth century whilst others are extremely 'modern'. Another work on a similar plan is *Judith* (1925).

Amongst other works that have attracted attention by their novelty of conception have been a 'mimed symphony', *Horace Victorieux* (1921); a locomotive tone poem, *Pacific 231* (1924); the very original lyric drama, *Antigone* (Brussels, 1927); a football tone poem, *Rugby* (1928); a choral–orchestral work (poem by René Bizet), *Cries of the World* (1931); a light opera, *Les Aventures du Roi Pausole*; an opera, *L'Aiglon* (after Rostand); and a ballet (with use of the voice), *Sémiramis* (1934), in which is used the Martenot Musical Wave instrument (see *Electric Musical Instruments* 1 f i), and incidental music to Claudel's *Jeanne d'Arc au bûcher* (1938). These are merely a few representative works of a very large and varied output.

See references as follows: *Beck, C.*; *Clarinet Family* 6; *Collaboration*; *Concerto* 6 c (1892); *Melodrama*; *Oratorio* 4, 7 (1921, 1940); *Electric* 1 i; *Opera* 24 f (1937).

HON. G.S.M.; HON. R.A.M.; HON. R.C.M. See *Degrees and Diplomas* 2.

HOOK, JAMES. Born at Norwich in 1746 and died at Boulogne in 1827, aged eighty-one. He was organist successively at Marylebone Gardens and at Vauxhall Gardens, for over half a century in all, performing concertos nightly and composing over two thousand songs, a number of which remain in use, such as the mock-Scotch 'Within a mile of Edinbro' Town' (q.v.), and the English 'Lass of Richmond Hill' (q.v.).

Dean Hook of Worcester and Theodore Hook, the humorous writer and practical joker, were his sons, and Dean Hook of Chichester, the high-church divine, was his grandson. (For this last see *Anglican Parish Church Music* 7.)

See references under *Scotch Snap*; *Ballad Opera*.

HOPAK. See *Gopak*.

HOPE-JONES, ROBERT (1859–1914). Very inventive organ-builder, active first in England, and then in the United States. See references under *Organ* 6, 9, 14 I.

HOPKINS.

(1) EDWARD JOHN. Born in London in 1818 and died there in 1901, aged eighty-two. He was for fifty-five years organist of the Temple Church, London, a great authority on organ construction, a tasteful composer for that instrument, a fine choral trainer, and a composer of anthems and service music that are valued in English cathedrals and churches.

See references under *Presbyterian Church Music* 3, 6; *Improvisation* 2; *Holland* 3.

(2) JOHN LARKIN. Born at Westminster in 1819 and died at Ventnor, Isle of Wight, in 1873. Cousin of the above. He became organist of Rochester Cathedral (1841) and Trinity College, Cambridge (1856). Some of his church music remains in use.

(3) EDWARD JEROME. Born at Burlington, Vermont, in 1836 and died at Athenia, N.J., in 1898, aged sixty-two. He had an active career as organist and musical lecturer and journalist, and also as composer of an enormous quantity and variety of music. He is liable to be confused with Edward John Hopkins, on account of the similarity of name and of occupation, the coincidence of period, and the fact that both wrote church music.

(4) ANTONY (original name Reynolds). Born in London in 1921. He was trained at the Royal College of Music, and later joined the staff of Morley College. He is a pianist and composer whose works include piano sonatas, chamber music, songs, etc. His one-act opera, *Lady Rohesia*, was produced at Sadler's Wells Theatre in 1948; there is also other stage music, as also music for film and for radio.

(5) REVD. J. H. See *Carols*.

(6) JOHN (d. 1570). See references under *Sternhold*.

HOPKINSON.

(1) FRANCIS (p. 1040, pl. **169.** 1, 5). Born in Philadelphia in 1737 and died there in 1791, aged fifty-three. He played the harpsichord, invented a metronome, composed songs, practised law, wrote prose and poetry, and signed the Declaration of Independence.

He seems likely, according to the authoritative Oscar G. Sonneck, 'to stand as the first native poet–composer of the United States'. His song, 'My days have been so wondrous free' (1759), is the earliest extant secular song by an American. His set of *Seven Songs for the Harpsichord or Forte-piano* (1788) was dedicated to George Washington. In it he asserts his claim to be 'the first native of the United States who has produce a Musical Composition'.

See references under *United States* 3; *Concert* 15; *Harpsichord Family* 5; *Farnaby* 1; *Pianoforte* 17.

(2) JOSEPH. Son of the above. See *Hail, Columbia!*

HOPSER. See *Galop.*

HOQUET. Same as *Hocket* (q.v.).

HORN. See *Horn Family.*

HORN.

(1) KARL FRIEDRICH. Born in Saxony in 1762 and died in 1830. He early settled in England and became music-master to Queen Charlotte and her daughters. He collaborated with Samuel Wesley (q.v.) in the popularization of Bach and published an English edition of the '48'. He also published some sonatas, etc., and a book on figured bass.

(2) CHARLES EDWARD. Born in London in 1786 and died at Boston, Mass., in 1840, aged sixty-three. He was son of the above. He left the British people an inheritance of simple pleasant songs—*Cherry Ripe* (q.v.), *I've been roaming*, the duet *I know a bank*, and the like. He wrote profusely for the London stage and sang upon it also. When about forty he emigrated to the United States, becoming conductor of the Handel and Haydn Society at Boston, Mass.

(3) A German instrument-maker from whom the Basset Horn is said by some to take its name. See under *Clarinet Family* 4 f.

(4) CAMILLO. Born at Reichenberg, Bohemia, in 1860 and died in Vienna in 1941. He was a pupil of Bruckner in Vienna and remained in that city as music critic, choral conductor, and teacher.

He composed orchestral, choral, and other works. See a reference under *Horn Family* 4.

HORN BANDS. See *Horn Family* 3 (towards end).

HORN DIAPASON STOP. See *Organ* 14 I, III.

HÖRNER (Ger.). Horns.

HORN FAMILY

1. Construction, Tone, etc. 3. History. 5. Nomenclature.
2. Members of the Family. 4. Repertory.

(For illustrations see p. 140, pl. 26. 1–3.)

1. Construction, Tone, etc. The modern horn is a long tube (normally over 11 feet), very narrow at one end (¼ inch), widening as a long-drawn-out cone to the other, and ending in a large bell (11–14 inches); it has characteristically a funnel-shaped mouthpiece, but some modification in the direction of a cup-shaped mouthpiece is now becoming common.

In all these characteristics it differs from the trumpet, which is a much shorter tube of cylindrical bore throughout its length until actually approaching the bell, with that bell much smaller in diameter—and having, moreover, a cup-shaped mouthpiece.

The pitch of the natural horn (for 'Natural' see below) is, with the exception of the high one in B flat, an octave below that of the natural trumpet in the same key, and its tone (in consequence of all the other factors mentioned, but especially that of the wide bell) is much smoother. Horns of German make are (being wider in bore) heavier in tone and less bright than those of French or British make.

The principle of performance is (as with all the brass-wind instruments) that of the obtaining of the *Harmonic Series*. The player's lips serve as a 'reed' (see *Reed*) and set in wave-motion the air-column within the tube; by varying the tension of the lips he is able to provoke that air column to vibrate in halves, thirds, etc., and so to produce, at will, one harmonic or another (see *Acoustics* 8). The fundamental tone (i.e. the tone which would be produced if the air-column vibrated as a whole) is, from the shape of the instrument, obtainable only in the higher-pitched horns, and when obtainable is (with one slight exception) of no musical service.

The horn exists in two main forms, the *Natural Horn*, restricted to the notes of the harmonic series, and the *Valve Horn*, capable of playing at will any note of the chromatic scale by instantaneously switching over from the harmonic series at one pitch to that series at another (see 2 b and c below).

The modern horn (the valve horn) is valuable either in solo melody or, when several are present, in harmony. It can be used, then, either to play a principal part or merely to enrich the general web of tone. Long-held notes are very effective. The range of intensity from the softest effects to the loudest is a particularly wide one. It combines in tone well with the bassoon, in chords.

The horn has the reputation of possessing the most difficult technique of all the instruments of the orchestra; every regular concert-goer has experienced the shock of hearing even famous players 'crack' on a note.

Discussion arises from time to time as to the nature of *Horn Chords* (several notes simultaneously from a single horn); these are indicated in the cadenza of Weber's Concertino for horn and orchestra and in Ethel Smyth's Violin and Horn Concerto. The theory has been advanced that Weber meant his chords to be played in arpeggio, which would remove them from the realm of freakish acoustical phenomena. As for instances where chords are unmistakably intended to be played as such, the intention is that the performer shall make use of a trick that has been known from near the end of the eighteenth century. A single tube cannot, of course, produce more than a single note at a single moment, but if the player sounds a note on his instrument and hums another appropriate note there may be heard a further note or two notes ('resultant tones'— 'summation' and 'difference'; see *Acoustics* 10), which, with a room of suitable acoustical properties and other kinds of luck, can produce the effect of a true horn chord. The same trick is possible with the trombone (and possibly other instruments).

Burney, in his *History*, mentions a player named Creta, who in 1729 in London 'blew the first and second treble on two French horns in the same manner as is usually done by two persons'.

Like other brass instruments, the horn possesses a pear-shaped mute (see *Mute*) for insertion in the bell when soft ethereal sounds are wanted—or loud horrific ones. Double and triple tonguing (see *Tonguing*) are effective.

2. Members of the Family.

(*a*) **Hunting Horn** (p. 140, pl. 26. 1). This was the big coiled form of the *Natural Horn*, i.e. the horn that the player placed over his shoulder or over his head and under one arm, carrying (but not playing) it in this position. Its mouthpiece was shallow; it thus approached the trumpet pattern (the name *Trompe* was generally used in France) and as a consequence its tone was loud and brilliant.

(*b*) **French Horn—'Natural' but with Crooks** (p. 140, pl. 26. 2). This was the smaller form of the natural horn (smaller because less wide in the circles of its coils—not shorter as a tube), the one which the player could not place over his head and arm. In its more developed eighteenth-century form, as a real orchestral instrument, it was provided with *crooks* which could be inserted in order to add to its tubular length and hence to change its fundamental note—and with that, necessarily, the whole pitch of the harmonic series available to the player. The effect of the various crooks upon the notation was as follows:

B flat alto[1]—music written a major 2nd higher.
A   „   „   minor 3rd   „
A flat   „   .„   major 3rd   „
G   „   .„   perfect 4th   „
F   „   „   perfect 5th   „
E   „   „   minor 6th   „
E flat   „   „   major 6th   „
D   „   „   minor 7th   „
C   „   „   an octave   „
B flat basso[1] „   „   a major 9th   „

(Very occasionally crooks in A basso and A flat basso may be found indicated.)

By a convention, when there occurred notes low enough to demand the bass clef, these were written an octave below what the true transposition demanded.

Another convention required that all horn parts should be written as if in the key of C, i.e. the flats and sharps were inserted not at the beginning of the stave, but as accidentals: this, of course, is different from the practice with re-

gard to, say, the clarinet (q.v.), but is the same as the practice with regard to the trumpet (cf. *Trumpet Family* 2 b).

The **Compass** of the horn, with all these crooks, was three octaves or less—varying somewhat with the crook (high notes in the harmonic series being more easily obtainable on low crooks) and also with the skill of the player (first horn players being accustomed to higher ascents than second horn players). Thus the compass to be expected from a capable first horn player was up to the sixteenth harmonic on crooks below G, and the twelfth harmonic on the G and higher crooks, from a second horn player a major third or fourth lower. But any general statement is subject to exceptions.

It will be realized that on this instrument no continuous scale is obtainable, the harmonic series being an ascending series of intervals, at the bottom wide and, as the series ascends, progressively narrower—like a ladder with many rungs missing at the bottom and fewer and fewer missing towards the top, until at last none is missing. Thus on that imaginary C-crooked horn, which figures as the notational representative of all the crooks, the notes available were merely:

2   3   4   5   6   7   8   9   10 11 12 13 14 15 16

The four notes given in black are not in perfect tune with any musically employed scale (see *Temperament*), but there is a means available of modifying the pitch by inserting the hand in the bell of the instrument, one hand being free for the purpose. By thus using the hand the pitch of a note can be either lowered or raised. The raising can be to the extent of a semitone and the lowering to that of a semitone or tone, and thus not only can the out-of-tune notes be brought into tune but the smaller gaps of the series can be filled in. The process of lowering has been long known; that of raising has been more recently recognized.

The notes thus modified are known as **Stopped Notes**.

(*c*) **French Horn—with Valves** (p. 140, pl. 26. 3). This is the horn as our orchestras know it today. Normally it is pitched in F (i.e. it corresponds to the natural French horn with the F crook in use), though higher pitches are also in use and a 'Double Horn' (Ger. *Doppelhorn*) has latterly come into almost universal use, built in both F and B flat alto. The valve horn has the immense advantage of an ungapped series of notes—indeed a chromatic series, for three valves add instantaneously to the air column a length corresponding respectively to a semitone, two semitones, and three semitones, and as any two or all three of these valves can be used simultaneously any note in the harmonic series can be lowered by anything up to six semitones (i.e. an augmented fourth). What this means to the player's

---

[1] *Alto* in the sense of high; *basso* in the sense of low; the B flat alto crook was rare later than Haydn and Mozart.

convenience will be realized when it is stated that, with the form of the instrument described above under (*b*), Mozart indicated thirty-five changes of crook in the opera *Don Giovanni*.

There is now, evidently, no need of 'stopped notes' so far as the completion of the scale is concerned, but they are still sometimes used by composers, either blown softly to obtain an ethereal effect, or blown loudly to obtain a harsh, blaring effect—an effect largely overdone in some later music. Such notes as these latter are called '*brassed*' (see 5 for other terms).

The notation of this horn is nominally the same as that of the natural horn in F shown above, i.e. its music is written without key signature a perfect fifth higher than it is to sound; but there is now a strong tendency to adopt the practice of inserting a key-signature, which when it appears has, of course, one flat less or one sharp more than that of the non-transposing instruments in the same score (see *Transposing Instruments*).

The compass of the valve horn in F (i.e. its actual compass in sound) may be taken as from B natural below the bass staff to F at the top of the treble staff.

Beside the valve horn in F and the double horn above mentioned, the following valve horns, all of which are intended to facilitate playing the higher parts, are sometimes met with:

The horn in F with an 'ascending' third valve, i.e one which, when pressed down, raises the pitch a tone, putting the instrument into G instead of lowering it three semitones. This century-old device is popular with French players.

The horn in B flat (rarely C) alto, used chiefly in Belgium. The horn in B flat alto now usually possesses an extra valve manipulated by the thumb, adding a semitone to its downward range and so converting it into a horn in A.

3. History. The horn was anciently what its name implies, the actual horn of an animal, and for long it continued to be simply a curved, conical, end-blown tube of some substance or other. It played a great part in medieval communal life, being used to call together assemblies, to give signals, to indicate the approach of the watch, etc. Several municipalities in England still possess their ancient ceremonial horns, as for instance Ripon, where the instrument is blown at nine o'clock every night before the mayor's door and at the town cross, so perpetuating the former announcement of the setting of the watch. The later horns used for hunting and other purposes were not of the original shape, but circular, thus allowing of a much longer tube and consequent greater variety of notes, and also permitting the carrying of the instrument round the head and part of the body (see 2 a above). It is from this circular form that the modern more definitely musical instrument has developed. In France, where the details of the hunt were highly organized, most elaborate codes of horn signals

were devised and standardized: in England the hunting use of the horn was usually simple, except in the first half of the eighteenth century. It is possibly partly the great development of the use of the horn in France that led to the early name, still current, of 'French Horn'.

The horn as a mere tube (the so-called 'Natural' horn) being necessarily limited to the notes of the harmonic series of the one key in which it was pitched, attempts were probably early made to discover some means of overcoming the limitation. Efforts at the invention of a more versatile horn are recorded in Germany in the eighteenth century. Dr. Burney states that 'the Messings were the first who pretended to perform in all keys in England, about the year 1740', but his meaning is not clear—perhaps merely that they introduced a larger series of available crooks. The problem of rendering the instrument capable of performing in 'all keys' seems, in any case, to have been solved in anything like a satisfactory way only in 1754, when a Dresden player named Anton Joseph Hampel improved the principle of the already attempted detachable crooks (see 2 b above); these crooks, of course, enabled the player to change the key of his instrument at will but still left him at the mercy of the gapped harmonic series within that key.[1] To some extent the latter limitation was, however, overcome by further improvement—Hampel's accidental discovery of stopped notes (see 2 b, above), which came to his notice in his efforts to invent an effective mute for the instrument. The application of the discovery involved a change in the manner of holding the horn: formerly it had been held in hunting fashion, with the bell upward; now, in order to bring the bell within reach of the hand, it was held downwards. From this time the term *Handhorn* (alluding to the method of stopping) becomes common.

The name given to Hampel's instrument was *Inventionshorn* (q.v.).

In 1788 the Irishman Charles Clagget, a musician in London theatres (see also *Trumpet Family* 3), took out a patent for 'a method of uniting two trumpets or horns, one in D and the other in E flat, so that the mouthpiece might be applied to either instantaneously, thereby getting the advantages of a complete chromatic scale'. Here we see, apparently, the first dim dawn of the idea which led to the invention of the present instrument, in which the

[1] An authority who has read this article thinks it desirable to explain in what way Hampel improved the principle of the crooks. He says: 'This is the point: With the earlier crooked horns, furnished with terminal crooks, it might be necessary to put one crook on top of another. In fact, the Hellier horns of 1735 had two crooks which could be put directly into the socket of the horn, and four others which had to be used between the first-named crooks and the socket. The effect of this was that the relative positions of the mouthpiece and the horn-bell were continually varying. This did not matter until it became necessary to use the hand in the bell. Therefore Hampel designed a horn with the mouth-pipe fixed and always in constant relation to the bell. The crooks were inserted by a double slide into the body, and in fact gave rise to the all-important tuning-slide. These were the *Einsatzbogen*, as opposed to the older *Aufsatzbogen*.'

impact of the vibrations of the player's lips may be at will and immediately directed to a longer or shorter wind column, so enabling the player not merely to play in all keys but to play *all notes in all keys*. The fuller application of this principle is described above (2 c).

The first introduction of the horn into the orchestra (otherwise than as a mere concomitant of hunting scenes, etc.) is said to be found in the score of R. Keiser's opera *Octavia* (Hamburg, 1705). Handel was in early life a member of Keiser's orchestra in the Hamburg opera, and he used horns in his *Water Music* (about 1717)—but this was, of course, for open-air use; he afterwards used them, however, in *Radamisto* (1720), henceforward continuing to use them rather freely. Bach uses horns in thirty of his church cantatas, etc.

The horn found in the scores of Bach, Handel, Haydn, Mozart, Beethoven, and Mendelssohn and his contemporaries is the 'Natural' one with crooks; so it is in those of some much later French works, e.g. Gounod's *Faust* (1859) and Bizet's *Carmen* (1875). In the period from Bach to Mozart the notes used are the 'open' ones, the principle of 'stopped' notes not being drawn upon except in such works as Mozart's Horn Concertos, etc., where the employment of a virtuoso was implied. From Beethoven onwards the 'stopped' notes are in use, but Beethoven himself calls on them only in cases where he feels them to be really necessary.

Bach, making use of the higher range of harmonics in both trumpets and horns, although he knows nothing of stopped notes, is yet able to demand of his players some melodic passages (see the scheme of the harmonic series, p. 487); later, the use of this higher range diminished, and the horn and trumpet in later composers are, in consequence, very much restricted to those few chords in the tonic and dominant keys which permit the use of the lower notes of the harmonic series. In effect, indeed, this meant the limitation of the instrument to those passages of reiteration of tonic and dominant harmony that were so commonly used in those days, especially at the end of a movement or the section of a movement (cf. *Trumpet Family* 3).

The normal number of horns in an orchestra was then two, but once or twice four are found in Handel and, later, in Haydn and Mozart. Beethoven used three in the 'Eroica' Symphony and sometimes used four, directing two to 'crook' in one key and two in another, and, availing himself of the now accepted fact of the properties of 'stopped' notes, was able to free the horn very considerably from the bondage to a couple of chords in which Haydn and Mozart had found and left it.

In 1820 Weber used eight horns in *Preciosa* (but some of these for stage purposes). Wagner at first used two hand-horns and two valve-horns: later he used only valve-horns. In *Tannhäuser* (1845) he used sixteen horns (but twelve of these on the stage), and later he came to use eight as a regular thing.

The horn was long looked upon as a purely open-air instrument. Its tone evoked romantic associations, and it is fairly common in eighteenth-century literature to find instances of its use as one of the adjuncts of country-house life (e.g. in Richard Graves's novel *The Spiritual Quixote*, 1726—'The French-horns which were played by two servants in the opposite woods now ceased').

A development of this romantic use took place in Russia where, in the middle of the eighteenth century, proprietors of large estates established **Horn Bands**, much on the principle of our present-day handbell ringing, each player being provided with one instrument of appropriate size for the easy production of one note, so that the whole body, ranged in order, could produce the complete scale. The horns were straight ones (not circular) and had really little in common with the kind of horn we have been discussing. They ranged from 9 inches in length at one end of the row to 12 feet (with a supporting tripod) at the other. Horn bands of this sort toured Europe, and musical memoirs of the earlier nineteenth century (e.g. Spohr's) often refer to them. The American piano-dealer Morris Steinert speaks of hearing such a band in St. Petersburg in the 1850s, conducted by the great dance-composer, Joseph Gung'l. Dalyell (*Musical Memories of Scotland*) speaks of hearing one in Scotland in 1833, when the concert opened with the performance of the *Old Hundredth*—evidently in harmony, since a blind gentleman present exclaimed, 'What a fine organ!' The inventor of this species of entertainment was one J. A. Maresch, a horn player in the service of the Empress Elizabeth. His band in its later development comprised sixty-four instruments, covering a compass of over five octaves.

The present-day horn is, of course, as useful in the purely wind band as in the orchestra.

4. Repertory. From the nature of the instrument it might appear that (once its high-note technique, comparable to that described under *Trumpet* 3, had become obsolete) it could not play a very important solo part until the post-Beethoven days, when the introduction of valves made the chromatic scale available. Yet the hand-horn, properly utilized, could be a fairly efficient solo instrument. Even after the introduction of valves, however, the provision of opportunities for the display of the horn's qualities outside the orchestra has not been very lavish. The following incomplete list gives at any rate an idea of the extent and nature of the repertory:

Handel has a Trio for corno da caccia (see 5 a) and two clarinets. Bach's first Brandenburg Concerto makes very prominent use of two horns.

Haydn has a Trio for horn, violin, and violoncello; **Mozart**, a fine Quintet for horn, violin, two violas, and violoncello, three Divertimenti for strings and two horns, and other things; **Beethoven**, a notable early

Sonata for horn and pianoforte, a Sextet for strings and two horns, a Sextet for two clarinets, two horns, and two bassoons, and an interesting posthumous Rondino for wind instruments.

Spohr has an Octet for strings, clarinet, and two horns (important and difficult parts for the last).

Schumann has an Adagio and Allegro for horn and pianoforte and a *Concertstück* for four horns and orchestra, both of exceptional difficulty.

Brahms has a Trio for horn, violin, and pianoforte (spoken of as 'the greatest piece of chamber music for horn'); **Rheinberger** has a Sonata for piano and horn. So have **Camillo Horn, Hindemith,** and **York Bowen.**

N. Tcherepnin has six quartets for horns.

Of concertos the following may be mentioned:

Handel, one for trumpets and horns and one for horns and side-drums; **Mozart,** four for horn; **Haydn,** three for one horn and one for two horns. **Weber,** a Concertino for horn; **Strauss** and **Hindemith,** Concertos for horn; **Ethel Smyth,** a Concerto for violin and horn.

5. Nomenclature.

Horn (the general term). *Cor* (Fr.); *Corno* (It.); *Horn* (Ger.).

'Natural' Horn (the general term). *Cor simple* (Fr.); *Corno naturale* (It.); *Naturhorn* (Ger.).

(*a*) **Hunting Horn.** *Cor de chasse, Trompe,* or *Trompe de Chasse* (Fr.); *Corno da caccia* (It.); *Jagdhorn*[1] (Ger.).

(*b*) **French Horn** (pre-valve). *Hand-horn; Cor d'harmonie*[2] (Fr.); *Corno* (this seems to be the term Bach used for this instrument); *Corno a mano* (It., i.e. 'hand-horn'); *Waldhorn*[1] (Ger.).

(*c*) **Valve Horn** (the term 'French Horn', or simply 'Horn' nowadays, implies this). *Cor à pistons, Cor chromatique* (Fr.); *Corno ventile, Corno a pistoni, Corno a macchina, Corno cromatico* (It.); *Ventilhorn* (Ger.).

'Stopped Notes' and **'Brassed Notes'.**
Evidently these are not synonymous, since a stopped note gently played is not 'brassy' in tone, and, moreover, notes 'brassy' in tone can be produced without 'stopping'. But the terms indicating the effects have in current practice become very muddled.

Properly the following mean **'Stopped'**—*Bouché* (Fr.—the ordinary term for the stopping of a hole of any kind); *Chiuso* (It., 'closed'); *Gestopft* (Ger., 'stopped'). The sign + is also used for 'stopped', as the sign O is sometimes used for 'open'.

And properly the following mean **'Brassed'**—*Cuivré* (Fr.—'cuivre' being one word in French for 'brass'); *Schmetternd, Stark blasend, Mit Dämpfern und stark anblasen,* and similar terms (Ger., respectively 'blared', 'strongly blown', and 'with mutes and blow strongly').

For instruments called horn, though not belonging to the Horn Family in the sense in which the term is used here, see as follows:

Alpenhorn (or **Alphorn,** or **Cor des Alpes**): under *Alphorn.*

Althorn: under *Saxhorn and Flügelhorn Families* 2 c d; *Tuba Group* 5.

Basset Horn: under *Clarinet Family* 2, 4 e f, 5, 6.

Bass Horn: under *Cornett and Key Bugle Families* 2 e, 3 e, 4 e.

Coach-horn: under *Posthorn.*

English Horn (or **Cor Anglais**): under *Oboe Family* 3 b.

Flügelhorn: under *Saxhorn and Flügelhorn Families* 3.

Horn Diapason: under *Organ* 14, I, III.

Hornpipe: under *Stockhorn.*

Keyed Horn: same as bass horn above.

Klappenhorn: same as bass horn, above.

Nachthorn: under its own name.

Posthorn: under its own name.

Saxhorn: under *Saxhorn and Flügelhorn Families* 2.

Stierhorn: under its own name.

---

[1] Some of these distinctions between *Jagdhorn* and *Waldhorn*, etc., are made on the authority of the late Professor C. Sanford Terry (*Bach's Orchestra*), who has minutely discussed the subject. It must not be taken, however, that any of the distinctions shown in the present list are observed by *all* writers or composers, the terminology of the horn being of extremely fluid usage and differing from place to place, period to period, and individual to individual. A curious indication common in Bach is that of *Corno da tirarsi* (i.e. 'slide-horn'); no such instrument is known to have existed and Canon Galpin suggested that a slide-trumpet (see *Trumpet Family* 2 a) was used, but supplied with a horn mouthpiece, so giving something approaching horn tone.

A close student of the whole subject, to whom the above has been shown, comments on it as follows:

'The distinction between Jagdhorn and Waldhorn is reasonably clear, though there may be examples that it is difficult to assign to one class or the other. The Jagdhorn was a smaller and high-pitched instrument, with a narrower bell and not capable of being slung over the body. The Waldhorn was the longer and larger belled horn of later origin, which could be worn round the body—the French horn proper. This name was given to it whether it was used in the hunting-field or not, so that the term, exactly like our "French horn", means

either a Corno da caccia or a Cor d'harmonie. Anybody who doubts this has merely to look at old German books relating to the chase. Writing in 1700, Kuhnau, in *Der musikalische Quacksalber,* says "*Die wilden Thiere ergötzen sich an einem Wald- und Jäger-Horne*" ("Wild animals delight in a Waldhorn or Jagdhorn"), showing that both forms were used out of doors. Bach's use of the term "Corno da caccia" for the instrument used in the B minor Mass shows that a large Waldhorn was meant, because no Jagdhorn could possibly have played the part. Now there was no difference between the Waldhorn and the early orchestral horns, except such as might be made for convenience. An authentic eighteenth-century Cor de chasse will, if played in the orchestral manner, give the same quality of tone as the orchestral horn.

'I should, however, point out that, though the above distinction between Jagdhorn and Waldhorn is that accepted by experts, it is not universally observed. The word Jagdhorn, meaning merely "hunting horn", can be applied to any horn used for that purpose. Thus in one German work on instruments, which, however, does not consider them in their historical aspects, the Jagdhorn is described as a kind of Waldhorn, somewhat larger and usually standing in D or E flat.'

[2] The French term *Cor d'harmonie* own tends to be applied also to the valve horn.

Stimmhorn: see *Stimme*.

Stockhorn: under its own name.

Tenor Horn: under *Saxhorn and Flügelhorn Families* 2 c d.

Vamp Horn: under its own name.

The 'Russian Horns' mentioned near the end of 3, above, might also, as some would say, be included in this list.

See also *Slug-horn*.

Note that in modern jazz parlance 'Horn' is a general term for almost the whole range of wind instruments.

HORNPIPE. The word has two meanings: (1) An obsolete instrument, consisting of a wooden pipe with a reed (single 'beating', see *Reed*) and a horn bell (cf. *Stockhorn*). It was common in all the Celtic parts of Britain.

Picture, p. 545, pl. **100. 5**.

(2) A dance once popular in the British Isles and apparently not elsewhere known, to which this instrument was originally the usual accompaniment. Properly it is a solo dance. The earlier music is in three-in-a-measure, but by the end of the eighteenth century the time had completely changed to two-in-a-measure. Hornpipes are now chiefly kept up amongst sailors, but that is just as it happens to have come about: they had no seafaring associations originally (see *Matelotte*).

Hornpipes can be found in the works of Purcell and occasionally in those of Handel.

HORNPIPE CONCERTO. See *Nicknamed* 10.

HORN STOP. See *Organ* 14 VI.

'HORSEMAN' QUARTET (Haydn). See *Nicknamed Compositions* 12.

HORSLEY, WILLIAM. Born in London in 1774 and died there in 1858, aged eighty-three. He was a London organist who wrote, amongst other things, a large number of pleasant glees much admired by his friend Mendelssohn; some of these (e.g. 'By Celia's arbour') are still popular. He was one of the band of London musicians who in 1813 founded the Philharmonic Society. He was son-in-law of J. W. Callcott (q.v.). The painter J. C. Horsley, R.A., and the musician Charles Edward Horsley (1822–76), of London, Melbourne, and New York, were his sons.

HORST WESSEL SONG. This was the great song of the German National Socialist or 'Nazi' party. The words are by a student, Horst Wessel, who was born in 1907 and was killed in 1930 in a Communist quarter of Berlin in which he lived as commander of a Storm Troop section of the Nazi forces. There are various stories of the incident of his death, for which three persons, in their turn, suffered death at the hands of Nazi justice.

The tune was that of a music-hall song popular amongst the German troops in 1914.

HORTENSE, QUEEN. See *Partant pour la Syrie*.

HOSANNA. A Hebrew exclamation of praise to God, adopted also into the Greek and Latin languages. It was the cry of the multitudes on Christ's entry into Jerusalem (Matthew xxi. 9) and has been taken into many liturgies, as into the Roman Catholic Mass.

See *Mass* 3 d.

HOSCHKE, FREDERICK ALBERT. See *Electric* 4.

HOSTINSKY, O. (1847–1910). See *Bohemia*.

HOTETERRE Family. During the greater part of the seventeenth and eighteenth centuries they were active in Paris as makers and players of, composers for, and compilers of tutors for, various wood-wind instruments (flute, hautboy, bassoon, bagpipes)—and some of them the hurdy-gurdy (q.v.) and other stringed instruments. The most illustrious member of the family was Jacques (also known as Jacques Martin, and as 'The Roman'—on account of residing for some time in Rome.)

Cf. *Bagpipe Family* 6.

HOTHBY, JOHN. Died in England in 1487. He was an English Carmelite monk (said to be a graduate of Oxford) who travelled a good deal and lived for some years in various parts of Italy, teaching music and other subjects for a part of the time in a monastery at Lucca. He enjoyed fame as a theorist and left several theoretical treatises (still often cited and some now printed); a little music by him, sacred and secular, also remains. The name is sometimes found as 'Octobi', 'Otteby', and 'Octobri'.

See reference under *England* 2.

HOT JAZZ. See *Jazz* 3.

HOTTETERRE. See *Hoteterre*.

HOTZ, FR. See *Reed-Organ Family* 3.

HOURS. See *Divine Office*.

HOVHANESS (originally CHAKMAKJIAN), ALAN. Born at Somerville, Massachusetts, in 1911. Of Armenian descent, he was trained at the New England Conservatory. Many of the works on his very long list of compositions (1,200 by 1960) show the results of his long study of Asiatic and Middle-Eastern music.

'HOW DO YOU DO?' QUARTET. See *Nicknamed* 12.

HOWARD DE WALDEN, LORD. See *Holbrooke*.

HOWARD, JOHN TASKER (1890–1964). Composer, author, and an authority on Stephen Foster and the history of American music generally.

HOWELL, DOROTHY. Born in Birmingham in 1898. She studied at the Royal Academy of Music, London (whose staff she joined in 1924), and has appeared before the public with a piano concerto and other works.

HOWELLS, HERBERT (p. 352, pl. **55. 5**). Born at Lydney, Gloucestershire, in 1892. His early student life was spent as an articled pupil to Brewer (q.v.), the organist of Gloucester

Cathedral, his later as the holder of scholarships at the Royal College of Music, whose staff he later joined. As a composer he first came before the London public with a Mass composed for Westminster Cathedral (1912). Amongst the many works that have followed are *Sine Nomine* for two solo vocalists, organ, and orchestra (1922); a piano concerto (1924) and a cello concerto; a Requiem (1935); the *Hymnus Paradisi* (1950); a piano quartet and a clarinet quintet and several sonatas for violin and piano. He often shows originality in the resources he employs and he has a light touch.

He succeeded Holst in 1934 as director of music at St. Paul's Girls' School and is active as an adjudicator at competitive festivals, and occasionally as a writer on music.

See references under *Mechanical Reproduction* 13; *Clarinet Family* 6; *Competitions* 3.

HOWES, FRANK. Born at Oxford in 1891. He was educated at St. John's College, Oxford. In 1925 he became an assistant music critic of *The Times* and, after the death of Colles (q.v.), from 1943 to 1960 its chief critic. He was a lecturer in the History of Music at the Royal College of Music and active as an author and in the committee work of various national organizations for the good of music. He died in 1974.

HOWLAND, HORACE. See *Criticism* 5.

HOWLAT, BOOK OF THE. See *Scotland* 3.

HOW SWEET THE NAME OF JESUS SOUNDS. See *Hymns and Hymn Tunes* 6.

Hptw. in German organ music = *Hauptwerk* ('Chief work'), i.e. 'Great Organ'.

Hr. Short for horn.

Hrf. Short for *Harfe*, i.e. Harp.

HROTTA. Sometimes used for 'crwth' (q.v.).

HUBAY (or Huber), JENÖ (or Eugen; p. 480 pl. 83. 2.). Born at Budapest, Hungary, in 1858 and there died in 1937, aged seventy-eight. He was an eminent violinist, the pupil at the Berlin Conservatory of Joachim, the successor at the Brussels Conservatory of Wieniawski, and the teacher of Vecsey, Szigeti, Jelly d'Arányi, and many others of the most notable violinists of the day. From 1919 to 1931 he was director of the conservatory of his native city. He composed symphonies, concertos, operas, many songs, etc.

HUBBARD, ANTHONY. See *International Music Association*.

HUBER, HANS. Born near Olten, Switzerland, in 1852 and died at Locarno in 1921, aged sixty-nine. He was head of the Conservatory of Basle and a vigorous and varied composer whose works include eight symphonies, a new Well-Tempered Clavier (forty-eight preludes and fugues in all the keys; cf. *Temperament* 5), several operas and oratorios, masses, etc.

HÜBSCH (Ger.). 'Pretty', dainty.

HUCBALD (*c.* 849–930). A monk of St. Amand, near Tournai (Belgium). He wrote a treatise *De institutione harmonica*. Other treatises were in the eighteenth century printed as by him and have since been reprinted, but they are now attributed to some 'pseudo-Hucbald' —or sometimes to Otger (q.v.).

HUDDERSFIELD CHORAL SOCIETY. See *Clubs*.

HUDSON, GEORGE. See under *Opera* 13 a.

HUE, GEORGES ADOLPHE. Born at Versailles in 1858 and died in Paris in 1948, aged ninety. He studied at the Conservatory of Paris and at twenty-one won the Rome Prize. He wrote chiefly stage music, but orchestral music and a good many songs also. He was a member of the Institute.

HUGHES.

(1) HERBERT. Born in Belfast in 1882 and died at Brighton in 1937. He was educated at the Royal College of Music and worked as music critic, helped to found the Irish Folk Song Society, and published quantities of effective settings of Irish folk songs as well as light-handed original songs.

(2) ANSELM. Born in London in 1889, and died at Nashdom Abbey in 1974. Anglican Benedictine, Prior of Nashdom Abbey (1936–45), and long the active spirit of the Plainsong and Mediaeval Music Society, for which, amongst other valuable work, he edited manuscripts. He was an editor of the *New Oxford History of Music*.

See references under *Old Hall Manuscript*; *Anglican Chant* 6 (end).

(3) CEIRIOG. See under *God bless the Prince of Wales*.

(4) DAVID EDMUND, physicist. See under *Broadcasting* 2.

(5) CHAS. See *Jazz* 3.

HUGH THE DROVER. See *Stilt*.

HUGO, VICTOR. See *Bagpipe* 1; *Symphonic Poem*; also p. 893, pl. 152. 4.

HUGUENOTS AND MUSIC. See *Hymns and Hymn Tunes* 4; *France* 4.

HUIT (Fr.). 'Eight'; hence *Huitième*, 'eighth'.

HULAK-ARTEMOVSKY, SEMEN (1813–73). He was a Russian Ukrainian vocalist and composer. Glinka admired his singing and secured him a position in the Czar's chapel; for twenty years he sang at the Imperial Opera in St. Petersburg. He was composer of the Ukrainian folk opera, *The Cossack beyond the Danube*, frequently performed in the many Ukrainian-settled parts of Canada.

HULLAH, JOHN PYKE (p. 976, pl. 163. 3). Born at Worcester in 1812 and died in London in 1884, aged seventy-one. He became enamoured of the Paris pedagogue Wilhem's (fixed-doh) method of teaching sight-singing and held classes in and near London to teach it —with enormous initial success, the system being one of those that are attractively easy for the beginner and reveal their difficulties only later. The St. Martin's Hall in London, built

1. PREACHING AND SINGING AT PAUL'S CROSS, LONDON (See *Community Singing* 2). James I and his Queen are in the projecting part of the balcony. Above them, to the extreme left, is a slight white patch which in the original is seen to be the surpliced choir

2. THE METRICAL PSALMS IN AN 18TH-CENTURY LONDON CHURCH—led by the Parish Clerk, with Organ and Charity Children in the Gallery. (Hogarth's *Industrious Apprentice*)

1. AINSWORTH'S PSALTER, Amsterdam, 1612—the Psalm Book of the Pilgrim Fathers. See *Hymns and Hymn Tunes* 11

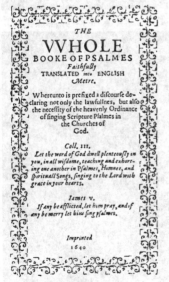

2. THE BAY PSALM BOOK, Cambridge, Mass. 1640. See *Hymns and Hymn Tunes* 11

3. COTTON MATHER'S 'ACCOMPLISHED SINGER', Boston, 1721

for his work, was burnt to the ground, and this temporarily ruined him. Mr. Gladstone's casting vote as Rector of Edinburgh University shut him out from the professorship he sought there, but he received a solatium some years later when the Government made him inspector of music in training colleges. His sight-singing system at last collapsed before Curwen's more psychologically true tonic sol-fa.

He wrote books on musical history and an opera (on a libretto by Dickens) which ran for sixty nights in London and was running in Edinburgh when a fire destroyed all the copies of the music. Some of his songs enjoyed a long popularity—especially his setting of poems by his friend Charles Kingsley, as, for instance, *The Three Fishers* and *O that We Two were Maying!*

See references under *Tonic Sol-fa* 1; *Oratorio* 5; *Grand Opera*; *Gathering Note*.

HUME, TOBIAS. Died in 1645. He attained the rank of captain in the army, and then, during his latter years, was a 'poor brother' (or pensioned inmate) of the Charterhouse. He was reputed for his skill on the viola da gamba, and wrote music for voices and for viols that is still sometimes to be heard, especially his tender song, 'Fain would I change that note'.

HUMFREY (or **Humphrey** or **Humphrys**, etc.), **PELHAM.** Born in 1647 and died at Windsor in 1674, aged twenty-seven. This is Pepys's 'Little Pelham Humphreys . . . an absolute monsieur as full of form and confidence and vanity, and disparages everything and everybody's skill but his own'—a sad testimonial and unfortunately better known to the world than the more modest one they cut seven years later, on his tomb in Westminster Abbey.

When the Commonwealth came to an end and Charles II returned as King, the Chapel Royal services began anew (see *Cooke*), and Humfrey was one of the very remarkable first batch of children of the Chapel (cf. *Wise*; *Blow*; *Turner*; *Purcell*).

By the time he was seventeen, anthems of his were evidently in use, since a book of anthem-words of that date includes five. In the same year he was sent by the King to France and Italy to study. There he picked up that declamatory style (see *Recitative*) and those rhythmic qualities in which Charles during his own involuntary stay on the Continent had taken pleasure. On his return Pepys recorded the impression with which the present notice began, but it is fair to add that he greatly praised his lute playing, and on another occasion a 'fine anthem' of his.

He succeeded his teacher (and father-in-law) Cooke as Master of the Children of the Chapel Royal and became the colleague of Thomas Purcell, as orchestral composer to the Court ('Composer in Ordinary for the Violins to his Majesty').

England probably lost much by his early death, but after it he continued to exercise his influence through his contemporaries and successors. We rarely hear a composition of Humfrey's (except the famous 'Grand Chant' to be found in all Anglican chant collections, and one or two anthems), but we hear many a composition which we might never have possessed but for his able teaching.

See references under *Chapel Royal*; *Anthem*, Period II; *France* 6.

HUMMEL, JOHANN NEPOMUK (p. 797, pl. 136. 4). Born at Pressburg (or Pozsony, now known as Bratislava) in 1778 and died at Weimar in 1837, aged nearly fifty-nine. He was a pupil of Mozart, living for two years in his house in Vienna. He then, aged nine, toured northern Europe as a prodigy-pianist in the care of his father, and settled in London for a year, where he received lessons from Clementi. In after life he used to recall his pleasure when, after playing a sonata of Haydn in the Hanover Square Rooms, London, the composer, who was in the audience, tipped him a guinea. He returned to Vienna and studied composition with Schubert's great teacher Salieri, with Beethoven's teacher Albrechtsberger, and with Haydn.

Further travels followed and then for some years he was the occupant of that post of musical director to the Esterházy family earlier long held by Haydn, and of one or two similar posts. He was one of the many friends of Beethoven who had to regret a quarrel with him, and only after many years, as the greater composer lay on his death-bed, was friendship restored.

Amongst his piano pupils were Czerny, Henselt, and Thalberg. He had a remarkable gift for extempore performance. He wrote a great 'Piano School' and a multitude of piano pieces, as well as compositions of other kinds. Perhaps his greatest importance is as one who helped to develop the art of piano playing. His is a great name in the history of music—and now little but a name.

See *Pianoforte Playing* 2, 3; *Improvisation* 2; *Sonata* 10 d (1803); *Roman Catholic Church Music in Britain*; *Concerto* 6 b (1778); *Meyerbeer*.

HUM NOTE. See *Bell* 1.

HUMORESQUE (Fr.), **HUMORESKE** (Ger.). A term applied by some composers to a lively instrumental composition—often not so much humorous as good-humoured. Schumann, Dvořák, Grieg, and others have pieces so entitled—generally short single-movement pieces, but Schumann's op. 20 is one of his longest piano works and is, in fact, a sort of suite.

HUMPERDINCK, ENGELBERT (p. 401, pl. 70. 4). Born near Bonn in 1854 and died at Neustrelitz in 1921, aged sixty-seven. He was an habitué of the Bayreuth circle and helped Wagner in the first production of *Parsifal*. As a composer he leapt into world recognition in 1893 with his opera *Hänsel and Gretel* (q.v.), perhaps the only fine work in the operatic repertory to which one can take a child with the definite certainty of gratitude. His other operas (several of them, also, upon fairy-tale libretti) have had less success.

HUMPHREY, HUMPHREYS, etc. See *Humfrey.*

HUMPHRIES, JOHN. Born in 1707 and died about 1730, aged twenty-two or twenty-three. He was a violinist who, at his youthful decease, had published a good deal of music for his instrument, some of which has lately been reissued. (See reference under *Sonata* 10 c.)

There is another composer for the violin of similar name and of about the same period, J. S. Humphries, of whom little is known.

HUMSTRUM. See reference under *Rebec.* But apparently the word has been variously used. Some writers use it as a synonym for hurdy-gurdy (q.v.) and others apparently (see *Shorter Oxford Dictionary*) for any instrument 'of rude construction or out of tune'.

HUNCHBACK OF ARRAS. See *Adam de la Halle.*

HUNDOEGGER, AGNES. See *Tonic Sol-fa* (end of article).

HUNEKER, JAMES GIBBONS (1860–1921). See reference under *Criticism* 5.

HUNGARY. The Hungarians are Finno-Ugrian in origin and their remotest ancestors are believed to have come from the river-valleys of the Obi and Kama in the western slopes of the Ural Mountains. There had been Mongolian and chiefly Turkic intermixture before they reached the Carpathian Basin in A.D. 896, subduing the pre-Magyar 'Huns' who had inhabited south-eastern Europe since the fourth century. In the thirteenth century German colonists were introduced, accounting for the German-speaking communities of pre-1918 Hungary.

In the Middle Ages Hungary was a country of peasants, governed by the king and a number of noble families. The presence of foreign musicians in Hungary from the twelfth century onwards is a sign that the music of the Troubadours (see *Minstrels* 4) and the German Minnesingers (see *Minstrels* 7) was cultivated by the Court. King Mathias Corvinus (1458–90), a great supporter of the arts, had at his Court Italian and Burgundian musicians and, for a time, the Fleming, Willaert.

The Papal Nuncio reported in 1483 that the choir of the royal chapel was the finest he had anywhere heard.

The Battle of Mohács, in 1526, in which the Turks were victorious, brought for a time ruin upon the country; Turkish influence is, after this date and for some time, perceptible in popular music. The Reformation, later in the century, affected church music; the Huguenot metrical psalms of Marot had some vogue and led to imitations. Some reaction took place, however, in the following century—after 'a good deal of cruel fighting.

A famous song composer was **Tinódi**, other-wise 'Sebastian the Lute Player', who lived in the first half of the sixteenth century (died about 1559) and wrote historical chronicles set to music. His music shows a mixture of in-fluences—the folk song of the period, church song, Turkish music. The national spirit of his songs carried them into popular use and a few of them are still known and sung, though to other words than the original. The English poet Sir Philip Sidney, in his *Defense of Poesie* (1583), records his experiences in Hungary and dwells on the popularity of the country's heroic songs, the music of which, he says, often existed in printed form.

The lute was greatly cultivated at this period: **Valentine Greff Bakfark**, born in Transylvania, ranks among the great composers for the lute.

At a slightly later period the English virginal composers are said to have enjoyed a consider-able vogue in the castles of the nobility; a few manuscripts exist (e.g. one of 1680) which show Hungarian folk tunes treated for virginals in much the same way as those of the English composers of a slightly earlier period. (See *Harpsichord Family* 3; *Pianoforte* 20.)

In the eighteenth century a good deal of Italian and German influence is evident in the adoption respectively of the solo Cantata (see *Cantata*) and the Lied (see *Song* 5). A national type of Lied was introduced by the monk **Ferenc Verseghy** (1755–1822), but it is strongly infected with German romanticism (see *Romantic*).

Organization of Hungarian culture took place under Maria Theresa (reigned 1740–80); national literature acquired new strength and schools of music were multiplied. In the article *Bohemia* will be found an account of the re-markable cultivation of music in the common schools during the late eighteenth century; Burney, who gives us this account from his own experiences, tells us that similar conditions obtained in Hungary.

Hungarian opera first appeared at the very end of the eighteenth century. In the mid-nineteenth century were heard the operas of **Ferenc Erkel** (1810–93), some of which are still popular. **Mosonyi** (1814–70; real name Michael Brandt) was an instrumental com-poser who adopted a national style.

Certain Hungarian dance styles have become widely known abroad (see *Csárdás*; *Verbunkós*). Haydn (who spent thirty years in Hungary as Capellmeister to the noble family of Esterházy), Beethoven, Schubert, and other great com-posers have based instrumental movements on such dances, the designation '*All'Ongarese*' becoming for a time fashionable. The high rhythmic variety and melodic force of Hun-garian folk tune were, in particular, made familiar to the world by Liszt (q.v.) in his Hun-garian Rhapsodies. Brahms, also, has used Hungarian tune. An enormous collection of such tunes was made on some 15,000 discs, by Bartók and Kodály who traversed the country in all directions in the course of researches that then greatly influenced the compositions of these two composers.

The so-called 'Gipsy Music' of Hungary is really Hungarian music composed by Hungarians and performed and propagated by gipsy violinists and orchestras (who often embellish it almost out of recognition). There is a genuine gipsy music amongst the Hungarian rural gipsies, but it differs greatly from what we call 'Hungarian Gipsy Music'. There is also a Hungarian peasant music, and this, though it has exercised much influence on Hungarian composers of today, is, again, quite distinct from the so called 'Hungarian Gipsy Music'. These are the conclusions of Bartók (q.v.), who thoroughly investigated the subject, and they completely overturn those of Liszt in his book (1859) on *The Gipsies and their Music in Hungary*, which credited the gipsies with a very much more serious role in the musical production of the country. (Cf. *Magyar*.)

The important position that gipsy musicians occupy in Hungarian life was made clear to the outer world in 1930, when reports appeared in the papers of the funeral ceremony at Budapest of a leading player, Béla Radics. He was played to the 'Grave of Honour' (granted him by the municipality) by a body of 500 gipsy musicians, and 50,000 people were present. Three months later there was held an open-air memorial ceremony for which special trains were run from all over Hungary. In this an orchestra of over 1,000 gipsies took part. Included in the orchestra were twenty-six examples of the cymbalon, the national instrument of Hungary (see *Dulcimer*; and for another distinctive Hungarian instrument, the tárogató, see an allusion under *Clarinet Family* 4 h).

Budapest is one of the great musical centres of Europe. Its school is famous and has trained very many well-known violinists and other performers (e.g. there have come out of it several string quartets known throughout Europe and America).

For a long time German influence has reigned in Hungarian composition; with Dohnányi, to some extent, and with Bartók and Kodály to a much greater extent, this influence is thrown off. The (German born and trained) composer-teacher Hans Koessler (q.v.) has had these and most of the leading living composers through his hands and is looked upon as the foster-father of modern Hungarian music.

Hungarian composers treated in this volume under their own names are as follows: Bartók; Czibulka; Dohnányi; Frid; Goldmark; Gung'l; Heller; Hubay; Jemnitz; Joachim; Kéler-Béla; Kodály; Korbay; Lajtha; Lehár; Liszt; Nováček; Rózsa; Franz Schmidt; Seiber: Weiner; Zádor.

HUNT.

(1) THOMAS. In the early part of the sixteenth century he composed church music. A madrigal of his is still in use, as also a short service.

(2) ARABELLA (d. 1705). Noted vocalist, lutenist, and teacher of singing, for whom Purcell, Blow, and others of the chief composers of her period composed songs.

See reference under *Cold and Raw*.

(3) JAMES HENRY LEIGH (1784–1859). Essayist, poet, and music-lover.

See quotation under *Street Music* 2.

HUNTINGTON LIBRARY. See *Libraries*.

HUNTING HORN. See *Horn Family* 2 a, 3, 5 a.

'HUNT' QUARTET. See *Nicknamed Compositions* 12, 15.

'HUNT' SYMPHONY (Haydn). See *Nicknamed Compositions* 11.

HUON DE BORDEAUX. See *Minstrels*, etc. 5.

HÜPFEND (Ger., with various terminations according to case, etc.). 'Hopping', i.e. 'springing bow'—same as *Spiccato* (q.v.).

HURDY-GURDY (p. 417, pl. **72**. 5–7). A stringed instrument somewhat of the violin type, played by turning with the right hand a handle which operates a rosined wheel (in effect a circular bow), and by depressing with the left hand a few finger-keys like those of the piano. These latter operate an internal mechanism functioning somewhat like the fingers of the left hand of a violinist; this mechanism suggests the tangent principle of the clavichord (q.v.), which is possibly partly derived from it.

Two of its strings (the one or the other of which is allowed to be in use at any given moment, according to the key of the composition) produce a continuously sounding low note (the keynote), and hence resemble in function the drone of a bagpipe (see *Bourdon*; *Harmony* 24 p); the other strings (i.e. those operated by the finger-keys) supply the melody. Some instruments possess also 'sympathetic strings' (q.v.).

This ancient and once highly respectable instrument is probably still alive in some parts of France. The present writer saw it more than once during the second decade of the twentieth century in the London streets; in the early part of the previous century it was very commonly heard there. It had a high popularity amongst all grades of society in France (under the name 'Vielle' or 'Vielle à roue', i.e. wheelvielle) during the later part of the seventeenth and early part of the eighteenth century (cf. *Bagpipe* 6), and it is said still to be played at village festivities in Auvergne (see under *Bourrée*), Morvan, and Berry, and also throughout Spain.

It must not, then, be thought that the vielle is a mere plaything or street instrument. Serious 'Methods' existed for it, as also collections of music, including suites by the French eighteenth-century composer Charles Baton. Haydn wrote for the King of Naples three concertos and eight nocturnes for two hurdygurdies with other instruments. (For Leopold Mozart's use of it see *Bagpipe* 7.)

Its music is satirically described in Bonnell Thornton's burlesque *Ode on St. Cecilia's Day* (cf. *Saltbox*; *Marrow-bones and Cleaver*; and *Jew's Harp*):

> With dead, dull, doleful, heavy hums,
>   and dismal moans,
>   and mournful groans,
> The sober hurdy-gurdy thrums.

The hurdy-gurdy in a large size was, under the name *organistrum,* once popular as a church instrument (say about the year 1000 and onwards).

Other names for the hurdy-gurdy are *Symphony, Symbal* (English, seventeenth century), *Chifonie* (early French), *Symphonie* (French, seventeenth century), *Lyra, Leyer,* or *Leyre, Drehleier, Radleier, Bauernleier* (German), *Bawren Leyer* (Old German) and *Lira organizzata* (Italian).

The vulgar application of the name 'hurdy-gurdy' to the once popular street piano (see *Mechanical* 12) arises probably from the facts (*a*) that the latter largely superseded the former as a means of street entertainment and (*b*) that both are operated by turning a handle. A form of hurdy-gurdy played with a bow (i.e. having the finger-keys but no wheel) has been popular in Scandinavia (p. 417, pl. **72.** 7).

See *Chédeville.*

HURÉ, JEAN. Born at Gien (Loiret, France) in 1877 and died in Paris in 1930, aged fifty-two. He was a fine pianist, founder of a school of music, editor of a journal for organists, author of books on piano and organ playing, etc., and composer of masses, piano sonatas, cello sonatas, symphonies, etc.

HURLSTONE, WILLIAM YEATES. Born in London in 1876 and died in 1906, aged thirty. He had a brilliant student career at the Royal College of Music, whose staff he later joined. He was establishing himself as one of the most promising young composers of his period when death overtook him.

See *Oboe Family* 6.

HURTIG (Ger.). 'Nimble', agile.

HURWORTH. See *Cornett and Key Bugle Families* 3.

HUS. See *Huss.*

HUSK, WILLIAM HENRY (1814–87). See *Cecilia, St.*

HUSS, JOHN (1373–1415). See *Bohemia; Hymns and Hymn Tunes* 17 a. Also p. 108, pl. **19.** 1, 2.

HUSSEY, DYNELEY. Born in India in 1893 and died at Cheltenham in 1972, aged seventy-nine. He graduated at Oxford and served as a music critic on the London *Times* (1924–47) and later became critic of the *Saturday Review, Spectator,* and *Listener.* He wrote books on Mozart, Verdi, etc.

HUTCHINGS, ARTHUR JAMES BRAMWELL. Born at Sunbury-on-Thames in 1906. He became a schoolmaster but pursued musical studies and activities and in 1947 was appointed Professor of Music at the University of Durham. He has written several books (on Schubert, Delius, Mozart's Concertos, etc.) and done some composition.

HUTCHINSON, VICTOR HELY-. See *Hely-Hutchinson.*

HUTSCHENRUYTER Family.

(1) WOUTER. Born at Rotterdam in 1796 and there died in 1878, aged eighty-one. He was violinist, horn-player, composer, conductor, musicologist, and man of high general musical activity and usefulness.

See a reference under *Concerto* 6 b (1796).

(2) WOUTER (grandson of the above). Born at Amsterdam in 1859 and died in 1943, aged eighty-four. Conductor and teacher; also known as a composer and as the author of valuable books on musical subjects.

HÜTTENBRENNER, ANSELM. He was born at Graz in 1794 and died near there in 1868, aged seventy-three. As a composer he was a pupil, with Schubert, of Salieri. He became a friend of Beethoven and was with him when he died. He was appreciated as a pianist and as the composer of almost innumerable songs, male-voice quartets, etc., as well as of music for orchestra, chamber music, piano music, etc.

Hw., in Ger. organ music = *Hauptwerk,* i.e. great organ.

HWYL. See *Wales* 3.

HYDRAULIKON. See *Hydraulus.*

HYDRAULUS, HYDRAULIS, or **WATER ORGAN.** This is the most ancient form of organ known, yet nevertheless it resembles in a startling degree our present instrument. It was introduced by Ctesibius the Egyptian, a famous inventor of about two and a half centuries before Christ, and though representations of it occurred upon coins, etc., and certain treatises described it, no modern expert could gather the nature of the mechanism until, in 1885, Father Delatre, Director of the Museums at Carthage, called attention to a terra-cotta model of the instrument that had been dug up there. From this Canon F. W. Galpin, the English authority, was able to construct a working model, which was shown at the Worshipful Company of Musicians' Exhibition of Musical Instruments in London in 1904. In 1931 some remains of an actual specimen of an hydraulus of date A.D. 228 were discovered in the ruins of a Roman station near Budapest. At the same place was found an inscription of a soldier of the second legion in memory of his wife. He describes himself as a player of the hydraulic organ and says that his wife, also, played it admirably.

In general appearance the hydraulus is like any small organ of today. There are, in the Galpin model, three ranks of pipes, giving the scale in three octaves (like our Diapason, Principal, and Fifteenth), the pipes of each rank ranging in order of length, from little to big. There are about twenty finger-keys, each about

us in the right and true singing of the Tunes that are already inUse in ourChurches ; which, when they first came out of the Hands of the Composers of them, were sung according to the Rules of the *Scale of Musick*, but are now miserably tortured, and twisted, and quavered, in some Churches, into an horrid Medly of confused and disorderly Noises. This must necessarily create a most disagreable Jar in the Ears of all that can judge better of Singing than these Men, who please themselves with their own ill-founding *Echoes*. For to compare small Things with Great, our *Psalmody* has suffered the like Inconveniencies which our *Faith* had laboured under, in case it had been committed and trusted to the uncertain and doubtful Conveyance of *Oral Tradition*. Our Tunes are, for Want of a Standard to appeal to in all our Singing, left to the Mercy of every

1. THE STATE OF NEW ENGLAND PSALMODY in 1721 —from Dr. Thos. Walter's *Grounds and Rules*. See pp. 503, 507

2. A BILLINGS ENTERPRISE of 1792. See pp. 504, 507

1

2

To the P U B L I C K.
A large Committee having been selected by the several Musical Societies in Boston and its vicinity, beg leave to solicit the attention of the publick to the following

P R O P O S A L S
For Publishing a Volume of Original
AMERICAN MUSICK,
COMPOSED BY
WILLIAM BILLINGS, *of Boston.*

THE intended Publication will consist of a number of Anthems, Fuges, and Psalm Tunes, calculated for publick social Worship, or private Musical Societies. — A Dialogue between MASTER and SCHOLAR will preface the book, in which the Theory of Harmony, grounded on Question and Answer, is adapted to the most moderate capacity. — Also an elegant FRONTISPIECE, representing the ARETINIAN ARMS, engraved on Copperplate.

3. FROM AN AMERICAN BOOK OF 1798—'*The Easy Instructor; or, A New Method of Teaching Sacred Harmony, containing,* I THE RUDIMENTS OF MUSIC *on an improved Plan, wherein the Naming and Timing of the Notes are familiarized to the weakest capacity.* II A choice Collection of PSALM TUNES and ANTHEMS, from the most celebrated Authors, with a number composed in Europe and America, entirely new; suited to all the Metres sung in the different Churches in the United States,' By WILLIAM LITTLE and WILLIAM SMITH. (By 'Flat Key on A' is meant the key of A minor. It will be noted that this is what Billings, in his books, called a 'fuge', and that the principal line is that of the tenor)

4. A CAMP MEETING—at Sing Sing, New York, 1859. See p. 504

5. MOODY AND SANKEY. See pp. 184, 504

PLATE 90   MUSICAL IMPRESSIONISM—THE PARALLEL IN PAINTING

IMPRESSIONISM—A comparison of Frith's *Railway Station* (1862) with Monet's *Gare St. Lazare* (1877) graphically conveys the change which came over painting with the Impressionistic movement, a change which had its counterpart in the sister art of music. Monet's *View of the Thames in London* still further emphasizes the coming into existence of a 'new eye' at this period— to be followed ere long by the coming into existence of a 'new ear'

2 inches wide, each acting on a slider which goes under the appropriate pipe. There is a device corresponding to our 'stop' for each rank of pipes.

The blowing apparatus of the hydraulus was not unlike that of today. Water was applied to the wind reservoir, in an ingenious manner, for the compression of the air (as to the details of this authorities at present differ), and that gave the instrument its name. The Greeks called it 'Hydraulikon', the Romans 'Hydraulus', the Hebrews 'Magrepha'. (There seems to have been one variety in which air was forced into the pipes by the flow of water.)

Some of these organs described by ancient writers had as many as ten ranks of pipes or stops.

According to old records the tone of such instruments was enormously powerful. It is even stated that it carried for sixty miles and that the players were compelled to plug their ears to avoid danger to them. They were used in the open, at gladiatorial shows and the like. The Emperor Nero (A.D. 37–68) was a notable organist and this was the type of instrument on which he performed.

It was probably a combination of poverty and of repugnance due to the associations of this instrument that long deterred the Christian community from applying the organ to the purposes of worship. When they did admit the organ into the services it was of this very type.

The whole subject of the hydraulus was, in 1931, thoroughly rediscussed in H. G. Farmer's *The Organ of the Ancients from Eastern Sources, Hebrew, Syrian, and Arabic*, to which Galpin contributed a preface.

HYDRODAKTULOPSYCHICHARMONICA. See *Harmonica 1*.

HYMN OF THE SOVIET UNION. See under *Internationale*.

HYMNS ANCIENT AND MODERN. See below, 2, 6.

HYMNS AND HYMN TUNES (INCLUDING METRICAL PSALMS)

(For illustrations see p. 484, pls. 85, 86; 492, 87, 88; 496, 89.)

1. Definition. Many definitions of the hymn are possible, such as would include or exclude various classes of poetical production. For the purposes of this article St. Augustine's definition will be adopted:

'A hymn is the praise of God by singing. A hymn is a song embodying the praise of God. If there be merely praise but not praise of God it is not a hymn. If there be praise, and praise of God, but not sung, it is not a hymn. For it to be a hymn, it is needful, therefore, for it to have three things— praise, praise of God, and these sung.'

This excludes the wonderful body of pagan song, and also Hebrew and Christian poems not intended for song. But it includes several classes of song, some of which hardly existed in St. Augustine's day (354–430), which it is not intended to treat here under this head, and so a little further definition is necessary—'For it to be a hymn it is needful for it to have *four* things—praise, and praise of God, and these sung, and sung by a congregation of people.' (It is perhaps even necessary to define a little further. 'Praise of God' is to be understood in a very wide sense—not necessarily jubilation.)

Hymns coming within the definition were a part of the worship of the Hebrew church (see *Psalm*) and the practice of singing such was taken up by both the Eastern and Western branches of the Christian Church. Up to the present day the office of the Eastern Church is embellished by innumerable hymns.

2. Latin Hymns. Amongst the many famous Latin hymns are the following, most of which (cf. *Office Hymn*) are in common use in the English translations mentioned:

Conditor alme siderum. Advent: possibly by St. Ambrose, fourth century. ('Creator of the starry height.')
A solis ortus cardine. Christmas: by Sedulius (fourth century). ('From east to west.')
Pange lingua. There are two hymns so opening. See entry *Pange lingua*.
Ave maris stella. Feasts of the Blessed Virgin Mary. ('Hail, O star that pointest.')
Te lucis ante terminum. Service of Compline. ('Before the ending of the day.')
Iste confessor. Feasts of Confessors.
Ut queant laxis. Feast of St. John the Baptist. See reference under *Hexachord*.
Vexilla regis. By Fortunatus, end of sixth century. ('The royal banners forward go.')
Te Deum. See separate article.

St. Ambrose, Bishop of Milan in the fourth century, to whom so many innovations and reforms are attributed (see under *Plainsong 3*; *Modes 2, 4*; *Te Deum*), is considered to be the great founder of hymnody in the Western Church (some references to factors that led to hymnal development in the Latin Church will be found under both *Sequence* and *Trope*).

The class of hymns above mentioned dates from before the use of harmony as we today know it, and most of such hymns date even from a period when music was purely melodic. They quickly acquired their own plainsong melodies, and, most of them being metrical, they brought into existence a type of plainsong tune that, in greater or lesser measure, still has a place in almost every hymn-book—though nowadays either harmonized for four voices or, at least, provided with an organ accompaniment.

It is not always realized how much the Latin hymns have entered into the life of some branches of Protestantism (see *Chorale*). One of the most popular hymnals, *Hymns Ancient and Modern*, includes translations of one hundred and eighty of them (out of a total of 780 hymns in the whole collection), whilst in addition sundry special books of hymns of this character, with plainsong tunes, have been issued (see *Neale, J. M.*).

Five great medieval Latin hymns are mentioned elsewhere in this volume (see *Sequence*); it will be realized that they are but some of the most important examples from a huge body of such poetry composed from the fifth to the fifteenth century, and their prominence is partly due to their having been retained in the missal when other similar poems were deleted.

3. The Reformation and the Chorale. The Reformation in Bohemia (q.v.) in the fourteenth and early fifteenth centuries, and in Germany, France, and England in the sixteenth, gave a very marked impetus to hymn writing and hymn-tune composition. Huss wrote many hymns, and the first hymn-books published in any vernacular are said to have been the collections of his followers, who in 1501 and 1505 issued books containing 89 and 400 hymns respectively.

In Germany Luther made great use of hymns: he was himself a musician and he was greatly helped by his musical colleague, Johann Walther, cantor at one of the north German courts. The first Lutheran hymn-book appeared at Wittenberg in 1524; it was very tiny —only eight hymns. Other books quickly followed. The tunes set to these hymns were partly adaptations of the ancient plainsong, partly arrangements of folk song and partly original (see some remarks on these tunes in article *Rhythm* 6). One hymn of Luther himself, to be found in the official hymn-book of every Protestant body throughout the world, is *Ein' feste Burg* ('A safe stronghold'—p. 484, pl. 85. 2), a rendering of the forty-sixth Psalm; the tune also is Luther's; it became the battle-song of the Reformation. Other Lutheran hymns (not by Luther himself) that have entered into the religious life of every Protestant community are *Nun danket alle Gott* ('Now thank we all our God') and *O Haupt voll Blut und Wunden* ('O sacred Head surrounded', or, in some versions, 'O sacred Head once wounded'; the German is itself a translation from the Latin); but there are many such, and as a rule they are still sung to their original German melodies.

The poetry and tunes of these German hymns (see *Chorale*) have been a high source of inspiration to German composers. The mind of Bach, two centuries after Luther, was soaked in this influence; he followed the custom of his period in introducing the now traditional chorales very freely, sometimes, apparently as a sort of 'people's part', into his Church cantatas and his settings of the Passion (but by 'people's part' it is not meant that he always intended the congregation actually to join in the singing), and also in writing upon their melodies many organ 'Chorale Preludes' (q.v.) for use in church as a prelude to the congregational singing. He also harmonized very many of them for four-part singing; Professor Sanford Terry's complete edition of the Four-Part Chorales of Bach contains nearly five hundred harmonizations, though in many cases three or four together are different harmonizations of the same tune. (See remark on some of Bach's less effective treatments under *Melody* 5.)

It would be difficult to over-estimate the importance of the place which the chorale has taken in German life (chiefly, of course, in the Protestant north, but also in the Catholic parts of the country, which have also adopted the chorale). The chorales have been continually heard in the homes as much as in the churches. It was customary for centuries for church choirs to perambulate the streets during the week, singing them before the houses. In the 1880s Steinert, the Boston piano dealer, revisiting his native Bavarian town after an absence of forty years, found the night-watchman in the streets still marking the hours by singing his hymn verses to their old chorale tune, as he does in another Bavarian town in Wagner's *Mastersingers*. The chorale, indeed, permeated German religious, communal, and domestic life.

For some further remarks on the subject see *Chorale*.

4. The Genevan Metrical Psalms. The Calvinistic reformers also greatly used hymns, or rather, in their case, metrical versions of the psalms, and in France those made by Marot and Béza and set to music by Goudimel (q.v.) (p. 484, pl. 85. 4), Bourgeois, and others, supplied the Huguenots with the inspiration to fight and to suffer. The Genevan and French versions had much influence in other countries. A German Calvinistic version based upon that of Marot and Béza was issued by Lobwasser, the Genevan melodies being attached; later, one by Becker came into use in Saxony, and Schütz (q.v.) in 1661 issued a musical setting of it (further editions in 1676 and 1712).

Compare *France* 4; *Calvin, John*.

5. The Psalms and Psalm Tunes of England and Scotland. To Geneva, the headquarters of Calvinism, many English and Scottish divines fled to escape the persecutions of the times. They took there some of the English psalm paraphrases and their tunes and brought back other tunes; from Geneva thus came a number of the metrical psalm tunes now most endeared to the hearts of English and Scottish congregations. Of these some examples are the *Old Hundredth* (but see 17 c), the *Old 113th*, the *Old 124th*, and others frequently found in hymn-books of today, the names just mentioned referring of course to the psalms to whose metrical versions they were originally attached. (It was really Day's publication mentioned below that fixed the canon as to what was 'Old'.)

It is to be observed that Calvinistic practice, unlike Lutheran, restricted congregational singing to metrical versions of the psalms; 'human hymns' were not considered to be admissible; this restriction operated in England and for a much longer period in Scotland (cf. *Baptist Churches and Music* 3; *Presbyterian Church and Music* 3). The love of the metrical psalms in sixteenth-century England is clear to us from many accounts of their singing by huge crowds at Paul's Cross, London.

The hymn tunes of this period are (in the form as printed then) necessarily mainly modal (see *Modes*): many of them, too, are in what we now call free rhythm, i.e. if one tries to apply barring and time-signatures to them the latter will have to be changed several times in the course of the tune (whether German or Genevan or English the tunes were quantitative like plainsong, not accentual like the hymn tunes of today—which are often the old tunes tamed). Both these qualities are, of course, found in many of the English folk tunes collected four hundred years later by Cecil Sharp and others.

The metrical psalter of Sternhold and Hopkins, completed and published by John Day in London in 1562 (p. 485, pl. **86**. 1, 2; see 17 e for earlier issues of Sternhold and Hopkins), was the great treasury of sacred song of Englishmen in the sixteenth and seventeenth centuries. Day published it with melodies taken from French and German sources, and the following year brought out a harmonized edition of the tunes. Other tune books that followed as companions for Sternhold and Hopkins's version were Este's (1592), Ravenscroft's (1621), and Playford's (1677). Playford's was the first popular book to put the melody in the treble, though Day's book, mentioned above, had one tune in the treble, and other books, in the century that followed Day, had experimented further. (The same thing is seen in other countries: Goudimel's psalter of 1565 has eighteen tunes in the treble and the rest in the tenor.) Presumably in an ordinary congregation those who could sing in parts would do so, the others singing the main tune in the octaves suited to their voices and so duplicating the tenor part. But this was a period when sight-singing was a common accomplishment.

Sternhold and Hopkins was the chief book authorized in the Church of England for a century and a third, i.e. up to 1696, when Tate and Brady's version appeared and was used by a number of churches in preference, though many continued to use Sternhold and Hopkins

for over a century longer, its phraseology having acquired almost the authority of Holy Writ, so that it passed through 600 editions. (It should be noticed that some other versions had popularity; the Bay Psalm Book, so called, of Massachusetts, had forty editions in England and Scotland; see sections 11 and 17 f below.)

Sternhold and Hopkins was after 1696 spoken of as the 'Old Version' and Tate and Brady as the 'New Version', and this 'New Version' (or rather, we may say, the two versions together) held the field right up to the introduction of the modern hymn-book. Both were often abused. From the Restoration onwards the various versions of the metrical psalms were a target for the shafts of superior people. Isaac D'Israeli (a Jew with a racial proprietary interest in the psalms) in the early nineteenth century called them 'scandalous compositions', and others have agreed with him.

It should be noted that in all the above discussion of psalm singing and psalm tunes the liturgical use of the psalms in the Church of England is not in question. The psalms for the day were in ordinary churches read in prose, in alternation of minister and parish clerk, or, in cathedrals, sung to the Anglican chants (see quotation at the end of the article *Anglican Chant*): a metrical psalm would be sung in a service as a sort of religious relaxation (p. 492, pl. **87**. 2). The settings in some of the books were more in a motet style (or simple anthem style) than in that of the straightforward hymn tune of today (see *Reports*).

It is, perhaps, not generally realized to what a great extent psalm books contributed to popular musical education. From Day's complete psalter of 1562, and onwards for about 250 years, almost all the psalters of England and many of other countries open with theoretical instructions designed to equip the singer for the reading of vocal music by the use of some form of sol-fa (p. 960, pl. **161**. 4). The same is true of the American Colonies from the date when they reached the point of being able to produce a musical psalter literature of any importance. An examination of these introductions was made by Sir John Stainer in 1900 as a study of the development of ideas on the theory of music and of methods in sight-singing during this long period from Queen Elizabeth I's day almost to Queen Victoria's (cf. *Lancashire Sol-fa* for the common British and American system of the whole period).

Further, during the eighteenth century itinerant psalmody teachers were extremely common and were often engaged by village communities to give a course of class lessons in singing for the benefit of the younger people, who were often extremely enthusiastic psalm singers. Gibson, Bishop of London, in his directions to his clergy in 1724, warns them against 'the inviting or encouraging those idle instructors who of late years have gone about the several counties to teach tunes uncommon and out-of-the-way (which very often are as ridiculous as they are new)' and recommends the use of merely 'five or six of the plainest and best known tunes', so that the whole congregation can take part in the exercise. (For a similar warning by another Bishop of London, sixty years later, see *Anglican Parish Church Music* 4.)

For the extraordinary elaboration of 'graces' in the singing of psalm tunes see 11 and compare 10. For the Interludes often played between lines and verses see *Interlude*.

6. The English Hymn. Many beautiful religious lyrics were meanwhile written, some of which are to be found in present-day hymnbooks, but they were not at that time much used in public worship. James I, in 1623, gave the poet George Wither a patent to have his *Hymns and Songs of the Church* bound with Sternhold and Hopkins, but the combination came to nothing (see 17 e (xv)) and it was not until about a century later that what we should now call 'hymn-books' appeared.

Dr. Watts published his first book in 1707 and John Wesley's first such publication appeared in 1737 in Charleston, South Carolina. The latter contains metrical psalms, translations from the Greek and the German, six lyrics of George Herbert, thirty-seven hymns by Watts and some others: this mingling of sources makes it the first hymn-book of the modern type. The Methodist movement made enormous use of hymn singing and the many later publications of the Wesleys kept it abundantly supplied. They had, on the whole, a high poetical standard (see a remark or two in the article on *Church Music*); John Wesley protested against 'the scandalous doggerel of Sternhold and Hopkins'. The total number of hymns written by Charles Wesley is over 6,000, and amongst them are such universal favourites as 'O for a thousand tongues to sing' and 'Jesu, lover of my soul'. Handel wrote three hymn tunes for the Methodists, of which one (*Gopsal* to 'Rejoice, the Lord is King') is still in frequent use, and will be found in other than Methodist books.

This was, indeed, the great flowering period of English hymnology. Such hymns as those just quoted, with Toplady's 'Rock of Ages', Newton's 'How sweet the Name of Jesus sounds', Watts's 'O God, our help in ages past' and 'When I survey the wondrous cross', Doddridge's 'Hark the glad sound', and Cowper's 'Hark, my soul! it is the Lord' and 'O for a closer walk with God' (which all represent either eighteenth-century Nonconformity or Evangelical Anglicanism), seem now to be woven into the very mental texture of English-speaking Protestantism.

The hymn-tune books of this period are rather disappointing. Some of the fine old Genevan and other psalm tunes are there (often much disfigured), but there are many florid tunes of a very secular character, and some of secular origin (the promotion of secular tune to this sacred use is not, however, confined to any one period or country; for an example see *Rule, Britannia!*). 'Fugueing Tunes', i.e. tunes in which a voice or two fell momentarily silent and then came in with an imitation of some preceding voice, were also introduced amongst the hymn-singing denominations; they may still be heard occasionally in England; they have come to be called 'Old Methodist Tunes', but this is a misnomer, as being too limiting. These tunes were popular in the American Colonies, which produced many of their own (see 11, below). Some tunes involved much repetition of the words, often very arbitrarily, and the tales still current of the ludicrous distortions of sense sometimes involved may be no exaggeration: ('He's our best bul-, He's our best bul-, He's our best bulwark still'; or 'Bring down Sal-, Bring down Sal-, Bring down Salvation from the skies'; or 'And catch the flee-, And catch the flee-, And catch the fleeting hour'—this sort of thing *must* have sometimes happened). Nevertheless, there is a body of eighteenth-century hymn tunes that is both melodious and dignified and so retains what looks likely to be a permanent place in the use of the churches. Examples are Croft's *St. Anne* (usually sung to 'O God, our help') and his *Hanover* (usually sung to 'O worship the King'), and Miller's *Rockingham* (an adaptation of a somewhat earlier tune and now usually sung to 'When I survey').

From this point onwards hymn writers and hymn-tune composers became so numerous that it is difficult to summarize their activities. Just as the Evangelical movement of the eighteenth century had inaugurated the popularity of the hymn, so the High Church (or Oxford) Movement of the early and middle nineteenth century gave it renewed vigour, for the Anglican church had at last accorded hymns, as distinct from metrical psalms, general acceptance—long after the nonconforming bodies had all done so. In 1861 appeared *Hymns Ancient and Modern*, which (with many additions and revisions) is still a very popular book in the Anglican communion (during the first ninety years of its publication a hundred million copies were sold). With it are associated the names of such composers as W. H. Monk (q.v.), Dykes (q.v.), and Stainer (q.v.); the best of their tunes are worthy, but the second-best fall into the class rather of part song than of hymn, depending overmuch on sweetness of harmony (they have been brutally called 'the strawberry jam of music'; cf. *Carols*) and owing little to strength and shapeliness of melody—the latter the true mark of a good hymn tune, which, in the main, is to be sung in unison or in quasi-unison. A thoroughly revised edition of this book in 1904 was unfortunately very badly supported, and the old editions, with some additions, outdistanced it in popularity. An attempt at a genuinely congregational selection of tunes for the Anglican Church, with less frequent tendency to the sentimental, was, however, made in the publication of the *English Hymnal* in 1906 (new edition 1933); both plainsong (see 2) and folk-song melodies were freely introduced; this book has had considerable success. All existing books, however, are open to criticism somewhere—and receive it.

There is now a tendency to restore to the older tunes some of the rhythmic variety they once possessed; it is argued that few of them ought to appear as that unbroken series of notes of one length to which from the middle of the nineteenth century they were reduced.

Passing mention must be made here of the appearance of a small school of Roman Catholic hymn writers, contemporary with the High Church Anglican hymn writers of the nineteenth century. Faber (1814–63; p. 485, pl. 86. 7) and Caswall (1814–78) are the most important of these: very many of their hymns are to be found in Protestant hymnals (sometimes with neat doctrinal changes). Faber was an Oratorian and the founder of the Brompton Oratory, London, and, true to the practice of his order, made great use of popular music (see references to St. Philip Neri under *Laudi Spirituali* and *Oratorio* 2). Unfortunately his taste in music was poor and many of his hymns were wedded to trivial tunes.

7. The Most Popular Hymns. Julian's *Dictionary of Hymnology*, which supplies particulars of well over 400,000 hymns, states that the following four stand at the head of all in the English language as to popularity in English-speaking countries.

Ken's Morning Hymn, 'Awake, my soul' (1695).

Watts's 'When I survey the wondrous cross' (1707).

Charles Wesley's 'Hark! the herald angels sing' (1739).

Toplady's 'Rock of ages' (1775).

This was written in 1892. Probably after this lapse of time a somewhat different list would be offered, including, certainly, 'Abide with me' and 'O God, our help', 'Jesu, lover of my soul', and perhaps 'Lead, kindly Light'.

8. 'Lining-Out' (or in America 'Deaconing'). The practice of having each line read (by minister, parish clerk, or precentor) before it was sung by the congregation probably dates from the earliest days of the introduction of metrical psalms into public worship. It received official status in England in the early days of the Puritan régime, when Parliament (1644), in an Ordinance settling matters concerned with the service, laid down a rule as follows:

'That the whole congregation may join herein, every one that can read is to have a psalm-book, and all others, not disabled by age or otherwise, are to be exhorted to learn to read. But for the present, where many in the congregation cannot read, it is convenient that the minister, or some fit person appointed by him and the other ruling officers, do read the psalm line by line before the singing thereof.'

It will be observed that the practice was regarded as a temporary concession to an ignorance that was expected to disappear, but, once established, it came to possess that sanctity that attaches to all ecclesiastical custom and it was exceedingly difficult to get rid of it. It lingered in a few Anglican churches of England up to the 1860s or 1870s and probably rather longer in some of the Nonconformist churches there and in the Presbyterian churches of Scotland. In 1860 the governing body of Wesleyan Methodism, the Annual Conference, passed a resolution deploring the growing practice of discontinuing 'our long-established custom of giving out the verse in successive portions'. Latterly, in many churches of different denominations, the custom was to read two lines at a time, or even a whole verse—or the whole hymn (Mark Twain records the last method as in vogue in the United States as late as 1878— see remark in *A Tramp Abroad*. It is still in vogue in the Reformed Church in France).

Lining-out had been introduced into the American Colonies not with the first settlement but as late as 1681 (Plymouth) and is said not to have been general until about 1750. At Worcester, Mass., a public meeting decided on its abandonment in 1779, but in some places it continued for nearly a century longer and was dropped only after a bitter opposition. It has been stated that the American practice was for the precentor or an elder to *sing* a line and for the congregation to sing it after him. This may have been so in some places (for mention of such a practice in the Highlands of Scotland see *Modes* 5), but it would seem that they were exceptional and that reading in the spoken voice (or on a monotone, as in some parts of Scotland in the nineteenth century) was the usual custom of the precentors.

The maintenance of pitch under any system of 'lining-out' must surely have often been difficult. It was also, of course, destructive of both literary and musical sense. Moreover, it sometimes caused a parish clerk to forget what was the tune he had set. And Leman in *A New Method of Learning Psalm Tunes* (1730) complains that on the 'lining-out' system the congregation's thoughts are so intent upon what the clerk is going next to deliver that they in great measure forget the preceding part of the tune, and doing thus one line after another may be one reason why the whole tune is remembered in but a very imperfect manner.

9. Organ Accompaniment. This was for long very crude. Mace in his *Musick's Monument* (1676) says:

'Let the parish clerk be taught to pulse or strike the common psalm-tunes for a trifle—20s., 30s., or 40s. (a year). This will lead to business for the clerk for he will be so doated on by all the pretty ingenuous children and young men of the parish that they will beg a shilling from their parents for a lesson on how to pulse the psalm-tune, which they may learn in a week or fortnight's time very well, and so in a short time the parish will swarm with organists, and no parent will grutch the money so given.'

Most probably Mace had nothing more in view than the playing of the melody (i.e. tenor) —or, at most, melody and bass, which was considered a proper way of playing psalm tunes for a century later. Hymns were taken extremely slowly, so that 'execution' did not come in. Further, from six to twelve came to be considered a sufficient number of tunes for any ordinary church (this is true of the American Colonies as much as of the mother country).

The better equipped organist, where lining-out did not prevail, nevertheless broke the hymn and tune into fragments by the practice of a long shake at the end of every line, or a few measures of trivial interlude (see p. 485, pl. 86. 3), and played quite long interludes between the verses, or, at any rate, before the last one. 'A jig for three or four minutes' is a description given in 1810. Barrel organs (see *Mechanical Reproduction* 10) came into use in very many churches and these duly provided the shake, which thus could not be dispensed with even if the line of the words ended with a preposition or conjunction.

A hint or two may here be offered to the young organist of today. (*a*) If a verse or line is played before the hymn is sung it should be remembered that the purpose is not merely to let the congregation know the tune, but also the speed, and, moreover, to inspire them with a sense of rhythm. (*b*) The playing of many organists in the course of the hymn itself is nothing like as steadily rhythmic as they imagine it to be. (*c*) A 16-foot pedal kept going throughout throws away a fine opportunity of contrast. (*d*) When the singing is going well an unaccompanied verse, or part of a verse, is often effective. (*e*) A verse which the choir have been told to sing in unison offers opportunities for varied organ harmonies—which should not be startling. (*f*) A treble descant can offer a great variety (see *Descant*). (*g*) The meticulous and disconcerting expression marks found in certain hymn-books should often be ignored. (*h*) Finally, the playing and singing of the hymn is as well worthy of the best effort of those concerned as is the playing and singing of any other part of the service: indeed, to some members of any congregation the hymns mean more than any other part of the music of the·service, and this should be remembered.

10. Further Facts on Psalm and Hymn Singing in Scotland. The following facts may be added to those given incidentally above. The Scottish refugees from Geneva brought with them the incomplete Psalter published there in 1561 for the use of the Anglo-Scottish Church, completed it, and issued their edition at Edinburgh in 1564. It appeared in many later editions and served the churches for a century. The early editions had melodies only; the edition of 1635 had harmonized tunes (see reference in 17 e below, and also in article *Reports*). This book, in its various editions, is known as 'The Old Psalter' or 'John Knox's Psalter'.

In the middle of the seventeenth century the psalm versions of Francis Rous, Provost of Eton, Speaker of the House of Commons, were adopted (with much revision, however), and many metrical psalms that are to be found in Scottish hymn-books today, and that have become a part of national life, retain lines or stanzas from that English collection. This book, unfortunately, never had tunes printed with it, and it is said that a musical decline followed its appearance.

In addition to the psalms, paraphrases of other portions of scripture have from the later eighteenth century been sung—though some have objected to these (see *Presbyterian Churches and Music* 3). Hymns (mere 'human compositions') were not commonly allowed until near the end of the nineteenth century, after which a number of hymn and tune books, almost indistinguishable from their English contemporaries, appeared.

A peculiarity of Highland musical life has been the extraordinary way the old psalm tunes have been lengthened out with roulades and grace notes (cf. *Modes* 5) until they have become unrecognizable save by the expert: this is very much like the florid elaboration of plainsong (an extraordinary example will be found under *Ornaments* 1; cf. also *Plainsong* 3; *Machicotage*. For the psalm-tune elaborations that took place in England and New England see mention in next section of present article).

The 'Precentor', or leader of the church singing, has been a power in Scotland. Latterly he had a pitch-pipe (see *Pitch* 6 a and c)—the only instrument heard in Scottish Presbyterian churches until near the end of the nineteenth century (and some objected to even this). The singing in old times was funereally slow. The Church of Scotland has today a special committee under which music for the services is carefully fostered. In particular it has issued a *Revised Church Hymnary* which is in wide use, and helped with *The Church Anthem Book* and *Children Praising*.

For an allusion to the nature of some of the tunes in the 1635 book see *Reports*.

11. Psalms and Hymns in America. Nothing seems to be known of the singing of the earliest settlers—those of Virginia from 1607 onwards; their cares were harassing, but presumably they sang, and most probably from the book of Sternhold and Hopkins to the tunes that Day's books of 1561 and 1562 had made popular, with possibly some from Este or Alison (see 17, below).

Almost immediately, in the north appeared the Pilgrim Fathers, bringing with them the Psalter to which they had become accustomed in Holland, that of Ainsworth, their minister at Amsterdam, *The Booke of Psalmes englished both in prose and metre* (published in 1612—eight years before the sailing of the *Mayflower*, p. 493, pl. 88. 1). Ainsworth said:

'Tunes for the Psalms I find none set of God, so that each people is to use the most grave, decent and comfortable manner that they know how, according to the general rule.'

He gave thirty-nine tunes, which he stated came from English, French, and Dutch sources. (He could not have used entirely English tunes because of his great variety of metres—as he explained in his preface.) Ainsworth's hymns and tunes, in various editions, served the Plymouth community for twenty years (the Massachusetts Bay Colony also used them, but generally preferred Sternhold and Hopkins, presumably with Day's settings, and perhaps those of Este and Ravenscroft, brought by individuals). Then, in 1640, a better version was desired and a clerical committee (Revds. John Eliot, Thos. Weld, and Richard Mather) compiled it, and printed it in the house of the President of Harvard College, at Cambridge, Mass., on a press given by Puritan friends in Holland but sent from England (1638). This was the first actual book produced in the North American Colonies—unless a trifling almanac be counted.

This book, known familiarly as 'The Bay Psalm Book' (p. 493, pl. **88.** 2), had immense popularity, which did not die out for a century and a third, the last edition (of about 70) appearing in 1773. England adopted it to some extent (18 editions; last in 1754) and Scotland (22 editions; last in 1759); these editions were based not on the original edition but on the edition by Dunster and Lyon ten years after the first edition.

The book at first contained only psalms, but as early as 1647 a few hymns were included.

A curious attempt to supply something better was made nearly eighty years later (1718) when the great Cotton Mather, grandson of one of the compilers of the 'Bay' book, brought out one—with two kinds of type and brackets so applied to the psalms that either long- or short-metre tunes could be used: this was probably found to be one of those inventions that are too ingenious for the service of man.

About this time arose a great clamour on the subject of 'Singing by Note', also called 'Regular Singing' (i.e. singing by rule), which simply meant singing the tunes as printed—cf. *Methodism and Music* 4. For the most part those who advocated it were ministers or had many ministers on their side; several ministers wrote vigorously on the subject, as Revd. Thos. Symmes, of Bradford, Mass. (*The Reasonableness of Regular Singing or Singing by Note*, 1720); Revd. Thos. Walter, of Roxbury, Mass. (*The Grounds and Rules of Musick explained, or an Introduction to the Art of Singing by Note fitted to the meanest capacity. Recommended by several Ministers*, Boston, 1721); and Revd. John Eliot (*A Brief Discourse concerning Regular Singing, showing from the Scriptures the Necessity and Incumbency thereof in the Worship of God*, Boston, 1725). The 'Several Ministers' mentioned on Walter's title-page were fifteen in number; their names are given, and they include some of the most honoured (one of them is the Revd. Cotton Mather above mentioned).

The points are always the same. The tunes, being learnt only by ear, have diminished in number down to eight or ten in some congregations or half this in others; so many graces have been introduced that the tunes have become unrecognizable; the graces differ so much that no two congregations sing a tune in the same way; for want of knowledge of the notes the various members of a congregation do not keep together, and so on. Tunes, says Walter (p. 496, pl. **89.** 1), are now 'miserably tortured, and twisted, and quavered, in some churches into an horrid medly of confused and discordant Voices', 'much time is taken up in shaking out the Turns and Quavers, and beside no two men in the Congregation quavering alike, or together, which sounds in the Ears of a Good Judge like five hundred different Tunes roared out at the same Time', and so on.

Here an interpolation may be made. This New England controversy is often mentioned in books on the history of American music, but it may be surmised that few readers today realize what was involved in the proposed reform that aroused such vigorous opposition. It can be simply illustrated by an example from old England, where such a reform was evidently still needed thirty years later. Arnold's *Compleat Psalmodist* (1750), a very popular book, with many editions, tells the singers how to carry out the adornment of their tunes. 'The first and most principle Grace necessary to be learned is the Trill or Shake; that is, to move or shake your voice distinctly on one syllable the distance of a Whole Tone.' For this the following example is given:

He then explains what he calls 'the Grace of Transition'; that is 'to slur or break the Note, to sweeten the Roughness of a Leap, of which we see the following example:'

All the English psalm books of this period give instructions as to graces (sometimes as many as eight different kinds), with, apparently, no thought of the inevitable effect when the members of a choir or congregation, performing in concert, individually attempt to interpret and apply these instructions. It would really appear that the Colonies were before the Old Country in the awakening of a desire for more seemly psalmody (for similar abuses in Scotland see 10 above; also *Ornaments* 1. Cf. also *Methodism and Music* 4).

The protests and attempts at reform met with the most violent opposition, but in the end good sense prevailed and the new ideas spread over all the settled parts of the North American continent. The consequence was the bringing into existence of many sight-singing text-books, singing schools, and at last church choirs. (For sight-singing instructions in the early

American psalm books see some remarks near the end of 5.) Harmonized tune selections became common, though at this time and for a good deal longer the compilers mostly take their harmonies, without acknowledgement, from the various books of Playford (see 5 above and 17 e (xviii) below).

The wrenching away from the idea of an officially limited body of sacred song tune and the development of ability in singing opened the field for the first American composers. William Billings (p. 496, pl. 89. 2) was one of these. Billings (1746–1800) was self-taught but he flew high, even into what he called 'fuges' (cf. 6, above). And just as Tate and Brady in England, a century earlier, ingeniously paraphrased certain psalms so as to turn them against the enemies of William and Mary, so Billings now managed to turn pious sentiments against George III:

> Let tyrants shake their iron rod,
> And Slavery clank her galling chains;
> We'll fear them not, we'll trust in God;
> New England's God forever reigns.

Thus, by the exercise of a talent for simple tune, choral effect, and easy versification, with an appropriate topical allusion here and there, Billings won great favour: incidentally, he had a good deal to do with the introduction of pitch pipes into churches, and the consequent lessening of unhappy incidents in the choice of pitch, and he even fought for the bass viol, which so, in time, earned the honourable title of 'the Lord's fiddle'. His musical importance lies largely in the facts that (a) discarding the traditional psalm tunes, he actually *composed*, and that (b) following the English example of Watts and Wesley, he wrote hymns and not mere psalm paraphrases. The work of Billings, then, marks the beginning of modernity in church song in America.

There was a reaction against Billings (and the Billings school, for he had many imitators) during the first two decades of the nineteenth century. Taste was rising; the compositions of Handel and Haydn were becoming known: people wanted something better than they then had. (For the introduction of organs into American churches see under *Organ* 9.)

Later came such enthusiasts as Thomas Hastings (1787–1872), who wrote many hymns and tunes and did enormous work in developing choral activities in New York State, and Lowell Mason (1792–1872), who, as organist at Dr. Lyman Beecher's church in Boston, as one of the founders of 'musical conventions', as a trainer of singers and a composer of hymn tunes, and as a purveyor for the young, exercised an enormous influence. Certain of Mason's tunes are in most British hymn-tune books and from this period a proportion of the new tunes introduced in Britain (e.g. those of Dykes and Barnby) found their way into American books. New British and American hymns also often quickly became common property. Thus, in a fair measure, the repertory is the same on both sides of the Atlantic, and the remarks made above in discussing British hymns and hymn tunes apply to those of America also.

There was some decline in the old tradition of American psalmody from about the middle of the nineteenth century, due (a) to the leaders being more and more those of foreign birth and (b) to the replacement of amateur choirs by quartets of professional singers. These influences seem now to be waning. Certainly, hymn and psalm singing were far and away the most vital musical activity in America up to near the end of the nineteenth century.

It was stated by Dean Peter Lutkin, of North Western University, in 1930, as it has been stated by others before and since, that the standard of musical value in the hymn tune was still too low—'We are years behind England, where the best hymnals make little or no concession to popular taste and yet enjoy a considerable sale.' Dean Lutkin called attention to the fact that, whilst the average hymnbook contains 400–500 hymns, the ordinary congregation sings only fifty or sixty. There is, however, probably a weakness in this matter in England also.

Horatio Parker's book, for use in the Episcopal Church (1903), maintained a very high standard.

12. The 'Gospel' Hymn. A special phase of American hymnology has been the Mission Hymn. It came at last into world prominence with the work of the Evangelist Moody and his musical colleague, Ira D. Sankey (p. 496, pl. 89. 5), which was actively pursued in the United States and Britain during the 1870s, 1880s, and 1890s, during which period it has been claimed that they 'reduced the population of Hell by a million souls'. Like Orpheus rescuing Eurydice, they accomplished this achievement largely by means of music—but music unfortunately of the lowest class. Contrary to what is often believed, Moody did not himself write the words of any hymns. Moreover, in the widely circulated *Sacred Songs and Solos* Sankey is as much compiler as composer, drawing largely on a type of tune that had already become popular in the United States, the type with a lively rhythm and a harmonization consisting of little more than alternations of the three chief chords of the key (tonic, dominant, and subdominant). To this type the American W. B. Bradbury (1816–68) had been a considerable contributor, publishing many collections (his *Fresh Laurels* had a sale of 1,200,000 copies). A few of the hymns and tunes of this class are genuinely touching and stirring, but the bulk of them are commonplace reiteration of one or two sentimental ideas set to fitting music. The Salvation Army, founded by William Booth in 1878, has made this type of hymn and tune familiar to the members of almost every race in the world. When its history comes to be studied it will probably be found that behind Sankey and Moody lies the powerful influence of the American Camp Meeting (p. 496, pl. 89. 4).

13. Hymn Metres. In many hymn-tune books figures are attached to hymns and tunes, either in the body of the book or in the index, to show the number of syllables in the lines, and so to facilitate the fitting of tunes to hymns, e.g. the metre known as 'six-eight', or 'six-lines-eight', appears as 8 8 8. 8 8 8. or 8 8. 8 8. 8 8. according as the poet has arranged his lines (as to rhymes) in the one way or the other.

The following metres have distinct names:

8 6. 8 6. Common Metre (also called Ballad
 Metre from its being that of the old English ballads).
6 6. 8 6. Short Metre.
8 8. 8 8. Long Metre.

The variety of metres is now astonishing, as many as 100 to 120 being found in some hymn-books.

Returning to the subject of the two 'six-eights', which are metres much found in the hymns of the brothers Wesley, it may be re-marked that organists have been known who could ally a hymn in one of these metres to a tune in the other without apparently being troubled by the strange effect.

14. Accentuation in Hymns. It seems strange that hymn poets, knowing that their hymns are to be sung to fixed tunes, the same for every verse, do not trouble to avoid those irregularities of accentuation that do not matter in a poem only intended to be read or intended to have each stanza set separately. As things are, a hymn tune, if specially written for a par-ticular hymn, usually fits the first verse and probably no other. However, a poet of high distinction and great delicacy of rhythmic feel-ing and some musical knowledge (and a British Poet Laureate), Robert Bridges, wrote (letter to a friend in 1911, published by the Church Music Society):

'I think that the intelligent hymn-singer is get-ting much too squeamish on this head. I do not find that an occasional disagreement between accent of words and of music offends me in a hymn. A fine tune is an unalterable artistic form, which pleases in itself and for itself. The notion of its giving way to the words is impossible. The words are better suited if they fit in with *all* the quantities and accents of the tune, but it is almost impossible and not necessary that they should. Their *mood* is what the tune must be true to; and the mood is the main thing. If the tune also incidentally re-inforces important words or phrases, that is all the better, and where there are refrains, or repetitions of words, the tune should be designed for them; but the enormous power that the tune has of enforcing or even creating a mood is the one invaluable thing of magnitude which overrules every other con-sideration.'

15. Quality in Hymns. Some general re-marks on quality in the music of worship will be found in the article *Church Music*. A word may be added here on the subject of the words of hymns. Some of these are true poems; many are not. It is unfortunate that much crude thought and expression is to be found in hymns that, by their doctrinal significance or their response in some other way to the needs of worshippers, have been carried down the years and have acquired the sanctity of tradition. The crudity is in certain instances so great that it might be expected that even worshippers with little literary experience would discover it, but, in church, as in the opera-house, the human being becomes very uncritical. There is a gradual but noticeable tendency to drop such hymns out of the books of the various religious bodies, but new hymns sometimes appear that, if less crude in their thought and wording, are weakly sentimental. The worst doggerel is usually put into the mouths of little children, and many Sunday-school hymnals require drastic revision.

In favour of the exercise of taste in hymno-logy it may be suggested that people who are not conscious of quality in poetry will at any rate accept the good, whereas those who are so conscious cannot accept the bad; thus, merely on the practical grounds of 'the greatest good to the greatest number', poor hymns should be dropped—or, if new, never introduced.

In Wesley's historic hymn-book of 1780, hymns from which are now found in every Protestant hymn-book of the English-speaking world, he appealed to 'men of taste', as to 'whether there be not in some of the following hymns the true spirit of poetry, such as cannot be acquired by art or labour, but must be the gift of nature'. Too often in later periods (even amongst his followers) the opinions of 'men of taste' have been disregarded.

16. The Composition of New Tunes. The corpus of fine hymn tunes (Lutheran, Calvin-istic, Old and Modern English and American) is now so great that there is no need for new ones, except to accompany the rare new hymns that are written in original metres or otherwise call for special treatment. It is much to be desired therefore that organists would, as much as in them lies, and unless they are sure of the possession of very special gifts, refrain from the composition of tunes, and, above all, from the not infrequent practice of composing new tunes for hymns that already have fine tunes wedded to them by long association. It is to be observed that (going perhaps too far in the practice of a good principle, let us admit) Ger-man Protestantism has, since the early eigh-teenth century, been content to regard its hymn-tune repertory as complete (see *Chorale*). Compare with this the activity of Dr. Gauntlett (1805–76), who believed he had composed as many as 10,000 English hymn tunes; it may be admitted that his standard was high, but what purpose has been served by such excessive production? (This number may be doubted and the present writer does not guarantee its accuracy; but remember that one poet has written 6,000 hymns! See 6.)

A new activity has come into existence dur-ing the twentieth century—the writing of descants, also sometimes called Faburdens or Fauxbourdons (see *Descant 2* and *Faburden*

9), for hymn tunes, thus introducing a welcome variety into the performance of a long hymn without making any increased demand upon the congregation: collections of such descants have been published and some ordinary hymn-tune books also provide a proportion of tunes so embellished.

17. Summary of Early Hymn and Psalm Publications.

(a) **Bohemian.** The followers of the Bohemian Reformer John Huss published Czech hymn-books in 1501 and 1505, and a collection in the German language, by Michael Weiss, with tunes, appeared in 1531. Luther much approved of these books.

(b) **German.** (i) The first of Luther's books, *Etlich cristlich lider Lobgesang* (eight hymns, five tunes), edited by Walther, appeared at Wittenberg in 1524. (ii) In the same year appeared at Erfurt (in two editions) *Enchiridion*, by Jonas and Lange, with twenty-five hymns and sixteen tunes, and (iii), at Wittenberg, *Geistliche gesangk Buchleyn*, with thirty-two hymns and thirty-five tunes, set in five parts by Walther, and with a preface by Luther (the first book to which he wrote a preface). (iv) In 1529 appeared at Wittenberg *Geistliche Lieder auffs new verbessert*, with tunes. (v) In 1545 appeared at Leipzig *Geystliche Lieder mit einer newen Vorrhede*, with 101 hymns (some by Hans Sachs) and tunes; this contained every hymn Luther had written and was the last hymn-book prepared under his supervision, for he died the next year.

Many books now appeared. The first one to give harmonized settings with the tune in the treble was that of Osiander, *50 Geistliche Lieder*, at Nuremberg, 1586.

(c) **Dutch.** In 1539, at Antwerp, appeared a book of 259 hymns, with tunes, the title of which may be given in brief as *Gheestelijke Liedekens* ('Little Spiritual Songs'). The following year the same printer produced a different work. *Souter Liedekens* (i.e. 'Little Psalm-songs'; see also *Holland* 2). This latter is a psalter, not a hymn-book, and the first complete metrical one in any language. The tunes are those of 158 Dutch and other folk songs, etc., and the work is the best original source for the study of the folk music of the Netherlands. The *Old Hundredth* (q.v.) appears to derive from one of the tunes. The book had enormous popularity and thirty-three editions are known (the last in 1618), some with settings for four voices. What some consider to be the original of the English *Lilliburlero* appears in this book. (See also reference under *Publishing of Music* 3.)

(d) **Genevan.** (i) in 1538 Calvin published his first psalter, at Strasbourg: it contained metrical psalms by Marot and by himself, with tunes. (ii) In 1542 and 1543, in Geneva, he published larger books: Béza contributed psalms to some of these. (iii) In 1552 he published the complete psalter, with syllabic tunes, adapted by Bourgeois, including the *Old Hundredth* (see

'Dutch' above) exactly as it now generally appears. (iv) In 1564 and 1565 harmonized versions appeared. (v) In 1565–6, Goudimel's settings in motet style appeared. (Note this, in view of the frequent statement that Calvinistic Protestantism approved only of unison singing.) These are some of the chief books; the one numbered (iii) was that which influenced British psalm setting and singing.

(e) **British.** (i) In 1539 appeared Coverdale's *Goostly Psalms*, an adaptation of German hymns and tunes at once suppressed by Henry VIII. (ii) In 1549 appeared Crowley's Psalms, complete and with four-voice music (as to which see *Anglican Chant* 2), and in the same year (iii) Sternhold's nineteen Psalms, with no music, and in the same year still (iv) Sternhold and Hopkins's forty-four Psalms, again with no music; this last quickly went into many editions. (v) In 1556, at Geneva, appeared the first Anglo-Genevan book, an edition of Sternhold and Hopkins, with tunes; other editions followed. (vi) In 1561 Day started publication with an edition of Sternhold and Hopkins, with tunes and an 'Introduction to Learn to Sing', and (vii) in 1562 he brought out a Sternhold and Hopkins, completed (i.e. all the Psalms), with sixty-five tunes. This is the standard book that went through very many editions. (viii) In 1563 Day published a harmonized tune book to the last (or rather, four books, one for each voice), with 143 compositions; sometimes the same tune is set differently by two or three composers. (ix) In 1579 appeared Damon's four-voice settings, unauthorized by him, so in 1591 were published two authorized books, one with the tune in the tenor and the other with it in the treble. (x) In 1592 Este's book appeared—the whole book of Psalms, with four-voice tunes set by ten of the best composers of the day (Dowland, Farnaby, etc.), some settings plain and some motet-like; three tunes have place-names attached—the beginning of this practice. (xi) In 1599 appeared Alison's Psalter (published by Barley), with four-voice settings and accompaniments for lute or other stringed instruments. (xii) In 1615 appeared Andro Hart's Scottish Psalter, with tunes. (xiii) In 1621 appeared the first Psalter in the Welsh language, that of Archdeacon Prys, with a few tunes. (xiv) Also in 1621 appeared Ravenscroft's Psalter, with four-voice settings; forty tunes have place-names attached which established Este's innovation henceforth. (xv) In 1623 Wither's book appeared and James I gave it a patent for fifty-one years and recommended that it should be bound with prayer books; the Stationers' Company opposed it and it failed; it included sixteen tunes by Orlando Gibbons (treble and bass only). (xvi) In 1635 appeared the Scottish Psalter with twenty-seven varieties of metre and much rhythmic freedom; it included Psalms in 'Reports' (see *Reports*); a scholarly reprint by the Revd. Neil Livingston appeared in 1864. (xvii) In 1638 appeared a new version of the Psalms by Sandys, with twenty-four tunes by Lawes (tune and bass only). (xviii) In 1671 the famous name of Playford appeared upon a not very successful four-voice edition of Sternhold and Hopkins, and in 1677 he brought out a three-voice edition, with the tune in the treble, and this during the next eighty years or so went into twenty editions. (xix) In 1696 appeared the Tate and Brady version of the Psalms. Many tune books followed (e.g. *Chetham's Psalnody*, 1718, which went through innumerable editions right down to nearly the end of the nineteenth century).

(*f*) **American.** (i) In 1640 appeared *The Whole Booke of Psalmes faithfully translated into English Metre, whereunto is prefixed a discourse declaring not only the lawfullnes, but also the necessity of the heavenly Ordinance of singing Scripture Psalmes in the Churches of God.* This is the 'Bay Psalm Book'. Last edition in America (70th) 1773; last in England (18th) 1754; last in Scotland (22nd) 1759. There were no tunes until 1698, and then only thirteen, given as air and bass (the oldest American printed music). (ii) In 1712 appeared Tuft's *Very Plain and Easy Instruction*, with twenty-eight tunes; in 1714, the same compiler's *Introduction to the Art of Singing Psalms*, with

three-voice tunes borrowed from Playford and a new method of letter notation. (iii) In 1721 appeared Walter's *Grounds and Rules of Music*, with three-voice tunes borrowed from Playford. (iv) In 1761 appeared Lyon's *Urania, or a Choice Collection of Psalm Tunes, Anthems and Hymns—in Two, Three and Four Parts* (the music is borrowed from various English compilations). In 1767 appeared Law's *Select Number of Plain Tunes*; in 1778 his *Select Harmony*; in 1779 his *Collection of Best Tunes and Anthems*, and so on (many such compilations by him). (v) In 1770 appeared Billings's *New England Psalm Singer*; in 1778 his *Singing Master's Assistant*; in 1779 his *Music in Miniature*; in 1781 his *Psalm Singer's Amusement*; in 1786 his *Suffolk Harmony*; in 1794 his *Continental Harmony*.

(It is hoped that the above summary will be useful to students, in view of the confused way in which the subject is often presented. It has been carefully compiled from the best sources. First-hand study of the subject is impossible to any but specialists, as many hymn-tune collections exist in only two or three, or even single copies, and these are widely scattered about Europe. A series of reprints of the most typical books is greatly to be desired.)

HYMN SOCIETY OF GREAT BRITAIN AND IRELAND. A Society founded in 1936 for the study of hymnology and the encouragement of the use of hymns and tunes of a high standard. Its officers and members are drawn from the ministry and laity of all the Protestant churches. Amongst its tasks is the very large and important one of an eventual revision of

Julian's *Dictionary of Hymnology* (see *Julian* and *Hymns and Hymn Tunes* 7).

HYMNUS EUCHARISTICUS. See *Rogers, Benjamin*.

HYOID BONE. See *Voice* 21.

HYPOAEOLIAN; HYPODORIAN; HYPO-IONIAN; HYPOLOCRIAN; HYPOLYDIAN; HYPOMIXOLYDIAN; HYPOPHRYGIAN. See *Modes* 6, 7.

I

I (It.). 'The' (masc. plural).

IAMBUS, IAMBIC. See *Metre*.

IBBERSON, MARY. See *Rural Music School Movement*.

IBÉRIEN, IBÉRIENNE (Fr., masc., fem.). As often loosely used this means 'Spanish', but properly it means this plus 'Portuguese'—the ancient Iberia comprising the whole peninsula.

IBERT, JACQUES (p. 388, pl. **65**. 2). Born in Paris in 1890 and died there in 1962, aged seventy-one. He studied at the Paris Conservatory under Fauré and others, and in 1919 won the Rome Prize. He composed half a dozen operas, symphonies, ballets, and other orchestral works, and also choral and chamber music, together with incidental music for plays and films. His style attaches him to the Impressionistic School (see *Impressionism*) in rather its Ravel than its Debussy manifestations (see *Debussy* and *Ravel*). From 1937 to 1953 he was Director of the French Academy at Rome (see *Prix de Rome*).

Cf. *Collaboration*; *Flute Family* 6; *Saxophone*; *Concerto* 6 c (1890); *Opera* 24 f (1937).

IBSEN, HENRIK. See *Grieg*.

ICELAND. See *Scandinavia* 5; *Harmony* 4.

IDÉE FIXE (Fr.). The 'Fixed Idea' in music was a device of Berlioz and will be found briefly explained in the article devoted to him.

IDELSOHN, ABRAHAM ZEVI (1882–1938). See *Jewish Music* 8.

IDYLL. In literature a description (prose or verse) of happy rural life, and so sometimes applied to a musical composition of peaceful pastoral character (e.g. Wagner's *Siegfried Idyll*).

IDZIKOWSKI. See *Ballet* 9.

I KNOW A BANK. See *Horn, C. E.*

IL (It.). 'The' (masc. singular).

'IL DISTRATTO' SYMPHONY (Haydn). See *Nicknamed Compositions* 11.

ILEBORGH, ADAM. See *Organ* 8.

ILES, JOHN HENRY (1872–1951). See *Competitions* 3.

IL FAUT (Fr.). 'There is (or are) needed'—such and such a player or players, etc. Or 'It is necessary to' (followed by a verb), or 'One must'.

I'LL SING THEE SONGS OF ARABY. See *Clay*.

IL TROVATORE. See *Trovatore*.

IMBRIE, ANDREW WELSH. Born in New York in 1921. He was educated at Princeton and the University of California, where he later taught, and he was a pupil of Sessions and Nadia Boulanger. His compositions include a violin concerto, choral music, and chamber music, mostly in a dissonant, but basically tonal, contrapuntal idiom.

IMITATION. See *Canon*; *Counterpoint*.

IMITAZIONE, ARIA D'. See *Aria*.

IMMER (Ger.). 'Ever', always, still, e.g. *Immer belebter*, 'ever more lively', or 'getting livelier and livelier'; *Immer schnell*, 'always quick', 'still quick'.

IMMORTAL HOUR, THE. See *Boughton*.

IMPAIR (Fr.). 'Odd' (numbers)—as opposed to *pair*, 'even'.

IMPAZIENTE, IMPAZIENTEMENTE (It.). 'Impatient', 'impatiently'.

IMPERFECT CADENCE. See *Cadence*.

IMPERFECT INTERVALS. See *Intervals*.

'IMPERIAL' MASS (Haydn). See *Nicknamed Compositions* 13.

IMPERIAL SYMPHONY (Haydn). See *Nicknamed Compositions* 11 (53).

IMPERIOSO (It.). 'Imperious.'

IMPETO (It.). 'Impetus', 'impetuosity'.

IMPÉTUEUX (Fr.). 'Impetuous.'

IMPETUOSO, IMPETUOSAMENTE, IMPETUOSITÀ (It.). 'Impetuous', 'impetuously', 'impetuosity'.

IMPONENTE (It.). 'Imposing'; so *imponenza*, an imposing style.

IMPONIEREND (Ger.). 'Imposing' in style.

IMPRESSIONISM. This is a word borrowed from painting, in connexion with which latter art it was adopted as a nickname for the style exemplified in the works of Manet, Monet, Degas, Renoir, Pissarro, Sisley, and Cézanne.

The origin of the nickname (applied by a critic, Louis Leroy, in the Paris journal *Charivari*) was a picture of Monet, exhibited in Paris in 1863 at the historic 'Salon des Refusés'—a picture bearing the title 'Sunrise; an Impression'. The idea of the word 'impression' here is that the painter records what a quick glance can take in, i.e. he does not unnaturally assemble on one canvas a mass of minute details each one of which could have been observed only by its special and particular glance. In practice impressionist painting reproduces less the appearance of objects as such than the play of light upon objects—in representing the minute nuances of which the impressionist painters became very adroit. (For some illustrations of impressionist painting see p. 497, pl. **90**.)

The Manet or Monet of music is Debussy (q.v.), whose treatment of effects of tone resembles that of Monet's treatment of effects of light. He may be said to seek shapes less, and tints and tinges more than his predecessors (though if his works be examined carefully the formal substructure will be found to be very ably contrived). Also, the strong and direct dramatic expression of much of the work of the previous romantics (see *Romantic*) is replaced in his work by a kind of expression that seems to hint rather than state; on this side such music approaches the methods of the contemporary French Symbolist School of poetry exemplified in the work of Verlaine and Mallarmé, and it will be remembered that in *The Afternoon of a Faun* ('L'Après-midi d'un Faune') Debussy actually transferred to expression in tone what Mallarmé had expressed in words—achieving in the new medium the same allusive vagueness that characterizes the original; it will also be remembered that Debussy set as songs very many of the poems of the symbolist poets, especially Verlaine (see *D bussy*).

Symbolism in poetry, impressionism in painting, and impressionism in music, then, represent one movement, the work óf a little group of Parisian artists in words, colours, and tones. The movement began later in music than in the other arts, and may be dated from 1887, when Debussy, returning from residence in Rome, settled again in Paris.

It would be beyond the scope of the present work to discuss the technical methods by which the painter impressionists obtained their 'atmospheric' effects. These methods have, however, a close counterpart in the harmonic system of Debussy, and especially in his use of the whole-tone scale (see *Scales* 9; *Harmony* 14) with its lack of the semitones which definitely mark the middle and top of the major and minor scales, this lack producing an effect of dreamy vagueness. The parallel thirds, fourths, and fifths of both Debussy and Ravel, the parallel ninths of the former and the parallel sevenths of the latter, contribute to this misty effect. Ravel, the second great exponent of the impressionist style, is less 'atmospheric' than his elder contemporary; he uses the whole-

tone scale hardly at all, and his lines are often more evident. Nevertheless, he must be classed as a practitioner of the impressionist style, and if the list of poets whose verses he has set to music be examined his general artistic sympathies will be evident.

Other French composers more or less closely allied with the impressionist school are Dukas, Florent Schmitt, Roussel, Ibert, and Sévérac. Delius was clearly much influenced by this school; so to some extent was Vaughan Williams. There are strong suggestions of impressionist influence in much of the music of Bax and in some of that of Ireland. Cyril Scott, too, shows leanings that way. The Alsatian–American, Loeffler, had a distinctly impressionist trend.

Some of the Italian and Spanish composers (e.g. Respighi, Falla) incline towards Impressionism. The German composers do so hardly at all.

See a reference under *Harp*; and cf. *Hill* 4.

IMPROMPTU. An instrumental composition of a character nominally (but by no means always really) suggesting improvisation (q.v.). The best-known examples are those for piano by Schubert (but the name may have been given by his publisher), Chopin, and Schumann.

The word came into use in the early nineteenth century, and the first to use it are believed to have been the Bohemian composer Woržischek and the Saxon composer Marschner, who, in 1822, both brought out pieces so entitled.

Cf. *Voluntary*.

IMPROPERIA. The Reproaches of the Roman Catholic Liturgy, sung on Good Friday morning. They consist of passages from the prophets, responded to by the Trisagion (q.v.). The music properly is plainsong, but there are some 'fauxbourdons' (q.v.), very simple four-part settings of Palestrina used in the Sistine Chapel and long kept for that place alone (cf. *Miserere*). They were first published by Burney (1771) and then reproduced in various other editions, but Casimiri discovered Palestrina's own manuscript and published it (1919), and it shows differences.

IMPROVISATION OR EXTEMPORIZATION

This is a branch of the musical art that was for centuries considered to be of the highest importance yet has now dwindled to insignificance amongst serious musicians (though it is still ably practised by jazz musicians and by the gipsy orchestras of the eastern countries of Europe, as also by all oriental musicians—see *Oriental Music*).

1. Various Historic Types of the Im-

provisatory Element. From the twelfth to the seventeenth centuries the art of descant was in process of development—a free vocal part interwoven by its singer or singers (more or less on the spur of the moment) with the existing fixed strand of the traditional plainsong carried by another voice (see *Descant*; *Modes* 9; and, for a cognate practice that still survives, *Wales* 5).

In the early days of the evolution of instrumental music much of it was improvised, and 'Toccata', 'Fantasia', 'Prelude', and other titles often met with today as those of published compositions remind us of their original predecessors, relatively few of which ever reached paper.

The once popular *Divisions* (q.v.), or extemporary 'breakings-up' of an air, by string players, are an example of the improvisatory element in the seventeenth century.

During that and the next century there was an important partially extemporary element in the *Figured Bass* (q.v.) part played by the harpsichordist as the background of all solo vocal, choral, string, and orchestral music.

The *Ornaments* (q.v.) that were so freely introduced by both player and singer at the period are another element of the same kind; however many of these might be written by the composer in his text the performer had a well-acknowledged right to add more, and often exercised this right very boldly.

The preludes to keyboard suites were often left by composers of the Bach and Handel period as mere successions of chords out of which the performer was to develop an introductory movement on his own lines; Handel's keyboard suites as published today offer examples, though in some editions the editor has added a written-out suggestion as to the treatment. (The practice of expecting the player to work out his own prelude originated earlier with the lute.)

In the earlier eighteenth century a great part of 'expression' on the part of the performer consisted in a filling in of details such as is with us assumed to be amongst the duties of the composer. So we find Burney in the third volume of his *History of Music* (1789) noticing the change to the more modern conception, in these words:

'It was formerly more easy to compose than to play an *adagio*, which generally consisted of a few notes that were left to the taste and abilities of the performer; but as the composer seldom found his ideas fulfilled by the player, *adagios* are now more *chantant* and interesting in themselves, and the performer is less put to the torture for embellishments.'

The *Cadenza* (q.v.) near the end of movements of the concerto is a quasi-extemporary element that remains today. Up to the nineteenth century it was customary to leave the performer entirely free at this point. (Brahms's Violin Concerto is a late instance—1879.)

The chorale preludes, extemporized in many German churches as introductions to the singing of the congregation, are another example (see *Chorale Prelude*).

Handel's cantata *Il Pensieroso*, at the words (declaimed by the full chorus) 'Let the pealing organ blow', has a blank marked 'Organ ad lib.', and so after every line of the chorus—until at the end we find 'Org⁰ ad Libᵐ; il soggetto della Fuga seguente', meaning that, arrived at this point, the organist is to go on extemporizing as long as he likes upon the subject of the following choral fugue. Such confidence had composers in those days in the ability of keyboard players!—unless we are to take it that Handel expected to be himself the organist in all performances, which seems hardly likely. (Cf. *Ives, Charles*, for a modern parallel.)

Most of these things have now entirely or virtually vanished, and with them the capacity for their execution, so that when we hear the older music in which the extemporary element was originally prominent we hear what the composer has written plus the work of some specialist editor carried out according to what he (sometimes after too little inquiry) believes to have been the practice of the period when the music came into being.

2. The Great Days of Keyboard Improvisation. The eighteenth century and early nineteenth century may be looked upon as the high period of the art of improvisation at the keyboard. Every keyboard player was, as a matter of course, expected to be able to play 'out of his own head'. Bach would improvise for two hours without stopping, and all upon one hymn-tune theme, working up out of it first a prelude and fugue, then a movement in thinner harmonies such as a trio, then a chorale prelude, and finally another fugue—of course combining with the original theme such new themes as occurred to him. His son, C. P. E. Bach, has told us that the published organ compositions offer no idea of the grandeur of the organ extemporization—which puts perhaps some strain on our credulity.

In Mozart's day the tradition was fully maintained. We hear of him performing at fourteen before the Philharmonic Society of Mantua and including in the programme an 'Air sung and composed extempore on words not previously seen by him, accompanied by himself on the harpsichord'. At twenty-one we find him at Augsburg, bombarded for hours by a bishop and dean with subjects for fugues. At Prague ten years later he is seen in the opera-house playing a half-hour extemporary fantasia and, recalled by a delighted audience, returning to the platform to play another, and then, recalled afresh, sitting down again and, on some member of the audience calling out '*Figaro*', reeling off a dozen brilliant variations on 'Non più andrai'.

With Beethoven extemporization was just as important. With paper before him he was one of the slowest and most laborious composers who ever lived, but with his fingers on the instrument he dashed away. His pupil Czerny says of him: 'His improvisations were most beautiful and striking. In whatever company he might chance to be he knew how to produce such an effect upon every hearer that frequently not an eye remained dry and many would break out into loud sobs.' This remarkable testimony is confirmed by other observers. Any chance theme served his purpose—a second violin part might be snatched from a music stand and its first few notes used as the theme, or a cello part turned upside down and a few notes from it similarly adopted.

Beethoven had many rivals as an improviser —Wölfl, Hummel, Steibelt, and others. Often friendly (or even not very friendly) competitions were arranged, the two antagonists taking turns to astonish the auditory.

Amongst later improvisers of high reputation were Moscheles, Liszt, and Ferdinand Hiller. Moscheles's last public extemporization was at the St. James's Hall, London, in 1865, at a concert of Jenny Lind's, when he extemporized for twenty minutes on 'See the conquering hero comes'. Liszt was famous as a boy extemporizer. At eleven we find him in Vienna, deferentially begging of Beethoven 'a theme on which to play a fantasia at his concert to-morrow', and at twelve at Manchester advertising 'An Extemporary Fantasia on the Pianoforte by Master Liszt, who will respectfully request a written theme from any person present'. In 1895 Miss Marie Wurm gave a complete recital in London in the form of extemporizations upon themes handed her by members of the audience.

Franck's organ extemporization is said to have been of the highest interest. Saint-Saëns was a very notable late nineteenth-century extemporizer on both piano and organ. Dupré stands high amongst twentieth-century organ extemporizers (more perhaps for his easy fluency than for invariable good taste) and has written a book on the subject of extemporization. Widor, Bonnet, Tournemire, Mulet, and Vierne are other French organists who have won a reputation as improvisers. The Roman Catholic Church offers, of course, many opportunities for extemporary performance, particularly in the Verset (q.v.); perhaps this is why improvisation of variations, a fugue, etc., is required of contestants for the Paris Conservatory prize for organ playing. According to Burney, writing about 1805, at English competitions for organists' places fugue subjects for improvisation were often given to the candidates—'which if the judges are profound and severe is a trial of abilities and courage in which few are able to acquit themselves with satisfaction'.

Amongst English organists notable for extemporary performance have been T. S. Dupuis, J. C. Beckwith, Samuel Wesley and his son Samuel Sebastian Wesley, Herbert Oakeley, E. J. Hopkins (whose extemporized voluntaries at the Temple Church, London, were a delight for more than half a century, as were those of his successor there, Walford Davies), Parratt, Lemare, Hollins, Wolstenholme, and W. G. Alcock.

Samuel Sebastian Wesley, Oakeley, and some others have been famous for fugue extemporization, but unless the subject of the fugue is handed up on the spot by some person present doubts creep in. Browning (The Englishman in Italy) tells of the festival sermon:

. . . the off-hand discourse which (all nature, no art)

The Dominican brother, these three weeks, was getting by heart.

And the late Dr. Harford Lloyd (himself a notable improviser) said at a meeting of the Musical Association in London in 1919:

'Wesley I had the privilege of hearing in the last year of his life. It was at Gloucester. I asked him to extemporize a fugue, which he did. A few months later (he had died in the meantime) I was talking to one of his sons about this extemporization. The son said "Can you remember the subject?" I gave it to him. "Yes," remarked the son, "that was a favourite subject of my father's to extemporize upon."'

Now Wesley was undoubtedly a marvellous extemporizer, but it seems likely that certain of his themes were very deliberately chosen for their malleability, and used over and over again, so that the extemporary element became gradually less and less important. No doubt this has been so with many famous improvisers. (For fugue extemporization see also entries under Mornington and Beckwith.)

Much of the 'extemporization' with which church organists today introduce and round off items in the service and fill the gaps that occur here and there can hardly be called extemporization at all.

It has been said (Sir James Swinburne, F.R.S., Proceedings of the Musical Association, January 1919), 'Extempore playing is very rapid composition in which a player imagines music and then plays it by ear. . . . Nearly every organist can make the noise called extemporizing, and does so, but the proportion able to extemporize even a definite march or minuet or anything that is clear-cut in form seems small.' (The definition in the first part of this extract is, by the way, probably the neatest possible.)

3. Duet Improvisation. This has occasionally been tried and, according to accounts, with some success. Instances of it have been related in the association of Mozart and Clementi, Beethoven and Wölfl, Moscheles and Mendelssohn, Ouseley and Parratt, and other notable pairs of pianists, and of Beethoven and Ries with pianoforte and violin.

The general plan seems to have been that first one player and then another would take the lead, a good deal of the performance being alternation rather than combination, the opportunity for the latter occurring chiefly at cadences and in passages where one harmony was obviously going to be continued for a few measures. In long stretches of a great deal of composed and printed music up to the time of Mendelssohn, an experienced musician can feel by instinct what is coming next and formal 'passage work' occupied many measures together.

Nevertheless, neat duet extemporization must always call for a very keen musical sense and great alertness. It may seem unkind to suggest that the present day, when so many unaccustomed harmonies are heard in written composition, offers a particularly favourable occasion for duet extemporization.

4. Machines for Recording Improvisation.

An enormous number of such machines have been invented, from the mid-eighteenth century (perhaps earlier) onwards.

One Creed, a London clergyman, in 1747, read to the Royal Society in London a paper (printed in its *Philosophical Transactions*) entitled 'A Discussion of the Possibility of Making a Machine that shall write Extempore Voluntaries or other Pieces of Music'. A mechanic called Hohlfeld (mentioned by Burney in his *Travels*) was another early inventor; his scheme has since been a very usual one—cylinders with a moving band of paper, a keyboard, and pencils attached to the keys. Electricity was brought into operation in 1863 in Fenby's 'Electro-Magnetic Phonograph'—anticipating (with another sense) Edison's use of the last word by fourteen years.

The gramophone and tape-recorder, like the earlier reproducing piano (see *Mechanical Reproduction* 13) today offer almost perfect means of recording extemporization, and the only question is—Have we much fine extemporization to record?

5. What is gained in Extemporization?

The world would certainly be the richer had a few of the best extemporizing efforts of Bach, Mozart, and Beethoven been preserved, and it would probably prove very instructive if we had this opportunity of comparing their style in extempore playing with that in their written music. It may be surmised that we should find the texture of the extemporary music less closely knit, so that a good many extemporizations which would impress us at first hearing might do so less and less if recorded and repeated. But, on the other hand, we might find a gain in spontaneity. Many people have never reflected on the intolerable loss of time in notating musical thoughts. A passage that in performance is to go through like a flash may take ten or fifteen minutes (or much more!) to notate; indeed, there is no Largo so slow that to

play it takes as much time as to notate it. Hence, in composing, the musician has to be in two minds at once—that which imagines the performance and that which laboriously undertakes to record its details, and it is possible that this conflict of speeds is an embarrassment (conscious or unconscious) to many composers, reducing their effectiveness by a percentage—at any rate, in the more emotional types of composition. It is doubtless for this reason that some composers (e.g. Elgar in his time) have formed the habit of working out all minute details in their minds before setting them on paper, and it is quite possible that some of the greatest composers, when expressing themselves in immediate sound, have done so in a different way from that of the lamp and the study. (For further discussion of this subject see *Composition*.)

A teacher of composition of high reputation, Frederick Corder (long at the Royal Academy of Music), in his book on Liszt, has said:

'It seems curious to our more informed minds what wonder and delight was in those days evoked by the simple art of improvisation. It is an art of the same kind as that of the mob-orator or the divine, who reels off the commonplaces of thought and speech so glibly as to make the hearer believe that what he hears is direct inspiration from on high.'

But it is incredible that all the greatest minds in music over a period of three centuries (say 1550–1850) should have themselves practised, and admired in their colleagues, an art that could fairly be described in those terms.

In conclusion, it may be recalled that there is one educational system today which requires the development of the extemporizing faculty in all its teachers, the Dalcroze system (see *Jaques-Dalcroze*), and that, in the United States, at all events, the attempt has been made to teach composition through extemporization —on the analogy (probably false) of our learning first to speak our own language freely and afterwards to write it.

SOME ARTICLES ON COGNATE SUBJECTS. *Descant; Harmony; Composition; Voluntary; Cadenza; Improvisatore; Jazz; Ornaments; Metamorphosis of Themes.*

IMPROVISATORE (It.; plural *Improvisatori*). One who practised the art of poetical improvisation, often with musical accompaniment.

Such performers seem to have been almost confined to Italy, Spain, Portugal, and Wales (see *Wales* 5), though cruder manifestations of the same art have probably been practised everywhere at some period or another. They were very active in Italy in the eighteenth century.

One of the most famous was a woman, Maddalena Morelli, celebrated all over Europe as 'Corilla', a name given her by the Arcadian Academy of Rome in 1775 when she was honoured there 'in the presence of the first nobility and men of letters and science'; next year she was 'solemnly crowned in the Campodoglio, as

Petrarch was in the 14th century' (Burney in Rees's *Cyclopædia*). She produced 'the most elegant verses' on whatever subject and in whatever metre was suggested, and sang them to simple tunes, accompanying herself on a violin held in her lap.

Rousseau in his *Dictionary of Music* (1767) says: 'Nothing is more common in Italy than to see during the Carnival, two masks meet, defy, challenge and attack each other in verse and answer, stanza by stanza, to the same air, with a vivacity, dialogue, melody, and accompaniment which without the having been present is difficult to comprehend.' Some Spanish gipsy musicians today make a living by extemporizing songs in competition with each other, on subjects given them by the frequenters

2. MUSICAL GLASSES TAPPED WITH RODS (in acoustical experiment) from the treatise of Gaforio, *Theoria Musicae*, 1496

1. MUSICAL GLASSES PLAYED WITH FINGERS, in a caricature by Gillray, 1790 —probably much as Gluck played them in London forty years earlier. The performer is 'Anne Ford'. See *Harmonica* 1

3. KAFFIR PIANO
The *Marimba* (q.v.) of South Africa

5. MARIMBA (q.v.) of Mexico

4. FRANKLIN AND HIS 'ARMONICA' about 1760. See *Harmonica* 1. Examples of this instrument can be seen in the museum at Pittsburgh, and in other museums in Europe and America

6. BLADDER AND STRING (q.v.)
With Bagpipes, Jew's Harp, Saltbox, and Dulcimer (Hogarth)

8. BELLOWS AND TONGS (q.v.)

7. MARROW-BONES AND CLEAVERS (q.v.). Celebration of the wedding of Hogarth's 'Industrious Apprentice'

9. THE SALTBOX (q.v.) The player is the famous clown Grimaldi (1779–1837)

For other pictures of old or uncommon instruments see pages 417, 449, 465, 513, and 544–5

2. TOM-TOMS

3. TURKISH CRESCENT
From an engraving of 1840 representing the procession
in Paris on the occasion of the translation of the remains
of Napoleon

1. DISTIN'S MONSTER DRUM was first introduced to the musical public
at the Crystal Palace Handel Festival of 1857. It was 7 feet in diameter and
its skin was said to be the largest buffalo hide ever imported, reduced by
machinery from its original thickness of a quarter of an inch. The rim
consisted of 30 dovetailed pieces

5. PANPIPERS AT VAUXHALL GARDENS (*c.* 1800)
The five members of the band, in addition to their percussive activities, are all absorbedly blowing. Their Panpipes are respectively marked *Primo, Secondo, Tenore, Basso,* and *Contrabasso*

4. PANPIPES
11th-century carving
outside the Cathedral
of Chartres

For other pictures of old or uncommon instruments see pages 417, 449, 465, 512, and 544–5

of inns, and much the same thing may be found in Parisian cafés; there were formerly occasional practitioners of this art to be heard in British music halls.

The great opera librettist Metastasio (see *Metastasio*; *Libretto*; *Opera* 9 b) was at five years old an able improvisatore, but, as he told Burney, 'this exercise was found to exhaust him so much that a physician assured his patron that if he continued the practice it would destroy him, for at such times he was so truly *afflatus numine* that his head and stomach swelled and became inflamed, whilst his extremities grew cold'. In later life Metastasio spoke of the practice as ruinous to the poetical faculty, 'the mind and genius, accommodating themselves to inaccuracies and absurdities, not only lose a relish for labour, but for everything that is chaste and correct'.

Wagenseil's book (1697) on the Mastersingers of Nuremberg (from which Wagner drew all his information) speaks scornfully of their inferior contemporaries, the Spruchsprecher —in English 'pithy talkers', or something of that kind (difficult to translate)—who attended weddings and social functions and extemporized doggerel, their object being merely, he says, to earn money and 'a good drink'. These Spruchsprecher were still to be heard up to about 1820.

See also *Improvisation*.

IM VORAUS (Ger.). See *Voraus*.

IN ALT, IN ALTISSIMO. See *Pitch* 7 i.

INCALCANDO (It.). Getting faster and louder.

INCALZANDO (It.). 'Pressing forward', hastening.

INCIDENTAL MUSIC to plays has always been an important side-line of the art and business of the composer. It dates back in one form or another as far as we have any record of the drama (Greek, Roman, Medieval) and is very important in the Elizabethan Age (see reference under *Shakespeare*).

Purcell wrote a great deal of music of this kind. So did Beethoven (Goethe's *Egmont*, Kotzebue's *The Ruins of Athens*, etc.). Mendelssohn's music to *A Midsummer Night's Dream* is a well-known and successful example. Towards the end of the nineteenth century, London theatre managers gave many commissions to the best contemporary composers for such music. Amongst British composers, the chief twentieth-century specialist in the art of providing suitable music for spoken plays was Norman O'Neill (q.v.). Delius's music to Flecker's *Hassan* (1923) contributed greatly to such success as that play enjoyed. One of the most developed examples of incidental music is that of Bizet to Daudet's *L'Arlésienne* (1872). This, like Grieg's music to Ibsen's *Peer Gynt* (1875) and other examples by various composers, was afterwards cast into the suite form for concert use.

A classical instance of the affecting power of a piece of suitable incidental music well played is that recorded by Pepys in his Diary, in connexion with a performance of Dekker and Massinger's *The Virgin Martyr* at the King's Theatre in London (27 Feb. 1668):

'Not that the play is worth much . . . But that which did please me beyond anything in the whole world was the wind-musique when the angel comes down, which is so sweet that it ravished me and, indeed, in a word, did wrap up my soul so that it made me really sick, just as I have formerly been made in love with my wife, that neither then, nor all the evening going home, and at home, I was able to think of any thing, but remained all night transported, so that I could not believe that ever any music hath that real command over the soul of a man as this did upon me; and makes me resolve to practice wind-musique, and to make my wife do the like.'

(This, it will be observed, refers to a piece of music in the actual course of a play. During overtures, entr'actes, and the like, London audiences have, it is believed, always talked— and seem unlikely ever to change their ways.)

INCISO (It.). 'Incisive.'

INCLEDON, CHARLES BENJAMIN (1763–1826). The leading tenor vocalist of his time, famous in opera, oratorio, and concert performance (see reference under *Lass of Richmond Hill*).

INCOMINCIANDO (It.). 'Commencing.'

INCORPORATED ASSOCIATION OF ORGANISTS. The formation, in Britain, of associations of organists (without distinction as to whether they were professional or amateur) seems to have begun at Wakefield, Yorkshire, in 1889. In 1913 the then existing associations federated under the title 'National Union of Organists' Associations' and in 1929 the Union became a legal corporation under its present title. It holds annual conferences, carries on a journal, etc. (Address, 37 John Dalton Street, Manchester.)

INCORPORATED SOCIETY OF AUTHORS, PLAYWRIGHTS AND COMPOSERS (otherwise, 'The Society of Authors'; 84 Drayton Gardens, London, S.W. 10). See *Copyright and Performing Right*.

INCORPORATED SOCIETY OF MUSICIANS (48 Gloucester Place, London, W. 1) See *Profession of Music* 10.

INDEBOLENDO (It.). 'Becoming weak.' So *Indebolito*, 'having become weak'.

INDECISO (It.). 'Undecided', capricious.

INDEPENDENTS. See *Congregational Churches*.

INDEPENDENT TELEVISION AUTHORITY. See *Broadcasting* 3.

INDIA. See the following: *Oriental*; *Scales* 8, 10; *Bagpipe Family* 7; p. 465, pl. 82 (for some instruments); *Clubs*.

INDIAN (AMERICAN). See *United States of America* 7.

INDICATO (It.). 'Indicated', i.e. prominent.

INDY. See *d'Indy*.

INFINITE CANON. See *Canon*.

INFLEXION. In plainsong, the general name given to such parts as are not in monotone, i.e.

Y

including the intonation, mediation, and ending, and excluding the recitation.

See *Plainsong* 2 and *Anglican Chant* 1.

INFRA (It.). 'Below.'

INGEGNERI, MARCO ANTONIO. He was born about 1545 at Verona and died in 1592 at Cremona, of whose cathedral he was choirmaster.

He was a pupil of Vincenzo Ruffo (q.v.), and master of Monteverdi, and published a number of books of church music and of madrigals which established his reputation as a composer of high originality and deep sensitivity.

See *Misattributed* (Palestrina).

INGEMISCO. See *Requiem*.

INGHELBRECHT, DÉSIRÉ ÉMILE. Born in Paris in 1880 and died there in 1965, aged eighty-four. He was a student at the Paris Conservatory and a friend of Debussy. He was an able conductor (especially of ballet) and the composer of ballets, symphonic poems, chamber music, songs, etc.

See reference under *Harp* 4.

INGLESE (It.). 'English.'

INGOLDSBY LEGENDS. See *Ballad* 5.

IN MODO DI (It.). 'In the manner of.'

INNIG (Ger.). 'Inmost', i.e. heartfelt. So the noun *Innigkeit*.

INNO (It.). 'Hymn.'

INNOCENZA (It.). 'Innocence.'

IN NOMINE. This name is attached to a very large number of sixteenth- and seventeenth-century English (*exclusively* English) contrapuntal compositions for viols or (less frequently) keyboard; they are practically instrumental motets and are constructionally much the same as fancies (see *Fancy*).

The Hon. Roger North, in his *Memoires of Musick* (written 1728), says of the *In Nomine*:

'It was onely descanting upon the eight notes with which the syllables ("In nomine domini") agreed [on this point see below]. And of the kind I have seen whole volumes, of many parts, with the severall authors names inscribed. And if the study, contrivance, and ingenuity of these compositions to fill the harmony, carry on fuges, and interspers discords, may pass in the account of skill, no other sort whatsoever may pretend so more. And it is some confirmation that in two or three ages last bygone the best private musick, as was esteemed, consisted of these.'

In the Fitzwilliam Virginal Book (q.v.) are several *In Nomines*, all constructed on one same piece of plainsong (the Trinity Sunday antiphon, *Gloria Tibi Trinitas Aequalis*); and, indeed, this is the invariable basis.

There are a few so-called *In Nomines* that are not upon this (or perhaps any) plainsong basis, but it seems certain that they are misnamed. Nobody yet has been able conclusively to explain the reasons why this particular bit of plainsong had such a fascination for composers, from Taverner to Purcell; nor until 1949 could it be discovered why, in view of the fact that the words associated with the plainsong are *Gloria tibi* (North being wrong on this point; he was a Protestant and ill-informed as to plainsong), the compositions should be termed *In Nomine*.

Glo - ri - a ti - bi.

As regards the first point the reader's attention may be called to the articles *Folía* and *Mass* 5 (allusion to *L'homme armé*), where a similar puzzle is posed. As regards the second point it has at last been simultaneously noticed by several musicologists that the prototype, an instrumental work by Taverner, is identical with the setting of the words *In Nomine Domini* in the Benedictus of that composer's Mass, *Gloria Tibi Trinitas* (of which all the movements are based on the *Gloria Tibi* plainsong): thus the pioneer instrumental composition of the kind was called *In Nomine* and other composers, in adopting the form, adopted also the name.

INNS AND TAVERNS AS PLACES OF MUSIC-MAKING. As shown in the article on the Concert (q.v.), the practice of providing music for the public at fixed prices and for money taken at the doors dates back no further than the end of the seventeenth century. But before this, and from time immemorial, there had been plenty of music to be heard in public places by those who wished for it, and a multitude of references in English literature show us that the inn was one of the buildings where it was constantly to be enjoyed (probably the same thing would be found in the literatures of most Continental countries if they were searched).

Thus Chaucer (died 1400) shows us the inns of a town haunted by the parish clerk, famed for his dancing and singing and his performances on two instruments, a bowed string instrument and plucked string one—the rubible or rebec (see *Rebec*) and the gittern or cittern (see *Cittern*):

In al the toun nas [was not] brewhous ne taverne
That he ne visited with his solas. (*Miller's Tale*.)

In Shakespeare (*Henry IV, Part II*) we find a tavern servant ordering his underling to 'find out Sneak's noise' because 'Mistress Tearsheet would fain hear some music' ('noise' = simply band of musicians). Sneak and his companions, probably regularly employed in going from tavern to tavern in the district, are quickly found and brought. They give a brief performance, and, with a 'Pay the musician, Sirrah!' from Falstaff (who has now come in) to his page, the party turns to its conversation again.

In this case the music had to be sent for, but that was just as it chanced, for it was common form for the musicians to poke their heads into a room and ask 'Would you have any music, Gentlemen?' So in a novel by a contemporary of Shakespeare (Deloney's *Jack of Newbury*) we find:

'To the Tavern they went . . . The old man called for wine plenty, and the best cheere in the house. . . . They had sitten long, but in comes a noise of Musitians in tawny coats, who (putting off their caps) asked if they would have any musicke.'

A custom that constantly turns up in sixteenth- and seventeenth-century literature is that of having music over one's meals in an inn. Thus Pepys at Marlborough in 1688 says: 'Then to supper and had musique, whose innocence [i.e. simplicity] pleased me, and I did give them 3 shillings. So to bed.'

Often the local waits (q.v.) acted in this way (p. 993, pl. 166). One meets with a good many allusions to the Cambridge waits and gathers that they were very diligent in their attention to business. Thus Judge Sewall, of Boston, Mass. (see *United States* 2), being in England in 1689, was entertained with music at Cambridge—'Mr. Littel dined with us at our Inn: had a Legg Mutton boild and Colly-Flowers, Carrets, Roasted Fowls, and a dish of Pease. Three Musicians came in, two Harps and a Violin, and gave us Musick.'

The local musicians kept in touch with the inn servants and, for a consideration (probably a percentage commission), were informed of all new arrivals. So Bishop Earle in his satirical sketch of 'A Poore Fidler' (*Microcosmographie*, 1628) says: 'He is in League with the Tapsters for the worshipfull of the Inne, who he torments next morning with his art, and has their names more perfit than their men' (knows the visitors' names better than their own servants know them, that is).

The object of thus getting the information was to greet the travellers in the morning, before they were up, by calling their names at their bedroom doors and then giving them a tune or two. Pepys at Reading, forty years after the date of Earle's book, would not trouble to get up to reward some musicians who both played badly and got the names wrong— 'Musicke, the worste we had had, coming to our chamber door, but calling us by our wrong names we lay.'

At various periods there existed laws (or rules of the musicians' guilds) against musicians playing to inn guests unless they were definitely sent for, but apparently these laws were generally ignored. During the Commonwealth a musician's apprentice named Hosier appealed to the Middlesex sessions to release him from his indentures, and it was given as one of his claims to release that the master had been 'commonly used to send Hosier up and down to proffer musick in taverns and alehouses, being not sent for, contrary to law'.

All the instances quoted above are anterior to the establishment of the practice of holding public concerts and tend to support the suggestion that before concert halls existed the inns and taverns offered the main public opportunities for enjoying musical entertainment.

In Massinger's play, *The Fatal Dowry* (printed 1632), we find a character, 'Aymer, a Singer and Keeper of a Musick House'. It is not clear that this establishment was an inn. Certainly Aymer was not an ordinary innkeeper, since he is described as 'a gentleman (for his quality speaks him) well received amongst our greatest gallants'. Yet, apparently as a matter of course, he serves refreshment to those who come to hear his music, so that his establishment did not differ altogether from an inn; it probably represented a step in advance made at that period—instead of meat and drink with music as a subsidiary, music with meat and drink thrown in.

Another step in advance was taken when, during the Commonwealth (as mentioned under *Music Halls* 1), organs removed from churches were bought by keepers of taverns, where they remained for some time after the Restoration. Such 'Musick Houses' (apparently generally with a small orchestra also) had, it seems, great popularity—especially in riverside resorts within easy reach of London. Thus in 1663 Pepys records, of a visit to Greenwich: 'To the musique house, where we had paltry musique till the master organist came . . . and he did give me a fine voluntary, and so home by water.' (By voluntary here is meant an extempore performance; see under *Voluntary*.)

Stepney had also a place of this kind with an organ and a band of fiddlers and hautboys. So had Wapping, where, according to Ned Ward (1698), the 'Musique House' possessed 'a most stately apartment', with 'gilding, carving, colouring and every good contrivance'; the upper end, where were the 'fiddlers and hautboys with a hum-drum organ', was divided off by a rail 'like a chancel' and the body of the room fitted with 'seats like pews', and all 'tippling conveniency'.

Information as to provincial 'Musique Houses' is not easy to find, but it is probable that they existed. There is record of an organ in the Globe Inn, Exeter, in 1697.

In all these 'Musique Houses' apparently there was no charge for admission. You ordered what food and drink you liked and, if generous, before leaving you tipped the musicians who had entertained you.

The next stage was to make a definite charge for admission to rooms set out 'alehouse-fashion' and still providing refreshments (but sometimes, at any rate, including them in the entrance price), and to maintain a daily musical programme at fixed hours. Then the 'alehouse-fashion' tables and the refreshments were abandoned and the concert as we know it had come into being (but for these later phases see *Concert* 3–5).

It is very observable that during the eighteenth century and, indeed, into the nineteenth, some of the regular concert rooms of London and of provincial cities were situated on inn premises, so maintaining an association that goes back for many centuries.

It seems likely that the eighteenth-century

London 'Mughouses' (taverns partaking somewhat of the nature of clubs, where all the habitués had their own mugs, where songs were sung, and where a harpist played) derived from the 'Musique Houses'. These 'Mughouses' had a political complexion. The last 'Mughouse' building to disappear was the Barley Mow, in Salisbury Court, Fleet Street, which used to be a Whig meeting-place. It was pulled down in 1936.

For some treatment of cognate subjects see the articles (or parts of them) on *Concert*; *Music Hall*; *Clubs or Music-Making*; *Barber Shop Music*; *Waits*; *Mealtime Music*; *Fairs and their Music*.

INNSBRUCK, I MUST FORSAKE THEE. See *Germany* 3; *Isaac* 1.

INQUIET (Fr.), **INQUIETO** (It.). 'Unquiet', restless.

INQUISITION. See *Belgium* 2.

INSENSIBILE (It.). 'Imperceptible.'

INSIEME (It.). 'Together', 'ensemble' (q.v.).

INSPIRATION. See *Composition* 4.

INSTÄNDIG (Ger.). 'Urgent.'

INSTANTE (It.). 'Urgent'. So *Instantemente*, 'urgently'.

INSTRUMENTATION. The study of the characteristics of the various instruments. Sometimes the word is used as meaning scoring for an orchestra, but it is best to apply to this the term 'Orchestration'.

INSTRUMENTS. The nervous excitation which we call sound is the result of atmospheric vibrations impinging on the drum of the ear (see *Acoustics* 2 and *Ear and Hearing*). What we may call 'natural' means of promoting such vibrations are the use of the voice, whistling, and the clapping of the hands or stamping of the feet. Thus man may be said to have possessed from his creation wind and percussion instruments, and to have merely imitated these in various more or less complex mechanisms, so bringing into being the great number of wind and percussion instruments that have at various ages existed.

A further class was invented at some period of high and unknown antiquity—a class in which the agent setting in motion the atmospheric vibrations is a stretched string.

All instruments fall into one of these three classes, string, wind, and percussion, with the exception of one or two oddities and of a new class that began to appear during the twenties of the twentieth century and may in time possibly prove the death of all the others—the class in which electrical excitation furnishes the vibrational basis (see *Electric Musical Instruments*).

Stringed Instruments fall into four classes; (*a*) those in which the string is set into vibration by *plucking*; (*b*) those in which it is set in motion by the *friction of a bow*; (*c*) those in which it is set in motion by the *impact of a hammer*; and (*d*) one instrument (the aeolian harp) in which the string is set in vibration by wind (a curious case, since pressure of the surround-

ing air itself causes vibrations which are then communicated to the surrounding air). Descriptions of such instruments will be found in this volume under the following heads:

(*a*) **Plucked.** *Lyre*; *Psaltery*; *Harp*; *Clàrsach*; *Bell Harp*; *Zither*; *Lute Family*; *Vihuela*; *Cittern*; *Guitar*; *Dital Harp*; *Banjo*; *Balalaika*; *Gusli*; *Mandolin*; *Ukelele*; *Victalele*; *Harpsichord Family*.

(*b*) **Bowed.** *Crwth*; *Rebec*; *Hurdy-gurdy*; *Tromba Marina*; *Viol Family*; *Violin Family*; *Arpeggione*; *Japanese Fiddle*.

(*c*) **Hammered.** *Dulcimer*; *Zimbalon*; *Pantaleon*; *Schlagzither*; *Clavichord*; *Pianoforte*. (Bowed instruments when played *Col legno* come into this class.)

(*d*) **Blown.** *Aeolian Harp*.

Wind Instruments may be conveniently divided into three classes: (*a*) those in which the air of the instrument is set in vibration by simple blowing into a tube (with or without a mouthpiece); (*b*) those in which it is set in vibration by means of reeds (see *Reed*) which are themselves set in vibration by blowing; and (*c*) those in which the lips of the blower himself serve as such reeds, i.e. the brass instruments and certain others which, though made of different material, are on the same lines. Descriptions of such instruments will be found in this volume under the following heads:

(*a*) **Mere Tubes.** *Recorder Family*; *Flute Family*; *Fife*; *Whiffle*; *Panpipes*; *Nightingale*. For the most part, the *Organ* also belongs to this group.

(*b*) **Reed Type.** *Oboe Family*; *Bombard*; *Clarinet Family*; *Saxophone Family*; *Bagpipe Family*; *Quail*; *Stockhorn*. The Reed Stops of the *Organ* belong to this family.

(*c*) **Brass Type.** *Brass*; *Whole Tube and Half Tube*; *Horn Family*; *Trumpet Family*; *Trombone Family*; *Saxhorn and Flügelhorn Family*; *Tuba Group*; *Cornet*; *Cornett Family*; *Bugle*; *Posthorn*; *Alphorn*; *Oliphant*.

Percussion Instruments fall into two classes: (*a*) those with determinate pitch and (*b*) those with indeterminate pitch. Descriptions of such instruments will be found under the following heads:

(*a*) **Determinate Pitch.** Percussion Family 2, 4, 5; *Bell*; *Marimba*; *Deagan Instruments*; *Glass Dulcimer* (see *Harmonica* 2).

(*b*) **Indeterminate Pitch.** *Percussion Family* 3, 4, 5; *Tarbouka*; *Turkish Crescent*; *Bones*; *Marrowbones and Cleaver*; *Tongs and Bones*; *Salt Box*.

Obviously other classifications are possible, but the above, based on method of tone-production, seems the most logical, and it embraces nearly everything, though one or two oddities are left unplaced, e.g. *Wind Machine*; *Thunder Stick*; *Nail Fiddle*; *Musical Glasses* (see *Harmonica*); *Jew's Harp*; *Mirliton*; *Monocord*; *Ocarina*; *Terpodion*. The hammered stringed instruments could, of course, be classified under percussion.

To instruments of all the above classes automatic means of performance have, at one time or the other, been applied. See *Mechanical Reproduction of Music*.

For a general discussion of the keyboard see articles *Keyboard*; *Pedalier*. For the nature of the human voice as an instrument see *Voice* 2, 3, 4, 6. For the various

2. PALESTRINA (1525–94) and the Pope

3. GESUALDO (1560–1613) with his uncle, Carlo Borromeo, standing

1. THE SISTINE CHAPEL, ROME
he Choir Gallery is at the right. See references
nder *Miserere*; *Belgium* 2; *Voice* 5; *Singing* 3;
Tonic Sol-fa 10

5. ALLEGRI (1582–1652)

4. MONTEVERDI (1567–1643)
a contemporary portrait

6. FRESCOBALDI (1583–1643)

7. A. SCARLATTI (1660–1725)

8. D. SCARLATTI (1685–1757)

1. VIVALDI (c. 1676–1741)

2. GEMINIANI (1687–1762)

3. PERGOLESE (1710–36)

4. PICCINI (1728–1800)

5. CIMAROSA (1749–1801) at the harpsichord

6. CLEMENTI (1752–1832)

7. CHERUBINI (1760–1842)

8. SPONTINI (1774–1851)

9. DIABELLI (1781–1858)

instruments *d'Amore* see entry under that word. For the use of the word *Double* in connexion with instruments see that word.

A great deal of the fundamental scientific principle underlying the construction of instruments will be found under *Acoustics*.

The question is sometimes asked whether (*a*) Invention introduces new instruments and then composers learn to use them, or (*b*) Composers feel the need of new instruments and call on Invention to supply them. It is really as impossible to answer that question as to answer the similar question 'Which came first, the Hen or the Egg?' Hens are always producing eggs and eggs are always producing hens. (Samuel Butler said that a hen was merely an egg's way of producing another egg.) And inventors are always producing instruments which lead to new activities on the part of composers, and composers are always indulging in new activities that call forth efforts on the part of inventors.

There has been a regrettable tendency on the part of composers once they have taken up a new instrument to allow some corresponding instrument to fall out of use. The flute family superseded the recorder family, the violin family the viol family, the pianoforte the harpsichord and clavichord. One great inconvenience resulting is that the older music can then no longer be performed by the medium for which it was intended and with the original timbres, etc. There has, however, during the twentieth century, been a marked reaction against this tendency and the old instruments of all classes are gradually coming back into use. All instruments that have been or are likely to be revived have received treatment in the present volume.

For an illustration of an eighteenth-century instrument-maker's workshop see p. 417, pl. **72**. 1.

Numerous illustrations of the more uncommon instruments will be found on p. 417, pl. **72**; 449, **77**; 465, **82**; 512, **91–92**; 544, **99–100**; and 785, **132**.

For instruments classified by their vibrating agencies see *Acoustics* 5.

For dictionaries of musical instruments see *Dictionaries* 6.

INTAVOLATURA. 'Scoring.' Used in Elizabethan times of the 'arrangement' of madrigals, etc., for keyboard performance—the choral originals having circulated merely in parts, not in score.

INTENSITY OF SOUND. See *Acoustics* 4.

INTERLUDE, of course, means anything inserted in an entertainment, and in sixteenth-century English means specifically the short play often interpolated in a banquet or between the acts of a Mystery, Morality, etc. (see *Mystery Plays*, etc.; *Chapel Royal*). Singing often made a part of the interlude, so that the Act of Parliament 24 Henry VIII prohibits acting *or singing* in interludes anything contrary to the established religion.

An instrumental passage inserted between verses of a hymn or lines of a verse is also called an interlude, and in the late seventeenth and eighteenth centuries such passages (to judge from published specimens) were of a very florid and banal character (p. 485, pl. **86**. 3). Lowell

Mason in his *Musical Letters* (1854), speaks of long interludes between the verses of hymns as though they were the rule in American churches.

See also *Chorale* 2.

INTERMEZZO (It.), **INTERMÈDE** (Fr.), **INTERMEDIO** (It.). Literally 'in the middle'. Obviously anything interposed in the middle of anything else can have these names attached to it, but as will be seen later this sense is sometimes lost.

(1) The first prominent use of the word in a musical connexion is in the sixteenth century in Italy, where the practice grew up of interpolating lighter entertainment between the sections of heavier, such as solo songs or madrigals between the acts of plays. This practice continued, and two centuries later we find Rousseau in his *Dictionary of Music* (1767) defining *Intermède* as 'A piece of music or dance inserted at the Opéra or sometimes at the Comédie between the acts of a big piece, to cheer and repose in some measure the spirit of the spectator, saddened by thoughts of the tragic and strained by its attention to matters of gravity'. (By 'Opéra' and 'Comédie' he means the royal opera-house in Paris, founded 1669, and the Comédie Française, or royal theatre for the spoken play, founded 1680.)

He goes on to complain of the practice being overdone: 'There are some Intermèdes which constitute true comic dramas, or burlesques, thus interrupting the main interest by an interest of a different sort, tossing and tugging the attention of the spectator, as one might put it, in a contrary direction, and this in a manner strongly opposed to good taste and good sense.'

He proceeds to make it clear that he does not object to the intercalation of entertainment, as such, but does to the alternation of two plots—a reasonable position and one which others also took up increasingly. As most tragedies had three acts, and comedies were played between these, it follows that comedies had in general two acts. Practically all the eighteenth-century Italian composers wrote intermezzi.

(2) It was as *intermezzo* or *intermède* that the comic opera grew up, and even when this type of piece had attained independence (generally as a one-act musical play with spoken dialogue) the term continued to be used. Pergolese's *The Servant as Mistress* ('La Serva padrona', Naples, 1733). Rousseau's own *The Village Soothsayer* ('Le Devin du village', Paris, 1752), and Cimarosa's *The Italians in London* (Rome, 1779) all bore on their title-pages or their programmes the description 'Intermezzo' or 'Intermède'; these are three of the most important works so designated. Pergolese's work, in its French edition, has as sub-title *Intermède à deux personnages* ('Intermezzo for two actors'); it is often looked upon as marking the beginning of the true *Opera buffa* or comic opera. A. Scarlatti was a great writer of intermezzi.

The importance of the *Intermezzo* or *Intermède* in the history of both ballet and comic opera is, then, evident. The Spanish *Tonadilla* (q.v.) also grew up in the middle of the eighteenth century as a sort of intermezzo, a few soloists (with sometimes a choir also) singing a little string of pieces between the acts of a serious play.

(3) Nowadays 'Intermezzo', in a theatrical application, means usually a musical passage interposed in an opera but having some connexion with its general scheme. Thus in Mascagni's *Cavalleria Rusticana*, an opera having only one act and hence offering no intervals to suggest the passage of time, the well-known intermezzo, played whilst the villagers are in church, serves this purpose and also that of maintaining the 'atmosphere' during the period of waiting.

(4) The Germans sometimes apply the term 'intermezzo' to the optional items of the suite (q.v.)—those that, in addition to the usual allemande, courante, sarabande, and gigue, are inserted between the last two of these.

(5) Some composers have latterly used the term for a movement in a sonata, symphony, etc. As an example may be mentioned the second Piano Quartet of Mendelssohn, where the movement so designated is presumably intended to be looked upon (and listened to) as an intercalation in the work of which it forms a part: the use of the word, then, appears to have a psychological significance, suggestive of the original use of it in connexion with stage works. Brahms, too, has an Intermezzo in his G minor Piano Quartet. Schumann in several works seems to use the term as a mere synonym for 'trio' (in the old 'Minuet and Trio' sort of sense).

(6) From this it is a slight step to independence (again as with the stage works), and so we find Schumann (op. 4, Six Intermezzi), Brahms (op. 117, Three Intermezzi), and others publishing separate little piano pieces under the name. Here the word has practically lost all definite meaning.

INTERNATIONAL COMPOSERS' GUILD. See *Varèse*.

INTERNATIONALE. The former official Communist song, words by Eugène Pottier, a woodworker of Lille; music by Pierre Degeyter (1849–1932). The words, in their original French, begin:

> Debout, les damnés de la terre!
> Debout, les forçats de la faim!
> La raison tonne en sa cratère;
> C'est l'éruption de la fin.
> Du passé nous faisons table rase.
> Foule esclave, debout! debout!
> Le monde va changer de base:
> Nous n'étions rien—donc, soyons tout!

This, then, was, as its name implies, an *international* anthem. On the first day of 1944 Russia abandoned it, substituting a *national* anthem, *The Hymn of the Soviet Union*, the first stanza and refrain of which, roughly translated (by Andrew Rothstein in the *Spectator* of 28 January 1944), run as follows:

'A Union unbreakable, of free Republics, has been welded forever by great Russia. Long live the Soviet Union, created by the will of the peoples, one and mighty! Glory to our free Fatherland, safe bulwark of the friendship of peoples. The Soviet banner, the people's banner—let it lead us from victory to victory!'

INTERNATIONAL FOLK MUSIC COUNCIL. Founded in 1940 at a conference representing twenty-eight countries. The first President was Vaughan Williams.

INTERNATIONAL INVENTORY OF MUSICAL SOURCES. See *Libraries*.

INTERNATIONAL MUSICAL SOCIETY. See *Musicology*.

INTERNATIONAL MUSIC ASSOCIATION OF GREAT BRITAIN. This was founded in London in 1944 by Anthony Hubbard, under the presidency of Sir Adrian Boult, to promote collaboration between musicians in the different countries and to encourage research and the exchange of information. In 1951 it opened a club house in London (14 South Audley Street, W. 1).

INTERNATIONAL MUSICOLOGICAL SOCIETY (or International Society for Musical Research). Founded in 1927 to resume the work of the International Musical Society (1899–1914). The headquarters are at Basle and it issues a journal, *Acta Musicologica*. See *Musicology*.

INTERNATIONAL PITCH. See *Pitch* 5.

INTERNATIONAL SOCIETY FOR CONTEMPORARY MUSIC. See *Festival* 3; *Germany* 9.

INTERPRETATION in music is simply the act of performance with the implication that in this act the performer's judgement and personality necessarily have their share.

Just as there is no means by which a dramatist can so write his play as to dictate to the actors the precise way in which his lines are to be spoken, so there is no means by which a composer can so notate his compositions as to dictate to the performer the precise way in which they are to be sung or played. Thus, no two performers adopt exactly similar treatments of any given composition, and the differences of speed, intensity, etc., produce a difference of effect similar to the slight difference of emphasis and shade of meaning in the declamation of a speech by two actors.

There have even been cases where a composer has admitted that a performer's interpretation was not merely different from but better than the one he himself had in mind when composing.

The fact that latitude necessarily exists for the exercise of judgement and the expression of personality often leads a certain class of performer (including, decidedly, the conductor) to seek deliberately the unusual and extreme in manner of interpretation.

See also *Expression*.

INTERRUPTED CADENCE. See *Cadence*.

INTERRUPTION OF SOUND. See *Concert Halls* 7.

INTERVALS. By an interval in music is meant the difference in pitch between any two notes. Precise measurement of such difference is expressible acoustically by statement of the vibration numbers (see *Acoustics* 3), but for ordinary purposes, which concern only the notes found in the various major and minor keys of our normal system (or, as we may say, the twelve notes of the piano under their various names), the major scale is taken as the most convenient measuring-rod.

The intervals between the keynote and the fourth, fifth, and octave of the scale are all called **Perfect**; they have a hollowness (and perhaps we might say purity) that is quite different from the effect of the other ('Imperfect') intervals.

The remaining intervals from the keynote (i.e. second, third, sixth, and seventh) are all **Major**.

If any major or perfect interval be chromatically increased a semitone it becomes **Augmented**. For instance, C to G and C to A are respectively a perfect fifth and a major sixth; thus C to G sharp and C to A sharp are augmented fifth and sixth respectively (so are C flat to G and C flat to A—for here again we have widened the interval by one semitone).

If any major interval be chromatically reduced a semitone it becomes **Minor**. For instance, C to D and C to A are respectively major second and major sixth; then C to D flat and C to A flat (or C sharp to D and C sharp to A) are minor second and sixth respectively.

If any minor or perfect interval be chromatically reduced a semitone it becomes **Diminished**. For instance, C to F is a perfect fourth and therefore C to F flat (or C sharp to F) is a diminished fourth. And C to E being a major third, C to E flat (or C sharp to E) is a minor third, whilst C to E double flat (or C double sharp to E) is a diminished third.

Thus all the intervals are accounted for—since we can here leave out of account such rarities as doubly augmented or doubly diminished intervals.

Note that, whilst C to A flat and C to G sharp are on the piano keyboard identical, that does not affect their names. C to A flat is the major sixth (C to A) reduced to a minor sixth; C to G sharp is the perfect fifth (C to G) increased to an augmented fifth. The notes G sharp and A flat are really distinct, and a good violinist can recognize and reproduce them as such (but see *Temperament* 10); the distinction must be maintained for the sake of accurate theory, although on keyboard instruments (and the harp) it is a distinction without a difference. Such intervals as those between G sharp and A flat are called **Enharmonic Intervals**.

Compound Intervals are simple ones plus an octave. For instance, C to the D next above it is a second; C to the D an octave-and-a-second above it is a compound second, otherwise a ninth.

And so with compound thirds or tenths; compound fourths or elevenths; fifths or twelfths, etc.

Inversion of Intervals is the reversing of the relative position of the two notes between which the interval lies, so that the lower becomes the higher and the higher the lower. In other words, whilst the upper one remains in its original place the lower one steps over its head, taking a pitch an octave higher than it had, or, conversely, whilst the lower remains the upper steps over it, taking a pitch an octave lower than it had.

To calculate the span of the new interval we must now reckon up from the new lower note. For instance, the interval C to G is a perfect fifth; to find the nature of its inversions we must run up the scale of G until we reach C, when we find the new interval to be a perfect fourth. So, of course, the inversion of a perfect fourth is a perfect fifth, and it becomes clear to us that fifths inverted become fourths, that fourths inverted become fifths (*total nine*), and that perfect intervals remain perfect.

Taking now a major interval, say a major third, C to E; the inversion E to C we find, by running up the scale of E major, to be a minor sixth (*total nine*).

By a little experiment we shall find that all major intervals inverted become minor and consequently all minor major, all diminished augmented and consequently all augmented diminished.

And we shall find that seconds become sevenths and sevenths become seconds (*total nine*), just as thirds become sixths and sixths become thirds; fourths become fifths; fifths become fourths (*always total nine*, for a reason that will be seen on a little reflection).

Intervals are necessarily either **Concordant** or **Discordant**. As explained in the article *Harmony* 21, this distinction is more or less a matter of convention, but the convention is a thoroughly recognized one and (despite all modern improvements in harmony!) is still one that is to an extent endorsed by most ears.

The Concordant Intervals are the following:

All perfect intervals.

Major and Minor Thirds and Sixths.

The Discordant Intervals are:

All Diminished and Augmented intervals.

All Seconds and Sevenths.

It will be realized that a concordant interval when inverted remains concordant and a discordant one remains discordant, inasmuch as (see above) all perfect remain perfect, all major become minor and vice versa, and all diminished become augmented and vice versa.

IN THE MIDST OF LIFE (from English Prayer Book). See *Sequence*.

INTIME (Fr.), **INTIMO** (It.). 'Intimate.' So the (It.) superlative *Intimissimo*.

INTONATION. (1) The opening phrase of a plainsong melody (see *Plainsong* 2), perhaps so called because it was often sung by the precentor alone and gave the pitch and (in the Psalms) the 'tone' (see *Gregorian Tones*) of what was to follow.

Cf. *Intoning*, below.

(2) The act of singing or playing in tune. Thus we speak of a singer or violinist's 'intonation' as being good or bad.

INTONING (i.e. 'Monotoning'). The singing upon one tone or note, as is done by the clergy in parts of the Roman, Anglican, and other liturgies.

Cf. *Intonation*, above.

INTRADA. The Spanish equivalent of *Entrée* (q.v.); cf. *Entrata*.

INTREPIDO, INTREPIDEZZA (It.). 'Bold', 'boldness'. So also *Intrepidamente*, 'boldly'.

INTRODUZIONE (It.). 'Introduction.'

INTROIT. In the Roman Catholic Church it is a passage normally consisting of an antiphon (q.v.) with one verse of a psalm and the Gloria Patri, sung at High Mass while the Celebrant recites the preparatory prayers at the foot of the altar steps, or said at a Low Mass by the Priest after these prayers. It varies according to the Mass celebrated. There is no Introit on Good Friday.

In the Anglican Church the word is used in the same sense, and in certain other Protestant churches it is used for a short piece of choral music opening a service.

'INTRUSIVE H.' See *Voice* 13.

INVENTION. This is the name given by Bach to fifteen short compositions for the domestic keyboard instrument. They are in two parts or voices, and these in follow-my-leader imitation of one another. Each 'invention' is the working out of a simple but characteristic melodic figure or two, and apparently the word has relation to this; they are meant as exercises in performance but also as models for contrapuntal extemporization. '*To learn . . . to acquire good ideas* ["Inventiones" is the word he uses here], *but also to work them out themselves . . . and at the same time, to gain a strong predilection for composition*' is to be a part of the purpose of the students who practise them, according to the composer's rather long-winded letter (1723) attached to his autograph copy of what he calls 'an honest guide' for 'lovers of the keyboard'.

Bach is not, as is sometimes stated, the only, or even the first, composer to use the title 'Inventions' for musical composition. A. F. Bonporti some years earlier (1714–15) published at Trent and Amsterdam *La Pace: Invenzioni o Dieci Partite a Violino e Continuo* ('Peace: Inventions: or Ten Partitas for Violin and Figured Bass'); four of these, being found in Bach's handwriting, were actually printed in the German Bach Society's edition as of his composition. It seems evident, then, that he picked up the title from his Italian contemporary.

Bonporti's 'Inventions' are of the nature of suites; Bach has, then, taken merely the name from him, just as, one composer having adopted 'Ideas' or 'Notions' as a fancy sub-title for one type of composition, another might do so for another type of composition.

In addition to Bach's fifteen 'Inventions' in two parts or voices he has also fifteen (exactly similar in style) in three parts, but, strangely, he calls these not 'Inventions' but 'Symphonies' —using the word doubtless in the etymological sense of 'sounding together'. (In modern editions the title 'Inventions' is usually applied to both sets.)

In an earlier autograph (1720) of some of these pieces he calls the two-part ones 'Préambules' and the three-part ones 'Fantasias'. They are not in any well-recognized form of the day; they do not fall into the customary two sections of the simple binary form (see *Form* 5) then so prevalent, but run on continuously, as fugues do. The uncertainty over the name and the final adoption of a very unusual one may, perhaps, be accounted for by the novelty of the form.

The origin and meaning of this rarely used term 'Invention' has been rather fully treated here on account of the inaccuracies and inconsistencies of some books of musical reference, and also of certain works on Bach.

INVENTIONSHORN, INVENTIONSTROMPETE. The prefix 'Inventions-' has been used to characterize several novelties. For the 'Inventionshorn' see *Horn Family* 3. As for the term 'Inventionstrompete', it seems to have been applied not only to the trumpet equivalent of the Inventionshorn but also to two earlier novelties—one a short horn in F with crooks for every key down to B flat, and the other the 'Italian Trumpet' (coiled into horn shape).[1]

INVERSION, CANON BY. See *Canon.*

INVERSION OF CHORDS. See *Harmony* 3, 24 f.

INVERSION OF INTERVALS. See *Interval.*

INVERSION OF MELODIES. In this process all the intervals remain the same as to *numerical value* (e.g. a downward 3rd becomes an upward 3rd) but not necessarily the same as to *quality* (e.g. a minor 3rd may automatically become a major 3rd). In fugal writing this device is a good deal used.

INVERTED CADENCE. See *Cadence.*

INVERTED MORDENT. See *Mordent*; Table 12.

INVERTED PEDAL. See *Harmony* 24 p.

INVERTED TURN. See Table 15.

INVERTIBLE COUNTERPOINT. See *Counterpoint.*

INVITATORY. In the Roman Catholic

[1] The assertion about the application of the name *Inventionstrompete* to the 'Italian Trumpet' comes from the trumpeter J. E. Altenburg (q.v.), a younger contemporary of Bach. The authority, the late W. F. H. Blandford, however, suspected 'a simple mistake on his part'.

Church a short passage of Scripture or versicle sung before, between the verses of, and after the Venite (q.v.) to indicate the character of the service according to the season (omitted from the Church of England Prayer Book but nowadays sometimes introduced).

The term Invitatory Psalm, or Invitatorium, is also applied to the Venite itself (Psalm 94 in Roman usage, 95 in the English Bible and Prayer Book; see *Venite*).

IOLANTHE, or THE PEER AND THE PERI (Sullivan). Produced at the Savoy Theatre, London, in 1882. Libretto by W. S. Gilbert.

ACT I

SCENE: *An Arcadian Landscape*

Fairies, led by **Celia, Leila,** and **Fleta,** lament that their Queen has banished Iolanthe for having, twenty-five years before, married a mortal. They beg the **Fairy Queen** (*Contralto*) to pardon her. **Iolanthe** (*Mezzo-Soprano*) appears from the stream where she has dwelt, and is forgiven. She lived in the stream in order to be near her son **Strephon** (*Tenor*), a shepherd, born after she left his father, who does not know that he has a son. Strephon, who is half fairy and half human, is in love with Phyllis, a shepherdess and a Ward in Chancery. The Lord Chancellor will not consent to their marriage.

Phyllis (*Soprano*), to whom many peers are attentive, has decided to marry Strephon now, before she is of age. A procession of peers, led by the **Lord Chancellor** (*Bass*), enters. They want him to allow her to marry one of their number. The **Earls of Tolloller** and **Mountararat** plead their love, but Phyllis says her heart is given to Strephon. The Lord Chancellor is adamant, but Iolanthe encourages her son. She will lay his case before the Fairy Queen: for Strephon is in the peculiar position of being, as a fairy down to the waist, able to defy humans so far, whilst, being a mortal as to his lower half, he can be seized and imprisoned.

The peers, by misinterpreting remarks made 'aside' by each of the lovers, persuade Phyllis to think Strephon false to her. She promises to marry one of the peers. Strephon, distracted, calls the fairies to his aid. The Queen decides that he shall go into Parliament, and by his fairy arts work ruin to their political schemes. Phyllis begs Strephon to repent, but he casts her off.

ACT II

SCENE: *Palace Yard, Westminster*

After the **Sentry's** (*Bass*) famous song the fairies tell of the success of their plot. Strephon in Parliament is irresistible. The peers beg the fairies to stop him, but they cannot.

Phyllis is engaged to two earls, neither of whom can decide what to do. In spite of Strephon's revealing to her that he is half a fairy, she decides to marry him. It turns out that the Lord Chancellor is the mortal whom Iolanthe married; he believed her to have died childless, and she is bound, under penalty of death, not to undeceive him. The fairy pleads for her son and learns, to her horror, that the Chancellor believes Phyllis to be his promised bride. The only resource is for Iolanthe to reveal herself to him as his wife, even at the cost of losing her life. But when the other fairies tell their Queen that they have married peers, and thus sinned also, she relents and decides to marry the Sentry, first turning him into a fairy and then transforming all the peers. So away they all go to Fairyland.

IONIAN. See *Modes* 6, 7, 8.

IPPOLITOF-IVANOF (Ippolitow-Iwanow, etc.), MICHAEL. Born at Gatchina in 1859 and died in Moscow in 1935, aged seventy-five. He was a pupil of Rimsky-Korsakof at the Conservatory of St. Petersburg and later became a professor and director of that of Moscow. He made a special study of Caucasian music and wrote a book on the *National Songs of Georgia*. From 1923 he bore the title of 'People's Artist of the Republic'.

He composed a great quantity of music, including six or seven operas, orchestral music, chamber music, and songs. A *Caucasian Suite* is his most popular work.

See reference under *Percussion Family* 4 b (near end).

IRA (It.). 'Ire', wrath. So *Irato*, 'irate', i.e. with angry feeling, and its adverb *Iratamente*. So, too, *Iracondamente*, 'angrily'.

IRELAND

(For some illustrations see p. 481, pl. 84; 64, 8. 1; 65, 9. 3.)

The present article is designed merely to offer a brief conspectus of Ireland as a musical country, further information on almost every branch of the subject mentioned, as on the personalities, being given under the appropriate heads scattered throughout the book. A list of the chief of these heads appears at the end of the article. The article ignores the political division of the island into Eire (Republic of Ireland) and Northern Ireland.

1. Folk Song and Minstrelsy. That the Irish are a naturally musical race is evident from the beauty of their folk music, which is abundant and varied (see *Melody* 10). There are competent students of folk music, not themselves Irish, who describe it as the finest that exists (see, for instance, Dr. Ernest Walker's *History of Music in England*).

The minstrel or bard class seems always to have been held in peculiar honour in Ireland and to have been largely the means of the diffusion of popular song. One of its later representatives was the blind **O'Carolan** (1670–1738; see also section 5, below), who on horseback, with an attendant, travelled the country; he showed a remarkable facility in the improvisation of both poetry and music.

To the outside world the treasures of Irish folk melody probably first became known through the inclusion of Irish tunes in the English country-dance books of the eighteenth century. In the early part of the nineteenth century they became thoroughly accessible through the work of the highly popular poet **Thomas Moore** (q.v.), who wrote new lyrics to many of the tunes; behind Moore's work lay the painstaking collecting of Petrie and others, and associated with Moore as musical collaborator was Sir John Stevenson (q.v.).

The publication of Irish folk tune (which began with a book issued by Burk Thumoth, probably about 1745) was in the twentieth century systematically undertaken by an Irish Folk Song Society.[1]

2. The Church and Music. The first essays of Irish art music, like those of other races, were stimulated by the ritual requirements of religion, and it appears as though in the early stages of composition Irish musicians were at least well abreast of those of the rest of Europe and in advance of those in many parts of it. Irish monastic culture was, from A.D. 500 onwards, very advanced; Irish missionaries spread over a great part of Europe, and Irish monasteries were everywhere centres for the cultivation of music. The Benedictine abbey of St. Gall in Switzerland (founded by an Irish saint), in which in the late ninth and early tenth centuries the versatile Irish artist–monk Tutilo lived and worked, offers an outstanding example of the influence of Ireland in church music; it made a great contribution to the musical culture of Europe (see *Trope*).

It may be presumed that the later development of composition by the churchmen followed much the same course in Ireland as in the rest of Europe, but there exists no corpus of music of the high period of polyphonic de-

velopment corresponding with that of England in the sixteenth century.

3. Effect of the Reformation. The Reformation was, of course, imposed on, rather than accepted by, Ireland. The monasteries suffered the same suppression as in England and Scotland, and the churches and cathedrals, turned to the purposes of Protestant worship, were, unlike those on the adjacent island, deserted by all but a small fraction of the population. The resources for fine musical performance were left in the hands of a largely alien body, and an artificial condition was created that could not be very favourable to religious or artistic development. English organists and vicars choral were often imported for the cathedrals.

The great English madrigal period had no counterpart in Ireland, except that Farmer and Bateson, English organists of Christ Church Cathedral, Dublin, published some fine works in this kind.

As to the local limitations of the English madrigal school, see some remarks under *Scotland* 8.

4. The Commonwealth and the Restoration. During the Commonwealth and Protectorate the same suppression of church music took place in Ireland as in England, and at the Restoration the same replacement of choirs and organs occurred. The revenues of the Church, however, though excessively large, were greatly misapplied, and this militated against progress; in some cathedrals the service was in time reduced to that of a mere parish church. Certainly there was no production of worthy church music comparable with its continuous production in England. In secular music, also, there is little evidence of creative activity.

5. Instrumental Developments. The instrumental accomplishment of the Irish was in the late twelfth century particularly praised by Giraldus Cambrensis, who was in Ireland in 1185. They excelled on the **Bagpipe**: in early times the instrument in use seems to have been much like the Scottish Highland bagpipe, but since the sixteenth century that form of it which is blown by a bellows beneath the arm has been universal (see further information under *Bagpipe Family* 5).

The harp (p. 481, pl. 84. 1, and p. 481, pl. 84. 3), perhaps because it was capable of use as an accompaniment to the voice and so was seen in the hands of the bards, came to be looked upon as the representative instrument; hence it was adopted as the national symbol, appearing in the British coinage, flag, etc., as it does now on the coins of the Republic of Ireland (founded in 1921), also remaining in the British Royal Standard. Unlike the similar instruments in most other countries, the Irish harp had wire strings and was played with the finger-nails. The great harper O'Carolan (1670–1738) composed many melodies still famous. Towards the end of the eighteenth century Harp Festivals were instituted with the object of bringing together the harpers and so making possible

---

[1] A close student of Irish tune writes as follows:

'For my part I have ceased to think of Irish music as folk-music. It is altogether too elaborate, too complex in form, too subtle in feeling. Obviously the finest tunes are the work of the great harpers, who were professional musicians to the Courts exactly as Lully was in France. :.. There is, however, a folk-music in Ireland (the dances and ballad tunes make up a great part of it) but it can be shown that many of the so-called folk-tunes are really corrupted versions of art-music. [He then mentions a number of examples.] The curious changes brought about by this process were sometimes for the better but generally much for the worse. Bunting's volumes show clearly that the harpers had a highly elaborate technique of playing and ornamentation, comparable to that of Couperin and Bach and the harpsichordists.' (For Bunting see 5 below.)

the collection of the traditional tunes; the Belfast Festival of 1792 is particularly famous. The chief name associated with this movement is that of Edward Bunting (1773–1843), who studied and then published the music. At the beginning of the nineteenth century the harp in Ireland (as in England at the same period) became a popular instrument for ladies (see *Harp* 2).

There was some **Instrument Manufacture** in Dublin during the eighteenth century, and also a fair amount of music publishing—the latter assisted by the absence of any copyright restrictions such as would have checked the Irish reprinting the publications of English firms.

As to the Belfast Anacreontic Society, for orchestral practice mitigated by conviviality, see *Clubs for Music-Making*.

6. Music in the Capital. Dublin, as the capital city and the seat of government, was at that time a considerable centre of musical culture generally. Musical societies existed (e.g. the Hibernian Catch Club, 1680, and the Academy of Music, 1757) and composers and performers from England often paid visits lasting some weeks or months. Thus Handel was there from November 1741 to August 1742, and *Messiah* had its first performance during his visit (p. 448, pl. **76.** 4). Arne and his wife (the vocalist Cecilia Young) paid several long visits. Fine musicians such as Geminiani and Dubourg settled in Dublin for periods of years. The Roseingrave family were settled there from 1698. Altogether Dublin in the eighteenth century appears to have been one of the musical centres of Europe. This period came to an end with the Union of 1801 and the consequent disappearance of Dublin's residential importance as the seat of parliament.

The Lord Lieutenant possessed the power of conferring knighthood, and on a number of occasions honoured not merely native musicians but, curiously, English visitors. The earliest recognition of British musicianship by knighthood was thus due to Ireland, Parsons, master of the band of George III (a comparatively insignificant musician, as he now looks in retrospect), being the absolute first recipient of the honour (1795).

The foundation, in 1764, of a chair of music at Trinity College, Dublin, is an event of some importance. The first professor was the active composer of glees and other vocal music, Lord Mornington: this chair was maintained only for ten years, the present professorship being a revival (1847) and chiefly concerned with the conduct of examinations for musical degrees—which (despite the long absence of any actual professorship) have been granted since the beginning of the seventeenth century. There are now professorships of music at two of the constituent colleges of the National University of Ireland (Dublin and Cork).

Dublin music owes a good deal to the work of the Robinson family. In 1810 Francis Robinson (the elder) founded 'The Sons of Handel', probably the earliest choral body in Ireland, for the practice of oratorio (as distinct from glees, catches, and the like). Robinson's four sons and the wife of one of them (Joseph, the most active) held leading positions in musical life during the nineteenth century. The Royal Irish Academy of Music, which owes much to this family, dates from 1848. The national musical competition, the Feis Ceoil, founded in 1897, has usually been held in Dublin.

Commendatore Michele Esposito (1855–1929), a Neapolitan who migrated to Dublin, was for years the centre of musical life in that city and in Ireland. He was composer, conductor, pianist, violinist, and publisher, gave innumerable orchestral concerts of his own productions, and was head of the Royal Irish Academy. Sir Hamilton Harty owed much to his advice.

It is worthy of note that Dublin, in the palmy days of ballad opera (q.v.), was a considerable centre of activity in that department of musical life. The Irish dramatist Coffey, author of the famous *The Devil to Pay*, etc., began his career in Dublin (*The Beggar's Wedding*, 1729).

7. Irish Composers. The chief composers of Irish origin are mentioned in the list below (9). For the most part they have lived and worked in London—as have composers born in the English provinces and in Scotland.

The pianist **Field** (1782–1837), the introducer of the nocturne and the composer of long-famous piano concertos, is, perhaps, the most notable figure in the annals of Irish musicianship, but two opera composers, **Balfe** (1808–70) and **William Vincent Wallace** (1812–65), held high European fame in their day.

In the work of **Stanford,** at the end of the nineteenth century and beginning of the twentieth, was often seen a serious attempt to develop themes from the Irish folk-tune repertory. **Harty,** conductor and composer, was of Irish birth and sympathies. The career of both these musicians was, however, in England.

8. Some Doubtful Claims. Dr. Grattan Flood, in his *History of Irish Music*, 1905, and many subsequent writings, stated, with great satisfaction to himself, that the practice of descant was of Irish origin, that the Eisteddfod was introduced into Wales by Irish musicians, that *Sumer is icumen in, God save the Queen*, and other tunes usually considered English, were variants of Irish airs, that certain composers generally considered English (e.g. Dowland) were really Irish, and so forth. These statements have by English scholars been admitted to reflect credit upon their author's vigorous patriotism, but it is usually considered that the racial gift for music of the Irish is sufficiently established in other ways.

9. List of Articles amplifying the present one. In order to amplify the information on various points mentioned above the following articles should be consulted:

a. *Song*; *Folk Song* 3; *Minstrels*; *Bagpipe Family* 5; *Festival* 1; *Knighthood*; *Competitions* 2 (for Feis

Ceoil and Oireachtas); *Cathedral Music* 2.
b. COMPOSERS, etc.: *Ap Ivor*; *Balfe*; *Bunting*; *Field*; *Harty*; *Hughes*; *Moore*; *Mornington*; *O'Carolan*; *Osborne*; *Petrie*; *Roseingrave*; *Stanford*; *Stevenson*; *Stewart*; *Wallace*; *Wood, Charles*; *Hempson*; *Joyce*.

IRELAND, JOHN NICHOLSON (p. 337, pl. **54**. 7). Born at Bowdon, Cheshire, in 1879 and died in Washington, Sussex, in 1962, aged eighty-two. He grew up in a literary home, for his parents (Alexander and Anne Elizabeth Ireland) were well-known authors, and Carlyle, Leigh Hunt, Emerson, and other men of letters had been familiar friends.

At the age of fourteen he entered the Royal College of Music (where he later taught from 1923 to 1939). He studied composition with Stanford, and quickly came before the public as the composer, especially, of serious chamber music. It was, however, his second violin and piano sonata, when he was already approaching forty, that securely established his reputation.

Before and after this date he wrote numerous piano compositions of great delicacy, sensitiveness, and (sometimes) humour, notably a fine piano sonata (1920) and many grateful shorter pieces, at the same time maintaining himself as an organist. In the early part of his career he wrote some organ music which achieved a wide popularity amongst organ recitalists. His choral works include a number of part songs and a little church music.

He wrote fewer orchestral pieces, but these include a pianoforte concerto and some other large-scale works. His songs number some ninety, all showing fastidious literary taste; they include the setting of Masefield's 'Sea Fever', in which his perfect reproduction of the poet's thought captured the British public's imagination so that to far too many of its members John Ireland for a long time meant 'Sea Fever' and 'Sea Fever' John Ireland. He was a slow and, in the old sense of the word, 'painful' composer and his opus list is hence not enormous. The last fifteen years of his life produced no new work, and latterly he was much neglected. A 'John Ireland Society' was formed in 1959.

See *Competitions* 3; *Chamber Music* 6 c Period III (1879); *Impressionism*.

IRISH ACADEMY OF MUSIC. See *Ireland* 6.

IRISH FOLK SONG SOCIETY. See *Ireland* 1; *Folk Song* 4.

IRISH ROUND. See *Round* 2.

IRON CHAINS (as musical instrument). See *Percussion Family* 4 d.

IRONICO, IRONICAMENTE (It.). 'Ironic', 'ironically'.

IRREGULAR CADENCE. See *Cadence*.

IRRESOLUTO (It.). 'Irresolute', undecided in style.

ISAAC (or **Isaak**, or **Ysach**, etc.).
(1) HEINRICH (born before 1450; died 1517). He was apparently of Flemish descent and birth, though in Italy, where he spent most of his professional life, he was known as 'Arrigo il

Tedesco' (Harry the German). In Florence he was in the employ of the great Lorenzo de' Medici and also had charge of the music in various churches.

In 1484 began his association with Innsbruck, and the one piece of music with which his name is connected that is universally known today is the melody *Innsbruck, ich muß dich lassen* ('Innsbruck, I must forsake thee'— probably a folk song), which he harmonized in four parts; this half a century later was used as a hymn, *O Welt, ich muß dich lassen* ('O world, I now must leave thee'), and as such is familiar to every musician in its various harmonizations by Bach.

Later he lived in Vienna, in Constance, and again in Italy, and he died in Florence.

His works, sacred and secular, vocal and instrumental, are very numerous. He ranks as one of the most notable composers of his period. His *Choralis Constantinus*, containing nearly sixty offices for the ecclesiastical year (completed by his pupil Ludwig Senfl, and published in three volumes 1550-5) has been said to be 'one of the greatest documents not only in the history of music but also in the history of art' (Alfred Einstein).

See reference under *Germany and Austria* 2.

(2) Dancing-master of the same name. See *Country Dance*.

ISLANCIO, CON (It.). 'Impetuously.'

ISLE OF MAN. See *Flute Family* 4.

I.S.M. Incorporated Society of Musicians (Britain). See *Profession of Music* 10.

ISORHYTHMIC (from Gr. *isos*). 'Of equal rhythm'—a modern musicological term applied to fourteenth-century choral works in which the tenor *canto fermo* (or sometimes an upper part) is many times repeated as to its rhythmic features, the pitch of the notes, however, being varied each time it appears.

ISOTONIC NOTATION. See *Notation* 7.

ISOUARD, NICOLO (1775-1818). French composer of very many operas. See *Collaboration*.

ISRAEL. See *Jewish Music*.

ISTE CONFESSOR. See *Hymns and Hymn Tunes* 2.

ISTESSO. See *Stesso*.

ISTRUMENTO D'ACCIAIO (It.). Mozart's name for his glockenspiel in *The Magic Flute*. See *Percussion Family* 4 e, 5 c.

ITA. See *Broadcasting* 3.

ITALIAN CONCERTO. See *Concerto* 5.

ITALIAN OVERTURE. See *Overture* 1.

ITALIAN SIXTH. See *Augmented Sixth*.

ITALIAN TRUMPET. See *Inventionshorn*, *Inventionstrompete*.

ITALIA PRIZE. See *Broadcasting* 4.

See the Articles under the individual names

1. ROSSINI (1792–1868)

2. DONIZETTI (1797–1848)

3. BELLINI (1801–35)

4. VERDI (1813–1901)

5. BOITO (1842–1918)

6. PUCCINI (1858–1924)

7. LEONCAVALLO (1858–1919)

8. MASCAGNI (1863–1945)

9. BUSONI (1866–1924)

1. RESPIGHI (1879–1936)

2. PIZZETTI (1880–1968)

3. MALIPIERO (1882–1973)

4. CASELLA (1883–1947)
By Giorgio de Chirico

5. CASTELNUOVO-TEDESCO (1895–1968)

6. DALLAPICCOLA (1904–75)

7. PETRASSI (b. 1904)

8. NONO (b. 1924)

ITALY

(For illustrations see p. 516, pls. **93, 94**; 524, **95, 96**; 65, **9**. 5; 544, **99**. 3.)

The present article is designed to offer merely a brief conspectus of the history of music in Italy, further information on almost every branch of the subject mentioned, as on the individual composers, being given under the appropriate heads scattered throughout this volume. A list of some of the chief of these heads appears at the end of the article.

1. General Considerations. From the break-up of the Roman Empire until 1870 the Italian peninsula was divided into a number of states of shifting ownership and rule. There was the bond of a common language, however, from which the more marked of the regional differences tended to disappear from the fourteenth century onwards, when a magnificent vernacular literature came into existence as a further tie.

There was, of course, also a common religion, little broken by the great conflict that divided other countries, and so employing throughout the country much the same musical resources in much the same way. And the courts and cities developed a cultural life that was much the same in all of them.

For the purposes of a short article we may, then, treat Italy as a unit.

2. Early Poetry and Song. A feature of musical life in Italy has been the popularity of secular song. The folk song (in the sense of peasant song), though widely prevalent and varied, has affected the art of music less than in some other countries. From the middle of the thirteenth century to the middle of the fifteenth the courtly Troubadour (in Italian, 'Trovatore') class, settlers from southern France (and perhaps first introduced by visiting Provençal royalties) was active, as was the more plebeian Jongleur (in Italian 'Giocolino') class, also French in origin (see *Minstrels*). A simple sort of part-singing early developed (see, for instance, *Frottola, Chanson, Canti Carnascialeschi, Laudi Spirituali*), culminating in the wonderful Italian madrigal school of the late sixteenth century.

Poetry went hand in hand with music. The fourteenth century was the first great flowering time of Italian vernacular; it saw Dante at work, and, a little later in the century, Petrarch; their lyrics, and those of their contemporaries, were set by the composers of the day and freely sung.

3. The Beginnings of Choral Music. Three light choral forms were common at this period: the **Ballata**, to be sung and danced simultaneously; the **Madrigal** (an early use of the word, here meaning a type in which the uppermost part had the chief melody, and not excluding instrumental accompaniment); and the **Caccia** (the word means 'chase' or 'hunt'), a lively two-voice hunting-song in canon in the unison or octave, sometimes with an independent lowest part, and intended to be accompanied on bright reed instruments (this style was revived and developed in the sixteenth century).

The poems of these three forms had their distinctive metrical characteristics. The music was remarkable for its rhythmic variety, necessitating a series of note-divisions much more elaborate than that of other countries at the same period, and a consequent special manner of notation. It was the opinion of the late Professor Johannes Wolf, who investigated this music, that a great variety of instruments was, at different times, called on to take part in the performance of these compositions. Figures of accompaniment had not yet been invented, and where voices and instruments combined they did so on substantially equal terms and on the lines of voices in a chorus. The greatest composer of this period was the blind **Landino** (*c.* 1325–97); Florence, his place of birth and work, was the centre of poetical and musical composition.

For the general change that came over composition at this period see *Ars Nova*.

4. Early Foreign Relations. The Italian influences upon the development of the ritual chant of Christendom can be traced under *Plainsong*. Missionary musicians carried the Roman scheme of church song to Britain (seventh century), to the court of Charlemagne (early ninth century), and to other parts of Europe. The art of composition had first developed largely out of the attempts to devise accompanying choral parts for plainsong, and in this development Italy had its full share.

With the return of the Papal Court from Avignon (where it had been situated during the period of seven Popes, from 1309 to 1377) a renewed French influence (see 2) was brought into Italy and the special Italian rhythms and notation decayed.

In the early fifteenth century **English Methods** had their effect, and there is significance in the fact that when, in the late nineteenth century, research was made into the work of Dunstable, the main repositories of his compositions were found to be in Trent, Modena, and Bologna.

The skill of the **Flemish School** of the early sixteenth century gave it great prestige in Italy. The maestri and the singing men were imported from Flanders, to the eclipse of native composers and performers, and such names as those of Willaert, Arcadelt, de Rore, and Lassus belong almost as much to the history of music in southern Europe as to that of northern Europe. Not only was the conduct of the church music of Rome, Florence, Venice, and other important centres largely in their hands, but they became the first composers of the **Italian Madrigal** (in the later and more usual sense of the word), though this form was quickly taken up by the Italian composers, who as the century advanced were asserting their right to be heard in their own country and beginning to be known outside it.

The pure unaccompanied (*a cappella*) style of church music simultaneously reached its zenith, the greatest name associated with it being, of course, that of **Palestrina**, who lived and worked in Rome and died there in 1594.

At the opening of the seventeenth century a change came over the texture of music in all countries—a change from the contrapuntal style to the harmonic, most plainly evident in the Italian invention of **Opera** and **Oratorio**. It was, in some measure, a late result of the Italian literary renascence, with its study of the dramatic methods of Ancient Greece, but it summed up changes of technical method that had for some time been developing. Important as it is, it need not be much discussed in the present article, as it is treated under the headings *Opera*, *Oratorio*, etc. (see the list below, under 10 a). To hint at the general nature of the change in two or three words (carrying wide implications), choral singing now sank to a secondary place and the solo voice became all-important.

5. The Solo Voice and the Opera. The seventeenth and eighteenth centuries were, indeed, the great centuries of the cultivation of the technique of the solo voice, and in this Italy was the leader (see *Singing* 2), so that, in return for the hospitality her churches had for two centuries offered to foreign singers, her own (male and female) were now treated as the pampered pets of every opera-house audience in Europe. The Italian Metastasio, from Vienna, in the eighteenth century, supplied the world with opera libretti. Such operas as the Italians did not write they influenced. The Italian language was used and the Italian methods were followed. In Italy itself opera was popular with all classes, instead of being, as in most countries, a diversion of the wealthier classes: thus operatic melodies tended to swamp the native folk song. (Cf. *Melody* 10.) The great contribution that Italy has made to the development of opera from the early seventeenth century to recent times is discussed in the article *Opera*, to which reference should be made for Rossini, Donizetti, Bellini, and Verdi.

6. Instrumental Music in the Seventeenth and Eighteenth Centuries. In **String Music** Italy was inspired by the wonderful productions of the Cremona violin maker (especially the **Amati** family in the sixteenth and seventeenth centuries, and the **Guarneri** and **Stradivari** families in the seventeenth and eighteenth; see *Violin Family* 4), and did notable work in laying out the primitive lines of the earlier sonata, concerto, and similar forms, and of the orchestral symphony. The names of **Corelli** (1653–1713), **Tartini** (1692–1770), and **Vivaldi** (c. 1676–1741) may be mentioned, but they are only three out of a large number. In harpsichord music **Domenico Scarlatti** (1685–1757) ranks high: after his day, which lasted to the middle of the century, harpsichord playing was a good deal neglected in Italy. The **Pianoforte**, which was introduced near the beginning of the eighteenth century but became common only towards the end of it, ranks as an Italian invention (by Cristofori of Florence; see *Pianoforte* 2, 3, 10, 13). But the greatest pianists have not usually come from southern Europe.

7. The Instrumental Decline and Revival. The fame and profit which Italian musicians reaped from their skill as composers for and performers upon the stage tended to lessen the national interest in 'absolute' music. It was the German composers who in the late eighteenth and early nineteenth centuries carried to its logical conclusions the instrumental experimentation of the Italian composers of the preceding period. It was only towards the end of the nineteenth century that a reaction took place, promoted largely by **Sgambati** and **Martucci**—a reaction which became accentuated as the twentieth century dawned. Such composers as **Pizzetti**, **Respighi**, **Casella**, and **Malipiero** have made it clear, both in letterpress and musical notation, that they felt the necessity of breaking with the immediate Italian past. They did not despise opera, but when they composed it they scorned the prevalent seventeenth- to nineteenth-century way of treating it as an opportunity for vocal display, and they devoted much attention to instrumental music. Some brief quotations from their opinions and the expression of their purposes will be found in the articles bearing their respective names (see also 8 below).

It may be pointed out that some of the nineteenth-century musical 'movements' that have affected the rest of Europe have passed over Italy's head, hardly touching her: such are the Nationalist movement and the Impressionist movement. The Italian Futurist movement in literature and art, initiated by Marinetti about 1907, with its demand for the development and minute differentiation of 'noise-sounds' as distinct from the contemned 'musical sounds', seemed to have little result, though there are passages in the following paragraphs that have a familiar ring in the sixties.

Marinetti, praised by Mussolini as 'the fearless soldier who offered his country a dauntless passion consecrated by blood, he who instilled in me the feeling of the ocean and the power of the machine', was, however, created a Senator and put in charge of the cultural side of Fascism. One of his tenets (see his *I Manifesti del Futurismo*, vol. iii, p. 114) is 'Il bello non ha niente a che fare con l'arte'—'Beauty has nothing to do with art.'

A prominent colleague of Marinetti in his propaganda was Russolo (q.v.), who issued at Milan as early as 1913 a manifesto laying down the principles of the 'Art of Noises'. The full text of this appears in the Appendix to Slonimsky's *Music since 1900*, the following being a brief extract:

'Let us then wander through a great modern city with our ears more attentive than our eyes, and distinguish the sounds of water, air, or gas in metal pipes, the purring of motors (which breathe and pulsate with an indubitable animalism), the throbbing of valves, the pounding of pistons, the screeching of gears, the clatter of streetcars on their rails, the cracking of whips, the flapping of awnings and flags. We shall amuse ourselves by orchestrating in our minds the noise of the metal shutters of store windows, the slamming of doors, the bustle and shuffle of crowds, the multitudinous uproar of railroad stations, forges, mills, printing presses, power stations, and underground railways.'

In 1913 Russolo conducted a concert in Milan in which he used such instruments as Thunderclappers, Exploders, Crashers, Splashers, Bellowers, Whistlers, Hissers, Snorters, Whisperers, Murmurers, Mutterers, Bustlers, Gurglers, Screamers, Screechers, Rustlers, Buzzers, Cracklers, Shouters, Shriekers, Groaners, Howlers, Laughers, Wheezers, and Sobbers. The concert room became a battlefield, for, whilst Russolo continued to conduct his strange orchestra, Marinetti and four of his partisans 'were seen to come down from the stage and to invade the circle and, with punches and walking sticks, to attack the "pastists", drunk with stupidity and traditional rage'. The 'pastists' had eleven wounded who had to be taken to the first-aid station. (Marinetti's account in the Paris *Intransigeant*, 29 April 1914.)

8. Italian Music in the 1930s and after.
The following is the composer Casella's estimate of the position of Italian music in 1932 (*Musical Courier*, 24th December of that year):

'Since the war our music has freed itself completely from all foreign influence and has assumed a national outlook, which characterizes it strongly and makes it independent in the midst of all other European music. The energetic affirmation of tonality, the absolute refusal to adopt the "atonal" formula, the influence of Gregorian models, the exploitation of folktune, the creation of new forms emanating directly from the Italian forms of the seventeenth and eighteenth centuries, a deep study of the past, a new valuation of the opera of the last century, the interpretation in fact of that admirable prophetic lesson left to us by Verdi which is called *Falstaff*: all this, joined to perfect serenity and impartiality in the face of contemporary foreign music, characterizes the present-day Italian music, and guarantees for it great liberty of movement in the troublous times in which we are living.'

A curious feature in Italian musical life has been the comparative lack of general musical literature. There have been one or two admirable musical journals but, as a writer in *Vita e Coltura Musicale* (March 1935) said:

'If in any of the Italian cities in which symphony concerts and opera performances take place a member of the public enters a book shop in quest of books on Wagner or Beethoven or Brahms, he learns with surprise that none are available except in foreign languages. A few days ago a translation of Kretzschmar's booklet on Bach appeared: it is the first book on the subject in the Italian language.'

The Fascist government in a number of ways encouraged musical activity, and under its aegis and with its financial support International Congresses of Musicians and Musicologists were held in Florence on several occasions. As will have been gathered, it had none of that antagonism to the 'modernistic' spirit in music that was so marked in the other 'Dictator' state north of it.

In post-Fascist Italy both Government and municipal support continues on as large a scale as ever.

Important centres for modern music are Venice, the home of Luigi Nono, and Milan, where the radio station houses an important electronic studio presided over by Luciano Berio and Bruno Maderna. Rome, with Petrassi as its best-known figure, is more conservative. Palermo has an annual festival of the avant-garde. Musical training in Italy is thorough, with a ten-year government-operated training course for composers.

9. Italy's Achievements summarized.
It is interesting to attempt to sum up Italy's distinctive, major, and permanent contributions to music. They include (a) the orderly recasting of the Church's plainsong in the fourth and sixth centuries and the devising of a system of sight-singing in the eleventh (see *Hexachord*); (b) Petrucci's invention of a practical music-printing process at the end of the fifteenth century (see *Printing of Music*); (c) the development of the madrigal in the sixteenth century; (d) the development of the violin family in the sixteenth and seventeenth centuries; (e) the introduction of opera and oratorio in the seventeenth century; (f) the practice of figured bass, which for about two centuries provided the background to almost every type of composition and greatly influenced the course of musical evolution; (g) the development of solo singing and the *bel canto* in the seventeenth and eighteenth centuries; (h) the introduction of schools of music—both the earlier school of church music (*schola cantorum*) and the later general school of music (*conservatorio*); (i) the invention of the pianoforte in the eighteenth century.

It will be seen that music's debt to Italy is as great as that of painting.

The most notable influences exerted by direct Italian example upon English music were perhaps those of the madrigalists upon the musicians about the courts of Elizabeth I and James I, and those of the violin composers and string sonata writers, nearly a century later, upon the musicians of the London of Charles II (i.e. the influence of Corelli and his colleagues upon Purcell and his). The eighteenth- and earlier nineteenth-century English obsession with Italian opera, which was unmeasured, can hardly be considered a pure benefit. (The same may be said of the Spanish obsession. A somewhat similar, though necessarily less powerful, obsession grew up in North America, and is alluded to under *Opera* 21.)

The German debt to Italian music is of course enormous; despite a general difference of mentality and a corresponding difference in the general 'flavour' of their music, the German composers up to the end of the eighteenth century were constantly picking up the devices of Italian technique; in this connexion it will be sufficient to instance Bach and Mozart.

France in the seventeenth century submitted to imported operatic influences which are mentioned under *Opera*.

10. List of Articles amplifying the above. In order to amplify the information given above the following articles should be consulted:

a. *Liturgy*; *Church Music*; *Plainsong* 3; *Mass*; *Hymns and Hymn Tunes* 2; *Carols*; *Laudi Spirituali*; *Sacre Rappresentazioni*; *Oratorio* 2; *Stabat Mater*.

b. *Ars Nova*; *Frottola*; *Canti Carnascialeschi*; *Chanson*; *Cantata*; *Napolitana*; *Madrigal* 1, 8 *b*; *Gondola Song*; *Street Music* 4, 7; *Jewish* 4; *Harmony* 4.

c. *Masque*; *Stile Rappresentativo*; *Opera* 1–8, 17, 21; *Recitative*; *Aria*; *Libretto*; *Intermezzo*; *Opera Buffa*; *Bouffons*; *Pasticcio*; *Ritornello*; *Figured Bass*; *Melody* 10.

d. *Singing* 2–7; *Bel Canto*; *Coloratura*; *Fioritura*; *Messa di Voce*; *Prima Donna*; *Castrato*; *Song* 10 *a*; *Ornaments*; *Shake*; *Applause* 2, 3, 5, 6, 7.

e. *Saltarello*; *Tarantella*; *Siciliano*; *Romanesca*; *Bergomask*; *Courante or Coranto*.

f. *Chamber Music* 6; *Canzona*; *Sonata* 1–3, 5, 10; *Suite* 1–5; *Overture* 1; *Symphony* 1–3, 8; *Concerto* 2, 6; *Orchestra* 1.

g. *Minstrels*, etc. 1, 4; *Schools of Music*; *Schola Cantorum*; *Sight-Singing* 1, 2 (for Guido d'Arezzo and his work); *Improvisatore*; *Street Music* 4.

h. *Printing* 1; *Publishing* 1; *Copyists*; *Hexachord*; *Prix de Rome*; *Concert* 14; *Broadcasting* 3.

i. *Violin Family* 4; *Bagpipe Family* 7; *Harpsichord* 9; *Pianoforte* 2.

j. *England* 3; *Spain* 5; *Belgium* 1 *a*; *Poland*.

k. CHRONOLOGICAL CONSPECTUS OF COMPOSERS—arranged by century of birth.

10th CENTURY: Guido d'Arezzo.

14th CENTURY: Landino.

15th CENTURY: Festa.

16th CENTURY: Allegri, the brothers Anerio, Banchieri, G. Bassani, Caccini, Cavalieri, Cifra, Ferrabosco, Frescobaldi, A. and G. Gabrieli, Gagliano, Galilei, Gastoldi, Gesualdo, Ingegneri, Marenzio, Marini, Monteverdi, Palestrina, Peri, Rossi, Ruffo, Vecchi, Viadana, Vicentino, Zarlino.

17th CENTURY: Albinoni, Ariosti, Astorga, G. B. Bassani, G. B., G. M., and M. A. Bononcini, Bonporti, Caldara, Carissimi, Cavalli, Cesti, Corelli, Durante, J. B. Farinelli, P. A. and G. H. Fiocco, Geminiani, L. Leo, Locatelli, Lotti, Manfredini, Marcello, the brothers Mazzochi, Milanuzzi, Picchi, Porpora, the brothers Sammartini, Sarti, A. and D. Scarlatti, Steffani, Stradella, Tenaglia, Torelli, Valentini, Veracini, Vinci, G. B. and T. A. Vitali, Vivaldi.

18th CENTURY: Alberti, Algarotti, Boccherini, Cherubini, Cimarosa, Clementi, Diabelli, Donizetti, Duny, Galuppi, Giardini, Giordani, Jommelli, Martini, Mayr, Mercadente, Nardini, Pacini, Paer, Paesiello, Paganini, Paradies, Pasquini, Pergolese, Piccini, Pugnani, Raimondi, Rauzzini, Rossini, Sacchini, Salieri, Spontini, Tartini, Viotti, Zingarelli.

19th CENTURY: Alaleona, Alfano, Arditi, Bellini, Boito, A. F. and M. E. Bossi, Bottesini, Busoni, A. Casella, Castelnuovo-Tedesco, Catalani, Cilea, Costa, Denza, Drigo, Franchetti, Ghedini, Giordano, Gnecchi, Labroca, Leoncavallo, Longo, Malipiero, Martucci, Mascagni, Massarani, Montemezzi, Papini, Perosi, Petrella, Pick-Mangiagalli, Pinsuti, Pizzetti, Ponchielli, Poniatowski, Pratella, Puccini, Respighi, the brothers Ricci, Rieti, Russolo, Sabata, Scontrino, Sgambati, Sinigaglia, Sivori, Smareglia, Tommasini, Toselli, Tosti, Verdi, Wolf-Ferrari, Zandonai.

20th CENTURY: Berio, Dallapiccola, Gavazzeni, Maderna, Mortari, Nono, Petrassi, Sanzogno, Turchi.

See also *Dictionaries* 4 *e*.

I'VE BEEN ROAMING. See *Horn, C. E.*

IVES.

(1) SIMON (1600–62). Otherwise 'Ive'. Organist, singing teacher, and composer of songs, catches, and instrumental works.

See reference under *Monopolies*.

(2) CHARLES (p. 1057, pl. **172.** 1). Born at Danbury, Conn., in 1874 and died in New York in 1954, aged seventy-nine. He was the son of a musician, but himself, though engaging in composition, successfully followed a business career until, in his late forties, ill health caused its abandonment—as it later did, for a time, of his composition.

His methods as composer were often startling. He wrote microtonal music, music in which liberty is left to individual players to follow their own feelings and even almost to extemporize portions (cf. Handel's practice under *Improvisation* 1)—and so on. His compositions include symphonies, choral works, chamber works, etc. Critics of high standing gradually came to take these very seriously. One of them (Nicolas Slonimsky) writes as follows:

'In the opinion of many American musicians, Ives is perhaps the only 20th-century American who developed an individual method of composition deeply rooted in national music. Every piece he wrote bore a reference to some aspect of American life as indicated by the titles: *Three Places in New England*, *Fourth of July*, *Lincoln—the Great Commoner*, *Concord Sonata* (the latter divided into four movements, titled "Emerson", "Hawthorne", "the Alcotts", and "Thoreau"). To represent the multiplicity of American moods, Ives often introduced a free counterpoint on national tunes, taken at different *tempi* and played in different keys. Even hymns and sacred songs were occasionally treated in this manner. Long before atonality, polytonality, and rhythmic devices became *le dernier cri* and even *le premier cri* of modern music, Ives applied these to portray the vital integration of American patterns—*e pluribus unum*. Polyrhythmic structures built by Ives are of such complexity that he abandons on occasion the uniformity of the bar and notates the tunes in different simultaneous metres. In such instances, the conductor is compelled to beat two different times with the two hands. The improvisational element is also inherent in Ives's writing when one

1. HEBREW LYRE-PLAYER of the time of Joseph (*c.* 1700 B.C.), from an Egyptian painting at Beni Hassan, supposed to represent the arrival of Jacob's family in Egypt

2. HEBREW TRUMPETS of A.D. 70—a triumphal procession after the fall of Jerusalem, on the Arch of Titus, at Rome. See *Jewish Music* 2

4. SOUNDING THE SHOFAR, or ancient Synagogue horn

3. THE ANCIENT SYNAGOGUE AT WORMS —dating from what the English-speaking peoples call the 'Norman' period of architecture

5. SYNAGOGUE AT VIENNA where the 19th-century reform of Jewish ritual music took its rise. See *Jewish Music* 6

6. SALOMON SULZER, the great Viennese Chazzan praised by Liszt. See *Jewish Music* 6

PLATE 98

JAZZ

See the Article *Jazz*, on pages 532–6

1. 'FLAT-FOOT FLOOGIE GOES HIGH HAT'—in New York's home of
'classical' music, Carnegie Hall, 1938

2. 'TRAPS'

3. A POPULAR ENGLISH JAZZ BAND OF THE 1930's—that of Henry Hall

4. ASSEMBLING AN ENGLISH TOWN HALL ORGAN which combines the orthodox instrument with
the full jazz band effects

instrument is give a repeated refrain, such as fiddlers employ in folk dances.

Ives was not averse to using simple triads in harmony and simple rhythms, in the manner of American ballads. Thus it is impossible to describe his style as essentially dissonant, for dissonance and consonance are used according to the mood.

Yet Ives went through a rigorous discipline of academic training; his early symphony is entirely within the tenets of traditional usage. And his music is free of all elements of sensationalism: he did not publish any of it until many years after these works were written. He printed his music at his own expense and distributed it gratis to anyone asking for copies: a note to that effect is inserted in his collection of 114 songs, which is now a bibliographical rarity.

Ives never participated in musical life; he rarely if ever attended concerts—even those at which his own works had their infrequent performances. He did everything in his power to keep fame away from his door. In later years, publishers vied with each other to secure rights to his many unpublished manuscripts; despite the difficulties in performing his orchestral music, many conductors in America placed it on their programmes. Conservative critics do not hesitate to apply the word "genius" when speaking of Ives. As a prophet of new American music, he received at the end full recognition.'

See *United States* 8.

J

JABO (Sp.). A solo dance in a slow three-in-a-measure rhythm. (In old Spanish, *Xabo*.)

JÁCARA. An old Spanish song-dance. (In old Spanish, *Xácara*.)

JACK. See *Harpsichord 2*.

JACKSON.

(1) WILLIAM (called 'Jackson of Exeter'). Born at Exeter in 1730 and died there in 1803, aged seventy-three. His father was master at the workhouse at Exeter and he himself became organist of the cathedral. He left behind him quantities of music of all kinds, of which one item (stated by one authority, however, not to be by him) appears to possess eternal life—'the' Te Deum in F, a composition that rises to the height of a curious sublimity of commonplace.

He had a career as a stage composer, one of his operas (the libretto of which was by General Burgoyne, who perhaps found in its compilation an anodyne for his trials after Saratoga a year or two earlier) holding the London stage for half a century.

He was also an author of books of essays and a painter and the friend of a greater one, the music-loving Gainsborough.

See *Catch*; *Te Deum*; *Davy 2*; *Ballad Opera*; *Conducting 4*.

(2) WILLIAM (called 'Jackson of Masham'). Born at Masham in Yorkshire in 1815 and died at Ripon in 1866, aged fifty-one. He was a self-taught musician who made some instruments and played more—fifteen, it is said.

He added to his activities those of a tallow chandler, but later settled at Bradford as a music-seller, becoming the organist of various places of worship, in turn the conductor of several famous choirs, and the choirmaster of the musical festival.

He wrote a choral symphony, oratorios, glees, and church music; and country choirs in the north of England have, perhaps, not yet quite forgotten him.

(3) GEORGE PULLEN (1874–1953). See *Lancashire Sol-fa* (end).

JACOB.

(1) alias JACOB POLAK, alias JACOB LE POLONAIS, alias JACOB DE REYS. See *Poland*.

(2) BENJAMIN (1778–1829); p. 784, pl. **131. 2**. Famous London organist, much associated with Samuel Wesley in the introduction of Bach's works.

See *Organ 12*; *Congregational Churches 4*.

(3) GORDON (p. 352, pl. **55. 9**). Born at Nor-wood, near London, in 1895. After war service from 1914 and a period as a prisoner of war, he entered the Royal College of Music, where he is now a professor of composition. He has written piano, violin, oboe, and horn concertos and other orchestral works, chamber music, etc., and a manual of orchestral technique, on which subject he is considered an authority. C.B.E. 1968. See *Oboe 6*.

JACOBI.

(1) GEORGE. Born in Berlin in 1840 and died in London in 1906, aged sixty-six. After a successful career in Paris he came to London, where for a quarter of a century he conducted at the Alhambra Theatre, composing for it over a hundred ballets which then went all over the old and new worlds.

(2) FREDERICK. Born in San Francisco in 1891 and died in New York in 1952, aged sixty-one. He was brought up in New York and studied there (under Rubin Goldmark, q.v.) and in Berlin. He lived much amongst the American Indians of New Mexico and Arizona, composing certain works based on their melodies. He further wrote music for the Jewish service. He produced much orchestral, chamber, and choral music, and took an interest in modern developments of the art.

JACOBSON, MAURICE. Born in London in 1896 and died at Brighton in 1976, aged eighty. He won an open scholarship in composition at the Royal College of Music, studying under Stanford and Holst. He wrote a good deal of incidental music for Shakespearian production at the 'Old Vic' Theatre, London. From 1933 he was a director (later chairman) of the Curwen publishing firm.

JACOPONE DA TODI. See *Stabat Mater*.

JADASSOHN, SALOMON (1831–1902). Long eminent in Leipzig as teacher and conductor. Composer of very many orchestral, choral, etc., works, and author of a number of theoretical books.

JAELL, ALFRED. Born at Trieste in 1832 and died in Paris in 1882, aged nearly fifty. He had a European reputation as a fine pianist and was also known as the composer of popular piano compositions now forgotten (see *Pianoforte 22*). His wife (Marie; 1862–1925) was also a fine pianist; she left not only compositions but a long series of serious pedagogical writings, chiefly on pianoforte playing.

JAGDHORN (Ger.). Hunting horn. See *Horn Family 2 a, 3, 5 a*.

JAGDQUARTETT. See *Nicknamed 15*.

JÄGER (Ger.). 'Hunter.'

JAHN, OTTO (1813–69). Distinguished archaeologist and philological scholar; author of articles and books on various composers and especially of a standard life of Mozart (1865–9 and later editions).

JAHNN, HANS HENNY. See *Organ* 10.

JALEO. A Spanish solo dance in a slow three-in-a-measure time. (In old Spanish, *Xaleo*.)

JALOUSIESCHWELLER (Ger.). 'Venetian-blind swell', i.e. the organ swell pedal mechanism.

JAMES.

(1) **RICHARD** (1592–1638). Anglican clergyman, poet, and scholar. See *Russia* 1.

(2) **PHILIP** (1890–1975). He was active in New Jersey as organist and composer and on the staff (chairman from 1933 to 1955) of the music department of New York University.

He composed orchestral, chamber, choral, organ, and piano works.

(3) **EVAN** (Ieuan ap Iago), and his son, James James (Ieuan ap Ieuan; 1833–1902). See *Land of my Fathers*.

JAMES I OF SCOTLAND (b. 1394; inherited the throne 1406 but a prisoner in England until 1424; d. 1437). See *Scotland* 6; *Bagpipe Family* 4.

JAMES III OF SCOTLAND (b. 1451; came to throne 1460; d. 1488). See *Scotland* 6.

JAMES IV OF SCOTLAND (b. 1473; came to throne 1488; d. 1513). See *Scotland* 6.

JAMES V OF SCOTLAND (b. 1512; came to throne 1513; d. 1542). See *Scotland* 6.

JAMES VI OF SCOTLAND and I OF ENGLAND (b. 1560; came to two thrones 1567 and 1603; d. 1625). See *Chapel Royal*; *Scotland* 6; *Minstrels* 3; *Masque*; *Italy* 9; *Hymns and Hymn Tunes* 6; *Parish Clerk*; *Volta*; *Jew's Harp*; *Composition* 3.

JAMES II OF ENGLAND and VII OF SCOTLAND (b. 1633; came to throne 1685; fled 1688; d. 1701). See *Scotland* 6; *Lilliburlero*; *Purcell*.

JAMESON, D. D. See *Colour and Music* 10.

JAMMERND, JÄMMERLICH (Ger.). 'Lamenting', 'lamentable'.

JANÁČEK, LEOŠ (p. 109, pl. **20.** 1). Born in 1854 at Hukvaldy (or Hochwald) in Moravia (then in Austrian territory, now in Czechoslovakia) and died at Ostrau (or Ostrava), Moravia, in 1928, aged seventy-four. He was the son of a village schoolmaster on the border of Moravia and Silesia, in a district that always remained 'home' to the composer; there he was born and there he spent all his holidays in the cottage of his birth, and from this, during one of them, he was taken to hospital and died.

At ten he became a choir-boy at Brno (Brünn), where he was much influenced by the monk Křížkovský, a composer of strong nationalistic tendencies, to whose position as choirmaster of the monastery he succeeded when only sixteen. He then studied in Prague and (at twenty-five) Leipzig, at the latter place producing a composition at the famous Ge-

wandhaus concerts. Approaching thirty he settled in Brno, which became henceforth the centre of his manifold activities as conductor, teacher, student of folk tune, and composer. He developed theories based upon his study of the sounds of nature and of the rhythmic and melodic traits of peasant speech and was the author of various essays and treatises.

In 1904 his opera *Jeji Pastorkyňa* was produced in Brno, but it had no further performance until 1916 when it was performed at Prague. Under the new title of *Jenůfa* it reached Vienna and fame in 1918 (New York, 1924). This is merely the most generally known of a number of operas of very national character and very personal expression, of which *Katya Kabanova* (based on Ostrovsky's *The Storm*) and *The Cunning Little Vixen* are the best known. There also exists a considerable quantity of chamber, orchestral, and choral music, and a Slavonic folk mass, of very original type.

See reference under *Opera* 19.

JANES, ROBERT (1806–66). See under *Anglican Chant* 6.

JANIEWICZ (also spelt Yaniewicz), **FELIX.** Born at Vilna in Poland in 1762 and died in Edinburgh in 1848, aged eighty-five or eighty-six. He was a remarkable violinist, who lived in Italy and then in turn in Paris, London, Liverpool, and Edinburgh. He wrote concertos, and trios for two violins and cello. He was one of the original founders of the Philharmonic Society of London.

JANISSARY MUSIC, JANITSCHAREN-MUSIK (Ger.). The Turkish type of military music at one time popular in the European armies (see *Military Band*; *Percussion Family* 4). The Janissaries were the Sultan's bodyguard, disbanded, after revolt, in 1826.

JANKO KEYBOARD. See *Keyboard* 4.

JANNEQUIN, CLÉMENT. Born at Châtellerault after 1472 and died in Paris about 1560. His personality and life are very obscure. He was almost certainly of French (not Netherlands) nationality and was a pupil of Josquin des Prés. He is an early writer of vocal part-music who is remarkable for the whole-hearted expression of 'programmatic' ideas (see *Programme Music*). Thus he wrote choral pieces (*Chansons*) with such titles as 'The Battle of Marignan' (he is thought to have been present at this battle), 'The Capture of Boulogne', 'The Siege of Metz', 'The Cries of Paris', 'The Lark', 'The Song of the Birds', 'The Hunt', 'The Chattering Women'.

In addition he composed masses, motets, etc., and a large number of simple melodic songs in which a strong rhythmic feeling is characteristic.

Brief references to this composer and his type of composition will be found under *Madrigal* 8 d; *Chanson*; *Programme Music* 5 a; *Street Music* 2.

JAPAN. See *Oriental*; *Broadcasting* 3.

JAPANESE FIDDLE. A one-stringed instrument—sometimes seen in the hands of English street performers and the like.

See also *Stroh Violin*, etc.

JAQUES-DALCROZE, ÉMILE (p. 864, pl. **147.** 5). A Swiss, born in Vienna in 1865, who died in Geneva in 1950, aged nearly eighty-five. After a school and university course at Geneva he studied music at the Conservatories of Vienna and Paris, Delibes being his principal teacher in the latter city. In his twenties he became a member of the staff of the Conservatory of Geneva, and it was there that he undertook the experiments which afterwards led to the foundation of a definite and carefully worked-out system of musical training through physical movement which he called Eurhythmics ('eu' = Greek 'good', 'well').

From 1910 until the outbreak of the first World War the centre of his activities was Hellerau, near Dresden; then he returned to Geneva, which remained his headquarters, though his Institute there now has branches in many parts of the world.

He was the author of several books explaining the principles and practice of Eurhythmics, and was also a voluminous and popular composer, his compositions taking various forms, from that of the simple quasi-folk-song to that of the extended work for the stage.

See *Eurhythmy*; *Improvisation* 5; *Concerto* 6 c (1865); *Education* 2.

JARMAN, THOMAS (c. 1788–1862). See under *Baptist Churches and Music* 4.

JARNACH, PHILIPP. Of Spanish parentage but born at Noisy, in France, in 1892. He is the son of the Catalan sculptor of the same name. His musical education was received chiefly in Paris. From 1914 for seven years he was on the staff of the Conservatory of Zürich. Thereafter he lived in Berlin, until in 1949 he became head of the Hamburg Conservatory.

He was the friend and disciple of Busoni, and his composition has been greatly influenced thereby; when Busoni died leaving his opera *Doctor Faust* unfinished, the completion of this work was entrusted to him.

He has written chamber music, songs, orchestral music, etc.

Cf. *Oboussier*.

JÄRNEFELT, ARMAS (p. 896, pl. **153.** 8). Born at Viipuri (otherwise Viborg), Finland, in 1869 and died at Stockholm in 1958, aged eighty-eight. He studied in Berlin with Busoni and in Paris with Massenet. After some experience in Germany he returned to his native city as conductor of the orchestra there. Later he became director of the opera and head of the Conservatory at Helsinki, then migrating to Stockholm, where he became opera and court conductor, and in 1932 returning to Helsinki.

He wrote orchestral and choral music and a little chamber music and piano music. A very popular little Praeludium for orchestra has made his name known even amongst simple-minded music-lovers. (See *Scandinavia* 6.) He married the sister of Sibelius.

JARVIS, CHARLES. See *Pianoforte* 5.

JAWS HARP. See *Jew's Harp*.

JAZZ

1. Historical Introduction.
2. The Melodic Element.
3. The Element of Extemporization.
4. The Orchestral Element.
5. Some Classics of the Movement.
6. Swing Music.
7. Boogie-Woogie and Bebop.
8. Factors in the Success of this Class of Music.

(For illustrations see p. 529, pl. **98**.)

1. Historical Introduction. Historians hesitatingly trace the roots of Jazz to American Colonial days, the ultimate source, via the Caribbean islands, being the native music of the African Negro slaves, blended with the simpler kind of mission hymns and the spontaneous work songs of the field hands and convict chain-gangs. The usual starting-point for the modern history of jazz is in the licensed brothel district of New Orleans, known as 'Storyville', and founded in 1897 as a social experiment in legalized prostitution. Here Negro musicians entertained the customers; these 'jazzmen' were largely musically illiterate improvisers, with a background of playing in street marching bands, the instruments they used being often relics of the Civil War. Thus there is no surviving evidence of their work. In 1917 Storyville was formally closed by the naval police, and the jazzmen dispersed, taking their art with them to Chicago, Kansas City, and elsewhere, like the scholars after the fall of Constantinople. (Or so read the usual accounts.)

The earliest gramophone records of jazz seem to have been made about 1916; by the early 1920's the jazz craze replaced the era of Ragtime (q.v.). For some time records were made primarily for the Negro market; but their popularity spread, and eventually jazz was adopted into the world of mass entertainment and ministered to a dance mania perhaps even more general and more violent than the manias for the waltz and the polka in the previous century. But in addition to its application to the dance, jazz came into a fairly general acceptance as one of the amenities of social life.

Jazz also appeared in the concert-room, though, like many of those who there appear, it changed its name to do so, figuring usually under some such euphemistic description as 'Symphonized Syncopation'.

It began to be taken seriously by a certain number of composers (see 5), and its rhythmic, harmonic, and orchestral elements crept into suites and other orchestral compositions, as also into operas. One or two operas were 'jazzed-up': *The Beggar's Opera* was re-written by Kurt Weill, and Sullivan's *Mikado*, by the kindly hands of another German musician, was similarly transformed (Berlin, 1927).

Some optimists in the United States, looking upon jazz as a distinctively national product, began to declare that in it was to be found the basis of a national 'school' of composition: this was certainly going too far, and indeed, on the whole, French and (especially) central European composers have made quite as much use of superficial jazz elements in serious composition as those of the United States. Apart from the definite and deliberate use of such elements, jazz must have more subtly influenced composition by accustoming a public's ears to rhythms of a kind to which they had hardly been led to give attention previously, and, especially, to orchestral colouring of a pungency that if it had been introduced directly into serious music, instead of coming to it via the music of pleasure, might have shocked them. Moreover, though the worst of jazz (like the worst of any type of music) is conventional, yet the best shows the able use of novel resources and is thus capable of adding to the technique of composers a few really valuable procedures.

2. The Melodic Element. The melodic element of jazz is of relatively little significance, being as often as not borrowed from some popular tune of the day, much as, in the thirteenth to fifteenth centuries, the early church composers took their themes from plainsong or from some previously existing composition, and treated them according to the devices of the technique of the period.

Owing to the incorporation in dance music of existing vocal melodies a custom quickly grew up of jazz dance players bursting into song. The practice of dancers doing this is ancient and respectable (see very many of the articles on the traditional dance forms in this volume); that of the players doing it seems to be more novel.

3. The Element of Extemporization. The word 'break' is important in the vocabulary of jazz. It means a passage interjected to fill the gap between the ending of one eight- or sixteen-measure section of a jazz tune and another. Such passages were generally extemporized by some performer. Extemporization necessarily played an all-important part in the development of the technique of jazz—a bigger part than it had played in that of any branch of music since the palmy eighteenth-century days of the Italian opera, when it was an understood thing that a great deal of the reputation of a vocalist depended on his or her ability to decorate the composer's melodic outline (see *Ornaments*).

One derivation of the word 'jazz' (given by Irving Schwerké in his *Kings Jazz and David*) is from the French *jaser* or *jasser*, to gossip. French was, of course, the language of the early white inhabitants of several of the Southern States and became, perforce, that of the slaves there. The Negro, both during and since the period of slavery, has found his pleasure in music, often with home-made instruments played in a carefree improvisation, with snatches of song and rhythmic clapping of hands from any who collected to listen. 'Each participant had unrestricted play and contributed towards an ensemble of unpremeditated harmony, rhythm, and melodic ideas.' Such performance was of the nature of a free conversation, in fact the verb *jaser* ('to gossip, to chat together') aptly fitted it. Still more probable, in view of the jazzmen's original function as players of a rather specialized form of background music, is the link with Negro slang for the sex act.

For other claims to the introduction of the much discussed term, see Slonimsky's *Music since 1900*, p. 170. It is stated that the first instrumental combination to adopt the word was the 'Original Dixieland Jazz Band' (Chicago, 1914) and that the first use of the word by a gramophone company was by Victor in 1917 (on a record made by that band).

The early jazz bands consisted of banjo, piano, violin, saxophone, motor-horns, whistles, rattles, and drums and other percussion instruments ('traps') *ad libitum*. The music (if any) before the players of these instruments would be a mere sketch, which they would proceed to fill in. They might take some existing song known to them all and 'jazz it', which was probably very much what the early Negro players had done. This principle of extemporization persisted, so that a well-known woman jazz pianist, writing to the author of the present book in 1926, said:

'We have had rehearsals and even performances of numbers that *none* of us had ever seen in print. Or, as a great treat, there might be for me a melody MS. copy, with a "harmony" cued in here and there. I was asked to play it, and as I began to *feel* what it was all about, to "fill it out". Then the boys would chip in, by ear, a trombone here, a trumpet there (muted, oh yes, but what muted playing—like the Lorelei combing her golden hair!); then the banjolin would stroke a chord or two, and put in a little trickly run, and that was "The Birth of the Blues". The result was that, although the general structure was the same, the performance sounded like an impromptu any time we did it.'

The technical name applied to the process just described was 'putting in the dirt'.

The same artist explains 'dirt' a little further:

'It is pure fun. The pianist will often play a 9th. instead of an 8ve., or sometimes the 8ve. and 9th. together, for a specially silly effect, or, converting a "straight" run into a tonal run, will finish a tone or so higher than was expected. All this is Piano Dirt, but is a branch only. We have sometimes played number after number, if not actually "straight", at least quietly and in orderly fashion, and then one of us would hear the call of the wild and put in a handful, and then the circus starts! In the old days it used to be a great game to "superimpose", i.e. to find another theme that has the same "vamp", or harmony, and put that in. Great ingenuity was shown at times.'

That phase, however, passed—to some extent. 'Nowadays' (1926), says that writer, 'we are so keyed up to play the difficult symphonic arrangements that we perforce behave.'

Broadly speaking, the terms *Straight Jazz* (or *Sweet Jazz*) and *Hot Jazz* applied respectively to jazz played as written and jazz in which the extempore element is prominent. The difficulty of attaching a definite significance to such terms is, however, considerable, as the practitioners of this branch of the musical art, and their journalistic following, do not seem to have used them at all precisely. So we find Louis Armstrong stating in 1934:

'There'll probably be new names for it, that's all. There have been several names since I can remember way back to the good ol' days in New Orleans, Louisiana, when Hot Music was called "ragtime music". So you see instead of dying out, it only gets new names'.

It was Louis Armstrong, again, who was once asked by a woman reporter on behalf of her readers, 'Just what *is* Jazz?' He looked at her for a moment and replied, 'Honey, you tell 'em if they gotta ask, they ain't ever going to know'.

4. The Orchestral Element. The composition of the jazz orchestra has varied. On the plantation it consisted of home-made makeshifts, and adaptations of non-orchestral material (motor-horns and the like) distinguished the first professional orchestra. The saxophone, in its various sizes, soon became important and by and by was the most sold instrument in the United States (and perhaps in some other countries). Strings were looked on as relatively unimportant. Trombones were useful, especially for a lurching glissando which no other brass instrument could supply; trumpets, especially muted and with an addition to their very highest notes, were acceptable; horns were apparently felt to be too tame. The piano and banjo, with their punctuating powers and ability to supply chords, were important. Percussion was infinitely varied (see *Traps*). Nearly all the players in the band had at least two instruments, and could make rapid changes. (See p. 529, pl. **98.** 3.)

The general aim was, not to merge orchestral colours but to make them 'stand off' (the same idea as that of Stravinsky and certain other serious composers at that period).

5. Some Classics of the Movement. It is said that the first conductor to provide a complete set of parts and insist on adherence to them was Paul Whiteman in 1920. Anyhow; it was Whiteman who 'brought jazz into the concert hall' and became the leader of this new development (much deprecated by many serious jazz lovers, it must be said). He brought about a wider and more considered attention to the claims of his art by concerts in the United States and Europe and by commissions to composers of standing. Thus came

into existence the famous *Rhapsody in Blue* of George Gershwin (1898–1937)—but orchestrated by Whiteman's right-hand man, Ferde Grofé; the work was required at short notice and was completed in three weeks, according to the dates on the manuscript. This composition was greatly praised by some at the time, but to others it appeared to be merely commonplace.

Most of the Whiteman creations are in the *genre* 'Straight Jazz' or 'Sweet Jazz'—not that of the wilder 'Hot Jazz'. Duke Ellington (1899–1974) early gained a reputation as 'the greatest musician that Swing Music (see 7) has up to the present produced'. The following extract from Constant Lambert's considerable treatment of this composer in *Music Ho! A Study of Music in Decline* (1934) may be quoted as showing the estimation in which Ellington is held:

'Ellington is a real composer, the first jazz composer of distinction, and the first Negro composer of distinction. His works (apart from a few minor details) are not left to the caprice or ear of the instrumentalist; they are scored and written out, and though, in the course of time, variants may creep in (Ellington's works in this respect are as difficult to codify as those of Liszt) the first American records of his music may be taken definitively, like a full score, and are the only jazz records worth studying for their form as well as their texture. Ellington himself being an executant of the second rank has probably not been tempted to interrupt the continuity of his texture with bravura passages for the piano, and although his instrumentalists are of the finest quality their solos are rarely demonstrations of virtuosity for its own sake.

'The real interest of Ellington's records lies not so much in their colour, brilliant though it may be, as in the amazingly skilful proportions in which the colour is used. I do not mean skilful as compared with other jazz composers, but as compared with so-called high-brow composers. I know nothing in Ravel so dexterous in treatment as the varied solos in the middle of the ebullient *Hot and Bothered* and nothing in Stravinsky more dynamic than the final section. The combination of themes at this moment is one of the most ingenious pieces of writing in modern music.'

(See portrait, p. 1068, pl. **175.** 4.)

From the earlier 1920s, serious composers have adopted some of the superficial characteristics of jazz; another work of Gershwin is a Piano Concerto in F, played under Damrosch in 1926. Other American jazz works that have attracted attention are Gruenberg's *Jazzberries* and *Daniel Jazz*, Deems Taylor's *Circus Day*, Sowerby's *Monotony* and *Synsonate*, Grofé's *Mississippi* and *Broadway at Night*, Carpenter's *Skyscrapers*, Bernstein's *Age of Anxiety*, Copland's Piano Concerto, Hill's *Study for Two Pianos*, Antheil's *Jazz Symphony* (1925), and Morton Gould's *Swing Symphonette*.

Amongst European compositions influenced by or based on ragtime or jazz are Debussy's *Golliwogg's Cake Walk* (1908), *Minstrels* (1910), and *General Lavine—Eccentric* (1910), all for piano; Ravel's slow movement (*Blues*) in his Violin Sonata; Stravinsky's *Ragtime for eleven Solo Instruments* (1918–19), *The Soldier's Story* (1918), and *Ebony Concerto*; Hindemith's *Chamber Music No. 1* (op. 24, atonal) and Piano Suite (1922); Wiéner's *Syncopated Sonatina*; Kurt Kern's *Jazz Symphony*; Weill's light opera, *Mahagonny* (1927–9); Erwin Schulhoff's *Partita* and *Jazz Sonata*; Křenek's opera *Jonny spielt auf* (1927); Milhaud's *Bœuf sur le toit* and *Création du monde*; Tansman's *Sonate transatlantique*; Constant Lambert's orchestral–choral piece, *The Rio Grande* (1929). Of these the Debussy works may be looked on as precursors, since the ragtime mania was hardly established when those were written.

These are just a few as samples. How far composition in jazz idiom will go remains to be seen. The general verdict after forty years is that the experiment was unworkable and of little more final significance than the spicing of 'Spanish' or 'Oriental' flavours in the music of an earlier generation. Certainly few of the works mentioned (with the notable exception of Stravinsky's) are heard today except as curiosities.

In the later 1950s experimenters, often followers of the school of Webern, made serious attempts to write in a style ('Third Stream'—see *History* 9) compounded of jazz and Western European music, with results much discussed but for the most part of limited appeal for the wider audience.

6. Swing Music. This term became current about 1935 as descriptive of the phase into which Jazz had then passed. Many definitions were attempted, but they were realized to be vague and it was freely stated, by leading exponents of Swing themselves, that the type was indefinable. An examination of a series of gramophone records of the most popular current examples, supplied by the various gramophone companies for the purposes of the original version of the present article, showed that there was, in reality, no difficulty whatever in exactly defining the particular quality called 'Swing'.

All such music consisted apparently of a *simple harmonic basis* supplied largely by guitars, piano, percussion instruments, etc. (what is called the rhythm section of the orchestra—if the last word can be used for the small combination employed) *with a melodic thread superposed*, this last being assigned to some one instrument (occasionally more)—saxophone, trumpet, etc. The accompanimental-harmonic part was played in strong rhythm, rigid, unvarying; the melodic part (often improvised or so much 'decorated' in performance as to take on an improvisatory character) used a free rubato (q.v.). The contrast between the two was piquant and constituted the charm which the devotees of this branch of popular musical art so clearly recognized without, apparently, being capable of the slight intellectual effort required to analyse the nature of their enjoyment.

Obviously two conditions necessary to the style were: (*a*) an accompanimental part using such simple and rarely changed chords that a melody note might anticipate or outlast its legal accompaniment chord without producing a clash (see the reference to Chopin under *Rubato* 2), and (*b*) an assignment of the melody (usually) to a single instrument so that the rubato could be carried out with that pleasing unanimity with which any one individual always agrees with himself in matters of taste.

In 1937 a new term was introduced—**Jam Music.** It was understood that music so described was to be accepted as simultaneously extemporized by all the participants, an occasion on which this is to be done being described as a **Jam Session.** Further in the United States there were **Rippling Rhythm** orchestras, the name of which derived from their inclusion of a new technique of 'blowing through a straw into a glass of water'.

7. Boogie-Woogie and Bebop. A development of jazz (beginning about 1938) was **Boogie-Woogie.** 'Its main characteristic is a more or less rigid harmonic pattern in a twelve-bar period—four bars of tonic harmony, and then two bars each of subdominant harmony, tonic harmony, dominant harmony, and tonic harmony again.' This harmonic pattern was established by means of an ostinato (q.v.) figure in the bass—which related Boogie-Woogie to the classical passacaglia and chaconne. 'The time is always quadruple (four crotchets to the measure), with the general rhythmic pattern running in quavers or in dotted quavers and semiquavers—a type suggested by the title of an early example (1940), *Beat me, Daddy, eight to the Bar*. While the bass line runs steadily on, the right hand may provide a variety of syncopation and polyrhythmic figuration.'

Towards the end of the second World War another new Jazz style was developed in New York City—specifically in night clubs on 52nd Street. It received the name 'Rebop', later changed to 'Bebop', or simply 'Bop'. The term is said to have had its origin in a characteristic figure of two quavers, which suggested the two percussive syllables. The high priest of the cult was the Negro trumpet player, Dizzy Gillespie, and its temple was the 'Royal Roost', a fried-chicken restaurant which became known as the 'Metropolitan Bopera House'.

The technique of Bebop depends on modern harmony with dissonant chords as its core. The melodic line (largely improvised) uses components of these chords. Often the harmonic schemes of old jazz classics are re-used with new melodies attached. A literature of Bebop was brought into existence with as its chief item a full-length book, *Inside Bebop* (1950).

It should be emphasized that the technique of Jazz, Swing, Boogie-Woogie, and Bebop is not so much a technique of composition as one of performance. What Louis Armstrong (cf. 3) said of Swing may be applied to Boogie-Woogie and Bebop—'Any average musical performer can play through a score, but it takes a swing player, and a real good one, to be able to leave that score and to know, or to feel, just when to leave it and when to get back to it.'

The history of jazz is one of successive waves of new styles, seized on by an inner circle of initiates and discarded on reaching wider popularity.

Jazz terminology shares with other private languages (Negro slang, adolescent jargon, underworld argot) the characteristic of constant change. Swing, Bebop, Hot, Cool, and many other words have begun as labels for the latest developments in the small 'in' group; then, following the commercial exploitation of the new trend, the 'in' group drops the label in distaste and goes on to something else.

Any article such as this must necessarily consist of attempts to catch on the wing and pin down in the pages of a dictionary definitions of terms out of date long before they are set in type.

Of late years, younger Negroes have rejected the more popular side of jazz as contributing to the 'Negro as entertainer' stereotype: hence a school of aloof, solemn players, many of them with a conservatory background.

By the 1960s the jazz world seemed to have disintegrated into a large number of small groups, each devoted to one style and contemptuous of most others.

8. Factors in the Success of this Class of Music. To a large degree the amazing success of jazz in the twenties was undoubtedly due to the desire for distraction of a war-wearied world. Ragtime cake-walks and 'Coon Songs' had become popular before the first World War began, and before it ended jazz in full panoply entered the field and, peace declared, was soon helping impartially on both sides, inspiring new courage—or at any rate dispensing forgetfulness.

Jazz compositions usually have a short life and a merry one. No other successful music has ever had so ephemeral an existence as the average piece of successful jazz; it ranks as journalism, almost as daily journalism, not as literature.

The commercial side of jazz needs to be taken into account when considering its success. As soon as it showed itself capable of appealing to a large public a great deal of both brain and capital were put behind it.

The remuneration of really able players of the jazz instruments rose at one time to lofty figures. Many an expert symphonic performer, with a lifetime of experience and a knowledge of the whole 'straight' orchestral repertory, earned at this period one-third or one-quarter of the income of a jazz-band player. Naturally, then, the jazz movement secured the advantage of a great deal of very fine performance.

In general, however, it must be said that the life of a jazz musician is hazardous in the extreme. In addition, he is often regarded as something of an 'outsider' in the conventional music world. As a sociological footnote it may be mentioned that the number of jazz musicians making occasional or regular use of drugs such as marijuana or even heroin has been shown beyond dispute to be very large.

For some remarks on the rhythmic claims of jazz see *Rhythm* 10 (near end). And see also *Ragtime*; *Blues*; *Swing*; and *United States* 8.

JAZZ-STICK. See *Percussion Family* 4 d.

JE (Ger.). 'Always', 'ever', 'each', etc. (a difficult word to translate exactly).

JEBB, JOHN. Born at Dublin in 1805 and died at Peterstow, Heref., in 1885. He was an Anglican clergyman (D.D., Canon of Hereford) who published important books on the Cathedral Service (1841) and Choral Responses and Litanies (2 vols. 1847–57).

JEDOCH (Ger.). 'Still', 'nevertheless', 'yet'.

JEFFRIES, GEORGE. Said to have died in 1685. He was a gentleman of the Chapel Royal of Charles I and served him as organist during the period of his war-time residence in Oxford. He composed great quantities of church music, of secular songs, string compositions, etc.

JELINEK, HANNS. Born in Vienna in 1901. He studied with Schönberg and became a convert to that composer's method of the Note row (q.v.). His published works include a *Sinfonia Ritmica* for orchestra (1932) and a series of piano pieces (*Zwölftonwerk*—'12-note opus').

JENA SYMPHONY. See *Nicknamed* 3.

JENKINS.

(1) JOHN. Born at Maidstone in 1592 and died at Kimberley in Norfolk in 1678, aged eighty-six. He was a long-active, extremely voluminous, and much valued composer of the fancy (q.v.) for viols, as also of the sonata for the then popular combination of two violins, bass bowed instrument, and keyboard, of the lighter rant (q.v.), and of catches, songs, etc. He was a good performer on several instruments (a virtuoso on the lyra viol) and was one of the royal musicians both before and after the Commonwealth, though he spent most of his life resident in the houses of certain noble families, including that of the Norths (q.v.). Some revival of interest in this once celebrated composer occurred in the early 1950s—almost the only composition of his previously generally known being the round, 'A boat! a boat! Haste to the ferry'.

See references under *Sonata* 10 b; *Wales* 10; *Rant*.

(2) DAVID. Born at Trecastle, Brecon, Wales, in 1848 and died at Aberystwyth in 1915, aged sixty-six. He was a pupil of Joseph Parry (q.v.) and a graduate in music of Cambridge University. He became Professor of Music at the University College of Wales, Aberystwyth. He took a great part in Eisteddfod activities and edited (with David Emlyn Evans, q.v.) the journal *Y Cerddor* ('The Musician'). His

compositions include an opera, *The Enchanted Island*, an operetta, oratorios, and various church music.

(3) CHARLES FRANCIS (1867–1934). A great American physicist and specialist in cinematography.

See reference under *Broadcasting* 6.

JENNEVAL. See *Brabançonne*.

JENSEN.

(1) ADOLF. Born at Königsberg, East Prussia, in 1837 and died at Baden-Baden, in the Rhineland, in 1879, aged forty-two. He was a pupil of Liszt and others, and a notable song composer of the stamp of Schumann (whom he greatly admired), both his vocal and his pianoforte parts having distinction and interest. Beyond many songs and some piano music he composed hardly anything. He resided at different times in Russia and Denmark, studying in Copenhagen (with Gade) and at Königsberg and Berlin, and then, for his health, living in Dresden, Graz, and Baden-Baden—a good many changes for a short life. His brother is treated below.

(2) GUSTAV. Born at Königsberg in 1843 and died at Cologne in 1895, aged fifty-one. He was brother of the above and a pupil of Joachim. His name is very well known to string players, if not as a composer of chamber music, then, at least, as a very active and serviceable editor of old music.

(3) LUDVIG IRGENS. Born in Oslo in 1894. He has written songs (usually to his own texts, which are often amusing), an opera, an oratorio, chamber music, orchestral music, etc.

JEPPESEN, KNUD (1892–1974). See *Scandinavia* 3 (near end).

JEREMIAH, ABRAM. See *Harp* 2.

JEROME, SAINT. See *Church Music* 4; *Psalm* (end).

JEROME OF MORAVIA. See *Voice* 14.

JERSEY, LADY (1785–1867). See *Quadrille*.

JERUSALEM. See references to this city under *Jewish*; *Oriental*.

JERUSALEM. The boldly idealistic song known by this name, which from the 1920s assumed almost the position of a secondary British National Anthem, is a setting by Hubert Parry of words by the poet–painter William Blake (1757–1827). The setting dates from 1915 or 1916 and was made on the suggestion of Robert Bridges, the then Poet Laureate, who wanted it for a meeting of the 'Fight for Right' movement in the Queen's Hall, London; and it later made a great impression when sung at a meeting in the Royal Albert Hall, in March 1918, to celebrate the attaining of the final stage in the 'Votes for Women' campaign—on which occasion the composer was in charge of the music. It was afterwards adopted by the Federation of Musical Competition Festivals, the National Federation of Women's Institutes, etc., and hence became very widely known.

The words (which, without direct mention, recall to our minds the days of infant factory labour, child chimney-climbing sweeps, farm labourers at ten shillings a week, and men transported for life for poaching a hare) are not to be confused with Blake's longer poem 'Jerusalem'.

JESSIE, THE FLOWER OF DUNBLANE. The poem is by Robert Tannahill, of Paisley (1774–1810); the air is a Scottish folk tune.

JESU, BLESSED WORD OF GOD INCARNATE. See *Ave Verum Corpus*.

JESU, LOVER OF MY SOUL. See *Hymns and Hymn Tunes* 6.

JESUS CHRISTUS UNSER HEILAND. See *Chorale*.

JEU (Fr., plural *Jeux*). 'Game'. 'play', etc. Also stop (organ), e.g. *Jeux d'anche*, reed stops; *Jeux de fonds*, foundation stops; *Grand jeu* or *Plein jeu*, full organ.

JEU DE CLOCHETTES (Fr.). Glockenspiel. See *Percussion Family* 2 c, 4 e, 5 c.

JEU DE ROBIN ET DE MARION. See *Adam de la Halle*.

JEU DE TIMBRES (Fr.). Same as *Jeu de Clochettes* (q.v.).

JEUNE, LE. See *Claudin*.

JEUNE FRANCE, LA. A Paris group of composers banded for mutual support and propaganda. It was formed in 1936, its members being Messiaen, Jolivet, Baudrier, and Lesur.

JEUNEHOMME, MADEMOISELLE. See *Nicknamed Compositions* 15.

JEUNESSES MUSICALES. This extension of the Music Appreciation idea was begun in 1940 by Marcel Cuvelier, Director-General of the Brussels Philharmonic Society. By 1945 there were 11,000 members in Belgium alone. In 1941 a French counterpart was begun by René Nicoly of Paris; the French organization had 200,000 members by 1946. The movement spread to Israel, Mexico, Scandinavia, Germany, Austria, and many other countries. The general idea of the organization is to have activities organized for and by young people, though with some adult guidance.

The children's concerts organized in London by Sir Robert Mayer since 1925 were affiliated to Jeunesses Musicales in 1955.

In the United States a branch was formed in 1964 with the help of a grant from the Ford Foundation.

JEU ORDINAIRE (Fr.). Ordinary way of playing—countermanding some behest to play in an unusual way, such as *Sur la touche*, 'near the fingerboard' (violin, etc.).

JEUX. See *Jeu*.

JEWEL, JOHN (1522–71). Bishop of Salisbury. See reference under *Community Singing* 2.

JEWISH MUSIC

(For some illustrations see p. 528, pl. 97.)

1. A Great Musical Tradition. The difficult task of sketching the musical development of various European countries in such articles of this volume as those upon England, France, Germany, Italy, Spain, Russia, etc., is far exceeded by that of sketching the musical development of a race boasting a recorded history of nearly 4,000 years and of dwelling-places covering a large part of the habitable globe.

At every stage of that history we come upon references to musical activities. In the Patriarchal period we find Laban reproaching Jacob on his departure with '*Wherefore didst thou . . . not tell me, that I might have sent thee away with mirth, and with songs, with tabret and with harp?*'[1]

The Hebrews' escape from the Egyptians is celebrated by the vividly descriptive Song of Moses, sung by the children of Israel to the accompaniment of Miriam's dancing and timbrel playing, upon the shore of the Red Sea.

In the struggle for the Promised Land the walls of Jericho fall to the strains of the priests' martial music.

When that land is occupied we read of much music. Saul's distemper is soothed by performance upon the harp. And the Ark of the Covenant of the Lord is '*brought up with shouting, and with sound of the cornet, and with trumpets, and with cymbals, making a noise with psalteries and harps*', David '*dancing and playing*' before it. (For the priestly trumpet and Shofar see p. 528, pl. 97. 4.)

In the Temple of Solomon '*The Levites which were the singers . . . being arrayed in fine linen, having cymbals and psalteries and harps, stood at the east end of the altar, and with them an hundred and twenty priests sounding with trumpets*' (cf. *Psalm*).

Through the ancient history of the Jewish people, then (and the Talmud is just as eloquent on the subject as the Bible), we find music mentioned perhaps more often than in the history of any other people. Every sort of popular rejoicing is accompanied by music; returning conquerors are welcomed with music and with it are celebrated coronations and royal marriages; the company of the prophets march together to the sound of a psaltery, a tabret, a pipe, and a harp, and it is to the playing of a minstrel that the hand of the Lord comes upon Elisha so that the future becomes clear to his eyes.

When the ten tribes that revolted and formed the Kingdom of Israel disappear into the As-

syrian captivity, never more to find their way back to the pages of history, the two that formed the Kingdom of Judah and remain in our sight are seen to retain their love of music. They, too, at last succumb to an invader, and in their Babylonian captivity the pathetic image in which their grief is imperishably preserved to us is that of a cessation of music—'*We hanged our harps upon the willows in the midst thereof. . . . How shall we sing the Lord's song in a strange land?*'

When at last they are allowed to return, the rebuilding of the Temple of Jerusalem is undertaken. 'The singers' are restored to the functions their forefathers had exercised, and at the laying of the foundations it is recorded that there were present, '*the priests in their apparel with trumpets, and the Levites, the sons of Asaph with cymbals, to praise the Lord after the ordinance of David the King of Israel, and they sang together by course in praising and giving thanks unto the Lord*'.

The importance of the existence of a large class of professional musicians in any nation is evident: fixed scales, tunes, rhythms, etc., thus tend to be developed. Under King David, out of 38,000 Levites, 4,000 were appointed as musicians. Flavius Josephus talks of 500,000 musicians in Palestine; this is an obvious exaggeration, but it serves to indicate the importance of music under the old régime.

2. The Synagogue and its Music. It is now, apparently, that the institution of the Synagogue system comes about (though some trace its beginnings earlier), so that those who cannot take part more than the statutory three times a year in the worship of the Temple at Jerusalem may have their regular and frequent local worship. Every village has its synagogue, and a ritual is laid down which, after the destruction of Jerusalem under the Roman rule in A.D. 70 (pl. 528, p. 97. 2), is to develop the vocal part of the Jewish musical traditions in all the Mediterranean lands and, at the greater dispersal that followed, to carry it into every part of the civilized world. But a dispersed Jewry was a sorrowing Jewry, and in the synagogues that were now to be found almost everywhere in the known world an abstention from instrumental music served as a lasting reminder of the glories of the Temple worship of the past, which should, it was confidently believed, after a period of patient waiting some day be renewed.

3. The Chazzan (or Cantor) and his Cantillation. The reading of the scriptures by cantillation was a great feature of synagogue

---

[1] The quotations from Scripture in this article are taken from the Authorized (King James) English version, in which the names of instruments are, of course, merely the approximations of the seventeenth-century translators.

worship. Those books which it is obligatory to read publicly had acquired traditional tunes of a highly decorative character, in free rhythm and on a system strongly resembling that of the modes used in Christian worship (see *Modes*) and, indeed, including most of these; different modes were used for different occasions and were deemed to express different characteristic moods, much as with the Greeks. When Jesus went into the synagogue and publicly read the prophecies of Isaiah (Luke iv) he probably used cantillation of this character.

It is, by the way, significant that the singing of the Book of Esther, which had pathetic significance for a race everywhere persecuted, from an originally simple system of tune became greatly enriched; it offers an example of a tendency that was very general amongst the Ashkenazic Jews (i.e. those with their original headquarters in Germany, as distinct from the Sephardic Jews, those with their original headquarters in Spain and Portugal) to accumulate popular tunes of the peoples amongst whom they lived, incorporating them in their synagogal cantillation so that they became part of the tradition.

This cantillation was the duty of the **Chazzan** (or Hazzan) of a synagogue, at first a mere beadle who added ritual chanting to other communal duties such as that of the ritual slaughtering for the community.

The position of the chazzan tended in time to become musically important; a fine tenor (or tenorized baritone) voice, the ability to use it effectively, and a large and attractive repertory of cantillation (traditional, semi-traditional, and for some of the scripture passages and prayers, original or quasi-original) would win a high reputation and lead to a position of standing in the community. In eastern Europe, where the Jews multiplied exceedingly and lived apart from the Gentiles, the singing of the chazzanim (plural of chazzan) supplied the place of concert and opera. The faculty of melodic improvisation often became wonderfully developed, as did the art of florid coloratura (q.v.).

At times of persecution many chazzanim adopted a wandering life and became almost as minstrels, going from one Jewish community to another and seeking popularity and a livelihood. At the present time there are a few chazzanim (or cantors) whose names are everywhere known and who travel a good deal in the practice of their sacred art. In the eighteenth century a practice obtained of reinforcing the services of the chazzan by the appointment of two assistants, a bass and a descant (alto or soprano); apparently they sang in turn—melodically, therefore, not harmonically.

The traditional cantillations for the reading of the Law have always required to be completely memorized, as no signs are permitted in the Scrolls containing it; those of the Prophets, however, are sung from a printed book, bearing signs which are in many cases very strikingly similar to the Neumes from which our staff notation developed (see *Nota-*

tion 2). When Christian plainsong and Jewish cantillation are compared some resemblances can be seen, and, moreover, a few passages in common. It would seem probable, therefore, that the early Christians took over into their new worship some part of their old Jewish musical tradition.

Cantillation is in some measure used in the Jewish home on the first two nights of the Passover, when the story of the redemption from Egypt is sung from the Haggadah (the book of prayers and songs for these two nights) by the master of the house, with the participation of his family.

4. An Italian Development of the Sixteenth Century. A very interesting development of the synagogue music took place in the late sixteenth century in Italy, where a number of Jewish musicians came to hold high favour amongst the Gentile community. One of these, **Salomone de' Rossi,** who was engaged at the court of Mantua from 1587 to 1628, not only published many books of madrigals and canzonets and did notable work in the development of instrumental music, but also set psalms in the contrapuntal style in four to eight voices, issuing them in Hebrew for use in the synagogue. There is nothing Jewish about this work; it is purely Italian; apparently it did not remain very long in use, but it had some indirect influence upon German developments. The use of a choral setting was, of course, at that period a great innovation. An Italian rabbi and scholar, of the same period, **Leone Modena,** was a great champion of the idea of the modernization of the synagogue service. It is notable that the Italian composer Marcello, in making his famous settings of fifty psalms (1724–7), used over a dozen tunes from the Ashkenazic and Sephardic synagogues in Venice (they are not tunes of long tradition, however, but rather Jewish borrowings from other sources).

5. The Partial Reintroduction of Instrumental Music. Allusion has been made above to the prohibition of instrumental music in the synagogues. The second Temple (completed 515 B.C.) had possessed a very large organ (*Magrepha*) of the type of the Hydraulus (q.v.). Apart from the desire to reserve instrumental music until the return to Zion, those who controlled the worship in the synagogues had two other motives in refraining from the introduction of organs—the fact of their association with Christian worship, and the fact that no Jew could lawfully perform on an instrument on the Sabbath. Various reform movements have, however, brought organs into synagogues, the last-mentioned difficulty being sometimes overcome by the use of Gentile organists. A new synagogue built in Prague in 1594 (i.e. at the same period as the Italian innovations above mentioned) was equipped with both an organ and an orchestra, and its Friday (i.e. Sabbath Eve) services were elaborated by the addition of something like a concerto. Such concerts were then introduced into most of the nine synagogues of that city: they eventually fell off because the performers formed the habit of over-running the time and so violating the sanctity of the Sabbath.

In the eighteenth century a number of German synagogues introduced instrumental music. There seems to have been a considerable cultivation of instrumental music amongst the Jewish communities in the late eighteenth and early nineteenth centuries. In reading the lives of the Russian composers, from Glinka onwards, we often find mention of the attraction towards music they experienced in youth as the result of hearing the private orchestras of Jewish musicians attached to the country houses of the Russian aristocracy.

6. The Nineteenth- and Twentieth-century Reform Movement. The very definite Reform Movement that began in 1810 at Seesen in Westphalia led to a considerable introduction of the organ into worship. Reform synagogues sprang up in which reading was substituted for cantillation, whilst choral setting of some parts of the service, with organ accompaniment, further approximated the musical conditions to those prevailing in Christian churches.

Amongst prominent leaders in the Reform Movement was Sulzer of Vienna (1804–90; p. 528, pl. **97.** 6), much praised by Liszt, who used to go to hear him sing. It was his policy to preserve the ancient music, to do away with second-rate accretions of later centuries, and to add good modern music. Almost every modernized synagogue in central Europe accepted his reforms and modelled its music on that of the synagogue in Vienna of which he was chazzan. He brought dignity back to the service, but the music he composed was German rather than Jewish.

Another great reformer was **Louis Lewandowski** (1821–94) of Berlin, who arranged services for the entire year to organ accompaniment and in his turn was looked on as the head of the profession of chazzan. His compositions are somewhat more Jewish than Sulzer's and, with Sulzer's, are now regularly used in both the Orthodox and the Reform synagogues. Amongst the numerous other composer-chazzanim are Mombach (1813–80), whose works are popular in England and elsewhere, and Wasserzug (1822–82), who in Poland introduced choral singing in place of cantillation (for an English Jewish composer see *Salaman*).

The movement has gone very far in the United States, where there are many Reform synagogues (generally called 'Temples') with prayers and hymns in English, an abandonment of cantillation, mixed choirs (often largely of Gentiles), with anthems and solos taken from the Old Testament part of the Christian musical repertory, and organs with Gentile organists. The chazzan has in these places receded into the background or altogether disappeared. The orthodox synagogues, of course, retain the chazzan and the traditional song, but the conditions of life (constant influx of new members of the Jewish community, of all European languages and of all social grades and degrees of education, etc.) have made conformity to any one settled convention almost impossible.

Jewish communities, then, throughout the world, are today divided into Orthodox and Progressive (or Reform) bodies, and the presence or absence of an organ in the synagogue may be looked upon as the most obvious symbolical and distinguishing sign.

7. Jewish Popular Song. Some brief allusion must, of course, be made to Jewish popular song.

It would appear that in the earlier periods music and poetry were, with the Jews, very closely allied. In the childhood of Hebrew poetry (as, possibly, in the childhood of the poetry of every race) all poems were chanted. The oldest and the greatest book of songs now in use anywhere in the world is, of course, that of which some brief particulars will be found in the article *Psalm*.

Jewry has naturally, in its long career in so many parts of the world, accumulated a great body of folk song, though it has probably lost again much more than it has retained. The poems of Hebrew song have in general, but not exclusively, a religious and ethical tendency, as many early spiritual leaders were opposed to secular song and, also, the suffering of continual persecution was not favourable to a spirit of light-heartedness. There are many songs on the Elijah *motif*, songs in praise of the Sabbath, and domestic songs for religious festivals and weddings. Their tunes often show evidence of great age and an oriental origin. An early collection of such songs is that of **Israel Najara,** called *Zemiroth Israel* ('Hymns of Israel'), published at Safed (North Palestine) in 1587 and reissued a few years later in Venice: this had great popularity in the Near East. Najara borrowed a good many tunes from various Eastern nations and composed a few. The melodies of the collections must be called oriental rather than specifically Jewish.

The Jews of Ashkenaz, from the sixteenth century to the middle of the nineteenth, accumulated a song literature of their own. They were confined to their ghettos and thus cut off from entertainment, and song met a social need: largely, however, they used not original tunes but tunes borrowed either from the synagogue or from the German popular song repertory. The influence of the prohibition of owning land and of confinement to the ghetto is seen in the fact that the words of the song never show, as those of other races do, a love of country life (in this differing from some of the Psalms and Israeli folk song).

The eastern Jews used songs of a more genuinely Jewish cast. It is notable that the songs of the Ashkenazim strongly favour the major mode and those of the Sephardim, and also of the Jews of the East, a mode with two augmented seconds—between either second and third or third and fourth degrees, and between sixth and seventh. The Sephardic Jews in North Africa, the Balkans, Turkey, and elsewhere have songs in Ladino (a Spanish Yiddish) recalling the centuries spent in Spain before the catastrophe of the expulsion in 1492.

From the early years of the great dispersion of the Jews under Titus until the middle of the nineteenth century a profession of *Badchonim*, or jester–singers, existed in central Europe, and in eastern Europe it lasted still later. From the fifteenth century, travelling Jewish bands playing at Christian festivals have been common —though harassed with many governmental restrictions.

The subject of Jewish song is an immense one and any summary of it is difficult to achieve.

8. Some Modern Investigations and Opinions. The first writer to make any serious attempt to describe accurately the ancient Hebrew music was Forkel, in his *History of Music* (1788). The earliest rational description of the ancient instruments was that of the philosopher Moses Mendelssohn (grandfather of the composer) in his great German translation of the Pentateuch (1783); there is a good description of them in the *Jewish Encyclopedia*. The founder of serious modern scholarship was A. Z. Idelsohn, who made long research in many countries; in 1914 he began publication (in German, Hebrew, and English editions) of a great thesaurus of Hebrew–Oriental melodies, and in 1929 published a very careful and detailed study, *Jewish Music in its Historical Development*, to which (as also to the several long articles in the *Jewish Encyclopedia*, and to other works) the present brief sketch is indebted.

Another learned investigator is Dr. Solomon Rosowsky of the Hebrew University at Jerusalem; he has especially devoted himself to research as to the traditional systems of cantillation as represented by the signs attached to the words in the Hebrew Bible.

Cantor Mayerowitsch contributed valuable musical matter to the (Hebrew–English) edition of the Pentateuch prepared by J. H. Hertz, late Chief Rabbi of the British Empire.

Other modern scholars include Dr. Eric Werner of the Hebrew Union College in New York (one of the three training centres for Cantors), Robert Lachmann, and Peter Gradenwitz, a specialist in modern Israeli music.

9. Some Jewish Musicians. Amongst composers claimed to be Jewish or partly Jewish are the following: Ferdinand Ries, Meyerbeer, Halévy, Mendelssohn, Ferdinand Hiller, Moscheles, Offenbach, Ferdinand David, Rubinstein, Goldmark, Bruch, Cowen, Moszkowski, Korngold, Mahler, Dukas, Schönberg, Schreker, Ornstein, Milhaud, Kurt Weill, Lourié, Eisler, Toch, Frankel, Jacobi, William Schuman, Diamond, Lukas Foss, Leonard Bernstein, Gruenberg, Blitzstein, Alexander, Julian, and Gregory Krein, Maximilian Stein-

berg, Castelnuovo-Tedesco, Morton Gould, Bernard Herrmann, Lopatnikof, Schillinger, Elie Siegmeister, Weinberger, Gniessin, Tansman, Saminsky, Achron, Copland, Bloch, Irving Berlin, and George Gershwin.

The violin seems to make a strong appeal to Jewish musicianship; amongst famous Jewish violinists are: Reményi, Joachim, Auer, Kreisler, Huberman, Heifetz, Elman, Zimbalist, Seidel, Menuhin. New violin prodigies are constantly appearing, and they are largely Jewish. Amongst cellists may be mentioned Popper, Feuermann, and Piatigorsky.

Amongst Jewish (or partly Jewish) pianists must be named Anton and Nicolas Rubinstein, Godowsky, Bauer, Moritz Rosenthal, Fanny Bloomfield Zeisler, Sauer, Ignaz Friedman, Artur Rubinstein, Schnabel, Serkin, Lhevinne, Solomon, Moiseiwitsch, Harold Samuel, Horowitz, Myra Hess, Irene Scharrer, and Harriet Cohen.

The Jewish singers are very numerous— Pasta, Braham, Schorr, Selma Kurz, Kipnis, Tauber, Henschel, etc.

Almost all schools of music, throughout the world, have many Jewish students.

Amongst Jewish or partly Jewish conductors are Damrosch, Hertz, Walter, Klemperer, Leo Blech, Ronald, Koussevitzky, Szell, Monteux, and Dobrowen.

Jewish musicologists and music critics have been very numerous, especially in Germany. A few whose names spring to mind are Kalisch, in England, and, in Germany and Austria, Adler, Alfred Einstein, Curt Sachs, Paul J. Bekker, and Hornbostel.

In 1948 the British mandate was ended, and Israel became an independent state.

Among the composers prominent in Israel may be mentioned Menahem Avidom, Aviassaf Barnea, Paul Ben-Haim, Oedon Partos, and Karl Salomon. Contributors to modern Jewish religious music include Milhaud, Arthur Berger, Leonard Bernstein, David Diamond, and Kurt Weill.

Many Israeli composers are firmly western in their cultural background: their attempts to introduce a national flavour in Israeli music seem to have produced a pastiche 'Eastern Mediterranean' style, with melodic and rhythmic echoes of the near and middle East.

An Opera Company gives regular performances, using libretti translated into Hebrew. There are a number of schools of music (that of Jerusalem, opened in 1948 with one hundred students, by 1950 had eight hundred); chamber music is cultivated and concerts of all types are very frequent. The Israel Philharmonic Orchestra was founded (as the Palestine Orchestra) by the violinist Huberman in 1936; the first concert was conducted by Toscanini. By 1943 it was giving 200 concerts a year. Considering the small size of the country and its limited resources, the development of musical life has been very rapid and complete.

For music during the earlier Christian period, see *Church Music* 4.

JEW'S HARP—or Jews' Harp or Jews Harp (p. 544, pl. **99.** 1, 2). This simple instrument is one of the most ancient and widespread. It is found throughout Europe and Asia. A Chinese work of the twelfth century shows it in much its present shape. The Stearns Collection of Musical Instruments at the University of Michigan includes examples from Japan, the Philippines, Formosa, New Guinea, and Borneo; the Metropolitan Museum, New York, has a specimen from Siberia; other museums have specimens from parts of the world very remote from these and from each other. A woodcut in Virdung's *Musica getutscht* (1511) shows the instrument exactly as it exists today. Mersenne, in his *Harmonie Universelle* (1636), also pictures it. A sculpture on the minstrels' gallery in Exeter Cathedral (fourteenth century) shows a player of what appears to be this instrument: it is also seen on the crozier of William de Wickwane (Archbishop of York, 1279–85). It appears in several of the pictures of Breughel (1525–69) and other Flemish painters and engravers.

The Jew's harp is a harmonic instrument, i.e. it produces only the natural harmonic scale (see *Acoustics* 8), and to this extent it resembles the brass instruments and the tromba marina (q.v.). It is a small iron frame open at one end, in which a single strip of steel vibrates. This frame is held between the teeth and the strip of steel then twanged by the finger. The strip itself is, obviously, capable of producing only one note, but the harmonics of this note become available by resonance, through various shapings of the cavity of the mouth (see *Voice* 6, 7; also *Acoustics* 20); some people have learnt to tap tunes with a pencil on their teeth and the general principle of this production of the various notes is the same.

In the seventeenth and eighteenth centuries this instrument was a good deal used in Scotland for dancing; and it is said that its use was known much earlier, preceding that of the bagpipe (see *Bagpipe Family* 4); when James VI of Scotland (afterwards James I of England) took part in a trial of witches (1591), he caused one of the accused to play before him on this instrument a tune which she admitted having played for dancing at a Witches' Sabbath. The fact that the twanging of the fundamental note is heard throughout may have endeared the instrument to a race that delights in the drones of the bagpipe.

In the late eighteenth and early nineteenth centuries there were some very celebrated travelling virtuosi on the instrument, such as Franz Paul Koch, and Eulenstein (q.v.). Some of these would play on two instruments together, presumably with vibrating strips of differing lengths or tension. Possibly the two cavities of the mouth, as used in the production of the various sounds (see *Voice* 7), would be brought into play, so that two notes (not more) could by an adroit performer be produced together; it is more likely, however, that the two harmonic series available were used merely in alternation to fill up one another's gaps and so to facilitate the performance of melodies. The Tyrolese peasants used to have (possibly still have) a practice of using two of these instruments together, one tuned a fourth or fifth above the other, so giving them a more complete melodic scale. Eulenstein is reported to have played on sixteen instruments, but this could, of course, only be in rapid alternation, not simultaneously. Probably they were fixed on a frame, so that one or another could quickly be brought into action as desired. Apparently bands of Jews' Harps have occasionally existed. The village of Dacre, in Nidderdale, Yorkshire, had one.

The name 'Jew's Harp' is very ancient and is not (as some dealers make out in the wish to avoid hurting the susceptibilities of their Jewish customers now that the instrument has descended to humble spheres) a corruption of *Jaws Harp*. The name *Jew's Trump* was in slightly earlier use (the *Oxford English Dictionary* gives 1545 and 1584 as the earliest dates that have been found for the use of these two terms) and is still the regular term in Scotland, where, however, it is often abbreviated to *Trump* (or *Tromp*). In the German language the instrument has one name that is the exact equivalent of Jew's harp, viz. *Judenharfe*. Nevertheless, no connexion with Jewry has ever been traced and some mystery of ancient false etymology is presumably concealed in the name.

Other German names are *Maultrommel* ('mouth-drum'), *Brummeisen* ('buzzing-iron'), and *Mundharmonika* ('mouth harmonica'—which name is, however, also used for the mouth organ).

French names are *Guimbarde*, *Trompe de Béarn* (hence a name occasionally found in eighteenth-century English writings—'trompe de Berne'), *Trompe de laquais* ('lackey's trumpet') and, in earlier literature, *Rebute* (as in fifteenth-century Scottish *Ributhe*).

The Italian names are poetical—*Scacciapensieri* ('chase-thoughts'), *Spassapensieri* ('distract-thoughts'), and *Aura* ('breeze' or 'breath').

A Northumbrian name is said to be *Gew-Jaw*, as in the proverbial saying, 'He's swopped his fiddle for a Gew-Jaw'. The Welsh is *Styrmant*.

Medieval Latin names are *Crembalum* (retained as late as 1619 in the *Syntagma musicum* of Praetorius) and *Cymbalum orale* (e.g. in Mersenne, 1588–1648).

In the seventeenth century the Jew's harp was used by the English settlers as a regular object of barter with the American Indians, and Professor Percival R. Kirby, late of the University of Witwatersrand, reports that he has found traces of its similar use in South Africa; curiously, the native races of America and Africa seem nowadays to be amongst the very few peoples who do not know the instrument.

In 1935 the Department of Commerce of the United States reported that all the Jew's harps of the world were then being made by one firm in Birmingham, England, that one order just given from the United States to this firm was for 160,000 instruments, and that the firm in question, though making 100,000 a week, was unable to keep up with the world demand owing to a lack of skilled 'tongue-setters'.

JEW'S TRUMP. See *Jew's Harp*.

JIG. As a dance the jig was once popular in England, Scotland, and Ireland, in the last of which its popularity lasted longest, so that probably many people today look upon it as something specifically Irish. But Shakespeare (*Much Ado about Nothing*, II. i) says, 'Hot and hasty like a Scotch Jig'.

During the late sixteenth and the seventeenth centuries the word 'Jig' or 'Jygge' was applied in the London playhouse to a lively song-and-dance item, of comic character, used to terminate performances. Celebrated solo performers such as Richard Tarlton (d. 1588) or the equally famous Will Kemp (q.v.), of slightly later date, took part in the jig, which developed into a sort of farcical ballet or almost a ballad opera (q.v.) with strings of songs. The English jigs taken by English actors to Germany became the foundation of the Singspiel (q.v.). There is a mass of allusions to the jig in English literature of the period in question, often very condemnatory on account of the loose character of the performers.

The *Oxford English Dictionary* does not accept the commonly held idea that 'jig' comes from the Old French 'gigue', a fiddler (cf. Ger. *Geige*); it suggests that the dance 'gigue' derives its name from English 'jig' and not from that Old French word. See *Gigue* for the nature of the dance's music and its incorporation into artistic composition.

JIG FUGUE (Bach). See *Nicknamed Compositions* 1.

JIM CROW. See *Negro Minstrels*.

JINGLING JOHNNY. See *Turkish Crescent*.

JIRÁK, KAREL BOLESLAV. Born at Prague in 1891, and died at Chicago in 1972. He was trained under Novák and Foerster.

He did much choral conducting and was long a professor of composition at the Conservatory of Prague. In 1949 he became head of the theory department of Roosevelt College, Chicago.

He composed an opera, symphonies, chamber music, and other things. He ranks high amongst the composers of his original nationality.

JOACHIM, JOSEPH (p. 1097, pl. **182**. 6). Born in 1831 near Pressburg (otherwise Pozsony, then in Hungary, now in Czechoslovakia and known as Bratislava), and died in Berlin in 1907, aged seventy-six.

After early violin lessons under various masters he entered, at twelve years old, the Conservatory of Leipzig, then under Mendelssohn's direction. At thirteen he visited England, where to the end of his life he remained, of all violinists, the greatest public favourite.

At eighteen he was leading violin under Liszt at Weimar, and for a time he was an adherent of the school of the 'New Music', or 'Music of the Future', of which Liszt and Wagner were the great champions, but by temperament he really belonged to the Mendelssohn–Schumann–Brahms party (which we may call the 'classical-romantic' school), and in 1860 he definitely and publicly separated himself from the innovators (cf. *Brahms*).

Amongst official positions he held at various times were several in Berlin, where he helped greatly to develop the present Hochschule, or official conservatory of music.

In that city, in 1869, he founded the Joachim Quartet, which for over thirty years occupied the premier position all over Europe: his colleagues in the later phases of the work of the quartet were Halir, Wirth, and Hausmann. During the early years of the present century the annual visits of this quartet to London were amongst the most eagerly anticipated of all musical events: the London programmes were exclusively German, ranging from Haydn to Brahms (p. 173, pl. **36**. 2).

There was a high idealism in all that Joachim did, combined with great technical skill and deep interpretative insight. Amongst elderly concert-goers he long ranked as the greatest solo violinist and the greatest quartet leader that their world had ever known.

His compositions (which some hold to be greatly too much neglected) include three violin concertos and five overtures.

See *Acoustics* 10; *Temperament* 10; *Concert* 7, 8; *David, Ferdinand*; *Marteau*; *Piatti*; *Brahms*; *Franz*; *Cadenza*; *Pianoforte Playing* 8; *Concerto* 6 b (1831); *Hellmesberger*.

JOCKEY'S DELIVERANCE. See *Bonnie Dundee*.

JOCULATOR. See *Minstrels*, etc. 1.

JODEL. *Jodelling* is the practice, common in Switzerland and the Austrian Alps (Tyrol), of singing without words and, in doing so, passing often from the normal voice to the falsetto (see *Voice* 5). The effect is very gay.

The word *Jodel* is used as both verb and noun, and with the same spelling in both French and German Switzerland and in the Tyrol. In English it is usually spelt *Yodel*, which suggests its accurate pronunciation (long 'o').

A song introducing jodelling is sometimes called a **Tyrolienne**. (But see also *Ländler*.) British concert-goers in 1829 made acquaintance with this sort of music when a family of three brothers and a sister came to London from the Zillerthal, under the sponsorship of Moscheles, and had a great success. There is a Tyrolienne in Rossini's *William Tell*.

JOHN XIX, POPE. See *Hexachord*.

JOHN XXII, POPE. See *Church Music* 4; *Faburden*; *Ornaments* 1.

JOHN ANDERSON, MY JO. The poem of

this song is by Burns, superseding several old poems, of various dates, which begin with the same words. The origin of the tune is disputable, there being several old tunes that resemble it. ('Jo' is not short for John as English people sometimes think, but means 'sweetheart'.)

JOHN BROWN'S BODY. The following account of the genesis of this song has been supplied by Mr. Nicolas Slonimsky, and supersedes the account given in the earliest editions of this *Companion*, which represents the story long generally accepted.

In the 1880s, one James Beale, of the 12th Massachusetts Volunteer Infantry, published a paper, *A Famous War Song*, which he had read before the United Service Club in Philadelphia. This paper (printed by himself in 100 copies only), gives an apparently authentic story of the origin of the song. Here is the essential part of it:

Somewhere in the late fifties a fire-company in Charleston, S.C., commissioned a Philadelphia musician to write a 'chantey' for their use on a proposed excursion. They received a song, the opening words of which were *Say bummers will you meet us?* Acting on the maxim, sometimes attributed to John Wesley, 'Don't let the Devil have all the good tunes', the Methodists promptly appropriated the tune and, with but slight modification, the words, the new version being *Say brothers will you meet us?* This became a very popular camp-meeting and revival hymn.

The firing on Fort Sumter, and consequent rally to arms, caused Fort Warren, Boston Harbour, to be occupied by a military force—the Second Battalion of Massachusetts Infantry, commonly known as the 'Tigers'. They found the Fort in a very unfinished state, work on it having been stopped when Jefferson Davis was Secretary of War, and as a natural result 'fatigue-parties' were very numerous. After the day's work was over, a favourite amusement was singing, for there were excellent voices in the company, notably one quartet: Chas. E. B. Edgerly, James Jenkins, Newton J. Purnette, and John Brown.

This last, a Scotsman, was the subject of many jokes owing to the identity of his name with that of the famous anti-slavery warrior, John Brown, of the Harper's Ferry attack, then recently hanged by his antagonists.

The story goes that one evening, when two of this quartet were returning to the Fort, John Brown and the other being seated near the sally-port, the query was shouted, 'What's the news?' Promptly came the retort, 'Why, John Brown's dead'. Someone added, 'Yet he still goes marching round'.

By dark the camp-meeting song had undergone revision, for the 'Tigers' were chanting *John Brown's body lies a-mouldering in the grave, But his soul goes marching on.*

On 25 May 1861 the 'Tigers' left Fort Warren, but as on 7 May the Twelfth Massachusetts Volunteers had reached the Fort, many of the 'Tigers', including the members of the quartet, enlisted in this regiment, called the 'Webster Regiment'. They carried their song with them, and it became the fashion after dress-parade for the regiment to strike up the song and march around the parade-ground. Thus the second verse, *John Brown's knapsack's strapped upon his back, As we go marching on.*

Chaplains in those days were very fond of styling the Volunteers 'the army of the Lord'. So the third verse, *He's gone to be a soldier in the army of the Lord.* The regiment frequently styled itself 'Webster's cattle': thus the fourth verse, *His pet lambs will meet him on the way,* which they used to do every evening while marching round the Fort. Soon the tune was played on dress-parade as accompaniment to the eleven hundred voices of the regiment. Copies of the song were given to Gilmore's Band and the Germania Band; then Ditson published it, and thus the John Brown Song became known everywhere.

JOHN CLEMENTI COLLARD FELLOWSHIP. See under *Minstrels*, etc. 3.

JOHN KNOX'S PSALTER. See *Hymns and Hymn Tunes* 10; *Presbyterian Church Music* 1.

JOHN OF DAMASCUS, SAINT. See *Greek Church* 3.

JOHN OF FORNSETE. (Living at the beginning of the thirteenth century.) He has been credited with the composition of *Sumer is icumen in* (q.v.), on the ground of its being found in his handwriting in a calendar for which he, as a keeper of the records of Reading Abbey, was responsible.

JOHN PEEL was a fox-hunter of the English Lake District where, from the nature of the ground, the hounds were followed on foot. The poem was written by his friend John Woodcock Graves, about 1820, to an old folk tune *Bonnie Annie*. The 'coat so gay' of many printed versions is, in the original, 'coat so grey'. Modern feeling against cruel sports now begins to frown on the use of this song, hence alternative words have been published.

JOHNSON.

(1) ROBERT (early sixteenth century). See *Scotland* 5.

(2) EDWARD. End of sixteenth and beginning of seventeenth centuries. Little is known of him, but he composed madrigals and virginal pieces, of both of which two or three remain. He was a contributor to *The Triumphs of Oriana* (see *Madrigal* 4).

(3) ROBERT. Born in London about 1583 and died about 1634. He was one of the 'Musicians of the Lute' to James I and Charles I, and of high reputation as a musician. It is thought that his 'Where the bee sucks' and 'Full fathom five' (still sometimes to be heard) were written for the first production of Shakespeare's *The Tempest*. (The later settings of these poems,

See the general Article on pages 516–17; also entries under *Jew's Harp*, *Effects*, and *Russolo*

1. A SCOTTISH JEW'S HARP PLAYER
By Sir David Wilkie, 1809

2. JEW'S HARPS AND THEIR CASES
(French, 18th century)

3. FUTURIST NOISE MACHINES IN 1913
The inventor, Russolo, manipulates a 'Howler' at the left and his assistant
a 'Buzzer' at the right. See *Italy* 7

'EFFECTS'

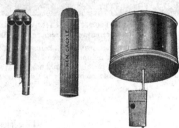

4. *Siren Whistles* (top left); *Type-writing Effect* (top middle); *Cow Bawl* (right); *Bear Growl or Lion Roar* (bottom)

5. *Ship's Siren*, 3 notes (top left); *Hen Cackle* (top middle); *Dog Bark* (top right); *Cuckoo* (bottom left); *Locomotive* (bottom right)

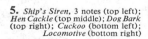

4

5

For other pictures of old or uncommon instruments see plates at pages 417, 449, 465, 512–13, and 545

1. VAMP HORN
In the church of East Leake, Notts. (nearly 8 feet in length)

There are eight of these strange instruments in English village churches. See the brief
article on p. 1071 and compare the picture below

3. ALPHORN
Above Grindelwald, Switzerland,
1930

2. TOWN WATCHMAN'S HORN
In the church tower of Freiburg-im-Breisgau today

The juxtaposition of pictures 1 and 2 here seems at last to settle the long-
debated problem of the manner of use of the English church Vamp Horns.
They were, apparently, merely megaphones, and as such could be used for
purposes of alarm and many other parish purposes. See *Vamp Horn*

4. A TRUMPETER IN KENYA

5. PIBCORN (or Hornpipe). The Scottish STOCKHORN (q.v.) resembled this

For other pictures of old or uncommon instruments see plates at pages 417, 449, 465, 512–13, and 544

respectively by Arne and Purcell, are today better known.)

See *Misattributed Compositions* (Locke's music to 'Macbeth').

(4) SAMUEL (1709–84). Lexicographer. See *Ballad* 5; *Burney, Charles*; *Criticism of Music* 6; *Methodism* 2; *Beggar's Opera*; *Hay*; *Bagpipe Family* 4; *Hawkins, John*; *Saltbox*.

JOIO. See *Dello Joio*.

JOLIVET, ANDRÉ. Born in Paris in 1905 and died there in 1974, aged sixty-nine. He studied with Varèse (q.v.), from whom he learned the art of employing various percussive effects. He wrote music for electrophonic instruments, several 'radiophonic suites', and some chamber music. He was musical director (1943–59) of the Comédie française.

See *Jeune France*; *Concerto* 6 c (1905); *History* 9.

JOMMELLI (or Jomelli), NICCOLÒ (or Nicolà). Born near Naples in 1714 and died in that city in 1774, aged nearly sixty. He was one of the most famous of the opera composers of his period, and also wrote much church music. For fifteen years he was in Germany, and on his return, having germanized his style (i.e. having introduced more subtle harmony, modulation, and orchestration) was hissed by his countrymen, whereupon he retired from his profession, had an apoplectic stroke, and shortly after died.

See references under *Oratorio* 7; *Passion Music* 6; *Requiem*; *Harmonica* 1; *Goethe*; *Giardini*; *Malipiero*.

JONES.

(1) ROBERT. End of sixteenth and beginning of seventeenth centuries. He directed the 'Children of the Revels of the Queen within Whitefryers'; that is, he was a theatrical entrepreneur, with a royal licence, in the days when boys' acting was relished. He wrote madrigals and ayres with lute accompaniment, and these are valued today by lovers of such music.

See *Wales* 10.

(2) INIGO (1573–1652). Celebrated architect and designer of masques (see *Masque*).

(3) RICHARD. Beginning of eighteenth century. He was leader of the orchestra at Drury Lane Theatre, London, and wrote sonatas, suites, and the like for violin and harpsichord.

See mention under *Sonata* 10 c; *Nicknamed Compositions* 10 ('Harmonious Blacksmith').

(4) EDWARD. Born in Merionethshire in 1752 and died in London in 1824. He was a famous performer on the Welsh harp and bard to the Prince of Wales. See reference under *Sibyl*.

(5) SIDNEY. Born in London in 1861 and died at Kew in 1946, aged eighty-four. He began professional life as a military bandmaster and then conducted travelling opera companies in Britain and Australia. He made a name as a popular composer in 1892 with the song *Linger Longer, Loo*, and followed this with a number of highly successful musical comedies and operettas (*A Gaiety Girl*, *The Geisha*, etc.).

(6) ROBERT HOPE. See *Hope-Jones*.

(7) DANIEL. Born 1881. Professor Emeritus of Phonetics at University College, London. See reference under *Voice* 7 (last par. but one).

(8) DANIEL. Born at Pembroke in 1912. Composer, etc. He was educated at University College, Swansea, and at the Royal Academy of Music and has composed an opera, five symphonies, concertos, etc., and choral and chamber works and a sonata for three kettledrums unaccompanied.

(9) ARTHUR TABOR. See *Pitch* 7 g.

(10) HENRY FESTING (died 1928). See *Butler, Samuel*.

JONGEN (The Brothers).

(1) JOSEPH. Born at Liège, Belgium, in 1873 and died near there in 1953, aged seventy-nine. He studied at the Conservatory of his native place, later joined the staff, and from 1920 to 1939 was head of the Conservatory of Brussels.

He wrote, especially, chamber music, but orchestral music, piano music, songs, etc., also came from his pen.

(2) LÉON. Born at Liège in 1884. Like his elder brother, he studied at the Conservatory of Liège and succeeded him as head of the Brussels Conservatory, resigning in 1949. He has written chiefly for the stage, though songs, piano pieces, and chamber compositions have also appeared.

JONGLEUR. See *Minstrels, etc.* 1.

JONNY SPIELT AUF. See *Křenek*.

JONSON, BEN (c. 1573–1637). Dramatist and poet. See *Masque*; *Barber Shop Music*; *Drink to me only with thine eyes*; *Opera* 13 a.

JOOSS, KURT. See *Ballet* 5.

JORA, MICHEL. Born at Jassy, in Moldavia, Rumania, in 1891. He studied at Leipzig and in Paris. He has written chamber and orchestral music, the latter including *Scenes of Moldavia*.

JORDAN.

(1) DOROTHEA or DOROTHY (1762–1816). Noted actress. See reference under *Blue Bells of Scotland*.

(2 and 3) ABRAHAM (Father and Son, with same Christian name). Eighteenth-century London organ builders (see *Organ* 8).

JOSQUIN DES PRÉS (p. 96, pl. 15. 3). Born, probably at Condé, in Hainault, about 1440 and died at that place in 1521, aged about eighty-one. He was a pupil of Ockeghem and became one of the most learned, able, and sensitive of the contrapuntists of the fifteenth century. Luther said of him, 'He is master of the notes; others are mastered by them.'

It is probable that in his younger manhood he travelled a good deal in Italy, and he is known to have been in Rome, in the Pope's service, from 1486 to 1499. Here he was one of the many northern musicians who left their influence and who may be considered the precursors of the genuine Italian Choral School which culminated in Palestrina. Afterwards he was in the service of Louis XII of France and of the Emperor Maximilian I.

Like many others of the Netherlands musicians he took orders, and he died a Canon of Condé. He left a quantity of masses, motets, and secular songs (see under *Chanson*). His work was long forgotten, but in the late eighteenth century was rediscovered by Burney, the historian of music.

See references to his period and himself under *History* 2; *Belgium* 1; *Mass* 4; *Stabat Mater*; *Miserere*; *Anglican Chant* 2; *Chanson*; *Holland* 9; *Publishing* 1; *Mouton*; *Ave Verum*.

JOSTEN, WERNER. Born at Elberfeld in 1885 and died in 1963. In his early thirties he went to the United States, was appointed to the staff of Smith College, Northampton, revived there many seventeenth- and eighteenth-century Italian operas (Monteverdi, Handel), and from 1929 became known as a composer. He composed ballets, orchestral music, chamber music, choral music, many songs, etc.

See *Concerto* 6 c (1885).

JOTA. This is a dance of northern Spain and especially of Aragon. It is danced by one or more couples, who also sing. The time is three-in-a-measure, the speed is rapid; the steps are much like those of the waltz but with more variety; the castanets (see *Percussion Family* 3 q, 4 c, 5 q) are used.

The poetry sung to the jota is that of the *cuarteta*—the four-line stanza with eight syllables to a line, in lines 1 and 3 of which assonance (agreement of vowels) is used instead of rhyme (but in the jota the four lines are extended to six by repetitions).

The jota form and style have been used by Glinka in his orchestral *Jota Aragonesa*, part of the result of his stay in Spain. Liszt has a Jota for piano. Saint-Saëns has one for orchestra; Albéniz one for piano; Falla has one in his ballet *The Three-Cornered Hat*; Balakiref has one. Raoul Laparra has an opera *La Jota*.

Different parts of Spain have their own form of the dance. That of Aragon is the most important. In Valencia the jota is danced at funerals. (In old Spanish the spelling is *Xota*.)

Cf. *Tango*.

JOUBERT, JOHN. Born in Cape Town in 1927. He was trained at the Royal Academy of Music, and in 1951 joined the staff of University College, Hull, later moving to Birmingham University. His compositions include operas, concertos for piano and for violin, chamber music, and other things.

JOUER (Fr.). 'To play.'

JOURNALS DEVOTED TO MUSIC. Newspapers began to be published in the early seventeenth century—Germany 1609, England (*Weekly Newes*) 1622. Periodicals other than newspapers date from 1665, when the French *Journal des Sçavans* (still existing) began, quickly to be followed in England by the *Philosophical Transactions* of the Royal Society (1665), which existed to report on research, invention, and discovery. What we may call magazines date from the early eighteenth century, when England has the credit of leading with *The Tatler* (1709) and *The Spectator* (1711), which were, of course, of an essay character.

It was not long before specialist musical journals appeared. Of these the earliest are German, Mattheson's *Musica Critica* (1722) and Telemann's *Der getreue Musik-Meister* (1728); a number of others followed, and by 1766 Germany had a weekly musical paper, the *Wöchentliche Nachrichten* (Leipzig). In the same year France saw its first musical review, *Sentiments d'un harmonophile sur différents Ouvrages de musique* ('Feelings of a Lover of Harmony on various Musical Works'; two issues only).

English musical periodical literature begins later, with the *New Musical and Universal Magazine* (monthly; 1774–5), the *Monthly Musical Journal* (1801, four issues only), the *Quarterly Musical Register* (1812, two issues only), and the *Quarterly Musical Magazine* (1818–28). Closely following these came the *Harmonicon* (1823–33) and the *Musical World* (1836–90). The oldest British musical journal now existing is the monthly, *Musical Times* (1844), and next to that are the *Monthly Musical Record* (1871–1961) and *Musical Opinion* (1877).

The earliest musical journal in the United States was the *American Musical Magazine* (New Haven, 1786; really no more than a selection of music). 'Gilbert's Musical Magazine', sometimes mentioned, was a music shop. A very important journal in the latter half of the nineteenth century was *Dwight's Journal of Music* (Boston, 1852–81).

Present-day quarterlies of serious value are in the United States the *Musical Quarterly* (1915), *Notes* (organ of the Music Library Association), and *Perspectives of New Music* (1962), and in Britain *Music and Letters* (1920) and *The Music Review* (1940). In most countries there are important publications devoted to the recording of research, issued by the various musicological societies; there are also a multilingual international journal of this type, *Acta Musicologica*, the organ of the International Musicological Society, and another, *Musica Disciplina; a Journal of the History of Music* (American Institute of Musicology, Rome; appears at irregular intervals).

No complete list of existing musical journals in the various countries is here attempted, as such a list would be very long, and quickly out of date. Throughout the history of musical journalism the starting, stopping, and amalgamation of journals have been incessant, and by the time this article is in print it may be no longer entirely trustworthy.

Enormous circulations in musical journalism

were reached in the United States. The weekly *Musical Courier* (1880–1962) and *Musical America* (1898–1964) had circulations far beyond those of any musical journals in Britain or perhaps in Europe. The circulation of the monthly *Étude* (1883–1957) at one time reached 250,000.

It would be ungrateful to close this article without referring to the high degree in which the present work is indebted to many of the journals, current and extinct, mentioned above, and to others whose names have not been cited. There is an enormous amount of useful information preserved in periodical musical literature such as has never found its way into books.

See also *Criticism of Music*.

JOYCE.

(1) PATRICK WESTON. Born at Ballyorgan, Co. Limerick, in 1827; died in Dublin in 1914, aged eighty-six. He grew up amidst opportunities of hearing Irish folk melodies and in adult years made a habit of keeping music paper by his bedside so that he might record such as came to his memory. In 1872 he published a volume of *Ancient Irish Music* and in 1909 a much more comprehensive and very valuable collection. He was also the author of books on Irish Social History, Irish Grammar, Irish Place-names, etc., and the translator of Irish classic tales. He was a professor in the Government Training College for Teachers and an LL.D.

Cf. *Bunting*.

(2) JAMES. See *History* 9.

JOYEUX, JOYEUSE (Fr., masc. and fem.). 'Joyous.'

JUBELND (Ger.). 'Jubilant.'

JUBILATE (1). The 100th Psalm, *Jubilate Deo* ('O be joyful in the Lord, all ye lands'); see *Common Prayer*.

(2) See *Alleluia*.

JUBILEE SINGERS. See *United States of America* 6.

JUBILI. See *Pneuma*.

JUDENHARFE (Ger.). 'Jew's harp' (q.v.).

JUDGE, JACK. See *Tipperary*.

JUGGLER, JUGLERE, etc. See *Minstrels*, etc. 1.

JUHAN, JAMES. See *Pianoforte* 5.

JUILLIARD FOUNDATION. See *United States of America* 5 f; *Patronage* 7; *Publishing* 9.

JUIVE, LA. See *Halévy*.

JUKE BOXES are automatic coin machines installed in American (and other) inns, etc., for the playing of gramophone records of the customer's choosing. 'Juke' is a southern name for a local inn, apparently ultimately derived from the Chaucerian English *jowken*, 'to rest or sleep'.)

JULIAN, REVD. JOHN (1839–1913). Author of the immense and valuable *Dictionary of Hymnology* (1892). See *Hymns and Hymn Tunes* 7; *Hymn Society*.

JULLIEN or **JULIEN, LOUIS ANTOINE** (1812–60; p. 240, pl. 44. 4). He was a French composer of dance music, and conductor of that and every other sort of orchestral music and of opera. His London Promenade Concerts had great popularity. He made immense sums and died in poverty and lunacy.

See *Quadrille*; *Concert* 7.

His full name was very imposing—'Louis George Maurice Adolph Roch Albert Abel Antonio Alexandre Noé Jean Lucien Daniel Eugène Joseph-le-brun Joseph Barème Thomas Thomas Thomas-Thomas Pierre-Cerbon Pierre-Maurel Barthelemi Artus Alphonse Bertrand Dieudonné Emanuel Josué Vincent Luc Michel Jules-de-la-plane Jules-Bazin Julio César Jullien.'

The explanation is as follows. He was born at the little French town of Sisteron, in the Basses Alpes. His father, Antonio, a good violinist, was invited to play a concerto at a concert of the Philharmonic Society.

'Meanwhile the good curé insisted that the child should be baptised, and Antonio thought it would be only polite to ask one of the members of the Philharmonic Society to stand as godfather. A difficulty arose when every member claimed this privilege, for there were thirty-six of them. So after much discussion it was decided that the baby should be held at the font by the secretary, and that he should be christened with the names of all the members of the society. Thus it was that the future great conductor acquired the long string of Christian names which in the future he found so useful when he required pseudonyms under which to publish some of his musical compositions.' (Carse, *Life of Jullien*, 1951).

'JUNGFERN' QUARTETTE (Haydn). See *Nicknamed Compositions* 12 (37–42).

'JUPITER' SYMPHONY (Mozart). See *Nicknamed Compositions* 15.

JUSQU'À (Fr.). 'Until.'

JUSTE (Fr.). 'Just' in sense of exact (e.g. in time or tune). So *Justesse*, 'exactitude'.

JUST INTONATION. See *Temperament* 7, 9.

K

K (followed by a number). See *Köchel*.

KABALEVSKY, DMITRI. Born in St. Petersburg in 1904. He is a pupil of Miaskovsky and thus a member of the Moscow group. He has written several symphonies, choral music, chamber music, etc., and is also a music critic.

KAFFIR PIANO. See *Marimba*; *Acoustics* 20; p. 512, pl. **91**. 3.

'KAISER' QUARTETT (Haydn). See *Emperor's Hymn*; *Nicknamed Compositions* 12.

KAJANUS, R. See *Scandinavia* 6.

KALDALÓNS. See *Scandinavia* 5.

KALEIDACOUSTICON. See *Composition* 14.

KALEVALA. See *Scandinavia* 6.

KALINNIKOF (Kalinnikov, Kalinnikow, etc.), VASSILY. Born in the government of Orel in 1866 and died at Yalta in 1901, aged thirty-five. He had a youth of poverty during which were sown the seeds of the consumption that brought about his premature death. After a short time as an assistant conductor of opera at Moscow he retired on grounds of health and devoted himself to composition, making his name, especially, with his effective first symphony, which has been much played in different parts of the world. A second symphony exists, as also chamber music, songs, etc.

For music in the Russian Church, to which he contributed, see *Greek Church* 5.

KALKBRENNER, FRIEDRICH WILHELM. Born in Germany in 1785 and died near Paris in 1849, aged sixty-three. He was a renowned pianist and teacher, and his fellow Parisian pianist, Chopin, dedicated to him his Concerto in E minor.

See reference under *Pianoforte* 18, 21; *Pianoforte Playing and Teaching* 2; *Clementi*; *Albéniz, Pedro II.*

KALLIWODA, JOHANNES WENCESLAUS. Born at Prague in 1801 and died at Karlsruhe in 1866, aged sixty-five. He was a violin virtuoso who held for over thirty years the position of Kapellmeister at the court of Donaueschingen. He wrote seven symphonies and much other music—at one time much played.

See reference under *Roman Catholic Church Music in Britain.*

KAMIENSKI, MATTHEW (1734-1821). See *Poland.*

KAMINSKI, HEINRICH. He was born near Waldshut in the Black Forest in 1886 and died near Munich in 1946. His composition was of a very polyphonic character. He wrote orchestral works, chamber music, choral music, etc., but is especially known by his opera *Jürg Jenatsch*, which is considered to be a work of unusual dramatic force and musical invention.

KAMMER (Ger.). 'Chamber.' So *Kammercantate*, 'Chamber cantata' (see *Cantata*); *Kammerduett*, *Kammertrio*, 'chamber duet', 'chamber trio' (i.e. for a room rather than a concert hall); *Kammerconcert*, *Kammerkonzert*, either 'chamber concert' or 'chamber concerto'; *Kammermusik*, 'chamber music'; *Kammersymphonie*, 'chamber symphony' (i.e. one for a small orchestra).

KAMMERTON. See *Pitch* 3.

KANDINSKY. See *Colour* 10; *Expressionism.*

KANON (Ger.) 'Canon.' For *Kanon in der Umkehrung* see *Umkehrung.*

KANTELE. Finnish variety of the gusli (q.v.), plucked with the fingers (see *Scandinavia* 6).

KAPELLE, KAPELLMEISTER, KAPELLMEISTERMUSIK. See *Chapel.*

KAPELLTON. See *Pitch* 8.

KARAPETOFF. See *Electric Musical Instruments* 2 b.

KARG-ELERT, SIGFRID. Born at Oberndorf-am-Neckar in 1877 and died at Leipzig in 1933, aged fifty-five. At first he was a pianist, then he turned composer and devoted himself particularly to the organ, for which he wrote a number of ingeniously contrived compositions, a good deal played and discussed. He wrote also for the harmonium, for the piano, stringed instruments, voices, etc.

See *Chorale Prelude*; *Reed-Organ Family* 9; *Clarinet Family* 6 (towards end); *Oboe Family* 6; *Flute Family* 6.

KARPELES, MAUD (1885-1976). See p. 364, pl. **59**. 6.

KARSAVINA. See *Ballet* 5, 9.

KASSATION or **CASSATION** (Ger.). See *Suite* 7.

KASTAGNETTEN (Ger.). 'Castanets.' See *Percussion Family* 3 q, 4 c, 5 q.

KASTALSKY (Kastalski, etc.), ALEXANDER. Born in Moscow in 1856 and died there in 1926, aged seventy. He was the son of a priest and became a great authority upon Russian church music and a prominent composer of it. (His other works are now practically forgotten.)

KASTNER, JEAN GEORGES (1810-67). See *Saxhorn* (note 1); *Saxophone Family.*

KATE O' GOWRIE. See *Lass o' Gowrie.*

KATHLEEN MAVOURNEEN. The words of this favourite song are by an Irishwoman, Mrs. Julia Crawford (of whom little is known), the tune by the Englishman F. N. Crouch (q.v.), who used to sing it himself with great success—as in 1892 at a banquet held in his honour at Portland, Maine, to celebrate his eighty-fourth birthday, and again in public at eighty-eight. He sold the song to a London publisher for £10 and the publisher made, it is said, £15,000 profit.

KATSWARRA. See *Kotzwara*.

KATUAR. See *Catoire*.

KATZENMUSIK. See *Charivari*.

KAUFMANN, J. G. and F. K. See *Mechanical Reproduction of Music* 9.

KAUM (Ger.). 'Barely.'

KAY, ULYSSES. Born at Tucson, Arizona, in 1917. A Negro who studied at the University of his native place and at the Eastman School, and then at the Berkshire Music Center and the Yale School of Music. During the second World War he served in the U.S. Navy, and on return to civil life he won a number of important awards, including the Rosenwald Fellowship. His work includes chamber music, choral music, and a considerable amount of orchestral music.

KAZOO. See *Mirliton*.

KB. Short for *Kontrabass*, i.e. 'double bass'.

K.B.E., K.C.V.O. See *Knighthood and other Honours* 3.

KEACH.

(1) BENJAMIN (1640–1704). See *Baptist Churches and Music* 2.

(2) ELIAS. See *Baptist Churches and Music* 6.

KEATS, JOHN. See *Choral Symphony*.

KECK (Ger.). 'Audacious.' So *Keckheit*, 'audacity'.

KEEL ROW. This song is closely associated with the district of Newcastle and Tyneside generally, though its first appearance in print seems to be in an Edinburgh publication (*A Collection of favourite Scots Tunes*; about 1770). There is thus a contention as to its origin.

'Keel' means a boat, and the Tyneside words represent a lassie singing 'Weel may the keel row . . . that my laddie's in'.

The tune resembles several English country dances, including one printed in a *Choice Collection* of 1748. The tune of a song called 'The Dumb Waiter', printed 1751, is evidently another version.

KEEN. See *Caoine*.

KEEP THE HOME FIRES BURNING. This song, popular with British and American soldiers and civilians during the first World War, is, as to the music, the work of the actor–playwright–filmwright–composer Ivor Novello (1893–1951). He wrote it at the request of his mother, the well-known choral conductor Clara Novello Davies, who felt that 'Tipperary' (q.v.) had 'become tiresome through months

of iteration'—which, it may be suggested, this substitute became in its turn.

The verses are, in the main, the work of an American lady in London, Mrs. Lena Guilbert Ford, to whom the composer supplied the tune with the first line of the words, leaving her to do the rest. It is said that half an hour accounted for the fashioning of both music and verses, and that the composer made just about £16,000 out of it. Mrs. Ford was killed in a London air raid in 1918.

KEGELSTATT-TRIO (Mozart). See *Nicknamed* 15 (K. 498).

KEINESWEGS (Ger.). 'In no way.'

KEISER, REINHARD. Born near Leipzig in 1674 and died at Hamburg in 1739, aged sixty-five. He is of historical importance on account of his long association with the opera at Hamburg; he composed not only operas, however, but oratorios, some remarkable settings of the Passion, etc.

See references under *Opera* 9 a; *Passion Music* 4; *Folia*; *Horn Family* 3; *Scandinavia* 2.

KEITH PROWSE. See *Publishing of Music* 7.

KÉLER-BÉLA (originally Albert von Keller). Born in 1820 at Bartfeld (Bardiov) in Hungary (now in Czechoslovakia), and died at Wiesbaden in 1882, aged sixty-two. He was a famous waltz-conductor in the tradition of Gung'l and Lanner. His works are of the better 'popular' order, and they still have wide currency.

KELLIE, EDWARD. See *Scotland* 6.

KELLY.

(1) MICHAEL. Born in Dublin in 1762 and died at Margate in 1826, aged sixty-three. He was an Irish tenor singer and theatre composer, friend in Vienna of Mozart, and participant in the first performance of *Figaro*. His *Reminiscences* (2 vols., 1826; compiled for him by Theodore Hook) are a useful, though not uniformly reliable, source of information on the period.

See reference under *Waltz*.

(2) EARL OF (Thomas Alexander Erskine; p. 945, pl. **160**. 2.). Born in 1732 and died in Brussels in 1781. He was a violinist and a prolific and much-performed composer of symphonies, overtures, sonatas, etc. (a pupil of Stamitz). As a loyal Scot he was active in Edinburgh music-making, but he also travelled much abroad, where, as in Britain, his music (much of which was published) seems to have been appreciated.

KELWAY (The Brothers).

(1) THOMAS. Probably born at Chichester, and died there in 1744 (not 1749—a mistake due to a careless repair of his tombstone). As a boy he was a chorister in Chichester Cathedral, as a man its organist. Some of his church music is in regular use in the English Church.

(2) JOSEPH. Died probably in 1782. He was

a very noted organist, admired of Handel; he published harpsichord sonatas. He is sometimes spoken of as a son of Thomas, but this appears to be an error.

See reference under *Wesley Family* 3.

KEMP (or **Kempe**), **WILLIAM**. Famous dancer and comic actor of the late sixteenth and early seventeenth centuries, a colleague of Shakespeare, and a performer in his plays (Peter in *Romeo and Juliet*; Dogberry in *Much Ado*). His book *Kemp's Nine Daies Wonder, Performed in a Daunce from London to Norwich* records his most famous dancing feat.

See *Morris*; *Jig*; *Scandinavia* 2.

KEN, BISHOP (1637–1711). Bishop of Bath and Wells. See references under *Tallis's Canon*; *Doxology*; *Hymns and Hymn Tunes* 7.

KENNEDY-FRASER, MARJORY (p. 364, pl. **59**. 2). Born at Perth in 1857 and died in Edinburgh in 1930, aged seventy-three. She was a daughter of David Kennedy (1825–86), a singer of Scots songs known all over the British Empire and the United States, with whom, and with other members of the family, she journeyed (often as his accompanist) on many of his travels. Her life-work was the collection, arrangement, and publication of the songs of the Hebrides, of which she also gave innumerable recitals. She published an autobiographical volume of great interest. One of her sisters was the wife of Tobias Matthay (q.v.).

See *Scotland* 1; *Clàrsach*; *Melody* 5. Also p. 452, pl. **78**. 7; p. 945, pl. **160**. 4.

KENNEDY SCOTT, CHARLES. See *Scott*.

KENT BUGLE. Key bugle. See *Cornett and Key Bugle Families* 1, 2 h, 3 h, 4 h.

KENT, JAMES. Born at Winchester in 1700 and died there in 1776, aged seventy-six. He was organist of Trinity College, Cambridge, and then of Winchester Cathedral and College. He wrote church music (and stole other people's, incorporating long sections in his own works, e.g. movements of Bassani, q.v.). He is still to be heard in cathedrals. His 'Hear my prayer' used to be a great favourite.

See *Anthem*, Period III; *Bassani, G. B.*

KEPPEL, LADY CAROLINE. See *Robin Adair*.

KERAULOPHON. See *Organ* 14 II, III.

KERLE, JACOBUS VAN. Born at Ypres c. 1531–2 and died at Prague in 1591. He composed motets, masses, etc., and by the triweekly performance at the Council of Trent (in its later sessions, 1562–3) of his clear and impressive *Preces speciales*, induced the cardinals and bishops to retain in use polyphonic music.

KERLL (or **Kerl**), JOHANN CASPAR. Born at Adorf, Saxony, in 1627 and died in Munich in 1693, aged sixty-five. After studying in Italy (probably under Frescobaldi) he became celebrated as organist and composer for the organ and for other instruments, and for

the voice, his compositions including operas, masses, and motets. His working life was divided between Munich (where he was court Capellmeister) and Vienna (where he was court and cathedral organist). His works influenced Handel, whose 'Egypt was glad' in *Israel in Egypt* is 'borrowed' from one of his canzone.

See *Temperament* 5.

KERMAN, JOSEPH. Born in London, of American parents, in 1924. He studied at Princeton, and from 1951 taught at Berkeley, Calif. Professor of Music at Oxford, 1971. He has written books on the Elizabethan madrigal, on opera, and on Beethoven's quartets.

KERN, JEROME (1885–1945). See p. 1060, pl. **173**. 3.

KERNSTOCK, OTTOKAR. See *Emperor's Hymn*.

KES, WILLEM. Born at Dordrecht in 1856 and died at Munich in 1934, aged seventy-eight. He was a violinist and the first conductor of the Concertgebouw orchestra of Amsterdam (see *Holland* 9), for two years (1896–8) conductor of the Scottish Orchestra, afterwards holding positions in Moscow, Dresden, and Coblenz. He composed orchestral and other music.

KETÈLBEY, ALBERT W. Born at Birmingham in 1875 and died at Cowes, I.O.W., in 1959, aged eighty-four. At the age of thirteen he won a scholarship in composition at Trinity College, London. His early musical career was largely as a theatre conductor. He composed chamber and orchestral works, and then turned to the production of instrumental works of a much lighter and more 'popular' type: *In a Monastery Garden*, *In a Persian Market*, etc. These have had a world success. He also used the pseudonym of 'Anton Vodorinski'.

He also worked as music editor, and as music director of the Columbia Graphophone Co.

KETHE, WILLIAM (died about 1608). See *Old Hundredth*.

KETTLEDRUM. See *Percussion Instruments* 2 a, 4 a, 5 a.

'KETTLEDRUM' MASS (Haydn). See *Nicknamed Compositions* 13.

KEY. Key is a quality that gradually crept into European music during the sixteenth century and began gradually to creep out of it from the beginning of the twentieth. So far, then, from being, as many people have taken for granted, a fundamental element in music it appears (alarmingly to some) to be a mere passing phenomenon. But Time has not yet fully declared its intentions.

The principle of key is that of the construction of melody and harmony, at any given moment, out of a scale of which all the notes bear a strong and easily recognized allegiance to a chief note ('key-note' or 'tonic'). The same scale can be taken at different pitches, and consequently any melody or harmony in one key can be taken also in another key, the effect being precisely the same but for pitch. The melody or series of harmonies may move from key to key ('modulate'), but the piece will return to its original key to end. In fact, the feeling of 'home' is the essence of key. The key-note is the home note of the scale and the opening key of a composition is the home key. There are two modes of every key, the major and the minor; they differ from one another merely by two notes—the third and sixth being a semitone lower in the minor than in the major. For the principle of 'related keys' see *Modulation*.

There are ways of using incidental notes extraneous to the key without destroying the 'home' feeling; such notes are called 'Chromatic', the notes of the key itself being 'Diatonic'.

The key of a piece is often stated for purposes of identification (e.g. 'Sonata in A minor') and in the case of a piece in several movements it is that of the first movement (usually the same as that of the last one) that governs the designation.

For side-lights on the whole general question of key see *Scales* (whatever relates to the major and minor); *Modulation*; *Harmony*; *Diatonic*; *Colour and Music*; *Form*; *Tonic Sol-fa*.
For key in suites see *Suite* 2, 3, 4, 5.
A cognate subject is that of *Modes* (q.v.).

KEY, FRANCIS SCOTT. See *Star-spangled Banner*.

KEYBOARD

(For illustrations see p. 560, pl. **101**.)

1. Introduction. The purpose of keyboards is to enable the hand (hurdy-gurdy, accordion), the two hands (pianoforte, harmonium, etc.), or the hands and feet (organ) readily to control the sounds from a much larger number of strings, reeds, or pipes than could otherwise be controlled.

One standardized keyboard has been universally adopted. It is by no means the most convenient imaginable, but the conservatism of musicians will probably refuse to part with it until some drastic change in the scales used in music (e.g. by the acceptance of quarter tones, see *Harmony* 19, 23; *Microtones*) compels them to do so.

One very obvious and enormous disadvantage is the number of different fingerings the keyboard imposes for the different scales. The explanation for this is that the original keyboard came into existence when music was mainly vocal and of a far simpler character, and that the few additions afterwards introduced had to be adapted to what already existed.

2. The Course of Evolution. The earliest keyboard was that of the organ, on which at the time of its introduction merely the simplest *melodies* (single lines of notes) were played. Passing over the early days when each key was so broad and heavy as to require the blow of a fist (hence the name 'organ-beater' for organist), and coming to later times when something like our present finger-keyboard had come into use (thirteenth to fourteenth centuries), we find ourselves, so far as the material of music is concerned, still in the period of the Modes; the series C, D, E, F, G, A, B, C was, then, the basis of music, and the earliest keyboards represented this, being made up of what today we should call the 'white' finger-keys.

As explained in the article *Modes* (q.v.) and *Musica Ficta* (q.v.), the interval of an augmented fourth from F to B was felt to be ob-noxious and the objection was often removed by lowering or 'flattening' the B. This brought an extra note into music, and on the keyboard room was found for it by cutting away a part of the A and B and placing the B flat, as a short narrow finger-key, between these (p. 560, pl. **101**. 1). It appears from a statement of Praetorius (q.v.) that a few keyboards of this kind were actually still to be seen at the time he wrote (1619).

As explained in the article *Modes*, after the B flat the following notes were successively introduced, probably in this order: F sharp, E flat, C sharp, and G sharp, and then the modal system began to break up and our modern key-system to be recognized. These notes were provided for on the keyboard as the B flat had been, i.e. by insertion of short finger-keys between the longer existing ones.

Thus came about our keyboard as we have it today, which, despite the enormous changes in the nature of the music to be played by its means, has itself undergone no change whatever since about 1450 save a little variety in the width of the finger-keys and the colouring of the short and long keys respectively as white and black or black and white.

3. The Missing Enharmonics. Apart from the inconveniences already mentioned, it is clear that many notes were not represented on the keyboard at all. If C sharp is there, where is D flat? If E flat is there, where is D sharp? If F is there, where is E sharp? And so on (see *Enharmonic Intervals*).

To supply all the naturals, flats, sharps, double flats, and double sharps would, of course, be impossible. Experimental keyboards which did this have been devised by ingenious acousticians (see *Vicentino* for a forerunner of these), but they are not sufficiently capable of manipulation to be of practical value to the artist. General Perronet Thompson in the mid-nineteenth century (p. 560, pl. **101**. 5), and Bosanquet in the 1880s made harmoniums for scientific purposes, with seventy-two and eighty-four finger-keys to the octave respectively. Keyboard music must, apparently, always remain under restrictions.

One main restriction, then, up to the middle of the eighteenth century was that of the number of keys in which an organist, harpsichordist, or clavichordist could play. If the harpsichord music of, say, Purcell, Couperin, Rameau, or Handel, or the organ music of Bach, be examined it will be found that the pieces are set in a narrow range of keys and that their modulations are more limited than those of today. In using even these few keys some falsification (and consequent pain to the ear—greater or lesser according to its sensitiveness) was inevitable, since no system of tuning could give perfect results in even this somewhat limited number (cf. *Temperament* 5).

In Bach's *Well-Tempered Clavier* (see *Temperament* 5) we see the whole range of twelve major and twelve minor keys boldly adopted, but this was achieved by a system of compromise-tuning which gave no key dead in tune but all equally, if slightly, out of tune (see *Temperament*, in which some apparent predecessors of Bach in this reform are incidentally mentioned). Our ordinary notation provides for seven each of naturals, sharps, flats, double sharps, and double flats, i.e. thirty-five notes in all, and the Equal-Temperament system makes all equally available by the use of twelve finger-keys.

It is evident that the development of music had been very much limited by the faults of the keyboard and that Bach's plan (not that he was the first to think of it: see the article referred to above) is merely a common-sense evasion.

Essentially this kind of fault (as distinct from the kind of fault mentioned earlier; see 1) springs from he fact that, for practical purposes, the octave must be brought within the comfortable average span of the thumb and little finger (i.e. about 7 inches) and that the finger-keys between these extremes must be few enough and broad enough for easy use. Ideally the octave-span should accommodate many more finger-keys than at present, and these would all be equal in width, height, and length (and hence in leverage): but this ideal is forever unattainable. The hand is man's best tool for the making of instrumental music, but it is clearly not fully suited to its task.

At one period (see *Temperament* 8) a slight alleviation as to tuning was attempted by cutting one or more of the short finger-keys in two so that the back and front portions could bring into play two different strings or pipes, and thus for any short key so divided an extra note could be added to the series (for instance, A flat was thus added to G sharp and D sharp to E flat). This expedient was abandoned when the more comprehensive one of Equal Temperament was realized to be practicable.

4. Modern Attempts at Perfection. Attempted improvements of the keyboard from the point of view of easier manipulation have often taken the shape of placing one or more others behind it, so arranged as to distance and height as to be readily accessible, the fingers passing freely from one to another or even one finger playing on one keyboard and another or others of the same hand on another keyboard simultaneously.

The first such attempt was made as early as 1555 or 1560. And possibly since then there has never been a time when somebody was not worrying over the problem. The most elaborate attempt so far has been that of the Janko Keyboard, patented in 1882 by the Hungarian Paul von Janko, devised on the general basis of the suggestions (1862) of the Viennese musician H. J. Vincent. This (p. 560, pl. **101**. 2) had six rows of short finger-keys so placed in relation to one another that the fingers could easily wander anywhere on them, as they do on the several rows of a typewriter keyboard, any particular note being playable from three of them. On each row the notes were arranged as a whole-tone series, in three of them C, D, E, F sharp, G sharp, A sharp, C, and in the other three C sharp, D sharp, F, G, A, B, C sharp. The C rows and the C sharp rows were alternated with one another in order, i.e. the first, third, and fifth rows had the C series and the second, fourth, and sixth the C sharp series. All the finger-keys were of the same length and width, but those which on the normal piano are short had a black band down them, as a concession to pianists accustomed to find their way about the normal keyboard. The finger-keys were narrow and the span of the octave was much diminished; consequently wider intervals could be spanned and large chords were easy. All major scales had the same fingering and so had all minor scales. Transposition became so easy that any infant player could play equally well in any key any piece within his capacity. Public demonstrations were given to show the increased facility offered and much interest was aroused. Liszt and Rubinstein praised the system. It was quite believed by many musicians for some years that the Janko Keyboard would supersede the existing one; in Vienna a society for its promotion long hopefully survived, a number of German manufacturers being prepared to supply their instruments fitted with it. It has had supporters in the United States.

Other attempts followed the Janko (e.g. the Adam Keyboard, 1901; the Durand Keyboard, 1904; the Kuba Keyboard, 1907; and the Nordbo Keyboard, 1915). The 'Clavier Hans' (1917; p. 560, pl. **101**. 6) was an intelligent attempt by a Belgian engineer to profit by some of the main principles of the Janko Keyboard, whilst reducing the rows of keys to two and bowing to tradition by retaining the appearance and long-and-short key arrangement of the traditional keyboard.

A French invention of the 1870s aimed, very logically, at rectifying the mistake of nature in providing pianists with hands in which the fingers are arranged in reverse order; each hand had its own keyboard (one above the other) and the finger-keys of the left-hand keyboard were what we may call a mirror-reversal of those of the right-hand keyboard (which was our normal one). Thus, whilst a scale on the right-hand keyboard ascended from left to right, on the left-hand keyboard it ascended from right to left: hence, any passage or chord whatever was fingered identically by both hands. The inventor of this instrument was E. J. Mangeot, and he created a sensation with it at the Paris Exhibition of 1878.

The piano of Emanuel Moór (1863–1931) has two rows of keys, both of them just like those of the normal instrument. The upper row operates an octave higher than the lower. The two rows are so placed in relation to one another that the hand can pass easily from one to the other and even play on both together; by the latter device scales of tenths can be played as scales of thirds, and so forth. The two keyboards can be instantaneously coupled so that a passage in single notes becomes one in octaves. The Moór invention was introduced in 1921 and was demonstrated with success in Europe and America. It suffered the disadvantage of appearing at a time of severe economic depression. The instruments were manufactured by Messrs. Blüthner and had some use. Obviously this keyboard does not profess to offer all the advantages sought by some of its predecessors, but, on the other hand, it offers certain advantages foreign to them.

Dumb keyboards have been used from time to time for piano practice painless to the neighbours and also (especially since about 1920) for class-instruction in piano playing.

For the Clutsam Keyboard, curved and concave (one of several concave keyboards that have at various periods been introduced) see p. 560, pl. **101**. 4.

5. Keyboard Compass. The earliest clavichords had only about two and a half octaves; in the seventeenth century they had up to four (Bach's compass in his '48': his first book has not so big a compass as his second—if we take into account all autograph copies. It is, of course, not certain which of the compositions in the two books are intended for clavichord and which for harpsichord).

Instruments of the harpsichord family tended to exceed the compass of the clavichord; in the South Kensington Museum there is an actual harpsichord of 1521 (the oldest known) with a compass of nearly four octaves. Bach's (described under *Harpsichord* 6) had over five.

English organs, up to the middle of the nineteenth century, often had a compass beginning at G an octave below the bass stave; when pedals became common the lowest notes were cut off and C below the bass stave became the lowest note.

For the compass of the domestic keyboard instruments at various times see *Pianoforte* 13.

For a peculiarity of the lowest part of the keyboards of old organs, harpsichords, etc., see the article *Short Octave and Broken Octave*.

For systems of fingering at different periods see *Fingering*, sections 1–3.

KEY BUGLE or **KEYED BUGLE.** See *Cornett and Key Bugle Families* 1, 2 h, 3, 4 h; *Cornet* 2.

KEYED HARMONICA. See *Harmonica* 3, 6.

KEYED HORN. See *Cornett and Key Bugle Families* 2 e, 3 e, 4 e.

KEYED TRUMPET. See *Trumpet Family* 3.

KEY-NOTE. The principal (and lowest) note of the scale out of which a passage is constructed. Same as *Tonic*.

KEYS, IVOR CHRISTOPHER BANFIELD. Born at Littlehampton in 1919. He was educated at Christ Church, Oxford and the Royal College of Music. In 1947 he became Lecturer in Music at Queen's College, Belfast, and in 1951 Professor there. 1954, Nottingham University; 1968, Birmingham. His compositions range over various forms.

KEY SIGNATURE. See *Signature*. Also Table 8.

KHANDOSHKIN, IVAN (1747 or 1748–1804). He was the son of a Russian peasant but, by the generosity of a wealthy man, was given the opportunity of studying violin and composition in Italy—the former with Tartini at Padua. He adopted a style similar to that of J. S. Bach.

KHATCHATURIAN, ARAM (p. 913, pl. **156**. 7). Born at Tiflis, in Georgia, in 1903; died 1978. He was by parentage an Armenian. He

was trained at the Conservatory of Moscow and became one of the most widely known Soviet composers (*Poem for Stalin*, 1938; Stalin Prize for the ballet, *Gayaneh*). His works include symphonies, concertos for piano, for violin, and for violoncello, etc.

See *Concerto* 6 c (1903); *Russia* 8.

KHRENNIKOF, TIKHON. Born at Eletz, Russia, in 1913. He has written two symphonies and an opera, *In the Storm*. In 1948 he became a dominant political power and violently attacked Prokofief for an alleged decadence in his style and a lack of Soviet consciousness.

See *Opera* 25 f (1939); *Russia* 8.

KIDSON, FRANK (p. 364, pl. **59**. 1). Born at Leeds in 1855 and died there in 1926, aged nearly seventy-one. Without any definite musical training, but possessed of enormous enthusiasm and a small independent income, he gave his whole life to the collection and study of early British song and dance music, whether traditional or composed. He published very valuable books on British Music Publishers (see *Dictionaries* 4), *The Beggar's Opera*, etc.

See references under *Folk Song* 3; *Scotland* 1; *Moffat, Alfred*; *British Grenadiers*; *Ye Banks and Braes*; *Camp-*

bells are coming; Monk's March; Brenhines Dido; St. Patrick's Day; Bells of Aberdovey; Barley Shot; First of August.

KIELFLÜGEL (Ger.). Harpsichord (*Kiel* = 'quill'; *Flügel* = 'wing'. Alluding to the plucking medium and the general shape).

KIENZL, WILHELM. He was born at Waizenkirchen, in Austria, in 1857 and died in Vienna in 1941, aged eighty-four. He studied at the Conservatory of Prague and then at Munich under Rheinberger. He was encouraged by Liszt, who saw his promise, and for a time associated with Wagner, whose influence is to be seen in his operas. *Der Evangelimann* ('The Apostle'; 1894) has had enormous popularity, as has *Der Kuhreigen* ('Ranz des Vaches', q.v.; 1911).

He wrote choral, orchestral, and chamber music, many songs, a book on Wagner, an autobiography, etc.

KIEPURA, JAN. See *Encore*.

KILPINEN, YRIÖ. Born at Helsingfors in 1892 and died there in 1959, aged sixty-seven. He studied in Berlin and Vienna and then taught in the Conservatory of Helsingfors. The Finnish Government gave him a small life-pension (cf. *Sibelius*) so that he might devote himself to composition. He wrote over 800 songs (more than Schubert), and several sonatas and other works for the piano. His idiom is not that of his own generation, but rather that of the 1890s.

KIND, KINDER (Ger.). 'Child', 'children'.

KINDERGARTEN MOVEMENT. See *Education* 1.

KINDERSTÜCK (Ger.). 'Children's piece.'

KINDERSYMPHONIE. See *Toy Symphony*.

KINDLICH (Ger.). 'Childlike.'

KING.

(1) WILLIAM I (1624–80). He was chaplain of Magdalen College, Oxford, and then organist of New College. He wrote some church music and songs.

(2) WILLIAM II (1663–1712). The miscellaneous writer and judge. See reference under *Barber Shop Music*.

(3) CHARLES (1687–1748). He was Master of the Choristers of St. Paul's Cathedral, London, and the composer of services and anthems.

(4) ROBERT. An active composer of the late seventeenth and early eighteenth centuries (B.Mus., Cambridge, 1696; living in 1711). He composed many songs and set Shadwell's *Ode on St. Cecilia's Day*.

(5) ALEXANDER HYATT. Born at Beckenham in 1911. He was educated at Cambridge. Since 1934 he has been a member of the staff of the British Museum and since 1945 in charge of its collection of printed music. He is Hon. Secretary of the Council of the Union-Catalogue of Printed Music, Chairman of the Executive Committee of the British Institute of Recorded Sound, a Vice-President of the International Association of Music Libraries, and the author of many articles in musical periodicals.

KING JAMES'S MARCH. See *Lochaber no more*.

KING OF THE MINSTRELS. See *Profession of Music* 3.

KING'S CONCERTS. See *Concert* 6.

KING'S LYNN. See *Minstrels* 3.

KINKELDEY, OTTO. Born in New York in 1878 and died at Orange, N.J., in 1966, aged eighty-seven. Distinguished musicologist. He held important professional positions in the United States and in Germany, was Chief of the Music Division in the New York Public Library, and Librarian and Professor of Cornell University, N.Y. (retired 1946).

KINLOCK, WILLIAM. See *Scotland* 7.

KIPLING, RUDYARD. See *Agincourt Song*.

KIRBY, PERCIVAL ROBSON. Born at Aberdeen in 1887. Professor of Music in the University of the Witwatersrand, Johannesburg, retiring 1949. Author of *The Musical Instruments of the Natives of South Africa* (1934), *The Kettle-drums* (1930), etc.

See references under *Jew's Harp; Harmony* 4.

KIRBYE, GEORGE. Died at Bury St. Edmunds in 1634. He was apparently house-musician to a gentleman of Bury St. Edmunds, and he wrote a considerable number of fine madrigals and some church music—beyond which what is known of him is not of importance or of interest except to the most fanatical antiquary.

KIRCHE (Ger.). 'Church.'

KIRCHENCANTATE (Ger.). 'Church cantata' (see *Cantata*).

KIRCHER, ATHANASIUS (1602–80). See *Colour and Music* 6; *Composition* 14.

KIRCHNER, (1) THEODOR (1823–1903). He was a German composer of the Schumann lineage. His songs and his piano works constitute his most notable contribution to the repertory.

(2) LEON. Born in Brooklyn, New York, in 1919. He is a pupil of Schönberg and Roger Sessions. After teaching in California he joined the staff of Buffalo University in 1959. His compositions include a piano concerto, songs, and chamber music.

KIRKWALL, EARL OF. See *Mechanical Reproduction of Music* 11.

KIRNBERGER, JOHANN PHILIPP (1721–83). He was a pupil of Bach, a violinist, composer, and theorist. He left a variety of compositions and (especially) many theoretical works.

See references under *Mechanical Reproduction of Music* 5; *Composition* 14.

KISSENTANZ (Ger.). 'Cushion dance' (q.v.).

KIT. A small bowed stringed instrument used

by eighteenth- and early nineteenth-century dancing-masters. It was literally a pocket fiddle and the French name *Pochette* (from 'poche'— pocket) records the fact (though 'Kit' seems properly to have referred to a true violin in small size and 'Pochette' to a long, narrow type with rounded back).

KITSON, CHARLES HERBERT. Born at Leyburn, Yorks., in 1874 and died in London in 1944, aged sixty-nine. He was organist of Christ Church Cathedral, Dublin (1913–20), and Professor of Music at Dublin University (1920–35), and later taught at the Royal College of Music, London. His various textbooks in different branches of composition, and especially *The Art of Counterpoint*, had great influence in introducing less academic methods of training.

KJERULF, HALFDAN CHARLES. Born at Oslo (then Christiania), Norway, in 1815 and died there in 1868, aged nearly fifty-three. He was a very successful composer of songs, men's voice choral music, and (in a lesser measure) pianoforte music. His art had a national character and was praised by Grieg.

He began life as a law student, turned to music, like Grieg received a government grant for study abroad, and (again like Grieg) became a friend of the national poet Björnson and strove ardently for a higher musical culture in the capital of his country.

When he died the nation lamented.

See *Scandinavia* 3.

Kl. Short for *Klarinette*, i.e. 'clarinet'.

KLAGEND, KLÄGLICH (Ger.). 'Lamenting.'

KLANGFARBE. See *Colour and Music* 3.

KLAPPENHORN (Ger.). Key bugle (*Klappen* means 'keys'). See *Cornett and Key Bugle Families* 2 h, 3 h, 4 h.

KLAR (Ger.). 'Clear', distinct (various grammatical endings, as *klare*, *klaren*).

KLARINETTE, KLARINETTEN. 'Clarinet', 'clarinets'. See *Clarinet Family* 5.

KLAVARSKRIBO. See *Notation* 7.

KLAVIATUR (Ger.). Keyboard.

KLAVIATURHARMONIKA. See *Harmonica* 1, 6 b.

KLAVIER or CLAVIER. German for 'keyboard instrument'. The word is used familiarly for whatever domestic keyboard instrument is in fashion; thus at one period it means 'harpsichord' and at a later period 'pianoforte'. Sometimes the word is used specifically for 'clavichord'. Often it means clavichord or harpsichord indifferently and perhaps early piano, also—at the period when all these instruments were in common use. It is also used for the manuals of the organ (q.v.).

Bach's *Wohltemperirtes Klavier* (the title of his '48' Preludes and Fugues; see *Temperament* 5) has been thought by most authorities (e.g. Dolmetsch, q.v.) to be a clavichord, but by others (e.g. Landowska, q.v.) to be a harpsi-

chord (see *Clavichord* 5). Probably it was neither specifically. When a word is loosely used, sometimes for a generic and sometimes for a specific description, confusion is bound to occur. (Some editors have substituted 'Clavichord' for 'Klavier' in the title of this work; this is certainly unwarranted.)

In German parlance of today, *Klavier* meaning 'pianoforte', *Klavierstück* means 'piano piece'; *Klavierauszug*, 'piano arrangement'; *Klavierübungen*, 'piano exercises', etc.

KLEČKI. See *Kletzki*.

KLEIN.

(1) HERMAN (1856–1934). Well-known London singing-master, and music critic in New York (1902–9) and London, who was associated with the Garcias (q.v.).

(2) ADRIAN BERNARD. Son of the above. See *Colour and Music* 10.

KLEIN (Ger.). 'Small' (or, of intervals, 'minor').

KLEIN DISCANT ZINK. See *Cornett and Key Bugle Families* 4 a.

KLEINE FLÖTE or KLEINFLÖTE. See *Flute Family* 5 b; *Organ* 14 II.

KLEINE ORGELMESSE (Haydn). See *Nick-named Compositions* 13.

KLEINE TROMMEL. Literally 'small drum', i.e. the side drum; otherwise 'snare drum'. See *Percussion Family* 3 i, 4 b, 5 i.

KLEMPERER, OTTO (1885–1973). See *Germany* 9 a.

KLENAU, PAUL AUGUST VON. Born in Copenhagen in 1883 and there died in 1946, aged sixty-three. He had a successful career as opera and orchestral conductor, first in Germany and then in his native country, and wrote operas, orchestral works, choral works, piano works, etc., somewhat lyrical in style and sensitive in their expression of mood. He lived for a time in London and wrote a 'Hampstead Heath Bank Holiday' Scherzo.

See *Opera* 24 f (1937).

KLENGEL.

(1) AUGUST ALEXANDER. Born at Dresden in 1783 and there died in 1852, aged sixty-nine. He was a pupil of Clementi and (like Field, q.v.) accompanied him to St. Petersburg and there remained for a time.

He became court organist at Dresden and won special renown as a writer of (amongst much other music) quantities of canons and fugues—including two sets in all the twenty-four keys—like Bach's '48'. (Cf. *Temperament* 5.)

(2) PAUL. Born at Leipzig in 1854 and there died in 1935, aged eighty; brother of Julius (below). He was a composer of songs, pianist, violinist, conductor, and writer on music.

(3) JULIUS. Born at Leipzig in 1859 and there died in 1933, aged seventy-four; brother of Paul (above). He was a notable cellist and composer of string music—especially music for his own instrument.

KLENOVSKY.

(1) NIKOLAI SEMENOVITCH (1857–1915). He was a Russian composer of ballets and other stage music, cantatas, orchestral works, etc.

(2) PAUL. A pen-name of Sir Henry Wood (q.v.)—a whimsical borrowing from the Russian (Klen = 'maple tree', Klenovsky meaning 'one of the family of the maple tree').

KLETZKI (KLECKI), PAUL. Born at Łódź, Poland, in 1900, and died at Liverpool in 1973. He played in public at thirteen, as a violinist, then studied at the University of Warsaw, the State Conservatory there, and the Hochschule at Berlin. His early career as conductor took him to many of the chief cities of Europe and in 1932 he was nominated by Furtwängler as conductor of the Berlin Philharmonic Orchestra, but owing to the coming into power of the Nazi party he became an exile. After the second World War he entered on a new career as an international conductor. His compositions, which have been widely performed, include two symphonies, a *Prelude to a Tragedy*, violin and piano concertos, chamber music, etc.

Kl. Fl. Short for *Kleine Flöte*, i.e. piccolo.

KLINDWORTH, KARL. Born at Hanover in 1830 and died at Stolpe-bei-Oranienburg in Prussia in 1916, aged eighty-five. His name is known to pianists as that of a painstaking editor of the classics (particularly of Chopin) and the official 'arranger' for piano of Wagner's *Ring*. For fourteen years in earlier life he lived and worked in London.

KLINGEN (Ger.). 'To sound.' So *Klingend*, 'resonant'.

KLOSÉ, HYACINTH ELÉANORE (1808–80). Born at Corfu, he spent his life in France, where he had great repute as a clarinettist and writer of tutors for clarinet and saxophone.

See reference under *Clarinet Family* 2.

KNARRE (Ger.). Rattle. See *Percussion* 3 r, 5 r.

KNECHT, JUSTIN HEINRICH (1752–1817). He was a well-known organist, composer, conductor, and concert manager, and a voluminous theatrical writer. He is now remembered by two circumstances: (*a*) he composed a symphony, a piece of programme music of which the scheme anticipates that of Beethoven's 'Pastoral' Symphony, and (*b*) he was a pioneer of the annotated programme (see *Annotated Programmes* 2).

KNEIFEND (Ger.). 'Plucking' (same as *Pizzicato*).

KNEISEL QUARTET. See *United States* 4.

KNELLER HALL. See *Degrees and Diplomas* 2; *Military Band*.

KNIGHT, G. H. H. See *Royal School of Church Music*.

KNIGHTHOOD AND OTHER HONOURS. For the history of knighthood and particulars of the order in various countries the article 'Knighthood and Chivalry' in the *Encyclopædia Britannica*, or similar articles in general works of reference, may be consulted.

The two knighthoods that most commonly come to notice in connection with music seem to be the Papal Order of the Golden Spur, which dates from 1559, and British knighthood (usually but not invariably that of 'Knight Bachelor', i.e. not involving membership of any order). It is impossible in this short article to discuss other knighthoods than these.

Amongst musicians upon whom the Knighthood of the Golden Spur has been conferred are Orlandus Lassus (1571), A. Scarlatti (1716), Gluck (1756), Dittersdorf (1770), Mozart (1770), and Paganini (1827).

Probably the list could be very greatly extended, as this order was very freely conferred at certain periods. Some of the recipients do not seem to have made much use of the distinction. Mozart hardly did after boyhood (he was a knight at fourteen!); on the other hand, Gluck on his title-pages punctiliously styled himself 'Chevalier' or 'Ritter von Gluck'. Some of these musicians received higher honours in addition. Orlandus Lassus, for instance, had already received an hereditary patent of nobility from the Emperor Maximilian, with 'the grant of a coat of arms' (in which the sharp, flat, and natural signs figured).

The first British knighthoods to be conferred upon musicians seem to have been due to the Lord Lieutenant of Ireland (see *Ireland* 6).

The first British knighthood, other than Irish, conferred on a musician seems to have been that conferred on the composer Henry Bishop by Queen Victoria in 1842.

Since that date music has come to have its fair share of recognition in the honours lists (generally issued twice annually, Queen's Birthday and New Year), and many composers, university professors of music, heads of musical institutions, and cathedral organists have received knighthood. The sovereign acts upon the recommendation of the Prime Minister.

Readers other than British may care to know that etiquette demands that a knight be addressed by the prefix 'Sir' and his first name —thus 'Sir Adrian Boult' or (in conversation with him) 'Sir Adrian'. The only known exception is Paderewski, who (a law to himself in all things), though in 1925 he accepted knighthood at the hands of King George V, apparently never made use of the title.

The wife of a knight is a 'Dame', but in ordinary use is addressed as 'Lady', followed by the surname.

Since 1917 the honour of 'Dame' (corresponding to 'knight') has been separately conferred, Clara Butt, the popular contralto, who had done much valuable war service, being the first musician to receive it (1922) and the composer Dr. Ethel Smyth the next (the same year). The title of 'Dame', conferred in this way, implies a rank in an order such as that of the 'British Empire' ('Dame Commander'); the letters D.B.E., etc., after the name are proper. And we say 'Dame Ethel Smyth' or 'Dame Ethel', not 'Lady'.

A knighthood is not hereditary; a baronetcy is. Baronetcies are, however, rarely conferred on musicians. Sir Hubert Parry was raised from knighthood to baronetcy by King Edward VII in 1903; so was Elgar by George V in 1931. There have been a few other baronet musicians, but they have mostly inherited the title. A baronet is, like a knight, addressed as 'Sir', but, in addition, the abbreviation 'Bart.' or 'Bt.' is placed after his name in writing it in any formal way.

No example has yet occurred of a musician being created a peer (i.e. a baron, viscount, earl, marquis, or duke) and thus enabled to represent his art in the House of Lords.

Alphabetical suffixes to musicians' names that are, have been, or may be found, representing membership of some royal order, are as follows (alphabetically arranged):

C.B.E., Commander of the Order of the British Empire.
C.H., Companion of Honour.
C.V.O., Commander of the Royal Victorian Order.
D.B.E., Dame Commander of the Order of the British Empire.
D.C.V.O., Dame Commander of the Royal Victorian Order.
G.B.E., Knight (or Dame) Grand Cross of the Order of the British Empire.
G.C.V.O., Knight (or Dame) Grand Cross of the Royal Victorian Order.
K.B.E., Knight Commander of the Order of the British Empire.
K.C.V.O., Knight Commander of the Royal Victorian Order.
M.B.E., Member of the Order of the British Empire.
M.V.O., Member of the Royal Victorian Order.
O.B.E., Officer of the Order of the British Empire.
O.M., Order of Merit—this being the highest distinction awarded (limited to twenty-four recipients in the whole country, these chosen for high service in the army or navy, science, literature, or art; Elgar, Vaughan Williams, Walton, and Britten have been honoured in this way, the first being also a baronet).

KNIGHT OF THE ROSE. See *Rosenkavalier.*

KNIPPER, LEV. Born at Tiflis in 1898. He studied in Berlin (under Jarnach) and his work is in the Russian manner but on broad diatonic lines. He has written many symphonies, several operas, chamber music, etc. In 1932 he was appointed music instructor to the Soviet army and navy.

See *Russia* 8.

KNORR, IWAN. Born at Mewe, in West Prussia, in 1853, and died at Frankfort-on-Main in 1916, aged sixty-three. He was brought up in Russia, but at fifteen entered the Leipzig

Conservatory and was eventually appointed professor of composition at the Conservatory of Frankfort-on-Main.

He wrote textbooks and composed. Amongst his pupils were a number of British youths who afterwards became known to the public— Norman O'Neill, Cyril Scott, Roger Quilter, and Balfour Gardiner.

KNOX, JOHN (1505–72). See *Common Prayer* (near end of article).

KNOX'S PSALTER. See *Hymns* 10; *Presbyterian Church Music* 3.

KOCH.

(1) FRANZ PAUL (b. 1761). See *Jew's Harp.*
(2) DR. LUDWIG (1882–1974). See *Bird Music.*

KÖCHEL, LUDWIG VON. Born near Krems in 1800 and died in Vienna in 1877, aged seventy-seven. He was a botanist and mineralogist and, thus familiar with the principles of scientific classification, was shocked at the disorder in which the works of non-opus-numbered composers lay (see *Opus*). He took in hand those of his beloved Mozart, studied their chronology, helped towards the production of the first complete edition, and established that Köchel numeration ('K. 91', etc. or 'K.V. 91', 'V' meaning *Verzeichnis* = list) which is now almost universally used as a means of identification in concert programmes and in all writings upon the works of the composer: various revisions of it were undertaken—notably by Alfred Einstein (q.v.) in 1937; a thorough recasting appeared in 1964.

See *Misattributed Compositions* (s.v. Mozart); *Opus.*

KOCZWARA. See *Kotzwara.*

KODÁLY, ZOLTÁN (p. 480, pl. **83.** 6). Born at Kecskemét in Hungary in 1882 and died in Budapest in 1967, aged eighty-four. He studied at the Conservatory of Budapest and at twenty-four joined its staff as a teacher of composition. Like Bartók (q.v.), with whom he was associated and who expressed the highest opinion of him, he collected Hungarian folk tunes, and like him he was both national in spirit and 'modern' in his harmonies and general methods —in other words, in no way controlled by conventions.

He was not greatly attracted by the orchestra (the suite *Háry János*, from a comic opera completed in 1926, is, however, well known), but wrote a certain amount of chamber music, piano music, vocal music, choral music (*Psalmus Hungaricus*, 1923), etc. A sonata for cello alone (1915) appears to exhaust the very utmost powers of that instrument.

See *Hungary; Zimbalon; Dulcimer; Psalm; Concerto* 6 c (1882); *Opera* 24 (1948).

KOECHEL. See *Köchel.*

KOECHLIN, CHARLES (p. 384, pl. **64.** 6). Born in Paris in 1867 and died in Var in 1950, aged eighty-three. He was of Alsatian parentage. He was trained at the Paris Conservatory under Massenet and then Fauré. He wrote a large amount of music for piano, for chamber combinations, for orchestra, and for voice. In this he made no claim to popular qualities, being content to let the public ordained for him duly find him at the time ordained. A certain number of connoisseurs and critics found his reticent simplicity, his lyrical vein, and his freedom of rhythm very congenial, and some expressed great enthusiasm.

He wrote important theoretical treatises.

See *Electric Musical Instruments* 1 f; *Flute Family* 6.

KOENIG, RUDOLPH. See *Pitch* 6 b.

KOENIG HORN. (1) See *Posthorn*; (2) a sort of saxhorn with downward bell.

KOESSLER, HANS. Born at Waldeck, Bavaria, in 1853 and died at Ansbach in 1926, aged seventy-three. He was a pupil of Rheinberger at Munich. From his thirtieth year he lived in Budapest, where, as professor of composition at the Conservatory, he had as pupils Dohnányi, Bartók, Kodály, and most of the members of the younger school of Hungarian composers (see *Hungary*). His own compositions include symphonies, chamber music, choral music, an opera, etc.

KÖHLER, LOUIS (in full, Christian Louis Heinrich). Born at Brunswick in 1820 and died at Königsberg in 1886, aged sixty-five. He is chiefly remembered by his piano studies.

KOKETT (Ger.). 'Coquettish.'

KOLLMANN, A. F. C. See *Cadence*, n. 1.

KOLOMYIKA. A quick Polish dance in two-in-a-measure time, popular amongst the mountain peasants of Poland.

KOLOPHON (Ger.). 'Colophony', i.e. bow resin.

KOMBINATION (Ger.). 'Combination.' In organ music applied to any mechanical device for preparing registration.

KOMISCH (Ger.). 'Comic.'

KOMPONIERT (Ger.). 'Composed.'

KONIUS. See *Conus* (it is a French name and 'Conus' is correct).

KONTRABASS. German for double-bass—generally the stringed one.

KONTRABASSKLARINETTE. See *Clarinet Family* 5.

KONTRABASSPOSAUNE. Double-bass trombone. See *Trombone Family* 2 f.

KONTRABASSTUBA. See *Tuba Group* 4 c.

KONTRAFAGOTT. See *Oboe Family* 5 d.

KONTSKI, ANTOINE DE. Born at Cracow in Poland in 1817 and died in Lithuania in 1899, aged eighty-two. He was a piano pupil of Field. He lived in Paris, Berlin, St. Petersburg, and London, and travelled in the United States, and, indeed, everywhere. Of his many popular drawing-room compositions one or two are still to be heard—and avoided (especially *The Awakening of the Lion*).

See reference under *Pianoforte* 22.

KONUS, KONIUS, KONYS. See *Conus* (it is a French name and 'Conus' is correct).

KONZERT. German for both 'concert' and 'concerto'. So *Konzertstück*—same as *Concertstück* (q.v.).

KOPPEL (Ger.). 'Coupler' (organ).

KORBAY, FRANCIS ALEXANDER. Born at Budapest, Hungary, in 1846 and died in London in 1913, aged sixty-six.

He was an opera singer at Budapest who, his voice temporarily failing, took to the piano and, advised by his fellow Hungarian and godfather Liszt, toured and taught in Europe and America. Then he returned to song as recitalist, teacher, and composer, and became a professor of the Royal Academy of Music, London. Some of his settings of Hungarian songs are very widely known.

KOREAN TEMPLE BLOCKS. These are an oriental addition to the twentieth-century dance-band drummer's equipment. Skull-shaped hollow blocks of wood (p. 789, pl. **134**. 9) are struck with the drum-stick or one of several kinds of special mallet. A set of the blocks consists of five, approximating in pitch to C, D, E, G, and A—i.e. the pentatonic scale (see *Scales* 10). The Chinese Temple Blocks are similar.

KORNETT (Ger.). The modern cornet or the old cornett—either. See *Cornet* and *Cornett and Key Bugle Families*.

KORNGOLD, ERICH WOLFGANG. Born at Brno (Brünn), Moravia, in 1897 and died in Hollywood, Calif., in 1957, aged sixty. He was the son of Julius Korngold, the Viennese music critic. For some time following his twelfth year, when his first stage work appeared, he was the subject of discussion, largely on account of his then 'modern' harmony. Some of his operas have been much performed, e.g. *The Dead City* (1920). From 1935 he lived mainly in California where he composed much incidental music for films.

See references under *Pianoforte* 21; *Jewish* 9.

KÖSELITZ, HEINRICH. See *Nietzsche*.

KOSLECK, JULIUS (1835–1905). See *Trumpet Family* 2 e.

KOSTELANETZ, ANDRÉ (born 1901). See *Broadcasting* 4.

KOSTENKA. A Serbian dance type.

KOTELETTEN WALZER. See *Chopsticks*.

KOTONSKI, Wlodzimierz. See *Poland*.

KOTZELUCH, J. A. (1738–1814). Same as 'Kozeluch'. See *Bohemia*.

KOTZWARA (Koczwara, or Kats warra) FRANZ. Born at Prague in 1730 and died in London in 1791, aged sixty-one. He lived for some time in Germany and Holland and then in Dublin, where he played the violin in a theatre band. About 1790 he settled in London as a double-bass player at a theatre, but soon after hanged himself in a house of ill-fame.

He wrote a certain amount of chamber music and music for piano. Parke, in his *Musical Memoirs* (1830), says that he made himself very useful to the London musical publishers by his ability to imitate the style of Haydn, Pleyel, and others, so enabling them to perpetuate some lucrative frauds.

His name would now be utterly perished but for the accident of his composing a piece of 'programme music' for piano (with optional parts for some other instruments) called *The Battle of Prague*. This, though exceedingly commonplace, became immediately popular and was published and republished all over Europe. Mark Twain heard it from one of his countrywomen in an hotel at Lucerne in 1878 a century after its first appearance ('she turned on all the horrors of *The Battle of Prague*, that venerable shivaree, and waded chin deep in the blood of the slain'). It still has a certain sale and is from time to time reprinted. (See under *Programme Music* 4; *Pianoforte* 22.)

KOUIAVIAK, KUJAWIAK. A slow Polish dance in three-in-a-measure time. See reference under *Mazurka*.

KOUKOUZÉLES, JOHN. See *Greek Church* 3.

KOUSSEVITZKY (Kussevitsky), SERGEI. Born near Tver, Russia, in 1874 and died in Boston, Mass., in 1951, aged seventy-six. He was a Russian virtuoso on the double-bass and, in the earlier part of his career, the public-spirited publisher of contemporary music, but he attained yet higher international fame as an orchestral conductor (Boston Symphony Orchestra 1924–49). In 1942 he created, as a memorial to his first wife, the Natalie Koussevitzky Foundation, which (amongst other activities) commissions works by composers on either side of the Atlantic. The work of the Foundation was continued by his second wife, Olga, and by 1965 135 commissions had been announced.

See *Concerto* 6 c (1874); *Expression* 6; *Tempo*; *Violin Family* 9; *Copland*; *Oriental* (end).

KOVEN, DE. See *De Koven*.

KOZACHOK. A Cossack dance, in a pretty quick two-in-a-measure time, and often in the minor. The speed increases as the dance proceeds. There is a fine one for orchestra by Dargomijsky.

KOZELUCH (Kozeluh) (Uncle and Nephew).

(1) JOHANN ANTON (1738–1814). See *Bohemia*.

(2) LEOPOLD. Born at Welwarn in 1752 and died at Prague in 1818, aged sixty-five. The earlier part of his life was spent in Vienna as a popular composer of ballets, etc. Then, in 1792, he became Court Composer at Prague. His output was varied, including symphonies, cantatas, etc.

See *Misattributed* (Beethoven's Pianoforte Duets); *Bohemia*.

KOZLOWSKI, JOSEPH (1757–1831). See *Poland*.

KRAFT (Ger.). 'Strength', vigour. So *Kräftig*, 'strong', vigorous.

KRAFT.

(1) ANTON. Born near Pilsen, Bohemia, in 1752 and died at Vienna in 1820. He was a cellist in Haydn's orchestra at the court of Prince Esterházy (see *Haydn*) and then at that of Prince Lobkowitz, and composed a good deal of fine music for (or including) his instrument. For his son see below.

Cf. *Misattributed*, s.v. 'Haydn's Violon cello Concerto'.

(2) NICOLAUS. Born at Esterházy in 1778 and died in 1853. Like his father (above) he was an admirable cellist and a gifted composer for his instrument. He held, at various times, positions in the courts of Prince Lichnowsky, Prince Lobkowitz, and the King of Württemberg. He was esteemed by Beethoven.

KRAKOVIAK, KRAKOWIAK. See *Cracovienne*.

KRAMER, A(RTHUR) WALTER. Born in New York in 1890 and died there in 1969, aged seventy-eight. He was on the staff of *Musical America* from 1910 and served as editor 1929–36, later becoming managing editor of the Galaxy Music Corporation. He composed orchestral and chamber music, songs, and other things.

KRATZENSTEIN, CHRISTIAN GOTTLIEB (b. 1723). See *Reed-Organ Family* 6.

KREBS, JOHANN LUDWIG. Born in Thuringia in 1713 and died in the same state in 1780, aged sixty-six. He was Bach's show pupil and assistant. 'Krebs' means 'cray-fish' and Bach means 'brook', and the prophet (by no means above an occasional joke) used to speak of his disciple as 'the best *Krebs* in the whole *Bach*'.

Some of Krebs's organ music may still be heard.

KREBSGANG. German name for any composition (sometimes a canon, q.v.) which produces the same effect when played either backwards or forwards.

KREBSKANON. See *Canon*.

KREHBIEL, HENRY EDWARD (1854–1923). See *Criticism* 5; *Folk Song* 5.

KREIN.

(1) ALEXANDER. Born at Nijni-Novgorod in 1883 and died in Moscow in 1951. He came of a Jewish family which boasts more than ten considerable musicians. Two are mentioned below, and the celebrated violinist David Krein is his brother.

He studied violoncello at the Conservatory of Moscow and, turning to composition, became one of the most gifted representatives of the Russian-Jewish school. He used the ancient tunes of the synagogue, treating them in a modern harmonic style.

His works include operas (*Zagmuk*, 1930; *Daughter of the People*, 1946), a symphony, a cantata (*Kaddish*), a funeral ode for Lenin, a piano sonata, etc.

(2) GRIGORY. Born in 1879 at Nijni-Novgorod. He is a brother of the preceding. He studied composition under Max Reger in Germany and violin at the Moscow Conservatory. His music is not so definitely racial as his brother's, but equally modern in style and very complex in structure. His compositions include much chamber music, piano sonatas, violin sonatas, the symphonic poems, *Saul and David* and *David's Song*, etc.

(3) JULIAN. Born in 1914 in Moscow. He is the son of Grigory, inherited the family gifts, and has been a composer since the age of four. His first sonata, published in 1926, is written in the last manner of Scriabin. Some of his orchestral music has been performed by the Philadelphia Orchestra under Stokowski.

KREIS (Ger.). 'Circle', cycle. So *Liederkreis*, 'song cycle'.

KREISLER, FRITZ (p. 1097, pl. **182.** 9). Born in Vienna in 1875 and died in New York in 1962, aged nearly eighty-seven. He studied violin playing under Hellmesberger in Vienna (winning the gold medal of the Conservatory at the age of ten), and then with Massart in Paris. Having acquired a technique adequate to the high demands of the expression of an unusually refined artistic temperament, he toured and re-toured the world until 1950, playing with skill and feeling a curiously restricted repertory of the greater classics, almost ignoring contemporary composers of standing, and entertaining an enormous and infatuated public with trifles of his own composing or arranging—attractive bits of melody either original or picked up here and there in the classical repertory and recast.

In 1935 he aroused universal controversy by revealing the fact that practically all the pieces which appear in the series 'Classical Manuscripts' to which he had attached the names of seventeenth- and eighteenth-century composers were really of his own composition. The items of the list he supplied to the press (which does not quite tally with his publishers' advertisements of his 'Classical Manuscripts') are included elsewhere in the present volume (see *Misattributed Compositions*). He also published a string quartet and a booklet, *Four Weeks in the Trenches: the War Story of a Violinist* (1918). An operetta, *Appleblossom*, was performed in New York in 1919, and another, *The Marriage Knot*, in 1923.

See *Jewish* 9.

KŘENEK, ERNST (p. 416, pl. **71.** 7). Born in Vienna in 1900. He is of Czech origin (partly German also), though this does not show itself in his compositions. He studied composition under Schreker at Vienna and Berlin, and married (as his first wife) Mahler's daughter, and for a time his works were influenced by the neoromantic tendencies of these composers (see *History* 8).

There followed a 'neo-classic' phase of vigorously dissonant contrapuntal writing, this in turn being succeeded by another in which the rhythmic and coloristic influence of jazz is prominent, as in his much-played opera *Jonny spielt auf* ('Johnny strikes up'; dedicated to his second wife, Berta Hermann, the well-known actress). There are also many other operas.

His instrumental works are numerous. They include symphonies, concertos, string quartets, and modern specimens of the old form of the concerto grosso (see *Concerto* 2). He has also written a number of songs. In 1938 he emigrated to the United States, becoming Professor of Music successively at Vassar College and Hamline University, St. Paul, Minn., and in 1947 settling in Hollywood. His *Studies in Counterpoint* (1940) explains the Note-row (q.v.) technique.

Cf. *Jazz* 5; *Clarinet* 6; *Opera* 24 f (1938).

KRENZ, JAN (b. 1926). See *Poland* (end).

KREUTZER, RODOLPHE. Born at Versailles in 1766 and died at Geneva in 1831, aged sixty-four. He was a fine violinist. In Vienna he won the favour of Beethoven, who dedicated to him that sonata for violin and piano (op. 47) which is now universally known as the 'Kreutzer' Sonata—a work which, though to most listeners it appears reasonably measured in expression, was heard by Tolstoy, ninety years later, as passionate and exciting, and imagined by him as leading to the dire events related in his novel named after it. (It is said that the dedicatee of this sonata never publicly played it.)

Kreutzer wrote about forty operas and about twenty violin concertos, but, apart from the glory Beethoven conferred on him, is best remembered today by his still valuable technical studies for the violin.

See *France* 9; *Étude*; *Concerto* 6 b (1766); *Collaboration*.

KREUZ (Ger., 'cross'). The sign of the sharp (Table 7).

KRIEG (Ger.). 'War.' So *Kriegerisch*, 'warrior-like', 'martial'.

KRIŽKOVSKY, PAUL (1820–85). See under *Janáček*.

KROHN, I. H. R. (1867–1960). See *Scandinavia* 6.

KROMMER, FRANZ (1759–1831). Moravian violinist and wholesale composer of music for wind band and other combinations (sixty-nine string quartets and quintets, some quartets and quintets for flutes, symphonies, masses, etc.).

KRUMHORN or **KRUMMHORN** (sometimes corrupted into 'Cromorne', q.v., or 'Cremona'). A widespread and popular medieval instrumental family with a double reed (like our Oboe family, q.v.) and a cylindrical tube (like our Clarinet family, q.v.). The end of the instrument was recurved (hence the French name, *Tournebout*) and the reed was usually beneath a perforated cap (i.e. not taken actually into the player's mouth).

KRUMMBOGEN, KRUMMBÜGEL (Ger., 'bent-arch'), or **Stimmbogen** ('tuning-arch').

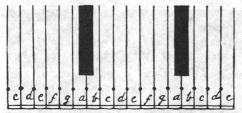

1. EARLY 16TH-CENTURY KEYBOARD—with the added B flat. From Virdung's *Musica Getutscht*, 1511. See *Keyboard* 2

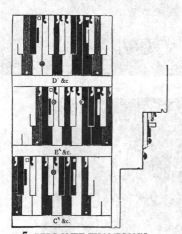

2. JANKO KEYBOARD. See *Keyboard* 4

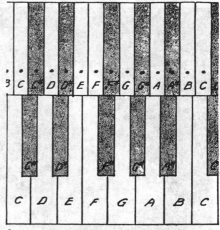

3. STOEHR QUARTER-TONE KEYBOARD (1924)
See *Microtones*

4. THE CLUTSAM KEYBOARD, curved and concave, taking account of the fact that the arms move in arcs on two planes. See the short article on page 199

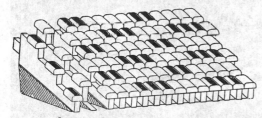

5. PERRONET THOMPSON'S ENHARMONIC ORGAN
with 72 notes to the octave
See *Keyboard* 3

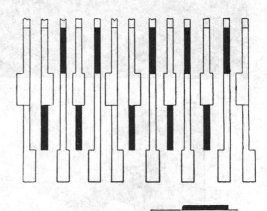

6. CLAVIER HANS—the keys here separated to show the system. See *Keyboard* 4

HOW DID THE KEYBOARD ORIGINATE—i.e. a means of playing an instrument by levers adapted to fingers? In figure 1 above we see the earliest pictorial representation of such a thing and in the other figures a few bold modern attempts at its improvement

1. A CONCERT. By Ercole Roberti (1450–96)

2. A NINTH-CENTURY LUTENIST
(From the *Psautier de Lothaire*)

3. AN ARCHLUTE
See *Lute Family* 2

Crook—of a brass instrument. See *Brass*; *Trumpet Family* 2 b, 3; *Horn Family* 2 b.

KRUMMHORN. See *Krumhorn*.

KRUMPHOLZ (or **Krumpholtz**), **JOHANN BAPTIST** (*c.* 1745–90). See *Bohemia*; *Harp* 3, 4.

KUBA KEYBOARD. See *Keyboard* 4.

KUBELIK, JAN (1880–1940). See *Bohemia*.

KÜCKEN, FRIEDRICH WILHELM. Born in Hanover in 1810 and died at Schwerin in 1882, aged seventy-one. He long enjoyed tremendous popularity as the composer of tuneful songs.

KUHAČ, FRANK XAVER (1834–1911). See *Folk Song* 5.

KUHE, WILLIAM. Born at Prague in 1823 and died in London in 1912, aged eighty-eight. He had a European reputation as pianist. From his early twenties he lived in England, chiefly at Brighton, where for twelve years (1870–82) he held an annual Musical Festival. For some time he was a professor of the piano at the Royal Academy of Music. His compositions were of the salon variety.

See allusion under *Pianoforte* 22.

KUHLAU, FRIEDRICH. Born in Hanover in 1786 and died in Copenhagen in 1832, aged forty-five. He was a professional flute-player of high attainment and some of his music for his instrument is still played, as are certain compositions for piano (sonatinas, etc.) now used as 'teaching pieces'.

See references under *Flute Family* 6; *Scandinavia* 2; *Chamber Music* 6, *Period III* (1786); *Sonata* 10 d (end).

KUHNAU, JOHANN. Born at Geising, in Saxony, in 1660 and died at Leipzig in 1722, aged sixty-two. He was Bach's immediate predecessor as cantor of the Thomas School at Leipzig and his greatest forerunner as a composer for clavichord and harpsichord. He has two special titles to fame in that he was one of the early composers to write sonatas, as distinct from suites, and that he was one of the early writers of 'programme music'. The latter allusion is to the *Biblical Sonatas*, in which in close musical detail are depicted 'The Combat between David and Goliath' and other stirring events from Holy Writ.

He also wrote a satirical novel, *The Musical Charlatan* ('Der musikalische Quack-Salber').

See *Composition* 10; *Sonata* 4, 10 d (1695); *Programme Music* 5 b; *Conducting* 2; *Horn Family* 5 a (footnote).

KUHREIHEN or **KUHREIGEN** (p. 880, pl. **147**. 1.). See *Ranz des Vaches*.

KUJIAVIAK, KUJAWIAK. Other spellings of Kouiaviak (q.v.).

KULLAK, THEODOR. He was born at Poznan in 1818 and died in Berlin in 1882, aged sixty-three. He is the most notable member of a musical family. His life was that of a leading piano teacher in Berlin (Moszkowski was his pupil), and he is specially remembered today by his scholastic piano compositions.

See *Pianoforte Playing and Teaching* 7.

KUNST (Ger.). 'Art.' So *Künstler*, 'artist'; *Kunstkenner* ('art-knower'), connoisseur.

KUNST DER FUGE. See *Art of Fugue*.

KUNST HARMONIUM. See *Reed-Organ Family* 9.

KUNSTLIED (Ger.). Literally 'Art Song', i.e. in contradistinction to 'Folk Song'—a distinction probably based on that of the similar terms *Kunstdichtung* ('Art Poem') and *Volksdichtung* ('Folk Poem').

KUNZEN, F. L. A. (1761–1817). See *Scandinavia* 2.

KURPINSKI, CHARLES (1785–1857). See *Poland*.

KURTH, ERNST. Born in Vienna in 1886 and died in Berne in 1948, aged sixty-two. Musicologist and teacher, active in Berne. His *Foundations of Linear Counterpoint* (1917) had much influence on the younger generation of composers.

KURZ, KURZE, etc. (Ger.; various grammatical terminations). 'Short.'

KURZER VORSCHLAG. See *Vorschlag*.

KUSSEVITZKY. See *Koussevitzky*.

K.V. (followed by a number). See *Köchel*.

KVEDA RIMUR. See *Scandinavia* 5.

KWALWASSER, JACOB. See *Tests and Measurements*.

KYASHT. See *Ballet* 9.

KYRIE. See *Mass* 2 a, 3 a, and *Requiem*. The ejaculation of the Greek words *Kyrie Eleison* and *Christe Eleison* was very common in Germany down to the tenth century—on pilgrimages, on going into battle, at funerals, and so forth.

KYTSON, SIR THOMAS. See *Wilbye*.

L

L' (Fr., It.). 'The' (masc. or fem. sing.).

LA (It., Fr.). 'The' (fem. sing.).

LA. The sixth degree of the major scale, according to the system of vocal syllables derived from Guido d'Arezzo (q.v.), and so used (spelt 'Lah') in Tonic Sol-fa (q.v.—in which system it is also the name of the first degree of the minor scale). In French and Italian usage, however, the name has become attached (on 'fixed-doh' principles) to the note A, in whatsoever scale or other association this may occur (see Table 5). For still another use of 'La' see *Lancashire Sol-fa*.

L.A.B. See *Degrees and Diplomas* 2.

LABAN, RUDOLF VON (1879–1958). See *Ballet* 5, 8.

LABIALSTIMME (Ger.). Flue stop. The plural is *Labialstimmen*.

LABLACHE, LUIGI. Born in Naples in 1794 and died there in 1858, aged sixty-three. He was of French and Irish parentage but Italian birth and upbringing. He became the greatest operatic basso of his day (in two senses, for his bulk was abnormal).

See references to his extraordinary powers of breath control under *Voice* 3; *Thalberg*.

LA BOHÈME (Puccini). See *Bohème*.

LABORDE. See *Partant pour la Syrie*.

LABYRINTH. See *Ear and Hearing* 1.

LÄCHELND (Ger.). 'Smiling.'

LÂCHER (Fr.). 'To loosen' (e.g. snare of drum).

LACHMANN, ROBERT (1892–1939). See *Jewish* 8, 9.

LACHNER.

(1) FRANZ. Born at Rain, in Bavaria, in 1803 and died at Munich in 1890, aged eighty-six. In early life, in Vienna, he was an intimate friend of Schubert. He was successful as an opera conductor and is the best remembered of a once important musical family. As a composer he won abundant laurels that have now faded.

(2) IGNAZ. Born at Rain in 1807 and died at Hanover in 1895, aged eighty-seven. He was brother of the above and, like him, an opera conductor; as a composer he was in repute for his operas, symphonies, and other works.

(3) VINCENZ. Born at Rain in 1811 and died at Karlsruhe in 1893, aged eighty-one. He was brother of the two above and an eminent organist, orchestral conductor (chiefly at the court of Mannheim), and composer.

(4–6) THEODOR, THEKLA, and CHRISTIANE (half-brother and two sisters of all the above) were also eminent in their day—altogether a remarkable family!

LACOMBE.

(1) LOUIS TROUILLON (not 'Brouillon', as often printed). Born at Bourges, in central France, in 1818 and died at St. Vaast la Hougue, near Cherbourg, in 1884, aged sixty-five. He was a prominent touring pianist, Paris teacher, and composer of operas, orchestral and chamber compositions, songs, etc.

(2) PAUL. Born at Carcassonne in 1837 and died in 1927, aged nearly ninety. He was a friend and disciple of Bizet. He composed a large amount of orchestral and chamber music, piano and vocal music. He was not related to (1) above.

LACRIMOSA. See *Requiem*.

LACRIMOSO, LAGRIMOSO (It.). 'Lacrimose', tearful.

LACY, ROGER DE (d. 1212). See *Minstrels* 2.

LADRÉ. See *Ça ira!*

LADY NEVELLS BOOKE, MY (or My Lady Nevill's Book). This is a manuscript collection of virginal music dating from 1591. It consists of forty-two pieces by Byrd, who may have been the teacher of the lady—out of whose hands it must have quickly passed, however, for 'Lord Abergavenny, called the Deafe, presented it to the Queene' (Elizabeth I). It has been copied and published by Hilda Andrews.

See mention under *March*.

LAGE (Ger.). 'Position' (e.g. in string playing).

LAGNOSO, LAGNEVOLE (It.). 'Doleful.' So the adverb *Lagnosamente*.

LAGRIMANDO, LAGRIMOSO (It.). 'Lacrimose', 'tearful'.

LAH. See *La*.

LAHEE, HENRY CHARLES (1856–1953). See reference under *Madrigal* 8 d.

LAI, or LAY. A fourteenth-century French song form, usually consisting of twelve unequal stanzas sung to different tunes. Examples from later periods are in several voices.

LAIRD O' COCKPEN. The poem is by Lady Nairne (q.v.); the tune is the traditional Scottish one of *When she-cam ben she bobbit*.

LAISSER (Fr.). 'To allow', 'to leave'. *Laissant*, 'allowing', 'leaving'. *Laissez* is the imperative.

LA JEUNE FRANCE. See *Jeune France*.

LALANDE, MICHEL RICHARD DE. Born in Paris in 1657 and died at Versailles in 1726, aged sixty-eight. In the time of Lully, and after, he was one of the musical favourites of Louis XIV, directing the musical education of his daughters and for a long period serving as Superintendent of Music to the court. He wrote much church music (chiefly motets, which the king caused to be sumptuously printed) and also a good many ballets.

LALO, ÉDOUARD (in full, Victor Antoine Édouard; p. 369, pl. **62.** 5). Born at Lille in 1823 and died in Paris in 1892, aged sixty-nine. He studied at the Paris Conservatory. He first composed drawing-room ballads, then chamber music. Then for ten years, disgusted at the French public's lack of interest in music other than opera, he composed nothing. At forty-four he tried his hand at an opera, which had little success. He now turned to orchestral composition; his 'Spanish Symphony' for violin and orchestra, and other works, at last made his name, and his opera, *The King of Ys*, years after, confirmed it.

His masterpiece is considered to be the ballet-pantomime *Namouna* (also existing in the modified form of an orchestral suite), which awakened the enthusiasm of Debussy, d'Indy, and others, and influenced them a good deal. Dukas, also, owed a good deal to him. Deft orchestration was one of Lalo's strongest points. He left some excellent songs.

See Aubade; *Concerto* 6 b (1823); *France* 13.

L.A.M. London Academy of Music. See *Degrees and Diplomas* 2.

LAMARTINE (1790–1869). See *Romantic*; *Symphonic Poem*.

LAMB, CHARLES (1775–1834). See *Tremolo*; *Publishing* 7.

LAMBERT.

(1) MICHEL. Born at Vivonne, Poitou, about 1610 and died in Paris in 1696, aged about eighty-six. He was a skilful singer, song composer, and choir trainer at the court of Louis XIV. Lully (q.v.) married his daughter.

See *Ballet* 5.

(2) CONSTANT (p. 353, pl. **56.** 6). Born in London in 1905 and there died in 1951 aged nearly forty-six. He was trained at the Royal College of Music. In 1925 and 1927 he was commissioned to write ballets for Diaghilev (see *Ballet* 5), and later he became Musical Director of the ballet for the Old Vic–Sadler's Wells enterprise in London.

His vivid and original *Rio Grande*, for chorus, pianoforte, and orchestra (1929), with some jazz influence, further drew attention to him, and he also produced a concerto for piano and nine orchestral players, a choral–orchestral work, *Summer's Last Will and Testament* (1936), and other things, as well as editing symphonies of William Boyce, engaging in a good deal of musical journalism and publishing a book, *Music Ho! A Study of Music in Decline* (1934).

His stature as a composer was perhaps lessened by the energy he devoted to conducting and other activities.

See *Nationalism* (near end of article); *Jazz* 5; *Broadcasting* 4.

LAMBETH DEGREES. See *Degrees and Diplomas* 1.

LAMENT. A piece of traditional music of an elegiac character. The Scottish clans had their laments, reserved for occasions of the death of a member of the clan; they were generally bagpipe pieces, but sometimes songs. There were also laments in Ireland.

LAMENTANDO, LAMENTABILE, LAMENTEVOLE, LAMENTOSO (It.). In lamenting style.

LAMENTATIONS. In the Roman Catholic Church the Lamentations, based on the words of the prophet Jeremiah, are sung in the service of Tenebrae (q.v.).

'LAMENTATIONS' SYMPHONY (Haydn). See *Nicknamed Compositions* 11.

LAMENTAZIONE, LAMENTO (It.). 'Lamentation', 'lament'.

LAMOUREUX, CHARLES (1834–99). Famous Parisian conductor. See under *d'Indy*; *Chabrier*; *Concert* 14 (end).

LAMPE.

(1) JOHN FREDERICK. Born in Saxony in 1703 and died in Edinburgh in 1751, aged forty-seven or forty-eight. He was a bassoon player in London who composed theatre music and songs, as also tunes for his friend Charles Wesley, the hymn writer (p. 624, pl. **108.** 4). His wife, the vocalist Isabella Young, was sister-in-law to Arne.

See *Methodism and Music* 2.

(2) CHARLES JOHN FREDERICK. He was son of the above, and also a composer.

(3) FREDERICK ADOLF (1683–1729). See *Percussion* 4 b.

LANCASHIRE BAGPIPES. See *Bagpipe Family* 3.

LANCASHIRE SOL-FA (p. 976, pl. **163.** 5). This is the name latterly given to a method of sight-singing that apparently continued longer in Lancashire than elsewhere in Britain. It might more properly be called 'Old English Sol-fa', since it was at one time universal in England, to which country, according to Rousseau (*Dictionary of Music*, 1767) it was peculiar (see *Hymns and Hymn Tunes* 5—reference to psalters and musical education).

The principle of the method is to call, in every major scale, the first three notes *fa*, *sol*, *la*, and the second three notes (which are exactly like them as to intervals) also *fa*, *sol*, *la*. This leaves one note to be accounted for, and it is called *mi*. Thus in key C major the notes would run C = *fa*, D = *sol*, E = *la*; F = *fa*, G = *sol*, A = *la*; B = *mi*. And thus in all other scales, the first and fourth notes being always *fa*, the second and fifth *sol*, the third and sixth *la*, and the seventh always *mi*. The minor is treated as a mode of the major and (as in Tonic Sol-fa, q.v.) the raised seventh note of the minor mode is called *se* (being *sol* sharpened).

This method is recommended by Campian (q.v.) in his *New Way of Making Four Parts in Counterpoint* (1613) and by Charles Butler in his *Principles of Music* (1636). It is found in Playford's *Introduction to the Skill of Musick* (1655 and subsequent editions) and Christopher Simpson's *Compendium of Practicall Musick* (1677, etc.), and also in most of the many musical introductions to collections of metrical psalms published in England and the American Colonies during the late seventeenth century and the eighteenth.

The most recent British expositions of the method are probably John Fawcett's *Lancashire Vocalist: a Complete Guide to Singing at Sight* (London, 1854) and James Greenwood's *The Sol-fa System of Teaching Singing as used in Lancashire and Yorkshire* (first published 1879), which latter was up to at least the late 1930s still on sale as one of Novello's Music Primers, though probably no longer anywhere used. Greenwood, born in Lancashire in 1837, went to Bristol as a lay-clerk in the cathedral and died there in 1894; he taught the system there and, according to a 'Narrative of Facts' he includes in his book (signed by five of the chief musicians of the city), he obtained good results.

The system lacks several of the most characteristic features of Tonic Sol-fa, as, for instance, the reliance upon the 'mental effect' of each note of the key, the rhythmic system, and the special notation. As regards the last, it will be realized that a tune set out solely in this *fa-sol-la* system would be unintelligible, there being no means of distinguishing whether these syllables belong to the lower or upper part of the scale. The 'Lancashire Sol-fa' is, therefore, merely a method of solmization applied to the normal staff notation.

To American musicians it may be of interest to note that the system above described is that used in the ninth edition of the famous 'Bay Psalm Book', i.e. the first edition to contain music (Boston, 1700). In this book sol-fa names appear under the staff notation. The same system (nicknamed 'fasola' and formerly often called 'Patent Notes') is found in use throughout the eighteenth and well into the nineteenth century, latterly often with a form of music type which gives differently shaped heads (triangular, round, square, diamond) for the *fa, sol, la, mi*, so facilitating sight-reading. This novel feature (nicknamed 'buckwheat notation') possibly makes its first appearance in *The Easy Instructor, or a New Method of Teaching Sacred Harmony* (Philadelphia; probably 1798), and is found in such books as *The Western Lyre* (Cincinnati, 1831) and *The Missouri Harmony* (1837)—to mention some examples of the collections of hymn tunes then so popular (p. 976, pl. **163**. 6).

The latest book to be printed in this combination of 'fasola' and 'buckwheat' was *The Social*

Harp (Philadelphia, 1855). One of these books is still on the market and in large use, *The Sacred Harp* (which first appeared in Philadelphia in 1844).[1] Thus the ancient English system of sol-fa is by no means dead. It has, however, since 1832 (see *Tonic Sol-fa* 10) been a good deal superseded by a seven-note 'buckwheat' system corresponding to the later Tonic Sol-fa. The 'Bible Belt' or 'Fundamentalist Region' of the Southern States is nowadays the home of these two systems, the continued existence of which was little known to musicians elsewhere until the appearance of George Pullen Jackson's study, *White Spirituals in the Southern Uplands* (1933), which records a number of popular annual Singing Conventions in which the systems are maintained.

For reference to the use in Scotland of the old system of sol-faing see *Presbyterian Church Music* 4.

LANCERS. See *Quadrille.*

LANCIO (It.). 'Gusto.'

LANDINO (or Landini), FRANCESCO, called 'Il Cieco' (the blind), 'Francesco degli Organi' ('of the organs'), etc. Born in Florence about 1325 and died there in 1397, aged about seventy-two. He was a highly renowned organist and composer and, in addition, played famously on the lute, the flute, and other instruments. His reputation led to his being invited to visit Venice, where he was greatly honoured. For the contemporary developments in composition in which he took his part see *France* 3 ('Ars Nova'); also *Tunsted*. He was versed in philosophy and was a skilful astrologer.

See references under *Italy* 3; *Madrigal* 1; *Opera* 1 (footnote).

LÄNDLER. This is the popular German dance which is most probably the true original of the waltz (q.v.) and is much like it, but not so quick. Mozart, Beethoven, Schubert, and other German composers have written Ländler.

Schleifer ('slider') was another name for Ländler; it refers to the action of the feet, an action preserved in the waltz. *Tyrolienne* was still another name (but see *Jodel*).

LÄNDLICH (Ger.). 'Country-like', rustic.

LAND OF MY FATHERS ('Hen Wlad fy Nhadau'). The poem of this song (which is the National Anthem of Wales) is by Evan James, of Pontypridd, the tune by James James. Both poem and tune first appeared in print in 1860 in John Owen's *Gems of Welsh Melody*.

For a detailed study of the history of the song, with the varying accounts that have been given of the circumstances of its composition, see the present writer's paper in the *National Library of Wales Journal* III. i, Summer 1943.

[1] This book makes large claims, for its cover bears a statement that its words and music 'are in accord and keeping with the sacred music in the Bible from Jubal 160 A.M., 1,500 years before the Deluge, from Abraham, Moses, the Children of Israel, the Prophets, Levites, David, Solomon, down to Jesus Christ, his Disciples, and the founding of his Church and to the present'.

LAND O' THE LEAL. The poem is by Lady Nairne (q.v.); the tune is the traditional Scottish one of *Hey, tutti tatti*—also sung to Burns's *Scots wha hae* (q.v.). The song was written about 1798 and first published soon after 1800.

LANDOWSKA, WANDA. Born at Warsaw in 1877 and died at Lakeville, Conn., in 1959, aged eighty-two. She was a virtuoso of the harpsichord and an authority on the older keyboard music. She lived in Berlin (1912), near Paris (1920), and near New York (1940).

LÁNG, PAUL HENRY. Born in Budapest in 1901. At the Conservatory of his native city he was a pupil of Kodály (q.v.) and Weiner (q.v.), and he became one of the conductors of the opera of that place. He settled in the United States, holding various academic posts (Assistant Professor, Columbia University, 1933; Professor of Musicology 1939–70). His musicological writings are important (e.g. *Music in Western Civilization*, 1941; *Handel*, 1966); he is editor (since 1945) of the *Musical Quarterly*, and was music critic (1954–63) of the New York *Herald Tribune*.

LANG (Ger.). 'Long.'

LANGE-MÜLLER, PETER ERASMUS. Born at Frederiksberg (now part of Copenhagen), in 1850, and died at Copenhagen in 1926, aged seventy-five. He studied at the Conservatory of Copenhagen and then took rank as a composer of strong nationalist tendencies, composing orchestral music, operas, much choral music, many songs, etc.

LANGER. See *Electric Musical Instruments* 1 j.

LANGER VORSCHLAG. See *Vorschlag*.

LANGLEIK. See *Scandinavia* 3.

LANGOUREUX, LANGOUREUSEMENT (Fr.). 'Languorous', 'languorously'.

LANGSAM (Ger.). 'Slow.' So *Langsamer*, 'slower'.

LANGSPIL. See *Scandinavia* 5.

LANGTON, STEPHEN (d. 1228). Archbishop of Canterbury. See *Veni sancte spiritus*.

LANGUE D'OC AND LANGUE D'OÏL. See *Minstrels*, etc. 4.

LANGUENDO, LANGUENTE, LANGUE-MENTE (It.). 'Languishing.'

LANGUEUR (Fr.). 'Languor.'

LANGUIDO, LANGUIDAMENTE (It.). 'Languid', 'languidly'.

LANGUISSANT (Fr.). 'Languishing.'

LANGUORE (It.). 'Languor.'

LANIER, (Laniere, Lanyer, etc.—many spellings).

(1) A numerous family of this name of French origin was active in English musical life (especially about the Court) for well over a century, ending with the death of Thomas Lanier some time after 1686. A Nicolas Lanier (one of three bearing that same Christian name;

p. 289, pl. **51.** 1) is the only member of this branch of the family whom it is necessary to include in a book of the scope of the present one. He was born in 1588, was Master of the King's Musick to Charles I, and after the Commonwealth served Charles II in the same capacity as he had served his father. He was also Marshal of the Corporation of Music. He left songs and vocal dialogues. For his introduction of recitative into England see *Opera* 13 a.

There is another brief reference to him under *Masque*.

(2) It would be unintelligent to introduce this family into a book of reference intended partly for American use without mention of the fact that a member of the family, Thomas (probably a grandson of Nicolas), settled in Richmond, Va., in 1716 and founded a branch there that has distinguished itself in many ways, but especially in the person of Sidney Lanier (1842–81), the delicate and accomplished poet. In him the musicality of the family was still aflame, as witness the subject-matter of a good deal of his literary work and its decidedly musical flow. For some years, indeed, he earned a part of his living as first flute in the symphony orchestra at Baltimore, making a great impression by his concerto playing.

LANNER, JOSEPH FRANZ KARL. Born near Vienna in 1801 and died there in 1843, aged forty-two.

The Lanner and Strauss families were the generators of the early nineteenth-century waltz fever, which they unremittingly fed with fresh excitements. At the outset Lanner was the conductor of a little orchestra, for which he wrote waltzes and other dances, and Johann Strauss the elder was his violin player. So the craze began. There have been many worse dance-music crazes since!

See *Waltz*.

LANZA, MARIO (1921–59). See *Cinematograph*.

LANZENTANZ (Ger.). Same as *Pordon Danza* (q.v.).

LAODICEA, COUNCIL OF. See *Greek Church and Music* 2; *Singing* 3.

LAPARRA, RAOUL. Born at Bordeaux in 1876 and killed in an air-raid in Paris in 1943, aged sixty-six. He won the Rome Prize in 1903 and in 1908 attained celebrity with the performance at the Paris Opéra Comique of his *La Habanera*, which was followed in 1911 by *La Jota* (see *Habanera*; *Jota*). He wrote orchestral and other music and engaged in musical journalism, etc.

'LA PASSIONE' SYMPHONY (Haydn). See *Nicknamed Compositions* 11.

'LA POULE' SYMPHONY (Haydn). See *Nicknamed Compositions* 11.

LARBOARD WATCH. See *Britannia, the Pride of the Ocean*.

'LA REINE' SYMPHONY (Haydn). See *Nicknamed Compositions* 11.

LARGAMENTE (It.). 'Broadly', i.e. slowish and dignified (cf. *Largo*, below).

LARGE (Fr.). 'Broad', i.e. slow and dignified (cf. *Largo*, below).

LARGEMENT (Fr.). 'Broadly' (same as It. *Largamente*; see above).

LARGEUR (Fr.). 'Breadth.'

LARGHETTO (It.). The diminutive of *Largo* (see below). Slow and dignified, but less so than *Largo*.

LARGHEZZA (It.). 'Breadth' (cf. *Largo*, below).

LARGO (It.). 'Broad', dignified in style; so *Largo di molto*, 'very slow and dignified'—and similar expressions of which the separate words will be found in their alphabetical positions.

LARIGOT. See *Organ* 14 IV.

'LARK' QUARTET (Haydn). See *Nicknamed Compositions* 12.

LAROON. See *Street Music* 2.

'LA ROXOLANE' SYMPHONY (Haydn). See *Nicknamed Compositions* 11.

LARSSON, LARS ERIK. Born in Sweden in 1908. He studied at the Conservatory of Stockholm and then in Vienna with Alban Berg. He is known in Sweden as a conductor, critic, and composer (operas, orchestral and chamber music, etc.).

> See *Saxophone Family*—near end.

LARYNGOSCOPE. See *Singing* 11; *Garcia Family* 2.

LARYNX. See *Voice* 7, 8, 21.

LASCIARE (It.). 'To allow to . . .' So the imperative *Lasciate*.

LASSEN, EDUARD. Born in Copenhagen in 1830 and died at Weimar in 1904, aged seventy-three. He succeeded Liszt as musical director at Weimar and remained in the position for over thirty years, being the second conductor in the world to undertake the perilous venture of performing Wagner's *Tristan*. He composed operas, symphonies, etc., and is now chiefly remembered by a song or two.

LASSO. See *Lassus*.

LASS OF RICHMOND HILL. The poem of this popular song is by a barrister, Leonard McNally (q.v.), and the lass commemorated (of Richmond, Yorkshire, not Richmond, Surrey) became his wife in 1787. The music is by James Hook (q.v.). It was first publicly performed at Vauxhall Gardens (see *Concert* 12) in 1789 by Incledon.

LASS O' GOWRIE. The poem is by Lady Nairne (q.v.), but is founded on an earlier one, 'Kate o' Gowrie', by William Reid. The melody is an old Scottish one.

LASS O' PATIE'S MILL. The poem, highly praised by Burns, is by Allan Ramsay (q.v.); it appears in his *Tea-Table Miscellany* (1724–7). The air is an old Scottish one.

LASSÚ. See *Czardas*.

LASSUS, ORLANDUS—or **Orlando Lasso**, or **di Lasso**, not Roland de Lattre as often stated (p. 96, pl. **15**. 7). Born at Mons about 1532 and died at Munich in 1594, aged about sixty-two. He is the greatest representative of the Flemish school, as his contemporaries Palestrina, Byrd, and Victoria are of the Italian, English, and Spanish schools. All these men represent the culmination of what had been long in progress—that development of choral technique by which at length the sense of pure musical beauty and the desire for the musical expression of man's emotions found one of their highest manifestations (see an allusion under *Chanson*). Of this the settings by Lassus of the Penitential Psalms offer one of the most striking examples.

He wrote enormously and travelled adventurously and widely, everywhere welcomed at the courts of princes, as at the Sacred City, where for a time he was maestro of the Lateran. His fame as a composer was equalled by his fame as a choirmaster; he 'gave the time with such steadiness, that like warriors at the sound of the trumpet, the expert singers needed no other orders than the expression of that powerful and vigorous countenance to animate their sweetly sounding voices'.

The last thirty-four years of his life were spent at Munich in the service of Albert V of Bavaria and his successor William V. The Emperor Maximilian raised him to the nobility and Pope Gregory XIII conferred on him the order of the Golden Spur (see *Knighthood*). Through over-exercise of his intellectual faculties he latterly fell into a settled melancholy.

His four sons all became musicians and after his death they piously published many of his works. The family musical talent persisted into a third generation.

> For references to the conditions and musical style of his period, and to him personally, see as follows: *History* 2; *Belgium* 1; *Italy* 4; *Harmony* 8; *Passion Music* 2; *Magnificat*; *Psalm*; *Chanson*; *Cecilia*; *Publishing* 2; *Competitions in Music* 1; *Eccard*; *Madrigal* 8; *Counterpoint*; *Lechner*; *De profundis*; *Knighthood*.

LASS WITH A DELICATE AIR. See *Arne, Michael*.

LAST JUDGEMENT. See *Spohr*.

LAST POST. In the British Army a bugle call, the *First Post*, at 9.30 in the evening, draws all men back to barracks for the calling of the roll. Then, at 10 o'clock, the *Last Post* (formerly known as the Watch-setting) ends the labours and pleasures of the day. By a natural and poetical association of ideas it has become the custom to sound the same call at every military funeral.

> See also *Tattoo*.

LAST ROSE OF SUMMER. The poem is by Thomas Moore and first appeared in his *Irish Melodies* (1813). The air is that of a previous Irish song, 'The Groves of Blarney', by R. A. Millikin (about 1790), which in its turn was that of a song called 'Castle Hyde'; but Moore altered it.

Beethoven made a setting of the air as part of his contract with George Thomson (q.v.),

Mendelssohn wrote a piano fantasia on it, and Flotow used it in his opera *Martha*.

LÁSZLÓ, ALEXANDER. Born in Budapest in 1895. Pianist and composer. See *Colour and Music* 10.

LATES.

(1) JOHN JAMES (d. 1777). He was an Oxford violinist and composer. See *Sonata* 10 c.

(2) CHARLES (d. about 1810). He was an organist and composer of songs, sonatas, etc.

LATIN AMERICA, COMPOSERS OF. See under the following heads: *Castro*; *Ginastera*; *Williams, Alberto* (Argentine). *Fernandez*; *Guarnieri*; *Villa-Lobos* (Brazil). *Allende*; *Santa Cruz* (Chile). *Uribe-Holguin* (Colombia). *Carrilo*; *Chávez*; *Ponce*; *Revueltas* (Mexico). *Sas* (Peru). *Fabini* (Uruguay). See also *Dictionaries* 4 j.

LA TRAVIATA. See *Traviata*.

LATTRE. See *Lassus*.

LAUB, T. L. (1852–1927). See *Scandinavia* 2.

LAUBER, JOSEPH (1864–1952). He was resident in Geneva, where he was a member of the staff of the Conservatory. His compositions are very varied and numerous.

'LAUBE' SONATA (Beethoven). See *Nicknamed Compositions* 5.

LAUD (Sp.). See under *Cittern* (near end).

LAUD, WILLIAM. Born in 1573, executed in 1645. After a number of increasingly important ecclesiastical preferments he became Bishop of London in 1628 and Archbishop of Canterbury in 1633. His high-church views, expressed in forcible ways, had much influence upon the conduct of the musical part of the services. See references under *Common Prayer* (end of article); *Anglican Parish Church Music* 1, 2.

LAUDAMUS TE. See *Mass* 3 b.

LAUDA SION. One of the four Sequences (q.v.) allowed to remain in the liturgy of the Roman Catholic Church when the Council of Trent (1545–63) abolished the rest. It has its traditional plainsong, but has also been set by composers, as by Palestrina (eight voices) and by Mendelssohn (who used the plainsong, but in a degraded form).

The words are by St. Thomas Aquinas (*c.* 1264); they were written for the feast of Corpus Christi (on which they are still sung) at the request of Pope Urban IV.

LAUDI SPIRITUALI (more correctly 'Laude Spirituali'). Popular devotional songs, the poems in Italian, composed for the 'Laudisti', a singing confraternity of Florence at the end of the thirteenth century and later, and for similar confraternities that sprang up in other cities of Italy. These confraternities continued at least as late as the Napoleonic period. Collections of the Laudi have been published.

It was the performance of Laudi in the oratory, at Rome, of St. Philip Neri, founder of the order of Oratorians, that led to the introduction of the form of oratorio (q.v.).

See references under *Church Music* 2; *Canti Carnascialeschi*; *Oratorio* 2; *Street Music* 4.

LAUDISTI. See *Laudi spirituali*.

'LAUDON' SYMPHONY (Haydn). See *Nicknamed Compositions* 11.

LAUDS. The second of the Canonical Hours or services of the day of the Roman Catholic Church; formerly sung at sunrise (cf. *Matins*; *Prime*; *Terce*; *Sext*; *None*; *Vespers*; *Compline*).

LAUFWERK. See *Mechanical Reproduction* 5.

LAUSANNE CONFERENCES. See *Concert Halls* 9.

LAUT (Ger.). 'Loud.'

LAUTE (Ger.). Lute. See *Lute Family*.

LAUTENMACHER (Ger.). Same as *Luthier* (q.v.).

LAVALLÉE, CALIXA (1842–91). See *United States* 8; *O Canada!*

LAVENDER CRY. See *Street Music* 2.

LAVOIX, HENRI MARIE FRANÇOIS (1846–97). Notable writer on music. See *Clarinet Family* 4 f (note).

LAVOLTA, LAVOLTE. See *Volte*; *Courante*.

LAW, ANDREW (1749–1821). Connecticut psalmodist. See *Hymns* 17 f iv; *Organ* 9.

LAWES (The Brothers; p. 817, pl. **140.** 3).

(1) HENRY. Born at Dinton, Wiltshire, in 1596 and died in London in 1662, aged sixty-six. He was a Gentleman of Charles I's Chapel Royal. He wrote the music for Milton's masque of *Comus*, for the famous performance at Ludlow Castle on Michaelmas Night, and to him Milton addressed his famous sonnet, 'To Mr. H. Lawes on his Aires':

> Harry, whose tuneful and well-measured song
> First taught our English music how to span
> Words with just note and accent . . .

He also composed the Christmas songs in Herrick's *Hesperides*, and Herrick and others of the poets of his day greatly valued his settings of their words—presumably on the grounds made clear by Milton's encomium (the soundness of which, however, is to be questioned; see a discussion of the subject in Ernest Walker's *History of Music in England*).

See allusions to him under *Masque*; *Opera* 13 a; *Hymns and Hymn Tunes* 17 e xvii.

(2) WILLIAM. Born at Salisbury in 1602 and killed at the siege of Chester in 1645 fighting on the Royalist side. He was brother to Henry and, like him, Gentleman of the Chapel Royal. He wrote 'Gather ye rosebuds while ye may' and other vocal and instrumental pieces. His music for viols is especially important. He may be regarded as the experimental composer of his day, revelling as he did in bold and discordant counterpoint, and is a more striking composer than his brother as to warmth and nobility of feeling.

See *Monopolies*.

LAY CLERK, LAY VICAR. See *Vicar Choral*; *Anglican Parish Church Music* 1.

L.B.C.M. See *Degrees and Diplomas* 2.

A a

LE (Fr.). 'The' (masc. sing.). (It.). 'The' (fem. plur.).

LEADER. The British 'first violin', called in America the 'concertmaster', is also called in Britain the 'leader of the orchestra'. But in America the conductor is sometimes called the 'leader' and the verb 'to lead' is often used for the English 'to conduct'.

The first violin of a string quartet, etc., is also (in both countries) called the 'leader', and in vocal combinations the terms 'leading soprano', etc., are used.

LEADING MOTIF (Ger., *Leitmotiv*, plural *Leitmotive*; Fr., *Motif conducteur*; It., *Motivaguida* or *Tema fondamentale*). This term, which is associated with Wagner's processes of composition, was introduced not by him but (shortly after his death) by one of his commentators, Hans Paul von Wolzogen (1848–1938), Wagner's own term being *Grundthema*. The meaning of the term is sufficiently explained in the articles *Motif* and *Wagner*.

It should be observed that, though no composer before Wagner made such continuous and systematic use of the leading motif principle, the device cannot be considered as of his actual invention. We see at least the germ of it in Mozart, for instance, when, in *Don Giovanni*, the warning by the statue of the Commendatore in Act II, Scene iii, and its ghostly reappearance in Act II, Scene v, are linked in significance by the use of the same orchestral theme. We see it also in Mendelssohn's *Elijah*, when the same theme appears in connexion with the famine-chorus 'The harvest now is over', and, later, Elijah's expression of his longing for the Lord as a thirsty land for water. We can even trace this device of a recurrence of musical themes in connexion with a recurrence of dramatic thought as far back as the earliest days of the opera in Monteverdi, and in Peri and Caccini. It is, indeed, such an obvious means of connexion between related passages of the libretto that it was bound to be introduced so soon as opera and oratorio were born: it is perfectly possible to write with dramatic effectiveness without it, yet its usefulness was sure to occur to some composers, and it did so occur to very many.

The *idée fixe* ('fixed idea') of Berlioz (see *Berlioz*) and the 'Metamorphosis of Themes' of Liszt (see *Liszt*; *Metamorphosis of Themes*), both of which were developed independently of Wagner, have obviously the same root idea underlying them.

Since Wagner the leading motif system has been a great deal used. Each of Elgar's oratorios is largely a string of such motifs, and the thought of *The Kingdom* is bound to that of its predecessor *The Apostles* by the recurrence of many of these.

LEADING NOTE. The seventh degree of the major scale—and of the minor scale too, when that degree lies a semitone below the tonic. It is called 'leading note' because of its suggestion of a tendency to rise to the tonic.

When, as sometimes in the minor, it is temporarily lowered it loses this suggestion; it is then called the 'flattened leading note'.

LEADING SEVENTH. The chord of the minor seventh on the leading note, i.e. in key C major, B–D–F–A. (It will be realized that this chord can occur only in the major keys; in C minor the corresponding chord would be B–D–F–A flat, i.e. the chord of the diminished seventh.)

LEBENDIG (Ger.). 'Lively.' So *Lebendiger*, 'livelier'.

LEBHAFT (Ger.). 'Lively.' So *Lebhafter*, 'livelier'; *Lebhaftigkeit*, 'liveliness'.

LECAIL, CLOVIS. See *Trombone Family* 4.

LECHANTRE, MLLE. See *Pianoforte* 17.

LECHNER, LEONHARD. Born in the Austrian Tyrol *c.* 1550 and died at Stuttgart in 1606. (From the place of his birth he sometimes added to his name the word 'Athesinus'.) He was a choir-boy at Munich under Lassus (q.v.) and in later life part of his service to the art consisted in his publication or re-publication of certain works of his one-time master. But the publication of his own works, composed during his occupation of positions at Nuremberg, Hechingen, Tübingen, and Stuttgart, constitute an almost equal service. These are numerous, and, by the skill and feeling with which they are written, stamp him as a worthy forerunner of Schütz (q.v.), whose work was soon to follow.

LECLAIR, JEAN MARIE (p. 1096, pl. **181.** 4). Born at Lyons in 1697 and died in Paris in 1764, aged sixty-seven. He was a famous violinist and composer for the violin. His early professional career was connected with the ballet. It is said that he was a dancer at Rouen and it is certain that in his twenties he was a ballet master at Turin; in his early thirties, however, he held a position of importance in Paris as a violinist. Then, in his forties, he gave himself entirely to composition. By the high technical demands of his violin works he materially forwarded the powers of the instrument; some of them are frequently heard today, and there is decidedly nothing in *them* to explain why their writer should have been murdered—as he was in the streets of Paris, close to his own door.

LECOCQ, CHARLES (in full, Alexandre Charles). Born in Paris in 1832 and died there in 1918, aged eighty-six. He was trained at the Paris Conservatory and then made a painful living as a teacher, organist, and writer of sacred songs. Gradually he forced his way into the wider field of comic opera composition, and in his mid-thirties had there attained a reputation which later blossomed into fame. Of his fifty-odd operas *Madame Angot's Daughter* ('La Fille de Madame Angot') is the most celebrated. It ran for five hundred consecutive nights in Paris and had great success in London (both in

1873). The vitality of this composer's melodies made the chief ingredient in his success.

See *Opera* 24 e (1872).

LE DÉSIR ('Beethoven'). See *Nicknamed Compositions* 18—under Schubert's 'Mourning Waltz'.

LEDGER LINES. See *Leger Lines*.

LEEDS. See *Festival* 1; *Wesley, S. S.*; *Methodism* 8; *Alto Voice*.

LEER (Ger.). 'Empty'; applied to open strings of violin, etc.

LEEVES, WILLIAM (1748–1828). Composer of 'Sacred Airs', etc. See *Auld Robin Gray*.

LEFÉBURE-WÉLY (original name **Lefébre**), **LOUIS JAMES ALFRED.** Born in Paris in 1817 and died there in 1869, aged fifty-two. He was an infant prodigy who was publicly playing the organ at eight. For eleven years he was organist of the Madeleine and he died organist of St. Sulpice. His ability as an improviser was outstanding. He was not oppressed by the traditional dignity of the instrument, and both his playing and his composition exhibited brilliant immediate effectiveness.

In his day high hopes were entertained of the artistic usefulness of the recently improved harmonium, and he wrote for it (as did César Franck and other composers of standing).

See reference under *Pianoforte* 22.

LEFEBVRE, CHARLES ÉDOUARD. Born in Paris in 1843; died at Aix-les-Bains in 1917, aged seventy-four. He was a student of the Paris Conservatory and won its Rome Prize in 1870. He composed operas and some orchestral, chamber, and church music.

LEFEUILLET. See *Dance* 10.

LEGATO, LEGANDO, LEGABILE (It.). 'Bound', 'binding', 'in a binding fashion', i.e. performed with a smooth connexion between the notes (opposite of *Staccato*). *Legatissimo* is the superlative.

LEGATURA (It.). (*a*) Tie, (*b*) slur, (*c*) syncopation.

LÉGER, LÉGÈRE (Fr., masc., fem.). 'Light.' So *Légèreté*, 'lightness'. *Légèrement*, 'lightly', slightly.

LEGER LINES (sometimes spelt 'Ledger Lines'). These are short lines added below or above the staff when notes occur that are too high or too low to be accommodated within the staff itself.

LEGGIADRO, LEGGIADRETTO (It.). 'Graceful.' So *Leggiadramente*, 'gracefully'.

LEGGIERO, LEGGERO (It.). 'Light.' So *Leggermente* or *Leggiermente*, 'lightly'; *Leggerezza*, *Leggeranza*, 'lightness'; *Leggerissimo*, 'as light as possible'.

LEGGIO (It.). Music desk (from 'leggere', to read).

LEGNO (It.). 'Wood.' Used in the expression *Col legno* ('with the wood')—i.e. tapping the strings with the stick of the bow instead of playing on them with the hair of it. So *Bacchetta di Legno*, wooden-headed drum-stick (see *Percussion Family* 2 a; *Strumenti di Legno, Stromenti di Legno*, 'wood [wind] instruments').

LEHÁR, FRANZ (p. 480, pl. 83). 3. Born in 1870 at Komarno (or Komorn or Komaron), then in Hungary, now in Czechoslovakia, and died at Bad Ischl in 1948. His father was a military bandmaster. He himself was trained as a violinist (at the Conservatory of Prague), but soon took up his father's calling, serving in various parts of the Austro-Hungarian Empire. His first efforts at fame as a composer were in the domain of serious opera, but from these he turned, and *The Merry Widow* (1905) saw him launched into the highest popularity as the purveyor of a lighter type of stage work. Amongst many other triumphs have been *The Count of Luxemburg* (1909) and *Frederica* (1928). There are also dance compositions, marches, piano music for the young, sonatas, and a violin concerto.

His work always abounds in melody and is piquantly orchestrated. There is some Southern Slav folk-tune influence. In his earlier and middle-aged works he made much use of the 'song-and-dance' type of solo; latterly he tended to curtail this and also the spoken dialogue, so departing from the 'musical-play' tradition and approaching nearer to the true comic opera style.

LEHMANN, ELIZABETH NINA MARY FREDERIKA (called 'Liza Lehmann'). Born in London in 1862 and died at Pinner, Middlesex, in 1918, aged fifty-six. She was granddaughter of Robert Chambers, the Edinburgh publisher, daughter of Rudolf Lehmann, the painter, and Amelia Lehmann (the one-time popular song composer 'A. L.'), and wife of Herbert Bedford (q.v.), the composer and miniature painter. She had a fine career as a public singer (soprano) and then took to song composition, specializing in cycles of songs which pleased the wide public as not being too heavy and the connoisseur as not being too light.

LEIBOWITZ, RENÉ. Born in Warsaw in 1913, and died in Paris in 1972. He studied with Webern and Schönberg and was a devoted follower of the dodecaphonic method of composition (see *Note-row*), on which he wrote an extensive treatise (*Introduction à la musique de douze sons*), as he also wrote a more general one on Schönberg and his school. He composed orchestral and chamber works and conducted in many countries.

LEICHT (Ger.). Two senses—(*a*) light in style, (*b*) easy.

LEICHTFERTIG (Ger.). 'Giddy', 'frivolous'.

LEICHTIGKEIT (Ger.). (*a*) 'Lightness', (*b*) 'easiness'.

LEID (Ger.). 'Sorrow.' **LEIDENSCHAFT**, 'passion'; *Leidenschaftlich*, 'passionately'.

LEIFS (the spellings 'Leif', 'Lief', and 'Liefs' seem also to be current), JÓN. Born at Solheimar, Iceland, in 1899. Considered Iceland's leading composer, though he studied and for some time worked as a conductor in Germany. He has composed operas and orchestral works, some using Icelandic folk material.

LEIGH, WALTER. Born at Wimbledon in 1905; killed in action in Libya in 1942, aged thirty-six. He studied at Cambridge and under Hindemith in Berlin. He wrote piano music, songs, jazz music, a sonatina for viola and piano (International Musical Festival, Vienna, 1932), comic operas (e.g. *Jolly Roger*, Birmingham and London, 1933), and other things.

See *Harpsichord* 9.

LEIGH HUNT. See *Hunt, James Henry Leigh.*

LEINENTROMMEL. See *Percussion Family* 5 i.

LEIPZIG. See *Concert* 13; *Copyist*; *Printing* 5; *Publishing* 8; *Conducting* 5; *Schools*; *Bach, J. S.*; *Mendelssohn*; *Kuhnau*; *Rust, W.*; *Schein.*

LEISE (Ger.). 'Soft', gentle. So *Leiser*, 'softer'.

LEISTEN (Ger.). 'To perform.' So *Leistung*, 'performance'.

LEITGEBISCHES QUINTETT (Mozart). See *Nicknamed* 15 (K. 407).

LEITMOTIV (Ger.). Literally, 'leading-motif'. See under *Leading Motif*; *Motif*; *Wagner.*

LE JEUNE. See *Claudin.*

LEKEU, GUILLAUME (p. 97, pl. **16.** 3). Born near Verviers, in Belgium, in 1870 and died at Angers, in France, in 1894, aged twenty-four. He was a pupil in Paris of Franck and d'Indy and composed chamber music and other things that showed great promise, especially a sonata for violin and piano that has been much performed. His death (from typhoid) the day after his twenty-fourth birthday probably robbed the world of a great composer.

LEKPREVICK, ROBERT. See *Printing* 1.

LEMAN. See *Hymns and Hymn Tunes* 8.

LEMARE, EDWIN HENRY. Born at Ventnor in the Isle of Wight in 1865 and died in the United States in 1934, aged sixty-nine. He was trained at the Royal Academy of Music, London, and after holding church organ posts gave himself up to a recital career. He was successively organist at the Carnegie Institute, Pittsburgh, municipal organist at San Francisco, and municipal organist at Portland, Maine. He was a popular writer and (especially) arranger of music for his instrument.

See references under *Improvisation* 2.

LEMMENS, NICOLAS JACQUES. Born near Westerloo, in Northern Belgium, in 1823 and died near Malines in 1881, aged fifty-eight. He was the son of an organist and himself devoted to the organ from earliest years. After study at the Conservatory of Brussels he was sent by the Belgian Government to Breslau to study under Hesse, who after twelve months declared he had nothing to teach him. Appointed professor of organ at his old school, he exercised a remarkable influence upon the whole development of the art of organ playing

in his native country and, indeed, in a far wider territory. For a time (married to Miss Sherrington, the soprano, hence known as 'Lemmens-Sherrington') he lived in England. In his very last years he carried on an institution at Malines for the training of church musicians.

He wrote a great *Organ School* and an important work on the accompanying of plainsong. His organ compositions are numerous and are often played. If organists must play 'Storms' let them keep to the one he left!

Cf. *Organ* 13.

LEMMENS-SHERRINGTON. See under *Lemmens.*

LENE, LENO (It.). 'Gentle.' So *Lenezza*, 'gentleness'.

LENKOVITCH, BERNHARD (born 1927). See *Scandinavia* 2.

LENT (Fr.), **LENTO** (It.). 'Slow.' So *Lentando, Lentato*, 'slowing', 'slowed' (same as *Rallentando*); *Lentement* (Fr.), *Lentamente* (It.), 'slowly'; *Lenteur* (Fr.), *Lentezza* (It.), 'slowness'; *Lentissimo*, 'very slow'.

LEO.

1) LEONARDO. Born near Brindisi in 1694 and died at Naples in 1744, aged fifty. He wrote sixty comic and serious operas, some fine church music, and also various works for harpsichord and organ. Some of his music is still played and sung.

(2) OF MODENA. See *Jewish Music* 4.

LEONCAVALLO, RUGGIERO (p. 524, pl. **95.** 7). Born at Naples in 1858 and died near Florence in 1919, aged sixty-one. After an early life in café music he succeeded in getting his *Pagliacci* (q.v.) on to the boards of Milan (1892). This was his first and last great success (cf. *Mascagni*), but some have preferred his *La Bohème* to that of Puccini.

See reference—*Music Hall* 4.

LÉONIN (or **LEONINUS**). See *France* 2.

'LEONORA' OVERTURE. See *Fidelio.*

LEOPOLD OF ANHALT-CÖTHEN. See *Puritans* 3.

LERCHENQUARTETT (Haydn). See *Nicknamed Compositions* 12.

LE ROY. See *Publishing* 2.

LERTES. See *Electric Musical Instrument* 1 k.

LES (Fr.). 'The' (plural).

LES ADIEUX (Beethoven Sonata). See *Nicknamed Compositions* 5.

LESCHETIZKY, THEODOR (LESZETYCKI, TEODOR). Born in 1830, of Polish parents, near Lemberg (then in Austrian territory, now in Russia—Lwow), and died in 1915 at Dresden, aged eighty-five. He was a pianist and composer (chiefly of piano music of the lighter type), but, above all, a teacher of piano.

For eighteen years he was attached in this last capacity to the Conservatory of St. Petersburg. and then he settled in Vienna, where there flocked to him, from all parts of the world, innumerable pupils. Many of these (e.g. Paderewski, Gabrilowitch, Fanny Bloomfield-Zeisler, Katharine Goodson, Ethel Liggins or Leginska, Mark Hambourg, Moiseiwitsch, Schnabel) became famous, and three of them (Essipoff, Benislavska, Rozborska) became respectively his second, third, and fourth wives: the last-named is the Madame Leschetizky who was widely known as a piano recitalist.

He disclaimed the often-used term 'Leschetizky Method', saying that he applied nothing so describable, but studied the needs of each pupil individually. The main bases of his teaching were, in technique, a very close analysis of muscular movements and, in interpretation, an intense concentration on detail.

See references under *Pianoforte Playing* 7; *Fingering* 5.

LESGINKA. Same as *Lezginka* (q.v.).

LESLIE, HENRY DAVID. Born in London in 1822 and died near Oswestry in 1896, aged seventy-three. He began musical life as violoncellist and ended it as the most famous British choral conductor of his day, 'Henry Leslie's Choir' (a London organization) winning the first prize in the Paris International Contest in 1878. His part songs (admirably laid out for the voices) are still sung, his other compositions almost forgotten.

See reference under *Absolute Pitch*.

LESQUERCADE (Fr.). This word, which is seen as a movement-title in several lighter orchestral suites (e.g. Delibes, Hahn, Röntgen) appears to be unknown to the musical dictionaries, the French dictionaries, or the many French musicologists who have been questioned. It is found to be Languedoc patois for 'a maiden in love'.

LESSER DOXOLOGY. See *Doxology*.

'LES SIX.' See *France* 11.

LESSON. See *Suite* 1.

LESTO (It.). 'Quick.' So *Lestamente*, 'quickly'; *Lestissimo*, 'very quickly'.

L'ESTRANGE, SIR ROGER (1616–1704). See references under *Puritans* 4; *Clubs for Music-Making*.

LESUEUR, JEAN FRANÇOIS. Born near Abbeville in 1760 and died in Paris in 1837, aged seventy-seven. The first quarter-century or so of his musical life was passed in the practice of church music, in which he quickly ran through the whole gamut of activity from choir-boy in his native Abbeville to the musical control of Notre Dame in Paris.

In this last position his methods were novel. He employed all the resources of a full orchestra, introduced dramatic and picturesque effects of every kind, and set out, successfully, to attract crowds to the place of devotion. It is significant that the grandiose Berlioz, who was one of his pupils at the Conservatory (years later, of course), speaks of these methods with sympathy; some of the clergy, however, were distressed (if only on the grounds of the expense involved); a short pamphlet war ensued, and he retired from his position. This was in 1788, so that in any case the Revolution would before long have brought his church work to an end.

He passed four years in retirement and then opened a new career—as opera composer. He had various battles to fight in this field also, but he emerged triumphant in 1804 when Napoleon, as First Consul, appointed him his musical Director. This position he held throughout the period of the Empire, and on the accession of Louis XVIII in 1814 he was offered and accepted a similar position at his court.

As a teacher at the newly founded Conservatory he did work of high value. Twelve of his students gained the Rome Prize, and these included Berlioz, Ambroise Thomas, and Gounod.

See references under *Oratorio* 4, 7 (1826).

LESUR, DANIEL. Born in Paris in 1908. He is an organist, professor of counterpoint at the Schola Cantorum (q.v.), and composer—a member of the little group with which Messiaen (q.v.) is associated (see *Jeune France*).

LESZETYCKI. See *Leschetizky*.

LETTER V SYMPHONY (Haydn). See *Nicknamed* 11.

LETZT (Ger.). 'Last' (various terminations according to gender, number, case).

LEUTGEBISCHES QUINTETT. See *Nicknamed* 15.

LEVALTO. See *Volta*.

LEVARE (It.). 'To lift' or take off. So *Si levano i sordini*, 'the mutes are taken off'. The past participle *Levato* (plural *Levati*) occurs. Also the imperative *Levate*, 'lift off'.

LEVERIDGE, RICHARD. Born in London about 1670 and died in 1758, aged about eighty-eight. He was a bass singer who at sixty offered to sing a bass song with any man in England for a hundred guineas. And he not only sang songs but made them, including 'All in the Downs', 'The Roast Beef of Old England', and 'Black-eyed Susan' (q.v.).

He fell into poverty, and it would have gone hardly with him in old age had he not been supported to the end by friends and admirers who maintained an annual subscription list on his behalf.

See reference s.v. *Misattributed* (Locke's Music to 'Macbeth').

LEVET. A piece of music for the rising out of bed. See, for instance, this entry in the diary of Judge Sewall of Boston, New England, on New Year's Day 1696: '*One with a Trumpet sounds a Levet at our window just about break of day, bids me good morrow and wishes health and happiness to attend me.*'

Cf. *Reveille* and *Aubade*.

LEVEZZA (It.). 'Lightness.'

LEVI, HERMANN (1839–1900). He was one of the most famous opera conductors of his period, especially renowned for his Wagner interpretations at Bayreuth and elsewhere, and, in addition, the composer of a piano concerto, songs, etc., and the editor of German editions of some of Mozart's Italian operas, some French operas, etc.

LEVIDIS, DIMITRI. See *Electric Musical Instruments* 1 f.

LEWANDOWSKI. See *Jewish* 6.

LEWIS, ANTHONY. Born in Bermuda in 1915. He studied at Cambridge and then in Paris under Nadia Boulanger. In 1935 he joined the staff of the BBC. After war service he was (1947) Professor of Music at Birmingham University and (1968) Principal of the R.A.M. He was knighted in 1972. He has written on various musical subjects, has edited old music, and composed orchestral and other works.

LEY, HENRY GEORGE. Born at Chagford, Devon, in 1887 and died in 1962, aged seventy-four. He was a chorister at St. George's Chapel, Windsor, who, after holding scholarships at the Royal College of Music (on whose staff he later served) and Keble College, Oxford, passed to the organistship of Christ Church Cathedral, Oxford (1909), and was then from 1926 to 1945 Musical Director ('Precentor') of Eton College. He published songs, part songs, church music, etc.

See *Anglican Chant* 6.

LEZGINKA (Russian). A dance of the Mohammedan tribe, the Lezghins or Lezghians (on the Persian border).

L.G.S.M. See *Degrees and Diplomas* 2.

L'HOMME ARMÉ. See *Mass* 5.

LIADOF (Liadoff, Liadov, Liadow, etc.), **ANATOL** (p. 912, pl. **155.** 1). Born in St. Petersburg in 1855 and died there in 1914, aged fifty-nine. He came of a line of professional musicians and after studying with his father was placed under Rimsky-Korsakof at the Conservatory of St. Petersburg, of which he later became a professor.

As a composer he is best known by his attractive brief piano compositions and by the tone poems *Baba Yaga* and *Kikimora*. He did good service in the collection and publication of Russian folk music.

See also allusions to him under *Chopsticks*; *Belaief*; *Mechanical* 7.

LIAISON (Fr.). 'Binding.' Three senses: (1) smooth performance: (2) the slur that indicates such performance; (3) the tie or bind.

LIAPUNOF (Liapunov, Liapounow, etc.), **SERGE** (p. 912, pl. **155.** 2). Born at Yaroslavl in 1859 and died in Paris in 1924, aged nearly sixty-five. He was a friend of Balakiref and an adherent of the Russian national school of composition. He wrote orchestral music and some very difficult and effective virtuoso music for piano (*Studies in Transcendental Execution* —suggested obviously by Liszt's work in the same field; two Concertos). He did good ser-

vice as a collector and editor of Russian folk music.

LIB. See *Ad libitum*.

LIBEL. See *Criticism* 10.

LIBERA ME. See *Requiem*.

LIBERAMENTE (It.). 'Freely', i.e. as to tempo, rhythm, etc.

LIBER SCRIPTUS. See *Requiem*.

LIBERTÀ (It.). 'Liberty', freedom.

LIBERTY SONG. See *Heart of Oak*.

LIBITUM (Lat.). See *Ad libitum*.

LIBRARIES OF MUSIC AND MUSICAL LITERATURE. From a very early period in the history of the Christian Church collections of the manuscript copies of the music in use naturally accumulated in the abbeys and cathedrals of Europe and some of these still remain and are a valuable source of material for historians and for editors of early compositions. Royal and noble personages likewise amassed material—in their case chiefly of instrumental and other secular music: a familiar late instance of this last is the royal collection due largely to the very musical George III and his queen, now in the British Museum.

Highly important stores of musical material in **Britain** are those in the British Museum, the Fitzwilliam Library, Cambridge, and the Library of Cambridge University, the Bodleian Library of Oxford University, the National Library of Scotland (Edinburgh), the libraries of the Royal College and Royal Academy of Music, the Manchester Public Library (based on the private collection of the late Dr. Henry Watson), the Bournemouth Music Library (based on the collection of the late Dr. J. B. Camm), the library of St. Michael's College, Tenbury (based on that of Sir Frederick Gore Ouseley (q.v.)), and the rapidly growing Central Music Library (based on the collection of the late Edwin Evans); this last is housed in a branch of the City of Westminster Public Libraries in Buckingham Palace Road, London, and was founded and endowed in 1947 by the pianist, Mrs. Winifred Christie Moór (1882–1965). The 'British Union-Catalogue of Early Music printed before 1801' (1957) covers the contents of over 100 British libraries, including many private ones (cf. *King, Alexander Hyatt*).

In **Eire** the library of Trinity College, Dublin, is very important. Under the British Copyright Act this Library, the University Libraries of Oxford and Cambridge, the British Museum, and the National Library of Scotland are entitled to a free copy of every book and every piece of music as published.

In the **United States** important collections are those of the Library of Congress (Washington), the Libraries of Harvard and Yale Universities, the Public Libraries of New York, Chicago, and Boston, the library of the Curtis Institute and the remarkable Fleisher Library (both in Philadelphia), that of the Eastman

School at Rochester, N.Y., and the Huntington Library, San Marino, California.

In **Germany** there is the Prussian State Library (Berlin): in **Austria** the Library of the Gesellschaft der Musikfreunde (Vienna): in **France** the Library of the Conservatoire and the Bibliothèque Nationale, Paris, and that of the Paris Opéra: in **Belgium** the Royal Library and the Conservatoire Library (both in Brussels); and in **Italy** the Vatican Library, that of the Santa Cecilia, Rome, and that of the Liceo Musicale of Bologna (this last based on the collection of Padre Martini—see *Martini* 1). These are just a few of the many great libraries that exist.

As regards Britain and the United States it may safely be said that every city and every town of any size now possesses a larger or smaller collection of music and books on music —these being available not merely for reference on the spot but also for borrowing. Public libraries also have an arrangement by which if they do not possess a publication desired by a reader they will procure the loan of it from some other library in the country. (The books and music in the Central Music Library above mentioned are thus available to borrowers in all parts of the country).

Microphotography and xerography have now come to the aid of musicology and unique or rare manuscripts or early printed volumes can be quickly and cheaply reproduced—with the double advantage of making them widely accessible to students and of avoiding irreparable loss to the musical world in case of fire or of war destruction. The extension of this practice to the reproduction of works protected by copyright is understandably regarded with mixed feelings by authors and others whose livelihood seems, however mildly, threatened.

Mechanical recordings now form an increasing part of the resources of many libraries, e.g. at the Library of Congress there is a large collection of American folk music thus preserved, and this is continually growing.

For extended and comprehensive lists of the more important music libraries of the world and of their chief contents the following should be consulted: Grove's *Dictionary of Music and Musicians*, the *International Cyclopedia of Music and Musicians*, and the *Harvard Dictionary of Music*. For the location of unique or rare copies of works of particular composers consult, under the composer's name, Eitner's *Biographisch-bibliographisches Quellen-Lexikon der Musiker und Musikgelehrten* (ten volumes, 1900–4, and many supplementary brochures— extremely useful). For a general discussion of the subject of the management of music libraries there is available a work by E. T. Bryant—*Music Librarianship* (1959). There is in progress an *International Inventory of Musical Sources*, which is intended eventually to replace 'Eitner'.

The following advice may be offered to any young reader who is desirous of building up a useful personal collection of musical literature —(*a*) Buy any useful book as soon as it appears, as many books are quickly sold out and their publication not repeated; (*b*) if, however, you wish to procure any older work which has already gone off the market ask a second-hand bookseller to insert a notice in the private trade paper which circulates throughout the whole trade.

See *Dictionaries* 15; *Gramophone* 7.

LIBRARY OF CONGRESS. See *United States of America* 5 a; *Libraries*.

LIBRE, LIBREMENT (Fr.). 'Free', 'freely'.

LIBRETTO (It.; literally, 'little book'). The 'book of words' of an oratorio or opera. It is necessarily a very important ingredient in the work. A bad librettist has often brought failure on the work of a good composer, as did Wilhelmina von Chezy, the librettist of Weber's *Euryanthe*. Yet sometimes a good composer has triumphed over the poverty of an incompetent librettist, as Verdi did in *Il Trovatore*.

Wagner was his own librettist. Boito wrote not only his own libretti but those of a number of operas set by other composers—especially those of Verdi's *Othello* and *Falstaff*.

Certain librettists have supplied the needs of a number of composers. Thus Rinuccini (d. 1621) wrote the books for several of the operas of the Florentine pioneers (see *Opera* 1, 2) and so may be called the Father of the Libretto.

In the eighteenth century the name of Apostolo Zeno (1668–1750), of Vienna and Venice, is prominent, but the universal provider was Metastasio (1698–1782), who wrote about fifty opera and oratorio libretti, some of which were set over and over again, and occasionally by as many as twenty or thirty different composers. Opera-goers all over Europe came to know many of his 'books' by heart. He was the King of the Librettists, and held his court at Vienna. The Englishman Burney compiled his life and letters in three volumes (1796). He reports that the German composer Hasse (1699–1783) told him that he had set all but one of Metastasio's libretti and some of them he had set two, three, and four times (see *Metastasio*; *Opera* 9).

Sometimes a particular librettist has become associated with a particular composer, so that they have come to think together, as it were. This was so with Calzabigi and Gluck, who collaborated in *Orpheus*, *Alcestis*, and *Paris and Helen*; with Hofmannsthal and Strauss, who collaborated in *Electra*, *The Knight of the Rose*, *Ariadne in Naxos*, *The Woman without a Shadow*, *The Egyptian Helen*, and *Arabella*; and, of course, supremely, with Gilbert and Sullivan, who in some future years may come to merge in the public mind into one personality, like, in another department of literature, the novelist-collaborators Erckmann–Chatrian.

For references to the Towers *Dictionary of Opera Libretti* and the Schatz Collection of libretti see *Opera* 26.

LICENZA (It.). 'Licence', freedom (in such expressions as *Con alcuna licenza*—'with some licence', i.e. freedom as to tempo and rhythm).

LICHFIELD CATHEDRAL. See references under *Cathedral Music* 2, 7; *Este, M.*; *Alcock, John* (I).

LICHFILD, HENRY. End of the sixteenth century and beginning of the seventeenth. Little is known of him except that he left madrigals behind him. It is surmised that he was an amateur musician.

LIE, SIGURD. Born at Drammen, Norway, in 1871 and died there in 1904, aged thirty-three. He studied in Leipzig and Berlin and practised as a violinist and choral conductor in Bergen and Christiania (now Oslo).

His works (for orchestra, choir, solo voice, etc.) have qualities that render his early death deplorable.

LIÉ (Fr.). 'Bound', i.e. (*a*) slurred, or (*b*) tied.

LIEBE (Ger.). 'Love.'

LIEBERMANN, ROLF. Born in Zürich in 1910. He studied under Wladimir Vogel and Scherchen. He has been in turn musical director of the local radio network, head of the orchestral division of Swiss radio, manager of the Opéra in Paris, and (from 1973) director of the Hamburg State Opera. His works include the operas *Leonore 40/45* (1952); *School for Wives* (1955), a Concerto for Jazz Band and Symphony Orchestra, and other orchestral and chamber works.

LIEBESGEIGE (Ger.). Viola d'amore (see *Viol Family* 4 f).

LIEBESOBOE (Ger.). Oboe d'amore (see *Oboe Family* 5 f).

LIEBLICHFLÖTE. See *Flute Family* 5.

LIEBLICH GEDACT. See *Organ* 14 I, II.

LIED, LIEDER (Ger.). 'Song', 'songs'. (For the special connotation of these terms, as used nowadays by musicians, see *Song* 5.) So *Liedchen*, *Liedlein*, 'little song'; *Liedercyklus*, 'song cycle'; *Liederkreis*, 'song circle', i.e. song cycle; *Liederreihe*, 'song series', i.e. song cycle; *Lied ohne Worte* (not 'Wörter' in this connexion, though sometimes so misspelt), 'song without words' (q.v.).

LIEDERTAFEL (Ger.; literally 'song-table'). A common name for the male-voice singing society. Originally the singing was done sitting round a table with refreshments, but the aims later became more definitely artistic. It has long been understood that the Liedertafel movement was founded by Zelter (q.v.) in Berlin, in 1808 or 1809, and English and German books of reference confirm this. On the other hand, the Liedertafel Association of Germany (10,000 members) celebrated its centenary in 1931 and on that occasion it was stated that 'the first society of this type was founded at Nienburg-on-the-Weser by some singers who came from Bremen and Hamburg, other groups quickly forming in neighbouring towns'.

A *Männergesangverein* ('Men's Song Society') is much the same as a Liedertafel (see *Orphéon* for the analogous French movement).

England (see *Clubs for Music-Making*) was, as German and French books of musical reference admit, the pioneer in this type of activity.

LIED OHNE WORTE (Ger.). 'Song without words' (q.v.).

LIEFS, JON. See *Leifs*.

LIÈGE. See *Belgium* 2, 5.

LIETO (It.). 'Joyous.' So *Lietissimo*, 'very joyous'; *Lietezza*, 'joy'.

LIEVE (It.). (1) 'Light', (2) 'easy'. So *Lievezza*, 'lightness'; *Lievemente*, 'lightly'.

LIFAR, SERGE. See *Ballet* 9.

LIFE FOR THE CZAR. See *Glinka*.

LIFE ON THE OCEAN WAVE. See *Russell, Henry*.

LIGATURE.

(1) The mark which in plainsong notation binds several notes into one group (see *Notation* 3). There have been very complicated rules as to the interpretation of the time-values in ligature.

(2) The slur which, in modern notation of vocal music, shows that the notes it affects go to one syllable of the words.

(3) The tie or bind (q.v.) is sometimes called a 'ligature', but there seems no purpose in giving it a third name which also belongs to a different thing entirely.

(4) The adjustable metal band securing the reed to the mouthpiece in instruments of the clarinet type.

LIGHT, EDWARD. See *Dital Harp*.

LIGHT-KEYBOARD. See *Colour and Music* 11.

LIGHT OPERA. Opera of which the subject-matter is cheerful and the musical treatment such as calls for little effort on the part of the listener.

LIGHTWOOD, JAMES THOMAS (1856–1944). He was an authority on the history of the hymn tune and long editor of the monthly periodical *The Choir*. See *Methodism* 10; *Descant*.

LILLIBURLERO. This tune first appeared in print in 1686 in a book of 'lessons' for the recorder or flute, where it is styled merely a Quickstep.

Next year it became popular set to some grotesque and satirical verses (with the mock Irish word 'Lilliburlero' as a refrain) referring to the appointment to the Lord Lieutenancy of Ireland of General Talbot, just created Earl of Tyrconnel, whose name they several times mention.

This was the period when the Roman Catholic James II was becoming very unpopular, and the song was a bitter party one ridiculing Talbot and the Irish Roman Catholics. It played a part in the events leading to the discomfiture of James II and the landing of William in Northern Ireland and has remained a tune of the Orange party to this day, set to another song, 'Protestant Boys'. In the intervening period this tune has had many such songs of militant Protestantism attached to it.

Apparently the song 'Lilliburlero' was sometimes sung not to the tune in question but to another well-known tune, *Cold and Raw* (q.v.), with which it is associated in a ballad broadside of the time: if so, it would seem that the present tune quickly superseded this.

It is thought that Purcell may be the author as, in 1689, in John Playford's *Music's Handmaid*, it appears, with Purcell's name attached, under the title 'A New Irish Tune', as a tiny piece for the harpsichord: Purcell also used it as a ground bass (q.v.) in music for a play, *The Gordian Knot unty'd*, in 1691. The probability seems to be that Purcell was simply using a popular air of the day. (For an alleged Dutch origin for the tune, a century and a half earlier, see *Hymns and Hymn Tunes* 17 c.)

Some English children now know the tune as that of the nursery rhyme 'There was an old woman tossed up in a blanket, Seventy times as high as the moon'.

'L'IMPÉRIALE' SYMPHONY (Haydn). See *Nicknamed Compositions* 11.

LINCOLN CATHEDRAL. See *Cathedral Music* 2; *Acoustics* 2 (footnote). Musicians who receive notice in this volume are (with their periods of office): *Byrd* (organist 1563–72); *J. Reading* ('Poor Vicar' 1667; Master of the Choristers 1670).

LINCOLN CENTER. A cultural centre opened in New York in 1962, and finally including concert hall, opera house, theatre, music school, etc. First President (1961–8), William Schuman.

See *Opera* 23; p. 721, pl. **120**. 3.

LINCOLN'S INN FIELDS THEATRE. See *Fairs and their Music*; *Beggar's Opera*.

LIND, JENNY (1820–87). See *Scandinavia* 4; *Benedict*.

LINDBERG, O. (1887–1955). See *Scandinavia* 4.

LINDEMAN, L. M. (1812–87). See *Scandinavia* 3.

LINDSAY, LADY ANNE (1750–1825). See *Auld Robin Gray*.

LINEAR COUNTERPOINT. Counterpoint with emphasis on the individual strands of the musical fabric rather than on their harmonic implications.

LINING-OUT. See *Hymns and Hymn Tunes* 8.

LINKE HAND (Ger.). 'Left hand.' *Links* means the same.

LINLEY Family of Bath and district. They are too numerous to detail here, but the following must be noticed:

(1) THOMAS (Senior). Born in 1732 and died in London in 1795, aged sixty-three. He was a carpenter who, being sent to do a job at a duke's, heard some good playing and singing, determined to become a musician, studied first under the organist of Bath Abbey and then under Paradies at Naples, and set up as a singing-master and concert-giver in Bath, becoming famous for the Handel works he performed with the help of his talented family.

Sheridan married his daughter, Elizabeth Ann, the famous soprano ('The Maid of Bath'), and when the son-in-law took over the management of Drury Lane Theatre the father-in-law accepted charge of the music there.

He was a popular stage composer, and music of his is found in song-books today.

See reference under *Oratorio* 5.

(2) THOMAS (Junior). Son of the above. Born at Bath in 1756 and died at Grimsthorpe in Lincolnshire in 1778, aged twenty-two.

He was the bosom friend of Mozart at Florence, when both were there as boys of fourteen, Mozart travelling with his father and Linley studying the violin with Nardini. Burney, in the account of his Italian tour, records, 'The *Tommasino*, as he is called, and the Little Mozart, are talked of all over Italy as the most promising geniuses of this age'.

On his return to England he was active in composition and might possibly have realized the Italians' expectations had he not lost his life through a boating accident. The song (from *The Tempest*) 'O bid your faithful Ariel fly' is by him.

(3) WILLIAM (another son of Thomas, senior). Born at Bath in 1771 and died in London in 1835, aged sixty-four. He was in the service of the East India Company, but in his thirties left it and settled in London where he composed glees, anthems, songs, etc., and wrote novels and verses.

LINLEY, GEORGE. Born in Leeds in 1798 and died in London in 1865, aged sixty-six or sixty-seven. He wrote operas and polite popular songs such as 'Ever of thee I'm fondly dreaming'. In bolder mood he stood up to the critics in a satirical volume, *Musical Cynics of London*.

LINTERN. See *Nicknamed Compositions* 10 ('Harmonious Blacksmith').

'LINZ' SYMPHONY (Mozart). See *Nicknamed Compositions* 15.

LIRA. See *Lyra*.

LIRA ORGANIZZATA. *Hurdy-gurdy* (q.v.).

LIRICO (It.). 'Lyric.'

LIRONE, LIRONE PERFETTO. See under *Lyra* 3.

LISCIO, LISCIA (It., masc., fem.). 'Smooth.'

LISLE. See *Rouget de Lisle*.

LISLEY, JOHN. All that is known of him is that a madrigal of his is to be found in *The Triumphs of Oriana* (see *Madrigal* 4).

LISTENIUS, NICOLAUS. See *Notation* 3 (end of section).

L'ISTESSO (It.). 'The same', e.g. *L'istesso tempo*, maintain the same speed as before. (But see *Stesso*.)

LISZT, FERENCZ—or Franz (p. 480, pl. **83**. 1; 797, **136**. 8; 893, **152**. 4; 801, **138**. 6). Born at Dobr'jan (otherwise Raiding), Hungary, in 1811 and died at Bayreuth, Bavaria, in 1886, aged seventy-four. He was born in 'the year of the great comet', and his career was that of a brilliant phenomenon. For half a century he illuminated the world of music as pianist, astonishing and delighting the greatest auditory any public musical performer had yet attached to himself, and earning fabulous sums which he freely dispensed in generous charity.

As composer he introduced new processes, and he counts as the inventor of the symphonic poem. A special device of his was that called *Metamorphosis of Themes* (q.v.). A piece of programme music would be based upon some theme or themes representative of some person or idea, and, as the music progressed and the circumstances imagined altered in accordance with the underlying literary or dramatic scheme of the composition, the theme would change in character. This is obviously akin to the *Idée fixe* of Berlioz (q.v.) and the *Leading Motif* (q.v.) of Wagner.

As teacher of piano he had through his hands nearly all the most brilliant young people of his day. As teacher of composition he did not regularly practise, but the young men of the period flocked to him with their scores and if they showed promise he encouraged them, and, by his influence with publishers and conductors, launched them in their careers (see, for instance, under *Brahms, Grieg,* and *MacDowell* —merely three examples out of a very large number).

He prominently represents the progressive tendencies in the music of the mid-nineteenth century; the term 'The Music of the Future' was coined in his house. He was the noblest and most powerful champion of Wagner, who became his son-in-law, and his daughter Cosima, after twenty years of life with that composer, lived on at Bayreuth, and for about double that period, until age at last laid her aside, continued to maintain the Wagner cult in its central temple and to sustain the authentic traditions of performance (she died in 1930, aged ninety-two).

A brief summary of his life may now be given. His father was steward to that family of Esterházy that had shortly before had Haydn in its service, and was a good amateur musician and his son's first teacher. Then the boy was taken to Vienna, where he studied piano under Czerny and composition under Salieri, the former teacher of Schubert, with whom the boy became acquainted. At eleven, in Vienna, his amazing abilities were greeted by Beethoven with a public kiss.

He passed on to Paris, where Society, Literature, and Art fêted him, and where, still a child, he produced his only opera; in England at the same period he had a brilliant reception.

During his Paris period he was much in touch with the writers of the flourishing Romantic School—Hugo, Lamartine, George Sand, Sainte-Beuve, and others, as also with their painter colleagues such as Delacroix, and this marks the greatest influence in his life.

Approaching forty (in 1849), he settled at Weimar as musical director to the Prince, and here he remained for ten years, reviving the fame which that capital had enjoyed under its great intellectual and artistic dictator, Goethe. It was here that he enjoyed and exercised his greatest opportunity of pushing forward rising genius. Wagner's *Lohengrin* had its first performance under his baton, and the works of Berlioz were prominently brought before the public.

From about his fiftieth year he made Rome his centre. He still carried on activities at Weimar and, to some extent, at Budapest (for the Hungarians were proud of him and took means to entice him to their capital), but he had turned to religion, taken minor orders in the Church, and become known as the Abbé Liszt; his compositions from now onwards took a religious trend.

It is impossible to discuss the career of Liszt without reference to the women whom in turn he loved and who in turn influenced him. He was more ardent than constant. Omitting minor episodes, there must be mentioned his intimacy with the Countess of Agoult (later known as a novelist under the name of 'Daniel Stern'); Cosima Wagner, already referred to above, was one of his children by her.

The Princess Sayn-Wittgenstein was his companion at Weimar and in Rome, and their relations were coloured by a curious mixture of passion and piety. The Prince being still alive, there were obstacles to marriage; it was hoped that the Pope would remove them, but after a long consideration of the case he unexpectedly refused.

Of works bearing Liszt's name there are about 1,300, of which 400 are original and the rest 'transcriptions'—for he was a great 'transcriber' or 'arranger' for the piano (see *Arrangement*). His playing overshadowed his composing, and though the influence of his compositions (especially of the spirit and technical processes of his symphonic poems) is seen in the work of such various writers as Wagner, Raff, Tchaikovsky, Rimsky-Korsakof, Borodin, Saint-Saëns, Smetana, Scriabin, and Strauss, yet his works have never, in themselves, come to occupy the position their creator and his admirers (of his own time and of the present) have thought to be their due.

Articles or passages bearing on or mentioning the work of Liszt will be found as follows:

Albéniz, Isaac; Arrangement; Balakiref; Ballade; Bartók; Bell 6; *Berlioz; Borodin; Brahms; Bülow; Campanella; Chopsticks; Cinematograph; Composition* 12; *Concert* 8; *Concerto* 6 b (1811); *Cornelius; Criticism* 5; *Danse Macabre; Étude; Fingering* 5; *Folia; Folk Song* 5; *Franck; Franz; García* 4; *Glazunof; Grieg; Harp* 3; *Hexameron; History* 7; *Holland* 7; *Hungary; Improvisation* 2; *Jewish* 6; *Joachim; Jota; Keyboard* 4; *Kienzl; Korbay; Leading Motif; Liapunof; Lohengrin; Mac-Dowell; Mass* 4; *Metamorphosis of Themes; Nationalism; New Music; Oratorio* 1, 3, 7 (1865, 1876); *Organ* 13; *Paganini; Patronage* 6; *Percussion Family* 4 b (Bass Drum, Triangle); *Pianoforte* 13, 14, 20, 21, 22; *Pianoforte Playing* 6, 7; *Programme Music* 1, 5 d; *Rákóczy March; Recital; Rhapsody; Romantic; Rubinstein, Anton; Rumania* (3, Adolf Flechtenmacher); *Sonata* 10 d (1854); *Song without Words; Spain* 10; *Strelezki; Symphonic Poem; Symphony* 8 (1811); *Wagner.*

LITANIAE LAURETANAE, or Litany of Loretto, is a thirteenth-century litany in honour

PLATE 103

LISZT THE TRAVELLER

By Batt

ALTHOUGH Liszt was lionized and fêted wherever he went he was at heart an unhappy man. Two opposing forces were continually at war within him. He revelled in the glamour he created, but when satiated with all this he would shut himself away from the world, full of disgust, the desire to write great works strong upon him. Then his delight in the world's applause would prove too strong; he longed again to see fashionable society at his feet and he would emerge again from his isolation.

In his last years his raking discontent made him more than ever restless. He travelled incessantly, urged on, it would seem, by a burning desire to make amends, for he gave his services wherever they could be applied to a useful purpose, as he had for long given all his lessons free of charge. He was, at heart, a grand old man, yet ever haunted by the spectre of 'the idle uselessness that frets me'.   B.

of the Virgin Mary. It is sung every evening at Loretto and is much sung in Italy generally. It is frequently used at Benediction (q.v.) after the O Salutaris (q.v.). Palestrina composed many settings of it and modern composers too many.

Cf. *Litany*, below.

LITANY. A supplication. The Roman Catholic Church and the Anglican Church each possesses a long litany consisting of very brief expressions by the priest, each followed by some such response from the people as 'Deliver us, O Lord', or 'We beseech Thee, hear us'. The Anglican Litany (see *Common Prayer*) is a free translation and adaptation of the chief Roman Litany. It first appeared (in English) as a separate Book under Henry VIII (1544) and in his Primer of the following year was called the 'Common Prayer of Procession'; litanies, with their rhythmical alternation of prayer and refrain, being considered specially suitable for processional use. (Cf. *Litaniae Lauretanae*.)

LITHOGRAPHY. See *Printing of Music* 4.

LITOLFF, HENRY CHARLES. Born in London in 1818 and died near Paris in 1891, aged seventy-three. He was of Alsatian descent. His first fame was as a widely travelling virtuoso pianist, his second as an enlightened and enterprising music publisher, his third as a composer. In the last capacity he is now forgotten save for one or two things, notably the *Concerto symphonique* for piano and orchestra.

See references under *Publishing* 8; *Pianoforte* 22.

LITTLE SYMPHONY (Schubert). See *Nicknamed* 18.

LITURGY. By liturgy is properly meant the service of the Christian Eucharist, but in ordinary usage of the English language it is now applied to the written and officially authorized form of religious service of any church which employs such a form. The evolution of liturgies, and the forms in which they have finally become standardized, have had a very great effect on the development of music, especially since for many centuries the only literate musicians were those of the church, and the only fully organized music that of its services.

During the first few centuries of the Christian Church liturgies were innumerable, being largely local or territorial. There were Syrian, Egyptian, Persian, Byzantine, Hispano-Gallican, and other rites. In addition to all these there is, of course, the Roman Rite which now prevails throughout the Roman Catholic Church of the world, with a few exceptions; amongst these exceptions are the Ambrosian Rite which is still in use in Milan, though every fresh Archbishop modifies it a little so that it must in time disappear (see reference to the influence of St. Ambrose on music in the articles *Plainsong* and *Modes*), and the Mozarabic Rite, which is still maintained in Toledo in Spain (see *Spain* 2; *Dance* 7).

The first Christian churches at Rome were Greek-speaking and had a Greek liturgy; the origin of the Latin liturgy of Rome is unknown. It overspread Europe from the seventh to the eleventh century, though local differences remained (see reference to the influence of Charlemagne in the article *Plainsong*). It is comprised for the main part in two volumes, the **Missal** (compiled about 900; many revisions since), which gives the service of the Mass or Eucharist, and the **Breviary** (compiled in the eleventh century), which gives other services—i.e. the Divine Office for each day. The **Ritual**, giving the special services (baptisms, marriages, funerals, etc.), and the **Pontifical**, giving services only to be performed by bishops (as that of ordination), complete the series.

The Mass being the principal service of the Roman Catholic Church, the Missal has had the greatest part in directing the activities of church composers (see article *Mass*).

Until the second half of the twentieth century the Roman Catholic liturgy remained unique amongst liturgies in the general conformity of its language throughout the world, that of the Greek (or Orthodox Church) being in use in Old Greek, Old Slavonic, Arabic, and Georgian and other languages (see *Greek Church and Music*), and that of the Anglican Church (so far as it is used outside English-speaking countries) in innumerable translations according to the country in which it is being used. (It has already been mentioned that within the Roman Catholic Communion other rites than the Roman are in use, and it may here be added that other languages than the Latin are in use in certain ancient churches, especially in Slav countries and in the Near East.) In the 1960s the Roman Catholic Church at last gave official encouragement to the use of the vernacular.

The Greek Church admits no instrument into its services. Some particulars of its music will be found in the article *Greek Church and Music*, while the music of the Roman Catholic Church will be found discussed under *Mass* and similar articles on details of the service, and that of the Anglican Church under *Common Prayer*.

The Lutheran liturgy, as its author left it, was largely a translation, with omissions, of the Latin liturgy—and with an increased opportunity for the congregation to take part.

For examples of the interpolations by which the Roman liturgy was gradually expanded see *Trope, Alleluia*, and *Sequence*.

For related subjects see *Divine Office; Mass; Common; Common Prayer; Use of Sarum; Litany; Psalm; Canticle; Hymn; Respond; Accentus; Antiphon; Antiphonal; Tract; Caeremoniale; Creed; Improperia; Requiem; Te Deum*.

LIUTO (It.). Lute. See *Lute Family*.

LIVERPOOL. See *Temperament* 6; *Best; Peace; Organ* 5; *Concert* 10; *Abraham*.

LIVINGSTON, REVD. NEIL. Presbyterian divine (Free Church minister at Stair, Ayrshire, 1844–86). See *Hymns and Hymn Tunes* 17 e xvi.

LIVRE (Fr.). 'Book.'

LLANDAFF CATHEDRAL. See *Cathedral Music* 2, 7.

LLANOVER, LADY. See *Wales* 7 a.

L.L.C.M. See *Degrees and Diplomas* 2.

LLOYD.

(1) **CHARLES HARFORD.** Born at Thornbury in Gloucestershire in 1849 and died at Slough in 1919 on his seventieth birthday. He was educated at Oxford. In his twenties he succeeded S. S. Wesley (q.v.) as organist of Gloucester Cathedral; in his thirties, Corfe as organist of Christ Church Cathedral, Oxford; in his forties, Barnby as 'Precentor' (i.e. organist and chief music master) of Eton College; and in his sixties he moved to the Chapel Royal, St. James's. His compositions are mostly of the English festival-cantata or Anglican Service class. They have the charm of melody, and are 'well written'.

(2) **JOHN AMBROSE.** Born at Mold, Flintshire, in 1815 and died in Liverpool in 1874, aged fifty-nine. He was a commercial traveller who composed hymn tunes, anthems, and part songs that attained high general favour and are still popular, as well as a sacred cantata, *The Prayer of Habakkuk*, said to be the first such work to be produced in Wales (cf. *Owen, John*, and *Stephen, Edward*). He helped to methodize congregational singing and published collections of tunes.

(3) **GEORGE.** Born at St. Ives, Cornwall, in 1913. He came into notice in 1935 with the performance in London of his opera *Iernin* (libretto by his father), produced the previous year at Penzance, and of his third symphony—his first and second having been previously heard at Bournemouth. His opera *John Socman* was produced in Bristol in 1951.

(4) **JOHN MORGAN.** Born at Ystradyfodwg, Wales, in 1880, and died at Barry in 1960, aged seventy-nine. He studied at University College, Cardiff, where from 1920 he was Lecturer in Music and from 1939 Professor. He conducted the Cardiff Musical Society and frequently adjudicated at the National Eisteddfod. His published works are mainly choral.

(5) **LLEWELYN SOUTHWORTH.** Born in Cheshire in 1876 and died in Birmingham in 1956. Researcher and writer on acoustical questions. He held an important position in the Department of Scientific and Industrial Research (1917–43) and was Chairman of the British Standards Institution Committee on Standard Pitch (1946–50). He published some organ compositions.

LLWYN ONN. See *Wales* 2.

L.MUS. See *Degrees and Diplomas* 2.

L.MUS.L.C.M. See *Degrees and Diplomas* 2.

L.MUS.T.C.L. See *Degrees and Diplomas* 2.

LOBWASSER, AMBROSIUS (1515–87). See *Hymns and Hymn Tunes* 4.

LOCATELLI, PIETRO ANTONIO. Born at Bergamo in 1695 and died at Amsterdam in 1764, aged sixty-eight. He was a pupil of Corelli and himself a great violinist. A considerable part of his life was spent in Holland. He advanced violin technique by the introduction of novel effects, and wrote sonatas (i.e. in the earlier form), concerti grossi (see *Concerto* 2), and other things. Many of his works remain in the violinist's repertory and a few others in the repertories of the violoncellist and the flautist.

LOCHABER NO MORE. The words are by Allan Ramsay (q.v.). The tune is a variant of an old Irish one, *King James's March to Ireland*, said to have been composed by the harper Miles O'Reilly (born 1635). Scottish regiments use this tune as a lament.

LOCH LOMOND. The poem is attributed to Lady John Scott (compare *Annie Laurie*). The tune may also be by her.

LOCKE (or **Lock**).

(1) **MATTHEW.** Born at Exeter about 1630 and died in London in 1677, aged about forty-seven. He was a chorister of Exeter Cathedral and has left permanent marks of his choristership in the shape of his name cut into the stone organ-screen at some time when the vergers were not about (cf. *Ebdon*). When at the Commonwealth all cathedral services ceased, he zealously continued his musical studies and came well to the front, so that part of the first opera ever heard in England, Davenant's celebrated *Siege of Rhodes* (1656), was of his composition and his singing.

Pepys in his diary records a dinner, in 1659, with Locke and 'Mr. Pursell' (father or uncle of the greater Purcell) after which the approaching return of the king was celebrated by the singing of a loyal canon composed by Locke. When Charles II returned, Locke composed the band music for the royal progress through the city and was appointed 'Composer in Ordinary' to the king. In this capacity he was the cause of a notable dispute by his setting of the responses to the Commandments in such a way that the music varied after each: the conservative-minded choir disliked this innovation and not only protested, but, as the composer asserted, spoilt the music in performance.

For the well-known *Macbeth* music, long attributed to him, see *Misattributed Compositions*. This was not his; he did, however, compose a good deal for the Restoration stage. He left anthems, songs, music for viols, and other things. When he died Purcell composed an ode or elegy 'On the death of his Worthy Friend, Mr. Matthew Locke'.

See references under *Masque*; *Opera* 13 a; *Notation* 7; *Percussion Family* 4 a; *Arrangement*; *Consort*.

(2) **JOHN.** Physician and philosopher. See reference under *Education and Music* 2.

LOCO (It.). 'Place', used after some sign indicating performance an octave higher or lower than written and reminding the performer that the effect of that sign now terminates. Often the expression used is *Al loco*, 'at the place'.

LOCRIAN. See *Modes* 6.

LODER, EDWARD JAMES. Born at Bath in 1813 and died in London in 1865, aged fifty-one or fifty-two. He came of a distinguished family. In the forties, fifties, and sixties of last century his operas (particularly *The Night Dancers*) had great popularity in England.

Cf. *Opera* 24 d (1846).

LODGE, SIR OLIVER JOSEPH (1851–1940). See *Broadcasting of Music* 2.

LOEFFLER, CHARLES MARTIN TORNOW. Born at Mulhouse, in Alsace, in 1861 and died at Medfield, Mass., in 1935, aged seventy-four. After a boyhood spent partly in Russia and Hungary, and after study with Massart and Joachim for violin and Kiel and Guiraud for composition, he went to America as first-desk violinist of the Boston Symphony Orchestra, from which body he resigned in 1903.

His list of compositions is a long one, the best known being a *Pagan Poem* for piano and orchestra after an Eclogue of Virgil. There is also much chamber music.

See also *Concerto* 6 c (1861); *Patronage* 6; *Impressionism*; *Symphony* 8 (1861); *Programme Music* 5 e.

LOEILLET.

(1) JOHN (JEAN BAPTISTE). Born at Ghent in 1680 and died in London in 1730, aged forty-nine. In 1730 he settled in London, where his surname sometimes appears as Lullié or Lully. He was an oboist and composer.

(2) JACQUES (JACOB). Younger brother of (1). Born at Ghent in 1685 and died at Versailles in 1748.

(3) JEAN BAPTISTE. Cousin of (1) and (2). Born at Ghent in 1688 and died *c.* 1720; also known as 'Loeillet de Gant'.

LOEWE, CARL (in full, Johann Carl Gottfried, p. 400, pl. **69.** 1). Born near Halle in 1796 and died at Kiel in 1869, aged seventy-two. He was both a singer and a composer for singers. In early life he attracted the attention of Napoleon's brother, Jérôme, King of Westphalia, who gave him an annuity which enabled him to devote himself to musical study. He created something like a new genre in art-song —the vividly descriptive or dramatic ballad, his 'Edward' being an example well known to present-day audiences, whilst his *The Erl King* is a worthy companion setting to that of Schubert.

He travelled widely, singing his ballads, and won much favour and many official honours. In addition to ballads he wrote oratorios, operas, and musical textbooks. When he was nearly seventy he fell into a trance that lasted six weeks and some years later into another from which he never awakened.

He is highly esteemed by all who have studied the history of song.

See *Ballad* 5.

LOEWENBERG, ALFRED. Born in Berlin in 1902 and died in London in 1949, aged forty-seven. He studied at the University of Jena (D.Phil.) and in 1934 migrated to London, where he brought into existence his invaluable comprehensive book of reference, *Annals of Opera* (1943; revised 1955).

LOGIER, JOHANN BERNARD. Born in the Palatinate in 1777 and died in Dublin in 1846, aged sixty-eight. He came to Britain at the age of ten and became a military bandmaster, pianist, organist, and music seller in Ireland. He promoted a system of teaching the piano to a dozen or more pupils at a time and thus amassed a considerable sum (see *Chiroplast*). He composed piano sonatas, etc., and wrote a textbook of harmony that was internationally known and from which Wagner imbibed his first instruction.

LOHENGRIN (Wagner). Produced at Weimar in 1850 under Liszt's direction. Libretto by the composer.

ACT I

SCENE: *A Meadow by the River, near Antwerp. Time, early in the tenth century*

King Henry I of Germany ('Henry the Fowler') (*Bass*), coming to gather his men against Hungarian invasion, finds that Gottfried of Brabant has mysteriously disappeared, and that **Count Frederick of Telramund** (*Baritone*), the regent, has claimed the throne. The count accuses **Elsa** (*Soprano*), Gottfried's sister, of having made away with her brother in order to usurp his place. The king commands that her case shall be decided, according to ancient custom, by Ordeal by Combat between her accuser and some knight who shall defend her. No champion is forthcoming from among the assembled knights; but on the river appears a boat drawn by a swan. In it is a strange knight, **Lohengrin** (*Tenor*). He will be her champion, and if he wins she will be his betrothed. She must never ask his name or whence he comes. If she does, he must at once depart for ever. The combat is held and the stranger is the victor. **Ortrud,** Frederick's wife (*Mezzo-Soprano*), encourages him to seek the ruin of Lohengrin.

ACT II

SCENE: *The Fortress at Antwerp, with the Knights' and Ladies' Palaces, and the Cathedral. Night*

Frederick and Ortrud have been banished, but the woman, who has uncanny powers, is determined to have revenge. Craftily she arouses the pity of Elsa and plants in her mind a seed of doubt about her strange lover.

The king's ban upon Frederick is announced. Ortrud, furious, openly shows her hatred of Elsa, and her husband accuses Lohengrin of sorcery; the latter will not reveal his name.

ACT III

SCENE 1: *The Bridal Chamber*

After the famous 'Bridal Chorus', Elsa and Lohengrin, being alone, sing of their love. She begs him now to tell her his name and everything about himself. She will never reveal it to another. He, knowing the penalty they both must pay, is distraught, but still refuses.

At this moment Frederick and some of his friends rush upon them. Lohengrin strikes the count dead. The nobles then yield themselves to him, and Lohengrin tells them that he will reveal the truth about himself, in the king's presence.

SCENE 2: *The River-bank. Morning*

Before all the assembly the stranger knight tells his secret: he is Lohengrin, a Knight of the Holy Grail and son of Parsifal. He who is chosen as the Grail's servant is invincible, but only so long as he remains unknown. Now he must depart. The swan reappears, and Ortrud asserts that the bird is really Elsa's brother, whom she has enchanted into this shape. As the white dove of the Holy Grail flies down, the swan changes into the youth Gottfried, whom Lohengrin hails as the rightful heir of the land, before stepping into the boat, which is led by the dove down the river. Elsa falls lifeless to the ground.

See under *Encore* reference to an incident at the first London performance of this opera; further references will be found under *Opera* 21 k; *Liszt*; *Prelude*; *Overture*; *d'Indy*.

LOIN, LOINTAIN (Fr.). 'Distant', i.e. faint.

LOMAX, JOHN AVERY. See *Folk Song* 4.

LONDON. A large amount of information illustrating the musical life of London is scattered about this volume, e.g.:

(*a*) For Concerts, Concert Rooms, etc., see *Concert* 2–8; *Festival* 1; *Conducting* 4, 5.

(*b*) For Opera see *Opera* 13; *Beggar's Opera*; *Ballad Opera*; *Fairs*.

(*c*) For Church Music see *Cathedral Music*; *Anglican Parish Church Music*; *Parish Clerk*; *Westminster Abbey*; *Saint Paul's Cathedral*; *Roman Catholic Church Music*; *Organ*; *Congregational Churches*; *Methodism*.

(*d*) For various other subjects see *Minstrels*, etc.; *Waits*; *Profession of Music*; *Fairs*; *Inns*; *Street Music* 2, 3, 7; *Community Singing* 2, 4, 5; *Printing* 1; *Publishing*; *Puritans* 4, 5.

LONDON, BISHOPS OF. See *Oratorio* 5; *Anglican Parish Church Music* 4, 5.

LONDON COLLEGE OF MUSIC. See *Degrees and Diplomas* 2.

LONDONDERRY AIR. This most beautiful Irish melody is first found in print in the Petrie collection of 1855, where it appears with the indication that the name of the composer is unknown. It is understood to be a genuine folk tune and bears all the marks of this. It was given to Petrie by Miss Jane Ross, of Limavady, who, with her sister, made a practice of taking down tunes from the peasants who came to that town on market day.

The first words known to have been set to it were 'Would I were Erin's apple blossom o'er

you', by Alfred Perceval Graves; the second setting was 'Emer's Farewell', by the same poet. The words generally sung to it now ('Danny Boy') are by F. E. Weatherly.

The melody has become popular all over the English-speaking world and elsewhere. It is published in 'arrangement' for every possible voice, instrument, and combination, and finds a place in some collections of hymn tunes. It figures in Stanford's first Irish Rhapsody.

As a study in what Walker in his *History of Music in England* calls 'emotionally organized design of quite exceptional power' this tune repays close examination. Parry spoke of it as 'the most beautiful tune in the world'. Plunket Greene, than whom no singer was more notable for beautiful phrasing, said that it 'is a perfect example of pure phrasing far beyond the powers of that most limited instrument, the human voice. Only the violin can begin to do it justice and rise to its wonderful climax with every note serenely true. None of the great singers have tried to sing it; they know better.'

In the Journal of the English Folk Dance and Song Society for December 1934 will be found an argument (by Miss Anne G. Gilchrist) for the theory that the original must have been not in four-in-a-bar but in three-in-a-bar, and that Miss Ross, misled by the singer's rubato (q.v.), misunderstood the rhythm. For this theory is the fact that the tune as now sung does not fit any known Irish metre, and against it the fact that Miss Ross was a very competent and practised collector of Irish folk songs.

LONDON IS A FINE TOWN. See *Vicar of Bray*.

LONDON SCHOOLS' MUSIC ASSOCIATION. A body founded about 1920 to secure co-ordinated effort in promoting greater efficiency in the musical activities of London schools.

LONDON SOCIETY OF MINSTRELS. See *Minstrels* 3.

'LONDON' SYMPHONIES (Haydn). See *Nicknamed Compositions* 11.

'LONDON WAITS' TUNE. See *Waits*.

LONG (note). See *Notation* 3, 4.

LONG DRUM. Tenor drum (but sometimes the name is applied to the bass drum). See *Percussion Family* 3 j, 4 b, 5 j.

LONGHURST, WILLIAM HENRY (1819–1904). See *Organ* 8.

LONG METRE. See *Hymns and Hymn Tunes* 13; *Rhythm* 7.

LONGO, ALESSANDRO. Born at Amantea in 1864 and died in Naples in 1945, aged eighty. He was a pianist, composer of piano music, and editor of a piano journal (*L'Arte pianistica*). His name is well known in connexion with the keyboard works of Domenico Scarlatti, of which he published a complete edition.

LÖNNROT, ELIAS (1802–84). See *Scandinavia* 6.

LONTANO (It.). 'Distant', e.g. *Come da lontano*,

'as if from a distance', i.e. faintly. So *Lontananza*, 'distance'.

LOPATNIKOF (Lopatnikov, Lopatnikow, etc.), NICOLAI. Born at Revel (later Tallinn, the capital of Estonia) in 1903 and died in Pittsburgh in 1976, aged seventy-three. A Russian exiled from his country; after living for some years in Germany (1920–33), where he qualified as an engineer, he settled in the United States. He was awarded a Guggenheim Fellowship in 1945, and later became Professor of the Carnegie Technical Institute, Pittsburgh. His music displays vigorous ideas skilfully treated in a conservative idiom.

LOPOKOVA. See *Ballet* 5, 9.

LORD, FOR THY TENDER MERCIES' SAKE. See under *Farrant, Richard.*

LORETTO, LITANY OF. See *Litaniae Lauretanae.*

LORINE. See *Country Dance.*

LORIS, HEINRICH = 'Glareanus' (1488–1563). See *Modes* 6.

LORRAINE, DUKE OF (in early seventeenth century). See *Cornett Family* 3; *Trombone Family* 3.

LORTZING, GUSTAV ALBERT. Born in Berlin in 1801 and died there in 1851, aged forty-nine. He lived the theatre life, married an actress, and wrote many comic operas which in Germany are still often heard (from 700 to 800 performances annually in the early 1930s—about the same as the operas of Mozart). *Zar und Zimmermann* ('Czar and Carpenter') is one.

See *Opera* 21 j.

LOS (Ger.). 'Loose', free in style.

LOTTI, ANTONIO. Born probably in Venice about 1667 and died there in 1740, aged about seventy-two. He was for a time organist of St. Mark's, Venice. He composed church music, operas, and other things, and enjoys the esteem of those students who know his works.

LOUDON. See *Nicknamed* 11, no. 69.

LOUIS XIII OF FRANCE (reigned 1610–43). See *Cornett Family* 3; *Opera* 11 b; *Volta*; *Rigaudon*; *Ballet* 2.

LOUIS XIV OF FRANCE (reigned 1643–1715). See *France* 6; *Chapel Royal*; *Anthem*; *Opera* 11 a b; *Military Band*; *Dance* 6 b; *Ballet* 3; *Branle*; *Courante* 2; *Gavotte*; *Minuet*; *Passepied*; *Rigaudon*; *Bagpipe Family* 6; *Eccles* 4; *Lully*; *Conducting* 2; *Pantaleon.*

LOUISE (Charpentier). Produced in Paris, 1900. Libretto by the composer.

Act I

SCENE: *A Room in Louise's Home. Spring*

Louise (*Soprano*), a Parisian seamstress, loves **Julian** (*Tenor*), an artist whose studio window she can see from her room. They talk together across the area. The lover has written to ask her father's consent to their marriage,

and even if it is refused, she says, she will come to him. Louise's **Mother** (*Contralto*) overhears, and nags at her daughter. She considers artists wastrels. The **Father** (*Baritone*) comes in. He is doubtful about the match, yet kindly. Influenced by the malicious mother, he ends by begging Louise to have done with Julian.

Act II

SCENE 1: *A Street in Montmartre. Early Morning*

Julian, with some of his friends, plans to kidnap Louise from her mother, guarded by whom she duly appears, on her way to her workroom. Left there, she is seized on by Julian, but fears to go with him, and returns to her work.

SCENE 2: *A Dressmaker's Workroom*

The workgirls talk about their sweethearts. They joke about Louise, who is serenaded by Julian, with whom she goes off.

Act III

SCENE: *A little Garden in Montmartre*

The lovers have set up house together. Louise's mother has given her up, but Louise is uneasy, in the midst of her happiness, in thinking of her father's grief. Julian turns her thoughts to the bright future, and as voices outside are heard singing of freedom, they join in a passionate love-duet as night comes on.

Bohemian friends of Julian decorate the house with bunting and lanterns, and a festive scene is worked up. In the midst of the fun the mother appears, telling Louise that her father is ill and pining for her, who alone can make him happy and save his life. Louise goes home with her mother, promising to return to Julian.

Act IV

SCENE: *Louise's Home*

The mother refuses to let Louise go back to her lover, and the father adds his plea for the sacrifice. He hates the garish city that he feels is drawing her away from home. But Paris and love are calling. The parents in their wrath turn her out, the father, too late, crying to her to come back; but she has gone to seek happiness in her own way.

LOULIÉ.

(1) ÉTIENNE. Latter part of seventeenth century. A noted Paris music-master who wrote theoretical treatises. His importance comes from the fact that he was the first inventor of a metronome; but as his instrument was 6 feet high it did not come into much use. He is mentioned here only to remove the possibility of confusion with his namesake (below).

(2) L. A. (names unknown). Born in Paris about 1775 and died probably in the thirties of the next century. He was a Paris violinist who left various string works, one or two of which are sometimes heard today. The less carefully drafted kind of recital programme occasionally

confounds him with Lully (q.v.); avoid also confusion with the above or with Loeillet (q.v.).

LOURD, LOURDE (Fr., masc., fem.). 'Heavy.' So *Lourdement*, 'heavily'; *Lourdeur*, 'heaviness', weight.

LOURE. The word has two (connected) meanings.

(1) An old Normandy bagpipe (q.v.). The word *loureur*, meaning a bagpiper, will be found in French dictionaries.

(2) A rustic dance, apparently once accompanied by the bagpipe (q.v.). Its music was usually like that of the gigue (q.v.), but the speed was slower. It was in three-in-a-measure or six-in-a-measure time. An accented short note followed by a long note (e.g. a one-beat note at the opening of the measure followed by a two-beat) was a feature. In Bach's fifth French Suite is the best-known example of the use of the loure rhythm and style in artistic composition.

Cf. *Louré*, below.

LOURÉ. A kind of string-instrument bowing, possibly derived from the manner of playing or dancing the loure (q.v.). Several notes are played in one movement of the bow, but slightly detached from one another and with a separate pressure on each. The verb *lourer* means to play in this manner.

LOURIÉ, ARTHUR VINCENT. Born at St. Petersburg in 1892. He is of Jewish descent. In the early days of the Russian revolution he became Commissar of Music, but in 1922 he settled in Paris, and from 1940 he has been a resident of New York. His early compositions were adventurously modernist: his later ones tend to be influenced by his Roman Catholic faith (*Liturgical Sonata*, 1928; *Concerto Spirituale*, 1929; etc.).

See *Microtones*.

LOUVAIN. See *Publishing* 3; *Belgium* 2.

LOVE IN A VILLAGE. See *Saint Patrick's Day*.

LOVE FOR THE THREE ORANGES. See *Prokofief*.

LOVE OF THE THREE KINGS. See *Montemezzi*.

LOVER, SAMUEL. See *Rory O'More*.

LOWE.

(1) EDWARD (c. 1610–82). See *Cathedral Music* 6; *Anglican Chant* 4.

(2) CLAUDE EGERTON (1860–1947). Author of many educational works, overseas examiner for Trinity College of Music, and lecturer. Quoted under *Memory* 6; *Mazurka*; *Polonaise*.

LOWER RHINE FESTIVAL. See *Festival* 3.

LOWERY, HARRY (1896–1967) See *Tests and Measurements*.

LOWLAND SCOTTISH BAGPIPE. See *Bagpipe Family* 4.

LOW MASS. See *Mass* 1.

L.R.A.M., L.R.S.M. See *Degrees and Diplomas* 2.

L.T.C.L., L.T.S.C. See *Degrees and Diplomas* 2.

LUDFORD, NICHOLAS. Lived *c*. 1485–*c*. 1557. He was a member of St. Stephen's Chapel, Westminster, and one of the more important English composers of church music of his day.

LUDLOW. See *Masque*.

LUENING, OTTO. Born at Milwaukee in 1900. He is a flautist, opera conductor, etc. He won a Guggenheim Fellowship in 1930, and was then on college musical staffs (Columbia University and Barnard College, 1944). His works include orchestral and chamber music, etc., and also an opera, *Evangeline* (1932). He has done much experimental work involving electronic means.

LUFTIG (Ger.). 'Airy.'

LUGUBRE (It. and Fr.). 'Lugubrious.'

LUIGINI, ALEXANDRE CLÉMENT LÉON JOSEPH. Born at Lyons in 1850 and died in Paris in 1906, aged fifty-six. He was a fine violinist and a conductor, and composed amongst other things a good deal of ballet music, of which the *Egyptian Ballet* is everywhere known.

LULLIÉ. See *Loeillet*.

LULLY (or **Lulli**), JEAN BAPTISTE (p. 368, pl. **61**. 1). Born in Florence in 1632 and died in Paris in 1687, aged fifty-four. He was of humble birth. Managing somehow to get instruction in guitar playing, he at the age of fourteen caught the attention of the Chevalier de Guise, who took him to Paris and placed him in the service of his cousin, Mademoiselle d'Orléans (he is often said to have been at first given the duties of a kitchen-boy, but this is untrue). By his violin playing and by his talent for the dance he soon became celebrated, and at the age of twenty he passed to the service of Louis XIV, whose composer of dance music he became in 1653. Soon a special and additional body of string players was formed and put under his direction, and now, as violinist, conductor, and composer, he attracted much attention.

The composition of the court ballets, in which the king himself was wont to dance, was soon largely left in his hands, and the bestowal of various high and lucrative official positions rewarded his success in this branch of work.

At twenty-nine he married the daughter of Lambert (q.v.), another high musical official of the court. The association with Molière is an important event; it led to the composition of music for several plays (as, for instance, *Le Bourgeois Gentilhomme*) and to the dramatist and composer joining forces in the preparation of many of the mythological ballets then in vogue. Lully himself often acted and danced in his own productions, sometimes with the king as a companion. Another collaborator was Quinault, who frequently served him as opera librettist. (See p. 688, pl. **115**. 3, 4).

He then bought from the poet Perrin his monopoly for the performance of opera in the

French tongue (Perrin then being at logger-heads with his colleagues and in prison for debt). His position as king's favourite he used to the utmost to preserve himself from any infringement of his rights and privileges. He succeeded in securing a patent of nobility and also an appointment as one of the king's secretaries. He amassed much money and bought much property in and about Paris. His fine house there is still to be seen.

The court of France was then a hotbed of vice of every imaginable kind, some of which went too deep into the mire for even Louis XIV to tolerate. Lully hobnobbed with the worst of the offenders and probably nothing but his genius saved him from serious punishment. There is a picturesque life of him by the great authority Henry Prunières (1929).

The death of Lully was from an abscess induced by his striking his foot with his long baton whilst conducting a Te Deum (see *Conducting* 2).

The artistic importance of Lully lies in the many improvements he introduced in French opera. He abandoned *recitativo secco* (see *Recitative*) and substituted recitative with artistic and well-designed accompaniment. In the setting of music to words he was careful to secure proper accentuation. In his ballets he introduced many quicker dances than had been customary. He established the form of French overture (see *Overture* 1). In everything he aimed at 'effect', and his instinct generally enabled him to attain it. At the outset his style was based on that of his countrymen Rossi (q.v.) and Cavalli (q.v.), but little by little he assimilated the French style, instrumental and vocal, and he then created a new and original way of writing that was much imitated throughout Europe, notably in Germany. Purcell's instrumental pieces show its indirect influence.

A complete edition of the works of Lully is now in preparation. It will take many years to complete.

See references, of greater or lesser importance, as follows:

Bagpipe 6; Ballet 2, 7; Bouffons; Canaries; Chaconne; Chapel Royal; Conducting 2; De Profundis; Flute 4; France 6; Gavotte; God save the Queen 10; Grand Opera; Guédron; History 4; Military Band; Minuet; Miserere; Monopolies; Opera 11 b, 24 b (1673, 1676); Overture 1, 7; Passepied; Pastoral; Percussion 4 (Kettledrums); Publishing 2; Recitative; Rhythm 5; Singing 8.

(Note that Jean Loeillet, q.v., was sometimes called 'Lully' on the title-pages of his published works, and that concert programmes sometimes credit to Lully works by L. A. Loulié, q.v.).

LUMINEUX (Fr.). 'Luminous.'

LUNGO, LUNGA (It., masc., fem.). 'Long.' So *Lunga Pausa*, (a) 'long pause', (b) 'long rest'.

LUOGO (It.). Same as 'Loco' (q.v.).

LUR. (1) A prehistoric bronze trumpet. See *Scandinavia* 2.

(2) A wooden trumpet-like instrument used today by herdsmen in Scandinavia, as the Alphorn (q.v.), which it somewhat resembles, is in Switzerland.

LURLINE. See *Wallace, W. V.*

LUSIGANDO. A term that appears sometimes in Debussy's music. Apparently a mistake for *Lusingando* (q.v.).

LUSINGANDO (It.). 'Flattering', i.e. play in a coaxing, intimate manner. So, too, *Lusinghevole, Lusinghevolmente, Lusinghiero, Lusingante.*

LUST (Ger.). 'Pleasure'. So *Lustig*, 'cheerful'; *Lustigkeit*, 'cheerfulness'; *Lustspiel*, 'comedy'.

LUTE FAMILY

1. Construction.
2. Members of the Family.
3. Notation.
4. History.
5. Nomenclature.

(For illustrations see p. 561, pl. 102.)

1. Construction. This is a family of stringed instruments of which the strings are plucked by the fingers (without plectrum). They have rounded backs, their shape being something like that of a pear cut in half from its stalk downwards. They have not (like the violin family, etc.) a bridge, the vibrating length of the strings extending the whole way from the top of the finger-board nearly to the bottom of the sounding board. Each string except the top one is duplicated in unison (some of the bass strings are sometimes in octaves); the number of the strings has varied in different periods and countries. The finger-board has frets, or raised lines indicating the position of the semitones (cf. the modern banjo or mandoline, or the viol; usually, as in the case of the viol, the lute's frets are pieces of catgut tied round the neck at the appropriate places). The head, containing the peg-box, is generally bent back at an angle from the neck.

Vincenzo Galilei, of Florence, says in 1581 that the English-made lutes are the best. Chambers's *Cyclopædia* (1728) says, 'Those of Bologna are esteemed the best, on account of the wood'.

2. Members of the Family. The family has included individuals of various sizes, the largest being the **Theorbo** and **Archlute** and one of the smallest the **Mandora** or **Mandore**. The theorbo and archlute (p. 561, pl. 102. 3) had double peg-boxes, the strings attached to one peg-box passing over a finger-board (q.v.) and being 'stopped' in the normal way, and the longer strings attached to the other having no finger-board and being plucked merely as 'open strings'. Two instruments of the theorbo kind, the largest archlute and (not quite identical) the **Chitarrone,** corresponded to the bowed double-bass in our modern orchestra; it had a small body (normal lute size) but a long neck that made it as tall as a man; it was distinguished from the other lutes by having wire strings (on account of its great length); in addition to these open strings it had stopped ones of normal length.

3. Notation. A special notation, or **'Tablature'**, was used for the lute. The principle of this was a staff with a space for every string, and small letters (*a*, *b*, *c*, etc.) placed within the spaces, indicating which fret of the string was to be used and thus defining the note (the letters being the names of the frets, not those of the notes produced by those frets); small marks above the staff, resembling the tails of our present notes, gave the duration of the sound. The system varied somewhat in various ages (e.g. numbers sometimes taking the place of letters), but the above is roughly true for the palmy days of the instrument—the sixteenth and seventeenth centuries.

4. History. The lute is of unknown antiquity and of almost universal habitat in the whole eastern hemisphere. Its name is Arabian, and it is still greatly cultivated amongst the Arab peoples. English literature over a long period of time (Chaucer, Shakespeare, Pepys, etc.) continually testifies to the popularity of the lute; Alison's Psalter of 1599 (see *Hymns and Hymn Tunes* 17 e xi) has lute accompaniment. We get an idea of the degree of popularity the instrument attained when we read in the autobiographical memoirs of the Puritan lawyer and statesman, Whitelocke, that in 1633, arranging the music for a masque for the entertainment of Charles I and his queen, he 'engaged forty lutes, besides other instruments and voyces'. The great characteristic of lute music is its contrapuntal character. The lute was, indeed, the most serious solo instrument of the sixteenth century. (Cf. *Suite* 1, 2.)

In the early examples of orchestration connected with the first opera performances in Italy (1600 onwards) lutes of various sizes were largely drawn upon. Later, lute tone became a merely occasional ingredient in orchestral colouring; Bach included it in his scoring of the *St. John Passion* (1722) and *Trauer Ode* (1727), and with Handel's last opera, *Deidamia* (1741), it made what was probably its final orchestral appearance.

Bach wrote for solo lute four suites, one or two fugues, and a little other music. Haydn contributed a piece for two lutes, and two trios for lute, violin, and violoncello.

It would appear that the lute family fell out of use earlier in France than elsewhere, for the President de Brosses, travelling in Italy in 1739, speaks of having heard a theorbo adroitly played and of being by that convinced that 'no better step was ever taken than to drop the use of these instruments'.

The British court had an official lutenist as late as 1752, actually, and 1846, nominally. Perhaps the day may yet come when the office will be brought into existence again, for a revival of the lute has taken place during the twentieth century, and its characteristic silvery tones and the music of its sixteenth- and seventeenth-century composers are gradually becoming familiar to music-lovers. Possibly no instrument that has ever existed, except the pianoforte, has possessed so large a repertory as the lute. But its technique is difficult and unless the tone is well produced it loses its warmth and resonance, so gaining for one of the finest instruments a bad name.

A special value of the lute today is for the accompaniment of the many fine songs of the sixteenth and early seventeenth century that were written to be so accompanied (see *Song* 3, 10). The works of all the British 'Lutenist Composers' of that period have now been republished, including those of the most famous of any nation, John Dowland.

Entries referring to these composers will be found as follows: *Bartlet*; *Campian*; *Dowland*; *Ford, Thomas*; *Greaves*; *Johnson*; *Rosseter*; *Wilson*. For lute exponents of a somewhat later period see *Humfrey*; *Mace*.

For a reference to the cultivation of the instrument in Scotland, see *Scotland* 7 (end).

5. Nomenclature.

(*a*) **Lute.** *Luth* (Fr.); *Liuto* (It.); *Laute* (Ger.); *Laud* (Sp.).

(*b*) **Forms of Smaller Lute.** *Mandora* or *Mandore*; *Bandola*; *Lutina*.

(*c*) **Forms of Large Lute.** *Theorbo, Archlute* or *Arciliuto*; *Chitarrone* (the common identification of Archlute with Chitarrone is uncertain).

(*d*) **Lute-Guitar.** See separate entry under *Vihuela*.

(*e*) **Harp-Lute.** See *Ditiyal Harp.*

The player of a lute is a **Lutenist** or **Lutanist** (perhaps the latter spelling is the commoner). In the seventeenth century we find *Luthist* for either a maker or player of the instrument.

For 'Luthier' and 'Lutherie' see *Luthier*.

LUTH (Fr.). Lute. See *Lute Family*.

LUTHER, MARTIN (p. 484, pl. 85. 2, 3). Born at Eisleben in Saxony in 1483 and died there in 1546, aged sixty-two. Like Wesley, Rowland Hill, General Booth, and a number of other religious leaders, he was the first to utter the famous dictum that the devil should not have all the best tunes, and in this faith he lived and died.

He was a practical musician, playing the lute

and the flute, and the associate of musicians, whom he freely called in to help him in the provision and arrangement of suitable music for the reformed service. He approved of the use of professional choirs, but loved to hear the congregation sing.

The first Protestant hymn-book (1524) has not yet ceased its influence. He wrote the words of certain hymns which are now sung all over the world, and possibly in a few cases the music also. The composition of the north German contrapuntal school of the early eighteenth century is saturated with the influence of the Lutheran chorale or hymn tune which he introduced, and it is perhaps worthy of remark (at any rate as a mnemonic) that the birth dates of the chorale's originator and its greatest exponent as the material of developed art, Luther and Bach, are separated by almost exactly two centuries (1483–1685).

See references to Luther and the Lutheran Church under *Germany* 3; *Church Music* 2; *Liturgy*; *Mass* 3; *Veni Creator Spiritus*; *Hymns and Hymn Tunes* 3, 5, 16, 17 a b; *Chorale*; *Pope and Turk Tune*; *Street Music* 5; *Walther, Johann*; *Presbyterian Church Music* 1; *Education and Music* 1; *Bohemia*; *Poland*; *Scandinavia* 2, 4, 5; *Josquin des Prés*; *Rhythm* 6.

LUTHIER (Fr.). The word comes from 'luth' (lute) and long meant a maker of stringed instruments in general (lutes, harps, viols, etc.); nowadays it usually implies a maker of instruments of the violin family in particular. The trade of the luthier is *lutherie*. The Germans, similarly, use *Lautenmacher*, literally 'lutemaker', in a wider sense than the word itself implies.

LUTKIN, PETER CHRISTIAN (1858–1931). See reference under *Hymns and Hymn Tunes* 11.

LUTOSŁAWSKI, WITOLD. Born at Warsaw in 1913. He has become one of the leaders of the modern school of Polish composers, and in 1960 was elected vice-president of the I.S.C.M. His *Funeral Music* (1958) is considered outstanding.

See *Poland*.

LUTTO (It.). 'Mourning.' So *Luttoso* or *Luttuoso*, 'mournful'; *Luttosamente*, 'mournfully'.

LUTYENS, ELISABETH. Born in London in 1906 (daughter of the well-known architect and widow of Edward Clark the conductor). She studied at the Royal College of Music and has become known as a composer of orchestral and chamber music, etc., in which she employs the Note-row (q.v.) technique. C.B.E. 1969.

See *Concert* 6 c (1906).

LUX AETERNA. See *Requiem*.

LVOF (Lvov, Lwoff, Lwow, etc.), **ALEXIS.** Born at Revel in 1798 and died near Kovno in 1870, aged seventy-two. (Some authorities put the birth a year later.) He was the son of the director of music in the Imperial Court Chapel at St. Petersburg. He entered the army, in which he rose to high rank, and then turned to music, succeeding to his father's position. He was a good violinist and the leader of a famous string quartet, and also the composer of a large amount of unaccompanied choral music for the Russian Church (see *Greek Church* 5).

The official national anthem from 1833 until the end of the rule of the Czars was of his composition, and by its bold melody (to be heard as a hymn tune in Britain and elsewhere) he was known all over the world.

LYDGATE, JOHN. Early fifteenth-century poet. Quoted under *Street Music* 2.

LYDIAN MODE. See *Modes* 6, 7, 10.

LYDIAN TETRACHORD. See *Scales* 5.

LYON, JAMES. See; *American Musical Terminology* 1; *United States* 3 (end); *Hymns and Hymn Tunes* 17 f iv.

LYRA, LIRA. Properly the word means 'Lyre' (see next article), but in the Middle Ages it was applied loosely to a considerable variety of instruments whose one common feature was the possession of strings.

(1) In German it became an early name for the hurdy-gurdy (q.v.).

(2) In Italian the **Lira, Lira moderna,** or **Lira da braccio** was one of the earliest European bowed instruments, and it continued in use until the end of the sixteenth century. It was played resting on the arm, whence *Lira da braccio* (cf. *Braccio and Gamba*, and see p. 1073, pl. **178.** 1). It had four or five strings, according to period, or seven in the *Lira da sette corde*. The pegs were inserted in the top (not at the side) of a characteristic heart-shaped head. This is the bowed instrument most frequently depicted in thirteenth- to sixteenth-century religious art and it was, with the Rebec (q.v.), one of the contributory ancestors of the violin.

(3) The **Lira da gamba** (in French simply **Lyre**) was a bass form of the above, but with far more strings (11–15). It was also called **Lirone, Lirone perfetto,** and **Arciviola** or **Arciviola da gamba.**

For Lyra Viol (not of the same family as the above) and the lyra way of playing see *Viol Family* 4 c. For Bell-Lyra see that word.

LYRE. (1) An instrument of the ancient Greeks, Assyrians, Hebrews, etc. (p. 528, pl. **97.** 1), long obsolete and included here mainly on account of some confusion of it (especially on the part of poets) with the lute (q.v.). It was, in effect, a small harp, but it differed from the normal harp in two essential particulars—the strings were stopped (by the left hand), and it was played not with the fingers but with a plectrum (right hand). (See also p. 452, pl. **78.** 1.)

(2) The name was later, with some looseness, applied to certain plucked and bowed instruments. See under *Lyra*.

LYRE-BIRD PRESS. See *Patronage* 7; *Greek Church* 4.

LYRIC. Properly this term is applied to poetry of the simpler type of personal expression, in stanzas and lending itself to, or suggesting, treatment as song. It excludes the ballad, the sonnet, the epic, etc. The following are some uses common amongst musicians:

(1) The word, as a noun, has come to have a specialized application to the type of poem used for the songs interpolated in plays, so constituting these 'musical plays'. Thus we used to find in the British *Who's Who* one of the most admired of the practitioners of this special art recorded as having won the Chancellor's Medal for English Verse at Cambridge and written lyrics for *San Toy*, *The Merry Widow*, *Lilac Time* (or *Blossom Time*), etc.

And another well-known poet constantly advertised himself in the British musical press as 'Lyric Author . . . 2,000 songs . . . not one failure to give great pleasure . . . Lyrics written for Cinema Films'.

The word is also used for the poems of popular songs.

(2) **Lyric Drama**. Another name for opera, covering all kinds. The term is applied not so much to any particular work as to the whole class—i.e. opera as distinct from the spoken play.

(3) **Lyric Opera**. A rough general term meaning opera in which the singing counts for rather more than the drama.

(4) **Lyric Piece** (or in German *Lyrisches Stück*). A title probably originated by Grieg, who attached it to a number of short compositions for piano. It carries no special connotation as to form.

(5) **Lyric Soprano, Lyric Tenor**. See *Voice* 19.

LYRIQUE (Fr.), **LYRISCH** (Ger.). 'Lyrical.'

LYRISCHES STÜCK (plural, *Lyrische Stücke*). See *Lyric* 4.

M

MA (It.). 'But.'

MAAS, ADOLF. See *Trombone* 4.

MAATSCHAPPIJ TOT BEVORDERING DER TOONKUNST. See *Holland* 9.

MACABRE. See *Danse Macabre*.

MACARTHUR. See *Bagpipe Family* 4.

MACBETH MUSIC. See *Misattributed* (Locke).

McBRIDE, ROBERT GUYN. Born at Tucson, Arizona, in 1911. He won a Guggenheim Fellowship in 1937. He has composed both works of jazz tendency and serious orchestral and chamber works, etc.

MACCARTHY, MAUD. Born in Clonmel, Ireland, in 1882. See *Microtones*; *Foulds, John*.

MACCHINA (It.). 'Machine, mechanism.' So *Macchina a venti*, 'wind machine' (q.v.); *Corno a macchina*, valve horn (see *Horn Family* 2 c, 5 c); *Tromba a macchina*, valve trumpet (see *Trumpet Family* 2 c, 3).

MACCRIMMON. See *Bagpipe Family* 4.

MACCUNN, HAMISH (p. 945, pl. **160.** 7). Born at Greenock in 1868 and died in London in 1916, aged forty-eight. He was one of the first batch of pupils at the opening of the Royal College of Music, London. When he was nineteen he sprang into prominence by a romantic overture, *Land of the Mountain and the Flood*. Later he became active as a conductor of operas and as a composer of them too (*Jeanie Deans*, etc.). He wrote a number of cantatas and orchestral pieces, chiefly on Scottish subjects.

MACDERMOTT, K. H. See *Anglican Parish Church Music* 4; *Oboe Family* 2.

MACDONALD, McDONALD.

(1) **MACDONALD**, KEITH NORMAN. See *Scotland* 1.

(2) **McDONALD**, HARL. Born near Boulder, Colorado, in 1899 and died at Princeton, N.J., in 1955, aged fifty-five. After study in the United States and Germany he held positions on the music staffs of schools and on that of the University of Pennsylvania. He wrote chamber, orchestral, and choral music.

(3) **MACDONALD**, PATRICK. See *Scotland* 1.

MACDOWELL, EDWARD ALEXANDER (p. 1041, pl. **170.** 7). Born in New York in 1861 and there died in 1908, aged forty-six. He showed early talent and studied piano under Teresa Carreño. At fourteen he was admitted to the Paris Conservatory, and later to that of Frankfurt, where he was Raff's pupil in composition. He was appointed chief piano teacher at the Conservatory of Darmstadt, and from the age of twenty-one, when Liszt commended his First Piano Concerto, began to gain recognition as composer amongst the German people.

At twenty-six he returned to America and settled in Boston; at thirty-five he moved to New York as Professor of Music at Columbia University. He found the drudgery of academic work excessive and after eight years resigned. Brain trouble followed, and after four years more he died. His former pupil and devoted companion, the pianist Marian Nevins (1857–1956), gave her long widowhood to activities tending to widen the knowledge of his music and to help young American artists of all kinds by offering them the opportunity of quiet work at their art in the MacDowell Colony, established on the small estate the composer had bought for his own work, at Peterborough, New Hampshire.

The music of MacDowell reflects the literary influences of the nineteenth-century Romantic school, as also his Celtic descent and temperament and his love of nature. Well-known are his Second Piano Concerto, his four Piano Sonatas (*Tragica*, *Eroica*, *Norse*, and *Keltic*), some of his very poetical shorter piano pieces, and some songs.

See *United States* 7; *Programme Music* 3, 5 d; *Absolute Pitch*; *Gilbert, H. F. B.: Colour and Music* 4; *Schindler, Kurt*. For mention of the MacDowell Colony see *Patronage* 7.

MACE, THOMAS (p. 389, pl. **66.** 3). Born in York (?) about 1620 and died about 1710. He was a lay clerk of Trinity College, Cambridge, and is well remembered today for his quaint and useful book, *Musick's Monument* (1676), which treats of church music and also of the lute and the viol and their music.

See quotations under *Hymns and Hymn Tunes* 9; *Cebell*.

McEWEN.

(1) JOHN BLACKWOOD (p. 945, pl. **160.** 8). Born at Hawick in 1868 and died in London in 1948, aged eighty. In his early twenties he studied at the Royal Academy of Music. Then he returned to Scotland, where, however, no Scotsman who has once tasted London seems able to live, so that at thirty he was back at the Royal Academy, this time as a professor. From

1924 to 1946 he was Principal of this institution. He was knighted in 1932.

Amongst his compositions are the 'Solway' Symphony, the overture *Grey Galloway*, and many other orchestral works, a number of piano pieces, and a good deal of chamber music.

He wrote theoretical works and made several thoughtful and Scottishly argued contributions to music aesthetics.

See *Symphony* 8 (1868).

(2) ROBERT FINNIE. See *Use of Colmonell*.

MACFARLANE, WILLIAM CHARLES. See *America the Beautiful*.

MACFARREN.

(1) GEORGE ALEXANDER. Born in London in 1813 and died there in 1887, aged seventy-four. He was the son of a dramatist and theatrical manager who was himself a good amateur musician. He was trained at the Royal Academy of Music, London, and became a professor and then Principal of that institution.

For nearly half a century he was enormously successful as a composer, at first of operas and then of oratorios and festival cantatas, as also of orchestral and other instrumental music: all now forgotten, along with his textbooks of harmony and counterpoint, once in universal use in his own country.

All his later artistic, educational, and administrative work was bravely carried out under the hampering condition of total blindness. For the last twelve years of his life he was Professor of Music at Cambridge.

He was knighted four years before his death.

See references under *Oratorio* 7 (1873–77–83); *Harmony* 20; *Flute Family* 4; *Day, Alfred*.

(2) NATALIA, whose name is seen as translator on the title-pages of oratorios, operas, and songs, was the wife of the above. She was a German by birth and, although she married at 17, had previously had an international career as vocalist.

(3) WALTER CECIL. Born in London in 1826 and died there in 1905, aged seventy-nine. He was for nearly sixty years a professor of the Royal Academy of Music, and published much graceful music, especially for the piano, some of which survives. He was also widely known as an editor of the piano classics. He was brother of G. A. Macfarren (see above).

McGILL CONSERVATORY (Montreal). See *Schools of Music*.

MACHAUT (or Machault), GUILLAUME DE. Born about 1300 at Machaut in the Ardennes and died in Rheims about 1377. He was a learned priest and a graceful poet. He lived successively at the courts of John of Luxembourg, the Duchess of Normandy, and Charles V of Navarre (for whose coronation he composed a notable Mass). Latterly he settled in Rheims, of whose cathedral he was a canon. His compositions (sacred and secular) are numerous and important. The oldest still existing polyphonic setting of the Mass is his, and he was the last of the French poets of the age of the troubadours to write not merely the words but also the music of his songs. A complete edition of his works was begun in 1926, but later abandoned.

See *France* 3.

MACHICOTAGE. The process, once common in France, of ornamenting the solo parts of plainsong in the way of adding 'vocalises' (q.v.), or of inserting passing notes (see *Harmony* 3), or of making leaps of a third before going on to the next note, and the like. This was done in an extemporary way by the priest, and so in time led to corruption in the written texts, which corruptions have now been swept away by the official adoption of the Solesmes version (see *Plainsong* 3). The term sometimes covers also the addition of an improvised part by a second voice.

Cf. *Ornaments or Graces*.

MACHINE À VENT (Fr.). 'Wind machine' (q.v.).

MACHINE DRUM. See *Percussion Family* 2 a.

MÄCHTIG (Ger.). 'Mighty', powerful.

MACKENZIE.

(1) ALEXANDER CAMPBELL (p. 945, pl. 160. 5). Born in Edinburgh in 1847 and died in London in 1935, aged eighty-seven. He came of a musical family, his great-grandfather being a member of a militia band, and his grandfather and father being professional violinists.

When he was ten he was sent to Germany to study music. There he learnt to play the violin and to compose. When he returned at fifteen he had to relearn his native language. He then won a scholarship at the Royal Academy of Music, and on leaving it settled for a time in Scotland as choral conductor, precentor of an Edinburgh church, and general musical practitioner. A period devoted to composition in Italy followed, and at forty-one he was appointed Principal of the Royal Academy, where for thirty-six years he ruled with mingled firmness and sympathy.

His compositions include operas (several of which had successful production in Germany), oratorios, and cantatas, orchestral pieces, a piano concerto, a violin concerto, and most other things.

Queen Victoria knighted him in 1895 and King George V made him a Knight Commander of the Victorian Order in 1922. He held seven honorary doctorates.

For names and dates and places of first performance of his operas see *Opera* 24. For other references see *Nationalism*; *Oratorio* 5, 7; *Concerto* 6 b (1847); *Melodrama*; *Rule, Britannia!*; *Ecossaise*; *England* 7; *Oratorio* 8 (1884); *Pibroch*. Also p. 705, pl. **118**. 6.

(2) COMPTON (1883–1972). Novelist and enthusiast for the gramophone. Knighted 1953.

See reference under *Gramophone* 7.

McKIE, WILLIAM NEIL. Born at Melbourne, Victoria, in 1901. He was trained at the Royal College of Music (later on its staff) and Worcester College, Oxford. He became successively Director of Music at Clifton College (1926), City Organist of Melbourne (1931), organist of Magdalen College, Oxford (1938), and organist of Westminster Abbey (appointed 1941, but took over in 1946, after his war service). As a composer he is a pupil of Gustav Holst. Knighted 1953.

MACKINTOSH, ROBERT, known as 'Red Rob Mackintosh' (1745–1807). Violinist and composer. See *Scotland* 3.

MACKLEAN, CHARLES. Eighteenth-century Edinburgh violinist and composer. See *Sonata* 10 c.

MACLEAN family.

(1) **CHARLES DONALD**. Born at Cambridge in 1843 and died in London in 1916, aged seventy-three. After an Oxford career he became musical director of Eton College and then spent nearly a quarter of a century in the Indian Civil Service. Returning to England, he occupied himself with valuable musical organizing work, especially in connexion with the International Musical Society.

(2) **ALEXANDER MORVAREN** (Alick). Born at Eton in 1872 and died in 1936, aged sixty-four. He was a son of Charles Donald (above). His career was that of a theatre and light-orchestra conductor (for his last twenty-four years at Scarborough) and a composer of songs, operas, and choral–orchestral works.

Cf. *Opera* 24 e, f (1895, 1906-09-20).

(3) **QUENTIN MORVAREN**. Born in London in 1896 and died in Toronto in 1962, aged sixty-six. He was son of Alexander Morvaren (above). He was a cinema organist and composer of light music; he lived in Canada from 1939.

MACLEOD, ANNIE. See *Skye Boat Song.*

MACLOUGHLIN, F. (Medical-man composer). See *Programme Music* 4.

MACMILLAN, ERNEST CAMPBELL. Born near Toronto in 1893, and died there in 1973. He took his A.R.C.O. at 13. He studied music at Edinburgh, and wrote, and had accepted, his Oxford D.Mus. exercise while interned at Ruhleben. He later wrote much other music. He was Principal of the Toronto Conservatory (1926–42), Dean of the Faculty of Music at Toronto University (1926–52) and Conductor of the Toronto Symphony Orchestra (1931). He was knighted in 1935.

McNALLY, LEONARD (1752–1820). Playwright, barrister at Irish Bar, and political informer. See *Lass of Richmond Hill.*

McNAUGHT.

(1) **WILLIAM GRAY** (1849–1918). See *Competitions* 5.

(2) **WILLIAM** (1883–1953). Son of the above. He was an Oxford graduate and a music critic attached to various important journals. From 1939 till his death he edited the *Musical Times.*

MACONCHY, ELIZABETH. She is of Irish extraction but was born at Broxbourne, Herts.,

in 1907. She studied at the Royal College of Music and then abroad. She won recognition as a composer by a piano concerto (first performed at Prague, 1930), by a *Comedy Overture*, and by her chamber music (string quartets, a quintet for oboe and strings, etc.).

McPHEE, COLIN. Born at Montreal in 1901 and died in Los Angeles in 1964, aged sixty-two. A composer of modernist tendencies, he settled in the United States. He spent the years 1931–7 in anthropological-musical research in Bali and published papers on the subject. His compositions include theatre music, orchestral and chamber music, etc. In several works he made use of Balinese idioms.

MACPHERSON.

(1) **(CHARLES) STEWART** (p. 32, pl. **3. 4**). Born in Liverpool in 1865 and died in London in 1941, aged seventy-six. He was a distinguished pupil and afterwards professor of the Royal Academy of Music. After a career as conductor and composer, he devoted himself to raising the level of the educational treatment of music throughout the country, writing many valuable textbooks and producing practical editions of pianoforte music.

See *Appreciation; Ear Training.*

(2) **CHARLES** (1870–1927). He was a choir-boy of St. Paul's Cathedral, London, who later became its assistant organist and then (1916) its organist. He composed music for church and concert-room.

See *Anglican Chant* 6.

MADAM BUTTERFLY (Puccini—*Madama Butterfly*). Produced at Milan in 1904. Text by Giacosa and Illica, founded on the story by J. L. Long, and the drama by David Belasco.

ACT I

SCENE: *A House on a Hill near Nagasaki*

Lieut. Pinkerton (*Tenor*), of the American Navy, is being shown by **Goro** (*Tenor*), a marriage broker, over a house which he has taken for his Japanese bride-to-be, Cho-Cho-San, known as 'Madame Butterfly'. He meets **Suzuki** (*Mezzo-Soprano*), Butterfly's maid.

The American consul, **Sharpless** (*Baritone*), tries in vain to dissuade Pinkerton from the marriage, which he appears to take lightly, while Sharpless knows that Butterfly and all her friends consider it fully binding. She has even given up her religion for it.

Now **Butterfly** (*Soprano*) enters, with her relatives, and the marriage is celebrated, not without opposition from a **Bonze** (priest; *Bass*), Butterfly's uncle, who denounces her for forsaking her faith. Pinkerton clears the house and comforts Butterfly, and as the stars come out they sing of their love.

ACT II

SCENE: *Inside Butterfly's House*

Three years have passed, and Butterfly has a little boy, who has never seen his father, for

Pinkerton, recalled to America, has not returned to Japan, in spite of his promise. Butterfly is sure he will come. Sharpless arrives, to try to tell her that Pinkerton has married an American girl, with whom he will soon be visiting Nagasaki; but Butterfly is so excited at hearing Pinkerton's name that she does not listen to the explanation, and Sharpless has to leave without undeceiving her.

Prince Yamadori (*Baritone*) comes to seek her hand, but she insists that she is married to Pinkerton, and refuses him. The consul tries once more to tell her that Pinkerton will not come back into her life, but she is sure he will if he knows about his little boy. Sharpless sadly leaves, unable to do more.

A cannon shot from an American ship in the bay attracts the notice of Butterfly and Suzuki, who decorate the house and then watch for the coming of Pinkerton. As the night draws on Suzuki falls asleep, but Butterfly stays awake.

Act III

Scene: *Same as before*

At dawn Butterfly goes off to rest a little. Pinkerton and his American wife appear, with Sharpless, but on realizing the position the lieutenant cannot bear to stay. Butterfly hears without apparent emotion that Pinkerton wishes to adopt her child, and replies that in half an hour he may take the boy away. Left alone, she embraces the child, falls upon her father's sword, and dies as Pinkerton and Sharpless rush in.

MADDOX. See *Opera* 17 b.

MADELON, LA. This was the favourite song of the French soldiers during the latter part of the first World War, corresponding to the British 'Tipperary' (q.v.). Its composer was Camille Robert. He wrote it in 1914 for a vocalist called Bach and its popularity began when this vocalist first sang it at a soldiers' concert in the battle area two years later. When peace was proclaimed a new version was issued —*Madelon de la Victoire*, with the substitution of 'Foch, Joffre, et Clemenceau' for 'Madelon, Madelon, Madelon' in the final stanza.

MADERNA, BRUNO. Born in Venice in 1920, and died in Darmstadt in 1972. An active conductor and composer, he was a pupil of Scherchen and Malipiero. His works include a piano concerto and other things. He was considered one of the leaders of the Italian group of advanced experimental followers of Webern.

MADRIALE. See *Madrigal* 1.

MADRIGAL

1. The Madrigal in Italy. The word 'madrigal', as the title of a musical composition, is found from the late thirteenth and fourteenth centuries, when in Italy it was applied to secular unaccompanied vocal compositions for two or three voices, in the simple harmony of the day.

It should be noted that the earliest composer known to have written madrigals under that name is Dante's friend Pietro Casella (died some time before 1300), of whose music he speaks as—

... That amorous song
Which erst was wont my every care to lull
(*Purgatorio*, Canto II).

Amongst other madrigal composers of this period was the organist, Francesco Landino (q.v.).

Unlike most of the choral music of this period, the madrigal was free composition, i.e. it was not a mere addition of free parts to a fixed part (or 'Canto Fermo'; see *Harmony* 6, 7), but was free in every part.

After the fourteenth century the term seems for a time to have dropped out of musical use (although, of course, the thing itself continued to exist and to develop) and to have been applied to that fairly definite type of lyrical poetry of a pastoral or idyllic or amorous character which had formed the subject of the musical settings. The form of the word used was usually *madriale* or *mandriale*. Petrarch (1304–74) was one of the chief of those who developed and perfected the poetical form of the madrigal; D'Annunzio was one of those who in the twentieth century took up the form again, and the literary application of the word is not entirely extinct, since poets today sometimes use it as a description of any kind of light-handed lyric.

The re-emergence of the word in its musical sense came in the sixteenth century, when the Flemish composers who abounded in Italy (being the chief church musicians there at that period) and the Italian composers themselves wrote secular unaccompanied choral compositions under the title, such as may be looked upon as representing the previous type carried out according to the methods of a period that enjoyed the results of two centuries of additional experiment and achievement in the technique of composition. The Flemish and Italian madrigal repertories of this period are of very great importance.

For some further remarks on the Italian madrigal see *Italy* 2, 3, 4; *Jewish Music* 4; *Opera* 1. An exhaustive and scholarly account of the origins and history of the madrigal is Einstein's *The Italian Madrigal* (3 vols., 1949).

2. The Madrigal in England. From Italy this type of composition travelled to England, where in 1588 and 1597 Nicholas Yonge (q.v.)

published *Musica transalpina* ('Music from across the Alps'), a collection of Italian madrigals with the words translated into English. These were not the first madrigals to be imported, but they established the madrigalsinging habit. Yonge was a singing-man of St. Paul's Cathedral and had a house not very far away where he used to gather 'a great number of Gentlemen and Merchants of good accompt (as well of this realme as of foreine nations) . . . for the exercise of music daily'. From this time on the English composers began to be active in writing madrigals, and they quickly equalled their Flemish and Italian models.

Except for the frequent use of a lighter touch, the madrigals of these, the palmy days of the type, do not differ greatly from the church music (e.g. the Continental motets and English anthems) of the same period. Both are for unaccompanied voices, but the madrigals were intended for only one voice to a part (this conflicts with the assertion of several other books of reference but is believed to be correct); both are contrapuntal in style (see *Counterpoint*) and abound in points of imitation (see under *Canon*). The number of parts written for varies from two to six or more.

The poems set are often either pastoral or amatory, or both: they abound in classical allusions and are often fanciful and high-flown—in fact, they are touched with the contemporary euphuism; they are charming but artificial. The English madrigals (like the contemporary English lute songs) are a mine of poetry; their words have sometimes been republished in modern times purely as poetry and apart from the music, and are as such relished by people of literary taste whose interest in music has never been awakened.

The setting of the notes to the words has almost invariably been done with high skill; not only are changes of mood closely reflected, but definite point is given to every expression of the poet, so far as possible. The whole corpus of English madrigal poetry was collected by Dr. E. H. Fellowes in one volume in 1920, and from 1913 to 1924 he similarly issued the whole of the music in thirty-six volumes. He also wrote the exhaustive work *The English Madrigal Composers* (1921), and the small work *The English Madrigal* (1925). Thus this great national heritage of choral song, of which considerable portions had been published at various periods by the care of various editors, is now fully at the nation's service.

As the high period of madrigal writing was the period when the influence of the modes (q.v.) was by no means extinct, many madrigals will be felt at once to be modal rather than written according to the modern key system: it is this, more than anything, but also the rhythmic freedom and independence of their separate voice-parts, that give so many of them, as heard by present-day ears, a touch of archaism and quaintness.

For the restricted area from which came the British madrigal composers see *Scotland* 8. For slight passing allusions to madrigal publication in England see *Printing* 3; *Publishing* 4; *Puritans* 7. For the pitch at which the old madrigals should be sung see *Pitch* 2.

3. The Three Classes of Madrigal. The English madrigals can be divided into three classes (and the same divisions apply in a large measure to the madrigals of other nations):

(*a*) *The Madrigal proper* (published in part-books for the separate voices), contrapuntal, with many points of 'imitation': conversational in its musical style, so to speak. It is a general characteristic of the madrigal proper that each line or thought of the poem is introduced in some voice to a new phrase of music which is then taken up by other voices. (For some remarks on its rhythmic freedom see *Notation* 4.)

(*b*) The *Ayre*, which (if a true ayre and not a specimen of the madrigal proper to which the composer has carelessly attached an unsuitable name) is less contrapuntal (see *Counterpoint*) and more like a soprano song with accompanying vocal or instrumental parts (often lute; p. 609, pl. **107**. 6). Moreover, it repeats the music for the different verses of the poem instead of being 'through-composed'. It was not published in part-books, like the madrigal proper, but in a large book around which the performers could sit or stand (though in many cases it might be sung by only one performer—to his own lute accompaniment).

(*c*) The *Ballett* resembles the ayre in that it is verse-repeating, but it has a dance-like lilt and a 'fa-la' refrain. It was probably often danced to by the singers. This type was directly taken from the corresponding Italian type. It was usually published in part-books like the madrigal proper (p. 609, pl. **107**. 5).

Despite the fact that the English madrigals were, as above stated, very closely detailed and expressive settings of poems, they were often used without words and purely as instrumental music, or some strands might be sung and others played according to the resources available at the moment: some collections were even published with the description 'Apt for Voyces or Vyols' (see *Viols*; *Chamber Music* 5, 6—Period I).

4. 'The Triumphs of Oriana.' A highly important book of English madrigals is *The Triumphs of Oriana*, a collection of twenty-nine madrigals generally considered to have been composed in praise of Queen Elizabeth I, by twenty-six different composers, under the editorship of Thomas Morley (q.v.).

About ten years before (1592) there had appeared in Venice a collection of twenty-nine madrigals, by twenty-nine different composers, called *Il Trionfo di Dori*. Palestrina and all the finest Italian composers of the day contributed to this. Each madrigal ends with the words 'Viva la bella Dori!' Who Dori was is now unknown: it is thought by some authorities that she was a lady of the house of the Sanudi in Venice, but she may have been merely an impersonation of Italian womanhood. The idea was taken up in England and turned to the praise of Queen Elizabeth under the name of Oriana (the heroine of the ancient romance of *Amadis of Gaul*), which name appears in the refrain of each madrigal as that of Dori had done in the earlier publication. 'Long live fair Oriana'—so ends each of the twenty-nine compositions, but it was not to be, for when the collection (dated 1601 on its title-page) came to actual publication (in 1603) the Queen was already dead. The best known of these Oriana madrigals is Weelkes's 'As Vesta was from Latmos hill descending'.

5. Choral 'Chamber Music'. The madrigal was originally home music. Just as Nicholas Yonge and his friends sang such music daily in his parlour in the parish of St. Michael's, Cornhill, so in many a parish up and down England, and especially in the great houses where families of education and refinement lived and entertained their guests, people were singing. To be able to read one's part at sight in a new madrigal, when the part-books were handed round after supper, was then (according to a statement of Morley in his *Plaine and Easie Introduction*, 1597—a statement of which one would like a little confirmation) almost a necessary part of the equipment for social life. The madrigal, it will be gathered, was not a popular but an aristocratic (or at least a bourgeois) form of musical art.

The fact that madrigals were considered one-voice-to-a-part compositions (a form of 'chamber music', like the string quartet) probably comes merely from the fact that they were the choral music of private gatherings. Choral societies did not then exist; now that they do so madrigals are often sung by many voices to a part, though some admirable one-voice-to-a-part groups are still to be heard.

The first English society definitely founded for the cultivation of madrigal singing was the Madrigal Society, which was founded in 1741 (a century after the true madrigal period had ended) and is still active, meeting regularly in the City of London to eat a dinner together, after which the madrigals are passed round the table, choir-boys are brought in to take the treble parts, and the singing begins. There is no audience; the meeting is not for the display of choral skill but for the pleasure of choral performance. This is believed to be the oldest musical society in the world.

Another old and still existing body is the Bristol Madrigal Society, founded in 1837. R. L. de Pearsall (see 7) was one of its first members.

6. Exceptional Names and Types of Madrigal. Some English composers have written madrigals under other names, such as *Canzonet* (q.v.), *Pastoral* (q.v.), *Neapolitan* (see *Napolitaine*), or even, vaguely, *Air* or *Song*. The word *Motet* was also used by Orlando Gibbons.

Although the madrigal has been spoken of several times in this article as having secular

words, and although this is roughly true, yet some examples are settings of serious poems or even scriptural passages and are, of course, little distinguishable from anthems or motets.

In Italy madrigals were a good deal used as intermezzi in stage plays. As mentioned at the beginning of the article *Opera*, a few plays were actually set to madrigal music throughout.

Some Italian madrigals had very lascivious words, and as a protest, or in reaction from this, *Madrigali spirituali* were written by Palestrina and others.

7. The Decline of the Madrigal. With the coming of the monodic style (see *Monody*, *Recitative*, *Opera*, and *Oratorio*) the madrigal disintegrated: the word was still used, but it was allied to compositions that no longer maintained the traditional madrigalian attributes of contrapuntal writing, freedom from instrumental accompaniment, etc. Monteverdi (d. 1643), for instance, wrote madrigals with solos and accompaniment—really incipient choral cantatas, and in the eighteenth century vocal duets with accompaniment of figured bass (q.v.) were sometimes so designated. Such madrigals as have been written since about 1630 are either not madrigals at all or are deliberate imitations of a style no longer current. The English composer de Pearsall (1795–1856) was a skilful and expressive nineteenth-century writer of sixteenth-century madrigals; his work may be compared to (say) Pugin's nineteenth-century Gothic architecture. (See 5; also *Pearsall*.)

8. A Conspectus of Madrigal Composers. The following composers of madrigals in the high period of madrigal production (sixteenth and early seventeenth centuries) are all treated under their own names in this volume.

(a) **Netherlandish.**

(The brief references to Italian residence and professional occupation have been added as being of significance to the history of the development of the madrigal form and style.)

Willaert (c. 1480–1562). Maestro of St. Mark's, Venice.

Verdelot (first half of sixteenth century). Singing-man of St. Mark's, Venice, and then Maestro of St. John's, Florence.

Arcadelt (c. 1514–67). Singing-man of the Sistine Chapel, Rome.

de Rore (c. 1516–65). Maestro of the court at Parma and of St. Mark's, Venice.

Waelrant (1518–95). Said to have studied in Venice.

Filippo di Monte (c. 1521–1603).

Lassus (c. 1532–94). Maestro of the Lateran, Rome.

Giaches Wert (1535–96). Worked chiefly in Mantua.

(b) **Italian.**

(It will be noted that in general the lifetimes of these composers fell a little later than those of the Flemings and Walloons above mentioned, from whom they largely learnt their art: indeed, all but five of the Italian composers here listed

1. AN ELIZABETHAN MASQUE. At the marriage of Sir Henry Unton (*c.* 1580)

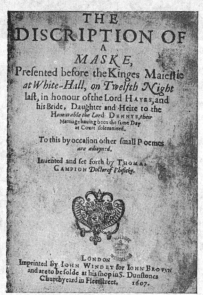

THE
DISCRIPTION OF
A
MASKE,
Presented before the Kinges Maieſtie
at White-Hall, on Twelfth Night
laſt, in honour of the Lord HAYES, and
his Bride, Daughter and Heire to the
Honourable the Lord DENNYE, their
Marriage hauing been the ſame Day
at Court ſolemnized.

To this by occaſion other ſmall Poemes
are adioyned.

Inuented and ſet forth by THOMA.
CAMPION Dollor of Phiſicke.

LONDON
Imprinted by IOHN WINDET for IOHN BROWN
and are to be ſolde at his ſhop in S. Dunſtones
Churchyeard in Fleetſtreet. 1607.

2. A MASQUE BY CAMPION—performed
before James I in 1607

3. DESIGN FOR A SCENE IN A MASQUE by Inigo Jones, who
provided the scenery of masques for James I

PLATE 105

MEALTIME MUSIC

See the Article on pages 609–10

1. CHRISTMAS FEASTING. From a rare print of 1525

2. A ROYAL FEAST IN 14TH-CENTURY
ENGLAND

3. A BANQUET AT BERGAMO. By Romanino (early 16th century)

Psal. 150. Laudate Dominum in tympano & choro:
laudate eum in chordis & organo.

4. IN 16TH-CENTURY GERMANY

5. AT A FRENCH COURT
From a wood-engraving (16th century)

were born later than the last-born of the Netherlandish list.)

Festa (c. 1490–1545); A. Gabrieli (c. 1510–86); Vicentino (1511–72); Ruffo (born c. 1520); Palestrina (c. 1525–94); Ingegneri (c. 1545–92); Vecchi (1550–1605); Marenzio (1553–99); Gastoldi (c. 1556–1622); F. Anerio (c. 1560–1614); Gesualdo (1560–1613; a 'modernist', introducing surprising harmonies: see separate article); Gagliano (c. 1575–1642); Monteverdi (1567–1643); D. Mazzocchi (1592–1665).

(c) **English.**

(Arranged in decades, as to birth.)

20s; Edwards (c. 1523–66); a precursor—prior to the Italian influence.

40s; Byrd (c. 1542–1623).

50s; Morley (1557–c. 1603); Carlton (c. 1558–1638).

60s; Cobbold (1560–1639); John Hilton, senior (c. 1560–1608); Pilkington (c. 1562–1638); John Milton, father of the poet (c. 1563–1647); Dowland (1562–1626); Cavendish (c. 1565–1628); Campian (1567–1620).

70s; Marson (c. 1570–1632); Nicholson (c. 1570–1639); Bateson (c. 1570–1630); Peerson (c. 1572–1651); Tomkins (1573–1656); Ellis Gibbons (1573–1603); Wilbye (1574–1638); Rosseter (c. 1575–1623); Weelkes (c. 1575–1623); Daniel Norcombe (b. 1576).

80s; Orlando Gibbons (1583–1625).

90s; Vautor (born c. 1590); John Hilton, junior (1599–1657).

Birth dates unknown:

Alison; Bennet; Farmer; Farnaby; Greaves; W. Holborne; John Holmes; Hunt; Edward Johnson; Robert Jones; Kirbye (d. 1634); Lichfild; Lisley; Patrick (d. 1595); Philips (died c. 1628); Ward; Youll.

The greatest amongst the above are probably Weelkes, Wilbye, Byrd, Gibbons, Morley, Tomkins, and Bateson.

For a pioneer of the Ayre see *Whythorne.*

(d) **Other Nationalities.**

The above are the chief madrigal-composing nations.

In **France** many of the *chansons* (q.v.) were much like madrigals and one French composer created a new genre, the descriptive madrigal, as we may call it— Jannequin (q.v.) in his *The Battle*, *The Hunt*, and *The Cries of the Birds.*

In **Germany** (see also *Germany* 2) the principal madrigalist was Hassler (1564–1612); he had his training in Italy and the words of many of his madrigals are Italian.

Spain (see also *Spain* 5) has some madrigal composers and the villancico (q.v.) approached the madrigal in style. The greatest Spanish composer of the period, Victoria (c. 1549–1611), did not write any madrigals—which seems odd considering his long Italian residence, but he had a religious scruple as to the secular use of music.

The **American Colonies** came into existence only at the very end of the madrigalian period, and the busy colonists were, in any case, little inclined for musical composition. Thus America lies right outside the field of this branch of art. It seems curious that in Lahee's *Annals of Music in America*, which gives a long list of musical organizations founded between 1720 and 1920, not one madrigal society (so designated) is included. The United States has, however, participated in the late nineteenth and early twentieth centuries' revival of the practice of singing madrigals, and has cultivated madrigal singing in a number of universities and high schools, many of which became equipped with excellent *a cappella* choirs.

MADRIGALI SPIRITUALI. See *Madrigal* 6.

MADRIGAL SOCIETY. See *Madrigal* 5.

MADRILEÑA (Sp.), **MADRILÈNE** (Fr.). A Spanish dance type deriving from the province of Madrid.

MAELZEL, JOHANN NEPOMUK (1772–1838). See *Mechanical Reproduction of Music* 8, 9; *Metronome.*

MAESTÀ, MAESTADE (It.). 'Majesty', 'dignity'. So *Maestevole, Maestevolmente*, 'majestic(ally)'.

MAESTOSO. 'Majestic'. So *Maestosamente*, 'majestically'.

MAESTRALE (It.). 'Masterly.' This adjective is sometimes applied to a fugue stretto (see *Form* 12 c) in strict canon.

MAESTRO (It.). 'Master', 'teacher', etc. *Maestro di capella* (see *Chapel*) means 'chief musician' or 'musical director' and nowadays (usually abbreviated to merely 'Maestro') 'conductor'.

MAGAZINES. See *Journals.*

MAGER, JÖRG (Georg Adam). Born in 1880 at Eichstätt, Bavaria, and died in 1939 at Aschaffenburg. He began life as a schoolmaster–organist, studied at the Mannheim Conservatory, became interested in the subject of microtonal music, constructed a quarter-tone harmonium, passed on to electrical experiment, and invented the Sphärophon and then the Partiturophon (see *Electric Musical Instruments* 1 c).

MAGGIOLATA (It.). 'May Song', or Spring Song—either traditional or composed.

MAGGIORE (It.). 'Major.'

MAGGOT. In older English, a fanciful idea, and so, by extension, a pleasant piece of music —generally a country dance (q.v.) with somebody's name attached, presumably in a complimentary way, e.g. 'My Lady Winwood's Maggot'.

MAGICAL USE OF MUSIC. See *United States of America* 7.

MAGIC FLUTE, THE (Mozart—*Die Zauberflöte*). Produced at Vienna in 1791. Libretto by Schikaneder (q.v.) and Giesecke.

Act I

(For an allusion to the overture see *Overture* 3.)

Scene 1: *A Rocky Place by a Temple*

Tamino (*Tenor*), an Egyptian Prince, is rescued from a huge serpent by **Three Ladies**

(*Soprani* and *Contralto*), attendants of the Queen of Night. They give him a portrait of the Queen's daughter, Pamina, and he at once determines to seek her. She, it seems, is in the power of Sarastro, High Priest of Isis and Osiris.

Papageno (*Baritone*), a bird-catcher, pretends that he killed the serpent, but the ladies padlock his lying tongue. **The Queen of Night** (*Soprano*) tells Tamino that she relies on him to rescue her daughter, and the ladies give him a magic flute which will preserve him from all evil; Papageno, whom the queen has commanded to go with the prince, is given a chime of magic bells.

SCENE 2: *A Room in Sarastro's Palace*

Monostatos (*Tenor*), the blackamoor slave of the Temple, is pestering **Pamina** (*Soprano*), the queen's daughter. On Papageno's appearing in his bird-like costume, the slave, terrified, runs away. Papageno tells Pamina that the prince is in love with her and is coming to rescue her.

SCENE 3: *The Entrance to the Temple*

Three Genii (*Soprani* and *Contralto*) bring on Tamino, who defies a **Priest** (*Bass*), but learns from him that Sarastro is not cruel, but benevolent. Meanwhile, Papageno and Pamina, captured by Monostatos and his followers, escape: for when Papageno sets the magic bells jingling the slaves cannot but dance, forgetting all their duty.

Now **Sarastro** (*Bass*) appears. Pamina confesses that she tried to escape. He tells her that her life would be wrecked if she were given over to her mother, and that she needs a man to guide her to wisdom. Tamino, with joy, finds her, and Sarastro decides that the two lovers must undergo probation before they can know the secret of the holy life.

ACT II
SCENE 1: *The Sacred Grove*

Tamino is accepted by the priests as worthy to undergo the ordeals. Papageno is told that he, too, is to find happiness—in a wife, feathered like himself, Papagena. But neither he nor Tamino must speak to any woman during the trials.

SCENE 2: *The Courtyard of the Temple*

The ladies tempt them to speak, but without success.

Next, **Papagena** (*Soprano*) enters, disguised as an old woman; but as she throws off her disguise the priests drive her away. Pamina, finding that Tamino will not speak to her, thinks he no longer loves her.

SCENE 3: *A Garden*

Monostatos, again pursuing Pamina, is scared away by the Queen of Night. She, hearing from Pamina that Tamino has joined the initiates of the Temple, is furious, and gives her daughter a dagger, bidding her kill Sarastro.

Pamina tells the High Priest, who replies that within those sacred walls no evil thought can dwell.

SCENE 4: *A Hall in the Temple*

Pamina is further submitted to ordeal by being told that Tamino is to take his last farewell of her. But Sarastro hints that all is not so dark as it appears for them.

SCENE 5: *An Open Place*

Poor Pamina, intending to take her life, is prevented by the Genii, who bid her hope.

Papageno, having lost *his* ladylove, prepares to hang himself, but the Genii tell him to set his bells ringing and he shall see his bride. So it happens, and they go off happily together.

SCENE 6: *A Doorway before the Place of Ordeal*

Tamino and Pamina pass through fire and water (he playing his magic flute) and are welcomed to the fellowship of the Temple.

SCENE 7: (*Sometimes omitted.*) *Before the Temple*

The Queen, her ladies, and Monostatos, plotting to destroy the occupants of the Temple, find themselves powerless before Sarastro, and vanish, never to reappear.

FINAL SCENE: *The Entrance of the Temple*

The faithful lovers are acclaimed, having found the high places of Wisdom.

See *Overture* 3; *Panpipes*; *Opera* 9.

MAGINTY, E. A. See *God save the Queen* 1.

MAGNA (It.). Fem. of *Magno*, 'great'.

MAGNARD, ALBÉRIC (in full, Lucien Denis Gabriel Albéric). Born in Paris in 1865, killed in 1914, aged forty-nine. His general education was received partly at Ramsgate, England, and his musical at the Paris Conservatory under Dubois and Massenet. He left these teachers and went to d'Indy, whose artistic ideals were more congenial to him and to whom he always felt the greatest indebtedness; in other words, he belongs to the school of Franck.

His opera *Yolande* was given in Brussels in 1892, and gradually his work became known, but its dignity and even severity are perhaps a lasting bar to any wide popularity. His chamber music and symphonies are of value.

He was a man of wealth and possessed an estate near Senlis. He died defending it at the outbreak of the first World War.

See *Ropartz*.

MAGNIFICAT. The hymn of the Virgin Mary ('My soul doth magnify the Lord') as given in the gospel of St. Luke. It forms a part of the text of the service of Vespers (q.v.) in the Roman Catholic Church and of that of Evensong in the Anglican Church (see *Common Prayer*). It has its traditional plainsong but is more often sung to an Anglican chant in the latter and has also been set innumerable times by composers as a part of the musical Evening Service. It has also been set in Latin many times (Palestrina, Lassus, Marenzio, Morales, Bach, etc.).

MAGNO, MAGNA (It., masc., fem.). 'Great.'

MAGREPHA. See *Jewish Music* 5.

MAGYAR. The Magyars are a Mongol race now chiefly found in Hungary. So 'Magyar' is sometimes used for 'Hungarian', but the Hungarian music best known to the world being that of the Hungarian gipsies, this is the usual musical association. (But cf. *Hungary*.)

MAHLER, GUSTAV (p. 401, pl. **70.** 6). Born in 1860 in Bohemia and died in Vienna in 1911, aged fifty. Like Brahms, he may be styled a classical-romantic, for he wrote symphonies yet expressed the typical German romantic feeling. He was influenced by Bruckner, still another 'classical-romantic', and greatly, also, by the spirit and technique of Wagner.

His musical education was received in Vienna and then he held in turn a number of important opera conductorships—including that at Vienna, where he ruled for ten years and carried out many reforms.

He conducted a German opera season in London in 1892, and from 1908 spent a good deal of time in America, especially in New York, where he was chief conductor at the Metropolitan Opera House and also director of the Philharmonic Orchestra.

His symphonies (some with voices), have always been taken seriously in Germany and Holland, in the latter through the influence of J. W. Mengelberg (q.v.), and from the late 1940s they became part of the standard concert repertory in Britain and the U.S.A. His forty-two songs are of importance.

Mahler's Symphonies are as follows: No. 1, in D (1888). No. 2, in C minor, 'Resurrection' (1894); with solo voices and chorus. No. 3, in D minor (1895); with solo contralto, and boys' and female choruses. No. 4, in G (1900); with solo soprano. No. 5, in C sharp minor (1902). No. 6, in A minor (1904). No. 7, in E minor (1905). No. 8, in E flat (1907); with 7 solo vocalists, 2 mixed choruses and boys' chorus, and organ. No. 9, in D (1909). No. 10 was completed by Deryck Cooke and performed in 1964. There is also *The Song of the Earth* (*Das Lied von der Erde*), a Symphony with solo voices.

(In 1938 it was announced that Mengelberg had discovered the autographs of four juvenile and hitherto unknown symphonies by this composer.)

See references under *Germany* 9 b; *Percussion* 4 e; *Saxophone*; *Scordatura*; *Křenek*; *Orchestra* 5; *Bruckner Society*.

MAIDEN QUARTETS (Haydn). See *Nicknamed Compositions* 12 (37–42).

MAILLART, LOUIS (or Aimé). Born at Montpellier in 1817 and died at Moulins in 1871, aged fifty-four. At the Paris Conservatory he won the Rome Prize. He is known as the composer of a number of operas, particularly *Les Dragons de Villars* ('Villars Dragoons').

MAILLOCHE (Fr.). Stick of bass drum.

MAIN, MAINS (Fr.). 'Hand', 'hands', e.g. *Main droite* (or *M.D.*), 'right hand'; *Main gauche* (or

M.G.), 'left hand'; *Deux mains*, 'two hands'; *Quatre mains*, 'four hands' (in piano music).

MAINZ. See *Minstrels* 8; *Printing* 1.

MAINZER, JOSEPH (p. 976, pl. **163.** 1). Born at Trier (Trèves) in 1801 and died at Salford, Manchester, in 1851, aged fifty. In his career he was by turns a mining engineer, a priest, an opera composer in Brussels, a music critic, and a promoter and teacher of sight-singing classes in Paris and then all over Britain. (He published as a textbook for his classes *Singing for the Million*, 1842.) His successive places of British resident activity included London, Edinburgh (in response to a petition signed by the Lord Provost and about one hundred of the principal inhabitants), and Manchester (in response to a similar petition). At Edinburgh he met with some opposition, a public placard posing the momentous question 'Ought Christians to encourage Evening Classes in Singing?' He was an enterprising man of high public spirit.

See a quotation from him under *Ornaments* 1.

MAIS (Fr.). 'But.'

MAITLAND, J. A. FULLER. See *Fuller Maitland*.

MAÎTRE (Fr.). 'Master.'

MAÎTRISE. French for a choir school (the place where the boys come under the direction of a *maître*, or master). By extension, the word is often applied to the body of choir-boys of a church. (The term *Manécanterie* is in certain places used for a choir school, but the term *Schola Cantorum*, q.v., tends to supersede all other names.)

MAJESTÄTISCH (Ger.). 'Majestic', majestically.

MAJESTUEUX, MAJESTUEUSE (Fr.; masc., fem.). 'Majestic'; so *Majestueusement*, 'majestically'.

MAJEUR (Fr.). 'Major.'

MAJOR BASS. See *Organ* 14 I.

MAJOR COMMON CHORD. See *Harmony* 24 d.

MAJOR FLUTE. See *Organ* 14 II.

MAJOR INTERVALS. See *Interval*.

MAJOR SCALE. See *Scales* 6.

MAL (Ger.). 'Time', in such connexions as 'First Time' (*Das erste Mal*), 'Twice' (*Zweimal*), etc.

MALAGUEÑA. A kind of fandango (q.v.) of Malaga, in southern Spain. It has some more or less improvised singing. Its harmony, particularly at the cadence, is a feature: the mode is minor and the bass of the last four chords is nothing but the descending upper half of the scale (with flattened leading note), so terminating on the dominant (or soh), not the tonic (or doh). Above this scale in the bass the upper parts proceed in parallel thirds, fifths, and octaves.

The poetry sung to the malagueña is in the same metre and style as that of the jota (q.v.).

Cf. *Granadina*; *Murciana*.

MALBROUCK S'EN VA-T-EN GUERRE.
This is an eighteenth-century French nursery ditty said to have become widely fashionable through being sung as a cradle song by the nurse of one of the children of Louis XVI and Marie Antoinette. The tune is in Britain sung to both 'For he's a jolly good fellow' and 'We won't go home till morning'. It has had a great popularity all over Europe, to many different sets of words.

It is usually stated that 'Malbrouck' is the great Duke of Marlborough, but this is doubtful; the name 'Malbrouck' is found in the *Chansons de Gestes* (eleventh to fourteenth centuries) and other literature of the Middle Ages.

MALCOLM, ALEXANDER. Born in Edinburgh in 1687 and died in 1763 in Maryland. In 1721, at the age of thirty-four, he published in Edinburgh his important *Treatise of Music, Speculative, Practical, and Historical* (new editions in 1731 and 1776); he also published two books on arithmetic. He emigrated to America, where he had a career as schoolmaster and as Anglican parson. He was an M.A. (probably of Edinburgh) and he played the flute and violin.

MALDER (or Maldere), PIERRE VAN. Born in Brussels in 1724 and there died in 1768, aged forty-four. He enjoyed, in his day, high reputation as a composer of symphonies and of sonatas of the type popular in his youth, i.e. for two violins, cello, and figured bass. He also wrote operas.

MALE ALTO. See *Voice* 5, 17.

MALE VOICE CHOIR OR CHORUS. See *Choir or Chorus*.

MALE VOICE QUARTET. See *Quartet*.

MALIBRAN. See *Garcia* 3; *Festival* 1.

MALINCONIA, MALINCONICO (It.). 'Melancholy.' So *Malinconoso, Malinconioso, Malinconicamente*, in melancholy fashion.

MALIPIERO, FRANCESCO (in full, Gian Francesco; p. 525, pl. **96**. 3). Born in Venice in 1882, and died in Treviso in 1973. He was a pupil of Bossi (the statement in several British and American works to the effect that he was also a pupil of Max Bruch is definitely incorrect). He wrote instrumental music, including symphonies, but interested himself especially in problems of the combination of music and drama, experimented in operas of a very original kind, and edited the complete works of Monteverdi, and works of Corelli, Tartini, Jommelli, Galuppi, Frescobaldi, etc. In support of his ideas he carried out a good deal of effective journalistic propaganda. He also wrote valuable books and many polemic articles.

See references under *Italy* 7; *Mechanical Reproduction* 13 (near end); *Strambotto*; *Opera* 24 f (1938).

MALIZIA (It.). 'Malice.'

MALLARMÉ, STÉPHANE (1842–98). Like Verlaine, a leader in the symbolistic phase of French poetry. For his influence on French music see *Impressionism*.

MALLET (originally **Malloch**), **DAVID** (*c.* 1705–65). Scottish poet and miscellaneous writer. See *Rule Britannia!*

MALLING.
(1) JÖRGEN. Born in Copenhagen in 1836 and there died in 1905, aged sixty-eight. He composed operas, piano music, songs, etc., and became well known as the Danish champion of the Chevé method of sight-singing (see *Sight-Singing* 2).

(2) OTTO VALDEMAR. Born in Copenhagen in 1848 and there died in 1915, aged sixty-seven. He was a pupil of Gade and J. P. E. Hartmann (see *Scandinavia* 2), and then became an organist, choral conductor, and teacher at the Conservatory of Copenhagen, of which, from his early fifties, he was director. He wrote a symphony, a piano concerto, and other orchestral works, chamber and choral music, piano music, songs, etc., and is particularly favourably known for his organ works.

MALLOCH, DAVID. See *Mallet, David*.

MALTMAN, THE. See *Sir Roger de Coverley*.

MAN (It.). Short for *Mano* (q.v.). But in German organ music *Man. I* = Great Manual; *Man. II* = Swell; *Man. III* = Choir; *Man. IV* = Solo. This, it will be seen, is a numeration in order of importance. There is another numeration (in less use) which is based on the position of the manuals: *I* = Choir; *II* = Great; *III* = Swell; *IV* = Solo.

MANCANDO, MANCANTE (It.). 'Dying away.'

MANCANZA (It.). 'Lack.'

MANCHEGA. The local type of seguidilla (q.v.) that is danced in La Mancha—Don Quixote's province of Spain. It is bright and lively and is looked upon as the original form of the dance.

MANCHESTER (England). See *Concert* 10; *Flute Family* 4; *Wainwright*; *Schools of Music*; *Festival* 1.

MANCHESTER CATHEDRAL. Organists who receive notice in this volume are (with their periods of office): *Wainwright, J.* (1767–8); *Wainwright, Robert* (1768–75); *Wainwright, Richard* (1775–82); *Bridge, J. F.* (1869–75); *Nicholson, S. H.* (1908–18).

MANDOLINE or MANDOLIN. An instrument of somewhat the same type as the lute (q.v.) but much less artistically valuable, being now in use for the most part by people who wish to play simple music without much trouble. There are, in the type known as 'Neapolitan', eight wire strings tuned in pairs to the same notes as those of the violin; in the type known as 'Milanese', ten tuned on a similar system. They are set in vibration not by the fingers but by a plectrum, a tremolo being the usual motion: the sustaining of the sound by this device distinguishes the mandoline from such instruments as lutes and guitars, in which the string is plucked and the sound at once begins to die away.

A few of the considerable composers have written on occasion for the mandoline, generally as a concomitant in some dramatic incident, e.g. Handel in his oratorio *Alexander Balus* (1748), Grétry in *The Jealous Lover* (1778), Paesiello in his *Barber of Seville* (1780), Mozart in *Don Giovanni* (1787). Mozart also wrote two independent songs with mandoline accompaniment. Beethoven wrote at least five pieces for the mandoline and piano, of which one can be seen in full in the first edition of Grove's *Dictionary*, under 'Mandoline' (for another see the *Revue Musicale S.I.M.*, Dec. 1912):

SONATINE

(*Pour mandoline et piano.*)

DÉDIÉ À MLLE CLARY   L. VAN BEETHOVEN.
Allegro.

The mandoline was at one time to be found in some orchestras; it disappeared from that of Stuttgart only in 1755. Sonatas for mandoline and violin, mandoline and violoncello, two mandolines and violoncello, etc., were in vogue in the eighteenth century.

See also *Stroh Violin*, etc.; *Pandurina*; *Tablature*; *Electric Musical Instruments* 2 d.

MANDORA or MANDORE. See *Lute* 2, 5.

MANDRIALE. See *Madrigal* 1.

MANÉCANTERIE. See under *Maîtrise*.

MANÉN, JOAN DE. Born at Barcelona in 1883. He is a violinist and the composer of operas, orchestral works, chamber music, etc.

MANFREDINI, FRANCESCO (1688–1748). He was born at Pistoia, and returned there towards the end of his life, having held positions as violinist in various cities. He published trio sonatas, some string concertos, and other things.

MANGEOT family.

(1) EDWARD JOSEPH (1834–98). Piano maker. (See *Keyboard* 4.) He founded the journal *Le Monde musical*.

(2) AUGUSTE, long editor of *Le Monde musical*, was son of the above.

(3) ANDRÉ, also son of (1), was born in Paris in 1883, made his home in London, where he died in 1970, aged eighty-seven. He was a well-known violinist. He edited the Purcell String Fantasies.

MANI (It.). 'Hands.'

MANICA (It.). Shift, on violin, etc. (see *Position*).

MANICHORD. See *Clavichord* 7; *Monochord*.

MANICO (It.). Finger-board (violin, etc.).

MANIEREN (Ger.). Ornaments or 'graces' (q.v.).

MANN.

(1) ARTHUR HENRY. Born at Norwich in 1850 and died at Cambridge in 1929, aged seventy-nine. Under Zechariah Buck (q.v.) he was a chorister and then assistant organist at Norwich Cathedral, and after holding various positions as organist was given that of King's College, Cambridge, in 1876, holding it to his death. He had a high reputation as a choir trainer, as a student of Handel, and as a musical antiquarian.

(2) JOHANN CHRISTOPH. See *Monn, Georg Matthias*.

(3) THOMAS (1875–1955). German novelist and essayist of high international reputation, whose keen musical interests show themselves in his writing. In 1947 his *Doktor Faustus* aroused special attention from the fact that the character of its hero is clearly based on that of Schönberg, and that the hero's processes of composition (minutely described) are exactly those of the Schönbergian Note-row (q.v.). Against this Schönberg strongly protested and in compliance with his demand an 'Author's Note' was appended to all future copies of the book in all languages, beginning—'It does not seem supererogatory to inform the reader that the type of musical composition delineated in Chapter XXII, known as the twelve-tone or row system, is in truth the intellectual property of a contemporary composer and theoretician, Arnold Schönberg. . . .'

This raised worse trouble, articles by the composer strongly protesting against the terms of the statement and included the tart observation: 'He has added a new crime to his first in his attempt to belittle me: he calls me "a [a!] contemporary composer and theoretician": of course in two or three decades one will know which of the two was the other's contemporary.'

MÄNNER (Ger.). 'Men.' So *Männerchor*, 'men's choir'; *Männerstimmen*, 'men's voices'; *Männergesangverein*, 'men's singing society' (see *Liedertafel*).

MANNHEIM. See *Expression* 5; *France* 7; *Clarinet Family* 2; *Conducting* 6.

MANNI, MARCELLO. See *Giovinezza*.

MANNS, AUGUST. See under *Concert* 7; *Scotland* 10; *Annotated Programmes* 5. Also p. 289, pl. 51. 4.

MANO, MANI (It.). 'Hand', 'hands'.

MANSFELDT, EDGAR. See *Pierson*.

MANTUA. See *Orchestra* 1; *Opera* 2; *Monteverdi*; *Jewish* 4.

MANUAL. See *Organ* 1, and also (for the German indications) under *Man*.

MANUALKOPPEL (Ger.). 'Manual coupler', i.e. (usually) 'Swell to Great'.

MAPLE LEAF FOR EVER ! This Canadian national song was written and composed in 1867 by a schoolmaster, Alexander Muir (born in Scotland 1830, died 1906). Since 1887 it has been officially used in Ontario schools; in Quebec 'O Canada!' (q.v.) is preferred.

MARACAS. These are dance-band instruments made from the dried shell of a Cuban gourd, with beans or beads inside and a handle by which they can be shaken to produce a rattling effect (sometimes they are made of plastic and have lead shot inside, so giving a stronger effect).

MARAIS, MARIN (p. 1073, pl. **178**. 4). Born in Paris in 1656 and died there in 1728, aged seventy-two. He was a very fine player of the bass viol (some say the finest who ever lived) and in composition a pupil of Lully. He wrote successful operas and a good deal of instrumental music, some of which is still occasionally to be heard. Two of his sons published music for viols.

See reference under *Folia*.

MARBECK. See *Merbecke*.

MARCANDO, MARCATO (It.). 'Marking', 'marked', i.e. each note emphasized. *Marcatissimo* is the superlative.

MARCELLO, BENEDETTO. Born in Venice in 1686 and died in Brescia in 1739, aged nearly fifty-three. He was a Venetian lawyer and official, a violinist, singer, composer, poet, and polemic writer, who published, amongst other things, settings of fifty Psalm-paraphrases (a most celebrated work) and a notable satire on the opera of his day—*Il teatro alla moda*.

See *Psalm*; *Jewish* 4; *Oratorio* 7 (1670); *Chopin*.

MARCH. Music designed to promote orderly marching, and to enliven the spirits and so minimize fatigue, has been used from early times. The earliest march music preserved in notation is that with which Arbeau in 1589 begins his *Orchésographie* (see *Dance*); it is for drums (for which he gives a vast number of different rhythms) and fife, this latter improvising in a way of which he gives specimens. This gives us the French practice.

About the same period, in 'My Lady Nevell's Booke' (q.v.), a manuscript collection of virginal music, is a group of pieces with such titles as 'The Marche before the Battell', 'The March of Footemen', 'The March of Horsmen', 'The Irishe Marche', and 'The Marche to the Fighte', which, presumably, gives us something of the British practice, although the actual tunes shown may be original.

Many marches in operas, and even in oratorios, show us the style of march music in vogue in the army at the time these works were written, as for example, Handel's 'Dead Marches' in *Saul* and *Samson*, and his famous march in the opera *Scipio* (1726). Indeed these marches sometimes passed into actual army use, as happened with the 'Dead March' in *Saul* and the 'March' in *Scipio* just mentioned, the former being used for army funerals and the latter being from Handel's day to the present the regular parade march of the Grenadier Guards, so that the Guards have come to claim that it was composed for them and only later introduced into the opera.

March music necessarily differs little in general rhythm in different periods, and as for melody and harmony the necessity for simplicity prevents any startlingly rapid changes here.

The usual time is four beats in a measure, three being practically impossible unless played so quickly that a whole measure goes to a single step. The form is usually that of a kind of rondo (see *Form* 9), a chief tune coming round again and again with intervening tunes (called, as in the minuet, 'trios'; see *Trio*): necessarily a strict system of four-bar phrases is maintained throughout, for marches, like dances, must be regular. A Trio is, of course, in some related key (usually dominant or subdominant) so that the rather common practice of bandmasters of ending with it, instead of with the chief section, is disturbing.

There was an American ebullition of march music towards the end of the nineteenth century, when Sousa's band, playing all over the world, popularized his vigorous creations (over 100 marches—see *Sousa*). Elgar has written marches (*Pomp and Circumstance*) intended equally for the concert-room (in their original orchestral scoring) and for the British Army.

Marches still find a fairly frequent place in opera, the action of which often provides military or ceremonial occasions for music. One of the most moving marches ever written is the death march in Wagner's *The Dusk of the Gods*.

The march is not unknown as a movement in the suite, the sonata, and the symphony, and several famous examples of its so figuring will occur to every musician.

The speeds of marches in the British Army are defined as follows (though, in practice they differ considerably in different branches of the service):

Slow march: 75 steps per minute.

Quick march: 108 steps per minute.

The **Quickstep** is another name for the latter.

It should be remembered that the word 'march' in British Army history often connotes merely a traditional drum rhythm, as in the case of 'The English March', 'The Scots March', and 'The Grenadiers' March'. 'The English March' was described in a warrant of Charles I as 'the March of this our English Nation, so famous in all the honourable achievements and glorious warres of this our kingdom in foreigne parts, being by the approbation of strangers themselves confest and acknowledged the best of all marches'. Allusion is made to the 'ancient custome of nations' to 'use one constant forme of March in the warres, whereby to be distinguished from one another', and this 'English March' is then set out in musical notation to redress the corruptions that had crept in through 'the negligence and carelessness of drummers'. It will be seen from the allusion to the use of march rhythms for distinction of one army from the other that they have at one time served an intention similar to that which brought into existence the art and practice of heraldry.

MARCHAND, LOUIS (1669–1732). See *Competitions* 1.

MARCHANT, STANLEY. Born in London in 1883 and died there in 1949, aged sixty-five.

He was trained at the Royal Academy of Music (of which in 1936 he became Principal) and was associated with St. Paul's Cathedral from 1916. In 1937 he became Professor of Music in the University of London. In 1942 he was knighted. He composed church music and other things.

See *Anglican Chant* 6 e.

MARCHE (Fr.). 'March.'

MARCHE AUX FLAMBEAUX (Fr.). 'Torch-light procession.'

MÄRCHEN (Ger.). 'Tale' or 'tales'—often with some suggestion of the traditional or legendary.

MARCHING THROUGH GEORGIA. This song commemorates General Sherman's famous march of 1864. He hated it because he considered it had unduly glorified one particular episode in the war and distracted attention from more important factors; he is even reported to have said (doubtless with a smile), 'If I'd thought my march would have inspired that piece I'd have marched *round* the state'. It is difficult, however, when reading the account of this march, to enter into his feelings.

Both the stirring, rhythmic verses, with their mixture of enthusiasm and humour, and the fine swinging tune are by Henry Clay Work (1832–84). They never existed in manuscript; he was, at the time of the song's composition, a letterpress and music compositor by trade, and set both in type straight away.

MARCIA (It.). 'March.' So *Alla marcia*, 'in march style'.

MARCONI. See *Broadcasting* 2.

MARCOTONE. See *Colour and Music* 5.

MARENZIO, LUCA. Born near Brescia in 1553 and died in Rome in 1599, aged forty-six. He held important positions in Rome and Warsaw and was so much admired, especially as a composer of madrigals, as to earn the nicknames of 'The Sweetest Swan' and 'The Divine Composer'. He adopted a more chromatic style than had been usual heretofore and tended to the abandonment of the modes (q.v.) and the use of the major and minor scales, and in these ways he prepared the road for the new Monteverdian school. Some of his madrigals were published in England (1590) and had their effect on taste there. Others were published at Antwerp, Nuremberg, Paris, etc.

See references under *Harmony* 22; *Magnificat*.

MAREPPE. See *Mechanical Reproduction* 9.

MARESCH, J. A. See *Horn Family* 3 (end).

MARIANA, FATHER. See *Sarabande*; *Dance* 7.

MARIA THERESA SYMPHONY (Haydn). See *Nicknamed Compositions* 11 (48).

MARIAZELLERMESSE (Haydn). See *Nicknamed Compositions* 13 (8).

MARIMBA (p. 512, pl. **91**. 5). A Mexican and Central and South American instrument (especially popular in Southern Mexico and Guatemala) consisting of strips of wood of different length with (tuned) resonators underneath (see *Acoustics* 19), the whole fixed in a frame and struck with drumsticks—in fact, a super-xylophone large enough for four players (or *Marimberos*), sitting side by side, to perform on together.

A feature of this instrument is a piece of bladder attached to each resonator, which by its vibration intensifies the sound and also contributes a buzzing effect to the lower notes.

The South African natives possess instruments of the same sort as the marimba (sometimes called by Europeans 'Kaffir Pianos', but one native name is *Malimba*), and these are doubtless the originals, the slave trade being responsible for the present-day presence of this type in the New World (p. 512, pl. **91**. 3).

Compare *Vibraphone*. For adaptations of the marimba to orchestral use see *Percussion* 2 g h; *Deagan Instruments*.

MARIMBA GONGS. See *Percussion Family*.

MARIMBAPHONE. See *Deagan Instruments*.

MARIMBEROS. See *Marimba*.

MARINE TRUMPET. See *Tromba Marina*.

MARINETTI. See *Italy* 7; *Applause* 5.

MARINI, BIAGIO. Born in Brescia in 1597 and died in Venice in 1665, aged sixty-eight. He was a violinist–composer and pupil of Monteverdi, who held posts in various courts of Italy and Germany. His output of vocal and chamber music is more exacting in performance than was usual in his day, and includes the earliest known sonata for solo violin (1617).

MARINUZZI, GINO. Born at Palermo in 1882 and died at Milan in 1945. He had a very varied and successful career as opera conductor in Italy, Spain, France, the United States, and South America, and composed a number of operas, symphonic works, and a Requiem.

MARITANA. See *Wallace, W. V.*

MARIUS, JEAN. Paris harpsichord-maker of early eighteenth century. See *Pianoforte* 3.

MARKEVICH, IGOR. Born at Kief in 1912. His life was at first lived mainly at Vevey in Switzerland, and in Paris, where his various orchestral, choral, and chamber works had their early performances, arousing keen discussion.

His productions include ballets, choral works, orchestral and chamber music, etc.

As an orchestral conductor he has acquired an international reputation.

MARKIERT (Ger.). 'Marked', i.e. (*a*) clearly accented, or (*b*) brought out, e.g. a melody to be emphasized, as compared with the accompaniment.

MARKIG (Ger.). 'Vigorous.'

MAROT, CLÉMENT (p. 484, pl. **85**. 4). Born at Cahors, France, about 1496 and died at Turin in 1544, aged about forty-eight. He was a poet and courtier of the time of Francis I who took up the task of producing French metrical versions of the Psalms.

See references under *Hymns and Hymn Tunes* 4, 17 d i; *Old Hundredth*; *Publishing* 2; and for the group of musicians associated with the Huguenot movement to which Marot's work contributed see *France* 4.

MARPURG, FRIEDRICH WILHELM. Born in Brandenburg in 1718 and died in Berlin in 1795, aged seventy-six. In Paris he became acquainted with the theories of Rameau, d'Alembert, etc., and on return he published books on keyboard performance and keyboard-instrument tuning, composition, fugue, etc., as also some keyboard works and songs.

MARQUÉ (Fr.). 'Marked', i.e. emphasized (cf. *Markiert*).

MARRIAGE OF FIGARO, THE (Mozart). Produced in Vienna in 1786. Libretto by Lorenzo da Ponte, after Beaumarchais's comedy. (The work continues the story partially told in Rossini's *Barber of Seville*, q.v.)

ACT I

SCENE: *A Room in the Palace of Count Almaviva. Time, seventeenth century*

Figaro (*Baritone*), the popular barber of Seville, has entered the service of the count and wants to marry **Susanna** (*Soprano*), the countess's maid. The count, however, is running after the maid. Figaro once promised to marry another—**Marcellina** (*Soprano*), the elderly housekeeper to **Dr. Bartolo** (*Bass*), and she appears to claim her due, backed by the doctor.

Cherubino (*Soprano*), a young page-boy whom the count has dismissed, comes to ask Susanna's intercession with his master. Hearing the **Count** (*Baritone*) coming, he hides. His master is making advances to Susanna when **Don Basilio** (*Tenor*) comes in, and, not seeing the count, talks freely of Cherubino's flirtations with the countess, and with **Barbarina** (*Soprano*), the gardener's daughter. Cherubino is discovered, and, as he knows of the count's carryings on, he is sent away to join the army.

ACT II

SCENE: *The Countess's Chamber*

The **Countess** (*Soprano*) is sad at her husband's intrigues. He will not allow Figaro to marry Susanna, because he wants to continue his flirtations with the maid. Figaro devises a plan: the count is to be made to believe, first that the countess is going to meet a lover, and second that Susanna is going to meet *him*. Instead of Susanna, Cherubino, in one of her dresses, will attend. Then the countess is to surprise her husband. The count interrupts the plot but does not discover it, for Cherubino, in his woman's dress, jumps from a window into the garden, unseen by anyone outside the plot, except the gardener, **Antonio** (*Bass*), who, after a little extra complication, is left unsuspicious.

Marcellina pursues her action against Figaro, and the count, glad of an excuse to keep the valet from marrying Susanna, says he will investigate the matter.

ACT III

SCENE: *A Hall decorated for Wedding Festivities*

It turns out that Figaro is the son of Marcellina and Bartolo, so the path of his marriage to Susanna is smoothed.

The count is to be taught a lesson. Susanna is to send him a note appointing a meeting, and the countess, exchanging clothes with her maid, is to confront her fickle husband.

ACT IV

SCENE: *The Garden*

The plot is effective, and is again complicated a little by Figaro's and Cherubino's ignorance of the deception. All is cleared up, and the count asks forgiveness.

See references under *Opera* 9; *Fandango*; *Improvisation* 2; *Harmony* 11.

MARROW-BONES AND CLEAVERS (p. 512, pl. 91. 7). The traditional music of the butchers of England and Scotland. It is still occasionally heard at London weddings of members of the fraternity—or was until very recently.

'Hark, how the banging marrow bones
Make clanging cleavers ring.'
(Bonnell Thornton, 1763.)

Cf. *Saltbox*, *Jew's Harp*, and *Hurdy-gurdy*; also *Bellows and Tongs*; *Tongs and Bones*; *Bladder and String*.

MARSCH (Ger.). 'March.'

MARSCHMÄSSIG (Ger.). See *Mässig*.

MARSCHNER, HEINRICH AUGUST. Born in Saxony in 1795 and died at Hanover in 1861, aged sixty-six. He was encouraged in composition by Beethoven and was a loyal colleague of Weber in the conductorship of the opera at Dresden, and to Weber's school of National German Romantic Opera he may be said to belong. *Hans Heiling* is the most famous of his operas. He is one of the many influences behind Wagner.

Cf. *Impromptu*.

MARSDEN, NEWTON. See *Newton Marsden*.

MARSEILLAISE. See *Rouget de Lisle*; *Carmagnole*.

MARSHALL, WARDENS, AND COMMONALTY. See *Minstrels*, etc. 3.

MARSHALL, WILLIAM. Born at Fochabers, Moray (= Elginshire), in 1748 and died at Craigellachie, in Banffshire, in 1833, aged eighty-four. He enjoyed great fame as an admirable violinist and as a composer of attractive strathspeys (of which he left over 100), reels, jigs, hornpipes, and the like. He was also for thirty years butler to the Duke of Gordon, was a good surveyor and architect, an astronomer and clockmaker and general mechanician, a farmer, factor of several estates, and a justice of the peace.

Collections of his music were published in 1781 and 1821, and certain pieces were also pirated by Niel Gow senior (q.v.). (Cf. *Scotland* 3.)

MARSICK.

(1) MARTIN PIERRE JOSEPH. Born near Liège, Belgium, in 1848 and died in Paris in 1924, aged seventy-six. He was a notable violin virtuoso (see *Belgium* 5), trained at the Conservatories of Liège and Paris and then (at the expense of the Belgian government) under Joachim. His compositions are for his own instrument and include three concertos.

(2) ARMAND. Born at Liège in 1877 and died in Brussels in 1959, aged eighty-three. He was a pupil of d'Indy and others, who became a conductor and teacher at Athens (1908), Bilbao (1927), and Liège (1927–39). He composed operas, symphonic poems, etc.

MARSON, GEORGE. Born about 1570 and died at Canterbury in 1632, aged about sixty-two. He was organist of Canterbury Cathedral, and a lively madrigal of his is in *The Triumphs of Oriana* (see *Madrigal* 4).

MARTEAU (Fr.). 'Hammer.' Cf. *Martelé, Martellando.*

MARTEAU, HENRI. Born at Rheims in 1874 and died in Lichtenberg in 1934, aged sixty. From his tenth year he was before the public as a virtuoso violinist, travelling widely in Europe and America. He was a member of the staffs of the Conservatories of Prague, Berlin (where he succeeded Joachim), and Geneva.

His compositions are mainly for strings and include a good deal of chamber music and a violin concerto.

MARTELÉ (Fr.). 'Hammered'—referring to the manner of playing bowed instruments by a series of short, sharp blows with the bow upon the strings. Use the point of the bow for this process unless the heel is indicated by the expression *Martelé au talon* (see also *Détaché*).

MARTELLANDO, MARTELLATO (It.). 'Hammering', 'hammered', often meaning heavy staccato bowing of a stringed instrument (same as *Martelé*, above), though the words are sometimes applied to pianoforte playing and even singing. It may be added that Liszt's imagination was strong enough to allow him to use this term in organ music.

MARTENOT, MAURICE (born 1898). See *Electric Musical Instruments* 1 f.

MARTIN.

(1) P. J. (partner of Mozart in a concert speculation). See *Concert* 13.

(2) GEORGE CLEMENT. Born at Lambourn, Berkshire, in 1844 and died in London in 1916, aged seventy-one.

In his forties he succeeded his master, Stainer, as organist of St. Paul's Cathedral, London. He wrote some dignified music for the Anglican Church, including a great Te Deum sung on the steps of the cathedral when Queen Victoria celebrated her Diamond Jubilee. She knighted him. He is buried in the crypt of the cathedral.

(3) FRANK (p. 880, pl. **147.** 8). Born at Geneva in 1890 and died at Naarden, Holland, in 1974, aged eighty-four. He was a Swiss composer whose works first became known through the festivals of the International Society for Contemporary Music. They include much orchestral and chamber music, a mass, incidental music to Greek plays, etc., personal in style and untrammelled by harmonic or other conventions. In some of his works he employed the Note-row (q.v.) technique. See *Concerto* 6 c (1890).

(4) JACQUES. See *Hoteterre.*

(5) CONSTANT. See *Electric* 4.

MARTINI.

(1) GIAMBATTISTA, or Giovanni Battista—called Padre Martini (p. 389, pl. **66.** 4). Born at Bologna in 1706 and died there in 1784, aged seventy-eight. He was a Franciscan friar who became a composer and the most learned musical scholar and most famous teacher of composition in the eighteenth century, so that his residence in Bologna made that city a place of pilgrimage for musicians of all countries so long as he lived.

See references under *Opera* 17 b; *Descant*; *Sonata* 1od (1741); *Harmonica* 1; *Misattributed Compositions*; *Libraries.*

(2) MARTINI IL TEDESCO (i.e. 'Martini the German'; real name, Johann Paul Aegidius Schwarzendorf; 1741–1816). He was a German who settled in Paris, wrote music for military band, symphonies, operas, church music, etc. In 1814, on the restoration of the Bourbons, he became director of the court music.

See *Percussion Family* 4.

MARTINON, JEAN (1910–76). A pupil of Roussel and Charles Munch, he conducted the Paris Conservatoire Orchestra (1944), the Bordeaux Orchestra (1946), and the Chicago Orchestra (1963–7). His own compositions include orchestral pieces, an opera, and chamber music.

MARTINŮ, BOHUSLAV (p. 109, pl. **20.** 6). Born in 1890 in a belfry in Polička, Czechoslovakia, and died near Basle in 1959, aged sixty-eight. A pupil of Suk and Roussel, he composed music in virtually all forms. He had a long struggle to make his way, and his vast output is of startlingly uneven quality. He lived in Paris (1923), the U.S.A. (1940), and Prague (1945).

See *Concerto* 6 c (1890); *Opera* 24 b (1938).

MARTIN Y SOLER. See *Spain* 6.

MARTUCCI, GIUSEPPE. Born at Capua in 1856 and died at Naples in 1909, aged fifty-three. He was a pianist and a capable and enterprising orchestral conductor (the first in Italy to conduct Wagner's *Tristan*), and director in turn of the Conservatories of Bologna and Naples.

As composer he belonged to the 'New Music' school of Liszt and Wagner. His works include symphonies, piano concertos, chamber music, six volumes of piano music, and other things.

(Paolo Martucci, born in 1883, who has practised as pianist and teacher in London, Cincinnati, and New York, is his son.)

See reference under *Italy* 7.

MARTY, EUGÈNE GEORGES. Born in Paris in 1860 and died there in 1908, aged forty-eight. He was a student under Massenet at the Paris Conservatory and won the Rome Prize in 1882. His professional activities were largely those of a choral trainer and orchestral and operatic conductor, and he held a number of important positions in these branches. His compositions reflect the influence of his teacher; they include operas and orchestral works.

MARX.

(1) **ADOLPH BERNARD.** He was born at Halle in 1795 and died in Berlin in 1866, aged seventy-one. He was a lawyer who turned musicologist, started a musical journal, became Professor of Music at the University of Berlin, founded (with Kullak and Stern) the Berlin institution now known as the Stern Conservatory, published a long series of learned writings, chiefly on musical aesthetics (his 4-volume treatise on practical composition was long in use amongst students), and produced a certain amount of music (oratorio, opera, etc.) of no high importance.

He helped to elucidate Beethoven to the public and was appreciated by him, and he encouraged the young Mendelssohn.

(2) **JOSEPH.** Born at Graz, Austria, in 1882 and died in 1964, aged eighty-two. He took his Ph.D. at the University of Graz with a thesis on the alarming subject of 'The Functions of Intervals in Harmony and Melody for the Comprehension of Time-Complexes', and then took up pedagogic duties, becoming successively professor of theory at the Academy of Music in Vienna, Director (1922) of that institution, and (1925) Rector of the Hochschule. He acquired a high reputation as composer, especially of songs and chamber music of a romantic cast.

MARY I OF ENGLAND (b. 1516; came to throne 1553; d. 1558). See brief references under *Chapel Royal*; *Anglican Parish Church Music* 1; *Cathedral Music* 3; *Ballad* 1.

MARYLAND, MY MARYLAND. The words are by James Ryder Randall of Baltimore and, dating from 1861, express the sentiments of the Southern cause. The tune is the German *Der Tannenbaum* (cf. *Red Flag*).

MARYLEBONE GARDENS. See *Concert* 12.

MARYON, EDWARD (1867–1954). See *Colour and Music* 5.

MARY, QUEEN OF SCOTS (1542–87). See reference under *Scotland* 1, 6.

MARZIALE (It.). 'Martial.'

MASCAGNI, PIETRO (p. 524, pl. **95.** 8). Born at Leghorn in 1863 and died in Rome in 1945, aged eighty-one. He was the son of a baker, and was a 'prentice lawyer who took music lessons by stealth. Then, his musical bent admitted, he studied at the Milan Conservatory, but not for long, since the academic teaching irked him. He joined a travelling operatic company as conductor, and after some years married and settled down as the piano teacher of a small town. At twenty-six he leapt into the limelight with his prize-winning one-act opera *Cavalleria Rusticana* (q.v.), produced at the Costanzi Theatre in Rome. Of his many later operas not one has had a similar international success, though *L'Amico Fritz* (1891), *Zanetto* (1896), and *Iris* (1898) won some esteem and *Nero* (1935) was enthusiastically received. He is to the British public, at any rate, like Leoncavallo (whose *I Pagliacci* appeared only a year or two later and has since kept *Cavalleria* company on many an evening's programme), a one-opera composer.

See references under *Community Singing* (end); *Intermezzo* 3; *Samisen*.

MASCARADE (Fr.). In earlier use this means masque (q.v.) and in later use masquerade, i.e. masked ball.

MASCHINENPAUKEN (Ger.). Mechanically tuned kettledrums. See *Percussion Family* 2, 5 a.

MASKE. Old spelling of *Masque*, but sometimes found attached to (say) a virginals piece, and then generally implying, probably, a dance of a character fitting it for use in a masque.

MASKELYNE FAMILY (illusionists). See reference under *Mechanical Reproduction* 9.

MASKENSPIEL. See *Masque*.

MASON, WILLIAM (1724–97). Poet, and Precentor of York Minster. See *Mechanical Reproduction of Music* 10; *Oratorio* 5; *Copyists*; *Pianoforte* 15.

MASON family of Massachusetts.

(1) **LOWELL** (p. 1040, pl. **169.** 2). Born at Medfield, Mass., in 1792 and died at Orange, New Jersey, in 1872, aged eighty. He was a great musical educational pioneer, especially in the schools of Boston, and a foremost promoter of choral singing. He wrote much simple church music.

See references under *Hymns and Hymn Tunes* 11; *Education in Music* 3; *God save the Queen* 14; *Competitions in Music* 1; *Interlude*; *Cathedral Music* 8; *United States* 4.

(2) **WILLIAM** (p. 1040, pl. **169.** 6). Born at Boston in 1829 and died in New York in 1908, aged seventy-nine. He was a famous pianist, a pupil of Liszt, and a highly popular teacher.

See reference under *Yankee Doodle*.

(3) **DANIEL GREGORY** (p. 1056, pl. **171.** 8), a grandson of Lowell Mason (born at Brookline, Mass., in 1873 and died at Greenwich, Conn., in 1953, aged eighty) was a refined composer of orchestral and chamber music, etc., a thoughtful author, and a discerning critic. He was long Professor of Music at Columbia University, New York.

See references under *Clarinet Family* 6; *Elgar*; *Harp* 4; *Appreciation*.

MASON AND HAMLIN. See *Reed-Organ* 7.

MASQUE or MASK (Fr., *Masque*; Ger., *Maskenspiel*. The masque was a ceremonial social entertainment of the aristocracy. It consisted of a combination of poetry, vocal and instrumental music, dancing, acting, costume, pageantry, and scenic decoration, applied in the most lavish and expensive way to the representation of mythological or allegorical subjects.

Its origin was probably in processions on horseback of men with torches, in masks and fantastic costumes (sometimes to represent mythological personages), accompanied by musicians; such processions would visit the hall of some noble acquaintance, where they would dance and act in dumb show and then invite the host and principal guests to join the dance. This mingling of the two parties was an important element in the masque. We see something very like this in Shakespeare's *Henry VIII* (Act I, Sc. iv), in the visit to Wolsey's palace of the 'noble troops of strangers ... habited like shepherds, with torch bearers', one of whom turns out, when the moment of unmasking comes, to be the King himself.

From this beginning developed a more elaborate performance, with prepared scenery and a more or less definite plot, and of this we see an example in the masque which Shakespeare has introduced into *The Tempest* (Act IV, Sc. i)—a masque which Prospero conjures up as a vision before the bridal pair and the theatre audience, wherein Juno and Ceres sing a marriage blessing and nymphs and reapers join in 'a peaceful dance'. Cervantes has a vivid description of a masque in his account of the wedding of Camacho in *Don Quixote*.

The masque was developed simultaneously out of indigenous materials in several countries, but Italy cultivated it especially and England, learning from Italy, carried it to its highest pitch of artistic elaboration. It was a diversion of noble amateurs, but a professional element later entered with the speaking parts and the introduction of contrast in the form of grotesque **Antimasques** consisting of dances by professionals. (For a satirical touch see an allusion under *Monopolies*.)

Some of the greatest authors of masques in England in Elizabethan times were Ben Jonson, Fletcher, Chapman, Beaumont, Dekker, and Ford. Jonson's work was partly done with the collaboration of the celebrated Inigo Jones as designer of the decorations and the machinery (p. 592, pl. **104**. 3). James I's queen, with the ladies, danced in his *Masque of Blackness* at Whitehall in 1605; he counts as the supreme master of the English masque.

The English masque composers of this period were sometimes half-amateurs, though able at their art—men such as the physician-poet–musician Campian or Campion (q.v.), who more than once wrote both words and music (p. 592, pl. **104**. 2). Coperario (q.v.), Nicholas Lanier (q.v.), and Alfonso Ferrabosco, junior (q.v.) were notable masque composers. From a literary point of view the most famous masque ever written is Milton's *Comus* (written for performance at Ludlow Castle, 1634); it comes near the end of the true masque period and is not on the traditional lines; its music was written by Henry Lawes (q.v.). Shirley's *Cupid and Death* (1653) is a still later and very notable masque; the music was by Matthew Locke (q.v.) and Christopher Gibbons (q.v.); in general dramatic scheme (naturalistic rather than mystically allegorical) and in music (use of recitative, for instance) such a work as this is as near opera as masque. Indeed, it was out of the English masque that the English opera grew, and the border-line is a very fine one. It will be noted from the last date mentioned that masques continued during the Puritan régime; the one referred to was performed by order of Cromwell in honour of the Portuguese ambassador.

Later masques still (for the form did not cease to exist) are Blow's *Venus and Adonis*, written in the 1680s for the entertainment of the court (this again is practically an opera) and Arne's *Alfred* (1750), written for performance in the garden of the Prince of Wales and ending with the soon-to-be-famous song of 'Rule, Britannia!' (q.v.).

The French Ballet de Cour (see *Ballet* 2) was practically the masque, and the eighteenth-century English pantomime (see *Pantomime*) was really a masque with harlequinades. The masque element is strong in the stage works of Purcell. Obviously much modern ballet (q.v.) has something of the masque about it, the main difference being the absence of literary and lyrical elements.

The orchestral resources used in the English masque of the late sixteenth and early seventeenth centuries were often considerable, groups of players of different types of instruments being dispersed through the scenes in association with different groups of mythological or other personages: perhaps this led to a perception of varieties of available tone-colourings and so helped forward the study of orchestral treatment.

A valuable contemporary description and criticism of the masque in its high period is Bacon's essay (1625) *Of Masques and Triumphs*.

MASQUERADE. Masked ball.

MASS

1. The Three Types of Mass Service. Owing to the importance it holds in the minds of worshippers and the opportunities it offers for musical participation, the Roman Catholic service of the Mass, or celebration of the Eucharist, has exercised an enormous influence upon the development of music. The service may take any one of three forms:

(a) **High Mass** ('Missa Solennis' or 'Missa Solemnis'), performed by a priest with the assistance of deacon, subdeacon, and other ministers, together with a choir, the music consisting of five passages of plainsong (the 'Proper of the Mass', for which see 2 below) and five other extended passages from the congregation's part (the 'Ordinary of the Mass', or 'Common of the Mass'), which latter are often set in a more or less elaborate choral way.

The above is theoretically the normal form of Mass, but there are also (b) **Sung Mass** ('Missa Cantata'), practically the same as the above but without deacon and subdeacon; and (c) **Low Mass** ('Missa Privata' or 'Missa Lecta'; i.e. Private Mass, or Read Mass), performed by a priest and one clerk (but hymns are in some places sung during its progress by the congregation); see 5 ('Folk Mass').

2. Musical Settings of High Mass. The **Proper of the Mass** (i.e. the parts which vary from season to season and even from day to day —*Introit, Gradual, Offertory,* and *Communion*) has naturally usually been left to its traditional plainsong treatment. The Ordinary of the Mass is invariable whatever the seasons of the Church's year.

The five passages which are frequently set for chorus (or for chorus and soloists) and which, as a collection, constitute what a musician means by a 'Mass by' such-and-such a composer, are as follows:

(a) *Kyrie*	Lord, have mercy ...
(b) *Gloria in excelsis Deo*	Glory be to God on high ...
(c) *Credo*	I believe ...
(d) *Sanctus* (with *Benedictus* properly as part of it, but in practice often separated)	Holy, holy ...
(e) *Agnus Dei*	Lamb of God ...

The above, as already stated, are really the congregational parts of the Ordinary of the Mass, but so soon as harmony began (see article *Harmony*) attempts were made to devise part-settings of those passages to take the place of the unison plainsong settings. The highest point was reached at the end of the sixteenth century, when the period of unaccompanied choral contrapuntal music reached its apogee: no music has ever been written more movingly beautiful than the Masses of the Italian Palestrina, the Englishman Byrd, the Spaniard Victoria, and others of their period.

The introduction of instrumental accompaniment in the seventeenth century, and the high development of solo singing (including that of women singers) in Italy and elsewhere, were not favourable to the maintenance of a solemn and dignified style in the Mass, and the Masses of the later eighteenth-century and early nineteenth-century Roman Catholic composers, such as Haydn, Mozart, Weber, and Schubert, however musically effective, have not the devotional quality of those of a century and a half to two centuries earlier. Yet those just mentioned 'drew the line', as some of their contemporaries did not. Mozart, hearing Doles (1715–97), one of Bach's successors at the Thomas School at Leipzig, praise a very lighthearted Mass by a certain comic opera composer, took away the parts and brought them back with humorous words of his own written in, distributed them to a party of singers, and was answered by approving laughter when he cried, 'Now, doesn't that go better?'

From the eighteenth century onwards the Mass became accepted as one of the great opportunities of composers who felt themselves able to rise to the heights of sublimity to which the words called them. Indeed, the five texts above mentioned became a sort of oratorio libretto to be set over and over again, often with the intention that the settings should be used on great ecclesiastical occasions but also with a view to concert performance.

3. The Movements of the Bigger Settings. Lutheranism took over the choral parts of the Mass, as shown above (still in Latin), and Bach and other Protestant composers set them, often very elaborately, the texts tending to become subdivided, so as to yield material for a variety of movements. Haydn, Mozart, and others of the Viennese school adopted this unliturgical practice in Masses intended for liturgical use, the practice being at last definitely forbidden by Pius X in 1903 (see *Motu Proprio*), to the great regret of many good Roman Catholic musicians who did not realize that they had come to regard as normal on the greater occasions in the larger Roman Catholic churches what was a distinctively Protestant treatment. Any or all of the following divisions (and sometimes others also) are, then, found in the larger settings, from Bach downwards:

(a)	*Kyrie eleison*	Lord, have mercy
	Christe eleison	Christ, have mercy
	Kyrie eleison	Lord, have mercy
(b)	*Gloria in excelsis Deo*	Glory be to God on high
	Laudamus te	We praise Thee
	Gratias agimus tibi	We give Thee thanks
	Domine Deus	Lord God
	Qui tollis peccata mundi	Who takest away the sins of the world
	Qui sedes ad dexteram Patris	Who sittest at the right hand of the Father
	Quoniam tu solus sanctus	For Thou only art holy
	Cum sancto Spiritu	With the Holy Spirit
(c)	*Credo in unum Deum*	I believe in one God
	Patrem omnipotentem	Father almighty
	Et in unum Dominum	And in one Lord
	Et incarnatus est	And was incarnate
	Crucifixus	Crucified
	Et resurrexit	And rose again
	Et in Spiritum sanctum	And [I believe] in the Holy Spirit
	Confiteor unum baptisma	I confess one baptism

(d) *Sanctus* — Holy
Hosanna in excelsis — Hosanna in the highest
Benedictus qui venit — Blessed is he that cometh

(e) *Agnus Dei* — Lamb of God
Dona nobis pacem — Give us peace

The above are the divisions adopted by Bach in his great Mass in B minor. The movements shown are variously for chorus, vocal solo, and vocal duet. The whole vocal and instrumental resources of the period are employed, and the result is one of music's most impressive masterpieces, such as it took the world a little time to appreciate (first German performance of the work as a whole in Berlin in 1835; first British performance in London in 1876; first American performance at Bethlehem, Pa., in 1900). But such a large-scale Mass as this of Bach, or the *Missa Solennis* in D of Beethoven, is not properly a ritual Mass and is almost always performed (whether in concert room or church), without the intervening liturgy. It may be said, indeed, that the Bach Mass in B minor inaugurated a new form—the Concert-Mass or Oratorio-Mass.

4. The Different Periods of Mass Composition. The musical history of the Mass (already roughly outlined) may be more precisely set forth as follows:

I. **The Plainsong Period,** up to, say, A.D. 900.

II. **The Period of the Growth of Unaccompanied Choral Music,** from 900 to, say, 1500, including at its close composers of genius like the Flemings Dufay, Ockeghem, and Josquin des Prés. It had now become usual to give unity to the music by basing all the movements upon the same musical theme.

III. **The Period of the Climax of Unaccompanied Choral Music,** from, say, 1500 to 1625, with, at its close, such great men as Palestrina (93 Masses), Victoria (18 Masses), and Byrd (3 Masses).

Then comes a fall in artistic values due to the introduction of a new and experimental style of harmony (see *Harmony* 9), with the use of instruments and the development of solo singing (see *Singing* 4), and consequent tendency to display. At last dignity returns with—

IV. **Bach's B Minor Mass,** which may be said to stand alone, on a solitary and lofty peak.

V. **The Viennese Period,** of tuneful gracious music of no high dignity, represented by the fourteen Masses of Haydn and the fifteen of Mozart, the seven of Schubert, and so forth. High above all these towers the great Mass in D of Beethoven, one of the greatest masterpieces of the world. Thence onward it is hardly possible to speak of 'periods'. A proportion of the composers of every country in western Europe continued to set the words of the Mass—Weber 2; Cherubini 11; Schumann 1; Liszt 4, including the Graner Mass; Franck 2; Bruckner 4; Gounod many, and so on.

Certain composers of more modern times have introduced novel forms and styles. Widor has used a four-part mixed choir and a unison choir, with two organs; Vaughan Williams (q.v.) has returned to the past in writing for voices without accompaniment and in adopting some of the practices of choral composers of the early days of harmonic writing.

5. Names of Masses. In the early days of harmonic music and up to the end of the sixteenth century many Masses will be found with names such as *Ave Maria*, or even secular names such as *L'homme armé* ('The Armed Man'; see entry, *Homme armé*), *Les nez rouges* ('Red Noses'), *La Basse Danse* (q.v.), or *Westron Wynde* ('Western Wind'). These names remind us that the earliest harmonized music was based upon a plainsong or other existing musical theme, either set out note for note in one of the parts or, in later times, used as a theme to be developed in various ways in the different parts; the title, then, is that of the tune used for the purpose. All these works date from the time when it was customary to base the whole of the five movements of the Mass upon various treatments of one short musical theme, so giving it a desirable unity. (The Mass of Palestrina known as *Assumpta est Maria* is a later instance.)

As the practice of using a secular musical theme as a part of the texture of a piece of devotional music has often been a good deal misinterpreted in textbooks of musical history, it may be explained that composition in the period was usually nothing but the art of adding choral lines to an existing line or 'canto fermo' (see *Harmony* 4, 5, 6; *Modes* 9). As a variant on the practice of using a piece of plainsong as the canto fermo, a secular tune might be taken, but this tune was (as Ambros has put it) comparable merely with the light iron framework on which a sculptor models his clay, i.e. it was lost under the vocal lines that overlaid it. Moreover, it was often so elaborated in rhythm and floriated in line as to be barely identifiable with its original self by any ordinary ear. Further, it was usually a tune that was already out of date and forgotten, e.g. the *Homme armé* canto fermo was used by about thirty known composers, from Dufay in the fifteenth century to Carissimi in the seventeenth, but was antiquated when the first of these composers used it; its words were no longer current and beyond a few lines have proved to be irrecoverable.

The *Westron Wynde* was used by Shepherd, Willan, Taverner, and Tye, and appears to offer the only case now discoverable of English composers writing Masses on a secular theme.

The expression **Missa sine Nomine** ('Mass without name'), sometimes met with, refers to a Mass composed upon an original musical theme, in contradistinction to such Masses as those just mentioned: Palestrina and others have Masses so described.

Missa ad Fugam, or **Ad Canones,** meant a Mass in a fugal or canonic style (see *Canon*).

Missa Quarti Toni ('Fourth Mode Mass'

—see *Modes*), **Messe du Premier Ton** ('First Mode Mass'), and similar titles were other attempts to frame a somewhat distinctive description. **Missa supra Voces Musicales** ('Mass on the musical notes') means a Mass in which the theme is merely a fragment of a scale, the six notes of the hexachord (q.v.).

Missa Brevis usually simply means a short Mass, i.e. not one so musically elaborate as to take a long time to perform, and hence suitable for ordinary occasions as distinct from high ceremonial occasions on which a Missa Solennis would be performed. Sometimes, however, 'Missa Brevis' is used for a mere setting of the Kyrie and Gloria, as customary in the Lutheran service: Bach's B Minor Mass began as this form, but he later extended it; he left, however, four Masses of this kind. Still a third meaning is a Mass in which the breve was the time unit, as Palestrina's *Missa Brevis*.

A **Votive Mass** is one offered with a particular 'intention', or one offered in honour of a saint on some day other than the feast of that saint. A **Nuptial Mass** is, of course, offered as a part of the ceremony of marriage. The **Mass of the Presanctified** is that of Good Friday, in which the priest does not consecrate afresh but uses the Host reserved from the Mass of the previous day. The liturgical and musical changes in these Masses are not such as call for particularization here.

The **Missa de Angelis** is a particular plainsong Mass, very popular both in Roman Catholic and some Anglican churches; it seems to be largely of fourteenth- and fifteenth-century provenance, considerably modified in the seventeenth century and possibly the eighteenth; it does not, then, altogether represent the true spirit of plainsong.

A **Folk Mass** is properly Low Mass (that is, Mass said, not sung) which proceeds whilst the congregation sing hymns in the vernacular: the term has also been applied to a type of setting so simple that congregations can sing their part. In the 1960s, as part of the tendency towards the use of the vernacular and the greater participation of the congregation, 'Jazz Masses' and Masses using popular musical features were heard.

For the Missa pro Defunctis ('Mass for the dead') see the article *Requiem*. For the following portions of the Mass, not included in usual settings as discussed above, see under their respective names: *Introit*; *Gradual*; *Alleluia*; *Prose*; *Sequence*; *Offertory*; *Communion*; *Grail*. For the pronouncement of Pope Pius X on the music of the Mass (1903) see *Motu Proprio*.

MASSÉ, VICTOR (real name Félix Marie Massé). Born at Lorient in 1822 and died in Paris in 1884, aged sixty-two. He was a student of the Paris Conservatory who won the Rome Prize in 1844, and, back from his travels, made a great name as a composer of songs and of operas, usually of the lighter type.

See *Carnival of Venice*.

MASSENET, JULES ÉMILE FRÉDÉRIC (p. 384, pl. **63.** 2). Born at St. Étienne, in the Department of the Loire, in 1842 and died in Paris in 1912, aged seventy. He studied at the Paris Conservatory, helping his parents towards the expense by playing drum and triangle in a theatre orchestra. At twenty-one he won the Rome Prize.

On return to Paris he gradually made headway as an opera composer, producing *The King of Lahore* in 1877, *Herodias* (in England called 'Salome') in 1881, *Manon* in 1884, *Werther* in 1892, *Thaïs* in 1894, and *Sappho* (a 'lyric play)' in 1897. These are but a few items from the long list of his stage works.

During the eighteen years 1878–96 he was a professor of composition at the Conservatory and a great number of the younger composers passed through his hands.

His work is facile and melodious and some of it maintains a high popularity. Certain orchestral compositions are still heard, including some of a series of suites called 'Scenes'—*Hungarian Scenes* (1871), *Picturesque Scenes* (1874), *Neapolitan Scenes* (1876), *Fairyland Scenes* (1879), *Alsatian Scenes* (1881). There are also some overtures, a piano concerto, some cantatas and oratorios, a good deal of incidental music to plays, and a couple of hundred songs.

See references: *Bruneau*; *Charpentier, G.*; *Chausson*; *Grand Opera*; *Opera* 11 d; *Oratorio* 4, 7 (1873–5); *Opus*; *Concerto* 6 b (1842).

MÄSSIG (Ger.). (*a*) 'Moderate', 'moderately'; (*b*) 'in the style of' (e.g. *Marschmässig*, 'in march style'). *Mässiger*, 'more moderate'; *Mässigen*, 'to moderate'.

MASSIMO, MASSIMA (It.; masc., fem.). 'The greatest.'

MASSINE. See *Ballet* 5, 9.

MASSINGER, PHILIP (1583–1640). Dramatist. See references under *Incidental Music*; *Tonic Sol-fa* (end of article); *Inns and Taverns*.

MASTER OF THE QUEEN'S (King's) MUSICK. See *Chapel Royal*.

MASTERSINGERS. See *Minstrels* 8; *Colour and Music* 2; also following entry.

MASTERSINGERS OF NUREMBERG, THE (In German, *Die Meistersinger von Nürnberg*. Wagner). Produced at Munich in 1868 under von Bülow. Libretto by the composer.

ACT I

SCENE: *The Interior of St. Katharine's Church at Nuremberg. Time, the Sixteenth Century*

(For an allusion to the overture see *Overture* 4.)

Walther von Stolzing (*Tenor*), a young knight of Franconia, has fallen in love at sight with **Eva** (*Soprano*), daughter of Pogner the goldsmith. **Magdalena** (*Mezzo-Soprano*), Eva's maid, is in the way when, after church service, Walther tries to get a word with the girl. **David** (*Tenor*), apprenticed to **Sachs** (*Baritone*), the shoemaker, and in love with Magdalena, is preparing for a meeting of the Mastersingers, the solemn company of burgher-minstrels.

Magdalena tells Walther that Eva's hand is to be the prize at the contest of song on St. John's Day. Now the Mastersingers assemble for a preliminary trial; **Pogner** (*Bass*) announces his prize, and Walther begs to be allowed to sing a trial song there and then. He does so, and the ill-conditioned **Beckmesser** (*Bass*), the 'marker', who is aiming for the same charming prize as Walther, sees to it that his song is pronounced badly made, according to the Masters' strict rules. But Sachs knows how promising it was.

ACT II

SCENE: *A Street in which are Pogner's House and Sachs's Shop*

Pogner brings Eva home. She does not yet known the result of the trial. She finds it out from Sachs, cobbling in the open air outside his shop in the cool of the evening, who in turn finds out that she loves Walther. He has always been fond of her and has wondered if her affectionate friendship for him might ripen some day. But he unselfishly determines to further her love-affair with Walther.

Walther comes to beg Eva to elope with him. She is prepared for that, but Sachs, who has gone into his shop and dimmed his lamp, suddenly causes it to shine on the road they must go by: for he knows that way of escape will bring them no happiness, and is bent on helping them to a better betrothal.

Beckmesser arrives to serenade Eva, and Sachs, who has come outside again, insists on banging in nails, 'marking' the errors in his song. The noise arouses the neighbours. David drubs Beckmesser, thinking that he has come to serenade Magdalena. Amid the hubbub Sachs takes Walther into his house. The folk go to bed again, and a watchman is left in the quiet street, calling out the hour.

ACT III

SCENE 1: *In Sachs's Workshop. St. John's Day*

David confesses to Sachs, who is meditating, his love for Magdalena. Walther sings the cobbler a song he dreamt last night, and Sachs copies it down. They go out, and Beckmesser, entering, steals the song, which he thinks is the cobbler's composition. Sachs gives him leave to sing it at the trial.

Eva, with a pretext about her shoes, comes in and inspires Walther to complete his song there and then. They all go off to the feast.

SCENE 2: *An Open Meadow by the River, near the City*

The various tradesmen's guilds sing their songs. At the trial, Beckmesser nervously flounders in the stolen song, and when he says it is Sachs's, the cobbler answers 'No', and calls upon Walther to sing the piece rightly. This

he does, and becomes at once a Mastersinger and Eva's betrothed. With some wise advice from Sachs, whom all hail as their city's truest poet, the curtain falls.

See *Hanslick* for an allusion to Beckmesser; and see also *Opera* 21 k; *Ballet* 7.

MATASSINS. Same as the dance *Bouffons* (q.v.).

MATELOTTE (Fr., from *matelot*, 'sailor'). A sailors' hornpipe (see *Hornpipe*).

MATHER.

(1) RICHARD (1596–1669). See *Hymns and Hymn Tunes* 11.

(2) COTTON (1663–1728). See *Hymns and Hymn Tunes* 11.

MATHIS DER MALER. See *Hindemith*.

MATIEGKA. See *Guitar*.

MATINS. The first of the Canonical Hours or services of the day in the Roman Catholic Church, and Morning Prayer in the Anglican Church (see *Common Prayer*). In the Roman Catholic Church Matins was originally recited or sung in the early morning; it is now sometimes forestalled on the previous evening or afternoon. It consists of one or more 'Nocturnes' or 'night watches', generally of three of them, each with Psalms, Paternoster, scripture, and responses (cf. *Lauds*; *Prime*; *Terce*; *Sext*; *None*; *Vespers*; *Compline*).

'MATIN' SYMPHONY (Haydn). See *Nicknamed Compositions* 11.

MATTACHINS. Same as the dance *Bouffons* (q.v.).

MATTEI.

(1) FILIPPO ('Pipo'). Early eighteenth-century violoncellist and composer in London. See *Pasticcio*.

(2) TITO (1841–1914). He was an Italian pianist who in early life settled in London and became a popular composer of songs, piano pieces, etc.

MATTEIS.

(1) NICOLA. He was an Italian violinist who came to England about 1672 and astonished all connoisseurs of violin playing by his amazing technique (mentioned in Evelyn's *Diary* and North's *Memoires of Musick*). He published some fine violin compositions in London, as also songs and a theoretical treatise for guitar players. His influence upon the development of violin technique was probably important.

(2) NICHOLAS. Died at Shrewsbury about 1749. He was a son of the above who went to Vienna for a time but returned and lived at Shrewsbury, where he was one of Burney's teachers.

MATTHAY, TOBIAS (p. 289, pl. **51.** 6). Born in London in 1858; died at Haslemere in 1945. He was a student and then a professor of piano at the Royal Academy of Music. He developed, by close observation of the workings of both physical and psychological laws, a system of piano teaching which found its expression in a school organization of his own and in a series of books. Very many of the leading British pianists were his pupils.

See references under *Pianoforte Playing and Teaching* 7; *Rubato* 1; *Memory* 4; *Swinstead*; *Kennedy-Fraser*.

MATTHESON, JOHANN (1681–1764). See *Sonata* 10 d (1704, etc.); *Criticism* 2; *Journals*; *Voice* 5; *Temperament* 5; *Recorder* 2; *Singspiel*; *Froberger*; *Dictionaries* 3.

MATTINATA (It.). A morning song, or a piece with that suggestion, i.e. the same as *Aubade* (Fr.), *Alborada* (Sp.), and *Morgenlied* (Ger.).

MATTINS. See *Matins*.

MAULTROMMEL (Ger.). Jew's harp (q.v.).

MAUNDER, JOHN HENRY. Born in London in 1858 and died in 1920. His musical career was chiefly that of organist and choirmaster of various churches on the outskirts of London, though an extension of his interests is shown in his employment as choir-trainer to the Lyceum Theatre. Of his compositions the apparently inextinguishable cantatas, *Penitence, Pardon, and Peace* and *From Olivet to Calvary* long enjoyed popularity and still aid the devotions of undemanding congregations in less sophisticated areas.

MAURESCO (Sp.), **MAURESQUE** (Fr.). 'Moorish.' See also *Moresca*.

MAURI. See *Ballet* 9.

MAW, NICHOLAS. Born at Grantham, Lincs., in 1935. He studied at the Royal Academy of Music and under Nadia Boulanger. His compositions include songs and choral works, chamber music, and operas.

MAXIMA. See *Notation* 4.

MAXIXE. A rather strenuous Brazilian dance in two-in-a-measure time, which had some European popularity in the early years of the nineteenth century and then reappeared about 1911–13 in a somewhat different form as the tango (q.v.): both these dances had more popularity as exhibition dances than as ball-room dances.

MAXWELL, JAMES CLERK (1831–79). See *Broadcasting* 2.

MAYER, CHARLES. See *Misattributed* (Chopin).

MAYEROWITSCH. See *Jewish Music* 8.

MAY FAIR. See *Fairs and their Music*.

MAYNARD.

(1) JOHN. He was a lutenist of the early seventeenth century who composed twelve songs (poor ones) called *The XII Wonders of the World*, in which he musically depicts the characters of twelve men and women of different professions and states.

(2) JOHN. Bass singer. See *Scandinavia* 2.

(3) WALTER. See *Beale, Thomas Willert*.

MAYR, SIMON—properly Johann Simon Mayr. Born in Bavaria in 1763 and died at Bergamo in 1845, aged eighty-two. He was a composer, chiefly of operas, of which he pro-

duced a great number and with which he had great success until those of Rossini somewhat pushed his into the shade. He was also a church musician and a teacher (director of the music at the chief church in Bergamo and of the conservatory there). His most eminent pupil was Donizetti (q.v.).

MAYRHOFER (eighteenth-century instrument-maker). See *Clarinet Family* 4 f (note).

MAYSEDER, JOSEF. Born in Vienna in 1789 and died there in 1863, aged seventy-four. He was a great violinist and violin teacher, and a composer, especially for his instrument.

MAZARIN, CARDINAL (1602–61). See *Opera* 11 a; *Rossi, Luigi*.

MAZAS, JACQUES FÉRÉOL (1782–1849). He was a notable Paris violinist, travelling far afield as a virtuoso, and he also wrote operas and (especially) violin music of all types.

MAZÉR, JOHAN. See *Scandinavia* 4.

MAZERSKA. See *Scandinavia* 4.

MAZURKA. One of the traditional national dances of Poland—originally sung as well as danced. It spread to Germany in the mid-eighteenth century, then to Paris, and in the early part of the nineteenth to Britain and so to America. The London *Observer* of 25 April 1830 gives a description of it as just 'introduced or intended to be introduced into this country'.

It is in three-in-a-measure time, with a certain accentuation of the second beat and an ending of the phrases on that beat (with a tap of the heel): dotted notes are a feature. It is a round dance and is properly performed by either four couples or double that number. There is some latitude for improvisation in the step. The speed is not great and a certain pride of bearing, and sometimes a wildness, sharply differentiate its mood from that of the more sensuous waltz. C. Egerton Lowe contributed the following, based on his observations of Tyrolese and Polish dances in the early 1880s: 'The Mazurka being an improvised dance the male dancer has to be on the look out for *unexpected* accents on any beat. He then clinks his spurs together, stamps on the floor, claps his hand, gives a suitable facial expression, etc. (I have seen some of the dancers with rows of medals all round their bodies—won in competitions).'

This dance has entered into instrumental composition a good deal, especially with Chopin, who wrote over fifty mazurkas for piano. He refines the style greatly, sometimes varies from the usual tempo and rhythm, and combines some of the characteristics of a related dance, the kuiaviak. Musically it would seem as if the two dances are almost local forms of the same thing—the mazurka that of the province of Mazovia and the kuiaviak that of the province of Kujavein. Glinka, Tchaikovsky, and other Russian composers have written mazurkas. The Pole Szymanowski wrote many for piano.

1. FRENCH 'TABATIÈRE A MUSIQUE' of mid-19th century. See *Mechanical Reproduction* 7

2. HAYDN FLUTE-CLOCK OF 1792
See *Mechanical Reproduction* 5

3. DROZ'S MECHANICAL HARPSICHORDIST OF 1774. See *Mechanical Reproduction* 9

4. BARREL ORGAN, by Bryceson, in Rowde Methodist Church, Wiltshire, *c*. 1800. See *Mechanical Reproduction* 10

5. METHOD OF PRICKING BARRELS FOR CHIMES OR ORGANS (from Tans'ur's *Elements of Musick*, 1766)

6. MECHANISM OF A BARREL ORGAN of about 1800 (illustrating Burney's article 'Organ' in Rees's *Cyclopædia*)

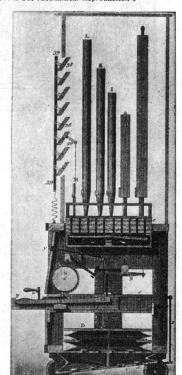

A PSALM-TUNE *for* SIX BELLS.

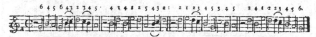

The same Tune, prick'd on a Moduli-Campanarum, or Chime-Barrel

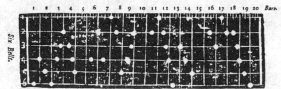

Note, That the *White Lines* at each End shew where the Paper meets, when wrapped round the *Barra*; where you may allow what Time you please before the Tune begins again.

6

PLATE 107

THE MONOCHORD

See the Article on pages 655–6

1. GUIDO D'AREZZO explaining his use of the Monochord to Bishop Theobald. He has a quill in one hand, to pluck the strings, and a blunt knife in the other, to stop them at the proper places, these places being marked on the side of the monochord—but wrongly, the artist evidently not being a musician

2. MOVABLE BRIDGES for determining the various intervals

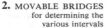

MIRACLE PLAYS

See the Article *Mysteries, Miracle Plays, and Moralities* on pages 669–70

3, 4. MIRACLE PLAYS—in church and in the open, No. 3 being an illustration in *Till Eulenspiegel*, 1532

THE MADRIGAL

See the Article on pages 590–3

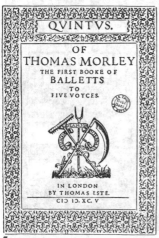

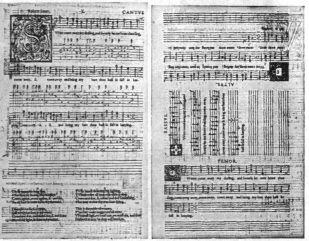

5. Title-page of a part-book of Morley's Balletts (1595), each voice having a separate book

6. An opening of Robert Jones's Songs and Ayres (1600); here all the parts are printed in one book, as explained under *Madrigal* 3 b. There is a lute accompaniment in tablature. See *Tablature*

The **Polka-Mazurka** is a different thing from either of the dances that combine in its name: it differs from the polka (q.v.) in having a three-in-a-measure time and from the mazurka in having an accent on the third beat of the measure.

MAZZINGHI, JOSEPH. Born in London in 1765 and died in Bath in 1844, aged seventy-eight. He was a pupil of the 'English Bach' (Johann Christian Bach, q.v.) and a popular composer both of operas and of piano music. Two of his compositions were not long ago everywhere known in Britain and probably still linger in country places—the humorous duet 'When a little farm we keep' and the pleasant glee 'The Wreath' (or 'Ye shepherds, tell me').

MAZZOCHI (The Brothers).

(1) DOMENICO (1592–1665). He wrote madrigals, etc., and particularly an oratorio, performed in Rome in 1631. *Querimonia di S. Maria Maddalena* ('Plaint of St. Mary Magdalen'), which had a very powerful effect on all who heard it. He is also said to have been the first to use in scores terms of expression such as *forte* and *piano* (1638).

See *Expression* 1.

(2) VIRGILIO (1597–1646). He was brother of the above, choirmaster of St. Peter's in Rome, and composer of published sacred music.

M.B.E. See *Knighthood and other Honours*.

Mc. For names beginning 'Mc' see under 'Mac'.

M.D. *Main droite* (Fr.) or *Mano destra* (It.), i.e. 'right hand'.

ME. In the Tonic Sol-fa system (q.v.), the name for the third degree of the major scale (and the fifth degree of the minor scale). In French and Italian usage, however, the name has become attached to the note E, in whatever scale or other association it may occur.

Cf. *Mi*.

MEADOWS WHITE, MRS. See *Smith, Alice Mary*.

MEALTIME MUSIC (p. 593, pl. 105). The practice, often considered modern, of providing music at mealtimes is in reality very ancient. As Izaak Walton in his *Compleat Angler*, wishing to exalt fish, tells us, 'The Romans at the height of their glory . . . had music to usher in their sturgeons, lampreys, and mullets'.

The British custom of eating to music is of great antiquity. We get a glimpse of it in the sixteenth century when we find Sir Francis Drake's chaplain reporting of one of his voyages, 'Neither had he omitted to make provision also for ornament and delight, carrying with him for this purpose expert musicians', and when we find a Spanish captain whom Drake took prisoner writing, 'He has all possible luxuries. . . . He dines and sups to the music of viols.' Before Drake set out on his 1589 expedition he sent to the mayor and council of Norwich to borrow 'the waytes of this citie' (see *Wait or Wayte*), and of the body of six only two returned.

The Elizabethan novelist Deloney tells us of one of his heroes, the great clothier Tom Dove, 'It was as sure as an Act of Parliament that he could not digest his meat without musick', and in several of his novels shows music as commonly accompanying meals at inns (see *Inns and Taverns*).

There was in 1606 enacted a rule of the London Musicians' Company (see *Profession* 1) that 'at banquets . . . within the City of London, suburbs or precincts' the performers engaged should not be 'under the number of four, in consort or with violins', the fine inflicted on members of the Company who condescended to appear in lesser force being three shillings and fourpence.

One of Cromwell's distinguished guests wrote: 'The musick played all the time we were at dinner' (which was quite in the traditional custom of royalty in England and Europe generally). Twenty years later Pepys, dining at the Dolphin as the guest of 'Mr. Folz, the ironmonger', complains, 'I expected musique, the missing of which spoiled my dinner', and later, when dining at the same hostelry with the Commissioner of Ordnance, is careful to record, 'Good musick at my direction'.

The New England notability Judge Sewall, in entering in his diary the incident of his presence at the Council Dinner at Boston, complains, 'Had no musick, though the Lieut. Govr. had promised it'. And when visiting the Old Country he sometimes had musicians to play to him whilst he ate in the inns.

Such examples as the above could be multiplied indefinitely so far as the sixteenth and seventeenth centuries are concerned, and probably also the eighteenth century; there was much eating to music in the several 'Gardens' in this century, as novelists of the period frequently reveal (for the Gardens see *Concert* 12). Defoe, in his *Tour through England* (1724–6), tells us that the Duke of Chandos, to whom Handel had just ceased to be chief musician, had musicians 'to entertain him every day at dinner'.

In the twentieth century the difficulty is not to find examples of eating publicly to music but to find places where one can eat without it; in this epoch, when rest for the ear is more difficult of attainment than ever before in the world's history, restaurants have been known to advertise as an attraction, 'No Music'. In 1932 Messrs. Lyons, the London caterers, stated that they were employing, at their various establishments, 300 musicians in 30 orchestras, at an annual cost of over £150,000. This implies an average salary of £10 per week (at that time a comfortable income), and presumably a corresponding quality of musicianship. Thirty years later the restaurant orchestra was a thing of the past, but the vacuum had been filled by recorded music of the type of 'Muzak' (q.v.).

Cf. *Jazz* 1.

MEAN-TONE TUNING. See *Temperament* 7.

MEANY, STEPHEN JOSEPH (d. 1890). See *Britannia, the Pride of the Ocean.*

MEASURE. (1) The most part of music since the mid-seventeenth century falls into a regular scheme of beats—groups of two, three, four, etc., with a strong accentuation of the first of every group. The time-space of a group, i.e. between one strong accent and another, is called, in the terminology of older British writers, in that of John Curwen and his followers (see *Tonic Sol-fa*), and in that of all modern American writers, a measure.

The measures are, in notation, marked off from one another by 'bars' or 'bar lines' before each of the strongly accented beats. As a consequence, the British have come to use the word *bar* for 'measure', which is illogical and yet seems to cause little confusion.

It may be noted that a fair amount of wrong barring exists in music, composers not always sufficiently considering where the principal accents really fall. As instances may be suggested Chopin's Nocturne in E flat, op. 9, no. 2 (where it may be maintained that the lines should properly come in the middle of the measures as at present printed), and his Study in D flat, op. 25, no. 8 (where it may be maintained that each present measure should properly be cut in two). A considerable proportion of hymn tunes are wrongly barred. There are many examples of contrapuntal music, however, for which no possible barring could be devised that would properly indicate the accentuation of all the parts or voices.

For a discussion of the nature and function of the measure see *Rhythm*; for something of the history of bar lines see *Notation* 4.

(2) Any dance tune, in older English, is called a Measure.

MECHANICAL REPRODUCTION OF MUSIC

(For illustrations see p. 608, pl. **106**; 17, **2**. 6.)

1. Introductory. The history of the mechanical reproduction of music, which many consider to be a recent phase of musical activity, is, in reality, a long one. For at least 600 years inventors of all European races have been busily employed in attempts to provide mechanical means for the easy dissemination of music. As will be seen by the present article, they have sometimes been inspired rather by the desire to astonish than by definitely artistic aims, but that the latter have not been absent is seen by the support they have received from some of the great composers—Handel, Emanuel Bach, Haydn, Mozart, Beethoven, and others.

It will be found, in reading what follows, that for five centuries the simple principle of the barrel-and-pin held the field. Then, in the nineteenth century, the introduction of pneumatics brought with it the perforated roll. At the very end of that century Edison's discovery of a means of recording and reproducing sound waves began the era of the wax cylinder and the vulcanite disk. Later still came the recording of sound waves on a continuous film or magnetic tape.

The last three methods are not included in the present article, being treated under *Gramophone.*

It should be understood that in the space available it has been impossible to discuss all the almost innumerable applications of the barrel-and-pin and perforated roll to the production of music, but enough is perhaps given here to illustrate the immense activity that these two devices have provoked amongst inventors.

2. Clock Chimes and Carillons. The first of all mechanical instruments seems to be the public clock. Clocks are said to date from A.D. 996, but they were a long time in becoming common; however, as soon as they came into being there existed a mechanism the application of which to quasi-musical purposes was inevitable.

The earliest time-marking bells were struck by men with hammers who ascended the towers for the purpose, and the mechanical human figures that are seen striking bells in so many of the cities of Europe recall the custom to mind. Such mechanical figures were to be seen marking the hours before dial clocks were in outdoor use. It was during the second half of the fourteenth century that the weight-drawn clock reached the stage of development that made possible its use in towers, and at this period came into much greater prominence the machine-impelled performers beating drums, blowing horns, or striking bells. The bells struck by the figures (or *jacks*) were usually two in number: when they became four the term carillon was applied and some etymologists actually derive this word from the Low Latin 'quatrino', a group of four. As carillons are treated in this volume under the heading *Bell,* it is unnecessary to discuss them under the present heading. It is, however, desirable to mention them here, since it is clear that in the introduction of the mechanism of a revolving barrel with pins operating a chiming or ringing apparatus, we have the historical basis of all that has followed in the way of the mechanical performance of music—up to the advent of the paper-operated pneumatic piano-playing and organ-playing mechanism and the recording of sound vibrations by means of a diaphragm and a stylus which led to phonographs and gramophones.

3. A Mechanical Virginal. The application of the barrel-and-pin principle to keyboard instruments was an obvious step to take and not a long one. Amongst the fine collection of instruments left by Henry VIII (q.v.) at his death (1547) was 'a Virginal that goethe with a whele without playing uppon'. Whether this was a unique specimen or merely the representative of a class is not now to be discovered, but it was clearly a barrel instrument.

4. Sixteenth-century Mechanical Organs, etc. Half a century later we find the daughter of the last-named monarch interesting herself in the application of the mechanical principle to the organ.

In 1599 Queen Elizabeth sent to the Sultan of Turkey a number of presents, designed to propitiate him and to facilitate the operations of the 'Company of the Merchants of the Levant' —which company, it is permissible to guess, paid for the presents. One of these presents was an organ with carillon combined, operated by keyboard or by touching a spring and also by the automatic action of a clock (apparently on the twenty-four-hour system of striking, by the way) which released the spring normally every six hours. The queen herself inspected this instrument before it left London—which it did in the personal charge of its builder, Thomas Dallam, a member of a firm that was active and in great reputation during the whole of the seventeenth century. Dallam's long and vivid account of his voyage and stay at Constantinople is extant, and a brief quotation from it shall be made here, as offering probably the earliest description of a mechanical instrument of elaborate construction.

'All being quiett, and no noyes at all, the presente began to salute the Grand Sinyor; for when I lefte it I did alow a quarter of an houre for his cominge thether. Firste the clocke strouke 22; than the chime of 16 bels went of. and played a songe of 4 partes. That being done, tow personagis which stood upon to corners of the seconde storie, houldinge tow silver trumpetes in there handes, did lifte them to theire heades, and sounded a tantarra. Then the musicke went of, and the orgon played a song of 5 partes twyse over. In the tope of the orgon, being 16 foute hie, did stand a holly bushe full of blacke birds and thrushes, which at the end of the musick did singe and shake their wynges. Divers other motions thare was which the Grand Sinyor wondered at. Than the Grand Sinyor asked the Coppagawe [the Sultan's secretary] yf it would ever doo the like againe. He answered that it would

doo the lyke again at the next houre. Cothe he: I will se that. In the meane time, the Coppegaw, being a wyse man, and doubted whether I hade so appoynted it or no, for he knew that it would goo of it selfe but 4 times in 24 houres, so he came unto me, for I did stand under the house sid, where I myghte heare the orgon goo, and he asked me yf it would goo againe at the end of the next houre; but I told him that it would not, for I did thinke the Grand Sinyor would not have stayed so longe by it; but yf it would please him, that when the clocke had strouk he would tuche a little pin with his finger, which before I had shewed him, it would goo at any time. Than he sayde that he would be as good as his worde to the Grand Sinyor. When the clocke began to strick againe, the Coppagaw went and stood by it; and when the clocke had strouke 23 he tuched that pinn, and it did the lyke as it did before. Than the Grand Sinyor sayed it was good. He satt verrie neare unto it, ryghte before the Keaes [keys] wheare a man should play on it by hands. He asked whye those keaes did not move when the orgon wente and nothinge did tuch them. He Tould him that by those thinges it myghte be played on at any time. Then the Grand Sinyor asked him yf he did known any man that could playe on it. He sayd no, but he that came with it coulde, and he is heare without the dore. Fetche him hether, cothe the Grand Sinyor and lett me se how he dothe it.'

Perhaps the earliest example on record of a great musician providing music for such an instrument as this is that of Peter Philips (q.v.), who arranged a madrigal by Striggio for the famous inventor Salomon de Caus. At all events, this work appears in de Caus's book, *Les Raisons des forces mouvantes* (1615), in which he describes his barrel organ worked by water power.

About the same period we find the great German composer Hans Leo Hassler (q.v.) much occupied with the commercial production of musical clockwork instruments and involved in legal combats concerning them.

5. Clockwork Instruments of the Eighteenth Century. The instrument of 1599 is curiously like three of two centuries later (1772, 1792, and 1793; see p. 608, pl. **106.** 2), made by Father Primitivus Niemecz, librarian to Prince Esterházy, for which the Prince's chief musician, Haydn, provided a series of pieces (published in 1932 by Nagel of Hanover, under the title of *Werke für das Laufwerk*—'Laufwerk', or 'barrel-work', being Haydn's name for such an instrument). Some of these pieces are specially composed for the instruments and others are arrangements of movements from Haydn's quartets and symphonies, etc.; one of them is a three-part fugue. Mozart's two well-written Fantasias in F minor (1790–1) were written for an instrument of this kind, for which another name is *Flötenuhr* ('flute-clock', referring to the nature of the mechanism rather than to the presence of an actual clock, which is not invariable); both of these now often figure in organ recital programmes. Amongst other composers of repute who have written for instruments of this class are Michael Haydn, Emanuel and Friedemann Bach, Quantz, Graun, and Kirnberger. Beethoven, in the early nineteenth century, used to frequent a Vienna café where there was such an instrument and used often to call for a performance of the overture to Cherubini's *Medea*.

Actual watches and clocks were sometimes made to perform tunes. In the early part of the eighteenth century (1716–17) litigation took place in London between Charles Clay and Daniel Quare, who both claimed to be inventors of such timepieces. In 1736 Clay exhibited to Queen Caroline his 'surprising musical clock'. It played its tunes on both bells and organ pipes, and Handel wrote and arranged for it a large number of pieces (mostly in two parts, but with occasional chords); these are set out in full in the *Musical Quarterly* of October 1919.

6. The Orgue de Barbarie, Serinette, etc. The name of this organ does not refer either to Barbary or the barbaric; it is said that 'Barbarie' is a corruption of 'Barbieri', the name of an Italian instrument-manufacturer who in the latter part of the eighteenth century invented it—though 'adapted' would surely be a better word than 'invented', in view of the fact that no positively new mechanical principle seems to be involved.

In a small portable case are one or two rows of small organ pipes of wood or metal (or some of each). The turning of a handle sets in motion both a bellows and a barrel, so bringing about the performance of a few short tunes. Right down to the beginning of the twentieth century instruments of this sort were common in the London streets.

A very simple form of this instrument was used in France for teaching the canary ('serin domestique') to sing; it was called the *Serinette*, and the verb 'seriner' remains in French dictionaries as 'to teach birds to sing by means of the serinette', with secondary (but nowadays more common) meanings to 'din an idea into any one', 'to thump out a passage on the piano', and so forth. The same thing was in use in Britain under the name *Bird Organ*. The *Merline* was a similar instrument, somewhat more powerful, for teaching the blackbird ('merle'). And there was the *Turlutaine* which took its name from the curlew ('turlu') and, as nobody, surely, ever tamed and taught a curlew, was probably used as an instrument of enticement by bird catchers (a common expression today is 'C'est sa turlutaine', meaning 'He's always harping on the same string'). These, then, may be considered as items of educational or attractional apparatus rather than as real musical instruments, but it appears that almost any kind of small organ-like instrument played by a handle came to be called a serinette, as were also, at a later date, instruments of the type of harmonium (see *Reed-Organ Family* 6), i.e. pipeless organs, and, further, handle-played instruments of the musical-box order, having neither pipes nor reeds but combs of metal the teeth of which were set in vibration by the pins of a barrel (see section 7).

The son of a Parisian manufacturer of seri-nettes (the *real* serinettes), one Davrainville (b. 1784), developed the instrument remarkably, so that it could 'execute four overtures with a single cylinder'. From this he went on to the construction of barrel organs for dance purposes and to mechanical trumpet-fanfare instruments and the like—including one for the then newly introduced vehicle, the omnibus (1827) which enabled the driver to play coach-horn melodies by the action of his feet, and another that executed all the cavalry calls and served for instructional purposes in the army.

A number of other inventors were similarly busy in France and elsewhere at the end of the eighteenth and beginning of the nineteenth centuries, and the important development of the barrel-and-pin principle at the period was recognized by the publication of a very serious work of an Augustinian monk, M. D. J. Engramelle (1727–81), who elevated the practice of the principle to the level of an art and gave it a well-sounding name—*La Tonotechnie, ou l'art de noter les cylindres* ('Tonotechnique, or the art of placing the notes on cylinders'; Paris, 1775). He also contributed material on the subject to the famous work on organs of the Benedictine monk F. Bédos de Celles, *L'Art du facteur d'orgues* ('The Organ-builder's Art', 1766–78; see *Bédos*), still a classical work on its subject; the inclusion of treatment of the barrel-and-pin device in this latter work is noteworthy as an indication of the growing employment of the barrel organ (see section 10) in France.

7. Metallic Comb Instruments (p. 608, pl. 106. 1). The application of the barrel-and-pin mechanism to a comb of metal, of which the teeth, being of different lengths, yielded different notes, seems to have come in at the end of the eighteenth century, and the 'Musical Box' on this principle (sometimes 'Musical Snuff Box'; in France, *Tabatière à musique*) remained popular almost throughout the nineteenth century. The *Musical World* of 1837 reports the misadventure of a 'gentleman who had a snuff-box that played *Drops of brandy* and *The glasses sparkle on the board*', and who, having it in his pocket at church, accidentally touched the spring. Such boxes were largely manufactured in the watch- and clock-making country of Switzerland, where they are, indeed, still on sale to travellers. Sometimes the spring is disengaged by the opening of the lid of the box; chairs which strike up a tune when sat upon, wine decanters which surprise a guest by offering him musical as well as liquid refreshment, and other fanciful devices of the kind, are also to be seen in the shop windows of tourist resorts.

The musical box has given its name to a class of simple piano compositions which, by the use of the upper part of the keyboard, imitate its effect; about 1830 a 'Snuff-Box' Waltz was extremely popular; Liadof's *Tabatière à musique* is the best-known piece of the type.

The automatically performing doll musicians

of the penny-in-the-slot machines on the piers of British seaside resorts are of this metal comb tribe. Possibly, too, of the same type was the patent automatic 'bustle' reported to have been presented by an ingenious inventor to the music-loving Queen Victoria in celebration of her year of Jubilee (1887); this was so designed as to provide a performance of the National Anthem ('God save the Queen') whenever the wearer sat down—which the august recipient of the gift must have found very gratifying.

8. Maelzel's Inventions. The inventions of Beethoven's one-time friend, Maelzel, demand a separate notice. He is remembered today as (a) the inventor of the clockwork metronome (q.v.); (b) the inventor of the ear-trumpet that was so useful to Beethoven; (c) the improver and exploiter of the world-famous mechanical chess player which forms the subject of one of Poe's essays; and (d) the maker of the *Panharmonicon*, a mechanical orchestra for which Beethoven wrote his *The Battle of Vittoria* (1813).

This last-named instrument was by no means his only one of the sort. A mechanical trumpeter was an earlier invention of his, and it seems to have been supposed that the human figure of which it consisted actually produced the sounds from the trumpet it held; in view of the difficulty of producing the various degrees of the harmonic series from a single tube, however, and remembering Poe's acutely argued doubts as to the complete automatism of the chess player, one may question whether the trumpet placed to the mouth of the figure actually produced the sounds and may suspect a concealed group of separate tubes of the organ-reed character.

The Panharmonicon included flutes, clarinets, trumpets, violins, violoncellos, drums, cymbals, triangle, and strings struck by hammers. It would appear to be the ancestor of that numerous body of mechanical orchestras that today enliven the fair-grounds of Europe. Maelzel, born in 1772, spent the latter part of his life in exploiting his inventions in the United States and died on the American brig *Otis* in 1838, when on a voyage to the West Indies.

The following appeared in the London *Times* in October 1829. It professes to relate to the brother of Maelzel, but may be suspected to relate to Maelzel himself:

'A mechanician, brother to the celebrated Moelzel [sic], of Vienna, has constructed at Boston a set of musical automata, no less than 42 in number, which compose a complete orchestra, and execute several of the most difficult pieces of music in the most perfect manner: among others, the overtures to *Don Juan*, *Giovanni* [sic], *Iphigenia*, and *La Vestale*. Those which excite the most admiration and wonder are the violin-players, which execute their portion of the music precisely as if they were living performers—viz., by the motion of their fingers, etc. A company of Americans have offered the artist 300,000 dollars for this extraordinary and unrivalled piece of mechanism; but the price demanded is 500,000 dollars, and it seems probable that it will be obtained.

9. Automaton Violinists, Flautists, and the like. It may be doubted whether the violin players mentioned above actually performed in the manner described. A concealed set of strings with wheel-bow mechanism (the only type that has in more recent times approached success as a means of playing instruments of the violin family) may be suspected. Similarly, it may be permitted to doubt the exact truth of the following account of Mareppe's automaton violinist, exhibited at the Paris Conservatory in 1838:

'On entering the saloon I saw a well-dressed, handsome figure of a man, apparently between forty and fifty, standing with a violin in his hand, as if contemplating a piece of music which lay on a desk before him. . . . I had but little time for observation before the orchestra was filled by musicians, and on the leader taking his seat, the figure instantly raised itself erect, bowed with much elegance two or three times, and then turning to the leader, nodded as if to say he was ready, and placed his violin to his shoulder. At the given signal he raised his bow and applying it to the instrument, produced *à la* Paganini, one of the most thrilling and extraordinary flourishes I ever heard . . . with a degree of rapidity and clearness perfectly astonishing.'

The automaton played a fantasia containing a rapid movement on the fourth string; it included in its performance 'double and single harmonics', arpeggios on the four strings, and a 'prestissimo movement played in three parts throughout'. The writer now under citation, one Bruyère, felt as if lifted from his seat, and burst into tears, 'in which predicament were most persons in the room'. Of the three-part prestissimo he says:

'This part of the performance was perfectly magical. I have heard the great Italian [Paganini], I have heard the greater Norwegian [Ole Bull], I have heard the best of music, but I never heard such sounds as then saluted my ear. It commenced *ppp*, rising by a gradual *crescendo* to a pitch beyond belief; and then gradually died away, leaving the audience absolutely enchanted.'

The inventor, Mareppe, told the audience at the Conservatory that he had made this automaton in emulation of Vaucanson's flute players. This implies a long-lasting fame, as the two flute players, one sitting and the other standing, had been exhibited a century before: it is said that the flutes were actually operated by winds that came from the mouths of the automata and the pressure of their fingers on the holes of the instrument. Each of them played twenty pieces. The inventor published a description of his mechanism in Paris, it was repeated in the great French *Encyclopédie* of Diderot and d'Alembert, and an English translation was issued by the Prince of Wales's chaplain under the title, *An Account of the Mechanism of an Automaton or Image playing on the German Flute*. A German translation also appeared. Vaucanson was a man of standing who held a post under government as an inspector of manufacturers, and he was elected a member of the Royal Academy of Science. In view, then, of the wonders this inventor unquestionably performed, some reader may feel inclined to dissent from the suspicions just passed as to one or two other inventors, and it may be admitted that an inventor who today appeared in one of the great British, American, or Continental schools of music with a fake automaton violinist would be unlikely to reduce his audience to the 'predicament' mentioned.

One of the best assurances we have as to the credibility of these descriptions of old-time automata is the fact we occasionally find of their sale to persons of importance who may be supposed to have inspected them carefully. These flute players came into the possession of a then famous German physicist, chemist, and surgeon, Beireis.

Other renowned musical automata instruments are the harp and flute clockwork apparatus of J. G. Kaufmann (1789), a trumpeter automaton he constructed with the help of his son F. K. Kaufmann (1808), and the *Orchestrion* of the son of the latter (i.e. the grandson of the first named), apparently something on the lines of Maelzel's Panharmonicon, and introduced to an astonished British public at the Exhibition of 1851. The inventions of the three generations of the Kaufmanns were at one time on exhibition in what was intended to be a permanent collection attached to their music factory at Dresden.

Another inventor family was that of the Swiss P. J. Droz (1721–90), who constructed clocks with carillon and flute mechanism and whose son H. U. J. Droz, in 1774, made a stir in Paris with a harpsichord-playing young lady who, compact merely of cogs and springs, yet breathed and, moreover, possessed a repertory from which she was always prepared to play, following the music copy carefully with her eyes and head, and at the end rising to acknowledge the applause of the audience (p. 608, pl. **106.** 3). The appliances of the two Droz are said now to be in America.

In 1838, one Veckelen of Breda exhibited a figure 'who on the machinery being set in motion, takes out a clarinet, wets the reed once or twice with his lips, and then performs compositions by de Bériot, Weber, Beethoven, and other composers, with the most extraordinary precision, the inventor accompanying on the pianoforte'.

In the 1880s Maskelynes were exhibiting in London, at their famous Egyptian Hall, a mechanical cornet player and a mechanical euphonium player. Jasper Maskelyne assured W. T. H. Blandford (cf. *Clarinet Family*, 4 f, note), who heard these automata and reported that they were very lifelike, that the sounds were actually produced by the instruments.

10. The English Barrel Organ (p. 608, pl. **106.** 4–6). During the late eighteenth and early nineteenth centuries the application of the barrel-and-pin mechanism to the organ became very common in England. Messrs. Flight of

London advertised barrel organs as early as 1772. Hundred of instruments of this type came to be used in the churches, gradually superseding the orchestras which at that time existed almost everywhere—both the barrel organs and the remaining orchestras at last disappearing before the harmonium (see *Reed-Organ Family* 6) and, as manual and pedal skill became more common, the hand-played pipe organ.

These barrel organs (called *Hand Organs* in distinction from 'Finger Organs') were, as a rule, capable only of mechanical performance, their mechanism being internal and undetachable; but in addition there existed a class of organ that possessed both a keyboard and a separate barrel arrangement, the latter, when brought into use, operating on the keys much as the early 'Pianolas' were to do at a later date. The purely barrel type of instrument was, for some inscrutable reason, called a *Dumb Organist*.

Most of the barrel organs proper possessed five or six stops and three to five interchangeable barrels, each with about ten of the most popular metrical-psalm and hymn tunes of the day. (For their shakes between the lines see *Hymns and Hymn Tunes* 9.) Some provided also for the use of the Anglican Chant (which must have required an adroit stopping and restarting of the motion of the handle in order to accommodate the reciting note): in late specimens a setting of the responses to the Commandments was also included. But it must be remembered that such complications as the chanting of the Psalms and canticles and musical responses were, until the Oxford Movement (the 1830s onwards), almost confined to the cathedrals (see *Anglican Chant*, concluding paragraph), so that barrel organ accompaniment was little called for.

Many of the organs were, for economy, not supplied with a full chromatic series of pipes, and the tunes were therefore restricted to two or three keys.

An inquiry in 1953 showed that a surprising number of these instruments still remained in the churches of England (all in the south, with Essex predominant), that most were not in order for use, that a few were occasionally used, and that one or two were in regular weekly use. One such is in the tiny church of Shelland, Suffolk (p. 17, pl. **2.** 6). Its maker was Bryceson of London (who made a great many) and its date is probably about 1815. It has three barrels, each with twelve tunes, and six stops —open diapason, stopped diapason, principal, twelfth, fifteenth, tierce. The 'full organ' ought, with those stops, to sound very bright, but the congregation in 1934 (when this article was first written) never had a means of judging, for the organist, who had then been in office nearly half a century, said, 'I have had the same two out for years; I am not one for fiddling with the stops'. A similar model in the church of Brightwell Baldwin (Oxon.) is in regular use but only for a voluntary before the service.

We are apt today to think lightly of the possibilities of the barrel organ. The famous Dr. Burney, however, in his long treatment of the instrument in Rees's *Cyclopædia* (written about 1805) declares that 'the recent improvements of some English artists have rendered the barrel capable of producing an effect equal to the fingers of the first-rate performers'—and Dr. Burney, himself an organist, had travelled half over Europe listening critically to the 'first-rate performers' in every department of music. Moreover, the very musical poet Mason, who was Precentor of the Cathedral of York from 1763 to 1797, in his *Essays, Historical and Critical, on English Church Music* (1795), says that he prefers 'the mechanical assistance of a Cylindrical or Barrel Organ to the fingers of the best parochial Organist'.

Half a century earlier Handel had not disdained to compose for an instrument of this class. The Earl of Bute employed one Langshaw, an organist and mechanician of merit, to add cylinders to a fine organ he possessed (a task which took a dozen years, so that we may imagine that it was largely experimental), and engaged Handel to write some pieces specially for these cylinders. Apparently Handel's amanuensis, John Christopher Smith, had something to do with the transference of this music to the barrels and it is related that 'the barrels were set in so masterly a manner that the effect was equal to that of the most finished player'.

It is possible that the Earl of Bute's enterprise may have been inspired by the wide publicity accorded to the efforts of 'Mr. Henry Bridges, a carpenter of Waltham Abbey, who, by nine years study, prepared and finished a musical machine, or surprising Microcosm or musical clock, whose performance to the most curious has given general satisfaction, nay even beyond common fame or belief'. (Here, as often, by 'clock' mere clockwork seems to have been meant.) This Microcosm, to use the name given it by its deviser, was for about forty years carried by him 'through most parts of Europe and the English America' (*Gentleman's Magazine*, 1796). The date of the introduction of the Microcosm was somewhat prior to 1735, in which year a description of it appeared.

Some legend as to the devotion of the English to barrel-made music apparently lingered on the Continent, for the very reputable *Dictionnaire pratique et historique de la musique* of the erudite 'Michel Brenet' (q.v.) gives the following under the rubric 'Orgue Mécanique': 'Cette industrie est grandement développée en Angleterre, où il est d'un usage constant de se servir dans les églises d'orgues mécaniques, qui ont un répertoire étendu d'hymnes, de chants religieux et de fantaisies' ('This trade is greatly developed in England, where it is the regular thing to make use in the churches of mechanical organs, which possess an extended repertory of hymns, religious songs, and fantasias').

That appeared in 1926!

11. The Apollonicon. The most elaborate barrel organ ever built was probably that of Messrs. Flight & Robson, called the *Apollonicon*. It was from 1817 to about 1840 exhibited in London, in a special building erected for it near Regent's Park, and attracted crowds to its performances. It was played either by three barrels or by anything up to six performers at six consoles ('These, acting in concert, develop the various powers of the organic construction, and operate on the nerves and feelings of the auditors in a truly surprising manner', writes Dr. Busby in 1825). There is in Rees's *Cyclopædia* a very elaborate description from the pen of Dr. Burney (written about 1805) of another large and important instrument, built by the same firm for the Earl of Kirkwall; this article, with its diagrams, constitutes perhaps the best source of reference on the mechanical construction of such instruments. Burney, alluding to a performance of Mozart's *Magic Flute* Overture, etc., before the Prince Regent, says: 'The machine produces the various accompaniments of a whole band of music, in such dulcet as well as forcible tones, that no one would credit without an opportunity of hearing it.'

An instrument of a similar kind, apparently, was the *Euterpion*, which, also, was exhibited in London; its performance of Weber's *Oberon* Overture is highly praised in the *Musical World* of 1837.

12. The Street Piano. This is said to have been first made by one Hicks, of London, in the early nineteenth century. It is simply a barrel-and-pin-operated pianoforte, with no proper claim to the name, however, since no 'piano' or gradation of tone-quality is in any way possible, the hammers having hard leather heads and there being no means of modifying the force of their blows. Similarly there are no dampers, a deprivation that is little felt in the open air where, exclusively, the instrument is heard. The manufacture of these instruments drifted entirely, or almost so, to Italy, and the performers of them, popular throughout the alleys and courts of all British cities, then came from that country. After the advent to power of Mussolini, in 1922, their cheering influence tended to disappear from British urban life, as, understandably jealous for the dignity of his race, he recalled all Italians engaged in street musical activities. Since then the instrument has been rarely seen.

The application of the colloquial term 'Barrel Organ' to this instrument is evidently due to mere association of ideas at the time it became popular.

13. The 'Pianola' and other Perforated Paper-Roll Instruments. Attempts at mechanical means of playing the pianoforte have been fairly common since the close of the eighteenth century, as readers of the old musical journals can testify. Dr. Busby in his *Concert Room Anecdotes* describes the appliances that had come into existence about the time that this work appeared (1825). One was the 'Self-acting Pianoforte' of Messrs. Clementi, Collard & Co., which apparently included also in its construction a normal pianoforte, so that, if desired, the two could be heard together, the one played by hand and the other by 'a horizontal cylinder similar to that of a barrel-organ and set in motion by a steel spring'—which latter was capable of performing 'the most intricate and difficult compositions', and of continuing for half an hour without re-winding.

'The time in which it executes any movement may be accelerated or retarded at pleasure; and while by the delicacy and perfection of the mechanism the *piano* and *forte* passages are given with correctness and effect, the *forzandi* and *diminuendi* are produced by the slightest motion of the hand applied to a sliding ball at the side of the instrument.'

The other was the 'Cylindrichord', invented by Courcell; it was 'found to be an admirable and efficient substitute for a first-rate performer on the pianoforte'. We are told that:

'In small or family parties, where dancing to the music of the pianoforte is practised . . . a person totally unacquainted with music, a child or a servant, may perform, in the very best and most correct style, quadrilles, waltzes, minuets, country dances, marches, songs, overtures, sonatas, choruses, or indeed any piece of music, however difficult. This instrument is extremely simple and differs altogether from the barrel or self-playing pianoforte; it can be accommodated to the height or dimensions of any pianoforte, and when not in use for that purpose, forms a piece of elegant furniture.'

Apparently, then, the 'Cylindrichord' acted upon the keys of the instrument, like some of the church barrel-organs of the day (see section 10) and like the 'push-up' (early twentieth-century) form of the 'Pianola' (see later in this article). It was almost certainly operated by means of a barrel with pins, as was also the 'Self-acting Pianoforte'. This was the normal method in all such instruments.

A step forward was taken when, following the introduction of the pneumatic lever as a substitute for the old tracker action in organ building (first tried 1827), it was realized that perforated sheets of cardboard or rolls of paper could be used to control apparatus and so to produce tunes. A patent for applying this idea was taken out in France in 1842. Small instruments of the organ or harmonium kind operated by this means played simple hymn tunes in the London streets up to the early twentieth century. A handle was turned by the operator and it both worked a small bellows and effected the progression of the perforated cardboard or paper. A patent for the application of a 'perforated note-sheet' to the organ was taken out in London in 1846 by Alexander Bayne, but it is not known that it was ever exploited. In 1878 a domestic instrument, a table appliance with a handle, was put on sale in New York—the 'Organette'. Later its principles were applied, as an auxiliary, to reed organs of the regular hand-played parlour type. It was with the sale of the Organette that began the Æolian Company, later the makers of the 'Pianola', etc.

In 1887 the Welte-Mignon Company, of Freiburg-im-Breisgau, patented a pneumatic paper-roll contrivance applied to the pianoforte. About 1890 Thibouville-Lamy, of Paris, was manufacturing the 'Pianista', a cabinet apparatus with felted fingers, to be placed before the keys of the pianoforte. A handle supplied the motive power; if it were turned quickly the music came out loud and fast, if it were turned slowly the music came out soft and slow; there was no detaching these associations!

The 'Pianola' was patented by an American, Mr. E. S. Votey, in 1897. It was for long a 'push-up' contrivance to be wheeled to the pianoforte when its services were desired. Gradually it was improved in many ways, and especially in the conceding of the opportunity for a higher expressiveness on the part of the performer. The actual notes were provided in the form of perforations on a roll passing over a 'tracker-bar' which had corresponding holes (at first for only the 66 notes in the middle of the keyboard; later for 88) communicating by an array of tubes with the normal hammer mechanism of the pianoforte. The main control over dynamic force, accentuation, etc., was by finesse in the foot-operated blowing, but hand-levers greatly aided this.

Essentially this is the 'Pianola' as later perfected, though for long it was invariably built in as a part of the instrument. The player's control eventually became so perfect that when he was musical by nature and had troubled to acquire the technique of his instrument the effect was, in most types of composition, barely distinguishable from the finest hand playing. By certain devices it was even possible to 'bring out' a melody whether in the top, bottom, or middle part of the music. In the early years of the present century there was introduced the 'Reproducing Piano', of which the 'Welte-Mignon' make, the 'Ampico' (*Am*erican *Pi*ano *Co*.), and 'Duo-Art' (Æolian Co.) are well-known examples. Such instruments repeat the complete performances of an artist photographically, as a gramophone record does, the roll having been mechanically produced from his playing and in such a way that both his tempo nuances and his dynamic nuances are copied. Of a London performance of a Liszt Rhapsody, in which passages were performed alternately by Cortot himself and by a 'Duo-Art' roll as recorded by Cortot (the whole being so dovetailed that the effect was continuous) the English critic, Ernest Newman, said, 'With one's eyes closed it was impossible to say which was which'.

It is of interest to note that in 'Duo-Art' rolls sixteen degrees of dynamic intensity are sufficient to cover all extremes of *fortissimo* and *pianissimo* and to produce the most finely graded *crescendos* and *diminuendos*: Mr. Guy Montrose Whipple discussed this subject in the *Journal of Applied Psychology* of April 1928 and came to the conclusion that sixteen is too many, seven being sufficient to satisfy the finest ear:

this surprising statement will be doubted by most pianists.

Composition direct for the Player-piano (so ending the limitations inherent in composition for the mere ten fingers of the human hand) has been undertaken by Stravinsky, Malipiero, Hindemith, Casella, Goossens, Herbert Howells, and others.

In 1920 70 per cent. of the 364,000 pianos manufactured in the U.S.A. were player pianos. By 1932 the combined inroads of radio, gramophone, and the Depression had made the instrument all but extinct, though rolls could still be bought. In the late 1950s it made a remarkable come-back and many old pianolas were repaired and put back into commission.

The application of the perforated paper-roll device to both the reed-organ and the pipe-organ became very common. Particularly in the United States many of the finest concert and domestic organs were supplied with this device as an auxiliary.

For a legal point concerning mechanical reproduction of music see *Copyright and Performing Right*.

MECK, NADEZHDA VON. See *Tchaikovsky*; *Cinematograph*.

MEDESIMO (It.). 'Same', e.g. *Medesimo movimento*, 'the same speed'.

MEDIANT. The third degree of the major or minor scale. So called as midway between the tonic and the dominant.

MEDIATION. See *Plainsong* 2; *Anglican Chant* 1.

MEDICEAN EDITION. See *Plainsong* 3; *Cecilian Movement*.

MEDICI FAMILY. See *Ballet* 2; *Caccini*.

MEDLEY. See *Overture* 5.

MEDTNER, NICHOLAS (p. 416, pl. **71**. 2). Born in Moscow in 1880, of German parents, and died in London in 1951, aged seventy-one. He was trained at the Conservatory of Moscow —in piano playing under Safonof, who helped him to become an exceptionally brilliant performer. After a career as touring recitalist he settled in his native country and city as a professor of piano at his old school. He appeared in America and Britain, and then resided in Paris and (1930 to death) London.

Medtner composed much piano music, songs, two piano concertos, and a little chamber music; he did not show any interest in the orchestra or in opera. He expressed little Russian national feeling, and was indeed hardly a Russian composer, but rather a German composer born in Russia; Brahms was a considerable influence in his music—at all events as to its general sentiment and its 'bigness' of style.

He wrote a *Sonata-Vocalise* (voice and piano, the former using merely vowels and attempting an instrumental, almost violin-like type of expression).

The spelling 'Metner', sometimes seen, is an incorrect transliteration; when the Russian alphabet is not used the name should, of course, revert to its original German form.

MEGAPHONE. A large speaking-trumpet. Also a device introduced by Edison for listening at a distance of some miles without the use of wires or electricity—practically an improved ear-trumpet on a large scale.

MEHR (Ger.). 'More.' Also 'many', in compounds such as *Mehrstimmig*, 'many-voiced', i.e. polyphonic.

MEHRERE (Ger.). 'Several.'

MÉHUL, ÉTIENNE NICOLAS—or Étienne Henri (p. 368, pl. **61**. 6). Born at Givet (Ardennes) in the extreme north of France in 1763 and died in Paris in 1817, aged fifty-four. He was born in poverty but, combining native talent for music with a determined will, contrived by the time he was ten to launch himself on a professional career as organist of a convent. At fifteen his abilities attracted the benevolence of a wealthy music-lover who gave him the advantage of musical training in Paris. There he heard and was overwhelmed by the music of Gluck, and made the acquaintance of that master himself, who encouraged and helped him. He threw himself into opera composition and at twenty-seven found himself famous.

The Revolution was now in progress, and some of its stirring events were marked by compositions of his, as were some events of the succeeding Napoleonic epoch. He received official honours, and was connected with the Paris Conservatory from its foundation.

He died of consumption, leaving a mass of work behind him, most of it remarkable especially for its dramatic power and for the novelty and effectiveness of its orchestration, in which last particular he was often an innovator.

The work best remembered today (and it is still performed) is the sacred opera *Joseph* (1807); it is considered his masterpiece.

See *Belgium* 4; *Rouget de Lisle*; *Bochsa*; *Bohemia*; *Collaboration*.

MEIKLE, WILLIAM. See *Oboe* 4 h.

MEINERT, JOHN. See *Scandinavia* 2.

MEISTERSINGER SONATA (Brahms). See *Nicknamed Compositions* 7.

MEISTERSINGER VON NÜRNBERG, DIE. See *Mastersingers of Nuremberg*.

MELA, EUGENIA. See *Voice* 17.

MELARTIN, ERKKI GUSTAV. Born in east Finland in 1875 and died at Helsinki in 1937, aged sixty-two. After study under Wegelius (see *Scandinavia* 6), and then in

Vienna, he became a Professor of the Conservatory of Helsinki and later its Director. He composed symphonies, symphonic poems, chamber music, piano music, an opera, many songs and other things, and published books of Finnish folk songs.

MELBA, NELLIE. Born near Melbourne, Australia, in 1861 and died in Sydney in 1931, aged sixty-nine. Her original name was Helen Porter Mitchell, her married name Armstrong, and her professional name was derived from that of her native place. She had a long and brilliant international career as an operatic soprano. She was created a Dame of the Order of the British Empire.

See reference under *Gramophone* 6.

MELBOURNE, VICTORIA. See under *Cathedral Music* 8 (end); *Schools of Music*.

MELISMA (a Greek word meaning 'song'; plural *Melismata*). A term used of passages in plainsong (see *Plainsong* 2), or in other song, in which one syllable flowers out into a passage of several notes. It means much the same, then, as *Coloratura*, *Fioritura*, or *Divisions* (q.v.). The melisma is a feature of eighteenth-century vocal music, often used merely for display purposes but also descriptively and for emotional expression (Handel, 'Rejoice greatly' and 'Thou shalt break them' in *Messiah*; Bach to such words as 'wept' and 'scourged' in his Passions). Sometimes a vocal cadenza (q.v.) is spoken of as a melisma.

MELISMATA (1611). See under *Round*; *Street Music* 2; *God save the Queen* 3; also above.

MELLERS, WILFRID HOWARD. Born at Leamington in 1914. He is a writer on music and the composer of orchestral and chamber music, songs, etc.

He was educated at Cambridge University and has taught successively there, at Birmingham University, and at York University (1964). He has collaborated in a history of music and has written a large-scale book on Couperin. After a period in the U.S.A. he produced *Music in a New Found Land* (1964), an account of modern American music. He has composed orchestral and chamber music, songs, and other things.

MELLERTION. See *Electric Musical Instruments* 1 h.

MELLISH, COLONEL (born about 1777). See *Drink to me only with thine eyes*.

MELLOPHONE. A synonym (U.S.A.) for the tenor horn. (See *Saxhorn and Flügelhorn Families* 2 c d.)

MELLOR, HUGH. See *Wales* 2 (end).

MELODEON. See *Reed-Organ Family* 7.

MELODIA. See *Organ* 14 II.

MELODICA. See *Reed-Organ Family* 6.

MELODIC MINOR SCALE. See *Scales* 6.

MELODICON. See *Reed-Organ Family* 6.

MELODIC SEQUENCE. See *Sequence*.

MELODRAMA. (1) A play, or a passage in a play, or a poem, in which the spoken voice is used against a musical background. Beethoven has used the device in a movement of his music to Goethe's *Egmont*, and in his opera *Fidelio* (the grave-digging scene). Weber has used it in his incantation scene in *Der Freischütz*, Schumann in parts of his music to Byron's *Manfred*, Mendelssohn in his *Midsummer Night's Dream* music, Bizet in his incidental music to Daudet's *L'Arlésienne*.

Before all these, famous examples exist in the works of Benda (*Ariadne* and *Medea*, both 1775), and though he is not the first to use the device, his success has led to his being considered its virtual introducer. Mozart as a young man heard *Medea* at Mannheim and wrote to his father: 'Nothing ever so much surprised me, for I had always fancied that no effect could be thus produced. . . . I will tell you an opinion of mine—that the greater part of the recitatives in opera should be treated in this manner, and only those sung of which the words are really suitable for musical expression.' Thus he would, apparently, have substituted it for 'Recitativo secco' (see *Recitative*).

Earlier than Benda was Rousseau, for one, with his much discussed *Pygmalion* (written 1762, performed 1770). Some of the first tentative efforts towards what we now call opera involved a very curious combination of the speaking voice with a choral background (see *Opera* 1).

Richard Strauss's setting of Tennyson's *Enoch Arden* (1898), with piano, is a modern example of melodrama. Mackenzie set a number of recitations to piano accompaniment, and set Joseph Bennett's *The Dream of Jubal* with orchestra (1889). Stanley Hawley (1867–1916) put piano accompaniment to Poe's 'The Bells' and 'The Raven', Hood's 'The Song of the Shirt', etc. Fibich (q.v.) has written many melodramas. Schönberg's *Pierrot lunaire* might be called a sort of semi-melodrama, since a half-speaking voice is used on definite notes indicated in the score. Honegger's *King David* has a good deal of melodrama. Bliss's *Morning Heroes* (1930) is partially a melodrama (subtitle, 'A Symphony for Orator, Chorus, and Orchestra'), and so is Milhaud's *Christophe Colomb* (see also *Rebikof*).

Altogether, then, there has been a good deal of experimentation with this combination of music and speech, yet it has perhaps never quite established itself—some people say because speech and music will not combine.

Melodrama for one speaker is **Monodrama**; for two, **Duodrama**.

(2) The word has come to have another sense, that of a highly sensational spoken play—as when the scene-shifter congratulated Sir Henry Irving ('I 'ave 'eard many play 'Amlet, Sir, but you 'ave raised it to the level of a mellerdrammer'). This is nowadays the sense in which the words 'melodrama' and 'melodramatic' are used in ordinary conversation.

MELODY

1. Introductory. Melody has been called the surface of music. This is not merely in the sense that it is often what we call the 'top' part; in whatever part of the music it may for the moment be it is what catches the ear as the surface of an object catches the eye. Melody without harmony is all surface; it is like painting without perspective, and just as the element of perspective entered into the art of painting late in its history so did the element of harmony into the art of music (cf. articles *History of Music* and *Harmony*), unaccompanied melody being, broadly speaking, the only music everywhere until comparatively recent times. Indeed, just as part of the population of the world still lacks the element of perspective in its painting, so part (the greater part, indeed) lacks that of harmony in its music. Harmony is, then, not a necessity to musical art; melody is, and the man in the street who demands that music must have melody before everything else is right in principle—though in practice he often goes wrong by failing to see melody where it most abounds, that is to say in contrapuntal music and especially the fugue.

2. Origin of Melody. Probably melody originated in the natural inflections of speech (compare *Scales* 3). All speech possesses the two constituents of melody, (*a*) pitch variation and (*b*) rhythm. The student of linguistics calls (*a*) *pitch accent* (but his use of the word 'accent' here is misleading to a musician) and (*b*) *stress accent*, together with *quantity*. The last two, stress and quantity, make up rhythm—'quantity' in the sense in which the word is applied to the classical languages, not in the quite different and incorrect sense in which it has unfortunately been transferred to English. (See *Metre*.)

Everybody in speaking any phrase speaks some syllables on a higher note and some on a lower note (pitch), some more loudly and some more softly (stress), and some more lingeringly and some more curtly (quantity). This *is* melody.

We are, in fact, though we may think ourselves mere conversationalists, actually all operatic artists, and we habitually declaim to a great variety of melodies, using several different ones to the same words. There are many tunes to the simple phrase 'I beg your pardon'—as, for example, the three which give it the respective meanings of 'I deeply regret having stepped on your toe', 'I didn't hear what you said; please repeat it', and 'I don't agree with you at all; you're a fool!' (Incidentally, the varieties of tone quality, facial expression, and gesture that go with those three senses of the phrase help to justify the above suggestion that we are all operatic artists.)

The tunes to which we perform our daily dialogues vary a great deal according to the district from which we come. The English intonations and rhythms differ from the Scottish; those of southern England from those of northern England, the latter using a much more frequent change of note, a wider range of intervals, and more of a singing voice. The English-speaking population of one of the Commonwealth countries has an upward turn at the end of sentences where the population of the home country has a downward one; the southern population of the United States has a different set of melodic curves from the northern or western. It is difficult adequately to account for the varieties. Race and environment supposedly enter—and, it may be, mere chance, if Science admits the existence of such a factor in establishing the world's varied habits and customs.

In the Chinese language the meaning of individual words is affected by the intonation, so that adult foreigners have difficulty in learning the language unless possessed of a quick ear and retentive musical memory. Melody here has become very definitely attached to meaning.

Any human being compelled to repeat the same phrase many times daily inevitably sets it to a very distinct melody, such as could in many cases be recorded in musical notation, though in others it does not sufficiently conform to our accepted scale system for this to be possible. Thus the fatherly English railway porters who used to pass along the platform of a station protecting passengers from the embarrassments of their own ignorance or forgetfulness developed a folk-tune repertory that might have been worth collecting. Phrases like the following were common:

Change here for Hal - i - fax! all change.

(As mentioned in the article *Street Cries*, the traditional fragmentary melodies of itinerant vendors in London and Paris were appreciated as attractive thematic material by composers of the sixteenth century.)

We may then plausibly look for the origin of melody in human speech.

3. Construction of Melody. The melodies of primitive races are often mere alternations of two short motifs (each of them, as a unit, the equivalent of one of the street cries just discussed), one being sung two or three times and then relieved by the other. Some races will chant in this way for hours, and it may be remarked that certain birds have developed their music to this point. Simple as such music may be it embodies the apparently essential principle of economy of material. Almost any good melody will, if closely examined, be found to consist of an exploitation of some brief motif. A glance through a book of English hymn tunes or of the traditional German chorales will show this, as will a glance through any collection of folk tunes.

The following beautiful Welsh air ('All through the night') is a very obvious example:

The lines placed underneath the notes here call attention to the tiny motif of three stepwise descending notes which make up the staple of the tune. The lines above the notes show this motif both reversed in direction and changed in rhythm. The dotted lines in the middle section of the music show the motif appearing once changed as to the notes and three times changed as to the rhythm. After this section we are ready for the motif in its original form, and the first line is thus brought into play again.

The attainment of a higher pitch-level in the middle section is an element in the variety achieved. Note that the climactic note (E) is only once touched, so that its effect is not weakened: it is like the point of highest light in a painting. Note too the effective use of sequence (q.v.) in the middle section.

By all these means, instinctively applied, there has come into existence a melody of extreme coherence and unity, yet of sufficient variety. It consists of nothing but ten repetitions of a motif of three notes, varied in pitch, rhythm, and direction.

As an example of a modern composer the opening melody of Stravinsky's *Rite of Spring* may be quoted:

Here again the opening motif (C–B–G–E–B–

A) is repeated, in whole or in part, several times.

(The marks are inserted on the same principle as those of the previous example: they do not correspond with the composer's phrasing.)

Again it will be seen that the note of climax has been touched only once, and hence is not cheapened. An example in which the point of climax is a low note is at the end of Beethoven's Ninth Symphony, which the reader can analyse for himself on the principles just exemplified.

(Again the marks inserted do not indicate the phrasing but the structure.) The way in which the composer has varied the incidence of the motif in relation to the stress accent (generally beginning it on the first beat of the measure, but sometimes, also, on the second and third beats) and the several rhythms in which he presents it are elements in the melody's effectiveness.

4. Rhythm as an Element in Melody. Rhythm (q.v.) is, indeed, a highly important element in melody—whether it be the freer rhythm of plainsong, some folk song, and Stravinsky and other modern composers, or the equal-measured rhythm of most music of the classical period (say 1650–1900). So important is it, indeed, that recognition of a melody often fails if its notes be reproduced in altered rhythm, whereas if the bare rhythm be tapped it is often at once recognized.

Many people would fail to recognize a certain well-known tune played to them in the following form:

But most would at once recognize it played in this form:

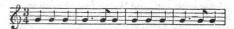

The rhythmic organization of many fine melodies will be found, on careful inspection, to be extraordinarily subtle. Both as to linear shape and as to rhythm the subjects of Bach's fugues are worthy of study. Some are, of course, mere melodic motifs and others complete melodies.

The study of Beethoven's sonata subjects, both on first appearance and on their appearances as re-worked material in the development portion of the movement, is interesting. No composer has taken greater pains than Beethoven in the elaboration and perfecting of his melodic material, and another example of his processes of thought will be given shortly.

One hears it suggested that the genius of Bach and Beethoven frequently enabled them to make a fine composition out of insignificant material. This may be contested. The primary melodic themes of their compositions may often be simple but are almost always well shaped and rhythmically strong. Just as Bacon's essays often open with a striking aphorism leading to a closely argued debate, so do very often the first movements of Beethoven's sonatas and symphonies.

5. Harmony as a Basis of Melody. Beethoven's melodies are often plainly harmonic in their structure (consider the opening of the 'Eroica' Symphony as one obvious example). From the beginning of the seventeenth century, when harmony *qua* harmony began to be understood (see *Harmony* and *History of Music*), harmonically shaped melodies became very common. Bach's are often strongly harmonic. It is impossible to think of some of them that he conceived them as bare melodies; they came to him clothed with harmony. In his compositions for a single bowed instrument the harmony is often not merely implied or suggested, but as fully present as if it were given to an accompanying keyboard instrument. The following, from the opening of the Courante of the first Partita for violin alone, will illustrate this:

The evolution of a system of harmony, with its requirement of definite chords for the cadences at the end of phrases and sentences (i.e. as a part of the punctuation of the music), necessarily very greatly affected the idiom of melody, whose sections became as clearly marked off as if by a series of commas, semicolons, colons, and full stops. At all times melody has been a series of short flights and fresh starts, a continuous line being unimaginable, but the stopping and starting were now emphasized by the new harmonic reinforcement. The increased interest shown in the setting to music of lyrical poetry, and the adoption of dance forms as one of the chief bases of the earlier instrumental

music (up to the mid-eighteenth century), tended to emphasize this element of clear-cut division.

It is sometimes rather pathetic to see Bach involved in unavoidable clumsiness in the attempt to harmonize for Protestant church use, as a chorale, what is in origin (though he probably never heard it as such) a pre-harmony plainsong melody which was not framed for the purpose. He has to force the tune to accept cadences of a kind that were never contemplated when it came into existence.

Despite the beauty of much of the melody written since the harmonic age began it must be admitted that the sense of melody *qua* melody (i.e. of curves and rhythms independent of any chordal structure or harmonic cadences) has a good deal decayed. The late Mrs. Kennedy-Fraser, the collector of the *Songs of the Hebrides*, complained that she found that some sophisticated people had no power to appreciate a bare melody (i.e. of the unharmonic type that she found in the remote islands of the western seas); she showed great skill in supplying the tunes she published with a piano accompaniment, but such a process is, in a sense, a concession.

The melody of Wagner and others who followed him was often very chromatic, and its shape and details were influenced by the system of accented chromatic passing-notes and the like which formed a part of their harmonic technique. There is often a very simple underlying harmonic structure, the complexity lying in its elaborate ornamentation. (See the example from Wagner under *Harmony* 13.)

Of course Wagner occasionally made very effective use of unaccompanied melody (opening themes of *Parsifal*; sailor's song and herd-boy's piping in *Tristan*). Mélisande's beautiful unaccompanied solo in *Pelléas and Mélisande* shows that Debussy too could create one-dimensionally. And there is Stravinsky's music for clarinet alone—and so forth. Earlier there are the many purely melodic movements of Bach for violin unaccompanied and violoncello unaccompanied, already alluded to.

6. Form in Melody. Extending what has been said above about the way in which melodies fall into distinct sections, attention may be called to the formal element in much melody. Apart from the use of *motifs* as a unifying influence, the principles of order are often met by the adoption of definite forms such as the ternary (see *All through the night* and the Beethoven Ninth Symphony example above).

7. Quality, Originality, Popularity. The element of originality in melody is rather intangible. Apparently it lies mainly in mere detail. The Welsh folk song and the Beethoven Ninth Symphony theme given above may be said to grow out of the same motif (though in the one it begins as an upward motif and is afterwards heard as a downward one, and in the other vice versa).

Edwin Evans called attention to the strong

resemblance in the opening phrases of many of the most popular melodies of the nineteenth century:

Highland Laddie (Scots Folk Song).

'Wait till the clouds roll by' (Victorian popular song).

The Holy City (Victorian 'Sacred' Song).

Soldiers of the Queen (time of Boer War).

Land of Hope and Glory. ELGAR.

Wedding March. MENDELSSOHN.

It would appear that to become immediately and widely popular a melody must possess just as much difference as will confer a sense of novelty, and no more. Indeed, any immediately popular song will be found to be little beyond some previously popular melody refurbished. Dr. Sigmund Spaeth, in his study of the popular ballads of the nineteenth century in the United States (*Read 'em and Weep*, New York, 1927), gives as one of the chief theories of the American song-writer of that period the following: 'That a tune which suggests or definitely imitates one which has already been popular has just that much more chance of success.' As an example of the principle (taken from the British repertory) the following may be given. It is Miss Brahe's song, 'I passed by your window', which in the early 1920s became violently epidemic all over the British Empire, but which was (probably quite unconsciously) based on a most popular organ voluntary of a quarter of a century earlier, Batiste's Andante (see *Batiste*).

BRAHE.

BATISTE.

Memory is, then, a strong ingredient in the enjoyment of melody—90 (or 95) per cent. memory and 10 (or 5) per cent. novelty is probably something like the proper proportion for immediate success with the public at large. (Cf. *Composition* 12.)

It is difficult, sometimes, to see what it is in a melody that ensures it a long life. The famous one mentioned in the article *Folía* is attractive, but one cannot quite grasp the reason why it became so universally diffused and enjoyed such a long-continued popularity with composers and public—as it still does in one of its reincarnations, given below:

1st time.

2nd time.

The whole melody is nothing but a little motif repeated nine times at various levels within the meagre compass of a perfect fifth. It is set out above as it appears in Corelli's twelfth Violin Sonata. For nearly two centuries this melody was made use of in one way and another by composers in Italy, France, Germany, and England—amongst them Frescobaldi, Lully, Keiser, Vivaldi, Bach, Pergolese, Grétry, and Cherubini. What gives the air its 'haunting' quality? What, indeed, constitutes the 'haunting' quality of melody in general?

For that matter what constitutes 'quality' in general? What is the difference between a good and a bad tune? Some of the attributes of a good tune are economy and logic in the use of materials; avoidance of any cheapening of the climax note; sufficient, but not too much variety, and so forth. But whether by the compilation of a list of such attributes one could put the student in the way of composing tunes infallibly good is a different matter.

8. A Melody in the Making. Certainly by the analysis of melody, somewhat on the lines of that carried out in this article but with more detail, the student of composition and the listener may improve respectively their powers of polishing a melody and of appreciating the fine points of a composer's melodic products in the state in which he finally presents them. Beethoven's polishing processes have been mentioned above; here is an example to which Stanford called attention in his treatise *Musical Composition*, i.e. in the first state, as it appears in one of Beethoven's rough 'sketch books', and in the final state as it appears in the Sonata in F for Violin and Piano (op. 24):

Sketch state.

a

b

Final state.

b   *b*

a

b

b

c   *c*   *b*

b   *b*   *b*

c   *c*

c   *c*

By a few adroit touches here the effect has been enormously enhanced. One imagines the mental processes to be somewhat as follows: (1) The germ of the whole thing springs to the composer's mind in the passage here marked (*a*); (2) by one of the commonest practices in melody composition it is at once repeated at a different pitch-level, and this brings the tiny motif (*b*) into existence as a link; (3) in continuing the melody the composer evolves the motif (*c*), and on second thoughts feels dissatisfied with it, the interest of the melody being felt to diminish, instead of to increase, towards its end; (4) he also feels dissatisfied with the want of climax—the highest note (D) as it appears near the end is on a weak part of the measure and has been anticipated at the opening; (5) he sees the possibilities of the motif (*b*) that had originated so incidentally, decides to introduce this at the very opening and then to use it to build up a really effective climax in what had previously been the weakest part of the melody, and what should be the strongest—the measures towards the end; (6) in doing so he brings the spot-light on to the high note G, which is touched just this once in the whole course of the melody, the bustling short notes in the preceding measures working up excitement to which it becomes the culmination.

Here it may be remarked that if the popular song and dance 'hits' of the day be examined it will frequently be found that they fail at just the place where Beethoven's melody was failing until he strengthened it, i.e. they often fall into some commonplace cliché towards their final cadence. This may partly account for their ephemeral existence.

9. The Inexhaustibility of Melodic Resources. The miracle of melody is that so much can be accomplished with so little. The resources available seem so limited that thinkers have sometimes predicted the exhaustion of melody, but in the light of experience there appears to be no reason for alarm. The great philosopher, John Stuart Mill, in his *Autobiography* (1873) amuses himself by recalling his early fears:

'I at this time first became acquainted with Weber's *Oberon*, and the extreme pleasure which I drew from its delicious melodies did me good, by showing me a source of pleasure to which I was as susceptible as ever. The good, however, was much impaired by the thought, that the pleasure of music (as is quite true of such pleasure as this was, that of mere tune) fades with familiarity, and requires either to be revived by intermittence, or fed by continual novelty. And it is very characteristic both of my then state, and of the general tone of my mind at this period of my life, that I was seriously tormented by the thought of the exhaustibility of musical combinations. The octave consists only of five tones and two semitones, which can be put together in only a limited number of ways, of which but a small proportion are beautiful: most of these, it seemed to me, must have been already discovered, and there could not be room for a long succession of Mozarts and Webers, to strike out, as these had done, entirely new and surpassingly rich veins of musical beauty.'

A little mathematical calculation might have set Mill's mind at ease. The shortest type of composition in use is, perhaps, the Single Anglican Chant, which requires but ten notes; but assuming that those ten notes were all different they could be arranged in over one hundred-and-fifty million different orders. This does not mean that it is easy to create highly original Single Chants (or Double ones either), for the harmonic conventions limit one severely in such compositions, but considering melody *qua* melody quite a lot can still be done with Mill's 'five tones and two semitones'.

10. Character of Melodies. Melody may be said to divide itself, like music in general, into two classes, that which lays more emphasis on the beauty of pattern and that which lays more on depth of expression—the classical and the 'romantic' types.

Racial and national feeling expresses itself very strongly in melody. English melody, whether bluff or tender, is in general downright, plain, and straightforward; Lowland Scottish melody is often pathetic, Highland fiery; Welsh has mostly, perhaps, not the depth of feeling of that of other parts of the British Isles (though there are many striking exceptions), but is often very beautiful in its curves;

Irish is sometimes wild and sometimes more deeply emotional than, perhaps, any other in the world (see *Londonderry Air*).

Scales, intervals, and rhythms particular to various races or nations make it often easy immediately to recognize the provenance of a folk melody—Spain offering itself as one obvious example. Italy in the eighteenth and nineteenth centuries was supposed to hold a pre-eminence as the land of melody, but this was due rather to her composers having established and then satisfied a liking for facile, flowing, and readily followed tune (with much use of elaborate vocal embellishment) than to any actual superiority; in the late eighteenth century the traveller–historian Burney, a great lover of Handel whose vocal style was formed

in Italy, yet declared, when writing his Italian experiences, that melody was 'much refined' since Handel's time—'It is more graceful, more pathetic, and even more gay'. In this judgement was shown little beyond conformity to fashion, and the melodies of the composers whose operas Burney enjoyed in Rome, Naples, and Venice, are now mostly completely forgotten.

There is a growing interest in Oriental melody (see *Oriental Music*), which is, of course, uninfluenced by harmonic associations, often employs scales and intervals unknown to the West, and makes much of subtle rhythmic figures.

The following articles deal with subjects cognate to that of the present one: *Song*; *Folk Song*; *Scales*; *Modes*; *Cadence*; *Sequence*; *Phrasing*; *Bird Music*; *Fioritura*.

MÉLOPÉE (Fr.). 'Melopoeia' (the art of composing songs; the musical side of dramatic art); the term covers declamatory song, recitative, etc.

MELOPHONE. See *Reed-Organ Family* 6.

MÊME (Fr.). 'Same', e.g. *Même mouvement*, same speed.

MEMORY IN MUSIC

1. Memory as a Basis of all Musical Activity. It is obvious that the whole of musical composition, performance, and enjoyment depends upon memory. The Composer could not write with effect the simplest passage if he had not before heard at least the units of the progression of which it is made up and could not subconsciously recall them so as to imagine them in their new relationships. The Performer likewise is directed by his memory of music previously heard or performed which that before him resembles or from which, in some degree, it differs. The enjoyment of the Listener in even the simplest composition is conditioned by his familiarity with (i.e. his remembrance of) similar melodic and harmonic passages, based on the same tonal relationships (i.e. key-material): it is not even possible to hum a tune without calling for an exercise of memory, since no note will be correctly sounded in pitch and in rhythm unless its immediate predecessors in the tune are kept in mind. Musical memory, then, lies at the base of every musical activity.

2. All Memory implies Association. The one indispensable tool of memory is 'Association'. Nothing in music or elsewhere can be remembered where there is not some previous memory to which it can (consciously or subconsciously) be attached—by similarity, contrast, or some other factor. The mind is as a large room with its walls covered with hooks but with no floor. What is merely thrown in falls through; what has a hook provided for it, and catches upon it, remains. When the teacher gives the pupil something that he cannot retain

it is because he has gone beyond the supply of hooks or has failed to avail himself of their presence. There may be individuals who seem to be capable of assimilating disconnected facts, but that the facts are disconnected is an illusion based on the connexion being overlooked; we may take it that the *subconsciousness* of these individuals is so expert in finding appropriate 'hooks' as not to need to inform the *conscious* of what it is doing. Some can even memorize a page of the dictionary—and if it baffles others it is precisely because of the difficulty they experience in creating 'associations'.

Associations may be *visual*, arising from similarities or observed differences of appearance, or may be *significant*, arising from similarity or difference of meaning. In order to remember with security most of us need to bring the new facts into some sort of relationship both to each other and to facts already known; they then help one another, on the principle of 'united we stand; divided we fall'.

The above principle is that upon which all general or musical systems of 'Memory Training' are founded.

Certain people, sometimes not good musicians in any other way, possess a natural musical memory so perfect that nothing ever leaks from it. After hearing a piece of music they can sit down at the piano and correctly repeat it (though not usually so entirely correctly as they imagine, perhaps). Probably such people will do well not to attempt to analyse their gift—not to render conscious what is at present subconscious. Others can cultivate memory by conscious processes, gradually relegating these

1. JOHN WESLEY (centre) in the streets of Edinburgh, 1790

2. CITY ROAD CHAPEL, London, in 1786
See *Methodism* 4, 8

4. FROM 'SACRED HARMONY', 1821, by Charles Wesley, junior
See *Methodism* 2, near end

3. CHARLES WESLEY—author of over 6,000 hymns

5. ONE OF WESLEY'S PREACHERS—JOHN BEAUMONT. See *Methodism* 6. He is seen in the chapel at Newark

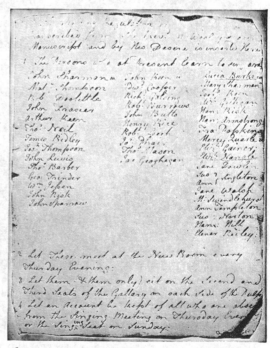

6. JOHN WESLEY'S 'RULES FOR THE SINGERS' at Dublin

PLATE 109

THE MILITARY BAND

See the Article on pages 638–9

2. MUSICIANS OF THE KING'S GUARD
France, 18th century

1. ROMAN BUCCINA (with straight support resting on shoulder)

3. BANDMASTER, ROYAL MARINES (1830); he holds an oboe

4. MILITARY BAND OF LATE 18TH CENTURY (before St. James's Palace, London)

5. A NEW ZEALAND MILITARY BAND

to the subconsciousness—which is the method of all education, from learning to walk onwards.

3. Three Forms of Association in Piano Performance. In order to cultivate a memory for piano performance (to take an example) three forms of observation should be applied so that three forms of association may be set up: (*a*) observation of the *manual processes* involved, the 'feel' of the passage, the length of a leap, and so forth; (*b*) observation of the *look* of the music as printed; and (*c*) observation of the constructional features of the music (melodic, harmonic, and formal).

The first two forms of observation come so naturally to many people that they depend almost entirely on one or both of them when memorizing and do not consciously apply (*c*).

Memory resulting from the first form of observation we may call **Tactile Memory**. It depends on a habit. Once the limbs or fingers have become accustomed to going through any series of actions in a stated order they have only to perform the first of these actions for the rest to follow automatically, each provoking the next one. Thus a man who is accustomed to take a certain route to business every morning may intend on some occasion to deviate from it, but unless he consciously checks himself (breaks the association) at the point where he should take a turn in the unaccustomed direction his legs will carry him along the usual route.

Memory resulting from the second form of observation may be called **Visual Memory**. We all possess it in some degree, or we could not recognize one another; many of us, wishing to know how a word is spelt, have to write it in two or more ways to see which 'looks right'. Musicians sometimes have this form of memory so strongly developed that in playing or conducting without score they involuntarily 'see' each page before them and in imagination turn it at the right moment.

Memory resulting from the third form of observation, i.e. **Analytical Memory,** is probably the most susceptible of conscious cultivation. It demands a certain theoretical knowledge and skill in formal and harmonic analysis. The repetition of a passage (changed or unchanged as to key, etc.) is then recognized, whilst the underlying harmonies, often surprisingly simple, are seen as the canvas upon which the melodic or contrapuntal pattern has been embroidered. Certain formulae (scales, arpeggios, broken chords, etc.) are welcomed as familar by a glance similar to that by which we take in a word without needing to see its separate letters, or even a phrase without needing to see its separate words. This form of observation is, for most players, equally a basis of secure memory and of good sight-reading.

Probably one of the most useful subsidiary labours for a pianist who wishes to cultivate the memory is to practise the playing, without copy, of harmonic progressions heard—as, for instance, simple songs and hymn tunes of which the customary harmonies are familiar to him. He may not attain the proficiency of Mozart and Mendelssohn, both of whom, when young, wrote down Allegri's celebrated *Miserere* after hearing it at St. Peter's at Rome, but every degree of ability gained will prove a help to memorizing. Sir Frederick Gore Ouseley once played Beethoven's Septet on the piano, stating the instruments to which each passage was assigned, and this after only two hearings of it, one of them ten years before (and never having seen the score).

4. The Obstacle of Self-consciousness. It should be borne in mind that conscious effort is apt to defeat memory. If we are suddenly asked for a name, and *try* to recall it, it often only the more eludes us, so that in order to recall it we have to turn to some other thought, when, after a time, the subconscious produces the missing fact without our conscious volition. Unselfconsciousness should be cultivated. If one can play a particular piece from memory when practising by oneself one can play it with an audience of a single familiar friend; if one can play it with that audience one can play it with an audience of six or a dozen or a thousand. The player and the music being the same, there is no more real difficulty in playing the piece in public than in playing it in private, and if a difficulty supervenes that is merely the result of 'bad suggestion'. The player imagines himself failing, and then does so; if he took success as a matter of course he would succeed.

The remedy for fear of the future moment is concentration on the present one. Matthay (*On Memorizing*) relates the following:

'At one of our private concert meetings one of the performers broke down after playing about 16 bars. She then started again and broke down after playing only eight bars. Again she tried, and again stopped herself, after four bars now. Finally, after being urged to play again, she was only able to play the first four notes. I then pulled her together by speaking to her from the audience, saying: "Do not *try* to remember, but just think the music, and let the music take you along." She then started once more and quite successfully played the same little Purcell piece to the end, without hesitation. She had been *preventing* the natural memory-action of her mind, and *stopping* it by asking herself: "What is the next note?" '

To this may be added that the cultivation of the habit of thinking of the music and not of the audience will automatically cure all stage-fright and most memory-failure.

Old-fashioned pianoforte teachers used to discourage playing from memory as tending to incorrectness. Nowadays some teachers are actually carrying their child pupils to a certain point of advancement before they trouble them with notation, and this is probably psychologically right, if only on the principle, 'the thing first and then the sign'. Students so started tend to take dependence on memory as a matter of course.

5. Anomalies in the Customs of the Day. There are some curious anomalies in current practice. Pianists now almost invariably play from memory (not in every case to the advantage of the music); organists rarely do so. Solo vocalists show their ability to memorize in opera yet generally use a copy of the music in oratorio. Choralists rarely memorize, though experience shows that many of them can easily do so and that this brings a great gain in increased attention to the conductor; orchestral players practically always have the music before them. Solo string players always play from memory, but when they combine into a trio or quartet they use music copies: even a pianist and a violinist playing a sonata will use notes, although in playing a mere solo with or without piano accompaniment the violinist would not do so and in playing a pianoforte solo the pianist almost certainly would not, nor in playing a concerto!

In fact, a code of somewhat too tyrannical convention has come into existence. It has undoubtedly a tendency to restrict the repertory —players to whom secure memorizing is not natural or easy preferring to repeat the classics that already form a part of their stock-in-trade rather than to learn by heart new works which they may not in future be frequently called upon to perform.

6. Orchestral Conductors and Players. Orchestral conductors sometimes conduct without score, and probably most experienced orchestral players could go through the regular repertory without parts, although, as above mentioned, they rarely do so. C. Egerton Lowe recorded:

'When I was in Leipzig (1878–1882) Dr. Hans von Bülow brought his Meiningen orchestra on one occasion, and gave a concert to "avenge" an indifferent performance of a Brahms Symphony at the Gewandhaus, under Reinecke. The programme was the *Leonora* Overture, No. 3, and the Seventh Symphony in A (Beethoven) and the Pianoforte Concerto in D minor and the Second Symphony in D (Brahms). Bülow played the Concerto. Not a single music-stand or sheet of music was on the platform during the whole performance. I was present on the occasion, and this is the only time I know when a whole orchestra played an evening's programme from memory.'

A good deal of memory conducting is, however, alleged to be mere swank. A good orchestra will not allow its performance to be wrecked by a conductor's slips—and any member of such an orchestra can, in moments of candour, tell strange tales!

7. Von Bülow and Others. Von Bülow's musical memory may be called perfect. Beringer records hearing him one evening play nearly the whole of Brahms's piano works from memory. On his first American tour he gave 139 concerts without looking at the printed page. On his second American tour he occupied sixteen consecutive evenings by playing from memory every one of Beethoven's piano works. Bülow once memorized Stanford's 'Irish' Symphony in the train between Hamburg and Berlin and then conducted it without score at a

concert of the Berlin Philharmonic Society. On one occasion, when he was to give a piano recital at Brighton, he discovered that it was Sterndale Bennett's birthday. In the morning, before setting out from London, he went to a music shop, asked for some music of Bennett's, was given the *Three Musical Sketches*, memorized these in the train, and played them without ever having heard them. The first performance of Wagner's *Tristan and Isolde* was conducted by Bülow at Munich in 1865, entirely without the score.

In Bülow's day the practice of playing without music copy was still new and provoked remark. Even as late as the early 1870s the London *Daily Telegraph* critic could acidly remark, 'He plays without the book and the public act as if an astounding memory demonstrated astounding musical capacity'. When Hallé, in London in 1861, set out to play the whole of the Beethoven piano sonatas the adverse criticism of *The Times* at his daring to do this without book led to his placing the music on the desk from the third recital onwards—but he continued to play from memory. One of the first pianists to play from memory in London was Arabella Goddard (1836–1922) in the 1850s; however, when playing with orchestra she always used notes (Clara Schumann, who was before the public for sixty years from 1828, also always used notes when playing with orchestra, even in her husband's concerto). Rubinstein's wonderful memory weakened after his fiftieth year (sometimes with catastrophic result), yet some time after this he gave in various cities of Europe his famous series of seven historical recitals, with programmes taking in examples from Byrd to that day, and did this without music. Tausig could play from memory any piece of value in the whole pianoforte repertory. Brahms could play Bach and Beethoven complete, Moriz Rosenthal could play all Chopin from memory, and Harold Samuel could play all Bach.

Sir Walter Parratt, organist of St. George's Chapel, Windsor Castle, once successfully played at chess, and without seeing the board, two other players in consultation, meantime performing continuously on the piano, from memory, compositions asked for from Bach, Mozart, Beethoven, Mendelssohn, or Chopin. Memory came naturally to him; at ten he was able to play without book the whole of Bach's '48'.

One of the most remarkable cases of musical memory on record is that of the Negro 'Blind Tom', who was an idiot and incapable of reading a note of music, yet in the 1850s–60s travelled America playing from memory programmes made up of anything he had once heard. (For another remarkable case of the memorizing of music heard, see under *Stanley*.)

But all these wonderful doings dwindle in importance when one comes across the record of Mr. Napoleon Bird, barber of Stockport, Cheshire, who in 1894 won the World's Record for what has been called 'Pianofortitude' by publicly playing for forty-four hours without repeating a composition; from 11 p.m. to 3 a.m. he played dance music for hundreds of couples, and, during the subsequent forty hours, whenever any vocalist or instrumentalist appeared and asked to be accompanied, the mere statement of the title of the piece and the key required were sufficient.

8. Mozart and Others. A curious case of a concerted composition that, for the most part, existed at its first performance only in the mind of its composer is that of Mozart's Sonata for pianoforte and violin in B flat (Köchel Catalogue 454). This was composed in Vienna at the request of an Italian woman violinist, Signora Strinasacchi, on the night before she was to play before the Emperor. Mozart wrote her out the violin part, so that she could practise it on the morning of the concert, and it was publicly performed by the composer and her without rehearsal. The Emperor, having watched the performance through his opera glasses, sent for the piano part and found it to be a sheet of mere blank manuscript paper. (A living composer to whom this article has been shown says that he has several times done the same thing; he regards it as no extraordinary feat.) Many of Mozart's orchestral compositions had originally no parts for the brass instruments: when these were wanted he wrote them, on a separate sheet of paper without reference to the score.

It has been stated that the first published pianoforte score of Haydn's *Creation* was made by a Vienna musician who had merely heard the work several times and had no other help to his memory than a copy of the book of words. This was Clement, conductor of the Theatre 'An der Wien'; his arrangement was published with Haydn's approval.

There appear to be no limits to the musical memory and where in a particular individual the faculty seems to be at all narrowly limited, that individual would do well to assure himself that he is not either allowing it to rust for want of exercise or (a very probable explanation) inhibiting it by fear.

9. A Practical Hint. Inasmuch as the subconscious plays an important part in memory and as it never sleeps, but, on the contrary, works most actively when the conscious mind is at rest, it is probable that last thing at night is a good time for playing over what one desires to remember. There is an unexpectedly early hint of this device in Moritz's autobiographical novel *Anton Reiser*, published in 1785. Speaking of the learning of certain Latin exercises he says:

'This he always did in the evening before going to sleep, and in the morning when he awoke he found the ideas far better and more clearly arranged in his memory than the evening before, as though his mind had continued to work during sleep and had completed at leisure what it had once begun, during the whole time his body was at rest. Everything that Reiser committed to memory he used to learn by heart in this way.'

This is in accordance with modern psychological teaching and could certainly be applied to musical study.

For memory as an ingredient in the appreciation of music see *Melody* 7.

For Musical Memory Contests see *United States of America* 5.

MEN (It.). Same as *Meno*, 'less'.

MENC. See *Education* 3.

MENDEL, HERMANN (1834–76). See references under *Chorale*; *Dictionaries* 1.

MENDELSSOHN, FELIX (in full Jacob Ludwig Felix) (p. 400, pl. **69.** 2). Born at Hamburg in 1809 and died at Leipzig in 1847, aged thirty-eight. He, Chopin, and Schumann (these two born the following year), make up the trinity of early nineteenth-century romanticism of the less expansive (see *Berlioz* and *Liszt*) and non-theatrical type (see *Wagner*). His music is charmingly written but never very deep, sometimes extremely beautiful and occasionally facile and commonplace.

He was the grandson of the philosopher, Moses Mendelssohn, and the son of a cultured and prosperous banker; the grade of society to which he belonged, then, was that of educated people in easy circumstances.

His genius declared itself early and was quickly recognized. He had sound teaching under the great Berlin teacher, Zelter, and as a boy became a friend of the old Goethe. Before he was fifteen years of age he had written as many symphonies, as well as an opera and other things, all later to be discarded.

From twenty to twenty-four he travelled to see the world, becoming a great favourite in England. A little later he became town director of music at Düsseldorf and at a festival there produced his oratorio *St. Paul*. At thirty-six he settled in Leipzig as conductor of the famous Gewandhaus Concerts and director of the Conservatory, of which latter he was the founder (see reference under *Germany* 9). His influence on musical conditions in Germany was throughout admirable, and the mid-nineteenth-century revival of Bach was largely due to him.

At the age of thirty-seven, at the Birmingham Festival, he produced his oratorio *Elijah* and in the next year he died.

He wrote important works in all the forms except opera (in which he left only an early effort and an unfinished later one), and for all the usual instruments and combinations of instruments. He was one of the first to write independent concert-overtures and his *Fingal's Cave* (or *Hebrides*) Overture is a perfect example both of that type and of the romantic temper in music. And he had a genius for the scherzo. In a sense he may be placed amongst the 'classic-romantics', since he used the classical forms and paid great attention to polishing the details of his music *qua* music.

The original name of the family was Mendelssohn and the name 'Bartholdy' was taken by the father when he abandoned Jewry: hence the name Mendelssohn-Bartholdy on many editions of the son's works.

See references as follows: *Germany* 6, 9 a b; *Romantic. Additional Accompaniments*; *Alto Voice*; *Amen*; *Arioso*; *Cantata*; *Chorale*; *Oratorio* 1, 3, 7 (1836–40–46); *Part Song*; *Psalm*; *Venite*.
Bergomask; *Cadenza*; *Chamber Music* 6, *Period III* (1809); *Composition* 5, 9; *Concert* 6, 8; *Concerto* 6 b (1809); *Form* 6; *History* 7; *Improvisation* 3; *Incidental Music*; *Intermezzo* 5; *Leading Motive*; *Melodrama*; *Overture* 6, 8; *Programme Music* 5 d; *Quality* 3; *Saltarello*; *Scherzo*; *Sonata* 9, 10 c d e; *Symphony* 8; *Tarantella* (at end); *Toy Symphony*; *Voluntary* 5 (at end).
Gondola Song; *Last Rose of Summer*; *Lauda Sion*; *Nicknamed* 1 (St. Anne's Fugue), 11; *Song without Words*; *Wedding March*.
Clarinet Family 4 f, 6; *Cornett and Key Bugle Families* 3 d g; *Gramophone* 6; *Harp* 3; *Horn Family* 3; *Organ* 8, 13; *Pianoforte* 20, 22; *Pianoforte Playing* 5, 10.
Jewish 8; *Wales* 4.
Applause 2; *Appreciation* (and cf. *Quality* 7); *Colour and Music* 4; *Conducting* 5; *Criticism* 5; *Memory* 3; *Publishing* 7; *Tempo*; *Whistling*.
Attwood; *Baillot*; *Bennett, Sterndale*; *Cherubini*; *David, Ferdinand*; *Franz*; *Gade*; *Horsley*; *Marx, A. B.*; *Smart, Sir George*; *Wesley, Samuel*; *Zelter*.

MENDELSSOHN QUINTETTE CLUB. See *United States of America* 6.

MENDELSSOHN SCHOLARSHIP. This British benefaction was founded shortly after Mendelssohn's death in 1847, the first holder (Arthur Sullivan) being appointed in 1856. It was originally awarded to a young performer or composer, but is now reserved to the latter. It is awarded biennially and the present (1969) value is £450. The beneficiary may pursue his education either at home or abroad.

MÉNESTREL, MÉNESTREL DE GUERRE, MÉNESTREL DE BOUCHE. See *Minstrels* 1.

MÉNESTRIER AND MÉNESTRANDIE. See *Minstrels* 1.

MENKE, WERNER. See *Trumpet Family* 2 e.

MENNIN, PETER (originally Mennini; p. 1069, pl. **176.** 9). Born in Erie, Pennsylvania, in 1923. He was trained at Oberlin Conservatory and the Eastman School. He taught at the Juilliard School (1947–58) and became director of the Peabody Conservatory; in 1962 he was made president of the Juilliard School. His compositions have won many awards; they are mainly orchestral, and include concertos, seven symphonies, and choral and chamber music.

MENO (It.). 'Less.'

MEN OF HARLECH. See *Wales* 2.

MENOTTI, GIAN CARLO (p. 1069, pl. **176.** 2). Born at Cadigliano, Italy, in 1911, but went to the United States in boyhood, and there studied five years at the Curtis Institute, Philadelphia (later on the staff). In 1947 he was awarded a Guggenheim Fellowship. His compositions include operas which have been performed in New York (some also in London), e.g.; *Amelia goes to the Ball* (1937); *The Island God* (1942); *The Medium* (1946); *The Telephone*

(1947); *The Consul* (1950); *Amahl and the Night Visitors* (1951, see *Broadcasting* 6); *Maria Golovin* (1958); *The Labyrinth* (for television), *The Last Savage* (1963); *Martin's Lie* (1964).

He has retained Italian citizenship, and is the prime mover in the successful annual summer festival at Spoleto.

See *History* 9.

MENSURAL MUSIC, or 'Cantus Mensuratus'. See *Plainsong* 1.

MENTER, SOPHIE. See *Popper*.

MENUET, MENUETT, MENUETTO (this last common spelling being incorrect). See *Minuet*.

MENUHIN, YEHUDI. Born in New York in 1916; début as violinist 1924. See reference under *Enesco*.

MERBECKE (or **Merbeck**, or **Marbeck**), JOHN. Born in Windsor about 1510 and died about 1585. He was organist of St. George's Chapel, Windsor Castle, and in the reign of Henry VIII, having embraced the doctrines of Calvin, he was condemned to be burnt as a heretic, but pardoned (it is said on account of his musical abilities) and allowed to return to his organ stool. He figures interestingly in Foxe's *Martyrs*, but as Foxe had drawn the account of the proceedings from the heretic himself he should not have made the slip (as he did in the first edition) of describing his actual death at the stake.

He published the first Concordance of the whole English Bible, and a number of theological and controversial volumes, and, more to the point so far as a musical work of reference is concerned, *The Booke of Common Praier Noted* (see *Common Prayer*; *Plainsong* 4; *Responses*). This latter is an adaptation to the prayer book of Edward VI of the music of the Roman ritual, and subtly modifies the plainsong, according to the requirements of the accentuation of the English language, as well as introducing some original music in the plainsong idiom (p. 816, pl. **139.** 5, 6). His system has latterly been much revived in the Office of Communion, and his contrapuntal church music (a five-part Mass and some Latin motets) has come into some use again.

See *Tallis*.

MERCADANTE, GIUSEPPE SAVERIO RAFFAELE (the Christian name is sometimes stated as 'Francesco Saverio', or simply 'Saverio'). Born at Altamura, in South Italy, in 1795, and died at Naples in 1870, aged seventy-five. He was a composer of European reputation, living in turn in most of the chief cities of Italy, in Madrid, Lisbon, Paris, and Vienna, and directing the performance of his operas. His orchestral and other instrumental works earned for him the title of 'the Italian Beethoven'.

See reference under *Spain* 10.

'MERCURY' ('MERKUR') SYMPHONY (Haydn). See *Nicknamed Compositions* 11.

MERIKANTO, Father and Son.

(1) OSKAR. Born at Helsinki, Finland, in 1868, and died there in 1924, aged fifty-five. He studied in Germany and then established himself in his native city as organist and, later, opera conductor. He composed a number of operas (including some of the popular comic opera class) and other works.

(2) AARRE. Born and died at Helsinki (1893–1958; aged sixty-five). He composed orchestral and piano works and was Professor of composition at the Helsinki Conservatory from 1951.

MERKEL, GUSTAV. Born near Bautzen, in Germany, in 1827 and died at Dresden in 1885, aged nearly fifty-eight. He was a fine organist and wrote organ works that remain in use.

'MERKUR' SYMPHONY (Haydn). See *Nicknamed Compositions* 11.

MERLIN, JOSEPH. Famous late eighteenth-century London piano-maker and man of mechanical ingenuity in various fields. See *Pianoforte* 5, 15, 21.

MERLINE. See *Mechanical Music* 6.

MERRY WIDOW. See *Lehár*.

MERRY WIVES OF WINDSOR. See *Nicolai*.

MERSENNE (or **Mersennus**), MARIN (p. 389, pl. **66.** 1). Born in Maine, France, in 1588 and died in Paris in 1648, aged near sixty. He was a theologian, philosopher, mathematician, and musician, who wrote a number of books on musical theory, of which the *Harmonie Universelle* (1636–7) is greatly valued by musicologists today for the information it conveys on contemporary instruments. (Cf. *Oboe Family* 2; *Cornett Family* 3 d; *Jew's Harp*; *Temperament* 5.)

MERULO, CLAUDIO (1533–1604). Famous organist of St. Mark's, Venice (later of Mantua and of Parma), composer of organ music, motets, and madrigals, and music publisher. See reference under *Competitions* 1.

MESSA DI VOCE. This does not mean (as young students have quite naturally sometimes thought) a 'Sung Mass', nor has it anything whatever to do with 'Mezza Voce' (q.v.).

The term was greatly used by Italian singing-masters of the eighteenth century (the palmy days of Bel Canto, q.v.) and is still used by their successors in all countries. It means literally a 'placing of the voice', and actually a crescendo-plus-diminuendo on a long-held note. It was considered in the eighteenth century to be both one of the best means of exercising and gaining control of the voice and one of the greatest beauties in vocal performance; every long note (irrespective of the sense of the words) was expected to bear a *messa di voce*. See references under *Singing* 4, 6; also under *Aria*—description of 'Aria di Portamento'.

Burney, speaking of Farinelli's visit to London in 1734, says: 'In the famous air *Son qual nave*, which was composed by his brother, the first note he sung was taken with such delicacy, swelled by minute degrees to such an amazing volume, and afterwards diminished in the same manner to a mere point, that it was applauded for full five minutes.' (For the eighteenth-century custom of interrupting a song in such a way see *Applause* 3.)

Cf. *Filar la voce*.

MESSAGER, ANDRÉ CHARLES PROSPER (p. 384, pl. **63.** 5). Born at Montluçon, in central France, in 1853 and died in Paris in 1929, aged seventy-five. He was a pupil of Saint-Saëns who early carried off many public honours and then endeared himself to a large public by light-handed operas and operettas.

Amongst these are *La Béarnaise* (his first outstanding success, performed in both Paris and London in 1885), *La Basoche* (1890), *Madame Chrysanthème* (1893), *Mirette* (written for the Savoy Theatre, London, 1894), *Les P'tites Michu* (1897), *Véronique* (1898), and *Monsieur Beaucaire* (also written for England, 1919).

He had a high reputation as a stage conductor and for five years (1901–6) was in general charge of the music and stage management at Covent Garden, which post was followed by a similar one at the Paris Opéra.

He married an Englishwoman, the song composer Hope Temple (d. 1938), but they separated. In 1918 he toured the United States and Canada with an orchestra.

The *Pelléas and Mélisande* of Debussy was dedicated to him and he was its first conductor.

Cf. *Opera* 11 d.

MESSA PER I DEFUNTI (It.), **MESSE DES MORTS** (Fr.). Requiem Mass (see *Requiem*).

MESSE DU PREMIER TON (Fr.). See *Mass* 5.

MESSIAEN, OLIVIER EUGÈNE PROSPER CHARLES (p. 388, pl. **65.** 5). Born at Avignon in 1908. He studied at the Paris Conservatory under Dukas and Dupré. He became a professor of the Schola Cantorum (see *d'Indy*; *France* 10) and later of the Conservatory. In 1931 he was appointed organist of the church of the Holy Trinity. He is a religious mystic of the extremest type, his works (choral, organ, and orchestral) reflecting this, as they do also his highly personal theories on the methods of composition (explained in two volumes entitled *Technique de mon langage musical*, 1947). He has had a strong influence on some of his younger colleagues.

See *Jeune France*; *History* 9; *Bird Music*.

MESSIAH. See *Oratorio* 5; *Overture* 1; *Arne, Michael*; *Carols*; *Ireland* 6; *Hallelujah Chorus*.

MESSING (Ger.). 'Brass.' So *Messinginstrumente*, 'brass instruments'.

MESSINGS. (Horn players.) See *Horn Family* 3 (second paragraph).

MESSNER, CHR. See *Reed-Organ Family* 3.

MESTO (It.). 'Mournful', sad. So *Mestizia*, 'sadness'.

MESURE (Fr.). (1) Measure, bar. (2) Time; e.g.
À la mesure = A tempo. Mesuré, In time.

METÀ (It.). 'Half.'

METALLIC COMB INSTRUMENT. See
Mechanical Reproduction of Music 7.

METAMORPHOSIS OF THEMES. The
nature of this process in composition (especially
in that of the symphonic poem) is briefly described under *Liszt.*

It has, with the twentieth-century decline of
Programme Music (q.v.), suffered some diminution of popularity, but for a time a new use for
it came about through the use of the organ in
the cinema ('Movie'). The following remarks on
a type of extemporization are an extract from
How to Play the Cinema Organ, by Dr. George
Tootell:

'In "metamorphosis of themes" the player will
either devise variants of the theme itself, or utilise
portions which lend themselves to development,
such metamorphoses being designed in accordance
with the characteristics of the scene portrayed, or
the ideas suggested on the screen; and in this the
organist must bring to bear upon his work all his
ingenuity in melodic interest and harmonic contrast, remembering that effect is not obtained by
melodic means alone, but frequently (if not more
frequently) by harmonic designs and decoration.
The more extensive his knowledge of harmony and
counterpoint, the more effective his variants of the
theme become, and the more he can develop and
extend them. Such a player will never feel at a loss
as to what course to pursue, and can always find
means by which to express an idea.'

Liszt anticipated this. He composed, we
may say, to an imaginary film.

Cf. *Leading Motif* and see the mention of 'Idée fixe'
under *Berlioz.*

METASTASIO, The Abbé—real name
Pietro Trapassi (p. 704, pl. **117.** 3). Born in
Rome in 1698 and died in Vienna in 1782, aged
eighty-four. He was a grocer's son who, being
heard at the age of eleven publicly improvising
verses in the street (see *Improvisatore*), was
adopted and educated by a wealthy man of
learning, Gravina, who later left him a fortune.

He now climbed rapidly, devoting himself
particularly to the provision of texts for music,
and becoming the most celebrated librettist in
Europe—almost The Librettist, for his dramas
were universally accepted as the perfection of
their kind, some of them being set by twenty
or thirty different composers, so that their
every word was known in advance to the
audiences of the day, as regular church-goers
know their book of prayers. Gluck, Handel,
Haydn, and Mozart were amongst his clients.
Hasse set all his libretti once and some twice.

His poetical works other than those for music
were translated into many languages. For over
half a century he lived in Vienna as court poet'

See references under *Italy* 5; *Opera* 9 bc, 17a;
Libretto; *Composition* 10; *Oratorio* 2; *Passion Music* 6;
Improvisatore.

METER. The American spelling of *Metre* (q.v.).

METHODISM AND MUSIC

1. Introductory. The Methodist movement of the eighteenth century has had considerable influence on musical culture amongst
the masses and especially, for a long period, on
the more congregational part of the church
music of the English religious bodies. And
some of the hymns the movement produced
are still amongst the most loved by the whole
of the Protestant English-speaking peoples of
the world (of which the Methodists have long
formed the largest body).

There is some reason for considering the
founders of Methodism as being, in some fair
degree, musical. Both John and Charles Wesley
showed a considerable appreciation of music.
John Wesley (p. 624, pl. **108.** 1) was friendly
with Pepusch, the famous theorist and arranger
of the music in *The Beggar's Opera,* and enjoyed conversation with him about music.
Charles Wesley (p. 624, pl. **108.** 3) had two
sons who were child prodigies as musicians,
and who attained eminence (the one temporary
eminence and the other permanent). As youths
Charles Wesley junior (q.v.) and Samuel

Wesley (q.v.), from 1779 to 1785, gave annual
series of subscription concerts at their father's
house in Marylebone, attended by the titled
rank and fashion of the day; the Lord Mayor
of London was a subscriber, so was the Bishop
of London, and the Archbishop of Canterbury
is known to have been present on occasion.
Charles became organist of various London
churches; Samuel Wesley (q.v.; p. 209, pl. **41**)
is now remembered as the composer of the
magnificent eight-voice motet *In Exitu Israel,*
as the first prominent champion of Bach, and
as the father of Samuel Sebastian Wesley (q.v.).
Another relative, and constant attendant at
these concerts and habitué of the Wesley home,
was the composer, Garrett Colley Wellesley,
afterwards Earl of Mornington (see *Mornington*)
and Professor of Music at Dublin University.

For a slight further treatment of the subject of the
Wesleys and music see *Puritans* 9; see also allusion to
Moravian influence under *Bohemia.* And see also the
article *Wesley Family.*

2. The Methodists a Singing People.
The general recognition of the high reputation

for singing which the Methodist body obtained is seen in a letter of the Archbishop of Canterbury in the 1760s, commending the design of a country clergyman to bring out a new psalm and hymn book with tunes: 'Something must be done', he said, 'to put our psalmody on a better footing; the Sectarists gain a multitude of followers by their better singing.'

Such expressions as these become exceedingly common towards the end of the eighteenth century. The Revd. Dr. Dodd, Chaplain-in-Ordinary to George III, in alluding to Methodist singing in 1769, urged that 'it is lawful to learn even from an enemy'. And if (since he later, despite Dr. Johnson's efforts, came to be hanged for forgery) he is not to be counted, we may cite Dr. Miller, the celebrated organist of Doncaster Parish Church, in *Thoughts on the Present Performance of Psalmody addressed to the Clergy*—who makes comparison between Anglican and Methodist singing, much to the disadvantage of the former. It seems certain, from the frequency of such allusions, that the example of the Methodists must have had an influence in promoting a better standard in the music of the Established Church.

The fondness of the Methodists for singing led to their Cornish nickname of 'the Canorum'; a title that may have been given them in the first instance by some classically educated clergyman, or more likely is derived from the Cornish 'canor', a singer.

East Anglia, too, looked on the Methodists as a singing people. *A Letter to a Country Gentleman on the Subject of Methodism* (Ipswich, 1805), by a clergyman, condemns the practice of hymn-singing in the home, as 'injurious to the domestic economy of the poor':

'The labourer of this class returns from his day's work nearly exhausted with it; but instead of taking the rest so much wanted, in the chimney corner, he immediately takes his wife and children from the wheel and other useful employments in the house; which is not unfrequently kept up at the expense of fire and candle to an unseasonable hour. I have often heard this singing in some of our poorest cottages at so late an hour as nine, and sometimes later of a winter's evening.'

The first Methodist tune book was one published by John Wesley in 1742 (see *Hymns and Hymn Tunes* 6); it gave melodies without harmonies, and these so notated as to show that the founder of Methodism, however naturally musical, was completely lacking in technical knowledge of the art. It was sold at 3*d*. Other and better books were later issued—always at low prices, so as to be within the reach of all. Handel, about 1750, wrote three tunes for the Methodists (see *Hymns and Hymn Tunes* 6). Battishill (q.v.) and Lampe (q.v.) were other composers of tunes for the Methodists. Charles Wesley, junior, in 1821 prepared for the Methodist authorities a new edition of John Wesley's tune book of 1789, *Sacred Harmony* (p. 624, pl. **108**. 4). His greater brother, Samuel, took pride in disinterring in the Fitzwilliam

Museum, Cambridge, in 1826, Handel's Methodist tunes, and, two years later, published at his own expense, at the Methodist Conference Office, a set of *Original Hymn Tunes, adapted to every metre in the Collection of the John Wesley*.

3. The 'Old Methodist Tunes'. The present-day demand by the leaders of Anglican church music for non-syllabic tunes and varieties of rhythm was anticipated by the eighteenth-century Methodists and others who came under their influence. Many of the Methodist tunes of that century and the early years of the following one are extremely florid; others are of a 'fugueing' type (cf. *Reports*), but not to the extent of obscuring the words; no doubt the popularity of Handel's choruses was reflected in this type of tune. The last line of the words was often repeated in such a way as to be taken up by the men and women in succession and then by both together. Some tunes have a section for two vocal parts only, with an instrumental bass; others have a chorus after each verse or a Hallelujah refrain extending to twenty, thirty, or even forty measures. Tunes of this type are often spoken of today (for some of them are still in a degree of use) as 'the Old Methodist Tunes', but they were by no means exclusively Methodist in origin and certainly not in the places of their use. *Parochial Music Corrected* (1762), by William Riley, a parish clerk, complained that Anglican admiration of the Methodists' singing was going so far that their tunes were 'creeping into the Churches', and alleged that on certain occasions Anglican congregations would 'pay the Clerk and Organist to stay away, that two of their people may supply their places; by which Means they have every Thing performed in their own Way'.

The remarkable variety of metres in the hymns of the Wesleys lent itself to bright rhythms and was probably felt as a relief by such Church of England congregations as had been brought up on the prevalent common-metre of Sternhold and Hopkins. This variety of metres may to some extent have arisen from the Wesleys' associations with the Moravians and experiences of the German chorale tunes (see *Choral or Chorale*), which, likewise, are much more varied than the tunes current in England when the Methodist movement began, i.e. those sung to the 'Old Version' and 'New Version' of the Psalms (Sternhold and Hopkins; Tate and Brady); John Wesley's copy of Freylinghausen's *Gesangbuch* is still in existence.

The elaborate and almost anthem-like tunes of the period, in which often (as already described) a line of the words was sung by one part and another part of the choir in turn, were evidently in the mind of the Conference of 1796, which decreed—'Let the women constantly sing their parts alone. Let no man sing with them unless he understands the notes and sings the bass as it is pricked down in the book.' Clearly some of the men had been at fault, and in future, if they could not, in their eagerness, bring themselves to remain silent during the singing of the strings of melodious thirds and sixths of the lines allotted to sopranos and contraltos, they were to be allowed to double the instrumental bass part, but that only. (As will be seen later, it was a common arrangement in those days for men and women to occupy different sides of the building.)

John Wesley hated slow and dragging singing. He constantly inveighed against it—'This Drawling Way naturally steals on all who are lazy'. It is not generally remembered that he published (about 1770) a pamphlet, *The Grounds of Vocal Music*. It gives the necessary theoretical instruction and seven 'Lessons for exercising the voice'; whom Wesley employed to compile this is unknown. For the choir at Dublin Wesley wrote a sheet of pretty severe 'Rules for the Singers' (p. 624, pl. **108**. 6).

4. The Use of 'Graces' in Singing. Apparently the eighteenth-century Methodists (like the Anglicans in England and the Presbyterians in Scotland at the same period) were inclined to embroider their tunes with 'graces'. That is probably the meaning of the demand of the Conference (the annual official gathering of preachers) in 1763. The question was asked *'What can be done to make the people sing true?'* And the pointed answer was given, *'Learn to sing true yourselves'*. Two years later the preachers are exhorted to teach the congregation to 'sing by note', which expression, as in New England about the same period (see *Hymns and Hymn Tunes* 11), does not mean to sing at sight, but to keep to the authentic tune, without interpolating shakes and passing notes, and the like. The demands of the Conference on this point were, apparently never continuously complied with, for the precentor of City Road Chapel, London (p. 624, pl. **108**. 2), as late as the 1870s, was able to recall the time when if the melody leapt a third the women invariably added the intervening note, and if it leapt more than a third they glided up or down, *portamento*, then giving the coming note in anticipation (cf. *Presbyterian Church Music* 4). He said that such practices were common until about 1860.

5. Early Methodist Choirs. There are many anecdotes showing that the Methodist preachers of the late eighteenth and early nineteenth centuries had at times as great difficulties with their choirs as had the Anglican clergymen of the period. Both strikes and lock-outs occurred. The scholarly Adam Clarke was troubled on one occasion with a newly formed choir that attended the services but manifested its displeasure at the position allotted to the 'singing pew' by refusing to utter a sound and leaving him to 'raise' the hymns himself: the trustees of the chapel thereupon immediately engaged a precentor and dispensed with the choir. Samuel Bradburn on one occasion announced to the congregation that he had nailed up the door of the singing gallery.

('These fellows . . . shall either conduct the singing in a manner different from what they have done or they shall not conduct it at all.') This celebrated orator probably liked the sound of his own voice better than that of the voices of the singers (unlike John Wesley, who rarely exceeded twenty minutes in a sermon, he was known on occasion to preach for three hours), and in 1803 he stopped a performance of 'The horse and his rider', which was being performed with 'trumpets, horns, violins, hautboys, bassoons, bass viols, and double bass', with the cry, 'Put that horse into his stable; we've had enough of him for today'.

Methodist choirs right up to the end of the nineteenth century, and particularly in the north of England, tended to concentrate a good deal of their energy on the organization of special gala performances. The Conference of 1800 complained of 'Bands of Music and Theatrical Singers being brought into our chapels when charity sermons are preached'. Evidently, the prohibition was not effective, for five years later an anathema was similarly officially thundered against 'Music Festivals, or, they are sometimes called, Selections of Sacred Music, and Pieces, as they are called, in which *recitatives* by single men, *solos* by single women, *fugueing* (or different words sung by different voices at the same time) are introduced'.

6. Early Methodism and Anthems. Wesley's appreciation of a good anthem (provided it was not fugal, so obscuring the words) is evident from a number of entries in his Journal. On several occasions he records the words of the anthem at St. Paul's Cathedral and elsewhere. At Monymusk, near Aberdeen, in 1761, he heard in the Presbyterian Church (see *Presbyterian Church Music* 4) 'thirty or forty sing an anthem after sermon with such voices as well as judgement that I doubt whether they could have been excelled in all England'. Simple anthems were introduced in some of his hymn-tune books, including the then (and long after) highly popular *Vital Spark* of Harwood—a setting of Pope's 'Dying Christian to his Soul'. On one occasion (Bolton, 1787) he says, 'I desired forty or fifty children to come in and sing *Vital spark of heavenly flame*. Although some of them were silent, not being able to sing for tears, yet the harmony was such as I believe could not be equalled in the King's Chapel.'[1]

One of Wesley's preachers, John Beaumont (p. 624, pl. **108**. 5), had as a boy in Yorkshire been brought up as a musician, and was to the end of his days credited with a taste for 'a blood horse and a fine psalm tune'; he published, amongst other things, a book of anthems (1793), avoiding 'fuges [*sic*] where different parts are

[1] The present writer being in his youth (the very last years of the nineteenth century) organist of a village Methodist Chapel in Yorkshire, was called upon to accompany *Vital Spark* on the Sunday following the funeral of any member of the congregation. It is quite possible that this Spark is not yet quite snuffed out.

performing different words at the same time', and was pleased to think (as his preface tells us) that they could thus 'be introduced into any place of worship without shocking the feelings of the most delicate mind'. (One of Beaumont's hymn tunes was included in the 1904 edition of *Hymns Ancient and Modern*; like much of the eighteenth-century Methodist music it is little on paper, or played on a keyboard instrument, but thrilling when thundered in harmony by a large body of voices.)

7. Methodist Orchestras. In the use of orchestral instruments in worship the practice in the Methodist chapels at the very end of the eighteenth century and the early part of the nineteenth was much the same as that of the Anglican Church. Apparently, however, they were not officially approved, for in 1805 the Conference decreed, 'Let no instruments of music be introduced into the singers' seats, except a bass viol, should the principal singer require it'. This exception seems curious today, but it was a common practice in all churches of the seventeenth and eighteenth centuries (on the Continent as well as in England and in Catholicism as well as Protestantism) to strengthen the bass of a choir by the use of the bass viol (i.e. violoncello), the serpent, etc. The bass viol was the first instrument the New England Puritans introduced into their churches.

8. Organs and Voluntaries. The Conference in 1780 said, 'Let no organs be placed anywhere till proposed in Conference', and as late as 1808 refused for the future to 'sanction or consent to the erection of any organs in our chapels', decreeing that where they already existed they were no longer to 'overpower or supersede' the congregational singing. No voluntaries were to be played 'during the time of divine service', which suggests that the Anglican practice of having a long voluntary in the middle of the service (whilst the clergyman was in the vestry changing his gown for the sermon) had somehow spread to Methodism (where no gown-changing justified it). An organ surreptitiously introduced into a Liverpool chapel shortly after was ruthlessly condemned to be taken down again. Another Liverpool chapel, three years later, obtained special permission to install an organ, after a four hours' debate in the Conference on a petition the congregation had submitted; voluntaries were again banned, however, and the organ was to be 'constructed on the simplest plan and with such stops as will assist congregational singing'. In 1820 the Conference met at Liverpool and the meeting-place may have significance as concerns a more tolerant resolution passed that 'in some of the larger chapels, where some instrumental music may be deemed expedient in order to guide the congregational singing, organs may be allowed'. Seven years later (1827) the erection of a very large organ in Brunswick Chapel, Leeds, by the trustees of the Chapel but against the wish of many of the congregation, led to disturbances that spread elsewhere. The Conference supported the trustees, and the affair took on a legalistic colouring as to rights of self-government. Hundreds of adherents left the mother body of Methodism and formed a separate body called the Protestant Methodists, and this put a stop to the erection of organs for some years. The original objection seems, from pamphlets then issued, to have been the old one of the Continental Calvinists and English Puritans, i.e. instruments, as such, were not in the least objected to, but their use in public worship was considered to be unscriptural and inexpedient.

As bearing on the subject of voluntaries, certain words of the founder of Methodism may be recalled. He described the ordinary mid-service voluntary of the Church of England as an 'unreasonable and unmeaning impertinence', as no doubt it usually was, to judge by the published specimens of the English organ music of the period that remain, most of which are so trivial that they would never be tolerated in any place of worship today. (It must be remembered that the whole German repertory was unavailable, as English organs had then no pedals.) Yet of a visit to a church at Manchester in 1751 he says, 'I found an uncommon blessing when I least expected it—namely, while the organist was playing a voluntary', and at a church at Macclesfield, thirty-one years later, whilst helping the resident clergyman to administer the Communion on Good Friday to thirteen hundred persons, he heard a 'low, soft, solemn sound, just like that of an Æolian harp', which 'so affected many that they could not refrain from tears'; and he exclaimed in his diary, 'Strange that no other organist (that I know) should think of this'. He told the organist, 'If I could ensure a similar performance to yours this afternoon I would have an organ introduced into every one of our chapels'. Only three organs were, however, erected in Methodist chapels during Wesley's lifetime—at Bath (the first, about 1780), Keighley, and Newark (about 1790). The Bath organ (which still exists in a developed form) is believed to have been the earliest organ in England in which the old G downward compass was abandoned for the now universal C.

A tiny and not very important puzzle may here be put forward. Although at the time Handel wrote his Methodist hymn tunes (see 2), and for thirty years afterwards, no Methodist place of meeting contained an organ, he yet in one of these tunes (the one known as *Gopsal* and sung today to its original hymn, 'Rejoice, the Lord is King') introduced a tiny three-note interlude between two of the lines. It is true that it is not essential (indeed, many tune books of today, regrettably, omit it). And possibly it implies rather the presence of stringed instruments than of an organ.

No organ was introduced into what may be called the cathedral church of Methodism, City Road Chapel, London (p. 624, pl. **108.** 2), until the 1880s. In the years before 1850 a flute, clarinet, bass viol (i.e. cello), and double-bass were in use, and after that, the players having seceded owing to some dispute, the precentor already mentioned led the singing without instrumental aid.

It is noted that the annual Methodist Conference, although every building in which it meets is now equipped with an organ, still sings unaccompanied at its official meetings. A precentor, chosen from amongst the ministers, starts the tunes and leads the singing most effectively.

9. Whitefield and Music. Whitefield, the quondam associate of the Wesleys, who founded the Calvinistic branch of the Methodist church, as against their Arminian branch, made as great use of psalmody as they. We hear of his journeying from Evesham to Tewkesbury escorted by a hundred horsemen and six thousand people singing psalms and hymns. (An association of ministers at Weymouth in 1745 condemned his practice of 'singing hymns in the public roads when riding from town to town'.) He had studied sight-singing seriously with a party of young singers. He published both a hymn book (1753) and a tune book (1754). Some dialogue hymns are included, adapted to the arrangements of his Tabernacle, where the men occupied one side and the women the other, as was common in those days.

10. The Present Day. Writers in the later nineteenth century gave the impression that Methodist singing had largely fallen off, owing to the dependence on organs and choirs. Doubtless this was so in many places. Refinement had crept in and heartiness had gone out, and the judgement of any critic depended on the respective values he gave to these two qualities. On special occasions, as those of the annual missionary services in that chapel whose erection of an organ once cost the society so many members (see 8), the singing was, then, such as 'to lift the roof off'.

The adaptation of the Book of Common Prayer which John Wesley, to the last a clergyman of the Church of England, made for his congregations is still in use amongst some of them. The singing of canticles and psalms to Anglican chants has now long been common. There is certainly now no Methodist church of any size without an organ, and none at all without some form of keyboard instrument. In 1932 the various Methodist bodies that had at various periods come into existence by fission from the original and largest body all joined with it into one united church.

A society for the advancement of Methodist music, formed in 1934, tries, by conferences of ministers and musicians and in other ways, to bring about the more satisfactory outcome. A new hymn and tune book for the united body was published in 1933.

METNER. See *Medtner*.

METRE is the rhythmic element in poetry. The term covers:

(a) The number of lines in a stanza.
(b) The number of syllables in a line.
(c) The arrangement of the syllables as to accentuation (or in the ancient languages their arrangement as to 'quantity', i.e. relative amount of time involved in the enunciation of the various syllables—the nature of these languages being different from that of the modern languages).

Concerning (a) and (b) something will be seen under *Hymns and Hymn Tunes* 13. Concerning (c) the following succinct statement is offered:

The unit or group in the rhythmic make-up of a poem is called a **Foot**.

A foot consisting of an unaccented syllable plus an accented one (in ancient poetry a short plus a long) is an *Iambus*, and any metre made up of such feet is **Iambic**.

'The *dusk-* | y *night* | rides *down* | the *sky.*'

(All the examples in this article should, of course, be read in their natural rhythm as poetry, uninfluenced by any tunes that may have become attached to them in the reader's mind.)

A foot consisting of an accented syllable plus an unaccented (in ancient poetry a long plus a short) is a *Trochee*, and any metre made up of such feet is **Trochaic**.

'*Jack* and | *Jill* went | *up* the | *hill.*'

A foot consisting of an accented syllable plus two unaccented (in ancient poetry a long plus two shorts) is a *Dactyl*, and any metre so made up is **Dactylic**.

'*Here's* to the | *maiden* of | *bashful* fif- | *teen.*'

A foot consisting of two unaccented syllables with an accented one between them (or in ancient poetry two short with a long between) is an *Amphibrach*, and a metre so made up is **Amphibrachic**.

'Come *cheer* up | my *lads* 'tis | to *glory* | we *steer.*'

A foot consisting of two unaccented syllables plus an accented (or in ancient poetry two shorts and a long) is an *Anapaest*, and a metre so made up is **Anapaestic**.

'There are *hills* | beyond *Pent-* | land and *lands* | beyond *Forth.*'

It will be noticed that the division of a line of poetry into feet is much like the division of a phrase of music into bars, but that, whereas the conventional barring system of music divides the beats into groups each beginning with an accent, the conventional metrical arrangement divides them into groups each beginning *as the line began* (i.e. the first rhythmic unit in the line is taken as the first foot and the others are like it; the system allows of no incomplete feet at the beginning of lines, like the incomplete bars at the beginning of musical phrases). The conception of the metrical foot being very ancient and universally accepted, it is curious (but fortunate) that when, in relatively modern times, a musical barring system began (see *Notation* 4) it was not influenced thereby, but was based on a more rhythmically logical principle.

It must be added that while the poetic metres in use are comprised within the above description an infinitely varied rhythmic variety can be and is superposed on them. For instance, just as in music a bar may have its beats subdivided, so in poetry a foot may have its syllabic arrangements broken into. Two simple examples will suffice:

'*Charlie* | *is* my | *dar-* | *ling*, the | *young* | *Cheva-* | *lier.*'

Here in the third and fifth feet of a trochaic metre a single syllable, by dwelling on it, is made to do duty for two.

'I *come* | down *dah* | wid my *hat* | caved *in.*'

Here in the third foot of an iambic metre two syllables are 'trotted over' in the place of one.

It should be observed that in setting metrical poetry to music there is no obligation on the composer to follow the poet's metrical scheme in its simplest form. He is not compelled to set iambic and trochaic poems in duple time and dactylic, amphibrachic, and anapaestic in triple. The only metrical obligation is that he shall bring the accented syllables of the poetry on to the accented parts of his bars. For modern metre is a matter of accentual (not of quantitative) arrangement.

The whole science of versification is comprised under the term **Prosody.**

For the development of metrical variety by the Troubadours see *Minstrels*, etc. 5.
For *Anacrusis* see entry under that word.

METRE OF BALLADS. See *Ballad* 2.

METRES OF HYMNS. See *Hymns and Hymn Tunes* 13.

METRICAL PSALMS. See *Hymns and Hymn Tunes* 5; *Modes* 5; *Presbyterian* 3.

METRONOME (Fr. *Métronome*; It. *Metronomo*; Ger. *Taktmesser*). An apparatus for fixing tempi. Many different forms of such apparatus have been in use since the first (invented by Loulié in 1696). The commonest form now in use is the clockwork one of Maelzel (1772–1838), for some time the friend of Beethoven, who took much interest in it. (Maelzel, however, seems to have stolen the principle from one Winkel.) It is the often-seen small pyramidal instrument, with a beating rod in front, and sometimes a bell that can be made to strike at every second, third, or fourth beat. From the use of this metronome came the practice of using the letters 'M.M.', as in 'M.M. ♩ = 100', i.e. Maelzel's Metronome set at 100 beats to a minute and each representing a crotchet or quarter-note.

About 1945 a pocket metronome, shaped like a watch, was introduced in Switzerland. Metronomes designed to synchronize irregular rhythms (three against five, and the like), such as are found in much modern music, have also been devised.

Metronome marks, even when they originate with the composer and not merely some editor, are not to be understood as rigidly binding. Brahms said in a letter to Henschel: 'As far as my experience goes every composer who has given metronome marks has sooner or later withdrawn them.' Some of Schumann's marks are almost impossibly fast, suggesting that his own metronome was not in good order.

To practise to a metronome (unless for some quite special purpose) is unnecessary and harmful. The instrument should normally be used only in order to realize the speed at which a composition is intended to be taken. Beyond that one's mental metronome should suffice.

A watch of which one knows the tick-speed (generally 5 per second) can be quite conveniently used as a metronome. William Turner (*Sound Anatomized*, 1724) says that in what we now call 'Alla breve' time the crotchets are 'counted as fast as the regular motions of a watch'—which implies that all watches ticked alike in his day (as they now do not), and that all crotchets had the same value (as they now have not).

In 1756 Bremner, in his *Rudiments of Music*, concerns himself to propagate a method by which 'the Time in all Churches may be equal'. He says that a pendulum 8 feet 8 inches long will by its double vibration suitably fix the length of the semibreve, and tells us that this length was arrived at by experiment 'at a meeting of the *Musical Society* and *Music Masters* in Edinburgh'. He suggests that such a pendulum should be 'hung at the End of all schools where Church music is taught'. Such were the expedients before Maelzel bestowed his convenient contrivance on the waiting world.

In metronomizing one's own compositions (or in testing whether one's speed in other compositions is about right) the most comfortable method is to play naturally for 15 seconds, count up the beats, and multiply by four to bring it to the normal manner of statement.

For some general remarks on the question of speed in performance see *Tempo*.

The metronome has been introduced into composition by the Brazilian composer Villa-Lobos, who in one of his works uses three metronomes ticking at different rates of speed.

See *Loulié* 1.

METROPOLITAN BOPERA HOUSE. See *Jazz* 7.

METROPOLITAN POLICE ACT, 1864. See *Street Music* 7.

METTENLEITER, The brothers, JOHANN GEORG (1812–58), DOMINICUS (1822–68). See *Cecilian Movement*.

METTERE (It.), **METTRE** (Fr.). 'To put'; hence *Mettete il sordino*, 'Put on the mute'. *Mettez* (Fr. imperative) often means 'put into action' an organ stop.

MEYER, (1) B. v.d. SIGTENHORST-. See

Holland 8. (2) CONRAD (of Philadelphia; d. 1881). See *Pianoforte* 9; *Toy Symphony.*

MEYERBEER, GIACOMO, his real name, however, being Jacob Liebmann Beer (p. 397, pl. **68**. 9). Born in Berlin in 1791 and died in Paris in 1864, aged seventy-two. His family resembled that of Mendelssohn, a little later—a wealthy German-Jewish business family. He was a fellow pupil of Weber's under Vogler (q.v.).

His early reputation was as a pianist. Hearing Hummel play the piano he felt humiliated and went for some months into retirement to practise playing and composing for the instrument.

He soon turned to opera, however, and in this branch of composition found his life work. At first he wrote Italian operas and with some success had them performed in Italy. Then he settled in Paris and wrote for the Paris stage in the pageant-like and highly coloured style that it preferred. After a time he was appointed Royal Director of Opera at Berlin and divided his time between the two capitals.

The other romantics looked on Meyerbeer with suspicion. Wagner called him 'a Jew banker who composes music', and Schumann said, 'I place him with Franconi's circus people.' He had, however, great success with his operas *Robert the Devil, The Huguenots, The Prophet, The North Star, Dinorah, L'Africaine*, etc., and he occupies a place of his own from the adoption of an individual method and style. He had high ability and, if vulgar, the courage of his vulgarity; hence he was effective.

See *Opera* 9 c, 11 d, 21 g, 24 d (1836–49); *Singing* 10; *Ballet* 7; *Jewish* 8, 9; *Percussion Family* 4 a (Kettledrums), 4 e; *Viol Family* 4 f; *Halévy*; *Fife*; *Saxophone*; *Grand Opera.*

MEYEROWITZ, JAN. Born at Breslau in 1913. He studied under Zemlinsky in Berlin and under Casella, Respighi, and Molinari in Rome. He went to the U.S.A. in 1946, becoming naturalized in 1951, and taught at Tanglewood and at Brooklyn College. His many compositions include five operas.

MEZZA (It.). 'Half' (fem. of *Mezzo*), e.g. *Mezza voce*, 'Half-voice', i.e. half the vocal (or instrumental) power possible. (Not to be confused with *Messa di voce*; q.v.).

MEZZO (It.). 'Half', e.g. *Mezzo forte*, 'half-loud', i.e. neither loud nor soft.

MEZZO CARATTERE, ARIA DI. See *Aria.*

MEZZO-SOPRANO VOICE. See *Voice* 17.

M.G. = *Main gauche* (Fr.), i.e. 'left hand'.

MI. The third degree of the major scale, according to the system of vocal syllables derived from Guido d'Arezzo (q.v.), and so used (spelt 'Me'; q.v.) in Tonic Sol-fa. In French and Italian use, however, the name has (on 'fixed-doh' principles) become attached to the note E, in whatever scale or other association this may occur (see Table 5).

For another use of 'Mi' see *Lancashire Sol-fa.*

MIASKOVSKY (Miaskowski, Myaskovski, etc.), NICOLAS (p. 913, pl. **156**. 3). Born at Novo-Georgievsk (then in Russia, now in Poland) in 1881 and died at Moscow in 1950. He was born in a fortress, the son of a general in the Russian army, and himself trained for the army, in which he fought from 1914 to 1916. He had had a good musical education at the Conservatory of St. Petersburg under Rimsky-Korsakof and others, and on the conclusion of the War became a professor of composition at the Conservatory of Moscow. He wrote twenty-seven symphonies and some sonatas and other things.

His musical style shows the influences of both Glazunof and Tchaikovsky, and emotionally he approaches the latter in his pessimistic and even neurasthenic outlook—his manner, however, being necessarily more modern (cf. *Russia* 8). See *Kabalevsky.*

MICE, SINGING. See *Singing Mice.*

MICKIEWICZ, ADAM (1798–1855). See *Romantic.*

MICKLE, WILLIAM JULIUS (1734–88). Poet, brewer, purser on a man-of-war, corrector to the press for the publishers of the present work—and other things. See *There's nae luck aboot the hoose.*

MI CONTRA FA. The tritone (q.v.).

MICROCOSM. See *Mechanical Reproduction of Music* 10.

MICROPHONE. See *Broadcasting of Music* 1.

MICROTONES (p. 356, pl. **57**. 5–7) are any intervals smaller than the semitone. During the late nineteenth and the twentieth century a good deal of experimentation has gone on in the use of microtones in composition.

G. A. Behrens-Senegaldens, of Berlin, in 1892, patented a quarter-tone piano and published a pamphlet on quarter-tone music.

The Moravian Aloys Hába has written quarter-tone music for string quartet and for small orchestra, and also for quarter-tone harmonium and quarter-tone piano: in 1931 he produced a quarter-tone opera. He has also used sixth-tones and has published a book on microtonic composition, demonstrating the value of third-, fourth-, sixth-, and twelfth-tones. Some of his orchestration demands the use of quarter-tone clarinets, trumpets, etc. His brother, Karel Hába, has also written microtonal music.

The German R. H. Stein has written for a quarter-tone piano and a quarter-tone clarinet; his earliest quarter-tone music dates from 1906.

The Italian Gnecchi in his opera, *La Rosiera*, and Enesco in his *Œdipe* use occasional quarter-tones.

The Mexican Carrillo has composed music based on quarter-, eighth-, and sixteenth-tones, and has constructed instruments on which to play it and has introduced a special notation; the conductor Stokowski, of Philadelphia, appeared in 1927 as champion of his music (see *Carrillo*).

The Swiss-American composer Ernest Bloch has introduced quarter-tones into the string parts of his piano quintet.

The Englishman J. H. Foulds used quarter-tones. His wife, Maud MacCarthy, the violinist, who had studied Indian music, once broadcast a lecture in which she sang up and down the Hindu scale of twenty-two notes to the octave. The present writer tested her on the piano on starting, on reaching the upper octave, and on returning, and found her perfectly accurate. Dr. Ernest Walker reported that during a lecture at Oxford she performed the same feat, undisturbed by the tolling of Great Tom, the big bell of Christ Church. It is said, however, that Hába went further than this, having brought himself, by assiduous practice, to the point where he can accurately sing five divisions of the semitone, i.e. sixty in the octave. This demonstrates that musicians' ears can be trained to the recognition of microtones, but whether the ears of the general public would ever feel the difference between deliberate microtones and mere out-of-tune performance is another matter.

Dr. Moritz Stoehr of New York built a quarter-tone piano in 1924 (see p. 560, pl. **101.** 3). Quarter-tone harps and guitars have been heard.

The Russian Vyschnegradsky, of Paris, is one of the several inventors of a quarter-tone piano and has written quarter-tone music for string quartet, etc. The Russian Lourié has also composed quarter-tone music. Hans Barth (1897–1956), of New York, made a quarter-tone piano, and in 1930 played a concerto of his own on it with the Philadelphia Orchestra; the American Charles Ives wrote music for Barth's programmes.

This list could be lengthened, but it is enough to show that there has been a good deal of activity in the microtonal field.

It should be remembered that the idea of microtonal composition is far from new. It was apparently much discussed in the seventeenth century in England, for in Christopher Simpson's *Compendium of Practical Musick* (1667) we read, 'I am slow to believe that any good musick (especially in many parts) can be composed in Quarter-Tones, although I hear some talk much of it'.

As early as that the principle of microtones was in some small measure instrumentally recognized. Simpson mentions the 'splitting of some keys in Harpsichords and Organs, as also the placing of a Middle Fret near the Top or Nut of a Viol or Theorbo, where the space is wide'.

But this was merely to provide alternatives (as G sharp and A flat) in the days before equal temperament (see *Temperament* 8).

See further references to Microtones under *Scales* 8; *Tonality*; *Harmony* 19, 23; *Electric Musical Instruments* 1 c, f; *Spain* 1; *Oriental*; *Mager*.

MIDDELSCHULTE, WILHELM. Born in Westphalia in 1863 and died there in 1943. He came to Chicago in his late twenties, and there enjoyed a high reputation as organist and as composer for his instrument—often in a very contrapuntal style.

MIDDLE C. See *Pitch* 7.

MIDDLE REGISTER. See *Voice* 4.

MIDGLEY-WALKER ORGAN. See *Acoustics* 7.

'MIDI' (Symphony of Haydn). See *Nicknamed Compositions* 11 (6–8).

MIESSNER PIANO. See *Electric Musical Instruments* 3 d.

MIGNON. See *Thomas, A.*

MIGOT, GEORGES. He was born in Paris in 1891. He studied with d'Indy and Widor, was wounded in the first World War and for some years was an entire invalid, and slowly (and then but partially) recovered. He has since, as composer, taken a high place in the esteem of many French critics, who praise his technique as remarkable, and claim much originality for his music. He has written orchestral, chamber, choral, piano, and theatre music, and also some small books on musical subjects. He is, further, a competent painter. A strong nationalistic spirit underlies all his activities.

MIHALOVICI, MARCEL. Born at Bucharest, Rumania, in 1898. Like a number of other Rumanian composers he studied with d'Indy in Paris, but later he attached himself to the younger French and Russian group in that city. He has written a good deal of chamber music, a little orchestral music, an opera, and some vivid and forceful ballet music.

See references under *Clarinet Family* 6 (end); *Oboe Family* 6 (end).

MIKADO, THE, or THE TOWN OF TITIPU (Sullivan). Produced at the Savoy Theatre, London, in 1885. Libretto by W. S. Gilbert.

ACT I

SCENE: *Courtyard of the Palace of Ko-Ko, Lord High Executioner of Titipu, in Japan*

Nanki-Poo, son of the Emperor (Mikado), is disguised as a wandering minstrel, in order to seek Yum-Yum, one of Ko-Ko's wards, with whom he is in love. He tells **Pish-Tush,** a nobleman, that though Yum-Yum was betrothed to her guardian when Ko-Ko was a tailor, he has heard that Ko-Ko has been condemned to death for flirting, and so he himself has come back to pursue his suit. But Ko-Ko was reprieved, it seems, and is now that much-to-be-feared personage, the executioner: judge as well, for that is the Mikado's decree—'every judge his own executioner'. **Pooh-Bah,** who tells Nanki-Poo this, is eight high officials rolled into one. Yum-Yum is to wed Ko-Ko today, he adds.

Ko-Ko appears, with his 'little list' of people 'who will none of 'em be missed', and then the 'three little maids from school' come in—his three wards, **Yum-Yum, Pitti-Sing,** and

Peep-Bo. Nanki-Poo, made known by them to Ko-Ko, is quickly dismissed by the lordly one as insignificant.

When Nanki-Poo and Yum-Yum can be alone, he tells her that he is really the Mikado's son, who fled because his father ordered him to wed an elderly lady of the court, Katisha. They kiss, and for the time part.

Ko-Ko is commanded by the Mikado to find somebody to behead within the next month, on pain of losing his post, or even (as he is under sentence of death for flirting) his life. Luckily Nanki-Poo enters, intent on putting an end to *his* existence, because Ko-Ko is to marry the girl he adores. Ko-Ko represents to him the great advantages of being beheaded instead, and Nanki-Poo agrees to be on hand a month hence—if he may marry Yum-Yum tomorrow. At the month-end she will be a widow, ready to marry Ko-Ko. The Executioner is agreeable, and the bargain is struck.

But **Katisha** comes to claim her perjured lover. She tries to tell the crowd that Nanki-Poo is the Mikado's son, but they will not hear her, and she rushes off to have her vengeance by letting the Mikado know that his son is found.

ACT II

SCENE: *Ko-Ko's Garden*

Yum-Yum is preparing for her marriage. She and Nanki-Poo try to forget that they will have only a month of wedded bliss. Ko-Ko makes things worse by informing them that he has now discovered an ancient regulation that when a married man is beheaded his wife is buried alive. Nanki-Poo is in a dilemma: if he marries Yum-Yum, she must die with him. If he does not marry her, Ko-Ko will. He determines to kill himself at once. But this terrifies Ko-Ko, for if Nanki-Poo is not there in a month, the Executioner will be beheaded instead: and the Mikado's coming is announced. Nanki-Poo says, 'Well, behead me now!'; but Ko-Ko is nervous: he dare not try; he cannot kill anything!

Ko-Ko persuades Pooh-Bah to make a false affidavit that Nanki-Poo has been executed, but actually to marry him to Yum-Yum, in order to get him out of the way.

Now the **Mikado** appears with Katisha, bent on being married to the ruler's son. Ko-Ko produces the affidavit of execution. So far all is well. The Mikado is seeking his son, who, Katisha has told him, is going about in disguise. But Katisha has read the affidavit, which the Mikado did not, and it appears that it is the heir to the throne who has been beheaded. The Mikado orders that the punishment for 'compassing the death of the Heir Apparent' shall be carried out. There is nothing in the law about 'accidents'.

The only hope is to bring Nanki-Poo to life again. He has married Yum-Yum, and so cannot marry Katisha, who will certainly then insist on his death, which will involve his wife's. Ko-Ko solves the problem by offering his hand to Katisha, who accepts him; and the end comes with the revelation to the Mikado of his son's being alive and well.

See reference under *Opus.*

MILÁN, LUIS. See S*pain* 8; *Song* 3.

MILANUZZI (or **Milanuz**), **CARLO.** An Augustinian of the early seventeenth century, who held many positions as organist, etc., and composed much church music.

See reference under *Folia.*

MILFORD, ROBIN (p. 353, pl. **56.** 4). Born at Oxford in 1903 and died at Lyme Regis in 1959, aged fifty-six. He was the son of Sir Humphrey Milford, publisher to the Oxford University Press, and studied under Holst, Vaughan Williams, and R. O. Morris, later becoming a schoolmaster. He was a fluent and prolific composer and in an unassuming way an individual one. Besides choral works, such as *A Prophet in the Land* (1930) and *A Pilgrim's Progress* (1932) he wrote much orchestral and chamber music.

MILHAUD, DARIUS (p. 388, pl. **65,** 4). Born at Aix-en-Provence in 1892, and died at Geneva in 1974. He was educated at the Paris Conservatory. When, after the 1914 War, Europe saw six Paris composers momentarily banded together for mutual support he was found amongst them (see *France* 11). His art was then already taking a 'modernist' direction, and he later worked on polytonal lines (see *Harmony* 17). His works are numerous and varied, including chamber and orchestral music, ballets, incidental music to Greek plays, a 'satiric drama', a 'musical novel', symphonies, concertos, etc. Amongst his chamber works are (1949) two string quartets (nos. 14 and 15) which can be played either independently or combined as an octet. From 1922 he spent much time in the United States (from 1940 on the staff of Mills College, California).

He collaborated several times with the mystical poet and dramatist, Claudel, as in the remarkable *Christophe Colomb*, wherein all manner of original stage artifices are employed, and the spoken voice is used by certain characters, with accompaniment either of orchestra or of mere percussion instruments.

See *Harmony* 17; *Ballet* 5; *Concerto* 6 c (1892); *Oratorio* 7 (1947); *Opera* 24 f (1950); *Jazz* 5; *Melodrama*; *Singing Saw*; *Electric Musical Instruments* 1 f; *Saudades*; *Jewish Music* 9; *History* 9; *Harpsichord* 9.

MILIEU (Fr.). 'Middle'; hence *Milieu de l'archet*, 'middle of the bow'—and so forth.

MILITAIRE (Fr.), **MILITARE** (It.), **MILITÄR** (Ger.). 'Military.'

MILITÄRTROMMEL (Ger.). Side drum; see *Percussion Family* 3 i, 4 b, 5 i.

MILITARY BAND (p. 625, pl. **109**). The term is today freely used in Britain either for actual regimental bands or for bands on their model, i.e. comprising both wood-wind and brass instruments.

The history of military music is too long to be told here, but a few leading facts may be mentioned. From earliest times some association between music and military evolutions has been maintained, but in the later seventeenth and eighteenth centuries it became more definite and more organized under the influence of such music-loving warriors as Louis XIV and Frederick the Great.

Louis (reigned 1643–1715) employed Lully (q.v.) to organize his bands and to compose music for them; the bands consisted of hautboys of four sizes (or hautboys of three sizes plus bassoon) and drums. Frederick (reigned 1740–86), coming later, naturally went further; he fixed the constitution of his bands (1763) as two hautboys, two clarinets, two horns, and two bassoons, with, presumably, drums. (It should be remembered that the hautboys of the seventeenth and eighteenth centuries were much louder instruments than the present-day oboes.)

Of British bands of the same period that of the Royal Regiment of Artillery (1762) consisted of two trumpets, two horns, four hautboys (or clarinets; see *Clarinet Family* 2), and two bassoons: the players (it was laid down) were also to be capable of playing stringed instruments, which was a condition common amongst the municipal Waits (q.v.) of the day and one observed in some British and other bands today.

A madness for percussion instruments, shrieking fifes, and other noisy instruments was epidemic throughout Europe during the later years of the eighteenth century, as was also a penchant for a Negro time-beater and for Negro drummers. (The drummers of British military bands still wear leopard skin—a relic of the day when they were Negroes, and often slaves, dressed as exotically as possible.) Music employing these elements was called 'Turkish Music', and both Mozart and Beethoven have left evidence in their works that they had noted its peculiarities—Mozart in a piano sonata and Beethoven in his *Ruins of Athens* music.

The great public fêtes of the French revolutionary and Napoleonic period (from 1789 onwards) greatly favoured band development. Enormous bodies of musicians performed at these fêtes and much music was composed for them. Infantry regiments under Napoleon had bands consisting of one piccolo, one high clarinet and sixteen ordinary clarinets, four bassoons, two serpents, two trumpets and one bass trumpet, four horns, three trombones, two side-drums and one bass drum, one triangle, two pairs of cymbals, and two Turkish crescents, making in all forty-two. The great modern movement in military music dates from this period and from French example. (For brief descriptions of any unfamiliar instruments in the above list see under their own heads in this dictionary.)

During the mid-nineteenth century wind instruments were greatly improved by Sax and others, and this had much influence upon the development of the band and its music.

The composition of a military band is not a fixed thing. It varies in different countries and even in different regiments. As indicating roughly the British standard, the following specification of an ordinary British regimental band may be offered; the number of clarinets will be noted; they have come to be 'the violins of the band': (*a*) piccolo (or flute, or both), oboe, small clarinet, twelve to fourteen ordinary clarinets and two bass clarinets, alto and tenor saxophones, two bassoons; (*b*) four horns, two baritones, two euphoniums and four bombardons; (*c*) four cornets, two trumpets, three trombones; (*d*) two drummers with a variety of instruments of percussion. A stringed double-bass or two is a not unusual alternative to the same number of bass wind-instruments when the conditions of performance permit. American bands differ only in detail from the above general scheme.

The ordinary orchestral notation is used in the military band (not in the brass band, q.v.).

Until the gramophone and radio came to take orchestral music into every home the military band and brass band were the instrumental combinations heard by far and away the biggest and most frequent audiences; yet serious composers have always neglected them and a large part of their repertory has always consisted of either somewhat trivial music specially composed or more valuable music 'arranged' for the combination (cf. *Brass Band*—end of article; and see *Competitions* 3).

A peculiarity of the sound of a military band is its weakness at the upper and lower extremes of the range. There are many thick-sounding instruments of baritone range. Works contributed by such composers as Hindemith, Schönberg, and Stravinsky are as a rule written for the wind section of a normal orchestra.

The training school for British military bandmasters is Kneller Hall, Twickenham, near London (founded 1857).

Bands are much developed in American schools and there is a very high standard of performance.

A good deal of further information bearing directly or indirectly on the subject of military bands will be found under the following heads; *Flute Family*; *Oboe Family*; *Clarinet Family*; *Saxophone Family*; *Brass*; *Trumpet Family*; *Cornet*; *Horn Family*; *Trombone Family*; *Tuba Family*; *Saxhorn Family*; *Pitch* 5; *Percussion Family* 4; *Brass Band*; *Degrees and Diplomas*; *Sousa*.

For a concerto for piano and this combination see *Rowley*.

MILITARY MUSIC. See *March* and *Military Band*.

'MILITARY' SYMPHONY (Haydn). See *Nicknamed Compositions* 11.

MILL, JOHN STUART (1806–73). Philosopher and music-lover. For his fears as to the future of music see *Melody* 9.

MILLER.

(1) EDWARD (p. 485, pl. 86. 4). Born at Norwich in the 1730s (precise date variously stated) and died at Doncaster in 1807, in his later seventies. He was a pupil of Burney (q.v.), and from 1756 was organist of Doncaster Parish Church. He composed harpsichord music,

songs, etc. Southey in *The Doctor* has allusions to him.

See *Hymns and Hymn Tunes* 6; *Methodism and Music* 2.

(2) JAMES. See *Ye Banks and Braes*.

(3) DAYTON CLARENCE. Born at Strongsville, Ohio, 1866 and died at Cleveland, 1941. Distinguished physicist, who did much research in acoustics, especially in problems connected with the flute. See *Phonodeik*.

MILLER OF THE DEE, THE. The words were first printed in 1762, when they appeared in Arne's opera *Love in a Village* (see *Ballad Opera*); but it is almost certain that the song was then an old one.

The tune exists in many versions as an English folk song, set to various words. It is found in several of the early eighteenth-century ballad operas from 1728 onwards.

Saint-Saëns, who has ingeniously introduced the Scottish clans into the ballet of his opera *Henry VIII*, makes them enter to this tune—presumably confusing the Scottish Dee with the English one.

MILLIGAN FOX. See *Folk Song* 3.

MILLIKIN (or Milliken), RICHARD ALFRED (1767–1815). Poet. See *Last Rose of Summer*.

MILLÖCKER, KARL. Born in Vienna in 1842 and died near there in 1899, aged fifty-seven. He was a prolific and popular composer of tuneful operettas of the typical Viennese stamp. For some years he issued a monthly album of piano compositions.

MILLS, RICHARD (1809–44). He came of a musical family and was one of the earliest Welsh musical theorists. He composed and edited collections of hymn tunes and anthems.

MILNER, ANTHONY. Born in Bristol in 1925. He was trained at the Royal College of Music and took lessons from Seiber. He has made a name as a lecturer, writer, and pianist, and has composed a number of works, chiefly choral.

MILOPHONE. Mouth organ. See *Reed-Organ Family* 3, 10.

MILTON.

(1) JOHN I. Born at Stanton St. John, near Oxford, in 1563 and died in London in 1647, aged eighty-four. He was the father of the poet and the composer of church music and of a few madrigals, of which one appears in *The Triumphs of Oriana* (cf. *Madrigal* 4).

(2) JOHN II. The poet (1608–74).

See references under *Puritans* 5; *Copyists*; *Masque*; *Symphony* 1; *Recorder Family* 2; *Bagpipe Family* 1; *Lawes, Henry*; *Education and Music* 2; *Congregational* 2; *Appreciation*.

MIME. A play in dumb show or an actor of such (cf. *Pantomime*). Obviously a great deal of ballet (q.v.) includes miming as an ingredient. The connotation of farce is generally present.

MIMODRAMA. Any play (musical or other) which is carried on in dumb show (cf. *Pantomime*). The genre and term are sometimes used by composers; for instance, Roger-Ducasse's *Orpheus* (1913) is called 'a mimo-drama'.

MINACCEVOLE, MINACCEVOLMENTE (It.). 'Menacing', 'menacingly'. So also *Minacciando, Minaccioso, Minacciosamente*.

MINDER (Ger.). 'Less.'

MINEUR (Fr.). 'Minor.'

MINIATURE SCORE. See *Eulenburg*.

MINIM ($\downarrow$). The 'Half-Note'—i.e. half the time-value of the Semibreve or 'Whole-Note'; see Table 1.

MINIMA. See *Notation* 4; Table 3.

MINISTER OF MUSIC. A dignified American term sometimes officially adopted by a church for its organist–choirmaster.

MINNE (Ger.). 'Love'; so *Minnelied*, 'Love-song'.

MINNESINGERS. See *Minstrels* 7; *Notation* 1; *Form* 6.

MINOR CANON. In an English cathedral of the 'New Foundation' (see *Cathedral Music* 2) a clergyman whose duty is to intone the priest's part in the choral services (cf. *Vicar Choral*).

MINOR COMMON CHORD. See *Harmony* 24 d.

MINORE (It.). 'Minor.'

MINOR INTERVALS. See *Intervals*.

MINOR SCALE. See *Scales* 6.

MINSTRELS, TROUBADOURS, TROUVÈRES, MINNESINGERS, MASTERSINGERS

1. Jongleurs and Minstrels.
2. The Minstrel in English History.
3. Guilds and Companies of Minstrels.
4. Troubadours and Trouvères.
5. The Nature of the Troubadour's Art.
6. Academies for the Encouragement of the Art.
7. Minnesingers.
8. Mastersingers.

All these names, coming from various parts of Europe and various periods, call up the concept of the cultivation of music by distinct groups of men who have set themselves apart for the purpose, and it will perhaps save confusion if they are treated in one place in this encyclopedia, with cross-references from the other places where the separate treatments are likely to be looked for. In this way the distinctions will become plain.

1. Jongleurs and Minstrels. In every age and country there has been some class of men professionally devoted to musical amusement.

The Roman name for such a person was **Joculator**, which points to some exercise of

1, 2. ANGLO-SAXON GLEEMEN. See *Minstrels* 1, 2

3, 4. TWO FAMOUS MINNESINGERS—Reinmar the Elder and his pupil Walther von der Vogelweide. For Minnesingers see *Minstrels* 7

5. HANS SACHS. See *Minstrels* 8: also *Mastersingers of Nuremberg*

6. FRAUENLOB—founder of the Mastersingers, 1311 See *Minstrels* 8

7. A MASTERSINGER CANDIDATE AND HIS 'MARKERS' See *Minstrels* 8

PLATE 111

THE MUSICAL MOZARTS IN 1763 AND 1780

See the Article on pages 662–3

1. LEOPOLD MOZART WITH HIS CHILDREN (Maria Anna, or 'Nannerl', and Wolfgang), as they appeared before the public in 1763

2. THE FAMILY SEVENTEEN YEARS LATER
(The Mother's portrait on the wall)

the art on its lighter side. From this came the French Joglar, later **Jongleur**, the German **Gaukler**, the Italian **Giocolino**, the Spanish **Juglar**, and the English **Juggler**. The words 'Gaukler' and 'Juggler' descended in dignity and came to refer merely to the lighter side of the professional work of the public entertainers in question, who numbered in their ranks the actors, the bear-leaders, the conjurers, and the acrobats of the Middle Ages, as well as the musicians.

Such a division of duties and of dignity asserted itself early. By the tenth century it was well recognized. The play-acting, tumbling, conjuring *jongleurs* were frequently condemned by the Church; the *jongleurs de gestes* (*Gestes* or *Chansons de geste* were the long, traditional or original, narrative poems recounting the deeds of national heroes) were received with respect in the monasteries and castles of the day.

This difference of social grade was marked in the fourteenth century by the introduction of a new term for the higher-class public entertainers, the musician class—that of **Ménestrier** (akin to 'minister' and thought by some to allude to the duty of attending on the Troubadours with instrumental accompaniment; see 4 below), which was really at this time pretty well the equivalent of 'professional musician'. The profession itself was known as that of *ménestrandie*.

Soon the word **Ménestrel** grew out of the former word, with subdivisions of the profession described by such terms as *Ménestrel de bouche* for a singer, *Ménestrel de guerre* for a player of a military instrument, and so forth.

Necessarily very wide differences of social importance existed even amongst the Ménestrels. There were humble wanderers and there were the well-rewarded permanent servants of great nobles or of royalty; in fact it may be said that the range was as wide as that today between the needy-looking individual who plays the banjo and sings a little outside the doors of London public-houses (saloons) and the 'Master of the Queen's Musick'.

England had always had musical entertainers of the various grades, as, for instance, the Saxon 'gleemen' (p. 640, pl. **110**. 1, 2), and the close political connexion with France brought to it the name used in that country, which in England changed slightly into 'minstrel'.

2. The Minstrel in English History. The musical profession, by whatever name it was called, had been important in England. The Saxon Gleemen have been alluded to above, and it will be remembered that in the Norman Invasion of 1066 William the Conqueror was accompanied by his warrior-bard, Taillefer, who obtained permission to strike the first blow at the Battle of Hastings, advanced singing of Charlemagne and Roland and throwing his sword in the air and catching it (a jongleur's trick), and was there killed. This gives some idea of the importance attached to the position of jongleur by the Norman monarchs.

Rahere (d. 1144), who founded the Priory and Hospital of St. Bartholomew in London (the Priory Church still, in part, exists and the hospital, 'Barts.', is still on the same site), was at one time a musician, jongleur, or, as would later be said, 'minstrel' to Henry I. By the time Rahere was enabled to show his munificence he had deserted music and entered the Church and thrived therein; but in any case we see in him a representative of the higher ranks of the profession.

We get a glimpse of the lower ranks in an incident of nearly a century later—Earl Randulf of Chester, being in 1212 besieged by the Welsh in his castle of Rhuddlan in Flintshire, sent word to Roger de Lacy, known for his ruthlessness as 'Roger of Hell', Justiciar and Constable of Chester, who, the annual fair of that city being then in progress, collected the jongleurs of various kinds there assembled and marched them off under his son-in-law Dutton, when their very numbers perceived in the distance were enough to drive the Welsh away. In return for this a Royal Charter gave the Duttons jurisdiction over the minstrels of Cheshire for ever. This right was recognized so long as minstrelsy lasted—and even beyond. Two and a half centuries later we find Edward IV, when granting a charter to the fraternity of Minstrels of England (1469), carefully excepting 'the County of Chester'; and three centuries after that the Duttons were still holding a court at Chester every Midsummer Day, receiving four flagons of wine and fourpence-halfpenny (or its equivalent) from applicants, and issuing licences to practise the profession for the coming twelve months. The last such court was held in 1756.

3. Guilds and Companies of Minstrels. Control of the profession of minstrel in another way—the formation of a fraternity, or guild (see also *Profession of Music* 1), seems to have begun in London at least as early as 1350, and various ordinances and Royal Charters are in existence (1500, 1518, 1574, etc.) which detail the objects sought and the conditions imposed. One of the main objects was the exclusion of 'foreign' musicians (i.e. those who were not Londoners). Another was the prevention of competition from amateurs ('as tayllers, shoemakers, and such others', singing 'songs called Three Mens Songs in the Taverns, Innes, and such other places of this Cytie, and also at weadings', etc.; 1555). Still another was the avoidance of overcrowding of the profession, by the prohibition of the taking of too many apprentices. Other cities besides London had these guilds, such as York, Beverley (ruling the minstrels between Trent and Tweed), and Canterbury.

In 1604 James I granted a new charter to the 'London Society of Minstrels', and they became 'The Master, Wardens, and Commonalty of the Art or Science of the Musicians of London'. This charter was revoked by Charles I, in 1636, with the allegation that the previous one had been obtained from his father 'by untrue suggestion'. Charles then chartered a new body, 'the Marshall, Wardens, and Cominalty of the Arte and Science of Musick in Westminster in the County of Middlesex'. Westminster was merely their seat. Whereas the 1604 body had powers only within the City of London and three miles therefrom, the new one had powers over the whole of England—except, of course, Cheshire, which, as already mentioned, enjoyed autonomy.

The further history of the legal control of musicians is obscure. In 1657 some of Cromwell's musicians petitioned the Council of State, which had appointed a 'Committee for the Advancement of Musick'. They said that they wished to found a 'Corporation or Colledge of Musitians . . . in all things to regulate the profession of musick'. This is very curious, as such a corporation (as we have just seen) already existed. Nothing much seems to have come of the petition (Cromwell died within eighteen months), and after the Restoration we, strangely, find the 'Westminster' body, chartered a quarter of a century earlier by Charles I, at last active; there seems to be no record of its doing anything until now, when it sent deputations into various counties and apparently began seriously to try to organize the profession. So far as we can find, this body was active only from 1661 to 1679 and then quietly died.

In 1700 we find the Common Council of the City of London conferring power on a company, and in 1763 an action was successfully fought before the Recorder of London against one Hudson, who had employed as musicians at a Lord Mayor's banquet persons not 'free of the company'. This company possessed powers over teachers as well as performers and could fine non-members four pounds if they dared to give lessons within the London area.

The present Worshipful Company of Musicians (see also *Profession of Music* 1) had, from the late eighteenth century, claimed to be working on a Charter of James I, granted in 1604, though no continuous records of its history date back further than 1772.

An application for a new Royal Charter was made, and duly granted in December 1949.

The members of the Company are nowadays active not merely in dining regularly and amicably together, as of old time, but also in offering prizes for composition (including the John Clementi Collard Fellowship of £300 a year for a maximum of three years), and in other useful ways (see a reference under *Hydraulus*). It is believed that all the present-day members are true to the regulations of 1604 not to 'unseemly revile, rebuke, smite, or abuse any brother of the same Fellowship', not to 'sing any ribaldry, wanton or lascivious songs or ditties', not to 'go in any open street from house to house with an instrument uncased or uncovered, to be seen by any passing by', and even to the earlier regulation of 1535 'not to play upon any instrument in the open streets, lanes, or alleys of the city between the hours of ten at night and five in the morning'.

From the regulation forbidding night music, by the way, the **Waits** (q.v.) were expressly exempted. The word represents one side of a town minstrel's work—the patrolling the streets at night, with a wind instrument, generally of the oboe kind. There are still corners of England (e.g. the precincts of Canterbury Cathedral) patrolled by a Wait calling the hours of the night and announcing the state of the weather, but no musical instrument is now played. (For more on the Waits see separate article *Wait or Wayte*.)

Minstrels' galleries exist in many Tudor mansions. They seem to be designed for instrumentalists, and, indeed, by the late fifteenth century the name had come to be nearly so restricted. In St. Mary's Church, Beverley, is a Minstrels' Pillar, given by the local guild of minstrels and with carvings of minstrels playing different instruments. On a tomb at King's Lynn are shown minstrels performing on various instruments at a fifteenth-century banquet, and, curiously, exactly the same design appears in a manuscript in the National Library at Paris. Exeter Cathedral has a music gallery, with minstrels and their instruments carved on the front.

There is abundant evidence of the importance of the calling of jongleur or minstrel from the faint dawn of civilization in Europe down to, say, the sixteenth century, when the musical profession found other directions for development, and two Acts of Queen Elizabeth I, aimed at all strollers, declared minstrels to be 'rogues and vagabonds'.

For a half-satirical representation of minstrel life in a set of keyboard compositions see under *Couperin Family*.

4. Troubadours and Trouvères. The activity of the jongleurs and minstrels, as has just been seen, can be traced from almost the beginnings of history down to comparatively modern times. That of the troubadours was of much briefer duration, being only about two hundred years—from the end of the eleventh century to the end of the thirteenth.

The art of the jongleurs and minstrels was exercised in all parts of Europe; it had no one country as its headquarters. That of the troubadours and trouvères was confined to the south of France, with overflows into northern Spain and northern Italy (wherever the Provençal tongue was spoken, in fact) and central and northern France—so confined, that is to say, except as far as those who exercised it travelled at times to other countries, and to some extent inspired these with the desire of imitation (see *Minnesingers* below).

The professional standing of the jongleurs and minstrels just discussed varied from that of the itinerant street performer to that of the chief entertainer of a court; the standing of the troubadours was higher—indeed, their activities often altogether transcended those of a profession, becoming rather the occupation of certain gifted members of the nobility, and they even numbered kings among their practitioners (e.g. Richard Lion Heart of England, who was partly Provençal by origin). There were a very few female troubadours.

The troubadours and trouvères both exercised the same art, that of the Poet–Composer. The words troubadour and trouvère mean exactly the same thing—'finder' or 'inventor'. ('Such as found out musical tunes and recited verses in writing.' So the phrase of the Book of Ecclesiasticus, in its catalogue of 'famous men', described such people.)

The distinction between troubadour and trouvère is one of locality and language. The troubadours lived in southern France, in Provence, and used the Provençal tongue, the *langue d'oc*. The trouvères were in central and northern France and spoke the French tongue —the *langue d'oïl*—'oc' and 'oïl' being the respective words for 'yes', and serving as a handy term of distinction of these two branches of the Latin tongue.

The troubadours were the earlier in the field, and were active from the end of the eleventh century to about the end of the thirteenth. The persecution (and indeed almost complete destruction) of the sect of Albigenses, who numbered nearly all the southern nobility in their ranks, was the greatest factor in the decline of the troubadours (Albî, north-east of Toulouse, from which the heretics took their name, was a nest of troubadours). Another factor was the spread of the French language and decreasing importance of the Provençal language in which they had developed their verse-forms and rhyming devices. The decay of chivalry, of which the art of the troubadours and trouvères was the poetical and musical expression, was the chief cause of the decline of the trouvères a little later, and would in any case have brought about that of the troubadours had not the other causes operated previously. Roughly it may be said that the activity of the trouvères began and ended half a century later than that of the troubadours.

See an allusion under *Form* 14.

5. The Nature of the Troubadour's Art.
The art of the troubadours and trouvères represents one of the greatest refinements in the processes of poetry that the world has ever seen. Nine hundred different metres and forms of stanza are to be found in the remaining body of their poetry. They developed the lyric, especially, and the effect of this intensive study of its possibilities is to be seen in the literature of almost every country of Europe. The praise of woman was their principal subject. Every troubadour had his particular female divinity to whom he expressed an idealistic devotion in high-flown rhetoric. But he also celebrated heroism, the greatness of princes, and national pride, and took sides in political disputes and preached crusades in song (for *Chansons de geste* see 1). Whatever the subject chosen, the troubadour poetry is charged with rhapsody and passion.

As for the music, it should be remembered that almost all poetry was in those days intended for singing, so that the maker of the words of a poem had done only half his task until a tune was wedded to them. Some troubadours are spoken of as making good words and poor tunes, and vice versa, but at any rate they all had to provide both (though they sometimes borrowed the tune). A fair body of troubadour music remains (that to about one-tenth of the poems); it is expressed in the contemporary Gregorian notation of plainsong (q.v.), and the determination of its rhythms is a matter of debate in the case of every melody. No accompaniment is given in any of the manuscripts, so this was presumably extemporized by the instrumentalist. Necessarily the troubadours employed the Modes (q.v.), but it is noticeable that a good many of their tunes are in that mode which is the same as our major scale.

The troubadour was, then, both poet and composer, but it was not expected that he should necessarily be also performer. He might or might not have a good voice, and might or might not care to appear in courts and halls in the capacity of singer. If he did so appear he probably used the services, as instrumental accompanist, of a jongleur attached to his service. If he did not so appear he used such services both for the singing and the accompaniment of his songs—and by his jongleurs, to whom he taught them, they would be spread abroad, and if appreciated, become widely known. A jongleur of creative gifts could rise to the rank of troubadour, and a needy troubadour has been known to descend to the rank of jongleur.

One of the greatest of all troubadours was Bernard de Ventadorn (*c.* 1130–95), who praised Eleanor of Aquitaine, later the wife of Henry II of England. She went to England in 1154 and he is thought to have followed her.

A good deal of our knowledge of the troubadour life comes from Dante, whose period (1265–1321) closely followed that of the troubadours and whose poetical technique shows their influence. The love of Dante for Beatrice very perfectly represents the ideal of the troubadours. Chaucer (*c.* 1340–1400) shows the influence of troubadour verse in English poetry.

A trouvère who should be mentioned by name, even in so brief a sketch as the present, is **Adam de la Halle** (q.v.), composer of the play of *Robin and Marion*.

The subject of one troubadour *chanson de geste* is known to French schoolchildren of today—that of Huon of Bordeaux, which existed in many versions. It supplied Weber with the plot of his opera *Oberon*.

6. Academies for the Encouragement of the Art.
After the periods mentioned the art still lingered faintly and attempts were made to maintain or revive it. One such was the foundation at Toulouse, in 1323, of an academy which held competitions and awarded prizes for the best productions: from 1694 the French

language has been admitted. This institution still functions, under the name of Academy of Floral Games ('Académie des Jeux Floraux'; a golden violet was the original prize): troubadour activity may, then, be said to be not quite extinct even today. Barcelona, in Spain, had for some centuries a similar academy. Puy Notre Dame (near Saumur) had founded a sort of troubadour academy as early as the twelfth century, and it was widely copied elsewhere, giving its name to similar institutions; in the thirteenth century London had a musical society called 'Le Pui', and it held competitions.

See a further reference to the Puys under *Competitions in Music* 1.

7. Minnesingers (from *Minne* = love). These were the German counterpart of the troubadours and trouvères, with whom they were contemporary, though they began a little later, and from whom their art derived, though it assimilated also native folk influences. Like the troubadours and trouvères, they were largely of knightly rank. They sang of heroism, love, and nature, and their general tone was rather more idealistic than that of their Provençal-speaking and French-speaking brothers, their reverence for womankind being more natural and genuine. In their metres and verse-structures they show the troubadour influence. Their melodies (of which a good many remain) show the same influences; they are written in the same notation and offer the same difficulty in rhythmic interpretation.

There were two chief schools, that of the Danube valley and that of the Rhine valley—the two great highways, by the former of which many of the troubadours and those who had learnt their songs travelled to the Crusades, so spreading their art.

Wagner, in *Tannhäuser*, has shown us a tournament of Minne-song. Tannhäuser and his opponent Wolfram of Eschenbach are historical figures, chosen to represent the lower and higher types of Minnesinger character. It was Wolfram of Eschenbach's version of the Parsifal legends from which Wagner chiefly drew the material for his great sacred music-drama, whilst the material for *Tristan* he found in Godfrey of Strasbourg's version of the legend of the lovers (beginning of thirteenth century).

The art of the Minnesingers declined about the same time as that of the troubadours and trouvères, i.e. the end of the thirteenth century.

8. Mastersingers (in German, *Meistersinger*). After the decline of the aristocratic Minnesingers the trader and craftsman classes took up their dual art and practised it, with added complexities and under very academic regulations. This began at Mainz at about the same time (or a little earlier) as the attempt was made at Toulouse to save the dying art of the troubadours by the founding of the academy above mentioned, and the object was the same. Henry of Meissen, otherwise known as 'Frauenlob' or 'Woman's Praise' (p. 640, pl. **110.** 6),

is regarded as both the last of the Minnesingers and the first of the Mastersingers; it was he who founded the guild or corporation at Mainz (1311), which was soon imitated all over Germany, so that almost every city had its similar guild. Throughout the fourteenth, fifteenth, and sixteenth centuries, and into the seventeenth century, these guilds were active, and that of Ulm was dissolved only in 1839, its last member (the last of the Mastersingers) dying in 1876.

The subjects treated by the Mastersingers were largely Biblical and the meetings were usually held in churches. The membership of the guilds was organized in a series of grades, culminating in that of 'Master', and admission and promotion were by examination. Contests were held. Rules of a pedantic character had to be observed: they bore the name 'Tablature'. 'Markers' officiated at a contest, watching for infractions of these rules.

In fact, the conduct of a Mastersingers' Guild was very much what Wagner has shown us in *The Mastersingers of Nuremberg* (q.v.), and the very names of the characters of that opera are for the most part those of actual personages (p. 640, pl. **110.** 7).

Hans Sachs (p. 640, p. **110.** 5), the dignified and genial elder hero of Wagner's music-drama, lived from 1494 to 1576, i.e. he came near the end of the Mastersinger period. He was a prolific poet, playwright, and composer. He himself gives the number of his productions as 4,275 master songs, 1,700 fables and tales, 208 plays, and so forth, but as he lived for nine years after he compiled these statistics they are well below his final totals. Three big folio volumes were published during his own lifetime, and the whole is now available in twenty-three volumes. Some of his naïve farces are still occasionally acted in Germany.

Certain of the themes in Wagner's music-drama are actual Mastersinger tunes and are taken, with the rules and other details, from Wagenseil's curious book on the Mastersingers (1697).

See an allusion to minstrels, etc., under *Modes* 11.

MINUET (Eng.), or **MENUET** (Fr.), or **MINUETTO** (It.), or **MENUETT** (Ger.). (The spelling 'Menuetto' does not exist in any language, though Beethoven and others have used it.)

Of all the hundreds or thousands of dances in Europe this is the one that made the greatest mark upon music. The name is said to come from the small (French, *menu*) steps it used.

It began as a rustic dance in France, probably as a variant of the branle (q.v.) or the galliard. Lully (q.v.) and other composers in France took it up and it came to court and became refined, so that its invention is sometimes credited to Beauchamp, Louis XIV's great dancing-master (see *Dance* 6 b). Soon it spread to other countries, and in the England of the later seventeenth and the eighteenth centuries it became a part of the life of the country, declining from about the year 1790 after about 120 years of high favour.

During the whole period of its court and assembly-room popularity the minuet was looked upon as a training in and a test of deportment. Thus we find Lord Chesterfield writing to his son in 1748, 'I would have you dance a minuet very well, not so much for the sake of the minuet itself (though that, if danced at all, ought to be danced well), as that it will give you an habitual genteel carriage and manner of presenting yourself'.

The minuet was early taken up, as other dances had been, by composers of instrumental music, and it became one of the optional dances of the suite (q.v.). The suites of Purcell, Handel, and Bach, for instance, sometimes include minuets. It also found its way into overtures, even oratorio overtures, as those of Handel's *Samson* and *Jephtha* (not *Messiah*, though there is a tradition that for that, too, Handel wrote a minuet for use on occasions when the overture was played as an independent concert piece). In the next period it was seen in some of the sonatas, string quartets, and symphonies of Haydn and Mozart and their contemporaries.

In Vienna in Mozart's day it was a concert custom for the orchestra to play minuets between the appearances of solo players and singers, and this explains the existence of some of the detached works of this kind in the list of Mozart's compositions—though he wrote also many actual dancing minuets for the balls of Vienna. The minuet appears sometimes in the sonatas, etc., of Beethoven, though with him it is often supplanted by the scherzo, which may be a glorified and speeded minuet or may be something quite different. After the time of Beethoven the minuet appears only in compositions designed to possess a flavour of the archaic; its day was done, but it could be revived now and again.

The minuet is in three-in-a-measure rhythm, and, as danced, was in an unhurried tempo. Its phrases, in the older examples, usually begin on the first beat of the measure and in the newer ones frequently on the third beat. It is normally (after its earliest day) in a ternary form, a first stanza, a second, and the first again. With it is usually associated another minuet in a related key—called Trio, from the old practice of Lully and others of sinking here, for variety, from the tone of the full orchestra to that of three instruments, generally two oboes and bassoons (see *Trio*). After the trio the first minuet reappears. So that each of the two minuets is in ternary form, and the two taken in combination fall into that form also.

See allusions to the minuet under *Overture* 7; *Sonata* 7, 8; *Symphony* 6; *Scherzo*; *Suite* 3; *Pavan and Galliard.* For an early specimen, in binary form, see *Form* 5.

MINUIT, CHRÉTIENS. See *Adam, A.*

'MINUTE' VALSE (Chopin). See *Nicknamed Compositions* 8.

MIRACLE PLAYS. See *Mysteries, Miracle Plays, and Moralities.*

'MIRACLE' SYMPHONY (Haydn). See *Nicknamed Compositions* 11.

MIRLITON. The French name for what English children call (or used to call) 'Tommy Talker', or 'Kazoo'. It is a tube with a membrane at each end and two holes into one of which holes one sings in one's natural voice, the tone issuing in a caricatural fashion (see also *Bigophone*). It is of ancient origin and has been known as the *Eunuch Flute* or (from the source of the membrane in the skin of an onion) the *Onion Flute.*

MIRROR CANON. See below.

MIRROR FUGUE. (*a*) One which when played from the end to the beginning sounds the same as when played from the beginning to the end.

(*b*) The above is the obvious application of the term, but certain theorists have applied it to an equally recondite type of fugue in which all the voices can invert all their intervals (upward intervals becoming downward and vice versa) and also the position of their voices (upper voices becoming lower and vice versa), the new fugue thus brought into existence being as effective as the old. For a reference to 'Mirror Fugue' of this type see *Art of Fugue.*

The word 'Mirror' can be applied to canon in the same two ways as to fugue.

MISATTRIBUTED COMPOSITIONS

(Alphabetically arranged by putative composers.)

Arcadelt's Ave Maria. This is an adaptation (apparently first published 1845) of Arcadelt's three-voice Chanson 'Nous voyons que les hommes' (published 1557). For full particulars see *Musical Times*, October 1933.

Arne's 'The Lass with a Delicate Air'. See *Arne, Michael.*

Arne's Mass in D. By Alphonse d'Eve (1662–1727).

C. P. E. Bach's 'Battle of Rosbach'. A keyboard piece; not by him.

J. C. Bach's 'Battle of Bergen'. A keyboard piece; not by him.

J. C. Bach's Concerto for harpsichord and strings in A; not by him.

J. S. Bach's 'Willst du dein Herz mir schenken'. This song, often confidently accepted as Bach's, is certainly not his (see Spitta's *Bach*).

J. S. Bach's Motets. *Lob und Ehre* ('Blessing and Honour') is not Bach's, the composer being Georg Gottfried Wagner (1698–1756), one of Bach's violinists at Leipzig, afterwards a cantor elsewhere. *Jauchzet dem Herrn, alle Welt* ('Rejoice in the Lord, all the World') may be in part Bach's. Some other motets ascribed to Bach are doubtful; they may be early works of his or they may be by some contemporary.

J. S. Bach's St. Luke Passion. See under *Passion Music* 5.

W. F. Bach's 'Grave' for violin. By Kreisler (q.v.).

W. F. Bach's Organ Concerto in D minor. Really a violin concerto of Vivaldi arranged by J. S. Bach.

Beethoven's 'Adieu to the Piano' (once very much played and still extant) is decidedly not by Beethoven.

Beethoven's 'Le Désir'. See *Nicknamed Compositions* 18 (under 'Mourning Waltz').

Beethoven's Funeral March in B flat minor. A discussion about this composition arose in 1910 through its being heard in the funeral procession of King Edward VII (see *Weekly Graphic* of 24 May and *Musical News* of 4 and 11 June). It was alleged to be a very commonplace thing, such as Beethoven would never have written, and to be the work of one Walch, Kapellmeister of Gotha in the early nineteenth century. Its first attribution to Beethoven is said to have been in Graz about 1830.

Beethoven's Pianoforte Sonatinas in F and G. These were not published until after Beethoven's death and their authenticity is not established. (Nottebohm's standard work on Beethoven's compositions, the British Museum catalogue, etc., class them as 'doubtful'.)

Beethoven's Piano Duets. *Gavotte in B flat* and *Funeral March in C minor*. These, and one or two other less important pieces, have long appeared in the British Museum catalogues as by Mozart, but have been by some authorities confidently credited to the young Beethoven. They are now shown (O. E. Deutsch in *Music and Letters*, Jan. and April 1946 and Jan. 1952) to be by Kozeluch.

Beethoven's 'Concertstuck in D' or 'Pianoforte Concerto in D in one Movement'. This appears in Breitkopf and Härtel's collected edition of Beethoven's works and has, at intervals over a long term of years, been played in London, and doubtless elsewhere, as the work of Beethoven, and is included in many books on Beethoven. It is really the first movement of a concerto by the Hungarian composer J. J. Rösler (1771–1813; slightly incorrect dates given by some authorities). The attribution to Beethoven is due to a copyist's mistake. It was published during Beethoven's lifetime (1826) as by Rösler (see *Beethoven Jahrbuch*, 1925).

Beethoven's 'Dream of St. Jerome'. The story of this once-popular piano piece seems to be as follows:

(*a*) Thomas Moore (q.v.), as one of his *Sacred Melodies* (*c.* 1820), wrote a poem with this name, to an adaptation (printed with it) of the first theme of the slow movement of Beethoven's Second Symphony.

(*b*) Thackeray, in *The Adventures of Philip*, in the *Cornhill Magazine*, forty years later (1861–2) alluded to this: 'Miss Charlotte . . . went to the piano and played us Beethoven's "Dream of St. Jerome" . . . which always soothes me and charms me', and so forth.

(*c*) Readers of the popular *Philip* naturally went to their music shops and asked for Beethoven's piano piece, *The Dream of St. Jerome*. A publisher thereupon instructed his then assistant, Brinley Richards (see *God bless the Prince of Wales*; *Pianoforte* 22), to supply the demand. Richards hastily knocked up two movements, an 'Andante affettuoso' (being the melody of Beethoven's song *Love of our neighbours*, op. 48, no. 3) and an 'Allegretto' (being a Welsh folk song, *Megan's Daughter*). For some years this pastiche circulated widely as a true work of Beethoven and it may possibly still be found on the music desks of the green-silk-faced pianos of very old ladies in remote parts of the country.

Beethoven's 'Jena' Symphony. Probably by Friedrich Witt, though some parts of a set discovered in 1909 bear Beethoven's name.

Boccherini's Allegretto. By Kreisler (q.v.).

Boccherini's Violoncello Concerto in B flat. The familiar version of this work is to a great extent re-composed by the cellist Grützmacher, whose name appears as editor. It is a pot-pourri of four Boccherini manuscripts in the Dresden State Library.

Boyce's Pan and Syrinx and **The Power of Music.** By John Stanley.

Byrd's Non Nobis Domine. Not certainly by Byrd. See separate entry under the name of the composition.

Cartier's 'La Chasse'. By Kreisler (q.v.).

Chopin's Fugue, in the Universal Edition of his pianoforte works. Arthur Hedley, in his book on Chopin, says, 'There is evidence that the fugue published under Chopin's name was composed by Cherubini'.

Chopin's Variations for Flute on a Theme from Rossini's 'Cenerentola'. The authority mentioned above doubts the authenticity of this attribution also.

Chopin's Polonaise in G flat major. Niecks, in his *Life of Chopin*, says, 'Nothing but the composer's autograph would convince one of the genuineness of this piece'.

Chopin's Mazurka in F major (not

op. 25 or op. 68). E. Pauer has shown that this is by Charles Mayer.

F. Couperin's 'Aubade Provençale'. By Kreisler (q.v.).

L. Couperin's Chanson Louis XIII and Pavane. The first eight measures are a traditional melody; the rest is by Kreisler (q.v.).

L. Couperin's 'La Précieuse'. By Kreisler (q.v.).

Debussy's song, *Chanson d'un fou*, is really the work of Émile Louis Fortuné Pessard (1843–1917) and was published under his name in 1873 (cf. *Musical Times*, Sept. 1932). And the song also attributed to Debussy, *Ici-bas tous les lilas meurent*, is by the Hillemacher brothers and was originally published as by 'P. L. Hillemacher' (q.v.).

Dittersdorf's Scherzo. By Kreisler (q.v.).

'Dvorsky's' Various Compositions. Really by Josef Hofmann—Dvorsky being a fictitious personage. (The word is a literal translation into Russian of the German words 'Hof' and 'Mann'.)

Farrant's 'Lord, for Thy Tender Mercies' Sake'. See under *Farrant, Richard*.

Francœur's Sicilienne and Rigaudon. By Kreisler (q.v.).

Handel's Viola Concerto, edited by Marius Casadesus. This must be regarded as, at any rate, a doubtful work.

Haydn's 'Ox' Minuet. This is the work of a musician called von Seyfried (1776–1841) who provided music for a Singspiel (q.v.) on a supposed incident in the life of Haydn. The music of the Singspiel was, for the most part, taken from Haydn, but not this item. The various anecdotes related to account for the name are inventions.

Haydn's Symphonies. Thirty-eight symphonies by over twenty different composers have been mistakenly credited to Haydn. There are also thirty-six credited to him of which the authorship is doubtful. It is naturally impossible to list all these works here.

Haydn's Toy Symphony. Probably part of a longer work by Leopold Mozart (see ' *Toy' Symphony*).

Haydn's Violoncello Concerto (op. 101). It was at one time considered probable that this was not by Haydn but by Kraft (q.v.) but the discovery in 1954 of the autograph of the work in Haydn's own hand seems to show that the attribution to Haydn, is, after all, correct.

Henry VIII's 'O Lord, the Maker of all thing' (not 'things'—cf. 'everything'). This anthem is in all probability by William Mundy (d. *c.* 1591), a Vicar-choral of St. Paul's Cathedral and a Gentleman of the Chapel Royal (not to be confused with John Mundy, d. 1630).

Locke's Music to 'Macbeth'. This is claimed by some authorities for Purcell, by others for Eccles (q.v.), by still others for Leveridge (q.v.).

It was not printed until the middle of the eighteenth century, when Boyce (q.v.) edited it and attributed it to Locke. This he did, probably, on the statement of Downes (in *Roscius Anglicanus*, 1708), who had been prompter at the performance of *Macbeth* under Davenant (q.v.) in 1672. But Downes is a man of proved unreliability in detail, and, moreover, even if Locke did contribute the music to that performance there is nothing to show that this is the particular music in question.

The theory that Purcell was the composer rests on the existence of a copy in his handwriting—and of many other old copies bearing his name as composer. But, as the late Dr. Cummings (one of the leading champions of the attribution to Purcell) averred, the music is 'clearly an elaboration and development of a series of short movements by the considerably earlier composer Robert Johnson (not the priest-composer of that name) for Middleton's play of *The Witch*, so that it is, in any case, in its entirety neither Locke's nor Purcell's'.

(It will be remembered that music of Purcell was performed at court from his eleventh year, so that his ability to recast simple music for a theatrical performance when he was fourteen need not constitute a real difficulty.)

See an allusion to this music under *Arrangement*.

Lully. See references under *Lully, Loulié, Lœillet*.

Martini's Andantino. By Kreisler (q.v.).

Martini's Preghiera. By Kreisler (q.v.).

Mozart Works. The authoritative collected edition of Mozart's works excludes as spurious or doubtful thirty-four Masses and a large quantity of other vocal and instrumental work, much too great to be catalogued here they are listed in the later editions of Köchel (q.v.). The two following must, however, be mentioned:

Mozart's Twelfth Mass. This ought certainly not to be considered a work of Mozart, though it may contain some material by him. It may be a pastiche, put together after his death (published in 1821 from a manuscript supplied by the composer Carl Zulehner—a dubious personage); it seems at one time to have been known as 'Müller's Mass'.

Mozart's Requiem. This was the last work the composer undertook and he left it in some measure unfinished. Franz Xaver Süssmayr (1766–1803) was entrusted with its completion. The Sanctus, Benedictus, and Agnus Dei are usually thought to be composed (or completed, or perhaps only orchestrated) by Süssmayer, and he completed other movements from Mozart's sketches. The whole question of the authorship of various portions of this work has, however, been often discussed, and somewhat different opinions will be found in various works on Mozart (see especially the later editions of Köchel mentioned above).

Mozart's 'Wiegenlied' ('Schlafe mein Prinzchen'). Really by Bernhard Flies (born

Berlin 1770) and first published 1795 as by him. (See Max Friedlander in Peters's *Jahrbuch*, 1896; also Eitner's *Quellenlexikon*, s.v. 'Flies'.)

Mozart's 'Adelaide Concerto' for violin. This was published by Marius Casadesus in 1934 with the suggestion that it was composed by Mozart at Versailles, at the age of ten, for the use of the eldest daughter of Louis XV, Princess Adelaide (to whom the manuscript bears a dedication—whence the name Casadesus gave it). This manuscript, stated to be 'in a private collection in France', is on only two staves giving merely the solo part and a line of bass with occasional fragmentary hints of other parts, the remainder of the published score being the work of Casadesus himself. If genuine this concerto would precede all other concertos of the composer (for whatever instrument) by seven years.

Objections raised by the greatest Mozart expert, Alfred Einstein, are (*a*) That Mozart was not at Versailles at the date given on the autograph (26 May 1766), the carefully kept diary of his father showing that he and his children did not arrive there until two days later; (*b*) That Mozart at that age could not have written a work 'on a form and scale like that', and that though the material used is Mozartian in style, yet, if Mozart's, it clearly belongs to a later period of his development; (*c*) That if he *had* written such a work he would never have done so in the shape of a score of merely two lines; (*d*) That in 1768 (i.e. about two years after the date given on the manuscript) Mozart's father made a catalogue of the works of the boy and did not include this work. To this may be added the curious fact that neither Einstein, whose knowledge of the composer's handwriting was unique, nor yet the publishers of the Casadesus score (Schott), were allowed to see the autograph or a photograph of any part of it.

Pending further light on the subject it has seemed proper to include this work amongst the 'Misattributed'; it may possibly include passages taken from some manuscript of the putative composer, but in the shape in which it has been published and performed does not appear to be safely described as a Mozart concerto.

Mozart's Musical Dice-Game. See *Composition 14*.

Palestrina's 'Adoramus Te'. In addition to the composition printed in the complete edition of Palestrina's works, of which the genuineness has not been questioned, there is a work wrongly credited to Palestrina. It was, apparently, first published in 1838, by Friedrich Rochlitz in his *Sammlung vorzüglicher Gesangstücke*, vol. 1, and is there attributed to Palestrina—an attribution that appears to have been accepted for a century following. Its uppermost voice-part and much of its harmony are taken from an *Adoramus Te* by Rosselli (*Maestro di cappella* of St. Peter's, Rome, 1548–50).

Palestrina's Responsoria (vol. 23 of Haberl's collected edn.). By Ingegneri.

Pergolese's 'Tre giorni son che Nina'. This is probably by Legrenzio Vencenzo Ciampi (1719–62), being found in his opera *Gli tre cicisbei ridicoli*.

Pergolese's concertinos for strings, his trio-sonatas, and dozens of vocal works attributed to him, are certainly by other composers.

Porpora's Minuet. By Kreisler (q.v.).

Pugnani's Praeludium and Allegro. By Kreisler (q.v.).

Purcell's 'Passing By'. See *Passing By*.

Purcell's Trumpet Voluntary. Really by Jeremiah Clarke (q.v.). It was published in *A Choice Collection of Ayres for the Harpsichord or Spinet* (1700) as 'The Prince of Denmark's March' and described as a 'Round O' (i.e. Rondo). The Prince of Denmark was, of course, Queen Anne's Consort. The attribution to Purcell is first seen in a collection of organ arrangements which appeared in the 1870s, and which was the source of the famous arrangement by Henry Wood.

Purcell's anthems *By the waters of Babylon, O Lord rebuke me not, Turn Thee again*, and *Turn Thou us, O good Lord*, are all not his.

Schubert's 'Adieu'. This song, found in some of the most respectable publishers' albums of 'Songs of Schubert', is by A. H. von Weyrauch, who, as he is otherwise forgotten, might at least be allowed this slight claim to remembrance.

Schubert's 'L'Abeille' ('The Bee'). See *Schubert, Franz* (2).

Schubert's Quartet for flute, viola, guitar, and violoncello. Schubert added the cello part to an existing trio ('Nocturne') by W. Matiegka.

Stradella's 'Pietà, Signore'. By Rossini —written by him as a joke.

Tartini's Variations on a Theme by Corelli. By Kreisler (q.v.).

Vivaldi's Violin Concerto in C. By Kreisler (q.v.).

Wagner's 'Eagle' March. This commonplace composition (given, for instance, in *The Advanced Montessori Method*) is probably by one Rudolf Wagner.

Wagner's 'Nibelungen' March. This composition, impudently described on some band programmes and record labels as 'by Wagner', should rather be described as 'containing a little Wagner' (two short themes from *Siegfried* in the middle).

Weber's Last Waltz (known on the continent of Europe as 'Weber's Last Thought'). Really the work of K. G. Reissiger (1798–1859), being No. 5 of his *Danses brillantes*, op. 26. He played these dances to Weber in February 1826, just before Weber left for London, where he was to die. Weber, for some reason, asked for a copy of this one of the dances and Reissiger wrote one out on the spot.

It was found in London amongst Weber's possessions at his death, supposed to be his, and published under the name it has since retained. The error was revealed to the actual composer of the music when J. P. Pixis (1788–1874) innocently sent him a copy of one of his (i.e. Pixis's) own compositions—'Fantasia on Weber's Last Thought'.

MISE (Fr.). 'Placing' (noun). *Mise de voix = Messa di voce* (q.v.).

MISERERE. The fifty-first Psalm (fiftieth in the Roman Catholic enumeration), *Miserere mei Deus* ('Have mercy upon me, O God'). In the Roman Catholic Church it is sung in the service of *Lauds* (q.v.). On the Thursday, Friday, and Saturday of Holy Week *Matins* and *Lauds*, taken together, are called Tenebrae, and the *Miserere* forms a part. In the Sistine Chapel at Rome (p. 516, pl. **93**. 1), Allegri's nine-voice setting (two choirs, one of four, the other of five voices, singing alternate verses) is used, the Pope and Cardinals kneeling. This composition was long kept as the exclusive property of the papal choir (compare *Improperia*), but the boy Mozart memorized it and so made a copy (see *Memory* 3). It was later published by Burney and others.

Other famous *Misereres* are those of Josquin des Prés, Palestrina, F. Anerio, and Lully—this last more a concert setting, though written for the chapel of Louis XIV.

MISSA AD CANONES. See *Mass* 5.

MISSA AD FUGAM. See *Mass* 5.

MISSA BREVIS. See *Mass* 5.

MISSA CANTATA. See *Mass* 1.

MISSA DE ANGELIS. See *Mass* 5.

'MISSA IN TEMPORE BELLI' (Haydn). See *Nicknamed Compositions* 13.

MISSAL. See *Liturgy*.

MISSA LECTA. See *Mass* 1.

MISSA PRIVATA. See *Mass* 1.

MISSA PRO DEFUNCTIS. The *Requiem* (q.v.).

MISSA QUARTI TONI. See *Mass* 5.

'MISSA SANCTI NICOLAI' (Haydn). See *Nicknamed Compositions* 13.

MISSA SINE NOMINE. See *Mass* 5.

MISSA SOLENNIS (or Solemnis), See *Mass* 1.

MISSA SUPRA VOCES MUSICALES. See *Mass* 5.

MISTERO (It.). 'Mystery.' So the adjective *Misterioso* and the adverb *Misteriosamente*.

MISTICO (It.). 'Mystic.'

MISURA (It.). 'Measure' (*a*) in the English sense of 'bar', (*b*) in the general sense of regularity. So *Alla misura*, 'in strict time'; *Senza misura*, 'without strict time', free in time. And so, too, *Misurato*, 'measured', i.e. strictly in time.

MIT (Ger.). 'With.' Very many terms of expression begin with this word. The adjectives and nouns which follow it in such terms of expression will be found in their alphabetical positions.

'MIT DEM HÖRNERSIGNAL', (Symphony, Haydn). See *Nicknamed* 11 (31).

MITCHELL, DONALD. Born in London in 1925. As a critic he specialized in modern music, and founded and edited the periodical *Music Survey*. He has edited books on Britten and Mozart, and has written a large-scale biography of Mahler. He is director of Faber Music Ltd.

MITLEIDIG (Ger.). 'Pitiful.'

MITTE (Ger.). 'Middle', e.g. *Auf der Mitte des Bogens*, 'in the middle of the bow'.

MIXED CADENCE. See *Cadence*.

MIXED MODES. See *Modes* 9.

MIXED VOICES. A term used in choral music meaning men's and women's voices, together, as, for instance, in the normal soprano, alto, tenor, and bass ('S.A.T.B.') combination.

MIXOLYDIAN. See *Modes* 6, 7.

MIXTURE STOP. See *Organ* 2 c, 14 V; *Harmony* 4.

MIZLER, LORENZ CHRISTOPH (1711–78). See *Criticism* 2.

MJÖEN, REIDAR. See *Scandinavia* 3.

M.K. = *Manualkoppel* (Ger.), i.e. 'Manual Coupler' (in organ music—followed by an indication of the particular manuals to be coupled).

M.M. See *Metronome*.

M.MUS. See *Degrees and Diplomas* 1.

MOD. See *Scotland* 1.

MODAL. Pertaining to the modes (q.v.).

MODE. See *Modes*.

MODENA, LEO OF. See *Jewish Music* 4.

MODERATO (It.), **MODÉRÉ** (Fr.). 'Moderate' (i.e. in point of speed). So the adverbs *Moderatamente*, *Modérément*.

MODES

1. Introductory.
2. History of the Modes.
3. The Nature of a Mode.
4. The Ambrosian Modes.
5. The Gregorian Extension.
6. The System of Glareanus.
7. A Note on Terminology.
8. Added Notes and the Break-up of the Modal System.
9. How to Identify the Mode of a Piece of Music.
10. Use of the Modes by Composers of the Non-modal Period.
11. The Term 'Church Modes'.

1. Introductory. A knowledge of the modes (sometimes called the 'Church Modes' or the 'Ecclesiastical Modes') is essential to the intelligent lover of music because they completely dominated European music for eleven hundred years, then continued (in a decreasing measure) to influence composers for another four hundred, after that still reappeared occasionally in composition, and have now again been brought into considerable use by composers. This prevalence of the modes and modal influence might be set out thus:

(a) The plainsong of the Western Christian Church, probably always modal in character, was, from, say, A.D. 400, systematically based on the modes; it still is, as is also much of the folk song of Europe.

(b) The earlier harmonized music (say, A.D. 900 to 1500) is entirely based on them.

(c) Later harmonized music is influenced by them up to the time of Palestrina and Byrd —and even of Bach and Handel, but with them the influence becomes rare and faint.

(d) Occasional appearances of the modes still continue to occur (see 10 below).

(e) In the late nineteenth and the twentieth centuries they have tended to come into use again (in a free treatment) as, for instance, in much of the work of Vaughan Williams.

2. History of the Modes.[1] The long history of the modes may be looked upon as the record of an attempt to put and keep in order the available material of music, i.e. the scheme of notes that had come to be accepted. The history begins in Greece, and a hint of its foundations there may be seen in the article *Scales* (see the reference to Pythagoras and the succeeding passages).

The material of music at the period when the modes became accepted was that which we would now speak of as represented by the white notes of the pianoforte or organ. Those notes constitute the scale which Pythagoras and the Greek thinkers of his time worked out scientifically (see *Scales* 5), whilst the black keys represent later additions (Pythagoras's tuning was a little different, but the above statement is true enough for the ordinary reader and is the conception which even the advanced student carries in his mind as a guide).

In the second century of the Christian era the Greeks were using their scale in seven ways or modes. Greek influence was strong in the early Christian Church, and when the famous Bishop of Milan, St. Ambrose (c. 340–97), took upon himself to set the music of the Church in order he accepted the Greek scale, but laid it out in four modes, or manners of using its notes. Pope Gregory (St. Gregory the Great, c. 540–604) took the matter in hand again (it is usual to credit him with the good work: at any rate, it was accomplished about the time of his papacy) and left the system substantially as it has remained ever since. To the four modes of Ambrose he added four others that were perhaps not so much new modes as additional ways of using the old ones (for further references to

[1] The account this condensed 'History of the Modes' gives is that long traditionally accepted, and is convenient as affording a clear and logical classification. Some modern students of the subject, however, consider the roles it assigns St. Ambrose and St. Gregory to be of doubtful validity. Pending a definitive agreement on the subject by deep students of the matter the account is left unchanged (i.e. as it appeared in previous editions of the *Companion*).

the work of SS. Ambrose and Gregory and their reforms see 4 and 5 below, and *Plainsong*).

To these eight modes four others were later added, so that the whole series with which the student of today needs to be acquainted consists of twelve.

3. The Nature of a Mode. These twelve modes are not *keys*. All our major keys are, except for pitch, precisely alike; a listener with an excellent ear cannot tell one from another unless he happens to possess the gift of 'absolute pitch' (q.v.). The difference between one mode and another is not the kind of difference which exists between C major and D major but that which exists between C major and C minor or D major and D minor, i.e. a difference of the arrangement of tones and semitones, and hence, necessarily, of the width of some of the other intervals. It may be called a difference of *flavour*, so that a keen ear, well accustomed to modal music, should be able to tell in what mode a piece of plainsong or a piece of early harmonized music lies.

4. The Ambrosian Modes. What the four modes of Ambrose sounded like may be heard by playing in the pianoforte octave scales of white notes beginning on the following four notes, D, E, F, G. If any little melody be composed within the limits of one of those scales, and then transferred to another of them, it will be found to change considerably in character owing to the different disposition of the tones and semitones.

The fifth note and the first note of an Ambrosian mode were treated as notes of special importance. The interval of the fifth is one of the most fundamental intervals (see *Scales* 4), and it seemed natural, when there was a passage of the liturgy to intone, to use, as a general formula, those two notes, the fifth of the mode as a reciting note and the first of the mode as a dropping of the voice, or 'cadence'. Thus *Dominant* and *Final* came about.

An Ambrosian mode, then, consists of a series of eight notes of which the fifth dominates and the bottom note serves as a point of rest, and the Ambrosian series is as follows:

D to D, with Dominant A
E to E,   ,,   ,,   B (later C)
F to F,   ,,   ,,   C
G to G,   ,,   ,,   D

The dominant of the mode E–E, coming logically on what was considered the unstable note B (a note which the spiritual guides of our ancestors looked upon as barely respectable; cf. *Musica Ficta*), was later changed to C.

Out of those four modes could be fashioned (and was fashioned) a great variety of plainsong for the service of the Church.

5. The Gregorian Extension. Gregory's re-ordering of the plainsong, at the end of the sixth century, had as one object the provision of greater variety, for he added to the above (which he called the *Authentic Modes*) another set of four (which he called the *Plagal Modes*).

Each of the plagal modes was a new form of a corresponding authentic mode. It was simply the same mode taken in another compass, so as to lie between its former dominant and dominant (with the final in the middle) instead of, as before, between final and final (with the dominant in the middle).

A piece of plainsong in a plagal mode would come to a close on the same final as a piece of plainsong in the corresponding authentic mode, but its range would be different, and in order not to have the reciting note at the bottom or top of the compass a new one was appointed, lying three notes below the old one.

Lest any misconception should arise, it may here be added that in certain more elaborate plainsong no one note was used for what may be called the 'recitation', but whatever notes were given to it would be likely to circle around the dominant, to touch on it fairly often, and to throw it into relief in the mind of the listener.

It is interesting to note that the Presbyterian precentors of the Scottish Highlands in the mid-nineteenth century were using a similar system in 'lining out' the metrical psalms for the congregation to sing. They frequently gave out a line of the words of the psalm on a vague melody of their own, circling about the dominant, after which the congregation sang those words to a line of the proper psalm tune—and so through the psalm (see *Hymns and Hymn Tunes* 8).

The whole series of modes may now be set out as follows:

Mode I	D–D, with Dominant A
„ II	A–A, „ „ F
„ III	E–E, „ „ C
„ IV	B–B, „ „ A
„ V	F–F, „ „ C
„ VI	C–C, „ „ A
„ VII	G–G, „ „ D
„ VIII	D–D, „ „ C

(The dominant of Mode VIII should logically be B, but this is avoided for the same reason as operated in the case of Mode III, explained under 4.)

It will be seen that in this system of numeration the odd-numbered modes are authentic and the even-numbered plagal. Occasionally the wide compass of a melody would be such that it took in a good deal of both the authentic and the plagal form of its mode, and then it would be said to be in a '*mixed mode*' (referred to again later).

6. The System of Glareanus. Nine hundred and fifty years after Gregory, a Swiss monk, Henry of Glarus (Henricus Glareanus), a friend of Erasmus, was studying and writing about music. He brought forth the theory (in his *Dodecachordon*, 1547) that there should be not eight but twelve modes, adding a mode on A (the Aeolian) with its plagal and one on C (the Ionian) with its plagal, four new ones in all (he rejected the idea of a mode on B with its plagal, sharing the objection already mentioned to any prominence of that note). To some ex-

tent these new modes already existed, for composers had gone ahead of theory, but the plainsong of the Church was, and still is, restricted to the eight modes of Gregory. As a great part of Glareanus's argument was derived from what he understood of Greek theory, he gave to the modes what he thought to be their Greek names. His nomenclature is incorrect, but it has established itself, and although the system of numbering is better than the pseudo-Greek naming both are now in use, and hence both are shown in the table below, which gives the complete modal system as gradually built up by Ambrose in the fourth century, Gregory in the sixth, and Glareanus in the sixteenth.

In looking at this diagram it should be clearly understood that modes are not a question of *pitch*. Any mode (whilst preserving the order of tones and semitones which give it its individual character) can be taken at any pitch. It is usual, however, to show the modes at what we may call their original pitches, and this helps to make their memorizing simple.

THE MODES

(Showing the groups of five notes common to the Authentic and the Plagal form of each)

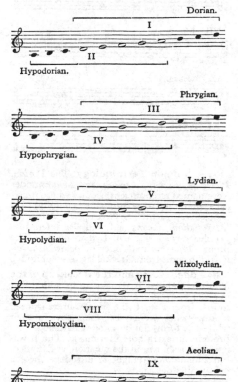

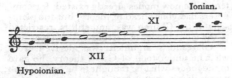

Ionian.

XI

XII

Hypoionian.

(Sometimes as XI and XII are shown the Locrian and Hypolocrian, with B as final, but these modes barely existed. When they appear the Ionian and Hypoionian are numbered XIII and XIV: some prefer always to use this latter numeration.)

THE AUTHENTIC MODES

(Shown uniformly with C as final—with the semitones marked)

I. Dorian.

III. Phrygian.

V. Lydian.

VII. Mixolydian.

IX. Aeolian.

XI. Ionian.

7. A Note on Terminology. The *Dorian, Phrygian, Lydian, Aeolian,* and·*Ionian* modes were named after ancient peoples whose musical system they were (probably fancifully) supposed to represent. The Greek prefix '*Mixo-*', in '*Mixolydian*', means half, and also refers to a people (they spoke a 'half-Lydian' dialect). The prefix '*Hypo-*' means 'under' or 'below'. '*Plagal*' is said to come from Greek 'Plagios'—'oblique'.

8. Added Notes and the Break-up of the Modal System. It remains to be added that in order to avoid the interval of the augmented fourth from F to B (i.e. in the untransposed modes—what we may call the modes in their white-key form) the B was often flattened. This brought an extra note into music. The B was not always shown, in the notation, as flattened, but singers were taught to introduce the flat on suitable occasions.

The recognition of B flat as a note made it possible to notate a piece of music a fifth lower or a fourth higher without disturbing the relative positions of the notes (i.e. the intervals).

For a long time B flat was the only 'key signature' (as we should now say) additional to the open key.

F sharp was later added and then E flat, C sharp, and G sharp (see *Musica Ficta*); and then, naturally, the modal system began to break up. The Aeolian and Ionian modes (our present minor and major scales) were more suitable for harmony and by the aid of these accidentals other modes began to assimilate themselves to these two. Finally, the whole system went to pieces, so far as harmonic music was concerned, and composers wrote on a key system, with two modes in every key, and a large number of keys, only limited by certain difficulties of tuning keyboard instruments, which difficulties were at length overcome (see *Temperament*), so that they were soon using twelve keys in two modes each, or twenty-four in all—but *only* two modes instead of four, eight, or twelve; thus (since flavour is a more distinctive ingredient in music than pitch) there was loss as well as gain. It is curious to reflect that of the two modes that survived, the Ionian (exactly our major) had been styled the 'wanton mode' (*modus lascivus*), having before Glareanus's day crept into secular music, especially that of the troubadours in the eleventh to thirteenth century (see *Minstrels*, etc. 4, 5).

9. How to Identify the Mode of a Piece of Music. In order to discover in what mode a piece of plainsong lies, look first at its last note, which is the Final of the mode. If, for instance, this last note is D then the mode is either the First or the Second (Dorian or Hypodorian). Examine now the range of the melody. If it lies (with possibly the exception of an odd note or two) between two finals this mode is Authentic; if between two dominants it is Plagal. Thus in the case just imagined of a melody in the First or Second Mode (Dorian or Hypodorian), if it lies between D and D the mode is the First (or Dorian); if between A and A the Second (or Hypodorian).

The case of melodies of extended compass has already been mentioned (end of 5); if they cover the range of an octave and a fourth, which represents the two forms of the mode together (e.g. from A to the D twelve notes above) they are said to be in a *Mixed Mode*.

Sometimes a plainsong melody is preceded by a B flat signature. This indicates its transposition. Mentally retranspose the melody a fourth lower 'from Key F' (as we should say) 'to Key C', and proceed as before.

When we read modal music of the period where varied key-signatures begin, or when we are using modern transposed editions, it is necessary mentally to transpose the music to 'Key C' (to use modern terms), and then calculate as before.

The statement that a piece of harmonized music is in such-and-such a mode is only relative. Obviously it would be impossible to keep all the voices of a four-voice composition within the same octave limits. Roughly speaking, the natural range of the alto voice lies a fourth or fifth below that of treble and that of the bass a fourth or fifth below that of the tenor. Generally, then, if the treble and tenor are authentic, the alto and bass will be plagal, and vice versa. During the first five hundred years of harmonized music, say A.D. 900–1400 (see *Harmony*), church composers rarely or never discarded plainsong, their composition being of the nature of a harmonization of a piece of plainsong, which is generally in the tenor part (so called because it 'holds' the plainsong, whilst the others stray around it); Palestrina and others of his period, although quite accustomed to free composition, would, on occasion, revert to the old practice. In such cases it is the nature of the tenor part that decides the mode in which the whole composition is said to lie.

In free composition (that is composition not written around a plainsong tenor) it is still the nature of the tenor that decides the mode, but in such music glance first at the bass of the last chord, as the final is now to be looked for there, the harmony demanding this.

Obviously the naming of the mode in the case of a harmonized composition is something of a convention. A four-part or five-part composition may be felt to be in the Dorian Mode, but whether it is in the Dorian proper or the Hypodorian (the first mode or the second) the ear cannot decide. It is just 'Dorian' (because the intervals in all the parts fall into a more or less Dorian–Hypodorian order, and because the dominant and final, D and A, are prominent).

10. Use of the Modes by Composers of the Non-modal Period. Allusion has already been made (section 1) to the occasional use of modes by composers of the post-modal period. Beethoven's String Quartet in A minor (op. 132) has, it will be remembered, a slow movement headed 'Song of Thanksgiving to the Deity on Recovery from an Illness; written in the Lydian Mode'. The last words of this description are, however, only partly true. The 'Incarnatus' of the Mass in D, on the other hand, is pretty definitely Dorian. Mozart's Mass, K. 258, at the end shows a strong Mixolydian influence. And there are a good many other instances in late eighteenth-, nineteenth-, and twentieth-century compositions.

Bach's so-called 'Dorian Mode' Fugue for the organ (see *Nicknamed Compositions*) is, however, not in the mode mentioned, but in D minor, though the original copy omitted (as was then common) the B flat signature, and so suggested the mode. As a matter of obvious fact, a fugue of the Bach period, with its alternation of tonic and dominant in the very exposition, and its modulatory episodes and entries afterwards, could hardly be written in a mode: even the fantasias or early fugues of a century before Bach show as a rule little modal influence. Some of the modal chorales (see

Chorale) that Bach arranged for four-part choir he harmonized in a quite un-modal way. Hauptmann has pointed out modal influences here and there in Handel, as in *Israel in Egypt*, where the chorus, 'And I will exalt him', is essentially Dorian, and the chorus 'Egypt was glad' (taken by Handel from the somewhat earlier composer Kerll) essentially Phrygian.

Dr. Wm. Pole, the scientist and musician, in his *The Philosophy of Music* (1879), discussing the modes, made a shrewd prophecy: 'It is by no means impossible that composers of genius might some day open for themselves a considerable field for novelty and originality by shaking off the trammels of our restricted modern tonality; and that they might find scope for the development of the art in some kind of return to the principles of the ancient forms [of scale], which at present are only looked down upon as obsolete remnants of a barbarous age.' This prophecy has had a degree of fulfilment.

In Stanford's *Musical Composition*, the student is urged to practise writing in the modes ('instead of two scales he has six, every one of them different in constitution—i.e. in the succession of tones and semitones; he has, therefore three times the variety of the contrapuntist who bases himself on the ordinary major and minor scales'). In the Bodleian Library, Oxford, is a series of anthems by Maurice Greene (q.v.), representing, in its intentions, apparently, an early eighteenth-century anticipation of the above early twentieth-century suggestion.

11. The Term 'Church Modes'. Finally a word may be added in removal of what seems to be a rather common misconception. Because of the association of the names of great ecclesiastical figures like Ambrose and Gregory with the modes, and the connexion of modes with plainsong, it is sometimes assumed that the modes are a church possession. They are often spoken of as 'the Church Modes' or 'the Ecclesiastical Modes'. Now the Church helped to classify them and codify the system of their employment, but held no monopoly in them. The minstrels, troubadours, and the like, used them (see *Minstrels*, *Troubadours*, etc.)—and no other scales, for no others were known. Many of the folk-song melodies collected in English villages have been found to be in a mode, not a modern scale. Folk songs in the scales are either more recent in origin or are old ones that have conformed to later fashion, so somewhat changing their melodies, or are to be regarded as in the Ionian or Aeolian Mode.

For a reference to the modal influences in sixteenth-century harmony see *Harmony* 8 and for one to the influence of harmony in destroying the modes see *Harmony* 17.

For a reference to a popular survival of modal influence (even in our cities) see *Street Music* 2.

MODINHA. A type of song popular in Portugal—not a folk song but a sort of composed song which has been popular from the eighteenth century onwards. It varies from simplicity to considerable elaboration.

MODO (It.). Either (*a*) 'manner' (*In modo di*, 'in the manner of'), or (*b*) 'mode' (see *Modes*).

MODULATION. This is a term which, as generally used, is connected with the system of key (q.v.) which began to rule music from the latter part of the sixteenth century, soon ruled it completely, and may be said to have continued to do so until the late nineteenth century still doing so in a considerable measure.

According to that system there are two modes, the major and minor, either of which may be taken at any pitch, i.e. commencing on any one of the twelve different notes from C to B, there being thus twelve major and twelve minor keys. Any piece of music written according to the system adopts one of the twenty-four keys as its main one, starts in that key and ends in it. But unless the composition be one of the very tiniest dimensions it will not throughout its course remain constant to that key. The needs of variety will be met by changes of key, tactfully effected by the process called modulation.

Modulation may be familiarly defined as a method of key-change without pain. The adoption of the new set of tonal conditions is softened, or at any rate made intelligible. For instance, the 'take-off' into the new key may be judiciously managed from a chord that is common both to it and the old key. Or a single note that is common to the old key and to the chord which is to effect the modulation may be sounded and dwelt upon until the ear has thoroughly accepted it, whereupon the said chord supervenes and effects the change. Or a chord of the old key may be regarded as changed in notation so that it becomes one of the defining chords of the new one.

The last is called **Enharmonic Modulation** (see *Enharmonic Intervals*, also *Diminished Seventh* and *Augmented Sixth*).

The simplest modulations are the following (to what are called the 'Related' or 'Attendant' keys):

To the Relative Minor (or Major, as the case may be).
To the Dominant Key and its Relative Minor (or Major).
To the Subdominant Key and its Relative Minor (or Major).

All these five keys have many notes in common with the original one, so that the music, in removing, takes most of its furniture with it, and thus quickly feels at home. For instance, the key of the dominant has all the notes of the original key except one (its seventh is sharpened), the subdominant the same (its fourth is flattened). Taking Key C major as our example the scheme of relationship is:

C major and A minor
G major and E minor F major and D minor.

Taking the key A minor as our example the scheme is:
A minor and C major
E minor and G major D minor and F major.

Probably the tonic major and minor (e.g. C major and C minor) should also, properly, be considered to be 'related keys', as modulation from one to the other is very easily and naturally effected; they are not, however, usually spoken of as such.

Generally speaking, the modulations of the period after the modes had gone and the key system taken their place (the period that takes in Purcell and Corelli, Bach and Handel, Haydn and Mozart, and their many important contemporaries) is confined to these related keys. Then came Beethoven, a brusquer man and musician, who not only changed key more frequently but, on occasion, leapt, with little notice to the listener, into unrelated keys (*Extraneous Modulation*), and from his time this greater freedom was commonly exercised. For one of the influences that long operated in restraint of freedom in modulation read the article *Temperament* (especially section 6).

MODULATOR. See *Tonic Sol-fa*.

MODUS LASCIVUS. The Ionian mode, same as our major scale of C. See *Modes* 8.

MOERAN, ERNEST JOHN (p. 352, pl. 55. 8). Born near London in 1894 and died in Co. Kerry in 1950, aged fifty-five. He was of Irish descent but of Norfolk residence and mixed Irish and East Anglian sympathies. He collected English and Irish folk tunes and composed orchestral and chamber music, choral music, songs, and other things, much of it showing the folk-tune influence. Larger-scale works include a Symphony (1937) and a Sinfonietta (1944), a Violin Concerto (1942), a Cello Concerto, and a Piano Concerto, a Rhapsody for pianoforte and orchestra (1943), and an Overture for a Masque (1944).

See *Concerto* 6 c (1894).

MOFFAT, ALFRED. Born in Edinburgh in 1866 and died in London in 1950, aged eighty-three. He devoted himself to the revival, by publication, of old and neglected compositions, vocal and instrumental and of various nationalities and periods, but especially those of the eighteenth century (see a reference under *Sonata* 10 c), and also of the traditional songs of the different parts of the British Islands—this last occasionally in collaboration with Frank Kidson (q.v.). Cf. *Ravenscroft, John*.

MÖGLICH (Ger.). 'Possible.' Thus *So rasch wie möglich*, 'as quick as possible'. The superlative is *möglichst*.

MOINS (Fr.). 'Less.'

MOIR, D. M. See *Canadian Boat Song*.

MOITIÉ (Fr.). 'Half.'

MOKE, MARIE. See *Pleyel*.

MOLIÈRE (1622–73). See references under *Opera* 11 b; *Ariadne*; *Charpentier, M. A.*

MOLIQUE, WILHELM BERNHARD. Born at Nuremberg in 1802 and died near Stuttgart in 1869, aged sixty-six. He early showed remarkable ability as a violinist, took lessons from Spohr, and in youth and younger manhood held orchestral positions in Vienna, Munich, and Stuttgart. Then he came to London, where he won high popularity and remained until his retirement a few years before his death.

His compositions, which include a number of violin concertos and a considerable amount of chamber music, show the influence of his old master, Spohr, and also of Mendelssohn. They are now little heard.

See reference under *Reed-Organ Family* 5.

MOLL. German for 'minor' in the sense of key, e.g. *A moll*, 'A minor'; *Moll Ton*, or *Moll Tonart*, 'minor key'. See Table 9.

MOLLE, MOLLEMENTE (It.). 'Gentle', 'gently'.

MOLTO (It.). 'Much', 'very', e.g. *Molto allegro* 'very quickly'. *Moltissimo* is the superlative.

MOMBACH. See *Jewish Music* 6.

MOMENT MUSICAL (Fr.). This is one of the many terms introduced in the early nineteenth century, when pianoforte composition was being developed on the romantic side, as titles for short compositions for that instrument. It owes its introduction, apparently, to Schubert. (In some editions the term appears in the older spelling, i.e. in the plural 'Momens'.)

MOMPOU, FEDERICO. Born at Barcelona in 1893. He is the composer of piano music of poetic quality, showing the influence of the modern French school (cf. *Spain* 7), and in 1921 took up residence in Paris. He has evolved a style to which he gives the name 'primitivista' (no bar lines, no key signatures, etc.).

MONDONVILLE, JEAN JOSEPH CASSANEA DE. Born at Narbonne in 1711 and died near Paris in 1772, aged sixty. He was a noted Paris violinist, Superintendent of the Music to Louis XV, and composer of motets, oratorios (see *Oratorio* 4), instrumental music, and (especially) operas. In the famous fight of 1752–4 between the lovers of French music and those of Italian music, known as the *Guerre des Bouffons* (see *Bouffons*), he was one of the chosen champions of the national school.

MONDRIAN. See *History* 9.

MONET, CLAUDE (1840–1926). French painter. See references under *Romantic; Impressionism.*

MONIUSZKO, STANISLAW. Born at Minsk, White Russia, in 1819 and died at Warsaw in 1872, aged fifty-three. He was an organist who became musical director of the Warsaw opera house and professor at the Conservatory. He wrote operas (e.g. *Halka*), masses, over 270 chamber works, songs, etc. In his own country (cf. *Poland*) he has great reputation.

MONK. The two contemporaries (apparently unrelated).

(1) EDWIN GEORGE. Born at Frome, in Somerset, in 1819 and died at Radley, near Oxford, in 1900, aged eighty. He was organist and music-master of Radley College, and then, for nearly a quarter of a century, organist of York Minster. He wrote church music, and his name (like that of W. H. Monk, see below) was much seen as editor of hymn-books, chant-books, and the like, he being one of the prominent workers in the Victorian Anglican musical revival.

(2) WILLIAM HENRY. Born in London in 1823 and died there in 1889, aged sixty-five. He was organist and professor of vocal music at King's College, London, and held other official appointments. Like his namesake above, he was active in the Victorian Anglican musical revival and edited hymn-books and the like. Notably he was one of the musical editors of *Hymns Ancient and Modern*.

See references under *Hymns and Hymn Tunes* 6; *Presbyterian Church Music* 3; *Steggall*.

MONK'S MARCH, THE, or THE MONKS OF BANGOR'S MARCH. This 'Welsh folk song', claimed as the tune of the monks of Bangor when they marched into Chester in 603, is first found in Playford's *Dancing Master* (1665), where it figures as the march of General Monk —a very different thing, involving a difference of period of a thousand years! The connexion with Bangor or Wales is a myth dispelled by the great authority on British songs, Frank Kidson, in an article in the *Musical Times*, February 1911. Amongst the many misled was Sir Walter Scott, who wrote to the tune words treating of the massacre of the monks of Bangor.

MONN.

(1) GEORG MATTHIAS. Born in Lower Austria in 1717 and died at Vienna in 1750, aged thirty-two or thirty-three. He was organist of a Vienna church and composed symphonies, chamber music, etc. His dates show him to be a younger man than the composers of the Bach–Handel school and to have preceded those of the Haydn–Mozart school. He was born, indeed, about the same time as the father of the sonata, C. P. E. Bach, but died nearly forty years before him. The style of his music conforms to the expectations aroused by these considerations, i.e. it is transitional. Schönberg made performing arrangements of some of his works.

There is a doubt in the ascription of certain works to him, as he had a namesake, variously described as 'Johann Christoph Monn' and 'Giovanni Matteo Monn', or 'Mann'. (This particularly applies to a symphony in E flat.)

(2) JOHANN CHRISTOPH. See above.

(3) GIOVANNI MATTEO. See *Monn* (1).

MONNET, JEAN (1703–85). See *Bouffons.*

MONOCHORD (p. 609, pl. **107**. 1, 2). This is a scientific instrument more than a musical one. It was in use amongst the Ancient Egyptians and the Ancient Greeks and is in use amongst physicists today under the name of *Sonometer*.

Fundamentally it is nothing but a sound-box over which is stretched a single string which can be divided at any point by a movable bridge, the position of which can be accurately determined by a scale of measurement marked on the surface over which it moves. The ratios of intervals and many others of the facts that make up the very foundations of the science of acoustics were discovered by its use, and for five thousand years it gave rise to intricate mathematical calculations, the results of which may be seen expressed in tabular form in many old scientific musical treatises.

It is always said that in medieval times the monochord was used not only scientifically but also didactically—in teaching intervals to singers: this may have been so, but it must have been a very clumsy piece of apparatus for such a purpose. It is also said to have been used for giving the pitch to a choir, but as so much depends on variable factors, such as the tension of the string, here again its use cannot have been very practical. Tans'ur (1772) says that in his time the English bell-founders were using the monochord to tune their bells.

The principle of obtaining variously pitched sounds from one string was later adopted into keyboard music by the invention of the clavichord (q.v.) in which, at first, each string was so treated, and which, hence, we sometimes find described as a monochord (or *Manichord*).

The one-string principle is also applied to the *Tromba marina* (q.v.), but here the sounds obtained are all harmonics. The principle of the movable bridge is found in the Norwegian *Langleik* (see *Scandinavia* 3).

MONODRAMA. Same as melodrama (q.v.) with the restriction that it is for a single speaker.

MONODY. See *Recitative*; *Opera* 1.

MONOPHONIC. Having one 'line' of notes —as distinct from *Homophonic* (several lines of notes but moving together as chords, and without individuality in the lines) and *Polyphonic* (several lines of notes, each with individuality and moving with some independence).

Cf. *Polyphony*.

MONOPOLIES in musical activities of various kinds constitute an element in the history of music that is often overlooked. Craft and commerce were everywhere in Europe based on the monopoly principle until the very end of the sixteenth century and in some parts for long after that, the gradual destruction of the monopoly system being one of the revolutionary successes of the centuries which followed.

In England, trade with large tracts of the earth's surface was granted in monopoly to companies especially chartered for the purpose, and at home the sale of great numbers of commodities was granted in monopoly to various individual or groups of individuals. There was pointed reference to the evils of this system in the masque given in 1633 by the lawyers of the Inns of Court before Charles I and his queen, to which Ives and William Lawes wrote the music, ridiculous incidents being introduced in one of the sections of the masque, such as that of a projector begging 'a patent of monopoly to feed capons with carretts'. The evil only gradually died out and, years after, Charles II offered one to a man who had stood on his head on the top of a steeple—'to prevent any one doing it but himself'.

Nearly all musical activity, up to this period, was covered by monopoly. For its application in the control of the musical craft or profession, see *Profession of Music*. For its very hampering effect upon the issue of musical publications see *Printing of Music* 1; *Publishing of Music* 4; also *Scotland* 9. For a passing reference to the operatic monopoly in France see *Lully*.

The principle of monopoly is today, happily, maintained only in unavoidable instances. Musical copyright and the patenting of improvements in instruments are forms of monopoly of an obviously legitimate and necessary kind. The British government originally granted a monopoly of radio musical performance to the British Broadcasting Corporation (see *Broadcasting* 3), in order to avoid a clash of interests and a multiplicity of broadcasting stations and wave-lengths that, in a small area like that of Britain, would have led to impossible confusion.

In addition to the references above given, note *Publishing of Music* 1 (for Petrucci's monopoly at Venice) and *Plainsong* 3 (for Papal privileges in editions of plainsong). Also *Cambert*; *Lully*; *Morley*; *Barley*.

MONOTONING. See *Intoning*.

MONS, PHILIPPE DE. See *Monte*.

MONSIGNY, PIERRE ALEXANDRE. Born near St. Omer in 1729 and died in Paris in 1817, aged eighty-seven. He was a man of 'good family', who held various official positions in Paris, including that of inspector-general of canals. He played the violin well and enjoyed fame as a composer of comic operas for about twenty years during the latter part of the reign of Louis XV and the earlier part of the reign of Louis XVI, after which he ceased composition.

He counts as one of the most eminent of the contemporaries of Grétry, Philidor, and Duny. His greatest musical gift was attractive melody.

See references as follows: *Opera* 21 a, 24 c (1769); *Opera Buffa*; *France* 8.

MONTE, FILIPPO DI, or Philippe de Mons (p. 96, pl. **15.** 5). Born at Mechlin about 1521 and died at Prague in 1603, in his early eighties. He was one of the later of the composers who, by their compositions and their labours in many parts of Europe, contributed so greatly to the musical fame of the Netherlands; indeed, he was spoken of as the rival of Palestrina. For about thirty-five years he was musical director at the court of the Holy Roman Empire, first at Vienna and then, when it was moved, at Prague. He was very prolific, publishing over one thousand madrigals as well as many masses and motets. A complete edition was begun in 1927.

See *Belgium* 1; *Bohemia*; *Italy* 10 (end); *Composition* 10.

MONTÉCLAIR, MICHEL PINOLET DE. Born about 1667 at Andelot (*not* Chaumont) in north-eastern France and died near Paris in 1737, aged nearly seventy. He began life as a choir-boy, then travelled in Italy as music-master to a prince, and for the last thirty years of his life was a double-bass player in the Paris opera orchestra, practising likewise as a teacher of the violin. He wrote operas, ballets, cantatas, instrumental music (including a quantity for flute), and educational works.

MONTEMEZZI, ITALO. Born near Verona in 1875 and died there in 1952, aged seventy-six. Beginning life as a student of engineering he took up music late, studied at the Conservatory of Milan, and at thirty appeared as an opera composer. At thirty-eight he achieved some international fame with the opera *The Love of the Three Kings* ('L'Amore dei tre re'), a work of which a characteristic is an abundance of Italian melody.

MONTER (Fr.). 'To raise.' So the imperative, *Montez.*

MONTESSORI. See *Education* 1 (near end).

MONTEVERDI (or Monteverde), CLAUDIO (GIOVANNI ANTONIO) (p. 516, pl. **93**. 4). Born at Cremona in 1567 and died at Venice in 1643, aged seventy-six. He boldly applied, with artistic insight and ingenuity, the ideas of 'The New Music' (see *Opera* 1, 2; *Peri*; *Caccini*). His harmonic invention, freedom and richness of his orchestral accompaniments, and the increased effectiveness of recitative in his hands, give him a place of the highest importance in the history of music, and, in particular, of opera.

He travelled in Hungary, Flanders, and elsewhere. For eleven years he was attached to the court of Mantua, where his important opera *Orpheus* (p. 688, p. **115**. 1) was produced (1607). His *The Coronation of Poppaea* (1642) is a masterpiece. For his last thirty years he directed the music of St. Mark's, Venice.

See *History* 4; *Opera* 2, 7, 24 (1607, 1642); *Leading Motif*; *Aria*; *Madrigal* 7; *Toccata*; *Orchestra* 1; *Trumpet Family* 2 a, 3; *Trombone Family* 3; *Malipiero*; *Ingegneri*; *Reed Organ*; *Publishing* 1.

MONTHLY MUSICAL RECORD. See *Journals*; *Abraham.*

MONTPELLIER BOOK. See *Plainsong* 3.

MONTRE. See *Organ* 14 I.

MONTREAL. See *Schools of Music.*

MONTRÉSOR (or Montressor). See *Opera* 21 f.

MONUMENTA MUSICAE BYZANTINAE. See *Greek Church and Music* 4.

MOODY AND SANKEY. See *Church Music* 2; *Hymns and Hymn Tunes* 12; p. 496, pl. **89**. 5.

MOOKE, MARIE. See *Pleyel.*

'MOONLIGHT' SONATA (Beethoven). See *Nicknamed Compositions* 5.

MOÓR, EMANUEL (1863–1931). Hungarian composer of symphonies, operas, chamber music, etc.; and instrumental inventor (see *Keyboard* 4; and for his wife see *Libraries*).

MOORE.

(1) THOMAS (p. 481, pl. **84**. 4). Born in Dublin in 1779 and died at Bromham, Wiltshire, in 1852, aged seventy-two. Like Scott, he made his native country romantic. He came, as a young man, to England and quickly became a social and literary success, playing and singing his way, a modern troubadour, into the hearts of drawing-room audiences.

From 1807 onwards he rose ever higher in fame by writing, under the general title of *Irish Melodies* (at one hundred guineas apiece, or nearly thirteen thousand pounds in all), poems for the collection of Irish folk tunes published under the musical editorship of Sir John Stevenson. (This is today still popular, re-edited by Stanford.) Other series of songs followed—*Sacred Songs, Popular National Airs,* and the like.

His reputation as a poet was so overwhelming that the firm of Longman agreed to pay him the highest lump sum ever given for a poem, that of three thousand pounds for 'Lalla Rookh', which rivalled in popularity the contemporary productions of Scott and Byron and was translated into almost all European languages. That and other large-scale works are now almost forgotten, but their author is not, nor can he be so long as singers and listeners continue to value such simple yet elegant, impassioned yet sincere poems as 'The Harp that once through Tara's Halls', 'Let Erin Remember', ''Tis the last Rose of Summer', and 'The Minstrel Boy'.

See references under *Ireland* 1; *Last Rose of Summer*; *Saint Patrick's Day*; *Eileen Aroon*; *Berlioz*; *Folk Song* 3; *Canadian Boat Song*; *Misattributed Compositions*, s.v. 'Beethoven's "Dream of St. Jerome"'.

(2) DOUGLAS STUART. Born on Long Island in 1893 and died there in 1969, aged seventy-five. He studied at Yale and in Paris (with d'Indy and Nadia Boulanger), and at Cleveland under Bloch: Pulitzer and Guggenheim awards enabled him to further his studies in Europe. He wrote *Moby Dick*, a *Barnum Suite*, and other pieces for orchestra, a violin sonata, etc., and six operas, including *The Devil and Daniel Webster* (1938), *Giants in the Earth* (1951), *The Ballad of Baby Doe* (1956), and *Wings of the Dove* (1961).

In 1926 he became Associate Professor of Music in Columbia University, New York, and in 1940 succeeded Daniel Gregory Mason as Professor and Head of the Music Department, retiring in 1962.

(3) THOMAS (seventeenth century). See *Printing of Music* 2.

(4) THOMAS (eighteenth century). See *Presbyterian* 4.

MOORS AND MUSIC. See *Spain* 1, 2, 3.

MOQUEUR (Fr.). 'Mocking', 'waggish'.

MORALES.

(1) CRISTÓBAL (p. 977, pl. **164.** 1). Born at Seville *c.* 1500 and died at Malaga in 1553. In his twenties, being then a priest, he was a singer in the pontifical chapel at Rome; in his thirties, for a period, director of the music in the cathedral of Toledo. He then held various other church positions, but his life is a little obscure and it is evident that he was somewhat of a wanderer.

He held a high place amongst his contemporaries and his countrymen as a composer of church music, and this reputation has been confirmed by succeeding ages and by the best judges everywhere of the sixteenth-century contrapuntal music. A fair number of his Masses, motets, and the like were printed in his own country, in Venice, and in Paris and Lyons. His settings of the Magnificat were famous.

See *Spain* 5.

(2) OLALLO JUAN MAGNUS. Born at Almeria, Spain, in 1874 and died at Tällberg in 1957, aged eighty-two. His mother was Swedish and he was first educated at Stockholm. He joined the staff of the Stockholm Conservatory and also worked as a music critic. He wrote orchestral and chamber music, etc.

(3) PEDRO GARCÍA. Born at Huelva, in southern Spain, in 1879, and there died in 1938, aged fifty-nine. He was a poet, composer, violinist, conductor, and propagandist of Spanish music and dance, well known especially in London, where he studied at one time at the Royal College of Music, and where he long resided. His compositions are chiefly vocal.

MORALITIES. See *Mysteries.*

MORASCO. Same as *Moresca* (q.v.).

MORAVIAN BRETHREN. See *Bohemia; Concert* 15; *United States of America* 3.

MORBIDO, MORBIDEZZA (It.). Soft or gentle; softness or gentleness. (The translations 'morbid', 'morbidity', given in some books, are misleading; cf. the use of the term 'morbidezza' in painting, for delicacy of reproduction of flesh tints.)

MORCEAU (Fr.). 'Piece'. So *Morceau symphonique,* 'symphonic piece'.

MORDENT. This ornament, in both its forms, Lower (standard) and Upper (inverted), is shown in Table 12 at the opening of the volume. The German name for the *Lower Mordent* has always been simply 'mordent'. The *Upper* Mordent was thoroughly out of fashion during most of the seventeenth century and the first half of the eighteenth, and its use in music of those periods, though frequent in modern performances, is generally incorrect. The Berlin school of C. P. E. Bach restored its social status under the name of *Inverted Mordent,* or alternatively *Schneller.* The modern German name is *Pralltriller. Prall* is a German adjective meaning 'tight'; *Pralltriller* means literally 'compact trill', and has been used in both early and modern times for the half-shake, which can be likened to an upper mordent with

an extra note, namely the upper note, added at the beginning. But the two ornaments are not really the same, and it is typical of the confusion into which both the names and the performance (not to mention the signs) of most ornaments have fallen that the methodical Germans should let them share the same name. It is, however, interesting that the Germans confine the name 'Mordent' to the *Lower* Mordent, thus confirming that this is alone the standard form.

Further varieties of Mordent found in early music are generally (but not, unfortunately, always reliably) set out in full by modern editors. The chief are the *Double Mordent* (two 'waggles' of the fingers instead of one, i.e. four notes instead of two) and the *Prolonged Mordent* or *Extended Mordent* (further 'waggles' and notes). Occasionally extra 'waggles' in the sign indicate the additional 'waggles' of the fingers; but unfortunately this sensible convention has been chiefly honoured in the breach. *Lower Mordents,* whether 'Single', 'Double', or 'Extended', are of frequent occurrence in Bach's keyboard works, the choice depending on the musical context, since Bach himself, like most early composers, was lamentably casual in the use of signs.

MORE, HANNAH. See *Education and Music* 2.

MOREAU, JEAN BAPTISTE. Born at Angers in 1656 and died in Paris in 1733, aged seventy-six or seventy-seven. After a short career as cathedral organist in the provinces he went to Paris and crept into favour at court, composing dramatic divertissements and, for the famous academy for young ladies at Saint Cyr, music to Racine's *Esther* and to biblical plays by other authors.

He was a renowned singing-master and song composer.

MORELLI, MADDALENA. See *Improvisatore.*

MORENDO (It.). 'Dying.'

MORESCA, MORESCO, or **MORISCO.** 'Moorish.' A Moorish dance. The name was common from the fifteenth to the seventeenth century, but it is difficult to see that it had any settled implication as regards rhythm and style. Amongst other applications the word had one of any rough and ready, grotesque dance, employing costumes representing animals, savages, etc.

For the alleged connexion between the Morris (q.v.) and the Moresca, etc., see *Dance* 5.

MORESQUE. Same as *Moresca* (q.v.).

MORGENBLÄTTER (Ger.). This can mean either 'Morning Leaves' (i.e. foliage), or 'Morning Papers'. It occurs in musical use by the waltz composer Johann Strauss II, who, it is clear from the picture on the original edition and from the dedication to the Vienna Journalists' Association, intended the second meaning.

MORGENLIED (Ger.). 'Morning song.'

MORHANGE. See *Alkan.*

MORHOF, D. G. (1639–91). See reference under *Acoustics* 2 (end).

MORISCA, MORISCO. Same as *Moresca, Moresco* (q.v.).

MORISQUE. Same as Morris (q.v.); the old French form of the dance. Or this word may sometimes mean merely 'Moorish Dance'.

MORITZ, CARL PHILIPP (1757–93). See *Memory* 9; *Street Music* 5.

MORLEY, THOMAS. Born in 1557 and died about 1603, aged forty-six. He was organist at St. Paul's Cathedral, London, and, like so many of the great musicians of his place and time, a Gentleman of the Chapel Royal. He was probably a friend of Shakespeare, for whose plays he composed certain songs. Queen Elizabeth I's government gave him a monopoly of music-printing. (The monopolists, in turn, were, 1575 Byrd and Tallis; 1585 Byrd alone; 1598 Morley; 1603 to about 1614, Barley: then this restriction on trade seems to have lapsed; see *Monopolies*.)

He wrote a *Plaine and Easie Introduction to Practicall Musicke* (1597) which was popular for two hundred years and is now one of the best sources of information about sixteenth-century methods of composition and performance and musical life in general (reprinted 1937 and 1952). Better still, he wrote church music, instrumental music, lute songs, and many of the finest madrigals of the great madrigal period, excelling especially in the light, rhythmic style of the ballet (see *Madrigal* 3 c and p. 609, pl. **107.** 5).

For some references to Morley see *Descant*; *Canzonet*; *Anglican Chant* 3; *Service*; *Chapel Royal*; *Barber Shop Music*; *Publishing* 4; *Gastoldi*; *Madrigal* 4, 5; *Voluntary*.

MORMORANDO, MORMORANTE, MOR-MOREVOLE, MORMOROSO (It.). 'Murmuring.'

MORNINGTON, EARL OF (Garrett Colley Wellesley). Born at Dangan Castle, County Meath, Ireland, in 1735 and died in London in 1781, aged forty-five. He was a remarkable child musician, playing violin, harpsichord, and organ, and extemporizing fugues, who grew into a man of genuine musical learning and, approaching thirty, became Professor of Music at Trinity College, Dublin (see *Ireland* 6). His lasting fame as a composer comes from his glees, such as 'Here in cool grot', and, in a lesser degree, through certain compositions for the Anglican Church.

His eldest son, Richard, was Pitt's famous Governor-General of India, a younger son was the still more famous Duke of Wellington, and his youngest son the great diplomatist, Henry, Lord Cowley. The English Wesley family, which included fine musicians, was closely related to the Irish Wellesleys.

Lord Mornington, when in London, used to go every week to breakfast with Charles Wesley, the hymn-writer, to make music with the Wesley boys, Charles and Samuel (see *Wesley Family* 3 and 4). Like his more famous son, the hero of Waterloo (see reference s.v. *Wellington*), he was a man of cool courage, for he is reputed to have been the first member of the British aristocracy who dared to walk through the London streets openly and unashamedly carrying a violin case.

MORRIS. See the general article *Dance*, under the sub-heading 'English Folk Dances'. Most Morris dances are in two-in-a-measure or four-in-a-measure time, but three-in-a-measure, though very rare, also exists. Sometimes the dancers are accompanied by persons dressed to represent certain characters such as the Queen of the May, the Fool, etc. (symbolic figures of former ritual significance). The local municipal authorities formerly often equipped Morris troupes. There are a number of troupes still in existence in England. Arbeau, in 1589 (see mention of him under *Dance* 6), describes the Morris as if he knew it in France in his youth.

Shakespeare (*All's Well that Ends Well*, II. ii) speaks of 'a Morris for May Day'. Kemp (q.v.), the famous comic actor and dancer who acted with Shakespeare before Queen Elizabeth I in 1594, a few years later added to his renown by dancing a Morris all the way from London to Norwich. The mayor of that city rewarded him with a pension of forty shillings a year for life. He also danced the Morris in many Continental cities. A one-man Morris is, strictly, impossible, but solo performers like Kemp used the Morris step and wore the Morris dress and bells (p. 272, pl. **48.** 1, 3).

For the alleged connexion between the Morris and the Moresca (q.v.) see *Dance* 5.

MORRIS.

(1) REGINALD OWEN. Born at York in 1886 and died in London in 1948, aged sixty-one. He was educated at Harrow, New College, Oxford, and the Royal College of Music, where he was on the staff, as he was for a time at Oxford, and at the Curtis Institute of Music, Philadelphia. He published original-minded theoretical works, including *Contrapuntal Technique in the 16th Century* (1922) and *The Structure of Music* (1935). His compositions include orchestral works, chamber music, etc.

(2) HAROLD. Born at San Antonio, Texas, in 1890 and died in New York in 1964, aged seventy-four. He studied at the University of Texas and the Cincinnati Conservatory, and later taught at the Juilliard School (1922–39) and Columbia University. A pianist himself, he wrote a piano concerto, a symphony, chamber music, etc., some of these much influenced by Scriabin.

MORROW, WALTER. See *Trumpet Family* 2 e; *Cornet* 2.

MORTARI, VIRGILIO. Born near Milan in 1902. He is a pianist and composer who has written a good deal of music for various instrumental combinations, as well as songs and some operas.

MORTON, THOMAS (d. 1646). See *Puritans* 8.

MOSCHELES, IGNAZ (p. 797, pl. **136.** 6). Born at Prague in 1794 and died at Leipzig in

1870, aged seventy-five. He was a neat and brilliant pianist. He was resident in London from 1826 to 1841 and then, on Mendelssohn's invitation, became head of the piano department in the Conservatory at Leipzig. Of his many compositions the piano studies are the best remembered.

See *Pianoforte* 22; *Pianoforte Playing* 2, 4; *Improvisation* 2, 3; *Sonata* 10 d; *Étude*; *Concerto* 6 b (1794); *Cadenza*; *Concert* 8; *Jodel*.

MOSONYI. See *Hungary*.

MOSS, MARSHALL. See *Electric* 2 b.

MOSSO (It.). 'Moved', e.g. *Più mosso*, 'more moved' = quicker.

MOSSOLOF, ALEXANDER. Born at Kief in 1900. He was trained at the Conservatory of Moscow. He is an accomplished pianist and a daring composer of works expressive of the intellectual and social ideas of his milieu. His *Iron Foundry* (1927), though later condemned as 'formalistically depraved', has been heard in various countries; like others of his works, it embodies novel effects of sonority.

In 1935 the Union of Soviet composers expelled this member, accused of 'defects of character, drunkenness, and misconduct', since when he has held a series of minor appointments in remote places.

MOSZKOWSKI, MORITZ (p. 800, pl. **137.** 9). Born in 1854 at Breslau, German Silesia, and died in Paris in 1925, aged seventy. He lived, as teacher and performer, in Berlin and then for nearly thirty years in Paris, where he died in poverty owing to the loss of his savings through war-depreciation.

He had a great reputation as solo pianist and as composer, especially of that much-needed class of piano music that is at once attractive to a wide public and acceptable to musicians of taste. He wrote also a symphony and other orchestral music, a violin concerto, a piano concerto, an opera, and other things, and many of these were performed under the best auspices, in different parts of Europe and America.

MOTET. The church choral form of the motet superseded that of the conductus (q.v.). From the thirteenth century into the fifteenth or early sixteenth both were in use: then the conductus gradually died out and the motet continued and, in a greatly developed form, may be said to be alive today.

The motet from the first had more contrapuntal freedom than the conductus. Its parts moved in different lengths of notes according to the rigid rhythmic schemes of the day, which cannot be gone into here.

Sometimes a motet would be constructed by the crude experiment of putting together different existing tunes (sacred or secular), with perhaps some little adjustments, and driving them along the same road in double, triple, or quadruple harness. Frequently, however, the plan was to give the tenor a piece of plainsong or folk song to sing, and to place above it two other parts ('motetus' and 'triplex') moving in quicker notes. Usually the different parts had different words.

By the fifteenth century the form had taken on modern refinements; the conflict of words had gone, and the form might be described simply as that of a not very long piece of unaccompanied choral counterpoint to Latin words.

When we come to the period of Palestrina and Byrd we find the motet grown into a great medium of the most able expression of the finest musical thought. Palestrina wrote about 180 motets. An alternative for 'motets' frequently used at this period is 'Cantiones Sacrae'.

The motet was not a setting of any part of the ordinary or proper of the Mass (see *Mass* 2) but had its place as what Protestantism today calls an anthem (q.v.). Indeed, we may say that the anthem is but the motet turned Protestant, and the most suitable distinction, so far as the English Church is concerned, is that which calls the older anthems in Latin motets, and motets in English anthems. This nomenclature is, however, a mere local convenience.

It may be said that at the time when it attained maturity (the sixteenth century) the motet was the church counterpart of the domestic madrigal. Both were unaccompanied choral compositions with very freely moving voice parts woven into a contrapuntal texture, and a serious madrigal to sacred words would be a motet—indeed, Gibbons, Pierson, and one or two others so used the word.

Bach wrote six magnificent motets, all in German, and four of them are for eight voices: the great *Singet dem Herrn* ('Sing ye to the Lord') is one of them. These are for voices unaccompanied (i.e. with no written accompaniment, though some think that an instrumental support doubling the voice parts was given), but by this time choral works with independent accompaniment were taking on the name, and indeed the word is henceforth very loosely applied—even to pieces for solo voice with accompaniment. The true motet continued to be written, however.

The moments when motets may be introduced into the Roman Catholic service are at the Offertory, during the Elevation of the Host, and during processions and other ceremonies for which the liturgy does not prescribe any particular text to be sung.

There was a 'Motet Society' in London from 1841 to about 1857. It was restricted to members of the Church of England and met weekly to practise the works of the pre-seventeenth-century composers. It also published old church music under the editorship of Dr. E. Rimbault.

For the resemblance of some madrigals to motets see *Madrigals* 6.

MOTETUS. See *Motet*; *Voice* 17.

MOTHER GOOSE SONGS. This is an old American term for what the British call 'Nursery Rhymes'.

The information supplied by various

authorities concerning the identity of 'Mother Goose' is conflicting. It is circumstantially stated by some that she was a real personage, an Elizabeth Foster, a native of Boston, Mass., who became the wife of one Isaac Goose, that she was born in 1665 and died in 1757, and that Thos. Fleet, her brother-in-law, printed and published the first edition of her *Songs for the Nursery, or Mother Goose's Melodies* in 1716 (also stated as 1719—but anyhow no copy of this publication can now be traced).

The affirmation has been made with equal confidence that the name 'Mother Goose' has merely been taken from Perrault's book of children's stories, *Contes de ma Mère l' Oye* (1697), which in its turn took it from earlier French literature, and that *Mother Goose's Melodies* was first brought out by the famous English publisher of children's books, Newbery, about 1760. It has been conjectured (but never proved) that Newbery's friend Oliver Goldsmith edited this book.

The repertory of 'Nursery Rhymes' or 'Mother Goose Songs' includes many of English folk-song origin, and in some cases the words have become so corrupted as to lose all tangible meaning; this, however, does not diminish their charm for children.

In both Britain and the United States, but especially the latter, stern-faced moralists have at different periods protested against children being told 'Mother Goose Stories' or allowed to sing 'Nursery Rhymes'. And, indeed, it must be admitted that these are not 'true'— as is, of course, everything written, spoken, sung, or read by the moralists themselves. Moreover it has been objected that 'half of them are full of death and violence'. In an 'average collection of two hundred' the founder of the British Poetry-Drama Guild has found one hundred that 'harbour unsavoury elements', including 'eight allusions to murder, two of choking to death, three of death by drowning, and one each of death by devouring, cutting a human being in half, decapitation, squeezing, shrivelling, starvation, boiling, and hanging'. He sadly adds that 'the above facts also apply to nearly all rhyme collections in other languages'.

MOTIF (Fr.), **MOTIV** (Ger.), **MOTIVO** (It.), **MOTIVE** (Eng.). The briefest intelligible and self-existent melodic or rhythmic unit. It may be of two notes or more. Almost any piece of music will be found, on close examination, to be developed out of some figure or figures, repeated—at different pitches, and perhaps with different intervals, yet recognizably the same (see *Melody* 3; *Suite* 5).

The development of the *Motif* finds a great expansion in the Wagnerian texture (see *Wagner*), but a Wagner motif (*Leitmotiv*, i.e. Leading motif, q.v.) is not necessarily so atomic as the above definition of 'Motif' in general would suggest; it may be merely two or three notes or, on the other hand, an extended phrase.

For the use of a sort of motif system in much of the music of the East see *Oriental Music*.

MOTION is a convenient term based on the linear appearance of music as notated. In the combination of any two 'voices' or 'parts' of a composition at a given moment, if they run in the same direction they are in *Similar Motion*, if they are both moving in such a way as to diverge progressively they are in *Contrary Motion*, if one is stationary (i.e. holds to or repeats the same note) and the other moves in a direction away from it there is *Oblique Motion*. Similar Motion when the two 'parts' move by the same intervals is called *Parallel Motion*.

In the shaping of a single 'voice' (i.e. part) at a given moment *Conjunct Motion* means progress by step, *Disjunct Motion* progress by leap.

MOTION PICTURE MUSIC. See *Cinematograph and Music*.

MOTIV, MOTIVE, MOTIVO. See *Motif*.

MOTO (It.). 'Motion', e.g. *Con moto*, 'with motion' = quickly.

MOTO PERPETUO. See *Perpetuum Mobile*.

MOTO PRECEDENTE (It.). 'Preceding motion' (i.e. same speed as what has just gone before).

MOTTEGGIANDO (It.). 'Bantering.'

MOTTL, FELIX (1856–1911). Great orchestral conductor, of Viennese birth and training, occupying important positions at Karlsruhe and Munich, conducting at Bayreuth, London, New York, etc.

See reference under *Percussion Family* 4 e (allusion to Bell Machine).

MOTTO THEME. A device akin to 'Leading Motive' (see *Wagner* and *Motif*), 'Idée Fixe' (see *Berlioz*), and 'Metamorphosis of Themes' (see under that head and under *Liszt*). It arises by attaching some symbolic significance to a musical theme which reappears at intervals in the course of a piece of 'Programme Music' (q.v.) and is supposed to bring that significance to the mind of the listener whenever it is heard.

MOTU PROPRIO. Literally, 'of his own motion'. A sort of Bull issued by the Pope, reserved for the internal administrative affairs of the Church. The word is often heard in connexion with church music on account of the Motu Proprio of Pius X, issued in the year of his becoming Pope (1903). It was of the nature of an Instruction upon Sacred Music; it laid down general principles recognized everywhere by cultured, intelligent, and devout musicians as being sound, and placed emphasis especially upon the importance of the traditional plainsong and of the 'classical polyphony' of the time of Palestrina which ultimately derived from it. Church music of a theatrical style was strongly condemned and forbidden, its great nineteenth-century vogue (especially in Italy) being deplored. Modern compositions were not prohibited, but they were to be such as 'by their merit and gravity are not unworthy of the liturgical functions'. Nothing was to be omitted from the liturgy 'except when the rubrics allow the use of the organ to replace several verses of the text whilst these are merely recited in the choir of the church' (see *Verset*). The Kyrie, Gloria, and Credo, in composed masses, were not to be divided up into separate movements (see *Mass* 3). Solo treatment of portions of the liturgy was not entirely forbidden but was to form but a small portion of the section in which they occurred. Boys, and not women, should be used for the soprano part. Instruments other than the organ were not to be employed without the bishop's special permission, and the organ was to play a modest role of accompaniment and not to be allowed to cover up the singing; long organ preludes or interludes were reprehended. The practice of the *Verset* was not to be abused. The piano and instruments of percussion were not to be employed in church. Wind bands were not to take part in church music, except in special cases recognized by the bishop, and then their music was to be of a grave style, exactly identical with that proper to the organ. In fine, music was to be at the service of the liturgy and not the liturgy at the service of music.

To watch over all these things, each bishop was to appoint a special commission of competent people, well versed in sacred music. Theological students were to receive instruction in the music of the Church. The ancient 'Scholae Cantorum' were to be revived and attached to the principal churches everywhere (see *Schola Cantorum*).

About the same time as this Motu Proprio was issued the papal support was definitely given to the monks of Solesmes in their long-continued labours for the purity of plainsong (q.v.) and the official Vatican edition was the result.

In 1928 Pope Pius XI issued a constitution commanding the restoration to the congregation of their part of the Common of the Mass (see *Mass* 2; *Common*).

See also *Cecilian Movement*; *Roman Catholic Church Music in Britain*.
For a provision in the Motu Proprio of 1903 for the use of harmonized passages alternating with plainsong see *Faburden* 2.

MOUNTED CORNET. See *Organ* 14 V.

MOURET, JEAN JOSEPH. Born at Avignon in 1682 and died at Charenton in 1738, aged fifty-six. He held various official musical posts in Paris and composed operas, ballets, motets, and music for stringed and wind instruments—of great delicacy combined with strong vitality.

'MOURNING' SYMPHONY (Haydn). See *Nicknamed Compositions* 11.

MOURNING WALTZ (Schubert). See *Nicknamed Compositions* 18.

MOUSSORGSKY. See *Mussorgsky*.

MOUTH HARMONICA or **MOUTH ORGAN.** See *Reed-Organ Family* 3, 10 b.

MOUTH MUSIC. Same as *Port à Beul* (q.v.). Cf. *Diddling*.

MOUTHPIECE of brass instruments. See *Brass*; *Horn Family*; *Trumpet Family*; *Trombone Family*; *Saxhorn and Flügelhorn Families*; *Tuba Group*; *Cornet*.

MOUTON, JEAN. Born towards the end of the fifteenth century and died in 1522—at St. Quentin, of whose church he had become a canon. He was pupil of Josquin des Prés and master of Willaert. For some part of his earlier career he was a musician at the court of Louis XII and his successor Francis I. He left many masses, motets, and the like, and the reputation of a master of choral effect.

MOUVEMENT (Fr.). 'Movement' (either in the sense of motion or in the derived sense of a section of a composition). *Mouvement perpétuel* is the same as *Perpetuum mobile* (q.v.). *Mouvt.* is an abbreviation of *Mouvement*; sometimes (as in Debussy) the meaning is 'Return to the proper speed' (e.g. after 'Rit.').

MOUVEMENTÉ (Fr.). 'Bustling', animated.

MOVABLE DOH. See *Tonic Sol-fa*; *Hexachord*.

MOVEMENT. The word is used in respect of 'cyclic forms', i.e. forms consisting of several contrasting compositions strung together as one longer composition: each of these contrasting compositions is called a 'movement', from the fact that one chief element in the contrast is that of speed (hence we speak of 'the Slow Movement' of a sonata, etc.).

In some other languages the idea is the same—French, **Mouvement**; Italian, **Tempo**. The Germans, however, use the word **Satz**, a word which in everyday parlance has such various meanings as 'set', 'sentence', 'thesis', 'proposition' (of Euclid), 'batch' (of bread), etc.

MOVENTE (It.). 'Moving.'

MOVIMENTO (It.). 'Motion.'

MOZARABIC RITE. See *Liturgy*; *Dance* 7; *Spain* 2.

MOZART.

(1) LEOPOLD (1719–87). See references under *Mozart, W. A.*, below; *Bagpipe Family* 7; *Trumpet Family* 4; *Dot*; *Symphony* 8 (1719); *Rubato* 2; *Toy Symphony*.

(2) WOLFGANG AMADEUS (p. 641, pl. **111**). Born at Salzburg in 1756 and died in Vienna in 1791, aged nearly thirty-six. In natural gifts he was one of the most perfectly equipped musicians who ever lived. As a child his ear was so accurate and his musical memory so strong that he was said to detect a difference of an eighth of a tone and recall it next day (but see reference to this incident under *Absolute Pitch*).

Of all the instrumental music ever written his is perhaps the most 'pure' in the sense that, *qua* music, i.e. apart from its emotional associations and significance, it is perfect in melodic shape, in rhythmic interest, in natural yet original harmonic colouring, in form, and (if orchestral) in the piquancy yet propriety of its instrumental treatment. Wagner, whose art was so different (in that it was invariably applied, often in the most detailed way, to the expression of literary meaning, and charged with the most powerful emotions), wrote of Mozart that he was 'the greatest and most divine

PLATE 112

MOZART AT THE BILLIARD TABLE

By Batt

BALL games, particularly billiards and bowls, were greatly to his liking. There is little doubt that he pursued these games not merely for their own sake but because he found in the movement and control of a rolling ball a congenial accompaniment to the movement within his own copious and productive mind.

Instances are recorded of his stopping in the middle of a game to make notes, or of his humming, as he played, a theme which was later found in one of his works. Moreover, he was particularly fond of playing billiards alone, keeping his note-book handy—though the notes he made were always the briefest indication of an idea, for he did his actual composing 'in his head'.

The ever-flowing rhythms in his mind induced him incessantly to tap his fob, a table, a chair-back, or anything to hand, and there is no doubt that he spent some of his most fruitful hours alone at the billiard table.   B.

genius'. The word 'classical' finds its most apt musical application in speaking of the work of Mozart. (See *Classical* 1.)

His life was brilliant at its dawn and clouded at its close. His father, Leopold Mozart, himself a gifted and cultured musician (of some European reputation as the author of a violin 'school'), was an intelligent teacher and a wise parent, and gave him that firm foundation of sound musical and general instruction which his natural endowment deserved.

At six (p. 641, pl. **111.** 1), with his gifted sister (four years older than himself), he began his travels, the performances of both children, but especially those of the younger, arousing enthusiasm in the courts of Europe as they visited them in their father's company. At fourteen the Pope knighted him, as he had knighted Gluck fourteen years before. Gluck henceforth called himself 'Chevalier de' or 'Ritter von' Gluck, but we hear no more of Mozart's knighthood—after a short period during which his father made him sign his compositions as 'Cavaliere Amadeo' (see *Knighthood*).

In later youth, touring alone or with his father or mother, he found some decline in the public interest, the ripening of his musical mind not compensating the public for the loss of the attraction of infant accomplishment.

Then came much vexation and sorrow. He settled down as a member of the Archbishop of Salzburg's household, and he who had in childhood played with Marie Antoinette and received gifts from monarchs now dined at the servants' table, and, as 'the villain, the low fellow', suffered hard words from the patron at whose private concerts he was expected to shine. In the end this 'vile wretch' was discharged by the Archbishop and kicked out of the room by the Court Marshal. In Vienna, however, he was morally supported by many members of the nobility and by the Emperor, and as the composer of several operas he had achieved a wide public reputation.

We have now arrived at his twenty-sixth year. He had but ten more years to live. He married and lived sparsely, with occasional cheering periods of success and public triumph. His series of great operas began. *Figaro* appeared in his thirtieth year, *Don Giovanni* in his thirty-second, *The Magic Flute* in his thirty-fifth—the year that was to see the ending of his efforts. *The Magic Flute* has spoken dialogue and is in the German language: it may be taken as having a nationalistic aim and as constituting a glorification of the German 'Singspiel' (q.v.).

In his thirty-second year (1788) he composed the three symphonies that rank as his greatest (and amongst the greatest ever written)—the one in E flat, the one in G minor, and the one in C, now called 'Jupiter'. To him composition seemed as effortless as to Beethoven it was painful. He poured out, during his brief career, nearly fifty symphonies, nearly twenty operas and operettas, over twenty piano concertos, twenty-seven string quartets, about

forty violin sonatas, and a quantity of other music.

He sometimes meditated settling in England, and at one time he and his wife had their belongings packed to do so, but just then the Emperor bestowed a small place and pension and the plan dropped.

His death was probably from uraemia. Near the end he made his wife promise to keep his death secret until his friend Albrechtsberger should have had time to put in an application to succeed him in a post that had recently been given him—that of Capellmeister of the Cathedral. The severest economy marked his funeral; few friends accompanied the coffin; the burial took place in the common grave allotted to paupers—and nobody even marked the position.

His last work had been his *Requiem* and he had seen in the commission that prompted it an evil omen.

In the history of music the mutual relation of Mozart and Haydn is probably unique. Mozart's art was founded on that of Haydn, as that of Haydn had been on that of Emanuel Bach. Then, as Mozart came to maturity, applying his gifts ever more and more triumphantly to the forms and style for which Haydn was so largely responsible, in some refinements he surpassed his master, who in turn learnt from him and again strode forward.

Many references of greater or lesser importance are necessarily scattered through this work. They will be found as follows:

Absolute Pitch; Acoustics 8; *Alberti Bass; Cadenza; Composition* 5, 7, 10, 11, 12, 13, 14; *Dot; Expressionism; Figured Bass; Finale; Harmony* 4, 11, 20, 23; *History* 6, 7; *Improvisation* 2, 3, 5; *Leading Motive; Modes* 10; *Pitch* 4; *Scales* 9; *Syncopation; Tierce de Picardie.*

Additional Accompaniments; Annotated Programmes 4 (1st Perf. of *Requiem* in Britain); *Ave Verum; Cecilian Movement; Doxology; Mass* 2, 3, 4 V; *Misattributed Compositions; Miserere; Oratorio* 3; *Requiem; Roman Catholic Church Music in Britain.*

Aria; Broadcasting 2 (allusion to *Magic Flute*); *Cavatina; Comic Opera; Glyndebourne; Grand Opera; Holland* 6 (allusion to *Don Juan*); *Melodrama; Opera* 9 b c g, 10, 19, 21 d e f, 24 c (1786–87–91); *Opera Buffa; Singspiel; Vaudeville; Schikaneder* (allusion to *Magic Flute*). Also plots, etc., as follows: *Abduction from the Seraglio; Così fan tutte; Don Giovanni; Magic Flute; Marriage of Figaro.*

Chamber Music 6, Period III (1756); *Coda; Concerto* 3, 4, 6 b; *Development; Fantasia* 1; *Form* 2, 7, 9, 10, 11; *Nachtmusik; Overture* 3; *Serenade; Sonata* 2, 6, 7, 8, 10 c d; *Symphony* 4, 6, 8 (1756).

Allemande 2; *Ballet* 3, 7; *Country Dance; Fandango; Ländler; Minuet; Polonaise; Ridotto; Waltz.*

Acciaio; Bell 6; *Brass; Clarinet Family* 2, 4 f, 6; *Flute Family* 4, 6; *Harmonica* 1; *Harp* 3; *Horn Family* 2 b (note), 3, 4; *Mandoline; Mechanical Reproduction of Music* 5, 11; *Military Band; Oboe Family* 2, 3 a b, 6; *Panpipes; Percussion Family* 2 a c, 4 a b e; *Recorder* 3; *Trombone Family* 3; *Trumpet Family* 2 b, 3.

Coloratura; Expression 5; *Fingering* 3, 4; *Fioritura; Harpsichord* 7; *Memory* 3, 8; *Organ* 13; *Ornaments* 6; *Pianoforte* 12, 13, 17, 18, 20, 21; *Pianoforte Playing* 2, 3; *Recitative; Rubato* 2; *Singing* 10.

Applause 2; *Arrangement; Bird Music; Colour and Music* 2; *Competitions* 1; *Concert* 6, 13; *Copyists; Knighthood; Misattributed* (Adelaide); *Nicknamed* 15; *Opus; Patronage* 6; *Profession* 8.

Bohemia; France 7; *Holland* 6.

Attwood; Bach, C. P. E.; Bach, J. C.; Balakiref; Beethoven; Clementi; Hahn; Hummel; Jahn; Kierkegaard; Köchel; Levi, H.; Linley 2; *Pleyel; Salieri; Sarti; Storace.*

MP. = *Mezzo-piano*, 'half-soft'.

M.S. = *Mano sinistra* (It.), 'left hand'.

M.S.M. See *Degrees and Diplomas* 3.

M.T.N.A. Music Teachers' National Association (see *Profession of Music* 10; *United States* 8).

MÜDE (Ger.). 'Tired', languid in style.

MUDGE, REVD. RICHARD. Born at Bideford, Devon, in 1718 and died near Birmingham in 1763. He was the son of Dr. Johnson's friend, the Revd. Zachary Mudge. After graduating at Pembroke College, Oxford, he was ordained to the curacy of a parish near Birmingham and later given the living of Bedworth (Warwicks.), where, however, he never resided. Some of his 6 concerti (Walsh, 1749) have been exhumed and found to be effective compositions of the pre-Haydn period. No other works survive.

MUELLER. See *Müller*.

MUFFAT.

(1) GEORG, born at Megève, Alsace, in 1653 and died at Passau in 1704, aged fifty; and (2) his son GOTTLIEB, born at Passau in 1690 and died in Vienna in 1770, aged eighty. The father held important musical positions at Strasbourg, Salzburg, and elsewhere, travelled widely, and published instrumental music that is still to be heard. It is said that he was of Scottish descent. The son spent nearly all his professional life in the royal service in Vienna and published organ and harpsichord music that has been reissued and re-welcomed in modern times. (Cf. *Toccata*.)

MUFFLING (of drums). See *Mute* 3 and *Percussion Family* 2 a, 5 a.

MUGHOUSES. See *Inns and Taverns*.

MÜHELOS (Ger.). 'Effortless.'

MÜHLFELD, RICHARD (1856–1907). See *Clarinet Family* 6 (end).

MUIÑEIRA (or *Muñeira*). A type of Spanish dance and song in six-in-a-measure time. It is popular in Galicia. Another name for it is *Gallegada* (i.e. a Gallic dance, Galicia being the Celtic or Gallic province of Spain).

MUIR, ALEXANDER. See *Maple Leaf for Ever*.

MULCASTER. See *Education and Music* 2.

MULET, HENRI. Born in Paris in 1878. Paris organist and composer for organ and orchestra. See mention under *Improvisation* 2.

MÜLLER.

(1) Author of Trombone Method. See *Trombone Family* 1.

(2) IWAN (1786–1854). See *Clarinet Family* 2.

(3) WENZEL (1767–1835). See *Opera* 26.

MULLINER MANUSCRIPT. The contents of this book, which is in the British Museum, consist of more than one hundred instrumental and vocal compositions (sacred and secular) by sixteenth-century composers. In 1951 they were published by the Royal Musical Association under the editorship of Denis Stevens. The compiler is assumed to have been Thomas Mulliner, an organist of St. Paul's Cathedral in the mid-sixteenth century.

MUNDHARMONIKA (Ger.). 'Mouth harmonica', i.e. mouth organ. See *Reed-Organ Family* 3, 10 b.

MUNDY (Father and Son).

(1) WILLIAM. Latter half of sixteenth century. He was a Gentleman of Queen Elizabeth I's Chapel Royal, and left some Anglican church music that is still sung and possesses considerable value (see under *Henry VIII*; *Anthem*, Period I).

(2) JOHN. Died in 1630. He was organist of Eton College and of St. George's Chapel, Windsor. He left madrigals (including one in *The Triumphs of Oriana*, see *Madrigal* 4) and keyboard pieces amongst which is one of the classic early examples of 'Programme Music' (q.v.), a sort of meteorological fantasia representing 'Faire Wether', 'Lightning', 'Thunder', and the like (in the Fitzwilliam Virginal Book, q.v.).

MUÑEIRA. See *Muiñeira*.

MUNTER (Ger.). 'Lively.'

MURCIANA. A kind of fandango (q.v.), of Murcia, in southern Spain, with the same peculiarity as the malagueña (q.v.).

MURIS (or **Murs**), JOHANNES DE. See *France* 3.

MURISIANO, JACOB. See *Rumania*.

MURMELND (Ger.), **MURMURANDO** (It.). 'Murmuring.'

MURRAY, DOM GREGORY. See under *Cecilia, Saint*.

MURRAY'S HYMNAL. See *Adeste Fideles*.

MURRILL, HERBERT HENRY JOHN. Born in London in 1909 and there died in 1952, aged forty-three. He studied at the Royal Academy of Music and at Worcester College, Oxford, and held organ posts in London. He then engaged in broadcasting work and in 1950 became head of the BBC's music department. His many compositions include an opera (*Man in Cage*, 1929), incidental music for the theatre, orchestral music, a string quartet, piano music, songs, etc.

  See *Clarinet Family* 6.

MURS (or **Muris**). See *France* 3.

MUS.B.; MUS.D. See *Degrees and Diplomas* 1.

MUSCADIN. A term occasionally found in English virginal music; apparently it is a kind of hornpipe (q.v.).

MUSETTA (It.), **MUSETTE** (Fr.). See *Bagpipe Family* 6; *Gavotte*.

MUSGRAVE, THEA. Born in Edinburgh in 1928. She studied at Edinburgh University and under Nadia Boulanger, and has become known as the composer of orchestral and chamber music and songs, as well as much incidental music for television and films.

MUSICA ALLA TURCA (It.). See *Percussion Family* 4 b.

MUSICA COLORATA (It.). See *Musica figurata* 2.

MUSICA DISCIPLINA. See *Carapetyan*; *Journals*.

MUSICA ENCHIRIADIS. See *Harmony* 4, 5.

MUSICA FALSA (It.). Literally 'false music'. Same as *Musica ficta* (below).

MUSICA FICTA (Lat.). Literally 'feigned music'. The old modes (q.v.) were written as sections of what we should call the scale of C major. In the first mode (or 'Dorian Mode'), for instance, the notes ran from D to D, with D as the final or tonic, and A as the dominant, and a composition in that mode would use only the seven different notes, D, E, F, G, A, B, C, ending on the tonic, D. And so with the other modes.

This system gradually received tiny modifications, of which the following are examples:

The interval of the augmented fourth, F–B, and its inversion B–F, were objectionable to the ears of those days, and so the B was often flattened or sometimes, later, the F sharpened (see *Modes* 8; *Tritone*; *Keyboard* 2).

When harmony was introduced, from the tenth century onwards, there was a disposition at the cadence, in modes that had a full tone (i.e. major second) between the seventh and eighth notes, to reduce this to a semitone by sharpening the seventh, so making what we call a 'leading note'—i.e. leading up to the final or tonic.

When the third note of a mode in an upper part made a minor third with the tonic in the lowest part there was a disposition to sharpen it in the final chord, so that the ear should rest upon a major third and not a minor (see *Tierce de Picardie*).

When a voice part descended one degree and then returned, or ascended one degree and then returned, there was a disposition to sharpen the middle note in the first case and flatten it in the second, so as to make a semitone step instead of a tone (in modern times some choir singers are a little apt to do this involuntarily).

The following (opening of *Vexilla Regis*) is an example of a melody which on two of the grounds above mentioned took the flattened B:

Here the F and the B are prominent in their relation to one another as the lowest and highest notes of a passage, so the B would be flattened; but in any case this would probably be done, since the A rises to the B, which then falls to A again.

And so changes occurred in the modes, which changes at first (in the days when ecclesiastical authority closely controlled church music, or tried to do so) were rather winked at than permitted, and so were not shown in the notation but inserted by the singers, much in the way that many points of 'expression' not indicated in the copy may today be supplied by the singers under the direction of the choirmaster.

The introduction of these modifications, be-ginning in the days when music was purely melodic, increased enormously as the art of contrapuntal composition developed, until at last, towards the end of the sixteenth century, it broke down the modal system and turned it into our present key system.

The shamefacedness or timidity of composers, or their fear to insult their singers by inserting in the copies what a good performer was supposed to be able to insert for himself as he went along, has led to insuperable difficulties for modern editors of music of the eleventh to the sixteenth centuries; if two modern editions of an ancient piece of music be examined it will probably be found that the two editors have taken different views as to the introduction of accidentals in certain places.

Compare *Fa Fictum*.

MUSICA FIGURATA (It.), or **FIGURAL-MUSIK** (Ger.). The term has two meanings:

(1) (The commoner meaning.) Contrapuntal music in which the various melodic strands move more or less independently, shorter notes in one against longer in others—as distinct, that is, from mere 'note against note' counterpoint.

(2) (The less common meaning.) Decorated melody in plainsong, etc., as distinct from the more sober type. (Such decorated plainsong is also known as *Musica colorata*—'coloured music'. Cf. *Coloratura*.)

For other entries beginning *Musica* see later, in due alphabetical order.

MUSICAL AND UNMUSICAL SOUNDS. See *Acoustics* 9.

MUSICAL BANQUET (1651). See under *Round*.

MUSICAL BOX. See *Mechanical Reproduction* 7.

MUSICAL COMEDY. The term seems to be applied to any sentimental-humorous play with plenty of light music in it (cf. *Operetta*).

MUSICAL COMPETITIONS. See *Competitions in Music*.

MUSICAL COURIER. See *Journals*.

MUSICAL CRITICISM. See *Criticism of Music*.

MUSICAL FUND SOCIETY. See *United States of America* 4.

MUSICAL GLASSES. See *Harmonica* 1, 5 a c.

MUSICAL GRADUATES' MEETING. See *Graduates' Meeting*.

MUSICAL MEMORY CONTESTS. See *United States of America* 5.

MUSICAL QUARTERLY MAGAZINE. See *Journals*; *Engel, Carl* II; *Láng*.

MUSICAL SAND. The phenomenon of sounds emitted by masses of sand (described in various different circumstances as a 'booming', a 'singing', or a 'wail like that of a trombone') is observable in the deserts of Arabia, in over seventy recorded places on the North American Atlantic coast, at Studland Bay, Dorset, on the west coast of the island of Eigg in the Hebrides, and elsewhere, and has often been discussed by scientists. It has been explained as due to the rubbing together of millions of clean and incoherent grains of quartz, free from angularities or roughness. Though the vibrations emitted by the friction of any two grains might be inaudible, those emitted from millions, approximately of the same size, would give an audible note. A small portion of such sand in a basin will emit the note when stirred, but moistening or the addition of flour immediately 'damps' the sound out of existence. (This is the traditional explanation of the phenomenon and it is apparently still accepted as correct.)

MUSICAL SAW. Same as *Singing Saw* (q.v.).

MUSICAL SNUFF-BOX. See *Mechanical Reproduction* 7.

MUSICAL SWITCH. A popular type of 'café-music' composition constructed out of snatches of popular tunes dovetailed into each other so that the attention is no sooner running on one line than it is 'switched' to another.

MUSICAL TIMES. See *Journals*; *Gramophone* 1.

MUSICAL UNION. See *Annotated Programmes* 4.

MUSICAL WORLD. See *Journals*; *Annotated Programmes* 4.

MUSIC AND LETTERS. See *Journals*.

MUSICA PARLANTE (It.). Literally, 'talking music'. A term used by the early Florentine opera composers (see *Opera* 1, 2) to describe their invention, *recitative* (q.v.).

MUSICA RESERVATA. This term first appears in a work by Adrianus Petit Coclico (1551). Its significance is disputable. One theory (see Lowinsky, *Secret Chromatic Art in the Netherlands Motet*, 1946) applies it to what may be called an extreme form of *Musica ficta* (q.v.), resulting in chromaticism and in modulation through all the keys and so destroying the modal effect which the actual notation indicated. The 'secrecy' thus exemplified is ascribed to the necessity of providing against official ecclesiastical antagonism to innovation. Other theories apply it to music employing a greater reserve than had become usual in the use of figuration and ornaments, or as merely to music 'written for classes of high cultural standing' (see *Harvard Dictionary of Music*, 1944).

MUSICA TRANSALPINA. See *Madrigal* 2; *Clubs for Music-Making*.

MUSIC BOOTHS. See *Fairs and their Music*.

MUSIC DRAMA. See *Wagner*.

MUSIC EDUCATORS' NATIONAL CONFERENCE. See *Education* 3; *Profession* 10.

MUSIC HALL

1. The Remote Origin.
2. The 'Free and Easy' and the 'Saloon Theatre'.
3. The True 'Halls' begin.
4. The Musical Attractions.
5. Modern Invention creates a Rival.

1. The Remote Origin. The genealogy of this long-popular institution goes back (strangely, as some may think) to the days of the Puritan régime of the seventeenth century, when organs, being banished from churches, were bought by tavern keepers. In Pepys and other writers of the period we find evidence of the existence of tavern organs and organists, and a French traveller whose work was translated and published by Evelyn in 1659 says:

'That nothing may be wanting to the height of luxury and impiety of this abomination, they have translated the organs out of the Churches to set them up in taverns, chaunting their dithyrambics and bestial bacchanalias to the tune of those instruments which were wont to assist them in the celebration of God's praises.'

Right through the eighteenth century certain taverns continued to be places of popular musical entertainment, and up to the end of the nineteenth century it was common all over England to see on a public-house a notice of weekly entertainment, in some such terms as 'A Free and Easy kept here every Tuesday evening'. In all these cases the object was the sale of refreshment—as in a German beer garden and similar places of amusement all over the civilized world. Another English name for this kind of public-house musical meeting was 'Harmonic Club'.

A circumstance that long tended to prevent the development of music halls apart from taverns was the restriction (dating from Stuart times) of theatrical performances in London to the few houses that possessed a Royal Patent. This limited the variety of the 'turns'. It was not until the Theatre Act of 1843 that this restriction was partially removed, and not until 1866 that prosecutions of what were called 'Saloon Theatres', for exceeding their legitimate programmes, finally ceased. In 1912 the restriction was at last formally dropped.

2. The 'Free and Easy' and the 'Saloon Theatre'. The programme in a 'Free and Easy' or 'Harmonic Club' was not printed. Each item or 'turn' was introduced by a chairman, showily dressed (with a display of diamonds, or what glittered just as brightly) and imposing in manner; he sat in an armchair with his back to the stage, and with a table in front of him at which guests to whom he wished to show honour might be invited to sit. The rest of the company also sat at tables.

It must be emphasized that this was not a 'low' nineteenth-century custom but essentially a survival of the early and respectable English concert custom, as will be realized by a reference to the contemporary description of Banister's late seventeenth-century concerts given under *Concert* 3 (see, too, under *Concert*

4, the description of Britton's similar series, where also refreshments were supplied to the company).

Evans's Supper Rooms (mentioned under *Annotated Programmes* 4) was a nineteenth-century survival of this, the earliest, type of concert—at which the hearing of good music was combined with the taking of food and drink. Thackeray's 'Cave of Harmony' in the opening chapter of *The Newcomes* gives a living description of this or some similar place: to judge by his description, the singing of the good old English ballads provided the staple of the programme, and members of the audience were allowed to step up to the platform and offer their vocal contributions.

3. The True 'Halls' begin. The institution of the chairman was continued in the earlier Victorian music halls of London, but these grew in size, developed printed programmes instead of depending on a chairman, and admitted the public by payment at the doors instead of making their profits solely out of refreshments.

At length there blossomed out of these the 'Palaces of Variety', 'Palladiums', 'Tivolis', 'Oxfords', 'Coliseums', 'Empires', 'Pavilions', 'Hippodromes', and 'Alhambras', with their gorgeous furnishings and decorations, their attendants in uniforms rivalling those of field-marshals, and their 'stars' paid more highly than cabinet ministers. Capitalist impresarios developed a system of circuits, or chains of such entertainment palaces in different parts of the country, to which they could transfer their artists and their programmes.

4. The Musical Attractions. Performers on freak instruments, and on 'ten-thousand pound' organs that could be dismantled and moved to another city in a day or two, were amongst the attractions, with singers of vocal and histrionic talent who popularized in a few nights some song that then came to be hummed or whistled by every errand-boy in the kingdom and played on street pianos in every west-end street and every slum.

Many of the songs were very poor, but others had honest poetical sentiment of a simple kind or genuine wit, and sound tunes such as musicians would be glad to find in the mouths of street boys of today. Some of these songs, good and bad, went all over the world: 'Ta-ra-ra-boom-de-ay', introduced by Lottie Collins, could be heard by travellers in foreign lands, for years after, from people white, black, and yellow. In general, certain sides of the life of the times were faithfully depicted, and a fairly adequate compendium of British lower-class manners during the period could be compiled from these productions; the contributions of Albert Chevalier, the coster-impersonator, offer an example. Solo or ensemble dancing was also a feature of these entertainments, and in some places the ballet corps was well organized and important.

Large orchestras were often employed and composers of some standing would occasionally be induced to appear, as, for instance, Leoncavallo conducting a shortened version of his opera *Pagliacci*. Occasionally well-known conductors would be engaged to direct items of the more popular part of the 'classical' repertory.

When in the late 1920s the Cambridge University Madrigal Society made a number of appearances in a London 'hall' it was but reviving part of the earlier tradition by which in some of the 'Harmonic Clubs', etc., a 'glee party' was a feature.

5. Modern Invention creates a Rival. It is interesting to note the earliest public appearances of the cinematograph (then called 'Vitagraph') and of the gramophone (then called 'Phonotoscope') in programmes of 1896 and 1897 respectively: of the latter it is announced that 'This wonderful Machine stands in the centre of the Stage, talks as a Human Being, Sings Comic and Sentimental Songs, plays Piccolo and Cornet Solos, also a Full Brass Band Selection—a Modern Miracle'.

This introduction of the cinematograph and phonograph marks the beginning of the end of the music hall. Soon the cinema possessed its own halls in every town, and even in the larger villages, and, like the 'Gardens' (see *Concert* 12), which enjoyed nearly two centuries of varying prosperity, the music hall at last succumbed.

MUSIC HOUSES. See *Inns and Taverns as Places of Music-Making.*

MUSICHROME. See *Colour and Music* 10.

MUSICIANS' BENEVOLENT FUND. See *Profession* 10; *Cecilia.*

MUSICIANS' COMPANY. See *Minstrels*, etc. 3; *Profession* 1; *Cecilia.*

MUSICIANS' UNION. See *Profession* 10.

MUSICK BOOTHS. See *Fairs and their Music.*

MUSICK HOUSES. See *Inns and Taverns as Places of Music-Making.*

MUSICK MEETINGS, MUSIQUE MEETINGS, etc. See *Clubs for Music-Making*; *Concert* 5.

MUSICKS' MONUMENT. See *Mace.*

MUSICO. One eighteenth-century term for a castrato—soprano or alto (*Voice* 5).

MUSIC OF THE FUTURE. See *Germany* 7; *Liszt.*

MUSICOLOGY. This is a word of comparatively recent adoption into the English language (from the French *musicologie*), so that up to the end of the first third of the twentieth century many English dictionaries did not include it.

It may be said to cover all study of music other than that directed to proficiency in performance or composition—though even such study as this has to call on musicology for light on some of its problems.

Amongst the divisions of musicology are acoustics; the physiology of voice, ear, and hand; the psychology of aesthetics and, more directly, of musical appreciation and of musical education; rhythm and metrics; modes and scales; the principles and development of instruments; orchestration; form; theories of harmony; the history of music; the bibliography of music; terminology—and so forth. To the study of cultural anthropology or ethnology so far as it bears on music is given the name 'comparative musicology' or **ethno-musicology**.

The International Musical Society (1900–14) had as its purpose the promotion of musicological study, and its post-war successor made its purpose clear in its name—Société Internationale de Musicologie (founded 1928; organ, *Acta Musicologica*). There are also national musicological societies in many countries. An American Musicological Society was founded in 1934, the first President being Dr. Otto Kinkeldey. During the 1940s and early 1950s there took place in the United States so much activity on the historical side of musicology (in particular) as may be said to have made this the leading country in that branch of study. (For the British society see under *Royal Musical Association*.)

In Germany many universities have chairs of musicology (Musikwissenschaft—literally 'Musical Knowledge'); in France one or two; in Holland two (Utrecht and Amsterdam). The first American university to establish such a chair was Cornell (1930). The Royal College of Music has a degree of 'Master in Music (Research)', and a good deal of musicological work is privately carried on in the universities and elsewhere.

MUSIC REVIEW. See *Journals*.

MUSIC SETTLEMENTS. See *United States* 5.

MUSIC TEACHERS' ASSOCIATION. See *Profession* 10; *Appreciation*.

MUSIC TEACHERS' NATIONAL ASSOCIATION. See *Profession of Music* 10; *United States* 8.

MUSIC WEEKS. See *United States of America* 5.

MUSIKWISSENSCHAFT. See *Musicology*.

MUSIQUE À LA TURQUE. See *Percussion Family* 4 b.

MUSIQUE CONCRÈTE. See *History* 9.

MUSIQUE HOUSES. See *Inns and Taverns*.

MUSIQUE MEETINGS, MUSICK MEETINGS, etc. See *Concert* 5; *Clubs for Music-Making*.

MUS.M. See *Degrees and Diplomas* 3.

MUSSOLINI. See *Italy* 7;

MUSSORGSKY (Musorgsky, Moussorgski, etc.), **MODESTE** (p. 897, pl. **154.** 8). Born in the government of Pskov in 1839 (not 1835, as often stated) and died in St. Petersburg in 1881, aged just forty-two. Like some other Russian musical pioneers (cf. *Glinka*; *Balakiref*) he got much of his inspiration from folk music heard in childhood, and the folk tales he also heard gave him the literary basis for much of his composition.

He came early in touch with Dargomijsky (q.v.) and all his life tried to apply his principles. In his works musical realism attains its culmination. His songs are very characteristic of him; they are sardonic, humorous, or tender, and 'go straight to the mark'.

His greatest works are operas, *Boris Godunof* (1869) and *Khovanstchina* (1886), now of world-reputation, though having no success during the lifetime of their composer. The version of *Boris* long used was one that had been (like other things of this composer) 'touched up' by Rimsky-Korsakof; the original version was published in 1928 and tends now to be adopted. (For the plot, etc., see *Boris Godunof*.)

In early manhood he was an officer in the guards; then he entered the civil service. His life was not admirable; he was slovenly and waged a long losing fight against the drink habit. His personal weaknesses were redeemed only by a great public purpose—to produce an art that should illuminate the life of many. In his determined nationalism he was the most typical member of 'The Five' (see *Russia* 5, 7), as he was not the least gifted of them.

For further references to Mussorgsky and his period see *Composition* 13; *Opera* 17 c d, 21 m, 24; *Ballet* 7; *Rhythm* 10; *Gopak*; *Nationalism*; *History* 7.

MUSTEL ORGAN. See *Reed-Organ Family* 8.

MUT, MUTH (Ger.). 'Courage.' So *Mutig* or *Muthig*, 'bold'.

MUTA. Italian for 'change', e.g. of kettledrum tuning. *Muta D in C* means 'change tuning from D to C' (thus no connexion with the word 'mute'). So also for change of crook in brass instruments.

MUTANO (It.). 'Change' (third person plural—'[they] change'). Cf. *Muta*.

MUTATION (in the sense of a sort of modulation). See *Hexachord*.

MUTATION STOP. See *Organ* 2 c, 14 IV.

MUTE. A silencer, or partial silencer.

1. In **Stringed Bowed Instruments** it is a small clamp placed on the bridge, with the effect of rendering the tone soft and silvery.

2. In **Brass Instruments**, on the other hand, it is a pear-shaped stopper to be pushed into the bell, modifying the tone in a somewhat similar manner to the above—unless overblowing be indicated by the composer, when the effect is clanging or piquant. A similar method is sometimes also applied (though not so effectively) to **Wood-Wind Instruments**. (In *Lélio* Berlioz mutes a clarinet by putting it into a bag.)

Apparently the use of mutes for brass instruments became common only towards the end of the eighteenth century, for in 1780 we find Mozart in Munich (whither the famous Mannheim orchestra was now transferred) writing to his father in Salzburg for 'some *sordini* for trumpets and horns of which there are none here. Send me some by the next diligence that I may get others made from them.'

3. With the **Kettledrums** the effect of muting was formerly obtained by placing a cloth over the parchment (we speak, however, generally of 'muffling' rather than 'muting'). Nowadays the usual plan is merely to use sponge-headed drumsticks.

4. With the **Pianoforte** something of the same effect is obtained by a pedal that (*a*) causes the hammers to strike one string less for each note, or (*b*), in old instruments, interposes a piece of felt between hammers and strings, or (*c*) reduces the ambit (and so the force) of the hammer's blow.

MUTE CORNETT. See *Cornett and Key Bugle Families* 1, 4.

MUTH, MUT (Ger.). 'Courage.' So *Muthig*, *Mutig*, 'bold'.

MUZAK. Programmes of background music supplied via telephone circuits for use in restaurants, industrial plants, and the like. In the United States Muzak is said to be heard by some sixty million people daily.

M.V.O. See *Knighthood and other Honours*.

MYASKOVSKI. See *Miaskovsky*.

MY AUNT MARGERY. See *Sir Roger de Coverley*.

MY COUNTRY, 'TIS OF THEE. See *God save the Queen*.

MY LADY NEVELLS BOOKE. See *Lady Nevells Booke*.

MYSLIVICZEK, JOSEPH. Born near Prague in 1737 and died in Rome in 1781, aged forty-three. He was the successful composer of over thirty Italian operas, as well as instrumental works, and was much admired by Mozart.

MYSTERIES, MIRACLE PLAYS, AND MORALITIES. Very early in the history of the Christian Church there grew up the custom of teaching the stories of the Old Testament and the life of Christ by means of sacred plays, often in church. At first these were performed by the priests and so came, in later times and in France, the name *Ministère*, from which 'Mystery' is derived. (This is the usual statement: perhaps, however, the word 'mystery' is used of handicrafts—see reference later to the trade gilds, or 'guilds', as the actors of the plays.)

Properly 'Mystery' is applied to plays representing scriptural story (p. 609, pl. **107**. 3, 4), whilst 'Miracle' is applied to representation of stories from the lives of the saints, but the two words are loosely used and have become almost interchangeable.

A 'Morality' is a play in which the virtues and vices, etc., are personified; it is, then, an allegory; the play *Everyman*, still occasionally revived, is a fine example.

Religious plays of the Mystery type are recorded as early as the fourth century. The earliest remaining record of the performance of one in England is in 1110 (at Dunstable, in Bedfordshire) and the latest record of a fully staged example is in 1599 (at Newcastle-on-Tyne); but even after this date relics of the Mystery survived, and the present writer has seen of the north of England (about 1890) a crude performance of what is still remembered of the Miracle Play of St. George and the Dragon (cf. Thomas Hardy's novel *The Return of the Native*). It appears that this was still in the 1930s played at Rochdale in Lancashire, Midgley in Yorkshire, and a few other places, and possibly it continues.

The palmiest days of the Mystery, Miracle, and Morality were probably those of the end of the fifteenth and beginning of the sixteenth century. At York during the fifteenth century as many as fifty plays would be performed in the course of the year. The text of some of the York, Wakefield, Chester, Coventry, and Cornish plays can easily be obtained ('Everyman's Library').

Corpus Christi (instituted 1264 by Pope Urban IV) became throughout Christendom a great occasion for the giving of plays. They were often organized by the various trade guilds. At Chester twenty-four plays were performed in one day on wheeled pageant stages, moved, play by play, to different streets: i.e. each play would be performed at each 'stand' and then move on, being followed by the next of the series, so that every 'stand' had every play in turn.

Sometimes appropriateness was attained in the allotting of the plays; for instance, at Chester the Water Drawers of the Dee played 'The Ark and the Flood'; at York the Shipwrights were responsible for the play of the building of the ark, the Mariners for that of the voyage of the ark, the Chandlers for that of the star in the east, the Goldbeaters for that of the three kings offering gifts, the Vintners for that of the miracle of turning water into wine, and the bakers for that of the Last Supper.

In some parts of Europe the plays were suppressed by authority, having become an occasion of irreverence (for a great deal of comedy crept into them—as, for instance, when Noah's wife refused to enter the ark and had to be placed in it by main force). The ranting and raving of Herod was proverbially an opportunity to 'split the ears of the groundlings', as Shakespeare's Hamlet puts it; when he speaks of the type of actor who 'out-herods Herod' he is alluding to the Mystery performances. The devils of the plays were favourite comic characters.

A play for which special permission to continue was successfully obtained (reforms being first introduced) was that of the Passion at Oberammergau, in Bavaria, which is still to be seen once every decade, drawing spectators from all over the world; and there are a few others in various countries. The *Pastorales* of the Basques are also a survival of the old mysteries.

Necessarily a good deal of singing came into some of the plays, and so we may see in them one of the ancestors of both oratorio and opera. The Coventry Christmas Play, for instance, has the song of the Angels, songs by the Shepherds, and a Lullaby by the mothers of the Innocents. The Wakefield Christmas Play, belonging to the traditionally musical Yorkshire, has an amusing example of musical criticism (favourable) of the singing of the herald angel—

First Shepherd: 'Say what was his song?
      Heard ye not how he cracked it?
      Three breves to a long?'
Second Shepherd: 'Yea, marry, he hacked it.
      Was no crotchet wrong,
      Nor no thing that lacked it.'

(For 'breve' and 'long' see *Notation*.)

A very happy picture of Christmas singing, dancing, and acting in church (cf. *Dance* 7; *Seises*) is the following from Barnabe Googe (1540–94):

'Three masses every priest doth sing upon that
  solemne day,
With offerings unto every one, that so the more
  may play.
This done a wodden childe in clowtes is on the
  altar set,
About the which both boyes and gyrles do daunce
  and trymly jet:
And carols sing in prayse of Christ, and, for to
  help them heare,
The organs answer every verse with sweete and
  solemne cheer.
The priest do rore aloud; and round about their
  parents stand
To see the sport, and with their voyce do help
  them and their hande.'

For an account of cognate musical–dramatic activities see *Masque*; *Oratorio* 2; *Passion Music* 1; *Opera*. For instances of mystery plays and moralities in London in medieval times see *Parish Clerk*.

MYSTERIÖS (Ger.). 'Mysterious.'

MYSTERY. See *Mysteries*.

N

NABOKOF, NICOLAI. Born at Lubcha, near Minsk, White Russia, in 1903. He studied under Rebikof and in Berlin under Juon and Busoni and has lived in Paris, the USA, and Berlin. He has written ballets (at first for Diaghilef), orchestral, choral, chamber, and piano works, etc. Amongst his works are a ballet on American song themes called *Union Pacific* (1934) and *Vita nuova* (after Dante: 1951), also a book, *Old Friends and New Music* (1951). He is the cousin of Vladimir Nabokof, the writer.

NACAIRES (Fr.). See *Percussion Family* 4.

NACH (Ger.). 'After', 'in the manner of', 'according to', 'towards', 'to'. *Nach und nach*, 'bit by bit'; *Nach Es*, etc. '[Tune now] to E flat', etc.

NACHDRUCK (Ger.). 'Emphasis.' So *Nachdrücklich*, 'emphatically'.

NACHGEHEND (Ger.). 'Following.'

NACHLASSEND (Ger.). 'Leaving behind', i.e. slackening in speed.

NACHSCHLAG (Ger.). Literally 'after-stroke', and in that sense applied to two different things:

(*a*) To the two notes that end a shake, which, with the two notes immediately preceding, form the turn with which the shake terminates (some authorities consider only the former of the two notes that end the shake to be entitled to the description 'Nachschlag', since it is the only one foreign to the shake itself).

(*b*) To any ornamental note or notes indicated as to be added after another note (for the varieties and their manner of indication, a specialist book on ornaments should be consulted).

The application of the term in this second sense is, from one point of view, illogical. The idea intended to be conveyed is, presumably, that the note or notes are 'after' the note preceding them in the sense that their time-duration is a deduction from the time-duration of that note, but since their *ornamental function* always concerns the note that follows, they are, aesthetically considered, rather *vor* ('before') than *nach* ('after').

NACHSPIEL (Ger.). Literally 'afterplay', and so the equivalent of Postlude (q.v.).

NACHTANZ (Ger.). Literally, 'after-dance'. The term is applied to the second of the two dances in the contrasted pairs that were so common in the fifteenth to seventeenth centuries, i.e.:

> Pavan and Galliard,
> Passamezzo and Saltarello,
> Allemande and Courante,
> Sarabande and Gigue.

Especially it is applied to the Saltarello (q.v.). Another name is *Proporz* or *Proportz*.

When two dances were thus connected, usually one was danced by the participants in two facing lines and the other was a round dance.

NACHTHORN (Ger.). 'Night-horn', i.e. the organ stop also known as *Cor de nuit*. See *Organ* 14 I.

NACHTMUSIK (German for 'night music'). The term is applied to a composition of a serenade character, and especially to a suite intended for a serenade (see *Serenade*). Thus Mozart's suite with the description *Eine kleine Nachtmusik* (' a small piece of night music').

NACHTSTÜCK (German for 'night piece'). The term is used:

(1) As the equivalent of Nocturne (q.v.), the type invented by Field and perpetuated by Chopin, with a much ornamented melody in the right hand and broken-chord accompaniment in the left.

(2) As a title for any piece of music of a solemn character such as one can imagine to have been inspired by the feeling of night in the open air.

NACH UND NACH (Ger.). 'Bit by bit.'

NACH WIE VOR. 'After as before', i.e. 'As on the previous appearance'.

NAEGELI. See *Nägeli*, below.

NAENIA. (Lat.). 'Dirge.'

NAGEL, WILIBALD (1863–1920). He was a German musicologist, author of a long list of monographs, including two on English music.

See reference under *White, Robert*.

NAGELGEIGE. See *Nail Fiddle*.

NÄGELI, HANS GEORG (1773–1836) (p. 880, pl. 147. 4). Zürich musician, educationist, and publisher—influential in all these capacities. He was in touch with the composers of the day, including Beethoven, some of whose work first saw the light in his edition. He published Bach's 'Forty-eight' in a better version than any that had previously appeared, from an original copy, in Bach's handwriting, in his possession.

See *Education* 3; *Appreciation*.

NAG'S HEAD SWELL. See *Organ* 8.

NAHE (Ger.). 'Near.'

NAÏF, NAÏVE (Fr.), **NAIV** (Ger.). 'Artless.' So *Naïvement* (Fr.), 'artlessly'.

NAIL FIDDLE or **NAIL VIOLIN** or **NAIL HARMONICA** (Ger. *Nagelgeige*). In a semicircular sounding-board nails are fastened around the curve, graduated in size so as to produce the different notes. This board is held in the left hand and the nails are made to vibrate by the use of a bow held in the right hand.

This instrument was invented in the eighteenth century and for a time was more or less popular—probably, however, generally rather as a 'stunt' than as a means of serious music-making. It was widespread in Europe, and in New York in 1786 we find Peter Van Hagen (formerly of Rotterdam) publicly performing 'a solo upon iron nails, called *Violin Harmonika*'. Another name is *Semi-luna* ('half-moon').

NAIRNE, BARONESS (1766–1845). After Burns (and not too far after), Lady Nairne (*neé* Oliphant) is the foremost of the poets who have composed poems for the old Scottish tunes. See under *Caller Herrin*'; *Charlie is my Darling*; *Laird o' Cockpen*; *Land o' the Leal*; *Lass o' Gowrie*; *Will ye no come back again?*

NAJARA, ISRAEL. See *Jewish* 7.

NAKERES, NAKERS. See *Percussion Family* 4.

NÄMLICH (Ger.). (*a*) 'The same'; (*b*) 'namely'.

NAPLES. See *Singing* 7; *Schools of Music*; *Opera buffa*; *Belgium* 2; *Scarlatti, A.*; *Cimarosa*; *Napolitana*.

NAPOLITANA (It.), **NAPOLITAINE** (Fr.). A light and simple type of madrigal, presumably of Neapolitan origin, and pretty much the same as the Villanella (q.v.). The most correct description of it is 'Canzone alla Villanesca' (*Villanesca* = 'rustic'). Its greatest master was Giovanni Domenico del Giovane da Nola (died at Naples 1570) and there are three-, four-, five-, and six-voice examples by other composers of the period.

Some of the English madrigal composers used the term *Neapolitan* (see *Madrigal* 6).

During the twentieth century a certain type of music-hall song came to be called a 'Napolitana'. It appears that a usual characteristic was that of verses in the minor with choruses in the major.

NAPRAVNIK (**Naprawnik**), etc., ED-WARD F. Born in Bohemia in 1839 and died in St. Petersburg in 1916, aged seventy-seven. He studied music in Prague and at length became chief conductor of the Court Opera House at St. Petersburg. He identified himself so thoroughly with Russian life that his compositions took on the national character, and he counts as a Russian composer. His operas have had a great success. He composed also some orchestral music and a good deal of chamber music, songs, and piano music.

NARDINI, PIETRO. Born at Leghorn in 1722 and died at Florence in 1793, aged seventy or seventy-one. He was in his day one of the most reputed violinists. He composed for his instrument, and his music is still played.

See mention under *Linley, Thomas (Junior)*.

NARES, JAMES. Born at Stanwell, Middlesex, in 1715 and died in 1783, aged sixty-seven.

He was organist of York Minster, and then of George the Third's Chapel Royal. He composed music for the Anglican Church (which is still sung), as also music for harpsichord, catches, glees, and other things.

See references under *Anthem*, Period III; *Organ* 13.

NARRANTE (It.). 'Narrating', i.e. in a declamatory manner.

NARVAEZ, LUIS DE. See *Spain* 8.

NASAL RESONANCE. See *Voice* 6.

NASAL VOICES. See *Voice* 12.

NASARD, NAZARD. See *Organ* 14 IV.

NASO, NASETTO (It.). Literally 'nose', 'little nose'—the point of the bow.

NATIONAL ANTHEMS AND OFFICIAL TUNES. Taking the texts of National Anthems in general, it can hardly be said that they reach a high poetical or, indeed, ethical level.

Those which are of the nature of prayers for a monarch, such as the old Austrian anthem and the British anthem, are, however admirable and however suitable for many occasions, hardly wide enough to merit the title 'national'. Eliza Flower's 'Now pray we for our country', or Parry's 'Jerusalem', or Katharine Lee Bates's poem 'America the beautiful' (q.v.) is more fully 'national' than 'God save the Queen', and some song like this might well be adopted as a secondary national anthem in those countries which at present possess one of the narrowly personal sort.

An equally faulty type is that of the song which arose out of some particular event of war or revolution and, whilst well worthy of being retained in the national repertory of song as a valuable historical relic, has lost its application and is, in any case, like the monarchical type, too narrow for its present purpose. A criticism that was passed upon 'The Star-spangled Banner' by the Music Supervisors' Conference of America, at the time when this song was on the point of being elevated to the position of the official national anthem of the United States (1931), might be applied with equal force to such songs as the 'Marseillaise' and 'The Watch on the Rhine'—'the text of the song is largely the reflection of a single war-time event which cannot fully represent the spirit of a nation committed to "peace and good-will"': the resolution on the subject continued that 'whilst recognizing the legitimate place of *The Star-spangled Banner* as one of our historical songs, the Conference still vigorously opposes its adoption as our national anthem'.

These wise sentiments, uttered in America, were disregarded, as are similar sentiments occasionally heard in Europe, and the millions of children in school are being taught, as the highest and oftenest repeated expression of their school life, that narrower type of patriotism which, without such stimulus, quite naturally arises in moments of national crisis.

This is certainly opposed to Christian teaching (or the teaching of any idealistic religion) and cannot be for the good of the world.

See the Articles *Reed* on pages 862–3 and *Clarinet Family* on pages 190–3

1. OBOE REEDS AND BASSOON REED

2. CLARINET MOUTHPIECE

3. CLARINET REEDS

4. OBOE

5. CLARINET

6. OBOE

7. COR ANGLAIS

8. BASSOON

9. DOUBLE-BASSOON

10. CLARINET

11. BASS CLARINET

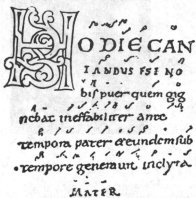

1. TENTH-CENTURY NEUMS, from a MS. at St. Gall, Switzerland. See *Notation* 1, end; 2

2. NEUM NOTATION (above) and its translation, according to Solesmes, below

3. TABLE OF NEUMS—compiled by H. B. Briggs, 1898

And as there is six strings on your Violl, so the Lessons which are set down for your Violl, are prickt or Printed on six Rules or Lines, the Letters being placed on those sixe Lines doe answer the six strings on your Violl. For example:

In this Example you see the places of the Letters as they are stopt on the neck of your Violl.

4. TABLATURE FOR THE BASS VIOL, 1652. It is played 'Lyra way' (i.e. from Tablature instead of from Notation). The 6 lines represent the 6 strings and the 8 letters, *a* to *h*, the open string and 7 frets. See *Tablature* (p. 1004) and *Viol Family* (pp. 1079–81, section 4 c)

The tunes of national anthems vary greatly in merit. Sometimes a relatively poor tune, on being officially adopted, gains a permanency that it could not otherwise have won. In the main, however, the tunes have merit. Some of them have served other purposes before being allied with their present words. Few have been specially written, and of these the best is assuredly Haydn's *Emperor's Hymn*.

The following national anthems and quasi-official national songs are separately treated in this volume— *God save the Queen*, otherwise *My Country, 'tis of thee*; *Land of my Fathers*; *Rule, Britannia!*; *God bless the Prince of Wales*; *Star-spangled Banner*; *Hail, Columbia!*; *America the Beautiful*; *O Canada!*; *Maple Leaf*; *Marseillaise*; *Brabançonne*; *Deutschland über Alles*; *Watch on the Rhine*; *O Deutschland*; *Horst Wessel*; *Emperor's Hymn*; and the *Internationale*, which till 1944 served Soviet Russia in place of a national anthem, and which (as the name implies) a school of political thought would have liked to see serving other countries in the same capacity.

NATIONAL ASSOCIATION OF SCHOOLS OF MUSIC. An American organization, founded 1924. Of 184 members, 102 are departments of colleges, 55 are schools of universities, and 27 are independent institutions. Its purposes are to secure a better understanding between schools, to establish a more uniform system of granting credits, and to set minimum standards for the granting of degrees and diplomas.

NATIONAL BROADCASTING CORPORATION. See *Broadcasting of Music* 3.

NATIONAL BUREAU FOR THE ADVANCEMENT OF MUSIC. See *United States of America* 5 f.

NATIONAL COUNCIL OF MUSIC FOR WALES. See *Wales* 9.

NATIONAL FEDERATION OF MUSIC CLUBS. An American women's organization incorporated in 1898 'to bring into working relation with one another music clubs and other musical organizations and individuals directly or indirectly associated with musical activity for the purpose of aiding and encouraging musical education, and developing high musical standards throughout America'. Its members are active in raising funds for worthy musical purposes, and annual Festivals are held for young musicians, as well as auditions and substantial awards for artists beginning their careers.

NATIONAL FEDERATION OF MUSIC SOCIETIES. This is a British organization, originally brought into existence in 1935 by the Incorporated Society of Musicians, with important initial financial help from the Carnegie Trust, and now independent. It aims at encouraging and supporting choral societies and the like and is entrusted with the administration, by way of grants and guarantees, of the sums provided by the Arts Council (q.v.).

NATIONAL GRAMOPHONIC SOCIETY. See *Gramophone* 7.

NATIONAL HIGH SCHOOL ORCHESTRA. See *United States* 5 b.

NATIONALISM IN MUSIC. It is a generally accepted fact that the folk music of various races and nations (even when so near one another as those of Europe) differs in some more or less subtle way that can be accepted as expressing distinctions in national or racial feeling. This difference is inevitably carried into the work of the composers of those races and nations when they have not stultified their racial or national characteristics by adopting a mere cosmopolitan convention. There is a sense in which it may paradoxically be said that the most original composer is normally the most national, just as 'the greatest genius is the most indebted man'—for, instinctively keeping himself free from conventions, he allows free play to the feelings within him, and these are necessary largely racial and national.

The more conscious expression of national feeling, and the deliberate adoption, to that end, of the melodic and rhythmic idiom of folk song and folk dance, dates from the middle of the nineteenth century, when composers of the Northern nations, who (many of them trained at Leipzig) had for some time been under strong German influence, began to assert their right to express their own native temperament and the emotions of their own native life. A distinctively nationalist movement began (see also *Folk Song* 5), of which the motive may be said to have been dual, corresponding to the wave of national political feeling that went through Europe at this period and to the desire to get nearer the primitive sources of life: it was, then, at one and the same time a 'my country' motive and a 'back to the land' motive.

The 'movement' was a branch of that larger one which we call the Romantic Movement (see *Romantic*), the promoters of which sought vivid emotional expression rather than classic beauty, and which achieved at least this—the introduction into music of an immensely increased variety of rhythmic, melodic, and harmonic phraseology, so preparing the way for the apparently almost complete freedom from rule and convention of the period that has followed.

Amongst earlier composers of this period who may be called Nationalists are Schumann, nurtured on German literature and music and expressing, intensely and naturally, the German spirit, and (with more sense of purpose, because actuated by conscious patriotism) Chopin, of mixed Polish and French origin, sometimes adopting Polish dance rhythms and forms and yet likewise exhibiting the French grace; in certain of Liszt's compositions there was, similarly, the attempt to express the Hungarian spirit.

But more decidedly and (perhaps one may use the term) *narrowly* nationalistic were a group of somewhat later birth—Smetana and Dvořák in Bohemia, Grieg in Norway, Glinka, Balakiref, Borodin, Mussorgsky, and Rimsky-Korsakof in Russia, and Albéniz, Granados, Falla, and Turina in Spain. All these adopted, of set purpose, idioms derived from the folk music of their native countries.

A British nationalistic trend began when Parry the Englishman, Mackenzie the Scot, and Stanford the Irishman showed in their work the characteristics of their countries— Parry expressing the bluff straightforwardness of his countrymen, and Mackenzie and

Stanford, on occasion, basing their music on themes taken from the folk-music repertories of the countries of their birth. In the opening years of the twentieth century some of the younger contemporaries of these three composers were extremely nationalistic. Under the influence of the folk-song and folk-dance collecting movement of the day they frequently adopted folk melodies as the material of their composition. For a time this process was overdone, tended to become an affectation, and discouraged individuality, but nevertheless it served its purpose (cf. *Enesco*).

The work of the Finnish composer, Sibelius, is, of course, very nationalistic—perhaps more obviously so in his earlier works.

Attempts have been made at nationalistic expression in American music (see *United States* 8), by the use of Negro or American-Indian themes (which when used by white composers have no racial connexion at all), and occasionally by the effort to represent in music a reaction to 'the American scene'. It would seem that there is some artificiality in all these expedients; but the American problem is very debatable and has been much discussed (see *United States* 8).

Extreme views have been expressed by younger composers (those born, say, within the twentieth century) as to the desirability or possibility of nationalism remaining an influence in artistic expression. So Constant Lambert wrote in 1931, 'The slogan of nationalism will die as soon as it is realized that each nation is aiming at the same ideal of mechanized civilization'. If during the twentieth and twenty-first century national aspiration and ideals die out and racial differences of temperament disappear, and the world becomes one big family, Latin and Teuton and Celtic, black and yellow, then we may, indeed, expect national distinctions in art to vanish. But a period which has seen some great historic empires split into their racial constituents, and a jealous attempt to conserve their political and linguistic independence, seems hardly the period in which one can safely utter such prophecies.

Cognate subjects treated in this volume appear under the following heads: *Folk Song*; *England*; *Scotland*; *Wales*; *Ireland*; *Italy*; *France*; *Bohemia*; *Germany*; *Spain*; *Belgium*; *Holland*; *Poland*; *Hungary*; *Scandinavia*; *United States*.

NATIONAL MUSIC SUPERVISORS' CONFERENCE. See *Education* 3.

NATIONAL UNION OF ORGANISTS' ASSOCIATIONS. See *Incorporated Association of Organists*.

NATURAL (♮). (1) A note that is neither raised ('sharpened' or 'sharped') nor lowered ('flattened' or 'flatted'). (2) The sign which, after a note has been raised by a sharp or double-sharp or lowered by a flat or a double-flat, restores it to its original pitch. After a double-sharp or double-flat the change to a single one is indicated by either the single one, or sometimes ♮♯ or ♮♭ (see Table 6).

'NATURAL' BRASS INSTRUMENTS. See *Horn Family* and *Trumpet Family*.

NATURALE (It.). 'Natural' (one sense being 'in the natural or usual manner'—in rescinding some direction to perform in an unusual manner).

NATURAL HARMONICS. See *Acoustics* 8.

NATURAL HEXACHORD. See *Hexacord*.

NATURAL NOTES (of Brass Instruments). See *American Musical Terminology* 5; *Brass*.

NATÜRLICH (Ger.). 'Natural' (in same sense as given under *Naturale*).

NATURTÖNE. See reference s.v. *American Musical Terminology* 5.

NAUMANN, JOHANN GOTTLIEB (1741–1801). He was a successful opera composer in Saxony (of which he was a native), Italy, Sweden, and Prussia. He wrote also much church music, etc. (including the 'Dresden Amen').

See references under *Harmonica* 1; *Amen*.

NAUTCH DANCE. See *Dance* 3.

NAVA. See *Voice* 20.

NAVARRAISE. A Spanish dance type deriving from the province of Navarre.

NAYLOR, DR. E. W. See *Fitzwilliam Virginal Book*.

NAZARD. See *Organ* 14 IV.

NAZI RÉGIME AND MUSIC. See *Germany* 9; *Oboussier*; *Paderewski*; *Nietzsche*; *Einstein*; *Eisler*; *Gebrauchsmusik*; *Kletzki*; *Schreker*; *Weill*.

NE (Fr.). If the word 'pas' follows immediately or with the interruption of a verb, this is the simple negative. So too with the word 'point' (a little more emphatic).

If the word 'jamais' follows the meaning is 'never'; if the word 'que' the meaning is 'only' (e.g. in organ music, 'Ne laissez que', followed by the name of a stop, means 'Leave [in use] only' that stop).

NEAL, MARY (1860–1944). See *Folk Song* 3; *Country Dance*.

NEALE, JOHN MASON (1818–66). High Church Anglican divine, poet, and remarkable linguist, who wrote hymns and translated many more from the Latin and Greek, one-eighth of the contents of the original *Hymns Ancient and Modern* being his.

See *Pange Lingua*; *Veni Sancte Spiritus*; *O Salutaris Hostia*.

NEAPOLITAN. See *Napolitana*.

NEAPOLITAN SIXTH. The Chord of the Neapolitan Sixth is one of the chromatic chords (q.v.), i.e. it includes an element that is not a part of the key. It is the major common chord on the flattened supertonic, in its first inversion. Thus in key C (major or minor) it is as follows: F–A flat–D flat. (But why Neapolitan? It is surely no special characteristic of what is called the Neapolitan School, i.e. A. Scarlatti, Pergolese, etc.; and it was in use long before their day.)

NEARER, MY GOD, TO THEE. See *Flower, Eliza*.

NEBEN (Ger.). 'Near', 'at the side of', etc. But in a number of compound words the meaning is 'additional', 'accessory', 'subsidiary', 'secondary', etc. So *Nebenthema*, 'subsidiary theme'; *Nebenstimmen* or *Nebenregister*, the mutation stops of an organ.

NEBENSATZ. See under *Satz*.

NEBST (Ger.). 'Together with', 'including'.

NECK. The projecting portion of a violin, etc., that carries the fingerboard and terminates in the peg-box.

NEDBAL, OSCAR. Born in 1874 at Tabor, in Bohemia, and died at Prague in 1930, aged fifty-six. He had a career as chamber music player (viola in the famous Bohemian Quartet) and orchestral conductor, and wrote chamber and orchestral music, many ballets and operettas, etc. His life became clouded by financial anxiety and he brought it to an end.

NEEFE, CHRISTIAN GOTTLOB (1748–98). See *Conducting* 3; *Beethoven*.

NEGLI (It.). 'In the', 'at the', etc. (masc. plur.).

NEGLIGENTE, NEGLIGENTEMENTE (It.). 'Negligently', i.e. with insouciance.

NEGRI. See *Dance* 10.

NEGRO MINSTRELS. The Negro Minstrel type of entertainment had about sixty years of popularity. Its origin is said to have been in the singing of the song 'Jim Crow' by Thomas Rice, at Pittsburgh, in 1830.

From 1843 there became popular in the United States a troupe called the Virginian Minstrels—with which was connected Dan Emmett, who for it composed 'Dixie' (q.v.). Their type of programme became an accepted public entertainment. The performers were white men with blacked faces, singing what purported to be Negro songs, imitating the Negro speech, cracking Negro jokes, playing the banjo and the bones (q.v.), dancing, etc. Many composers catered for them, writing simple melodies to sentimental or humorous verses. The most famous of such composers is Stephen Foster (q.v.), and with his name is associated that of Christy, who introduced his songs by means of his famous 'Christy Minstrels' troupe.

Towards the end of the nineteenth century Negro Minstrels were a feature of every considerable British coast resort, performing many times daily on the sands. The supersession of these in Britain by 'Pierrots' began about 1890 as a by-product of the performance in London of the wordless play *L'Enfant prodigue* ('The Prodigal Son'; see article *Pantomime*), in which the traditional Pierrot make-up costume (whitened face and white clothes) was used. This play made a sensation. Clifford Essex (1859–1946), a law student and banjoist, was impressed and took a troupe of performers so made up and clothed to Henley Regatta, with the consequence that within a few years such troupes were to be found in summer on the sands of every English seaside resort.

(The traditional Pierrot was a personage of the ancient Italian Impromptu Comedy.)

The 'minstrel shows' declined in the U.S.A. from about 1900. By 1930 the last of the old-style troupes had closed down.

The 'Negro Minstrels' have made just one or two entries into the world of artistic music. Debussy's piano pieces *Minstrels* and *Golliwogg's Cake Walk* record his interest in them. More significantly, they introduced the early Ragtime (q.v.).

NEGRO MUSIC AND MUSICIANS. See *United States* 6; *Jazz* 1.

NEGRO SPIRITUALS. See *United States* 6.

NEHMEN (Ger.). 'To take.'

NEI (It.). 'In the' (see *Nel*).

NEL (It.). 'In the.' Other forms (according to gender, number, etc.) are *Nello, Nella, Nell', Nelle, Nei, Negli*.

NELSONMESSE (Haydn). See *Nicknamed Compositions* 13.

NENIA (It.). 'Dirge.'

NEO-BECHSTEIN PIANO. See *Electric Musical Instruments* 3 a b c.

NEO-CLASSICAL. See *History of Music* 8; *Romantic* (near end); *Stravinsky*; *Germany* 8; *Hindemith*.

NEO-ROMANTIC. See *History of Music* 8; *Romantic* (near end); *Germany* 8.

NE . . . PAS (Fr.). 'Not' (the two words are usually separated by the verb).

NERA (It.). 'Black', i.e. the Crotchet or Quarter Note (Table 3).

NERI, ST. PHILIP. See *Oratorio* 2; *Laudi Spirituali*; *Palestrina*. Also p. 738, pl. **121.** 1.

NERNST, W. See *Electric Musical Instruments* 3.

NERO, EMPEROR. See *Hydraulus*.

NERVEUX (Fr.). 'Nervous', 'sinewy'.

NET, NETTE (Fr., masc., fem.). 'Clear'; so *Nettement*, 'clearly'.

NETHERLANDS. See *Belgium*; *Holland*; also references there given.

NETTA, NETTAMENTE. See *Netto*.

NETTE, NETTEMENT. See *Net*.

NETTO, NETTA (It., masc., fem.). 'Clear'; so *Nettamente*, 'clearly'.

NEUF (Fr.). 'Nine'; hence *Neuvième*, 'ninth'.

NEUKOMM, (Chevalier) SIGISMUND VON. Born at Salzburg in 1778 and died in Paris in 1858, aged seventy-nine. He was a favourite pupil of Haydn, and attained a high position in the musical and fashionable worlds. He spent a good deal of his time in France and England, composing, amongst immense quantities of other things, songs and oratorios of a brief but astounding popularity.

See reference under *Oratorio* 7 (1834); also p. 738, pl. **121.** 2.

NEUMA, NEUMAE (medieval Latin), **NEUMS, NEUMES.** See *Notation* 1 (end), 2.

NEUN (Ger.). 'Nine.'

NEUPERT. See *Harpsichord Family* 5 (end of section).

NEUVIÈME (Fr.). 'Ninth.'

NEVIN (The Brothers).

(1) ETHELBERT WOODBRIDGE (p. 1041, pl. **170**. 8). Born at Edgeworth, Pa., in 1862 and died at New Haven, Conn., in 1901, aged thirty-eight. He wrote many graceful piano compositions of the better 'salon' type and many songs of shapely melody and pleasing sentiment. His song 'The Rosary' (1898) had an enormous vogue (six million copies sold in the first thirty years; £80,000 royalties to the composer and his heirs). A piano piece of a shallow but graceful sort, *Narcissus*, for long dominated the market of American music for that instrument. He had a very real though ephemeral talent, acceptable to the musical dilettantism of his period. In certain moments he composed with a considerable degree of passion and sensuousness.

(2) ARTHUR FINLEY. Born at Edgeworth, Pa., in 1871 and died at Sewickley, Pa., in 1943, aged seventy-two. As a composer he was much influenced by American-Indian music.

See *United States* 7 (end); *Opera* 24 f (1918).

NEVINS, MARIAN. See *MacDowell*.

NEWBERRY MUSIC LIBRARY, CHICAGO. See under *Patronage* 7.

NEWBERY. See *Mother Goose Songs*.

NEWBOULD, HERBERT. See *Contra-Violin*.

NEWCASTLE (England). See *Street Music* 3; *Keel row*.

NEW ENGLAND. See *Puritans* 8; *United States* 2. See also under *Boston*; *Cambridge* (*Mass*.).

NEW ENGLAND CONSERVATORY. See *Schools of Music*.

NEW FOUNDATION. See *Cathedral Music* 2.

NEWMAN.

(1) ERNEST. Born at Liverpool in 1868 and died at Tadworth, Surrey, in 1959, aged ninety. He was music critic successively of the *Manchester Guardian* (1905), *Birmingham Post* (1906), *Observer* (1919), and *Sunday Times* (1920), as well as being connected with other journals. His books are numerous, those on Wagner being especially notable for the original research and thought they embody; he translated Wagner libretti and other things. His original name was William Roberts.

See *Mechanical Reproduction* 13; *Jazz* 5; *Composition* 6.

(2) ROBERT. See *Concert* 7.

NEW MEXICO COWBOY SONGS. See *Folk Song* 4.

NEW MUSIC. There have been at least three periods at which the term 'New' has been applied to music—about 1300 (see *France* 3); about 1600 (see reference to 'Nuove Musiche' under *Opera* 1; *Caccini*); and after 1850, when the music embodying the revolutionary principles of Liszt and Wagner (q.v.) was often spoken of as 'The New Music' (though more usually as 'The Music of the Future').

NEW MUSIC (journal). See *Cowell*.

NEW ORLEANS. See *Opera* 21 a e, 23.

NEW PHILHARMONIC PITCH. See *Pitch* 5.

NEWTON.

(1) SIR ISAAC (1642–1727). The great natural philosopher. See *Colour and Music* 5, 6.

(2) JOHN (1725–1807). Sea captain, Evangelical clergyman, and author (with Cowper) of the 'Olney Hymns'. See *Hymns and Hymn Tunes* 6.

NEWTON MARSDEN, ERNEST OCTAVIUS (1881–1954). East London music-teacher and experimenter in questions of piano touch. See *Pianoforte* 14.

'NEW' VERSION. See *Hymns* 5.

NEW YORK. See *Opera* 21, 23; *United States* 4; *Cecilia*; *Concert* 15; *Publishing* 9; *Journals*; *Schools of Music*; *Patronage* 7; *Applause* 7; *Arrangement* (end).

NEW ZEALAND. See *Cathedral Music* 8; *Broadcasting* 3.

NIBELUNGEN MARCH. See *Misattributed*, s.v. 'Wagner'.

NIBELUNGENRING. See *Ring of the Nibelung*.

NICENE CREED. See *Creed*.

NICETAS, BISHOP. See *Te Deum*.

NICHOLL, HORACE WADHAM. Born near Birmingham in 1848 and died in New York in 1922, aged nearly seventy-four. After a short career as organist in his native country he went, in his early twenties, to the United States, where he held positions at Pittsburgh and New York. He served as reader to the firm of Schirmer and himself wrote organ music, a mass, several oratorios, orchestral music, songs, and other things.

NICHOLSON.

(1) RICHARD (or 'Nicolson'). Born about 1570 and died at Oxford in 1639, aged about sixty-nine. He was connected with Magdalen College, Oxford, it is thought as organist, and was the first University Professor of Music. He left church music, a good many madrigals, and a three-voice setting of a poem, which may be called *The Wooing of Joan and John*, in eleven sections; this has been claimed to be the earliest example of the song cycle (q.v.).

(2) SYDNEY HUGO. Born in London in 1875 and died at Ashford in 1947, aged seventy-two. He was educated at Oxford, the Royal College of Music, and Frankfurt-on-Main; and then held organist's positions (Carlisle Cathedral, 1904; Manchester, 1908; Westminster Abbey, 1918–28). He devoted himself especially to the improvement of church music, and in 1928 founded, to this end, St. Nicolas College and the associated School of English Church Music (see *Royal School of Church Music*). He wrote a good deal of church music, etc. In 1938 he was knighted.

See reference under *Anglican Chant* 6.

NICHT (Ger.). 'Not', e.g. *Nicht gedämpft*, 'not muted'—countermanding an earlier direction.

NICKNAMED COMPOSITIONS

(i.e. Compositions with Unauthorized Titles)

1. Bach's Organ Fugues.
2. Various Works of Bach.
3. Beethoven's Orchestral Works.
4. Beethoven's Chamber Music.
5. Beethoven's Piano Works.
6. Boccherini.
7. Brahms.

8. Chopin.
9. Dvořák.
10. Handel.
11. Haydn's Symphonies.
12. Haydn's String Quartets.
13. Haydn's Masses.

14. Mendelssohn's 'Songs without Words'.
15. Mozart.
16. Purcell.
17. D. Scarlatti.
18. Schubert.

1. Bach's Organ Fugues

Alla Breve Fugue (D major). So nicknamed because in 'Alla Breve' time—a foolish title, as many other fugues have an equal claim to it.

Corelli Fugue (B minor). So nicknamed because it is made out of two subjects taken from Corelli (op. 3, no. 4).

Dorian (or **Doric**) **Toccata and Fugue** ('In modo dorico'). Really in D minor and nicknamed Dorian for a reason explained under *Modes* 10.

Fiddle Fugue (D minor). So nicknamed because it exists also for violin solo (the violin solo setting came first—despite the assertions of several authorities).

Fuga alla Giga (or 'Jig Fugue', G major). Not so named by the composer, apparently, though the description is correct enough. Probably composed for a two-manual and pedal harpsichord.

Giant Fugue (D minor). Merely a nickname due to the stalking figure in the pedal. The name was given by George Cooper (1820–76), the London organist who did much to popularize Bach's organ works in Britain. The recurring pedal theme suggested to him the song of Polyphemus, 'O ruddier than the Cherry', in Handel's *Acis and Galatea*.

St. Anne's Fugue (E flat major). The title has been given by some English writer, or grown up amongst English organists, from the chance that the first subject is the same as the first line of Croft's hymn tune *St. Anne* (first published 1708 and so called because Croft was organist of St. Anne's, Soho, London; see *Croft*). The same phrase is found in two movements of Handel's Chandos Anthem *O praise the Lord with one consent*. Harvey Grace (*The Organ Works of Bach*, 1922) points out that but for the first two notes changing places the phrase is also the first line of the chorale *Was mein Gott will*; and it may be that in some variants these notes are in the same order as in the fugue subject, so that the fugue may be, in effect, a sort of chorale prelude (q.v.).

The Prelude to this fugue has no association with it in the original publication (the *Clavierübung*). Thus we find Mendelssohn writing to his mother from England: 'Ask Fanny [his sister] what she thinks of my intention of playing Bach's organ Prelude in E flat major with the Fugue at the end of the same book. I suppose she will disapprove of this, yet I think I am right.'

Little Fugue (G minor). The one in Peters Edition, vol. iv, no. 7.

Wedge Fugue (E minor). Merely a nickname due to the melodic shape of the subject, which, beginning by alternating notes (in a rocking style) a minor third apart, expands its alternations step by step. In Germany it is known as the **Scissors Fugue**.

2. Various Works of Bach

Bach's Brandenburg Concertos. So called from their being dedicated (1721) to Duke Christian Ludwig of Brandenburg.

Bach's '48'. No. 9 of Book II, in E major, was, from its dignity and triumphant feeling, nicknamed by Samuel Wesley, **Saints in Glory**.

Bach's French Suites. These seem to have acquired their nickname from the fact that they are considerably lighter in style than the other two sets of suites for the domestic keyboard instruments and in that way somewhat akin to the suites of Couperin and other French masters.

Bach's English Suites. These were not published in the composer's lifetime. It is said that in a manuscript copy of them the first (of which the prelude is an expansion of a gigue by Dieupart, who lived in London from 1707 to his death thirty-three years later) bore the words 'fait pour les Anglais', and it is thought that this may have been understood by someone to apply to the whole set. Bach's first biographer, Forkel (q.v.), however, states (1803) that they were composed for an Englishman of high standing.

Bach's German Suites. This nickname for the Partitas for the domestic keyboard instrument seems to have been given them:

(*a*) by analogy, since the other sets had been nicknamed 'French' and 'English', and

(*b*) because Bach's own designation, 'Partien' (a purely German term) suggested that the composer himself regarded them as conforming in style to the German tradition.

Bach's Goldberg Variations. These thirty variations for double-keyboard harpsichord, forming the fourth book of the *Clavierübung*, have taken their nickname from the circumstance related under *Goldberg, Johann Gottlieb*.

Bach's Art of Fugue. This was published two years after the composer's death and the name was probably given by C. P. E. Bach. (In the original manuscript the word 'fugue' is not used, the pieces being called merely 'counterpoints'.)

3. Beethoven's Orchestral Works

Emperor Concerto. The Piano Concerto in E flat, op. 73, written in 1809. It is unknown who dubbed it 'Emperor' (J. B. Cramer has had the 'credit'). The name is unknown in Germany.

Beethoven's Jena Symphony. A symphony discovered in Jena in 1910 by Fritz Stein and considered by some to be a youthful work of Beethoven. It has been published by Breitkopf and Härtel. (The **'Eroica'** and **'Pastoral'** Symphonies, Nos. 3 and 6 respectively, were so named by the composer.)

4. Beethoven's Chamber Music
(alphabetically arranged).

Archduke Trio. This is the Piano Trio in B flat (op. 97) dedicated to the Archduke Rudolph.

Harp Quartet. This is the String Quartet in E flat, op. 74. The nickname has become attached to it because of some pizzicato arpeggios in the first movement that suggest a harp. It is misleading, as uninformed concert-goers naturally expect to see on the platform, if not four harps, at least one (with three bowed instrument companions).

Kreutzer Sonata. See under *Kreutzer, Rodolphe.*

Rasoumoffsky Quartets (or 'Rasumov-ski', or 'Rasoumowsky'.) This name is commonly given to the three string quartets numbered op. 59, dedicated to Count Rasoumoffsky (Russian Ambassador at Vienna and a keen quartet player).

Spirit Trio ('Das Geister Trio'). This is the nickname (commoner in Germany that elsewhere) of the Pianoforte Trio in D, op. 70, no. 1. The mysterious opening of the second movement has, apparently, suggested the idea. (There is a tradition that this movement had some connexion with sketches for spirit music in projected incidental music to *Macbeth*.)

Spring Sonata. This is a German name ('Frühlingssonate') for the Sonata in F for piano and violin (op. 24). The nicknamer is unknown.

The Storm. Quintet in C, op. 29.

5. Beethoven's Piano Works

The only piano sonatas to which Beethoven himself gave titles are the op. 13, *Grande Sonate Pathétique* (so entitled by him—in French), and the op. 81a, *Sonate caractéristique: Les Adieux, l'Absence, et le Retour* (again so entitled by him in French—in deference to the wishes of his publisher, who objected to a German title). The following (alphabetically arranged) are, then, mere nicknames.

Appassionata Sonata. This was so called by the publisher Cranz, without authority yet with a certain propriety.

Dramatic Sonata. The Sonata in D minor, op. 31, no. 2, is sometimes so called.

Hammerklavier Sonata. If we call the Piano Sonata op. 106 by this title so we should call the Sonatas op. 101, op. 109, and op. 110. Hammerklavier ('Hammer-keyboard') means the pianoforte as distinct from the harpsichord. It was the old German name for the instrument, and in an access of patriotism Beethoven adopted it on the manuscript of all these four works, that is he called each *Sonate für das Hammerklavier* ('Sonata for the Hammer-keyboard').

Laube Sonata. Another fancy title for the so-called 'Moonlight' Sonata (see below). 'Laube' ('arbour' or 'bower') represents a popular tradition as to the place of its composition.

Moonlight Sonata. The composer called this simply *Sonata quasi una fantasia*, op. 27, no. 2, as he described the preceding one as *Sonata quasi una fantasia*, op. 27, no. 1. A critic called Rellstab wrote that the opening movement reminded him of moonlight on the Lake of Lucerne and the idea stuck (see also above and s.v. *Harpsichord* 7).

Pastoral Sonata. This is op. 28 (D major). The name 'Pastoral' was given it by the publisher Cranz, without authority. (But it has a certain fitness—to the first movement, at any rate.)

Waldstein Sonata. Op. 53 (C major). The composer did not call the sonata by this name, but he dedicated it to his friend Count Waldstein and so there is little harm in the nickname.

Rage over a Lost Penny. Op. 129. This is a youthful unfinished piano piece published after the composer's death. It was originally headed in Italian, *Alla ingharese* [sic], *quasi un capriccio* ('In Hungarian style; a sort of Capriccio'), to which the composer later added the German sub-title *Leichter Kaprice* ('Easy Capriccio'). The author of the present fancy title is unknown. Beethoven's autograph copy was discovered (about 1947) in the United States.

For 'Beethoven's Adieu to the Piano' see *Misattributed Compositions.*

6. Boccherini

La Divina. The Sinfonia in D minor. The name doubtless arises from the fact that it is more serious and reflective than most of Boccherini's works.

L'Uccelliera ('The Aviary'). Quintet in D.

7. Brahms

Meistersinger Sonata. This is the second sonata for violin and piano in A, op. 100. The first theme slightly resembles the 'Preislied' of the music drama that has given it its name.

Rain Sonata ('Regen Sonate'). The sonata for violin and piano in G, op. 78. So nicknamed from its use of the theme of the composer's

Rain Song ('Regenlied'—one of the eight songs of op. 59).

Thuner-Sonate. The sonata for pianoforte and violin in D minor, op. 108, composed at Thun, in Switzerland, 1888 (1st perf. by Brahms and Joachim, Vienna, 1889).

8. Chopin

Butterfly's Wings Étude. This is no. 9 (in G flat) of his Twelve Études, op. 25. There is no authenticity in the title.

Cat Valse. This is op. 34, no. 3. The title recalls a legend that the composer's cat jumped on the keyboard as he was composing and, running up and down, suggested to him the appoggiatura passage in the fourth section (cf. Scarlatti's 'Cat's Fugue', under 14 below).

Dog Valse. This is op. 64, no. 1 (D flat)—the most popular of all the composer's valses. The story that supports the nickname is of 'George Sand's' dog running round and round after its own tail and Chopin sitting down and improvising a valse to represent the incident (see 'Minute Valse' below). However, a pianist writes—'I am sure the number given is incorrect. Pachmann told us the story to the Valse in F, and I had heard it so dozens of times'.

Minute Valse. Same as the above (i.e. op. 64, no. 1) and so nicknamed because it is supposed to take a minute to play (it really takes a minute and a half if it is to make its effect).

Raindrop Prelude. This is no. 15 (in D flat) of his op. 28, Twenty-four Preludes. No. 6 was written whilst rain was falling on the roof (the monastery of Valdemosa); Chopin denied that this had influenced him, but his companion, the novelist 'George Sand', seems to think that it had done so without his realizing it. It has been supposed that in this no. 15 prelude he further elaborated the same idea.

Revolutionary Étude. This étude (op. 10, no. 12) is said to express the composer's feelings on hearing of the taking of Warsaw by the Russians in 1831 and the partition of his native Poland amongst Russia, Austria, and Germany. Hence the nickname.

Shepherd Boy Étude. This is no. 1 (in A flat) of his op. 25, Twelve Études. The composer did not attach the name, but it is authentic to this extent—'he told a pupil that he had imagined a little shepherd taking refuge in a grotto from a storm and playing a melody on his flute'.

Winter Wind Étude. This is no. 11 (in A minor) of his Twelve Études, op. 25. There is no authority for the title.

9. Dvořák

American Quartet (the String Quartet in F, op. 96). This was written at Spillville, Iowa, and, like other of the composer's works of the American period, uses some thematic material with characteristics found in Negro song (e.g.

pentatonic scale, syncopation), hence the one-time English nickname 'Nigger Quartet', now happily no longer heard.

10. Handel

The Harmonious Blacksmith. This is an air and variations from Handel's fifth Harpsichord Suite of his first set (1720), and he gave it no fancy title whatever. There is no foundation for the story that Handel heard the air sung by a blacksmith at Edgware, near London, nor justification for the exhibition of the anvil upon which the man beat time as he sang, nor for the inscribing of a portion of the air upon the tombstone of a blacksmith in a graveyard at Edgware.

The Edgware Blacksmith story was first floated by the notoriously inventive Richard Clark (q.v.) in his *Reminiscences of Handel* (1836). In 1889, in the first edition of Grove's *Dictionary of Music*, the following appeared from the pen of William Chappell (1809–88):

'A few months after Clark's publication the writer saw the late J. W. Winsor, Esq., of Bath, a great admirer of Handel and one who knew all his published works. He told the writer that the story of the Blacksmith at Edgware was pure imagination, that the original publisher of Handel's lesson under that name was a music-seller at Bath, named Lintern, whom he knew personally from buying music at the shop, that he had asked Lintern the reason for this new name, and he had told him that it was a nickname *given to himself* because he had been brought up as a blacksmith, although he had afterwards turned to music, and that this was the piece he was constantly asked to play. He printed the movement in a detached form, because he could sell a sufficient number of copies to make a profit.'

Chappell was a careful and conscientious musical antiquarian and this story is probably true, but there is no copy of Lintern's edition of the piece in the British Museum and Mr. Wm. C. Smith, late of that Museum, a Handelian specialist of high standing, said that the earliest copy of the piece that he had yet (1940) been able to find under the name *The Harmonious Blacksmith* was that published by the British Harmonic Institution, arranged as a pianoforte duet, the paper of which bears the watermark '1819'.

Equally there is no foundation for the statement that the air is by Wagenseil (who was only five years old when it was first printed), and some other attributions have been shown to be equally baseless.

Almost the same air, but in the minor, is found in a bourrée by Richard Jones (1680–1740), and it is not known whether the publication of this preceded or followed that of Handel's suite. But a passage in Handel's opera *Almira*, written 1704, is very like the 'Harmonious Blacksmith' tune, so it is more than likely that the latter was his own.

Beethoven has used much the same theme for the subject of a two-part organ fugue—probably an unconscious reminiscence.

Hallelujah Organ Concerto, no. 9 in

B flat (set 2, no. 3). The opening phrase of the 'Hallelujah Chorus' appears a good deal in the first movement, whence the designation.

Hornpipe Concerto. This name has been given to the Concerto Grosso no. 12, in B minor.

11. Haydn's Symphonies

A number of these have nicknames and it is not easy to know which of them were authorized by the composer; hence what is believed to be a complete list of symphonies possessing titles is given. In order to assist identification the list gives key, time-signature, and tempo indication of the opening movement, and also date; the numbers prefixed (and the arrangement is numerical) are those of Mandyczewski's edition of Haydn's complete works (Breitkopf & Härtel), which has been slowly appearing since 1907. The name as first given is in the form generally used in Germany— i.e. whether in German, French, or Italian, it is as seen in most German editions.

For 'Haydn's Ox Minuet' see *Misattributed Compositions*.

6–8. Le Matin ('Morning'). D, 4/4, Adagio. **Le Midi** ('Midday'). C, 4/4, Adagio. **Le Soir** ('Evening': it bears sometimes another name, **La Tempesta**—'The Storm'). G, 3/8, Allegro molto. All about 1761.

22. Der Philosoph ('The Philosopher'). E flat, 4/4, Adagio. 1764. The character of the opening is said to have given it the name.

26. Weihnachtssymphonie ('Christmas Symphony', also called **'Lamentations'**). D minor, 4/4, Adagio assai. About 1765. It is said that this is rather an 'Advent Symphony' than a 'Christmas' one, and that this explains its general tone of solemnity.

30. Alleluia. C, 4/4, Allegro. (Has only three movements.) 1765. Incorporates part of a plainsong alleluia.

31. Auf dem Anstand ('At the Hunting-place') or **Mit dem Hörnersignal** ('With the Horn Call'). D, 3/4, Allegro. 1765. This has many horn fanfares.

43. Merkur ('Mercury Symphony'). E flat, 3/4, Allegro. Before 1772.

44. Trauersymphonie ('Mourning Symphony'). E minor, 4/4, Allegro con brio. Before 1772.

45. Abschiedssymphonie ('Farewell Symphony'). F sharp minor, 3/4, Allegro assai. 1772. Explained by the well-known story of the desire of the members of the orchestra to get away from the Esterházy country estate to their homes in Vienna. The score is so designed that in the last movement the players can, one by one, blow out their candles and depart, until none are left. It is said that the Prince took the hint.

48. Maria Theresia ('Maria Teresa'). C, 4/4, Allegro. 1772. So called because when the Empress Maria Teresa visited Esterházy in 1773 this piece greatly pleased her.

49. La Passione ('The Passion'). F minor, 3/4, Adagio. Before 1773.

53. L'Impériale ('The Imperial'). D, 3/4, Largo maestoso. Before 1774.

55. Der Schulmeister ('The School-master'). E flat, 3/4, Allegro molto. 1774. Said to have received its name from the character of the second movement.

59. Feuersymphonie ('Fire Symphony'). A, 4/4, Presto. Before 1776. May have been intended as the overture to a drama, *Die Feuersbrunst* ('The Conflagration'), known to have been performed at Esterházy.

60. Il Distratto ('The Absent-Minded Man'). C, 2/4, Adagio. The six movements of this symphony were originally the overture and incidental music to a comedy, *Der Zerstreute* (same meaning), produced in Vienna in 1776.

63. La Roxolane. C, 3/4, Allegro. 1777. There is some mystery which the present writer has not been able to clear up. Apparently this symphony was originally the Overture to the opera buffa of 1777, *Il Mondo della Luna* (see Grove's *Dictionary*, first edition; Schnerich, *Joseph Haydn und seine Sendung*, etc.). Tenschert (*Joseph Haydn*) speaks of the Allegretto of Symphony no. 63 as a 'variation movement on the French song, *Roxelane*'.

69. Loudon. C, 4/4, Allegro vivace. Before 1779. The name honours the famous Austrian field-marshal, Baron Gideon Ernst von Loudon (not 'Laudon'; 1717–90).

Kindersymphonie ('Children's Symphony'). C. 1788. See separate article, '*Toy*' *Symphony*.

73. La Chasse ('The Hunt'). D, 3/4, Adagio. 1781. The last movement is responsible for the name; this movement had previously appeared in an opera.

82. L'Ours ('The Bear'). C, 3/4, Allegro vivace. 1786 (First 'Paris' Symphony). The name comes from the bagpipe-like theme of the finale, which suggests the music of a bear-leader. (Others have heard a 'growling' theme in the bass in the same movement.)

For 82–87 see lower down.

83. La Poule ('The Hen'). G minor, 4/4, Allegro spiritoso. 1786 (Second 'Paris' Symphony). The first movement's second subject was thought by the Parisians to suggest a hen's cluck.

85. La Reine ('The Queen'; often called 'The Queen of France'). B flat, 4/4, Adagio. About 1786 (Fourth 'Paris' Symphony). Much approved by Marie Antoinette, whence the nickname.

88. Letter V. G, 3/4, Adagio.

(The alphabetical designation refers to the catalogue of the Philharmonic Society of London.)

92. Oxford. G, 3/4, Adagio. 1788. This was not composed for Oxford but was performed in 1791, when the composer was there to receive his honorary D.Mus.

For 93–104 see lower down.

94. Paukenschlag (literally, 'Drumstroke';

in English called 'Surprise' Symphony). G, 3/4, Adagio cantabile. 1791 (Third 'London' Symphony). So called because of the humorous sudden breaking of the peace of the slow movement. (Not to be confused with 'Paukenwirbel'; see 103.)

96. **The Miracle.** D, 3/4, Adagio. 1791 ('London Symphonies', no. 4).

100. **Militär** ('Military'). G, 4/4, Adagio. 1794 (Twelfth 'London' Symphony).

101. **Die Uhr** ('The Clock'). D, 3/4, Adagio. 1794 (Eleventh 'London' Symphony). The slow movement suggests 'tick-tack'.

103. **Paukenwirbel** ('Drum-roll'). E flat, 3/4, Sostenuto. 1795 (Eighth 'London' Symphony). The slow introduction opens with a kettledrum roll, which appears also later in the movement, of which it is a feature. (Not to be confused with 'Paukenschlag'; see 94.)

82–87. **Paris Symphonies.** These are a set of six, written for the famous Concert Spirituel (see *Concert* 14. Brenet's *Haydn*, however, speaks of the six 'Paris' Symphonies as written in 1764 for the 'Concert de la Loge Olympique', and not for the Concert Spirituel). It is sometimes stated that there are twelve 'Paris' Symphonies, but this is an error.

93–104. **Salomon Symphonies** or **London Symphonies.** These are Haydn's last twelve symphonies, written for the London violinist and impresario Salomon (q.v.). As will be seen above, four of the twelve possess nicknames. For some reason no. 7 of the set (in D) has come to be called by many people 'The London Symphony', but it is really no more 'the' than the other eleven.

12. Haydn's String Quartets

The numbers prefixed below are those generally used, and the order of arrangement is numerical. (For the opus numbers of Haydn's works see remark under *Opus*.)

1. **La Chasse** ('The Hunt'). B flat, 6/8, Presto ('Op. 1, no. 1'). So nicknamed from the horn-call character of the opening phrase.

31–36. **Sonnenquartette** ('Sun Quartets'; cf. no. 78 below). So called from the first publisher's trade-mark, which appeared on the copies.

They are sometimes described as op. 20, nos. 1–6, and sometimes as **Die Grossen Quartette** ('The Great Quartets').

37–42. **Die Russischen Quartette** ('The Russian Quartets'). The reason for the name is not apparent. The group is also known by the Italian name of **Gli Scherzi** ('The Scherzos' or 'The Jokes'), because all the minuets are quicker than usual and bear the description 'Scherzo' or 'Scherzando'. Another name is **Jungfernquartette**, i.e. 'Maiden Quartets'.

39. **Vogelquartett** ('Bird Quartet'). C, 4/4, Allegro moderato. (One of the 'Russian Quartets'—see above; sometimes known as op. 33,

no. 3.) It seems to have taken some of its thematic material from bird-calls (see *Bird Music*).

41. **'How do you do?'** G, 2/4, Vivace assai ('Op. 33, no. 5'). The words fit the first motif of the music.

48. **Dream.** F, 2/4, Allegro moderato ('Op. 50, no. 5'). It is the Adagio movement that gives it the nickname.

49. **Froschquartett.** ('Frog Quartet'). D, 4/4, Allegro. (Sometimes described as op. 50, no. 6.) The title comes from the character of the chief theme of the finale. This quartet is also known as **The House on Fire** and **The Row in Vienna**—doubtless from the vigour of the opening phrase.

57–68. **Tostquartette.** There are two series (of six each), written 1789–90. They are so called because dedicated to Johann Tost, merchant and violinist of Vienna. (They are sometimes described as op. 54, nos. 1–3; op. 55, nos. 1–3; op. 64, nos. 1–6.) The word 'Tost' is on some copies misprinted 'Dort'.

See also opp. 61 and 67 below.

61. **Rasiermesserquartett** ('Razor Quartet'). F minor, 4/4, Andante. (Sometimes described as op. 55, no. 2.) This is no. 5 of the 'Tostquartette' (see above). The tale is of Haydn, when shaving, crying 'I'd give my best quartet for a new razor', and of his visitor, the London publisher Bland, taking him at his word.

67. **Lerchenquartett** ('Lark Quartet'). D, 4/4, Allegro con spirito (no. 11 of the 'Tostquartette'; see above). Sometimes described as op. 64, no. 5. The opening accounts for the nickname. It is also sometimes, from the character of the last movement, called **Hornpipe Quartet.**

74. **Rittquartett** or **Reiterquartett** ('Horseman Quartet'). G minor, 3/4, Allegro. (Sometimes described as op. 74, no. 3.) The rhythm of the first movement suggests the nickname.

75. **Farmyard.** G, 2/2, Allegro con spirito ('Op. 76, no. 1').

76. **Quintenquartett** ('Fifths Quartet'). D minor, 4/4, Allegro. (Sometimes described as op. 76, no. 2.) The name comes from the bold leaps of the interval of a fifth in the chief theme of the first movement. The remarkable minuet is sometimes called **Hexenmenuett** ('Witch Minuet'). This quartet is also known as **The Bell,** or **The Donkey.** The falling fifths of the opening phrase have evidently suggested a bell-peal motif to some and 'Hee-haw' to others.

77. **Kaiserquartett** ('Emperor Quartet'). C, 4/4, Allegro. (Sometimes described as op. 76, no. 3). See under *Emperor's Hymn*.

78. **Sunrise.** B flat, 4/4, Allegro con spirito. In England the above name is sometimes given, apparently from the nature of the opening (cf. 31–36).

82. **'Wait till the Clouds roll by.'** F, 4/4,

E e

Allegro moderato ('Op. 77, no. 2'). So called in Britain from some slight resemblance of the opening phrase to that of the old song.

13. Haydn's Masses

(The order is by the numbers generally applied.)

4. Grosse Orgelmesse ('Great Mass with Organ'). In E flat. 1766. The nickname comes from the fact that the organ plays an important solo role. (Haydn inscribed it, *In hon. Beatae Mariae Virginis*.) See also below.

5. Kleine Orgelmesse ('Little Mass with Organ'). In B flat. 1770. The reason for the nickname is the same as in the case of 4. (Haydn inscribed it *Missa brevis Sti. Joannis de Deo*.)

6. Sechsviertelmesse ('Six-four-time Mass'). In G. 1772. The opening ('Kyrie'), being of a pastoral character, is in 6/4 time. (Haydn himself inscribed this *Missa Sti. Nicolai*.)

8. Mariazellermesse ('Mariazell Mass'). In C. 1782. Mariazell, 60 miles from Vienna, is the most famous place of pilgrimage in Austria. There is a Benedictine monastery there for which it is to be supposed the person known to have commissioned the Mass intended it.

9. Heiligmesse ('Holy Mass'). In B flat. 1796. The nickname comes from a noteworthy treatment of the words 'Holy, Holy', in the Sanctus. (Haydn himself inscribed it *In hon. b. Bernardi de Offida*.)

10. Paukenmesse ('Kettledrum Mass'). In C. 1796. (Haydn himself called this *Missa in tempore belli*, i.e. 'War-time Mass'.)

11. Nelsonmesse ('Nelson Mass'). In D minor. 1798. The composer gave this Mass no name, but it was said that a certain passage (the entry of trumpets at the beginning of the Benedictus) was connected in his mind with the battle of Aboukir, of which the news was received whilst he was at work on the Mass. Another explanation is that it was performed on the occasion of Nelson's visit to Eisenstadt in 1800. In England it is called the **Imperial Mass** and often spoken of as 'No. 3'.

12. Theresienmesse ('Theresa Mass'). In B flat. 1799. The name, which is not Haydn's, has aroused various surmises. It was not, as sometimes thought, composed for the Empress Maria Theresa, who died nineteen years before its composition, but probably for the wife of Francis II.

13. Schöpfungsmesse ('Creation Mass'). In B flat. 1801. The nickname comes from the fact that in the 'Qui Tollis' there appears a theme already familiar in *The Creation*.

14. Harmoniemesse ('Wind Band Mass'). In B flat. 1802. The nickname comes from a fuller use of wind instruments in the orchestra (see *Harmonie*) than is usual in Haydn's masses.

14. Mendelssohn's 'Songs without Words'

The following titles are authentic—and no others: *Gondola Song* (three with this same title), *Duetto*, *Folk Song*.

Neither *Spinnlied* ('Spinning Song'; usual German title) nor *Bee's Wedding* (usual English title for the same piece) is authentic. Nor are *Spring Song* and *Funeral March*.

An earlier nickname for the *Spring Song* was *Camberwell Green*—from its composition in a house in what is now Ruskin Park.

For Mendelssohn's *Funeral March* see under *Colour and Music* 4.

15. Mozart

The numbers prefixed are those of Köchel and the order is numerical. (For 'Mozart's Twelfth Mass' see *Misattributed Compositions*.)

K. 66. Dominicus Mass or **Pater Dominicus Mass**. In C. 1769. The name may, perhaps, be considered as more or less authorized, since the composer's father alludes to what appears to be this work, in a letter of 1773, as the 'P. Dominicus Mass'. It was written for the first celebration of mass by a young family friend who had become a Benedictine—Cajetan Hagenauer, now become Father Dominicus.

K. 220. Spatzenmesse ('Sparrow Mass'). 'From the characteristic violin figure in the Allegro of the Sanctus' (Köchel–Einstein).

K. 250. Haffner Serenade. Suite in D. Written in 1776, for a wedding in the family of the burgomaster of Salzburg, Sigmund Haffner. The composer was then 20 (compare K. 385).

K. 257. Credo Mass. In C. 1776. The nickname is easily accounted for. Of all the Credos of Mozart the one in this mass is perhaps that in which he has the most sincerely striven to find a fitting musical expression for the text. He uses a device he has already used (though not with such fine effect) in his Mass in F (K. 192). The word 'Credo', whenever it occurs, is given out to a simple theme of its own, always in unison, which remains distinct from the general musical texture of the movement.

K. 259. Organ Solo Mass. In C. 1776. The Benedictus has an important organ solo passage. In a letter, eighteen months after the composition of this mass, Mozart's father writes of it as 'Wolfgang's Mass with the Organ solo'.

K. 271. Jeunehomme Concerto for Pianoforte. In E flat. 1777. Mozart, in a letter ten months after the composition of this work, concerning three of his concertos, familiarly distinguishes this as 'the one for the Jenomy'. He means Mademoiselle Jeunehomme, a celebrated French pianist who in one of her tours had evidently visited Salzburg, and whose name has become permanently connected with the work.

K. 297. **Paris Symphony.** The Symphony in D, which Mozart wrote when, at the age of twenty-two, he was in Paris with his mother.

K. 317. **Coronation Mass.** In C. 1779. The name has been retained, apparently, from the association of some performance of it with the annual ceremony of crowning the miracle-working representation (*Gnadenbild*) of the Virgin at Maria-Plain, near Salzburg.

K. 385. **Haffner Symphony.** The Symphony in D, composed in less than a fortnight, in 1782, to please the Haffner family (compare K. 250).

K. 407. **Leutgebisches (Leitgebisches) Quintett.** In E flat, for violin, two violas, cello, and horn. The horn player for whom it was composed was one Leutgeb (Leitgeb).

K. 425. **Linz Symphony.** The Symphony in C, composed 'at breakneck speed' for Count Thun in that city in 1783.

K. 458. **Hunt Quartet** (or 'Jagd Quartett', or 'La Chasse')—from the character of the opening subject.

K. 465. **Dissonanzen Quartett, Les Dissonances.** These are the German and French nicknames for the String Quartet in C—on account of its much-discussed introduction.

K. 498. **Kegelstatt-Trio** ('Skittle-ground Trio'). 'Because Mozart wrote it whilst playing at skittles' (Köchel–Einstein).

K. 504. **Prague Symphony.** This is the Symphony in D, composed in Vienna in December 1786 and received with enthusiasm in Prague in January 1787.

K. 537. **Coronation Concerto** (piano). In D. 1788. Performed at a concert the composer gave at Frankfurt, in 1790, on the occasion of the coronation of Leopold II.

The Concerto K. 459 in F was performed on the same occasion and, like K. 537, was published as 'Exécuté à l'occasion du Couronnement de l'Empereur Léopold II'.

K. 551. **Jupiter Symphony.** The greatest of the eight symphonies in C major.

The designation 'Jupiter' appears to have been first attached to the work in British programmes and has been attributed to J. B. Cramer. An early (and perhaps the earliest) use of it is in the programme of the Edinburgh Festival in October 1819. It is also found in the programme of a Philharmonic Concert in March 1821.

K. 576. **Trumpet Sonata.** The Pianoforte Sonata in D. So nicknamed from the opening of the first movement's first subject.

K. 581. **Stadler Quintet**—in German, *Stadlers Quintett* or *Stadler-Quintett* and in French, *Quintette Stadler*. This is the Clarinet Quintet. The composer himself, who wrote it for the distinguished clarinettist Anton Stadler (not, as sometimes stated on programmes, for

the Benedictine Abbot, musical theorist, and historian, Maximilian Stadler), used the nickname in a letter of 8 April 1790.

16. Purcell

Bell Anthem. So called from the scale passage on which the instrumental introduction is based. The name occurs in two contemporary manuscripts. The words begin 'Rejoice in the Lord alway'.

Golden Sonata. The ninth of the 'Sonatas of Four Parts'.

17. D. Scarlatti

The Cat's Fugue. This is a harpsichord fugue by Domenico Scarlatti. Behind the nickname lies a story as to the origin of the subject of the fugue in notes played by the composer's cat in walking over the keyboard (cf. Chopin's 'Cat Valse', under 8 above).

18. Schubert

Death and the Maiden Quartet. The String Quartet in D minor. The second movement consists of variations on the composer's song 'Death and the Maiden', and some think that the whole work is inspired with the poetic idea of this song.

Trout Quintet. The Piano Quintet in A, op. 114. The fourth movement (of five) consists of variations on the composer's song 'The Trout', and the whole was written at the request of a friend who admired that song.

Mourning Waltz (*Trauerwalzer*), or **Sad Waltz** (*Valse Triste*). It was the publisher who conferred the German and French names on this composition (op. 9, no. 2) and when Schubert heard of it he exclaimed 'What kind of jackass ever composed a "Valse Triste"?' It appeared in 1821, and five years later it reappeared, mixed up with a waltz of Himmel and so made into a *Sehnsuchts Walzer* ('Longing Waltz'—also known by a French title, *Le Désir*) by 'Beethoven'!

Tragic Symphony. The one in C minor (1816).

Little Symphony. The one in C major composed in 1817–18.

Unfinished Symphony. The one in B minor (1822).

Symphony of Heavenly Length. The one in C major (1829)—Schumann's name for it.

Gastein, or Gmünden, Symphony. Supposed to have been composed at Gastein or (more likely) Gmünden, Upper Austria, in 1825, but now lost. In the centenary year of Schubert's birth the Columbia Graphophone Co. fruitlessly offered a reward of £200 for its discovery. The theory has been advanced that the 'Grand Duo' for pianoforte is an arrangement of this symphony.

NICODÉ, JEAN LOUIS. Born near Poznán (Posen), in Poland, in 1853 and died at Dresden in 1919, aged sixty-six. He left Poland for Germany as a child, studied and then taught in Berlin, and settled in Dresden, where he held several important appointments as teacher and conductor. He also toured as a pianist. His works are chiefly either for piano or for orchestra, and amongst them are two of a choral symphony stamp, *The Sea* and *Gloria*.

See *Double Sharp*.

NICOLAI.

(1) KARL OTTO EHRENFRIED. Born at Königsberg in 1810 and died in Berlin in 1849, aged nearly thirty-nine. He was a flourishing opera conductor and composer in Italy and Germany, whose career was suddenly cut short by apoplexy. His *The Merry Wives of Windsor* (1848) is his best-known work. He founded the Vienna Philharmonic Society (1842), which, under him and his sucessors (Georg Hellmesberger, Dessoff, Richter, Mahler, Joseph Hellmesberger, Schalk, Muck, Mottl, Richard Strauss, Weingartner) has done much to raise the general standard of orchestral performance and to widen the orchestral repertory. It has been the custom to close the orchestral season with a 'Nicolai Concert', the proceeds of which are devoted to the orchestra's pension fund.

(2) WILLEM. See *Holland* 7.

NICOLAU, ANTONI. Born in Barcelona in 1858 and there died in 1933, aged seventy-four. He was director of the school of music in his native place, and wrote choral and orchestral music, operas, etc.

NICOLSON, RICHARD. See *Nicholson*.

NICOLY, RENÉ. See *Jeunesses musicales*.

NIECKS, FREDERICK. Born at Düsseldorf in 1845 and died in Edinburgh in 1924, aged seventy-nine. He was a violinist who in his early twenties settled in Edinburgh. A man of fine general and musical culture, he became the author of important books on Chopin and on Programme Music, etc. From 1891 to 1914 he was Professor of Music at Edinburgh University.

See references under *Scotland* 10; *Polonaise*; *Macmillan*.

NIEDER (Ger.). 'Down.' So *Niederdrücken*, 'to press down'.

NIEDERMEYER, ABRAHAM LOUIS. Born at Nyon, Switzerland, in 1802 and died in Paris in 1861, aged nearly fifty-nine. At twenty-one he settled in Paris, where he attempted an operatic career, but then turned to church music, studying especially that of the sixteenth to eighteenth centuries (including that of Bach), and founding the school for its study and practice which still exists with his name attached to it and which has been the place of training of a number of eminent French musicians (Fauré, Messager, etc.). His church music is in use in France and elsewhere. (Cf. *Gigout*.)

NIEDERSCHLAG (Ger.). 'Down-beat' ('up-beat' being *Aufschlag*), or 'Down-stroke' (of the bow).

NIEDERSTRICH (Ger.). 'Down-stroke' (of the bow).

NIELSEN, CARL AUGUST (p. 896, pl. **153.** 3). Born on the Danish island of Funen in 1865, and died at Copenhagen in 1931, aged sixty-six. He began his musical life as a boy bugler in the army, and was then, on the strength of early compositions, taken up by Gade, who secured him a good musical education at Copenhagen. He rose to be opera conductor and director of the musical society of that city, where, also, he enjoyed a high reputation as composer—a reputation which has continued to grow and spread.

His works, which are numerous, include operas, symphonies, a violin concerto, choral compositions, string quartets, and other chamber music, piano compositions, and other things.

NIEMECZ. See *Mechanical Reproduction* 5.

NIENTE (It.). 'Nothing', e.g. *quasi niente*, 'almost nothing' (in point of tone).

NIETZSCHE, FRIEDRICH. Born at Röcken, Saxony, in 1844 and died at Weimar in 1900, aged fifty-five. From the age of twenty-five to that of thirty-five he occupied the chair of Classical Philology at the University of Basle. Wagner, with whom he was already acquainted and whom he already admired, had some time before settled at Lucerne, and for the year or two of overlapping of the two men's residence in Switzerland there was a close association between them.

It was during this period (1872) that Nietzsche published his *The Birth of Tragedy from the Spirit of Music, or Hellenism and Pessimism*, in which he greeted Wagnerian Music Drama as the modern successor of Greek tragedy.

In that same year Wagner settled in Bayreuth and four years later (1876) there appeared Nietzsche's *Richard Wagner in Bayreuth*. These two works released a turbulent flood of argument that swept through German philosophical and musical circles.

Five or six years of physical weakness (during which period were produced works of original thought which continued to stir opinion but which do not call for mention in a book of musical reference) were followed by a change of philosophical orientation. Amongst the works which characterized the close of this period was the allegorical prose-poem *Thus spake Zoroaster* (1883–5), which was, a decade later, to inspire the young composer Strauss to the composition of his symphonic poem of the same name, and, by its teaching of the doctrine of the 'Superman', to become one of the incitements to Germany's greatest crimes and one of the causes of Europe's greatest distresses. An adaptation of selected passages from this same work was set to music by Frederick Delius (q.v.) in 1905 for soloists, chorus, and orchestra, under the title of *A Mass of Life* (first performed in 1909).

For some time before this Nietzsche's attitude to the Wagnerian ideals had been changing, and in *The Case of Wagner* (1888) and *Nietzsche versus Wagner* (1889) he turned from the heavy romanticism of his country, and (living, in his renewed bad health, much at Genoa and Nice) cried, 'We must Mediterraneanize music', and set up Bizet's *Carmen* as his ideal (see reference to this in the article *Bizet*). He also exalted the music of one Peter Gast (real name Heinrich Köselitz, 1854–1918) who had been his pupil, friend, and secretary at Basle, and who after his death became the keeper of the 'Nietzsche Archives' at Weimar.

The remaining eleven or twelve years of life were years of insomnia, drug-taking, egotism, hysterical literary outbursts, and mental collapse.

Nietzsche was himself a musician, with a reputation in friendly circles as an extemporizer on the piano, and he left behind him a mass of amateurish and conventional musical compositions, of which in 1924 complete publication was hopefully undertaken.

NIGHTINGALE. An instrument that imitates the song of the nightingale and is used in an oratorio of Alessandro Scarlatti, and then in Toy Symphonies (q.v.) such as those of Haydn and Romberg. The imitation is evidently very faithful, since the compiler of this volume has known a community, in a year when, quite exceptionally, the local nightingale did not appear, perfectly satisfied for weeks by surreptitious nightly performance on this instrument.

NIJINSKY. See *Ballet* 5, 9.

NIKISCH, ARTHUR. Born in Hungary in 1855 and died at Leipzig in 1922, aged sixty-six. He was an extraordinary youthful prodigy who, after a career as violinist, turned conductor and won world fame, being for almost the whole of the last forty years of his life connected with Leipzig but making short residences in, or passing visits to, other centres of Europe and America. His wife (Amélie Heussner) was an operatic singer and composer, and their son Mitja (1899–1936) was a pianist of repute and latterly conductor of a famous jazz orchestra.

See *Clarinet* 4 h.

NILSSON, CHRISTINE. See *Scandinavia* 4.

NIN, JOAQUÍN (Nin y Castellanos). Born (of Spanish parents) at Havana, Cuba, in 1879 and there died in 1949, aged seventy. He was a pupil in Paris of Moszkowski and d'Indy, and was associated as student and teacher with the Schola Cantorum.

As a pianist he devoted himself with particular enthusiasm to the old keyboard writers, whose music he played throughout Europe. He opposed, however, the reintroduction of the harpsichord. His compositions, which are not numerous, have a Spanish nationalist tinge; they include a mimo-drama, piano music, and

music for violin and piano. He edited some books of Spanish songs and wrote polemical treatises enforcing his somewhat unusual views as to the old music. (His daughter was the author Anais Nin, 1903–77; for his son see below.)

NIN-CULMELL, JOAQUÍN. Born in Berlin in 1908 but is a Cuban citizen, brought up in Spain, New York, and Paris. He is a pupil of Dukas and Falla, for the latter of whom he expresses the warmest admiration. His published music is mostly for piano. He is son of Joaquín Nin (see above).

NINETEENTH. See *Organ* 14 IV.

NINFALI (It.). The Regal. See *Reed-Organ Family* 2, 10.

NINNA-NANNA, NINNARELLA (It.). 'Cradle song.'

NINTH. See *Interval*. A 'Chord of the Ninth' is a Common Chord (see *Harmony* 24 d) plus the seventh and ninth.

NIPKOV. See *Broadcasting* 6.

NOBILE (It.). 'Noble.' So *Nobilmente*, 'nobly'; *Nobiltá*, 'nobility'.

NOBLE, THOMAS TERTIUS. Born at Bath in 1867 and died at Rockport, Mass., in 1953, aged nearly eighty-six. He was assistant to Stanford when the later was organist of Trinity College, Cambridge, and then organist successively of Ely Cathedral, York Minster, and St. Thomas's Church, New York. His dignified church music was much sung in its day.

See reference under *Chorale Prelude*.

NOBLEMEN'S AND GENTLEMEN'S CATCH CLUB. See *Clubs for Music-Making*; *Glee* 3.

NOBLEZZA (It.). 'Nobility.'

NOCH (Ger.). 'Still', 'yet', in the sense of continuance or of 'even', e.g. *Noch leise*, 'still softly', *Noch leiser*, 'still more softly'.

NOCHE (Sp.). 'Night.'

NOCTURNE (Fr., and now Eng.), **NOTTURNO** (It.).

(1) Any composition which suggests the romantic beauty of night may be so described. The name is at least as early as Haydn, who has a Notturno for flute, oboe, two horns, and strings, and several for two hurdy-gurdies (see *Hurdy-Gurdy*) combined with other instruments, and Gyrowetz (q.v.), who wrote sixteen for various combinations.

But, more specifically, the name is given to a type of slow piano piece in which a graceful and often much embellished melody in the right hand is accompanied by some form of broken chords in the left. This type (which is essentially a thing of the piano, with its sustaining pedal—not of the earlier harpsichord or clavichord) belongs to the Romantic period in music. It was originated by the Irishman John Field (q.v.) and perfected by the French Pole Chopin. In general, such a piece is in three sections, the last being much a repetition of the first. A certain sentimentality (not necessarily excessive) marks the type.

(2) For reference to the ecclesiastical use of the word see *Matins*.

NODE. This word, when it occurs in connexion with music, means the point of rest between two wave motions of a vibrating string, etc. (cf. *Acoustics* 6; last par. of 8, etc.). From a practical point of view a node is the place where the player lightly touches the string to obtain a harmonic (see *Acoustics* 8).

NŌ DRAMA. See *Dance* 3.

NOËL (Fr.) or **NOWELL** (Eng.). The word means 'Christmas', and is also used as meaning a Christmas carol (see *Carol*).

NOIRE (Fr.). The English 'crotchet' or American 'quarter-note'. (Table 3.)

NOISE (= band of musicians). See *Inns and Taverns as Places of Music-Making*.

NOISE, EXCLUSION FROM ROOMS. See *Concert Halls* 8.

NOISE, ITS NATURE, EFFECT, etc. See *Acoustics* 9.

NOLA, GIOVANNI DOMENICO DA (died 1570). See *Napolitana*.

NOLLEKENS, JOSEPH (1737–1823). Sculptor. See reference under *Street Music* 2.

NOMINE, IN. See *In Nomine*.

NON (Fr., It.). 'Not.'

NON-COMPETITIVE FESTIVALS. See *Competitions in Music* 7.

NONE. The sixth of the Canonical Hours or services of the day of the Roman Catholic Church. Properly it takes place at the 'ninth hour', i.e. 3 p.m. (cf. *Matins*; *Lauds*; *Prime*; *Terce*; *Sext*; *Vespers*; *Compline*).

NONET (Eng.); **NONETTE** (Fr.); **NON-ETTO** (It.); **NONETT** (Ger.). Any combination of nine instruments or any piece of music composed for such. Such compositions are comparatively rare.

NONNENGEIGE (Ger.). The Tromba Marina (q.v.).

NON NOBIS DOMINE. This famous vocal canon is traditionally attributed to Byrd (q.v.), but cannot definitely be traced to him. The version usually sung (sometimes at banquets as a 'grace') is in three parts, the top voice entering first, the middle voice entering at the fourth below, and the bottom voice entering at the octave below the first one. A surprising number of 'solutions' of the canon are, however, possible in various numbers of parts and at varying pitch and time intervals, and even with the melody inverted (see *Canon* for 'inversion').

The opening phrase of the melody is a very common one in the music of the sixteenth, seventeenth, and eighteenth centuries (see *Hallelujah Chorus*).

NONO, LUIGI (p. 525, pl. **96**. 8). Born in Venice in 1924. He studied law in Padua and

has been a pupil of Maderna and of the conductor Hermann Scherchen, though he is largely self-taught. One of the more radical and widely performed of the advanced Italian followers of Webern, he first came to attention with his *Il Canto sospeso* (1956) for soloists, choir, and orchestra. His method of composition involves much mathematical calculation and results in flowing vocal lines abounding in tritones and ninths. He is a son-in-law of Schönberg.

See *Italy* 6; *Opera*.

NORCOME (or **Norcombe**), **DANIEL.** Born at Windsor in 1576 and died before 1626. He was a member of the choir of St. George's Chapel, Windsor Castle, who turned Roman Catholic and transferred (as an instrumentalist) to the royal chapel at Brussels (see *Belgium* 9). He is known today by a madrigal and some music for viols.

(Certain difficulties in the recorded facts concerning this composer incline Pulver, author of the valuable *Biographical Dictionary of Old English Music*, etc., to the view that there were two contemporaries of the same name.)

NORDBO KEYBOARD. See *Keyboard* 4.

NORDRAAK, RICHARD. Born at Christiania, Norway, in 1842 and died in Berlin in 1866, aged nearly twenty-four. Despite the brevity of his life he is of importance in the history of national expression in general and that of his native country in particular, not only for his own compositions, which are naturally few, but for his influence on Grieg, who was closely associated with him and who wrote a notable funeral march for him (performed also at Grieg's own funeral).

He counts as one of the founders of the Norwegian national school. (Cf. *Scandinavia* 3.)

NORGAARD, PER (born 1932). See *Scandinavia* 2.

NORHOLM, IB (born 1931). See *Scandinavia* 2.

NORMAN-NERUDA. See *Hallé, Charles*.

NORTH.

(1) FRANCIS, LORD GUILFORD (1637–85). Lord Chief Justice and then Keeper of the Great Seal, a keen musician, and author of an *Essay on Musick* (1677). See *Bagpipe Family* 3.

(2) THE HONOURABLE ROGER (1653–1734). Brother of the above. Attorney-General, a good musician (pupil of John Jenkins, q.v.), and author of *Memoires of Musick* (written 1728, published 1846; *The Musicall Gramarian*, published 1925, is really an early draft of part of this work). See *Concert* 3; *Cornet Family* 3; *In Nomine*; *Matteis* I.

NORTHUMBRIAN BAGPIPES. See *Bagpipe Family* 3.

NORWAY. See *Scandinavia* 3.

NORWICH. See allusions under *Waits*; *Street Music* 3; *Morris*; *Cathedral Music* 2; *Festival* 1; *Temperament* 6; *Alto Voice*; *Concert* 12. Organists of the Cathedral who receive notice are (with their periods of office): *Cobbold* (1598–1608); *Beckwith* (1808–9); *Z. Buck* (1819–77).

NOSKOWSKI, ZYGMUNT. Born at Warsaw in 1846 and died at Wiesbaden in 1909, aged sixty-three. He was for many years one of the leading personalities of his native city. His compositions include operas, three symphonies and other orchestral works, cantatas and other choral works, songs, piano music, string quartets, etc., and he also wrote (in Polish) some theoretical works and invented a musical notation for the blind.

NO SURRENDER! This is a tune used by the Protestants of Northern Ireland (cf. *Lilliburlero*), having a traditional connexion with the siege of Londonderry. The present words date only from 1826, being by Mrs. Charlotte Elizabeth Tonna, who wrote other Orange party songs and also anti-Catholic tracts.

NOTA CAMBIATA. See *Changing Note*.

NOTATION AND NOMENCLATURE

1 Early History.
2. The Neums (or Neumes).
3. Proportional Notation.

4. The Present Staff Notation.
5. The Limitations of Notation.

6. Special Defects of the Staff Notation.
7. Attempted Reforms of Notation.

(For tables explanatory of the various elements in the musical notation in use today see beginning of book.)

1. Early History. It is quite possible for an elaborate musical system to grow up and survive for centuries with a large and enlarging repertory and yet no means of writing it down —just as there have been, and are, racial literatures (national history, legend, poetry) handed down the generations without any knowledge of the art of writing. Examples of great bodies of music preserved in this way are the folk songs (see *Folk Song*) of the various races and the early music of the Christian Church (see *Plainsong*).

Yet races and organizations that have developed an intellectual life generally wish to record their music. Thus Europe had musical notation even before the invention of polyphony (the art of combining melodies so that different persons might sing together in different 'parts'), and polyphony, of course, made the possession of a means of writing music almost essential if correctness of performance was to be achieved and compositions preserved and disseminated.

The Ancient Greeks possessed two systems, one for instrumental and one for vocal music. One of these was based (as so many later systems have been) on the use of the letters of the alphabet as attached to the series of sounds. The Romans also used an alphabetical system.

At the end of the Roman period Boethius (c. A.D. 470–525), the confidential adviser and chief statesman in the court of Theodoric the Great and the last great Roman student of the Greek learning, wrote five books on music, which remained as standard textbooks throughout Europe during the Middle Ages and beyond. (The University of Oxford examined in a knowledge of them from its foundation and retained such knowledge as a nominal requirement for musical degrees until after 1856.) Boethius was a theoretician rather than a practical musician and he needed a means of referring to pitches somewhat as a physicist needs it today. The official and recognized working range of sounds in those days was two octaves, i.e. fifteen notes, and he attached to these the first fifteen letters of the alphabet. This may have been original with him or it may have been current at that time. It did not, as he used

it, constitute a true notation, though the term 'Boethian Notation' is applied to it.

A commoner system, in the time immediately following, was to use the letters A–G as we do today, i.e. repeating them for every octave. Small letters were used for the second octave and double small letters for the one beyond that. The scale being extended downwards by a note (i.e. an extra G being added), the Greek G, or gamma, was attached to it, and from this recognized beginning of the scalic series came the present French and former English words for scale, *gamme* and *gamut*.

As explained under *Modes* 8, the B early existed in two forms. Two signs were, therefore, needed for it, and to the lower B ('B flat', as we say) was attached the round B (b) and to the upper one ('B natural') the square or Gothic B (♮). The one of these remains with us today as the flat sign and the other, slightly modified, as the natural. The sharp sign, introduced later, is in origin a 'b' with a stroke through it—called the 'cancelled b' (a stroke to indicate sharpening is used in figured bass to this day). The name H, which the Germans use for B, comes from the natural sign being made in such a way that it resembled an 'H'.

The letter system of nomenclature continues in use today in Britain, Germany, the United States, and elsewhere. The French, Italians, and others have dropped it in favour of a series of names (*ut, re, mi*, etc.) derived by Guido d'Arezzo (c. 995–1050—see *Guido d'Arezzo*; *Sight-Singing* 1) from a Latin hymn.

The systems so far alluded to were, as already hinted, more theoretical than practical, and were indeed rather nomenclatures than notations. Meantime the practical musicians of the Church were developing a more graphic means of recording the traditional plainsong tunes— the system of Neums. This system was adopted not merely by the musicians of the Church but also to some extent by secular musicians, e.g. some of the songs of the Minnesingers (see *Minstrels*, etc. 7) of the end of the fourteenth century are recorded in the Neum notation.

2. The Neums (p. 673, pl. **114.** 1–3). The **Neums** (or **Neumes**), signs for notes or groups of notes, are found from about the seventh century, and they are still to be seen in the plainsong manuals of the Church. They are now precise, at all events as to pitch, so that an instructed singer can 'read' from them a melody as yet unknown to him, but for long they were not so, being merely good for indicating to a singer which of the plainsong melodies already known to him he was expected to sing, and for reminding him of the general curves and the general rhythms of the melody.

The present exactitude as to pitch is effected by the addition of the device of the **Staff** or **Stave**, which began as a single line and then had companion lines added to it. These defined the exact pitch of the notes. In time they became standardized, for plainsong purposes, as a stave of four lines, and this stave is still universally used for plainsong. In the early days the device of different colours for the different lines was a good deal used.

A special purpose of the Neums was to record time-values, but the record was only approximate, since the values were affected by all manner of conditions—the number of syllables in the group, the position of the group in the phrase, and the like. Exactly fixed time-values are not sought in plainsong and the Neum system hence does not provide for these, merely giving those approximate rhythmic shapes (so to speak) which the singer is expected to render in a free and flowing manner.

The original generating forms of the Neums were simply the grave and acute accents plus a horizontal line. The period during which they were developing was considerable, and the scribes engaged in writing music by their means very scattered; naturally, then, they took on widely dissimilar appearances. The signs for the Trill and the Turn, as used today, are relics of the Neum system of notation.

The Neums as printed today represent the research and selection of the Benedictines of Solesmes (see *Plainsong* 3), who during the late nineteenth century so fruitfully investigated the whole subject of plainsong.

3. Proportional Notation.

During the ninth and tenth centuries interest began to be shown in the idea of a notation that should record time-values with some exactitude, and when, in the tenth and eleventh centuries, polyphonic music began to develop, such a system became an urgent necessity (see reference to Franco of Cologne under *France* 2).

Something approaching our present scheme of note-shapes now came into existence, there being in early days four such shapes, as follows:

double long ◤
long ◥
breve ■
semibreve ◆

Each of these is theoretically the third or half of the preceding one—according as 'perfect' or 'imperfect' time is in use (i.e. what we should call 'triple' and 'duple' times). But, as a matter of fact, the time-durations were affected by the character of the previous and next notes, and by other conditions.

This variability grew more extensive, so that at the end of the thirteenth century a breve might be of the time-value of anything from two to seven semibreves, according to circumstances, and later of anything between two and twelve. Many new signs were inserted by those who used the notation, in order to make it clearer, and Walter de Odington complained (c. 1300) that there were as many new signs invented as there were music copyists in the world. (For a further brief reference to *Proportion* see the entry under that word.)

Ligatures, joining notes together, were devised in order to bind into a unity a rhythmic or melodic group of syllables. Their use grew into a very complex system. Listenius, in 1533, published at Wittenberg a compendium of music which gave ten mnemonic verses as a help to recalling the effects of ligatures in the different circumstances in which they might appear.

4. The Present Staff Notation.

With the *Ars Nova* (q.v.) period of the fourteenth century the system grew into something colourably like that of today.

◢ maxima
| longa
■ brevis
◆ semibrevis
𝅗 minima
𝅘 semiminima
𝅘𝅥 fusa
𝅘𝅥𝅮 semifusa

Time signatures were in use, in the shapes of the Circle for perfect (i.e. triple) time and the Semicircle for 'imperfect' (i.e. duple) time. The semicircle remains in use today and, having by chance and the decorative instinct of scribes and engravers come to resemble a C, is taken by many young students to stand as the initial letter of 'common time'. We now associate time signatures with measures (i.e. bars). At the period in question the time-signatures now referred to had a different significance from those of the full-barred-music period; they indicate division of the Long into three Shorts or two (see section 3).

Changes were constantly taking place, and during the fifteenth century, whilst the note shapes such as above were retained in use, the heads were left white, except that black heads were used for the purpose of indicating changes of values or rhythms in the course of a composition. Enormous complications were again added, e.g. time-signatures of circle or semicircle with or without a dot, up to twenty-four different varieties, indicating the high rhythmic complexity of much of the music of the day.

2. SCENE IN ROSSI'S 'ORPHEUS', 1647. See *Opera* 11 a

1. MONTEVERDI'S 'ORPHEUS'—performed 1607. See *Opera* 2

3. LULLY'S 'PHAETON'—extraordinary stage scene of 1683, showing the skill of the machinists of the period

4. A LULLY OPERA AT VERSAILLES IN 1674
See *Opera* 11 b and *Lully*

5. OPERA IN LONDON, *c.* 1728
Farinelli, Cuzzoni, and Berenstadt, in Handel's *Flavio.*

THE
SIEGE
OF
RHODES

Made a Reprefentation by the Art of Pro-
fpective in Scenes, And the Story fung in
Recitative Mufick.

At the back part of *Rutland*-Houfe in the upper
end of *Alderfgate*-Street,
LONDON.

LONDON,

Printed by *F. M.* for *Henry Herringman*, and are to be fold at his
Shop, at the Sign of the *Anchor*, on the Lower-Walk
in the *New-Exchange*, 1656.

The Story Perfonated.

Solyman		Capt. *Henry Cook.*
Villerius		Mr. *Gregory Thorndell.*
Alphonfo		Mr. *Edward Coleman.*
Admiral	by	Mr. *Matthew Lock.*
Pirrhus		Mr. *John Harding.*
Muftapha		Mr. *Henry Perfill.*
Ianthe		Mrs. *Coleman,* wife to Mr. *Edward Coleman.*

The Compofition of *Vocal Mufick*
was perform'd

	First Entry		Mr. *Henry Lawes.*
	Second Entry		Capt. *Henry Cook.*
The	Third Entry	by	Capt. *Henry Cook.*
	Fourth Entry		Mr. *Matthew Lock.*
	Fifth Entry		Mr. *Henry Lawes.*

The Inftrumental *Mufick* was compos'd by
Dr *Charles Coleman,* and Mr *George Hudfon.*

1. OPERA BEGINS DURING THE PERIOD OF PURITAN CONTROL
The list of composers and performers is an impressive one
See the Article on *The Puritans and Music,* pp. 844–7

2. SIR WILLIAM DAVENANT (1606–68). With *The Siege of
Rhodes* he introduced to England the Italian art of Opera (1656)
See pp. 709–11

3. THOMAS BETTERTON (c. 1635–1710), famous actor,
dramatist, and manager. He was associated with Davenant in
some of his many enterprises. He is buried in Westminster Abbey

It is very regrettable that such frequent changes took place in the system of notation and that regional differences were so marked. As a result of this the de-coding of old music is exceedingly difficult and the versions of modern editors sometimes differ widely.

Bar lines gradually became common during the sixteenth and seventeenth centuries. The earliest use known is in a book of organ preludes dated 1448, now in the Curtis Institute in Philadelphia. They did not at first, as at present, cut the music up into equal time-lengths marked by regular accents, but were more or less casually drawn here and there as aids to the eye and then only in the *scores* of concerted choral or instrumental music (i.e. they were not inserted in the *parts* used by the player), or in solo instrumental music which used several moving parts in combination (e.g. lute, virginals). Where they are inserted in modern editions of madrigals and the like they often, if interpreted in the modern way, falsify the accentuation of the music, which was much freer in its rhythm than music later became, and which did not necessarily, at any point, accentuate simultaneously all the different voices or parts, but followed instead a varying accentuation based, in vocal music, upon the natural accentuation of the words being sung (not necessarily at a given moment the same in all the voices), and, in instrumental music, upon the varying demands of the musical phrases. (To avoid misunderstanding it may be added that the choral music of this period usually has a pretty steady metrical progression in its harmonies, the accentuation of the *separate voice parts* not altogether following this progression.)

The device of the **Staff** was differently used by various composers contemporary with one another. In the organ music of Frescobaldi (1583–1643) we find a right-hand staff of six lines and a left-hand of eight; in that of Sweelinck (1562–1621) we find two staves of six lines; in that of Scheidt (1587–1654) we find four staves of five lines each. These are just examples. At last the five-lined staff became universal (with the exception of plainsong's four-lined staff already mentioned).

The **Clef** (in Latin *Clavis*; in Italian *Chiave*; in German *Schlüssel*—all these words mean 'key') was an early and important device which appeared first in the Neum system. It fixes the pitch to be understood as attaching to one of the lines of the staff and thus fixes also that attaching to all the other lines and spaces. There have been many clefs used, in many positions; only three now remain in use, and of these two appear always in the same position and the third wanders as need arises.

The movable clef is the C clef (║ or ║), fixing the place of middle C. It is found in present-day or comparatively recent music in three places: (a) On the bottom line of the staff, as the *Soprano Clef* sometimes seen in German and other vocal music at least as late as Brahms; (b) on the third line, as the *Alto Clef*,

used for the viola and alto trombone and also up to about the mid-nineteenth century for the alto voice; (c) on the fourth line up, as the *Tenor Clef*, long used for the tenor voice, for the higher range of the violoncello, for the tenor trombone, etc.

The convenience of the movability of the C clef is, of course, that when one has higher music to write one can move the clef lower and when one has lower music to write one can move the clef higher (or, alternatively, one may consider that the clef remains stationary and the staff moves). Thus the music is brought within the limit of the staff, and the use of many short extra lines (*Leger Lines*) above or below the staff is avoided.

The two fixed clefs give the notes respectively five notes above and five notes below the middle C, i.e. G and F. The G or Treble clef (𝄞) is now always placed on the lowest line but one of the staff and the F or Bass clef (𝄢 or 𝄢:) on the highest line but one. (The choice of the three notes C, F, and G as those giving their significance to the clefs is explained by the fact of these being the three principal notes of the old hexachordal system. See *Hexachord*.)[1]

Amongst them these three clefs give a range of three octaves, nearly covering the normal choral compass; for higher or lower notes the leger lines just mentioned are used, or if an extended high or low passage is written for some instrument it may be notated an octave too low with the indication *8va*, meaning that it is to be played an octave higher than written, or may be notated an octave too high with the indication *8va bassa*, meaning that it is to be played an octave lower than it is written. In this way the whole range of recognizable pitches useful in music may be represented. See *Great Staff*.

5. The Limitations of Notation. Allusion has been made above to the difficulties that are found in the attempt to interpret the notation of the Middle Ages. To an extent that difficulty persists when we attempt to interpret the music of the following period—say the sixteenth to eighteenth centuries. There is now less difference of practice in different parts of Europe, but the conventions that have grown up and that change from time to time necessitate severe and comprehensive study of the music of any period before the interpreter can feel any great certainty that he is able to play or sing a composition in the precise way its com-

[1] It is customary today to use the G clef for the tenor voice, with the understanding that the notes sung shall be an octave lower than shown. A better plan (to avoid all ambiguity) is to use this clef modified in the form 𝄞̸. Sometimes we see the clef doubled, as 𝄞𝄞 with the same effect.

It may be added, for completeness, that when tenors sing from short score they are compelled to use not the G (or treble) clef, as mentioned, but the F (or bass) clef. Thus a church choir tenor will use the G clef in an anthem and the F clef in a hymn. Alone of all the four voices in the choir the tenors are expected to be able to sing from two clefs—which is hardly fair.

poser intended. The great French harpsichord writer Couperin, in the eighteenth century, complained 'We write one thing and play another'. Any vocalist who has studied the recitative (q.v.) of Bach or Handel is able to support Couperin's statement from experience of another branch of the art. A large amount of 'tradition' is woven in with notation in this period, and this has to be mastered by the would-be interpreter.

The most outstanding examples of the incompleteness of notation in the period 1600–1800 are (a) Recitative, as mentioned above; (b) Figured Bass (q.v.); and (c) 'Graces'. All those leave a great deal to the performer's knowledge of the musical customs of the day, and also to his good judgement.

As concerns the graces—the music of this period was heavily loaded with indications for shakes, mordents, and the like; the precise way in which these are to be rendered is often a matter of doubt and sometimes a matter of dispute, even between experts.

The existence of innumerable sixteenth-, seventeenth-, and eighteenth-century textbooks instructing students how to interpret notation and to insert the graces, and of such modern compilations as Arnold Dolmetsch's (q.v.) *The Interpretation of the Music of the XVIIth and XVIIIth Centuries revealed by Contemporary Evidence* (1915), with its accompanying album of illustrative compositions, F. T. Arnold's monumental *The Art of Accompaniment from a Thorough-Bass* (1931), and Robert Donington's *The Interpretation of Early Music* (1963) is proof of the very partial degree in which notation, in itself, reveals the intention of composers. (For an example of points which require in the performers a knowledge of the notational customs of the different periods see *Dot, Dotted Note.*)

As a further consideration it may be observed that there are elements in music which no notation can ever represent. General indications of intensity and of speed may, it is true, be given, but there are nuances which paper and ink afford no means of representing and without which the music does not 'live'; and 'tempo rubato' (see *Rubato*) entirely eludes the art of writing.

6. Special Defects of the Staff Notation.

It will be evident from what has just been said that our present universal notation has 'grown up' rather than been designed, and that, moreover, its main features were fixed at a period when music was merely melodic and in some other respects enormously simpler than at present. Musicians generally are so accustomed to it that they do not stop to reflect upon its defects, a few of which are listed in the following:

'Everyone knows the advantage we possess in the beautiful notation of Number which the Arabians have given us. It proceeds on one simple uniform principle, is easily recognized and easily combined; while the old Roman numerals adopt various and heterogeneous contrivances for denoting numbers, expressing some by the direct symbol, others by a multiplication of symbols and others again by a curious sort of subtraction and addition of symbols. The old notation of music is of kindred structure with the latter. Heterogeneous and indirect, it exhibits the pitch of notes partly by the inaccurate *pictorial* appearance of the staff, and partly by the *symbols* of flat and sharp; it shows the length of notes sometimes by one symbol, and sometimes by another, without any direct relation to the regular recurring accents, which are the only true measures of time; and instead of making obvious and prominent the simple and beautiful relationships of key, on which the whole framework of music rests [this was written in 1875], it shrouds them in mystery, and keeps them in constant subserviency to the incomparably less important indications of pitch.

'Now, let the reader think, what would become of arithmetic if we were compelled to work all our sums by help (!) of the old Roman numerals? Would it not be made, like music, the possession of the few to whom lengthened practice has given a facility, which is the fruit more of instinct than reason, instead of being, as it now is, the common attainment of the people? What would be said of the signs of Algebra if "plus" were sometimes represented by a cross, and sometimes by a round O—that same round O, moreover, being occasionally used for "minus"? And yet this is just the position of "sharp", "flat", and "natural" in the old notation!' (John Curwen, *Teachers' Manual.*)[1]

7. Attempted Reforms of Notation.

Reference has been made in the article *Keyboard* to the many attempts at reform of that item in the apparatus of musical performance, and to the fact that none of these has yet been able to establish itself. A still greater number of attempts have been made to reform the staff notation, but they have invariably failed and probably always will do so until a change in the whole musical system brings about an unavoidable corresponding change in the methods of representing music on paper. The enormous amount of capital locked up in the world's stock of printed music, and the conservatism of musicians (many of whom confusedly look upon the familiar notation as 'music' and cannot effect a mental dissociation) are two formidable obstacles in the way of the adoption even of the simpler reforms.

A glance at a page from, say, a work of Boulez or Stockhausen, should be convincing to any musician who maintains that the present notation is 'good enough'. It is certainly *not* 'good enough', and just as the Spelling Reformers maintain that the adoption of the reform would 'save a year of school life', and the advocates of the metric system that the adoption of their reform would do the same, so the inventor of any reasonably thought-out reformed staff notation can claim that he is offering the means of saving several years of music study or, alternatively, of freeing students from reading difficulties in order that

[1] As a matter of fact, such divergences in the meaning of arithmetical and algebraical signs do exist as between different European countries, and a child having its education partly in one country and partly in another must be very much inconvenienced.

they may devote themselves more completely to other aspects of their work. Yet apparently nothing can be done, and the reading of music remains many times more difficult than it has any need to be.

As but one example, 'accidentals' may be cited. The very notion of 'accidentals' as a departure from a 'key' becomes obsolete in non-tonal or twelve-note (see *Note-row*) music. In many modern compositions more than half the notes have before them some accidental. Already in Schönberg's *Pierrot lunaire* (1912) there are pages with 98 per cent. of the notes inflected by accidental signs. That the rhythmic part of the notation has also its difficulties has been discovered by many a young student struggling to read so comparatively simple a composition as the slow movement from one of Beethoven's pianoforte sonatas. Many composers of the sixties have felt obliged to include with the printed score of their music a glossary of *ad hoc* notational symbols.

It has often been claimed by unthinking defenders of the system that it gives a picture or graphic diagram of the sounds. It is true that perpendicular distance is, in this system, associated with pitch and horizontal distance with time, but since the same distance perpendicularly may represent anything from a single half-step (semitone) to six half-steps (an extreme case, of course), and the same distance horizontally anything from a whole-note (semibreve) to a 32nd note (demisemiquaver), it is evident that the diagrammatic value of the system is slight. (Cf. *Tonic Sol-fa* 3.)

There have often been (and are and always will be!) attempted reforms based on the general principle, in itself sound (if the tempered scale be admitted as the basis; see *Temperament*) of allotting one line or space to every note—white or black, to use pianist's language. Thus sharps, flats, naturals, double sharps, and double flats are abolished. The argument is that, as there are twelve notes in the octave, so there should be twelve places for notes on the stave.

Proposals for making the notes on all staves (treble, bass, etc.) correspond to one another have been common. One such put forward by Revd. Thos. Salmon in 1672 (*An Essay to the Advancement of Musick, by casting away the perplexity of different Cliffs, and uniting all sorts of Musick in one universal character*) generated great heat in the subsequent discussion by Matthew Locke and others.

A French attempt at reform, of the twentieth century, is André Piaceski's *Clef unique* ('Single Clef') system. For all instruments and voices it uses the ordinary treble or G clef for that octave which on the piano lies in the middle of the keyboard, placing single, double, and triple strokes above or below it for the various octaves above and below. Nothing could be more simple or practical at first sight, but the objection arises that an embarrassingly frequent repetition of the clef sign would apparently be necessary as the music moves into fresh octaves. This is not the first time such a system has been proposed—and dropped.

The *Notation musicale continue* of Pierre Hans, a Belgian engineer, observed a similar general principle, worked out into a very detailed and complete system. It has been warmly commended by leading Belgian musicians.

Klavarskribo is the invention of a Dutch engineer, Cornelius Pot. This carefully thought-out notation is based (as its name suggests) on the appearance of the pianoforte keyboard. The arrangement of the stave is at right angles to the normal, so that successive notes are read downwards instead of horizontally: all semitones of the chromatic scale have equal status and the time element is indicated graphically by the space allotted to each note, as in Tonic Sol-fa. Clefs, accidentals, and differentiated symbols of note-value are thus abolished. The inventor (evidently a man of some means) had produced by 1951 a catalogue of some 10,000 items, embracing both a large proportion of the classical repertory and a number of more ephemeral works.

A very simple and apparently practical reform is that embodied in the *Isotonic Notation* of Dom John Stéphan, O.S.B. Everything is left much as in the accepted notation except that the sharp and flat signs, etc., disappear, their place being taken by differently shaped heads to the notes. The impression one gets from examination of examples of music in this notation is that a pianist (for instance) could become accustomed to it in a very few hours and that thereafter if music printed in the notation were available he would find the process of reading simplified—especially as an inflected note continues to show its inflexion every time it appears, which is not the case with the present notation. Moreover, his facility in the use of the music in the present notation would not suffer.

Schönberg put forward a proposal for a special notation more fitted for the harmonic system of himself and his followers, a system which allows equal rights to every note of his 12-note scale.

What is curious is the general neglect by would-be reformers of the extremely illogical provision of the orthodox staff notation for the recording of rhythm. A reform that could be carried out by convention between publishers of different countries and immediately applied, with no inconvenience and nothing but advantage to all concerned, would be the adoption of one note-value (say the crotchet) as the beat in all new music.

It is probably impossible to establish a completely or almost completely new notation at the present date, when tons of music plates exist engraved in the old notation and the system itself is, equally, engraved in the minds of all the world's musicians. What could be done, however, would be judiciously to 'tinker with' the notation in various ways, introducing improvements such as do not involve the learning and practising of a new system and the casting aside of existing stocks of printed music.

The only reformed notations that up to the present have ever established themselves have been certain notations for choral music. The chief of these are mentioned in the article *Tonic Sol-fa*.

The above article, it will be seen, is concerned chiefly with the development and present state of the staff

notation. To complete the study of the general subject of notation the following articles should also be read: *Proportion*; *Tablature*; *Tonic Sol-fa*; *Lancashire Sol-fa*.

For the peculiarities of the staff notation as applied to music for the larger combinations of instruments see *Transposing Instruments* and the articles on the various orchestral instruments, and for the notation of ornaments see *Ornaments or Graces* 5, 6; Tables 12–16.

NOTE. The ordinary English dictionary definition of this word is threefold: '(1) Written sign representing pitch and duration of a musical sound; (2) key of pianoforte, etc.; (3) single tone of definite pitch made by musical instrument, voice, etc.' (*Concise Oxford Dictionary of Current English*).

This gives the word three distinct musical meanings. To a pianist, for instance, according to this, the widely accepted usage, the sign on the paper before him is a 'note', the finger-key he then presses is a 'note', and the sound which thereupon ensues is a 'note'.

British musicians often express objections to the second of these meanings ('key of pianoforte', etc.) and feel that 'note' should be limited to the two meanings of the 'written sign' and the 'single tone of definite pitch'. In the present work the keyboard 'note' is, to avoid confusion, spoken of as a 'finger-key'.

American musicians have during the later nineteenth century come to reject both the second and third of these meanings and to use the word 'note' merely in the first sense, 'written sign representing pitch and duration of a musical sound'. For further remarks on the subject see *American Musical Terminology* 1.

For a table of the notes (i.e. 'written signs representing pitch and duration of a musical sound') see Table 1.

NOTE-ROW (Ger., 'Tonreihe'; Amer., 'Tone-row'). This is a method of composition first formulated by Hauer, and developed by Schönberg in his later period (from about 1924, after an 'atonal' period beginning in 1907 during which he wrote such works as *Pierrot Lunaire*) and practised by some of his followers (see list on next page).

All the twelve notes of the octave are employed in every composition, and all the notes are treated in such a way as to enjoy an equal footing, i.e. there are no notes with special qualities such as those which in the major and minor scales, and even the chromatic scale, lead to their being called 'tonic', 'dominant', 'sub-dominant', 'leading note', etc.: for this reason the theorists of the Schönberg school prefer to call his method not a chromatic one but 'Dodecaphonic' (twelve-note; see *Scales* 7). Schönberg's own phrase was 'a method of composing with the twelve notes'.

Every composition is fabricated out of one theme or formula and in this theme each of these twelve notes occurs (once and once only), the order of occurrence in it being predecided by the composer. This formula is used both 'horizontally' (i.e. melodically or contrapuntally) and 'perpendicularly' (i.e. in chords), and

throughout the composition the notes, whether used singly in a melody or combined in an accompaniment, occur in the same order. If used as an ordinary accompaniment ('perpendicularly') they may occur as chords—complete, or possibly as six in one chord and the next six in another, or three in one chord and the remainder in following chords, and so on, the point being that there should be no departure from the order until the series has been entirely exhausted and can begin again. Thus any chords following one another make up, as a whole, the original set of twelve notes in their original order.

For variety, however, the series may occur in four different ways as follows: (1) As first formulated; (2) With this order reversed so that the first note becomes the last and vice versa—i.e. in 'retrograde motion'; (3) Inverted, i.e. with each ascending note now descending by the same interval and vice versa; (4) With this last also reversed, i.e. in retrograde order. Here is an example:

The theme:[1]

The theme in retrograde order:

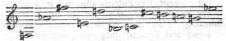

The theme in inversion:

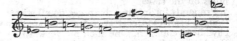

The inversion in retrograde order:

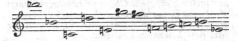

So far as rhythm is concerned there is perfect freedom throughout: this can be varied at any moment according to the composer's desire. Another relaxation from the rigour of the method lies in the fact that any note of the series can appear in any octave; thus a downward leap can be turned into an upward one

---

[1] Observe that every note in a Note-row has before it a sign of sharp, flat, or natural, and that double-sharps and double-flats are not needed, since it is understood that so long as the notation used represents the *sound* to be heard nothing else matters.

and vice versa. Moreover, the whole note-row in any of its four forms may be used at any pitch-level (or two or more pitch-levels may be in use together in a strange kind of imitative counterpoint), so giving further variety.

It will be seen, however, that the principle of perfect equality, already referred to, is maintained.

As will be realized after a moment's thought, each statement of the formula being possible at twelve pitch-levels, there are, in all, forty-eight forms of it available.

Obvious characteristics of the system are as follows: (1) With the disappearance of the Tonic effect, the Dominant effect, etc., the diatonic *Cadence* also vanishes, except so far as devices of rhythm and volume can provide the feeling of such. (2) There is, equally, no means of obtaining real *Modulation*: where the pitch-level of the formula is changed this is done without any process other than that of abruptly lifting it or lowering it. (3) The contrast of *Concord and Discord* is practically unobtainable. (4) Inasmuch as the simplest and best-known tune played backwards is practically unrecognizable the use of *Retrograde motion* serves little auditory purpose: indeed it may be said that, so far as the ear is concerned, not one formula is employed, but two, each of them in direct motion and inverted. (The palindrome in music hardly ever 'comes off'.)

Composers who have followed the system in greater or lesser degree, and with closer or less close adherence to Schönberg's rules, are led by Schönberg's fellow-Austrians and pupils, Berg and Webern, together with very many of their juniors. Indeed, of the still younger generation it may be said that the use of some form of the system is the rule rather than the exception.

The acceptance of the system by audiences is, however, still something short of complete.

See also the following: *Schönberg*; *Hauer*; *Mann, Thomas*. Also the following: *Berg*; *Dallapiccola*; *Eisler*; *Křenek*; *Leibowitz*; *Lutyens*; *Martin*; *Pisk*; *Riegger*; *Searle*; *Seiber*; *Thomson, V.*; *Vogel*; *Webern*; *Wellesz*.

NOTES (Journal of the American Music Library Association). See *Journals*.

NOTKER. See *Sequence* 2.

NOTTEBOHM, MARTIN GUSTAV (1817–82). A noted German piano teacher (long settled in Vienna), a minor composer, and a musicologist of high rank, with an especial fame as the author (or editor) of valuable works on Beethoven. Amongst these are Beethoven's harmony exercises under Haydn; some of his 'sketch books', in which he jotted down musical themes for possible future use; a careful thematic list of all his published works, etc. (His similar list of Schubert's works was in 1951 superseded by that of Deutsch.)

NOTTINGHAMSHIRE BAGPIPES. See *Bagpipe Family* 3.

NOTTURNINO (It.). A miniature nocturne (q.v.).

NOTTURNO. See *Nocturne*.

NOVÁČEK, OTTOKAR EUGEN. Born in 1866 at Fehertemplon (or Weisskirchen), Hungary, and died in New York in 1900, aged thirty-three. He was a brilliant violinist, compelled to relinquish performance by heart weakness, which soon brought about his death. His compositions include string quartets, a piano concerto, violin music, etc.

NOVACHORD. See *Electric Musical Instruments* 4.

NOVÁK, VITĚZSLAV (p. 109, pl. **20**. 5). Born in 1870 at Kamenice-on-Lipa (or Kamenitz) in Bohemia and died near Prague in 1949, aged seventy-eight. He was a pupil of Dvořák at the Conservatory of Prague, of which institution he became a professor. As a composer he was first influenced chiefly by the ideals and style of the German romantics, by Schumann, Brahms, and others. Later he absorbed nationalistic sentiments and studied native folk tune, using it as the basis of his composition.

His works include several operas (see *Opera* 24 f (1937)), symphonic poems, piano music, and a good deal of solo vocal and choral music.

NOVE (It.). 'Nine.'

NOVELETTE. A word introduced into music by Schumann as the general title for the eight pieces of his op. 21 for piano. They have no individual titles, but each novelette has its own character and is, says the composer, to be taken as the musical equivalent of a 'romantic story'. A few other composers (e.g. Gade) have, since Schumann, used the term. It carries with it no special connotation of form. A novelette can be in any form; it is the spirit that entitles it to the description. (The German spelling is 'Novellette'; plural 'Novelletten'.)

It may be added that Schumann's happy introduction of a pleasant and suitable term originated in a sort of pun, and was based on an association of ideas such as, perhaps, it needs the romantic early nineteenth-century German soul properly to appreciate. According to two letters to his future wife, Clara Wieck (quoted in Niecks's *Schumann*, p. 201), in the pieces he called by this name she 'appeared in every possible attitude and situation'. He said, 'I assert that the Novelettes could only be written by one who knows such eyes as yours, and has touched such lips as yours'. He then explains that, this being so, he would have liked to embody her name in the title, but that, considerations of euphony intervening, he had come as near as he could to his wish by substituting the name of another musical Clara, Clara Novello (q.v.), then touring Germany with high success—'I have called the whole *Novelleten* because your name is Clara and *Wiecketten* would not sound well'.

NOVELLO Family. A gifted musical family of which the most important members are the following:

(1) VINCENT (1781–1861; p. 289, pl. **51**. 3)

He composed much church music and revived much more, including Purcell's Sacred Music in five volumes. For further information see *Publishing of Music* 6; *Roman Catholic Church Music*; *Figured Bass*.

(2) JOSEPH ALFRED (1810–96). Son of Vincent. He succeeded to the publishing business founded by his father. He was also a singer and choir trainer. See *Publishing* 7; *Copyists*.

(3) CLARA ANASTASIA (1818–1908). Daughter of Vincent and one of the most celebrated soprano singers of the mid-nineteenth century. (See *Applause* 2; *Novelette*; *Cabaletta*, and p. 140, pl. **26**. 4.)

NOVELLO, IVOR (1893–1951). See *Keep the Home Fires Burning*.

NOVELLO DAVIES. See reference under *Keep the Home Fires Burning*.

NOVERRE, JEAN GEORGES. See *Ballet* 3, 9; *Dance* 10.

NOWELL (Eng.) or NOËL (Fr.). A Christmas carol (see *Carol*). The word means 'Christmas'.

NOWOWIEJSKI, FELIX. Born in 1877 in East Prussia and died in 1946 in Poland, aged sixty-eight. He studied in Berlin and at Regensburg, and won many prizes for composition. Then he taught and served as conductor in Berlin, Cracow, Warsaw, and Posen.

His dramatic oratorio *Quo Vadis* was successful; other oratorios and operas followed, as also orchestral works, piano works, organ works, unaccompanied choral music, and a Mass (*Missa Pacis*).

NOW PRAY WE FOR OUR COUNTRY. See *Flower, Eliza*.

NOZZE DI FIGARO (Mozart). See *Marriage of Figaro*.

NUANCE. The ordinary English dictionary definition is 'Delicate difference or shade of meaning, feeling, opinion, colour, etc.'. The musical meaning of the word is presumably comprised within the 'etc.' and covers the 'delicate differences' of intensity and of speed which, very largely, make up the 'life' of music. Nuance is thus closely bound up with *Phrasing* (q.v.).

N.U.I. National University of Ireland.

NUNC DIMITTIS. The Song of Simeon in St. Luke's Gospel ('Lord, now lettest Thou Thy servant depart in peace'). It is a part of the Service of Compline in the Roman Catholic Church and of that of Evensong in the Anglican Church. It has its traditional plainsong in the former and is sung to this, or more often, to an Anglican Chant in the latter, but it has also been set innumerable times by composers as part of an 'Evening Service'. (See *Service*.)

NUN DANKET. See *Hymns and Hymn Tunes* 3.

NUN'S FIDDLE. The Tromba Marina (q.v.).

NUOVE MUSICHE. See *Opera* 1; *Caccini*.

NUOVO, NUOVA (It., masc. and fem.). 'New.' Hence *Di nuovo*, 'anew'.

NUPTIAL MASS. See *Mass* 5.

NUR (Ger.). 'Only.'

NUREMBERG. See *Recorder Family* 2.

NURSERY RHYMES. See *Mother Goose Songs*.

NUT. (1) In a stringed instrument this is the slightly projecting ridge over which the strings pass on leaving the pegs—their sounding portion being that which lies between the nut and the bridge (q.v.).

(2) The same name is used for that end of the bow at which it is held, where there is a screw by which the tension of the hair is adjustable.

NUTRENDO, NUTRITO (It.). 'Nourishing', 'nourished'—metaphors for 'sustaining', 'sustained'.

NUTTALL FAMILY OF ROSSENDALE. See *Baptist Churches and Music* 4.

NYSTROEM, GÖSTA. Born at Silfberg, Sweden, in 1890. He studied in Paris and became a painter (of the school of Picasso), a music critic, and a composer of high standing in his own country—with a leaning towards French impressionism.

O

O, OD (It.). 'Or.'

OAKELEY.

(1) **HERBERT STANLEY.** Born near London in 1830 and died at Eastbourne in 1903, aged seventy-three. He was Professor of Music in the University of Edinburgh and Composer to Her Majesty in Scotland. In 1876 Her Majesty knighted him. He was a fine organist with a special gift for extemporization. He left church music which is still sung, and other compositions.

See references under *Cathedral Music* 7; *Absolute Pitch*; *Improvisation* 2.

(2) **CANON FREDERICK.** See reference under *Adeste Fideles*.

OATES, DR. J. P. See *Trumpet Family* 3.

OBBLIGATO. Italian for 'obligatory'. Sometimes, but incorrectly, spelt 'obligato' (French, *obligé*; German, *obligat*). This word, attached to the part of any instrument in a score, obviously means that that part is essential to the effect. For instance, one may have a song with 'Violin Obbligato', in which case the violin must not be omitted. In the contrary case, that of an optional violin part, the term would be 'Violin ad libitum'.

Unfortunately, thoughtless musicians, seeing the word attached to what looked to them like an *extra* part, have come to use it for any such part, and even to reserve its use for an *ad libitum* part, and so one finds songs published 'With Violin Obbligato' meaning 'With Violin ad libitum'—a clear case of *Lucus a non lucendo*. The consequence is that when one sees these words upon a piece of music one has to examine its structure to find out whether they mean what they should mean, or its very opposite.

O.B.E. See *Knighthood and other Honours*.

OBEN (Ger.). 'Over', 'above'.

OBER (Ger.). 'Over', 'upper'.

OBERAMMERGAU. See *Passion Music* 1; *Mysteries*, etc.

OBEREK. The folk form of the Obertas (q.v.).

OBERTAS, OBERTASS. One of the national dances of Poland. It is a round dance of a rather wild character in a quick three-in-a-measure time (see *Drabant*).

OBERTUS. See *Obrecht*.

OBERWERK (Ger.). 'Over work', i.e. upper work, swell organ. (Abbreviated. 'Obw.' or 'O.W.'.)

OBLIGATO, OBLIGAT, OBLIGÉ. See *Obbligato*.

OBLIQUE MOTION. See *Motion*.

OBLIQUE STRINGING. See *Pianoforte* 16.

OBOE. See *Oboe Family*.

OBOE, BASSET. See *Oboe Family* 5 i.

OBOE DA CACCIA. See *Oboe Family* 4 e, 5 e, 6.

OBOE D'AMORE. See *Oboe Family* 4 f, 5 f, 6.

OBOE FAMILY

1. Construction.
2. History.
3. Chief Members of the Family today.
4. Other Members of the Family.
5. Nomenclature.
6. Repertory of the Family.

(For illustrations see p. 672, pl. 113.)

1. Construction. The distinguishing characteristics of this family are two—a double reed (see *Reed*) and a conical tube. Both these characteristics differentiate it from the clarinet family, which has a single reed and a cylindrical tube. The oboe family, on account of its conical tube, overblows at the interval of an octave as flutes do, whilst the clarinet family, with its cylindrical tube, overblows at the interval of a twelfth. This affects the whole mechanism for obtaining the upper notes.

Because of the position of the reed in the mouth of the player, and its small size, double and triple tonguing (see *Tonguing*) are difficult, and in this the oboe, with other reed instruments, differs from the flute family and the brass.

2. History. The type is very ancient and widespread. At Bridgeness, on the Forth, on a stone in the Antonine Wall (built by the Romans early in the second century A.D.) a young man is depicted playing an instrument somewhat of this sort. By the sixteenth century the type had blossomed elaborately into a group of six (see plate), capable of sustaining the whole performance of a composition, two upper instruments, usually called **Shawms** or **Schalmeys,** and four lower ones, often called **Pommers** and **Bombards**—though 'Shawm' was a quite common name for the whole family. There were also the **Curtall** and **Double Curtall,** which were early forms of smaller (tenor) and larger bassoon.

The upper instruments came to be called the

'high-wood' (or just possibly loud-wood) instruments, *hautbois*, and the lower the big-wood, *gros-bois*. (However, it must be admitted that the name 'hautbois' turns up fairly indiscriminately for any size of the sixteenth- and seventeenth-century shawm.)

The next stage is that of the **Hautboys** (an anglicization of *hautbois*) and **Bassoons** of the seventeenth and eighteenth centuries, and the last stage that of the **Oboes** and **Bassoons** of today.

All these instruments possessing the double reed and the conical bore, their differences are only those of detail, especially in a progressive refinement (some say emasculation) of tone and improvement of mechanism.

The early hautboys were loud and brilliant. Mersenne in 1636 speaks of them as the loudest of all instruments except the trumpet. At this period Louis XIV adopted them for his military bands, and some years after, in Britain, hautboys and bassoons with percussion instruments superseded the previous drum and fife bands (see *Fife*).

In the orchestra of the eighteenth century (e.g. Bach and Handel) the hautboys and bassoons played an important part. They were often very numerous, doubled the strings in loud passages, and sometimes played antiphonally with the trumpets (see *Orchestra*).[1]

Judging from Handel's orchestration (e.g. *Acis and Galatea*) the same performer often played flute and oboe, since the two instruments do not appear together; this is also true of some of Mozart's Divertimenti and Serenades (cf. *Loeillet Family* for two instances of this doubling of roles).

The present generation of the oboe family may be said to date from roughly the time of Haydn and Mozart, though it is impossible to fix a date, as the changes that have brought the instruments to their present state, and made the upper members of the group (at any rate) perhaps the most sensitive and expressive wind instruments of the orchestra, have been gradual.

It may be of interest to state that, whilst the bassoon was in the early nineteenth century a

---

[1] Dr. B. Hague, of the Engineering Departments of the University of Glasgow (who made a special study of the acoustics and history of the Oboe Family, and is himself a player), supplied the material for this account. He writes:

'Although the hautboy of Bach's day may have been strident in tone (in tuttis it is often set in competition with trumpets) and imperfect in intonation, I think there is little doubt that the best players of the time could coax a softer and more expressive tone from their instruments —quite sufficient to make clear to Bach that the refinement that his greatest obbligati require could at some time (perhaps not even in his own lifetime) be realized, as has in fact come about today. By the time of Mozart there were many players (e.g. Ramm and Ferlendis) who were noted for their refined and expressive style, just as there were others (like Fischer) whose style and tone he calls "impudent". There are these distinctions even today; compare Léon Goossens with any ordinary theatre player. It is largely a question of over-blowing and insensitive lip control; if you think of the oboe as a trumpet you can easily make it as noisy as one.

'It is, of course, quite true that Bach makes very much use also of the oboe in its *ripieno* capacity.'

common instrument in the English villages, the oboe seems never to have obtained any real footing there—or, if it did, to have been ousted by the clarinet. The Revd. K. H. Macdermott, in *Sussex Church Music of the Past* (1923), states that he was able to find still-existing memories of twenty-two village church orchestras with bassoons (one with five and another with nine), but of only three with oboes—against forty-seven with clarinets!

The tone of the members of the modern oboe family differs considerably with the breadth of the reed: generally speaking, the German players use a broader reed and produce a 'thicker' tone than the French and others who share their preference for delicacy.

It may be mentioned that the twentieth-century revival of old instruments (viols, lutes, recorders, etc.) has brought the occasional suggestion that the older generation of the oboe family might be worth revival. (By reference to the separate entry *Bombard* it will be seen that they have never quite died out.)

3. Chief Members of the Family today. The family is represented in the orchestra of today by the following:

(*a*) **Oboe** (p. 672, pl. **113**. 4, 6). Its natural scale is D, but like the flute, which has the same scale, it is written for at the actual pitch, i.e. not treated as one of the 'transposing instruments' (q.v.). Its compass is of about two octaves-plus-a-sixth from B natural or B flat below the treble stave. The lower limit, for any good modern oboe, is B flat; those oboes descending merely to B are usually old instruments, generally for military use.

The tone is peculiarly penetrating but not shrill, and the instrument's value in the orchestra is much more for its frequent passing solo contributions than as a part of the ensemble. Up to Mozart's time one oboe was often considered enough in an orchestra; then two became the rule, and since Wagner three are sometimes found.

(*b*) **Cor Anglais** or **English Horn** (p. 672, pl. **113**. 7). This is an alto oboe, its range lying a fifth below that of the oboe itself, but descending practically always merely to B (sounding E), instruments with the B flat (cf. Oboe above) being rare. It is treated as one of the transposing instruments (q.v.), its music being written in a key a fifth higher than it is intended to sound. As the instrument is necessarily longer than the oboe, and would be a little too long to be held in the same way, the reed is placed in a metal tube which is bent back to meet the player's mouth: earlier examples had their whole tube curved in something approximating a semicircle, or else bent at an angle in the middle, with the same object (whence the perhaps fanciful derivation from the adjective *anglé*, afterwards corrupted into *anglais*). It had a narrower bore in proportion, and therefore a yet more colourful tone.

It should be pointed out that the oboe has an open, slightly flaring bell, whereas the bell of the cor anglais is pear-shaped and constricted at the opening. The oboe is clearly shown in Plate **113** (4 and 6), but the picture of the cor anglais in Plate **113** (7) does not show the lower part of the instrument well.

The cor anglais was occasionally used in the orchestra of Gluck and of Mozart and his contemporaries, but became a regular member of the orchestra only from the time of Wagner. It is often entrusted to the second (or third) oboe player. It excels in the interpretation of slow expressive melody.

(c) **Bassoon** (p. 672, pl. **113**. 8). This, since a true bass oboe is not in use, is by courtesy counted in the family, and in the orchestra always serves as the family's bass member. As its tube is much too long to be handled as a straight line it is bent back on itself, the reed then being brought within reach of the player's mouth by a curved metal tube like that of the cor anglais but much longer. The compass is wide—about three-octaves-plus-a-fifth from the B flat below the bass stave.

To the other members of the oboe family the bassoon is what the violoncello is to the violin family. It both supplies the bass and is capable of effective melodic passages. It blends well with the horns, and in chords is used frequently to merge with them. Played quickly and staccato it often becomes comical, and its use by some composers for humorous purposes has earned it the very one-sided description of 'the Clown of the Orchestra'.

The bassoon is written for at its proper pitch, i.e. it is not one of the 'transposing instruments' (q.v.).

Note: There is an instrument called the *Russian Bassoon* which is not a bassoon at all. See *Cornett and Key Bugle Families*, 2 f, 3 f, 4 f.
For an odd old instrument of the bassoon type see *Rackett*.

(d) **Double Bassoon** (p. 672, pl. **113**. 9). This is to the bassoon much what the stringed double-bass is to the cello, but it is very much more rarely employed. Its range is roughly an octave below that of the bassoon. It is, like the stringed double-bass, written for an octave above the pitch desired, in order to avoid excessive use of leger lines.

The first introduction of the double bassoon into Britain seems to have been by Handel. It is used in Haydn's *Creation*. (He brings it in with a low note fortissimo on the last word of the phrase, 'By heavy beasts the ground is *trod*'.) Beethoven's occasional use if it first gave it a more or less stable position. Unlike its companions of the family it has never reached a standard form.

4. Other Members of the Family.

(e) **Oboe da Caccia.** The name means 'Oboe of the Chase', i.e. 'Hunting Oboe', presumably from one of its old uses when the tone of the oboe family was more strident than it is now. Its pitch is below that of the normal oboe and it is, indeed, the predecessor of the cor anglais.

Bach used it freely but from his period it fell into oblivion so that its part in any old score is nowadays entrusted to the cor anglais.

The *Taille* which appears in some of Bach's scores was a tenor oboe of the same pitch as the Oboe da Caccia but somewhat different in shape, and hence, possibly, in bore, and, if so, then also in tone.

(f) **Oboe d'Amore.** This is intermediate in pitch between the oboe proper and the cor anglais; the three instruments therefore standing in the relations of soprano, mezzo-soprano, and alto. It is to be found in the scores of Bach and his contemporaries and in a few modern scores, such as that of Strauss's 'Domestic' Symphony, where it is played by one of the regular oboists. It is written for as one of the transposing instruments (q.v.), in a key a minor third higher than the effect desired. Its part in the performance of old music is often taken by the ordinary oboe.

It is very important to bear in mind the essential feature of the narrower bore of the oboe d'amore, upon which its tone colour depends. Also, although it is true that in old music its part is often taken by an ordinary oboe, this is much to be deplored; its timbre is something quite individual and incapable of replacement by any other orchestral voice. Instruments are not uncommon (though often badly out of tune).

In the examples of its use since Bach the Strauss *Sinfonia Domestica* is usually quoted by books on orchestration—as it is above. This is seldom heard, however; but the ordinary listener to broadcasts of Ravel's *Bolero* can hear the instrument, solo, from bar 77 onwards. Mention should also be made of Tovey's adaptation of the A major Piano Concerto of Bach as a concerto for oboe d'amore.

(g) **E Flat Oboe.** This is a high-pitched instrument, corresponding to the clarinet in E flat and, like that, used (but very much more rarely) in military bands. It is a transposing instrument, written for a minor third lower than its sound.

(h) **Tenoroon.** English name for what the French call *Basson quinte*. A small bassoon a fourth or fifth higher in pitch than the ordinary instrument, now virtually obsolete. Confusion occurs, however, as, quite independently, there was another instrument, of brief life, to which the name was attached (invented by a Scotsman, William Meikle, about 1830); this latter had a single reed and belonged to the clarinet family—or perhaps, more properly, it was a precursor of the saxophone family.

(i) **Heckelphone.** This is a sort of baritone oboe, i.e. its pitch lies between that of the cor anglais and that of the bassoon. Strauss and Delius have used it. It takes its name from its German inventor, Heckel, who introduced it in 1905, and its first public appearance was in Strauss's *Salome* in that year. It is generally written for in the treble clef an octave higher than the sounds desired.

There seems to be a great deal of vagueness in books on the relation between the hautbois baryton (bass oboe) and the heckelphone. The only feature they have in common is that they stand an octave below the ordinary oboe. They are constructionally and tonally very different.

The baryton is of French descent. It is of narrow scale, with a slow-tapered, conical bore, an elongated pear-shaped bell, and a light reed of the cor anglais type. In fact, the instrument is made and played like a large cor anglais and partakes somewhat of its tone colour, which is sweet, sensitive, and expressive like a baritone voice. It is admirable for solo work and for chamber music, but its light timbre is easily lost in the orchestra unless great care is taken with the scoring.

The heckelphone is of German design. It has a wide-scale tube with a pronounced conical bore; not only is the tube twice as long as that of the oboe, but it is also twice the diameter. It terminates in a spherical bell, closed at the end and provided with a foot upon which the instrument stands; sound holes are bored in the sphere at front and sides. It is played with a reed similar to that of a bassoon, much shorter and stiffer than that used for the baryton. This fact and the wide scale of the tube make a smooth, sonorous, and powerful tone, excellent in the orchestra as an oboe bass, quite unlike the bassoon, but rather too rough and 'solid' for chamber music use. It descends to A. Some American dance bands include it. When modern scores specify 'bass oboe' it is probably generally the heckelphone that the composer has in mind; certainly this was so in the case of German composers like Strauss, Weingartner, Hindemith, etc., or others like Delius and Holst who probably heard it in German orchestras or perhaps in the London Symphony Orchestra, which used to possess one.

(j) **Sarrusophone.** This is acoustically related to the oboe family (much as the saxophone is to the clarinet family) but is made of brass. It is a military band instrument (making very rare appearances in the orchestra) and exists in six sizes, roughly ranging from the pitch of the oboe to that of the double bassoon. The keys of these, in ascending order, are alternately E flat and B flat—the two favourite keys for military band instruments. They are all treated as transposing instruments (q.v.).

The name comes from the French bandmaster, Sarrus; he introduced his invention in 1863, his idea being apparently to supplant the oboes and bassoons in bands by instruments of a power and quality of tone more in keeping with those of the other instruments. (See also *Rackett*.)

5. Nomenclature.

(a) **Oboe** (plural, properly *Oboi*, the word being Italian, but it is usual to say *Oboes*). *Hautbois* (Fr.); *Hoboe* (Ger., but Germans also often spell the word 'Oboe').

(b) **Cor Anglais** (Fr., and generally adopted in Britain). *English Horn* (American and tending to become adopted in Britain); *Corno inglese* (It.); *Englisches Horn* (Ger.).

The more correct term *Althoboe* ('Alto Oboe') is used by Wagner in the score of *Parsifal*—probably suggested by a remark in Berlioz's *Instrumentation*.

(c) **Bassoon.** *Basson* (Fr.); *Fagotto* (It., 'bundle', from its appearance, two tubes bound together); *Fagott* (Ger.). An early English name for the bassoon (sixteenth century) was *Curtall* for a sort of tenor bassoon, and *Double Curtall* for one corresponding to our bassoon of today.

(d) **Double Bassoon.** *Contrabassoon.* *Contrebasson* (Fr.); *Contrafagotto* (It.); *Kontrafagott* (Ger.).

(e) **Oboe da Caccia.** *Hautbois de chasse* (Fr.).

(f) **Oboe d'Amore** (It.). *Hautbois d'amour* (Fr.); *Liebesoboe* (Ger.).

(g) **Tenoroon.** *Tenorbassoon* (Eng.); *Basson Quinte* (Fr.); *Quintfagott* or *Tenorfagott* (Ger.).

(h) **Heckelphone.** *Baritone Oboe, Basset Oboe* (Fr.); *Heckelphone* (Ger.).

6. Repertory of the Family. The surviving repertory may mostly be said to begin with the eighteenth century. **Bach** makes some solo use of the normal hautboy, though its tone was pungent, and he uses it largely in an orchestral way, often scoring an aria for merely three hautboys plus continuo. To the oboe, the oboe d'amore, and the oboe da caccia he often gave a solo position in his cantatas, etc.; the Sinfonia of the *Christmas Oratorio* is a well-known instance, and that of Church Cantata 156 (*Ich steh' mit einem Fuss im Grabe*) another. He used the Bassoon frequently; it has, for instance, a part in many of his cantatas. Note that his C minor Concerto for two harpsichords began life as a Concerto for violin, hautboy, and strings.

With **Handel** we find the hautboy greatly in use: he left six Hautboy Concertos, three Sonatas for hautboy and harpsichord, and three Sonatas for two hautboys and harpsichord. In addition there are in existence six Sonatas for two hautboys and a bassoon, written at the age of eleven (when shown these in after years he laughed and said, 'I used to compose like the devil in those days, chiefly for the hautboy, which was my favourite instrument'), as also six so-called Hautboy Concertos that are really Concerti Grossi.

There are two Sonatas for hautboy and continuo by **Telemann** and two by **John Loeillet** (see *Loeillet Family*), the latter also providing two Trios for flute, hautboy, and continuo.

Haydn wrote an Oboe Concerto and a Divertimento for oboe, strings, and keyboard; **Mozart** an Oboe Concerto (long lost but now published), a Quartet for oboe and strings, a Quintet for oboe, clarinet, bassoon, horn, and pianoforte, a Bassoon Concerto, a Sonata for bassoon and piano, one for bassoon and cello, and other things. He uses the double bassoon in his Serenade No. 10 (K. 361), which is for two oboes, two clarinets, two basset horns, two waldhorns, two bassoons, and double bassoon. **Beethoven** left two Trios for two oboes and cor anglais (one being a set of variations), three Duos for clarinet and bassoon, a Trio for flute, bassoon, and pianoforte, and a Quintet for oboe, clarinet, bassoon, horn, and pianoforte; and **Weber** a Bassoon Concerto, and a Hungarian Adagio and Rondo for bassoon and orchestra—the latter work was originally written for viola and orchestra.

From this period composers, whilst increasingly developing the orchestral use of the members of the family, do not seem to have troubled very much as to their solo or chamber music use. However, at a somewhat later period we find **Schumann** writing three Romances for oboe (or violin, or clarinet) and pianoforte; **Glazunof** a 'Pathetic' Trio for clarinet, bassoon, and pianoforte; **Reinecke** a trio for oboe, horn, and pianoforte; **Saint-Saëns** a Sonata for oboe and pianoforte and also one for bassoon and pianoforte; and **Hurlstone** another for bassoon and pianoforte; **d'Indy** a Fantasy on French folk tunes for oboe and full orchestra; **Karg-Elert** a Trio for oboe, clarinet, and cor anglais; **Tovey** a Trio for violin, cor anglais, and pianoforte; **Hindemith** a Sonata for bassoon and pianoforte (1938), and

a Sonata for cor anglais and pianoforte (1942); **Dunhill** a Lyric Suite for bassoon and pianoforte; **David Stanley Smith** a Sonata and **Mihalovici** a Sonatina for oboe and pianoforte; **Poulenc** a Sonata for clarinet and bassoon, and a Trio for oboe, bassoon, and pianoforte; **Bax** a Quintet for oboe and strings; and **Bliss, Bowen, Eugene Goossens**, and a few other British composers, stimulated by the artistry of the oboist Léon Goossens, providing him with chamber works in which his instrument can take part, and his brother and **Gordon Jacob** each providing him with an Oboe Concerto. **Boughton** and **Vaughan Williams** have written concertos for oboe and strings and **Milford** a Suite for the same. **Benjamin Britten** has written an Oboe Quartet and **Elizabeth Maconchy** an Oboe Quintet. **Gordon Jacob** has written a concerto for bassoon. **Prokofief** has a Scherzo Humoristique for four bassoons (1935), and **Dubensky** a Fugue for eight bassoons.

A work employing the Heckelphone is **Hindemith's** op. 47, Trio for viola, heckelphone, and piano. A late work by **Strauss** (1946) is his Oboe Concerto.

OBOE STOP. See *Organ* 3, 14 VI.

OBOUHOF, OBUKOF, etc. NICOLAS (1892–1954). See *Scales* 13; *Electric Musical Instruments* 1 g.

OBOUSSIER, ROBERT. Swiss composer of Lausanne descent. Born at Antwerp in 1900 and died at Zürich in 1957, aged fifty-six. He studied at Heidelberg, Mannheim, Zürich, and Berlin—at the last two places with Jarnach. He worked successively in Florence, Munich, and Paris as conductor and critic. Later he occupied himself similarly in Berlin, but owing to lack of sympathy with the Nazi government he left in 1938 and settled in Zürich. He composed chamber and orchestral music, piano music, and choral and solo vocal music, and an opera *Amphitryon* (Berlin, 1951).

OBRECHT (or Hobrecht, or Obertus, or Hobertus), JACOB. Born at Berg-op-Zoom (not Utrecht) in 1453 and died at Ferrara in 1505, aged about fifty-two. He held important church music positions in the Low Countries (especially at Bruges, Cambrai, and Antwerp—all great centres of musical activity). Like other musicians of his race at this period (see *Belgium* 1) he spent a good deal of time in Italy, and there, at last, plague caught him and he died. A great deal of his music survives and has been republished; it is of high importance.

See reference under *Holland* 1, and for the famous Passion long ascribed to him see *Passion Music* 1.

OBUKOF, etc. See *Obouhof*.

Obw. (in German organ music) = *Oberwerk*, i.e. 'Swell Organ'.

O'BYRNE, DERMOT. See *Bax*.

O.C. = *Organo corale* (It.), i.e. 'Choir Organ.'

O CANADA! One of the national songs of that dominion, popular especially amongst the French-Canadian population. The music, by Calixa Lavallée (see *United States* 8), written in 1880, was originally a hymn in honour of St. John the Baptist. The tune is officially adopted for regimental bands in Canada. In the non-French part of Canada the alternative national song, 'The Maple Leaf for Ever!', remains very popular. (See *Maple Leaf*.)

O CAN YE LABOUR LEA. See *Auld Lang Syne*.

OCARINA. A more or less egg-shaped small instrument made of metal or of earthenware.

It can be said to be the only instrument in use that is on the principle of Helmhotz's Resonators (see *Acoustics* 20; *Voice* 6, 7), i.e. the air within a closed chamber is set in vibration from without. There are eight finger-holes and the pitch is affected not as in the flutes and other tube-shaped instruments by the particular hole or holes left open but (much more, at all events) by the number of holes left open, i.e. if one hole is open it does not much matter which, and so with more than one. It is (like the harmonica and the tin whistle) sold in small shops all the world over, for boys and others who want to make a little simple music without much expense or trouble (see reference under *Tablature*).

The Ocarina has its prototype in certain instruments of various uncivilized races, as, for instance, an African instrument made out of the dried shell of the 'Kaffir orange'. It was first introduced into Europe by the Italians in the 1870s. The name seems to be a diminutive of *Oca*, 'goose' (perhaps from the shape).

O'CAROLAN, TURLOUGH (p. 481, pl. **84**. 2). Born at Newtown, County Meath, Ireland, in 1670 and died at Alderford, County Leitrim, in 1738, aged sixty-eight. See references under *Ireland* 1, 5.

OCCULTISM. See *Colour and Music* 12.

OCKEGHEM (Okeghem, Ockenheim, etc.), JEAN DE (p. 96, pl. **15**. 2). Born about 1430 at Dender in east Flanders and died at Tours about 1495. He was, as a boy, a chorister in Antwerp Cathedral, and as a young man in the chapel of the Duke of Bourbon. In 1454 he is found at Paris as composer and chaplain in the service of Charles VII. He is then found at Tours, as treasurer of the Abbey of St. Martin; and there he remained until his death. He left masses, motets, chansons, etc., and in them he shows very strikingly the progress that polyphonic composition was making at the period—a progress to which he greatly contributed (see remarks under *Belgium* 1; *Mass* 4). Josquin des Prés and Busnois were his pupils.

OCTANDRE (Fr.). Term used by Varèse (q.v.) for octet (real meaning: an eight-stamen plant).

OCTAVE. See *Hexachord*; *Scales* 4, 5.

OCTAVE FLUTE. See *Flute Family* 3 b.

OCTAVE QUINT. See *Organ* 14 IV.

OCTAVES GRAVES, OCTAVES AIGUËS in French organ music mean respectively the sub- and super-octave couplers.

OCTAVIN (Fr.), **OCTAVINA** (It.), **OKTAVIN** (Ger.).

(1) The piccolo.

(2) The 'fifteenth' stop of the organ (so *Octavin harmonique*, 'Harmonic Piccolo').

(3) A very small portable spinet of restricted range, sounding an octave higher than the normal instrument.

(4) A small guitar pitched an octave above normal.

(5) An odd instrument resembling the saxophone.

OCTET (Fr., *Octuor* and *Octette*; It., *Ottetto*; Ger., *Oktett*). Any combination of eight performers or any piece of music composed for such.

The normal String Octet is for four violins, two violas, and two cellos. Various octet combinations of wind and strings exist.

OCTO-BASS or **Octobasse** (p. 1088, pl. **179**. 8). An immense stringed double-bass, 10 ft. high, invented by the great *luthier* J. B. Vuillaume in the 1840s, apparently at the suggestion of Berlioz. As the finger-board was above the head of the player and its stretches were, in any case, too great for the fingers, the stopping was effected mechanically by means of levers operated by left hand and feet, the player bowing meanwhile with the right hand.

OCTOBI. See *Hothby*.

OCTUOR. See *Octet*.

OD (It.). 'Or.'

ODDINGTON. See *Odington*.

ODE. Properly a chorus in a Greek play. Any exalted poem in the style of an address, generally of moderate length.

ODER (Ger.). 'Or.'

O DEUTSCHLAND, HOCH IN EHREN ! ('O Germany, high in honours'). A song, the music by the Englishman Henry Hugh Pierson (q.v.), which (curiously, considering this origin) became a war-song of the German people in 1914 and the following years. The poem is by Ludwig Bauer (1832–1910), a schoolmaster of Augsburg, and was written in 1859. Pierson's tune was written as a sea-song and Bauer adopted it.

ODINGTON, WALTER DE. He was a monk of Evesham (hence often called Walter de Evesham), who lived at the end of the thirteenth century and the beginning of the fourteenth. He left important treatises on mathematics and astronomy, and one (*De speculatione musice*) on music.

See *France* 2; *Notation* 3.

ODO DE CLUNY (or **Clugny**). Died at Cluny in 942. Abbot of Cluny (near Mâcon). He was an important musical theorist and reformer of notation, and is the reputed author of the *Dialogus de Musica* (or *Enchiridion Musices*).

ODOUR AND MUSIC. The idea of a scale of perfumes was worked out in 1865 by S. Piesse, the Parisian manufacturer of them.

In his book *Des Odeurs*, he claimed, 'there is an octave of odours, as there is an octave of notes', and he set out in musical notation a range of 6½ octaves, every note of which had its own perfume, from patchouli on the lowest C of the piano to civet at its highest F. He said that bouquets ought to be grouped like the notes of a chord, and described the chord C–E–G–C as follows—geranium, acacia, orange-flower, and camphor. There was about as much science and sense in this as in some of the colour-scale theories mentioned in the article *Colour and Music*.

In 1891 there was given in Paris a public performance which combined music, colour, and odour. The work performed was *The Song of Solomon, a Symphony of Spiritual Love in Eight Mystical Devices and Three Paraphrases*, the 'book' being by Paul Roinard and the 'musical adaptations' by Flamen de Labrely. The programme set out the nature of each of the eight 'devices' in the following style—'First Device: orchestration of the word in I illuminated with O; orchestration of the music, D major; of the Colour bright orange; of the Perfume, white violet', and so forth. The meaning of this seems to be that in the recitation the vowels I and O predominated; that the music was in D major; that the stage decoration was of a bright orange colour; that a perfume of white violet was disseminated meanwhile.

The following year New York also experimented in a bold combination of appeals to the various senses in *A Trip to Japan in Sixteen Minutes conveyed to the Audience by a Succession of Odours*. This was claimed to be the 'First Experimental Perfume Concert in America', and also as 'A Melody in Odours (assisted by two Geishas and a Solo Dancer)'.

As explained in the article *Colour and Music*, the attempts at combination of appeal to the eye and the ear by a play of colours connected with simultaneous sounds have usually been based on analogies connected with the fact that both sound and light are vibratory stimuli conveyed by so-called 'waves': there is not even this basis for attempts to bring the sense of smell into the combination, as odours are conveyed by the dispersion of (infinitely tiny) particles of the material of the odoriferous substance.

ODUM, HOWARD WASHINGTON (b. 1884). See *Folk Song* 5.

O.E. = *Organo espressivo* (It.), i.e. 'Swell' organ.

OEHLENSCHLÄGER, A. G. See *Scandinavia* 2.

ŒUVRE (Fr.). 'Work.'

OFFEN (Ger.). 'Open.'

OFFENBACH (real name **Wiener**[1]), JACQUES or JAKOB (p. 369, pl. **62.** 3). Born at Cologne, Germany, in 1819 and died in Paris in 1880, aged sixty-one. He was the son of a Jewish cantor. As a boy he settled in Paris, and he lived there ever after. His early career was that of a violoncellist and as such he earned his living in the orchestra of the Opéra Comique, after a time becoming conductor at the Théâtre Français. Gradually he became known to the wide public as a composer of light and humorous operettas, very melodious and 'taking'. He visited America and Britain, and his multitudinous works had great popularity everywhere.

Amongst them are *Orphée aux Enfers* ('Orpheus in the Underworld', produced in England as 'Orpheus in the Underground'), *The Grand Duchess of Gérolstein*, and the more ambitious *Tales of Hoffman* (q.v.), the production of which was in preparation when he died—three months too early to witness its reception, an experience to which he had ardently looked forward.

See *Opera* 24 e (1858–67–81), 26; *Comic Opera*; *Opera buffa*.

OFFERTORY, OFFERTOIRE, or **OFFERTORIUM.** The Offertory of the Mass consists of an Antiphon (q.v.), a part of the Proper (see *Common*) of the Mass, sung just after the Credo, whilst the Priest is preparing the bread and wine and offering them upon the altar. The plainsong setting of the Antiphon is generally insufficient to occupy the time, so there may be interpolated a motet (sometimes one which repeats the words of the antiphon

just heard), or an organ voluntary. Palestrina set the Offertory Antiphons for the whole of the Church's year, in order to provide for this need. Organ music written to supply the need has often been of the tawdriest character, especially that of some French and Italian composers.

In the Anglican service the place of the Offertory is now usually taken by a hymn.

OFFICE. The 'Hour Services' of the Roman Catholic Church ('The Divine Office'). Also used for Anglican Matins and Evensong, and (though loosely) in the phrase 'The Office of the Holy Communion'.

OFFICE HYMN. A liturgical hymn appointed for the Office, or Service of the day (see above). The Office Hymns of the Roman Breviary were not transferred to the English Prayer Book, apparently merely because of the difficulty of translation. They have now gradually been translated and many of them find their place in Anglican hymnals. Their traditional tunes ('proper' melodies) have also been made available for Anglican use.

ÖFFNEN (Ger.). 'To open.'

OFICLEIDE (It.). Ophicleide. See *Cornett and Key Bugle Families* 2 g, 3 g, 4 g.

O FOR A CLOSER WALK. See *Hymns* 6.

O FOR A THOUSAND TONGUES TO SING. See *Hymns and Hymn Tunes* 6.

OFYDD. See *Wales* 7.

O GIN I WERE FAIRLY SHUT OF HER. See *Barley Shot*.

OGNI (It.). 'All', 'every'.

O GOD, OUR HELP. See *Hymns and Hymn Tunes* 6.

O HAUPT VOLL BLUT UND WUNDEN. See *Hymns and Hymn Tunes* 3; *Hassler*.

OHNE (Ger.). 'Without', e.g. *Ohne Dämpfer*, 'without mute'.

OIL OF BARLEY. See *Cold and Raw*.

OKEGHEM. See *Ockeghem*.

OKTAVE (Ger.). 'Octave.' So *Oktavflöte*, 'Octave Flute', i.e. Piccolo (see *Flute Family* 3 b); *Oktavkoppel*, 'Octave Coupler' (see *Organ* 2 e).

OKTAVIN. See *Octavin*.

OKTETT. See *Octet*.

OLD FOUNDATION. See *Cathedral Music* 2.

OLD HALL MANUSCRIPT. This is a manuscript presented to St. Edmund's College, Old Hall, near Ware, Hertfordshire, in 1893, first described by W. Barclay Squire in 1903 and bought for the British Museum in 1973. The contents were edited by the Revd. A. Ramsbotham, H. B. Collins, and Dom Anselm Hughes (q.v.) and published by the Plainsong and Medieval Music Society (3 vols., 1933–8).

The manuscript is the work of four copyists of the early fifteenth century. It offers a most valuable means of studying the church music

---

[1] This from information supplied by his granddaughter to the Editor of the *Radio Times* (29 January 1932). Grove's *Dictionary* gives 'Levy', Riemann's *Musiklexikon* gives 'Eberscht'. And there are other discrepancies in books of reference.

and the choral style of a period from about 1415 to about 1430.

See *Henry V of England* and compare *Eton College Choirbook*.

OLD HUNDRED. See *Old Hundredth*.

OLD HUNDRED-AND-THIRTEENTH. See *Hymns and Hymn Tunes* 5.

OLD HUNDRED-AND-TWENTY-FOURTH. See *Hymns and Hymn Tunes* 5.

OLD HUNDREDTH (English name) or **OLD HUNDRED** (American name). A metrical psalm tune that holds pre-eminence throughout the English-speaking Protestant world on account of its age, traditions, and dignity.

Its origin, despite much research, remains uncertain (cf. *God save the Queen* 9). Its name indicates that it was set to the hundredth psalm in the 'old' version of the metrical psalms, i.e. Sternhold and Hopkins as distinct from Tate and Brady (see *Hymns and Hymn Tunes* 5); the edition of this version in which it first appeared was Day's of 1563 (see *Hymns and Hymn Tunes* 5).

But the history of the tune goes back rather further—to Marot and Béza's Geneva Psalter of 1551 (see *Hymns and Hymn Tunes* 4, 17 d), in which it is attached to the 134th Psalm.

A form of the tune appears even earlier than that, in the Antwerp collection, *Souterliedekens* (see *Hymns and Hymn Tunes* 17 c). In some German and other settings it appears in three-in-a-measure rhythm: Bach in his Church Cantata No. 130 gives such a version of it (this is one of four harmonizations of it by him that remain). In hymn-books of today it appears sometimes in even notes and sometimes with notes of double value at the beginning and end of each line; this latter resembles the authentic Genevan treatment. (But see *Gathering Note—end*.)

The *Old Hundredth* is not only now the 'proper tune' (to use the old psalm-book term) to the metrical version of the psalm ('All people that on earth do dwell', by Wm. Kethe, one of the refugees in Geneva; published 1561), but is also in England always sung to the metrical doxology (see *Doxology*).

OLDMAN, CECIL BERNARD. Born in London in 1894 and died there in 1969, aged seventy-five. After study at Oxford he joined the staff of the British Museum, becoming (1948–59) Keeper of the Printed Books. He was a learned musicologist and bibliographer. C.B. 1952.

OLD METHODIST TUNES. See *Hymns and Hymn Tunes* 6.

OLD PSALTER. See *Hymns and Hymn Tunes* 10; *Presbyterian Church Music* 3.

OLD VERSION. See *Hymns and Hymn Tunes* 5.

'OLD VIC'. See *Victoria Hall, Royal*.

OLE (Sp.). A gipsy type of Seguidilla (q.v.), also known as *Polo*.

OLIPHANT. The word is Old English for 'elephant' and the thing was a hunting or signalling horn made of ivory, often very beautifully carved. It was in use as far back as A.D. 800—perhaps earlier.

OLSEN, OLE. Born at Hammerfest, Norway, in 1850 and died at Oslo in 1927, aged seventy-seven. He studied in Leipzig and then, settling in Christiania, served as piano teacher, conductor, inspector of army music, music critic, etc.

His compositions, which are considered to belong to the national school (cf. *Grieg*), have high reputation; they include operas, symphonic poems, and songs.

O.M. See *Knighthood and other Honours*.

ONDEGGIANDO, ONDEGGIANTE, ONDEGGIAMENTO (It.). 'Undulating', i.e. tremolo or vibrato, or (also) any swaying effect.

ONDES MUSICALES, ONDES MARTENOT. See *Electric Musical Instruments* 1 f.

ONDŘÍČEK, FRANZ (1859–1922). See *Bohemia*.

ONDULÉ (Fr.). 'Undulating', i.e. tremolo or vibrato, or (also) any swaying effect.

O'NEILL, NORMAN. Born in London in 1875 and died there as the result of a street accident, in 1934, aged nearly fifty-nine. He cut out a special niche for himself as a theatre conductor and composer, many of the most artistic dramatic productions in London owing much to his direction and to the incidental music provided by him. He wrote other than theatre music, but it is secondary in public interest.

See *Knorr*; *Incidental Music*.

ONE-STEP. A ballroom dance of American origin that overspread the world during the early twentieth century. It is rather more vigorous than the fox-trot and is in two-in-a-measure time.

ONGARESE (It.). Hungarian. (See *Hungary* for the one-time popularity of this term.)

ONION FLUTE. See *Mirliton*.

ONSLOW, GEORGE. Born in 1784 at Clermont-Ferrand, in Auvergne, and died there in 1853, aged sixty-nine. His father was a member of the English aristocracy, his mother a Frenchwoman. He became a fine pianist and wrote operas, symphonies, and other music in enormous quantities. In his mid-forties, whilst boar-hunting (or wolf-hunting; historians differ), he sat down to record a musical theme that had just come into his head, when a bullet struck him and injured his ear, leaving him ever after partially deaf. The theme was later worked up into a quintet (*The Bullet Quintet*) of which each portion represented some stage in the illness his accident had brought him, as 'Fever and Delirium', 'Convalescence', 'Cure', and the like. (Cf. *Programme Music* 4, end.) In his fifties he inherited a great fortune and was also elected to the Institute of France in succession to Cherubini.

His compositions, which once had frequent

performance, are now unheard, except, rarely, a few of those for chamber combinations. He specialized in string quintets, of which he wrote over thirty.

OP. Short for *Opus* (q.v.). For the plural *Opp.* is often used.

OPEN DIAPASON. See *Organ* 3, 14 I.

OPEN HARMONY. See *Harmony* 24 h.

OPENING SYMPHONY. See *Symphony* 1.

OPEN NOTES. The notes on the unstopped strings of any bowed or plucked instrument.

OPEN PIPES (Diapason, etc.). See *Organ* 3.

OPEN STRING. A string of a bowed or plucked instrument when not 'stopped' by the fingers.

OPER (Ger.). 'Opera.'

OPERA

<table>
<tr><td>1. The Renaissance takes Effect in Music.</td><td>11. Opera in France.</td><td>21. Opera in the American Colonies and the United States.</td></tr>
<tr><td>2. Some Early Opera Composers.</td><td>12. Chronological List of French Opera Composers.</td><td>22. Opera Composers of other Nationalities than the above.</td></tr>
<tr><td>3. The Triumph of the Singer.</td><td>13. Opera in Britain.</td><td>23. Opera-houses.</td></tr>
<tr><td>4. The Aria.</td><td>14. Chronological List of British Opera Composers.</td><td>24. A Survey of Historical First Performances.</td></tr>
<tr><td>5. Gluck.</td><td>15. Opera in Spain.</td><td>25. A Bird's-eye View of the World's Chief Opera Composers.</td></tr>
<tr><td>6. Nineteenth-century Italian Opera.</td><td>16. Chronological List of Spanish Opera Composers.</td><td>26. How many Operas have been Written?</td></tr>
<tr><td>7. The Late Nineteenth-century and Twentieth-century Italians.</td><td>17. Opera in Russia.</td><td>27. Articles in this Volume upon Subjects cognate to Opera.</td></tr>
<tr><td>8. Chronological List of Italian Opera Composers.</td><td>18. Chronological List of Russian Opera Composers.</td><td></td></tr>
<tr><td>9. Opera in the German Countries.</td><td>19. Czech Opera.</td><td></td></tr>
<tr><td>10. Chronological List of German Opera Composers.</td><td>20. Chronological List of Czech Opera Composers.</td><td></td></tr>
</table>

(For illustrations see p. 688, pl. **115–16**; 704, **117–18**; 720, **119–20**. For a list of dictionaries of Opera see *Dictionaries* 8.)

The beginning of the setting of stage plays to music is always very definitely dated at 1600, and it is true that at that time novel works were composed and produced that formed the basis for a course of evolution that was to go on to the present day and is still going on. But there was abundant stage music before this, and if opera began in 1600 it had many precursors, of which may be especially mentioned the aristocratic *Masques* (q.v.) and the more popular *Mysteries, Miracle Plays, and Moralities* (q.v.) and *Sacre Rappresentazioni* (q.v.).

1. The Renaissance takes Effect in Music. Towards the very end of the sixteenth century, when the madrigal (q.v.) had been brought to its highest perfection and popularity, certain attempts were made in Italy to apply this to the stage, a string of madrigals carrying on the story behind the scenes whilst actors recited and acted before them (cf. *Melodrama; Pantomime*). But such attempts did not satisfy acute minds, since an elaborate choral style cannot closely adapt itself to dramatic situations, and obviously any simultaneous mixture of singing and speech is confusing. And so in Florence during the last decade of the century efforts took place in the direction of a totally new type of writing.

The group who made these efforts belonged largely to the more aristocratic intelligentsia of the city, and what they brought into existence may be looked upon as a late, but nevertheless pretty direct, result of the Renaissance. This had begun a century and a half earlier, with the capture of Constantinople by the Turks (1453) and the dispersal of Greeks of learning, who fled in all directions taking with them many of the ancient manuscripts upon which this learning was based, and so disseminating widely a love of the literature, drama, and philosophy of antiquity.[1]

It is, of course, from that epoch that is usually dated Europe's definite transition from medieval to modern thought. Art, architecture, literature, philosophy, and education were all pretty quickly remodelled upon a Greek framework. Humanism began, and, as John Addington Symonds has put it, 'Europe after having lived in the shadow of Antiquity lived in its sunshine once again'.

The most universally visible fruit of the Renaissance, and the one which even today cannot escape the most casual eye, is the change in architecture. Gothic expired and the classical forms, proportions, and orders came back to the world. St. Peter's at Rome, St. Paul's in London, and the Capitol at Washington (whatever their varying dates), and similar pillared and domed buildings in every large city throughout Europe and America, are, for any knowledgeable man who strolls through the streets of those cities, reminders of the Renaissance; and to the instructed musician any passage of a recitative in a Handel oratorio, a

---

[1] The Renaissance can be, of course, variously dated, according to the narrower or wider sense one attaches to the word.

One sense in which the word is used carries it very far back to the mid-fifteenth century—to the earliest glimmers of dawn after the long night of medievalism. There is also a definite tendency now amongst historians to decry the importance of the results of the capture of Constantinople in 1453; nevertheless that date has been accepted here as, at least, a prominent landmark in the movement towards the study of Greek literature—a movement one result of which was, undeniably, to bring about the attempt to find and apply afresh the principles of Greek dramatic performance, thus leading to the development of a new art, that of opera.

This pushing back of the Renaissance has caused some authorities to consider Landino (q.v.) and his contemporaries to mark the start of Renaissance music.

Rossini comic opera, or a Wagner music drama can be just as much so.

In their infatuation for everything Greek the little aristocratic group already mentioned tried to restore the Greek presentation of drama. Taking Greek mythological subjects, and casting them into dramatic and poetical form, they then made settings of them, in what, from their reading, they imagined (not altogether wrongly) to be the historical Greek fashion, that in which the plays of Aeschylus and Euripides had originally been presented.

They discarded the elaborate choral polyphony of the madrigal style as barbaric, and set dialogue or soliloquy for single voices, imitating more or less the inflexions of speech, and accompanying the voice by playing mere supporting chords (see *Figured Bass*). Short choruses were interspersed, but they, too, were homophonic rather than polyphonic, i.e. they moved not like the madrigal, as an interweaving of melodies, but straightforwardly in blocks of chords.

Putting it briefly, counterpoint was now discarded, at all events by those bold spirits, and the harmonic aspect of music came to the fore.

This new type of music received various names. Sometimes it was called 'the New Music' (*Le Nuove musiche*, 'The New Musics', was the title of a book of songs of Caccini, published in 1602), sometimes a play set in this way was called a 'Drama by means of Music' (*Dramma per musica*). A handy later term to describe the principle of one voice accompanied (instead of the old one of many voices intertwined) is *Monody*.

2. Some Early Opera Composers. The early operatic examples of this new style are Peri's *Daphne* in 1597 (now lost) and his *Eurydice* in 1600. In this last certain portions were supplied by Caccini, and this composer then immediately reset the whole text (also 1600). The *Eurydice* by Peri with parts by Caccini is nowadays generally spoken of as the first opera, and can be conveniently considered as such.

(The facts have been as clearly as possible stated here, as in many books a good deal of confusion occurs: sometimes 'the first opera' is spoken of as *Daphne*, sometimes as *Eurydice*, and sometimes *Eurydice* is spoken of as by Peri, sometimes as by Caccini, and sometimes as by the two of them. The precise statement above can be relied upon.)

The leading composers of this early period of opera were the two just mentioned, with also Monteverdi. The performance of Monteverdi's *Orpheus* at Mantua, in 1607 (p. 688, pl. 115. 1), is a landmark in the history of opera, as is also that of his *The Coronation of Poppaea* in Venice (where he was long resident), in 1642. In the meantime he had developed the style very greatly.

All through history it is found that once a drastic reform is accomplished the reformers' first ideas begin to weaken and the practices of the previous period tend to return, more or less modified by the new ideas. It was so with opera. Polyphony and continuous melody had been expelled with a hayfork, but they soon began quietly to creep back—polyphony never regaining all its lost ground (so far as the stage is concerned), but melody more than doing so. The purely speaking or recitative style at once began to be diversified with melodic passages. One of Caccini's daughters, Francesca (see also reference later—11 a), was a celebrated singer, and took part in the performances of his works, and for her he included not only suave melodic passages, but also florid passages of vocal display. And with Monteverdi we find a great step forward towards the Italian Aria—soon to be almost completely conventionalized (see *Aria*). Human nature is very unvarying, and the demand for 'tune' and for the showy display of the voice, though it may be abandoned in some mood of severity, is quickly put forward again.

3. The Triumph of the Singer. In the next period (we now reach the end of the seventeenth century and the beginning of the eighteenth) the supremacy of the singer was fully established and the desire for dramatic strength and truth about extinguished. A race of highly paid and thoroughly spoilt public favourites had arisen. An adult male soprano voice, only obtainable by a surgical operation, had come into existence (see *Voice* 5), and those who possessed it were commonly the vainest and most exigent of the whole vocal tribe. (An artificial alto similarly existed.)

The gymnastic possibilities of the human voice were during the eighteenth century exploited to the full by a school of vocal teachers such as the world has perhaps never since seen, and moreover (if accounts are to be believed) a standard of vocal tone was attained that we should be very glad to recover today (see *Bel Canto*).

With all this the opera had, rather naturally, degenerated into something like a costume concert. Italian audiences listened to and applauded the big songs of their favourite singers, and in the intervening stretches of the performances, comfortably seated in their boxes, they were served with supper, or had little conversation parties, or played cards. The President de Brosses (q.v.), writing from Rome in 1793, tells of playing draughts (checkers) in his box at an opera house, remarking humorously, 'Draughts are an admirable invention—just the thing to fill up the gaps whilst the long recitatives are being sung, as music itself is to relieve the pressure of a too great devotion to draughts'.

4. The Aria. The great medium of vocal display of those days was the aria already mentioned. It had settled into a practically invariable form of first section, second section, and first section repeated (essentially an undramatic form). For a description of the various types of aria see the article *Aria*; they included (amongst others) the *Aria cantabile*, smooth and sustained, the *Aria di bravura*, agile and

1. A HANDEL TITLE-PAGE

2. FRONTISPIECE OF GLUCK'S 'ORPHEUS', 1764

3. METASTASIO

4. THE COVENT GARDEN RIOT OF 1763. Members of the audience are climbing on to the stage with bludgeons and rapiers; the orchestra cower to avoid missiles. The opera is Arne's *Artaxerxes*; the grievance is the abolition of half-price after the third Act

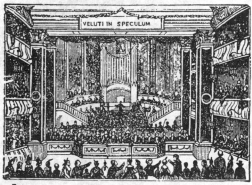

5. COVENT GARDEN IN THE LATE 18TH CENTURY
(An oratorio performance)

6. THE MORNING AFTER THE FIRE OF 1808

2. M. W. BALFE (1808–70)

3. W. V. WALLACE (1812–65)

1. SIR H. R. BISHOP (1786–1855)

4. SIR ARTHUR SULLIVAN (1842–1900). By Millais

5. SIR WILLIAM SCHWENCK GILBERT (1836–1911)

6. SIR ALEXANDER MACKENZIE (1847–1935) and SIR
EDWARD GERMAN (1862–1936)

7. RICHARD D'OYLY CARTE (1844–1901)
Impresario of the Gilbert and Sullivan operas

brilliant, the *Aria parlante*, rather more in the recitative vein, and so on. These had to be used according to an obvious principle of variety, no two of a kind consecutively. More than that, every principal singer in the cast must have both his or her prominent appearance in every Act and his or her appearance in different types of aria, so exhibiting versatility. The rules that came to be accepted are too many and complicated to be set out here, but it will be readily seen that in the hands of a routine composer they could be, so far as dramatic expression was concerned, disastrously crippling. (However, they were not always rigorously observed.)

It was under these conditions that lived and worked, during the first half of the eighteenth century, some of the greatest composers of the whole history of opera; in their own day they won fame and sometimes wealth, but not one of their operas has any place in the operatic repertory now, partly (*a*) from the requirement of the male soprano, a requirement that can, happily, no longer be met, partly (*b*) from the present-day lack of interest in their subjects (which were still always classical and mythological), but chiefly (*c*) from the excessive formality of their treatment. In spite of occasional revivals, it is unlikely that the world at large will come to take pleasure again in these one-time favourites.

For the elaborate decoration of passages in the arias by the singers, see *Ornaments* 1 (near end).

5. Gluck. And so the current repertory begins not with Handel, A. Scarlatti, and their very numerous active contemporaries and successors, but with a composer who boldly dared to return to dramatic truth—Gluck.

Thus far we have been considering Italian opera; a German composer has been mentioned (a German whose work was, however, almost all done in England—Handel), but every opera whose existence has been implied in the general description so far offered has been by either an Italian or an Italian-trained and Italianate composer, working in the Italian tradition, and using the Italian language.

Gluck's first operas were in that language and that tradition; he had studied in Italy and his early works were written for Italian opera-houses. Then he suffered a change of heart and came boldly into the open with a banner on which was inscribed (for this is what it came to) '*Back to 1600!*'

He wanted poetry and dramatic truth, and less of this pandering to the vanity of singers and to the love of vocal display of fashionable audiences. He began to write for Paris, where a tradition of opera in the native language had come into existence and where opera had been developing on lines a little different from those of Italian opera (we will return to this in a moment). His *Orpheus* (first written as an Italian opera in 1762, and so performed in Vienna that year and in Paris two years later, and then recast for Paris and performed there

in French in 1774) is the earliest full-length opera of any composer still to maintain a regular place in any repertory. His *Alcestis*, written (also in Italian) for Vienna in 1767, and performed in an adapted and translated form in Paris in 1776, marks the real turning-point, for its preface is a plain manifesto of the new principles, which as already hinted are in effect a return to the old ones. His *Iphigenia in Aulis* (to a French text), written for and produced in Paris in 1774 (the same year as the French version of *Orpheus*), is of high importance as the first opera he wrote originally in the French language, and as embodying many valuable innovations.

The general principles of Gluck may be summarized (from his preface to *Alcestis*) as follows:

(*a*) The music to be secondary to the poetry and drama, not to weaken them by unnecessary ornaments—to be, in fact, something like the addition of colour to drawing, giving more life to the figures without changing their shapes.

(*b*) Halts in the poetry and action for the sake of any kind of display to be particularly avoided, whether such halts be for the sake of vocal display or for that of the added interest of interpolated instrumental passages ('ritornelli').

(*c*) The overture to be of such a character as to prepare the audience for the drama to follow.

(*d*) The orchestration to vary according to the degree of interest and passion in the words.

(*e*) Too great a disparity between recitatives and arias to be shunned.

Gluck, then, stands as the Great Reformer of opera. He still clung to the old classical subjects (p. 704, pl. **117.** 2)—how many times was the tale of Orpheus and Eurydice set during the period 1600–1800? But his gods and men were living, active, and feeling, not lay figures with voices.

Gluck, however, was a German; he starts a line that runs through Mozart to Weber, to Wagner and Strauss, and to follow that we shall have in a moment to turn back to him; the Italian opera continued meanwhile in very much its old course. We will for the time leave out of account the *Opera buffa*, or humorous and less formal opera, that had been growing up out of a practice of interspersing lighter works between the acts of the opera proper, merely saying that it exercised a healthy influence from the very fact that its success depended less on vocal effect than on dramatic, and that it therefore introduced an element of less sophistication.

6. Nineteenth-century Italian Opera. At the beginning of the nineteenth century, graceful melody and vocal pyrotechnics were more than ever in cultivation in Italy, both for home use and for export to the opera-houses of all the capitals of Europe, where they were eagerly accepted. Donizetti (1797–

1848), Bellini (1801–35), and Rossini (1792–1868) are the greatest names, and they lead us onward to the earlier work of the long-lived Verdi (1813–1901), who, in that period, shows himself an Italian of the Italians, rejoicing in melodramatic situations and expressing the emotions arising out of them in easy-flowing melody and passages of laryngeal athletics. Then with *Aida* (1871), written for Cairo, he turns to a more genuinely dramatic treatment, with a great emphasis on the element of spectacle, and with *Othello* (1887) he rises to true greatness of scope and vision, expressing a noble drama in appropriate music, and adopting some of the technical resources of his contemporary Wagner, of whom we shall read shortly. *Falstaff* (1893—he was now in his eightieth year) shows him full of the high spirits of youth, freely adopting Wagnerian devices quite foreign to his earlier and middle styles, and endowing the world, at an age when some men are senile, with a work that abounds in touches of real genius, and all through holding to the finest ideals of those who first introduced the opera and those who, from time to time, had tried to reform it.

The work of the Donizetti–Bellini–Rossini era is not contemptible: it offers much good music (shapely melody on a simple harmonic basis), but the dramatic side comes secondary to the musical; the motive that takes audiences to hear it is that of enjoying singing rather than that of enjoying the art of musical drama. The later work of Verdi, whilst it is still definitely Italian in its high vocal quality and its ease of movement, is infinitely deeper as music and worthier as literature and drama.

7. The Late Nineteenth-century and Twentieth-century Italians. To complete this brief survey of Italian opera reference must be made to one or two of the younger contemporaries and successors of Verdi. Puccini is the one who stands highest. In him we see a remarkable adaptability. The Italian love of melody is provided for without too much sacrifice of other qualities. The sense of dramatic movement is strong, the subjects are often 'melodramatic' and melodramatically treated, but the characters are alive and, simply as plays, the operas have such interest that it is possible for the auditors to imagine their success (with the necessary recasting) even if the music were removed. There is in Puccini a good deal of that *verismo* (or violent, passionate realism) that is more often accredited to his contemporaries, Mascagni and Leoncavallo.

Orchestration is an important ingredient of the operatic art that has been deliberately neglected throughout this article because it is impossible to pursue many lines of thought simultaneously, but it may be said that the history of orchestration in opera is much the same as that of orchestration in symphony. In Peri and Caccini we have the tiniest little (apparently chance) collection of instruments (Peri's *Eurydice* had merely a harpsichord, a viola da gamba, and two or three lutes—and flutes once); with Monteverdi the force is greatly enlarged (in his *Orpheus*, only seven years later than Peri's *Eurydice*, he used over thirty instruments; and so the development goes forward, what we now consider the Handel type of orchestra, the Haydn type, the Beethoven type, and the Wagner type being in turn employed (see article *Orchestra and Orchestration*).

In Italian opera in the twentieth century there has been another attempt to recapture the old ideals. Pizzetti offers an outstanding example. He has laid it down that the ideal drama for music is one in which the music can enhance the significance of every word and thought and action; with him opera has turned again largely from the later Italian ideal of lyricism to the earlier Italian ideal of a flexible recitative, and he has reduced the importance of the orchestra.

Of course opera suffers from a permanent business handicap. It is very expensive and, even with lavish subsidy by municipalities and governments, it calls for large audiences if it is to pay its way. This tends to embarrass composers of originality or of strong views, for the big public is not very intelligent nor very eager for progress. It likes opera to run along in the old tracks, or, at any rate, not to deviate into very unfamiliar country. This is particularly true of the Italian public, and the lot of the true innovator in Italy is rather discouraging. It was only in old age that Verdi reached the point where *Othello* or *Falstaff* might be ventured, and Puccini never got so far as that—if he wished to do so.

It should be noted that the whole of the opera discussed in this article to the present period is what is traditionally called 'Grand Opera'—opera in which the music is continuous, i.e. without the use of the spoken voice. That has always been the Italian ideal in serious opera, as it has not always been in French, German, or English opera.

8. Chronological List of Italian Opera Composers. Italian opera composers who receive notice in this volume under their own names are (ranged in order of birth):

Caccini (*c.* 1546–*c.* 1618); Peri (1561–1633); Monteverdi (1567–1643); Gagliano (1575–1642); Rossi (1597–1653); Cavalli (1602–76); Carissimi (1605–74); Cesti (1623–69); Pasquini (1637–1710); Stradella (1642–82); G. B. Bassani (1657–1716); A. Scarlatti (1660–1725); Ariosti (1666–1740); Lotti (*c.* 1667–1740); Bononcini (1670–1747); Leo (1694–1744); Galuppi (1706–85); Pergolese (1710–36); Jommelli (1714–74); Piccini (1728–1800); Sacchini (1730–86); Pugnani (1731–98); Paesiello (1740–1816); Cimarosa (1749–1801); Salieri (1750–1825); Cherubini (1760–1842); Paër (1771–1839); Spontini (1774–1851); Rossini (1792–1868); Mercadante (1795–1870); Donizetti (1797–1848); Bellini (1801–35); L. Ricci (1805–59); F. Ricci (1809–77); Verdi (1813–1901); Poniatowski (1816–73); Bottesini (1821–89); Arditi (1822–1903); Ponchielli (1834–86); Boito (1842–1918); Scontrino (1850–1922); Catalani (1854–93); Smareglia

(1854–1929); Leoncavallo (1858–1919); Puccini (1858–1924); Mascagni (1863–1945); Busoni (1866–1924); Giordano (1867–1948); Wolf-Ferrari (1876–1948); Alfano (1876–1954); Respighi (1879–1936); Pizzetti (1880–1968); Malipiero (1882–1973); Pick-Mangiagalli (1882–1949); Zandonai (1883–1944); Castelnuovo-Tedesco (1895–1968); Rieti (born 1898); Dallapiccola (1904–75); Nono (born 1924).

9. Opera in the German Countries.

(a) The Florentine experiment had its repercussion in Germany thirty years later, Peri's *Daphne*, originally produced at Florence in 1597, being performed (in a German translation and somewhat adapted) to celebrate a royal wedding at Torgau, in Saxony, in 1627. The adaptation was made by the versatile and able Schütz; the music, like that of the original, is now lost and to what extent Schütz's own work came into it is debatable.

There is interest in the fact that this work was heard in German, for in this it stood for a long time almost alone so far as concerns 'grand opera'. Italian and Italianate opera soon became a fashionable and popular entertainment in Germany as elsewhere. The Italian composers and singers were very active in German courts and other centres of artistic activity right through the latter half of the seventeenth century and the whole of the eighteenth, and German composers of 'grand' opera adopted the Italian language and style.

Keiser for over forty years (1694–1739) reigned as opera king at Hamburg, composing for the theatre there over one hundred operas; most are in Italian and on the usual mythological subjects, but he made an attempt (without lasting success) to establish German opera on popular subjects.

Graun, Frederick the Great's Kapellmeister in Berlin, wrote over thirty Italian operas; Hasse, long attached to the court of the Elector of Saxony, at Dresden, wrote over one hundred; Handel, a German by birth, after the beginnings of his operatic career in Germany and Italy, settled in England and composed Italian opera for the London aristocracy.

(b) The court of the Emperor at Vienna was a great centre of operatic activity; a long line of important men occupied the position of director of the opera-house (including Gluck from 1754 to 1764 and Salieri from 1774 to 1792). The most wholesale opera librettist who ever lived, the Italian Metastasio (see *Libretto* and p. 704, pl. **117**. 3), was settled there for over half a century (1730 to his death in 1782), and from that centre were issued the libretti (see *Libretto*) which, put to music over and over again by innumerable ambitious composers, all anxious to go one better than their predecessors, came to be household words to opera-goers in every European capital. The close connexion of Gluck (p. 396, pl. **67**. 7) with Vienna lasted, with intervals, from 1754 to his death in 1787. The service he rendered opera has been alluded to in the discussion of Italian opera above.

Mozart (forty years Gluck's junior) was in and out of Vienna all his life, and resident there for his last ten years (i.e. 1781–91). Two of his three greatest operas were written there—*Figaro* (1786) and *The Magic Flute* (1791); the other one, *Don Giovanni*, was written during the same period, but at Prague. It will be noted that none of these three was a setting of one of the customary classical mythological plots, and *The Magic Flute* was actually in the German language; it is not, however, 'grand' opera, i.e. it has spoken dialogue. In Mozart we find a great development. The technique of composition is much more ably applied; there are high melodic charm, subtle harmony, more effective orchestration, a wonderfully more elaborate building up of the finales of the acts, and a fine musical characterization of the various dramatis personae.

(c) There followed Beethoven's *Fidelio*, in German, and with the full Romantic period (see *Romantic*) came Weber, with his operas in German and on popular subjects. The Italian language was now entirely cast aside by German composers and so were the old mythological plots. Mozart set a book of Metastasio (*The Clemency of Titus*, Prague, 1791); after that, we may say, Metastasio's influence was great enough for Burney to think it worth while to issue his *Life and Letters* in three volumes, and up to the 1830s composers of standing occasionally reset his libretti (e.g. Meyerbeer's *Semiramide*, 1819). But despite his enormous one-time fame he is unknown to the opera-goer of today, and his poetical works, of which over forty editions, in all the languages of Europe, were published in his own lifetime, are now read only by students of the Italian language and literature.

(d) From Weber we step to Wagner, who owes much to him, and as Wagner's work is briefly summarized in the article under his own name, space may be saved here if the reader will turn to it. It will be found that in essence the reforms of Wagner embody the same ideals as those of Gluck, and hence the same as those of the Italian group who first introduced opera to the world. Wagner abhorred musical display and sought to intensify the drama by allying it with music.

For the work of Meyerbeer see under his own name.

(e) Strauss we may look upon as Wagner out-Wagnered in the sense that the enormous new harmonic and orchestral resources of Wagner are exceeded; for the purposes of a short sketch like the present this composer is merely a Wagner born half a century later than the original one: his technical methods (for instance, use of the Leading *Motif*, q.v.) are those of Wagner. Since Wagner there has been a strong disposition amongst German (and other) composers to adopt his general principles, and his flexible Leading *Motif* method, and the somewhat heavy Wagnerian type of romantic feeling (a very German thing) clings about much subsequent German opera.

(f) Young composers are constantly arising who apply the modern harmonies and orchestration. One of these, Alban Berg (1885–1935), in 1925 produced an opera, *Wozzeck* (q.v.), which created a great stir (first performance in Berlin after one hundred and thirty-seven rehearsals; stopped by the police in Prague, owing to rioting amongst the audience, 1926; enormous success at Philadelphia and New York in 1931). Its specialities are the use of an atonal harmony, a very accomplished orchestration of the non-merging type, and its division into a large number of tiny scenes, each based musically upon some special form ('fugues, inventions, suites, sonatas, variations, passacaglias'), all of which, the composer stated, were intended to increase the logical consistency of a work so divided into sections, without drawing the attention of the auditor from the dramatic purpose of the combination. The literary basis of this opera (founded on a drama of Büchner, 1813–37) is decidedly of the old-fashioned sentimental German type—however 'objective' the music may be.

Many others of the more recent German operas will be found briefly alluded to under the names of their composers.

(g) One very important side of German opera (and for half a century its most definitely German side) is the *Singspiel*. It is treated separately in this volume under its own name, and the article devoted to it should be read if a complete bird's-eye view of the subject of German opera and opera in Germany is desired. It is to be noted that some of the finest German composers of 'grand' opera (e.g. Mozart, Weber, Beethoven) have not disdained to give the spoken voice a place in their schemes.

10. Chronological List of German Opera Composers. German and Austrian opera composers who receive notice in this volume under their own names are:

Schütz (1585–1672); Handel (1685–1759); Hasse (1699–1783); C. H. Graun (1701–59); Gluck(1714–87); Haydn (1732–1809); J. C. Bach (1735–82); Dittersdorf (1739–99); Mozart (1756–91); Beethoven (1770–1827); Hoffmann (1776–1822); Spohr (1784–1859); Weber (1786–1826); Meyerbeer (1791–1864); Marschner (1795–1861); Loewe (1796–1869); Schubert (1797–1828); Lortzing (1801–1851); Benedict (1804–85); Nicolai (1810–49); Flotow (1812–83); Wagner (1813–83); Suppé (1819–95); Cornelius (1824–74); Goetz (1840–76); Millöcker (1842–99); Knorr (1853–1916); Humperdinck (1854–1921); Moszkowski (1854–1925); Wolf (1860–1903); Reznicek (1860–1945); Thuille (1861–1907); Weingartner (1863–1942); Strauss (1864–1949); d'Albert (1864–1932); Pfitzner (1869–1949); Siegfried Wagner (1869–1930); Zemlinsky (1872–1942); Schönberg (1874–1951); Schreker (1878–1934); Braunfels (1882–1954); Berg (1885–1935); Toch (1887–1964); Hindemith (1895–1963); Orff (born 1895); Korngold (1897–1957); Křenek (born 1900); Weill (1900–50); Blacher (1903–75); Fortner (born 1907); Liebermann (born 1910); Einem (born 1918); Henze (born 1926).

11. Opera in France. (The first section of what follows is concerned with the spread of opera from Italy to France in the mid-seventeenth century. Before it is read the reader may care to turn to a reference to a French thirteenth-century protoype of the opera—Adam de la Halle's *Robin and Marion*, performed in Italy about 1280; see *Adam de la Halle*.)

(a) The particular circumstances in which what we usually call 'the first opera', Peri's *Eurydice*, was performed were not mentioned above, as not being essential to the story of Italian opera. It is now desirable to refer to them. The occasion was the marriage, in Florence, of Henry IV of France to Mary de' Medici. Apparently the opera pleased the bride (a great lover of art) and the bridegroom, for the author of the drama, Rinuccini, was frequently invited to Paris during the following five years, and was appointed a Gentleman of the King's Chamber. He seems to have made some efforts to introduce the new art of opera to Paris, but without great success. Caccini, with his daughter (see section 2), the famous singer, visited Paris in 1605. Further attempts were made after the death of Henry IV in 1643, by the Prime Minister, Mazarin, himself an Italian and animated partly by some political aim; again there were not very satisfying results. The Italian composer Luigi Rossi was invited to Paris by Mazarin in 1647 to superintend the performance of his *Marriage of Orpheus and Eurydice*, and was allowed to bring twenty singers with him. His work was performed in Italian, but Mazarin was so thoughtful as to distribute to the audience (it was, of course, a court performance) an analysis, in French, of the action, scene by scene. A few other attempts to acclimatize the opera in France were made, and at last, in 1660, for the occasion of the marriage of Louis XIV, Cavalli was invited to come from Venice and produce his opera *Xerxes*: two years later he came again and produced his *Hercules as Lover*; both of these were, of course, in Italian.

(b) The moment had now arrived when the art, after fifty years of preparation, was definitely to strike root in France. Ballet (q.v.), in origin, we may almost say, a French type of entertainment, had been very popular at court during the latter part of the reign of Louis XIII, and the accession of Louis XIV, himself a dancer, had given it greater glory. The Italian-born but thoroughly naturalized Lully (q.v.), head of the king's instrumental forces and court composer, was the leader in the provision of this type of entertainment, and he was engaged to add to Cavalli's opera what to French eyes it lacked—the element of *divertissement* (p. 76, pl. **12**. 1). The king, queen, princes, and nobles danced publicly in the performance to the ballet music he added. The recitative of Cavalli won Lully's admiration, and he adopted its formulae in incidental music he wrote for the plays of Molière and others.

For the moment Lully did not write anything for the theatre beyond ballet (with some vocal music) and *intermèdes* (see article *Intermezzo*);

other composers did so. Then in 1672 began the series of Lullian operas which continued until his death, fifteen years later, and which is looked upon as the solid rock foundation of French opera (p. 688, pl. 115. 3, 4). Lully's texts were in French; he considered the French taste by including plenty of ballet (see *Ballet* 7); he greatly developed accompanied recitative (that of the Italians having been *recitativo secco* —see *Recitative*); he adopted the aria much as he found it in Cavalli; but he made a definite innovation in the overture, which with him became a form of several varied movements (see *Overture*) instead of a mere brief prelude.

(c) Rameau, born four years before Lully died, was his greatest successor. He, also, used the French language. It is impossible to particularize his qualities here, but one may be mentioned—he was definitely French in his style, not attempting to imitate the characteristics of contemporary Italian operas. Towards the end of his reign (as we may call it) the performance in Paris of Pergolese's *The Servant as Mistress* (first heard at Naples some years earlier) brought about the establishment of a flourishing school of humorous opera, of which the story is briefly traced in the articles *Intermezzo* and *Opera buffa*. A violent war between a nationalist and an anti-nationalist group broke out over the introduction of this form (see *Bouffons, Guerre des*; also *Vaudeville*).

(d) It is possible now to proceed more rapidly in our consideration of the evolution of opera in France. The influence of Gluck has already been mentioned (5). It was in Paris that he dared his greatest experiment; and Paris appreciated and rewarded him.

Rossini and all the great Italians had influence on the Paris taste, their works being very frequently performed. The work of the German, Meyerbeer, brilliant and heavily spectacular, was largely composed for Paris, where people like to have something to look at as well as something to listen to.

Berlioz (1803–69) is one of the very biggest figures in French operatic history, but he was not recognized as such. The facile, sentimental, but undoubtedly effective Gounod and the light-handed Bizet were at work towards the end of the nineteenth century. Massenet, Charpentier, Messager, and Saint-Saëns are names that all stand for something in the history of French opera, but not something of the greatest: however, they have dramatic sense and tunefulness, and those are two fine things.

(e) Some brief reference to the operas of d'Indy, Debussy, and Ravel will be found under their own names. The *Pelléas and Mélisande* of Debussy (1902) stands alone in the whole opera repertory as the most determined and consistent attempt ever made to apply the foundation principles of the Florentine initiators of opera, of Gluck, and of Wagner, i.e. the subjection of music to drama rather than the use of drama as a motive for the provision of music. To attain his object Debussy largely

discarded the contrapuntal and symphonic style of Wagner, as he also did all purely melodic considerations. He produced a fluid score, the current of which followed without deviation the bed carved for it by the drama.

There is, of course, an active young modernist school in France, as in Germany; it has, however, on the whole been taken less seriously, and it has certainly had a smaller chance of establishing itself, owing (apart from any other causes) to the relatively small number of well-equipped opera-houses in France.

To complete the consideration of French opera read not only the articles above mentioned, but also that on *Opéra-comique*. For French opera in Russia see section 17 of present article.

12. Chronological List of French Opera Composers. French opera composers who receive notice in this volume under their own names are:

Cambert (1628–77); Lully (1632–87); M. A. Charpentier (1634–1704); Marais (1656–1728); Campra (1660–1744); Montéclair (1666–1737); Destouches (1672–1749); Mouret (1682–1738); Rameau (1683–1764); Duny (1709–75); Mondonville (1711–72); Jean-Jacques Rousseau (1712–78); Dauvergne (1713–97); F. A. Philidor (1726–95); Monsigny (1729–1817); Lesueur (1760–1837); Méhul (1763–1817); Boïeldieu (1775–1834); Auber (1782–1871); Benoist (1794–1878); Panseron (1796–1859); Halévy (1799–1862); Berlioz (1803–69); F. David (1810–76); Ambroise Thomas (1811–96); Maillart (1817–71); Louis Lacombe (1818–84); Gounod (1818–93); Offenbach (1819–80); Weckerlin (1821–1910); Massé (1822–84); Lalo (1823–92); Reyer (1823–1909); Lecocq (1832–1918); Saint-Saëns (1835–1921); Delibes (1836–91); Guiraud (1837–92); Dubois (1837–1924); Bizet (1838–75); Audran (1840–1901); Bourgault-Ducoudray (1840–1910); Chabrier (1841–94); Massenet (1842–1912); Lefebvre (1843–1917); Fauré (1845–1924); Planquette (1848–1903); Godard (1849–95); d'Indy (1851–1931); Messager (1853–1929); Bruneau (1857–1934); Huë (1858–1948); Bemberg (1859–1931); G. Charpentier (1860–1956); Marty (1860–1908); Debussy (1862–1918); Pierné (1863–1937); Ropartz (1864–1955); Dukas (1865–1935); Magnard (1865–1914); Erlanger (1868–1943); Bréville (1869–1949); Schmitt (1870–1958); Rabaud (1873–1949); Hahn (1875–1947); Ravel (1875–1937); Laparra (1876–1943); Ladmirault (1877–1944); Aubert (1877–1968); Gabriel Dupont (1878–1914); Milhaud (1892–1974); Delannoy (1898–1962); Poulenc (1899–1963).

13. Opera in Britain. (a) Recitative seems to have been first heard in England in 1617, when Nicolas Lanier (q.v.) used it in the music for a masque by Ben Jonson (see *Masque*). After this little is heard of recitative for forty years.

The new art of opera reached England in 1656, half a century later than it was heard for the first time in France or Germany. This was the time of the Commonwealth, when the spoken play was forbidden, but there was, from the year mentioned until the Puritan rule ended, regular opera of a kind in London.

The performances began with what was called *The Firste Dayes Entertainment at Rutland House by Declamation and Musick; after the manner of the Ancients*, which last words might be thought to point to recitative and the same classical intention that had inspired the Florentine group in 1600, though this was not so. Sir William Davenant (p. 689, pl. 116), the promoter of this enterprise, had probably heard some of the Italian operas in Paris, for he had spent much time in France in attendance on the queen of the executed Charles I, but this 'First Day's Entertainment' was but a trial trip, apparently, to see whether it would pass with authorities who had suppressed the ordinary play. This, then, was an approach to the Florentine opera, but come to London via Paris and treated in an individual way. Davenant later became Poet Laureate and he was not altogether unwilling that people should believe a common rumour that he was the son of Shakespeare. The 'libretto' was by himself; it was printed and consists merely of four long speeches by Diogenes and Aristophanes, who discuss the propriety of dramatic entertainment, and by a Parisian and an Englishman who each abuse the other's city. Instrumental and vocal music was interpolated.

A few months later Davenant began a series of performances of what is always considered to be the first real opera in England, *The Siege of Rhodes* (p. 689, pl. 116. 1); the dialogue was apparently set to music throughout, and this music was by five composers—H. Lawes (q.v.), H. Cooke (q.v.), Locke (q.v.), C. Coleman, and G. Hudson. Recitative was used, but what it was like it is now impossible to guess. Davenant speaks of recitative as 'unpractised here, though of great reputation among other nations'.

Some similar entertainments followed, until the Restoration in 1660, and the consequent withdrawal of the Puritan embargo on the spoken play, made it possible to reopen the regular theatre, after which opera performances were merely occasional. It will be noted that there was no imitation of the classical mythological subjects of the Italian and French. Two of the operas performed during the Commonwealth were on subjects of national interest, *The Cruelty of the Spaniards in Peru* and *The History of Sir Francis Drake*.

(*b*) Some further opera performances were given under various auspices, and at last was composed a true and valuable opera, in every sense, and one that is still heard frequently and always with delight—Purcell's *Dido and Aeneas*. The dialogue of this is in recitative and the speaking voice is never heard. There is some dancing (see *Ballet* 7). Other so-called operas of Purcell are not true operas, being rather of the nature of incidental music, or operatic insertions in plays. The influence of the masque (q.v.) is very evident in these, and, indeed, it is often said that opera in England is an outgrowth of the masque.

(*c*) The arrival of Handel who visited London and performed his opera *Rinaldo* there in 1711 and settled permanently there from 1712, was the beginning of an almost complete Italian opera conquest of England (see *Handel*).

Throughout the century the aristocracy applauded and overpaid Italian men and women singers, and invited composer after composer of Italian opera to come over and help to administer the fashionable pleasure. There was practically no national element in all this; the language was Italian and the composers and performers were cosmopolitan migrants as much at home in one of the capitals of Europe as another.

(*d*) A national protest against this came in the Ballad Opera (q.v.), beginning with the famous *Beggar's Opera* (q.v.) in 1728. Out of Ballad Opera grew the more pretentious type known as 'English Opera', which term, in its technical sense, means practically the same as the French term *Opéra-comique* (q.v.) or the German term *Singspiel* (q.v.), i.e. it is a musical setting with an admixture of spoken dialogue. Bishop, Balfe, Wallace, and Benedict were some composers of this kind of opera in the middle part of the nineteenth century.

(*e*) 'Grand Opera' (see 7, end) from the pen of the British composer really only begins in the mid-nineteenth century, and then there is not much of it. Towards the end of the nineteenth century Goring Thomas, Mackenzie, and Stanford produced able works, as later did Ethel Smyth, Holst, Vaughan Williams, Walton, Tippett, and above all Britten. But in general the later nineteenth- and twentieth-century British opera-goer has wanted to hear the standard Italian, German, and French works—or, sometimes, apparently, rather to hear famous singers *in* those works.

Britain is not an operatic country: a proportion of the population loves opera, but in the main orchestral, choral, and piano music have usually enjoyed more support. Perhaps if the native type of opera had been followed up things might have been different. There was great popularity for the old Ballad Opera and 'English Opera', from the *Beggar's Opera* in 1728 down to the palmy days of Bishop, Balfe, and Wallace; and after that there is to be found no native opera enjoying a widespread and lasting popularity except the Gilbert and Sullivan series—which belongs to that very type. Theoretically 'Grand' opera is a higher artistic type than opera with spoken dialogue, because more homogeneous; yet it seems to suit the British taste less well—partly perhaps because the words are less clearly heard and the action is slower, and probably because it is more pretentious—less intimate. Cost comes in, too; up to 1930, when Mr. Philip (later Viscount) Snowden, as Chancellor of the Exchequer in a Socialist Government, offered a small subsidy (later withdrawn), opera in Britain had to be self-supporting, whereas Continental governments and municipalities have always given large annual grants. However, with the coming into existence of the Arts Council (q.v.), a welcome financial backing became available. Thanks largely to this support, opera is no longer confined to London but is provided in some measure elsewhere by tours of the

Sadler's Wells company; by seasons given by the Scottish Opera and the Welsh National Opera, and by various 'intimate' or 'shoe-string' groups.

14. Chronological List of British Opera Composers. British opera composers who receive separate notice under their own names are:

Henry Cooke (1616–72); Locke (1630–77); Purcell (c. 1658–95); Weldon (1676–1736); Carey (c. 1690–1743); Greene (1695–1755); Arne (1710–78); Boyce (1710–79); W. Jackson (1730–1803); T. Linley, senior (1732–95); Battishill (1738–1801); Samuel Arnold (1740–1802); Dibdin (1745–1814); Shield (1748–1829); Storace (1763–96); Attwood (1765–1838); Mazzinghi (1765–1844); Braham (1777–1856); T. S. Cooke (1782–1848); Hawes (1785–1846); Horn (1786–1849); Bishop (1786–1855); G. Linley, junior (1798–1865); Balfe (1808–70); Hullah (1812–84); Wallace (1812–65); Loder (1813–65); Pierson (1815–73); Sullivan (1842–1900); Cellier (1844–91); Mackenzie (1847–1935); Goring Thomas (1850–92); Cowen (1852–1935); Stanford (1852–1924); Smyth (1858–1944); German (1862–1936); Delius (1862–1934); Drysdale (1866–1909); Bantock (1868–1946); MacCunn (1868–1916); Vaughan Williams (1872–1958); Alex. M. Maclean (1872–1936); Holst (1874–1934); Tovey (1875–1940); Martin Shaw (1875–1958); Holbrooke (1878–1958); Boughton (1878–1960); Goossens (1893–1962); Walton (born 1902); Tippett (born 1905); Britten (1913–76); Williamson (born 1931); Goehr (born 1932): Crosse (born 1937).

15. Opera in Spain. In the eighteenth century Italian opera was everywhere, Spain included, and in such a city as Barcelona the composers whose works were heard were much the same as those whose works were heard in (say) Naples, Vienna, or London. But the Spanish had native popular forms of their own. The *Zarzuela* (q.v), an immensely popular type of theatrical performance (generally one act and humorous in character), with a very long history yet still quite alive today, resembles 'English Opera' (q.v.), or perhaps, more closely, the old French *Vaudeville* (q.v.), or the German *Singspiel* (q.v.), i.e. it has spoken dialogue, interspersed with songs, choruses, and dances.

Amongst modern composers of the Zarzuela are Tomás Bretón (1850–1923) and Ruperto Chapí (1851–1909).

Pedrell (q.v.) wrote several operas, but they are very little known. Later operas have been composed by Granados (q.v.) and, especially, Falla (q.v.). The much discussed *Goyescas* of Granados (first production, New York, 1916) is, curiously, a series of piano pieces recast into an opera; it has an intensely national flavour. Falla's *Brief Life* ('La Vida breve', 1905) and his short *Master Peter's Puppet Show* ('Il Retablo de Maese Pedro', first performed 1923) are also expressions of national feeling in national idiom; they are much more 'modern' in their technical methods than the work of Granados.

For more on opera in Spain see *Spain* 6, *Albéniz*.

16. Chronological List of Spanish Opera Composers. Spanish opera composers who are the subject of separate notices in this volume are:

Eslava (1807–78); Pedrell (1841–1922); Bretón (1850–1923); I. Albéniz (1860–1909); E. Granados, senior (1867–1916); Falla (1876–1946); Turina (1882–1949); Esplá (1886–1976); E. Granados, junior (1894–1928).

17. Opera in Russia. (a) Like other countries, this one had certain native dramatic-musical entertainments similar to the mysteries, masques, etc. But the actual opera came to this country, as to others, from Italy. The influence of the Florentines approached Russia in 1635, when the libretto (possibly the music, too) of Peri's *Daphne*, after forty years, reached Poland; it was there performed, in the original Italian, in Warsaw, and also published in several editions, and early in the eighteenth century was translated into Russian and published in St. Petersburg; possibly it was performed there.

A permanent opera was founded by the Empress Anne, who in 1734 imported an Italian company with the Neapolitan Araja (1700–70); a great many of this composer's operas were performed during the next fifteen years, some of them to the usual libretti of Metastasio. A few of Araja's operas were translated into Russian and sung in that language by a native company. Nearly all were treatments of the regular classical subjects; it is curious to see how automatically and for how long a period every country accepted the idea that opera was a classical art revived and that the suitable subjects were those from classical mythology and history.

From this time there was a steady coming and going between the operatic centres of Italy and the Russian capital. Singers and composers were constantly posting along this route. Amongst the leading Italians who resided in Russia were Galuppi (1706–1785), Traetta (1727–79), Sarti (1729–1802), Paesiello (1740–1816), and Cimarosa (1749–1801). All these held lucrative court positions in St. Petersburg, as did a host of lesser men. Some Russian composers were sent to Italy for training, and their operas, in the Italian style, were performed there.

(b) Under Catherine the Great (reigned 1762–96) not only was the Italian opera continued but a measure of native activity arose. Fomin (1761–1800) was one of the first Russian composers, but it is worthy of notice that he was sent to Italy for training, and that the opinion of the famous Padre Martini was asked before his setting of a libretto by the Empress herself was put into rehearsal. However, with Fomin, treatment of Russian subjects in the Russian language became accepted, and henceforth native composers, trained in Italy and writing in an Italian style, enjoyed a good deal of popularity and were apparently allowed to use Italian or Russian indifferently. A French company was for a long time supported by the court, and at the beginning of the nineteenth century there were three companies active together in the capital, Italian, French, and

Russian—all under the direction of the Italian, Catterino Cavos (1776–1840), who composed operas for them in the three languages; he was over forty years in St. Petersburg and there died.

From 1776 to 1805 an Englishman, Maddox, successfully carried on an opera-house in Moscow, where he produced a large number of Italian and French operas, and also a good many by Fomin and other native composers.

Gradually native pride began to exert influence on opera and native composers to become more common; Verstovsky (1799–1862), a pupil of the Irishman Field and others, became director of the Moscow opera in 1823 and composed a number of Russian operas, and he is only one of several who came to the front about this time.

(c) Verstovsky was a contemporary of the composer who now, on account of his higher abilities and his greater national feeling, is looked upon as the true founder of Russian opera—Glinka. His *A Life for the Czar*, on a thoroughly national subject, and with some folk influence showing in the music, was produced in St. Petersburg in 1836 (see *Glinka*); this work became a great source of national pride; in its first forty-three years it had 500 performances, and its jubilee was celebrated by performances in every opera-house in Russia. *Ruslan and Liudmila* followed.

Dargomijsky, emulating Glinka and directly influenced by him, in his *Russalka* (1856) and *The Stone Guest* (performed in 1872—after his death), really surpassed his model in the element of what we call 'truth' in dramatic representation: his ideals are much those of Gluck (or of his contemporary Wagner, of whose works he knew nothing).

Rimsky-Korsakof's *Ivan the Terrible* (or 'The Maid of Pskof', 1873), Mussorgsky's *Boris Godunof* (1874), and Borodin's *Prince Igor* (1890) are a few other landmarks: further information as to the activities of these composers should be sought under their own names.

(d) Russian opera first penetrated to the Western world in 1908 when Diaghilef (see *Ballet* 5) produced Mussorgsky's *Boris Godunof* in Paris, with Chaliapin as a member of his company. In March 1913 this opera was heard at the Metropolitan Opera House in New York,[1] and three months later it was heard at Drury Lane Theatre in London as a part of the programme of the wonderful series of Russian ballet and opera performances given there by Diaghilef under the auspices of Sir Joseph Beecham. Thence onward Europe and America became more or less familiar with Russian musical stage activities—unfortunately from thirty to forty years later than they should have begun to do so. The oriental tinge in the stage settings and the music, the vigour of the acting, the beauty of much of the singing, and

above all, the freshness of outlook due to the Russian nationalist school having so largely grown up in deliberate isolation—all these made a very powerful impression. (See also an allusion to Russian opera under *Ballet* 7.)

The more 'modern' outlook and technique are seen in the works of Stravinsky and Prokofief; other composers, such as Shostakovich, who have remained in their own country have tended to a degree of conservatism (see Russia 8).

18. Chronological List of Russian Opera Composers. The following is a list of the Russian opera composers who have received separate treatment in this volume:

Alabief (1787–1851); Verstovsky (1799–1862); Glinka (1804–57); Dargomijsky (1813–69); Serof (1820–71); A. Rubinstein (1829–94); Borodin (1833–87); Cui (1835–1918); Mussorgsky (1839–81); Napravnik (1839–1916); Tchaikovsky (1840–93); Rimsky-Korsakof (1844–1908); Taneief (1856–1915); Ippolitof-Ivanof (1859–1935); Arensky (1861–1906); Gretchaninof (1864–1956); Rebikof (1866–1920); Rachmaninof (1873–1943); Glière (1875–1956); Stravinsky (1882–1971); A. A. Krein (1883–1951); Prokofief (1891–1953); Knipper (born 1898); Kabalevsky (born 1904); Shostakovich (1906–75); Dzerzhinsky (born 1909); Khrennikof (born 1913).

19. Czech Opera. It is obviously impossible in a volume of this size to describe the development of opera in every country (and indeed it would be difficult to find a volume of any size where so comprehensive a treatment as that is to be seen). One more European country, however, has a definite right to a few words —Bohemia. The importance of Prague as an operatic centre is of long standing. Under the Austrian domination, which lasted for three centuries (1620–1918), national aspirations were not encouraged. An opera-house was founded in Prague in 1725; it welcomed the leading composers of the eighteenth century; some of Gluck's operas and Mozart's *Don Giovanni* had their first performances there. In 1860 the country won a new constitution, the Czech language was made compulsory in schools, and a National Opera House came into existence (1862). The Czech composer Smetana, from 1866 to 1882, produced a series of eight works in the Czech language and on national subjects (see *Smetana*); these form the basis of Czech opera as Glinka's *A Life for the Czar* does of Russian opera.

Dvořák, from 1874 to 1904, produced a similar series of nine operas, and the Czech race was now supplied with a national repertory.

Janáček followed. His *Jenufa* (this is the German title by which it is known abroad, the Czech title being 'Jeji Pastorkyna'—'Her Foster-daughter') had a performance in Brno in 1904, but had to wait twelve years for one in Prague, after which it became widely known both in and out of its native country (New York, 1924). It is very original in style, influenced neither by Smetana nor by the generally prevailing post-Wagnerism of the period.

---

[1] This opera-house had already performed Tchaikovsky's *Queen of Spades* in 1910, and before this Damrosch had given a concert performance of the same composer's *Eugen Onegin*.

Four or five other operas followed, all very novel in conception and treatment.

20. Chronological List of Czech Opera Composers. The Czech opera composers who receive separate treatment in this volume are as follows:

Smetana (1824–84); Dvořák (1841–1904); Brüll (1846–1907); Fibich (1850–1900); Janáček (1854–1928); Foerster (1859–1951); Novák (1870–1949); Jirák (1891–1972).

21. Opera in the American Colonies and the United States. (a) When opera first reached North America it was a purely English product imported into the English colonies. The period when it began to make its appearance was that of the advent of the ballad opera type in England (cf. *Ballad Opera*).

The first opera performed is thought to have been *Flora, or Hob in the Well*, in the courtroom of Charleston, South Carolina, in 1735. This had been both performed and published in London six years before. Its authorship is uncertain. It was in two acts and had twenty-four songs. It was on the general lines of *The Beggar's Opera*; the title-page of the London publication called it 'Mr. Dogget's Farce of the Country-Wake, alter'd after the manner of the Beggar's Opera'. It was O. G. Sonneck who unearthed the facts as to its performances; there are some who think that further research may bring to light prior performances in the American colonies of *The Beggar's Opera* itself, whose triumphant vogue in England would, one imagines, be likely to cause its appearance in America earlier than 1750, the year of the first performance there as yet discovered (in the 'Theatre in Nassau Street', New York; this performance took place no less than twenty-two years after the production in London).

English ballad opera had apparently a clear run, without rival, of fifty-five years, i.e. from 1735 to 1790, and then in the French-speaking part of America **French Opera** began, New Orleans becoming the headquarters of a body of French actors who left it from time to time to visit Charleston, Baltimore, Philadelphia, and New York, performing the operas of Rousseau, Dalayrac, Monsigny, Grétry, and others.

The first mention of **Italian Opera** is in 1794, when Paesiello's *Barber of Seville* was given (but in English) in Baltimore, Philadelphia, New York, and some other centres.

(b) The first **American Operas** seem to have been James Hewitt's *Tammany* (New York, 1794) and B. Carr's *The Archers of Switzerland* (New York, 1796), but these composers were not American-born; they had arrived from England only a few years earlier. Their work was on the lines of the English Opera of the period, which at this time and later was popular in America—that of Arne, Arnold, Storace, Shield, Dibdin, etc. (for complete lists see Sonneck's *Early Opera in America*). An opera called *Disappointment*, by Andrew Barton, was published in Philadelphia in 1767 but not performed.

Another American opera followed in the same year as Carr's and in the same city, the *Edwin and Angelina* of Pélissier, a French horn-player active in theatrical music. It has been suggested that 'the first successful American opera' was *The Saw-Mill, or a Yankee Trick*, by Micah Hawkins (New York, 1824).

(c) In 1819 Rossini's *Barber of Seville* was played (in English) at New York: this was pretty prompt for those days, as its original production (in Rome) had taken place only three years previously. Probably the English version used in New York was that used shortly before in Covent Gardent Theatre. It is worthy of notice that New York heard Rossini's *Barber* six months after London and six months before Paris. In 1825 New York heard this same opera in Italian; it was the first opera ever to be sung in that language in that city.

Another prompt importation was Bishop's *Clari, the Maid of Milan*, which was heard at Covent Garden in May 1823 and at New York the same year. The author of the libretto was John Howard Payne (1791–1852), the notable American actor and dramatist, then resident in Paris. He took the plot from a French piece with a similar name. His lyric 'Home, Sweet Home' (q.v.) appears for the first time in this opera; Bishop's music to it had appeared to other words in an album of national melodies.

(d) An opera of Mozart was heard in North America for the first time two years later (1825) —Mozart's *Figaro*, not as Mozart wrote it, however, but in an English adaptation by that same Bishop. It was at New York that this was given. Two years later (1827) Weber was heard at New York—his *Marksman* ('Freischütz'), in English.

In that same year, 1825, Rossini enjoyed quite a vogue in New York, for Manuel Garcia's famous company appeared there with not only his *Barber of Seville* (which, as already stated, had been heard there six years previously), but also his *Tancredi, Semiramide, The Turk in Italy*, and *Cinderella* ('La Cenerentola'). Mozart's *Don Giovanni* was also given—really a wonderful opera festival. Garcia's company included his son, Manuel junior, and his daughter (soon to be known as Malibran), and his son's wife. The party travelled on to Mexico, where brigands stripped them of all they possessed.

(e) New Orleans continued to be a centre of French opera, and its company travelled to Philadelphia, New York, and other cities, and thus about this time some of the operas of Boïeldieu became familiar to music-loving Americans. His *The White Lady* ('La Dame blanche'), produced in Paris in December 1825 and at London in January 1827, was heard in these American cities in July 1827. It will be seen that, once what we may call the Mozart period was over, America, so far as first performance was concerned, kept pace with

Europe better than has sometimes been realized.

Weber's *Oberon* was heard at Philadelphia in 1827, Mozart's *Magic Flute* in the same place in 1832.

(*f*) In this latter year occurred the noteworthy Italian opera performances at New York organized by da Ponte (1749–1838), the quondam storekeeper of Elizabethtown, New Jersey, and distiller of Sunbury, Pennsylvania, now a teacher in New York. He was the proud librettist of Mozart's *Figaro*, *Don Giovanni* (whose New York performance mentioned above he had been instrumental in bringing about—'my Don Giovanni', he called it), and *Così fan tutte*. He was successful in inducing an Italian troupe, directed by one Montressor or Montrésor, to come and give a season at New York. In 1833, at da Ponte's instigation, a luxurious Italian Opera House was built in New York. It soon turned into an ordinary theatre, but Italian opera had been established in the American mind as a desirable entertainment and the records of the following years show many performances.

(*g*) The name of Meyerbeer apparently figures for the first time in the list of American theatrical activities in 1834, when his *Robert the Devil* (then three years old) was given in English in New York. Beethoven's *Fidelio* was heard there in 1839.

About the 1840s we see a good deal of Auber and Donizetti in the lists. Balfe's *Bohemian Girl* was given in 1844, one year after its production in London.

(*h*) It is surely now about time that a native example of 'grand' opera should appear, and it does so in 1845—William H. Fry's *Leonora*, given at Philadelphia, the composer's native city (born 1813; died 1864).

Wallace's *Maritana*, produced in London in 1845, was heard at Philadelphia in 1848. America had now quickly made acquaintance with the two typical English operas of this period—Balfe's *Bohemian Girl* and Wallace's *Maritana*.

(*i*) 'Grand' opera began to reach out West in the early fifties. It got to Chicago in 1850; Bellini's *The Sleepwalker* ('La Sonnambula') was the first 'grand' opera heard there. San Francisco began to learn what operas were in 1853 —Verdi's *Ernani* was the first. Verdi had been heard in New York in 1850 (*Attila* and *Macbeth*) and henceforth his fame may be considered as established in America.

(*j*) German opera in the German language seems to have begun at New York in 1855 with a series including Weber's *The Marksman* ('Der Freischütz'), Flotow's *Martha*, and Lortzing's *Czar and Carpenter* ('Zar und Zimmermann'). In this year another native opera attracted attention, the *Rip Van Winkle* of George F. Bristow (1825–98). He was a friend of Fry, the production of whose *Leonora*, ten years earlier, has been mentioned above, and the two of them carried on the campaign in favour of the American composer—who at that

period was hardly numerous enough to be capable of backing up his defenders, but was soon to emerge in some force (though not at all prominently in opera).

(*k*) Extracts from Wagner had been by this time heard in the concert-room, and in 1859 his *Tannhaüser* (produced in Germany fourteen years earlier) was thus performed at New York under the devoted conductor Bergmann. His *Flying Dutchman* (produced in Germany sixteen years earlier) had a concert performance under Theodore Thomas in the same city three years later. A concert selection of *The Mastersingers* was given in New York in 1870.

Lohengrin was given its first American stage performance in New York in 1871 (see *Conducting*); it reached Boston in 1874.

The Flying Dutchman was heard in 1876 in Philadelphia (in Italian). *Rienzi* and *The Valkyrie* were given in New York the following year (Bizet's *Carmen* reached the same city that year).

In 1883, the year of Wagner's death, the Metropolitan Opera House, New York, was opened, but still the hearing of most of the bigger things of Wagner was delayed, until in 1886 *The Mastersingers* was given there under Anton Seidl. *Tristan* was given the same year. In 1888 *The Ring* was given complete, under the same conductor. These were the palmy days of German opera in New York, the chief influence in leading taste in that direction being Dr. Leopold Damrosch.

(*l*) In this year Verdi's *Othello* was also given in New York, so now the greater Wagner and the greater Verdi had both had recognition. *Othello* had been heard in Italy only the previous year and England did not hear it until the next year. In 1895 the same composer's *Falstaff* (then two years old) was given.

The nineties saw the beginnings of the taste for Puccini (*Manon* in Philadelphia, 1894; *La Bohème* in San Francisco and New York in 1898); after this all the Puccini operas were heard in America very quickly after their appearance in their own country.

(*m*) In 1913, the copyright of Wagner's *Parsifal* expiring, his intention that it should be reserved strictly for Bayreuth was ignored and it was given in New York and forty-six other American cities, to say nothing of other countries.

Strauss's *Salome* was heard in New York in 1907 and his *Elektra* in 1910—two years and one year respectively after their initial performances in Germany. The New York *Salome* performance led to an uproar (on moral and religious grounds) without precedent, and performance in Boston was for a time forbidden.

Russian opera began to be a little heard in America about the same time as in England—Mussorgsky's *Boris Godunof*, 1913; Borodin's *Prince Igor*, 1915; Rimsky-Korsakof's *Golden Cockerel*, 1918 (all in New York).

Debussy's *Pelléas* was heard in 1908, six years after the Paris production, and Ravel's

Heure espagnole in 1920, nine years after the Paris production.

But all this (or nearly all) refers to exotic opera. The dates of first productions of a number of native operas will be found in the general table appended, but until the mid-twentieth century neither the United States nor Great Britain could claim a single work in the regular repertory of the world's opera-houses. Nevertheless by 1959 there was a distinct school of American opera composers writing in an idiom deriving partly from the Broadway 'musical' and partly from Italian opera.

An enormous upsurge was stimulated in 1959 by the Ford Foundation, which gave a total of $950,000 for the commissioning of 18 operas over the next decade, with the object of establishing an American repertory. Most of the commissions went via New York's City Centre, the remainder via the Metropolitan and the Chicago and San Francisco companies.

It will be noticed on glancing over the above list that for the first century or more of operatic activity the centres were New Orleans and New York and the cities that lie between them. New England's interest awoke later, and the West took to opera as its settlement and civilization developed.

Though over 450 opera-performing organizations are listed, by far the greater number of these are on a very small scale, usually amateur. There are two companies with long regular seasons, the Metropolitan and the City Centre, both in New York. Chicago and San Francisco both have brief seasons, and there are short summer festivals in Santa Fe, Dallas, and elsewhere.

22. Opera Composers of other Nationalities than the above. The following receive brief separate treatment in this volume under their own names:

(*a*) **Belgian.** Gossec (1734–1829); Grétry (1741–1813); Gresnick (1755–99); Campenhout (1779–1848); Blockx (1851–1912); Tinel (1854–1912); Gilson (1865–1942); De Boeck (1865–1937). See also *Belgium* 4, 6.

(*b*) **Danish.** Heise (1830–79); Nielsen (1865–1931).

(*c*) **Finnish.** Merikanto (1868–1924).

(*d*) **Hungarian.** Goldmark (1830–1915); Czibulka (1842–94); Dohnányi (1877–1960); Bartók (1881–1945).

(*e*) **Norwegian.** Olsen (1850–1927); Sinding (1856–1941).

(*f*) **Polish.** Paderewski (1860–1941); Szymanowski (1882–1937).

(*g*) **Rumanian.** Enesco (1881–1955).

It will be understood that many of the lists of opera composers given above include the names of men who have needlessly complicated the task of lexicographers by not being born in the country of their race or by carrying on their work in some country of neither their birth nor their race. An effort has been made to place these individuals under the most appropriate classification, but in a few cases what that is may be a legitimate cause for difference of opinion.

23. Opera-houses (p. 720, pls. 119–20). At first opera (like its predecessor the masque) was a fashionable ceremonial festive entertainment, but it quickly reached the general public, and special theatres for it were opened as follows: 1637, Venice; 1656, London; 1669, Paris; 1671, Rome; 1678, Hamburg. After that such houses became very common. The many petty German princes had them, and often opened them to the public. (See also *Poland*.)

In America New Orleans had the Théâtre St. Philippe in 1808, New York the Italian Opera House promoted by da Ponte in 1833 (see 21 f above).

Covent Garden Theatre, London, was opened in 1732, and the present house (opened 1858) is the third on the site, the previous houses having been burnt.

The Metropolitan Opera House, New York (see section 21), was opened in 1883 and rebuilt in 1893, the previous one having been burnt (it may almost be said that all opera-houses are sooner or later destroyed by fire). It was replaced by a building in the Lincoln Center (q.v.) in 1966.

See also under *Victoria Hall*; *Sadler's Wells*.

24. A Survey of Historical First Performances. This list includes (i) works that have influenced the development of opera, (ii) works that retain an important place in the repertory, and (iii) works by British and American composers that represent the efforts of these two nations to establish a permanent footing in the field of operatic composition.

(*a*) **Sixteenth Century.** 1597 Peri's *Daphne* in Florence.

(*b*) **Seventeenth Century.** 1600 Peri's *Eurydice* in Florence (some portions by Caccini). 1607 Monteverdi's *Orpheus* in Mantua. 1627 Schütz's *Daphne* in Torgau (first German opera—an adaptation of Peri's). 1642 Monteverdi's *The Coronation of Poppaea* in Venice. 1647 Rossi's *Marriage of Orpheus and Eurydice* in Paris. 1671 Cambert's *Pomone* in Paris (first French opera). 1673 Lully's *Cadmus and Hermione* in Paris. 1676 Lully's *Atys* in Paris. 1678 Theile's *Adam and Eve* in Hamburg (precursor of Singspiel) *c.* 1689. Purcell's *Dido and Aeneas* in a London school for young ladies.

(*c*) **Eighteenth Century.** 1711 Handel's *Rinaldo* in London. 1728 *The Beggar's Opera* (book by Gay; music chosen by Pepusch) in London. 1733 Pergolese's *The Servant as Mistress* ('La Serva padrona') in Naples; Rameau's *Hippolytus and Aricia* in Paris. 1737 Rameau's *Castor and Pollux* in Paris. 1739 Rameau's *Dardanus* in Paris. 1752 Rousseau's *The Village Soothsayer* ('Le Devin du village') in Fontainebleau. 1753 Dauvergne's *The Hucksters* ('Les Troqueurs') in Paris. 1762 Arne's *Artaxerxes* in London; Gluck's *Orpheus and Eurydice* in Vienna (revised version in Paris twelve years later). 1767 Gluck's *Alcestis* in Vienna (revised version in Paris nine years later). 1769 Monsigny's *The Deserter* in Paris. 1774 Gluck's *Iphigenia in Aulis* in Paris. 1777 Gluck's *Armida* in Paris. 1779 Gluck's *Iphigenia in Tauris* in Paris. 1784 Grétry's *Richard Cœur de Lion* in Paris. 1786 Mozart's *The Marriage of Figaro* in Vienna. 1787 Mozart's *Don Giovanni* in Prague. 1791 Mozart's *The Magic Flute* in Vienna. 1792 Cimarosa's *The Secret Marriage* in Vienna. 1796 Carr's *The*

Archers of Switzerland in New York; Pélissier's *Edwin and Angelina* in New York.

(*d*) **Nineteenth Century—First Half.** 1800 Cherubini's *The Water Carrier* ('Les Deux Journées') in Paris; Boïeldieu's *The Caliph of Baghdad* in Paris. 1805 Beethoven's *Fidelio* in Vienna. 1807 Spontini's *The Vestal Virgin* in Paris; Méhul's *Joseph* in Paris. 1816 Rossini's *The Barber of Seville* in Rome. 1821 Weber's *The Marksman* ('Der Freischütz') in Berlin. 1823 Weber's *Euryanthe* in Vienna. 1826 Weber's *Oberon* in London. 1828 Auber's *Masaniello* ('La Muette de Portici') in Paris. 1829 Rossini's *William Tell* in Paris. 1830 Auber's *Fra Diavolo* in Paris. 1831 Hérold's *Zampa* in Paris; Bellini's *The Sleepwalker* ('La Sonnambula') in Milan; Bellini's *Norma* in Milan; Meyerbeer's *Robert the Devil* in Paris. 1835 Halévy's *The Jewess* ('La Juive') in Paris; Donizetti's *Lucy of Lammermoor* in Naples. 1836 Meyerbeer's *The Huguenots* in Paris; Glinka's *A Life for the Czar* in St. Petersburg. 1840 Donizetti's *The Daughter of the Regiment* in Paris. 1841 Auber's *The Crown Diamonds* in Paris. 1842 Glinka's *Ruslan and Liudmila* in St. Petersburg; Wagner's *Rienzi* in Dresden; Verdi's *Nebuchadnezzar* in Milan. 1843 Wagner's *The Flying Dutchman* in Dresden; Donizetti's *Don Pasquale* in Paris; Balfe's *The Bohemian Girl* in London. 1844 Verdi's *Ernani* in Venice. 1845 Fry's *Leonora* in Philadelphia; Wagner's *Tannhäuser* in Dresden; Wallace's *Maritana* in London. 1846 Loder's *The Night Dancers* in London. 1847 Flotow's *Martha* in Vienna. 1849 Nicolai's *The Merry Wives of Windsor* in Berlin; Meyerbeer's *The Prophet* in Paris.

(*e*) **Nineteenth Century—Second Half.** 1850 Wagner's *Lohengrin* in Weimar. 1851 Verdi's *Rigoletto* in Venice. 1853 Verdi's *The Troubadour* ('Il Trovatore') in Rome; Verdi's *La Traviata* in Venice. 1855 Bristow's *Rip Van Winkle* in New York. 1856 Dargomijsky's *Russalka* ('The Water Sprite') in St. Petersburg. 1858 Cornelius's *The Barber of Baghdad* in Weimar; Offenbach's *Orpheus in the Underworld* ('Orphée aux Enfers'; recast in 1874) in Paris. 1859 Gounod's *Faust* in Paris. 1862 Benedict's *The Lily of Killarney* in London. 1863 Berlioz's *The Trojans at Carthage* in Paris (i.e. Part 2 of *The Trojans*; for Part 1 see 1890). 1864 Fry's *Notre Dame de Paris* in Philadelphia. 1865 Wagner's *Tristan and Isolde* in Munich. 1866 Smetana's *The Bartered Bride* in Prague; Ambroise Thomas's *Mignon* in Paris. 1867 Gounod's *Romeo and Juliet* in Paris; Offenbach's *Grand Duchess of Gérolstein* in Paris; Sullivan's *Cox and Box* in London. 1868 Wagner's *The Mastersingers of Nuremberg* in Munich; Boito's *Mephistopheles* in Milan. 1869 Wagner's *The Rhinegold* in Munich. 1870 Wagner's *The Valkyrie* in Munich. 1871 Verdi's *Aïda* in Cairo. 1872 Lecocq's *Madame Angot's Daughter* in Brussels; Dargomijsky's *The Stone Guest* in St. Petersburg. 1873 Rimsky-Korsakof's *Ivan the Terrible* ('Pskovitianka') in St. Petersburg. 1874 Mussorgsky's *Boris Godunof* in St. Petersburg; Goetz's *The Taming of the Shrew* in Mannheim; Johann Strauss's *The Bat* ('Die Fledermaus') in Vienna. 1875 Bizet's *Carmen* in Paris; Sullivan's *Trial by Jury* in London (beginning of the Gilbert and Sullivan partnership); Goldmark's *Queen of Sheba* in Vienna. 1876 Wagner's *The Ring of the Nibelung* complete (i.e. including *Siegfried* and *The Dusk of the Gods* now first performed) in Bayreuth; Ponchielli's *La Gioconda* in Milan. 1877 Saint-Saëns's *Samson and Delilah* in Weimar; Sullivan's *The Sorcerer* in London. 1878 Sullivan's *H.M.S. Pinafore* in London. 1879 Tchaikovsky's *Eugen Onegin* in Moscow; Sullivan's *The Pirates of Penzance* in Paignton. 1881 Sullivan's *Patience* in London; Offenbach's

The Tales of Hoffmann in Paris; Stanford's *The Veiled Prophet* in Hanover. 1882 Rimsky-Korsakof's *Snow Maiden* ('Snegoúrotchka') in St. Petersburg; Wagner's *Parsifal* in Bayreuth; Sullivan's *Iolanthe* in London. 1883 Mackenzie's *Colomba* in London; Delibes's *Lakmé*. 1884 Stanford's *Savonarola* in Hamburg; Stanford's *The Canterbury Pilgrims* in London; Massenet's *Manon* in Paris; Sullivan's *Princess Ida* in London. 1885 Goring Thomas's *Nadeshda* in London; Sullivan's *The Mikado* in London. 1886 Mussorgsky's *Khovantchina* in St. Petersburg; Mackenzie's *The Troubadour* in London. 1887 Verdi's *Othello* in Milan; Sullivan's *Ruddigore* in London. 1888 Sullivan's *The Yeomen of the Guard* in London. 1889 Sullivan's *The Gondoliers* in London. 1890 Mascagni's *Rustic Chivalry* ('Cavalleria Rusticana') in Rome; Borodin's *Prince Igor* in St. Petersburg; Berlioz's *The Taking of Troy* (first part of *The Trojans*; for second part see 1863) in Karlsruhe; Tchaikovsky's *The Queen of Spades* ('Pique Dame') in St. Petersburg. 1892 Massenet's *Werther* in Vienna; Leoncavallo's *I Pagliacci* in Milan. 1893 Verdi's *Falstaff* in Milan; Humperdinck's *Hänsel and Gretel* in Weimar; Sullivan's *Utopia Limited* in London; Puccini's *Manon Lescaut* in Turin; Bruneau's *Attack on the Mill* in Paris. 1894 Massenet's *Thaïs* in Paris; Strauss's *Guntram* in Weimar. 1895 Alick Maclean's *Petruccio* in London. 1896 Stanford's *Shamus O'Brien* in London (Breslau, 1907); Wolf's *The Corregidor* in Mannheim; Giordano's *André Chénier* in Milan; Puccini's *La Bohème* in Turin; Sullivan's *The Grand Duke* in London (end of the Gilbert and Sullivan partnership). 1897 d'Indy's *Fervaal* in Brussels; Mackenzie's *His Majesty* in London. 1898 Giordano's *Fedora* in Milan.

(*f*) **Twentieth Century.** 1900 Puccini's *Tosca* in Rome; Charpentier's *Louise* in Paris. 1901 Dvořák's *Russalka* (the favourite of all his operas, amongst his countrymen) in Prague; Strauss's *The Fire Famine* ('Feuersnot') in Dresden; Stanford's *Much Ado about Nothing* in London (Leipzig following year). 1902 Smyth's *Der Wald* ('The Forest') in Berlin (London same year); Cilèa's *Adriana Lecouvreur* in Milan. Debussy's *Pelléas and Mélisande* in Paris. 1903 d'Albert's *Tiefland* in Prague. 1904 Puccini's *Madam Butterfly* in Milan; Delius's *Koanga* in Elberfeld. 1905 Strauss's *Salome* in Dresden; Coerne's *Zenobia* in Bremen (first European production of an American opera). 1906 Converse's *The Pipe of Desire* in Boston; Gatty's *Greysteel* in Sheffield; Alick Maclean's *Die Liebesgeige* in Mainz; Smyth's *The Wreckers* in Leipzig (London, 1909). 1907 Delius's *A Village Romeo and Juliet* in Berlin; Dukas's *Ariadne and Bluebeard* in Paris. 1909 Strauss's *Elektra* in Dresden; Rimsky-Korsakof's *The Golden Cockerel* in Moscow; Gatty's *Duke or Devil* in Manchester; Wolf-Ferrari's *Susanna's Secret* in Munich; Alick Maclean's *Maître Seiler* in London. 1910 Puccini's *The Girl of the Golden West* in New York. 1911 Strauss's *The Rose Cavalier* in Dresden; Ravel's *The Spanish Hour* ('L'Heure espagnole') in Paris; Wolf-Ferrari's *The Jewels of the Madonna* in Berlin; Converse's *The Sacrifice* in Boston; Herbert's *Natoma* in Philadelphia. 1912 Horatio Parker's *Mona* in New York; Schreker's *The Distant Tone* ('Der ferne Klang') in Frankfurt; Strauss's *Ariadne in Naxos* in Stuttgart (new version in 1916). 1913 Walter Damrosch's *Cyrano de Bergerac* in New York; Falla's *Brief Life* ('La Vida breve') in Nice. 1914 Stravinsky's *The Nightingale* in Paris; Herbert's *Madeleine* in New York; Mackenzie's *The Cricket on the Hearth* in London; Boughton's *The Immortal Hour* in Glastonbury. 1916 Granados's *Goyescas* in New York; Boughton's *Bethlehem* in Glastonbury; Smyth's *The Boatswain's Mate* in

London; Holst's *Sāvitri* in London; Stanford's *The Critic* in London; Boughton's *The Round Table* in Glastonbury. 1917 de Koven's *The Canterbury Pilgrims* in New York; Pfitzner's *Palestrina* in Munich; Busoni's *Harlequin* and *Turandot* in Zürich. 1918 Bartók's *Duke Bluebeard's Castle* in Buda-Pesth; Nevin's *A Daughter of the Forest* in Chicago; Puccini's *The Cloak* ('Il Tabarro'), *Sister Angelica* ('Suor Angelica'), and *Gianni Schicchi* in New York; Cadman's *Shanewis* in New York; Schreker's *The Branded* ('Die Gezeichneten') in Frankfort. 1919 Strauss's *The Woman without a Shadow* in Vienna; Delius's *Fennimore and Gerda* in Frankfurt-on-Main; Gatty's *Prince Ferelon* in London; Boughton's *The Birth of Arthur* in Glastonbury. 1920 d'Indy's *The Legend of St. Christopher* in Paris; Korngold's *The Dead City* in Hamburg; de Koven's *Rip Van Winkle* in Chicago; Hadley's *Cleopatra's Night* in New York; Gatty's *The Tempest* in London; Alick Maclean's *Quentin Durward* in Newcastle-on-Tyne. 1922 Boughton's *Alkestis* in Glastonbury; Stravinsky's *Mavra* and *Renard* in Paris; Pizzetti's *Deborah and Jael* in Milan. 1923 Holst's *The Perfect Fool* in London; Smyth's *Fête Galante* in Birmingham. 1924 Mackenzie's *The Eve of St. John* in Liverpool; Boughton's *The Queen of Cornwall* in Glastonbury; Boito's *Nero* in Milan; Vaughan Williams's *Hugh the Drover* in London; Schreker's *Fitful Flames* ('Irrelohe') in Cologne; Strauss's *Intermezzo* in Dresden. 1925 Ravel's *L'Enfant et les sortilèges* at Monte Carlo; Berg's *Wozzeck* in Berlin; Busoni's *Doctor Faust* in Dresden; Holst's *At the Boar's Head* in Manchester; Smyth's *Entente Cordiale* in London; Stanford's *The Travelling Companion* in Liverpool. 1926 Puccini's *Turandot* in Milan. 1927 Weinberger's *Schwanda the Bagpiper* ('Švanda Dudák') at Prague; Stravinsky's *Oedipus Rex* ('opera-oratorio') in Paris; Deems Taylor's *The King's Henchman* in New York; Křenek's *Jonny spielt auf* in Leipzig. 1928 Strauss's *The Egyptian Helen* in Dresden; Schreker's *The Singing Devil* in Berlin; Weill's *Dreigroschenoper* in Berlin. 1929 Goossens's *Judith* in London; Tovey's *The Bride of Dionysus* in Edinburgh; Vaughan Williams's *Sir John in Love* in London. 1931 Deems Taylor's *Peter Ibbetson* in New York. 1933 Strauss's *Arabella* at Dresden. 1934 Hanson's *Merry Mount* in New York. 1935 Strauss's *Silent Woman* ('Die Schweigsame Frau') in Dresden. 1936 Vaughan Williams's *The Poisoned Kiss* at Cambridge. 1937 Goossens's *Don Juan de Mañara*; Vaughan Williams's *Riders to the Sea* in London; Klenau's *Rembrandt van Rijn* in Berlin and Stuttgart (same day); Respighi's *Lucretia* in Milan; Schoeck's *Massimilla Doni* in Dresden; Honegger and Ibert's *L'Aiglon* at Monte Carlo; Novák's *Signorina Gioventù* in Prague; Menotti's *Amelia goes to the Ball* in Philadelphia; Casella's *Il Deserto tentato* in Florence; Berg's *Lulu* (not completed) in Zürich; Blitzstein's *The Cradle will Rock* (opera-revue) in New York; Dzerzhinsky's *Soil Upturned* in Moscow; Weinberger's *Wallenstein* in Vienna. 1938 Kabalevsky's *Colas Breugnon* in Leningrad; Martinů's *Juliette* in Prague; Malipiero's *Anthony and Cleopatra* in Florence; Hindemith's *Mathis der Maler* in Basle; Giannini's *The Scarlet Letter* in Hamburg; Křenek's *Charles V* in Prague; Strauss's *Der Friedenstag* in Munich and his *Daphne* in Dresden; Egk's *Peer Gynt* in Berlin. 1939 Wolf-Ferrari's *La Dama Boba* in Milan; Menotti's *The Old Maid and the Thief*, broadcast in U.S.A. (staged in Philadelphia in 1941); Douglas Moore's *The Devil and Daniel Webster* in New York; Khrennikof's *In the Storm* in Moscow. 1940 Villa Lobos's *Izaht* in Rio de Janiero; Dallapiccola's *Volo di notte* in Florence; Prokofiev's *Simeon Kotko* in

Moscow; Blitzstein's *No for an Answer* in New York. 1942 Dzerzhinsky's *The Blood of the People* in Tchkalov (by the company of the evacuated Leningrad Opera); Deems Taylor's *Ramuntcho* in Philadelphia; Menotti's *The Island God* in New York; Randall Thompson's *Solomon and Balkis* at Harvard University; Walter Damrosch's *The Opera Cloak* in New York. 1945 Britten's *Peter Grimes* in London. 1946 Britten's *The Rape of Lucretia* at Glyndebourne; Healey Willan's *Deirdre of the Sorrows* broadcast from Toronto. 1947 B. Rogers's *The Warrior* in New York; Menotti's *The Telephone* in New York; Sessions's *The Trial of Lucullus* at the University of California; Virgil Thomson's *The Mother of us All* at Columbia University, New York; Poulenc's *Les Mamelles de Tirésias* in Paris; Britten's *Albert Herring* at Glyndebourne; Einem's *Danton's Death* in Salzburg. 1948 Kodály's *Czinka Panna* in Budapest; Kurt Weill's *Down in the Valley* at Indiana University; Werner Egk's *Circe* in Berlin. 1949 Blitzstein's *Regina* in Boston; Douglas Moore's *White Wings* at Hartford, Conn.; Carl Orff's *Antigone* in Salzburg; Douglas Moore's *The Emperor's New Clothes* in New York; Pizzetti's *Vanna Lupa* in Florence; Hans Werner Henze's *Das Wundertheater* at Heidelberg; Burkhard's *Die schwarze Spinne* ('The Black Spider') at Zürich; Ghedini's *Billy Budd* in Venice; Bliss's *The Olympians* in London. 1950 Kabalevsky's *The Family of Taras* in Moscow; Menotti's *The Consul* in New York; Françaix's *La Main de gloire* at Bordeaux; Dello Joio's *The Triumph of Joan* at Bronxville, N.Y.; Milhaud's *Bolivar* in Paris; Lukas Foss's *The Jumping Frog* at Bloomington, Ind.; Dallapiccola's *Il Prigioniero* in Florence; H. Andriessen's *Philomela* in Amsterdam; A. Gretchaninoff's *The Marriage* in Paris. 1951 Robert Oboussier's *Amphitryon* in Berlin; Douglas Moore's *Giants in the Earth* in New York; Vaughan Williams's *The Pilgrim's Progress* in London; Pizzetti's *Ifigenia* in Florence; Roberto Gerhard's *The Duenna* at Wiesbaden; Stravinsky's *The Rake's Progress* in Venice; Britten's *Billy Budd* in London; Wellesz's *Incognita* at Oxford; Menotti's *Amahl and the Night Visitors* (televised) New York. 1952 R. Strauss's *Die Liebe der Danaë* at Salzburg; Henze's *Boulevard Solitude*. 1953 Britten's *Gloriana* in London; Einem's *Der Prozess* ('The Trial') in Salzburg. 1954 Britten's *Turn of the Screw* in Venice; Liebermann's *Penelope* in Salzburg; Copland's *Tender Land* in New York; Walton's *Troilus and Cressida* in London. 1955 Prokofiev's *Fiery Angel* in Venice; Carlisle Floyd's *Susannah* in Florida; Tippett's *Midsummer Marriage* in London. 1956 Bergsma's *Wife of Martin Guerre* in New York; Henze's *König Hirsch* in Berlin. 1957 Fortner's *Blood Wedding* in Cologne; Gardner's *Moon and Sixpence* in London; Hindemith's *Harmonie der Welt* in Munich; Poulenc's *Dialogues des Carmélites* in Milan; Schönberg's *Moses and Aaron* in Zürich. 1958 Barber's *Vanessa* in New York; Britten's *Noye's Fludde* at Aldeburgh; Pizzetti's *Murder in the Cathedral* in Milan. 1960 Britten's *Midsummer Night's Dream* at Aldeburgh; Henze's *Prinz von Homburg* at Hamburg; Tate's *The Lodger* in London. 1961 Falla's *La Atlántida* in Barcelona; Henze's *Elegy for Young Lovers* at Schwetzingen; Nono's *Intolleranza* in Venice; Ward's *The Crucible* in New York; R. R. Bennett's *The Ledge* in London. 1962 Tippett's *King Priam* at Coventry. 1963 Hindemith's *Long Christmas Dinner* in New York. 1964 Einem's *Der Zerrissene* at Hamburg; Ginastera's *Don Rodrigo* in Buenos Aires. 1965 Henze's *Der junge Lord* in Berlin. 1966 Henze's *Bassarids* in Salzburg. 1967 Walton's *The Bear* at Aldeburgh.

See also *Dictionaries* 8.

25. A Bird's-eye View of the World's Chief Opera Composers

(shown in half-centuries from 1600).

ITALY	FRANCE	GERMANY AND AUSTRIA	GREAT BRITAIN	RUSSIA	BOHEMIA	U.S.A.
1600 Peri Caccini Monteverdi	1600	1600	1600	1600	1600	1600
1650 A. Scarlatti	1650 Cambert Lully	1650	1650 Purcell	1650	1650	1650
1700 A. Scarlatti (contd.) Pergolesi Jommelli	1700 Rameau	1700 Keiser Hasse	1700 Handel (German) Bononcini (Italian) *The Beggar's Opera* and its many successors	1700	1700	1700
1750 Paesiello Cimarosa Piccini Sacchini Salieri	1750 Rousseau Philidor Monsigny Grétry Piccini (Italian)	1750 Hasse (contd.) Gluck J. A. Hiller Dittersdorf Mozart	1750 Arne Dibdin Arnold Hook Shield	1750 Fomin	1750	1750
1800 Rossini Donizetti Bellini	1800 Cherubini Spontini (both Italian) Méhul Boïeldieu Auber Hérold Halévy Meyerbeer (German) Berlioz	1800 Weber Beethoven (one opera) Meyerbeer Flotow Nicolai	1800 Bishop Balfe Wallace	1800 Glinka	1800	1800 Fry
1850 Verdi Boito Mascagni Leoncavallo Giordano	1850 Ambroise Thomas Lecocq Gounod Bizet Offenbach Saint-Saëns Massenet	1850 Johann Strauss Suppé Wagner R. Strauss Cornelius Humperdinck	1850 Balfe (contd.) Wallace „ Benedict Sullivan Stanford	1850 Dargomijsky Rimsky-Korsakof Mussorgsky Borodin Tchaikovsky	1850 Smetana Dvořák Fibich	1850
1900 Puccini Wolf-Ferrari Pizzetti Malipiero Respighi Dallapiccola	1900 Charpentier Debussy (one opera) Dukas d'Indy Ravel Poulenc	1900 R. Strauss (contd.) Schreker Pfitzner Korngold Busoni (Italian) Berg Hindemith Orff Henze	1900 Delius Smyth Boughton Holst Vaughan Williams Britten	1900 Stravinsky Prokofief Glière Kabalevsky	1900 Janáček Foerster Hába Martinů	1900 Converse Parker Damrosch Cadman Taylor Menotti
1950 Nono	1950 Milhaud	1950 Blacher Egk Einem Henze	1950 Bennett Tippett Williamson Walton	1950 Shostakovitch	1950	1950 Bernstein Moore Weisgall Schuller

It should be noted that where a composer's work falls into two half-centuries it has usually been thought sufficient to enter his name under that half-century in which most of his work or his more important work was done.

Where a composer worked for a considerable period, or in such a way as to exert great influence, in a country other than his own, his name has been entered under that country, with his nationality indicated in brackets.

All the above composers receive some treatment in this volume under their own names.

26. How many Operas have been Written? As a conclusion to this article one may ask this unanswerable question. In 1911 John Towers of Pennsylvania announced his Dictionary Catalogue of 28,015 Operas and Operettas. Thereupon a German researcher, G. Steiger, took upon himself to demonstrate its incompleteness. Taking the titles 'Aaron' to 'Achilles', between which Towers gave 165 other titles, Steiger added 114 (counting only those composed up to 1905), so that apparently this great dictionary contained only about two-thirds of the possible total. According to this, information of one sort or another can be found of over 42,000 operas and operettas.

The Schatz collection of Opera Libretti in the Library of Congress, Washington, as increased by other acquisitions, includes about 25,000 works. As to the most fecund composers of opera Towers reports eight whom he knows to have composed over 100 apiece—Antonio Draghi (1635–1700), Galuppi (1706–85), Pietro Guglielmi (1727–1804), Piccini (1728–1800), Paesiello (1740–1816), Wenzel Müller (1767–1835), Bishop (1786–1855), Offenbach (1819–

80). Their average lifetime is rather over seventy years—say fifty years' working life with a steady output of two a year.

27. Articles in this Volume upon Subjects cognate to Opera.

Aria; Ballad Opera; Ballet; Beggar's Opera; Bouffons, Guerre des; Comic Opera; Drame lyrique; Dramma per musica; Extravaganza; Festspiel; Finale, Grand Opera; Incidental Music to Plays; Intermezzo; Libretto; Light Opera; Lyric Drama; Masque; Melodrama; Mime; Mysteries, Miracle Plays, and Moralities; Musica parlante; Opera buffa; Opéra comique; Opera seria; Pantomime; Pastorale; Pasticcio; Recitative; Scenario; Singspiel; Stile rappresentativo; Trittico; Vaudeville. (See also the articles on the various countries.)

The similar early history and somewhat parallel development of oratorio are treated in the article so headed.

OPERA BUFFA (It.), **OPÉRA BOUFFE** (Fr.). These are merely the Italian and French terms for Comic Opera (in the English sense of the words, not the French *Opéra-comique*, q.v.): such opera admits spoken dialogue, though the practice in Italy was anciently to use 'recitativo secco' (see *Recitative*).

The origin of the form may be gathered by turning to the article *Intermezzo*. In that article Pergolese's *The Servant as Mistress* ('La Serva padrona') is mentioned as the typical developed example of the form once it had secured an independent status: there had been plenty of humorous musical entertainments before, but the success of this one won a new standing. It was first performed at Naples in 1733 and was performed at Paris in 1746 and 1752; here it served as the basis for a national school of Opéra bouffe, of which the leading exponents were Duny, Monsigny, F. A. Philidor, and Grétry (all of them treated under their own names in this volume): Duny, a Neapolitan but settled in Paris, is sometimes spoken of as the founder of French *Opéra bouffe*. We may, then, look upon the form as Italian in origin and French by adoption.

In the first half of the nineteenth century it was customary in Paris to speak of the theatre given up to this type of work as 'les Bouffes' and to use the same term for the performers there. When in the middle of the century Offenbach opened a theatre for the performance of his works he called it **Bouffes Parisiens**. But 'Opéra bouffe', in the Offenbachian sense, makes a closer approach to farce than is necessarily implied by 'Opera buffa'—which latter term covers such works as Rossini's *Barber of Seville* and even Mozart's *Don Giovanni*.

Serious opera learnt several things from its lighter rival, amongst them the concerted finale.

For the eighteenth-century 'Guerre des Bouffons' in Paris see *Bouffons, Guerre des*.

OPÉRA-COMIQUE (Fr.) does not mean 'Comic Opera' (the subject may, indeed, be tragic, as for example in Bizet's *Carmen*), but opera in which the spoken voice is used.

The reason for the anomaly is historical. In the eighteenth century there were in Paris two fairs which were the annual occasion of much theatrical performance. It was at one of these fairs (that of St. Germain) that, in 1715, the announcement 'Opéra-comique' was first employed, and the idea was that of a humorous satirical imitation, or parody, of the grand opera—the Académie de Musique, with its official monopoly of the sung drama. A little singing was held not to infringe that monopoly, but the staple of the entertainment was to be spoken dialogue; a legal agreement with the official and monopolistic house confirmed this and consecrated the title 'Opéra-comique'. (But see an allusion under *Community Singing* 3.)

This opera was, then, comic in its subject-matter and the treatment of it, and it also used the spoken voice, and the latter characteristic came to be regarded as the more defining quality.

The present 'Opéra-comique', with its official and government-subsidized building, is the descendant of this annual fair entertainment. Some operas without spoken dialogue are now included in its repertory, so that the application of the term is again confused.

See also *Adam de la Halle*.

OPERA SERIA (It.). 'Serious' opera, as distinguished from *Opera buffa*.

OPERETTA. (1) A short opera. (2) A light opera—this being now the common sense of the word, and generally with the implication of spoken dialogue; the word is now, indeed, often almost a synonym for 'Musical Comedy' (q.v.).

OPHIBARYTON. See *Cornett and Key Bugle Families* 2 f.

OPHICLEIDE (Eng.), **OPHIKLEIDE** (Ger.). See *Cornett and Key Bugle Families* 2 g, 3 g, 4 g; *Organ* 14 VI.

OPIE, MRS. AMELIA. See *All through the Night*.

OPP. Abbreviation for the plural of *Opus* (q.v.), 'Op.' being the singular.

OP. POST. See *Opus*.

OPUS (Latin for 'work'). The custom of composers numbering their works as they appear 'opus 1' (or 'op. 1'), and so on, is of convenience both as a means of identification and as an indication of the place a particular work occupied in a composer's process of development. Unfortunately, owing to the unsystematic application of the device, neither purpose is as fully served as it should be.

The system began in the early seventeenth century. Cifra (q.v.), for one, used it. Later Corelli (1653–1713) and Vivaldi (c. 1676–1741) are two of the composers who adopted it. With them, and with other composers of this period and of the one succeeding, the numbers are not applied to single works; it was usual in those days to publish sonatas, etc., in books of six or twelve and to give one opus number to each book. Corelli's books, and consequently his numbers, run only to six (each of twelve works) and those of Vivaldi to twelve (mostly of six works). Modern composers usually adopt the single-work numeration but even so they often make an exception for a book of short pieces or songs, and Reger's 'op. 76' (a book of songs) contains no fewer than sixty compositions. When one opus number includes several compositions it is common nowadays to use designations such as 'op. 1, no. 1', 'op. 1, no. 2', etc.

A few only of Handel's works (and these all instrumental) bear opus numbers—added by his publisher Walsh.

J. C. Bach uses opus numbers in the Corelli group fashion, but omits most of his vocal works from the numeration (moreover, he has two separate 'opp. 6'). Other composers have done this and still others have numbered only their vocal works, but not their instrumental.

There are many anomalies in the numeration of the works of Haydn, owing to different publishers (contemporary and subsequent) taking upon themselves to add numbers; thus some works appear in different editions under different numbers. In some cases publishers' catalogue numbers have become attached as opus numbers.

The confusion in the numbering of Mozart's works was complete until it was largely cleared up by Köchel (q.v.).

There is also some confusion about two or three of Beethoven's works, especially the latest string quartets.

Occasionally books on music have been included in the opus numeration of a composer: thus Berlioz's treatise on orchestration is his 'op. 10'.

Massenet has no 'op. 13', superstitiously preferring 'op. 12 b'.

Only two of Wagner's works bear opus numbers, op. 1 being a piano sonata of 1831 and op. 2 a four-hand piano polonaise of 1832. (It can, of course, be taken that opus 1 is never a composer's first work but, at most, only the first that, in his youth, he was able to bring before the public.)

Busoni's opus numbers well illustrate the various muddles that occur in connexion with opus numeration.

'As a boy he numbered each work as he wrote it, whether it was published or not. After reaching Op. 47 at the age of 17 he gave the numbers of unpublished *juvenilia* to new works; later he started again at Op. 30, adding an *a* to Op. 30–6. The Pianoforte Concerto he numbered in Roman figures as Op. xxxix. From Op. 41 onwards the numbering proceeds regularly, though some works appeared without opus number' (Dent, *Busoni*).

'Op. Post.' indicate a posthumously published work.

ORAGEUX, ORAGEUSE (Fr.; masc., fem.). 'Stormy.'

ORA PRO NOBIS. 'Pray for us'—a litany response in the Roman Catholic Church.

ORATORIO

(For some illustrations see p. 738, pl. 121.)

1. Introductory. The term 'oratorio' is difficult to define, as it has taken so many meanings at different periods and in different countries. Usually it is nowadays understood to mean an extended setting of a religious libretto for chorus, orchestra, and vocal soloists, and for either concert or church performance, i.e. without scenery, dresses, or action. But in its beginnings, at the opening of the seventeenth century (see 2), it had action, scenery, and dresses, and so it sometimes had in the eighteenth century. Further, many works not religious have at various periods been called oratorios, apparently on the ground that they had the choral, orchestral, and solo features and so were on the general lines of an oratorio, and could not be called opera since they were not intended for stage performance (Handel's *Semele* is an instance; it was always announced as an 'oratorio', and Haydn called his *Seasons* by that name, though its lapses into piety are infrequent).

Miscellaneous concert programmes have been called 'oratorios', as for instance those given in London in Lent towards the end of the eighteenth century. Even single-movement sacred vocal compositions have had the name applied to them; that, according to Mr. Sonneck (*Early Opera in America*), was probably the nature of the 'oratorio' mentioned in the announcement at New York in 1751 as to be sung between the acts of *The Beggar's Opera*!

In the common parlance of choral singers, a Mass, a Requiem Mass, a 'Passion', a setting of the *Stabat Mater* or of the *Seven Last Words*, etc., are all oratorios. Such things as these are

1. COVENT GARDEN THEATRE—as depicted by Rowlandson (*c.* 1810)

2. COVENT GARDEN THEATRE—a late-19th-century undress rehearsal (from the *Illustrated London News*)

PLATE 120 OPERA HOUSES IN NEW YORK

1. PARK THEATRE, NEW YORK—opened 1798, burnt down 1820, rebuilt and again burnt 1848—this last house, in its turn, suffering the same fate

2. CASTLE GARDEN, NEW YORK—Sontag, Salvi, and Badiati in Donizetti's *Lucia di Lammermoor*. This house began as a music hall in 1845 and was burnt down in 1876

3. THE LINCOLN CENTER, New York. Left: New York State Theater. Centre: Metropolitan Opera. Right: Avery Fisher Hall

separately treated in the present work, as having distinct characters: yet admittedly, as frequently set by composers, they differ but little from certain oratorios in the usual sense of today, and any limits laid down as to the use of the term must, in the nature of the case, be reckoned as a matter of convenience rather than of exact definition.

As already mentioned, some early oratorios were given with dresses and action like operas, and it may be added that some more modern oratorios (e.g. Berlioz's *Childhood of Christ*, Mendelssohn's *Elijah*, and Liszt's *St. Elizabeth*) have been found capable of bearing the same treatment, being, in fact, on occasion, staged as operas.

2. Oratorio in Italy. Like the opera the oratorio began in Italy, and like it, it had an ancestry scattered over Europe in the *Mysteries*, *Miracle Plays* and *Moralities* (see *Mysteries*).

The good priest Philip Neri (1515–95; later canonized and now known as St. Philip Neri; p. 738, pl. **121.** 1) began in Rome, in 1556, popular services, especially designed to attract and hold the attention of youth. He imported elements from the popular plays on sacred subjects alluded to above, and also from the *Laudi Spirituali* (q.v.), interpolating addresses between the acts of the plays. The building he used for this purpose was not a parish church but an oratory, and he was led to found an order of priests called the Congregation of the Oratory (Oratorians), of which he became superior. After some years he rebuilt the Church of Santa Maria in Vallicella, in Rome, and this then became the headquarters of the Order. This Order still survives and a brief reference to the musical traditions of one of the present-day English oratories will be found under *Hymns and Hymn Tunes* 6 (end).

The oratorio, in the musical sense, is always spoken of as originating in the church above mentioned five years after the death of St. Philip Neri, i.e. in the year 1600. This is the same year as that usually accepted for the first opera (see *Opera* 1, 2), which the first oratorio preceded by about ten months.

Florence was the birthplace of opera and Rome of oratorio, but both sprang from the same Florentine attempt to introduce (or revive) a method of direct and dramatic vocal statement in music (see *Recitative*). Cavalieri, composer of the first oratorio, had been an active member of the group of musicians and dilettanti who had been working out the problems of the new art of opera at Florence, and musically his work, *La Rappresentazione dell' anima e del corpo* ('The Representation of Soul and Body'), looks much the same as his Florentine colleague Peri's opera *Eurydice*.

The first oratorio was to be given with dresses and action, and a (hidden) orchestra of much the same kind as that used in the first opera. The composer's directions gave a final dance as optional (see *Dance*). The characters are Time, Life, World, Pleasure, Intellect, Soul, and Body—in fact, it was a Mystery Play set to music. Nearly all (perhaps all) the Mystery Plays had some music mixed with their use of the speaking voice; this one had no use of the speaking voice at all, and that was the main difference. The ancient Mystery is, then, the true source of the early oratorio and the didactic purposes of the two are absolutely identical.

It is possible that both words and music, which are in a mixture of styles, are a pasticcio of existing material.

Soul and Body was Cavalieri's last work; he was unable to follow up his experiment, as he would doubtless have done had he lived, and his immediate imitators were neither very clever nor very numerous. Such imitators did, however, exist, and a few of them were successful in expressing religious feeling and moral teaching in a sensitive way.

Towards the middle of the century we come to a very great name in the history of the oratorio, that of **Carissimi** (*c.* 1605–74). He wrote five oratorios of which one at least, *Jephtha*, is still kept in print and in an ordinary performing edition, and is, therefore, presumably still in some use. The original text is Latin; it comes partly from the Scriptures, but there are lyrical rhymed passages for solo and chorus. The characters speak in their own voices, but there is the connecting link, whenever necessary, of the declamation of 'Historicus', a personage who is the exact equivalent of the Narrator in such a work as a Bach Passion (see *Passion Music*), which, indeed, in general scheme, *Jephtha* closely resembles. The practice of actual dramatic representation was now ceasing.

Thence onwards very many Italian composers essayed to write Oratorio (see list under 7). The most notable is **Alessandro Scarlatti**, who, as in his operas, used both recitativo secco and accompanied recitative (see *Recitative*) and the developed aria (q.v.); both in style and in feeling his oratorios are barely distinguishable from his operas, and indeed it may be said that vocal display and musical enjoyment, in place of dramatic truth, had become a characteristic of both: oratorio had, then, slipped from its early ideals, as opera had—and it had, if anything, slipped further, since it had originally a religious as well as a dramatic ideal and this was now largely lost. It is of interest to note that Scarlatti has one oratorio on the life of the very founder of oratorio, St. Philip Neri: it was performed at Foligno in 1713, but this may not have been the first performance.

The great opera librettist, Metastasio (q.v.), wrote eight or nine oratorio libretti which were repeatedly set by Italian (and sometimes other) composers during the eighteenth century.

A decline in Italian oratorio was now in full being, and it is hardly necessary to trace its steps. In general the development of Italian oratorio was on the same lines as that of Italian opera, which is fully enough described in the article *Opera*. In the main, Italian oratorio had become entertainment, and how lightly it was sometimes taken as much as a century later can be seen by a glance at the reference to **Rossini's** *Moses in Egypt* in the list below (section 7—1818).

At the end of the nineteenth century and beginning of the twentieth a determined attempt was made by Dom Lorenzo **Perosi** (q.v.), musical director of the Sistine Chapel at Rome, to revive the dignity and influence of that Roman form, the oratorio. His works are included in the list given below; they combine the influence of plainsong, of the Palestrina school of choral composition, and of modern practice, and, partly from the incompatibility of these elements, cannot be said to have altogether attained their great end.

3. Oratorio in Germany. The great popularity in Germany of the Passion Music and, especially, of the Church Cantata, doubtless to some extent satisfied the need that might otherwise have been met by Oratorio proper.

The work of **Schütz** (1585–1672) is alluded to under the heading *Passion Music*, and the facts of his Italian training and circumstances are there set out. He was a master of the new Recitative style, with an inclination to adopt in it, on occasion, something very like the style and formulae of plainsong. This is seen in his oratorio *The Story of the happy and triumphant Resurrection of our only Redeemer and Saviour, Jesus Christ* (1623). This work, like Carissimi's *Jephtha* rather later, has a Narrator, in this case called 'Evangelist'. In this and in other ways the oratorio resembles the contemporary and later German Passion settings and, indeed, it is the same sort of thing adapted to the occasion of Easter. It shows a good deal of sense of drama. Unlike the same composer's Passions, it has instrumental accompaniment (strings and organ); the Evangelist's part is always accompanied by four bass viols (viole da gamba).

Bach, a century after Schütz, wrote no oratorios (if we accept the rather narrow definition on which we are at present working). His oratorio-like treatment of the forms of the *Mass, Passion,* and *Cantata* is briefly described under those heads. His so-called *Christmas Oratorio* is really a sequence of six cantatas for separate performance (see 7). His *Easter Oratorio* ('Kommt, eilet und laufet') and his *Ascension Oratorio* ('Lobet Gott in seinen Reichen') must also be mentioned.

His son **Carl Philipp Emanuel Bach** wrote not only two Passions and a Passion Cantata (1770) but also two oratorios *The Israelites in the Wilderness* (1775), and *The Resurrection and Ascension of Jesus* (1787). Of *The Israelites in the Wilderness* Sir Henry Hadow, who made a study of it, says (*Oxford History of Music*, vol. v): 'Up to the first two numbers of the second part this oratorio deserves our most careful consideration; not only for its intrinsic merit—and it is eminently worth reviving at the present day—but for its remarkable resemblance to Mendelssohn's *Elijah*. We can

hardly doubt that it served in some degree as a model for that noble though unequal composition.'

The oratorios of **Handel** were written in England for the English taste and are, therefore, treated in the English section of this article.

The one or two oratorios of **Mozart** are youthful and negligible. His *Requiem* is mentioned under that head.

Haydn's *The Return of Tobit* has a poor libretto and some good music; a modern edition of it was published in the early twentieth century and it was given a performance at an English festival (Newcastle-on-Tyne, 1909—its first British hearing!). His *Creation* (1798) is his masterpiece in the line of oratorio. Some of it is naïve and childlike, but it has many forceful moments, much charming solo melody, and some grandly effective choral writing. His *The Seasons* is referred to under 1.

Beethoven wrote one oratorio, *Christ on the Mount of Olives,* which he himself in after years thought to be too operatic; Christ sings a duet with an angel and there are other features that British taste has tried to mitigate by four or five new libretti, including the one long popular of *Engedi, or David in the Wilderness.* One chorus from this work, the 'Hallelujah', is well known in Britain and America.

Schubert's cheerful *Song of Miriam* is brief and he never orchestrated it. His *Lazarus* (which includes some fine music) is unfinished and its libretto is rather sickly.

Spohr's oratorios had high popularity in Germany, Britain, and America, but have now, like all his music, practically vanished except for *The Last Judgement,* their rather relaxing chromatic idiom being too pervasive for modern taste.

J. C. F. Schneider (1786–1853) wrote fifteen or sixteen oratorios which enjoyed very great reputation in their day and are now totally unknown.

And so we come to **Mendelssohn,** whose Bach researches show their influence in the contrapuntal choruses and the interpolated reflective chorales of *St. Paul* (1836). *Elijah* (1846) is a very dramatic work and, as already stated, has actually been staged successfully, on occasion, in England. It was written for England and has had a popularity there perhaps not even second to that of Handel's *Messiah. The Hymn of Praise* is called 'a Symphony-Cantata'; the first portion of it is purely orchestral—a novel scheme with some resemblances to that of the Choral Symphony of Beethoven. *Christus* was never finished.

Wagner's *The Love Feast of the Apostles* in his only contribution to the oratorio repertory. It is, naturally, for male choir. It is an early work (1843), and, by comparison with his music-dramas, quite unimportant.

Liszt's *Christus* (in Latin) and his *St. Elizabeth* had a vogue at the time they were written, and there are serious critics who maintain that they are well worthy of being retained in the choral repertory.

Dvořák's *St. Ludmila* (1886) is now rarely to be heard, but his *Stabat Mater* has still a considerable following; the works of Raff and Bruch seem to have gone for ever. (The Czech composer Dvořák would object to being treated in the German section of this article. Convenience must be the apology: Liszt, the Hungarian, could also complain, but probably would not trouble to do so.)

4. Oratorio in France, Belgium, and Switzerland. Oratorio has never taken very strong root in France, i.e. it has not enjoyed the popularity there that it has done in Germany and, especially, England.

M. A. Charpentier, a pupil of Carissimi, and a famous opera composer in the time of Lully, introduced the form at the end of the seventeenth century. He wrote twenty or more oratorios in the Latin language. He used the terms *Sacred Stories* ('Histoires sacrées') and *Spiritual Tragedies* ('Tragédies spirituelles'). In the next century J. J. C. **Mondonville** (1711–72) was active as an oratorio writer. He directed the famous *Concerts spirituels* in Paris (see *France* 7; *Concert* 14) and wrote for them *The Israelites at Mount Horeb*, and one or two other works.

Gossec (1774) wrote a *Nativity*, with a choir of angels singing at a distance.

Lesueur, chief musician to Napoleon and himself a grandiose Napoleon of church music, aimed at dramatic descriptive effects: he wrote a number of oratorios, but some of his works called by this name are mere motets. **Berlioz** and **Gounod** were among Lesueur's pupils and he was a teacher who exercised a strong influence on those under him. No doubt Berlioz's Requiem (see *Requiem*) shows the Lesueur touch; his Christmas Oratorio, *The Childhood of Christ*, is a gentler and sensitive work. Gounod's oratorios are somewhat tainted by sentimentality, but are effective and had great popularity in England, where, indeed, he spent five years of his life.

Franck wrote four oratorios, *The Beatitudes, Rebecca, Ruth,* and *Redemption*, and his pupil, **d'Indy,** a work that impressed many critics when it was produced in 1915—*The Legend of St. Christopher*.

Pierné specialized in oratorios using (as a part of their vocal resources) children's choirs —*The Children's Crusade* and *The Children of Bethlehem*. The Belgian, **Benoît,** wrote a *Children's Oratorio*. Probably more could be done with children's oratorios if composers would try: Haydn, Berlioz, and others have recorded the deep impression made on them by the singing of the large choir of charity children at St. Paul's Cathedral, London.

Massenet, Dubois, and **Tinel** are other names that occur in thinking of oratorio in France and Belgium.

Honegger, a Parisian Swiss, as he may be called, made a stir with *King David* in 1921. It uses the speaking voice of a sort of narrator, with choruses, etc., interspersed (so reverting to the early practice of Passion Music), and was originally written for stage action (again reverting to the early Italian type of oratorio).

5. Oratorio in Britain (p. 738, pl. **121.** 4, 5, 6). Oratorio came late to Britain—and then won a popularity more triumphant than in any other country.

So far as the present writer is aware nothing that could be called oratorio exists in the archives of British music before Handel. His 'masque' of *Haman and Mordecai*, written for the private chapel of the Duke of Chandos in 1720, and rewarded, it is said, by a fee of £1,000 (the Duke had made millions by doubtful practices as Paymaster of the Forces during Marlborough's campaignings, and could afford to pay lavishly for pious stimulus), slightly adapted became the first British oratorio (*Esther*). It was performed with scenery and dresses. Twelve years later Bernard Gates, Master of the Children of the Chapel Royal, pleased Handel on his birthday by giving a performance of a good section of it, by the children, at his own (Gates's) house in Westminster —with scenery, dresses, and action; this succeeded and the performance was repeated on two nights at the Crown and Anchor tavern in the Strand for the members of the Academy of Ancient Music. The Princess Royal then expressed a wish to see the work performed at the Opera House, but the Bishop of London (who was Dean of the Chapel Royal), refused to allow his choristers to appear there in a sacred work in costume—even though the concession was offered of their holding books in their hands. It was these circumstances and the publicity the work received that led first to a pirate performance and then to an official one by the indignant composer, 'By His Majesty's Command', with the instructions 'N.B. There will be no acting on the stage, but the house will be fitted up in a decent manner for the audience. The Musick to be disposed after the manner of the Coronation Service' (which 'Coronation Service' is a series of four great anthems, composed for George II's accession five years earlier). Six crowded houses resulted in the popularity of English oratorio, performed in what we now consider to be the oratorio manner, and led to the long and fine series of works which were, more than any others of Handel's composition, to keep his fame as a composer bright amongst coming generations. Thus the Concert Oratorio was born.

And here attention may be called to the outstanding differences between the Handel oratorio and the various German works of the preceding and contemporary period, such as the Schütz *Resurrection* Oratorio and Passions and the Bach Passions. These latter are definitely *devotional* works. They have a thread of narration, with the dramatic element entering in the dialogue of the various passages, and meditation in the shape of reflective arias and chorales. Handel's oratorios are not primarily devotional, but either dramatic or epic. They are nearer to the Carissimi model than the Schütz or Bach model, but they are essentially English—the natural religious recreation of a Bible-loving and chorus-singing nation.

The special business function of the oratorios was to fill up profitably the Wednesdays and Fridays of the period of Lent, at which period theatrical performances were forbidden by law. After Handel's death these Lenten oratorios were continued by his amanuensis J. C. Smith, and the famous blind organist Stanley (q.v.); after Smith's retirement by Thomas Linley (see *Linley* 1) and Stanley; after Stanley's death by Dr. Samuel Arnold and Linley; and then from 1795 a rival series directed by J. Ashley and afterwards by his son carried on the tradition. It is a somewhat curious occupation for a spare five minutes to sum up the various religious, social, and commercial accidents and elements that entered into the firm establishment in England of this great art form.

From London the love of oratorio permeated the country until the poet Mason (canon and precentor of York Minster) could write, towards the end of the century and thirty-six years after Handel's death, 'the rage for oratorio has spread from the capital to every market town in the Kingdom' (*Essays on English Church Music*, 1795). From Mason's county and the adjoining county of Lancashire it was in his period (say from 1770 to 1805) common to import women chorus singers for the great performances of London, the Birmingham and Three Choirs Festivals, etc.

The greatest of the Handel oratorios are, as every one would unite in declaring, *Israel in Egypt* (1738), with its magnificent double choruses, and *Messiah* (1741), with its intense and sincere religious feeling.

The annual and triennial choral festivals of England, and the choral societies—these last largely fostered by the nineteenth-century sight-singing systems and organization of Hullah (q.v.) and, especially, Curwen (q.v.)—increased the hold of oratorio and particularly Handel on the English people. A glance through the list below will give a hint as to the large number of works, British and foreign, which came into being at the demand of festival committees. The monster triennial Handel Festivals of the Crystal Palace began a century after Handel's death and continued into the late 1920s.

The large majority of the British oratorios of the later eighteenth and the nineteenth centuries were mere academic exercises, or popular examples of what may (now that the composers are dead) be called choir-fodder. They served their day and generation and then fell on sleep —like an almost equal proportion of Italian and German operas or German symphonies of the same period (or of any period).

In the late nineteenth and early twentieth centuries, with men of the sincerity and sound taste of Parry, Stanford, and Mackenzie, a better type was brought into existence, and the works of Elgar (see list below) lifted the Eng-

lish oratorio form to a level it had not reached for a century and a half. These last-mentioned works were modern in harmonic and orchestral idiom: they largely abandoned the old set divisions into arias, choruses, etc., they employed the Leading Motif (q.v.) system, and, indeed, it may be said that they applied to oratorio the ideals and methods of Wagnerian music-drama. They were intensely mystical in feeling—and yet strangely English. They were felt by most British musicians to constitute a national monument.

Few oratorios have since been written and the form appears to be either definitely extinct or to be awaiting a new awakening by some great master—probably in a period of religious revival, for, in the last analysis, the new order of thought initiated by Darwin and Huxley has probably, more than any other single cause, been the death of oratorio in Britain.

6. Oratorio in the United States. Oratorio was reaching the end of its popularity before the United States had yet had time to pull herself together as a composing nation. During the last century-and-a-quarter of the Oratorio Period (which period, let us consider, runs from 1600 to 1900) choral societies were gradually coming into existence in the United States. The first, the Handel Society of Dartmouth College, dates from four years after the signing of the Declaration of Independence. The foundation of the Handel and Haydn Society of Boston in 1815 was important for the popularization of oratorio in the United States, as the list subjoined shows. Some of the principal oratorios composed in the United States are shown in that list. Europe was first invaded, in any marked way, just at the end of the nineteenth century, when the work of Horatio Parker (q.v.) won recognition from some of the old-established and influential English festivals.

From the early years of the twentieth century onwards the position of oratorio in the United States has been nearly the same as that in Britain. The great classical oratorios and some of the more modern works have been kept before the public by the devotion of the choral societies, but there has been no great effort on the part of composers to maintain oratorio as a living art-form.

Few American composers are interested in choral music, and only one oratorio written since 1930 has endured as a repertory piece—Randall Thompson's *The Testament of Freedom* (1943), to a text from the writings of Thomas Jefferson.

7. A Historical List of Oratorios, showing the chief works of importance either intrinsically, or as influencing the development of the form, or as representing the taste or spirit of their period, especially in Britain and the United States—the date of first performance in those two countries being given wherever possible. The dates before the titles are those of the works' first coming into public use.

1600. Cavalieri's *Soul and Body*, at Rome.

1623. Schütz's *The Resurrection*, at Dresden.

c. 1630–70. Carissimi's *Jephtha* and many other works, at Rome (in Latin).

1631. D. Mazzocchi's *The Plaint of St. Mary Magdalene*, at Rome. (See *Mazzocchi*.)

1664. Schütz's *Christmas Oratorio*, at Dresden.

c. 1670–1800. A host of Italian compositions, mostly operatic in style, by such as Colonna (born about 1640), Stradella (born 1645), Caldara (born 1670), Marcello (born 1686), Leo (born 1694), Pergolese (born 1710), Jommelli (born 1714), Piccini (born 1728), Sacchini (born 1730).

c. 1680–1720. A. Scarlatti's many oratorios (of which eighteen remain), at Naples and Rome.

c. 1690. M. A. Charpentier's *The Denial of St. Peter*, at Paris.

1720–52. Handel's English oratorios, of which the most important are *Saul* (1739), *Israel in Egypt* (1739), *Messiah* (1742), *Samson* (1743), *Occasional Oratorio* (1746), *Judas Maccabaeus* (1747), *Joshua* (1748), *Solomon* (1749), *Theodora* (1750), *Jephtha* (1752). All of these had their first performance in London, except *Messiah* in Dublin. In America *Messiah* was performed in part in New York in 1770 and as a whole in Boston in 1801—most of the Handel oratorios that have been performed in America first reached there during the 1840s and Boston was usually the city of first performance.

1734–5 (Christmas Day 1734 to 5 January 1735), Bach's *Christmas Oratorio* (really six separate cantatas for performance on six days from Christmas to Epiphany), at Leipzig. First British performance, London, 1861; first American performance, Boston, 1877—in part.

1761. Arne's *Judith*, at London.

1770 and 1775. C. P. E. Bach's *The Israelites in the Wilderness* and *The Resurrection and Ascension*, at Hamburg.

1775. Haydn's *The Return of Tobit*, at Vienna (Newcastle-on-Tyne, 1909).

1780 and 1781. Gossec's *The Nativity* and *The Ark of the Covenant*, at the Concerts Spirituels, Paris.

1798. Haydn's *Creation*, at Vienna (London, 1800; partial performance at Bethlehem, Pa., in 1811; complete performance at Boston in 1819).

1803. Beethoven's *Christ on the Mount of Olives*, at Vienna (London, 1814).

1812. Crotch's *Palestine*, in London.

1818. Rossini's *Moses in Egypt*, in Naples. London, as an Italian opera, *Peter the Hermit*, 1822; as an oratorio with scenery and dresses, *The Israelites in Egypt, or the Passage of the Red Sea*, parts of Handel's *Israel in Egypt* being incorporated, 1833. What appears to have been this same Rossini–Handel mixture in Boston, 1842; the pure Rossini work (translated) in the same city, 1845. As an Italian opera *Zora*, in London, 1850; at last the pure Rossini work (translated), in London, 1878.

1823. Schneider's *The Deluge*.

1825. Spohr's *The Last Judgement*, at Cassel (Norwich Festival, 1830; Boston, 1842).

1826. Lesueur's *Christmas Oratorio*, at Paris (many other oratorios before and after this, including an 'Oratorio for the Coronation of Sovereign Princes', composed for that of Napoleon, 1804).

1834. Neukomm's *David*, at the Birmingham Festival (Boston, 1836—twelve times in this year by the Handel and Haydn Society, in 1839 the Society gave it fourteen times. The same composer's *Sinai* also found great British and American favour).

1835. Spohr's *The Last Hours of the Saviour* (London, 1837, as 'Calvary', the name by which it is known in Britain).

1836. Mendelssohn's *St. Paul*, at Düsseldorf (Liverpool, 1836; New York, 1838).

1840. Mendelssohn's *Hymn of Praise*, in Leipzig (Birmingham Festival, same year; Boston, 1862).

1842. Spohr's *The Fall of Babylon*, at the Norwich Festival.

1843. Wagner's *The Love Feast of the Apostles*, in Dresden.

1846. Mendelssohn's *Elijah*, at the Birmingham Festival (Hamburg, 1847; Boston, 1848); in 1927 Chicago gave it with a new text by Messrs. Mannusovich and Deutsch, representing the prophet as 'freed from the mantle of religion and stepping forth as the leader of the eternal revolt of the masses against injustice, tyranny, and oppression'.

1854. Berlioz's *The Childhood of Christ*, in Paris—the first performance of the work as a whole (Manchester, 1880; a selection in New York, 1884).

1855. Costa's *Eli*, at the Birmingham Festival.

1863. Schubert's *Lazarus* (unfinished and dating from 1820), at Vienna (Three Choirs Festival, Hereford, 1909).

1864. Costa's *Naaman*, at the Birmingham Festival.

1865. Liszt's *St. Elizabeth* (London, 1886; New York, 1911; as an opera, 1918).

1866. Benoît's *Lucifer*, in Brussels (Paris, 1883; London, 1889).

1867. Brahms's *German Requiem*, in Vienna (completed version, 1869, Leipzig; London, 1873; New York, 1877). This is an oratorio—not a setting of the Requiem Mass.

Sterndale Bennett's *The Woman of Samaria*, at Birmingham.

1869. Sullivan's *The Prodigal Son*, at the Three Choirs Festival, Worcester (Boston, 1879).

1870. Benedict's *St. Peter*, at the Birmingham Festival.

1873. Sullivan's *The Light of the World*, at the Birmingham Festival.

Macfarren's *St. John the Baptist*, at the Bristol Festival.

Franck's *Redemption*, in Paris.

Paine's *St. Peter*, at Portland, Maine.

Massenet's *Marie Madeleine*, in Paris (afterwards arranged as an opera).

Liszt's *Christus*, at Weimar.

1875. Massenet's *Eve*, in Paris.

1876. Saint-Saëns' *The Deluge* (Boston, 1880).

1877. Macfarren's *Joseph*, at the Leeds Festival.

1878. Stainer's *The Daughter of Jairus*, at the Three Choirs Festival, Worcester.

Dubois's *Paradise Lost*, in Paris (Glasgow, February 1900; New York, the following month).

1879. Franck's *The Beatitudes*, in Paris.

1880. Sullivan's *The Martyr of Antioch*, at the Leeds Festival.

1882. Gounod's *Redemption*, at the Birmingham Festival (New York, same year).

Gaul's *The Holy City*, at the same Festival.

1883. Macfarren's *David*, at the Leeds Festival.

1884. Mackenzie's *The Rose of Sharon*, at the Norwich Festival.

1885. Gounod's *Mors et Vita*, at the Birmingham Festival.

1886. Dvořák's *St. Ludmila*, at the Leeds Festival.

1887. Cowen's *Ruth*, at the Three Choirs Festival, Worcester.

1888. Cowen's *Song of Thanksgiving*, in Melbourne, Australia.

Tinel's *St. Francis*, at Brussels (New York, 1893; Cardiff, 1895).

Parry's *Judith*, at Birmingham.

1889. Lee Williams's *The Last Night at Bethany*, at the Three Choirs Festival, Gloucester.

1890. J. F. Bridge's *The Repentance of Nineveh*, at the Three Choirs Festival, Worcester.

1891. Stanford's *Eden*, at Birmingham.

Parry's *De Profundis* (psalm), at the Three Choirs Festival, Hereford.

1892. Parry's *Job*, at the Three Choirs Festival, Gloucester (repeated at the same Festival at Worcester and Hereford in the two years following).

Lee Williams's *Gethsemane*, at the Three Choirs Festival, Gloucester.

1893. Horatio Parker's *Hora Novissima*, in New York (Three Choirs Festival, Worcester, 1899).

1894. Bridge's *The Cradle of Christ*, at the Three Choirs Festival, Hereford.

1895. Cowen's *The Transfiguration*, at the Three Choirs Festival, Gloucester (Düsseldorf, 1902; Chicago, 1903).

1896. Elgar's *The Light of Life*, at the Three Choirs Festival, Worcester.

1897-9. Perosi's trilogy, *The Transfiguration*, *The Raising of Lazarus*, and *The Resurrection of Christ*, in Rome (London, 1899; the first of the three works at Boston a month earlier).

1898. Horatio Parker's *The Legend of St. Christopher*, in New York (in part at Three Choirs Festival, Worcester, 1902; whole at Bristol Festival, same year).

1900. Elgar's *The Dream of Gerontius*, at the Birmingham Festival (Chicago, 1903).

1901. Brewer's *Emmaus*, at the Three Choirs Festival, Gloucester.

Perosi's *Moses*, at Rome.

1902. Perosi's *Leo the Great*, at Rome.

1903. Elgar's *The Apostles*, at the Birmingham Festival (New York, 1904; Cologne, 1904).

Coleridge-Taylor's *The Atonement*, at the Three Choirs Festival, Hereford.

Wolf-Ferrari's *La Vita nuova* (New York, 1907).

1904. Brewer's *The Holy Innocents*, at the Three Choirs Festival, Gloucester.

Walford Davies's *Everyman*, at the Leeds Festival.

Perosi's *The Last Judgement*, in Rome.

Pierné's *The Children's Crusade* (New York, 1906).

1906. Elgar's *The Kingdom*, at the Birmingham Festival (New York, 1907).

1907. Pierné's *The Children of Bethlehem* (New York, 1908).

1910. Cowen's *The Veil*, at the Cardiff Festival (Chicago, 1915).

1913. Saint-Saëns's *The Promised Land*, at the Three Choirs Festival, Gloucester.

1915. H. R. Shelley's *Death and Life*, in New York.

1920. d'Indy's *The Legend of St. Christopher*, in Paris.

1921. Honegger's *King David* (first produced as a play at Mézières, Switzerland).

1931. Walton's *Belshazzar's Feast*, at the Leeds Festival.

1935. Vogel's *Wagadu Destroyed*, in Brussels.

1936. Berkeley's *Jonah*, in London.

1940. Honegger's *La danse des morts*, at Basle.

Tippett's *A Child of our Time*, in London.

1944. Bernard Rogers's *The Passion*, at Cincinnati.

1947. Schönberg, Stravinsky, Toch, Milhaud, Castelnuovo-Tedesco, and Nathaniel Shilkret (who commissioned the work), joint oratorio, *Genesis*, at Portland, Oregon.

1949. Martin's *Golgotha*, at Geneva. Badings's *Apocalypse*, at Rotterdam.

1953. Beck's *Death in Basle*, at Basle.

1958. Fricker's *Vision of Judgement*, at Leeds.

1961. Britten's *War Requiem*, at Coventry.

The encouragement that the British festivals have given to the composition of oratorio is evident from the above. Birmingham's record is especially to be noted.

ORATORIANS. See *Oratorio* 2; *Hymns and Hymn Tunes* 6.

ORCHESTRA AND ORCHESTRATION

(For illustrations see p. 739, pl. **122**; 752, **123-4**; 756, **125-6**.)

The idea of combining instruments is probably as old as instruments themselves, but the principles of what may be called systematic combination (and the art of orchestration is just that) were very slowly realized. To illustrate the gradual development of the principles we will take the four approximate dates of 1600, 1700, 1800, and 1900.

1. The Monteverdi Period. In the year 1600 (period of the early operas; see *Peri*; *Caccini*; *Monteverdi*; *Opera* 1, 2) an orchestra was an occasional and varying collection, apparently conditioned partly by the chance of such and such instrumentalists being available on such particular occasion.

The instrumental force for Monteverdi's opera *Orpheus* (1607), at Mantua, included practically all the instruments known (except drums, strangely!)—fifteen viols of three different sizes and two violins; two large flutes, two ordinary flutes, two hautboys; two cornetts (the old wooden instrument, see *Cornett and Key Bugle Families*); four trumpets and five trombones; a harp and two harpsichords, two little organs and a regal (a small portable reed-organ; see *Reed-Organ Family* 2), forty in all. Monteverdi here was evidently simply calling upon the instrumentalists whom his patron, the Duke of Mantua, had in his employ, and in the effort to do so with effect he would necessarily discover valuable combinations and striking contrasts, and also suitable associations between certain tone colours and certain dramatic situations or emotional states, and so help forward the young art of orchestration. The important place taken by the bowed instruments in the above list is to be noted.

Many records of the fifteenth and sixteenth centuries mention large groups of musicians assembling for special purposes, such as weddings. Monteverdi's orchestra in *Orpheus* is a late example of such a 'Renaissance orchestra', rather than an invention of his own.

The beginnings of the modern orchestra are recognizable in France in the later sixteenth century. The king's band of 22 violins and 12 wind instruments was regularly established by 1609. From these beginnings developed the 'Baroque orchestra', founded on bowed strings.

2. The Bach Period. By the year 1700 progress had been made. Some instruments had been improved (as also, in many cases, the technique of performance on them), and some effective combinations had been worked out—with a growing tendency to standardize the central string section exactly as we have it today.

As a background to everything a keyboard instrument was used—a harpsichord or organ, playing from the bass line of the score, which was usually supplied with figures more or less completely indicating the harmonies to be drawn upon by the extemporizing player (see *Figured Bass*); the player was usually responsible for controlling the instrumental force and was then in effect what we should today call the conductor (see *Conducting* 3). The violin family (q.v.) was now fast replacing the old viol family, and though members of the latter still appeared for special effects they no longer formed the string basis of the force. Bach's *Magnificat* (first version, 1723), which was written for use in church, where a comparatively small force was available, has parts for strings (first and second violins, violas, cellos, and double-basses); two flutes, two oboes and two oboes d'amore, three trumpets and drums, and keyboard instrument. The figured bass (i.e. the organ, in church performance) is present throughout, but the other instruments vary from movement to movement and never once are they all heard together. A chorus will be accompanied by strings, oboes, trumpets, and figured bass, or by strings, trumpets, and figured bass, or by strings, oboes, and figured bass, or (the final brilliant *Gloria*) by strings, oboes, trumpets, drums, and figured bass. A solo will be accompanied by strings and figured bass, or by figured bass alone, or by flute and figured bass. The aim is variety of 'colour' *between one movement and another*. Evidently, too, some of the players were 'double-handed' or even treble-handed; it is noticeable that of the three couples of wood-wind instruments (flutes, oboes, and oboes d'amore) never more than one couple is in action in any movement of the work.

In a purely orchestral composition Bach will often have more instruments in action together, but he and his contemporaries had arrived at no standard orchestra, and it is noticeable that the instrumental forces required for his six Brandenburg Concertos are identical in no two of them; another point that strikes one about these works is that the functions of the various instruments are comparatively little differentiated, wood-wind instruments, brass, and strings playing the same types of passage, and even handing a passage imitatively from one to another.[1]

3. The Modern Orchestra Emerges. By 1800 a change of conception has taken place. The keyboard instrument has gone and the string tone is accepted as the invariable basis (save in passages of special effect).

A strong differentiation of function has taken place, according to the natural genius of the different families of instruments. The brass instruments are different from what they were, and their technique has changed; they no longer attempt florid passages (see the remark above). No longer do instruments or groups of instruments drop out for whole movements; generally speaking, all are at hand throughout; delicacy of combination has been studied and there is often now a kaleidoscopic play of orchestral colour, the changes occurring from moment to moment, instead of from movement to movement; the orchestra is a standardized combination of violins (divided into firsts and seconds), violas, cellos, and double-basses (these last two usually duplicating one another at an octave distance and so supplying a firm bass), a pair each of flutes, oboes, clarinets, bassoons, trumpets, and horns, with kettle-drums (score of Beethoven's First Symphony, performed 1800). This is the real beginning of the modern orchestra. Whatever changes have taken place since have observed the same principles and merely amplified the forces.

4. Orchestration at the Beginning of the Twentieth Century. We now come down to 1900. We might take as our key work Strauss's tone-poem, *A Hero's Life* (1898), or his 'Domestic' Symphony (1903).

In the score of the former he demands no fewer than sixty-six stringed instruments. Of wood-wind there are three flutes and a piccolo; three oboes and a cor anglais; two clarinets, a high clarinet, and a bass clarinet; three bassoons and a double-bassoon. Of brass there are eight horns, five trumpets, three trombones, a tenor tuba, and a bass tuba. Of percussion we have not only the kettledrums but bass drum, side drum, military drum, and cymbals, and there are two harps.

Between the Haydn–Mozart period and the Strauss period have come the work of the later Beethoven and of Wagner, and this great expansion of orchestral media, with its consequent enhanced variety, increased dynamic power, and greater aptitude for dramatic characteriza-

[1] For the balance of forces in the orchestras of the period see remarks under *Additional Accompaniments*. For the treatment of the oboe family in Bach's day, as compared with its treatment today, see *Oboe Family* 2.

tion, represents the influence of the Romantic movement (see *Romantic*) plus that of the efforts of instrument-makers during the greatest age of invention the world has yet seen. It will be realized that the increased variety and increased differentiation just mentioned have necessarily brought with them a somewhat changed attitude on the part of the composer towards his score; a process which at one time could be described as colouring a sketch separately conceived has now largely changed to a process in which outline and colour of any passage are simultaneously conceived, so that the actual melodies, harmonies, and forms of the composition are in some degree dictated by the other element of colour.

5. In the 1930s and after. From the date just given until the date of the first writing of this article a third of a century had passed. Looking at its changes in a broad general way the main developments seemed to have been as follows: (1) An occasional tendency deliberately to use instruments out of their 'proper' style, giving them feats to perform for which (as Haydn, Beethoven, and even Wagner would have said) Providence never intended them: this is the element of brutality in Strauss carried further; (2) a development of a contrary kind—the increasing use (now plainly typical of the age) of smaller forces and more minute refinements; (3) an unceasing effort to discover yet new colours and combinations (as an example may be mentioned the occasionally experimental introduction of the human voice, wordless and simply 'as an instrument').

The process numbered (2) above may be readily seen by comparing one of Stravinsky's earlier scores with one of his later. His *Rite of Spring* ('Le Sacre du Printemps', 1911–13) calls for almost every conceivable instrument (thirty-nine instruments in addition to a huge force of strings and lavish percussion) and deliberately assaults the unaccustomed ear by such effects as blacksmith blows with a heavy mallet on a huge gong; his *The Soldier's Tale* ('L'Histoire du Soldat', 1918—not so much later, but there had been a change of heart meanwhile) is scored for only six instruments plus percussion, seven players in all (one each of violin, double-bass, clarinet, bassoon, cornet, trombone, and eight percussion instruments in the hands of one player).

Undoubtedly European penury after the first World War was one influence behind the tendency to see what beauties could be obtained from smaller resources; the Lilliputian orchestra cost only a tiny fraction of the Brobdingnagian and a new work for the former stood a better chance of coming to a hearing than one for the latter. But there is no doubt that the tendency of musical development leant towards a certain sparseness of style to which a rather small orchestra was more suitable than the very large one for which the last of the Romantics, like Strauss and Mahler, found such fitting and effective use.

What the future of the orchestra will be nobody can say. Sir Henry Wood's ideal festival orchestra, of which he laid out the specifications in a very fine article on orchestral colour in the *Dictionary of Modern Music and Musicians* (1924), called for 200 players and used every suitable existing instrumental resource. It should, he said, 'inspire music that would be a wonder of colour'. Since he wrote composers in all countries have exhibited a spirit of adventure (both harmonic and orchestral) such as the world of music had never before seen and their methods have been so various and personal as to make any generalization extremely difficult.

Probably what will come next will be a new period of invention. The present orchestra, with all its amazing resources, is but a combination of instruments that are no more than improvements upon instruments originally separately evolved through the ages, without much thought of their combination. It is conceivable that a root-and-branch reformer with high courage, ingenuity, skill, and unlimited financial resources could give the world's composers a far more logically conceived and effective orchestra than any that has yet been heard. And developments in the realms of physics and electronics have revealed opportunities of perfecting means of producing all tones at all pitches and in all colours without the need of our present complicated and varied mechanism.[1] (See *Electric Musical Instruments*.)

6. The Reading of Orchestral Scores. From the period of Beethoven onwards the orchestral score has been more or less standardized. It is usual to set it out as follows, reading downwards—Wood-wind; Brass; Percussion; Strings.

If the harp appears it is placed under the percussion; if voices, they are generally (rather foolishly perhaps) placed above the bass strings (for violoncellos and double-basses); if there is an organ it is placed immediately below the voices (if there are any) and in any case (with very few exceptions) immediately above the bass strings.

In concertos the solo instrument is generally placed immediately above the strings.

[1] The high authority to whom the scrutiny of this article, in its revised form, has been submitted registers a protest. He says, 'I do not believe in this "new period of invention". The main acoustic highways (and endless side routes, and even blind alleys as well) were explored centuries ago. It is in *combinations* that changes have mostly occurred and might be expected again to occur. True, some wind families at present incomplete could acoustically (and should ideally) be given their missing members to fill the gaps—not so that composers could use more instruments at once but to increase the *choice* of tones complete in all registers.

'Electric instruments may be invented, of course, but not, I hope, as substitutes for the present ones. For one thing the technique (bow-attack, tonguing, etc.) on present instruments contributes largely to their musical individuality and to improve such idiosyncrasies away would be artistic loss, not gain. There has been a certain amount of that (or of loss balancing gain) in the present history of orchestral instruments, anyway. However, really *new* electric instruments are always, in theory, a possibility. I mean such as would produce new sound-colours, not merely reproduce old ones by other means.'

A rough general principle as to the arrangement within each group is to observe pitch order, but it is *only* a general principle. Thus the wood-wind group (if very full) will be found to include instruments in this order reading downwards: piccolo, flutes and bass flute; oboes, cor anglais; clarinets, bass clarinet; bassoons, double bassoon.

Then come the horns, which are reckoned to have some affinity to the wood-wind and so are placed next to them.

After this we see the following:

Trumpets, trombones, tuba.

Kettledrums, bass drum and cymbals, side drum, and any other percussion instruments.

Harp, if any.

First violin, second violin, viola.

Solo voice or voices and chorus, if any.

Organ, if any.

Violoncello; double-bass.

In the wood-wind and brass it is usual that the 'first' and 'second' of any instrument shall share a stave; in the strings this is not so, the first and second violins possessing separate staves. In older scores violoncello and double-bass usually share a stave and play the same notes (sounding an octave apart); in modern scores they are separately accommodated.

The novice in score-reading will do well to rule a line or two on every page, for example, between wood-wind and brass and between percussion and strings. This is particularly desirable as the engravers of scores, in the desire to economize paper, often exasperatingly omit from a page the staves of any instruments that do not happen to be in use on that particular page. Thus the number of staves on a page may vary widely and if one is trying to follow a performance with a score, and the composition is at all a quick one, before one has got one's bearings on a new page one has to turn to one still newer.

Thus in a popular cheap score (not at all an exceptional one) at the moment before the present writer the number of staves per page within one and the same movement varies from 7 to 20, and an instrument that has the fifth line down on one page has the second on another and the tenth on still another. Moreover, when an unusually large number of instruments is in use, the engraver turns the pages sideways and rules the staves at right-angles to their normal position, treating the two facing pages as one big page. Obviously these proceedings add enormously to the difficulty of score reading, and it is to be regretted that the simple plan of engraving thick lines between each two groups of instruments (wood-wind, brass, percussion, strings) is not adopted, as it would offer, at any rate, *some* guidance to the eye.

The next difficulty in reading comes from the multiplicity of clefs—treble, alto (for the violas, at all events), tenor (for the tenor trombones, and the upper notes of cellos and bassoons), and, in a Continental-printed score, possibly soprano (i.e. the C clef on the lowest line) for soprano voices and, also, the alto and tenor clefs for these voices—with, of course, too, the bass clef for bass voices and various instruments.

But the greatest difficulty for the novice lies in the notation of the transposing instruments, which gives the uninitiated the impression that many of the instruments are playing individualistically in keys remote from that of the bulk of their fellows. For an explanation of this peculiarity see *Transposing Instruments*.

It may be admitted that by the beginner some of these anomalies may be disregarded if his object is merely to 'follow' a performance with the score, i.e. to use the score as a means of enabling him to note more completely the details of the orchestration. When his ear catches a melody from the orchestra his eye may catch it on the score by its general contour and its rhythm, undisturbed by the fact that, if it be one of the 'transposing instruments' that is playing it, the notation represents it in a wrong key. Indeed, for the ordinary listener a score is little more than an aid to disentangling coloured threads and may be frankly treated as such without one's feeling that expenditure on its purchase has been wasted. As for the more serious student, he will set himself to learn the art of exact score-reading by playing on the piano first, perhaps, simple minuets and slow movements from the early string quartets, then movements from Haydn and Mozart symphonies (taking care to use modern scores in which the instruments appear in the now accepted order); then movements from Beethoven's symphonies and so on to Wagner and to the moderns.

Both the mere listener and the serious student must acquire the knack of distinguishing what may be called the leading voices of the moment. If the First Oboe has a melody the eye must automatically gravitate to that; if the melody is then taken up by the Clarinet the eye must follow it on the other stave. And so on— the stave of the First Violins being looked upon, however, as the one which most consistently maintains the position of leading actor in the play of sound.

Other articles supplementing this one are as follows:

Violin Family; *Flute Family*; *Oboe Family*; *Clarinet Family*; *Saxophone Family*; *Brass*; *Trumpet Family*; *Cornet*; *Horn Family*; *Trombone Family*; *Tuba Group*; *Saxhorn Family*; *Cornett Family*; *Recorder Family*; *Viol Family*; *Lute Family*; *Percussion Family*; and various articles on separate instruments, ancient and modern. Also *Conducting*; *Symphony* 3; *Opera* 7; *Ornaments* 4; *Chamber Music* 2 (for 'Chamber Orchestra'). The question of conductorless orchestras is discussed under *Conducting* 7.

ORCHESTRAL COLOURS. See *Colour and Music* 3.

ORCHESTRAL SCORE. See *Score*; *Orchestra and Orchestration* 6.

ORCHESTRAS IN CHURCH. See *Anglican Parish Church Music* 4; *Methodism and Music* 7.

ORCHESTRATION. The art or act of scoring for an orchestra (cf. *Instrumentation*).

ORCHESTRE DE GENRE. This term, which during the 1930s became common in French-speaking countries, appears to mean the same as *Tipica Orchestra* (q.v.).

ORCHESTRION. See *Mechanical Reproduction of Music* 9. (But there have been many instruments called by this name.)

ORDER OF GOLDEN SPUR. See *Knighthood and other Honours.*

ORDINAIRE (Fr.). 'Ordinary', normal; sometimes to rescind some direction to play in an unusual way.

ORDINARIO (It.). 'Ordinary', normal, e.g. *Tempo ordinario* (q.v.).

ORDINARY. See *Mass* 2.

ORDO EXSEQUIARUM. See *Rituale.*

ORDRE. See *Suite* 1, 3.

OREFICE, GIACOMO. Born at Vicenza in 1865 and died at Milan in 1922, aged fifty-seven. He composed operas, ballets, orchestral suites, chamber music, piano music, etc., occupied an important position as a teacher of composers (Milan Conservatory), and served as newspaper music critic.

O'REILLY, MILES. See *Lochaber no more.*

ORFEO ED EURIDICE. See *Orpheus and Eurydice.*

ORFF, CARL. Born at Munich in 1895. He is an influential Munich teacher ('rhythmical education through the dance'), conductor, editor of works of Monteverdi, etc., and composer. His many works include a 'scenic cantata', *Carmina Burana* (1938; frankly eschewing counterpoint, development, and all but the most elementary harmony, and gaining its effects through the exploitation of simple rhythms, reiterated short motifs, and plain-song-like declamation), and a number of other choral works, as also operas, and orchestral compositions. His 5-vol. text, *Das Schulwerk* (1930–54), gives expression to his views as a teacher of young children, with much stress on the use of tuned percussion instruments.

See *Harpsichord Family* 9 (end); *Opera* 24 f (1949).

ORGAN

(For illustrations see pp. 764, 768, 781, pls. **127–32**.)

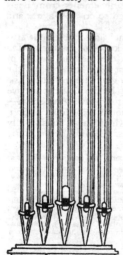

Since many music-lovers other than organists have a curiosity as to the construction of the instrument, the attempt will here be made to explain this in an entirely untechnical way, and certain more technical information will be added, in list form, at the end. The older, mechanical type of organ is taken as the basis of the description that follows, as offering a simple means to a fundamental understanding; but the manner in which mechanism has in modern organs been superseded is indicated throughout.

1. The Fundamentals. The old Scottish name, invented in derision at the time when Calvinistic piety objected to the introduction of machinery for the worship of God, was 'Kist o' whistles' (i.e. 'chest of whistles', or 'box of whistles'). This is a good description, so far as the foundational principle of the instrument is concerned (up to the 1930s, but see *Electric Musical Instruments* 4).

A number of pipes, little and big, are placed upon a box (or **Wind Chest**).

The whistles are in several rows, each row, or **Rank**, comprising a complete set of whistles of some special tone-character, etc.

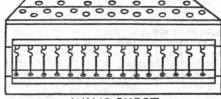

WINDCHEST

The box is furnished with an even supply of wind from a **Bellows** supplied by **Feeders** or, in modern organs, a rotary fan, electrically driven.

In order that all the ranks shall not sound

together unless desired, **Sliders** of wood are made to pass under their mouths, each slider

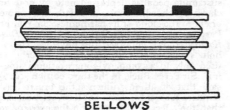

BELLOWS

controlling one rank. They have holes in them to coincide with the mouths of the pipes, and being pushed in, the holes no longer coincide and the rank is out of action, or 'stopped';

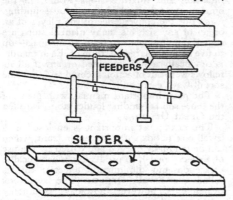

FEEDERS

SLIDER

hence the word **Draw-stop**, or merely **Stop**, for the knob which controls a slider, and hence, by usage, the additional employment of the word 'Stop' to signify a rank of pipes, i.e. a set of pipes, affected by one such knob. Such a set is also called a **Register.** In modern organs the sliders are often replaced by a valvular gear, and the draw-stops by tiny balanced slips of ivory. In order that all the notes of a rank shall not

sound together, the mouth of each pipe in the rank is supplied with a hinged lid under it, a **Pallet,** operated by a series of rods, called **Trackers** and **Stickers,** or, in modern organs, pneumatic or (more usually now) electric connexions, these constituting the '**Action**' ('Tracker Action', 'Pneumatic Action', or 'Electric Action'). The action is attached to a hand-keyboard, or **Manual,** and (some of the ranks) to a foot keyboard or **Pedal Board.**

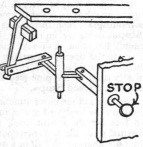

STOP

Now imagine the organist at work on a simple instrument. He pulls out those particular stops whose pipes will give him the tone-colours he wants (*their* pipes are then capable of action, whilst the others are restrained by the sliders). He puts his fingers and one or other of his feet upon the keys which will give him the notes of the chord he wants (the pallets in question then open the mouths of the pipes concerned, the wind enters, and they sound). That is essentially all there is in the mechanics of organ playing.

The whole ensemble of keyboards and stops is called the *Console.*

PALLET

TRACKER

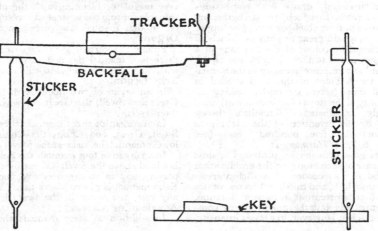

TRACKER

BACKFALL

STICKER

STICKER

KEY

2. The Details (p. 764, pl. **127.** 1). Imagine now the following refinements:

(*a*) The variety of 'Stops'. Most of the pipes are mere whistles, tubes of wood or metal with a mouthpiece, and *their* ranks are called **Flue Stops**. But a certain number have a tongue of metal like that of a toy trumpet, vibrating against the open (or partially open) side of a little brass tube called *eschallot* or *shallot*) at the bottom of the pipe (see *Reed*), and these are called **Reed Stops**.

(*b*) Some of the pipes attached to a particular note on the keyboard are of the normal length (8 feet for the lowest one), sounding at the normal pitch like the corresponding notes on a piano. Others are of half or a quarter the length (4 feet and 2 feet for the lowest note), sounding one octave and two octaves above, respectively. Still others are of double or even quadruple the length (16 feet and 32 feet for the lower note, sounding one octave and two octaves below, respectively (64 feet *has* occurred, sounding three octaves below). Thus on depressing a particular note of the keyboard the organist may, if he draws the appropriate stops, hear not merely a note of the normal pitch but that note duplicated in several octaves—the addition of lower octaves adding dignity and that of higher octaves brilliance.

A stop of which the notes are of the normal pitch is called an **Eight-Foot Stop**, and so, too, we have a **Four-Foot Stop** and a **Sixteen-Foot Stop**, a **Two-Foot Stop** and a **Thirty-two-Foot Stop**.

(*c*) This last principle (the principle of providing pipes of other than normal pitch) is in any large instrument carried further. There is a type of stop, called a **Mutation Stop**, which sounds not an octave or two octaves higher but some other harmonic (as, for instance, the interval of the fifth above the octave), and there is another type, called a **Mixture Stop**, in which each note is provided with several such pipes (of pitches corresponding to certain of the natural harmonics of that note: see *Acoustics* 2. Such stops are invariably drawn with some stops of normal pitch, to which, by strengthening one or more of their chief harmonics or 'upper partials', they add great brightness. Much of the characteristic colour of the full tone of a large organ is due to the superposition of the 'mutation' and 'mixture' tones upon the normal pitched tones. Stops of this kind existed in medieval times (often, curiously, making up the majority of the stops of an instrument), and, amazingly, anticipated Helmholtz's theory (proved by his invention of the Helmholtz Resonators) by five hundred years (see *Acoustics* 6, 8, 20; *Harmony* 4).

Purists have occasionally protested against the presence of such stops, on the grounds that they produce a succession of parallel intervals of the octave, fifth, and third, and even seventh, etc., such as, written out in musical notation, would appal any but the most modern composition teacher. However, in a lesser intensity, the same parallel intervals are produced from the piano when, as is frequently the case, the sustaining pedal is depressed note by note or chord by chord, so releasing with every note or chord the cloud of its harmonics. Sir Walter Parratt, in the second edition of Grove's *Dictionary* (1907), endorsed the physicist Helmholtz's view that mixtures 'can properly be used only to accompany congregational singing'. Sir Percy Buck, in the third edition (1927) said that of all instruments the organ least requires the reinforcement of its overtones, and that 'the effect is distressing in the extreme to all but hardened organists'. Berlioz is quoted as objecting to the effect. However, Bach's ear approved and the ear of almost every organist since has done so, and a large organ without mutation and mixture stops would, in the opinion of most people, be very dull-sounding.

(*d*) For the convenience of the player of an organ of any size his many manual stops are shared out amongst two or more manuals—up to five in a very large instrument. Each manual is practically a self-contained organ: if all its fellows were out of action it could still, in some sort of way, 'carry on'.

The most important manual, with many of the more solid-sounding louder stops, is called the **Great Organ**.

The next most important is enclosed in a 'swell box' (a box with shutters in front, which can be gradually opened and closed by the use of a special pedal, so producing, mechanically, crescendo and diminuendo effects): this is called the **Swell Organ**. (The swell-box principle is, however, nowadays commonly applied to other manuals, though rarely to the Great Organ.)

The next most important, possessing a number of sweet-toned softer stops, is useful for accompanying purposes, and is hence called **Choir Organ**: in nineteenth-century British organs it was very undeveloped, but it now tends to be full and complete, like the corresponding 'Positif' in French organs.

Certain stops of an orchestral quality, not very useful for blending with the others but valuable for solo use against an accompaniment on another manual, are placed in the **Solo Organ**.

Finally, in certain very large instruments there is a manual devoted to delicate stops, with a far-away sound, and this is called the **Echo Organ**.

In an organ of two manuals there will be Great and Swell, the Great below (i.e. nearer the player).

In an organ of three manuals there will be Swell, Great, and Choir, the Choir as the lowest manual (i.e. nearest the player).

In an organ of four manuals the Solo manual is added above the Swell (i.e. furthest from the player), and in an organ of five manuals the Echo manual is placed above that. (This is, at any rate, the order in the best British and American instruments.)

In addition to these manuals there is, as

already explained, the **Pedal Organ.** Its normal pitch is not that of the manuals but an octave below, i.e. whilst the chief stops of the manuals are 8-foot stops, the chief stops of the pedal organ are 16-foot stops, giving 'depth' to the general effect, like the double-basses in an orchestra, and like them sounding an octave lower than the notation indicates. To these stops, of course, are added others of octave pitches (8-foot and occasionally 4- and 32-foot, and very rarely indeed the 64-foot already mentioned).

(e) By a system of **Couplers** two manuals can be connected, so that playing on one keyboard has the effect of playing on the two. And similarly the pedal organ can be 'coupled' to any one of the manuals, and indeed it is usually so coupled to the manual at the moment in use.

There are often, also, couplers causing the notes an octave below or an octave above to sound with the ones played (sub-octave and super-octave couplers).

(f) Certain of the stops can be 'drawn' in groups, by means formerly of special pedals, but nowadays usually of pistons pressed by thumb or foot. Pistons fall into two classes—'Ordinary' pistons affecting selected groups of stops of each of the manuals or the pedal organ, and 'General' pistons affecting groups of stops and couplers of the entire organ. Both classes of piston can be arranged or adjusted by the player in advance to affect the particular stops he requires for quick 'registration'. This adjustment can be instantly effected in the modern organ by means of a 'locking piston' placed for convenience in the key-slip of the Choir (third) manual, i.e. in the strip of wood below it. This much facilitates any quick changes of **'Registration'** ('Register' = 'Stop', as explained above, and 'registration' simply means the choice of stops to give the tone-colouring desired). Such stop-changing pedals as those described are called **Combination Pedals,** or **Composition Pedals,** and the pistons **Combination Pistons** or **Composition Pistons.**

3. The Tone-Colours and the Means by which they are Produced (pl. 127. 3, 4). Some explanation may now be given of the chief organ stops and the conditions affecting their tone. (See also *Acoustics* 7.)

The basic tone of the organ is its **Diapason** tone. This is the tone which every British or American church-goer recognizes as characteristic of an organ. Every organ has at least one **Diapason Stop,** and large organs have many, differing in their **Scale** (a confusing word which here means simply size of diameter of pipe) and so varying in their loudness, and also differing in their material (wood or metal) and in other details, so giving subtle varieties of diapason tone.

There are two kinds of diapason, **Stopped** and **Open** (and this applies also to some other varieties of stop). By a stopped pipe (a slightly confusing term in view of the other use of the word 'stop') we mean one which has a cover at the top; by an open pipe we mean one without a cover. The effect of the cover on a pipe is not merely felt in the tone quality, but also in the pitch, which becomes an octave lower than in a corresponding pipe left open; thus an 8-foot open diapason is actually 8 feet in length (i.e. in its lowest pipe), whilst an 8-foot stopped diapason is really 4 feet in length (i.e. in its lowest pipe), though as it sounds at 8-foot pitch we still *call* it an 8-foot stop. (To be quite accurate it should be stated that the stopped diapason approximates in tone to the flute type mentioned below.)

The important pedal stop, the **Bourdon,** is a sort of stopped diapason; its lowest pipe is 8 feet in length, but it is *called* a 16-foot stop.

Next in importance, perhaps, to the diapasons are those stops bearing the pleasant name of **Flute.** Some of these are, constructionally, stopped diapasons but they are so voiced (**Voicing** is the subtle adjusting of the tone-producing part of the pipe, a highly skilled occupation for specialists) as to cause a smooth flute-like tone. One type of flute is the **Harmonic Flute:** its pipes are of double the nominal length, though by means of a small hole pierced half-way up they are made to sound at their proper flute pitch, but with a peculiarly delightful hollow, silvery quality. (Cf. the octave harmonic on a violin string, produced by touching it gently at half its length. See *Acoustics* 8.)

The **String-Toned Stops** are important. The form of their pipes is so contrived as to produce more or less of an imitation of the tone of the violin and viol families. The various kinds called **Gamba** (cf. *Viol Family* 3) are the most important.

All the above are 'flue' stops. The **Reed Stops** (cf. *Acoustics* 5) are of great variety. By means of their varying Scale (i.e., as already explained, the diameter of their tubes), of the width and shape of their reeds, the thickness and curvature of their tongues, the degree of **Wind Pressure** applied, and of other variable details, they exist in great diversity, some more or less successfully imitating orchestral reed and brass instruments, as the oboe stop, the clarinet stop, the trumpet stop, and the like. The term **Chorus Reeds** is applied to those not so generally put to solo use.

Stops which interest the public more than their musical value quite warrants are the **voix céleste** (or vox angelica) and the **vox humana.** Strictly to justify their names these should imitate respectively the vocal tone of Heaven and Earth.

The voix céleste has its pipes tuned slightly 'out', so as to 'beat' (see *Acoustics* 16) with one of the normal soft stops of the same manual (dulciana or salicional), which stop is automatically brought into action whenever the voix céleste stop itself is drawn. The slight 'wave' thus produced causes a pleasant mysterious effect: possibly angels do thus sing, but if so a few minutes' musical entertainment by angels would be sufficient, as the effect soon palls.

The vox humana is a reed stop with a tone which, if it imitates the voice of humanity at all, imitates only that of humanity in advanced age; usually, however, the imitation is rather that of a discouraged goat. (The great Dr. Burney, at the end of the eighteenth century, said 'No such stop, in the treble part, has ever reminded me of anything human, so much as the cracked voice of an old woman of ninety, or, in the lower parts, of Punch singing through a comb'.)

With the vox humana is commonly drawn the **Tremulant**—not a 'stop' at all, strictly speaking, but a very ancient device causing a vibration or fluctuation in the tone of whatever stop is drawn with it, which, effective for a movement, becomes extremely irritating if long continued.

4. Range, Wind-pressure, etc. The range of the organ keyboards is now normally as follows: Manuals, five octaves above C on second leger line below bass stave; Pedal from same note to F two and a half octaves above, or to G above that (in U.S.A. always to G).

So far as keyboards are concerned the organ's range is, then, about an octave less each way than that of the piano, but its actual range is enormously greater, because of the varying 'feet-length' of pipes in the different registers. The pipes in the very largest organs ever made range from 64 feet to ⅛ inch, and reach the very limits of audibility in each direction. No other instrument has anything like this compass.

Scaling (i.e. the width of a pipe in proportion to its length, already referred to) greatly affects tone.

The tone produced from a given pipe can vary a good deal according to the degree of **Wind Pressure** applied: it is commonly arranged that the reed-pipes shall be subjected to about double the pressure of the flue pipes, and certain reed-pipes (those of the Tuba variety; see list of stops below) even to as much as eight times that of the flue-pipes.

The **Detached Console**, i.e. the keyboard and stop part of the apparatus placed away from the sounding parts, where it is more convenient for the player (with a view to hearing his own effects, being in touch with his choir, etc.), is an improvement made possible by the application of electrics to the action.

5. Some Large Organs (p. 769, pl. **130**. 1–3). How complex is the machinery placed under the organist's control may be seen by an examination of the specification of some of the later large organs, e.g. that of Breslau (1913), which has 5 manuals, 187 stops, a great array of composition pistons, and 30 composition pedals, and that of Passau, with 5 manuals and 208 stops. At Philadelphia in 1917 was erected an organ of 283 stops. At the Liverpool Anglican Cathedral has been gradually built up an organ of 168 actual 'speaking stops' (we so call the stops which really sound, as distinct from other devices, such as couplers, operated by similar outward mechanism and sometimes dubbed 'stops' by courtesy).

The organ in the Chicago Stadium has 6 manuals and 828 stop-keys. The organ in the Convention Hall at Atlantic City, N.J., goes beyond this, being planned as a seven-manual instrument with 1,200 stops.

For a five-manual instrument in the early eighteenth century see mention of Notre Dame, Paris, in section 8.

6. The Unit Organ. This type of organ (developed by Casson, Compton, Hope-Jones, and others) had little vogue so long as the organ was chiefly a church instrument, but gained enormously during the period when it was also a cinema instrument. Both American and British builders, then, contributed to the unit organ's evolution, which the modern expansion of ellectrical application greatly favoured.

The principle is that of the fullest use of a comparatively small number of ranks of pipes, so avoiding needless duplication with its consequent expense and loss of space. Thus, instead of four flute-stops of 16-foot, 8-foot, 4-foot, and 2-foot tone respectively, one rank will be provided, but extended upwards and downwards, so enabling the flute tone to be taken from it at all these four pitches. What thus appears at the console and in the organ specification as four stops is seen on inspection of the interior of the instrument as only one, but that of greater range than normal. Many apparently fair-sized two-manual organs are thus built with only five or six ranks of pipes, and three-manual organs with only ten or so. Not only the octave stops but also the mutation and mixture stops are applications of the unit principle, i.e. they have no separate ranks of their own but are entirely 'derived'. The term *Extension Organ* is sometimes seen and its applicability is obvious.

Whatever economic advantages may be claimed for the unit organ, it is denied by none of its adherents that the principle of relying on mechanical means for the production of a build-up of pure organ tone is fundamentally unsound. A pipe cannot do duty in more than one place at once, and it is inevitable that in the playing of contrapuntal music irrational gaps and missing notes must occur when a unit organ is used as the medium of interpretation —irrational because they occur here and there at odd intervals in the contrapuntal texture without the consent of the player, so to speak. Further, it is not possible to obtain correct balance between 16-, 8-, 4-, and 2-foot pitches, as in a straight organ where these ranks are properly scaled and voiced to fit into the tonal architecture.

Moreover, any mutation stops obtained by unification are, of course, tempered (see *Temperament*), which is incorrect, as they no longer correspond with the natural harmonics of the keyboard notes (see *Acoustics* 8).

The Hope-Jones principle of the double-touch is usually applied in these instruments;

thus upon one and the same manual a solo and accompaniment may be played, by preparing one stop (say a clarinet) on the second touch (i.e. depressing the keys to the full extent of their fall) and a small group of suitable accompaniment stops on the first touch (i.e. depressing the keys merely to their first resistance, part-way down). The principle is applied to the pedals, as well as the manuals, so enabling the player to change from a light accompanying pedal to a heavy solo pedal when he wishes to bring out a particular passage, or to change the weight of his pedal when he moves his hands from one manual to another. It is generally felt that the use of the double-touch device is prejudicial to the finger technique of the executant, which is a reason why it is practically confined to the cinema organ.

A special application of the principle of double touch is occasionally made to the stop-tablets (for there are no draw-stops on the cinema-type organ); on pressing a tablet to the bottom not only is the stop in question brought into action, but all other stops on that manual are put out of action. Thus when this effect is desired, one motion of the hand serves for two.

Cinema organs of the unit type were usually entirely enclosed within swell boxes. As a rule they were so arranged that any stop could be played from any keyboard.

The great object of the cinema organ was orchestral imitation; it generally lacked diapason tone, and hence 'body'.

The widespread impression amongst a section of the musical public that a unit organ consists of about a dozen vox humanas and a powerful tremulant is based upon observation of the performances of the injudicious.

7. The Pipeless (Electrophonic, Electrotonic) Organ (p. 769, pl. 130. 4, 5). This type of instrument (which dates from 1930) is discussed under *Electric Musical Instruments* 4.

8. History of the Organ in Europe (p. 765, pl. 128). There are records of the existence of an instrument of this class from long before the beginning of the Christian era (see *Hydraulus*; *Jewish Music* 5). By the tenth century after Christ the art of organ building had got so far as is indicated by the specification (in which, however, allowance must be made for poetic hyperbole) of the famous Winchester Cathedral instrument—two manuals (played by two performers), each manual of twenty notes, each note having ten metal pipes, making 400 pipes in all. It is said to have required seventy blowers, and the organists' practice must have been expensive.

Possibly the twenty notes were those of the 'Hard' and 'Natural' Hexachords (see *Hexachord*) which the singers were using. If in any instrument the 'Soft' Hexachord, with its B flats, was provided for, the number would be twenty-two. Possibly some organs had that number. (At a later date they certainly did.)

The twenty keys for the twenty notes would be very broad and each would require the pressure of the whole fist to depress it; or quite as probably there was, instead of a key, a slider affecting the pipes of *each note*, the melody being produced by adroit (but necessarily slow) manipulation of the sliders.

By a reference to *Harmony* 4 it will be seen that this instrument would be sufficient for the needs of the time; it would merely thunder out the plainsong melodies of the service, and so lead the singing.

This organ was famous as being of giant size. For long after its date there were few organs that could not more or less easily be moved about the church. Those that could be less easily moved were called **Positive Organs** (i.e. organs of fixed *position*)[1] and the others (which were often carried in procession slung from the neck of the player, who manipulated the keys with one hand and the bellows with the other) were **Portative Organs**. A particular kind of tiny portative organ was the **Regal** (p. 884, pl. **149**. 2), which possessed merely one set of pipes, and these reed-pipes (see *Reed-Organ Family* 2).

Reeds first came into use in the fifteenth century. It is surprising to learn that mutation stops were in use three centuries earlier.

Organ-building in Britain took a new start from the restoration of Charles II (1660). Many of the previously existing church organs had been destroyed by Puritan principle (see *Puritans and Music* 3; *Inns and Taverns*) during the Civil War and Commonwealth. This led to the settling in England of foreign-born organ-builders, especially Schmidt (q.v.), often called 'Father Smith', and his two nephews from Germany, and Renatus Harris (of English parentage) from France. These became leaders in the revival of the craft.

The organ developed early in Northern Germany, and by the seventeenth century had assumed something very like its present character (save for a much clumsier mechanism), so that from that period date the organ compositions that were soon to form the foundation upon which built the great Sebastian Bach, e.g. those of Reinken (1623–1722), Buxtehude (1637–1707), and Pachelbel (1653–1706).

A special feature of organ building and playing in Germany and the Netherlands was the provision (perhaps as early as the fourteenth century) of a pedal department and the surprisingly high development of a pedal technique. The first compositions to show a separate pedal part are some preludes of Adam Ileborgh, dated 1448: they are in a manuscript now in the library of the Curtis Institute, Philadelphia (see also *Notation* 4). It is one of the most amazing facts in musical history that

[1] The name 'Positive Organ' was about 1887 adopted by Thomas Casson for a miniature instrument designed by him for small churches where space or money for a larger instrument is lacking. There were devices by which the lowest note of each chord played could, if desired, be reinforced (giving the effect of pedalling), and the highest similarly reinforced (giving the effect of the melody played on a second manual).

most countries other than the German ones so slowly adopted the pedal-board. France added a pedal-board to some of her organs in the early seventeenth century, and in the eighteenth her bigger organs were well furnished with pedal-pipes. The organ of Notre Dame, Paris, in 1773, had a pedal-board of nearly three octaves with seven stops—four of them flues and three of them reeds (this was a five-manual instrument).

These early pedals, both in Germany and France, were of the clumsy sort called 'toe-pedals' (p. 739, pl. **122. 6**). The following statement by Schweitzer (*My Life and Thought*, 1931) will surprise some organists who have wrestled with Bach's more elaborate pedal passages:

'In pedalling, Bach could not use the heel because the pedals of his day were so short; he had to produce every note with the point of the foot. Moreover, the shortness of the pedals hindered the moving of one foot over the other. He was, therefore, often obliged to let his foot glide from one pedal on to its neighbour, whereas we can manage a better legato than was possible for him by moving one foot over the other, or by using foot and heel alternately.

'When I was young I found the short pedal of the Bach period still existing in many old village organs. In Holland many pedals are even to-day so short that to use the heel is impossible.'

England was more than three centuries behind Germany in adopting pedals. Fifteen years after Bach's death his countryman Herschel (q.v.), afterwards the great astronomer, won the position of organist of Halifax Parish Church by 'faking' a simple pedal effect. He placed leaden weights on the lowest finger-key of one of the manuals and on its octave, and extemporized as on a 'tonic pedal' (see *Harmony* 24 p), obtaining 'such a volume of slow solemn harmony' as nobody could account for.

The question of the precise date of the introduction of organ-pedals into England, however, is one which has been much discussed and the confident statements made from time to time by various authorities seem to be open to question.

W. L. Sumner, in his authoritative *The Organ* (1952), quotes a record of a payment of £20 in 1720–1 to 'Xtopher Shrider' for supplying 'the Pedal and its Movements' to the organ of St. Paul's Cathedral. But this seems to be a quite isolated instance, and the provision of pedal-boards in England in any numbers was delayed for another seventy years.

Dr. C. W. Pearce (*The Evolution of the Pedal Organ*, 1927) says:

'Six short toe-pedal keys have been found in an old organ (built by Snetzler in 1756) at Sculthorpe Church, Norfolk. This may have been an experimental production of pedals, made by Snetzler shortly after his arrival in England [really 16 years after, since he arrived in 1740], but a tentative commencement not immediately followed up.'

Some other examples of early pedals:

(a) Tans'ur's *Elements of Music Displayed*, in its 'Book III', published in London in 1767, speaks as if at that date pedals had become fairly common:

'To play on an organ, is, to press down the several Keys with the Fingers (*or if Pedals, with the Feet*) . . . .'

(b) Still earlier Chambers's *Cyclopædia* (1728) says that large organs have pedals and Grassineau's *Musical Dictionary* (London, 1740), in its article 'Organ', says:

'Usually the longest pipe is sixteen feet; tho' in extraordinary Organs 'tis thirty-two: *the pedal tubes are always open though made of wood and of lead.*'

Admittedly this work is largely a pirated translation of a foreign one (Brossard's *Dictionary*, Paris, 1703), and the allusion may have passed from the one book to the other by inadvertence. But the opening page bears an endorsement by Dr. Pepusch, organist of the Charterhouse, and Dr. Greene, organist of St. Paul's Cathedral and the Chapel Royal ('We whose names are herinto subscribed do approve the following sheets'), and it is curious if they have let 'get by them' a passage concerning their own special domain, yet not applicable for their country.

(c) Two of Handel's organ concertos, published by Walsh in 1740 and 1760, include a pedal part.

(d) Burney's *Commemoration of Handel* (London, 1785), referring to the Dr. Greene just mentioned, says:

'From Greene's great admiration of this master's manner of playing, he had sometimes literally condescended to become his bellows-blower, when he went to St. Paul's to play on that organ, for the exercise it offered him, in the use of the pedals.'

Now Handel first visited England in 1710 and settled there in 1712. Greene became organist of St. Paul's in 1718. Burney came to London in 1744 and knew Handel and, we may be sure, Greene. Greene died in 1755 and Handel in 1759.

Whilst all this calls for explanation it may be admitted that 1700 appears to be the really important date in the provision of pedal-boards in England, as several London organs acquired them about this date. It is said that the active pedal part in the service 'Cooke in G', which is of this date, was written to display the pedals at Westminster Abbey, of which the composer was organist.

It should be noted that when pedal-boards were adopted in England they were for long rudimentary contrivances, often with merely a single octave of pedal keys which pulled down the corresponding manual keys. The name 'German Pedals' was applied, but it is not clear to the present writer whether this term was applied to any pedal-board as such or merely to the later ones, which possessed pipes of their own (but see next paragraph).

Rees's *Cyclopædia* (article by Burney, c. 1805) speaks of 'large church organs' as being supplied with pedals, and says 'these command certain pipes, which, to increase the harmony, are tuned an octave below the diapason'. It complains that 'scarce two organs in the kingdom have their pedals alike, either in respect of number or position', and gives a diagram of the pedal-board at St. Paul's Cathedral, which 'might serve as a model for all other English organs'. This pedal-board has a range of two octaves, C–C. At this time many pedalboards reached down only to G (bottom line of bass stave). The fully developed pedal-keyboard was not at all common in England until about 1830–40, and could not always be found even then: the London papers of June 1844 announced: 'The organ in the Hanover Square Rooms being found by Dr. Mendelssohn not to have the German pedals, he is prevented giving the Organ Performance, as previously announced'. Probably this organ had merely a few pedals; it had only nineteen when built a quarter of a century earlier. As late as 1884 Dr. Longhurst, Organist of Canterbury Cathedral, wrote to the *Musical Times* saying that his organ had only one octave of pedals (and a swell organ descending merely to Tenor C).

Many older English organists would to the end of their days not touch the pedals, so that the seventy-five-years-old Sir George Smart (q.v.), organist of the Chapel Royal, on being asked at the famous London Exhibition of 1851 to try one of the organs there, replied, 'My dear Sir, I never in my life played on a gridiron'. This state of things was one of the main obstacles to the introduction of Bach's organ music into England, and the much-needed raising of the general artistic standard in organ playing (see *Wesley, Samuel*); when Bach's works did begin to be heard they were often spoken of comprehensively as 'The Pedal Fugues'.

If England lagged as to the provision of its organs with pedals, the swell device, on the other hand, is probably a purely English invention (Jordan, 1712, in the organ of St. Magnus the Martyr, London Bridge).[1] It was slowly taken up abroad, so that when Dr. Burney made his famous tour in Germany in 1772, sixty years later, he came across only one organ supplied with it. For some years after the introduction of the swell it was of the clumsy type called 'Nag's Head' (a shutter rising and falling); then the English builder, Green, introduced the present 'Venetian' type (louvres, like those of a Venetian blind; see p. 608, pl. **106**. 6).

The pneumatic action, which at last almost entirely replaced the necessarily clumsy and often heavy mechanical action, is also of British origin (Booth, 1832; Barker, 1837); and so is the Composition Pedal (Bishop, 1809). During the latter half of the nineteenth century Henry Willis (1821–1901), the leading British organbuilder, introduced a large number of both mechanical and tonal refinements, rebuilding nearly half the cathedral organs of his country, building the most notable concert-hall organs (St. George's Hall, Liverpool; Albert Hall, London, etc.), and establishing a new standard.

[1] A claim for priority on the part of Spain has been made. See *Spain 8*.

British organ-builders now rank very high. In France during the same period Cavaillé-Col (1811–99) rendered similar services.

For the out-of-order arrangements of the lowest notes in early organs—up to the beginning of the nineteenth century—see *Short Octave and Broken Octave*. For references to the introduction of Equal Temperament in the Organ see *Temperament*.

9. History of the Organ in America. The following are a few of the main facts:

The first organ may have been that in Gloria Dei (Swedish) Church, Philadelphia, which it is thought may have been installed in 1694.

The King's (Episcopal) Chapel, Boston, Massachusetts, had an organ in 1714; it had been offered to, but refused by, Brattle Square (Independent) Church there, which could not overcome its prejudices and did not possess an organ until nearly eighty years later. It is now in St. John's Chapel. Portsmouth, New Hampshire (p. 768, pl. **129**. 6).

Christ Church, Philadelphia, had an organ in 1728, and Trinity Church, Newport, Rhode Island, one in 1733. The first organ to be actually built in America (i.e. not imported from England) was that of John Clemm in Trinity Church, New York City, in 1737: it had three manuals and twenty-six stops. Early in the 1740s there were two organs in the Moravian Church, Broad Street, Philadelphia (see *Bohemia*).

A treatise on organ playing (apparently the first) appeared in the United States in 1809 (Andrew Law's *Art of Playing the Organ*; Cheshire, Connecticut); it went into a second edition ten years later. Dr. Edward Hodges (of Bristol, England), organist of the new Trinity Church, New York, when it was rebuilt in 1846, had a good deal of influence on organ playing and organ building in the United States of America. The organ in the South Reformed Church, New York, about this time, is said to have been the first in America to possess an independent pedal department, pneumatic action, and a vox humana stop. The placing of a fine German organ in the Boston Music Hall, in 1863 (see 10, below), gave a great impetus to the arts of organ building and organ playing.

The subsequent popularity of the organ in the United States has been remarkable. Large and fine organs abound. Unlike Britain, however, the United States has a dearth of organs in rural districts in some parts of the country.

A good many innovations, in both Britain and America, were, between 1890 and 1914, due to the Englishman Robert Hope-Jones (1859–1914)—new devices in electric action, double touch, and tonal novelties (see 6 and references in the list of stops at the end of this article). During the late nineteenth century the artistry of the builders Roosevelt in the United States and Cassavant in Canada set a new standard.

10. A Reconstruction of the Seventeenth-Century Organ. More recently it is contended that just as to form a correct impression of the domestic keyboard music of the sixteenth and seventeenth centuries we must hear it on the harpsichord and clavichord, and not on the piano, so to form a correct impression of the early organ music we must hear it on an instrument of the time, which differed as much from the modern instrument as the harpsichord and clavichord do from the piano. Reconstructions of 'baroque' organs have been made by various makers, and performances on them show the music of that period in an altogether different light. The general tonal principle is individuality of stops, rather than smooth ensemble.

11. Old Organs still in Use. A few weeks before first drafting this article the author stood behind the organist of a famous German cathedral and admired his adroit accompaniment of the plainsong on an organ of three manuals ('Echo', 'Manual', 'Positif') and pedal, with 'tracker' action, with the stop-handles all placed above the player's head, so that he could not change them except when the music ceased, with no couplers, no composition pedals, no swell box, and an almost total lack of diapason tone (practically nothing but string-toned stops, flutes, and mutation stops). And this was in a church (Aachen) famed for its music all over Christendom eleven hundred years ago.

There is a good deal of old pipe-work remaining in many organs, but, in general, many new stops have been added and the mechanism many times renewed. Of 'Father Smith's' work the organ retaining most was probably that of the Temple Church, London, but this was, unfortunately, entirely destroyed by enemy action in 1941.

Many early organs were actuated mechanically. There are one or two such still in use in England (see *Mechanical Reproduction* 10).

12. Organ Playing. The foundational principles of artistic performance on the organ are the same as those on every other instrument (see *Interpretation*). But special to the organ are, (1) its pedal technique; (2) the player's inability to mark accent by applying greater force—calling for an even greater attention than in other instruments to the niceties of phrasing and rhythm; (3) the need for the discriminating use of a colour palette which ranges far beyond that of any other single instrument and approaches that of the orchestral composer; (4) the wide differences between the resources and the mechanical apparatus of individual instruments, calling for a remarkable suppleness of adaptation.

Point (3) is of particular importance. There is no instrument which offers so much encouragement to the rowdy player who wishes to make a loud noise or to the sentimental player who wishes to tickle the sensuous susceptibilities of his hearers. (He who inherits the greatest wealth has the greatest power to do good or harm.) Much use should be made of single stops, of families of stops (diapasons, flutes, etc.) as such, and of combinations without pedal. Couplers should not be over-used.

The **Touch** of the organist is totally different from that of the pianist. The facts that a note, once depressed, goes on sounding until released, and once released immediately ceases sounding, call for the practice of exactness and the acquirement of an extreme legato—which can, however, be effectively abandoned on good cause.

The wholesale adoption of electric mechanism by many modern builders has already influenced the technique of organ playing to a large extent. Crispness in the key touch (which had suffered during the period when tubular-pneumatic action held the field) has now been restored to its former excellence, and today the touch of the manual keys in the modern electric organ approximates to that of the better 'tracker' organs of 100 years ago. The essential feature of this delightful touch is the *top resistance* of the keys. That is to say, in the course of its travel the key first offers a resistance equivalent to a weight of $4\frac{1}{2}$ oz.; when this has been overcome and the key is pressed down, the resistance offered is only 2 oz., and a slightly higher pressure by the finger will then be enough to hold it down. Clean playing in rapid runs and scales is thus rendered an easy matter on the modern organ.

In the same way stop-control of the various tonal resources of the instrument has been reduced to a fine art, thanks to the facilities offered by the quick-acting accessories of the modern electric console. Fundamental changes of stops over the whole organ can be effected in a flash by simply pressing *one* of the general pistons, or by operating the 'General Crescendo' pedal, or, if a sforzando is required, by pressing on and off with the foot the 'Full Organ' reversible pistons. The net result of all these progressive developments in organ-building is to place the organist more on an equal footing with the pianist in the matter of controlling the machine at his disposal and to make organ playing a more fluid and intimate matter.

The British public tends perhaps to take the organ player's art a little cheaply, probably from the fact that it can, without payment, hear so much organ playing in church and elsewhere. But a fine organist is a fine artist. Beethoven said (letter to Freudenberg): 'If an organist is a master of his instrument I rank him amongst the first of virtuosi.' Competent British artists of the organ today must sometimes wish they had been born a little earlier, when though their instrument was much inferior their public was more appreciative. In the early nineteenth century Surrey Chapel, London, holding 2,000, used to be crammed to hear Samuel Wesley and Benjamin Jacob give a four hours' performance (40 to 50 items) on an organ of thirteen stops, with only $1\frac{1}{2}$ octaves of pedals (and only one octave of these supplied with independent pedal-pipes).

13. The Organ Repertory. No instrument except the piano has a more varied solo repertory than the organ. Its beginnings date back to

ORATORIO OF DAVID. NEUKOMM'S celebrated Sacred Dramatic Oratorio of David, now performing with unprecedented success by the Handel & Haydn Society, has been published by them, and may be obtained at DITSON'S Music Store, 107 Washington street, by the dozen or single.   152w   ● march 30

2

1. ST. PHILIP NERI, founder of the oratorio (By Zuccaro, 1593). See *Oratorio* 2

2. A BOSTON ORATORIO ADVERTISEMENT OF 1835. (See *Oratorio* 7—1834; also *Neukomm*). This oratorio enjoyed amazing popularity both in Britain and America. Boston heard it 12 times in 1836 and 14 in 1839

3. THE HOME OF THE BOSTON HANDEL AND HAYDN SOCIETY IN 1850. See *Oratorio* 6

1   3

4. HANDEL WATCHING THE REHEARSAL OF AN ORATORIO. The conductor is at a two-manual harpsichord. The solo vocalists stand at his left. The main body of the orchestra is behind him and the choir in front of h.m to the left. At his left are the principal instrumentalists—2 Violins, Flute, and 'Cello
(Contemporary print in British Museum)

N.B. Every Ticket will admit either one Gentleman, or Two Ladies.

COVENT-GARDEN.
By SUBSCRIPTION.
The Ninth Night.

AT the Theatre-Royal in Covent-Garden, Wednesday next, will be perform'd
A NEW SACRED ORATORIO.
A CONCERTO on the ORGAN,
And a Solo on the Violin by Mr. DUBOURG.
Tickets will be deliver'd to Subscribers on Tuesday next, at Mr. Handel's House in Brook-street.
Pit and Boxes to be put together, and no Person to be admitted without Tickets, which will be deliver'd that Day, at the Office in Covent-Garden Theatre, at Half a Guinea each. First Gallery 5 s. Upper Gallery 3 s. 6 d.
The Galleries will be open'd at Four o'Clock. Pit and Boxes at Five.

For the Benefit and Increase of a FUND *esta-blish'd for the Support of Decay'd* MUSICIANS, *or their Families.*

5. ORATORIO AS SEEN BY HOGARTH, 1734

6. FIRST LONDON PERFORMANCE OF 'MESSIAH', 1743

1. BATON CONDUCTING IN THE LATER 15TH CENTURY—a remarkable anticipation of modern practice by one of Melozzo da Forlì's musician angels from the church of SS. Apostoli, Rome (now in the Vatican). See *Conducting* 2

2. LATE 16TH-CENTURY CHOIR AND ORCHESTRA. 2 Boy and 3 Men Singers, Virginals, Violin, Bass Viol, Lute, Transverse Flute, 2 Sackbuts, 2 Cornetts. Joint conductorship by Virginalist and Treble Viol player—his instrument strangely held, this possibly not being a very exact picture. (Cf. *Conducting* 1, 2)

3. A GERMAN PERFORMANCE OF 1620. Bassoon, Trombones, and Singers, with Organ (other instruments are in galleries not here shown). The conductor beats time with the left hand. See *Conducting* 2

4. A VENETIAN ORCHESTRA AND CHOIR IN THE 18TH CENTURY. The conductor has a roll of paper (cf. *Conducting* 2) and has his back to his forces. Strings are on each side of him and Brass and Kettledrums in galleries. Singers at left

5. SCHÜTZ'S CHOIR AND ORCHESTRA IN THE 1670's (from *Geistreich Gesang-Buch*, published just after his death). He can be seen amongst his singers, at the left of the desk, beating time with his hand. The orchestra is in the organ gallery and is hardly to be seen in this reduction

6. A NORTH GERMAN CHURCH CANTATA PERFORMANCE (from Walther's *Lexicon*, Leipzig, 1732). The conductor holds a thick baton or roll of paper in each hand. He faces his singers (not here included) but has his back to his players. The Violoncello (no peg at that date) is next to the Organ to support the figured bass. Note the old convex bows and the clumsy organ pedals. Conductor and organist are probably using the same score (very inconveniently placed!). See *Conducting* 2

the sixteenth and early seventeenth centuries (when, however, organ music was little differentiated from virginal music), with such composers as the Englishman Bull, the Italian Frescobaldi, and the Dutchman Sweelinck. In the later seventeenth century and the earlier eighteenth century the Dane Buxtehude was important, and the Germans became prominent, with Pachelbel, Bach, and others—Bach today remaining, in the eyes of every organist, the greatest master of organ composition the world has ever seen.

Organ composition is not, unfortunately, a great feature of the succeeding period (the period of orchestral development under Haydn, Mozart, and Beethoven). The eighteenth-century and the early nineteenth-century English organ composers (e.g. Stanley, Nares, Samuel Wesley, Crotch, and Thomas Adams) are, however, by no means to be overlooked; there has, happily, been a considerable republication of English organ works of this period (see *Voluntary* 5).

In the Romantic Period Mendelssohn was a notable organ player and composer: his organ works are not of the deepest but they suit the instrument and sound well. Liszt and Brahms, in their different styles, wrote some organ music (see under *Chorale Prelude*). In England Samuel Sebastian Wesley left worthy compositions.

The French and Belgian schools developed greatly in the latter half of the nineteenth century and early years of the twentieth, the works of Franck and Saint-Saëns, Guilmant, Widor, Lemmens, and Vierne being outstanding. Much French organ music is brilliant rather than solid, reflecting the French organ, which lacks diapason tone but has many flutes and fine reeds. On the other hand, much English organ music is solid and dignified rather than brilliant. When the French falls into defect it is flimsy; when the English does so it is dull. (This is merely a broad generalization.) In Germany, Merkel, Rheinberger, and Reger added notably to the repertory, and Karg-Elert, later, made a considerable reputation. All the composers mentioned and many other organ composers (including the more modern British and American) will be found treated under the headings of their own names.

The neglect of the organ by so many great composers, combined with its ability to reproduce, with more or less fidelity, many of the colours of the orchestra, led to a great expansion of the repertory in the way of transcriptions or 'arrangements' of orchestral works. Thousands of such arrangements were issued, many of them the work of the greatest organists, such as W. T. Best, of Liverpool (1826–97). Obviously even if every stop of the organ were a perfect replica of some orchestral instrument, and if all the instruments were thus represented, an exact reproduction of an orchestral performance would be still unobtainable, since the number of keyboards and human limbs available is far too few. But a fair imitation can be got and sometimes something a good deal better—a genuine *translation* of the orchestral score into terms of the new medium. We have here an opportunity for the exercise of the highest skill and the most refined taste: no instrument offers a greater.

Organ concertos have had a limited popularity. Handel wrote a number. A good many people, however, have felt with Berlioz that the organ playing with the orchestra produces a 'detestable effect', and the number of such works has remained small. Generally speaking, when organ is added to orchestra only the diapason stops are of value, as all the rest have more effective counterparts in the orchestra itself; the pedal, of course, can make a real contribution.

14. A Student's Classified List of Organ Stops. No list of unarguable accuracy and completeness is possible, since not only are new names sometimes introduced by organ-builders but the older names vary in their significance with different periods, different countries, and different individual builders. It is hoped, however, that the following, which is the outcome of a good deal of time spent in the study of British and American organ specifications, old and new, and of consultation and comparison of a large number of authorities (often greatly at variance), may be found to provide for all ordinary requirements of readers. The classification adopted is, in the main, an artistic rather than a scientific one, i.e. it is often based less on the constructional principles of the pipes of the various stops than on their tonal effect. It is in fact in some parts a player's classification rather than an organ-builder's classification. Doubtful cases have been decided according to a balance of experience, as, for instance, the classification of certain stops, the tone of which in some organs partakes more of a true diapason quality and in others more of a string or flute quality.

The length and pitch mentioned are (except when otherwise mentioned) those normal to the stops in question when found on the manuals; on the pedals they will usually be of double the length and an octave lower in pitch.

The stops most commonly met with in smaller organs have in this list their names in heavy type. (In the very large instruments almost every stop name existing comes into use, and even then organ-builders seem to feel a shortage in their nomenclature.)

I. Stops with Diapason Quality of Tone.

Open Diapason. The characteristic stop of the organ; if an organ of only one stop can be imagined this would be the stop, and the organ would still sound like an organ, and like no other instrument whatever. As a manual stop it is generally of metal, but as a pedal stop often of wood. It is normally of 8-foot length and pitch, but an organ may include additional examples of half or double the length, and thus an octave above or below the normal pitch. It is not uncommon to find more than one Open Diapason on the same manual, sometimes as many as four, of contrasting and complementary tone quality.

Stentorphone (from 'Stentor', the Greek warrior in the Trojan War, who could shout as loud as fifty ordinary men). A very powerful type of open diapason, with wide mouth and on high pressure.

Montre. An open diapason on a special raised sound-board of its own, generally so placed as to form the front of the organ case ('Montre' is French for 'shop window'; cf. *Prestant*, later, in this connexion).

Double Open Diapason. An open diapason of 16-foot length and pitch. (For 'Double Diapason' see later.)

Major Bass. Generally a 16-foot open diapason on the Pedals.

Horn Diapason. See under III. 'String Quality of Tone'.

Violin Diapason. See under III. 'String Quality of Tone'.

Geigen Principal. See under III. 'String Quality of Tone'.

Principal. In British and American organ parlance this means an open diapason of 4-foot length and pitch on the manuals or of 8-foot length and pitch on the pedals. It is used to add brightness to the 8-foot diapasons. In German parlance it normally (and quite properly) means the principal stop on the organ, i.e. the 8-foot open diapason on the manuals (but the German organs have also 4-foot and 16-foot principals).

Prestant. Same as 'Principal' (i.e. the British–American principal, not the German; see above). The word comes from Latin *Praestare*, 'to stand before', and alludes to position in the organ case (cf. *Montre* in this connexion).

Octave. Same as 'Principal'.

Fifteenth. A diapason speaking two octaves (fifteen notes) above the normal, i.e. it is of 2-foot length and pitch on the manuals and 4-foot length and pitch on the pedals.

Bourdon. The characteristic dull-toned, booming stop, especially on the pedals. If a small organ has only one pedal stop it is this. It is usually of wood, and has stopped pipes of 8-foot length and 16-foot pitch. (See 'Double Diapason' below.) It is of the Stopped Diapason family (see below). 'Bourdon' in French is, amongst other things, a name for the bee, and also means the drone of a bagpipe. As regards the quality of sound thus fancifully attributed to the stop, note that the Bourdon of French organs suggests this less than that of English organs, being a clear-toned Stopped Diapason of either 16-foot or 8-foot pitch.

Sub-bourdon. A (pedal) Bourdon of 16-foot length and 32-foot pitch.

Sub-bass. Same as 'Bourdon'.

Untersatz (literally 'Under-position', i.e. lower than normal pitch). This is the German for a 'Sub-bourdon'.

Double Diapason. Sometimes this term is met with, applied to a 16-foot manual bourdon (see above).

Quintatön. A bourdon (usually of metal) of which the scale and construction are such that the harmonic octave-fifth (i.e. the twelfth) is faintly heard with the normal sound. Occasionally a bourdon is unintentionally so made as to have something of this effect and it is then, in organist's slang, 'fifthy'.

Quintadena. Like the quintatön (see above), but with its tone more strongly tinged with the octave-fifth.

Cor de nuit (literally 'night horn', i.e. watchman's horn). A stop of 4-foot length and 8-foot pitch of the stopped flute or the quintatön class (see above), of large scale and thin metal and very individual tone-quality.

Dulciana. In Britain a small-scaled, soft, open metal diapason; the most generally useful soft stop on the organ. Usually of 8-foot length and pitch, but sometimes of 4- or 16-.'In the United States the dulciana belongs to the string quality type (see III later).

Dolce (literally 'sweet'). A small-scaled, soft-toned, 8-foot metal stop, the pipes being of inverted conical shape. It tends, from this constructional feature, to be somewhat unsteady in tone.

Dolcan. Same as 'Dolce'.

Dulcet. A dulciana of 4-foot length and pitch.

Stopped Diapason. A diapason of 4-foot length and 8-foot pitch. It may be argued that the quality of tone in many examples would rather justify the name 'Stopped Flute'.

Gedact or **Gedeckt** (literally 'covered', or 'roofed'). A soft-toned metal 'stopped' stop of small scale. It somewhat approaches flute quality (hence included in the list of flute-toned stops following), or, very occasionally, clarinet quality.

Lieblich Gedact ('Lieblich' means 'lovely'). Same as above with a compliment added. See also II. 'Flute Quality', later.

Salicional. In Britain a quiet-toned 8-foot metal stop of slightly reedy quality (Latin *salix*, 'willow'). In the United States this stop belongs to the string quality group.

Salicet. Same as 'Salicional' (see above), but 4-foot.

Cor-Oboe. A stop of 8-foot length and pitch, with a tinge of the quality of the reed stop oboe.

Voix céleste (or *Voix célestes*) or **Vox Coelestis** (literally 'Heavenly Voice'). Already explained in section 3 of this article.

Vox Angelica (literally 'Angelic Voice'). Usually much the same as voix céleste. Occasionally, however, the name is given to a single-rank stop of soft dulciana quality.

Unda Maris (literally 'Wave of the Sea'). Much the same as voix céleste.

Diaphone. A loud type of diapason, of Hope-Jones's invention. Each pipe has a vibratory apparatus (of varying form), which gives the stop its characteristic quality—i.e. a peculiar lack of definiteness of timbre. It is of 32-, 16-, or 8-foot length and tone.

Diapason Phonon. An open diapason with the lips of the pipes leathered, so 'refining' the tone. The name is that given by Hope-Jones. But there are many leathered diapasons in existence without this name.

Phoneuma. A very soft stopped dulciana, with a quintatön effect. Of Hope-Jones's introduction and little used.

II. Stops with Flute Quality of Tone.

Hohlflöte (literally 'hollow flute', i.e. hollow-sounding). A metal or wood stop of 8-foot length and pitch. Nearly the same as clarabella, claribel, and keraulophon.

Clarabella. See above (Latin, *clarus*, 'bright', and *bellus*, 'beautiful').

Clarabel or *Claribel Flute.* As above.

Keraulophon. As above. (See under III. 'String Quality'.)

Suabe Flute (Latin, *suavis*, 'sweet'). Very like Hohlflöte, but usually of 4-foot length and pitch.

Harmonic Flute. A metal stop, of 8-foot length but a 4-foot pitch, the latter being the effect of a hole bored half-way up, which causes it to sound its octave harmonic (see *Acoustics* 6, 7), and gives it the characteristic silvery tone of harmonic sounds. (Sometimes of 16-foot length and 8-foot pitch.)

Rohrflöte or **Rohr Flute** (literally 'Reed Flute', but 'reed' here means a tube). Of metal stopped pipes, with a slender tube through the stopper (hence the name).

Flûte à cheminée (literally 'Chimney Flute'). The same.

Spitzflöte (literally 'Pointed Flute'). Of metal, with slightly conical shape (hence its name). It may be 8-foot, 4-foot, or 2-foot in length and pitch.

Zauberflöte (literally 'Magic Flute', cf. Mozart's opera). A pleasant-sounding metal stop usually of 8-foot pitch. It is really a kind of harmonic flute (see above), but has stopped pipes, not open ones, and the hole is pierced in such a place that the third harmonic (i.e. the twelfth) is the note heard, not the second harmonic (i.e. the octave)—the length of the pipe being adjusted accordingly.

Grossflöte (literally 'Large Flute'). The name is probably intended to distinguish it from 'Kleinflöte' (see below). A metal stop of 8-foot length and pitch.

Fernflöte (literally 'Far-flute' or 'Distant Flute'). A soft stop of metal of 8-foot length and pitch.

Flauto traverso. Supposed to resemble the ordinary orchestral flute (the 'cross flute', as distinct from the old flageolet or recorder, i.e. from the end-played flute). Of 4-foot length and pitch.

Waldflöte (literally 'Woodland flute'). Like the clarabella (see above), but often of 4-foot length and pitch and with inverted mouth.

Clear Flute. Much like the above.

Flûte d'amour (literally 'Love-Flute'.) In Britain a soft stop of 8- or 4-foot length and pitch; in the United States of 2-foot length and 4-foot pitch and of small scale.

Flauto amabile. The same.

Gedact or **Gedeckt**. This stop (given already under I. 'Diapason Quality') sometimes approaches flute quality.

Stopped Diapason. The same may be said.

Lieblich Gedact (literally 'lovely and covered' or 'lovely and lidded'). A Gedact of 8- or 4-foot length and pitch. It has often a pretty pure flute quality. (It also has been given under I. 'Diapason Quality'.)

Lieblich Flöte (literally 'Lovely Flute'). Same as above, but of 4-foot length and pitch.

Piccolo. A metal or wooden flute stop of 2-foot length.

Harmonic Piccolo. This stands to the piccolo as the harmonic flute does to the ordinary flute. Of 4-foot length and 2-foot pitch.

Kleinflöte (German for 'Little Flute'). Same as piccolo.

Flageolet. A soft piccolo.

Gemshorn (literally 'Chamois Horn'). A light-toned stop, with conical pipes of 8-, 4-, or 2-foot length and pitch (generally of 4-).

Flautina. A gemshorn of 2-foot length and pitch.

Doppelflöte (literally 'Double Flute'). A wooden stop, the stopped pipes having two mouths (hence the name). Of 8-foot length and 4-foot pitch as a rule. It was at one time particularly popular in the United States.

Tibia. A large-scaled, loud type of stop, not brilliant, but full-toned. The tibia in anatomy is the shin-bone, and the shin-bone of birds was supposed by the ancients to have supplied the material for early flutes. The word 'Tibia' has been applied to stops in organs on the Continent for some centuries; in Britain and the United States it owes its use largely to Hope-Jones.

Tibia Major. A loud-toned flute of 8- or 16-foot length and pitch.

Tibia Minor. Its name is given to several rather different types of flute stop, generally open but sometimes stopped and of 8- or 4-foot pitch.

Tibia Plena. A very loud flute, of 8-foot length and pitch, introduced by Hope-Jones.

Tibia Profunda. Something like tibia plena, but of 16-foot pitch.

Tibia Dura. Of 4-foot length and pitch; hard-toned. One of the Hope-Jones inventions.

Tibia Clausa. A large-scale stop of 4-foot length and pitch introduced by Hope-Jones.

Clarinet Flute. A stop of 4-foot length and 8-foot pitch, having a hole through the stopper which gives it a slightly reedy quality.

Block Flute (German, *Blockflöte* = recorder; see *Recorder Family*). A metal stop of unusually large scale and of 2-foot length and pitch, a sort of very robust piccolo.

Flûte à pavillon (literally 'Tented Flute'). A muted stop of which the pipes end in a sort of bell-tent structure. Of 8- and 4-foot shape and pitch.

Melodia. A stop popular in the United States, of 8-foot length and pitch, of the same type as the Hohlflöte.

Major Flute. A loud flute of 8- or 16-foot length and pitch.

Bass Flute. A rather foolishly named 8-foot flute on the pedal; should be named 'Flute 8'.

Concert Flute. The name is sometimes given to a harmonic or other flute, usually on the solo manual.

Corno dolce. A not very common type, of nondescript soft flute colour ('Corno' is a misnomer as a rule).

Flauto dolce. Much the same as dolce (see I. 'Diapason Quality'), but a little more fluty.

Salicional. See remark on this stop under I. 'Diapason Quality'.

III. Stops with String Quality of Tone.

Gamba (in full 'Viola da Gamba'; see the mention of that instrument under *Viol Family* 3). An agreeable and much-used stop with a very fair imitation of string tone. The pipes are of metal, often tapering somewhat towards the top, and then sometimes widening again into an inverted bell (thus sometimes called *Bell Gamba*). They are usually of 8-foot length and pitch, but sometimes of 4- or 16-. Some gambas have a small roller in front of the mouth of each pipe: these are called *Bearded Gambas*.

The Gamba of French organs has a much smoother tone than that of British organs, so that in registering French organ music some stop of the Violin Diapason type represents it better.

Viola da Gamba. See above.

Bell Gamba. See above.

Echo Gamba. A soft gamba.

Keraulophon (from three Greek words, meaning 'Horn-Pipe-Voice'). Constructionally a sort of salicional (see I. 'Diapason Quality'); its tone may sometimes approach string quality (it appears also in the list of flute-toned stops above). It is almost obsolete.

Violone. A small-scaled stop of 8-foot length and pitch; or (much more usually and more properly, the instrument the 'Violone' being the double-bass) of 16-foot length and pitch.

Violoncello. Like the above; 8-foot length and pitch.

Contrabass. Much the same as 'Violone'.

Viola. A stop of 8-foot length and pitch.

Violino. A metal stop of 4-foot length and pitch (sometimes 8-foot) with a challenging title.

Geigen Principal or **Geigen** (Ger. *Geige*, 'fiddle'). A sort of slightly string-toned diapason of 8- or 4-foot length and pitch—or sometimes 16-.

Horn Diapason. A stop of 8-foot length and pitch and of string-like tone, the word 'horn' being a little misleading.

Terpodion. A sort of wide-mouthed gamba, probably imitative of the tone of one of the now obsolete instruments of this name (see separate article *Terpodion*).

Violin Diapason. A small-scaled diapason of 8-foot length and pitch.

Viole d'Amour. Much like the above. In the United States the pipes are usually tapered slightly.

Viole d'Orchestre. A small-scaled gamba of somewhat biting quality.

Fugara. A rather rough-toned variety of gamba.

Aeolina or *Aeoline*. Of 8-foot length and pitch; a soft stop supposed to imitate the tone of the Aeolian harp (q.v.). Sometimes it is tuned to 'beat' with another soft stop, like the céleste: other names are given it occasionally, always beginning with 'Aeol'. It is sometimes of gamba quality and sometimes of dulciana quality.

Erzähler. A soft stop of 8-foot length and pitch; the pipes are those of the gemshorn (see II. 'Flute Quality'), tapered so that the top is only one-quarter or even one-fifth of the diameter of the pipe near the mouth. When properly voiced the first harmonic (i.e. the octave) is almost as strong as the fundamental. Two of them together make a good céleste. This stop was introduced by the Skinner firm and is a feature of many organs in the United States. (The word *Erzähler* is German for 'narrator'—a fanciful idea!)

Dulciana. See remark on this stop under I. 'Diapason Quality'.

Salicional. See remark in section I of this list.

IV. Mutation Stops (i.e. Single Rank). All are open, metal stops.

Quint. See *Acoustics* 10.

Twelfth. It sounds an octave and a fifth above the normal, i.e. the interval of a twelfth. Length and pitch 2⅔-foot.

Nazard. Same as above.

Octave Quint. Same as above.

Seventeenth. It sounds two octaves and a third above the normal, i.e. the interval of a seventeenth. Length and pitch 1⅗-foot.

Tierce. Same as above.

Nineteenth. It sounds two octaves and a fifth above the normal, i.e. the interval of a nineteenth. Length and pitch 1⅓-foot.

Larigot (the old name for Flageolet). Same as above.

Flat Twenty-first. It sounds two octaves and a minor seventh above the normal, i.e. the interval of a minor twenty-first.

Septième. Same as above.

These and similar single-rank stops, drawn with one or two carefully chosen stops, produce some new 'colours' (see *Timbre* for the explanation of this).

When these stops appear on the pedal their length and pitch are double (sometimes quadruple).

V. Mixture Stops (i.e. Multiple Rank).

The following are old or modern names for various types of stops of this kind, from two ranks to five. Note that most of them 'break back' at certain points in their compass, i.e. their various ranks, instead of continuing indefinitely up the scale and so arriving at last at very shrill notes, return (preferably not all the ranks of a stop at the same time) to a lower octave. Note too that it is a feature of the Cornet that its ranks do *not* 'break back'.

Mixture. Full Mixture. A mixture of diapason scale.

Cornet. On this, as a solo stop, florid solo pieces, called 'Cornet Voluntaries', were much played in the eighteenth century (see *Voluntaries*). It now usually has 4–5 ranks.

Mounted Cornet ('Mounted' = placed high on a sound-board of its own, so as to be well heard).

Echo Cornet. Of slight calibre and gentle tone.

Furniture, or *Fourniture*. A powerful mixture.

Cymbel. A brilliant loud mixture, resembling either 'Furniture' or 'Sharp Mixture' (see below). It 'breaks back', i.e. repeats itself, every octave.

Sesquialtera. Properly a two-rank mixture of a twelfth and tierce, but any kind of mixture came to be so called.

Dulciana Mixture. A soft mixture generally on swell or echo manual.

Harmonics. A type of mixture stop, usually of four ranks (seventeenth, nineteenth, flat twenty-first, twenty-second).

Grave Mixture. A two-rank mixture (twelfth and fifteenth); the name, rare nowadays, indicates the effect.

Sharp Mixture. A mixture of high-pitched pipes and bright tone. The name, likewise rare nowadays, indicates the effect.

Plein Jeu. A sort of mixture, including only the unison, octave, and fifth.

Ripieno maggiore and *Ripieno minore*. Types of mixture stops, respectively voiced louder and softer. (For normal meaning of *Ripieno* see under that head elsewhere in this volume.)

Carillon. A three-rank mixture (twelfth, seventeenth, twenty-second). It is chiefly found in the United States and is very piquant in its effect.

Stops of the mixture family can generally be used only against a good backing of normal-pitched stops (whatever was done in earlier days), and their highest value is as an ingredient in the effect of 'Full Organ'.

VI. Reed-Stops. The pitch of a reed pipe depends on the length of the reed and not on the length of the pipe, which serves merely as a resonator—though generally made to scale. The pipes are mostly conical, not cylindrical.

Oboe. The commonest and most useful of all reed stops, and when avowedly imitative (as in the *Orchestral Oboe*) a very fair reflection of its instrumental counterpart. Of 8-foot pitch.

Hautboy. Same as above.

Cor Anglais. A type of oboe stop and, like it, of 8-foot pitch, or sometimes of 16-.

Bassoon. A 16-foot pitch oboe stop (usually in the pedal department).

Fagotto. Same as above.

Double English Horn. A 16-foot pitch chorus reed-stop of Hope-Jones's invention: it is very brilliant in tone.

Clarinet. Smoother toned than the oboe. Of 8-foot pitch (occasionally 16-foot). The pipes (cylindrical, not conical) are only half length.

Corno di bassetto. Much the same as clarinet but of broader tone, and, like it, of 8-foot pitch. The pipes sometimes have conical bells fitted to the top of the resonators.

Cremona. Much like the clarinet, and, like it, of 8-foot pitch (the name has nothing to do with the famous violin-making town, being a corruption of Cromorne; see *Krumhorn*).

Trumpet. A powerful stop of 8-foot pitch. 'Horn' and 'Cornopean' (see below) are practically synonymous with 'Trumpet'.

Clarion. Much the same as trumpet, but of 4-foot pitch.

Cornopean. Much the same as trumpet, but generally softer, though smoother. Of 8-foot pitch.

Horn. Much the same as trumpet, but fuller and smoother in tone. Of 8-foot pitch.

Tuba. Something like the trumpet but on high pressure and very sonorous. Of 8- or 16- or 4-foot pitch. The pipes are, for the most part, double the usual length.

Tuba Major. A variety of the above.

Tuba Minor. A small smooth-toned tuba.

Tuba Mirabilis. A variety of the loud tuba.

Tuba Sonora (Hope-Jones). A variety of the loud tuba.

Tromba. A variety of the loud tuba.

Ophicleide. A variety of the loud tuba.

Bombarde, Bombardon. A powerful stop of 16-foot pitch, often on the pedal; sometimes it is of 32-foot pitch. Presumably originally an imitation of the instruments of the same name (q.v.). But for *Clavier des bombardes* see next section (15).

Trombone. A 16-foot counterpart of the 8-foot tromba or tuba—generally on the Pedal Organ.

Posaune. A broad 'splashy' kind of old-fashioned reed-stop, often on light wind pressure. (The word is German for trombone.) Of 16-foot pitch.

Harmonic Trumpet. A trumpet stop embodying (in its upper pipes, at any rate) the principle of the harmonic flute. (All chorus reeds have harmonic trebles nowadays, and the prefixed epithet should indicate a stop 'harmonic' from Tenor F sharp upwards.) Of 8-foot pitch.

Vox Humana. A sort of clarinet stop with pipes of bigger bore and very short (usually only one-eighth the normal length). Of 8-foot pitch.

15. A List of Foreign Terms found in Organ Music (alphabetically arranged). This list is a mere selection of a few of the most commonly used terms. About two hundred and fifty such terms will be found dispersed through the book in their alphabetical positions.

Buffet d'orgue. French for organ case.

Clavier de récit. French for swell organ keyboard. 'Récit' originally meant any sort of a composition for one voice, being the word invariably used until the Italian word 'solo' superseded it. (The word is *not* an abbreviation of 'recitative', as sometimes imagined.) Originally in French organs

the manual which we call 'swell' was supplied with stops chiefly intended for melodic use accompanied by harmonies on another manual.

Clavier des bombardes (French). Keyboard of the Bombardes, i.e. the organ manual to which are attached the powerful trumpet and tuba stops (the French organs excelling in the reed department); in other words, the solo organ.

Echoklavier (literally, 'Echo Keyboard'). German for choir organ.

Grand Chœur. French for full organ.

G.O. or **G.** (= 'Grand Orgue') means 'Great'.

Grand Orgue. French for great organ.

G.P. (= 'Grand-Positif'), means 'Great and Choir coupled'.

G.R. (= 'Grand-Récit'), means 'Great and Swell coupled'.

Hauptwerk (literally, 'Chief-work'), or **Hauptmanual.** German for great organ.

H.P.W. or **H.W.** = 'Hauptwerk'.

Oberwerk (Ger.; literally 'upper-work') means 'Swell'. It is sometimes abbreviated 'Obw.' or 'O.W.'

P. (= 'Positif') means 'Choir'.

Pedalklavier (literally 'Pedal Keyboard'). German for pedal board.

Plein Jeu. French for 'Mixture' or for 'Full to Mixtures' (without reeds).

Positif. French for choir organ. The name perpetuates the idea of the old 'Positive' organ.

Principale. Italian for great organ.

Récit. See 'Clavier de récit', above.

Schwellwerk (literally 'swell-work'). German for swell organ.

Soloklavier (literally 'solo keyboard'). German for solo organ.

Unterwerk (literally 'under-work'). German for choir organ.

U.W. = 'Unterwerk'.

I, II, III, IV in German organ music. See separate entry, s.v. *Man.*

16. List of References to the Organ in other Articles.

Sound production in Organ—*Voice* 2; *Acoustics* 5.

Tuning of Organ by Mean Tone and Equal Temperament—*Temperament* 5, 6, 7. Divided Finger Keys for certain notes—*Temperament* 8; *Keyboard* 3. Organ Keyboard—*Keyboard*; *Short Octaves and Broken Octaves*. Position of Organ in Churches, etc.—*Concert Halls* 11.

Stopped Diapason's relative freedom from Harmonics—*Timbre*. Flue and Reed Pipes in early Organs—*Reed-Organ Family* 2. Invention of Harmonic Flute—*Spain* 8. Nature of Harmonic Flute—*Acoustics* 8. Acoustic Bass (or Resultant or Harmonic Bass)—*Acoustics* 10. Invention of Swell Box—*Spain* 8. Production of Drum Effects—*Acoustics* 16. Freedom from 'Key Colour' of Organ Music—*Colour and Music* 4. Organ of Bach's time—*Barocco*.

Pitch of Organs in Bach's time and in nineteenth century—*Pitch* 3, 4, 5. Pitch Names of Organ Builders, etc.—*Pitch* 7. Vibration Numbers of Organ Pipes of various lengths—*Acoustics* 15. Difficulty of distinguishing Pitch of Lowest Pedal Notes—*Acoustics* 17. Highest Sounds (Mixture Stops)—*Acoustics* 17.

Double Organ—*Double*.

Role of the Organ in old and modern 'Service Settings'—*Service*. Accompaniment of Plainsong—*Plainsong* 5. Accompaniment of Hymns in seventeenth century and today—*Hymns and Hymn Tunes* 9; *Gathering Note.* Organ Preludes and Interludes to Hymns—*Chorale*.

Official Position of Organist in 'Old' and 'New' Cathedrals—*Cathedral Music* 2; *Precentor.* Cathedrals as Training Schools for Organists—*Cathedral Music* 1. Neglect of Organ in Cathedrals during eighteenth and earlier nineteenth centuries—*Cathedral Music* 7. S. S. Wesley on position of Cathedral Organists—*Cathedral Music* 7. Salaries of Cathedral Organists in twentieth century—*Cathedral Music* 7, 8. Organists of Chapel Royal—*Chapel Royal*.

Puritan Objections to Church Organs—*Cathedral Music* 3, 5; *Anglican Parish Church Music* 2; *Puritans and Music* 3, 4. Organ Building at Restoration—*Cathedral Music* 6; *Anglican Parish Church Music* 3. Organ in Parish Churches at various periods—*Anglican Parish Church Music.* London Parish Clerks' Company's Organ—*Parish Clerk.*

Organ in Roman Catholic Church—*Motu Proprio; Roman Catholic Church Music in Britain; Verset.* Organ in various churches—*Congregational Churches* 4, 5; *Presbyterian Church Music* 2, 3, 6; *Baptist Churches* 5; *Methodism and Music* 8. Organ in Jewish Synagogue—*Jewish Music* 5, 6. Objection to Organ in Greek Church—*Greek Church* 2. Quaker Objections to Organ in seventeenth century—*Quakers and Music.*

Spain's Contribution to the Organ—*Spain* 8. Germany and the Organ—*Germany* 4. Scotland and the Organ—*Scotland* 6, 11; *Presbyterian Church Music* 2, 3, 6.

Organs in Taverns, Early Concerts and Music Clubs—*Concert* 4; *Clubs; Music Hall* 1. Mechanical Organs—*Mechanical Reproduction of Music* 4, 5, 6, 10, 11, 13. Various types of Organ Music—*Form* 12 (for fugue); *Chorale Prelude; Voluntary; Sonata* 10 e; *Arrangement; Improvisation.* Unauthorized titles of some of Bach's Organ Fugues—*Nicknamed Compositions.* Old Organ Notation—*Tablature.* Royal College of Organists—*Anglican Parish Church Music* 7; *Degrees and Diplomas* 2.

For dictionaries of organs and organists see *Dictionaries* 6 c.

ORGANETTE. See *Mechanical Reproduction of Music* 13.

ORGANINO. See *Reed-Organ Family* 6.

ORGANISTRUM. The hurdy-gurdy (q.v.).

ORGANISTS, INCORPORATED ASSOCIATION OF. See under *Incorporated*.

ORGANO (It.). Organ. *Organo d'eco*, echo organ (see *Organ* 2 d). *Organo d'espressione*, swell organ (see *Organ* 2 d). *Organo di coro* or *Organo Corale*, choir organ (see *Organ* 2 d). *Organo di legno*, (1) flue stops (see *Organ* 2 a); (2) xylophone (see *Percussion Family* 2 f, 4 e, 5 f). *Organo pieno*, 'full organ'.

ORGAN POINT. See *Point d'Orgue*.

ORGAN SOLO MASS (Mozart). See *Nicknamed Compositions* 15.

ORGANUM. See *Harmony* 4, 5.

ORGATRON. See *Electric* 4.

ORGEL (Ger.). 'Organ.' So *Orgelwalze*, 'organ cylinder', i.e. a clockwork organ, functioning by means of a barrel (see *Mechanical Reproduction* 5).

ORGELMESSE (Haydn). See *Nicknamed Compositions* 13.

ORGIA (It.). 'Orgy.'

ORGUE (Fr.). 'Organ.'

ORGUE DE BARBARIE. See *Mechanical Reproduction of Music* 6.

ORGUE EN TABLE. Regal (see *Reed-Organ Family* 2, 10).

ORGUE EXPRESSIF. See *Reed-Organ Family* 6.

ORGUE PLEIN. 'Full organ.'

ORGUE POSITIF. 'Choir organ' (see *Organ* 2 d) or positive organ (see *Organ* 8).

ORIANA. See *Madrigal* 4.

ORIENTAL MELODY. See *Melody* 10.

ORIENTAL MUSIC (p. 465, pl. 82). Until the second half of the twentieth century, 'Music' to the ordinary listener meant European music (for the most part written after 1700). Modern communications and the enormous development of the gramophone have combined to broaden our musical horizons immeasurably, and we can with little trouble find out for ourselves the widely differing characteristics of the musics of North and South India, Java and Bali, Japan and China, and so on. Each of these needs an extended article of its own, such as can be found in the first volume of the *New Oxford History of Music*. But there are certain qualities common to the music of all the races, nations and tribes included in the term 'oriental', and this makes it possible, in a brief article, to treat the subject in a general way.

Oriental music is purely melodic (but see explanation below) and is usually in free rhythm, i.e. not in a system of equal beats and measures; measured rhythms are, however, used for dancing (this distinction exists, of course, in much European music up to the early seventeenth century and again in the twentieth century). The rhythmic appeal is often a very strong feature, instruments of a purely rhythmic kind being common and some of the rhythms used being exceedingly complex.

The scale systems (see *Scales* 8) often use *microtones* (q.v.)—generally quarter-tones, so than an octave has as many as twenty-four steps instead of the series of twelve on which, until recently, occidental music has been almost entirely based. This, however, does not mean that so many notes as that are used in any one scale, the scales being merely different sets of notes chosen from the series of twenty-four. Moreover, some races (e.g. in the hill countries of India, and in China and Japan) use the primitive pentatonic scale, found also in some Scottish songs (the scale which corresponds to the black keys of the piano, beginning F sharp), and, so far from being microtonic, this scale has not even semitones (see *Scales* 10).

Very many oriental tunes have not so wide a *range* as an octave, merely ringing the changes on the notes within a section of half an octave or a little more.

Amongst some oriental races there is a system of modes, in the sense of the association of short groups of notes with particular scales (cf. *Motif*). A tune is nothing but an arrangement of these groups in a desired order, with added decorative notes and sometimes shiftings from one mode to another.

Decoration is a great feature of much oriental music, long notes being adorned with tremolo or blossoming into ornamental passages of shorter notes.

The element of *Improvisation* is important in much oriental music. It has to be skilfully carried out within the chosen mode, and may either consist of entirely original material or be merely an embellishment of a traditional tune (the principle of the western variation form, indeed).

It has been said above that oriental music is purely melodic. This is true in that there is no sense of harmonic combination. But, for vocal convenience, tunes, or portions of them, are sometimes sung in fourths or fifths, as was done in Europe in the beginning of the harmonic period (cf. *Harmony* 4), or even in seconds or other dissonant intervals. Also instrumental drone basses (of the kind to which the bagpipe still accustoms western ears) are common.

The *Forms* of the music are very simple. Tunes are short and mostly consist of only two or three phrases. Such music is comprehensible by all, and thus the latter-day western division of a people into those who can and those who cannot appreciate music does not exist. We may say that in oriental countries the art is in the folk-song stage, and like our western folk music it is transmitted orally.

Instruments are, of course, relatively uncomplicated in construction, and in the main they are used for the accompaniment of the voice rather than for independent performance. It should be remembered that at an early period the oriental influence was strongly felt in the development of musical instruments in Europe.

The words 'lute', 'rebec', 'guitar', and 'naker' (the old word for kettledrum; see *Percussion Family* 4) are all in origin Arabic—*'al-'ūd, rabāb, quitāra,* and *naqqāra.*

The oriental taste in vocal tone is very different from the occidental, and the smooth and refined voice-production which is the aim of the European and American vocal teacher and pupil is unknown in eastern countries.

Large claims are made for the general influence of Arabian theory and practice upon European musical evolution in the Middle Ages.

Oriental influence has, of course, often come again into occidental music from the later nineteenth century onwards, but a good deal of what is intended (in opera, tone-poems, etc.) to represent the East does so very superficially; indeed, there is an accepted convention of a theatrical kind that can hardly be considered to be more than a bag of melodic and orchestral tricks. The larger part of Russia (q.v.) is Asiatic, and an oriental tinge is seen in much Russian music. Spanish music inherits an oriental tinge from the Moorish conquerors who were expelled only in the fifteenth century. Jewish music (q.v.) is of course a branch of oriental music. The spirit of the arabesque in certain French works, such as Debussy's *Afternoon of a Faun,* is probably of oriental origin.

With the twentieth century a great danger has come about that the oriental races may partially or entirely lose their native music. This danger was recognized in a practical way by the foundation in 1930 of an International Society for the Investigation of Oriental Music ('Gesellschaft zur Erforschung der Musik des Orients'), with its seat in Berlin. One object was to make phonograph records of the music of the different races of the Near and Far East. Owing to political events it lived only until 1937, its record collection being then transferred to the Oriental Institute of the Hebrew University at Jerusalem.

In parts of the Far East the danger is just as pressing. The radio station of Tokyo broadcasts very largely programmes of the western classics, symphonic and operatic. The leading European phonograph firms possess associated houses in the East, to which they have for years sent pressings of all their disks, and many of their European recordings are thus remanufactured and issued in the East within a few weeks of their original appearance.

Just at the moment, then, when Western civilization is beginning to realize that oriental music is something better than the barbaric noise it has long thought it to be, the oriental nations are in grave danger of losing interest in it, and as it has been conveyed from generation to generation not by the arts of writing and printing, but orally, so soon as that interest is gone the art itself, unless special measures are taken, will have entirely evaporated—that is, will be for ever irrecoverable. One would wish East and West to study one another's music, whilst pursuing independent courses in their own, but that seems to be impossible.

ARTICLES ON COGNATE SUBJECTS. *Jewish Music; Russia; Spain* 1–3; *Plainsong; Rhythm* 10 (for oriental rhythmic influence in twentieth-century occidental music); *Harmony* 24 p; *Percussion Family* 4; *Applause* 2.

ORIGINALITY IN MUSIC. See *Composition* 12; *Quality in Music* 3.

ORNAMENTS OR GRACES

1. Their Universality.
2. Conventionalization of many Graces.
3. The Eighteenth-century Keyboard 'Doubles'.
4. Gracing in Chamber Music and Orchestral Music.
5. Variability of Notation of Graces.
6. The Decline of the Practice.

(See also Tables 12–16, pp. liii–lv.)

1. Their Universality. By ornament in music is meant melodic decoration.

The instinct to elaborate a melody is usual. So notorious have the eighteenth-century singers become for their elaboration of the composer's melodic line, and so heavily did some of the harpsichord composers of that century overload their music with 'graces', that it is sometimes absent-mindedly taken for granted that the practice of ornamentation is chiefly an eighteenth-century practice. From the earliest times, however, the tendency to ornament has been very marked. The existence of the vocal trill or shake is recorded as early as the third century. (For a reference to vocal ornament in Spain in the nineteenth century see *Singing* 1; *Spain* 1.)

Much of the church's plainsong, as we have it today, is quite evidently an embroidery upon a much simpler original (see *Plainsong* 3; *Machicotage*). There is early record of such embroideries. Indeed, the primitive notational system of Neumes (see *Notation* 2) provided for a decorative element. Apparently, as we should expect, the Italian singers were particularly active in its practice, for Guido d'Arezzo (c. 995–1050) advises singers other than Italian that if they find difficulty in what comes easily from Italian throats they should make no effort about it but leave their plainchant plain. Three centuries later that very uncompromising Pope John XXII (reigned at Avignon 1316–34) formally decreed the abolition of all such decoration, but without lasting effect.

When out of the unisonous plainchant there developed the combination of voices, each singing its own strand, and the whole weaving into a polyphonic tissue, the practice of embroidering at first continued, and we find that Hieronymus of Moravia (thirteenth century) in his *Tractatus de musica* has a chapter on ornament in the polyphonic music of his day.

How long the practice of embroidering in choral singing continued it is difficult to say. Obviously when the art of harmony had developed to a certain point of refinement and exactitude, any extreme deviation from the written note would, even if there were only one voice to a part, produce a clash between the parts; yet apparently the singers risked it (cf. the orchestral example in section 4 of this article).

In 1591 Giovanni Bassani, singer in the choir of St. Mark's, Venice (and later director of the music there), published a book of motets, arranged for organ with an optional part for a voice. Amongst them is a motet of Palestrina of which the style of treatment is sufficiently indicated by the following brief extract (remember that Palestrina was still alive):

(1) PALESTRINA.

(2) PALESTRINA-BASSANI.

This perpetuates the practice of lute- and organ-players and composers for a century or so before and reminds one of the practice of the viol-players of the period (see *Divisions* and *Ground*). We find just the same process going on in the song of certain less sophisticated Christian communities right up to the nineteenth century. The great class-singing teacher Mainzer (q.v.) noted down at Strathpeffer, Ross-shire, Scotland, some of the hymns of the Presbyterian Church as sung there, and published them under the title *Gaelic Psalm Tunes* (1844). Below are shown the first six notes of the well-known tune *Dundee* or *French* (1) as it first appeared in the early Scottish psalters and as it is heard today, and also (2) as sung by the Highland congregation whose singing Mainzer gives us.

(1)

(2)

(The crosses are added to help the reader to find his landmarks amidst the luxuriant jungle-growth of ornament.)

This seems almost incredible, but Mainzer's witness is unimpeachable, and it is, moreover, confirmed by many other observers. In the American colonies during the eighteenth century a similar exaggeration of 'gracing' prevailed (see *Hymns and Hymn Tunes* 10, 11; and compare *Methodism and Music* 4). It may be mentioned that older Irish folk-song singers treat their tunes somewhat in this way today and that many Spaniards are incapable of humming the simplest tune without embellishment.

In the solo vocal singing of the early seventeenth to the early nineteenth centuries the addition of embellishments to the music was a permitted and admired practice. The composer himself prescribed many such embellishments and it was understood that he left full liberty for the addition of others. Indeed, at the final cadences these were expected. If one of the more florid airs of Bach or Handel be examined it will be seen how often a passage fundamentally simple has blossomed out into runs and other decorative features. But vocalists did not stop at what the composer had written; the following is recorded as a contemporary reading of what in its unadorned state we now consider one of the most touching vocal movements in Handel's *Messiah*:

(a) Original.

Com — — fort ye

(b) Improved.

There exists a cadenza for the ending of the following movement, 'Every valley':

the crook-ed straight, and the rough

pla — — ces plain.

The singer of the earlier twentieth century who thus made the plain places rough and the straight crooked would have been listened to with amazed indignation and never re-engaged, yet this cadenza is recorded in the handwriting of Smith, Handel's confidant and amanuensis, and may be pretty safely taken to have had the composer's own sanction. Nowadays there is a strong movement towards the restoration of vocal ornament along with other features (smaller forces, authentic instrumentation) of performance.

The Italian opera at this period gave the greatest opportunities. Here the most elaborate shakes and roulades were interlarded with the text, and the final cadenzas assumed astonishing dimensions and attempted to prove the vocalist capable of safely negotiating the most acrobatically alarming difficulties. When we read of Farinelli singing to the King of Spain the same four songs every evening for ten years (see *Voice* 5) we must bear in mind that he probably varied their gymnastic element continually.

The instrumental music of the seventeenth and eighteenth centuries likewise abounded in the element of decoration. The comparative lack of sustaining power of the lute and harpsichord was always an encouragement to expansive composers and performers, who found, as it were, blank spaces to fill. The several 'initial ornaments', as they may be called (acciaccaturas, appoggiaturas, mordents, turns, etc.), at the beginnings of notes served also to mark the accent, otherwise not very easily marked in the case of the harpsichord.

2. Conventionalization of many Graces. To a large extent the graces became conventionalized in different countries, some, of course, being common to all. To print them out in full would have entailed much extra expense in engraving, and would, moreover, have obscured the main melodic lines of the composition, and so an extensive system of signs was evolved which told the performer where to embellish and, to a large degree, what was to be the nature of his embellishment.

As the practice of different countries and even of different composers within these countries varied greatly, many books of instrumental music opened with a table of the graces, explaining the interpretation of the signs used by the composer. Such a table is, for instance,

found in the book of Purcell's harpsichord music, published by his widow the year after his death, and Couperin's *Art de toucher le clavecin* ('Art of Playing the Harpsichord', 1717) has also a list. Bach profited much by the study of Couperin's keyboard works, but, as his biographer Forkel says, 'He considered them affected in their excessive use of ornaments, scarcely a single note being free from them'; with this criticism many pianists of today must be in sympathy. Bach's most famous son, Carl Philipp Emanuel Bach, in his *Versuch über die wahre Art das Klavier zu spielen* ('Attempt at the true manner of Keyboard-Playing', 1753), goes fully and very systematically into the whole subject of ornamentation in no fewer than eight chapters. He says (abridging some of his passages a little):

'Nobody doubts the necessity of ornaments. They are quite indispensable. They connect the notes and give life to them. When necessary they add to them a particular expression and weight. They render the meaning clearer; be it sad or merry or otherwise they contribute something towards it. An indifferent composition is made tolerable by them and the best melody, without them, is empty and lacking in significance. . . . Those performers who possess sufficient ability may insert ornaments beyond these I prescribe, but they must be careful to do this in the proper places and without doing violence to the general expression of the composition.'

He goes on, conservatively, to say that many notes require no addition and that, just as good architecture can be spoilt by overloading it with decorative features, or good cooking by too much condiment, so music, too, can be ruined by injudicious embellishment.

3. The Eighteenth-century Keyboard 'Doubles'. The keyboard composers of the eighteenth century provided one special opportunity for the display of skill in the neat performance of elaborate decorations. Every pianist is acquainted with Bach's first English Suite with its 'Courante avec deux Doubles' (i.e. with two extra versions filled out quite on the general principles of the elaborated Palestrina motet and the Scottish psalm tune quoted above), and likewise with his second and third English Suites, with their sarabandes followed by a version, 'Les Agréments de la même sarabande' (i.e. 'the Decorations of the same Sarabande'). These are examples of a common practice of a day when a real delight was taken in the adroit embellishment of a tune, as it was in the florid decorative treatment of the architecture of a great part of Europe at this period of Baroque.

4. Gracing in Chamber Music and Orchestral Music. It will be seen, then, that both composers and performers at that period indulged freely in the art of decorative additions. Even in the playing of chamber and orchestral music there were cases where such additions were tolerated (cf. the practice of dance-music players of today as mentioned under *Jazz* 3), and in a violin concerto or sonata it was taken for granted that when a 'subject' was repeated the solo player would elaborate his part so that the same passage should not be heard without the advantage of some new interest (see *Fioritura*).

How far decoration could go in orchestral music we see from an incident related by Spohr in his reminiscences; it occurred as late as 1813. He conducted an orchestra consisting of the best musicians in Rome. Ornamentation in the old Italian vocal style had become so much second nature with them that nothing he could say would induce them to keep to the copies before them. Thus at the end of a phrase for horns and clarinets the parts blossomed out something as follows:

5. Variability of Notation of Graces (cf. *Notation* 5). As already mentioned, a kind of shorthand came gradually into existence for the indication of the commonest of the ornaments. But it was never standardized, and there are examples of one sign being used with seven or eight different meanings by different composers, whilst one meaning may be found expressed by seven or eight different signs. Hence

in the preparation of modern performing editions of the pre-nineteenth-century classics some editors apply a good deal of research and careful exercise of judgement to the full elucidation of all but a few signs that have come to be fairly well understood as possessing definite meanings, these few being left in their shorthand and the others translated into detail.

It must be stated, however, that other editors show themselves to be culpably lacking in any large body of information on the practices of composers of various periods, and that too rarely do either the good or the bad editors adopt the scholarly (and indeed only honest) practice of making clear to the performer which are ornaments written out in full by the composer himself and which are their own translations of his shorthand into longhand.

6. The Decline of the Practice. With the period of Haydn and Mozart we get far less decoration than in the period of Bach and Handel, and with Beethoven still less. Moreover, the tendency has been for the composer to trust less to conventional signs and to write out most of his decorative passages in full, exactly as he wishes them to be performed. Chopin, however, did not keep to his own notation. When playing his own compositions 'he would introduce *fioriture*, always varying them, when repeated, with new embroideries, according to the fancy of the moment' (reported by his English friend G. A. Osborne, q.v.).

The element of decoration still persists and probably always will do so. To take a modern instance, the piano music of Albéniz and Granados embodies a very definite decorative element derived from the guitar playing of their native Spain.

As regards the interpretation of the conventional signs for ornaments the plan of the present volume is to give, at the opening, tables showing the commonest signs of ornaments and their interpretation (Tables 12–16). In addition there will be found in the body of the volume brief entries under such heads as *Shake, Mordent, Appoggiatura, Bebung*.

ORNITHOPARCUS (real name Andreas Vogelsang). Author of celebrated theoretical work, *Musicae activae micrologus* (Leipzig, 1516), of which John Dowland (q.v.) published an English translation a century later (1609).

ORNSTEIN, LEO (p. 1061, pl. **174**. 4). Born (of Jewish ancestry) at Krementchug, Russia, in 1895, but has lived since early childhood in the United States, where he has acquired citizenship. He is a piano virtuoso and has composed in large as well as small forms. His methods of composition at one time appeared more radical than they do today.

Cf. *Concerto* 6 c (1895).

ORPHARION. See under *Cittern*.

ORPHÉE ET EURYDICE. See *Orpheus and Eurydice*.

ORPHÉON. The French name for a male-voice choral society—generally not of very lofty

artistic ambitions. The Orphéoniste Movement began about 1835. From 1852 to 1860 Gounod was director of the Paris societies. By 1880 there were 1,500 societies with a membership of 60,000 and supporting several journals.

For the similar movement in Germany see *Liedertafel*.

ORPHEOREON. See under *Cittern*.

ORPHEUS AND EURYDICE (Gluck). Vienna, 1762; new version in Paris, 1774. Libretto by Calzabigi, after the Greek legend.

ACT I

SCENE 1: *A Grotto containing the Tomb of Eurydice*

Orpheus (*Contralto*: all the parts are now played by women) mourns, with his friends, for his wife Eurydice. **Amor,** the God of Love (*Soprano*), descends to console him. The bereaved husband, he says, may go down to the abode of the dead, to seek to prevail upon its guardians with his touching music. If he succeeds, he must on no account look upon Eurydice's face as he returns, or explain why he must not, or her life will be forfeit.

Scene 2: *The Abode of the Furies*

Orpheus seeks the aid of the Shades. His music and his sorrow move them to pity, and they open to him the gates leading to the Valley of the Blest.

Act II

Scene: *The Happy Valley*

Eurydice (*Soprano*) and the blest spirits sing of their joys. Orpheus is welcomed, and his appeal for Eurydice is answered. Avoiding her face, he leads her forth.

Act III

Scene: *A Wood*

Eurydice, at first transported with joy, cannot understand why her husband will not look at her, and he dare not tell her. She thinks he does not love her, and wishes again to die. Moved beyond endurance by her lamenting, he clasps her and looks into her face. As he does so, the penalty is paid and the life is rapt from her.

To Orpheus, now in the most bitter grief, appears Amor. This was but a trial of his faith: Amor restores Eurydice to life once more, and the two faithful hearts to their rapture.

See *Chaconne*.

ORR.

(1) C(HARLES) W(ILFRID) (1893-1976). Critic and the composer of a number of songs, especially to words by Housman.

(2) ROBIN. Born at Brechin in 1909. He studied at Cambridge and at the Royal College of Music, and in Paris under Nadia Boulanger. He has held the posts of organist of St. John's College, Cambridge (1938); Professor at the R.C.M. (1950), at Glasgow University (1956), and at Cambridge (1965). His compositions include orchestral, choral, and chamber music, songs, etc.

ORTHODOX CHURCH. See *Greek Church and Music*.

ORTIZ, DIEGO. A sixteenth-century Spanish composer of church music, lute music, etc., and the author of a famous book (1553, republished 1913) on the art of playing divisions (q.v.) on the bass viol. (Cf. *Concerto* 5.)

O SALUTARIS HOSTIA. A hymn sung at the service of Benediction (q.v.) and in certain other services: it is sometimes introduced between the *Sanctus* and the *Agnus* at High Mass (see *Mass* 2). It has a very elaborate traditional plainsong borrowed from the hymn for Ascension-tide, *Aeterne Rex altissime*. It has also been set by various composers either chorally or for solo voice. J. M. Neale's transla-

tion is now an official alternative to *Gloria in Excelsis* in the Communion Office of the Protestant Episcopal Church of America.

OSANNA. Italian form of 'Hosanna' (q.v.).

OSBORNE, GEORGE ALEXANDER. Born at Limerick in 1806 and died in London in 1893, aged eighty-seven. At twenty he went to Paris, where he studied under Kalkbrenner and others and became the close friend of Berlioz and Chopin, of whom in after years he had many interesting reminiscences. In his thirties he settled in London, where he had a high reputation as a teacher and as a composer of chamber music (some of it, for piano and violin, written in collaboration with de Bériot), and of piano music as little like the work of his two friends above mentioned as imaginable, as witness the once ubiquitous *Pluie de Perles*.

See references under *Pianoforte* 22; *Ornaments* 6.

OSSERVANZA (It.). 'Observation', hence 'care'.

OSSIA (It.). 'Or' (literally, 'Or maybe'). This expression is attached to passages added by the composer (or some editor) as alternatives to the original—often on grounds of greater facility (hence the ingenious bad guess of some young musicians that 'Ossia' means 'Easier').

OSTINATO (It.). 'Obstinate', 'persistent'. *Basso ostinato*, ground bass (q.v.).

OSTRČIL, OTTOKAR. Born in 1879 near Prague and died there in 1935, aged fifty-six. He was a school-teacher who turned musician and had a career in his native city as conductor and as composer of operas, symphonies, and chamber music. His style always inclined to the polyphonic and, indeed, in general the intellectual side of music appealed most to him.

OSWALD, JAMES. Born in Scotland about 1710 and died at Knebworth, Herts., in 1769, aged about fifty-nine. He was a dancing-master, violinist, and composer who settled in London, ran a music-publishing business, and became Chamber Composer to George III.

See *God save the Queen* 10.

OTELLO (Verdi). See *Othello*.

ÔTER (Fr.). 'To take off.' *Ôte, ôtent* are the third person sing. and plur., [he] 'takes off', [they] 'take off'. *Ôtez* is the imperative, 'take off'. So *Ôtez les sourdines*, 'take off the mutes'.

In organ music this verb means to throw out of use some stop up to that point in use.

O THAT WE TWO WERE MAYING. See *Hullah*.

OTHELLO (Verdi). Produced at La Scala, Milan, in 1887. Libretto by Boito, from Shakespeare's play.

Act I

Scene: *A Tavern by the Quay of a Seaport in Cyprus. Time, end of the Fifteenth Century*

Cassio (*Tenor*) and other officers and gentlemen welcome as governor the Moor **Othello** (*Tenor*), who is a general in the army of Venice. **Iago** (*Baritone*) tells **Roderigo** (*Tenor*) how he hates Othello, because others have received preferment over him. Finding that Roderigo loves Othello's wife, Desdemona, Iago sees a hope of hurting the Moor. He plies Cassio with drink, and when the latter picks a quarrel with **Montano** (*Bass*), former governor of Cyprus, and wounds him, Othello dismisses Cassio from his service. Alone together, Othello and **Desdemona** (*Soprano*) sing of their love.

ACT II

SCENE: *A Hall in the Castle*

Iago, bent on making Othello jealous of his wife, advises Cassio to ask Desdemona to plead for his reinstatement. This she does. Then Iago draws Othello's attention to Cassio's conduct, saying 'Look to your wife!' Iago makes a tool of his wife **Emilia** (*Mezzo-Soprano*). Getting Desdemona's handkerchief into his possession, he swears to Othello that Cassio lately had it, and promises to aid the Moor in vengeance upon Desdemona.

ACT III

SCENE: *The Great Hall of the Castle*

Desdemona innocently pleads for Cassio's reinstatement, but her husband angrily repulses her and goes out. Iago warns Othello to listen to his conversation with Cassio, and by dexterously leading Cassio on, and placing Othello where he cannot clearly hear the whole of it, further inflames the Moor's jealousy—not least by causing Cassio to show the handkerchief, which Iago has taken care shall come into the lieutenant's hands. Othello now determines to poison his wife, whilst Iago shall kill Cassio. (But the crafty Iago will order Roderigo to strike the blow.)

Messengers from Venice come to announce that Othello is recalled and his governorship given to Cassio.

ACT IV

SCENE: *Desdemona's Bedchamber*

Desdemona has a foreboding of evil. When Othello charges her with guilt, and she denies it, he strangles her. Emilia brings the news that Cassio has killed Roderigo. She reveals her husband's wickedness, and Othello, unwilling to live when he has destroyed what was dearest to him, stabs himself.

See *Opera* 21 l.

OTTAVA (It.). 'Octave.' So *All'ottava*, 'at the octave' higher (occasionally in orchestral scores the term is used to show that one instrument should play in octaves with another); *Ottava alta*, 'high octave' (same as last); *Ottava bassa*, 'low octave' (i.e. at the octave lower); *Ottava sopra*, 'octave above'; *Ottava sotto*, 'octave below'; *Coll'ottava*, 'with the octave', i.e play in octaves.

In all these expressions *Ottava* is sometimes abbreviated to *8va*.

OTTAVINO. See *Flute Family* 5 b.

OTTO (It.). 'Eight.'

OTTOBI, OTTEBY. See *Hothby*.

OTTONE (It.). 'Brass.'

OU (Fr.). 'Or.' **OÙ** (Fr.). 'Where.'

OULIBICHEF. See *Balakiref*.

'OURS' SYMPHONY (Haydn). See *Nicknamed Compositions* 11.

OUSELEY, FREDERICK ARTHUR GORE—Sir Frederick Gore Ouseley, Bart. (p. 165, pl. **34**. 9). Born in London in 1825 and died at Hereford in 1889, aged sixty-three. He came of a family distinguished in war, travel, and diplomacy, and of ample means. After Oxford he entered the Church, but his musical leanings and capacities had to find vent. They had been manifested in a remarkable way at an early age ('Only think, papa blows his nose in G', cried he at five; at six he played a piano duet with Mendelssohn and as an undergraduate he was a remarkable extemporizer of fugues).

Before he was thirty he had begun the building of St. Michael's College, Tenbury, which he munificently endowed and of which he for the rest of his life served as warden; here a full cathedral service is maintained and well-chosen musical boys receive an education that fits them to become leaders in the maintenance of a higher standard of music in the Anglican Church—as many of them have done.

He was for thirty-four years Professor of Music at his old university. He left a large quantity of church music of all kinds, some of which is still heard.

See references under *Absolute Pitch*; *Memory* 3; *Degrees* 1; *Anthem* IV.

OUVERT, OUVERTE (Fr., masc., fem.). 'Open.'

OUVERTURE (Fr.). Overture. (See *Overture* 7 for Handel's and Bach's use of the term.)

OUVRIR (Fr.). 'To open.' The imperative is *Ouvrez*—often used in organ music in connexion with the swell box or in the sense of to put into action some stop mentioned.

OVERBLOWING. See *Bagpipe Family* 2; *Cornet* 1; *Clarinet Family* 1; *Acoustics* 8.

OVERDAMPER. See *Pianoforte* 16.

OVERTONES. See *Acoustics* 6, 8; *Partials*.

OVER THE SEA TO SKYE. See *Skye Boat Song*.

OVERTURE

1. The 'Italian' and 'French' Overtures.
2. Gluck's Innovation.
3. The Mozartian Type.
4. The Overture as the Beginning of the Work's Train of Thought.
5. The Medley Overture.
6. Overtures to Plays.
7. The Overture as an Independent Suite.
8. The Nineteenth-century 'Concert Overture'.

The term 'Overture' has come to have two meanings: (*a*) a piece of instrumental music composed as an introduction to an opera, oratorio, or similar work, and (*b*) a piece of instrumental music (generally keyboard or orchestral) modelled on one of the types of opera or oratorio introduction but intended for perfectly independent performance. It will tend to clarity if (*a*) and (*b*) are separately treated here.

1. The 'Italian' and 'French' Overtures. The early operas and oratorios (i.e. in the years immediately following 1600—see articles *Opera* and *Oratorio*) had either no instrumental introduction at all or a mere flourish of trumpets or other very brief call to attention. But soon this was felt to be insufficient for the preparation of the listener, and as opera and oratorio developed and became more definitely organized the introduction developed with them until it became a standard type, or rather two types.

These two types have been called the *Italian Overture* and the *French Overture*, and have been associated with the names of A. Scarlatti (1660–1725) and Lully (1632–87), who, if they did not actually initiate them, at least so popularized them as to come to be fairly considered responsible for their survival.

Both were in more than one movement (see *Movement*). The Italian was made up as follows:

A quick movement.
A slower movement.
A quick movement.

The French was made up as follows:

A slow movement (played twice).
A quick movement.
(Often) a moderately slow dance type of movement, such as a minuet; or it might be that the slow movement, or a part of it, was repeated here.

The Italians claimed superiority for their type of overture, says Rousseau in his *Dictionary o Music* (1767), because 'a big audience always makes much noise and to constrain them to silence a loud, striking opening is necessary', and they pointed out, it appears, the danger of the grave opening of a French overture being confounded in the minds of the audience with the tuning of the instruments that had just preceded it. (There is surely some confusion here between speed and force; the grave opening of the French overture was not necessarily soft.)

The French type is familiar to many people today, since Handel very generally adopted it for his oratorios. Thus *Messiah* begins with two instrumental movements, a slow, grave one (in 'dotted' rhythm) coming to no proper conclusion of its own but with an imperfect cadence (see *Cadence*) leading straight into a quick movement in fugal style (see *Form* 12). The 'dotted' rhythm of the slow movement and its imperfect cadence, and the fugal style of the quick movement, are all taken direct from the French overture; they belong to the Lullyan convention. (For a tradition concerning a further movement see *Minuet*.) Handel's *Samson* and *Jephtha* (to take two further examples) have similar overtures, with a slowish dance movement to end—in *Samson* a minuet, in *Jephtha* a gavotte.

The Italian type is hardly so familiar today, but it will be seen that its general plan closely resembles that of the classical sonata, symphony, and string quartet, of which it is, indeed, one of the ancestors. It is to be noted that the name often given to it was '*Sinfonia*' —a tradition still maintained when we speak of the 'opening symphony' of a song, etc. (See *Symphony* 1–end.)

2. Gluck's Innovation. It will be realized that both the Italian and French types constituted in effect little *Suites* (q.v.), and that though their music might be in general spiritual consonance with what was to follow (the *Messiah* Overture is a good example), yet there was no organic connexion between the introduction and the thing introduced. Gluck (q.v.) showed a better way. To his later operas he prefaced an overture designed, as he himself said, 'to prepare the audience for the plot of the play', i.e. he sought a more intimate correspondence between the two things. To secure this he often let his overture, instead of coming to a full stop, merge at its close into the beginning of the first act. His overture to *Iphigenia in Tauris*, with its 'distant storm', 'approaching storm', 'very violent storm', and 'rain and hail' merging into the first scene, is the obvious prototype of the Prelude to Wagner's *Valkyrie*.

3. The Mozartian Type. With the operas of Mozart we find the overture carried out on the lines of the prevailing instrumental form, that of the first movement of the sonata or symphony, often with a slow opening passage and sometimes with a similar interpolation somewhere, and without the conventional immediate repetition of the 'Exposition' of the sonata form proper of the period (see *Form* 7) —i.e. the form is (*a*) Exposition, (*b*) Development, (*c*) Recapitulation.

And we also find a disposition to quote in advance some striking passage from the work to follow, as, for instance, in the overture to *Don Giovanni*, which prepares us (by a brief reference) for the statue music of the last scene, and in that of *The Magic Flute* where the trombones allude to the three masonic knocks on the door of the Temple of Wisdom, to be introduced later.

Such allusions as these have, perhaps, their greatest significance when the work has been previously heard, helping, by the reminder they offer, to pull one's frame of mind into shape for the drama to follow. In Beethoven's four wonderful attempts at an overture for his opera *Fidelio* (q.v.) are similar allusions, and so there are in Weber's opera overtures. Wagner's great *Mastersingers* Overture is a magnificent example of the anticipatory type.

4. The Overture as the Beginning of the Work's Train of Thought. In Haydn's 'Chaos' Overture to his oratorio *Creation*, and in Wagner's river music preceding *Rhine Gold*, and his thunderstorm music before *The Valkyrie*, we have another idea: here the overture actually *begins* the work, as we may say, and the opening words of the libretto merely continue a train of thought already in progress.

The general tendency during the nineteenth and twentieth centuries has been for the overture to diminish in length and in independent importance, so much and no more being retained as will serve to awaken the expectation and proper mood of the audiences. If a distinction of name be desired, the words *Symphonic Prologue* can be adopted for this type.

It may be of interest to list Wagner's instrumental introductions to his dramatic works, as showing the trend:

Rienzi (1840) and *The Flying Dutchman* (1841); long independent overtures.

Tannhäuser (1845); extended overture in definite form in the Vienna version of 1875 (not, as usually stated, the Paris performance of 1861) merging, on the opening of the first scene, into a great dramatic ballet.

Lohengrin (1848); short but independent prelude. The four *Ring* dramas (1853–74); all comparatively brief prefatory orchestral preludes leading into the first scene.

Tristan (1859); shortish prelude leading into the first scene.

The Mastersingers (1867) and *Parsifal* (1882); full-length and important overtures, but leading into the first scene.

The preludes to later acts of Wagner's works are sometimes almost as important as those to the first acts.

Wagner often used the word *Vorspiel* ('Foreplay' or 'prelude') for his instrumental introductions to music dramas.

5. The Medley Overture. A cheap but not always ineffective type of opera overture is that of the pot-pourri or medley—little more than a string of tunes from the work to follow. The French composers Boïeldieu, Auber, and Hérold had a good deal to do with the popularization of this easy-going type. Sullivan's comic opera overtures usually belong to it.

6. Overtures to Plays. Many fine overtures have, of course, been written to spoken plays, such as Beethoven's to Goethe's *Egmont*, to von Collin's *Coriolanus*, etc., and Mendelssohn's to Shakespeare's *Midsummer Night's Dream* (though this was at first intended as an independent work).

7. The Overture as an Independent

Suite. The Lullyan or French type of overture was soon taken as a model for a kind of instrumental suite, or for the opening part of such.

Thus Handel's seventh harpsichord suite is a French overture (the word 'Ouverture' is used at the beginning) with a number of short pieces tacked on to it at the end. Bach's fourth partita (where the word 'Ouverture' is again used) is on exactly the same model. It is possible to consider these either as extended overtures or as suites beginning with overtures. The sixteenth of Bach's 'Goldberg' Variations is called 'Ouverture' and consists of a slow movement and a quick one, quite on the Lully plan.

Bach has four orchestral compositions which go indifferently under the name 'suite' and 'overture'. They are on the same lines as his partitas above mentioned; for instance, the third consists of a long slow movement leading into a quick one in fugal style, these being followed by quite brief pieces as follows: Air, Gavotte, Bourrée, and Gigue.

The confusion which sometimes occurs in the minds of younger students on finding 'Overture' and 'Suite' apparently interchangeable terms in certain instances has now, it is hoped, been cleared up: the explanation, it will have been seen, is an historical one. The minuet or gavotte or other light dance which often ended the French overture was extended into a little chain of such dances, and so the overture became assimilated to the suite.

The true symphony, when it came, at first sometimes bore the name 'Overture'. The programmes of Haydn's concerts when he appeared in London in 1791 used this term.

8. The Nineteenth-century 'Concert Overture'. A totally different type of independent overture is that of the concert overture of which Mendelssohn is considered to be the inventor (his *Hebrides* Overture, Dvořák's *Carnival* Overture, Brahms's *Academic Festival* Overture, etc.). This is really but the later type of opera overture (like Beethoven's *Leonora* overtures) but composed for purely concert performance. In many cases such a work is in the same form as the first movement of the classical symphony (usually without the repeat of the 'exposition'); in others it is rather a *Symphonic Poem* (q.v.).

OVVERO (It.). 'Or.'

O.W., in German organ music = 'Oberwerk', i.e. the Swell Manual.

OWEN.

(1) DAVID. Welsh harper (1720–49), otherwise *Dafydd y Garreg Wen* (see under this heading and under *Rising of the Lark*).

(2) JOHN (Owain Alaw). He was born at Chester in 1821, became an organist there, and died there in 1883, aged sixty-one. He composed an oratorio of Handelian texture,

Jeremiah; a cantata, *The Prince of Wales* (said to be the first Welsh secular cantata—cf. *Lloyd*, *John Ambrose*); and many glees, anthems, and the like. His collections of Welsh national airs were popular (see *Land of my Fathers*).

(3) His son WILLIAM HENRY was born at Chester in 1845 and was killed in a railway accident at Abergele in 1868. Some of his Welsh anthems, etc., were published by his father.

O WORSHIP THE KING. See *Hymns and Hymn Tunes* 6.

1. ORCHESTRA OF A VENETIAN 'OSPEDALE' in the 18th century. Detail from a picture by Guardi, 1712–93. Cf. *Schools of Music*

2. A LONDON ORCHESTRA OF THE EARLY 18TH CENTURY —Harpsichord, 2 Violins and Viola, 'Cello, Double-bass, Flute, and Oboe, and one unidentifiable player. The conductor uses his hand (From a concert ticket designed by Hogarth)

3. THE HALL OF THE CONSERVATOIRE, PARIS, in 1843 The conductor (using a violin bow as baton, as could be seen in the unreduced picture; cf. *Conducting* 4) has a solo violinist (or the First Violin) beside him. He faces the orchestra but has his back to most of the chorus

4. THE HANOVER SQUARE CONCERT ROOMS, London, in 1843. The orchestra is probably that of the Philharmonic Society

5. THE SACRED HARMONIC SOCIETY, in Exeter Hall, London, 1848, only five years later than the performance shown in the previous picture. Costa is conducting

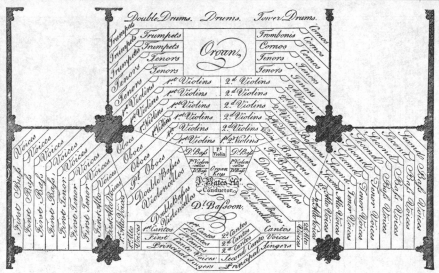

THE HANDEL COMMEMORATION IN WESTMINSTER ABBEY, 1784

The conductor (Joah Bates) at a detached organ console
Orchestra (of 250) between him and the organ and to right and left
Singers (264) in front and in galleries out of sight
'Cantos' are soprano singers. 'Tenors', as distinct from 'Tenor Voices', are Violas)
See the Article *Festival*, pp. 350–1

OXFORD. See *Clubs*; *Concert* 9; *Cecilia, Saint*; *Degrees and Diplomas*; *Notation* 1; *Act Music*; *Dictionaries* 11.

University Professors of Music who receive notice in this book are (with their periods of office): *R. Nicholson* (1626–39); *J. Wilson* (1656–61); *Edw. Lowe* (1661–82); *W. Hayes* (1741–77); *P. Hayes* (1777–97); *Crotch* (1797–1847); *H. R. Bishop* (1848–55); *Ouseley* (1855–89); *Stainer* (1889–99); *C. H. H. Parry* (1900–8); *Parratt* (1908–18); *Allen* (1918–46); *Westrup* (1947–71); *Kerman* (1971).

Organists of the cathedral (see *Cathedral Music* 2, 6, 7) who receive notice are (with their periods of office): *Taverner* (1526–30); *Edw. Lowe* (*c.* 1630–82); *Crotch* (1790–*c.* 1807); *C. H. Lloyd* (1882–92); *Harwood* (1892–1909); *Ley* (1909–26); *W. H. Harris* (1928–33); *Armstrong* (1933–55).

Other Oxford musicians who receive notice are: *Aldrich*; *R. Davy, R. Edwards*; *W. Ellis*; *J. Farmer II*; *Hadow*; *D. Purcell*; *J. Varley Roberts*; *B. Rogers*; *Turner*; *Weldon*; *E. Walker*; *Walond*; *J. Dykes Bower*.

OXFORD MOVEMENT. See *Anglican Chant* 6; *Hymns* 6; *Cathedral Music* 8.

OXFORD PSALTER. See *Anglican Chant* 6.

OXFORD SYMPHONY (Haydn). See *Nicknamed Compositions* 11; *Concert* 9.

OXFORD UNIVERSITY MUSICAL CLUB AND UNION. See *Clubs for Music-Making*; *Concert* 9; *Applause* 2.

OXFORD UNIVERSITY PRESS. See *Publishing* 7.

OXON. Oxford—from 'Oxonia', latinized name of 'Ox(en)ford'.

P

P. short for *piano* (It.). 'Soft.' See *PP*.

P. in French organ music is sometimes used for *Pédales*, i.e. pedals, and sometimes for *Positif*, i.e. choir organ.

PAAR (Ger.). When this word is used as an ordinary noun (with a capital letter) it means 'pair', 'couple'; otherwise it means 'few' (*Ein paar*, 'a few').

PACATO, PACATAMENTE (It.). 'Placid', placidly.

PACCHIEROTTI, GASPARO (1744–1821). See *Singing* 6.

PACHELBEL.

(1) JOHANN. Born at Nuremberg in 1653 and there died in 1706, aged fifty-two. He held various important positions as organist, including that of St. Stephen's Cathedral, Vienna, and those at the courts of Eisenach and Stuttgart, and his keyboard compositions are of high importance as influencing his younger contemporary, J. S. Bach. A good many of his works are available in modern editions but the complete issue, though attempted, remains unfinished.

See references under *Chorale Prelude*; *Organ* 8, 13.

(2) WILHELM HIERONYMUS (*c.* 1685–1764). His life closely resembled that of his father, above, as did his type of work (of which, however, not much is now available).

(3) CARL THEODORE (surname also given as 'Percival'), son of (1) above. Born at Stuttgart in 1690 and died at Charleston, S.C., in 1750, aged fifty-nine. In his early forties he emigrated to Boston, then passed on to Newport, R.I., and Charleston, holding positions as organist in these places. Only one of his compositions appears to be extant—a Magnificat in eight voices in the State Library of Berlin.

PACINI, GIOVANNI. Born at Catania in 1796 and died at Pescia in 1867, aged seventy-one. He wrote about ninety operas, as also many other compositions, including a *Dante* Symphony and some string quartets. He was also a great teacher of composition, to whom pupils flocked from far and near, and for them he published textbooks. He studied the human voice and wrote well for it, but neglected orchestration. *Sappho* (Naples, 1840) was his most famous creation.

PACIUS, F. (1809–91). See *Scandinavia* 6.

PACK UP YOUR TROUBLES IN YOUR OLD KIT BAG AND SMILE! SMILE! SMILE! This song, which must have been worth many thousand men to the British

Empire and American troops during the first World War, was the work of two Welsh brothers, as poet and composer, George Henry Powell (1880–1951) and Felix Powell (died 1942). (The former was known as 'George Asaf'.)

PADEREWSKI, IGNACY JAN (not Ignaz Josef, as often given; p. 801, pl. **138**. 1). Born at Kurilowka, Podolia, Russian Poland, in 1860 and died in New York in 1941, aged eighty. After study at the Conservatory of Warsaw he toured as a solo pianist, taught at his old place of education, and then returned to the student life in Berlin and in Vienna under Leschetizky and his wife, Essipoff, to which couple (with an equal debt to his own iron perseverance) he owed his dazzling technique. By this possession, and by those of a romantic personality, high interpretative qualities, and an amazing head of hair, he established a position with the crowd and with the connoisseurs without parallel since the times of Rubinstein and Liszt.

His father was a Polish patriot who at one time suffered exile in Siberia, and he himself for half a century longed and worked for the freedom of his native country, which he at last (1918) had the happiness to see, becoming its first Prime Minister (not, as often stated, President).

When, in 1939, his country, having been attacked simultaneously by Nazi Germany and Bolshevist Russia, was shared between them and its government was temporarily re-formed at Angers in France, 'the great Polish Patriot and First Citizen of Poland', now in his eightieth year, was the first to be summoned there to occupy a seat in its Parliament of which, at the first meeting, he was elected 'Speaker'.

His later pianism (a resumption, in 1923, after some years of entire silence) came under criticism on account especially of the quality of tone.

As a composer he is known to an enormous public through one or two favourite trifles, like the piano Minuet, but he composed more important works than these, as, for instance, a piano concerto and an opera.

See references under *Cracovienne*; *Germany* 9 a; *Yankee Doodle*; *Knighthood*; *Pianoforte Playing* 9; *Virtuoso*; *Criticism* 10.

PADIGLIONE (It.). 'Pavilion', 'tent'; hence (from the shape) the 'bell' of a wind instrument. (But for *Padiglione cinese* see *Turkish Crescent*.)

PADOVANA. See *Pavan and Galliard*.

PADRE BOËMO. See *Bohemia*.

PADUANA. See *Pavan and Galliard*.

PAEAN. A song of triumph or of praise (originally one to Apollo).

PAËR, FERDINANDO. Born in Parma in 1771 and died in Paris in 1839, aged sixty-seven. He wrote over forty operas and served as musical director at the Court of Napoleon I.

PAESIELLO (or **Paisiello**), **GIOVANNI.** Born at Taranto in 1740 and died at Naples in 1816, aged seventy-six. He was a great opera composer about the courts of Ferdinand IV, of Joseph Bonaparte and Murat at Naples, of Catharine the Great at St. Petersburg, and of Napoleon I in Paris. He composed one hundred operas, in which, with great taste, he used a charming simplicity and introduced some definite innovations of plan. (Cf. *Opera* 17 a.)

PAGANINI, NICCOLÒ (p. 1097, pl. **182.** 1). Born at Genoa in 1782 and died at Nice in 1840, aged fifty-seven. He was a poor boy who, born with a natural talent for the violin, exhibited a madness of perseverance in its development which brought him to high honour and abundant fortune. The amazing stories of his technical feats invested his person with a glamour almost of the supernatural, so that the London mob is reported to have followed and touched him to see if he were flesh and blood.

He had annoyances over his attempt to found a gambling-house, the 'Casino Paganini', in Paris, began to suffer from an affection of the throat, and died—improvising marvellously during his last hours on his Guarnerius and leaving it to his native city of Genoa, where it may be seen reverently preserved in the museum.

For five years the Church, disturbed as to his orthodoxy, refused his body interment in consecrated ground, and then it was laid to rest in a village graveyard on his own Italian estate.

His chief gift to music is his extension of the technique of stringed instruments, from which more serious composers than he himself (for he was a composer) have been able richly to profit. Some of his violin music has supplied the basis for piano music by Schumann, Liszt, Brahms, and Rachmaninof.

See *Guitar*; *Concerto* 6 b (1782); *Chamber Music* 6, Period III (1782); *Campanella*; *Carnival of Venice*; *Bull*, *Ole*; *Ernst*; *Gluck*; *Cinematograph*; *Knighthood*; p. 893, pl. **152.** 4.

PAGET, SIR RICHARD ARTHUR SURTEES, Bart. (1869–1955). Barrister, patent expert, physicist, song poet–composer, and original investigator in linguistics. See *Voice* 7; also p. 1089, pl. **180.** 7.

PAGLIACCI, I (Leoncavallo). Produced at Milan in 1892. Libretto by the composer. (Title = 'The Clowns'.)

Act I

SCENE: *A Village in Calabria. Time, about 1865–70*

In the famous prologue, **Tonio** (*Baritone*), a clown in a company of travelling players, reminds us that actors have their joys and sorrows, like the rest of us.

The head of the troop, **Canio** (*Tenor*), introduces to the villagers his wife, **Nedda** (*Soprano*). Tonio, for giving his hand to Nedda to help her to alight, gets a buffet from the fiery-tempered, jealous Canio, and is laughed at by the villagers —his own people, for this is his native place. He goes away, muttering about revenge. We also meet **Beppe** (*Tenor*), another member of the company.

Left alone with Nedda, who, we gather, is untrue to Canio, Tonio tries to make love and is repulsed. He swears vengeance. Now her lover, **Silvio** (*Baritone*), appears. He is a villager, with whom she arranges to run away. Tonio overhears, and brings Canio. They surprise the lovers, but Silvio manages to get away without Canio's knowing who he is. Nedda will not tell him. Tonio suggests that the lover is sure to come to the evening performance. Canio must watch her then.

Act II

SCENE: *The Strollers' Theatre ready for the Play*

The play is given before the villagers. Canio's part is that of a husband who, returning home, suspects his wife of infidelity. In the miserable reality which faces him he forgets his lines and demands from his wife the name of her lover. She tries to pass off his agitation as part of the play. At last her husband loses all control of himself and stabs her to death. Silvio rushes up, and Canio, recognizing him as her lover, kills him also. The horrified villagers seize Canio, who sobs out 'The comedy is ended!'

See *Music Hall* 4.

PAINE, JOHN KNOWLES (p. 1041, pl. **170,** 2). Born at Portland, Maine, in 1839 and died at Cambridge, Mass., in 1906, aged sixty-seven. He enjoyed a thorough musical training in Germany. Later he became successively instructor, assistant professor, and (in 1875) full Professor of Music at Harvard University, which, indeed, in that year created for him the first definite Chair of Music in any American university.

He composed much serious music, but his enduring influence works through the many students he trained and the evidence he provided as to the value of music as an element in the university curriculum and as a part of cultural life.

See *Symphony* 8 (1839); *Oratorio* 7 (1873).

PAINTING AND MUSIC. See *History of Music* 1; *Belgium* 3.

PAIR (Fr.). 'Even' (numbers)—as opposed to *Impair*, 'odd'.

PAIR OF. See *Clavichord* 7; *Harpsichord* 3.

PAISIELLO. See *Paesiello*.

PALABRA (Sp.). 'Word.'

PALADILHE, ÉMILE. Born at Montpellier in 1844 and died in Paris in 1926, aged sixty-one. He won the chief piano prize at the Paris Conservatory at the age of thirteen and the Rome Prize at the age of sixteen. He developed into a successful composer—especially of operas.

PALATE and SOFT PALATE. See *Voice* 21.

PALCOSCENICO (It.). 'Stage.'

PALÉOGRAPHIE MUSICALE. See *Plainsong* 3.

PALÉOPHONE. See *Gramophone* 1.

PALESTINE. See *Oriental* (near end of article); *Jewish Music*.

PALESTRINA, GIOVANNI PIERLUIGI DA (p. 516, pl. **93.** 2). Born at Palestrina, on the edge of the Campagna Romana (whence his name), probably in 1525, and died in Rome in 1594, aged probably sixty-eight or sixty-nine. His reputation is that of the greatest, though by no means the representative, composer of the age of contrapuntal composition for un-accompanied chorus (mostly church music but also a quantity of madrigals).

At about eighteen he was organist and choir-master of the cathedral in his native town. Six or seven years later his bishop became Pope and made him choirmaster of the Julian Chapel at the Vatican. He published (1554) a book of masses dedicated to the Pope, the first ever so dedicated by an Italian—the famous school of Flanders (see *Belgium* 1) up to about that time supplying the chief city of Christendom with its singers and its composers.

Henceforward he held for longer or shorter periods various important positions in Rome, his life being prosperous and happy and en-riched with friendships, amongst which must be especially mentioned that of the founder of the oratorio (q.v.), St. Philip Neri, as whose musical director he for some time served.

This places him in a historical position that faces two ways. He stands on a peak which looks over the long slope that had led up from choral music in mere consecutive fifths and octaves to the perfections of the unaccompanied choral music of Byrd, Victoria, Lassus, himself, and others of various nationalities; and which looks, likewise, over the long further slope that stretches in front to the equal glories of the orchestrally accompanied Passions and Masses of Bach and the oratorios of Handel.

See *History* 2, 5; *Italy* 4; *Spain* 5; *Harmony* 8; *Counter-point*; *Modes* 1 c, 9; *Rhythm* 10; *Composition* 12, 15; *Singing* 3; *Ornaments* 1; *Church Music* 1; *Plainsong* 3; *Mass* 2, 4, 5; *Requiem*; *Motet*; *Improperia*; *Lauda Sion*; *Offertory*; *Stabat Mater*; *Litaniae Laurentanae*; *Magni-ficat*; *Madrigal* 4, 6, 8 b; *Cecilia*; *Roman Catholic Church Music in Britain*; *Cathedral Music* 8; *Patronage* 2; *Parody*; *Josquin des Prés*; *Monte, Filippo di*; *Bourgault-Ducoudray*.

PALESTRINA, ALLA (It.). 'In the style of Palestrina', i.e. *A Cappella* (q.v.).

PALINDROME. The dictionary definition is 'A word or verse, that reads the same back-wards as forwards', e.g. *Subi dura a rudibus*, *Able was I ere I saw Elba*, or the word *Madam*. The term is sometimes applied to a composi-tion on this principle.

It doubtless interests a composer to apply this principle occasionally, but, since there is probably no human ear that can recognize even *God save the Queen* ('America') when so played, its artistic value would appear to be slight or nil. There are examples of this device in the works of some of the fifteenth-century school, in Haydn, Mozart, Schönberg, Hinde-mith, etc. (Cf., s.v. *Canon*, the explanations of 'Cancrizans', 'Recte et Retro', and 'Retro-grade Canon'; and also *Rovescio*; *Note-row*.)

PALLET. See *Organ* 1.

PALMER.

(1) CLEMENT CHARLTON (1871–1944). Organist of Canterbury Cathedral, 1908 to 1936, and composer of church music. See *Chorale Prelude*.

(2) LORD (formerly Sir Ernest) (1858–1948). See *Patronage* 7.

(3) JOHN (eighteenth-century Philadelphia concert-giver). See *Concert* 15.

(4) REVD. GEORGE HERBERT (1846–1926). See *Plainsong* 4.

(5) ROBERT. Born at Syracuse, N.Y., in 1915. He studied at the Eastman School and under Copland and Roy Harris, later joining the staff of Cornell University. He is a composer whose chamber works, especially, have enjoyed con-siderable performance.

PALMGREN, SELIM (p. 896, pl. **153.** 9). Born at Björneborg, Finland, in 1878 and died in Helsinki in 1951, aged seventy-three. He studied for four years at the Conservatory of Helsinki (otherwise Helsingfors) and passed on to Germany, working with Busoni and others in Berlin, and to Italy. He then returned to his native country, serving as choral con-ductor, composing choral works, and success-fully producing his first opera *Daniel Hjort*. In his thirties he for a time abandoned other work in order to develop his composition and to tour as pianist—latterly accompanied by his wife, a singer of high reputation.

During the first World War he was resident in Copenhagen, and later he lived for a time in Rochester, New York, as a teacher of com-position in the Eastman School of Music.

The greater part of his compositions reflect his interest in the piano and his skill as a pianist. Much of his work has a national flavour. He favours the smaller forms and gives his com-positions fanciful titles.

PALOTACHE (properly *Palotás*). A Hungarian type of instrumental piece in dance style (two-in-a-measure or four-in-a-measure)—a derivative of the Verbunko (q.v.).

PAMMELIA (1609). See under *Round*; *Street Music* 2.

PANDEAN PIPES. See *Panpipes*.

PANDIATONICISM. This is a term which was introduced by Nicolas Slonimsky and has now found its way into musical literature. Slonimsky's own definition is as follows: 'Pandiatonicism is the technique of free use of all seven degrees of the diatonic scale,

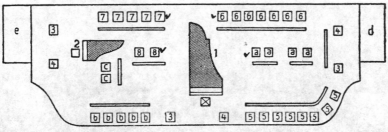

1. THE DRESDEN ORCHESTRA IN 1753

1, Capellmeister's Harpsichord (cf. *Orchestra* 2)
2, Accompanist's Harpsichord
3, Violoncellos (three, dispersed)
4, Double-basses (three, dispersed)
5, First Violins (eight)
6, Second Violins (seven)
7, Oboes (five)
8, Flutes (two)
a, Violas (four)
b, Bassoons (five)
c, Horns (two)
d, e, Platforms for Trumpets (two or more) and Kettledrums (two pairs)

Note that all the players looked inwards to the Capellmeister, those at the front having their backs to the audience

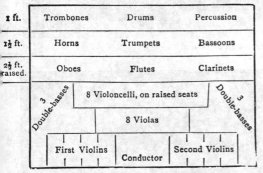

WAGNER'S ARRANGEMENT OF THE ORCHESTRA AT MANNHEIM CONCERT (all the back rows raised stepwise as usual today)

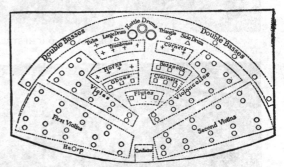

3. NEW YORK PHILHARMONIC SOCIETY, 1897, under Anton Seidl (note Cornets, not Trumpets, and cf. *Cornet* 3)

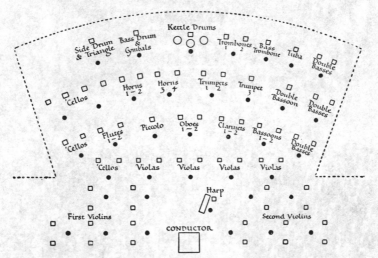

4. A COMMON 20TH-CENTURY PLACING OF THE ORCHESTRA. (A frequent variant of this arrangement places the Second Violins adjacent to the Firsts (on the Conductor's left and the 'Cellos on the Conductor's right, with the Double-basses behind them)

PLATE 126   THE ORCHESTRA IN AMERICA

See *United States* 4

1. THE GERMANIA ORCHESTRA, 1850—Carl Bergmann, Conductor

2. THE CLEVELAND ORCHESTRA, 1968

melodically, harmonically, or contrapuntally. Wide intervalic skips are employed, and component voices enjoy complete independence, while the sense of tonality is very strong due to the absence of chromatics. Visually, a page of pandiatonic music looks remarkably clean. C major is favoured by most composers writing in this style. The opening pages of Prokofief's Third Piano Concerto, Casella's *Valse Diatonique*, Stravinsky's *Pulcinella*, and certain pages of Malipiero are characteristic examples of pandiatonic writing. The added sixth and ninth, widely used in popular American music, are pandiatonic devices.'

PANDORA, PANDORE. See under *Cittern*.

PANDURINA. A very small instrument of the lute type, strung with wire—probably the ancestor of the mandoline (q.v.).

PANGE LINGUA. These are two hymns so opening:

(1) *Pange lingua gloriosi praelium certaminis.* Passion hymn by Venantius Fortunatus (530–609). A modification of J. M. Neale's translation of this is often sung—'Sing, my tongue, the glorious battle, Sing the last, the dread affray'.

(2) *Pange lingua gloriosi corporis mysterium.* By St. Thomas Aquinas, written 1263, and modelled on (1). A translation based on J. M. Neale and E. Caswall is often sung—'Now, my tongue, the mystery telling'. This hymn was written for the feast of Corpus Christi, as a part of the Office (q.v.) for that day which St. Thomas compiled at the request of Pope Urban IV, who first ordered the observance of this feast by the whole church. *Tantum ergo* (q.v.) is a part of the hymn.

Each of the above has its own plainsong tune.

PANHARMONICON. See *Mechanical* 8, 9.

PANMURE HOUSE MANUSCRIPT. See *Scotland* 1, 7.

PANORGUE. See *Reed-Organ Family* 6.

PANPIPES, PANDEAN PIPES, or **SYRINX.** A series of small wooden whistles, graduated in size to give the different pitches (p. 513, pl. **92.** 4). It is held in front of the mouth (the sound being produced from each whistle in the same manner as one produces it by blowing across the hollow end of a key) and moved from left to right and right to left according to the note required. This ancient instrument is still used in an elementary way by British and other exhibitors of Punch and Judy shows; in Hungary and Rumania it is played with amazing virtuosity and made to produce really musical effects.

Mozart has made a slight humorous use of it (on the stage) in *The Magic Flute*. In Rees's *Cyclopædia* a plate of about 1805 shows a band at Vauxhall Gardens, London, consisting of five persons playing panpipes of various sizes (marked 'Primo', 'Secondo', 'Tenore', 'Basso', and 'Contre Basso') and each, in addition,

manipulateing some percussion instrument (p. 513, pl. **92.** 5).

No wind instrument is more ancient and none more widespread than the panpipes. The Greeks gave it the name it still bears, for they evolved the legend of the god Pan pursuing the nymph Syrinx, of her being changed in the nick of time by the Naiades into a bundle of reeds, and of the god Pan, noticing how the wind made these musical, cutting them down and playing upon them.

PANSERON, AUGUSTE MATHIEU. Born in Paris in 1795 and died there in 1859, aged sixty-four. He was a student at the Paris Conservatory (Rome Prize) and then a professor there, who wrote a large number of vocal exercises which are still in use, textbooks of singing, operas, church music, and many songs.

Cf. *Singing* 9.

PANTALEON, PANTALEONE, or PANTALON. This was a much elaborated form of dulcimer (q.v.) invented towards the end of the seventeenth century by a German named Pantaleon Hebenstreit, who composed concertos and overtures for it and travelled giving performances. The instrument is referred to in a Worcester (England) newspaper of 1767 as follows:

'Mr. Noel will perform several Grand Overtures on the newly invented instrument, the Pantaleone. The instrument is eleven feet in length and has 276 strings of different magnitudes.'

Obviously at this date the instrument was not 'newly invented', but it may have been new to Britain. It is said to have been Louis XIV who gave it as its name the Christian name of its inventor.

In the earlier days of the pianoforte the name was, by analogy, transferred to a German horizontal variety of this in which the hammers struck from above. It was also applied to a certain stop found in some harpsichords—one which put the dampers out of action, leaving the strings free to vibrate, as they are necessarily left in instruments of the dulcimer class like the pantaleon.

See an allusion under *Pianoforte* 3.

PANTHEON, LONDON. See *Concert* 8.

PANTOMIME. The word is from the Greek and means 'all-imitating'. The Greeks, and after them the Romans, had a species of entertainment in which an actor performed in dumb show whilst a 'chorus' described the purport of his action and outlined and commented on the plot (cf. the sixteenth-century Italian experiments; *Opera* 1): with the Romans the 'chorus' was at one time a singer declaiming recitative to the accompaniment of a pipe. The actor was masked and so his means of expression were by bodily movements and especially the hands. The mask was changed from time to time according to the character of the play represented at the moment. The subjects were mythological and were well known to the audience. In Roman times persons of high position appeared in this way, e.g. the emperor Nero. The word 'Pantomime' as used by the Romans had the same significance as it has in its primary use in French today, i.e. it signified the actor, not the play. In English the word now generally signifies the play.

Any action without speech can be legitimately called pantomime, as, for instance, 'The Dumb Show' in Shakespeare's *Hamlet* (ACT III, Sc. ii).

Obviously pantomime closely approaches the *Ballet d'action* (see *Ballet* 3), the difference being that in the latter the motions are made rhythmic and conventionalized into dance. The true pantomime has been subjected to a good deal of musical development. A notable instance is *The Prodigal Son* ('L'Enfant Prodigue') of the French composer Wormser (1851–1926), produced in Paris in 1890 and then toured in England and elsewhere (see *Negro Minstrels*). It was revived later and will probably continue to be revived from time to time as a classical example of its form. Bartók has a pantomime, *The Miraculous Mandarin* ('Der Wunderbare Mandarin', 1926). Strauss calls his *Legend of Joseph* (1914) a pantomime and his *Whipped Cream* ('Schlagobers', 1924) a 'Ballet-Pantomime'. Gluck often uses the word 'Pantomime' in the scores of his operas, and Berlioz uses it in that of his opera *The Taking of Troy* (1856), where Andromache and her son Astyanax silently lay flowers at the foot of the altar (the chorus meanwhile commenting sympathetically).

The common use of the word pantomime in England is as the description of a Christmas theatrical entertainment bearing the title of some traditional children's fairy tale ('Mother Goose' story—to use the American term) or the like, but constituting in effect nothing much beyond an extravagant variety entertainment with music largely consisting of humorous and sentimental songs. Until well into the nineteenth century it made a good deal of certain characters borrowed from the Italian 'Commedia dell'Arte' (or play with written plot and extemporized dialogue); amongst these were Harlequin, Columbine, and Pantaloon. The clown's importance in such 'Pantomime' is said to have been established by the great Grimaldi (1779–1837). This type of pantomime is of very slight musical importance, except that it floats (or used to float) into popularity the songs to be popular in the streets of cities for the next twelve months or so.

This English pantomime at one time had more coherence and enjoyed the musical services of the best native composers (Arne, Dibdin, Shield). It is based on the entertainments, first of John Weaver (q.v.) at Drury Lane in 1702, and then of Rich (of the Lincoln's Inn Fields Theatre and later of Covent Garden), who developed it about 1716 and was himself (under the name of 'Lun') a very famous Harlequin.

PANTOUM (also 'Pantum', 'Pantun'). This occurs as the heading to the scherzo in Ravel's Piano Trio. Properly it is the name of a peculiar type of poem, introduced by Victor Hugo and used by others of the French Romantic poets of the nineteenth century (based on a Malay type).

PAPER ROLL INSTRUMENTS. See *Mechanical Reproduction of Music* 13.

PAPINI, GUIDO. Born near Florence in 1847 and died in London in 1912, aged sixty-five. As violinist and teacher he lived latterly in Dublin and London. Some of his tuneful music, solo and concerted, is still enjoyed by violin students.

PÂQUE, DÉSIRÉ (in full, Marie Joseph Léon Désiré). Born at Liège in 1867 and died at Besancourt in 1939, aged seventy-two. He was trained in the conservatory of his native place and then settled as a teacher, for short periods, in various cities of Bulgaria, Greece, Portugal, and Germany. He was long resident in Paris and in 1927 became a naturalized Frenchman. His compositions, to which he latterly entirely devoted his time, include eight symphonies, a Requiem, a great quantity of chamber music, and other things. Four sonatas (*c.* 1911) are early examples of the atonal style.

PARADIES (or **Paradisi**), PIETRO DOMENICO. Born at Naples in 1707 and died at Venice in 1791, aged eighty-four. He was a harpsichord player and composer who lived for some time in London. His composition best known today is a certain very sparkling Toccata.

See *Linley, Thomas (Senior)*; *Sonata* 10 d (*c.* 1754).

PARALLEL MOTION. See *Motion*.

PARAPHRASES. (Scripture) See *Presbyterian Church Music* 3. (Piano) See *Chopsticks*.

PARAY, PAUL. Born at Le Tréport in 1886. He studied at the Paris Conservatory, won the Rome Prize, and became known as a conductor (Lamoureux, 1923; Colonne, 1944; Detroit, 1952–63). He has composed choral and orchestral works, chamber music, songs, etc.

PARDESSUS DE VIOLE. See *Viol Family* 4 e (for *Pardessus de viole d'amour*, 4 f).

PAREJA, RAMOS DE. See *Spain* 9; *Temperament* 5.

PARIS. See *France* (passim); *Ars Nova*; *Harmony* 6; *Opera* 11, 23; *Opera buffa*; *Opéra comique*; *Concert* 14; *Conducting* 2; *Schools of Music*; *Singing* 8; *Printing* 1, 2; *Publishing* 2; *Community Singing* 3; *Street Music* 7; *Organ* 8; *Belgium* 4; *Spain* 7, 8; *Rumania*.

It is hardly possible to list the composers the articles upon whom refer to Paris—*Lully*; *Couperin*; *Rameau*; *Gluck*; *Chopin*; *Franck*; *Saint-Saëns*, etc. For 'Paris' symphonies of Haydn and Mozart see *Nicknamed Compositions*.

PARIS, AIMÉ (1798–1866). See *Sight-Singing* 2; *Tonic Sol-fa* 9.

PARISH-ALVARS, ELIAS (1810–49). See *Harp* 4.

PARISH CHURCHES AND MUSIC. See *Anglican Parish Church Music*.

PARISH CLERK. This important official is habitually ignored by dictionaries of music, yet for centuries he exercised a strong musical influence in England.

Originally the word 'clerk' was applied only to men in holy orders (including minor orders), but by a natural extension it came to be also applied to others. Thus 'till quite lately [*Catholic Dictionary*, 1883] the server at Mass used to be called the "clerk", because he did clerks' work, just as the boys at Mass are called "acolytes", though not really so, because they do acolytes' work'. After the Reformation the term was used for a number of minor functionaries in the Church (as regards cathedral lay clerks see *Vicar Choral*). The parish clerk was an important functionary. He was lower than the rector or vicar but higher than the sexton, and these three constituted the salaried officials of the parish church (p. 172, pl. **35.** 1).

Amongst the duties the parish clerk came in time to perform were those of making or leading the responses in the service, pronouncing a loud 'Amen' at the end of every prayer and of the sermon, and giving out the metrical psalm, and, when on great occasions there was an anthem, that also. He would act as precentor, giving the note for the psalm tune (or the four notes for the four voices) on his adjustable pitch-pipe. Often he taught the choir: occasionally he played the 'barrel organ' or 'finger organ' (see *Hymns and Hymn Tunes* 9 and *Mechanical Reproduction of Music* 10). He was, indeed, in many cases the chief musical functionary, and so Benjamin Payne, clerk of St. Anne's, Blackfriars, London, in his *The Parish Clerk's Guide* (1685), speaking of Playford's Psalmody (1671 and 1677; see *Hymns* 5, 17 e xviii), calls its author 'one to whose memory all parish clerks owe perpetual thanks for their furtherance in the knowledge of psalmody'. Playford was himself a clerk (though not technically a parish clerk, for the Temple Church, London, where he officiated, is extra-parochial); his *Introduction to the Skill of Musick* (1654) came out in edition after edition, and perhaps Payne was thinking partly of this when he recalled Playford's services to the profession.

The London Parish Clerks constitute one of the City Livery Companies; it has now been in existence for seven hundred years, for they were incorporated by Henry III in 1232. They had a fine hall in Bishopsgate that was taken from them, another in Broad Lane that was burnt in the fire of London in 1666, and from 1671 were in their hall in Silver Street. This last was destroyed during an air-attack on London in January 1941. With it were lost the interesting old organ (dating from 1737) pictured on plate **35** (p. 172), the furniture, the windows containing the arms of Masters of the Company, and other precious relics (the silver, charters, and deeds, being stored at a bank, were saved).

When James I and then Charles II renewed their Charter it was laid down that 'Every person that is chosen Clerk of a Parish shall first give sufficient proof of his abilities to sing at least the tunes which are used in parish churches' (see *Anglican Parish Church Music* 1). In 1762 William Riley, in *Parochial Music Corrected*, says this test is no longer applied, but he makes it clear that the London clerks were not forgetful of their musical duties, for he says they hold weekly meetings in their hall 'where they sing psalms, accompanied by an organ, for about an hour'.

The *Parish Clerk's Guide*, already alluded to, was a publication appearing periodically, and in it was an official list, made by the company, of the metrical psalms best suited to each Sunday in the year, so that they might enforce the teaching of Collect, Epistle, and Gospel.

The arms of the company (p. 172, pl. **35.** 3) have a musical interest—'The feyld azur, a flower de lice goulde on chieffe gules, a leopard's head *between two pricksong books* of the second, the laces that bind the books next, and to the creast upon the healme, on a wreathe gules and azur, an arm, from the elbow upwards, *holding a pricking book*' (from a description in 1582). These arms stood over the court-room door, with the motto 'Pange lingua gloriosi'.

The passages italicized have reference to the ability to read and write music. Pricksong was music 'pricked down' or composed, in distinction from the merely unison plainsong and from descant performed extemporaneously. In 1559 'Sir Thomas Pope was buried at Clerkenwell with two services of pryke song and two masses of requiem and all the Clerkes of London with the choir of St. Paul's Cathedral joined to them'.

The mention of Clerkenwell recalls the fact that this district of London got its name (when it was still open fields) from the fact that the parish clerks came there once a year to perform mystery plays and moralities. They used to give *The Creation of the World* and *The Passion of our Lord*, and the like, and their drama (not unlike that of the peasants of Oberammergau, which still goes on) lasted several days. In 1391 King Richard II and his Queen went to see them; in 1409 'the most part of the nobles and gentles of England'. The influence of the mystery plays upon the development of drama and of music is important. (See *Mysteries, Miracle Plays, and Moralities.*)

Today the English parish clerk barely exists. All his musical functions have gone, and, indeed, he takes no part in the church's services. An Act of Parliament of 1844 robbed him of nearly every duty, in favour of the curate, and another in 1894 left him nothing to do but look after certain maps and documents that are now taken from him and handed to that purely secular functionary, the clerk of the parish council.

The parish clerk, then, is now nobody, but he can look back to the days of metrical psalms and pitchpipes, and sometimes, too, of a barrel organ or even a little orchestra in the gallery under his direction—to say nothing of the dignity of singing and dining in his own City Hall and officially drafting the metrical psalms for the year and the weekly Bills of Mortality. He has no present and probably no future (though there are those who press for his return)—but he has certainly an important past.

> *The Vocal Powers here let us mark*
> *Of* PHILIP, *our late Parish Clerk:*
> *In Church none ever heard a Layman,*
> *With a clearer Voice say Amen.*
> *Who now with Hallelujah's Sound*
> *Like Him can make the Roof rebound?*
> *The Choirs lament his Choral Tones,*
> *The Town—so soon Here lie his Bones.*
> *Sleep undisturb'd within thy peaceful shrine*
> *Till Angels wake thee with such notes as thine.*

MEMORIAL OF PHILIP ROE (died 1815) in BAKEWELL CHURCH, DERBYSHIRE.

For a reference to Chaucer's description of a fourteenth-century musical parish clerk see *Inns and Taverns*.

PARISH PSALTER. See *Anglican Chant* 6 d.

PARISIAN TONES or **PARISIAN GREGORIANS.** The Gregorian Tones (q.v.) supposedly according to the ancient Use of Paris (cf. *Use of Sarum*) but actually more according to the Use of Rouen. In the latter half of the nineteenth century they had considerable popularity in 'high' Anglican circles.

'PARIS' SYMPHONIES (Haydn and Mozart). See *Nicknamed Compositions* 8, 12.

PARKE, WILLIAM THOMAS. See *Kotzwara*.

PARKER.

(1) ARCHBISHOP. See *Tallis's Canon*.

(2) MARTIN. See *You Gentlemen of England*; *When the King enjoys his own again*.

(3) HORATIO WILLIAM (p. 1056, pl. **171.** 1). Born at Auburndale, Mass., in 1863 and died at Cedarhurst, N.Y., in 1919, aged fifty-six. His *Hora Novissima* (1893), had a great vogue both in England (Three Choirs Festival, Worcester, 1899), and in America.

In 1894 he was appointed Professor of Music at Yale University.

In addition to his choral music he composed two prize operas. Of these the first, *Mona*, was produced by the Metropolitan Opera Company, New York, in 1912, the second, *Fairyland*, at Los Angeles in 1915.

See *United States* 8; *Oratorio* 6, 7 (1893–8); *Hymns* 11 (end).

PARLANDO, PARLANTE (It.). 'Speaking'—either literally or in style of performance; for the latter see *Aria*; *Recitative*.

PARLATO (It.). 'Spoken.'

PARMA, ILDEBRANDO DA. See *Pizzetti*.

PARODY. In its application to a musical composition the word is often applied in its more general sense, i.e. without the implication of ridicule or caricature, and meaning simply *in the style of* some previous work, or *making use of thematic material from* such a work. For instance Palestrina composed 'Parody Masses'

and 'Parody Madrigals', based on works of Cipriano de Rore and others.

PARRAMON. See *Viole-Ténor*.

PARRATT, WALTER. Born at Huddersfield in 1841 and died at Windsor in 1924, aged eighty-three.

He held various posts as organist, settling in Oxford in 1872 (Magdalen College) and in Windsor ten years later (St. George's Chapel), and was, later, Master of the royal music. He was Professor of Music at Oxford 1908–18. He was knighted in 1892. His influence upon British organ playing was great and valuable.

His compositions are few and unimportant.

See references under *Absolute Pitch*; *Memory* 7; *Organ* 2 c; *Chorale Prelude*.

PARRIS, HERMAN, M. (Medical-man composer). See *Programme Music* 4.

PARROTT, (HORACE) IAN. Born in London in 1916. He studied at the Royal College of Music and New College, Oxford (M.A., D.Mus.), and in 1947 became Lecturer in Music at Birmingham University. In 1950 he was appointed Professor of Music at the University College of Wales, Aberystwyth. His compositions for various forms include orchestral, vocal, chamber, and piano music.

PARRY.

(1) JOHN ('Blind Parry'). Died 1782. A famous Welsh harper and collector–editor of Welsh airs. (See *Brenhines Dido*.)

(2) JOHN ('Bardd Alaw'). Born at Denbigh in 1776 and died in London in 1851, aged seventy-five. He composed much theatre music, wrote a book on the harp, published collections of Welsh melodies, served as a London music critic, and made himself generally useful. His son is mentioned immediately below.

(3) JOHN ORLANDO. Born in London in 1810 and died at East Molesey in 1879, aged sixty-nine. He was the son of the above, and was a highly successful humorous composer and singer. Amongst his admirers are recorded the names of Liszt, Chopin, and Mendelssohn. His 'Flow gently, Deva' and a few other things may still occasionally be heard.

(4) JOSEPH. Born at Merthyr Tydfil in 1841 and died at Penarth in 1903, aged sixty-one. He was born in poverty but, by the subscriptions of men of his race in his own country and in the United States (where he had spent some time), was enabled when nearing thirty to enter the Royal Academy of Music, London. He took his Mus.D. at Cambridge, held posts in Welsh university colleges, composed operas, oratorios, cantatas, songs, and other things, and at the National Eisteddfod of 1896 received a gift of six hundred pounds for his services to his country's music. His is a name still held in high honour amongst Welsh music-lovers, and several of his hymn tunes are widely current—notably 'Aberystwyth'.

(5) HUBERT (in full, Charles Hubert Hastings)

(p. 336, pl. **53.** 2). Born at Bournemouth in 1848 and died at Rustington, Sussex, in 1918, aged seventy. He was the son of the artist and English country gentleman, Gambier Parry. He began to compose at eight. At Eton he led in musical activities and he took his Oxford B.Mus. whilst still at school. As an Oxford undergraduate he was equally active.

At the end of his university course he entered business, but ardently pursued music under Dannreuther, whose house was a great centre of musical culture in the London of those days. By compositions for festivals he became known as a composer, and at thirty-five he joined the staff of the Royal College of Music, under Grove, whom he succeeded as Director at forty-six. At fifty-two he added to this appointment that of Professor of Music at Oxford. He was knighted in 1898 and created a baronet five years later.

As a composer he was essentially English, not in the sense of using native folk-song themes, but in the sense that the typical national qualities markedly express themselves in his work. His music has a Miltonic character, and it is significant that one of his finest achievements as a composer (*Blest Pair of Sirens*) is a setting of Milton. His list of compositions is very varied and regrettably long: less work and more patient would have been better. Certain critics warmly admire his solo songs and towards the end he wrote a number of unaccompanied motets of great beauty. His literary works are of importance, especially his *Evolution of the Art of Music* (which brought in a new way of looking at the subject), his *Bach*, and his *Style in Musical Art*.

He was prominent in almost every branch of athletics and constantly ran into every kind of danger that land and water afford, suffering almost all possible injuries short of the immediately fatal. His geniality, generosity, moral character, and artistic ideals were of great influence; indeed he was everything that one would like the world to consider as implied in the description 'English gentleman'.

See *England* 7; *Nationalism*; *Oratorio* 5, 7 (1888, 1891–2); *Te Deum*; *Part Song*; *Chorale Prelude*; *National Anthems*; *Londonderry Air*; *Jerusalem*; *Symphony* 8 (1848); *Cadenza*; *Knighthood*.

PARSIFAL (Wagner). Produced at Bayreuth in 1882. Libretto, founded on medieval legends, by the composer. The work was by him designated 'A Stage Dedication Festival Play'.

ACT I

SCENE 1: *A Forest at Monsalvat.* (For a reference to the Prelude see *Overture* 4.)

We are to know that the Knights of the Holy Grail guard within the Castle of Monsalvat the vessel from which the Saviour drank at the Last Supper, and the spear with which His side was pierced at the crucifixion. The old ruler of the knights, Titurel, has appointed his son Amfortas to succeed him; but Amfortas has yielded to the beguilements of the enchantress Kundry, who, having mocked at the Saviour,

is torn between service to the Grail and the evil service of a magician, Klingsor, who seeks to overthrow the knights.

When Amfortas yielded to sin, Klingsor wounded him with the Sacred Spear. The wound will not heal, and the brotherhood of knights grieves. Only one, it has been revealed, can win back the Spear and with it heal the wound—one free from guile, and guided by pity. For him the brotherhood waits and longs.

As the sacred drama opens **Gurnemanz** (*Bass*), an old knight, is telling two young followers about Amfortas, to whom, as he is being carried to bathe, in the hope of relief from his wound, **Kundry** (*Mezzo-Soprano*) offers balsam.

Parsifal (*Tenor*) is brought on, having, in his innocence, killed a wild swan. Gurnemanz, finding him ignorant of his parentage and country, hopes that he may be the guileless one appointed to bring peace to them. Kundry knows a little of his upbringing as a fearless youth. Gurnemanz takes him to the Castle.

SCENE 2: *Panoramic change to a Hall in the Castle*

The knights enter, and the aged **Titurel** (*Bass*) calls upon his son **Amfortas** (*Baritone*) to perform his sacred office, the remembrance of which, and of his sin, tortures Amfortas. The communion is celebrated. Gurnemanz, anxious to discover whether Parsifal is indeed their deliverer, asks him if he understands what he has seen, but the youth can only shake his head. The old man, disappointed, thrusts him roughly forth.

ACT II

SCENE: *Inner Keep of a Tower in Klingsor's Enchanted Castle*

Klingsor (*Bass*) calls up his slave Kundry in the likeness of a beautiful maiden, and commands her to use her fascinations upon Parsifal, who has made his way, so far victorious, through Klingsor's defending knights. The tower keep vanishes, and a 'transformation scene' brings us to

The Magic Garden

Parsifal remains untempted by Klingsor's Flower Maidens, and when Kundry seeks to entrap him with a kiss, his mission is suddenly revealed to him: he understands everything he saw at the Castle of the Grail. He sees that he is to bring redemption even to Kundry. Klingsor appears, and hurls the Holy Spear at Parsifal; the youth seizes it, unharmed, and makes the sign of the cross. The castle vanishes, the garden withers.

ACT III

SCENE 1: *A Wood near the Castle of the Grail. It is the early morning of Good Friday*

Years have passed. Parsifal, a knight, unrecognized in black armour, greets Gurnemanz and the penitent Kundry. When Gurnemanz sees the Holy Spear in Parsifal's hand, he knows that salvation is near. Kundry washes the feet and anoints the head of the visitant, and he baptizes Kundry, freeing her from sin.

SCENE 2: *The Hall of the Grail*

Titurel has died, and Amfortas can no longer endure the spiritual and physical agony that has racked him for so long. The knights urge him to uncover the Grail, but he dare not. Parsifal enters and touches the wound with the Sacred Spear. Immediately it is healed, and he, recognized as the means of salvation, takes the Grail from its long-closed shrine. It glows with heavenly light, the knights kneel in homage, and Kundry, her weary pilgrimage accomplished, sinks lifeless before it.

See references under *Overture*; *Ballet* 7; *Amen*; *Harmony* 13; *Percussion* 4 e; *Electric* 1 c; *Oboe* 5 b; *Opera* 21 m.

PARSLEY (Parslie, Persley, and other spellings), OSBERT. Born in 1511 and died in 1585, aged seventy-four. He was for over half a century a choir-man of Norwich Cathedral and a composer of church music, some of which exists also in arrangements for viols. There is a highly eulogistic epitaph to him on one of the pillars of the nave of the cathedral.

PARSONS.

(1) ROBERT. Born at Exeter (date unknown) and died by drowning in the Trent at Newark in 1570. He was a Gentlemen of the Chapel Royal and had especial fame as a church composer.

(2) SIR WILLIAM (1746–1817). See under *Ireland* 6. He was Master of the King's Musick from 1786. (A useful man but not a great composer, he was said to be knighted 'more on the score of his merits than on the merits of his scores'.)

(3) SIR CHARLES A., O.M., F.R.S. (1854–1931). Celebrated British engineer. See *Auxetophone*.

PART (Fr., *Partie* or *Voix*; It., *Parte* or *Voce*; Ger., *Part* or *Stimme*). A part song (q.v.) is, in the general sense of the term, a song for several groups each singing its own line of notes, as distinct from a solo song; and the groups are often called 'parts', as are the separate sheets of music for each voice, when there are such.

So, too, in music for instruments, each instrument has its 'part' (or it may be each group of instruments, for there may be many 'first violins', etc., playing the one part).

By part-writing we mean that aspect of composition which consists in the devising of suitable melodic lines for each instrument or group, i.e. *Counterpoint* (q.v.).

The word is also sometimes (confusingly) used for 'section', e.g. Binary Form is spoken of as 'in two parts', Ternary Form as 'in three parts'.

PARTANT POUR LA SYRIE ('Departing for Syria'). This song passed as the composition of Queen Hortense (Hortense de Beauharnais, daughter of Josephine by her first marriage), and was appointed as the official march for festival use during the reign of her son, Napoleon III, so superseding for a time the Marseillaise.

It is now thought that the real author of the words was Count Alex. de Laborde (1774–1842), and that the music was largely the work of the Dutchman Philip Drouet (1792–1873), a solo flute player to the Court of Holland under Hortense's husband, Louis Napoleon, and then to the court of Napoleon Bonaparte in Paris, and afterwards a flute manufacturer in London, conductor at the Court of Coburg, and for a time resident in New York. At all events, Drouet, who was a notable composer for his own instrument, claimed to have put Queen Hortense's tune into shape for her.

PARTE, PARTI (It.). 'Part', 'parts'. So *Colla parte*, 'with the (solo) part', i.e. much the same as *Col canto* (see *Canto*); *A tre parti*, 'in three parts' (i.e. three vocal or instrumental strands).

PARTHENIA (Gk. 'Maidens' Songs'). A famous book of music for the virginals (see *Harpsichord* 3), the first to be printed in England (1611; republished 1613 and at intervals up to 1689, after which it was not republished again until 1847, and thereafter in 1908). The title-page (p. 193, pl. **39.** 5) claimed that this was the first music ever printed for the virginals; it was actually the first such music printed from engraved plates in Britain (see *Printing* 3), and possibly it was the first music of any kind there so printed, though Gibbons's *Fantasias of Three Parts for Viols* contests the priority.

The music of *Parthenia* was 'composed by three famous Masters, William Byrd, Dr. John Bull, and Orlando Gibbons, Gentilman of his Maties. most Illustrious Chappell'. It consists largely of Pavans and Galliards (see *Pavan and Galliard*; *Suite* 2).

A companion work, which appeared later, was *Parthenia Inviolata*, of which only one copy is known to exist—that in the New York Public Library. The bass line here is shared with a viola da gamba.

As regards the title of these two publications see remarks under *Harpsichord* 3, and note that in 1579 Puttenham, author of *The Arte of English Poesie*, presented to Elizabeth I, the Maiden Queen, a series of poems called *Partheniades*.

Compare *Fitzwilliam Virginal Book*; *Benjamin Cosyn's Virginal Book*; *Will Forster's Virginal Book*; see references under *God save the Queen* 4.

PARTHIE, PARTHIEN. See *Partita*.

PARTI (It.). See *Parte*.

PARTIALS. An acoustical term reflecting the conception of any individual note heard as being in reality the combined effect of a simultaneous sounding of not only the note itself (the 'fundamental') but also the 'overtones', in most cases those of the 'harmonic series' (see *Acoustics* 6, 7, 9, 14). The overtones are called the *Upper Partials* (the fundamental note being a Partial but not an 'upper' one).

'Upper Partial' is, then, a synonym for 'Overtone', and it is often used as a synonym for 'Harmonic'—which is not quite correct, since, though all harmonics (except the fundamental tone) are 'upper partials', not all upper partials are harmonics. For example, the tuning-fork and the bell produce upper partials that do not correspond with the harmonic series—'Inharmonic Upper Partials'.

Note that in numbering the harmonic series the fundamental (or generating) note is the 'First Harmonic' or 'First Partial' and that its octave (the following note in the series) is the 'Second Harmonic' or 'Second Partial', but the 'First Overtone' (it is also the 'first *upper* partial', but this description is not in use).

PARTIE. See *Partita*; *Suite* 1. The same word means 'Part', e.g. *Partition et Parties*, 'Score and Parts'.

PARTITA (It.), **PARTIE** (Fr.), **PARTHIE** (Ger., plur. *Parthien*). (1) In most cases this means 'Suite'. (2) It is also sometimes found as meaning 'Air with Variations'.

In connexion with both these applications of the word it may not be too fanciful, perhaps, to point out that in Italian one common use of the word is in the sense of 'quantity', or 'lot' (of goods); thus *in partita* means 'wholesale'.

See *Suite* 1 and *Chorale Prelude*.

PARTITION (Fr.), **PARTITURA** or **PARTIZIONE** (It.), **PARTITUR** (Ger.). 'Score.'

PARTITO (It.). 'Divided.'

PARTITUROPHON. See *Electric* 4.

PARTOS, OEDON. See *Jewish Music* 9.

PART SONG. Etymologically any song for several voices could be called a part song; actually the meaning is more restricted.

The three great schools of English choral composition are those of the Madrigal (late sixteenth and early seventeenth centuries), the Glee (late eighteenth and early nineteenth centuries), and the Part Song (nineteenth and early twentieth centuries).

All these are compositions for unaccompanied singing. The madrigal and glee were intended, properly, for singing by soloists, i.e. one voice to a part; the part song belongs to the period of development of large choral societies and is intended for singing by many voices to a part. This, however, does not define the difference, since it little affects the style of composition.

What does mark the part song as compared with the madrigal (q.v.) is that it is not inherently contrapuntal in style, i.e. it is much of the nature of a melody in the top part accompanied by harmonies in the other parts.

And what marks it as compared with the glee (q.v.), properly a male-voice type, is that it may be for either mixed or male or female voices (it really represents the period of the active participation of women in public choral performance), and that it is not divided into little separate self-contained movements, each reproducing closely the feeling of the section of the poem it is treating. Moreover, as already stated,

there is no implication that it is intended for solo voices, i.e. it is sung by many voices to a 'part'.

The nearest resemblance is to that modified form of madrigal called the Ayre, and it resembles this also in being usually strophic (i.e. a setting of a number of verses all to the same music), which the madrigal and glee are not. Really we might define the part song as a developed and extended hymn tune.

The greatest popularity of this type of composition has always been in Britain, and, indeed, we might almost consider it, like the glee and round, as a specially British type of musical enjoyment. (But see below as to other countries.)

Parry and Stanford did notable work in the late nineteenth century, developing a more contrapuntal texture. With Elgar the English part song took on higher musical qualities than ever before: he made full use of the advance of choral technique, usually chose texts of high literary quality, and attained a great expressiveness.

It is impossible to list the part-song composers, for during the nineteenth century it was as inevitable that every English organist should write a few part songs as that he should write a few anthems. Amongst the most important are the following (they are arranged in order of birth): Pearsall (1795–1856); Goss (1800–80); Hatton (1809–86); Henry Smart (1813–79); G. Macfarren (1813–87); Walmisley (1814–56); Barnby (1838–96); Parry (1848–1918); Stanford (1852–1924); Elgar (1857–1934).

Some German composers have produced compositions on much the lines of the English part song, as, for instance, Schubert, Schumann, Abt, Mendelssohn, and Cornelius; the *Songs for the Open Air* of Mendelssohn (1839) were probably the result of his visits to England and his friendship with William Horsley (q.v.), the popular composer of glees and part songs.

There are many American composers of effective part songs.

It has been stated above that the part song, like the madrigal and glee, is for voices only. The term 'Accompanied Part Song' or 'Part Song with Accompaniment' is, however, sometimes used to describe a short secular work for chorus having a part for pianoforte or orchestra, etc.

PAS (Fr.). (1) 'Not', 'not any' (see also *Ne pas*). (2) 'Step' (see below).

PAS DE BASQUE (Fr.). See *Basques*; *Ballet* 8.

PAS DE DEUX. A stage dance for two performers. There is also a particular dance so called—something like a gavotte; it dates from the beginning of the nineteenth century.

Cf. *Pas de quatre*; *Pas seul*; *Action*; *Écharpe*.

PASDELOUP, JULES ÉTIENNE (1819–87). He was an able orchestral conductor and organizer of concerts, whose popular series of weekly performances ran from 1861 to 1884, and introduced to the public of Paris a quantity of fine music, native and foreign, hitherto there unheard. Thirty years after Pasdeloup's death the 'Concerts Pasdeloup' were revived by Rhené-Baton.

PAS DE QUATRE. A stage dance for four performers. In 1845 there was a famous one danced at the request of Queen Victoria by the greatest dancers of the day—Taglioni, Cerrito, Grisi, and Grahn ('the greatest sum total of choreographic ability that has ever been brought together').

PAS GLISSÉ. See *Ballet* 8.

PASO DOBLE. A kind of one-step (q.v.), though the words mean 'double step'. It is in $\frac{2}{4}$ or $\frac{6}{8}$ time. It became popular about 1926.

PASPY. See *Passepied*.

PASQUALI. See *Figured Bass*.

PASQUINI, BERNARDO. Born near Lucca in 1637 and died in Rome in 1710, aged nearly seventy-three. He wrote operas, oratorios, and (especially important) works for harpsichord and for organ. He occupied positions in Rome as organist of St. Maria Maggiore and, later, as chamber musician to Prince Borghese and director of the concerts of Queen Christina of Sweden, and enjoyed fame not only as a performer but also as a teacher.

See *Sonata* 10 d (1704, and at end); *Pianoforte* 21; *Folia*; *Bird Music* (near end).

PASSACAGLIA (It.), **PASSACAILLE, PASSECAILLE** (Fr.). See *Chaconne and Passacaglia*; *Jazz* 7.

PASSAGE WORK. In general the word 'passage' in a musical connexion means much what it does in a literary connexion. One speaks of a particular passage in Bach as one speaks ot a passage in the Bible.

But the word has another application—to 'passages' in musical works that are such and little more; that have no particular value or interest but serve as 'padding', offering also an opportunity for brilliant display on the part of the performer. This is the type of 'passage' that is intended in the term 'Passage Work', which generally implies rapid execution of 'scale passages' or of some form of 'arpeggio-passage'.

PASSAMEZZO or **PASSEMEZZO.** There is a good deal of doubt as to the nature of this old dance. From its name it is presumed to be of Italian origin and, by some, to have had a pace-and-a-half feature in its steps. It was popular in the sixteenth century in England, France, and Germany. Originally the air was sung by the dancers. It was in two-in-a-measure time and was often followed by a Saltarello (q.v.) in triple time.

Some writers have considered the Passamezzo as a variety of the Pavan (q.v.)—merely a quicker form of it. Sir Toby Belch (*Twelfth Night*, v. i) speaks of 'a passy-measures pavin'. The spelling *Passo e mezzo* is found.

PASSECAILLE (Fr.). 'Passacaglia.' See *Chaconne and Passacaglia*.

PASSEMEZZO. See *Passamezzo* above.

PASSEND (Ger.). 'Fitting.' Cf. *Comodo*.

PASSEPIED (Fr.) or **PASPY** (Eng.). This was, in origin, a gay, rapid dance, very popular in Brittany. It appears to derive from the branle (q.v.). It was in three-in-a-measure time, and its phrases generally began on the last beat of the measure.

Like so many other dance types it crept into instrumental music, becoming one of the optional items in the suite (q.v.). Bach occasionally thus uses it. Sometimes there were contrasted sections in major and minor, or two Passepieds (I, II, and I repeated), similarly contrasted (see Bach's Fifth English Suite, for instance).

As with other dances of rural origin, so the Passepied was promoted to the salon and the court. Louis XIV and his courtiers were fond of it and Lully and other French composers of the period introduced it into their operas. It appears in Gluck's *Iphigenia in Aulis* (written for Paris) as late as 1774. Debussy has a Passepied in his *Suite Bergamasque* for piano (but in two-in-a-measure). The name ('pass-foot') obviously refers to a feature in the technique of the dance; in England it became 'Paspy'.

PASSEREAU. A Paris composer of chansons who lived in the earlier sixteenth century.

PAS SEUL. A stage dance for one performer.

PASSINGALA. See *Chaconne and Passacaglia* (end).

PASSING BY. This song is not, as often stated in programmes, by Henry Purcell, but by 'Edward C. Purcell', really E. Purcell Cockram, who also wrote songs under his true name. He died in 1932. The words are not, as often stated, by Herrick, who was only sixteen when (1607) they appeared in their original musical setting in Ford's *Musick of Sundry Kinds*.

PASSING NOTE. See *Harmony* 3.

PASSING SHAKE. Another name for *Upper Mordent* (see Table 12).

PASSIONATO, PASSIONATAMENTE (It.). 'Passionate', 'passionately'. *Passionatissimo* is the superlative.

PASSION CHORALE. See *Hassler*.

PASSIONE (It.). 'Passion.'

'PASSIONE' SYMPHONY (Haydn). See *Nicknamed Compositions* 11.

PASSION MUSIC

1. Origin and Earlier Development. The practice of setting to music the Passion of Christ, for performance during Holy Week, has two connected origins.

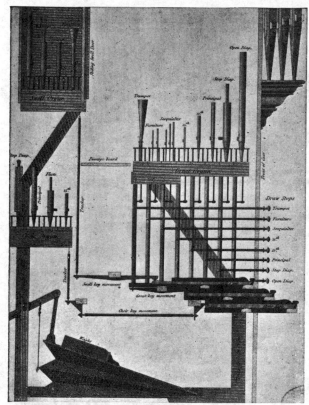

2. GIANTS AND DWARF (Atlantic City). The man is holding the organ's smallest pipe between his hands. The pipe behind is 2 feet in diameter and 40 feet high

1. DIAGRAMMATIC REPRESENTATION OF ORGAN MECHANISM, *c.* 1800, supplied by Dr. Burney to Rees's *Cyclopædia*, and substantially representing the organ as it was often found until near the end of the century. For a general explanation see *Organ 1, 2*

The GREAT stops are (r. to l.) Open Diapason, Stopped Diapason, Principal, 12th, 15th, Sesquialtera (3 ranks), Furniture (2 ranks), and Trumpet

The SWELL stops are (l. to r.) Open Diapason, Stopped Diapason, Principal, Hautboy. The Swell box is on the old sliding door or shutter principle (see *Organ 8*). The CHOIR stops are (l. to r.) Stopped Diapason, Principal, Flute, 15th

There is no Pedal Organ. See *Organ 8*

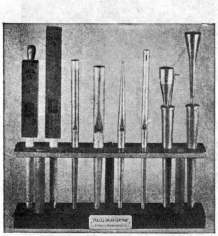

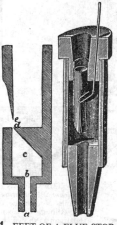

3. PIPE SHAPES. From l. to r. these are Gedact, Clarabella, Harmonic Flute, Diapason, Gemshorn, Salicional, Vox Humana, Oboe. See *Organ 14*

4. FEET OF A FLUE STOP AND A REED STOP
See *Organ 2 a*

5. A PIPE FOR ST. PAUL'S CATHEDRAL, LONDON. Being too long for its position, it is bent round on itself

1. ELEVENTH-CENTURY POSITIVE ORGAN. The simple-minded German artist of the period has left out such details as bellows and wind chest and has provided only 6 sliders for 14 pipes

2. POSITIVE ORGAN ABOUT THE YEAR 1500. From the designs, by Dürer, for *The Triumph of Maximilian*. The organist shown is the Emperor's chief musician, Hans Hofhaimer. For other examples of the Positive Organ see 4 below and also p. 593, pl. **105.4**

3. FOURTEENTH-CENTURY PORTATIVE ORGAN, the player being Francesco Landino (q.v.). For the type of instrument see *Organ* 8

5

4. FIFTEENTH-CENTURY POSITIVE ORGAN (See *Organ* 8). Engraving by Israhel van Meckenham, who died in 1503

6

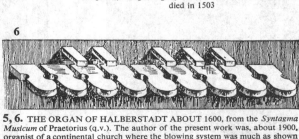

5, 6. THE ORGAN OF HALBERSTADT ABOUT 1600, from the *Syntagma Musicum* of Praetorius (q.v.). The author of the present work was, about 1900, organist of a continental church where the blowing system was much as shown here (though on a smaller scale, with only one blower), but the keyboards of the organ as shown above (tne naturals over 3 inches wide and struck with the fists; see *Organ* 8) must have been quite out of date even when these pictures were published in 1619

The old mysteries (see *Mysteries, Miracle Plays, and Moralities*) are obviously one of them. Passion plays have been given from early times, and in all parts of European Christendom. In Rome in 1264 a Compagnia del Gonfalone ('gonfalone' = banner) was licensed with the purpose of acting the sufferings of Christ during Passion Week; in the fifteenth century it was performing Passion plays in the Coliseum; in 1554 it was still active and its statutes were printed. In France a 'Confrérie de la Passion' was in 1402 given royal privileges, i.e. a monopoly of performances of such plays.

One at least of the old German Passion plays survives, that at Oberammergau in Bavaria, enacted every ten years. Britain also had plays of this kind.

These plays were naturally often under the control of the priests, and in some cases they were performed in churches. Some plainsong would doubtless creep into them and perhaps a little simple choral singing. Every type of dramatic performance tends in time to absorb a certain amount of music, and thus in the Passion plays we can doubtless see one of the sources of the later Passion music.

A more direct and obvious source, however, is found in an ecclesiastical custom. There is a very ancient Holy Week practice of reading or reciting in church, in a more or less dramatic fashion, the story of the Passion of Christ. It is known to have existed in the fourth century; by the eighth its character is determined as follows: a priest recited the story of the Passion from one of the Gospels, in a speaking voice except for the words of Christ, which he gave out to a traditional plainsong.

By the twelfth century the general method had become a little more elaborate. Three of the clergy took part, a tenor as Narrator, a bass as Christ, and an alto as the Crowd (Turba). Right through the Middle Ages this was continued, the story from the four gospels being thus recited on four days in Holy Week.

By the fifteenth century, the art of composition being now advanced to a sufficient point, Passions of a somewhat more elaborate character, musically, became common in various parts of Europe, the motet type of chorus being used either for the utterances of the crowd, to which it had an obvious dramatic suitability, or even for those of all the personages (by 'crowd' is meant the disciples asking 'Where wilt Thou that we prepare for Thee to eat the Passover?', the mob crying 'Crucify Him', and the like). We know that in 1437 Binchois composed some 'Passions in a New Style' for the Duke of Burgundy, to whom he was then chaplain, but the earliest complete example that still remains is a setting long (but it is now thought wrongly) ascribed to Obrecht (died 1505). It embodies traditional plainsong, but it is harmonized in motet style. Its text is drawn from all the four gospels, in such a way as to incorporate the whole of the Seven Words from the Cross; like the texts of all the settings hitherto mentioned it is in Latin.

2. The Influence of the Reformation. The Reformation brought a further development of the Passion. The French or Calvinistic reformers made no use of the form, but the German or Lutheran reformers, who were very much more conservative in their treatment of old liturgical customs, turned it to good account. According to their principle that the people should be able to follow the words of the service, they adapted it to the German language. Johann Walther (1496–1570), Luther's friend and chief musical helper, some time during the 1520s produced the first Passion in the vulgar tongue: it had a great vogue and was still in use in one or two places at the opening of the nineteenth century. It employs a modified plainsong for the narrative and the voices of individual characters, with very simple harmony for the ejaculations of the crowd.

A parting of the ways had now come. The old Latin form remained in use in Roman Catholic countries, the modern form in Germany and northern Europe generally. Amongst those who set the Passion in Latin during the sixteenth century were Orlandus Lassus, Victoria, and Byrd. The last-named merely set the chorus for the crowd—*Turbarum Voces in Passione Domini Nostri secundum Joannem* ('The Voices of the Crowds in our Lord's Passion according to St. John'); the intention obviously was that the priest (or several priests) should recite or chant the story in dialogue, the choir breaking in with collective utterances.

3. The Passions of Schütz. Outstanding examples of the German type of Passion are the settings of Schütz (1585–1672). He had been trained in Italy, studying at Venice with G. Gabrieli at the very period when the new Italian school of composition was active. As Capellmeister to the court at Dresden for the greater part of his long working life he was constantly in touch with Italian music and musicians, who were much in favour there. He adopted a type of recitative that doubtless derived from the new Italian style (see *Recitative, Opera*, and *Oratorio*), but that also had considerable affinity with the old plainsong. The whole works are without any instrumental parts, so presumably this recitative was to be sung unaccompanied, though some think that an organ was used. The various characters are allotted to different vocal soloists. The choruses are frequently dramatic in character, but are contrapuntal. The music is very austere in feeling.

4. The Influence of Oratorio and Opera. Soon after the death of Schütz (i.e. towards the end of the seventeenth century) new elements creep into the Passion. To the narrative and the dialogue of its personages is added matter commenting, or rather reflecting, on the various occurrences, in the shape of lyrical poetry set to music and chorales (q.v.) to be sung by the congregation. Recitative is still used (with an accompaniment of figured bass, q.v.), the choruses are made more pointedly dramatic, and the orchestra is introduced. In effect, the

Passion has now passed right away from its liturgical origins and become an oratorio. In some instances it may almost be said to have become an opera—a sacred opera without costume and action. Such examples as those of the great Keiser, of Hamburg (under whom the young Handel worked), are somewhat of this type: Keiser composed 100 operas and the opera style and feeling were natural to him, yet there is much devotionally expressive music in his Passion settings. Handel himself (1704 and 1716) wrote a couple of settings, much in this style. One of them, like one of those of Keiser, was a setting of a certain text written about this time which was set by more than twenty composers. The author was one Brockes, of Hamburg. His text is rhymed throughout and is rather naïve in its expression. For a time it was the standard text and Bach used portions of it in one of his Passions.

5. Bach's Settings. The Passion reached its highest point with the work of Bach. He wrote five settings, including one according to each gospel, of which only those of St. Matthew and St. John and a part of that of St. Mark are now extant (there is a *St. Luke Passion*, partly in his handwriting, which is not thought to be a work of his).

The *St. Matthew Passion* is, by general consent, technically, emotionally, and devotionally the greatest work of its kind ever written, as it is, and must ever be, the most performed. The forces employed are large—soloists, double chorus (with in one case an additional unison chorus of sopranos), double orchestra, and organ. Chorales are interspersed as reflection or personal application by the congregation of the lessons of the events of the story; it is uncertain whether these were intended to be sung by or merely to the congregation—most likely by them; they are, however, very subtly harmonized.

The Narrator is a tenor. When he comes to the words of any of the characters these are taken up by singers representing them (e.g. Jesus, St. Peter). There are reflective arias, allotted largely to an imaginary 'Daughter of Jerusalem'. The words of Jesus have an invariable accompaniment of strings only, so distinguishing them from those of every other personage. The chorus sometimes represents the crowd and sometimes the whole body of Christendom in reflective mood.

Whether the recitatives, the arias, or the choruses be looked at, each is seen to attain the utmost height of expressiveness. The cries of the crowd, the rending of the veil of the temple, and the earthquake are thrillingly realistic; yet there is no such striving after effect as to give the work any tinge of insincerity. Everything is felt yet everything controlled. Since the time of Palestrina and Byrd music had never been so worthily employed in the service of religion as it was in this and its sister work in another form—the same composer's Mass in B minor.

The text of this Passion is the compilation of Henrici (otherwise known by his pen-name of 'Picander'), a postal official of Leipzig and Bach's frequent literary collaborator. The narrative and dramatic dialogue is expressed in the words of scripture, but the lyrics and the general arrangement are the work of this writer.

The *St. John Passion* is considerably shorter than the *St. Matthew*, is more dramatic in style, and ranks only just lesser as a work of genius.

6. The Post-Bach Passions. As the *St. Matthew Passion* of Bach is the greatest so it is practically the last of the Passions of the classical type. A work of Graun, *The Death of Jesus* (1755), is still heard in Germany and occasionally in England and possibly America. Bach's son, Carl Philipp Emanuel, wrote twenty-one cantatas on parts of the story of the Passion. Jommelli and others set an Italian text of Metastasio. And there are settings of the *Seven Last Words* (q.v.), as that of Haydn (1785), and oratorios on the story of the Passion, as that of Dubois (1867) and the 'Sacred Trilogy' of Perosi (1899).

A second-rate yet sincere little work that has had enormous vogue in the British Commonwealth and United States is Stainer's *The Crucifixion*. It follows the later classical model in providing reflective hymns for the congregation.

Cognate subjects are discussed under the following heads: *Oratorio*; *Cantata*; *Seven Last Words*; *Mysteries, Miracle Plays, and Moralities*. See also *Davy, Richard*.

PASSO E MEZZO, PASSY MEASURES PAVIN. See *Passamezzo*.

PASTICCIO. Italian for 'pie' or 'pasty'. As applied to music it usually means a medley, especially an operatic medley in which the favourite airs from many operas (generally, but not necessarily, by different composers) are taken and worked into a new scheme, with its own new libretto. Such *pasticci* were extremely common in all the opera-houses of Europe during the eighteenth century. Ballad opera (q.v.) may be considered a variety of this type of pasticcio.

A different application of the term is to an opera of which each act has been written by a different composer, as, for instance, the famous *Muzio Scevola* (London, 1721), of which the three acts were written by Mattei, Bononcini, and Handel respectively.

The term has also been applied to instrumental music, as, for instance, the piano variations which the Vienna music publisher Diabelli organized in 1823, and which were to be written, one apiece, by fifty composers—Beethoven's well-known 'Diabelli Variations' representing his share, considerably overdone so far as the original scheme was concerned.

Anything, in fact, can be called a pasticcio which has this medley character. It is worthy of mention, perhaps, that in painting and literature, too, the word (in its French form, 'pastiche') is frequently used, but usually with a slightly different sense—a work in which the creator has imitated the style of another writer or artist.

Another word for 'Pasticcio' in the first sense just given would be *Cento*, and, in fact, the French *Centon* and the Italian *Centone* were sometimes in the eighteenth and early nineteenth centuries applied to oratorios and operas made up on the 'pie' principle, with many tasty ingredients.

It is perhaps just worth mention that in the west of England the name of one particular *pasticcio* opera has come to be used as a general synonym for 'medley' by people who have no knowledge of the origin of the term they are using; thus the writer has heard a lady speak of her workbox, which had been shaken, as 'a regular beggar's opera' and found she had never heard of a musical work of that name (see *Beggar's Opera*).

PASTICHE (Fr.). Same as It. *Pasticcio* (q.v.).

PASTORAL (Eng.), **PASTORALE** (Fr., It.), **PASTOURELLE** (Fr.). (1) The name was, in the fifteenth to eighteenth centuries, given to a type of stage work embodying music, ballet, etc. It was really a forerunner of the opera, yet continued after the opera had come into being. The word implies a rural subject, and a mythological element also usually entered: there are many important examples in France during the late seventeenth century (Cambert, Lully, etc.). An allusion to the word in England in the eighteenth century will be found under *Beggar's Opera*.

(2) The name Pastorale is often applied to an instrumental composition, generally in a six-in-a-measure or twelve-in-a-measure time, and with something of a musette (bagpipe) suggestion. Handel's 'Pastoral Symphony' in *Messiah* is a perfect example of the type, being based upon an actual bagpipe tune heard by the composer as played by Italian shepherds. The *Siciliano* (q.v.) is much the same style of composition.

One or both of the two elements (notes flowing along in groups of threes and a drone bass suggestion) will usually be found somewhere in compositions to which the adjective 'Pastoral' has been applied either by the composer or by common usage, e.g. Bach's 'Pastoral Symphony' in his *Christmas Oratorio* and Beethoven's 'Pastoral' Sonata for piano (see *Nicknamed Compositions*) and his 'Pastoral' Symphony. There was an old dance-type of the name and the term probably came into instrumental music from that, e.g. Bach's Pastorale in F, for organ.

See also *Madrigal* 6; *Suite* 3.

PASTOSO (It.). Literally 'soft' or 'sticky' (from *Pasta*, 'paste', 'dough'). The application of this adjective to musical performance calls for an effort of the imagination: 'mellow' is a suggestion given in most musical books of reference in English.

PATENT NOTES. See *Lancashire Sol-fa* (near end).

PATER DOMINICUS MASS (Mozart). See *Nicknamed Compositions* 15.

PATETICO (It.). 'Pathetic.' So *Pateticamente*, 'pathetically'.

PATHÉPHONE. See *Gramophone* 8.

PATHÉTIQUE (Fr.). 'Pathetic' (see *Nicknamed Compositions* 5). So *Pathétiquement* 'pathetically'.

PATHETISCH (Ger.). 'Pathetic.'

PATIENCE, or BUNTHORNE'S BRIDE (Sullivan). Produced at the Opéra Comique, London, in 1881. Libretto by W. S. Gilbert.

ACT I

SCENE: *The Exterior of Castle Bunthorne*

A chorus of languishing, aesthetic maidens is led by the Ladies **Angela** (*Mezzo-Soprano*), **Ella** (*Soprano*), **Jane** (*Contralto*), and **Saphir**, rivals for the love of the fleshly poet Reginald Bunthorne, who loves, not them but **Patience** (*Soprano*), the dairymaid, who now appears, innocent (she thinks) of any longing for love, a sentiment which she does not understand.

They go off, and the men of the 35th Dragoon Guards enter, with **Colonel Calverley** (*Bass*). Once the languishing girls were in love with them, but since then their maidenly tastes have been etherealized.

Enter the **Duke of Dunstable** (*Tenor*), an officer in the Guards. He is tired of having an income of £1,000 a day, and too much flattery. **Bunthorne** (*Baritone*) and attendant ladies enter. The dragoons, neglected, sniff at the aesthete, regarding the maidens' preference for such creatures as an insult to the uniform.

Bunthorne, alone, admits he is a sham. To Patience he avows his love. She is not interested, and he goes off, desolate.

A new-comer is **Archibald Grosvenor** (*Baritone*), an idyllic poet, a friend of Patience's early days, who has always loved her. They are about to become engaged, but she is deterred by thinking how selfish it would be to monopolize one whom all women delight in. Yet, as she is unattractive, there can be no harm in *his* unselfishly loving *her*. So matters stand, when Bunthorne enters with his **Solicitor**, who has advised him to put himself up to be raffled for. Patience approaches. She will not take a ticket for the raffle, but, having reasoned that a maiden who loves the unattractive Bunthorne cannot be selfish, she offers herself to him. The other girls find in Grosvenor their next object of affection, to his horror and Bunthorne's jealousy.

ACT II

SCENE: *A Glade*

Lady Jane bemoans her friends' desertion of Bunthorne, whom she, ageing, longs for. Grosvenor, who cannot get rid of the maidens, pities them and sighs for Patience.

When he sees her alone, she reminds him

that she is another's, but still has a fancy for *him*. Duty calls her, however, and she *will* love Bunthorne, though she weeps to think of it.

Bunthorne, aided by Jane, decides to be insipid, like Grosvenor, and see if the damsels will again follow him, since they now find him too highly spiced.

The dragoons, in turn, have decided on a change, and are got up as aesthetes, to show their devotion to the languishing ladies.

Bunthorne complains to Grosvenor of being neglected since the latter came. Grosvenor would be glad to escape the girls' attentions, and, to escape something he thinks even worse —Bunthorne's curse—he promises to put aside his poetic affectations and become a perfectly ordinary, matter-of-fact young man. Bunthorne, relieved, decides to be henceforth good-natured and only mildly, pastorally, aesthetic. Finally, Patience decides that, as there can be nothing unselfish in loving so perfect a being as he will become, she can and does love a

commonplace suitor, so she and Grosvenor fall into each other's arms.

PATIMENTO (It.). 'Suffering.'

PATREM OMNIPOTENTEM. See *Mass* 3 c.

PATRICK (or **Pattrick**).

(1) NATHANIEL (died 1595). He was organist of Worcester Cathedral and active as a church composer during the latter half of the sixteenth century. He wrote madrigals, but they are lost. Some of his church music is preserved in modern editions, and is in use today.

(2) RICHARD. He was a lay-vicar of Westminster Abbey from 1616 to about 1625 and is mentioned here merely to clear up the confusion between him and Nathaniel, the credit of whose church music he has often received.

(3) MILLAR (1868–1951). Ecclesiastic, hymnologist, and chief originator of the *Scottish Students' Song Book* (1891). Author of the monumental *Four Centuries of Scottish Psalmody* (1948).

PATRONAGE

1. Necessity of finding a Patron in Early Times. Like literature, painting, and the other arts, music has only in comparatively recent times come into the position of being able to rely for its support and encouragement upon the suffrages of some large section of the population. Until the beginning of the eighteenth century, it may be said, composers were almost entirely dependent for their livelihood upon the appreciation and goodwill of royal or noble personages or upon definite regular employment by some municipality or by the church (see *Profession of Music*). Thenceforward a gradual emancipation took place, with the growth of public concert and operatic activities, the increase in size of the enlightened musical public, and the development of printing and publishing facilities, which provided an additional source of revenue.

It must be remembered that the first public Opera House was opened only in 1637 (see *Opera* 23), that no such thing as a public concert is recorded earlier than the late seventeenth century (see *Concert* 3), and that almost to the end of the eighteenth century copying by hand remained nearly as important as printing, the copyist of a work often making more money out of it than the composer (see *Copyists*; *Publishing of Music*); moreover, so far as printing and publishing were concerned, these could not be securely lucrative until the introduction of copyright laws, which became general in Europe only during the eighteenth century. (See *Copyright and Performing Right*).

2. The Church as Patron. The most consistent patron of music has been the Church

(for long the chief patron also of painting). It is hard to see how the development of music could, from the tenth century to the end of the sixteenth, have been possible without her help. It was within the Church that there was evolved a means of permanently recording the thought and work of composers (see *Notation*), and that the principles were formulated upon which, instead of the unison singing formerly universal, contrapuntal and harmonic combinations might be carried out. The first great definite stage in the evolution of music as we know it today, the stage of the evolution of an unaccompanied choral style, may be said to have ended about 1600 with Palestrina, who was all his life in the service of and dependent on the Church, like his colleagues in various countries, practically all of them similarly employed. Bach and others, in the century which followed, owed much to the dependable revenue which they derived from their tenancy of ecclesiastical positions, and right down to the present day it has remained the practice for a large proportion of musicians at any rate to begin life in the service of this mistress—who, however, has never paid them any too well and at present, in nearly all countries, offers them a smaller sum per hour for the time she exacts than they may expect to gain in any other musical occupation whatever.

3. The Monarch as Patron. During the whole of the above-mentioned first great period of the development of the art, the patronage of aristocracy and royalty was also important. Monarchs have in all times kept a musical establishment as a part of their royal state

1. BACH'S ORGAN AT ARNSTADT (1703). For this he composed his earlier Fugues, &c.

2. BEETHOVEN'S ORGAN AT BONN (1783). The stops are all above the player's head. See *Organ* 11

3. COUPERIN'S ORGAN AT PARIS, with 5 manuals and 25 stops. François Couperin was organist of the church of St. Gervais, from 1696 to his death in 1733. Nine Couperins were in turn organists of this church— *c.* 1650–1850

4. A SCHUBERT ORGAN AT VIENNA (1814), in the Lichtenthal Church

5. S. S. WESLEY'S ORGAN AT GLOUCESTER (1865–76). See remarks under *Wesley Family* 5

6. THE ORGAN REACHES AMERICA (1714). The famous Boston organ, which the Independents of the Brattle Square Church refused but the Anglicans of the King's Chapel accepted. It is now in St. John's Chapel, Portsmouth, New Hampshire. See *Organ* 9

1. ST. GEORGE'S HALL, LIVERPOOL
As rebuilt by Willis in 1931

2. THE WORLD'S LARGEST ORGAN
Atlantic City, U.S.A.

3. ORGAN OF THE U.S. MILITARY ACADEMY (West Point)

4. A COUPLEUX AND GIVELET ELECTRO-
-PHONIC ORGAN, 1933
See *Electric Musical Instruments*

5. A HAMMOND ORGAN. See *Electric Musical Instruments* 4

(p. 172, pl. 35). As they have also always given official recognition to religion, a good deal of the employment of musicians was of a dual character, contributing to the grandeur and the pleasure of the court and also to the solemnity of the court worship (see *Chapel Royal*). The chief theorist of the fifteenth century, the Belgian, Tinctoris, ascribes the great advance in composition at that time to the establishment of royal chapels and particularly mentions the happy innovations of Dunstable (q.v.) attached to that of Henry V of England. For an example of a country whose music has suffered from the absence, throughout its whole period of civilization, of a monarch, see 'Finland', under *Scandinavia* 6.

4. Patronage and Opera. It will be recalled that the childhood of the English drama was supported by patronage. It began in the Church, and when secular drama developed in the sixteenth century the law decreed that no company of players could exist unless under the responsible patronage of the court or of some great noble.

From 1600 onwards the notable developments in music are concerned with opera and with instrumental music. As already stated, opera (with the example of the spoken drama before it) quickly found a means of appealing to the support of the general public, but, simultaneously, it was accepted as one of the most attractive diversions of court life, so that the taste of the courts of Italy, the court of France, and the many courts of Germany exercised a considerable influence over the development of this branch of musical art. Many of the German courts maintained their opera-houses at great expense, and the system by which in various countries today opera lives largely upon a subsidy from the government is a relic of the days of absolute government, when the prince made it his business to support artistic enterprise, partly for the supply of his own pleasures and the maintenance of regal state, and partly from paternal motives of public welfare.

5. Patronage and the Development of Instrumental Music. The enormous development of instrumental forms and styles during the late sixteenth, seventeenth, and eighteenth centuries was almost entirely associated with court and aristocratic support. A great artistic advancement in keyboard music is to be credited to the musicians of the courts of Queen Elizabeth I of England (herself a keyboard player) and of the first two Stuart kings.

It is interesting to note the practice of naming keyboard music after royal or aristocratic supporters. Over twenty pavans and galliards in the Fitzwilliam Virginal Book (q.v.) bear names such as 'The Queene's Alman, The Duke of Brunswick's Alman, Sir John Grave's Galliard, Lady Riche, Pavana of the Lord Lumley'. From this and other virginal collections of the time (p. 193, pl. **39.** 5) it would be almost possible to compile a little directory of music's patrons at the end of the sixteenth century and the beginning of the seventeenth.

For examples of English musicians actually resident in the houses of their patrons see *Ward, John*; *Wilbye*.

Such forms as those of the string quartet, the sonata, and the symphony have owed very much to the experiment and effort of the composers who were attached to the many German courts, small and great.

The question is sometimes raised as to why England, which had previously on several occasions led the way in musical adventure and progress, took almost no part in that of the eighteenth century, and the answer probably largely lies in the greater opportunity that Germany offered. England had one court and one capital and hence one more or less well-equipped laboratory for musical experiment. Germany, with its over 300 states and courts (very many more if the tiniest ones are counted), possessed many such centres; some of these states were insignificant and their rulers relatively poor, but a good many were extensive and their rulers wealthy and lavish in expenditure on whatever conduced to their glory. Naturally at a period when the orchestra, with the necessary employment of quite a corps of musicians, was offering the opportunity for the next great development, the country with the many centres had an overwhelming advantage over the country with the few, or (as in the case of France and England) but one.

6. The Beginning of Emancipation. At the end of the eighteenth century and the beginning of the nineteenth we see the musician emancipating himself from royal control. Mozart, treated with indignity by his employer, takes his life in his hand and essays henceforth to subsist on such moneys as he can draw from the appreciation of the public at large—never, however, getting out of touch with the aristocracy whose approval and support still remain a necessary background for the musician's larger operations. We see Beethoven, likewise brought up as a court servant, casting off the bonds and taking up a free life in a great city, but, like Mozart, still dependent largely upon aristocratic favour (and indeed drawing a yearly pension from the pockets of three noble admirers). The tragedy of Schubert's life, at the same period and in the same city, is perhaps due to his having no fixed position with church or court and moving always in a bourgeois circle which could not offer him substantial recompense for the pleasures with which he supplied it.

The tradition of dependence upon the willingness of some royal lover of music to contribute to the support of the art is still seen, though in rapidly diminishing measure, up to the middle of the nineteenth century and later. Wagner, in difficulties that might well have made him despair of ever accomplishing his life's work, is rescued (1864) by the eighteen-year-old King of Bavaria. Liszt, in no money difficulties but seeking a retreat where he might steadily devote himself to the furthering of the operatic and orchestral branches of the art, settles at the court of Saxe-Weimar (1849–59). Brahms gains a sufficient subsistence and leisure for composition by taking service (1854–8) at the court of Lippe-Detmold.

The earlier life of Loeffler offers us an interesting example of the primitive type of patronage surviving well into the nineteenth century (the late 1870s and early 1880s). The following (from Howard's *Our American Music*) recalls Haydn and his companions in the service of Prince Nicholas Esterházy, and moving with him, according to the season of the year, from the town house in Vienna to the country house at Esterház.

'He was engaged for the private orchestra of Baron Paul von Derweis, who spent his summers at his castle near Lake Lugano and his winters at Nice. Whenever the court moved from summer to winter quarters, three special trains were needed to carry the family, the guests, and the tutors for the children, the servants and the horses, and the orchestra of seventy and the mixed choir of forty-eight singers. Loeffler was a favourite with the Baron and he was often asked to help in the performance of chamber music by members of the family.'

If the lives of the composers who created the great nineteenth-century Russian school of music be studied, it will be found that they all came (unlike nearly all those of other countries) from the 'gentle' classes, and that several of them received the initial impetus that carried them through their life-work from the hearing of the private orchestras then often maintained by the aristocracy of Russia as one of the amusements of life on their country estates (see *Russia* 3).

A rather curious American development of the early twentieth century was the fashion amongst millionaires for the possession of a domestic organ and organist. The *Diapason* records of the year 1911:

'Among prominent private organists for famous men were: Archer Gibson, who played for Henry C. Frick; Harry Rowe Shelley, who played for John D. Rockefeller, William K. Vanderbilt, Jr., E. C. Converse and Louis Tiffany; Walter C. Gale, who played every morning for Andrew Carnegie while the latter took his bath and dressed; Homer Norris, for whom J. Pierpont Morgan was building a country house with an organ all his own; Dr. William C. Carl and Arthur Scott Brook, who had been selected by ex-Senator William A. Clark to play at his mansion.'

7. The Present Day. At the present day the court support of musicians has almost ceased. Courts have diminished greatly in number and those that remain have probably generally diminished in wealth, and the public provision of musical performances is taken advantage of by kings as by commoners. The phase of royal patronage is then, apparently, over, and an important chapter in the social history of music closed. In Russia the Soviet Government has, as a matter of course, taken over the patronage of music formerly exercised

by the Tsars and the aristocracy (with this, however, goes a degree of control—see *Russia*), whilst in Italy prizes for new operas, instrumental works, etc., are offered by a number of state-supported institutions.

In Britain there are nowadays many examples of the better side of the spirit of patronage wisely applied, as for instance the work of the Arts Council (q.v.), the British Council (q.v.), the Carnegie United Kingdom Trust (see *Scotland* 11), and the late Lord Palmer's endowment of the 'Patron's Fund', which since 1903, under the management of the Royal College of Music, has offered to young composers a chance of an experimental hearing of their orchestral works—as to young performers and conductors an opportunity of a semi-public appearance.

The Corporation of the City of London maintains its Guildhall School of Music and, of course, the Royal Academy of Music and College of Music both receive some financial help from the national government. Some very valuable schemes are financed and carried on by generous, active, and practical individuals. A British (Australian) woman, Mrs. Hanson Dyer, organized in Paris, at her own expense, a wide-ranging enterprise (the Lyre-Bird Press) of publication of older music (especially French) such as has been long unobtainable; to this has been added a further activity in the production of gramophone records of such music (see also *Greek Church* 4).

In the United States instances of all these types of patronage are common. Schools of music are founded and generously endowed— as the Eastman School at Rochester (see reference to its publishing scheme, under *Hanson, H. H.*), the Curtis Institute in Philadelphia, the Juilliard School (for advanced studies and entirely on a scholarship basis) and Manhattan School in New York, and the American Academy at Rome (see *Prix de Rome*). Akin to these is the Presser Foundation, which gives scholarships to needy students in eighty or more musical colleges throughout the country (as well as maintaining an admirable 'Home for Retired Music Teachers'). Libraries are helped or endowed (as the Newberry Music Library at Chicago and the very complete Edwin A. Fleisher Music Collection in the Public Library of Philadelphia). And there are 'fellowships' or 'prizes' offered to young composers, as to other young artists, to enable them to do a period of creative work uninterruptedly in Europe or elsewhere, such as the Pulitzer Prize, the Guggenheim Fellowships, the Elizabeth Sprague Coolidge and Fromm Foundation commissions to composers, and Koussevitzky's memorial to his first wife, which takes the form of commissions for symphonic and operatic works.

There is also the MacDowell Colony, at Peterboro, New Hampshire, which (in memory of the composer and for 40 years directed by his widow) offers a place of quiet work for musicians and other artists. The expenditure of over $6,000,000 by Carnegie (and more since his death by his trustees) in grants of half the cost of the erection of organs in the United States and Britain must be considered a notable example of modern 'patronage'. (Cf. *Scotland* 11; *Presbyterian Church Music* 2.)

These examples, from Britain and America, are but a few of those that could be mentioned.

The great increase in the cost of maintaining an orchestra in the mid-twentieth century created great difficulties everywhere. In Britain few halls would hold a sufficiently large audience to pay the expenses of an orchestral concert, so that subsidies from city councils, etc., became necessary. In the United States orchestras such as those in New York, Philadelphia, Chicago, Detroit, Minneapolis, Cincinnati, St. Louis, San Francisco, and Los Angeles are supported by very large voluntary contributions from local citizens, over and above the sale of tickets. These contributions, formerly donated by a few of the very wealthy (some orchestras, such as those of Boston and Cleveland, were at one time kept going by virtually a single patron), come increasingly in the form of very numerous relatively small amounts raised by committees of energetic women (cf. *National Federation of Music Clubs*.) By the mid-sixties extensive Federal support for the arts was well on its way.

With the abandonment of royal and aristocratic patronage of the old type there has, it is to be hoped, been a gain of dignity. It is not pleasant to think of genius in livery, and to recall the fulsome poems Purcell cast as 'Welcome Songs', Bach's servile Birthday Cantata for his Prince, or even the dedicatory letter of the thirteen-year-old Beethoven 'deposing the first-fruits of my young labours on the steps of your throne'.

8. Some Examples of Musicians with Royal or Aristocratic Patrons.

Dunstable (died 1453); Tallis (died 1585); Byrd (c. 1542–1623); Morley (1557–c. 1603); Bull (c. 1562–1628); Gibbons (1583–1625); Humfrey (1647–74); Blow (1649–1708); Purcell (c. 1658–95); Croft (1678–1727); Greene (c. 1695–1755); all (with many other notable British musicians) on the staff of the Chapel Royal.

Victoria (1549–1611). In the service of the Spanish Court at Madrid.

Dowland (1562–1626). Lutenist to the King of Denmark, then to Lord Walden, and finally one of the six lutenists of Charles I.

Wilbye (1574–1638). For over forty years household musician to the Kytson family of Hengrave Hall, Suffolk.

Orlandus Lassus (1532–94). Capellmeister to the Duke of Bavaria.

Lully (1632–87); Couperin (1668–1733), and many other notable musicians. In the service of Louis XIV of France.

Rameau (1683–1764), in the service of Louis XV of France.

Corelli (1653–1713). Over thirty years resident in the house of Cardinal Ottoboni at Rome as his chief domestic musician.

A. Scarlatti (1660–1725). In the service of Queen Christina of Sweden in Rome, and of the Viceroy of Naples, etc.

D. Scarlatti (1685–1757). In the service of Ferdinand de' Medici at Florence and of the Queen of Poland in Rome, etc.

J. S. Bach (1685–1750). For some years in the service of the Municipalities of Arnstadt, Mühlhausen, and Leipzig, and also of the courts of Saxe-Weimar and Cöthen.

Handel (1685–1759). In the service of the Elector of Hanover and pensioned for life by Queen Anne of England, the pension being increased by the said Elector as George I. For a time in the private service of the Duke of Chandos.

C. P. E. Bach (1714–88); Quantz (1697–1773) and others. In the service of Frederick the Great at Potsdam (C. P. E. Bach was afterwards a municipal official at Hamburg).

Haydn (1732–1809). Thirty years in the service of Prince Esterházy.

Mozart (1756–91). For a time in the service of the Archbishop of Salzburg.

Beethoven (1770–1827). In early life in the service of the Elector of Cologne, at Bonn; later supported by a sort of little committee of the Viennese aristocracy.

Weber (1786–1826). Conductor of the King of Saxony's German Opera at Dresden.

Wagner (1813–83). Greatly helped by King Ludwig II of Bavaria.

This list could, of course, be enormously extended, and if all the musicians who enjoyed church patronage were included it would take in almost every composer of note from the beginning of the history of European music down to the opening of the nineteenth century.

For the effect of the lack of Patronage in the American colonies in their earlier period see *United States* 2.

PATRON'S FUND. See under *Patronage* 7.

PATTER SONG. A type of song in which the rapid iteration of a string of words, requiring alertness on the part of singer and listener, constitutes a good deal of the attraction. Rossini's 'Room for the Factotum' ('Largo al Factotum') in *The Barber of Seville*, and Mendelssohn's 'I'm a roamer', offer refined examples. Gilbert and Sullivan have provided many favourites in this genre.

PATTI, ADELINA (1843–1919). She was the most celebrated soprano vocalist of the long period 1860 to 1906, in which latter year she retired. See reference under *Home, Sweet Home*.

Carlotta Patti (1835–89), her elder sister, was also a soprano. **Carlo** (1842–73), their brother, had an American career as an orchestral violinist.

PATTRICK. See *Patrick*.

PAUER, ERNST (1825–1905). See *Opera* 25 (at end); *Dictionaries* 6 b.

PAUKEN (Ger.). 'Kettledrums' (plural of 'Pauke'). See *Percussion Family* 2 a, 4 a, 5 a.

'PAUKENMESSE' (Haydn). See *Nicknamed Compositions* 13.

'PAUKENSCHLAG' and **'PAUKENWIRBEL'** **SYMPHONIES** (Haydn). See *Nicknamed Compositions* 11.

PAUMANN, CONRAD. See *Germany* 4.

PAUSA (It.). 'Rest' (not 'Pause', which is 'Fermata').

PAUSE (Eng.). The sign ⌒ indicating that the note, chord, or rest over which it appears is to be prolonged at the performer's will. It is occasionally placed over a bar-line, indicating a short silence. Another use sometimes made of the sign is to intimate that the composition is finished; it is then placed over the final double bar and corresponds to 'finis' in a book.

PAUSE (Fr.). (1) 'Pause'; (2) rest, especially (*a*) semibreve rest—thus *Demi-pause* means minim (half-note) rest, (*b*) measure (bar) rest.

PAUSE (Ger.). 'Rest' (not 'Pause', which is *Fermate*).

PAVAN AND GALLIARD. This association of two dance-types (see *Nachtanz*) is very common in the instrumental music of the late sixteenth century, as, for instance, in that of the English Elizabethan composers. We have here the beginning of the suite (see *Suite* 2).

The pavan is a dance of Italian origin; occasionally the name appears 'Padovana' (or 'Paduana'), indicating Padua as the home of the dance (the derivation from the Latin *Pavo*, a peacock, is now generally discredited).

It had a four-in-a-measure (just occasionally two-in-a-measure) rhythm of a majestic slow swing, and was processional and spectacular. At one time its air was sung by the dancers. At weddings and solemn feasts a pavan was frequently played by wind instruments.

This dance became popular in Spain, so that for long it was assumed to be of Spanish origin. Ravel has recalled an old custom of dancing a solemn pavan in memory of the dead in his *Pavane pour une Infante défunte* ('Pavan for a Dead Infanta'). He has also included a pavan in his *Mother Goose* suite, whilst his countryman, Fauré, has written one for vocal quartet with piano accompaniment. Vaughan Williams has a 'Pavane of the Heavenly Host' and a 'Galliard of the Sons of the Morning' in his ballet *Job*.

So the pavan is still a living form, but its real importance is in the musical life of three hundred to four hundred years ago.

An interesting influence of the pavan is that seen in the slow opening movement of the 'French Overture' (see *Overture*), e.g. that of Handel to *Messiah*, to take a very familiar example.

Varied forms of the word pavan are often seen in old music, e.g. *Pavin, Pavyn, Pavane, Pavana, Paven*, etc.

The **Galliard**, in striking and immediate contrast with the pavan, was in three-in-a-measure time and its steps were rapid and complex. It was of Italian origin ('Gagliarda') and its name indicates the intention of gaiety. The popularity of the galliard in the England of Elizabeth I is evident by the many allusions to it in literature: Shakespeare makes many references to it, e.g. 'I did think by the excellent constitution of thy leg, it was formed under the star of a Galliard' (*Twelfth Night*, 1. iii). Another name for galliard was one which arose from its five steps, *Cinque passi* (It.), *Cinque pas* (Fr.), *Cinque-pace*, or '*Sink-a-pace*' (Eng.). The five steps were fitted to six beats, the fifth beat being without a step (cf. *God save the Queen* 2).

The names of Elizabethan pavans and galliards are of interest. Sometimes they arise from the origin of the musical theme treated, e.g. *Pavana Lachrymae*. Sometimes they indicate a courtier musician's dedication to some patron, e.g. *The Lord of Salisbury his Pavan*.

In a certain number of cases associated pavan and galliard will be found to be different treatments (duple time and triple time respectively) of the same musical theme. This is an interesting early example of the effort to attain unity which was made again by various sonata and symphony composers in the nineteenth century.

As dances, the pavan and galliard lost their popularity at the beginning of the seventeenth century in England, and a little sooner in France and Italy, when the pavan was superseded by the Branle and the galliard by the Courante (later by the Minuet).

PAVEN. See *Pavan and Galliard*.

PAVENTATO, PAVENTOSO (It.). 'Timid.'

PAVILLON (Fr.). 'Pavilion', 'tent'; hence (from the shape) the 'bell' of a wind instrument. But for *Pavillon chinois* see *Turkish Crescent*.

PAVIN. See *Pavan*.

PAVLOVA. See *Ballet* 5, 9.

PAXTON (The Brothers).

(1) STEPHEN. Born in London in 1735 and died there in 1787. He was a violoncellist and a famous composer of part songs and glees.

(2) WILLIAM. Born in 1737 and died in 1781. He also was a violoncellist and composer. His glee *Breathe soft, ye winds* (sometimes wrongly attributed to his brother Stephen) is not forgotten.

PAYNE.

(1) BENJAMIN. See *Parish Clerk*.

(2) JOHN HOWARD (1791–1852). See *Opera* 21 c.

(3) ALBERT (1842–1921). He was the son of an Englishman who was in business in Leipzig as a music publisher. After professional training as a musician he entered the family business and brought into existence the series of miniature scores of orchestral and chamber music, etc., that bore his name (see *Eulenburg*).

PAY TV. See *Broadcasting* 6.

PEABODY CONSERVATORY. See *Schools of Music*.

PEACE, ALBERT LISTER. Born at Huddersfield in 1844 and died at Liverpool in 1912, aged sixty-eight. From the age of nine he held organ positions, in 1897 reaching that of St. George's Hall, Liverpool (in succession to W. T. Best, q.v.). He left church and organ music.

See reference under *Presbyterian Church Music* 3.

PEACHAM, HENRY (*c.* 1576–*c.* 1643). School-master, heraldist, mathematician, composer, and author of *The Compleat Gentleman* (1622). See *Harmony* 22; *Reports*.

PEAL OF BELLS. See *Bell* 2.

PEARCE.

(1) CHARLES WILLIAM (1856–1928). Organist, theorist, etc., and prominent in con-nexion with the Royal College of Organists and Trinity College of Music. Composer of organ and church music, etc.

See *Anglican Chant* 6; *Pitch* 7; *Organ* 8; *Cadence.*

(2) REVD. E. H. See *Festival* 1.

PEARL, CORA. See *Crouch.*

PEARS, PETER (born 1910). See *Britten.*

PEARSALL, ROBERT LUCAS DE. Born at Clifton in 1795 and died at Wartensee, on Lake Constance, in 1856, aged sixty-one. He came of a well-established English family and at first practised at the Bar. He settled in Germany, studying the works of the English madrigal school and composing (often finely) upon their model, as well as composing church music, choral ballads, and other things.

He was of romantic temper, joined the older branch of the Western Church, and added the prefix 'de' to his name. He had literary gifts, often wrote the poems for his own com-positions, and published English translations of Schiller and Goethe.

His most widely known compositions are his setting of *In dulci jubilo* and the little part song 'O who will o'er the downs so free?'.

See *Madrigal* 7.

PEARSON, HENRY HUGO. See *Pierson.*

PEAU (Fr.). 'Skin' (of a drum-head).

PEDAL. The word is used in various senses (some of them rather odd).

1. For **Piano Pedals** and **Pedalling** see *Piano-forte* 12; *Pianoforte Playing* 5, 9.

2. For the **Pedal Piano** see *Pianoforte Playing* 15.

3. For **Harp Pedals** see *Harp* 1.

4. For **Organ Pedals, Pedal Board, Pedal Organ** see *Organ* 2 d e; (also for *Combination Pedals* or *Composition Pedals* 2 f, and for *Swell Pedal* 2 d).

5. For **Pedal** (or Pedal Point) **as a term in Harmony** see *Harmony* 14, 24 p; *Form* 12 d.

6. For **Pedal Clarinet** see *Clarinet Family* 4 g, 5.

7. 'Pedal C' on the various members of the sax-horn family (q.v.) is the C below middle C (nota-tionally, that is, for its actual pitch differs with the different members of the family). And so for other notes in this range, Pedal D, etc.

8. For **Pedal Notes on the Trombone** see *Trombone Family* 1, 2 b c d.

9. **Pedal Notes on the Horn** (barely obtainable); apply the explanation given under *Trombone Family* 1.

10. **Pedal Drums** (Ger. *Pedalpauken*) are those in which the changing of pitch is effected by pedals. See *Percussion Family* 2 a, 5 a.

PEDALCOPPEL (Ger.). 'Pedal coupler' (organ).

PEDALE (It.). 'Pedal' or 'pedals'.

PEDALFLÜGEL (Ger.). 'Pedal piano' (grand).

PEDALGEBRAUCH (Ger.). Literally 'pedal-use' (in piano playing).

PEDALIER. The word is applied to either the pedal-board of the organ or to a similar pedal-board occasionally in old days attached to the harpsichord and now to the piano. Bach had a two-manual harpsichord with pedalier, and his Trio Sonatas and Passacaglia in C minor were written for it. Schumann and others have written compositions for the piano with pedalier, but in the main this is used merely as a means of getting home-practice of organ music.

As a rule there are no separate strings for a piano pedalier: the keys operate on the manual action.

PEDALIERA (It.). 'Pedal-board.'

PEDALKLAVIER. See *Organ* 15.

PEDALPAUKEN (Ger.). Mechanically tuned kettledrums (tuned by pedals). See *Percussion Family* 2 a, 5 a.

PEDRELL, FELIPE (p. 977, pl. **164**. 3). Born at Tortosa in 1841 and died at Barcelona in 1922, aged eighty-one. He was the inspirer of the nineteenth-century Spanish national movement in composition and the most dili-gent worker on its behalf. (See *Spain* 7, 9.)

He began his career as a choir-boy in the cathedral of his native place, was a diligent and self-taught student of his art, and first came prominently before the public as a composer, in his thirties, with an opera performed at Barcelona. Cf. *Opera* 15.

For about thirty years he was a member of the staff of the Conservatory of Madrid and then he lived in Barcelona until his death.

His compositions include some cantatas, church music, and orchestral music, a little chamber music, and songs. They have never attained any wide popularity, and his influence was mainly exerted in other directions. He was the founder of several periodicals de-voted to the interests of Spanish music, the writer of a number of books on various aspects of that subject, and the editor of much of the older music, including the complete works of Victoria (q.v.). By his cultivation of an under-standing of, a taste for, and a pride in, Spanish folk tune and the Spanish music of the great sixteenth-century school, and by his en-couragement and earnest training of his younger contemporaries amongst the com-posers of his country, he helped towards the casting off of foreign (and especially Italian) influences and the rebuilding of the nobler national tradition.

PEEL, GRAHAM (in full, Gerald Graham). Born near Manchester in 1877 and died at Bournemouth in 1937. He wrote a large number of attractive and popular songs.

PEEL, JOHN. See *John Peel.*

PEERSON, MARTIN. Born about 1572, probably near Ely, and died in London in 1651, aged about seventy-eight. He was organist of

St. Paul's Cathedral, London, and a composer of Ayres, instrumental music, and other things. His dates place him between the true madrigal school and the later English school that culminated in Purcell, and the style of his music accords with this position.

PEETERS, FLOR. Born at Thielen, Belgium, in 1903. He is a recital organist who has been on the staff of the Ghent Conservatory (1931) and Director of the Antwerp Conservatory (1952). He is an active composer for his instrument and the author of an exhaustive organ method, *Ars organi*.

PEINE (Fr.). The expression *à peine* means 'scarcely', 'hardly at all'.

PELAGIUS II (POPE). See *Singing* 3.

PÉLISSIER, VICTOR. See *Opera* 21 b.

PELLÉAS AND MÉLISANDE (Debussy). Produced in Paris, 1902. A setting of the play by Maurice Maeterlinck.

ACT I
SCENE 1: *A Forest*

Golaud (*Baritone*), one of the two grandsons of King Arkel of Allemonde, finds **Mélisande** (*Soprano*) weeping over some sorrow she will not reveal, and over a diadem, lying at the bottom of the well by which she grieves. They go off together.

SCENE 2: *A Hall in the King's Castle*

Geneviève (*Contralto*), Golaud's mother, reads to **King Arkel** (*Bass*) a letter from her son telling of his marriage to Mélisande six months ago. The letter, though meant to reach the king's ear, is written to Golaud's half-brother Pelléas. Golaud wants to know if his grandfather will welcome Mélisande. **Pelléas** (*Tenor*) enters, and hears that the old man will do so.

SCENE 3: *Before the Castle*

Mélisande walks with Pelléas. She is oppressed by the castle's gloom. A storm is rising.

ACT II
SCENE 1: *A Fountain in the Park*

Mélisande, talking with Pelléas, loses in the water the ring that Golaud gave her. She knows that it will never be found again.

SCENE 2: *A Room in the Castle*

Golaud has been thrown from his horse in another part of the wood, at the same time as Mélisande lost his ring, the absence of which he notices. Though she had told Pelléas that she would speak the simple truth to her husband, she does not, saying that she lost the ring in a cave by the sea.

Golaud bids her ask Pelléas to go with her and seek it.

SCENE 3: *Before the Cave*

The two seekers find some old beggars in the cave. Mélisande is afraid, and the two soon go away.

ACT III
SCENE 1: *A Tower in the Castle*

Pelléas comes to say farewell to Mélisande for a time. As she, within, combs her hair at the window, it falls over the head of Pelléas, outside. He claims her as his love. Golaud, coming upon them, only chides them nervously for what he calls their childishness.

SCENE 2: *The Vaults beneath the Castle*

A very short scene, in which Golaud, increasingly 'on edge', shows Pelléas a well, from which comes an odour as of death.

SCENE 3: *A Terrace near the Vaults*

As they come out into the fresh air, Golaud warns Pelléas not to excite Mélisande, for she is about to become a mother.

SCENE 4: *Before the Castle*

Golaud, uneasily realizing how much older he is than his wife, questions his little son **Yniold** (*Soprano*), the child of his former marriage, about the association of Pelléas and Mélisande. The child, frightened, can tell him little.

ACT IV
SCENE 1: *A Room in the Castle*

Pelléas asks Mélisande to meet him for a last farewell by the fountain. He fears that they are overheard.

SCENE 2: *Same as before*

Arkel asks Mélisande why she is sad. Golaud comes in, his jealousy afire. He abuses Mélisande, and drags her about by her hair.

SCENE 3: *A Fountain in the Park*

Little Yniold has lost his ball beneath a stone, which he is trying to lift. Sheep are being folded, and he wonders where they are going.

SCENE 4: *Same as before*

Pelléas and Mélisande, taking leave of each other for the last time, declare their love. Golaud discovers them and kills Pelléas. Mélisande runs away from her husband.

ACT V
SCENE: *A Room in the Castle*

A **Doctor** (*Bass*) tries to comfort Golaud about Mélisande, who is very ill, by telling him that no blow from him could have been the cause of her sickness. Golaud asks her forgiveness but is still tortured by his fears about her love for Pelléas. She dies, and King Arkel speaks her epitaph: 'Only a little peaceful soul that has suffered and did not complain . . . a frail, mysterious being, like all humanity.'

See *Recitative*; *Opera* 11; *d'Indy*; *Messager*.

PENBROCK. See *Bagpipe Family* 7 (Norway).

PENCERDD. See *Wales* 7 a.

PENDANT (Fr.). 'During.'

PENDULUM, action of. See *Acoustics* 4.

PÉNÉTRANT (Fr.). 'Penetrating.'

PENILLION. See *Wales* 5.

PENITENTIAL PSALMS. See *Psalm.*

PENNILLION. See *Wales* 5.

PENNY WHISTLE. See *Recorder Family* 1, 3 b.

PENTATONIC SCALE. See *Scales* 10; *Harmony* 4; *United States* 6, 7.

PEPUSCH, JOHN CHRISTOPHER (p. 101, pl. **18.** 3). Born in Berlin in 1667 and died in London in 1752, aged eighty-four or eighty-five. When over thirty he settled in London and was occupied as an orchestral player, as a composer and adapter of stage musical works, as an organist (Handel's predecessor as organist at Cannons and finally organist of the Charterhouse), as a founder and director of the Academy of Ancient Music (see *Concert* 6), and as a learned theorist and teacher of composition. He became Mus.D., Oxford, and a Fellow of the Royal Society, married a wealthy woman,

the great singer Margarita de l'Épine, and is favourably remembered today by the fact that it was he who chose and arranged the music for the famous *Beggar's Opera.*

See *Ballad Opera*; *Beggar's Opera*; *Methodism* 1; *Organ* 8; *Concert* 4, 9; *Grassineau.*

PEPYS, SAMUEL (1633–1703). Admiralty official, diarist, and music-lover. See quotations and references as follows:

Bagpipe Family 1, 3; *Ballad* 5; *Barber Shop Music*; *Branle*; *Clubs for Music-Making*; *Composition* 14; *Cooke, Henry*; *Courante*; *Dulcimer*; *Gamut*; *Greensleeves*; *Gresham Professorship*; *Harpsichord Family* 4; *Humfrey, Pelham*; *Incidental Music*; *Inns and Taverns*; *Locke, Matthew*; *Lute Family* 4; *Mealtime Music*; *Music Halls* 1; *Profession* 9; *Recorder Family* 2, 3; *Tarantella*; *Triangle*; also p. 224, pl. **42.** 1.

PER (It.). 'By', 'in order to', etc.

PERCHIVAL. See *Pachelbel* 3.

PERCOSSA (It.). 'Percussion.' See *Percussion Family.*

PERCUSSION BAND. See *Rhythm Band.*

PERCUSSION FAMILY

1. Introductory.   3. Instruments of Indefinite Pitch.   4. History.
2. Instruments of Definite Pitch.   5. Nomenclature.

(For illustrations see p. 788, pl. **133**; 789, **134.**)

1. Introductory. This may be the oldest instrumental family in existence, and decidedly certain of its representatives in the modern orchestra are the most primitive members of that community. Many members of the family contribute to the rhythm, colour, and dynamic force of any combination with which they are associated without being able to contribute to its melodic or harmonic elements; others can make a greater or lesser contribution on the latter side. On this distinction can be based a logical classification as shown below, which takes first the class which is capable of the fuller contribution.

2. Instruments of Definite Pitch. (*a*) The **Kettledrum** (p. 788, pl. **133.** 1, 2) consists of an inverted bowl of metal with a membrane stretched over the open end, this being capable of being increased or lessened in tension (and hence tuned to particular notes) by means of screws around the circumference, or sometimes by a handier mechanical method. The frequent changes of tuning demanded by composers often keep the player very busy. The mechanically tuned kettledrums have been in existence since 1837 ('Machine Drums' of various kinds); they permit of instantaneous tuning, so that even a fairly rapid chromatic melody can be played on them, but (on account of real or imagined deficiencies of tone and of exactness in tuning) they are not yet so universally adopted that a composer can confidently write his kettledrum part with them in mind.

The kettledrums are played with two sticks, the heads of which may be of various materials according to the quality of tone desired.

The orchestra up to and including Beethoven normally had two kettledrums; the present-day orchestra normally has three to five (under the hands of one player), so both permitting of a considerably increased range and facilitating changes of tuning.

The chief effects obtainable from kettledrums are those of punctuation by repeated notes and the roll. Melodic passages, also, though limited in variety, can be remarkably effective, the tone produced by a skilful drummer from fine kettledrums being very definite in pitch and beautiful in timbre. Kettledrums were formerly 'muffled' (the equivalent of 'muting' in stringed or wind instruments) by placing a piece of cloth over the membrane: the modern method is merely to use sticks with heads of softer material.

The kettledrums up to and including Mozart were (almost always, Handel being an exception) treated as transposing instruments (q.v.). Their part was written in key C and the composer's intimation at the opening of a movement 'Timpani in D, A' (or whatever the notes might be) brought about the correct tuning which automatically transposed the part into its proper key: the player read C, G, but his tuning caused him to play D, A.

The later and current method is to intimate as before, at the beginning of a movement (or at the beginning of any passage in it), 'Timpani in D, A' and to write D, A. There is one small exception from the strictness of this principle of writing the actual notes: sharps or flats, whilst necessarily included in the preliminary *intimation*, are not generally included in the actual *notation*. Thus a composer will write

'Timpani in D, A flat', and the player will tune his instrument accordingly; but, this being done, the composer will not think it worth while to show the flat in his notation and will simply write D's and A's, knowing that the tuning of the instrument will of itself ensure all the A's being flattened.

The usual compass of drum tunings nowadays extends from E below the bass staff to a minor ninth above that note, but slightly lower and higher notes are demanded, some of the latter calling for the use of special smaller-sized instruments.

For kettledrum concertos see *Tausch* and *Cleather*; for a sonata see *Jones* 8.

(*b*) **Bells.** Their normal form is that of the **Tubular Bells** (p. 789, pl. **134.** 1) hung on a wooden frame: a scale of about an octave in a middle register is usually provided for, generally (and especially with military bands) the diatonic scale of E flat, but occasionally a chromatic scale. Thus actual tunes can be played if desired. (Other forms of bell occasionally appear; see *Bell* 6; *Cowbell*.)

(*c*) **Glockenspiel** (German for 'Bell-Play'). This is a set of steel plates (p. 789, pl. **134.** 4), played, dulcimer-wise, with two little hammers. The effect is bright and agreeable. Glockenspiels of a somewhat different kind (with real bells) were used by Handel and Mozart (see 4 e).

There is a form of glockenspiel in use today which has tubes, instead of plates, and is operated from a keyboard; it is called the **Tubophone.** There is another form (see *Vibraphone*) with resonating perpendicular metal tubes under each bar and vibrations continued by electrical means.

(*d*) **Celesta** (p. 789, pl. **134.** 2). Like the glockenspiel, it is a set of steel plates, but each has attached to it a resonator of wood, which gives the tone a peculiarly ethereal quality and also supplies sustaining power, and there is a complete set of hammers operated from a keyboard. Mustel invented it about 1880 and Tchaikovsky was one of the first to make use of it. (The French seem sometimes to use the word 'Celesta' or 'Céleste' as a name for either what we call 'Celesta', or for the glockenspiel or the dulcitone—all very vague and unsatisfactory!)

(*e*) **Dulcitone** (rarely used orchestrally). It is like the celesta in being operated from a keyboard, but the sound-producing agents are a series of tuning-forks. A French name is **Typophone.** The tone resembles (but is inferior to) that of the celesta.

(*f*) **Xylophone** (p. 788, pl. **133.** 5). It consists of a graduated series of bars of hard wood played by means of two hard beaters held in the hands. Saint-Saëns uses it in his *Danse macabre* to represent rattling bones, which sufficiently suggests its tone quality.

There is a variety in existence today that, with a change of material and somewhat of tone, has changed its name—*Aluminophone*.

Many xylophones today possess resonators, and so fall into the class described below (*g*).

(*g*) **Marimba** (p. 512, pl. **91.** 5). A sort of xylophone (see above). It has bars of wood (rather thinner than those of the xylophone) cut to tune with various notes, and each bar has a gourd (in the primitive instruments) or a metal resonator (in the sophisticated ones) proportioned to the bar, i.e. tuned to it. The tone is mellower than that of the xylophone, because of the softer beaters used. It seems to be taken seriously in the United States, and Percy Grainger used it in one or two compositions. At the Chicago Exposition of 1931 appeared a band of 100 marimbas. The American composer, Paul Creston, has a Concertino for marimba and orchestra; Milhaud has a Concerto (1947).

See *Marimba*; *Deagan Instruments*; *Vibraphone*.

(*h*) **Marimba Gongs.** They are something like the marimba but with metal plates instead of bars of wood, so resembling the glockenspiel and the celesta.

3. Instruments of Indefinite Pitch. (*i*) **Side Drum** or **Snare Drum** (p. 788, pl. **133.** 3). This is a small cylindrical drum, with parchment at both ends, one end having strings (called 'snares') across it to produce a rattling effect (and so to add a dry brilliance to the tone), the other end being left clear for the use of the two drum-sticks. Rolls and other combinations may be played; single notes are not effective. Its technique is difficult to acquire.

The snares may be switched off by means of a lever, or the instrument may be muted by placing a handkerchief between the snares and the parchment, or a wooden wedge is used for the same purpose. The name 'side drum' alludes to its being slung to the side of the player.

For some less common varieties see 5 (*i*) in this article.

(*j*) **Tenor Drum.** This is a middle-size drum, i.e. intermediate between side drum and bass drum, and slung to the side of the player like the one invidiously styled 'side'. It has no 'snares' (see above). It is little used in the orchestra.

(*k*) **Bass Drum** (p. 788, pl. **133.** 4). This is the biggest drum used. It has no 'snares' (see *i* above). Its effects can be thunderous, it can be quietly awe-inspiring, or it can descend to mere carpet-beating. Single notes and rolls are played. A shallower, single-headed variety is used by some orchestras.

(*l*) **Tabor** or **Taboret.** See *Pipe* 3. A form of this ancient instrument is occasionally used orchestrally. Apart from its orchestral adaptation this instrument still plays a part in the popular musical life of Provence.

(*m*) **Tambourine** (p. 789, pl. **134.** 6). A very ancient and primitive instrument (the Romans had it in almost precisely its present form) consisting of a shallow wooden hoop with a parchment head. Inserted in its side are small circular metal plates or 'jingles'. It is played by striking with the knuckles, by shaking (so as to produce a continuous sound from the 'jingles'), and by rubbing the thumb over the parchment (which also sets in motion the jingles). In the English version of the Psalms this instrument is called the Tabret.

(n) **Triangle** (p. 789, pl. **134.** 3). It is a steel bar bent into three-cornered shape, one corner being left open. The sound is produced by striking with a small metal rod. Its indefinite pitch (see *Acoustics* 9) has the property of assimilating itself uncannily to any harmonies that are being played by the rest of the orchestra.

(o) **Cymbals** (p. 788, pl. **133.** 6). These are plates of metal, with leather handles. They can be held in the two hands and clashed together (or sometimes fixed in a contrivance worked by the foot for the same purpose), or one can be fixed to the side of the drum and the other clashed on to it, or they can be rattled together at the edges; or a single cymbal can be struck with a drum-stick or suspended and a roll performed upon it with drum-sticks, or it can be vibrated by a wire brush, or with a wooden, rubber, hard felt, or metal beater. Although these instruments are here included amongst those of indefinite pitch, yet examples tuned to particular notes are not quite unknown; Berlioz has used such (called 'Ancient Cymbals').

For Choke Cymbals, Chinese Crash Cymbals, Sizzle Cymbal, Sting Cymbal, see separate entries under those terms.

(p) **Gong** (p. 789, pl. **134.** 8). It is a big round plate of heavy metal, turned up at the edge so as to form a sort of dish. The best specimens are imported from the East. It is beaten with a soft drum-stick. The **Tam-tam** is the same thing.

For 'Marimba Gongs' see 2 (h), earlier in this article.

(q) **Castanets** (p. 789, pl. **134.** 5). They are a distinctively Spanish and oriental instrument ('Castanuelas') consisting of two small hollow pieces of wood attached to the finger and thumb of each hand and so clacked together, or (in the orchestra) fastened to the end of a stick which can be taken up and shaken as required. They are mostly used in Spanish dance music, or music posing as such or based upon such. The *Crotales* (Fr.; made of wood or metal) are a variety of castanet.

See also *Spain* 8; *Seguidilla*; *Bolero*.

(r) **Rattle.** This is of the usual children's pattern, and the same as the alarm signal of the old watchmen. A small frame bearing strips of wood is revolved so that they catch in the cogs of a wheel. Beethoven uses it in *Wellington's Victory* (as gunfire) and Strauss in *Till Eulenspiegel*.

(s) **Anvil.** An imitative instrument of steel bars and a striker, used by Wagner (in *Rhine Gold*, where eighteen, in three different sizes, are demanded by the score), and occasionally by other composers—including those who write jazz.

For some other instruments see 4 d; also *Chinese Wood Blocks*; *Korean Temple Blocks*; *Bongos*; *Claves*; *Effects*; *Bell*; *Wind Machine*.

4. History. Although the use of instruments of percussion is universal, yet it would appear that the European development of that use is largely due to the influence of Asia and Africa, in which continents their variety and popularity have always been very great.

For three distinct periods mark the introduction of new percussion processes into European music—that of A.D. 1100 to 1300, when the Crusades were apparently responsible for the importation into Europe of the kettle-drums (by far the most important members of the percussion family); that of the eighteenth century, when a craze for 'Turkish Music' in European armies added a variety of more noisy instruments to military band and orchestral resources; and that of the first World War when, in the universal weakening of social conventions, Afro-American elaborations of rhythm and noise, suited to the accompaniment of the dances of the period, were carried over the world and, under the influence of a highly commercialized sophistication, still further elaborated. In each case what has been introduced as an adjunct to movement (in the first two periods, marching; in the third, dancing) has in a measure tended to pass over into the opera and concert orchestra and become a part of the apparatus of both descriptive and 'pure' music—as such to pursue an evolution adapting it more and more to avowedly artistic purpose.

It is proposed, in the sections immediately following (a to e), to sketch the development of the percussion element in western music.

(a) The eastern origin of the **Kettledrums** is sufficiently attested by the name they bore for some centuries. The English word 'kettledrum' is not earlier than the sixteenth century; what Shakespeare, in *Hamlet*, calls 'kettledrums' Chaucer, in *The Canterbury Tales*, had called 'nakeres'. And 'nakeres' or 'nakers' (or in French, *nacaires*), the name by which these instruments were always known from the Crusades onwards to the mid-sixteenth century, is but the 'naqqareh' of the Turkish and Arabic languages.

The custom of providing the drummer with two instruments of this sort, a smaller and a bigger, sounding a higher and a lower note, is also Eastern, and the European cavalry musician who carries his two drums in front of him on the two sides of a horse has had his counterpart in the armies of the East, where the two drums were carried on each side of a camel. This military custom was, apparently, not brought direct into Britain at the time of the Crusades; it penetrated into Hungary (so constantly at war with Turkey), and thence it was imported by Henry VIII (q.v.), who in 1542 sent to Vienna for drums that could be played on horseback 'after the Hungarian manner'. The Hussars, or light cavalry, it was who introduced the horseback kettledrums, and 'hussar' is a Hungarian word.

The early experimenters in orchestral combination (e.g. Monteverdi) do not seem to have realized the orchestral possibilities of percussion, and the adoption of that military instrument, the kettledrum, into the orchestra does not seem to have taken place until near the end of the seventeenth century. It is generally said that the event occurred in Paris, in the performance of Lully's *Thésée*, in 1675, but the Englishman Locke's *Psyche*, of two years earlier, had called for kettledrums. It is impossible to fix exactly a priority which involves questions of comparative dates not only of publication but of first performance and of composition; it is enough to state that the 1670s in France and England were marked by this innovation and that henceforward it was often followed up. So in Purcell's *Fairy Queen* (1692) we find, in the prelude to one of the acts, the kettledrums actually taking a brief solo part. And in Bach's cantata *Tönet, ihr Pauken! erschallet Trompeten* ('Sound out, drums and trumpets'—a chorus of which the joyous music also appears in the *Christmas Oratorio*) we find another brief solo treatment, as we do, too, in Handel's *Semele* at the impressive moment of Jupiter's oath.

In these last two cases the kettledrums obviously serve a directly dramatic purpose. Their more purely musical use at this period was relatively humble; when they appeared for a more narrowly musical purpose it was almost always in association with the trumpets (or occasionally the horns), to which they supplied the bass in passages of simple tonic and dominant harmony, being tuned to the two notes of tonic and dominant.

The instruments then in use were, according to some authorities, 'thudding' in tone, not resonant as ours of today, and they were mostly reserved for loud passages in works of a festive or ceremonial character. Bach generally has them tuned to D and A, and when he wishes to use them writes the movements concerned in key D. He never changes the tuning during the course of a work; if there happen to come movements or passages in other keys the kettledrums must remain silent. He uses them in many cantatas, but not in his Passions, and in orchestral music only three times. To his ears, evidently, the kettledrum was a joyous instrument particularly serviceable as a co-opted member of the brass group in choral accompaniment.

Handel treated the kettledrums in much the same fashion. He who 'sighed for a cannon' probably looked on the kettledrums as a welcome loan from militarism to music: it is said that from the battle of Dettingen (1743) onwards he used a pair captured on the field. And the military association of the instrument lasted thirty years after his death, for in 1784, at the great Handel Commemoration in Westminster Abbey, the kettledrums were borrowed from the Tower of London, being those captured on the field of Malplaquet seventy-five years earlier (to these were added another huge pair of 'double kettledrums', specially made—see 5 (a).

In Handel's performance of the 'Firework Music' in 1749 he is said to have used no fewer than sixteen kettledrums and twelve sidedrums: but this was a matter of a wind-band playing in the open air, and open-air windbands were very naturally looked upon as entitled to a large allowance of rhythmic noise. Thus in the next period we find Mozart, in a Divertimento (about 1773), scoring for two flutes and five trumpets with four kettledrums tuned to four notes, G–C, A–D. Such elaborate tuning as this was very rare then and for some time afterwards.

The kettledrum in the days of Haydn and Mozart was by no means the enrolled member of the orchestra that it afterwards became; there must be more orchestral works by these composers without kettledrums than with them. And the kettledrum, when it did appear, was still held to be under contract to support the brass in all loud passages.

The kettledrum roll (used by Bach, but rarely by Handel) now became commoner: it will be remembered that one of Haydn's symphonies opens with this effect and is in consequence known as the 'Paukenwirbel' (i.e. 'Drum-roll') Symphony. It is at this period that the first known instance is found of two notes played simultaneously—a device sometimes attributed to the ingenuity of Beethoven but apparently really due to that of the composer known as Martini il Tedesco (q.v.), whose opera *Sappho* (1793) offers an example.

The tone of the kettledrum prior to Beethoven (or perhaps, in a measure, up to Berlioz) was probably hard and unresonant: the military conception still prevailed, apparently. Again and again in the later years of the eighteenth century and earlier years of the nineteenth we find Burney, one of the best judges of music in Europe, protesting against 'the eternal din of double drums and trombones'.

However, the early years of the nineteenth century saw a considerable refinement in the use of the kettledrum. Piano treatment and crescendo became more common, and the two instruments were no longer necessarily tuned to tonic and dominant. Beethoven's independence and enterprise were largely the inspiration for such developments as these. In a movement of the opera *Fidelio* he tunes his kettledrums to a diminished fifth (A–E flat); in a movement of his Seventh Symphony to a minor sixth (A–F); in movements of his Eighth and Ninth Symphonies to an octave; he was also the first to use double notes to real artistic purpose. His opening his Violin Concerto with four notes of kettledrum solo is often credited to him as his invention, but, as we have seen, Purcell, 114 years earlier, had anticipated that, and Bach, later, had thought of it too.

A colleague and friend of Beethoven, Anton Reicha, went in one direction much further than he. Beethoven never used more than two kettledrums, although Weber in *Peter Schmoll*

(1801) had shown the way to using three and Mozart, as we have just seen, used four. But Reicha, in a setting of an ode of Schiller, employed eight kettledrums tuned to a section of the chromatic scale. This, however, was probably looked on as a 'stunt', and soon after it was out-stunted by Berlioz, who for the performance of his *Requiem* (1837) demanded sixteen kettledrums operated by eight kettledrummers; the original manuscript specifies double these numbers, but even Berlioz had at times to cut his coat according to his cloth. Previous to this he had in his 'Fantastic' Symphony (1831) scored for four kettledrums with four players and given them chords—even chords to play as rolls.

Berlioz, who made a minute study of every detail of orchestral resources, was the first to investigate closely the possibilities of obtaining variety of tone quality from the kettledrums; in his book on orchestration (1843), discussing the respective qualities of drum-sticks with wooden ends, with ends covered with leather, and with sponge ends, he says that 'the use of these so changes the nature of the sound of the drum that it is worse than negligence on the part of composers if they fail to indicate in their scores the kind which they desire the performer to use'.

Berlioz is usually stated to be the first composer in whose scores change of tuning is indicated during the course of a movement—though in his textbook, in his usual generous spirit, he intimates that this should not be necessary, since two pairs of drums and two drummers should properly be present 'in all orchestras'.

Berlioz was not the only experimenter in kettledrums at this period. Whilst he was engaged on his 'Fantastic' Symphony, Meyerbeer was engaged on his *Robert le Diable*, in which figures a genuine and attractive tune for kettledrums—four of them, later parsimoniously reduced to three in the printed score and there eked out by the double-basses. Three and more kettledrums were at this period not uncommon amongst the rather adventurous spirits who then flourished, especially amongst opera and oratorio composers. Spohr, in *Calvary* (1833), had six, tuned so as to supply chromatically moving basses.

Glancing over the above dates, the reader will realize that the period of the 1830s and 1840s, so disturbed a period politically throughout Europe, was a period of considerable revolution in the orchestra. Towards the end of the period the young composer Wagner was becoming known, and the entirely fresh eye with which he was to look at the whole subject of orchestration, together with a 'stick-at-nothing', spirit in the financial and technical demands he was prepared to make when penning a score, were to affect the percussion department of the orchestra, as all other departments; if his innovating tendency had less definite effect on the development of kettledrum usage than on that of some other instruments, we may put it down to the thoroughness of the explorations already effected by his elder contemporary, Berlioz.

The modern treatment of the kettledrums has pushed out a little in various directions; we find Schönberg, in his Five Pieces (1909), writing a semitone shake, Glazunof in *Stenka Razine*, Holst in the *Planets*, and others carrying solo passages further than their predecessors (the last-named work has six kettledrums). Rimsky-Korsakof, Strauss, and Stravinsky have called for small kettledrums to produce higher notes. Elgar has prescribed a roll with side-drum sticks in the *Enigma* Variations. And so on—these are just examples.

One or two concertos for kettledrum exist—e.g. that of Pietro Pieranzovini (1814–85) for that instrument and strings (the composer was a great virtuoso of the instrument and author of a famous 'method') and two works of Julius Tausch (q.v.; see *Concerto* 6 for one or two other examples).

(*b*) We pass to the consideration of the collection of instruments that the French call the **batterie**, which formerly they often called *Musique à la turque*, as the British called it *Turkish Music*, the Italians *Musica alla turca* or *Banda turca*, and the Germans *Türkische Musik*, or *Janitscharenmusik* (the last name alluding to the Sultan of Turkey's famous bodyguard, the janissaries).

Military bands on the Turkish model (oboes and fifes with kettledrums, tenor drums, bass drums, cymbals, and triangles) were in the 1740s adopted in Austria-Hungary, Prussia, and France, and Britain followed later (Royal Artillery Band 1786 or before). As a result of all this public display, a quasi-Turkish style came to be looked upon as a piquant element in music. Pianofortes were made with attachments operated by pedals bringing into play an apparatus of jingling and clashing. Mozart imitated this effect in a 'Turkish Rondo' in one of his pianoforte sonatas, and in his *Seraglio* (1782) he obtained the same Turkish atmosphere, but more potently, by the use of bass drum, cymbals, and triangle; Haydn, in his 'Military' Symphony (1794), evoked army associations by the use of bass drum, cymbals, and triangle; Beethoven concocted a Turkish March out of the same ingredients for his *Ruins of Athens* music (1812); and on the score of the chorus of dervishes in this work he wrote, 'At this point add all the noisy instruments possible, castanets, cymbals, etc.'. And, wishing to attain the extreme of ebullient utterance in certain passages in the finale of his Ninth Symphony (1823), Beethoven called up his Turkish forces once more (indeed, an early sketch of the work actually bears the words 'end of the symphony with Turkish music').

The examples just cited cover a period of forty years, during which the Turkish-military element was often called upon for oriental 'atmosphere' and also, on occasion, for the expression of warlike feeling or mere happy abandon.

Naturally, certain instruments making up

the 'Turkish Band' sometimes appeared without their fellows. **Bass Drum** and **Cymbals**, however, generally kept company. Gluck used both the bass drum (at that period sometimes called 'Turkish Drum') and the cymbals in his *Pilgrims of Mecca* (1764), so that Berlioz is wrong in crediting the orchestral introduction of the bass drum to Spontini (*La Vestale*, 1807, and *Fernand Cortez*, 1809), though perhaps it was Spontini's example that proved effective in popularizing the instrument as one for occasional orchestral use. Beethoven used bass drums as cannons for the opposing armies in his *Battle of Vittoria* (1813). Later came Berlioz's Hungarian March in his *Faust*, and the works of Rossini and the Rossini school, who were apt to overdo these adjuncts. Wagner in *Rienzi* and *Tannhäuser* made use of the bass drum, and also in *The Mastersingers* (but here played with kettledrum sticks).

As concerns the cymbals, constructionally one of the simplest instruments imaginable, it may be mentioned, as a curiosity, that in 1703 F. A. Lampe, a theologian, issued a book of no less than 450 pages on the use of this instrument in ancient times, and in 1715, with Teutonic thoroughness, embodied fresh discoveries and theories in still another book. Whether Berlioz a century later knew this book or not one cannot say, but he showed an interest in the subject, reviving the ancient smaller-sized cymbals (small enough to be tuned to definite notes, as the big ones are not), and using them in his *The Trojans* and in *Romeo and Juliet*. Some other French composers, as Gounod and Saint-Saëns, have followed him in this. Recent composers have much elaborated cymbal technique, instituting ingenious practices such as striking one suspended cymbal with a wooden drum-stick, a metal triangle-stick, etc., or executing a roll upon it with sponge-headed sticks; all these sticks they minutely prescribe as heavy or light; they also make use of an effect of the two cymbals shuffled together instead of clashed. (Cf. 3 o.)

An old implement has latterly been revived for use with the bass drum; this drum was formerly struck on both sides at once, on the one side with a drum-stick and on the other (this usually for the unaccented beats) by a switch of birch twigs (see p. 513, pl. **92.** 5); Strauss, Mahler, and others have prescribed, in places, the use of a switch much of this old type (Ger. *Rute*). Bass-drum rolls, which possibly began with Liszt (*Ce qu'on entend sur la montagne*, 1849), are now quite common.

It seems as though it was Gluck who, having successfully introduced the bass drum into the orchestra, then gave the **Side Drum** the same leg-up in the social scale, for that instrument appears in the score of his *Iphigénie en Tauride* (1779).

Nearly forty years later Rossini reintroduced the side drum orchestrally (*La Gazza ladra*, 1817); one assumes he was mistakenly looked on as a pioneer in the matter, since his action brought him the nickname of 'Tamburossini'.

It will be seen from the above that Gluck was the first active orchestral employer of the oriental and military platoon. The use of the **Triangle** by Haydn, Mozart, and Beethoven has been mentioned, but Gluck had anticipated them in that, too, for in the opera just mentioned (*Iphigénie en Tauride*, 1779), three years before Mozart's use of the instrument, he employed a triangle. All these exotics, however, remained for a time largely operatic cultures; Schumann's Symphony in B flat (the 'Spring' Symphony, 1841) has a triangle, however, as, forty years later, has Brahms's in E minor (1883); it was Liszt who dared to allow the tinkle of a triangle to sound in a concerto—his Pianoforte Concerto in E flat (1849), in which it figures solo, i.e. entirely without accompaniment. As for the tenor drum, it seems to have gained an orchestral position rather late—1831, when Meyerbeer gave it a place in the score of *Robert le Diable*, to be followed by Wagner in *Rienzi* (1842) and *Lohengrin* (1850).

For eastern colour, right through the nineteenth century, composers often demanded instruments that conductors found it difficult to supply (or even, sometimes, to identify), such as Ippolitof-Ivanof's 'Piccoli timpani orientali' in his *Caucasian Sketches*, Delibes's 'Petites timbales en La-Mi' in his *Lakmé*, and Berlioz's 'Tarbouka' (a flower-pot shaped drum from North Africa) in the Slave Dance of his *The Trojans*.

(c) Experience and experiment with the instruments of the *batterie* naturally led to an enlargement of this section of the orchestra. The **Gong** has been in occasional use since Steibelt's *Romeo and Juliet* (1793), or possibly a little earlier; Spontini's *La Vestale* (1807) and Halévy's *La Juive* (1835) demand it; all three were written for the Parisian public, and Paris, as will have been noticed, was at that time (as she has always been) a centre of research in percussion effects. Cherubini's *Requiem* was another Parisian work of the period that introduced the gong (at the opening of the *Dies Irae* —it was at that time usually to moments of dread or deep sorrow that the gong made its emotional contribution; Gossec used it in his funeral music for Mirabeau, as, long years after, Tchaikovsky did, with ominous effect, in the despairing finale of his 'Pathetic' Symphony).

The rustic **Tabor**, or Tambourin (as distinct from the very different tambourine), must have been one of the earliest 'local colour' instruments to be admitted to the orchestra, since that of the Paris opera, as early as 1750, had a tambourinaire attached to it, and so had that of the Comédie Italienne. A teacher of galoubet (three-holed pipe) and tambourin, Alphonse Châteauminors, settled in Paris from 1772, made the instrument fashionable, and wrote a 'method' for it. It still appears, generally to add a touch of Provençal colour, as in Bizet's *L'Arlésienne* music and Wallace's tone-poem *Villon*; Stravinsky's use of it in *Petrouchka* is effective.

The **Tambourine**, which also was taken into military service, is spoken of by Berlioz, in his treatise (1843), as being in considerable orchestral use and 'of excellent effect employed in masses to strike like cymbals and with them mark a rhythm in a scene of dance and orgy'. The gipsy scenes in Weber's *Preciosa* (1820) offer a typical example of its use. It is one of the oldest instruments in the world and is today exactly as pictured on ancient monuments.

In the late eighteenth and early nineteenth centuries the tambourine was a favourite instrument amongst British and other ladies. In some cities there were teachers of the instrument. In 1800 Joseph Dale (1750–1821) published a *Favourite Grand Sonata for the Piano-Forte and Tambourine*. (He also published an instruction book.) Clementi published *Twelve Waltzes for the Piano-Forte with an accompaniment for a Tambourine and Triangle* (c. 1798) and Steibelt a *Grande Marche de Buonaparte* for piano and tambourine (Paris, c. 1800).

The **Castanets**, another 'local colour' instrument, though apparently not unknown in earlier use seems to have won its occasional place in the orchestra through the nationalistic movement of the late nineteenth century, which brought Spanish music into notice. Bizet's quasi-Spanish opera, *Carmen* (1875), offers a well-known example of its use for national 'atmosphere'. It goes back beyond modern Spain, however, and Saint-Saëns is guilty of no historic absurdity in introducing it into *Samson and Delilah*.

As for the **Anvil**, it may be that Auber can claim the honour of importing its contribution into a musical score (*Le Maçon*, 1825); other uses have been in Berlioz's *Benvenuto Cellini* (1838); Verdi's *Il Trovatore* (1853); Wagner's *Rhine Gold* (1853); Gounod's *Philemon and Baucis* (1860); Bizet's *Fair Maid of Perth* (1867); Goldmark's *Queen of Sheba* (1875). It is of course usually in opera that this instrument appears, and then, more often than not, on the stage rather than in the orchestra; in fact, the anvil is generally found occupying the position of a stage property that happens to be capable of producing a musical note.

(*d*) We now come to the most recent extension of what may be called, without disrespect, the 'rhythmic-noise' department of the orchestra. With the advent of jazz anything became possible—the **Jazz-stick**, or slap-stick of flapping wood, the **Chinese Wood Blocks** and **Chinese** and **Korean Temple Blocks**, the **Rustling Tin Sheet**, the **Thunder-Stick** (q.v.), the swishing **Wire Brushes** (p. 789, pl. **134.** 7) for the snare drum, cymbals, etc., and even, in at least one or two recorded instances (e.g. Satie in *Parade*), the tapping **Typewriter** —And so on! The influence of jazz has not been merely in the introduction of unaccustomed instruments, but also in the discovering of ways of evoking from accustomed instruments unaccustomed sounds. This tendency had begun to manifest itself before the advent

of jazz. Albéniz, who died in 1909, had actually in one of his scores instructed a member of the percussion department to *beat with drum-sticks on the music-desk*—and this is the same jazz spirit that prompts the obtaining of tone from a carpenter's saw. Schönberg, in his *Gurrelieder* (1911), made use of six kettle-drums, bass drum, tenor drum, side drum, cymbals, triangle, tam-tam, rattle, xylophone, glockenspiel, and '*some big iron chains*'—and the word 'chains' for once indicates complete emancipation.

New ways of attacking percussion instruments are constantly being devised. We may take two examples out of many. The score of the Fugue for Eight Percussion Instruments (1933) by William Russell, offers such instructions to its performers as these:

'Handkerchief over drum head' [of snare drum]. 'Sweep wire brush stick across head near rim' [timpani]. 'Scratch strings, lengthwise along winding, with a coin held like a banjo pick' [piano]. 'Pizzicato on the strings of piano with fingertips.' 'Place a piece of paper over drum head' [snare drum]. 'Pizzicato with back of finger nail' [piano]. 'Rub resined glove or cloth over a snare drum stick.'

And Roberto Gerhard's *Concerto for Orchestra* (1965) calls for cymbals to be played with screw-rods and cello bows, as well as the more usual soft and hard sticks.

For forerunners of some of the modern jazz-percussion instruments see *Marrow-Bones and Cleavers* and *Salt box*; for the *Wind Machine* see separate entry.

(*e*) One section of the percussion community has been left out of the above historical survey —the most cultivated section of that community (if one may say so without offence to the kettledrums, which, in their post-eighteenth-century refinement, approach it closely).

The **Bell-Glockenspiel-Celesta Type** (p. 789, pl. **134.** 2, 4) stands apart from its percussion companions in its varied powers of melody and harmony. True, it has its simpler-minded manifestations—Bach's mere two bells so feelingly used in his death-hour cantata (*Schlage doch*; 'Strike then, longed-for hour'); the enormous bell of the Paris Opéra specially cast in 1836 to sound the tocsin of bloody St. Bartholomew in Meyerbeer's *Les Huguenots*; the 7 a.m. and 7 p.m. glockenspiel taps in Strauss's *Domestic Symphony* (1905); and the 'jingles' in Vaughan Williams's *London Symphony* (1914). But it passes into subtler expression in the impressive bell effects of *Parsifal* (1882), to obtain which various expedients have been used, including Mottl's *Bell Machine*, with sets of six heavy pianoforte wires for each note—later abandoned in favour of big tubes (see *Bell* 6, and also *Electric Musical Instruments* 1 c).

And then we have the three- and four-part keyboard-operated subtleties of Handel's **Glockenspiel** in *Saul*, in 1738 ('a queer instrument which he calls "Carillon" and says some call it Tubalcain, I suppose because it is both in the make and tone like a set of hammers striking upon anvils', wrote one of his friends,

Jennens, in a letter), and the similar passages fifty years later in Mozart's *Magic Flute* (1791). After this the Glockenspiel disappears for a space, to come to light again in the second half of the nineteenth century inexplicably robbed of its keyboard, with a shorter compass, and parsimoniously limited to the merely melodic —but to do good service notwithstanding, in Wagner's 'Entry of the Apprentices' in *The Mastersingers* (produced 1868), and in his *Valkyrie* 'Fire Music' (produced 1870) and his *Siegfried* 'Woodland Murmurs' (produced 1876). And allied to this are the **Dulcitone** of d'Indy's *Song of the Bell* (1883), an instrument which marks distinct progress by something very like a return to Handel, and the **Celesta** of Widor's *La Korrigane* (1880), soon to become world-known as a participant in Tchaikovsky's delightful colourings in his *Nutcracker* (1892).

This leaves us for notice only a humbler relation of these bell-like hammered instruments. The **Xylophone** (p. 788, pl. **133.** 5) was perhaps first made widely known by one M. J. Gusikof (1800–37), who won an enormous reputation as a travelling virtuoso and actually died whilst playing it in public at Aix-la-Chapelle. Then there was (about 1870) the Parisian, Charles de Try, who reintroduced the instrument in slightly altered form as the 'Tryphone' and who also enjoyed fame as a virtuoso. Perhaps as a result of de Try's demonstration Saint-Saëns rattled the bones of the dead to its music in his *Danse macabre* (1874), and thirty years later Mahler conferred on it the dignity that attaches to a position in the symphonic orchestra (Sixth Symphony, 1904).

Looking through this attempt at a summary sketch of the development of percussion effects in music, one cannot but be struck again with the importance of the encouragement Paris has consistently given. A very large proportion of the first and other early appearances of the various percussion instruments recorded here is due to the opportunities offered by the Paris opera stage or concert platform (but especially the former) during a period of nearly two and a half centuries. The materials may come from less 'civilized' countries, but to a great extent it is sophisticated Paris that has shown how to turn them to artistic account.

5. Nomenclature.

(*a*) **Kettledrums** (or in late eighteenth-century and early nineteenth-century English literature sometimes *Double Drums*; sometimes, however, at that period, we find 'Double Kettledrums' for a rare kind then occasionally used, an octave below the ordinary); *Timbales* (Fr.); *Timpani* (It.; the spelling 'Tympani' is incorrect); *Pauken* (Ger.).

The mechanically tuned kettledrums, *Machine Drums*, or *Chromatic Drums*, are in Italian *Timpani a pedali*, and in German *Pedalpauken* or *Maschinenpauken*.

The expression *Timpani coperti* (It. 'covered kettledrums') is sometimes used for 'muffled drums'.

(*b*) **Bells.** *Cloches* (Fr.); *Campane* or *Campanelle* (It.); *Glocken* (Ger.); *Glöckchen* (Ger. diminutive of *Glocken*).

(*c*) **Glockenspiel.** *Carillon, Jeu de clochettes* or *Jeu de timbres* (Fr.; 'timbre' means bell); *Campanetta* (It.; Mozart, in *The Magic Flute*, calls it *Istrumento d'acciaio*, i.e. 'steel instrument'); *Glockenspiel* (Ger.).

(*d*) **Celeste** or **Celesta** is also called *Celesta-Mustel* (from the original maker).

(*e*) **Dulcitone.** One sort is called Typophone, and this name seems to be in general use on the Continent; the *Gabelklavier* ('fork-keyboard') is much the same thing.

(*f*) **Xylophone.** *Xylophone, Claquebois, Échelette*, or *Harmonica de bois* (Fr. 'Claquebois' = 'clack-wood', 'Échelette' = 'little ladder'); *Xilofono, Organo di legno* (It. 'Organo di legno' = 'Organ of Wood'); *Xylophon, Strohfiedel*, or *Holzharmonika* (Ger. 'Strohfiedel' = 'Straw Fiddle', the wooden blocks formerly resting on ropes of straw; but see also under *Stroh Violin*; 'Holzharmonika' = 'Wood-Harmonica').

A French form of the instrument is called *Tryphone*—see previous column.

(*i*) **Side Drum** or **Snare Drum.** *Caisse claire* (Fr.; 'caisse' = box, and 'claire', clear—alluding to the sound, which is not dull and booming like that of the snareless tenor drum); *Tamburo militare* (It.); *Kleine Trommel* ('little drum') or *Militärtrommel* (Ger.); *Rührtrommel* (Ger. 'rühren' simply means to beat) is sometimes also used, but this means properly tenor drum; see below.

There is a shallow French variety, the *Tarole* (*Tarolle*) or *Tarole Grégoire* (used in Satie's *Parade*). The *Tambour militaire* is a deep shell drum, tightened by cords and braces. It corresponds to the British *Guards' Model* and the German *Leinentrommel*. There is also the *Caisse plate*, a shallow drum tightened by rods and screws; it is commonly seen in such British military bands as do not use the *Guards' Model*. (The name 'Caisse plate' is, apparently, sometimes also given to the Tarole.)

(*j*) **Tenor Drum** or *Long Drum* (but see below, under (*k*)). *Caisse roulante* (Fr. 'rolling box') or *Caisse sourde* (Fr. 'dull drum'; cf. 'Caisse claire' under (*i*)); *Tamburo rullante* (It. 'rolling drum'); *Wirbeltrommel, Rolltrommel,* or *Rührtrommel* (Ger. 'wirbeln' is to roll, trill, whirl; for 'Rührtrommel' see also above, under (*i*); Wagner introduced the name 'Rührtrommel' and applied it to this drum, *not* the side drum).

(*k*) **Bass Drum** (sometimes called *Long Drum*—but see above). *Grosse caisse* (Fr. 'big box'); *Gran cassa, Cassa grande* (It. 'big box'; sometimes simply *Cassa* is used; and in older scores *Tamburo grande,* or *Gran tamburo* or *Tamburo grosso*); *Grosse Trommel* (Ger. 'big drum').

(*l*) **Tabor** or *Taboret, Tambourin, Tambourin de Provence, Tambour de Provence,* or *Tambourin genre Watteau* (Fr.—the last name alluding to the appearance of this instrument in many of Watteau's paintings); *Tamburino* (It.), *Tambourin* (Fr.); *Tambourin* (Ger. Unfortunately in Italian and German the same word is used for Tabor and Tambourine).

(*m*) **Tambourine.** *Tambour de Basque* (Fr.); *Tambourin, Tamburino,* or *Tamburo basco* (It.); *Baskische Trommel, Handtrommel, Schellentrommel,* or *Tambourin* (Ger.; the 'Schellen' are the 'jingles'). It will be noticed that three languages credit the Basques with the use of this instrument, which, however, they are said not to possess. For the double use of *Tamburino* in Italian and *Tambourin* in German see (*l*).

(*n*) **Triangle.** *Triangle* (Fr.); *Triangolo* (It.); *Triangel* (Ger.).

(*o*) **Cymbals.** *Cymbales* (Fr.); *Piatti* or *Cinelli* (It.; 'piatti' means plates); *Schallbecken* or simply *Becken* (Ger.; 'schallen' is to sound and 'Becken' are basins).

(*p*) **Gong.** *Tam-tam* (Fr., It., and Ger.).

(*q*) **Castanets.** *Castagnettes* (Fr.); *Castagnette* (It.); *Kastagnetten* (Ger.).

(*r*) **Rattle.** *Crécelle* (Fr.); *Knarre* (Ger.).

(*s*) **Anvil.** *Enclume* (Fr.); *Amboss* (Ger.)

For an important eighteenth-century book on drum playing see *Altenburg*.

PERCY, THOMAS (1729–1811). Bishop of Dromore, editor of *Reliques of Ancient English Poetry* (1765). See *Ballad* 5; *Ballade*; *Folk Song* 1; *Rumania*.

PERDENDO, PERDENDOSI (It.). 'Losing', 'losing itself', i.e. gradually dying away. *Se perdant* (Fr.) means the same.

PEREGRINE TONE or *Tonus Peregrinus*. See *Anglican Chant* 2.

PERFECT CADENCE. See *Cadence*.

PERFECT FIFTH, Nature of: see *Temperament* 1, 2. As a part of most scales: see *Scales* 4.

PERFECT INTERVALS. See *Interval*.

PERFORATED PAPER ROLL INSTRUMENTS. See *Mechanical Reproduction of Music* 13.

PERFORMING RIGHT, PERFORMING RIGHT SOCIETY. See *Copyright and Performing Right*.

PERGETTI. See *Voice* 5.

PERGOLESE (or **Pergolesi**), GIOVANNI BATTISTA (p. 517, pl. 94. 3). He was born at Jesi, near Ancona, in 1710 and died near Naples in 1736, aged twenty-six. In a brief lifetime he gave the world fifteen operas, with twelve cantatas (in the older sense of the term —see *Cantata*) and much sacred music. His most famous opera is *La Serva padrona* ('The Servant as Mistress', 1733), and his most famous piece of sacred music his *Stabat Mater* (1736), still to be heard. References to *La Serva padrona* (a work of great historic importance owing to the influence of its Paris performances on French music) will be seen in the articles *Bouffons, Guerre des*; *Opera buffa*. It was first heard in England in 1750.

A number of romantic legends have gathered about his meteoric career and (owing to the cupidity of eighteenth-century copyists) a good deal of music by minor composers has his name attached to it. In particular, much of the instrumental music attributed to him is of doubtful authenticity.

See references under *Opera* 11 c; *Oratorio* 7 (1670–1800); *Intermezzo* 2; *Applause* 5; *Concert* 8; *Opera buffa*.

PERI, JACOPO. Born at Rome in 1561 and died at Florence in 1633, aged nearly seventy-two. He was a great musician of the days of the Medicis, and an intimate of the circle of progressive artists and writers gathering regularly in certain great houses in Florence which discussed the possibility of a revival of Greek drama. Experimenting in musical declamation to a supporting accompaniment, he became one of the first composers of recitative and produced the world's first regular operas, *Daphne* (now lost) and *Eurydice* (1600).

See considerable reference to Peri and the movement with which he was connected under *History* 4; *Harmony* 9; *Opera* 2, 7, 9 a, 11 a, 17 a; *Recitative*; *Oratorio* 2; *Composition* 12; *Leading Motif*; *Bohemia*.

PÉRIGOURDINE. An old French dance in a quick six-in-a-measure time: the dancers sang the tune. Its native home was Périgord, now forming the Department of Dordogne and part of that of Lot-et-Garonne.

PERIODICALS. See *Journals*.

PERMANENT COUNCIL FOR INTERNATIONAL CO-OPERATION OF COMPOSERS. See *Atterberg*; *Kilpinen*; *Reznieček*; *Różycki*.

PERÒ (It.). 'However', 'therefore'.

PEROSI, LORENZO. Born at Tortona in 1872 and died in Rome in 1956, aged eighty-three. He was an Italian priest–musician who, in the closing years of the last century and the opening years of the present one, made a great stir in his own country and elsewhere, with a series of oratorios.

He was for some time in charge of the music in St. Mark's, Venice, and later of that in the Sistine Chapel in Rome.

It is said that his influence had something to do with the admirable (but a good deal neglected) regulation of Pius X, tending to the restoration of dignity in the music of the Roman Catholic Church (see *Motu Proprio*).

See *Oratorio* 2 (end), 7 (1897, 1901–2–4); *Passion Music* 6.

PÉROTIN-LE-GRAND (or 'Perotinus Magnus'). Born *c.* 1160 and died *c.* 1220. He was in charge of the music in the church on the site of which Notre Dame de Paris now stands. We owe to him compositions which led to a higher development of the then juvenile art of polyphonic composition—its first great climax. He is an important representative of the 'Ars antiqua' (cf. *Ars nova*).

See *France* 2 for a brief statement as to the group of musicians to which he belongs.

PERPETUAL CANON. See *Canon*.

PERPETUO. See under *Perpetuum Mobile* below.

PERPETUUM MOBILE (Latin, 'perpetually in motion'). This name, or the same in Italian, i.e. *Moto Perpetuo*, is given to a rapid instrumental composition that proceeds throughout in notes of the same value—a variety of toccata (q.v.), one may say. Weber, Mendelssohn, Paganini, and others, use the term.

PERRET, WILFRED. See *Temperament* 9.

PERRIN, PIERRE (c. 1620–75). See *Ballet* 2; *Lully*.

PERRONET THOMPSON, THOMAS (1783–1869). See *Keyboard* 3.

PERRUQUE, STYLE DE. See *Zopf*.

PERRY. Mid-nineteenth-century London violinist. See *Conducting*.

PERSIAN. A languorous, melancholy type of dance, e.g. in Delibes's *Lakmé*.

PERSICHETTI, VINCENT. Born in Philadelphia in 1915. He is a pianist, composer, and conductor, and as such a pupil of Olga Samaroff, Roy Harris, Fritz Reiner, and others. He has taught at the Philadelphia Conservatory (1942) and the Juilliard School (1948). His very numerous works include seven symphonies, chamber and piano music, and songs, and a book on twentieth century harmony.

PERSIMFANS. See *Conducting* 7; *Russia* 8.

PERSLEY. See *Parsley*.

PERSONAL TASTE IN MUSIC. See *Quality in Music* 7.

PERSPECTIVES OF NEW MUSIC. See *Journals*.

PES (Latin for 'foot'). See *Sumer is icumen in* for an explanation. The word is found with the same signification in the manuscript of that work and in a few manuscripts of later date. It is also sometimes found with a totally different signification—as a synonym for *podatus*, a particular melodic figure of plainsong as indicated in the old neume notation.

PESANT (Fr.), **PESANTE** (It.). 'Weighing', i.e. heavy, heavily. So, too, *Pesamment* (Fr.), *Pesantemente* (It.), 'heavily'.

PESTALOZZI. See *Education* 1, 3.

PETENERA. A sort of traditional Spanish song (so called after a nineteenth-century singer). It is in a fairly brisk three-in-a-measure, but the guitar 'breaks' which go by the same name frequently alternate with this a six-in-a-measure.

PETER, JOHANN FRIEDRICH. Born (of German parentage) in Holland in 1746, and died at Bethlehem, Pa., in 1813. He migrated to America in 1770 and became organist, in turn, of various Moravian churches in Pennsylvania and North Carolina, settling finally as that of the American Headquarters church at Bethlehem. He composed chamber music, anthems, etc.

PETER AND THE WOLF. See *Prokofief*.

PETERBOROUGH CATHEDRAL. See *Alto Voice*.

PETER GRIMES. Opera by Benjamin Britten; Libretto by Montagu Slater, derived from Crabbe's poem *The Borough*. Produced at Sadler's Wells Theatre, London, in 1945.

PROLOGUE

A Coroner's Inquest in a small fishing town on the East Coast of England. **Swallow** (*Bass*), Mayor and Coroner, is examining **Peter Grimes** (*Tenor*), a fisherman, as to the death of his apprentice during a recent fishing trip. **Mrs. Sedley,** an assertive widow, momentarily intervenes and the **Chorus** makes its comments. **Mrs. Ellen Orford** (*Soprano*) gives some evidence. The inquest ends with a verdict of accidental death coupled with a warning to Grimes not to get another boy apprentice. **Hobson** (*Bass*), a carrier and constable, cries 'Silence', and eventually, 'Clear the Court'. Peter and Ellen Orford are left alone and Ellen expresses herself sympathetically. Grimes is in love with Ellen.

ACT I

SCENE 1: *A Street by the Sea*

Captain Balstrode (*Baritone*), a retired merchant skipper, is looking out to sea with his glass. Fishermen enter the 'Boar' inn where the landlady, known as **Auntie** (*Contralto*), serves them. **Robert Boles** (*Tenor*) and Mrs. Sedley are seen going to the church. Fishermen disembark. The apothecary, **Ned Keene** (*Baritone*), tells that in the workhouse of the neighbouring place is a boy who could be obtained as apprentice for Grimes. Hobson, the carrier, has to be persuaded to call for him with his cart and Ellen Orford agrees to accompany him. A conversation takes place between Grimes and Balstrode as to Peter's position in local opinion, the coming new apprentice, and Grimes's ambition to marry Ellen Orford.

SCENE 2: *Interior of the 'Boar' inn, where fisherfolk are sheltering from a violent storm*

From the excited conversation we learn of the storm's ravages. Brawls occur amongst the pub's customers. Grimes enters and then the carrier, with Ellen Orford and the new apprentice. Peter takes the boy and goes out to his hut.

ACT II

SCENE 1: *The Street again. It is a sunny Sunday morning*

Ellen Orford and the boy enter and sit down by the breakwater. Whilst Ellen talks to the boy, and notes with distress signs of his having been roughly treated by Grimes, there are heard snatches of the service in the neighbouring church. Peter enters and insists on

See the Articles under their respective names

1. STANLEY, 1713–86. The famous London blind organist

2. BENJAMIN JACOB, 1778–1829. A leader of the early English enthusiasts for Bach

3. GUILMANT, 1837–1911. Organist, composer, and editor of early organ music

4. THE INFANT CROTCH

5. BEST, 1826–97. Britain's great concert organist

6. VIERNE, 1870–1937. The celebrated blind organist of Notre Dame

7. WIDOR, 1844–1937. The world-famous organ player, composer, and Bach editor

PLATE 132   THE ORGAN, VI. PLAYING TO A WHOLE REGION

THE ORGANIST OF KUFSTEIN (in the Tyrol)

He sits at his console in a little building 250 feet below the narrow rectangular orifice near the tower roof, whence the music issues (the distance
involved creates a difficulty for the player, whose fingers must always be in
advance of his ears)

There are recitals every midday—and sometimes also in the evening

the boy coming with him to the pursuit of a shoal of fish that is in sight. He and Ellen quarrel. Grimes and the boy depart. The Rector and Swallow appear and, with a number of the townspeople, set off to Peter's hut to see what is happening.

SCENE 2: *Peter's Hut*

The boy staggers into the room and Peter follows. The townspeople are heard approaching, but Peter quickly drives the boy before him to embark. The people enter but find the hut empty.

ACT III

SCENE 1: *The Street again on a summer evening; a dance is in progress at the Moot Hall and the music can be heard*

Keene, the apothecary, comes out of the hall and Mrs. Sedley tells him that the apprentice has disappeared. We learn that his jersey has floated ashore. Various characters discuss the matter animatedly, and then set off on a search.

SCENE 2: *The same place: there is a fog at sea*

The people are still looking for the boy. Peter staggers in, apparently demented. Balstrode urges him to get again into his boat, sail away, sink her, and destroy himself. He embarks. Soon after the news goes round that the coastguard report a boat far out at sea sinking. The curtain falls.

PETERKIN, NORMAN. Born at Liverpool in 1886. He is of Scottish–Irish descent. In music he is self-taught. He has composed (reticently and when the spirit has moved him) songs, piano pieces, and chamber and orchestral music, all of sensitive feeling and delicate texture.

PETERS.

(1) REVD. SAMUEL. See *United States* 2.

(2) Publishing firm. See *Publishing* 8.

PETERSEN, WILHELM. Born at Athens in 1890 and died at Darmstadt in 1957, aged sixty-seven. He was trained at the academy of Munich, and wrote sonatas, symphonies, etc.

PETERSON - BERGER, OLOF WILHELM. Born at Ullanger, Sweden, in 1867 and died at Oestersund in 1942, aged seventy-five. He studied in Sweden and Germany and then devoted himself to writing music in a definitely Swedish idiom—dramatic, orchestral, chamber, and vocal. He also took some rank as a poet, served as music critic, translated works of Wagner into Swedish, and directed the Wagner performances at the Stockholm operahouse.

PETIPA. See *Ballet* 9.

PETIT, PETITE (Fr., masc., fem.). 'Small', 'little'.

PETIT BUGLE. See *Saxhorn and Flügelhorn Families* 3 a b.

PETIT DÉTACHÉ. See *Détaché*.

PETITE FLÛTE, PETITE FLÛTE OCTAVE. See *Flute Family* 5 b.

PETITS DROITS. See *Copyright and Performing Right* 1 (note).

PETRARCH (1304–74). See *Italy* 2; *Madrigal* 1.

PETRASSI, GOFFREDO (p. 525, pl. **96**. 7). Born at Zagorolo, near Rome, in 1904. After a period of employment in a music firm, he began at twenty-one to study organ and composition at the St. Cecilia Academy in Rome and became known as the composer of choral, orchestral, and chamber works, as also of a one-act opera, *Morte dell' Aria*, and other things. For a time his output showed the influence of Casella and Hindemith, but he has at various times shown himself susceptible to a variety of influences.

See *Italy* 8; *Harpsichord* 9.

PETRELLA, ENRICO (1813–77). He was a highly successful Italian opera composer. A Dead March by him (from the opera *Ione*) is still often heard at Italian funerals.

PETRESCO. See *Greek Church* 4.

PETRIE, GEORGE. Born in Dublin in 1789 and died there in 1866, aged seventy-six or seventy-seven. He was an eminent painter and a painstaking and ingenious antiquary (the first to establish the origin of the Irish round towers), as well as an amateur violinist. All his life he collected Irish folk tunes, and his work must ever remain the basis for the study of that branch of music. His complete collection has been republished, partly under the editorship of Stanford (q.v.).

See *Londonderry Air*; *Bunting*.

PETRUCCI, OTTAVIANO DEI (1466–1539). See *Printing* 1; *Publishing* 1; *Suite* 2; *Ricercare*; *Frottola*; *Strambotto*; p. 832, pl. **141**. 4.

PETTO (It.). 'Chest', e.g. *Voce di Petto* 'chest voice'.

PETZOLD (or **Petzel**), **JOHANN CHRISTOPH.** Born at Glatz in 1639 and died at Bautzen, in Saxony, in 1694, aged fifty-four. He was town musician of Bautzen and was active as a composer for wind instruments.

PEU (Fr.). 'Little.' So *Peu à peu*, 'little by little'.

PEVERNAGE, ANDREAS. Born at Courtrai in Flanders, in 1543 and died at Antwerp in 1591, aged about forty-eight. He was choirmaster of the cathedral of Antwerp. He published masses and books of his own motets and chansons and edited a book of madrigals (*Harmonia celeste*, 1583 and later editions).

PEZZO (It.). 'Piece.' The plural is *Pezzi*.

PFEIFE (Ger.). 'Pipe.' **PFEIFEREI.** See *Street Music* 5 (end).

PFEIL, V. A. See *Electric Musical Instruments* 2 b.

PFENNINGER, RUDOLF. See *Electric Musical Instruments* 5 c.

PFERDEMUSIK (Beethoven). See *Galop*.

PFIFFIG (Ger.). 'Artful.'

PFITZNER, HANS (p. 401, pl. **70**. 7). Born

in Moscow in 1869 and died in Salzburg in 1949, aged eighty. Despite his birthplace his parents were German and his life was passed in Germany, where he was active as opera conductor and composer. He accepted the influence of Wagner and may be said to have belonged to the neo-romantic German school—if, however, the 'neo' can be prefixed with propriety in this case (see *Romantic*). His opera *Palestrina* (Munich, 1917) and his very elaborate romantic cantata *Of the German Soul* ('Von deutscher Seele') are works which move his admirers to reverence. He philosophized about music a good deal and engaged in controversy, particularly in opposition to Busoni. At the age of sixty-three he produced his first symphony—an orchestration based on his string quartet of seven years earlier. Two years later a cello concerto appeared.

PHAGOTUM. An elaborate instrument, with wind-bag and bellows, invented by Canon Afranio in the early sixteenth century. For long it was quite mistakenly supposed (probably on account of its name) to have been the original of the bassoon (fagotto).

PHALÈSE. See *Publishing* 3.

PHANTASIE, plural *Phantasien* (Ger.). The word simply means 'fancy', 'imagination', or 'reverie', and when used as a title for a piece of music has no connotation more definite than that. *Phantasiren* in German means to indulge one's imagination or, when applied to music, to improvise. **Phantasiestück** (plur. *Phantasiestücke*) and **Phantasiebild** (plur. *Phantasiebilder*) are probably best translated literally as 'Fantasy Piece' and 'Fantasy Picture'. Schumann uses 'Phantasiestück' a good deal. (Some of these words will sometimes be found spelt with an 'F' instead of 'Ph'.)

Cf. *Phantasy*.

PHANTASY. In the first years of the twentieth century, Walter Willson Cobbett, a keen amateur devotee of chamber music, offered prizes and commissions to British composers for single-movement pieces, without conditions as to the form to be employed. To these (on the advice of the Musicians' Company) he applied the name 'Phantasy', taking the suggestion from the sixteenth-century English Fancy (q.v.). Over forty of these compositions were heard between 1905 and 1930.

Cf. *Phantasie*.

PHARYNX. See *Voice* 21.

PH.D. See *Degrees and Diplomas* 1.

PHILADELPHIA. See *United States* 3; *Concert* 14; *Pianoforte* 5, 9; *Harpsichord Family* 4; *Publishing* 9; *Patronage* 7; *Organ* 5, 9; *Schools of Music*.

PHILHARMONIC PITCH, OLD AND NEW. See *Pitch* 5.

PHILHARMONIC SOCIETY (LONDON). See *Concert* 6, 8; *Conducting* 5.

PHILHARMONIC SOCIETY (NEW YORK). See *United States of America* 4.

PHILHARMONIC HALL (NEW YORK). See *Concert Halls* 14.

PHILHARMONIE (HALL), BERLIN. See *Concert Halls* 14.

PHILIDOR Family (real name 'Danican'). They resemble the Purcells, the Couperins, and the Bachs in the family possession of musical gifts. Their lifetimes, in their three generations, covered the period of about 1600 to 1800. They were largely instrumentalists in the service of Louis XIV and Louis XV; two of the favourite family instruments were the krumhorn (q.v.) and the so-called tromba marina (q.v.), but there were also oboists (especially), fifers, drummers, and fiddlers amongst them. From ten to fourteen of them will be found biographically treated in the larger works of musical reference, and even that does not include all the musicians of the family.

The most important member of the whole tribe is **François André,** who was born at Dreux (Eure-et-Loire) in 1726 and died in London in 1795, aged nearly sixty-nine. His first fame was as a chess player, and before he was twenty he had begun his extensive travels as a virtuoso of the board. He came much to London, where he was welcomed by the Chess Club, which gave him a regular pension, apparently in return for annual visits. There, as an emigré from the Revolution, he died.

Along with his chess he assiduously practised music. As a page in the French Chapel Royal he had lessons from Campra (q.v.); then for a time he earned his living as a music teacher and copyist. He heard Handel's oratorios in London, from 1749 onwards, and composed choral music in Handelian style. In the year Handel died he turned to comic opera (see a reference under *Opera buffa*), and produced a series of highly successful works in Paris at the time when Grétry, Monsigny, and Duny were also popular there. His dramatic ensembles constitute one of his titles to an important place in the history of the development of operatic art.

See references to A. D. Philidor (the founder of the Concert Spirituel in Paris) under *Concert* 14; *France* 7.

PHILIP II OF SPAIN (b. 1527; d. 1598). See *Spain* 5, 8; *Belgium* 2; *Holland* 2; *Sarabande*.

PHILIPP, ISIDORE (1863–1958). Famous Hungarian pianist and trainer of pianists at the Paris Conservatory. He lived in New York, 1941–55.

PHILIPPE DE VITRY. See *France* 3.

PHILIPS, PETER (p. 164, pl. **33.** 3). Born in England in 1561 and died at Brussels in 1628, aged about sixty-seven. His life-history is obscure, but it is certain that he held important musical positions in the Spanish Netherlands, including that of organist of the Royal Chapel at Brussels (see allusion under *Belgium* 9). He was in holy orders and held certain canonries. He wrote madrigals, church music, and instrumental music, much being published at Antwerp. His fame, high in his own day, was in the early twentieth century revived by the performance of his sacred music under R. R. Terry (q.v.) at Westminster Cathedral, his madrigals (to Italian words) being later made known by broadcast performances under the same direction.

See *Mechanical Reproduction* 4 (end); *Germany* 4.

PHILLIPS, BURRILL. Born in Omaha in 1907. He was trained at the Eastman School, Rochester, N.Y., and later joined its staff. He has composed a variety of orchestral, chamber, piano, and stage works.

'PHILOSOPHER' SYMPHONY (Haydn). See *Nicknamed Compositions* 11.

PHILOSOPHICAL PITCH. See *Acoustics* 15; *Pitch* 5.

PHILOSOPHICAL TRANSACTIONS. See F.R.S.

PHONAUTOGRAPH. See *Gramophone* 1.

PHONEUMA. See *Organ* 14 I.

PHONODEIK. A very ingenious and delicate apparatus, invented by Professor Dayton C. Miller (q.v.) of the Case School of Applied Science, Cleveland, Ohio, to cause sounds to produce, photographically, diagrams representing their so-called 'wave' forms (see *Acoustics* 12).

PHONOFIDDLE, etc. See reference under *Stroh Violin*.

PHONOGRAM, PHONOGRAPH. See *Gramophone* 8.

PHONOMANDOLIN, etc. See reference under *Stroh Violin*.

PHONON. See *Organ* 14 I.

PHONOPHOTOGRAPHY. See *Folk Song* 3.

PHOTO-ELECTRIC CELL. See *Electric Musical Instruments* 5; *Gramophone* 4; *Broadcasting* 6.

PHOTOGRAPHON, PHOTOPHONO-GRAPH. See *Gramophone* 4.

PHOTONA. See *Electric Musical Instruments* 5 b.

PHOTOPHONE. See *Electric Musical Instruments* 5 b.

PHRASE AND SENTENCE. If any simple four-line folk tune, hymn tune, etc., be hummed through, it will be felt to fall definitely into two halves; these are musical *Sentences*. If one of these sentences be now hummed it will be felt to fall again into two halves; these are musical *Phrases*. In this analysis two 'Phrases' form a 'Sentence' but some theorists would prefer to call the 'Sentence' the group of the *four* 'Phrases': there is no accepted understanding amongst musicians on this point but all are pretty well agreed as to the meaning of the word 'phrase', though in analysing any particular composition one theorist might on occasion prefer to consider as one phrase a particular passage which another would prefer to consider as two phrases.

The simplest type of composition was taken as the example above so as to demonstrate the principle, which can, obviously, be applied to longer compositions. Indeed, every composi-

tion whatever will be found on examination to fall into a series of phrases (not necessarily of equal lengths), it being as natural for the composer to conceive of his melody and harmony as broken continually at more or less regular intervals by some sort of *cadences*, as for a speaker to take breaths at more or less regular intervals or for a writer to give intelligibility to his thought by the use of the various signs of punctuation. Indeed, no such thing as a continuous melody seems to be conceivable by the mind of man.

The normal length of a phrase is four measures, but three-measure phrases are not uncommon, and what has obviously been first conceived by the composer as a four-measure phrase is often found to have been extended by him to five measures. There is thus no rule as to phrase-length, and indeed the introduction of a change of length often gives a very acceptable variety.

The phrase itself, short as it may be, is not the lowest unit; closely examined it will often be found to fall into half-phrases and these into *motifs* (see *Motif*).

The building up of a long movement in composition is then from the *motif* to the *half-phrase*, to the *phrase*, to the *sentence*, to the *subject*, to the *section* (e.g. the Exposition, or Development, or Recapitulation of a movement in 'Compound Binary Form'—see *Form* 7), and so to the movement or composition as a whole.

See also *Phrase Marks* and *Phrasing* below.

PHRASE MARKS in musical notation are the slurs, etc., placed over or under the notes as a hint towards the manner of performance. They are usually very illogically used even by the greatest composers (Schumann is sometimes cited as an honourable exception), there being a great confusion between the slur which indicates the limits of a phrase and that which indicates the composer's (or editor's) desire for legato. Thus the young performer, instead of being helped, is often puzzled, and is largely thrown back on his own common sense and artistic feeling.

Various means have been suggested for getting rid of this anomaly, one being the using of straight lines (square-ended or curve-ended) to show the actual phrase lengths, with, inside these, the curved lines, dots above or below notes, and the like, to indicate legato and staccato (or, in bowed instruments, the 'bowing').

PHRASING (see the article *Phrase and Sentence* above). Phrasing in performance is the neat and artistic observance of the cadences at the ends of phrases, and also of the half-phrases and motifs, not necessarily by any pronounced 'break' (Couperin, in 1722, introduced the use of the comma to mark the end of phrases), but by that judicious accentuation and nuance that gives intelligent 'point' to the melodic and harmonic structure of the music. It may almost be called the last refinement in 'interpretation'. Mechanically carried out, as the result of mere study of the structure, it may be deadening; artistically carried out, as a result of study plus intuition or feeling, it is one of the greatest charms in performance.

For the vocal performer there is frequently a special problem. He has, at one and the same time, to give 'point' to the words and to make clear the musical structure. This sometimes involves a compromise, but it is one which the greater singers achieve triumphantly.

See also *Phrase Marks*; *Agogic*.

PHRYGIAN CADENCE. See *Cadence*.

PHRYGIAN MODE. See *Modes* 6, 7.

PHRYGIAN TETRACHORD. See *Scales* 5.

PHYSHARMONICA. See *Reed-Organ Family* 6. There is on some German organs a soft reed-stop of this name (8-foot or 16-foot).

PHYSICAL GROUPS. See *Fingering* 5.

PIACERE (It.). 'Pleasure.' So *A piacere*, 'at pleasure', i.e. the same as *Ad libitum* (q.v.).

PIACESKI, A. See *Notation* 7.

PIACEVOLE (It.). 'Agreeable.' (Not 'peaceful', as sometimes supposed.)

PIAE CANTIONES. See *Scandinavia* 6.

PIANAMENTE (It.). 'Softly.'

PIANGENDO, PIANGENTE (It.). 'Weeping', i.e. 'plaintively'.

PIANGEVOLE, PIANGEVOLMENTE (It.). 'Plaintive', 'plaintively'.

PIANINO. See *Pianoforte* 6.

PIANISSIMO (It.). The superlative of *Piano*, soft.

PIANISTA. See *Mechanical Reproduction of Music* 13.

PIANO (It.). 'Soft.'

PIANO-ACCORDION. See *Reed-Organ Family* 4.

PIANO À QUEUE (literally 'tailed-piano'). French name for grand piano.

PIANOFORTE

(Literally 'soft-loud'; commonly spoken of as 'Piano' for short; often abbreviated pf.; German *Klavier*; French and Italian as in English.)

1. Introductory.
2. The Invention of the Pianoforte in Italy.
3. Claims to German and French Invention.
4. The German Development of the Instrument.
5. The English Developments.
6. The Three Shapes of Pianoforte.
7. The Viennese Action.
8. The French Developments.
9. An American Contribution—the Iron Frame.
10. The Strings and Hammers.
11. The Sound-board.
12. The Pedals.
13. The Compass of the Pianoforte.
14. 'Touch' in the Pianoforte.
15. Special and Experimental Instruments.
16. Some Terms found in Makers' Catalogues, etc.
17. Early Public Appearances of the Instrument.
18. Early Compositions for Pianoforte.
19. The 'Crimes' of the Pianoforte.
20. The Pianoforte Repertory.
21. Four-hand Music, One-hand Music, Crossing-hand Music.
22. The Growth of Public Taste in Pianoforte Music.

(It will be noted that Pianoforte Playing and Teaching are treated in a separate article following the present one.)

(For illustrations see p. 796, pl. **135**.)

1. Introductory. The pianoforte is really nothing but a keyed dulcimer (q.v.), but it came into existence under the guise of an improved harpsichord (q.v.).

At the opening of the eighteenth century the domestic keyed instruments were the clavichord, which had high expressive qualities but was very faint in tone, and the harpsichord, which was louder and more brilliant but of which the tone-force could be substantially modified only by mechanical means—the passing from one manual to another (in a two-manual instrument), the bringing into or out of action of one or more of the sets of strings, and the like; other defects of the harpsichord were its inability to sustain tone and hence its incapacity for cantabile, and its frequent needs of re-quilling—a tiresome and time-consuming operation.

The natural desire seems to have grown up for a keyboard instrument combining the clavichord's power of accentuation, crescendo, diminuendo, and cantabile with the force and brilliance of the harpsichord. We find something distantly suggesting this desire expressed by the great French harpsichordist and com-poser, François Couperin (q.v.), in the preface to his first book of Harpsichord Pieces, 1713:

'The Harpsichord is perfect as to its compass, and brilliant in itself, but *as it is impossible to swell out or diminish the volume of its sound* I shall always feel grateful to any who, by the exercise of infinite art supported by fine taste, contrive to render this instrument capable of expression.'

(Here Couperin is not, as at a hasty glance might appear, actually demanding the invention of an improvement in the instrument itself, which may not have occurred to him as possible, but is calling for the extreme practice of 'the art that conceals art'—of such refinement in phrasing and delicacy in all the details of performance as may, by the naturalness of their effect, cause the hearers to overlook the constitutional defects of the medium—to seem to 'render it capable' of a form of expression it really lacks.)

2. The Invention of the Pianoforte in Italy. As a matter of fact, unknown to Couperin, the physical means of 'swelling out or diminishing the volume of sound' were already in existence when that preface was

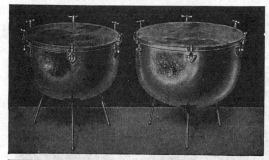

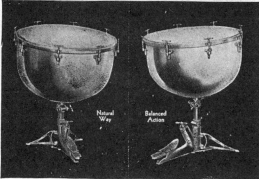

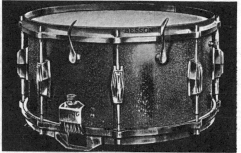

3. SNARE DRUM OR SIDE DRUM
See *Percussion Family* 3 a, 4 b, 5 i

1, 2. TIMPANI. Hand-tuned and Pedal-tuned. See *Percussion Family* 2 a, 4 a, 5 a

4. BASS DRUM
See *Percussion Family* 3 k, 4 b, 5 k

5. XYLOPHONE, DULCIMER, TAMBOURINE, SIDE DRUM, AND CYMBALS

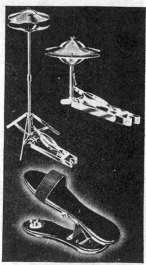

6. CYMBALS
See *Percussion Family* 3 o, 4 b, 5 o

PLATE 134 THE PERCUSSION IN SOME OF ITS VARIETIES, II

1. TUBULAR BELLS
See *Percussion Family* 2 b, and *Bells* 7

2. CELESTA. See *Percussion Family* 2 d, 4 e, 5 d

3. TRIANGLE. See *Percussion* Family 3 n, 4 b, 5 n

4. GLOCKENSPIEL
See *Percussion Family* 2 c, 4 e, 5 c

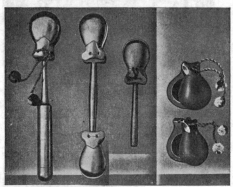

5. CASTANETS
See *Percussion Family* 3 q, 4 c, 5 q

6. TAMBOURINE
See *Percussion Family* 3 m, 4 c, 5 m

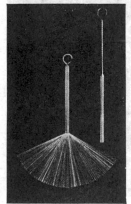

7. WIRE BRUSH
See *Percussion Family* 4 d

8. GONG, or Tam-Tam
See *Percussion Family* 3 p, 4 c, 5 p

9. CHINESE WOOD BLOCKS (q.v.)

written. Cristofori in Florence had already produced (about 1709) what he called a '*gravicembalo col piano e forte*', i.e. a 'harpsichord with soft and loud' (p. 796, pl. **135**. 1). For the plucking of quills of the harpsichord he had substituted hammers, and now, by greater or less force applied to the finger-keys, louder or softer sounds could be produced at will.

Cristofori's mechanism was ingenious. There was an **escapement** by which immediately any hammer struck a string it returned, so leaving the string free to vibrate; and there were **dampers** which, on finger-keys being released, fell at once upon the string and suppressed its vibration, bringing the sound to an immediate end.

Two, and only two, of Cristofori's instruments still remain: one (dated 1726) is at Leipzig, and the other (dated 1720) is in the Metropolitan Museum at New York. They are surviving ancestors of a progeny that has spread all over the world.

Although Cristofori is universally spoken of as the inventor of the pianoforte there were apparently occasional experimental instruments of the pianoforte type made before his day and then forgotten. One known example is dated 1610—a century before Cristofori. It is of Dutch origin. It has small hammers attached to the keys but no dampers. It was in the collection of Mr. René Savoye, of Paris, when inspected by Dolmetsch in 1913. It seems to be an isolated example, resulting from a passing experimental fit on the part of some ingenious maker. It is said to have been made for a French nobleman. A manuscript of about 1430 (an astonishingly early date!), in the Bibliothèque Nationale of Paris, seems to describe an instrument on the pianoforte principle (i.e. with hammers). However, it was only with Cristofori that the principle established itself.

3. Claims to German and French Invention. When any need is widely felt many minds set to work in the effort to find a means of meeting it, and so it is a common thing to find priority of invention disputed. This priority as to the invention of the pianoforte is now seen (apart from the abandoned Dutch attempt) to belong undoubtedly to Italy, but at one time it was claimed for both France and Germany.

The French claim was based on the fact that one Marius in 1716 submitted models of an instrument of the pianoforte kind to the Academy at Paris, and the German claim on the fact that one C. G. Schroeter, in 1721, submitted such models (devised four years earlier—1717) to the Court of Saxony. It will be seen that Cristofori has a priority of date to both of these, and moreover he actually made four instruments at that date, whereas Marius is not certainly known ever to have made an instrument, and Schroeter, an organist and general musical practitioner, decidedly never did.

Marius called his invention a *Clavecin à maillet* (mallet-harpsichord, or hammer-harpsi-

chord); Schroeter looked upon his rather as a developed dulcimer, having, as he said, been inspired with the idea of it by his experience of the performances of the renowned Pantaleon Hebenstreit upon the enlarged dulcimer called 'Pantaleon' (q.v.), of his invention. The relationship of the pianoforte to the dulcimer was long kept in mind in Germany by the use of the name 'Pantaleon' for certain kinds of pianoforte.

In one respect the French and German inventions were very obviously inferior to the Italian. The French model, like the early Dutch one, possessed no dampers, so that once a string had been struck it remained sounding until the vibration died away; and the German model had dampers which fell the moment the hammer had struck and had 'escaped', so making all sostenuto impossible and indeed compelling the use of a continuous staccato. Cristofori's hammers 'escaped' immediately they had struck their blow, but his dampers remained away from the strings until the player's finger allowed the key to rise: that has, of course, been the principle ever since. In every way, then, Cristofori is the true father of the pianoforte as we know it.

4. The German Development of the Instrument. Schroeter's models seem to have led to nothing, and indeed they were not capable of leading to much. Cristofori's invention, however, was taken up in Germany and intelligently exploited by the famous organ-builder and clavichord-maker, Gottfried Silbermann (1683–1753), who had apparently heard of it in 1725 through the appearance of a German translation of an Italian account of it.

In 1726 Silbermann made two pianofortes and a few years later he submitted them to John Sebastian Bach, who hurt him by pointing out serious defects—heavy touch and weakness of the higher notes. Later instruments of his Bach was able to praise, and it is on record that when in 1747 Bach visited Frederick the Great at Potsdam he played upon Silbermann pianofortes, of which the king possessed a number.

All pianofortes up to this point were of the harpsichord shape—what we now call the 'grand', with the strings horizontal and in a line with the finger-keys.

For an influence of the development of the pianoforte upon German composition see *Song* 5; *Germany* 6.

5. The English Developments. The wars of the mid-eighteenth century and especially the Seven Years War (1756–63) drove many German workmen to England. Amongst these was one of Silbermann's pupils, Zumpe, who, on coming to London, at first worked for the great Swiss harpsichord maker Tschudi or Shudi and then set up for himself and became famous all over Britain and France as the inventor and manufacturer of the so-called Square (really oblong) Piano, which he introduced about 1760 (p. 796, pl. **135**. 2). The account given by Dr. Burney (Rees's *Cyclopædia*, article 'Harpsichord') connects the

I i

English development with the settling in London, in 1762, of J. S. Bach's son, John Christian Bach, who had fame as a pianist. He says:

'After the arrival of John Chr. Bach in this country, and the establishment of his concert, in conjunction with Abel, all the harpsichord makers tried their mechanical powers at piano-fortes; but the first attempts were always on the large size, till Zumpé, a German, who had long worked under Shudi, constructed small piano-fortes of the shape and size of the virginals, of which the tone was very sweet, and the touch, with a little use, equal to any degree of rapidity. These, from their low price and the convenience of their form, as well as power of expression, suddenly grew into such favour, that there was scarcely a house in the kingdom where a keyed-instrument had ever had admission, but was supplied with one of Zumpé's piano-fortes, for which there was nearly as great a call in France as in England. In short he could not make them fast enough to gratify the craving of the public. Pohlman, whose instruments were very inferior in tone, fabricated an almost infinite number for such as Zumpé was unable to supply. Large piano-fortes afterwards receiving great improvement in the mechanism by Merlin and in the tone by Broadwood and Stoddard, the harsh scratching of the quills of a harpsichord can now no longer be borne.'

Zumpe's square pianoforte was later greatly improved by Shudi's son-in-law and former workman, John Broadwood (1732–1812), who became his partner and then successor (cf. *Absolute Pitch*). At this period the London makers were undoubtedly the finest in Europe.

Great numbers of English pianos were imported into the United States in the period following the revolution. The Shudi–Broadwood firm shipped quantities to John Bradford of Charleston, S.C. Early American makers were John Brent (1774), Behrent (1775; ? the same as the last), John Belmont (1775), Charles Jarvis (1785), James Juhan (1786); all were in Philadelphia, which seems to have been the first great centre of the manufacture in America.

6. The Three Shapes of Pianoforte. The Square Piano (or Table-Piano—from its appearance) must be familiar by sight to many readers (p. 796, pl. **135. 2**), as, though very few examples remain in use, many are to be seen in houses, museums, and second-hand furniture shops, in which latter they are, in England, always called 'spinets', a description which gives them an air of saleable antiquity but is entirely incorrect, the spinet being, of course, a form of harpsichord.

In the square piano the strings, like those of the clavichord and the virginals, run at right angles to the finger-keys. But, as in the previous (or 'grand') form, they still lie horizontally.

Another form had been experimented with in Germany and England, the Upright Piano, in which the strings ran perpendicularly (p. 796, pl. **135**. 3). The necessary practical adjustments required by this form, for mechanical success, were made in 1800 by Isaac Hawkins of Philadelphia (p. 796, pl. **135**. 5) and by the Englishman Robert Wornum (junior) of London (1811; perfected 1829) and others; the

existing upright model is largely based on Wornum's. (For Hawkins's pianoforte see also 9.)

It was the perfecting of the upright type (called 'cottage piano', 'piccolo piano', 'pianino', and various other names) that, after the middle of the nineteenth century, drove the once popular square piano from the field, from which it at present looks as though it may itself be driven by the 'small grand'.

The **Grand Piano**, the earliest type of all, is the only one that not only persists today but seems to be unshakable; other types only gain a domestic footing on the ground of smaller cost and smaller space required. Constructionally the 'grand' has certain definite advantages. The sound-board of the grand (see 11) is in a better position for sonority, not being placed, as is usually the case with that of an upright, against a brick wall but parallel to a wooden floor and at an acoustically suitable distance from it; the dampers fall by gravity and not by spring and are hence more efficient. And there are other advantages.

It will be realized that the three shapes of piano mentioned all had their prototypes in the harpsichord family—the harpsichord proper supplying the model for the grand; the virginals for the square; and the clavicytherium, or erect spinet, for the upright (see *Harpsichord* 4).

A curious point about the earlier square piano is that the damper-lifting action, which is today operated by means of a pedal (see section 12 of this article), was in them worked by a hand-stop like the stop of an organ. Evidently, then, the dampers were raised or lowered not note by note (as so often today) but over passages of some length (of course the instruments of those days had much less resonance—which is, incidentally, the explanation of some of Beethoven's otherwise inexplicable pedal indications in his early works, e.g. the slow movement of the C Minor Concerto).

7. The Viennese Action. It should be noted that a distinct type of instrument became associated with Vienna, the names of the makers Stein and Streicher (Stein's son-in-law) being prominent in its development. The action was different from the English and French types, the touch lighter and the tone less sonorous. The 'Viennese' and the 'English' pianofortes were recognized as two competing types and they bred two different schools of performer (see *Pianoforte Playing* 2) and even of composer.

8. The French Developments. As already stated there is no evidence that Marius, claimed as one of the inventors of the pianoforte, ever actually made anything more than models of his proposed action. It is usually considered that no pianoforte was made in France for sixty years after this, i.e. until 1777, when Sebastian Erard (1752–1831) made a square pianoforte in imitation of the English instruments. Erard worked for some time in London, where he established a branch in 1786, and he adopted the 'English Action' for his grand pianos, soon, however (several patents from 1809 to 1823), introducing an action of his own, with means for easy and quick repetition—a double-escapement which marked a definite step on the road towards the present-day action. The grand piano of today owes much to Erard.

In Erard's day the harp ran the pianoforte very close in the race for musical popularity as a domestic instrument; he introduced great improvements and sold astonishing quantities.

Pleyel (the composer and performer–pupil of Haydn) was another important Paris maker of those days and founded the firm which, long after, in 1931, was amalgamated with that of Erard.

A characteristic of French pianos today is a markedly 'thinner' tone than that of German and British pianos. This is apparently a matter of national taste. The German and British makers have striven unceasingly for greater resonance, regarding 'fullness' or 'roundness' as one of the principal criteria of perfection, sacrificing both clarity and colourfulness in some degree as the price, for inescapable acoustic reasons.

9. An American Contribution—the Iron Frame. Vital improvements subsequent to those already mentioned have largely depended on the strengthening of the framework of the instrument. How necessary strength is in this part of the instrument will be realized when it is stated that the strings of the very largest grands of today may have an aggregate 'pull' of as much as 30 tons, with the requisite weight of framework to stand it—times having changed since Zumpe's porter used to carry the instruments to the homes of London purchasers on his back.

A pioneer in the introduction of iron in piano construction was John Isaac Hawkins, an Englishman resident in Philadelphia, whose upright pianoforte (mentioned under 6) had a full iron frame (p. 796, pl. **135.** 5). Alpheus Babcock, also of Philadelphia, made further improvements in 1825, as did Conrad Meyer of that city in 1832 and Jonas Chickering, of Boston, in 1837; and in 1855 Steinways, of New York, made such an advance as constituted one of the landmarks in the history of the art of piano making. Largely, then (but by no means completely), the successful application of iron to the framework of the pianoforte is due to American enterprise and invention. The Steinway principle was first exemplified in a square instrument, but the next year (1856) the firm made its first grand.

Iron is the best metal existing for the skeleton work of the pianoforte, since it shrinks least on cooling after casting (about 1 per cent.); the fine adjustment of spaces and sizes in a pianoforte is of the highest importance and even this small shrinkage has to be very accurately allowed for in the design of an instrument. The casting of a piano frame is, indeed, one of the most delicate operations in foundry practice.

The fuller tone of the modern piano is largely due to the use of thicker wire, such as on the old tension would have given a much too low pitch. Brought up to the proper pitch, the tension would have laid the old wooden frame in ruins before all the strings were on.

The difference in the stability of the old wooden-framed piano and of the modern iron-framed (or steel-framed) one will be realized when there is recalled the former concert custom of sending a tuner on to the platform in the mid-programme intermission.

10. The Strings and Hammers. The pitch of a string depends on its length, its diameter, the density of its metal, and the tension to which it is subjected. The tension of a single string today may be 180 to 200 lb.; the enormous total of tension sometimes reached has already been mentioned. The diameter varies from one-thirtieth to one-third of an inch (including the copper coiling of the bass strings shortly to be mentioned).

The stress on the frame can be distributed by **overstringing,** i.e. one large group of wires is made to cross another large group more or less diagonally—a method introduced with the object of providing a requisite length of string and at the same time enabling instruments to be constructed of a reasonable height (in the 'upright' shape) or length (in the 'grand' shape). The principle seems to have been first adopted in the pianoforte about 1835, but there had been occasional overstrung clavichords.

The harpsichords of the eighteenth century had more than one string to a note, and Cristofori's piano had two to each note throughout the compass. The piano of today has one string for each lowest note, two for middle notes, and three for upper notes; the higher we go the less resonance a string possesses, hence the increase in number as we proceed. Even with their three strings the very highest notes of all (ending with a mere 2 inches of sounding length) have so little resonance that no dampers are provided.

The length of the strings is not strictly proportioned to their pitch; if it were, the lowest bass strings would make the instrument far too long for any ordinary room. As above explained, length is only one of four factors controlling pitch and it is largely by an adjustment in the other three that the deeper pitches are obtained (cf. *Acoustics* 3). The lowest strings of all are wrapped with a copper coiling, to increase their mass without too greatly reducing their flexibility.

The tension of the strings being so high, much softer hammers are used than formerly and the hard tone that would otherwise result is thus avoided. The striking surface is of wool felt. The making of pianoforte hammers is an independent trade, the felting of them being a very special process. The piano manufacturers, then, do not make their own hammers: nor do they make their own actions, that also being a specialized trade.

11. The Sound-board. The strings would produce little tone were it not for the sound-board or belly—the broad expanse of wood which lies under them in a grand or behind them in an upright. It fulfils the same function as the body of a violin and is connected with the strings in the same way, i.e they press upon a wooden bridge, which in turn presses upon it. The sound-board is strengthened by wooden bars, the position of which has been carefully calculated.

It seems curious that no application of the idea of a double sound-board, box-like as that of the bowed instruments, has ever proved successful. It was tried by Broadwood as early as 1783.

As everybody knows, a violin gains in beauty of tone with years, so that the oldest violin is (other things being equal) the most desirable, whereas a pianoforte loses tone with years, so that the oldest piano is (other things being equal) the least desirable. Where does the difference come in? It is said, almost purely in the sound-board. The shape of the violin sound-board is permanent; time brings no loss of tone in that quarter. The shape of the pianoforte sound-board, which is at first somewhat arched, tends to be bent back into flatness by the pressure of the strings, communicated (by the very long bridge) to its whole breadth. The board does not then bear against the body of strings as it should; the delicate adjustment of the two pressures, one to another, which has been a matter of elaborate care on the part of the designer of the instrument, is increasingly disturbed.

As better and better means are discovered of strengthening the sound-board without adding to its rigidity this defect should disappear.

12. The Pedals. The harpsichord had made use of certain pedals for various purposes and it was natural to apply the device to the pianoforte. Some applications have been stupid, as, for instance, that fairly common in the early nineteenth century which brought into action drum and cymbal effects, to be employed in playing Turkish Marches and the like (see *Percussion Family* 4 b).

Pianofortes today have never less than two pedals, with sometimes a third.

Of the two pedals the more important (Broadwood's invention, 1783) is the right or **Sustaining Pedal,** often improperly called 'Loud Pedal'.

This (imitating an earlier contrivance, worked by the knee—see a letter of Mozart, October 1777) removes the whole series of dampers from the strings, whereas depressing a finger-key removes the damper from the strings of only the one note. The consequences of this complete removal are twofold: firstly, any note one may play is given a longer duration, irrespectively of whether the finger remains on the key (making many beautiful effects possible, such as two hands on a keyboard could not otherwise compass), and,

secondly, the whole of the strings of the instrument are made available for sympathetic resonance, on principles explained elsewhere (*Acoustics* 20 a; *Voice* 6). The harmonics of a string (see *Acoustics* 8) are then enriched by the sounds awakened from the strings corresponding to them, and the tone becomes much fuller; this, in a modern instrument, compensates for the doublings in the octave below and octave above obtainable by the use of certain 'stops' on the harpsichord—effects which players must surely have abandoned with some regret.

A greatly increased power is obtainable when desired, by means of this pedal, but its effects are as much used in soft as in loud passages and indeed a good player is using this pedal so continuously (save in very involved and contrapuntal music where clashes would be unavoidable) that he rarely takes his foot off it. This is the pedal to which Rubinstein alluded —'The more I play the more I am convinced that the pedal is the soul of the pianoforte'.

It is, of course, normally, important to release this pedal and depress it afresh at a change of harmony, as otherwise confusion will result. The sustaining pedal has naturally much greater influence over the lower notes of the instrument than over the higher, both because the longer strings, with their greater amplitude, are capable of a longer-lived tone, and because there are so many other strings higher up the compass and hence capable of being awakened to sympathetic resonance (as has been explained above). When the sign 'Ped.', or any similar sign, occurs, this is the pedal intended: the sign to release it is usually a star. It does not always follow that the pedal is not to be lifted between the two signs; the player has to use his discretion, based on a sound knowledge of harmony (see *Pianoforte Playing* 5). The lower strings require more 'damping' than the higher, and if the pedal, after being lifted, be depressed again too quickly it will be found that the lower strings are still sounding; this effect of *half-pedalling* is sometimes purposely used in passages where it is desired to sustain a bass note or notes whilst playing changing harmonies in the treble.

To make a similar effect more easy an extra **Sostenuto Pedal,** the middle pedal of the three, is attached to most pianos made in the United States and Canada, but rarely to others (it was perfected by Steinways in 1874). This operates an apparatus which catches any dampers at the moment they are raised and maintains those particular dampers in their raised position until the pedal is released: thus one may play a note or chord and allow it to continue sounding whilst passing on to some succession of notes or chords which, whilst each compatible with the note or chord held over, are incompatible with one another. Music of the kind which, without any disrespect either to Chopin or to the composers of popular waltzes, we may call the 'jab-and-jump' order offers an obvious opportunity for the use of this pedal.

An inferior variety of this middle pedal is one which operates on the whole of the dampers of the lower two octaves of the instrument, leaving the other dampers untouched.

The **Soft Pedal** may act in one of several ways: (a) in 'grands', by moving keyboard and hammers sideways, so as to leave unstruck one string of each note—cf. *Corda*; (b) in 'uprights', by moving the whole set of hammers in their position of rest, nearer to the strings, so that when any of them are brought into action they give a less powerful blow; or (c) by interposing a piece of felt between the hammer and strings (this last being the crudest way and now little used).

Method (a) has the advantage that the string or strings not struck are left free to act sympathetically, thus producing a sweeter, soft tone of somewhat silvery quality. This was the method understood to be normal when the signs for the use and disuse of the pedals were invented—*Una corda* and *Tre corde*, i.e. 'One String' and 'Three Strings'. (See *Due* and *Tutte le corde*).

13. The Compass of the Pianoforte. Of the two existing specimens of Cristofori's instruments one has a compass of four octaves and the other of four and a half. This compass was gradually increased. Mozart's Concert Grand piano, now in the Mozarteum at Salzburg, has five octaves. In 1790 Broadwood made the first pianoforte with five and a half octaves, and in 1794 the first with six octaves. Liszt in 1824 was still playing, in Paris, on an Erard with six octaves, and the works of Schumann and Chopin require nothing beyond six and a half octaves. The present usual compass is seven and a quarter octaves (88 notes), but some instruments have only seven octaves: instruments with eight have been sold.

The inconvenience of the too short compass of Beethoven's time can be seen in certain of his sonatas where some long ascending passage appears in two ways according to the key it is in (as, for instance, in the exposition of a movement and the recapitulation, respectively), breaking back upon itself before its ascent is concluded when in the higher key, but ascending unbroken when in the lower key. In such instances it is surely permissible, on the modern piano, to play rather what Beethoven wished than what he wrote and modern editors often observe the principle, which Liszt, with the increased compass of his later years, was the first to practice; however, the principle cannot be blindly carried out, as sometimes Beethoven, compelled to adopt an altered shape of passage, has introduced a new effect which should not be sacrificed.

14. 'Touch' in the Pianoforte. This word has two distinct meanings. As applied to the instrument it means the weight of the resistance offered by the finger-keys to the fingers, and as applied to the performer it means the manner in which he operates the finger-keys—a manner 'heavy' or 'light', varied or unvaried.

Using the word in the first sense, it may be said that the touch of the pianoforte became heavier as more power was sought, until it reached 3 to 5 oz. when playing as softly as possible at the very edge of the finger-key.

Investigations by E. O. Newton Marsden, of London, showed that: (i) The best upright pianos have graduated resistances, from between 3 and 4 oz. for the lowest bass notes, to between 2½ and 3 oz. for the highest treble notes, grands being slightly heavier. (ii) In most pianos the black keys are heavier than the white; this sometimes produces two distinct levels of touch-weight. (iii) In some pianos adjacent keys differ by as much as two or more ounces, making the touch very irregular. (iv) Most pianos have a sudden lightening at the undamped notes. (v) Some pianos are too light throughout their entire keyboard, which condition engenders key-squeezing. These grave defects are greatly embarrassing to the teacher, and present difficulties to the pianist, though he may not recognize their origin.

Liszt, according to von Lenz, had a practice pianoforte made for him with so heavy a touch that he 'could play ten scales when he played one'. To anyone with modern sensitiveness to fine tone this craze for muscular development seems ridiculous and casts doubt upon Liszt's ideals.

Of touch in the sense of the player's manner of manipulating the keyboard it may be said that there is a vital point concerning it in dispute. This is discussed under *Pianoforte Playing* 8.

For the differences of 'key colour' in different keys, enabling certain keen-eared listeners to tell in what key a pianist is playing (and this whatever the pitch at which the instrument is tuned), see *Colour and Music* 4.

15. Special and Experimental Instruments. The number of modifications of the pianoforte that have been brought into existence without achieving permanency is enormous.

Following the precedent of the harpsichord, **Pianofortes with more than one Keyboard** were early produced. Mozart played one, by Tschudi of London, in 1765.

There have been many attempts to produce a **Pianoforte with Longer Sounds** or sounds of unlimited duration. Most of these have invoved the application of a revolving wheel or other imitation of a violin bow, in place of hammers, so abandoning the real pianoforte principle. Sir Charles Wheatstone, the inventor of electric telegraphy, in 1836 attempted to secure duration by the device of a small aperture at the end of each string through which passed a current of air tending to keep the string in vibration after the hammer had left it. About 1925, J. H. Hammond, of Gloucester, Mass., a well-known electrical engineer, devised an instrument in which, by means of reflection, the sounds could be prolonged at will and even increased in volume. (For various twentieth-century inventions serving this purpose see *Electric Musical Instruments* 3.)

There have been many **Pianofortes made with Tuning-forks** or metal bars in place of stretched strings, so avoiding the necessity of tuning, and such as are on sale at the present time (see references to Dulcitone, etc., under *Percussion* 2 e, 4, 5 e). Their tone, owing to the acoustic properties of their sources of sound, is excessively colourless, being grossly deficient in upper harmonics. But they need no tuning!

An absurd invention of Daniel Hewitt, patented in 1854, provided for the saving of the expense of a pianoforte framework by attaching the strings to the wall of the house.

A patent of the Pleyel firm provided for the performance of music for two pianofortes by building **Two Grands as one**, the two triangles fitting into one rectangle and the players facing one another from keyboards at the two ends.

Combinations of other Instruments with the Pianoforte have been fairly common, as, for instance, that of percussion instruments (see 12). In 1722 the Paris organist Balbastre brought out a combined pianoforte and flute (the addition of the flute had previously been attempted with the harpsichord); this probably really meant the playing of a one-stop organ from the same keyboard, since the French used the verb 'organiser' for such attempts. The poet Mason, in 1755, writes of buying in Hamburg a clever combination of harpsichord and piano. The London maker Merlin, in 1774 introduced a two-keyboard, combined harpsichord and piano, and a combination of clavichord and piano has also been attempted. The Moór Pianoforte (see *Keyboard* 4) has a device enabling the player to obtain a harpsichord effect if he so desires.

A **Damage-resisting Pianoforte**. An extremely robust type of instrument was in 1951 introduced by a London firm and brought into use in army canteens during the Korean War. It was described as follows:

'Among the innovations are the following. The lid has a double slope like a house-top, so that no drinks can be stood upon it. For a similar reason the lid of the piano has no level part. The woodwork above the pedals is reinforced with brass plates to receive kicks. The wood itself is solid oak, with rounded corners for the mutual protection of heads, shins, and the piano frame. Keyboard ends are made of copper to counteract smouldering butts. The ivory surfaces are bevelled so that they cannot be picked off. The instruments are also made to withstand tropical weather and damage in transit.'

Quarter-tone Pianofortes have been made to acommodate those modern composers whose music requires them (see *Harmony* 19, 23; *Microtones*).

The **Neo-Bechstein** or **Siemens-Bechstein Pianoforte** is described under *Electric* 3 a.

Various experiments have been made of late years in the **Production of Piano Tone from Stringless Instruments** by electric devices operated from a piano keyboard, and it would appear quite possible that something on these lines may eventually succeed the piano as the world at present knows it.

There have been, and are, many **'Pedal Pianos'**—pianofortes with playable pedals like those of an organ. Their chief use is for practising organ music, but Schumann, Alkan, Boëly, and others have written compositions specially for such instruments (see *Pedalier*).

For the 'Pianola' and all forms of mechanically operated pianofortes see the article *Mechanical Reproduction* 13; for various experimental types of keyboard see *Keyboard* 4; for the 'prepared piano' see under *Cage, John*.

16. Some Terms found in Makers' Catalogues, etc.

Aliquot Scaling. An arrangement whereby the weak upper notes of the instrument have each an extra free string, tuned to the octave above the proper pitch and acting, as 'sympathetic' strings on certain older bowed and plucked string instruments did, by mere resonance. In this way a fuller tone is obtained (cf. *Duplex Scaling* below). This device is the speciality of the Blüthner firm.

Baby Grand. Simply a grand pianoforte on a small scale—sometimes nowadays on so small a scale (length of strings not enough for full flexibility) as to lose much of the 'grand' advantage and to be inferior to a good upright.

Barless. Applied to grand pianoforte, iron frames made to be sufficiently strong and rigid without the usual strengthening bars believed to be inimical to tone (Broadwoods).

Cabinet Piano (obsolete). A tall cupboard-like upright piano.

Concert Grand. A grand pianoforte of the largest size.

Console Piano. This term is used by some American manufacturers for a type of miniature instrument.

Cottage Piano. A small upright.

Duplex Scaling. A system whereby those two portions of the strings that are normally dumb (i.e. on each side of the main or vibrating portion) are left free to vibrate also, and so arranged as to length that they correspond with, and thus (by sympathetic resonance) strengthen, some of the harmonics of the main portion (cf. 'Aliquot Scaling', above).

Full Trichord (or **Tricord**). Three strings to each note (except the lowest ones).

Giraffe. The tall upright pianoforte often to be seen in German museums. The shaping of the upper part of the case to the strings as they diminish in size from left to right, produces a form that readily explains the name.

Oblique. A term applied to upright pianofortes which have the strings running at an angle instead of perpendicularly, so as to secure greater length, and hence greater fullness of tone.

Overdamper. Cf. 'Underdamper' below, from which the meaning of the term can be deduced.

Pedal Piano. See *Pedalier*.

Spinet. Sometimes used (misleadingly) of a small upright. See 6.

Underdamper. Applied to uprights in

which the dampers are placed lower down than the hammers (where the amplitude of vibration of the strings is greater and the damper hence, presumably, more immediately effective).

Upright Grand. The term has meant different things at different periods. It now usually means a large upright, overstrung, and with all improvements.

17. Early Public Appearances of the Instrument. The first pianoforte heard in Britain is said by Burney to have been made by an English monk in Rome, Father Wood, for Burney's friend Samuel Crisp, who brought it back with him. The date of his return does not seem to be known (probably about 1760 or rather earlier), and there seems to be some possible claim to priority on the part of another friend of Burney, the poet Mason (see section 15).

The first public performance on the pianoforte, so far as is known, took place at Covent Garden Theatre a few years later, in 1767, when it was announced that Dibdin would use, in the accompaniment of a song, 'a new instrument called piano-forte'.

The following year, 1768, saw what are believed to be the first British appearances of the instrument in a public solo way, the performers being Henry Walsh, in Dublin, on 19 May 1768, and two weeks later, in London, J. C. Bach—that son of J. S. Bach, already mentioned, who, during his residence in London for the rest of his life (died 1782), contributed much to the popularization of the instrument (there is evidence in his banking account, which Dr. Sanford Terry searched, of his buying a pianoforte of Zumpe in the very month before this concert, the price being £50; we may suppose, then, that the instrument was a 'square').

Clementi set out from London for a Continental concert tour (Paris, Strasbourg, Munich, Vienna) in 1781, and Messrs. Broadwood's books show that they shipped to Paris for him both a harpsichord and a pianoforte. (In Vienna he met Mozart and, at the instigation of the Emperor Joseph II, competed with Mozart in performance; both played pianofortes and as a part of the entertainment they improvised on them in duet.)

As already stated (5, 8) the pianoforte reached France via England. There is mention of the sale of a pianoforte in Paris in 1759 (probably a solitary imported specimen), but the first recorded appearance does not seem to be until 1768, when a Mademoiselle Lechantre played at the Concert Spirituel (see *Concert* 14) a 'Clavecin [i.e. Harpsichord] forte-piano'. This was one year after the instrument's first public appearance in England. The next year (1769) a boy of nine, son of Virbès, organist of St. Germain-l'Auxerrois, played under the same auspices a 'new instrument, with hammers, a sort of harpsichord in the form of those of England'. The father had made this instrument and it had been described in the press three years earlier (1766).

It is not known when the pianoforte was first imported into America, but it was evidently rare in the 1770s, since Behrent of Philadelphia (see also end of section 5), advertising in 1775 what was certainly one of the first made in that continent, proclaimed that he had 'just finished an extraordinary instrument by the name of Pianoforte, made of mahogany, being of the nature of a Harpsichord, with hammers and several changes'.

The earliest mention of the pianoforte in O. G. Sonneck's *Early Concert Life in America* occurs in connexion with a concert at Philadelphia in 1786, when Reinagle played a 'Sonata Piano Forte' of his own composition and another curiously defined as by 'Haydn and Reinagle'. Francis Hopkinson's *Seven Songs* (Philadelphia, 1788) were advertised as having accompaniments for 'harpsichord or forte-piano'.

18. Early Compositions for Pianoforte. It took the pianoforte just about a century from its birth (to about 1800) to oust the harpsichord and clavichord, for the newer type was only slowly subject to improvements and the older were in their full glory of perfection. It is a pity that the pianoforte did so oust its predecessors, for the three instruments have different qualities, and though one house will not as a rule suitably hold the three, or one household make use of them all, yet for the music composed for their capacities and their technique the harpsichord and clavichord are irreplaceable.

The earliest known compositions for the pianoforte are the work of an Italian, Luigi Giustini, who published at Florence, in 1732, *12 Sonate da cembalo di piano e forte detto volgaramente dei martellati* ('12 Sonatas for the soft-and-loud harpsichord, commonly called the one with hammers'). This work stands alone for some years.

It is convenient to remember the growth of the popularity of the pianoforte as synchronizing with the growth of the new 'homophonic' school of domestic keyboard composition. Bach and Handel, contrapuntists and the heroes of the fugue and the suite, were harpsichord–clavichord men, and though Bach (certainly) and Handel (possibly) played the pianoforte on occasion they never wrote a note for it; by Bach's sons, Haydn, and Mozart, the heroes of the classical sonata, the pianoforte was increasingly used. Bach's ninth son Johann Christoph Friedrich, about 1757, wrote a sonata described on its title-page as 'For Harpsichord or Pianoforte', but this was certainly an abnormal instance of a description that was later to become very usual. The common title-page phrase was at last changed to 'For Pianoforte or Harpsichord', and this lingers on some of Beethoven's works as late as 1802 (see *Harpsichord* 7).

We may say, then, that for over forty years composers often seemed to take little account of the differing qualities and capabilities of the two instruments, yet from the first sonatas of Clementi, published in London in 1773, we do find the distinctive powers of the pianoforte increasingly recognized. Mozart was acquainted with the pianoforte from boyhood and his later sonatas (as Haydn's also) obviously take account of its special powers. But it was Beethoven who really set the instrument on its feet. His keyboard music, from the first, however labelled, is obviously pianoforte music. In Schumann and Chopin (both born 1810) we have two composers who expressed themselves, the one largely and the other practically entirely, by means of the domestic keyboard instrument, and nobody looking at any page of their keyboard works could imagine that this instrument was anything but the pianoforte.

It has been said above that it is convenient to remember the growth of the popularity of the pianoforte as synchronizing with the growth of the new homophonic school. This synchronization seems to have begun by chance, since the invention of the pianoforte, about 1709, took place well before there began the development of the new style (the classical Sonata Form and the like—see article *Sonata*). Yet it would appear that the expressive pianoforte was almost essential to any developed keyboard treatment of the new style. The Sonata Form, with its strong contrasts, is essentially dramatic, as we see when Beethoven appears; it is impossible to imagine one of the later Beethoven sonatas effectively performed with the quiet though sensitive tone of the clavichord or the largely mechanical tone contrasts of the harpsichord. It would seem, then, that the parallel development of the domestic keyboard instrument and of instrumental form, though independent, proceeded from one general human impulse of the times.

It is rather remarkable that so many eminent players of the pianoforte and composers for it have also been manufacturers (e.g. Clementi, Kalkbrenner, Pleyel, Herz); this cannot have been without effect in the simultaneous development of the three techniques of pianoforte playing, pianoforte composition, and pianoforte manufacture, and the adapting of each of them to the suggestions of the other two.

19. The 'Crimes' of the Pianoforte. From time to time some purist springs to his feet with objections against the pianoforte. Sometimes he is a lover of the keyboard music of the late sixteenth, seventeenth, and early eighteenth centuries (i.e. from the Elizabethan virginalists to Bach), and is influenced by his wish to hear this music in the medium that inspired it and for which it is obviously most fitted. Or he may be a 'modernist' of the type which decries sentiment in music and may feel an objection to the rich colourings of pianoforte tone and the expressive nuances of pianoforte playing. Or he may be a person of delicate sensibility who has become offended by the thunderings of athletic touring virtuosi evoked from super-powerful concert grands. Or he

may be a person of keen harmonic sense who has been listening too keenly for comfort to the inevitable clash of harmonics (the 'hash of sound' it has been called) which arises when an instrument of so many strings and so well-designed a sound-board is played upon. Or he may be a specialist in the older music who deplores the introduction by Bach and others of Equal Temperament and imagines that perfect tune is obtainable and obtained from stringed instruments and voices when not led astray by their accompanist (see remarks on unaccompanied choral and string quartet performance in article *Temperament*). Or he may be a caviller who is worried by the instrument's lack of a complete sustaining power, making its 'singing' of a melody a makeshift, or by the fact that the uppermost two octaves are weak in tone relative to the rest of the compass. Or he may realize (what used to be comparatively true) that the instrument is too all-pervading, that its presence in the house as a piece of furniture leads to the whole of the children learning to play it whereas some of them should, of course, be learning to play other instruments.

And so on! There is no lack of objections to the instrument—yet it remains the handiest home representative of the art of music, with the finest repertory of any instrument, and able, at a pinch, to give a good account, with two or four hands, of orchestral music, etc.

It seems impossible to 'down' an instrument which Beethoven, Schumann, Chopin, and Debussy have taken so seriously; every musical instrument has limitations and imperfections; the pianoforte, which is one of the youngest instruments in use, has as many as most, but under the hands (and feet) of a fine player they can be readily forgotten.

The greatest enemy of the pianoforte in recent times has been radio broadcasting. In 1919 the number of pianofortes sold in the United States was 230,000, in 1929 only 92,000; but in this latter year the country spent a record sum on radio sets. By 1936 the sales of pianos showed, however, a fairly strong upward trend again. In 1964 sales were reported as 220,000.

After the second World War, the production of new instruments in Great Britain for the home market was for long very limited; veteran instruments had to continue doing full service long after they would normally have been due for 'retirement', and a large part of the trade's activity was devoted to the reconditioning of such instruments.

20. The Pianoforte Repertory. The repertory of the pianoforte is larger than that of any other instrument and it is infinitely varied. It is generally regarded as taking in all the music written for the clavichord and for the harpsichord family.

The following list gives the names of merely the most outstanding contributors to the repertory and barely enters on the difficult discrimination necessary when the names of living

1. THE EARLIEST EXISTING PIANOFORTE—by Cristofori. See *Pianoforte* 2

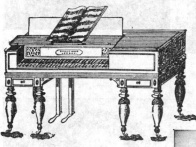

2. 'SQUARE' PIANO. See *Pianoforte* 5, 6
From the title-page of Haydn's *Grand Overture for the Piano Forte*, published in 1800 at Philadelphia 'by G. E. Blake who has always on hand an *eligant* assortment of Piano Fortes'

3. UPRIGHT GRAND OF 1800
By William Stodart of London. 'Hammers and dampers returned by weight, trichord stringing and 5½ octaves compass.' (For the Upright Piano see *Pianoforte* 6)

4. HAYDN'S CONCERT GRAND

5. THE FIRST IRON FRAME PIANO— 1800. By Hawkins of Philadelphia. See *Pianoforte* 9. The front boards are removed to show something of the frame

6. CABINET OR 'GIRAFFE' PIANO, by Van der Hoef of Amsterdam, *c.* 1810. The six pedals are Bassoon (bringing a strip of parchment in contact with the strings), Drum-stick (hitting the belly of the instrument), Celeste (Soft Pedal, interposing a strip of felt), Bells, Shifting Soft Pedal (moving the keyboard), Damper Pedal (much as today). See *Pianoforte* 16

7. BEETHOVEN'S BROADWOOD
Presented to him by the makers in 1818

1. CLEMENTI (1752–1832)

2. STEIBELT (1765–1823)

3. J. B. CRAMER (1771–1858) by J. C. Horsley, R.A. See *Horsley*

4. HUMMEL (1778–1837)

5. CZERNY (1791–1857)

6. MOSCHELES (1794–1870)

7. HERZ (1803–88)

8. LISZT playing to Berlioz and his own teacher Czerny (these two behind), Kriehuber (left), and Ernst (right)

men are introduced (a rather fuller list of composers of the clavichord and harpsichord period will be found under *Harpsichord* 9).

The English Sixteenth- and Early Seventeenth-century Virginal Composers.

Byrd, Bull, Gibbons, Farnaby, etc.

They wrote variations on popular tunes, etc. (and so developed the technique of keyboard composition and performance), incipient suites (pavans and galliards), and incipient fugues (fantasias), etc. For an example of their wide influence see *Hungary*.

The Late Seventeenth-century and Earlier Eighteenth-century Clavichord and Harpsichord Composers.

In *England*: Purcell, and later, Handel (German).
In *France*: Couperin and Rameau.
In *Italy*: Domenico Scarlatti.
In *Germany*: J. S. Bach.

Purcell, Couperin, Bach, and Handel wrote suites of many movements; Bach wrote preludes and fugues. Scarlatti wrote sonatas (single movement compositions, not like the later sonata).

The Later Eighteenth-century Composers.

C. P. E. Bach, Mozart, Haydn.

They developed the modern type of sonata (see *Sonata* 6), in several movements, one at least of these in what we call 'Sonata' or 'First Movement' form (see *Form* 7). Their earlier works were written for the harpsichord, some of their later works for the pianoforte.

Late Eighteenth- and Early Nineteenth-century Study and Sonata Composers.

Hummel, Clementi, Cramer, Czerny, Beethoven, Schubert, Weber, Field.

Clementi, Beethoven, and Schubert wrote many sonatas, Beethoven carrying the form and spirit of this type of music to the highest point they have ever attained (see *Sonata* 8). Clementi and Cramer wrote much technical practice material—'Studies' (see *Étude*); Schubert many pieces in smaller one-movement forms (impromptus, moments musicaux, waltzes, etc.). Field introduced the nocturne.

The Mid-Nineteenth-century Composers.

Chopin, Schumann, Mendelssohn, Liszt, Franck.

They developed especially the shorter, one-movement pieces (Chopin's nocturnes, studies, preludes, waltzes, mazurkas, and polonaises, Schumann's Novelettes, Mendelssohn's Songs without Words are examples). Schumann wrote strings of such pieces, with a connected idea (*Carnaval, Papillons*, etc.). Liszt wrote 'Hungarian Rhapsodies' and dozens of fantasias on operatic airs, etc., as well as bigger things. Franck imported a serious organ feeling into pianoforte music.

The Late Nineteenth-century Composers.

Brahms, Grieg, Balakiref, Albéniz, MacDowell.

Essentially they wrote the same type of piece as the composers in the previous group. (It will be understood that throughout this summary nothing beyond a generalized impression is being attempted.) Grieg, Balakiref, and Albéniz introduced a strongly nationalistic element (Norwegian, Russian, and Spanish, respectively); see *Nationalism in Music*, also *Scandinavia, Russia, Spain*).

Twentieth-century Composers.

Scriabin, Debussy, Ravel, Reger, Dohnányi, Granados, Turina, Falla, Ireland, Bax.

Scriabin wrote a great number of preludes, etc., inspired, in the first instance, by Chopin; he also wrote a series of sonatas of very advanced workmanship and passionate emotional expression. Debussy and Ravel wrote in the delicate French impressionistic style (see *Impressionism*), Granados, Turina, and Falla, like Albéniz, exploited Spanish idiom (see *Spain*).

All the above composers are, of course, treated under their own names, as are the various types of composition mentioned.
See also *Dictionaries* 6 b.

21. Four-hand Music, One-hand Music, Crossing-hand Music. The earliest known keyboard music for two players at one instrument is Nicholas Carlton's *A Verse for Two to Play on One Virginal or Organ*, in the British Museum (this may have been written about the middle of the sixteenth century). *A Fancy* for two players, by Thos. Tomkins (q.v.), is in the same volume (Tomkins lived from 1573 to 1656).

The earliest such music to be printed appears to be Burney's *Four Sonatas or Duets for two performers on one. Pianoforte or Harpsichord* (1777) and Theodore Smith's (q.v.) nine sonatas (Berlin, 1780). But before these composers published their work a good deal of duet music probably existed in manuscript. Mozart and his sister, when in England in 1764–5, did much duet-playing in public. The great period of piano duet composition may be said to have begun with Mozart and ended with Schubert.

An eighteenth-century difficulty in playing harpsichord duets is mentioned by Burney himself (Rees's *Cyclopædia*, s.v. 'Ravalement'). He says that 'the ladies at that time wearing hoops which kept them at too great a distance from one another, [he] had a harpsichord made by Merlin, expressly for duets, with six octaves' and goes on to say that, such duets then being composed 'by all the great masters of Europe', the extended compass became general.

The earliest known piece for two keyboard instruments is Giles Farnaby's Piece for two virginals in the Fitzwilliam Virginal Book (Farnaby, q.v., lived from about 1560 to about 1640). Pasquini (1637–1710), Couperin, J. S. Bach, and others, have left works for two harpsichords, and Bach, of course, wrote concertos for anything up to four harpsichords and orchestra. For two pianos Mozart wrote two sonatas and one fugue.

It would appear that England was a pioneer in the composition of duet keyboard music, for one instrument or two.

During the nineteenth century there was composed a great deal of fine music both for two players at one instrument and two players at two instruments, and, in addition, hundreds of pieces of chamber music and orchestral music were arranged for two players—generally at one instrument. Stravinsky and Poulenc have written concertos for two pianos.

There is a two-piano sonata by York Bowen. Bax composed a good many pieces for this medium.

A considerable amount of music has also been written for one hand, either as practice material for pianists in general, or as a *tour de force* of composition, or for the use of one-armed players, who have sometimes shown themselves capable of surprising execution. Some examples are the following:

Kalkbrenner, a Sonata for left hand; Scriabin, a Prelude and a Nocturne for left hand; Brahms, arrangement of the Bach Violin Chaconne for a left-hand pianist; Janáček, Capriccio for piano left hand and wind quintet; Ravel, Prokofiev, Franz Schmidt, and Erich Korngold, concertos for left-hand pianists; Strauss, *Parergon* (a concerto-like treatment of themes from his *Domestic Symphony*); Britten, 'Diversions on a Theme', for left-hand pianist and orchestra; Bax, a Concertante for the same; Demuth, a Concerto and a Legend for this combination.

Godowsky (q.v.), who pleaded for a fuller cultivation of the left hand by both-handed players (see his short article in the *Musical Quarterly*, July 1935), has published left-hand music including *Six Waltz Poems*, *Six Miniatures*, a *Suite*, and a *Prelude and Fugue*.

There is other music for left hand besides this, and some (e.g. by Alkan) for right hand. York Bowen includes a Caprice for right hand in his *Curiosity Suite*.

Perhaps the most famous one-armed pianist was the Hungarian, Count Zichy (1849–1924), a pupil of Liszt and an active recitalist and composer; his compositions include a book of studies for left hand alone, to which Liszt contributed a preface. Other one-armed players are the German composer and writer on music, Hermann W. S. von Waltershausen (born 1882), who lost his right arm (and foot) when a boy, and the Austrian Paul Wittgenstein (1887–1961) who lost his right arm in the first World War. A French left-hand pianist, Charles Gros, gave successful recitals in London in 1899. Willem Coenen (q.v.), possessing both hands, enjoyed fame for left-hand performance and published music for it.

The device of crossing hands is introduced by Rameau in *Cyclops*, in his book of harpsichord pieces of 1724. Domenico Scarlatti (1685–1757) uses it a great deal. Bach uses it only once or twice (e.g. in the Gigue of the Par-

tita in B flat). In modern pianoforte composition it is a common (and convenient) device.

22. The Growth of Public Taste in Pianoforte Music. The improvement in the taste of audiences during the period that has elapsed since the pianoforte became a concert recital instrument is astonishing.

The clavichord was not played in public (being too gentle in tone), the harpsichord (as a solo instrument) comparatively little, though plenty of commonplace rondos and variations were written for domestic entertainment. And it is certain that players of reputation on those instruments did not play rubbish. But with the coming of the pianoforte into popularity, and the bringing into existence of a new class of travelling keyboard virtuoso performing in large public halls, a serious decline of taste seems to have taken place amongst performers, or rather, perhaps, they bent down to the level of a larger and less cultured public.

It is somewhat surprising today to learn that when Chopin first played his Concerto in F minor in his native city of Warsaw, in 1830, it was felt to be necessary to divide it into two by a piece of light music on the horn, and on another occasion by a violin solo. At both these concerts Chopin played potpourris on national melodies.

When Clara Wieck (later Clara Schumann) played Beethoven's sonatas in public in Germany about the same period she used to ease her audience by the concession of some piece of bravura fly-about stuff between the movements; it was at that time considered that to play a whole sonata without break would impose altogether too heavy a strain on the patience of any audience.

Liszt made his début in St. Petersburg in 1842 with a programme largely of his own arrangements (Beethoven's song 'Adelaide', Schubert's song 'The Erl-King', the fantasia on airs from *Don Giovanni*, ending with his showy *Chromatic Galop*). This was a quite good programme for him, and is not too poor in its way, perhaps, but a Liszt of today would offer a programme exclusively of real and valuable piano music.

At a Birmingham Festival (one of the most serious events in British musical life) Moscheles played his *Recollections of Ireland* (this was in 1846, when Mendelssohn was present to conduct the first performance of *Elijah*).

Beringer gave daily pianoforte recitals at the Crystal Palace, London, from his thirteenth year to his twenty-second (1857–1866). His programmes consisted of compositions by Kuhe, Döhler, Alfred Jaell, Osborne, Ascher, and Brinley Richards, with Thalberg's variations on 'Home, Sweet Home' (which he says became a nightmare to him by the constant repetition demanded), a few of Mendelssohn's Songs without Words, and one or two of Chopin's nocturnes and waltzes. This was *his entire repertory*. In 1861, at one of the famous Saturday orchestral concerts of the Palace (then reckoned the best series in Britain), he played Kuhe's 'Fantaisie de Concert' on airs from Flotow's *Martha*, and the critics singled this out as the best item in the programme.

One of the most famous European pianists in the 1850s and 1860s was Arabella Goddard. She was the first to play Beethoven's Sonata op. 106 in England, but her special favourites were Thalberg's operatic fantasias, especially the one on airs from Rossini's *Moses in Egypt*.

Sterndale Bennett, wishing to wean the public from the operatic fantasias, played some of his friend Mendelssohn's Songs without Words at his first London concert and continued to do so at every future concert (1838 to about 1848).

The first player to popularize the Beethoven sonatas in Britain was Charles Hallé, who played the whole thirty-two in a series of recitals in the St. James's Hall, London, in 1861, and repeated the series in 1862 and 1863.

The Songs without Words and three of the Beethoven sonatas (the 'Pathetic', the so-called 'Moonlight', and the A flat with the Funeral March) soon after this began to 'catch on' with amateur pianists, as did Mendelssohn's *Rondo Capriccioso*, Chopin's Valse in D flat (op. 64), Nocturne in E flat (op. 9), and Fantaisie Impromptu in C sharp minor, Rubinstein's Melody in F, Grieg's *Norwegian Wedding March*, and Litolff's *Spinning Song*.

This was the pabulum of the highest circles in amateur musicianship. Lower circles were still satisfied with Badarzewska's *Maiden's Prayer*, Osborne's *Pluie de perles*, Brinley Richards's *Warblings at Eve* and *Warblings at Dawn*, Lefébure-Wély's *Cloches de monastère*, and the like (sentimental melodies, a harmonic scheme of about three chords and the tritest modulations, with runabout passages and twiddles), plus a few tarantellas and gavottes. These last two were 'coming in' in the '60s and won an extraordinary popularity, so that hundreds of them were composed; Sydney Smith's tarantella and the infinitely more refined Stephen Heller's were popular teaching-pieces for another forty years or more, and so were a number of the gavottes which enterprising publishers had taken out of Bach's suites because they were non-copyright and could be had for nothing. A few of Dussek's

rondos were played, a few easier things of Clementi's, with Handel's *Harmonious Blacksmith* (q.v.) and Kotzwara's *Battle of Prague*, a battle which long continued to be waged in the back parlours of lower middle-class suburbs.

In America de Kontski's *The Awakening of the Lion* and Gottschalk's *Dying Poet* (like Charles II, 'unconscionably long in dying') were being freshly recorded by the makers of one of the highest class 'reproducing pianos' as late as 1928. (Most of the above popular composers will be found, by the curious, to enjoy the honour of entries under their own names.)

The long-lasting triumphs of bad taste in the pianoforte repertory may perhaps be put down largely to (*a*) the attractions that athletic manipulation of the instrument has always had for people of very slight musical instinct, which for long put evil pressure on public pianists, and (*b*) the fact that the instrument gained recognition as a piece of furniture essential to the respectability of the home, thus often promoting a sale of music amongst the unmusical, and retained this recognition until the gramophone and the radio set entered as competitors. (See remark near end of 19.)

Had it not been for the existence of a large mass of really tuneful music (some of it not difficult to play—in a sort of way) amongst the compositions of the early nineteenth-century 'romantic composers' (Chopin, Schumann, Mendelssohn), the supremacy of bad taste would necessarily have endured still longer, for the 'classical' style of Haydn, Mozart, and Beethoven would have gained ground slowly amongst the lovers of what they can recognize as 'a tune'.

There is much trumpery music still in the shops today, but the sales of the finer things (including, decidedly, Bach) are now immense, and show the existence of thousands of genuinely musical homes amongst all social classes, whilst, of course, recital programmes are almost impeccable, so far as the quality of their music is concerned, erring only by over-repetition of the same few great compositions and by their tendency to ignore the later nineteenth-century and the twentieth-century music.

PIANOFORTE PLAYING AND PIANOFORTE TEACHING

(For illustrations see p. 797, pl. 136; 800, 137–8.)

1. Introductory. The history of the development of methods of playing the domestic keyboard instruments is extremely interesting. Such methods had to accommodate themselves to the successive developments of the instrument, which should be studied in the articles *Clavichord*, *Harpsichord Family*, and *Pianoforte*. As, essentially, the art of playing the pianoforte is the art of applying fingers to a keyboard, the article *Fingering* should also be read.

By the time the pianoforte was slowly winning popularity (second half of the eighteenth century) something like ·a technique of finger movement more or less suitable to it had already been developed by the greater harpsichord and clavichord players. They were at last using all five fingers fairly freely (whereas for over two centuries it had been customary to allow three fingers to undertake most of the work) and they were beginning to recognize the value of the thumb as a pivot for the shift of the hand to a higher or lower position on the keyboard. But they did not require (and hence tried to avoid) much movement at the wrist, elbow, or shoulder joints. A musician who had played the clavichord had probably cultivated evenness of touch; a player of the harpsichord had less need to think of this, as the tones produced were in any case approximately even in degree of force; moreover, with the harpsichord anything which could be called a 'singing tone' (cantabile), in the full sense of the term, was barely possible. The motions required were all gentle. Burney records of Handel's playing (which he often heard):

'His touch was so smooth and the tone of the instrument so cherished that his fingers seemed to grow to the keys. They were so curved and compact that when he played no motion and scarcely the fingers themselves could be discovered.'

Of J. S. Schroeter, an early exponent of the pianoforte whom Burney describes as 'the first who brought into England the true art of treating that instrument' (this was in 1772), he says:

'His manner of playing was so quiet that when the hand seemed doing nothing he surpassed all other great players in rapidity.'

See also *Harpsichord Family* 7.

With the growing understanding of the real nature of the pianoforte this was changed: a 'truer art' than Schroeter's· had to be built up. The thumb, finger, wrist, elbow, arm, and body give the hand a power of accommodating itself to surfaces such as no other organ of the body possesses, and the play and interplay of all the joints and muscles involved had to be studied.

It took some time before the study was completed, and indeed that stage can hardly be said to have been reached before the opening of the twentieth century, though gifted musicians had sometimes arrived at a partial or complete application of the proper principles by instinct or by empirical methods.

2. The Two Early 'Schools' of·Pianism. Pianists, for a period at the end of the eighteenth and opening of the nineteenth century, fell into a classification by 'schools'—the 'Viennese' and the 'English' schools. Methods of playing were conditioned by the different action, touch, and tone of the two types of instrument mentioned under *Pianoforte* 7, and in some measure methods of composition for the instrument were similarly influenced.

The light touch and tone of the Viennese (Stein–Streicher) type of instrument was re-

flected in the playing (and pianoforte compositions) of Mozart, for example. In the modern sense of the word 'pianist', he can hardly be said ever to have become one, beautiful as his pianoforte playing is reported to have been. A host of brilliant pianists followed him —Hummel (1778–1837; p. 797, pl. **136.** 4), Czerny (1791–1857; p. 797, pl. **136.** 5), and Moscheles (1794–1870) being outstanding examples, still remembered today not only by the partial survival of their reputation as performers but also by the part they took in the provision of an ample repertory for the instrument, a repertory of both student material and artist material. They sought in their playing (providing for it also in their compositions) equality and purity of tone, delicacy of nuance, lightness, and speed. They had not great 'depth' as performers or composers, and their style of playing and composition tended towards the *bravura* style of such younger men as Herz (1803–88), whose work has now been completely put aside.

The deeper fall of the keys of the English pianoforte, with the greater ambit of the hammers, its fuller tone and higher capacity for cantabile ('singing tone'; apparently C. P. E. Bach was the first to use such a term) made it, with the French models based on it (the Broadwood–Erard types, we may say), attractive to players and composers who had more serious aims.

Clementi (1752–1832; p. 797, pl. **136.** 1), one of the first composers to write definitely for the new instrument (see *Fingering* 4), was brought up on the English instruments and became a maker of them himself. His pupil Field (1782–1837; p. 48, pl. **84.** 5), employed by him to show off his instruments·in his London warehouse, developed in a high degree the singing style and became the inventor of the nocturne (q.v.) and thus the exemplar of Chopin.

The style and methods of Beethoven's very dramatic pianoforte sonatas are based on those of the sonatas of Clementi (see *Sonata* 8), and though Beethoven, as an almost life-resident in Vienna, long played the Viennese type of instrument, his idiom and performance must always have been too 'big' for it, and we know with what delight, when he was forty-eight, he welcomed the gift of a Broadwood.

Dussek (p. 108, pl. **19.** 5) and J. B. Cramer (p. 797, pl. **136.** 3) are other names associated with the more solid type of pianism and pianoforte composition. Dussek (1760–1812) was celebrated for his declamatory and 'singing' style. Cramer (1771–1858) wrote music which Beethoven greatly admired, prescribing the famous 'Studies' as an essential part of the technical and artistic basis of his nephew's musical education, and considering them to offer the best possible preparation for the playing of his own works.

Up to the early decades of the nineteenth century there was a difference of opinion on many quite important points in pianoforte technique. Even the position of the player's

See the Article *Pianoforte Playing* on pages 799–804 and the Articles on the individuals

1. THALBERG (1812–71)

2. HENSELT (1814–89)

3. CLARA SCHUMANN (1819–96)

4. SIR CHARLES HALLÉ (1819–95)

5. GOTTSCHALK (1829–69)

6. ANTON RUBINSTEIN (1829–94)

7. TAUSIG (1841–71)

8. BERINGER (1844–1922)

9. MOSZKOWSKI (1854–1925)

1. PADEREWSKI (1860–1941)

2. BUSONI (1866–1924)

3. ONE-ARMED PIANISM—Paul Wittgenstein
(1887–1961). See *Pianoforte* 21

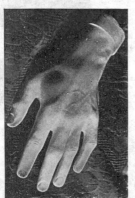
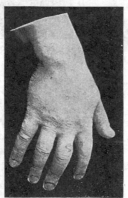
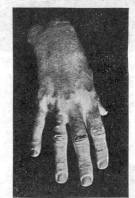

4, 5, 6. HANDS OF CHOPIN, RUBINSTEIN, AND LISZT

7. THE HANDS OF RACHMANINOF (1873–1943)

8. THE HANDS OF BUSONI

stool was unsettled. Mozart relates (1777) how he heard the child prodigy Nanette Stein (daughter of one great pianoforte maker and later to be wife of another and also the helper of Beethoven)—'She sits right up in the treble, instead of in the middle of the instrument, so as to be better able to move about and to make grimaces'. C. P. E. Bach (still flourishing at this date) sat in the very centre of the instrument: Dussek sat to the left of it, to gain power for the left hand. Kalkbrenner (1785–1849) sat to the right, because the compass of the instrument had now been extended and the new upper notes were important. Standardization in pianoforte technique was long in coming—in fact, we may almost say that, in some features, it has never yet come but is still the subject of vigorous discussion.

3. Beethoven as Pianoforte Teacher and Pianist.

The position of piano technique at the turn of the eighteenth to nineteenth centuries can be seen by Czerny's description of the teaching he received as a boy from Beethoven. From this we learn that the use of the thumb (see *Fingering* 1, 2) was still not universally understood, and certainly not by Czerny's father, his previous teacher (born 1750), and that the new possibility of legato was not yet being adequately exploited.

'During the first lessons Beethoven kept me altogether on scales in all the keys, and showed me (something at the time still unknown to most players) the only correct position of the hands and fingers, and, in particular, how to use the thumb, rules whose usefulness I did not learn fully to appreciate until a much later date. Then he went over the studies belonging to this method with me, and, especially, called my attention to the *legato*, which he himself controlled to such an incomparable degree, and which at that time all other pianists regarded as impossible of execution on the fortepiano, for even after Mozart's day the choppy, short, detached manner of playing was the fashion. In later years Beethoven himself told me he had heard Mozart play on various occasions and that Mozart, since at the time the invention of the fortepiano was still in its infancy, had accustomed himself to a mode of playing on the claviers then more frequently used, which was in no wise adapted to the fortepiano. In course of time I also made the acquaintance of several persons who had taken lessons from Mozart, and found this remark justified by their playing.' (Translation from *Beethoven —Impressions of Contemporaries*.)

Czerny says that Beethoven's playing had 'tremendous power, character, unheard-of brilliance and facility'. He says that Hummel's supporters said that Beethoven was noisy (Cherubini used the word 'rough') and that Beethoven's supporters said that Hummel was dull.

4. The Peaceful Wrist Idea.

At this period and for half a century later there were many great pianists who still adhered to the principle of the unmoving wrist and of the fingers as the sole source of the tone. That the Viennese school and their followers did so we can well imagine. Moscheles, up to the 1860s, was still teaching that one should be able to play passages with a glass of water balanced on one's wrist. Clementi had been in the habit of placing a piece of money on a pupil's wrist, and a few people still living have known their teachers apply the same test, for the tradition has taken long to die.

5. The Romantic Period and the Sustaining Pedal.

The sonatas of Beethoven, representing classical form applied to the expression of dramatic feeling, were supplemented by those of Schubert and by the numerous short, characteristic pieces of the latter, 'Impromptus', 'Moments Musicaux', waltzes, and the like. In these, and in the 'Studies' of the Czernys, Moscheleses, and Cramers of the day, all sides of the technique and expressive capabilities of the instrument as it then was were worked out. With the romantic trio, Schumann, Chopin, and Mendelssohn, the still expanding powers of the instrument were enthusiastically exploited. The sustaining pedal, by which Beethoven had been the first greatly to profit (much more, his contemporaries tell us, than the markings in his published copies betray), took in their work a position of high importance, and the pianoforte became an instrument played not merely by the hands but also by the feet. The teaching of Moscheles (and he was ranked as one of the very finest teachers of Europe) was that a good pianist uses the pedals as little as he can. 'Why should he try to provide an effect by his feet instead of his hands?' said Moscheles; 'a horseman might as well rely on the spur instead of the bridle.' To the end of his life he refused to play Chopin, partly on the grounds of objection to tempo rubato (see *Rubato*), but probably also because the reliance upon the pedal which the works of Chopin demand seemed to him a negation of pianism.

A little-known fact bearing upon the proper interpretation today of Chopin's pedal-markings seems worthy of mention here. Examination of a piano that belonged to him in his later years shows that the resonance of its pedal ceases to take effect about an octave lower than that of our modern instruments, so that he could keep the pedal down continuously through middle-keyboard passages in his works in which such treatment is not now possible without producing confusion. In playing music by Beethoven and his more immediate successors the pianist must always read the pedal markings (provided the modern editor has reproduced them textually) merely as indications of an intended effect; the ear, and not merely the eye, must control the feet.

Since Chopin's period the importance of the pedal has become more and more recognized; it has enabled composers to produce effects akin to those of a third hand (Thalberg, particularly, developed a type of composition in which a melody in the middle of the compass of the instrument was shared between the hands, whilst the hand that happened to be at any moment unoccupied made brilliant excursions to the upper or lower reaches, as the case might be). But beyond the use of the pedal in enabling a hand to establish an alibi (which, of course, so far as the left hand is concerned we owe largely to Field and Chopin), it has developed an elaborate technique for enriching the tone (see *Pianoforte* 12; *Acoustics* 8). By the pedal, more than by any other means, does the instrument reveal its 'soul', and if we were to be asked what is the one characteristic that most strongly differentiates pianoforte playing from harpsichord playing, or even the pianoforte playing of today from that of 1800, we should have to reply—the use of the sustaining pedal. The poetry of pianism lies largely in fine pedalling.

6. The Palmy Days of the Virtuoso. Since the days of Bull and the Elizabethan virginalists there has never been a period when keyboard virtuosity has been despised, but it was with the nineteenth-century exploitation of the pianoforte that the keyboard artists began to win the fame and cash reward which the vocal artist had enjoyed for a couple of centuries. Such names as those of Liszt (1811–86), Thalberg (1812–71; p. 800, pl. **137**. 1), Tausig 1841–71; p. 800, pl. **137**. 7), and Rubinstein (1829–94; p. 800, pl. **137**. 6) stand for something very definite in the social history of music. These were all men with a huge command over the keyboard, which is something the public highly values; they keenly studied keyboard effect, and they all did something to extend the technique of pianoforte performance and composition.

Liszt's style was essentially the 'grand' style —on a scale suited to large halls. He had extreme velocity and immense power, with a strong tinge of the sentimental upon which he could rely as a relief from the heroic. He could (and did) break hammers and strings when his full forces were unleashed, and this suggests that his fortissimo tone (whatever our grandfathers may tell us) must have been brutally rough. There probably never has been so masterly ·a pianist as Liszt, and apart from his pianism both his musicianship and his showmanship were of the highest order. Moreover, he had a generosity of nature that won people to him and, incidentally, led to his giving instruction free to half the musically talented youth of Europe and America, and so to his perpetuating his ideals and his style to the present day—a doubtful benefit, as those may think who argue 'Plus fait douceur que violence'.

A fine musician, who knew his playing well (Oscar Beringer, in *Fifty Years' Experience of Pianoforte Teaching and Playing*), has said:

'Words cannot describe him as a pianist—he was incomparable and unapproachable. I have seen whole rows of his audience, men and women alike, affected to tears, when he chose to be pathetic: in stormy passages he was able by his art to work them up to the highest pitch of excitement: through the medium of his instrument he played upon every human emotion. Rubinstein, Tausig, and Bülow all admitted that they were mere children in comparison with Liszt. Wagner said of his playing of Beethoven's Sonatas Opus 106 and Opus 111 that "those who never heard him play them in a friendly circle could not know their real meaning. His was not a re-*production*—it was a re-*creation*".'

There is some justification, then, for those who look upon Liszt as the greatest pianist who ever lived. The pianoforte had in the days of the height of his recital career (about 1839–49) reached a stage of development which lent itself to virtuoso handling on the big scale, and though with the greater use of metal in its framework it now possesses enhanced capacity for enormous tonal effects, no one, we may take it, has ever surpassed Liszt in the power exercised over an impressionable public.

Tausig, Liszt's favourite pupil, unfortunately died at twenty-nine (1841–71). In technique he is recorded as having been head and shoulders above everybody else but his master; the most difficult feats he executed with a rigidly careful concealment of all effort. He cultivated great beauty of tone and his memorized repertory included every important work in the whole harpsichord–clavichord–pianoforte literature as it then existed.

Tausig's career opened after Liszt's short active recital career had closed (for Liszt gave himself after 1849 to conductorship and composition); Rubinstein's career partially overlapped Liszt's and then continued through a long period (up to about 1886) during which he ranked as the world's greatest pianist. He had enormous technique yet could play simple things movingly. He was very unequal, because subject to the impulse of the moment, but at his best he was overwhelming.

The existence of such names as these is a reminder of the tremendous development that had taken place in so short a time. From Cristofori's small and feeble-toned instrument to the enormous 'concert-grand' (from the coracle to the ironclad, so to speak) in a century and a half!

7. The Teaching of Pianoforte Playing. It may be supposed that there has been no advance in actual pianoforte playing since the days of the giants just mentioned. There may have been an advance in taste, and if Liszt were living and playing today there are, it may be admitted, certain types of music he would no longer play and perhaps certain ways of playing he would no longer practise. But there can be few devices in the piano technique of today that were not known to and used by him. There has, however, been an advance in the teaching of the instrument, and whilst the greatest players of the instrument of recent times may be no greater than those of a century earlier, yet the *average* of piano-playing must be enormously higher.

It is common knowledge that, so far as technique is concerned, the great players just mentioned were not great teachers. They had accomplished much by the light of nature, by experiment, and by hard work, and had not analysed their processes. Liszt expected the pupil to have his technique before he came to him and to go on improving it in his own way. It is said that Rubinstein, when he wished to explain to a pupil a point in his own technique, would go to Leschetizky (when they were both at the Conservatory of St. Petersburg, presumably) and ask 'How do I produce such and such an effect?'—whereupon Leschetizky would gravely explain to him his own methods. Leschetizky is only one of a number of modern teachers who have applied an analytical mind to the process of piano-playing.

This is a feature of modern musical education. There was no teaching whatever of piano touch and technique at the Conservatory of Leipzig in the 1860s. Plaidy, who had quarrelled with the authorities and left the Conservatory, taught these subjects privately, and students who felt the need of expert guidance went to him. He had the reputation then of being the world's best master of the subject, but since his time there has been a great advance which might perhaps be described by saying that not only have finger, wrist, arm, and body movements been analysed and synthesized, but the ear has been applied to the study of tone qualities and the mind to the study of the principles of interpretation. One result of this is that at the time when this was written (the 1950s) there were young players who essentially were finer artists than some of the surviving players of great reputation of an earlier generation. The larger public is slow to recognize this, but then the larger public is very much influenced by 'suggestion' and accepts the favourable verdict of the past as valid so long as its subject lives.

If Liszt came back he might have to go to school with one of the young players of today before he could adequately play Debussy and Ravel, who carried Chopin's reliance on tone quality and pedal effects further than Chopin himself, and with whom the piano had almost ceased to seem like a percussion instrument.

The general principles accepted today, as underlying all good technique, are the use of weight rather than pressure, the treatment of the whole playing mechanism from finger-tip to shoulder as one (instead of the old insistence on the finger as the working part of the mechanism and the rest as the mere means of carrying it to its work), and the utter absence of stiffness (i.e. 'relaxation'). These principles were very competently laid down by Matthay (q.v.), of London, in his *The Act of Touch* (1903), and in rather similar terms at about the same time (1904 and 1905) by Steinhausen, a German army surgeon who applied himself in a keenly specialist spirit to the study of the muscular movements connected with the playing of various instruments. Kullak, in 1876, in his *Aesthetics of Pianoforte Playing*, was probably the first to realize the importance of arm and hand weight; in that work he speaks of 'the *fall* of the finger' (which, since the finger in itself has not enough weight to depress the key,

implies the doctrine just alluded to). The avoidance of useless pressure (i.e. pressure once the key has spoken) was a point with Plaidy.

How completely have changed the ideas as to the best way of getting from the pianoforte the kind of tone every refined ear wishes to receive can be seen by the report of one of the pupils of Sterndale Bennett (1816–75), whose own playing was, according to all contemporary reports, admirable—'He often said that when the *fingers* are tired it is a sign that one has practised well, and he constantly warned me from letting any other part of my body become engaged in the work. It took, he said, "from the strength that ought to be in the fingers".' This is dead against modern doctrine!

8. The Problem of 'Touch' as related to Tone Quality. That 'heavy' and 'light' touch is found in different players everybody has noticed, but do different players get a more pleasant or less pleasant quality or a greater or less variety of 'colour' or 'timbre', and if so how?

It is the contention of one party that such a difference is very noticeable as between players; of another party that this must be imagination, since the only variations of movement in the hammer of the piano are variations of speed and weight, resulting in mere variations of loudness. A moment's inspection of the action of any piano will show that the hammer is out of the player's control long before it comes into contact with the string; he does not, indeed, so much *strike* a string with a hammer as *throw* a hammer at a string. But it may be maintained that there are different ways of throwing, resulting in a different behaviour of the hammer when it reaches the string; it is possible to throw a cricket ball so that it arrives with a 'twist' and it may, by rough impact, be possible to throw a piano hammer in such a way that it slightly 'rakes' the string. The cause of good tone and bad tone is the awakening of one series of harmonics or another (or of certain harmonics more loudly than others), and the manner in which the hammer strikes the string may have great influence upon this factor (see the treatment of harmonics under *Acoustics* 7).

Pianoforte tone-quality and 'colour' is, admittedly, largely made by the piano-manufacturer; it comes in great part from the relative length, thickness, tension, and density of the strings, the kind of covering of the hammer, the efficiency of the sound-board, etc. But when the manufacturer has done the best he can (for the particular sum paid him) there remains something for the player to do in the matter of tone-quality, as can be proved by the following experiment: With right pedal down repeat a chord many times, beginning very softly and working up gradually to very loudly; do this first with the utmost rigidity of arm and fingers and then with the utmost suppleness of all these parts: in the first instance the tone will be found to be hard and harsh, and in the second to be round and pleasant. The reason why this difference of quality occurs is a subtle question, probably involving a good many factors and still open to discussion, but there seems no question of the existence of the difference, which is the basis of the demand for muscular relaxation in pianoforte playing.

Bülow (than whom, surely, no musician has possessed a more delicate ear) actually goes so far in his edition of Beethoven's sonatas as to mark passages 'Quasi Clarinet', 'Quasi Horn', etc. He once advised his pupils to imitate in their piano playing the violin tone of Joachim rather than that of Sarasate. Are we, not satisfied with accusing Bülow, perhaps, of a little exaggeration, to believe that all he suggests is nothing whatever but a mad illusion on the part of one of the greatest pianists and conductors who ever lived?

It may be added that another great pianist, d'Albert, in his edition of Beethoven's Sonatas, uses the expressions *Quasi corni* ('as if horns'), etc.

There *is* surely such a thing as 'bad' and 'good' touch producing a 'bad' and 'good' tone in piano playing, though how it comes to exist may continue to be a matter of earnest, friendly dispute for some time yet. And beyond 'good' and 'bad' there are varieties of 'colour', though the way in which these are brought about may be still more debatable.

For another aspect of 'Touch' see *Pianoforte* 14; *for the existence of good and bad touch even in the playing of the more purely mechanical harpsichord see* Harpsichord Family 2.

9. Playing with the Ear. If any thoughtful critic were asked what is the greatest fault of pianists today he would probably reply—careless listening. This fact is particularly noticeable not so much with the young artist as with the routined one who has played the same programmes dozens or hundreds of times. To take one single example, carefully study of the performance of many pianists will show that they are not pedalling as they intend to do and believe themselves to be doing, their release of the sustaining pedal not coming at the effective moment, but before or (more generally) just after this. This was noticed with, for instance, Rubinstein and with Paderewski. And so with every feature of their playing. Busoni, in a communication to the great teacher of the Paris Conservatory, I. Philipp, laid heavy stress on this fault:

'In my opinion, we could learn a great deal more than we do by listening intently to our own playing, by judging with the utmost severity every sound we produce, from the beginning to the end of the piece. How many artists, as well as pupils, there are who lose valuable time by working mechanically, that is to say, without thinking! They pay no more attention to the sounds they produce than does a deaf man. At a concert no one listens to me more attentively than I do myself. My mind is fixed on hearing and judging every note; indeed, my atten-tion is so concentrated that I am incapable of thinking of anything else. I try to give the most faithful interpretation along with my own personal conception of the work I am playing. I am continually discovering new beauties, and sometimes there flash upon me details of interpretation of which I had never dreamt before.'

10. The Coming Pianism? There are signs of a revulsion from the view that the pianoforte is a singing instrument (the view which finds support in Beethoven's slow movements, Chopin's nocturnes, Mendelssohn's Songs without Words, and thousands of compositions since these). The school of composers that professes to have revolted against all that is 'expressive' in music, and to want to achieve an uninflected music free from what they consider 'sentimentalism', regards the pianoforte as capable of reclamation. The old-time pianists aimed at avoiding just what some new-time composers aim at attaining. Rubinstein used to say to his pupils, 'Forget you are striking the notes; imagine you are *singing* them'; Béla Bartók, with the cimbalom or dulcimer of his native Hungary as his apparent ideal, wrote music calling for a percussive touch, and himself performed it with this touch—very trying to the unaccustomed ear. His style was the opposite of all that has been taught since the pianoforte first gained recognition. If the ideals of a Bartók were right, then the ideals of a Busoni were wrong—and to many people the playing of Busoni (1866–1924) remains in memory as the extreme of artistry and the most successful employment of the natural qualities of the instrument that they have ever heard.

Or is it just possible that the pianoforte may be capable of two uses, equally legitimate, though opposed?

Then there is the American, Henry Cowell (p. 1061, pl. **174.** 8), who invented innumerable new effects—'tone clusters', sometimes played by the fist or the elbow, a foot-length of notes played by the fore-arm, strings plucked by the player's hand, and the like (not all new, since Dandrieu, who lived from 1682 to 1738, has, in a battle piece, an indication that to express the cannon's roar the player may strike with his flat hand all the lower notes of the harpsichord).

It remains to be seen whether the art of pianism, whose technique had appeared to be practically completed by the middle of the nineteenth century, is capable of receiving additions on the original lines just mentioned, which amounts to a bold denial of the whole ideal of the treatment of the instrument built up during the first century and a half or two centuries of its existence.

See also the following articles: *Fingering*; *Expression*; *Interpretation*; *Accompaniment*; *Mechanical Reproduction of Music*.

PIANOFORTE TRIO, QUARTET, QUINTET. See *Chamber Music* 2, 3.

PIANOLA. See *Mechanical Reproduction of Music* 13.

PIANO SCORE. See *Score*.

PIANO, STREET. See *Mechanical Reproduction of Music* 12.

PIANTO (It.). 'Plaint', lamentation.

PIATTI (It.). Cymbals. See *Percussion Family* 3 o, 4 b, 5 o.

PIATTI, ALFREDO CARLO (1822–1901). He was a very famous Italian violoncellist who wrote a number of sonatas and concertos for his instrument and collected and edited old music for it. He associated much with Joachim, and in 1894 a celebration of the fiftieth anniversary of the appearance in London of the two artists was organized—for they had made their London débuts at the same concert as one another in 1844 (p. 1088, pl. **179**. 4).

See references under *Bergomask*; *Violin Family* 3 h.

PIBCORN or **PIBGORN**. A Welsh instrument, much the same as the stockhorn (q.v.) of Scotland (p. 545, pl. **100**. 5).

PIBROCH. See *Bagpipe Family* 4, 9. The pibroch style has appeared in the concert-room in the suite of that name by Sir Alexander Mackenzie (1889) for violin and orchestra—much played by Sarasate and others. Similarly Granville Bantock has a pibroch for violoncello and harp (or piano).

PICANDER. See *Passion Music* 5.

PICARDIE, TIERCE DE ('Picardy Third'). See *Tierce de Picardie*.

PICCHETTATO, PICCHIETTATO, PIC-CHIETTANDO (It.). 'Knocked', 'knocking', i.e. (in the playing of bowed instruments) detaching the notes (cf. *Spiccato*).

PICCHI, GIOVANNI. Early seventeenth-century composer for harpsichord. His work abounds in consecutive fifths (see *Harmony* 4, 22) and the tritone (q.v.), deliberately used.

PICCINI (Picinni or **Piccinni), NICOLA** (p. 517, pl. **94**. 4). Born at Bari, in south Italy, in 1728 and died at Passy, near Paris, in 1800, aged seventy-two. He was a favourite pupil of Leo and Durante. In 1754 he suddenly created a furore at Naples with an opera, and soon was known throughout Italy and in 1776 warmly invited to Paris.

In that city Gluck was then at the height of his popularity, and there began one of those feuds between the followers of two eminent composers (compare Bononcini and Handel or Brahms and Wagner) which from time to time have enlivened the musical activities of a city and provided its inhabitants with a source of division almost as sharp as the divisions of politics and religion.

In this campaign Gluck was the victor, but Piccini bore no rancour and, indeed, declared himself one of his rival's warmest admirers. He remained in Paris until in 1789 the Revolution drove him back to Naples, where the authorities, suspecting him of republican views, kept him for four years under guard, though in his own house.

Some years later he returned to Paris and there was appointed to the staff of the new Conservatory, which position he held only a few months before death claimed him.

He left behind him 139 operas, not one of which can now be heard; yet they deserve respect. Their style is largely that of melody with simple accompaniment—as compared with Gluck's more dramatic methods. He also wrote oratorios.

PICCOLO, PICCOLA (It., masc., fem.). 'Little.'

PICCOLO. See *Flute Family* 3 b, 5 b; *Organ* 14 II.

PICCOLO PIANO. See *Pianoforte* 6.

PICINNI. See *Piccini*.

PICKELFLÖTE. Piccolo. See *Flute Family* 3 b, 5 b.

PICK - MANGIAGALLI, RICCARDO. Born at Strakonice, in Bohemia, in 1882 and died in Milan in 1949, aged nearly sixty-seven. Despite his birthplace, he was an Italian. He composed a number of operas and ballets that had success in his own country and many well-known piano pieces.

PIED (Fr.). 'Foot' (used in connexion with organ stops; see *Organ* 2 b).

PIED EN L'AIR (Fr.). 'Foot in the air'—a particular motion in the Galliard (see *Pavan and Galliard*).

PIENO, PIENA (It., masc., fem.). 'Full.' E.g. *Organo pieno*, 'full organ'; *Coro pieno*, 'full choir' (as contrasted with passages for quartet, etc.); *A voce piena*, 'with full voice'.

PIERANZOVINI, PIETRO (1814–85). See *Percussion Family* 4 a (end); *Concerto* 6 b.

PIERNÉ, GABRIEL (in full, Henri Constant Gabriel). Born at Metz in 1863 and died at Ploujean, Finistère, in 1937, aged nearly seventy-four. He was a student of the Paris Conservatory, where he won the Rome Prize when nineteen. When César Franck (q.v.) died in 1890, he succeeded him as organist of St. Clothilde, and when Colonne died, twenty years later, he succeeded him as conductor of the Colonne Concerts.

As a composer he was prolific—operas, ballets, incidental music to plays, orchestral music, chamber music, piano music, songs, and the remarkable musical legend, *The Children's Crusade* (1902), which makes much use of children's voices, as does also the similar work, *The Children of Bethlehem*.

See references under *Oratorio* 4, 7 (1904, 1909), *Trumpet Family* 4.

PIERROTS. See *Negro Minstrels*.

PIERSON, HENRY HUGO (originally 'Pearson'). Born at Oxford in 1815 and died at Leipzig in 1873, aged fifty-seven. He was the son of the Dean of Salisbury and was educated at Harrow and at Cambridge. In his early twenties he went to Germany, where he became known to Mendelssohn, Schumann, and others of the leading composers of the day. Schumann in his musical magazine praised some of his early songs.

Before he was thirty he had become Professor of Music at Edinburgh University, but he soon resigned the position, returning to Germany, marrying a German lady, and changing the spelling of his name (probably to secure the correct pronunciation).

His oratorios, operas, songs, and instrumental works had success in his day, some of them in Germany and others in England. (Some of them were published under the name of 'Edgar Mansfeldt'.) His incidental music to the second part of Goethe's *Faust* had a wide currency and was greatly admired.

See *O Deutschland*.

PIESSE. See *Odour and Music*.

PIETÀ, PIETOSO, PIETOSAMENTE (It.). 'Pity', 'piteous', 'piteously'.

PIFFERO, PIFFERARI. See *Bagpipe Family* 7.

PIJPER, WILLEM (p. 97, pl. **16**. 5). Born at Zeist, near Utrecht, Holland, in 1894 and died at Leidschendam in 1947, aged fifty-two. He served as music critic of a Utrecht newspaper, directed the Utrecht Wind Sextet, taught in the Amsterdam Conservatory, and composed symphonies, chamber music, a 'symphonic drama', songs and other things—latterly in an 'atonal' idiom.

See reference under *Holland* 8, and for atonality see *Harmony* 18.

PIKE (of Charleston). See *Concert* 15.

PIKIEREN (Ger.). To play spiccato (q.v.).

PILGRIM FATHERS. See *Puritans* 8; *United States* 2; *Hymns and Hymn Tunes* 11.

PILKINGTON, FRANCIS. Born about 1562 and died at Chester in 1638. He was in orders and a minor canon of Chester Cathedral, and wrote a good many ayres and madrigals—of high value.

PILSS, KARL. Born in Vienna in 1902. Composer of chamber music, etc. See reference under *Trumpet* 4.

PINAFORE. See *H.M.S. Pinafore*.

PINCÉ (Fr.). 'Pinched', i.e. pizzicato (there was also an old mordent called by this name).

PINCHERLE, MARC (1888–1974). He was educated at the Sorbonne; directed the Pleyel concerts from 1927 to 1955; was president of the French musicological society 1948–55, and professor of music at the École Normale. He did much research on the history of the violin, and wrote important works on Vivaldi and Corelli.

PINEAL GLAND. See *Colour and Music* 12.

PINSUTO, CIRCO. Born near Siena in 1829 and died at Florence in 1888, aged fifty-eight. He studied in England under Cipriani Potter (q.v.) and at Bologna under Rossini, and from his nineteenth year until his retirement was busy in England as a fashionable singing-master and composer of songs and part songs, etc., and in Italy as an opera composer.

PIOBAIREACHD. See *Bagpipe Family* 4.

PIPE (1) Poetically the word is used for any of the less noisy wind instruments. (2) In the mouth of a Scotsman it stands for 'bagpipe' (q.v.), as 'piper' for 'bagpiper'. (3) In 'Pipe and Tabor' it means the small flageolet-like instrument held to the mouth in old times with the left hand whilst the right played the tabor, or small drum, hanging from the body; see *Recorder Family* 3 c. (4) In modern educational parlance it stands for *Bamboo Pipe* (q.v.).

PIPERS, TOWN. See *Bagpipe Family* 4.

PIQUÉ (Fr.). Literally 'pricked'. A bowed instrument term—same as It. *Spiccato* (q.v.).

PIQUIREN (Ger.). To play spiccato (q.v.).

PIRATES OF PENZANCE, THE; or THE SLAVE OF DUTY (Sullivan). First produced (merely for copyright purposes) at the Bijou Theatre, Paignton, in 1879, and then at the Fifth Avenue Theatre, New York, the same year and the Opéra Comique, London, the following year. Libretto by W. S. Gilbert.

Act I

Scene: *A Rocky Seashore off the Coast of Cornwall*

Frederic (*Tenor*), a former apprentice pirate, is now out of his indentures and proposes to leave the band. **Ruth** (*Contralto*), their present maid-of-all-work and formerly Frederic's nurse, being told, years ago, to apprentice the lad to a pilot, misheard, and bound him to a *pirate*. Once free, he will feel bound, he tells them, to seek their destruction. He bids the **Pirate King** (*Baritone*) farewell. As he has for so long seen no woman but Ruth, he is inclined to accept her word that she is handsome; but when some maidens appear he is undeceived: all those he can see are lovely, and Ruth is not. He renounces her.

Not wishing to be seen as a pirate, Frederic hides whilst the maidens, among whom are **Kate, Edith, Isabel,** and **Mabel** (*Sopranos*), the four daughters of Major-General Stanley, prepare to paddle. Frederic seeks a plain, dutiful maiden. Such is Mabel. While she and Frederic are exchanging confidences the pirates come back. So does **General Stanley** (*Tenor*). On hearing that the pirates propose to marry the maidens, among them his daughters, he pleads that he is an orphan, and the daughters his sole remaining joy. This is a lie, but it works. The pirates let them go, and elect them honorary members of the band.

Ruth returns and begs Frederic to remember her, but he bids her go.

Act II

Scene: *A Ruined Chapel by Moonlight*

The general repents his lie at the tombs of his ancestors—or rather, the ancestors he bought with the estate a year ago. Frederic plans to capture the pirates and win Mabel as his reward. Police appear, led by a **Sergeant** (*Bass*). When they go off, leaving Frederic alone, he is surprised to see the Pirate King and Ruth, who cover him with pistols. They have come to tell him that as his birthday is on 29 February, and he can only have one in every four years, he is really only about five-and-a-quarter years old, and so not out of his apprenticeship to piracy. Conscience compels him to rejoin the band, and also to tell the leader that General Stanley is *not* an orphan. The pirate, disgusted, determines to attack the general's mansion that night.

When he and Ruth are gone, Mabel enters, and Frederic swears to return and claim her when, according to strict leap-year reckoning, he comes of age—which means in something like sixty years!

The police now gather, concealing themselves. The pirates appear, and in turn hide as the general enters in his dressing-gown, soon followed by his daughters, also in night attire. They wonder what has caused their father to do this. The pirates spring upon the general, who, seeing Frederic, bids him summon his men and capture his assailants. He cannot. The police now jump out, but the pirates overpower them. But when the sergeant charges the pirates to yield, in the Queen's name, they do so, their loyalty being too much for them. Ruth reveals a last secret—that the pirates are all noblemen, and the rest kneel to them, for, 'with all our faults, we love our House of Peers'. The general says 'Take my daughters!' and all is over.

PIROUETTE. See *Ballet* 8.

PISK, PAUL AMADEUS. He was born in Vienna in 1893. He earned his doctorate at the University of Vienna, with a musicological thesis, took up musical journalism, and pursued study in composition under Schreker and Schönberg, conducted theatre orchestras, became secretary of a Schönberg Society, and has composed orchestral and chamber works, choral, piano, and organ music, songs, etc. In 1937 he settled in the United States.

See *Note-Row.*

PISTON. In a brass instrument, a type of valve consisting of an elongated cylinder or 'pump' bored with passages, which, when it is depressed within its casing, deflect the air-way passing through it into the valve tubing. See *Brass*; *Trumpet Family* 2 c; *Cornet* 2, 3.

Or, in French and German, the word may mean the ordinary Cornet (q.v.).

See also *Organ* 2 f.

PISTON, WALTER HAMOR (p. 1060, pl. 173. 9). Born at Rockland, Maine, in 1894 and died at Belmont, Mass., in 1976, aged eighty-two. He studied at Harvard and in Paris, became a member of the Harvard music staff (Naumburg Professor 1948–60) and was the author of textbooks on harmony and on counterpoint. As a composer his thinking was contrapuntal rather than harmonic. His works include eight symphonies (both the third and the seventh won the Pulitzer Prize), a violin concerto, chamber music, and a ballet, *The Incredible Flutist* (from which an often-performed suite has been made), but no vocal music.

PISTONE, PISTONI (It.). 'Piston', 'pistons'. Used in connexion with the brass instruments. *Pistone* is also a name for the high (E flat or F) cornet (see *Cornet*). **Corno a Pistoni** is the valve horn (see *Horn Family* 2 c, 3, 5 c).

PISTONS, BUGLE À (Fr.). See *Saxhorn and Flügelhorn Families* 5.

PISTONS, TROMBONE À. (Fr.). See *Trombone Family* 5.

PITCH

1. Introductory. As explained in the article *Acoustics* (section 3), the phenomenon of varying pitch of sounds depends on variety of vibration-frequency in the sounding body. Different vibration-frequencies have been associated with the same note of the stave at different periods and in different countries, and even for different classes of music at the same period and in the same country. There is practical importance in the understanding of this matter, and it will be discussed here under heads covering three important periods of which the music is still freely performed. It is not possible to treat of various countries in detail, but enough can be said to offer a general guide to (for instance) the choral conductor whose repertory includes the sixteenth- and early seventeenth-century English madrigals, the works of Bach and Handel, Mozart and Beethoven, and the more modern choral music.

2. The Tudor Period in England. There is a common statement that pitch in the sixteenth and early seventeenth centuries (the important period of the madrigals and the early keyboard music) was about three semitones lower than the pitch of today, so that when we play or sing from the original notation music of that period it is heard a minor third higher than its composers intended. The main basis of this statement lies in certain evidence that the domestic keyboard instruments of the day possessed this low pitch.

The whole question was thoroughly examined by Dr. E. H. Fellowes in his book *The English Madrigal Composers*, and the conclusion worked out convincingly that not one but three pitches existed:

(a) *Domestic keyboard pitch*, about three semitones lower than our standard pitch of today.

(b) *Secular vocal pitch*, much the same as the pitch of today.

(c) *Church music pitch*, more than two semitones higher than the pitch of today.

There was thus a discrepancy of about five semitones between the pitch of the virginals and that of the church organ.

It will, then, be seen that, whereas the madrigals of the period should be sung as they stand in the music copies, the church music should be transposed a tone higher—and this latter practice has, in fact, long been customary amongst choirmasters, for practical reasons of comfort in singing and of effectiveness.

On the other hand, pianists, harpsichordists, or clavichordists are entitled, if they desire, to transpose the music of the period a minor third lower, and possibly viol and recorder players might do the same,[1] whilst the little organ music of the period that exists may properly (on the assumption that it was written for church organs) be transposed higher by any modern editor who feels it thus gains in effectiveness.

For in all these classes of music (domestic choral, domestic keyboard, and ecclesiastical choral) we may take it that the composers notated their music according to the intended medium of its performance.

3. The Period of Bach and Handel. A high pitch for church music seems to have obtained in Germany, where it was known as the *Cornett-Ton* (to be explained later) or the *Chorton* (i.e. choir-pitch). Quantz, whose book on flute playing (1752—just after Bach's death) tells us so much more than its title promises, says that this high pitch had reigned in Germany for 'some centuries', and that the old organs still existing proved this. He says that the other instruments (and he gives a list pretty well covering the whole series—bowed, wood-wind, and brass) had also formerly been made to this high pitch but that the French, who had improved the wood-wind instruments, had adopted a lower pitch, and that as a result of their example a strong tendency had set in to adopt this in Germany, where it was known as *Kammerton* (i.e. 'Chamber Pitch'). He says that this tendency was shown in the making of the more modern organs to this lower pitch.

This statement is borne out by an examination of the parts of many of Bach's church choral works. His organs and strings being at the high pitch and his other instruments at the low, he perforce wrote with this discrepancy in mind, writing his string parts and organ part (the 'continuo' or 'figured bass', q.v.) in a lower key in order to be in tune with the other instruments. The voices he usually sets in the

[1] A specialist authority on the instruments of this period writes:

'The sixteenth century viol music tends to lie too low if anything; the seventeenth century music to be just right. There is no clear evidence on viol pitches at this time, but on practical grounds I do not endorse the general idea that downwards transposition is a possibility. (Upwards perhaps for, for example, some of the Byrd pieces.) However, the whole early pitch issue tends to become more and more curious.'

same key as the strings and organ part. (It is clear that there is nothing final about the pitch of strings and voices; strings can tune to any pitch, without limits, and voices, in effect, do likewise; but the pitch of wood-wind is of the nature of a fixed element.)

Thus, for instance, we may find in some cantata the voice, string, and organ parts in key A or B flat and the wood-wind parts in C. The exact amount of the discrepancy in the notational pitch of the parts depended upon the church where the work was to be performed, for its organ might be pitched at the *Cornett-Ton* (the town-pipers' pitch in older times adopted for convenience of the church performances of those functionaries) or the *Chorton*, which was a semitone lower. Moreover, the other instruments might be pitched at the *Hoch Kammerton* ('high chamber pitch') or, occasionally, at the *Tief Kammerton* ('low chamber pitch').

Taking the Hoch Kammerton as the norm (and when we say 'Kammerton' without prefix this is the one we mean), the other pitches were related to it as follows: *Cornett-Ton*, three semitones higher; *Chorton*, two semitones higher; *Tief Kammerton*, one semitone lower.

In view of the several pitches used by Bach it is clearly impossible to lay down any general rule as to the pitch at which his music should be performed today; obviously every work must be considered separately, and in a choral work the lie of the soprano and bass will offer the best guidance. It would, however, seem that any organist who feels equal to transposing preludes and fugues up two or three semitones is entitled to do so, for the *Cornett-Ton* and *Chorton* of Bach's organs were a good deal higher than the pitch of our organs today.

(Before leaving this subject the student may be warned that a good many books of reference have somehow got the relative position of *Chorton* and *Kammerton* reversed. It will be clear from what has been said above that the *Chorton*, in Bach's day, was the higher. See C. S. Terry, *Bach's Orchestra*, p. 155.)

As to Handel's pitch for the works he wrote in England, we have definite evidence in his tuning-fork (see below), which gives a pitch somewhat lower than that of today.

4. The Period of Haydn, Mozart, and Beethoven. It will be clear from what has just been quoted from Quantz and shown as to Bach's practice that a movement was on foot towards a lowering of the pitch and a standardizing of it. The existence of old organs in the churches was the great obstacle. Bach's at St. Thomas's and St. Nicholas's, Leipzig, were respectively a century and a century and a half old when he was born, and though there had necessarily been renovations the very costly process of altering the pitch had never been undertaken. Gradually, however, this condition altered. As old organs finally wore out they were replaced with new ones at the low pitch (as happened at both of the churches above mentioned after Bach's death), and examination of newer instruments has shown that, roughly speaking, the pitch of Handel's English tuning-fork, which still exists, represents the pitch at which eighteenth-century composers expected to hear their works performed. This fork gives the pitch A as 422·5 vibrations per second, Mozart had a piano tuned to A 421·6, and the eighteenth-century pitch in general may be taken as A 415 to A 430.

This is the pitch which ought to have been retained in order that the works of Haydn, Mozart, Beethoven, and their contemporaries might be heard as they intended them.

For a reference to the pitch for which the early eighteenth-century Italian violins were intended see *Violin Family* 4.

5. The Nineteenth Century and after.

Unfortunately during the nineteenth century the pitch tended everywhere to rise by a semitone and more, especially in Britain, and an A of 452·5 vibrations per second, adopted by the London Philharmonic Society (superseding its original, 1813, pitch of 423·7 and its later pitch of 433·2), became one of the accepted standards, under the name of *Philharmonic Pitch*.

Many attempts were made in various countries to get a standard pitch adopted and to fix it at a lower figure than this, and at the end of the nineteenth century the official French government *Diapason Normal* (called in U.S.A. 'French Pitch', or 'International Pitch') of 435 vibrations for A was generally adopted in Britain—very slightly raised to 439 vibrations (at 68° Fahrenheit). This was in Britain called the *New Philharmonic Pitch* and it was in almost universal British use. Military bands unfortunately remained at the Old Philharmonic Pitch of A = 452·5, so making it impossible for any of their players to take part in orchestral work unless they possessed a second instrument. Very strenuous attempts, made by Col. J. A. C. Somervell and others, to get the military band pitch brought down to the orchestral pitch (incidentally enabling British bands to play with British organs, most of which now stood at this pitch, and also enabling British and French bands to play together) failed for a long time, owing to the expense involved in the alteration of instruments, but in 1929 they were successful.

A = 440 is now the standard British pitch; it has been accepted in most countries by piano makers, orchestral instrument makers, and official bodies as the result of an international conference in 1939. It may be noted that in a concert hall the pitch may rise by four or five vibrations—in the well-heated halls of the United States probably more; the standard pitch is really a little too high, but it must now remain, and the convenience of the existence of a universally accepted standard must, by any who have traced the fluctuations, be regarded as a triumph of human co-operation.

The vague expression 'Concert Pitch' may require some elucidation. English dictionaries define it as 'slightly higher than the ordinary (*Oxford Concise Dictionary*), 'rather higher than usual' (Professor H. C. Wyld's *Universal Dictionary of the English Language*). This sense, being that in which the general public understands it, has led to its becoming a common metaphor (e.g. applied to health).

Probably the distinction implied is between the ordinary domestic piano, possibly old and low in pitch, and a piano intended for public use, which, if played with an orchestra (as in a concerto), would require to be tuned to A = 440, and even if not played with an orchestra would need to be tuned as high as that in order to produce the expected brilliance of effect. The expression 'Concert Pitch', then, if interpreted exactly means 'A = 440' and if interpreted loosely means merely 'high in pitch'.

For purposes of acoustical calculation and statement (as in the article *Acoustics* in this work) what is called 'Philosophical Pitch' (meaning 'Scientific Pitch') is adopted. This is always stated in terms of C, not A, and puts the C on the treble staff at 512 vibrations per second. This figure gives a lower pitch than the Diapason Normal (it implies an A of nearly 427—a 'Classical Pitch', i.e. a pitch of the Haydn–Beethoven period), but has the advantage of offering ease in calculation; it implies an imaginary low C at 1 vibration per second (really a quite inaudible note, of course), the next C above having, of course, 2, and so on through 4, 8, 16 (where audibility may be said to begin), 32, 64, 128, 256, and (at the ninth octave) 512.

6. Pitch-carrying Instruments.

(*a*) **Pitch-pipe (Flue).** This is a small wooden organ pipe of square section, about 18 inches long, with a whistle mouthpiece. In its most developed form, in which it was greatly used during the eighteenth century, and as it is described in Rousseau's musical dictionary (1767), it has a wooden stopper that can be pushed in to shorten the pipe and hence raise the pitch: on the side of this stopper are marked the positions to which it should be pushed in order to procure the specified notes. It was especially in starting psalm tunes in church, in the absence of any instrument, that the pitch-pipe was used in Britain, and the following from the *Scots Magazine* of 1755 will show the method:

'As the tune must begin on a pitch neither too high for the tenor and other upper parts ascending to the highest notes the tune requires, nor too low for the bass, the leader must begin with striking such a sound as will answer this end. With this all the performers join in unison; and then the several parts ascend or descend to the notes upon which the respective parts of the tune begin, and after a little pause proceed to the tunes. This is called *pitching*.

'As it required great practice and skill, all at once, and without premeditation. to strike a sound precisely proper for the pitch, and in order to ascertain this in the beginning, and before such expert performers can be had in a parish as are capable of doing it, an instrument is used commonly called a *pitch-pipe*, which, by moving a slider properly divided, gives all the notes, with their subdivisions, which are proper for the *tenor-part* [i.e. the part with the tune itself]. Upon this the leader gives one sound, acute or grave as the tune requires; with which all the performers immediately strike in; and the instrument is laid aside. Those who are offended at this (as a gentleman observed upon hearing the objection) might as well be offended at a parson's hemming to clear his throat before he begins, which is often done by some precentors with many affected airs.'

The last sentence alludes to the severity of the Calvinistic objection to the use of instruments, even the simplest, in worship (see *Hymns and Hymn Tunes* 10).

In some parts of the south of England the name *Spoke Pipe* was used, and it was customary in the preliminary process as above described to make use of the word 'Praise' or the phrase 'Praise ye the Lord'.

It is difficult to decide at what period the pitch-pipe came into use. From an anecdote related below under *Tuning-fork* it was evidently the common aid to the tuning of stringed instruments at the beginning of the eighteenth century, and, moreover, Handel's pitch-pipe is still in existence, as well as his tuning-fork, which, supposedly, superseded it.

On the other hand, Tans'ur, in his *Elements of Music Displayed* (1772), says 'I went several miles to see the first I heard of', and tells us that before the introduction of a pitch-pipe a bell was used (cf. p. 961, pl. **162**. 2). Probably the novelty of the type of pipe Tans'ur went to see lay in the graduated scale of the stopper: the pre-existing pitch-pipes probably (like the bells he mentions) sounded only one note.

It is said that the introduction of the pitch-pipe into American church life was due to the active choral promoter William Billings (1746–1800: see references under his name).

In England pitch-pipes remained in use in the churches until, at the end of the eighteenth century, church orchestras came in. In Scotland, which enjoyed no church orchestra phase, they lasted much longer.

It will be seen that the vogue of the pitch-pipe overlapped that of the tuning-fork by a considerable period. No doubt this was due to the adjustability of the former, which enabled a Scottish precentor or English parish clerk to give the exact keynote of any psalm tunes without preliminary calculation.

(*b*) **Tuning-fork (Pitch-fork).** This was invented in 1711 by John Shore, Sergeant Trumpeter to the court and also lutenist in the Chapel Royal. His trumpet playing had long been famous (the florid trumpet parts in many of both Purcell's and Handel's works were written for him), but it was naturally in his lutenist capacity that he made use of his tuning-fork. The name now sometimes used, 'pitch-fork', was introduced by him in the form of a pun—'He was a man of humor and pleasantry, and was the original inventor of the tuning-fork, an instrument which he constantly carried about him and used to tune his lute by, and

which whenever he produced it gave occasion to a pun. At a concert he would say, "I have not about me a pitch-pipe, but I have what will do as well to tune by, a pitch-fork" ' (Hawkins).

Handel possessed one of Shore's forks (as well as the pitch-pipe alluded to under 4 above), and, as already mentioned, this still exists.

The tuning-fork as we have it today embodies refinements due to the mid-nineteenth-century scientist Rudolph Koenig, of Paris. Physicists make great use of the tuning-fork in various sizes and forms, often mounted on resonance chambers and sometimes made to sound continuously by means of an electro-magnet.

The tone of the tuning-fork is particularly clear, from the facts that the only harmonics plainly heard (see *Acoustics* 6, 8, and *Timbre*) are the very high ones, and that reinforcement of the tone by the use of a resonance chamber or by placing the foot of the fork on a wooden table practically leaves only the fundamental tone.

J. H. Scheibler (q.v.) made valuable experiments in tuning by means of *Tonometers* consisting of over fifty forks, giving that number of fixed pitches within the octave.

Deagan, of Chicago, in the late nineteenth century, introduced steel bars. The *Deagano-meter* is a set of six of these tuned respectively from A 435 to A 440.

(*c*) **Pitch-pipe (Reed).** This had a nineteenth-century popularity as 'Eardsley's Patent Chromatic Pitchpipe'. It consisted of a small metal pipe (about 2 inches long) with a reed the vibrating length of which was adjustable by means of a graduated curved piece of metal on which were marked the names of the notes. Such instruments are still on sale. Sets of small metal reed pipes each tuned to a different note have also been in use, as have double pipes which, blown at one end or the other, sound different notes. The tuning-fork is, however, the most reliable pocket indicator of pitch that has yet been introduced.

(*d*) **Resonoscope.** This is an electrical pitch-carrying instrument (see *Temperament* 11, end), introduced in 1936 in the United States and the following year in Great Britain. It sounds any note desired of the chromatic scale, at the same time showing it in visual terms as a wave form on a small screen. Any attempt to sing or play the same note can also be shown as a wave form and checked by comparison. The construction of the instrument is partially described as follows:

'The Resonoscope ingeniously combines a set of twelve master tuning-forks electrically actuated, and their notes are translated into corresponding electrical terms, with microphone, amplifier, loudspeaker, and cathode-ray tube. The tuning-forks are mounted on a wheel which in turn is rotated by the main dial knob, so that any fork corresponding to the desired note can be brought in position between the electro-magnets.'

7. Means adopted for Indicating the Notes of Different Octaves. Some handy means of speaking and writing of the notes of the different octaves is obviously necessary. Every book on acoustics or on the organ, etc., makes use of such a means. Unfortunately there is no one generally accepted convention. This would not greatly matter if the different conventions used totally different terms, but unfortunately they nearly all use the same terms, applying them in different ways—to the bewilderment of the reader, who, on passing from one book to another, may very easily and without blame be an octave out in his understanding of some of the statements he reads.

Even the same book will sometimes use differing terms for the same octave. For instance, Pearce's valuable *Notes on English Organs of the Period 1800–10* haphazardly uses five different names for the same octave, scattering two or three such names on the same page.

Many books of musical reference give no explanation of pitch names and it seems urgently desirable that the subject should be worked out once for all and the chief of the various systems put on record as some help to readers. The information that is shortly to be given is the result of many hours' exasperated grappling with quantities of books on various musical subjects in the endeavour to discover their methods of pitch statement. Before giving it, it may be remarked that, such confusion having arisen, it would be well if future authors wishing to quote the notes of the various octaves would abandon *all* systems of great and small letters, single letters and double letters, letters with strokes and numbers, and the like, and speak of the octaves by the organ-pipe length of the C which begins each, i.e.:

Thus one would speak of '4-foot E', meaning E in the octave whose lowest note is of 4-ft. pipe length, and so on. If this system is used there can be no possible misunderstanding.

Also the following names of particular notes can safely be used, as they do not vary in the usage of different authors (they are at present perhaps, especially, names used by organists):

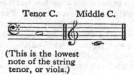

(This is the lowest note of the string tenor, or viola.)

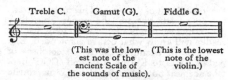

(This was the lowest note of the ancient Scale of the sounds of music).   (This is the lowest note of the violin.)

Or one can use clumsy but exact terms such as 'G, second line on treble clef' (as has been done generally throughout the present work) or, in conversation with a scientist, be very precise and give vibration numbers. Beyond those various ways there is no security that one will be accurately understood, but the following methods (and others) are in common use. (In every case the lowest note of the octave is given, the other notes of the octave (excepting, of course, the top one, which begins a new octave) being indicated in exactly the same way):

(*a*) What is called the 'Helmholtz Notation' (described in Helmholtz's *The Sensations of Tone*, 1875):

(*b*) What is often called the older English organ pitch notation:

and so on.

(*c*) The same as either of the two ways (*a*) and (*b*), but instead of c′ and c″ there are used the signs 'cc', 'ccc', and so on: or the signs c^1, c^2, etc., may be used—in two different ways, unfortunately, c^1 and c^2 sometimes meaning the same as c′ and c″ and sometimes the same as c and c′.

(*d*) The same as the preceding way (*b*), but instead of CC the sign C_1 is used, instead of CCC the sign C_2, and so on—or instead of CC the sign C_2 is used and instead of CCC the sign C_3.

(*e*) In the older books on the organ (e.g. the standard Hopkins and Rimbault) a system deriving from the old *Gam* (scale) of Guido d'Arezzo is in use. Here the octave, instead of running from C to C, runs from G to G.

and so on.

(*f*) Present-day organ builders in their specifications generally use system (*b*) so far as the lower limit of the range of manuals or pedals is concerned, but for the upper limit they generally use merely a letter, assuming that the reader will know what octave is intended. E.g. 'compass of Manuals CC to C; compass of pedals CCC to E' (the 'CC' and 'CCC' here take account not of the notation of organ music but of the fact that the normal pitch of the lowest note of the manuals is 8-foot and of that of the pedals 16-foot).

(g) From *Sound*, by Prof. Arthur Tabor Jones (1937); in frequent use in the United States, as, for instance, in articles in the *Journal of the Acoustical Society of America*. It begins with the bottom note of the organ manuals.

C_1 C_2 C_3 C_4 C_5

(h) Proposed in the United States 'Report of Committee on Acoustic Standardisation' in the *Journal of the Acoustical Society of America*, ii, 318 (1931). C_4 = Helmholtz C_{11} (see (a), above); C_5 = Helmholtz C_1, etc., so that C_8 = Middle C (Helmholtz c^1). In this system C_6 is the same as C_1, in example (g) above, and so on.

This is based on 'Philosophical Pitch' (see *Pitch* 5, end of section), in which all C's are powers of 2, i.e. Middle C is 2^8, or 256.

(i) Certain high notes are often spoken of as *in alt* or *in altissimo*. Here again the practice varies.

'In Alt', the octave above this being 'In Altissimo'.

'In Alt', the octave above this being 'In Altissimo'.

or (rarely)

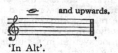

and upwards.

'In Alt'.

8. Terminology.

Pitch. *Hauteur* (Fr., 'height'); *Altezza* (It., 'height'), or *Altezza sonora*, or *Diapason* (It.); *Tonhöhe* (Ger., 'tone-height').

Pitch-Pipe. *Diapason de bouche* (Fr.); *Corista* or *Diapason* (It.; both also used for tuning-fork); *Stimmflöte* (Ger., 'tune-flute'), *Stimmhorn* (Ger., 'tune-fork').

Tuning-Fork (Pitch-Fork). *Diapason* (Fr.); *Corista* or *Diapason* (It.; both also used for pitch-pipe); *Stimmgabel* (Ger., 'Gabel' = fork).

Choir Pitch. *Chorton, Chorstimmung, Chormässige Stimmung, Kapellton* (all Ger.); *Corista di coro* (It.).

Chamber Pitch. *Kammerton* (Ger.; occasionally spelt 'Cammerton'); *Corista di camera* (It.). After a certain conference in Vienna in 1885, when the pitch of A = 435 was adopted, this pitch took over the old name of *Kammerton* (see 3): it will be noticed that this is practically the 'New Philharmonic' pitch.

For Absolute Pitch see article under that head.
For Relative Pitch see *Absolute Pitch.*
For Pitch Accent in Linguistics see *Melody* 2.
For the faculty of pitch perception see *Ear and Hearing* 4.

PITCH-PIPE. See *Pitch* 6 a c, 8; *Hymns and Hymn Tunes* 10.

PITFIELD, THOMAS BARON. Born in Lancashire in 1903. He had a brief training at the Royal Manchester College of Music and then earned his living as a woodworker and designer of lino-cuts and lettering, also giving himself to the activities of a poet and composer. He has published piano, choral, chamber, and orchestral works, etc.

PITUITARY BODY. See *Colour and Music* 12.

PIU (It.). 'More.'

PIUS IV. See *Church Music* 4.

PIUS IX. See *Cecilia, Saint.*

PIUS X. See *Plainsong* 3; *Psalm*; *Motu proprio*; *Roman Catholic Church Music in Britain*; *Faburden* 2.

PIUS XI. See *Motu proprio* (end).

PIUTTI, CARL (1846–1902). Organist and composer for the organ, etc. See *Chorale Prelude.*

PIUTTOSTO (It.). 'Rather' (cf. *Tosto*).

PIVA (It.). Bagpipe. See also *Suite* 2.

PIXIS, JOHANN PETER (1788–1874). Pianist and popular composer for his instrument. See *Misattributed Compositions* (Weber); *Hexameron.*

PIZZ. See *Pizzicato.*

PIZZETTI, ILDEBRANDO (p. 525, pl. 96. 2) (known also as Ildebrando da Parma). Born at Parma in 1880 and died in Rome in 1968, aged eighty-seven. After study and teaching in the conservatory of his native place he became professor of harmony in that of Florence, of which institution he later became director, in 1924 passing to that of Milan and then to that of Rome (1936–52).

As an opera composer he began by practising the traditional conventions of his nation, but quickly turned to a style in which the claims of homogeneous dramatic expression were accepted as paramount. He was a wide reader and a skilful writer and developed theories which he was able clearly to set forth in magazine articles and in several volumes of essays upon musical subjects.

It should be noted that his theory demands self-abnegation on the part of both poet and composer, since he called upon the former to sacrifice passages which do not essentially require musical setting in order to produce their fullest effect, and the latter to abandon all striving after purely musical charm, and to reduce the function of the orchestra to that of enforcement of the dramatic emotions (see also *Opera* 7).

His opera *Fedra* ('Phaedra') (first performed 1915) is a setting of d'Annunzio's text; it clearly marks his new direction. *Deborah and Jael* (first performed 1922) proceeds further in that direction: other stage works followed (bringing the total to twelve), notably *La Figlia di Jorio* (1954) and *Assassinio nella cattedrale* (1958). In general he was his own librettist.

In addition he wrote orchestral works, church music (a *Requiem*, 1922) chamber music, songs, and other things.

See *Italy* 7; *Opera* 24 f (1949–51).

PIZZICATO (It.), generally abbreviated to *Pizz.* 'Plucked', i.e. pluck the strings (violin, etc.) with the fingers instead of bowing them. The plural is *Pizzicati*.

PK. (1) Short for *Pauken*, i.e. kettledrums.

(2) *Pedalkoppel*, i.e. 'Pedal Coupler' (in organ music—followed by an indication of the particular manual to be coupled to the pedal).

PLACIDO, PLACIDEZZA (It.). 'Placid', 'placidity'. *Placidamente*, 'peacefully'.

'PLACING' OF VOICE. See *Voice* 14.

PLACITO (It.). 'Pleasure.' So *A bene placito*, 'at [one's] good pleasure'—same as *Ad libitum* (q.v.).

PLAGAL. See *Modes* 5, 6, 7; *Cadence*.

PLAGIARISM in music. See *Composition* 12; *Melody* 7.

PLAIDY, LOUIS (1810–74). Able and devoted Leipzig piano teacher and compiler of famous book of technical studies. See *Pianoforte Playing* 7; *Fingering* 5 c.

PLAINCHANT. Same as *Plainsong* (q.v.).

PLAINSONG

(For some pictorial illustrations see p. 816, pl. 139.)

1. Definition. The word is applied to the large body of traditional ritual melody of the Western Christian Church. It is a translation of *Cantus planus*—in contradistinction to *Cantus figuratus* (florid song, implying a counterpoint added to the traditional melody) or *Cantus mensuratus* (measured song, implying the regularity of rhythm associated with harmonic music). The term 'Plain' then may be taken in the literal sense of unadorned, and as obviously dating from the period when harmonic accompaniment to the church's ritual music was beginning (see article *Harmony*) so that a distinction had become necessary. *Plainchant* and *Gregorian Chant* (see 3) are common synonyms, the latter for a reason that will become evident later in this article. The Eastern (or 'Greek') branch of the Christian Church (see *Greek Church*) and the Jewish Church (see *Jewish Music* 3) have similar bodies of melodic ritual song, but the term *Plainsong*, as ordinarily used, does not include them.

2. Nature of Plainsong. The simpler plainsong springs, one may suppose, from the natural tendency of a reader or speaker (especially in a large building) to utter his words on one note, with some dropping of the voice at the ends of sentences or verses (cf. 'Hwyl', under *Wales* 3). Plainsong rhythm is the free rhythm of speech, i.e. the beats fall irregularly, not as in poetry; it is a prose rhythm, which of course arises from the unmetrical character of the words to be recited—psalms, prayers, and the like.

In character, plainsong falls into two essentially distinct groups—the responsorial (developed from recitation of psalms round a 'dominant'), and antiphonal (developed as pure melody).

The character of the psalmodic plainsong is best seen in the familiar simple psalm tone. Usually there will be found an opening note or two ('intonation'), leading to a monotone ('reciting note'), which is retained for some time and then merges into a cadence (here called 'mediation'); the monotone is then resumed and another cadence (called the 'ending') closes the verse. The intonation is, in the Psalms, used for the first verse only. The 'reciting note' is always the dominant of the mode (see *Modes*).

Tone 1, ending D.

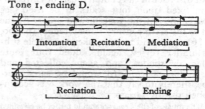

To readers more familiar with Anglican chanting than with plainsong, it will occur that this is the general scheme of that also, a scheme in which, however, the opening intonation has disappeared, whilst, of course, the introduction of harmony, and a more rigid framework, disguise the origin (see *Anglican Chant*). It will be realized that the frequent parallelisms in Hebrew poetry led naturally to this binary form of melody.

Many pieces of psalmodic plainsong that are not marked by the comparative simplicity just described will be found on examination to circle round or touch frequently upon one special note (clearly the original reciting note), and then to drop to a cadence in some sort of a florid figure. Such a figure is called a 'melisma'; this word is used for any decorative passage in which the music is spun out with more than one note to a syllable (see *Ornaments* 1). For the ancient scales represented by plainsong and for the influence of the reciting note in creating the idea of a scale 'dominant' see the article *Modes*. Each mode naturally developed its own type of cadence and melisma.

The repertory of plainsong is very large. The round of daily services includes:

(a) First and foremost, the florid and beautiful chants of the Proper of the Mass (see *Mass* 2)—Introit, Gradual, Alleluia, Tract, Offertory, and Communion.[1]

(b) The settings of the Ordinary of the Mass (q.v.), most of which is posterior to the activities of Charlemagne.

(c) The Antiphons for the Psalms and Canticles, also the Responds, of the Breviary.

(d) The hymns from the same book.

(e) The eight 'tones' or chants, with their variable endings, to which the Psalms and Canticles themselves are sung.

(f) The traditional 'reading-tones' of the Accentus (q.v.), e.g. the Preface tone.

(g) Sundry items to complete what is needed, e.g. the chant of the *Te Deum*.

The traditional notation of plainsong still in use (see *Notation* 2) employs a stave of only four lines, instead of five.

For an allusion to form in plainsong see *Form* 14.

3. History of Plainsong. The history of plainsong is of the highest interest. It grew up during the first centuries of Christianity, influenced possibly by the music of the Jewish synagogue and certainly by the Greek modal system (see *Modes*). At the end of the fourth century Ambrose, Bishop of Milan, finding a great disorder in the church music of Christendom, fixed upon four scales to be used (see *Modes*) and set the repertory in order. At the end of the sixth century Pope Gregory (p. 960, pl. **161**. 1) is said to have taken the whole subject under review again, added four more scales, or modes, and again collected and recast the repertory (it would be safer, perhaps, merely to say that the work was accomplished during Gregory's papacy).[2]

[1] The music of the *Sequence* should rather be classified with (d) the hymns.

[2] As to the codification attributed to Saints Ambrose and Gregory, see footnote to *Modes* 2.

One difference between Ambrosian Chant and Gregorian Chant is that the Gregorian has developed a more consistent use of the principle of a dominant or reciting note; in the Ambrosian psalm system there was some variety as to the note used in this capacity; further, the Ambrosian chants had no mediation and the Gregorian had this. Altogether, then, the latter system was more definite, and its greater number of modes made it more varied.

In the late eighth century and early ninth century the influence of Charlemagne was powerful. He invited singers from Rome to his court at Aix-la-Chapelle (Aachen), founded a school of song, and personally supervised the work of this. It is said that one of the monks sent to him at his request from Rome fell ill in crossing the Alps and, resting at the monastery of St. Gall, in Switzerland, was allowed by Charlemagne to remain. At all events that monastery became a great centre for the cultivation and dissemination of ecclesiastical song. The earliest manuscripts date from this period, and so do the earliest theoretical treatises.

The introduction (we might almost say the 'invention') of composition (see *Harmony* 4), which at first meant the provision of accompanying contrapuntal parts for a plainsong tenor part, or Canto Fermo (see references under *Canto Fermo*), accustomed singers to a more rigid performance, for when a number of singers are to be kept together in a combination of melodic parts freedom of rhythm is practically impossible. A period of some decline may, then, be said to date from about the year 1000; other adverse influences operated, and a low point as to authenticity of text and artistry of performance was reached in the sixteenth, seventeenth, and eighteenth centuries.

A reform was attempted at the end of the sixteenth century, but the results were disastrous. Palestrina was charged with the work of revising the plainsong of the Gradual, Antiphonal, and Psalter, but died almost immediately after accepting the commission. His son professed to have the manuscript of the revision, but it was seen to be a forgery; a lawsuit followed, and in the end the manuscript found its way to the pawnshop. Felice Anerio and Soriano then undertook the work, and their edition was published by the Medicean Press in two volumes in 1614–15. This Medicean Edition, as it is called, with its addition and suppression of melismata, its altered melodies, and its new ones, became the basis for many cheaper performing editions.

In the eighteenth century there was a craze for introducing grace notes and passing notes into the plainsong (called in France *Machicotage*, q.v.). In the nineteenth there was another cry for reform and the famous Ratisbon (Regensburg) editions appeared—unfortunately based on the Medicean Edition (see *Cecilian Movement*). Years of controversy followed, for the Benedictine monks of Solesmes (p. 816, pl. **139**. 3), in France, had long been at work in the most scientific spirit, photographing innumerable manuscripts in all the libraries of Europe, collating them, and setting the text by the almost mathematical principle of 'what the greatest number of manuscripts say must be the correct reading'. As an example of their resources and their method they published one piece of plainsong in 200 versions from different periods and different parts of Europe. They had been greatly helped by the discovery, in 1847, of the Montpellier book, with the plainsong in two notations, throwing light on certain problems of deciphering, and, in 1848, of a St. Gall manuscript that is probably the earliest existing. After about half a century of investigation they published their *Gradual* in 1883 and their *Antiphonal* in 1891. Their enormous series of volumes of facsimiles, etc. (*Paléographie musicale*) began to appear in 1889. It was interrupted 1940–50 and then publication was resumed. The Ratisbon edition had had papal privileges conferred upon it, but in 1903 these expired and in the same year Pius X was chosen Pope and he at once issued his famous *Motu Proprio* on church music, laying down, amongst other things, the importance of plainsong and the necessity of taking it from early and pure sources.

Amongst the reforms of the Solesmes monks (who, temporarily driven from France by anti-clerical legislation in 1901, carried on their work until 1922 in the Isle of Wight) was the introduction of a better manner of performance, lighter and more rhythmic—for plainsong is essentially rhythmic, though the basis of its rhythm is that of speech, not of metrical song.

4. Plainsong in England. The introduction of the authorized plainsong into England took place in the time of that very Pope Gregory whose name is connected with it in the word 'Gregorian' and whose supposed reorganization of the plainsong system has been previously mentioned. Augustine, whom he sent to convert King Ethelbert and his subjects (A.D. 597), approached the king in the Isle of Thanet singing a certain piece of plainsong. St. Gregory was the first of fifty Benedictines who have occupied the papal throne, and Augustine was the first of the many Benedictine Archbishops of Canterbury. In 1897, English Benedictine monks commemorated the thirteen hundredth anniversary of Augustine's arrival by singing in the same spot the same words to the same music, *Deprecamur te, Domine*.

Canterbury, the court of Ethelbert and the see of Augustine, quickly became a centre for the study of the Gregorian plainsong; to it monks from many other abbeys flocked to learn. The Abbey of Wearmouth in County Durham was another great centre; Benedict Biscop (*c.* 628–90), its founder and a great traveller, brought with him, from one of his visits to Rome, John, Archcantor of St. Peter's, whose teaching became very influential.

At the time of the Norman Conquest attempts were made to introduce the French manner of singing. In the Anglo-Saxon Chronicle (the Peterborough–Canterbury or 'E' MS., which is very outspoken about Norman misdeeds) it is stated that in 1083 Abbot Thurston of Glastonbury stationed Norman archers in the clerestory and when rebellious monks persisted in singing in the way by them regarded as native and authentic, they were shot as they sang the holy office.

The English Reformation of the sixteenth century greatly reduced the musical interest of the plainsong used in the churches, as it was a point with Cranmer and his party to abolish ornament and to establish as far as possible a note-for-syllable principle, in order to achieve the ideal that the words of the service, now in the native tongue, might be fully and easily 'understanded of the people'. In 1550 Merbecke (q.v.) set the new English Prayer Book (*The Boke of Common Praier Noted*). Tallis (q.v.) and others provided harmonized versions of the simpler elements of this, leaving Merbecke's *canto fermo* in the tenor, with the result that Tallis's added treble part is now taken by many people to be the proper plainsong (see *Responses*).

The growth of Anglican chant out of plainsong has already been mentioned (2).

Beyond the Versicles and Responses of the Prayer Book little plainsong was heard in the Anglican Church between the Reformation and the Oxford Movement of the nineteenth century, but since the beginning of that movement it has gradually gained large ground. In addition to its use for the Psalms and in the liturgy generally it has found its way, in the shape of the later metrical melodies, into many hymn books (see *Hymns and Hymn Tunes* 2), and this has accustomed the ears of congregations to its modal and rhythmic characteristics, and prepared the way for its larger adoption, which has been fairly widespread.

In America numerous Roman Catholic churches have made plainsong familiar to a large public; from about 1925 it has seemed that the interest in it was greatly widening.

Research in plainsong has been stimulated and guided in Britain by the Plainsong and Mediaeval Music Society (founded in 1888), who have published facsimiles of the Sarum Gradual and Antiphonal and performing editions of the Ordinary and Proper of the Mass to English words, as also by the lifelong study and the publications of the Revd. George Herbert Palmer, D.Mus. (1846–1926), Editor of the Sarum Psalter, and the Right Revd. Walter Howard Frere (1863–1938), Editor with H. B. Briggs of the *Manual of Plainsong*. The Revd. Francis Burgess (1879–1948), and Dr. John H. Arnold have had great influence on the British Plainsong Movement.

5. Accompaniment of Plainsong. Plainsong is complete in itself; it is pure melody and needs no instrumental accompaniment, for it belongs to a pre-harmonic age. It is true that in large churches in early days it sometimes had organ accompaniment, but this was merely a unison doubling, thumped out by the player's fists on the broad keys of the simple organs of the day as a means of keeping the singers together. It is now customary, however, both for the assistance of the performers and the satisfaction of the hearers, to support it with a background of organ harmonies. If simple concords are used (in root position and first inversion), the modal style of harmonization observed, and a chord-to-a-note method largely avoided in favour of a less laboured manner, in which chords are set only at the rhythmic points, and if only the lighter 8-foot stops are called upon (rarely 16-foot, even on the pedals), then the accompaniment is unobtrusive and is felt by most people to be in keeping. Nevertheless, it is, properly, an anachronism.

For *Parisian Tones* see entry under that head.

PLAINSONG AND MEDIAEVAL MUSIC SOCIETY. See *Plainsong* 4.

PLAISANT (Fr.). 'Merry.'

PLANCHETTE RONFLANTE. See *Thunder Stick.*

PLANQUETTE, ROBERT. Born in Paris in 1848 and died there in 1903, aged fifty-four. He was a student of the Paris Conservatory who made a reputation as the composer of gay songs for café concerts and from thence graduated to the writing of operettas, which won wide popularity up and down the world. The best known of these is *The Bells of Corneville* ('Les Cloches de Corneville'), sometimes known in the United States as *The Chimes of Normandy* or *The Bells of Normandy.*

PLAQUÉ (Fr.). A keyboard and bowed instrument term applied to chord playing, meaning to play all the notes simultaneously, avoiding 'spreading'. (The reverse of this meaning is sometimes given; it has, however, been carefully checked in reliable French works and may be accepted as accurate.)

PLATEAU, PLATEAUX (Fr.). 'Plate', 'plates' (of cymbals).

PLATO. See *Education and Music* 1; *Appreciation.*

PLAUDERND (Ger.). 'Chattering', 'babbling'.

PLAYERA (Sp.). A Gipsy Seguidilla (q.v.), sung and danced. Another name is *Seguidillas gitanas.*

PLAYER-PIANO. See *Mechanical Reproduction* 13.

PLAYFORD (Father and Son). They were the great London publishers of music in the second half of the seventeenth century.

(1) JOHN I (p. 849, pl. **144**. 3). Born in 1623 and died in 1686 or 1687, aged about sixty-four.

See *Publishing* 5; note also information under *Profession* 9; *Dance* 7, 10; *Country Dance*; *Scotland* 1; *Parish Clerk*; *Hymns and Hymn Tunes* 5, 11, 17 e xviii, f ii, iii; *Puritans* 6; *Anglican Chant* 4; *Reports*; *Round*; *Descant*; *Monk's March*; *Cold and Raw Cittern*; *Lancashire Sol-fa.*

(2) HENRY. Born in 1657 and died in 1706 or (as some say) 1710, in his later forties or early fifties. He was son of John I, and actively carried on his father's business.

See references under *Clubs*; *Publishing* 5.

(3) JOHN II. Born in 1655 and died in 1685, aged twenty-nine or thirty. He was a nephew of John I and was a printer employed by his cousin Henry on the production of all his musical publications.

PLAY OF ROBIN AND MARION. See *Adam de la Halle.*

PLECTRUM. The small piece of wood, metal, ivory, or other material, used to actuate the strings of the mandoline, zither, and one or two other instruments. The quills of the harpsichord are, of course, plectra.

PLÉIADE. See *Concert* 2.

PLEIN, PLEINE (Fr.; masc., fem.). 'Full.'

PLEIN JEU (Fr.). 'Full play', i.e. the whole power of the organ (or harmonium). But see *Organ* 15.

PLENO (It.). 'Full.'

PLEYEL, IGNAZ JOSEPH (p. 397, pl. **68**. 4). Born near Vienna in 1757 and died in Paris in 1831, aged seventy-four. He was a favourite pupil of Haydn who settled in Strasbourg as choirmaster of the Cathedral, but, as German-born, was compelled by considerations of prudence to slip away from there when, in the third year of the Revolution, France had her back to the wall against foreign opposition. When things were quieter he settled in Paris as a music publisher and (later) piano-maker.

He wrote an immense quantity of instrumental music of every kind, some of it (the earlier compositions) greatly admired by Haydn and Mozart. His sixty-four string quartets are not yet all dead, though they are played chiefly by amateurs for the sake of pleasant practice; for the most part, however, Pleyel, as composer, is today known to violin pupils, and to them through his fresh-sounding easy compositions for two violins.

His son CAMILLE, who took on his business, was also a composer. Camille's wife, MADAME PLEYEL (Marie Moke, or Mooke) had a European reputation as a piano virtuoso (see *Berlioz*).

See *Pianoforte* 8, 18; *Concerto* 6 b (1757); *Chamber Music* 6, Period III (1757); *Harpsichord Family* 5; *Harp* 1 (the Pleyel form).

PLINY (THE YOUNGER). See *Church Music* 4.

PLÖTZLICH (Ger.). 'Suddenly.'

PLUGGING. A twentieth-century term, presumably derived from the nineteenth-century slang expression, 'plugging away' for 'persisting perseveringly'. It is applied to the practice of so incessantly introducing an attractive melody (generally a song), by radio, cinema, etc., as to make it universally known, thus widely sold, and hence commercially profitable.

PLUIE DE PERLES. See *Osborne, G. A.*

PLUS (Fr.). 'More.'

PNEUMA. Literally 'breath' or a 'breathing' (Greek). The term is applied to the florid

1. GREGORY THE GREAT, with his Father and Mother
From a 7th-century fresco. See *Plainsong* 3

2. CHOIR OF CATHEDRAL OF CONSTANCE, 1513
The Capellmeister's baton will be noticed, as also the wearing of hats in church (Town Library, Lucerne)

3. THE BENEDICTINE ABBEY OF SOLESMES. See *Plainsong* 3

4. DOM POTHIER (d. 1923)—guiding spirit in the Solesmes researches. See *Pothier*

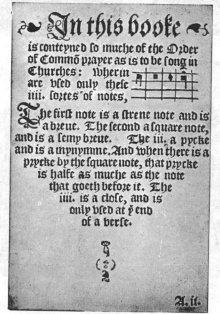

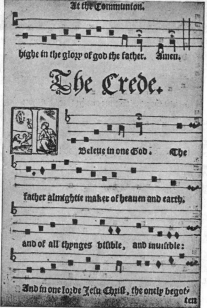

5, 6. MERBECKE'S *Booke of Common Prayer Noted*, 1550. See *Merbecke*

1. THE 'OWN HANDE' OF DOWLAND (1562–1626)

2. JOHN WILSON (1595–1674)

3. HENRY LAWES (1596–1662)

4. HENRY CAREY (*c.* 1688–1743)

5. CHARLES DIBDIN (1745–1814)

6. WILLIAM SHIELD (1748–1829)

7. J. L. HATTON (1809–86)

8. HENRY RUSSELL (1812–1900)

passages sung to a single vowel at the end of certain pieces of plainsong. The last vowel of 'Alleluia' in the traditional plainsong setting of this word is an example. Such final vocalizes were also known as *Jubili*, indicating their intention as expressions of pious joy.

et ge - ne - ra - ti - o - nem

PNEUMATICS APPLIED TO MUSIC. See *Mechanical Reproduction of Music* 1, 13; *Organ* 8.

POCHETTE (Fr.). See *Kit*.

POCHETTO, POCHETTINO (It.). 'Very little', 'very little indeed' (cf. *Poco*).

POCHISSIMO (It.). Diminutive of *Poco*, 'little' i.e. 'the least possible'.

POCKRICH, RICHARD. See *Harmonica* 1.

POCO (It.). 'A little', i.e. rather, e.g. *Poco lento*, 'rather slow'. *Poco a poco* means 'little by little', e.g. *Poco a poco animando*, 'becoming lively by degrees' (cf. *Pochetto, Pochissimo*).

POÈME SYMPHONIQUE (Fr.), **POEMA SINFONICO** (It.). Symphonic poem (q.v.).

POETRY IN SONG. See *Song* 3, 8.

POGGIATO (It.). 'Dwelt upon', 'leant upon'.

POI (It.). 'Then', e.g. (after some direction for the repetition of a passage) *Poi la Coda*, 'then the Coda'.

POIDS (Fr.). 'Weight.'

POIKILORGUE. See *Reed-Organ Family* 6.

POINT (of bow of violin, etc.). The end opposite to that at which it is held. Cf. *Heel*.

POINT D'ORGUE. This French term has several related meanings:

(1) Simply the **Pause Sign** ⌢.

(2) A harmonic **Pedal**, i.e. a passage in which one bass note continues whilst varied upper parts are executed over it (see *Harmony* 24 p; *Form* 12 d). The origin of the expression is probably to be found in the use of the sign over a note in the pedal part of an organ concerto at a place where the organist was expected to extemporize a passage over that note held down.

(3) A **Cadenza** in a concerto, probably so called because the sign that such an excursion on the part of the solo instrument is expected is the printing of a pause over the parts for the other instruments—as in (2). When in a French publisher's catalogue we see the term it means

a Cadenza, e.g. 'Points d'orgue pour le Concerto en mi bémol de Mozart, par C. Saint-Saëns' (Cadenzas for Mozart's E flat Concerto, by C. Saint-Saëns).

See *Cadenza*.

POINTÉ (Fr.). 'Pointed', 'detached'.

POINTE (Fr.). 'Point', as *Pointe d'archet*, 'point of the bow'.

POINTING. See *Anglican Chant* 6.

POIRIER (Vocalist). See *Ca Ira!*

POLACCA. See *Polonaise*.

POLAK, JACOB. See *Poland*.

POLAND. Very little is known of the music of Poland in its pre-Christian era (i.e. before the tenth century). With Christianity (of the Roman branch) came its traditional plainsong. From the eleventh century some amount of vernacular religious song came into existence.

A type of minstrel became common during the fifteenth century, called the 'rybalt'; he concerned himself largely with sacred song and with the popular plays and ceremonies of the festival seasons: after rather more than two centuries of useful activity in spreading a love and knowledge of the national repertory of song he fell into disrepute (as did his equivalent in other countries), became a mere class of vagabond, and disappeared.

In the sixteenth century the polyphonic music of the Church reached a high state of cultivation in Poland, as elsewhere; there was some importation of Italian and other foreign musicians for the royal chapel. In 1543 a school of song was founded by Sigismund I at Cracow (then the capital), and it continued until near the end of the eighteenth century, serving as a centre for the study and practice of church music ('College of the Roratistes'—from 'Rorates', the name of the daily service). In the following century many similar establishments were founded by various ecclesiastical personages, for the improvement of church music in their regions.

The great composer of the period was **Nicolaj Gomólka** (c. 1539–1609), who, in his polyphony, abandoned all merely scholastic complications and attained a more direct effectiveness than had previously been common. His works are still performed and highly valued.

The Lutheran reform had a good deal of influence in Poland and a number of books of metrical psalms and of hymns, with tunes, appeared towards the end of the sixteenth century. As originally in France, the cultivation of metrical vernacular psalmody was not confined to the Protestant part of the community. Gomólka, attached to the royal chapel, published a famous collection of psalm tunes.

Another important composer of church music of this period was **Nicolaj Zielenski** (c. 1550–c. 1615), who was attached in some way to St. Mark's, Venice, and in that city published, in 1611, a collection of about 120 of his works, largely for double choir, with two organs and groups of instrumentalists, in the St. Mark's style; the collection also including coloratura vocal duets, etc., and some instrumental music.

A Polish lutenist of international reputation was the one known as **Jacob Polak**, Jacob le Polonais or Jacob de Reys (c. 1545–1605), who spent all the latter part of his life in Paris. He composed much music for his instrument.

When the introduction of opera took place in Italy (see *Opera* 1, 2) Poland did not long lag behind. A royal opera-house was inaugurated at Warsaw by Ladislas IV (reigned 1632–48). The works performed were almost exclusively Italian (opening with Caccini) and they were sung in the Italian language. Some of the rich nobles emulated this example, but the invasions of the Swedes, the risings amongst the Cossacks, and the other troubles that overtook a country whose lot has never been one of peace, brought them to an end after a few years. Despite these troubles music other than that requiring the initiative and support of a wealthy aristocracy continued to flourish. Church music went on and a number of theoretical treatises appeared, the first in the Polish language (earlier treatises having been in Latin) being the *Tablatura* of **Alexander Gorczyn** (Cracow, 1647).

It is clear that Polish music had some international vogue during the early eighteenth century, since Bach, in a letter to the council of Leipzig, mentions that his choir was accustomed to perform it (he mentions also, in this connexion, the music of Italy, France, and England).

The leading composer of the eighteenth and early nineteenth century was **Joseph Kozlowski** (1757–1831). His production was considerable—a great deal of theatre music, cantatas, choruses, songs, and hundreds of polonaises (some of high popularity; one was, strangely, used for a time as the Russian national anthem and is alluded to in Tchaikovsky's opera *The Queen of Spades*), etc. For a great part of his life he was attached to the Russian court, for which most of his music was written. He wrote some ecclesiastical music, however, not for the church of the country of his adoption (i.e. not for the Greek rite) but for that of his native country (i.e. for the Roman rite), amongst it being a Requiem Mass in E flat minor (commissioned by the king, Stanislas Augustus, shortly before his death in 1798), which remains famous.

The monarch just mentioned erected a public opera-house in Warsaw. As in Russia so in Poland, the musicians employed to direct and compose for this house were often Italians. The first native opera composer of Poland (i.e. composing operas in the Polish language) was **Matthew Kamienski** (1734–1821); some of his works enjoyed high favour. **Joseph Elsner** (1769–1854; Chopin's teacher) was for a time in charge of the opera-house, for which he composed a variety of operas of varying types,

as well as composing chamber music, symphonies, songs, church music, etc., and a celebrated setting of the Passion. He was the first director of the first Conservatory of Warsaw, which, however, owing to the political troubles of the period, remained in existence only from 1821 to 1830.

Charles Kurpinski (1785–1857) was a popular composer of operas, church music, polonaises, etc., a theoretician, and an active teacher.

Ignacy F. Dobrzynski (1807–67), Chopin's friend and fellow pupil under Elsner, was a fine pianist, an outstanding orchestral conductor, and an active composer, especially of instrumental works.

For **Chopin** himself, as well as for **Moniuszko** and other Polish composers, see the separate articles mentioned in the list below.

With the beginning of the twentieth century an increased activity in composition became manifest and a society called 'Young Musical Poland' was in 1905 formed to foster modernistic and nationalistic tendencies. The acknowledged leader in this new school was **Szymanowski** (p. 209, pl. **41. 4**).

During the late nineteenth and the twentieth centuries the Polish race has produced a large number of fine interpretative artists—singers, pianists, violinists, etc., of international fame.

Certain of the dance styles of Poland have strongly impressed themselves upon the universal musical consciousness. Particulars of these should be sought under *Polonaise, Mazurka, Cracovienne, Kouiawiak, Obertass, Kolomyika, Drabant*. For a reference to one of the frequent accompaniments of the dances see *Bagpipe Family* 7.

A circumstance that can hardly escape mention in such an article as this is that when, after the successive partitions of Poland in 1772, 1793, and 1795, and the dishonouring arrangements of the Congress of Vienna in 1815, Poland at last regained her individuality and independence, it was a musician, Paderewski (p. 801, pl. **138.** 1), who became her first prime minister (January to December 1919).

After the second World War Poland disappeared for some ten years behind the Iron Curtain. Political changes in 1956 relaxed the controls on musical activity, and composers rapidly put themselves in touch with Western musical developments. Prominent names of this period include **Witold Lutosławski** (born 1913; q.v.), **Kazimierz Serocki** (born 1922), **Włodzimierz Kotonski** (born 1925), **Tadeusz Baird** (born 1928), **K. Penderecki** (born 1933), and **Henryk Gorecki** (born 1933). The 'Warsaw Autumn' is among the most comprehensive and tolerant of international festivals.

POLISH MUSICIANS WHO RECEIVE SEPARATE ATTENTION IN THIS VOLUME—arranged according to century of birth.
18th CENTURY: Janiewiecz.
19th CENTURY: Badarzewska, Chopin, Godowsky, de Kontski, Landowska, Leschetizky, Moniuszko, Nicodé, Noskowsky, Paderewski, Różycki, Statkowsky, Szymanowski, Tansman, Wieniawski.
20th CENTURY: Kletzki, Leibowitz, Lutosławski.
See also *Dictionaries* 4 i.

POLAROLI. See Pollaroli.

POLDOWSKI. Pen-name of Lady Dean Paul, whose maiden name was Irene Regine Wieniawska (daughter of Henri Wieniawski, q.v.). Born Brussels 1880; died London 1932. She composed, especially, graceful songs, appearing as her own interpreter, as singer and accompanist.

POLE, WILLIAM. Born in Birmingham in 1814 and died in London in 1900, aged eighty-six. He was for seventeen years Professor of Civil Engineering at University College, London, for thirty organist of a London church (D.Mus., Oxon.), and for eleven years one of the examiners for musical degrees at London University. He was a distinguished scientist (F.R.S.) and, amongst other things, wrote a work on *The Philosophy of Music* (1879 and 1924) which is still valuable and valued.

See references under *Temperament* 10; *Modes* 10.

POLKA (p. 273, pl. **49.** 6). A Bohemian dance which originated early in the nineteenth century and in its forties spread over Europe like an epidemic, so that streets and public-houses (saloons) were named after it. *Punch* (October 1844) says 'Can you dance the Polka?—Do you like the Polka?—Do you know the new Polka? —Polka—Polka—Polka—Polka—it is enough to drive me mad!'

The dance is a round one, and the time is a pretty quick two-in-a-measure. There are steps on the first three half-beats and a sort of rest on the fourth. The music has some resemblance to that of the Schottische (there is no relationship between Polka and Polacca: see *Polonaise*).

The great national Bohemian composer, Smetana (q.v.), composed some polkas; there is one in his opera, *The Bartered Bride*. He has also an orchestral specimen, one in his string quartet, *From My Life*, and a good many for piano. The pretty story sometimes seen as to the polka being the invention of a Bohemian peasant girl is itself an invention.

There was a particular kind of polka introduced in Paris in the eighteen-forties, called **Polka tremblante, or Schottische bohème.**

For Polka-Mazurka see under *Mazurka*; for German Polka see *Schottische*.

POLLAROLI (Polaroli, Pollarolo), CARLO FRANCESCO (1653–1732). Composer of church music, instrumental music, and operas. See *Sonata* 5.

POLLY. See *Beggar's Opera*.

POLNISCH (Ger.). 'Polish.' For *Polnischer Bock* see *Bagpipe Family* 7.

POLO. A type of Spanish folk song in three-in-a-measure with syncopation. Bizet has used one in the prelude to the fourth act of *Carmen*. Or a sort of seguidilla (q.v.).

POLONAISE (in German *Polonäse* and in Italian *Polacca*). One of the national dances of Poland, which in the hands of Chopin was made to express patriotism and chivalry and became a sort of pageantry in tone. It is in a moderate three-in-a-measure time and is perhaps rather to be described as a procession than as a dance proper. Mr. C. Egerton Lowe stated that in his student period at Leipzig, in the late 1870s, all balls opened with a Polonaise, which was purely processional. Partners were chosen and then a promenade was made concluding with a Waltz. Niecks in his *Chopin* (ii, 240), says, 'Strictly speaking, the Polonaise, which has been called a *marche dansante*, is not so much a dance as a figured walk, or procession, full of gravity and a certain courtly etiquette'.

Certain rhythms are characteristic and often occur, such as the frequent division of the first beat of the measure with an accentuation of its second half, the division of this second half in the accompaniment into halves again, the ending of the phrases on the third beat of the measure, and so on.

The legend sometimes quoted to the effect that the polonaise originated out of a processional ceremony in connexion with the accession of Henry III of Anjou to the throne of Poland (1573) is of doubtful authenticity. It may, however, have happened that one of the existing national peasant processional dances (Polski) was adapted and elaborated or turned to ceremonial use for this occasion; processional folk dances are not uncommon in Europe (cf. *Farandole*). What is probably true is that the French word 'Polonaise' originated on this occasion.

During the eighteenth century the polonaise, in an earlier type, began to appear as an occasional member of the suite. Bach so uses it on two or three occasions, and his eldest son, Friedemann, wrote, as independent pieces, a number of rhythmically intricate polonaises that had great popularity in northern Germany and are still published.

It has been noted, however, that to Bach, Telemann, and their contemporaries the words 'polonaise' and 'polacca' do not seem to imply a specifically Polish character but are rather 'collective names for all kinds of East European folk music'. Handel, Mozart, Beethoven, Schubert, Weber, and Wagner have also written polonaises (Wagner's is a very bad one for piano duet), and of course many Polish composers have done this, as have many Russian composers also. With Chopin (who wrote thirteen examples) the form was an outlet for the pent-up national feeling of an exile from an oppressed fatherland. Schumann as a youth wrote a number of polonaises (rediscovered 1928). Mozart in his Sonata 6 (in D) has a 'Rondeau en Polonaise'.

The Cracovienne (q.v.) is in its figures and style (not its music) a sort of simpler polonaise.

See also *Fackeltanz*; *Poland*.

POLONÄSE. German for 'polonaise' (q.v.).

POLSKA. A Scandinavian dance in three-in-a-measure time. It is of Polish origin (hence its name), deriving from the mazurka and dating from the union of the crowns of Sweden and Poland in 1587.

POLSKI. 'Polonaise' (q.v.).

POLSTERTANZ (Ger.). 'Pillow Dance'; same as *Kissentanz* or *Cushion Dance* (q.v.).

POLYPHONY, POLYPHONIC. The words are applied to 'many-sound' or 'many-voice' music, i.e. to music in which instead of the parts marching in step with one another, and without particular interest in their individual melodic curves, they move in apparent independence and freedom though fitting together harmonically.

Frequently the terms are applied in a restricted way to the music of the great age of unaccompanied choral song, i.e. the age which rose to its climax with Palestrina, Byrd, Victoria, and their contemporaries at the end of the sixteenth century (see *Harmony* 8; *History of Music* 2, 4, 5).

'Counterpoint' (q.v.) has the same meaning but tends to an academic use, i.e. in connexion with study of the technique of polyphonic writing.

'Homophony', 'Homophonic' ('like-sounding') are the converse terms.

See also *Monophonic*.

POLYTONALITY. See *Harmony* 17.

POMMER. See *Oboe Family* 2.

POMO D'ORO, IL. See *Cesti*.

POMPEUX, POMPEUSE (Fr.,; masc., fem.). 'Pompous.'

POMPOSO (It.). 'Pompous.'

PONCE.

(1) JUAN. See *Folía*.

(2) MANUEL M. Born in Fresnillo, Mexico, in 1882 and died in 1948, aged sixty-five. He studied in Italy and Germany and then returned to win, in time, high regard as composer, as collector of Mexican folk song, and as orchestral conductor. His song *Estrellita* won universal popularity. He composed for Segovia (q.v.) a guitar concerto.

PONCHIELLI, AMILCARE. Born near Cremona in 1834 and died at Milan in 1886, aged fifty-one. His operas have had enormous success—especially *La Gioconda* (1876).

PONDEROSO, PONDOROSO (It.). 'Ponderous.'

PONIATOWSKI (PRINCE), JOSEPH MICHAEL XAVIER FRANCIS JOHN (known as 'Joseph'). Of Polish descent but born in Rome in 1816 and died at Chislehurst, Kent, England, in 1873, aged fifty-seven. He was grand-nephew of the last King of Poland and nephew of Napoleon's famous marshal. His father settled in Italy and he himself became Prince of Monte Rotondo. He attached himself warmly to the Emperor Napoleon III, whom he followed into exile, dying six months after his friend and at the same place.

Although an aristocrat by birth and a diplomat by profession, he practised music with assiduity, composing a dozen operas and some smaller things, of which latter one is still (or

used lately to be) frequently heard—*The Yeoman's Wedding Song*.

PONTE, LORENZO DA (1749–1838). See under *Opera* 21 f, 23; *Marriage of Figaro*; *Don Giovanni*; *Così fan tutte*.

PONTICELLO (It.). Literally, 'little bridge', i.e. the bridge of a stringed instrument. *Sul ponticello* ('on the bridge') means play with the bow as close to the bridge as possible—so greatly diminishing the intensity of the lower overtones (see *Acoustics* 7; *Timbre*) in favour of the higher.

PONTIFICAL. See *Liturgy*.

POOR MARY ANN. See *All through the Night*.

POOT, MARCEL. Born near Brussels in 1901. He was a pupil of Paul Gilson, won the Rubens prize, and was enabled to study in Paris under Dukas. He is a member of the group of seven Belgian modernists known as the Synthétistes (q.v.), editor of the *Revue Musicale Belge*, and music critic of *Le Peuple*. His compositions, which have received performance both in Britain and the United States, include operas, ballets, and a number of orchestral and chamber works. In 1949 he became Director of the Brussels Conservatory.

POPE, ALEXANDER (1688–1744). Poet. See reference under *Methodism and Music* 6.

POPE AND TURK TUNE. The tune of Luther (one of the few that can with confidence be assigned to him) to his own hymn for the young. This tune and a translation of the hymn appeared in a good many of the English psalters of the sixteenth and seventeenth centuries and were very well known. The hymn began:

Preserve us, Lord, by Thy dear Word;
From Turk and Pope defend us, Lord.

The tune is still in some British (and possibly American) hymn-books under the name of *Spires*.

POPOV, ALEXANDER. See *Broadcasting* 2.

POPOVICI, TIMOTEI. See *Rumania*.

POPPER, DAVID (p. 1088, pl. **179**. 5). Born at Prague in 1843 and died near Vienna in 1913, aged sixty-nine. He studied as cellist, under Goltermann, at the conservatory of his native place, and then travelled as a virtuoso, occupying for short periods various important posts, as, for instance, that of solo cellist to the court of Vienna. The pianist Sophie Menter was for fourteen years his wife and they travelled widely together. Latterly he was professor of cello at the Conservatory of Budapest. His compositions for his instrument have had great currency. (Cf. *Bohemia*.)

'POPS', 'POPULAR CONCERTS' IN LONDON. See *Concert* 7.

PORDON DANTZA (Basque). A dance of men with lances (so the German name, *Lanzentanz* or *Stabtanz*), formerly performed on the day of St. John of Tolosa in commemoration of a military victory. The accompaniment was by guitar or bandurría and also, often, by voice.

PORPORA, NICCOLO ANTONIO. Born at Naples in 1686 and died there in 1766, aged eighty. He was a great opera composer and still greater singing-master, many of the most celebrated singers of the eighteenth century being his pupils. Haydn profited by his instruction in Vienna, being engaged by him in youth as accompanist and valet. His vocal method is now lost, but as so many singing teachers advertise their full knowledge of the 'Old Italian Method' the vocal world can still roll on.

See *Singing* 5, 9; *Misattributed Compositions*.

PORT Á BEUL. A type of vocal performance used in the Highlands of Scotland when it is desired to dance and there is no instrumental performer. The words are often improvised and sometimes personal and humorous.

Cf. *Diddling*.

PORTAMENTO (It.). Literally, 'carrying'. (1) Applied to the voice or a bowed instrument, it means carrying on the tone from note to note without gaps (hence very legato and momentarily sounding pitches in between the two indicated by the notation: see Table 22); the same effect is possible on the trombone. (2) In connexion with the piano, *Portamento* means (curiously) a half-staccato.

For *Aria di Portamento* see *Aria*.

PORTANDO, PORTATO (It.). 'Carrying', 'carried'. The same (usually) as *Portamento* (q.v.).

PORTATIVE ORGAN. See *Organ* 8.

PORT DE VOIX (Fr., literally 'the carrying of the voice'). A vocal *portamento* (q.v.). One or two obsolete 'graces' also bore this name, either as it stands or with some added adjective.

PORTÉ, PORTÉE (Fr.). 'Carried.' Same as *Portamento* (q.v.). As a noun, however, *Portée* means 'stave', or 'staff'.

PORTER.

(1) WALTER. Died in 1659. He was a Gentleman of the Chapel Royal of James I and Charles I, who published (1632 and possibly 1639) what he called *Madrigals and Ayres*, but what, with their instrumental interpolations, no longer correspond to the old implications of the title. Later he published motets, etc. He is said to have been a pupil of Monteverdi (q.v.).

(2) QUINCY. Born at New Haven, Conn., in 1897 and died there in 1966, aged sixty-nine. He studied composition under Horatio Parker at Yale, under d'Indy in Paris, and then at Cleveland under Bloch. He was in 1928 awarded a Guggenheim Fellowship. He was Dean of New England Conservatory, Boston (1938), and Professor of Music at Yale (1947–65), and composed much chamber music, orchestral music, etc.

See *Concerto* 6 c (1897).

PORTER LA VOIX (Fr.). 'To carry the voice' i.e. to use the vocal *Portamento* (q.v.).

PORTEUS, BEILBY (1731–1808). Bishop of Chester (1770) and then of London (1787). See *Anglican Parish Church Music* 4, 5.

PORTUGAL. See *Harmony* 4; *Bagpipe* 7.

PORTUGUESE CHAPEL, LONDON. See *Roman Catholic Church Music in Britain*.

PORTUGUESE HYMN. See *Adeste Fideles*.

PORTUNAL, PORTUNALFLÖTE (Ger.). An organ stop of open wooden pipes wider at the top than the bottom. It has a smooth tone.

POS., in French organ music = *Positif*, i.e. 'choir organ'; in violin music, etc., it means *Posizione* (It.), *Position* (Fr.), i.e. 'position' (q.v.).

POSAUNE (Ger.). Trombone. See *Trombone Family*; *Organ* 14 VI.

POSEIDONIUS OF APAMEA. See *Wales* 1.

POSÉMENT (Fr.). 'Steadily', 'sedately'.

POSITIF (Fr.). Choir organ; see *Organ* 2 d.

POSITION. (1) The left hand in the playing of stringed instruments is moved from time to time so that its four fingers may fall on a different set of places on the fingerboard (q.v.) and so produce a different set of notes. Each of these locations is a 'position'—'First Position', 'Second Position', etc. 'Shift', means the same thing (It. *Manica*). But for 'Position naturelle' see *Pos. Nat.*

(2) For position in trombone playing see *Trombone Family* 1.

POSITIVE ORGAN. See *Organ* 8.

POSIZIONE (It.). 'Position' (q.v.).

POS. NAT. = *Position naturelle* (Fr.). Used in string parts to countermand (say) *Sur la touche*. See *Touche*.

POSSIBILE (It.). 'Possible.' Generally used in some such connexion as *Il più forte possibile*, 'as loud as possible'.

POSTHORN. A straight or oblong-coiled (on the continent of Europe, circular-coiled) brass instrument, with no valves or other means of producing any notes but those of the harmonic series (see *Acoustics* 8). Its name comes from its old-time use by the guards of the mail coaches to announce their arrival in the villages and towns on their routes. The cornet was developed from it (see *Cornet* 2). The once famous *Posthorn Galop* of Koenig was played on a straight instrument of this sort ('Koenig-Horn'). The larger varieties of the posthorn came to be known as the coach-horn, a later term which, though in general use, has not found its way into many dictionaries.

POSTLUDE. Converse of prelude (q.v.). Anything played as an afterpiece to anything else can be so called. Especially is the term used in organ music as an equivalent of 'concluding voluntary'.

POSTON, ELIZABETH. Born at Highfield, Herts., in 1905. She is the composer of many songs, of music for films, etc., and is a frequent broadcaster—as pianist or as speaker.

POT, CORNELIUS. See *Notation* 7.

POTHIER, DOM JOSEPH (see p. 816, pl. 139. 4). Born near Saint-Dié in 1835 and died at Conques in 1923. A Benedictine monk, he became a professor of theology at the monastery of Solesmes and the leader in the researches into Plainsong there carried out. (See *Plainsong*

3; *Notation* 2; *Machicotage*; *Spain* 2; *Roman Catholic*). Pope Pius X appointed him as chairman of the committee controlling the preparation and publication of the Vatican Edition of the church's liturgical chant. His own publications on and of Gregorian music are numerous and valuable.

POT-POURRI (Fr., literally 'rotten-pot'). From its original application to a jar in which are kept rose petals and spices the term has come to be applied to a composition that consists of a string of favourite tunes with the slightest connecting links and no development (see *Overture* 5). Thus one may have a pot-pourri 'on' some popular opera, etc. The term has been used in this way since the beginning of the eighteenth century.

POTTER, PHILIP CIPRIANI HAMBLY (generally known as 'Cipriani Potter'). Born in London in 1792 and died in 1871, aged nearly seventy-nine. He held a commanding position as pianist, composer, and principal of the Royal Academy of Music (1832–59). Beethoven respected him as a man and composer, and so did Wagner.

See *Conducting* 5 (end); *Elgar* (note).

POTTIER, EUGÈNE. See *Internationale*.

POUCE (Fr.). 'Thumb.'

POULENC, FRANCIS (p. 388, pl. **65**. 4). Born in Paris in 1899 and died there in 1963, aged sixty-four. He was a disciple of Satie and a friend of the poet Cocteau, and was a member of the group called 'The Six' so long as that group survived (see *France* 11). His principle was one of opposition to the 'romantic', and to avoid it he sometimes goes a long way round, arriving perhaps at romanticism in another form, as, for instance, in the influence of the bar and the circus. His compositions include ballets, orchestral works, chamber music, much piano music (he was himself a very capable pianist), songs and part-songs (some of them for children). There are also a 'comédie bouffe', *Le Gendarme incompris* (1920), an 'opéra burlesque', *Les Mamelles de Tirésias* (1947), a tragic opera, *Dialogues des Carmélites* (1957), and the one-act *La Voix humaine* (1958).

See *Ballet* 5; *Clarinet Family* 6; *Trumpet Family* 4; *Trombone Family* 4; *Harpsichord Family* 9; *Oboe* 6; *Concerto* 6 c (1899).

'POULE' SYMPHONY (Haydn). See *Nicknamed Compositions* 11.

POULSEN, VALDEMAR. See *Gramophone* 4.

POUR (Fr.). 'For.'

POUSHKIN. See *Russia* 4; *Salieri*; *Boris Godunof*; *Coq d'Or*.

POUSSÉ (Fr.). 'Pushed', i.e. 'up-bow' (as contrasted with *Tiré*, 'pulled', i.e. 'down-bow').

POWELL, JOHN. Born at Richmond, Virginia, in 1882 and died at Charlottesville, Virginia, in 1963, aged eighty. He made a mark as a concert pianist but produced certain compositions which smack invigoratingly of

the soil. Among them are a *Negro Rhapsody* for piano and orchestra, 1918 (see *United States* 8–end), *In Old Virginia*, *Natchez on the Hill*, a *Virginia Symphony*, chamber music, piano pieces, etc.

POWER, LIONEL. Died at Winchester in 1445. He was a famous composer of church music, a contemporary of Dunstable (q.v.), and he left an important theoretical work, a *Treatise on the Gamme* (reprinted by Hawkins in his *History of Music*).

PP, PPP, etc. Abbreviations for *Pianissimo*, i.e. very soft.

P.R. (in French organ music) = *Positif-Récit*, i.e. 'choir-swell' (swell to choir coupler).

PRÄCHTIG, PRACHTVOLL (Ger.). 'Grand', 'grandly', with high dignity, pompously.

PRÄCIS (Ger.). 'Precise' (in rhythm).

PRACTICE CLAVIER. See *Virgil Practice Clavier*.

PRAELUDIUM. Prelude. The use of the word in music dates back as far as the English Elizabethan virginal composers, who often use it for the opening movement of their rudimentary suites. It is sometimes used today as a title for a single and independent composition such as might, presumably, be played suitably at the opening of a programme.

PRAETORIUS (real name Schulz, Schultz, or Schultze). The larger books of reference give particulars of quite a number of sixteenth-and seventeenth-century German musicians using this latinized form of their name. In the present work the only one demanding notice is Michael Praetorius (1571–1621), author of *Syntagma musicum* (Wolfenbüttel, 3 vols., 1615–19), which valuably summarizes the musical knowledge of his period, and also a considerable composer.

See allusions under *Keyboard* 2; *Jew's Harp*; *Sonata* 10 a; *Organ* 10; *Harp*.

PRAGUE. See *Bohemia*; *Opera* 19; *Concert* 13; *Jewish* 5; *Dvořák*; *Hába*; *Jirák*; *Novák*; *Smetana*; *Schools of Music*.

'PRAGUE' SYMPHONY (Mozart). See *Nicknamed Compositions* 15.

PRALLTRILLER. See *Mordent*.

PRÄLUDIUM (Ger.). 'Prelude.'

PRATELLA, (FRANCESCO) BALILLA. Born in the Romagna in 1880 and died at Ravenna in 1955, aged seventy-five. He was a composer of operas, orchestral music, etc., and a musical writer and lecturer of futuristic views.

PRATT.

(1) SILAS GAMALIEL. Born at Addison, Vermont, in 1846 and died at Pittsburgh in 1916, aged seventy. He composed a number of operas, and a good deal of orchestral music, some of which enjoyed considerable temporary success. He deserves immortality, if only for the alleged conversation with Wagner, when Wagner said, 'You are the Richard Wagner of

the United States', and the polite rejoinder was made, 'And you, Sir, are the Silas G. Pratt of Germany'.

(2) WALDO SELDEN (1857–1939). See references under *United States* 4; *American Terminology* 1; *Dictionaries* 1.

PRAYER BOOK. See *Common Prayer*.

PRÉAMBULE. A term occasionally used as a substitute for 'Prelude'. See, for instance, Bach's use of it, mentioned under *Invention* and under *Suite* 4.

PRÉCÉDEMMENT (Fr.). 'Previously.'

PRECENTOR. The term (as old as the fourth century) means 'First Singer', and is attached to the official in charge of the song in a cathedral or monastic establishment or a church. In the English cathedrals the dignity of the precentor varies. For a discussion of this subject see *Cathedral Music* 2.

The cathedral precentor sits opposite the dean, whence the name for the two sides of the choir, Decani (i.e. 'of the Dean') and Cantoris (i.e. 'of the Precentor').

In the Presbyterian Churches of Scotland (see *Presbyterian Church Music*), which until the latter part of the nineteenth century had no organs, the precentor was formerly a very important official (see *Hymns and Hymn Tunes* 10). He was supplied with a pitch-pipe (see *Pitch* 6 a, *Hymns and Hymn Tunes* 10), and gave out and led the metrical psalm. Sometimes he was called the 'Uptaker of the Psalms'.

In the earlier settled parts of America the precentor has also had a place in the life of the religious community. As late as 1902 Professor Edward Dickinson, in his *Music in the History of the Western Church*, alludes to churches where the congregation 'led by a precentor with voice or cornet assumes the whole burden of song' (see *Hymns and Hymn Tunes* 11).

For the precentor in English nonconformity see *Hymns and Hymn Tunes* 8; *Methodism and Music* 4, 5, 8; *Baptist Churches and Music* 5.

PRECES (plural of *Prex*, 'prayer'). In liturgical worship these are short petitions uttered by the priest and responded to by the congregation (or by the choir representing the congregation). In the Church of England the prayers of this character that precede the Creed are called *Preces* and those that follow it *Versicles*; the plainsong settings of the Preces differ somewhat in different churches; Tallis's setting (see *Plainsong* 4; *Responses*) having never been uniformly followed.

PRECIPITATO, PRECIPITOSO, PRECIPITOSAMENTE, PRECIPITANDO, PRECIPITANDOSI, CON PRECIPITAZIONE, etc. (It.). 'With precipitation', i.e. impetuously.

PRÉCIPITÉ (Fr.). 'With precipitation', i.e. impetuously.

PRECISO, PRECISIONE (It.). 'Precise', 'precision' (in the sense of time).

PREFACE. The name for the Versicles and Responses which precede the *Sanctus* in the Roman Catholic Mass (q.v.). In the Anglican Communion Service 'Proper Prefaces' are sung by the celebrant only on special festivals. A traditional plainsong is, of course, in both cases, used.

PREGANDO (It.). 'Praying', i.e. in a devotional style.

PREGHIERA (It.). 'Prayer.'

PRELUDE. Any piece of music played as a preliminary to any other piece or before any play, ceremony, etc., can obviously be called a prelude (in Fr., *Prélude*).

The chief uses of the word can be exemplified from three composers as follows:

(1) **Bach.** Each fugue of the '48' is preceded by a prelude. Such preludes may be in differing forms and style, the only conditions to be met being that they shall be in the same key and form a suitable preparation of the listener's ear and mind for what is to follow. (For Bach's preludes to some of his suites see *Suite* 3, 4.)

(2) **Chopin.** He so denominated his set of twenty-four piano compositions, one in each major and minor key, of very diverse form and style. Apparently the idea was that they are the kind of thing that an able pianist would extemporize before a performance of a set programme or of a particular piece, a sort of 'trying the piano' (but the idea is rather far-fetched in view of the perfect finish and elaboration of some of the compositions). Many composers for piano have taken the title from Chopin (Scriabin, Rachmaninof, etc.).

(3) **Wagner.** He sometimes dispenses with the long, formal overture and replaces it with a shorter and less formal introductory orchestral piece. Thus *Lohengrin*, the four evenings of *The Ring* (and later acts thereof). He uses the word *Vorspiel* ('fore-play' or overture) for both the longer formal introductions and the shorter informal ones; in English translation the word 'prelude' is generally substituted for the shorter ones (occasionally for the longer ones too).

PRÉLUDER (Fr.). 'To prelude'; often also 'to tune up' or 'to play a few introductory chords in an extemporary manner'. So the present participle *Préludant*.

PRELUDIO (It.). Prelude (q.v.).

PREMIER, PREMIÈRE (Fr.; masc., fem.). 'First.' So *Première fois*, 'first time'.

PRENDRE (Fr.). 'To take.' *Prenez* is the imperative.

PREOBRAJENSKA (1871–1962). See *Ballet* 9.

PREPARATION of Discords. See *Harmony* 21, 24 k.

'PREPARED PIANO.' See *Cage, John*.

PRÈS (Fr.). 'Near', e.g. *Près de la touche*, 'near the finger-board'—of the violin, etc. (referring to manner of bowing).

PRÉS, JOSQUIN DES. See *Josquin des Prés*.

PRESANCTIFIED, MASS OF THE. See *Mass* 5.

PRESBYTERIAN CHURCH MUSIC

1. Introductory. The Presbyterian Church, in England and Scotland, taking its inspiration and ideas largely from the church of Calvin, adopted from the outset the Genevan ideals as to church organization and the conduct of the church service. Thus it rejected control of the church by bishops, substituting a more democratic system, and in worship it refused a place for whatever could be held to obscure the words, as elaborate choral music, or to constitute a distraction, as instrumental music, which latter was said to find no warrant in scripture except, under an older dispensation, in the one Temple at Jerusalem. The same ideas were accepted by the 'Reformed' Church in Germany but not by the Lutheran Church, which like the Anglican Church tried to salve from the older methods of worship all that was not, from the new doctrinal point of view, definitely objectionable.

Presbyterianism was, then, a more 'thorough' reform than Anglicanism and Lutheranism and a considerable degree of austerity marked the conduct of its services. There was amongst the Calvinists of Switzerland, France, and Germany, Holland, England, and Scotland no objection to the delights of music in the home, but (except in a very simple form) it was looked upon as out of place in the Church. The position is exemplified very typically in Bach's experience when in charge of the music at the court of Coethen from 1717 to 1723; this was, ecclesiastically, a Calvinistic or 'Reformed' state, and (a century and a half after Calvin's death) it had, like parts of Switzerland, progressed so far as to use the organ to accompany congregational singing, but that was the limit to which the musical adornments of the worship extended. Bach's court activities, then, lay otherwhere than in the court chapel. For the court concerts of the very musical monarch he composed abundantly, and Schweitzer's opinion is that 'The six years that Bach passed in this small capital were the pleasantest in his career'. The point that the Calvinistic form of Protestantism was in no way opposed to music as such is worth making here, as the attitude to music of the Presbyterians in Scotland and England has, in this matter, often been seriously misrepresented.

2. The Exile and Return of the Organ. The organ, which had been in use in the larger churches in Roman Catholic Scotland did not reappear in Presbyterian Scotland until the nineteenth century—in church that is; it existed in concert-halls from the mid-eighteenth century, and possibly in private houses continuously from the period of the Reformation, when churches are known to have sought private buyers for their organs. It was, indeed, not until near the end of the nineteenth century that organs became common in the Presbyterian churches of Scotland, and when they did so the organists had largely to be attracted from Anglican and other churches in the north of England by the relatively high salaries offered. When in the early twentieth century the Scottish-American millionaire, Andrew Carnegie (cf. *Patronage* 7), made his benevolent gesture to music, organs became common everywhere in Presbyterian churches, British and American, with the exception of certain smaller Presbyterian bodies which still rigidly exclude all use of instruments (for a long time even a pitch-pipe was an abomination).

The official dates of the permission to install organs in churches in Scotland are as follows: Established Church, 1866; United Presbyterian Church, 1872; Free Church, 1883. There is a very considerable Scottish Presbyterian literature on the question of the use of the organ in church; it dates largely from the 1860s to the 1880s, when the above-mentioned permissions were being debated or becoming operative, to the distress of many older or older-minded adherents.

3. Metrical Psalms, Paraphrases, Hymns. The metrical psalm constituted Presbyterianism's only church music for about two and a half centuries and still remains much endeared to all Presbyterians. One might have supposed that the Anglican chant would have appealed to the Scottish people, as enabling them to sing the Psalms one degree nearer to the original, i.e. without the inevitable twisting and turning of a translation hampered by the demands of English metre and rhyme. But this apparently never occurred to anybody at that time, the Anglican chant then being an exercise exclusively limited to the trained cathedral choirs and accompanied by the cathedral organs —and nothing was more definitely anathema to the Presbyterian mind than the cathedral choir and organ.

Then if not the Anglican chant, why not the plainsong tones? Apparently nobody either in Geneva or what we may call its Scottish suburbs ever thought of them. They were associated with the old ecclesiastical régime and the Latin language. The Anglican Church made an adaptation of much of the plainsong to the new English service and the Lutheran Church also adapted some of it, but the Calvinistic churches did not do anything of the sort.

The general history of the Metrical Psalm and of the often strange manner of its performance can be gathered from the article *Hymns and Hymn Tunes* 4, 5, 8, and especially 10 (see also *Precentor*). It will also be seen from that article that at length an additional element came into the musical part of Presbyterian worship—the metrical paraphrase of portions of scripture other than the Psalms. Such paraphrases began to be used in certain congregations from 1745, but their use was not authorized until 1781. A further extension of liberty—the permission to use 'human hymns'—came to the body known as the Relief Church in 1833; this church shortly afterwards became part of the United Presbyterian Church which formally authorized the use of hymns in 1852. The Established Church of Scotland authorized the use of hymns in 1861, the Free Church of Scotland ('disrupted' from the Established Church in 1843) did the same only in 1873. Some of the smaller and more rigid of the Scottish Presbyterian bodies still exclude both paraphrases and hymns.

It is noticeable that the editors employed for the first tune books of these various bodies were Englishmen and organists in the Anglican Church—Henry Smart (for the United Presbyterian Church), W. H. Monk and A. L. Peace successively (for the Established Church), E. J. Hopkins (for the Free Church). Presumably the reason was the same as that for the employment of English organists a little later—Scotland's lack, at that time, of musicians with the right kind of experience. In 1898 the three churches mentioned combined to produce *The Church Hymnary*, employing Sir John Stainer to edit the music; *The Revised Church Hymnary* was issued under the editorship of the Welsh musician David Evans in 1927.

The statement has often been made that Presbyterianism long opposed part-singing—that all singing of the Psalms was in unison. This is not a fact. The 1564 Psalter (known as the 'Old Psalter' or 'John Knox's Psalter'; see *Hymns and Hymn Tunes* 10) gives, it is true, only the melodies of the tunes, but there is evidence that harmonized versions were sometimes made and used from manuscript; moreover, in 1635 an edition with a four-voice harmonization appeared. In addition to the normal psalm tunes this volume contains eight of those more elaborate tunes called Reports (q.v.). There exists other conclusive evidence that Scottish Presbyterians at this date delighted in part-singing.

It is said that the period immediately following 1635 was Scotland's Golden Age for metrical psalm singing. The fact that the later official book which in 1650 superseded the one just mentioned had no tunes printed with it, and that no official tune book was ever published as a companion to it, is said to have led gradually to a great decline—the number of tunes in use dwindling to ten or twelve, and in some places fewer, and the manner of singing becoming very crude. The omission of tunes from the 1650 book seems to require some explanation; possibly the political excitements of the time may account for it.

The Pre-Reformation Sang Scuils of Scotland (see *Scotland* 4) suffered at first from the effects of the Reformation but were revived and for some time trained the young in instrumental music (chiefly the virginals) and vocal music—but latterly little beyond the singing of the metrical psalms. An Act of 1579 had urged provosts and councils of boroughs to restore these schools and maintain them in full vigour. There are seventeenth-century records of such schools in Glasgow, Aberdeen, Dundee, and very many other places (indeed practically every town of any size). As late as the end of the nineteenth century the precentor of the parish church of Dunfermline (the precentors usually held school positions and the boys led the 'praise') was enjoying an annual salary of £8. 6s. 8d. as 'Master of the Song' in the Sang or Grammar School—his position by that date, however, being treated as a sinecure. Apparently the schools gradually drifted from their original purpose and became mere elementary or grammar schools, not concerned with music.

4. The Various Movements for Reform. Musical interest awakened in the churches about the middle of the eighteenth century, when the livelier fashion of singing that had become common in England (see *Methodism and Music* 3) was introduced by soldiers of General Wolfe's regiment, quartered in Aberdeen. One of these soldiers, Thomas Channon, in 1753 was granted his discharge from the army, on the request of a number of ministers, in order that he might comply with the request to teach psalm-singing in the parishes. His methods were to organize choirs, placing the members together in a gallery; to abolish useless 'graces' in the melodies (to sing them 'plain, without quavering'); to introduce a brisker tempo; to restore part-singing (which had apparently fallen into disuse); and to bring into use the pitch-pipe. All this was soundly buttressed by sight-singing instruction on the method of sol-faing then in use (see *Lancashire Sol-fa*). He began in the parish of Monymusk. Under *Methodism and Music* 6 will be found an account by John Wesley of the singing he heard at this place; he was, in effect (though he does not say so and perhaps did not realize it), experiencing the result of an English influence with which his own Methodist movement had a good deal to do. From Monymusk Channon was invited to Aberdeen, and the example of that city led to similar revivals of interest in the musical rendering of the psalms in Edinburgh and elsewhere. In 1755 the Corporation of Glasgow engaged Thomas Moore of Manchester, a well-known teacher of psalmody and compiler of books of psalm tunes (resigned 1787; died 1792). The Edinburgh music publisher, Bremner (see *Publishing of Music* 6), issued, in 1756, a work designed, evidently, to assist the movement for the revival of musical psalm singing. It is called *The Rudiments of Music; or a Short and Easy Treatise on that Subject, to which is added a Collection of the best Church Tunes, Canons and Anthems*. A point made by Bremner is the stupidity of the 'graces and quavers' with which the old tunes had become defaced. (As will be seen under *Hymns and Hymn Tunes* 11 and *Methodism and Music* 4, the tendency to these tasteless embellishments was during the eighteenth century as strong in England as in Scotland.) Bremner was evidently against Channon and his followers in one matter; he opposed sol-faing and his encouragement of singing by ear may have been one cause why the movement eventually accomplished less than had been expected.

This movement thus inaugurated by Channon and supported by Bremner was for some years the cause of bitter controversy, as has been, at the outset, every successive attempt to change what had become established in popular usage in the Presbyterian Churches in Scotland.

Smollett in *Humphry Clinker* (1771) speaks of an Edinburgh attempt to improve psalmody, 'which is here practised and taught by a professor from the cathedral of Durham'.

There was another movement in the years just before and after 1820, led by R. A. Smith, a silk weaver of Paisley but born and brought up at Reading, England, where he had had experience as member of a church choir and of the band of a regiment of volunteers. He became a celebrated choir-trainer, settling finally at St. George's, Edinburgh, which he made the centre of a great musical activity. His publications (books of psalm tunes, anthems, an *Introduction to Singing*, etc.) were very numerous, and many of them were in full use until after the middle of the century. In view of what has been said under 2 above it seems strange that many of his works should be supplied with 'A Thorough-bass for the Organ or Pianoforte', but possibly this was intended for use in the home. Some of his simple anthems, such as 'How beautiful upon the mountains', came to have a popularity with English choirs. (He also published books of Scottish songs—traditional and original.) Smith's minister at St. George's, Dr. Andrew Thomson, also a composer, took a vigorous part in the general effort to improve church music in Scottish Presbyterianism.

A still further movement came into being in 1854, when a Psalmody Improvement Association, numbering fifty or sixty precentors, was founded under the direction of William Carnie, an Aberdeen precentor and journalist who published collections of psalm tunes and anthems, etc. Later the tonic sol-fa movement (see *Tonic Sol-fa*) had a valuable influence in improving church singing.

5. Music in Twentieth-century Scottish Presbyterianism.

From what has been said it will be seen that (*a*) in the early days of Scottish Presbyterianism the standard of music was high, within the limits possible in a church that then frowned upon any musical elaboration in worship; that (*b*) from the middle of the seventeenth century it declined; and that (*c*) from the middle of the eighteenth century there were frequent efforts to raise the standard

again, which efforts widened out with the admission of hymns and organs in the later nineteenth century.

By the opening of the twentieth century the Anglican chant (q.v.) had become common (the metrical version of the psalms has, however, never dropped out of use), and in many churches there was little to distinguish the musical part of the service from that in an Anglican Church—though where the psalms were chanted the version used was that not of the Anglican Prayer Book but of the Authorized (King James) Version of the Bible. Loss as well as gain has, of course, accrued, though not necessarily permanently. *Music in the Church*, by the Revd. G. Wauchope Stewart, reported the position in 1914 as follows:

'For three centuries metrical Psalms were the sole musical pabulum of our congregations. Then suddenly they had set before them a musical feast of fat things in the shape of hymns, anthems, chants and organ music. Naturally the tendency was to make too free use of the new material to the neglect of the old. The metrical Psalms fell into disfavour and hymns now held the field. Those who had any claim to musical skill revelled in their new-found freedom. The choir began to assert itself more and more in the service of praise. But the danger was that in this new enthusiasm for a richer musical service the interests of the congregation would be neglected. As a set-off to the general improvement of Church music we must admit a tendency to decline in congregational praise.'

6. England and America.

It is hardly possible here to outline the musical activities of Presbyterianism in England. For a few years (1647–52) it was the legally established religious system.

It is interesting to notice that in 1673 Richard Baxter, in his *Ecclesiastics*, expressed the view that the use of the organ was lawful, though he would avoid its introduction where this would lead to disputes. He was strong in his condemnation of people who were opposed to singing, but equally of those who would leave the singing to a choir, so depriving the congregation of their rights.

The Scottish Psalter of 1650 came into use in England and remained in use for about two centuries. Many of the churches, however, drifted to Independency (see *Congregational Churches*) and more to Unitarianism. In 1836 most of the remaining orthodox churches founded 'The Presbyterian Church in England', which in 1857 published a book of hymns and paraphrases; in 1867 the Scottish Psalter was practically superseded by a book containing both psalms and hymns, the music of which was edited by Dr. Rimbault; this book had a wide circulation all over the British Empire. In 1876 this church was joined by the many English congregations of the United Presbyterian Church of Scotland, changing its name slightly to the 'Presbyterian Church of England', and shortly after it adopted a new hymnal, *Church Praise*, the music of which was edited by E. J. Hopkins. The use of instrumental music was strictly forbidden until 1870, but is now general, as is also the use of the Anglican chant, etc.

The Presbyterian Church in the United States, though it has many sources, finds perhaps its chief one in Maryland, where at the end of the seventeenth century there settled many refugees from the later Stuart persecution. The Presbyterians of Kentucky and Tennessee played a large part in the Camp Meeting activities of the beginning of the nine-

teenth century, which left their mark on religous song. There are now several million communicant members of Presbyterian churches in the United States, and their worship, so long deprived of organs, choirs, and hymns, now differs in no material way from those of other non-episcopal bodies. (One 'die-hard' section, however, the American Reformed Presbyterian Church, still rigorously bars all these things.)

PRESBYTERIAN CHURCH OF ENGLAND. See *Presbyterian Church Music* 6.

PRESIDENT'S MARCH. See *Hail, Columbia!*

PRESQUE (Fr.). 'Almost.'

PRESSANDO, PRESSANTE (It.), **PRESSANT** (Fr.). 'Pressing on' (= accelerando). Sometimes the Fr. infinitive is used, *Presser.*

PRESSER. See *Publishing* 9.

PRESSER FOUNDATION. See under *Patronage* 7; *United States* 5 f.

PRESSEZ (Fr.), **PRESSIEREN** (Ger.). 'Press on' (= accelerando).

PRESS GANG FOR CHOIR-BOYS. See *Chapel Royal.*

PRESTANT. See *Organ* 14 I.

PRESTO (It.). 'Quick.' So *Prestezza*, 'quickness'; *Prestamente*, 'quickly'; *Prestissimo*, 'very quick'; *Prestissimamente*, 'very quickly'.

PRICE, JOHN. See *Scandinavia* 2.

PRICK SONG. To 'Prick' is an obsolete English synonym for to 'mark'. Thus Shakespeare (*Julius Caesar*, iv. i): 'These many then shall die; their names are pricked. . . . Your brother, too, must die. . . . Prick him down, Antony.'

Thus Shakespeare, again, speaking of written song as distinct from traditionally conveyed song (i.e. *Plainsong*) or improvised song (see *Descant*): 'He fights as you sing prick-song, keeps times, distance and proportion, rests me his minim rest, one, two and a third in your bosom' (*Romeo and Juliet*, ii. iv).

The term was long current for any sort of written or printed music. See the article *Parish Clerk*, and note that the arms of the Parish Clerks' Company in London, in Shakespeare's day, included, as a sign of their musical duties and skill, three prick-song books.

The official expression 'Pricking for Sheriffs' is still current in England, and though 'prick' in its musical sense has gone we still have a similar idea surviving in the 'point' of counterpoint (q.v.).

PRIÈRE (Fr.). 'Prayer.'

PRIEST, JOSIAS or JOSIAH. See *Dido and Aeneas*; *Profession of Music* 1.

PRIMA (It.). 'First' (feminine form of 'Primo'). Thus *Prima donna* (q.v.), 'first lady'; *Prima volta*, 'first time' (see Table 20); *Prima vista*, 'first sight'; *Come prima*, 'as at first'.

PRIMA DONNA (It., 'First Lady'; plural, *Prime Donne*). The term came into existence

during the first century of opera (i.e. some time before 1700), as the purely vocal demands of that form of art became greater and the prominence of its performers more marked. At this period the term 'Primo Uomo' ('First Man') was also in use—for the leading castrato performer (see *Voice* 5). The self-contradiction of the admission of two 'prime donne' into an opera soon became common. Later the term 'Prima Donna' became accepted by the general public as meaning simply a highly-paid public woman singer, and more recently the word has, in the mouths of the more thinking members of the musical public, taken on a half-humorous, half-caustic meaning in which it is now occasionally applied to those orchestral conductors whose deportment seems to suggest a full recognition, on their own part, of their gifts and of the public favour they enjoy. (The child who in an examination paper misspelt the term 'Prim Madonna' was very young.)

The remuneration of Prime Donne has been the cause of malignant envy on the part of mere composers and instrumentalists, as, of course, of music critics, the compilers of musical dictionaries, and the like. The boy Storace (q.v.) in 1775, being put to copy music for Agujari, was, in his childish innocence, so astonished at her receiving 50 guineas for singing a song that he counted the notes and worked them out at four shillings and tenpence apiece, a single passage of flourish coming out at eighteen pounds eleven shillings (but she sometimes got 100 guineas a song, so we can double these figures).

Prima Donna Autobiography is a class of literature to itself and is equally relished by sentimental young females and men of the world with a sense of humour.

DUKE (in *The Gondoliers*, 1889): 'And now there is a little matter to which I think I am entitled to take exception. I come here in state with her Grace the Duchess and her Majesty my daughter, and what do I find? Do I find, for instance, a guard of honour to receive me? No. The town illuminated? No. Refreshments provided? No. A Royal salute fired? No. Triumphal arches erected? No. The bells set ringing? Yes—one—the Visitors', and I rang it myself.'

TETRAZZINI (in *My Life of Song*, 1921): 'How different was my arrival in London from that to which I had been accustomed for many years past! In the capitals and most of the other towns of the Latin Republics the governors and mayors and the town bands were at the station to accord me a ceremonial welcome, as though I were a queen or a foreign representative of high rank. But chilly London!'

A frequently used synonym for 'Prima Donna' is *Diva* (Goddess). The term *Prima donna assoluta* ('absolute first lady') is sometimes used to make perfectly clear the position of the *very* most important woman member of an opera company.

There exist what we may call male 'Prime Donne Assolute'. When Wieniawski and Rubinstein were touring America together, the latter's name was on some occasion displayed on the posters in larger type than the former's. As a result of this indiscretion they publicly played the 'Kreutzer' Sonata together more than seventy times without ever speaking to one another.

PRIMARIUS. See *Corno Alto* and *Basso*.

PRIMARY TONES. See *American Musical Terminology* 5.

PRIME. (1) The third of the eight Canonical working Hours or services of the day of the Roman Catholic Church, properly sung at 6 a.m. (i.e. the first hour of the working day; cf. *Matins*; *Lauds*; *Terce*; *Sext*; *None*; *Vespers*; *Compline*).

(2) The word has also some theoretical applications—to (*a*) the lower of two notes forming an interval; (*b*) the root of a chord; (*c*) the generator of a series of harmonics—see *Acoustics* 8; (*d*) a unison; (*e*) the first note of a scale; (*f*) the interval formed by two notes which are written on the same line or space, e.g. F and F sharp.

PRIMO (It.). 'First', e.g. *Primo uomo*, 'first man', or leading male singer in an opera cast; *Tempo primo*, 'first tempo', i.e. same speed as at the beginning: *Primo violino*, 'first violin'.

PRINCE IGOR (Borodin). Produced in St. Petersburg in 1890. Libretto by the composer, on suggestions from the critic Stassof. The work, left unfinished, was completed by Rimsky-Korsakof and Glazunof.

PROLOGUE

The Market Place of Putivle. Time, 1185

Prince Igor Sviatoslavitch of Seversk (*Baritone*), starting on an expedition against the Polovtsy tribe, is warned by his wife, **Yaroslavna** (*Soprano*), and by others, that an eclipse of the sun is of ill omen. Igor goes off with his son **Vladimir** (*Tenor*). **Prince Galitsky** (*Bass*), the treacherous brother of his wife, is left behind to govern the town.

ACT I

SCENE 1: *The Courtyard of Prince Galitsky's House*

Galitsky has won over the people, aided by **Scoula** (*Bass*) and **Eroshka** (*Tenor*), deserters from Igor's army. Some girls come to ask the Prince to use his authority in compelling his men to bring back a maiden whom they have carried off, but he cynically refuses.

SCENE 2: *A Room in Yaroslavna's Apartments*

The girls appeal to Igor's wife. She questions Galitsky, but he treats her disdainfully, and she imperiously bids him leave her.

Disturbing news comes: Igor and his son are captives, and the Polovtsy are going to attack the city. Its leaders promise to defend it and their queen.

ACT II

SCENE: *The Camp of the Polovtsy. Evening*

Igor's son Vladimir is in love with the daughter, **Kontchakovna** (*Contralto*), of his conqueror, the **Khan Kontchak** (*Bass*). Vladimir dare not approach his father on this matter, but the maiden is sure *her* father would consent.

To Igor comes **Ovlour** (*Tenor*), one of the Khan's men, offering to help Igor to escape, but the Prince will not do so. Kontchak himself says that Igor may go free if he will not make war on the Polovtsy again. But Igor will not consent. Each respects the other, and the Khan orders songs and dances for his captives' entertainment.

ACT III

SCENE: *Part of the Camp*

In order to save his city Igor decides to accept Ovlour's offer of help in escaping. Vladimir is prevented by Kontchakovna from going with his father. The Polovtsy, enraged, wish to kill Vladimir, but the Khan thinks it wiser to hold him by the love of his daughter, to whom he weds the youth.

ACT IV

SCENE: *The Square at Putivle*

Prince Igor is reunited to his wife. Eroshka and Scoula decide to save their skins by shouting with the crowd, by whom Igor and his wife are acclaimed.

PRINCESS IDA, or CASTLE ADAMANT (Sullivan). Produced at the Savoy Theatre, London, in 1884. Libretto by W. S. Gilbert, described as 'a respectful operatic per-version of Tennyson's *Princess*'.

ACT I

SCENE: *Pavilion attached to the Palace of King Hildebrand*

Soldiers and courtiers, with **Florian** (*Baritone*), a friend of King Hildebrand's son Hilarion, are awaiting the coming of King Gama and his daughter Ida, who from the age of one has been betrothed to Hilarion.

Hildebrand (*Bass*) announces that if Gama does not appear with Ida by sunset, there must be war between the two kingdoms. He dreads meeting Gama, 'a twisted monster', whom he has not seen for twenty years.

Hilarion (*Tenor*) has heard that Ida, with a band of women, has shut herself away from the world, to study philosophy. Now Gama's three sons appear, boasting of their fighting powers, and then **Gama** (*Light Baritone*) himself, who has a talent for being disagreeable. He says that his daughter runs a woman's university in Castle Adamant, which contains no men. Gama and his sons are held as hostages, and Hilarion, with his friends **Cyril** (*Tenor*) and

Florian, set out to prove their quality to the haughty ladies.

ACT II

SCENE: *The Gardens of Castle Adamant*

Lady Psyche (*Soprano*), Professor of Humanities, is teaching her class. **Lady Blanche** (*Contralto*), Professor of Abstract Science, announces some of the stern princess's punishments—one for a girl who brought a set of chess*men* into the castle. The **Princess** (*Soprano*) herself gives us a sample of her man-hating mind, and declares that a hundred of her maidens have sworn to humiliate the tyrant Man.

Hilarion and his friends steal in, put on robes that the girls have left, and, being surprised by the princess, pretend to be new students, and are so received. When she has gone, Lady Psyche enters and recognizes Florian as her brother. **Melissa** (*Mezzo-Soprano*), Lady Blanche's daughter, who has never before seen men, is attracted by Florian, and, when her mother pierces the youths' disguise, pleads with her for them and plays on her jealousy of the princess in order to win her sympathy.

At lunch, Cyril drinks too much, insults the princess, quarrels with Hilarion, and gives away the secret of the visitors' identity. Ida, horrified, misses her footing by the stream, falls in, and is rescued by Hilarion. She, however, will show no mercy, and the three are arrested.

But Hildebrand and his army have come to enforce the marriage bargain: the gate is down, the game is up; if Ida does not marry Hilarion by tomorrow her three brothers will be executed. Yet Ida defies the invaders. Who will win?

ACT III

SCENE: *Outer Walls and Courtyard of Castle Adamant*

Ida's maidens, outwardly bold, are secretly frightened. They shrink from the carnage of battle, and would prefer that of tongues. Ida, her rock turned to sand, loses hope. To her comes her father on parole, with a suggestion from Hildebrand that Ida's three brothers should be pitted against Hilarion, Florian, and Cyril. Gama, tortured by Hildebrand's craftily giving him everything he wants so that he cannot exercise his capacity for grumbling, begs his daughter to yield. She consents. The three sons of Gama fight Hilarion and his two friends, and are defeated. It is the end; Ida gives in, acknowledges her error, and gives her hand to Hilarion, whilst his friends pair off with Melissa and Lady Psyche.

PRINCESS ROYAL. See *Arethusa*.

PRINCIPAL. See *Organ* 14 I.

PRINCIPALE. See *Organ* 15; *Trumpet Family* 5.

PRINTING OF MUSIC

1. The First Century.
2. The 'Tied Note' Improvement.
3. Engraving.
4. Lithography.
5. Modern Type-printing.

1. The First Century. The art of printing was practised in China and Japan for centuries before it was to be found in Europe. The first European printing began about 1425, with a sort of crude woodcut process, possibly introduced from China by the Venetian traders. The introduction of movable type is usually considered to date from the publication, about 1450-5, of Gutenberg's Mainz Bible, which was, at all events, the first big volume to be so printed. Printing in Britain began with Caxton in 1477.

At the time that British letterpress printing began, there began the application of the process to music—in Conrad von Zabern's *Opusculum de monochordo* (Mainz, *c.* 1462-74); and in the plainsong of a Gradual possibly printed at Augsburg about 1473 a handsome type was used.

Early music printing, owing to the awkwardness of getting staves and notes together from type, was done in two separate processes (the notes often being printed in black and the stave in red). There was an obvious difficulty in correct 'registering' (i.e. bringing the second printing exactly into place with the first), so sometimes only the stave was printed and the notes written by hand, or the notes printed and the staves afterwards ruled. Soon these plans were abandoned, and staves and notes were cut in wood and printed at one process.

The famous **Petrucci**, of Venice (began printing 1501), then discovered means of doing the double printing accurately, and **Haultain** (or Hautain) of Paris, in 1525, showed how to do the whole thing at one printing, his plan being the one still used in music type printing—that of using type in which small fragments of the stave are combined with the notes and the whole combination of staves and notes then built up. Yet for 300 years the double-printing process still emerges at intervals, as, for instance, in a music book printed by Coghlan of London as late as 1788. Note that Petrucci, with all his skill, never dared to go beyond the printing of single vocal and instrumental parts, i.e. he never attempted to print in score. We may almost say that score printing had to wait for the application of engraving to music (see 3).

The first instance of British music printing is very insignificant. In 1482 Caxton printed a book (Higden's *Polychronicon*) which required a certain music illustration of eight notes. He left a space for this and had it filled in by hand (some copies were missed, for the one in the British Museum has merely the blank space). Thirteen years later the book was republished by **Wynkyn de Worde**, and he ingeniously made up the short stretch of stave by the use of ordinary printing 'rules', and for the notes used the square under-surface of ordinary type, i.e. he turned pieces of letter-type upside down, using the print of the square bottom as a note (p. 832, pl. **141.** 2). The earliest British music printing was, then, a pure makeshift. The next instance comes a good deal later (about 1516), being a black-letter ballad sheet with music, printed by John Rastell, M.P. (q.v.), of which a fragment is in the British Museum. The first actual music book printed in England is a collection of songs which appeared in 1530 (p. 832, pl. **141.** 3).

Gradually music printing from movable type became common in various countries and improvements were introduced. **Pierre Attaignant** of Paris was the first in France to use it (from 1528). His publications are important and numerous. Scotland had movable-type music printing in 1564, in *A Forme of Prayers* printed by **Robert Lekprevick** of Edinburgh.

It may be remarked that it was a fortunate thing for the world that music printing came into existence simultaneously with the rise of the wonderful polyphonic schools of the Netherlands, Italy, Spain, and England, as otherwise much of the work of these schools would undoubtedly have been only locally known and then lost to posterity. But English music printing and publication were somewhat hampered during the late sixteenth and early seventeenth centuries (precisely the most important period in the whole history of British musical composition) by being created a monopoly. Queen Elizabeth I conferred the sole right of music printing and importing, for twenty-one years, on two of her Gentlemen of the Chapel Royal, Byrd and Tallis. This helped them to eke out their official Chapel Royal salary of sevenpence a day—but was not for the good of the art, since it impeded the free circulation of printed music (see *Monopolies; Publishing* 4).

Music printing was particularly active in England during the Commonwealth (see *Puritans* 6). For music printing in Scotland during the late seventeenth century see note under *Scotland* 9.

2. The 'Tied Note' Improvement. A great improvement came into music printing with the introduction of what was in England called 'the new tied note', i.e. the method of joining the tails of such notes as had them, as is done today. **Thos. Moore** of London, in 1681, seems to have been the first English printer to use it, and other printers improved it. But it had appeared on the Continent earlier. **Ballard** of Paris (see *Publishing* 2) had it forty years before, so it is not, as sometimes believed, an English invention.

3. Engraving. Up to this point, we may almost say, all the music printing described has been with movable types. The many madrigal publications of English composers which appeared from about 1590 to 1620 were all so printed. Now begins the era of engraving—at first the incising by hand but soon the punching of staves and notes on a sheet of metal, and the taking of the impressions from that. Music

printing from engraved plates began in Rome in 1586; the first British publication so printed was Orlando Gibbons's *Fantasies* (about 1606).

Music type now tended to disappear and by the opening of the eighteenth century had almost gone. It will be remembered that Bach engraved some of his own music; so did his contemporary Telemann. One obvious reason why movable type was discarded was the enormously increased complexity of musical composition, which made it difficult to reproduce it by means of a number of separate small pieces of metal. It was easier to use a set of punches for the many different signs than to fit together these signs in the form of loose type, and a more uniform and sightly effect would be produced by the use of the punches in the hands of a good workman.

In America music printing from engraved plates took place in 1721, but with plates imported from England; the actual engraving of plates there began in 1764 and one of the first music engravers was no other than **Paul Revere**. Music printing from type had taken place in Mexico in 1556.

4. Lithography. The commonest process of actual printing of today is lithography, and it began in 1796, when Senefelder, a German actor and dramatist who wished to reproduce his own plays, introduced the process. It was based on the traditional antagonism of oil and water. Senefelder wrote or drew on smooth stone with greasy ink and then ran a gum-thickened water over the stone. The inked portions of the surface refused the water; the blank spaces accepted it. He could then renew the ink indefinitely by running an inked roller over the stone. The inked surface, of course, accepted more ink but the wetted surface refused it. This is essentially the process of lithography as still practised, but the present process incorporates improvements, some of which quickly came about, whilst others are more recent. The chief of these is that instead of writing or drawing on the stone we engrave with punches on a sheet of metal, take an impression on paper, and lay it down on the stone, which 'stone', though the word is still used, is now zinc. (Mostly the camera is used today for 'laying-down', the old paper transfer being superseded by the photograph.) The metal then remains as a permanent record that can be taken down from its shelf at any time for the printing of a fresh edition. Thus the bulk of music today is produced by a process (only partially described above) that combines engraving and lithography.

Senefelder (1771–1835) is always spoken of as the 'inventor' of this whole process of printing by lithography, but it is interesting to note that he alleged that the idea came to him from seeing as a child, piles of stones inked with music, and thrown away by a printer after use. It would appear, then, that he had some predecessor and that the art of lithography actually began with music.

Senefelder himself quickly applied his process to music, for the minor composer Gleissner financed him and composed for his reproduction by the process a set of songs.

The composer Weber, as a boy, assisted Senefelder, introduced some improvements in his process, and injured himself by accidentally drinking some of the acid used in the work (Senefelder's first idea had been to use acid to eat away the uninked portions of the stone, so leaving the inked portions elevated).

About 1850 the Cylinder Power Press was applied to music lithography and this gave it a great impetus. In Britain the firm of Augener were (1853) pioneers in the use of lithography (pp. 833, 848, pls. 142–3).

5. Modern Type-printing. Music printing from movable type has never completely died out and, indeed, it took a new lease of life from the middle of the eighteenth century when the Leipzig printer Breitkopf greatly improved the method. His plan was to cast type consisting of a number of small portions of notes and staves made to a uniform measure and so capable of being easily fitted into the strange mosaic of which music setting necessarily consists. But printing direct from type was given up when stereotyping was perfected. In 1847 J. Alfred Novello issued a pamphlet, *Some Account of the Methods of Musick Printing, with specimens of the various sizes of Moveable Types*, and Novellos continued to use this method for their octavo choral music until early in the twentieth century. The cost of type-setting and of making a stereotype plate from type was heavy, being about double the cost of an engraved plate, but the subsequent machining cost was much lower. With improvement in lithographic printing in the early 1900s this advantage disappeared, and type proving too rigid to meet the increasingly elaborate demands of modern music, typesetting gradually fell into disuse. To some extent, however, it is still to be found, chiefly in music examples associated with letterpress.

The London firm of Clowes has, since about 1820, been famous for its artistic use of music type.

For cognate subjects see the articles *Copyists* and *Publishing of Music*.

PRINZIPALE. See *Trumpet Family* 5. But in German organs the word *Prinzipal* means the same as English 'Diapason'.

PRIVALOF. See *Balalaika*.

PRIX DE ROME.

(1) **France.** The Academy of Fine Arts (of the Institute of France) has since 1803 awarded annually, after prolonged and severe competitive examination, what would in English be called 'bursaries' or 'exhibitions' or 'scholarships', entitling the winners to live in Rome for four years, engaged in study and creative work. The subjects in which the competition is held are painting, sculpture, engraving, architecture, and music, and an award is annually made in each of these. The winner of a first prize (who henceforth styles himself 'Premier Grand Prix de Rome') receives a gold medal and resides in the French Academy, the Villa Medici. The form of the competition in music is the composition of a cantata on a given subject, the competitors being locked up (*en loge*) for some days to carry out their task.

Two consolation prizes are given, but these consist merely of gold medals.

Many of the most distinguished composers of France have won the 'Grand Prix de Rome' —and others, equally distinguished, have competed yet failed (see *Ravel*).

For some of the winners of the prize see s.v. *Berlioz*; *Bizet*; *Boulanger, Nadia*; *Boulanger, Lili*; *Caplet*; *Charpentier, Gustave*; *Debussy*; *Delvincourt*; *Dubois*; *Théodore*; *Gaubert*; *Gounod*; *Guiraud*; *Huë*; *Ibert*; *Laparra*; *Lefebvre*; *Maillart*; *Marty*; *Massé*; *Pierné*; *Rabaud*; *Ravel*; *Schmitt, Florent*; *Thomas, Ambroise*.

(2) **Belgium** has a similar prize, under the same name, but it is competed for only once in two years and the winner is not necessarily tied to residence in Rome during the tenure of his prize.

(3) **The United States** in 1920 instituted a similar Rome Prize, the winner of which resides at the American Academy in Rome.

PROCESSIONALE. See *Ritual*.

PROCOPIUS. See *Bagpipe Family* 1.

PRODIGAL SON. See *Pantomime*.

PROEMIO. 'Preface'; so 'Prelude'.

PROFESSIONAL CONCERTS. See *Concert* 6.

PROFESSION OF MUSIC

1. The Guild System in England. A comprehensive history of the musical profession has, apparently, never been written, and a bird's-eye view of the subject is difficult to attain.

The first conception of music as a distinct vocation seems to have been that of minstrelsy, and in all countries this was early regulated more or less rigidly by bodies on the lines of the craft guilds. The following summary of the constitution and object of craft guilds in general (Chambers's *Encyclopædia*, 1925 edition) is in every word as accurate for the craft of the musician as for any other craft, be it that of a carpenter, blacksmith, cobbler, or what not.

'The inner organization of the guilds rested on the arrangement of the workers into master, journeyman, and apprentice. The right to the independent exercise of a trade depended on being member of a guild, and guild membership carried with it the privileges of citizenship. On the one hand, the guild had its own particular branch of industry reserved to it and a local market for its produce secured; on the other hand, the guild had to see that its members possessed the due qualifications, moral and technical, and that the work they turned out was of fair and reasonable quality. In other words, the interests of producers and consumers were supposed to be reconciled on equitable terms. Those objects could be attained and the guild organization generally could be maintained only by a system of regulations, which were often very minute.'

A brief account of the various English guilds, companies, and corporations officially entrusted with the regulation of the performance and teaching of music will be found under *Minstrels*, etc., 3, where it will be seen that we have evidence of the continuous existence of such bodies (one succeeding another as reconstitutions were found necessary) for at least 500 years, and that one of them still existing, the 'Musicians' Company' (or Worshipful Company of Musicians), long claimed to be in their distinct and unbroken line. If this claim had been justified, very wide legal powers of control of the musical profession within the London area would still exist; for instance, it would be (legally, at any rate) quite possible for them to set on foot proceedings such as are recorded in the following (28 June 1669):

'Warrant to apprehend George Smyth, Francis Pendleton, Mosse, Caesar Duffil, and Josiah Priest, for teaching, practising, and executing music, in companies or otherwise, without the approbation or lycence of the Marshall and Corporation of musick, in contempt of His Majesty's authority and the power granted to the Marshall and Corporation.'

(See *Inns and Taverns as Places of Music-Making* for a further instance of the guild control of the profession.)

2. The Waits. For some centuries an important branch of musical activity in England and elsewhere was that of the Waits (q.v.)—bodies of municipal musicians, whose members patrolled the streets at night, playing on some instrument to mark the hours, and awakening the chief citizens in the morning by music before their windows, giving public band performances on Sundays and holidays, greeting strangers to the town by playing before their inns, and so forth. The Waits wore a uniform with silver chains and badges.

3. The Organization of Musicians in France and the Netherlands. On the continent of Europe the organization of the craft of music was very similar to that in England. A Corporation of Minstrels was founded in France in 1321. It included women. Its

head was called its 'King', and the last 'King of the Minstrels' abdicated as late as 1773. As early as 1335 this corporation built a hospital for poor musicians. In the sixteenth century it was organized as a series of branches in the chief towns: in the seventeenth it was insisting upon a four years' apprenticeship, and its 'King' had the right to imprison musicians breaking its laws, and to destroy their instruments. In that century began a series of struggles with dancing-masters and also with clavecinists and organists, these classes of practitioners claiming to be outside its jurisdiction, and this period in all countries seems to mark the beginning of the breakup of the general system. In 1742 the 'King', being in the position of music-master to the Dauphin, had influence enough to be able to limit the music-making of street musicians: he insisted that they should never use a four-stringed violin, but only the more primitive three-stringed rebec. Presumably this was done in order to reduce the force of their competition with the more regular type of musicians, and also to mark their inferior social and artistic position.

The abdication of the last of the 'Kings' (which, as above mentioned, took place quite late in the eighteenth century) followed a failure some years earlier to secure endorsement by the highest legal authority of his right to license and demand fees from the musicians of France.

The Netherlands possessed a system of corporations or guilds similar to that of France.

4. The Organization in Germany. As an instance of organization in Germany we may take the formation of a College or Union of Instrumental Musicians of the District of Upper and Lower Saxony in 1653, presumably replacing some earlier body. Its very elaborate series of statutes was submitted to and approved by the Emperor Ferdinand III. It controlled the movements of musicians, not allowing one to settle in the territory of another to the hurt of the latter. It forbade a musician, on accepting office with a town, to agree to a lower wage than his predecessor in that office. It insisted on a five years' apprenticeship (no master to have more than three apprentices at one time), with periodical examination of apprentices by officers of the union and a period of status as journeyman between that of apprenticeship and that of master. It forbade its members to sing improper songs, to play the less dignified instruments, as 'bagpipes, sheep-horns, hurdy-gurdies, and triangles', or to consort with low company, as jugglers, bailiffs, or hangmen, or to take as apprentices sons of such. It protected its members in old age, by insisting that they should continue to receive half their municipal salary, the other half going to a deputy, and in case of disputes between members it appointed a board of six to settle them, its decisions to be binding.

It will be recognized from all the above that

vocales ordine natali posite notule sut mucates cui voci lra sit accomo
da etia p deplshone et eleuaco; ad instar game natal sol/fa/mi/re/ut/
Aut ponat ordo nature vocaliu deptis asonantibs ut p; in hac figura·

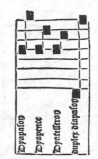

1. EXAMPLE OF MUSIC PRINTING
In Gerson's *Collectorium*, 1473

2. EARLIEST EXAMPLE OF BRITISH MUSIC PRINTING
By Wynkyn de Worde, 1495
See *Printing of Music* 1

3. FROM THE FIRST MUSIC BOOK PRINTED IN BRITAIN
1530. See *Printing of Music* 1

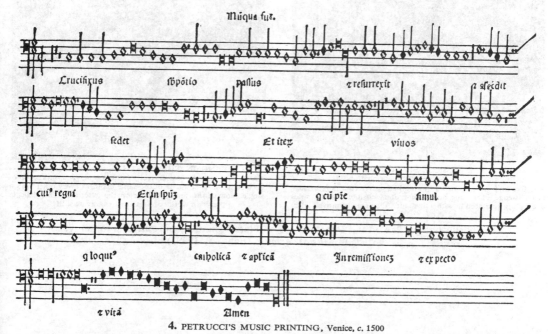

4. PETRUCCI'S MUSIC PRINTING, Venice, *c.* 1500

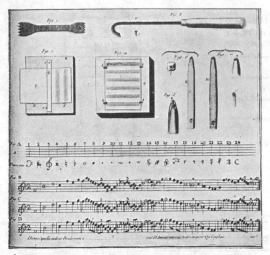

1. EIGHTEENTH-CENTURY TOOLS AND PROCESSES OF MUSIC ENGRAVING

This illustration comes from a valuable early source of information on such subjects: the *Dictionnaire des arts* (Volume XXII). It shows that towards the end of the 18th century the processes used were much like those of the present day

2. A BOUQUET OF DIES

Of hardest steel, these bits of musical notation cut into the engraving plates and leave their impressions. This picture of the process of printing music and the pictures which follow were taken at the century-old American firm of Robt. Teller Sons and Dorner

3. INCISING THE MUSICAL STAFF in the making of the engraving plate for one page of printed music

The five lines are cut with a five-toothed graver run along a steel straight-edge. Then the approximate final positions of the notes are lightly scratched in with a fine knife (they may be moved later)

4. STAMPING IN THE WORDS—letter for letter, and backwards in order to appear correctly in the proof. The impression of each letter must be made of the same depth as every other with a single blow of the small hammer on the letter die. This delicate precision work requires great engraving skill

(The illustrations 2–4 on this Plate and 1–5 on Plate 143 are taken from an informative article in *Musical America* (February 1949))

the practice of music rarely until comparatively recent times possessed a 'free-lance' character, and that the late nineteenth- and twentieth-century organizing of orchestral players on Trade Union principles, as in Britain and the United States, is historically sound.

5. Musicians in Domestic Service. The guilds and corporations just described were often founded and largely directed by musicians in the service of the monarch. Such service represented the height of professional advancement until well into the nineteenth century. Prince-Bishops, nobles, and the highly placed generally, maintained a musical organization as a part of their dignity and a contribution to their pleasure. This division of the subject will be found to be discussed under *Patronage* and *Chapel Royal*.

6. The Church as Employer. The earliest church musicians were priests and monks, but a separate class of lay musicians in time emerged. For a treatment of this part of the subject see *Cathedral Music*; *Vicar Choral*; *Parish Clerk*; *Patronage*.

7. Opera and Concerts. Opera-houses began to be erected (first in Italy) during the early part of the seventeenth century and public concert-schemes developed towards the end of that century. With these, new opportunities for professional activity necessarily came into existence. For this division of the subject see various parts of the articles *Opera*; *Concert*; *Singing*; *Bel Canto*; *Prima Donna*; *Conducting*.

8. The Vocation of Composer. It is only with the development of music printing and publishing that composition, as such, can be said to have declared itself as a separate and potentially self-supporting branch of the musical profession—and then it did so only very slowly. Up to the beginning of the nineteenth century most of the great composers held positions such as those described under *Patronage*, and composition was with them a part of the work done in return for a regular salary. Some (but not all) of the Italian opera composers were free-lances, as were Handel and some others in England; Mozart threw up a regular position and became one, but his financial position was precarious; effectively we may consider Beethoven, who abandoned a court position in early life, to be the first great free-lance composer other than operatic, but even he was partly supported by a syndicate of wealthy admirers. Some light will be thrown on this subject by a reading of the articles *Copyists*; *Printing*; *Publishing*.

At the present time the number of composers is enormous, but comparatively few of them (unless engaged in the production of 'popular' ephemeral music) are able to maintain themselves purely by composition. Many of them are engaged in teaching or some form of musical administration—devoting to composition what scant time and energy remain.

9. The Music Teacher. Teaching has always constituted a financially important part of the work of the musician. We find Byrd in a petition to Queen Elizabeth I (1577) calling attention to the loss he has sustained by his position as a Gentleman of the Chapel Royal —'By reason of his daily attendance in the Queen's service he is letted from reaping such commodity by teaching as formerly he did'.

There is a list of the chief London music teachers of Commonwealth times in Playford's *Musical Banquet* (1651). It mentions nine for 'Organ or Virginall' and eighteen for 'the Voyce or Viol', but intimates that there were many others.

Fees of teachers (other than those in the first rank) do not seem to have been high. Anthony Wood, at Oxford, in the mid-seventeenth century, paid his Violin master 2*s*. 6*d*. 'entrance fee' and 10*s*. a quarter; Pepys, in 1661, paid his singing-master 20*s*. 'entrance' and 20*s*. a month. The practice of charging an 'entrance fee' was customary until at least the end of the eighteenth century. Thus Dr. Burney in London used to take a guinea entrance fee, and Van Hagen in New York advertised (1789) that he taught harpsichord, violin, viola, cello, flute, oboe, clarinet, and singing (some teachers were then very versatile, particularly in America, where as yet musicians were somewhat few), at a fee of 6 dollars per month of twelve lessons, with a guinea entrance fee. (The British guinea circulated in the United States until 1792, although the dollar was introduced in 1787; professional fees in Britain are still commonly reckoned by the guinea, i.e. twenty-one shillings, in preference to the pound of twenty shillings, although the guinea as a coin ceased to exist in 1817.)

What appears to be the first attempt at legal control of fees for music teaching was that of a German Government (1936); it fixed the minima as 8 marks or 5 marks a week, according as the lesson lasted one hour or half an hour, the payment to be on a basis of fifty-two weeks in the year, but holidays to be given corresponding with those in the State schools. Teachers accepting lower fees would be forbidden to practice. (Such fees would seem to have been prohibitive for the poorer classes.)

For further information on the history of music teaching see *Education and Music*. For the organization of schools of music (which, except in Italy, dates only from the eighteenth century) see the article *Schools of Music*. For official qualifications of teachers see *Degrees and Diplomas in Music*.

Until the early twentieth century a general defect in the preparation of the musician for his task as teacher was the lack of facilities for his learning something of the art of teaching, as distinct from the art of music. This lack is (especially in the U.S.) now supplied, most musical colleges now taking the subject within their purview.

10. Modern Professional Societies, etc. The loss of the craft-guild system has been, to an extent, made good in every country by the bringing into existence of professional societies, such as, in Britain, the Royal College of Organists (1864), the Incorporated Society of Musicians (1882, reconstituted 1928), the Music Teachers' Association (1908), the Musicians' Union (1921), and the Composers' Guild (1945), and in America the Music Teachers' National Association (1876), the American Guild of Organists (1908), and the Music Educators' National Conference (first held 1907).

Benevolent organizations must also be considered as partly supplying the place of one side of activity of the craft guilds. Of these the oldest in Britain is the Royal Society of Musicians, founded in 1738, Handel being one of the foundation members. A modern organization is the Musicians' Benevolent Fund (1921).

For cognate subjects see *Education and Music*; *Schools of Music*; *Degrees and Diplomas*; *Pianoforte Playing and Teaching*; *United States* 5; *Concert* 16; *Mealtime Music* (end).

PROFONDO (in 'Basso Profondo'). See *Voice* 19.

PROGRAM, PROGRAMME. The original English spelling of this word (seventeenth century) was 'program', as in American English at present. Apparently 'programme' was intro-

duced into English from the French in the early nineteenth century, but Scott, Carlyle, and others use 'program'—and even Browning as late as 1869 in *The Ring and the Book*.

For *Annotated Programmes* and *Programme Music* see entries under those heads.

PROGRAMME MUSIC

1. Liszt's Definition of the Term.
2. A Question of Emphasis on Design or on 'Meaning'.
3. 'Suggestive Music.'
4. The Cruder Kinds of Programme Music.
5. An Historical List of Programme Compositions.

1. Liszt's Definition of the Term. The term 'Programme Music' (Ger. *Programmusik*; Fr. *Musique à programme* or *Musique programmatique*; It. *Musica a programma*) dates from the time of Liszt, who defined 'programme', in this application, as 'any preface in intelligible language added to a piece of instrumental music, by means of which the composer intends to guard the listener against a wrong poetical interpretation, and to direct his attention to the poetical idea of the whole or to a particular part of it'. As an example of what he meant by such a 'preface' or 'programme' we may reproduce the following, which is the concluding passage from that to his symphonic poem, *Tasso*:

'Tasso loved and suffered at Ferrara; he was avenged at Rome; his glory is yet living in the popular songs of Venice. These three stages are inseparable from his immortal memory. To render them in music we have first conjured up the great shade of the hero, even as it appears to us to-day, haunting the lagoons of Venice; we have then caught sight of his haughty, saddened countenance as he glides through the fêtes of Ferrara, where his masterpieces first saw the light of day; finally we have followed him to Rome, the Eternal City, which in crowning him glorified in him the martyr and the poet.'

It will be seen that here Liszt not merely outlines in advance the scheme of *emotion* which his listeners are to find successively expressed in his music but also gives them a series of *pictures* which are likely to recur to their mental eye as the three sections of this Tone Poem are performed.

2. A Question of Emphasis on Design or on 'Meaning'. The foregoing is an example of what is meant by 'Programme Music' (which need not, as the term is nowadays used, have a 'preface' or detailed printed 'programme', a mere 'fancy title' often sufficing). It is music

which, instead of being based, purely or primarily, upon a formal scheme of contrasting themes, development of them, repetition of them, etc. (see *Form*), is based upon a scheme of literary ideas or of mental pictures, which it seeks to evoke or recall by means of sound. The formal scheme is rarely or never entirely absent, even from the most advanced 'programme' composition, just as the poetic form (metre, etc.) is not absent from some passage of Shakespeare in which his main object is the evoking of a mental picture rather than the creation of beauty by the choice of words or by their effective arrangement in rhythm. But in music of the kind we are now considering a literary or pictorial 'programme' is first in the composer's mind and he expects it to be first in that of his listeners. He is aiming at beauty, yet emotion, and, more than that, drama or mental visualization is for the moment his major interest.

The opposite of 'Programme Music' is **Absolute Music** or **Abstract Music**—a prelude and fugue of Bach, a sonata of Mozart or Beethoven, in writing which the composer has worked to no literary or pictorial scheme, but has based his work upon the principles of formal beauty and, in a greater or less degree, upon that of a play of emotional contrasts, of emotions freed from material associations, of *sublimated* emotions. Here the composer has achieved what some extremists hope for in the sister art of poetry, as Edith Sitwell, who at a meeting of the 'Sitwell Society' in 1931 declared 'the poem comes first and it is not necessary that it should have any meaning'.

Not all music we are accustomed to call 'abstract' is *entirely* unprogrammatic, since in the act of composition images are apt to come to the composer's mind and to express themselves in sound (and, indeed, in any case he is representing a series of moods); and, similarly, there is no purely programmatic music, since, however much one may work to a literary or pictorial scheme the principles of form will assert themselves and demand recognition. But there is a vast quantity of music in which the dramatic or pictorial element, if it is present at all, is negligible and, also, there is a considerable quantity in which the dramatic or pictorial element quite obviously dominates.

It may be observed further that inasmuch as the creation of music on a mere wallpaper-pattern basis seems to be wellnigh impossible (i.e. music constructed entirely as *design*), and as some play of emotions seems to be inseparable from the act of musical creation, so almost any composition, however, 'abstract' or 'absolute' in the composer's intention, is capable of having a story or series of pictures read into it by an imaginative listener. Indeed, certain composers have found such stories or pictures occur to their minds *after* the composition of the music, and have given their works titles accordingly. Schumann says of his *Scenes of Childhood* ('Kinderscenen') that he did not work to a picture, e.g. 'place a crying child before me and then seek for tones to imitate it'. He says: 'It is the other way round . . . the superscriptions came into existence afterwards and are, indeed, nothing more than delicate directions for the rendering and understanding of the music.' The separate titles of the *Scenes of Childhood* are, 'Of Foreign Parts and People', 'Strange Story', 'Catch me if you can', 'Entreating Child', 'Dreaming', 'The Knight of the Hobby Horse', 'Child Falling Asleep', etc., and they fit the music so well that, had we not Schumann's word for it, it would probably never have occurred to us that he had not actually composed to the titles.

As a corollary to what has just been said it may be remembered that there are some people who seem to enjoy 'Absolute Music' best when they mentally add to it a more or less detailed programme of their own devising, and others who seem to enjoy 'Programme Music' best when they put the composer's programme entirely away from them. These two types of musical mind probably have always existed and always will exist.

Cf. *Composition* 5 on this whole general subject.

3. 'Suggestive Music.' Between the two extremes of 'Absolute Music' (so far as it is possible) and full 'Programme Music' of the Liszt type lies a large domain to which Mac-Dowell, who worked much therein, gave the name 'Suggestive Music'; in this a pictorial or literary title defines the mood and its source, but there is no detailed phrase-by-phrase following out of a programme.

Obviously, in this kind of music (as, indeed, in much programme music proper) the listener would rarely guess the actual literary idea of the music if the title were not there to tell him. Francesco Berger (1834–1933) once wrote a pianoforte piece and invited three brother composers to hear it and tell him what it 'meant'.

The 'meanings' suggested (according to him, quite seriously) were (1) 'Daybreak as seen from the lowest gallery of a Welsh coal mine'; (2) 'A boar-hunt in Russia'; (3) 'An enamoured couple whispering love vows'. And the intention of the composer had been musically to illustrate 'The discovering by Pharaoh's daughter of the infant Moses in the bulrushes'. The wide difference between Rimsky-Korsakof's intentions in his orchestral suite *Sheherazade* and the story applied to it by the great ballet impresario, Diaghilef, is notorious.

4. The Cruder Kinds of Programme Music. A great deal of programme music that has enjoyed a temporary popularity in uncultured circles is, of course, of the crudest kind, attempting to imitate actual sounds, bird-singing, cannon-firing, storms, and the like. Kotzwara's long-popular piano piece, *The Battle of Prague*, is an instance; Kotzwara (q.v.) hanged himself in London in 1791, yet his *chef d'œuvre* is still on sale there, so is, presumably, still 'done on the piano by females of energy', as Carlyle in his day reported. The 'Celebrated Storm in the Alps' played by the organist of Lucerne Cathedral to admiring visitors is another. One of the earliest American composers, James Hewitt, in 1792 performed in New York an orchestral 'Overture' of his composition 'in 9 Movements expressive of a Battle', and at the same concert a colleague of his, Jean Gehot, presented an 'Overture in 12 Movements expressive of a Voyage from England to America'. These might more properly be called descriptive suites; the movements included in the one case 'The Charge for the Attack', 'The Enemy Surrender', etc., and in the other 'Preparation for sailing, carpenters' hammering, crowing of the cock, weighing anchor', and 'Dance on Deck by the Passengers', etc. Such compositions as those mentioned in this paragraph do not in the slightest justify themselves as music and so there is nothing to be said for them save as entertainment.

And even as an entertainment they surely do not rank high. Agesilaus, king of Sparta, replied to one who asked him to hear a man that could imitate the nightingale, 'I have heard the nightingale himself'. What would he have said to Dr. Forde McLoughlin, of Toronto, who in 1932 entertained his fellow members of the Canadian Medical Association by a performance of his *Influenza—a Tone Poem*, or to Dr. Herman M. Parris of Philadelphia, who in 1948 similarly gave pleasure to the Doctors' Orchestral Society of New York by employing their musical–medical insight upon a ten-movement suite, *The Hospital*, descriptive of a young woman's appendectomy, including movements such as 'A Nurse' (*Allegro e amabile*), 'A Pre-operation Prayer' (*Andantino*), 'The Operating Room' (*Allegro* and then *Molto agitato*), and 'Anæsthesia' (*Presto*), etc.? (For a forerunner of these pathological composers see *Onslow, George*.)

5. An Historical List of Programme Compositions. As it has been stated above that the *term* 'Programme Music' originated with Liszt in the mid-nineteenth century, the impression may have been given that the *thing* then originated also. This is not so, and to illustrate the prevalence of this type of music in all ages a few examples (out of hundreds available) are mentioned below, in a chronological arrangement.

(*a*) **Sixteenth and Early Seventeenth Century.**

Jannequin's descriptive choral pieces, *The Battle, The Hare Hunt, The Song of the Birds*, etc.
John Mundy's Fantasia for virginals, with 'Lightning', 'Thunder', 'Calm Weather', etc.
Byrd's virginals piece with 'The March before the Battle' ('Here the Battle be joined', etc.).[1]

(*b*) **Seventeenth Century.**

Schütz's many realistic passages (cock crowing, the stone rolled away from the Sepulchre, etc.) in the Passions and Oratorios. This is of the nature of 'word-painting'.
Kuhnau's *Biblical Histories in Six Sonatas for the Keyboard* (with 'The Combat between David and Goliath', 'Hezekiah sick unto Death and recovered of his Sickness', etc.).

(*c*) **Eighteenth Century.**

Couperin's harpsichord pieces such as *The Butterflies, The Frightened Linnet, The Little Windmills, Jugglers, Tumblers, and Mountebanks with their Bears and Monkeys* (this last an item in his 'Records of the Grand and Ancient Minstrelsy'). In his piece *Les Tricoteuses* ('The Knitters') he has a passage in the minor for 'Mailles Lâchées' ('dropped stitches').
Handel's Frogs and Flies, Hailstones, etc., in the oratorio *Israel in Egypt*.
Bach's Rending of the Veil of the Temple in the *St. Matthew Passion*, his keyboard *Caprice on the Departure of his Dearest Brother* (with 'Cajolery of his friends to dissuade him from his journey', 'Fugue in Imitation of the Postilion's Horn', etc.). There is in his vocal music much 'word-painting'.
Haydn's introduction to the oratorio *The Creation*, entitled 'Chaos', and other passages in that work and in *The Seasons*. The *Seven Last Words* for orchestra ('Seven Sonatas with an Introduction and at the end an Earthquake'—see article *Seven Last Words*), etc.
The works of Hewitt and Gehot (New York, 1792).

(*d*) **Nineteenth Century.**

Beethoven's 'Battle' Symphony (*Wellington's Victory in the Fight near Vitoria*), much of his 'Pastoral' Symphony, etc.

[1] An even earlier category than the music of the sixteenth and seventeenth centuries might have preceded this list, for the principle is found applied in the plainsong period, certain antiphons in the old English service books abounding in examples that are sometimes astonishing.

Mendelssohn's *Midsummer Night's Dream* Overture, his *Hebrides* Overture, etc.
Schumann's *Carnival* and many other piano compositions.
Berlioz's 'Fantastic' Symphony (with its Ball Scene, its March to the Scaffold, its Witches' Sabbath, etc.), and many other works of this composer.
Liszt's 'Faust' Symphony and other orchestral works and much of his piano music (such as *St. Francis preaching to the Birds*).
Franck's tone-poem, *The Accursed Hunter*, etc.
MacDowell's *Heroic Sonata* for Piano (on the Arthurian Legend, with a Scherzo suggested by 'a picture of Doré's showing a Knight in a wood surrounded by elves'), etc.
Grieg's piano pieces, *Bridal Procession, March of the Dwarfs*, and many other things.
Smetana's autobiographical string quartet, *From my Life*, his series of six symphonic poems, *My Fatherland* (one of which sketches the course of the river Moldau), etc.
Saint-Saëns's symphonic poems (*Danse macabre, Omphale's Spinning Wheel*, etc.).
Rimsky-Korsakof's symphonic poems, *Sadko* and *Antar*, his symphonic suite, *Sheherazade*, etc.
Strauss's tone-poems, *Don Juan, Death and Transfiguration, Till Eulenspiegel's Merry Pranks, Thus Spake Zoroaster, Don Quixote, A Hero's Life*; his *Domestic Symphony* and *Alpine Symphony* (the last two come into the twentieth century).

(*e*) **Twentieth Century.**

Strauss. See above.
Elgar's symphonic study, *Falstaff*, etc.
Wallace's symphonic poems, *Wallace* (see *Wallace*), *Villon*, etc.
Bax's symphonic poems, *The Garden of Fand*, etc.
Honegger's orchestral works, *Horatius Victorious, Pacific 231* (a locomotive impression), *Rugby* (a football impression), etc.
Loeffler's orchestral works, *The Death of Tintagiles, Memories of my Childhood*, etc.
Copland's symphonic poem, *El Salón México*.
Respighi's symphonic poems, *Pines of Rome* and *Fountains of Rome*.

Some of the above are rather 'descriptive' or records of 'impressions' than detailed 'programme' pieces. But it is usual to collect all such music under the one title, as no clear dividing line is possible. Necessarily a great deal of song and song accompaniment (e.g. that of Schubert's *Erl-King* with its galloping horse) and of instrumental music in stage works (e.g. the 'Woodland Murmurs' in Wagner's *Siegfried*) is of the nature of Programme Music.

Subjects cognate to that of Programme Music are treated in the following articles, which should, for completeness, be read—*Romantic, Classical, Symphonic Poem, Metamorphosis of Themes; Motto Theme; Expression 5; Expressionism; Cinematograph*. Also refer to the article on Berlioz for 'Idée Fixe' and that on Liszt for 'Metamorphosis of Themes'. And see *Composition 5*.
All the composers mentioned above have articles devoted to them in this volume.

'PROGRESS' IN MUSIC. See *Composition* 15.

PROGRESSION. See *Harmony* 24 c.

PROGRESSIVO, PROGRESSIVAMENTE (It.). 'Progressive', progressively.

PROKOFIEF (Prokofieff, Prokofiev, Prokofyeff, etc.), **SERGE** (p. 913, pl. **156.** 5).

Born at Sontsovka, renamed Krasnoye, in the government of Ekaterinslav in 1891 and died in Moscow in 1953, aged sixty-one. He was a pupil at the St. Petersburg Conservatory of Liadof, Rimsky-Korsakof, and others. He became widely known as a brilliant pianist and applied his knowledge of the piano in his compositions, at twenty-three winning the Rubinstein prize with his First Piano Concerto. His appearances were usually as the interpreter of his own compositions. For some years he lived in exile, travelling on a League of Nations passport. He visited Russia in 1927 and 1929 and again in 1932, finally settling in Moscow with his family in 1934.

His style may be described as the antithesis of that of Scriabin. He aimed at the realization of primitive emotions, and playfulness and satire are also characteristics. His sympathies and taste inclined towards the classical but his manner was independent.

Among his works are the *Scythian Suite*, for orchestra, the ballets, *Chout* (or 'The Buffoon'), *The Prodigal Son*, *Romeo and Juliet*, and *Cinderella*, eleven operas, including *The Love for Three Oranges* (the libretto after Carlo Gozzi), *War and Peace*, *The Flaming Angel*, etc., a fairy tale for children, *Peter and the Wolf* (a monologue in the spoken voice with orchestral accompaniment; 1936), five piano concertos, violin concertos, symphonies, the brief piano pieces *Sarcasms*, nine piano sonatas, songs, etc.

In 1948 Prokofief along with other leading musicians came under censure by the Soviet authorities for the alleged 'formalistic distortions and anti-democratic tendencies of his music', and he promised to begin 'a search for a clearer and more meaningful language'.

He died on the same day as Josef Stalin. In 1957 his Seventh Symphony was posthumously awarded a Lenin Prize.

For Prokofief's period in Russian music see *Russia* 7, 8. See also *Oboe* 6 (end); *Clarinet* 6; *Ballet* 5; *Khrennikov*; *Broadcasting* 4; *Viol Family* 4; *Opera* 24 f (1955).

PROLOGUE, SYMPHONIC. See *Overture* 4.

PROLONGEMENT HARMONIQUE. This is a device applied to some organs and instruments of the harmonium type whereby the duration of a note may be indefinitely prolonged without occupying one of the hands or feet.

PROMENADE CONCERTS. See *Concert* 7; *Jullien.*

PROMPTEMENT (Fr.). 'Promptly.'

PRONTO (It.). 'Ready', 'prompt'. So *Prontamente*, 'promptly'.

PRONUNCIATION. See *Voice* 7, 8.

PROPER. See *Mass* 2; *Common.*

PROPHECY. See *Accent* 2.

PROPORTION. A conception that pervades medieval musical theory. It concerns both the relations between the vibration numbers of notes and those between their time-lengths. There are allusions to it in several theoretical works of the sixteenth century and the complex and sometimes very arbitrary cross-rhythms (see *Rhythm*) of a few instrumental pieces of that period are late relics of its use. Thereafter it disappears. For some of the complications of

the period of Proportion see *Notation* 3, under the heading 'Proportional Notation'.

PROPORTION AND FITNESS IN MUSIC. See *Quality in Music* 5.

PROPORZ. See *Nachtanz.*

PROSA or **PROSE.** The older name for *Sequence* (q.v.) in the liturgy of the Roman Catholic Church.

PROSE RHYTHM. See *Rhythm* 6.

PROSKE, KARL (1794–1861). See *Cecilian Movement.*

PROSODY. See *Metre.*

PROTESTANT BOYS. See *Lilliburlero.*

PROUT, EBENEZER. Born at Oundle in 1835 and died in London in 1909, aged seventy-four. He had a long and active career as organist, conductor, composer, music critic, and Professor of Composition at the Royal Academy of Music, Professor of Music at the University of Dublin (1894), and, especially, author of a long series of theoretical works, the most valued of their period, because the most exact and complete.

See references under *Colour and Music* 3; *Cornet* 1; *Additional Accompaniment*; *Day, Alfred*; *Congregational* 5; *Tonality*; *Dot.*

PROVENÇALE (Fr.). Apparently a vague name for any dance of Provence.

PROVENÇAL LANGUAGE, PROVENCE, TAMBOURIN DE. See *Minstrels*, etc. 4, *Tambourin.*

PROWSE, KEITH. See *Publishing* 7.

PRUNIÈRES, HENRY (1886–1942). Distinguished French musicologist—author of important works on Monteverdi, Lully (q.v.), etc. and founder (1919) and editor of *La Revue musicale.*

PRYS, EDMUND (c. 1541–1624). See *Hymns and Hymn Tunes* 17 e (xiii).

PS. Short for *Posaunen*, i.e. trombones.

PSALM. The Book of Psalms is the oldest book of songs still in use. The word 'Psalm' means a hymn accompanied by stringed instruments. Some of the various Psalms are definitely accredited to particular authors; their titles give seventy-three to David, twelve to Asaph, and so on. These attributions are later than the poems themselves, and some are demonstrably incorrect, but they have their interest. Asaph was amongst the Levite musicians whom 'David set over the service of song in the house of the Lord, after that the ark had rest' (1 Chron. vi. 31 et seq.), i.e. he was one of the pre-Temple musicians (see *Jewish Music* 1).

The dates of the Psalms are much debated by authorities: probably a number of collections of them, corresponding to our modern hymn-books, were in use. The present 'Book of Psalms' is an anthology, or rather a collection of previously existing anthologies. It falls into five volumes, as follows: 1–41, 42–72, 73–89, 90–106, 107–50. (But see reference to the system of numeration below.) Each of the books ends with a Doxology or liturgical formula of praise, the last four psalms constituting an extended Doxology to the whole collection.

The Psalms form the backbone or essential part of the Offices (Matins, Vespers, etc.) of the Roman Breviary and to some extent (following this tradition of a thousand years) of Morning and Evening Prayer in the Anglican Church.

Single Psalms, and groups of them, have repeatedly been set by composers, as, for instance, the Seven Penitential Psalms by Orlandus Lassus (published 1565) and the setting of the first fifty Psalms by Marcello (1724–7), these latter being treatments of Italian paraphrases; Schütz, Bach, Mendelssohn, Franck, Florent Schmitt, Kodály, and, indeed, perhaps one may say most composers in history, have set psalms, and psalm texts naturally form a large proportion of the texts of German and other motets and English and American anthems.

The **Penitential Psalms** referred to above are in the English Authorized Version, 6, 32, 38, 51, 102, 130, and 143, and in the Latin Version (Vulgate), 6, 31, 37, 50, 101, 129, and 142. The numeration of these two translations differs from No. 10 onwards, 10 and 11 of the English version being put together as one Psalm in the Latin. The English version agrees with the Jewish prayer book.

The **verse system** of the Psalms is that peculiar to Hebrew poetry. It is not to a great extent metrical, even in the original, and there is no rhyme: its rhyme and rhythm are, so to speak, those of thought rather than of words, expressing themselves especially in parallelism of thought. This parallelism should be grasped by all who are concerned with the musical rendering of the poems. It consists either in two balanced clauses of a verse, expressing the same or a similar thought, or in an antithesis between two clauses, or by a second clause stating the result of the first. This can be best studied in the two volumes of the Psalms in the *Modern Reader's Bible*, edited by the late Professor R. G. Moulton of the University of Chicago, where not only is the original personal or liturgical intention of each Psalm explained but all are set out according to their logical divisions into lines and (with indentations and other devices) stanzas, according to our present usual system of displaying lyrical verse. A fresh meaning comes into the Psalms when their historical meaning and their lyrical construction are both grasped.

The music attached to the Psalms in services of the Christian Church is referred to under *Gregorian Tones* and *Anglican Chant*. They are sung antiphonally either (as often in the Roman Catholic Church) by priest and choir, or, as in the Anglican Church, by the two sides of the choir. This antiphonal treatment is traditional and dates from the time of Solomon's Temple, as a number of biblical references show.

The place of the Psalms in the Anglican Liturgy is referred to under *Common Prayer*. The attempted revision of 1927, there mentioned, provided for reforms in the use of the Psalms, including permission to omit the Imprecatory Psalms (e.g. 69, 109, 137). The Roman Catholic Church, by a Constitution of Pius X (1911), has restored its previous rule of a weekly recitation of the whole Psalter in order, which the multiplication of Saints' offices, etc., had broken into. (There was a time, in the early centuries of Christianity, when certain orders recited the whole Psalter daily; it has also been the practice to go through it on certain occasions—as when the Chapel Royal of Edward IV, in 1483, sang 'the holl sauter' over his corpse.)

The English version of the Psalms sung in churches (the 'Prayer Book Version') dates from the sixteenth century, having as its basis the sixteenth-century translations of Tyndale and of Coverdale, these being revised by Cranmer for the 'Great Bible' (1539), and being retained in the Prayer Book when the present Authorized Version of the Bible was issued in 1611. The Latin versions in use in the Roman Catholic Church are two, known as the Roman and the Gallican. Both were made by St. Jerome, as part of the Vulgate, at the end of the fourth and beginning of the fifth century; the Gallican (so called from its circulation in Gaul) represents his later revision and is in use everywhere except St. Peter's in Rome, St. Mark's in Venice, and Milan.

The **Metrical Psalm,** or verse paraphrase, holds a very important place in the history of English-speaking Protestantism; it is treated in this volume under *Hymns and Hymn Tunes* 4, 5, 10, 11.

PSALMODY. By this term is generally meant the study of the tunes for metrical versions of the psalms and for hymns, but it can, obviously, have a wider range of meaning.

See *Hymns and Hymn Tunes*; *Psalms*; *Plainsong*; *Gregorian Tones*; *Anglican Chant*.

PSALMODY IMPROVEMENT ASSOCIATION. See *Presbyterian Church Music* 4.

PSALTER NEWLY POINTED. See *Anglican Chant* 6.

PSALTERY (p. 447, pl. 77. 1, 2). An early stringed instrument, like a dulcimer but played by plucking with a plectrum or with the fingers, instead of being hammered. It was extremely widespread in the fourteenth and fifteenth centuries, as attest the innumerable references in European literature and representations in pictures and ecclesiastical sculptures. The sixteenth-century English translators of the Bible were evidently acquainted with it.

There has been much variety in its shape at various times and in various places. It is an obvious forerunner of the harpsichord (with its plucked strings), as the dulcimer is of the pianoforte (with its hammered strings). It may also be considered a type of harp with resonance box, or a simpler form of zither (q.v.). The English Bell Harp (q.v.) is of the same type.

PSAUME (Fr.). Psalm (in old spelling *Pseaulme*).

p.s.m. See *Degrees and Diplomas* 2.

PTOLEMY. See *Colour and Music*.

PUBLICATION. See *Publishing*.

PUBLISHING OF MUSIC

(For illustrations see p. 849, pl. **144.**

As stated in the article *Printing of Music*, the printing of musical notation followed hard on the introduction of letterpress printing. Printing implies publishing, and the publishing of music was in active swing during the early part of the sixteenth century.

1. Venice. The great commercial importance of Venice at this period, together with the musical activities connected with the cathedral of St. Mark, no doubt combined to make it the first centre of the music publishing business, the name of **Petrucci** (see *Printing of Music* 1) standing at the head of the roll of the music publishers of the world. Music had been published before this, but it was mostly nothing beyond the plainsong and service books. Petrucci obtained from the government of Venice a twenty years' monopoly of the printing of figured music (i.e. non-plainsong), including music in the tablature of organ and lute. His first publication appeared in 1501 and thenceforward he poured out a series of fine collections of church music, lute music, etc.—all beautifully printed. This was the period of the supremacy of the Flemish church composers in Italy and it was largely their works that Petrucci published (three volumes of Josquin des Prés, for instance). In 1511 he returned to his native place of Fossombrone, in the Papal States, obtaining from the Pope a fifteen years' monopoly of music printing in those states. The work of Petrucci has been of high value in preserving unaccompanied choral compositions of the Flemish period, some of which would doubtless, but for it, have been lost.

The firm of **Gardano** (see also 3) published in Venice from 1537 to 1650. Its production was enormous and comprised the unaccompanied choral works of the Flemish school and of the similar succeeding Italian school, and also some of the early operatic works which followed these.

The important firm of **Amadino** (for its first three years Amadino and Vincenti) existed from 1583 to 1615, and its publications included the *Orfeo* of Monteverdi and others of that composer's works.

2. Paris. The next great publishing enterprise after that of Petrucci is that of **Attaignant** of Paris (cf. *Printing of Music* 1), who was publishing there 1527–49. Like Petrucci he published on a large scale—masses, motets, dances, lute music, and thirty-five books of four-part songs comprising nearly 1,000 in all (a precious treasury of the North French and Flemish music which was at the height of its flowering at this period).

From 1540 **Le Roy** was at work; he was a friend of Orlandus Lassus and published some of his music. From 1552 his brother-in-law, **Ballard** (cf. *Printing of Music* 2), was in partnership with him and the Ballard family henceforth held almost a monopoly of the trade in France. They were actually still publishing almost up to the beginning of the nineteenth century and had the same type in use for over two hundred years. They began in the period of the Flemish and Northern French school and published Marot's Psalms and the works of Orlandus Lassus and Claude Le Jeune, went on, the next century, to publish Lully, and in the eighteenth century published Couperin and others. Their three great (successive but overlapping) series of songs. *Chansons pour danser et à boire* ('Dancing and Drinking Songs') and *Airs de différents auteurs* and *Airs sérieux et à boire* ran from 1627 to well into the eighteenth century—at first appearing annually and then for over thirty years monthly, many of the numbers being often reprinted.

3. Antwerp and Louvain. An interesting case of a professional music copyist turned printer and publisher is that of **Susato** of Antwerp, who changed his occupation in 1543, and during the next eighteen years published over fifty volumes of music, most of them including something composed by himself. (For his 'psalm-ditties' or 'Souterliedekens' see *Hymns and Hymn Tunes* 17 c.) Like Petrucci and Attaignant he published a quantity of the music of the then popular Flemish school.

The important firm of **Phalèse** published at Louvain and later at Antwerp, 1545–1674. It had, after a time, a working arrangement with the Venice firm of Gardano, already mentioned, whereby a great deal of Italian music published in Venice was republished at Antwerp and thus made known in northern Europe: this returned the compliment of an earlier day when the Flemish works were mostly issued from Italy.

4. Britain in the Sixteenth Century. Music publishing as a recognized branch of commerce first comes into prominent notice in British musical history with the Psalm Book publications of John Day (p. 849, pl. **144.** 1)—especially that of Sternhold and Hopkins, 1562 (see *Hymns and Hymn Tunes* 5, 17 e), and then with the monopoly which Queen Elizabeth I in 1575 granted to two Gentlemen of her Chapel Royal, the composers **Tallis** and **Byrd** (see *Printing of Music* 1; *Monopolies*); this gave them the right to control both printing and importation of music and music-ruled paper for twenty-one years. When Tallis died, ten years later, the rights belonged to Byrd alone, and at the expiration of his rights the composer **Morley** got the grant of the monopoly (1598), also for twenty-one years—'with forfeiture of £10 by every person offending against the grant' (see also *Barley, William*).

The general principle of monopolies was, of course, much and rightly objected to at that period, and in the early years of the seventeenth century Parliament interfered, but the music monopoly went on (perhaps not considered worth troubling about). Thus for over forty years, and this, as it happened, a period of high and valuable activity in British music, one or two composers were given the control of all the musical publications of their native brethren, and even of their brethren abroad so far as the publishing of their works in Britain was concerned.

Tallis and Byrd did not publish much in their own name, and when the rights came into Byrd's hands alone he assigned them to a printer, **Thomas Este or East** (p. 849, pl. **144.** 2). The wonderful flow of English madrigal compositions was just beginning. It was Este who, in 1588, published Yonge's *Musica Transalpina*, the collection of Italian madrigals that inspired the English composers (see *Madrigal* 2). And on the title-page of practically all the many books of English madrigals that were published Este's name will be found (see under *Este*, and for a reference to his psalm-tune publications see *Hymns* 5, 17 e).

5. Britain in the Seventeenth Century. The next music publishers of importance (and the first to make a special and separate business of music publishing) are the bookseller **John Playford** (p. 849, pl. **144.** 3) and, succeeding him, his son **Henry Playford**. John was clerk of the Temple Church, London, and had a shop by it. In 1650 (i.e. during the Commonwealth; see *Puritans and Music* 6) he published his *English Dancing Master*, which in the next seventy years had eighteen editions and remains a most valuable compilation. The days of official monopoly were over but the Playfords' business skill gave them a virtual monopoly. They published all the most important theoretical treatises, instrumental instruction books, collections of catches, music for viols, Psalm Books (see *Hymns and Hymn Tunes* 5, 17 e), and indeed everything musical. They were the first publishers of Purcell's music. When the elder Playford died (about 1686) Purcell set to music the elegy upon him written by Nahum Tate (of Tate and Brady—see *Hymns and Hymn Tunes* 5), and ten years later the younger Playford published Blow's setting of Dryden's *Ode on the Death of Purcell*. Here were pleasant relations between publisher and composer.

6. Britain in the Eighteenth Century. The Playford business finally declined about 1705, under the competition of **Walsh**, for whom composers would perhaps gladly have written elegies in a different frame of mind— if he would only have given them occasion a

little earlier. He is today remembered especially as Handel's publisher. The first work published was the opera *Rinaldo* and Handel wrote to Walsh, 'My dear Sir, As it is only right that we should be on an equal footing, you shall compose the next opera and I will sell it.' Walsh was in the habit of giving Handel only £20 for the right to publish an oratorio. Walsh and his son, who succeeded him, profited greatly by the eighteenth-century enthusiasm for Italian operas, publishing very many books of songs from them. They also published the catches so popular then, many collections of country dances, and collections of songs sung at the entertainment gardens (see *Concert* 12). And they reprinted in England a number of valuable Continental publications, such as the works of Corelli. The firm flourished until the death of the younger Walsh (very rich) in 1766.

Bremner was a very important publisher in the period following. He started business in Edinburgh and then came to London in 1762, where he was active until his death in 1789. He took the place of the Walshes as the publisher of books of songs from the fashionable Italian operas of the day, and published a good many books of country dances and of Scots songs and dances, as well as much instrumental music, theoretical works, psalm tunes, etc.

There was a little British provincial music publishing in the eighteenth century, but it was unimportant. The two capitals of Edinburgh and Dublin issued a good deal, however (see *Ireland* 5).

7. Britain in the Nineteenth and Twentieth Centuries. The oldest existing British firm is, apparently, that of **Joseph Williams** (founded 1808), five generations of the same family having already been engaged in its management.

Other prominent existing firms are **Chappell** (founded 1810); **Boosey** (founded 1816; began as one of the few houses engaged in the importation of foreign music and had long a speciality in Italian opera; from the 1930s, after an amalgamation with Hawkes and Co., as **Boosey and Hawkes** rapidly became a leading international publisher of contemporary music); **Cramer** (founded in 1824, by the pianist and composer, J. B. Cramer, q.v.); **Keith Prowse** (earliest date obtainable being that of an advertisement of 1835).

The story of modern choral-music publishing in Britain may be said effectively to begin with the firm of **Novello**. It was based on the enterprise of the Roman Catholic organist, Novello (p. 289, pl. **51.** 3)—Vincent Novello, the hero of his friend Lamb's *Chapter on Ears* (see reference under *Roman Catholic Church Music in Britain*). He could find no publisher for a collection of 'Sacred Music' he had compiled, so, in 1811, issued it himself, and in it introduced the innovation of writing out the organ part in full, instead of giving the mere figured bass (see *Figured Bass*); in this he was much opposed by some organists of the day.

His son, J. Alfred Novello (began business 1829), was just as enterprising and knew how to turn to business account the nineteenth-century British enthusiasm for choral singing. Up to this time the members of such choral societies as existed had either to buy large-sized and expensive scores of the oratorios or to sing from manuscript copies of their own vocal parts made by themselves. In the 1820s a copy of Handel's *Messiah* cost two guineas (then about 10 dollars); in the 1830s it cost a guinea; in 1846 Novello published it in twelve monthly numbers at 6*d.* each (12 cents), and this he did also with other oratorios, including Mendelssohn's *St. Paul* a few years after its first appearance. In 1859 *Messiah* and *Israel in Egypt* could be bought for one shilling and fourpence (35 cents) and later one shilling (25 cents) became the established price.

Another firm whose success was based upon the choral movement was that of Curwen, associated with *Tonic Sol-fa* (q.v.); it began in 1863. Like the firm of Novello, that of Curwen is still active.

Some other prominent firms are **Augener** (founded 1853; see *Printing of Music* 4); **Chester** (founded at Brighton in 1860, but the present business, reconstituted by Kling, largely interested in the publication of and agency for contemporary music and managed from London, may be said to date from 1915); and the **Oxford University Press** (the Press dates from 1478 but the music department only from 1924). There have been and are a large number of other firms of importance, but they cannot be listed in an article of this scale and the above are sufficient to present an outline of British music publishing activity. Generalizing very roughly it may be said that after the eighteenth century the British music publishing trade has been largely based upon choral and didactic publications. The great developments in composition during the later eighteenth and the nineteenth centuries were in Germany, and this gave it a pre-eminence as a centre of musical publication. There has in British music necessarily been a much greater import than export trade.

A very curious custom that persisted into the twentieth century was the double-pricing of sheet music. Thus an ordinary song or piano piece would bear the printed price 4*s.* but be sold at 2*s.* (indeed, lavish discounts often reduced the price still lower—even to 1*s.* 3*d.*). Possibly George Walker, in the early nineteenth century, was the first to introduce this cheap-jack method.

8. Some Continental Firms. It is not possible here to discuss the publishing activities of all periods and countries, but something must be said of the eighteenth- and earlier nineteenth-century German enterprises that gave the German music trade its undisputed primacy. As above mentioned, it largely arose, naturally, out of the German leadership in musical composition during the same period.

Breitkopf (of Leipzig) is the first great name. He was a printer and general publisher who took to music printing in 1754. His business success was largely founded on the introduction of improvements in music type (see *Printing of Music* 5). **Härtel** bought the firm in 1795, and then began that publication of great series of the complete works of various composers for which the house is still famous. The records of the firm contain a great deal of most interesting material concerning the long series of famous composers (Beethoven, etc.) with whom they have had business associations. Their premises suffered war destruction in 1943 but were afterwards rebuilt.

A few other historic German and Austrian firms (of many) are **Artaria**, of Vienna (1778–1932); **Schott**, of Mainz (*c.* 1770); **André**, of Offenbach (1774); **Simrock**, of Bonn and later Berlin (1790); **Cranz**, of Hamburg (1813); **Peters**, of Leipzig (1814); **Diabelli**, of Vienna (1824); **Schuberth**, of Hamburg (1826); **Bote and Bock**, of Berlin (1838); **Litolff**, of Brunswick (1851); **Steingräber**, of Leipzig (1878); **Universal Edition**, of Vienna (1901); **Bärenreiter**, of Kassel (1924).

For the special conditions that led to the foundation of the Russian publishing house of Belaief see that name.

Space cannot be found in this article for the French and Italian firms today. A few words seem due, however, to the activities of the firm of **Ricordi**, founded 1808 by a music copyist, Giovanni Ricordi. It has always specialized in the publication of the works of Italian composers, naturally, therefore, in opera publication—Rossini, Bellini, Donizetti, Verdi, Boito, and the composers of the twentieth century. Its headquarters have always been at Milan. In 1943 the entire Ricordi establishment was wiped out by an air-raid. The stock and more than three hundred thousand engraved plates of musical publications were thus lost.

9. United States of America. Music publishing in the American colonies was necessarily very restricted, indeed for long almost confined to books of psalm tunes (see *Hymns and Hymn Tunes* 11, 17 f; also p. 493, pl. 88) and treatises for singing-class work designed to train singers to take their part in religious worship. Music of a scope beyond this was largely imported from England. However, towards the end of the eighteenth century there came a gradual widening. In the 1790s members of the Carr family, musicians from England, established music shops and publishing businesses in New York, Philadelphia, and Baltimore; it would appear that they had had experience of the business before emigrating to America. They issued songs from the ballad operas, pianoforte sonatas of Haydn, etc.

Gradually, from the end of the eighteenth century onwards, a number of publishing firms came into existence, and the issue of music (especially didactic material) is now enormous.

Some leading older figures are the following:

Oliver Ditson (Boston 1835; in 1931 his entire catalogue of 52,000 items was handed over to the Presser firm—see below); Schirmer (New York 1861—continuing an earlier firm); John Church (Cincinnati 1854); J. Fischer (New York 1864); Carl Fischer (New York 1872); Arthur P. Schmidt (Boston 1877); Witmark (New York 1885); Summy (New York 1888); Theodore Presser (Philadelphia 1888); B. F. Wood (Boston 1893); H. W. Gray (New York 1894); C. C. Birchard (Boston 1900). A few of these dates of foundation may be open to question, as some of the firms were in business earlier as music-sellers and the exact period of their starting publishing is not always easy to determine.

From 1930 a very considerable movement towards the amalgamation of music publishing firms took place. Several of the above firms were affected; and in addition there is a strong tendency for other interests such as broadcasting and the cinema to enter the field. A difficulty has been found in the United States, as in certain other countries, in securing publication of good work of native composers, such as could not, from its nature, be expected to enjoy a remunerative sale. To remedy this Arthur Farwell (q.v.) in 1901 founded the Wa Wan Press, supporting it partly by sales on a subscription basis and partly by his own lectures and performances. In 1912 Messrs. Schirmer took this over. The Society for the Publication of American Music was founded by B. C. Tuthill in 1919, chiefly for the publication of chamber music. The Eastman organization of Rochester, N.Y., and the Juilliard Foundation of New York have also helped towards the publication of native works. And the serial, *New Music*, founded by Henry Cowell in 1927, for a number of years carried on the publication of contemporary compositions.

A useful enterprise has, from 1935, been undertaken by the Music Division of the New York Public Library. From old orchestral and chamber music 'parts' in its possession, of works of which the scores have never been issued, it makes scores and then reproduces them by a cheap process for sale to any who desire them for performance. In this way much late sixteenth-, seventeenth-, and eighteenth-century music is made available for study and performance. For cognate subjects see *Copyists; Printing of Music.*

10. An Undesirable Method of Publication. A few words may well be added upon a common yet generally undesirable activity—that of publication at the composer's expense. There are in Britain, and possibly in other countries, firms which confine their activities to this form of publishing (though 'firm' is too complimentary a term for what may turn out on inquiry to be a man and a girl typist working in one or two rooms). Some of the old-established and reputable publishers, especially if they are also music-printers, will accept commissions to publish at composers' expense work which they feel they cannot accept for their regular catalogue, and if it be decided to adopt this method of publication negotiations should be confined to them.

It should, however, be understood by the amateur or professional musician who has written a song or pianoforte piece that if none of the many regular firms of publishers available will accept it on the usual terms of publication at their own expense, with payment of the composer by a sum down or by royalty, then it is probably not worth publication.

It should also be understood that a publisher who has at the outset been spared any expenditure on production has none to recoup, so that one strong motive for 'pushing' sales does not exist. Further, firms which *confine themselves* to the 'composer's expense' form of publishing rarely or never possess the organization and contacts with retailers that are necessary for the adequate putting of a publication on the market.

PUCCINI, GIACOMO (p. 524, pl. **95. 6**) (in full Giacomo Antonio Domenico Michele Secondo Maria). Born at Lucca in 1858 and died at Brussels in 1924, aged sixty-five. He represents the fifth generation of a family of professional musicians holding official positions of some importance in Italy.

He was trained at the Milan Conservatory, his chief teacher being Ponchielli.

His first opera to reach performance was *Le Villi* (1884), and thenceforward there was a procession of works at rather long but fairly regular intervals—*Edgar* (1889); *Manon Lescaut* (1893); *La Bohème* (1896); *Tosca* (1900); *Madam Butterfly* (1904); *The Girl of the Golden West* (1910); *La Rondine* ('The Swallow', 1917); the 'Trittico' (q.v.), a series of one-act operas, unconnected in subject, made up of *Il Tabarro* ('The Cloak'), *Suor Angelica* ('Sister Angelica'), and *Gianni Schicchi* (1918); *Turandot* (finished after his death by Alfano, 1926).

In all these works the music is essentially Italian in its easy-flowing melody, its clearly pointed dramatic effect, and its brightly coloured orchestration. In his harmonies the composer was usually just original enough to rouse to attention the conventional operagoer; perhaps it may be said that he employs not so much his own system of harmony as that of his immediate predecessors served up with new condiments.

Only two or three of Puccini's operas ever failed and perhaps the reason of his success may be generalized as follows. As hinted above, he never bored by blandly repeating old formulae (melodic, harmonic, orchestral), nor shocked by introducing entirely new ones, and he showed a strong sense of stage effect.

See references under *Alfano; Samisen; Carner; Opera* 7, 21 l, 24 (1893 onwards); also for plots, etc., *Bohème; Madam Butterfly; Tosca; Trittico; Turandot.*

PUCKERIDGE, RICHARD. See *Harmonica* 1.

PUGNANI, GAETANO. Born at Turin in 1731 and died there in 1798, aged sixty-six. He was a great violinist and composer for strings, of the best eighteenth-century stamp. He also wrote operas and other works. (The familiar *Praeludium and Allegro* in E minor, for violin, attributed to him by its 'editor' Kreisler, is now admitted to be entirely the work of this latter.)

PUI or PUY. See *Minstrels*, etc. 6; *Cecilia, St.; Competitions* 1.

PUJOL.

(1) **JUAN.** Born at Barcelona in 1573 and there died in 1626. He was choirmaster of the cathedral of his native place and composed valuable church music.

(2) **JUAN BAUTISTA.** Born at Barcelona in 1835 and there died in 1898, aged sixty-three. He was a pianist, pianoforte teacher, composer of piano music, and author of a book on piano playing.

(3) **EMILIO.** Born in Lérida in 1886. He is a world-touring guitarist (see *Vihuela*).

PULITZER PRIZE. See under *Patronage* 7.

PULSE. A term sometimes used as a synonym for 'beat', but a distinction is sometimes made, e.g. six-eight time may be said to have six pulses but two beats (cf. Table 10).

PULT, PULTE (Ger.). 'Desk', 'desks' (i.e. music stand, stands—each desk having two players). So *Pultweise*, 'Desk-wise', i.e. in order of the players' desks (for instance, in directions that a stringed instrument part's mutes are to be added by its players gradually—not all at one moment, which would involve a moment's silence of the whole body of the instruments concerned).

PULVER, JEFFREY. See mention under *Norcome; Dictionaries* 4.

PUNTA (It.). 'Point', e.g. *A punta d'arco*, 'with the point of the bow'.

'PUNTO' (= J. W. Stich). See *Bohemia*.

PUNTO CORONATO, PUNTO D'ORGANO (It.). Literally 'crowned point', 'organ point' (see *Point d'orgue*), i.e. the sign ⌢.

PUPITRE (Fr.). 'Desk', i.e. music stand.

PURCELL.

(1) **HENRY** (p. 864, pl. **145**). Born in London in 1658 or 1659 and there died in 1695, aged thirty-six. He was the son of a Gentleman of the Chapel Royal (either Thomas or Henry Purcell; more probably the latter) and himself became a boy of that Chapel. Here his masters would be, successively, Captain Henry Cooke (q.v.) and Pelham Humfrey (q.v.). Possibly he was also a pupil of John Blow (q.v.).

At about fourteen, apparently (probably on his voice breaking), he became assistant keeper, maker, mender, repairer, and tuner of the regals, organs, virginals, flutes, recorders, and other wind instruments, possibly being apprenticed to John Hingston (q.v.), the principal keeper of those things. The Treasurer's accounts of Westminster Abbey show that from 1675 to 1678 he received annual sums for tuning the organ there; there are also records of his receiving sums in 1676 and 1688 for copying music (but he did not, as has often been stated, hold any official position as copyist). In 1679 he was appointed organist of the Abbey at ten pounds per annum.

The Lord Chamberlain's records show that in 1677 (when he was only eighteen or nineteen) he was appointed to the Chapel Royal as 'Composer in Ordinary with fee, for the Violins' (i.e. for the orchestra there. See *Chapel Royal*). In 1682 he became organist of the Chapel.

In 1683 he succeeded Hingston as keeper of the instruments, at an annual salary of £60—but had some difficulty at times to get his money.

At the coronation of James II in Westminster Abbey he provided (possibly in his capacity of keeper of the royal instruments or possibly in that of organist of the Abbey) a small additional organ, receiving payment for this; at the coronation of William and Mary he again provided a supplementary organ. On these occasions the Abbey choirs sat by the permanent organ and the Chapel Royal Choir by the temporary one. For admission of spectators to the great organ loft in 1689 he took money, but the Chapter made him hand it over to them, giving him only two days in which to do so ('And in default thereof his place to be declared to be null and void. And it is further ordered that his stipend or salary due at our Lady Day last past be detained in the hands of the Treasurer untill further order').

Six years later a newspaper (*The Flying Post*, 23–6 Nov. 1695) records a kinder resolution of the Chapter:

'Mr. Henry Pursel, one of the most celebrated Masters of the Science of Musick in the kingdom and scarce inferiour to any in Europe, dying on Thursday last; the Dean of Westminster knowing the great worth of the deceased, forthwith summoned a Chapter, and unanimously resolved that he shall be interred in the Abbey, with all the Funeral Solemnity they are capable to perform for him, granting his widow the choice of the ground to reposit his Corps free from any charge, who has appointed it at the foot of the Organs, and this evening he will be interred, the whole Chapter assisting with their vestments; together with all the Lovers of that Noble Science, with the united Choyres of that and the Chappel Royal, when the Dirge composed by the Deceased for her late Majesty of Ever Blessed Memory, will be Played by Trumpets and other Musick; And his place of Organist is disposed of to that great Master, Dr. Blow.'

His official duties led him to the composition of a large amount of church music, some of it grave and polyphonic, in the old English style, and other of it gay and rhythmically simple, in the lighter and more modern French style beloved of his master Charles II (cf. *Humfrey*).

He wrote many royal odes, and a good deal of theatre music, the former now unperformable on account of the courtier-like extravagance of its words, and the latter chiefly kept in public remembrance by the performance of isolated songs—many of them of great spirit or of a rare gentle beauty. His instrumental music includes fresh and delightful (if simple) harpsichord suites, admirably expressive sonatas for two violins, cello, and harpsichord, and very beautiful string fantasias. There is also one sonata for solo violin and keyboard. His choral style in his principal works is magnificent, and it is supposed to have influenced Handel when he settled in England.

His early death must ever be regarded as a national calamity.

Reference will be found as follows:

1. Historical Position, etc. *History of Music* 5; *England* 5, 6; *Italy* 9; *France* 6; *Puritans* 3.

2. Range of Keys, etc. *Keyboard* 3; *Suite* 4; *Modulation*.

3. Manner and Types of Composition, etc. *Composition* 10; *Figured Bass*; *Form* 5, 6; *Sonata* 3, 6, 10 b; *Suite* 3, 4, 5; *Allemande*; *Sarabande*; *Courante*; *Minuet*; *Rigaudon*; *Cebell*; *Canaries*; *Chorale Prelude*; *Ground*; *Fancy*; *Hornpipe*; *In Nomine*; *Recitative*; *Tremolo*; *Arrangement*; *Voluntary*.

4. Church Music. *Chapel Royal*; *Copyists*; *Te Deum*; *Anthem*; *Bell* 6 (for 'Bell Anthem'); *Hallelujah Chorus*; *Cecilia*; *Cathedral Music* 8.

5. Theatre Music. *Opera* 13 b, 24 b (1688); *Masque*; *Incidental Music*; *Ballet* 7; *Dido and Aeneas*.

6. Instruments. *Flute Family* 1, 4; *Trumpet Family* 3; *Trombone Family* 2 a; *Percussion Family* 4 a; *Reed-Organ Family* 2.

7. Theoretical Teaching, etc. *Descant*; *Harmony* 20; *Ornaments* 2; *Expression* 1; *Reports*.

8. Various. *Street Music* 2; *God save the Queen* 6, 7, 8,

9, 15; *Lilliburlero*; *Cold and Raw*; *Passing By* (wrongly attributed to him); *Locke, Matthew*; *Roseingrave, Daniel*; *Weldon, John*; *Patronage* 7 (end); *Stradella*; *Lully*; *Publishing* 5; *Pitch* 6 b; *Nicknamed* 16; *Misattributed* (Locke's 'Macbeth'); *Ballad*; *Beggar's Opera*; *Bird Music*; *Novello*; *Dictionaries*; *Gesamtausgabe*.

(2) DANIEL. Born about 1660 and died in 1717, aged about fifty-seven. He was the son of Thomas Purcell and thus possibly the younger brother of Henry (see 1 above). For a time (1688–93) he was organist of Magdalen College, Oxford. He then returned to London and became a popular composer for the theatres. A book of psalm tunes with interludes between the verses throws light on the organ-playing customs of the day.

See reference under *Recorder Family* 2.

PURCELL COCKRAM, E. See *Passing By*.

PURCELL SOCIETY. This is a British organization founded in 1876, its main purpose being the editing and publication (by Messrs. Novello) of the composer's works. The thirty-first and final volume appeared in 1959.

PURDAY, CHARLES HENRY (1799–1885). Vocalist, London Presbyterian precentor, lecturer, song composer, music publisher, and other things. His hymn tune *Sandon* is still much sung.

See *Annotated Programmes* 4.

PURITANS AND MUSIC

(For some illustrations see p. 865, pl. **146.**)

1. Introductory. The word Puritan has come to possess two connotations. The present article accepts that definition of Webster's Dictionary which describes the Puritan as:

'One who, in the time of Queen Elizabeth and the first two Stuarts, opposed traditional and formal usages, and advocated simpler forms of faith and worship than those established by law; originally a term of reproach. As a political party the Puritans were in the ascendant during the Commonwealth period (1649–60). Many before that time had emigrated to New England, forming the bulk of the early population.'

That is the strict and historically accurate definition. In addition to this the word is often loosely applied to any person or body standing for adherence to principle in religious or social life.

2. The Objection to Elaborate Church Music. Puritanism, in either sense of the word, has been antagonistic to music as such only in the case of certain quite exceptional individuals or sects. But it has always been somewhat strict in what concerns music as a part of, or aid to, worship. It is an error to suppose that this kind of musical Puritanism has been confined to certain Protestant bodies or

to the Anglo-Saxon peoples. Throughout the whole history of the Christian Church it has reappeared at intervals, and certain Popes and Councils have been in this sense amongst the most rigid Puritans. (A brief discussion of this branch of the subject will be found under *Church Music* 4.) Nevertheless, the churches whose doctrines and practices have most closely followed those of the church of Calvin at Geneva have the most steadily held to the stricter view.

3. The Complete Acceptance of Music other than in Church. When Bach was in the service of Prince Leopold of Anhalt-Cöthen (1717–23) his compositions were not of the nature of organ music or church music of any kind, but of chamber music. This was because the Prince was a Calvinist (belonging to the 'Reformed' Church of Germany, and not the Lutheran Church); no music beyond simple chorales was required in the church service, and Bach's musical energies, though fully employed, were so employed in the provision of music for the court's entertainments (see *Presbyterian Church Music* 1).

This was much the position in the English

Puritanism of the previous century. There was no objection to music; indeed, secular music flourished as never before. But there *was* an objection to elaborate church music, with church organs and professional choirs. Simplicity and sincerity were aimed at, but no doubt we must consider that a misreading of scripture, and consequent prejudice, was a factor in excluding so much that was beautiful from the service of the church. To the organ as such there was no objection; domestic organs were common and so were, apparently, tavern organs (see *Music Hall* 1).

There is evidently not the very slightest ground for the often repeated statement that the Commonwealth and Protectorate (1649–60) 'killed' English music, as the career of the great Purcell immediately followed this period.

For London music teachers during the Commonwealth see *Profession*, etc. 9.

4. Cromwell as Music-lover.
The Puritan leaders of the nation loved the recreation of music. Cromwell is recorded to have entertained distinguished foreign guests with music at meals (Report of one of the Dutch ambassadors, 1654). When he sent an embassy to Sweden, under Bulstrode Whitelocke (1653), he included musical performers in the party, and they were so successful in pleasing those to whom the embassy was sent that the Queen of Sweden demanded that on their return they should send her copies of the English music performed. Cromwell had a particular liking for the Latin motets of Deering (q.v.) and used to have them performed before him. He removed the organ from Magdalen College, Oxford (where its presence was no longer needful), to his own palace of Hampton Court, where his private organist, Hingston, often performed on it before him. He employed Hingston as music teacher to his daughter at the then very high salary of £100 per annum. Hingston and four other musicians petitioned the Council of State for the establishment of a 'Corporacion or Colledge of Musitians . . . in all things to regulate the Profession of Musick'. This petition does not seem to have been granted, but on 19 Feb. 1656/7 one of the items on the agenda of the Council was 'The Advancement of Musick' and as a result it appointed a Committee of six to receive any suggestions and report to the Council. When one of Cromwell's daughters was married he entertained his guests with a very large orchestra (as a contemporary newsletter tells, 'they had forty-eight violins and much mirth with frolics, besides mixt dancing'), and when another was married he himself took part in a vocal duet.

It was alleged against the Royalist Roger l'Estrange (afterwards Sir Roger), who returned from exile in 1653 and was pardoned, that he had obtained this grace by playing upon Cromwell's love of music, having gained admission to the Protector by bribing the servants, carrying his fiddle under his cloak. From this legend he received his nickname 'Noll's Fiddler'. His reply to the charge was 'Truly my Fiddle is a Bass Viol, and that's somewhat a troublesome instrument under my cloak' (see *Clubs for Music-Making*).

In 1658 Cromwell sent a Mandate to the Vice-Chancellor and Senate of Cambridge University requiring them to waive some of the regulations for admission as Bachelor of Music in the case of Benjamin Rogers (q.v.).

See further references under *Chapel Royal*; *Minstrels* 3; *Clubs for Music Making*; *Street Music* 3; *Dance* 7.

5. Milton and Bunyan.
Cromwell's Latin secretary was the poet Milton, the son of a good composer (a contributor to *The Triumphs of Oriana*; see *Madrigal* 4). Milton's own love of music is evident from many a page of his works —for instance, the poem *At a Solemn Musick*, and the sonnet on Henry Lawes, the Latin sonnet to his father, the *Tractate of Education* (which allots music a quite important place), and the *Areopagitica*.

If anyone today is asked for the name of a Puritan divine of the period he will first mention that of Bunyan, Roundhead soldier and Baptist minister. His *Holy War* and his *Pilgrim's Progress* offer sufficient testimony of approval of the recreation of music. In the dining-room of the Interpreter's House there is a pair of virginals and the guests hear music at meals. Christiana plays the viol and her daughter Mercy the lute. When Giant Despair's prisoners are released they fall to dancing. Cast into Bedford Goal after the Restoration, Bunyan solaced himself by playing on a flute of his own making, which still exists, as does also a violin of iron bearing his name and probably made by him during his early life as a metalworker (p. 865, pl. 146. 5, 6).

6. Publication of Music
(p. 865, pl. 146. 3, 4). A very large quantity of music was published during the Commonwealth and Protectorate, which (perhaps through the suppression of spoken stage plays and church music activities) released a great flood of secular musical publication. Playford's famous *Dancing Master* (see *Dance* 7; *Publishing of Music* 5) then first appeared and during this period it went into three editions, each time enlarged by the addition of extra tunes and dances. Rounds and catches, madrigals, string fantasias, collections of 'Lessons' for lute and for viol, tunes for the violin, books on the theory of music, and other musical works of every possible kind, were poured out in a profusion much greater than that of the periods immediately preceding or immediately following. Some books that were looked on as the standard works on their subjects well into the eighteenth century (such as Playford's *Brief Introduction to the Skill of Musick*) first appeared during the Puritan régime.

7. Masque, Opera, Madrigal.
The masque (q.v.) was one of the occasional diversions of the period and opera first began in Britain then (see *Opera* 13 a).

L l

It is often charged against the *Puritan control* of the country that *a cappella* compositions, and particularly the madrigal, ceased to be written about this time, but this is equally true of the same period in Italy, Germany, France, and other countries, and is to be put down to the general change of fashion explained in the article *Opera* and elsewhere in this volume.

The facts above (2–7) are, strangely, still unknown to many general historians, as they were to the older historians of music, but they are perfectly well known to every seriously equipped student of the musical life of the period, who could easily support them by the statement of many similar facts.

8. The Puritans in America. (The word is here used in the same general sense as in the preceding part of the article and not in the special sense sometimes attributed to it in the United States, i.e. it takes in the Separatist Puritans, who landed in 1620, the non-Separatists who landed in 1628, and any other similar parties, and the immediate descendants of all of them.)

The Pilgrim Fathers of 1620, and those who followed them, had their attention taken up with work and the anxieties of winning a living and of self-defence, and they do not seem to have practised the arts to any high degree. It is often stated in books on American music that they strongly objected to music; but no supporting evidence can be found for his statement, which seems to be a mere reflection of that one which attributes such an objection to the Puritans in England. It is hardly likely that at a time (1649–60) when, under Puritan rule in England, musical activity was flourishing as hardly ever before, the successive parties that left England would arrive long-faced and music-hating.

The Pilgrim Fathers themselves were Brownists, i.e. Independents (Congregationalists), and they could certainly have drawn no hatred of music from their founder Robert Browne, who, though like other Puritans he inveighed violently against elaborate music in church, was 'a singular good lutenist' and taught his children to perform.

Six years after the Pilgrims' landing at Plymouth Thomas Morton arrived there and scandalized them by his celebration of the First of May with singing and dancing round the maypole in the old English fashion. There was great complaint made, but as the song sung was decidedly Bacchanalian ('Drinke and be merry, merry, merry, boyes'), and as the Indians were drawn into the celebration, and as, moreover, Morton was selling guns and ammunition to the Indians, it is probable that there were good practical reasons for the objections made to his residence in the colony, altogether apart from any dislike of music and merriment. Anyhow, the colonies that were not Puritan showed themselves as anxious for the suppression of Morton and his companions as did those that were Puritan, so that the meaning of this incident has clearly been completely misstated by many American historical writers.

For further discussion of this general subject see *United States* 2.

9. The Evangelical Movement and Music. Whilst to some extent the misconception as to the feeling towards music of the English seventeenth-century Puritans is due to a mistaken deduction from the fact that they disliked elaborate music in church, yet to some extent it is doubtless also due to a confusion with an objection to music that did exist in some degree amongst the eighteenth- and nineteenth-century Evangelicals. The Puritans began as a reforming party within the Church of England and wished to stay within that church, but circumstances led to their leaving it: the earliest of the eighteenth-century Evangelicals, the Methodists, have a similar history. The descendants of both today, the Congregationalists, Baptists, and Presbyterians, on the one hand, and the various Methodist bodies on the other, are all now alike Nonconformists, and all alike have been charged with a contempt for art, for which some evidence can be found.

The founders of Methodism, John and Charles Wesley, it is true, had no dislike of music (see *Methodism and Music*) and they appreciated the value of church music, even of the more elaborate kind. Indeed, three anthems in St. Paul's Cathedral may be considered to have formed a part of the immediate influence which led to John Wesley's conversion. Charles Wesley, the hymn-writer, had two sons of high musical talent, Charles Wesley Junior and Samuel Wesley (q.v.), and this talent he fostered to the utmost. It is curious to find Charles Wesley Senior writing to the wife of Oliver Cromwell (the last male descendant of the Protector) to reassure her as to her daughter's musical occupations. He says, 'If Miss Cromwell should prove by and by one of the first players of England it will not hinder her shining among the Harpers above, with the Sweet Singer of Israel, and thousands of the best men of all ages.' This letter was written because Mrs. Cromwell had had her mind disturbed by some scruples of certain religious people, and it contains an admission that 'All Quakers and some of the Dissenters' have 'an aversion to music'.

Such an aversion was, in fact, traditional on the part of the Quakers and had now come to be felt also by numbers of people belonging to the other dissenting bodies. The late eighteenth- and early nineteenth-century Church of England Evangelicals too (the so-called Clapham Sect, for instance, though its prominent member William Wilberforce is an exception) in general perhaps felt music to be 'worldly' and 'a snare' (like novel-reading, dancing, card-playing, and play-going) and likely to lead to 'bad company'.

This feeling has now almost disappeared, but at one time pious families could be found who excluded the piano from their homes but admitted the reed-organ, presumably because this latter had limitations that tended to confine it to 'sacred' music.

Such a manifestation of intolerance (springing, let it be admitted, from high ideals) must be regarded as a late eighteenth-century and a nineteenth-century phenomenon. As has been shown above, it is not to be associated with historic Puritanism, though, in the widest sense of a word whose sense has by custom now become very much over-widened, it can be called 'Puritanical'.

See *Wales* 2 for an allusion to the disappearance of the Welsh folk dances owing to the eighteenth-century Evangelical movement.

10. List of Articles on Cognate Subjects.
With the present article may be read *Cathedral Music* 5 (for the destruction of organs, etc., by the Puritans); *Anglican Parish Church Music* 2 (for the same); *Chapel Royal* (for the same); *Congregational Churches and Music*; *Presbyterian Churches and Music*; *Baptist Churches and Music*; *Methodism and Music*; *Quakers and Music* (the Quakers, who were in their early days strongly inimical to all the Puritan sects, being the only British religious body that was opposed to recreation and the arts—including the art and recreation of music); *Ballad* (for the allegation that the Puritans suppressed ballad singing and selling); *Minstrels*, etc., 3; *Carol* (for the discouragement of Christmas celebration); *Profession of Music* (for London music teachers during the Commonwealth); *Waits* (for the full continuance of these municipal bodies of musicians during the Commonwealth); *Music Hall* 1 (for the use of the organ in taverns during the Commonwealth); *Clubs for Music-Making* (for the weekly gatherings of amateur and professional musicians at Oxford and elsewhere); *Street Music* 3 (for the waits during the Commonwealth), 6 (for legislation against ballads); *Fairs and their Music* (for continuance during the Commonwealth); *Inns and Taverns as Places of Music-Making* (for the development of their musical resources during the Commonwealth); *Dance* 7 (for the allegation that Puritanism abominated dancing); *Russia* 2 (for an analogy).

PUSHKIN. See *Russia* 4; *Coq d'or*; *Salieri*; *Boris Godunof*; *Glinka*.

PUY. See *Minstrels* 6; *Cecilia, St.*; *Competitions in Music* 1.

PYRRHIC DANCE. See *Dance* 2.

PYTHAGORAS. See *Modes* 2; *Scales* 5, 10; *Tetrachord*.

PYTHAGOREAN COMMA. See *Temperament* 3.

PYTHIAN GAMES. See *Competitions in Music* 1.

Q

QUADRAT (Ger.). The sign of the Natural (Table 7).

QUADRIBLE. See under *Treble*.

QUADRILLE. This dance became popular first in France at the court of Napoleon I. In 1816 it was brought to England by Lady Jersey, one of the leaders of fashion at that time, and at once became popular to the point of madness. Everybody wrote quadrilles, generally basing the music on something popular at the moment, as, for instance, an opera. The practice persisted for a long time, so that Chabrier (born 1841), as a joke, was able to compose a set of quadrilles on themes from *Tristan*.

As the name implies, the quadrille was a square dance. Its music had five movements, as we may call them, in different kinds of time. The Quadrilles of Jullien (q.v.), played at his concerts, were famous; sometimes he would have six military bands and a full orchestra playing simultaneously in them. The **Lancers**, introduced in the middle of the nineteenth century, was a variant of the quadrille.

QUADRIVIUM. See *Education and Music* 1.

QUADRUPLE CHANT. See *Anglican Chant* 5.

QUADRUPLE CONCERTO. See *Concerto* 6 a.

QUADRUPLE COUNTERPOINT. See *Counterpoint.*

QUADRUPLE-CROCHE. French for 'Quadruple Hook'—the Hemidemisemiquaver or sixty-fourth-note (Table 3).

QUADRUPLE FUGUE. See *Form* 12 f for 'Double Fugue' and apply the explanation.

QUADRUPLET. See Table 11..

QUADRUPLE TIME. See Table 10.

QUADRUPLIN. See *Voice* 17.

QUAIL. An instrument that imitates the cry of the bird of that name and is used in Toy Symphonies (q.v.) such as that of Haydn. See also *Wachtel*.

QUAKERS AND MUSIC. The Society of Friends, to whom has remained attached their early nickname, was founded by George Fox during the Commonwealth. He taught the doctrine of the 'inward light' and opposed all formalism and sacerdotalism, refused to show such signs of respect as removing the hat, addressed high and low equally by the familiar 'thee' and 'thou', would take no oath, assumed a sober clothing, and denounced all amusements. He was both a religious and a social reformer. He had many followers and both he and they were frequently in prison, where many died; to some extent Fox and the Quakers of his lifetime drew persecution on themselves, as they were violent in their attacks on all who differed from them, and often disturbed their religious services. Four were hanged (not burnt, as often stated) at Boston, Mass., in 1661. The peaceful behaviour and pacifist views of the Friends of a later day were not typical of those of the earliest beginnings. The Friends (numbering some 200,000 in 1967) have always been active in education and philanthropy.

The detail in the history of the Friends which justifies their admission to a book of reference on music is their original and long-continued opposition to this (as to all) art. They were the one sect who opposed it, and they continued to do so until recent times. George Fox, in his journal for 1649, says '*I was moved to cry out against all kinds of music*', and the 'Yearly Meeting and Epistle' of the Friends in Great Britain for 1846, two centuries later, speaks of the 'acquisition and practice' of music as '*unfavourable to the health of the soul*' and as leading to '*unprofitable and even pernicious associations, and, in some instances, to a general indulgence in the vain amusements of the world*'.

There was a little singing in some of the meetings in George Fox's day, but for two centuries after that Friends seem to have used no music whatever in their worship. There does not, at first, appear to have been an absolute objection to the singing of the metrical psalms (see *Hymns and Hymn Tunes* 4, 5), which it may be presumed (since nothing else would seem at that date to be available), are what George Fox himself sang when, in 1653, his jailer '*fetched a fiddler . . . thinking to vex me thereby; but while he played I was moved in the everlasting power of God to sing; and my voice drowned the noise of the fiddle and made the fiddler sigh and give over fiddling and pass away in shame*'. (See another reference to Fox under *Fairs and their Music*.) Barclay's *Apology* (1676), the standard exposition of the doctrines of the Friends, speaks of 'the singing of psalms' as 'a part of God's worship, and very sweet and refreshing', but opposes the 'formal, customary way of singing' on the grounds (amongst others) that 'all manner of wicked people take upon themselves to personate the experiences and condition of the blessed David, which are not only false, as to them, but also as to some of more sobriety, who utter them forth'. This would seem to allow of individual song on the part of a believer prompted to such by his feelings, and perhaps even collective song in meetings known to be purely of believers, but to forbid singing in any mixed congregation.

See the Article *Printing of Music* on pages 829–31

1. THE NOTES ARE HAMMERED IN after the words, perhaps having to be moved slightly from their original scratched position in order to coincide. The scratch marks will then be smoothed away by polishing.

This is the first plate of the Christmas carol, *Silent Night*. It will later be corrected after a proof has been read, the engraver turning the plate on its back and hammering the incorrect impressions back into the plate. Then the new letters and notes are inserted

2. TAKING A PROVISIONAL PROOF. After the plate has been completely engraved and inked with green ink (green being considered easier on the proof-reader's eyes) it is put into the printing press and a sample proof is struck off. It is carefully pulled from the plate and given to the proof-reader for correction. Here, the proof is the reverse of the final page of printed music in that the dark or printed areas will be light or unprinted in the final form. The process is half complete

3. A FINAL PROOF IS DRAWN on a special slightly moist laminated paper of very soft quality and pressed into the inked crevices of the plate by a heavy roller. This serves as the original, from which a photographic negative is made. From this a printing plate is made to allow for greater speed in mass printing

4. A CHEMICAL PROCESS

Negatives of plates needed for one printing unit of sixteen pages. Having been set up precisely, exposed to powerful mercury lights and printed on the zinc plate below, these plates are placed on a revolving drum and treated with the chemical poured from this dipper. Everything but the notated surface is eaten out

5. THE PRESS AT LAST COMES INTO ACTION

After the etched plate, which is not much thicker than paper, is wiped clean it is fitted on presses which, with every turn, produce impressions of sixteen pages each

1. JOHN DAY IN 1562
See *Publishing* 4

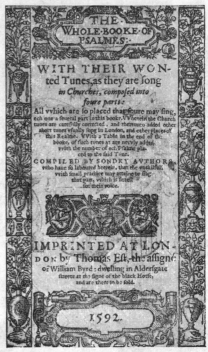

2. ESTE'S BEAUTIFUL PRINTING IN 1592
See *Publishing* 4

3. THE FATHER OF BRITISH MUSIC
PUBLISHING—JOHN PLAYFORD in
1660. He holds in his hand Byrd's *Non Nobis*
See *Publishing* 5

M U S I C K.
Lately received, and SOLD at
E. BATTELLE's Book-Store,
STATE-STREET,

A VALUABLE Collection of
MUSICK BOOKS, consisting of Airs,
Songs, Country-Dances, Minuets and Marches.
—Symphonies, Quartellos, Concertos, Sonatas, Divertimentos, Duettos, Solos, Trios,
Oratorios, &c. for the Organ, Harpsichord,
Clarinett, French-Horn, Hautboy, Flute,
Violin, Violincello, Harp, Piano-Forte,
Voice, &c.

P S A L M O D Y.
Massachusetts Harmony.
Law's elect Harmony.
——'s Collection of Hymns,
——'s Rules of Psalmody with Tunes and
Chaunts annexed.
——'s Select tunes.
N. B. Books and Stationary as usual.

4. A BOSTON ADVERTISEMENT in the late 18th
century—apparently of imported publications
Cf. *Publishing* 9

Barclay then goes on to take common ground with the Puritan bodies in objecting to '*artificial* music, either by organs, or other instruments, or voice, as we have neither example nor precept for it in the New Testament' (cf. *Puritans and Music*; *Eccles*, *Solomon*).

There must also be taken into account here the historic Quaker principle of avoiding programme or pre-arrangement of any kind, which principle is still observed at the meetings for worship. Apart from any other point this would, of course, bar the development of a musical service.

The traditional general attitude of the Friends to all amusements and art, including music, began to weaken about 1870 (perhaps first in the United States) and has now disappeared. Indeed, it may be said that the Friends in general now realize both the social value of music and its value as an aid to devotion, and make use of it much as do other religious bodies. Hymn singing at many of what we may call the 'extra' meetings is now common, instrumental accompaniment also being used (in Britain apparently usually or always that of a piano).

(The term 'Singing Quakers' sometimes found in late seventeenth- and early eighteenth-century English and American writings does not refer to any section of the Society of Friends, but to another sect, also known as the Rogerenes.)

See *Eccles*.

QUAKER'S OPERA. See *Vicar of Bray*.

QUAL (Ger.). 'Agony.' So *Qualvoll*,'agonized'.

QUALITY IN MUSIC

1. Introductory.
2. Vitality.
3. Originality.
4. Workmanship.
5. Proportion and Fitness.
6. Feeling.
7. The Element of Personal Taste.
8. The Test of Time.

1. Introductory. As to the nature of 'goodness' or 'badness' in music (to say nothing of the 'goodness' or 'badness' of particular compositions) there have probably always been debates—and probably always will be. There are even people who deny that 'goodness' and 'badness' exist, thinking it to be a mere matter of taste; but in that case music would ·stand alone as the one thing in the world not possessing quality, and, anyhow, there is no musical person of experience who does not assert the existence of grades of value in the musical repertory. The thoughtless division of music into 'what I like' and 'what I don't like' is too easy-going. Music, like everything else, has its standards.

In any discussion of the subject it seems well, at the outset, to clear the platform of the encumbrance of a common confusion. The categories 'good' and 'bad' are altogether independent of the categories 'complex' and 'simple': there is 'good' simple music and 'good' complex music, and 'bad' simple and 'bad' complex. Similarly, the categories of 'good' and 'bad' have no real connexion with the categories of 'classical' and 'popular': not only are there good symphonies and bad but there are good waltzes and bad. Untutored music-lovers are met with who appear to care only for 'bad' music, but on closer examination it will often be found that what they like is simple (and, as they would say, tuneful) music—whether it be good or bad. (No doubt there are 'perverted tastes' in music as in everything else, but they are probably rarer than is usually supposed.)

And the factors that, in their sum, constitute goodness and badness in a complex composition equally constitute it in a simple and 'popular' one. The same standards apply throughout.

There are many possible ways of stating these standards, the following being one attempt (for a further account of the principles here discussed see Sir Henry Hadow's epoch-making *Studies in Modern Music* in 1892). Good music possesses all the characteristics now to be mentioned; bad music lacks one or more of them and is, on that account, bad.

2. Vitality. First, good music has vitality and bad music often has not. It is easier to recognize this characteristic than to define it. A melody which wanders aimlessly is not vital. Compare with such a melody the opening phrase of any one of Beethoven's sonatas, symphonies, or string quartets—a phrase which in every instance arrests the attention, as does the opening phrase of so many of Bacon's essays. We feel ourselves at once to be in the presence of *life*.

And in a 'good' piece of music this feeling (provided we ourselves are equipped, by natural powers and experience, to follow the composer's processes) continues to the end of the composition. There may be, and indeed must be some lowering of the intensity here and there, but every passage is felt to be significant and not mere 'padding'. It is recognized by all composers and critics that it is infinitely easier to make an effective and rapid scherzo than an effective slow movement, for the reason that in the former, even without much intrinsic vitality, mere speed carries one along. A really vital adagio is the achievement of a master.

Probably not one-tenth of either the 'popular' or the more serious music produced, at the present or at any period, possesses this characteristic, the presence or absence of which is what causes one to feel a work to be 'inspired' or merely 'made'.

3. Originality. We may say that good music is 'individual' and 'personal'. Music lacking vitality is generally found (at once or on close examination) to be a diluted extract of that of some other composer, or perhaps of so many other composers that no one composer can be named; or it may even be a thickened extract, for if there has been poured out upon the world much Mendelssohn and Water, there has equally been poured out much Wagner and Glue. Thus, after the triumphs of a genuinely original composer there come the failures of a host of unconscious imitators who have merely adopted an idiom and not originated one. Vitality and originality are, then, very near akin, and not easily separable under any critical analysis.

Originality is necessarily relative. There has never been an entirely original composer, for the most original one conceivable has to begin at the point where others before him have left off. The only way of producing completely original composition would be to bring up a child suspected of musical genius entirely segregated from all musical experience—and then, presumably, the child would produce nothing beyond the unsophisticated rattlings or warblings of the remotest prehistoric period.

Beethoven was a Haydn–Mozart widened and deepened; Wagner was Beethoven carried further and applied in the dramatic branch—and so on. Thus the early works of any composer are always found to be imitative; personality in a good composer emerges more and more as the middle works are studied, and only with maturity does the composer become truly himself. Beethoven's finest works are his most original, and these are the ones of the third period, where the melodies, the harmonies, the form, and (in the orchestral works) the treatment and combination of the instrumental colours are found to differ most from anything of the pre-Beethoven period. This phenomenon is, of course, common to all the arts.

A composer is always at his best when he is most himself, and this is the reason that the finest works of so many composers have proved to be the most difficult for the public to assimilate. The very originality which in the end firmly establishes a work in the regular repertory may, when it first appears, be an obstacle to its getting there—the ear being a conservative member.

By far the major part of all music put forth has been not so much composed, as remembered, and this, if it be competently written, secures it an easy and pleasant youth—at the same time dooming it to an early death.

It should be noted that, like vitality, originality may be found equally in simple and complex music. And as, according to the proverb, 'a live dog is better than a dead lion', so a Viennese ball-room waltz with a touch of originality must be worth more to the world of art than any unoriginal symphony.

4. Workmanship. There is an allusion above to music that is 'inspired' and music that is merely 'made'. This is not intended to reflect adversely upon the process of 'making'. Music may be 'inspired' in the sense of possessing vitality and originality in all its material, but the handling of the material is a matter for solid workmanship. There have been composers (Dvořák is an excellent instance) whose musical material was strikingly vital and original yet whose workmanship sometimes showed, if not carelessness, at any rate a lack of judgement, and their music must be classified as 'good' or 'bad' according as its 'good' characteristics are or are not sufficiently powerful to enable us (at least partially) to overlook the 'bad'. A sonata-form movement may have two excellent 'subjects', yet these may be connected by material so commonplace (and later, perhaps, may be developed in so clumsy a way) as greatly to diminish the net 'goodness' of the movement.

If 'inspiration' shows itself most obviously in the musical material out of which a composition is fashioned, workmanship, then, shows itself chiefly in the treatment of this material. 'Style' and 'finish' are as necessary characteristics of 'good' music as of 'good' painting or 'good' prose or 'good' poetry.

Sometimes capable workmanship is applied to inferior material, and, indeed, the well-trained and adroit but uninspired workman is a pathetically common figure in musical life. To take an example: church music abounds in instances of dull though well-constructed music —perhaps music with sound and well-knit harmonies and ingenious and effective interweaving of the various voice parts (i.e. good counterpoint), with, nevertheless, a weakness and lack of originality in the melodic phrases out of which the tissue is woven and perhaps also in the harmonies and rhythms—and nowhere any flash of imagination.

Bad workmanship sometimes shows itself in a lack of fitness of means to ends; means suitable for dance music have before now been applied to church music and means suitable to the pianoforte have been applied to the brass band; or we may find a string quartet in many respects 'good' yet spoilt by the 'bad' characteristic of being 'too orchestral'.

5. Proportion and Fitness. This could, perhaps, be considered part of workmanship; in fact, the categories throughout this article often overlap one another.

A composition that, kept within the limits prescribed by its material and its purpose, would have been 'good' may be felt to be 'bad' because it has transgressed those limits.

Or a part of the composition may be felt to be too long in relation to the other parts or to the whole.

Or the intellectual element (akin to the element of workmanship) may be felt to be overdone in relation to the emotional, as a preacher, by over-labouring a point, may diminish the spiritual force of what he has to say.

Or the composer may have over-orchestrated his music, as a painter may heavily treat in oils a subject that is really suitable for treatment only as a light sketch in water-colours.

Or the music may transgress against fitness

by attempting imitation of the sounds of nature or of humanity or, by a sort of symbolism, the telling of a story or the painting of a picture (see *Programme Music*), and by doing this too regardless of the general musical value of the composition. In a sense this, too, is a defect of proportion, the narrative and pictorial elements certainly not being illegitimate in themselves but being liable to be overdone.

6. Feeling. Inasmuch as, in some mysterious way, music can express a big range of emotions, there is always the possibility of defect in the emotional implications of the music.

Up to about the end of the nineteenth century it was common for preachers who had some knowledge of music and were called on for 'choir sermons', sermons at cathedral musical festivals, and the like, to make the statement that music was 'the purest of the arts', since it alone, of all of them, could not 'depict evil'. With the extension of harmonic and orchestral idiom that statement, if it was then true, can hardly be said to remain so. In latter times works have been written that seemed very definitely to suggest some of the baser emotions, as, for instance, a morbid eroticism. It may be said, then, that a characteristic exists in music akin to moral soundness or unsoundness.

But a commoner fault is the expression of vulgarity or a weak sentimentality, as in much dance music, popular drawing-room ballads, and (sometimes) 'religious' music. In this respect, indeed, music has at least equal capacity for 'badness' with painting and literature.

One frequent sort of vulgarity is that of an overdone rhetoric or false eloquence, very conformable with that of the tub-thumper.

Another sort comes from the frequent repetition of a musical catch-phrase, some sequence of notes or chords of no particular significance but of an ear-arresting character. This sort is particularly common in popular dance and song, and seems to be infectious, such a phrase or series of chords becoming common for a time, and then giving place to another.

7. The Element of Personal Taste. Personal preferences must exist in music as in every other human activity. It is as impossible to imagine music free of this influence as of distinctions of 'quality'. But it is often possible for the connoisseur to distinguish between his preferences and genuine deficiencies of quality —to say, for instance, 'I can feel that this composition is good, but it is not of a kind to appeal to me', or, 'I like that composition whilst at the same time realizing that it has small substantial value, that it will not endure, and that with sufficient hearing I am likely to tire of it'.

Taste, naturally, changes with growth. A man may like one type of composition at one age and another at a later age. The power of discrimination also develops, so that many music-lovers have found themselves coming to enjoy a deeper kind of music as their experience

both of music and of life has become wider. Further, it is quite possible for a person in early life to despise some lighter phase of the art and in later life to arrive at the point where he can tolerantly admit that there is good in that too.

These phenomena occur also, of course, in connexion with literary taste. Indeed, all the phenomena of quality are seen equally in connexion with all the arts, and such rules as can be formulated, if broadly enough drafted, appear to apply equally to all.

Many errors of taste arise from insufficient experience. Often the tiro adventuring into the field of art seems to be like the yokel setting out into the world; he is at first easily taken in and then progressively less so. On matters of 'quality' and 'taste' those with the widest experience have the greatest right to pronounce.

Nothing trains taste more rapidly than the thoughtful playing several times through of the *whole of the mature output* of a composer, which serves magnificently towards the cultivation of a generalizing ability. Goethe, perhaps the most widely cultured man of his time, made the young Mendelssohn play to him the whole of the more important works of Bach, Handel, Haydn, and other composers, in chronological order.

8. The Test of Time. Time is the Court of Last Appeal in matters of artistic taste and quality, and one has to wait for its verdicts.

Whilst the person of abundant musical experience can always put aside a vast quantity of the music he hears as of no conceivable permanent value, yet there is other music about which he cannot be sure, since it may, by its novelty or lack of novelty, be either attracting or repelling him unduly, according to his personal temperament.

Few composers (as few novelists) remain in good standing during the period immediately following their death. New styles appear and take the public attention, and the older style seems old-fashioned. After a sufficient period of lingering in the background the really fine composer comes to the front again, and then (if the world's comparatively short experience of developed music can be depended on) his position is assured. There exists, perhaps, as yet, no instance of a composer being widely 'revived' and re-appreciated and then dropped again, though it may be that along with his finer works some poorer ones are revived and that these then drop for ever.

Bach (largely unpublished) fell a good deal out of sight during the later eighteenth century, then re-emerged (and was published in full), and now appears to be permanently established. So, too, with the sixteenth-century madrigal school. In the history of architectural taste we see a parallel in the decline of interest in Gothic during the late sixteenth, seventeenth, and eighteenth centuries, and its supersession by 'Renaissance'; in the nineteenth century Gothic came to be understood and valued again, and now the masterpieces of Gothic and Renaissance architecture enjoy a popularity side by side, which popularity it seems impossible to imagine will ever decline again.

The Bills of Mortality in the music population are astoundingly heavy, and for most members of that population there is, it is to be feared, no resurrection. The programmes of some of the serious concerts of London and New York around the turn of the century make sad reading, and the glowing newspaper criticisms of some of the 'new works' of that period still sadder. But the most ephemeral music of all is that which is momentarily acclaimed by the largest number. Twelve months is the lifetime of much of this. The writer being, about 1925, on the pier of Blackpool (the Coney Island of England) and glancing over the windows of a music shop there, heard one girl say to another with disgust—'Just look at these songs. All last year's!' Yet Schubert had then been dead about a century and still endured.

Probably bad popular music now lasts a shorter time than ever before, since its incessant repetition by radio, television, juke-box, cinema, and taped music tends to speed the judgement of Time.

As regards more serious music, the judgement of Time can in doubtful cases often be anticipated by analytical study according to the categories listed above. It is a mistake to suppose that analysis can 'kill' a good composition: if interest exists at first but does not survive analysis the composition is certainly not good.

There is no acid test for 'goodness' in music. The thoughtful consideration of a trained taste must be applied, directed by some such method of analysis as that indicated above. It may not be possible by such means to prove a composition to be a masterpiece, but, at all events, great masses of second-rate music can thus be put aside.

Not all short-lived music is to be utterly condemned, for soundly-written journalism is a kind of literature. But it *must* be soundly written. There is, in fact, no excuse (beyond the commercial) for really 'bad' music in any place or for any purpose.

QUALITY OF SOUND, HOW CAUSED. See *Acoustics*, 6, 8, 9.

QUANTITY. See *Melody* 2; *Metre*.

QUANTO (It.). 'As much', 'so much'.

QUANTZ, JOHANN JOACHIM (p. 396, pl. 67. 3). Born near Göttingen in 1697 and died at Potsdam in 1773, aged seventy-six. He was a mighty flute player and flute composer before that other ardent practitioner, Frederick the Great (q.v.), in whose service he remained for over thirty years. His book on *The True Art of Flute Playing* (1752; many later editions, including 1906 and 1926) is valuable beyond the promise of its title, offering much general information as to the musical ideas of the period.

See *Fingering* 2; *Rubato* 2; *Pitch* 3; *Flute Family* 6; *Mechanical* 5; *Appreciation*; *Chamber Music* 6, Period II (1697); *Concerto* 6 a (1697); *Sonata* 10 f.

QUARE, DANIEL. See *Mechanical Reproduction* 5.

QUARTAL HARMONY. This term became commonly current in the 1930s and 40s as distinguishing a chordal system based on the interval of the fourth, as the long traditional system was on the interval of the third.

QUARTERLY MUSICAL MAGAZINE. See *Journals*.

QUARTER-NOTE (Amer.). 'Crotchet' (Table 3).

QUARTER TONES. See *Harmony* 19, 23; *Microtones*.

QUARTET (Fr. *Quatuor*; Ger. *Quartett*; It. *Quartetto*; an additional French name is *Quartette*, but this is rarely employed). Any body of four performers, vocal or instrumental, or any piece of music composed for such, is a quartet.

The normal **Vocal Quartet** ('Mixed Voice Quartet') consists of soprano, alto or contralto, tenor, and bass (often abbreviated 'S.A.T.B.'): a *Double Quartet* consists of this with two to each part (occasionally, however, the term is misleadingly used for 'Vocal Octet'). The *Male Voice Quartet* usually consists of either alto, first tenor, second tenor, and bass, or first tenor, second tenor, first bass, and second bass (the qualification 'with alto lead' or 'with tenor lead' expresses the distinction). A vocal quartet may or may not have accompaniment.

The normal **String Quartet** consists of two violins (called 'First' and 'Second', but the instruments are the same), viola, and violoncello.

Piano Quartet is the illogical name for a combination of three stringed instruments (violin, viola, and cello) with piano. So, too, with **Flute Quartet** and similar expressions.

There is clumsiness in the practice of using the word quartet to mean either (*a*) a type of composition or (*b*) those who play that type of composition. Thus we have to say 'a Beethoven String Quartet was played by the London String Quartet', and so on.

QUARTETT (Ger.). 'Quartet.'

QUARTETTO (It.). 'Quartet.'

QUARTO (It.). 'Fourth.'

QUARTUS CANTUS. See *Voice* 17.

QUASI (It.). 'As if.' So (often) 'almost'.

QUATRE (Fr.). 'Four'; hence *Quatrième*, 'fourth'. (For 'Quatrième Position' see *Position*.)

QUATTRO (It.). 'Four', e.g. *Quattro mani*, 'four hands'; *Quattro voci*, 'four voices'.

QUATUOR (Fr.). 'Quartet.'

QUAVER (♪). The eighth-note, i.e. one-eighth the time-value of the whole-note or semibreve. See Table 1.

QUE (Fr.). 'That', 'as'.

QUEEN ELIZABETH'S VIRGINAL BOOK. See *Fitzwilliam Virginal Book*.

'QUEEN OF FRANCE' SYMPHONY (Hay n). See *Nicknamed Compositions* 11 (85).

QUEEN OF SHEBA. See *Goldmark*.

QUEEN'S COLLEGE, OXFORD. See *Carol*.

QUEEN'S HALL. See *Concert* 7, 8.

QUEEN SYMPHONY (Haydn). See *Nicknamed Compositions* 11 (85).

QUELQUE, QUELQUES (Fr., sing., plur.). 'Some.'

QUERFLÖTE. See *Flute Family* 5 a.

QUESTO, QUESTA (It., masc., fem.). 'This.' The plurals are *Questi, Queste*.

QUEUE (literally 'tail'). 'Piano à queue' is the French name for 'grand piano'.

QUICKSTEP. See *March*.

QUID SUM MISER. See *Requiem*.

QUIETO (It.). 'Quiet', 'calm'. *Quietissimo* is the superlative.

QUILL. See *Harpsichord Family*; *Plectrum*.

QUILTER, ROGER (p. 337, pl. **54.** 4). Born at Brighton in 1877 and died in London in 1953, aged seventy-five. After school-days at Eton he studied music in Germany. With a touch at once light-handed and distinguished he wrote effective songs and some incidental music for plays. His orchestral *Children's Overture* (favourite old tunes adroitly strung together) has given abundant pleasure. His light opera *Julia* was produced in London in 1936.

  See *Knorr*.

QUINCEY, THOMAS DE (1785–1859). English essayist and music-lover. See references under *Anglican Parish Church Music* 3; *Wales* 4.

QUINIBLE. See under *Treble*.

QUINTA. See *Quinto*.

QUINTADENA. See *Organ* 14 I.

QUINTATÖN. See *Organ* 14 I.

QUINTENQUARTETT (Haydn). See *Nicknamed Compositions* 12 (76).

QUINTET (Fr. *Quintette, Quintuor*; It. *Quintetto*; Ger. *Quintett*). Any body of five performers, vocal or instrumental, or the music composed for such.

  The normal **String Quintet** is for two violins, two violas, and cello, but sometimes the combination two violins, viola, and two cellos is used, and also (very rarely) the combination string quartet plus double-bass.

Piano Quintet is the illogical name for the combination of piano and string quartet.

  The **Clarinet Quintet** is not uncommon— one clarinet plus string quartet.

  Many other instrumental quintet combinations occur.

  Vocal quintets are usually for two sopranos, contralto, tenor, and bass, or soprano, contralto, two tenors, and bass.

QUINTO, QUINTA (It., masc., fem.). 'Fifth.'

QUINTSAITE (Ger.). E string of violin.

QUINT STOP ON ORGAN. See *Acoustics* 9.

QUINTUOR (Fr.). 'Quintet.'

QUINTUPLE COUNTERPOINT. See *Counterpoint*.

QUINTUPLET. See Table 11.

QUINTUPLE TIME. See Table 10 (notes at end).

QUI SEDES. See *Mass* 3 b.

QUI TOLLIS. See *Mass* 3 b.

QUITTER (Fr.). 'To quit', 'leave'.

QUODLIBET (Lat. 'What you please' or 'what pleases'). A collection of different tunes or fragments of composition brought together as a joke, either (*a*) successively (as in the 'Musical Switch' of today, in which a bit of one tune is heard but 'switches off' into another, and so on indefinitely) or (*b*) simultaneously, tunes being found which, without too much pain to the listener, can be made to 'go together'. This latter kind is often for choral performance, and it was popular from the fifteenth century to the eighteenth. The numerous family of musical Bachs used to sing quodlibets at their annual reunions, and J. S. Bach has introduced the device at the end of his famous Goldberg Variations, where two popular tunes of his day, 'Long have I been away from thee' and 'Cabbage and Turnips', are made to run in double harness.

  The name 'Quodlibet' probably comes from an early practice of letting the performers work into the web of the music any tune they liked.

  In medieval 'disputations' (formal debating exercises), a *quodlibet* was a question brought up only to arouse spirited discussion among the participants. The French word 'quolibet' current today has the sense of a pleasantry.

  Cf. *Ensalada*.

QUOIQUE (Fr.). 'Although.'

QUONIAM. See *Mass* 3 b.

R

R. (in French organ music) = *Récit*, i.e. swell organ. Cf. *Organ* 15.

RABAUD, HENRI (p. 385, pl. **64.** 9). Born in Paris in 1873 and there died in 1949, aged seventy-five. He was a pupil of Massenet, who at twenty-one won the Rome Prize and later made a public name with several operas, especially *Mârouf*. In 1920 he became director of the Paris Conservatory.

RABBIA (It.). 'Rage.'

RACHMANINOF (Rachmaninov, Rachmaninow, Rakhmaninoff, etc.**), SERGEI VASSILIEVICH** (p. 912, pl. **155.** 8). Born in the government of Novgorod in 1873 and died in California in 1943, aged seventy. He studied at the Conservatories of St. Petersburg and Moscow, his teachers including Arensky and Taneief. He left Russia in 1917.

As a pianist he toured the world extensively, as a conductor he was much respected, and as a composer he made a mark with a number of works, very skilfully written, but for the most part inspired by no very strong national or personal feeling, being cosmopolitan and general in their expression. They include operas, 3 symphonies, 4 piano concertos (of which the second remains one of the most popular of all), pieces for piano solo, songs, etc. Probably some of his best work was put into the smaller piano pieces and the songs, many of which are perfect in their kind.

In 1931 his music was banned in Russia as representing 'the decadent attitude of the lower middle classes' and 'especially dangerous on the musical front in the present class war'.

Later the danger seems to have been bravely faced, since in 1939 the composer was reported to have said that his works were 'receiving most appreciative treatment' in the Soviet Union, and when he died there was great lamentation.

For the music of the Russian Church, to which Rachmaninof contributed, see *Greek Church* 5. For a reference to the popular 'Prelude' see *Arrangement*. And see *Concerto* 6 c (1873); *Symphony* 8 (1873); *Folia*; *Prelude*. Also p. 801, pl. **138.** 7.

RACKETT (or **RANKETT**). An old instrument of the bassoon kind; but in form a thick wooden cylinder with ten channels, connected so as acoustically to make one tube. The German name was *Wurstfagott* ('Sausage Bassoon'), the French, similarly, *Cervelas* ('Sausage').

RADDOLCENDO, RADDOLCENTE (It.). 'Sweetening', i.e. becoming gentler, calming down. So, too, *Raddolciato*, 'calmer'.

RADDOPPIARE (It.). 'To double.' Hence *Raddoppiato*, 'doubled'; *Raddoppiamento*, 'doubling'.

RADICAL CADENCE. See *Cadence*.

RADICS, BELA. See *Hungary*.

RADIO. See *Broadcasting of Music*.

RADIO TIMES. See *Broadcasting of Music* 1 c, 5.

RADIOTONE. See *Electric Musical Instruments* 2 c.

RADLEIER. See *Hurdy-gurdy*.

RAFF, (JOSEPH) JOACHIM (p. 400, pl. **69.** 6). Born at Lachen, Switzerland, in 1822 and died at Frankfort-on-Main in 1882, aged sixty. He fought his way up, poor and self-taught but encouraged by Mendelssohn, Liszt, and von Bülow, until at last he stood prominent in the music of Germany; then he died, and the slow up-hill progress of his fame was followed by a swift downhill rush, so that soon his many orchestral, chamber, and piano works and songs were almost entirely unheard, and the public knew him by a tiny trifle, 'Raff's Cavatina'.

See *Symphony* 8 (1822); *Oratorio* 3; *Concerto* 6 c (1822).

RAFFRENANDO (It.). From *Freno*, 'brake'. So 'putting on the brake', i.e. checking the speed.

RAGA. See *Scales* 8.

RAGEUR (Fr.). 'Ill-tempered.'

RAGE OVER A LOST PENNY. See *Nicknamed* 5 (Beethoven).

RAGTIME. The Ragtime era began just before the twentieth century. As distinct from Jazz (q.v.), which is an art of improvisation, ragtime was essentially composed music, usually played on the piano, with many printed and published examples: characteristically piano ragtime consisted of regular melodic lines, simply syncopated over a four-square march-style bass. Its popularity with an enormous international audience lasted until the early 1920s, by which time it had been replaced by jazz.

See *Negro Minstrels*.

RAHERE. See *Minstrels* 2.

RAIMONDI, PIETRO. He was born in Rome in 1786 and there died in 1853, aged sixty-six. This was a musician with whom composition was almost a branch of large-scale engineering. His diligence and skill in putting before his public 64 operas, 21 ballets, etc., sink into insignificance before such feats as (*a*) The fashioning of fugues for four voices, capable of being performed either singly or four or six of them simultaneously; (*b*) A fugue for sixteen four-part choirs (i.e. sixty-four independent voice parts); (c) Three oratorios performable separately or in combination; (d) An opera seria and an opera buffa which could be performed separately or together (these latter presumably as a kindly time-saving device in the interests of over-worked music critics).

'RAINDROP' PRELUDE (Chopin). See *Nicknamed Compositions* 8.

RAINIER, PRIAULX. Born in Natal in 1903. She is a violinist and composer, trained at Cape Town, in Paris under Nadia Boulanger, and at the Royal Academy of Music, where since 1942 she has been on the staff. Her works include string quartets and other chamber music and songs.

RAIN SONATA. See *Nicknamed* 7.

RAKMANINOFF, RAKHMANINOFF, etc. See *Rachmaninof*.

RÁKÓCZY MARCH. Francis Rákóczy was the leader in the Hungarian insurrection of 1703–11, and ranks as one of the great heroes of his nation. The march named after him dates from 1809, but is based on old Hungarian airs (it is said of the period of Rákóczy). It was composed by János Bihari, a typical Hungarian gipsy violin virtuoso (see *Hungary* for this kind of musician) specially for the use of a Pesth regiment about to march against Napoleon, and arranged for military band by one Nicolas Scholl, to whom he played it. Scholl published it in Vienna under his own name as composer. It then fell into oblivion until 1838, when Liszt included it in the programme of a recital tour in Hungary, and the arrangement of Berlioz (*Marche Hongroise*; 1846) established it in full favour. Berlioz then added it to his *Scenes from 'Faust'*, published seventeen years earlier and now remodelled as *The Damnation of Faust*, taking the liberty of making Faust travel to Hungary and see the passage of a Hungarian army across a plain where he was walking.

There is another (but apparently less trustworthy) attribution of this march which credits it to an amateur flautist, Karl Vaczek (d. 1828), who based his work on an earlier melody, and later gave the manuscript to a violinist and military bandmaster, Wencelas Ruzsicska (1758–1823), who rearranged it.

RALENTIR (Fr.). 'To slow down.'

RALLENTARE, RALLENTANDO, RALLENTATO (It.).'To slow', 'slowing', 'slowed' (in each case gradually). So the noun *Rallentamento*.

R.A.M. Royal Academy of Music (London). See *Schools of Music*; *Degrees and Diplomas*.

RAMEAU, JEAN PHILIPPE (p. 368, pl. **61.** 4). Born at Dijon in 1683 and died in Paris in 1764, aged nearly eighty-one. His father was organist of Dijon Cathedral. At seven the boy could read any piece of harpsichord music put before him, but this was about all he would read, which did not please his headmaster, who asked his father to remove him.

Little more is known of his early years, the tales usually told being efforts of imagination rather than the results of research. It is certain however, that he received some education from the Jesuits of Dijon, that at eighteen he travelled in Italy, and that he then roamed about France with a troupe of actors.

He afterwards became organist at Avignon, at Clermont, at Paris, at Lyons, and again at Clermont. Here he had leisure and began to study Acoustics and Musical Theory, accomplishing the first real systematization of harmony and putting this into a book which he went to Paris to publish (1726); in this book first appeared the suggestion of 'inversions' of chords, i.e. that E–G–C and G–C–E are the same chord as C–E–G, and so on. Later he published other scientific-musical treatises, and his work in this branch is the foundation of musical theory today. In Paris he again held an organ post, and he took a position of importance as a fashionable harpsichord teacher; his harpsichord music is of value.

At the age of fifty he became famous as a theatrical composer with the opera of *Hippolyte et Aricie* (1733), and thence onwards until his death he turned out a succession of operas and ballets (twenty-four in all), which are of great importance in the history of French music, and received the recognition of an appointment at court and a pension from Louis XV.

See *France* 5, 6, 7, 9; *Opera* 11 c, 24 (1733–7–9); *Bouffons*; *Form* 9; *Keyboard* 3; *Pianoforte* 20, 21; *Chaconne*; *Courante*; *Gavotte*; *Tambourin*; *Clarinet Family* 2; *Rhythm* 5; *Bird Music*; *Bourgault-Ducoudray*; *Dukas*; *Rousseau*; *Saint-Saëns*.

RAMSBOTHAM, ALEXANDER. Born in Leeds in 1862 and died in London in 1932. He was a distinguished musical scholar who from 1912 to his death was 'preacher' of the Charterhouse. He edited the 'Old Hall Manuscript' (q.v.) for the Plainsong and Mediæval Music Society and was an editor of the Carnegie edition of Tudor Church Music (see also *Anglican Chant* 6).

RAMSAY, ALLAN (1686–1758). He was an Edinburgh wig-maker and then bookseller, a poet, and an editor of ancient Scots poems. In 1725 he published his 'Scots Pastoral Comedy', *The Gentle Shepherd*. This, in its first edition, had only four songs; it seems to have suggested to Gay the writing of his *The Beggar's Opera* (q.v.), and that in turn led to an expansion of the musical element in Ramsay's work, to which he added an additional fourteen songs. In this enlarged state it first reached performance, by amateurs at Haddington, in 1729, i.e. eight months after the first performance in Scotland of *The Beggar's Opera*, in the same place. Strangely, no professional performance of *The Gentle Shepherd* seems to have been heard in Scotland until the year of its author's death, nearly thirty years later. In time it became widely known, being much performed during the late eighteenth century, and even reaching New York, Philadelphia, and Jamaica. In the twentieth century it had a notable revival during the Edinburgh Festival of 1950, when nine performances took place—all beginning at midnight!

See *Scotland* 9; *Ballad Opera*; *Beggar's Opera*; *Lass o' Patie's Mill*; *Lochaber*; *Clubs*.

RANDALL, JAMES R. See *Maryland.*

RANDULF, EARL. See *Minstrels*, etc. 2.

RANELAGH. See *Concerto* 12, 13; *Saltbox*; *Ridotto.*

RANGER, RANGERTONE. See *Electric* 4.

RANGSTRÖM, T. See *Scandinavia* 4.

RANK. See *Organ* 1.

RANKETT. See *Rackett.*

RANT. The rather mysterious name of an old dance of not clearly determined character. The word is chiefly found in use amongst the works of John Jenkins (q.v.). He has the *Peterborough Rant*, the *Fleece Tavern Rant*, etc.

RANZ DES VACHES (p. 880, pl. **147.** 1) is the name given to a type of Swiss mountain melody sung or played on the Alphorn (q.v.) to call the cows for milking or for any other purpose. The derivation of the patois word 'Ranz' is much discussed, but in general it is taken that the French-Swiss name as above is the equivalent of the German-Swiss name **Kuhreihen** or 'Cow-rank', i.e. 'Cow-procession'.

It is, strictly, not correct to speak of 'the' *Ranz des Vaches*, as every district has its own version and over fifty such versions have been said to exist, these differing in both music and words. Even so there are many variants in actual performance, as an element of improvisation enters. The most celebrated version is that of the district of Gruyère, which bears the name (from its opening line) of *Les Armaillis des Colombettes* ('Armaillis' are the men who spend the summer in the high mountains, taking charge of the cows sent there by the peasants of the neighbouring valleys, milking them, making cheese of the milk, and crediting the owners of each cow with the amount of cheese to which he is entitled). The Gruyère version is set out in full in the first edition of Grove's *Dictionary of Music.* Of this Dean Bridel (1757-1845), the great preserver of the folk-lore of French-speaking Switzerland, was the first to collect versions of the words and to settle a definitive version which was henceforth generally accepted. It is thought that the tune was originally one for Alphorn and that the words were a later addition, and the broken nature of the music, the intervals used, etc., support this view. In general style the tune in its various forms resembles that of the pipe of the shepherd boy in *Tristan*; a few short motifs are much reiterated, creating a slightly hypnotic effect.

There are many legends concerning the power of the *Ranz des Vaches* to awaken an overwhelming feeling of homesickness in the Swiss peasants. Boswell in his *Johnson* alludes to 'that air, which instantly and irresistibly excites in the Swiss, when in a foreign land, the *maladie du pais*'. He says that it has 'no intrinsick power of sound', and puts down its effects purely to 'association of ideas'. This may be true of the cows and of some humans, but the music *has* some 'intrinsick power'.

Rousseau in his *Dictionary of Music* (1767), alluding no doubt to the eighteenth-century employment of Swiss mercenaries in several of the armies of Europe, says that it 'was forbidden on pain of death to play it amongst the troops, because it caused those who heard it to burst into tears, to desert, or to die—so much did it arouse in them the longing to see their country again'. (This story can be traced back as far as Zwinger, 1710.)

The *Ranz des Vaches* has been introduced into operas, etc. The Overture to Rossini's *William Tell* has an example. Beethoven has a version at the opening of the last movement of his Sixth ('Pastoral') Symphony. Other versions are features of Schumann's *Manfred* music and Berlioz's 'Fantastic' symphony. Still another figures in Strauss's symphonic poem, *Don Quixote.*

RAPIDO, RAPIDAMENTE, RAPIDITÀ (It.). 'Rapid', 'rapidly', 'rapidity'.

RAPPROCHER (Fr.). 'To bring closer together.' So the present and past participles *Rapprochant*, *Rapproché.*

RAPSODIA (It.). 'Rhapsody' (q.v.).

RAPTAK. A whirlwind type of dance that appears in Delibes's opera *Lakmé.* Another name is *Rektah.*

RASCH, RASCHER (Ger.). 'Quick', 'quicker'.

RASIERMESSERQUARTETT (Haydn). See *Nicknamed Compositions* 12.

RASOUMOFFSKY QUARTETS (Beethoven). See *Nicknamed Compositions* 4; *Russia* 1.

RASTELL, JOHN (d. 1536). Lawyer, printer, Member of Parliament, Protestant reformer. See *Printing of Music* 1.

RATHAUS, KAROL. He was born at Tarnopol, then in Austria, in 1895 and died in New York in 1954, aged fifty-nine. He studied composition in Berlin under Schreker and produced a number of operas (including *Fremde Erde*—'Strange World', depicting a modern American city), symphonies, choral works, string quartets, film music, etc. His style, which is individual, inclines to atonality.

From 1932 he was in London and from 1934 in Paris. From 1938 he was head of the music department of Queen's College, Flushing, N.Y.

RATISBON EDITION. See *Plainsong* 3.

RATSCHE (Ger.). 'Rattle.'

RATTENERE, RATTENENDO, RATTENUTO (It.). 'To hold back', 'holding back', 'held back' (in each case gradually).

RATTLE. See *Percussion Family* 3 r, 5 r.

RAUH (Ger.). 'Rough', coarse.

RAUSCHEND (Ger.). 'Rushing', dashing. But perhaps more commonly 'rustling'.

RAUZZINI, VENANZIO. Born at Camerino in 1746 and died at Bath in 1810, aged sixty-three. He was a famous tenor singer and singing teacher, concert organizer, and composer of operas, pianoforte sonatas, string quartets, etc. He spent the latter part of his life in London and Bath.

RAVEL, MAURICE (p. 388, pl. 65. 1). Born in 1875 at Ciboure, near St. Jean de Luz, and died in Paris in 1937, aged sixty-two. He spent his childhood in or near Paris and then entered the Conservatory. There he was a pupil in composition of Fauré and Gédalge, who taught him the value of classic form, as Chabrier, whom he met and greatly admired, taught him the charm of vivacious melody, bright rhythms, and clear orchestration. Another influence was that of Satie, a born iconoclast, who opposed the 'heavy' Wagnerian style of those days, as unsuited to the Latin temperament.

When just turned thirty Ravel became the hero of a public agitation of high interest. He had competed repeatedly for the Rome Prize. At twenty-six he won the second prize (which does not qualify for residence in Rome) and that was as near as he ever got. At twenty-eight his failure aroused strong protests in which his teacher, Fauré, took part, and at thirty, when already known as the composer of such things as the refined yet popular piano compositions *Pavan for a Dead Infanta* and *Fountains* ('Jeux d'eau') and, most important, of the fine String Quartet, he was actually refused permission to sit, the results of the preliminary test not being considered satisfactory. A stirring newspaper campaign followed, with the resignation of Dubois, the director of the Conservatory, and the election of Fauré in his place.

Amongst the works that followed those just mentioned are (for piano) the set of pieces, *Mirrors*, the *Sonatina*, three pieces constituting *Gaspard de la Nuit* (based upon strange poems of Bertrand), the five pieces, *Mother Goose* (later orchestrated and turned into a ballet), and the suite called *The Tomb of Couperin*, the ballet *Daphnis and Chloe*, the humorous opera (the name not easily translatable) *L'Heure espagnole* (1911), and the opera *L'Enfant et les sortilèges*, the orchestral *Bolero*, and many songs.

The music of Ravel is often spoken of as akin to that of Debussy, and the suggestion is just, provided it be understood that the younger composer is no mere disciple of the elder (indeed if the dates of their respective compositions are compared he is seen as in some ways to have forestalled him), and certainly no mere cheaper edition of him, but an artist of pronounced individuality and originality. Reference should be made by the reader to the description of the Impressionist School of composition which opens the article upon Debussy in the present volume (as also to the article *Impressionism*), and then the distinction

may be made that the music of Ravel is less fluid than that of Debussy, firmer in its harmonies and part-writing, clearer in its outlines, more formal, more 'classic', as some would say—more 'objective' where Debussy's is more 'subjective'. Ravel makes no use of the whole-tone scale of Debussy, and that, in itself, is accountable for some of the difference of effect. (See reference to whole-tone scale in Debussy article and also *Harmony* 14.) And with him, as with Stravinsky, musical values are reduced to a simple question of technique.

Like Debussy, Ravel was a great inventor of novel procedures both in the technique of piano composition and in that of orchestration. The literary influences in Ravel's art are much the same as those in that of Debussy. Both steeped themselves in the poetry of the symbolists (again, see article on Debussy), and many of Ravel's songs are settings of Mallarmé, Verlaine, Verhaeren, etc.

Ravel accepted the Hon. D.Mus. of Oxford University (1928). He twice refused the Legion of Honour.

References of greater or lesser importance will be found as follows:

Alborada; *Ballet* 5, 6; *Bériot, C. W. de*; *Bolero*; *Chabrier*; *Chamber Music* 6, Period III (1875); *Composition* 4; *Concerto* 6 c (1875); *Falla*; *Flute Family* 4; *Forlana*; *France* 10; *Harmony* 17; *Harp* 4; *Jazz* 5; *Oboe Family* 4 f; *Opera* 21 m; *Pantoum*; *Pavan*; *Pianoforte* 20, 21; *Pianoforte Playing* 7; *Prix de Rome*; *Rigaudon*; *Satie*; *Sonata* 10 c (1922); *Sonatina*; *Spain* 10; *Waltz*.

RAVENSCROFT, THOMAS. Born about 1590 and died about 1633, aged about forty-three. He was a chorister of St. Paul's Cathedral and then music master of Christ's Hospital, and published books of rounds and catches, etc. (*Pammelia, Deuteromelia*, and *Melismata*), a theoretical work, and a famous book of metrical psalm tunes. The last of these has brought his name into all modern Protestant English hymn-books, and rounds from his collections (e.g. 'Three Blind Mice') are still constantly sung.

See references to him under *Round*; *Three Blind Mice*; *Hymns and Hymn Tunes* 5, 11, 17 e xiv; *Song Cycle*; *Street Music* 2; *God save the Queen* 3.

RAVVIVANDO, RAVVIVATO (It.). 'Quickening', 'quickened'.

RAWDON, LORD. See *Bagpipe Family* 5.

RAWSTHORNE, ALAN (p. 353, pl. 56. 7). Born at Haslingden, Lancashire, in 1905 and died in Cambridge in 1971, aged sixty-six. He was trained at the Royal Manchester College of Music (pianoforte, violoncello, and composition) and then abroad (pianoforte under Egon Petri).

His *Symphonic Studies* attracted attention at the ISCM Festival at Warsaw in 1939: later, other works of his were heard at this Society's festivals. Amongst the more important items of his output are a Concerto for clarinet and string orchestra (1936), two concertos for piano (1942 and 1951), one for oboe and string orchestra (1947), two for violin (1948 and 1956), one for cello (1966), one for string orchestra (1949), and three symphonies (1950, 1959, and

1964). His style, which remained remarkably consistent, may be briefly summarized as one of terseness and tension. His later works included a good deal of vocal and chamber music. C.B.E. 1960.

RAY. See *Re*.

'RAZOR' QUARTET (Haydn). See *Nicknamed Compositions* 12.

RCA VICTOR CO. See *H.M.V.*; *Electric Musical Instruments* 1 d.

R.C.M. Royal College of Music (London). See *Schools of Music*; *Degrees and Diplomas*.

R.C.O. Royal College of Organists (Britain). See *Degrees and Diplomas*.

RE. The second degree of the major scale, according to the system of vocal syllables derived from Guido d'Arezzo (q.v.), used (spelt Ray) in tonic sol-fa (q.v.), in which latter system it is also the fourth degree of the minor scale. In French (Ré) and Italian usage, however, the name has (on 'fixed-doh' principles) become attached to the note D in whatever scale or other association it may occur (Table 5).

REA, WILLIAM. Born in London in 1827 and died at Newcastle-on-Tyne in 1903, aged nearly seventy-six. He became organist to the corporation of Newcastle-on-Tyne, where also he carried on choral and orchestral concerts and promoted the love of music in every active way. A few of his anthems are to be heard.

READ.

(1) ERNEST. Born near Guildford in 1879 and died in London in 1965, aged eighty-six. London organist, conductor, etc. He was trained at the Royal Academy of Music and taught there from 1914 until 1959. His activities covered many branches of musical educational work—including the system of Jaques-Dalcroze (q.v.). He was the author of books of high educational value and promoter and conductor of orchestras for young people. C.B.E. 1956.

See *Ear Training*.

(2) GARDNER. Born at Evanston, Ill., in 1913. He studied at the Eastman School of Music and then, in 1939, in Europe. He has composed orchestral, chamber, organ, and piano works. His first symphony won the prize of the New York Philharmonic Society in 1937. He has held various academic positions and in 1948 became Professor of Composition at the Boston University College of Music. His comprehensive *Thesaurus of orchestral devices* appeared in 1953.

READING, JOHN. Date and place of birth unknown; died at Winchester in 1692. He was a vicar-choral of Lincoln Cathedral, and then successively organist of Winchester Cathedral and Winchester College, for the last of which places he composed the famous school song, *Dulce Domum* (q.v.).

It may be worth adding that the musician here mentioned had several namesakes of inferior importance, of whom particulars can be found in those works of musical reference, British and German, which run to many volumes.

READING ROTA. See *Rota*; *Sumer is icumen in*.

REAL ANSWER in Fugue. See *Form* 12.

REAL FUGUE. One in which the 'Answer' is 'real', not 'tonal' (see *Form* 12). The designation is rather absurd as, even if the answer is tonal, it may not continue to be such beyond the mere exposition.

REAL SEQUENCE. See *Sequence* 1.

REAY, SAMUEL. Born at Hexham in 1822 and died at Newark in 1905, aged eighty-three. He held many organistships in different parts of the country, was the first to perform Bach's *Peasant* and *Coffee* Cantatas in England (1879), and wrote church music and part songs that remain in use.

See *Wedding March*.

REBEC or **REBECK** (p. 1073, pl. **178. 2**). One of the earliest bowed instruments and one of the contributory ancestors of the violin—like which it existed as a family of various sizes roughly corresponding to the soprano, alto, tenor, and bass voices. The tenor instrument remains in use in Greece and Crete to this day, under the comprehensive name of *Lyra* (q.v.) and is (or was, at any rate until recently) to be found in some remote parts of Spain. But already in the sixteenth century its social status was in decline.

It is sometimes stated that the *Ribible* or *Rubible* was the same as the Rebec and that the *Humstrum* (q.v.) was related. (See references to the rebec under *Inns* and *Oriental*.)

REBEL.

(1) JEAN FÉRY (1661–1747). A celebrated Parisian violinist, opera manager, and composer of violin music, operas, etc. See reference under *Sonata* 10 b (p. 368, pl. **61. 2**).

(2) FRANÇOIS (1701–75). Son of (1). Also a Paris violinist, opera manager, composer of operas and other things (cf. *Collaboration*).

REBIKOF (Rebikow, Ryebikoff, etc.), VLADIMIR (p. 912, pl. **155. 6**). Born in Krasnoyarsk, Siberia, in 1866 and died in the Crimea in 1920, aged fifty-four. He studied in Moscow and Berlin and then lived and worked in various parts of Russia and in both Berlin and Vienna.

As a composer he is notable for having experimented energetically with the whole-tone scale (see *Scales* 9) and also for having written 'Musical Psychological Sketches', as for instance the short opera *The Christmas Tree* (widely performed in different parts of Russia and in some countries bordering on it), in which opera the states of the rich and the poor are contrasted.

He also introduced a type of pantomime called 'melo-mimic'. Some of his piano pieces are often heard.

For the music of the Russian Church, to which Rebikof contributed, see *Greek Church* 5.

REBOP. See *Jazz* 7.

REBUTE (Fr.). Jew's harp (q.v.).

RECAPITULATION. See *Form* 7.

RECHT, RECHTE (Ger.; masc., fem.). 'Right.'

RECHT CHOR ZINCK. See *Cornett and Key Bugle Families* 4 b.

RECIO, MLLE. See *Berlioz.*

RECIT. Short for *Recitative* (q.v.).

RÉCIT (Fr. for 'Swell Organ'). Note that this is not, as stated in some English books, an abbreviation of 'Récitatif', but a complete word in itself.

RECITAL. The word 'Recital' has been referred to under *Concert* 1. It is applied to a programme given by one instrumental or vocal performer, or perhaps by two (as 'Piano and Violin Recital', in which the two participants play sonatas, etc., together). According to a statement in Grove's *Dictionary* which seems to have been accepted by the compilers of musical works of reference in various languages, the first application of the word to music was made by Liszt at a performance in London in 1840, but in a way a little different from that now current: 'M. Liszt will give Recitals on the Pianoforte of the following works.' The word was suggested to him by Frederick Beale of the music firm of Cramer, Beale, and Addison, whose son, Thomas Willert Beale, author of *The Enterprising Impresario* (1867), records the fact. Shortly after this (from about 1850 onwards) Hallé's 'Pianoforte Recitals' were popular in Britain.

As the word 'recital' implies an element of personal display, more or less innocent, it is perhaps worth while to record that the first solo pianist to place his instrument in such a position that his interesting profile might be in view was Dussek (q.v.). Dussek, however, did not give 'one man shows'; Liszt is always regarded as the pioneer in this form of enterprise—with the exception of a few musical entertainers, of the Dibdin type. Liszt's 'recitals' had an element of informality about them. He would get up between the items and walk about and chat with members of the audience.

The use of the term 'Organ Recital' apparently became common in England from the 1860s; for instance, it appears on Best's programme at Union Chapel, Islington, in 1867.

For 'Song Recital' see *Song* 7.

RECITANDO, RECITANTE (It.), **RÉCITTANT** (Fr.). 'Reciting' (i.e. more like speech than song). So also *Recitato,* 'recited'.

RECITATIVE (in It. *Recitativo*). A style of vocal composition in which melody and (to a greater or lesser extent) fixed rhythm and metre are largely disregarded in favour of some imitation of the natural inflections of speech.

It adapts itself to rapid changes of thought or emotion, as set song cannot, and is particularly suitable as a vehicle for prose. In an opera or oratorio it commonly serves for narrative, dialogue, or dramatic expression, where the formal song or 'Aria' (q.v.) serves for extended soliloquy and the more lyrical kind of expression: the two are frequently heard in sequence and it may be said that after recitative states the case aria reflects or comments on it.

Recitative is, *par excellence*, the rhetorical element in music and, as such, is occasionally imitated for short passages in purely instrumental music (e.g. in Bach's *Chromatic Fantasia* and some passages in his organ works; also in some passages in Beethoven's pianoforte sonatas and his Ninth Symphony).

For the purpose behind the original introduction of Recitative *see Opera* 1. The earliest operas (beginning of seventeenth century), it may almost be said, *were* Recitative (see also *Oratorio* 2).

In seventeenth- and eighteenth-century opera there are two distinct types of Recitative, *Recitativo secco* (literally, 'dry recitative') and *Recitativo stromentato* (literally, 'instrumented recitative').

Recitativo secco or 'Recitativo semplice' (the word 'secco' appears for the first time in this connexion in 1831 in a German dictionary) is a quick-moving kind; it gets over the ground almost (or sometimes quite) as rapidly as speech. It has an accompaniment, but this is the merest background, of which the listener is barely aware; it serves to keep the singer on the pitch and little else. This is the original kind of recitative and it was in much use for a couple of centuries. The quick action of Mozart's *Figaro* proceeds largely by recitativo secco.

Properly the accompaniment of this kind of recitative is simply a series of chords from the harpsichord, with the string basses to thicken and sustain the lowest line of the music. In the score it appeared as a mere figured bass (q.v.). In the late eighteenth and early nineteenth centuries, when the harpsichord was going or gone from the orchestra, the harpsichord part of the accompaniment was (at any rate in Britain) given to a cello, which turned the chords into arpeggios.

Recitativo stromentato began to come in when the first unsophisticated phase of opera was passing, and in Venice (a great centre of operatic development) more attention was being given to its definitely musical interest as against its dramatic interest. As dates, 1600 may be given for the introduction of recitativo secco and 1630 (approximately) for that of recitativo stromentato. The latter was accompanied not by the mere harpsichord but by the orchestra— hence the name. Necessarily in this type of recitative the singer cannot have the same rhythmic freedom in his rendering, or he would throw the orchestra into confusion.

For handy illustrations of the two types of recitative, turn to Handel's *Messiah*. Such a recitative as 'Behold, a virgin shall conceive' is pure secco. It serves merely to make an announcement which becomes the motif for an elaborate aria following ('O thou that tellest'): in Handel's original score this recitative is accompanied by nothing beyond a figured bass (for the string bass players and harpsichordist). 'Comfort ye' is at first stromentato and then (at 'The voice of one') secco. 'Thus saith the Lord of Hosts' is fully stromentato. Such recitatives as this last are little removed from the 'aria parlante' (see *Aria*); note, for example, the long divisions (q.v.), which have left the method of mere speech-imitation far behind.

Recitative took a large place in the early French opera (see *Opera* 11). Lully's recitatives (end of seventeenth century and beginning of eighteenth) are remarkable for their freedom of rhythm; some of them have the time-signature changed at almost every bar.

From France the practice of writing recitatives became common in England largely through the work of the youth Pelham Humfrey (q.v.), who was sent by Charles II to study under Lully. He it was who, on return, first introduced it into English church music, so that henceforth it took an important place in the Anthem (q.v.): Purcell was Humfrey's disciple in the matter of French developments in composition. Recitative was also used in the masque *Cupid and Death*, 1653, and the first English opera, *The Siege of Rhodes*, 1657; both of these somewhat precede Humfrey's activities. Nevertheless, it perhaps was Humfrey who really established it. (For an isolated example of the use of recitative as early as 1617, see *Opera* 13.)

No form of musical setting can become so perfunctory as recitative, and perhaps no form can become more dramatic. Tartini, in 1714, heard a piece of recitative that inspired him to an eloquent descriptive passage:

'In the fourteenth year of the present century in the drama that was performed at Ancona, there was at the beginning of the third Act a line of recitative accompanied by no instrument but the basses. By this passage both performers and listeners were thrown into such a commotion of spirit that they all looked the one into the face of the other, struck by the change of colour they saw. The sense was not one of complaint (I remember very well that the words were disdainful), but of a certain rigour and cold-bloodedness that disturbed the very soul. Thirty times was that drama performed and always with the same universal effect.'

To trace the history of recitative through the three centuries and more that have passed since its introduction would be beyond the scope of this volume, but a few references to modern developments must be made. Wagner carried recitativo stromentato to a very high point of expressiveness, both as regards the dramatic declamation of the voice part and the elaboration of the orchestral accompaniment (see *Wagner*). With him, in his later work, there was hardly any set division into recitative and aria; the vocal part might be said to be in recitative

almost throughout, rising in lyrical moments, but without break, into the more continuous and flowing style, and sinking at narrative moments and moments of pure dialogue into something nearer recitative proper.

Debussy's *Pelléas and Mélisande* may almost be called one long recitative (see *Debussy*; *Opera* 11 e). Some work of Schönberg (see *Schönberg*; *Melodrama*) is directed to be declaimed in a half-speaking voice; if recitative may be considered as lying half-way between speech and song, this style may be regarded as lying half-way between speech and recitative.

Early names for recitative are *Musica parlante* ('speaking music') and *Stile rappresentativo* (q.v.); by the latter term reference is made, apparently, to the power of this form of song closely to reproduce the play of emotion. *Monody* (really an ode sung by a single actor in the ancient Greek tragedy) is a term used in connexion with the early opera, in distinction from the style of polyphony ('many-voiced music')—the madrigal style in which previous stage music had been written (see *Opera* 1).

It may be of interest to point out that *Plainsong* (q.v.) shows a similar development to recitative, beginning about a thousand years earlier. In its early form it corresponds much to recitativo secco, then it develops through a style corresponding to that of recitativo stromentato (though the term is inapplicable, since no accompaniment was intended) to something very like the continuous aria style—even taking on metrical rhythms when used for versified hymns. This process of development is, then, natural, and the world will probably see it happen all over again in some other way.

The performance of recitative is governed by long-standing traditions that sometimes involve considerable deviation from the plain implication of the composer's notation (see *Notation* 5). How much authenticity these traditions possess is a matter of dispute. There are other problems for the singer. He must, whilst preserving an effect of spontaneity, not neglect (as many tend to do) the steady rhythm of the passage. And he is sometimes called on to decide whether he shall adopt a narrative or a dramatic manner. (See *Cavatina*.)

As for the accompaniment, note that the conventional final pair of chords (dominant and tonic), in earlier recitative, though printed with the last note of the voice part, are not to be sounded until that part has finished.

RECITING NOTE. See *Modes* 4, 5; *Plainsong* 2; *Anglican Chant*.

RECORDARE. See *Requiem*.

RECORDER FAMILY

(For illustrations see p. 881, pl. **148**.)

1. Introductory. Under this heading, for the purpose of convenience, are here included all flutes of the whistle-mouthpiece, end-blown type, as distinct from those of the side-blown type, which are treated earlier in this book under the heading *Flute Family*.

Flutes of the end-blown variety are, as a general description, known as **Fipple Flutes** ('Fipple: the plug at the mouth of a wind instrument by which its volume was contracted': *Shorter Oxford Dictionary*).

They had an enormous vogue in musical life for centuries (Iron Age sheep-bone specimens exist, as one found in a burial mound in west Yorkshire and now in the Leeds Museum), but at last fell into almost complete disuse, save for the humble *Tin Whistle* (or *Penny Whistle* as it used to be called in the days of cheaper commodities). The actual recorders are, however, now revived, as a feature of the movement for the bringing into use again of the sixteenth- and seventeenth-century English and other music, and from the late 1920s have been on sale in many countries, the revival beginning with the work of Arnold Dolmetsch in England.

No instrument of this type has formed any regular part of the orchestra since the days of Bach and Handel (who both used it freely), though occasional appearances in later scores can be found (see *Flute Family* 4). Handel sometimes demands as many as four of these instruments.

2. The True Recorders (p. 881, pl. 148. 1.) The instruments of this important group have eight holes (three for the middle fingers of each hand, plus one for the thumb of one hand and one for the little finger of the other). Sometimes in the larger ones the mouthpiece is placed at the end of a metal tube bent back along the instrument so as to bring it within reach of the player—like a bassoon mouthpiece. The bore is mainly conical.

The recorder, besides much solo use, was, from the amplitude of its family range, capable of being used in sets of three, four, or five of different sizes (compare the old 'Chest' of viols, or the members of the violin family today). Apparently no more than two such sets are known to remain in existence now. There is a complete set in the museum of Chester, which is of eighteenth-century date, and there is another set in Nuremberg, which dates from the sixteenth century but lacks one of its instruments. The Chester set consists of four instruments, treble, alto, tenor, and bass. The recorder may have been of English origin, and the English instruments were famous on the Continent.

The sizes of recorder in the eighteenth century may be laid out somewhat as follows. (As regards the pitch, the lowermost C shown in the table is middle C; the one shown above is the C in the middle of the treble stave; the other notes can be calculated accordingly. It will be seen that the lowest notes of the whole series cover two octaves.)

The enormous popularity of the recorder during the sixteenth and seventeenth centuries is realized when one recalls the frequent references to it in English literature (Shakespeare, Milton, Pepys, etc.). Henry VIII (q.v.) was a recorder player and possessed seventy-six recorders, as well as seventy-eight transverse (i.e. side-blown) flutes. The twentieth-century revival of the instrument has assumed considerable proportions in England, Germany, and elsewhere. It has perhaps been helped in England by the movement for the revival of the folk dance, which has adopted it as a convenient means of performing the old tunes, and by the encouraging fact that of all true musical instruments this one is the cheapest, and the easiest to learn. In Germany, under the old German name of *Blockflöte* (apparently the same as 'Fipple Flute', the 'Block' referring to the plug or stopper in which the mouthpiece is inserted), the instrument has a great vogue.

Name	Key	Remarks
Sopranino Recorder	F	Handel's *Flauto Piccolo*.
Sixth Flute . .	D	
Descant Recorder or Fifth Flute	C	Now called *Sopran* in Germany.
Fourth Flute .	B flat	
Third Flute . .	A	
Flauto d'Eco (may be the same as the one below)	..	As indicated by Bach in his fourth Brandenburg Concerto.
*Treble Recorder or Flauto	F	Now called *Alt* in Germany.
*Alto Recorder .	D	
*Tenor Recorder .	C	Now called *Tenor* in Germany.
*Bass Recorder .	F	Now called *Bass* in Germany.

The four marked * constitute the quartet of recorders preserved at Chester.

The modern German Blockflöte differs, however, from the English recorder (the traditional instrument as revived by Dolmetsch) in the size and position of the holes, and this difference severely limits the capabilities of the German type. Hence the use of 'English fingering' as a distinguishing term.

Much music has been published for the modern instrument, both solo and concerted—original recorder music (English and German) and arrangements of other music of seventeenth- and eighteenth-century date. In the original recorder period, apparently, amateur players largely used solo vocal and choral music (songs, madrigals, etc.), and also that large class of music whose title-page indicated that it was equally suitable for various stringed and wind instruments. But there exist for treble recorder such works as four sonatas by Handel and six by Daniel Purcell, three by Telemann, and many by lesser composers. Sonatas for two recorders by various English composers are fairly common, and there are some for three recorders by Mattheson. All this music was provided with a figured-bass keyboard part. Bach's second and fourth Brandenburg Concertos use the end-blown instrument, and it should be noted that at this period that instrument was ordinarily intended, unless in the score the flute part was marked 'Traversa' or 'Flauto Traverso', etc.; thus the 'Flauto Piccolo' of Handel in *Acis and Galatea* is the little sopranino recorder, an octave above the treble one (or possibly the flageolet was used). If the piccolo as we understand the word today had been intended Handel would have written 'Traversa piccola'.

Another German name is *Schnabelflöte* ('Schnabel' being the beak of a bird); this corresponds to the English *Beak Flute*, French *Flûte à bec*, and Italian *Flauto a becco*. The French term *Flûte douce* is also sometimes used, and the Italian *Flauto d'eco* (or Flauto d'echo—Bach's term in the fourth Brandenburg Concerto). Other names are *Direct Flute* or *Flauto diritto*; *English Flute* (the side-blown flute being known in the eighteenth century as the 'German Flute'—see *Flute Family* 4) or *Flûte d'Angleterre*, and *Common Flute* (the side-blown variety, at the time it became fashionable, being apparently considered more 'select'). For comparison with the names given to the side-blown flutes see *Flute Family* 5.

The German names *Bassetflöte* and *Bassflöte* have been applied to a recorder of low pitch.

A peculiarity of recorders is that they tend to give the impression of sounding an octave lower than their actual pitch—probably owing to the relative paucity of their high harmonics (see *Acoustics* 6, 7).

3. Other Members of the Family.

(*a*) **Flageolet** (p. 881, pl. **148**. 3). Two of the six holes of the seventeenth-century or 'French' instrument are at the back and are closed with the thumbs, and this is its main distinguishing feature from the recorder.[1] Handel and other composers have introduced it into their scores

[1] The nineteenth-century (or 'English') instrument has seven finger-holes and one thumb-hole.

(see *Flute Family* 4, for an instance in Mozart). It was long a favourite instrument with amateurs (see, for instance, Pepys). Grove's *Dictionary*, as late as its third edition (1927), says it 'survives only in dance music, and that only in a limited and diminishing use', but that was surely incorrect; it had gone long before then (with the Victorian 'Quadrille Bands'). Sullivan used it as late as 1877 in *The Sorcerer*, but that was only to accommodate the Vicar with an instrument he could play.

At the beginning of the nineteenth century double flageolets and triple flageolets were in use (the two or three instruments terminating in a single mouthpiece).

(*b*) **Tin Whistle or Penny Whistle.** This, like the early flageolet, has six holes, but, unlike it, has them all at the front. A wooden form of this instrument called *Stockflöte, Schulflöte* ('school flute'), or *Czakane* had, from the 1930s, a vogue amongst German school children.

(*c*) **Pipe and Tabor (or Galoubet and Tambourin).** This simple combination of wind and percussion (played by one performer) was for centuries very popular in Britain and on the Continent for rustic dancing and other purposes. The names above given are the English and French respectively; another English name was *Whittle and Dub*. The pipe having only three holes could be played with one hand, leaving the other free for the drum (p. 881, pl. **148**. 2). By the cunning use of overblowing to the high harmonics a remarkable variety of notes can be produced. (Cf. *Bamboo Pipe*.)

RECTE ET RETRO, or RECTUS ET INVERSUS. See *Canon*.

RECUEILLI (Fr.). 'Collected', 'meditative'.

REDEND (Ger.). 'Speaking', hence same as *Parlando* (It.).

RED FLAG. The author of the words of this Socialist song was Jim Connell, Secretary of the Workmen's Legal Friendly Society, who described himself in *Who's Who* as 'sheepfarmer, dock labourer, navvy, railwayman, draper, journalist, lawyer (of a sort), and all the time a poacher'.

The original tune used was that of *The White Cockade*. Later the German tune of *Der Tannenbaum* (sometimes known as *Maryland*, q.v.) was adopted. It was criticized by the socialist George Bernard Shaw as being unlikely to inspire any one to action and more suited to drive all who hear it 'to crawl under a bedstead', and as suitable only for 'the funeral march of a fried eel'.

REDFORD, JOHN. He was an eminent organist and composer who died in London in 1547. For some time he was organist of St. Paul's Cathedral, and his most important compositions seem to have been written for his own playing or for the singing of his choir. As a

part of his duties he was concerned in the preparation of the choir-boys for play-acting, and a play which he wrote for them is available still.

REDLICH, HANS FERDINAND. Born in Vienna in 1903 and died in 1968, aged sixty-five. A conductor and musicologist, he studied at the universities of Vienna, Munich, and Frankfurt. From 1939 he lived in England; in 1962 he was appointed Professor of Music at Manchester University. He was an authority on Monteverdi and Handel.

REDOUBLER, REDOUBLEMENT (Fr.). 'To double', 'doubling'.

REDOUTE, REDOUTENSAAL, REDOUT-ENTÄNZE. See *Ridotto*.

REDOWA. A Bohemian dance in a pretty quick three-in-a-measure time. It resembles the Polish mazurka. See also *Rejdovăčka*.

RÉDUIRE (Fr.), **REDUZIEREN** (Ger.). 'To reduce', 'arrange'.

REDUNDANT ENTRY. If at the beginning of a fugue (see *Form* 12), after all the 'voices' have entered with the Subject or Answer, one of them re-enters, this term is applied.

REED. The sound-producing agent (of thin cane or metal) in a good many musical instruments.

A reed which vibrates against an air-slot is called a *beating reed*; one which vibrates through the slot (i.e. from one side of it to the other) is called a *free reed*. (For such reeds as those of the oboe, which has no air slot, see below.)

Reeds may be either *single* or *double*, i.e. two reeds placed together with a slight orifice between.

Here are examples:

(*a*) The **Clarinet Family** (q.v.) have single beating reeds, vibrating against a slot in the mouthpiece (p. 672, pl. **113**. 3).

(*b*) The **Oboe Family** (q.v.) have double reeds, the two halves of the reed themselves constituting the mouthpiece; as these vibrate against each other they may be considered to be beating reeds (p. 672, pl. **113**. 1).

(*c*) The **Bagpipe** (see *Bagpipe Family*) has usually double reeds for the 'chanter' and single reeds for the 'drones'.

(*d*) The **Mouth Organ, Concertina, Accordion, Harmonium,** and **American Organ** (see *Reed-Organ Family*) have a separate free reed for each note.

(*e*) Certain **Organ Pipes** (see *Organ* 2 a, 3, 14 VI) have beating reeds. So had the **Regals** (see *Reed-Organ Family* 2).

(*f*) The **Human Voice** has a pair of free reeds in the vocal cords (unique in that the pitch is altered from moment to moment by tension), and all the brass instruments have a pair in the lips of the player. But we do not (though we logically might) call tenors or trumpets 'Reed Instruments'.

REED-ORGAN FAMILY

1. Introductory.
2. Regal.
3. Mouth Organ.
4. Accordion and Bandoneon.
5. Concertina.
6. Harmonium.
7. American Organ.
8. Mustel Organ, Estey Organ, etc.
9. General Remarks on Instruments of the Larger Reed-Keyboard Class.
10. Nomenclature.

(For illustrations see p. 884, pl. **149, 150**.)

1. Introductory. It has seemed both logical and conducive to clear understanding to group together in one article here all those instruments of which the sounding principle is purely the reed (see *Reed*) and which provide a separate reed for each note.

Of the instruments now to be described one is ancient, being out of use since the seventeenth century. The others are modern and date from the early nineteenth century. The ancient one applies the principle of the 'beating reed'; the others the principle of the 'free reed' (see the entry *Reed*, above, for this distinction).

The various instruments included in this article appear to have a common predecessor or even ancestor in the Chinese *Cheng* or *Sheng* (p. 884, pl. **149**. 1). This is a sort of 'mouth organ', with pipes supplied with free reeds. There is record in the fourteenth century of a form of this instrument in which the reeds were 'beating', instead of free, and in which bellows and sliders (like those of early organs) were added. This is clearly a forerunner of the regal described below under 2. Later the reeds were 'free' ones and a chromatic scale was introduced, so making the instrument the forerunner of the harmonium described below under 6.

The original simple form of the cheng was introduced into Europe in the late eighteenth century, and, apparently, led to the successive invention of all the instruments described under 3–8 below. It is said that the Abbé Vogler (q.v.), who had seen the cheng in Russia, was ultimately responsible for all these developments.

2. Regal (p. 884, pl. **149**. 2). This is an instrument that came into use in the fifteenth century and remained popular through the sixteenth and into the seventeenth. It was in appearance a tiny portable one-manual organ, but the pipes (short and sometimes entirely concealed within the instrument) were reed pipes, and so the instrument has some resemblance to the harmonium type that came into existence in the late eighteenth century. The reeds of the harmonium group of instruments are, however, 'free' reeds (and without pipes), whereas those of the regal were 'beating' reeds (see *Reed* for this distinction). The pipes of the regal were too short to influence the pitch, which was determined by the reeds themselves, but they contributed to the timbre.

At the time of the regal's introduction organs had merely 'flue' pipes (see *Organ*), but the example of the regal led to the addition of reed pipes; in gratitude the organ gave the regal, in its later developments, an occasional row of flue pipes. Thus it becomes difficult to distinguish between regal and chamber organ, but it seems most logical to restrict the name 'regal' to specimens in which there is no flue work at all, or, at any rate, in which the reed work predominates.

A handy type of regal which folded in two like a book was called *Bible Regal*. The meaning of the term *Double Regal*, occasionally met with, is disputed; it seems most likely that it meant one whose bass extended into the region where pitch is indicated by double letters, as CC or GG (see *Pitch* 7). No regals of double keyboard are known.

One of Purcell's (q.v.) court positions, given him when his choir-boy voice left him, was that of 'keeper, maker, mender, repayrer, and tuner of the regalls, organs, virginalls, flutes, and recorders'; this post was, however, possibly by that date a sinecure, so far as regal-keeping was concerned, though it nominally existed until 1773.

The name 'regal' is not supposed to have any connexion with royalty; one suggested derivation is from the Latin 'regula'—having reference to the instrumental 'ruling' or 'regulating' of ecclesiastical plainsong performance (see *Harmonica* 6 d for 'Harmonica regula' as a name for the monochord).

The regal, being, in its small forms, easily portable, could be used in processions.

In Monteverdi's *Orpheus* (1607; see *Opera* 2) the regal appeared in the orchestra—to accompany the singing of Charon.

The term *Regalwerke* is sometimes applied in Germany to either the reed stops of an organ or, more specifically, the vox humana. See *Organ* 3, 6, 9, 14 VI.

3. Mouth Organ (in Germany, U.S.A., and elsewhere 'Harmonica'—but see under that word for other applications of it). This little instrument (p. 885, pl. **150.** 1) is one of the simplest possible applications of the principles of the free reed (see *Reed*). A number of small metal reeds of graduated size are fixed within slots in a plate of metal a few inches in length, placed within a sort of narrow box. Each reed has its own channel for wind within the box, and the channels run in two parallel rows at right angles to the edge of the box. This is placed against the lips and moved in one direction or the other according to the note desired; as the mouth accommodates four holes it is necessary that the tongue should cover the ones not needed. The instrument is practically a harmonium or accordion simplified to the last point possible.

A peculiarity is that alternate notes of the scale are obtained by blowing and by suction. The scale being diatonic, this brings it about that contiguous channels, laterally considered, produce notes a third apart, and when a simple harmony is desired two contiguous holes can be left uncovered by the tongue to produce it.

Note that during the 1930s a number of chromatic models came on to the market. These are really two diatonic instruments put together—for instance, one C Harmonica and one C-sharp Harmonica: by a special spring lever the air channels opening the notes of the C Harmonica can be shut, and, automatically, the corresponding notes on the C-sharp Harmonica are opened. Instruments with up to four complete chromatic octaves are available, as also special bass instruments for band work.

The instrument is, to a point, easily learnt, but feats of virtuosity are possible only to the talented and persevering. The claims for its use in educational institutions are based on (*a*) its simplicity and cheapness; and (*b*) the expectation that a proportion of children thus introduced to instrumental performance may be led to proceed to some instrument of more definite artistic possibilities. Milhaud (*c.* 1942) composed a Suite for mouth organ, for performance by a great performer of the day, Larry Adler (q.v.); he later added a concerto for the instrument. Vaughan Williams and Arthur Benjamin composed for the same player.

The invention of the instrument is often attributed to Sir Charles Wheatstone (the virtual inventor of the electric telegraph, the inventor of the concertina, etc.; see also 4 and 5), the date 1829 being mentioned. However, it is also claimed that in 1827 the Chr. Messner firm started its manufacture at Trossingen, Württemberg (where the Hohner factory is now situated), that in 1825 Fr. Hotz began making them in Knittlingen (his factory being now absorbed in the Hohner organization), and that in 1829 J. W. Glier founded the Klingenthal mouth-organ industry. The Hohner firm has for many years enjoyed almost a world monopoly.

4. Accordion (or Accordeon) and Bandoneon. The sound-producing principle of the accordion (p. 885, pl. **150.** 4) is that of the 'Mouth Organ' (see 3), but it differs in the provision of bellows, of buttons for producing the notes (and often of a keyboard like that of a small piano—up to 3½ octaves), all these being so designed that the instrument can be held in the two hands. The right hand has the melody studs (or keyboard) and the left operates the bellows and also certain buttons which provide an accompaniment of major or minor common chords (with which, in some sort of a way, every note of the diatonic scale may be harmonized), and, in the more expensive instruments, the chords also of the dominant and diminished seventh. In some cases, too, there are octave couplers (cf. *Organ* 2 e).

A peculiarity of one type, resembling that of the mouth organ, is that two different reeds (or groups of unison or octave reeds) are put into action by each key of the right-hand keyboard—one when the bellows is compressed and the other when it is expanded (i.e. one by blowing and the other by suction). But whereas in the mouth organ these reeds produce different notes of the scale, in one type of accordion they differ in power or in timbre.

The inventor of this developed mouth organ was Damian of Vienna and the date 1829, or, alternatively (authorities differ), Buschmann of Berlin and the date 1822: the latter attribution seems the likelier, as in 1829 Sir Charles Wheatstone invented the concertina (see 5) as an improvement on the accordion, which he could hardly have done if the latter had itself been invented only that year. The larger and more expressive accordions of today have improvements derived from Wheatstone's concertina.

The early accordions were all provided with buttons like those of the concertina (see below), as very many are still; but the application of the above-mentioned piano keyboard (hence the term 'Piano Accordion') was made by Bouton, of Paris, in 1852, and about 1920 became common. It much added to the popularity of the instrument, which has attained a great height, accordion bands being common in many

PURCELL IN HIS LAST YEARS
By Closterman

THE OPENING BARS OF PURCELL'S 'GOLDEN SONATA'
From his own manuscript in the British Museum

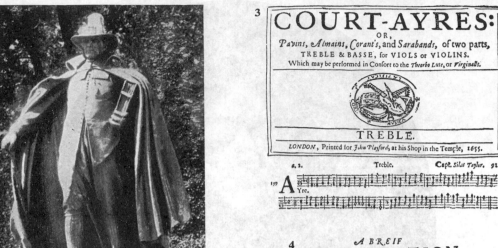

3 COURT-AYRES:
OR,
Pavins, Almains, Corant's, and Sarabands, of two parts,
TREBLE & BASSE, for VIOLS or VIOLINS.
Which may be performed in Consort to the *Theorbo Lute,* or *Virginalls.*

TREBLE.

LONDON, Printed for *John Playford,* at his Shop in the Temple, 1655.

1. THE JOYLESS PURITAN OF LEGEND
Statue by St. Gaudens

Thus having briefely set downe these few necessary and easie principles of the theorick part of Musick, I shall with you good successe in the practick part, which will soone bee obtained by the helpe of an able Master, this City being at present furnished with many excellent and able Masters in this Art and Science, some of whose names for information of such as desire to become Practitioners therein, I have heere inserted.

For the Voyce or Viole.		For the Organ or Virginall.
Mr. *Henry Lawes.*	Mr. *Edward Colman.*	Mr. *Richard Portman.*
Mr. *Charles Colman.*	Captaine *Cooke.*	Mr. *Christopher Gibbons.*
Mr. *William Webb.*	Mr. *Henry Farabosco.*	Mr. *Randall Jewet.*
Mr. *John Birtenshaw.*	Mr. *John Harding.*	Mr. *John Cobb.*
Mr. *George Hudson.*	Mr. *Jeremy Savile.*	Mr. *John Hingston.*
Mr. *David Mell.*	Mr. *John Goodgroome.*	Mr. *Farmelon.*
Mr. *Thomas Bates.*	Mr. *John Esto.*	Mr. *Brian.*
Mr. *Stephen Bing.*	Mr. *William Paget*	Mr. *Benjamin Sandley,*
Mr. *Thomas Maylard.*	Mr. *Gregory.*	Mr. *Benjamin Rogers.*
	Cum multis aliis.	*Cum multis aliis.*

2. LONDON MUSIC TEACHING DURING THE
PURITAN RÉGIME. See *Profession* 9

4 *A BREIF*
INTRODUCTION
To the Skill of
MUSICK:
FOR
SONG and *VIOL.*

In two Books.

First Book contains the *Grounds* and *Rules* of
Musick for *Song.*
Second Book, *Directions* for the Playing on the
Viol de Gambo, and also on the *Treble-Violin.*

By *J. Playford,* *Philo-Musico.*

London, Printed by *W. Godbid,* for *John Playford,*
at his Shop in the *Inner-Temple,* neer the
Church dore. M. DC. LVIII.

3, 4. MUSIC PUBLISHING DURING THE PURITAN
RÉGIME. See *Puritans and Music* 6 and *Playford.* The composer, Silas Taylor (see the music-type example above),
was one of Cromwell's captains

5, 6. BUNYAN'S FIDDLE AND FLUTE
See *Baptist Churches and Music* 2; also *Puritans and Music* 5

countries and the accordion probably being the most commonly purchased instrument in the world save the mouth organ. A frequent and not ineffective combination for dancing in mountain villages in Switzerland is that of clarinet, accordion, and stringed double-bass.

In 1947, at a concert in the Royal Albert Hall, London, the Norwegian accordionist, Tollefsen, introduced a concerto for his instrument by an American, Pietro Deiro, who is credited with introducing the instrument to the U.S.A. in 1909. The American Accordionists' Association commissions new works by serious American composers such as Roy Harris and Paul Creston.

The **Bandoneon** is an Argentinian type of accordion. There is no keyboard—merely buttons. And the left-hand buttons produce not chords but single notes, so that to produce chords several buttons must be depressed.

5. Concertina (p. 884, pl. **149.** 4). This instrument was invented in 1829 as an improvement on the early accordion by Sir Charles Wheatstone (already mentioned under 3 and 4 above). His family were London musical instrument makers and the firm still exists and still makes the instrument. It differs from the accordion in having hexagonal ends and a series of studs (i.e. finger pistons) instead of the keyboard which the present-day accordion often has. It produces only one note from each piston whether the action of the bellows be, at the moment, that of blowing or suction. This latter characteristic is at any rate true of the English concertina—the German concertina, a far inferior instrument, being like the mouth organ in that important detail; other inferiorities are that the German instrument can play only in two keys whilst the English is chromatic; further, the accompanying chords are severely limited in the German one (cf. 4 above). There is also an Anglo-German form of the instrument, with some advantages over the pure German. Messrs. Wheatstone make their instruments in three sizes, 'Treble', 'Tenor-treble', and 'Baritone'.

A good player of the English instrument (much the more difficult to play) can do surprising things, and at one time this instrument was popular in high circles of British society and possessed several professors of virtuoso ability. The British statesman, Lord Balfour, a great authority on Handel, was during the early and middle part of his lifetime an ardent performer on the concertina.

Quartet families of the instrument exist, corresponding in compass roughly to the stringed bowed instruments.

There are concertos for the concertina by Molique and Regondi (one of its greatest public exponents); sonatas have been written for it and it has had music provided in which it formed a part of various chamber music combinations with stringed instruments. Tchaikovsky included four concertinas in the score of his second orchestral suite, op. 53. Percy

Grainger and one or two other more recent composers have also made use of it. Edward Silas was a very active concertina composer: his works include an Adagio for eight concertinas, trios, a quartet and a quintet for combination of concertina, strings, and pianoforte, and many works for concertina and pianoforte, including two sonatas.

A curious practice of some players is the swinging of their instrument as they play, which they maintain improves the tone (for a similar practice by the players of an older instrument of another type see *Bell Harp*).

6. Harmonium. The introduction of this type of instrument is apparently due to one Kratzenstein, a medical man and acoustician of Copenhagen, and to G. J. Grenié (1756–1837) of Paris, both of whom made experiments suggested by a consideration of the Chinese cheng (see 1 above). Grenié's invention, the *Orgue Expressif*, became the parent of a progeny including the *Adelophone, Aelodicon, Aelophone, Aeoline, Aerophone, Apollonicon, Harmonicum, Harmonikon, Harmonine, Melodica, Melodicon, Melophone, Organino, Panorgue, Physharmonica, Poikilorgue, Seraphine, Terpodion* (this last with reeds of wood, instead of metal)—little more than the names of most of which survive to remind us what a demand suddenly sprang up for a simple and inexpensive domestic–ecclesiastical means of music-making. The original name of 'Orgue Expressif' is still in some use in France as one of the names of the harmonium.

The various good and bad points of these multifarious efforts were studied by Debain of Paris, who in 1840 began to register a series of patent rights relevant to the subject. His great innovation was the introduction of wind channels of varying sizes leading to the different sets of reeds, the tone-colour of which was individualized by the differing wind-pressures thus contrived. This is the principle still used to give individuality to the various 'stops' (for the term see 'Organ') of the harmonium and American organ. It was Debain who originated the name *Harmonium*.

Other inventors followed, of whom the most important was Alexandre, also of Paris, who is sometimes, but obviously incorrectly, spoken of as the 'inventor' of the harmonium. His special service was the introduction of the *Expression* device, by which, on drawing a stop-handle, the air is made to short-circuit the reservoir through which it otherwise passes, and to proceed direct to the reeds; this places the most delicate control of the volume of tone under the feet of the player, and calls for a good deal of practice on his part—practice which apparently only a proportion of the lovers of the instrument are prepared to undertake, since many of them are utterly disconcerted if this stop is drawn, and consequently never use it.

Details of importance in the larger harmoniums are two 'knee swells', one of which, by a lateral pressure of the knee on a projecting piece of wood, brings into action the full power of the instrument, whilst the other operates on the principle of the swell pedal of the organ (see *Organ* 2 d).

7. American Organ. One of the workmen in Alexandre's harmonium factory (see 6 above) discovered and applied a new principle—that of suction instead of compression of the air. Alexandre applied this to experimental instruments but was dissatisfied with the result, whereupon the inventor left his service and went to the United States. Hence came into existence the *Melodeon* (or *Melodium*), which from 1854 in Boston, under the hands of a new firm, Messrs. Mason & Hamlin, developed into the 'American Organ', to use the English name, or 'Cabinet Organ', to use the American name. Many refinements were gradually introduced, including varied devices for modifying the tone-colour of the various sets in place of Debain's device mentioned above.

This instrument is easier to play than its elder sister, but its usual lack of the 'expression' stop is a disadvantage; its tone is less pungent and, in some stops, much more like that of a pipe-organ, but the variety of tone-colour is less. On account of the absence of the expression device the feet of the player can be used for a keyboard of actual speaking pedals like those of the pipe-organ, and so complete two-manual-and-pedal models (blown by hand or electricity) can be made, which afford practice opportunities for pipe-organ players.

8. Mustel Organ, Estey Organ, etc. Another of Alexandre's employees (see 6 and 7 above), having set up for himself, introduced an important series of detailed improvements in the harmonium in the 1860s and the instrument that resulted is known as the Mustel Organ. The Estey Organ is another popular modern example. But there are now many such instruments (p. 884, pl. **149.** 7).

9. General Remarks on Instruments of the Larger Reed-Keyboard Class. The swell device (cf. *Organ*) has been applied to all these types of instruments. In an instrument with several rows of reeds (i.e. 'stops') not all are of normal pitch, some (cf. *Organ*) being of the pitch of an octave above, for brightness, and others of the pitch of an octave below, for dignity. A very great disadvantage in many instruments is that the stops are 'divided', i.e. the whole 'register' or 'set of reeds' cannot be put in action by drawing one stop handle, but only by drawing two, one at the right hand controlling the higher notes and one at the left the lower. The ostensible reason for this division is to allow a few very adroit performers to play a melody on one stop on one half of the keyboard and the accompaniment on another; for instance, when playing a right-hand melody, by drawing a 4-foot stop (i.e. one an octave above normal pitch; see *Organ* for explanation of 'feet') at the left hand of the keyboard, and playing an accompaniment on this an octave

lower than the notation of the composition prescribes, one has in effect an 8-foot stop, equivalent to that second manual on a pipe-organ on which one might accompany a melody played on another manual: but the contrivance necessary to dodge the trespass of the left hand upon the right hand's reserve, and vice versa, calls for more musicianship than is usually available, and it is to be feared that the multiplication of stop handles (as likewise a disproportionate expenditure of money upon fancy carpentry) has more of a commercial than an artistic motive behind it.

Another misleading device is the provision of a stop of 16-foot pitch (i.e. one an octave below normal pitch) operating over only the lower portion of the keyboard. Plausibly this represents the 16-foot pitch of the pedal department of the pipe-organ, and should be used to produce a similar effect, but in practice the playing of even a simple hymn-tune with this stop drawn may become a feat beyond the ordinary player, since unless careful watch is kept, and the score judiciously departed from, the tenor part may stray into the 16-foot region (with an unhappy sudden thickening of the effect), or the bass part stray out of it (with an equally unhappy sudden thinning of the effect).

Another deception (whatever the motive behind it) is the use of one set of reeds for two stops, the same reeds being acted upon in a different way by, say, both the 'diapason' stop and the softer 'dolce', and even sometimes by a third stop, perhaps called 'dulciana'. This gives two or three somewhat thinly demarcated varieties of tone for separate use, but when all are drawn together there is nothing heard beyond the original 'diapason', so that the 'full organ' effect of the instrument is by no means what its array of stops would lead one to suppose. Taking into account the 'division' principle above mentioned, it will be seen that for full organ effect one may pull out six stop handles and only get the equivalent of a single stop on the pipe-organ. If automobile manufacturers attempted to practise upon their customers' credulity in this way they would soon be out of business, but the less educated amateur musician is a docile creature!

The player of a harmonium in a place of worship should know that the volume of sound diminishes very rapidly with distance, so that what he hears is no criterion as to what is heard in the back pew; in the 'American' or 'Cabinet' organ this peculiarity is not so marked.

A defect of the harmonium is its slow 'speech', making rapid performance ineffective.

It is not always remembered by musicians that the reed-organ has been taken very seriously by a number of composers of high standard. Amongst those who have provided for its players are Dvořák, Franck, Reger, and Karg-Elert; the last of these, in addition to several serious compositions for the instrument, wrote a book (in German) on *The Art of Registration on the Harmonium*, and toured as a recitalist on a two-manual instrument, a *Kunst-*

Harmonium (or 'Art-Harmonium'). Berlioz, when the instrument was still in comparative infancy (1844), treated it with great respect in his *Treatise of Instrumentation*, and more modern writers, as Widor in his *New Treatise of Instrumentation*, do the same. As showing the wide popularity of the instrument Gevaert quotes the title of a harmonium tutor in his library 'printed in Hindustani and in the musical notation of Bengal (Hârmaniyamsûtra, Calcutta, 1874)'. This is, perhaps, less surprising that it seems. Small harmoniums have in modern time achieved phenomenal popularity throughout most of the Indian sub-continent— with lamentable effect on the native musical traditions.

The fact that the pitch of the harmonium's reeds remains practically constant under varying conditions of temperature, etc., has given it a place in physical laboratories, and has caused its employment for experimental keyboards providing for more than the usual twelve semitones to the octave (see *Microtones*).

The harmonium has occasionally had a use in chamber music (as in Dvořák's Bagatelles for harmonium, two violins, and violoncello) and in orchestral music (as in the Nocturne of Strauss's *Schlagobers*, where it provides a background for a violin solo).

10. Nomenclature.

(a) **Regal**, and **Bible Regal**. *Book Organ*; *Régale*, or *Régale à vent* (Fr.; there is a quite different instrument with metal plates, called 'Régale à percussion'); *Orgue en table* (Fr.); *Regale* or *Ninfali* (It.); *Regal, Bibelorgel, Bibelregal* (Ger.).

(b) **Mouth Organ**. *Aeolina* (original name, 1829); *Harmonica, Mouth Harmonica*, or *French Harp* (U.S.A.); *Harmonica, Flûte harmonique, Mélophone, Milophone* (Fr.). 'Flûte harmonique' is also the name of a totally unrelated organ stop, as also of an old instrument consisting of two flutes made in one and tuned a third apart. And 'Melophone'—see below. *Harmonika* or *Mundharmonika* (Ger.— 'Mund' = 'mouth'; cf. 'Ziehharmonika' below).

(c) **Accordion**. *Accordéon* (Fr.). *Accordeon* or *Armonica a manticino* (It., 'manticino' = a little bellows). *Akkordeon, Ziehharmonika* ('drawing-out harmonica'), *Handharmonika, Klavier-harmonika* (applied to the modern form of the instrument, with keyboard), *Chromatische-harmonika* (Ger., the last is applied to the modern form with chromatic keyboard).

(d) **Concertina**. *Bandonnier* (Fr.); *Konzertina* (Ger.).

(e) **Harmonium**. Eng. and Fr. and Ger. all have the same word (pronounced different ways); the term *Orgue expressif* is also used in France. Italian has *Armonium*. For a selection of the various fancy titles given to this instrument by different makers see 6.

(f) **American Organ**. *Cabinet Organ* (U.S.A.).

REED STOP. See *Organ* 2 a, 3, 14 VI.

REEL. A dance common in Scotland and Ireland (and a little used in north Yorkshire also, where it forms a part of the sword dance).

It is one of the two national dances of Scotland, the other being the strathspey (q.v.); the strathspey is slow, whilst the reel is quick. It is danced by two couples or sometimes more. The music, like that of the strathspey, is in four-in-a-measure time, but unlike that of the strathspey it is in a smoothly flowing rhythm. The *Highland Fling* is a particularly vigorous form of the Scottish reel. At the end of the eighteenth century an adaptation of the Scottish reel was popular in English ball-rooms.

The *Irish Reel* is quicker than the Scottish.

Similar dances are common in other northern countries, and especially Scandinavian (e.g. the Halling, q.v.). There is an American variety called the *Virginia Reel* which, it is said, is the same as the English *Sir Roger de Coverley* (q.v.).

REES.

(1) REVD. ABRAHAM (1743–1825). Compiler of *The New Cyclopædia* (1819) in forty-five volumes, for which Burney (q.v.) supplied the musical articles; these, many of which are quoted in the present work, were written about 1805.

(2) DAVID. See *Baptist Churches and Music* 2.

REESE, GUSTAVE. Born U.S.A., 1899, died 1977. He was at various times editor of the *Musical Quarterly* and director of publications of G. Schirmer (1940) and Carl Fischer (1945), while teaching at New York University. He was an active force in the American Musicological Society, and the author of the scholarly *Music in the Middle Ages* (1940).

REFLECTION OF SOUND. See *Acoustics* 18.

REFORMATION AND MUSIC. See *Germany* 3; *Cathedral Music* 1, 2, 3; *Anglican Parish Church Music* 1; *Service*; *Hymns and Hymn Tunes* 3; *Passion Music* 2; *Roman Catholic Church Music in Britain*; *Scotland* 4–6; *Ireland* 3; *Hungary*; *Poland*; *Scandinavia* 2, 4, 5, 6; *Presbyterian Church Music* 1; *Education and Music* 1.

REFRAPPER (Fr.). 'To strike again.'

REFRET. See *Ritornel* 3.

REGAL, BIBLE REGAL, DOUBLE REGAL. See *Reed-Organ Family* 2, 10 a.

REGALE (It.), **RÉGALE, RÉGALE À VENT** (Fr.). 'Regal'; see *Reed-Organ Family* 10.

RÉGALE À PERCUSSION (Fr.). See *Reed-Organ Family* 10.

REGALWERKE. See *Reed-Organ Family* 2.

REGENSBURG EDITION. See *Plainsong* 3.

REGENSONATE (Brahms). See *Nicknamed* 7.

RÉGENY, RUDOLF WAGNER-. See *Wagner-Régeny*.

REGER, MAX (p. 401, pl. **70**. 9). Born in

Bavaria in 1873 and died at Leipzig in 1916, aged forty-three. Like Brahms he might be described as a classical-romanticist in his sympathies and in his general methods.

He held academic and executive positions in Wiesbaden, Munich, Leipzig, Meiningen, and elsewhere, and received many academic honours, all the while turning out compositions at a rate and in a style that gave evidence of great facility and perfect mastery of all the technical resources. Largely owing to the work of Straube, of the Thomas Church, Leipzig, his elaborate organ works attracted much attention.

Appointed director of the historically famous Meiningen Orchestra, he was incited to the composition of a quantity of serious orchestral music.

His traffic with his fellows was honest, his dealings with his art sincere, and he earned and won large admiration. How much of so extensive an output, produced during so short a life, will prove weighty enough to withstand the winnowing of time cannot with any confidence be guessed. There is a curious contrast between the solidity of his larger works and the sentimentality of some of his songs.

See *Chorale Prelude*; *Clarinet Family* 6; *Reed-Organ Family* 9; *Violin Family* 10; *Concerto* 6 c (1873); *Opus*; *Tempo*; *Temperament* 6.

REGINA COELI LAETARE. See *Antiphons of the Virgin Mary*.

REGISTERS OF ORGAN. See *Organ* 1.

REGISTERS OF VOICE. See *Voice* 4, 14.

REGISTRATION. See *Organ* 1, 2 f.

REGISTRATION OF MUSIC TEACHERS. See *Profession of Music* 10.

REGISTRIEREN, REGISTRIERUNG (Ger.). 'To register', 'registration'. See *Organ* 1, 2 f.

REGISTRO (It.). 'Register.' See *Organ* 1, 2 f.

REGNAL. See *Erlanger*.

REGONDI, GIULIO (1822–72). He was a great performer, at first on the guitar and then on the concertina, who from the age of nine toured Europe, his virtuosity arousing everywhere the greatest admiration.

See reference under *Reed-Organ Family* 5.

REGULAR SINGING (in American Colonies). See *Hymns and Hymn Tunes* 11.

REICHA, ANTON JOSEPH. Born at Prague in 1770 and died in Paris in 1836, aged sixty-six. He was a youthful friend of Beethoven, a flautist, and a prolific composer who became also an author upon the art of composition. The greater period of his working lifetime was spent in Paris, where as professor of counterpoint and fugue in the Conservatory he had innumerable composers through his hands.

See *Percussion* 4 a; *Chamber Music* 6, Period III (1770).

REICHARDT, JOHANN FRIEDRICH (1752–1814). He was a pianist, violinist, composer (particularly of songs and operas), a

theorist, and Kapellmeister to Frederick the Great. His writings on music were numerous.

See references under *Song* 5; *Annotated Programmes* 2; *Folia*.

REICHE, GOTTFRIED (1667–1734). See *Trumpet Family* 2 (note).

REID, JOHN (1721–1807). General; amateur flute player and composer. See *Scotland* 10.

REIGEN, REIHEN (Ger.). Round dance, or (more casually used) merely 'dance'. So such compounds as *Elfenreigen*, 'Elf Dance'; *Gnomenreigen*, 'Gnome Dance'.

REIN (Ger.). 'Pure.'

REINCKEN. See *Reinken*.

REINE, LA (Symphony by Haydn). See *Nicknamed Compositions* 11 (85).

REINECKE, CARL HEINRICH CARSTEN (p. 401, pl. **69.** 7). Born at Altona in 1824 and died at Leipzig in 1910, aged eighty-five. He was a younger member of the Mendelssohn–Schumann circle. For thirty-five years he was conductor of the famous Gewandhaus Concerts at Leipzig, and later, he became director of studies at the Conservatory there. His career as pianist and as a teacher of pianists was a successful one. As a composer he was a reactionary-romantic (see *Romantic*). Some of his easier pieces are well known to piano pupils and he was a notable editor of the classics of his instrument.

See *Concerto* 6 b (1824); *Oboe Family* 6; *Cadenza*; *Harp* 3; *Toy Symphony*.

REINKEN (or Reincken), JOHANN ADAM (or Jan Adams, i.e. 'Jan the son of Adam'). Born in Lower Alsace in 1623 and died at Hamburg in 1722, aged ninety-nine. His boyhood and early manhood were spent at Deventer, in Holland, where he became an organist. He then moved to Hamburg, where he succeeded the great Scheidemann at St. Catharine's Church, and was, in addition, later connected with the opera-house founded there in 1677. His skill as an organist was high enough to lead Bach (on several occasions from his fifteenth to his thirty-fifth year) to walk considerable distances to Hamburg to hear him, and it was on the last of these occasions that Reinken, hearing Bach extemporize on a chorale, uttered the often quoted exclamation, 'I though this art was dead, but in you it still lives.' Of his organ and other compositions few are now extant.

See passing references under *Chorale Prelude*; *Holland* 3; *Bull, John*; *Organ* 8.

REISS, GEORG (1861–1914). See *Scandinavia* 3.

REISSIGER, KARL GOTTLIEB (1798–1859). After residence in many places he settled at Dresden as opera conductor. He composed operas, masses, orchestral and chamber music, etc., and a quantity of songs.

See references under *Misattributed Compositions* ('Weber's Last Waltz'); *Chamber Music* 6, Period III (1798).

REITERQUARTETT (Haydn). See *Nicknamed Compositions* 12.

REIZENSTEIN, FRANZ. Born at Nuremburg in 1911 and died in London in 1968, aged fifty-seven. He was a pianist, composer, and conductor, trained at the Berlin Conservatory under Hindemith, etc., and at the Royal College of Music under Vaughan Williams. His compositions include piano and chamber music, piano and cello concertos, etc.

REJDOVÁČKA, REJDOVÁK. A Bohemian dance, in two-in-a-measure time, somewhat resembling the polka, yet considered to be a variant of the *Redowa* (q.v.).

REJOICE, THE LORD IS KING. See *Hymns and Hymn Tunes* 6.

RÉJOUISSANCE (Fr.). 'Rejoicing', 'Merry-making' (as an example of the word's musical use—Bach and Handel have used it as the title of a movement in a suite).

REKTAH. See *Raptak*.

RELÂCHÉ (Fr.). 'Loosened' (e.g. snare of drum).

RELATED KEYS. See *Modulation*.

RELATIVE MAJOR AND MINOR. See Table 8.

RELATIVE PITCH. See *Absolute Pitch*.

RELATIVE PITCH THEORY OF TIMBRE. See *Acoustics* 6.

RELIGIEUX, RELIGIEUSE (Fr., masc., fem.). 'Religious.' So *Religieusement*, 'religiously'.

RELIGIOSO, RELIGIOSAMENTE (It.). 'Religious', 'religiously', i.e. devotional in feeling.

REMÉNYI, EDUARD. Born in Hungary in 1830 and died at San Francisco in 1898, aged sixty-seven. His name is familiar to every reader of the life of Brahms on account of their touring together, as violinist and pianist, at the very outset of Brahms's career. He afterwards won enormous fame all over the world as a virtuoso violinist. He was Jewish by descent but strongly Hungarian by sympathy, and the Hungarian element in some of Brahms's works is ascribed to his early influence.

REMETTRE (Fr.). 'To put back.' Hence the imperative *Remettez* in French organ music means to replace some stop that had been temporarily put out of action.

RENAISSANCE AND MUSIC. See *Opera* 1; *Education and Music* 1.

RENFORCER (Fr.). 'To reinforce', increase. The imperative is *Renforcez*.

RENTRÉE (Fr.). 'Re-entry.'

RENVOI (Fr.). The 'sending back', i.e. the sign to repeat.

RÉPÉTITEUR (Fr.), **REPETITORE** (It.), **REPETITOR** (Ger.). Chorus-master of an opera-house. (In ordinary French it means 'assistant teacher', 'coach', etc.). The Fr. *Répétition* and It. *Repetizione* mean 'rehearsal'.

REPIANO. See *Ripieno*.

REPLICA (It.). 'Repeat.'

REPLICATO (It.). 'Doubled.'

REPORTS or **RAPPORTS** (apparently from French 'rapporter', to carry back). 'Report', in seventeenth-century musical parlance, was the equivalent of 'imitation' today. It meant the taking up by one voice or 'part' of a melodic phrase just heard from another. In Playford's *Introduction to the Skill of Musick*, twelfth edition, 1694 (embodying revisions by Purcell), the word is found in the phrase 'Imitation or Reports'. Peacham in his *Compleat Gentleman* (various editions, 1622 to 1661) uses the word in this same sense.

In the Scottish Psalter of 1635 (see *Hymns and Hymn Tunes* 17 e xvi, and *Presbyterian Churches and Music*) appeared some tunes with the heading 'Heere are some Psalmes in Reports'. These are really little motets, or anthem-like treatments. The psalm tune proceeds in one part (generally the tenor), with longish rests between the lines of the poetry, enabling the other voices to enter in imitation, sometimes of a rather vague kind. It need hardly be pointed out that the existence of such music in Scotland at this date conclusively disproves the common statement that Calvinism in general and British Puritanism in particular were antagonistic to any church singing other than in unison.

It may be mentioned here that this type of treatment, though perhaps unusually elaborate, was not entirely new. Many of the settings in the English and Scottish psalm Books of the sixteenth and seventeenth centuries were in a motet style, giving evidence of the prevalence of a higher standard of sight-reading ability than is now common amongst the congregations of places of worship.

REPOS (Fr.). 'Repose.'

REPRENDRE (Fr.). 'To take up again.' *Reprenez* is the imperative.

REPRISE (Fr.). (1) A 'repeat', (2) 'recapitulation section' (see *Form* 7), (3) a 'revival'.

REPROACHES. See *Improperia*.

REPRODUCING PIANO. See *Mechanical Reproduction of Music* 13.

REQUIEM. The word is generally used as meaning the Mass for the Dead (*Missa pro defunctis*), which begins with the introit 'Requiem aeternam'. The text is much the same as that of the normal Mass (q.v.), with the more joyful parts (as the *Gloria in excelsis*) and the *Credo* omitted, and the long thirteenth-century hymn *Dies Irae* (by Thomas of Celano) interpolated: in describing the musical settings of the normal Mass it was mentioned that certain parts are rarely set by composers, as being variable from day to day through the Church's year; in the Requiem Mass these passages are fixed, and consequently can be set (the opening introit which gives its name to the Mass is an example). Certain small changes occur in the text of some sections: in the *Agnus*, instead of the words 'Miserere nobis' ('Have mercy upon us') are the words 'Dona eis requiem' ('Give them rest'). The text, then, may be described as the same as that of the normal Mass with the omission of certain joyful passages and the addition of a good deal of thought of death and the last things.

The traditional plainsong setting of the *Missa pro defunctis* is very beautiful. Naturally, after composers had learnt to replace portions of the normal mass with harmonized settings they began to do the same with the mass for the dead. The development of style was exactly the same as that outlined under *Mass*. Some celebrated settings are here mentioned—

Palestrina's in five parts (printed 1571); Victoria's in six parts, considered by many to be his greatest work (1605); Cavalli's (d. 1676), written on plainsong themes with the use of a double choir, and intended for his own death; Jommelli's (1756), long famous for its solo airs and orchestral accompaniments; Gossec's (1760), in which the *Tuba mirum* is set for two orchestras, one of strings in the church and one of wind in some adjoining place; Mozart's, written on his death-bed and completed by Süssmayr; Cherubini's two, greatly admired in their day and since; Berlioz's tremendous work (1838)—see under that composer; Schumann's (his last opus number; 'A Requiem is a thing one writes for oneself', he said); Dvořák's, Bruckner's, and Verdi's, the last (1874) written on the death of Manzoni, the famous Italian poet and novelist. The settings of Saint-Saëns, Fauré, Sgambati, Stanford (1897), Henschel (1902), and Pizzetti (1922) may also be mentioned. Britten's *War Requiem* (1961) uses the text intercalated with the poems of Wilfred Owen.

As a typical disposition of the text in a large-scale setting, upon what may be called oratorio scale, we may take Verdi's:

(a) Requiem aeternam and 'Rest eternal' and
    Kyrie eleison   'Have mercy'.
(b) Dies Irae—divided into movements as follows:
    Dies irae   'Day of wrath.'
    Tuba mirum   'Hark the trumpet.'
    Liber scriptus   'Now the record.'
    Quid sum miser   'What affliction.'
    Rex tremendae   'King of Glories.'
    Recordare   'Ah! remember.'
    Ingemisco   'Sadly groaning.'
    Confutatis   'From the accursed.'
    Lacrimosa   'Ah! what weeping.'
(c) Domine Jesu Christe 'Lord Jesus.'
(d) Sanctus   'Holy.'
(e) Agnus Dei   'Lamb of God.'
(f) Lux aeterna   'Light eternal.'
(g) Libera me   'Deliver me.'

Liturgically the Requiem Mass has its place at funerals and memorial services and on All Souls' Day (2 November). Certain works called 'Requiem' are not Requiem Masses, e.g. that of Brahms, which is a setting of passages from the German Bible, and that of Delius, which is not Christian. The word 'Requiem' appears fairly frequently as a song-title, attached to settings of poems concerned with death.

In French the name for Requiem Mass is *Messe des Morts*, in Italian *Messa per i defunti* (or *pei defunti*), and in German *Totenmesse* (all of which terms mean 'Mass for the Dead').

RESEARCH. See *Ricercare*.

RÉSOLUMENT (Fr.). 'Resolutely.'

RESOLUTION OF DISCORD. See *Harmony* 24 i.

RESOLUTO, RISOLUTO (It.). 'Resolute.'

RESOLUZIONE (It.). 'Resolution.' Firmness and steady rhythm.

RESONANCE. See *Acoustics* 20; *Concert Halls*; *Ocarina*. For vocal resonance see *Voice* 6.

RESONOSCOPE. See *Pitch* 6 d.

RESPIGHI, OTTORINO (p. 525, pl. **96. 1**). Born at Bologna in 1879 and died in Rome in 1936, aged fifty-six. He studied in his native city, in St. Petersburg under Rimsky-Korsakof, and in Berlin under Max Bruch. He was for a few years (1923–5) head of the St. Cecilia Conservatory of Rome.

He wrote six or seven operas (including one charming little work for marionettes) and a little chamber music, also several effective orchestral pieces of the descriptive or 'characteristic' kind—especially *The Pines of Rome* and *The Fountains of Rome*.

See *Italy* 7; *Impressionism*; *Bird Music*; *Opera* 24 f (1937).

RESPOND. Same as *Responses* (q.v.) but the word is specifically used as a name for the long and elaborate plainsong or choral settings sung by the choir, in answer to passages by the priest, as a part of the chanting of psalms. Such settings occur both in the Mass (between the Epistle and the Gospel) and in the other services of the Church; the description *Responsorium Graduale* (or, briefly, 'Gradual') is applied to that sung in the Mass, whilst *Responsorium*, without the addition of 'Graduale', means one sung in the ordinary services.

RESPONSES. The replies of the congregation (or the choir, representing them) to the Preces (q.v.) or Versicles (q.v.) of the priest, in the Roman and Anglican services.

The traditional Anglican settings are the ancient plainsong, adapted by Merbecke (q.v.) to the English words at the time of the Reformation. In Elizabethan times various composers made 'harmonized' versions of the responses, often, though not invariably, taking Merbecke's 'plainsong' notes as a *canto fermo* in the tenor part. The best known of these settings are those by Byrd, Morley, and Tomkins, and two distinct, though to some extent similar, versions by Tallis. These are now usually known as the **Festal Responses.** The **Ferial Responses** (see *Ferial*) have the plainsong in the treble, the harmonization being by any of the thousand-and-one organists who have undertaken to produce a version.

RESPONSORIAL. (1) Alternation of singing (plainchant, etc.) by a soloist and a chorus—as distinct from alternation of two half-choruses (which is 'antiphonal').

(2) Old name for Gradual—i.e. the book 'Gradual'.

(3) A collection of the solo passages of the Mass.

RESPONSORIO. A sort of motet in which a soloist and the choir sing responsively—in English a sort of 'Solo Anthem'.

RESPONSORIUM. See *Respond*.

RESSORTIR (Fr.). 'To come out.' So used of making a melody prominent.

RESTEZ (Fr.). 'Remain', e.g. remain on a note—not hurry off it; or (in string music) remain in the same 'position'.

RESTORATION OF BRITISH MONARCHY AND MUSIC. See *Anglican Parish Church Music* 3.

RESTS. See Tables 2, 3.

RESULTANT BASS ON ORGAN. See *Acoustics* 10.

RESULTANT TONES (Differential and Summational). See *Acoustics* 10, 13; *Electric Musical Instruments* 1 b. Also p. 16, pl. **1**. 8.

RETARDANDO (It.). Same as *Ritardando* (q.v.).

RETARDATION (in two senses). See *Harmony* 24 l; *Rubato* 2.

RETENANT, RETENU (Fr.). 'Holding back', 'held back' (immediately, like ritenuto—not gradually, like rallentando).

RETIRER (Fr.). 'To withdraw.' The imperative *Retirez*, in French organ music, means 'withdraw from use' the stop in question.

RETROGRADE. See *Canon*.

RETROUVEZ (Fr.). 'Find again', re-attain.

RETURNING TONE. See *Changing Note*.

REUBKE, JULIUS (1834–58). Son of a well-known German organ builder. He was a pupil of Liszt and composed piano music, songs, and (especially) a remarkable organ sonata, programmatically based on the 94th Psalm, which has since exercised influence on organ composition. His early death was a loss to music.

RÉUNIS (Fr.). 'United', 'reunited' (e.g. after *Divisés*). In organ music it means 'coupled'.

REUTTER, HERMANN. He was born in Stuttgart in 1900. He has been Director of the Frankfurt Hochschule (1936–45), etc., and a composer of solo vocal and choral works of a romantic tendency, and also of some experimental chamber operas.

REVEILLE (from *réveil*, Fr., 'wakening'). The military signal beginning the day (in the British Army pronounced 'revelly' or 'revally').

REVENIR (Fr.). 'To return.' *Revenez* is the imperative.

REVERBERATION. See *Concert Halls* 1.

REVERE, PAUL. See reference under *Printing* 3.

RÊVEUR (Fr.). 'Dreamy.' So the adverb, *Rêveusement*.

REVIDIERT (Ger.). 'Revised.'

'REVOLUTIONARY' ÉTUDE (Chopin). See *Nicknamed Compositions* 8.

REVUELTAS, SILVESTRE. Born at Santiago Papasquiaro, Mexico, in 1899 and died in Mexico City in 1940, aged forty. He was a violinist, conductor, and composer and was trained in Mexico City and Chicago. He composed orchestral and other music influenced by Mexican idiom, though without using actual folk material, including a good deal of film music and music for children.

REX TREMENDAE. See *Requiem*.

REYER (original name 'Rey'), ERNEST (in full Louis Étienne Ernest). Born at Marseilles in 1823 and died near Hyères in 1909, aged eighty-five. He became known both as composer and as critical writer, winning the praise of Berlioz in the former capacity and in the latter attaining to the position Berlioz had once held, that of the music critic of the *Journal des Débats*. In both capacities he showed himself an admirer of Wagner, and his choice of the subject of *Sigurd* for one of his operas indicates this. It is but one of a number of operas he wrote, and he left also songs, choral works, and other things.

Sigurd was first performed, at Brussels, in 1884 and two years later was given at Covent Garden, London. When it reached the Paris Opéra it was reduced in length, and the composer walked out of the house in protest. The opera which bears the reputation of being his best is *The Statue* (1861; re-written 1903); *Salammbô* (1890) is often heard in France.

REYNOLDS. See *Hopkins, Antony*.

REZITATIV (Ger.). 'Recitative.'

REZNIČEK, EMIL NIKOLAUS VON. Born in Vienna in 1860 and died in Berlin in 1945, aged eighty-five. After studentship in various places, including the Leipzig Conservatory, and a number of theatrical, orchestral, and military band conductorships (including Mannheim, 1896–9), he settled in Berlin, where he directed a series of orchestral concerts, for two years (1909–11) conducted at the Comic Opera, and then became a member of the staff of the State Conservatory, or 'Hochschule'. He had success as a conductor in Russia and in England.

His compositions are numerous. They include a number of operas, of which the humorous operas *Donna Diana*, 1894, and *Ritter Blaubart* ('Knight Bluebeard'), 1920, have been particularly successful; an operetta, five symphonies, and a number of other orchestral works; a Requiem, a Mass, chamber music, organ works, etc.

A gay satirical touch is a frequent characteristic of his work.

RF., RFZ. = *Rinforzando* (q.v.).

RHAPSODY. 'Epic poem, or part of it, of length for one recitation, high-flown utterance or composition, emotional irregular piece of music' (*Concise Oxford Dictionary*).

The introducer of the use of the word in the last of its dictionary senses is generally said to have been Liszt—in his fifteen *Hungarian Rhapsodies* (1853–4)—but, as a matter of precision, the Bohemian composer Tomaschek published at Prague just half a century earlier six rhapsodies for piano.

Usually the rhapsody is a free-ranging and ebullient fantasia on folk or folk-like melodies, e.g. the *Slavonic Rhapsodies* of Dvořák.

Departing from this idea, Brahms has a Rhapsody for contralto with male choir and orchestra and, further, three ballade-like piano pieces (see *Ballade*) called Rhapsodies. None of these uses folk-music material. Dohnányi and many others have followed Brahms.

RHEINBERGER, JOSEF GABRIEL (p. 401, pl. 70. 2). Born in Liechtenstein in 1839 and died at Munich in 1901, aged sixty-two. He was an able general practitioner of music, and the devoted teacher of a whole generation of composers, as a composer himself best known by his organ works and especially his twenty organ sonatas, some of which every competent organist has in his repertory.

See *Horn Family* 4; *Toccatina*; *Concerto* 6 b (1839).

RHEINGOLD ('The Rhine Gold'). See *Ring of the Nibelung*.

RHENÉ-BATON (really René Baton). He was born in Normandy in 1879 and died at Le Mans in 1940, aged sixty-one. After completing his training at the Paris Conservatory he held various posts in Paris and in provincial cities, and in Paris won a high position as orchestral conductor (Pasdeloup Orchestra). He wrote orchestral music, chamber music, songs, etc.

RHUMBA. See *Rumba*.

RHYFELGYRCH GWŶR HARLECH. See *Wales* 2.

RHYTHM

1. Good Rhythm in Performance.	5. Irregularities of Grouping.	8. The Beat and the Lapse of Time.
2. The Rhythmical Analogy between Music and Poetry.	6. 'Prose Rhythms' and 'Verse Rhythms' in Music.	9. Emotional Effects of Rhythm.
3. Rhythm as 'Grouping'.	7. Harmony and Rhythm.	10. The New Rhythmic Impulse in Twentieth-century Music.
4. Accent as the Defining Factor.		

The word 'Rhythm' is used in several senses, hardly any two works of musical reference agreeing; some of the senses are comprehensive and some limited. In its fullest sense (the sense adopted in this volume as the most rational) it covers the ensemble of everything pertaining to what may be called the *time* side of music (as distinct from the *pitch* side), i.e. it takes in beats, accents, measures or bars, grouping of notes into beats, grouping of beats into measures, grouping of measures into phrases, and so forth.

1. Good Rhythm in Performance. When in ordinary speech we speak of a performer's rhythm being good what we mean is that every requirement connected with all these time-features has been met with accuracy and judgement. One effect of such perfection concerning the various time-considerations of music is that the listener experiences a feeling of onward motion, and the presence or absence of this feeling on the part of the listener testifies to the performer's good or bad 'sense of rhythm', as those words are used by every music teacher and music critic.

The words 'accuracy and judgement', used above, represent a necessary combination. Flagrant contravention of (for instance) the demands of the regularity of the beats would destroy rhythmic feeling. So would sternly relentless, machine-like observance of these demands. So would, also, petty deviations arbitrarily made with the object of avoiding relentless observance. There is to be accuracy —but it is not to be pedantic; there is to be liberty—but it is to be within the law. And, throughout, there must be purpose.

The rise and fall of the intervals of the melody, and the greater or lesser pungency of the chords of the harmony, create in the mind of the genuinely musical performer and listener a desire for tiny hurryings and lingerings such as could never be expressed in any notation (see *Agogic* and *Rubato*). These operate to modify the demands of regularity without destroying the feeling of regularity; such slight but purposeful departures from regularity suggest life as opposed to mechanism.

As such modifications, though following general principles that would perhaps be susceptible of codification, are yet infinite in their variety of possible detail, rhythmic treatment of a composition offers one of the most notable means of the unconscious expression of personality and of mood. It is certain that no two master-performers have ever yet performed the same composition in the same rhythmic manner, and it is even doubtful whether any master-performer has ever performed the same composition twice in quite the same way.

2. The Rhythmical Analogy between Music and Poetry. There is a close analogy between musical performance and the reciting of English verse. Each line of a normal poem has a fixed number of strong accents (e.g. five in a normal line of Shakespearian blank verse) and the verse could be 'barred', as music is, by drawing a line before each strong accent. What falls within each measure could, then, readily be expressed in musical notation, as

$$\frac{2}{4} \; \; \downarrow \mid \downarrow \; \; \downarrow \mid \downarrow \; \; \downarrow \mid \downarrow \; \; \downarrow \mid \downarrow \; \; \downarrow \mid \downarrow$$

for '*I pray thee, gentle mortal, sing again*'. No actor with a feeling for the meaning of words would adopt so jog-trot a rhythm, yet no actor with an ear would fail to make that rhythm felt as *underlying* his words. (More actors have a sense for meaning than an ear, as it happens, and so it is the rhythm rather than the sense that usually suffers.)

In good recitation of English verse, then, (whether blank or rhymed) there is a compromise—a freedom within a regularity. And (but usually in a less marked degree) this is so with musical performance.

We may now consider rhythm defined, so far as the ordinary sense of the word is concerned. In this sense its realization is the highest attribute of the executive musician (singer, player, or conductor), a very important part of whose business is to give *life* to the varieties of rhythmic grouping of notes included in the composer's notation.

3. Rhythm as 'Grouping'. The chief parts of rhythm were listed above as 'beats, accents, measures, grouping of notes into beats, grouping of beats into measures, grouping of measures into phrases, and so forth'.

It appears that the human ear demands of music the perceptible presence of a unit of time—the feeling of a metronome audibly or inaudibly ticking in the background, which is what we call the *Beat*. Unless this is present it is doubtful if any music can be said to exist, for even in the free rhythm of plainsong it can be felt. (Cf. 6.)

And, the ticks being felt, it is a further necessity that they shall be grouped into twos or threes. Indeed, the mind cannot accept regularly recurring sounds without supplying them with some grouping, if they have not already got it: in listening to a clock ticking the mind hears either *tick*-tack or *tick*-tack-tack; this is so definite that it is hard to believe that the ticking is really quite accentless, yet that this effect is purely subjective is seen in the fact that a very slight conscious effort turns the effect from the one grouping to the other and then back again. It is the listener and not the clockmaker who is responsible.

This grouping of beats forms what we have called the 'measures' or 'bars', marked off from one another in musical notation by bar-lines, each line being drawn just before an accented 'tick' or beat. Two-beat measures and three-beat measures are, in a sense, the only real units possible, for all others are combinations of these—two or more measures thrown into one as $4 = 2+2$; $6 = 3+3$; $9 = 3+3+3$; $5 = 2+3$, or $3+2$; $7 = 2+2+3$, or $3+2+2$, or $2+3+2$; and so forth.

From these groupings we can work both 'downwards' into smaller ones and 'upwards' into larger ones. Just as the measure can be divided into beats, the beat can be subdivided into sub-beats (to coin a necessary word)—and in very slow music each *nominal* beat may well be felt as the *real* measure. So if Bach's Sarabande from the Partita in C minor be played to a listener who does not know it he is liable to fail at first to realize that it is a sarabande (a type of dance-piece with three slow beats in a measure), and to regard it as some sort of a fairly quick piece with four beats to a measure

(each of the actual beats throughout being divided into four short even notes). In fact, the distinction between measure and beat is merely conventional—a matter of convenience.

Similarly, working upwards—just as the beats are grouped into measures so the measures are grouped into phrases, each phrase being, so to speak, a super-measure (to coin another necessary word). The most common grouping is first into twos, and then two twos into fours, 'four-measure phrases', as we call them, being the norm. In very quick music the phrases may well be felt as the *real* measure, the nominal measures being felt as the real beats.

In fact, just as the distinction between beat and measure is conventional, so is that between measure and phrase. All these things are really of the same order. They are all groupings demanded by the ear for the sake of intelligibility, and differ in size (i.e. time-duration), and in no other way whatever. It would be possible in some compositions to show that just as the measures group themselves into phrases, so the phrases group themselves into sections consisting of several phrases; and if whilst the grouping can go on 'downward' to infinity the upward grouping is usually considered to end at the phrase, it is because the listener's memory does not readily retain the longer stretches and so, beyond the point of the phrase, any degree of regularity becomes less important to the ear.

4. Accent as the Defining Factor. It is, as already implied, accent that defines all these groupings. Theoretically a four-measure phrase is the recognition of a scheme of accentuation something like this:

And the measures and beats themselves, if subdivisions occur, show a similar scheme of accentuation, e.g.:

It is not possible to have a group of two notes, two beats, or two measures together without one of them being felt to bear a greater stress than the other. But if there are three beats together then two of them may have practically the same stress, as:

—and similarly with a grouping of three measures to a phrase, the opening of the first will bear a heavy stress and the openings of the other two lighter and practically equal stresses.

5. Irregularities of Grouping. The ear does not demand that a grouping once established shall continue quite undisturbed. Provided the normal grouping be sufficiently obvious for departure from it to be felt as such, the ear is satisfied. Occasional deviations are welcomed as a pleasant variety. Thus we may have:

etc.

And similarly a composer may effectively turn from a grouping of four measures to the phrase to one of three measures to the phrase, as, for instance, Beethoven has done in the rapid Scherzo of his Ninth Symphony, where he has called the attention of the conductor and players to the need for proper accentuation by the Italian words 'Ritmo di tre battute' and 'Ritmo di quattro battute' ('Rhythm of three measures' and 'Rhythm of four measures'; see *Battuta*).

The barring of French operatic recitatives (and in a less degree the airs) of the seventeenth and earlier eighteenth centuries (Cambert, Lully, Rameau, etc.) is marked by constant changes as to the number of beats in a bar, with a consequent lavish sprinkling of time-signatures over the pages; here the effort is to represent dramatically and with rhetorical force the varying rhythms of human speech. Twentieth-century composers have often, likewise, a great many changes of measure-values, and hence of time-signatures, in their music, whether vocal or instrumental. Such devices as these suggest an effort after the effect of prose rhythms as distinct from that of verse rhythms.

6. 'Prose Rhythms' and 'Verse Rhythms' in Music. (For some remarks on the early history of musical rhythms see *France* 3; *Italy* 3). If a piece of fine English prose be read it will be found to have beats and accents—amounting to measures but with the beats not grouped in either invariable twos or invariable threes. It is one of the qualities of fine prose to have perceptible and dignified rhythm; it is, indeed, largely this that *makes* it 'fine'. Plainsong (q.v.) is a musical setting largely of prose (always fine prose), and in its beginnings it doubtless shaped itself in a simple and direct manner on the rhythm of the words: later the decorative element (see *Ornaments* 1) became very pronounced and the original rhythms in many cases a good deal overlaid. The rhythms of plainsong are very marked, but they are prose rhythms, not verse rhythms.

The early harmonized music consisted of the addition of one or more free vocal parts to a plainsong in the tenor (see *Modes* 9) and the prose-rhythm quality persisted. When metrical psalm singing came in with the Reformation there was still (despite the now regularized rhythms of the words) no idea of maintaining a steady two-beat or three-beat measure right through the music, and the tunes of both the Calvinistic and the Lutheran branches of the Protestant Church, as first in use, have what we should now call a very 'irregular barring'. The treatment of the words was quantitative rather than accentual, and so we may find two-in-a-measure and three-in-a-measure mixed.

During the late sixteenth and earlier seventeenth centuries these tunes were drilled into regularity, thereby probably losing as well as gaining. By the time of Bach they are all so drilled, and his many harmonizations of the old German Chorale melodies show these reduced to *regular rhythms* (cf. remarks under *Chorale*).

Choral music generally, right up to the end of the great 'a cappella' period (i.e. to about 1600), was free in rhythm, and consequently either the copies were left unbarred or if bars appeared they were a mere convenient guide to the eye (cf. *History of Music* 5).

The only choral music of the period of which this cannot be said is that of the nature of ayre and ballett (see *Madrigal* 3), which, being probably influenced by the popular ballad singing and dancing of the day, is regular in its grouping of notes into beats and beats into (implied) measures.

The keyboard and other instrumental music of this period is also often regular in its barring, being likewise often so based (variations on folk songs, pieces in the style of pavans and galliards, etc.). Here printed bar-lines were used to mark the measures.

This period (say 1600–20), then, represents the line of division, so far as one is possible, between the old system of prose rhythms in music and verse rhythms in music (cf. *History of Music* 5). In the earlier part of this article mention was made of the imaginary metronome that seems to form a part of the mental equipment of every human being. But it will be realized that the period during which this imaginary (and uninvented) metronome was most mechanically obeyed began only with the seventeenth century—and the freedom shown by composers from the beginning of the twentieth century onwards (see 10) makes it look as though mechanical obedience has been a mere phase, lasting only three to four centuries or so out of all the long history of music. But rhythm always has been and always will be present in music, whether it be of the more steady or the freer kind: it is inescapable.

One curious and exceptional freedom of rhythm during the period when regularity of rhythm was normal is seen in the suites of courantes in the French type of earlier eighteenth-century keyboard music (see *Courante*). But regularity was now the ordinary thing and expected by the ear, so that when Couperin wished to portray 'Coquetry' in a little harpsichord piece he was able to get his effect by six changes of time-signature in his sixteen measures.

Occasional examples of cross-rhythm are to be found in compositions throughout the regularized-rhythm period. For instance, the Minuet of Bach's fifth keyboard Partita has a conflict of two-against-three almost throughout.

7. Harmony and Rhythm. The relation between harmony and rhythm is too big a subject to be discussed here. Roughly speaking, it is normal for a cadence to consist (harmonically) of a chord 'looking forward to' another chord, and for the latter to fall upon a strong beat (the 'first of the measure'). Considerations of this sort tended, as harmonic music developed, to regularize rhythm, and the gradual change to the new harmonic conception (as distinct from the contrapuntal), which culminated about 1600, coincided with the change from the irregular grouping (or 'barring'—though bars were then less used) to the regular (see *Harmony* and *History of Music*).

A curious little deviation from correct portrayal in notation may here be mentioned in passing. Hymn-tune books wrongly bar long-metre tunes, placing the strong final chord of each of the four cadences in the middle of the measure instead of on the strong first beat. But a careful study of the tunes in any hymn-book will bring to light some unexpected problems. (Bach in his harmonization of the traditional German chorales seems to follow no settled principles and his accentuation of the words is often quite careless.)

8. The Beat and the Lapse of Time. A strange rhythmic phenomenon is the power of the beat to maintain itself as unit. Suppose a composition to be proceeding in regular phrases, each of four measures (i.e. the normal thing). Suppose the composer gives only three measures to one of his phrases (perhaps the last one in the piece), the fact that he has done so is still recognized by the ear although the performer may introduce a slackening of speed (i.e. *rallentando*) which causes this three-measure phrase to occupy as much time as the preceding four-measure phrases have occupied. Similarly if he uses a five-measure phrase a hastening (i.e. *accelerando*) will not hide the fact. It is the beat that is the felt unit, and not any particular lapse of time such as the second or quarter-minute.

This comparative negligibility of the strict time-factor explains why all the little hurryings and delayings mentioned at the beginning of this article as a feature of fine performance do not destroy the feeling of rhythmic progression. As long as no excess or extreme abruptness characterizes the time-variations introduced the onward pressure of the system of beats and measures is still felt. Metronomes and clocks are in a sense misleading analogies for the regularity of beat, measure, and phrase, and the inevitable yet flexible regularity of the waves of the sea really offers a better one.

9. Emotional Effects of Rhythm. A slow tempo with long notes gives the impression of nobility, dignity, or peace; a rapid tempo with many short notes gives the impression of excitement—pleasurable or otherwise according to the other features of the music. This is the merest hint of an analysis that might be made of the emotional effects of rhythmic processes, or, to state it the other way, of the manner in which emotions express themselves in rhythms.

Every composer in every age has made use of what we may call the 'symbolical' suggestions of rhythm (though they are really too natural and instinctive for the word 'symbolical' to be quite in place). But with the advent of Beethoven and the romantics who followed him (see article *Romantic*) a very much more subtle use was made of such suggestions. Whereas formerly (see the suites of Bach) a composition had often proceeded sturdily in one sort of rhythm from beginning to end, now very many changes of rhythm were introduced. Beethoven's frequent device of working up to a climax by using quicker notes (i.e. more and more in a measure) is an example. So is his way of increasing the emotional tension by repeating a phrase several times at different pitches, then repeating the first half of the phrase similarly, then the first half of that, and so forth (see article *Development*). Here he is bringing the repetitions of some musical thought (the opening of the phrase in question) nearer and nearer together—a rhythmic device equivalent in its way to the using of quicker and quicker notes.

This may be the best place in this article to mention that, though for convenience the measure has been spoken of as a unit, the word 'measure' is not in this connexion to be understood always and necessarily as meaning the music enclosed between two bar-lines, i.e. beginning with a strong accent and ending with a weak one. The ear accepts, we may say, rather a measure's-worth than an actual measure as the unit, as (to take some very simple instances) in the gavotte where the measure-unit throughout is:

or the bourrée, where the unit is:

Analogies with the 'feet' of classical poetry are often introduced in discussing this subject, but for the ordinary reader (and in a brief treatment) they are rather confusing than helpful, and so they have been omitted here (see *Metre*).

10. The New Rhythmic Impulse in Twentieth-century Music. At the end of the nineteenth century and beginning of the twentieth a new rhythmic impulse came into music, largely through the study of European folk music and still more of oriental and other exotic music in which instruments of percussion play a very important part. Thus we find Debussy profiting by an exhibition in Paris to study the rhythms of Javanese musicians and writing eagerly of the rhythmic freedom and complexity of their performances: 'If, setting aside European prejudice, we pay heed to the charm of their percussion instruments we are compelled to admit that in comparison ours produce nothing better than the barbaric noise of a travelling circus.' And alluding to the combination of rhythms he says: 'The music of Java is based on a counterpoint beside which that of Palestrina is child's play.' (For an allusion to the intricacies of American Indian rhythms see *United States* 7.)

The important nineteenth-century Russian school (see *Russia* 5, 6, 7) offers a good example of the revitalizing of European music by the inspiration of exotic rhythm, the oriental side of the Russian temperament expressing itself both in the vivid orchestral colourings and in the forceful rhythms of the music of such composers as Balakiref, Mussorgsky, and (later) Stravinsky. It is significant that Spanish music, with its strong guitar and dance rhythms (of Moorish, and hence oriental origin), greatly attracted some of the Russian composers (see *Spain* 10), and such rhythms also came more

directly into notice through the work of such Spanish composers as Albéniz, Granados, and Falla.

Africa influenced European and American music during the period that immediately followed the first World War by the pungent rhythms of the Negro dance (see *Jazz*).

ARTICLES ON COGNATE SUBJECTS. *Melody* 4 (for relative importance of melodic shape and rhythm).
Tempo; *Rubato*; *Agogic*; *Syncopation*; *Courante*; *Proportions*.
Ars Nova (fourteenth-century rhythm).
Dot, Dotted Note; *Duplet*.
Jaques-Dalcroze.
Scotch Snap; *Jazz*; *Metre*.
For instruments whose main or only purpose is rhythmic see *Percussion*. See also the following tables at the beginning of the book: 1–3, 10, 11, 24.

RHYTHM AND BLUES. See *Blues*.

RHYTHM BAND or **PERCUSSION BAND.** A type of communal activity introduced largely into infant schools during the 1920s and 1930s (though it was not unknown earlier). A variety of percussion instruments is put into the hands of the children and a sort of percussion orchestration achieved, the melody and harmony being supplied by a piano. Music is published for such bands and many of the classics (even whole symphonies) are arranged for them.

Cf. *Dulcimer*.

RHYTHM BRUSHES. Same as *Wire Brushes*. See *Percussion Family* 4 d.

RHYTHMÉ, RHYTHMIQUE (Fr.). 'Rhythmic.'

RHYTHMICON. See *Electric Musical Instruments* 5 a.

RHYTHMIC PROPORTIONS. See *Notation* 3.

RHYTHMISCH (Ger.). 'Rhythmic.'

RHYTHMUS (Ger.). 'Rhythm.'

RIBIBLE or **RUBIBLE.** See under *Rebec*.

RIBUTHE (Scottish). Jew's harp (q.v.).

RICCI (The Brothers).

LUIGI was born at Naples in 1805 and died at Prague in 1859, aged fifty-four, and FEDERICO was born at Naples in 1809 and died at Conegliano in 1877, aged sixty-eight.

They were prolific and successful opera composers. Luigi's *Crispino e la Comare* (Venice, 1850), in which Federico to some extent collaborated, holds especially high rank, being looked on as one of the best comic operas ever composed in Italy.

RICERCARE. An Italian verb with both the same suggestion as the English 'research' and the same suggestion as the French 'recherché', i.e. it means literally 'to seek out' and implies effort in the seeking. In music the verb is used as a noun and applied (sixteenth to eighteenth centuries) to a composition in the fugue style using the most elaborate contrivances of counterpoint, all variations of canonic writing,

augmentation, diminution, inversion, etc. (see *Canon* and compare *Fancy*).

Like many other musical terms this one has had different meanings. Burney (1805, in Rees's *Cyclopædia*) says of **Ricercata** (which is the same verb in the past participle), 'a research, a flourish, a prelude, an impromptu, a voluntary', and under the heading 'Research' says:

'A kind of prelude or voluntary played on the organ, harpsichord, violin, etc., in which the composer seems to search or look out for the strains and touches of harmony, which he is to use in the regular piece to be played afterwards. This is usually done off-hand. When in a motetto the composer takes the liberty to use any thing that comes into his head, without applying any words to it, or subjecting himself to the sense or passion of it, the Italians call it *fantasia ricercata*, the French *recherché* and the English *research* and *voluntary*.'

This definition Burney seems to have taken very much from Rousseau's *Dictionary of Music* (1767).

To complete the definition of this word it should be mentioned that in early Italian music for the lute (e.g. the book published by Petrucci in the first decade of the sixteenth century) the title is applied to short preludes to transcriptions of songs. Here the word seems to imply not a search for elaborate ways of developing a theme but a search and establishment of the key in preparation for a piece to follow.

Bach has used (acrostically) the word 'Ricercar' (in the sense of a piece of research). Composing at Leipzig certain complex pieces upon a theme given him by Frederick the Great when he visited him in Potsdam (the series known as the 'Musical Offering') he sent it to the King with this inscription on its title-page, *Regis Iussu Cantio Et Reliqua Canonica Arte Resoluta* ('the theme given by the King's command, with additions, resolved according to the canonic style').

RICH, JOHN (*c.* 1682–1761). Noted theatrical manager. See *Pantomime*.

RICHARD I of England, 'Cœur de Lion' (b. 1157; came to throne 1189; d. 1199). See *Minstrels*, etc. 4; *England* 2.

RICHARD II of England (b. 1367; came to throne 1377; d. 1400). See *Parish Clerk*.

RICHARD III of England (b. 1452; came to throne 1483; d. 1485). See *Chapel Royal*.

RICHARDS, HENRY BRINLEY (1817–85). See *Pianoforte* 22; *God bless the Prince of Wales*; *Misattributed Compositions*, s.v. 'Beethoven's "Dream of St. Jerome"'.

RICHARDSON (alias Heybourne), **FERDINANDO HEYBOURNE** (c. 1558–1618). See *Suite* 2.

RICHARDSON'S MELODRAMA. See *Fairs and their Music*.

RICHETTATO (It.). Same as *spiccato* (q.v.).

RICHTER.

(1) **ERNST FRIEDRICH EDUARD** (1808–79). He was cantor of the Thomas School at Leipzig and author of a long series of theoretical works.

See reference under *Harmony* 20.

(2) **HANS** (1843–1916). He was a horn player who, taken by Wagner as his copyist and general assistant, became the leading Wagnerian conductor. His popularity and influence in England were immense, and from 1897 to 1911 he was resident in Manchester as conductor of the Hallé Orchestra.

See reference under *England* 7.

RICHTIG (Ger.). 'Right', 'precise'.

RICOCHET (Rebound). Musically applied this is a sort of bowing on the violin, etc., in which the upper part of the bow is, so to speak, thrown on to the string, so that in playing a series of notes it will bounce. Cf. *Volante*.

RICORDI. See *Publishing* 8.

RIDEAU (Fr.). 'Curtain.'

RIDOTTO (It.). (1) 'Reduced', i.e. arranged.

(2) An entertainment (in Fr. **Redoute**) extremely popular throughout the eighteenth century, consisting of a mixture, in varying proportions, of music performed to the company and dancing performed by them—the company often being masked.

Busby, in his *Concert Room and Orchestra Anecdotes* (1825), says, speaking of London: 'The year 1722 was distinguished by the introduction of a new species of entertainment called a *Ridotto*, consisting of select songs, followed by a ball, in which the performers were joined by the company, who passed from the front of a house, over a bridge connecting the pit with the stage.'

That was one kind of ridotto. Ridottos on somewhat different lines were popular occasional features of the annual bill of fare at the London gardens, i.e. Vauxhall, Ranelagh, and similar places of entertainment (see *Concert* 12).

In Vienna there is a great *Redoutensaal* ('Ridotto-room'), in fact two of them, a small and a big, attached to the palace of the Hofburg. Some of the most famous concerts in history have been given there, especially during Beethoven's time, and for the actual ridottos there held Haydn, Mozart, Beethoven, and others of the Viennese school have written dance music (*Redoutentänze*).

In Britain the original Italian form of the word has generally been used (i.e. 'Ridotto'), in Germany the French form of it (i.e. 'Redoute').

RIDUZIONE (It.). 'Reduction', arrangement.

RIEGGER, WALLINGFORD (p. 1060, pl. 173. 4). Born at Albany, Georgia, in 1885 and died in New York in 1961, aged seventy-five. He studied in New York and Berlin, then holding positions as opera conductor in Germany, and on return to his own country became active as a cellist and as a teacher of composition in various universities, etc. His compositions for the modern stage are many and he composed also orchestral and chamber music, often using the Note-row (q.v.) technique. It was only in his later years that his music won understanding applause in America. He made a study of electrophonic musical instruments and learned to play a cello of this class (cf. *Electric Musical Instruments* 1 d).

See *Bird Music*.

RIEGO, TERESA CLOTILDE DEL—Mrs. Leadbitter. Born in London in 1876 and died in 1968, aged ninety-one. She was the composer of some 300 songs (e.g. *O dry those tears*), also of (largely unperformed) works of a more ambitious kind.

RIEMANN, (KARL WILHELM JULIUS) HUGO (1849–1919). He was Professor of Music at the University of Leipzig and one of the most diligent and productive musicologists and theoreticians of his period, the long list of his works covering every branch of the subject and including a valuable musical lexicon (1882 and later editions in various languages; cf. *Einstein*).

See references under *Classical*; *Concert* 13; *Agogic*; *Colour and Music* 4; *Country Dance*; *Art of Fugue*; *Anglebert*; *Cornett* 3 d. Also *Expression* 2 (music example).

RIENZI, THE LAST OF THE TRIBUNES (Wagner). Produced at Dresden in 1842. Libretto by the composer, after Bulwer Lytton's novel (1835).

Act I

SCENE: *A Street in Rome, with Rienzi's House. Time, the mid-fourteenth century*

(For an allusion to the overture see *Overture* 4.)

Rienzi, a Roman Tribune and Papal Notary, filled with pride of birth and country, dreamed of releasing his native city from the hands of the nobles and making it once again the leader of the world. This dream, alike patriotic and, to the Tribune, religious, wrought within him so that his duty became a passion.

As the opera opens, one of the patrician leaders, **Orsini** (*Bass*), is attempting to abduct **Irene** (*Soprano*), Rienzi's sister. **Colonna** (*Bass*), another patrician, with his son, **Adriano** (*Mezzo-Soprano*: played by a woman), rescues her. Adriano loves Irene.

Rienzi (*Tenor*) appears. He seeks peace, but the tyrannous nobles must be put down. **Raimondo** (*Bass*), the Papal Legate, encourages him, as do **Cecco** (*Bass*) and **Baroncelli** (*Tenor*), leading citizens. Adriano, though the son of a noble, takes his stand on the side of democracy, with Rienzi. After a love scene for Adriano and Irene, Rienzi accepts the leadership, at the people's behest.

Act II
Scene: *A Hall in the Capitol*

Rienzi has conquered and is receiving messengers of peace, with the nobles, who are still haughty. They plot against him who has humbled them and are overheard by Adriano, who is torn between two loyalties, but warns Rienzi. When the nobles, in their treachery, attempt Rienzi's life, they are overpowered and condemned to die. Adriano pleads for his father's life, which Rienzi spares. The nobles are to renew their oath of fealty.

Act III
Scene: *A Public Square*

The nobles break their oath and revolt once more. Adriano, mindful of his father, again pleads to Rienzi for mercy upon him, but this time the Tribune resolves to extirpate the patricians or reduce them to complete submission. Colonna is killed, and now begins the estrangement of Adriano from Rienzi.

Act IV
Scene: *The Square of St. John Lateran. Night*

The Emperor has taken sides against Rienzi, and Baroncelli raises the people's anger by suggesting that Rienzi has betrayed them. Adriano supports Baroncelli and attempts to stab his former friend. The Pope excommunicates the Tribune. Adriano begs Irene to go away with him, but she, loyal to her brother, refuses.

Act V
Scene: *Before the Capitol*

This opens with the famous 'Prayer', in which Rienzi seeks aid in his despair. Irene's faithfulness, in spite of his advice to flee, inspirits him. She will not listen to Adriano's fervent pleading, denouncing him as a betrayer of his native city. Lonely, Rienzi and his sister face the maddened mob, who fire the Capitol and stone them. Adriano, rushing into the building to try to save Irene, dies with them when it falls in ruins.

RIES Family. From five to nine members of this distinguished German musical family receive notice in the larger works of reference. The most important three are the following:

(1) FRANZ ANTON (1755–1846), a good violinist of Bonn, who greatly helped the young Beethoven with moral and material support and intelligent teaching.

(2) FERDINAND (p. 397, pl. **68**. 7, 1784–1838). Son of the above, befriended and taught by Beethoven. (Cf. *Composition* 5.) After much struggle and poverty he settled for a time in London, marrying an Englishwoman: there, as pianist and composer, he had great success. Cf. *Concerto* 6 b (1784).

(3) HUBERT (1802–86). Also a son of Franz Anton. He is remembered today especially for his violin 'School' and his studies.

RIETI, VITTORIO. Born at Alexandria, Egypt, in 1898. He is of Italian parentage and his studies were carried out at Milan and Rome, in the latter place under Respighi. He wrote the ballets *Noah's Ark* and (for Diaghilef's Russian troupe) *Barabau* and *The Ball*. Other works include symphonies, a concerto for wind instruments, a sonata for four wind instruments and piano, a *Neapolitan Concerto* for violin and orchestra, a concerto for harpsichord and orchestra, and a musical drama in five parts, *Orpheus*, from the work of that name by Poliziano (Politian). In 1939 he took up residence in New York, where he returned in 1953 after three years teaching composition at Chicago Musical College.

RIGAUDON or RIGADOON. An ancient Provençal dance, in a two-in-a-measure (or four-in-a-measure) time. Usually, the phrases beginning on the last quarter of the bar, or just before or after it, there is a certain resemblance to the bourrée (q.v.).

The rigaudon was gay and lively until its promotion from the village green to the aristocratic ball-room and the court, when it took on dignity. It was popular at the courts of Louis XIII, XIV, and XV. It had a certain degree of popularity in England also. Composers sometimes took it into the suite (q.v.) as one of the optional members. 'Rigaudon' is the French name; 'Rigadoon' the English.

Amongst Purcell's harpsichord lessons is a rigadoon whose phrases begin on the first of the measure. There are rigaudons in Ravel's *The Tomb of Couperin* and Grieg's suite *From Holberg's Time*. One by Raff was long popular.

RIGHT LITTLE, TIGHT LITTLE ISLAND. See *Rogue's March*.

RIGOLETTO (Verdi). Produced in Venice in 1851. Libretto by Piave, after Victor Hugo's play *Le roi s'amuse*.

Act I
Scene 1: *A Room in the Palace of the Duke of Mantua. Time, the Sixteenth Century*

The profligate **Duke** (*Tenor*) is inquiring of his man **Borsa** (*Tenor*) concerning a 'fair unknown' whom he is pursuing. The courtiers' conversation reveals the duke's character. **Count Ceprano** (*Bass*), whose wife the Duke has been pursuing, defies him, unavailingly. **Rigoletto** (*Baritone*), the duke's hunchbacked jester, who aids his master's designs, cynically mocks his victims. Led by Ceprano, some of the noblemen decide to make Rigoletto, in turn, a prey. Enter the aged **Count Monte-**

rone (*Baritone*), whose daughter has been dishonoured by the Duke and who frightens Rigoletto by laying a curse upon him.

SCENE 2: *The Street outside Rigoletto's House*

Rigoletto meets **Sparafucile** (*Bass*), an assassin, ready to do murder for any one; but he does not at the moment require his services. Sparafucile departs, and **Gilda** (*Soprano*) appears. She, Rigoletto's daughter, is closely tended by her father, who forbids her to go about, except to church. But there she has been seen by the duke; she is his 'fair unknown', and he now comes to make love to her, under a false name.

Seeing the two together, the spying noblemen assume her to be the jester's mistress. They abduct her, and even get Rigoletto to help by telling him that she is Count Ceprano's wife. Too late, the jester finds that he has been deceived. The curse is taking effect!

ACT II

SCENE: *The Duke's Palace*

Rigoletto, keeping up a pretence of mirth, is bitterly seeking his daughter, who is in the palace. He breaks down, and admits to the courtiers his knowledge of their fraud. Gilda appears and tells him the sad truth. He vows vengeance on the duke.

ACT III

SCENE: *A Lonely Inn near Mantua, kept by Sparafucile. Night*

Gilda is still in love with the duke, though her father shows her the profligate amusing himself in the inn with **Maddalena** (*Contralto*), Sparafucile's sister. Here is sung the famous Quartet, in which Gilda is mortified, the duke gallant, and Maddalena coy, whilst Rigoletto mutters of revenge.

The jester bargains with Sparafucile to murder the duke, whose identity the assassin does not know. Gilda, anxious for her lover, with whom she is still fascinated, overhears Maddalena, who is also attracted by the duke, begging her brother Sparafucile not to do the murder. But the honest assassin must earn his money: there must be a victim. He promises that if a guest comes to the inn before midnight he will kill him instead.

The infatuated Gilda determines to sacrifice herself to save the duke, returns to the inn, disguised, and is stabbed.

Rigoletto comes to claim his victim, and as he receives the body in a sack is amazed to hear the duke singing outside. Opening the sack, he finds his daughter, dying. With her last breath she asks his pardon. As she dies, he sinks down, murmuring 'At last the curse is fulfilled!'

RIGORE, RIGOROSO (It.). 'Rigour', 'rigorous' (referring to exactitude in point of time).

RIISAGE, KNUDAGE. See *Scandinavia* 2.

RILASCIANDO, RILASCIANTE (It.). 'Releasing' or 'relinquishing', i.e. getting gradually slower; the equivalent of *rallentando*. *Rilassando, Rilassato* mean the same thing.

RILEY, WILLIAM. See *Parish Clerk*; *Methodism* 3.

RIMBAUD, ARTHUR. See *Colour and Music* 1.

RIMBAULT, EDWARD FRANCIS (1816–76). London organist and never-resting musical antiquarian researcher and editor of old music, etc.

See *Motet*; *Presbyterian* 6; *Holland* 3.

RIMETTENDO, RIMETTENDOSI (It.). 'Putting back' (in the sense of resuming the old tempo).

RIMINGTON, PROF. A. WALLACE; **RIMINGTON COLOUR ORGAN**. See *Colour and Music* 7, 8.

RIMONTE. See *Ruimonte*.

RIMSKY-KORSAKOF (**Korsakov, Korsakow**, etc.), NICHOLAS (p. 897, pl. **154**. 9). Born in the government of Novgorod in 1844 and died at Lyubensk, near St. Petersburg, in 1908, aged sixty-four. Like others of the Russian nationalists (cf. *Glinka, Balakiref, Mussorgsky*) he was of 'gentle' birth and was reared in the country, so enjoying the early advantages of a soaking in folk tune.

His early manhood was spent as an officer in the navy, and the first symphony Russia ever produced was partly written when on duty. The qualities of this work and of Russia's first symphonic poem, *Sadko* (an orchestral setting of a legend of the sea; 1867), led to his being offered the post of professor of composition at the Conservatory of St. Petersburg. He felt himself far from sufficiently equipped for such a post, but by dint of hard study he acquired the principles and the technique of his art and, indeed, made himself the best theorist of the whole group of 'The Five' (see *Russia* 5).

He was a strong nationalist and a devoted student of the folk tune of his native country. He was urged by a powerful dramatic impulse, with much rhythmic force and a vivid sense of orchestral colour. The last characteristic allies him with Berlioz, whose successor in this line he may almost be considered (as he may, likewise, be considered the predecessor of Stravinsky and others of the moderns); his own treatise on instrumentation is, like that of Berlioz, now a classic.

He composed freely and copiously. His fifteen operas include *Ivan the Terrible* (otherwise 'The Maid of Pskof', original version 1872; third and last version 1892), *The Snow Maiden* (1881), *Sadko* (1896; also the subject of a symphonic poem—see above), *Kitesh* (1906), and *The Golden Cockerel* (1908). He wrote three symphonies, the symphonic suite *Sheherazade* (1888), choral music, songs (especially important), and other things.

On the break-up of the group of 'The Five' he became the centre of another circle of similar aims, to which belonged Belaief and Glazunof.

For Rimsky-Korsakof's period in Russian music see *Russia* 5 and *Opera* 17 c. For references to him and his work see *Akimenko*; *Alborada*; *Aubade*; *Ballet* 6, 7 (near end); *Belaief*; *Bird Music*; *Borodin*; *Chamber Music* 6, Period III; *Chopsticks*; *Clarinet Family* 2; *Colour and Music* 4, 9; *Concerto* 6 b (1844); *Coq d'Or*; *Dargomijsky*; *Folk Song* 5; *Glazunof*; *Greek Church* 5; *Gusli*; *Mussorgsky*; *Nationalism*; *Percussion Family* 4 a (Kettledrum); *Prince Igor* (Borodin); *Programme Music* 3, 5 d; *Salieri*; *Scales* 12; *Spain* 10; *Trombone* 4.

RIMUR. See *Scandinavia* 5.

RINCK, JOHANN CHRISTIAN HEINRICH. Born in Thuringia in 1770 and died at Darmstadt in 1846, aged seventy-six. He was a noted organist and organ composer, and of his many organ works some are still in the repertory.

RINFORZANDO, RINFORZATO (It.). 'Reinforcing', 'reinforced', i.e. stress applied to individual notes or chords. So *Rinforzo, Rinforzamento*, 'reinforcement'.

RING DANCE. See *Round Dance*.

RINGING OF BELLS. See *Bell* 3.

RING OF THE NIBELUNG, THE (*Der Ring des Nibelungen*—Wagner). A Festival Play for Three Days and a Preliminary Evening. Libretto by the composer.

Produced, as a whole, at Bayreuth in 1876. The first two portions had been produced several years earlier. (See *Opera* 21 k; *Klindworth*; *Prelude*.)

I. THE RHINE GOLD

('Rheingold'). Produced at Munich in 1869.

SCENE 1: *At the Bottom of the River Rhine*

To the three river maidens, **Woglinde** (*Soprano*), **Wellgunde** (*Soprano*), and **Flosshilde** (*Mezzo-Soprano*), comes the dwarf **Alberich** (*Baritone*), who belongs to the race of underworld gnomes. They tell him about their treasure of gold. Any one who shall fashion a ring from it shall be master of the world—but only if he forswears love. Alberich, willing to pay this price, steals the gold.

SCENE 2: *An Open Space on a Mountain Top, near Valhalla, the Home of the Gods*

The King of the gods, **Wotan** (*Baritone*), and his wife, **Fricka** (*Mezzo-Soprano*), see with joy the completed Valhalla, home of the gods. But its price must be paid to the giants who built it; and that price is the goddess of Youth, **Freia** (*Soprano*). The giants, **Fasolt** (*Baritone*) and **Fafner** (*Bass*), lumber in to claim their pay. Wotan haughtily bids them choose some other recompense, and Freia's brothers, the gods **Donner** (*Baritone*) and **Froh** (*Tenor*), with **Loge** (*Tenor*), their crafty colleague, conspire to defeat the simple giants. Loge, having heard of the gold which Alberich has stolen, and of the ring, counsels a second theft to restore the joys which, with the departure of the goddess of Youth, would pass from the gods. Wotan feels that he cannot stoop to such meanness, but when the giants' cupidity is roused, and they say that they will give up Freia if Wotan will get the gold for them, he agrees. Already the gold is working its evil, for the chief of the gods has fallen low indeed. The giants take Freia away as ransom, until the gold is delivered to them, and the gods know that their youth goes with her. Wotan plots with Loge to steal the gold.

SCENE 3: *Nibelheim, the Home of the Dwarfs, below the Earth*

Alberich, already a master in his underworld, by virtue of the ring's power, bullies his brother **Mime,** a cowardly smith (*Tenor*), who has made him a magic helmet which enables its wearer to change himself into any shape he pleases.

By flattery the gods persuade Alberich to transform himself; first he becomes a serpent, and then a toad. In an instant Wotan's foot is upon the toad, and Loge's hand on the magic helmet. As Alberich resumes his own shape they bind him and bear him away to their world.

SCENE 4: *Valhalla*

The price of Alberich's freedom is to be all his gold—and the ring, which he swears will carry a curse of death with it.

The giants reappear with Freia. Wotan would retain the ring, but the earth-goddess, **Erda** (*Contralto*), rises from the ground to warn him to yield it and flee from its curse. He gives it up, and Freia and the surety of youth return to the gods. The ring's curse is immediately at work, for the giants quarrel over the spoil, and Fafner kills Fasolt.

Donner ascends a high rock, smites it, and clouds disperse, showing a rainbow bridge, over which the gods pass to their new home.

See *Overture* 4; *Scordatura*.

II. THE VALKYRIE

('Die Walküre'). Produced at Munich in 1870.

ACT I

SCENE: *Hunding's Hut*

We are to know that the Valkyrie, the wild horsewomen of the air, appointed to bear to Valhalla the bodies of dead warriors, are the nine daughters of Wotan and Erda. Wotan must get back the ring, because if he does not the race of gods cannot endure; but Fafner, the remaining giant, has transformed himself into a serpent, and guards the gold on earth. In the hope that a son of a god born upon earth may regain the gold, Wotan has become the father of sons by a woman of earth. Upon these children is visited in turn the curse of the stolen gold.

Siegmund (*Tenor*), one of these children, now a man, is fleeing, in a thunderstorm, from enemies. In the hut of Hunding, husband of **Sieglinde** (*Soprano*), he takes refuge. The two, not knowing that they are brother and sister, are stirred by love. **Hunding** (*Bass*) gives Siegmund refuge, though he is his enemy. Sieglinde guesses who the stranger may be, though he does not recognize her, since she was carried away by raiders when young; and he has lost his father—though whether he is dead or alive, Siegmund knows not. Sieglinde puts into Hunding's drink a sleeping potion.

See the Articles mentioned on page 998

Er Appenzeller Kureien Lobelobe.

1. RANZ DES VACHES—the Appenzell version, as published by G. Rhaw in 1545. Over fifty regions in Switzerland are said to possess their own versions of the music and words. See the article on p. 856

2. GLAREANUS, whose treatise *Dodecachordon* 1547 codified the modal system. See *Modes* 6

3. ROUSSEAU (1712–78). His teachings, philosophical and social, supplied the foundations of a new humanism. As a musician he was active and prominent as Theorist, Lexicographer, and Composer. See pp. 892–3

4. NÄGELI (1773–1836). Musician, Educationist, and Publisher, who from his Zürich headquarters exercised valuable influence. See the Articles *Nägeli, Education,* and *Appreciation*

5. JAQUES-DALCROZE (1865–1950) He developed a system of musical training through physical movement ('Eurhythmics'). His headquarters were at Geneva, but branches came into existence in many countries

6. GUSTAVE DORET (1866–1943) Composer and writer on musical subjects

7. HONEGGER (1892–1955). Composer of many and varied works

8. FRANK MARTIN (1890–1974) Composer with a personal style and freedom from conventions

PLATE 148   THE RECORDER FAMILY

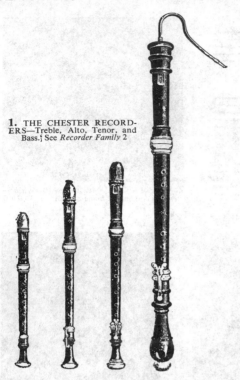

1. THE CHESTER RECORD-
ERS—Treble, Alto, Tenor, and
Bass. See *Recorder Family* 2

2. PIPE AND TABOR—Richard Tarlton
See *Tarlton* and *Jig*

3. NINETEENTH-
CENTURY
FLAGEOLET

Gauote pour les Fluſtes douces.

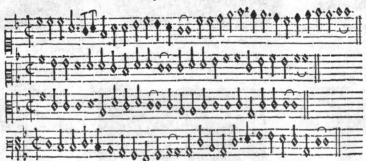

4. GAVOTTE FOR FOUR FLAGEOLETS—from the *Harmonie Universelle* of Mersenne
(q.v.), 1627. See 5 below for modern notation of part of the passage

6. FLAGEOLET PLAYER
From Greeting's *Pleasant Companion*, 2nd edition, 1673

In the roof-tree of the hut is embedded a sword, which a stranger [Wotan] had placed there on Sieglinde's wedding-day, declaring that he who could draw it forth should possess it. No one has ever been able to secure it. Siegmund, inspired, wrenches it forth. Sieglinde is now sure of his destiny, and of hers; and the two rush forth together into the night.

ACT II

SCENE: *A Wild, Rocky Place*

Wotan (*Baritone*) commands **Brünnhilde** (*Soprano*), one of the Valkyrie maidens, whom he loves dearly, to shield Siegmund in the fight which he must wage with the pursuing Hunding. Wotan's wife, **Fricka** (*Mezzo-Soprano*), demands that Siegmund shall be punished for his profanation of Hunding's wedlock. His wife's reproaches cause Wotan to change his purpose: he realizes that his fetters were forged by himself, in first yielding to wrong-doing. Though he now orders Brünnhilde to give Hunding the victory, she attempts to save Siegmund; but Wotan's interposed spear, at the critical instant, allows Hunding to deliver the decisive stroke. Siegmund dies. Brünnhilde lifts Sieglinde on to her horse and flees, whilst Wotan, grieved at the loss of Siegmund, contemptuous of Hunding, and wrathful at the defeat of his will by Fricka's, takes his revenge upon Hunding by striking him dead.

ACT III

SCENE: *The Summit of a Rocky Mountain*

'The Ride of the Valkyries' shows the warrior-maidens gathering. Brünnhilde brings Sieglinde, and, telling her that she is to become the mother of another hero, urges her to escape into the forest from Wotan's wrath. She does so, and the god decrees Brünnhilde's punishment for her disobedience: she is to be no more a goddess, but a woman only. He causes her to fall into a trance, from which she may be awakened, and taken as wife, by whatever man shall find her. He grants a last request—that she may be surrounded by fire which only a fearless hero shall penetrate. The fire is invoked, and the scene closes in.

See *Overture* 4.

III. SIEGFRIED

Produced at Bayreuth in 1876.

ACT I

SCENE: *Mime's Forge*

We are to know that Sieglinde died in giving birth to her son Siegfried, who, found in the forest by the cunning dwarf Mime, has been brought up by him. Mime hopes that the youth may win for him the ring.

We find **Mime** (*Tenor*) trying to forge a sword wherewith the guardian of the gold may be slain. The pieces of the sword belonging to Siegmund, which Hunding shattered, he cannot unite. **Siegfried** (*Tenor*) forces Mime to tell him of his birth and parentage. **Wotan** (*Baritone*) comes in the guise of a Wanderer, seeking shelter. He and Mime question each other. Mime finds that the Wanderer knows of the three races: the Nibelung below the earth, the giants upon it, and the gods above it; and Mime, Wotan finds, is aware of the vital importance of the forging of the sword, but does not know who can forge it. Wotan reveals that a fearless hero shall not only make the sword but shall be the cause of Mime's death.

Siegfried, coming back, is questioned by Mime as to his knowledge of fear. He does not understand what it can be, and the dwarf realizes that here is the fearless one. And, indeed, Siegfried is he, for he forges the sword there and then.

ACT II

SCENE: *The Cavern Home of Fafner*

We remember that the giant Fafner turned himself into a dragon, to guard the gold for which he killed his brother. **Alberich** (*Baritone*), who first, by stealing the treasure, brought on the curse, lies in wait to secure it again. Wotan watches and comments. **Fafner** (*Bass*) will on no account give up anything. Mime brings Siegfried to the dragon's lair, but that does not inspire him with fear. Siegfried slays the guardian of the gold, and, having by accident tasted the dragon's blood, becomes able to understand not only what the birds say, but what Mime plots in his evil heart—the death of Siegfried. The hero kills the treacherous dwarf, thus fulfilling Wotan's prophecy. A bird reveals to him his immediate destiny— that he shall rescue Brünnhilde, and led by it he goes upon this adventure.

ACT III

SCENE 1: *At the Foot of the Mountain*

Wotan, seeking advice from **Erda** (*Contralto*), the earth-goddess, finds no hope, and decides to will that 'twilight of the gods' which, he realizes, cannot be avoided. Siegfried and Brünnhilde are the appointed rulers of the future, not the old gods. It is fate. When Siegfried appears, the progress of that fate is clearly attested by the hero's breaking with his all-conquering sword the spear with which Wotan once ruled the fate of Siegmund. Siegfried plunges into the fire, to Brünnhilde.

SCENE 2: *Brünnhilde's Rock*

Siegfried, with a kiss, awakes the slumbering **Brünnhilde** (*Soprano*)—no longer a goddess —and places on her finger the ring he has won. The penultimate drama of the cycle ends.

IV. THE TWILIGHT OF THE GODS

(Or 'Dusk of the Gods'—*Götterdämmerung*). Produced at Bayreuth in 1876.

PRELUDE

SCENE: *Valkyries' Rock* (as in the last Act of *The Valkyrie*)

The **Three Norns** (*Soprano, Mezzo-Soprano, Contralto*) predict the fate of the gods, whose home, Valhalla, is to be destroyed when the curse of the Ring is ended.

Brünnhilde (*Soprano*) sends **Siegfried** (*Tenor*) to seek adventure. He has her horse Grane, upon which he is to go to further proofs of his love.

ACT I

SCENE 1: *The Hall of the Gibichungs, by the Rhine*

We find **Hagen** (*Bass*), son of Alberich the dwarf, plotting with his half-brother **Gunther** (*Baritone*) to secure the ring, of whose resting-place he has knowledge. Gunther is to possess Brünnhilde, whom Siegfried, by a magic potion, is to be caused to forget; instead, he will love **Gutrune** (*Soprano*), Gunther's sister. Then Gunther will insist that before he weds Gutrune, Siegfried shall secure Brünnhilde for Gunther, who does not know that she had already been won by the hero.

Siegfried (*Tenor*) comes, drinks what he presumes to be a horn of mead, and the philtre at once works its spell. Siegfried and Gunther swear the solemn oath of blood-brotherhood, and go off to find Brünnhilde.

SCENE 2: *Brünnhilde's Rock*

Waltraute (*Mezzo-Soprano*), one of the Valkyrie sisters of **Brünnhilde** (*Soprano*), has come to beg her to return the ring to the Rhine maidens from whom was stolen the gold that made it. Waltraute has heard Wotan, now grown sad, say that the curse would be lifted if that were done. But Brünnhilde will not give up Siegfried's pledge of love.

Waltraute departs, in despair, and Siegfried appears, but in the form of Gunther—a magic helmet has made the transformation. The ring cannot protect her, and she must be Gunther's bride.

ACT II

SCENE: *An Open Space before the Gibichungs' Hall*

Alberich (*Baritone*), who first stole the gold, exhorts his son Hagen to win for him the ring, and count not the cost.

Siegfried, now in his own form, announces that Gunther is bringing home his prize, Brünnhilde. The **Vassals** (*Chorus*) gather to greet them. Brünnhilde is amazed and grieved to see Siegfried about to be wed to Gutrune, for the ring (so she believes) was taken from her not by the hero, but by Gunther, and here is Siegfried wearing it. He is a traitor to her, and to Gunther and Gutrune, for is he not wedded to her, Brünnhilde? Poor Siegfried is unconscious of any fraud, and dismisses Brünnhilde's rage as groundless, roused 'by some demon's evil craft'.

Her love turned to hate, Brünnhilde plots with Hagen and the unhappy Gunther to murder Siegfried when he is hunting.

ACT III

SCENE 1: *A Rocky Valley by the Rhine*

The three **Rhine Maidens** (*Sopranos* and *Mezzo-Soprano*) seek the ring from Siegfried, but he will not give it up. They warn him that evil will befall him. The rest of the hunt comes up. Hagen pours into Siegfried's drink a potion which brings back the hero's memory, and he tells how he first found Brünnhilde. Hagen stabs him and he dies, calling upon Brünnhilde with his last breath. To the great 'Funeral March' music he is borne upon the shields of the vassals to the Gibichungs' hall.

FINAL SCENE: *The Hall of the Gibichungs*

Hagen tells Gutrune that he has murdered Siegfried. He now demands the ring. Gunther refuses it, and Hagen kills him. Again the curse of the ring is working. As Hagen is about to take the ring from the dead man's hand, the arm is raised threateningly. It is Brünnhilde's, and hers alone. She, who has heard from the Rhine Maidens the truth, bids the vassals build a funeral pyre. She bids her farewell to the hero, mounts the horse Grane, and rides into the heart of the flames. They blaze up, fill the whole scene, and then subside, whilst the Rhine overflows, extinguishing the fire. The Rhine Maidens, borne upon the flood, seize the ring. Hagen, rushing to try to gain it, is drawn by them into the depths. Valhalla is seen in the distance in flames—final illumination of that twilight of the gods which is now to darken into eternal night.

See March.

RINUCCINI. *See* Libretto; Opera 11 a.

RIPETIZIONE (It.). 'Repetition.'

RIPIANO. An erroneous form of 'ripieno' (see below). The word thus spelt means a staircase landing.

RIPIENO (It.). Literally 'full'. (1) The term is used in the older music, to make a distinction between passages to be played by some solo performer, or group of solo performers, and passages to be played by the whole orchestra. The latter are *Ripieno*. The players of secondary skill, who in the seventeenth- and eighteenth-century concertos (see *Concerto* 2) performed only in the full passages, were the Ripieno players, or the *Ripienists*. The antithetical term is *Concertante*, and old scores were often marked alternately with the terms *Concertante* (see also *Concertino* 1) and *Ripieno*. (In cases where a single instrument took the principal part, instead of *Concertante* the word *Solo* would be used.)

(2) In more modern music the word is still in some use, and in a similar sense, e.g. in a brass band (q.v.) a Ripieno cornet (generally misspelt *Ripiano* or *Repiano*) is a player who takes part only in the full passages.

(3) In Italian organ music the word means 'mixture' (see *Organ* 14 V).

RIPOSO, RIPOSATO (It.). 'Repose', 'reposeful'. So *Riposatamente*, 'with a feeling of repose'.

RIPPLING RHYTHM ORCHESTRAS. See *Jazz* 6.

RIPPON, REVD. JOHN (1751–1836). See *Baptist* 3.

RIPRENDERE (It.). 'Take up again', i.e. resume (e.g. the original tempo).

RIPRESA (It.). 'Repeat' (of a section of a composition). Also 'recapitulation section' (see *Form* 7). Also 'revival' (of an opera, etc.).

RISCALDANO (It.). From *Caldo*, 'warm'. Literally 'they warm up', i.e. the players are to become more lively.

RISE, COLUMBIA ! See *Rule, Britannia !*

RISING OF THE LARK. This is the old Welsh song 'Codiad yr Ehedydd' said to have been composed by the harper David Owen (see *Dafydd y Garreg Wen*) as, going home from a long-extended feast at three in the morning, he saw a lark mount and heard it herald the break of day. The truth of this origin of the melody is held to be attested by the existence of a stone which is still shown.

RISOLUTO, RISOLUTAMENTE (It.). 'Resolute', 'resolutely'. So the superlative *Risolutissimo*.

RISPETTO. A type of Italian folk song—with eight lines to the stanza. The plural is *Rispetti*. Wolf-Ferrari, Malipiero, and others have written music under this title.

RISTRINGENDO (It.). 'Drawing-together', i.e. quickening.

RISVEGLIATO (It.). 'Wakened up', i.e. animated.

RIT. Short for *ritardando* (see below).

RITARDARE, RITARDANDO, RITARDATO (It.). 'To hold back', 'holding back', 'held back' (gradually, i.e. the same as *rallentando*).

RITARDO (It.). The act of holding back (i.e. of gradually diminishing the speed).

RITE (Ambrosian, Roman, Gallican, Mozarabic, etc.). See *Liturgy*.

RITENENDO, RITENENTE (It.). 'Holding back' (= *Rallentando* and *Ritardando*).

RITENUTO (It.). 'Held back', i.e. slower (immediately, not gradually as with *Ritardando* and *Rallentando*; but it may be that some composers have not observed this distinction).

RITMICO (It.). 'Rhythmic.'

RITMO (It.). 'Rhythm.'

RITMO DI TRE BATTUTE (It.). See *Battuta*; *Rhythm* 5.

RITORNEL (Fr. *Ritournelle*; It. *Ritornello*; Ger. *Ritornell*). The Italian form of this word is the original and most common and means anything 'returned to' in music. The following applications of the word have been brought about:

(1) In the older verse-repeating type of Italian madrigal the refrain was so called.

(2) A certain type of Italian folk song (3-line stanzas with the rhyme of the first line returning in the third—one supposed origin of 'terza rima' in fact) was also so called.

(3) When in the early seventeenth century song with instrumental accompaniment was developed in Italy, the return of the purely instrumental portions was so called, and this use is common today, the word even being applied to the introductory instrumental portion (which is no 'return' whatever). Here 'Ritornello' becomes a synonym for 'Symphony' in one of its senses (see *Symphony* 1). *Refret* is another name.

(4) In the classical concerto the return of the full orchestra after a solo passage used to be so called. Here 'Ritornello' becomes a synonym for 'tutti'.

(5) The word is sometimes (logically) found in the simple sense of 'Da capo' (q.v.).

RITORNO (It.). 'Return' (noun).

RITTER, ALEXANDER (1833–96). See *Symphonic Poem*.

RITTERLICH (Ger.). 'Knightly.'

RITTQUARTETT (Haydn). See *Nicknamed Compositions* 12.

RITUALE. In the Roman Catholic Church the book containing the Rites for the administration of the Sacraments, Burial Service, Processions, and Blessings. The second and third ('Ordo Exsequiarum' and 'Processionale') are also separately published.

RIVERSO, AL (It.). By contrasting motion, i.e. the upward intervals of a melody all turned into downward intervals of the same numerical value, and vice versa.

RIZZIO (or Riccio), **DAVID** (*c.* 1533–66). Son of an Italian musician and himself such, secretary and favourite of Mary Queen of Scots and murdered by her jealous husband, Darnley. See *Scotland* 1.

RK. = 'Rank', referring to the 'mixture' stops of an organ. See *Organ* 1, 2 c, 14 V; *Harmony* 4.

R.M.C.M. Royal Manchester College of Music. See *Schools of Music*.

ROAST BEEF OF OLD ENGLAND. See *Leveridge, Richard*.

ROBERT, CAMILLE. See *Madelon*.

ROBERT DE SABILON. See *France* 2.

ROBERTON, HUGH S. (1874–1952). See *Scotland* 11.

ROBERTS.

(1) JOHN (Ieuan Gwyllt). He was born near Aberystwyth in 1822 and died at Caernarvon in 1877, aged fifty-four. He exerted one of the greatest influences on Welsh musical life of the past century, introducing Bach, Handel, and Mendelssohn to Welsh choirs, curbing the extravagances of the old florid hymn tunes, and making known the German chorales (q.v.); his collection of hymn tunes, indeed, marks an epoch in Welsh religious musical life, and a tune of his own composing, *Moab*, is spoken of by Sir Henry Hadow as 'one of the seven greatest tunes in the world'—but he also published a translation of Sankey and Moody's hymns which had a wide popularity.

He edited the musical monthly *Cerddor Cymreig*; and, for a time, a Welsh newspaper in Liverpool. And he was a preacher in the Welsh Calvinistic Methodist Church.

(2) JOHN VARLEY. Born at Stanningley, near Leeds, in 1841 and died at Oxford in 1920, aged seventy-eight. He was for nearly forty years organist of Magdalen College, Oxford, and wrote church music, a *Method of Training Choristers*, etc.

ROBIN ADAIR. The tune of this song, commonly thought to be Scottish, is in reality the old Irish one of *Eileen Aroon* (q.v.). It appears to have been popularized in Scotland about 1715 by the famous blind Irish harper, Hempson (q.v.), then touring there.

The first introduction of the name 'Robin Adair' seems to have been in a parody which in 1734 welcomed to Puckstown (County Dublin) an Irish M.P. of the name. This version, too, travelled to Scotland, where 'Puckstown' became 'Paxton'.

The words now used date from about 1750 and are by Lady Caroline Keppel, being addressed (this is curious and confusing!) to another Robin Adair, a young Irish surgeon, with whom she was in love, and whom (after a long fight with her relatives) she married in 1758; he became Surgeon-General to George III. Presumably the name 'Robin Adair' in the song as then circulated suggested to her a version with a personal application.

The Scotch Snap (q.v.) which pervades the song is no part of the original, and dates only from the early nineteenth century; it may have been added by the great singer Braham, who at that time popularized the present version of the song.

ROBIN ET MARION. See *Minstrels* 5, etc.; *Adam de la Halle*.

ROBIN GRAY. See *Auld Robin Gray*.

ROBINSON Family of Dublin (see *Ireland* 6).

(1) FRANCIS I. Baritone singer, etc. See *Ireland* 6. The following are his sons:

(2) FRANCIS II. Eldest son of Francis I (c. 1800–72). Tenor vocalist, Vicar-Choral of Christ Church and St. Patrick's Cathedrals, Dublin, organist of the latter (1828–9), composer of church music, etc.

(3) WILLIAM. Bass singer. Member of same choirs as Francis II.

(4) JOHN (c. 1812–44). Tenor singer and organist of the two cathedrals above mentioned. (For another John Robinson see below.)

(5) JOSEPH (1816–98). Baritone singer (p. 481, pl. 84. 6). Great choral conductor, Professor of Singing at Royal Irish Academy of Music, composer, founder of the Ancient Concerts (1834–64). His wife (Fanny Arthur) was a leading pianist and a composer; she died in 1879.

ROBINSON.

(1) JOHN (1682–1762). Organist of Westminster Abbey from 1727. See *Anglican Chant* 5. (For another John Robinson see above.)

(2) THOMAS. See *Scandinavia* 2.

ROBUSTO (It.). 'Robust' (e.g. *Tenore robusto*—

a powerful tenor voice; see *Voice* 19). So *Robustamente* = in a robust spirit.

ROCHBERG, GEORGE. Born at Paterson, N.J., in 1918. He studied at the Curtis Institute, Philadelphia, where he was on the staff from 1948 to 1954. He became chairman of the Music Department of the University of Pennsylvania in 1960. His compositions include two symphonies.

ROCHESTER CATHEDRAL. See references under *Cathedral Music* 2, 7, 8.

ROCHESTER, New York. See *Schools of Music*.

ROCK AND ROLL. See *Blues*; *Festival* 2.

ROCK HARMONICON. See *Dulcimer*.

ROCKINGHAM. See *Hymns and Hymn Tunes* 6.

ROCK OF AGES. See *Hymns and Hymn Tunes* 6, 7.

ROCKSTRO (originally 'Rackstraw') WILLIAM SMYTH (1823–95). Pupil of Sterndale Bennett and friend of Mendelssohn, musical theorist and archaeologist, authority on plainsong, author of a valuable life of Handel, etc.

See reference *Tonic Sol-fa* 10 (end).

ROCO (It.). 'Raucous.'

ROCOCO. In French, the word conveys the idea of a kind of fancy rock-work (*rocaille*) in architecture as found in the period of Louis XV. In older English usage the meaning is usually 'tawdry' or 'tastelessly florid'; in music it is applied to the light and diverting 'galant' or homophonic style (see *Style galant*) of composers such as Telemann, the sons of Bach, and the early Haydn and Mozart (roughly 1730–70).

It has been said that the aim of baroque is to astound, that of rococo to amuse.

RODE, JACQUES PIERRE JOSEPH (p. 1096, pl. 181. 7). Born at Bordeaux in 1774 and died there in 1830, aged fifty-six. His youthful talent as a violinist led to his being accepted as a pupil of Viotti, and then to his appointment at sixteen as chief second violin in a theatre orchestra in Paris. At twenty he toured as a virtuoso in northern Europe, and soon after in Spain. When he was twenty-six Napoleon, then First Consul, appointed him his solo violinist.

He toured in Russia and spent some time at Vienna, where Beethoven composed a Sonata (op. 96 in G) for him. For some years he lived at Berlin.

The example of his polished style as a performer had great influence upon Spohr and other contemporaries and hence is not lost today. There was a tragedy in his life in that his playing quite evidently declined, and this led to his abandoning public performance and, it is said, contributed to his death.

His violin concertos and his twenty-four caprices (one in each major and minor key) have had great celebrity and are still in use amongst students. His string quartets have too much the nature of a first violin part with

See the Article *Reed-Organ Family* on pages 863–7

2. REGAL and BIBLE REGAL—the latter folding in the middle. See *Reed-Organ Family* 2

3. SIR CHARLES WHEATSTONE. Inventor of the Concertina. See *Reed-Organ Family* 4

1. CHINESE CHENG
(see *Reed-Organ Family* 1)

4. ENGLISH CONCERTINA

5. DOMESTIC MUSIC IN THE MID-19TH CENTURY

6. PULLMAN CAR DEVOTIONS IN THE 1870's (Sunday morning on the 6-day journey from New York to San Francisco)

7. REED-ORGAN (English, 1935)

1. MOUTH-ORGAN OR HARMONICA
See *Reed-Organ Family* 3

2. MOUTH-ORGAN CLASS IN GERMANY
Early 20th century

3. AMERICAN HARMONICA BAND at Philadelphia, 1922–38; Albert N. Hoxie, Director

4. AT AN INTERNATIONAL CHAMPIONSHIP COMPETITION (London, 1937)
The English Accordion Band here shown came from Norwich

accompaniment, and are now forgotten. A famous show piece of his is still to be heard in the set of Variations in G.

See *France* 9; *Étude*.

ROECKEL Family. They were well known throughout the nineteenth century. The father, JOSEPH AUGUST (1783–1870), was a notable singer and opera director in Germany, Paris, and London.

Of his sons, AUGUST (1814–76) was Wagner's colleague in the opera of Dresden and his companion revolutionary, less lucky than Wagner since he suffered thirteen years in prison. EDWARD (1816–99) lived nearly all his life in Bath, England, and poured out piano music of no particular importance. JOSEPH LEOPOLD (1838–1923) lived at Clifton, England, and composed melodious songs for the Victorian drawing-room.

ROGER-DUCASSE, JEAN JULES AIMABLE. Born at Bordeaux in 1873 and died there in 1954, aged eighty-one. He was a pupil of Fauré at the Paris Conservatory, and his style derives from that of his master. His compositions include chamber, orchestral, and choral music, and a good deal of piano music, with a little music for the stage (especially a mimodrama, *Orpheus*) and a few songs.

He served as inspector of singing in the schools of Paris from 1909 and in 1935 succeeded Dukas as a professor of composition at the Paris Conservatory.

ROGERENES. See *Quakers* (end).

ROGER IN AMAZE. See *Fairs and their Music.*

ROGERS.

(1) BENJAMIN. Born in Windsor in 1614 and died at Oxford in 1698, aged eighty-three or eighty-four. Before the Commonwealth he was organist of Christ Church Cathedral, Dublin, and after it organist of Eton College and then of Magdalen College, Oxford. He composed a good deal of church music, some of it still in regular use, and also of music for strings, then considered of high value but now unobtainable and forgotten. The *Hymnus Eucharisticus*, sung every May Day from Magdalen Tower, Oxford, is his.

For a reference to Cromwell's interest in him see *Puritans* 4. Allusions to his church music will be found under *Cathedral Music* 7 and *Anthem*, Period II.

(2) WILLIAM. See an allusion under *Scotland* 6.

(3) BERNARD (p. 1060, pl. **173**. 8). Born in New York in 1893 and died at Rochester, N.Y., in 1968, aged seventy-five. He studied with Bloch and then with Nadia Boulanger and Frank Bridge. His many and varied works include a one-act opera *The Warrior* (Metropolitan Opera, New York, 1947), a Passion (Cincinnati 1944), and five symphonies. He was on the staff of the Eastman School.

ROGER'S FAREWELL. See *Auld Lang Syne.*

ROGER THE CAVALIER. See *Sir Roger de Coverley.*

ROGUE'S MARCH. This tune is almost identical with that of the well-known *Right little, tight little Island* of Dibdin (q.v.). Its origin is unknown; there are many printed copies in the eighteenth century but, apparently, none earlier.

In the British Army it was used in the ceremony of expelling (or 'drumming out') a soldier from the army—hence its name.

(It is sometimes stated that *The Rogue's March* was only a drum-beat. This is incorrect. See a description of one of the last 'drummings out' in the British Army in Lieut.-Col. Mackenzie-Rogan's *Fifty Years of Army Music* —where the tune is given.)

ROH (Ger.). 'Rough', 'coarse'.

ROHR (Ger.). 'Reed'. *Rohrflöte, Rohrflute,* see *Organ* 14, II. *Rohrwerk, Rohrstimmen,* the reed department of the organ.

ROLLAND, ROMAIN (1866–1944). Valuable French writer on musicological subjects—notable also as novelist, dramatist, biographer, political writer, etc. His many-volumed novel *Jean Christophe* (1904–12) depicts the life of a musical genius. His great book on Beethoven is important. See reference under *Fidelio* (footnote); *Dupin.*

ROLLER. See *Waltz.*

RÖLLIG, K. L. See *Harmonica* 1.

ROLLSCHWELLER (Ger.). The 'General Crescendo' pedal of an organ (the one which gradually brings out all the stops).

ROLLTROMMEL (Ger.). Tenor drum; see *Percussion Family* 3 j, 4 b, 5 j.

ROMALIS (Sp.). A sort of Seguidilla (q.v.). Other names are *Ole* and *Polo.*

ROMAN, J. H. (1694–1758). See *Scandinavia* 4.

ROMAN CATHOLIC CHURCH MUSIC IN BRITAIN. A fair general idea of the development of music in the Western Christian Church before, in the sixteenth century, it divided into its present Protestant and Roman Catholic sections (as also the general basis of musical treatment of the Roman service) can be gathered from other articles in this volume, as, for instance, *Liturgy, Mass, Plainsong, Psalm, Hymns and Hymn Tunes* 2. Articles concerned with the early evolution of harmonized music (e.g. *Harmony* 4–8) may also be consulted. The purpose of the present article is to supply a parallel to those articles in which is briefly sketched the history of post-Reformation music in the Anglican Church and the various Nonconformist bodies, and thus to complete, in some measure, the survey of the general subject of the treatment of music as a part of British religious life during the past four centuries.

The Reformation in Britain, which may be dated from 1534, entailed the destruction of a vast number of buildings in which church music was carried on at various degrees of efficiency (600 in England alone from 1536 to 1539). Henceforth the tradition of a high musical culture was confided entirely to those comparatively few buildings retained as cathedrals for the new national church. Except for the five years of Queen Mary's reign (1553–8) the Romanists, who had formerly sternly suppressed heresy, were now regarded as heretics themselves, and this and their real or supposed allegiance to a foreign power led to their worship being prohibited, so that for long the Mass could be celebrated only in secrecy or quasi-secrecy. Gradually, towards the very end of the eighteenth century, the disabilities of Roman Catholics were removed by a series of Acts, affecting in turn England and Wales, Ireland, and Scotland. Complete freedom came only with the Catholic Emancipation Act of 1829. Up to this date, though Roman Catholic churches had been gradually brought into existence, they were usually built in back streets, to avoid undue public observation, and they were merely tacitly tolerated, not openly permitted, the only legal places for the celebration of the Romanist rites being the chapels of foreign embassies, which thus took on a public importance they would not otherwise have had and do not nowadays retain. It will be seen that but for these Embassy Chapels Roman Catholic service music may be said to have been necessarily non-existent in Britain for about 300 years.

A series of able English-born musicians latterly directed the music at some of these embassies, as Samuel Webbe senior (q.v.) at the Sardinia Chapel, Lincoln's Inn Fields, and perhaps too, at the Portuguese Chapel, Grosvenor Square; Samuel Webbe junior (q.v.) at the Spanish Chapel, Manchester Square; and Vincent Novello (see *Publishing of Music* 7 and p. 289, pl. **51**. 3), who in turn had posts as chorister or as organist at all these three chapels. The period represented by the work of these three musicians probably represents much the highest point that what we may call Catholic Embassy music had so far reached since the Reformation. They all published a good deal of music for the use of their choirs, and, though not always inspired, it possesses dignity.

Two of these musicians lived to see the happier times for their faith, Novello then becoming organist of the Roman Catholic Pro-Cathedral, Moorfields, London, and Samuel Webbe junior, organist of Roman Catholic churches at Liverpool.

The Roman Church on the Continent was then passing through what we may consider a bad phase musically. The Masses most valued were not those of the high polyphonic period of Palestrina, Victoria, and their immediate predecessors and contemporaries, but the orchestrally accompanied Viennese Masses of Haydn, Mozart, Weber, Hummel, Beethoven, and their contemporaries, or those of Kalliwoda (1801–66) and others of his period, in all of which the spirit is rarely that of the church and more often that of the concert-room or even of the opera-house, and in all of which the form is quite unliturgical (see *Mass* 3). One of the three musicians mentioned, Vincent Novello, founded the music-publishing house that still

bears his name (see *Publishing* 7), and amongst his issues were many Masses of this type, which henceforth dominated Catholic music in Britain until well into the twentieth century. When British Catholic musicians themselves wrote Masses these were their models. Later came Gounod and other composers whose Masses, whatever their musical attractions or value, were in no real sense church music.

The use of music of this sort was by no means the only, or, indeed, the worst abuse. Both in Britain and on the Continent, until the nineteenth century was far advanced, the organ music was often entirely unsuitable. The columns of the musical and Catholic press during this period frequently record startling examples of bad taste, as in *The Tablet* of 27 November 1875, where a London church is mentioned at which, after a Mass the music of which was 'only fit for a singing saloon or a circus', the organist 'wound up with the overture to Boïeldieu's *La Dame Blanche*', and another where 'the organist played quite coolly at Mass a selection from Balfe's opera *Il Talismano* and ended the Mass with the overture to *Zampa*'.

The vernacular hymns sung in Roman Catholic churches until near the end of the nineteenth century were usually not on a high level. The Webbe–Novello period left behind it a small supply of sound diatonic tunes, which, however, dropped almost out of use when, in the middle of the century, the hymns of Faber (see *Hymns and Hymn Tunes* 6, also p. 485, pl. **86**. 7) came into use and popularized a type of tune of much slighter worth. *The Crown of Jesus* was the popular tune-book of the period; many of its tunes were adaptations from operatic music, Beethoven's piano sonatas, and other varied compositions never designed to appear in places of devotion, and the accompaniments were often of a trumpery kind. When at the end of the century better tunes were introduced they were largely those of Anglican nineteenth-century provenance and of the very type which Anglicans of better taste were even then beginning to try to eliminate.

In the middle of the nineteenth century a change of taste, form, and spirit in continental Catholic music came about as the result of the movement in Germany promoted by the Cäcilienverein (or St. Cecilia Society), but the influence of this movement, partly good and partly bad, though it extended to Britain, left many churches untouched, and in any case the new music introduced, though not objectionable, as the old had been, showed few positive virtues (see *Cecilian Movement*).

The change of ideal that has now happily largely come about dates from the issue of a Motu Proprio on the subject, by Pius X, in 1903, (see *Motu Proprio*) and the appointment of Richard Terry in 1901 to the newly-erected Roman Catholic Cathedral at Westminster, where, during the following quarter-century, a remarkable revival took place not only of the works of Palestrina and his continental predecessors and contemporaries but also of English music of the same periods, the bulk of which existed only in manuscript parts at the British Museum and elsewhere, so that much research and labour of scoring was necessary before it could be brought into use.

The authority given by Pius X to the plainsong publications of the monks of Solesmes (see *Plainsong* 3), in the same year as that of his Motu Proprio, naturally supported this movement for a higher standard of music and of performance in the Catholic Church in Britain—a movement that is not yet exhausted and, indeed, has still much to accomplish.

In the 1960s approval was given to the increasing use of local vernacular, encouraging the 'active participation' of the faithful, and cautiously opening the door to Lutheran chorales, folk music, 'jazz masses', and the like. At the same time, instruments commonly accepted as suitable for secular music only (such as electric guitars and so on) were excluded from liturgical celebration and popular devotions.

It will be seen that the difficulty has been twofold: (*a*) the complete loss of the British Catholic musical tradition by three centuries of enforced silence, and (*b*) the unfortunate fact that, at the moment when the resumption of Roman Catholic musical activities came about in Britain, Catholic churches on the Continent offered bad models.

ROMANCE. In French, 'song' ; in Spanish a type of ancient ballad; in English often a song-like instrumental piece.

ROMANCE SANS PAROLES (Fr.). Literally 'Song without Words'.

ROMANCERO. See *Spain* 4.

ROMANESCA (It.) or **ROMANESQUE** (Fr.). (1) Same as a galliard (see *Pavan and Galliard*), according to the writer 'Arbeau' (see *Dance* 6). Probably it was a kind of galliard originally danced in the Romagna.

(2) The word also appears as the name for a certain melody much used as a ground bass (q.v.) in the seventeenth century (it is given in full in the 1929 edition of Riemann's *Lexikon*).

(3) a type of song (e.g. by Monteverdi).

ROMAN MUSIC (Ancient). See *Notation* 1.

ROMAN RITE. See *Common Prayer*.

ROMANTIC (for illustrations see p. 892, pls. 151–2). The ordinary dictionary definition of 'Romantic' is 'Imaginative, remote from experience, visionary; in music subordinating form to theme [i.e. to some literary or pictorial subject-matter]; in literary and artistic method preferring grandeur or picturesqueness or passion or irregular beauty to finish and proportion; subordinating whole to parts, or form to matter'. This is compressed from the definition in the *Concise Oxford Dictionary*. It sufficiently outlines the implications of the word, as applied to music, and to anyone who is acquainted with a sonata of Haydn and a nocturne of Chopin,

or an opera air of Mozart and a scene from a Wagner music drama, it is clear enough that, though there is 'romance' in both, the later work is more completely permeated by it than the earlier (see *History of Music* 7).

By the 'Romantic School' in music is meant the group of active spirits in that movement which began in Germany with Weber (born 1786) and was taken up by his fellow Germans, Mendelssohn (born 1809), Schumann (born 1810), and Wagner (born 1813), by the Frenchman Berlioz (born 1803), by the French-Pole Chopin (born 1810), by the Hungarian Liszt (born 1811), and so on.

Or it can be carried back as far as Schubert (born 1797) and Beethoven (born 1770), but it is, for purposes of generalization, sometimes considered that the classical element (see *Classical*) in the work of those two was strong enough to rank them as the last of the Classicists rather than as the first of the Romanticists, i.e. their work is then regarded as constituting the culmination of that of Haydn and Mozart, the symphonic classicists *par excellence*.

No exact defining lines can be drawn anywhere in the history of music, or in that of any art, and categories such as 'Classical' and 'Romantic' are devices of convenience. All music has an element of romance, and it is a matter for intelligent decision at just what period that element becomes so predominant that we may speak of the beginning of the Romantic Epoch. It must in any case be placed somewhere not long before or after the year 1800.

The Romantic Movement in music which began at this period was not, of course, an isolated phenomenon; it was merely part of a general romantic movement which, all over Europe, but perhaps especially in Germany and France, affected all the arts. Its advent in English literature (see *Ballad* 5) may be conveniently dated from Wordsworth, Coleridge, and the 'Lake Poetry', and the novels of Sir Walter Scott, which last had their influence on continental literature. It is noticeable that at this period the arts of literature and painting began to exercise, more directly and powerfully than ever before, an influence upon that of music. Such composers as Weber, Schumann, and Wagner had strong literary interests. Weber and Wagner were attracted by the legends of northern Europe; Schumann by the pseudo-philosophic romantic literature of his own day; Chopin by his national Polish poet Mickiewicz (1798–1855); Berlioz by the greater earlier romantic poet Shakespeare; Liszt by the contemporary French romantic poet Lamartine and by various French romantic painters with whom he associated—and so on (cf. *Song* 5).

Thus a fertilization of music by poetry, fiction, philosophy, and painting took place (see *Programme Music*), and with it was associated a further fertilization by the spirit of nationalism, which was then, at the end of the Napoleonic domination, gaining ground rapidly all over

Europe, so that Weber, Schumann, and Wagner were definitely conscious of expressing the German spirit, and Chopin of expressing the passionate rebelliousness of an enslaved Poland, whilst Liszt attempted to express national feeling through Hungarian Rhapsodies (see *Nationalism in Music*). Later came other romantic-nationalistic composers, in whom the national element was the more evident from a frequent and conscious use of the idioms of the folk-music of their native countries. Dvořák (Bohemian, born 1841) and Grieg (Norwegian, born 1843) are examples of this tendency that will occur to every reader.

The Romantic Movement continued right into the opening years of the twentieth century (Strauss, Elgar, MacDowell, etc.). By this time an Impressionistic School, founded by Debussy (see *Impressionism*), had arisen as an offshoot of it; this also had affiliations with contemporary painting (e.g. Monet) and poetry (e.g. Mallarmé).

Then there came about in certain quarters a revulsion from romanticism, and a definite Anti-Romantic and Anti-Impressionistic or Neo-Classical Movement may be said to have begun with Stravinsky (Russian, born 1882) and Bartók (Hungarian, 1881–1945), a movement which attempted to abolish the expression of strong emotion in music, as also literary associations and implications in instrumental works, and to adopt a less emotional harmony and a more pungent and forceful rhythm, with an orchestration in which the 'colours' of the instruments employed would stand off sharply from one another instead of blending. (Here again was an obvious parallelism between the 'movement' of the day in music and those in poetry and in painting.)

Meanwhile a Neo-Romantic school (though perhaps not anxious to adopt the title) flourished in Germany and Austria, and here we may consider Schönberg (1874–1951) as the representative personage.

Romanticism, it will be seen from the above, is the predominant artistic 'ism' of the nineteenth century. But, as aforesaid, the romantic element is found in music of all ages and any attempt to introduce a practice which denies this can probably never have any greater ultimate result than the shifting of balance—a lesser stress upon poetry and a greater upon pattern.

With this article should be read *History of Music* 7, 8, where will be found a further short treatment of the whole subject with chronological lists of the composers concerned in the movement in various countries; and also *Opera* 9 c and e; *Ballet* 4; *Song* 5; *Expression* 5; *Scandinavia*; *Wales* 7; *Rousseau*.

ROMANZA (It.). A song or song-like instrumental composition.

ROMBANDO (It.). 'Humming.'

ROMBERG Family.

(1) ANDREAS JAKOB (p. 1088, pl. **179**. 3). Born at Münster in 1767 and died at Gotha in 1821, aged fifty-four. He was an eminent violinist and composer of quantities of operas, choral works, symphonies, violin concertos, and all other forms of music. (Cf. *Chamber Music* 6, Period III (1767).) His *Lay of the Bell* cantata used to be a favourite with choral societies. He is now (ironically!) remembered by most people simply by one lesser work—a Toy Symphony.

There were ten other Rombergs who were close relations of this one and some of them of fair importance, but particulars of them must be sought in some larger work than the present.

(2) BERNHARD (1767–1841) was a very great cellist and played much with Beethoven.

See *Concerto* 6 b (1767).

ROMBERG, SIGMUND (1887–1951). A popular composer of operettas (over 70, including *The Student Prince*, 1924) and, in later years, film music.

ROME. See *Italy*; *Opera* 23; *Plainsong*; *Singing* 2; *Belgium* 2; *Cecilia*; *Prix de Rome*; *Applause* 3.

RONALD, LANDON (originally Landon Ronald Russell). Born in London in 1873 and died there in 1938, aged sixty-five. He was the son of Henry Russell, the song composer (q.v.), and displayed musical ability at an early age. He studied at the Royal College of Music. After a period as conductor of opera and of musical comedy, as Melba's accompanist on her American tour, and in miscellaneous ways he became known as an able orchestral conductor. He specialized as an interpreter of the music of his friend Elgar. As a composer he is known through his songs and some theatrical incidental music. He was Principal of the Guildhall School of Music from 1910 to 1937 and was knighted in 1922.

RONDA, RONDALLA (Sp.). Young men making their evening rounds in the streets to play and sing before people's houses. (For Ronda, the place, see *Rondena*.)

RONDE (Fr. 'Round'). The Whole-Note or Semibreve (Table 3); also a round dance to which the music is supplied by the dancers' singing.

RONDEAU. (1) A thirteenth- and fourteenth-century type of song—sometimes accompanied by dance. In it a solo voice and choral refrain alternated. The music tended, as time went by, to become polyphonically complex. In the earlier part of the period it was cultivated by the Troubadours and Trouvères (see *Minstrels* 4, 5). 'Rondel' is another form of the word, and the Virelay, or Virelai, was much the same thing.

(2) An instrumental form possibly deriving (as to the arrangement of its sections) from the above. The earlier and simpler type of Rondo (see *Form* 9).

RONDELLUS. A round, in medieval church services usually associated with festive occasions. The form was much cultivated in the period 1250–1350, and then dropped from sight.

RONDEÑA. A kind of fandango (q.v.) of southern Spain, with the same harmonic peculiarity as the malagueña (q.v.). It takes its name from Ronda in Andalusia.

RONDO, RONDO FORM. See *Form* 9, 10, 13, 14.

RONDO-SONATA FORM. See *Form* 10.

RONDS DE JAMBE. See *Ballet* 8.

RONSARD, PIERRE DE (1524–85). See *Concert* 2.

RÖNTGEN, JULIUS. Born at Leipzig in 1855 and died in Holland in 1932, aged seventy-seven. He was of Dutch parentage and from his early twenties lived in Amsterdam, where he occupied many important positions, including latterly that of head of the Conservatory. His operas, orchestral works, piano works, songs, etc., have had high repute in many countries. He was the friend of Liszt, Brahms, and, especially, Grieg.

See references to him and the period in Dutch musical progress he represents, under *Holland* 8; *Lesquercade*.

ROOSEVELT.

(1) THEODORE (1858–1919; President of U.S.A., 1901–9). See references under *United States* 7; *Ballad* 3.

(2) New York organ-building firm, in business 1872–93. See *Organ* 9.

ROOT, ROOT POSITION (of a Chord). See *Harmony* 24 f.

ROOT, G. F. See *Battle Cry of Freedom*.

ROOTHAM, CYRIL BRADLEY. Born at Bristol in 1875 and died in Cambridge in 1938, aged sixty-two. At nineteen he entered St. John's College, Cambridge, and at twenty-six he returned to it as musical director. His published compositions are not very numerous, but they have character.

ROPARTZ, GUY (in full Joseph Guy Marie; p. 384, pl. 63. 8). Born at Guingamp, in Brittany, in 1864 and died there in 1955, aged ninety-one. He was a pupil of Massenet at the Paris Conservatory, and later of Franck. He devoted a good deal of his energy to educational work, as director first of the Conservatory of Nancy and then, when Alsace again became French at the end of the first World War, of that of Strasbourg. He also did a good deal of conducting, and as an enthusiast for the works of his late friend Magnard, did his best to bring them into notice.

His compositions, frequently tinged with the folk idiom of his native Brittany, were largely for the stage, but there is a considerable list of orchestral and chamber works and of church music (including some for organ), and, further, one or two volumes of critical writing and three or four of poems.

ROPER, EDGAR STANLEY. Born at Croydon in 1878 and died in London in 1953, aged seventy-four. He was Assistant Organist of Westminster Abbey, Organist of the Chapel Royal (1919–53), and Principal of Trinity College of Music (1929–44). He appeared little in public as a composer but did valuable service as editor of the older English church music. C.V.O. (1943).

See reference under *Anglican Chant* 6.

RORATISTES, COLLEGE OF. See *Poland*.

RORE, CIPRIANO DE (or 'Van Rore'). Born at Antwerp (or perhaps Malines) in 1516 and died at Parma in 1565, aged forty-eight or forty-nine. He was one of the later of the many Flemish composers who, by their compositions and their activities abroad, contributed to the musical fame of their country. He held positions in St. Mark's, Venice, where he was a pupil of Willaert (q.v.), at Ferrara, and at Parma. He succeeded his old master in Venice, but returned to Parma, where he lies buried in the cathedral. He published madrigals and motets.

See *Belgium* 1; *Italy* 4; *Parody*.

RORY O'MORE. The words and air of this popular Irish song are by the novelist–poet–painter, Samuel Lover (1797–1868). He wrote it as the result of a challenge to make something better than the Irish comic songs of which he complained—'a pig and a poker, expletive oaths, *hurroos* and *whack fol de rols*'. The popularity of the song became such that he was able to boast that 'on the day of Queen Victoria's coronation every band along the line of procession to Westminster Abbey played Rory O'More during some part of the day, and finally, it was the air of the band of the Life Guards played as they escorted Her Majesty into the park on her return to Buckingham Palace'.

As a good business-man he based a novel on the song and a play on the novel, and these were equally successful.

ROSA, (1) CARL AUGUST NICOLAS—really 'Karl Rose'. 1842–89. Violinist and, with his wife, opera impresario and organizer of the 'Carl Rosa Opera Company' which until its demise in 1958 was the chief means of bringing opera to British provincial centres.

(2) SALVATOR (1615–73). Painter, satirist, poet, and musician. Most or all of the songs long attributed to him have been shown to be by other composers.

ROSALIA. See under *Sequence*.

ROSEINGRAVE or **ROSINGRAVE**.

(1) DANIEL. Died in Dublin in 1727. He was a pupil of Purcell and organist successively of the Cathedrals of Gloucester, Winchester, Salisbury, and Dublin (both of St. Patrick's and Christ Church; cf. *Ireland* 6). Most of his compositions are lost.

(2) THOMAS. Born at Winchester in 1690 and died in Ireland in 1766, aged seventy-five or seventy-six. He was son of the above, but studied in Italy, where the two Scarlattis were his friends. He carried on some theatre activities in London, and was organist of St. George's, Hanover Square. He fell in love with a pupil, was refused by her father, and thereafter was intermittently mad. He published organ and harpsichord music, etc.

(3) RALPH. Born at Salisbury about 1695 and died at Dublin in 1747, aged about fifty-two. He, also, was a son of (1), whom he succeeded

as organist of Christ Church Cathedral, Dublin. He wrote church music.

ROSENBERG, HILDING C. Born at Bosjökloster, Sweden, in 1892. He studied in Stockholm and in Berlin, Vienna, and Paris, and then became known in his own country as a conductor (Stockholm Opera, etc.). His orchestral and chamber music, etc., shows leanings in the direction of Expressionism (q.v.). His opera, *Joseph and his Brethren* (1948), based on Thomas Mann's *Joseph*, takes eight hours in performance.

ROSENKAVALIER, DER, i.e. 'The Knight of the Rose' (Strauss). Produced at Dresden in 1911. Libretto by Hugo von Hofmannsthal.

ACT I

SCENE: *A Room in the Palace of the Princess von Werdenberg. Morning. Time, Eighteenth century (reign of Maria Theresa). Place, Vienna*

Whilst the husband of the Princess (*Soprano*) is away she has been receiving the attentions of the youth **Octavian, Count Rofrano** (played by a woman: *Mezzo-Soprano*). **Baron Ochs of Lerchenau** (*Bass*), a coarse fellow, cousin to the princess, is announced, and Octavian retires into another room. The Baron's errand is to seek someone who shall carry the customary token of the time, a silver rose, to his betrothed, Sophie von Faninal, whose father has recently risen swiftly from a humble position.

Octavian re-enters, disguised as a chambermaid, and the Baron flirts with the pretty 'servant'. Before the princess attends to Ochs's business she receives many morning callers—a singer (*Tenor*), a flautist, several tradesmen, people seeking assistance, and the like; among them an intriguer, **Valzacchi** (*Tenor*), and his so-called 'niece', **Annina** (*Contralto*).

After the reception-hour, the princess promises Ochs that she will find him a rosebearer, and he goes off. She has decided that Octavian is to be the knight; but she realizes that she may lose her lover to some younger woman.

ACT II

SCENE: *Room in Herr von Faninal's House*

Faninal (*Baritone*) is delighted to have captured a baron for a son-in-law. His daughter **Sophie** (*Soprano*), with her attendant **Marianne** (*Soprano*), awaits her betrothed anxiously, and with timidity. Octavian presents the silver rose, and he and the girl are at once attracted to each other. The baron's uncouthness infuriates Octavian, and disgusts Sophie. When the baron has gone out, the two declare their love. The intriguer and his companion spy on them, and inform the baron. He and Octavian take to their swords, and the baron is slightly wounded. Sophie's father, however, insists on making sure of the grand son-in-law, and Octavian goes out to plan the boor's downfall. In this he makes use of Valzacchi and Annina, getting the latter to give the baron a note from the princess's 'chambermaid', making an appointment for the next night.

ACT III

SCENE: *A Private Room in an Inn near Vienna*

Here the baron meets his charmer, to whom he makes love. He is plagued by mysteriously appearing figures (part of Octavian's plot), and Annina comes in with several children, pretending to be his deserted wife. The police arrive, and the baron, in danger of disgrace, declares that the 'girl' he is with is Sophie, his wife-to-be. Octavian's plot has included the bringing on the scene at this point of Sophie's father, whom the badgered baron, near the end of his tether, pretends not to know. Last of all appears the princess. Octavian explains to the police his masquerade, the baron has to pay a huge bill to the innkeeper, Sophie's father refuses to allow her to marry the oaf, and the princess, who realizes that her young lover has found his true mate in Sophie, resolves not to come between the two.

ROSENMÜLLER, JOHANN (*c.* 1620–84). See *Sonata* 10 b.

ROSENTHAL, MORIZ (1862–1946). Polish pianist of high reputation. See references under *Memory* 7; *Jewish* 9.

ROSLAVETS (Roslavyets, etc.), NIKOLAI. Born in the district of Chernigov in 1881 and died in 1930. The son of a peasant, he received his training as a composer at the Moscow Conservatory and for a time prided himself on his modernist style and his avoidance of the emotional. For this he abjectly apologized in 1930 in the *Proletarian Musician*, but, apparently unforgiven, is stated to have been sent to Siberia in the year mentioned and there to have died.

See *Harp* 4; *Chamber Music* 6, Period III (1881).

RÖSLER, JOHANN JOSEF (1771–1813). See *Misattributed Compositions* s.v. 'Beethoven's Concertstück, or One-movement Concerto in D'.

ROSOWSKY, SOLOMON. See *Jewish Music* 8.

ROSS, JANE. See *Londonderry Air.*

ROSSETER, PHILIP. Born about 1575 and died in London in 1623, aged about forty-eight. He was a lutenist and writer of songs and ayres and instrumental chamber music. He was active in Queen Elizabeth's court theatricals and was a friend and collaborator of Campian (q.v.), who left 'all that he had unto Mr. Philip Rosseter, and wished that his estate had bin farr more'.

ROSSI.

(1) LUIGI. Born at Torremaggiore (Foggia), in south Italy, in 1597 and died in Rome in 1653, aged fifty-five or fifty-six. He was a singer, organist, and composer who, popular in Rome and elsewhere in Italy, in the early years of the reign of Louis XIV became popular also in Paris, having been there invited by his countryman Cardinal Mazarin, under whose patronage he produced the first Italian opera

there heard, *Orfeo* (1647—see *Opera* 11 a and p. 688, pl. **115**. 2). Later he returned to Rome.

His compositions are numerous. They include sola arias, or cantatas, in the improvement of which form he was active. (Cf. *Lully*.)

There are very many other Rossi's of some degree of eminence in the art of music, but for these the larger works of reference should be consulted.

(2) SALOMONE. See *Jewish* 4.

ROSSINI, GIOACCHINO ANTONIO (p. 524, pl. **95**. 1). Born at Pesaro in 1792 and died near Paris in 1868, aged seventy-six. His father was a town trumpeter and inspector of slaughter-houses, who, on the appearance of Napoleon's troops in northern Italy, showed a disposition to welcome them, was removed from these high positions, and was cast into jail. The mother thereupon took the child to Bologna and began to earn a living for the two of them as leading lady in comic opera. It is evident, then, that the future composer enjoyed at least those advantages that come from the possession of parents of independent thought and sturdy character.

After a childish apprenticeship to the boards he entered the Conservatory of Bologna as a student of cello and composition. The music of Mozart was a particular cult with him and his companions called him 'the little German'.

On emerging from pupilage he quickly made a name as an opera composer, greatly helped by two qualities very properly dear to the public—a sense of melody and a sense of humour. In his early twenties he was already director of the great San Carlo Theatre of Naples and composer of *The Barber of Seville* (1816), which immortal opera was hissed on its first performance.

At thirty-seven he wrote *William Tell* (1829), which made his thirty-sixth opera in nineteen years. Then, tired or lazy, he stopped, and for the remaining forty years of his life never wrote another opera—unless we unkindly speak of his *Stabat Mater* as such.

He thoroughly understood the human voice, and also the various instrumental voices and how to combine them in an orchestral score. This, with the two qualities before mentioned, account sufficiently for his enormous success.

See *Opera* 6, 11 d, 21 c d; *Barber of Seville*; *Oratorio* 2 (near end), 7 (1818); *Stabat Mater*; *Ranz des Vaches*; *Jodel*; *Cornet* 2; *Percussion Family* 4 b (Bass Drum; Side Drum); *Composition* 5; *Chamber Music* 6, Period III (1792); *Opera Buffa*; *Cabaletta*; *Cavatina*; *Alabiev*; *Auber*; *Balfe*; *Misattributed* (Stradella); *Figured Bass*; *Collaboration*; *Mayr*. Also p. 893, pl. **152**. 4.

ROTA (1) A round (q.v.); 'Sumer is icumen in' (q.v.) is often called the 'Reading Rota' (from its place of composition). (2) A Latin name for the hurdy-gurdy (q.v.).

ROTE or ROTTE. Another name for crwth (q.v.), though it may sometimes mean harp, perhaps. It occurs in Chaucer, etc.

ROTONDO (It.). 'Round', i.e. full in tone.

ROUGET DE LISLE, CLAUDE JOSEPH. Born near Lons-le-Saulnier, in Franche-Comté (now in the Department of the Jura, France), in 1760, and died at Choisy-le-Roy, near Paris, in 1836, aged seventy-six. Composer of the *Marseillaise*. He was an engineer officer in the French Army, stationed in Strasbourg when, in 1792, the first and more peaceful stages of the Revolution accomplished, France, already challenged by Austria, was about to be opposed by the First Coalition, and was angrily bidding her neighbours defiance.

Chancing to hear the Mayor of Strasbourg express in conversation his regret that the young soldiery had no patriotic song to which to march, he spent the night of 24 April in the composition of words and music of a song for this purpose, helping himself to the tune by means of his violin. The song was sung by the mayor next day, hastily arranged for military band, and played at a review the day after, and then, two months later, sung at a patriotic banquet at Marseilles. Here so high an enthusiasm was engendered that the idea came of printing copies and giving them to the volunteers just about to leave for Paris. Cheered by this song, they 'accomplished the astounding feat of traversing France, drawing cannon with them, at the rate of eighteen miles a day, in the height of a torrid summer, for close on a month on end. There is no parallel to such an effort in the history of war' (Hilaire Belloc). And Paris the Marseillais volunteers duly entered singing their song, and with it, too, they marched to the Tuileries on 10 August, on the morning of the day when the gallant Swiss Guard were annihilated and Louis XVI and Marie Antoinette driven to take refuge with the Parliament.

Rouget de Lisle's composition is, then, for ever associated in men's minds with the event that at length weighted the quivering balance and set it heavily down on the side of republicanism. Yet he himself was a royalist, and, the fate of the King and Queen having been decided, refused to take the oath of allegiance to the new constitution, was stripped of his uniform and imprisoned, and escaped the guillotine only by happy accident. When the spirit of excess subsided, he re-entered the army, fought in the Vendée and was wounded, retired to povery, was pensioned (but inadequately) on the defeat of Napoleon and the accession of Louis XVIII, and in old age subsisted partly by the charity of old friends.

On different occasions he wrote other patriotic hymns, and he published a volume of essays and poems which he dedicated to Méhul.

See a reference to the 'Marseillaise' under *Schumann* (end of the article). And cf. *Carmagnole*.

ROUGH MUSIC. See *Charivari*.

ROULADE (Fr.). Much the same as a vocal *Division* (see *Divisions* 2).

ROULANT, ROULANTE (Fr.; masc., fem.). 'Rolling.' *Caisse roulante* is a tenor drum. See *Percussion Family* 3 j, 4 b, 5 j.

ROUMANIA. See *Rumania*.

ROUND. (1) A short vocal canon (q.v.) for unaccompanied singing. The canonic imitation is always at the unison (or octave).

An example known to nearly every one is 'Three Blind Mice', which has been popular in England since the days of Queen Elizabeth.

The round is a simple social form—for domestic and convivial use. The melody being the same in all parts is quickly picked up and thus people who cannot read the simplest music at sight can yet take their share in the enjoyment of contrapuntal choralism. In the Elizabethan and early Stuart period, when in the aristocratic houses of England the madrigal was in high favour, the round (and especially the humorous type of it; see *Catch*) was in equal favour amongst the common people—though not limited to them. This popularity lasted right on through the nineteenth and early twentieth centuries, and is not yet extinct, though the use in school singing-classes is now perhaps the strongest factor in keeping the form alive.

Ravenscroft's *Pammelia; Musickes Miscellanie, Or Mixed Varietie of Pleasant Roundelayes and delightfull Catches of 3, 4, 5, 6, 7, 8, 9, 10 Parts in one* (1609) ,was the first published collection of rounds. A second part, *Deuteromelia*, appeared the same year, and a third part, *Melismata* (brief madrigals as well as rounds), two years later. These publications seemed to satisfy the needs of singers until, during the Commonwealth, John Playford published his *Musical Banquet* (1651), after which a flood of similar publications poured out for a century and a half (p. 145, pl. **30**).

(2) A round dance, i.e. one in which the dancers formed a circle. One sees allusions in old literature to Cheshire, Shropshire, and Irish rounds, and comes across tunes so denominated. There is a tune called **Cheshire Rounds** in the later editions of Playford's *Dancing Master*, and Burney, who was under the impression that no folk music existed in England, said, 'The English have not a melody that they can call their own except the hornpipe and the Cheshire Round'.

It is clear that though the dance might be originally a round one the tune and steps were also used for solo dancing, for in the late seventeenth and early eighteenth century are to be found London advertisements such as the following: 'In Bartholomew Fair . . . you will see a Black that dances the Cheshire Rounds to the admiration of all spectators.'

In Hone's *Every-Day Book* is a letter dated 1825 in which the Cheshire Round is spoken of as an old tune in use at that date for Welsh May-dancing ceremonies.

ROUND DANCE. A dance in which the performers turn round or (more common use of the term) a dance in which they move round in a circle (i.e. a ring dance). Cf. *Square Dance*.

ROUND-O. See *Form* 9.

ROUS, FRANCIS (1579–1659). See *Hymns and Hymn Tunes* 10.

ROUSSEAU, JEAN JACQUES (p. 880, pl. 147. 3). Born at Geneva in 1712 and died near Paris in 1778, aged sixty-six. He was the son of a Geneva watch-maker and dancing-master; deserted by his father, he entered on a vagrant career, one phase of which shows him as a music teacher in Lausanne, though hardly able to play a tune, and as the inventor of a system of musical notation which he took to Paris and submitted to the Academy of Sciences, to be told that it was 'neither new nor useful'.

At forty he appeared in the most distinguished way as a composer, his opera *Le Devin du village* ('The Village Diviner' or 'Village Soothsayer') being performed both before the court of Louis XV at Fontainebleau and, more publicly, in Paris. The success of this work led to its introduction into England twelve years later, translated and arranged by Burney (q.v.) as *The Cunning-Man*; there it made no great effect, though it was heard repeatedly at the Paris Opéra for the following seventy-five years, having four hundred performances there in all.

The year after his opera was first heard appeared the *Letter upon French Music*, the trend of which is sufficiently indicated by the fact that its author was burnt in effigy in Paris.

He consorted with Diderot and d'Alembert and supplied articles on music and on political economy for the famous *Encyclopedia*. Rameau (q.v.) published three pamphlets on the musical errors of this publication.

At fifty-five (1767) he published his *Dictionary of Music*, which shortly after appeared in an English translation. There were other writings on music and a few compositions other than those mentioned above.

At fifty-eight (1770) he produced his famous *Pygmalion*, a one-act melodrama (see *Melodrama* 1); his responsibility for the music is, however, disputed.

For the stormy life of Rousseau, and for his philosophy, more general works of reference should be consulted, but it should be said here that his ideas on social justice were the foundation of a new humanism, and as such were a huge contributing force to the art of Beethoven and of the musical Romantics (see *Romantic*), as they were to the art of Wordsworth and the English poetical Romantics. He was an explosive agent, who shattered in fragments notions of the rights of kings and aristocracies and so cleared the way for the French Revolution that broke out a decade after his death. And with the old régime in politics went the old formal rules in art. 'Back to Nature' is the best brief statement of a creed that needed volumes to express. The implication is very wide: 'Those who boast they grasp the whole of it', said Rousseau himself, 'are cleverer than I am.' The treatment of Rousseau in dictionaries of music is commonly confined to his compositions and his writings directly upon music. That is surely the expression of much too narrow a view and the above hints as to the artistic implications of his philosophy, though brief, may serve to set the minds of some readers upon a new track of thought.

1. THE EMBARKATION OF THE QUEEN OF SHEBA (by Claude, 1600–82)

2. DIDO BUILDING CARTHAGE (by Turner, painted 1815)

Claude's picture has for two centuries been an inspiration to landscape painters by the beauty of its sky and of the sunlight shining on the water. Turner's has been a similar inspiration in its delicate colourings and its emotional suggestion. Turner bequeathed his picture to the National Gallery on condition that it should be hung beside Claude's masterpiece, as a perpetual challenge. Here, then, we have similar subjects treated in the 'Classical' manner and in the 'Romantic'—affording a comparison as to aim and feeling that can by analogy be applied to music

PLATE 152   THE CLASSICAL AND THE ROMANTIC, II

1

3. ROMANTIC OPERA—as *Punch* saw it in 1844. His picture is headed '*Der Freischütz' at the Haymarket*, and is of the nature of a suggestion based upon the fact that 'the stage, under its Shakespearian meridian, boasted no other scenery than mere placards'

2

1, 2. The Romantic Spirit and the Neo-Classical Spirit, as expressed in the home

4. A ROMANTIC GALAXY. Liszt playing to Dumas and George Sand (seated), Victor Hugo, Paganini, and Rossini (behind them), and the Countess d'Agoult (by the piano). Painting by Danhauser. The bust of Beethoven, from which the player seems to be drawing inspiration, is probably the one which the artist himself made after Beethoven's death. (It was he who took the death-mask of Beethoven and this he later gave to Liszt)

Information on most of the points above mentioned and on some others is scattered through the pages of the present work and can be found by means of the following list of references:

I. HIS LIFE AND WORK: *Copyists*; *Education* 1; *Criticism* 3; *Bouffons*; *Opera* 21 a, 24 (1752); *Intermezzo*;

Zopf; *Melodrama*; *Rousseau's Dream* (below).

II. HIS ANTAGONISM TO FRENCH MUSIC: *Bouffons*; *Overture* 1; *Singing* 9; *Conducting* 2.

III. HIS DICTIONARY AND QUOTATIONS FROM IT: *Dictionaries* 2 (and at end); *France* 8; *Entrée*; *Overture* 1; *Arioso*; *Chanson*; *Ballet* 7;

Sonata 1; *Divertissement*; *Copyists*; *Descant*; *Tierce de Picardie*; *Improvisatore*; *Boutade*; *Ricercare*; *Fantasia*; *Country Dance*; *Ranz des Vaches*; *Barocco*; *Cantata*; *Capriccio*; *Pitch* 6 a.

IV. HIS VIEWS ON MUSIC IN EDUCATION, etc.; *Education* 1; *Sight-Singing* 2; *Lancashire Sol-fa*.

ROUSSEAU'S DREAM. This tune comes from Rousseau's opera *Le Devin du village* (1752; see *Rousseau*), where it appears without words, to accompany action. The title *Rousseau's Dream* was given by J. B. Cramer (q.v.). The tune appears in many hymn collections.

ROUSSEL, ALBERT (p. 385, pl. **64**. 7). Born at Tourcoing, in the north of France, in 1869 and died at Royan in 1937, aged sixty-eight. He began life in the navy and (like Rimsky-Korsakof) began the practice of composition when on his voyages. He afterwards studied under Gigout and also under d'Indy at the Schola Cantorum, of which institution he later became a professor.

He composed orchestral music (four symphonies), ballet music, songs, and other things. His work is poetical and refined. It is influenced by the Impressionist (q.v.) School, and, in his later works, harmonically, by Stravinsky, yet it expresses a definite individuality.

His travels are reflected in several works of an Eastern tinge.

In 1929 a Roussel Festival was held in Paris, and attracted a good deal of attention in the press of all countries.

See references under *Harp* 4; *Ballet* 6; *Concerto* 6 c (1869).

ROVESCIO, AL (It., 'In reverse'). (1) By contrasting motion, i.e. the upward steps of a melodic passage all turned into downward steps of the same numerical value, and vice versa.

(2) In addition to this application mentioned there is another one—to compositions on the principle of the *Palindrome* (q.v.).

ROWALLAN MANUSCRIPT. See *Scotland* 1.

ROWLEY, ALEC. Born in London in 1892 and died there in 1958, aged sixty-five. He studied at the Royal Academy of Music. He was a fluent and original composer of songs, chamber music, organ music, a concerto for piano and military band, etc., and his piano music included much attractive material for young performers.

He was vice-principal of Trinity College of Music, London.

'ROXOLANE' SYMPHONY (Haydn). See *Nicknamed Compositions* 11 (63).

ROYAL ACADEMY OF MUSIC, LONDON. See *Schools of Music*; *Degrees*, etc.; and for a reference to the early eighteenth-century operatic institution of this name see under *Ariosti*.

ROYAL ACADEMY OF MUSIC, PARIS. See *Community Singing* 3.

ROYAL ALBERT HALL. See *Concert* 8.

ROYAL COLLEGE OF MUSIC, LONDON. See *Schools*; *Degrees*, etc.

ROYAL COLLEGE OF ORGANISTS. See *Profession of Music* 10; *Degrees*, etc.; *Anglican Parish Church* 7.

ROYAL FESTIVAL HALL. See *Colour* 10; *Concert* 8; *Electric* 4.

ROYAL IRISH ACADEMY OF MUSIC. See *Ireland* 6.

ROYAL KENT BUGLE, KEY BUGLE. See *Cornett and Key Bugle Families* 4 h.

ROYAL MANCHESTER COLLEGE OF MUSIC. See *Schools*.

ROYAL MILITARY SCHOOL OF MUSIC. See *Schools*; *Degrees and Diplomas* 2.

ROYAL MUSICAL ASSOCIATION. Founded in London in 1874 'for the investigation and discussion of subjects connected with the art and science of music'. The Association was incorporated in 1904 and given leave to use the title 'Royal' in 1944. See *Musicology*.

ROYAL PHILHARMONIC SOCIETY, LONDON. See *Concert* 6, 8; *Conducting* 5.

ROYAL SCHOOL OF CHURCH MUSIC. This was founded by Sir Sydney Nicholson (q.v.) in 1927. Its aim is to promote and maintain a high level in the church music of the country. In 1950 the number of choirs affiliated was reported as just on three thousand (including some in Canada, Australia, New Zealand, etc., and a few in the United States). Its headquarters are at Croydon and it maintains there a training centre for organists and choirmasters, the College of St. Nicholas (Director, Gerald H. H. Knight, formerly Organist of Canterbury Cathedral).

See *Schools*; *Anglican Parish Church Music* 7.

ROYAL SCHOOLS OF MUSIC. See *Degrees and Diplomas* 2.

ROYAL SCOTTISH ACADEMY OF MUSIC. See *Schools*; *Degrees and Diplomas* 2; *Scotland* 1.

ROYAL SOCIETY OF LONDON. See *F.R.S.*

ROYAL SOCIETY OF MUSICIANS. See *Festival* 1; *Profession of Music* 10; *Festing, M. C.*

ROYALTY BALLAD. See *Ballad* 6.

ROYAL VICTORIA HALL. See *Victoria Hall*.

ROYAL WESTMINSTER AQUARIUM. See *Concert* 8.

RÓZSA, MIKLÓS. Born in Budapest in 1907. He studied at the Leipzig Conservatory and then settled successively in Paris, London, and Hollywood (1940), in which last place he won recognition as a highly effective composer of film music.

RÓZYCKI, LUDOMIR. Born at Warsaw in 1883 and died at Katowice in 1953, aged sixty-nine. He had a brilliant career at the conservatory of his native place, studied at Berlin under Humperdinck, occupied various teaching positions in Germany, and returned to the place where he began as a member of the staff of the conservatory of which he was a former pupil.

He wrote five or six operas, a number of tone-poems (chiefly on Polish subjects), a piano concerto, chamber-music, songs, etc. He was considered to be one of the leading members of the Polish school.

RUBATO (or TEMPO RUBATO)

1. Its General Nature.   2. The Doctrine of the Inexorable Bass.   3. Certain Old Uses of the Term.

1. Its General Nature. There can be no term whatever of which the definition is more troublesome to a conscientious musical lexicographer than this, because there is none which has been used with more diverse meanings by previous writers, and none which is more diversely used today. The term *Tempo rubato* has been attached (and still is by some) to *elasticity in tempo and rhythm* in general, i.e. to the sum of all possible kinds of deviation from a strict clock-work regularity of beat from the beginning to end of a performance. And it has been applied to various kinds of such deviation singly.

It does not appear to be very suitable to apply the term in the wide general way, for which an abundant choice of ordinary English terms already exists, positive terms such as 'elasticity', 'flexibility', and 'freedom', and negative terms such as 'avoidance of mechanical regularity', and so forth.

And in applying it in a more particular way it seems wisest to reserve it for that important variety of elasticity which would otherwise lack a distinctive name.

It is suggested that rallentando, ritardando, accelerando, the dramatic pause, etc., should be considered as adequately described by their own names, and as not coming within the scope of tempo rubato, and that, following the growing modern custom, this term should be reserved as the name of that type of flexibility which consists of a *'give and take' within a limited unit of the time-scheme*.

In performance that is both deeply felt and sanely controlled this latter type of flexibility does undoubtedly constantly occur within the phrases of the music, the 'give and take' principle operating to bring the phrase back to the beat as it ends.

For thirty years a similar definition was before the public in the first two editions of Grove's *Dictionary of Music*, with the very essential difference that the unit just mentioned was not the phrase but the measure. However, the phrase, not the measure, is the musical unit that the ear accepts as such, and certainly a flexibility that was exercised and then (almost necessarily sharply) corrected over such a short period as the measure would hardly suggest flexibility to the listener, but rather sound to him merely erratic. In point of actual experience no artist exercises such a variation from the beat and return to it within the measure, but every fine artist (whether he realizes it or not) does so within the phrase.

It is admittedly difficult to prove this latter statement to any determined doubter, since it is difficult to find performances where there are no rallentandos and accelerandos over longer stretches, superposed on the tempo rubato of the shorter ones. Theoretically and mathematically, according to the definition of tempo rubato just adopted, all phrases of equal length within a single movement of a composition should occupy the same number of seconds, but in actual practice this is prevented by the fact of the presence of rallentandos and accelerandos, and also by the fact that an artistic principle may exist as a principle, and offer valuable guidance to the student, without there being any great probability that it will ever be carried out by human beings with exactness.

Keenly analytical performers and listeners are, as already stated, aware that the phrase, as the unit in music, has its own elasticity and that a stretching out is compensated by a drawing in and vice versa, with a consequent 'return to the beat'. (There is also a return to the beat in the case of rallentando or accelerando, but it is to a beat which occurs later or sooner than it would normally have done; we are not back where we were, for time has been permanently lost or gained.)

A good deal of the charm of rubato seems to come from this 'return to the beat', which over a longer stretch than a phrase would probably not be felt at all. A suggestion is communicated of 'free time' but not 'bad time'; 'bent but not broken', as Matthay has put it, and thus, paradoxically, only a very good time-keeper can be a very good 'rubatist' (if the word may be allowed).

When the art of tempo rubato is practised in an accomplished way probably only the most analytical-minded listener is consciously aware of it. To others the effect is simply that of abundant 'life' in the performance.

Defined as above, the 'robbery' (for that is what the Italian word 'Rubato' means) is honest robbery. It is a 'robbing of Peter to pay Paul', and as those early Christians had 'all things in common' nobody is the richer or the poorer for the crime. The slow backwash of a wave is made up by a succeeding quicker wash forward and the tide is all the time steadily flowing in at the rate of the same number of feet per minute. For some of the melodic, harmonic, and other factors which suggest to the sensitive artist's subconscious or conscious mind the slight lingerings that have afterwards to be 'made up', see the article *Agogic*.

2. The Doctrine of the Inexorable Bass. There is a doctrine that the bass should proceed regularly, beat by beat, whilst the treble varies as the accompaniment proceeds. This doctrine is often stated, occurring in Tosi's famous book on singing (1723), in Quantz's equally famous book on flute playing (1752), in C. P. E. Bach's still more famous book on harpsichord, clavichord, and pianoforte playing (2 vols., 1753 and 1762), in the *Violin School* of Mozart's father (1756), in a letter of Mozart's to his father (1777), in Nissen's life of Mozart (1828), in Türk's *Clavier School* (1789), in the accounts of Chopin's teaching given by one or two of his pupils (about 1840), and probably in very many other documents.

Any detailed discussion of the (at first sight) rather startling view of these various high authorities would involve the quotation of the actual passages in which the view is stated, in order that their very wording might be taken into account, and is therefore out of the question here, but it will be realized that the literal application of the principle they lay down could be made only to certain limited types of composition, or grave harmonic clashes would result. (For a contemporary objection to Chopin's music on account of the rubato it demands see *Pianoforte Playing and Pianoforte Teaching* 5.) Further, in contrapuntal compositions, with their frequent imitation (q.v.) any application of tempo rubato of this sort would be quite out of the question, since it would involve the same bit of melody being played in different rhythmic shape by the two hands.

Türk, in the work above mentioned, gives examples in musical notation showing that it actually was customary in his day to apply tempo rubato (he uses this term) to an upper part, whilst leaving the lower one unchanged, and in such a way as actually to produce in the harmony a series of 'Anticipations' or 'Retardations' (see *Harmony* 24 l m). But he wisely adds the proviso, 'This *Tempo Rubato* must be applied cautiously for it might easily render the harmony faulty'. His examples and those of some earlier writers are given in Dolmetsch's (q.v.) *The Interpretation of the Music of the Seventeenth and Eighteenth Centuries*, which should be studied by all who wish to know how much freedom was allowed and expected by the composers of that period.

Such playing would, of course, be more in keeping with the qualities of the non-sustaining (or, at any rate, only slightly sustaining) harpsichord or the thin-toned early pianoforte (to which Mozart is alluding in the passages above mentioned) than with those of the modern pianoforte.

So far as Chopin is concerned it would be easy to account for the pronouncement by saying that, like many other great pianists, he could not accurately analyse his own rhythmic actions, and this we know to be a fact, since both Berlioz and Hallé, independently, state that in his mazurkas instead of three beats in a measure he played four, and that when the fact was mentioned to him he was incredulous about it. However, we have the testimony of more than one of Chopin's pupils to the fact that he actually did use a rubato of this kind, and this being so we can only suppose that he confined the practice to those of the compositions of himself and others which consist of florid melodic passages in the right hand over one or two harmonies per measure defined by the left hand. (Chopin, by the way, is one of the few composers who actually print the direction 'rubato' on the scores of some of their compositions.)

It will be observed that the ground principle of this alleged rigid-left-hand, free-right-hand kind of tempo rubato is the same as that of the kind previously described—that of not losing sight of the beat. When tempo rubato does that it has ceased to be tempo rubato and becomes a mere drunken muddle.

3. Certain Old Uses of the Term. Sometimes in old treatises we find the term tempo rubato applied to certain customary variations in performance from the conventional notation of the day—in passages which in many cases, but for tradition, could just as well have been notated as they should be played. It is very necessary that all who intend to play or sing the old music should understand the various notational conventions, but they hardly offer instances of rubato in any present-day sense of the word.

One application of the term which still lingers in some works of reference is to a mere shifting (by the use of the accent sign) of the tonic accent, as, for instance, in a measure of four-time from the first and third beats to the second and fourth. This is rubato only in the sense that notes have been 'robbed' of their accent; nowadays we should call it simply one form of *Syncopation* (q.v.).

For cognate subjects see *Expression*; *Rhythm*; *Agogic*; *Syncopation*; *Jazz* 6. For an allusion to rubato in orchestral playing see *Conducting* 5.

RUBBRA, EDMUND (p. 356, pl. **56**. **2**). Born at Northampton in 1901. His early opportunities of musical study were slight. At the age of twelve he was working after school hours as an errand boy, and from fourteen to nineteen he was a railway clerk. His first piano lessons were given by his mother, later ones by Cyril Scott and Howard Jones. He then won a music scholarship at the University of Reading and a year later one in composition at the Royal College of Music, where he had the advantage of the teaching of Holst, Vaughan Williams, and R. O. Morris. In 1937 he was awarded the Collard Fellowship of the Worshipful Company of Musicians.

His output has been steady and large.

It includes to date well over a hundred works, with eight symphonies, concertos for piano, violin, and viola and orchestra, a 'Festival Overture', chamber music, a Mass for double choir for performance at Canterbury Cathedral (*Missa Cantuarensis*), many songs, and good deal of choral music, including madrigals. His style, which inclines to polyphonic treatment, is sincere, forcible, and austere, and firmly rooted in tradition.

He was a lecturer on the staff of the music faculty of Oxford University. C.B.E. 1960.

RUBENS, PAUL (1876–1917). Highly popular composer of songs for musical comedies (*Country Girl* 1902, *Miss Hook of Holland* 1907, etc.).

RUBIBLE or **RIBIBLE**. See under *Rebec*.

RUBINI, GIOVANNI BATTISTA (1794–1854). See *Tremolo*.

RUBINSTEIN (The Brothers).

(1) ANTON (p. 800, pl. **137.** 6). Born in the government of Podolsk, Russia, in 1829 and died at Peterhof in 1894, aged sixty-four. He received his musical education in Moscow and then, at twelve, appeared as pianist in many of the chief cities of northern Europe. In Paris he met Liszt, who helped him. He studied composition in Germany and lived for some years in Austria, but at nineteen he was back in Russia, where he continued his studies diligently, both as pianist and composer.

By the time he was twenty-four two Russian operas of his had been performed, and then, at frequent intervals, he took up his pianistic travels again, visiting, amongst other countries, Britain and the United States (see anecdote under *Prima Donna*), and winning everywhere the highest fame—except, perhaps, that reserved for the one and only Liszt.

In his early thirties he did a great deal for the music of his country by founding the Conservatory of St. Petersburg and for some years he served as its principal.

The composer Rubinstein has been overshadowed by the pianist Rubinstein, as the composer Liszt was for a time by the pianist Liszt. Both great players felt that, whatever the welcome given to their compositions (and it was sometimes considerable), it was less than their due.

The list of works of Anton Rubinstein is a long one. It naturally includes a great many things for the piano, but also twenty operas (some of them on sacred subjects), symphonies, piano concertos, chamber music, and songs. Roughly speaking, only the small-scale compositions remain in the repertory today; a few of the piano pieces and songs have great popularity.

In the development of Russian music Rubinstein (a Jew by parentage) stands for cosmopolitanism or Teutonicism, and he was an antagonist of Nationalist composers such as 'The Five' (see *Russia* 5, 6).

See references under *Russia* 6; *Pianoforte* 12 (pedalling); *Pianoforte Playing* 6, 7, 9, 10; *Memory* 7; *Keyboard* 4; *Jewish* 9; *Symphony* 8 (1829); *Chamber Music* 6, *Period* III (1829); *Concerto* 6 b (1829); *Concert* 8; *Clavichord* 6; *Albéniz, Isaac*; *Yankee Doodle*.

(2) NICHOLAS. Born in Moscow in 1835 and died in Paris in 1881, aged forty-five. As a composer he was not notable, leaving only a few piano pieces of virtuoso and salon character, but, like his brother, he was a fine pianist; like him, too, he stood for the cosmopolitan and academic view, as opposed to national and more 'instinctive' principles of 'The Five' (see *Russia* 5, 6). About the same time as the elder brother founded the Conservatory of St. Petersburg the younger founded that of Moscow.

RUCKERS. See *Belgium* 8; *Harpsichord Family* 5; *Concert* 4.

RÜCKSICHT (Ger.). 'Consideration.'

RUDDIGORE, or THE WITCH'S CURSE (Sullivan). Produced at the Savoy Theatre London, in 1887. Libretto by W. S. Gilbert.

ACT I

SCENE: *The fishing village of Rederring (in Cornwall). Early Nineteenth Century*

Rederring's corps of professional bridesmaids daily put on their gay and official garb in the hope that **Rose Maybud,** the belle of the village, will get married that day. But all the young men, though madly in love with her, are too shy to propose. The only one upon whom she looks with favour is **Robin Oakapple,** a young farmer, but the book of etiquette which is her constant guide and mentor prevents her from giving him any encouragement.

Robin is really Sir Ruthven Murgatroyd, Baronet of Ruddigore, but twenty years ago he fled from home and assumed the character of a country boy. His younger brother, Despard, believing him to be dead, succeeded to the title, and to the family curse, about which we hear from Rose's aunt, **Dame Hannah.** (The first Baronet, Sir Rupert, was a ruthless persecutor of witches, and one of them, when burning at the stake, cursed him thus: '*Each lord of Ruddigore, Despite his best endeavour, Shall do one crime, or more, Once, every day, for ever! . . . should he stay his hand, that day In torture he shall die!*' The prophecy came true, and each succeeding Baronet committed crime after crime until, overwhelmed by remorse, he cried 'I'll sin no more!' and on that day died in agony.)

Robin's seafaring foster-brother, **Richard Dauntless,** visits the village and undertakes to propose to Rose on Robin's behalf, but on seeing her he himself falls in love with her and asks her to marry him, whereupon Rose, after consulting her etiquette book, consents.

Robin, though heartbroken, forgives Richard because he has only followed his guiding principle—to act according to his heart's dictates—but now Rose, realizing that Robin really loves her and remembering that he is, moreover, a prosperous farmer, changes her mind so that Richard has to resign her to Robin.

See the Article *Scandinavia* on pages 919–24, and the Articles under the individual names

1. J. A. P. SCHULZ, 1747–1800
(Norway)

2. GADE, 1817–90
(Denmark)

3. NIELSEN, 1865–1931 (Denmark)

4. SVENDSEN, 1840–1911 (Norway)

5. GRIEG, 1843–1907 (Norway)

6. SINDING, 1856–1941 (Norway)

7. SIBELIUS, 1865–1957 (Finland)

8. JÄRNEFELT, 1869–1958 (Finland)

9. PALMGREN, 1878–1951
(Finland)

1. GLINKA (1804–57)

2. DARGOMIJSKY (1813–69)

3. BORODIN (1833–87)

4. BALAKIREF (1837–1910)

5. BELAIEF (1836–1904)

6. TCHAIKOVSKY (1840–93)

7. CUI (1835–1918)

8. MUSSORGSKY (1839–81)

9. RIMSKY-KORSAKOF (1844–1908)

Mad Margaret, a victim of the faithless Sir Despard Murgatroyd, appears on the scene. So, shortly after, does **Sir Despard** himself, accompanied by a party of Bucks and Blades. The village girls are terrified of Sir Despard, who looks 'thoroughly bad', but who (to do him justice) tries to minimize the guilt of his crimes by getting them over early in the morning and doing good all the rest of the day.

Richard, in order to prevent Robin from marrying Rose, betrays Robin's secret to Sir Despard, who interrupts the wedding preparations to expose his brother. Again Richard's dictatorial heart wins him forgiveness for his treachery. Rose now rejects Robin, who has to assume his rightful title, and offers herself to Despard: but he, now no longer under the curse but a virtuous person, insists on keeping his old vow to Margaret, so Rose turns again to Richard, 'the only one that's left'.

ACT II

SCENE: *Picture Gallery in Ruddigore Castle. The walls are covered with full-length portraits of the Baronets of Ruddigore*

Robin, very much changed for the worse, enters, with his faithful servant, **Adam.** Robin, after a visit from Richard and Rose, whom he contemplates throwing into a dungeon but to whose marriage Rose persuades him to give his consent, appeals to the portraits of his Ancestors for mercy. The portraits come to life and the last deceased Baronet, **Sir Roderic,** acts as spokesman. He warns Robin that they are not satisfied with his crimes and unless he carries off a lady at once he will perish in inconceivable agony. Robin is reluctant, but a little torture persuades him to send Adam to fetch some maiden from the village. He follows him out, and Sir Despard and Margaret enter, both dressed in sober black of formal cut—a very respectable married couple, though Margaret is still inclined to get a little excited.

Robin returns and is reminded that he is now responsible for all Sir Despard's crimes as well as his own. He decides to defy his Ancestors and, by courting death, to atone for the infamy of his career. At this moment Adam enters with the village maiden—he has brought Dame Hannah, who is armed with a dagger. Robin, alarmed, calls upon his ghostly uncle, Sir Roderic, for help. Sir Roderic appears and recognizes Hannah as his old love, who many years ago broke off their engagement when she discovered who he was, and a love scene follows between the elderly couple.

Finally Robin ingeniously finds a way out of his difficulties: for a Baronet of Ruddigore to refuse to commit his daily crime is certain death; such a refusal is, therefore, tantamount to suicide; but suicide is itself a crime, so there is no need for him to die, and Sir Roderic ought never to have died: hence Sir Roderic can regard himself as practically alive and marry Hannah, and Robin can give up his criminal

career and marry Rose, who is, of course, ready to desert Richard in his favour.

Richard at once finds another lady, and so all ends happily.

RUDEMENT (Fr.). 'Roughly.'

RUDHYAR, DANE. Born in Paris in 1895 (original name, Daniel Chennevière).

At the age of eighteen he published a book on Debussy, at twenty-one he settled in the United States, and at twenty-five he won the Los Angeles Orchestra prize of a thousand dollars with his tone-poem *Surge of Fire.* Other compositions have followed—mostly of a somewhat recondite and abstract order. He has published books on astrology, etc., and edits a *Bulletin of Spiritual Reconstruction.*

RUDOLPH II. See *Bohemia.*

RUEDA. A Spanish round dance in five-in-a-measure time. It is popular in Castile. Cf. *Zortziko.*

RUFFO, VINCENZO. Born at Verona, probably about 1505, and died at Sacile, near Udine, in 1587. He became choirmaster of the cathedral of his native place and then of those of Milan (1563), Pistoia (1572), and Milan again. Beginning in 1539 he published many books of church music and of madrigals, and is looked upon as one of the most accomplished of the many accomplished masters of his time.

RUGGLES, CARL (p. 1057, pl. **172.** 3). Born in Massachusetts in 1876 and died at Bennington, Vt., in 1971, aged ninety-five. He underwent the Harvard training, then superposing a close study of Schönberg and developing an individual attitude towards harmony, counterpoint, and orchestration, and inclining noticeably towards the perturbing and the riotous.

Amongst his handful of orchestral works are *Men and Angels, Men and Mountains, Portals,* and *Sun Treader* (a tremendous orchestral score of shattering effect). He was also a painter.

RUHE (Ger.). 'Peace.' So *Ruhig,* 'peaceful'; *Ruhelos,* 'peace-less'.

RUHEPUNKT, RUHEZEICHEN (Ger.). 'Rest-point', 'rest-sign', i.e. the sign ⌢.

RÜHRTROMMEL (Ger.). Tenor drum. See *Percussion Family* 3 i j, 4 b, 5 i j.

RÜHRUNG (Ger.). 'Feeling.'

RUIMONTE (or **RIMONTE**), **PEDRO.** Born at Saragossa. He was a Spanish composer of the late sixteenth and early seventeenth century who was attached to the court at Brussels and wrote madrigals, masses, etc.

For the background to his career, see *Spain* 5.

RULE BRITANNIA! The music of this is by Arne (q.v.) and the words by James Thomson (of *The Seasons, The Castle of Indolence,* etc., 1700–48). It was first performed in the masque *Alfred* (see reference under *Masque*), produced in the grounds of the Prince of Wales, Frederick (Cliefden House, Maidenhead), on 1 August 1740. The words of the masque were published three weeks later. The

N n

song with its music was published a few months later still in an appendix to Arne's music to Congreve's *Judgement of Paris*, which also was performed at Cliefden on the same occasion.

Both words and music are very bold and flowing, and they seem to have 'caught on', since in Handel's *Occasional Oratorio*, six years after *Alfred* was produced, he introduced the opening strain, evidently confident that the audience would recognize it. (Schoelcher in his life of Handel accuses Arne of plagiarism in this matter; but the boot is on the other foot.)

Alfred was revived in 1745 as an opera and performed in Dublin. The announcement promised that it would conclude with an Ode beginning, 'When Britain first at Heaven's command'.

Wagner is reported to have said of this tune that the first eight notes expressed the whole character of the British nation, or words to that effect—which certainly simplifies that character somewhat but nevertheless leaves it some sterling qualities. He wrote an overture based upon it (an early work; 1837).

Beethoven wrote piano variations on the tune (poor ones), and many composers who were no Beethovens have done the like. Beethoven also introduced it into his 'Battle' Symphony ('Wellington's Victory at the Battle of Vitoria', 1813). It appears also in Attwood's anthem *O Lord, grant the King a long life*.

Mackenzie (q.v.) has a brilliant *Britannia* Overture, partly based on the tune.

Various people at various periods have felt sure that they could improve on Thomson's words. The eighteenth-century Jacobites sang:

> Britain, rouse at Heav'n's command
> And crown thy native Prince again!

Some later eighteenth-century and early nineteenth-century English hymn-books had a sacred parody, to the same tune, by the Revd. Rowland Hill. It began:

> When Jesus first at heaven's command
> Descended from his azure throne,

and had 'Hail Immanuel!' for 'Rule, Britannia!' in the chorus. This was written for a service of Volunteers, and no doubt they had a hearty sing. (For Rowland Hill see *Congregational Churches and Music* 4.)

In 1794 an Americanized version of the song appeared—'Rise, Columbia!' by Robert Treat Paine.

It is sad to have to admit that the chorus of 'Rule, Britannia!' is the only part of it the ordinary British man, woman, or child can repeat when called upon, and then he, she, or it makes the confident but unauthorized statement, 'Britannia *rules* the waves', instead of uttering the poet's stern advice or nowadays somewhat wistful command, 'Britannia, rule the waves!'

It is just possible that the above ascription to Thomson is incorrect, as he had a partner in the writing of the masque, the dramatist David Mallet or Malloch (c. 1705–65), but it is thought that this particular song was Thomson's because its sentiment had already appeared in two poems of his and seems to be a personal speciality.

RULE OF THE OCTAVE. This was a simple formula (possibly of French introduction) for harmonizing diatonically an octave of ascending and descending scale in the bass. It was learnt, as a foundational exercise, by perhaps every harmony pupil in Europe during the eighteenth and earlier nineteenth centuries. To quote Burney, 'This rule, well known and practised in the 24 keys, major and minor, will enable students in thorough bass [see article *Figured Bass*] to figure a bass themselves, and to accompany music without figures'—an assertion very difficult to justify, since it did not provide for any progression of the bass other than by step. However, Rousseau and other eighteenth-century theoretical writers take the Rule just as seriously.

RULES IN HARMONY AND COMPOSITION. See *Harmony* 20, 21; *Composition* 3.

RULLANTE, TAMBURO. 'Rolling drum', i.e. tenor drum. See *Percussion Family* 3 j, 4 b, 5.

RUMANIA. Of all the countries of Europe now active in music the development of that of Rumania is perhaps the most recent. The country abounds in popular manifestations of the love of music, but it is only since the end of the nineteenth century that artistic achievements have been such as to attract any notice in other parts of Europe.

This is explained by geographical position and historical conditions. The ancient territory of Dacia was not merely subdued by the Romans (A.D. 101–6), but treated by them as an actual colony, so that the people remain largely Roman in physical type, and the language, despite an admixture of words of Slav origin, is rather nearer to Latin than is the modern Italian. Christianity, when it was adopted, was, however, of the Greek and not the Roman branch, and the music of the Church was thus left outside the current of that of western Europe. Hence Rumania was only very slightly influenced by the successive developments in harmonic writing, i.e. those (*a*) of the school of Paris (eleventh and twelfth centuries; see *France* 2); (*b*) of Florence (beginning of fourteenth century; see *Ars Nova*); (*c*) of England (beginning of fifteenth century; see *Dunstable*); (*d*) of Flanders (end of fifteenth and beginning of sixteenth century; see *Belgium* 1); and (*e*) of Italy (end of sixteenth century; see *Italy* 4). Although these had their influence almost everywhere else in Europe, and even in such neighbouring countries as Hungary, Bohemia, and Poland (see the articles on these countries), they affected Rumania little.

Add to this the fact of the partial control by Turkey of a large part of the country from the early seventeenth century, and its complete control during the eighteenth and well into the nineteenth, with consequent oppression and misgovernment and the lack of any court to serve as a centre of Western musical culture, and it will be seen that the country was, culturally, becalmed in a backwater.

In 1822, however, Turkish rule ceased, and in 1866 a ruling family was imported from Germany (that of Prince Carol of Hohenzollern-Sigmaringen, who married Elizabeth of Neuwied—'Carmen Sylva', a great encourager of Rumanian art and letters). From this period Rumania (this inclusive name for the several provinces had been adopted only in 1859) became a part of political and musical Europe. But in the meantime not only had the musical developments already detailed had their effect in other parts of Europe, but also the development of keyboard music from the sixteenth century onwards, the development of the orchestra and of symphonic writing during the eighteenth century, and the development of opera from the opening of the seventeenth century onwards. Thus, when Rumania was at last brought into touch with European musical civilization she had everything to learn—but she learnt it quickly.

The Russian development of a national music, which began in the first half of the nineteenth century (see *Russia*), served to some extent as an incentive to Rumanian musicians, who began to look into their own resource of folk legend and folk music and to find in it an inspiration, as had the Russian composers.

The folk music of Rumania is naturally, in view of the extent of the country and the races of differing origin it includes, very varied. Some of it is based on the modes that at one time prevailed over all western Europe—especially the Dorian, Phrygian, Hypodorian, and Mixolydian (see *Modes*); other of it is based on forms of Pentatonic Scale (see *Scales* 10), and still other on scales of what sound to the Western ear very strange intervals—the major scale with its fifth augmented and its seventh minor, the minor scale with its fourth augmented, the minor scale with its second minor, its fourth diminished, and its sixth minor. Then, in the Church's plainsong, under Eastern influence, occur microtones and glissandos from note to note capable of being represented in the Byzantine notation but not in that of western Europe; in 1928 there was founded in Bucharest a school of church song intended to preserve these traditional characteristics.

Amongst folk instruments are a sort of alphorn (q.v.), the Bucium; flutes and fifes (much in use); panpipes (very adroitly played); a type of bagpipe; the fiddle (especially amongst the gipsies); and a curious contrivance called the Buhaiu—which may be described as a small barrel, covered at one end with a skin through which project strands of horsehair, by sliding the fingers upon which a deep lowing sound is produced (the name of the instrument signifies 'bullock').

The first appearance of Rumanian folk tune in print was in a history of the country, by F. J. Sulzer, published in Vienna in 1781. The work of the poet **Vasile Alecsandri** (or Alexandri, 1821–90), who was inspired by a study of Percy's *Reliques* (see *Ballad* 5) to publish, in 1852, many of the ballads and popular songs of Rumania, stimulated interest, and towards the end of the nineteenth century and during the twentieth there has been a considerable collection and publication of folk music, in which the Hungarian composer Bartók took his part (confining himself, however, to those Transylvanian regions that before the first World War had been Hungarian). One of his several collections (nearly 400 songs of the district of Bihor) was issued by the Rumanian Academy in 1913: he has also published piano treatments of Rumanian songs and dances, and has thus given them some international vogue. The Rumanian Government in 1896 set an example to all the other governments of Europe by subsidizing the collection of folk tunes under the direction of Professor Breazul, whose phonographic records at the National Museum at Bucharest (including those of Bartók) number many thousands, scientifically classified.

This activity was if anything intensified after 1949, becoming part of the machinery of mass education and indoctrination.

The Rumanian writer Marcu Beza (Lecturer at King's College, London) has, in his *Paganism and Roumanian Folklore*, given many interesting particulars of ballads strangely resembling, in their themes, some of those of Scotland, of dances suggesting the English folk dances (with hobby-horse, wooden swords, and bells on the legs), and of a folk play very like the English one of St. George and the Dragon (see *Mysteries*, etc.). These affinities, suggesting a common origin (indefinably remote, of course), possibly merit more study than they have yet received.

Among the founders of the Rumanian school of composition the following were perhaps the most important:

(1) The Viennese musician, **Ludwig Anthony Wiest** (1819–89). He was brought to Bucharest in 1838 by Prince Alexander Ghika, Hospodar (governor) of Wallachia, who dismissed his Turkish band, wishing to reorganize his domestic music on Western lines. Wiest, a fine violinist and a capable conductor, adapted himself to the new conditions, composing fantasias on national airs and Rumanian theatre music.

(2) **Anton Wachiman,** first director of the Conservatory of Bucharest, and his son **Edward Wachiman** (1836–1909); the latter, after studying in Paris, composed piano music, church music, theatre music, etc., and inaugurated the first regular series of symphony concerts of the country.

(3) **Adolf Flechtenmacher** (born 1823), who studied in Vienna and Paris and wrote Rumanian songs, operettas, etc., and an opera *Baba Hirca*, on a nationalistic subject and with the use of folk-music themes, which became extremely popular. When in 1847 his overture *Moldova* was performed at a festival in honour of Liszt, at Jassy, Liszt sat down at once at the piano and extemporized brilliant variations on its themes.

(4) **Edward Caudella** (1841–1923), who studied in Germany and Paris, made Jassy a musical centre, was one of the first in Rumania to perform the symphonies of Mozart and Beethoven, and wrote many operas and operettas of national feeling and style.

(5) **George Dima** (1847–1925), who, educated at Vienna and Leipzig, founded at Sibiu (or Hermannstadt) an orchestra, took it on tour, popularized the great German classics, and performed Rumanian airs orchestrally arranged by himself. His works have been published by the Rumanian Ministry of Instruction.

(6) **Jacob Murisiano**, who studied at Leipzig and Vienna. He wrote a symphonic poem on national airs, and in 1888 started the first Rumanian musical journal.

(7) **Timotei Popovici**, who at Sibiu, in 1908, began publication of the first Rumanian dictionary of music; it is rich in descriptions of native dances, songs, instruments, etc.

It is perhaps of a little significance that some of the earliest names of importance in Rumanian music have a German appearance. For centuries there have been German settlements in northern Rumania, preserving their German language and their German ways of thought, and it may be assumed that these centres would the most quickly respond to the opportunity which the national musical development offered. French influence is also very strong, for the Latin descent of the greater part of the population has led it to look upon Paris as its most natural outside source of cultural training. In glancing down the list of Rumanian composers it is noticeable that nearly all of them have finished their musical education in Paris, and also that some of them, such as **Enesco** (1881–1955), the distinguished violinist, conductor, and composer, and **Golestan** (1872–1956), composer and music critic of *Figaro*, have had homes there. Enesco founded a national prize for composition.

For Enesco and Golestan see separate entries in this volume under their own names, as also for **A. Alessandrescu, M. Andrico**, and **M. Mihalovici**.

The revolution of 1947 brought the usual period of political isolation from Western Europe; however, accomplished younger composers continued to develop, influenced by their own folk music but also aware of the innovations of Stockhausen, Boulez, and Cage.

Opera was first performed in Rumania (by foreign performers) in 1847; from 1870 there have (with rare exceptions) been annual seasons. There is now a national opera-house, supported and directed by the government.

Bucharest with 850,000 inhabitants is the country's only big centre, no other place having more than 210,000 and only five in the whole country attaining a six-figure population. The greater musical opportunities of the country are, then, somewhat concentrated in one city—but one of an intense and well-directed musical activity. Nevertheless there are seven permanent opera companies and eighteen symphony orchestras.

Some reference should be made to the music of the Rumanian gipsies. For a long time, as in Hungary (q.v.), musical entertainment in the towns was almost left to them. They were not only to be found in all the cafés but aristocratic houses often had orchestras of them, importing musicians from the German centres of Transylvania (already alluded to) to train them. As in Hungary, so in Rumania, the gipsy café music is not gipsy in origin, but consists of native or foreign music embellished.

A curious personality of the early eighteenth century, who has not found mention above and is worthy perhaps of a word, is **Prince Demetrius Cantemir** (1673–1723), for a short time (under the Turks) ruler of Moldavia; he spoke eleven languages, introduced musical notation into Turkey (where apparently it was soon forgotten), wrote in Turkish a treatise on music said to be the first produced in Rumania, and left in the Rumanian language a manuscript *Introduction to Turkish Music*.

The above attempt to give a brief sketch of the musical history and conditions of Rumania is of course very general in scope. The size of the territory in question has varied greatly from period to period, as has the number of races represented in it. What we now call Rumania includes Hungarian communities (mostly Roman Catholic and with church music of a totally different style from the actual Rumanian); German communities (mostly Lutheran their music resembling that of the country from which their ancestors came as early as the twelfth century); a Jewish population; and there are Ukrainian Russians and other Slavs in the eastern portion of the country, with small bodies elsewhere of Turks, Bulgars, etc.

RUMBA. A Cuban dance of somewhat complex rhythm, which became popular in the United States and Europe from about 1930. The original and genuine (Negro) rumba is erotic and confined to the lowest classes—'*Not* suggestive, as has been alleged—since it leaves nothing to suggest'. Belonging to the rumba family are the *Son*, the *Danzon* and *Danzonetta*, and the *Conga*.

RUMBA BONGOS. Merely *Bongos* (q.v.); they are sometimes used in playing rumbas.

RUNNING SET. An English folk dance still in use in the Appalachian mountain region of North America—a very active dance in four-in-a-measure rhythm, with figures that can be varied in many ways, and a refrain that is unvaried. It is danced to any appropriate tunes or even to the mere thrumming of the bow on the fiddle. Vaughan Williams published a set of traditional dance tunes arranged for it.

RURAL MUSIC SCHOOL MOVEMENT. This was founded in 1929 as a consequence of the work of Mary Ibberson (long its Director). In a variety of ways it promotes musical activities in the villages and small towns of

England (with a tendency to extend to larger centres also—including some work in London). To this end it holds classes under the direction of county organizers. Its headquarters are at Hitchin, Herts. (the town in which its first operations were conducted).

RUSLAN AND LIUDMILA. See *Glinka*.

RUSSA (It.). See *Russo*.

RUSSELL.

(1) HENRY (p. 817, pl. **140**. 8). Born at Sheerness, in Kent, in 1812 and died in London in 1900, aged nearly eighty-eight. He was a pupil of Rossini in Italy, a singer on the London stage, organist at Rochester, N.Y., and then a famous travelling entertainer, singing his own songs, many of them of sterling worth, amounting in all to about eight hundred. 'Cheer, boys, cheer', 'There's a good time coming, boys', and 'A life on the ocean wave' are his. He was much associated with the robust and popular poet, Dr. Mackay. Landon Ronald (q.v.) was his son (really Landon Ronald Russell). The well-known singing teacher and operatic impresario, Henry Russell (1871–1937), was another son.

(2) WILLIAM. See *Percussion Family* 4 d.

RUSSIA

(For illustrations see p. 897, pl. **154**; 912, **155, 156**.)

1. Folk Music. Russia abounds in folk music. How varied this is in rhythm and melody and in the moods expressed may be guessed from the mere fact of the extent of Russian territory, which amounts to one-sixth of the land surface of the globe (European Russia constituting merely a quarter of the great area). There has been a praiseworthy attempt to harvest the musical wealth of this immense field, former governments having commissioned competent musicians to collect and compile it.

One of the earliest collectors of Russian folk-song poetry was an Englishman, the Revd. Richard James, who in the reign of Charles I accompanied as chaplain an English envoy to Russia; the poems he collected are *Bylini*, long epics, such as have been sung for centuries to the music of short snatches of tune repeated over and over again. Another type of folk song is choral in character, reminding one of the report of Giraldus Cambrensis, in the late twelfth century, concerning the people's songs of Wales and the north of England; the added parts in Russia are variants of the main melody and this may have been so in Britain. For a period edicts of the Czars forbade the singing of folk songs.

It will be recalled that Beethoven found some melodic themes for two of his 'Rasoumoffsky' string quartets in a collection of Russian folk tunes.

A popular peasant instrument has been a form of guitar, the balalaika (q.v.).

2. The Church and Music. The origins of Russian Church Music go back to the year 987 when Saint Vladimir accepted the Christian faith and made Christianity the religion in his state. He himself was baptized in the Dnieper, but he entrusted the conversion of his people to Byzantine monks. The chant of the Russian Church has, therefore, two sources, and at one time alternating choirs sang hymns in Greek with responses in Old Slavonic.

The Russian ecclesiastical attitude has always agreed with that of the seventeenth-century English Independents and Presbyterians (see *Puritans and Music*, end of section 4, and *Greek Church* 4) in the objection to instrumental music in church.[1] No Orthodox Church in Russia or other countries ever has an organ. As a consequence the arts of unaccompanied singing and of composing for the choral medium have been carried to a high perfection. The Russian bass voices are famous for their low range, which extends greatly below that common in other countries.

3. The Aristocracy and Music. The Russian nobles, in the eighteenth and nineteenth centuries, often enjoyed the services of small private orchestras in their town houses and on their country estates, and several of the Russian composers to be mentioned later in this article received their first stimulus towards creation from hearing such orchestras in the houses of their parents, relatives, or friends (cf. *Jewish Music* 5). The performers were mainly serfs and they were often bought and sold at prices corresponding to their degree of skill and artistry.

A type of band peculiar to Russia and developed on the estates of the aristocracy is the **Horn Band**, dating from the middle of the eighteenth century. The principle was that each performer produced only one note (see *Horn Family* 3).

4. Italian Influence and the Reaction therefrom; Glinka and Dargomijsky. During the eighteenth century the activities of

---

[1] In 1649 the Patriarch Joseph ordered a public fire of all the musical instruments of Moscow. There was also an objection to theatrical entertainments of all sorts.

the Russian court largely controlled musical taste in the capital, and those activities were mainly in the department of Italian opera. For a brief description of such activities the reader should turn to *Opera*, which has two sections (17, 18) devoted to Russia.

The reaction against Italianism in music is connected with the growth of patriotic feeling engendered by the Napoleonic Wars, and with the national literary revival initiated by the poet Pushkin (1799–1837), whose works were to furnish the basis of important operas during the next half-century. The reaction began with **Glinka** (1804–57), and the direct impulse came to him when, at the end of three years' travel and study in Italy, overdosed with music that, as he realized, had made no deep appeal to him, he began to suffer from what he called 'musical home-sickness'—the wish to hear music expressing the temperament of his own race. He set off for Russia, but in Berlin lingered to take some lessons from the great musicologist and theorist Dehn, who at the end of the course bade him 'go home and write Russian music'. In 1836 his opera *A Life for the Czar* had its first performance, and this and (still more) the following opera, *Ruslan and Liudmila* (from a poem of Pushkin), became the foundation-stones of a new national edifice. Their subjects and much of their musical idiom, partly derived from Russian folk song, are distinctly national.

Other works followed. For the inspiration and suggestion that Glinka and later composers received from Spanish folk music see *Spain* 10: that inspiration and suggestion led to the composition of Glinka's orchestral *Jota Aragonese* and *Night in Madrid*, based on Spanish folk themes, and then to that of the fantasia *Kamarinskaya*, based on two Russian folk songs; this fantasia became in its turn the stimulus to much vivid nationalist composition both in Russia and in Spain. Glinka by virtue of his operas and his orchestral pieces occupies an international pedestal as the father of conscious nationalism in music. (See separate entry under the name of this composer.)

Dargomijsky (1813–69), nine years Glinka's junior, followed up his work, and in 1872 (thirty-six years after Glinka's *A Life for the Czar*) there appeared Dargomijsky's posthumous opera, *The Stone Guest*, in which he sought to give a greater place to the dramatic element, as distinct from the conventionally operatic. From its shunning of the charms of melody *qua* melody it was described by an unkind contemporary as 'a recitative in three Acts'. It also, however, earned more flattering descriptions as 'The Gospel of the New School' and 'The Keystone of Modern Russian Music' (see separate entry under the name of this composer).

5. The Group of 'The Five'. The country pioneered by Glinka and Dargomijsky was settled by a group of younger composers, who are known as 'The Five'—**Balakiref** (1837–1910), **Cui** (1835–1918), **Borodin** (1833–87),

Mussorgsky (1839–81), and **Rimsky-Korsakof** (1844–1908), all of whom, of course, have separate treatment in this volume under their own names. The work of Cui stands apart, since, whilst associating intimately with the other four of the group and apparently fully sharing their nationalist views, his scores show little national colour, of which there is abundance in such things as Balakiref's piano rhapsody *Islamey*, Borodin's opera *Prince Igor*, Mussorgsky's opera *Boris Godunof* (both of these based on Russian history) or Rimsky-Korsakof's many operas and glowing orchestral pieces.

A notable fact about all these composers, from Glinka to Rimsky-Korsakof, is that they were not professional musicians. They came from the 'comfortable classes', and most of them who had to earn a living did so (at first or all their lives) by the practice of some other profession than that of music. Thus Cui was an army officer, rising to the rank of general and becoming an authority on fortification; Rimsky-Korsakof entered the navy and wrote part of the first symphony any Russian composer ever produced whilst on duty (at Gravesend), later joining the staff of the Conservatory of St. Petersburg; Mussorgsky was first an officer in a guards regiment and then a minor civil servant; Borodin was a medical man and professor of chemistry, burying himself in music in scanty hours of leisure; Balakiref was the son of a minor state official, the descendant of a very old family, and at first considered taking up a mathematical career, drifting, however, early into musical life as incitements and opportunities gradually offered themselves.

A circumstance about the work of the nationalist composers that is perhaps sufficiently curious to be just worth mentioning is the extent to which they left unfinished works of importance. Thus Dargomijsky's opera, *The Stone Guest*, was finished by Cui and Rimsky-Korsakof; Serof's opera *Rogneda* (see below) by his own wife; Borodin's opera, *Prince Igor*, by Rimsky-Korsakof and Glazunof; Borodin's Symphony in A minor by Glazunof. And Mussorgsky's opera, *Boris Godunof*, was (to the causing of much dispute in later years) drastically revised by Rimsky-Korsakof, to whom the composer had, before his death, entrusted the orchestration of his opera *Khovantschina*.

6. Partisans, Opponents, and Successors of 'The Five'. Associated with 'The Five' was the redoubtable writer **Stassof** (1824–1906). Opposed to them was another writer, almost as powerful, **Serof** (q.v.), an ardent Wagnerian and a composer first in the earlier Wagnerian style and then in that of Meyerbeer, and finally again in that of Wagner.

The official conservatories of music at St. Petersburg and Moscow, directed by Anton and Nicholas Rubinstein respectively, were of the 'anti' faction, and this supplied the motive for the foundation of the Free School of

Music. Very roughly generalizing, the conservatories stood for the cultivation of technique, whose fostering was very necessary in a country musically in arrears, and in conservatory circles the group of musicians just described were for some time looked upon as dilettantes. In time the two groups tended to merge, and the merger may be looked upon as finding its most palpable embodiment in **Tchaikovsky** (1840–93), who is at once cosmopolitan and nationalist—and a good deal more nationalist than is often admitted, the intense emotionalism of many of his works, with the love of extremes in both the bright coloured and the sombre, being a clear reflection of one prominent side of the Russian temperament. His pupil **S. Taneief** (1856–1915) inclined well to the cooler, classical side, and the accomplished **Glazunof** (1865–1936), a prolific composer, did not prove himself very distinctly national.

Very Russian, at any rate in his quasi-religious mysticism and forceful expression (though quite un-national in his musical idiom) was **Scriabin** (1872–1915), less so was the romantic-classic **Rachmaninoff** (1873–1943).

7. Modernist Russia of the Twentieth Century.
Definitely deriving from Glinka, Dargomijsky, and 'The Five' is **Stravinsky** (1882–1971), who showed himself to be strongly influenced by the melodic and rhythmic idioms of Russian folk music, as most of those men were; and to share their predilection for experiment in orchestral colour and, above all else, their fearlessness in disregarding tradition and conventions of every kind. The one of 'The Five' who most influenced him was undoubtedly the uncompromising Mussorgsky. In the work of the group of 'The Five' there was, as we have seen, a robust manifestation of the spirit of nationality. The Italian influence in Russian music had, with them, gone by the board; a German influence, however, in some measure, took its place. Stravinsky's ballet *The Rite of Spring* (1913, afterwards detached from its choreography and performed as an independent orchestral composition) may be looked upon as the manifesto of a school that has cast off German leading strings and walks in the light that shines from the folk element in Russian art and largely, moreover (to free itself the better from German influences), in a folk element from primitive pagan Russia. With this work something had definitely gone; civilization had been abandoned and a new area for artistic development staked out in barbarism. The result is unconventional (until the new style begins to grow into a convention of its own) and highly picturesque. The Slav soul is at last invited to come, without dressing up, into the theatre and the concert-hall. Paris, if only out of an instinctive readiness to take up with whatever opposes German culture, was the centre to give the new school its first welcome (see *Spain* 10 for the similar friendly reception it gave to the nationalist Spanish

School, which likewise smelt of the soil; the cult of the peasantry was a characteristic of advanced sophistication in the late nineteenth and early twentieth centuries). Debussy and impressionism (themselves not uninfluenced, by the way, by Russia and especially the art of Mussorgsky), in their attack on the accepted conventions, received a formidable ally in Stravinsky and this new type of anti-classicism and anti-Wagnerism.

Prokofief (1891–1953), like Stravinsky, was bold and outright; he, also, was attracted by primitive pagan Russia. (See, for instance, his *Scythian Suite* of 1916.)

The period lasting from, say, 1836 (Glinka's opera *A Life for the Czar*) to 1913 (Stravinsky's ballet *The Rite of Spring*) may be looked upon as the great formative period in Russian music. That stretch of about three-quarters of a century sees a wonderfully complete passage from dependence to liberty; artistically it was another Freeing of the Serfs.

For a reference to the gradual popularization of Russian opera in France, Britain, and the United States see *Opera* 17 d. For a brief treatment of the subject of Russian Ballet see *Ballet* 5.

8. The Soviet Period.
At the end of the first World War, and as a result of the new political conditions, Russian musicians became divided into two groups, those who remained in Russia and those who left it and settled elsewhere—generally in Paris and later in the United States. The home group was very much cut off from musical life in western Europe, whilst those in Paris or elsewhere tended to lose their national affiliation and to be absorbed into the general 'modernist' ranks (though this has been denied).

In 1917 the principal composers remaining on the post-revolutionary scene were Glazunov (who departed in 1928), Glière, and Miaskovsky.

The intention of the Government of the Soviet Republic to transform art in consonance with the new political ideals and organization has probably been more difficult to carry into effect in the case of the intangible art of music than in the case of literature and the plastic arts.

In the early years there was a period of nihilism during which there were proposals to do away with equal temperament by destroying all pianos, and attempts by composers such as Mossolov to glorify factory noises. The democratic experiment of a conductorless orchestra, 'Persimfans', was made in 1922 and lasted five years or so (see *Conducting* 7), and opera texts were transformed—Glinka's *A Life for the Czar* becoming for a time *For Scythe and Hammer* (later the composer's original name for it—*Ivan Susanin*—was used); *Tosca* taking place in the Paris of the French Revolution; *The Huguenots* becoming *The Decembrists*; and so on. The musical profession was reorganized by drastic regulations, and opera and concerts brought within the reach of all city dwellers. During the early twenties composers had relative freedom to write much as they wished, though an ideological basis was preferred. In the later twenties the (musically) progressive Association for Contemporary Music lost ground to the Association of Proletarian Musicians, devoted to the interests of the masses. In 1932 was founded the Union of Soviet Composers, at first with 150 members; this encouraged the production of music of optimistic content in easily accessible forms, preferably using national idioms.

Composers continued to have a fairly peaceful time, interrupted by incidents such as the severe official condemnation of Shostakovich's *Lady Macbeth of Mtsensk* in 1936. In 1948 came the notorious Zhdanov decrees, when Shostakovich, Prokofiev, Khachaturian, Shebalin, Miaskovsky, and others were accused of 'formalistic perversion', and 'failure to express Soviet reality'. In a context where all art, being supported by the State, is expected to display inspirational qualities such as warmth, nobility, and dignity, 'formalism' (the adherence to formulas such as dissonant harmony, bizarre orchestration, or note-row methods) is equated with pessimism. Realism is equated with optimism, and is characterized by euphony, diatonicism, and a concentration on subjects glorifying Soviet achievement. Operas and choral works on contemporary themes were preferred over quartets or symphonies. (It is worth noting that there is a gap of eight years between the eighth and ninth symphonies of Shostakovich.) In time the Zhdanov decrees were largely disregarded, and in 1958 the condemnation of Russia's leading composers was struck from the record. Works by previously banned composers such as Hindemith, Bartók, and even Stravinsky appeared on concert programmes, though the Party reserved the right to combat unhealthy alien phenomena and modernistic tendencies, including the use of the note-row.

The nineteen-sixties saw a period of many exchange visits between Russian musicians and their opposite numbers from Britain and the United States. Leading Soviet artists are treated as an *élite* and live well on high incomes. They are allowed to keep the fees earned on foreign tours.

The figure of Shostakovich dominates the scene. Among other names that are prominent

may be mentioned the politically active Khrennikov (born 1913), Khachaturian (born 1903), Shebalin (born 1902; principal of the Moscow Conservatory); Knipper (born 1898); Kabalevsky (born 1904); and Popov (born 1904). Others are Salmanov (born 1912); Lobkovsky (born 1912), and Galynin (born 1922); and of the younger generation Shchedrin (born 1934), Nikolaiev (born 1931), and Ovchinikov (born 1937) have achieved some note. Foreign visitors, however, report few works of striking originality. Links with the great Russian masters Mussorgsky, Tchaikovsky, and Rimsky-Korsakov are strong, with little evidence of the influence of Schönberg or the French Impressionists, though it is said that many composers are well aware of Webern, Hindemith, and Bartók, and privately write music that shows this. Composers have a strict five-year training, moving from State music school to music high school and finally to one of the 22 conservatories.

Much is made of the secretiveness of Soviet Russia, but it may be worth remark that as long ago as 1906 the American monthly *Musical Courier* complained that letters from its Russian correspondent were so heavily censored as to be useless.

In reading this brief sketch of Russian musical development, after reading elsewhere in this volume that of musical development in any other European country, one must be at once struck with a unique historical condition. Whilst artistic music in other countries passed through a series of stages, from the tenth century to the twentieth, that in Russia suddenly appeared in the nineteenth century, in the midst of the Romantic Movement (see *Romantic*), having skipped previous phases. And it at once displayed so striking a degree of novelty and merit as to win acceptance in all civilized countries.

Then within less than a century (dating from Glinka's *A Life for the Czar*, the first work of sufficient independence to mark the new era) there took place political changes of an unprecedented character the effect of which on the art it is yet quite impossible to forecast, but which must amount to an interruption of normal evolution.

RUSSIAN BASSOON. See *Cornett and Key Bugle Families* 2 f, 3 f, 4 f.

RUSSISCHE QUARTETTE ('Russian' Quartets of Haydn). See *Nicknamed Compositions* 12.

RUSSLAN AND LUDMILLA. See *Glinka*.

RUSSO, RUSSA (It.; masc., fem.). 'Russian.' So *Alla russa*, in the Russian style.

RUSSOLO, LUIGI. Born at Portogruara in 1885 and died in 1947. He was prominent as an apostle of the Italian Futurist movement, utilizing in his performances (from 1913) noise-instruments (*intonarumori*) of his own invention (see *History of Music* 9). In 1916 he published a book *L'Arte dei rumori* ('The Art of Noises'). (Cf. *Italy* 7.)

RUST.

(1) FRIEDRICH WILHELM (1739–96). He was a pupil of C. P. E. Bach and (in Italy) of Benda, Tartini, and Pugnani. The greater part of his working life was spent in Dessau, as director of the music in the theatre there. He composed operas, songs, piano music, violin music, church music, etc.

(2, 3) A son, WILHELM KARL (1787–1855), was a fine pianist and a Vienna intimate of Beethoven; and a grandson, WILHELM (1822–92), led an active career first in Berlin and then in Leipzig, where he was cantor of the Thomas School, edited some of Bach's works, and those of his grandfather (1 above), and composed.

RUSTLING TIN SHEET. See *Percussion Family* 4 d.

RUTE, RUTHE (Ger.). Literally 'rod'. A sort of birch brush used to beat the bass drum for a particular effect. See *Percussion Family* 4 b.

RUTHERFORD, DAVID and **JOHN.** London music publishers of last half of the eighteenth century. See *Saint Patrick's Day*.

RUTSCHER. See *Galop*.

RUUTH (Ruuta, Rwtha), T. P. See *Scandinavia* 6.

RUVIDO (It.). 'Rugged', 'harsh'.

RUYNEMAN, DANIEL (born 1886). Highly experimental Dutch composer. See *Electrophone* 2.

RUZSICSKA, WENCELAS. See *Rákóczy March*.

RWTHA. See *Scandinavia* 6.

RYEBIKOFF. See *Rebikof*.

RYTHME and **RYTHMIQUE** (Fr.). 'Rhythm' and 'Rhythmic'.

S

SABANEEF (Sabaneyeff, Sabanaïew, etc.), LEONID. Born in Moscow in 1881. An emigré Russian composer, writer, and critic, active (since 1926 mainly in France) as a champion of modernist developments in his art.

See *Colour and Music* 3, 5; *Cinematograph.*

SABATA, VICTOR DE. Born at Trieste in 1892 and died at Santa Margherita, Liguria, in 1967, aged seventy-five. He studied in the Conservatory of Milan and in his nineteenth year became known, both in Italy and abroad, by an orchestral suite. He later produced more orchestral music, some chamber music, and several operas, and won world fame as a conductor (La Scala, Milan, and elsewhere).

SABILON, ROBERT DE. See *France* 2.

SABINE, P. E. See *Concert Halls* 14.

SACBUT, or SACKBUT, or SAGBUT. Old name for trombone. See *Trombone Family.*

SACCADÉ (Fr.). Literally 'jerked', i.e. sharply accented.

SACCHINI, ANTONIO MARIA GAS-PARO. Born in Florence in 1730 and died in Paris in 1786, aged fifty-six. He became one of the most able and famous composers of his time. His life had many ups and downs; Marie Antoinette was unable to keep her promise to have one of his operas performed at Fontainebleau, so, heartbroken, he took to his bed and shortly died.

SACEM. See *Copyright* 3; *Auric.*

SACHS.

(1) KURT. Born in Berlin in 1881 and died in New York in 1959, aged seventy-seven. After gaining his doctorate at Berlin University he engaged in research there and as curator of the state collection of musical instruments; later he worked in Paris, and from 1937 he was a professor at New York University. His books and countless articles on the history of musical instruments, the dance, and kindred subjects, are important.

See *Dictionaries* 6 a.

(2) HANS. See *Minstrels*, etc., 8; *Mastersingers*; *Hymns and Hymn Tunes* 17 b.

SACKBUT, or SACBUT, or SAGBUT. Old name for trombone. See *Trombone Family.*

SACKPFEIFE. See *Bagpipe Family* 9.

SACRED HARMONIC SOCIETY. See *Concert* 6; p. 752, pl. 123. 5.

SACRE RAPPRESENTAZIONI (It.; 'Sacred Representations' or 'Sacred Dramas'). These were a kind of mystery or miracle play (see *Mysteries, Miracle Plays*, etc.), popular in Florence and elsewhere in Italy up to the middle of the sixteenth century, after which they declined. They have importance as precursors of opera, for in their last period of development they were entirely sung, not spoken, and they had the relief of interludes with dancing.

SADLER'S WELLS. A place of entertainment on the north side of London, dating from the 1680s. It takes its name from a Mr. Sadler, highway-surveyor of Clerkenwell, who by happy chance rediscovered a well that had in the Middle Ages been credited with miraculous powers and there set up a garden for the drinking of the waters combined with musical enjoyment (see *Concert* 12 for the London 'Gardens'). Later he erected in the grounds a 'Musick House' (see *Inns and Taverns*). The varied fortunes of the place are too long to be told here, but it may be said that at the opening of the nineteenth century Charles Dibdin (q.v.) was managing it as an 'Aquatic Theatre' (with a huge tank under the stage) and carrying out nautical dramas such as offered, no doubt, an opportunity for the introduction of his famous sea songs, and that in the 1840s the great actor Phelps was making it a noted centre of Shakespearian performance.

At the opening of the twentieth century this historic house (by then, as to its outward walls, possibly the oldest remaining theatre in Europe) was derelict. In 1926, by the efforts of Lilian Baylis supported by many lovers of drama and music, it was rebuilt as a sister house to the 'Old Vic' (see *Victoria Hall, Royal*), and after a short time the whole of the operatic enterprises of the 'Old Vic' were transferred to it, the 'Old Vic' itself retaining the spoken drama. Thus at last the capital of the Empire came to possess an all-the-year-round centre of opera in English, which steadily added to its repertory most of the standard works, as well as giving from time to time performances of many lesser-known ones. For an account of the admirable ballet company see under *Ballet* 5.

SAD WALTZ (Schubert). See *Nicknamed Compositions* 18.

SAETA. A sort of Spanish folk song, sung without the guitar or other instrument. (Cf. *Carcelera.*)

SAFONOF, VASSILY (1852–1918; p. 240, pl. 44. 9). Pianist and conductor. See *Conducting* 5.

SAGBUT, or SACBUT, or SACKBUT. Old name for trombone. See *Trombone Family.*

SAGITTARIUS. See *Schütz*.

SAINETE (Sp.), **SAYNÈTE** (Fr.). A sort of Spanish musical farce.

SAINT ALBAN'S ABBEY. See *Fayrfax*.

SAINT AMBROSE. See *Plainsong* 3; *Te Deum*; *Modes* 2, 4; *Liturgy*.

SAINT ANDREW'S PSALTER. See *Scotland* 5.

SAINT ANNE (Hymn Tune). See *Croft*; *Hymns and Hymn Tunes* 6; *Nicknamed* 1.

SAINT ANNE'S FUGUE (Bach). See *Nicknamed Compositions* 1.

SAINT ASAPH CATHEDRAL. See *Cathedral Music* 2; *Allen, H. P.*

SAINT BARTHOLOMEW FAIR. See *Fairs and their Music*.

SAINT CECILIA. See *Cecilia*.

SAINT CECILIA'S HALL, EDINBURGH. See *Concert* 11.

SAINT EDMUND'S COLLEGE, WARE. See *Old Hall Manuscript*.

SAINT GALL. See *Plainsong* 3; *Sequence*; *Ireland* 2.

SAINT-GEORGE, CHEVALIER. See *United States* 6.

SAINT GEORGE'S CHAPEL, WINDSOR. See *Chapel Royal*; *Cathedral Music* 2.

SAINT GREGORY. See *Plainsong* 3.

SAINT JAMES'S HALL. See *Concert* 7.

SAINT MATTHEW PASSION. See *Passion* 5.

SAINT MICHAEL'S COLLEGE, TENBURY. See *Ouseley*.

SAINT PATRICK'S DAY. This air, which was played by the Irish bagpipes at the battle of Fontenoy (1745), was a popular Irish patriotic song earlier than that. Its first appearance in print seems to be in Rutherford's *Country Dances* (an English publication) in 1749. Frank Kidson (q.v.) states that the same air is traditionally known in the north of England as *Barbary Bell*, and in the south of England as a morris dance tune, *Bacon and Greens*.

Moore (q.v.) wrote to the tune his song 'Though dark are our sorrows' (1811). Many different lyrics, Irish and English, had been previously sung to it, including one in the famous ballad opera *Love in a Village* (1762).

SAINT PAUL'S CATHEDRAL, LONDON. See under *Cathedral Music* (passim).

The following organists connected with the cathedral receive notice under their own names, their periods of office being here appended: *Redford* (early 16th century); *Morley* (? 1591–2); *Batten* (c. 1624–37); *Clarke, J.* (1695–1707); *Greene, M.* (1718–55); *Attwood* (1796–1838); *Goss* (1838–72); *Stainer* (1872–88); *Martin* (1888–1916); *Macpherson, Charles* (1916–27); *Marchant* (1927–36); *Bower* (1936–67). Also p. 764, pl. **127**. **5**.

SAINT PAUL'S CATHEDRAL PSALTER. See *Anglican Chant* 6 e.

SAINT-SAËNS, CAMILLE, or, in full, Charles Camille (p. 369, pl. **62**. 6). Born in Paris in 1835 and died at Algiers in 1921, aged eighty-six. He came of a Normandy family of some standing. He studied at the Paris Conservatory, and privately under Gounod. His first successes were as organist. For about twenty years he was organist of the Madeleine. He had composed a symphony at sixteen and from that age until his death seventy years later he never ceased composition, in which he had the greatest facility. He was also a considerable author, and delighted in polemic, defending the Romantics, Liszt, Berlioz, Wagner, later attacking Wagner on the ground of his Teutonizing influence on French music, and also demolishing 'modernist' young compatriots. Yet he himself had been in some sort a pioneer, for his *Omphale's Spinning Wheel* (1871) was the first symphonic poem ever written by a French composer.

He was one of the early members of the National Musical Society, and he was also a great champion of the earlier French composers, and especially Rameau. His was a curious temperament, versatility, cosmopolitanism, and narrowness being blended in an unusual way. His reminiscences, as published in several books, are human and entertaining. At Dieppe there is a Saint-Saëns Museum, in which are preserved relics largely presented by himself—his aunt's pin-cushion and his first copybook (or that kind of thing).

Saint-Saëns was a fine pianist. The bigger world has known him chiefly by his four symphonic poems (the one already mentioned, *Phaëton*, *The Youth of Hercules*, and *Danse macabre*), by one or two of his piano concertos, a violin concerto, and a cello concerto, his great Third Symphony (with organ and four-hand piano; 1886), his First Pianoforte Trio (in F; 1863), and (1877) his very successful opera *Samson and Delilah* (q.v.).

References, of more or less importance, will be found as follows: *Bird Music*; *Cadenza* 3; *Cinematograph*; *Clarinet Family* 6; *Concerto* 6 b (1835); *Criticism* 6; *Danse macabre*; *Dies Irae*; *France* 10, 12, 13; *Grand Opera*; *Harp* 4; *Improvisation* 2; *Jota*; *Miller of the Dee*; *Oboe Family* 6; *Opera* 11 d; *Oratorio* 7 (1876, 1913); *Organ* 13; *Percussion Family* 2 f, 4 b (Cymbals), 4 c (Castanets), 4 e (Xylophone); *Programme Music* 5 d; *Requiem*; *Samson and Delilah*; *Saxophone*; *Symphonic Poem*; *Symphony* 8 (1835); *Trumpet Family* 4.

SAITE (Ger.). String (plural *Saiten*; so *Saiteninstrumente*, 'stringed instruments').

SALAMAN, CHARLES KENSINGTON. Born in London in 1814 and died there in 1901, aged eighty-seven. He was a brilliant pianist and a popular piano teacher, also experienced as an orchestral and choral conductor and active in the organization of London musical life. A Jew by birth and a religious man by instinct and circumstances, he wrote music for the synagogue of the Reformed Congregation. He is remembered chiefly by his songs, and especially by his setting of Shelley's 'I arise from dreams of thee', written in his younger days (1836).

SALAMANCA. See *Degrees*.

SALAZAR.

(1) JUAN GARCIA. Died in 1710. He was a Spanish priest and a notable composer of church music.

(2) ADOLFO. Born at Madrid in 1890. He has composed piano music, songs, chamber and orchestral music, etc., has been music critic of a leading Madrid newspaper, and has published several books on music. In 1939 he emigrated to Mexico.

SALICIONAL, SALICET. See *Organ* 14 I.

SALIERI, ANTONIO (p. 397, pl. 68. 3). Born at Legnago (nr. Verona) in 1750 and died in Vienna in 1825, aged seventy-four. He was a much applauded conductor and composer of operas and other works who entered the royal service in Vienna in his early twenties and continued in it for the remaining half-century of his life. (Cf. *Opera* 9 b.)

He was the associate of Gluck and Haydn, and the teacher of Beethoven and Schubert. He is said to have disliked Mozart, who had become in some degree a rival of his in Vienna, but the story that he poisoned him, made by Pushkin the basis of a 'dramatic-duologue' which was then converted into an opera by Rimsky-Korsakof, has no foundation.

SALINAS, FRANCISCO. Born at Burgos in 1513 and died at Salamanca in 1590, aged seventy-six. Although blind from birth he became a good organist and a famous theorist.

See *Spain* 3, 9.

SALIS, BRINDES DE. See *United States* 6 (end).

SALISBURY CATHEDRAL. See references under *Cathedral Music* 2; *Acoustics* 16; *Cecilia*.

Organists who receive notice in this book are (with their periods of office): *J. Farrant* (1598–1602); *J. Holmes* (1602–10); *Wise* (1668–87); *D. Roseingrave* (1692–8); *W. G. Alcock* (1916–37).

SALLÉ, MARIE (1710–56). See *Ballet* 2.

SALLY IN OUR ALLEY. The poem is by Henry Carey (q.v.) So was the original music, but this was in 1790 replaced by a traditional English tune, *What though I am a Country Lass,* which is the tune we now know.

SALMO (It.). 'Psalm.'

SALMON, THOMAS (1648–1706). A Bedfordshire clergyman in the Church of England who was active in exploring the scientific side of music. See *Notation* 7.

SALOME (Strauss). Produced at Dresden in 1905. Libretto adapted (in German) from the play by Oscar Wilde. Time, about A.D. 30.

SCENE: *The Terrace of Herod's Palace. Evening*

We recall the brief history of the marriages of Herod Antipas, son of Herod the Great. He divorced his first wife in order to marry Herodias, wife—and murderess—of his halfbrother—an alliance that John the Baptist condemned. Salome was the daughter of Herodias.

When the opera begins we find John im-

prisoned for his presumption in a disused cistern in Herod's palace.

Narraboth (*Tenor*), Captain of Herod's guard, loves Salome, but she lusts after the Baptist (*Baritone*), who in the opera is named Jokanaan. From the cistern-prison his voice is heard, bidding the wicked repent. In Salome (*Soprano*) is the taint of her mother's lust. She burns to see the Prophet, and Narraboth, to gain her favour, disobeys orders, and brings forth John, who will have nothing to do with her, and denounces her and her mother. Narraboth, seeing her unbounded passion for the Prophet, in despair takes his own life.

Now Herod (*Tenor*) and his wife Herodias (*Mezzo-Soprano*) come out from the palace. The king desires Salome, but Herodias is watchful. She urges her husband to make an end of Jokanaan, whose voice of prophecy is again raised. Herod is afraid to do so. Various Jews dispute concerning the Prophet's inspiration.

Herod, to turn the situation, asks Salome to dance for him, promising her any reward she asks. She does so, and demands, as her price, the head of the Prophet. He tries to persuade her to take some other reward, but she insists, and he sends a soldier down into the cistern. His arm appears, bearing the severed head, over which Salome exults. Herod, maddened with horror, cries to his guard, 'Kill that woman!', and they crush her to death beneath their shields.

See *Opera* 21 m; *Oboe* 4 i.

SALOMÉ, THÉODOR CÉSAR. Born in Paris in 1834 and died near there in 1896, aged sixty-two. He was a student at the Paris Conservatory and at twenty-seven won the second Prix de Rome (q.v.). He became known to the public chiefly as an organist and as the composer of attractive organ music, some of which is still in considerable use in Britain and the United States, as well as in his own country.

SALOMON.

(1) JOHANN PETER (p. 464, pl. 81. 3). Born in Bonn in 1745 and died in London in 1815, aged seventy. He was a violinist who settled in London, where he became active as soloist, chamber music player, orchestral director, and concert manager. That part of his fame which endures attaches to him in the last-named capacity, in which he was instrumental in persuading Haydn to visit England and for it to compose his best symphonies and his *Creation.*

See *Concert* 6, 8; *Nicknamed Compositions* 11 (for the 'Salomon Symphonies' of Haydn); *Conducting* 4.

(2) KARL. See *Jewish Music* 9.

SALTANDO, SALTATO (It.). 'Leaping', 'leapt' (generally in connexion with bowed instrument playing—meaning with a springing bow, i.e. same as *Sautillé*, q.v.).

SALTARELLO. The word has two distinct meanings:

(1) It is the name of the after-dance (see *Nachtanz*) to the passamezzo (q.v.). It was

usually based on the same musical theme, treated not in duple time, as in the passamezzo, but in triple.

(2) It is the name of a Roman dance in three-in-a-measure or six-in-a-measure time, and something like the tarantella (q.v.), but the tune, instead of continuously running triplets, has a predominance of triplets made up of a longer note and a shorter. As the name suggests ('saltare', to jump) it embodies lively motions, and these are usually reflected in the music. Mendelssohn has called the last movement of the 'Italian' Symphony a saltarello; properly its first subject is a saltarello and a subsidiary subject a tarantella.

Some consider the saltarello to be a form of galliard (see *Pavan and Galliard*).

See reference under *Suite* 2.

SALTBOX (p. 512, pl. **91**. 9). One of the traditional handy domestic instruments for use when joyous music was to be extemporized. The mode of performance can be gathered from the following verse from Bonnell Thornton's burlesque ode (1749), *Ode on St. Cecilia's Day, adapted to the ancient British musick, viz. the salt-box, the jew's-harp, the marrow-bones and cleaver, the hum-strum or hurdy-gurdy,* etc.:

In strains more exalted the salt-box shall join,
And clattering and battering and clapping combine;
With a rap and a tap while the hollow side sounds,
Up and down leaps the flap, and with rattling re-
   bounds.

This is the stanza which Dr. Johnson once repeated with gusto and an expression of admiration, and, indeed, it is excellently onomatopoeic. (A few years later his friend Burney set the ode to music, his score including all the instruments it mentions, and it was performed with success at Ranelagh; see *Concert* 12.) Apparently the saltbox made on occasion some pretensions to real artistic powers, since J. T. Smith in his life of the sculptor Nollekens (1829) mentions of one Price (keeper of 'The Farthing Pie House', Tottenham Court Road, London) that 'he was an excellent salt-box player, and he has frequently accompanied the famous Abel when playing on the violoncello'. Now Abel was a celebrated musician, a pupil of John Sebastian Bach at Leipzig and the bosom-friend of John Christian Bach in London.

Smith's modern editor, Wilfred Whitten, has a footnote, 'The salt-box, a somewhat mysterious instrument, was beaten with a rolling pin in such a way as to produce sounds varying with the music'. Eighteenth-century prints show that this was sometimes so. It will be noticed that Thornton above speaks of a simultaneous 'clattering and battering'.

Cf. *Marrow-bones and Cleaver*; *Bellows and Tongs*; *Bladder and String*; *Jew's Harp*; *Hurdy-gurdy*.

SALVATION ARMY. See *Hymns and Hymn Tunes* 12; *Church Music* 2; *Dictionaries* 7.

SALVE REGINA. See *Antiphons of the Blessed Virgin Mary*.

SALZÉDO, CARLOS. Born at Arcachon, France, in 1885 and died at Waterville, Me., in 1961, aged seventy-six. He was a celebrated harpist, founder of the harp department of the Curtis Institute, Philadelphia, an inventor of new techniques in harp performance, an active propagandist for modern music, and the composer of many works for his instrument, for orchestra, chorus, etc.

See *Harp* 3; *Concerto* 6 c (1885).

SAMARA, SPIRO. Born at Corfu in 1861 and died at Athens in 1917, aged fifty-five. By parentage he was half Greek, half British. He was trained at the Paris Conservatory and he wrote operas to Italian libretti, nearly all being produced in Italy.

SAMAZEUILH, GUSTAVE. Born at Bordeaux in 1877. He is a pupil of Chausson and d'Indy and has served as a music critic and composed symphonic poems, chamber music, piano music, songs, etc.

SAMBA. A Brazilian dance in the major mode and in duple time. It exists in two forms, the urban and the rural—the urban form less varied in rhythm, the rural form employing a good deal of syncopation.

SAMINSKY, LAZAR (p. 913, pl. **156**. 4). Born at Odessa in 1882 and died in New York in 1959, aged seventy-six. After a mathematical and philosophical course at the University of St. Petersburg, he studied composition in the Conservatory of that city, under Rimsky-Korsakof and Glazunof, and then became a strong supporter of the Jewish national school of composition. From 1920 he worked in the United States (especially as conductor) in the cause of modern music. He was in charge of the music at the Temple Emanu-El, New York. He wrote several books freely expressing his opinions (good and bad) of various American composers. His compositions include opera-oratorios, ballets, mimo-dramas, songs, and symphonies.

SAMISEN. An instrument used in one or two Italian scores. It consists of hollow bronze vessels of graduated sizes, struck with a sort of drumstick. The instrument described is the one used in Puccini's *Madam Butterfly* and Mascagni's *Iris*. But the Japanese instrument to which this name is more properly applied is a three-stringed, rectangular affair. Both faces of the body are covered with cat-skin and it is played with a plectrum about the size and shape of a shoehorn.

SAMMARTINI (or **SAN MARTINI**), the brothers (1) GIUSEPPE (born at Milan about 1693 and died in London in 1751) and (2) GIOVANNI BATTISTA (born at Milan in 1701 and died there in 1775).

(1) GIUSEPPE was a hautboy player, the greatest ever heard up to his day. He was also an active and reputable composer. He passed a good deal of his life in London.

(2) GIOVANNI BATTISTA was organist of

Milan Cathedral and the fluent composer of two thousand works of all kinds. His symphonies prefigure those of Haydn. He was the master of Gluck.

See references: *Chamber Music* 6, Period II (1700), Period III (at beginning); *Symphony* 3, 8 (1700).

SAMMLUNG (Ger.). 'Collection.'

SAMSON AND DELILAH (Saint-Saëns). Produced at Weimar (not, as usually stated, under Liszt) in 1877. Banned from the English stage until 1909. Libretto by F. Lemaire, from the Bible story.

Act I

Scene: *A Square in Gaza, Palestine*

The Israelites groan under Philistine tyranny. **Samson** (*Tenor*) heartens them, prophesying deliverance. **Abimelech** (*Bass*), satrap of Gaza, jeers at their prayers and their God, and attacks Samson, who wrests from him his sword and slays him. The Hebrews go off.

Now the **High Priest of Dagon** (*Baritone*) exhorts his followers to revenge the Hebrews' insult. A **Messenger** (*Tenor*) brings the news that Samson is leading his countrymen in the destruction of the harvested grain. The frightened Philistines leave, and an **Aged Hebrew** (*Bass*), with others of his kind, welcome the victorious Samson and his countrymen.

But now **Delilah** (*Mezzo-Soprano*), with her song of 'Fair Spring', spins her web, which, in spite of the Aged Hebrew's warning, ensnares Samson again (for he has known her before), whilst the Priestesses of Dagon perform their languishing dances.

Act II

Scene: *Delilah's House in the Valley of Soreck. Night*

Delilah knows that Samson will come to her. She will be revenged on him for leaving her. First, the High Priest tells her of the Philistine disaster, and urges her to entrap him; but she needs no urging. Three times she has tried to discover the secret of his strength, and has failed. The Priest departs to make his preparations for taking the hero by surprise, and Samson comes to meet his fate. He intends to bid Delilah farewell, but she is stronger than he, and in spite of the thunder, in which he hears the voice of God, he yields to her. The Philistines creep up, and on Delilah's cry "Tis done!' rush into the house and overpower the shorn hero.

Act III

Scene 1: *The Prison at Gaza*

Samson, blinded and in chains, is turning a mill and praying for pity and pardon, while without the Hebrews lament his betrayal of their cause.

Scene 2: *Interior of the Temple of Dagon*

The Philistines rejoice in bacchanalian dances. Samson is led in and taunted by Delilah. He prays to God for one final mercy—the restoration, but for a moment, of his strength. As the carousing Philistines exult, Samson whispers to a child to lead him between the pillars of the temple, and, his prayer being granted, he exerts his strength for the last time, breaks the pillars asunder, and brings down the temple in ruins, destroying all within it.

SÄMTLICH (Ger.). 'Complete', 'collected'. So used of the works of a composer, the body of stops of an organ (*Sämtliche Stimmen*), etc.

SAMUEL, HAROLD (1879–1937). Fine pianist. See *Memory* 7; *Jewish Music* 9; *Ferguson, Howard*.

SAMUELS, BERNHARD. See *Aerophor*.

SANCTUS. 'Holy.' See *Mass* 2 d, 3 d; *Requiem*; *Common Prayer*; *Ter Sanctus*; *Trisagion*.

SANDBURG, CARL. See *Ballad* 3.

SANDS OF DEE, THE. See *Clay*.

SANDS, SINGING. See *Musical Sand*.

SANDYS, GEORGE (1578–1644). See *Hymns and Hymn Tunes* 17 e xvii.

SANFT (Ger.). 'Soft', gentle, gently. So, too, *Sanftmütig*.

SANG SCUILS, SANG SCHOOLIS. See *Schola Cantorum*; *Scotland* 4; *Presbyterian* 3.

SANKEY AND MOODY. See *Church Music* 2; *Hymns and Hymn Tunes* 12.

SAN MARTINI. See *Sammartini*.

SANS (Fr.). 'Without.' So *Sans les sourdines*, 'without mutes'.

SANTA CRUZ (or Santa Cruz Wilson), DOMINGA. Born at La Cruz, Chile, in 1899. His early career was that of a lawyer and diplomat. He studied music at Madrid and elsewhere, held important musical posts at the University of Chile and later undertook the direction of the government Institute of Musical Extension. He has been active as a composer.

SANTIR. See p. 465, pl. **82.** 7.

SANTLEY, CHARLES. Born at Liverpool in 1834 and died in London in 1922, aged eighty-eight. He was the greatest British baritone of his day—equally famous in oratorio and opera. He also did a little composition. In 1907, when he had been before the public fifty years, he was knighted.

See *Voice* 18, 20; *Singing* 12; *Gramophone* 6.

SANZ, GASPAR. He was a seventeenth-century guitar player and composer, and in 1694 published an important book on guitar playing.

See *Folía*.

SANZOGNO, NINO. Born in Venice in 1911. A composer and conductor, he is a pupil of Malipiero and Scherchen, and has written concertos for viola and cello and other works.

SAPORTA, MARC. See *History* 9.

SARABANDE or **SARABAND.** An ancient dance form, possibly originating in Spain or possibly of oriental origin and developed in Spain; it was once popular over a great part of Europe.

It is in three-in-a-measure time and its phrases usually begin on the first beat of the measure and go along at a sober, steady pace and with a degree of nobility. Handel's *Lascia ch' io pianga* is a good specimen of the sarabande and was originally written as one, the words being added in a later opera: the accent in the second beat in the measure is typical of this dance.

The sarabande commonly appears as one of the movements of the classical suite (q.v.). With Purcell it sometimes appears as the last movement but Bach and others follow it with the lively gigue (other movements often interposed). It is in simple binary form (see *Form* 5).

There exist pieces called 'Sarabande' that do not conform to the above description, but they are exceptions.

In view of the staid dignity which is such a marked feature of many of the sarabandes known to us it is curious that Father Mariana (1536–1623), in his *Treatise against Public Amusements*, speaks of it as 'a dance and song so loose in its words and so ugly in its motions that it is enough to excite bad emotions in even very decent people'. And he is by no means alone. Many authors of the period utter similar denunciations, and Philip II of Spain (reigned 1555–98) actually felt it necessary to suppress it. That the sarabande was in the eighteenth century a popular dance in England there is some evidence in an allusion to it under *Fairs and their Music*.

See also *Dance* 7; *Folia*; *Ornaments* 3.

SARASATE, PABLO DE (in full, Pablo Martin Melitón Sarasate y Navascuez; p. 1097, pl. **182**. 7). Born at Pamplona in 1844 and died at Biarritz in 1908, aged sixty-four. He was trained at the Paris Conservatory and made a world name as a violinist. (Cf. *Pianoforte Playing* 8.) He composed attractive music for his instrument and was the cause of others composing such.

SARDANA. The national dance of Catalonia, put into its present form in the 1850s by a village musician, Pep Ventura. It is danced to the Spanish equivalent of the pipe and tabor (see *Recorder* 3 c) and instruments of the oboe family. It may be in sections, partly two-in-a-bar, partly six-in-a-bar (occasionally only the former). There is movement with linked hands, as in the farandole.

SARDINIA CHAPEL, LONDON. See *Roman Catholic Church Music in Britain*.

SARGENT, (HAROLD) MALCOLM (WATTS). Born at Ashford, Kent, in 1895 and died in London in 1967, aged seventy-two. After a career as organist and composer, he gradually, during the early 1920s, made his way in a new career as choral, orchestral, and opera conductor, in which he attained eminence. From 1950 to 1957 he was conductor of the BBC Symphony Orchestra and thereafter continued as chief conductor of the Promenade Concerts. In 1947 he was knighted.

SARRUSOPHONE. See *Oboe Family* 4 j.

SARTI, GIUSEPPE. Born at Faenza in 1729 and died at Berlin in 1802, aged seventy-two. He was successively organist of the cathedral of his native place, opera conductor at Copenhagen, principal of a Conservatory at Venice, musical director at Milan Cathedral, and (for nearly twenty years) chief court musician at St. Petersburg. (See reference under *Greek Church* 5; *Opera* 17 a.)

He was a composer of operas, Masses, and sonatas, the pupil of Padre Martini and the master of Cherubini. His name often occurs in discussions of Mozart's string quartets, certain of which prompted him to write 'Music is bound to go to the dogs when such barbarians take it into their heads to compose'—in which condemnation, however, he was only one of many contemporary critics.

See *Scandinavia* 2.

SARUM GRADUAL AND ANTIPHONALE. See *Plainsong* 4.

SARUM USE. See *Common Prayer*; *Use of Sarum*.

SAS, ANDRÉ. Born in Paris (of Belgian and French descent) in 1900 and studied in Brussels. He settled in Peru and has taken rank as the leading composer of that country. His music shows Peruvian melodic and harmonic traits.

SASSOFONO (It.). 'Saxophone.' See *Saxophone Family*.

SATIE, ERIK (Alfred Eric Leslie Satie) (p. 385, pl. **64**. 4). Born at Honfleur, in Normandy, in 1866, and died in Paris in 1925, aged fifty-nine. He came of musical parents, both his mother (Scottish) and his father being composers. At seventeen he spent a year at the Paris Conservatory, and, at forty, three years at the Schola Cantorum under d'Indy (q.v.) and Roussel (q.v.); at this latter, in 1908, he took a diploma.

He was a composer who feared no man, but ever did what was right in his own eyes—unless, perhaps, the motive might be stated a little differently, to do what was wrong in the eyes of other people.

The tendency of French music in his early life might be stated generally as Wagnerian—big ideas developed on the Leading Motif system, with heavy orchestration. This he looked on as un-Latin; he stood for a greater directness. He influenced certain contemporaries. It is commonly said (but also denied) that Debussy, with whom he was intimate and who encouraged him, was one of these, as Ravel, to a certain extent, certainly was. As the second decade of the present century opened the young musical rebels of France discovered him and turned his garret into a Cave of Adullam, where the weapons of Polytonality and Atonality were sharpened, and their use practised preliminary to many a raid on the orthodox.

His whimsicality was one thing that stood in the way of any wide recognition—writing his scores in red ink without bar lines, and giving his compositions punning titles such as *Pieces in the Shape of a Pear* and *Limp Preludes for a Dog*.

Ravel tried for years to help him to some degree of public recognition, and that record is a testimonial of some value.

SATZ (Ger.). 'Movement' (q.v.). Also, bewilderingly, (*a*) 'Theme', 'Subject'; (*b*) 'Phrase'; (*c*) 'Composition', 'Piece'; (*d*) 'Texture'; (*e*) 'Style'. *Hauptsatz* means 'First Subject' and *Nebensatz* or *Seitensatz* 'Second Subject'. *Schlusssatz* means either 'Finale' or 'Coda'.

SAUDADES (Portuguese). Milhaud has written compositions under this title (short tango-like dances), and Heseltine ('Peter Warlock') a set of songs. It 'expresses the haunting sense of sadness and regret for days gone by'.

SAUGUET, HENRI. Born at Bordeaux in 1901. He was a pupil of Koechlin (q.v.) and then a member of the little group of French composers who gathered round Satie (q.v.) and were influenced by him. He came into some prominence in the early 1920s, with the production by Diaghilef (q.v.) of *La Chatte*, the first of some twenty ballets. In 1939 his operatic version of Stendhal's *La Chartreuse*

de Parme was produced in Paris, and after the second World War his second symphony (*Symphonie Expiatoire*), dedicated to the war's victims, was heard in Paris and broadcast from London. Song cycles and other works also reached early performance and tended to increase interest in him and his style and methods.

See *Ballet* 5.

SAURAU. See *Emperor's Hymn*.

SAUSAGE, SAUSAGE BASSOON. See *Rackett*.

SAUTILLÉ (Fr.). A type of staccato bowing (on the violin, etc.) in which the bow bounces from the strings. It seems to have been introduced by Paganini. (Same as *Saltato* and *Saltando*.)

SAVILE, JEREMY. A seventeenth-century musician known as composer of a few songs and part-songs, notably 'Here's a health unto his Majesty'.

SAVONAROLA. See *Canti carnascialeschi*.

SAVOY OPERAS. Operas of Gilbert and Sullivan (see *Sullivan*)—produced or revived at the Savoy Theatre, London, opened 1881. The band of artists associated with these performances dubbed themselves (or were dubbed) 'Savoyards'.

SAW, SINGING. See *Singing Saw*.

SAX. See *Belgium* 8; *Tuba Group* 1, 4; *Saxhorn and Flügelhorn Families* 2; *Saxophone Family*; *Trumpet Family* 3.

SAXHORN AND FLÜGELHORN FAMILIES

1. Introductory.
2. The Saxhorns.

3. The Flügelhorns.
4. The Flicorni.

5. Nomenclature.

(For illustrations see p. 140, pl. 26.)

1. Introductory. These two families are treated in many French and German works as identical, but a distinction can be made. Both are families of brass instruments with cup-shaped mouthpieces (like trumpets, trombones, and genuine tubas), not funnel-shaped mouthpieces (like the true horns, i.e. the 'French Horns'). Both are on the bugle model, with a conical bore like that of the true horns, not like that of the trumpets or trombones (which is cylindrical for the most part of the length). But the bore of the saxhorns is wider than that of the true horns, and that of the flügelhorns wider than that of the saxhorns.

That last detail (which affects the tone quality) constitutes one element of differentiation between the saxhorns and the flügelhorns. Another element of differentiation concerns the larger members of the two families: the bell of the larger saxhorns is held upward and that of the flügelhorns held forward.

The upper saxhorns and flügelhorns are almost entirely wind-band instruments.

The nomenclature of saxhorns and flügelhorns is in a state of complete confusion. The following is an attempt to introduce into the discussion of the subject a little more clarity

that is usual, but it must be confessed that a complete statement of the facts as to the instruments and their names is impossible; certain German and French names are included below, but they do not cover the ground, the names used in Austria differing in some respects from those used in Germany and those used in Belgium from those used in France. It may fairly be said that no two works on orchestration or works of musical reference, even those published within the boundaries of the same country, agree in their information.[1]

[1] Whilst the author of this work adheres to what he has written above, he thinks it fair to add the comment of a high authority to whom the article has been submitted:

'I am disposed to agree with the works that treat these two as identical, or, at all events, as showing only minor differences which do not entitle them to be separately classified. One can easily find differences between Sax's original designs and the Saxhorns of to-day. Each group of makers seems to have produced just such a conical bore as he thought gave the best results.

'In Britain the name "Flügelhorn" is understood to mean the Bugle of the pitch of a Cornet and built on its lines. It appears to be identical with Sax's "Bugle en si bémol perfectionné (ancienne forme, proportions nouvelles)"—"Perfected Bugle in B flat, old shape, new proportions". J. G. Kastner, *Manuel général de musique militaire*, Pl. 24, f. 3.

'Even abroad, the name is often limited to this one

See also Plates 154 and 156 on pages 897 and 913, and Articles under the individual names

1. LIADOF (1855–1914)

2. LIAPUNOF (1859–1924)

3. ARENSKY (1861–1906)

4. GRETCHANINOF (1864–1956)

5. GLAZUNOF (1865–1936)

6. REBIKOF (1866–1920)

7. SCRIABIN (1872–1915)

8. RACHMANINOF (1873–1943)

1. STRAVINSKY (1882–1971)

2. PICASSO AND STRAVINSKY, by Cocteau

4. SAMINSKY (1882–1959)

3. MIASKOVSKY (1881–1950)

5. PROKOFIEF (1891–1953)

6. ALEXANDER TCHEREPNIN
(b. 1899)

7. KHATCHATURIAN (1903–78)

8. SHOSTAKOVICH (1906–75)

2. The Saxhorns. This name is given to a set of seven instruments introduced by Adolphe Sax in 1845 (see *Belgium* 8), ranging from deep bass to high treble. The highest instrument of the lower-pitched three and the lowest instrument of the higher-pitched four are identical in pitch, so that, so far as compass is concerned, the seven instruments amount only to six, the practical difference lying in the rather fuller tone of the instrument belonging to the lower set.

The lower-pitched set of three, which are familiarly considered to be tubas and are used to play tuba parts in the orchestra, are treated in the present work under *Tuba Group* 4. The higher-pitched set of four are as follows:

(*a*) **Sopranino Saxhorn in E flat (or F)**; also called *Soprano Saxhorn*; also often miscalled *Soprano Flügelhorn* or *Flügelhorn piccolo*. This instrument is really not much different from the E flat cornet (see *Cornet*). The German name is *Kleines Kornett in Es* (or F), the French *Petit Bugle*.

The compass runs up chromatically about two octaves from E flat (or F) at the bottom of the treble staff, and (by means of the valves) down to six semitones from that note.[1]

(*b*) **Soprano Saxhorn in B flat or (C)**; also called *Alto Saxhorn*; also often miscalled *Alto-Flügelhorn*; in Germany called simply *Flügelhorn in B* (C) or *Kornett in B* (C); in France called *Contralto* or *Bugle*. This instrument is really not much different from the B flat cornet (see *Cornet*).

The compass runs up chromatically about two octaves from B flat (or C) just below the treble staff, and downwards (by means of the valves) six semitones from that note.

(*c*) **Alto Saxhorn in E flat (or F)**; also called simply *Saxhorn*, or *Tenor*, *Tenor Saxhorn* or *Tenor Horn*; also called *Alto* or *Althorn in E flat* or *Altkornett in Es* (F), or *Althorn in Es* (F), or *Bugle alto* (Fr.). There is a variety of this instrument called the Tenor Cor, made in the form of a horn.[2]

instrument, e.g. in H. Kling's *Populäre Instrumentationslehre*, p. 90. "Das Flügelhorn ist von etwas grösserer Bauart als das Cornet à Pistons, sein Ton daher voller und runder." ["The Flügelhorn is of somewhat bigger build than the Cornet, its tone, fuller and rounder."] No other type is referred to.'

[1] Outside Sax's categories is a Sopranino Saxhorn in B flat (C). In Germany it is known as *Oktavkornett* in B (C), in France as *Petit Bugle*. It is a still smaller instrument than the Sopranino Saxhorn in E flat (F) and an octave above the Soprano Saxhorn in B flat (C).

[2] The muddles of nomenclature in relation to this family of instruments are diabolic. An authority to whom the above has been submitted writes:

'There is a lot of confusion between the Ballad Horn and the Tenor Cor, and whatever is put down will be incorrect in some one's eyes. But I have lately made inquiries of both Boosey & Hawkes and W. Brown & Sons (well known to the professional brass player), and find that in their view the Tenor Cor is in F (or Eb) and the Ballad Horn in C (i.e. a fourth lower).

'The following are equivalents, or as nearly so as makers in different countries get them:

'Tenor Cor (in F or Eb) = Oktavwaldhorn (Ger.) of Eichborn; Primhorn (Aust.) of Cervený; Mellophone (U.S.A.) of Conn and others; Cor alto (Fr.) of Couesnon & Besson (not to be confused with Cor alto as denoting the performer).

The compass runs up chromatically about two octaves from the E flat (or F) near the middle of the bass staff, and downwards (by means of the valves) six semitones from that note.

(*d*) **Tenor in B flat (or C)**; also called *Baritone*, or *Baritone Saxhorn*; also called *Althorn in B flat*. In Germany often called *Tenorhorn in B* (C) or *Bassflügelhorn*; in France, *Bugle ténor*.

The compass runs up chromatically about two octaves from the B flat (or C) near the bottom of the bass staff, and downwards (by means of the valves) six semitones from that note.

The saxhorns in E flat and B flat are those in use in wind bands; those in F and C are occasionally used in orchestras.

The notation of the saxhorns regards them as 'transposing instruments' (q.v.), and notates as middle C the note just mentioned in connexion with each instrument as the pivot of its compass; the treble clef is used for the whole set of four instruments above shown (and, indeed, often for the lower set of three also. See *Tuba Family* 4).

3. The Flügelhorns. (The lettering of the paragraphs here is made identical with the paragraphs concerning the corresponding saxhorns, above.)

(*a*) **Soprano Flügelhorn in E flat.** Not often heard. A French name is *Petit Bugle*.

(*b*) **Flügelhorn in B flat**; also called *Alto Flugelhorn*, or simply *Alto*. It is used in wind bands amongst the cornets—usually only one in Britain but often more in other countries. Its tone is somewhat more mellow than that of the cornet. A French name is *Grand Bugle* (cf. *Petit Bugle* above); sometimes it is called simple *Bugle*.

(*c*) **Flügelhorn in E flat**, or *Tenor Flügelhorn*, or *Altflügelhorn in E flat*, or *Alto Flügelhorn in E flat*, or *Althorn in E flat*.

(Sometimes instead of being in E flat it is in F. This is the Flügelhorn that is sometimes used in Germany to play the upper tuba parts of Wagner; see *Tuba Group* 5.)

4. The Flicorni. A series of Italian band instruments corresponding to the saxhorns and Flügelhorns is that of the flicorni. Its keys, like theirs, are alternately E flat and B flat. (Cf. *Tuba Group* 5.)

5. Nomenclature. An attempt has been made, in what has just been stated, to give the names commonly in use. The student must, however, be prepared to meet with other names, e.g. in French books (some of which are in circulation in English translation—with many of the names of instruments unfortunately left untranslated). He may find such terms as *Bügelhorn* and *Bugle à pistons*, and from the context he must endeavour to discover what instrument is intended.

'Ballad Horn or vocal Horn (in C) = Tenor Cor of C. Sachs. I can't find at present that anything else is entitled to this name. America makes Ballad Horns in Bb.'

SAXOFONIA, SAXOFONO (It.), **SAXOFON** (Ger.). Saxophone. See *Saxophone Family*.

SAXOPHONE FAMILY (p. 140, pl. **26.** 6). This family was brought into existence by the Belgian instrument maker Adolphe Sax (cf. *Saxhorn*; *Belgium* 8), then of Brussels, in 1846. Its first public appearance seems to have been in 1841, in the French composer J. G. Kastner's Biblical oratorio *The Last King of Judah* (the frequent statement that Meyerbeer was one of the early composers to write for it appears to be inexact).

French military bands quickly adopted the family and it then gradually spread its activities until, with the rise of jazz (q.v.) in the United States, during the convulsion of 1914–18, these suddenly increased and multiplied so that the instrument became, of all instruments, the best known to that general public that frequents dance halls and likes to dine or sup to music. To the judicious this was a grief, as the members of the family were often made to perform feats for which providence had not intended them, and the tone quality that resulted was often trying to sensitive ears; later a degree of better taste showed itself and the true powers of the family began to be more widely realized.

The constructional principles of the saxophone family are very hybrid. They include the conical tube of the oboe family (q.v.) and the single reed of the clarinet family (q.v.), with a tube of brass. In the military type of band their tone forms a useful link between that of the wood-wind and the brass.

The complete family numbers twelve different instruments, big and little, but only two or three of these are in very general use. They are written as 'transposing instruments' (q.v.), being usually in the regular band keys of B flat and E flat.

There is comparatively little serious solo music for the saxophone. Debussy composed a Rhapsody for saxophone and orchestra (1903; posthumously published), and Jemnitz a Sonata for saxophone and banjo. Berlioz, in his textbook of orchestration, greatly praised the saxophone, and his compatriots, Bizet, Saint-Saëns, Delibes, d'Indy (in *Fervaal*, which has a quartet in D of saxophones), Debussy, Florent Schmitt, etc., have made a good deal of use of it. Strauss has a quartet of saxophones in the 'Domestic' Symphony ('to be considered *ad libitum* only in case of extreme necessity'). Mahler has used the saxophone in certain scores and it appears in Hindemith's opera *Cardillac* and in Holbrooke's symphonic poem *Apollo and the Seaman*; this last composer has written a concerto for the instrument, as have also Lars Erik Larsson, Norman Demuth, Ibert, and others. Vogel (q.v.) has written an oratorio with saxophones as the accompanying instruments. Eric Coates has written a *Saxo-Rhapsody* for saxophone and orchestra, and Phyllis Tate a concerto for saxophone and strings. Vaughan Williams uses the saxophone in his ballet *Job* to introduce Job's comforters.

The Fr. name is the same as the Eng., the It. (usually) *Saxofono* but sometimes *Saxofonia* or *Sassofono*, and the Ger. *Saxophon*.

For a precursor of the saxophone, the *Tenoroon*, see allusion under *Oboe Family* 4 h.

SBALZ., SBALZATO (It.). 'Jerk' or 'dash', 'dashed' (generally with the sense of impetuosity).

SCACCIAPENSIERI (It.). 'Jew's harp' (q.v.).

SCALA ENIGMATICA. See *Scales* 12.

SCALDS. See *Scandinavia* 5.

SCALE (in organ stops). See *Organ* 3, 4.

SCALES

1. Definition of the Word. By 'Scales' we mean stepwise, ordered arrangements, for theoretical purposes or the purposes of vocal or instrumental practice, of all the chief notes found in particular compositions or passages or in the music of a period or people.

The number of different scales that mankind has used and is using is enormous, and can, indeed, never be completely known, whilst the processes by which they have come to be adopted are various also, including intuition, scientific reasoning, and chance.

Apparently any combination of notes whatever may be adopted as the material from which a peasantry, or a composer, or a group of composers, may make their tunes, and there exists not even one interval common to all the scales of the world.

2. The Three Processes by which Scales come about. Three processes have been suggested above as those by which scales come into being: intuition, reasoning, and chance. The first is not unimportant; a large number of scales, even of quite early times, have been constructed, partially at least, on lines which the discoveries of science have later endorsed as being in accordance with acoustic principle, or, in other words, natural mathematical logic; this can be nothing but an instinctive recognition of natural fact. Other scales have been brought into existence by early scientists (as, for instance, those of Greece in the sixth century B.C.) as a consequence of theoretical research and reasoning, and have then imposed themselves, more or less (perhaps partly by instruments being constructed on their principles), upon a whole population. Still others, doubtless, have come about as roads have done; the inhabitants of a district having occasion to cross a tract of land adopt a route that, for no reason that one can completely trace, includes certain slight meanderings, and this in the course of ages gets trodden and worn and at last is accepted as the Queen's Highway.

3. Speech Inflexions as the Ultimate Origin. Probably the ultimate origin of scales is in speech inflexions (compare *Melody* 2). The theoretically possible number of these is almost unlimited, so that every man might, if he wished, develop his own and maintain it as a personal characteristic. Yet we find, in practice, that a whole nation will adopt a particular type of inflexion (the way of ending its sentences, for instance), so that an intelligent observer can often discover the nationality of a man by his inflexions alone (see *Melody* 2), although not a word he says may be caught. And within the system of national inflexion particular districts will unconsciously adopt particular characteristics, so that a Gascon can be quickly differentiated from a Picard, or a Yorkshireman from a Londoner.

And, similarly, nations and parts of nations adopt, in their music, characteristic idioms and inflexions that are reducible to scales. The relation between the territorial inflexions of speech and those of song, and between the scales of one and those of the other, will, perhaps, some day be considered a necessary foundation for the thorough study of racial and national musical characteristics.

This opening of the discussion will, it is hoped, remove the impression, still sometimes found to exist, that there are one or two special scales (such as our common major and minor) that have a value above all others, these scales possessing a scientific basis superior to those of other scales. The scales of the East and the West, diatonic scales, chromatic scales, the ecclesiastical modes, whole-tone scales, quarter-tone scales, and the recent scales invented by particular composers (see, for instance, under *Scriabin*) have an equal authority if it can be shown that they represent a basis for music that has proved capable of satisfying the ears and touching the hearts of some considerable body of men.

In reading what follows it will be well to remember that most scale systems are, in their origin, the outcome of melody; it is only within the last five hundred years (and then only amongst European races) that the combination of notes in harmony has begun to influence and limit the character of scales.

4. Certain Intervals common to many Scales. It has been said above that there is no interval common to all scales, nevertheless there are one or two intervals that are found in many. The octave from the lowest note is the most important of these. This is to be expected. The relationship of the two notes of an octave is so close (see *Acoustics* 8, 15) that men and women, or men and boys, singing the same tune do so at the interval of an octave, effortlessly and without giving thought to the fact that they are not uttering the same notes as one another.

The perfect fifth is also common to a good many scales. This, likewise, is an interval the two notes of which have a close acoustic relationship (see again *Acoustics* 8, 15), so much so that the street singers have occasionally been known to sing in fifths without being aware of it, apparently just as they might sing in octaves; further it is found that a certain proportion of people asked to whistle a tune that has been sung will unconsciously do so at the interval of a fifth (see *Harmony* 4; cf. *Scandinavia* 5). The fact that certain types of wind instruments when overblown sound their notes an octave plus a fifth above the normal pitch (for an instance today see *Clarinet Family* 1) might possibly also early accustom musicians to the interval.

The prevalence of the perfect fourth is perhaps not quite so easy to account for, yet this interval is one of those whose notes are in a simple acoustical relation (see below).

5. How our Western Note Series came about. It was Pythagoras who, about 550 B.C., formally introduced the octave, for it was he who first discovered the mathematical side of music. Experimenting with strings, he found that a division at the half raised the pitch an octave and accepted this as the most important relationship in music; that a division at the two-thirds raised the pitch by a perfect fifth and accepted this as the second most important relationship; that a division at the three-quarter raised the pitch by a perfect fourth—obviously another important relationship. Thus he placed in a position of pre-eminence the three notes which every banjoist, every accordion player, and every compiler of a 'Vamping Tutor', in a true Pythagorean spirit, exalts today by the prominence his basses give them.

The fourth and fifth being found, the interval between them received attention, and this interval, that of the tone, was then accepted as a standard. The larger interval between the first note and the fourth, and that between the fifth and the last were then divided by marking out two tones, and a half-tone was seen to remain in each case. So was very logically laid down a note-series of an octave, consisting of two tetrachords each of two tones and one semitone. There were obviously three possible arrangements, semitone-tone-tone (called the *Dorian Tetrachord*), tone-semitone-tone (called the *Phrygian Tetrachord*), and tone-tone-semitone (called the *Lydian Tetrachord*).[1] The

[1] It will be observed that these names do not correspond with the beginning notes of the Modes now similarly named. That is because in the sixteenth century a wrong system of nomenclature was applied to the Modes (see *Modes* 7).

double tetrachord of each of these 'modes' can be visualized by looking at them (so far as their arrangement of tones and semitones is concerned) as octaves of white keys of the piano, beginning respectively on E, D, and C.

6. Modes and Scales based on the Western Note Series. The above account of the Greek origin of our present series of notes is necessarily very compressed. Many facts are omitted, the only objects in view at the moment being (*a*) to show a process of reasoning applied to the practical end of providing a logical series of notes for the use of musicians, and (*b*) to show the starting-point of a system (discussed more freely in the article, *Modes*) which influenced all Western music, and still does so.

The birth of Christ five hundred years later brought about this influence. The note-series had naturally been adopted for the Greek instruments. One of these instruments, the organ, was taken into use in Christian worship. The plainsong to which the service was rendered was based on the note-series in its various 'Modes', and so it became familiar to all Christendom. (This may be thought by some to be an over-simplification of history, but is it so far out?) Some of these modes are today the commonplaces of every collector of the ancient songs of the English countryside; one of them is, of course, our everyday major scale. The reason that the major scale (the Lydian of the Greeks) has outdistanced other modes is its suitability for harmony. This is briefly explained in the article *Harmony*.

Our minor scale, or minor mode, is a slight adaptation for purposes of harmony of one of the modes that were later added to the Pythagorean system (see *Modes*; and for systems of tuning adopted in order to make these two modes, the major and the minor, more fully available for harmonic purposes, and especially for that comparatively modern practice called 'Modulation', see *Temperament* 9).

Major Scale (Semitones: 3–4 and 7–8—the Tetrachords thus being alike).

Minor Scale—'Harmonic' Form (Semitones 2–3, 5–6, 7–8; there is the interval of the Augmented Second, 6–7)

Minor Scale—'Melodic' Form (Semitones 2–3, 7–8 ascending; 6–5, 3–2 descending; this avoids the interval of the augmented second, whilst allowing the Leading Note to retain its function of 'leading' to the Tonic).

7. The Chromatic and Dodecaphonic Scales. The keyboard and other recognition of the semitone led in time to the adoption of a system whereby all the adjacent notes consisting of tones upon the keyboard had other notes (what we now call 'black' notes) placed between them, so that the major and minor modes could be begun at various pitches, all the notes necessary to complete the mode at such pitches being thus provided on the keyboard (see *Keyboard*). On stringed instruments and in vocal music the same principle was, of course, also applied. And thus there came into existence a series of notes each divided from the next by the interval of a semitone and constituting a potentia twelve-note semitone scale (the 'Chromatic Scale'). For long, composers used these extra notes merely as a means of taking the two scales at various pitches, as just mentioned, or as interpolations and embellishments to passages that quite plainly still belonged to one of those scales. This latter use, from the days of Wagner onwards, became very extensive, so that all but the simplest music embodied these semitonic embellishments, in the form of additions to the essential melodic shapes, or even in combinations as interpolated chromatic chords or as chromatic chords plainly substituted for the chords that would otherwise have stood in that place (see *Harmony* 24 a).

In the early part of the twentieth century an assertion of the power to use all twelve notes of the chromatic scale on equal terms and in their own right (not as mere embellishments or substitutes) began to be heard, and the name Dodecaphonic Scale has been given to the result (cf. *Bartók*; *Note-row*). The Chromatic Scale *is* the Dodecaphonic Scale, so far as actual notes are concerned, but when we use the latter term we imply that system just mentioned of an octave divided into twelve notes *of equal importance*, as distinct from an octave of seven different notes coloured here and there ('chromatic' means 'coloured'). We speak of Wagner's music as very chromatic, because it employs many of these semitone divisions, but it is certainly not dodecaphonic: it is diatonic music 'coloured', 'seasoned', 'gingered up'.

Chromatic Scale (in 'melodic' notation—raised notes upwards, lowered notes downwards; this notation economizes accidentals).

Chromatic Scale (in 'harmonic' notation).
The scheme is as follows: the notes of the key of the composition, plus those which differ according to the

signature of the tonic minor or major, plus the minor second and augmented fourth.

The above show the two ways of notating when the scale occurs in a composition in the key of C major. In other keys the existing key signature requires to be taken into account.

These two ways are those authorized by the textbooks, but it may be admitted that many composers (e.g. Beethoven) do not always trouble to observe any system but notate chromatic scale passages in any way that occurs to them at the moment of writing—sometimes in several ways in the same composition. (See, for instance, Beethoven's Piano Concerto in G, no. 4.)

8. Microtonal Scales. Later came the introduction of minuter divisions—scales of quarter-tones, and even smaller intervals were tried (see *Microtones*; *Hàba*; *Foulds*; *Carrillo*). The idea of microtonic divisions is not new. Some Oriental races have it. The Hindu system divides the octave into twenty-two, though it does not use all the notes in any one tune, but only a selection of them based upon one of the sixty or more ragas (a raga is roughly describable as a scale plus traditional regulations as to its use and the melodic turns to be associated with it in improvisation).

9. The Whole-tone Scale. A scale which is much associated with the name of the composer Debussy (see *Debussy*; *Impressionism*; and cf. *Rebikof*), since he made much use of it, is the Whole-tone scale. Liszt, Dargomijsky,

The Whole-tone Scale.

and some other composers had occasionally used it earlier—and even Mozart in a sextet (called, however, *A Musical Joke*). This scale allows, of course, of only six different notes within the limits of the octave, instead of seven. As there are no semitones to define position in the scale it conveys an impression of vagueness, and such is, indeed, perhaps a part of the purpose of its adoption. It has proved capable of much beautiful music, but as it lacks variety it is considered that its uses have been pretty well exhausted by its chief exponent, leaving little for others to do with it. A moment's reflection will show that it exists only at two pitches, that beginning on C and that beginning on C sharp (or D flat).

Other notations may be used, according to the key-signature in force at the moment. Equal temperament (see *Temperament*) is implied, as otherwise the varying size of the tones would prevent the scale ever reaching its starting-note an octave higher.

10. The Pentatonic Scale. The Pentatonic Scale is very widespread. As its name implies, it gives only five different notes to the octave, and in the most common form of the scale these follow the scheme that happens to be represented by the black keys of the piano, beginning on F sharp (or by the white keys beginning with C and omitting F and B). This scale is almost a tune in itself, and any order of the notes has beauty. Such scales, by comparison with the seven-note scales, are often called 'Gapped Scales', as though a mouth had had a tooth or two knocked out here and there; but they are just as complete as other scales, and perhaps in the days when microtonic scales have become common our present seven-note scales and even the dodecaphonic scale will be spoken of as 'gapped'.

The Pentatonic Scale (commonest order of the intervals).

The common form of the pentatonic scale just shown is the basis of tunes in many parts of the world. Many of the finest Scottish tunes are based upon it, as are Chinese tunes, Japanese tunes (e.g. the national anthem—though its German-born reviser has introduced one irregular note), the tunes of the primitive hill tribes of India (the well-known old hymn tune 'There is a happy land' is an Indian hill melody), many African tunes ('Nobody knows the trouble I've seen' is one of many American Negro songs based upon the ancestral scale), some American Indian tunes, and tunes from still other parts of the world. The make-up of the scale (Doh-ray-me-soh-lah-doh) suggests an instinctive acoustic sanction. Its framework is the familiar Doh-me-soh-doh, and these notes are (in an order that disperses them over a wider range) the first three that come into the natural harmonic series (see *Acoustics* 8). The *ray* and *lah* are possibly such embellishments as would naturally accrue in approaching the *doh* and *soh* from above, for primitive singers would not be likely to trouble to take notes 'cleanly'. The smallest interval in this scale is the tone; at the stage of development it represents the human ear is probably as incapable of grasping semitones as many ears are today of grasping quarter-tones: travelling in Basutoland in the early days of the twentieth century the present author found the Christian natives singing magnificently in their churches, in four parts from sol-fa tune books, but tunes with many semitones were beyond them, these being foreign to their native scale, the pentatonic.

Looking at the pentatonic scale in this way,

it is natural to regard it as another approach than the Pythagorean to our common diatonic system. Probably whilst Pythagoras was experimenting and reasoning people all over the world were instinctively moving in the same direction: where Pythagoras raced ahead was in a train of thought that led him to the definite acceptance of an interval, the semitone, that might otherwise not have received its sanction of widespread European popularity until centuries later. As was affirmed at the opening of this article, both reasoning and intuition have gone to the making of scales. (For some discussion of the gapped scales of the Negro races see *United States* 6; *Harmony* 4; for gapped scales among the American Indians see *United States* 7.)

11. A Bagpipe Scale. Finally, a very extraordinary scale in common use today requires a word, extraordinary in that it exists side by side with very different scales—the Scottish Highland Bagpipe Scale (see *Bagpipe Family* 4). The compass of the instrument extends from G on the treble stave to A above it. The notes are roughly those to which we are accustomed in the white notes of the tempered scale of the piano (see *Temperament*), except that the C and F are about a quarter-tone sharp.

The precise definition of notes used in music can be accomplished only by means of vibration numbers, and this, in the case of the tune-collector, means the use of the microphone and subsequent study of the records in the physical laboratory. Throughout this article, then, statements as to notes being common to scales can be only approximate, and there is, for instance, no guarantee that the third in the pentatonic scale above mentioned, as in use in different parts of the world, is exactly the same third in all, for the recording explorers or students of music of various countries may have notated it as the third to which they were accustomed at home. In the case of the Highland bagpipe we have, however, something more than a mere deviation of a few vibrations, and it is a somewhat romantic circumstance that one nation should have been able to preserve in actual use scales so different as the pentatonic, the diatonic major and minor scales, and the strange scale above mentioned. It is to be noted, however, that this last scale is in use only instrumentally, and it would be interesting to know whether any Scot but a bagpiper could, if called upon, *sing* it or its tunes correctly.

12. 'Artificial Scales.' What may, for convenience, be called by this name are the scales that have not 'grown up' but have been deliberately invented by individuals. Some of them have already found a place in the present article (e.g. the Whole-tone Scale, and the Microtonal Scales) and the nineteenth and twentieth century exploring mentality of rest-

less composers has led to the creation of others. Here are a few examples:

(*a*) Verdi, in the Ave Maria of his *Four Sacred Pieces*, made use of a *canto fermo* based on a so-called 'Enigmatic Scale' ('*Scala Enigmatica*')—C, D flat, E, F sharp, G sharp, A sharp, B, and C ascending, with the F sharp changed to F natural on descending.

(*b*) A scale of alternating tones and semitones has been used by many composers, notably the Russian school: in the symphonic interlude, 'Battle of the Kerzhenetz' (from the opera, *The Legend of the City of Kitezh*), Rimsky-Korsakof makes use throughout of this scale.

(*c*) Scriabin derived a six-note scale from his 'Mystic Chord', C, D, E, F sharp, A, B flat, C (or, set out as a series of superposed fourths, C, F sharp, B flat, E, A, D, C).

(*d*) Alexander Tcherepnin (q.v.) has introduced a nine-note scale, C, C sharp, D sharp, E, F, G, G sharp, A, B, C.

Several attempts have been made by the theorists to systematize artificial scales. **Busoni,** in his *New Esthetics*, states that he has invented one hundred and thirteen different scales of seven notes. The Italian, **Domenico Alaleona** (q.v.) suggested scales based on the equal division of the octave into several parts. **Alois Hàba** (q.v.) in his *Neue Harmonielehre*, gives a table of intervallic formations that generate new scales. **Joseph Schillinger** (q.v.) devised scales with several tonics. In 1947 **Nicolas Slonimsky** (q.v.) published a *Thesaurus of Scales and Melodic Patterns*, listing two thousand three hundred artificial scales and melodic progressions of his devising.

(For two particularly curious scales see references below.)

13. Conclusion. Summarizing the main points of this article: The number of scales existing or that have existed is enormous: there is no scale with higher authority than the rest, since all have served and are serving their purpose of allowing man to express his emotion and his sense of beauty. Active young composers of today often experiment with new scales of their own contrivance. Some of these are perhaps too artificial, and make demands on the ear that could be met only by the abnormally gifted. As an example may be mentioned the twelve-note scale promulgated by the Russian composer, Nicholas Obouhof (1892–1954), which consists of the normal major scale with an Oriental pentatonic scale superposed; the temperament (q.v.) of this latter differing from the temperament in European use, we get five notes doubly represented (so to speak) at slightly different pitches. For a curious scale not so extreme as this see under *Esplá*.

SCAMPANATA. See *Charivari*.

SCANDINAVIA

(For illustrations see p. 896, pl. **153**.)

1. Introduction. The name Scandinavia being variously applied, it is necessary to say at the outset of this article that it is here used in the most comprehensive sense, i.e. as taking in Norway, Sweden, Denmark, Iceland, Finland, and the various islands contiguous to their coasts. All these countries have some community of thought, resulting in some cases from racial relationship, in other cases from past or present political associations, common language types, a more or less common mythology and folk lore, or similarity of literary and artistic activity. They stand rather noticeably apart from the Teutonic, Latin, or Slav affiliations of most of the rest of Europe, and it is convenient to treat them as a group.

In general they have not been looked upon as very advanced musically. Music has always been cultivated, but the contribution to the world's repertory has not so far been comparable with that of France, England, the Netherlands, Italy, Germany, or Russia (arranging these countries in roughly the order of their periods of initial musical importance). It was, indeed, only during the nineteenth century that they began to attract the attention of the outside musical world, and it is perhaps of some significance, as reflecting upon the northern temperament, that it was only with the general European efflorescence of musical romanticism (see *Romantic*) that they began to inscribe a few names in the records of universal musical fame. It was the highly romantic quality of Scandinavian folk tune, when it was at last allowed to impregnate Scandinavian composition, that gave Scandinavia an admitted musical 'standing'.

Paradoxically it was the deepening of Scandinavian *national* consciousness in the early nineteenth century, with the formation of societies for the fostering of national art and literature and the collection of national folk material (including folk melody), that led to the extension of the musical map of Europe northwards.

Yet there is a possibility that the earliest progress towards that combining of different sounds that for us today *is* music took place in these very regions. Giraldus Cambrensis, writing in the twelfth century of the fact noticed by himself that in Britain it was in the northern parts that the common people sang not in mere unison but in a sort of harmony, says, 'I believe that it was from the Danes and Norwegians, by whom these parts of the island were more frequently invaded, and held longer under their dominion, that the natives contracted their mode of singing' (see also 3, below).

2. Denmark enjoys the distinction (shared to some extent with Sweden) of possessing tangible relics of the musical life of prehistoric times. In a museum of Copenhagen are no fewer than nineteen specimens, found in peat bogs, of a well-fashioned curved bronze trumpet-like instrument, the **Lur**. This instrument dates from the Bronze Age, which in northern Europe extended from about 1800 B.C. to 900 B.C. The notes that were played can only be conjectured; a present-day player can obtain the fundamental note of the tube and eleven harmonics (see *Acoustics* 8), and it is reasonable to guess that the prehistoric musician's technique was equal to the obtaining of at least two or three of these.

Of music in the earliest historic times little is now known. With the gradual acceptance of Christianity in the ninth, tenth, and early eleventh centuries the Gregorian plainsong naturally became familiar, and its influence can be seen in folk song today.

The development of church music presumably took much the same course here as in other parts of Europe. In the twelfth century it shows the influence of the School of Paris (see *France* 2). In the early sixteenth century Flemish musicians were invited to the court and there composed music similar to that which their countrymen were composing in Italy and elsewhere (cf. *Italy* 4). At this period, the most important in Denmark's musical history, native composers composed a good deal of church music, as also madrigals, etc. The Reformation which immediately followed, being Lutheran and not Calvinistic, did not destroy ecclesiastical musical activity any more than it did in Luther's own country.

The English lutenist and composer Dowland was from 1598 to 1606 an honoured (and highly remunerated) official of the court of the music-loving Christian IV. This king maintained young musicians in London and Venice for the purpose of study (a group of four promising young men was, for instance, sent to London in 1611).

Amongst the very considerable number of other English performers employed at the Danish court about this time were Thomas Simpson and William Brade (violists and composers), Thomas Robinson and Francis (or Thomas) Cutting (lutenists), Darby Scott (harpist), John Price (pipe and tabor player), John Meinert (? Maynard; bass singer), and William Kemp (the famous morris dancer); whilst from Germany, a little later, came the great composer Schütz (three visits, 1633-44).

In the eighteenth century opera was a court amusement. Reinhard Keiser was in Copenhagen in the 1720s, serving for a few years as the royal musical director, and in 1749 Gluck was welcomed there. A number of Italian musicians were imported, amongst them

Giuseppe Sarti, who directed the court theatre from 1770 to 1775.

Up to this point, it will be realized, the court was the great centre of musical activity, and courts seek their entertainers in whatever country they can find them.

When a more nationalistic turn was given to Danish musical activity it was, strangely enough, one or two foreign musicans who were responsible. The German J. A. P. Schulz (1747–1800; p. 896, pl. 153. 1), who was Court Musical Director in the late 1780s and early 1790s, was much influenced in his compositions by Danish folk music and wrote songs and Singspiele (see *Singspiel*) in that style. His work marks an epoch in Danish musical history and from his period the Sing-spiel remained for some time a very popular form of entertainment in Denmark.

Three other Germans who followed up this lead were Cristoph E. F. Weyse (1774–1842), who not only showed the influence of folk song in his opera, etc., but published a valuable pioneer edition of such song; Fried-rich Kuhlau (1786–1832), the flute player and composer, who used national song in an opera (*Elverhöi*, 1828; still popular in Scandinavia and elsewhere today); and Friedrich L. A. Kunzen (1761–1817), who wrote a series of Danish operas, published a collection of Danish songs, and was regarded as the leading musician of his period. All these settled in Copenhagen and there died. The period was that of the poet A. G. Oehlenschläger (1779–1850), whose pro-lific production was largely of a nationalistic trend, and to him must be credited, in part, at any rate, the growth of Danish national feeling which inspired these adopted sons of Denmark.

Weyse, the German musician just men-tioned, was the teacher of the first Danish musician whose name became widely known outside his own country, Gade (1817–90), to whom is devoted a separate short article which should be consulted. Gade was influenced by Danish folk song and has sometimes been spoken of as 'saturated with national senti-ment', but Grieg put his case as it appears to most students of the period today when he said that Gade's was but an 'effeminate Scan-dinavianism'. With Gade were associated his father-in-law, the long-lived J. P. E. Hart-mann (1805–1900), and his brother-in-law, Emil Hartmann (1836–98); both wrote operas on Danish subjects and in the Danish language, as well as other works of national inspiration. A pupil of Gade was the successful song and opera composer, Peter Arnold Heise (1830–79).

Thomas Linnemann Laub (1852–1927) did thorough work in the study and publica-tion of both the old Danish chorales and the folk songs and folk-dance music.

The most important remaining names are those of Eduard Lassen and Carl Nielsen (q.v.), and more recently Poul Schierbeck (1886–1949), a pupil of Nielsen and the com-poser of music somewhat influenced by Ravel

and Roussell; Knudage Riisage (1897–1974), the chairman of the Danish section of the International Society for Contemporary Music, who studied in Paris, and whose orchestral piece *Qarrtsiluni* is well known; Svend Erik Tarp (born 1908), also French influenced; Jøgen Bentzon (1871–1951); Finn Hoffding (born 1899); Vagn Holmboe (born 1909), and Niels Viggo Bentzon (born 1919).

Among the group of composers writing in the twelve-note idiom are Flemming Weiss (born 1898); Bernhard Lenkovitch (born 1927), Ib Norholm (born 1931), and Per Norgaard (born 1932).

A musicologist of distinction is Knud Jeppesen (born 1892), a pupil of Laub and Nielsen.

The one great cultural centre of Denmark is Copenhagen. It has an active musical life, with a Royal Theatre in which opera is given two or three times a week, a Conservatory of Music, and a university with a musical depart-ment.

Broadcasting in Denmark is under govern-ment control, much as in Britain.

3. Norway. The rapid sketch of Denmark's musical development that has just been given shows a continuous activity, largely dependent on royal support and foreign artistry, blossom-ing out in the nineteenth century into a more widespread and more national expression. The musical history of Norway, though it is be-lieved to show the existence of some precocity in the early stages of musical development, shows less in the middle stages, and then, like that of Denmark, a sort of release of the national musical spirit as soon as the Romantic Movement of Europe, already active in litera-ture and painting, touches also music.

The precocity alluded to is claimed by the distinguished Norwegian musicologist, Dr. Georg Reiss (1861–1914). Briefly, his findings go to confirm, after eight hundred years, the ingenious guess of Giraldus Cambrensis, alluded to at the opening of the present article. It is his theory that the practice of polyphony did indeed begin in Norway and Iceland in the age of the Vikings (see also 5, below) and he maintains, further, that a considerable instru-mental development occurred at this same early period.

In the later centuries, whilst music was, of course, cultivated in the several cities, it did not apparently develop much individuality, but depended, even more than was the case in Denmark, upon importations, German and Italian compositions usually supplying the staple of performance. It is suggested by Reidar Mjöen, in his thoughtful article in Adler's *Handbuch der Musikgeschichte* (1930), that 'The Classical style, with its objectivity and formalism . . . was rather far removed from the Norwegian temperament'. Romanticism, he says, 'offered greater liberty to the Nor-wegian instinct for free lyrical and subjective expression'.

Importance is attached to the work of **Valdemar Thrane** (1790–1828), who in 1824 roused his countrymen with a Singspiel of racial and national colouring, *Fjeldeventyret* ('Tales of the Mountain'), and to that of **L. M. Lindeman** (1812–87), a great organist (he gave recitals in London at the inauguration of the Albert Hall organ), who issued a collection of 600 Norwegian folk melodies, still a standard work.

Ole Bull (1810–80; p. 1097, pl. **182.** 3), the patriot violinist, is also a leading figure in this movement, as is **Kjerulf** (1815–68), especially famous for his songs, and, a little later, **Nordraak** (1842–66), who in his brief life accomplished much and inspired others to more.

At this point it may be considered that the Norwegian School is established, and for a little more information on the three personalities last mentioned, as well as on the greater ones of **Grieg, Svendsen,** and **Sinding,** the reader may be referred to the short articles on other pages of this volume (other Norwegian composers separately treated are Jensen, the Backer-Gröndahls, Sigurd Lie, and Ole Olsen).

The collection of Norwegian folk music has been fostered by the Norwegian government, which in 1898 made a grant to the composer **Catharinus Elling** (1858–1942), whose researches resulted in several useful treatises.

Norway possesses several distinctive instruments. The **Langleik** (also found in Iceland under the name *Langspil*), used until near the end of the eighteenth century, was a sort of developed monochord (q.v.): it had two strings controlled by movable bridges and plucked by a plectrum whilst the other (open) strings were plucked by the fingers (cf. *Zither* for a similar general arrangement). The **Hardangerfele** ('Hardanger Fiddle') is a violin with sympathetic strings (q.v.). It is short-necked and has a low bridge, making chord-playing easy; the oldest known example of the instrument is dated 1651. It is much used for dancing the halling (q.v.) and other Norwegian dances, and the player greatly embellishes his tunes, hardly playing them the same way twice.

The general style of Norwegian folk-song and folk-dance melody is known to the world through the work of Grieg, which, though not employing the actual folk tunes, is largely based on their characteristics. The device of the drone-bass is a good deal used in instrumental music (see references to 'Pedal' under *Form* 12 d; *Harmony* 14, 24 p; cf. *Bagpipe Family* 8).

4. Sweden. The general lines of the musical history of Sweden are much the same as those of that of Denmark.

Christianity was introduced in the ninth century. The plainsong of the Church in succeeding centuries developed certain particularities, some of which have been learnedly discussed by C. A. Moberg of Uppsala (*Über die schwedischen Sequenzen,* 1927). In the sixteenth century Flemish and Italian musicians were a good deal employed. The Re-

formation, which took place in 1527, was, as elsewhere in Scandinavia, Lutheran (see remarks under Denmark above). In the seventeenth century a number of English musicians are found visiting Stockholm. In 1637 Buxtehude was born in Helsingborg (then, however, Danish), where his father was organist, but he did not spend many years there.

Johan Helmich Roman (1694–1758) is called the 'Father of Swedish Music'. After study in London (under Ariosti and Pepusch), and a brief English career as violinist, he returned to Sweden and became director of the court music, living at times also in France, Italy, and, again, England. He was an active composer (with nothing of a Swedish style, however), and the translator of foreign theoretical treatises, of choral works of Handel, etc.

In the eighteenth and early nineteenth centuries French influence was rather strong.

King Gustaf III built a Royal Opera House at Drottningholm, near Stockholm, in 1773 and it is still preserved almost exactly in its original state—with thrones for the king and queen and benches in raised tiers for members of the court and officials, down to a stool for the king's barber.

Just as in Denmark we find German musicians first showing the way to a Danish musical nationalism, so in Sweden we find a French musician doing so—**J. B. E. L. C. Dupuy** (or Edouard Du Puy, or Camille Dupuy; 1770–1822), who produced the operas *Ungdom og Galskab* (1806) and *Björn Jernsida* (posthumous and incomplete).

But the first Swedish composer to strike the Swedish note at all loudly was **Ivar Hallström** (1826–1901), who based many of his operas and operettas on Swedish subject-matter and used folk tune as a principle. He has been called 'The Swedish Glinka'. At the same period **August Söderman** (1832–76) was active and won high approval.

A considerable patriotic activity made itself felt in musical ways about this period. There came into existence societies for the revival of folk dance and festivals of folk dance and folk song. There was also a movement towards the greater development of folk material in music composition, which, however, weakened under the growing popularity of Liszt and Wagner.

In 1881 **Andreas Hallén** (1846–1925) made an attempt at a Swedish music drama. His *Harold the Viking* was given at Leipzig in 1881 and at Stockholm in 1882, but it did not hold the boards. He also attempted tone-poems on Swedish subjects, but without lasting success. His activities were very varied and his production copious.

The number of nineteenth- and twentieth-century Swedish composers of serious value is rather large. The following have separate treatment in the present volume: **Atterberg, Natanael Berg, Berwald, Blomdahl, Broman, Larsson, Nystroem, Rosenberg, Sjögren, Wirén.**

Amongst others who have done distinguished

work are Wilhelm Peterson-Berger (1867–1942), Wilhelm Stenhammar (1871–1927), Hugo Alfvén (1872–1960), Ture Rangström (1884–1947), and Oskar Lindberg (1887–1955). A number of younger men are at work—many of them banded into an active Society of Swedish Composers.

Sweden has distinguished herself in the production of fine women sopranos—e.g. Jenny Lind (1820–87), Christine Nilsson (1843–1921), and Ellen Gulbranson (1863–1947).

There is a very active concert life in Stockholm, and the Royal Opera House is a fine one. There is also a Royal School of Music. The Royal Musical Academy, founded at the end of the eighteenth century, is a learned society responsible for the advancement of musical culture: the Royal School above mentioned is an offshoot from it. The Mazerska (named from Johan Mazér, a wealthy amateur violinist and violin maker), founded in 1849, continues its activities as a mixed professional and amateur society for the practice of chamber music on informal lines, with tobacco and refreshments. (Compare the similar seventeenth-century English activities under *Clubs for Music-Making*.)

The University of Uppsala has had a singing society since about 1625. The library of the university possesses a remarkable collection of musical manuscripts partly obtained through Sweden's ancient practice of seizing libraries in countries where she was at war, and partly by purchase (see *Young, William*). There is a famous series of duets (baritone and bass) depicting student life in Uppsala—the *Gluntarne* of Gunnar Wennerberg (1817–1901), politician, literary man, and musician.

In 1937 was published a collection of Swedish folk songs, initiated by Nils Andersson (1864–1921) and carried on by Olaf Andersson (born 1884; not related to his predecessor)—a selection from the more than 18,000 that had, by diligent work in the villages, been got together.

5. Iceland was colonized mainly from Norway from the ninth century onwards and the Icelandic language is the language formerly spoken in Norway, Sweden, and Denmark—Norraena. Whilst Danish and Swedish have changed (much as Italian and Spanish have changed from Latin), Icelandic has changed so little that the sagas of the twelfth and thirteenth centuries can easily be read today. The collection of rhymed and heroic songs called the *Edda* includes what amounts to an early version of that German *Nibelungenlied* which supplied Wagner with the basis of his cycle of music dramas. In early times Icelandic skalds (minstrels chanting the traditional epic and lyric poetry) were much employed at the Norse and Danish courts.

As the primitive language has remained, so has the music. The fifteenth-century Arnamagnaän Manuscript (now at Copenhagen) is the chief source for its historical study. The modes (q.v.) remain in force (the Lydian being

especially common; see example below), and the part-singing still, in places, at any rate, resembles that of other parts of Europe in the late tenth century. See *Harmony* 5 and compare the example there given with the following, as sung in Iceland today:

ÍSLAND, FARSÆLDA FRÓN.

(From an article by Mr. Eggert Stefansson in *World Radio*, 24 Feb. 1933; the harmonies seem to tally with those given in the *Icelandic Students' Song Book*, 1894.)

As bearing on the suggestion of Giraldus Cambrensis mentioned above under 1 (end) and 3, the reader may be reminded that there was a considerable coming and going between Iceland and the north of Scotland and Ireland in the tenth and eleventh centuries and that not only did Norwegians settle in those countries but Scotsmen and Irishmen settled in Iceland —which is a hundred miles nearer to Scotland than it is to Norway; the connexion between Iceland and Scotland was, then, in all probability a close one (as, by trade, it is today).

A custom popular to the end of the eighteenth century, then for a time somewhat neglected and now revived, is that of *kveda rimur*—the singing of a long traditional poem (such as that of Tristan and Isolde) to a short melody, varying the latter slightly at each verse. Particular individuals have a reputation as Rimur Tellers and on the long winter nights are to be found in one farm or another of their district. The priest and musician **Bjarni Thorsteinsson** at the end of the last century and the early part of the present one was busied in collecting the

Rimur and wrote a valuable book on the subject. The composer **Jon Leifs** has done similar work.

There has been a great increase of interest in more sophisticated types of music-making, such as choral singing of the kind found elsewhere in Europe; male-voice choirs are popular. The capital, Reykjavik (80,000 inhabitants —the total population of the country being only about 200,000), has now a concert life in summer. Popular composers of songs and choral music include Dr. Kaldalóns, Jón Laxdal and Pall Ísólfsson. Another outstanding composer, Leifs, has already been mentioned; in 1932 a society was formed for the publication of his work—no music having previously been published in Iceland. Other names are Hallgrímur Helgason, Jon Nordal, and Leifur Thórarinsson.

One of the traditional Icelandic instruments, the *Langspil*, has been alluded to above, under Norway. Another is the *Fidla*, also a stringed instrument.

Iceland, in the thirteenth and fourteenth centuries ruled by Norway, was in the latter century (with Norway) united to Denmark. In the early nineteenth century Norway regained its independence of Denmark, but Iceland did not. It has been since 1918 a completely independent and self-governing state, and is now a republic with its own president. Reykjavik possesses a flourishing conservatory and an active choral and orchestral society, as well as its own symphony orchestra and is often visited by performers of international reputation.

6. Finland. The Finns belong, for the most part, to a race different from that of the inhabitants of the other countries comprised in this article—i.e. to the Ugrian race; they have, racially, more affinity with the Hungarians than with the Swedes, Norwegians, or Danes (a considerable proportion of the most cultured Finnish nationals are, however, not racially Finns, being of Swedish descent).

Like Iceland, Finland possesses a vast literature of mingled history and myth in poetical form. After being orally transmitted for centuries, it was collected in 1835 by Elias Lönnrot, as *The Kalevala* (the title meaning much the same as the Walhalla of other Scandinavian legends). The publishing of the Kalevala, quickly recognized as one of the great epics of the world, was more than a literary event. It was both an expression and an 'inspiration' of a patriotism that was soon to affect all the arts, including music. It was followed by a collection of lyrical poetry, the Kanteletar. The **Kantele**, from which this takes its name, used to be the national instrument of Finland and can still be heard in the province of Karelia and, indeed, seems to be coming into general use again. It is a plucked stringed instrument of a simple type (somewhat like the zither), formerly with five strings (tuned G, A, B flat, C, D), later with as many as thirty. It has been

in use for 2,000 years and is much mentioned in the Kalevala. (See also *Bagpipe* 7.)

Finland began to accept Christianity in the twelfth century, largely by the efforts of two Englishmen, Bishop Henry of Uppsala, left behind by King Eric of Sweden, who had conquered the country (martyred and now Finland's patron saint), and Thomas. As time went on church music developed considerably in Turku (Swedish name, Åbo; the second city of Finland and its former capital), where the cathedral became a centre of musical activity.

A good many manuscripts of church music remain from the period of the Neumes (see *Notation* 2) onwards.

When the Reformation reached Finland in 1528 it was of the Lutheran type, which was favourable to the cultivation of church music. Gregorian chant and other existing church music were adapted to the Finnish language.

A collection of religious school songs in from one to four voices ('Piae Cantiones'), made by **Theodoricus Petri Ruuth** (**Ruuta** or **Rwtha**), was published in Germany in 1582, has gone through countless later editions up to 1776, and was republished in 1910. This book had, to some extent, an international character and circulation (especially in all the territories then administered by Sweden).

In the seventeenth century Turku had a Guild of Town Musicians, and in 1640, when its university was founded, music formed a part of the curriculum.

In 1790 Turku possessed a musical society, with an amateur orchestra and choral and chamber music activities. This lasted until 1835, when, on the transference of the capital (after a disastrous fire at Turku) to Helsinki (Helsingfors), a new society was there formed under the direction of **Fredrik Pacius** (1809–91).

The university had, in 1828, been transferred to the new capital and Pacius was appointed its Professor of Music. He was a German, a pupil of Spohr, an excellent violinist, and the composer of several operas (one of them on a libretto taken from the *Kalevala*), of patriotic songs, and other things.

Pacius was followed at the university by another German, **Richard Frederik Faltin** (1835–1918), who composed choral works, etc., fostered church music, and published arrangements of Finnish folk songs. He was a fine organist and choral and orchestral conductor, and contributed much to the success of the opera organization founded in 1870.

In 1882 a conservatory of music came into being in Helsinki. It was directed by **Martin Wegelius** (1846–1906), a Finn by birth but trained in Vienna and Leipzig. He has importance as the teacher of the new school of Finnish composers that shortly sprang into existence—**Sibelius, Järnefelt, Melartin, Palmgren,** to all of whom (as also to **Kilpinen** and **Merikanto**) short separate treatment is given on other pages of the present volume. Associated with him in the musical forward movement of Helsinki and of Finland in general was **Robert Kajanus** (1856–1933), another Finn, but trained at Leipzig, Paris, and Dresden; as composer (especially of symphonic poems based on incidents from the Kalevala), Professor of Music at the University, and conductor he exercised valuable influence. Under him the Helsinki orchestra attained an international status, giving at one period performances in Germany, France, Belgium, England, etc., and thus making Finnish music more generally known.

Finland has now an active band of young composers, some of whom will probably make their way gradually into the field of international recognition and call for notice in some future edition of this work. Development has been greatly helped by the generous attitude of the government, which has made grants that in some other countries would be considered lavish towards musical education, the support of composers (see *Sibelius*), etc.

The absence of a royal court (for Finland was a province of Sweden from the twelfth century to 1809 and attached to Russia thence onwards to 1917, when it became an independent republic) militated in earlier periods against the higher development of performance and composition (see article *Patronage* for a general discussion of this question; compare Denmark and Sweden above). Today royalty and the court life of a country count for little or nothing in the development of the arts, which depend upon wider suffrages, and musical Finland is holding her own.

Finnish folk tune has been said to show three clearly recognizable strata.

The earliest is of a recitative-like character, with narrow tonal range.

The second is the more developed type of the Rune melodies, with definite rhythms of considerable variety, of which the five-footed one (five measures to a phrase) is the most characteristic: in this stratum, also, the melodic range is slight, being often no more than a fourth or fifth. Runes such as the following

(from the Kalevala) were sung in a peculiar manner. Two singers sat on stools facing one another and with fingers interlocked. One sang a line and the other repeated it after him, whilst they rocked themselves backwards and forwards in time with the music. The repetition of each line was connected with the element of improvisation that entered into the recitation of the rune; it gave the narrating musician time to think out the form in which he would present the next line. (This feature and that of the metre were, of course, imitated by Longfellow in his *Hiawatha*.)

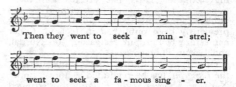

Then they went to seek a min - strel;

went to seek a fa - mous sing - er.

The stratum of latest formation employs a greater melodic range and much variety of rhythms and largely falls into the four-bar phrases that we nowadays consider the musical norm; like the folk music of many other northern countries it is often modal (see *Modes*); there are a good many religious songs.

The systematic collection of folk music began soon after 1800, and about 15,000 tunes have so far been collected. They are gradually being published in a great edition. The composer **Ilmari H. R. Krohn** (1867–1960) has published valuable studies of both the secular folk music of Finland and its traditional church song. The influence of Finnish folk tune on Finnish composition of the late nineteenth and twentieth centuries is very marked.

It may be added that the neighbouring Estonian people have a similar body of folk song. The *Eesti Runoviised*, published in 1930, containing over 2,500 runes, clearly demonstrates the racial and cultural relationship between Estonia and Finland.

SCARLATTI (Father and Son). The father, Alessandro, was born in Sicily in 1660 and died at Naples in 1725, aged sixty-five. The son, Domenico, was born at Naples in 1685, and died at Madrid (not Naples, as often stated) in 1757, aged seventy-one.

(1) ALESSANDRO (p. 516, pl. **93. 7**) was the great opera composer and founder of the Neapolitan school of opera. He was brought up in Rome, where, when he was about twenty-one, an opera of his attracted the attention of the self-exiled Queen Christina of Sweden, who made him her musical director. Four or five years later the Spanish viceroy at Naples appointed him to the same position in his court.

After about twenty years there, disappointed at the viceroy's musical taste and his treatment of him, he settled in Rome again, occupying

church posts and composing operas and some church music; but the Pope did not approve of opera, and life became a little difficult.

After a few years he was tempted back to Naples by the offer of increased salary and better treatment, and his brilliant period began, his best works being written now and his fame attaining great heights. It appears, however, that he later slipped back to Rome again, Naples having ceased to applaud him so generously as before. And so between those two cities he had for a lifetime alternated.

His great work lay in the realm of opera and that of the chamber cantata (see *Cantata*), of which latter form he wrote five hundred examples. His lifetime ended (1725) shortly before that of Haydn was to begin (1732), and this has significance, for his development of harmony and the devices of form prepared the way for the great achievements of the Haydn–Mozart period.

See *Oratorio* 2, 7 (1680); *Symphony* 2; *Chamber Music* 6, *Period* III (1660); *History of Music* 5; *Overture* 1; *Aria*; *Folia*; *Roseingrave, Thomas*; *Patronage* 8; *Intermezzo*; *Dukas*; *Knighthood*; *Nightingale*.

(2) DOMENICO (p. 516, pl. **93**. 8) was the great touring keyboard virtuoso of his age. He was born in the same year as Handel, and when they were twenty-three, being both in Rome, they competed together at the instigation and under the refereeship of the great lover of music, Cardinal Ottoboni; they were adjudged equal on the harpsichord, but Handel was considered the winner on the organ. Thenceforward they held each other in that mutual respect which forms the surest basis for a life friendship.

Domenico held several court positions of importance and was for a time musical director of St. Peter's at Rome, composing church music. He also spent his last twenty-eight years in Spain, thus influencing Spanish harpsichord composition.

His delightful compositions are very numerous. Quantities of them bear the name 'Sonata', but this word is not used in the modern sense (vide *Sonata* 5). They embody many points new in their day, including effects obtained by crossing the hands (though Domenico became very stout in old age and this effect, if not denied him, became at least difficult).

The techniques of keyboard playing and keyboard composition owe much to him. Like his father's, his life-work was foundational.

See *Italy* 6; *History* 5; *Spain* 8; *Harmony* 22; *Harpsichord Family* 5; *Étude*; *Cantata*; *Folia*; *Roseingrave, Thomas*; *Nicknamed Compositions* 17; *Capriccio*; *Patronage* 8; *Longo*; *Tommasini*.

SCEMANDO (It.). 'Diminishing', i.e. in volume of tone. Same as *diminuendo*.

SCENA. See *Cantata*.

SCENARIO. The skeleton libretto that precedes actual work on the writing of the full libretto of a play or opera: it shows the characters required, the number of scenes with a précis of each, the places where the chief dramatic and musical climaxes will occur, and so forth.

(**Scenarium**, in German, is a different thing: it is a complete libretto with the full directions inserted for the scenery of each act.)

SCHAEFFER, PAUL. See *History of Music* 9.

SCHÄFER, DIRK. Born at Rotterdam in 1873 and died at Amsterdam in 1931, aged fifty-seven. He studied in his native place and in Cologne and Berlin. He toured as a virtuoso pianist and composed much music for his instrument, as also chamber music, choral music, and orchestral music. He made Amsterdam his centre.

SCHALE, SCHALEN (Ger.). Cymbal, cymbals. See *Percussion Family* 3 o, 4 b, 5 o.

SCHALKHAFT (Ger.). 'Roguish.'

SCHALLBECKEN (Ger.). Cymbals.

SCHALMEY. See *Oboe Family* 2.

SCHARF (Ger.). 'Sharply' (in various connexions, as *Scharf betont*, given out with emphatic accent).

SCHÄRFE (Ger.). 'Sharpness', definiteness, precision.

SCHARWENKA (The Brothers).

(1) LUDWIG PHILIPP. Born near Posen, East Prussia, in 1847 and died at Bad Nauheim, Upper Hesse, in 1917, aged seventy. He studied and then taught in Berlin, latterly taking charge of the private conservatory founded there by his brother. His compositions include symphonies and other large-scale works, much chamber music, and many pleasant smaller piano pieces.

(2) XAVER (in full, Franz Xaver). Born near Posen, in East Prussia, in 1850 and died in Berlin in 1924, aged seventy-four. He, too, studied at Berlin. He then travelled as a piano virtuoso, having considerable success in England in both this capacity and that of composer. In 1881 he opened a conservatory in Berlin (see above), and ten years later a branch in New York.

He received royal honours in Germany and academic honours in America, and left behind him the reputation of an exceedingly fine pianist, of a gifted teacher, and of a fluent and graceful composer of symphonies, piano concertos, an opera (produced at the Metropolitan Opera House, New York), as well as a quantity of instrumental music, especially some attractive smaller pieces for piano.

SCHAURIG, SCHAUERIG, SCHAUERLICH (Ger.). 'Ghastly', 'gruesome'.

SCHEIBE. See *Criticism* 2.

SCHEIBLER, JOHANN HEINRICH (1777–1838). He was a silk manufacturer who applied himself to problems of tuning, making remarkable experiments and introducing ingenious inventions in connexion with the Jew's harp (q.v.) and then with tuning-forks (see *Pitch* 6 b).

SCHEIDEMANN, HEINRICH. Born in Hamburg about 1596 and there died in 1663. He was a very famous organist, the pupil of Sweelinck at Amsterdam and the predecessor of Reinken at St. Catherine's, Hamburg. He wrote keyboard music and religious songs.

SCHEIDT, SAMUEL. Born at Halle in 1587 and there died in 1654, aged sixty-six. He was a pupil of Sweelinck and a famous organist and organ composer. His *Tabulatura Nova* (1624) set a new standard in organ-playing, by showing how to make it less showy and more significant, more coherent and purposeful. His *Tablaturbuch* of 1650 is a series of harmonized chorales.

See references under *Notation* 4 (Staff); *Chorale Prelude*.

SCHEIN, JOHANN HERMANN. Born at Grünhain, Saxony, in 1586 and died at Leipzig in 1630, aged forty-four. A century before Bach he held the position of Cantor at St. Thomas's, Leipzig, being Bach's most illustrious predecessor there.

He was the very prolific composer of works of high importance in the history of the development of German music—important especially as profiting by Italian models. These included works for church choir, madrigals, instrumental compositions, etc. He edited an important book of chorales (his *Cantional*, 1627).

SCHELLE, SCHELLEN (Ger.). 'Bell', 'bells'.

SCHELLENBAUM (Ger.). 'Bell-tree', i.e. Turkish Crescent (q.v.).

SCHELLENGELÄUTE (Ger.). 'Bell-ringing', i.e. sleigh-bells.

SCHELLENTROMMEL (Ger.). 'Bell-drum', i.e. tambourine; see *Percussion Family* 3 m, 4 c, 5 m.

SCHELLING, ERNEST (p. 1057, pl. **172**. 4). Born at Belvedere, New Jersey, in 1876 and died at New York in 1939, aged sixty-three. He was a virtuoso pianist who benefited by the counsels of Paderewski, and the composer of effective (if derivative) compositions which are distinguished by facility and a degree of imagination.

In late years Schelling laboured industriously in the field of musical education, especially as conductor of the children's orchestral concerts of the New York Philharmonic Society and of other orchestral organizations in various American cities.

SCHELMISCH (Ger.). 'Roguish.'

SCHEMELLI HYMN-BOOK. This is the English title generally used for the *Musikalisches Gesang-Buch* (1736), of 954 sacred poems, compiled by a German cantor, Georg Christian Schemelli (*c.* 1676–1762). Its importance comes from the fact that he employed Bach as musical editor of the 69 tunes included. A certain small proportion of these were actually of Bach's own composition (how many and which being a matter of some difference of opinion amongst authorities). Many of the items are rather sacred songs than congregational hymns.

SCHENKER, HEINRICH. Born in Galicia in 1868 and died in Vienna in 1935, aged sixty-six. He was a pupil of Bruckner, a composer, an editor of the piano classics, and the author of voluminous theoretical works of a severely Teutonic philosophical nature and expressive of highly revolutionary views.

SCHERZ (Ger.). 'Fun', 'joke'; so *Scherzend*, *Scherzhaft*, 'jocular'.

SCHERZANDO, SCHERZANTE, SCHERZEVOLE, SCHERZEVOLMENTE (It.). 'Jokingly', 'playfully'; so the superlative *Scherzantissimo*.

SCHERZARE (It.). 'To joke.'

SCHERZETTO, SCHERZINO (It.). A short scherzo (q.v.).

SCHERZO, in Italian (plural 'Scherzi'), means a 'joke'. The use of the word in music goes back as far as Monteverdi, who in 1628 published some light and popular choral pieces under the title *Scherzi musicali* ('musical jokes'), and even

before that—indeed into the late sixteenth century. The suggestion of the word must not be taken too literally. There were actually published in 1614 *Scherzi sacri* (by Cifra, in Rome), so even at this early date the main musical connotation of the word was not actual humour but brightness.

Nowadays the word is applied solely to instrumental music, sometimes to independent pieces, but more commonly to that movement of the sonata (see *Sonata* 7, 8), symphony, string quartet, etc., which would otherwise be a minuet. It was Haydn who quickened the music of the minuet and reduced its resemblance to the rather sober and very formal dance to accompany which was its original function. He adopted the word 'Scherzo', in place of 'Minuet', first in an early piano sonata and then in certain string quartets (op. 33), but then reverted to the word 'Minuet' for a time.

Most (but not all) scherzos retain one relic of their minuet derivation—they are in three-beats-in-a-measure time. Their form is sometimes that of the minuet and trio (see *Form* 6 and *Minuet*); often, however, they are more extended.

Beethoven is looked upon as the father of the scherzo as we understand it today. He made his scherzos bustling pieces, often humorous and, indeed, sometimes droll, though (as in that of the Fifth Symphony) he could on occasion introduce a touch of deeply reflective or even mystical poetry. It is interesting to observe how, as he goes on, he increases the speed of the scherzo. Early ones are usually allegretto, and later successively allegro, allegro vivace, and presto (this last in the Seventh Symphony, where the word 'scherzo' is no longer used, though the movement occupies the place of the scherzo and is in its spirit). With and from Beethoven the triple time that derived from the minuet is often abandoned.

Mendelssohn has given us a delightfully feathery or fairy-like type of scherzo.

Chopin's four famous scherzos for piano are no jokes—they are full of a robust but gloomy vigour.

SCHERZOSO, SCHERZOSAMENTE (It.). 'Playful', 'playfully'.

SCHIERBECK, POUL. See *Scandinavia* 2.

SCHIETTO (It.). 'Sincere', 'unadorned'. So the adverb *Schiettamente* and the noun *Schiettezza*.

SCHIKANEDER, EMANUEL JOHANN (baptized Johannes Josephus; 1751–1812). He was a Viennese theatre director who compiled the libretto of *The Magic Flute* and persuaded Mozart, an old friend of Salzburg days and a brother Freemason, to write the music. He wrote a large number of libretti for other composers.

See *Magic Flute*.

SCHILLINGER, JOSEPH. Born at Kharkof in 1895 and died in New York in 1943, aged forty-seven. He was active as a teacher of composition and as a collector of Georgian folk song, and distinguished himself as a discoverer of 'the Principles of Automatic Composition applied to sound, light, and action', which principles 'are based on mathematics and provide a basis from which the graphic arts, sculpture, music, cinema, speech, and literature, can be executed'. Amongst his works are *The Schillinger System of Musical Composition; a Scientific Technique of Composing Music* (2 vols., 1600 pages; posthumous) and *Electricity, a Liberator of Music*.

He wrote a good deal of chamber and orchestral music. From 1929 he lived in the United States (see *Electric* 1 d), where he collected a large following. There are Schillinger courses in some American universities.

See also *Scales* 12.

SCHILLINGS, MAX VON. Born at Düren in 1868 and died in Berlin in 1933, aged sixty-five. He was a noted conductor and as composer has been described as 'a tasteful follower of the modern German direction'.

SCHINDLER.

(1) ANTON (1795–1864). He was a close friend of Beethoven and his first biographer. See reference under *Accent* 1.

(2) KURT. Born in Berlin in 1882 and died in New York in 1935. He was an orchestral and choral conductor, a composer, and a man of wide musical learning—in the last capacity devoting himself especially to studies in Russian and Spanish folk and other music, of which he published collections and on which he published treatises. He founded and conducted a choral society in New York—at first (1909) called the MacDowell Chorus and later the Schola Cantorum.

SCHIRMER. See *Publishing* 9; *Nicholls, H. W.*; *Sonneck*.

SCHKRAUP, FRANZ (1801–62). See *Bohemia*.

SCHLACHT (Ger.). 'Battle.'

SCHLAG (Ger.). 'Stroke', 'blow'.

SCHLÄGEL (Ger.). Drum-stick.

SCHLAGEN (Ger.). 'To strike.'

SCHLAGINSTRUMENTE (Ger.). Percussion instruments; see *Percussion Family*.

SCHLAGZITHER. 'Striking-zither', i.e. one in which the strings are struck instead of plucked, i.e. a form of dulcimer (q.v.), 'zither' being a misnomer.

SCHLANGENROHR (Ger.). Serpent. See *Cornett and Key Bugle Families* 2 d, 3, 4 d.

SCHLEGEL (Ger.). Drum-stick.

SCHLEIFER. See *Ländler*; *Slide*.

SCHLEPPEND (Ger.). 'Dragging' (generally used in the negative—*Nicht schleppend*).

SCHLUMMERLIED (Ger.). 'Slumber song.'

SCHLUSS (Ger.). 'Conclusion', end.

SCHLÜSSEL (Ger.). Clef. See *Notation* 4.

SCHLUSSSATZ. See under *Satz*.

SCHLUSSZEICHEN (Ger.). 'Close-sign', i.e. the double-bar with pause which indicates the end of a repeated portion which is to close a movement.

SCHMACHTEND (Ger.). 'Languishing.'

SCHMALTZ (from Ger. *Schmalz*—'fat'). The term employed in the United States for romantic sentimentality in general.

SCHMEICHELND (Ger.). 'Coaxingly.'

SCHMELZEND (Ger.). 'Melting', i.e. dying away.

SCHMERZ (Ger.). 'Pain', 'sorrow'. So *Schmerzlich, Schmerzhaft, Schmerzvoll*, 'painful', 'sorrowful'.

SCHMETTERND (Ger.). 'Blared' in horn-playing—notes produced as 'stopped' (i.e. with the hand inserted in the bell), combined with hard blowing. The usual indication with British composers is + together with an *ff*.

See *Horn Family* 5.

SCHMIDT.

(1) BERNHARD (organ-builder). See *Smith*.

(2) ARTHUR P. See *Publishing* 9.

(3) FRANZ. Born at Pressburg or Pozsony (now Bratislava) in 1874 and died near Vienna in 1939, aged sixty-four. He was originally a cellist, but his career included important educational positions in Vienna (director of the Hochschule, etc.) and he wrote operas, symphonies, chamber music, organ music, etc., and a delightful series of variations for piano (left hand alone) and orchestra.

SCHMITT.

(1) ALOYS. Born at Erlenbach-am-Main in 1788 and died at Frankfort in 1866, aged nearly seventy-eight. He was a notable piano pedagogue and young people of all civilized nations have passed millions of hours in his company by the medium of 'Exercises'—now largely discarded as lacking musical interest.

(2) FLORENT (p. 385, pl. 64. 8). Born at Blâmont, near Nancy, in 1870 and died at Neuilly in 1958, aged eighty-seven. He studied at the Paris Conservatory under Massenet, Fauré, and others, and won the second Rome Prize in 1897 and the first in 1900. At Rome he wrote his remarkable Psalm 46. His compositions are many and varied—orchestral, chamber, vocal, piano, and dramatic. In his earlier works (especially) he ranks almost as an Impressionist (see *Impressionism*). He was fond of writing on a large scale and often for large resources (he was a remarkable orchestrator), and as to subjects he had a taste for the powerfully dramatic.

See *Harp* 4; *Expression* 2; *Saxophone*; *Psalm*; *History* 9.

SCHNABEL, ARTUR (1882–1951). Austrian pianist and composer. See *Germany* 9 a.

SCHNABELFLÖTE. See *Recorder Family* 2.

SCHNARRE (Ger.). 'Rattle.' So *Schnarrtrommel*, snare-drum (see *Percussion* 3 i, 4, 5 i), *Schnarrsaite*, 'rattle-string', being the snare. But the *Schnarrwerk* of an organ is the reed department.

SCHNECKENBURGER, MAX. See *Watch on the Rhine*.

SCHNEIDEND (Ger.). 'Cutting sharply', defining.

SCHNEIDER, JOHANN CHRISTIAN FRIEDRICH. See *Oratorio* 3, 7 (1823). In addition to the activities there recorded he was a busy choral conductor and the author of several theoretical works.

SCHNELL, SCHNELLER (Ger.). 'Quick', 'quicker'. So *Schnelligkeit*, 'speed'.

But *Schneller*, in addition to its adjectival meaning of 'quicker', has a substantival application as another name for the *Upper Mordent*, or 'Pralltriller' (see Table 12; *Mordent*).

SCHOBERT, JOHANN. Born about 1720 at some place unknown, and died in Paris in 1767, aged about forty-seven. His works are no longer heard, but we still profit by his labours, since as harpsichordist and composer he exercised influence upon the development of the art of the Haydn–Mozart period.

He died of eating toadstools, and with him his whole household.

SCHOECK, OTHMAR. Born at Brunnen, on Lake Lucerne, in 1886 and died at Zürich in 1957, aged seventy. He had a high reputation as a choral and orchestral conductor, and composed a large number of songs (including several cycles), choral music, chamber music, orchestral music, and some operas (including *Venus*, 1922, and *Massimilla Doni*, 1937). Zürich was his centre of activities; in 1934 the orchestra of Berne gave a week's festival performance of his works.

SCHOELCHER, VICTOR (1804–93). He was a French literary man, politician, and musical amateur, who wrote an important life of Handel (1857). See reference under *Rule, Britannia!*

SCHOEMACHER, MAURICE. See *Synthétistes*.

SCHOENBERG. See *Schönberg*.

SCHOFAR. Same as *Shofar* or *Shophar*, the ancient synagogue horn of the Jews.

SCHOLA CANTORUM. Schools for church song are of very ancient origin (see under *Singing* 3). That of Rome is said to have been founded in the fourth century. St. Gregory (cf. *Plainsong* 3, 4, and *Modes* 2, 5, 6) at the end of the sixth century much developed the system. From the Roman School were sent out instructors (for a reference to one sent to England and two sent to the court of Charlemagne, see *Plainsong* 3, 4). It soon became the custom for cathedrals and abbeys to maintain such schools (the existing choir school of York Minster dates from 627), and in Church Latin the term is still in use to signify the choral body of such a foundation. In its earlier and more correct sense the term is used by Pope Pius X in his *Motu Proprio* (q.v.) of 1903—'Found wherever possible [in theological colleges] a Schola Cantorum with a view to the execution of sacred polyphony and good liturgical music', and 'It is not difficult for the clergy to found these schools, even in the small churches, and country churches . . . as a means of training children and young people for their own advantage and the edification of the population'.

The English song schools and the Scottish 'Sang Scuils' or 'Sang Schoolis' carried on the tradition up to the Reformation, and in some cases beyond (see *Singing* 3; *Presbyterian Church Music* 3; *Scotland* 4; *Education and Music* 1).

Modern institutions for the study or practice of sacred song have sometimes taken the name. See *d'Indy* and *France* 10 (also *Bordes*; *Guilmant*) for that of Paris, which is, however, a full-scale conservatory.

SCHOLES, PERCY ALFRED. Born in Leeds in 1877 and died at Vevey, Switzerland, in 1958, aged eighty-one. Largely because of early poor health, he was educated privately; he became an organist and schoolteacher, at the same time being active as a journalist and lecturer, gaining prominence in the 'Music Appreciation' movement. In 1908 he founded the *Music Student* (later the *Music Teacher*). He wrote for the *Evening Standard*, and later was appointed chief music critic of the *Observer* (1920–7, in succession to Ernest Newman) and the *Radio Times* (1923–9).

An advantageous contract to write annotations for pianola rolls enabled him to withdraw to Switzerland and tackle single-handed the task of writing the *Oxford Companion to Music*, which appeared in 1938, and by which he is best known. In addition to many books on music appreciation he produced several more scholarly works, including *The Puritans and Music* (1934) and *The Great Dr. Burney* (1948), with whom in breadth of interest and robust common-sense he perhaps felt an affinity.

See *Dictionaries* 1, 5, 15.

SCHOLIA ENCHIRIADIS MUSICA. See *Harmony* 5.

SCHOLL, NICOLAS. See *Rákóczy March*.

SCHÖNBERG, ARNOLD (p. 416, pl. **71**. 1). Born in Vienna in 1874 and died in Los Angeles in 1951, aged seventy-six. His musical development began early and showed itself chiefly in the playing of violin and cello and the composition of chamber music. Zemlinsky (q.v.) encouraged and guided him. He was long engaged in a struggle for bare existence, and supported himself by the orchestration of thousands of pages of other people's theatre music and by conducting theatre orchestras.

His romantically emotional string sextet, *Verklärte Nacht* ('Resplendent Night', 1899), and the enormous score of his choral–orchestral *Gurrelieder* ('Songs of Gurra', 1900–13; see under *Schreker*) are deeply tinged with Wagnerian idiom; on the strength of the latter Strauss awarded him the Liszt Fellowship and secured him a place on the staff of the Stern Conservatory in Berlin; Mahler was another of his supporters. There followed the symphonic poem, *Pelléas and Mélisande* in which his chromatic, polyphonic style reached the limits of tonality.

In his next period he developed a style of a quite uncompromising individuality, largely atonal, and the *Three Piano Pieces* and *Five Orchestral Pieces*, the drama with music *Die glückliche Hand* ('The Lucky Hand'; completed 1913), and the cycle of twenty-one poems, *Pierrot lunaire* (1912), show its growth, which, however, by no means ceased with the last-named works. From 1915 there were eight years of silence, during which he experimented privately with his 'method of composing with twelve notes' (see *Note-row*), which was his solution to the problem of organizing music without a tonal centre. In 1923 and successive years appeared the *Five Piano Pieces* op. 23, the *Serenade* op. 24, and numerous other works.

He emigrated to the United States in 1933, becoming naturalized in 1940. He lived in Los Angeles, and was on the staff of the University of California[1] (1936–44).

These last years saw his Violin Concerto (1936), the *Ode to Napoleon* (1942), the Piano Concerto (1942), and a string trio (1946), showing a more relaxed treatment of the Note-row technique. An opera, *Moses and Aaron*, remained unfinished, though two acts have been performed.

He wrote a *Manual of Harmony* (1911 and ater editions) and another of *Counterpoint* (1911), these on orthodox, traditional lines, and also a book *The Theory of Composition* (1940), and through his personal teaching and his example influenced many younger composers in Austria, Germany, and later in France, Italy, and the United States. He painted also, professing allegiance to the school of his friend, the founder of the Expressionistic School in painting, Kandinsky (see *Expressionism*). Moreover, he was (according to his own account of himself in *Who's Who*) active in 'tennis, ping-pong, and book-binding'.

As a child he was a Catholic. At eighteen he became a Protestant, and in 1933 assumed the Jewish faith. His personality was intransigent and uncompromising and he nursed grudges against those he considered his enemies. None the less he was loyally supported by many friends, and in turn gave his own affection, notably to his pupils Berg and Webern.

See *Arrangement*; *Berg*; *Cage*; *Chamber Music* 6, Period III (1874); *Colour and Music* 11; *Expressionism*; *Germany* 8, 9; *Harmony* 18, 21 (near end); *Hauer*; *History* 7, 8, 9 (note); *Jazz* 7; *Leibowitz*; *Mann, T.*; *Melodrama*; *Milhaud*; *Monn* 1 and 2; *Notation* 7 (three allusions); *Opera* 24 f (1957); *Oratorio* 7 (1947); *Percussion Family* 4 a (near end), 4 d (Iron Chains); *Pisk*; *Recitative*; *Romantic*; *Russia* 8; *Schreker*; *Song* 6; *Suite* 8; *Symphony* 8.

For paintings by him see p. 356, pl. **57**. 3, 4.

SCHONBERG, HAROLD C. Born in New York in 1915. He was educated at Brooklyn College and New York University, and worked as music critic on various newspapers, joining the staff of the *New York Times* in 1950 and becoming its chief music critic in 1960. He is the author of a historical book on pianists and another on conductors.

[1] During his last few years he adopted the spelling 'Schoenberg'.

'SCHOOLMASTER' SYMPHONY (Haydn). See *Nicknamed Compositions* 11.

SCHOOL OF ENGLISH CHURCH MUSIC. See *Anglican Parish Church Music* 7; *Schools of Music*.

SCHOOLS' MUSIC ASSOCIATION. This organization was formed in 1938 to carry on the work of the non-competitive schools' music festivals. It arranges courses, advises teachers, and organizes national festivals.

SCHOOLS OF MUSIC. The earliest schools of music were those organized by the church to secure the proper rendering of her plainsong (see *Education and Music* 1; *Schola Cantorum*).

The introduction of schools of music of the modern kind, in which a wide range of musical subjects is taught and a professional training given, occurred first in Italy. The first such schools were orphanages and the name 'Conservatorio' (with its French equivalent 'Conservatoire') records the fact; an Italian–English dictionary of today will be found under this head to include 'poor-house, girls' school, school of music', or some such series of meanings. Naples was the great centre for conservatories for boys, the first being founded in 1537, and Venice for those for girls, though these latter were at first called Ospedali, i.e. Hospitals. (Cf. *Singing* 7; p. 752, pl. **123**. 1.)

The Président de Brosses (q.v.) in his *Letters from Italy* (1739), gives a description of the music of the orphans of the Venetian 'Hospitals'. He says:

'They are educated and maintained at the expense of the State, and their sole training is to excel in music. Thus they sing like angels, and play the violin, flute, organ, oboe, violoncello, and bassoon—in fact there is no instrument so big as to intimidate them. They are cloistered like nuns. They perform without outside help, and at each concert forty girls take part. I swear there is nothing prettier in the world than to see a young and charming nun, in a white frock, with a spray of pomegranate flowers over her ear, conduct the orchestra and give the beat with all the exactness imaginable.'

In 1774 the English musician, Charles Burney (q.v.), having studied the organization of these institutions during his travels in Italy, issued a *Plan for a Music School*, his idea being to establish it in connexion with the Foundling Hospital in London. His 'Plan' was not well received, and the first professional school of music in England was not founded until almost a half-century later—the Royal Academy of Music (1822); it was not an orphanage, but pupils were at first admitted at an early age and all lived on the premises (p. 289, p. **51**. 5); it had a clergyman as 'Head-Master', as well as a principal (Crotch, q.v.). It is, of course, still active, in a very much enlarged and modernized form. The Royal College of Music followed a half-century after this (1873 as the National Training School of Music; reorganized 1882 under its present title). Trinity College of Music dates from 1872. These are national institutions situated in London, the first two of them operating on royal charters. The City of London maintains its own institution, the Guildhall School of Music (1880). Amongst schools of music outside London are the Royal Irish Academy of Music in Dublin (1848; re-organized eight years later), the Royal Manchester College of Music (founded by Hallé in 1893), and the Royal Scottish Academy of Music, Glasgow (founded in 1930 on the basis of the Glasgow Athenaeum School of Music, dating from 1890). Specialist schools are the Royal Military School of Music, Kneller Hall, Twickenham (1857), and the Royal School of Church Music (1929) with its associated College of St. Nicholas, both now at Croydon.

Apart from the Italian conservatories, some of them dating back to the days of the orphanage system, the earliest founded school of music now existing in Europe is the Paris Conservatory, founded, under another name, in 1784; it has had a very distinguished history. Many of the smaller cities of France have conservatories.

Central and northern Europe have many conservatories. That of Prague is one of the oldest (1811). The Vienna Conservatory dates from 1817 (a state institution only since 1909). The Leipzig Conservatory was founded by Mendelssohn in 1843; the list of its alumni is very imposing. The Berlin Conservatory was founded in 1850, as was that of Cologne. Geneva has had a Conservatory since 1835; Brussels (one of the oldest) since 1813. These are just a few. It will be seen from the dates given that, apart from the Italian orphanages, we may consider the conservatory as, in general, a product of the early nineteenth century.

There is an immense number of institutions of the conservatory kind in the United States of America, some of them independent and some attached to universities. It was in the 1860s that such institutions began to appear. That of Oberlin, Ohio, was founded in 1865, those of Boston (New England Conservatory), Cincinnati, and Chicago (Musical College), in 1867, the Peabody Conservatory, Baltimore, in 1868, and so on.

Amongst specially endowed institutions of this kind are the New York Institute of Musical Art (1904; since 1926 connected with the Juilliard Foundation); the Eastman School of Music, Rochester, N.Y. (1919); the Curtis Institute, Philadelphia (1924); and the Juilliard School of Music, New York (1924). Also in New York are the Manhattan (1917) and the Mannes (1916) Schools of Music. There is no other country in the world in which, at the present time, such generous provision is made for the training of talented young musicians (including those of small financial resources) as the United States.

In Canada notable institutions are the Conservatories of Montreal (McGill University) and Toronto. South Africa has a school of music at Cape Town, as well as smaller institutions. Australian conservatories attached to universities are Adelaide and Melbourne Sydney has one not so attached—the State Conservatorium of New South Wales; see references under *Bainton*; *Goossens* 3.

SCHÖPFUNGSMESSE (Haydn). See *Nick-named Compositions* 13.

SCHOTT. See *Publishing* 8.

SCHOTTISCHE. A round dance, a sort of slower Polka (q.v.). When first danced in England, about the middle of the nineteenth century (which was the period of the Polka invasion), it was called 'the German Polka'. It has no resemblance to the Écossaise, with which it is confused in some German dictionaries of music; the Écossaise (q.v.) is a country dance (q.v.) and the Schottische a round dance. Both are, however, in two-in-a-measure time.

The German word is *Schottisch* (meaning either 'Scottish' or the dance here in question), the final 'e' being an English, and sometimes French, addition.

For the *Schottische Bohème* see *Polka*.

SCHRAMMEL QUARTET. This is a popular Viennese type of instrumental quartet for light music. The name perpetuates the memory of Johann Schrammel (1850–93), a good violinist, who, with his brother (also a violinist), Danzer (a clarinettist), and Strohmeyer (a guitarist), won great fame for the performance (and composition) of Viennese waltzes, marches, etc. The accordion later took the place of the clarinet, as it still commonly does. Sometimes the combination expands somewhat, into a 'Schrammel Orchestra'.

SCHRAMMKAPELLE (Ger.). A combination of (generally) two violins and zither, playing folk songs. The word may be connected with the name of Johann Schrammel (see above) or may derive from *schrammen*, to scratch.

SCHREKER, FRANZ. He was born at Monaco in 1878 and died in Berlin in 1934, aged fifty-six. He studied at the Conservatory of Vienna, the violin being his major study.

His various compositions attracted notice and were early performed not only in Vienna but in other European centres. At thirty he was conductor of the Popular Opera House (Volksoper) at Vienna, had founded the Vienna Philharmonic choir (which gave performances of many modern works, including the first one of the elaborate and difficult *Songs of Gurra* of Schönberg), and had become a Professor of Composition at the Conservatory at which he was trained. He later became the head of the State High School of Music at Berlin, and then, in 1932, resigned this position, becoming a Professor of Composition at the Prussian Academy of Arts. When the Nazi government came into power in 1933, a suspicion arose that he was guilty of the crime of some measure of Jewish descent. The shock of events caused a stroke and he suddenly died.

PLATE 157

SCHUBERT LEAVING THE COFFEE HOUSE

By Batt

AMONG the haunts of Schubert's circle Bogner's Coffee House, in the Singerstrasse, was the favourite. The droll cry of a waiter there was always an attraction and greatly amused him. The interior of this Coffee House would sometimes present a strangely interesting spectacle, for there, sitting alone at a table in the corner, the solitary figure of Beethoven could be seen, quite unaware of the identity of the timid little Schubert, who, too scared to approach the formidable presence, would sit silently amongst his companions with reverent gaze fixed upon the lonely figure in the corner.

Above is pictured the Coffee House as it was in those historic days, with Schubert, as he must frequently have been seen, walking away from it.   B.

Schreker's fame as a composer is mainly based on his operas, which have been much performed in German and Austrian opera-houses (See *Opera* 24 f—1912–18–24–28.) He wrote his own libretti, which had an erotic tendency. He may be styled a Neo-Romantic (see *Romantic*) with a leaning to Expressionism (q.v.).

SCHRITTMÄSSIG, SCHRITTWEISE (Ger.). 'Step-style', 'step-wise', i.e. at a walking pace (= *Andante*).

SCHROEN, B. See *Trombone Family* 4.

SCHROETER.

(1) CHRISTOPH GOTTLIEB (1699–1782). See *Pianoforte* 3, 4.

(2) JOHANN SAMUEL (1750–88). See *Harpsichord Family* 7; *Pianoforte Playing* 1.

SCHTSCHERBATCHEW (and similar spellings). See *Stcherbatchef*.

SCHUBART, CHRISTIAN FRIEDRICH DANIEL (1739–91). Court music director at Stuttgart, author on musical subjects, and composer. See reference to one of his books under *Cornett and Key Bugle Families* 3 a–c.

SCHUBERT.

(1) FRANZ PETER (p. 944, pl. **159**). Born in Vienna in 1797 and died there in 1828, aged thirty-one. He was Beethoven's contemporary in Vienna (twenty-seven years his junior) and like Beethoven he represents the classical school of Haydn and Mozart carried forward into the opening of the 'Romantic Period'.

Like Beethoven, too, he wrote symphonies, sonatas, and string quartets, but, unlike him, he developed a special talent for that type of solo song which, whilst tuneful and musically delightful, yet seizes characteristically the meaning and flavour of the poem and expresses these aptly. This form of art (see *Zumsteeg* and *Loewe*) owes more to him than to any other one composer in history.

He composed with infinitely more ease and fluency than Beethoven and the list of his works seems very long when one considers the brevity of his lifetime; some of them show a weakness of form or content, due to rapidity and facility that were so great that on occasion he was known to fail to recognize his own work when it was put before him. His gift for pure and lovely melody is one of his greatest charms and in this he stands worthily beside Mozart.

He was the son of a schoolmaster with a small income, and his early life was not luxurious. But he had the advantage of being a member of an intensely musical family, whose string quartet playing was renowned in their suburb.

At eleven he was admitted to the choir school of the Royal Chapel, and here he received a good general and musical education, with insufficient food and little comfort. On finishing his course here he became for a time an assistant in his father's school, but his whole being was absorbed in music and soon he abandoned everything for it, living sparely and then only subsisting by the help of generous comrades who believed in him.

Some of these friends were afterwards famous as painters or poets; others belonged to the cultured bourgeois class. They were members of a different 'set' from the more aristocratic music lovers who in the same city and at the same period surrounded and supported Beethoven, and the elder and younger musicians met only as the former lay on his death-bed, when, as is recorded, he was moved to an expression of generous admiration and confident prophecy.

Schubert carried a torch at the high ceremonial of Beethoven's funeral and next year was buried beside him. He left worldly property of the tiniest value and a huge mass of lovely music—more, perhaps, than the world will ever have time to know.

Like Beethoven, Schubert was never married. His elder brother, Ferdinand, a schoolmaster–musician like the rest of the family, and a minor composer, was one of his most devoted supporters, and deserves here this word of recognition.

Schubert's Pianoforte Sonatas, as numbered in their various edns. and their mention in recital programmes, are in a very confused state. The following list rectifies this. It was supplied by Richard Capell in the *Daily Telegraph* on 12 Nov. 1938, being based by him on the researches of H. Költzsch (*Schubert in seinen Klaviersonaten*, 1927). No. 1, in E, 3 movements (1815). No. 2, in C, 3 movements; there may have been finale now lost (1815). No. 3, in E, 5 movements (1816; publ. 1843 as *5 Klavier-stücke*, '5 Piano Pieces'). No. 4, in A flat, with finale in E flat (1817). No. 5, in E minor, 2 movements (1817); an unpublished Scherzo may belong to it, and the Rondo called op. 145 may be its finale. No. 6, in E flat (op. 122, 1817); 1st publ. in 1830. No. 7, in F sharp minor (1817); unfinished, but completions exist by Heinz Jolles and W. Rehberg. No. 8, in B (op. 147, 1817). No. 9, in A minor (op. 164, 1817). No. 10, in C (1818); unfinished. No. 11, in F minor (1818); unfinished; completion exists by W. Rehberg. No. 12, in C sharp minor (1819); fragmentary. No. 13, in A (op. 120, 1819—not later as sometimes stated). No. 14, in A minor (op. 143, 1823). No. 15, in C (1825); minuet and finale unfinished, completions by L. Stark, E. Křenek, and W. Rehberg. No. 16, in A minor (op. 42, 1825). No. 17, in D (op. 53, 1825). No. 18, in G (op. 78, 1826). No. 19, in C minor (1828). No. 20, in A (1828). No. 21, in B flat (1828).

Schubert's Symphonies are as follows (but a few are sometimes differently numbered): No. 1, in D (1813). No. 2, in B flat (1814–15). No. 3, in D (1815). No. 4, in C minor, nicknamed the *Tragic* (1816). No. 5, in B flat (1816). No. 6, in C (1817 or 1818). No. 7, in E (1821); sketched out in 4 movements; it has been completed and orchestrated by J. F. Barnett (1883) and Weingartner (1935). No. 8, in B minor, the *Unfinished* (2 movements only, 1822 1st perf. 1865; publ. 1867); completions have been supplied by Frank Merrick and others. No. 9 in C (1829, sometimes called No. 7, sometimes No. 10—the latter counting the *Gastein* (see below) as No. 9). There is a mere sketch of one in E minor (1820). The *Grand Duo*, for piano (op. 140) has been scored as a symphony by Joachim, and also by Anthony Collins. There is supposed to be one lost symphony, called the *Gastein Symphony* from the place (in the Tyrol) of its composition; the date is thought to be 1825; some think the *Grand Duo* to be an arrangement of it.

References to him and his work are scattered through this volume as follows: *Accompaniment*; *Arpeggione*; *Arrangement*; *Atterberg*; *Ballad* 5; *Chamber Music* 6, Period III (1797); *Clarinet Family* 6; *Compositions* 6 (on his song-writing), 8, 10 (fecundity as composer); *Concerto* 6 b (1797); *Criticism* 6; *Écossaise*; *Flute Family* 6; *Germany* 5, 6; *Gesamtausgabe*; *Guitar*; *Harmony* 12; *Haydn, J. M.*; *History*, 6, 7; *Hungary*; *Impromptu*; *Lachner, Franz*; *Ländler*; *Liszt*; *Loewe*; *Mass* 2, 4; *Misattributed*; *Moment Musical*; *Nicknamed* 18; *Nottebohm*; *Oratorio* 3, 7 (1863); *Patronage* 6; *Pianoforte* 20; *Polonaise*; *Programme Music* 5 e (near end); *Romantic*; *Singing* 10; *Sonata* 10 d (1815); *Song* 5; *Song Cycle*; *Song Without Words*; *Stabat Mater*; *Symphony* 5, 8 (1797); *Trombone Family* 3, 4; *Waltz*; *Zumsteeg*. Also p. 768, pl. **129**. 4.

(2) FRANZ. Born at Dresden in 1808 and died there in 1878, aged sixty-nine. This Franz Schubert, a violinist, is of no serious importance, but ought to be mentioned in all works of musical reference on account of an error that constantly occurs, his busy, buzzing trifle *L'Abeille* ('The Bee') being assumed to be by the earlier and greater composer of the same name. (Sometimes, apparently in the effort to create a distinction, this Schubert is called 'François'; the best plan, however, would be to write of him as 'Franz Schubert of Dresden'.)

SCHUBERTH. See *Publishing of Music* 8.

SCHÜCHTERN (Ger.). 'Shy.'

SCHULFLÖTE. See *Recorder Family* 3 b.

SCHULHOFF.

(1) JULIUS. Born at Prague in 1825 and died in Berlin in 1898, aged seventy-two. He was a piano virtuoso who toured widely in Europe and America, and composed effective drawing-room music for his instrument (cf. *Carnival of Venice*), as well as some more serious compositions that have remained less known.

(2) ERWIN. Born at Prague in 1894 and died in a Nazi concentration camp in 1942. He was distantly related to the above, and a composer of 'modern' vein. His works are numerous and include music for *Le Bourgeois Gentilhomme* which employs jazz effects.

SCHULLER, GUNTHER. Born in New York in 1925, of a musical family, he was a professional horn player from the age of sixteen until 1959. The techniques of composition he largely acquired on his own, becoming a notable follower of the paths opened by Webern and an active propagandist of modern music, as also for jazz, on which subject he has written an important history.

See *History* 9.

'SCHULMEISTER' SYMPHONY (Haydn). See *Nicknamed Compositions* 11.

SCHULTZ, WILLIAM EBEN (b. 1887). See *Ballad Opera* (near end).

SCHULTZ, SCHULTZE, SCHULZ. See *Praetorius*.

SCHULZ, J. A. P. (1747–1800). See *Scandinavia* 2; p. 896, pl. **153**. 1.

SCHUMAN, WILLIAM HOWARD (p. 1069, pl. **176**. 1). Born in New York in 1910. He studied at Columbia University and joined the staff of Sarah Lawrence College, Bronxville, N.Y. In 1939 his promise as a composer gained him a Guggenheim Fellowship. He has composed seven symphonies as well as other large-scale orchestral works, chamber music, choral works, etc. For a period he was director of publications at G. Schirmer; in 1945 he became head of the Juilliard School of Music, New York, then from 1961 until 1968 he was President of Lincoln Center. He has been the recipient of many honorary degrees.

See *Concerto* 6 c (1910); *Ballet* 5.

SCHUMANN.

(1) ROBERT ALEXANDER (p. 932, pl. **158**). Born at Zwickau, in Saxony, in 1810 and died near Bonn in 1856, aged forty-six. He stands as the typical example of the influence of literature upon music in the early nineteenth-century German Romantic School. His father, who was devoted to the English romantic writers, especially Scott and Byron, was by profession a bookseller and publisher, and the boy breathed a thoroughly bookish atmosphere; he became devoted to the writings of the two German romantic writers, Hoffmann and Jean Paul (Richter), and the fantastic element in their work showed its influence on his ever after.

He received the regular classical education and was intended for the law, but at the university his surreptitious musical practice occupied more time than those legal studies in which duty was supposed to engage him. He became a friend and pupil of the great piano pedagogue, Wieck, whose daughter Clara, then a child, later became his wife, and, as one of the most accomplished artists amongst pianists of her time, was largely responsible for the world's knowledge of her husband's compositions. (She was also herself a by no means insignificant composer—chiefly of piano music and songs.)

He also engaged in journalism, founding and editing a musical paper which fought powerfully against the weaknesses and follies of the musical life of the day, and did enormous service by leading into the lighted circle of public recognition Chopin and some lesser yet worthy composers who might, without such help, have lingered much longer in outer darkness.

It has been customary to group together Chopin, Schumann, and Mendelssohn, not only because they were born within a period of eighteen months but because (though their individualities are pronounced) they represent the same general stamp of what we may call the more refined romanticism.

In various official positions Schumann's dreamy and unpractical nature precluded entire success, but as a composer he was winning serious recognition and as a critical authority

PLATE 158

THE INTROSPECTIVE SCHUMANN

By Batt

WHILE Schumann lived in Leipzig it was his custom, after the day's work, to retire to Poppe's 'Kaffeebaum', where students and others were wont to congregate in a spirit of good fellowship. There was a particular corner which attracted him because it was secluded. There he would sit at the table, with his beer and a pipe or cigar, and sometimes read the newspaper, but more often, perhaps, become lost in his own thoughts. On these latter occasions he would sit with his chin resting on his hand and gaze at the wall with half-closed eyes, his mouth pursed as if whistling: sometimes he actually did whistle, but softly and to himself. B.

exercising large influence, when he was struck down by a mental malady which led to attempted suicide, and at last, death in an asylum.

The works he left include quantities of piano music and songs, much chamber music, some choral music, four symphonies, and a fine piano concerto. The orchestral works are usually held to suffer a little from a thickness and lack of variety in the instrumental colourings.

Information about certain of Schumann's titles that sometimes puzzle Pianists.

Op. 2. **Papillons** ('Butterflies'). The name is a mere 'fancy title', suggesting lightness and grace, but the music was inspired by Jean Paul's novel *Die Flegeljahre* (i.e. 'Years of Hobbledehoyhood').

Op. 6. **Die Davidsbündler**, or *Davidsbündler-Tänze* ('The David's-Band', or 'David's-Band Dances'). The David's-Band was an imaginary group of opponents of all 'Philistines' that was often referred to in Schumann's periodical. 'Florestan' and 'Eusebius' were the chief individuals in it, and represent two sides of Schumann's own character—the active and the reflective. The pieces in this set were signed 'F' or 'E'. (The 'Davidsbündler' come into 'Carnival', also, in a 'March against the Philistines'.)

Op. 9. **Carnaval. Scènes mignonnes composées sur quatre notes** ('Carnival. Tiny Scenes composed on Four Notes'). A masked ball is the idea. The 'four notes' are A.S.C.H. ('S' = 'ES' = E flat; 'H' in German is B in English'; thus the four notes are A, E flat, C, B.) 'Asch' is the name of a town where the composer had a lady friend and the four letters happen also to be, he pointed out, 'the only musical letters in my name'. The 'Sphinxes' ('not to be played') which appear in one place in the course of the score represent 'SCHumAnn', AsCH (A flat = 'As' in German) and ASCH. The whole idea is very fanciful, but good music results.

Op. 16. **Kreisleriana**. Kreisler is a clever, wild, eccentric musician who figures as the hero of a fantastic romance of E. T. A. Hoffmann (q.v.).

Op. 21. **Novelletten** ('Novelettes'). The composer spoke of them as 'longish connected romantic stories'. (See *Novelette*.)

Op. 26. **Faschingsschwank aus Wien** ('Carnival Jest from Vienna'). The gay Vienna life is here, and the main point of the jest is in the first piece, where the *Marseillaise*, at that time forbidden in Vienna, finds its way into the music.

Schumann's Symphonies are as follows: No. 1, in B flat, the *Spring Symphony* (op. 38, 1841). No. 2, in C (op. 61, 1846). No. 3, in E flat, the *Rhenish* (op. 97, 1850; inspired by Cologne Cathedral). No. 4, in D minor (withdrawn after 1st performance in 1841; revised in 1851 and published as op. 120).

To these may be added the *Overture, Scherzo, and Finale* (op. 52, 1841; finale revised 1845).

References to Schumann, of greater or lesser importance, will be found as follows: *Germany* 6, 9; *History* 7; *Holland* 6; *Nationalism*; *Romantic*.
Accompaniment; *Mass* 4; *Melodrama*; *Requiem*; *Singing* 10; *Song* 5; *Song Cycle*.
Albumblatt; *Alternativo*; *Ballad* 5; *Burla*; *Chamber Music* 6, *Period III* (1810); *Characteristic Piece*; *Composition* 9; *Concerto* 6 b (1810); *Form* 5; *Harmony* 21; *Hoffmann, E. T. A.*; *Humoresque*; *Impromptu*; *Intermezzo*, 5, 6; *Manfred*; *Novelette*; *Phantasie*; *Polonaise*; *Programme Music* 2, 5 d; *Sonata* 9, 10 c d; *Symphony* (1810); *Toccata*; *Waltz*.
Clarinet Family 6; *Gramophone* 6; *Harp* 3; *Horn Family* 4; *Metronome*; *Oboe Family* 6; *Percussion* 4 b; *Scordatura*.

Expression 1; *Pedalier*; *Phrase Marks*; *Pianoforte* 13, 15, 18, 19, 20; *Pianoforte Playing* 5.
Absolute Pitch; *Ballet* 5; *Cinematograph*; *Colour and Music* 3; *Competitions* 1; *Composition* 5, 9; *Conducting* 5; *Criticism* 2, 4, 5, 6, 9; *Ear* 4.
Bargiel; *Bennett, Sterndale*; *Brahms*; *Bülow*; *Chopin*; *Franz*; *Heller*; *Jensen*; *Mendelssohn*; *Meyerbeer*; *Paganini*; *Vieuxtemps*.

(2) CLARA (1819–96) (p. 800, pl. **137**. 3). See under *Schumann, Robert*; *Pianoforte* 22; *Memory* 7; *Concert* 8; *Bargiel*; *Clavichord* 6.

SCHUNDA. See *Dulcimer*; *Clarinet Family* 4 h.

SCHUSTER, VINCENT. See *Arpeggione*.

SCHUSTERFLECK (Ger.). Rosalia. See *Sequence* 1.

SCHÜTT, EDUARD. Born in St. Petersburg in 1856 and died at Merano in 1933, aged seventy-six. He was a fine pianist, resident in Vienna, who published worthy piano music, as also chamber music, songs, a comic opera, etc.

SCHÜTTELN (Ger.). 'To shake.'

SCHÜTZ, HEINRICH (p. 396, pl. **67**. 2). Born in Thuringia in 1585 and died at Dresden in 1672, aged eighty-seven. His birth took place exactly a century before that of Bach, and he ranks as one of Bach's greatest precursors, bridging the gap between the earlier contrapuntal school of Palestrina, Byrd, Victoria, and their contemporaries in various countries (the school of the perfection of unaccompanied choral music) and the later contrapuntal school of Bach and Handel (the school of the perfection of accompanied choral music and of the definite laying of the foundations of modern instrumental music).

His very numerous works include psalms, motets, Cantiones Sacrae, Symphoniae Sacrae, madrigals, arias, etc. He composed the earliest German opera (*Dafne* 1627) but it is lost.

His settings of the Passion, in particular, prefigure Bach, but they have their own very high value in addition, and their composer stands forth sturdily as an artist and an historical personage in his own right. His complete works have been twice reprinted in modern times.

His life was spent, briefly, as follows. As a boy he was in the choir of the court chapel at Cassel. In early manhood he spent three years (1609–12) in Venice studying with Gabrieli (q.v.). Returning he became court organist at Cassel and then (1615) court Kapellmeister at Dresden. His middle life was, necessarily, much disturbed by the Thirty Years War (1618–48). He made frequent visits to Italy, keeping in touch with musical developments there.

The name 'Schütz' is also found latinized as 'Sagittarius.'

References will be found as follows: *Germany* 2, 3; *Gesamtausgabe*; *Oratorio* 3, 5, 7 (1623–64); *Passion Music* 3; *Cantata*; *Concerto* 1; *Seven Last Words*; *Psalm*; *Symphony* 1; *Hymns and Hymn Tunes* 4; *Programme Music* 5 b; *Opera* 9 a, 24 b (1627); *Scandinavia* 2; *Trombone Family* 3. Also p. 739, pl. **122**. 5.

SCHUYT. See *Holland* 3.

SCHWAB, FREDERICK. See *Criticism* 5.

SCHWACH, SCHWÄCHER (Ger.). 'Weak' (soft), 'weaker'. So *Schwächen*, 'To weaken'.

SCHWANKEND (Ger.). 'Swaying.'

SCHWARZENDORF. See *Martini* 2.

SCHWEBUNG (Ger.). 'Fluctuation.' So (*a*) the 'beats' between two notes nearly but not quite in tune (see *Acoustics* 16, *Harmony* 21); (*b*) tremulant stop of organ.

SCHWEIGEN (Ger.). 'Silence' or 'to be silent'. So *Schweigt = Tacet* (see *Tacere*). And *Schweigezeichen* ('silence-sign') = rest.

SCHWEITZER, ALBERT. Born at Kaysersberg, Upper Alsace, in 1875 and died at Lambaréné in the Congo in 1965, aged ninety. He was a philosopher and theologian of high distinction, a qualified medical man (founder and director of a hospital in Equatorial Africa), an organist, and one of the leading authorities on Bach. His many literary works, which cover all the above interests of his life, enjoy great repute and some have been translated into many languages. With his organ teacher, Widor, he prepared an edition of the organ works of Bach and his book on that composer is everywhere known.

See allusions under *Presbyterian* 1; *Organ* 8; *Arrangement*.

SCHWELLEN (Ger.). 'To swell', i.e. to increase in tone (*crescendo*). So *Schweller* is the swell of an organ, *Schwellwerk* being the swell organ and *Schwellkasten* the swell box.

SCHWER (Ger.). (*a*) 'Heavy' (in style), (*b*) 'difficult'.

SCHWERMÜTIG, SCHWERMUTSVOLL (Ger.). 'Heavy-hearted.'

SCHWINDEL. See *Schwindl* below.

SCHWINDEND (Ger.). 'Diminishing' (in tone, i.e. *diminuendo*).

SCHWINDL or **SCHWINDEL**, FRIED-. RICH. Born in Amsterdam in 1737 and died at Karlsruhe in 1786, aged forty-nine. He was a violinist, harpsichordist, flautist, and composer, who lived and worked, at various periods, in Holland, Switzerland, and Germany, his compositions (which enjoyed a good deal of favour) being published in several countries, including England.

See reference under *Symphony* 8 (1737).

SCHWIRRHOLZ. See *Thunder Stick*.

SCHWUNG (Ger.). 'Swing.' Hence *Schwungvoll*, 'full of go', 'vigorous'.

SCINTILLANTE (It.). 'Sparkling.'

SCIOLTO, SCIOLTAMENTE (It.). 'Not tied up', 'loosely', i.e. in a free and easy manner. So the corresponding noun, *Scioltezza*.

SCISSORS FUGUE. See *Nicknamed* 1.

SCIVOLANDO (It.). 'Sliding', i.e. *glissando* (q.v.).

SCONTRINO, ANTONIO. Born in Sicily in 1850 and died at Florence in 1922, aged seventy-one. He was an eminent double-bass player, composition teacher, and composer of operas, valuable chamber music, etc. His string quartets are of especial importance.

SCOOP. In singing, an exaggerated gliding from note to note.

SCORDATO (It.). 'Out of tune.' See *Scordatura*, below.

SCORDATURA (It.). Literally 'out of tuning', i.e. abnormal tuning of a stringed instrument for the purpose of producing some unusual note, facilitating some type of passage, or changing the general tonal effect. The most common instance remaining today is the tuning of the lowest string a semitone or tone lower in order temporarily to increase the compass. For instance, in the Andante of Schumann's Piano Quartet the C string of the violoncello is tuned down to B flat; in Wagner's *Rheingold* the E string of the double-bass is tuned to E flat; in the second movement of Mahler's Fourth Symphony a solo violin's strings are tuned A–E–B–F; and in Kodály's Sonata for unaccompanied violoncello the C string is tuned to B and the G string to F sharp.

For a composition for three violins and violoncello, using nothing but open strings in *scordatura* throughout, see *Franklin*.

Cf. *Biber*.

SCORE. A music copy which shows the whole of the music—as distinct from a mere 'part', which shows that of one performer.

A *Full Score* shows not only the whole, but each part separately displayed, i.e. it is a combination of all the parts, orchestral and vocal (if any) placed one above the other.

An *Orchestral Score* is the full score of an orchestral work.

A *Vocal Score* of a choral work shows all the vocal parts but with the orchestral parts reduced to a piano version.

A *Piano Score* is the reduction of an orchestral score to a piano version; a *Short Score* is the same, or a similar reduction, but not necessarily adapted for a piano performance.

A *Miniature Score* is a full score of pocket size.

Scoring has two meanings: (*a*) deciding upon and committing to paper the orchestration of a work already conceived, and (*b*) taking the separate parts of a work and assembling them as a score (as in the case of a sixteenth-century composition, for instance, which has been preserved only as a set of 'parts').

SCORRENDO, SCORREVOLE (It.). 'Scouring' (a country), etc. Hence (*a*) gliding from note to note = *glissando*; (*b*) in a flowing style.

SCOTCH CATCH. Same as Scotch Snap (see below).

SCOTCH SNAP. A short note (on the beat) followed by a long one (occupying the rest of the beat). It is a feature of the strathspey (q.v.) and is also found in some Scottish song-tunes, but there are a good many popular tunes of which it is a feature that are not of Scottish origin at all, but are merely relics of the London rage for Scottish balladry of the eighteenth century, which brought into existence many sham-Scottish melodies (see *Scotland* 1) for the theatres and for Ranelagh, Vauxhall, etc. (see *Concert* 12). James Hook (q.v.) was one of the chief manufacturers of these, but the Italian opera composers who came to London also con-

tributed. No Scottish song earlier than the eighteenth century seems to have the snap and the question of its provenance is at present difficult to answer.

See allusions under *Robin Adair*; *United States* 6 (for Negro use of the device).

SCOTLAND

1. Folk Songs.
2. Folk Dances.
3. Instruments.
4. Sang Scuils.
5. Church Music.

6. Music at Court.
7. Lack of Early Instrumental Music.
8. Lack of Madrigals.
9. Publication of Music.

10. Edinburgh as a Musical Centre.
11. Various Activities.
12. List of Articles amplifying the present one.

The present article is designed to offer merely a brief conspectus of the history of music in Scotland, further information on almost every branch of the subject being given under the appropriate heads scattered throughout this book. A list of some of the chief of these heads appears at the end of the article.

1. Folk Songs. Scottish folk song is abundant and beautiful; it is equally remarkable for pathos and vigour. The Highland songs approximate somewhat to the Irish, the Lowland to the northern English. The Hebridean songs, to which attention was called from the early days of the twentieth century by the active collecting and publication of Mrs. Kennedy-Fraser (q.v.), show an enormous range of expression; there are songs recording history and legend, religious songs, love songs, and songs setting the rhythm for the processes of various handicrafts. Earlier work in Scottish folk song is represented by the *Highland Vocal Airs* of Patrick Macdonald (1781), and in the collection of Keith Norman Macdonald (1895) and that of Frances Tolmie (*Folk Song Society's Journal*, 1911).

Some Scottish folk songs are modal (see *Modes*) and the pentatonic scale (see *Scales* 10) forms the basis of others. A good many songs often considered Lowland Scottish are, or have been, current in the English countryside also, and others are not folk songs at all, but are the products of a London drawing-room and theatre craze for Scottish song at the end of the seventeenth century and the early part of the eighteenth, to which craze popular English composers lent themselves; the beginnings of this movement can be seen as early as Playford's *English Dancing Master* issued during the Commonwealth. (Cf. *Scotch Snap*.)

Not so much as the title of any Scottish song is known prior to the fifteenth century, and the earliest remaining written records of the music are in the Rowallan, Skene, Straloch, and Panmure manuscripts (for the last three see 7), all belonging to the twenties of the seventeenth century; these manuscripts also include some English tunes (see also 7).

During the early 1930s, by the encourage-

ment of the British Broadcasting Corporation, the early Scottish musical manuscripts received a systematic examination such as they had never received before. The earliest printed collection of Scottish song appeared in the eighteenth century, and the manuscripts of the seventeenth century contain a considerable number of folk airs that have hitherto escaped printing. The result of the examination was the recovery of the primitive and least ornamented form of certain airs that are still known today and also of other airs that had been lost for centuries.

The idea was long current that the Italian musician David Rizzio, favourite of Mary Queen of Scots, was the composer of much of the Scottish popular song. This idea is now generally scouted as absurd, and though the great authority Frank Kidson, in Grove's *Dictionary*, gave a little support to the idea that Rizzio exercised some influence, it is usually considered that the Scots have shown themselves fully capable of providing their own literature of song.

The Highland Mod, corresponding somewhat to the Eisteddfod (see *Wales* 7), exists to foster the study and to encourage the preservation of the Gaelic tongue and Celtic minstrelsy. It is organized by An Comunn Gàidhealach (i.e. The Highland Association).

The institution of the Céilidh, or night-long informal social gathering, largely for song and instrumental music, is to some extent still maintained in the Highlands. (The Mod is made the occasion for the Céilidh also; p. 945, pl. **160. 1**).

2. Folk Dances. The national dance-literature is also very large. Its beginnings are in the lute and viol manuscripts of the seventeenth century. Much of it may be folk dance in the full sense of the word, but a great deal is the work of forgotten country fiddlers or of known composers like the famous Niel Gow the elder (q.v.). The reel and strathspey are briefly described in this book under their own heads. The 'Scotch Snap' (a short note on the beat followed by a long one off it; see separate entry), by some considered characteristic of

Scottish folk tune, rarely occurs except in the strathspey.

3. Instruments. According to Giraldus Cambrensis, who wrote in the latter part of the twelfth century, Scotland was at that time active in instrumental performance, in this department rivalling Ireland, and later records show that this unusual activity was fully maintained down to the sixteenth or early seventeenth century. A good score of instruments are mentioned in the *Book of the Howlat* and in Gavin Douglas's *Palice of Honour* (1501).

The Register of the Privy Council of Scotland for 1612 shows a scale of import duties for **Viols** and **Virginals** (and whistles for children), so evidently there was a sale for such instruments at that date. The remaining instrumental manuscripts of the seventeenth century are for lute and viol, with a few for virginals.

The instrument now usually considered typical of Scotland, the **Bagpipe,** was probably not of very early introduction there, as there is no trace of it before the early fifteenth century. It rose, however, to great importance. Chieftains had among their attendants pipers whose office, like that of their masters, was hereditary. In war and in sport, at funerals and at marriages, the bagpipe had its place. The pipers of a clan had their own piper-chief, and their school of piping. In the eighteenth century the bagpipe was in frequent use to regulate the simultaneous action of workers in road-making, boat-launching, harvesting, fulling cloth, etc. From 1781 onwards public competitions of pipers have been held, with the object of maintaining both the repertory and the standard of performance. (See also information under *Bagpipe Family* 4.)

The **Jew's Harp** (q.v.) was, from early times, an instrument of high importance in Scotland, and was a good deal used for the accompaniment of dancing. Some of the performers on this instrument seem to have been very accomplished. The eighteenth and nineteenth centuries saw a great rise of the **violin** for dance accompaniment. Two of the most eminent performers and composers for this instrument were Niel Gow senior (q.v.) and William Marshall (q.v.). Such men had little technical knowledge but could provide a vigorous tune and supply it with a simple bass. Another composer of this stamp was Robert Mackintosh (1745–1807), who migrated to London and was popular there.

For the **Highland Harp** see *Clàrsach*. Some chieftains (as also the greater ecclesiastics) maintained their private harpers, as did persons in a corresponding position in Ireland.

The profession of Town Minstrel existed in Scotland as in England and other countries (see *Wait*) and during the same long period.

4. Sang Scuils. The sang scuil played a great part in the early cultivation of music in Scotland; it provided a general elementary education together with that instruction in music that was necessary for the service of the church. From the thirteenth century onwards most cities and towns had a school of this sort, that of Aberdeen being especially famous. Some of the schools continued for two centuries or more after the Reformation. At the end of the sixteenth century James VI re-established several. (See *Schola Cantorum*; *Presbyterian Church Music* 3.)

5. Church Music. Of the extent and value of the pre-Reformation church music of Scotland we know little today, as record is lacking. Simon Tailler, an ecclesiastic who had studied music in Rome and Paris, is stated to have brought about great improvements during the thirteenth century, but we have nothing of his.

A very important manuscript, a source of much knowledge as to European church music in the thirteenth century, is the collection of music now known as the 'Wolfenbüttel Manuscript 677', whose provenance is now seen to be the Abbey of St. Andrews. The only Scottish composers of the polyphonic period of whose work any substantial remains exist are the early sixteenth-century **Robert Carver** and **Robert Johnson** (a priest), who show high accomplishment.

There is an important illuminated manuscript set of four part-books known as the *St. Andrews Psalter* (commonly called Wood's Psalter), unfortunately now scattered in libraries in Edinburgh, Dublin, and London; it includes not only psalm tunes but (and this in 1566, seven years after the Reformation) Latin motets and canticles, from which latter fact we may guess that it was intended for domestic use. The composers represented are the Robert Johnson above mentioned; David Peebles, a canon of St. Andrews, described as 'ane of the principale mussitians in all this land of his tyme'; Sir John Futhy, of Aberdeen, a priest and 'the first organist that ever brought in Scotland the curious new fingering and playing on Organs'; Andro Kemp, 'sumtyme maister of the sang scule in Sanctandrous'; John Angus, a monk of Dumfermline, and Andro Blakhall, afterwards Presbyterian minister. Peebles was responsible for the harmonizing of the psalm tunes.

Another composer of the sixteenth century is Patrick Douglas, described in a manuscript at Christ Church, Oxford, as 'Priste, Scotte borne'; a few motets of his remain.

It has been suggested that the marked absence of surviving specimens of church music is to be attributed to the destruction of manuscripts at the Reformation. To this the rejoinder has been made that England, too, had its Reformation and its consequent destruction (under Henry VIII, rather earlier than that of Scotland), and yet can produce a considerable corpus of pre-Reformation music.

Here the argument is usually allowed to end, but it seems easily possible to continue it. It is true that the Reformation in England entailed a destruction of the Abbeys and that their stores of music were largely destroyed or sent to the

Continent by shiploads for use in bookbinding. However, in England the Cathedrals remained; and such chapels as those of Windsor and Eton and the colleges of Oxford and Cambridge, with their libraries and collections of music, were untouched and their services with certain changes continued. Eighty years later their choral services, too, were brought to a stop, but the destruction of their choir books was only sporadic, and, moreover, printing of church music had by then at least begun (Barnard's Collection, 1641); further, a few years later the Restoration brought a resumption of the cathedral service everywhere, and so the stores of music which had been left on one side were carried into use again before neglect had been sufficiently prolonged to cause their gradual decay or dispersal.

The singing of metrical psalms has occupied an important place in Scottish life since the Reformation. Some remarks on Scottish psalters and psalmody will be found elsewhere in this book.

See list of Church Music articles under 12 c.

6. Music at Court. As in England, so in Scotland we find in the court records abundant evidence of the cultivation of music.

In the lists of 'Ordinare Feis and yeirlie Pensionis' (1538) we find many items of regular musical expenditure, as an allowance for two liveries a year to five 'Etalianis', quarterly stipends to four violists, sums for two tabourers and four performers on the 'trumpettis of weir' (war trumpets), a sum for a new lute and two dozen strings.

English musicians get a welcome, as is seen in these entries of three consecutive years:

1503. 'To VIII Inglis menstrales', and on the same day 'To the trumpetes of Ingland' and 'to the Erle of Oxfordis two menstrales', and a week later 'to the Inglis harparis'.
1504. 'To twa Inglise wemen that sang in the Kingis pailzeouse.'
1505. 'To the Inglis pipar with the drone' (i.e. an English bagpiper).

So, too, we find many other foreign musicians performing at court, Italian (fairly often), French, Irish, etc.

Sometimes municipalities are honoured by the King's enjoyment of their town music (or 'Waits', to use the English term); sums are paid 'to the commoun piparis of Abirdene'; 'to the commoun piparis of Edinborgh'. ('Piper' probably does not necessarily denote bagpiper; it was a common term for players of wind instruments—as in Germany and elsewhere.)

Itinerant musicians seem to be well received, such as (1490 and 1491) Blind Harry, the celebrated minstrel (reputed author of the great Wallace poem), the 'harpar with a [one] hand', and (1489) the 'Inglis pyparis that com to the castel yet [gate] and playit to the king'.

Many of the Scottish monarchs have been good musicians. The active-minded James I (reigned 1406–37), besides being a notable poet and a composer (as a captive in England, 1406–

24, he was there just at the time when Dunstable's innovations were being introduced), sang well and played the tabor, the flute, the trumpet, the shepherd's pipe, the psaltery, the lute, the organ, and (especially) the harp. The evening before his assassination was spent 'yn synging and pyping and harpyng and yn other honest solaces of grete pleasance and disport'.

His grandson, James III (reigned 1460–88), was also very musical. He founded the Chapel Royal at Stirling and endowed it richly so that its musical equipment should always be of the highest standard. Apparently his model was the Chapel Royal of the English king, Edward IV. He detained in Scotland a musical member of an embassy sent by Edward IV, William Rogers, and knighted him; Rogers is said, by his teaching, to have contributed greatly to the musical development of the country. The son of this monarch, James IV (reigned 1488–1513), doubled the number of the musicians in the Chapel Royal—apparently so that one-half might be prepared to travel with him whilst the other half maintained the services at home. On his wedding-day he entertained his bride by performing on the lute and clavichord. On his various progresses he often carried an organ with him.

His son, James V (reigned 1513–42), was also a music-lover, and this king's daughter, Mary Queen of Scots, sang well to her own lute accompaniment and also played on the virginals.

Her son, James VI of Scotland (reigned 1567–1625) and I of England (reigned 1603–25) tried several times to restore the musical glories of the Chapel Royal (now at Holyrood), where the Reformation, so much more thorough in Scotland than in England, had in 1560 abolished all but the simplest church music. In 1629 his son, Charles I, appointed as director of music Edward Kellie, who collected music, set up an organ, and provided flutes, viols, and pandores, engaged men and boys as singers, an organist and players on cornett and sackbut, etc. These arrangements implied the use of the Anglican Common Prayer instead of the Presbyterian order of service. For the twenty years 1617–37, then, the Chapel Royal at Holyrood maintained a service similar to that of the Chapel Royal, London (except that the service was not daily but only on Sundays). The Civil War ended all this and the Restoration of 1660 brought it back again. Various changes followed, and with the flight abroad in 1688 of James VII of Scotland and II of England the whole enterprise ceased.

7. Lack of Early Instrumental Music. Another problem concerning this same general period is a little more difficult. How is it that, whereas in England the end of the sixteenth century and beginning of the seventeenth constitute a period of ardent experiment in keyboard and string music and of high achievement in secular choral music, there is little evidence of the serious cultivation of composition in either of these branches of the art in

Scotland? The problem is accentuated by the fact that the Scottish court during several previous reigns is known to have encouraged music. Here again we may perhaps see the effect of the more drastic nature of the Scottish Reformation, as many of the Englishmen who have brought their country fame by their compositions at this period gained their sustenance largely by their activities in connexion with church music, and such a means of support was not open to musicians in Scotland. On the other hand, it may be that we merely lack information. It is thought by some that a careful search in some of the great houses of Scotland might reveal the existence of collections of music of the kinds just mentioned, and in support of this view is the fact that in 1934 such a search at Panmure House, Forfarshire (one of the seats of the Earls of Dalhousie), brought to light a book of virginal pieces of 1625—a few copied from Byrd and the rest composed by the owner of the book, William Kinloch (*Kinloch his ground, Kinloch his Almand, Kinloch his Pavane, Kinloch his Galliard, Kinloch his Battle of Pavia*, etc.). Another virginal book and several lute books were also discovered. A collection of lute airs and dance tunes is the *Skene Manuscript* of the reign of James VI (i.e. James I of England); about two-thirds of its contents are English or French: it has been published (Daunay's *Ancient Melodies of Scotland*, 1838). A collection of lute music still in manuscript is *An Playing Booke for the Lute . . . at Aberdein notted and collected by Robert Gordon in the year of our Lord 1627*. This is known as the *Straloch Manuscript* or *The Gordon Lute Book*. Its contents also are largely English.

A manuscript of more than common interest turned up at Panmure House. It is really three in one. The first part carries the date 1622 and contains the airs and sometimes the tenor part of choral songs; many of these can be traced to English madrigalists and lutenists, but quite a number have not been found in English sources: especially interesting are the airs associated in the manuscript with the poems of the Scottish writers of the sixteenth century, Alexander Montgomerie and Sir Alexander Scott. The second part is in a tablature for cittern and contains little but Scottish airs, many of which are found nowhere else; it is the only specimen of Scottish music for that instrument. The third section belongs to the second half of the seventeenth century and was compiled by a parish minister of Angus called Robert Edwards: it is for virginals and again contains unfamiliar Scottish airs. There are the usual psalm tunes, in harmony, for domestic use.

8. Lack of Madrigals. In considering such problems as that just raised it must be recognized that the element of accident may enter. The wonderful body of work of the English madrigal school came into existence apparently largely as the result of the stimulus given by Yonge's publication in 1588 of a collection of Italian madrigals (see *Madrigal* 2, 5), which had no counterpart in Scotland, and the period of English madrigal composition was over by about 1627: a stretch of forty years, then, saw the whole rise and decline of the English madrigal style, and, at a time of poor communications, it does not seem to have been long enough to have brought about anything beyond a rather local activity. If the list of the English madrigal composers be carefully examined it will be seen that all were resident in London, or attached to some south-country cathedral, or to some Oxford or Cambridge college, or to St. George's Chapel, Windsor, or else were household musicians employed by some south-country nobleman—with the exception of four who were resident in Chester and Dublin (two places then closely in touch with one another by geographical position, the one being the English place of departure for the other, and the traffic between the two being continual). We may, then, say that the madrigal was not produced north of Norwich and Lichfield except for the two places mentioned, which some chance had drawn into the movement. We speak of the 'English Madrigal School', but could speak of the 'Southern English Madrigal School', and the factor of remoteness, which probably in part explains the absence of such centres as York and Durham from the list of madrigal-producing localities, probably in an equal measure explains the absence of Edinburgh, Glasgow, and Aberdeen. It must be remembered that some other countries reveal no trace of having accepted the sixteenth-century Italian madrigal style, and that, indeed, England is the only country in which it became *fully* naturalized.

The above remarks are not intended as a complete discussion of a difficult subject, but they may suggest the desirability of further research before acceptance of the theory that little valuable musical activity was going on in Scotland at the time of highest activity in England—which so far as the present article is concerned is deliberately left an open question. Perhaps it is not fair so to leave it, however, without one more reflection—that this very period is the one concerning which all authorities on Scottish literature complain that they are suddenly left with nothing to show as against England's Spenser and Shakespeare, Sidney and Raleigh and Bacon.

A book known as the *Aberdeen Cantus*, printed by John Forbes in 1662 and again in 1666 and 1682, contains Ayres and Fancies, but they are English and Italian in provenance. It includes instructions for sight-singing, by Thomas Davidson, master of the Music School of Aberdeen (see 4), and is dedicated to the Lord Provost, Bailies, and Town Council, who are flatteringly described as constituting 'a harmoniously heavenly consort of as many musicians as magistrates'. It is modestly claimed that the musical fame of Aberdeen 'hath almost overspread all Europe'.

9. Publication of Music. The publication of music in Scotland was long greatly hampered by a monopoly granted by Charles II, which gave all printing into the hands of one individual. Activity in this department developed, however, during the eighteenth century, and both Edinburgh and Glasgow gradually became centres of a fairly considerable trade in music engraving, printing, and publishing. (Cf. *Publishing* 6; *Presbyterian* 4.)

In the early eighteenth century a work appeared in Edinburgh that may perhaps be considered as the foundation of the genre **Ballad Opera**—Ramsay's *Gentle Shepherd* (Edinburgh, 1725), which was interspersed with songs set to popular Scots airs and seems to have suggested the composition of Gay's *Beggar's Opera* (q.v.) three years later, and so to have led indirectly to various similar continental activities (see also under *Ballad Opera*).

10. Edinburgh as a Musical Centre. The position of Edinburgh as the great social centre of Scotland in the eighteenth century made it an active musical centre also. (For its first recorded concert, 1695, see under *Cecilia, Saint*; for its musical club see under *Clubs*.) The Musical Society, founded 1728, was in 1762 supplied with a home of its own in the long famous St. Cecilia's Hall, in the Niddry Wynd (see *Concert* 11). For a brief eulogy of Edinburgh musical amateurs of the period see Smollett's *Humphrey Clinker* ('Every man you meet plays on the flute, the violin, or violoncello'). Many foreign musicians, at this time, settled in the city for longer or shorter periods; orchestral activity was considerable. The will of General Reid (d. 1807) provided for the later foundation of a Professorship of Music at the University (1839). The last three professors have been Niecks (1891), Tovey (1914), and S. T. M. Newman (1940). The nineteenth century saw a cultivation of **Choral Music,** several important societies then coming into existence, and also of **Orchestral Music;** Bülow conducted the Choral Union's orchestra (founded 1874) in the season 1877–8, and August Manns conducted it for many years. The Scottish Orchestra founded in 1893 at Glasgow and giving regular concerts in Edinburgh also, superseded the above orchestra (first conductor, Henschel). It was succeeded in its turn (1950) by the Scottish National Orchestra. In 1915 Tovey brought into existence the Reid Symphony Orchestra, which long gave regular performances.

11. Various Activities. The conductorship of both these orchestras (the one founded in Glasgow and the one founded in Edinburgh) having been consistently in the hands of English or foreign musicians points, perhaps, to the lack of high training in music in Scotland. In 1930 the Glasgow Athenaeum School of Music, founded forty years earlier, was expanded and became, under Dr. W. G. Whittaker's direction, the **Scottish National Academy** (from 1944 Royal Scottish Academy of Music); at the same time a chair of music was founded at the University of Glasgow and the principalship of the school connected with it until 1952. The cultivation of choral music in Scotland was given a new impetus from the 1920s to 1951 by the increasing efficiency of the Glasgow Orpheus Choir (conductor, Hugh S. Roberton; knighted 1931, died 1952); and the Glasgow Musical Competition Festival, and similar festivals in other centres, exercised another important influence.

The reintroduction of **Choirs** and **Organs** into churches was gradual during the nineteenth century, towards the end of which a good many north of England organists were imported, pending the training of native performers. The generosity of a Scottish music-lover with an American-made fortune (cf. *Presbyterian* 2; *Patronage* 7), Andrew Carnegie, provided organs for many places of worship in Scotland as elsewhere in the British Isles, and in the grants made by the Carnegie United Kingdom Trust (established 1914) was found a means of bringing about the publication both of much contemporary music and of the English church music of that very period, above discussed, in which Scotland can show no comparable remains. Carnegie also made extensive gifts (1903) to his native town of Dunfermline, and the foundation of a school of music there was one of the results.

The most distinguished Scottish composers of recent time have been **Mackenzie, McEwen,** and **William Wallace** (all working in England, however). David Stephen, F. G. Scott, Erik Chisholm, Cedric Thorpe Davie, Thea Musgrave, and Ian Whyte (working in Scotland) enjoy a high reputation.

The annual Edinburgh Festival has provided an impetus to increased interest and activity in music in Scotland.

A Scottish Music Society, for research and publication of early music, was formed in 1936.

12. List of Articles amplifying the present one. In order to complete the information given above, the following articles should be consulted:

SCOTS CATCH. Same as *Scotch Snap* (q.v.).

SCOTS MARCH. See *March*.

SCOTS SNAP. See *Scotch Snap*.

SCOTS WHA HAE. The poem is by Burns; the air is the old traditional Scottish one of *Hey, tutti tatti*, also sung to Lady Nairne's 'Land o' the Leal'—a song of widely different sentiment, yet equally well fitted to this music—when the tempo and spirit of the performance are adjusted.

SCOTT.

(1) CYRIL MEIR (p. 352, pl. 55. 2). Born near Birkenhead in 1879 and died at Eastbourne in 1970, aged ninety-one. He studied at Frankfurt-am-Main and then settled for a time in Liverpool. At twenty-one he heard his *Heroic Suite* performed there and at Manchester, under Richter, and his first symphony performed at Darmstadt. Thence onwards his compositions became gradually familiar to the public.

He was a highly capable pianist and wrote effectively for his instrument, but his work covers almost all branches, including orchestral, chamber, solo vocal, choral, and operatic, though the success of his smaller pieces drew attention from his major works, which have seldom been performed.

His father, a business man, was an ardent and advanced student of New Testament Greek, in touch with and assisting some of the foremost authorities upon that subject. He himself was a student and writer of mystical poetry, a theosophist, and a bold promulgator of theories of art and life—and even of medicine (*Victory over Cancer*; booklet on cider vinegar as a cure for obesity, etc.).

See also references under *Colour and Music* 12; *Impressionism*; *Concerto* 6 c (1879); *Chamber Music* 6, Period III (1879); *Knorr*.

(2) CHARLES KENNEDY (1876–1965). Noted London choral conductor, authority on the English madrigals, and composer (*Everyman: a Mystery Play*, 1936).

(3) SIR WALTER (1771–1832). See *Ballad* 5; *Song* 5; *Bagpipe Family* 4; *Monks' March*; *Blue Bonnets*; *Bonnie Dundee*; *Dafydd y Garreg Wen*; *Berlioz*; *Canadian Boat Song*; *Romantic*; *Program*.

(4) LADY JOHN DOUGLAS (1810–1900). See *Loch Lomond*; *Annie Laurie*.

(5) E. L. See *Gramophone* 1.

(6) DARBY. See *Scandinavia* 2.

SCOTTISH NATIONAL ACADEMY OF MUSIC. See *Scotland* 11.

SCOTTISH ORCHESTRA. See *Scotland* 10.

SCOZZESE (It.). 'Scottish.'

SCRIABIN (Scriabine, Skryabin, etc.), ALEXANDER (p. 912, pl. 155. 7). Born in Moscow in 1872 and died there in 1915, aged forty-three. He inherited his musical instinct from his mother, who was a fine pianist.

He early showed a remarkable musical gift, being able, from the age of six onwards, to play on the piano almost anything he heard once performed. His education was received in the school for training military officers, but latterly he also attended the Conservatory of Moscow, where he studied under Taneief and Arensky. Then Belaief (q.v.), the patron-publisher of Russian music, took him up, planned recital tours for him, and published his compositions as they were finished. He taught in his old conservatory, but the claims of recital-travelling (in Europe and America) and of composition caused the relinquishment of this activity; for a time he lived in Brussels. He owed much to the help of the conductor Koussevitzky, who brought about many performances of his works.

In 1914 he was in London giving piano recitals. He was then suffering from a tumour of the lip and within about a year died.

His strange mystical theory, uniting aesthetics with religion and cosmogony, had much in common with theosophy, and some of the works devoted to its musical exposition may be described as a sort of philosophical programme music (see *Programme Music*). Amongst works so to be classified are the big orchestral compositions, including *The Divine Poem* and *The Poem of Fire* (or 'Prometheus', 1913); this last has a line in its score for a keyboard of light, throwing a play of colour on to a screen.

The piano writing of Scriabin is very able; he set out as a close student, admirer, and imitator (yet with great originality) of Chopin. Gradually his harmonic idiom changed, until at last he was making much use of a chord of his own, a chord of superposed fourths (e.g. C, F sharp, B flat, E, A, D). His melodic idiom also became very distinctive, particularly in the characteristic use of many upward leaps; his rhythms became extremely complex; the powerful expression of the most passionate moods became a notable feature of his works, and his climaxes were often overwhelming.

He did not use native idiom or attempt to express national thought or feeling, yet in the temperament that shows through his music he is essentially Russian (cf. *Tchaikovsky*).

See *Harmony* 15; *Scales* 12; *Colour and Music* 4, 11, 12; *Sonata* 9, 10 d (1896); *Pianoforte* 21; *Notation* 7; *Russia* 6, 8; *Prokofief*; *Symphony* 8 (1872); *Prelude*; *Feinberg*.

SCRIBE. See *Auber*.

SCUCITO (It.). Literally 'unsewed', so 'disconnected'.

SDEGNO (It.). 'Disdain.' So *Sdegnante*, 'disdaining'; *Sdegnoso*, 'disdainful'; *Sdegnosamente* 'disdainfully'.

SDRUCCIOLANDO (It.). 'Sliding' = *glissando* (q.v.).

SE (It.). 'If.'

SEANCHAIDH. See under *Corranach*.

SEARLE, HUMPHREY. Born in Oxford in 1915. He received his general education at Winchester College and New College, Oxford, and his musical training at the Royal College of Music and under Webern (q.v.). He was on the BBC staff from 1938 to 1948. His compositions are many and various, including concertos, opera, and five symphonies, and he has been one of the pioneer British followers of the Note-row system. He has written a good deal on music, and he is an authority on Liszt.

SEA SHANTY. See *Shanty*.

SEASHORE, CARL EMIL. Born in Sweden in 1866 and died at Lewiston, Idaho, in 1949. See *Tremolo*; *Tests and Measurements*.

SEBASTIAN THE LUTE PLAYER. See *Hungary*.

SEC, SÈCHE (Fr., masc., fem.). 'Dry', crisp; so *Sécheresse*, 'dryness'.

SECCO (It.). 'Dry', i.e. *Staccato*. But see also *Recitative*.

SECHS (Ger.). Six.

SECHSVIERTELMESSE (Haydn). See *Nicknamed Compositions* 13.

SECHZEHNTEL or **SECHZEHNTELNOTE** (Ger.). 'Sixteenth' or 'sixteenth-note'; semiquaver. See Table 3.

S.E.C.M. School of English Church Music. See *Anglican Parish Church Music* 7; *Schools of Music*.

SECOND. See *Intervals*.

SECONDA. See *Secondo*.

SECONDANDO (It.). 'Seconding', i.e. same as *Colla voce* and similar expressions (see *Col*).

SECOND INVERSION OF A CHORD. See *Harmony* 24 f.

SECONDO, SECONDA (It., masc., fem.). 'Second.' The respective plurals are *Secondi*, *Seconde*. For *Seconda volta* see Table 20.

SECOND VIOLIN. See *violin Family* 2 a.

SECUNDARIUS. See *Corno alto and Basso*.

SEDLÁK. The same as Furiant (q.v.).

SEELE (Ger.). 'Soul' (hence 'feeling'). Also the soundpost of a bowed instrument. *Seelenvoll* = 'soulful'.

SEGNO (It.). The 'sign'. See *Dal segno* and *Al segno*; also Table 20.

SEGOVIA, ANDRÉS. Born near Granada in 1893. He is a world-famous guitarist who has done much to bring his instrument back to the appreciation of the musical world. (See *Guitar*; *Ponce, M.*; portrait, p. 433, pl. **74**. 4.).

SEGUE (It.). 'Follows', e.g. *Segue la coda*, 'Here the coda follows'.

SEGUENTE, SEGUENDO (It.). 'Following.'

SEGUIDILLA. An ancient Spanish dance, possibly of Moorish origin. It is in a quick three-in-a-measure time, and much the same as the bolero except for its enhanced speed. A great deal of singing by the performers is a feature, the sung passages being called *Coplas*: they are in short lines, alternately of seven and five syllables, and have assonance (agreement of vowels) instead of rhyme. The Castanets (see *Percussion Family* 3 q, 5 q) are used.

This dance is in full use today, especially in Andalusia, though every province has it—in its own special style. Thus there exist the following: *Seguidillas Manchegas* (a lively type; see under *Manchega*); *Seguidillas Boleras* (a more dignified type—not related to the Bolero); *Seguidillas Gitanas* (a slower and more sentimental Gipsy type); *Seguidillas Taleadas* (an energetic type, with some relationship to the Cachucha).

To some extent the form has entered into artistic music. Albéniz (q.v.), for instance, has made effective use of it in piano composition, and it appears in Bizet's *Carmen*.

Cf. *Sevillana*; *Playera*.

SEHNSUCHT (Ger.). 'Longing' (noun). So the adjectives *Sehnsüchtig*, *Sehnsuchtsvoll*.

SEHNSUCHTSWALZER (Schubert). See *Nicknamed Compositions* 18.

SEHR (Ger.). 'Very', 'much'. *Zu sehr*, 'too much'.

SEI (It.). 'Six.'

SEIBER, MÁTYÁS. Born in 1905 in Budapest and died in a car crash near Johannesburg in 1960, aged fifty-five. He was trained as a cellist at the conservatory of his native city and was, for composition, a pupil of Kodály. He lived in Frankfurt from 1925 to 1933, and settled in London in 1935, becoming connected with Morley College. He composed chamber music, orchestral and choral compositions, etc. His cantata *Ulysses* is based on a scene from Joyce's novel of that name.

See *Note-row*.

SEIDL, ANTON (1850–98). One of Wagner's assistants at Bayreuth and later a great Wagnerian conductor. He spent much of the last decade of his life in New York. See *Opera* 21 k.

SEISES. The choir-boys who sing and dance and clash their castanets before the high altar in the Cathedral of Seville on great festival days (as they used to do also in the cathedrals of Toledo and Valencia). The name *Seises* comes from *seis*, 'six', but the boys are now ten (ritual dances of six boys are still performed at Jaca in Aragon, and in Majorca).

The music is quick but the motions of the boys slow. The music now used is of no antiquity and of no high value.

Cf. *Dance* 7.

SEITE (Ger.). 'Side', e.g. page of book or end of drum.

SEITENSATZ. See under *Satz*.

SEKLES, BERNHARD. He was born at Frankfurt-on-Main in 1872 and there died in 1934, aged sixty-two. He studied at the Hoch Conservatory at Frankfort, of which he later became Director (1923), being deprived of his post when the Nazi Government took power in 1933. As a composer he has had considerable success, especially with his Serenade for eleven instruments, which had one hundred European performances in its first year (1908–9). His works include operas, ballets, a symphony, chamber music, etc.

SELBY, WILLIAM. Born in England in 1738 and died in Boston, Mass., in 1798, aged fifty-nine or sixty. He was an accomplished harpsichordist and organist who went to America in 1771, sold groceries and liquor, performed and taught music, managed concerts and composed (from 1782) songs, anthems, 'Voluntaries or Fugues for organ or harpsichord', a Concerto for organ or harpsichord, and a Sonata for two violins and cello.

Sonneck suggests that 'Boston's musical history during the last thirty years of the eighteenth century may be said to have centred in the personality of this interesting and ambitious musician'.

SELF-ACTING PIANOFORTE. See *Mechanical Reproduction of Music* 13.

SEMEL. See *Gymel*.

SEMIBISCROMA (It.). Hemidemisemiquaver or sixty-fourth note. See Table 3.

SEMIBREVE (𝅝). The 'Whole Note', half the time-value of the breve (q.v.) and double the value of the minim or Half-Note. See *Notation* 3, 4; Table 1.

SEMICROMA (It.). Semiquaver or sixteenth-note. See Table 3.

SEMIDEMISEMIQUAVER (𝅘𝅥𝅲) or **HEMI-DEMISEMIQUAVER.** The sixty-fourth note, i.e. one sixty-fourth the time-value of the whole-note or semibreve. See Table 1.

SEMIFUSA. See *Notation* 4.

SEMIHEMIDEMISEMIQUAVER. The one-hundred and twenty-eighth note, i.e. a note of that fraction of a semibreve. See Table 1.

SEMI-LUNA. The nail fiddle (q.v.).

SEMIMINIMA. See *Notation* 4.

SEMI-PERFECT CADENCE. See *Cadence*.

SEMIQUAVER (𝅘𝅥𝅯). The sixteenth note, i.e. one-sixteenth the time-value of the whole-note or semibreve. See Table 1.

SEMITONE. The smallest interval used in normal European music (as distinct from Asiatic, etc.), e.g. B to C, C to C sharp, E flat to E natural, and so forth. For the distinction between diatonic and chromatic semitones cf. *Diatonic and Chromatic*.

SEMPLICE, SEMPLICITÀ (It.). 'Simple' (in all the English senses); 'simplicity'. So *Semplicemente*, 'simple'; *Semplicissimo*, 'extremely simple'.

SEMPRE (It.). 'Always', e.g. *Sempre legato*, the whole passage or composition to be played smoothly.

SENACHIE. See reference under *Corranach*.

SENALLIÉ (or Senaillé: the former spelling being found on printed copies of his music), JEAN BAPTISTE. Born in Paris in 1687 and died there in 1730, aged forty-two. He was a violinist, a pupil of various French teachers and then, in Italy, of Vitali. For some time in earlier manhood he was attached to the court of the Duke of Modena and in later life to that of Louis XV of France.

In his playing and his composition he combined the characteristics of the French and the Italian Schools. Some of his fifty sonatas are still to be heard.

SENEFELDER, ALOIS. See *Printing* 4.

SENFL, LUDWIG (c. 1490–1543). See *Germany* 2.

SENNET. The word occurs as a stage direction in Elizabethan plays and evidently means some sort of piece for wind instruments (cf. *Tucket*).

SENSIBILE, SENSIBILITÀ (It.). 'Sensitive', 'sensitiveness' (the *Nota sensibile* is the leading note).

SENTENCE. See *Phrase and Sentence*.

SENTITO (It.). 'Felt', i.e. with expression.

SENZA (It.). 'Without.'

SENZA ACCOMPAGNAMENTO. See *Aria*.

SENZA SORDINO, SENZA SORDINI (It.) 'Without mute', 'without mutes', as concerns bowed instruments; but for the pianoforte *Senza Sordini* means 'without dampers', i.e. use the right pedal, which throws this part of the mechanism out of action, leaving the strings to vibrate freely.

SÉPARÉ (Fr.). 'Separated.' In French organ music it means uncoupled.

SEPHARDIC JEWS. See *Jewish Music* 3.

SEPT (Fr.). 'Seven'; hence *Septième*, 'seventh'.

SEPTET (Fr. *Septette* or *Septuor*; It. *Settimino* or *Septetto*; Ger. *Septett*). Any combination of seven performers or any piece of music composed for such. The most famous septet in existence is the early work of Beethoven for violin, viola, cello, double-bass, clarinet, bassoon, and horn.

Very occasionally vocal septets are met with.

SEPTIÈME. 'Seventh.' See *Organ* 14 IV.

SEPTIMOLE, or **SEPTOLET,** or **SEPTU-PLET.** See Table 11.

SEPTUOR. See *Septet*.

SEQUENCE (1) in musical construction (for Sequence in Liturgical Music see below). The term is applied to the more or less exact repetition of a melody (with or without its harmony) at another level, higher or lower. If the repetition be only in the melody (the harmony being changed) it is a **Melodic Sequence**, if in the harmony also, a **Harmonic Sequence**. If the repetition is made without leaving the original key, which necessarily means that some of the intervals come out larger or smaller by a semitone, then the name used is **Tonal Sequence**. If in order to preserve the exact intervals the key is changed then the name given is **Real Sequence** (cf. the use of the words 'Real' and 'Tonal' in fugue: *Form* 12). Some sequences are real in some of their repetitions and tonal in others (in some instances to avoid carrying the modulation too far); these are **Mixed Sequences**.

When a sequence is of the nature of an exact repetition in another key of melody and harmony (i.e. when it is an 'harmonic real sequence') it is sometimes called **Rosalia**. In the more recent books of reference a condition sometimes laid down as a qualification for the designation is that the passage shall be repeated one degree higher, e.g. first heard in C, then in D, then in E, and so on—a very mechanical method of composing and an uncomfortable scheme of modulation through unrelated keys. In any case the word 'Rosalia' is almost a term of contempt, as its German equivalent **Schusterfleck** ('Cobbler's Patch') certainly is too.

The origin of the word *Rosalia* is explained in two equally plausible ways:

(*a*) It is 'derived from the name of a female saint, remarkable for repeating her "Pater Noster", and telling her beads. . . . An Italian cries out, upon hearing a string of repetitions, either a note higher or a note lower, of the same passage or modulation, "Ah: Santa Rosalia"' (article 'Richter', probably by Burney, in Rees's *Cyclopædia*, *c.* 1805).

(*b*) 'It comes from an old popular song, "Rosalia mia cara"' (see Grove's *Dictionary*, under 'Rosalia', where a snatch of the song, with a rising sequence, is shown); analogously there is a German term for this type of passage, **Vetter Michel**, from a popular song of that name which opens as follows:

Ge-stern A - bend war Vet-ter Mich - el hier
(Yesterday evening Cousin Michael was here)

(2) 'Sequence' was originally (to the ninth century) a musical term for the long melisma without words following the last syllable of the word 'Alleluia'. After that time it was used for the words set to the long melismas. It had become the habit to break up the melismas and to set to each note a syllable of a rhymed text. Notker Balbulus of St. Gall, Switzerland, was the first to suppress the word *Alleluia* and to replace it by short stanzas. In the following time new Sequences were composed—both music and words—modelled on the pattern of the already existing Sequences.

The *Dies Irae* (now a part of the text of the Requiem, q.v.) is a sequence, and so are the *Veni Sancte Spiritus* (q.v.), the *Victimae*

Paschali (q.v.), and the *Lauda Sion* (q.v.). These four were allowed to remain when all the other sequences were abolished by the Council of Trent (1545–63); and the *Stabat Mater dolorosa* was added later.

The passage in the English Prayer Book's Funeral service beginning 'In the midst of life we are in death' comes (via the Sarum Breviary —see *Use of Sarum*) from a sequence by Notker.

Some further remarks will be found under *Hymns and Hymn Tunes* 2.

SEQUENTIAL. Of the nature of sequence (q.v.), in melodic and sometimes also harmonic construction.

SERAGLIO (Mozart). See *Abduction from the Seraglio*.

SERAPHINE. See *Reed-Organ Family* 6.

SERENA. See *Serenade*.

SERENADE. French for 'evening music' (from Italian *sera* or French *soir*, or Provençal *Serena*, this last being a type of troubadour's song—cf. *Aubade*).

The most common suggestion of the word is that of a song by a lover beneath his lady's window, of which there are plenty of examples in opera literature and in the song repertory (e.g. Schubert). But it is also frequently applied to instrumental music, as, for instance, Mozart's orchestral 'Haffner Serenade', written to celebrate the wedding of the daughter of a Salzburg friend; or his many other serenades, some for orchestra, some for wind instruments only. Here the word seems to mean nothing more than a Suite in a good many movements and usually somewhat lighter in style than the Classical Suite (see *Suite*). Beethoven, Brahms, Dvořák, Elgar, and many others have also written serenades on more or less similar lines.

The German *Nachtmusik* ('Night Music') carries much the same suggestion, and so does the German *Ständchen* with the implication of something performed *standing*, and of brevity, -*chen* being a diminutive termination). The title 'Ständchen' is mostly applied to song, the term 'Nachtmusik' to instrumental compositions.

SERENATA. Not, as might be imagined, the same as Serenade, but either:

(1) A cantata, often of pastoral character and much like an opera without the stage concomitants. Handel's *Acis and Galatea* is a well-known example. This kind of serenata (nothing but a dramatic cantata, one may say) was, in the eighteenth century, much in vogue at the courts of Europe (e.g. that of the Emperor, at Vienna), as a complimentary offering on the occasion of the birthdays of royal persons—the subjects being chosen from mythological or ancient history in such a way as to suggest some flattering symbolical parallel.

(2) A sort of orchestral or wind-band suite, usually opening with a march and including a

minuet. It was of a lighter calibre, and, indeed, much the same thing as the *divertimento* or *cassation* (see *Suite* 7).

SERENATELLA (It.). Diminutive of *Serenata* (see above).

SERENO, SERENITÀ (It.). 'Serene', 'serenity'.

SERIA (It.). Fem. of *Serio*, 'serious'. E.g. *Opera seria*, serious (or tragic) opera, as distinct from *Opera buffa*, comic opera.

SERIAL TECHNIQUE = Note-row (q.v.) technique.

SERIAMENTE (It.). 'Seriously.'

SÉRIEUX, SÉRIEUSE (Fr., masc., fem.). 'Serious.'

SERINETTE. See *Mechanical Reproduction* 6.

SERIO, SERIA; SERIOSO, SERIOSA (It., masc., fem.). 'Serious.'

SERIOSAMENTE (It.). 'Seriously.'

SEROCKI, KAZIMIERZ (born 1922). See *Poland*.

SEROF (Serov, Serow, Sjeroff, etc.), ALEXANDER. Born in St. Petersburg in 1820 and died there in 1871, aged fifty-one. He entered the Civil Service, but unwillingly; and at length, defying his family, took to musical criticism and composition. At first violently anti-Wagnerian, he turned round in middle life, after a visit to Wagner at Lucerne, but his first opera, *Judith*, which had great success, is more influenced by Meyerbeer. In *Rogneda*, which followed, he approached the national tendencies of Glinka. His last opera, *The Power of Evil*, written on the subject of Ostrovsky's drama, 'The Storm', was left unfinished and was completed by his wife, Valentine Serof, a fine musician and herself the composer of several operas. In *The Power of Evil* he followed the national and realistic path of Dargomijsky.

His journalistic discussions with Stassof, the famous Russian art critic (1824–1906), rank amongst the most notable gladiatorial combats of music criticism (see *Russia* 6). Roughly, Serof represented the eclectic principle and Stassof the nationalist.

See *Russia* 5, 6 for a general description of the musical tendency of the period.

SERPENT, SERPENT D'ÉGLISE, SERPENT MILITAIRE. See *Cornett and Key Bugle Families* 2 d e, 3, 4 d.

SERPENTCLEIDE. See *Cornett and Key Bugle Families* 4 g.

SERPENTONE (It.). Serpent; see *Cornett and Key Bugle Families* 2 d e, 3, 4 d.

SERRANDO, SERRATO (It.)., **SERRANT, SERRÉ** (Fr.). 'Pressing', 'pressed', i.e. getting quicker.

SERVAIS.

(1) ADRIEN FRANÇOIS. Born at Hal near Brussels in 1807 and there died in 1866, aged fifty-nine. He had an enormous reputation as a violoncellist, travelling everywhere in Europe.

He also composed much music for his instrument.

(2) JOSEPH. Born at Hal near Brussels in 1850 and there died in 1885, aged thirty-four. His career and reputation resembled those of his father described above.

SERVICE. A service, in the Anglican Church musical vocabulary, implies a more or less elaborate and continuous setting of the canticles for Morning Prayer or Evening Prayer, or of the Communion Service (see *Common Prayer* and *Canticle*). A choir member in conversation will distinguish between a 'service setting' of these passages and the singing of them to mere Anglican Chants (see *Anglican Chant*) or *Plainsong* (q.v.). Strictly the use of such service settings (unless very simple) is proper only in cathedrals, college chapels, and the like, as in the parish church it is frequently, if not usually, desirable to give every member of the congregation the opportunity to participate audibly in the more important choral items (presuming on his part some moderate capacity for singing).

The effect of the Reformation on the composition of service music was mainly twofold: (*a*) the canticles had now to be set in the vernacular, and (*b*) they had to be set without lengthening by repetition of phrases and as much as possible on the principle of a syllable to a note—this last point apparently found unacceptable, or even impracticable, by the musicians, and, with the exception of Merbecke, Heath, and Tallis, totally disregarded from the start (in 1546) of vernacular composition. Some sixteenth-century English communion services exist in two forms: that of the Latin Mass and that of an adaptation, in English, to the new conditions. The terms *Short Service* and *Great Service* were often used by sixteenth- and early seventeenth-century composers, apparently to distinguish between the settings that faithfully followed the new regulations and those that passed beyond them into something like the old length and complexity. During the eighteenth century almost all services were composed on the 'short' principle; this was, however, in all ways, a period of poverty in service composition.

An antiphonal treatment (by the Decani and Cantoris sides of the choir; see *Precentor*) is a frequent feature in 'service' music. 'Verse' and 'Full' passages are also used (see *Verse*).

A rather curious feature of 'Service' music, as distinct from anthems, is the long observed tradition of writing it without independent organ part. Byrd, Morley, and Gibbons made experiments in the introduction of such a part, but after them such a thing is hardly found until the composition of 'Walmisley in D minor' two centuries later. Since Walmisley (q.v.) composers have made much effective use of the organ.

S. S. Wesley (q.v.) exercised a great influence on the composition of service music. The publication of 'Stanford in B flat', in 1879 (see *Stanford*), marked the beginning of a more

1. SCHUBERT'S BIRTHPLACE
In the Lichtenthal district of Vienna

2. SCHUBERT AT AGE 18

3. THE COMPOSER AND HIS WAITING AUDIENCE

4. DIGNITY AND HUMILITY
A humorous comparison of a famous exponent of
Schubert's songs and the humble composer thereof

1. A CÉILIDH OR NIGHT-LONG MUSIC-MAKING
See *Scotland* 1

2. THE EARL OF KELLY
Violinist and composer of repute (1732–81)
See p. 549

3. GEORGE THOMSON
In Edinburgh (1757–1851)
See *Folk-Song* 3

4. HEBRIDEAN FOLK SONG. Mrs.
Kennedy-Fraser (1857–1930), and one of
her Barra singers
See *Folk Song* 3; *Kennedy-Fraser*

5. SIR ALEXANDER MACKENZIE
(1847–1935)
Prolific composer and Principal of the Royal
Academy of Music

6. WILLIAM WALLACE (1860–1940)
Medical man, composer, and author of
thoughtful books on music

7. HAMISH MACCUNN
(1868–1916)
Active and much appreciated
composer

8. J. B. McEWEN (1868–1948)
Composer and Principal of the Royal
Academy of Music

economical and consistent use of material in service composition, a whole movement (and indeed the whole service) being bound together by a repetition of motifs, treated flexibly in something like the way in which Wagner often treats a Leitmotiv (see *Leading Motif*); the organ takes a large share in this treatment.

The successive styles and composers of service music being, in the main, the same as those listed under *Anthem*, need not be set out here, but it may be said that, as with the anthem so with the 'service', a great deal of purely conventional music has been brought into temporary existence. A common technical fault of such music is faulty accentuation of the words, which seems to go further here than in any other class of music produced by educated musicians; it probably results largely from the necessity for concision, which does not allow much 'elbow room'. From this last-mentioned condition effective composition in service music is perhaps more difficult to attain than effective composition in any other form. It is easy to set the words phrase by phrase, but flexibility, balance, and unity are hard of attainment.

The remark made at the end of the article *Anthem* as to the inevitable ignorance of continental European musicians of the fact of England's possession of a noble body of church music may be repeated here. It is a national possession for which the nation never gets and never can get credit.

SESQUIALTERA. A rhythmic proportion such as 3 : 2 or 4 : 3, where one element is greater by one than the other. See *Hemiola*; *Organ* 14 V.

SESSIONS, ROGER (p. 1061, pl. **174.** 6). Born at Brooklyn in 1896. He is a graduate of Harvard who also studied at Yale under Horatio Parker and was for some years on the staff of Smith College, Northampton, Mass. He then worked under Bloch, won a Guggenheim Professorship (1926) and worked at composition in Europe until 1933 as a winner of the American Rome Prize. He later held posts at Princeton (1935), Berkeley, California (1945), Princeton again (1953), and the Juilliard School (1965). His compositions are found by most listeners intellectual rather than ingratiating, in spite of their strongly lyrical element. The best known remains his early *Black Maskers* (1923); there are also four symphonies, several operas, a notable violin concerto (1935), and chamber music.

See *Concerto* 6 c (1896); *Opera* 24 f (1947).

SETTE (It.). 'Seven.'

SEUFZEND (Ger.). 'Sighing.'

SEUL, SEULE, SEULS, SEULES (Fr., masc., fem., sing., plur.). 'Alone.'

ŠEVČIK, OTTOKAR (1852–1934). He was a Bohemian violinist who elaborated a most complete course of training in violin and (with Prague as his centre for the most part) turned out a highly distinguished body of pupils. He published much material for the study of his instrument and many arrangements for violin.

SEVEN LAST WORDS. The last seven utterances of Christ are drawn some from one of the four gospels and some from another. The texts of Passion Music (q.v.) have sometimes been based on these, as, especially, that of Haydn (1785); this was commissioned for the Cathedral of Cadiz, for use on Good Friday, and was published in Vienna as 7 *sonate, con un' introduzione, ed al fine un terremoto* ('7 sonatas, with an introduction, and at the end an earthquake'), and had three opus numbers; op. 47 is in its original form for orchestra; op. 48, for strings; and op. 49 for pianoforte. After each of the Seven Words (given by Haydn to a bass in recitative) would come the bishop's commentary and exhortation, and then, whilst he prostrated himself at the altar, the appropriate 'sonata' would be played: in fact the music was a series of seven intermezzi in a sermon. Later the composer (or his brother Michael or some other person) turned the whole into a cantata.

Other settings of the Seven Words are those of Schütz (performed about 1645; first printed 1873) and Gounod.

SEVENTEENTH. See *Organ* 14 IV.

SEVENTH. See *Interval*.

SEVENTH, CHORDS OF. See *Dominant Seventh*; *Diminished Seventh*; *Harmony* 24 e f j.

SÉVÉRAC, DÉODAT DE (in full, Joseph Marie Déodat de Sévérac). Born at St. Félix de Caraman (Haute Garonne) in 1873 and died at Céret in the Pyrenees in 1921, aged forty-seven. He studied at the Paris Schola Cantorum under d'Indy and composed symphonic poems, chamber music, songs, piano and organ music, theatre music, etc. His music enjoys repute for the directness of its expression and its life. (Cf. *Expressionism*.)

SEVERO, SEVERAMENTE (It.). 'Severe', 'severely'. So also *Severità*, 'severity'.

SEVILLANA. A type of Spanish dance, originating in Seville. It is really the local type of the seguidilla (q.v.).

SEWALL (JUDGE), SAMUEL (1652–1730). See *United States* 2; *Inns*; *Levet*; *Mealtime*.

SEXT. The fifth of the Canonical Hours in services of the day of the Roman Catholic Church. Properly it takes place at the 'sixth hour', i.e. midday (cf. *Matins*; *Lauds*; *Prime*; *Terce*; *None*; *Vespers*; and *Compline*).

SEXTET (Fr. *Sextette* or *Sestuor*; It. *Sestetto*; Ger. *Sextett*). Any body of six performers, vocal or instrumental, or any composition for such.

The *String Sextet* is normally for two each of violins, violas, and cellos, but other combinations occur.

Sextets for various combinations of instruments, wind and string, also exist.

SEXTOLET. See Table 11.

SEXTUOR. See *Sextet*.

SEXTUPLET. See Table 11.

SEYFRIED, IGNAZ XAVIER RITTER VON (1776–1841). Pupil of Haydn, friend of Mozart and Beethoven. Successful composer and author of theoretical works. See reference under *Misattributed Compositions* ('Haydn's Ox Minuet').

SF. = *Sforzando, Sforzato* (q.v.). So Sff. means *Sforzatissimo.*

SFOGATO (It.). 'Freely given out'—i.e. light and easy in style (*Soprano sfogato* = light soprano voice).

SFOGGIANDO (It.). 'Flauntingly', 'ostentatiously'.

SFORZANDO, SFORZATO (It.). 'Forcing', 'forced', i.e. strongly accenting a note or chord. The letters Sf. are sometimes used in abbreviation. The superlative is *Sforzatissimo* (abbreviated, *Sff.*).

SFP. *Sforzato* (see above) followed immediately by *Piano.*

SFZ. = *Sforzando* (q.v.).

SGAMBATI, GIOVANNI. Born in Rome in 1841 and died there in 1914, aged seventy-three. He was an Italian ally of the 'Music of the Future' group of Wagner and Liszt, and as a composer much valued by them. His forty songs are important. His two piano quartets made a stir in their day and his string quartet is still played. His first symphony was a landmark in the Italian music of his period and in many ways he can be looked upon as the father of the modern musical movement in Italy (see references under *Italy* 7; *Concerto* 6 b (1841); *Requiem*). As a pianist and teacher of pianists he was also of high renown. He was English on his mother's side.

SGAMBATO (It.). 'Walked off one's legs', hence 'weary'.

SHADOWS, SOUND. See *Acoustics* 19.

SHAKE or **TRILL** (Fr. *Trille* or *Tremblant*; It. *Trillo*; Ger. *Triller*. See Table 16 at the opening of this volume). This is the most important of all the 'ornaments' (q.v.) and is found in music for all instruments capable of sounding two contiguous notes. Harpsichord and clavichord music abounds in it, and it is frequent in pianoforte music also. Books on instrumentation devote a good deal of space to tables and lists of the shakes possible and impossible with the various wind instruments, given their individual peculiarities of construction.

In vocal performance from the seventeenth to mid-nineteenth century the ability to make a good shake was valued very highly. A vocalist's reputation in those days depended much on the degree of perfection of his or her shake, but by the beginning of the nineteenth century the obligation to shake was beginning to be abrogated. So we find Burney (Rees's *Cyclopædia, c.* 1805) saying:

'The Italians call a bad shake, or no shake at all, but a quivering upon the same note, *tosse da capra*, a goat's cough. If the singer is not possessed of a true and good shake, he or she had best refrain from ever attempting it; and if accustomed to elegant melody, and possessed of good taste, and ornamental embellishments, the shake in songs of expression and pathos may be avoided with advantage. . . .

'A good shake well applied is certainly a great ornament; but it is a matter of brilliancy more than expression; *non dice niente*, it says nothing—according to modern Italian critics, and is seldom wanted except at the end of a formal close. Those who have a good shake, like persons with a fine set of teeth, are too ambitious of letting you know it.'

All the same, at this period it was high praise of a vocalist to say that he or she possessed a 'natural shake'.

A good shake has always been important to pianists and violinists and is a matter for special practice.

The manner of performing the shake has varied very greatly at various periods and with various composers. The general principles are made clear in the Table above mentioned.

For the use of the vocal shake in very early times see *Ornaments* 1.

For shakes in hymn singing see *Hymns and Hymn Tunes* 9, 10, 11.

SHAKESPEARE.

(1) WILLIAM I (1564–1616). His plays abound with musical references and he uses music very freely in his stage directions, not only in an 'incidental' way, i.e. for processions, war, festivity, etc., but also (and this obvious fact has been much overlooked by literary authorities) as a means of expressing or reinforcing the sense of mystery in situations calling for such, e.g. magic, death, etc. His many song lyrics, introduced into the plays, are admirable.

For references or quotations see the following: *Arne, T. A.*; *Bagpipe Family* 1, 3; *Balakiref*; *Ballad* 1; *Bergomask*; *Berlioz*; *Branle*; *Burden*; *Calino Casturame*; *Canaries*; *Carman's Whistle*; *Carols*; *Castelnuovo-Tedesco*; *Chapel Royal*; *Cittern*; *Community Singing* 4; *Composition* 6, 8, 12; *Consort*; *Cornett and Key Bugle Families* 3; *Courante*; *Dance* 6; *Dump*; *Edwards, Richard*; *Gamut*; *Giorgi Flute*; *God save the Queen* 11, 17; *Greensleeves*; *Hay*; *Hexachord* (at end); *History* 3; *Inns and Taverns*; *Jig*; *Johnson, Robert*; *Lute Family* 4; *Masque*; *Morley, Thomas*; *Morris*; *Mysteries*; *Pantomime*; *Passamezzo*; *Pavan and Galliard*; *Prick Song*; *Recorder Family* 2; *Romantic*; *Stevens, R. J. S.*; *Tongs and Bones*; *Volta*; *Whiffle*; *Wilson, John.*

(2) WILLIAM II (1849–1931). Noted singing teacher. See *Voice* 3, 7.

SHALLOT. See *Organ* 2 a.

SHANKS (and **CROOK**). See *Acoustics* 8; *Brass*; *Trumpet Family* 2 b, 3; *Horn Family* 2 b; *Cornet*.

SHANTY or **CHANTY** (in either case pronounced 'Shanty'). Many folk songs (see *Folk Song*) survived in the sea life of sailing-ship days. For amusement the sailor sang songs such as in no way differed from those of the landsman, but he had in addition to these a class of working songs, rhythmically fitted to seafaring processes, and sung by a 'shanty-man' set apart for the purpose whilst the rest of the workers engaged came in with the periodical refrain. Thus was attained unanimity in pulling ropes or pushing the capstan, and thus, at the same time, was work turned into a kind of game. 'The Rio Grande' and 'Blow the man down' are examples of well-known shanties. But there was always the element of extemporization in shanties, at all events as to the words, and they offered a recognized and tolerated occasion for letting the captain know of the good and bad points of the ship's commissariat and the like. Also a good many words and thoughts that could not be printed have found their way into the shanty, but always (says Sir Richard Terry, the best British authority) in the solo—never in the chorus, which could be heard all over the ship—and even so captains of passenger ships imposed a censorship.

There are in shanties many allusions to the American scene, and it would appear as though some of them have originated with American sailors. Nearly all maritime nations have shanties and they have been in use on the big rivers too, as for instance on the Mississippi. Shanties have been in much use in the lumber forests of Michigan, Wisconsin, and Minnesota, used in a similar way to those of the sea. The West Indian Negroes still use (or at any rate lately used) shanties when at shore work of a gang character.

SHAPE-NOTE SINGING. Same as 'Buck-wheat Notation'. See *Lancashire Sol-fa*.

SHAPERO, HAROLD SAMUEL. Born at Lynn, Mass., in 1920. He studied under Slinimsky, Křenek, Piston, Nadia Boulanger, and Stravinsky, and, thus equipped, embarked on the composition of strongly contrapuntal orchestral and chamber music, etc., in a neo-romantic style.

SHAPORIN, YURI. Born in Glukhov in the Ukraine in 1889 and died in Moscow in 1966, aged seventy-seven. He studied at the Conservatory of St. Petersburg and first became known as a composer of individual music to Soviet plays. He was inspired by Soviet ideology and his musical idiom is traditional. He wrote an opera, *The Decembrists*, and a symphony (1932) of which the first movement is headed 'Fact—or what occurred, 1917–20' and the fourth 'Campaign—signalizing the triumph of the Soviet Army'. This work employs not only a large orchestra but also a brass band, a piano, and a (wordless) choir.

SHARP (♯). The sign which, placed before a note, raises it in pitch by a half-step or semitone. (See Table 6).

In this connexion the British use the verb 'to sharpen', some Americans 'to sharp'. So in the British practice we get 'sharpened' and in the American 'sharped' (cf. *Flat*).

In early music a B with the sharp sign means B natural. Note, too, that in eighteenth-century writers (e.g. Burney) 'key E sharp' means 'E with the sharp third', i.e. E major.

As an adjective applied to performance (e.g. singing and violin playing) the word means a departure from exact intonation, on the upward side.

SHARP, CECIL JAMES (p. 364, pl. **59.** 3). Born in London in 1859 and died there in 1924, aged sixty-four. After completing his education at Cambridge he went to Australia. Returning to England he became head of the Hampstead Conservatory, occupying this position for nine years. He then gave himself to the collection, publication, and performance of the folk song and folk dance of his native land, and he, far more than any other single person, is responsible for the salving of this national heritage (p. 364, pl. **59.** 4–7). Towards the end of life he enjoyed a small pension from the government. In his memory has been built, in London, Cecil Sharp House—as headquarters for the English Folk Dance and Song Society.

See references under *Folk Song* 3; *Ballad* 3; *Country Dance*; *Écossaise*; and for the character of the English folk dances, as established by his investigations, see *Dance* 5.

SHARP MIXTURE. See *Organ* 14 V.

SHAW.

(1 and 2) MARTIN EDWARD FALLAS and GEOFFREY TURTON—Martin was born in London in 1875 (died at Southwold, Suffolk, in 1958), and Geoffrey in 1879 (died in London in 1943).

Their father was a Yorkshireman who became a well-known London organist. Geoffrey was a choir-boy at St. Paul's Cathedral and then won an organ scholarship to Cambridge. Martin studied at the Royal College of Music.

Geoffrey's chief public appointment was as Inspector of Music to the national Board of Education; Martin did a good deal of theatrical conducting and held a number of London organistships—always of a somewhat unconventional sort.

Both composed, Martin the more extensively and the more prominently. Both preached and practised composition informed with the English folk-tune spirit and idiom, and both worked for a revival of Purcell. They also connected themselves with the movement for a return to simple dignity in the music of the English Church.

Both wrote much about music and Martin's *Up to Now* (1929) is one of the few books of musical reminiscences possessing literary quality.

(3) GEORGE BERNARD (1856–1950). See references under *Criticism of Music* 7; *Red Flag*; *Composition* 7; *Copyright* 3.

SHAWM. See *Oboe Family* 2.

SHEBALIN, VISSARION YAKOVLEVICH. Born in Omsk in 1902 and died in 1963, aged sixty. Composer and teacher; director of the Moscow Conservatory until ousted in the 1948 purge (see *Russia* 8); composer of four symphonies, a two-hour choral symphony, *Lenin*, an opera, *The Taming of the Shrew*, and a completion of Mussorgsky's *Sorochintsky Fair*.

SHEDLOCK, JOHN SOUTH (1843–1919). London music critic and author of books of musical research. See *Sonata* 10 d; *Cramer, Johann Baptist*; *Dictionaries* 1.

SHEFFIELD CHURCH ORCHESTRA AND ORGAN. See *Anglican Parish Church Music* 4.

SHELLEY, HARRY ROWE (1858–1947). See *Patronage* 6.

SHENG. See *Reed-Organ Family* 1, 6.

SHEPHEARD, JOHN. See *Shepherd* (1).

SHEPHERD.

(1) JOHN (surname spelt in many ways). Lived in the first half of the sixteenth century. He was for a time a fellow and organist of Magdalen College, Oxford, and was a composer of church music. The remains of his work are, unfortunately, rather scanty, and in some instances fragmentary.

See references under *Henry VIII*; *Mass* 5.

(2) ARTHUR (p. 1057, pl. **172**. 6). Born at Paris, Idaho, in 1880, of English parents, and died at Cleveland in 1958, aged seventy-seven. He was a composer of considerable technical acquirements and marked individuality. He wrote large orchestral works (e.g. the symphony suite *Horizons*), some chamber music, and compositions in smaller forms. His style and idiom reflect memories of the English folk song and the cowboy songs of Idaho. He was a conductor, head (until 1950) of the music department of Western Reserve University, and a valued critic.

'SHEPHERD BOY' ÉTUDE (Chopin). See *Nicknamed Compositions* 8.

SHEPPARD (or **Shepperd**), **JOHN.** See *Shepherd* (1).

SHERA, FRANK HENRY. He was born at Sheffield in 1882 and died there in 1956, aged seventy-three. He held positions in various public schools, and was then from 1928 to 1948 Professor of Music at Sheffield University. He published several useful books on musical subjects.

SHE WANDERED DOWN THE MOUNTAIN SIDE. See *Clay*.

SHIELD, WILLIAM (p. 817, pl. **140**. 6). Born in County Durham in 1748 and died in London in 1829, aged eighty. He was a boat-builder's apprentice who studied music at Newcastle, under Avison (q.v.) and, being heard as violinist by Giardini (q.v.), was urged by him to take up music professionally. Later he succeeded Avison in some of his work at Newcastle, and then, on Giardini's invitation, went to London as a member of the orchestra of the Italian opera, long serving as one of the principal viola players of the capital.

He was appointed Master of the King's Musick (1817), had high success as a theatrical composer, and left many tuneful songs, such as *The Thorn* and *The Wolf*, that will long be relished by simple-minded music-lovers.

He was one of Haydn's many English friends.

See references under *Pantomime*; *Opera* 21 b; *Ballad Opera*; *Auld Lang Syne*; *Arethusa*.

SHIFT. See *Position*.

SHILKRET, NATHANIEL. Born in New York 1895. Orchestral player and then conductor, especially occupied in gramophone and film music. See *Oratorio* 7 (1947).

SHIMMY. A dance of American origin, popular about 1920. It was in two-in-a-measure ragtime (q.v.).

A learned German lexicographer derives the name from the colloquial word for 'chemise', and gives as the reason for the adoption of this name a shaking of the shoulders characteristic of the dance and in appearance designed to shake off that piece of apparel. Zez Confrey's *Kitten on the Keys* (set in four-in-a-measure, however) was looked on as the outstanding popular example of the music.

Hindemith used the name, rhythm, and style in a movement of his Piano Suite '1922' (op. 26), as did Wilhelm Grosz in his Second Dance Suite (op. 20).

SHINN, FREDERICK G. (1867–1950). See a reference under *Ear Training*.

SHIRLEY, JAMES (1596–1666). Dramatic poet. See *Masque*.

SHIVAREE. This word is an American corruption of 'Charivari' (q.v.).

SHOCK OF THE GLOTTIS. See *Voice* 3.

SHOFAR (or **Shophar**). The ancient synagogue horn of the Jews (p. 528, pl. **97**. 4).

SHOP BALLAD. See *Ballad* 6.

SHORE FAMILY. Mathias (d. 1700) and his two sons William (d. 1707) and John (d. 1752) were all famous trumpeters (for John, the most able of all, see *Trumpet Family* 3; *Pitch* 6 b). Catherine (d. about 1730) was a notable singer, pupil of Purcell, and wife of the actor-dramatist Colley Cibber.

SHORT, HORACE. See *Auxetophone*.

SHORT METRE. See *Hymns and Hymn Tunes* 13.

SHORT OCTAVE and **BROKEN OCTAVE.** Applied to the **Organ**, the *Short Octave* was a means of avoiding needless expenditure on the large pipes of the lowest part of the compass. In the days of unequal temperament certain notes on the instrument were impossible as key-notes (i.e. Tonics) because those keys would be out of tune (see *Temperament*), and were thus relatively unimportant. These notes were therefore often omitted from the bottom few inches of the keyboard.

The notes thus omitted were C sharp, D sharp, F sharp, and G sharp. A rearrangement was then effected, generally in the rather curious way shown below:

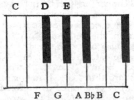

A short octave.

(Normal notes below; intruded notes above.)

The effect of this, it will be noticed, was that the lowest octave of the instrument consisted of C to C in naturals, plus the B flat.

This enabled the player to bring in the full-sounding deep final keynote of any composition in all keys in which he could possibly play the instrument, and avoided the spending of money on pipes for four notes not very likely to be much called for in that region of the keyboard, since they could not occur as keynotes, but only as incidentals.

The *Broken Octave* was a similar device. In it the normal lowest octave was complete from C to C, except that in the place of the lowest C sharp was the more useful note the A from below. Sometimes, too, a finger-key was added below the bottom C of the keyboard and allotted to the very useful note G. Other arrangements occurred, but those are the commonest.

The broken octave device was not extinct in English organ-building at the beginning of the nineteenth century.

Arrangements of a similar kind were often applied to the **Virginals, Spinet,** and **Clavichord.**

All the Italian domestic keyboard instruments, of any kind, up to the beginning of the eighteenth century had such an arrangement. The motive here was much the same as with the organ, presumably, i.e. to avoid needless cost—though in the instruments mentioned this was nothing like so large a matter as in the organ, where one pipe in the lowest octave takes as much metal as many pipes higher up the range. Possibly the practice began with the organ and was then rather unthinkingly copied in the other instruments.

Virginal music occasionally includes left-hand chords beyond the stretch of any hand, and their existence is explained by the fact that the lowest note was not in the keyboard position that a pianist of today expects.

In English harpsichords for a short period (about 1600–1725) the lowest two short finger-keys are sometimes divided, the back half given the proper note and the front half another note.

The distinction 'Short' and 'Broken' in these expressions is perhaps not very enlightening. In the 'Short Octave' two of the long finger-keys are omitted and the octave is therefore *visibly* 'short' of some of its notes. In the broken octave there was no *visible* omission but in playing up the chromatic scale a break would be noticed.

SHORT SERVICE. See *Service.*

SHOSTAKOVICH, DMITRI (p. 913, pl. **156. 8**). Born in St. Petersburg in 1906 and died in Moscow in 1975, aged sixty-eight. After study at the conservatory of his native city, under Maximilian Steinberg, he produced in quick succession a series of symphonies, operas (*Lady Macbeth of Mtsensk*—later *Katerina Ismailova,* 1934), piano works, film music, etc. These are a product of the relative artistic freedom of the earlier post-revolu-tionary years, though the titles of some works echo ideological preoccupations.

After being spoken of in such high terms as 'composer-laureate of the Soviet state', the composer, in 1936, fell into some degree of disgrace, the violently erotic *Lady Macbeth* offending several officials, including Stalin, when given a special performance in the Kremlin, and his music being suddenly discovered to be 'petit-bourgeois' and being officially dropped. This, however, proved to be a mere temporary eclipse.

His Seventh ('Leningrad') Symphony, 'dedicated to the ordinary Soviet citizens who have become the heroes of the present war', was heard in Russia, Britain, and the United States in 1942. Along with Prokofief and others (see *Russia* 8) he again came under criticism for ideological deficiencies in 1948. In 1960 he joined the Communist Party. His very long list of works, which includes fifteen symphonies and nine string quartets, is, not surprisingly, on varying levels of inspiration; nevertheless few would question his position as the leading composer of the U.S.S.R.

See *Electric* 5 (end); *Concerto* 6 c (1906); *Opera* 17; *Russia* 8.

SHROPSHIRE ROUND. See *Round* 2.

SHTCHERBATCHEV, etc. See *Stcherbatchef.*

SHUDI (or Tschudi), BURKHARDT. See *Harpsichord Family* 5; *Pianoforte* 5, 15.

SI. The seventh degree of the major scale, according to the system of vocal syllables derived from Guido d'Arezzo (q.v.). In tonic sol-fa (q.v.) it has, for a certain convenience, been changed to 'Te', which is also the second degree of the minor scale. In French and Italian usage 'Si' is now attached (on 'fixed-doh' principles) to the note B, in whatever scale or other association this may occur (see Table 5).

See *Hexachord.*

SI (It.). It is the mark of a reflexive verb, e.g. *Si replica,* 'it repeats itself', *Si segue,* 'it follows on', *Si tace,* 'it keeps silence' (i.e. silence is to be kept), and so on. (See also above.)

S.I.A.E. See *Copyright* 3.

SIBELIUS, JEAN (p. 896, pl. **153. 7**). Born at Tavastehus, in Finland, in 1865 and died at Järvenpää in 1957, aged ninety-one. He studied at the capital of his country, Helsinki (otherwise Helsingfors), and then in Berlin and Vienna. When he was thirty-two the State made him an annual grant for life, so that he might be free for composition. Later in his career (1930) it made arrangements for the gramophone recording of some of his works.

He found in his strong national feeling (see *Nationalism*) the inspiration of practically all his work. The austerity of a land of a long, hard winter, the charm of a land of a short but brilliant summer, are both found there. The influences of natural beauty and of national legend as preserved in the *Kalevala* (see *Scandinavia* 6) are equally evident; the mere names of his pieces show the latter, the list of them being largely made up of titles such as *A Saga*, *The Swan of Tuonela*, and *Lemminkäinen*.

His works include seven symphonies (long-current rumours of an eighth, whether completed or only projected, seem to have been unfounded), eight or nine tone-poems, and other orchestral pieces, a violin concerto, songs, etc. They are usually very individual in style and feeling, with a deep-seated, rather than a superficial, romanticism. His later works make no concessions to popular taste, but are downright, terse, personal documents.

See *Chamber Music* 6, Period III (1865); *Bell* 6; *Nationalism*.

SIBYL. This 'Welsh air' is in reality a *Cibel* (or *Cebell*, q.v.) in *Bremner's Harpsichord and Spinnet Miscellany* (Edinburgh, 1761). It appeared complete, treble and bass, in Jones's *Relicks of the Welsh Bards* (1784 and 1794), with the changed spelling of the title.

SICH (Ger.) .'Oneself', 'himself', 'herself', 'itself', 'themselves'.

SICILIANO, SICILIANA (It., masc., fem.). 'Sicilian.' So *Alla siciliana*, in the Sicilian style, or 'In the style of the Siciliano' (see below).

SICILIANO (It.), **SICILIENNE** (Fr.). An old dance type (supposedly of Sicilian origin), in slowish time and swaying rhythm, of six-or-twelve-beats-in-a-measure. It is often in the minor. The eighteenth-century composers used it for both instrumental and vocal compositions, but perhaps especially as the slow movement in violin suites and sonatas. In form the siciliano is generally tripartite, i.e. first section, second section, and first repeated. The *Pastorale* (q.v.) is much the same sort of thing; so is the *Gondoliera*.

SI CONTRA FA. See *Tritone*.

SIDE DRUM. See *Percussion Family* 3 i; 4 b, 5 i.

SIDNEY, PHILIP. See *Hungary*; *Ballade*.

SIEBEN (Ger.). 'Seven.'

SIEG (Ger.). 'Victory.' So several compounds such as *Siegesmarsch*, a march celebrating victory.

SIEGFRIED. See *Ring of the Nibelung*.

SIEGMEISTER, ELIE. Born in New York in 1909. He studied under Riegger and Nadia Boulanger, and at the Juilliard School, and started composing stage, orchestral, and chamber music, etc., modern in sound but intended to make a popular appeal, being often inspired by themes of American life. In 1949 he joined the faculty of Hofstra College.

SIEMENS-BECHSTEIN. See *Electric Musical Instruments* 3 a.

SIFFLÖTE (Ger.). 'Whistle-flute'—a high-pitched organ stop (2 ft. or 1 ft.).

SIGHT-SINGING

1. The Beginnings.
2. The Two Outlooks.

3. Teaching Difficulties.
4. Should all Pupils be taught?

5. The Phenomenon of 'Natural' Sight-singing.

(For illustrations see p. 960, pl. **161**; 961, **162**; 976, **163**.)

1. The Beginnings. In early days there was no sight-singing. The traditional plainsong of the churches was learnt by ear, and so passed down from generation to generation, and the notation was merely sufficient to indicate to the singer which piece of plainsong he was to take from his memorized store, and to remind him of its general shapes.

Definite sight-singing study and practice began, apparently, with the monk Guido d'Arezzo (lived about 995–1050; p. 960, pl. **161**. 1), in the monastery of Pomposa, near Ravenna. He devised the system of Hexachords, which held the field for about five centuries, and he improved the notation, developing the two-line staff into the present one of five lines.

His system (explained in the article *Hexachord*) was based upon a recurring group of notes, with the tones and semitones falling the same every time. This makes it, in a way, the ancestor of the movable-doh systems of today (see *Tonic Sol-fa*).

2. The Two Outlooks. When in the sixteenth and seventeenth centuries Guido's system broke down (owing to reasons explained under *Hexachord*) it was followed, after various attempts at adaptation in various countries, by a system in which the alphabetical names of the notes were the guide to the singer; in this system if d'Arezzo's names (ut-re-mi, etc.) were used, as they were in some countries, they were generally mere substitutes for the letter names, fixed to their actual pitches and not to positions in a group of notes or a key, i.e. 'sol' was always G, and so on. Such systems are the ancestors of the fixed-doh systems of today.

In the 'movable-doh' or 'tonic' systems, the general principle is always that described in the article *Tonic Sol-fa*. In the fixed-doh system the usual plan is to proceed by interval, calculating the extent of each leap or step before it is taken. (For a curious system everywhere taught in England from at least the beginning of the seventeenth century to the early nineteenth, and still current in the Southern United States, see *Lancashire Sol-fa*.)

Roughly speaking, the British Commonwealth and United States now use movable-doh systems and the continental European countries (and countries originally colonized from them) fixed-doh systems. But the Galin-Paris–Chevé movable-doh system is French and Tonika Do is German (see *Tonic Sol-fa*—end of article), and Poland has largely adopted movable-doh.

Galin, Paris, and Chevé were respectively a teacher of mathematics, a barrister, and a medical man. Theirs is a figure system, the keynote always being '1', the dominant always '5', and so on: this had been proposed by Rousseau in 1742 and by others before him. A rhythmic device which forms a more valuable part of the system is treated under *Tonic Sol-fa*.

A disadvantage of all fixed-doh systems is the progressive difficulty as keys take on more sharps or flats. The key of C is very easy; G and F are only a trifle harder; by the time the keys of four or five sharps or flats are reached the pupil has become discouraged. Movable-doh methods have, from the singer's point of view, only one key and hence are infinitely easier. On the other hand, they tend to break down in keyless music, for which fixed-doh methods, however difficult, are probably more suitable. Should microtonal divisions ever be applied to choral music (see *Microtones*) some totally new system will be needed: at present microtones only appear in such music without indication by the composer or the intention of the singers, and under the frown of the conductor.

The above discusses the difference between systems only on the side of pitch; they differ also in their treatment of rhythmic phenomena, but, roughly speaking, it may be said that movable-doh systems, as they regard the key and its degrees rather than the absolute names of sounds, so also regard the bar (measure) and the beat (pulse) rather than the absolute values; i.e. they talk of a one-beat note or a half-beat note rather than of minims, crotchets, and quavers, or half, quarter, and eighth notes, etc. The most logical and psychologically true presentation of rhythmic phenomena is undoubtedly that of tonic sol-fa (q.v.).

3. Teaching Difficulties. The teaching of sight-reading presents difficulties for the teacher, and, as a consequence, progress is often nothing like as rapid and sure as it ought to be. One failure is in not grading sufficiently minutely and even omitting essential steps: teachers of mathematics could have no success whatever if they graded their teaching as thoughtlessly as do many teachers of sight-singing. Another failure is in treating the class as the unit: in any class there will be present two or three musically-gifted individuals (see 5 below) who will lead the rest unless the teacher can detect them, tactfully silence them from time to time, divide and subdivide the class (perhaps with one section in friendly competition with another as the ostensible reason for the division), encourage occasional sight-singing by members of the class singly, set written tests in ear-training (the converse of sight-singing, offering exactly the same training of the ear), and in other ways ensure that *each individual* has the motive to think for himself and acquires the habit of doing so. When the whole class reads a test together the pupil who spoils the effect by boldly singing a wrong note is more praiseworthy than the many who merely go with the crowd. The occasional

occurrence of the accident of the crowd taking the wrong note together should open the eyes of teachers to the prevalence of the evil of crowd-singing, but, strangely, such symptoms are often ignored. Other failures in teaching are a lack of interest for the pupils (though sight-singing is properly a form of 'sport'), and a divorce of sight-singing from music—a treatment of it as a science and not as a branch of the art. Where the teacher of sight-singing is a good musician without training as a teacher he would do well to study books on class management and practical teaching; where he is a practical teacher but not a musician he should take means to increase his musicianship.

The definite laying-out of a scheme for the term, semester, or school year is an essential for good work, although, as the lessons proceed, it may be found necessary to modify it, owing to the class proving slower or quicker than expected. Every lesson should show a definite step forward on the two sides of rhythm and tune, unless a particular lesson be one deliberately reserved for revision. Further, every lesson should be prepared; the teacher should know exactly what he means to do and how many minutes he expects to take in doing it, as otherwise he will find himself labouring some point and extending one feature of the lesson to the necessary omission of some other features.

It is not usually advisable to use the class's intended repertory of songs as reading material, first because it is hard to grade the difficulties minutely, and secondly because in labouring over songs in sight-singing one diminishes the interest in them as music. Returning to and extending a thought expressed earlier in this article, treat sight-singing as sport and song-singing as art, and the pupils will enjoy both.

4. Should all Pupils be taught?—The question whether all school-children should be taught to sing at sight is sometimes debated: certain American observers say that only a proportion of them attain proficiency and that those who do not could have spent their time more profitably in other ways, such as a larger measure of song-singing. They consider that, by means of mental tests, the musical cream of the class should be skimmed off for separate treatment; mere milk, they say, can never make butter, and it is only annoying to it to be put in the churn; nor, they say, can butter be made so long as milk remains mingled with the cream. The opponents of this view say that a grasp of the principles of sight-singing is the rightful heritage of all, as is a grasp of the principles of reading one's own language, and that a child who can sing a song can learn to sing at sight. Undoubtedly a grading and re-grading of pupils according to natural ability and progress made is important (though in many schools difficult of attainment), but this does not necessarily imply that there is any grade incapable of useful work at sight-singing.

5. The Phenomenon of 'Natural' Sight-singing. In closing this article it may be admitted that a certain number of highly gifted musicians in every country need no methodical training in sight-singing; that possessing a sense of absolute pitch (q.v.) they seem to pick up the ability to read by some knack of direct association between the sign and the sound. Such persons are generally useless as teachers as they are incapable of putting themselves in the place of the ordinary pupil. Where they come into positions of official influence they are educationally dangerous on account of their impression that sight-singing is a simple matter of understanding notation (a mere intellectual process), whereas to 99 per cent. of pupils it is primarily a matter of training the musical ear.

In all probability, a really skilful sight-singer, by whatever method he has been taught, in actual practice makes use of a combination of means. The processes by which an advanced sight-singer works are probably, in the end, beyond analysis. This, of course, does not exempt the teacher from the duty of giving his pupils the best possible method as a foundation.

See *Dictionaries* 10; *Colour and Music* 13.

SIGNALHORN. See *Bugle*.

SIGNATURE. A 'sign' placed at the opening of a composition or of a section of a composition, indicating the key ('Key Signature') or the value of the beat and the number of beats in each measure ('Time Signature').

The 'Key Signature' consists of one or more sharps or flats (see Table 8), the 'Time Signature' usually of figures resembling a fraction (see Table 10).

SIGNATURE TUNE. The term appears to date from the 1920s when dance bands enjoyed enormous favour. It became the custom (when broadcasting at all events) for each band to pick a popular tune with which to sign its work, this tune being played at the end of every performance (sometimes at the beginning, too).

Max Beerbohm (*The Listener*, 22 Jan. 1942) says that R. G. Knowles ('The Very Peculiar American Comedian') in the 1880s and 1890s originated the custom, his appearance on the stage being always made to the accompaniment of the opening bars of Mendelssohn's Wedding March.

(Cf. *Wait* for an apparently similar practice in the sixteenth and seventeenth centuries.)

SIGTENHORST-MEYER. See *Holland* 8.

SIGURD. See *Reyer*.

SILAS, ÉDOUARD. Born at Amsterdam in 1827 and died in London in 1909, aged eighty-one. He was a boy prodigy, who, after studying at the Paris Conservatory, settled in London as a teacher and organist. His choral and orchestral works were produced at the Crystal Palace and elsewhere, and his piano works had popularity, but he is now chiefly remembered by his compositions for the organ.

See reference under *Reed-Organ Family* 5.

SILBERMANN, GOTTFRIED. See *Pianoforte* 4, 5; *Barocco*.

'SILENT' DOG WHISTLE. See *Ear and Hearing* 4; *Acoustics* 2.

SILENZIO (It.). 'Silence.'

SILVER BAND. A 'Brass Band' (q.v.) of which the instruments appear, or are reputed, to be made of silver.

SIMCOCK, JOHN. See *Bell Harp*.

SIMILAR MOTION. See *Motion*.

SIMILE, SIMILI (It., sing., plur.). 'Similar.' Some indication having been given, the composer avoids the necessity for constant repetition of it by thus intimating that its effect is to continue.

SIMPLE BINARY. See *Form* 4, 5, 8, 13, 14.

SIMPLE DUPLE. See Table 10.

SIMPLEMENT (Fr.). 'Simply', in a simple manner.

SIMPLE QUADRUPLE, SIMPLE TRIPLE. See Table 10.

SIMPLE TERNARY. See *Form* 4, 6, 8, 13, 14.

SIMPSON (or Sympson).

(1) CHRISTOPHER (p. 389, pl. **66.** 2). Died either in Lincolnshire or in London in 1669. He was a famous player of the viola da gamba (see *Viol Family* 3) and the author of important treatises such as *The Division Violist* (see *Divisions*), which continued to appear in new editions for sixty years after his death. His compositions are for viols.

See references under *Microtones*; *Descant*; *Divisions*; *Folía*; *Ground*; *Lancashire Sol-fa*; also p. 1073, pl. **178.**3.

(2) THOMAS (early seventeenth century). He held court positions as a violist in Germany and Denmark and published books of dances, etc., in Frankfurt and Hamburg (cf. *Scandinavia* 2; *Viol Family* 3).

SIMPSON, CANON ARTHUR S. See *Bell* 1.

SIMROCK. See *Publishing* 8; *Bohm*.

SIN' (It.). Abbreviation of *Sino*, 'until', e.g. *Sin' al segno*, 'until the sign'.

SINDING, CHRISTIAN (p. 896, pl. **153.** 6). Born at Kongsberg in Norway in 1856 and died in 1941, aged eighty-five. He studied at Christiania (now Oslo), and then, supported by his government, at the Conservatory of Leipzig and at Dresden, Munich, and Berlin. A good deal of his life was spent in Germany, but he also lived at Christiania, and at Rochester, New York, where he was for a brief period professor of composition at the Eastman School of Music.

He first made a name as a composer when he was nearing thirty, with his Piano Quintet, which was harshly discussed and then widely accepted. Later works included two violin concertos and a piano concerto (in earlier student days he played violin and piano), three symphonies, a symphonic poem, chamber music, an opera, violin music, piano music (including the ubiquitously popular *Rustle of Spring*), choral music, over two hundred songs, etc. He may be described as a nationalist-romantic.

See *Concerto* 6 c (1856).

SINE NOMINE. See *Mass* 5.

SINFONIA. See *Overture* 1; *Suite* 4.

SINFONICO, SINFONICA (It., masc., fem.). 'Symphonic.'

SINFONIETTA (It.). A symphony on a smaller scale—smaller as to length, or as to orchestral forces employed, or as to both.

SINFONISCHE DICHTUNG. *Symphonic Poem* (q.v.).

SINGAKADEMIE, BERLIN. See *Fasch, Carl Friedrich Christian.*

SINGBAR (Ger.). 'Singable', or 'in a singing style'.

SINGEND (Ger.). 'Singing' (cf. *Cantabile*).

SINGHIOZZANDO (It.). 'Sobbingly.'

SINGING

1. Introductory.
2. Italy as 'the Land of Song'.
3. Early Schools of Singing.
4. Bel Canto.
5. The Eighteenth-century Sing-ing-masters.

6. A Contemporary Description of a Great Eighteenth-century Singer.
7. The Eighteenth-century Con-servatories.
8. The French Ideals.

9. Printed 'Methods' of Singing.
10. The Decay of Bel Canto.
11. The Scientific Study of Song and Speech.
12. Some Hints to Young Singers.

(For illustrations see p. 960, pl. **161, 162**.)

1. Introductory. The art of singing has been cultivated in some sort of way amongst all peoples that have attained any considerable degree of ordered life. An interesting instance of early systematization of the art and of in-struction in it is found in the work of Ziryáb, who in the early ninth century left the court of Hárún-ar-Rashéd (the famous Caliph of Bagh-dad of *The Arabian Nights*) and established himself at Córdoba in Spain (then, of course, in Moorish occupation). His method has been set out in J. B. Trend's *The Music of Spanish History* as follows:

'As a teacher of singing he divided his instruction into three courses, rhythm, melody, and orna-mentation. The pupil had first to pass certain tests, one of which was to sing a prolonged *ah* on all degrees of the scale. Then he began by learning the words and metre; he spoke the words while he beat time with a tambourine, marking the strong and the weak accents, and the pace of different movements. Then he was taught the melody in its simplest form with no ornaments, and only when he could sing it perfectly was he allowed to study the shakes, vocalizes, scale-passages, and apog-giaturas with which the master embellished the song, and the nuances he introduced to give it expression and charm.'

2. Italy as 'the Land of Song'. But long before this period the definite cultivation of singing had begun in Rome, and we may almost say that from the fourth century to the present Italy has held a sort of primacy amongst the singing nations. The chief reasons for this seem to be as follows: (*a*) The language, with its many pure (i.e. undiphthongic) vowels and its absence of final consonants, lends itself to the singing use of the voice (see *Voice*, 9, 20). (*b*) From the birth of the Christian Church song was much used in its services, and from the early fourth century onwards Rome was recognized as the headquarters of the Western branch of that Church. (*c*) Opera and oratorio were both of them originally Italian forms of musical art and this led to the high cultivation

in Italy of the voice and of the technique of its improvement in the individual. (Cf. *Italy* 5.)

3. Early Schools of Singing. The growth of a large corpus of church song (see *Plainsong*), the necessity of memorizing it, and also of acquiring the breathing technique and the per-fect legato required for its performance, quickly led to the establishment in Rome of an official school of song. St. Sylvester (Pope from 314 to 336) may be regarded as the founder of this.

Probably the prohibition of congregational singing by the Council of Laodicea in 367, with the consequent increased importance of trained choirs, gave further impetus to the movement for the definite cultivation of singing.

In 580 the great monastery of Monte Cassino, founded by St. Benedict half a century earlier, was destroyed by the Lombards, and the monks took refuge in Rome, where, under Pope Pela-gius II, they opened schools for candidates for the priesthood and greatly developed the study of church song. St. Gregory (Pope from 590 to 604) was a strong protector of the Benedictine Order and also of church music (see *Plainsong* 3; *Modes* 5), and during his Papacy some recon-struction of the arrangements for the teaching of song took place in the development of the Schola Cantorum (q.v.), with a nine-years' course of study.

During the period of residence of Popes at Avignon (1309–77) the Flemish singers and composers (the same individuals fulfilled in those days both avocations) came to the front and were much employed at the Papal Court. On the return of the Popes to Rome their em-ployment continued, and in the later fifteenth and earlier sixteenth centuries the choir of the Sistine Chapel was almost entirely recruited from Flanders. (Cf. *Belgium* 1.)

It may be supposed, from the nature of the music composed during the period from Dufay (d. 1474) to the death of Palestrina (1594), that the technical cultivation of singing had reached

P p

a very high level. The implication is that a good command of the breath (giving the power to sing long phrases) and of the 'registers' (giving the power to pass from one to another without perceptible 'break') was recognized as a necessary qualification, together, also, with perfect flexibility.

Apparently boys were at this period in full use in the Roman choirs, but towards the end of the sixteenth century their voices were supplemented by those of Spanish falsettists (see *Voice* 5), and later of castrati (see *Voice* 5), the permanence of whose voices was, of course, a great advantage, the careful musical and vocal training of boys, to enjoy the mature use of their musical and vocal ability only for a year or two, being one of the great bugbears of choir-mastership from that day to this.

At the time of the introduction of opera (1600) there was, apparently, an abundance of vocal technique, ability, and experience to be drawn upon. Caccini, joint composer of the world's second opera, *Eurydice* (see *Opera*; *Caccini*), was himself an able singer, and his daughter, who sang the title-role of that opera, had an international reputation. A glance at Caccini's collection of vocal compositions, *The New Music* (1602), will show that nearly all the notoriously exacting demands of the great period of the Italian vocal compositions of the succeeding two centuries were already being made. Rapid and extended divisions are there in abundance, and the common impression that the continuity of long and smooth phrasing, an obvious requirement even in the more elaborate plainsong, yielded entirely to that of declamatory singing (see *Recitative*) is based on the reading of over-concise textbooks of the history of music and insufficient knowledge of the music itself.

4. Bel Canto. Thence onwards, it may be said, *Bel Canto* (q.v.) reigned with increasing authority, for, though the dramatic force of recitative was greatly valued, so was the beauty of pure, even tone and perfect control in the more lyrical sort of vocal composition, the highly virtuoso or gymnastic type of which gradually threw recitative somewhat into the shade and tended to relegate it to the position of a secondary element in opera and oratorio— a means of pushing on the dramatic plot in order that the audience might quickly again enjoy another ten minutes of the more definitely musical pleasure.

The Italian singing-master was a very important personage in the musical world from the days of Caccini onwards, and the writings of that singer–composer, and of many of his successors for the following two centuries and more, make it clear to us how seriously they took their duties and those of their pupils. A protracted devotion to solfeggi (see *Solfeggio*) was demanded, with a minute study of 'ornaments' (see *Ornaments or Graces*; *Coloratura*), especially the shake. Agility and the control of the breath, the practice of the various vowels, the interpretation of the words of the song—all

these were the subject of the greatest attention. The *Messa di Voce* (q.v.) was enormously practised. Slow practice in the earlier stages was insisted upon, with the avoidance of all strain, so that the jerry-built voice that collapses after a few years' service was then unknown. Volume was not an object, beauty of tone being put in the very first place.

Lastly, it may be said, the ideals of vocalism were then instrumental. The voice was, by training, to become a lovely flute. The music of those days (and indeed until the time of Beethoven and Wagner) expressed sorrow and joy but rarely violent passion, and perfection of tone was the first requisite.

5. The Eighteenth-century Singing-masters. The great teacher Tosi (died at some date after 1730) in his old age embodied his precepts in a volume in which he puts the proper order of study as: (1) 'placing' of the voice (see *Voice* 14); (2) gymnastic vocalization on vowels; (3) the study of ornaments (see *Ornaments or Graces*); (4) the singing of songs with words.

Porpora (1686–1766), who could claim amongst his pupils many singers whose names are still world-famous, is said to have confined his pupil Caffarelli for five years to exercises written on one sheet of paper and then sent him into the world with his blessing: 'Go, my son; I can teach you nothing more. You are the greatest singer in Europe.' Assuming that Caffarelli was made to pursue all the studies in composition, instrumental performance, and literature which then formed a part of the daily work of vocal students, he still had a vocal task which from its lack of variety must have called for the most determined perseverance. As vocal 'interpretation' would not seem to be adequately included in the curriculum on the ordinary understanding of the words 'a sheet of paper', it might be worth while to inquire in what sizes paper was made in those days and into how many pages a single sheet could be folded: perhaps, too, Porpora's writing was very microscopic; he may have been the inventor of the miniature score. Whatever be the explanation of this strange story, which is to be found in almost every dictionary of music and history of music, the moral implication with which it is told to every succeeding generation of vocal students is excellent—'make haste slowly'.

For a curious late eighteenth-century device for vocal development see *Herschel, Caroline.*

6. A Contemporary Description of a Great Eighteenth-century Singer. As an instance of the kind of singing that was valued in the eighteenth century there may be offered a short extract from the seven quarto pages which Burney, in his famous *History of Music* (1776–89) gives to one Italian singer, the castrato soprano Pacchierotti, who was a high favourite in London for the last twenty years of the eighteenth century:

'The natural tone of his voice is so interesting, sweet and pathetic, that when he had a long note, or *messa di voce*, I never wished him to change it, or do any thing but swell, diminish, or prolong it in whatever way he pleased, to the utmost limit of his lungs. A great compass of voice downwards, with an ascent up to B♭ and sometimes to C in alt, with an unbounded fancy, and a power not only of executing the most refined and difficult passages of other singers, but of inventing new embellishments which, so far as my musical reading and experience extended, had never then been on paper, made him, during his long residence here, a new singer to me every time I heard him. If the different degrees of sweetness in musical tones to the ear might be compared to the effects of different savours on the palate, it would perhaps convey my idea of its perfection by saying that it is as superior to the generality of vocal sweetness, as that of the pine apple is, not only to other fruits, but to sugar or treacle.' (*History of Music*, iv. 511.)

7. The Eighteenth-century Conservatories.

The great *conservatorios* of Naples and the *hospitals* (orphanages or foundling hospitals for girls; cf. *Schools of Music*) of Venice were in the eighteenth century two outstanding sources of Europe's vocal supply, and Burney gives very interesting descriptions of each. Of one of the Venice establishments he says, 'The young singers are absolute nightingales; they have a facility of executing difficult divisions equal to that of birds. They did such things in that way as I do not remember to have heard attempted before.' Of another he says, 'The girls played a thousand tricks in singing, particularly in the duets, where there was a trial of skill and of natural powers, as who could go highest, lowest, swell a note the longest, or run divisions with the greatest rapidity' (*Present State of Music in France and Italy*, 1771). The eighteenth-century ideals are pretty well expressed in these various extracts from Burney, whose judgement, taste, and knowledge were recognized all over Europe and whose books were known to musicians outside his own country by several translations.

The true *Bel Canto* method and skill applied to worthy musical material was a great possession for a singer, but, as Berlioz remarked later, many who acquired its technique were nothing beyond 'performers on the larynx'.

A large proportion of the 'Kings' and 'Queens' of Song still come from Italy. Largely they devote themselves to the more lucrative and glorious side of the profession—that of the opera stage. But now that the Wagnerian and post-Wagnerian works are in the repertory the Italians no longer enjoy an undisputed supremacy.

8. The French Ideals.

Whilst Italy was thus cultivating what may be called the airs and graces of song, France, on the initiative of the Italian-born Lully (1632–87), was paying more attention to that declamatory style which the Italians had founded about the year 1600 and then a good deal abandoned. But the decoration of the written notes by the singer's introduction of his own ornamental additions (*Agrémens*) was, as in Italy, highly cultivated and was carefully taught under the name 'goût

de chant' ('taste in singing'); there were singing teachers who specialized in this branch of the art and were known as 'Maîtres du Goût de Chant'. The popularity in Paris of the operas of the German-born Gluck, who was active there in the 1770s, with their high emphasis on dramatic feeling, much reduced the love of this tinsel and gilt of vocalism.

9. Printed 'Methods' of Singing.

It was much the fashion for French and English writers during the eighteenth century (e.g. Rousseau and Burney) to decry French singing (as also French composition) and to exalt Italian. The study of the vocal art in France has, however, been very thorough. In 1803 the professors of the Paris Conservatory issued a collective method of singing study. Panseron (1795–1859) is one of the most eminent authors of 'methods' and collections of solfeggi for singers. But such methods and collections have been freely issued by the singing-masters of all countries, and the publication, in 1927, by Sir Henry Wood, of four large folio-size volumes (*The Gentle Art of Singing*), containing 1,470 vocal exercises, showed that the faith in the value of extended and detailed study of carefully devised vocal passages (as distinct from the interpretative study of songs, which is, of course, also necessary) had not entirely given way before the pressure of modern impatience. (Perhaps in heaven there are interesting disputes between Porpora and Sir Henry Wood.)

10. The Decay of Bel Canto.

Quite obviously the vocal demands of such composers as Meyerbeer, Wagner, and Verdi (to name only three examples) are very different from those of the innumerable forgotten Italian composers of the eighteenth century or even of Bach, Handel, and Mozart; the vocal style of the later men derives largely from that of the earlier, but it lays, on the whole, greater emphasis on the expression of feeling. Crudely generalizing (and perhaps exaggerating), one may say that in the eighteenth century the composer was the slave of the singer, and that in the nineteenth the singer became the slave of the composer. Dramatic effect and strongly marked expression are now looked for, where beauty of tone and the other 'instrumental' qualities were formerly the first requirement. Power has become important in these days of heavy orchestral accompaniment, and in Italy itself, as would appear from any cursory study of the best-selling vocal gramophone records, the loud singer is now the good singer. Virtuosity is still recognized; it is, however, now no longer the old Italian virtuosity of the trapeze and tight-rope but that of the accomplished histrion.

At the same time a high fidelity to the detailed thought and emotion of the poet has become a demand since the rise of the German Lieder school (Schubert, Schumann, Wolf, etc.; see *Song* 5). Something has been gained and something lost.

11. The Scientific Study of Song and Speech. Science entered the vocal studio with the introduction of the laryngoscope by the great singing teacher Garcia in 1855, and the study of the functions and action of the vocal cords, by its use, together with a growing interest in vocal technique on the part of both physiologists and phoneticians, has made possible the accumulation of a body of scientific fact, of which a summary has been attempted in this volume under the heading *Voice*.

12. Some Hints to Young Singers.
(1) Remember that you can do nothing at interpretation until your technique is so sure that it has become practically entirely subconscious. Therefore persevere in pushing on every branch of your technique to that advanced stage.

(2) Most of the great singing teachers say that the less you know about the physiology of singing the better. Santley wrote (in *The Art of Singing*): 'Manuel Garcia is held up as the pioneer of scientific teachers of singing. He was—but he taught singing, not surgery! I was a pupil of his in 1858, and a friend of his while he lived [to 1906], and in all the conversation I had with him I never heard him say a word about larynx or pharynx, glottis, or other organ used in the production and emission of the voice.'

Nevertheless, as the great singing teachers themselves have taken care thoroughly to understand the physiology of singing, and as you will almost certainly one day yourself do some teaching, it may be well to acquire a rudimentary scientific knowledge, a knowledge both of the physics and the physiology of singing—an extension of what is given in this volume under the headings *Voice* and (to some extent) *Acoustics*. But do not come to rely on this or to introduce scientific reasoning into your practice; simply do what your teacher tells you (the reason for which you will now, perhaps, understand a little better) and expect the result he promises.

(3) Remember that the conquering of 'long phrasing' and other apparent difficulties is largely a matter of sufficient courage. Within large limits what you expect to be able to do you can do; faith can remove mountains.

(4) Do not practise to the point of physical exhaustion, but avoid this by taking up some other musical study which you have always at hand.

(5) Become not merely a singer but a musician. Take up another instrument (preferably not another purely melodic one like your own, but the piano). And by this means become acquainted with a musical literature other than that of song.

(6) Hear all the great singers possible, in the concert-hall or opera-house, or by means of recordings and radio. But do not try to copy features in their singing which are personal to them and may suit them but not you, and avoid their mannerisms. Hear also the great instrumentalists and try to find out what makes them great. Above all, in listening to either great singers or great players try, by close attention, to get a concept of what is meant by 'style'.

(7) Make it your ambition to acquire a big repertory inclusive of everything most valuable, of all ages or nations, that really suits your voice, physique, and temperament (see *Song*). But find out what type of song really does meet these conditions and do not waste time and energy over what is too big for your voice, or in other ways unsuitable.

(8) Do not sing in public until your teacher assures you you are fully ready to do so. You will be led to over-exert yourself and you will receive flattery or discouragement, either of which will be bad for you.

(9) In waiting for the word 'go' (as regards public solo appearance) sing in a choir—being careful, of course, never to sing with effort or undue force.

(10) Do not take up a course of study for the profession without seeking what you are sure will be totally unbiased advice—preferably seeking this in two or three different quarters for purposes of comparison. It is the deliberate opinion of a great conductor who is also a great singing-master that a fine wood-wind player's opinion of a singer is often worth more than another singer's or a singing teacher's.

(11) Finally, remember that good singing is much more than mere able use of the voice. The great baritone Ffrangcon-Davies (1855–1918), whose book *The Singing of the Future* gives the secrets of his own very moving art, perhaps adequately summarized those secrets in this concluding paragraph of one of his chapters:

'The whole spiritual system, spirit, mind, sense-soul, together with the whole muscular system from feet to head, will be in the wise man's singing, *and the whole man will be in the tone.*'

For a common fault in singing, and its causes, see *Tremolo and Vibrato*.

SINGING BY NOTE (in American Colonies). See *Hymns and Hymn Tunes* 11.

SINGING COMMERCIAL. Name adopted in United States broadcasting circles for a brief, pithy announcement of some commodity, set to a catchy musical phrase or two.

SINGING MICE. Wide interest in these performers was aroused in 1937 by a series of competitions held by radio in the United States, followed by an international competition, also by radio, in which eminent mouse vocalists of the United States, Canada, and Britain were heard in friendly artistic rivalry. A scientist's description of a prima donna examined by him ran:

'Its voice ranged through two octaves, the notes partly resembling the high tones of the lark, partly the long-drawn flute-like tones of the nightingale, and partly the deep, liquid trilling of a canary.'

Post-mortem examination of such performers has disclosed the disappointing fact that they do not, like the birds and the humans, sing out of the joy or sorrow of their heart, but merely out of an inflammation of their respiratory organs, their song being, in fact, merely an accidentally artistic wheeze.

SINGING QUAKERS. See *Quakers* (end of article).

SINGING SANDS. See *Musical Sand.*

SINGING SAW. This is an ordinary hand-saw which is held between the player's knees and played on by a violin bow; its blade is meanwhile bent, under a lesser or greater tension, by the player's left hand, so producing the different pitches. (Milhaud, in his book *Études*, 1927, describes the same process but with blows from a drumstick substituted for the friction of a bow.)

SINGLE CHANT. See *Anglican Chant.*

SINGLE CLEF SYSTEM. See *Notation* 7.

SINGLE-TONGUING. See *Tonguing.*

SINGSPIEL (literally 'Sing-play') is practically the German equivalent of 'English Opera' in the technical sense of the term (see under *Ballad Opera*), i.e. it has spoken dialogue broken by interpolated songs. It probably had its origin in the old religious plays (see *Mysteries, Miracle Plays, and Moralities*), but it received a powerful stimulus from the English Jig (q.v.) of the early seventeenth century and the Ballad Opera (q.v.) of the middle of the eighteenth century. A performance in Berlin, 1743, of a German version of the Englishman Coffey's ballad opera *The Devil to Pay* had little success, but that of another version in Leipzig in 1764 had a great run and led the authors of the version, the poet C. F. Weisse (1726–1804) and the composer of its music, J. A. Hiller (1728–1804; p. 396, pl. **67**. 8), to produce a number of such pieces of their own making. Hiller is, therefore, usually looked upon as 'The Father of the Singspiel'.

Meanwhile this same opera of Coffey's (it was going about the world a great deal just then, e.g. it was heard in New York in 1751) had reached Vienna (1767) in the form of a French version that had been given in Paris, and so the Singspiel started there also.

Obviously German *Singspiel*, French *Vaudeville* (q.v.) and *Opéra-Comique* (q.v.), and *English Opera* (see *Opera* 13 d) were in essence the same. With their intelligibility (use of the vernacular and comparative simplicity of music) they constituted a form of entertainment that was more accessible to a certain public than 'Grand Opera'. And some of the greatest composers have not disdained to write in this form, as, for instance, Haydn (*Philemon and Baucis*, 1773, and other works) and Mozart (*The Theatre Director*, 1786; *The Magic Flute*, 1791; and, above all, *The Abduction from the Seraglio*, 1782; the last-named actually bears the description 'Singspiel' on its title-page), Beethoven (*Fidelio*, 1805), and Weber (all his operas except *Euryanthe*, which is set to music throughout). Goethe wrote the libretti of four Singspiele for the theatre at Weimar.

It is, perhaps, doubtful, however, whether we ought to apply the description 'Singspiel' to such elaborate works as those of Mozart, Weber, and Beethoven. They are in the vernacular and they have spoken dialogue, but they have developed far beyond the original ideal of a spoken play complete in itself yet relieved by the insertion of simple songs.

One of the most popular *Singspiele* ever produced is Dittersdorf's *Doctor and Apothecary* (1786), which is still often to be heard in Germany; it may be said perhaps to belong to an intermediate type.

Note. Whilst the above information defines the term as generally understood it may be mentioned that Mattheson (q.v.), in the eighteenth century, seems in his writings to use the term as the equivalent simply of 'opera'—of any type.

SINIGAGLIA, LEONE. Born at Turin in 1868 and died there in 1944. His compositions have high repute; many of them are based upon folk melodies of his native Piedmont.

SINISTRA (It.). 'Left' (hand).

SINK-A-PACE. See *Pavan and Galliard.*

SINO, SIN' (It.). 'Until', e.g. *Sin' al segno* = Go on 'until the sign'.

SINUS. See *Voice* 6, 21.

SIR. See *Knighthood and other Honours.*

SIR ALEX. DON'S STRATHSPEY. See *Auld Lang Syne.*

SIR ROGER DE COVERLEY. This is an old English dance (see *Country Dance*), long used as the finale for a ball, and still in use. The tune is a variant of the Scottish one of *The Maltman*, sometimes also called *Roger the Cavalier*, but it is not proved that this is of actual Scottish origin.

In Virginia the same tune used to be (perhaps still is) known as *My Aunt Margery* and the dance is said to be the same as the 'Virginia Reel'.

SISTINE CHAPEL AND CHOIR. See *Belgium* 2; *Voice* 5; *Singing* 3; *Tonic Sol-fa* 10; *Miserere*; *Allegri*; *Cappella*. Also p. 516, pl. **93**. 1.

SISTRUM. A sort of tinkling instrument (rings on a metal frame with a handle by which to shake it), used by many ancient nations and occasionally revived by nineteenth-century composers.

SITOLE. See *Cittern.*

SITTRON. See *Cittern.*

SITWELL, EDITH (1887–1964). See references s.v. *Programme Music* 2; *Walton.*

SIVIGLIANO, SIVIGLIANA (It., masc., fem.). 'In the style of Seville.'

SIVORI, ERNESTO CAMILLO. Born at Genoa in 1815 and died there in 1894, aged seventy-eight. A widely-travelling violin virtuoso and a composer for his instrument. He had much popularity in Britain and North and South America.

SIX (Fr.). 'Six'; hence *Sixième*, 'sixth'.

SIX-FOUR CHORD. See *Harmony* 24 f.

SIX, LES. See *France* 11.

SIXTEEN-FOOT C, etc. See *Pitch* 7.

SIXTEEN-FOOT STOP. See *Organ* 2 b.

SIXTEENTH-NOTE (Amer.). 'Semiquaver' (Table 3).

SIXTH. See *Interval*.

SIXTH, ADDED. See *Added Sixth*.

SIXTH, AUGMENTED. See *Augmented Sixth*.

SIXTH, CHORD OF. See *Harmony* 24 f.

SIXTH FLUTE. See *Recorder Family* 2.

SIX-THREE CHORD. See *Harmony* 24 f.

SIXTY-FOUR FOOT STOP. See *Organ* 2 b.

SIXTY-FOURTH NOTE (Amer.). 'Hemi-demisemiquaver' (Table 3).

SIZZLE CYMBAL. This is much like the normal cymbal (see *Percussion Family* 3 o, 4 b, 5 o) with five or six small jingles ('sizzlers') lying on its upper surface, to which they are loosely attached. It is played with a special kind of snare drum stick. The dance band is the home of this instrument.

SJEROFF. See *Serof*.

SJÖGREN, EMIL (in full, Johann Gustav Emil). Born at Stockholm, Sweden, in 1853 and died there in 1918, aged sixty-four. He studied at the conservatory of his native place and then in Berlin. He then settled in Stockholm as a church organist, composing prolifically for solo voice, chorus, piano, organ, and violin.

He counts as a nationalist-romantic, with the greater emphasis on the latter word, perhaps, since the Scandinavian character of his music is not so pronounced as that of the music of (say) Grieg or Sinding.

SKALDS. See *Scandinavia* 5.

SKALKOTTAS, NIKOS. Born at Chalcis, Greece, in 1904 and died at Athens in 1949, aged forty-five. He studied under Weill and Schönberg, but on return to Greece he had difficulty in making his way, and his gifts became known only after his early death. His works include orchestral pieces, concertos, chamber music, and songs, in a style influenced by his teachers but individual none the less.

SKENE MANUSCRIPT. See *Scotland* 1, 7.

SKETCH (Fr. *Esquisse*; Ger. *Skizze*). A brief, slight instrumental composition, generally for piano, and, it may be, having some pictorial suggestion. (The term is also applied to a composer's first rough draft of a composition or of some of its material: thus we speak of Beethoven's celebrated 'Sketch Books'.)

SKILTON, CHARLES SANFORD. Born at Northampton, Mass., in 1868 and died at

Lawrence, Kansas, in 1941. He wrote piano, organ, orchestral, and choral works, some of which have had great popularity—especially his *Indian Dances*.

SKIZZE, SKIZZEN (Ger.). 'Sketch', 'sketches'.

SKRAUP (or **Skroup**), FRANZ. See *Bohemia*.

SKRYABIN. See *Scriabin*.

SKYE BOAT SONG. One half of the tune is a sea-shanty heard in 1879 by Miss Annie MacLeod (later Lady Wilson) when going by boat from Torran to Loch Coruisk; the other half is by Miss MacLeod herself. The words, by Sir Harold Boulton, Bart., date from 1884.

Later some other words were written to the tune by Robert Louis Stevenson, who apparently believed the tune to be a pure folk tune and in the public domain. This latter set of words has appeared in association with the tune in certain song books, by permission of Lady Wilson and Sir Harold Boulton, and a confusion has thus originated, particularly as both sets of words include the phrase 'Over the sea to Skye'.

SLANCIO (It.). 'Impetus', outburst, i.e. impetuosity.

SLAP STICK. See *Percussion Family* 4 d.

SLARGANDO, SLARGANDOSI (It.). 'Slowing up', i.e. rallentando.

SLEGATO (It.). 'Un-legato.' See *Legato*.

SLEIGH BELLS. See *Bell* 5 (end).

SLENTANDO (It.). 'Slowing' (from 'Lento', slow), i.e. same as *rallentando*.

SLIDE (Ger. *Schleifer*). An ornament consisting of a filling-in (generally upwards) of the interval between one note and another (cf. *Glissando* and *Portamento* and Table 22). It occurs more especially in violin music.

A curved line is sometimes the indication used, but Bach often uses the following sign:

SLIDER. See *Organ* 1.

SLIDE TRUMPET. See *Trumpet Family* 2 d, 3, 5.

SLONIMSKY, NICOLAS (p. 1061, pl. **174**. 1). Born at Petrograd in 1894. He studied at the Conservatory of his native place. After activity as pianist, conductor, and composer, when nearing thirty he went to the United States and became naturalized there. His compositions embody various experimental devices. He is known also as lecturer, journalist, and author, his *Music since 1900* (1937, 1938, 1949) being regarded as a very valuable record. In 1947 he published a large *Thesaurus of Scales and Melodic Patterns*, 'analogous in function with phrase books and dictionaries of idiomatic expressions'. He has, moreover, been responsible for revisions of Baker's *Biographical Dictionary of Musicians* and the *International Cyclopedia of Music and Musicians* and gave most valuable help in the preparation of the ninth edition of the present work by checking various features.

See references under *Bergomask*; *Cinematograph*; *Italy* 7; *Jazz* 3; *Pandiatonicism*; *Scales* 12; *Villa-Lobos*; *John Brown's Body*; *Gretchaninoff*.

SLUG-HORN (Browning), **SLUGHORNE** (Chatterton). No musical instrument of this name exists, poets with a taste for the archaic having apparently been misled by the old Border word 'sloggorn' ('slogan'—battle cry).

SLUR. The curved line used in musical notation for various purposes. It may:

(1) Indicate the extent of the phrases (see *Phrasing*).

(2) Intimate that the notes it affects are to be played smoothly.

(3) If combined with dots over the notes, show that they are to be played slightly detached.

(4) In music for bowed instruments, show that the notes it affects are to be played with one stroke of the bow.

(5) In vocal music, show that the notes so marked are to be sung in one breath.

(6) In vocal music, call attention to the fact that several notes are to be sung to one syllable.

(7) The same sign when placed over a note and its repetition indicates that they are to be performed as one unbroken note. The name is then 'Tie' or 'Bind'. To avoid confusion Sterndale Bennett and some others have used a straight tie instead of a curved, i.e. ⌐—⌐.

See also Table 22.

SMALL GRAND. See *Pianoforte* 6.

SMALL PIPES. See *Bagpipe Family* 3.

SMANIA (It.). 'Craze', 'frenzy'. So the adjective *Smaniato* and *Smanioso* and the adverb *Smaniante*.

SMAREGLIA, ANTONIO. Born at Pola, in Istria, in 1854 and died at Trieste in 1929, aged nearly seventy-five. He was trained at the Conservatory of Milan and, as a composer, appeared before the opera public there at about twenty-five. His nine operas have had favour especially in Germany, for with the lyrical charm of the Italian school he combined the constructive interest of the German. Brahms commended his work. In his middle forties he became blind.

SMART Family. No fewer than six members, representing six generations, are listed in the various books of reference. Only two call for mention here.

(1) GEORGE THOMAS (Sir George Smart). Born in London in 1776 and died there in 1867, aged ninety. He was a chorister of the Chapel Royal who became a noted conductor, was knighted by the Lord Lieutenant of Ireland, and was appointed one of the organists of the Chapel Royal. Through his father, who had seen Handel conduct, he inherited the traditions of Handelian singing; he visited Beethoven in Vienna, Weber died at his house in London, and after Mendelssohn's death he was one of the principal promoters of the movement for the bringing into existence of the

Mendelssohn Scholarship (q.v.). Some of his glees are still sung.

See references under *God save the Queen* 4; *Organ* 8.

(2) HENRY THOMAS. Born in London in 1813 and died there in 1879, aged sixty-five. He was nephew of the above. After five years as organist at Blackburn, in Lancashire, he settled in London, where, to the end of his life, he held a prominent place as organist, being noted perhaps especially for his extemporization. He successfully produced choral works at many of the English festivals, but is now remembered as a writer of part-songs and, still more, of flowing, effective organ and church choral music. For the last fifteen years of his life he was totally blind.

See reference under *Presbyterian* 3.

SMETANA, BEDŘICH or Frederick (p. 108, pl. 19. 6). Born at Litomyšl (or Leitomischl), in Bohemia, in 1824 and died at Prague in 1884, aged sixty. When, in the middle of the nineteenth century, nationalism became a consciously accepted element in music he made himself the champion of his native Bohemia.

He produced a series of operas definitely national in both literary subject-matter and musical style and material, the most popular of which is the humorous *The Bartered Bride* (1866), and wrote a set of six symphonic poems entitled *My Fatherland*, in which the scenery and legend of Bohemia are commemorated.

The mention of the term 'symphonic poem' is enough to suggest that, in addition to being an exponent of the new national ideas in music (see *Nationalism* and compare *Grieg*, *Dvořák*, *Glinka*, *Balakiref*, etc.), he was also an adherent of the contemporary school that dubbed itself that of 'The Music of the Future' (see *Liszt*).

It was he, more than any other composer, who gave the Czech musicians a new confidence in themselves, and for this, for his positive contribution to the repertory of the art, and for his vivid expression of patriotic feelings at a time when the Bohemians were still a subject race, he is honoured by his countrymen, who in 1924 celebrated with great rejoicings the centenary of his birth.

That birth took place in Southern Bohemia, where his father, manager of a brewery, was a keen amateur musician. The child showed unusually early ability, playing in a Haydn String Quartet at the age of five and later showing remarkable dexterity as a pianist. His further studies were carried out at Prague, where he established himself as a fashionable teacher. When the National Theatre was founded in 1862 he became connected with it, and four years later became its principal conductor; it was here that the operas already mentioned were produced.

(Before this there was an interval of four years when he was absent in Sweden as conductor of the Philharmonic Society at Gothenburg, life at Prague under Austrian rule having become uncomfortable to one of such pronounced national sympathies.)

His end was sad. He suffered for some time from a malady one symptom of which was the illusion of a constantly sounding high note. This he has hinted at in a movement of his string quartet *From my Life* (1876). In 1874 he suddenly became completely deaf, yet he continued to compose and four of the six symphonic poems mentioned at the opening of this article he himself never heard. He died in an asylum and was buried in a cemetery on the legendary site of Vyšehrad, the castle of the mythical foundress of Prague, Libuše, whom he took as heroine of one of his operas, as the castle itself is the subject of one of his tone poems.

In addition to the various types of composition above mentioned he wrote much fine choral and piano music.

See references under *Nationalism*; *Bohemia*; *Folk Song* 5; *Opera* 19; *Polka*; *Furiant*; *Ear* 4; *Dvořák*.

SMINUENDO, SMINUITO (It.). 'Diminishing', 'diminished' (in power), hence = *Diminuendo*.

SMITH.

(1) 'FATHER' (Bernhard Schmidt). Born in Germany about 1630 and died in London in 1708, aged about seventy-eight. On the return of the monarchy and triumph of episcopacy, with the consequent reintroduction of organ playing in the English Church, he emigrated to England, where he became organ-maker to Charles II and later to James II, William and Mary, and Anne, and built organs for St. Paul's Cathedral, the Temple Church, the Sheldonian Theatre, Oxford, and many other places. His nephews, who came with him to England, continued his work. Many of his and their pipes are retained in English organs today, and they are remarkable for purity of tone.

(2) JOHN STAFFORD. Born at Gloucester in 1750 and died in London in 1836, aged eighty-five or eighty-six. He was the son of the organist of Gloucester Cathedral and a choirboy of the Chapel Royal, London, where he was later appointed organist and Master of the Children. He had a high reputation as tenor singer, organist, antiquary, and composer of catches, glees, part-songs, and anthems.

The American national song, 'The Star-spangled Banner' (1814), was set to the tune of his 'Anacreon in Heaven', so that the nation defied has furnished the music for the defiance —a proceeding happily unresented by either party.

See reference under *Star-spangled Banner*.

(3) THEODORE. An English pianist and composer, who apparently lived for a time in Germany, as some of his works (many temporarily popular) were published there. His dates of birth and death are unknown; his period of publication was about 1770–1810.

See *Pianoforte* 21.

(4) SYDNEY (in full, Edward Sydney). Born at Dorchester in 1839 and died in London in 1889, aged forty-nine. He was a noted pianist and piano teacher in London and cleverly composed brilliant nothings for his instrument. They had enormous vogue for many years.

For a reference to his Tarantella see *Pianoforte* 22.

(5) ALICE MARY. Born in London in 1839 and died there in 1884, aged forty-five. She was in her own time well known as a composer of orchestral, chamber, and large-scale choral works, but is now remembered chiefly by a few songs. Her married name was Meadows White.

(6) DAVID STANLEY. Born at Toledo, Ohio, in 1877 and died at New Haven, Conn., in 1949, aged seventy-two. He was a graduate of Yale, the successor of Horatio Parker as head of the Music Department of that university, and the composer of substantial works in many forms, including symphonies and an opera.

See *Oboe Family* 6; *Chamber Music* 6, Period III (1877).

Brief references to other Smiths will be found as follows: (7) JOHN CHRISTOPHER SMITH (1712–95; Handel's amanuensis and general assistant): see under *Oratorio* 5; *Mechanical Reproduction of Music* 10; *Ornaments* 1. (8) R. A. SMITH (1780–1829; active Edinburgh musician): see under *Presbyterian Church Music* 4. (9) Revd. S. F. SMITH (1808–95; author of *My Country, 'tis of thee*): see under *God save the Queen* 14. (10) JOHN THOMAS SMITH (Nollekens's biographer): see under *Street Music* 2; *Saltbox*. (11) CAPTAIN JOHN SMITH (explorer): see under *United States* 7. (12) JOHN SMITH (founder of English Baptists; died 1612): see under *Baptist Church and Music* 2. (13) WILLIAM C. SMITH: see *Nicknamed Compositions* 10; *Dictionaries* 4.

SMITHSON, HARRIET. See *Berlioz*.

SMOLLETT, TOBIAS. See *Corranach*; *Presbyterian* 4.

SMORENDO (It.). 'Becoming by degrees softer and slower.'

SMORFIOSO (It.). 'Mincing', affected.

SMORZANDO (It.). Literally 'extinguishing', i.e. 'toning down', i.e. making the performance softer to extinction (abbreviated *Smorz.*). *Smorzato* is the past participle of the same verb.

SMYTH, ETHEL MARY (p. 336, pl. 53. 3). Born at Foots Cray, Kent, in 1858 and died at Woking, Surrey, in 1944, aged eighty-six. She long studied music in Germany and many of her earlier works first came to public performance there. Her mass in D had its first hearing (at the Albert Hall, London) in 1893 and its second and third (at Birmingham and at Queen's Hall, London) thirty-one years later. Her opera *The Forest* was given at Dresden in 1901, at Covent Garden in 1902, and at the Metropolitan Opera House, New York, in 1903; *The Wreckers* has been given in Leipzig (1906), Prague, and London. The comedy opera *The Boatswain's Mate* (London, 1916) has had very many British performances. *Fête galante* was first heard at Birmingham and Covent Garden in 1923 and *Entente cordiale*

2. TEACHING THE 'GUIDONIAN HAND'
(From Day's *Whole Book of Psalms*, 1563)

1. GUIDO D'AREZZO explains his system to Pope John XX (*c.* 1025)
See *Guido d'Arezzo, Hexachord, Sight-Singing* 2

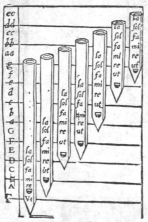

3. THE 'GUIDONIAN HAND'
See *Hexachord*

4. THE HEXACHORDS. As set forth
in the Sternhold Psalter of 1564

5. THE GAMUT. (From Playford's *Skill of Music*, 1654)
See *Gamut*

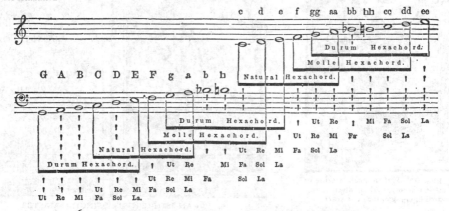

6. THE HEXACHORDS. As set forth in Hawkins's History of Music, 1776

1, 2. THEORETICAL AND PRACTICAL INSTRUCTION IN MUSIC in the 15th century (Gaforio, 1496)
(Note the bell which gives the pitch)

3. GERMAN SCHOOL OF THE 16TH CENTURY. With music class—right, top. (Music appears to be the only school subject which does not demand physical coercion!)

4. A SINGING CLASS
(Germany, early 19th century)

5. A MUSIC LESSON, 1501 (from the treatise of Prasperg, of Basle University, 1504, of which an edition appeared in Glasgow the same year)

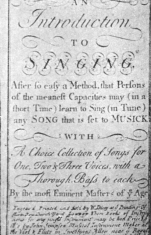

6. AN 18TH-CENTURY SINGING-MASTER

at Bristol in 1926. She wrote chamber music, orchestral music, a concerto for violin and horn (1927), and a little choral music, including the virile choral–orchestral *Hey Nonny No!*

She was the daughter of an artillery general and always ready to fire a shot in the interests of any cause she considered good, ever putting a special fervour into any fighting she might decide to undertake on behalf of national opera or of feminism. In 1911 she spent two months in one of His Majesty's jails as a militant suffragist and in 1922 received at His Majesty's hands the equivalent of knighthood, being henceforth known as 'Dame'. She published admirably written volumes recounting and reflecting upon her life experiences.

It is the opinion of some (as it was of herself) that had she been a man she would have been enabled more quickly to make her mark as a composer, and of others that she would with difficulty have made it at all. It is perhaps fair to consider that these views cancel out, leaving sex as no important factor in the sum.

See references under *Opera* 13 e—as to operatic conditions in Britain; *Opera* 24—giving dates and places of first performances; *Harp* 4; *Horn Family* 1, 4; *Bugle*; *Herzogenberg, H. von*; *Concerto* 6 c (1858); *Knighthood*.

SNAP. See *Scotch Snap*.

SNARE DRUM. Side drum. See *Percussion Family* 3 i, 4 b, 5 i.

SNELLO, SNELLAMENTE (It.). 'Nimble', 'nimbly'.

SNETZLER, JOHN. German organ-builder, settled in London in 1740. See *Organ* 8; *Bohemia*.

SNOWDEN, PHILIP, Viscount Snowden of Ickornshaw (1864–1936). See *Opera* 13 e.

SNUFF BOX, MUSICAL. See *Mechanical Reproduction of Music* 7.

SO (Ger.). 'As', 'so'.

SOAP OPERA. This term is applied to any broadcast daily-continued story designed to reduce the more sentimental part of the female population to pleasurable tears of sympathy and, concurrently, to keep bright in their memories the merits of some manufacturer's special product (originally soap). Certain popular masterpieces of this kind run for year after year, and the total number of daily listeners is many millions.

Cf. *Singing Commercials*.

SOAVE, SOAVITÀ (It.). 'Suave', suavity (or gentle, gentleness). *Soavamente*, 'suavely'.

SOBALD (Ger.). 'So soon as', and similar expressions. Sometimes 'should', in such phrases as 'should' a certain instrument not be able to do a certain thing.

SOCIETÀ ITALIANA DEGLI AUTORI, etc. See *Copyright* 3.

SOCIÉTÉ DES AUTEURS, etc. See *Copyright* 3.

SOCIÉTÉ FRANÇAISE DE MUSICOLOGIE. See *France* 14.

SOCIÉTÉ NATIONALE DE MUSIQUE. See *France* 13; *Bréville*; *Chausson*; *Franck*; *Saint-Saëns*.

SOCIETY FOR CONTEMPORARY MUSIC. See *Germany* 9 b.

SOCIETY FOR INVESTIGATION OF ORIENTAL MUSIC. See *Oriental Music*.

SOCIETY FOR THE PROMOTION OF NEW MUSIC (S.P.N.M.). Founded in 1943 as the Committee for the Promotion of New Music, by the Arrangers', Composers', and Copyists' Section of the Musicians' Union (first President, Vaughan Williams). It holds recitals, 'experimental rehearsals', etc., and after works have been tried out publishes periodical lists of recommended pieces.

SOCIETY FOR THE PUBLICATION OF AMERICAN MUSIC. See *Publishing of Music* 9.

SOCIETY OF AUTHORS, PLAYWRIGHTS, AND COMPOSERS. See *Copyright and Performing Right*.

SOCIETY OF MUSICIANS, ROYAL. See *Festival* 1.

SOCIETY OF TEACHERS, ROYAL. See *Profession of Music* 10.

SOCIETY OF WOMEN MUSICIANS. Founded in London in 1911. It possesses a library, a chamber music section, etc., and carries on a 'Composers' Conference'.

SÖDERMAN, AUGUST JOHANN. Born at Stockholm in 1832 and there died in 1876, aged forty-three. He was trained at Leipzig and then became attached to the opera-house at Stockholm as sub-conductor. He is known for various theatrical music, choral music, songs, etc. His *Peasant Wedding* for women's voices has long been popular, and a Mass of his is highly esteemed.

SOEBEN (Ger.). 'Just', in the sense of (*a*) 'barely', (*b*) 'a moment ago'.

SOFORT (Ger.). 'Immediately.'

SOFT HEXACHORD. See *Hexachord*.

SOFT PALATE. See *Voice* 21.

SOGGETTO. Italian for 'subject', meaning, in a musical sense, the subject of a fugue (see *Form* 12; also *Attacco* and *Andamento*).

SOGLEICH (Ger.). 'Immediately.'

SOH. See *Sol*.

'SOIR' SYMPHONY (Haydn). See *Nicknamed Compositions* 11.

SOL. The fifth degree of the major scale according to the system of vocal syllables derived from Guido d'Arezzo (q.v.), and so used (spelt 'Soh') in Tonic Sol-fa (q.v.). In French and Italian usage, however, the name has (on 'fixed-doh' principles) become attached to the note G, in whatever scale or other association this may occur.

For still another use of 'Sol' see *Lancashire Sol-fa*.

SOLA (It.). 'Alone' (fem. of *solo*).

SOLDATENZUG (Ger.). 'Soldiers' procession.' *Soldatenmarsch*, 'soldiers' march'.

SOLEÁ (plural *Soleares*). A type of folk song in Andalusia (Spain). Its poetry is in a three-lined stanza, with assonance (agreement of vowels, instead of rhyme) between the final syllables of the first and third lines.

SOLEMNIS, SOLENNIS (Lat.). 'Solemn.'

SOLENNE, SOLENNEMENTE, SOLEN-NITÀ (It.). 'Solemn', 'solemnly', 'solemnity'.

SOLENNEL, SOLENNELLE (Fr., masc., fem.). 'Solemn'; so *Solennellement*, 'solemnly'.

SOLENNIS, SOLEMNIS (Lat.). 'Solemn.'

SOLER.
(1) FATHER ANTONIO. See *Spain* 8.
(2) MARTÍN Y. See *Spain* 6.

SOLESMES. See *Notation* 2; *Plainsong* 3; *Machicotage*; *Spain* 2; *Roman Catholic*.

SOL-FA. See *Tonic Sol-fa*; *Lancashire Sol-fa*. For 'Sol-fa' as a conductor's baton see *Tonic Sol-fa* 10; *Conducting* 2.

SOLFEGGIO (It.), **SOLFÈGE** (Fr.). A type of vocal exercise, properly one in which the names of the notes, sol, fah, etc. are applied throughout—on the continental Fixed-doh system (i.e. G always being sol, F always fah, etc.), not the Tonic Sol-fa system. The object may be either voice exercise or sight-reading exercise.

The plural of 'Solfeggio' is *Solfeggi*. The diminutive *Solfeggietto* is also found.

Nowadays some confusion is apt to occur between Solfeggio and Vocalise (see *Vocalize*).

(*Solfège* is also sometimes loosely used as almost the equivalent of the English 'Rudiments' or 'Elements' or 'Theory' of Music, i.e. the knowledge of notation, intervals, etc.)

SOLI (It.). 'Alone' (plur. of *solo*, but in English 'solos' is now more accepted).

SOLITO (It.). 'Usual.' So *Al solito*, 'as usual'.

SOLLECITANDO (It.). 'Hastening forward.'

SOLLECITO (It.). 'Eager.'

SOLMIZATION. Singing a passage (i.e. reading it at sight) to the sol-fa syllables in any of the varying ways that have been used since Guido d'Arezzo introduced these syllables.

See *Hexachord*; *Tonic Sol-fa*; *Lancashire Sol-fa*.

SOLO (It.). 'Alone.' This word has now been adopted into most languages. (The plural in Italian is *Soli*, in English *Solos*.)

SOLO BELLS. A small glockenspiel (see *Percussion Family*, 2 c, 4 e, 5 c) of an easily portable type, used in dance bands, etc.

SOLOKLAVIER. See *Organ* 15.

SOLO ORGAN. See *Organ* 2 d.

SOLOVOX. See *Electric* 4.

SOLTANTO (It.). 'Solely.'

SOMBRE (Fr.). 'Dark', 'melancholy'.

SOMERVELL, ARTHUR. Born at Windermere in 1863 and died in London in 1937, aged seventy-three. He studied with Stanford and Parry and at the Berlin Hochschule. His larger compositions have been heard at English festivals and elsewhere, and some of his songs have enjoyed a wide popularity; there are four song-cycles, including the setting of Tennyson's *Maud*. For over a quarter of a century he was chief inspector in music to the national Board of Education, and on retiring from this position in 1929 he was knighted. He was a B.A., D.Mus., Cantab.

See reference under *Folk Song* 3.

SOMERVILLE, J. A. C. (b. 1872). Colonel in British Army (C.M.G., C.B.E.). Commandant of Royal Military School of Music, 1920–5. See *Pitch* 5.

SOMMESSO (It.). 'Subdued.'

SOMMO, SOMMA (It., masc., fem.). 'Utmost.'

SON, SONS (Fr.). 'Sound', 'sounds'. (*Son* also means 'his', 'her', 'its'.)

SONARE (It.). 'To sound', i.e. play. So *Sonante*, 'sounding', resonant.

SONATA

1. The Word 'Sonata'. The Italian word 'Sonata' is the past participle of the verb *sonare*, 'to sound', as 'Cantata' is of the verb *cantare*, 'to sing'. To the end of the eighteenth century the words 'si suona' and 'si canta' distinguished the instrumental and vocal passages in a song.

That was the idea at the time the words originated—the end of the sixteenth century, when an independent instrumental style was at last being developed, after a preliminary period in which instruments had been largely using choral style.

The distinction *Cantata—Sonata* was between a composition that was primarily a poem with music as its vehicle, and one that conveyed no thought but was mere sound.

There were, however, some few exceptions from this; Monteverdi, for instance, has a 'Sonata sopra Santa Maria' with an added voice part.

The word 'sonata' is the feminine form of the past participle in question. The noun at first used, then implied, and finally forgotten was *Canzona* (q.v.), a Canzona Sonata ('played canzona')—a vocal style adopted for instrumental use; compare such an expression today as 'Grand Chœur pour Orgue'.

The antithesis between 'Cantata' and 'Sonata', now generally somewhat out of sight, was for nearly two centuries recognized as the explanation of the words. As late as the period just after the death of Handel and Bach it was current, e.g. Rousseau's *Dictionary of Music* (1767) says, 'The Sonata is, for instruments, very much what the Cantata is for the voice'.

2. 'Chamber' and 'Church' Sonatas. From the article *Cantata* it will be seen that this early took on the form of a piece in several contrasted sections or 'movements' (so called from their varying speeds and rhythms) and that a differentiation was made between the *Cantata da Camera*, or 'Chamber Cantata', and the *Cantata da Chiesa*, or 'Church Cantata'. Similarly, the sonata was generally in several movements and took the name *Sonata da Camera* or *Sonata da Chiesa* according to its style and the intention as to its place of performance. Both of these were for strings with a keyboard background. The *Sonata da Chiesa* type has a frequent place in church ceremonies in the seventeenth and eighteenth centuries; Tartini played such pieces regularly for over thirty years in the famous church of St. Anthony in Padua—with organ accompaniment. For Salzburg Cathedral in the 1770s the young Mozart composed many examples of the 'Epistle Sonata', which was a feature of the service there—for organ and two violins, sometimes with other stringed or wind instruments added.

The most palpable difference between the chamber sonata and the church sonata was that the chamber sonata was ordinarily a series of movements in dance rhythms while the church sonata was a string of movements of a more abstract and serious character—usually four, a slow introduction, a quick fugal movement, a slow, expressive movement, and another quick movement.

3. The Instruments of the Early Sonatas. The early sonatas were for strings, with figured bass (q.v.) for harpsichord (Bach being the first to provide a fully written-out keyboard part); in fact the sonata is, in origin, a string form. Four-part sonatas were very common—for two violins, cello, and harpsichord (or organ, if given in church); Corelli's and Purcell's sonatas are mostly of this kind: they are often called *Sonate a tre*, or 'three-part Sonatas', because only the strings were counted in the title, the harpsichord, as the invariable background for all types of music at that period, being, apparently, taken for granted, and the cellist and harpsichordist having before them the same single line of bass notes—the former for melodic use, the latter as the basis on which to erect his scheme of chords directed by the line of figures. Purcell has twelve 'Sonnatas of III Parts to the Organ or Harpsichord' (1683—almost the first English works bearing the title 'sonata'), and ten sonatas of four parts (1697): they are identical as to the instruments required.

4. The First Solo Keyboard Sonatas. The harpsichord sonatas of Kuhnau (Bach's predecessor at Leipzig) are always considered to be the earliest for that instrument so titled (1692 onwards). Amongst these were 'Biblical Sonatas' of a curious descriptive character (see *Programme Music*).

5. The Eighteenth-century Use of the term 'Sonata'. During the late eighteenth century the term 'Sonata' became restricted to compositions for one instrument (e.g. harpsichord alone) or two (e.g. violin and harpsichord). Then the sonatas for three instruments were called 'Trios'; those for four, 'Quartets'; those for five, 'Quintets', and so on; whilst those for orchestra were called 'Symphonies' (see *Symphony*), and those making an antiphonal use of one chief instrument or group of instruments with the main body of the orchestra were called 'Concertos' (see *Concerto*). All these things, as generally found in the eighteenth century and since, are of several movements, and are, in fact, nothing but sonatas for different combinations of instruments.

A certain looseness in the use of the word 'Sonata' (as of nearly all musical terms) has to be reckoned with. Although a sonata is normally a composition in several movements, yet there have been a good many one-movement sonatas. The 545 sonatas of Domenico Scarlatti (contemporary with Bach and Handel) are largely such; the last of Corelli's twelve sonatas for violin and harpsichord is a single movement—an Air with Variations (see *Folía*). C. F. Pollaroli (1653–1722) has single-movement harpsichord 'Sonatas' that are nothing but fugues. But in general the title implies the contrast of three or four (sometimes only two) movements, in different rhythms at different speeds, and since the mid-eighteenth century in different keys—related keys as a rule, and with a return in the last movement to the key of the first one.

6. The Influence of C. P. E. Bach. John Sebastian Bach's ablest son, Carl Philipp Emanuel Bach (1714–88), is often spoken of as the Father of the Sonata, by which is meant the modern sonata. He wrote seventy sonatas for harpsichord. On looking at one of his sonatas and comparing it with the works of such predecessors as Purcell, Corelli, J. S. Bach, and Handel we notice a more harmonic (i.e. less contrapuntal) style (see *Counterpoint*); a great daring in the choice of keys for some of the movements; an originality of passage work, more definitely 'keyboard' in style than was often the case with his predecessors; and, above all, the emergence of a form that has been standardized and has come to be called '**First Movement Form**' or '**Sonata Form**', the one term unsatisfactory both because there exist sonatas with first movements in some other form and also because the form is often used in other than first movements, and the other still more unsatisfactory because it gives the impression that the form is that of the *whole* sonata. 'Sonata Form' is discussed in the article *Form* (7, 10). It is the most important form in the history of music and has served as the basis for innumerable great works from the time of C. P. E. Bach to the present.

With C. P. E. Bach the sonata had three movements—quick, slow, quick (cf. the Italian overture under *Overture* 1). The general tone of much of his work was distinctly lighter than that of his father's; the German eighteenth-century word for this style is 'galant' (they borrowed a French word), and the three main representatives of the *Style Galant* (q.v.), or *Galanter Stil*, are C. P. E. Bach and his younger contemporaries Haydn and Mozart. Certain of C. P. E. Bach's works leave the *Style Galant* behind and surprisingly anticipate Beethoven.

Note that in the early sonatas, as in the suites, all the movements were in one key (or at all events had the same key-signature, i.e. only varied within the limits of relative major and minor), whereas the new style of sonata had movements in contrasted keys.

7. The Interpolation of the Minuet or Scherzo. With Haydn and Mozart a former occasional element of the suite (which is related to the chamber sonata) curiously begins to take an occasional place in the sonata (the descendant of the old church sonata), and so the dance element comes back—in the form of the minuet as a substitute for the middle or final movement. At this period the minuet was enjoying a universal vogue in ball-rooms all over Europe and doubtless its steady three-in-a-measure swing and its graceful melodic contours were appreciated as a light relief after the more or less serious rapid first movement and the more deeply expressive slow movement. It quickly took on a heightened speed and brightness, and then in the hands of Beethoven tended to lose its dance character and was transformed into the playful, rapid scherzo—its very three-in-a-measure rhythm at last becoming not indispensable (cf. *Scherzo*).

8. The Movements in the Beethoven Sonata. Four movements may, from the days of Beethoven, be said to be normal, though there are very many exceptions. Beethoven's order is usually the following:

1. Quick extended movement in 'Sonata Form'.
2. Slower and more song-like movement, usually deeply expressive.
3. Minuet or scherzo—gay.
4. Extended rondo or movement in sonata form —rapid and lively.

Sometimes there is a slow introduction to the whole and sometimes the minuet or scherzo comes as number two instead of number three.

The greatest innovation of Beethoven is not one of form but one of spirit. He was an instrumental dramatist, and his impulse to express strongly felt emotion in music, and to indulge in violent contrast, found ample vent in a form which called for several contrasted moods (in the different movements) and allowed of them also within the limits of one movement by the use of different 'subjects'.

Two curious instances of the learner become teacher occur in the history of the sonata at the period. Haydn (born 1732) greatly influenced Mozart (born 1756) and, in turn, was influenced by him. Clementi (born 1752) greatly influenced Beethoven (born 1770) and then, in turn, was influenced by him. Clementi wrote 100 sonatas, of which 60 are for piano. Nobody who knows them well underrates his artistry.

9. The Romantic Period and After. The Romantic School who followed Beethoven were not at their greatest in the pianoforte sonata; Weber wrote brilliant, but not very deep, piano sonatas. Mendelssohn, Schumann, and Chopin also wrote some sonatas, but it was in single-movement 'characteristic' pieces that they excelled.

Brahms, in his sonatas, combined the 'classical' and 'romantic'. The dignity and scope of the Beethoven sonata were there, together with the romantic glamour of his friend and mentor Schumann. The spirit of Romanticism was carried into the sonatas of Grieg and MacDowell.

Scriabin (q.v.) found in his ten piano sonatas an opportunity of expressing the rapid development of both the musical and the poetic sides of his nature, and in the later ones the standard form was submerged in a bursting flood of vivid self-expression. With him and his contemporaries and successors the old formal connotations of the word tend to be lost.

During the late nineteenth century and the twentieth various devices have been tried for linking the movements by the use of the same material in all, or by the merging of the characteristics of several movements in one continuous so-called movement (not really one 'movement' at all, often, as both time and tempo may be greatly changed in the various sections).

There has also been a general tendency towards the gradual organic growth of a movement from short *motifs* instead of the clear statement of definite subjects of some length and their subsequent development and recapitulation—less like the plan of a building and more like the growth of a tree. (To the 'ordinary listener' a composition of the sonata class on these lines is necessarily a good deal more difficult to 'take in' at a first hearing than one on the older lines.)

It may be said that for nearly three centuries the sonata, always developing, has been recognized as the fittest medium for the musical expression of the longer trains of musical thought or emotion. If we include in the term those works of the same stamp and on the same scale which we call string trios and quartets, symphonies and concertos, etc., it may be said that the sonata ranks as far and away the most important type in instrumental music.

10. Historical List of Sonata Composers.

(a) *The Earliest Published Sonatas.*

1586. A. GABRIELI, Venice (possibly earliest use of the word, but the composition seems to be lost).
1597 and 1615. G. GABRIELI, Venice; fourteen

'Canzoni per sonar' and two Sonatas (in from three to twenty-two instrumental parts).

1619. M. PRAETORIUS of Wolfenbüttel.

All the above are in the canzona style. They represent the very origin of the sonata, though of course it took elements from other sources also.

1626. C. FARINA, Dresden; string sonatas for two to four instruments. He was a notable virtuoso and developed the technique of performance.

(b) String Sonatas of Later Seventeenth and Earlier Eighteenth Centuries.

1653. WM. YOUNG, Innsbruck; sonatas for two to five stringed instruments with figured bass. (These are the first printed English sonatas; they were republished as edited by W. G. Whittaker in 1931.)

1670 and 1682. J. ROSENMÜLLER, a German composer of importance, then in Venice; Sonate da Camera for two to five stringed instruments.

1676, etc. H. J. F. BIBER, Salzburg and Nuremberg; many sonatas for strings, including twelve for one violin with figured bass, said by the late Paul David to be 'the first German violin music of any artistic worth at all' (see Grove, under 'Biber').

1681, etc. CORELLI, Rome, Modena, and Bologna; five books of sonatas for one, two, or three stringed instruments with figured bass for keyboard. These may be said to have founded the notable eighteenth-century Italian String Sonata School.

There followed the many fine works of Vivaldi (c. 1676-1741), F. M. Veracini (1690-1750), Tartini (1692-1770), Locatelli (1695-1764).

1683 and 1697. PURCELL, London; twelve sonatas 'of Three Parts' and ten 'of Four Parts' (see 3 above). One sonata for solo violin and keyboard was discovered at the close of the nineteenth century.

1695. J. F. REBEL (French); sonata for violin alone.

From 1724 onwards. HANDEL. Many sonatas for one to three instruments and keyboard.

c. 1720 onwards. BACH. Six sonatas for violin unaccompanied (three are really partitas or suites), six for keyboard and violin, three for keyboard and gamba, one for two violins and figured bass.

These may be said to close the period of the Sonata da Chiesa or abstract type of the contrapuntal period. Nearly all these composers also wrote works of the Sonata da Camera (or dance) type (see *Suite*)—also contrapuntal in general character, of course.

(c) Later String Sonatas.

C. P. E. BACH (1714-88) wrote sonatas for keyboard and violin, for two violins, cello, and figured bass, etc. So did most of the composers of the period, this latter combination being very popular. HAYDN (1732-1809) wrote six for violin and viola and ten to twelve for violin and keyboard (the precise number is disputed). MOZART (1756-91) wrote twenty-eight for violin and keyboard; BEETHOVEN (1770-1827) ten for violin and piano and five for cello and piano. SCHUMANN (1810-56) wrote two (published 1852 and 1855); MENDELSSOHN (1809-47) wrote one for violin and piano and two for cello and piano. CHOPIN (1810-49) wrote one for cello and piano. BRAHMS wrote three for violin and piano (1880-9), and two for cello and piano. DVOŘÁK wrote a sonata and sonatina for violin and piano. GRIEG (1843-1907) wrote three for violin and piano and one for cello and piano; FRANCK one (1886) for violin and piano. ELGAR

wrote one for violin and piano (1919)—and so on; it is impossible to give anything like a complete list here.

Amongst many striking examples of modern works are KODÁLY's for cello alone (1915) and RAVEL's for violin and cello (1922).

It is worthy of note that there was during the eighteenth century a flourishing school of English writers of string sonatas—Lates, H. Eccles, Babell, Stanley, Collett, Arne, Richard Jones, Boyce, Macklean, Croft, Joseph Gibbs, J. Humphries, T. Vincent, etc. They were brought back to light by A. Moffat (q.v.), who republished specimens of their work in the series 'Old English Violin Music'.

(d) Harpsichord and Pianoforte Sonatas.

1695, etc. J. KUHNAU, Leipzig; the earliest keyboard sonatas—some of them of the nature of Scriptural 'Programme Music' (q.v.).

1704, etc. PASQUINI in Rome, Amsterdam, London, etc.; he had a good deal of influence, and J. S. Shedlock and others have republished his music.

HANDEL and BACH did not cultivate the keyboard sonata, preferring the suite, with its movements based on dance forms. Handel has a single-page Sonatina, a one-movement sonata of a forward-looking style (verging on that of a C. P. E. Bach first movement) and another forward-looking one of three movements. Bach has merely one youthful work and another that is a transcription of one of his violin solo sonatas.

Handel's boyhood friend MATTHESON wrote two or three harpsichord sonatas (1713-19), one of them 'dedicated to those persons who can play it best'; in a preface he laid stress on the importance of the player attaining vehemence, pathos, etc., in the different sections—presto, adagio, and so forth.

DOMENICO SCARLATTI's sonatas have been mentioned in the article above (5).

F. DURANTE (1684-1755) published a few sonatas for harpsichord and others left in manuscript have been considered worthy of publication in recent times.

1741, etc. G. MARTINI (Padre Martini), Amsterdam, Bologna, etc.: some of his sonatas have been republished in modern times.

ARNE (1710-78) wrote some very tuneful, light harpsichord sonatas.

c. 1754 onwards. PARADIES, Paris, London, Amsterdam, etc.; a good composer for the harpsichord.

ALBERTI (c. 1710-40); his sonatas are historical as having popularized the cheap 'Alberti Bass' (q.v.). The adoption of such a formula as this definitely marks a new conception of music—not the woven 'voices' of the older Bach but the chordal structure of his sons, who belonged to Alberti's generation, and of Haydn and Mozart and Beethoven, all of whom used the Alberti Bass, but with discretion.

1760, etc. G. C. WAGENSEIL, Nuremberg, London, Paris, etc.; Haydn studied his works. At this time Bach's sons Friedemann, Emanuel, Christian, etc., became active in keyboard sonata publication. They definitely took the new road away from the old Sonata da Chiesa influences and in the direction of the harmonic style and the 'sonata-form' first movement. The word 'Pianoforte' appears in some of their titles, e.g. Christian's set of 1768, 'Six Sonatas for the Harpsichord or Pianoforte'.

1767 onwards. HAYDN; fifty harpsichord or piano sonatas.

1773 onwards. CLEMENTI; sixty harpsichord or piano sonatas.

1774 onwards. MOZART; nineteen harpsichord

or piano solo sonatas, five duet, and one for two instruments.

DUSSEK (1760–1812); fifty-three sonatas for piano.

1796 onwards. BEETHOVEN; thirty-two sonatas (the earliest were published as for 'Harpsichord or Pianoforte').

1802 onwards. FIELD; four piano sonatas dedicated to his master, Clementi.

1803 onwards. HUMMEL; five sonatas.

KUHLAU (1786–1832) wrote, especially, a quantity of sonatinas now in considerable use as teaching material.

1812–22. WEBER; four piano sonatas.

1815 onwards. MOSCHELES; his sonata publications begin at this time with one celebrating Napoleon's defeat and called *The Return of the Emperor*. Most of his once popular piano works were, however, in smaller forms.

1815–28. SCHUBERT; twenty-one piano sonatas.

MENDELSSOHN left three piano sonatas, the earliest composed in 1826.

1836–54. SCHUMANN; six sonatas, three of them 'for the young'.

CHOPIN (1810–49); three piano sonatas.

LISZT. His one sonata dates from 1854.

1853–4. BRAHMS; three piano sonatas all published within two years (when he was 20–21).

GRIEG (1843–1907); only one piano sonata—an early work.

1873. STERNDALE BENNETT; two: the second a 'Programme' Sonata, *The Maid of Orleans*, based on Schiller's play. (This work is of little artistic but some historical importance.)

1893–1901. MACDOWELL; four piano sonatas, *Tragica, Eroica, Norse, Keltic*.

1896–1913. SCRIABIN; ten piano sonatas showing a progressive complexity in harmony and modification of the traditional form, and in the effort to express strongly felt emotion.

1910–21. BUSONI; six sonatinas.

Amongst notable British works are B. J. Dale's Sonata, on an original (and successful) scheme, using the variation form to cover three of the movements, John Ireland's Sonata and Sonatina, and the sonatas of Arnold Bax.

There are many sonatas for four hands at one harpsichord or piano (Christian Bach, Haydn, Hummel, Clementi, Dussek, Kuhlau, and later writers), and quite a number for two harpsichords or pianos (Pasquini, Friedemann Bach, Clementi, and later writers).

(e) Organ Sonatas.

Bach's so-called organ sonatas were apparently written for a double-manual-and-pedal harpsichord; they are trios, with one line of notes for each hand and another for the feet. Mendelssohn wrote six organ sonatas (without using 'Sonata Form' in any of their movements).

Reubke (1834–58) wrote a remarkable sonata, *The 94th Psalm*. Guilmant (1837–1911) wrote eight organ sonatas. Rheinberger (1839–1901) wrote twenty sonatas. Elgar wrote two—one (1898) as an offering to some visiting American musicians, and the other (1932) based on his 'Severn Suite'. Hindemith published two in 1937.

There are, of course, a number of others.

(f) Sonatas for Other Instruments.

Throughout the whole sonata period all instruments capable of serious and flexible musical expression have had their sonata literature. Bach wrote three for flute and harpsichord and one for two flutes and harpsichord, for instance. Handel wrote some also for flute and harpsichord, oboe and harpsichord, and other combinations. Quantz, at the court of Frederick the Great, wrote innumerable flute sonatas for his master's playing. Many sonatas will be found listed at the ends of the articles devoted to particular instruments.

SONATA A TRE. See *Sonata* 3.

SONATA DA CAMERA. See *Suite* 1; *Sonata* 2.

SONATA DA CHIESA. See *Suite* 1; *Sonata* 2.

SONATA FORM. See *Form* 4, 7, 8, 10.

SONATA-RONDO FORM. See *Form* 10.

SONATE (Fr., Ger.). 'Sonata.' The Ger. plur. is *Sonaten*, the Fr. plur. *Sonates*.

SONATINA. Usually the word means a shorter and easier sonata—often for the practice of younger instrumental students.

Sometimes, however, it means a sonata of a rather less serious character, or less developed, but by no means easy. Examples of this type are the piano sonatinas of Ravel, Busoni, and John Ireland.

Generally a sonatina has fewer than the four movements that are normal with the sonata since Beethoven (see *Sonata* 8).

Like other musical terms this is used inconsistently. There are 'sonatinas' that might well be called sonatas and 'sonatas' that might well be called sonatinas. And there is a one-page, one-movement harpsichord piece of Handel called 'Sonatina'. (See *Sonata* 10 d.)

SONATINE (Fr.). 'Sonatina' (q.v.).

SONEVOLE (It.). 'Sonorous', 'resonant'.

SONG

1. Song as Natural Self-Expression. No songless people has ever been discovered. The Stone Age still exists in parts of the Australian continent and tribes without musical instruments are said to exist amongst the aborigines, but they have well-developed songs. Song, then, seems to be instinctive amongst human beings, as it is amongst many specimens of birds (the reason why no animal but man and bird sings requires more consideration than can be given here; on the face of it the fact is a strange one).

Possibly the origin of organized human song may be looked for in a combination of the sense of rhythm, which seems to be likewise universal amongst men (and is shared in some measure by certain insects, birds, and animals), and the inflexions of speech. There are peoples whose ordinary speech is so varied in its pitch inflexion as almost to become song, and the development of this feature, together with the development of speech rhythms into metrical verse forms, sufficiently accounts for all types of traditional unaccompanied unisonous song folk song, that is. The same path of progress, then, may be said to have led from pure speech to poetry, on the one hand, and to metrical song on the other—the impulse to follow this path being the dual one of desire for symmetry in utterance and for a less ordinary means of expression for thought of the more romantic and imaginative types.

That song is a natural and instinctive means of self-expression is evident not only from its universality amongst the most primitive people, but also from its universality amongst children. A careful study of the musical phrases all children themselves unconsciously compose and hum or sing to themselves has been made by a musical parent (Pratt). As no children are brought up entirely away from the hearing of music it is dangerous to base very much theory on such a study, but it is interesting to note the development of music as the mind develops, and in that to trace some analogy to the development of music in the race.

Different races tend to develop different song idioms—the use of particular scales, melodic intervals, rhythmic motifs, etc. To some extent these may be the result of chance and of fashion, but in a considerable degree they seem to express the spirit of the race. To take an example, every musical Englishman must recognize in any collection of Irish folk song a frequent spirit of brooding and (as a contrast) a spirit of wild hilarity that are both of them foreign to his own folk song, and every musical Irishman must recognize in any collection of English folk song a frequent spirit of agreeable matter-of-factness and plain beauty (if the term be not a self-contradiction) that is foreign to his own.

2. Three Forces in the Development of Song. The development of song amongst European races has been greatly influenced by certain institutions. Thus the **Christian Church** early made use of song, cultivated it, and then from time to time sought to control it, as to the scales used and the melodies recognized, within limits fixed by tradition (see *Modes* 2, 4, 5; *Plainsong* 3; *Gregorian Tone*): the growth of a developing literature of harmonized song, or rather of simultaneous melodies, is also due to the Church (see *Harmony* 4–8).

The **Feudal System**, with its organization of a few great families, secure enough to attain a degree of culture, also had influence through the movement of the eleventh to thirteenth centuries associated with the names of the troubadours, trouvères, and minnesingers (see the article *Minstrels, Troubadours, Trouvères, Minnesingers, and Mastersingers*). This movement brought into existence a vast amount of love-poetry set to metrical tune.

The introduction of **Opera** (q.v.) at the beginning of the seventeenth century had an enormous effect upon the development of song, since it led to the devising of vocal forms and styles, such as those of the various types of recitative and of aria (q.v.), and also to the perfecting of methods of using the voice which made possible more highly elaborate and more varied styles of writing for it (see *Singing* 3–7).

Whilst all these and other institutions were coming into existence and affecting the development of song the cultivation of song amongst the unsophisticated peasantry went on continuously (see *Folk Song*; *Ballad*); it undoubtedly submitted to influences from above—from the Church, the court, and the opera-house, but on its part it also influenced these. In any case folk song is the obvious foundation of all song, as folk dance so largely is of instrumental music.

3. The Sixteenth-century Lute Songs. A great development in the direction of an original song-type with instrumental accompaniment took place in the sixteenth century, when the lute composers of various countries cultivated the art of singing to their instrument. The first book of accompanied songs ever printed is that of the Spaniard, Don Luis Milán, in 1536. Similar books later appeared in Italy, France, and England and other countries, and the English ayre with lute accompaniment reached its height in Dowland, whose first book appeared in 1597: the songs in this book have alternative accompaniments for lute and for three additional voices (see *Madrigal* 3 b).

A striking feature of the song books of this time is the fine poetry they contain. Any anthology of sixteenth- and early seventeenth-century lyrical poetry will be found to be largely made up from the contents of these books. Never since has there been so close a correspondence of high standard between the poetry and music of song, since the greatest composers of the later seventeenth, and the eighteenth and nineteenth centuries have often set words of very inferior value—whilst the lesser composers have, of course, often set words of no value at all.

For the introduction of recitative about the year 1600 see *Recitative*; *Opera*. For the development of the conventionalized Italian opera song see *Aria*.

4. Influence of the Ballad Opera. A feature of song production in many countries (but perhaps especially in England) during the eighteenth century is the perpetuation, in what we may call the professional repertory, of many of the qualities of the folk song—simple verse-repeating tunes being greatly in vogue as a result of the popularity of a form of opera consisting of spoken dialogue interspersed with musical entertainment (see *Vaudeville*; *Sing-*

spiel; *Ballad Opera*). Many of the most popular songs of the more hearty English type belong to this period. Some of the ballad operas were heard in the American colonies and the earliest composed American songs show their influence.

5. The German Lied. The Romantic Movement of the early nineteenth century (see *Romantic*) had a great effect upon the evolution of song. Schubert, basing his style upon one or two immediate predecessors or elder contemporaries, such as Zumsteeg (1760–1802), Zelter (1758–1832), and Reichardt (1752–1814), created a vast song-literature of his own of over 600 examples. On the one day, 13 October 1815, he wrote eight, and during that year he wrote 144. Some are tiny, some very long; some are verse-repeating and some through-composed; some have a very simple pianoforte accompaniment and others a highly elaborate and difficult one with remarkable harmonies and striking modulations; some are lyrical, others intensely dramatic. But all owe a good deal of their essential quality to two conditions of the period—the rise of the romantic school of poetry (Scott, Goethe, Heine, etc.) and the relative perfection and universal popularity (after nearly a century of development) of the pianoforte (cf. *Pianoforte* 6). The lyrical poems of Goethe, in particular, were a great source of inspiration to the composers just mentioned and their contemporaries.

A contemporary of Schubert, and one to whom a large share in the development of the dramatic ballad must be credited, is Loewe (q.v.).

Schumann, Franz, Brahms, and Wolf are other great names in the history of the German *Lied* (q.v.). This word is, properly, merely the equivalent of the English 'song'; it is, however, most often used not in this all-embracing sense but rather applied to the Austrian and German products of this very period (say 1780 onwards), the period of Romantic Verse, of the perfected pianoforte, of the discarding of figured bass (q.v.), and in place of it the careful elaboration of the harmonic and other details of the accompaniments as an essential part of the composition.

Since the opening of the period of the Lied (understanding the word in this sense) composers in Germany and all other countries have continued to write songs closely reflecting the spirit of the poems, and with the other attributions of the Schubertian Lied. Wagner's big dramatic demands and relatively small insistence on melody (in the old sense) and on the decorative vocal element have, of course, also had their influence.

The varying idioms and styles of the music in general have reflected themselves in song, as have the differing national temperaments. Information as to the various composers should be sought under their own names (see list below). The *Encyclopædia Britannica* gives valuable lists of the best of the modern British and American songs.

6. The Modern 'Sprechstimme' or 'Sprechgesang'. Amongst what may be recognized as experimental efforts have been the composition of songs for a half-speaking, half-singing voice ('Sprechstimme' or 'speech voice'; 'Sprechgesang' or 'speech-song', e.g. Schönberg's *Pierrot Lunaire*),[1] song to mere vowels (Medtner's *Sonata Vocalise*), and song without accompaniment.

7. The Song Recital. The interest in song as a distinct art form has shown itself in the inception and popularization of the song recital, in which a one-artist programme of nothing but songs entertains an audience for a whole evening. This implies a nineteenth-century development in expressive or interpretative singing equal to the eighteenth-century development in the cultivation of tone quality and agility which in those days found its opportunity in the opera-house. There are some singers of high reputation as recitalists who possess a relative lack of any natural charm of voice, this, however, outweighed by a great sense of poetry plus strong musical feeling. Amongst a large literature upon the subject the outstanding work is Harry Plunket Greene's *Interpretation in Song*.

See also *Accompaniment*.

8. Song an Art of Compromise. The essential difficulty in song composition and song interpretation is the fact that song is necessarily a compromise art. We can express emotions by the voice alone, in a meaningful tune without words; we can express thought by mere words without music. In song the two elements are mingled in widely varying proportions, and in singing there must be give and take between them. If the listener's pleasure in song be analysed it will be found to consist in satisfaction with (1) beauty of tone; (2) beauty of shape; (3) force and variety of rhythm; (4) significance of emotional expression; (5) force, significance, and beauty of accompanying harmonies and moving parts and (in the case of orchestral accompaniment) instrumental 'colours'. All these things have to be balanced, and in the balance is displayed a great part of the ability of the composer and the interpreter.

A prime consideration for both composer and interpreter is the relative importance to be attached to (*a*) details and (*b*) the poem and music as wholes. There again an intelligent compromise is called for, since it is quite possible by over-attention to details to kill the song as a whole, or by too exclusive a view of the thing as a whole to lose the interest which comes from due attention to details. The former danger is the more to be guarded against, the injunction 'Never stop the march of a song' being of vital importance.

Under the heading 'How to study a Song',

[1] 'Sprechgesang', the older term, is properly singing tinged with a speaking quality, whereas 'Sprechstimme' is rather speech tinged with a singing quality.

Plunket Greene, in the book above mentioned, gives the following rules:

1. Classify the song; in other words, find out what it is all about.
2. Find your fundamental rhythm and absorb it.
3. Learn the song in rough.
4. Memorize it.
5. Polish it musically first [i.e. before going into all the details of the varying treatment of the words].
6. Reconcile the phrasing to the text.
7. Absorb the accompaniment.

It seems to 'stand to reason' that the young singer's reading should include that of anthologies of poetry. A singer who is not acquainted with and an enthusiastic lover of the treasures of lyric poetry can obviously never become a first-rate interpreter of such poetry as set to music—and moreover will be very likely to take into his or her repertory examples of musical settings of inferior poems.

9. Other Aspects of Song. Many aspects of song have been either unmentioned above or else merely briefly treated, as being the subject of articles elsewhere in this volume. Amongst these are:

Types and Varieties of Song. See *Burden*; *Cantata*; *Canzonet*; *Catch*; *Chanson*; *Frottola*; *Glee*; *Madrigal*; *Napolitaine*; *Noël*; *Part Song*; *Romance*; *Round*; *Strambotto*; *Villanella*.

Church Application of Song, etc. See *Church Music*; *Alleluia*; *Anglican Chant*; *Anthem*; *Antiphon*; *Benedictus*; *Cantate Domino*; *Canticle*; *Cantor*; *Carol*; *Cathedral Music*; *Cecilian*; *Common Prayer*; *Gloria*; *Gradual*; *Gregorian Tone*; *Hoquet*; *Hymn*; *Introit*; *Kyrie*; *Lauda Sion*; *Laudi Spirituali*; *Litany*; *Liturgy*; *Machicotage*; *Magnificat*; *Mass*; *Miserere*; *Motet*; *Motu Proprio*; *Nunc Dimittis*; *Offertory*; *Oratory*; *O Salutaris*; *Passion Music*; *Plainsong*; *Psalm*; *Requiem*; *Respond*; *Response*; *Schola Cantorum*; *Sequence*; *Stabat Mater*; *Te Deum*; *Venite*.

Stage Application of Song, etc. See *Opera*; *Aria*; *Arietta*; *Arioso*; *Ballad Opera*; *Beggar's Opera*; *Bouffons*; *Cavatina*; *Comic Opera*; *Libretto*; *Light Opera*; *Opera Buffa*; *Opéra-Comique*; *Recitative*; *Ritornello*; *Singspiel*; *Stile rappresentativo*; *Vaudeville*.
The article *Accompaniment* should also be read.

10. The Chief Song Composers. Amongst the composers of (solo) songs who have separate entries in this volume are the following—arranged under nationalities in order of date of birth. It is not practicable to confine the list to composers of independent songs, since the opera composers have in many cases had great influence upon the development of song; composers of oratorios, etc., are for the same reason included. Not all the composers are of high artistic importance, the list being in part designed to give a conspectus of fluctuations of taste.

(a) **Italian.** Caccini (1546–1618); Peri (1561–1633); Monteverdi (1567–1643); Gagliano (1575–1642); Rossi (1598–1653); Cavalli (1602–76); Carissimi (1605–74); Cesti (1623–69); Stradella (1642–82); A. Scarlatti (1660–1725); Bononcini (1670–c. 1750); Astorga (1680–1736); Porpora (1686–1766); Leo (1694–1744); Pergolese (1710–36); Jommelli (1714–74); Piccini (1728–1800);

Sacchini (1734–86); Paesiello (1740–1816); Cimarosa (1749–1801); Salieri (1750–1825); Zingarelli (1752–1837); Cherubini (1760–1842); Paër (1771–1839); Spontini (1774–1851); Rossini (1792–1868); Mercadante (1795–1870); Donizetti (1797–1848); Bellini (1801–35); Costa (1808–84); Verdi (1813–1901); Ponchielli (1834–86); Sgambati (1841–1914); Boito (1842–1918); Tosti (1846–1916); Catalani (1854–93); Smareglia (1854–1929); Leoncavallo (1858–1919); Puccini (1858–1924); Mascagni (1863–1945); Busoni (1866–1924); Giordano (1867–1948); Alfano (1876–1954); Respighi (1879–1936); Pizzetti (1880–1968); Malipiero (1882–1973); Pick-Mangiagalli (1882–1949); Casella (1883–1947); Castelnuovo-Tedesco (1895–1968).

(b) **French.** Lully (1632–87); Campra (1660–1744); Rameau (1683–1764); Rouget de Lisle (1760–1836); Lesueur (1760–1837); Méhul (1763–1817); Boïeldieu (1775–1834); Auber (1782–1871); Panseron (1795–1859); Halévy (1799–1862); Berlioz (1803–69); F. David (1810–76); Ambroise Thomas (1811–96); Gounod (1818–93); Offenbach (1819–80); Weckerlin (1821–1910); Franck (1822–90; also included under Belgian); Massé (1822–84); Lalo (1823–92); Reyer (1823–1909); Lecocq (1832–1918); Saint Saëns (1835–1921); Delibes (1836–91); Guiraud (1837–92); Bizet (1838–75); Chabrier (1841–94); Massenet (1842–1912); Fauré (1845–1924); Duparc (1848–1933); Godard (1849–95); d'Indy (1851–1931); Messager (1853–1929); Bruneau(1857–1934); Chaminade(1857–1944); Huë (1858–1948); Bemberg (1859–1931); Bréville (1861–1949); Debussy (1862–1918); Pierné (1863–1937); Dukas (1865–1935); Magnard (1865–1914); Roussel (1869–1937); Rabaud (1873–1949); de Séverac (1873–1921); Roger-Ducasse (1873–1954); Hahn (1874–1947); Ravel (1875–1937); Aubert (1877–1968); Ladmirault (1877–1944); Delannoy 1898–1962); Poulenc (1899–1963).

(c) **Belgian.** Grétry (1741–1813); Campenhout (1779–1848); Franck (1822–90); P. L. Benoît (1834–1901); Gilson (1865–1942); J. Jongen (1873–1953); L. Jongen (b. 1884).

(d) **Swiss.** Jaques-Dalcroze (1865–1950).

(e) **Spanish.** Louis Milán (c. 1500–61); Pedrell (1841–1922); Bretón (1850–1923); Granados (1867–1916); Falla (1876–1946); Turina (1882–1949).

(f) **German and Austrian.** Schütz (1585–1672); J. S. Bach (1685–1750); Handel (1685–1759); Hasse (1699–1783); Graun (1701–59); Gluck (1714–87); Haydn (1732–1809); Mozart (1756–91); Zumsteeg (1760–1802); Beethoven (1770–1827); Spohr (1784–1859); Weber (1786–1826); Meyerbeer (1791–1864); Marschner (1795–1861); Loewe (1796–1869); Schubert (1797–1828); Benedict (1804–85); Mendelssohn (1809–47); Kücken (1810–82); Nicolai (1810–49); Schumann (1810–56); Flotow (1812–83); Wagner (1813–83); Clara Schumann (1819–96); Abt (1819–85); Theodor Kirchner (1823–1903); Cornelius (1824–74); Blumenthal (1829–1908); Brahms (1833–97); Adolf Jensen (1837–79); Humperdinck (1854–1921); Mahler (1860–1911); Wolf (1860–1903); Meyer-Helmund (1861–1932); Strauss (1864–1949); Pfitzner (1869–1949); Reger (1873–1916); Schönberg (1874–1951); Schreker (1878–1934); Joseph Marx (1882–1964).

(g) **Bohemian.** Smetana (1824–84); Dvořák (1841–1904); Fibich (1850–1900); Janáček (1854–1928); Foerster (1859–1951); Novák (1870–1949).

(h) **Hungarian.** Tinódi (died c. 1559); Liszt (1811–86); Goldmark (1830–1915); Korbay (1846–1913); Bartók (1881–1945); Kodály (1882–1967).

(i) **Dutch.** Pijper (1894–1947).

(j) **Russian.** Alabiev (1787–1851); Verstovsky

(1799–1862); Glinka (1804–57); Dargomijsky (1813–69); A. Rubinstein (1829–94); Borodin (1833–87); Cui (1835–1918); Mussorgsky (1839–81); Napravnik (1839–1916); Tchaikovsky (1840–93); Rimsky-Korsakof (1844–1908); Ippolitof-Ivanof (1859–1935); Catoire (1861–1926); Arensky (1861–1906); Conus (or Konius) (1862–1933); Gretchaninof (1864–1956); Kalinnikof (1866–1901); Rebikof (1866–1920); Rachmaninof (1873–1943); Medtner (1879–1951); Stravinsky (1882–1971); Prokofief (1891–1953).

(*k*) **Polish.** Chopin (1810–49); Szymanowski (1882–1937); Rózycki (1884–1953).

(*l*) **Scandinavian.** Kjerulf (1815–68); Gade (1817–90); Lassen (1830–1904); Svendsen (1840–1911); Grieg (1843–1907); Agatha Backer-Gröndahl (1847–1907); Olsen (1850–1927); Sjögren (1853–1918); Sinding (1856–1941); Nielsen (1865–1931); Lie (1871–1904).

(*m*) **Finnish.** Sibelius (1865–1957); Kilpinen (1892–1959).

(*n*) **British.** Morley (1557–*c.* 1603); Pilkington (*c.* 1562–1638); Dowland (1563–1626); Cavendish (*c.* 1565–1628); Daniel (*c.* 1565–1630); Campian (1567–1620); Cooper, or Coperario (*c.* 1570–1627); Rosseter (*c.* 1575–1623); A. Ferrabosco II (*c.* 1575–1628); Peerson (*c.* 1580–1650); Ford (*c.* 1580–1648); Robt. Jones (dates unknown); Maynard (dates unknown); Greaves (dates unknown); Corkine (dates unknown); Bartlet (dates unknown); Attey (died *c.* 1640); Hume (died 1648). These are the English lute-song composers.

R. Johnson (died *c.* 1634); John Wilson (1595–1674); Locke (*c.* 1630–77); Humfrey (1647–74); Blow (1649–1708); John Eccles (*c.* 1650–1735); Savile (dates unknown); Purcell (*c.* 1658–95); Clarke (*c.* 1659–1707); Leveridge (*c.* 1670–1758); Carey (*c.* 1690–1743); Greene (*c.* 1695–1755); Arne (1710–78); Boyce (1710–79); T. Linley, sen. (1732–95); Dibdin (1745–1814); Hooke (1746–1827); Shield (1748–1829); Davy (1763–1824); Storace (1763–96); W. Linley (1771–1835); Horn (1786–1849); Bishop (1786–1855); G. Linley, jun. (1798–1865); Balfe (1808–70); Crouch (1808–96); Hatton (1809–86); John Orlando Parry (1810–79);

Hullah (1812–84); Henry Russell (1812–1900); Loder (1813–65); Salaman (1814–1901); Pierson (1815–73); Sterndale Bennett (1816–75); Weiss (1820–67); 'Claribel' (1830–69); Coenen (1837–1918); Clay (1838–89); Sullivan (1842–1900); H. W. Nicholl (1848–1922); Parry (1848–1918); Goring Thomas (1850–92); Cowen (1852–1935); Stanford (1852–1924); Maude V. White (1855–1937); Elgar (1857–1934); Smyth (1858–1944); Wm. Wallace (1860–1940); German (1862–1936); Chevalier (1862–1923); Liza Lehmann (1862–1918); Delius (1862–1934); Somervell (1863–1937); Chas. Wood (1866–1926); Bantock (1868–1946); Walford Davies (1869–1941); Mallinson (1870–1946); Walker (1870–1949); Squire (1871–1963); Keel (1871–1954); Vaughan Williams (1872–1958); Ronald (1873–1938); Holst (1874–1934); Martin Shaw (1875–1958); Coleridge-Taylor (1875–1912); Graham Peel (1877–1937); Dunhill (1877–1946); Quilter (1877–1953); Boughton (1878–1960); Frank Bridge (1879–1941); Cyril Scott (1879–1970); Ireland (1879–1962); Harty (1879–1941); Hughes (1882–1937); Bax (1883–1953); Dale (1885–1943); Butterworth (1885–1916); Eric Coates (1886–1957); Peterkin (born 1886); Darke (1888–1976); Gerrard Williams (1888–1947); Gibbs (1889–1960); Bullock (born 1890); Gurney (1890–1937); Bliss (1891–1975); Howells (born 1892); Benjamin (1893–1960); Moeran (1894–1950); Heseltine ('Peter Warlock') (1894–1930); Britten (1913–76); ApIvor (born 1916).

(*o*) **United States of America.** Hopkinson (1737–91); Root (1820–95); Foster (1826–64); Dudley Buck (1839–1909); Foote (1853–1937); Chadwick (1854–1931); Shelley (1858–1947); de Koven (1859–1920); MacDowell (1861–1908); Loeffler (1861–1935); E. W. Nevin (1862–1901); Parker (1863–1919); Homer (1864–1953); Burleigh (1866–1949); Hadley (1871–1937); Farwell (1872–1952); D. G. Mason (1873–1953); J. R. Johnson (1873–1949); Handy (1873–1958); Oley Speaks (1874–1948); Ives (1874–1954); Carpenter (1876–1951); D. S. Smith (1877–1949); La Forge (1879–1953); Bloch (1880–1959); Cadman (1881–1946); Dett (1882–1943); O'Hara (born 1882); Griffes (1884–1920); Deems Taylor (1885–1966).

SONG CYCLE. A string of songs of related thought and congruous musical style, capable of being sung consecutively and being felt to constitute an entity.

Two very early examples (probably the earliest known) are the set of eleven songs 'I cannot come each day to woo' of Richard Nicholson (d. 1639) and a group of four songs included in the examples of Ravenscroft's *Brief Discourse* (1614). The first of these tells the wooing of Joane and John and the second that of Hodge and Malkyn.

The great *Lied* period of German song (see *Song* 5) established the song cycle (*Liederkreis* —'Song-circle'; *Liederreihe*—'Song Series'; *Liedercyclus*—'Song-cycle') as a definite feature in the vocal repertory. Notable examples of this period are Beethoven's 'To the Distant Beloved' ('An die ferne Geliebte', 1816), Schubert's 'The Beautiful Maid of the Mill' ('Die schöne Müllerin'; published 1823), 'Winter Journey' ('Winterreise', 1827) and 'Swan Song' ('Schwanengesang'; posthumous, the title was given by the publisher). Schumann's contributions are important, e.g. 'A Poet's Love'

('Dichterliebe'; pub. 1844), and 'Woman's Love and Life' ('Frauenliebe und Leben'; published 1843).

The song cycle is still a favourite form with composers. It may consist of lyrics of one poet (originally intended by him as a series or otherwise) or of lyrics of various poets, but similar in thought and feeling, brought together by the composer.

SONG FORM. Another name for simple ternary form (see *Form* 6), generally with a brief coda (q.v.), as used in the more lyrical type of instrumental piece (the description would hardly be applied to a minuet and trio, for instance, but would be to many a 'Song without Words' and 'Nocturne').

SONG LEADERS. See *Community Singing* 5.

SONG SCHOOL. See *Schola Cantorum*; *Scotland* 4; *Presbyterian Church Music* 3; *Education and Music* 1.

SONG WITHOUT WORDS. A term introduced by Mendelssohn to cover a type of one-movement pianoforte solo, throughout which a well-marked song-like melody progresses, with an accompaniment. The style was not new. Schubert's Third Impromptu (in G) of the op. 90 set and some of Beethoven's slow movements in his piano sonatas exemplify it, for instance. It is almost essentially a pianoforte type. Field's and Chopin's nocturnes are similar in style (Field even has one nocturne called 'Song without Words', but possibly the name was added by the editor, Liszt).

The German form of the term is *Lied ohne Worte*, plural *Lieder ohne Worte* (note: 'Worte', not 'Wörter', as sometimes printed). The French is *Chanson sans Paroles*.

For references to several of Mendelssohn's Songs without Words see *Nicknamed Compositions* 14.

SONNECK, OSCAR GEORGE THEODORE (1873–1928). He was chief of the Music Division in the Library of Congress, 1902–17, and a noted American musicologist and, later, publisher (Vice-President, G. Schirmer, Inc.).

See references and quotations under *Pianoforte* 17 (end); *Opera* 21 a; *Oratorio* 1; *Concert* 15; *Yankee Doodle*; *Hail, Columbia!*; *Star-spangled Banner*; *Hopkinson, Francis*; *Selby*; *Dictionaries* 8, 15.

SONNENQUARTETTE (Haydn). See *Nicknamed Compositions* 12.

SONNERIE (Fr.). 'Sounding.' Also a peal of bells, or a trumpet-call.

SONOMETER. See *Monochord*.

SONORE (Fr.), **SONORO** (It.). 'Sonorous'; so *Sonorité* (Fr.) and *Sonorità* (It.), 'sonority'; *Sonoramente* (It.), 'sonorously'.

SONS BOUCHÉS (Fr.). Stopped notes in horn playing (see *Horn Family* 2 b and 5; also *Gestopft* and *Schmetternd*).

'SONS OF HANDEL' SOCIETY. See *Ireland* 6.

SONS OF THE CLERGY. See *Festival* 1.

SOPRA (It.). 'On', 'above'. So *Sopra una corda*, 'on one string', of violin, etc. (for piano see under *Corda*); *Come sopra*, or *Come di sopra*, 'as above'.

SOPRAN (Ger.). 'Soprano.' See *Voice* 17, 19.

SOPRAN (recorder). See *Recorder Family* 2.

SOPRANA (It.). Fem. of Soprano. *Corda soprana*, highest string of violin, etc.

SOPRANINO RECORDER. See *Recorder Family* 2.

SOPRANINO SAXHORN. See *Saxhorn and Flügelhorn Families* 2 a.

SOPRANIST. See *Voice* 5.

SOPRANO. See *Voice* 17, 19.

SOPRANO CLEF. See *Notation* 4; Table 4.

SOPRANO FLÜGELHORN. See *Saxhorn and Flügelhorn Families* 2 a, 3 a.

SOPRANO SAXHORN. See *Saxhorn and Flügelhorn Families* 2 a b.

SOPRANO STAFF. See *Great Staff*.

SOPRANO VOICE. See *Voice* 17, 19.

SOR (or **Sors**), **FERNANDO** (1778–1839). See *Guitar*.

SORABJI, KAIKHOSRU SHAPURJI (originally Leon Dudley Sorabji). Born in Epping, Essex, in 1892, his father being a Parsee and his mother a Spaniard. He composes pianoforte pieces of a technical difficulty that denies approach to all but the most perfectly equipped performers and a complexity that repels all but the most receptive and persevering listeners, as also orchestral works that demand the largest and most expensive orchestra.

His *Opus Clavicembalisticum* is a two-guinea piano composition of 250 printed pages written in three or four staves throughout and without key-signatures; it is in twelve movements, including one theme with forty-nine variations and another with eighty-one, and fugues and canons of every variety known to musical science, and it takes over two hours to perform. Other works are two huge piano concertos and an organ symphony which occupies the time of a complete recital.

In view of the fact that the birth-date and birthplace of this composer as above given have been contested, and various other dates given, it may be added here that a close inquiry has been made and official confirmation obtained. (The composer, it appears, resents 'stupid and impertinent inquiries from lexicographical persons' and makes it a practice 'deliberately to mislead them as to dates and places'. Letter to the author of this book—22 Feb. 1952.)

SORDA, SORDAMENTE (It.). 'Subdued', muffled.

SORDINA (It.). Same as *sordino* (q.v.).

SORDINO, SORDINI (It.). 'Mute', 'mutes'. So *Sordini alzati* or *Sordini levati* means 'mutes raised', i.e. taken off.

But applied to the pianoforte *Sordini* means 'dampers': see *Senza sordino, Senza sordini*.

SORDO, SORDA (It., masc., fem.). 'Dull in tone', muffled.

SORDUN (Ger.). A quiet-toned wooden organ stop (8ft. and 16 ft.).

SORE, MARTIN. See *Agricola* (2).

SORGFALT (Ger.). 'Care'. So *Sorgfältig*, 'carefully'.

SORIANO (or **Suriano**), **FRANCESCO**. Born at Rome in 1549 and there died in 1620, aged seventy or seventy-one. He was a pupil of Palestrina and held important positions in various churches of Rome. He published motets, masses, madrigals, etc.

See a reference to him under *Plainsong* 3.

SORS, FERNANDO. See *Guitar*.

SORTIE (Fr.). 'Exit', 'departure', hence 'closing voluntary' and the like.

SOSPIRANDO, SOSPIRANTE, SOSPIREVOLE, SOSPIROSO (It.). 'Sighing', i.e. plaintive in style.

SOSTENENDO, SOSTENENTE (It.). 'Sustaining.'

SOSTENUTO (It.). 'Sustained.'

SOSTENUTO PEDAL. See *Pianoforte* 12.

SOTTO VOCE (It., literally, 'under the voice') The equivalent of the English 'under the breath' 'undertone', meaning in a barely audible manner. The term is, musically, applied to both vocal and instrumental performance.

SOUBASSE (Fr.). Contra-bourdon organ stop, 32 feet.

SOUBRETTE (Fr.). A secondary female part in comic opera, typically a lively and coquettish lady's maid.

SOUDAINEMENT (Fr.). 'Suddenly.'

SOUHAITTY. See *Tonic Sol-fa* 10.

SOUND, ITS NATURE. See *Acoustics.*

SOUNDBOARD. See *Pianoforte* 11.

SOUND FILM. See *Electric* 5 c.

SOUND-HOLES. The '*f* holes' cut in the belly (i.e. the upper surface) of a violin, etc.

SOUNDING-BOARDS. See *Acoustics* 18.

SOUND-POST. The piece of wood fixed within a violin, etc., to counter the downward pressure of the bridge (cf. *Âme, Anima*).

SOUND SHADOWS. See *Acoustics* 19.

SOUND WAVES. See *Acoustics* 12, 13, 14, 15.

SOUPIRANT (Fr.). 'Sighing.'

SOUPLE (Fr.). 'Supple', flexible.

SOURD, SOURDE (Fr., masc., fem.). 'Muffled.' So *Pédale sourde*, soft pedal.

SOURDINE (Fr.). This word is used in the same senses as It. *sordino* (q.v.).

SOUS (Fr.). 'Under.'

SOUSA, JOHN PHILIP (p. 1041, pl. **170**. 4). Born at Washington, D.C., in 1854 and died at Reading, Pa., in 1932, aged seventy-seven.

He was a bandmaster of international reputation and the composer of stirring marches (see *March*). His best marches (such as *The Stars and Stripes Forever, El Capitán, The Washington Post*) have in an extraordinary degree the youthful spirit, optimism, and patriotic feeling which animated the nation at the time they were composed: they are in fact vitally and distinctively American, though of the America of the 90's rather than that of later days. (It was his view that 'a march should make a man with a wooden leg step out'.) He also composed many light operas.

In 1880 he became leader of the Marine Band in Washington under Hayes's administration. Twelve years later he organized the celebrated Sousa's Band. This organization, with which he made a tour of the world (in addition to annual pilgrimages in his own country), had much to do with raising the entire standard of band playing in America.

The various statements as to Sousa's original name being 'So', 'Soucci', etc., have no foundation. His father was a Portuguese born in Spain and *Sousa* is a common name in Portugal. See a discussion of the subject in editions 3 to 8 of this book.

SOUSAPHONE. See *Tuba Group* 3 c.

SOUSEDSKÁ. A slow three-in-a-measure round dance of the Bohemian peasantry, often danced as a change after the Furiant (q.v.). At one time it was customary to give the Sousedská a devotional tinge by chanting a certain traditional Chorale.

SOUTENU (Fr.). 'Sustained.'

SOUTER LIEDEKENS. See *Hymn and Hymn Tunes* 17 c; *Holland* 2.

SOUTH AFRICA. See *Harmony* 4; *Broadcasting* 3; *Joubert; Rainier.*

SOUTH PLACE CONCERTS. This is a series of popular London Sunday chamber concerts of the highest class, beginning in 1887 and still continuing. For forty years the concerts were given in the chapel of the South Place Ethical Society, Finsbury Circus (destroyed 1927); they are now given in Conway Hall, Red Lion Square.

Cf. *Walthew; Concert* 7.

SOUTHWARK FAIR. See *Fairs and their Music.*

SOWERBY, LEO (p. 1061, pl. **174**. 3). Born at Grand Rapids, Michigan, in 1895 and died at Port Clinton, Ohio, in 1968, aged seventy-three. He had his early training in Chicago and then studied in Europe for three years, as the holder of an American Rome Prize. He was productive in most of the forms of composition. His organ music enjoys considerable favour. From 1962 he was Director of the College of Church Musicians in Washington, D.C.

See references under *Jazz* 5; *Concerto* 6 c (1895).

SPAETH, SIGMUND (1885–1965). See reference under *Melody* 7.

SPAGNOLETTO, SPAGNOLETTA, SPAGNILETTA, SPAGNICOLETTA. An old Italian round dance probably related to the pavan (q.v.). The male dancers clapped the rhythm with their hands against those of the female dancers. By its name it may have been borrowed from Spain—probably at the time when Spain held Naples.

The word is found in Elizabethan virginal music attached to pieces that are sometimes three-in-a-measure and sometimes four-in-a-measure.

SPAIN

1. Oriental Elements.
2. The Ancient Church Music.
3. Folk Song and Folk Dance.
4. The Romancero.
5. Composition in the Sixteenth Century.

6. The Stage and its Music.
7. The Nineteenth and Twentieth Centuries.
8. Some Spanish Instrumental Developments.

9. Contributions to Musical Theory.
10. Relations with other Countries.
11. List of Articles amplifying the above.

This article offers merely a brief conspectus of the history of music in Spain, further information on almost every branch of the subject mentioned, as on the individual composers, being given under the appropriate heads throughout this volume.

1. Oriental Elements. Spanish folk music and the modern Spanish music which accepts its influence are recognized by every one as having a distinctive 'flavour' of their own, and not merely a variety of any general European flavour. This is due to the **Moorish Occupation** of the southern part of the country, which lasted from the eighth century to the end of the fifteenth (say A.D. 732, when the Moors got as far north as Tours in France, and were driven back to the part of Spain they were able to occupy, and 1492, when the reconquest of Granada was effected under Ferdinand and Isabella, with the final expulsion of the Moorish remnant a century later).

During these seven centuries the complex Arabic rhythms, microtonic Arabic scales (the tone divided into three instead of two), Arabic instruments (especially the plucked string and percussion classes), and an oriental profusion of *fioriture* (see *Fioritura*) became the commonplaces of musical practice, especially in the southern province, where the Moors succeeded is confirming their conquest.

In the early ninth century Zirŷáb, a famous composer and singer, came from Baghdad and settled at Córdoba, where he taught song by very thorough methods, and enjoyed high fame. (See *Singing* 1.)

2. The Ancient Church Music. The Moors were tolerant to Christianity and the services of the Church continued, but just as Moorish influence affected Christian architecture so it did Christian music, the traditional plainsong now taking on a style of excessive ornamentation that continued until the papal decision of the early years of the present century, when the authentic primitive restoration of Solesmes (see *Plainsong* 3) was imposed. The actual **Mozarabic Rite** (that is the ancient rite of Christians living in Moorish territory) is still authorized in a chapel in the cathedral of Toledo and here continues, but the plainsong of this rite has some centuries since lost its former florid character and so the Mozarabic Church chant may be said to be now extinct.

3. Folk Song and Folk Dance. The folk tune of southern Spain retains the Arabic characteristics. An expert can easily recognize the provenance of Spanish folk melody; the song of the eastern provinces resembles that of the neighbouring Provence; the middle north and the central provinces have a song that has come down from the ancient Visigothic inhabitants, but with an oriental blend; along the north coast the oriental characteristics are almost entirely lacking and the tunes more resemble those in other parts of Europe.

Much of the song of Andalusia, in the south, comes under the description of **Cante Hondo** (q.v.), of which **Cante Flamenco** (q.v.) is a variety that has submitted to gipsy treatment. The gipsies first entered Spain in the middle of

the fifteenth century; it is a habit of their race to adopt the music of its hosts but to add an exaggeration or wildness to its performance, and this is what they have done in Spain. The vocal tone used by the singers of folk song is not at once acceptable to northern ears; it may be roughly described as tending to resemble the oboes where in other parts of Europe the vocal ideal is rather the flute. A good many folk-song tunes have measures of five or seven beats.

The native dances are exceedingly numerous (see list of some of them at end of this article; no country whose music is described in this volume has required anything like so many separate entries under heads representing dance and song). Two traditional Spanish dances passed into the sixteenth- to eighteenth-century suites, and became classical—the pavan (which, however, is thought to have come to Spain from Italy) and the sarabande. It is suggested that some of the rhythms of jazz are distinctly Spanish in origin and that the North American Negroes should have picked up and retained some of the characteristics of Spanish music does not seem to be impossible. The practice of public dancing in the street is still extant in Spain more than in any country in the world.

Folk tune has been occasionally collected and recorded in Spain since the days of the blind organist **Salinas** (1513–90). In 1922 the composer Falla held at Granada a great festival of folk song and dance and this gave some impetus to the study by musicians of the abundant material available. During the later nineteenth and the twentieth centuries no school of composers in Europe has more openly submitted to its native folk influence than the Spanish School. A great collection of tunes allied, at any rate, to folk tune was made at the end of the thirteenth century by Alfonso X of León and Castile ('Alfonso the Learned'), in two richly illuminated volumes of examples of the **Cantiga**—the popular religious song, the music showing the influence of the troubadours (see article *Minstrels, Troubadours*, etc.). This is one of the most precious and valuable collections of medieval music that the world possesses. The illuminations show that at Alfonso's court some of the musicians were Moors, with Moorish instruments.

4. The Romancero. There remain also quantities of examples of the Romancero, very like the French 'chansons de gestes', describing the deeds of heroes: they were disseminated by the 'juglares' (jongleurs; see article just mentioned) and were highly popular into the sixteenth century, and there exist two important collections made in that century, the *Cancionero musical* (preserved at Madrid) and the *Cantilenas vulgares* (preserved at Seville).

5. Composition in the Sixteenth Century. In the fifteenth century the English and Flemish methods of composition (see *England* and *Belgium* 2), which spread over Europe, penetrated to Spain, both English and Flemish musicians being welcomed in that country.

Then, with the coming to the Spanish throne of the Emperor Charles V, and the bringing under one crown of Spain and the Netherlands, the Flemish influence naturally increased. A music-loving monarch who inherited the Netherlands, Burgundy, Spain, and Naples and was elected Holy Roman Emperor, who thus had many capitals, each with its royal chapel, and was called upon to make many journeys, all of them with a full retinue of musicians, naturally, and in the mere course of official routine, brought the musicians of many countries into contact with one another. In his reign, and that of his son Philip II (the consort of Mary of England and the master of the Armada of 1588), music flourished.

These two reigns cover the period 1516 to 1598, and this was precisely the period of Spain's greatest musical glory. To a great extent local characteristics now disappeared. The special qualities of the dances and folk songs of Spain, as those of the compositions of the late nineteenth- and twentieth-century composers, are at once patent to any one who hears them, but only the experienced student of sixteenth-century music will notice anything specifically national in a mass or motet of this period. Towards the end of the period we may put much on a level as to both technical methods and artistry the skilful and moving polyphonic church music of Lassus, the Fleming (1532–94), Palestrina, the Italian (c. 1525–94), Byrd, the Englishman (c. 1543–1623), and **Victoria,** the Spaniard (c. 1549–1611).

That Italian type, the **Madrigal,** which was so successfully taken up in England, was in some measure adopted in Spain also. The native **Villancico** (q.v.), in its choral form, already approached the madrigal, and contact with Italy brought in the more developed true madrigal. This type never enjoyed, however, the popularity in Spain that it did in Italy and England.

Apart from Victoria, the most able composer of the period is his senior, **Cristóbal Morales** (c. 1500–53). Victoria wrote no secular music (from religious scruples), and Morales very little. **Francesco Guerrero** (1527–99) and his brother **Pedro** are of importance, as are also **Ruimonte** (or Rimonte; dates unknown) and **Mateo Flecha** (c. 1520–1604). **Comes** (1568–1643) was a writer of church music of a very grandiose type. But the number of names that could be cited is large, and choice amongst them for a brief article such as this is difficult. The age of Cervantes and Lope de Vega was, then, one of high musical achievement in Spain, as that of their contemporary Shakespeare was in England. And *Don Quixote* abounds with musical allusions, as do the works of Shakespeare.

6. The Stage and its Music (see also *Opera* 15–16). Poetry, music, and dancing have, perhaps, been less separable in Spain than in other countries.

The poet and dramatist **Enzina** (1469–1534)

introduced singing and dancing into his plays (it will be noticed by these dates that the Spanish theatre began somewhat earlier than the English). The music is by himself; where choral, it shows the influences of the Flemish school. His plays have little intrinsic merit, but he is looked on as both the founder of Spanish drama and that of Spanish opera. Lope de Vega, amongst his 1,500 plays, wrote in 1629 one (*La Selva sin amor*) to be sung throughout. The composer is unknown.

The **Zarzuela** (q.v.), the distinctively Spanish form of 'opéra-comique', dates from 1629 and is still being freely produced. The great dramatist Calderón (1600–81) wrote the words of many zarzuelas. A modern successful composer of zarzuelas is **Tomás Bretón** (1850–1923). **Joaquín Valverde** (1846–1910) and his son Quinito (1875–1918), who wrote more than fifty apiece, must also be mentioned.

It is very curious that a country possessing so many links with Italy should not have welcomed the **Italian Opera** until more than a century after its introduction. It was in 1703 that the first Italian opera troupe appeared in Madrid. Thenceforward, however, Italy dominated. Amongst Spanish composers of opera in the Italian language and style have been **Vincent Martín y Soler** (1754–1806), once popular throughout Europe, and **Carnicer** (1789–1855), who contributed in some ways to the founding of a national school, but was compelled by public opinion to set Italian libretti.

In the great days of Italian vocalism Spain opened her arms to all its great exponents—Farinelli, Caffarelli, Senesino, Cuzzoni, Faustina, and the rest. **Farinelli** (1705–82), as director of the royal music, naturally used his influence for Italian art, and on behalf of his countrymen and countrywomen. He himself was not allowed to sing in public, his only performances being those of the same four airs nightly for ten years to the king Philip V, a sufferer from melancholy who, strangely, thus found relief for a sick mind. (But cf. the reference to Farinelli and the king under *Ornaments* 1—near end.)

Barbieri (1823–94), a learned musician and musicologist and composer of comic operas, helped to establish a true Spanish type. **Ruperto Chapí** (1851–1909) has been successful, especially with comic operas.

The operatic situation in Spain is still spoken of by patriotic musicians as unsatisfactory. Falla, himself a composer of true Spanish opera, once complained: 'The best theatre in Madrid is at the mercy of Italian publishers. They are not unnaturally engaged in exploiting works of their own countrymen, compelling Spaniards to seek their premières in foreign countries' (his own were first heard in Paris, Nice, and London).

7. The Nineteenth and Twentieth Centuries. Amongst musicians of the early nineteenth century is **Arriaga,** who lived only to the age of nineteen (1806–25) but became a very accomplished contrapuntist: his three string quartets, somewhat in the Haydn style, were published in Paris the year before his death.

Hilarión Eslava, a priest, composed operas and, especially, church music (not very serious), wrote a treatise on composition, and earned the gratitude of students by publishing (1869) a ten-volume collection of Spanish music from the sixteenth century to the nineteenth; which remains the standard anthology. This monument to Spanish art came into existence as the result of the stay in Spain of the Belgian Gevaert and the report he wrote for his government (he was then in the enjoyment of a travelling scholarship) in which he pointed out the existence of a definite Spanish School of music—which had not previously been realized.

Pedrell (1841–1922) also published collections of national music. By research and composition and teaching he won a place as the acknowledged head of a definite national musical movement. A brief description of his manifold activities will be found under his own name, and likewise under their names are treated the successful nineteenth- and twentieth-century efforts to found a truly Spanish school of **Isaac Albéniz, Falla, Granados, Turina**, and others. Following these, a further group of active composers have come forward (**Mompou, Gerhard, Nin, E. and R. Halffter, Esplá**, etc.).

It is noticeable that contemporary Spanish musicians have in many cases studied in Paris, and have there first 'found their feet' as composers and received their first welcome. A National Society of Music, founded in 1915, has, however, latterly given many Spanish composers their first opportunity of being heard by their countrymen.

8. Some Spanish Instrumental Developments. There are some particularities about Spanish instrumental history that deserve a paragraph or two. The love of plucked-string instruments that came from the Moorish occupation has been mentioned. The typical instrument of this kind for some centuries was the **Vihuela** (q.v.) a sort of lute with some features of the guitar. It was the aristocratic instrument; every gentleman played it. The greatest vihuelist was **Luis Milán** (c. 1500–61), who left an important book of music for it: he developed varieties of accompaniment in his songs and worked out a truly instrumental technique of composition (see also an allusion under *Song* 3).

The **Guitar** was the popular instrument; it superseded the Vihuela about 1600 and became as much the regular domestic instrument as the piano in other countries: it 'caught on' in Paris, Vienna, and London, and then, in the eighteenth century, gave ground before the competition of the harpsichord and the harp.

A book of high importance on the use of a bowed instrument is that of Ortiz (1553) on the art of playing divisions (q.v.) on the **Bass Viol** (i.e. Viola da Gamba); with a **Lute** work by Narvaez, published in 1538, it gives Spain a strong claim to rank amongst the earliest countries to develop the instrumental variation style, which is apparently of English introduction (Hugh Aston's music for the virginals, somewhat earlier; see *Aston*).

It is probably little realized today that Spain at one time ranked high as a country of **Organ** building and organ playing. In the days of Spain's prosperity much money was spent on equipping churches with fine organs, and Spanish organ-builders became enterprising and inventive. The harmonic flute is said to be a quite ancient Spanish invention, and the swell box, long attributed to an English early eighteenth-century builder (see *Organ* 8), is now claimed to have been in use in Spain at a much earlier date. A great organist and early organ composer was the blind **Antonio de Cabezón** (1510–66), who in his work for organ and clavichord showed an advanced keyboard style; he is said to have passed some time in England with Philip of Spain (husband of Queen Mary of England; afterwards Philip II). He is, of course, one of the earliest of the world's composers for keyboard instruments. After his death his works were published (1576) by his son Hernando, also a royal musician. At this period and for some time later the **Clavichord** was in Spain preferred to instruments of the virginals, spinet, or harpsichord type.

In the eighteenth century **Father Antonio Soler** (1729–83) wrote a famous book on the organ. He also wrote harpsichord sonatas whose place of publication was London; they were written when Domenico Scarlatti was in Madrid and appear to have influenced him. Soler was an important theoretician.

It is worthy of note that a great book of Victoria's church choral music, published in 1600, has an organ accompaniment throughout—this merely duplicates choral parts, but is nevertheless a rare thing, if not unique, in those days.

Some very old organs are in use in places. The one presented to the Cathedral of Granada by Philip II (died 1598) is still regularly played. It has an incomplete set of pedals—like a row of door-knobs in the floor. Some visitors report hearing organs whose reeds do not give the impression of having been tuned since the days of the monarch mentioned.

On the whole the art of the organ-builder has, then, dropped behind, but the art of the organist is said to be fully maintained in certain quarters—contrapuntal improvisation being a feature. Organ composition in Spain is a good deal discouraged today by the almost total absence of concert organs and the clergy's non-approval of recitals in churches.

The Escurial, near Madrid, has a **Carillon** (see *Bell* 4), dating from the days when the same monarchs ruled Spain and the Low Countries.

Rustic instruments in use in parts of Spain today include the **Bagpipe** or **Gaita** (see *Bagpipe Family* 7). In some Basque towns the municipality maintains a troupe of four or five musicians playing instruments of the flute and drum kinds.

The **Castanets** (see *Percussion* 4 q) are, of course, a peculiarly Spanish instrument: they are used to accompany dancing.

In the latter part of the sixteenth century Spain produced (and supplied some of the Roman churches with) a type of adult soprano **Falsettist**, the voice being produced (without operation) by some peculiar process now lost.

9. Contributions to Musical Theory. There was an immense quantity of theoretical musical literature issued in Spain in the sixteenth, seventeenth, and eighteenth centuries, testifying to a wide and deep interest in the art of music. **Ramos de Pareja**, in *Musica Pratica* (published in Italy in 1482), discussed Equal Temperament and is thought to have been the first to do so (see *Temperament* 5). **Salinas**, a noted theorist, was Professor of Music at Salamanca and lectured daily. **Cerone** published in 1613 at Naples a book, *Melopeo y Maestro*, which gives a particularly comprehensive view of musical theory (even including an explanation of the music of the spheres!).

The conflict that arose between the partisans of the old and the new styles at the beginning of the seventeenth century (when the old contrapuntal ideal was weakening all over Europe and the newer harmonic aspect of music receiving attention) included in Spain a paper war of seventy-eight pamphlets.

An eighteenth-century theorist was the Jesuit priest **Eximeno**. On the expulsion of the Jesuits from Spain in 1768, he settled in Rome and published there a book showing how music aims to express emotion, and, also, that it should be based on national speech patterns (rather than folk song, as is often said). He encountered violent opposition: but his view was the one upon which Pedrell was later to base his propaganda.

10. Relations with other Countries. The musical relations of Spain with other countries through the centuries could be profitably discussed at great length. Some instances have already been mentioned.

Domenico Scarlatti passed nearly thirty years at the court of Spain (1729–57).

Boccherini, the violoncellist, was also there for a long period (1769 to his death in 1805).

Mercadante was director of the opera at Madrid in 1827–8 and then of Cadiz.

Haydn wrote his *Seven Words of Our Saviour on the Cross* for the Cathedral of Cadiz; his music was very popular in Spain and his chamber music was particularly so at Cadiz, then a great musical centre. (See *Seven Last Words*.)

Liszt visited Spain and introduced Spanish themes into several compositions.

The pianist Gottschalk (q.v.) had an enormous success there, and afterwards toured

other parts of the world playing his Spanish fantasias and so popularizing the Spanish idiom.

There is a somewhat unexpected connexion between Spain and the Russian school, which began with Glinka's stay in the country in 1845–7, and his composition of the orchestral *Jota Aragonese* and *Night in Madrid*; the resources awaiting employment in Spanish folk tunes were thus revealed by a foreigner (compare Gevaert's propaganda mentioned under 7) to the lasting advantage of native composition. Balakiref's *Overture on Spanish Themes* was the result of a suggestion of Glinka, and Rimsky-Korsakof's well-known *Spanish Capriccio* is another outcome. The sympathy the Russian composers of this period felt with Spanish folk music, and the stimulus it gave them towards the exploitation of their own music was doubtless due to the oriental element in much of the folk music of both countries.

Chabrier's orchestral rhapsody, *España*, and his pianoforte *Habanera*, Lalo's *Symphonie Espagnole* (written for the Spanish violinist Sarasate), and Debussy's *Ibéria, Soirée dans Grenade*, and a good many other compositions of his, testify to the French interest in the life and art of a neighbouring country. Ravel's pianoforte *Alborada del Gracioso*, his comic opera *L'Heure espagnole*, and his *Rapsodie espagnole* remind us that he was born on the borders of Spain. Berners and Walton have also written works in a consciously Spanish idiom.

Bizet's *Carmen* is not regarded very favourably by Spaniards, Mérimée's admirable picture of Spanish life being distorted in the libretto and the music rarely suggesting the authentic Spanish idiom.

Nineteenth- and twentieth-century Paris has warmly welcomed Spanish composers.

The above instances of foreign composers feeling the inspiration of Spain are worth recalling because no other country can show anything at all like it; it would not be unfair to say that in the nineteenth century Spain inspired a good deal more fine music than she produced —and this amongst composers of many widely differing European nationalities.

Spain has sent abroad many virtuosi—such as the great tenor Manuel García (1775–1832), his son Manuel (1805–1906), and his daughters Malibran and Viardot (see *García Family*), and in more recent times the violinist Sarasate, the violoncellist Casals (who, however, prefers to be considered a Catalan), the pianist Viñes (also of Catalan origin), and the guitarist Segovia.

11. List of Articles amplifying the above. In order to amplify the information given above the following articles may be consulted:

a. Madrigal 8 d; *Tono*; *Bagpipe Family* 7.
b. Liturgy (reference to Mozarabic Rite); *Motet*; *Schola Cantorum*; *Seises*.

c. Alalá; *Arada*; *Canto Flamenco*; *Cante Hondo*; *Cantiga*; *Carcelera*; *Copla*; *Ensalada*; *Entremés*; *Estribillo*; *Petenera*; *Polo*; *Saeta*; *Tonada*; *Tonadilla*; *Tor-*

nada; *Villancico*; *Villanesca*; *Zarzuela*.
d. Aurresku; *Baile*; *Bolero*; *Cachucha*; *Canaries*; *Chaconne*; *Fandango*; *Folía* (Folies d'Es-

1. MAINZER (1801–51)

2. MISS GLOVER (1785–1867). See *Tonic Sol-fa*

3. HULLAH (1812–84)
See *Tonic Sol-fa*

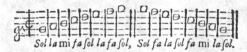

Sol la mi fa sol la fa sol, Sol fa la sol fa mi la sol.

Now you'll say, you know what all this means, only you cannot Tune you *Notes* right, nor can it be suppofed you ever will, without the affiftance of a Tunable Voice or Inftrument at the firft; all the Benefit you can reap without it, is to obferve what I now am going to lay down, in relation to the conftituted Sounds belonging to thofe eight Notes afcending and defcending. When a Sound is given to the firft Note, called *Sol*, you rife to *La*, (as the next in order above it) one whole Tone or Sound, and another whole Tone to *Mi*, from *Mi* to *Fa* is but half a Tone; from *Fa* to *Sol*, and *Sol* to *la*, are whole Tones; from *La* to *Fa*, but half a Tone; from *Fa* to *Sol*, a whole Tone; and you might afcend, if your Voice would permit you, Ten Thoufand *Octaves* in the fame Order as this one. The difference between whole Tones and half Tones, either rifing or falling is eafily diftinguifh'd, all whole Tones being *cheerful* to the Ear, but half Tones *melancholy*; and you'll always meet with two half Tones (either rifing or falling) within the compafs of eight Notes, and thofe two are call'd *Fa*; for to rife from *Mi* to *Fa*, and from *La* to *Fa*, are *melancholy* Sounds; alfo to fall from *Fa* to *La*, and from *Fa* to *Mi*, are *melancholy* Sounds. But let us look back on the Leffon of *Plain Song*, which you muft ma-

C   nage

4. CURWEN (1816–80). See the Articles listed under his name

Sol   Law   Mi   Faw

5, 6. LANCASHIRE SOL-FA. Playford's explanation in his *Skill of Musick* (1655 and many later editions) and the AMERICAN 'BUCK-WHEAT NOTATION', based on the same system, from the *Easy Instructor* (Philadelphia, *c.* 1798). See *Lancashire Sol-fa* (end)

PLATE 164

1. CRISTÓBAL MORALES
(c. 1500–53)

2. THE CENTENARIAN SINGING
MASTER, MANUEL GARCÍA (1805–1906)

3. PEDRELL (1841–1922)

4. THE GUITARIST, TÁRREGA
(1852–1909)

5. ISAAC ALBÉNIZ (1860–1909)

6. GRANADOS (1867–1916)

7. VIÑES (1875–1943)

8. FALLA (1876–1946)

9. TURINA (1882–1949)

pagne); *Granadina*; *Jácara*; *Jaleo*; *Jota*; *Malagueña*; *Manchega*; *Muiñeira*; *Murciana*; *Pavan*; *Rondeña*; *Rueda*; *Sarabande*; *Sardana*; *Seguidilla*; *Sevillana*; *Soléa*; *Tirana*; *Zapateado*; *Zortziko*.
e. *Singing* 3; *Voice* 5.
f. *Zarzuela*; *Opera* 15, 16.
g. *Rhythm* 10.
h. CHRONOLOGICAL CONSPECTUS OF

COMPOSERS. Arranged according to century of birth.

16th CENTURY: Flecha, P. and F. Guerrero, Luis Milán, C. Morales, Ortiz, J. Pujol, Ruimonte, Victoria.
18th CENTURY: Pedro Albéniz I and II, Arteaga, García.

19th CENTURY: Isaac Albéniz,

Barrios, Bretón, Conrado del Campo, Casals, Esplá, Falla, Garreta, Gerhard, Enrique and Edward Granados, Guridi, Manén, Mompou, O. J. M. and P. G. Morales, Nicolau, Nin, Pedrell, J. B. Pujol, A. Salazar, Sarasate, Turina, Vives.

20th CENTURY: E. and R. Halffter, Nin-Culmell.

SPANDENDO (It.). 'Expanding' (in power).

SPANISH CHAPEL, LONDON. See *Roman Catholic Church Music in Britain*.

SPARK, WILLIAM (1823–97). See reference under *Conducting* 4 (end).

'SPARROW MASS' (Mozart). See *Nicknamed* 15 (K. 220).

SPARTA, SPARTO, SPARTITA, SPARTITO (It.). 'Score.'

SPASS, SPASSHAFT (Ger.). 'Joke', 'jocular'.

SPASSAPENSIERI (It.). Jew's harp (q.v.).

SPASSHAFT (Ger.). 'Jocular.'

SPÄTER (Ger.). 'Later.'

SPATZENMESSE (Mozart). See *Nicknamed* 15 (K. 220).

SPEAKER-KEY in wind instruments. A key opening a hole which divides the wind column and so (by introducing a compulsory antinode) makes easier the production of the harmonics required in order to bring into use a high part of the register (see, for instance, *Clarinet Family* 2).

SPEAKING STOPS. See *Organ* 5.

SPEAKS, OLEY. Born at Canal Winchester, Ohio, in 1874 and died in New York in 1948, aged seventy-four. After beginning as a baritone soloist in a church choir, and as a teacher, he became known as a prolific composer of songs, some of which (such as *On the Road to Mandalay* and *When the Boys Come Home*) enjoyed enormous popularity. His works include also part songs and anthems.

SPECIES. See *Counterpoint*.

SPECTATOR. See *Criticism* 4; *Community Singing* 3.

SPEDIENDO (It.). 'Speeding', hurrying.

SPEECH. See *Voice* 20.

SPEECH INFLEXIONS, the source, scale of, and melody of. See *Scales* 3; *Melody* 2.

SPEED OF SOUND. See *Acoustics* 14.

SPERDENDOSI (It.). 'Fading out.'

SPHÄROPHON, SPHEROPHONE. See *Electric Musical Instruments* 1 c.

SPIANATO (It.—in the feminine form, *Spianata*). *Spianare* means to plane, and this adjective means 'planed', 'levelled', 'smoothed'.

SPICCATO. In treating of speech this Italian word means clear articulation of the syllables. In music it has a similar meaning, implying staccato effect, and, in the modern playing of the violin, etc., a loose bouncing movement of the bow. It should be noted that, despite the markings of present-day editors of Bach and his contemporaries, what we now call spiccato has, properly, no place in the music of that period, being then impossible owing to the lesser curve of the bridge.

SPIEGANDO (It.). 'Unfolding', becoming louder.

SPIEL, SPIELEN (Ger.). 'Play', 'to play'. So *Spielend*, 'playing', 'playful'; *Volle Spiel*, full organ; *Spieler*, 'player'.

SPIELMAN'S SUPER-PIANO. See *Electric Musical Instruments* 5 b.

SPINET. See *Harpsichord Family* 4; *Pianoforte* 16.

SPINETTI (or **Spinetus**). See *Harpsichord Family* 4.

SPINNEN DES TONS (Ger.). Same as *Filar la voce* (q.v.).

SPINNERLIED (Ger.). 'Spinner's song.'

SPINNING SONG (Mendelssohn). See *Nicknamed Compositions* 14.

SPINNLIED (Ger.). 'Spinning song.'

SPIRANTE (It.). 'Expiring', dying away.

SPIRITO (It.). 'Spirit', 'vigour'. So *Spiritoso*, 'spirited'; *Spiritosamente*, 'spiritedly'.

SPIRIT TRIO (Beethoven). See *Nicknamed Compositions* 4.

SPIRITUALS. See *United States of America* 6.

SPITTA, JULIUS AUGUSTE PHILIPP. Born at Wechold, in Hanover, in 1841 and died in Berlin in 1894, aged fifty-two. He held various professorial positions in Berlin. His musicological publications include the standard life of Bach (1873–80; in English 1884–5), the complete edition of the works of Schütz, an edition of the organ works of Buxtehude, and a selection of the compositions of Frederick the Great.

SPITZE (Ger.). 'Point.' Hence, in string playing, *An der Spitze*, 'at the point' (of the bow).

SPITZFLÖTE. See *Organ* 14 II.

SPITZIG (Ger.). 'Pointed', cutting.

SPOFFORTH, REGINALD. Born at Southwell, in Nottinghamshire, in 1770 and died in London in 1827, aged fifty-six or fifty-seven. He wrote a great number of fine glees which attained and retain a high popularity; one of them, 'Hail, Smiling Morn', is, of all glees ever written, the most generally known.

SPOHR, LOUIS (p. 397, pl. **68.** 5). Born at Brunswick in 1784 and died at Cassel in 1859, aged seventy-five. His life was that of a travelling virtuoso violinist and, also, of an opera conductor (in both capacities of high rank); and, further, that of a voluminous and, in his time, successful composer of the early nineteenth-century Romantic school.

There is a manneristic chromaticism in his compositions which has been a factor in their decline in popularity, his oratorios, *Calvary* and *The Last Judgement,* lingering perhaps longest in the repertory.

He wrote eleven operas, ten symphonies, fifteen violin concertos, eight overtures, thirty-four string quartets, and much other chamber music, a notable *Violin School,* and an autobiography that abounds in lively description of musical life towards the end of the period of royal patronage.

Stanford (born 1852) remembered the time when many musicians considered Spohr a greater composer than Beethoven.

See references under *Bagpipe Family* 7; *Chamber Music* 6, Period III (1784); *Clarinet Family* 6; *Concerto* 6 b (1784); *Concert* 8; *Conducting* 5; *Harp* 4; *Horn Family* 3, 4; *Oratorio* 3, 7 (1825, 1835, 1842); *Ornaments* 4; *Percussion* 4 a; *Rode*; *Symphony* 8 (1784); *Violin Family* 6.

SPOKE PIPE. See *Pitch* 6 a.

SPONTINI, GASPARO LUIGI PACIFICO (p. 517, pl. **94.** 8). Born at Jesi near Ancona in 1774 and died there in 1851, aged seventy-six. He was the son of a peasant, who studied at one of the music schools of Naples and before his course there was ended had begun to make a name as an opera composer.

At twenty-nine he tried his luck in Paris and by determination and patience established himself there in the teeth of chauvinistic opposition. In his early thirties (1807) he produced the opera *La Vestale,* a work in which he shed his former light Neapolitan style, and its success, with the support of Napoleon and Josephine, finally 'made' him.

In his forties he became chief director of music in Berlin, at an enormous salary, and he ranked as the supreme deity of the world of opera in Germany until, very shortly (1821), the appearance and immediate wildfire progress of Weber's *Freischütz* (a work of thoroughly German character, as opposed to the Italianism of his own style) threw him into the shade. Thereafter he led a career of alternating success and failure, which ended in litigation and his departure in 1842, after an occupancy of his high position lasting over twenty years.

A few years later he settled in his native place, where he devoted his time and money to good works, and, dying soon after, left his fortune to the poor.

In addition to his high fame in the history of opera he enjoys another in the history of orchestral conducting, for, by his masterful control and his keen attention to the slightest details, he helped to establish the modern standard.

See references under *Cornett and Key Bugle Family* 3 g (use of Ophicleide); *Percussion Family* 4 b (Bass Drum) c (Gong); *Grand Opera.*

SPÖTTISCH (Ger.). 'Mocking.'

SPREADING CHESTNUT TREE. See *Under the Spreading Chestnut Tree.*

SPRECHCHOR (Ger.). 'Speech-choir', i.e. 'Sprechgesang' (see *Song* 6) applied chorally. For a time there were 'speech-choirs' in Britain and other countries. (See *Vogel, Vladimir,* for an example.)

SPRECHEND (Ger.). 'Speaking.'

SPRECHGESANG, SPRECHSTIMME. See *Song* 6; *Schönberg.*

SPRINGAR. A popular dance in the Telemark district of southern Norway. It is danced by two people.

SPRINGDANS (or 'leaping dance', to distinguish it from the Gangar, or 'walking dance') is a Norwegian dance in three-in-a-measure time. Examples will be found in Grieg.

SPRINGEND (Ger.). 'Springing', hence *Mit springendem Bogen,* 'with springing bow'.

'SPRING' SONATA (Beethoven). See *Nicknamed Compositions* 4.

SPRING SONG (Mendelssohn). See *Nicknamed Compositions* 14.

SPRUCHSPRECHER. See *Improvisatore.*

SPUGNA, BACCHETTA DI (It.). Sponge-headed drum-stick. See *Percussion Family* 2 a.

SPURGEON, CHARLES HADDON (1834–92). See *Baptist* 3.

SPURIOUS COMPOSITIONS. See *Misattributed Compositions.*

SQUARE DANCE. A dance of which the ground plan, so to speak, is rectangular, as contrasted with the 'Round Dance' (q.v.).

SQUARE PIANO. See *Pianoforte* 5, 8.

SQUILLANTE, SQUILLANTI (It., sing., plur.). 'Clanging.' (Applied to cymbals, it means that they shall be suspended and struck with drum-sticks.)

SQUIRE.

(1) WILLIAM HENRY. Born at Ross-on-Wye, in Herefordshire, in 1871 and died in London in 1963, aged ninety-one. He won a scholarship at the Royal College of Music, London, and became one of the most popular cellists of his country. Of his compositions the many songs have had the greatest popularity.

(2) WILLIAM BARCLAY. Born in London in 1855 and died there in 1927, aged seventy-one. He spent his life in charge of the musical part of the contents of the library of the British Museum, adding to this such other tasks as would help to further the cause of musical scholarship. With his brother-in-law, J. A. Fuller-Maitland, he edited the Fitzwilliam Virginal Book (q.v.).

See references also under *Old Hall Manuscript*; *Eton College Choirbook*; *Écossaise*; *Benjamin Cosyn's Book*

STAATSKAPELLE (Ger.). State orchestra. See *Chapel*.

STABAT MATER DOLOROSA. A sequence (q.v.) of the Roman Catholic liturgy, appointed for the Friday of Passion Week and 15th September. Its authorship is unknown, but it is often attributed to Jacopone da Todi (*c.* 1228–1306), the Italian Franciscan. He is said to have been the author not only of the *Stabat Mater dolorosa*, describing the Mother at the foot of the cross, but also of a *Stabat Mater speciosa* (now disused), describing her at the cradle, which was in use in the thirteenth century.

Apart from its traditional plainsong the *Stabat Mater dolorosa* has had many composed settings, as by Josquin des Prés, Palestrina (eight voices), Astorga, Pergolese, Haydn, Schubert (two settings), Rossini (a very long operatic type of setting), Verdi, Dvořák, and Stanford. Some of the settings have had much concert performance.

STÄBCHEN (Ger.). Literally, 'little staff'—the beater for a triangle.

STABILE (It.). 'Stable', i.e. firm.

STACCATO (It.). 'Detached', i.e. the opposite of *legato*. The superlative is *Staccatissimo*. See Table 23 for the various signs used.

STADLER.

(1) ANTON. See *Clarinet Family* 6; *Nicknamed Compositions* 15.

(2) MAXIMILIAN. See *Nicknamed Compositions* 15 (K. 581).

STADTMUSIKER, STADTPFEIFEREI. See *Street Music* 5.

STAFF. See *Notation* 2, 4.

STAHLHARMONIKA. See *Harmonica* 5 b.

STAINER.

(1) (Violin Makers). See *Violin Family* 4.

(2) JOHN. Born in London in 1840 and died in Italy in 1901, aged sixty.

He was the son of a musical parish schoolmaster and became a choir-boy of St. Paul's Cathedral, and then, at sixteen, Ouseley's (q.v.) first organist at his college of Tenbury. Appointed organist of Magdalen College, Oxford, he meantime fulfilled his course as an undergraduate and took his degree in music and later that in arts, becoming also the recognized leader of the Oxford musical life.

In his early thirties he returned to St. Paul's Cathedral as organist, succeeding his old master, Goss (q.v.), and in his later forties he became Professor of Music at Oxford, succeeding Ouseley. In both these capacities he rendered high service, his achievement in bringing about a better standard of repertory and of performance in the music of the English Church being especially notable.

Queen Victoria knighted him in 1888, on the occasion of his relinquishing his position at St. Paul's on account of the weakness of his sight.

For many years he served as chief inspector in music to the national Board of Education, and he succeeded Sullivan as Principal of the National Training School (now Royal College) of Music.

He gave time to much valuable musical research (especially as to the music of Dufay), wrote textbooks, set a fine example as an organist by the good taste of his accompaniments, and composed service music, anthems, cantatas, and hymn tunes that remain in use, and some of them in high popularity. Two of his larger-scale choral works have enjoyed a great vogue, *The Daughter of Jairus* (1878) and *The Crucifixion* (1887). His style might be called 'better-Victorian', and might be more laboriously characterized as Bach much softened by Mendelssohn and then assimilated to the traditions of the Anglican church in the mood of its post-Tractarian spiritual propriety. (In later life he expressed himself as dissatisfied with the standard he had adopted.)

See references under *England* 7; *Passion Music* 6; *Anthem*, Period V; *Hymns and Hymn Tunes* 6; *Anglican Chant* 6; *Amen*; *Presbyterian Church Music* 3; *Harmony* 4, 20; *Harp* 2 (Stainer and Barrett); *Dictionaries* 2.

STAMITZ (STAMIČ) Family. During the mid- and late-eighteenth century, by their orchestral and composing activities (largely in Mannheim) they exercised an immense influence on the standard of orchestral playing and the composition of the symphony.

The chief members of this family (of Bohemian origin) were **Johann (Jan) Wenzel Anton** (1717–57) and his two sons **Karl** (1745–1801) and **(Johann) Anton** (1754–before 1809).

An idea as to the nature of their activities can be gained from the following articles: *Conducting* 6; *Expression* 5; *Symphony* 3, 6, 8 (1717, 1746); *Chamber Music* 6, Period II (1717); *France* 7; *Violin Family* 7; *Clarinet Family* 2; *Filtz*.

STAMPITA (It.). See *Estampie*.

STÄNDCHEN. German for 'serenade' (q.v.).

STANDHAFT, STANDHAFTIGKEIT (Ger.). 'Firm', 'firmness'.

STANFORD, CHARLES VILLIERS (p. 481, pl. 84. 8). Born at Dublin in 1852 and died in London in 1924, aged seventy-one.

His father, a Dublin legal official, was a keen amateur musician, and he himself showed early musical gifts, his first composition being a march which he composed at the age of eight, and which two or three years later was included in a pantomime at the Dublin Theatre Royal.

At eighteen he went to Cambridge where, at twenty-one, he became organist of Trinity College (M.A., D.Mus.) and, a little later, conductor of the University Musical Society; this under his direction gave many notable first British performances, especially of the works of Brahms, of whom he was always a great admirer, who later became his friend, and by whom he was a good deal influenced. His college on several occasions gave him leave of absence so that he might study in Germany, and of these opportunities he took the fullest advantage.

At the age of twenty-four, at Tennyson's request, he wrote the music for the production of *Queen Mary* at the Lyceum Theatre. Three years later he wrote the service known as 'Stanford in B flat', which, by its individual style and its unification of thematic material, at once attracted attention, gave its composer a high standing in English musical life, and set a new standard in Anglican Church music. Orchestral works, chamber works, oratorios (e.g. *Eden*, 1891), and operas followed, with many songs and part songs—some of high merit, and all notable for the effort shown to collaborate with the poet, living or dead, and not merely to profit by him. The flavour of Irish folk tune sometimes showed itself in his work, and his list of compositions includes six Irish rhapsodies, an Irish symphony, and an Irish opera, *Shamus O'Brien*.

Apart from his compositions he exercised influence as a choral conductor (Bach Choir, Leeds Festival, etc.), as an author (a fine book on composition, and other valuable things), as a collector and editor of Irish folk tune, and, especially, as a teacher. In the last capacity, at the Royal College of Music, he had through his hands many of the most important of his young contemporaries, and, whatever their subsequent views of life and art, they unanimously expressed gratitude for his pungent criticism and thoughtful guidance.

For nearly forty years he was Professor of Music at his old university, and in 1901 he was knighted.

See *England* 7; *Nationalism*; *Opera* 13 e, 24—for names, dates, etc., of operas; *Oratorio* 5, 7; *Requiem*; *Stabat Mater*; *Te Deum*; *Service*; *Symphony* 8 (1852); *Concerto* 6 c (1852); *Amen*; *Cathedral Music* 8; *Folk Song* 5; *Modes* 10; *Ireland* 7; *Petrie*; *Moore* 1; *Londonderry Air*; *Ballad* 5; *Part Song*; *Chorale Prelude*; *Clarinet Family* 6; *Flute Family* 4; *Bugle*; *Memory* 7; *Spohr*; *Graves*; *Bliss*; *Boughton*; *Noble, T. T.*

STANLEY, JOHN—not 'Charles John', as generally stated (p. 784, pl. **131.** 1). Born in London in 1713 and died there in 1786, aged seventy-three. A fall at the age of two rendered him totally blind, but notwithstanding this handicap he became so able an organist that at the Temple Church, where he officiated for over half a century, it was 'not uncommon to see forty or fifty other organists, with Handel himself, assembled to hear the last Voluntary'. His memory was so retentive that he would accompany a new oratorio after hearing it once played through. For the last fourteen years of his life he was Master of the Band to George III. Gainsborough (himself a great music-lover) painted his portrait.

Amongst his compositions are many organ voluntaries, and some of these are not infrequently included in recital programmes of today.

See also references under *Oratorio* 5; *Sonata* 10 c; *Concert* 15; *Organ* 13; *Misattributed* (Boyce).

STANTON, WALTER KENDALL. Born at Dauntsey, Wiltshire, in 1891. He spent many years as a school music master and in charge of the music department of the University of Reading. Then he had a period (1937–45) as Director of Music to the Midland Region of the B.B.C., and in 1947 became the first Professor of Music at Bristol University. His chief compositions are choral.

STARK (Ger.). 'Strong', loud; so *Stärker* 'stronger', louder.

STARK ANBLASEN, STARK BLASEND. 'Strongly blown'—in the playing of wind instruments (see *Horn Family* 2 c and 5, and compare *Schmetternd*).

STAR-SPANGLED BANNER, THE. This is the official national anthem of the United States, by a Bill which passed the Senate on 3 March 1931. Previous to this no official national anthem existed and in public custom this song shared the honours with 'Hail, Columbia!' (q.v.) and 'My country, 'tis of thee' (see under *God save the Queen*), being, however, long the official national anthem for use in the United States Army and Navy (the latter since the days of the Spanish-American War of 1898).

The words of this song, beginning 'O say, can you see by the dawn's early light What so proudly we hailed at the twilight's last gleaming?' first appeared as a handbill, hastily struck off the day after they were written. They then appeared in *The Baltimore Patriot*, on 20 September 1814, having been composed, in the circumstances there narrated, on 14 September, and this being the first reappearance of the journal after its official suppression for ten days.

'The following beautiful and animating effusion, which is destined long to outlast the occasion and outlive the impulse which produced it, has already been extensively circulated. In our first renewal of publication we rejoice in an opportunity to enliven the sketch of an exploit so illustrious, with strains which so fitly celebrate it—Ed. Pat.

'The annexed song was composed under the following circumstances: A gentleman had left Baltimore in a flag of truce for the purpose of getting released from the British fleet a friend of his who had been captured at Marlborough. He went as far as the mouth of the Patuxent, and was not permitted to return lest the intended attack on Baltimore should be disclosed. He was therefore brought up the bay to the mouth of the Patapsco, where the flag vessel was kept under the guns of a frigate, and he was compelled to witness the bombardment of Fort McHenry, which the admiral had boasted that he would carry in a few hours, and that the city must fall. He watched the flag at the fort through the whole day with an anxiety that can be better felt than described, until the night prevented him from seeing it. In the night he watched the bombshells, and at early dawn his eye was again greeted by the proudly waving flag of his country.'

The 'gentleman' was Francis Scott Key: the 'friend', Dr. Beanes—both of Baltimore. The peculiar metre adopted shows that the writer had in mind as the tune of his poem the one to which it was at once and is still sung, the 'Anacreontick Song' or 'Anacreon in Heaven', composed by John Stafford Smith (q.v.), of London, for the Anacreontic Society of London (see *Clubs for Music-Making*; *Flute Family* 4) and then popular in America as the official song of several Anacreontic Societies there.

This tune had, in America, been many times set to patriotic words and it was quite natural for Key to re-use it in this way.

The whole of the facts relating to the origin of the poem and tune are set out in Sonneck's *The Star-spangled Banner*, issued by the Library of Congress in 1914, and superseding, so far as this song is concerned, the publications mentioned under *Hail, Columbia!* and *Yankee Doodle*.

Other tunes have sometimes been written for the poem, but none has ever supplanted the original one. At an auction in New York in 1933 the original manuscript of the poem was sold for $24,000.

The adoption of the song as a national anthem was opposed on grounds mentioned under *National Anthems and Official Tunes*.

STASSOF. See *Russia* 6; *Serof*; *Prince Igor*.

STATE CONCERTS. See *Chapel Royal*.

STATIONERS' COMPANY. See *Hymns and Hymn Tunes* 17 e xv.

STATKOWSKI, ROMAN. Born near Kalisz, Poland, in 1860 and died at Warsaw in 1925, aged sixty-five. He studied in Warsaw and at the University of St. Petersburg. His compositions include operas, orchestral pieces, chamber music, and piano music.

STATT (Ger.). 'Instead of.'

STAUFER, G. See *Arpeggione*.

STAVE. Same as *Staff*. See *Notation* 2, 4.

STCHERBATCHEF (Stscherbatchew, Shtcherbatchev, Schtscherbatchew, etc.), VLADIMIR. Born at Warsaw in 1889 and died in Leningrad in 1952, aged sixty-two. He studied law at the University of St. Petersburg (Leningrad) and then music at the conservatory of that city. He wrote symphonies, chamber music, film music, etc.

See *Colour and Music* 10.

'STEADY-STATE NOTE.' See *Acoustics* 7.

STEDMAN, FABIAN. See *Bell* 2.

STEFANINI, GIOVANNI. See *Folia*.

STEFFANI, AGOSTINO (1654–1728). He was an Italian composer, singer, mathematician, theologian (a priest and eventually a bishop), and man of general learning and capacity, who spent all the later part of his life in Germany, occupying important musical positions at the courts of Munich and Hanover and also serving on occasion as ambassador to other courts. He composed operas, duet cantatas in immense quantity, church music (including a fine *Stabat Mater*), gavottes and minuets, etc.

His artistic influence was great. Handel and the other contemporary German composers, who were somewhat his juniors, show clear traces of it.

STEG (Ger.). Bridge—of violin, etc. Thus *Am Steg* = Sul ponticello (It.), i.e. 'bow near the bridge'.

STEGGALL.

(1) CHARLES (1826–1905). Active London organist, professor of the Royal Academy, and one of the founders of the Royal College of Organists. His church music has merit and he collaborated with W. H. Monk (q.v.) in an edition of *Hymns Ancient and Modern*. See reference under *Gathering Note*.

(2) REGINALD (1867–1938). Son of the above and having a similar career. Some orchestral music and a Mass enjoyed a measure of success.

STEIBELT, DANIEL (p. 797, pl. **136**. 2). Born in Berlin in 1765 and died in St. Petersburg in 1823, aged nearly fifty-eight. He was a famous pianist of the showy stamp, and a composer of operas and other works now forgotten—though occasional piano pieces come the way of the 'prentice pianist.

See references under *Improvisation* 2; *Percussion Family* 4 c (use of Gong and Tambourine).

STEIN.

(1) THE FAMILY. Early and important makers of pianofortes and musicians (pianists and composers), first at Augsburg and then at Vienna. A daughter of the family, Nanette Stein (1769–1838), a pianist, married J. A. Streicher (1761–1833), also a pianist, and they engaged in the business. In the end the concern split into two firms (both at Vienna and both famous), one under the name Stein and the other under the name Streicher.

See references under *Pianoforte* 7; *Pianoforte Playing* 2.

(2) RICHARD HEINRICH (1882–1942). Active German composer and author on music and a champion of modern music.

See *Microtones*.

STEINBERG, MAXIMILIAN. Born at Vilna in 1883 and died at Leningrad in 1946, aged sixty-three. He studied under Rimsky-Korsakof (whose son-in-law and literary executor he became) and Glazunof at the Conservatory of St. Petersburg, and later became a professor of composition there and, finally, its director (1934). He composed orchestral music (he was a master of orchestration), chamber music, ballets, etc.

See *Shostakovich*.

STEINER, RUDOLF. See *Eurhythmy*.

STEINERT.

(1) MORRIS (1831–1912). See references under *Hymns and Hymn Tunes* 3; *Barber Shop Music*; *Horn Family* 3 (near end).

(2) ALEXANDER. Born in Boston, Mass., in 1900 (nephew of the above). He graduated at Harvard in 1922 and then studied under Loeffler. In 1927 he won the American Rome Prize, since when a number of his orchestral and other works have been heard. He settled in Hollywood.

STEINGRÄBER. See *Publishing* 8.

STEINHARMONIKA. See *Harmonica* 5 b.

STEINHAUSEN, FRIEDRICH ADOLF (1859–1910). See *Pianoforte Playing* 7.

STEINWAY. See *Pianoforte* 9, 12.

STEINWAY HALL, LONDON. See *Concert* 8.

STELLE, STELLEN (Ger.). 'Place', 'places'.

STENDENDO (It.). 'Extending', i.e. spacing the notes out = rallentando.

STENHAMMAR, VILHELM EUGEN. Born at Stockholm in 1871 and there died in 1927, aged fifty-six. He studied at the conservatory at his native place and in Berlin. He then became attached as a sub-conductor to the opera-house at Stockholm and was also a member of the string quartet of Tor Aulin (q.v.). He composed much dramatic, orchestral, choral, and chamber music, piano works, and (especially) songs, and held high rank as an orchestral conductor.

STENTARE (It.). To 'labour', to play in a laborious way. So *Stentando*, 'labouring', 'retarding'; *Stentamento*, 'laboriously', slowly; *Stentato*, 'laboured' (i.e. held back and every note stressed).

STENTORPHONE. See *Organ* 14 I.

STEP-DANCING. See *Tap-dancing*; also *Figure* 2.

STÉPHAN, DOM JOHN. See *Notation* 7; *Adeste Fideles*.

STEPHEN.

(1) REVD. EDWARD (known as 'Tanymarian'). Born near (Blaenau) Ffestiniog in 1822 and died near Bangor in 1885, aged sixty-two or sixty-three. He was a Welsh Congregational minister who composed hymn tunes, anthems, and the first Welsh oratorio, *Ystorm Tiberias* ('The Storm of Tiberias'—revised by S. S. Wesley, Handelian but showing some personal character; cf. *Lloyd, J. A.*). He greatly encouraged singing amongst the Welsh Congregationalists, taking part in the preparation of several collections of hymn tunes. He was also a geologist.

(2) DAVID. Born in Dundee in 1869 and died in 1946. After a career as organist and choral conductor he became, in 1903, the first Director of Music to the Carnegie Trust at Dunfermline, retiring in 1927. His compositions include orchestral, choral, and chamber works, etc., and he edited albums of Scottish songs.

STERBEND (Ger.). 'Dying away.'

STEREOPHONIC SOUND REPRODUCTION. See *Concert Halls* 12; *Broadcasting* 4; *Gramophone* 2.

'STERN, DANIEL.' See *Liszt*.

STERNHOLD AND HOPKINS. Thomas Sternhold (d. 1549) and John Hopkins (d. 1570). See *Hymns* 5, 6, 11, 17 e (passim); *Methodism* 3; *Old Hundredth*; *Publishing* 4.

STERNUM. See *Voice* 21.

STESO (It.). 'Extended', spread out, hence 'slow'.

STESSO, STESSA (It. masc., fem.). 'Same.' The plurals are *stessi, stesse*. The word is used in such connexions as *Lo stesso tempo*, or *L'istesso tempo*, 'the same speed'—usually meaning that, though the nominal value of the beat has changed, its actual time duration is to remain the same. (For instance, the former beat may have been ♩ and the

new one ♩., and these are to have the same time-values.)

STETS (Ger.). 'Steadily', always.

STEVENS.

(1) RICHARD JOHN SAMUEL. Born in London in 1757 and died there in 1837, aged eighty. He was organist of the Temple Church and the Charterhouse concurrently, and Gresham Professor of Music. His permanent importance lies in his composition of admirable and ever-popular glees, especially some to words of Shakespeare, as 'Ye spotted snakes', 'From Oberon in fairyland', 'The cloud-capt towers', and 'Crabbed age and youth'.

(2) BERNARD. Born in London in 1916. He studied at Cambridge University and at the Royal College of Music (later on staff). He has composed a *Symphony of Liberation* (1945; *Daily Express* £250 prize), a Violin Concerto, an unaccompanied Mass, chamber music, piano music, film music, etc.

(3) DENIS (WILLIAM). Born at High Wycombe, Bucks., in 1922. Conductor and lecturer, especially on earlier music. He was on the staff of the BBC (1949–54), and made his home in the U.S.A. in 1962. Professor of Music, Columbia University.

See *Mullinar Book*.

(4) HALSEY. Born at Scott, New York, in 1908. A composer and teacher, he was trained at Syracuse University and under Bloch. He has taught at Syracuse (1935), Dakota Wesleyan University (1937), Bradley University (1941), and the University of Southern California (1946). His works include symphonies and other orchestral and choral works and chamber music, and he has written a book on Bartók and other critical pieces.

STEVENSON.

(1) JOHN ANDREW. He was born in Dublin in 1761 and died at Headfort House, Co. Meath, in 1833, aged seventy-one. He was a vicar-choral of the two cathedrals of Dublin and a composer of music for church and theatre, and edited and arranged the music for Moore's *Irish Melodies*. In 1803 he was knighted.

See *Ireland* 1; *Moore, Thomas*.

(2) ROBERT LOUIS (1850–94). Author. Amateur flute player, whose manuscript musical compositions have been in the market (for their autograph value).

See *Skye Boat Song*.

STEWART.

(1) ROBERT PRESCOTT (p. 481, pl. **84.** 7). Born in Dublin in 1825 and died there in 1894, aged sixty-eight. He occupied many musical positions in his native city, including those of organist of Christ Church Cathedral (from the age of nineteen) and Professor of Music in the University of Dublin (from the age of thirty-six). He was knighted by the Lord Lieutenant of Ireland.

His most successful works are choral, and they include many glees.

(2) CHARLES HYLTON (1884–1932). Organist of Rochester Cathedral, of Chester Cathedral, and (just before his death) of St. George's Chapel, Windsor, and a steady worker for a high standard of church music.

See *Anglican Chant* 6.

(3) REVD. G. WAUCHOPE. See *Presbyterian* 5.

STICH, J. W. (alias 'Punto'). See *Bohemia.*

STICKER. See *Organ* 1.

STIERHORN (Ger.). 'Cow-horn' (sounding only one note), e.g. the watchman's in *The Mastersingers.*

STILE RAPPRESENTATIVO (It.) means literally 'representative style'. The term was used by the early Roman composer of oratorio, Cavalieri, and the contemporary Florentine composers of opera (see *Opera* 1, 2; *Recitative*), to indicate the use of their invention of recitative (q.v.), which aimed rather at *representing* the sense and the natural inflection of the speaking voice than at providing the enjoyment of pure musical beauty.

STILL (Ger.). 'Quiet', calm.

STILL, WILLIAM GRANT (p. 1061, pl. **174.** 2). Born at Woodville, Mississippi, in 1895. He is a Negro composer who studied at Oberlin Conservatory (D.Mus.) and the New England Conservatory (under Chadwick) and with Varèse (q.v.), and in 1933 won a Guggenheim Fellowship, enabling him to work for a time in Europe. He has written several ballets and operas, music to films, and a number of orchestral works that reflect his racial interests —an 'Afro-American' Symphony (the first symphony by a Negro; several European performances).

STILLE. See *Gramophone* 4.

STILLER ZINK. See *Cornett and Key Bugle Families* 4.

STILT, THE. This is the name given in Hart's Psalter of 1615 to the well-known common metre tune now always called *York.* It moves by large steps, and doubtless this suggested the striding of a walker on stilts. Hawkins, in his *History of Music* (1776), says that this tune is 'so well known that within memory half the nurses of England were used to sing it by way of lullaby; and the chimes of many country churches have played it six or eight times in twenty-four hours from time immemorial'. Vaughan Williams introduces it as a village church clock tune in his opera *Hugh the Drover* (first performed 1924).

STIMMBOGEN. See *Krummbogen.*

STIMME (Ger.) and words derived therefrom. *Stimme* (plural *Stimmen*) means 'voice' and hence organ 'register' (i.e. 'stop'); for some fanciful reason it has also come to mean 'sound post' of a violin. The verb *stimmen* means 'to tune', and *Stimmung* means 'tuning'. But as the human spirit can be tuned in different ways according as the sun shines or does not, etc.,

Stimmung has also come to mean 'mood'. Some words connected with tuning in its more prosaic sense are *Stimmflöte, Stimmpfeife, Stimmhorn,* Pitch Pipe; and *Stimmgabel,* Tuning Fork. *Stimmzug* is the crook of a brass instrument.

A *Stimmungsbild* in painting is (literally) a 'mood picture' (Muret–Sanders Lexicon—'picture in harmony with the time of day, the state of weather, etc.', i.e. a picture in which the 'atmosphere' counts for more than the object depicted). And in music a **Stimmungsbild** (the word is sometimes used as a title by German composers) means much the same— the expression in music of some definite human mood. (The translation in certain musical dictionaries, 'tone-picture', is, then, wrong.)

STING CYMBAL. The normal cymbal (see *Percussion Family* 3 o, 4 b, 5 o), but made of specially tempered metal so as to give a hard tone.

STINGO. See *Cold and Raw.*

STINGUENDO (It.). 'Extinguishing', i.e. fading out.

STIRANDO, STIRATO; STIRACCHIANDO, STIRACCHIATO (It.). 'Stretching', 'stretched', i.e. making the music last out ═ ritardando.

STIRLING, ELIZABETH. Born at Greenwich in 1819 and died in London in 1895, aged seventy-six. She was a remarkable organist, holding important posts in London and giving fine recitals which exercised much influence. At a time when Bach was little played she included much of his work in her programmes. At forty-four she married a well-known London musician less than half that age, F. A. Bridge.

Women hold (or should hold) her in grateful remembrance for what she did, by her example, to open to them a wider door into the musical profession, and village choral societies for her legacy to them of a charming part song, 'All among the barley'.

STIRRUP BONE. See *Ear and Hearing* 1.

STOCK, FREDERICK A.—in full, Friedrich Wilhelm Augustus. Born in Prussia in 1872, became a naturalized citizen of the United States and died there in 1942, aged nearly seventy.

He was a leading conductor of America from 1905, when, after four years as assistant to Theodore Thomas as conductor of the Chicago Symphony Orchestra, he succeeded to his position. His compositions were numerous, but have not made a place for themselves in the concert repertory.

STOCKBRIDGE BOWL. See *Festival* 2.

STOCKEND (Ger.). 'Coming to a standstill', i.e. slackening the time gradually.

STOCKFLÖTE. See *Recorder Family* 3 b.

STOCKHAUSEN, KARLHEINZ (p. 416, pl. **71.** 8). Born near Cologne in 1928. As a composer he was trained in Cologne and Bonn and under Milhaud and Messiaen. He is a celebrated representative of the more advanced German followers of Webern and has made much study of electrophonic music. Some of his works are partly improvised by the performer, who selects the 'running order' of the various sections, playing them in sequence or simultaneously. He is active and successful as a lecturer, especially on the subject of his own music. He often engages in formidably technical discussions of the scientific basis of his art, in terms not always clearly understood by trained physicists.

See *Germany* 9; *History* 9.

STOCKHORN or STOCK AND HORN, or **STOCK IN HORN** (p. 545, pl. **100**. 5). An obsolete Scottish instrument. The stock is either a wooden tube, bored with finger-holes, or the thigh bone of a sheep similarly treated, the horn is a part of that of a cow, fixed to the end of the stock, at the other end of which is a mouth-piece with a reed (a single 'beating' reed on the principle of that of a Clarinet; see *Reed*). The name 'Hornpipe' is also sometimes used for much the same instrument. The Welsh Pibcorn is also much the same thing, and more or less similar instruments are found in the Spanish Basque provinces, Grecian Archipelago, Arabia, Persia, India, and China. The great interest of these instruments is in their distribution, which, it has been said, agrees with that of the megalithic monuments.

STODDARD. See *Pianoforte* 5.

STOEHR, MORITZ. See *Microtones*.

STOESSEL, ALBERT. Born at St. Louis in 1894 and died suddenly whilst conducting in New York in 1943. He studied at the Berlin Hochschule, and enjoyed an early career as a concert violinist. At twenty-six he was conductor of the New York Oratorio Society, and at twenty-nine head of the music department of New York University, which he later left to join the staff of the Juilliard School. He composed a number of orchestral and chamber works, piano music, etc.

STOJOWSKI, SIGISMUND. Born in Poland in 1869 and died in New York in 1946, aged seventy-seven. His education was largely received in Paris, where he studied at the Conservatory; he was also a pupil of Paderewski. In 1905 he settled in New York. His compositions include orchestral, chamber, and piano works, songs, etc.

STOKOWSKI, LEOPOLD ANTON STANISLAW. Born in London in 1882; died at Nether Wallop, Hampshire in 1977. He was trained at the Royal College of Music and graduated B.Mus., Oxon. He settled in New York in 1905 as organist, and was conductor of the Cincinnati Orchestra, 1909–12, and then of the Philadelphia Orchestra to 1936. He made a large number of orchestral transcriptions of Bach's organ and other works, and was engaged in film enterprises.

See *Colour and Music* 9; *Electric Musical Instruments* 1 a f; *Microtones*; *Conducting* 5; *Tempo*; *Krein, J.*

STÖLZEL (or **Stölzl**), HEINRICH (1780–1844). See *Trumpet Family* 3 (near end).

STONE, CHRISTOPHER REYNOLDS (1882–1965). Novelist and general writer, gramophone expert and radio talker (the first 'disc-jockey'); major in the first World War (M.C., D.S.O.) See *Gramophone* 7.

STOP. See *Organ* 1.

STOPPED DIAPASON. See *Organ* 14 I, II.

STOPPED NOTES. See *Horn Family* 2 b c, 3, 5; *Trumpet Family* 3.

STOPPED PIPES. See *Organ* 3.

STOPPING, on stringed instruments, is merely the placing of the tips of the fingers of the left hand so that they shorten the vibrating length of a string. Cf. 'Double Stopping' under *Double* 2.

STORACE, STEPHEN. Born in London in 1763 and died there in 1796, aged thirty-three. He was the son of an Italian double-bass player who settled in Dublin and then in London, and the brother of that **Ann (Nancy) Storace** who had great fame as a vocalist in Britain and on the Continent.

He was sent at twelve to study at Naples, toured Italy with his sister, and produced operas at Vienna, where he became a friend of Mozart and was imprisoned for quarrelling with an officer.

He struggled in London for a time as a drawing-master and then flourished for a few years as an opera composer, but was cut off early by gout.

Sheridan said he had literary talent, and he could boast the distinction of having had a string quartet played in Vienna, by Haydn, Dittersdorf, Mozart, and Vanhall. His ballads had fame.

See references under *Prima Donna*; *Opera* 21 b; *Tarantella*.

STORM, THE (Beethoven). See *Nicknamed* 4.

STORM EFFECTS (organ). See *Acoustics* 16.

STORM SYMPHONY (Haydn). See *Nicknamed Compositions* 11 (6–8).

STORNELLO (It.). A traditional type of Tuscan folk song often improvised by a *Stornellatore* (masc.) or *Stornellatrice* (fem.). The stanza has three lines. The plural of the word is *Stornelli*.

STOUGHTON MUSICAL SOCIETY, MASSACHUSETTS. See under *Concert* 15; *United States* 3.

STOURBRIDGE FAIR. See *Fairs and their Music*.

STOW, JOHN (c. 1525–1605). Chronicler. See *Community Singing* 2.

STRACCIACALANDO (It.). 'Prattling.'

STRACCINATO (It.). 'Stretched out', i.e. ritardando.

STRAD. See *Violin Family* 4.

STRADELLA, ALESSANDRO. Born in Rome in 1644 and died at Genoa in 1682, aged about thirty-eight. Tradition tells that he eloped with a Venetian lady whose lover, according to the custom of the place and time, sent assassins to seek him; that these entered the church where one of his oratorios was being performed under his direction, were touched by the music, warned the couple, and left them unharmed; and that further assassins, later engaged, either heard none of their intended victim's music, were less susceptible, or had more professional pride and sense of duty, since the deed was done.

Like Falstaff, who was not only witty in himself but the cause that wit was in other men, Stradella was not only a maker of music himself but the cause of others making it, as for instance Flotow and Niedermeyer, both of whom wrote operas on the above story (Marion Crawford wrote an excellent novel on it—*Stradella*, 1909).

Stradella's own music (operas, oratorios, cantatas, arias, string concertos, etc.) has high repute, yet little of it has been printed. There is a tradition that he was the favourite composer of his younger contemporary Purcell, and that the latter's extensive use of 'ground bass' (q.v.) was due to admiration of his hero's many fine examples of the device. Handel 'borrowed' a little from him.

For 'Pietà, Signore' see *Misattributed Compositions*.

STRADIVARI, ANTONIO (1644–1737), and his sons FRANCESCO (1671–1743) and OMO-BONO (1679–1742). See *Italy* 6; *Violin Family* 4.

STRAFF, STRAFFER (Ger.). 'Strict', 'stricter'. Also 'tight', 'tighter' (drum head, etc.).

STRAFFANDO, STRAFFATO (It.). 'Throwing off', 'thrown off'.

STRAIGHT JAZZ. See *Jazz* 3.

STRALOCH MANUSCRIPT. See *Scotland* 1, 7.

STRAMBOTTO (It.). An Italian renaissance poetical form, examples of which were often set to music on the lines of the *Frottola*. It had eight lines, each of eleven syllables and rhyming a b a b a b a c (or sometimes a b a b a b a b). See article *Frottola* and its reference to the collection of Petrucci; this included Strambotti. Malipiero has used the title. Cf. *Rispetto*.

STRANG, GERALD. Born in Alberta, Canada, in 1908. He was a disciple of Schönberg at the University of Southern California (1935), and is a modernist composer, working on harmonic and formal theories personal to himself.

STRANGWAYS. See *Fox Strangways*.

STRASCICANDO (It.). Same as *Strascinando* (q.v.).

STRASCINANDO, STRASCINATO (It.). 'Dragging', 'dragged' (e.g. heavily slurring notes in bowing, singing portamento, etc.).

STRATHSPEY. The slow dance of Scotland, as the reel (q.v.) is the quick dance. Its music is in four-in-a-measure time, with many dotted notes, and some use of the rhythmic peculiarity known as the 'Scotch Snap' (q.v.). It is really a slow reel with a less smoothly flowing rhythm.

The name comes from the Strath, or valley, of the River Spey—presumably the place of origin of the dance.

STRAUBE, KARL. Born in Berlin in 1873; died in Leipzig in 1950, aged seventy-seven. From 1902 he was organist of the Thomas Church, Leipzig, and from 1918 Cantor of the Thomas School. He was a well-known choral conductor, editor of organ music, etc. See *Reger*.

STRAUS, OSKAR. Born in Vienna in 1870 and died at Bad Ischl, Austria, in 1954, aged eighty-three. After a short career as conductor of theatre orchestras he became a very popular and prolific composer of light operas, e.g. *The Chocolate Soldier*.

STRAUSS Family (the dance composers).

With the Lanners (q.v.) they were the chief promoters and sustainers of the Vienna Waltz rage that long infected the world. No family in history has contributed more to 'the gaiety of nations' (p. 240, pl. **44.** 1–3).

Their names and dates are: Johann I (1804–49); his sons Johann II (1825–99), Joseph (1827–70), and Eduard (1835–1916); and Johann III (1866–1939), son of Eduard.

Johann II is the one whose waltzes (e.g. *The Blue Danube*) are most alive today.

See *Waltz*; *Comic Opera*; *Opera* 24 e (1874); *Morgenblätter*.

STRAUSS, RICHARD GEORG (p. 401, pl. **70.** 8). Born at Munich in 1864 and died at Garmisch-Partenkirchen, Bavaria, in 1949, aged eighty-five. He has proved to be the most vital and successful of the successors of Wagner. His operatic methods were based on those of his exemplar, his harmonies, naturally, as he developed, growing more 'modern' and individual, and his orchestration (which is masterly) more personal. Unlike Wagner, he wrote much independent instrumental music, usually in the form of highly 'programmatic' symphonic poems (see *Symphonic Poem* and *Programme Music*). His songs are noteworthy. As opera conductor he enjoyed the highest reputation and held the most important positions.

He was born into a musical circle, his father being first horn player in the court orchestra at Munich. He developed early, and at seventeen a symphony of his was publicly heard. At first, and until he definitely put aside parental influence on his art, he was of distinctly conservative tendencies; then the leaven of Wagner and Liszt began to work in him and quickly 'leavened the whole lump'.

It is a possible criticism of him that he sometimes went to excess in the violent expression of passionate emotion, and that at times his musical (and literary) material did not soar above the level of vulgarity. Most musicians looking down his long list of works would probably pick as the most purely enjoyable the symphonic poem *Till Eulenspiegel* and the opera *Der Rosenkavalier* (q.v.), so perhaps suggesting that he was greatest on his somewhat lighter side. He was fortunate in his association with a fine librettist in Hofmannsthal (*Elektra, Rosenkavalier, Ariadne auf Naxos, Die Frau ohne Schatten, Die Ægyptische Helena*, and *Arabella*).

Further information as to his compositions is dispersed in this volume under various heads and can be found by means of the list below.

History 7; *Germany* 7; *Romantic*.

Composition 9; *Symphonic Poem*; *Programme Music* 5 d; *Concerto* 6 c (1864); *Symphony* 8 (1864); *Chamber Music* 6, Period III (1864).

Opera 9 e, 21 m, 24 (1894 onwards—for names and dates of productions); *Libretto*; *Gnecchi*.

Melodrama; *Pantomime*; *Elektra*; *Salome*; *Rosenkavalier*; *Ariadne*; *Ballet* 7; *Waltz*.

Orchestra 4, 5; *Oboe Family* 4 f i, 6; *Clarinet Family* 2, 4 d g; *Horn Family* 4 (near end); *Percussion Family* 3 r, 4 a b; *Reed-Organ Family* 9 (end); *Thunder Machine*; *Viol Family* 4 f; *Harp* 3; *Aerophor*; *Ventilator*; *Saxophone*; *Tonguing*; *Pianoforte* 21; *Conducting* 6.

Ranz des Vaches; *Denza*; *Bartók*; *Nietzsche*; *Hindemith*; *Copyright*.

STRAVAGANTE (It.). 'Extravagant', fantastic.

STRAVINSKY (Strawinsky), IGOR (p. 913, pl. **156**. 1, 2). Born at Oranienbaum near St. Petersburg in 1882 and died in New York in 1971, aged eighty-eight. His father was an opera singer. He himself was trained for the legal profession, but at twenty, travelling in Germany, he met Rimsky-Korsakof and the impression received decided him to devote himself to music, which he did under that master's direction.

In his middle twenties he met the impresario of the Russian Ballet, Diaghilef, and henceforward Paris became his centre of public activity and his path was marked out for him. In the series of ballet scores which followed his individuality increasingly asserted itself; the most important of these were *The Fire Bird* (1910), *Petrushka* (1912), *The Rite of Spring* (1913), *The Nightingale* (1914; first an opera, out of the latter parts of which was fashioned a symphonic poem which became a ballet), *The Wedding* ('Les Noces'—composed 1917; first heard 1923), and *Apollo Musagetes* (first heard 1928).

The tussle with the public began with the vigorous and impressive *Rite of Spring*, which largely ignored existing conventions of harmony, rhythm, and form. Amongst its many successors have been the stage-works *Renard* (1915) and *The Soldier's Story* (1917), the so-called *Symphonies of Wind Instruments in Memory of Debussy* (1920; see *Symphony* 1), the opera *Mavra*, the secular oratorio, *Oedipus Rex* (1927), the choral-orchestral *Symphony of Psalms* (1930), the Violin Concerto (1933), the

opera–ballet *Persephone* (1934), and the ballet *Game of Cards* (1937), the Concerto in E flat for sixteen instruments (*Dumbarton Oaks*, 1938), Symphony in C (1940), *Danses Concertantes* (1942), *Symphony in Three Movements* (1945), *Ebony Concerto* (clarinet and swing band; 1946), Mass for chorus and double wind quintet (1948), and the opera *The Rake's Progress* (first performance in Venice in 1951).

In the early 1920s debate on this composer took a new turn, for in his Piano Sonata and Piano Concerto he deliberately abandoned the Russian characteristics of his earlier work and adopted a neo-classical style (see under *Romantic*); he had now reached a point where he claimed to have discarded all extra-musical influences and emotions. It may be pointed out that his works sometimes appeared in several successful forms (for instance first as ballets, then as operas, and then as orchestral pieces) and that their composer and his defenders have always claimed that, despite their original stage of 'programme', they were essentially 'Absolute Music' (q.v.).

He was long regarded as the antithesis of Schönberg in his musical sympathies. However, from about 1951 he became involved with serialism, and such late works as the *Canticum sacrum* (1952), *Agon* (1957), *Threni* (1958), *Movements* for piano and orchestra (1959), and *The Flood* (1962) make use of Note-row (q.v.) techniques.

Opinions as to the value of Stravinsky's later works are divided; as to that of the earlier ones little dispute remains. All are agreed as to his originality, personal force, and courage, and as to the wide influence he has exercised on younger composers.

He became a French citizen in 1934 but during the war that followed emigrated to the United States and was there naturalized in 1945.

Books by Stravinsky are *Chronicles of my Life* (1935) and *The Poetics of Music* (1947).

Stravinsky's second son, Soulima (b. 1910), is a pianist and has appeared in his father's works.

See *History* 8, 9; *Romantic*; *Harmony* 21; *Russia*, 7, 8; *France* 14; *Ballet* 5; *Expression* 6; *Melody* 3, 4, 5; *Rhythm* 10; *Symphony* 1, 8 (1882); *Suite* 7; *Jazz* 4, 5, 7; *Orchestra* 5; *Cornet* 2; *Trumpet Family* 4; *Trombone Family* 4; *Percussion Family* 4 a (near end), 4 c (Tabor); *Mechanical* 13 (near end); *Opera* 17 d, 24 f (1914–22–27–51); *Berners*; *Křenek*; *Concerto* 6 c (1882); *Holst*; *Oratorio* 7 (1947); *Harpsichord* 9; *Milhaud*.

STRAW FIDDLE. See *Percussion Family* 5 f.

STRAZIANTE (It.). 'Tearing.'

STREET CRIES. See *Street Music* 2.

STREET MUSIC

(For illustrations see pl. 992, p. **165**.)

1. Introductory. Slight as may be the present article, it is probably the first on its subject that has appeared in any musical work of reference. It is designed to call attention to the fact, often overlooked, that a great part of the musical life of the populations of European countries has been lived not in the concert-hall, opera-house, or church, but in the streets, where all, whatever their social position or wealth or poverty, could participate in its enjoyment.

It will be noted that the music of the streets has taken a very large range—from the traditional melodic 'cries' of the hawker (a branch of folk music) to four-part choral music and four-movement symphonies. Indeed, if with the present article be read the one on *Mysteries, Miracle Plays, and Moralities* it will be recognized that opera owes something to the one-time popular dramatic performance of the streets.

2. Street 'Cries' (p. 992, pl. **165.** 1). These constitute an interesting (and too little investigated) branch of folk music and have supplied the basis of a certain amount of composed music by musicians of repute.

The large trade done for centuries in the streets of all great cities by itinerant vendors and workers, all of whom cried their wares or services, led to the evolution of an accepted code of 'cries', most or all of which in time, moulded by the natural rhythms of the words and the natural cadence of the language, fell into different little tunes, these becoming so accepted that, very usefully, the distant approach of the vendor would be known even to those who only heard the music and could not catch the words.

An early record of the words of many of the London Cries is found in the poem, *London Lackpenny* (by John Lydgate, *c.* 1370–*c.* 1450). Each verse embodies different cries, as:

Then met I one cryed *Hot shepe's feete*;
One cryde *mackerell*; *rushes grene* another gan grete;
One bade me by a hood to cover my head;
But for want of money, I might not be sped.

Just as the cries are here worked up into a poem, so they have been worked up into several ingenious musical compositions, these using not only the traditional words of each cry but also its traditional music.

Italy, from the late fourteenth century, had simple choral compositions made from such cries (see *Italy* 3). The sixteenth-century French composer, Jannequin, has left a well-known motet bringing in the cries of Paris. Clapisson made use of Paris cries in a scene of his opera *La Fanchonnette* (1856) and Charpentier in a scene of *Louise* (1900).

Ravenscroft's *Pammelia* and *Melismata*, at the beginning of the seventeenth century, have a number of cries cleverly arranged as choral rounds, and there are pieces of the same period of the character of Fancies (q.v.) for viols with vocal parts added, and respectively by Weelkes, Orlando Gibbons, and Deering, which introduce the cries. In these last-named compositions there are 150 different cries represented, and as when the words are duplicated in the different compositions the same music is always associated with them in each, it is clear

that the traditional music is thus preserved. The cries include those offering fruit, vegetables, and fish, etc., and services—'Bellows to mend', 'Wood to cleave', 'Have you any work for a Tinker', and the like: civic officials like the Town Crier and the Watchman have their place in the chorus and so have beggars, the dentist, and the chiropodist. Deering also wrote one of these compositions on 'Country Cries'. That of Weelkes ends, 'Now let us sing and so we will make an end with Alleluia': that of Gibbons is in the form of an *In Nomine* (q.v.) and is for viols and voices.

Handel introduced street cries of his day into one of the movements of his opera *Serse* ('Xerxes'; 1738). Moreover, Lady Luxborough, writing to the poet Shenstone in 1748 (i.e. during Handel's lifetime), states, 'The great Handel has told me that the hints of his best songs, have several of them been owing to the sounds in his ears of cries in the street'.

The variety of vendor's melody to be heard in the street, even into the twentieth century, is very astonishing. In 1887 various readers of the *Musical Times* sent to that journal examples of such melody as they found in their respective districts, the following being one or two instances:

Who'll buy my sweet prim-ros-es? All in

bloom! all in bloom!

Lloyd's Week-ly News-pa-per! Pa-per!

Wa-ter-cress-es! Fresh wa-ter-cress!

The last example, it will be noted, suggests plainsong: like much other folk song it seems to imply a tradition of the old modes (q.v.) lingering amongst the people after it had disappeared from musicians' music.

As late as 1934 readers of the same journal were sending a few examples of such cries still in use. The 'Lavender Cry' of London (again modal) is particularly attractive; Vaughan Williams has introduced it into his London Symphony as follows:

['Who'll buy . . my sweet la-ven-der?']
[still heard in 1948]

In English literature there are a good many allusions to the London street cries showing the delight their melody and variety gave to all sorts of cultivated people. Leigh Hunt in his biography, in telling of his removal of his family to Chelsea about 1833, speaks of the abundance, 'quaintness and melodiousness' of the cries there as a great attraction, and tells us (strangely!) that they had 'the reputation of being composed by Purcell and others'. He adds, 'Nor is this unlikely when it is considered how fond those masters were of sporting with their art and setting the most trivial words to music in their glees and catches.' Nollekens, the once-famous sculptor (1737–1823), 'loved to imitate the cries of the itinerant vendors' as they were passing by whilst he was 'measuring the stone in the yard for a bust or figure' or 'improving the attitudes of his Venuses'. This leads his biographer, John Thomas Smith, to devote several pages to the subject of these cries, and to set out words and music of some of them. He gives one or two of a fairly elaborate nature.

'Besides the musical cries mentioned above, about sixty years back [i.e. about 1770], there were also two others yet more singular, which, however, were probably better known in the villages round London than in the metropolis itself. The first of these was used by an itinerant dealer in corks, sometimes called "Old Corks", who rode upon an ass, and carried his wares in paniers on each side of him. He sat with much dignity, and wore upon his head a velvet cap; and his attractive cry, which was partly spoken and partly sung, but all in metre, was something like the following fragment:

Spoken. Corks for sack
 I have at my back;
Sung. All handy, all handy;
 Some for wine and some for brandy.
Spoken. Corks for cholic-water,
 Cut 'em a little shorter;
 Corks for gin,
 Very thin;
 Corks for rum,
 As big as my thumb;
 Corks for ale,
 Long and pale:
Sung. They're all handy, all handy.
 Some for wine and some for brandy.

The other cry, which was much more musical, was that of two persons, father and son, who sold lines. The father, in a strong, clear tenor, would begin the strain in the major key, and when he had finished his son, who followed at a short distance behind him, in a shrill falsetto, would repeat it in the minor, and their call consisted of the following words:

 Buy a white-line,
 Or, a jack-line,
 Or, a clock-line,
 Or, a hair-line,
 Or, a line for your clothes here.'

It will be remembered that a famous series of colour prints, *The London Cries* by Francis Wheatley, R. A. (1747–1801), preserves for us the figures of the unconscious artists who performed these tiny vocal melodies, as they were to be seen in the late eighteenth century. An earlier set, and a much larger one, is that of engravings after drawings of Laroon, issued by the London printseller, Pierce Tempest, in 1711, which gives us the figures of about 60 of the singing vendors.

In France chair-menders, scissor-grinders, rag-and-bone dealers, etc., were known by tunes which they played on the mirliton (q.v.), each trade having its distinctive tune.

For an allusion to a Scottish Street Cry see *Caller Herrin*'.

3. The Waits. Information as to these bodies of instrumentalists (who in some cases were choralists too) will be found under the heading *Wait*. Street playing was amongst the duty of these municipal musicians. Thus when London came under Puritan control at the beginning of the Civil War the authorities decided (1642) to do away with Sunday street playing:

'That the City Waits shall cease to play at the Royal Exchange on the Sundays as heretofore hath been accustomed, but shall perform the said service every holiday hereafter and for the time accustomed.'

And after the Restoration (when Sabbatarianism was little, if at all, relaxed) the famous Norwich Waits were also restricted in the same way:

'To playe att the Crosses, but not upon the Lord's dayes.'

In 1648, at Newcastle, we find the Waits playing outside the Mayor's door to entertain Cromwell, who was visiting the city on his journey from Scotland.

In the eighteenth century the Bath Waits, as soon as they got wind of the arrival of a visitor, would play outside the house in which he was lodging.

The same customs, of course, obtained in other parts of England and in many continental countries.

4. Street Performances in Italy. Burney in Italy, in 1770, found street music everwhere. Thus at Turin a band of two girl vocalists, two violins, a guitar, and 'base' (probably a violoncello) performed on a stage in the public square and sold ballads, whilst in another part of the square a man and woman sang Venetian ballads (Burney says that the Italian street musicians were mostly Venetians), accompanied on a dulcimer. At Milan the same customs obtained.

At Brescia he heard outside his inn a band of two violins, a mandolin, a French horn, a trumpet, and a violoncello.

'And, though in the dark, they played long concertos, with solo parts for the mandolin. I was surprised at the memory of these performers; in short it was excellent *street* music, and such as we are not accustomed to; but ours is not a climate for serenades.'

At Vicenza he heard

'A psalm, in three parts, performed by boys of different ages, who were proceeding from their school to the cathedral, in procession, with their master, a priest, at their head, who sung the base. There was more melody than usual in this kind of music; and although they marched through the street very fast, yet they sung well in time and tune.

These boys are a kind of religious *press-gang* who, seize all other boys they can find in their way to the church, in order to be catechised.'

In Venice he heard a group of two violins, a violoncello, and a voice who, 'though un-noticed here as small-coalmen or oyster-women in England, performed so well that in any other country in Europe they would not only have excited attention, but have acquired applause, which they justly merited'.

From a barge on the Grand Canal (and the canals are, of course, the main streets of Venice) he heard 'an excellent band of music, consisting of violins, flutes, horns, bases, and a kettledrum'. It was 'a piece of gallantry, at the expense of an inamorato, in order to serenade his mistress'.

He was charmed with the singing of the gondoliers (see *Gondola Song*). Their superior performances he put down to the fact that they had free admission to the opera-houses.

At Bologna he found less street music and less good than at Venice, but nevertheless he was saluted on arrival at his inn, 'as every stranger is', with a duet, very well played by a violin and a mandoline, and later 'an itinerant band played under my windows several sym-phonies and single movements, extremely well, in four parts'.

In Florence, Burney heard the long-celebrated Laudisti (see *Laudi Spirituali*) 'in grand procession, dressed in a whitish uniform with burning tapers in their hands'. Outside the cathedral they sang 'a cheerful hymn in three parts, which they executed very well'.

'In this manner, on Sunday and holidays, the trades-people and artizans form themselves into distinct companies, and sing through the streets on their way to church. Those of the parish of S. Benedetto, we are informed by Crescimbeni, were famous all over Italy; and at the great Jubilee, in the beginning of this century, marched through the streets of Rome, singing in such a manner as pleased and astonished everybody.'

For the earlier singing of secular choral music in the streets of Florence see *Canti Carnascialeschi*.

In Burney's experience this Italy of the late eighteenth century was *par excellence* the country of street music of all kinds. 'It is not to be wondered at that the street music here is generally neglected, as people are almost stunned with it at every corner.'

The Spanish have always been great de-votees of music and dancing in the street, and still are.

For the 'Pifferari' of Italy, long a familiar occasional feature in British streets also, see *Bagpipe* 7.

5. Street Performances in Germany.
The street was long the popular concert-room of Germany. It will be remembered how Luther and his fellow choir-boys used at Eisenach to go from door to door collecting small doles by singing hymns and 'quartets at Christmas-time in the villages, carols on the birth of the Holy Child at Bethlehem'. This was apparently long a universal student and choir-boy custom in north Germany, both before and after the Reformation, and it con-tinued into the late eighteenth, and even the nineteenth century (p. 992, pl. **165**. 3). In 1782 Moritz (*Travels in England*) observes in the streets of London the Christ's Hospital boys in their blue cloaks, and expresses surprise that they are not heard singing in the streets, as the boys of such an institution would be in Germany.

Burney, in Munich, in 1772, found 'a very good concert in the street' at his inn door, and was told that they were 'poor scholars'. Next day he discovered that they were students of the music school and that their performance was intended as a compliment to him because he had been to the school to 'inform himself concerning the institution'. Next evening he heard the same performers elsewhere in the streets of the city. They had violins, a violon-cello, hautboys, French horns, and a bassoon; 'I was informed that they were obliged fre-quently to perform thus in the streets, to con-vince the public, at whose expence they are maintained, of the proficiency they make'.

In Frankfurt, too, he heard good street music, young theological students singing 'hymns in three or four parts attended by a chaplain . . . who in this manner excite the benevolence of passengers, that contribute to-wards their cloathing'. He also heard a band of street musicians who played several sym-phonies reasonably well, in four parts'. Passing into Austria, he heard music students from the Jesuit college at Vienna singing before the inn vocal duets and 'a kind of glees in three and four parts'.

Instrumental street music was for centuries of German town life supplied regularly by the municipal musicians, or 'Stadtpfeiferei' (pre-sided over by the 'Stadtmusiker'), correspond-ing very closely to the British waits. It will be recalled that many of Bach's ancestors and rela-tives were employed in this capacity.

6. The Attempted Suppression of Street Music in Former Times.
Street musicians (other than the authorized Waits) were sup-pressed by two Acts of Parliament of the reign of Queen Elizabeth I, they being declared rogues and vagabonds. And there were laws enacted against Ballad Singing and Ballad Hawking, in various reigns (see *Ballad* 1). The fact that such Acts were enacted during the Commonwealth has led thoughtless historians to put them down to Puritan feeling, but any Commonwealth laws on the point were only re-enactments or modifications of laws already existing. The suppression of ballad singers and hawkers was due to the frequently political nature of the ballads and the suppression (or attempted suppression) of other street musi-cians largely to that dislike of all wanderers and 'masterless men' that persisted through many centuries. (It will be remembered that under Elizabeth and the early Stuarts no bodies of actors could exist unless attached to the house-hold of some nobleman.)

In the eighteenth century Hogarth's well-known picture *The Enraged Musician* (p. 992, pl. **165**. 2) showed that room for a little useful legislation still remained.

7. Modern Attempts to control Street Music. In modern times there have been many attempts to restrain street music by law. Thus an English Act of Parliament early in Queen Victoria's reign gave London house-holders power to require street musicians to withdraw, on grounds of *'illness or other reasonable cause'*. In 1864 Mr. Michael T. Bass, M.P. (the brewer), led a campaign against street musicians, publishing a book entitled *Street Music in the Metropolis*, and introducing a Bill into Parliament. Members of the various professions presented petitions in favour of this Bill, including 'the leading composers and pro-fessors of music of the metropolis, who sent one with 200 signatures headed "The Street Organ Nuisance"', and complaining of the way in which 'our professional duties are seriously interrupted'. The main point of Mr. Bass's Bill was the removal of the clause about 'illness or reasonable cause', which latter phrase left far too much to the interpretation of the magistrate. Carlyle, Tennyson, Millais, Hol-man Hunt, and a great number of other distin-guished intellectual and artistic workers supported Mr. Bass by signing a document in favour of his Bill. Professor Babbage, the eminent mathematician and inventor of the Calculating Machine, considered (see *Diction-ary of National Biography*) that 'one-fourth of his entire working power had been destroyed by audible nuisances, to which his highly strung nerves rendered him peculiarly sensitive'. He had often prosecuted offenders in the police courts, under the existing unsatisfactory Act, spending on this attempt at defence during the first six months of 1861 alone the sum of £103. He sent Mr. Bass a list of 165 interruptions to his work in ninety days, including six brass bands and ninety-six street pianos and organs.

As a result of this well-justified agitation was passed the Metropolitan Police Act, 1864, which is still in force, but of which the relevant provisions do not operate as effectively as was hoped—owing partly to the provision which requires any householder complaining to 'accompany the constable who shall take into custody any person offending as aforesaid to the nearest police station house and there sign the charge-sheet'. Apparently many persons prefer to suffer rather than to make part of this interesting little group moving through the public streets, and, indeed, not every one can spare the time to carry through a prosecution. (For some *Punch* pictures illustrating the sub-ject see p. 992, pl. **165**. 5, 6.)

Apart from the metropolis it is competent for local authority to enact a by-law against street music under Section 23 of the Municipal Corporations Act of 1882: the reason London was left out of this Act is that the 1864 Metro-politan Police Act was supposed to provide adequately for that city.

The itinerant 'German Bands', formerly so common everywhere in Britain, were not heard after 1914. They numbered from six to fifteen performers—all Bavarians working at their trade at home in winter and migrating to various countries every summer. The 'one-man-band', playing simultaneously some sort of a wind instrument and (with elbows, feet, and head) a variety of percussion, was also at one time a feature of street life.

The unemployed in London and the pro-vincial cities in England, in the 1930s, with their Welsh choirs, bagpipes, and scratch bands, caused a temporary revival of street music in England, and the occasional accor-dionist or violinist can still be heard.

In the early 1930s some Parisians were deploring the rapid disappearance from their streets and courtyards of the singers formerly so common there.

'Si la chanson française ne doit pas mourir ce sont les chanteurs des rues qui doivent la perpétuer en apportant de la musique à ceux qui sont trop occupés ou trop indifférents pour aller à sa re-cherche. Mainte chanson qu'on entendait récem-ment par tout Paris aurait subi une mort préma-turée ne fût-ce que pour les musiciens de la rue.'

STREET PIANO. See *Mechanical Reproduction of Music* 12; *Street Music* 7.

STREICH (Ger.). 'Stroke' (of bow). Hence *Streichquartett*, 'string quartet', *Streichstimmen*, 'string-toned stops' (organ), and so on.

STREICHER, JOHANN ANDREAS. See *Pianoforte* 7; *Stein Family*.

STRELEZKI, ANTON (real name said to be Burnand; another *nom de plume* was 'Stepan Esipoff'). He was born at Croydon in 1859 and died in 1907, aged about forty-eight. He had a popularity as a pianist and a prolific composer of light piano music, and wrote a book record-ing his conversations with Liszt.

STRENG (Ger.). 'Strict.'

STRENS, JULES. See *Synthétistes*.

STREPITO, STREPITOSO, STREPITOSA-MENTE (It.). 'Noise', 'noisy', 'noisily'.

STRETTO (It.). (1) 'Drawn together', i.e. accelerando. (2) For Stretto in Fugue see *Form* 12 c.

STRICH or **BOGENSTRICH** or **ANSTRICH** (Ger.). A stroke (with a bow); hence *Mit breitem Strich*, 'with the breadth of the whole bow' and so forth. So also *Strichart*, 'manner of bowing', *Aufstrich*, 'up-bow', *Niederstrich*, 'down-bow'.

STRICT CANON. See *Canon*.

STRICT COUNTERPOINT. See *Counter-point*.

STRIKE NOTE. See *Bell* 1.

STRIKING REED. Same as 'Beating Reed'. See *Reed*.

STRIMPELLATA (It.). 'Strumming', 'scrap-ping', etc., a pejorative term.

STRINASACCHI, REGINA (1764–1839). Celebrated Italian violinist, praised by Mozart. See incident recorded under *Memory 8*.

STRING BAND and STRING ORCHESTRA. Properly both terms imply bodies exclusively of stringed bowed instruments, but in popular parlance 'string band' has often been applied to dance combinations and the like provided they *included* strings, i.e. the term has been used as a distinction between a band of this sort and one exclusively of wind instruments.

The distinction probably arose in the entertainment world—'String Band' *v*. 'Brass Band'. Thus we find that some British Army bands are prepared to provide an entertainment either in their normal military formation or as a String Band. The 'String Band of the Regiment' will usually or always be found to be a full orchestra manned by the same players as those of the regiment's wind band, who are thus what is called 'double-handed'.

STRINGENDO (It.). 'Squeezing', i.e. the time progressively quickening.

STRINGHAM, EDWIN JOHN. Born at Kenosha, Wisconsin, in 1890. He had held a number of educational positions when in 1929 he won a scholarship enabling him to study in Rome under Respighi. He later joined the staff of the Juilliard School, and has held, at various periods, many other educational positions. He has written a number of orchestral and choral works, as well as some books. He calls himself a 'Progressive Romanticist'.

STRING ORCHESTRA. See *String Band*, above.

STRING QUARTET. See *Chamber Music 2, 4* (end), 5; *Violin Family 2.*

STRING-TONE STOPS. See *Organ 3, 14 III.*

STRING TRIO. See *Chamber Music 2, 6.*

STRISCIANDO, STRISCIATO (It.). 'Trailing', 'trailed', i.e. smooth, slurred, etc., or, sometimes, Glissando (q.v.).

STROHFIEDEL (Ger.). Xylophone. See *Percussion Family 2 f, 4 e, 5 f*—and, to avoid confusion, compare *Stroh Violin*, below.

STROH VIOLIN, VIOLA, CELLO, MANDOLIN, GUITAR, and JAP FIDDLE. In these instruments the usual body of the instrument (sound box, etc.) is replaced by an ingenious mechanism connected with an amplifying horn. In the early days of gramophone recording the violins used were apparently of this sort (see Gaisberg, *The Music goes Round*, 1943).

Note that confusion is liable to occur between *Stroh Violin* and *Strohfiedel*; as German 'Fiedel' is English 'fiddle' it is natural to suppose these to be one and the same instrument. But 'Stroh' in the case of the 'Fiedel' means 'straw' (see *Percussion Family 5 f*), whilst as concerns the 'violin' it is the name of the inventor.

There is a series of 'Phono' instruments (*Phonofiddle, Phonomandolin*, etc.) on something the same principle (the Phonofiddle is sometimes played with a plectrum).

STROMENTO, STROMENTI (It.). 'Instrument', 'instruments'. See *Strumento* below.

STRONG, GEORGE TEMPLETON. Born in New York in 1856 and died in Geneva in 1948, aged ninety-two. His musical life was spent almost entirely in Europe, where he was a close friend of MacDowell and a number of the circles of Liszt (who valued his powers) and of Raff. From his early thirties he lived in Switzerland (latterly at Geneva, where he was greatly respected and where his ninetieth birthday was publicly celebrated). He composed much music (largely orchestral) and also painted a great deal in water-colours. His father (same Christian names; born 1820) was an active New York amateur; his musical diary was published in 1952.

STROPHIC. A song is sometimes spoken of as strophic, meaning in several verses (set to the same music—not 'through-composed'). The word comes from the terminology of ancient Greek literature, a Greek ode consisting of 'strophe', 'antistrophe', and 'epode', the first two corresponding in length and metre.

STRUMENTO, STRUMENTI (It.). 'Instrument', 'instruments'. So *Strumentato*, 'instrumented' (cf. *Recitative*).

> **Strumenti a Corde.** Stringed instruments.
> **Strumenti d'Arco.** Bowed instruments.
> **Strumenti di Legno.** Wood (wind) instruments.
> **Strumenti d'Ottone.** Brass instruments.
> **Strumenti a Percossa.** Percussion instruments.
> **Strumenti a Fiato.** Wind instruments.
> **Strumenti da Tasto.** Keyboard instruments.

STSCHERBATCHEW (and similar spellings). See *Stcherbatchef*.

STUART, LESLIE (real name, Thomas A. Barrett). Born at Southport in 1866 and died at Richmond, Surrey, in 1928, aged sixty-two. He began professional life with fourteen years as organist of Roman Catholic churches in Salford and Manchester, settling in London in 1895 and becoming highly popular as a composer of songs (e.g. *The Bandolero, Louisiana Lou, The Soldiers of the Queen, Little Dolly Daydream*) and musical plays (e.g. *Floradora*, 1899; *The Belle of Mayfair*, 1906).

STÜCK. (Ger.). 'Piece.'

STUCKEN, FRANK VALENTIN VAN DER. Born at Fredericksburg, Texas, in 1858 and died at Hamburg in 1929. See *United States 8*; *Concert 15*.

STUDENT'S COUNTERPOINT. See *Counterpoint*.

STUDIO, STUDY. See *Étude*.

STURBRIDGE FAIR. See *Fairs and their Music*.

STÜRMEND, STÜRMISCH (Ger.). 'Stormy', passionate.

STYLE DE PERRUQUE. See *Zopf*.

STYLE GALANT (Fr.), **GALANTER STIL** (Ger.). The light and elegant instrumental style of the harpsichord composers of the late eighteenth century, e.g. some of Bach's sons (Emanuel and Christian) and Haydn and Mozart (see *Sonata* 6). Sometimes the works of the earlier composers, Couperin, Rameau, and A. Scarlatti, are comprised within the term, and sometimes those of the later Clementi, but this seems to widen its scope rather too much for real significance.

Cf. *Galanterien*—the term applied to the lighter movements in the German suites of the period preceding the 'Style Galant' proper.

STYRMANT. See *Jew's Harp*.

SU (It.). (1) 'On', 'near'. It commonly occurs with various forms of the definite article (masc. and fem., sing. and pl.), as *Sul*, *Sull'*, *Sulla*, *Sui*, *Sugli*, *Sulle*, e.g. *Sul G* (in violin playing), 'On the G' (string).

(2) 'Up', e.g. *Arcata in su* means 'up-bowed'.

SUABE FLUTE. See *Organ* 14 II.

SUAVE, SUAVITÀ (It.). 'Suave', 'suavity'.

SUB-BASS. See *Organ* 14 I.

SUB-BOURDON. See *Organ* 14 I.

SUBDOMINANT. The fourth degree of the major or minor scale. 'Sub' here probably in the sense of 'less important'; from its functions this degree stands out as does the dominant, but less so. Subdominant then does not appear to mean 'under-the-dominant' (as supertonic means 'over-the-tonic'), but 'secondary dominant'—as 'submediant' means secondary mediant. The dominant proper lies five degrees above the tonic and this secondary one five degrees below, and the two mediants are the two half-way houses.

SUBITO (It.). Literally, 'suddenly', hence quickly, immediately, as in *Volti subito*, 'turn over immediately' (sometimes abbreviated to *V.S.*). *Subitamente* is another adverbial form.

SUBJECT in Fugue and Symphony, etc. (see *Form*, 7, 12). Any tune or musical theme or definite passage which recurs in a composition as part of the staple of its make-up is a 'Subject' of that composition. The subject of a fugue is a mere fragment of melody (i.e. a phrase of single notes); apart from fugue a subject is usually a fully harmonized and extended passage.

In the sense in which the terms 'First Subject' and 'Second Subject' are used in connexion with a movement of the sonata-form class (see *Form* 7) the subject is often a passage of some length, including several separate limbs. Indeed, in some cases we may describe the subject as not so much a 'tune' or 'theme' as a *group* of tunes or themes, and a study of the manner in which the 'exposition' is laid out as to key contrast is the only way in which to decide what are the 'Subjects' of the movement.

Compare *Subsidiary*.

SUBMEDIANT. The sixth degree of the major or minor scale. 'Sub' here means 'less important'. The mediant falls midway between the tonic and dominant and the submediant midway between the subdominant (i.e. less important dominant) and tonic. The one dominant lies five degrees above the tonic and the other five degrees below, and the two mediants are the two half-way houses.

SUBSIDIARY, or SUBSIDIARY THEME, or SUBSIDIARY SUBJECT. A term used (chiefly by the writers of annotated programmes for concerts) to designate one of the less important subjects (see *Subject*) in, for instance, a movement in sonata form (see *Form* 7). In such a movement, particularly in works by Beethoven or one of his successors, the 'First Subject' or 'Second Subject' may be a group of two or three distinct passages, almost capable of being considered independent subjects in themselves. In such instances the first of these passages is usually felt to be the most important and the other or others of the group to be subsidiary.

In a rondo subjects other than the first and most important may, instead of being called 'Episodes' (see *Form* 9), be called 'Subsidiaries' or 'Subsidiary Subjects'.

SUB-TONE CLARINET. See *Clarinet Family* 5.

SUCCENTOR. See *Cathedral Music* 2.

SUGGESTIVE MUSIC. See *Programme Music* 3.

SUGLI, SUI (It.). 'On the' (plur.).

SUITE

1. Introductory. Suite (French and English) is *Ordre* in old French, *Partie* or *Partita* in old German, *Sonata da Camera* in old Italian. A seventeenth- and eighteenth-century English term is 'Lesson', presumably implying an educational motive to the composition. All these things are one, and that one so similar in origin and so parallel in development with the sonata that for a complete view of the subject the article *Sonata* should be read with the present one. (As will be seen above, one name for *Suite* was *Sonata da Camera*, i.e. 'Chamber Sonata' as distinct from *Sonata da Chiesa*, or 'Church Sonata'.)

The two things suite and sonata represent different sides of the effort to find suitable forms

3. GERMAN SCHOOL CHOIR. Water-colour of *c.* 1800 in the Hamburg Historical Museum. See *Street Music* 5

Will you buy my dish of Eels?   Ha' ye an - y Rats or Mice to . kill?

1. OLD LONDON CRIES. See *Street Music* 2

5

2. LONDON STREET MUSIC IN THE 18TH CENTURY. Hogarth's *Enraged Musician*, 1741—the musician being Castrucci, First Violin of the Italian Opera. A Ballad Seller (left), an Oboe Player, and a Sow Gelder with his Horn are amongst the many performers. The bill on the wall announces *The Beggar's Opera*

4. 'A PROMENADE CONCERT' IN 1842 (from *Punch*)

5, 6. LONDON MUSICAL DELIGHTS OF 1891
(from *Punch*)

PLATE 166

THE WAITS—GERMAN AND ENGLISH

See the Article on page 1103

1. NUREMBERG TOWN BAND. Mural by Dürer in the Town Hall, painted about 1500

2. EARLY 17TH-CENTURY WAITS

3. WAITS OF BEVERLEY, YORKSHIRE
(From a pillar in St. Mary's Church there)

5. CHRISTMAS WAITS IN THE 16TH CENTURY

Lanthorne and a whole Candell light, hange out your lights heare

4. A TOWN WAIT ON HIS PERAMBULATION

CHRISTMAS MUSICIANS,
(Generally called WAITS.)

LADIES AND GENTLEMEN,
*To prevent Impoſtors from obtaining Money under
False Pretences.*

WE your old eſtabliſhed Muſicians preſume to ſolicit
your moſt worthy Favours, according to old eſtabliſhed Cuſtom, take this Method to inform you, that we
ſhall this Seaſon wear SILVER MEDALS, with the Impreſ-
ſion of the GEORGE and DRAGON, ſignifying the *Britiſh
Arms*; as witneſs our Hands.

J. LOYDE.   C. PHILLIPS.   T. DE MARK.

6. LONDON WAITS IN THE 18TH CENTURY

for instrumental music. Choral music had risen to its apogee in the sixteenth century and the turn of instrumental music had come. As has been shown in the article *Sonata*, one means of constructing effective instrumental music was found in an adaptation of the choral form of the canzona (q.v.); from this developed both the sonata and the fugue.

Another means was found, in the adaptation of dance forms. Lutenist and keyboard composers found in the ball-room custom of following a slower dance with a quicker, or a dance in two or four beats in a measure with one in three, a hint towards an independent instrumental form. In Italy a passamezzo was followed by a saltarello; in France, Germany, and England a pavan by a galliard—the two being in the same key.

Sometimes an organic connexion subsisted between the two dances, the same musical theme being treated in both, or at any rate, the two beginning with such.

2. The Earliest Suite Publications. Publications of music on these lines for the lute began as early as the opening of the sixteenth century, e.g. Petrucci, the great Venetian printer, brought out in 1507-8 four books of music for the lute, of which the fourth follows the pavan by a saltarello and then adds another piece called 'Piva' ('pipe' or 'bagpipe').

A number of such publications appeared in Italy during the sixteenth century, and frequently with that organic connexion between associated pieces spoken of above. In the early seventeenth century the German and French lute composers, also, were active. Some of them made series of four or five pieces growing out of the same fragment of generating tune.

The keyboard composers later adopted a similar scheme. *Parthenia* (1611), the first music printed for the virginals in England, has a number of pavans and galliards by Byrd, Bull, and Gibbons, and sometimes there is a 'Preludio', thus making up a little set of three movements. In the enormous manuscript collection made perhaps ten years or so later and now known as the Fitzwilliam Virginal Book (published 1894-9), a number of cases occur of groups of two pieces, generally pavan and galliard, and sometimes more than two, as for instance, two sets by Ferdinando Richardson of dances and variations on them—*pavana - variatio - galiardo - variatio*. In one of the sets the pavan and its variation are in the major and the galliard and its variation in the minor of the same keynote (G major and minor). Sometimes in this book there is the link of a common theme between pavan and galliard and sometimes not: there is no rule about this.

The nature of a suite is now clear. The word implies a set of two or more congruous yet sufficiently contrasting compositions, linked or not by some common thematic material, and always at this period and for a century and a half later by being in the same key—or exceptionally in the major and minor keys of the same keynote,

i.e. 'tonic' major and minor (later there are cases of 'relative' major and minor being used, i.e. the major and minor with the same key *signature*, C major and A minor and so forth).

3. The Second Period in the History of the Suite. There is fashion in dances, and when in the ball-room the allemand and courante superseded the pavan and galliard they soon tended to do so in the suite. Again we see a piece of slower speed and of four-in-a-measure time followed by one of quicker speed and of three-in-a-measure.

Gradually the suite became standardized as two groups of pieces in the allemand-courante relationship: allemand-courante-sarabande-gigue. Froberger (1616-67) is credited with having established this convention. One or two of these four dance types might have something else substituted, or other dance types might be intercalated in the scheme (see *Galanterien*; *Intermezzo* 4) but that four-square series was the norm from about 1650 to 1750, which was nearly the end of the classical period of the suite.

One or two examples from Italian, English, French, and German composers will show the way in which the suite, whilst still retaining these four dances as its most frequent concomitants, was yet varied by omissions or additions.

PURCELL, First Suite for harpsichord (*A Choice Collection of Lessons for the Harpsichord or Spinnet*, published the year after his death, 1696).

Prelude.
Almand.
Corant.
Minuet.

In all his suites the movements are short (shorter than, in the Elizabethan period, the pavans and galliards generally were); in this one they are exceptionally short—only sixty measures as a total.

CORELLI, Seventh Sonata for Violin and Harpsichord (A *Sonata da Camera*, published 1700).

Prelude.
Corrente.
Sarabande.
Giga.

COUPERIN, First Ordre for Harpsichord (published 1713; the French composers of this period were addicted to long suites and fancy titles for the different movements).

L' Auguste (The August Personage)—Allemande.
Première Courante.
Seconde Courante.
La Majestueuse (The Majestic Lady)—Sarabande.
Gavotte.
La Mylordine (The Great Dame)—Gigue.
Menuet.
Les Sylvains (Forest Deities)—Rondeau.
Les Abeilles (The Bees)—Rondeau.
La Nanette.
Les Sentiments—Sarabande.
Les Nonettes (The Young Nuns).

La Pastorelle (The Shepherdess—the word also meant a certain figure in a contre-danse).
La Bourbonnaise (The Lady of Bourbon).
La Manon.
L'Enchanteresse—Rondeau.
La Fleurie, ou la tendre Nanette (The Blooming Maiden, or Tender Nanette).
Les Plaisirs de St. Germain-en-Laye (The Pleasures of that town of royal residence).

One or two of these are followed by a variation, and the *Young Nuns* are divided into two —'First Part, The Blondes' and 'Second Part, The Brunettes'. The suite as a whole is in the key of G minor, but two or three movements are in G major.

BACH, First Partita (published 1731).

Prelude.
Allemande.
Courante.
Sarabande.
Menuet I and II.
Gigue.

All of these are in key B flat. Bach rarely changes key in a suite. When he does so he usually keeps the same keynote (i.e. goes to the tonic minor or major) and, very rarely indeed, the same key-signature (i.e. the relative major or minor). Compare Couperin above. Bach's six French suites and partitas have no changes at all, but the six English suites have them.

Handel, on his part, prefers the modulation to the relative (and not the tonic) minor or major. There is another interesting point about Handel's suites. He likes to have a thematic connexion, as some of the Italian lutenists and English virginal composers of long before did.

4. The Question of Key. The question of key just referred to is a curious one. The Elizabethan virginal composers generally kept to one key. So did Purcell. Couperin, and Bach, as has been seen, sometimes dropped into the *tonic* minor or major; Corelli and Handel sometimes, if they changed key, preferred the *relative* minor or major. But many suites did not even have these simple and obvious changes from major to minor and minor to major. Nor did many of the sonatas of the period. It is not until the sonatas of C. P. Emanuel Bach, Haydn, and Mozart (the earlier specimens of the modern form of sonata) that we find variety of key in the different movements regarded as essential.

The tendency to place some sort of a *Prelude* at the beginning of the suite will have been observed. It was, as a rule, the one movement not in a dance-rhythm style: often it was vigorous and rhapsodic. Different names were give to it: Bach called the opening movements of his partitas by six different names—*Prelude, Sinfonia, Fantaisie, Ouverture, Préambule, Toccata.*

5. The Form of the Separate Movements. Nearly all the movements in the suite of the period from Purcell and Corelli to the death of Bach and Handel were in simple binary form, i.e. a movement fell roughly into

halves, the first modulating to the key of the dominant (i.e. of one sharp more or one flat less), or if in the minor to the relative major, and the second half modulating back to the first key of the piece (see *Form* 5). Each half was repeated.

There was no attempt at variety of material within the limits of a movement. Certain figures or motifs were set in the opening measures and were adhered to throughout. It is the introduction of contrasted 'subjects', in contrasted keys, at the beginning of a movement, and the 'developing' and then repeating of these, that marks the modern sonata—the sonata type established by Bach's son, Emanuel, and by Haydn and Mozart.

There is thus a very great difference in aim and in method between the suite and the modern sonata, which largely took its place as it took that of the older sonata (see *Sonata* 2, 3). The variety both within a movement and as between movement and movement is much more limited in the suite. Many modern sonata movements partake of the nature of drama.

6. Relationship with the Overture. The old overture, though it had a different origin from the suite, assimilated itself to it, and the article *Overture* (1) should be consulted. Some of Bach's orchestral 'Suites', as they are called on their title-pages today, he himself called 'Overtures' (possibly meaning by 'Overture' rather 'Overture, etc.').

7. The Post-Classical Suite. As has been stated above, the period of the classical suite ended about the middle of the eighteenth century. Suites are, of course, written today, generally on very free lines. Occasionally they are attempts to evoke the spirit of the past, e.g. Grieg's *From Holberg's Time* (Holberg was the founder of modern Danish-Norwegian literature and a contemporary of Bach and Handel, and this suite consists of Praeludium, Sarabande, Gavotte and Musette, Air, Rigaudon). Or they are concert treatments of theatre music, e.g. the two suites from Bizet's *L'Arlésienne*, Grieg's two *Peer Gynt* Suites, Tchaikovsky's *Nutcracker* Suite, and Stravinsky's *Firebird* Suite. Or they are just strings of entertaining movements.

But in the second half of the eighteenth century, and later, strings of compositions of variable make-up and for a great variety of instrumental combinations were written (often recreative and for open-air use) under the names **Serenata** (q.v.), **Serenade** (q.v.), **Cassation, Cassazione,** and **Divertimento.** Thus Mozart's 'Haffner Serenade', composed for a wedding in 1782, consists of eight orchestral movements (of which the only ones in dance form are three minuets). Mozart wrote a considerable number of such things for varying combinations of instruments, and under the names just mentioned; it almost seems as though 'Divertimento' and 'Serenade' meant to him merely a suite in more than four movements. Haydn also has many such pieces under the name 'Divertimento'. Apparently during the Haydn–Mozart period this term generally implied a 'chamber' combination of stringed and wind instruments (i.e. only one stringed instrument to a part—*not* an orchestra).

Beethoven has two 'Serenades', one for string trio (op. 8, 1797) and one for flute, violin, and viola (op. 25, 1802). Later Brahms has a Serenade for full orchestra, and one for small orchestra (op. 11 and 16, both published 1860).

Dvořák, Elgar, Tchaikovsky, and many others have written 'serenades' of this same general type.

The term 'Cassation' is thought to come from the German *Gasse* ('street') and thus to imply the purpose of open-air entertainment.

8. The Oldest Cyclic Form. It will be realized that the suite is the oldest cyclic form. After 400 years it is still alive, and from the very nature of things, one would guess, will never die. Since the middle of the eighteenth century, however, it has ceased to be a regular medium for the deepest expression of composers, having, in this capacity, been superseded by the Sonata and Symphony; it seems likely henceforth to continue to maintain, for the most part, its later character of refined entertainment.

More or less serious keyboard suites are, however, still occasionally written, as, for instance, those of Schönberg and Hindemith.

The *Song Cycle* (q.v.) has an obvious relationship to the suite. A purely choral suite (mixed voices, without accompaniment) is Bantock's *A Pageant of Human Life*.

SUIVEZ (Fr.). 'Follow' (imperative).

SUK, JOSEF (p. 102, pl. **20.** 4). Born at Křečovice, in Southern Bohemia, then Austrian territory, in 1874 and died at Prague in 1935, aged sixty-one. He was a fine violinist, who at seventeen became one of the founders of the world-famous Bohemian String Quartet. He studied under Dvořák and married his daughter. She died early, and his thoughts on his loss of her and of her father inspired a symphonic poem, *Azrael* (the Angel of Death). He sought consolation in nature, and this also inspired some of his compositions. In the effort to approach nature more nearly he became, in a small way, a farmer.

Suk's earlier compositions are influenced by Dvořák's style; he later escaped from it and became freer both in rhythm and in harmony, sometimes approaching atonality.

SUL, SULL', SULLA, SUI, SUGLI, SULLE (It.). 'On the' (termination according to gender and number).

SUL G or **SUL IV** (It.). 'On the G', 'on the fourth' (string)—a term used in violin music.

SULLA TASTIERA (It.). Literally, 'on the fingerboard', i.e. bow on or near it. (*Sul Tasto* means the same thing.)

SULLIVAN, ARTHUR SEYMOUR (p. 705, pl. **118.** 4). Born in London in 1842 and died there in 1900, aged fifty-eight. His father was an army bandsman, and professor of clarinet at the Royal Military School of Music (Kneller Hall).

As a boy he sang in the Chapel Royal choir (see *Chapel Royal*); as a youth he won the Mendelssohn Scholarship, which enabled him to study at the Royal Academy of Music (under Sterndale Bennett, Goss, and others) and at the Leipzig Conservatory. At twenty his music to Shakespeare's *Tempest* was performed at the Crystal Palace and his name was already made.

He wrote orchestral music, oratorios, songs (sometimes poor ones), part songs, services, anthems, hymn tunes, and other things, held for a time an organistship or two, conducted at festivals, directed the National Training School (which later became the Royal College) of Music, received honorary degrees, and was knighted (1883), but his title to lasting fame was won by his happy combination of a sense of fun, a sense of rhythm, and gifts for melody, easy-going yet apt harmony, and piquant orchestration. These qualities first displayed themselves in his setting of Burnand's *Cox and Box* (1867), and later in the series written in collaboration with the satirical light-dramatist, Gilbert (p. 705, pl. **118.** 5)—*Trial by Jury* (1875), *The Sorcerer* (1877), *H.M.S. Pinafore* (1878), *The Pirates of Penzance* (1880), *Patience* (1881), *Iolanthe* (1882), *Princess Ida* (1884), *The Mikado* (1885), *Ruddigore* (1887), *The Yeomen of the Guard* (1888), *The Gondoliers* (1889), *Utopia Limited* (1893), *The Grand Duke* (1896).

His settings of librettos by other writers have not kept the stage. Gilbert was his man; he and Gilbert were born for each other, and their needless quarrel (ostensibly about a carpet in the Savoy Theatre, built for their work), which interrupted the series from 1890 to 1893, was looked upon as a national misfortune.

The dates of the more important non-Gilbert operas are here added for the sake of completeness and on the chance that time may bring some effort at their revival—Sydney Grundy's *Haddon Hall* (1892), Burnand's *The Chieftain* (1895), Pinero and Comyns Carr's *The Beauty Stone* (1898), Basil Hood's *The Rose of Persia* (1899), and his *The Emerald Isle* (completed by Edward German, 1901).

The 'grand' opera *Ivanhoe* (Julian Sturgis, 1891) had a run of 160 nights and then, probably through unfortunate temporary conditions, disappeared. The most important cantata is *The Golden Legend* (1886).

The music of Sullivan is often described as typically and completely English. It is true that the English folk song, Purcell, Arne, and the English ballad operas count for a good deal in him, but there are also the happy influences of Mozart and of French light opera, particularly Offenbach, and of the Italian opera composers (Bellini, Donizetti, etc.). It has been alleged that the musical quality of his Gilbert works (which keep the stage) and his non-Gilbert works (which do not) is identical, and that this involves 'a re-consideration and a lower estimate of Sullivan's own gifts' (Dr. Ernest Walker—footnote in the present writer's *Listener's History of Music*, vol. ii). The suggestion is here repeated, not with complete conviction, but for the reader's reflection.

It may be added that Gilbert's non-Sullivan works fail to keep the public eye.

See *Gondoliers*; *H.M.S. Pinafore*; *Iolanthe*; *Mikado*; *Patience*; *Pirates of Penzance*; *Princess Ida*; *Ruddigore*; *Yeomen of the Guard*. Also p. 705, pl. **118. 7.**
Anthem, Period V; *Auber*; *Ballad* 6; *Ballad Opera*; *Beggar's Opera*; *Cachucha*; *Coleridge-Taylor*; *Competitions* 3; *Composition* 6, 7; *Concert* 7; *Encore*; *Extravaganza*; *Jazz* 1; *Libretto*; *Mendelssohn Scholarship*; *Opera* 13 e, 24 (1875 to 1896); *Opus*; *Oratorio* 7 (1869–73–80); *Overture* 5; *Prima Donna*; *Recorder Family* 3; *Savoy Operas*.

SUL PONTICELLO (It.). 'On the bridge', i.e. bowing near the bridge (in playing the violin, etc.).

SUL TASTO (It.). 'On the touch' (meaning that the bow of the violin, etc., shall be kept over or near the fingerboard).

SULZER. See *Jewish* 6; p. 528, pl. **97. 6.**

SUMER IS ICUMEN IN. This is perhaps, of all musical compositions, the one that has been most discussed by historians, for it dates from the early part of the thirteenth century yet has a contrapuntal complexity that belongs to the fifteenth (see p. 145, pl. **30. 1**).

It is a spring song, with English words, for four tenor voices in canon in unison (see *Canon*), with two basses singing a short ground (q.v.), called 'Pes', also in canon at the octave. The melody is very folk-song-like in style: it may be an actual folk song (there are alternative Latin sacred words, but they fit badly). It is not in one of the old modes (see *Modes*), but in the later key of F, with the B flat duly marked at the beginning of every stave in the modern way. (If preferred, it may, of course, be said to be in the Ionian mode transposed, but the Ionian mode had little status at this period.)

The composition (sometimes called the Reading Rota, i.e. Round) is usually attributed to John of Fornsete, monk of Reading Abbey, where he was Keeper of the Cartulary (or records); the grounds for this attribution are the fact that it has been written into the book of records, and in what is evidently his handwriting. (For an insubstantial Irish claim to the melody see *Ireland* 8.)

The existence of this elaborately canonic work, of high musical value, has led many musicians to claim that the art of composition was at this date much more advanced than has been supposed. The difficulties are two: (*a*) other similar work of this period does not exist, and (*b*) if this had existed and been lost it is strange that such work of the period (and, indeed, of the century-and-a-half following) as has survived is so different.

In 1945 Dr. Manfred Bukofzer published in the United States a new study of the whole subject of the date and origin of this composition. He offered reasons for believing it to be of somewhat later date than had been previously suggested, and his argument was favourably received by some scholars though firmly rejected by others on palaeographical evidence, etc. Whilst placing its composition at not earlier than 1280 and probably as late as 1310 he admitted that 'the *rota* can still claim to be the first composition for six voices and the first specimen of canon as a form in its own right'.

See allusions s.v. *France* 2; *Annotated Programmes* 4; *Ground*.

SUMMATION TONES. See *Acoustics* 10, 13.

SUMMEND (Ger.). 'Humming.'

SUMMERS, JOSEPH (born 1843). English organist who migrated to Melbourne, Australia (D.Mus., Cantuar.). See *Copyists*.

SUMMY. See *Publishing* 9.

SUNDAY SCHOOL MUSIC. See *Hymns and Hymn Tunes* 15.

SUNG MASS. See *Mass* 1.

'SUN' QUARTETS and 'SUNRISE QUARTET' (Haydn). See *Nicknamed Compositions* 12.

SUO (It.). 'Its own.' (E.g. *Suo loco*, 'its own place' —after performing an octave higher or lower.)

SUONARE (It.). 'To sound' (*Sonare* being the more usual form of the word). So *Suonante*, 'Sounding'.

SUONO, SUONI (It.). 'Sound', 'sounds'.

SUPERBO, SUPERBA (It., masc., fem.). 'Proud.'

SUPER-PIANO. See *Electric Musical Instruments* 5 b.

SUPERTONIC. The second degree of the major or minor scale.

SUPERTONIC CHROMATIC CHORDS. Those generally recognized are (*a*) The major common chord on the Supertonic and its first inversion; (*b*) The Supertonic Chromatic Seventh (the above with a minor seventh added); (*c*) The Supertonic Chromatic Ninth (the major or minor ninth in the major key or the minor ninth in the minor key); (*d*) The Supertonic Chromatic Eleventh and Thirteenth; (*e*) To these may be added the Supertonic Diminished Triad in the major key, with or without a minor seventh and (*f*) The major common chord on the flattened supertonic in its first inversion (see *Neapolitan Sixth*).

SUPERTONIC SEVENTH CHORD. See *Added Sixth*.

SUPERVISOR SYSTEM IN SCHOOLS. See *United States of America* 5.

SUPPÉ, FRANZ VON—really Francesco Ezechiele Ermenegildo Cavaliere Suppé-Demelli (p. 400, pl. **69.** 5). Born at or near Split, in Dalmatia, in 1819 and died in Vienna in 1895, aged seventy-six. He was taken in boyhood to Vienna, where he early occupied a small post as theatre conductor. More important posts of the same sort followed, and for the last thirty years of his life he was in charge of the music at the historic theatre 'An der Wien'. He wrote operas, operettas, and the like to the number of over 150. One or two of his overtures (as *Light Cavalry* and *Poet and Peasant*) are everywhere known, and the opera *Boccaccio* is still occasionally produced; apart from these his works have had an almost solely Viennese popularity.

SUPPLIANT (Fr.). 'Supplicating.'

SUPPLICANDO (It.). 'Supplicating.'

SUPPLICHEVOLE, SUPPLICHEVOL-MENTE (It.). 'Supplicating', 'supplicatingly'.

SUPPLYING. See *Verset*.

SUPPRIMEZ (Fr.). 'Suppress.' In French organ music it means to put out of use the stop in question.

SUR (Fr.). 'On', or 'over'.

SURIANO. See *Soriano*.

SUR LA TOUCHE (Fr.). Literally 'On the fingerboard', i.e. (in violin playing, etc.) bow on or near it.

SUR LE CHEVALET (Fr.). 'On the bridge', i.e. (in violin playing, etc.) bow near it.

SURPRISE CADENCE. See *Cadence*.

'SURPRISE' SYMPHONY (Haydn). See *Nicknamed Compositions* 11.

SURREY GARDENS, LONDON. See *Concert* 8.

SURSUM CORDA. 'Lift up your hearts', included in all known Christian liturgies of all ages. The English words occur in the Communion Service of the Anglican Church.

SURTOUT (Fr.). 'Above all', especially.

SUSATO, TYLMAN. See *Publishing* 3.

SUSPENDED CADENCE. See *Cadence*.

SUSPENSION. See *Harmony* 3, 12, 13, 21, 24 k; *Appoggiatura*.

SÜSS (Ger.). 'Sweet.'

SUSSEX VILLAGE ORCHESTRAS. See *Anglican Parish Church Music* 4.

SÜSSMAYR. See *Misattributed Compositions* (s.v. 'Mozart's Requiem').

SUSURRANDO, SUSURRANTE (It.). 'Whispering.'

SVEGLIANDO, SVEGLIATO (It.). 'Awakening', 'awakened', i.e. brisk, alert.

SVELTO (It.). 'Smart', 'quick'.

SVENDSEN, JOHAN SEVERIN (p. 896, pl. **153**. 4). Born at Christiania (now Oslo), Norway, in 1840 and died at Copenhagen, in Denmark, in 1911, aged seventy. His father, a violinist and military bandmaster, gave him his first teaching and then he took up a similar career on his own account, attaining the position of bandmaster. The governments of Norway and Sweden (then united under one king) gave him an annual allowance that he might devote himself to study; he applied himself to the violin and then, a malady injuring the freedom of his hand, took up the study of composition in the conservatory of Leipzig.

He travelled much and passed a year or two in Paris towards the end of the reign of Napoleon III. He then spent a good deal of time in Germany, associating with Wagner and the group of the 'Music of the Future' (see *Liszt*).

His life was one of much travel, but he passed periods at Christiania occupying various important official posts, for a time having Grieg for his colleague as conductor.

He wrote two symphonies, a violin concerto, a cello concerto, songs, etc. His *Carnival at Paris*, for orchestra, is known to a wide public.

He was a national-romantic but, as a much-travelled cosmopolitan, a good deal less pronouncedly national than his countryman Grieg.

SVOLGIMENTO. See *Development*.

SWAIN, FREDA MARY. Born at Portsmouth in 1902. She had a brilliant early career as pianist, and at fourteen won a scholarship at the Royal College of Music for composition (later on staff). Her published and performed works include chamber music, a pianoforte concerto, songs, piano pieces, etc. In 1921 she married the pianist Arthur Alexander, with whom she toured the Commonwealth in two-piano recitals.

SWANSON, HOWARD. Born at Atlanta, Georgia, in 1909, of Negro parents. His early life was passed in Cleveland, Ohio. For a time he earned his living successively as a locomotive greaser, a letter carrier, and a mail clerk, studying meanwhile at the Cleveland Institute of Music. He won a Rosenwald Fellowship and was enabled to go to Paris, where he was a pupil of Nadia Boulanger (q.v.). During the second World War he was for a time in Spain and then in New York, where he obtained work in the Internal Revenue Department, composing meanwhile many settings of lyrics by American poets of today and a piano sonata; these gradually brought him into notice and were followed by a *Night Piece* for orchestra and a *Short Symphony* which was first performed in 1950 in New York and then at the Edinburgh Festival of 1951. With this symphony his name first became widely known.

SWEDEN. See *Scandinavia* 4.

SWEELINCK, JAN PIETERSZOON (p. 96, pl. **15**. 6). Born at Deventer (or Amsterdam) in 1562 and died at Amsterdam in 1621, aged fifty-eight or fifty-nine. He was a famous organist and the son of an organist, to whose post, at the Old Church of Amsterdam, he succeeded, occupying it until his death and crowding the church with a delighted auditory. Through his pupils, who came to him from Germany, Sweden, and elsewhere, the tradition of his playing was handed down, influencing the whole organ-playing art of northern Europe, including that of the great Bach himself. (When he died his son was appointed in his stead, and so for three generations, and probably for over a century, the Sweelinck family made music in the same building.)

His compositions are mostly for church use—organ and choral works. The organ works show almost the earliest examples of independent pedal playing, and include the first completely worked-out fugues for organ, the elements of the form and style of which he took from the ricercari and fantasias of his day. Here, again, he prepared the way for Bach—who was to be born sixty-four years after he died. These works show the influences of his personal friends, the English organists, John Bull and Peter Philips, respectively of Antwerp and Brussels. The choral works (sacred and secular) are numerous and important. He left a treatise on composition, in which, as one example, he included a canon by Bull—who wrote a fantasia based on a work of his.

See *Holland* 3, 5, 9; *History* 3; *Germany* 4; *Organ* 13; *Chorale Prelude*; *Hexachord*; *Notation* 4; *Bull, John*; *Hol*.

SWEET ADELINES. See *Barbershop Music*.

SWELL ORGAN. See *Organ* 2 d, 8.

SWIFT, JONATHAN (1667–1745). Ecclesiastic and satirist. See *Beggar's Opera*.

SWINBURNE, SIR JAMES, Bart., F.R.S., etc. (1858–1958). See *Absolute Pitch*; *Improvisation* 2.

SWING. This term, in common with most of those used in Jazz, is variously interpreted. It is generally taken as meaning that subtle form of rubato which renders a skilled performer acceptable to initiates.

In the 1930s 'Swing Bands' were widely popular, but in that connexion the term seems to have little clearly identifiable meaning.

SWINSTEAD, FELIX GERALD. Born in London in 1880 and died at Southwold in 1959, aged seventy-nine. He was trained under Matthay, Corder, and others, at the Royal Academy of Music, where he later taught. He published, especially, chamber music and a large number of works for piano.

SWISS PIPE. See *Fife*.

SWISS STAFF BELLS. See *Deagan Instruments*.

SWITCH, MUSICAL. See *Musical Switch*.

SWITZERLAND. See *Albicastro*; *Alphorn*; *Andreae*; *Beck*; *Binet*; *Bloch*; *Burkhard*; *Concert* 13; *Dictionaries* 4 g; *Doret*; *Education and Music* 1; *Gagnebin*; *Honegger*; *Huber*; *Jaques-Dalcroze*; *Lauber*; *Liebermann*; *Martin, Frank*; *Modes* 6; *Nägeli*; *Oboussier*; *Oratorio* 4, 7; *Plainsong* 3; *Ranz des Vaches*; *Rousseau*; *Schoeck*. Also p. 880, pl. **147.**

SWORD DANCE. See *Dance* 5.

SYLVESTER, SAINT (Pope). See *Singing* 3.

SYMBAL. See *Hurdy-gurdy*.

SYMBOLISM. See *Debussy*.

SYMMES, REVD. THOMAS. See *Hymns* 11.

SYMPATHETIC STRINGS. Strings which, on a bowed, plucked, or hammered instrument, are not played upon but merely vibrate by sympathetic resonance, so enriching the tone.

See *Acoustics* 20 a; *Viol Family* 4 d f; *Hurdy-gurdy*; *Tromba Marina*; *Scandinavia* 3 (for Hardangerfele); *Amore, Amour*; *Pianoforte* 12, 16 ('Aliquot Scaling', 'Duplex Scaling').

SYMPHONIC DANCE. An orchestral piece of serious value yet in dance rhythm and style.

SYMPHONIC POEM, or *Tone Poem* (Ger. *Sinfonische Dichtung* or *Tondichtung*; Fr. *Poème Symphonique*; It. *Poema Sinfonico*). At a certain point in the history of the symphony, the point at which, after a century of development, its composers had taken to themselves the harmonic and orchestral technique to make it expressive of the deepest and most romantic emotion (see *Symphony* 5), it gave birth to a new form, the symphonic poem.

The name and the thing are the legacy of Liszt (q.v.) and date from the mid-nineteenth century. Strongly influenced by the Romantic movement of his day, he brought into his music literary, dramatic, and pictorial elements: in other words, he wrote 'Programme Music' (q.v.). His two actual symphonies show this tendency, the one being a 'Dante' symphony (with movements 'Inferno', 'Purgatorio', and ('Magnificat' and the other a 'Faust' symphony (with movements 'Faust', 'Gretchen', and 'Mephistopheles'). He realized, however, that in a continuous one-movement work of a more or less free type he would be less bound by formal considerations and could, in fact, let the form mould itself to the thought: to this protean form (which usually somewhat resembles the first movement of a symphony, so far as it resembles anything previously existing) he gave the name 'Symphonic Poem'. Amongst works of this class by him are *Tasso* (after Byron and Goethe), *The Preludes* (after Lamartine's 'Poetic Meditations'), *Mazeppa* (after Hugo, who in turn was 'after' Byron), *The Slaughter of the Huns* (after a fresco by Kaulbach in Berlin), *The Ideals* (after a poem by Schiller), and *Hamlet*.

The Bohemian composer, Smetana, one of the most immediate followers of Liszt, eagerly seized upon the new idea and wrote a series of six symphonic poems with the general title *My Fatherland*.

Alexander Ritter (1833–96), an admirer of Liszt and Wagner and a practitioner of the 'New Music' (q.v.), wrote symphonic poems and greatly influenced his young disciple Strauss, whose *Don Juan* (1888), *Death and Transfiguration* ('Tod und Verklärung, 1889), *Till Owlglass's Merry Tricks* ('Till Eulenspiegels lustige Streiche', 1894), *Thus spake Zoroaster* ('Also sprach Zarathustra', 1895), and similar works were for a considerable period the principal representatives of the symphonic poem in the world's concert programmes.

The first symphonic poem by a French composer was Saint-Saëns's *Omphale's Spinning Wheel* in 1871; the first by a British composer (for Britain came late into this field) William Wallace's *The Passing of Beatrice* in 1892.

Elgar's *Falstaff* (1913), described by its composer as a 'symphonic study', is perhaps the most detailed programmatic treatment of a literary subject ever produced.

The fashion for the symphonic poem appeared to die down in the second decade of the twentieth century, the younger composers preferring, as a rule, a more abstract treatment of their art, that is, being more interested in music as music than in music as a means of interpreting literature or painting.

See also Concert Overtures under *Overture* 8.

SYMPHONIC PROLOGUE. See *Overture* 4.

SYMPHONIE. See *Hurdy-gurdy.*

SYMPHONIE BURLESQUE. See *Toy Symphony.*

SYMPHONIQUE (Fr.), **SYMPHONISCH** (Ger.). 'Symphonic.'

SYMPHONIZED SYNCOPATION. See *Jazz* 1, 5.

SYMPHONY

1. The Word 'Symphony'.
2. The Earliest Symphonies.
3. The Advent of the Symphony as we know it.
4. The Haydn–Mozart Symphony.
5. Beethoven's Contemporaries and Successors.
6. The Character of the Various Movements of a Symphony.
7. Later Developments in the Symphony.
8. A Historical List of Symphony Composers.

1. The Word 'Symphony' (Fr. *Symphonie*; It. *Sinfonia*; Ger. *Sinfonie* or *Symphonie*), from the Greek, means merely a 'sounding together'. In the Middle Ages it was applied to any consonant combination of two notes. Later it was applied to vocal or instrumental compositions in the early counterpoint—which implied the use of consonant combinations of notes. It has also sometimes been applied to instruments of which several notes were heard together, as, for instance, various forms of bagpipes (their melody notes 'sounding together' with their drones); indeed, the present-day Italian, Spanish, and Greek names for bagpipes, *Zampogna*, *Zampoña*, and *Zampouna*, are forms of the word, and the *Hurdy-gurdy* (q.v.) has also at various periods and in various places been called *Symphony* or *Symphonie*.

The original sense of the word, then, is that in which Milton, in 1644, uses it when pleading for music for schoolboys—'either while the skilful organist plies his grave and fancied descant, in lofty fugues, or the *whole symphony* with artful and unimaginable touches adorn and grace the well-studied chords of some choice composer'. It is somewhat in this sense that Schütz in Germany, at the same period, uses it on the title-page of his *Symphoniae Sacrae*, which are 'soundings together' of voices and instruments—vocal solos or duets, etc., with the instrumental parts treated on equal terms with the voices. Bach, a century later, uses it for a 'sounding together' of strands of tone, the original description of his three-part Inventions (q.v.), being *Symphonien*. Haydn called some of his string quartets symphonies. Stravinsky, two centuries beyond that, is still using the term in its old vague sense in his *Symphonies of Wind Instruments*.

In Italy, from the end of the sixteenth century, the word had come to be applied to any instrumental ensemble passages interpolated in plays, etc., and so when the opera and oratorio were introduced it passed over into them too. We still speak of a certain instrumental movement in the middle of Handel's *Messiah* as 'The Pastoral Symphony'. The term came to have a particular use as the title of the most impor-

tant instrumental piece in an opera and, as the 'Sinfonia avanti l'opera' (the symphony before the opera), was applied to the overture. (Old-fashioned people in England still often refer to the opening instrumental portion of a song as the 'Symphony' or 'the Opening Symphony', and this use is correct and classic.)

2. The Earliest Symphonies. At this point the reader who wishes to gain a clear general idea of the development of the symphony as we know it today should turn to *Overture* 1, when he will notice that the regulation Italian operatic overture of the eighteenth century (as often seen in the work of A. Scarlatti, for instance) has a very obvious resemblance to what we now call a symphony—consisting, as it does, of a quick movement, a slow one, and another quick one.

Highly developed compositions of this sort were too good to be reserved merely for use when an opera was performed and so were frequently played as independent orchestral pieces. From this came, naturally, a custom of composing pieces in the same form and style for independent performance, and so what we now call the symphony was born—a piece of self-sufficing orchestral music in several movements, an orchestral sonata, in fact.

Here the serious inquirer already postulated may care to turn to the article *Sonata* 1, when he will see that the sonata developed originally out of a vocal form, being at first much the same sort of thing as the canzona or the cantata but written purely for instrumental performance and later taking its own line of development. So, too, the symphony developed out of an earlier form, the overture, and took its own line of development.

Doubtless there was action and reaction all the time, the sonata (for one or a few solo instruments) and the symphony (for instruments of more than one to a part) influencing one another until at last (mid-eighteenth century) they were practically indistinguishable except as to the media employed. The concerto grosso (see *Concerto* 2) had also its influence on the symphony. In fact, to find any one clear line of ancestry for any particular musical form is always difficult.

In the earlier part of the eighteenth century the word 'symphony' still had a sense of overture. Bach sometimes used it in this sense, styling 'Sinfonie' the opening movement of a suite, for instance (see the opening movement of his second keyboard Partita), or, equally, so styling a whole orchestral suite, when its main movements had a likeness to those of the overture (generally the French, not Italian, type of overture—see *Overture* 1).

3. The Advent of the Symphony as we know it. The true symphony, as we understand the word today (i.e. the orchestral sonata, with the first movement, normally, in what we call 'first movement' or 'sonata' form—see *Form* 7), begins with the period of Bach's sons and their contemporaries in various countries. One of the earliest symphonists was the Milanese composer, **G. B. Sammartini** (1698–1775), whose works had a good deal of influence in fixing the style and form. The famous Mannheim Kapellmeister **Johann W. A. Stamitz** (1717–57) and his sons Karl Stamitz (1745–1801) and Anton Stamitz (1754–c. 1809) are also important figures in the early history of the symphony, as the Mannheim orchestra had been brought to a pitch of excellence far beyond any other in the world at that time, and had developed a tradition of expressive playing which suggested many effects to those fortunate enough to compose for it or to enjoy opportunities of hearing it. The first symphonist in France was **Gossec** (1734–1829), whose inspiration came from a visit to Paris of the elder Stamitz in the late 1750s.

There was at this period no settled constitution for the symphonic orchestra (see *Orchestra and Orchestration*). Sometimes it consisted merely of strings and sometimes a pair of flutes, oboes, or horns was added—or all of these, with perhaps bassoons as well (clarinets came a little later). Usually the traditional harpsichord was a part of the force, provided for by the composer by the use of a 'figured bass' (q.v.); this, whilst it apparently tended to disappear, to some extent lasted on into the next period.

4. The Haydn–Mozart Symphony. Carl Philipp Emanuel Bach (1714–88) is important in the early history of the symphony as in that of the sonata, but the title of 'Father of the Symphony' is usually conceded to Haydn (1732–1809), who as a youth earnestly pored over C. P. E. Bach's works.

Of the 107 symphonies that Haydn wrote, the only ones at all frequently heard today are the twelve written by him for English use (the two Salomon sets of six apiece, 1791 and 1794—Salomon being the London impresario who persuaded Haydn to visit England and to compose for his concerts). These twelve dominate the scene, in spite of the growing interest in his own previous efforts and of those of his contemporaries. The only prior symphonies now at all often performed are the best known

three of Mozart, written just before, in 1788, and one or two others of his.

The reciprocal influences of Haydn and Mozart are very interesting. Haydn, as the elder man by nearly a quarter of a century, had written many symphonies before Mozart became prominent as a composer, and undoubtedly Mozart learnt a good deal from these. Then Mozart wrote the three great symphonies just mentioned (the E flat, the G minor, and the so-called 'Jupiter'—written in three successive months, by the way), and the influence of these is certainly to be seen in the twelve great works of Haydn just referred to.

Looking over the pages of these fifteen symphonies, and considering what they stand for, one is struck at once with the serious intentions of their composers. Earlier symphony composers, and these two composers themselves in some earlier symphonies, had treated the form in a rather conventional and easy-going way, as a means of providing pleasant entertainment. The mood illustrated may be said to have varied from a joyous bonhomie to a tender melancholy. In the works under consideration there is often to be seen a greater depth—a force; also, the workmanship (alike in harmony, form, and orchestration) bears evidence of the highest skill and most thorough care of a devoted craftsman. Especially has the orchestration advanced, so that every instrument now contributes something individual to the effect (see *Orchestration*).

5. Beethoven's Contemporaries and Successors. For the purposes of a brief article such as the present it is not necessary to dwell upon the work of Beethoven's ablest contemporary, his junior, Schubert; or of his greatest legitimate successor in the symphonic line, Brahms, the first of whose four great symphonies was finished fifty-three years after the last of Beethoven's.

With these three composers we find a form that began as the somewhat perfunctory means of cheerful entertainment used as the vehicle for the expression of the most profound emotions (as well as, for relief, the lighter ones), so that today the composition of a symphony is regarded as perhaps the most serious task a composer can undertake.

Weingartner has, with astonishment, called attention to the fact that a mere six decades lie between the composition of Haydn's earliest symphony and Beethoven's latest—'the transformation of a gay pastime into a sublime tragedy'. Since 1824, when the latter work was written, nobody has expressed deeper emotion by means of music—and probably nobody ever will. Beethoven's Ninth Symphony remains the apogee of the orchestral art.

6. The Character of the Various Movements of a Symphony. The chief movement of a symphony, almost invariably the deepest in musical thought and the one which more than any other gives the whole work its character, is the first. It may or may not be preceded by a slow introduction, after which the movement proper (a quick one) is normally in that 'Sonata Form' or 'First Movement' form which is usually employed in the same position in a solo or duet sonata, a string quartet, etc. (see *Sonata* 8 and *Form* 7).

The next movement is usually a slower and expressively lyrical one. It is sometimes in 'Sonata Form' (or some abbreviation or modification of this) and sometimes in air-with-variations or some other form.

The third movement has often (in the Haydn period, at all events) a dance lilt. The number of movements gradually came to be normally four, instead of the original three, by the insertion at this point of that dignified yet light-hearted dance form that was paramount throughout Europe during the latter part of the eighteenth century, the minuet (q.v.). We find the minuet as an occasional part of the symphony as early as the elder Stamitz but Haydn was the first to make much use of it. Not by any means all the Haydn and Mozart symphonies possess a minuet, but most of those regularly heard have one, and in every case it is a charming feature of the work. With Beethoven the minuet is gradually freed from its dancing conventions and becomes the often unrestrained scherzo.

The fourth and last movement is a quick one of some considerable length, like the first, but often of lighter calibre—less full of meaning and more recreative, as befits what we may call the dessert course of the menu. It is often in rondo form (see *Form* 9), but it may be in 'Sonata Form', in air-with-variations form, or in any other.

The scheme, it will be seen, provides variety: it enables the composer to express several sides of his temperament and the listener to enjoy some rather widely differing types of musical entertainment—though, of course, there should be a certain homogeneity or correspondence amongst the four movements, so that the symphony may be capable of making an impression as a unity.

7. Later Developments in the Symphony. During the following period certain developments took place in all types of cyclic composition—sonatas, string quartets, symphonies, etc. One of these is the linking of movements by the use of some amount of material common to all of them. Another is the exploitation of literary, dramatic, or pictorial ideas. A good example of the two new principles applied together is Berlioz's 'Fantastic' Symphony, with its sub-title 'Episode in the Life of an Artist'; the scheme of this involves the employment of a 'fixed idea' (*idée fixe*), which is subjected to various modifications in order to adapt itself to the shifting requirements of something approaching a continuous narrative. This is an example of the application of the scheme of 'Programme Music' to what in origin was a purely abstract form.

At this point in the development of the symphony it gave birth to a child—the late nineteenth-century symphonic poem (q.v.), a more flexible form capable of carrying out a literary, dramatic, or pictorial programme with less constraint than that to which its parent was subjected.

As the twentieth century has advanced the symphony has shown a tendency similar to that alluded to under *Sonata* 9, i.e. towards the 'gradual organic growth of a movement from short *motifs* instead of the clear statement of subjects of some length and their subsequent development and recapitulation'.

The straightforward Mozart–Haydn–Beethoven style has, then, been left far behind, so far as contemporary composers are concerned, and a type requiring closer attention on the part of the listener has taken its place—the standard works of the older type fully retaining their interest, however, with both the more and the less sophisticated listening public.

The origin and growth of the symphony have now been sufficiently sketched in the general way appropriate to a book on the present scale, and details unmentioned here can in large measure be filled in by a study of the Historical List given below and by reference to the separate articles upon the chief of the various composers there mentioned.

8. A Historical List of Symphony Composers.

G. B. Sammartini (1698–1775), seventy-two still existing. **W. Friedemann Bach,** son of the greatest Bach (1710–84), nine. **Arne** (1710–78). **C. P. Emanuel Bach,** son of the greatest Bach (1714–88), eighteen. **G. C. Wagenseil** (1715–77). **Johann W. A. Stamitz** (1717–57), forty-five. **Leopold Mozart,** father of the greater composer (1719–87). **Toeschi** (c. 1723–88). **Abel** (1723–87). **Van Malder** (1724–68). **Cannabich** (1731–98), about fifty. **Haydn** (1732–1809), 107—the most important being the twelve of the 'Salomon' sets. **Gossec** (1734–1829), thirty to forty. **Schwindl** (1737–86). **J. Christian Bach**—'English Bach', son of the greatest Bach (1735–82), about fifty. **Michael Haydn,** brother of the greater composer (1737–1806), thirty. **Dittersdorf** (1739–99), about 115, including twelve based on Ovid's 'Metamorphoses'. **Boccherini** (1743–1805), twenty published. **Karl Stamitz,** son of Johann (1745–1801), seventy. **Clementi** (1752–1832), very many—now mostly lost. **Johann Anton Stamitz** (1754–c. 1809), thirteen. **Mozart** (1756–91), over forty, the most admired being the so-called 'Jupiter', the G minor, and the E flat. **Gyrowetz** (1763–1850), sixty—once famous. **Beethoven** (1770–1827), nine—of which the third (or 'Eroica'), the fifth, the seventh, and the ninth (with voices) are the most famous. **Spohr** (1784–1859), ten—including a number with novel ideas and fancy titles, such as the once-popular 'The Consecration of Sound'. **Weber** (1786–1826), two—of no importance. **Schubert** (1797–1828), ten—of which the 'Unfinished' and the C major are the favourites. **Berlioz** (1803–69), four—including the 'Fantastic' Symphony ('Episode in the Life of an Artist'), 'Harold in Italy', with viola obbligato, and 'Romeo and Juliet' (with voices). **Mendelssohn** (1809–47), five published—including the 'Scotch', 'Italian', and 'Reformation'. **Schumann** (1810–56), four—

in B flat, C, E flat, and D minor. **Liszt** (1811–86), two—'Dante' and 'Faust' (both with voices). **Wagner** (1813–83), one—early and unimportant. **Raff** (1822–82), eleven—including 'To the Fatherland', 'In the Alps', and others with fancy titles. **Franck** (1822–90), one. **Bruckner** (1824–96), ten. **Rubinstein** (1829–94), six—including the once-popular 'Ocean'. **Brahms** (1833–97), four—in C minor, D, F, and E minor. **Borodin** (1833–87), three—one being unfinished, however. **Saint-Saëns** (1835–1921), three. **Bizet** (1838–1875), one—first performed 1933. **J. K. Paine** (1839–1906), two—including the once-popular 'Spring'. **Tchaikovsky** (1840–93), six—plus 'Manfred' (a 'programme' symphony). **Dvořák** (1841–1904), nine—including the popular 'New World'. **Rimsky-Korsakof** (1844–1908), three—including the first symphony ever composed by a Russian. **Parry** (1848–1918), five. **D'Indy** (1851–1931), three. **Stanford** (1852–1924), eight. **Cowen** (1852–1935), six. **Chadwick** (1854–1931), three and a Sinfonietta. **Chausson** (1855–99), one. **Sinding** (1856–1941), three. **Elgar** (1857–1934), two. **E. Stillman Kelley** (1857–1944), two. **Mahler** (1860–1911), ten. **Loeffler** (1861–1935), one—in one movement and with men's voices. **Strauss** (1864–1949) three—an early one in F minor, the 'Domestic', and the 'Alpine'. **Sibelius** (1865–1957), seven (see *Sibelius*). **Glazunof** (1865–1936), eight. **Bantock** (1868–1946), three—the 'Hebridean' and two purely choral symphonies (i.e. *a cappella*), 'Atalanta in Calydon' and 'Vanity of Vanities'. **McEwen** (1868–1948), five—including the 'Solway'. **Roussel** (1869–1937). **Hadley** (1871–1937), four. **Scriabin** (1872–1915), five, the third being the 'Divine Poem', the fourth the 'Poem of Ecstasy', and the fifth 'Prometheus' (or 'The Poem of Fire'), the last two not always being considered to be symphonies. **Vaughan Williams** (1872–1958), nine—including 'A Sea Symphony' with voices. **E. Burlingame Hill**, (1872–1960), three. **Alfvén** (1872–1960). **Daniel Gregory Mason** (1873–1953). **Rachmaninof**

(1873–1943), three. **Schönberg** (1874–1951), Chamber Symphony for solo instruments. **Holst** (1874–1934), a Choral Symphony. **Tovey** (1875–1940). **Bloch** (1880–1959), two, of which the second, 'Israel', includes voices. **Miaskovsky** (1881–1950), twen ty-seven. **Zilcher** (1881–1948), five. **Stravinsky** (1882–1971), three (plus the choral–orchestral *Symphony of Psalms* and the work called *Symphonies of Wind Instruments*). **Malipiero** 1882–1973). **Szymanowski** (1882–1937), three. **Bax** (1883–1953), seven. **Dyson** (1883–1964). **Riegger** (1885–1961). **Toch** (1887–1964). **Martinů** (1890–1959). **Jirák** (1891–1972). **Bliss** (1891–1975), 'A Colour Symphony' and 'Morning Heroes', the latter with choir and a reciter. **Prokofief** (1891–1953), seven. **Honegger** (1892–1955). **(Milhaud** (1892–1974). **Goossens** (1893–1962). **B. Wagenaar** (1894–1971). **Moeran** (1894–1950). **Piston**(1894–1976). **Pijper**(1894–1947). **Sowerby** (1895–1968). **Hindemith** (1895–1963). Howard **Hanson** (born 1896). **Gerhard** (1896–1970). **Sessions** (born 1896). **Virgil Thomson** (born 1896). **Cowell** (1897–1965). **Tansman** (born 1897). **Roy Harris** (born 1898). **Randall Thompson** (born 1899). **Chávez** (born 1899). **Křenek** (born 1900). **Antheil** (1900–59). **Copland** (born 1900). **Rubbra** (born 1901). **Walton** (born 1902). **Rawsthorne** (1905–71). **Shostakovich** (1906–75). **William Schuman** (born 1910). **Barber** (born 1910). **Britten** (1913–76). **Irving Fine** (1914–62). **Searle** (born 1915). **Persichetti** (born 1915). **Diamond** (born 1915). **Gardner** (born 1917). **Rochberg** (born 1918). **Bernstein** (born 1918). **Fricker** (born 1920). **Bergsma** (born 1921). **Mennin** (born 1923).

Necessarily this list is but a roughly selected one. No two authorities would agree as to the names it should admit in its later portion. It is, however, sufficiently representative to give a general idea of the activity of symphony writers at various periods—which is its aim.

For a remark on the length of symphonies at various periods see *Form 2*.

SYMPSON. See *Simpson*.

SYNAESTHESIA. See *Colour and Music*.

SYNAGOGUE AND MUSIC. See *Jewish Music 2*.

SYNCOPATION is a displacement of either the beat or the normal accent of a piece of music.

Regular accent is a feature of most music since about 1600 (see article *Rhythm*). Recurring beats are felt and these group themselves irresistibly into twos or threes, the first of each group making itself felt as such by a slight extra stress. If, the feeling of regularity being thus established in the mind of the listener, irregularity is momentarily introduced, that is syncopation.

The feeling of regularity may be established by the succession of a number of normal measures, with the result that the listener's mind continues the regular throb or grouping and feels the disturbance of the new throb or grouping superposed on this, as it were; or it may be established and maintained by one part or voice of the music whilst another part or voice conflicts with it; or it may be established by a combination of these two processes,

It is, then, *rhythmic contradiction* that constitutes syncopation. Sometimes the effect of contradiction is brought about by the occurrence of rests on the normally accented parts of the measure, with notes on the unaccented; sometimes by notes being first sounded on the normally unaccented parts of the measure and then merely held on over the normally accented parts; sometimes by the introduction of a stress mark over notes that would normally be unstressed. In any case, the rhythmic effect is the same: there is a shifting of accent.

Syncopation may be applied in such a way as to cause one part or voice to proceed in a different number of beats per measure from the other voices (that is to say, its *actual* measures will be different from theirs, though for convenience the bar-lines are left in the same places).

All composers of all periods have used syncopation, and, being a very simple and natural device of artistry, it often occurs in the folk-song music of certain races. The Scotch Snap (q.v.) is a simple instance of syncopation, though here the normal divisions of the beat, rather than those of the measure, are contradicted. But this is little more than a matter of notation, for a beat is really a sub-measure, just as a measure can be considered merely a beat in that super-measure called the phrase. (It is all a question of taking a smaller or larger unit; see *Rhythm* 3.)

The prevalence of syncopation in African music, and hence in that of the American Negroes, brought about, early in the twentieth century, the existence of a world-wide dance-type, in music of which it is one of the principal elements (see *Ragtime*; *Jazz*).

The following is a conveniently comprehensive example of syncopation (the normal beats and accents being shown below):

MOZART, Sonata for Violin and Piano, No. 40.

Measure 1: A note held over from a normally weak to a normally strong beat—having the effect of a displacement of accent.

Measure 2: Rests filling in the normal beats with notes between—having the effect of a displacement of beat.

Measure 3: Notes sounded before beats and then held over beats—having again the effect of a displacement of beats

Cf. *Accent* 1.

SYNTHÉTISTES. Seven Belgian musicians whose music is 'a synthetized product of clas-sical forms and modern devices'. They are: Marcel Poot (q.v.; born 1901); René Bernier (born 1905); Gaston Brenta (born 1902); François de Bourguignon (born 1890); Théodore Dejoncker (born 1894); Jules Strens (born 1892), and Maurice Schoemaeker (born 1890).

SYRINX. See *Panpipes.*

SYVSPRING (literary 'Seven jumps'). A popular dance of Jutland.

SZYMANOWSKI, KAROL (p. 209, pl. **41**, 4). Born at Timoshovska, in the government of Eisavetgrad, in the Ukraine, in 1882 and died at Lausanne, Switzerland, in 1937, aged fifty-four.

Although born in Russian territory, he was of Polish race and studied at Warsaw, becoming Principal of the Conservatory there in 1927. Many assert him to be the greatest composer of Polish descent since Chopin.

He began by writing in a somewhat Chopin-esque manner, as did also the Russian Scriabin (q.v.), whose idiom for a time attracted him. Like both these composers, he was a masterly pianist and in his writing showed a perfect understanding of the powers of his instrument. In his later works he approached polytonality or even atonality (see *Harmony* 17, 18).

There are Polish and also oriental elements in some of his works. In general, though serious in import, they have a certain grace and lightness of texture. They include symphonies, symphonic poems, two violin concertos, two operas, chamber music, piano music (see reference under *Mazurka*), choral music, and songs.

See *Poland* (end).

T

TABARRO, IL (Puccini). See *Trittico, Il.*

TABATIÈRE À MUSIQUE. See *Mechanical Reproduction of Music* 7.

TABLATURE. (Fr. *Tablature*; Ger. *Tabulatur*; It. *Intavolatura*). Primitively the word means the representation of music by means of tabular forms, i.e. the bringing of the several 'voices' or 'parts' of the harmony into visual relation with one another—in other words, into score.

There have been very many ways of doing this, and after a time a distinction came about between those that used notes, which are regarded as systems of *notation*, and those that used (solely or partially) figures, letters, and similar signs, which are spoken of as systems of *tablature*.

These latter systems were very numerous from the mid-fifteenth century to the eighteenth and then they gave way almost entirely before the notation as we have it today. Tablature systems now linger only on the outskirts of musical art; simple tablature methods of learning easy instruments, limited in scope (e.g. ukeleles, zithers, ocarinas, mandolines, and the like), are often supplied in the small music shops of the poorer neighbourhoods: 'Vamping Tutors' for the pianoforte also sometimes use an order of tablature. Tablature has become, then, the exclusive province of two classes of musician, the learned one who is making a study of the old music for organ, virginals, lute, etc., and the ignorant one who is trying to acquire the ability to draw some sort of a tune out of some sort of an instrument.

During the high period of the use of tablature different countries used different systems, and the tablatures for the various instruments differed also. There was an organ tablature in use in Germany right down to Bach's day.

Some systems indicated (by either figures or letters) the actual pitch of the notes to be played, assimilating themselves in a degree to our notation so that it is doubtful whether the word 'tablature' is well applied to them. Others indicated the string, fret, hole in wind instrument, organ key, etc., and (often) the finger to be used. Frequently a stave something like the present one was the basis, and the lines or spaces represented the strings, finger holes, etc. (see p. 673, pl. **114**. 4; also p. 609, pl. **107**. 6).

A true tablature rather directed the player *what to do with his fingers* than what notes to play.

See *Lute* 3; *Viol Family* 4 c; *Wales* 4; and for 'Tablature' in a different sense (the rules of the Mastersingers) see *Minstrels*, etc. 8.

TABLE (of bowed instruments). See *Belly.*

TABLE MUSIC. See *Tafelmusik.*

TABLE PIANO. See *Pianoforte* 6.

TABOR, TABORET. See *Percussion Family* 3 l, 4 c, 5 l; *Recorder Family* 3 c.

TABORITE BODY. See *Bohemia.*

TABOUROT, JEHAN (otherwise 'Thoinot Arbeau'). See *Dance* 6 a and passing references under *Morris*; *Romanesca*; *God save the Queen* 2, 4.

TABRET. See *Percussion Family* 3 m.

TACERE (It.). 'To be silent.' So *Tace*, 'is silent'; *Tacciono*, 'are silent'. Often the Latin forms are used: *Tacet, Tacent.*

TAFELKLAVIER (Ger., literally 'table-keyboard'). The virginals or the spinet (either); for these see *Harpsichord* 3, 4.

TAFELMUSIK (Ger.). 'Table Music.' Music to be heard during a meal time. A cantata or opera might be composed for 'table' use on a special occasion but in general the term is attached to such music as the long light suites of Telemann (q.v.) so entitled.

TAGLIONI. See *Ballet* 4, 9; *Pas de Quatre.*

TAILLE. See *Oboe Family* 4 e.

TAILLEFER (eleventh century). See *Minstrels* 2.

TAILLEFERRE, GERMAINE. See *France* 11; p. 388, pl. **65**. 4.

TAILLER, SIMON. See *Scotland* 5.

TAKT (Ger.). (*a*) 'Time', (*b*) 'beat', (*c*) 'measure' (i.e. bar). So *Im Takt*, 'in time' (*A tempo*); *Ein Takt wie vorher zwei*, 'one beat as previously two' (one beat in the time of the previous two beats).

A good many compounds and derivatives of *Takt* are met with; e.g. *Taktart*, 'time-species', i.e. number of beats to a measure—duple, triple, etc.; *Taktfest*, 'time-firm' (in steady time); *Takt halten*, 'to hold [keep] time'; *Taktieren*, to 'beat time'; *Taktschlag*, 'time-stroke' (beat); *Taktzeichen*, 'time-sign' (signature); *Taktwechsel*, 'time-change'; *Taktmässig*, 'time-moderated' (generally meaning the same as *Tempo comodo*, q.v.); *Taktnote*, 'bar-note' (semibreve); *Taktpause*, 'measure-rest' (bar-rest); *Taktstock*, 'time-stick', i.e. baton; *Taktstrich*, 'bar-stroke' (bar-line); *Taktig*, 'bar-ish', in such connexion as *Drei-taktig*, 'three-bar-ish', i.e. in three-bar [three-measure] phrases.

TALBOT, RICHARD, EARL OF TYRCONNEL (1630–91). See *Lilliburlero.*

TALEADAS. The *Seguidillas Taleadas* (see *Seguidilla*) is a vigorous type, showing the influence of the cachucha (q.v.).

TALES OF HOFFMANN (Offenbach). Paris in 1881. Libretto by Barbier and Carré, based upon stories by E. T. A. Hoffmann (q.v.).

PROLOGUE

SCENE: *Luther's Inn in Nuremberg*

Councillor **Lindorf** (*Bass*) loves an opera singer, Stella, but she has once loved the poet **Hoffmann** (*Tenor*), to whom she sends a note asking him to meet her again. Lindorf gains possession of the letter and tries to quarrel with the poet, but the other convivial fellows would rather hear of Hoffmann's love affairs. Each of the acts represents one of these.

ACT I

SCENE: *A Room in the House of the Scientist Dr. Spalanzani*

Spalanzani (*Tenor*) has made an automaton, **Olympia** (*Soprano*), which he passes off as his daughter. Hoffmann falls in love with her, though his friend **Nicklaus** (*Tenor:* or *Soprano*) sees the truth—that Olympia is only a doll. But Hoffmann, blinded by love, cannot see it.

Coppelius (*Bass*), Spalanzani's partner, receives his price for his share in making the doll and departs. Olympia sings to the scientist's guests. Later Coppelius, finding he has been paid in worthless notes, returns, vowing vengeance. He smashes the doll, and only then does poor Hoffmann realize his folly.

ACT II

SCENE: *The Balcony of a Palace at Venice*

Giulietta (*Soprano*), a courtesan, is holding a reception (here comes in the famous 'Barcarolle'). Hoffmann loves her, but she prefers **Schlemil** (*Bass*). Nicklaus warns his friend in vain.

Schlemil is in the power of the magician **Dapertutto** (*Bass*), who steals people's shadows and their souls. Giulietta is his agent. She persuades the poet to part with his reflection (and so, she knows, his soul) as the price of her love. In the end Hoffmann kills Schlemil to get the key of the enchantress's door; but as he hastens to her room he sees her floating away in a gondola with—presumably—her next victim.

ACT III

SCENE: *A Room in the House of Councillor Crespel*

Crespel (*Bass*) is the father of **Antonia** (*Soprano*), who has inherited her mother's wonderful voice. But her father has forbidden her to sing, lest she, being delicate, should injure herself. She sings, however, with Hoffmann, to her father's concern, and his anger against the poet.

Now enters **Dr. Miracle** (*Bass*), whom Crespel hates, for he believes that the doctor's potions killed Antonia's mother. Though rebuffed, Miracle insists that Antonia *shall* sing, and by magic art causes a portrait of the mother to come to life and appeal to her daughter to do so. To Miracle's demonic fiddling the girl sings and falls dead. Miracle disappears into the earth, his devilish work done.

EPILOGUE

SCENE: *The Tavern, as in the Prologue*

These, then, are the tales of Hoffmann's loves and frustrations. In a final scene, sometimes omitted, Lindorf, who has made Hoffmann drunk, brings in the poet's former love, Stella, in order to disgust her with Hoffmann. This he succeeds in doing, and carries her off in triumph, while the poor poet lies in a stupor.

TALLIS, THOMAS (p. 164, pl. **33**. 2). Born probably between 1505 and 1510 and died at Greenwich in 1585, 'very aged', as he described himself eight years earlier. Many of the circumstances of his life are unknown, or only arrived at by conjecture. He was on the staff of Waltham Abbey, near London, probably as organist, but necessarily lost his position at the dissolution of the monasteries under Henry VIII.

He was a Gentleman of the Chapel Royal (q.v.) under that king and under Elizabeth, and the latter gave him, jointly with Byrd, a monopoly of printing music and music paper (see *Printing of Music* 1; *Publishing of Music* 4): at this time these two musicians were also serving jointly as organists of the Chapel Royal; in 1575 they published a book of their motets bearing a dedication to their royal mistress.

He arranged in harmony the plainsong responses of the English church service as adapted by Merbecke (q.v.), and his version is still in constant use, as is his famous setting of the Canticles 'in D minor' or 'in the Dorian mode' (see *Modes*). His admirable anthems were some of them written to Latin words and some to English words. His church music exists in great quantity and has been published, in the Carnegie Edition of Tudor Church Music, by the Oxford University Press. There is a motet in forty parts (cf. *In Nomine*, end). A little string music and keyboard music also remains.

The ever-popular hymn tune *Tallis's Canon* (see below) is an adaptation of a tune of his, and another tune, usually called simply *Tallis* (see *Form* 7), is in most hymn-books.

Cf. *Anglican Chant* 3; *Anthem* 1; *Plainsong* 4; *Responses; Common Prayer; Vaughan Williams.*

TALLIS'S CANON. This well-known tune dates from about 1567. It is one of the nine tunes (one in each of the eight modes, q.v., with an additional one) which Tallis (see above) composed for Archbishop Parker's metrical *Whole Psalter*, where it is attached to the 67th Psalm. The tenor and treble are in canon in the octave throughout. Nowadays the treble leads and the tenor follows at a measure's distance; in the original the tenor (then looked upon as the chief part in vocal harmony) led and the treble followed. The tune was, by repetition of each line, twice as long.

The words now long associated with the tune are those of Bishop Ken's evening hymn for the Winchester College boys, 'Glory to Thee, my God, this night' (1692). The earliest connexion of this hymn with the tune, in print, is 1732.

TALON (Fr.). 'Heel'—used for the nut end of the bow of the violin, etc.

TAMBORA. See mention under *Cittern*.

TAMBOUR (Fr.). Drum (see *Percussion Family*).

TAMBOUR DE BASQUE (Fr.). Tambourine (see *Percussion Family* 3 m, 4 c, 5 m.)

TAMBOUR DE PROVENCE (Fr.). See below.

TAMBOURIN. (1) The word 'Tambourin' in French usually implies the tabor: *Tambourin de Provence* and *Tambourin genre Watteau* are simply elaborations of this name. *Tambour de Provence* is the same thing (see *Percussion Family* 3 l, 4 c, 5 l). But *Tambourin de Béarn* is a sort of small dulcimer with its strings tuned only to the keynote and its fifth.

(2) Unfortunately the German and Italian languages use 'Tambourin' in two senses—either 'Tabor' or 'Tambourine' (see *Percussion Family* 3 l m, 4 c, 5 l m).

(3) The word is also the name of an old French (Provençal) dance, in which either of the instruments mentioned under (1) was used with, also, the galoubet (see *Recorder Family* 3 c). It is in two-in-a-measure time. Composers sometimes use the style for instrumental pieces, in which case the bass is generally largely in repeated notes in imitation of the percussion instrument—tonic pedal (see *Pedal*), with some dominant pedal variety, or a double pedal of the two notes. A harpsichord example by Rameau is very well known to pianists; he used this in *Les Fêtes d'Hébé*, and he has others in his famous operas *Castor and Pollux* (1737), *Dardanus* (1739), etc. In some cases Rameau, after having a tambourin played, has it sung.

TAMBOURINE. See *Percussion Family* 3 m, 4 c, 5 k.

TAMBOUR MILITAIRE (Fr.). Side drum. See *Percussion Family* 3 i, 4 b, 5 i.

TAMBURIN (Ger.), **TAMBURINO** (It.). Tabor or tambourine (either). See *Percussion Family* 3 l m, 4 c, 5 l m.

TAMBURO BASCO (It.). Literally 'Basque drum', i.e. the tambourine (see *Percussion Family* 3 m, 4 c, 5 m).

TAMBURO GRANDE or TAMBURO GROSSO, or GRAN TAMBURO (It.). Bass drum (see *Percussion Family* 3 k, 4 b, 5 k).

TAMBURO MILITARE (It.). Snare drum, side drum (see *Percussion Family* 3 i, 4 b, 5 i).

TAMBURONE (It.). Bass drum (see *Percussion Family* 3 k, 4 b, 5 k).

TAMBURO PICCOLO (It.). Literally 'little

drum', i.e. the side drum (see *Percussion Family* 3 i, 4 b, 5 i).

TAMBURO RULLANTE (It.). Tenor drum (see *Percussion Family* 3 j, 4 b, 5 j).

TAMPON (Fr.). Drum-stick. The *Tampon double* is a double-headed stick used occasionally with the bass drum for thunder effects.

TAM-TAM. Gong. See *Percussion Family* 3 p, 4 c, 5 p.

TÄNDELEI (Ger.). Same as *Badinage* (q.v.).

TÄNDELND. 'Playfully.'

TANEIEF (Taneieff, Taneyef, Taneyeff, Taneïew, etc.). Uncle and nephew.

(1) ALEXANDER. Born in St. Petersburg in 1850 and died there in 1918, aged sixty-eight. He held high office in the civil service of his country, studied music with Rimsky-Korsakof and others, and composed symphonies, string quartets, and other things.

(2) SERGE (= SERGEI IVANOVITCH). Born in the government of Vladimir in 1856 and died in Moscow in 1915, aged fifty-eight. He studied at the Conservatory of Moscow under Nicholas Rubinstein and Tchaikovsky, the latter of whom he succeeded as professor of counterpoint and composition, and the former, later, as the chief professor of piano and director. He had a great reputation as theorist and as pianist, and in the latter capacity toured in many countries; he gave especial study to the interpretation of Tchaikovsky, who had a great admiration and affection for him.

He wrote four symphonies, six string quartets, a piano quintet and a piano quartet, two string trios, several songs, the operatic trilogy *Orestes* (on the subject of the tragedy of Aeschylus), and two cantatas, *John of Damascus* and *After the reading of a Psalm*. As theorist, he was the author of two big treatises on invertible counterpoint and canon. Scriabin, Rachmaninof, and others of the Russian composers of the generation or two following him were his pupils.

See reference under *Russia* 6.

TANEYEF, TANEYEFF. See *Taneief*, above.

TANGENT. See *Clavichord* 2.

TANGLEWOOD. See *Festival* 2.

TANGO. An Argentine dance resembling the Cuban Habanera (q.v.), with which it has a common rhythmic figure. The dance called *Habanera del café*, which became popular during the Spanish-American War, was the prototype of the Tango. Stravinsky stylized the Tango in a movement of his *Histoire du soldat*.

TANNAHILL, ROBERT. See *Jessie, the Flower of Dunblane*.

TANNENBAUM. See *Maryland, my Maryland*; *Red Flag*.

TANNHÄUSER AND THE CONTEST OF SONG AT THE WARTBURG

(Wagner). Produced at Dresden in 1845. Libretto by the composer.

ACT I

SCENE 1: *The Abode of Venus (Venusberg). Time, the Thirteenth Century*

The knightly minstrel, **Tannhäuser** (*Tenor*), has for a year given himself up to **Venus** (*Soprano*), the Goddess of Love. Now he is yearning for the old pleasures of earth. She scornfully bids him begone, warning him that earth's joys will prove hollow.

SCENE 2: *A Valley by the Wartburg*

A Young Shepherd (*Soprano*) sings of spring. Pilgrims pass, going to Rome. Tannhäuser feels his guilt, and determines to seek heavenly pardon.

The **Landgrave of Thuringia** (*Bass*), with **Wolfram von Eschenbach** (*Baritone*) and other knights, his former associates, recognize him, remind him that Elizabeth, the Landgrave's niece, faithfully awaits him, and persuade him to rejoin them.

ACT II

SCENE: *The Hall of Song*

Elizabeth (*Soprano*) joyfully greets the returned knight. The Landgrave holds a contest of song; the prize to be his niece's hand. Wolfram, who also loves Elizabeth, sings of virtuous love, but in Tannhäuser's mind works the poison of Venus, and his shameless extolling of her love drives from the hall every woman save Elizabeth, who intervenes to protect Tannhäuser from the angry knights. The Landgrave, finding him penitent, orders him to seek, in Rome, the Pope's forgiveness.

ACT III

SCENE: *The Valley by the Wartburg, near Sunset*

Wolfram, who has put aside his own love for Elizabeth, comes with her to meet the pilgrims returning from Rome. They cannot find Tannhäuser, and Elizabeth sadly goes away. Wolfram, who has a foreboding of the end, waits on, and after a while Tannhäuser, ragged and weary, comes by. The Pope has told him that his sin can no more be forgiven than the staff he carries can burgeon with leaves. Hope is dead, and Tannhäuser is going to seek Venus once more. She appears to him in a vision, which the invocation of the name of Elizabeth dispels.

A funeral procession approaches, bearing the body of Elizabeth, whose heart has broken in sorrow and pity. Tannhäuser for the last time embraces her, and dies. Pilgrims enter, carrying the Pope's staff, which has put forth leaves and flowers: Tannhäuser's sin is purged.

See also *Ballet* 7; *Opera* 21 k.

TANSMAN, ALEXANDRE (p. 209, pl. **41**. 3). Born at Łódź, Poland, in 1897. He first came prominently before the public at a concert of his music in Paris in 1920, and he made that city the centre of his activities, thence travelling very extensively to perform (as a pianist) his works and to conduct orchestral performances of them. From 1941 to 1946 he was in the United States, then returning to Paris. His compositions include seven symphonies, several piano concertos, string quartets, songs, operas, ballets, etc. Both Polish and French characteristics are found in his style.

See *Jazz* 5.

TANS'UR, WILLIAM (1706–83). English provincial teacher of psalmody, composer and editor of psalm tunes, author of popular, useful (and rather odd) theoretical treatises, which had a wide sale not only in Britain but also in America. See *Pitch* 6 a; *Organ* 8; *Voluntary* (end); *Monochord*; *Dictionaries* 2.

TANT (Fr.). 'As much' (or sometimes simply 'much').

TANTO (It.). 'So much', 'as much', 'too much'. *Non tanto*, after an adjective or adverb, is a frequent expression, meaning 'But don't overdo it!' E.g. *Allegro non tanto*. *Tantino* is the diminutive— 'a very little'.

TANT SOIT PEU (Fr.). 'Ever so little.'

TANTUM ERGO SACRAMENTUM (in a familiar English version, 'Therefore we before Him bending, this great sacrament revere'). These are the opening words of the last section of St. Thomas Aquinas's Corpus Christi hymn, *Pange lingua* (q.v.). It is used in other services than that of Corpus Christi and especially in that of Benediction (q.v.). It has its own plainsong, but has often been set by composers.

TANZ, TÄNZE (Ger.). 'Dance', 'dances'. *Tänzchen* is a diminutive.

TAP BOX. See *Chinese Wood Block*.

TAP-DANCING is the present-day name for what was sometimes formerly known as 'Stepdancing' (though that term has also a wider sense; see *Figure* 2). Its merit is measured by the taps on the floor (indeed in competitions in the North of England the adjudicators used to be placed behind a screen). It may be said that the function and value of the taps are somewhat akin to those of the use of the castanets in Spanish dances. At the outset this kind of dance was performed in clogs, but it is now performed in the lightest of shoes, with toes and heels treated in some way to make their sounds audible (not noisy but audible).

TAPE-RECORDING. See *Gramophone* 4.

TARANTELLA (It.), **TARANTELLE** (Fr.). In the heel of Italy is the seaport Taranto. In the surrounding country is found a spider, hence called the Tarantula. The bite of this spider was supposed to cause a certain disease, hence called Tarantism. The malady was supposed to be curable by the patient's use of a particular very lively dance, hence called Tarantella. (It may be, however, that the spider and the dance were independently named after their place of origin, and that the similarity of the names thus given them set up in the Italian peasant mind a direct connexion between them.)

It has long been found that the bite of the spider is comparatively harmless, and modern research in the psychology of the subconscious suggests that the disease is merely hysterical: in any case a belief in the remedial power of music, or dancing, or anything else, if strongly enough held, might well be effective, on the principles of auto-suggestion.

Pepys, in 1662, records his meeting with a gentleman who 'is a great traveller and, speaking of the tarantula, he says that all the harvest long (about which time they are most busy) there are fiddlers go up and down the fields everywhere, in expectation of being hired by those that are stung'.

Three centuries ago there were great communal epidemics of tarantism and the musicians had a profitable period doing the work of the medical men. Such outbreaks had not totally ceased in the early twentieth century when the well-known London singing teacher, Albert Visetti, reported in a London paper how on a visit to his native Dalmatia he had seen 'the streets of the town teeming with dancers', all the people 'leaving their work and trades to give themselves up to unbridled dance'. In one town the cemetery, he says, was 'the principal centre of infection'. Here one could see 'girls, women, sick people of all ages, men falling to the floor as though they were real epileptics, some swallowing stones, pieces of broken glass, and burning coals'. The dance was 'conducted by an "abbot", who stood on a tomb and followed the scene from this point of vantage'. And then 'as a finale the abbot, with rare cleverness, would perform his favourite trick, the *saut de carpe* [somersault], which aroused in the onlookers an incredible enthusiasm'.

For Stephen Storace's remarkable account of his cure of a sufferer on the point of expiry in an Italian street, and a reproduction of the tune he was called upon to play, see the *Gentleman's Magazine* of September 1753 (partially reprinted in the *Oxford Junior Companion to Music*, s.v. 'Tarantella').

In the nineteenth century, whilst these occasional outbreaks of tarantism still occurred and the traditional remedy was applied, musicians made more money out of tarantellas by their merits as compositions than by their utility as therapeutic agents. Auber, Weber, Liszt, Chopin, Heller, Thalberg, Cui, Dargomijsky, and dozens of less important composers wrote tarantellas, the common features of all of which were six-eight time, great rapidity, and an approach to the *moto perpetuo*. The salterello (q.v.) is a similar type. Mendelssohn ends his 'Italian' Symphony with a movement that partakes of both.

Tunes recorded as curing tarantism in the seventeenth century are in common time and in a totally different style. A book of 1742, *La Théologie des insectes*, mentions a tune called *L' Air turchesca* as then the favourite curative tune of the Italians. Probably it does not matter what music is used provided one perspires freely in a mood of faith.

The American insect called 'Tarantula' is no relation of the Italian one.

TA-RA-RA-BOOM-DE-AY. During a fairly long period (from about 1890 onwards) the most popular street song in the English language, spreading widely, so that one could hear it sung and whistled all over the world. Its authorship and composition have been claimed for several individuals—Theodore Metz (responsible also for *There'll be a Hot Time in the Old Town To-night*), Richard Morton (died 1921), and Henry Sayers (died New York 1932).

TARBOUKA. A flowerpot-shaped drum from North Africa, used by Berlioz in the Slave Dance in his *The Trojans*.

TARDO, TARDA (It., masc., fem.). 'Slow.' So *Tardamente*, 'slowly'; *Tardando, Tardantemente*, 'slowing' (gradually); *Tardato*, 'slowed' (gradually).

TARLTON, RICHARD (d. 1588). Famous comic actor of Queen Elizabeth's court—and probably Shakespeare's Yorick. See *Jig*, and p. 881, pl. **148.** 2.

TAROGATO. See *Clarinet Family* 4 h; p. 481, pl. **84.** 8.

TAROLE (Tarolle) or **TAROLE GRÉGOIRE.** See *Percussion* 5 i.

TARP, SVEND ERIK (born 1908). See *Scandinavia* 2.

TÁRREGA (or **Tárrega Eixea**), FRANCISCO. See *Guitar*. Portrait, p. 977, pl. **164.** 4.

TARTINI, GIUSEPPE (p. 1096, pl. **181.** 2). Born at Pirano in 1692 and died at Padua in 1770, aged seventy-seven. He was the son of a wealthy nobleman and was educated by turns for the Church, for the law, and for the army, becoming moreover, meanwhile, a champion fencer and a skilful violinist.

He secretly married and, pursued by an angry cardinal, escaped to Rome in the disguise of a monk. He then spent a period of peace and study in hiding in the monastery of Assisi, and there discovered (but could not explain) the acoustical phenomenon of the 'third' sound or 'resultant tone', also called 'difference tone' or 'Tartini's tone'. He, further, invented improvements in violin strings and the violin bow, and, in imitation of a visitant who appeared to him in dream, composed his celebrated sonata called *The Devil's Trill*. Then, when he was playing the violin at a service, a careless ecclesiastic pulled aside the curtain that hid him, which led to his discovery, his forgiveness by the cardinal, and his return.

A very glorious career as a violinist, teacher of violinists, director of music, composer, and theorist followed, and in his house in Padua students of all nations sat at his feet.

See *Sonata* 2; *Violin Family* 4, 5; *Acoustics* 10; *Recitative*; *Misattributed Compositions*; *Bohemia*; *Malipiero*.

TASTE, TASTEN (Ger.). 'Key', 'keys' (in the sense of the finger-keys of a keyboard instrument).

TASTE IN MUSIC. See *Quality in Music* 7; *Church Music* 2.

TASTIERA (It.). This has the same two meanings as *Tasto*, below. Thus *Sulla Tastiera = Sul Tasto*. For *Tastiera per luce* see *Colour and Music* 11.

TASTO, TASTI (It., sing., plur.). (*a*) 'Key', 'keys', in the sense of the finger-keys of a keyboard instrument. Hence the expression 'Tasto solo' in old music with a figured bass (q.v.), meaning 'Play the key alone', i.e. the finger-key of the note marked, without adding chords by playing other finger-keys above it. In other words, the bass momentarily becomes a mere melodic part.

(*b*) *Tasto* also means the fingerboard of a violin, etc. Thus *Sul Tasto*, 'on the fingerboard', means that one is to bow on or near this.

TATE.

(1) **NAHUM** (1652–1715). Minor poet and Poet Laureate, associate of Purcell. Collaborator with Brady in a famous metrical version of psalms.

See *Hymns and Hymn Tunes* 5, 17 e, xix; *Old Hundredth*; *Publishing* 5; *Dido and Aeneas*.

(2) **PHYLLIS (MARGARET DUNCAN)**. Born at Gerrard's Cross, Bucks., in 1911. She was trained at the Royal Academy of Music. Amongst her output are three operas, a Concerto for Saxophone and Strings, a string quartet, a sonata for clarinet and cello, and much chamber music for instruments and voices. She is the wife of Alan Frank (q.v.).

See *Clarinet* 6; *Opera* 24 f (1960).

TATTOO. The music of bugles and drums recalling soldiers to their barracks at night. In the British Army it lasts for twenty minutes, beginning with the fanfare called the *First Post* and ending with that called the *Last Post*—which latter makes, also, the very impressive conclusion of a military funeral.

TAUBERT, WILHELM (in full, Karl Gottfried Wilhelm). Born at Berlin in 1811 and died there in 1891, aged seventy-nine. Pianist and conductor, and voluminous and graceful composer, praised by Mendelssohn, he is occasionally recalled to audiences today by some of his songs.

TAUBMANN. See *Electric* 1 d.

TAUSCH, JULIUS. Born at Dessau in 1827 and died at Berlin in 1895. He was conductor of orchestras in several German cities and a composer of orchestral and other works including a concerto for kettledrums and orchestra and a march and polonaise for the same combination.

See *Concerto* 6 b (1827).

TAUSIG, KARL (p. 800, pl. **137.** 7). Born at Warsaw in 1841 and died at Leipzig in 1871, aged twenty-nine. He was a member of the Liszt circle and one of the most agile athletes who ever touched the piano keyboard. He knew by heart (and here the word implies affection) the complete classical repertory, and showed his admiration for Bach, Scarlatti, Weber, Chopin, and other great men by 'transcribing' their works—naturally with added difficulties and 'effectivenesses'. He was one of the bold supporters of the fighting Wagner. His piano studies are still in use.

See reference under *Pianoforte Playing* 6.

TAVAN, ÉMILE. Born at Aix-en-Provence in 1849 and died at Gassicourt-près-Menthes, Département Seine-et-Oise, in 1930, aged eighty-one. He was the world's most active and most popular 'arranger' of masterpieces for performance by orchestras smaller than and otherwise different from those their creator had in view. In this capacity he has contributed notably to the pleasure of the patrons of seaside piers, cafés, cinemas, and other places of amusement. It is said that he was the inventor of the ingenious device of so laying out a score that the music would sound more or less complete provided that any reasonable number of instruments included in it happened to be present.

He was also the author of a *Practical Treatise of Orchestration*. For some time he was administrator of the French Society of Authors, and for nearly twenty years Mayor of Menthes.

TAVERNER, JOHN (p. 164, pl. **33.** 1). Born about 1495 and died at Boston, in Lincolnshire, in 1545, aged about fifty. He was Master of the Children of Cardinal College (now Christ Church), Oxford. Being accused, with others, of heresy, he was thrown by the founder of the college, Wolsey, into a cellar 'with a deep cave under the ground of the same Colledge, where their salt fyshe was layde, so that through the fylthe stincke therof, they were all infected'. However, he was pardoned by Wolsey, 'being but a Musitian'.

After three or four years at Oxford he forsook music, and settled in Boston, where, apparently, he was one of Thomas Cromwell's chief agents in the suppression of the monasteries and the martyrdom of religious opponents. He had, however, before this, composed much fine church music, and it has been published in the Carnegie Edition of Tudor Church Music by the Oxford University Press.

His work, though it abounds in technical ingenuities of the Flemish type (see *Belgium* 1), is virile and personal.

See *Mass* 5; *In Nomine*.

TAVERNS. See *Inns and Taverns as Places of Music-Making.*

TAYLOR.

(1) See *Coleridge-Taylor*.

(2) **DEEMS**—in full Joseph Deems (p. 1060, pl. **173.** 5). Born in New York in 1885 and died there in 1966, aged eighty. He composed some music for chorus, the fanciful orchestral suite *Through the Looking-Glass*, and other light orchestral works, and operas produced at the Metropolitan Opera House, New York—*The*

King's Henchman (1926) and *Peter Ibbetson* (1931). He also served as a New York music critic and engaged in radio and film activities.

See references under *Jazz* 5; *Opera* 24 f (1942).

(3) MESSRS. (Bellfounders). See *Bell* 1.

TCHAIKOVSKY (Tschaikowsky, Chaykovski, Chaikovsky, etc.), PETER ILICH (p. 897, pl. **154.** 6). Born in the government of Viatka in 1840 and died at St. Petersburg in 1893, aged fifty-three. Like so many of the Russian composers he began life as a civil servant. At twenty-three he gave up his official position and, in poverty, devoted himself entirely to music. He studied at the Conservatory of St. Petersburg under Anton Rubinstein, to whose moral and practical support he was long indebted.

When nearing his thirties he came under the influence of Balakiref and Rimsky-Korsakof, but he was never in full sympathy with the group of 'The Five' (see *Russia* 5, 6), of which they were the leading members. The sensitiveness and excitability of his temperament, as freely expressed in his music, are typically Russian, but he had no strong national aspirations, nor did he so often as his elder contemporaries seek to use national folk tune as his material or to adopt a Russian literary basis for his composition (cf. *Scriabin*).

His melodic vein, brilliant orchestral colour, and strong emotional expression quickly captured the ear of audiences in Britain and the United States, and in those countries, as in some others, he was the first Russian composer to become familiar to the public.

Amongst his works are ten operas, six symphonies, symphonic poems, suites, three piano concertos, a violin concerto, pieces for the violin and the violoncello, three ballets, three string quartets, a piano trio, a great many songs and small piano compositions.

His life includes some curious incidents, as, for instance, a marriage followed by a separation after only eleven weeks, his strange relationship with the wealthy widow, Nadezhda von Meck, whom he never once met (though they once passed in the street), yet who was for years his best friend, freeing him to devote himself to composition by the grant of a yearly allowance and entertaining him hospitably (in her absence) on her country estate.

His death came from imprudence. During a cholera epidemic, despite the warnings of friends who were present, he drank unboiled water and within a week was dead.

Tchaikovsky's Symphonies are as follows: No. 1, in G minor (op. 13, 1867); known as *Winter Dream*. No. 2, in C minor (op. 17, 1873); known as the *Little Russian* one. No. 3 in D, (op. 29, 1875); known as the *Polish*. No. 4, in F minor (op. 36, 1878). No. 5, in E minor (op. 64, 1888). No. 6, in B minor (op. 74, 1893); known as the *Pathetic*. There is also the *Manfred Symphony* (op. 58, 1885), which can be considered rather as a tone-poem, and is not numbered amongst the symphonies proper.

Tchaikovsky's Concertos are as follows: PIANOFORTE. No. 1, B flat minor (op. 23, 1875). No. 2, G (1880, revised 1893). No. 3, E flat (op. 75, left incomplete; the *Andante and Finale*, op. 79, belong to this work).

VIOLIN. D (op. 35, 1878).

Amongst Tchaikovsky's operas, *Eugene Onegin* (1878) and *The Queen of Spades* (1890) are very popular in Russia, and to some extent elsewhere. *Romeo and Juliet* (1870) and *Francesca da Rimini* (1876) are the best known of his tone poems. The Overture *1812* is very much played. The three ballets, *The Swan Lake* (1876), *The Sleeping Beauty* (1889), and *The Nutcracker* (1892) enjoy great popularity everywhere. Also popular is the *Italian Capriccio* (op. 45, 1880).

See *Arensky*; *Ballet* 6; *Bortniansky*; *Catoire*; *Chamber Music* 6, *Period* III (1840); *Cinematograph*; *Concerto* 6 b (1840); *Greek Church* 5; *Criticism* 6; *Knorr*; *Mazurka*; *Miaskovsky*; *Opera* 24 e (1879–90); *Percussion* 2 d, 4 c e (Celeste, Gong); *Reed-Organ Family* 5; *Russia* 6; *Suite* 7; *Taneief, S.*; *Waltz*; *Concert* 6.

TCHARDACHE. See *Czardas.*

TCHEREPNIN (Tcherepnine, Cheryepnin, etc.), Father and Son.

(1) NICHOLAS. Born in St. Petersburg in 1873 and died at Issy-les-Moulineaux in 1945. He was prominent as conductor in St. Petersburg and Paris, in which latter city he was attached to the Diaghilef ballet, then touring with it (1909–14). After a period in Russia proper he became head of the Conservatory of Tiflis, Georgia, and then (1921) lived in Paris. He composed ballets, operas, symphonies, symphonic poems, etc.

Cf. *Coq d'Or* (end).

(2) ALEXANDER (p. 913, pl. **156.** 6). Born in St. Petersburg in 1899 and died in Paris in 1977. He was son of the above and, like him, made Paris his headquarters. He composed symphonies, concertos, sonatas, and other things. In some of his later compositions he made use of a nine-note scale, consisting of three progressions of a semitone, tone, and semitone. He toured extensively as a piano recitalist. In 1949 he became instructor in theory at De Paul University, Chicago.

See *Horn Family* 4; *Scales* 12; *Concerto* 6 c (1909).

T.C.L. Trinity College of Music, London. See *Schools of Music; Degrees and Diplomas.*

TE. See *Si.*

TEACHERS OF MUSIC. See *Profession* 9.

TEACHING. See *Education; Composition* 13; *Singing; Pianoforte Playing; Appreciation.*

TECHNIQUE. As the word is used by musicians it means the skill necessary for execution as distinct from the mind expressed in 'interpretation'. So we speak of a pianist's technique, meaning his suppleness and speed in the use of wrists, fingers, feet in pedalling, etc., and of the technique of composition, meaning ability in harmony, counterpoint, orchestration, and general craftsmanship. Obviously a pianist might possess a perfect technique yet be a bad performer (which not infrequently happens), and a composer a

PLATE 167

TCHAIKOVSKY MUSES

By Batt

HE nears his end and, with the sensitiveness and tendency to periods of melancholy introspection natural to him, he perhaps has some instinctive knowledge of it.

His ten Operas, six Symphonies, four Concertos, Ballets, Chamber Music, Piano Compositions, and Songs have carried his name over the world and won appreciation by an un-usually wide public; indeed, few serious composers have reached a wider—for, apart from the qualities that appeal to cultured musicians, his works, by their tuneful melodies, their impressive harmonies, and their piquant orchestration have in them something that makes them readily accessible to the appreciative capacity of the concert-going or radio-listening multitude.

perfect technique and yet have nothing to express by its means (which, also, is not unknown).

For the technique of composition see *Composition* 8.

TEDESCA. Italian for 'German' (i.e. in the feminine singular—plural *Tedesche*; masculine singular and plural *Tedesco* and *Tedeschi*). The term has been used with different suggestions at different periods. In certain earlier instances *Alla tedesca* ('in the German style') has meant, 'in the style of the Allemande' (q.v.); in certain later ones 'in the style of the German (quick) Waltz' (e.g. 1st movement of Beethoven's Piano Sonata, op. 79; 4th movement of his great String Quartet, op. 130).

TE DEUM LAUDAMUS ('We praise Thee, O God'). The long hymn which constitutes the supreme expression of rejoicing in the Roman Catholic, Anglican, and other Christian Churches. The Roman Catholic Breviary calls it 'the Canticle of Ambrose and Augustine', from the legend that at the baptism of Augustine by Ambrose it was sung antiphonally, extempore, by the two saints. Actually it may have originated in the Gallic Church and its authorship has been put down both to Hilary, Bishop of Poitiers, in the fourth century and Hilary of Arles in the fifth, but in either case it seems as though portions of an older hymn have been taken into it; another ascription, now very generally accepted, is to Nicetas, a Dacian bishop at the opening of the fifth century. But its contents and arrangement clearly indicate that it is not a unity, and probably the minds and hearts of a number of writers of different places and periods express themselves in it.

In the liturgy of the Roman Catholic Church it finds a place as the outpouring of praise at the moment of climax of the service of Matins on the occasion of festivals; in the Anglican Church its English version is a part of the service of Morning Prayer, except when replaced by the *Benedicite* (q.v.).

The ancient traditional plainsong to the Latin hymn is of a very magnificent character; it has a great popularity amongst the peasantry of Italy. In the Anglican cathedrals and larger churches elaborate 'service' settings are used (see *Service*); in the smaller churches series of Anglican chants or, nowadays frequently, simple 'service' settings. The most popular *Te Deum* ever in use in England was that of Jackson of Exeter (1730–1803), in the service 'Jackson in F', which was for a century sung from every village choir loft; any musician of taste must call it trivial, yet there was something in the simplicity of its means and the broad effects obtained by them that carried it into the hearts of the whole church-going population of the nation (see *Jackson, William*).

Naturally the hymn has inspired innumerable composers of all periods and many of their settings, from the late seventeenth century onwards, have been on extended lines, with solos, choruses, and orchestral accompaniment, in the style of the oratorio. Amongst the important settings have been that of Purcell for St. Cecilia's Day (1694); that of Handel for the Peace of Utrecht (1712), his Chandos *Te Deum* (c. 1720), and that for the victory of Dettingen (1743); that of Graun (1756); that of Berlioz for the Paris Exhibition of 1855 (on a huge scale with three large choirs and large instrumental resources); and those of Bruckner (1884); Dvořák (1896); Verdi (1898); Stanford (1898); Parry (Latin original 1900; English adaptation 1913; another also for the Coronation of King George V in 1911); Walter Damrosch (Manila *Te Deum*, for Admiral Dewey's victory, 1898); Kodály (1936); Britten (1953); Walton (1953).

A solemn Te Deum is ordered on all occasions of rejoicing in Christian countries, so that throughout history nations opposed in war have used the same hymn to thank God for their alternating victories over one another.

TEETH-TAPPING. See *Voice* 7.

TEIL or **THEIL** (Ger.). 'Part', in the sense of 'portion' or 'section'. So *Teilen* or *Theilen* 'to divide'.

TELEGRAPH, ELECTRIC. See *Broadcasting of Music* 1.

TELEGRAPHONE. See *Gramophone* 4.

TELEMANN, GEORG PHILIPP (p. 396, pl. **67**. 5). Born at Magdeburg in 1681 and died at Hamburg in 1767, aged eighty-six. He held a large number of posts, as Kapellmeister and as church music director, and in his own day ranked very high as a composer, being one of the most fluent, versatile, and prolific who ever lived (e.g. over forty settings of the Passion, forty operas, six hundred overtures). Such of his works as are now performed from time to time are pleasing and tuneful without showing striking originality.

See *Composition* 10; *Expression* 1; *Colour and Music* 6; *Journals*; *Printing* 3; *Bagpipe Family* 7; *Recorder Family* 2; *Oboe Family* 6; *Chamber Music* 6, Period II (1681); *Tafelmusik*; *Bird Music*; *Dictionaries*.

TELEPHONE. See *Broadcasting of Music* 1.

TELEVISION. See *Broadcasting of Music* 6.

TELHARMONIUM, TELHARMONY. See *Electric Musical Instruments* (near opening).

TELLEFSEN, THOMAS DYKE ACLAND. Born at Trondheim, Norway, in 1823 and died in Paris in 1874, aged fifty. He was a pupil of Chopin, and, like him, composed nocturnes, mazurkas, valses, piano concertos, etc.

TELLER (Ger.). 'Plate' (e.g. of cymbal).

TELL ME, SHEPHERD. See *Mazzinghi*.

TE LUCIS. See *Hymns and Hymn Tunes* 2.

TELYN. See *Harp* 2 a.

TEMA (It.). 'Theme', i.e. a main subject of a composition. *Tema con Variazioni* is the same as 'Air and Variations' (see *Form* 11).

TEMPERAMENT

1. Introductory. Temperament means an adjustment in tuning in order to get rid of gross inaccuracy in the intervals between certain notes—an adjustment by the distribution of the amount of this inaccuracy over the intervals in general (or some of them), so that small disturbance to the ear results.

Any close discussion of the subject inevitably becomes highly mathematical, and mathematical treatment is aside from the scope and purpose of this book. An attempt will, then, be made here to avoid mathematics—even to the extent of almost silence as to such simple acoustical facts as that a perfect fifth (say C–G), which the semi-instructed might imagine from a glance at the pianoforte keyboard to include seven semitones, if *really* a 'perfect' one would include not an exact seven of our keyboard semitones but 7·019550008654 of them.

2. Perfection in Fifths. But what is a 'really' perfect fifth? It has been shown in the article *Acoustics* (section 8) that a sounding body tuned to give a note C is also giving, more faintly but still distinguishably to fine ears and demonstrably by the use of apparatus, the C an octave above and the G a fifth above that, as well as a host of other higher notes. This G (this naturally produced G) *is* a 'really' perfect fifth above the C it follows in the harmonic series, and an octave-plus-perfect-fifth above the fundamental note from which it derives.

In the same article (section 15) it is shown that if a string be tuned to produce a C the division of that string into two will give the C an octave higher, and the division of it into three will give the fifth above that. That upper C and G, thus naturally produced by division of the string at a half and a third respectively, are likewise at the interval of the really perfect fifth—as also, of course, are the lower C and G produced by the doubles of these lengths, i.e. the original length of string and a two-thirds length of it. It is this kind of fifth that comprises the seven-and-a-fraction of our present-day keyboard semitones, as just stated.

Now the perfect fifth is a very important interval—the second most important we possess. Exactly as every ear feels the octave to be a natural duplication of one sound, so does it feel the perfect fifth to be a sort of natural duplication—not a simple duplication, like the octave, but something approaching it.

Hence, as seen in the article *Harmony*, the first attempts at singing in any way other than in unisons and octaves were those at singing in perfect fifths.

Hence, too, the perfect fifth is an essential ingredient of what we call the common chords (e.g. C–E–G, or C–E flat–G, i.e. major and minor common chords respectively, but both with the perfect fifth; such chords at one time represented the only accepted chordal material of music). The perfect fifth, then, is a simple and 'natural' interval—a basic thing.

For a long time such simple material as those chords sufficed: harmonization in the modes (q.v.) was merely a matter of a few common chords, but when the modes gradually broke down and modern keys (with their system of modulation from one key to another) gradually took their place, trouble began—especially with keyboard instruments.

3. An Instrument-maker's Problem. Consider a keyboard instrument manufacturer setting to work to produce an instrument that will meet the demands of our modern modulatory key system.

He supplies a string for the lowest C and a series of other strings for all the C's above that, and so far there is no difficulty.

The natural thing might be next to supply a series of perfect fifths, so he might begin again at the same C and supply strings tuned to G, D, A, E, B, F sharp, C sharp, G sharp, D sharp, A sharp, E sharp, and B sharp. He could go on indefinitely, but here this imaginary experimenter may be brought to a pause. His B sharp is nearly but not quite the same as a C: as a matter of fact it is a little higher than C—higher by a tiny interval that we need not here define exactly (about a quarter of a semitone on the piano), called a *Pythagorean Comma*.

Any system of tuning by acoustically correct perfect fifths brings him to this difficulty. He will need separate strings on his instrument for the C and the B sharp, and as he pursues the system he will find other notes occurring in difficult and indeed impossible proximity until, if he pursues the system, he will soon find he needs enormous numbers of finger-keys in each octave (experimental instruments have actually been made with over fifty—e.g. Bosanquet's 'Generalized Keyboard Harmonium', in 1876, with fifty-three).

4. The Only Practical Solution. Obviously the C and B sharp are so near in pitch that one string (and one finger-key) ought, in practice, to be made to suffice for the two of them. And so with the other near neighbours. F sharp and G flat can share a string and so can E sharp and F, C flat and B and all the rest of these *enharmonics* as we call them.

And the obviously proper way for the manufacturer whose difficulties we are discussing to attain this end is to abandon his idea of tuning in acoustically perfect fifths, to make B sharp and C natural the same and then to do the same with the other enharmonics by dividing each octave into twelve equal semitones. Only the octave itself C–C will be perfectly correct; the rest will be all a bit 'out'—but not so much so that any ear once accustomed to the system will feel distress. His perfect fifth is now no longer 7·019550008654 times the 'size' of a semitone; it is just seven times the size (of our new practical kind of semitone)—i.e. as near as the tuner's ear can make it.

Imagine the tuner working up first in perfect fifths (*really* perfect ones—acoustically correct) from a low C, and down in perfect fifths (really perfect ones again) from a high one. The two processes would give him this conflict—up C, G, D, A, E, B, F sharp, C sharp, G sharp, D sharp, A sharp, E sharp, B sharp; down, C, F, B flat, E flat, A flat, D flat, G flat, C flat, F flat, B double-flat, E double-flat, A double-flat, D double-flat. We wipe out all that confusion of twenty-four different notes (and as already stated, if we pursued the system up and down we should have far more) by making one string, operated by one key on the instrument, serve for every neighbouring pair, and then, by making five of the finger-keys shorter than the others, and placing them between the others, we bring that important interval, the octave, within the reach of the normal adult hand.

Despite all Sunday-school teaching, life is necessarily a compromise; perfect truth is unattainable, and so is perfect tuning. If we are to mix among men we shall, in conversation, often have to be satisfied to utter and hear hasty generalizations (they are roughly true and do nobody any harm); and if in music we want to move easily amongst the keys (in both senses of the words 'keys'—the tonalities and the ivories) we shall have to accept approximations.

The system just outlined is that called, for obvious reasons, 'Equal Temperament'.

5. Bach's Support of the Solution. Because Bach tuned his domestic clavichords and harpsichords in this way and wrote two series of preludes and fugues, each series including all the twelve major and all the twelve minor keys, and because he made these two series a sort of public manifesto for the system by calling them (or, at any rate, the first of the two, 1722) *The Well-tempered Clavier*, many people have a vague idea that Bach himself invented the system; indeed this is sometimes stated by musical writers of good standing. It is, however, said to have been proposed by Aristoxenus (c. 350 B.C.) and to have been in actual use in China centuries before this (a difficult statement, however, in view of the fact that even in our day Chinese music uses the primitive pentatonic scale). The Spaniards seem to have used it in the placing of the frets on their guitars at least two centuries before Bach was

born—to judge by the instructions in the *Musica Practica* of Ramos de Pareja, 1482 (see another reference to the general subject under *Frets*); and the Italian Zarlino (q.v.), in the late sixteenth century, explains its application to the lute. Moreover, amongst the virginal works of the English Elizabethan composers, roughly a century before Bach, will be found two or three (notably by John Bull, q.v.) that go so far afield in modulation as to show that some of these composers, too, must have used a tuning system on the same lines. The celebrated organist J. C. Kerll (1627–93) wrote a duet on a ground bass, passing through every key; this certainly seems to imply a use of equal temperament, and that such temperament was in considerable use at this period is proved by a reference in Mersenne (1636). In the harpsichord works of Bach's contemporary, Handel, will be found some little use of extreme keys, showing that he, too, must have had his domestic instruments tuned in something the same way (cf. *Keyboard* 3). Mattheson in his *Organistenprobe* (1719) has a piece in every key. A little later than Bach's first book, the earliest pianoforte music ever published, Giustini's Sonatas (1732; see *Pianoforte* 18), modulate to such remote keys as G sharp major, so implying that their composer's instrument was tuned on the equal temperament system.

Bach was not even the only one to write a set of preludes and fugues called a *Well-tempered Clavier*, and taking in all the major and minor keys. An early eighteenth-century composer called Bernhard Christian Weber did the same thing (for modern instances see *Huber* and *Klengel, A. A.*; also cf. *Ashton, Algernon*); and Beethoven, in 1803, published his op. 39, being *Two Preludes through the twelve major keys*, for piano or organ.

As soon as instrumental music began to be developed and the modern scheme of twelve tonalities, all exactly similar in their intervals, to be dimly perceived as a convenient thing, the system of equal temperament became inevitable. The Flemish composer, Willaert, as early as 1550, had pleaded for such a system.

It will doubtless shock some readers to learn that despite all this propaganda on behalf of equal temperament from 1550 onwards some great English piano-making firms of nearly three centuries later had not adopted it. Broadwoods did so only in 1846 (see Hipkins, in *Musical Times*, Sept. 1898), so that one may take it that up to that date none of their clients, if keen-eared, could play through Bach's '48' with any satisfaction, to say nothing of Beethoven and Chopin, with their many keys and free modulations.

6. The Organ. Church music is generally relatively unprogressive—changes in that follow changes in secular music as a rule. And so organs were not usually tuned on the equal temperament system for long after it had been generally adopted for the domestic keyboard instruments, and it will be found that Bach's organ works normally range through no such wide field of key-signatures and modulations as his clavichord and harpsichord works. He wrote no 'Well-Tempered Organ' because few such instruments existed in his day, though nowadays every organ is well-tempered—and every organist, which would not be the case if the organist had to play (say) some of Max Reger's works on the instrument of his great-grandfathers.

Equal temperament came quite slowly to organs. German builders seem to have used it first: a few in north Germany as early as 1690, but only a few, apparently. Bach must have had an equally tempered organ in mind when he wrote his *Little Harmonic Labyrinth* which, starting in the key of C, continuously modulates (generally enharmonically) until it arrives home in C again. It was, however, not until well after the middle of the nineteenth century that British and American organ-builders universally adopted it, and then they were opposed by some eminent organists who preferred to play with relative purity in a small number of tonalities rather than to wander at will over all tonalities with none of them pure.

The famous organ of Exeter Hall, London, built in 1848, was tuned to equal temperament later (1852), but the still more famous organ of St. George's Hall, Liverpool, built in 1855 to the specifications of Dr. S. S. Wesley (q.v.), was, by his instructions, tuned unequally, and the great Best so played it for twelve years (to 1867) before he could take advantage of a rebuilding to have it altered. The organ of Norwich Cathedral was unequally tempered until the celebrated Zachariah Buck resigned in 1877 (many of these old organists had very conservative ears). The organ of St. George's Chapel, Windsor Castle, had unequal temperament until 1883, and the organ of Wells Cathedral until the same date or later.

Yet some of Wesley's compositions imply equal temperament (e.g. the anthem 'The Wilderness') and must have sounded very strange when accompanied on instruments tuned as he preferred. Music written since his day, of course, would be quite impossible with such tuning. The whole development of musical composition during the nineteenth century was based on the acceptance of the twelve equal keys into any one of which the composer could pass without let or hindrance. Wagner's chromatic harmonies, for example, necessarily imply an orchestra with its instruments tuned 'equally'.

An interesting experiment was tried at Trinity College, Cambridge, in 1911, when the organ was rebuilt. The choir organ, there called 'Positive', was tuned in unequal temperament (presumably 'mean-tone'—see below). After a short time the organist, Dr. Alan Gray, found the advantage illusory and that manual was retuned.[1]

[1] The general term 'unequal temperament' is used in this article, quite logically, for any form of temperament that is not equal, i.e. that does not treat all keys equally;

7. The Mean-Tone System. The organs of Bach's day and later were not tuned 'perfectly'; they were usually tuned in some *Mean-Tone* system—which term cannot be explained fully here; it refers to a system of temperament based on the major thirds being accurate and the other intervals adapted. In this system about six major keys and three minor were very good, but beyond that occurred a horrible out-of-tune-ness picturesquely nicknamed 'The Wolf'. Instead of the few big wolves of mean-tone temperament there are nowadays (in our equal temperament) a large number of little wolves—so little that their howls are unheard save by very keen-eared people.

A warning may be inserted here. Innumerable books for students state that prior to Bach the tuning system was that of 'just intonation'. Now, as we have seen, there were equal-temperament-tuned guitars, harpsichords, etc., before Bach, but in any case the system gradually displaced, owing to his propaganda and example, was not that of 'just intonation' (which with the ordinary twelve-note-to-the-octave keyboard could be accurate only for *one* key) but that of mean-tone temperament (which was reasonably accurate in about nine keys, counting major and minor, though painful in others).

8. Experiments with Divided Finger-keys. To give a rather bigger range of tonalities than the mean-tone system would normally do, and yet to avoid the wolf, experiments have been made in extra organ-pipes and corresponding finger-keys (see *Microtones*). In 1687 the new organ of the Temple Church, London, was supplied with pipes for both G sharp and A flat and D sharp and E flat, the finger-keys being cut across half-way and the back half raised, so that when the performer played on one half he got the sharp note and when the other the flat note. Said an old account: 'The Organ can play any tune, as, for instance, ye tune of ye 119th psalm [in E minor], and several services set by excellent musicians, which no other organ will do.'

Nearly a century later the organ of the Foundling Hospital (originally given by Handel) was fitted with extra pipes throughout for four notes in each octave; you decided in which key you were going to play, adjusted the instrument so that it would give you the notes desired (a different system from that of the Temple), and went ahead.

An instrument that retained mean-tone tuning until the 1860s was the English concertina: it had the same two extra notes as the old Temple organ, so that it had exactly the same range of practicable tonalities as that organ. There is a very interesting long passage on the English concertina in Berlioz's *Orches-*

thus it includes 'mean-tone' temperament, just to be described. Some writers, however, do not consider 'mean-tone' to be an 'unequal' temperament, on the grounds that it treats equally a certain number of keys, disregarding the others. This is, of course, purely a matter of terminology.

tration, in which he 'lets himself go' as to its 'barbarous scale'. The scale was, however, not 'barbarous'; it was very satisfactory—so long as the player avoided extreme keys.

The 'barbarous scale' effect of which Berlioz complained was due to players wrongly using the two extra studs that were provided: e.g. they might play A flat in a key where G sharp required. (These extra keys are still retained in the instrument, but are tuned as mere duplicates of two ordinary keys, serving merely to facilitate the fingering in certain types of passage.)

9. Present-day Dependence on and Opposition to Equal Temperament.

Composers everywhere have, of course, for long taken for granted the convention of equal temperament. The simplest enharmonic modulation in Beethoven implies a dependence on instruments tuned according to the equal temperament system (or, in a choral work, dependence on the ears of choralists whose training has been connected with the use of such instruments). The music of Wagner and all who have followed him would obviously become nonsense if robbed of its power to drift from key to key by means of enharmonic processes. Debussy's whole-tone scale (q.v.), Schönberg's dodecaphonic system (see *Note-row*)—these things imply a rigid mathematical division of the octave into twelve equal portions like the twelve inches of a foot rule, and Hába's quarter-tones (see *Microtones*) merely carry the process into a half-inch division.

It is difficult to see where this process is to stop, and there are those who would apply violent measures. From time to time such people make their voice heard—though it is, perhaps, no sooner heard than forgotten. Thus the incredibly detailed researches of Dr. Wilfred Perrett, of Cambridge, led up to 'a scheme for a Grand Organ in just intonation, to be heard by the unlimited audience of wireless' (to quote the statement of his publishers in 1932). Then there was Mr. H. Hunter, of Wimbledon, who advertised (1933) a 'Chorale and Pastorale of surprising strength and beauty, arranged in Just Intonation (true pitches) with diatonic and enharmonic contrasted tonality . . . arranged for three pianos tuned to a true scaling. . . . With full instructions how to tune three pianos to the scaling.'

The latter enthusiast announced that he had arranged a quantity of existing music for performance on the same lines as his own composition, but it is difficult to realize how a work of (say) Purcell, composed for performance on a mean-tone-tuned keyboard, or one of (say) Brahms, composed for performance on a keyboard tuned to equal temperament, could quite properly be transferred to a medium which must, apparently, to some extent ignore the principles of diatonic modulation implied in the music of the earlier of these composers and of diatonic and enharmonic modulation implied in the music of the later of them. (To this, however, it might be retorted that we are, in any case, today distorting works of the mean-tone period by performing them on equal-temperament instruments.)

As already shown, music for an instrument in just intonation, however many finger-keys it might possess, would have to confine itself to one key, or if it went beyond this, whilst it could contrast passages in various keys, would be destitute of means of passing unobtrusively from one to another—which is what we mean by 'modulation', since all modulation (diatonic or enharmonic) involves the use of linking chords, of which some note or notes are not, according to just intonation, of exactly identical pitch in the two keys, though they are of such identical pitch in the simpler keys in mean-tone tuning and in all keys in equal-temperament tuning.

Apparently, in addition to the knights-errant of just intonation there are some knights-errant of equal temperament, who fight for a more careful carrying-out of its principles. In May 1932 there appeared at Bow Street Police Court, London, Mr. Lennox Atkins, F.R.C.O., who, as honorary secretary of the 'Equal Temperament Committee', applied for a summons against the Associated Board of the Royal Academy and Royal College of Music, on the ground that they were not qualified to know whether music was being played in tune or not, and that, therefore, their certificates were valueless. The magistrate decided, mercifully, that this was not a matter for a criminal court.

10. Do String Players and Unaccompanied Choirs use Just Intonation?

One may be allowed to doubt the fairly frequent statement that bowed-instrument players with good ears tend to adopt just intonation. Obviously they could not (and should not) do so when playing with keyboard instruments or keyed wind instruments—the only media of accompaniment capable of just intonation being other bowed instruments, trombones, or voices, the performers in each case to be provided with ears as reliable as their own. Fuller Maitland, in his *Life* of Joachim (1905), defended that eminent violinist from the charge of playing out of tune, so frequently laid against him in the later part of his career, by the assertion that the truth of the matter was that 'in many intervals his intonation differed from that of the pianoforte' and went on as follows:

'It is only after realizing that the modern keyboard instruments are purposely tuned on a system which, in order to allow of the employment of all keys equally, makes almost all of the intervals a little out of tune, that the conviction dawns that possibly Joachim's intonation may be right and the piano keyboard wrong. This is, indeed, the plain fact of the matter; and it has been demonstrated by the greatest acoustician of modern times, von Helmholtz, that Joachim's playing is in "just intonation", and far nearer the point of exact scientific truth than that of any other violinist. The faultiness of the keyboard can be easily recognized by any one who can sing a note at even pitch, by this little experiment, going over no more than three intervals. Beginning with the notes C, D, E, the first three notes of the scale of C major, sing them mentally or audibly until they are perfectly in tune; it will be found that the middle note, D, has, in the key of C, to be made perceptibly nearer to the pitch of E than to that of the C; in other words, that the distance between the two intervals is not the same distance, as it is on the keyboard. Now, having secured the pitch of D and E, let the mind modulate into the key of D major, taking the same D as the keynote; if you sing the same E as before for the second note of the scale, it will sound too flat, and in readjusting the mind to the new key, a higher E will almost inevitably be taken unconsciously. This is the difference known as that between the major and minor tone, both of them being expressed by the same interval on the keyboard. In a single diatonic scale, without any modulation, there are seven intervals between adjacent notes, all of which vary slightly from those of the keyboard, and where modulation is introduced, as it is in all modern music, the difficulty of practically adjusting the intervals becomes so great that most violinists give up all attempt to play in true intonation, and just adopt the equal temperament of the pianoforte, or something not recognizably different from it. Joachim, the great master of just intonation in practical music, has often passed from a note to its enharmonic equivalent (from D sharp to E flat, for example) with an appreciable difference of pitch that a superficial hearer might easily mistake for an error in intonation, the fact being that the player is possibly the only violinist who has ever perfectly achieved this feat.'

Against this may be placed the statement of one of Joachim's own teachers, the distinguished theorist Moritz Hauptmann (1792–1868), himself a violinist of great eminence and reputed for the delicacy of his aural perception. He defended a 'psychical view of intonation', asserting that 'the mathematically true intonation does not suffice for an animated performance', and that 'an animated intonation' (on the violin) 'is just as little mathematically true as an animated time-keeping is strictly in accordance with the metronome'. He added, 'It is very easy to calculate that, as against C, C sharp is lower than D flat (this depends on the key of the piece), but when I use C sharp as a leading note, and D flat as a minor ninth, I take the former much higher than the latter.'

This is in accordance with the best teaching of the violin. As Dr. Pole (q.v.) stated in his *The Philosophy of Music* (1879): 'It is one of the most positive instructions to violin students that C sharp must be the nearest to D and D flat the nearest to C.' Courvoisier's *Foundations of Violin Technique* (Berlin, 1873), published under Joachim's patronage, says the same thing: 'C sharp is the leading-note in D major, and attaches itself closely to D; D flat, on the other hand, is the dominant 7th in A flat and attaches itself closely to the third of that key, i.e. C.'

Thus it will be seen that the practice of violinists is in conflict with scientific fact.

It would seem, then, that there is very little substance in the common impression that a fine violinist tends to play in just intonation. The truth would seem to be that when playing with a pianoforte or orchestra he largely (and necessarily) adopts the equal temperament of the keyed instruments, but that when playing in a string quartet (and this is especially true of players, of whom there are not a few, whose whole time is spent in quartet playing) his instinct forces him into an intonation that is neither 'just' nor 'equal' (and, indeed, to judge by the example offered by Hauptmann and Courvoisier, often a little more 'unjust' than is equal temperament). *Expressive Intonation* is the most descriptive term for this, and has been used by Casals and others.

At this point attention may be directed to a passage in the extract from Fuller Maitland above quoted—the statement that Helmholtz asserted that Joachim played in just intonation. In the second edition of Grove's *Dictionary of Music*, edited by Dr. Fuller Maitland, this is a little differently stated: 'Helmholtz found, by experiments with Dr. Joachim, that this distinguished violinist, in playing the unaccompanied scale, took the just and not the tempered intervals.' The point here lies in the words 'in playing the unaccompanied scale'. An unaccompanied scale, played under laboratory conditions, has no bearing upon the performer's practice (a) when accompanied by a tempered instrument or by the orchestra with its many tempered instruments, (b) when playing a passage full of chordal implications in (say) a string quartet (and, moreover, full of modulations, each of them implying, from a just intonation standpoint, a change of pitch of notes that remain notationally the same).

As a matter of fact, if Helmholtz had tested Joachim in some unaccompanied *composition*, instead of an unaccompanied scale (say in one of Bach's great unaccompanied sonatas or suites), he would have found that the player was using at least three differing C sharps (to keep to the same example we have been using earlier). In a plain scale he might find the note tuned according to just intonation corresponding to the position in the scale it occupied; in (say) a dominant seventh in the key of D he might find the C sharp a good deal higher than 'just'; and used in a decorative way, as, for instance, in a melodic passage such as D–C sharp–D, or a shake below D, he would almost certainly find it higher still. For a further study of this subject see Pole's *Philosophy of Music* or the long passage in Berlioz already alluded to (section 8), in which he imagines a violinist trying to play to the accompaniment of an English concertina.

The fact is that whilst in mathematics things are what they are, in aesthetics things are what they seem (cf. *Tempo*, below). In the plastic arts this is admitted. The Greek architects made all their pillars with a bulge so that they might appear straight. There are many bulges, of varying proportions, in fine violin playing.

The conclusion, then, is that the so-common statement that good string players use just intonation is incorrect. When playing unaccompanied by keyed instruments they deviate from equal temperament, but they do not drop into 'justness', except in certain appropriate passages, whilst in some other passages they (quite suitably) drop into a more pronounced 'unjustness' than any of which the modern pianoforte is mechanically capable.

And all that has just been said about string players applies equally to keen-eared choralists.

11. Methods of Pianoforte Tuners. It may be of interest to allude briefly to the methods adopted by modern piano tuners. They vary slightly, but have always the same basic principles—to tune, by fifths, octaves, and fourths, the middle section of the range of the instrument, and then to tune all the rest by octaves (testing also by fifths and fourths).

A tuner observed began by laying out the middle section as shown in the example here given. The tuner was careful to control his fifths (which he was in danger of making too acoustically 'perfect') by testing the notes in fourths and octaves; and as sixths and thirds became available he used these also for testing. Thus by empirical process of trial and error he arrived at the fair compromise which is equal temperament, or somewhere near it, for no tuner could achieve perfection in equal temperament or any other tuning without the use of the physicist's laboratory apparatus as a substitute for the human ear.

Such apparatus is now freely available and much used. The actual vibrations are counted electrically so that a stone deaf person can tune an instrument to any temperament specified. (Cf. *Pitch* 6 d.)

TEMPEST, PIERCE (1635–1717). See *Street Music* 2.

'TEMPESTA' SYMPHONY (Haydn). See *Nicknamed Compositions* 11.

TEMPESTOSO, TEMPESTOSAMENTE (It.). 'Tempestuous', 'tempestuously'.

TEMPLE BLOCK. See *Korean Temple Block*.

TEMPLE, HOPE. See *Messager*.

TEMPLE OF JERUSALEM AND ITS MUSIC. See *Jewish Music* 1, 2, 5.

TEMPO (It.; plural *Tempi*) usually means 'speed'. Upon the choice of the best speed the effect of the music greatly depends. Every composition may be said to have its correct tempo, but this is not capable of being minutely fixed without scope for variation, as to some extent circumstantial factors enter, such as the character of the instrument used (e.g. organs may greatly differ in their effect), and the size and reverberation of the room (a very reverberant room requiring a slower tempo if the music is to 'tell'). Moreover, the general character of the interpretation decided upon may affect the tempo: one performer may consider that a particular piece will be most effective if every detail be made clear (calling for a slower tempo) and another that it will be most effective if treated in a 'broad' style calling for a quicker tempo; and both these interpretations may be good ones. Further, a highly rhythmic performance at a slower tempo may give the impression of being quicker than a really quicker one with less rhythmic life. In fact, what

matters is not the tempo the performer actually adopts but the tempo that the listener is led to imagine he is hearing, for whilst in science things are what they are, in art things are what they seem. (Cf. *Temperament* 10, above.)

The following examples of the varying speeds of a typical Beethoven movement (the Funeral March from the 'Eroica' Symphony), as taken by various conductors, are from an article in the *Musical Times* of August 1935—a moment when a recent visit to London of the great conductor Toscanini was being discussed.

Beethoven's own marking: 12½ min. (i.e. ♪ = 80)
Koussevitzky . . 13½ " (i.e. ♪ = 74)
Beecham . . . 16 " (i.e. ♪ = 62)
Toscanini . . . 19 " (i.e. ♪ = 52)

Thus Toscanini took almost half as long again over the movement as the composer apparently intended—but everybody would agree that the composer's marking is too fast. Stokowski's gramophone recording of Debussy's *L'Après-midi d'un faune* lasts 8½ minutes, yet it was noted that at a performance in Bournemouth in 1951 it occupied 12½ minutes (Bournemouth *Winter Gardens Magazine*, Aug. 1951).

It has sometimes happened that when the tempo a composer has had in mind for his music has been disregarded by some performer the composer has admitted that the performer's tempo was the more effective one. Some composers' metronomic indications are clearly absurd, suggesting that they have fixed them with a metronome that was not in good order. Reger admitted to a friend that 'most' of his own metronomizations were wrong—being generally too fast; there may be a psychological explanation. (See also remarks under *Metronome*.)

In this connexion there may be recalled the very artificial conditions as to tempo under which the art of composition is necessarily practised. Musical invention and contrivance and the notating of music as composed (especially orchestral music) are relatively slow processes; a passage that is to go through in a flash when performed may take an hour or two to write and an element of confusion may enter from this too wide disparity between the two processes.

The high importance of tempo as a factor in effect has led to its receiving a good deal of attention at the hands of composers who have written on their art. Weber wrote a pamphlet on the subject. Wagner in his booklet *On Conducting* has a good discussion of the subject: he complains that the tempi adopted by the conductors for his music were sometimes wildly wrong (the *Tannhäuser* Overture under his own direction took twelve minutes, but he had known it take twenty under another conductor). Berlioz also treats this subject. He tells an anecdote of Mendelssohn's maintaining in conversation with him that the use of the metronome was unnecessary, as any musician worth his salt could himself judge of the proper tempo for a composition and, the next day, forgetting what he had said, sitting down at the piano to try a piece of Berlioz and asking him at what tempo it should go. Mendelssohn's idea was no doubt one with tradition behind it, since many older composers left much of their music without precise tempo indications. It was commonly said in Leipzig in Mendelssohn's day that he had quickened the tempi of all the works in the classical orchestral repertory.

A great many editions of the earlier classics embody tempo indications inserted by the present-day editor—and (criminally) often without any statement as to their lack of higher authority.

The general tempo of a composition has, since the seventeenth century, been usually indicated by the composer by the use of a series of Italian terms accepted by musicians in all countries (see *Expression* 1 for the introduction of these terms). All the chief of these appear in the present volume, in their due alphabetical positions.

The Italians use the word *Tempo* not only in the above sense but also in the derived sense of 'Movement' (in a sonata, symphony, etc.).

A great number of expressions include *Tempo* in the first sense, e.g. *A tempo*, 'in time' after *rall., accel.*, etc., and these which follow.

TEMPO ALLA BREVE (It.). See *Breve*.

TEMPO COMODO or **TEMPO COMMODO** (It.). 'Convenient speed', i.e. a speed convenient to the player.

TEMPO DI BALLO (It.). 'Dance speed', or a movement in dance style.

TEMPO DI MINUETTO (It.). 'Minuet speed' (and so for other dances).

TEMPO GIUSTO (It.). (1) 'Just' or exact *rhythm* or (2) the *speed* that the style of the music demands (usually *Moderato*).

TEMPO MAGGIORE (It.). The same as *Alla breve* (see *Breve*).

TEMPO MINORE (It.). The same as *Tempo ordinario* 3, below.

TEMPO ORDINARIO (It.). 'Ordinary time.' This expression is used in three different senses: (1) An ordinary rate of speed, neither fast nor slow, in fact *Moderato* or perhaps *Andante*; (2) the same speed as before, i.e. equivalent to *Tempo primo*; (3) a time in which the beats have their normal value, as opposed to *Alla breve* (see *Breve*).

TEMPO PRIMO (It.). Literally, 'first time', i.e. resume the original speed. (This is sometimes abbreviated to *Tempo 1mo.*)

TEMPO RUBATO (It.). See *Rubato*.

TEMPO WIE VORHER (Ger.). 'Time as before', i.e. resume or continue the original speed.

TEMPS (Fr.). 'Time', often in the sense of 'beat" See, for instance, *Deux Temps*.

TEN. Short for *Tenuto* (q.v.).

TENAGLIA, ANTONIO FRANCESCO. Apparently born in Florence in the early seventeenth century. Composer of arias, madrigals, cantatas, etc., a few of which have been republished in modern times.

TENBURY. See *Ouseley*.

TENDRE, TENDREMENT (Fr.). 'Tender', 'tenderly'.

TENEBRAE (Latin, 'darkness'). In the Roman Catholic Church the name applied to Matins and Lauds of the following day sung during the afternoon or evening from Wednesday to Friday of Holy Week. All the lights are extinguished, one by one, as the Penitential Psalms (see *Psalm*) are sung. This commemorates the darkness which is reported to have come over the earth at the time of the Crucifixion.

See references under *Miserere*; *Benedictus*.

TENEBROSO (It.). 'Dark', 'gloomy'.

TENENDO (It.). 'Sustaining' (e.g. *Tenendo il canto*, 'sustaining the melody').

TENERO (It.). 'Tender.' So, *Teneroso, Teneramente*, 'tenderly'; *Tenerezza*, 'tenderness'.

TENETE (It.). 'Hold out' (i.e. sustain).

TENNYSON, LORD ALFRED (1809–92). See references under *Ballad* 5; *Bell* 4; *Somervell*; *Stanford*.

TENOR. See *Voice* 17, 19; *Responses*; *Chorale*; *Hymns and Hymn Tunes* 5, 9; *Anglican Chant* 2; *Pitch* 6 a (the quotation from *Scots Magazine*); *Modes* 9; *Notation* 4.

TÉNOR (Fr.), **TENOR** (Ger.). The tenor voice (see above); or the viola.

TENOR C, etc. See *Pitch* 7.

TENOR CLEF. See *Table* 4; *Notation* 4.

TENOR COR. A high-pitched instrument of

horn-like character intended to take horn parts when proper horns are not available (see *Saxhorn and Flügelhorn Families* 2 c).

TENOR DRUM. See *Percussion Family* 3 j, 4 b, 5 j.

TENORE (It.). 'Tenor.'

TENORE LEGGIERO (It.). 'Light tenor.'

TENORE ROBUSTO (It.). 'Robust tenor.' See *Voice* 19.

TENOR FLÜGELHORN. See *Saxhorn and Flügelhorn Families* 3 c, and *Tuba Group* 5.

TENORGEIGE (Ger.). 'Tenor fiddle', i.e. viola.

TENOR HORN. See *Saxhorn and Flügelhorn Families* 2 c d.

TENOROON. See *Oboe Family* 4 h.

TENORPOSAUNE (Ger.). 'Tenor trombone.' See *Trombone Family* 2 c, 3, 5.

TENOR RECORDER. See *Recorder Family* 2.

TENOR SAXHORN. See *Saxhorn and Flügelhorn Families* 2 c.

TENOR STAFF. See *Great Staff.*

TENORSTIMME (Ger.). 'Tenor voice.'

TENOR TROMBONE. See *Trombone Family* 2 c, 3, 5.

TENOR TUBA. See *Tuba Group* 2 a, 3 a, 5.

TENOR VIOL. See *Viol Family* 3.

TENTH. See *Interval.*

TENU, TENUE (Fr., masc., fem.). 'Held.'

TENUTA (It., fem.). The Pause ⌒. (Probably short for *Nota tenuta*, i.e. 'held note'.)

TENUTO (It., masc.). 'Held', i.e. sustained to the end of its value (and perhaps sometimes a little more).

TEPIDO (It.). 'Tepid', 'lukewarm' (unimpassioned). So *Tepidità*, 'lukewarmness'; *Tepidamente*, 'in a lukewarm manner'.

TERANA. An oriental type of dance, introduced by Delibes in his opera *Lakmé*—a languorous six-in-a-measure occasionally lapsing into a three-in-a-measure—the time period of the two kinds of measure being equal. (Compare the old French *Courante* for a similar rhythmic peculiarity.)

TERCE. The fourth of the Canonical Hours, or services of the day of the Roman Catholic Church. Properly it takes place at the 'third hour', i.e. 9 a.m. (cf. *Matins, Lauds, Prime, Sext, None, Vespers,* and *Compline*).

TERMS AND SIGNS OF EXPRESSION. These, indicating speed and intensity (and generally the way of performance rather than the notes and their strict time values), will be found to have received some notice under the heading *Expression.* All the most usual terms of expression are also treated in this volume dispersed under their own heads. See also Tables 17, 18, 22–25.

TERNARY FORM. See *Form* 4, 6, 8, 13.

TERPODION.

(1) A keyboard instrument invented in 1816 by Buschmann of Berlin. The principle was that of the clavicylinder (q.v.) of Chladni, but the material and details were different. A cylinder of wood, in revolution, was in some way acted upon by apparatus controlled by the keyboard in such a way as to produce the different notes. It is now obsolete.

(2) See *Reed-Organ Family* 6.

(3) An organ stop, the tone quality of which presumably resembles that of one of the above instruments (see *Organ* 14 III).

TERPSICHORE. See *Dance* 2.

TERRY.

(1) RICHARD RUNCIMAN. Born at Ellington, Northumberland, in 1865 and died in London in 1938, aged seventy-three. He was from 1901 to 1924 director of the music at Westminster (Roman Catholic) Cathedral, where he revived much sixteenth-century music, especially English. He was also an authority on early Calvinistic hymn tunes, on carols, on sea shanties, etc. He was Hon. D.Mus., Durham, and was knighted in 1922.

See *Davy, Richard; Philips, Peter; Roman Catholic Church Music; Anglican Chant* 6; *Shanty.*

(2) CHARLES SANFORD. Born at Newport Pagnell (Bucks.) in 1864 and died in Aberdeen in 1936, aged seventy-two. Professor of History in the University of Aberdeen, author of many books on Scottish history, and of as many on various aspects of the life of Bach, upon which subject he became the world's leading authority. His comprehensive Bach collection is preserved intact in the library of the Music Faculty at Oxford.

See *Bach (the Family); Hymns and Hymn Tunes* 3; *Pianoforte* 17; *Horn Family* 5 (note); *Pitch* 3.

TER SANCTUS. Properly the same as Trisagion (q.v.), but sometimes improperly applied to the Sanctus as found in the Roman Catholic Mass or the Anglican Communion service (see *Mass* 2 d; *Common Prayer*).

TERTIS, LIONEL. See *Violin Family* 7.

TERTULLIAN. See *Dance* 7.

TERZA RIMA. See *Ritornello.*

TERZET or **TERZETTO.** See *Trio.*

TERZI TUONI. See *Acoustics* 10.

TESSITURA. See *Voice* 18.

TESTA (It.). 'Head.' So *Voce di testa*, 'head voice' (see *Voice* 4).

TESTO (It.). 'Text', e.g. Libretto.

TESTS AND MEASUREMENTS FOR MUSICAL CAPACITY. From the opening of the twentieth century an increasing interest has been taken in 'Applied Psychology', and one form which this activity has taken has been in the application of tests for the measurement of individual capacity for various branches of work. The old idea of the English Victorian phrenologist, lecturing on the shore at seaside resorts, that it was possible (for a suitable fee) to determine the relative fitness of a child for one vocation or another, is now accepted by many people, and scientific methods (differing, of course, from his) have been increasingly worked out and elaborated whereby this relative fitness may be discovered and more or less exactly stated.

In general the tests so far in use concern merely intelligence and capacities; it remains to be seen whether those traits of character and temperament which are such vital factors in success in life are susceptible of scientific measurement. Thus the methods so far adopted cover, as one may say, only one-half of the field, but this is already something. To turn back from the entrance gate of any profession those who, whatever their gifts of character, can meet with only disappointment if they enter, and to throw wide open the gates to those who, if they turn out to possess these gifts of character, can attain success, is obviously a good thing to do. And, similarly to direct school children towards or away from activities that correspond to their capacities and incapacities respectively is valuable—always bearing in mind in this latter case, however, that where there is a glimmer of capacity for any branch of activity, though only a glimmer, non-professional activity in that branch may be indicated—not with a view to the achievement of high attainment but as a means of widening the intellectual and emotional life of the individual.

To apply this to a particular field of musical work—every piano teacher must recognize that some plodding individuals are being encouraged to enter the musical profession who (especially in view of the highly competitive conditions of that profession today) should be persuaded rather to find in music a private domestic enjoyment; and that, on the other hand, many piano pupils of merely moderate capacity who are allowed to discontinue their studies who should be encouraged to continue them in order to develop that capacity to the point of enrichment of their lives.

It is clear also that the choice of an instrument may be more wisely made after the application of suitable tests; to take a simple example, a child markedly musical yet somewhat deficient in the discrimination of pitch should be directed rather to the piano than to the violin.

The study of psychological tests in relation to music was pioneered by American workers, notably Professor Carl Emil Seashore, of the University of Iowa (*The Psychology of Musical Talent*, New York, 1919; etc.) and Professor Jacob Kwalwasser, of the University of Syracuse, N.Y. (*Tests and Measurements in Music*, Boston, 1927; etc.). Professor Kwalwasser collaborated with Professor Peter Dykema of Teachers' College, Columbia University, New York, in the preparation of a series of gramophone records for testing purposes (Victor Co.), and Professor Seashore also

produced such a series (C. H. Stoelting Co., Chicago). The Kwalwasser–Dykema tests covered Memory for Related Notes, Discrimination of Tone-Qualities of Compared Instruments, Feeling for Tonal Movement, Time Discrimination, Rhythm Discrimination, Pitch Discrimination, Taste in Choosing between Compared Melodies, Discrepancies in Pitch Patterns between what is Written and what is Heard, and Discrimination similarly between Rhythmic Patterns.

Obviously such tests as these need to be very intelligently applied, for a music student of (say) fifteen years who had had abundant musical opportunity and well-directed training might earn a better marking than a potentially much more capable student of the same age whose opportunities had been more limited and his training inferior. Conditions of nervousness must also be allowed for.

° Dr. H. Lowery, of the South West Essex Technical College, maintained that the Seashore tests are too artificial, and he claimed to have evolved a more definitely practical series. Some American musicians of standing also express deep distrust of the value of such tests as at present elaborated.

The Education Departments of several British universities have experimented considerably with the Seashore and other tests.

Studies in the comparative enjoyment (specifically) of various types of music have been made and the subject has continued to be researched in the U.S.A. The *Journal of Research in Music Theory* (1957) has published the results of such work.

TETRACHORD. A Greek word applied to the four notes (covering a compass of a perfect fourth) of the early lyre. Terpander, about 670 B.C., added three more notes above, and the middle of the seven was looked on as common ground to two tetrachords. Pythagoras, a century later (see *Scales* 5), made the series of two tetrachords to consist of eight notes with no note common and the octave as the outward limit. These two tetrachords were, in any 'mode' (see *Modes*), not necessarily similar to one another as to order of tones and semitones, as the two tetrachords of our major scale are today.

TETRAZZINI, LUISA. See *Prima Donna*.

TEXAS COWBOY SONGS. See *Folk Song* 4.

THACKERAY. See references under *Misattributed Compositions*—'Beethoven's Dream of St. Jerome'; *Voluntary*; *Music Hall* 2.

THALBERG, SIGISMOND (p. 800, pl. **137.** 1). Born at Geneva in 1812 and died near Naples in 1871, aged fifty-nine. He enjoyed a brief, dazzling career as a touring pianist, both astonishing and touching crowded audiences all over Europe and in North and South America. He composed for his instrument, rather than used his instrument as a means of self-expression, and the contributions he made to the concert and domestic repertory have, hence, not maintained a place in it.

His wife was the daughter of the great bass singer Lablache.

See references under *Pianoforte* 22; *Pianoforte Playing* 5, 6; *God save the Queen* 16; *Hexameron*.

THAYER, ALEXANDER WHEELOCK (1817–97). An American enthusiast for the music of Beethoven, who, with small resources, contrived to pass many years in Germany and Austria, pursuing all possible means of research into the details of that master's life and producing at length what must ever remain his standard biography (published in a German translation 1866–79; final volume not until 1908: English edition, New York, 1921; revised 1964).

THEATER (Ger.). 'Theatre', but often used in the sense of 'stage', as distinct from 'auditorium'.

THEATRES. See *Fairs and their Music*.

THEIL or **TEIL** (Ger.). 'Part', in the sense of 'portion' or 'section'. So *Theilen* or *Teilen*, 'to divide'.

THEILE, JOHANN (1646–1724). He was a Saxon by birth, a pupil of Schütz, and a noted contrapuntist, and became eminent as one of the first German opera composers (see *Opera* 24 b), and also as a church composer.

THEMATIC MATERIAL. The whole body of musical subject-matter out of which a composition is constructed, including definite 'Subjects' or 'Themes' (see *Theme* below), but also covering less definite and important bits of melody, etc., used for constructional purposes. Physically considered, any composition consists of two elements—the element of Thematic Material and that of Constructive Treatment of this.

See *Composition* 7, 9; *Form*; *Metamorphosis of Themes*; *Leading Motif*.

THEME. Used of musical construction this word generally means the same as 'subject', as that term is applied, for instance, in speaking of a piece in the sonata form or rondo form (see *Form* 7, 9). Sometimes, too, the subject of a fugue is called its theme (see *Form* 12).

Theme with Variations (or, in Italian, *Tema con Variazioni*) is the same as air and variations (see *Form* 11).

See more on this subject under *Composition* 7, 9; *Thematic Material*.

THEME SONG. In 1928, in a film called *The Singing Fool*, there was introduced something like a sort of recurring Leitmotiv (see *Leading Motif*), a song called 'Sonny Boy'. This contributed greatly to the success of the film and was taken up, apart from this, by popular singers and café orchestras, etc., all over the world. Apparently the term 'Theme Song' was introduced in connexion with this film or the others which imitated it.

The Leitmotiv has been alluded to above as a precursor of the theme song, but we may almost say that there is an actual theme song in the Prize Song of *The Mastersingers*, which crops

up from time to time during the course of the action and, indeed, tends to dominate it. An earlier example is 'Home, Sweet Home' (q.v.), which pervaded Bishop's opera of *Clari, or the Maid of Milan* (1829).

THEORBO. See *Lute* 2, 4, 5 c.

THÉRÉMIN, THÉRÉMINVOX. See *Electric Musical Instruments* 1 d.

THERE'S A GOOD TIME COMING. See *Russell, Henry*.

THERESIENMESSE (Haydn). See *Nicknamed Compositions* 13.

THERE'S NAE LUCK ABOOT THE HOOSE. The poem, which Burns affirmed was 'the finest love-ballad of the kind in the Scottish or perhaps any other language', has been variously attributed to William Julius Mickle (1734–88) and to a schoolmistress, Jean Adams (1710–65), and no decision between these alternatives seems now to be possible. The air is the old Scottish one of *Up and waur at them a', Willie!*

THERE WAS AN OLD WOMAN. See *Lilliburlero*.

THESAURUS MUSICUS. See *God save the Queen* 8, 10, 13.

THESIS (Gr.). 'Down-stroke' (in conducting) for the strong beat of the bar. (This reverses the original sense of the word as applied to English poetical scansion.)

Cf. *Arsis*.

THIBAUT.

(1) **ANTON FRIEDRICH JUSTUS** (1774–1840). Professor of Law at various universities, great student of music (especially that of Palestrina and his school), collector of folk songs, and author of an important book mentioned under *Criticism* 2.

(2) **JEAN BAPTISTE.** See *Greek Church* 4.

THIBAUT DE COURVILLE, JOACHIM. See *Concert* 2.

THIBOUVILLE-LAMY. See *Mechanical Reproduction of Music* 13.

THIRD. See *Intervals*.

THIRD FLUTE. See *Recorder Family* 2.

THIRD INVERSION. See *Harmony* 24 e.

'THIRD PROGRAMME.' See *Broadcasting* 5.

THIRD STREAM MUSIC. See *History* 9.

THIRTY-SECOND NOTE (Amer.). Demisemiquaver (Table 3).

THIRTY-TWO FOOT STOP. See *Organ* 2 b.

THOMAS.

(1) **AMBROISE** (in full Charles Louis Ambroise). Born at Metz (then, and now again, in France) in 1811 and died in Paris in 1896, aged eighty-four. He was the son of a musician, and an infant prodigy. At the Paris Conservatory he carried off high honours, which culminated at twenty-one in the Rome Prize. Returning to

Paris he produced successfully a number of works both at the Opéra-Comique and at the (Grand) Opéra. The one by which he is most remembered today is the light opera *Mignon* (1866). Other famous operas are *A Midsummer Night's Dream* (1850), *Raymond* (1851), and *Hamlet* (1868). Some of his choruses are in the male-voice repertory in France.

At sixty, on appointment as head of the conservatory, he virtually abandoned composition.

See *Carnival of Venice*; *Chaminade*; *Bourgault-Ducoudray*.

(2) THEODORE (p. 1041, pl. **170**. 1). Born in Hanover in 1835 and died in Chicago in 1905, aged sixty-nine. He was one of the pioneers in orchestral activities in the United States, and as such will be ever remembered. Beginning as a conductor in New York, he then (from 1869) toured the country with his orchestra, settled in Cincinnati for a time, returned to New York, and finally (1891) founded what is now the Chicago Symphony Orchestra, conducting it with marked ability during the fourteen years of life that remained to him, He died three weeks after the opening of the fine hall specially built for his orchestra.

See references under *United States* 4; *Opera* 21 k.¹

(3) ARTHUR GORING. Born in Sussex in 1850, died in London in 1892, aged forty-one. He studied music first in Paris and then, for three years, at the Royal Academy of Music, London. In his early thirties he made his name by the production of the opera *Esmeralda* in London, Cologne, and Hamburg. His opera *Nadeshda* quickly followed (1885). He wrote also one or two pieces of the festival cantata class, as, for instance, *The Sun Worshippers* and *The Swan and the Skylark* (orchestrated by Stanford after his death). He had a light touch, somewhat influenced by his study in France. One composition of his frequently heard is the contralto air 'O, my heart is weary' (from *Nadeshda*). His life ended prematurely in the gloom of mental derangement.

For some references see *England* 7.

(4) THOMAS (known as Ap Thomas). Born at Bridgend, Glamorganshire, in 1829 and died at Ottawa, Canada, in 1913, aged eighty-four. He was brother to John Thomas (1826–1913; see 5 b, below), and like him a distinguished harpist. He played in many parts of Europe, including the famous Gewandhaus Concerts at Leipzig, and then, when approaching seventy, settled in America. He wrote a cantata, *The Pilgrim's Progress*, also many fantasias and other compositions for his instrument, and a history of it (1859).

(5) JOHN. There have been several musicians of this name, and some of these of lesser importance are included here in order to clear up confusion.

(*a*) Born near Carmarthen, Wales, in 1795 and died at Treforest, Glamorganshire, in 1871, aged seventy-six. He was a schoolmaster, a great promoter of choral singing, a poet,

a collector of the old Welsh minstrelsy, and a composer of airs that are to be found in collections of Welsh music. His bardic name was 'Ieuan Ddu'.

(*b*) Born at Bridgend, Glamorganshire, in 1826 and died in 1913, aged eighty-seven. It is he who is usually meant when 'John Thomas' is spoken of. He won a harp at an Eisteddfod at eleven and was sent to the Royal Academy of Music, London, where he spent eight years as student and many more as professor, afterwards joining the staff of the Royal College of Music. He toured Europe as a harpist and visited the United States, adjudicating at the Eisteddfod held in connexion with the Chicago Festival of 1893. He was harpist to Queen Victoria.

He was a composer of symphonies, operas, cantatas, harp concertos, and other things, and a collector and editor of the old Welsh melodies. At the National Eisteddfod of 1866 he was presented with a purse of five hundred guineas for his services to the music of his country. His bardic name was 'Pencerdd Gwalia' (see *Wales* 7).

(*c*) Born at Blaenanerch, Cardiganshire, in 1839 and died at Llanwrtyd Wells, Brecon, in 1922. Composed anthems, glees, part songs, and the like.

(*d*) JOHN R. Born at Newport, Monmouthshire, in 1829 and died in New York in 1896. He lived for some time in the United States. His songs, ''Tis but a little faded flower', 'Evangeline', and the like, once had high popularity.

THOMAS AQUINAS, SAINT (1226–74). See references under *Lauda Sion*; *Pange Lingua*; *Tantum Ergo*.

THOMAS OF CELANO. See *Dies Irae*; *Requiem*.

THOMPSON.

(1) RANDALL (p. 1068, pl. **175**. 3). Born in New York in 1899. He was educated at Harvard University, for three years enjoyed a Fellowship of the American Academy at Rome, and for two more a Guggenheim Fellowship. After holding various academic positions he became Director of the Curtis Institute (1939–41) and Professor in turn at the Universities of Virginia, Princeton, and (1948) Harvard. His compositions include symphonies and other orchestral and choral works. He is an Hon. D.Mus. of the University of Rochester, N.Y.

See *Oratorio* 6, last paragraph; *Opera* 24 f (1942).

(2) THOMAS PERRONET (1783–1869). See *Keyboard* 3.

THOMS, WILLIAM JOHN (1803–85). See *Folk Song* 1.

THOMSON.

(1) REVD. ANDREW MITCHELL (1779–1831). Divine. See *Presbyterian* 4.

(2) GEORGE (1757–1851). Collector and editor of Scottish, Irish, and Welsh airs. See

Folk Song 3; *Auld Lang Syne*; *Last Rose of Summer*; *Hogarth, G.* Also p. 945, pl. **160**. 3.

(3) JAMES (1700–48). Poet. See *Rule, Britannia!*

(4) JOHN (1805–41). Professor of Music at Edinburgh University and opera composer, etc. See *Annotated Programmes* 4.

(5) CÉSAR (1857–1931). Violinist. See *Belgium* 5; *Absolute Pitch*.

(6) VIRGIL (p. 1061, pl. **174**. 5). Born at Kansas City, Mo., in 1896. He graduated at Harvard University and, winning a Naumburg Fellowship, studied for some years in Paris. A friendship there with Gertrude Stein led to his setting some of her literary products to tonal accompaniment, and their opera, *Four Saints in Three Acts*, was in 1934 heard, performed by a cast of Negroes, at Hartford, Conn., and then in New York.

In addition he has written two symphonies, choral works, chamber music, a good deal of film music, etc. He has served as music critic of several journals (*New York Herald Tribune*, 1940–54).

See *Note-row*; *Opera* 24 f (1947).

THORAX. See *Voice* 21.

THORESBY, RALPH (1658–1725). Yorkshire antiquary. See *Bagpipe Family* 3.

THORN, THE (Song). See *Shield*.

THORNE, JOHN. Died in 1573. He seems to have been connected with York Minster—possibly as organist. A little of his church music survives, as also poems by him. Remarkable amongst poets and musicians, perhaps, he had sufficient reputation as logician for it to be thought worthy of mention on his tombstone ('Here lieth Thorne, musician; Most perfect in his art; In logic's lore who did excell; All vice who set apart', etc.).

THORNTON, BONNELL (1724–68). See *Hurdy-gurdy*; *Saltbox*.

THOROUGH-BASS. See *Figured Bass*.

THORSTEINSSON, B. See *Scandinavia* 5.

THOUGH DARK ARE OUR SORROWS. See *Saint Patrick's Day*.

THRANE, VALDEMAR (1790–1828). See *Scandinavia* 3.

THREE BLIND MICE. A round (q.v.) familiar to all children in Britain and most in the United States, and certainly the best-known round in the world.

It is found in the *Deuteromelia* (1609) of Ravenscroft (q.v.), but in the minor, in a shorter form, and with somewhat different words.

The tune is in certain quarters considered very 'unlucky', as, for instance, amongst circus folk. Were it played in a circus no performer would dare to do his turn—and if he did probably 'suggestion' would bring the dreaded result.

THREE CHOIRS' FESTIVAL. See *Festival* 1.

THREE FISHERS. See *Hullah*.

THREE-IN-ONE. See *Canon*.

THRENODY. Dirge.

THRING, EDWARD (1821–87). See *Education and Music* 2.

THRO' BASS. 'Figured Bass' (q.v.).

THROUGH - COMPOSED. See *Durchkomponiert*.

THUILLE, LUDWIG WILHELM ANDREAS MARIA. Born at Bozen (now Bolzano) in the Trentino (then Austrian, now Italian) in 1861 and died at Munich in 1907, aged forty-five.

He began life as a choir-boy in the monastery of Kremsmünster (Austria), and then studied at the Conservatories of Innsbruck, Munich (under Rheinberger), and Frankfurt. He afterwards became a professor of the Conservatory at Munich, where he was influenced by his friends A. Ritter (see mention under *Symphonic Poem*) and Richard Strauss.

He composed three operas, a little chamber music, music for men's voices, music for women's voices, and a few songs and piano pieces.

THUMOTH, BURK. See *Ireland* 1.

THUMP, THE. See *Viol Family* 4 c.

THUNDER MACHINE. This is called for by the score of Strauss's 'Alpine' Symphony and perhaps some scores by other composers; it is also in use in theatres. It usually consists of a big drum with balls of some material inside it; this is so fixed on pivots as to be capable of rotation, and the balls then strike the parchment.

THUNDER STICK, BULL ROARER, or WHIZZER. An instrument in use among the American Indians, the Australian aborigines, the natives of central Africa, etc., swung to produce a whirring noise, and rising or falling in pitch with the changing speed of the motion. It appears in chamber music in Henry Cowell's Ensemble for two violins, viola, two violoncellos, and two thundersticks.

The description given by Dr. Washington Matthews in his monograph, *The Mountain Chant*, is as follows:

'The Whizzer is a thin, flat, pointed piece of wood, painted black and sparkling with specular iron ore sprinkled on its surface. The Navajo Indians call it the *tsin-ce' ni*, or "groaning stick". It is most effective when made from the wood of a pine tree which has been struck by lightning. Wherever found its dimensions are practically the same, viz., 9 inches long, ¾ inch broad, and ¼ inch thick. A cord, about 2 ft. long, is attached to one end by which it may be swung so rapidly round the head that a very peculiar tone is produced.'

The German name of this instrument is *Schwirrholz* ('whirling-wood') and the French *Planchette ronflante* ('roaring board').

THUNER-SONATE (Brahms). See *Nicknamed* 7.

THYROID CARTILAGE. See *Voice* 21.

TIBIA (Major, Minor, Plena, Profunda, Dura, Clausa). See *Organ* 14 II.

TIBIA UTRICULARIS. See *Bagpipe Family* 9.

TIE or BIND. The curved line (or sometimes a straight one with rectangled ends) used over a note and its repetition, showing that it is intended that the two shall be performed as one unbroken note of the value of the total of the two.

The reason given for thus 'tying' notes is either (1) to get over the obstacle of an intervening bar-line, (2) within a bar, to draw attention to an internal accent past which a note is being continued, or (3) to make up a total value such as no single note could give: e.g. the value of five eighth-notes (quavers) might be made up by tying a half-note (minim) and an eighth-note.

The word 'Ligature' (q.v.) is sometimes used for Tie or Bind, but not wisely, this word having other meanings (see *Notation* 3).

 See also Table 22. Cf. *Slur* 7.

TIED NOTE. See *Printing of Music* 2.

TIEF (Ger.). 'Deep', 'low'.

TIEFGESPANNT. 'Deep-stretched', i.e. [of a drum] loosely braced, so as to give a low sound.

TIEF KAMMERTON. See *Pitch* 3.

TIEPIDO and derivatives. Same as *Tepido* (q.v.) and derivatives.

TIERCE (Fr.). 'Third' (the interval). And see *Organ* 14 IV.

TIERCE DE PICARDIE or TIERCE PICARDE. The major chord ending a composition in a minor key, or in any mode (see *Modes*) in which the third above the final or tonic is properly a minor third, e.g. in the key of C minor the last chord as C, E, G, instead of C, E flat, G; and similarly in the first (or Dorian) mode the last chord as D, F sharp, A, instead of D, F, A.

This idiom was common in the sixteenth and seventeenth centuries and the beginning of the eighteenth century.

It was felt to be unsuitable to bring the changing harmonies to rest on the interval of the minor third, since keen ears (*very* keen ones!) could detect the major third occurring as one of the harmonics of the keynote (see *Acoustics* 8); there are a few people today, indeed, who claim to do this. Probably the practice was initiated by stern theorists. It was perpetuated by the practice of *Musica Ficta* (q.v.), and so became a convention. The effect is pleasant, as of a bright ray breaking through the clouds as the sun sinks.

The reason for the name is unknown. Rousseau in his *Dictionary of Music* (1767) is very unconvincing: 'Tierce de Picardie because this way of ending survived longest in church music, and thus in Picardy, where there is music in a great number of cathedrals and other churches.' This explanation will be found copied into some other works of reference, sometimes word for word, for a half-century or more. (Most probably the name has something to do with the high development of contrapuntal choral music in the north of France and Flanders during the fifteenth century.)

The practice of using the Tierce de Picardie tended to die during the late sixteenth century and the seventeenth and had nearly vanished by the middle of the eighteenth century. Bach sometimes uses it and sometimes not. It is noticeable that in the first book of his *Well-Tempered Clavier* (1722; see *Temperament* 5), of the twenty-four minor movements (twelve preludes and twelve fugues) only one fails to end with a 'Tierce de Picardie', whereas in the second book written twenty-two years later (1744), fourteen end without it—some of these, however, using the evasion of ending on the unison. (The manuscripts differ a little in this matter, perhaps, but the general fact remains.)

A similar evasion to the one just mentioned was not uncommon, choral compositions in a minor key sometimes ending with a chord of the bare fifth. This is found from very early times and as late as early Mozart. An example from Tallis will be seen under *Form* 7.

(However it must be added that the omission of the third of the final chord is sometimes found also in compositions in a major key.)

TIETJENS (or Titiens), THERESE CATHLINE JOHANNA. Born at Hamburg (of Hungarian parents) in 1831 and died in London in 1877. Famous soprano. (See allusion under *Applause* 3.)

TILLYARD, HENRY JULIUS WETENHALL (1881–1968). At universities in England, Scotland, Wales, the Rand, and the Cape Province he demonstrated his versatility in posts as lecturer or professor of (in turn) Latin, Greek, and Russian, and in pursuing research into the literature of these languages and also into the notation and characteristics of Byzantine music, on which last subject he was one of the world's acknowledged authorities and the author of learned treatises.

 Cf. *Greek Church.*

TILOPHANE. See *Gramophone* 7.

TIMBALES (Fr.). Kettledrums. See *Percussion Family* 2 a, 4 a, 5 a. The term is also used for a small cylindrical drum used in Latin American dance music.

TIMBRE means tone quality—coarse or smooth, ringing or more subtly penetrating, 'scarlet' like that of the trumpet, 'rich brown' like that of the cello, or 'silver' like that of the flute. These colour analogies come naturally to every mind, as does the metaphorical term now becoming a commonplace as a synonym for 'timbre'—tone colour; the German for 'timbre' is *Klangfarbe*—literally 'sound-colour' (cf. *Colour and Music* 3).

The one and only factor in sound production which conditions timbre is the presence or absence, or relative strength or weakness, of overtones (see *Acoustics* 8). There is hardly such a thing as a single sound, in either nature

See the Article *United States of America* on pages 1059–69

1. THE MAYFLOWER, as she probably appeared

2. THE FIRST MEETING HOUSE

3. LATER MEETING HOUSE (at Hingham, Mass.; begun 1681)

No one shall read Common-Prayer, keep Christmas or Saints-days, make minced pies, dance, play cards, or play on any instrument of music, except the drum, trumpet, and jews-harp.

4. THE SOLE SOURCE OF AN ABSURD LEGEND. See *United States* 2

5. FROM EPHRATA CLOISTER. See *United States* 3

6. CHIPPEWA INSTRUMENTS, with Birch Bark Rolls containing Mnemonics of Songs. See *United States* 7

7. CHIPPEWA DOCTOR treating a patient

or art; almost all sounds are multiple, the ground-tone (or 'fundamental') and a number of its overtones being heard together (see *Bell* for a simple example of this easily within everybody's experience), and it is upon the variations in the details of this phenomenon that rest the varieties of tone colours of the different orchestral instruments and different makes of piano, the different qualities of tone that a beginner and a master respectively will elicit from one and the same piano or violin, and the different qualities of vocal production, from the almost pure tone of an English cathedral choir-boy (very few harmonics) to the rich tone of a fine contralto (many harmonics).

To take three examples from the wood-wind department of the orchestra—the pure upper tones of a flute are due to the fact that practically no overtones are really heard except the second harmonic (i.e. the octave above the fundamental); the rich, mellow tones of a clarinet are due to the fact that in clarinet tone, derived from a tube of cylindrical bore, the odd-numbered harmonics (see the diagram under *Acoustics* 8) are heard; the more pungent tones of the oboe and bassoon are due to the fact that the whole of the harmonics (with of course an upward limit) are heard. And so on. (But see *Acoustics* 6 for the modern 'formant' theory, bearing somewhat on this subject.)

The tuning-fork (see *Pitch* 6 b) comes as near to the absence of heard overtones as any instrument in ordinary use, and naturally, therefore, it will be found that there is practically no difference of timbre between one tuning-fork and another. The stopped diapason of an organ also approaches the condition of absence of overtones.

For examples of what may be called the modern synthetic production of desired timbres see *Electric Musical Instruments*. (Cf. *Organ* 14 IV.)

In the French language one meaning of timbre is 'bell'; hence *Jeu de timbres* for 'glockenspiel' (see *Percussion Family* 2 c, 4 e, 5 c).

TIMBREL. An ancient tambourine. See *Percussion Family* 3 m, 4 c, 5 m.

TIMBRER (Fr.). 'To stamp' (as, for instance, with a rubber stamp). So Debussy's *Doucement timbré*, 'softly accented'.

TIME. See *Tempo*; *Rhythm*; Table 10.

TIME AND RHYTHM. See *Rhythm* 8.

TIME, LAPSE OF, as the test of music. See *Quality in Music* 8.

TIME-NAMES, FRENCH. See *Tonic Sol-fa* 9.

TIME-SIGNATURE. See *Signature*; *Notation*; Table 10.

TIMES, THE (newspaper). See *Criticism* 4.

TIMIDO, TIMIDEZZA (It.). 'Timid', 'timidity'.

TIMORE (It.). 'Fear.' So *Timoroso*, 'fearful'; *Timorosamente*, 'fearfully'.

TIMPANI (*not* Tympani): Italian for 'kettle-drums' (plural of *Timpano*). See *Percussiom* 2 a, 4 a, 5 a.

TIMPANI COPERTI. See *Percussion* 5 a.

TINCTOR (TINCTORIS). See *Belgium* 1; *Patronage* 3; *Dictionaries*.

TINEL, EDGAR. Born at Sinay, in Flanders, in 1854 and died at Brussels in 1912, aged fifty-eight. He was trained at the Brussels Conservatory and won the Rome Prize. When nearing thirty he became head of the school for church music founded at Malines by Lemmens. His compositions, including two music-dramas and the oratorio *Franciscus*, were mostly of a religious character. He wrote a treatise on plainsong. For the last three years of his life he was head of the Brussels Conservatory.

See *Oratorio* 7 (1888).

TINÓDI. See *Hungary*.

TIN PAN ALLEY. See *Jazz* 2.

TIN SHEET (RUSTLING). See *Percussion* 4 d.

TINTER, TINTEMENT (Fr.). 'To tinkle', 'tinkling' (noun).

TINTINNARE (It.). 'To tinkle'; so *Tintinnando*, 'tinkling' (present participle).

TINTO (It.). 'Colour.' So *Con tinto*, 'colourfully', i.e. with expression.

TIN WHISTLE. See *Recorder Family* 1, 3 b.

TIPICA ORCHESTRA. This is a term which (with the necessary slight changes of spelling) became common in many European countries during the 1930s. Tipica is Italian and Spanish for 'typical', and orchestras bearing this name specialize in mixed programmes of music of markedly national and racial traits (Spanish, South American, Gipsy, etc.), claiming to play each type in its true native style. *Orchestre de genre* appears to be the same thing.

TIPPERARY. This song, beginning 'It's a long way to Tipperary' (composed in 1912), had an immense popularity in the British Army during the 1914 War, and also with the civil population of Britain.

One of the joint authors was a cripple, Harry J. Williams, who lived with his parents at the Plough Inn, Temple Balsall, Warwickshire. The first line of the song is inscribed on his tombstone. (Apparently another Harry Williams, an American, has sometimes been given the credit in error.)

The other author of the song was Jack Judge, a music-hall entertainer. The Editor of the *British Musician* wrote in 1933, 'We have stood outside his little 3- or 4-roomed house in Oldbury, a depressing, dirty, chemicals-manufacturing town a few miles out of Birmingham. Standing there, in the downstairs window we read a notice: *Mr. Jack Judge, Musician and Composer, Composer of Tipperary*; as in the window of an adjoining house we read *Boots Neatly Repaired*, and in the window of another house a little farther along the street, *Lodgings for a Respectable Young Man.*'

In 1928 Judge composed a sequel to the famous song—*It's a long way no longer*. (He died in 1938.)

TIPPETT, MICHAEL KEMP (p. 353, pl.

56. 8). Born in London in 1905. He was trained at the Royal College of Music and was later (1940–52) in charge of the musical organization at Morley College, London (cf. *Holst*). After producing some early works, most of which were later withdrawn, he came to general notice with his *Concerto for Double String Orchestra* (1939) and the oratorio, *A Child of our Time* (1940). There followed three operas, *Midsummer Marriage* (1955), *King Priam* (1962), and *The Ice Break* (1977), two symphonies (1945 and 1958), two piano sonatas (1956 and 1963), three quartets, and works for piano and other things.

He received the C.B.E. in 1959 and was knighted in 1966.

TIRANA. A Spanish song-dance popular in Andalusia.

TIRARE, TIRANDO, TIRATO (It.). 'To draw', 'drawing', 'drawn'. Used in connexion with the violin, etc., and implying the down-bow. *Tira tutto* ('Draws all') is the 'Full Organ' composition pedal or piston.

TIRASSE (Fr.). Coupler of organ—generally a pedal coupler.

So *Tirasse du Positif, du Récit, du Grand Orgue*, mean respectively 'Choir to Pedal', 'Swell to Pedal', 'Great to Pedal'.

These may be abbreviated *Tir. P.*, *Tir. R.*, and *Tir. G. O.*, whilst *Tirasse G. P. R.* means that all three couplers are to be used.

TIRER, TIRÉ (Fr.). 'To draw', 'drawn'. Used in connexion with the violin, etc., and implying down-bow (cf. *Poussé*). Sometimes *Tirez*, the imperative, is used.

TIR. G. O.; TIR. G. P. R. See *Tirasse*.

TIRO, TROMBONE A. See *Trombone Family* 5.

TIROLESE (It.). 'Tyrolese' (cf. *Jodel*; *Ländler*).

TIR. P.; TIR. R. See *Tirasse*.

TITELOUZE, JEAN. Born at St. Omer in 1563 and died at Rouen in 1633, aged sixty-nine or seventy. He was organist and a canon of Rouen Cathedral, famous as performer on and composer for his instrument, and an authority on organ building. He is looked upon as the founder of the French School of organ composition and his works have been patriotically republished under the editorship of Guilmant.

TITIENS. See *Tietjens*.

TITOF (**Titov**, etc.), **NICHOLAS.** Born in St. Petersburg in 1800 and died in 1875, aged seventy-five years. He was a lieutenant-general of the Russian army who composed songs and vaudevilles in a mixed Russian-Italian style that had influence upon his contemporaries, including even Glinka.

TOBEND (Ger.). 'Blustering.'

TOCCATA. The word is the past participle of the Italian *toccare*, 'to touch', and so means a keyboard piece that is 'touched' rather than played—in the sense of such rapidity that nothing is dwelt upon, the notes being left as soon as they are sounded. Often the toccata is a prelude to a fugue or some other piece that follows. Bach's fine organ toccatas (preceding

fugues) are the most famous of all existing pieces of this name; they are fantasia-like or rhapsodic in style and this is a frequent connotation of the word. Schumann has a fine toccata for piano (but in Sonata Form).

The above gives the usual definition, but it must be stated that there are various earlier works to which it does not quite apply. For instance, the earliest known use of the word is for a lute piece (Castelione, 1536), and the short prelude to Monteverdi's *Orfeo* (1607), which is a fanfare for trumpets, etc., is headed 'toccata'. Moreover, the instrumental prelude to a motet was in the early seventeenth century often so described; and Georg Muffat has a five-movement organ suite (1690) called a toccata. In all these early cases the idea seems to be 'played' (as distinct from 'sung'), the Italian 'toccare' having in this use the same sense as the existing French term 'toucher', for to play an instrument ('toucher du piano', etc.). Quite grave toccatas are sometimes found amongst the Italian keyboard composers of the earlier eighteenth century.

TOCCATINA, TOCCATINO. A miniature toccata (q.v.). Grove's *Dictionary* gives instances of the use of the word by Rheinberger and Henselt, but it goes further back that that. Burney in Rees's *Cyclopædia* (c. 1805) defines it as 'a short prelude on trial of an instrument'. Sixty years earlier Grassineau's *Musical Dictionary* (1740) says, 'A small research when we have not time to perform it in all its parts' (see *Ricercare*)—which is rather odd. Widor in one of his Organ Symphonies has a toccatina—a sort of *Perpetuum Mobile* (q.v.).

TOCH, ERNST (p. 1060, pl. **173.** 6). Born in Vienna in 1887 and died in Los Angeles in 1964, aged seventy-six. He was self-taught yet, nevertheless, as a young composer, won many prizes (Mozart Bursary, Mendelssohn Bursary, Austrian State Prize four times). After his middle twenties he lived in Mannheim as a teacher of composition: then in Berlin, for a short time in London, and afterwards in the United States, becoming naturalized in 1940.

His compositions are many and varied, and include eight string quartets, other chamber music (including many pieces for chamber orchestra), two piano concertos, three symphonies (the first at the age of sixty-three), four operas, and film music.

See *Oratorio* 7 (1947).

TODT (Ger.). 'Dead.' So such compounds as *Todtenmesse*, 'Mass for the dead', i.e. Requiem; *Todtenmarsch*, 'Dead march'; *Todtentanz*, 'Dance of Death' (cf. *Tot*; *Danse Macabre*).

TOE-PEDALS. See *Organ* 8.

TOESCHI, CARLO GIUSEPPE (c. 1723–88). An Italian violinist in the famous Mannheim orchestra under J. Stamitz, and a composer of chamber music, symphonies, etc.

TOGLI (It.). 'Take away' (imperative—used in organ music for the shutting off of any stop, etc.).

TOILE (Fr.). 'Curtain' (theatre).

TOLMIE, FRANCES. See *Scotland* 1.

TOMASCHEK, JOHANN WENZEL. Born at Skutsch, Bohemia, in 1774 and died at Prague in 1850, aged nearly seventy-six. He was a great piano teacher in Prague, with many distinguished pupils, and also a composer of all manner of instrumental and vocal works.

See reference under *Rhapsody*.

TOMASI, HENRI. Born at Marseilles in 1901, of Corsican parents and died in 1971. He studied in the conservatory of his native city and then in that of Paris, and in 1927 won the second *Prix de Rome*. He is known as the composer of much music of various types and as conductor of Radio-Paris.

TOMBEAU (Fr.). 'Tomb' (the term is fancifully used a good deal in compositions written in memory of some person).

TOM, BLIND. See *Blind Tom*; *Memory* 7.

TOM BOWLING. See *Dibdin*. (The name is originally that of a nautical character in Smollett's *Roderick Random*, 1748.)

TOME (Fr.). 'Volume.'

TOMKINS, THOMAS. Born at St. David's, Pembrokeshire, in 1573 and died at Martin Hussingtree, Worcestershire, in 1656, aged eighty-two or eighty-three. His father (also Thomas) was Precentor of Gloucester Cathedral, and his brother (also Thomas—which is confusing) was a lay-clerk of that cathedral. He himself was organist of the Chapel Royal (q.v.), London, and, for half a century, of Worcester Cathedral—until the discontinuance of organ and choir music with the coming into power of the Puritans (q.v.) deprived him of his position. He wrote instrumental music (see an allusion under *Pianoforte* 21), church music, and, especially, wonderful madrigals, which are much relished today by lovers of the superb musical art of the late sixteenth and early seventeenth centuries.

In addition to the brother above mentioned he had four others who were musicians. One of his nephews succeeded to his place as organist of Worcester Cathedral when the musical service was resumed after the Restoration.

The family is spoken of as that which 'produced more musicians than any other family in England'. There are actually twelve members of the family treated by Fellowes in Grove's *Dictionary*.

TOMMASINI, VINCENZO. Born in Rome in 1878 and there died in 1950, aged seventy-two. After classical study at the University of Rome, combined with musical study at the Conservatory of that city, he passed on to Germany, where he worked under Max Bruch, and to Paris, London, and New York.

One of his first works to attract attention was (1910) a String Quartet in F which received much praise. He followed this up by producing a good deal more instrumental music, and also

two or three operas and a ballet arranged from music by D. Scarlatti, *The Good-humoured Ladies*, which the Diaghilef company made widely known. He was an adherent of that modern Italian movement that sought to detach Italian music from the inevitability of its long-standing operatic association.

TOMMY-WALKER. See *Mirliton*.

TOM-TOM (p. 513, pl. **92**. 2). Native Indian or Chinese drum, or also gong (i.e. in the same sense as *Tam-Tam*; see *Percussion Family* 3 p, 4 c, 5 p). The true tom-tom (i.e. the drum type) is used in dance bands, etc.—in both a tunable and a non-tunable form.

TON (Fr., Ger.). (1) In **French** the word means:

(*a*) Pitch, as *Donner le ton*, 'to give the pitch'.

(*b*) 'Key', 'mode', as *Ton d'ut*, 'key C'; *Ton majeur*, 'major key'; *Ton d'église*, 'church mode'.

(*c*) Tone, in the sense of 'Gregorian Tone' (see *Gregorian Tones*). Somewhat akin to this are such expressions as *Ton de chasse*, 'hunting signal'—on the horn.

(*d*) 'Crook', as *Ton de trompette*, 'trumpet crook'; *Ton de cor*, 'horn crook'; *Ton de rechange*, 'spare crook' (or even simply 'crook').

(*e*) The interval 'tone', as distinct from *Demiton*, 'semitone'.

(*f*) 'Sound', 'note', etc. So *Ton aigre*, 'shrill sound'; *Ton bouché*, 'stopped note' of horn; *Ton doux*, 'sweet tone-quality'.

(2) In **German** (plur. *Töne*) the word means:

(*a*) Pitch, as *Den Ton angeben*, 'to give the pitch'.

(*b*) 'Key', 'mode', in compounds such as *Tongeschlecht*, 'tone-gender' (or some such idea), i.e. major or minor.

(*c*) 'Note', etc., as in such expressions and compounds as *Den Ton halten*, 'to hold the note'; *Tonabstand*, 'note stand-off' i.e. interval; *Tonfarbe*, 'tone-colour', i.e. timbre; *Tonfolge*, 'note-following', i.e. melody; *Tonfülle*, 'tone-fulness', i.e. volume of tone; *Tonhöhe*, 'note-height', i.e. pitch; *Tonlage*, 'note-lie', i.e. pitch, compass, register, etc.; *Tonleiter*, 'note-ladder', i.e. scale; *Tonreihe*, 'note-row' (q.v.), i.e. scale; *Tonmass*, 'tone-measure', i.e. 'time'; *Tonschlüssel*, 'note-key', i.e. keynote; *Tonsetzer*, 'note-setter', i.e. composer.

(*d*) 'Sound', 'music', in such compounds as *Tonkunst*, 'tone-art', i.e. knowledge, etc., of music; *Tonkünstler*, 'tone-artist', i.e. musician; *Tonlehre*, 'acoustics'; *Tonbühne*, 'music-stage', i.e. orchestra; *Tonbild*, 'tone picture'; *Tonmalerei*, 'music-painting', e.g. programme music (q.v.); *Tondichter*, 'tone-poet', i.e. 'composer'; *Tondichtung*, 'tone-poem' (see *Symphonic Poem*, and note that *Tondichter* and *Tondichtung* are not quite corresponding terms).

TONABSTAND (Ger.). See *Ton* 2 c.

TONADA (Spanish). The tune set to any poem or dance. Cf. *Tonadilla*.

TONADILLA (Spanish). The diminutive of tonada (q.v.). The word came, however, to mean a collection of verses sung to two or three tunes. By the middle of the eighteenth century the tonadilla had developed into a cantata, with solos and concerted vocal music and instrumental movements. Granados has composed tonadillas for solo voice and piano.

A great collection of tonadillas has been edited by José Subira and published under the auspices of the Royal Academy of Spain. For a hint as to the origin of the tonadilla see the article *Intermezzo*.

TONAL ANSWER in Fugue. See *Form* 12; *Tonal Fugue*, below.

TONAL FUGUE. One in which the answer is 'tonal', not 'real' (see *Form* 12). The distinction is rather absurd, as once the exposition is over the tonal treatment of the answer may cease.

TONALITY may be defined as loyalty to a tonic, in other words to the key scheme of a composition (see *Key*). As an example of the use of the word take the following—'*Without a clearly defined tonality music is impossible*'. That was written by Professor Prout in *Musical Form*, in 1893, at which time there were only just becoming known the mature works of Debussy, with their use of the whole-tone scale (which admits of no tonality in the sense intended by Prout). Since that time the methods of polytonality and atonality have been much explcited, to say nothing of microtonality—all of which are the negation of Tonality, in the proper sense of the word. (But see *Harmony* 18, footnote, for a somewhat conflicting view.)

For the sake of precision it may be added that the word 'tonality', although usually understood as above, may on occasion be used in a larger way—so as to have application also to the large body of composition (mostly preceding the late sixteenth century) in which the modes were strictly observed and no knowledge shown of what we call 'Key': such composition was based on a series of notes grouped about a chief one or 'tonic', and hence may be said to have expressed in a different way from that of the composition of the centuries that followed a sense of 'tonality'. One is compelled to think that Prout would give the term this wide definition, as otherwise the statement quoted would exclude a great body of fine music that was known to him.

The whole general subject is discussed under the headings *Scales* and *Modes*, and important considerations in reference to it are treated under the headings *Harmony* and *Form*.

TONAL SEQUENCE. See *Sequence*.

TONANTE (It.). 'Thunderous.'

TONART (Ger.). Literally 'Tone-kind' or 'Tone-type'; applied both to the modes (as Dorian, Lydian, etc.) and to the scales (as major and minor).

TONBILD, TONBÜHNE, TONDICHTER (Ger.). See *Ton* 2 d.

TONDICHTUNG (Ger.). Symphonic poem (q.v.).

TONDO (It.). 'Round', i.e. full-toned.

TONE. This is a word of several meanings.

(1) Musical sound. E.g. 'loud tone', 'soft tone', 'thin tone', 'poor tone', 'good tone'. For Tone Colour see *Colour and Music* 3; for Tone Poem see *Symphonic Poem*.

(2) The interval of the major second, i.e. of two semitones, e.g. C–D, E–F sharp, etc.

(3) A single sound of definite pitch. E.g. 'Tones may be either long or short'; and 'Tones may be either high or low' (John Curwen's *Teachers' Manual*, 1875). This is an accepted American use today, the British, for the most part, continuing to use the word 'note' (according to the immemorial practice of the English language), and so creating confusion with the word 'note' in its other meanings but (which is, perhaps, more important) avoiding it with 'tone' in the sense of a major 2nd (see *American Musical Terminology* 1).

(4) Gregorian tones (q.v.).

(5) Resultant tone (see *Acoustics* 10). This is really an instance where what is in general the American connotation of 'tone' (see 3 above) is accepted by British acousticians and musicians.

TÖNE (Ger.). Plural of *Ton* (see *Ton* 2), generally in the sense of 'sounds' or 'notes'.

TONE CLUSTERS. This is the term applied to complexes of notes played on the piano with forearms and fists. Henry Cowell (q.v.) introduced this style of playing and composed accordingly (including a concerto).

TÖNENDE HANDSCHRIFT. See *Electric Musical Instruments* 5 c.

TONE POEM. See *Symphonic Poem*.

TONE-ROW. See *Note-row*.

TONFARBE, TONFOLGE, TONFÜLLE (Ger.). See *Ton* 2 c.

TONGESCHLECHT (Ger.). See *Ton* 2 b.

TONGS AND BONES. A ready-to-hand domestic means of music-making once popular. 'I have a reasonable good ear in music; let's have the tongs and the bones' (Bottom in *A Midsummer Night's Dream*).

Cf. *Marrow-Bones and Cleavers*; *Bellows and Tongs*; *Saltbox*; *Bladder and String*.

TONGUING. In the playing of wind instruments the interruption of the wind stream by a movement of the tongue. Thus 'single-tonguing' (the normal method of playing) is effected by an action of the tongue equivalent to the enunciation of repeated T's, 'double tonguing' by the repetition of the group T K, and 'triple-tonguing' by the repetition of T T K, T K T, or some such group. (Consonants such as D and G are also used for a softer degree of articulation.) Double and triple tonguing allow of more rapid performance of passages or of repeated notes. See references under

Flute Family 2; *Oboe Family* 1; *Clarinet Family* 1; *Horn Family* 1; *Trumpet Family* 1; *Cornet* 1.

A variety of tonguing introduced by Strauss (applicable chiefly to the flute but also possible on the clarinet and some brass) is that of trilling an 'r' whilst playing a chromatic scale: he calls it *Flatterzunge* (i.e. *Flutter-tonguing*).

TONHÖHE (Ger.). See *Ton* 2 c.

TONIC. The first degree of the major or minor key. The 'key note' from which the key takes its name, as Key of A, etc.

TONIC ACCENT. See *Rubato* 3.

TONIC SOL-FA

1. Its History.
2. Its Root Principles.
3. The Modulator.
4. The Notation of Rhythm.

5. An Example of Tonic Sol-fa Notation.
6. The Simplification of Bar or Measure.

7. Mental Effects and Key.
8. The Minor.
9. Time Names.
10. Some Further Points.

1. Its History. This is a particular system of teaching sight-singing (q.v.) which in the mid-nineteenth century arose in England and quickly spread over the English-speaking world, and which has had some vogue in non-English-speaking countries.

The great protagonist of the movement was a Congregational minister, John Curwen (1816–80; p. 976, pl. **163.** 4). Himself considered to be without musical ear, he sought a method by which not only he but the young people in whom he was, as a minister, interested, might learn to sing at sight. He found a Norwich lady, Miss S. A. Glover (p. 976, pl. **163.** 2), teaching upon a *movable doh* method that made all keys alike and so might be said to reduce the labour by eleven-twelfths: this system seemed to him to be psychologically sound and he perfected it, and eventually founded a society, a college, and a publishing firm (now J. Curwen & Sons, Ltd.) for the carrying on of the work.

The system, whilst eagerly seized upon by many, was opposed by others. It did not attract musicians possessing the sense of absolute pitch, who do not need a system (see *Sight-Singing* 5), and it found an actual opponent in Dr. John Hullah (q.v.), who had recently imported from France the Wilhem system, based on the fixed doh, and who, from 1872, held the strategic position of government inspector of music in teachers' training colleges. The Hullah system eventually weakened and died, and the tonic sol-fa system triumphed. It had long, however, to struggle under the heavy weight of social inferiority; respectable society in Victorian Britain looked down upon anything that was concerned with religious nonconformity and was popular in the people's schools (or 'Board' schools, as they were then called, from the fact that they were governed by the elected School Boards). The naïvety and lack of musical taste of many of the leaders of the tonic sol-fa movement was also an impediment to its rapid recognition in cultured circles. The very fact that the system enabled elementary school teachers who had had themselves no regular musical education to do successful sight-singing work, and artisans to become efficient choralists, meant that there was quickly brought into existence a new musical class which possessed technical skill, without (at first) much artistic taste. Nevertheless the growth of choral society work, in itself, was a sufficient testimony to the value of the system, and from the eighties onwards it had few serious opponents (cf. *Wales* 6).

Although the system, as we have it, originated with Miss Glover and Mr. Curwen, it is a mistake to look upon it as altogether new. The root-difficulty in sight-singing which it was intended to remove was that of the aural conception of a note as a preliminary to its being sung, and the method by which this was secured was essentially the historical one, dating from the eleventh century and at one time universal over Europe (see *Hexachord* for an explanation), of considering the whole range of singable sounds as divided into groups exactly similar as to intervals and only differing in the pitch of the group as a group. This method had prevailed for nearly six hundred years and had then been discarded in face of new difficulties due to an enormously enhanced complexity in music itself and its gradual adoption of a system of twelve scales of seven different notes (our misnamed 'octave' system), with all the scales exactly alike as to order of tones and semitones, which inevitably clashed with an attempt to read music on a system of three six-note groups of notes, also alike in their order of tones and semitones. Had a Curwen been born in 1516 or even 1616, instead of 1816, he would doubtless have made the necessary adaptation, and tonic sol-fa (which borrows its very note names from the hexachordal system) would have continued the older system without break of continuity and perhaps without opposition.

It would appear (and so far as the present writer is aware the point has not previously been clearly brought out) that, in essentials, the Curwen system was slightly anticipated in America. D. Sower, in 1832 (eleven years before Curwen's first publication), issued in Philadelphia his *Norristown New and Much Improved Music Reader*, which applied the syllables 'do, re, mi, fa, sol, la, si' to the seven notes of the scale on tonic principles (i.e. with 'do' always for the keynote and the other names accordingly). The staff notation was used with a differently shaped note-head for each degree of the scale (see reference to 'Buckwheat Notation' under *Lancashire Sol-fa*—end of that article).

2. Its Root Principles. The general principle of the tonic sol-fa note-system is as follows.

The material for all simple singable tunes is more or less completely embodied in Diagram I, which represents just over two octaves of vocal range in any key.

DIAGRAM I

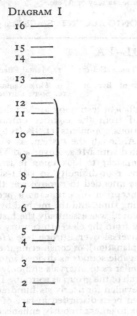

16 ——

15 ——
14 ——

13 ——

12 ——
11 ——

10 ——

9 ——

8 ——
7 ——

6 ——

5 ——
4 ——

3 ——

2 ——

1 ——

In this diagram the markings represent musical sounds ranged in relative pitch, and the spaces between the markings represent the intervals between the sounds, the wider spaces representing whole-tones, the narrower spaces semitones. The number of markings here shown, and the choice of the upper and lower limits of the diagram, are arbitrary, and the numbers attached to them are arbitrarily inserted for purposes of reference in this article. It will be seen that the pattern repeats itself at every eighth step; this is because every note has its 'octave' above and below. The diagram can be considered as potentially continued on this pattern upwards and downwards.

That a tune fits in with this framework can be demonstrated by comparing its pitch-intervals with the space intervals of the diagram. It will be found, for instance, that 'God save the Queen' corresponds to the series 5, 5, 6, 4, 5, 6, etc.; 'Charlie is my darling' begins 3, 4, 5, 6, 7, 10; the folk-song 'I'm seventeen come Sunday' (in the Dorian mode) runs 9, 10, 9, 10, 8, 6, 6, 6, etc. This suggests a means of co-operation between two persons. One can sing the notes of a tune and the other can point to the corresponding marks on the diagram. By a reverse process, one person can point to marks on the diagram and the other can (after some practice) sing the corresponding notes. We have thus arrived at a form of notation. To make it practical, some method other than pointing must be found for the indication of marks in

the diagram. The marks must have identification that can be set down in print. The most obvious suggestion is to identify them by a series of numbers (1 to 7); this has been tried and, in various ways, found wanting. Another suggestion is to attach names to the markings; this has been tried and found highly successful. It is, in fact, the tonic sol-fa system. An existing series of names that, as already mentioned, had been in use for a kindred purpose offered themselves as a basis, namely:

ut re mi fa sol la si

It was thought advisable to anglicize these and to make such changes that each name should consist of a consonant followed by a vowel, and that the seven consonants should be different. The series arrived at was:

doh ray me fah soh lah te

These words are used for the naming of notes by word of mouth. In printed notation the following abbreviations are used:

d　r　m　f　s　l　t

Only seven names are used because outside that range repetitions occur at the octave. Repetitions at the octave above are shown thus: **d^l r^l m^l** etc. Repetitions at the octave below are shown thus: **t$_l$ l$_l$ s$_l$** etc.

The name doh was attached to the note that happens to occur fifth in our diagram above. That diagram therefore now reads (from the bottom upwards):[1]

f$_l$ s$_l$ l$_l$ t$_l$ d r m f s l t d^l r^l m^l f^l s^l

The opening notes of 'God save the Queen' now become **d d r t$_l$ d r**; of 'Charlie is my darling' **l$_l$ t$_l$ d r m l**; of 'I'm seventeen come Sunday' **s l s l f r r r**.

So far we have considered only the diatonic (q.v.) scale, which is the general basis of singable tunes. But such tunes often make temporary departures from the scheme of Diagram I by the introduction of sharpened or flattened notes. The notes susceptible of sharpening are **d r f s l**, which become **de re fe se le**. The notes suceptible of flattening are **r m l t**, which become **ra ma la ta** (pronounced to rhyme with 'aw'). The minor scale (from l$_l$ to l) also makes departures which are not 'accidental' but essential. There are three forms of minor scale. One corresponds to Diagram I (and to the Aeolian mode, see *Modes*): **l$_l$ t$_l$ d r m f s l**. Another, the most frequently used (the 'harmonic' minor), substitutes **se** for **s** and runs **l$_l$ t$_l$ d r m f se l**. A third, used chiefly in ascending melodic phrases (the 'melodic' minor, ascending), sharpens both **f** and **s**; since the mental effect (see below) of the sharpened **f** (leading as it does to **se**) is different from that of the note **fe** (which leads to **s**), a new name is given to it, **ba** (called 'bay'). This form of the minor scale therefore runs:

<hr/>

[1] The notes which, when they are doh, are represented without an octave mark range from middle C and (C flat) up to the B above in soprano and contralto music. In tenor and bass music the range is an octave lower.

l₁ t₁ d r m ba se l. The notation of a scale, with its variants, is now complete, and Diagram I can be elaborated as follows:

DIAGRAM II

sˡ	or	sohˡ
fˡ		fahˡ
mˡ		meˡ
rˡ		rayˡ
dˡ		dohˡ
t		te
l		lah
s		soh
f		fah
m		me
r		ray
d		doh
t₁		te₁
l₁		lah₁
s₁		soh₁
f₁		fah₁

The following shows the connexion between the two notations, the keys being chosen arbitrarily:

DOH de RAY re ME FAH

fe SOH se LAH le TE DOHˡ

DOHˡ TE ta LAH la SOH

fe FAH ME ma RAY ra DOH

l₁ t₁ d r m ba se

l s f m r d t₁ l₁

The utility of the notation lies in the fact that a quick correspondence can be set up in the mind between a sol-fa syllable and the sound of the note which it represents. Each of the notes in Diagram I has a mental effect set up by its position relative to the other notes. The mention of a sol-fa syllable, or the sight of its printed initial, brings the mental effect, and as this mental effect is purely that of a sound, the voice is immediately directed to that sound (see 7).

Departures from Diagram I are not always temporary (i.e. 'chromatic'). When they are insistent they may dislocate the mental effects associated with the series. As a rule what such changes do is to set up an identically similar series in another position, as if Diagram I had been shifted so many degrees or half-degrees up or down. The music has changed key, or 'modulated'. In tonic sol-fa the mental effects become attached to their new positions, and in the notation a link has to be made where the change occurs. This is done by printing adjacently a small symbol for the mental effect of a note as approached in the earlier key and a full-sized symbol for the mental effect of the same note as quitted in the later key. Examples are shown in the musical extract on pp. 1034–5. The commonest modulations are those which lead to the dominant and subdominant keys. The former case occurs when fe is introduced instead of f and the substitution is maintained. The fe changes to t₁ (or t), the former s, a semitone above, becomes the new d (or dˡ), and the other changes fall into line. The latter case occurs when ta is introduced, and maintained instead of t. The ta becomes f (or f₁), and the former f, a fourth lower, becomes the new d (or d₁). These changes are known as one sharp remove and one flat remove (in the staff-notation they introduce one more sharp and one more flat respectively into the key-signature). There can be key-changes of two, three, four, five, or six sharp removes or flat removes, the last kind (t becoming f, or vice versa) being rare and difficult. Where, in the course of a piece of music that is set down in tonic sol-fa notation, a change of key occurs, a letter indicating the new key is printed over the notes that mark the change. By the side of this letter are printed indications of the notes that are newly brought into the scale by the change —to the left of the key-letter for flat removes, to the right for sharp removes. Thus, at change of key from G to E the newly introduced notes are D sharp, G sharp, and C sharp, which become the new t m and l. The indication of the change is thus: E. t. m. l. This somewhat cumbrous notation is academic rather than practical, and it has now been superseded. Instead of the new notes, the number of removes is indicated (the t and the f being, however, retained for single removes). Thus the above key-change would now be indicated by E. 3. Some examples follow: C to G is shown by G. t.; C to F by f. F; C to A flat by 4. A♭; A to B by B. 2.; B flat to E by E. 6.; A flat to E (eight sharp removes) by its equivalent (four flat removes) in the other direction, 4. E,[1] etc.

[1] Sometimes, more accurately, 4. F♭ = E, or 4 as E.

In a change to a minor key it is usual to indicate the new doh. Thus C to G minor is shown by 2. B♭. The numerals have a practical use, for an expert tonic sol-fa sight-reader knows the 'mental effects' of the various modulations and associates them with these figures, which act as a warning and a guide. Some tonic sol-fa printers do away with these complicated details altogether and simply put 'Key so-and-so' where a change occurs.

3. The Modulator. Early practice in the use of the tonic sol-fa names and in the changing of key is carried on by reference to a kind of map of the system known as a modulator. This can be more or less elaborate according to the stage at which it is used. A fairly simple example is shown in Diagram III.

DIAGRAM III				
l	r'	soh'	d'	f'
			t	m'
s	d'	fah'		
	t	me'	l	r'
f				
m	l	ray'	s	d'
				t
r	s	doh'	f	
		te	m	l
d	f			
t,	m	lah	r	s
l,	r	soh	d	f
			t,	m
s,	d	fah		
	t,	me	l,	r
f,				
m,	l,	ray	s,	d
				t,
r,	s,	doh	f,	
		te,	m,	l,
d,	f,			
t₂	m,	lah,	r,	s,
l₂	r,	soh,	d,	f,
			t₂	m,
s₂	d,	fah,		

The upright columns show a central key with adjacent keys, one sharp remove and two sharp removes on the right, one flat remove and two flat removes on the left. A complete modulator would show a whole cycle of keys, the sixth removes to the right and to the left being identical.[1] It must be borne in mind that the central key can be *any* key, just as Diagram I, of which Diagram III is an elaboration, can represent any key.

4. The Notation of Rhythm. The system

[1] Assuming the use of the tempered scale, as on all our keyed instruments (see *Temperament*).

of notating rhythm in the tonic sol-fa is as logical as the system of notating pitch, and here an actual visual representation is offered where the staff-notation offers none. The beat, or 'pulse', is the unit and occupies the same amount of horizontal space throughout a score, the half-beat occupying half this amount of space, a two-beat note occupying double, and so forth. Double dots (like a colon) separate beat from beat, single dots are used when necessary to divide the beat into half-beats, commas to divide the half-beats into quarter-beats and commas reversed to show triplets, lines are used to show that notes are held on and blanks indicate rests—and so forth.

5. An Example of Tonic Sol-fa Notation. The notational material of tonic sol-fa is largely exemplified in the piece of unaccompanied music for mixed voices on pp. 1034–5. This is shown in both notations in order that comparison between the two may indicate certain tonic sol-fa usages that are not here explained verbally.

6. The Simplification of Bar or Measure. The tonic sol-fa time-notation does not lend itself to the confusing alternatives that enter into the use of time-symbols in a staff-notation. Thus, a tonic sol-fa 'measure' of four pulses:

$$| \quad : \quad | \quad : \quad |$$

stands equally for a bar of $\frac{4}{2}$ $\frac{4}{4}$ or $\frac{4}{8}$ time to a conductor's beat. The only common exception to the general rule that a pulse is a beat occurs in fairly quick $\frac{6}{8}$ time, which is represented thus:

$$| \quad : \quad : \quad | \quad : \quad : \quad |$$

although it may be more natural to beat twice in a bar than six times. The triplet notation shown in the extract on p. 1034 is as a rule reserved for places where three notes temporarily occupy the time normally taken by two; thus:

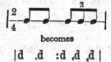

becomes

$$|d \ .d \ :d \ .d \ .d \ |$$

It will be noted, in the example, that ♪♪ is represented by **d .,d** : the characteristic appearance of which becomes associated with this strongly characteristic rhythmic effect.

7. Mental Effects and Key. In the elementary stages of teaching, when the pupil is first taught to associate the tonic sol-fa names with the aural conception of the notes, it is customary to aid the process by attributing certain emotional and picturesque qualities to certain notes—firmness to doh, sadness to lah, calmness to me, etc. These effects are felt only in the simplest uses of the notes of the major key (in which the earliest studies are made), and are discarded as soon as they have served their purpose. Such 'mental effects' are of a different order from the positional 'mental effects' referred to in 2 above, which are the permanent connexion between music and the tonic sol-fa notation.

8. The Minor. Owing to the prevalence of the major key in music the major tonic chord is taken as the first step in tonic sol-fa study, and it remains the basis of the notation in practice. This has led many educationists to suppose that 'doh = tonic' is the chief element in the principle of the notation. They argue from this that 'doh = tonic' should also be observed in the minor key, which, in its harmonic form, they would sol-fa thus:

$$d \ r \ ma \ f \ s \ la \ t \ d^l$$

This, however, does not tally with the system by which the tonic sol-fa names stand as identifications in Diagram I, and it departs from the tonic sol-fa system at that point, i.e. at its very foundation. This way of dealing with the minor scale is known as the 'doh minor'. The tonic sol-fa way is known as the 'lah minor'. It will be seen that the latter agrees with staff-notation practice in the use of key-signatures, which, for instance, gives the same signature to C minor and E flat major.

9. Time Names. A valuable teaching device, which does not appear in the actual notation of sol-fa but is much used in the classroom and choir practice room, is that of 'the time-names. These are borrowed from the Galin–Paris–Chevé system, used in France, though the ultimate origin may be in the various systems of syllables used from time to time to indicate drummers' rhythms (see, for instance, a tabulation of these in Arbeau's *Orchésographie*, 1588).

They are based on the principle that the ear measures time not by duration but by accents which mark off the duration. On this scheme (which is chiefly applied to definite rhythm exercises sung on one note, but can be referred to at any moment if rhythmic difficulty crops up in practice), the beginning of a beat is always called 'taa'; a beat extended into another beat becomes 'taa-aa'; a beat divided into two half-beats is 'taa-tai': a beat divided into four quarter-beats is 'ta-fa-te-fe', and so on. These names, when first introduced, are pronounced rhythmically and thereafter remain in the mind not merely as names but as rhythmic equivalents—as the *rhythm itself* expressed in words.

10. Some Further Points. Many are opposed to the sol-fa notation who accept the sol-fa system. Their opposition to the notation is usually based on the supposition (probably erroneous) that it takes more time to learn two notations than to learn one. In view of a large amount of vocal music not being published in sol-fa notation and practically no instrumental music being so published, the staff-notation has, they say, sooner or later to be learnt, and as well sooner as later! Those who take this view

apply the principles of tonic sol-fa to the staff-notation, without much difficulty. 'When doh is on a line', they teach, 'me is on the next line above and soh on the next above that, and top doh on the next space but one above soh'; and similarly with doh on a space. As for the question of where to find 'doh', that is simple. In a sharp signature the last sharp is 'te'; in a flat signature the last flat is 'fah' (or, if preferred, the last flat but one is 'doh'). This adaptation works very easily, but there is loss on the rhythmic side—which can be partly got over by freely using the French time-names.

Systems of **Hand Signs** for pitch and rhythm (useful in class work) are an ingenious element in the complete tonic sol-fa method and are equally applicable to movable-doh teaching by staff.

As already mentioned, a tonic method without the sol-fa names is sometimes used, with **Numbers** for the notes. (Numbers were perhaps first proposed by Father J. J. Souhaitty, of Paris, in his *Nouvelle Méthode*, 1665, and the plan was afterwards adapted by Rousseau and others.) It loses the advantage of the singable syllables and offers no other advantage in compensation. (See reference to Galin–Paris–Chevé, under *Sight-Singing* 2.)

The **Tonic Sol-fa Literature** is. copious and some of the older books are still decidedly worth study (especially those of John Curwen himself), for the early sol-faists, though rarely cultured musicians, were practical working psychologists, basing all their methods upon actual experience in the classroom, and past-masters in the art of grading their instruction by steps so small as to offer no obstacle.

The German system of **Tonika-do** is an adaptation of Curwen's system; the movement was started by Agnes Hundoegger (1858–1927); it is promoted by a society, which holds conferences and carries on a journal. There is another popular adaptation in Poland.

For the **old English method** of sol-faing (not included in this article, as it is not, completely, a 'tonic' system) see *Lancashire Sol-fa.*

It is worth noting, as an explanation of expressions found in older literature, that the time-honoured connexion of the sol-fa syllables with choral singing has led to the use of the word 'sol-fa' for a roll of music or baton used in time-beating, and, by an extension of metaphor, for any sort of beating or stern treatment. As late as 1880 we find Rockstro reporting of the Sistine Choir in Rome, 'The Conductor beats time with a roll of music called the Sol-fa'. And in the Italian language 'battere la sol-fa' has come to mean 'to be imperious or stern'. In Massinger's *New Way to Pay Old Debts* (published 1633) we find Overreach threatening to punish his servant with 'I shall sol-fa you, rogue . . . only fit for beating'.

This article was contributed to the first edition of this book by the late W. McNaught. In 1954 it was checked and approved by the late Mr. Frederick Green, of the Curwen Memorial College.

TONIC SOL-FA COLLEGE

TONIC SOL-FA COLLEGE. Founded in 1879 by John Curwen, a building being erected at Forest Gate, on the east side of London. In 1944 the College moved to Queensborough Terrace, W. 2., and took the additional name of 'Curwen Memorial College'.

See a reference under *Coward, Henry*.

TONIKA-DO. See *Tonic Sol-fa* (end of article).

TONITRUONE (It.). Sheet of iron, loosely hanging and shaken to produce a thunder effect.

TONKUNST, TONKÜNSTLER (Ger.). See *Ton* 2 d.

TONKÜNSTLERSOCIETÄT. See *Concert* 13.

TONLAGE (Ger.). See *Ton* 2 c.

TONLEHRE (Ger.). See *Ton* 2 d.

TONLEITER (Ger.). See *Ton* 2 c.

TONLOS (Ger.). 'Toneless.'

TONMALEREI (Ger.). See *Ton* 2 d.

TONNA, CHARLOTTE ELIZABETH (1780–1846). Irish Protestant writer. See *No Surrender!*

TONNERRE (Fr.). 'Thunder.'

TONO (It.). (1) Tone in general sense; (2) key, mode; (3) Gregorian tone (see *Gregorian Tones*); (4) thunder. The plural is *Toni*.

TONO (Sp.). A sort of Spanish part song or madrigal, of two or three verses, sung before a play in the time of the dramatist Calderón (1600–81)—a kind of choral overture or greeting to the public, often humorous.

TONOMETER. See *Pitch* 6 b.

TONOTECHNIE. See *Mechanical Reproduction of Music* 6.

TONREIHE (Ger.). 'Note-row' (q.v.).

TONSCHLÜSSEL (Ger.). See *Ton* 2 c.

TONSETZER (Ger.). See *Ton* 2 c.

TONSILS. See *Voice* 21.

TONUS (Lat.). (1) Mode; (2) Gregorian tone (see *Gregorian Tones*; and for *Tonus Peregrinus* see *Anglican Chant* 2).

TOOLE or TUTILO. See *Ireland* 2.

TOPLADY, AUGUSTUS MONTAGUE (1740–78). Anglican divine, controversialist, and hymn-writer. See *Hymns and Hymn Tunes* 6, 7.

TORCH DANCE. The name carries its own meaning (see also *Fackeltanz*).

TORCH SONG. This is described by a New York conductor of popular music as follows: 'I would say that the term is Negro in origin; the thing itself, not exclusively. 'Torch songs, anyway, are so called because of the subject, and torch singers are simply those ladies who have the right emotional flavour, voice, and personality to put over the sensations of un-requited love ["carrying the torch"] at full force.'

TORDION or **TOURDION**. See *Basse Danse*.

TORELLI, GIUSEPPE. Born at Verona in 1658 and died at Bologna in 1709, aged fifty. He was a violinist and composer of string music, of high reputation. He is considered to have been the first composer to write a concerto (in the sense in which the word is used in speaking of the works of Handel, etc.).

See reference under *Concerto* 2.

TORNADA (Sp.). A type of refrain in many of the folk songs of Catalonia.

TORNARE, TORNANDO (It.). 'To return', 'returning'.

TORONTO. See *Schools of Music*; *Macmillan*.

TORVO (It.). 'Grim.'

TOSCA (Puccini). Produced at Rome in 1900. Libretto by Illica and Giacosa, after Sardou's drama *La Tosca*.

ACT I

SCENE: *Sant' Andrea alla Valle, Rome. Time, 1800*

Cesare Angelotti (*Bass*) finds in the church a hiding-place in his escape from prison, where he has been confined for political offences. The painter **Mario Cavaradossi** (*Tenor*) enters, to resume work on his picture of Mary Magdalen. As a model he has used, unknown to her, a lady who comes daily to the church to pray. He does not know that she is Angelotti's sister. The **Sacristan** (*Baritone*) is shocked at what he considers a sacrilege. When he has gone, Angelotti comes out. Cavaradossi recognizes him as the Consul of the moribund Roman Republic. As the voice of **Floria Tosca** (*Soprano*) a famous singer, is heard seeking the painter, Angelotti again hides. Tosca, in love with Cavaradossi, is jealous of the unknown model. She leaves, and the painter arranges to help Angelotti to escape in woman's clothes. A cannon is heard. It gives news of the prisoner's escape.

Baron Scarpia (*Baritone*), the Chief of Police, who in his pursuit of Angelotti has come to the church, finds a fan left by Angelotti's sister, and the painter's lunch-basket, empty. The Sacristan knows Cavaradossi did not eat the food. Scarpia is suspicious. So is Tosca, whom Scarpia covets. He produces the fan, to make her jealously doubt Cavaradossi, his rival.

ACT II

SCENE: *Scarpia's Apartments in the Farnese Palace*

Scarpia is awaiting Tosca, who is to sup with him. His agent **Spoletta** (*Tenor*) brings in Cavaradossi, a prisoner. His plot to free Angelotti is known. As he will not confess, he is tortured, and Tosca, compelled to hear his cries, promises to tell where Angelotti is, if the painter be freed. He, being brought in, spurns her, and on hearing of the defeat of the royal

troops, defies Scarpia, and bids him beware. The Baron retorts that Cavaradossi shall be shot. The painter is taken out, and Scarpia begs Tosca to yield to him. She promises to do so if he will spare her lover. Scarpia lets her believe that he will—that blank cartridges will be fired at the 'execution'; but actually he does not intend to interfere. Scarpia claims his price, and Tosca stabs him to death.

ACT III

SCENE: *The Battlements of the Castle of Sant' Angelo*

A Shepherd (*Boy's voice*) greets the dawn. Cavaradossi writes his farewell to Tosca, but she soon comes with news of the pretended execution, as they believe it to be. They laugh over the scene when he is to fall, and lie very still, 'just like Tosca on the stage', until the soldiers have gone. But the bullets are real, and the painter is killed. Tosca at first will not believe that he is not acting, but when she discovers the truth, and finds that the murder of Scarpia is known, she defeats the agents who are coming up the stairs to arrest her by throwing herself over the battlements.

TOSCANINI, ARTURO. Born at Parma in 1867 and died in New York in 1957, aged eighty-nine. He stood at the very head of the list of the world's orchestral conductors. He had illimitable versatility (conducting equally well the works of widely different schools), a perfect memory (myopia obliged him always to conduct without the score), and a personality that dominated at need recalcitrant artists, a demanding public, or the authorities of a totalitarian State.

His activity was world-wide, but centred mainly on the opera-houses and concert plat-forms of Milan and New York.

See references under *Tempo*; *Germany* 9; *Jewish* 9.

TOSELLI, ENRICO. Born at Florence in 1883 and died there in 1926. He composed, especially, a good deal of instrumental music and his name is known all over the world through a Serenata of fabulous popularity.

TOSI. See *Singing* 5; *Rubato* 2.

TOSSE DA CAPRA. See *Shake*.

TOSTI, FRANCESCO PAOLO. Born in the Abruzzi in 1846 and died in Rome in 1916, aged seventy. He was singing-master to the queen of Italy and later to the British royal family, settled permanently in London, and was knighted. He wrote multitudes of graceful drawing-room songs (including *Good-bye!*), which enjoyed immense favour.

TOSTO (It.). 'Rapid', e.g. (1) *Più tosto*—'quicker'. (2) But note that *Più tosto*, or *Piuttosto*, as an ordinary Italian expression means 'rather', either in 'rather than' connexions (cf. the English 'sooner', which has come to be used for 'rather' in similar connexions) or in the sense of 'somewhat'. (3) And *Tosto* sometimes means 'immediately', 'without waiting'.

The superlatives are *Tostissimo* (adjective); *Tostissimamente* (adverb).

TOSTQUARTETTE (Haydn). See *Nicknamed Compositions* 12.

TOT. Modern spelling of *Todt* (q.v.).

TOTENTANZ (Ger.). 'Dance of Death.' Cf. *Danse macabre*.

TOUCH on Pianoforte, etc. See *Pianoforte* 14; *Pianoforte Playing and Teaching* 8; *Organ* 12.

TOUCHE (Fr.). Finger-board—of violin, etc., e.g. *Sur la touche*, bow over the finger-board.

TOUCHER. See reference under *Toccata*.

TOUJOURS (Fr.). 'Always.'

TOURDION or **TORDION**. See *Basse Danse*.

TOURNEMIRE, CHARLES ARNOULD (1870–1939). Notable French organist and composer of varied works. See reference under *Improvisation* 2.

TOURS, BERTHOLD. Born at Rotterdam in 1838 and died in London in 1897, aged fifty-eight. For the latter half of his life he was musical adviser to Messrs. Novello, of London, and through them he published neat and effective music for the English Church, songs, violin pieces, etc., which remain in currency.

TOURTE, FRANÇOIS. See *Violin Family* 5.

TOUT, TOUTE; TOUS, TOUTES (Fr.). 'All' (masc., fem. sing.; masc., fem. plur.).

TOUT À COUP (Fr.). 'Suddenly.'

TOUT À FAIT (Fr.). 'Completely.'

TOUT DE SUITE (Fr.). 'Immediately.'

TOUT ENSEMBLE (Fr.). The whole, the general effect.

TOVEY, DONALD FRANCIS (p. 337, pl. **54.** 3). Born at Eton in 1875 and died in Edinburgh in 1940, aged nearly sixty-five. From early childhood he showed remarkable musical talent. At twenty-five he definitely took up the musical life by appearing in London and on the Continent as a solo pianist—always with high success.

As a musician of great and varied activity, severe ideals, and enormous learning, he exercised great influence through his tenancy of the chair of music at the University of Edinburgh (1914 onwards) and through his writings, which include most of the musical articles in the fourteenth edition of the *Encyclopædia Britannica*—later collected as a book. His programme annotations for his Edinburgh concerts are amongst the best ever put forth and they, too, have been reprinted in book form. He composed much chamber music, a piano concerto, a cello concerto, a symphony, and an opera (*The Bride of Dionysus*, produced 1929). He also edited and completed Bach's *Art of Fugue* (see *Art of Fugue*). In 1935 he was knighted.

See *Flute Family* 6, *Clarinet Family* 6; *Garreta*; *Oboe Family* 4 f, 6; *Violin Family* 10.

TOYE. Occasional sixteenth- and early seventeenth-century title for any light type of virginal composition.

TOYE, THE BROTHERS.

(1) FRANCIS (1883–1964). Composer, voice-teacher, journalist, and the author of standard books on Verdi and Rossini.

(2) GEOFFREY (1889–1942). Conductor and composer.

'TOY' SYMPHONY (German *Kinder-symphonie*, i.e. 'Children's Symphony'. French *La Foire des enfants*, i.e. 'The Children's Fair'; or *Symphonie burlesque*). This type of entertainment was traditionally said to owe its origin to Haydn, who according to the story bought certain toy instruments at a fair, wrote a score utilizing them, and had it played by his orchestra at Esterházy (see *Haydn*). The symphony (now considered to be part of a larger work by Leopold Mozart) is still published and often played in schools (occasionally, too, by adults and sometimes by famous musicians as a joke). It is scored for two violins, double-bass, and keyboard instrument (these supplying the basis), with toys as follows: trumpet, drum, rattle, triangle, 'quail', cuckoo, and 'nightingale' (i.e. 'bird warbler').

A similar composition (but rather more elaborate) is the 'Toy' Symphony of Andreas Romberg (1767–1821), which also is kept in print today and often played.

Other composers also have written such things, e.g. J. André; Algernon Ashton; K. J. Bischoff; R. Blagrove; E. Grenzbach (Waltzes, etc.); J. Lachner; O. Lessmann (Waltzes); C. Meyer; H. Meyer; C. H. C. Reinecke, D. L. Ryan; Franklin Taylor; M. Wallenstein; (Mendelssohn wrote two, but they are lost).

TRACEY, HUGH. See *African Music Society*; *Harmony* 4.

TR. Short for *Trumpet*.

TRACHEA. See *Voice* 21.

TRACKER. See *Organ* 1.

TRACT. One of the psalmodic interludes in the Roman Catholic liturgy, occurring between the Epistle and the Gospel, replaced since the time of St. Gregory by the Alleluia (q.v.) and now only surviving in use from Septuagesima to Easter. It has, of course, its traditional plainsong.

TRADOTTO (It.), **TRADUIT** (Fr.). (1) 'Translated' ; (2) 'arranged' (see *Arrangement*); (3) 'transposed'.

TRADUZIONE (It.), **TRADUCTION** (Fr.). (1) 'Translation'; (2) 'arrangement' (q.v.); (3) 'transposition'.

TRAETTA, TOMMASO. Born at Naples in 1727 and died at Venice in 1779, aged fifty-two. He was a pupil of Durante (q.v.), who from his early twenties enjoyed fame as an opera composer. For seven years he was attached to the court of Russia (see *Opera* 17 a) and he then spent a little time in London. His operas numbered nearly forty, and he left also some church music and independent arias, etc. The historical importance of this composer tends to become more fully recognized.

TRAGIC SYMPHONY (Schubert). See *Nick-named Compositions* 18.

TRAINÉ (Fr.). 'Dragged.'

TRANQUILLO (It.). 'Tranquil.' So *Tranquilla-mente*, 'tranquilly'; *Tranquillità, Tranquillezza*, 'tranquillity'.

TRANSCRIPTION. See *Arrangement*.

TRANSFORMATION OF THEMES. Same as 'Metamorphosis of Themes' (q.v.).

TRANSIENT SHAKE. Another name for *Upper Mordent* (see Table 12).

TRANSIENT SOUNDS. See *Acoustics* 7.

TRANSITION. The term is often applied to a very brief and passing modulation. It is also sometimes applied in a different sense to a change of key effected with abruptness rather than by the regular process of modulation (see *Modulation*).

Curwen and the original tonic sol-faists used 'modulation' to mean a change of *mode* (major to relative minor or vice versa), reserving 'transition' for any other change of key.

TRANSMISSION OF SOUND. See *Acoustics* 11.

TRANSPOSE. See *Transposition*. Also *Transposing Instruments*, below.

TRANSPOSING INSTRUMENTS. This is the name for certain instruments which do not play at the pitch of their notation nor (mechanically and without the player's taking thought) transpose the music to a higher or lower pitch.

To put it in another way, they are instruments of which the music is not notated at the actual pitch desired.

A simple explanation of the principle may be given as follows. Imagine two pianos in one room and a composer who has to write music so that the two may be played together. He finds that one piano is at the normal pitch but that the other is (say) two semitones below that pitch. In copying out his music for the players he therefore notates the part for the first piano normally and the part for the second two semitones *higher*. The second piano has now become a 'transposing instrument', i.e. what the composer has transposed, on paper, from (say) key C to key D it transposes back, in sound, from key D to key C.

Had the composer not transposed the second piano part up the player would have had to do so, and this, unless he were a very accomplished performer, might have hampered him, every time he played the piece, in giving due attention to the technical and expressional features of the music. It is better, then, that the composer should do the work for him once for all.

Now take the ordinary clarinet as most commonly found in orchestras. For technical reasons that need not be gone into here it is found best to make it of such sizes that its easiest or normal keys are respectively B flat and A. To the player, then (taking the B flat instrument as our example), B flat is what the key of C is to the pianist, i.e. the key in which he plays all the notes without needing to introduce any of those modifications that we call sharps and flats. Composers therefore treat B flat as the C of the instrument. If they want key B flat they write in key C; if they want key C they write in key D, and so forth—always writing a major second above the sound they desire. Music for this clarinet is, then, treated exactly like music for the second of the pianos above imagined.

This system obviously helps the player, but constitutes a complication for the orchestral conductor, as also a bugbear for any score reader until he gets sufficiently practised mentally to perform all the transpositions required by the various instrumental parts concerned, which may amount to as many as ten or more in a score for very full orchestra.

Obviously, whilst the parts for the various instruments are, for the convenience of their players, notated as described above, it would be quite possible to consider the convenience of the conductor by giving him, in his full score, the whole of the music at the proper pitch. If this were done, however, he would be somewhat embarrassed in indicating errors, etc., to his players since score and parts would not correspond. Or so it is argued, though one would have thought that he might prefer mentally to transpose on the occasions when at rehearsal he has to mention a note by name rather than mentally to transpose right through all the rehearsals and the performance. Anyhow, the argument does not justify the production under the old system of the popular miniature scores intended for students, and a few sporadic experiments have been made in issuing such scores with all the parts shown in their proper keys (the first as long ago as 1876, by Messrs. W. A. Pond & Co., of New York)—unfortunately without as yet establishing the practice. This is, indeed, one of many instances where the skilled musician and the music publisher overlook the interests of the ordinary person.

For the manner of notation for the various transposing instruments see as below (instruments of which the notation, merely to avoid leger lines, differs by an octave from the actual pitch are not usually considered to be transposing instruments but have, for completeness, been included in this list, being, however, placed in brackets).

(PICCOLO. *Flute Family* 3 b.)
BASS FLUTE. *Flute Family* 3 c.
COR ANGLAIS. *Oboe Family* 3 b.
(DOUBLE BASSOON. ,, 3 d.)
OBOE D'AMORE. ,, 4 f.
OBOE IN E FLAT. ,, 4 g.
HECKELPHONE. ,, 4 i.
SARRUSOPHONE. ,, 4 j.
CLARINET IN B FLAT. *Clarinet Family* 3 a (sometimes called B Clarinet).
CLARINET IN A. *Clarinet Family* 3 a.
BASS CLARINET. ,, 3 b.
HIGH CLARINET IN E FLAT. *Clarinet Family* 4 c.
HIGH CLARINET IN D. *Clarinet Family* 4 d.
ALTO CLARINET IN E FLAT AND F. *Clarinet Family* 4 e.
BASSET HORN. *Clarinet Family* 4 f.
PEDAL CLARINET. ,, 3 g.

SAXOPHONES. *Saxophone Family.*
CORNETS. See *Cornet.*
HORNS. *Horn Family* 2 b c.
TRUMPETS. *Trumpet Family* 2 b e.
(BASS TRUMPET. *Trumpet Family* 2 f.)
SAXHORNS. *Saxhorn and Flügelhorn Families* 2; *Tuba Family* 4.
KETTLEDRUMS. *Percussion* 2.
(DOUBLE BASS. *Violin Family* 9.)

The brass band is a law to itself in the matter of transposing instruments. See *Brass Band.*

TRANSPOSITION. The changing of the pitch of a composition without change otherwise. For instance, a song may, for the convenience of the singer, be 'transposed' into a higher or lower key.

TRANSVERSE FLUTE. See *Flute Family* 1.

TRAPS (p. 529, pl. 98. 2). In the parlance of the players in jazz bands and the like, this means the otherwise nondescript collection of noise and rhythm producers played by the percussion expert, who is, hence, called a *Trap Drummer.* The origin of the word may be from the nineteenth-century colloquial 'traps' meaning 'baggage', of which the individual in question has necessarily a good deal (cf. *Effects*).

TRASCINANDO (It.). 'Dragging', i.e. holding back (= rallentando).

TRASCRIZIONE (It.). 'Arrangement' (q.v.).

TRATTENUTO (It.). (1) Held back; (2) sustained.

TRATTO (It.). 'Dragged' (used in the negative, *Non tratto,* 'not dragged').

TRAUER. German for 'sorrow', and so used in various musical titles, as *Trauermarsch* (funeral march), etc. (for Schubert's 'Trauerwalzer' and Haydn's 'Trauersymphonie', see *Nicknamed Compositions*). *Trauervoll,* 'sorrowful'.

TRAUERSYMPHONIE. See *Nicknamed* 11.

TRAUM (Ger.). 'Dream.' So *Traumbild,* 'dream-picture'; *Träumend,* 'dreaming'; *Träumerei,* 'reverie'; *Träumerisch,* 'dreamy', etc. And *Liebesträume,* 'love-dreams'.

TRAURIG (Ger.). 'Sad.'

TRAUTONIUM, TRAUTWEIN. See *Electric Musical Instruments* 1 e.

TRAVERS, JOHN. Born about 1703 and died in 1758, aged about fifty-five. He was a choir-boy of St. George's Chapel, Windsor, and then a pupil of Pepusch (q.v.). He became organist of the Chapel Royal (q.v.) and left church music which is still in use, as also organ voluntaries, secular songs, and other things.

TRAVERSA, TRAVERSO (It.); **TRAVERSIÈRE** (Fr.); **TRAVERSFLÖTE** (Ger.). See *Flute Family* 5.

TRAVIATA,[1] **LA** (Verdi). Produced at Venice in 1853. Libretto by Piave after the play 'La Dame aux Camélias', by Dumas the Younger.

[1] It is difficult to find an English equivalent for this title. It is a fem. past-participle meaning 'the led-astray'.

ACT I

SCENE: *Drawing-room in Violetta Valéry' House. Time, 1845.*

Violetta (*Soprano*), a courtesan, is receiving guests. **Alfred Germont** (Tenor) is introduced. He loves Violetta, and she, though accustomed to love lightly, wonders if his true affection is destined to cheer her life, now menaced by consumption. But she cannot believe that such love is for her: the life of pleasure is her destined path.

ACT II

SCENE 1: *A Room in a Country House near Paris*

Alfred has won Violetta, who has left her wild life behind. **Old Germont** (*Baritone*), Alfred's father, comes to beg her to give up her lover. Her association with him will ruin his career, and the good name of his sister. Violetta consents, but she cannot bear to tell her lover the truth. She goes away, leaving a note to explain that the old life is too strong for her: she must return to it.

SCENE 2: *A Room in the House of Flora Bervoix*

Flora (*Mezzo-Soprano*), Violetta's friend, is holding a costume ball. Violetta is there with a new protector, **Baron Douphol** (*Bass*). In loyalty to her promise, she keeps up, to Alfred, the heart-breaking pretence that she left him of her own will. Alfred, beside himself with grief and rage, publicly insults her, and, coming to his senses, goes sorrowfully away.

ACT III

SCENE: *Violetta's Bedroom*

Violetta is dying. The **Doctor** (*Bass*) tries to cheer her, but she knows the truth. A letter from the elder Germont tells her that Alfred, having challenged the Baron to a duel, is recovering from a wound. Alfred knows of Violetta's sacrifice, and is returning to ask her pardon. He comes in time for the two to realize the genuineness of their love. Violetta dies in his arms.

See *Brindisi.*

TRE (It.). 'Three.' So *A tre* means (*a*) in three parts, or (*b*) what have been three instrumental groups (e.g. three violins) now join together to play the same line of music (cf. *Due*; *Trois*).

TREBLE. The highest voice in choral singing and hence the equivalent of soprano (more especially applied to the boy's voice). But the names of clefs 'Treble' and 'Soprano' have differing significations (see *Notation* 4) and the former word is also applied to instrumental music, which the latter is not.

The derivation of the word 'Treble' is doubtful. It had apparent parallels, in the choral terminology of the Middle Ages, in Quadrible and Quinible, but these seem to have referred to singing in fourths and fifths respectively (see *Harmony* 4, 5).

TREBLE C, etc. See *Pitch* 7.

TREBLE CLEF. See Table 4.

S S

TREBLE RECORDER. See *Recorder Family 2.*

TREBLE STAFF. See *Great Staff.*

TREBLE TROMBONE. See *Trombone Family 2 a.*

TREBLE VIOL. See *Viol Family 3.*

TRE CORDE. See *Pianoforte 12.*

TREGIAN, FRANCIS (*c.* 1574–1619). Cornish musical amateur to whose interest and diligence we owe three very valuable compilations: (*a*) that known as the *Fitzwilliam Virginal Book* (q.v.); (*b*) a collection of over eleven hundred madrigals, etc., and instrumental pieces (British Museum, Egerton MS. 3665); and (*c*) a smaller collection similar to this last (New York Public Library).

He was the son of a Catholic exile, was educated in France, and became Chamberlain to Cardinal Allen, in Rome (1592–4). He returned to England to claim his father's estate in Cornwall. In 1609 he was convicted of recusancy and incarcerated in the Fleet Prison, London, where he died in 1619. It was during this period that he copied the manuscripts.

TREGIAN'S ANTHOLOGY. Another name for the Egerton MS. mentioned under *Tregian, Francis,* above.

TREIBEND (Ger.). 'Driving', i.e. hurrying.

TREMANDO, TREMANTE, TREMOLANDO (It.). 'With tremolo' (q.v.).

TREMBLANT (Fr.). Tremulant of organ.

TREMENDO (It.). 'Tremendous.' So the superlative *Tremendissimo.*

TREMOLANDO (It.). 'With tremolo.'

TREMOLANTE (It.). (1) 'With tremolo'; (2) name for organ tremulant.

TREMOLO AND VIBRATO. These two words seem customarily to be used in reverse senses in connexion with stringed instruments and the voice. This is unfortunate. It would be better that both in connexion with stringed instruments and voice 'Tremolo' should be the name for the effect caused by the tone-generator (bow, breath) and 'Vibrato' for that caused by the vibrating medium (string, vocal cords), *which latter involves a fluctuation of pitch.*

(1) In the parlance of the players and teachers of stringed instruments 'Tremolo' means a rapid iteration of one note by a motion of the bow, and 'Vibrato' that effect of waving of the pitch by a movement of the left hand much used by violinists and violoncellists (generally not sufficiently markedly to be objectionable), and occasionally to be found indicated in notation, as in the following from a Haydn symphony:

~ *Adagio* (solo violin).[1]

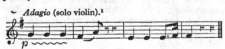

p ~~~~

[1] Note that the sign used by Haydn in the musical example given, and usually stated to indicate a vibrato (i.e. a waving of the pitch) is by some authorities (e.g.

By players of bowed instruments the word 'Tremolo' is also applied to two rapidly alternating notes (usually a third apart): this is called *Fingered Tremolo.*

(2) In the parlance of the vocalists and vocal teachers (when they show any knowledge of the existence of two distinct effects, which is not always) 'Tremolo' seems usually to mean the wavy, pitch-fluctuating effect, and 'Vibrato' the iteration of the one note.

Purcell has indicated the use of the Vibrato, for an obvious dramatic purpose, in the Frost Music of *King Arthur.*

To say that these effects are in the twentieth century tremendously overdone by a large number of vocalists is to speak mildly. They both have their place for purposes of emotional expression, corresponding to the unsteadiness that comes into the speaking voice of all of us in moments when we are exceptionally moved; but many vocalists so habitually use the effect that it becomes clear either (*a*) that they imagine it adds a beauty to the music as such, or (*b*) that there is a lack of control of the diaphragm or the tightening of certain muscles in the throat (see *Voice* 3). As confirming explanation (*b*) it may be added that very many singers addicted to the fault are, on inquiry, found to be unaware of it, so that it certainly does not result from their volition.

There is a very good psychological case for the abandonment of the practice of incessant tremolo or vibrato. One of the strongest bonds between a musical artist and his audience is the audience's unconscious recognition of the artist's confidence in himself. Now tremolo and vibrato (being associated with timidity and indeed often a symptom of actual 'stage fright') weaken this feeling; the audience does not analyse its experiences but that is what occurs. A clear, strong, melodic line brings into existence an impression of artistic purpose and quiet power, a wavering line one of doubt and insecurity. The 'suggestion' of the two is widely different.

The public at large detests the effect of tremolo and vibrato, as the numerous letters received by music critics and radio authorities testify. But many singers seem to be unaware of the feeling of the public, and adopt a convention that is accepted by inferior teachers and by many of their colleagues of the platform and stage. It is said that the tolerance of vibrato in such circles dates in Britain from the enormous popularity of Rubini, who spent much time in that country between 1836 and 1843; 'He was the first to use that thrill of the voice known as the vibrato, at first as a means of emotional effect and afterwards to conceal the deterioration of the organ'. It is said that Capoul (1839–1924) exercised a similar bad influence in France.

The most adroit description of vibrato in

Harvard Dictionary of Music, p. 758) interpreted as indicating merely a series of repetitions of the note concerned at moderate speed—say four to a crotchet (misleadingly called an *Undulating Tremolo*).

1. FRANCIS HOPKINSON
(1737–91)

2. LOWELL MASON (1792–1872)

3. W. H. FRY (1813–64)

4. DANIEL DECATUR EMMETT
(1815–1904)

5. THE EARLIEST AMERICAN SONG
By Francis Hopkinson in 1759

6. WILLIAM MASON (1329–1908)

7. STEPHEN FOSTER (1826–64)

8. 'THE OLD FOLKS AT HOME'
(Foster's mother and father)

9. LEOPOLD DAMROSCH (1832–85)
AND HIS SON WALTER (1862–1950)

For the plate 'Early American Musical Activities' see page 1024

1. THEODORE THOMAS
(1835–1905)

2. JOHN KNOWLES PAINE
(1839–1906)

3. ARTHUR W. FOOTE
(1853–1937)

4. SOUSA (1854–1932)

5. G. W. CHADWICK (1854–1931)

6. VICTOR HERBERT (1859–1924)

7. MACDOWELL (1861–1908)

8. ETHELBERT NEVIN (1862–1901)

9. WALTER DAMROSCH (1862–1950)

English literature is the following from Charles Lamb (*The Gentle Giantess*):

'The shake, which most fine singers reserve for the close or cadence, by some unaccountable flexibility, or tremulousness of pipe, she carrieth quite through the composition; so that her time, to a common air of ballad, keeps double motion, like the earth—running the primary circuit of the tune, and still revolving upon its own axis.'

The effect, says Lamb, 'when you are used to it' is agreeable, but of all English writers Lamb was (and by his own admission) the most totally lacking in musical 'ear', and wise singers will prefer to base their practice on the view of Wagner who never did get 'used to it' and spoke stingingly of Rubini 'with the sempiternal shake'.

Note that in the time of Bach the term 'Tremolo' was often applied to the ornament now called 'Shake'.

A thorough scientific study of the whole of the subject discussed in this article was made by Dr. Carl Seashore of the University of Iowa (2 vols. 1932, 1936).

See also Table 21.

TREMULANT. See *Organ* 3, 6.

TREMULO. Same as *Tremolo* (q.v.).

TREND, JOHN BRANDE (1887–1958). Professor of Spanish at Cambridge University and leading authority on Spanish music. See *Singing* 1.

TRENODIA (It.). 'Threnody', 'dirge'.

TRENT (including Council of Trent). See *Italy* 4; *Church Music* 4; *Sequence*; *Kerle*; *Lauda Sion*.

TREPAK. A dance popular in Russia and the Ukraine. It is in a two-in-a-measure time.

TRÈS (Fr.). 'Very.'

TRESCONE. A highly popular folk-dance of the district around Florence, something on the lines of the Cushion Dance (q.v.), but with the throwing of a handkerchief instead of a cushion. The music, in duple time, is very rapid and lively.

TRG. or **TRGE.** Short for *Triangle*.

TRIAD. See *Harmony* 3, 24 d.

TRIANGEL (Ger.). 'Triangle.' See *Percussion Family* 3 n, 4 b, 5 n.

TRIANGLE. (1) The tinkling orchestral instrument. See *Percussion Family* 3 n, 4 b, 5 n.

(2) A spinet was, from its shape, sometimes called a triangle—e.g. in Pepys and the later seventeenth- and early eighteenth-century literature (see *Harpsichord* 4).

TRIANGOLO (It.). 'Triangle.' See *Percussion Family* 3 n, 4 b, 5 n.

TRICHORD. See *Pianoforte* 16.

TRIHORY. A sort of branle (q.v.) formerly danced in Brittany. Arbeau (see *Dance* 6) describes it.

TRILL. See *Ornaments* 1.

TRILOGY (Eng.), **TRILOGIE** (Fr., Ger.), **TRILOGIA** (It.). A series of three works of art (e.g. operas, oratorios) on a common theme.

TRINITY COLLEGE, CAMBRIDGE. See *Agincourt Song*.

TRINITY COLLEGE, DUBLIN. See *Ireland* 6; *Libraries*.

TRINITY COLLEGE OF MUSIC, LONDON. See *Schools of Music* and *Degrees and Diplomas* (in addition to the activities there mentioned the College conducts examinations of pupil-grade all over the British Commonwealth).

TRINKLIED (Ger.). 'Drinking song.'

TRIO. (1) Any body of three performers, vocal or instrumental, or any piece of music composed for such.

A vocal trio may or may not have accompaniment.

The normal string trio consists of violin, viola, and cello.

Pianoforte trio is the illogical name for the combination of violin, cello, and piano.

The word *Terzett* (Ger.) or *Terzetto* (It.) is sometimes used, especially for a vocal trio.

(2) The middle portion of a minuet (or of the scherzo superseding the minuet). The name apparently recalls the old custom of writing this middle portion in three-part harmony, i.e. for three instruments, but it seems to date only from the end of the eighteenth century, the older custom being to call it 'Second Minuet', or 'Alternativo'. The object of the thinner harmonization and instrumentation was contrast. (Haydn's early String Quartet in F, op. 3, no. 5, gives one example of an actual trio at this point; so does Beethoven's First Pianoforte Sonata, in F minor.) See *Minuet*.

The middle section of a march is also called *Trio*—possibly simply by analogy.

After the trio, in both minuet and march, the first portion of the composition is repeated—sometimes as before and sometimes modified or supplied with a Coda. There are works in which after the repeat of the first portion a trio reappears (either the original one or a new one), to be followed by still another repetition of the first portion.

TRIOLET. (*a*) A type of poem—see English Dictionary. (*b*) A triplet (q.v.). (*c*) A short trio—this last use being regrettable, since as the title of a piece the word awakens expectations of some relationship with the poetical form mentioned under (*a*).

TRIONFALE, TRIONFANTE (It.). 'Triumphant.'

TRIPELKONZERT or **TRIPELCONCERT** (Ger.). 'Triple concerto.' See *Concerto* 6.

TRIPLE CHANT. See *Anglican Chant* 5.

TRIPLE CONCERTO. See *Concerto* 6.

TRIPLE COUNTERPOINT. See *Counterpoint*.

TRIPLE-CROCHE (Fr.). 'Triple hook', i.e. the demisemiquaver or thirty-second note (Table 3).

TRIPLE FLAGEOLET. See *Recorder Family* 3 a.

TRIPLE FUGUE. See *Form* 12 e, for 'Double Fugue', and apply the explanation.

TRIPLE SHARP. See under *Double Sharp.*

TRIPLET. A group of three notes, or its equivalent in notes or rests, to be performed in the time which two of that denomination would, in the composition in question, ordinarily take (cf. *Duplet*). The sign of a triplet is a '3' placed over the three notes.

TRIPLE TIME. See Table 10.

TRIPLE-TONGUING. See *Tonguing.*

TRIPLEX. See *Voice* 17; *Motet.*

TRIPTYCH (Eng.), **TRIPTYQUE** (Fr.). See description under *Trittico.*

TRISAGION or **TRISHAGION.** 'O holy God, Holy and mighty, Holy and immortal, Have mercy on us.' This is part of the liturgy of the Greek Church, and occurs also in that of the Roman Catholic Church in the service of the adoration of the cross on Good Friday, and in the ferial prayer at Prime for days of penitence; in the Roman Catholic use it appears in both Greek and Latin, sung antiphonally by two choirs, phrase by phrase, one uttering a phrase in Greek and the other repeating it in Latin to the same music. The word comes from the Greek *tris*, thrice, and *hagios*, holy. (Cf. *Improperia.*)

There are a number of well-known settings by Russian composers.

TRISTAN AND ISOLDE (Wagner). Produced at Munich in 1865. Libretto by the composer.

Act I

SCENE: *The Deck of a Ship*

Isolde (*Soprano*), an Irish princess, attended by **Brangäne** (*Mezzo-Soprano*), is voyaging from her home to Cornwall, there to become the bride of King Mark. Mark has sent his nephew **Tristan** (*Tenor*), a knight, to escort Isolde. He is accompanied by his retainer, **Kurwenal** (*Baritone*).

Tristan, having slain an Irish knight betrothed to Isolde, and been wounded, had been nursed by her. Each had grown to love the other. Isolde now resolves that poison is the only remedy for a hopeless passion, and Tristan agrees to share her doom. But Brangäne pours instead a love-philtre, which fills each with irresistible longing for the other. So they come to Cornwall.

Act II

SCENE: *King Mark's Castle*

The lovers meet while the King goes hunting. Kurwenal, coming to warn Tristan that the jealous courtier **Melot** (*Tenor*) has spied upon them and denounced them to Mark, is too late: the **King** (*Bass*) discovers them together. Tristan and Melot fight, and the former is wounded.

Act III

SCENE: *Tristan's Castle in Brittany*

In Tristan's native place he is tended by his faithful retainer, who has sent for Isolde, that with certain magic powers she possesses she may heal her lover. At last she comes; but Tristan, delirious, tears the bandage from his wound, and dies in her arms.

Brangäne had told King Mark the truth about the love-philtre, and the King has followed Isolde, with forgiveness in his heart. Kurwenal, however, thinking that the King and his men design to take the castle by storm, rallies its defenders, kills Melot, and is himself slain. Isolde's heart breaks, and she falls lifeless upon the body of Tristan.

See *Overture*; *Composition* 9; *Lassen, E.*; *Martucci*; *Quadrille.*

TRISTE (Fr.), **TRISTO** (It.). 'Sad.'

TRISTESSE (Fr.), **TRISTEZZA** (It.). 'Sadness.'

TRITONE. The interval of the augmented fourth, which is the product of a succession of three full tones. In the major scale it occurs between the fourth and seventh notes (the subdominant and the leading note), and so also in the minor, except in the descending form of the melodic minor. It is relatively difficult to frame in singing, and is in itself not a beautiful interval, and hence in early ecclesiastical music (fourth to sixteenth century) its melodic use was forbidden, as was also, though less stringently, its inversion, the diminished fifth. Early theorists called it the 'devil in music' (*Diabolus in musica*), and its avoidance was one of the motives of *Musica ficta* (q.v.). Another name for it was *Mi contra fa*. So the proverb called it:

> Mi contra fa
> Diabolus in musica.

We should call it *Si contra fa*, or *Te contra fah*, but the proverb dates from the period of hexachords (q.v.), when there was no 'Si' or 'Te' recognized in sight-singing practice, and a progression from B down to F natural meant going from the mi of the 'hard' hexachord (the one beginning on G) to the fa of the 'natural' hexachord (the one beginning on C).

In the melodic progressions of counterpoint exercises of today pupils are still urged to shun the devil and all his works, but modernist composers have made it a cornerstone of their atonal and polytonal practices.

For various allusions to the influence of the feeling against the tritone see *Modes* 4, 5, 6, 8; *Keyboard* 2; *Picchi*; *Hexachord.*

TRITTICO (It.). A triptych, or painting on three panels, such as is common over altars—the two side ones closing over the centre one. The word was adopted by Puccini in 1918 (see below) for his group of three one-act operas, not connected in subject-matter but originally intended to be performed together as one evening's entertainment.

Not the same, then, as *Trilogy*, q.v.

TRITTICO, IL ('THE TRIPTYCH'). Puccini's collective title for the three one-act operas, *Il Tabarro* ('The Cloak'), *Suor Angelica* ('Sister Angelica'), and *Gianni Schicchi*, which were produced together at the Metropolitan Opera House, New York, in 1918.

I. IL TABARRO ('THE CLOAK')

Libretto by Giuseppe Adami, from *La Houppelande*, by Didier Gold.

SCENE: *A Barge on the Seine. Sunset*

Giorgetta (*Soprano*) and her affectionate husband **Michele** (*Baritone*) see the labourers leave the barge after the day's work: all but **Luigi** (*Tenor*), who is Giorgetta's lover. After **Frugola** (*Mezzo-Soprano*), a rag-picker, has visited them, Luigi and Giorgetta talk of the life they might have together on shore. They arrange to meet again on the barge when Michele is asleep. The husband, in his slow way, is suspicious. He reminds his wife of the days when he wrapped her close in his cloak; but he feels she does not return his affection any more, and begins to hate her.

Wrapped in the cloak, Michele lights his pipe. Luigi, thinking the light his signal, jumps on the barge. Michele suddenly sees the truth, pinions Luigi, make him confess his love, and strangles him.

He holds the corpse to him, under the cloak, as Giorgetta comes on deck, looking anxiously around, and prepared to be coquettish and penitent for her harshness.. 'Don't you want me near you?' she asks, 'under your cloak?' Savagely Michele throws it open and the dead body falls at her feet; and she, thrown down by her husband, upon it.

II. SUOR ANGELICA ('SISTER ANGELICA')

Libretto by Gioacchino Forzano.

SCENE: *A Convent*

Various inmates of the convent are heard in their religious duties at sunset on a day in May, when the memories of the outside world come to some of them—to **Sister Genevieve** (*Soprano*), of the lambs she tended as a shepherdess; to **Sister Angelica** (*Soprano*), of the child that she left to the world; though she will not admit that she thinks of this.

Some members who have been out seeking tribute return well laden, and announce that a splendid coach is outside. It holds a visitor for Sister Angelica—her aunt, the **Princess** (*Contralto*), with a family document for Angelica to sign. The aunt, a hard woman, tells her that her baby son died two years ago.

Sister Angelica, her last hope gone, poisons herself, and, near to death, realizes the mortal sin she has committed. She prays for pardon, and a miracle is vouchsafed: from the church door, now glowing with mystic light, comes the Madonna with a child clad in white, who moves towards Sister Angelica as the spirit leaves her body.

III. GIANNI SCHICCHI

Libretto by Gioacchino Forzano, after Canto xxx of Dante's *Inferno*.

SCENE: *The Death Chamber of Buoso Donati. Florence, 1299*

This admirable comedy brings in a number of relatives of the dead Buoso, all of whom it is not necessary to name. They are after the departed's goods, and each of them is suspicious of the others. A pair of lovers, **Rinuccio** (*Tenor*) and **Lauretta** (*Soprano*), hope for a start in wedded life, from Buoso's will; but where *is* the will? Nobody can find it. At last it is discovered, and, amid much anticipatory lip-licking, read. But what misery! Buoso has left everything to charities!

Is there *no* hope? Somebody thinks of the clever **Gianni Schicchi** (*Baritone*), and he is fetched. His plan is to get into bed, pretend to be Buoso, and make a new will (for nobody outside the room yet knows that Buoso is not alive)

The Doctor, **Spinelloccio** (*Bass*), comes, and then the **Notary** (*Bass*), to whom Gianni dictates a will; but the rascal leaves a little to the relatives, and a great deal to himself, and menaces the furious relatives with exposure of their plot if they dare to object. When the notary has gone, they rush away with what they can grab, leaving the scheming Gianni master of the situation.

TRIUMPHS OF ORIANA. See *Madrigal* 4.

TRIUMPH TRUMPET. See *Trumpet Family* 2 e.

TRIVIUM. See *Education and Music* 1.

TROCHEE, TROCHAIC. See *Metre*.

TROIS (Fr.). 'Three'; so *À trois* means (*a*) in three 'voices', or (*b*) what have been three instrumental 'voices' (e.g. three violins) now join together to play the same line of music (cf. *Deux*; *Tre*).

TROISIÈME (Fr.). 'Third'; so *Troisième Position*, 'third position' (of the hand in playing stringed instruments'; see *Position*).

TROLLENS, CHARLOTTE. See *Folia*.

TROMBA (It.). Trumpet. See *Trumpet Family*; *Organ* 14 VI.

TROMBA A MACCHINA (It.). Valve trumpet. See *Trumpet Family* 2 c, 3, 5.

TROMBA BASSA. See *Trumpet Family* 5.

TROMBA CROMATICA (It.). Valve trumpet. See *Trumpet Family* 2 c, 3, 5.

TROMBA DA TIRARSI (It.). Slide trumpet. See *Trumpet Family* 2 d, 5.

TROMBA MARINA (It. for 'marine trumpet'). A performing variety of the scientific monochord (q.v.). Its body consisted of three tapering boards, say 5–6 feet long, usually placed together in such a way that in section they made a triangle. One of these was provided with a single string passing over a bridge —like that of a violin, but with only one foot of the bridge firmly placed, whilst the other, being slightly shorter, vibrated against the belly of the instrument, which was played with a bow (p. 417, pl. **72.** 4). The notes obtained were all harmonics (see *Acoustics* 8), produced by touching the string lightly with the thumb of the left hand between the bow and the bridge. Later specimens (late seventeenth century onwards) had sympathetic strings (q.v.) inside the instrument.

The tone was loud and brassy and this, apparently, together with the limitation to the notes of the harmonic series (cf. *Trumpet* 2 a), suggested the substantival part of the name, the adjectival part being, it is unplausibly alleged, due to the instrument being used for signal purposes in the Navy! (This seems quite absurd. What was wrong with instruments of the bugle and trumpet class that they should be put aside in favour of a sort of one-stringed double

bass, clumsy to carry, vulnerable to wet, and liable to the sudden breaking of its one string?)

The antiquity and long career of the tromba marina are notable. It goes back to the twelfth century at least, yet was still in use in the days of the young Mozart. Four or five of the family Philidor (q.v.) successively played this instrument at the Court of France.

The German names are *Nonnengeige* ('Nun's Fiddle'—probably from its use in convent chapels), *Trompetengeige* ('Trumpet-fiddle'), and *Trumscheit* or *Trumbscheit* ('Trumpet-plank') or *Brummscheit* ('Buzzing-plank').

The French is *Trompette Marine*.

TROMBA SPEZZATA (It.). Trombone. See *Trombone Family*.

TROMBA VENTILE (It.). Valve trumpet. See *Trumpet Family* 2 c, 3, 5.

TROMBONE FAMILY

(For illustration see p. 113, pl. **22.** 17.)

1. Construction, Tone, Notation, etc. The trombone (anciently called the Sackbut) is like a trumpet in consisting of a tube of *cylindrical bore*, a *moderate-sized bell*, and a *cup-shaped mouthpiece*.

It differs from the normal trumpet in possessing (as its means of extending the tube), not valves operated by pistons, but a sliding arrangement. It also differs from the trumpet in a small but important detail: its mouthpiece is larger, giving a more solemn tone quality (in the ancient instruments and in modern French ones it tends somewhat towards the funnel shape of the horn mouthpiece, which makes the tone in all but loud passages a little fuller and less penetrating).

Like all brass instruments the trombone is an application of the principle of the harmonic series (see *Acoustics* 8; also *Trumpet Family* and *Horn Family*).

The lips, in the mouthpiece, act as a vibrating reed and, according to the greater or less rapidity the player gives the vibrations, produce either the fundamental tone of the tube or a chosen one of the harmonics above this. As the harmonic series is, of course, a gapped one, what we may call the normal length of the instrument (i.e. its length with the tube at its smallest) is increased by successive extensions of that length by the sliding of the tubes, giving for each new length adopted a new pitch to the series of harmonics. There are seven recognized positions (six plus the original one), giving seven fundamentals and, thus, seven repetitions of the harmonic series at different pitches a semitone apart. In this way gaps are filled and, indeed, many a note is attainable in several different ways—as a higher harmonic of a greater-length position or as a lower harmonic of a lesser-length position.

The range for each position is one of about two octaves (rather more in the lower positions). The actual fundamental notes are not so easy to produce as the harmonics above them; they are spoken of as *Pedal Notes*—possibly because they are considered to be useful for the holding of a 'pedal', in the sense in which the word is used in the terminology of harmony (see *Harmony*, 14, 24 p), or else, as Berlioz suggests, from their resemblance to the low pedal notes of an organ. The reason why the fundamental notes, unusable on the trumpet, are yet, to some extent, obtainable on the trombone, lies in the greater relative width of the tube of this latter.

It will be realized that the difference between these slide instruments and the valve instruments (trumpets, horns, etc.), so far as the method of obtaining any desired note is concerned, is something like the difference between the violin, with its smooth finger-board, and the viol with its fretted one (see *Viol Family*); there is nothing except the player's own judgement to guide him to the point at which he should stop the motion of the slide, so that good intonation depends purely on that judgement.

It will also be realized that, as the movement from position to position occupies an appreciable fraction of a second, a true legato is not obtainable—though a glissando is (usually horrible, and used only for the production of a grotesque effect). It is especially in loud passages that the inescapable staccato of the trombone is most noticed by the hearer.

Valve Trombones have been made and used. Their tone is, however, less good, on account of the extra convolutions of the tube. They have usually, like the trumpets and horns, had three valves. For a time they were used in Italy; elsewhere they may be found in military bands.

A combined slide and valve trombone has

also been introduced, consisting of a slide trombone furnished with a single valve worked by the left thumb and lowering the pitch a fourth or occasionally a fifth. This facilitates certain passages by supplying an alternative to the more awkward positions, and extends the downward range.

The tone of the trombones is in general noble. It is perhaps most effective of all when they are playing chords in three-part harmony. The range of intensity from pianissimo to fortissimo is a very wide one.

The trombones, unlike most of their brass colleagues, are not 'transposing instruments', i.e. their music is written at its actual sounding pitch. In older scores, which often have three trombones of different sizes, three staves are generally allotted to them: in more modern scores, where three trombones of two sizes or (latterly) of only one are called for, two staves are considered sufficient, or sometimes merely one.

The trombones used in wind bands are identical with those used in orchestras and their notation is the same. The usual allowance in orchestras is two tenors and one bass (in France more often three tenors), and in general this allowance is the same in wind bands—whether 'military bands' or 'brass bands'.

A conical mute exists for insertion in the bell of the trombone—as in that of the horn, trumpet, etc.

For the trick of producing chords from a single trombone see reference under *Horn* 1 (near end). Müller's *Method* for the instrument gives a passage in three-part harmony to be played in this way.

2. Members of the Family.

(*a*) **Treble Trombone.** This, found in a few scores of Purcell, Bach, etc., is an octave above the tenor trombone (see *c* below). Berlioz, in 1843, speaks of it as still in some use in Germany.

(*b*) **Alto Trombone.** This is demanded by many classical scores, but no longer commonly exists (it went out because its range was so nearly that of the trumpet), so that its part is played by a tenor trombone, some players of which have acquired a special technique enabling them to reach the high notes, whilst by others the part has to be played an octave lower. Its music is notated either on a staff to itself, with the alto clef, or on the same staff as that of the tenor trombone and then, of course, in the tenor clef.

Its 'pedal' (or fundamental) notes were never used, being within the compass of the tenor trombone, which could give them with better quality. With the slide closed, i.e. in the first position, its fundamental note was E flat below the bass staff, and its next higher note (the second harmonic) the E flat in the middle of that staff. The latter note could be lowered chromatically six semitones by successive positions of the slide down to A at the bottom of the staff. Its upward compass can be considered as

extending two octaves above the second harmonic.

(*c*) **Tenor Trombone.** This is the most important member of the family. In the first position its fundamental is the B flat below the bass staff, consequently the B flat on the second line of that staff is its second harmonic and its chromatic compass runs normally two octaves up from that note and, by successive changes of position, six semitones down to E. In addition it is possible easily to sound four 'pedal' notes, the fundamental of the first four positions—the B flat, A, A flat, and G, below the bass staff; the other three are more difficult. (It will be realized that an unbridgeable gap necessarily occurs between the B flat fundamental and the E above it.) For reference to the tenor trombone with thumb-valve see 1.

The part of the tenor trombone is normally notated in either the tenor or bass clef, according to convenience. But occasionally, in old music, it joins the alto trombone on an alto-clef staff, or the bass trombone on a bass-clef staff. And occasionally all three instruments share one staff, with either the tenor or the bass clef.

(*d*) **Bass Trombone.** In the first position this has as its fundamental either the G, F, or (rarely) the E flat an octave below the bass clef. Its chromatic compass therefore extends upwards from the G, F, or E flat at the bottom of, or just below, the bass clef (its second harmonic) for two octaves, and, by successive changes of position, downwards for six semitones. The pedal notes, a very low-lying series, are sometimes stated to be of no practical use. They are very fine when produced by a first-rate player, but have seldom, if ever, been called for.

The G bass trombone is peculiar to Great Britain and the Commonwealth and has the disadvantage that its lowest note (exclusive of the pedals) is only C sharp, whereas C natural is required at times, as in the First Symphony of Brahms. It is therefore sometimes made as a combination instrument with a single valve lowering the pitch a fourth, and in this form is preferred by some players to the following instrument.

(*e*) **Tenor-Bass Trombone.** The instrument combines the bore of a bass trombone with the length of tubing of a tenor. It stands, therefore, in B flat and is furnished with a single valve which lowers the pitch a fourth (or sometimes an augmented fourth or fifth) when the slide is closed. By the conjoint use of the slide and valve, the chromatic scale of the tenor trombone can be carried on to a tone above the highest fundamental. In this way the unwieldy longest shifts of the true bass trombones are eliminated, while the sonority, if the bore is suitable, is retained. This type of instrument, first made in Germany in 1839, is in general use in many continental countries and America.

(*f*) **Contrabass Trombone, or Doublebass Trombone.** The largest of the family, having as fundamental the B flat (sometimes C) an octave below that of the tenor trombone. It was not, as sometimes stated, introduced by

Wagner, but is of ancient origin, being the **Octav-Posaun** of Praetorius (1618); examples contemporary with him still exist. Burney, in Rees's *Cyclopædia* (about 1805), says: 'Its use should be rare and its effects would be more striking' (but see also under 3 below). Early examples gave an incomplete scale because the great length of the shifts limited the positions of the slide to four at most. The difficulty was overcome in 1816 by the invention of the 'double slide', the tube being bent round twice to form two parallel slides working in conjunction. This principle, which has been several times 'reinvented', enabled Wagner to use it in the *Ring*, and a few other composers to follow his example. It is, however, very tiring to play —indeed, only a strong-lunged giant could perform on it with any sense of enjoying his task.

3. History. It is frequently stated that the history of the sackbut or trombone goes back to Roman times or earlier: this is, however, now questioned, owing to a closer scrutiny of the writings and pictorial representations that formed the documentary basis of the statement. What is certain is that by about the beginning of the fourteenth century the sackbut (in essentials indistinguishable from the present-day trombone) was well known in many parts of Europe. It became an important member of the ceremonial bands of princes. Henry VII, in 1495, had four 'Shakbusshes' attached to him; Henry VIII, a few years later, had ten. With the shawms and cornetts (see *Oboe Family* and *Cornett Family*) the sackbut made up an effective band, as it did at a later date with the trumpet and drums. It was also used in churches (e.g. Canterbury Cathedral) to support the plainsong of the choir (cf. Serpent under *Cornett and Key Bugle Families* 3).

In Germany sackbuts were used to accompany, in harmony, the singing of chorales on certain occasions, and also to play chorales from the church towers at stated hours of the day; their chromatic compass made them very useful for such duties, which were out of the power of the horns and trumpets, since (apart from slide trumpets) these could not change their fundamental and thus were limited by the gap of the harmonic series (see *Horn Family*; *Acoustics* 8).

At the end of the sixteenth century G. Gabrieli, at St. Mark's, Venice, was using trombones in his ecclesiastical compositions, and a century later there were still such instruments in use there. Monteverdi, in his opera *Orpheus*, produced at Mantua in 1607, made use of five trombones, providing two movements allotted merely to them plus two cornetts. At this period England seems to have enjoyed fame as a school of sackbut playing, since in 1604 we find the Duke of Lorraine sending his kapellmeister there to recruit players (compare *Cornett Family* 3). A normal set of sackbuts during the seventeenth century comprised three instruments corresponding to the alto, tenor, and bass (2 b c d), with, especially towards the end of the century, a fourth, high one, a 'Descant Sackbut' (see 2 a). Schütz and (once or twice) Purcell wrote effectively for the instrument.

Bach and Handel used the instrument, but used it conservatively. Bach never gave it a solo part, as he did practically every other instrument; for him it normally served as a support for the voices, merely doubling their parts. Handel, as a rule, did much the same: it appears in the scores of his oratorios *Saul*, *Israel in Egypt*, and *Samson*, and it was probably also used in *Messiah* and elsewhere, playing from the chorus parts (in *Samson* the score shows it in only one movement, and it would be unlike Handel, or any other practical man, to have such instruments present and to use them so little). At this period the association between the use of the voice and that of the trombones was strong; the latter constantly appeared in various countries in the performance of masses and oratorios and even of opera, but hardly ever in that of purely orchestral music. They seem to have been regarded as primarily useful for choral doubling, and secondarily for dramatic expression. Gluck used them effectively sometimes in the latter way (e.g. in the accompaniment of 'Divinités du Styx' in *Alceste*), but he does so only in special movements and then harmonically rather than melodically.

Handel having used the trombones, it is curious that, after his death in 1759, they seem to have almost disappeared. Twenty-five years later Burney records of the great Handel commemoration in Westminster Abbey:

'In order to render the band as powerful and complete as possible it was determined to employ every species of instrument that was capable of producing grand effects in a great orchestra and spacious building. Amongst these, the Sacbut or Double Trumpet was sought; but so many years had elapsed since it had been used in this kingdom, that, neither the instrument, nor a performer on it, could easily be found. It was, however, discovered that . . . in his Majesty's military band there were six musicians who played the three several species of sacbut; tenor, base and double base.'[1]

Burney then feels it necessary to describe the instrument, saying that the Italians call it 'Trombone'. The six players Burney mentioned were all Germans, and they 'played on other instruments when the Sacbuts were not wanted'.

After this date the instrument returned to full use again—now dropping its ancient name of sackbut and taking on the Italian one of trombone mentioned by Burney. About twenty years later (*c.* 1805) Burney rather libellously observes:

'Tromboni and double-drums are now so frequently used at the opera, oratorios, and in symphonies that they are become a nuisance to lovers of pure harmony and refined tones; for, in fact, the

---

[1] Is it just possible that Burney's nomenclature is at fault? It seems odd if there was no Alto Trombone in use at this festival, and yet the rare Contrabass. Can it be that his three Trombones are merely what we would call 'Alto, Tenor, and Bass'?

vibrations of these instruments produce noise, not musical sounds.'

Mozart's masterly employment of the trombone for special dramatic effect in *The Magic Flute* and *Don Giovanni* is well known. With Beethoven we see it appear in symphony—not often, however; merely in particular movements of the Fifth, Sixth, and Ninth Symphonies. Schubert used it in his later symphonies, and Weber, in opera, demonstrated the wonderful effect of trombones in very soft harmony.

Berlioz and Wagner, more than any others, helped to give the trombone a definite position, and after about 1860 its popularity grew enormously. Berlioz complained in 1843 that only the tenor trombone was in use; of the bass he said 'we have the misfortune, in Paris, to be utterly deprived of it; it is not taught at the Conservatoire, and no trombone player has yet been willing to acquire its familiar practice'. Whilst he would not speak quite so emphatically today (d'Indy has used even the double-bass trombone), yet it is a fact that French composers, down to and including Debussy and later, have preferred to write for three tenor trombones where their colleagues in most other countries except Italy write for two tenors and a bass. The abandonment of the bass instrument in France and Italy seems to date from about 1830, when the ophicleide (see *Cornett and Key Bugle Families* 2 g, 3 g) supplanted it, to be itself supplanted in turn by the tuba.

4. Repertory. From the character of the trombone one hardly expects to find a large repertory in which it takes a solo part.

Of works for trombones alone there are **Beethoven's** three short Equali (quartets), **Adolf Maas's** two Quartets (published 1920), and **Karl Bamberg's** Trio.

A least a few works for solo trombone with orchestra exist, e.g. **Ferdinand David's** Concertino, several concertos by the earliest travelling virtuoso of the instrument, **F. A. Belcke**

(1795–1874), and **Rimsky-Korsakof's** Concerto (1877). **Berlioz** entrusts his 'Funeral Oration' in his *Symphonie funèbre et triomphale* largely to a solo trombone: in Mozart's *Requiem* there is a big solo.

Sonatas with pianoforte are those of **B. Schroen** (1900) and **Hindemith** (1941).

Of chamber works for wind instruments there are **Poulenc's** Sonata for trumpet, horn, and trombone; **Glazunof's** Quartet for trumpet, horn, and two trombones; a 'Trumpet Sextet' by **Oscka Böhme**, for cornet, two trumpets, and bass trumpet, trombone, and bass tuba; a Septet for trumpets and trombones by **Clovis Lecail** (1921); **Stravinsky's** Octet for flute, clarinet, two bassoons, two trumpets, and two trombones; and **Schubert's** Nonet, *Eine kleine Trauermusik* (roughly—'A Little Dirge') for two clarinets, two bassoons and double bassoon, two horns, and two trombones.

5. Nomenclature.

Trombone (Eng., Fr., and It.—the plural in the last being 'Tromboni'. A less common Italian name is *Tromba spezzata*, i.e. 'Broken trumpet'—referring, of course, to the division of the instrument into two separate sliding portions); *Posaune* (Ger., plural 'Posaunen'),

Slide Trombone. *Trombone à coulisse* (Fr.); *Trombone a tiro* or *Trombone duttile* (It., i.e. 'Draw-Trombone' and 'Ductile Trombone'); *Zugposaune* (Ger., i.e. 'Draw-Trombone').

Valve Trombone. *Trombone à pistons* (Fr.); *Trombone a cilindri* or *Trombone a ventile* (It); *Ventilposaune* (Ger.).

Alto Trombone. *Trombone alto* (Fr.); the same or *Trombonino* (It.); *Altposaune* (Ger.).

Tenor Trombone. *Trombone ténor* (Fr.); *Trombone tenore* (It.); *Tenorposaune* (Ger.).

Bass Trombone. *Trombone basse* (Fr.); *Trombone basso* (It.); *Bassposaune* (Ger.).

For the organ stop, 'Trombone', see *Organ* 14 VI.

TROMBONINO (It.). Alto trombone. See *Trombone Family* 2 b, 3, 5.

TROMMEL (Ger.). Side drum (generally called 'Kleine Trommel', i.e. 'Little Drum'), or bass drum (generally called 'Grosse Trommel', i.e. 'Big Drum'). For these two instruments see *Percussion Family* 3 i k, 4 b, 5 i k.

TROMMELFLÖTE. See *Fife*.

TROMP, TROMPE, TROMPE DE BÉARN, TROMPE DE BERNE, TROMPE DE LAQUAIS. Jew's Harp (q.v.).

TROMPE. See *Horn Family* 2 a; *Jew's Harp*.

TROMPETE (Ger.). Trumpet. See *Trumpet Family*.

TROMPETENGEIGE (Ger.). See *Tromba Marina*.

TROMPETTE (Fr.). Trumpet. See *Trumpet Family*.

TROMPETTE À COULISSE (Fr.). Slide trumpet. See *Trumpet Family* 2 d, 5.

TROMPETTE À PISTONS (Fr.). The normal trumpet. See *Trumpet Famiiy*.

TROMPETTE BASSE (Fr.). Bass trumpet. See *Trumpet Family* 2 f, 5.

TROMPETTE CHROMATIQUE (Fr.). Valve trumpet. See *Trumpet Family*.

TROMPETTE D'HARMONIE. See *Trumpet Family* 5.

TROMPETTE MARINE. See *Tromba Marina*.

TROP (Fr.). 'Too much.'

TROPARY or **TROPER.** The collection of tropes (see below).

TROPE. In the liturgy of the Roman Catholic Church, an intercalation of music or words or both. The practice of embellishing the chants of the Mass (*Kyrie, Gloria, Sanctus, Agnus, Introit,* etc.) began about the ninth century. The first stage seems to have been the insertion of melismas (see *Melisma*), the second the setting of words to them. The tropes of the

Alleluia had a special name; they were called 'Sequentiae' (see *Sequence*).

The practice of introducing tropes was abolished in the fifteenth century. Such tropes as survive in use now lead a separate existence as a form of hymn.

Cf. *Farcing*.

TROPER or **TROPARY.** The collection of tropes (see above).

TROPPO (It.). 'Too much.' Generally used with a negative and as part of a warning, e.g. *Allegro ma non troppo*, 'quick, but not too much so'.

TROUBADOURS. See *Minstrels*, etc. 4; *Chanson*; *Modes* 11; *Form* 14; *Estampie*.

'TROUT' QUINTET (Schubert). See *Nicknamed Compositions* 18.

TROUVÈRES. See *Minstrels* 4.

TROVATORE, IL, i.e. **The Troubadour** (Verdi). Produced at Rome in 1853. Libretto by Cammarano, based on the drama by Gutiérrez.

ACT I ('THE DUEL')
SCENE 1: *The Palace of Aliferia in Spain. Time, the Fifteenth Century*

It is important to know what has occurred before the opera opens. This is told by **Ferrando** (*Bass*), Captain of the Guard to the Count di Luna, a young noble of Aragon. The count's younger brother, when a baby, was supposed to have been bewitched by an old gipsy woman. For this she was burned alive. Her daughter Azucena, in revenge, had meant to burn the baby, but had in mistake killed her own infant. The old count, dying, clung to the hope that the child yet lived, and laid upon his son, the present count, the charge to seek for the babe.

The child, now grown up, is the troubadour Manrico, who has been serenading Leonora, lady-in-waiting to a princess—a lady whom the count himself loves.

SCENE 2: *The Palace Garden*

Leonora (*Soprano*) tells her friend **Inez** (*Soprano*) that she loves the almost unknown troubadour. When the **Count** (*Baritone*) enters, she mistakes him for her lover, whom she hears singing. **Manrico** (*Tenor*) has been outlawed, and the count challenges him to a duel, which, to Leonora's horror, they go off to arrange.

ACT II ('THE GIPSY')
SCENE 1: *The Gipsies' Camp*

The gipsy woman **Azucena** (*Mezzo-Soprano*) tells Manrico the story of her mother's death, and bids him avenge it. In recalling the past Azucena forgets to conceal one fact, and Manrico now realizes that he is not her son. We learn that in the duel with the count he disarmed his opponent, but, moved by a strange feeling, did not kill him. (The listener, knowing the secret of their relationship, understands the hidden dramatic value of this fact.)

Ruiz (*Tenor*), a messenger from the Prince of Biscay, comes to deliver an order that Manrico shall command a fortress, and to tell the troubadour that Leonora, believing him to be dead, is about to enter a convent. Manrico goes to assure her that he lives, and loves her.

SCENE 2: *The Cloister of a Convent. Night*

The count comes to abduct Leonora, but Manrico prevents this.

ACT III ('THE GIPSY'S SON')
SCENE 1: *The Count's Camp, before Manrico's Fortress*

Ferrando has captured Azucena, believing her to be a spy. He recognizes her as the woman who (so all believe) cast into the flames the baby brother of the count. Azucena denies it, and calls upon Manrico to help her, naming him as her son. The count, delighted to have secured such a victim, orders her to be cast into prison.

SCENE 2: *A Room near the Chapel in the Fortress*

Manrico and Leonora are about to be married, when Ruiz rushes in with the news that Azucena is about to be burned. Manrico, telling Leonora that Azucena is his mother, goes with his men to rescue her.

ACT III ('THE TORTURE')
SCENE 1: *Part of a Prison*

Manrico failed to rescue his mother, and the count has condemned him to die. Leonora, coming to seek him, hears the 'Miserere' and the death-bell. She promises the count that if he will free her lover she will give herself to him; but rather than live without Manrico she privately vows to poison herself. This she does as she enters the tower in which Manrico is imprisoned.

SCENE 2: *In the Dungeon*

Azucena, her mind beginning to wander, sings of her mother's death, and then the pathetic air of 'Home to our mountains we yet shall go'. Leonora enters, and bids Manrico flee. He at first thinks she loves him no longer, but when he realizes what she has done for him, he begs her forgiveness. The poison does its work, and she dies. The count compels Azucena to watch her son's execution. She turns upon him: 'He was thy brother!' and with a cry of 'Thou art avenged, O mother!' she falls senseless, as the count with horror realizes the dreadful thing he has brought to pass.

See *Libretto*.

TROWELL, ARNOLD. Born at Wellington, New Zealand, in 1887 and died in 1966, aged seventy-nine. He was a violoncellist, professor of his instrument at the Guildhall School of Music (1924) and the Royal College of Music (1937), and composer of a number of concertos for it, as also of various chamber and orchestral works.

TRÜB, TRÜBE (Ger.). 'Sad.'

TRUMBSCHEIT (Ger.). See *Tromba Marina*.

TRUMP. See *Jew's Harp*.

TRUMPET FAMILY

1. Construction, etc.   3. History.   5. Nomenclature.
2. Members of the Family.   4. Repertory.

(For illustrations see p.112, pl. **21**. 1; 113, **22**. 15, 18; 140, **26**. 4; 528, **97**. 2; 545, **100**. 4.)

1. Construction, etc. The trumpet is a tube of narrow bore, *cylindrical* for about three-quarters of its length, then widening out to a *moderate-sized bell*; it has a *cup-shaped mouthpiece*. In all these respects it differs from the horn, which is a longer tube, more or less conical throughout its length, ending in a large bell and having a more or less funnel-shaped mouthpiece. In consequence of the difference in length the range of the modern trumpet lies much higher than that of the horn, and in consequence of the shape of the tube, the bell, and the mouthpiece, its tone is brighter and more ringing.

The principle of performance is the same as that of the horn (see *Horn* 1).

The hand-stopped notes of the horn are not possible on the trumpet, as its shape is such as to place the bell too far from the player. It can, however, like the horn, be muted by the insertion in the bell of a pear-shaped stopper or *mute* (see *Mute*) which may be used to subdue the instrument or, with severer wind pressure, to produce harsh and strident tone of a peculiar quality.

Double and triple *tonguing* (q.v.) are possible and are more effective on the trumpet than on any other wind instrument.

2. Members of the Family.

(*a*) **Natural Trumpet—Without Crooks** (p. 113, pl. **22**. 15). This is the simplest form of the instrument. Any individual instrument made in this form is capable of producing merely notes of the harmonic series (see *Acoustics* 8) in the one key corresponding to the length of the tube. At the beginning of the seventeenth century, when Monteverdi and others in Italy were making orchestral experiments, including the use of the trumpet, most trumpets were pitched in the key of D, which necessarily imposed a severe limitation: means adopted to shake off such limitations are described under (*b*) and (*c*). The natural trumpet without crooks is not now in use in any band or orchestra but is retained for cavalry signals and for such ceremonial purposes as, in England, that of the two players who by their fanfare signal the arrival of the judges at the assizes.

All the other trumpets of which the descriptions follow are, however, merely the natural trumpet with the addition of some means of lowering its pitch by various intervals, so producing the harmonic series at other levels.

(*b*) **Natural Trumpet—With Crooks** (p. 140, pl. **26**. 4). This is the instrument that was in use from the seventeenth century until well on in the nineteenth. The crooks were additional lengths of tubing, lowering the pitch of the tube as a whole to specified keys, and thus permitting the use of the harmonic series in any of those keys. But the player was still restricted to the few notes of that series, i.e. although the *variety of keys* in which the composer could use the trumpet was enlarged by the crooks the *variety of notes that he could use within any one of those keys* was restricted exactly as it had been with the natural trumpet without crooks.

In the early eighteenth century (Bach's period) a rather limited number of crooks was in use. The player had several instruments by him (generally G, F, D, and B flat), and by crooking down any of them a semitone or tone (or in some cases, inserting a mute in the bell, which raised the pitch), he could take part in performance in any of the keys then normally found in compositions.[1]

In Mozart's day a variety of actual instruments (C, D, E flat) was still in use, with a larger variety of crooks, lowering the pitch of the instruments by a larger variety of intervals.[2]

[1] [2] An authority to whom this article has been submitted comments as follows, on the two paragraphs marked.

'Although the statements in the text agree with Altenburg's enumeration of what instruments a trumpeter would require, to play in all keys (J. E. Altenburg, *Versuch einer Anleitung zur heroisch-musikalischen Trompeter- und Pauken-Kunst*, Halle, 1795, p. 85), I doubt whether the trumpeters of Bach's time possessed as a rule anything like the number. This I judge from the rarity in collections of any trumpets other than those in D or E flat (with a tone crook), and the rarity of parts requiring instruments in other keys.

'All but one of Bach's parts for the natural trumpet can be played on a D instrument, with a tone crook for C, and one of two tones for the two cantatas Nos. 5 and 90, which have parts for B flat trumpet. (As both these were composed after the death of Reiche [Bach's favourite trumpet player] in 1734, the new man may have brought a B flat crook with him.)

'The one exception is the part for F trumpet in the 2nd Brandenburg Concerto, which not even my respect for Bach's greatness prevents me from regarding as an unjustifiable and unaccountable freak. The only other early parts I remember for F trumpet (?) are the rather mysterious parts for Trombe da caccia in Telemann's Violin Concerto.

'I know of no parts for G trumpet, nor any ground for the old description of this as "the English trumpet". It is, however, possible that F and G trumpets were at times used for military and signalling purposes, and so trumpeters attached to princely houses or army corps may have had to use them. Thus at Weissenfels there appear to be mentioned in the records "Trombe, Trombe Francese, Trombe courte, Clarini", but it is impossible to say how far these were meant as synonyms. (A. Werner, *Städtische und fürstliche Musikpflege zu Weissenfels*, Leipzig, 1911, p. 68.)

'The E flat trumpet is not uncommon in collections and was written for. Telemann frequently uses it. (Incidentally, if Telemann's orchestral works were thoroughly studied, they would probably add to our knowledge of early orchestration.) I think the following passage represents the true state of affairs better than what you have in the text:

'"In the early 18th century (the period of Bach and Handel), the standard trumpet in use was that in D (or occasionally in E flat) with a single crook to put it into C. Trumpets in any other key were rarely used,

In Beethoven's day and onwards we find the following selection of crooks, involving the writing of the music in the fictitious pitches indicated (see *Transposing Instruments* and compare *Horn Family*):

F	Music written a	perfect 4th lower
E	„	„	major 3rd	„
E flat	„	„	minor 3rd	„
D	„	„	major 2nd	„
C	„	„	as sounded
B	„	„	a minor 2nd higher
B flat	„	„	major	„
A	„	„	minor 3rd	„

This is the table of transposition with which the student needs to be familiar in order to read the trumpet parts of classical scores. Note that trumpet parts are usually written without key signature, i.e. with sharps and flats inserted before the notes they inflect (cf. *Horn* 2 b).

(c) **Valve Trumpet** (p. 113, pl. **22**. 18). This is the natural trumpet, in some specified key, provided with a means of instantaneously increasing its speaking length and so of making available the harmonic series at a variety of pitches. The alteration of length is effected by pistons or rotary valves which admit the air column to additional lengths of tubing. The pistons are three in number, respectively lowering the pitch by two, one, or three semitones, and, also, by the depression of more than one piston at a time, allowing of a lowering of the pitch by four, five, or six semitones. Thus the valve trumpet may be said to be the equivalent of seven natural trumpets, or of a natural trumpet with six crooks and hence with seven levels of the harmonic series at the player's immediate command. So are filled in all the gaps in the instrument's 'natural' harmonic series, and the trumpet becomes chromatic.

The natural pitch of the modern valve trumpet, i.e. the pitch when none of the pistons is depressed, is, in B flat, alterable to A by a 'rotary change valve'. In some foreign orchestras only a trumpet in C, i.e. a tone higher, is used. Such instruments are only half the length of the old natural trumpets used down to and beyond the time of Beethoven; they are more flexible in tone production, though less colourful, and blend better with the orchestra. At the end of the nineteenth century a longer valve trumpet in F, or, for military band use, E flat, was in vogue. Its tone, though very fine, was more assertive in the orchestra and it was unsuited

except for signalling or military purposes. Bach writes only once for trumpet in F (in the second Brandenburg Concerto) and twice for one in B flat, probably a D trumpet with a long crook.

"'From the second half of the century it was customary, for orchestral purposes, to use a shorter trumpet with crooks for F and all lower keys down to B flat, which were sometimes inserted at the mouthpiece end of the instrument and sometimes, by a double slide, into the body [*Inventionstrompete*—cf. reference to Inventionshorn under *Horn Family* 3].

"'In or about Mozart's time, it became the custom not to use a variety of instruments, but to use a single instrument short enough to give the highest key required by composers, usually F, and with crooks to carry it down to the lowest key. There was no point in multiplying either trumpets or horns when the required result could be got by crooks.'"

for the complex parts written by modern composers for the shorter instruments. The use of such instruments, if they are still to be found in any European orchestra or military band, must be regarded as an interesting survival.

The present methods of writing for the trumpet as a transposing instrument are in a state of chaos. Some composers ignore the existence of the valve instrument and indicate any of the variety of crooks shown above under (b) and write their music accordingly, leaving the player to grapple with any problems of transposition involved. Others indicate one of the pitches of the valve instruments in use and write their music accordingly. The usual (and best) plan nowadays is, however, to write the actual pitch of the notes desired—which will be correct if the C instrument is in use, but will, of course, involve transposition by players who use the B flat, A, or F instrument.

(d) **Slide Trumpet.** From time to time trumpets have been designed the natural pitch of which can be altered, not by the use of valves, but by a sliding mechanism on the principle of the trombone. In the earliest kind, which goes back at least to the middle of the seventeenth century, the whole body of the instrument slides to and fro along a single tube which carries the mouthpiece. This, it is supposed, was the instrument written for by Bach under the name *Tromba da tirarsi* (It. = 'pulling-out trumpet'). At the end of the eighteenth century a slide trumpet was invented in England and used successfully down to within living memory; this had a short slide which was drawn backwards under the player's chin and returned to its original position by a spring. Yet another pattern, used in France, had a longer slide which was pushed forward, as in the trombone.

The reason that prevented these instruments from gaining a permanent position in the orchestra in spite of their tone (which, at least as regards the English variety, was as fine as that of the natural trumpet) was the fact that they were far more difficult to play than any valve trumpet, so that passages written by composers for the latter instrument were often impossible for the slide trumpet. There was, in fact, no place for it in modern music.

Returning to Bach's use of slide instruments, in his day the town bands which, amongst other duties, played chorales from the church tower at specified hours, were necessarily provided with such instruments, because the treble part of a chorale lies in that part of the harmonic series of the natural trumpet where the gaps are fairly large, so that with such a trumpet a tune of this kind could not be played.

For further remarks on Bach's use of the trumpet see below.

(e) **'Bach Trumpets.'** It is common knowledge that in the late seventeenth and earlier eighteenth centuries high-flying florid trumpet parts were commonly written (see 3, below)—such parts as are now looked upon as difficult to play.

In 1884, a Berlin trumpeter, Julius Kosleck,

introduced what was by some taken to be a reconstruction of the actual instrument of Bach's day, though he himself did not make this claim. It was a straight instrument, like a posthorn (but with valves), and pitched in A; the mouthpiece (which he kept secret) was funnel-shaped like that of a horn, not cup-shaped like that of other trumpets. As a result of Kosleck's being invited to England to take part in a Bach performance, the English trumpeter, Walter Morrow, copied this instrument, making some alterations, and brought forward his model at the Leeds Festival of 1886. It also was in A.

The Bach trumpet in A has generally given place to a shorter instrument in D, first brought out by the Brussels firm of C. Mahillon et Cie, which is still in use. In the 1930's a German designer, Werner Menke, introduced what is intended to be an exact copy of the trumpets of the Bach period, but with the addition of two valves, to enable the dissonant harmonics to be produced in tune. However, this instrument loses all the advantages of shorter length and consequently easier playing that are given by the A and D trumpets.

Trumpets identical with the 'Bach Trumpet' have been used of late years for fanfare purposes—apparently because they are supposed to look more effective than the folded trumpet. In American catalogues they are sometimes called 'Triumph Trumpets'.

For the special purpose of playing the trumpet part of the second Brandenburg Concerto, which is of unique difficulty, various small trumpets in high F have at times been made. Menke has, however, designed one in low F, corresponding to his other Bach trumpets in low D.

(f) **Bass Trumpet.** This was an idea of Wagner—an instrument for use in his *Ring*—but it was not a new idea, for bass natural trumpets were in use in the eighteenth century. Its tube would have been of enormous length, and it was to have been made in three keys. As this particular dream of Wagner's was found not fully realizable in waking moments, he had to put up with what, though called a bass trumpet, is (according to some authorities) more of the nature of a valve trombone. He treated it as a transposing instrument; with others it is pitched in key C and is thus not a transposing instrument (many composers, quite needlessly, write its music an octave higher than the sound desired). Up to about 1912, some continental military bands used bass trumpets in B flat and E flat—the usual wind-band keys.

3. History. The history of the trumpet goes back to the beginnings of human history. The Bible testifies to its importance in early religious ceremony, Homer to its use in battle. Earlier than Homer are the trumpets found in 1923 in the tomb of the Egyptian Pharaoh, Tutankamen (reigned 1358–1353 B.C.). These are still playable and, indeed, their tones have been broadcast. Four hundred years before Christ

the Greeks were holding a competition in trumpet playing as an item in the Olympic Games. This instrument is seen as a feature of processions on Roman sculpture (p. 112, pl. 21. 1). By the Middle Ages it had taken two clear forms, one of which (the *Claro*) has given us our trumpet family of today and the other (the *Buysine*) our trombone family (q.v.), though it, also, may be looked on as an ancestor of the trumpet.

The claro, at first a long straight tube, was later, for portability, crumpled into a zigzag shape; the name *Clarion* was now common, and, in one form or other, has never been abandoned.

The high importance of the trumpet in early instrumental bodies is seen in the fact that of the performers attached to Henry VIII fourteen (out of forty-two) were trumpet players.

The history of the orchestra begins, effectively, with the earliest years of the seventeenth century. The fact that the trumpet found a place in the experimental combinations of those days has already been mentioned (2). In Monteverdi's *Orpheus* (1607), there is a toccata for five trumpets in different registers. It has been suggested that the experiments made at the time in the use of the trumpet were not very successful, as little more use of it has been traced until the end of the century. It is more likely, however, that our knowledge of the music of the period is defective. Indeed, the fact that early in the seventeenth century appeared Fantini's *Modo per imparar a sonare di tromba*, 'Manner of learning to play the trumpet' (Frankfort, 1638), is significant. Towards the end of the century the trumpet was certainly well recognized.

At that period Purcell (to mention one composer) made considerable use of the instrument, as, for instance, in the opera *Dioclesian*, where he uses a trumpet and an alto voice in duet; he was writing for an able performer, John Shore, Trumpeter to the Court and a member of a family of trumpeters that remained famous for a century, and probably many of the difficult trumpet parts of the composers of the epoch were thus written for virtuosi whose competence to perform them was to be relied upon. By this time very many German composers were including the trumpet in orchestral combinations.

Handel, a little later, wrote florid high-lying trumpet parts, as in 'Let the bright seraphim' (*Samson*, p. 140, pl. 26. 4) and 'The trumpet shall sound' (*Messiah*). He marked his trumpet parts 'Clarino I, Clarino II, and Prinzipale', showing that the same general disposition of players as in the days of Monteverdi was still maintained. Bach also used the trumpet in a very florid way, and his parts, on the whole, are in a still higher range. It is, of course, only towards the top of the harmonic series that the notes lie near enough to one another for the performance of a part consisting of anything but a simple arpeggio, so that composers who wished to make a genuinely melodic use of the instrument were driven into altitude—which is perfectly feasible on the long (and therefore, basically low-pitched) trumpet of the period. There has been much speculation as to how players were able to produce these higher notes of the harmonic series and to negotiate such elaborate passages, and, as above recorded (see 2 e), it was for a time supposed that they were possessed of instruments essentially different from those of later periods. The true explanation seems to lie in the fact that players specialized in the performance of higher or lower trumpet parts; a 'Clarino' player spent his life playing high-lying parts and these became easy to him (cf. *Horn Family* 3). Modern players have found that with sufficient practice they also can play high-lying passages.

In general, the orchestral use of the trumpet in the period of Bach and Handel was less as a part of the general web than as a contribution to pointed expression. The instrument, as then used, did not merge well into the mass, but the fact that whenever it appeared it stood forward in its own limelight made it suitable for the occasions when a special effect of exultation (or, it might be, of Judgement-terror) was needed: in Bach, in such passages, we commonly find three trumpets.

After this period, however, the limelight was switched off and the instrument crept somewhat into the back stage. In Haydn and Mozart (with whom the modern orchestra may be said to begin) the trumpet tends to become much less a melodic instrument, much more a harmonic one: it no longer uses its high notes, lying adjacent one to another, but contents itself with its lower and more widely spaced ones, which, being mostly the notes of the tonic chord, limit it very much to a modest contribution to the general hurly-burly of coda-like passages at the ends of movements or of the sections of movements, and to similar relatively humbler uses. It becomes, in the orchestra, in fact, what it had always been elsewhere, the bosom companion of the kettledrums, which, restricted as they at that date are to the performance of two notes (the tonic and dominant), are similarly employed. The normal trumpet appeal is psychologically much the same as the fortissimo appeal, and as fortissimo passages were then largely constructed in a simple manner on a tonic and dominant chord (the very basis upon which the trumpet could find suitable employment for its lower and middle register) trumpet and fortissimo came to be closely connected.

Two trumpets per orchestra was now the regular allowance.

With Beethoven we find the role of both trumpet and drum somewhat widened, but so long as the 'natural' instrument, even with crooks, was the only one in use, the trumpeter could not take much part in the weaving of any contrapuntal web.

There were now various attempts to free the trumpet from its harmonic fetters and to release it into melodic freedom. In the late eighteenth century a *Keyed Trumpet* was tried (compare *Cornett Family* for the same principle) but soon abandoned. There were also tried trumpets so shaped as to bring the bell within reach of the player's hand and thus to allow him to add to his repertory the 'stopped notes' of the horn player (see *Horn Family* 2 b); such stopped notes, however, muffled as they have been accused of being in the case of the horn, seemed still more so in contrast with the brightness of the normal trumpet tone. As already recorded, the *Slide Trumpet* had some success in England, but hardly elsewhere. The Irishman Clagget, who, as recorded under *Horn Family* 3, ingeniously connected two horns of different pitch, supplying a valve for diverting the air-stream into one or the other, did the same with the trumpet. And other sanguine inventors brought forward other brilliant notions.

Two Germans, Blühmel and Stölzel (or Blümel and Stölzl,) in the early years of the nineteenth century, at last introduced the true valve principle; this was improved and ultimately perfected by Adolphe Sax, Périnet, and lastly Dr. J. P. Oates, and the present-day trumpet thus came into being—though improvements of detail have since been made and continue to be made. The first orchestral use of the valve trumpet seems to be that of Halévy in *La Juive* (1835); he used two valve instruments and two natural ones with crooks.

It will be seen that the valve trumpet was born in time to play a part in the chromatic music of Wagner, who was thus enabled to use trumpet tone freely in his highly contrapuntal style of composition.

During the later eighteenth century, as already mentioned, two trumpets had continued to be the normal orchestral allowance (except in the accompaniment of choral works, when three or four were often heard). Wagner regularly used three, so as to be able to produce complete trumpet chords; in *Tannhäuser* (for a special purpose) he used twelve. Since his day the trumpet has been very freely used by all orchestral composers, three being a common allowance.

It was Wagner, also, who first made substantial use of Muted Trumpet effects, though these can be traced back as far as Monteverdi.

4. Repertory. The trumpet, from its character, has necessarily been little used for solo or chamber music, especially in the earlier period when melody's thread was beyond its weaving except in the highest part of its compass. Its general popularity in the late seventeenth century has been mentioned, as also that seventeenth- and early eighteenth-century music in which voice and trumpet sing a bold duet. **Handel** has a Concerto for trumpets and horns. **Leopold Mozart** (1719–87) left a Trumpet Concerto in which the solo instrument moves almost as freely as a clarinet. **Haydn's** Trumpet Concerto (1796) must have been intended for the keyed trumpet, as it could not have been played on any other instrument in use at that date. It may be added that Weidinger, court trumpeter in Haydn's Vienna, introduced the year previous to Haydn's composition of this piece, i.e. in 1795 (*not* 1801, as often stated) a trumpet with five keys. Doubtless this invention and this concerto are connected in origin.

A few late nineteenth- and twentieth-century chamber works include the trumpet, as, for instance, **Saint-Saëns's** Septet for trumpet, five stringed instruments, and pianoforte, and **d'Indy's** Suite in the Olden Style for trumpet, two flutes, two violins, viola, and violoncello; **Stravinsky's** Octet for flute, clarinet, two bassoons, two trumpets, and two trombones; **Pierné's** Pastorale for flute, oboe, clarinet, two bassoons, horn, and trumpet; **Glazunof's** Quartet for trumpet, horn, and two trombones; **Poulenc's** Sonata for trumpet, horn, and trombone; **Hindemith's** Sonata for trumpet and piano (1939); and a Concerto for trumpet by **Karl Pilss** (1936). **Walton's** *Façade*, in its original version for 6 players, makes remarkable use of the trumpet. The French composers have provided a large proportion of such works as are available, probably on account of the earlier and greater popularity in France of the small trumpets in A, B flat, and C, as distinct

from the longer and less light and agile trumpet in F (see 2 c above).

The many courts of Germany and Austria, in the eighteenth century, maintained corps of skilled trumpeters as a part of their state, and there must have existed a large literature of trumpet solos, duets, etc., now lost to us.

5. Nomenclature.

Trumpet. *Trompette, Trompette d'harmonie* (Fr.); *Tromba* (It., plural *Trombe*); *Trompete* (Ger.); *Clarino, Tromba,* and *Principale* (It., seventeenth to mid-eighteenth century); *Prinzipale* (Handel's term for 3rd trumpet).

Valve Trumpet. *Trompette à pistons, Trompette chromatique* (Fr.); *Tromba ventile, Tromba a macchina, Tromba a pistoni, Tromba cromatica* (It.); *Ventriltrompete* (Ger.).

Slide Trumpet. *Trompette à coulisse* (Fr.); *Tromba da tirarsi* or *Tromba a tiro* (It.); *Zugtrompete* (Ger.).

Bass Trumpet. *Trompette basse* (Fr.); *Tromba bassa* (It.); *Basstrompete* (Ger.).

For trumpet stop see *Organ* 14 VI.
For mechanical trumpet see *Mechanical Reproduction* 8.
An important eighteenth-century book on trumpet playing was that of *Altenburg* (q.v.); and see 2 (b) above (note.)

TRUMPET SONATA (Mozart). See *Nicknamed* 15 (K. 576).

TRUMSCHEIT (Ger.). See *Tromba Marina.*

TRY, CHARLES DE. See *Percussion Family* 4 e; *Tryphone.*

TRYANGLE. Same as *Triangle* 2 above (Pepys spells it this way in his diary).

TRYPHONE. A French form of xylophone. Ch. de Try introduced it about 1870. See *Percussion Family* 2 f, 4 e, 5 f.

T.S. = *Tasto Solo* (q.v.).

TSCHUDI (or **Shudi**). See *Harpsichord Family* 5; *Pianoforte* 5, 15.

TSIGANE, TZIGANE (Fr.). 'Gipsy.'

TUBA GROUP

    1. Introductory.   3. The British Tubas.   5. The (Lower) Flügelhorns.
    2. The Wagner Tubas.   4. The (Lower) Saxhorns.

(For illustrations see p. 113, pl. **22**. 16.)

1. Introductory. To define 'tuba' is impossible. The name seems to be applied, in free-and-easy speech, to any sort of present-day bass-pitched brass instrument other than the trombones. Properly, for the sake of clear understanding, it would be well to limit the term (at the very least) to such of those instruments as are of *wide conical bore* and possess *cup-shaped mouthpieces*, but, as will be seen below, this has not been done.

All the instruments called by the name may, historically considered, be looked on as the artistic successors of the serpent, Russian bassoon, and ophicleide group. See *Cornett and Key Bugle Family* 1, 2 d e f g, 3.

Berlioz's treatise on orchestration (1843) must be the first, or one of the first, to recognize the tuba; he mentions, besides a primitive *Bombardon*, a *Bass Tuba in F*, a species of bombardon 'the mechanism of which has been improved by M. Wibrecht [W. F. Wieprecht,

1802–72], master of the King of Prussia's military bands'. He says that it is much used in north Germany, and praises its tone as 'incomparably more noble than that of ophicleides, bombardons, and serpents'. (This, however, was hardly fair to the serpent, a fine instrument when ably played.) He says that Adolphe Sax (see 4, below) in Paris is making bass tubas in E flat. In Berlioz's 'Fantastic' Symphony (1830) he had used an ophicleide, but in preparing, in the early 1850s, a copy for a German edition he wished to issue, he added a footnote authorizing the substitution of the tuba.

Gradually we find the tuba coming into use. Two of the earlier instances are an overture by Otto Bach (1858) and Wallace's opera *Love's Triumph* (1862).

It was Wagner's use of the tuba tribe, however, that gave it its sure position, and from 1869, when performances of the first drama of

The Ring were heard, its members began to take their place as normal constituents of the larger orchestra.

The various instruments that nowadays go under the name of tuba, or that undertake to play the tuba parts in a score, are a great source of confusion to the student, and the varying treatments of the subject in books on orchestration and works of reference add to the confusion. The following is an attempt at a systematic treatment; it is based partly on Forsyth's classification in his *Orchestration*, which 'seems to offer the clearest existing treatment, though not every authority approves it'. But the reader must be warned that not only have some instruments several names but that different instruments have, in some cases, the same names in different countries, whilst even in any one country names are often so loosely applied as to give only a more or less vague indication of what the speaker or writer is alluding to.

It will be noted in what follows that the indications '(*a*)', '(*b*)', and '(*c*)' are uniformly applied in the various sections, i.e. '(*a*)' in any one section is the instrument that can be (and sometimes is) replaced by '(*a*)' in any other section—and so, of course, with '(*b*)' and '(*c*)'. This method is, so far as is known, peculiar to the present work, and it may possibly prove helpful.

Conical mutes exist for insertion in the bells of the various members of the tuba group—as in those of other brass instruments.

It is common nowadays, where tubas do not otherwise figure in a score, for the composer to use one as a bass to the trombones, so making up a sort of low-bass brass quartet.

2. The Wagner Tubas. Wagner, desiring to be able to write eight-part harmony for horns in *The Ring*, added to the two pairs of horns of his previous orchestra two pairs of an instrument devised by him, and then, to thicken the bass, added another instrument which was capable of playing an octave below the normal bass of the set. He had thus nine instruments in all. The new instruments, which took the lower notes of his harmony, were as follows:

(*a*) **Tenor Tuba.** Of this he had two. They were not really tubas, their bore approaching the comparatively narrow bore of the horns, and their mouthpiece being much like the horn's funnel-shaped mouthpiece (not the tuba's cup-shaped one); and this approach to horn structure gave them an approach to the smooth horn tone.

Their fundamental key was that of B flat, and they had three valves, like those of the horns, plus a fourth one for correcting the intonation of the lowest octave.

(*b*) **Bass Tuba.** Of this also he had two. And these also were not true tubas, being reproductions of (*a*) with a fundamental key of F, i.e. the 'Bass Tuba' was the same as the 'Tenor Tuba', made bigger and with a range lying a perfect 4th lower. It may be noted that

Wagner's tenor and bass tubas corresponded in length and harmonic series with the true horns in B flat alto and F, of which they were, therefore, the wide-bore analogues.

(*c*) **Double-Bass Tuba** or **Contra-Bass Tuba.** Of this he had merely one. Unlike its companions it was a true tuba, with tuba bore and cup-shaped mouthpiece. Its fundamental key was C and its lowest note was the E flat five spaces below the bass staff.

What are sometimes heard today under the name of 'Wagner Tubas' represent a considerable modification of the above, so far as the tenor tuba and bass tuba are concerned, departing more from the French horn model as to bore, and approaching more to that of the saxhorn; they retain, however, the funnel-shaped mouthpiece of the horns.

Wagner's notation for these instruments was inconsistent and somewhat involved. It is explained in detail in the larger books on orchestration.

3. The British Tubas. What are usually played as 'tubas' in Britain are modelled on Wagner's one true tuba mentioned above (the term 'British Tuba' is not an accepted one, but is used here as conveniently distinctive). They are as follows:

(*a*) **Euphonium, or Tenor Tuba in B Flat.** In Germany, **Baryton**; in Italy (sometimes) **Bombarda.** The fundamental note is B flat, and there are four valves, making it possible to join up the fundamental note chromatically with the next harmonic and so providing an easy range of three octaves from B flat three spaces below the bass staff, some players attaining a range of over four octaves. For marching lightness this instrument is sometimes robbed of its fourth valve and the corresponding tube, and it is then reduced in compass at the bottom, reaching only E.

(*b*, i) **E Flat Bass Tuba** or **E Flat Bombardon, or EE Flat Bass Tuba.**[1] There are sometimes four valves, as in (*a*), and the range lies a perfect fifth lower; more commonly, however, only three are provided. This instrument is sometimes produced in a circular form for placing round the body of a marching bandsman, and is then called the *E flat Helicon.*

(*b*, ii) **F Bass Tuba.** This is a reproduction, two semitones higher, of (*b*, i), to which it is often preferred for orchestral use.

(*c*) **B Flat Bass Tuba, or B Flat Bombardon, or BB Flat Bass Tuba.**[1] This is, in fundamental note, an octave below (*a*) but, as it is usually provided with only three valves, its range, in reproducing that of (*a*), is shorter by an augmented 4th at the bottom (i.e. the bottom note, instead of being B flat, is only E—the fundamental B flat being barely possible). This instrument, like the one above, some-

---

[1] There is, properly, a difference between the E flat Bass Tuba and the EE Flat Bass Tuba and also between the B Flat Bass Tuba and the BB Flat Bass Tuba; the pitch is the same but the double letter indicates, in each case, a larger bore.

times takes the circular form; it is then called the *BB flat Helicon*.

All the above are written for at their proper pitch in the bass clef, i.e. they are *not* treated as transposing instruments.

A more recent American innovation is the **Sousaphone,** a form of (*b*, i) and (*c*) above, first made for Sousa's band in 1899 and now very popular. It is merely the Helicon form of the instruments, with the bell turned up through two right angles and terminating in an enormous flange about two feet across.

4. The (Lower) Saxhorns. These were introduced by the Paris wind-instrument maker Adolphe Sax, in 1845, as a part of his large family of saxhorns (see *Saxhorn and Flügelhorn Families*). They have cup-shaped mouthpieces, like the true tubas (the 'British'), not funnel-shaped ones like horns or the two upper Wagner tubas, and their bore approaches the wide tuba bore. They are treated here as members of the tuba group from their orchestral and band function of supplying bass parts. The association of the Wagner tubas, the British tubas, and the lowest three saxhorns in the mind of the student is necessarily a close one. The four highest saxhorns are treated elsewhere in this volume (see *Saxhorn and Flügelhorn Families*), primarily because they do not share this association, but also, secondarily, because they are structurally slightly different.

The *a, b, c* lettering below is, as before stated, made to correspond with that of the corresponding Wagner tubas and British tubas.

(*a*) **Bass Saxhorn in B Flat (or C).** This is practically the same as the euphonium (3 *a*) and is known in Germany as *Euphonion, Barytonhorn in B* (*C*) or *Baryton in B* (*C*) or *Tenorbass in B* (*C*), B being in German the name of our B flat; and in France as *Basse à pistons, Saxhorn baryton*, or *Saxhorn basse*.

(*b*) **Bass Saxhorn in E Flat (or F).** This is practically the same as the British E flat bass tuba, otherwise E flat bombardon (3 *b* i). It is known in Germany as *Basstuba in F* (*Es*) and in France as *Contrebasse à pistons, Saxhorn basse*, or *Saxhorn contrabasse*.

(*c*) **Double-Bass Saxhorn in B Flat (or C).** This is practically the B flat bass tuba (3 *c*), but it has four valves, not three, and so can carry its chromatic scale right down to the fundamental note, B flat. It is known in Germany as *Kontrabasstuba in B* (*C*) and in France as *Contrebasse à pistons, Saxhorn Contrebasse*, or *Saxhorn bourdon*.[1]

There is a peculiarity in the notation of these, the lower Saxhorns (cf. *Saxhorn and Flügelhorn Families* 2—end). Sometimes they are treated as non-transposing instruments and sometimes as transposing instruments. By some composers their music is written at its proper pitch and in the bass clef, but by others it is written in the treble clef and on the principle that the second harmonic (i.e. the octave of the fundamental) is represented always by middle C; to prevent mistake the pitch of that second harmonic is given here for the three instruments—(*a*) B flat near bottom of bass staff; (*b*) E flat one leger line below bass staff; (*c*) B flat three spaces below bass staff.

5. The (Lower) Flügelhorns. The tenor Flügelhorn in E flat (also misnamed 'Altflügelhorn', 'Alto Flügelhorn' or 'Althorn'; cf. *Saxhorn and Flügelhorn Families* 2 c d and 3 b c) is in Germany and elsewhere sometimes used to play the parts in Wagner which he allotted to what he called his 'Tenor Tuba'. See *Saxhorn and Flügelhorn Families* for more about this instrument.

An Italian variety of Flügelhorn is called **Flicorno** (plural 'Flicorni'); of tuba size there are the *Flicorno basso* (or *Bassflicorno*), the *Flicorno basso grave* and the *Flicorno contrabasso*, respectively in B flat, E flat, and B flat, like the saxhorns shown in section 4 of this article (compare *Saxhorn and Flügelhorn Families* 4).

[1] Besides those enumerated in the text, tubas have been occasionally constructed of still greater size and deeper pitch. Such are the German *Subbasstuba* in E flat or F, standing an octave below 3 (*b*, i) and 3 (*b*, ii) respectively, and *Subkontrabasstuba* in B flat or C, an octave or seventh below 3 (*c*). An American example of the latter instrument, called the BBB flat contrabass, stands about nine feet high, and its tube, apart from the valve tubing, is some 36 feet in length. But such enormous structures must be regarded as instrument-makers' curiosities rather than as subserving any useful purpose.

TUBA (Major, Minor, Mirabilis, Sonora). See *Organ* 14 VI.

TUBALCAIN. See *Percussion Family* 4 e.

TUBA MIRUM. See *Requiem*.

TUBA SONORA. See *Organ* 14 VI.

TUBO DI RICAMBIO (It. 'changing-tube'). Crook or shank of a brass instrument (see *Brass; Trumpet Family* 2 b, 3; *Horn Family* 2 b; *Cornet*).

TUBOPHONE. See *Percussion Family* 2 c.

TUBULAR BELLS. See *Percussion Family* 2 b, and *Bell* 7.

TUCKET. A preliminary flourish of trumpets—the word used by Shakespeare and his contemporaries.

TUDWAY, THOMAS (died 1726). He was a choir boy and then tenor in St. George's Chapel, Windsor; organist of King's College and Pembroke College, Cambridge; D.Mus. of the University and Professor of Music (1705); and Composer and Organist Extraordinary to Queen Anne. He is chiefly remembered today for his great manuscript collection of Cathedral Music, now in the British Museum.

See *Anthem*, Period II.

TUFT. See *Hymns and Hymn Tunes* 17 f (ii).

TUNE, as a noun, means a melodic succession of notes that 'makes sense', so to speak—notes that are felt to be in such relation to one another that the succession becomes a unit in itself. (Practically 'tune' means the same as 'Melody', q.v.) Often the word is used for the uppermost part in a single composition—'the tune and the accompaniment' or 'the tune and its harmonies'. Inexperienced listeners when they fail to detect a clear, comprehensible, and easily memorizable uppermost part say the composition 'has no tune'. Especially do they say this of contrapuntal compositions, such as fugues, which are, of course, *all* tune (i.e. in every part and not merely the uppermost).

As a verb 'tune' means to bring into correct intonation ('to tune a piano'). So 'to sing in tune'.

TUNING-FORK. See *Pitch* 6 b.

TUNING OF INSTRUMENTS. See *Temperament*.

TUNSTED (or Tunstede), SIMON. He was an English Franciscan friar who lived in the fourteenth century (thought to have died in 1369) and enjoys a reputation as an early writer on astronomy and music (though his authorship on the latter subject is not absolutely certain).

He is credited with a treatise codifying the principles of the 'Ars Nova' (see *France* 3) and thus considered to be a leader in the movement.

TUONO, or TONO (It.). 'Tone'—in all the various senses of the English word (q.v.). Also 'mode', 'key'; also 'thunder'. The plural is *Tuoni* or *Toni.*

TUPPER, MARTIN (1810–89). See *Broadcasting* 1 b.

TURANDOT. (Fantastic Chinese Opera by Puccini; completed after his death by Alfano, q.v.). Produced in Milan in 1926. Text by Adami and Simoni, based on Carlo Gozzi's eighteenth-century version of a widespread and ancient tale.

Turandot, daughter of the Emperor of China, feels herself bound to take revenge on the race of men for the dishonour suffered by a far-off ancestress at the hands of barbarian invaders. She will wed no one but the suitor who can give the answers to three riddles she propounds, and the penalty for failure in the ordeal is death.

Act I

Scene: *The Walls of Pekin, at Sunset*

A **Mandarin** (*Baritone*) announces to the crowd the fate of the latest of a long succession of suitors who is due to forfeit his life—the Prince of Persia. There is a clash between the bloodthirsty crowd and the guard, in the course of which a slave girl, Liù (*Soprano*), calls out that her aged master is being trampled on: an Unknown Prince (**Calaf,** *Tenor*) comes to his aid and recognizes him as his lost father, **Timur,** (*Bass*), the dethroned Tartar king. The execution of the Prince of Persia proceeds and Calaf curses the inhuman Turandot. But the moment the Princess herself appears on the scene he falls under her spell, and neither the cynical observations of the officials, **Ping**

(*Baritone*), **Pang**, and **Pong** (*Tenors*), nor warnings from the spirits of her former suitors, nor the entreaties of Liù (secretly in love with him) and Timur can prevent him from sounding the gong that proclaims him a suitor.

Act II

Scene 1: *A Pavilion*

The three ministers, Ping, Pang, and Pong, share out the duties of preparing for wedding festivities or funeral obsequies—whichever may be found necessary. They bemoan the present unhappy lot of China and evoke nostalgic memories of their distant country estates.

Scene 2: *The great Square in front of the Palace*

Calaf appears before the court and people to face his ordeal. The old Emperor, **Altoum,** (*Tenor*), tries without success to dissuade him, but he is firm in his resolve, and Turandot (*Soprano*), after recounting the story of her unfortunate ancestress, propounds her three riddles, all of which, to her consternation, are successively solved by the Prince. Appalled at the prospect of a dreaded union she implores her father to release her from her bargain. However, as the generous Prince does not want an unwilling bride, he once more offers his life if she can find out his name before the coming dawn.

Act III

Scene 1: *The Garden of the Palace*

Nobody is suffered to sleep in Pekin, where the whole populace is under a threat of death unless the name of the unknown Prince is discovered. Timur is dragged in with Liù, who claims to be the only possessor of the secret. She stabs herself before she can be put to the torture and dies predicting to the wondering Turandot that she, too, will be overcome by the power of love. Left alone with the Princess, Calaf tears her veil from her and embraces her; she is vanquished and confesses her love for him, but when he reveals his name, her fierce pride reasserts itself.

Scene 2: *The Exterior of the Palace*

But when the time comes for Turandot to give out the stranger's identity, she announces simply that his name is . . . 'Love'; and they embrace, amid the joyful acclamations of the people.

TURBA. See *Passion Music* 1.

TURCA, ALLA (It.). In the Turkish style. See the reference to 'Turkish Music' in *Military Band*; also *Percussion Family* 4 b.

TURCHANINOF, PETER (1779–1856). He was a priest and choir-master in the cathedral of St. Petersburg and elsewhere and wrote church music for the church in Russia (see *Greek Church* 5).

TURCHI, GUIDO. Born in Rome in 1916. As a composer he is somewhat influenced by the technique and style of certain of his

1. HORATIO PARKER (1863–1919)

2. AMY MARCY BEACH (1867–1944)

3. HENRY F. GILBERT
(1868–1928)

4. HENRY K. HADLEY (1871–1937)

5. FREDERICK S. CONVERSE
(1871–1940)

6. E. BURLINGAME HILL
(1872–1960)

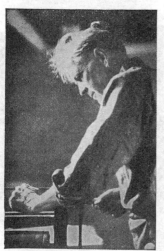

7. ARTHUR FARWELL as music
lithographer (1872–1952)

8. DANIEL GREGORY MASON
(1873–1953)

9. W. C. HANDY (1873–1958)

PLATE 172   AMERICAN MUSICIANS, IV

1. CHARLES IVES (1874–1954)

2. JOHN ALDEN CARPENTER
(1876–1951)

3. CARL RUGGLES (1876–1971)

4. ERNEST SCHELLING
(1876–1939)

5. ERNEST BLOCH (1880–1959)

6. ARTHUR SHEPHERD (1880–1958)

7. CHAS. WAKEFIELD CADMAN
(1881–1946)

8. PERCY GRAINGER (1882–1961)

9. CHARLES T. GRIFFES
(1884–1920)

Italian contemporaries (such as Petrassi, q.v.), and, later, of Bartók. He has written a good deal of choral music, as also piano music, chamber music, orchestral music, etc.

TURCO, TURCA (It., masc., fem.). 'Turkish.' See *Percussion Family* 4 b, *Military Band*.

TURINA, JOAQUÍN (p. 977, pl. **164.** 9). Born at Seville in 1882 and died in 1949, aged sixty-six. He studied at Seville and Madrid and then in Paris (whither most Spanish composers gravitated in their later student days) with d'Indy; here he associated also with Debussy, Ravel, and others of another school from that of his master.

He was a fine pianist and a capable conductor, and a prolific and admired composer of the genuine Spanish school (cf. *Pedrell* and *Falla*). He wrote a quantity of chamber music, many songs, a number of works for the stage and some orchestral music, of which the brilliant *Procesión del Rocío* ('Procession of the Lady of the Dew') is the most widely known and popularly appreciated item.

TÜRK, DANIEL GOTTLIEB (1756–1813). He was a popular German composer (in which capacity he is forgotten) and a writer of theoretical treatises (as which he is still remembered).

See passing reference under *Rubato* 2.

TURKEY AND MUSIC. See *Oriental*.

TURKEY IN THE STRAW. See *Guion*.

TÜRKISCH (Ger.). 'Turkish.' See *Percussion Family* 4 b; *Military Band*.

TURKISH CRESCENT or **TURKISH JINGLE** (p. 513, pl. **92.** 3, 5).

A noise maker introduced into military bands in Britain, France, and elsewhere at the time when there was a craze for 'Turkish Music' (see *Military Band*; also *Janissary Music*); it was long maintained in use in the German army.

A long stick is surmounted by a tent-shaped or hat-shaped construction, with an inverted crescent a little lower down the stick; from both of these are suspended small bells and the like. The mode of performance is simple— merely to shake the stick in rhythm.

Other names are *Pavillon chinois* (Fr.), *Padiglione cinese* (It.), i.e. 'Chinese Tent'— perhaps with some allusion to pagodas hung with bells, also *Chapeau chinois* ('Chinese Hat') and *Jingling Johnny*—the last name doubtless the invention of the British soldier. Also *Schellenbaum* (Ger.), i.e. 'Bell-tree'.

TURKISH MUSIC. See *Military Band*; *Percussion Family* 4 b.

TURLE, JAMES (p. 165, pl. **34.** 6). Born at Taunton, in Somerset, in 1802 and died in London in 1882, aged eighty. He was chorister at Wells Cathedral and then came to London, holding a number of organistships. For twelve years he was assistant organist at Westminster Abbey and for over fifty organist there (being

relieved, latterly, however, by Frederick Bridge, q.v.). He composed much church music, some of which will probably remain long in use.

See *Anglican Chant* 4.

TURLUTAINE. See *Mechanical Reproduction of Music* 6.

TURM-MUSIK, TURMSONATEN, TÜRMERMEISTER. See under *Wait*.

TURN. See Tables 14, 15.

TURNER, WILLIAM. Born at Oxford in 1651 and died in London in 1740, aged eighty-eight or eighty-nine. His father was cook of Pembroke College, Oxford, and he began life as a chorister of Christ Church, but was then removed to London, where, in the Chapel Royal, he served as chorister under Captain Cooke (q.v.), and joined his colleagues, Blow (q.v.) and Humfrey (q.v.), in the composition of a famous 'Club Anthem'. He remained a singer all his life, being attached to the establishments of the Chapel Royal, Westminster Abbey, and St. Paul's Cathedral.

He composed much music, of which some of that intended for the church remains in use, and dying a day or two after his wife, with whom he had lived nearly seventy years, was laid with her in the cloisters of Westminster Abbey.

See reference under *Anthem*, Period II; *Metronome*.

TURQUE (Fr.). 'Turkish.' See *Percussion Family* 4 b; *Military Band*.

TURTCHANINOW (and similar spellings). See *Turchaninof*.

TUSCH (Ger.). (1) A fanfare (q.v.). (2) A German orchestra's flourish of wind instruments and drums, as an expression of applause for an artist, sometimes called for by the audience.

TUTHILL, B. C. See *Publishing* 9.

TUTILO or **TOOLE.** See *Ireland* 2; *Trope*.

TUTTA, TUTTE (It.). 'All.' Fem., sing. and plur., of *Tutto* (below).

TUTTE LE CORDE (It.). 'All the strings', i.e. (in pianoforte music) cease to play *Una corda* (see *Pianoforte* 12).

TUTTI (It.). 'All.' Masc. plur. of *Tutto*. Used in the sense of 'all the performers now take part', after a passage in which only some did so. The word has come to be used as a noun. We speak of 'a tutti', meaning a passage for the whole force (compare *Ripieno*). In a modern concerto (see *Concerto* 4) the word means the passages for orchestra as distinct for those for the solo instrument (really then, often, 'all but one').

TUTTO, TUTTA (It., masc., fem.). 'All.' The word *Tutti* above is its masc. plural; *Tutte* is the fem. plural.

TWAIN, MARK. See references—*Hymns and Hymn Tunes* 8; *Kotzwara*.

TWELFTH. See *Intervals*; *Organ* 14 IV.

TWELFTH MASS. See *Misattributed Compositions* (Mozart).

TWELVE-NOTE SCALE. (*Dodecuple* or *Dodecaphonic* Scale). See *Scales* 7; *Temperament* 9; *Note-row*.

TWELVE-TONE SCALE. Misleading name for the above.

TWILIGHT OF THE GODS. See *Ring of the Nibelung*.

TWO-FOOT C, etc. See *Pitch* 7.

TWO-FOOT STOP. See *Organ* 2 b.

TWO-IN-ONE. See *Canon*.

TYE, CHRISTOPHER. Born probably in 1497 and died in 1572 or 1573, aged about seventy-five. He was D.Mus. of Cambridge and Oxford, master of the choristers at Ely Cathedral and a Gentleman of the Chapel Royal (q.v.) of Edward VI and Elizabeth. Concerning the latter a manuscript of Anthony Wood in the Bodleian tells the following story:

'Dr. Tye was a peevish and humoursome man, especially in his latter dayes, and sometimes playing on ye Organ in ye chap. of qu. Elizab. wh. contained much musick, but little delight to the ear, she would send ye verger to tell him yt he play'd out of Tune; whereupon he sent word yt her ears were out of Tune.'

Amongst his many compositions was a setting of his own translation into English metre of the Acts of the Apostles, 'wyth notes to eche Chapter to synge and also to play upon the Lute' (1553). This was a work for domestic consumption, but most of his music was for church use, and by it he exercised a great influence upon the development of the English school, being often styled 'The Father of the Anthem'.

The well-known tunes *Dundee*,[1] referred to

[1] This tune is in English hymn-tune books called *Windsor*. (What is in English books called *Dundee* is in Scottish books called *French*.)

in Burns's *The Cotter's Saturday Night*, and *Winchester Old*, commonly sung to 'While shepherds watched', are adaptations of tunes in his 'Acts of the Apostles' music.

In 1560 he took orders (resigning his musical position), and was given a living near Ely, to which two others were later added.

See *White, Robert*; *Anthem* I; *Farrant*; *Mass* 5.

TYERS, JONATHAN (died 1767), and his sons THOMAS (1726–87) and JONATHAN (d. 1792). They owned and successfully managed Vauxhall Gardens (see *Concerts*, 12, 13, 15; *Ridotto*) from 1732 to nearly the end of the century, the management of the family then continuing in the person of a son-in-law of Jonathan junior. It was this family that reformed the morals of the Gardens and developed their innocent musical pleasures. Thomas wrote the poems of many of the 'Vauxhall Songs' that circulated throughout the country.

TYMBAL. A frequent and long-standing misspelling of *Timbal* (Kettledrum; see *Percussion*, 2 a, 4 a, 5 a)—as 'Timpani' is often misspelt 'Tympany'.

TYMPANI. A common misspelling of *Timpani*, kettledrums. See *Percussion Family* 2 a, 4 a, 5 a.

TYNDALE, WILLIAM (d. 1530). Translator of the Bible. See *Psalm*.

TYPEWRITER (as musical instrument). See *Percussion Family* 4 d; p. 544, pl. 99. 4.

TYPOPHONE. A sort of dulcitone. See *Percussion Family* 2 e, 5 e.

TYROLIENNE. See *Jodel*; *Ländler*.

TYRWHITT, GERALD. See *Berners*.

TZIGANE, TSIGANE (Fr.). 'Gipsy.'

U

U. Frequent abbreviation of the German *Und*, i.e. 'and'.

ÜBER (Ger.). 'Over', 'above', 'too'.

ÜBUNG or **UEBUNG** (Ger.). 'Exercise' (plural *Übungen* or *Uebungen*).

U.G.M. Union of Graduates in Music (Britain). See *Degrees and Diplomas* 1.

UGUALE, UGUALI (It., sing., plur.). 'Equal.' So *Ugualmente*, 'equally'; *Ugualità, Uguaglianza*, 'equality'.

'UHR' SYMPHONY (Haydn). See *Nicknamed Compositions* 11.

UKELELE (p. 449, pl. **77. 7**). It has four strings and a very long finger-board, with or without 'frets' (q.v.). It was patented by the Honolulu Ad Club in 1917, from which date it gradually became very popular in the United States amongst people whose desire to perform was stronger than their willingness to acquire any difficult technique or their desire to make intimate acquaintance with any very elaborate music. It also had a place in some jazz bands (see *Jazz*). Its ultimate origin is Portuguese. The spelling 'Ukulele' is seen.

A similar instrument, though larger and often electrically amplified, is the *Hawaiian Guitar*; in this the six strings are stopped with a steel bar, giving the opportunity for a characteristically exaggerated portamento.

The Ukelele Banjo, or Banjulele, is another instrument related to the Ukelele and, like it, has four strings.

ULLOGAUN. A sort of Irish lament.

ULTIMO, ULTIMA (It., masc., fem.). 'Last.'

UMANO, UMANA (It., masc., fem.). 'Human.'

UMKEHRUNG (Ger.). 'Turning round', 'reversal'. Thus *Kanon in der Umkehrung*, 'Canon by Inversion' (see *Canon*).

UMORE (It.). 'Humour.'

UMSTIMMEN (Ger.). To tune in some special way (see *Scordatura*). So the noun *Umstimmung*.

UN', UNA, UNO (It.); **UN, UNE** (Fr.). 'A' or 'an'; 'one'.

UNACCOMPANIED SONG. See *Song* 6.

UNA CORDA. See article *Pianoforte* 12.

UNAUTHORIZED TITLES FOR COMPOSITIONS. See *Nicknamed Compositions*.

UND (Ger.). 'And.'

UNDA MARIS. See *Organ* 14 I.

UNDERDAMPER. See *Pianoforte* 16.

UNDULATING TREMOLO. See *Tremolo*.

UNESSENTIAL NOTES. See *Essential Notes*.

UNFINISHED SYMPHONY (Schubert). See *Nicknamed* 18.

UNGAR, UNGARISCH (Ger.). 'Hungarian.'

UNGEBUNDEN (Ger.). 'Free', unconstrained.

UNGEDULD (Ger.). 'Impatience.' So *Ungeduldig*, 'impatient'.

UNGEFÄHR (Ger.). 'About'—in the sense of approximately.

UNGESTÜM (Ger.). 'Impetuous.'

UNGEZWUNGEN (Ger.). 'Unforced', easygoing, natural.

UNGHERESE (It.). 'Hungarian.'

UNHEIMLICH (Ger.). 'Uncanny.'

UNI (Fr.). (1) 'United', (2) 'smooth'. The fem. is *Unie* and the plurals *Unis, Unies*.

UNIMENT (Fr.). 'Slurred together.'

UNION OF GRADUATES IN MUSIC. See *Degrees and Diplomas* 1.

UNION INTERNATIONALE DE RADIODIFFUSION. See *Broadcasting of Music* 3.

UNISONO, ARIA ALL'. See *Aria*.

UNITARY FORM. See *Form* 4.

UNITED PRESBYTERIAN CHURCH. See *Presbyterian Church Music* 3.

UNITED STATES OF AMERICA

1. The General Conditions when European Settlement began.
2. The Pilgrims and Puritans and Music.
3. Eighteenth-century Music-making.
4. The Nineteenth Century.
5. The Twentieth Century.
6. American Negro Music.
7. American Indian Music.
8. The Question of the American Composer.
9. List of Articles on Cognate Subjects.

(For illustrations see plates at pages 1024, 1040–1, 1056–7, 1060–61, 1068–9.)

1. The General Conditions when European Settlement began. The history of music in the United States is of unusual interest owing to the conditions under which the practice of the art has developed. We see a territory of three-and-a-half-million square miles completely occupied, in the course of little more than two centuries, by men of the most various

European races, each portion settled being, by the inevitable conditions of pioneer life, at first almost entirely deprived of all artistic opportunities, yet gradually bringing these into existence, so that by the end of the third century the practice of the art, in almost all its branches, is in almost every way according to the full contemporary European standard, and in some ways, perhaps, passing beyond it.

For the first two centuries those who emigrated to North America came principally from Britain. They settled the eastern seaboard, and up to the 1770s, when they claimed and won their independence, they had not got far behind this and its immediate hinterland. This, then, was the part of the country in which musical institutions first came into being—but much more slowly here than in parts further west, which were developed later, when the mechanical resources of civilization were more abundant, and in which the pioneer stage was, therefore, more quickly accomplished.

At the time when emigration to North America began European music had just risen to one of its high-water marks. Flemish, Italian, Spanish, and English composers had created a great corpus of *a cappella* choral music that today remains unsurpassed, and had made important and successful attempts at the bringing into existence of a specialized instrumental technique of performance and composition. We may say that the modern period of musical evolution had just opened and that England, from which the early emigrants came, was at this time well to the front.

In 1620 the great English composers of madrigals, *a cappella* church music, lute songs, and keyboard music were either still alive or only lately dead. Byrd, Weelkes, Gibbons, Wilbye, Dowland, and Bull (to pick merely a few great names) all died during the two decades following the sailing of the Pilgrim Fathers. English composers and performers were then popular on the continent of Europe. English music was published there. Important organ posts were occupied by Englishmen (as by Bull at Antwerp and Philips at Brussels), many royal courts included English violists, lutenists, and wind-instrument players amongst their musical retinues, and throughout the century London remained a recognized centre for the study of that favourite stringed instrument, the viola da gamba, so that students flocked to it from France, Germany, and other countries. Proficiency in music was common amongst cultured English people at this period, and the art formed one of the pleasures of the English home (see *England* 3).

These things being so, it may be asked why we have so little evidence of musical activities amongst the earlier of the English emigrants to America. To that the reply must be twofold: firstly, the records of the social life of the colonies are very fragmentary, and secondly, the conditions of life in a new colony are seldom favourable to the practice of the arts.

And apart from the fact that a pioneering people has not much opportunity for the production of art it should be remembered that neither has a rural people—and right down to the beginning of Washington's presidency, over a century-and-a-half after the beginning of colonization, 90 per cent. of the population of the American colonies was rural.

2. The Pilgrims and Puritans and Music. As the charge has repeatedly been made that in the Puritan colonies to the north music was frowned upon and even made the subject of oppressive legislation, it seems necessary to devote a little space to this special subject.

It may with the greatest confidence be affirmed that no colony whatever passed any law against music. Statements that this or that colony did so have been made and these are copied from book to book until the frequency with which one finds the charge, and the unanimity of the writers who make it, become imposing. All such statements can, however, be traced back to one source, and that a loyalist one, namely, *A General History of Connecticut by a Gentleman of the Province*, published in London in 1781 by the Reverend Samuel Peters. This author was a loyalist refugee in England: he was an episcopalian, with a strong bias against the republicanism and religious nonconformity of his native land and a complete disregard for truth on every occasion where falsehood would make more interesting reading. Peters's history (which includes the most amazing descriptions of natural phenomena, such as the Connecticut River pressed solid in a rocky defile and so rendered 'harder than marble') was in his own day and his own province known as 'The Lying History', and he has since been called 'The American Munchausen'. The book has long been discredited by every responsible historian of America, yet is constantly quoted, either consciously or unconsciously, in books on American music (p. 1024, pl. **168**. 4).

Few musical instruments are mentioned in early New England wills and inventories, but such documents will be found to ignore also many pieces of furniture and utensils that every household must necessarily have possessed. We find the much esteemed Puritan poetess, Ann Bradstreet (came to New England 1630; died 1672), freely making musical allusions, showing that she could depend on her readers both to understand these and to take them without offence. In 1699 the Puritan Judge Sewall records in his diary his call at a shop 'to enquire for my Wife's virginal', and by 1716 (less than a century after the landing of the Pilgrim Fathers) we see the Boston (Episcopalian) organist openly advertising that he tunes 'Virginalls and Spinnets', sells 'Flagolets, Flutes, Haut-boys, Bass Viols, Violins', etc., and teaches dancing—all of which suggests a considerable musical public in the capital of New England Puritanism. Proceedings in court may be found concerning music in taverns,

1. LOUIS GRUENBERG (1884–1964)

2. EDGAR VARÈSE (1883–1965)

3. JEROME D. KERN (1885–1945)

4. WALLINGFORD RIEGGER
(1885–1961)

5. J. DEEMS TAYLOR
(1885–1966)

6. ERNST TOCH (1887–1964)

7. FERDE GROFÉ (1892–1972)

8. BERNARD ROGERS (1893–1958)

9. WALTER PISTON (1894–1976)

PLATE 174   AMERICAN MUSICIANS, VI

1. NICOLAS SLONIMSKY (b. 1894)   **2.** WILLIAM GRANT STILL (b. 1895)   **3.** LEO SOWERBY (1895–1968)

4. LEO ORNSTEIN (b. 1895)

5. VIRGIL THOMSON (b. 1896)

6. ROGER SESSIONS (b. 1896)   **7.** HOWARD H. HANSON (b. 1896)   **8.** HENRY COWELL (1897–1965)

but music in places of alcoholic refreshment is restricted today in Britain (and probably in other European countries) without the legislators or magistracy or the religious leaders being suspected of any bias against music as such. There are passages in the writings of leading New England Puritan Divines (e.g. John Cotton and Increase Mather) that show a complete acceptance of domestic music.

No evidence exists of any widespread and deep objection in New England to dancing, as such, though a good many Puritans, both in England and New England, protested, apparently, against dancing of the sexes together, as then did some other English people who were not at all Puritans, and as did Calvinists in other countries. (For that matter Roman Catholic countries, also, often tried to control dancing.) Certain passages by seventeenth-century writers are often quoted and requoted which, it is alleged, proved that the New England Puritans showed an antagonism to dancing, but on closer observation it will always be found that these passages mention some special condition which formed the true grounds of the objection. Thus in 1685–6 a dancing master who attempted to set up a school in Boston was opposed by the ministers and had to retire, but he was a man of doubtful character and had moreover spoken scornfully of the ministers themselves and had chosen the 'Lecture Day' (the day of the mid-week sermon) as that of his operations.

The facts concerning this regrettable error in American history have been collected by the present writer in his *The Puritans and Music in England and New England, a Contribution to the Cultural History of Two Nations* (1933). For a brief reference to musical conditions in England during the seventeenth-century Puritan Commonwealth and Protectorate, see the article *England* (4) in the present volume, as also the special article *Puritans and Music*.

The one musical antipathy with which the English Puritans on both sides of the Atlantic can truthfully be charged is that to choir singing and organ playing *as a part of divine service*. This they inherited from Calvin and the Presbyterians of Geneva, from whence they derived their theology, but they had no objection to choral singing or organ playing as such (see article just mentioned) and organs were found in Puritan homes. (For early organs in American churches see *Organ* 9.)

The records of Virginia show rather more musical activity than those of the New England colonies, the landowning class here coming from a higher English social stratum than that of most of the New England settlers, and enjoying more leisure through the employment of indentured labour. There is, however, no distinction to be drawn between the laws of Virginia and those of the Puritan colonies; both are just as much or as little 'blue' (or severe), and neither condemns music.

In considering the extreme simplicity of most of the musical performances and productions during the whole colonial period it should be remembered that the colonists had left behind them two influential institutions upon the musical activities of which English music, up to the date of their leaving England and beyond, were largely built up—the cathedral and the court.

Although Anglicanism was strong in some of the colonies, its services necessarily reproduced the simple parish church type of the home country, with little music except the singing of a few metrical psalms, and the magnificent cathedral repertory of the Anglican service was unknown in America until in the nineteenth century it began very slowly to creep into a few churches wealthy and enterprising enough to make use of it. Up to the nineteenth century there can have been, in general, comparatively slight difference between the music of American Independency and that of American Anglicanism, except that organ accompaniment came into use more quickly in the latter.

As for the influence of court support, it remained important in England down to the death of Purcell, three-quarters of a century after the landing of the Pilgrim Fathers, and even during the Puritan Commonwealth and Protectorate the tradition was in some measure continued by Cromwell's maintenance of a small body of musicians and his official encouragement of music in several ways. The second half of the colonial period in America was the period when the great German school was establishing itself, and if the records of this school from Bach to Beethoven be examined it will be seen that every composer in it, at some time of his life and often for his whole life, was dependent upon the bounty of princes and earned his living by contributing to their enjoyments and their glory (see *Patronage*). Music in the American colonies was obliged by circumstances to antedate by about a couple of centuries that independence of social and financial props that came about in Europe during the nineteenth century, and this was, of course, a serious obstacle to development.

The early church song of the American colonies is discussed under *Hymns and Hymn Tunes* 11, 17 f.

3. Eighteenth-century Music-making. During the eighteenth century (conditions being now more settled, population greater, and city life better organized) musical activities grew, so that by the end of the century music in Boston, New York, Charleston, or New Orleans was much like that of the English cities other than London. The main facts concerning this period will be found chronicled under *Concert* 15 and *Opera* 21. New England saw little fresh immigration during the first half of the century, but into Pennsylvania, founded sixty years later, there flocked a number of Welsh, German, and Swedish settlers, who brought with them a love of music. Thus this colony (originally established by the

Quakers, the only English religious body, as it happened, whose principles were antagonistic to music) was at this period musically in advance of those colonies which had been settled by English people perhaps by nature equally musical with these Germans and others, but at a period when the conditions of colonial life had deprived the growing generations of musical influences.

A community of pietists on the Wissahickon River, near Philadelphia, was very active musically from 1694. Ephrata Cloister, fifty miles from Philadelphia, built by German Baptist Brethren, or 'Dunkers', in 1735 (some remains still existing), was another musical centre; beautifully written and illuminated books of chorales in many parts (up to seven), in a curious notation, copied by members of this latter body for their own use, may still be seen (p. 1024, pl. 168. 5). Johann Conrad Beissel (1690–1768), the founder of this sect, was one of the emigrants, and, on the grounds of his church music, has been claimed as the earliest American (though not American-born) composer; he and his companions published very many books of sacred songs (at least thirty between 1730 and 1800).

Bethlehem, a settlement of the Moravian sect (see Bohemia), was founded in 1742 by emigrants from a region that had by that time become one of the most musical in Europe. From almost the first service its church had an orchestra, and within four years of its foundation it had also an organ. A trombone choir, reminiscent of the civic musicians of Germany (see Wait or Wayte; also p. 993, pl 166. 1), was attached to the community, and on occasions of joy and sorrow played chorales: it continues to the present day. Benjamin Franklin records a visit to Bethlehem in 1756, and if his list of the instruments he heard is correct the clarinet was then in use there, a good deal earlier than it had become common in European orchestras (see Clarinet Family 2). A Collegium Musicum, a body of vocalists and instrumentalists on the lines of the organizations in central Europe bearing the same name (see Concert 15), was founded in 1748. When in the latter part of the century the chamber and orchestral works of Haydn and Mozart appeared they were imported and played at Bethlehem with little delay. At Bethlehem are to be seen a number of instrumental and choral compositions written and performed there during the later eighteenth century by the members of the Collegium (cf. Antes; Dencke, Peter).

The Bethlehem Bach Choir of today, notable for much admirable pioneer work, traces its direct descent from this eighteenth-century body.

Charleston, South Carolina, where many Huguenots settled at the Revocation of the Edict of Nantes in 1685, and where French refugees from Nova Scotia settled in 1755, was a centre of French taste, as was New Orleans, the capital of the French territory of Louisiana from 1721 and ceded to the United States in 1803. As mentioned under Opera 21, in the early part of the nineteenth century New Orleans had a French opera troupe that at times travelled up the coast to Charleston, Baltimore, Philadelphia, and New York.

A love of singing developed in New England out of the custom of the singing of metrical psalms in the churches. During the eighteenth century there appeared many books of psalm tunes, often with some theoretical material annexed. A list of the chief of these will be found under Hymns and Hymn Tunes 17 f. From 1770 onwards Billings, a tanner (see Hymns and Hymn Tunes 11), issued a number of books with tunes of a lively 'fuguing' type, and classes or societies for the singing of such music sprang up (p. 496, pl. 89. 2). The oldest existing choral society in the United States, the Stoughton Musical Society, is one of Billings's classes surviving in more elaborate form.

The high popularity of English ballad opera in America during a great part of the eighteenth century is mentioned under Opera 21. There also are given some particulars of the importations of Italian Opera from the last years of the century and of the earliest operas known to have been composed in America. The earliest genuinely American composer is considered to be Francis Hopkinson (q.v.), whose Ode to Music was composed in 1754 and whose song My days have been so wondrous free was composed in 1759; in this latter year James Lyon composed an Ode. (See reference to him under Hymns and Hymn Tunes 17 f (iv).)

For an ancient English method of sight-singing still current in a part of the United States, in combination with a very practical form of notation of specifically American character, see Lancashire Sol-fa (end of that article).

For an organist of some note see Pachelbel, Carl Theodore.

4. The Nineteenth Century. To a large extent the cult of the psalm tune and the simple type of solo song marked the first half of the nineteenth century, and the two typical names associated with these means of musical expression are those of Lowell Mason (1792–1872) and Stephen Foster (1826–64). Gottschalk (1829–69) was also an important figure as a popular composer for the piano. But more advanced music was also practised and it is rather surprising to note that Portland, Maine, had a Beethoven Society in 1819, i.e. eight years before Beethoven's death, and that the Handel and Haydn Society of Boston (see below) asked Beethoven for a composition.

An enormous increase in population took place during the first half of the nineteenth century, mainly as the result of fresh immigration. Central Europe was then in a very disturbed state, and many men of strength of character found themselves involved in charges of revolutionary activities, such as made it desirable to slip away. It will be remembered that in the great revolutionary year, 1848, Wagner became involved in political activities that caused his flight from Saxony; some lesser Wagners in different cities of Germany fled further than he and so enriched the musical life of a younger and freer country.

As an example of the fresh standard that was thus imported may be cited the Germania Orchestra (p. 757, pl. **126**. 1), whose members came to New York (largely from Berlin) in 1848. During the six years this organization lasted it gave 900 concerts all over the United States as they then existed, and by its extensive and well-rehearsed orchestral repertory and its co-operation with choral societies in various cities it accustomed the musical public to a higher type both of programme and of performance. From now on, the German element in the population and in the culture of the country became important, and before the end of the century it had become common for young American musicians to go to Germany to study.

The settling of the Middle West and then the Pacific slopes, with the consequent multiplication of cities, together with a simultaneous increase of population in the long-settled East, greatly enlarged the number of points at which musical activities could be conducted. Professional musicians became more in number and so did visiting virtuosi, the ever-extending railway mileage of the country greatly assisting.

Musical societies of high importance came into existence during the first half of the century, such as the Handel and Haydn Society of Boston (1815), the Musical Fund Society of Philadelphia (1820), and the New York Philharmonic Society (1842); the last two had permanent orchestras. Fine concert-halls were built in many cities.

Notable conductors who exercised a very high influence upon the development of musical taste towards the end of the century were Theodore Thomas (from 1864 onwards; p. 1041, pl. **170**. 1) and Leopold Damrosch (active from 1871; p. 1040, pl. **169**. 9): thenceforward many symphony orchestras of high quality came into existence. Professor Waldo Selden Pratt in his American Supplement to Grove's *Dictionary of Music*, edition of 1920, stated that by that date twelve or fifteen orchestras in the United States were holding daily rehearsals; this may be taken as the culmination of about a century's increasing activity in the orchestral domain. The development of the love and practice of orchestral music is, indeed, one of the most striking features in the American cultural history of the nineteenth century and the factor of the growing material wealth of the country must not be overlooked when the causes behind it are sought.

The first important chamber music organization in the United States was the Mendelssohn Quintette Club of Boston, which existed for nearly half a century (1849–95). Later organizations of high artistic merit were the Kneisel (1866–1917) and Flonzaley (1903–28) String Quartets; today there are innumerable groups, from world-famous ones such as the Juilliard

Quartet to ensembles based on university campuses and dividing their time between teaching and performing.

5. The Twentieth Century. The growth of musical activity, as the pioneering stage was everywhere gradually left behind and life became more orderly and settled, is strikingly shown in the census returns. In 1850 the population was 23 millions and the number of professional musicians of all kinds 3,550; in 1910 the population was 92 millions and the number of musicians 139,310, i.e. in those sixty years whilst the population was multiplied by four the number of people earning their living by music was multiplied by forty. As the methods of compiling the figures in 1850 were, however, somewhat different from those in 1910 we will take the census of 1880, when the methods were the same as in 1910. In that year the population was 50 millions and the number of musicians 30,500. Comparing this with the year 1910, we find that during the thirty years population less than doubled and the number of musicians more than quadrupled.

It is notable that in 1910 the number of male foreign-born 'Musicians', as distinct from 'Teachers of Music', was as great as the number of native-born 'Musicians' of native parentage, showing, apparently, to what a large extent the orchestras of the country were recruited from Europe (of 'Teachers of Music' the number of native-born far outbalanced the number of foreign-born: there was, however, an enormous number of native-born teachers of foreign parentage, i.e. whose parents were born abroad).

Massing together 'Musicians' and 'Teachers', 57,000 were in this year either immigrants or the children of immigrants—a phenomenon that has certainly never been paralleled in any country at any period and probably never can be repeated at any future period and in any country.

These figures emphasize a condition that is probably little realized by musicians in Europe.

The most musical ten cities (applying the number of musicians per thousand of population as the criterion) were by that date (1910) the following: Los Angeles, Denver, Boston, San Francisco, Seattle, Oakland, Kansas City, Portland (Oregon), Spokane, and Minneapolis. Of these, five are on the Pacific coast and only one east of the Mississippi. This demonstrates how, by the beginning of the twentieth century, the musical centre of gravity had moved westward.

Despite all the activity above indicated there remained fifty years later areas of the country very insufficiently supplied with musical amenities and musical workers, and while the best young musicians of every state have a tendency to migrate to New York and other great cities for their training, it is not easy to persuade those from certain states to return. 'The reason is that there are not enough musicians back there for them to feel comfortable, and there is no particular place to play. The musicians are all somewhere alse.'

Some features in American music that impress a European observer are the following:

(*a*) The lavish donations that have been made to it by wealthy men and women. Thus orchestras, schools of music, music libraries, etc., have been endowed in a way that is unknown elsewhere. Nationally supported is the admirable Music Division of the Library of Congress. This has an auditorium, built and endowed by Mrs. Elizabeth Sprague Coolidge, and here Chamber Music Festivals are held.

(*b*) The recognition of music as a part of general education, especially in high schools and universities—and the number of students in high schools and universities is extraordinary from a European point of view (it increased threefold between 1900 and 1930 and has gone on increasing). Specially commendable features are the provision of music departments in universities and colleges, and the 'Supervisor' system whereby groups of elementary and secondary schools secure the advantage of skilled oversight. The development of *a cappella* choirs and of full orchestras in high schools is a feature that greatly surprises the European visitor: it is made possible partly by the large enrolment of these schools, which often greatly exceeds that common in Europe. A national High School Orchestra organization brings together on certain occasions an orchestra with representatives from every state, and there are numerous summer camps for intensive orchestral practice.

Returning to the university provision for music—it appears to any European musician or university man or woman to be almost incredibly lavish. As just one example the School of Music of the University of Illinois was announcing in 1951 that it possessed 'over 100 practice rooms, 140 pianos, 8 organs, 300 other instruments, and audio-visual aids, recording and broadcasting facilities'.

(*c*) The financial aid freely given to talented young musicians out of the endowments mentioned in paragraph (*a*) above. With this may be mentioned the provision of 'Music Settlements' in some cities, whereby poor children of musical ability may secure training.

(*d*) The interest taken in musical activities by the women of the nation, the large attendance of women at the regular concert series of the great orchestras, etc., and the organization of women's music clubs (see *National Federation of Music Clubs*).

Incidentally, the growth of interest in orchestral music since the century opened is surprising. In 1900 there were in the whole country nine symphony orchestras, of which five were professional; in 1951 there were seven hundred, of which about thirty-six were professional (we have, of course, to allow for a considerable increase in population during the half-century).

(*e*) All kinds of ingenious devices for calling attention to the claims of music, as, for instance,

National Music Weeks, Musical Memory Contests, Initiatory Piano Lessons for adults by Radio.

(*f*) Institutions of kinds that many European nations do not possess, such as the American Academy in Rome; the American Summer School of Music at Fontainebleau near Paris; the Presser Foundation, financially buttressing music in many institutions throughout the country and maintaining a magnificent Home for retired Music Teachers; the Curtis Institute of Music, Philadelphia, and the Juilliard Foundation, New York, applying large funds to higher educational ends; the Guggenheim Fellowships for artists in all fields, including composition; the National Music Council (q.v); the system of Music Supervisors' regional conferences joining every two years in a great National Conference with anything from 5,000 members present. (For some of these activities see under *Patronage*.)

6. American Negro Music. It has always been considered that the Afro-American race possesses a great enthusiasm for and instinctive talent in music, and during the twentieth century the growing popularity amongst the white community of Negro religious songs ('Spirituals'—the term seems to date from the 1860s) and work songs greatly increased the public interest in its powers. A brief discussion of Negro song is therefore called for here.

The words of Negro spirituals are for the most part adaptations of passages from the Bible, though there are many instances where generations unable to read or write have lost the sense of particular words, retaining merely an approximation to the sounds, so that the meaning of certain lines can now no longer be even guessed. Many stanzas consist merely of several repetitions of a single line plus a line of refrain which occurs in every stanza and thus binds the song together. There is a frequent lack of continuity of thought from stanza to stanza. A great deal of song is half or wholly extemporized. Often one singer, serving as a kind of precentor, will give out a line or two in every stanza, the rest being added by the participating audience as a recurring refrain. (This is a typically African practice.) A great deal of extemporized song may be heard in Negro religious services. An apt and forceful phrase of the preacher may be seized upon by the congregation and sung, and thus developed into a 'spiritual'.

Many a 'spiritual' is of the nature of a cento. A stanza that has attained high popularity may find its way, often with considerable irrelevance, into several different songs. No definitive version of any song can be said to exist; indeed it might almost be said that no 'spiritual' is sung twice in exactly the same form. Responsive and confirmatory syllables such as 'um-u' are often inserted in the words of a work song, as a sort of refrain. Harmonized published versions are probably as a rule to be regretted.

There is a general flavour of sadness about

the words and music of Negro song. A European coming fresh to the subject would expect to find amongst a race that had suffered a quarter of a thousand years of slavery a good many rude poems of revenge allied to vigorous music. But in Negro song slavery is barely mentioned and overt hostility was until recently entirely absent, and instead of it is a spirit of gentle, patient melancholy and of longing and of a confidence in triumph in another world—both of these feelings largely expressed by the use of incidents and images from Scripture. Songs in which the words are joyous are sometimes sung in a spirit of sorrow —as though the words were little heeded and merely used as a vehicle for the dominant emotion. God, Christ, the Devil, and the heroes and heroines of the Old and New Testaments are dramatized in many songs, and become very real and present to the singers. At times marching occurs in Negro religious services. The benches are pushed to the wall and the company sing and march together—sometimes for hours. The term for this is 'Shout'. It is quite possible that in this religious exercise is a survival of something in pagan ceremonial brought from some part of the African continent, but it is now increasingly recognized by students of Negro song that in subject-matter and also in musical idiom, it owes a good deal to the early Baptist and Methodist revival meetings of the Negro's white masters.

A more vigorous spirit enters into the secular songs, which have during the twentieth century gained greatly in popularity. These songs may be classed as those of work and those of social enjoyment. The Negro uses music for work as other races do (cf. *Shanty*), only more readily and almost inevitably; it lightens his labour, times rhythmically recurring manual motions, and enables work done in company to be kept together in its motions.

The sources of the music of the American Negroes are many. A good many tunes are doubtless based upon the idiom of the Europeans with whom they have been so long and closely associated—chiefly of English descent but also of Spanish and French. Nevertheless, there is quite conclusive evidence that African characteristics survive. It is not possible to connect American Negro music with that of any one African people; the slaves were brought from many parts of Africa (there were even Moors) and spoke several totally different languages and many dialects of those languages, and their musics must, of course, have differed greatly. Little is known of the music of West Africa, the major source of supply.

The pentatonic scale (see *Scales* 10), upon which a great many American Negro melodies are founded, is common in parts of Africa. Other 'gapped' scales common in American Negro song are the ordinary major scale lacking either its fourth or its seventh (in other words, the pentatonic scale plus either the seventh or the fourth). These perhaps represent the original pentatonic scale extended under Euro-

pean influences. The ordinary major scale (which is very common) and the minor scale also represent the influence. Other less common scales, as the major with flattened seventh, and the minor with raised sixth, the minor without sixth and the minor with raised seventh are probably survivals of scales brought from various parts of Africa.

Rhythmically the most noticeable peculiarity of Negro music is its use of the *Scotch Snap* (q.v.)—a short note on the first of the measure followed immediately by a longer note. This, a species of syncopation, is the germ of 'Ragtime' (q.v.).

The manner in which Negro songs are performed is very interesting because of the suggestion that at once occurs to one of its probable resemblance to the extemporized counterpoint of the Welsh singers of the twelfth century as reported by Giraldus Cambrensis. His account runs:

'In their musical concerts they do not sing in unison like the inhabitants of other countries, but in many different parts; so that in a company of singers, which one very frequently meets with in Wales, you will hear as many different parts and voices as there are performers, who all at length unite, with organic melody, in one consonance.'

What Gerald heard (which could not, at that date, be 'harmony' or 'part-singing' in our modern sense) was probably something -like what W. E. Allen recorded seven centuries later (1867) in *Slave Songs of the United States*:

'There is no singing in *parts*, as we understand it, and yet no two appear to be singing the same thing; the leading singer starts the words of each verse, often improvising, and the others, who "base" him, as it is called, strike in with the refrain, or even join in the solo when the words are familiar. When the "base" begins the leader often stops, leaving the rest of the words to be guessed at, or it may be they are taken up by one of the other singers. And the "basers" themselves seem to follow their own whims, beginning when they please and leaving off when they please, striking an octave above or below (in case they have pitched the tune too high), or hitting some other note that chords, so as to produce the effects of a marvellous complication and variety and yet with the most perfect time and rarely with any discord. And what makes it all the harder to unravel a thread of melody out of this strange network is that like birds, they seem not infrequently to strike sounds that cannot be precisely represented by the gamut and abound in slides from one note to another and turns and cadences not in articulated notes.'

It will be realized that much this same method of free extemporization, applied to instrumental dance music, seems to have been the origin of Jazz (q.v.).

It appears a little curious that none of the distinctive African instruments has survived in America; presumably, however, they will in time disappear from Africa itself, driven out by the mechanically superior and more efficient European instruments. The banjo has never been used as much as is often believed; it belongs to the nineteenth-century 'Negro

T t

Minstrels' (q.v.) rather than the Negro; the guitar and violin, as already indicated, are common, and so are rhythmic instruments such as tambourines and bones (q.v.).

There is very little connexion between the songs the 'Negro Minstrels' popularized in America and Britain and the genuine Negro songs. The 'Negro Minstrels' songs were usually composed *ad hoc* by musicians like Stephen Foster (q.v.) and his imitators.

A general realization of the musical powers of the Negroes and of their possession of a fund of appealing tune came only when, in 1873, the 'Jubilee Singers' of Fisk University (a Negro institution) made their first concert tour. Crossing to Europe they sang in many countries, and when they appeared by invitation before Queen Victoria it was felt that Negro musicianship had 'arrived'. The Negro reputation for choral song was maintained and increased, and the accomplishment of an important stage in the progress was marked when in 1913 the students of the same university sang Elgar's *Dream of Gerontius*, with one of their own graduates in the title-role. Many Negro choral societies were started. The 1933 census showed the existence of nearly 8,000 Negro teachers of music (as against 4,000 in 1900). Amongst Negro composers under whose names entries will be found in this encyclopedia are Burleigh, Dett, Coleridge-Taylor (father African; mother English), W. G. Still, U. Kay, and Howard Swanson. The first symphony written by a Negro composer is said to have been that of Still (1929; performed 1931). Many Negro vocalists have become widely known to the American and European public (e.g. Roland Hayes, Paul Robeson, Marian Anderson). Bridgetower, for whom Beethoven wrote his Violin and Pianoforte Sonata in A, op. 47, i.e. the 'Kreutzer Sonata', and who performed it with him, was on his father's side an African Negro (p. 1096, pl. **181. 8**). Another Negro violinist was Brindes de Salis, born in the West Indies, court violinist to the Queen of Spain early in the nineteenth century. An earlier case was Chevalier Saint-George (1745–99), a half Negro, a pupil of Gossec; he had an opera, chamber music, etc. performed in Paris. Edmund Dédé, a New Orleans Negro, was trained at the Paris Conservatory and became conductor of the opera at Bordeaux. Joseph White, a Cuban Negro, studied at the same place and then taught there until his death in 1920.

Today the task of the Negro musician (by no means completed) is to be accepted as a 'musician' rather than as a 'Negro musician'. An 'all-Negro choir' is considered to have as little place in the scheme of things in the United States as an 'all-Jewish orchestra'.

For a brief reference to native African Negro harmony see *Harmony* 4.

7. American Indian Music. To discuss
in a brief general article the music of the North American Indian is difficult. The pre-sent size of the American Indian population is small (about 400,000 in the United States), but there is an inevitable diversity in the life and art of a race spread over so great a continent, speaking many languages, and differing considerably in customs.

Apparently there is some difference of function in music amongst this race as compared with other races. It is less used as mere entertainment and more associated with religious ceremonial, healing, and other of the higher activities. Indeed, there is (or has been) a strong magical suggestion about the Indian's musical practices, and these are closely bound up with his pantheistic creed. In general, songs are looked upon as inspirations, not as creations, and there is nothing corresponding to the popular song of the European races.

A great many of the songs are believed by the Indian medicine men to have come to them in dreams and to possess efficacy for the particular purposes for which they have been thus bestowed. It would appear that to the use of herbs and other material treatment the Indian doctors add the mental treatment that we today call 'suggestion', and that the singing of songs supposed to be endowed with specific powers is an essential part of the treatment (p. 1024, pl. **168. 7**). Songs are sung whilst games are played, and in the old days they were supposed to have their influence upon the success of the players. Ceremonial songs are sung only by men possessing the right to sing them, and the learning of the songs is a part of the initiation into the ceremonial office. At one time a horse was considered a reasonable fee to the teacher, for to convey a song was to confer its magical properties. Some singers know hundreds of songs.

Ceremonial songs are often sung by the community, sitting round a drum beaten by perhaps a dozen men. Some tribes have long cycles of song, describing the deeds of mythical personages; they are sung by a group of singers whilst another group dances. The singers surround the drum and the dancers circle about them.

An Indian dance (see *Dance* 4) is never a mere motion-pattern; it has a meaning, and presents certain dramatic pictures by means of conventional representative action. It is not a mere rhythmic movement of the limbs; the whole body becomes expressive.

Various types of drum (p. 1024, pl. **168. 6**) are the common accompaniment of Indian singing and it is notable that the drum rhythm (repeated over and over again) does not, as a rule, fit with the vocal rhythm. It is a debatable point whether such entire dissociation of the manual and the vocal on the part of one and the same performer argues a highly cultivated or a badly defective sense of rhythm.

Some observers have notated songs with drum accompaniment in a way that shows a correspondence of the measures, e.g. a song largely two-in-a-measure may be accompanied in three-in-a-measure, the time-length of the vocal and drum measures being, however, the same. One of the most experienced observers, however, Frances Densmore, has said, 'It is true that a song in duple time is frequently accompanied by a triple drumbeat, but, in my observation, there are no points of coincidence between the two, which suggests that a ratio between them is not present in the mind of the Indian'. It may well be that this is a matter in which the extent and variety of the field to be studied has led to different conclusions on the part of different observers.

The vocal rhythm is often very free, involving, when notated, the use of many time-signatures in one song; these time changes are rot temporary aberrations on the part of the performer but will be found to repeat themselves whenever the song is sung.

The words in Indian song are relatively unimportant; they are often supplemented by meaningless syllables and in some songs only the latter are used. The much-respected observer, Alice C. Fletcher, has said, 'To the Indian, song holds a place similar to that filled for us by wordless instrumental music'.

The actual instrumental art of the Indian is not very developed. To the drums already mentioned are added rattles, various whistles (some very ingeniously designed), and some reed instruments. The account given in 1606 by Captain John Smith, the pioneer of Virginia, shows accurate observation:

'For their musicke they use a thick Cane, on which they pipe as on a Recorder. For their warres they have a great depe platter of wood. They cover the mouth thereof with a skin, at each corner they tie a walnut, which meeting on the backside neere the bottome, with a small rope they twitch them together till it be so tought and stiffe, that they may beat upon it as upon a drumme. But their chief instruments are Rattles made of small gourds or Pumeons shels. Of these they have Base, Tenor, Countertenor, Meane, and Treble. These mingled with their voyces, sometimes twenty or thirtie together, make such a noise as would rather affright, than delight any man.'

The Ute Indians have a Bear Dance which they accompany with the growling sound of sheets of metal placed over a trench and made to vibrate by rasping a notched stick kept in contact with the metal. A game played by the Indians of British Columbia is accompanied by pounding on a plank raised a little from the ground.

Amongst the more marked mannerisms of Indian singers are the attacking of a note on its sharp side and then settling to the proper pitch, the use of an excessive tremolo, and the detachment of notes one from another by a curious contraction of the glottis.

The scale systems of the Indians are varied but there is a very general use of a pentatonic scale (see *Scales* 10), so common amongst primitive people. Care has to be exercised in reading the accounts of observers and studying the notated examples they offer; it must be remembered that inaccuracy and out-of-tuneness are as prevalent amongst Indian vocalists as amongst those of European races, and when

an example of extraordinary tonal complexity is found we might reasonably remind ourselves of the curious notational record and erroneous notions as to European music that a competent scientific visiting observer from another planet might on occasion take back with him from the opera-houses and concert-rooms of Europe and America.

A large majority of Indian songs descend throughout their whole course, i.e. beginning high, their successive phrases are at lower and lower pitches until the end.

The Indians have little idea of harmony; their music is practically all unisonous.

A very grave wrong was done to the Indian, and indeed to the American people, by the United States government's determination to crush out native characteristics. One of the best observers, the late Natalie Curtis, deeply deplored 'the past policy of our Government, which sternly set its face against all things Indian, believing that by stamping out everything pertaining to the native life the red man would be "civilised"'. In the preface to her *The Indian's Book* (2nd edition, 1922) it is recorded: 'Incredible as it now seems, when Miss Curtis first began her self-imposed task of recording Indian music, native songs were absolutely forbidden in the government schools. On one reservation she was warned by a friendly scientist that if she wished to record the Indian songs she must do so secretly, for if the government official should hear of it she would be expelled from the reservation; and on another the Indians were afraid to sing to her lest it should bring them into disfavour with the authorities.' It was the direct intervention of President Theodore Roosevelt that enabled her to overcome this obstacle, and there is, of course, now no trace remaining of official opposition.

It is, by the way, notable that scientifically-minded American women have played a large part in salving the musical treasury of the Indians. The three great authorities quoted in this article are all, it will have been noted, women. The labours of these researchers must have seemed a little surprising to the Indians, as Indian women take relatively little part in music, their magical powers being supposedly inferior.

Amongst white American composers who have made use of American-Indian melodic material in their compositions are MacDowell, Farwell, Gilbert, Arthur Nevin, Cadman, Lieurance, and Skilton. But there are a good many others.

8. The Question of the American Composer. The question is often raised as to the possibility of a genuinely distinctive 'American School' in composition, with definite and recognizable characteristics such as have, at various periods, marked the German, Italian, French, and English schools. This is a question easier to ask than to answer, for history provides no parallel for a country of so great a size with so large a population in which so many racial elements are represented. Because the art music of European nations has largely grown up out of the folk music of their own soils it was at one time assumed (e.g. by Dvořák when in America 1892–5) that the American composer must look round for a native folk music whose idiom he could adopt, and the American-Indian and Negro idioms were pointed out to him. Such an idiom might mean something to an American-Indian composer or a Negro one (at any rate if steeped in it from birth), but obviously it is, to a composer of European race, highly exotic. Similarly the English folk songs still orally preserved in the mountainous districts of the East (see *Folk Song* 3) and the other folk songs of later importation from Europe can be considered native only to small bodies of composers who by race and early environment feel them to be their own.

The increasing mixture of races since the opening of the twentieth century greatly complicates the question; after that date Italian, Polish, and Russian immigration much increased and outweighed the Teutonic and British. Speculation on the artistic outcome seems to be valueless. If any definitely American school is at last emerging its specific qualities or common denominator will probably represent what is distinctive in American ways of life and thought (and there is abundance of that) rather than a new raciality. And it will not come by deliberately adopting this idiom or that, for a national composer is such only in so far as he is personal in his expression and so far as his personality happens *naturally* to affirm a nationality.

The United States during the first World War and the following years gave to the whole world a new type of dance music, Jazz (q.v.), and there have been American writers who have maintained that in that were to be found elements of a new American musical aesthetic. If so, the rationale of the process would go no deeper than the simple notion that, a new popular idiom happening to have been brought into existence on American soil, it is marked out as quarry material for the building of the American composer, and would rest on the principle that, the American spirit having found apt if simple expression in a new idiom, the same spirit would naturally and inevitably represent itself in the same idiom in more advanced composition. A good deal of serious American music employing the jazz idiom has, as a matter of fact, been written, but whether it has sprung from the more superficial principle or from the deeper and more fundamental one above suggested remains to be tested by time.

The first group of American composers to make any deep impression upon the public mind was the New England group (compare the somewhat earlier New England literary group—Emerson, Hawthorne, Longfellow, Thoreau, Lowell, and Whittier). Apart from Paine (born 1839), the famous first Professor of Music at Harvard and the mentor of many young musicians, there were born between the 1850s and the early 1870s Foote, Chadwick, Whiting, Parker, Strong, Mrs. Beach, Gilbert, Converse, and Hadley. Contemporary with the middle members of this group was MacDowell, born in New York, who was the first American composer to attract any widespread attention in Europe. It is hard to see anything specifically American in the work of these composers: MacDowell, largely trained in Germany, was, despite some use of American suggestion in his titles, essentially a gifted member of the later German romantic school.

Charles Ives (1874–1954), on the other hand, may well be regarded as a forerunner, though a completely solitary one, of an 'American' tradition—his work was virtually complete by the early 1920s. The nineteen-twenties saw a host of active and individual composers, many of them still trained or at least 'finished' in Europe (France's Nadia Boulanger being a particular magnet). For the first time some names genuinely attained more than a merely national and local reputation. Some of these, such as Carl Ruggles (1876–1971), Wallingford Riegger (1885–1961), Henry Cowell (1897–1965), Edgard Varèse (1885–1965), and others maintained an avant-garde position to the end of their lives, while others such as Aaron Copland (born 1900), Virgil Thomson (born 1896), and Roy Harris (born 1896), explored the notion of 'American' works in a style compounded of melodic elements from folk-song, square dance, hymn tunes, and the like; much of this was written for the theatre, or as scores for the ballet or cinema.

At the same time, there continued to emerge able composers such as Howard Hanson (born 1896), Giannini (1903–66), Paul Creston (born 1906), Samuel Barber, and William Schuman, whose styles show relatively little of the influence of twentieth-century experiments.

In the later 1930s there was an influx of a number of European composers, particularly Hindemith and Schönberg, who by their teaching ensured that the central European experiments would continue in America while being interrupted elsewhere. Mainly as a result of this, the centre of gravity for the avant-garde shifted from Europe to the U.S.A.

The list of United States composers active in the 1960s seems endless, and though it may contain no composer of unassailably first-rate stature, certainly it contains some of the best-known experimenters (see *History* 9). But in addition there is an ever-growing army of highly trained writers of music of all grades of complexity, as will be seen from the chronological conspectus at the end of this article.

It is curious to learn that there is no record of any programme entirely devoted to the works of American composers earlier than 1883, when Mr. Calixa Lavallée (Canadian born and composer of the national song, *O Canada*, q.v.;

1. GEORGE GERSHWIN (1898–1937)

2. ROY ELLSWORTH HARRIS (b. 1898)

3. RANDALL THOMPSON (b. 1899)

4. 'DUKE' ELLINGTON (1899–1974)

6. GEORGE ANTHEIL (1900–59)

5. AARON COPLAND (b. 1900)

7. MARC BLITZSTEIN (1905–1964)

8. PAUL CRESTON (b. 1906)

9. SAMUEL BARBER (b. 1910)

PLATE 176   AMERICAN MUSICIANS, VIII

1. WILLIAM SCHUMAN (b. 1910)

2. GIAN-CARLO MENOTTI (b. 1911)

3. MORTON GOULD (b. 1913)

4. NORMAN DELLO JOIO (b. 1913)

5. DAVID LEO DIAMOND (b. 1915)

6. LEONARD BERNSTEIN (b. 1918)

7. WILLIAM BERGSMA (b. 1921)

8. LUKAS FOSS (b. 1922)

9. PETER MENNIN (b. 1923)

Paris-trained and not then long resident in the United States) organized one for the Music Teachers' National Association, meeting that year in Cleveland. This was a chamber concert, the first such orchestral concert being one given by Van der Stucken at New York, in the following year, and the second one given by the Music Teachers' National Association at that same city in that same year.

9. List of Articles on Cognate Subjects. In order to amplify the information given above the following articles may be consulted:

American Musical Terminology; *Folk Song*; *Mother Goose* 3; *Ballad* 3; *Nationalism*.

Church Music; *Hymns and Hymn Tunes*, 8, 9, 11, 12, 17 f.

Oratorio (section 6, on 'Oratorio in the United States', and section 7, giving a list of oratorios).

Opera 21; *Beggar's Opera*; *Ballad Opera*; *Concert* 14; *Cecilia, St.*; *Annotated Programmes* 6; *Festivals* 2; *Community Singing* 5; *Competitions* 4.

Organ; *Pianoforte* 9, etc. (various references to American improvements, etc.); *Gramophone* 8; *Broadcasting of Music*.

Printing 3; *Publishing*; *Copyright*.

Education (section 3, on the United States); *Schools of Music*; *Prix de Rome*; *Appreciation of Music*; *Jeunesses musicales*.

Patronage; *Criticism* 5.

Star-spangled Banner; *Yankee Doodle*; *God save the Queen* (= 'America') 14; *Hail, Columbia!*; *Dixie*; *Battle Cry of Freedom*; *John Brown's Body*; *Marching through Georgia*.

Jazz; *Barn Dance*; *Black Bottom*; *Blues*; *Charleston*; *One-Step*; *Shimmy*; *Breakdown*.

Jewish Music 6.

CHRONOLOGICAL CONSPECTUS OF AMERICAN COMPOSERS TREATED IN THIS BOOK, arranged according to date of birth, and including those who by residence rank as American though born in Europe.

1700–49 Antes, Billings, Dencke, Benjamin Franklin, Hopkinson, C. T. Pachelbel, Selby.

1750–99 Lowell Mason.

1800–49 Dudley Buck, Emmett, Foster, Fry, Gottschalk, E. Jerome Hopkins, Paine, Pratt.

1850–9 Chadwick, De Koven, Foote, Herbert, Kelley, Sousa, Strong, Van der Stucken.

1860–9 Mrs. H. H. A. Beach, H. T. Burleigh, W. Damrosch, Gilbert, Homer, Huss, Loeffler, MacDowell, E. Nevin, Noble, Parker, Skilton, A. B. Whiting.

1870–9 Borowski, Carpenter, Coerne, Converse, Mabel W. Daniels, Eichheim, Farwell, R. Goldmark, Hadley, Handy, Hill, Ives, LaForge, Lieurance, D. G. Mason, A. Nevin, Ruggles, Schelling, D. S. Smith, Speaks.

1880–9 Achron, Becker, Berlin, Bingham, Bloch, Branscombe, C. Burleigh, Cadman, Delamarter, Dett, Grainger, Griffes, Gruenberg, Josten, Powell, Riegger, Salzedo, Saminsky, Schindler, Shepherd, Taylor, Varèse.

1890–9 Bacon, R. R. Bennett, Cowell, Dawson, Donovan, Dubensky, Duke, Ellington, Elwell, Gershwin, Grofé, Guion, Hanson, Roy Harris, Jacobi, Philip James, H. Johnson, Kramer, McDonald, D. Moore, Morris, Ornstein, Piston, Porter, B. Rogers, Rudhyar, Schilkret, Schillinger, Sessions, Slonimsky, Sowerby, Still, Stoessel, Stringham, R. Thompson, V. Thomson, Wagenaar, Weiss.

1900–9 Armstrong, Antheil, Berezowsky, Blitzstein, Carter, Chasins, Copland, Creston, Dukelsky, Fiorillo, Fuleihan, Giannini, Luening, Nabokof, Phillips, Rozsa, Siegmeister, A. Steinert, Strang, Swanson, Van Vactor.

1910–19 Babbitt, Barber, Berger, Bernstein, Bowles, Cage, Dello Joio, Diamond, Fine, Gould, Haieff, Harrison, Herrmann, Hovhaness, Kay, Kirchner, McBride, Menotti, Meyerowitz, Palmer, Persichetti, Read, Rochberg, Schuman, R. Ward.

1920–9 Bergsma, Floyd, Lukas Foss, Imbrie, Mennin, Schuller, Shapero.

See also *Dictionaries* 4 b.

UNITI (It.). 'United.' E.g. after *Divisi* (q.v.), to revoke this direction.

UNIT ORGAN. See *Organ* 6.

UNIVERSAL EDITION (Vienna). See *Publishing* 8.

UNIVERSITIES. See *Education and Music*; *Degrees and Diplomas*; *Musicology*; *Wales* 9; *Notation* 1; *Act Music*.

UNMERKLICH (Ger.). 'Imperceptible.'

UNO, UNA, UN' (It.). 'A' or 'an', 'one'.

UN PEU (Fr.). 'A little' (often in the sense of 'rather').

UN POCO (It.). 'A little' (often in the sense of 'rather'). Sometimes shortened to *Un po'*.

UNPREPARED SUSPENSION. See *Harmony* 24 k.

UNRUHE (Ger.). 'Disquiet', 'lack of peace'.

UNRUHIG. 'Unpeaceful', restless.

UNSCHULDIG (Ger.). 'Innocent.'

UNTEN (Ger.). 'Under', 'below'.

UNTER (Ger.). 'Under', 'lower', 'beneath'; also 'amidst'.

UNTERSATZ. See *Organ* 14 I.

UNTERWERK. Choir organ.

UP AND WAUR AT EM! See *There's nae luck*.

UPPER PARTIALS. See *Partials*; *Acoustics* 6, 8.

UPRIGHT GRAND. See *Pianoforte* 16.

UPTAKER OF THE PSALMS. See *Precentor*.

URANIA. See *Hymns and Hymn Tunes* 17 f iv.

URANIAN CONCERTS. See *Annotated Programmes* 3.

URIBE-HOLGUÍN, GUILLERMO. Born at Bogotá, Colombia, in 1880. He studied composition in Paris under d'Indy and violin in Brussels under César Thomson. His compositions (orchestral, chamber, and piano, etc.), whilst showing the influence of Colombian native idiom, show also that of French impressionism.

URSPRÜNGLICH (Ger.). 'Original', 'originally'.

URTEXT (Ger.). Original text; usually taken to be an edition embodying the author's own final thoughts.

USE OF COLMONELL. Not an ancient 'use' like the 'Use of Sarum', etc., but merely an order of Presbyterian worship devised by Robert F. McEwen, laird and organist in the parish of Colmonell, Ayrshire, Scotland. By the enticements of certain provisions of his will he posthumously endeavoured, in the early twentieth century, to introduce it into other parishes also. McEwen was a semi-millionaire, well known as the organizer of local 'celebrity concerts', in which he would participate.

USE OF SARUM, HEREFORD, etc. The liturgy, ritual, and manner of performing the plainsong in the Diocese of Sarum (the cathedral and city of Old Sarum are now destroyed and replaced by New Sarum or Salisbury, on another site), Hereford, York, Bangor, etc. Some of these uses had acceptance out of the diocese in question. The English Prayer Book (see *Common Prayer*) had as one of its objects the introduction of uniformity—'And whereas heretofore there hath been great diversity in saying and singing in Churches within this Realm; some following Salisbury Use, some Hereford Use, and some the Use of Bangor, some of York, some of Lincoln; now from henceforth the whole Realm shall have but one use' (Preface to Book of Common Prayer).

We speak also of the Roman Use (or Rite), etc. See *Liturgy*. Cf. *Parisian Tones*.

U.S.F. = *Und so fort*, 'and so forth'. Same as *Simile* (q.v.).

U.S.W. = *Und so weiter*, 'and so further'. (Same meaning as *U.S.F.*)

UT. The keynote of the diatonic scale, according to the system of vocal syllables derived from Guido d'Arezzo (q.v.), replaced since the seventeenth century by the more singable syllable 'Do' in Italian use, and in the nineteenth by 'Doh' in the usage of the Tonic Sol-fa (q.v.), but retained in French use. The French and Italian names are, however, attached, not to the first note of the scale but to the fixed pitch of C in whatever scale this may occur. (The French use 'Ut' as the name of the note and the key, but now adopt the Italian 'Do' in solmisation.)

See also *Hexachord*; *Gamut*; Table 5.

UT QUEANT LAXIS. See *Hymns and Hymn Tunes* 2; *Hexachord*.

UTRAQUIST BODY. See *Bohemia*.

UVULA. See *Voice* 21 (end).

U.W. = *Unterwerk*, i.e. choir organ.

V

VA (It.). 'Go on', [it] 'goes on', i.e. 'continue', 'it continues' (e.g. *Va diminuendo*, 'it goes on getting softer').

VACILLANT (Fr.); **VACILLANDO** (It.). 'Wavering'—referring to the stringed instrument vibrato.

VACTOR. See *Van Vactor*.

VACZEK, KARL. See *Rákóczy March*.

VADÉ. See *Bouffons*.

VAGHEZZA (It.). (1) Longing; (2) grace, charm.

VAGO (It.). 'Vague.'

VALENTINE, ROBERT. See below.

VALENTINI. Of the numerous musicians, more or less obscure, who have borne this name the following may be mentioned: (1) GIO-VANNI (died in Vienna in 1649), court organist in Vienna and composer of church music; (2) GIUSEPPE (*c.* 1680–1740), accomplished violinist and composer of solo and concerted string music, some of which has been republished; (3) PIER FRANCESCO (died in Rome in 1654), theorist, and composer of vocal music and of canons of long-celebrated ingenuity and complexity; and (4) ROBERTO, a shadowy figure who flourished in Rome in the first part of the eighteenth century, and possibly the same as the **Robert Valentine** known in London at about the same time; sonatas for violin and for flute have appeared under both these names.

VALEUR (Fr.). 'Value.' So such expressions as Debussy's *La m.g. un peu en valeur sur la m.d.*, 'The left hand to have a little more value (importance, weight) than the right hand'. The same word also means 'valour'.

VALKYRIE, THE. See *Ring of the Nibelung*.

VALLÉE, RUDY. See *Crooning*.

VALORE (It.). Same two meanings as Fr. *Valeur*; see above.

VALSE. See *Waltz*. **VALSE TRISTE** (Schubert). See *Nicknamed Compositions*. (Sibelius later borrowed this title.)

VALVE INSTRUMENTS. See *Brass*; *Horn Family*; *Trumpet Family*; *Tuba Group*; *Cornet*. Also *Trombone Family* 1; *Acoustics* 8.

VALVERDE. See *Spain* 6; *Zarzuela*.

VAMP HORN (p. 545, pl. **100.** 1). This curious instrument (in varying shapes) seems to have been used in English churches. Examples survive in some eight villages. Apparently the use was merely as a megaphone: 'An old Sussex Parish Clerk, who formerly used the Ashurst Vamp Horn, stated that he merely sang or shouted down the instrument to make more sound for the singing.' Although to help the singing may have been one purpose of the instrument, its main use originally may have been rather in the tower than in the church itself. As will be seen by the pictures alluded to above, the vamp horn closely resembles an ancient instrument long used in some church towers in Germany—where its purpose was to give warning of fires, etc.

VAMPING. To vamp is to repair roughly, patch a shoe, etc., and especially, to put new uppers to old boots. Hence to 'vamp up a story' is to invent an explanation of some occurrence, probably in self-excuse, and to vamp a piano accompaniment is to extemporize a series of simple chords such as will support the tune of the singer. There are 'Vamping Tutors' sold; they deal chiefly (or entirely) with the three chief chords of the key.

See *Tablature*; *Scales* 5.

VAN DER STUCKEN. See under *Stucken*.

VAN DIEREN. See *Dieren*.

VAN HAGEN, PETER. See *Profession* 9; *Nail Fiddle*.

VANHALL (or **Wanhall**), JOHANN BAPTIST. Born in Bohemia in 1739 and died in Vienna in 1813, aged seventy-four. He had a high reputation in Vienna and elsewhere as a composer of symphonies (over 100), chamber music (over 100 string quartets), piano sonatas, Masses (over 20), etc. The successive advents of Haydn, Mozart, and Beethoven, however, threw him progressively into the shade.

See *Chamber Music* 6, Period III; *Storace*.

VAN MALDER or **VAN MALDERE.** See *Malder*.

VAN VACTOR, DAVID. Born at Plymouth, Indiana, in 1906. He began professional life as a flute player (Chicago Symphony Orchestra). His compositions include a symphony that in 1939 won the prize offered by the New York Philharmonic, and a variety of chamber music and orchestral and choral works.

VAPOREUX, VAPOREUSE (Fr., masc., fem.). 'Vaporous.'

VARÈSE, EDGAR (later EDGARD; p. 1060, pl. **173.** 2). Born in Paris in 1883 and died in New York in 1965, aged eighty-one. His father was French and his mother Italian. He studied mathematics and science in Turin, and at nineteen returned to Paris to work under Roussel and d'Indy. After a period in Berlin (1907–14) and war service he made his home in New York, becoming naturalized in 1926. He later founded the International Composers' Guild (1921–7), for the performance of the music of the day, and then served as Chairman of the Pan-American Association of Composers.

In his own compositions he exploited novel harmonic, rhythmic, and coloristic devices, in pursuit of his ideal of a music that should be *just sound* (freed from all the trammels of association and tradition). His works bear such titles as *Hyperprism*, *Intégrales*, *Ionization* (for percussion and two sirens), *Equatorial* and *Density 21·5* (this last for unaccompanied flute, being composed for Georges Barrère for the inauguration of his platinum flute—platinum being of the density stated). Performances of some of his works in Paris, Berlin, and Philadelphia have roused sections of the audience to indignant frenzy. Later he was rewarded by a measure of popular success and the evidence of solid influence on some contemporary composers, American and French.

Cf. *Jolivet*; *Octandre*.

VARIANTE (Fr., It.). 'Variant.'

VARIATIO. See *Suite* 2.

VARIATIONS. See *Form* 11; *Symphony* 6; *Composition* 14.

VARIATO, VARIATA (It., masc., fem.). 'Varied.'

VARIAZIONE, VARIAZIONI (It). 'Variation', 'variations'.

VARIÉ (Fr.). 'Varied.'

VARNISH. See *Violin Family* 4.

VARSOVIENNE. Originally a dance of Warsaw, a sort of mazurka (q.v.), which was popular in the ball-rooms about 1850–70.

VATERLÄNDISCH (Ger.). Having to do with the Fatherland, i.e. 'patriotic'.

VATER UNSER. See *Chorale*.

VAUCANSON. See *Mechanical Reproduction of Music* 9.

VAUDEVILLE. Originally a vaudeville was a satirical Paris street song. (Bourgeois, on the title-page of his psalter of 1547, stated that some of his tunes were 'familiers ou vaude-villes'.) Towards the end of the reign of Louis XIV the tunes of such songs, with topical words set to them, were intercalated into the comedies played by the two companies of the Paris fairs (see *Opéra Comique*) and these were called 'Comedies with Vaudevilles' and soon merely 'Vaudevilles'. Nowadays 'vaude-ville' (a word used, perhaps, more in the United States than in Great Britain) means a 'variety show', a theatre entertainment made up of anything whatever that can be considered entertaining, and is sometimes used in a derogatory

way, as when cheaply popular compositions are called 'vaudeville music'.

In musical literature the term may have any one of four meanings:

(1) A street song, or any simple song, harmonized simply (this is the common sixteenth- and seventeenth-century use).

(2) A type of ballad opera (q.v.), as one may perhaps describe it.

(3) A present-day music hall entertainment.

(4) A type of finale to a play or opera; e.g. Beaumarchais's play *The Marriage of Figaro* bursts into music at the end in what the author has himself called a vaudeville, a long song in which the characters express their sentiments by taking a verse in turn, and Mozart's *The Abduction from the Seraglio* ends similarly, the term being used in the score.

The accepted derivation of the word itself looks a bit far-fetched, but may have something in it: A fifteenth-century handicraftsman (Olivier Basselin) was celebrated for writing satirical songs; he lived in the valley, or 'Vau', de Vire, in Normandy, whence his songs became known as 'Vaux de Vire'; when such songs came to be popular in Paris the name changed to 'Vaux de ville'. Another derivation, quite as plausible, is from 'Voix de Ville' ('Voices of the town'). Volumes exist of mid-sixteenth-century 'Vaux de villes' and 'Voix de villes', both, so there is something to be said for each of the derivations.

VAUGHAN WILLIAMS, RALPH (p. 336, pl. **53.** 6). Born at Down Ampney, Gloucestershire, in 1872 and died in London in 1958, aged eighty-five. He was educated at Charterhouse and Cambridge, with the Royal College of Music interpolated for two years and then again added at the end of the period of formal education. He also studied with Max Bruch and had some advice from Ravel.

In the early nineties he began to be very active in the collection and study of English folk song, and this it was, more than anything apparently, that enabled him to shake off the influence of idioms acquired during his period of study, and, without relinquishing anything of his accumulated technical adroitness, courageously to adopt manners of expression that seemed definitely to assort with his temperament. Another such influence was that of the English Tudor music, sacred and secular: in his unaccompanied Mass 'in G minor' (1923) he has even gone behind this, freely adopting medieval tonalities and methods of counterpoint, and balking at no means of expressive treatment, even though it may involve the total ignoring of the code of prohibitions (as, for instance, of 'consecutives'; see *Harmony* 22) which was evolved as European music gradually standardized its system.

His orchestral music includes symphonies as follows : 1, *Sea Symphony* (1910; a choral-orchestral work, based on poems by Walt Whitman); 2, *London Symphony* (1914; revised version 1920); 3, *Pastoral Symphony*

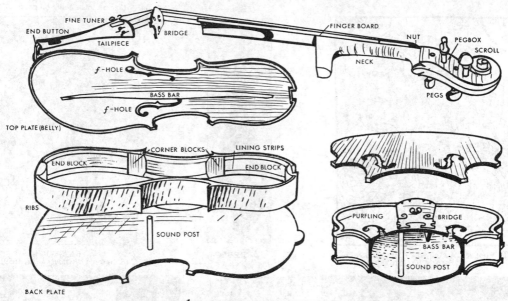

1. ANATOMY OF THE VIOLIN

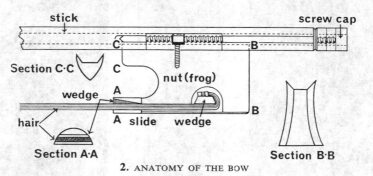

2. ANATOMY OF THE BOW

3. PUPPO of Edinburgh (d. 1827)
Note the old convex bow

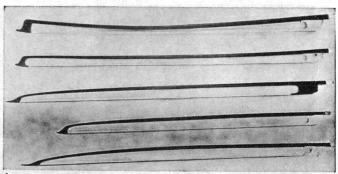

4. BOWS—from bottom to top, those of Treble Viol (17th cent.), do. (shortened), Bass Viol (17th cent.), Alto or Tenor Viol (18th cent.), and Violoncello (18th cent.)

For the Plates 'Some Famous Violinists' see pages 1096–7

1. VIOLA DA GAMBA AND VIOLA DA
BRACCIO (1516)

2. REBEC

3. BASS VIOL
(Simpson's *Division Violist*, 1659)

4. MARIN MARAIS WITH HIS BASS VIOL
See p. 598

5. BARYTON

6. ABEL WITH HIS BASS VIOL
(By his friend Gainsborough.) See p. 2

7. A CONSORT OF VIOLS—the Dolmetsch Family (*c.* 1929). See pp. 299–300

| RUDOLPH | CECILE | CARL | MRS. DOLMETSCH | ARNOLD | NATHALIE |
| Bass | Treble | Tenor | Bass | Treble | Tenor |

(1922); 4, in F minor (1935); 5, in D (1943); 6, in E minor (1948); 7, *Sinfonia Antartica* (1953); 8, in D minor (1956); 9, in E minor (1958). These are all intensely personal expressions, each original and strongly differentiated from its fellows, and they constitute a series of increasing power.

The *London* is vivid yet reflective; the *Pastoral* remote and mystical; the fourth, in F minor, when first heard, startled by its uncompromising directness; the fifth, in a time of peril (1943), seemed to express faith and confidence; the sixth, in E minor, impressed many hearers as one of the greatest works not only in the composer's output but in the twentieth-century international repertory.

The seventh symphony, the *Sinfonia Antartica* (1953), is rather of the nature of a programmatic suite, using material from his music to the film *Scott of the Antarctic* (see below). In it the composer makes striking use of his mastery of orchestral effects.

Other orchestral works include the popular early *Three Norfolk Rhapsodies* (1906–7), the *Fantasia on a Theme of Tallis* (for strings; 1909), the Piano Concerto (1934), the Suite for viola and orchestra (1934), and the Oboe Concerto (1944).

He wrote a number of choral–orchestral works of big dimensions which have considerable popularity and are perhaps amongst his most notable achievements, e.g. *Toward the Unknown Region* (Leeds Festival, 1907), *Flos Campi* (1925), *Sancta Civitas* (1926), *Benedicite* (1930), *Magnificat* (1932), *Five Tudor Portraits* (1936), *Dona Nobis Pacem* (1936).

His songs, some of which (e.g. the very early *Linden Lea*) quickly became popular favourites, and his chamber music show remarkable delicacy; the latter includes two String Quartets, a Piano Quintet, and a *Fantasy Quintet* for strings.

He adventured into the realm of stage music with the incidental music to *The Wasps* (1909), the operas (generally robust and thoroughly 'English') *The Shepherds of the Delectable Mountains* (1922), *Hugh the Drover* (1924), *Sir John in Love* (1929), *The Poisoned Kiss* (1936), *Riders to the Sea* (1937), and *The Pilgrim's Progress* (1951; incorporating the short work of 1922 above mentioned), as also with the ballet, *Old King Cole* (1923), and the 'masque for dancing', *Job* (1930). There is also a fair quantity of film music (*Scott of the Antarctic*, etc.). He published a thoughtful book on *National Music* (1935).

Throughout his life he showed much practical sympathy with popular movements in music, such as the Competition Festival movement and the Folk Dance movement, and edited *The English Hymnal*, etc.

In 1935 he received the Order of Merit.

See *Harmony* 16; *Modes* 1; *Folk Song* 3, 5; *English Folk Dance and Song Society*; *Ballad* 4; *Mass* 4; *Chorale Prelude*; *Oboe* 6; *Opera* 13 e, 24 f (1924–29–36–37–51); *Ballad Opera*; *Chamber Music* 6, Period III (1872); *Concerto* 6 c (1872); *Impressionism*; *Pavan*; *Stilt*; *Percussion Family* 4 e; *Saxophone*; *Running Set*; *Bird Music*; *Bliss*; *Street Music* 2; *Knighthood*; *Composer's Guild*; *Society for the Promotion of New Music*.

VAULTING. Effect on sound. See *Concert Halls* 4.

VAUTOR, THOMAS. In the early seventeenth century he was active as a madrigal composer of a decidedly original bent.

VAUXHALL. See *Concert* 12, 13, 15; *Ridotto*.

VC. Short for violoncello.

VECCHI, ORAZIO. Born in Modena in 1550 and died there in 1605, aged fifty-four. He was an ecclesiastic and chief musician of the Cathedral and the Court of Modena. His madrigals are of high importance, especially a series of them called *Amfiparnaso*, laid out in dramatic style, called a 'commedia harmonica', and grouped into acts (but not intended for the stage).

He also wrote motets, masses, etc.

VECKELEN. See *Mechanical Reproduction of Music* 9 (end).

VEEMENTE (It.). 'Vehement.'

VEGA, CARPIO, or **Lope de Vega** (1562–1635). See *Spain* 5, 6.

VELATO, VELATA (It., masc., fem.). 'Veiled.'

VELLUTI, GIOVANNI BATTISTA (1781–1861). See *Voice* 5 (near end).

VELOCE, VELOCEMENTE (It.). With velocity. *Velocissimo, Velocissimamente* are the superlatives. *Velocità* means 'velocity'.

VELOUTÉ (Fr.). 'Velvety.'

VENETIAN SWELL. See *Organ* 8.

VENICE. See *Italy* 4; *Singing* 7; *Schools of Music*; *Opera* 23; *Concert* 14; *Printing* 1; *Publishing* 1; *Ornaments* 1; *Belgium* 2; *Street Music* 4.

VENI CREATOR SPIRITUS. An eighth-century Whitsuntide hymn, of which translations exist in all languages (Luther, Dryden, etc.). The English translation generally used is the seventeenth-century one of Bishop Cosin ('Come, Holy Ghost, our souls inspire'). This is one of the only two metrical hymns included in the English Common Prayer, and thus officially authorized; the other belongs to an alternative translation given in the same place (The Ordering of Priests). The tune usually sung to Cosin's translation is a harmonized adaptation of the proper plainsong. Bach has several choral arrangements of the plainsong and a fine organ chorale prelude (see *Chorale Prelude*) based upon it—now often heard in a piano version.

The *Veni Creator Spiritus* is sung at the creation of a pope, the consecration of a bishop, the elevation or translation of a saint, and the coronation of a monarch (e.g. recent British monarchs), and on many other occasions.

VENI SANCTE SPIRITUS. A sequence (q.v.) of the Roman Catholic liturgy, appointed for Whitsunday. In medieval times it was called the Golden Sequence. The words date from the end of the twelfth century. It is one of the four sequences allowed to remain when the rest were abolished by the Council of Trent (1545–63). Its traditional plainsong is very beautiful. Both words and plainsong are now attributed by some good authorities to Stephen Langton, Archbishop of Canterbury (d. 1228).

Caswall's translation ('Come, thou Holy Spirit, come') is used in some hymn-books, and Neale's ('Come, thou holy Paraclete') in others.

VENITE. The 95th Psalm (in the Vulgate the 94th; see *Psalm* for the differing numeration), the Invitatorium or Invitatory Psalm, or, as it is called in Henry VIII's Prymer, 'A song stirring to the Praise of God'—*O come, let us sing unto the Lord*. In the Common Prayer (q.v.) of the Anglican Church it is sung as a prelude to the morning Psalms, and is, even where there is a good choir, chanted, not (except by some of the Elizabethan composers and a few others) 'set' with the rest of the 'Service' (see *Common Prayer*). Some elaborate settings of this psalm exist, not intended for liturgical use, e.g. Mendelssohn's.

The prayer book of the American Episcopal Church joins part of the Venite with part of the *Cantate Domino*.

VENOSA. See *Gesualdo*.

VENT (Fr.). 'Wind.' So *Instruments à vent*, 'wind instruments'.

VENTIL (Ger.). 'Valve.'

VENTILATOR. According to one score of Strauss's *Don Quixote* this is the English for 'Wind Machine' (q.v.). The author of the present volume has not elsewhere come across the word, but includes it as some score reader might think it to be a useful contrivance for supplying 'air' to music deficient in it.

VENTILE (It.). 'Valve.'

VENTILE, CORNO (It.). 'Valve horn.' See *Horn Family* 2 c, 3, 5.

VENTILE, TROMBONE (It.). 'Valve trombone.' See *Trombone Family* 1, 5.

VENTILHORN (Ger.). 'Valve horn.' See *Horn Family* 2 c, 3, 5.

VENTILPOSAUNE (Ger.). 'Valve trombone.' See *Trombone Family* 1, 5.

VENTILTROMPETE (Ger.). 'Valve trumpet.' See *Trumpet Family* 2 c.

VENTURA, PEP. See *Sardana*.

VENUSTO (It.). 'Pretty.'

VERACINI, ANTONIO (latter half of seventeenth century) and FRANCESCO MARIA (born at Florence in 1690 and died, perhaps at Pisa, in 1750 aged about sixty). They were uncle and nephew and both were violinists and composers of instrumental music.

Antonio spent his life in Florence. Francesco (p. 1096, pl. **181.** 3), whom Tartini (q.v.) at one time considered his own superior as a player, lived in Venice, Dresden, and Prague, and spent a good deal of time in London. At Dres-

den, from vexation at the behaviour of a rival or insanity (or both), he threw himself out of a high window; however, he merely lamed himself and lived for nearly another thirty years. Many considered him to be the world's greatest violinist.

See references under *Violin Family* 6; *Sonata* 10 b.

VERÄNDERUNGEN. 'Alterations', or 'changes'; a word sometimes used by Beethoven for Variations (see *Form* 11), as in *Veränderungen über einen Walzer von A. Diabelli* ('Alterations of—or Changes on—a Waltz by A. Diabelli').

VERBUNKO or **VERBOUNKOCHE.** A Hungarian dance, dating from the latter half of the eighteenth century and originally executed by hussars in uniform on public occasions as a recruiting attraction. It was danced to gipsy bands and not to those of the regiments. Later it became popular in the theatre, etc. The music has two contrasting elements, similar to those of the czardas (q.v.).

VERDELOT, PHILIPPE. Lived in the earlier part of the sixteenth century (dates unknown). He was one of the later members of the famous school of northern French and Flemish composers who practised their art in Italy. There he produced madrigals and motets which brought him great personal renown and still keep his name alive. With Willaert he exercised a great influence upon the development of the art of the madrigal (see *Madrigal* 8 a).

VERDI, GIUSEPPE (p. 524, pl. **95.** 4; p. 240, pl. **44.** 5). Born near Busseto, in the district of Parma, in 1813 and died at Milan in 1901, aged eighty-seven. He was the son of a village innkeeper. As a child he served as acolyte to the priest, who, finding him absorbed in listening to the organ instead of fufilling his ceremonial duties, kicked him down the altar steps so that he lay insensible at their base. Later he developed some skill as an organist, but he does not appear to have obtained any position as such.

Some years after he tried for a scholarship at the Conservatory in Milan, but was refused as lacking aptitude for music; he stayed in Milan, however, studying privately, and supported by a grant from a charitable institution in his native district. To that district he returned on completing his studies, there living the routine life of the general musical practitioner of a small town.

At twenty-four he returned to Milan with an opera; it was performed at the Scala but is now forgotten. Eighteen other operas followed, and *Rigoletto*, *Il Trovatore* ('The Troubadour'), and *La Traviata* ('The Misled'), written in 1851–3, still firmly hold their ground. They represent the culmination of the composer's early period, in which he was vigorous, tuneful, sometimes 'melodramatic', but with many hints of the greater work to come.

A middle period is represented by *Aida*, on an Egyptian subject and written for the Khedive of Egypt. It is spectacular and dramatic, and is musically more developed and more dignified than its predecessors; its orchestration is at once richer and more imaginative. It appeared in 1871, when its composer was fifty-eight.

A remarkable third period is the great phenomenon of Verdi's life. In 1877, when he was seventy-three, appeared *Othello*, often styled 'Wagnerian', because, undoubtedly influenced by his great contemporary (born in the same year, by the by), its composer has adopted a more 'symphonic' style, with some use of the principle of the 'leading motif' (q.v.). It has a gracious pendant in *Falstaff*, which followed six years later—a work of youthful high spirits in his eightieth year. Again we have 'music drama' rather than opera, and from its spirit and humour *Falstaff* may be called 'the Italian *Mastersingers*'.

Of the numerous other operas of Verdi no list can be given here. He wrote a string quartet (practically his only instrumental music) and some church music, including the great Requiem in honour of his compatriot, the poet and novelist Manzoni (a work that may be not unfairly called 'theatrical' yet is at once sincere and effective), and, in his eighty-fifth year, a *Te Deum*, a beautiful *Stabat Mater*, an *Ave Maria*, and *Laudi alla Vergine*.

In Verdi the nineteenth-century Italian school of opera composition reaches its very height. He took its gift for melody and its knack of the full use of vocal capabilities, and to them, in increasing measure as his genius matured, he added a richer harmony and orchestration and a greater sense of poetry, dramatic fitness, dignity, and truth.

See *Opera* 6, 21 i l, 24 (1844 onwards); *Comic Opera*; *Singing* 10; *Requiem*; *Te Deum*; *Stabat Mater*; *Form* 12; *Scales* 12; *Collaboration*; *Grand Opera*; *Percussion Family* 4 c (Anvil); *Italy* 8; *Gramophone* 6. Also *Aida*; *Falstaff*; *Othello*; *Rigoletto*; *Traviata*; *Trovatore*.

VERDOPPELN (Ger.). 'To double.' So *Verdoppelt*, 'doubled'; *Verdoppelung*, 'doubling'.

VEREENIGING VOOR NEDERLANDSCHE MUZIEKGESCHIEDENIS. See *Holland* 9.

VEREIN (Ger.). 'Society.'

VERGNÜGT (Ger.). 'Contented.'

VERHALLEND (Ger.). 'Dying away.'

VERHULST, JOHANNES JOSEPHUS HERMAN (1816–91). See *Holland* 6, 7.

VERISMO. See *Opera* 7.

VERKLÄRT (Ger.). 'Transfigured', 'glorified'.

VERLAINE, PAUL (1844–96). French poet of the Symbolist school, and hence one of the inspirers of musical impressionism (see *Impressionism*; *Bergomask*).

VERLAUF (Ger.). 'Course', 'continuance'.

VERLIEBT (Ger.). 'Loved', i.e. performed in a tender manner.

VERLIEREND (Ger.). 'Losing itself', i.e. dying away.

VERLÖSCHEND (Ger.). 'Extinguishing', i.e. dying away.

VERMEULEN, MATTHIJS. Born at Helmond in Holland in 1888. He occupied posts as music critic in Amsterdam from 1908 to 1920, and then settled in Paris, returning to Amsterdam in 1946. He has composed symphonies, chamber music, etc.

VERNEHMBAR (Ger.). 'Perceptible.'

VERSCHIEBUNG (Ger.). Soft pedal (literally 'away-shoving'—from the character of the mechanism).

VERSCHIEDEN (Ger.). 'Various.'

VERSCHWINDEND (Ger.). 'Disappearing', i.e. dying away.

VERSE, as contrasted with 'Full', is a term used in church music to mean a passage for solo voice, or for two or more voices (e.g. quartet), as contrasted with passages to be sung by the whole choir.

A 'Service' (see *Common Prayer*) or Anthem is called a 'Verse Service', 'Verse Anthem', 'Full Service', or 'Full Anthem', according as it has or has not some portion for solo voices. The words 'Verse' and 'Full' frequently occur in the scores of the eighteenth-century and other anthems, as an indication to the singers of the alternation of quartet and full chorus.

Some books of reference define a 'Verse Anthem' as one *beginning* with a part for solo voices, which seems to be a very useless indication and leaves no convenient term to describe an anthem which has (say) quartet passages elsewhere than at the opening: the absurdly contradictory term 'Full with Verse' is sometimes used by those who use 'Verse Anthem' in the way just deprecated.

Cf. *Anthem*; *Service*.

VERSEGHY, FERENC. See *Hungary*.

VERSE RHYTHM. See *Rhythm* 6.

VERSET. The word simply means 'verse', but has also a special application in the Roman Catholic Church to a verse of a psalm, during which the singers are silent, the organist plays, and the clergy, choir, and congregation repeat the words of the verse to themselves. Organ music intended for such performance is often published under the name of 'Versets'; frequently, however, the organist either simply plays the music omitted or extemporizes.

A similar practice is sometimes used in connexion with the performance of the Kyrie, Gloria, and Agnus Dei, the organ *supplying* (this is the technical term) alternate phrases. Similarly the Tract, Sequence, Offertory, and Communion may be 'supplied' by the organ and so may the repetition of the Introit. In some churches the verse of the Gradual is 'supplied'. The Antiphons at Vespers may be supplied on their repetition after the Psalm.

The object may be either to relieve the choir or to add to the exultation of a festival by brilliant outbursts of extemporization. The practice is much in use in the French cathedrals and large churches where there are fine organists. Organ versets were published as early as 1531, in which year Pierre Attaignant, the celebrated Paris publisher, issued two books of them (republished four centuries later—1925).

The practice is alluded to in the *Motu Proprio* (q.v.) of Pius X (1903)—'not to omit the prescribed texts in cases where the rubrics do not permit of replacing verses by the organ whilst they are simply recited in the choir'.

VERSETZUNG (Ger.). 'Transposition.'

VERSICLE. In the Roman or Anglican service a short verse spoken or chanted by the priest and responded to by the congregation (or the choir representing it). But see *Preces*.

VERSTÄRKEN (Ger.). 'To strengthen.'

VERSTÄRKT. 'Strengthened', i.e. same as rinforzando (q.v.).

VERSTOVSKY (Werstowsky, Verstovski, etc), ALEXIS. Born in Tambov, Central Russia, in 1799, and died in Moscow in 1862, aged sixty-three. He composed operas, of a somewhat amateurish kind, a good deal in the Italian style though with some admixture of the German (Weber) style and also some Russian elements. One of them, *The Tomb of Askold*, for a long period enjoyed immense favour.

His songs must also be mentioned.

VERT, JACQUES DE. See *Wert*.

VERTEILT, VERTHEILT (Ger.). 'Divided.'

VERWEILEND (Ger.). 'Delaying', i.e. rallentando.

VERZIERUNGEN. Embellishments. See *Ornaments or Graces*; also Tables 12–16.

VESPERAL. A Roman Catholic service book containing the liturgy and music for Vespers, and often for some of the other 'Hours' of the Church (see *Vespers* and *Divine Office*). It is merely an extract from the Antiphonal (q.v.) (see also below).

VESPÉRAL, VESPÉRALE (Fr., masc., fem.). As the title of a piece of music the word probably usually means 'Evening Mood' or something of that kind (see also entry above).

VESPERS. The seventh of the Canonical Hours, or services of the day of the Roman Catholic Church. Properly it is held at sunset. It is also known as Evensong (cf. *Matins, Lauds, Prime, Terce, Sext, None,* and *Compline*). This service has always been a favourite one with composers, and many (discarding the traditional plainsong of the various parts of the service) have provided elaborate settings.

VESTALE, LA. See *Spontini*.

VESTRIS Family.
GAETANO or GAËTAN (1729–1808); TERESINA (sister of Gaetano, 1726–1808); ANGIOLO (brother of Gaetano and Teresina, 1730–1809); VIOLANTE (sister of all the preceding, and a vocalist, 1732–91); AUGUSTE (son of Gaetano, 1760–1842); ARMAND (son of Auguste, 1788–1825). See *Ballet* 3 for mention of this family.

Note.—Some of the dates differ in various books of reference and the Christian names are sometimes given in Italian form and sometimes in French. Some of the wives of the above men were of importance as dancers or singers. The great contralto **Madame Vestris** (1797–1856) was for a time wife of Armand, above.

The names Vestris I, Vestris II, and Vestris III are often applied to Gaetano, Auguste, and Armand—three generations.

VETTER MICHEL (Ger.). See *Sequence*.

VEXILLA REGIS. See *Hymns and Hymn Tunes* 2.

VIA (It.). 'Away!' So *Via sordini*, 'Remove mutes'.

VIADANA (real name Ludovico Grossi). Born at Viadana near Mantua in 1564 and died at Gualtieri in 1645, aged eighty or eighty-one. He was a Franciscan who held at different times a number of positions in control of cathedral music, etc. He published many madrigals and much church music, including (1602) a collection of 100 motets with organ accompaniment, which he called 'concerti ecclesiastici' (see *Concerto* 1); as in this work he uses a figured bass (q.v.), he has been credited with the invention of the system, but this is inexact.

VIARDOT. See *Garcia Family* 4.

VIBRAPHONE, VIBRA-HARP. A sort of marimba (q.v.) of which the resonators (tuned ones) of the (metal) bars are fitted with lids kept in motion (i.e. opening and closing) by an electric motor. This give a pulsation to the sound coming from any bar of the instrument struck by the player and the speed of the pulsation can be regulated by the governor on the motor. In the 1920s and 1930s dance bands (especially) largely adopted this instrument. *Vibra-Harp* is an American name.

Perhaps the first use of this instrument in serious music is in Alban Berg's opera *Lulu* (1934) and in the suite made therefrom.

VIBRATIONS. See *Acoustics* (passim).

VIBRATO. See *Tremolo*.

VIBRER (Fr.). 'To vibrate.'

VICAR CHORAL. The term is peculiar to the Anglican Church and designates a cathedral singing man (see *Cathedral Music*). The position varies in the details of its conditions in different cathedrals, and at some the term 'Lay Clerk' or 'Lay Vicar' is used. The word vicar indicates that the duties are really those of the canons, done vicariously: at one time every canon had either a vicar choral or a minor canon (the latter being in orders) attached to him. The office, as it now exists, is one which sprang up at the time of the Reformation (1533–6). Formerly all these various 'Clerks' and 'Vicars' were in holy orders.

VICAR OF BRAY, THE. The hero of this song was a real personage who managed to keep his position through the reigns of Henry VIII (Roman Catholic and then Protestant), Edward

VI (Protestant), Mary (Roman Catholic), and Elizabeth I (Protestant). The Bray in question is in Berkshire and the poem expands a popular Berkshire proverb—'The Vicar of Bray will be Vicar still'. There were, however, at that period many clergymen (and even one or two bishops) just as adaptable.

The poem as we have it today is said to date from the early eighteenth century and treats events of the seventeenth (not those with which the actual Vicar of Bray was concerned —or rather unconcerned). An early poem on the same lines, which appears to have supplied the basis of the present one, is Ned Ward's 'The Religious Turncoat' (1712). This was sung to the tune of *London is a fine Town*.

The present poem was long sung to a Scottish tune, *Bessy Bell and Mary Gray*, but since about 1770 has been wedded to its present tune of *The Country Garden*, which still survives (or did recently) amongst English morris dancers, and apparently first appeared in print in *The Quaker's Opera* (1728).

VICENTINO, NICOLÁ. Born at Vicenza in 1511, and died in Rome in 1572, aged sixty or sixty-one. He was a pupil of Willaert who took orders and joined the household of Cardinal Ippolito d'Este at Rome. He became infatuated with the idea of reviving the ancient Greek modes, inventing multiple-keyboard instruments (capable of enharmonic distinctions), and writing madrigals in order to exemplify his ideas. He engaged in controversies, wrote theoretical treatises, and had fame as a keyboard player.

VICINO (It.). 'Near.'

VICTALELE. A simple form of zither, commercially announced as 'combining the playing of the ukelele, mandolin, harp, and guitar, all in one instrument, yet so simple that anybody can learn to play it in a few minutes'.

VICTIMAE PASCHALI. A sequence (q.v.) of the Roman Catholic liturgy, appointed for Easter day. It dates from the eleventh century and is one of the four allowed to remain when the rest were abolished by the Council of Trent (1545–63). It has, of course, its traditional plainsong.

VICTOR CO. See *H.M.V.*

VICTORIA, QUEEN. See *Mechanical Reproduction* 7; *God save the Queen* 17; *United States* 6.

VICTORIA, TOMÁS LUIS DE. Born at Avila, in Old Castile, probably in 1549, and died at Madrid in 1611, aged about sixty-two. From 1565 for about forty years he held various important posts in Rome, which accounts for the common Italianization of his name as 'Vittoria'. He was one of the greatest of the contemporaries of Palestrina (of whom he may have been a pupil) and like him a composer of unaccompanied church music in the contrapuntal style, then at its climax; but whereas Palestrina's music is serene that of Victoria is

charged with passionate mysticism. He wrote no secular music whatever.

See references under *History* 2; *Spain* 5, 8; *Mass* 2, 4; *Requiem*; *Passion Music* 2; *Harmony* 8; *Counterpoint*; *Composition* 12; *Patronage* 8; *Pedrell*.

VICTORIA HALL, ROYAL (or 'Old Vic'). This is a London theatre on the south side of the Thames, dating from 1818, which later became a low music-hall but was taken over in 1880 by Emma Cons, who converted it into a place of cheap, clean entertainment; in 1898 her niece, Lilian Baylis (afterwards, in recognition of her work, Hon. M.A. Oxon., Hon. LL.D. Birmingham, and C.H.; d. 1937), succeeded to the management and by adroit contrivance and perseverance made it a notable home of Shakespearian drama and of opera.

For a later development see under *Sadler's Wells*. See also *Competition* 2.

VICTOR TALKING MACHINE CO. See *Gramophone* 7; *Tests and Measurements*; *H.M.V.*

VICTROLA. See *Gramophone* 8.

VIDAL, PAUL ANTONIN. Born at Toulouse in 1863 and died in Paris in 1931. He won the French Rome Prize and after return became prominent and prolific as a composer and joined the staff of the Paris Conservatory (from 1910 a professor of composition) and was also eminent as an opera conductor and as an opera composer. He published three volumes of Cherubini's harmony lessons.

VIDE (Fr.). 'Empty.' Thus *Corde à vide* means 'open string'.

VIEL (Ger.). 'Much', 'many' (*viele, vielem*, etc., are other grammatical forms of the word).

VIELLE (Fr.). (1) A medieval precursor of the viol. (2) Short for 'vielle à roue', i.e. 'wheel vielle', i.e. hurdy-gurdy (q.v.).

VIENNA. See *Germany* 5; *Opera* 9 b; *Pianoforte* 7; *Concert* 13; *Jewish* 6; *Criticism* 2; *Street Music* 5; *Schools*; and a large number of personal entries: *Haydn, Mozart, Beethoven, Schubert, Brahms, Albrechtsberger, Nicolai* etc.

VIENNESE ACTION. See *Pianoforte* 7.

VIER (Ger.). 'Four.'

VIERFACH (Ger.). 'Fourfold.'

VIERHÄNDIG. 'Four-handed', i.e. piano duet.

VIERLING. See *Electric Musical Instruments* 2 a, 3 b c.

VIERNE.

(1) LOUIS VICTOR JULES (p. 784, pl. 131. 6). Born at Poitiers in 1870 and died in Paris in 1937, aged sixty-six. He was a pupil at the Paris Conservatory of Franck and Widor and at thirty became organist of Notre Dame. He composed much music for his instrument, for voice, for piano, for chamber music combinations, for orchestra, and for chorus, and had a high reputation as an organist and an improviser. All his life he suffered from blindness. He died on his organ stool.

See *Improvisation* 2.

(2) RENÉ. Born at Lille in 1878, killed in battle in 1918. He was brother of the above, was like him an organist, and composed music for organ and for harmonium.

VIERTE (Ger.). 'Fourth.' *Viertes, viertem, vierten* are other grammatical forms of the word.

VIERTEL or **VIERTELNOTE**. 'Quarter', 'quarter-note', crotchet (Table 3).

VIERUNDSECHZIGSTEL or **VIERUND-SECHZIGSTELNOTE** (Ger.). 'Sixty-fourth' or 'Sixty-fourth Note', hemidemisemiquaver (Table 3).

VIEUXTEMPS, HENRI (p. 1094, pl. **182. 5**). Born at Verviers, in Belgium, in 1820 and died in Algeria in 1881, aged sixty-one. At seven he played in public a violin concerto of Rode, at eight he toured as a virtuoso, and at nine he appeared in Paris under the auspices of his teacher, de Bériot. Very extensive concert journeys followed, and at fourteen Schumann heard him at Leipzig and wrote, 'When we listen to Henri we can close our eyes with confidence. His playing is at once sweet and bright, like a flower. His execution is perfect, masterly throughout.'

The years that followed were filled full with travel in Europe and America, study, and composition, the last, naturally, for his own instrument. For a time he lived in Russia as solo violinist to the Emperor and Professor at the Conservatory of St. Petersburg. Everywhere he was hailed as a marvel. In his early fifties he settled at Brussels as Professor of the Conservatory and then, suddenly, a dazzling career ended in an attack of paralysis.

His many works are magnificently written for the instrument, but lapse sometimes into the merely showy. Some of them, especially the six concertos, are still in much use.

He had two brothers in his profession—one a pianist and the other a cellist. They held good positions, but did not enjoy anything like the same fame as he did.

For a reference to the Belgian school of violin playing to which Vieuxtemps belonged see *Belgium* 5.

VIF, VIVE (Fr., masc., fem.). 'Lively.' *Vivement* is the adverb.

VIGUEUR, VIGOUREUX, VIGOUREUSE-MENT (Fr.); **VIGORE, VIGOROSO, VIGOROSAMENTE** (It.). 'Vigour', 'vigorous', 'vigorously'.

VIHTOL, JOSEPH. Born at Wolmar (in Russian territory, then in Latvia, and now again in Russia) in 1863 and died at Lübeck in 1948. He was a pupil of Rimsky-Korsakof at the Conservatory of St. Petersburg and later became a professor at this institution. After the first World War he founded the Latvian Conservatory at Riga, but in 1944 he settled in Germany. He wrote orchestral works, chamber works, songs, etc. (including arrangements of Latvian folk songs), and counts as the leading Latvian composer.

VIHUELA (p. 449, pl. **77. 6**). A Spanish instrument, strung and played like the lute (q.v.), but with a body resembling the guitar, of which it is the parent (see reference under *Guitar*).

In the sixteenth century the vihuela was the most serious solo instrument of the Peninsula, and the music of the Spanish player-composers ('Vihuelista' is the name applied to such an individual) remains important (see *Concerto* 5). Then it fell into complete disuse until, in the 1930s, one example of the instrument was found to be in existence in a museum in Paris. It served as a model from which others could be made and the eminent guitarist, Emilio Pujol, was able to revive the old technique and the forgotten compositions.

Fourteenth-century use of the term is wider than the above, including plucked and bowed forms, the latter being the viol—viol and vihuela are, indeed, the same word.

See *Guitar*.

VILLAGE BLACKSMITH See *Weiss* 2.

VILLA-LOBOS, HEITOR (p. 209, pl. **41. 6**). Born at Rio de Janeiro in 1887 and died there in 1959, aged seventy-two. He was the leading Brazilian composer, and wrote over two thousand works, including operas, an oratorio, symphonies, chamber music, piano music, etc., almost all strongly influenced by the melodies and rhythms of Brazilian folktune and sometimes embodying polytonal technique. He worked in Paris (1923–7); founded an orchestra in his native city; and became (1932) Director of Music in Education in his country, which last position led to his collection and composition of songs for children.

Some of his technical devices appear to be arbitrary and even eccentric, e.g. piano music in which one hand plays on the white keys and the other on the black, and 'millimetrization', the latter a method of extracting melodies from pictures:

'He traces the contours of a picture on graph paper, and then plots the melody, a semitone to a square of the graph in the vertical direction, and an eighth-note to a horizontal unit. Thus an ascending curve in the picture results in a melody going up, and a descending line produces a falling musical phrase. An undulating landscape is reflected in a florid cantilena.' (Slonimsky, *Music of Latin America*, 1945.)

At his radio début in New York, 'as a gesture of good will', he conducted an orchestral composition that he had based on the contours of a steamship company's panoramic photograph of the sky-line of New York City. Rather more comprehensibly, he composed a number of pieces in a style which he calls *Chôros*, 'in which are synthesized the different modalities of Brazilian, Indian, and popular music reflecting in its fundamental elements the rhythm and characteristic melodies of the people'.

See *Clarinet* 6; *Metronome*; *Opera* 24 (1940); *Harp* 4.

VILLANCICO (Spanish). The word comes from *villano*, 'rustic', and was used in the sixteenth century for a type of choral song of three or four lines to a verse (something like the English *Ayre*), which later grew into a sort of big anthem or cantata for Christmas or some other festival. It began and ended with a choral movement or *Estribillo*; the middle movements, for solo voices, are *Coplas* (q.v.). The best description in English is in Trend's *A Picture of Modern Spain* (1921).

See also *Spain* 5.

VILLANELLA (It.). Plural *Villanelle*. A sort of simple-minded, light-hearted Neapolitan madrigal, of easy-going rhythmic construction, popular in the sixteenth century. Like the *Frottola* (q.v.) and the English ayre and ballet, the villanella repeated the same music for many verses. All these forms were less contrapuntal than the normal madrigal. An apparently deliberate feature was the use of consecutive fifths here and there.

The *Villota* is practically the same as the villanella.

VILLANESCA (Sp.). 'Rustic.' Granados has a dance of this name. And see *Napolitana*.

VILLOTA or **VILLOTTA** (It.). Plural *Villote* or *Villotte*. Practically the Villanella (q.v.).

VINA (instrument). See p. 465, pl. **82.** 1.

VINCENT.

(1) THOMAS. English oboist and composer, of the latter part of the eighteenth century (see *Sonata* 10 c). But it appears that his father and son, also musicians, bore the same Christian name, and confusion exists.

(2) HEINRICH JOSEPH, originally 'Winzenhörlein' (1819–1901). A Viennese singer, opera composer, and theorist of very original ideas (see *Keyboard* 4).

VINCI, LEONARDO. Born in Calabria in 1690 and died at Naples in 1730, aged about forty. He was attached to the court of Naples and was a notable composer of operas in the style of Alessandro Scarlatti, as well as of church music. He had an influence upon the development of accompanied recitative and of the aria and left some instrumental music of interest and importance.

VIÑES, RICARDO (p. 977, pl. **164.** 7.) Born at Lérida, Spain, in 1875 and died at Barcelona in 1943, aged sixty-eight. He studied at the Conservatory of Paris and won high recognition as a pianist, particularly as an interpreter of the modern French school.

VIOLA. See *Violin Family* 2 b, 7; *Organ* 14 III.

VIOLA ALTA. A large-sized viola, in which the instrument is in just proportion to its pitch as compared with the violin, instead of being smaller (as in the normal viola); it has five strings. It was introduced by Hermann Ritter in 1876, and used by Wagner in the orchestra at Bayreuth, but the large stretch of the left hand which it demands has prevented its acquiring a permanent standing (cf. *Violeténor*). Its inventor gave it an alternative name, 'Altgeige' (but see this word).

VIOLA BASTARDA (It.). See *Viol Family* 4 c d.

VIOLA DA BRACCIO. See *Braccio and Gamba*.

VIOLA DA GAMBA. See *Braccio and Gamba*; *Viol Family* 3, 5.

VIOLA D'AMORE (It.). See *Viol Family* 4 f.

VIOLA DI BORDONE. See *Viol Family* 4 d.

VIOLA PARADON. See *Viol Family* 4 d.

VIOLA POMPOSA. See *Violin Family* 2 b.

VIOLE (Fr.). 'Viol' or 'viola'.

VIOLE (It.). Plural of *Viola* (see *Violin Family*). (See also one or two lower entries.)

VIOLE D'AMOUR. See *Viol Family* 4 f; *Organ* 14 III.

VIOLE D'ORCHESTRE. See *Organ* 14 III.

VIOLEN (Ger.). Plural of *Viola*.

VIOLENTO, VIOLENTAMENTE (It.). 'Violent', 'violently'.

VIOLENZA (It.). 'Violence.'

VIOLE-PARRAMON. See *Viole-ténor*, below.

VIOLE-TÉNOR (or Alto-Moderne). A large viola, tuned like the viola but held like the cello, introduced in the 1930s by R. Parramon of Barcelona and praised by Casals, Ravel, and others as avoiding the weakness of the normal viola (see *Violin Family* 2 b). Any of the music for either viola or cello can be played on it—the latter, however, being transposed up an octave.

VIOLET, ENGLISH. See *Viol Family* 4 f.

VIOLETTA. See *Violin Family* 2, and, for Violetta Marina, *Viol Family* 4 f.

VIOL FAMILY

| 1. Introductory. | 3. Chief Members of the Family. | 5. Date of Decline. |
| 2. Characteristics. | 4. Other Members of the Family. | 6. Music for the Viols. |

(For illustrations see p. 1073, pl. **178**; 33, **4. 5.**)

1. Introductory. This family preceded and then remained contemporary with the violin family (q.v.), which finally superseded it as the demand for public music superseded that for private, so that today the members of the viol family are used only by a small (but growing) body of devoted students of the older music who have revived them in order to give that music authentic performance. Like the instruments of the harpsichord family (which were superseded by the pianoforte) and the instruments of the recorder family (which were superseded by the side-blown flutes), viols are now again being made, as, for instance, by the

Dolmetsch group at Haslemere, England. The technique of the viol family is less exacting (at all events in its elementary stages) than that of the violin family, and the music that exists for it belongs to an age that demanded musicianship more often than virtuosity, hence the members of the former family are attractive to adult learners and others who have not time to devote to the acquirement of advanced executive skill—though for this also employment can be found.

2. Characteristics. The characteristics of the viol family are most conveniently defined by reference to those of the universally known violin family.

(a) The viol's back is usually flat, instead of convex.

(b) Its shoulders usually slope to the neck, instead of meeting this at right angles.

(c) Its wood is thinner and its ribs are deeper.

(d) Its normal number of strings is six, instead of four.

(e) Its finger-board is 'fretted', instead of smooth, i.e. it has raised lines marking the position of the semitones (cf. the mandoline, banjo, etc., today; in the viol, however, the frets take the form of pieces of gut tied round the finger-board and are hence capable of adjustment).

(f) The sound holes are usually of a 'c' shape instead of an 'f' shape.

(g) Its bridge is less arched, so allowing chords to be more easily played (this was, however, at first so with the violin).

(h) Its strings are thinner and less tense.

(i) Its bow stick curves outward from the hair (again facilitating chords), instead of inward to it as with the modern bow (the earlier violin bows, however, did the same).

Of these differences not all are of equal importance. The shape affects the tone much less than might be supposed. The thin wood and light construction are the primary differences, together with the thinner, less tense strings. These factors result in greater resonance but less volume; the tone sounds freer but less intense. The six strings, tuned mainly in fourths instead of altogether in fifths, encourage chord playing and tend to lead to a different technique. The frets, by cutting off the shorter length of string for stopped notes more sharply than does one's soft finger-end, contribute valuably to the characteristic tone. The outcurved bow, with its special technique, greatly influences the style and, to some extent, the tone produced. (Some modern players of the bass viol abandon both frets and outcurved bow, using instead the technique of the cello: the temptation can be understood but the result is 'neither fish nor fowl'.)

Note that all the viols were held *downwards*, the smaller ones resting between the knees, the larger ones between the legs. Note, too, that the hand was held *under* the bow, not over as today.

See under *Braccio and Gamba* for an explanation of some matters commonly misunderstood.

3. Chief Members of the Family. The sizes of the various members of the viol family are much like those of the violin family, i.e. they are (like the violin, viola, and violoncello of today) designed for the playing of the upper, inner, and lower parts of a composition. A complete **Chest of Viols** (meaning a domestic set of them, often kept in an actual chest fitted for their reception) might include the following: two trebles, two tenors (or one alto and one tenor), two basses (p. 1073, pl. **178.** 7).

There were other viols than those just mentioned (see 4), but those were the most generally employed and were what were required for a normal composition written for a **Consort of Viols** (see *Consort*).

The treble viol is sometimes called **Descant**, 'descant' (q.v.) having come to carry as one of its general meanings that of the highest part. It is also called (in French) **Dessus de Viole**.

The bass viol (p. 1073, pl. **178.** 3) was (and is commonly) called by the name **Viola da Gamba**, which is really proper to the whole family (cf. *Braccio and Gamba*): this is because it has always been by far the most important soloist of its group—just the opposite of the violin family.

The English were in the seventeenth century reckoned the best bass viol (viola da gamba) players in the world, and continental musicians often came to England for instruction. English bass viol players held positions at continental courts and published much of their music abroad, e.g. Thomas Simpson (q.v.) and William Brade (q.v.). When in New England literature we find, as we frequently do, mention of the 'bass viol' in church use, it is this instrument (or in later periods its successor the violoncello) that is referred to, not, as is often supposed, either the double-bass viol (violone; see 4 a below) or the more modern double-bass (see *Violin Family* 2 d).

4. Other Members of the Family. Amongst other members or pseudo-members of the family are:

(a) **Double-Bass Viol** or **Violone**, playing an octave lower than the bass viol. Bach in his cantatas almost always scores for the violone; indeed, it is not sure that he ever contemplated the use of the modern double-bass derived from it—which is still sometimes (perhaps chiefly in country places) described as Base (*sic*) Viol.

(b) **Division Viol**, a slightly smaller-sized bass viol, suitable for the playing of rapid variations.

(c) **Lyra Viol** (sometimes called the **Viola Bastarda**), a still smaller bass viol, intended for playing chordal and contrapuntal music rather of the lute type and played from tablature (q.v.), like the lute, instead of from the staff notation. Any size of bass viol, however, can be and sometimes was so played and this is the explanation of the frequent expression 'played lyra way'. The point of playing from tablature is that particular chords in a composition required particular tunings of the strings for those compositions, and that for such varied tunings the staff notation would impose an almost impossible strain on the player's memory and technique. Pizzicato (called 'The Thump') was a feature of 'lyra-way' performance.

(*d*) **Baryton** or **Viola di Bordone** or **Viola Paradon** (p. 1073, pl. **178**. 5), a sort of viol of bass (not double-bass) size, sometimes, but wrongly, considered to be identical with the **Viola Bastarda** (see *c* above). Like the viola d'amore (see *f* below) it had sympathetic strings, so that it is sometimes called in France **Basse de viole d'amour.** Haydn composed extensively for it, his patron, Prince Esterházy, being a performer.

(*e*) **Pardessus de Viole,** a smaller viol than the treble and tuned a fourth above it. It was an eighteenth-century French instrument and had often only five strings. It was held and bowed in the same way as the larger viols.

(*f*) **Viola d'Amore** (Viole d'Amour), literally 'love-viol', presumably from its affecting tone, which was modified by the existence of 'sympathetic strings' under the finger-board (see *Sympathetic Strings*), so that it stands in a class apart. It had no frets and was held upwards like the violins; indeed it belongs to their type almost as much as to that of the viols. Comparatively little music of importance was written for this instrument: Bach uses it twice in the St. John Passion and in four or five movements of other works. Vivaldi wrote a concerto for it and lute, with muted strings and organ. Ariosti wrote sonatas. Handel uses an instrument of this sort of higher pitch, sometimes called **Violetta Marina** (It.), **Pardessus de Viole d'Amour** (Fr.), or (by Leopold Mozart) **English Violet.** In more recent times Meyerbeer, Strauss, Prokofief, and others have made occasional use of the viola d'amore, and Hindemith contributed a sonata, as well as his

'Kammermusik No. 6'. The German word *Liebesgeige* ('love fiddle') occurs.

5. Date of Decline. The latest survivor of the viols (until the recent revival) was the bass viol (see 3), which long usurped and at last monopolized the name 'viola da gamba'; it was regularly heard in London concerts up to near the end of the eighteenth century (cf. *Abel, K. F.*), whereas the other viols began to be superseded gradually from the middle of the seventeenth century.

6. Music for the Viols. A vast quantity of music was composed for the viols and much of this still exists, though, unfortunately, with small exceptions, only in manuscript. The solo music frequently takes the shape of sets of 'divisions' (q.v.)—especially for the bass viol accompanied by a second bass viol, lute, or harpsichord. Concerted music for the viols abounds in manuscript in some of the great English libraries, in the form of fancies (q.v.) and music of lighter types. This early seventeenth-century English chamber music of the viols is as important and beautiful as the vocal chamber music of the period and it is now being increasingly explored. The Spanish concerted viol music of the sixteenth century, based on the extemporised ornamentation of what were originally vocal works, is also important.

Bach left three sonatas for the viola da gamba and harpsichord, and his sixth Brandenburg Concerto is for two viole da braccio and two viole da gamba, with violoncello and double-bass viol. References to English composition for the viols will be found under *Brade*; *Deering*; *Ferrabosco, Alfonso*; *Gibbons, Orlando*; *Hume*; *Jenkins, John*; *Lawes, William*; *Locke*; *Mace*; *Simpson*; *Weelkes*. For Spain see *Ortiz*. An interesting use of the bass viol (viola da gamba) by Schütz is mentioned under *Oratorio* 3.

See also *Chamber Music* 3; *Madrigal* 3 c (end).

VIOLINDA. A violin with various practical helps to the young learner, introduced in Britain in the 1930s, especially for class instruction. It is the invention of J. Hullah Brown.

VIOLIN DIAPASON. See *Organ* 14 III.

VIOLIN FAMILY

(For illustrations see p. 1072, pl. 177; 1088, **179**; 1096, **181, 182**.)

1. Introductory. This family emerges in the early part of the sixteenth century. The resemblance of its members to those of the viol family (q.v.) is only superficial and the two families (with the exception mentioned under 2 d below) are radically different: if they had a common ancestor (which some authorities now doubt) it must have been remote. The violins lived side by side with the viols in rivalry until the latter were largely ousted at the end of the seventeenth century. A comparison of the

characteristics of the two families will be found under *Viol Family* 2 (see also *Braccio and Gamba*).

2. Members of the Family. The members of the violin family are:

(*a*) The **Violin** itself (p. 1072, pl. **177**. 1). 'First Violin' and 'Second Violin' are mere distinctions of functions, like first soprano and second soprano in a choir. Cf. *Contra-Violin.*

(b) **Viola** (or **Tenor** or, better, **Alto**). Compared with the violin it is somewhat small in proportion to its lower pitch, and consequently its tone is rather less bright (cf. *Viole-ténor*). There was once a true tenor violin, in size a very small violoncello; it went out of general use at the end of the seventeenth century.

The **Viola Pomposa**, probably a large viola with five strings, is said (though there is no real evidence) to have been invented by J. S. Bach. It soon dropped out of use.

(c) **Violoncello** (p. 1088, pl. **179**) or, for short, cello.

(d) **Double-bass** (or *Contrabass*) (p. 1088, pl. **179**. 7, 9). Originally a much larger and more cumbrous instrument than the modern orchestral double-bass. It seems to have to have been early abandoned in favour of (or, at least, modified in the direction of) the more convenient and resonant violone (*Viol Family* 4 a), and from this our modern instrument is directly derived. All these instruments have four strings except the double-bass, which formerly had only three and now has four or sometimes five, and all have their strings tuned at the interval of a fifth apart except the double-bass, which has them tuned a fourth apart to avoid too long finger-stretch (a reminder, also, of its viol ancestry)—though varying tunings are adopted. The strings of these instruments are tuned as follows:

Violin   Viola   Violoncello

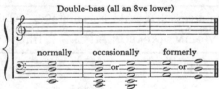

Double-bass (all an 8ve lower)

normally   occasionally   formerly

The strings of the *Violino Piccolo* were tuned an octave above those of the Viola.

A string quartet consists of first and second violin, viola, and cello. The normal employment of the family in the orchestra is as first and second violins, violas, cellos, and double-basses. The string quartet is the most versatile and (but for its loss of its true tenor) most perfectly homogeneous combination of solo instruments possible, and the string section of the orchestra has been its very basis from the seventeenth century to the present day; hence the family can claim the greatest importance of any instrumental family in existence.

In Bach's works we still find very occasion-ally (as in the first Brandenburg Concerto) a part for the **Violino Piccolo** (a smaller, higher pitched violin); he also once or twice prescribes the **Violetta** (an eighteenth-century name for our viola), and pretty frequently, the **Violoncello Piccolo** (a much smaller violoncello, with five strings).

3. Qualities of the Family. Some qualities of the family are as follows:

(a) Their tone is very pleasant and extremely sensitive, and can be varied with ease from very soft to loud.

(b) Their compass, from the lowest note of the double-bass to the highest possible on the violin, is nearly seven octaves.

(c) They have almost infinite powers of varying the effect of passages by different groupings of more or fewer notes within one bow and by different methods of applying the bow (see, for instance, *Spiccato, Martellato, Sul ponticello, Col legno, Tremolo*).

(d) They offer still another effect by the temporary abandonment of the bow and the substitution of plucking by the fingers (*Pizzicato*).

(e) Double notes and chords can be played—with considerable freedom and in considerable variety, though with some limitations (see *Double Stopping*).

(f) Flute-like 'harmonic' notes are possible (see *Acoustics* 8).

(g) The mute (a small clamp on the bridge) can be applied, so producing a curious silvery muffled tone.

(h) It may be noted that the end-pin of the violoncello is a comparatively modern innovation. The great nineteenth-century player Piatti (q.v.), for instance, never used it. Nor had it then become the custom to use the left arm and wrist in the manner of modern cellists to produce a vibrato (Fellowes, *Memoirs of an Amateur Musician*, 1946).

4. The Great Makers (p. 1072, pl. **177**. 2, 3). The greatest age in the making of these instruments was that of the various generations of the Amati, Guarneri, and Stradivari families (mid-sixteenth to early eighteenth centuries), all of **Cremona**, north Italy (see *Italy* 6). The Tyrolese Stainers, the London Hills (these last active throughout the eighteenth and nineteenth centuries and still in business today) offer other examples of the hereditary traditions of the craft.

The cause of the superiority of the old Cremona violin has been much discussed and has by many, from the late seventeenth century onwards, been thought to lie (apart from fineness of workmanship in every part and careful choice of wood) in the composition of the varnish. Experiments carried out in London, Paris, and elsewhere, have, however, shown it is quite possible today to produce an instrument which, played behind a screen in alternation with a genuine 'Strad', is indistinguishable from it in tone, even by experienced connoisseurs.

It is sometimes stated that the violin is exceptional amongst instruments in not having changed with time. This is inexact. As Dolmetsch pointed out, the original bass bar (the internal strip of wood supporting the pressure of the bridge) has been replaced by one longer and stronger; the neck has been lengthened, broadened, and thrown more backwards; the finger-board has been prolonged to reach extreme high notes; and the bridge has been raised and its curve increased so that the bow may press harder on one string without fear of touching the next. This last change has perhaps been carried unnecessarily far, with the result that three-part and four-part chords, which could on the old violins with their flatter bridges be well sustained (as, at least, the three-part ones could be), can now be played at all only with some violence. It may be added that in the days of Tartini (when the pitch was lower) the strain on the strings was 63 lb., whereas it is now 90—which has resulted in catastrophe to many fine old instruments.

Simple as a violin appears, it consists of eighty-four different pieces.

Editors of musical journals and music critics are continually receiving letters asking the monetary value of some violin bearing a label with the name of a famous old maker (p. 1072, pl. 177. 2); it should be understood that in 999 cases out of 1,000 this merely indicates the old model followed by a modern maker.

There are, on the continent of Europe, a number of villages that have for generations supported themselves by violin making. Such are Mirecourt in the Vosges, Mittenwald in Bavaria, Markneukirchen in Saxony, and Schönbach in Czechoslovakia. On a less extensive scale violin making goes on in all countries, and many amateurs engage in it as a hobby.

5. The Bow (p. 1072, pl. **177.** 5). The earliest bows for stringed instruments resembled in shape the weapon of the same name. Later bows, such as those of the viol family, retained in a slight measure the convex curve of the stick, i.e. when the hair was tightened by turning the nut: this was so with the bows of the violin family down to the time of the eighteenth-century players (Corelli, Tartini), etc., and that of Bach, Handel, and the younger Haydn and Mozart. The present violin, viola, and violoncello bow, received its standard form at the hands of François Tourte (1747–1835) of Paris. The curve is concave, the length a little longer than the previous average and the weight a little greater.

The modern bow has the advantage (*a*) for massive playing and (*b*) for certain special effects where it is allowed to spring on and off the string (*spiccato* bowings), these last effects being in any case freely employed by the seventeenth- and early eighteenth-century violinists.

The older bow has the advantage (*a*) for delicately articulated playing, neither quite smooth (so called *détaché*) nor quite springing (spiccato), and (*b*) for playing chords in such a work as (for instance) Bach's famous Chaconne, since owing to the slightly convex shape there is less danger of the stick itself being forced down on to the string when the bow is strongly pressed upon it. Excellent bows of a pre-Tourte pattern are now being made, so facilitating the playing of the old music.

See also *Bowing* and *Expression* 3.

6. Development of Violin Technique. The development of the technique of violin playing has been gradual. The most difficult compositions of the great Corelli (a deliberately classical composer) at the end of the seventeenth century and beginning of the eighteenth are, technically, almost child's play today. Yet he and his contemporaries and successors (see entries devoted to Matteis, Vivaldi, Veracini, Tartini) laid the foundations of all that followed, the supremacy of Italy in the making of the instrument being naturally associated with a general superiority in its intelligent and artistic application, though it must be admitted that some German composers (e.g. Biber, J. J. Walther) were in some respects ahead of them in expanding the technique, especially perhaps that of chord-playing.

For some later masters who developed the art see the entries in this volume, Giardini, Pugnani, Viotti, Geminiani, Nardini, Locatelli (all Italians); Francœur, Leclair, Kreutzer, Baillot, Rode (French school); Graun, Benda, Stamitz, Wilhelm Cramer (German school). More modern masters (also treated in this volume) are Mayseder, Spohr, Paganini, Sivori, de Bériot, Ernst, Vieuxtemps, Massart, Sarasate, Marsick, Wieniawski, Ferdinand David, Joachim, Wilhelmj, Hellmesberger, Auer, Ysaÿe, Kreisler, Elman, Heifetz, Kubelik (see also *Belgium* 5).

The technique of the instrument has now been analysed to the last degree, and set out in innumerable 'methods'; good teachers are common, and a year of well-directed study probably now accomplishes at least as much as two years did a century since. There are, however, certain older compositions the really effective playing of which still remains extremely difficult, as, for instance, J. S. Bach's sonatas and partitas for unaccompanied violin, including his well-known Chaconne, which is a movement in the D minor partita (see remarks under 5).

The manner of holding the violin was for long variable and generally defective. There was not even agreement as to whether the chin should be on the left or right of the tail piece. The chin-rest is said to have been introduced by Spohr (1784–1859) and as late as the end of the nineteenth century was decried by some players as a useless innovation.

7. Viola Playing has been relatively a somewhat neglected art. Mid-eighteenth-century composers commonly made the violas simply double the cellos and basses, and it was one of the reforms of Stamitz (q.v.) to give it again an independent part. Not a great deal of original composition has been provided for it. The Englishman Lionel Tertis (1876–1975) showed himself an enthusiast for this instrument, and carried its playing to heights perhaps never before reached; he increased its repertory by rearranging many violin compositions for it and persuading a large number of eminent composers to write special works for viola (sonatas, concertos, etc.). Hindemith (q.v.), beginning about twenty years later, showed himself to be a great virtuoso of the instrument.

The music for the viola is notated mainly in the alto clef, the treble clef being used for the higher notes.

8. Violoncello Playing. The development of violoncello playing has followed a similar path to that of violin playing. Amongst famous cellists who have contributed to it and who are treated in this volume are Duport, Romberg, Servais, Piatti, and Popper. In the twentieth century the influence of the Catalan virtuoso Casals has been important. See *Capotasto*.

9. Double-bass Playing has had its virtuosi in Dragonetti (1763–1846), Bottesini (1821–89), and Koussevitzky (1876–1951), the last also famous as an orchestral conductor; such solo players as these use a rather small-sized instrument, which can 'speak' more rapidly than the normal one and is easier to manipulate in passages of agility. The double-bass used for solo playing is often tuned up a tone for brilliance. The double-bass players were the last to discard the convex bow (see 5), which with them was still in general use at the opening of the twentieth century (in a very stiff and heavy form), and also a rather debased version of the viol method of bowing (see *Viol Family* 2 i). Even now in some German orchestras the older bow and bowing still persist.

The notation of the double-bass, in order to avoid excessive use of leger lines, shows the music an octave higher than its sound.

10. Repertory. The more important part of the repertory of the instruments of the violin family will be found described under the headings *Chamber Music* (which includes compositions of the type of sonata for one bowed instrument and pianoforte) and *Concerto*. In addition there exists a certain quantity of music for one instrument of the violin family without keyboard or other accompaniment, e.g. Bach's three sonatas and three partitas for violin alone and six suites for violoncello alone.

In modern times Reger has provided for violin alone seven sonatas and a number of preludes and fugues, Tovey sonatas for violin alone and violoncello alone (also one for two violoncellos), and so forth; indeed there has been a considerable amount of activity in this department of composition during the twentieth century. The double-bass repertory is of course small; a curiosity is Dubensky's Fugue for ten double-basses. For the position of the double-bass in chamber music see *Chamber Music* 2. Van Dieren (q.v.) left a string quartet (very difficult) with double-bass instead of violoncello.

11. References in other articles.

Italy 6; *Belgium* 5; *Pitch* 3; *Acoustics* 3, 11; *Sonata* 3, 10 a b c; *Concerto* 2, 6; *Electric Musical Instruments* 2; *Vuillaume*; *Viole-ténor*; *Stroh Violin*, etc.; *Violinda*; *Profession* 3; *Scandinavia* 3 (for Hardanger Fiddle).

VIOLIN HARMONIKA. See *Nail Fiddle*.

VIOLIN, MECHANICAL. See *Mechanical Reproduction of Music* 8, 9.

VIOLINO, VIOLINI (It.). 'Violin, violins.'

VIOLINO PICCOLO. See *Violin Family* 2.

VIOLIN PLAYING AND EQUAL TEMPERAMENT. See *Temperament* 10.

VIOLON (Fr.). 'Violin.'

VIOLONCELLE (Fr.). 'Violoncello.' See *Violin Family* 2, 8.

VIOLONCELLO (It.). See *Violin Family* 2, 8; *Organ* 14 III.

VIOLONCELLO PICCOLO. See *Violin Family* 2.

VIOLONE (It.). See *Viol Family* 4 a; *Violin Family* 2 d; *Organ* 14 III.

VIOTTI, GIOVANNI BATTISTA (p. 1096, pl. **181.** 5). Born in Piedmont in 1755 and died in London in 1824, aged sixty-nine. He was the son and pupil of a blacksmith and his first performances, at the age of eight, were given upon a small violin bought at the village fair. He lived to be regarded as the foremost violinist of his time and is looked upon as the father of modern violin technique. He played before Frederick the Great, Catherine the Great, and Marie Antoinette, served in the National Guard at the French Revolution, became a wine merchant in London, and helped to found the Philharmonic Society, was Director of the Opera in Paris under Louis XVIII, returned to London, and died in misery—heavily in money debt but leaving a rich legacy of fine instrumental compositions and a tradition of performance that, through his numerous pupils and theirs, has come down to the present day.

See *Concerto* 6 b; *Chamber Music* 6, Period III (1755).

VIRBÈS. See *Pianoforte* 17.

VIRDUNG, SEBASTIAN. In 1511, at Basle, he published his *Musica getutscht* (i.e. *Musica gedeutscht*), the most ancient book we possess describing the various musical instruments and hence (especially as it is illustrated) a very much valued source of musicological information. It has, in modern times, been reprinted in facsimile (1882).

See reference under *Jew's Harp*.

VIRELAI. A medieval French song-form (from *Vire*, in Normandy), with a refrain before and after each stanza.

See *Rondeau*.

VIRGIL PRACTICE CLAVIER. This is, in effect, a piano keyboard, without any sound-producing mechanism except that which can be used to provide a slight click on descent or ascent of the key, or on both descent and ascent, as desired. The merging of the upward click of one note and the downward of the next indicate absolute legato. The degree of resistance of the keyboard can be regulated at will.

The inventor was A. K. Virgil, an American, and he produced elaborate books of exercises to accompany its use. In the last years of the nineteenth century the apparatus had a vogue in Britain and it is still used there and in the United States.

VIRGINAL, VIRGINALS. See *Harpsichord Family* 3; p. 193, pl. **39.** 3, 4, 6, 7.

VIRGINAL, DOUBLE. See *Double* 1.

VIRGINAL, MECHANICAL. See *Mechanical Reproduction of Music* 3.

VIRGINIAN MINSTRELS. See *Negro Minstrels.*

VIRGINIA REEL. See *Sir Roger de Coverley.*

VIRTUOSO. The ordinary English dictionary meaning of the word is 'Person with special knowledge of or taste for works of art or virtu; person skilled in the mechanical part of a fine art' (*Concise Oxford Dictionary*).

In English usage the former part of this definition was the more in force during the eighteenth century and the latter part is the more in force at present—with a special application to music, which now rather tends to monopolize the term. The word is employed to designate (especially) an instrumental performer who can render the most difficult passages with the greatest ease and rapidity. Such an individual may or may not be at the same time a good 'interpreter' (see *Interpretation*).

There is a general inclination on the part of the big public to value virtuosity for its own sake, whereas it is, properly, a means to an end.

The reward of the instrumental virtuoso in glory and cash is among the greatest of any honest profession, and it has gone on increasing. In the late 1890s Paderewski made a record by returning from an American tour with a net gain of £46,000, but after the first World War (and after a period of five years during which, as he said, he had not touched the piano) he made in two years £208,000, and it was stated that the pianist Hofmann, the violinists Heifetz and Kreisler, and the vocalists Galli-Curci, Schumann-Heink, McCormack, and Chaliapin were about that time doing equally well.

In part, of course, this business success comes from the exploitation, by able concert agents, of the public's love of a personality in any sphere.

Music requiring an unusual technical skill for its performance is often spoken of as 'Virtuoso Music'—sometimes with such an inflexion of the voice as gives the expression a satirical tinge, suggesting that difficulty does not necessarily imply worth.

See also *Concerto* 3.

VISÉE, ROBERT DE (*c.* 1650–1725). See *Guitar.*

VISETTI, ALBERT (1846–1928). See reference under *Tarantella.*

VISHNEGRADSKY. See *Vyshnegradsky.*

VITALI, FILIPPO. Born in Florence about 1590 and died there in 1653. He was a priest, a member of the Vatican choir, and a composer of sacred music, madrigals, and an opera *L'Aretusa*, performed in Rome in 1620 and said to be the earliest one there heard. He is important in the history of the new style which came in with the beginning of the seventeenth century (see *Opera* 1, and cf. *Caccini*).

VITALI (Father and Son).

GIOVANNI BATTISTA (born at Bologna in 1632 and died there in 1692, aged sixty) and TOMASO ANTONIO (born at Bologna in 1663 and died in Modena in 1745, aged eighty-two. Both famous violinists and composers for strings. The father's sonatas (the early type of work bearing this name; see *Sonata* 2, 3) had influence on the development of form; the son is best known today by a much-played Chaconne.

VITALIAN, POPE. See *Church Music* 4.

VITALITY IN MUSIC. See *Quality in Music* 2.

VITAL SPARK. See *Methodism and Music* 6.

VITE, VITEMENT (Fr.). 'Quick', 'quickly'.

VITO (Sp.). A type of Baile (q.v.), danced in Andalusia.

VITRY, PHILIPPE DE (1291–1361). See *France* 3.

VITTORIA. See *Victoria.*

VIVACE (It.). 'Vivacious.' So *Vivacetto*, 'rather vivacious'; *Vivacissimo*, 'very vivacious'. *Vivacità*, *Vivacezza*, 'vivacity'.

VIVALDI, ANTONIO (p. 517, pl. **94.** 1). Born in Venice in 1678 and died in Vienna in 1741 (not, as usually stated, in Venice in 1743) aged sixty-three. He was a noted violinist and a prolific and evidently popular composer—Bach's contemporary and in some respects his model as to the composition of music for strings, etc. Especially important are his concertos (not such in the modern sense; see *Concerto* 2), nearly four hundred in number. Most of these are for strings but some are for oboe (about thirty known), for bassoon (about forty known), for flute, etc. He composed also at least forty operas, and, moreover, served as an active opera impresario. A Latin oratorio, *Juditha*, has dramatic qualities.

Vivaldi had the advantage of a musical father, who undertook his training. He took Orders and was known as *il prete rosso* ('the red-headed priest'), but he did not long continue to say Mass on account of an infirmity which hampered him. He was for thirty-six years in charge of the music of one of the famous Venetian conservatories for girls (for a description of these see *Schools of Music*), but he seems to have managed also to travel.

See *Violin Family* 6; *Sonata* 10 b (for his contemporaries, etc.); *Germany* 4 (influence on Bach, etc.); *Folia*; *Misattributed Compositions*; *Italy* 6; *Viol Family* 4 f; *Arrangement*; *Opus*; *Bird Music*.

VIVAMENTE (It.). In 'lively' fashion.

VIVE (Fr.). 'Lively' (*Vif* is the masculine form of the word; *Vivement* is the adverb). **VIVENTE** (It.). In 'lively' fashion.

VIVES, AMADEO (1871–1932). Spanish composer of a number of operas and over sixty zarzuelas.

VIVEZZA (It.). 'Life' (liveliness).

VIVIDO (It.). 'Vivacious', 'lively' (same as *Vivace*).

VIVO (It.). 'Lively'; *Vivissimo* is the superlative.

VL. Short for 'violin'.

VLADIGEROF, PANTSCHO. Born at Sofia in 1899. He studied at the conservatory of his native city, of the staff of which he later became a member. He has written piano and violin concertos and other orchestral works, including a *Bulgarian Suite*. All his work reflects the general character of the folk music of Bulgaria.

VOCAL CORDS. See *Voice* 2, 3, 4.

VOCALISE (Fr.). See below.

VOCALIZE. As a verb this means to sing on a vowel, as, for instance, in the French exercises called Vocalises (cf. *Solfeggio*), in the extended 'Divisions' (q.v.) of a Handel or Bach vocal solo, or the old Italian opera Arias (see *Aria*), in the similar passages of choral music (madrigals, eighteenth-century oratorios, etc.), or in plainsong (q.v.).

Vocalization in such music as the above has either a decorative or an emotional value or both: it can be a mere display of tight-rope performance on the vocal cords or it can express joy or even deep sorrow—as frequently in Bach and Handel (cf. *Coloratura*).

See a reference to a 'Sonata-Vocalise' under *Medtner*.

VOCALIZZO (It., plural *Vocalizzi*). Same as Fr. *Vocalise* (see above).

VOCAL SCORE. See *Score*.

VOCE, VOCI (It.). 'Voice', 'voices'. So *Colla voce*, 'with the voice', i.e. the accompanist carefully taking his time, etc., from the singer.

VOCE DI PETTO; VOCE DI TESTA. 'Chest voice'; 'head voice'; see *Voice* 4 (references to 'Registers').

VOCES AEQUALES (Lat.), **VOCI EGUALI** (It.). 'Equal voices' (q.v.).

VOCE UMANA ('Human Voice'). An eighteenth-century name for an instrument of the oboe family of the pitch of the present cor anglais.

VOCI. See *Voce*.

VODORINSKI, ANTON. See *Ketèlbey*.

VOGEL, VLADIMIR. Born in Moscow in 1896. His father was German, his mother Russian. He was in youth an associate of Scriabin and at a later period a pupil and then assistant of Busoni in Berlin. He has also resided in France and in Switzerland. His compositions (chamber music, orchestral, piano, etc.) first attracted wide notice through performances at the International Festivals of the Society for Contemporary Music. Some of his works are on a very large scale. He has introduced a new form which he calls *Ritmica*, 'consisting of a movement based on the development of an initial rhythmic figure'. The twelve-note system (see *Note-row*) is employed in some works.

VOGELQUARTETT (Haydn). See *Nicknamed Compositions* 12; *Bird Music* (towards end).

VOGELSANG, ANDREAS. See *Ornithoparcus*.

VOGLER, GEORG JOSEPH—known as Abbé or Abt Vogler.

Born at Würzburg in 1749 and died at Darmstadt in 1814, aged nearly sixty-five. A tireless experimenter in acoustics and inventor of instrumental devices, weaver of harmonic theory, organist, composer, teacher, and author. Amongst his pupils were Weber and Meyerbeer. Half a century after his death Browning so idealized him in a poem that he is now immortal.

See reference under *Reed-Organ Family* 1.

VOGLIA (It.). 'Longing.'

VOICE

(For illustrations see p. 1089, pl. 180.)

1. Introductory. The voice is a musical instrument, like any other, but with the additional power of framing the sounds called words and allying these with its tones.

Any scientific study of the voice has to include these two sides of its activity, i.e. we can look on the voice as a tone-producing instrument with a word-producing apparatus attached, or (perhaps not so scientifically) as a word-producing instrument with a tone-producing apparatus attached.

The singer has, in the training he undergoes, to take account of both functions, and weakness on either side brings failure with one or other of those two classes of listener, (a) the class which thinks most of the 'tune' of a song, and (b) the class which thinks most of the poem—and, of course, too, with that third class which keeps its mental balance and demands that the compromise (for song is a compromise) shall be fairly carried out.

The mechanism of the instrument and the functioning of this mechanism are briefly treated in the present article, which is, then, in nature scientific—artistic considerations in the use of the instrument being treated in the article *Singing*, and types of music for performance on the instrument in the article *Song*.

2. The General Plan of the Instrument (pl. **180.** 1–5). In looking for another musical instrument with which to compare the human voice the organ seems most suitable—or rather that part of an organ known as a reed pipe (see *Organ*).

A reed pipe has as its sound-producing agent a vibrating strip of metal. Beneath is the apparatus for wind-supply (wind-chest, bellows, etc.); above is the pipe itself which, as a resonating cavity, modifies the sound of the vibrating reed, so that instead of being a mere squeak this becomes a fully audible and pleasant musical sound. Similarly the human voice consists of a sound-producing agent (two vibrating strips of cartilage—the 'Vocal Cords'), with below it an apparatus for wind supply (lungs) and the tube from this to the vocal cords, and above it the resonating cavity (mouth, nose, and upper part of throat).

(3) Pipe ↑	(3) Mouth and nose, ↑ etc.
(2) Reed ↑	(2) Vocal cords ↑
(1) Bellows and wind-chest supplying	(1) Lungs
ORGAN	VOICE

The vocal cords are enclosed in a sort of box which is (especially in men) to be seen projecting at the front of the throat and is colloquially called the 'Adam's Apple', from the fancy that a piece of that fatal fruit stuck at that particular spot—and perhaps that a good deal of sin still originates there.

The human reed instrument has two very obvious elements of superiority over its mechanical counterpart, the organ reed pipe:

1. The organ reed can produce only one fixed note, so that a whole row of reed pipes, appropriately tuned, is necessary to produce the musical scale, whereas the human reeds can, by changes of tension, produce any note within a wide compass.
2. The organ reed, whilst it takes on both character and power from the addition of

the resonating chamber, the pipe, has only one fixed character of tone and one fixed power, whereas the power of the human reed can be increased or diminished by a greater or smaller air pressure from below, and its character of tone modified in an infinite number of ways by changes of shape in that part of what corresponds to the pipe of the organ reed which we call the mouth.

The differences, then, are those we often find when a natural thing and its artificial counterpart are compared—the natural is the more versatile, flexible, adaptable (the four legs of a deer and the four wheels of an automobile; the wings of a swallow and the propeller and wings of an aeroplane; the human hand, with its thousand uses, and any piece of machinery, necessarily designed for one use—and so on).

At the same time we must, in justice, recognize a third difference, in which the human-made apparatus has an advantage over the nature-made—in the organ the intake and outgo of air occur at two different parts of the instrument, and so can go on uninterruptedly, whereas with the human voice the same air passages and apparatus serve for both intake and outgo, and hence these two operations can occur only in alternation. Thus the sustaining power of an organ reed is infinite, whereas that of the human reed is limited to a few seconds.

It is now our business to consider the three parts of the instrument separately, restricting, so far as possible, the statement of physiological and acoustical fact to what will be found interesting and enlightening by the singer and teacher of singing. We will take in turn: (a) the Wind Supply, (b) the Sound-Producer, and (c) the Resonating Agents, i.e. (a) the Lungs, etc., (b) the Vocal Cords, and (c) the Upper part of the Throat, the Mouth, and the Nose.

3. The Wind Supply. There is no necessity, in a short article in such a work of reference as the present, to describe in detail the method by which this is obtained.

The quantity of air needed in singing is much greater than that needed in ordinary breathing (which is why special exercises are desirable).

As air is taken in, the diaphragm (or partition between the upper and lower portions of the body) descends and the ribs expand, and thus space is provided for the inflated lungs. The proper relation, in breathing-in, between the descent of the diaphragm and the expansion of the lungs ('Diaphragmatic breathing' and 'Costal breathing') is important and must be studied under a master or from books. There are anatomical reasons why diaphragmatic breathing is more pronounced in men and costal in women; both, however, use both methods simultaneously and all the time.

In breathing-out this relation is also important, both from considerations of health (the abdomen must not be put under too great pressure, especially by women) and on account of the necessity of delicate control of force (production of all degrees of loud and soft tone at will) and that of steadiness (avoidance of involuntary 'tremolo').

Capacity and control have to be developed both because in singing the emission of breath has often to be maintained over a long period for a sustained note or a group of notes, and also because breath must often be taken in abnormally quickly in order to interrupt the music as little as possible.

There is a particular method of breath emission the value of which has been much insisted on in the past but is now discredited by many teachers and even held to be harmful. Above the true vocal cords are two membranes called the *False Vocal Cords*. They can be closed and then quickly released, which constitutes the action of coughing. This action can be used as a method of attack of a note, but it associates a slight coughing sound with the commencement of the note, and, though many fine singers use it, is said to impose a strain. It is called the *Coup de Glotte* or 'Shock of the Glottis' (the glottis being the opening between the true vocal cords). It may be called 'unnatural' in the sense in which an attempt to control the stopping and starting of an automobile solely by the use of the brake would be unnatural—and like that it is a desperate wearer of the mechanism, as teachers who have pupils sent to them by throat specialists for curative lessons are always finding.

The sound method is the unvaried use of the control of air pressure from the source of air supply, i.e. an 'open-throat control'.

A good lung-capacity and perfect control of the breath are amongst the most valuable assets of any singer, and some of the great singers have possessed them to a remarkable degree. The teacher, William Shakespeare told of a feat of the famous bass Lablache (1794–1858), narrated by one who was present. At a dinner one day he 'sang a long note from piano to forte and back to piano; then drank a glass of wine without having breathed; then sang a chromatic scale up the octave in trills, still in the same breath; and finally blew out a candle with his mouth open'.

For a fault in singing often resulting from imperfect control of the breathing see *Tremolo and Vibrato*.

4. The Sound-Production. The elastic vocal cords are tiny—roughly half an inch in length in a man and less in a woman or child. During the intake of breath they are wide apart; during the outgo, when sound is to be produced, they are brought close together, and the passage between (or 'Glottis') being thus constricted the friction of the air is considerable enough to cause vibration—or, in other words, a series of very rapid puffs occurs.

The varying of the tension (tighter for high notes; slacker for low) is one of the amazing phenomena of nature. By some mysterious means, a particular note being imagined, the cords are immediately and subconsciously adjusted to the exact tension required; the breath is then expelled and the imagined note is produced. This is the equivalent of a violinist turning the pegs of his instrument without sounding the strings, then starting to play and finding the strings perfectly tuned.

'Inflexibility' or 'flexibility' in a voice results from the presence of thick, clumsy cords or lighter, more easily adjustable ones.

The good or bad quality of the tone produced, as also its personal characteristics (which enable us to recognize a friend in the dark by the mere sound of his voice), depend upon the number and identity and the relative strength and weakness of the upper partials heard (this is so with all instruments: see *Partials*; *Acoustics* 8). To some extent, apparently, the manner in which the cords vibrate, influencing this factor, can be controlled by the singer—again very mysteriously. But various upper partials are reinforced (partly involuntarily and partly under the control of the will) by the resonating chambers, to be discussed shortly. The differences of quality between one voice and another, or between one voice before training and the same after training, are all a matter of the production or non-production, and the greater or lesser reinforcement of those upper partials which create an agreeable timbre and those which do not.

The same general cause lies behind the differences of quality in different parts of the compass of a particular voice—called its 'Registers'. The physiological means by which these different registers are produced are much debated. It is a common thing for musicians who are not singing teachers to smile at those who are, on account of their striking differences of opinion as to methods of training and the obstinacy with which they oppose one another's views. But there is this excuse—that the physiologists and phonologists (trained men of science, not 'temperamental' artists) differ just as widely and as determinedly. As they are now supplied with devices (the laryngoscope, X-rays, and films) enabling them actually to see the vocal cords at work it seems strange that any differences of opinion can exist. (It may even be stated that individual observers, such as E. G. White, have maintained that the vocal cords are not the seat of origin of vocal sound, and have won a certain measure of support.)

As a familiar example of the phenomenon of 'register' may be instanced the striking difference between the quality of the lower and higher notes of the boy's voice. The lower notes are robust and 'deep-coloured', the upper notes are 'pure' and 'silvery'. (The difference almost amounts to that between the tone of an oboe and that of a flute.) The position of the 'break' between these two registers depends greatly on training, the usual effort being to keep it as low as possible so as to have uniform tone for the most used part of the compass of the voice. It may be about C (first line below treble stave), but in singing an upward scale it is likely to occur higher and in singing a downward one to occur lower, whilst the degree of loudness also

See *Violin Family* 8 and 9 on page 1084

1. THE 'CELLO IN 1850—with no tail pin. (The player is Sebastian Lee.)

2. J. L. DUPORT (1749–1819)—a famous player who laid the foundations for the modern system of fingering

3. BERNHARD ROMBERG (1767–1841). Touring performer of high repute, composer of 'cello concertos, &c., and author of a 'Method'

4. PIATTI (1822–1901). Celebrated virtuoso, from 1844 much associated with Joachim; composer and editor of 'cello music

5. POPPER (1843–1913). Of high repute as player and composer of 'cello music

6. CASALS (1876–1973). The greatest 'cellist of the 20th century; also conductor and composer

7. BOTTESINI (1821–89). The most accomplished double-bass player ever known

8. THE OCTO-BASS, invented by J. B. Vuillaume (1850) and praised by Berlioz

9. LINDLEY AND DRAGONETTI in 1836—the famous Yorkshire 'cellist and Venetian Double Bass—close friends who for half a century were seen playing at the same desk in all the chief London and provincial concerts

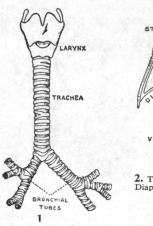

LARYNX

TRACHEA

BRONCHIAL TUBES

1

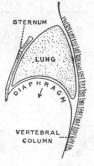

STERNUM

LUNG

DIAPHRAGM

VERTEBRAL COLUMN

STERNUM

LUNG

DIAPHRAGM

VERTEBRAL COLUMN

2. THE LUNGS before and after contraction of the Diaphragm. The black portion shows the increase in lung volume

4, 5. THE LARYNX as seen with the Laryngoscope

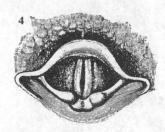

4

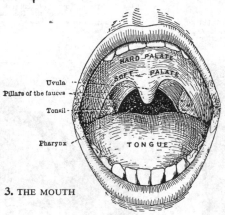

HARD PALATE

SOFT PALATE

Uvula
Pillars of the fauces
Tonsil
Pharynx

TONGUE

3. THE MOUTH

Median glosso-epiglottic fold
Tuberculum epiglotticum   Dorsum of tongue   **5**

Plica vocalis

Vallecula

Ventriculus laryngis

Recessus piriformis

Ary-epiglottic fold

Processus vocalis of arytænoid cartilage   Rings of trachea

Epiglottis

Plica ventricularis

Tuberculum cuneiforme

Tuberculum corniculatum

AI

EE

AH

NASAL CAVITY

PALATE

TONGUE

OH

OO

Pharynx

Larynx

6. THE MOUTH CAVITY when uttering the five vowels

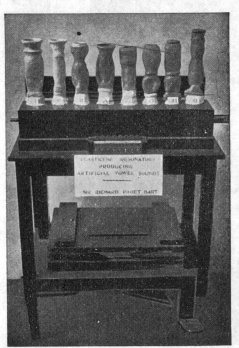

7. ARTIFICIAL VOWEL PRODUCTION by Sir Richard Paget's Plasticine Models on Lord Rayleigh's Organ

affects it, it being easier in soft singing to avoid dropping into the robuster and rougher type of tone.

The terms 'Head Register' and 'Chest Register' are often given to the higher and lower ranges of the voice with their characteristic tone-colourings. This does not imply that the head and chest, respectively, play any differing part in the production of tone of the two qualities and of the two pitches, but merely that sensation can be felt in head and chest respectively when the two registers are in use. A 'Middle Register' is also spoken of and there are other terms in use. These are handy terms—nothing more; unfortunately they often mislead.

For higher notes more pressure of air is required than for medium or low; this is because the vocal cords are tauter, and hence require more force to set them in vibration, and is the explanation of the sense of effort connected with the singing of high notes. The often considerable upward and downward extension of compass by means of training is probably due to the acquiring of the knack of setting into vibration the cords when they would be, normally, too tightly stretched or too slack to respond to the air pressure by any regular vibration.

An explanation may here be given of what is known as 'breathy' singing. Properly the bringing together of the vocal cords and the emission of the breath should be simultaneous. If the emission of the breath slightly precedes the bringing together of the cords some air necessarily escapes workless, and thus causes the effect mentioned. More definitely and violently carried out this kind of breathy singing degenerates into the use of unintentional aspirates (see 13 below).

If whilst the vocal cords are vibrating they are never properly brought together, the 'gas escape' effect is heard not merely at the opening of every note but continuously.

5. Falsetto and Castrato Production; the Boy's Voice.

There is a peculiar type of tone (thin and colourless) called falsetto. It is possible only in the higher range of a voice, generally beginning where the more natural tones leave off. It is usually said to be produced by the vibration of the mere edges of the vocal cords, and with a high larynx position. The adult male alto is a tenor or bass who by practice has obtained facility in the use of his falsetto range. This voice is principally found in Britain, being in use in church and cathedral choirs. A considerable repertory of English church music and glees is based on its availability (see Alto Voice; Glee).

The jodelling of Switzerland and the Tyrol is merely an ingenious mixture of the normal and falsetto voices, a tune for jodelling being provided with lower and higher notes or passages, enabling the two registers to be used in alternation.

Male altos were a feature of the nineteenth-century American Negro troupes of entertainers.

During the sixteenth century a special type of falsettist adult male soprano, producing his effects by some method of which the secret is now lost, was common in Spain. The Sistine Choir in Rome imported such singers in the days before, at the opening of the seventeenth century, it stooped to the use of Castrati (see below).

Normally at puberty the boy's voice becomes for a period more or less uncontrollable, owing to the sudden but unequal growth of the vocal cords and associated ligaments and muscles. Then it settles into a voice of roughly an octave lower than before. No corresponding important change takes place in the girl's voice, though the vocal cords lengthen a little; some authorities say that there is a period of unsettlement with girls also, and others deny it. This is one of the many disputed points in vocal science, as, in vocal practice, is that of whether boys and girls should be allowed to sing during the period of puberty.

On this last point it may be added that, extensive experiments having been carried out in several places, it has come to be seen that, broadly speaking, boys whose voices gradually *slide* lower at puberty may be allowed to continue singing in a quiet way, whilst those whose voices *break*, i.e. change suddenly and considerably, should not sing until the adult voice, with some measure of control, has been attained. (See Alto-Tenor.)

During the seventeenth and eighteenth centuries a class of voice now extinct was common—the artificial male soprano or contralto: this was obtained by an operation in boyhood upon the sexual organs, which prevented the development of some of the characteristics of manhood including that of the lengthening of the vocal cords and corresponding changes of the surrounding parts. Thus the boy's voice was perpetuated. So popular was this type of voice that it led to a considerable neglect of the natural man's voice; there were even operas in which the whole of the male singers were 'Sopranists' and 'Contraltists' (Musico was another name for a man of this type). Handel's early friend Mattheson, writing of the years when they were associated in the Hamburg opera-house (1703–6), says, 'At that time no man was called a great singer unless he had this sort of voice' (note in his translation of Mainwaring's Handel). Probably the last two of these artificial freaks were the famous Velluti (1781–1861), who was heard in London in 1829, and Pergetti, who was heard there as late as 1844.

The most famous castrato singer who ever lived (and perhaps, without qualification, the most famous singer) was Farinelli (1705–82), who spent a quarter of a century at the court of Spain, and during the last ten years of the lifetime of Philip V sang to him every evening the same four songs and nothing else (see Ornaments or Graces 1; also p. 688, pl. 115. 5).

6. The Resonating Agents. Before this section of the article is read it is recommended that the reader should turn to the article *Acoustics* and read there at least the section devoted to the subject of 'Resonance' (20).

Just as the reed of a toy trumpet, if removed from the trumpet, becomes a mere squeaker, so do the vocal cords without the resonating passages attached to them. That portion of the neck which lies between the vocal cords and the mouth is of great importance as adding fullness to the tone, and so are the mouth and nose. It has sometimes been stated that it is an error to suppose that the chest has much resonating influence, as the spongy character of the lungs would seem to be necessarily unfavourable to resonance; yet it must be admitted that in speaking and singing at a low pitch a strong sense of vibration can be felt in the chest.[1] The frontal sinuses (or open spaces lying above the nose and communicating with it by small orifices) have apparently considerable value as resonators: it is said that the Australian aborigines have a great want of resonance in their speech due to the small size of these sinuses.

All the resonating chambers or passages mentioned above as of importance are in direct communication with the air which has passed through the vocal cords, i.e. they are not mere recipients of vibration communicated through solid bodies (as the resonating chamber of a drum) but are also the recipients of vibrations communicated by the air stream itself after this has been set in vibration by the vocal cords.

From a study of sections 6 and 8 in the article *Acoustics* it will be seen that no ordinary sound communicates a mere single frequency. Almost every sound is compound; there are many different vibration-frequencies superposed on one another—the vibration-frequency of the various upper partials of a musical note being combined with the main (less rapid) vibration-frequency, that of the 'fundamental' from which these others derive. A resonating chamber such as the special globular resonators devised by Helmholtz is tuned to a special note; thus if a set of these resonators be placed where they will be affected by a neighbouring sounding body, those will come into action which are in unison with either the fundamental note sounded or any of its upper partials.

To illustrate this point we may turn for a moment to a set of tuned resonators of another kind to be found in any house—the strings of a piano when the right pedal is depressed (the strings being thus freed from the dampers).

[1] A medical authority to whom this article has been submitted writes as follows: 'The thoracic cavity possesses a considerable quality of resonance (instance the 'drumming' of certain apes on their chests, the character of stethoscopic or phonedoscopic sounds). The nature of the lung tissue does not enter into this; the organs are permeated by a system of branching tubes of decreasing diameter (the bronchi and bronchioli), which lead ultimately to the actual air-sacs. Moreover, the skeletal framework of the thorax (the so-called 'cage') forms a structure of a highly resonant nature (circular hoops—ribs—of semi-rigid bone attached to the spine and the sternum, but free to move at their sides).'

Sing a note into the opened piano and you will hear not only your fundamental note (the note you *intended* to sing) reproduced by resonance from the string corresponding to it in pitch, but also the many upper partials that you have involuntarily created—the octave, the fifth above that, the double octave, the third above that, and so on (see *Acoustics* 7), with possibly some other and non-harmonic upper partials if your voice is a harsh one and your tone thus includes upper partials that do not belong to the authentic harmonic series.

It will be possible for acute ears to verify, by this use of the piano strings as resonators, the facts that in bright voices the upper partials of higher pitch are prominent, in 'full' voices those of lower pitch, whilst in voices of very smooth quality the upper partials of lower and higher pitch are pretty equal in intensity.

The passage of the neck, above mentioned, is to some extent capable of unconscious tuning so as to respond to a tone sung, or to some of its upper partials. The spaces of the nose and the sinuses cannot be so tuned, but will always find some upper partials of the tone to which to respond. The mouth is a very delicately tuneable resonator, or rather pair of resonators, and must in a moment be specially considered.

A point of some importance to vocalists is this—that a badly tuned resonator in any instrument is able to 'work back' to the original sounding body, and to deflect it somewhat from its proper pitch (cf. *Acoustics* 5). In the instrument called the human voice this imposes a strain on the muscles of the vocal cord in order to counteract the influence, which is fatiguing and damaging to the organ. That a singer should acquire the knack of listening as much as possible to his resonances seems, then, to be important.

7. The Production of Vowel Sounds (p. 1089, pl. **180.** 6). The mouth itself constitutes two resonators by virtue of the use of the tongue, which in speech assumes a more or less arched position, dividing the space into two distinct but connected cavities. By a wonderfully delicate but subconscious adjustment of the tongue the size of each of these two resonators can be increased or diminished. (It is well that nature has relegated the duty to the subconscious, as the conscious could never undertake so complex a function.)

It is by this adjustment that all the varieties of vowel sounds are created. The reason why, despite the differences in the mouth cavities of the two sexes, and also of children and adults, the vowel-producing notes (and hence the vowels themselves) remain the same, is that the note of a Helmholtz resonator (or a resonator on its principles) differs not according to its size but according to its size *in relation to its opening*, and as the mouth capacities of the two sexes and various ages differ so the mouth openings differ with them, thus maintaining the same proportions.

The nature and origin of vowel sounds has

been under investigation since the beginning of the nineteenth century. In 1828 Professor Robert Willis (q.v.), of Cambridge, proved that each vowel was connected with a particular upper partial note evoked by resonance in the cavity of the mouth. In 1860 Helmholtz, having introduced his detective resonators (see allusion under *Acoustics* 20), found that certain of the vowels depended upon *two* resonances set up simultaneously in the mouth. In 1924 Sir Richard Paget, in a paper read to the Musical Association of London (later greatly amplified in his book, *Human Speech*), showed, as a result of more minute experimentation, that *every* vowel is the result of two such resonances.

These resonances are sounds of *definite pitch*, that is to say, a particular vowel effect is not the result of such and such numerically defined upper partials of the note at the moment being reproduced by the vocal cords (it might be the third and twelfth upper partials of such a note, or the ninth and the eleventh), but the result of two sounds in *absolute pitch*, evoked by the passage of air from the throat and also, by resonance, by whichever of the upper partials of the note is capable of evoking them (and, amongst the large number of upper partials present in any given note sounded, the right one to set in action any particular resonator can generally be found). With the agency of absolutely pitched sounds in the production of vowels compare a similar agency in the production of timbre (under *Acoustics* 6).

The association of vowel effect with fixed pitches can easily be demonstrated by every one in a personal experiment. It may be that the unpractised ear will detect only the principal of the two sounds, but that will be enough for the present purpose. Here are the three experiments:

1. Frame the mouth as if to sound *ah* (but without sounding it) and then tap on the teeth with a pencil ; a low tone is heard. Now frame it as if to sound *ee* and tap again; a higher tone is heard. Alternate the two shapes of the mouth and the difference of pitch will be clearly perceived.

2. Frame the mouth again, alternately on each of these two vowel sounds and clap the hand smartly upon the mouth after each, so as to drive air into it; again the low note is heard from the one shape and the high from the other —but acute ears with a little practice will also hear a note below each of these.

3. (The best of the three experiments.) Frame the mouth again alternately for *ah* and *ee* and merely breathe through the mouth, i.e. whisper. It will be found that each of these vowels has its fixed pitch, the *ah* a low one and the *ee* a high one, and that this pitch cannot be varied by any effort whatever. The whispers, but greatly magnified, are, as we may say, what attach themselves to our tone when we are speaking or singing and enable us to utter distinctive vowels.

From a speech point of view the utility of the larynx (the 'voice box', with its vocal cords) is

purely as adding *power* to the vowels. Everything that can be said can be whispered (which requires no larynx at all), but whispered sounds carry only one-tenth to one-twentieth of the distance of those which have even a little laryngeal tone added.

In all the above experiments a little practice may be necessary, as the ear does not easily pick out the pitch of sounds of an unfamiliar character, but after a few minutes' trial the experiments should be conclusive. (In any attempt to identify the actual notes associated with particular vowels the reader should beware of the tendency to think them an octave lower than they really are.)

The following scale of most vowel-notes has been worked out from a table given by Sir Richard Paget, one compiled from observation of his own speech. Necessarily it is only approximate, for we all differ from one another in pronunciation, at least slightly and sometimes considerably, and even differ from ourselves, pronouncing what is nominally the same vowel somewhat differently in different words:

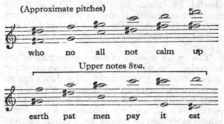

(Approximate pitches)

who   no   all   not   calm   up

Upper notes 8*va.*

earth   pat   men   pay   it   eat

If the reader will whisper these words in turn (but try the first and last to begin with) he will at any rate perceive the rising scale of the upper notes, and in some cases at least feel that there are other notes below them, though he may not be able to identify these latter.

William Shakespeare, in his *Plain Words on Singing*, says, 'When, by assiduous practice, we succeed in correctly tuning these whispers, we have an exact pattern of the shape of the spaces which should form themselves . . . during singing', and he 'gladly testifies' to the great assistance he and his pupils have derived from the practice of tuning these whispers. He suggests the following sentence for memorizing the vowels: 'Who knows aught of art must learn, and then take his ease' (the second clause of this sentence being, however, morally questionable).

It should be added, in reference to the adaptation of the scale of Sir Richard Paget given above, that this being a compilation from that investigator's table in which he shows merely the limits between which can range each note of the two notes producing the vowel, the proper *relation* of these two notes is probably not accurately shown. If this table were compiled afresh so as to show not the limits within which the notes can vary but the actual notes produced by a fine singer of delicate ear and very pure vowels, the two notes would

U u

probably be shown as being in some simple relation to one another, as octave, perfect fifth, major or minor sixth, and so on, since (as Dr. Aikin has pointed out) a double resonator can work perfectly only when the notes produced by the two parts are simply related.

Regarding the variations possible in vowels, it may be added that phoneticians recognize in the various languages of the world over seventy different vowels, many of these, of course, being close approximations to one another. In the English language there is no definitely accepted standard of vowel or other pronunciation. In England itself a fairly stable standard for educated people has established itself by the practice of the upper classes, for some centuries past, of sending their boys to be educated together in the historic boarding schools called 'Public Schools' (the term having different significances in Britain and the United States): this standard has been recorded by means of the International Phonetic transcription in the *English Pronouncing Dictionary* of Professor Daniel Jones of the University of London and should be useful to singers. The standard amongst educated people in Scotland is very different from that of those in England. It is a matter of convention; there is no right or wrong.

The exact vowels of foreign languages are scarcely to be reproduced by a singing student unless he has learnt the foreign language in early youth from natives of its country or else been taught it by an expert in practical phonetics. We all tend to substitute for a vowel which is new to us its nearest familiar equivalent. If a Cockney child who says 'pyper' for 'paper' be asked to imitate the correct pronunciation he will usually repeat 'pyper', and on being told to try again and say 'paper' will exclaim indignantly, 'I *did* say pyper!' There is a hint here for singers, and the type of practice recommended by Mr. Shakespeare (and also some study of phonetics) seems to be indicated.

For Sir Richard Paget's apparatus see p. 1089, pl. 180. 7.

8. A Difficulty in Vocal Pronunciation.

An important difficulty in vocal pronunciation arises from the fact that the two resonators to which the production of vowel notes are assigned must be brought into action by vibration frequencies emanating from the original impulse of the vocal cords. Take as an example a soprano who is trying to sing the vowel *o* (as in 'no') on a fairly high note. As the notes which produce that vowel lie low (see scale on page 1091), and as the notes of the 'Harmonic Series' are in its lower range few and widely spaced, there may be no harmonic existing, in the series produced by the note sung, to provoke to activity a resonator shaped to a broad *o*. The harmonics from the note B in Handel's 'O Sleep, why dost thou leave me?' (*Semele*)

O . . . . Sleep,

are as follows:

None of these is low enough to excite to action the necessary notes, which may be given as approximately:

The broad *o* is therefore physically impossible.

At this point the writer breaks off and tries three gramophone records of the song. In two cases where it is sung by women the vowel produced is some sort of an *aw* (as in 'all') or short *o* (as in 'not'); apparently, then, the singer is inadvertently making use, for the upper note of the vowel, of the upper partial B, an octave above the note sung, lying between the approximate G sharp necessary for 'aw' and the approximate C necessary for the short *o* (see table, p. 1091, and what happens as to the lower vowel only a physicist with his apparatus of minutely tuned Helmholtz resonators could decide. Probably the vowel resonances produced are the lower B (from the original note sung) and its octave (the first upper partial), and this gives as near an approximation as the singer can get, and has to content the audience.

In the third record the singer is a tenor, singing the song an octave lower, and he gets a little nearer a true broad *o*: as his original note lies low so does the whole set of upper partials arising from it, and he could probably give the exact vowel recognized did he try, but unfortunately the physical necessity of faking some of their vowels accustoms many singers to acceptance of their second best.

It will be deduced from this that in the matter of purity of words music critics should allow more latitude to women than to men, more to sopranos than to contraltos, more to tenors than to basses, and so on. The physical fact of vowel sounds being at fixed pitches causes little difficulty in speech, where the range of pitch drawn upon for the tones of the voice is limited and at the moment-by-moment subconscious choice of the speaker, but in singing it creates a curious and rather distressing situation which is certainly not understood by all music critics and adjudicators at solo vocal and choral contests, judging from their remarks. Nor is it sufficiently remembered by composers in setting words to music; it is obvious that if a composer writing for a high voice were to try to place every one of the poet's vowels at a pitch where it could be accurately sung he would be limiting himself so much that the music would suffer, but composers should at least try to avoid placing vowels on long-held notes at impossible pitches, as they then become very noticeable. Keeping to the example of the long *o* and to Handelian instances, a further recourse to the gramophone shows that singers are no more successful with their vowel in 'O thou that tellest' and 'O had I Jubal's lyre' than in 'O Sleep', but here the vowel is passed over so quickly that no distress ensues: in 'I *know* that my Redeemer liveth' the case is a little worse.

A gramophone experiment that may be tried as confirming the statement that vowel effects are produced by fixed pitches is the following: Take any record which has a long-held note and by means of the speed regulator transpose the performance higher or lower. It will be found that not only does the note change in pitch but that the vowel changes also. Thus an exceptional singer who may be producing his or her vowels as purely as physically possible when the record is played at the proper pitch will be found to be distorting them badly at any considerably different pitch. And thus in the gramophone language-courses now common, unless the speed of the gramophone is properly adjusted the student has a bad model of vowel pronunciation.

Conversely a singer who in vain tries to get a particular vowel and has to be satisfied with the second best may be helped to the true vowel (in certain cases, at least) by a slackening of speed and consequent lowering of pitch of the record. Thus the sopranos who in the two records already mentioned have failed to get the *o* in 'O Sleep', get it pretty nearly when the pitch of the record is lowered about three semitones. It may be pointed out that the vowels through which the singer in this case is made to range by changes of pitch (*aw, oh, oo*) are such as have their two sounds roughly parallel (see section 7), which makes it possible to pass from one to another by pitch changes.

An interesting further experiment with the piano may now be mentioned. Repeating the experiment previously mentioned (6), but varying the vowels sung, it will be found that the piano can reproduce them all. The explanation, of course, is that the upper partials responsible for each vowel, amplified by the mouth cavities, are prominently enough 'heard' by the selective piano strings series to stand out and so to create the vowel anew.

On one and the same note sing successively two vowels (say long *o* and *ah*); an acute dissonance will be found to result from the clashing of the vowel harmonics—it must be from them, since the other upper partials (those deriving from the *note* sung) are unchanged.

Other experiments on these lines will doubtless suggest themselves to the reader, and if they be repeated at intervals until the ear acquires a knack of picking out sounds from the mass some interesting results may be obtained.

There is one type of voice which, whatever the care in enunciation taken by its possessor, offers difficulty to the listener in the following of the words sung. This is the over-resonant voice in which the upper partials from the notes sung, as reinforced by the various resonators, overwhelm those of the vowels.

An as yet not fully explained fact should be mentioned here lest the experimenting reader should discover it and think it has been shirked: When the mouth resonators are shaped for the various vowels, movements, in some way apparently characteristic of each, take place in the larynx. This can be felt from outside by the finger. It may be that they are simply mechanical accommodating movements; they do not appear to affect the vowels, since these can be produced by mechanical apparatus that has no corresponding movements: probably the fact that the tongue and the larynx are both attached to the hyoid (or tongue) bone, a bone which is free, i.e. not attached to the skeleton of the body, results in every movement of the tongue causing some movement of that bone, which is then passed on to the larynx. The discovery that every vowel is the result of fixed notes (or restricted regions of pitch) suggests that the faculty of absolute pitch (q.v.) is, in some mysterious way, called in for the recognition of vowels— which is amazing, considering the rarity of its possession as tested in other ways.

9. Diphthongs. A singer's difficulty in conveying accurately the words of his poet has just been alluded to. Another is the large use of diphthongs in the English language (modern French has none whatever).[1] Even the vowel *o*, in 'no', just taken as an example, is not quite pure, as careful listening will reveal a touch of an *oo* sound at the end. To represent such a sound as this quite accurately in musical notation, then, two chords of two notes each (and not one as in the table in section 7) would have to be used.

The vowel *i*, in 'night', is a more marked example, being clearly *ah-ee*. In singing the word 'night' to a long note, then, a difficulty is created for the audience since the note has perforce to be sustained on the *ah*, the *ee* which completes the diphthong only occurring at the very end. Thus for an appreciable length of time the audience, though it does not realize what is bothering it, is uncertain of the word which is in course of utterance.

Similarly the vowel *a*, in 'hay', is not strictly a pure vowel but a diphthong, being *e* in 'men' plus *i* in 'it': its position in the above table shows it as midway between these two sounds, probably indicating that in practice people in

[1] The statement as to the French language being devoid of diphthongs having been questioned on the authority of various French dictionaries, which certainly include the word 'Diphtongue' and give examples from the French language, it may be pointed out that what the French consider to be a diphthong is not what is here meant by the word. See Professor L. M. Brandin (*Encycl. Brit.* ix, 762), 'Modern French contains no diphthongs or triphthongs', and compare the following definitions—which will explain his assertion—
Concise Oxford Dictionary: 'Union of two vowels *pronounced in one syllable.*'
Larousse Universel: 'Réunion de deux sons *entendus distinctement, mais d'une seule émission de voix.*'
The difference is most accurately defined as one of the speed with which, in the two languages, the second vowel sound follows the first, and from the point of view of the singer who wishes to 'get his words over' this difference is very important.

general incline the first part rather towards the *i* in 'it', so that the ear barely notices the change when at the conclusion that 'i' is heard.

Of the five vowels *a, e, i, o, u* (pronounced as in reciting the alphabet) one alone is a quite pure vowel—the second. The last of the five (*u = ee-oo*) is a diphthong of a different nature from the others, since in it the last part is the part sustained in slow speech or song, whereas in the others mentioned it is the first part which is so sustained.

As showing how compound is a sound that we are accustomed to consider simple, we may take the word 'you' in Handel's 'Behold I bring you good tidings' (*Messiah*). The note sung is C sharp in the middle of the treble stave. From this arises a series of upper partials, each of which in its turn promotes another series of its own, and so *ad infinitum*. Coincident with this is the combination, or two-note chord, which the mouth-resonators provide for the vowel *ee*, before the note ends, quickly followed by the combination that produces the vowel *oo* (or something as near it as possible, this vowel not being physically obtainable with exactitude at that pitch); and then, of course, there are the various series of upper partials that each of these brings into existence, and so, also, *ad infinitum*. The mind is staggered at the consideration of the cloud of notes in the complex that we are accustomed to consider as a single note.

In singing a diphthong to a note of any length or to a passage of several notes, the prolongation demands a decision as to the division of the duration of the note or notes between the two vowels of the diphthong. In most cases it will be found that to obtain anything like a natural effect the first vowel must have all the time given to it except what is enough for a momentary flick of the second vowel at the very end. But there are exceptions: in 'beauty', 'you', etc., the *u* sound consists of *ee-oo*, and it is the first of these that should have the 'mere flick', so that the vowel the more characteristic of the word (and the more musical) should be the more heard.

It may be mentioned here that the theory of vowels just set forth as a process of analysis can be checked by a process of synthesis ; two resonators or two small organ pipes, tuned to the two notes above mentioned as constituting any vowel, will, when sounded together, be found to produce that vowel. Indeed, investigation has now gone far enough to make it possible to imitate speech mechanically with considerable perfection, and with a sufficient expenditure of money a lazy congregation could now bring into existence some sort of an organ that would not only play its hymns but also sing them. (Some day we may come to see the term 'Choir Organ' take on a new meaning!) The application of electronic means to these principles has made it possible to transfer the spoken word to print.

10. A List of English Vowels and Diph- thongs. It may be of interest here to list the vowels which a standard English dictionary finds sufficient for its indication of current pronunciation. The keywords used for this purpose from the *Concise Oxford Dictionary* are as follows (italics indicate that the vowels are, or incline to, diphthongs):

mate	rack
mete	reck
mite	rick
mote	rock
mute	ruck
moot	rook

These give the related 'long' and 'short' vowels. In addition there are

caw, *cow*, bah and *boil*

and the indistinct sound which has resulted from the laziness of generations of British and American talkers, and which is found in such varied representations as the first vowel of 'again', the second vowel of 'moment', the vowel of 'earth' and the first vowel of 'support', the second vowel sound of 'jealous', etc.—especially when these words are uttered quickly.

11. Consonants. Consonants may for the purposes of a brief article like this be looked upon as merely ways of beginning and ending vowels. Most of them (*p, b, t, d,* etc.) are momentary, but the nasals (*m, n,* etc.) have a possibility of a sort of humming continuation, and the rolling *r* is also continuous. The movements of the tongue, lips, etc., by which the consonants are produced, are sufficiently familiar to everybody, or can be discovered by a few moments' experiment.

12. 'Nasal' Voices. The mention of nasal sounds suggests a reference to so-called nasal voices. Europeans often allude to the nasality of American speech. Very many Americans (indeed probably the majority) are, however, entirely free from what is so described, and where this particularity is found it will, on closer observation, be discovered to result not from excessive nasal resonance but from some particular form of resonance in the chamber of the throat. In most normal English vowels little nasal resonance is possible, as the nasal passage is almost completely closed by the soft palate. If whilst an *oh* or *aw* (for instance) is being sung the reader will pinch his nose he will find the quality of the sound unaffected: if, however, he sings an admitted nasal sound (an *m* or an *n*) and does the same he will find a change occur.

The precise method by which nasal tone comes into existence has not yet been entirely agreed upon, but it seems pretty safe to say that it is the result of too low a soft palate, causing a lessening of mouth resonance and an increase of nose or naso-pharynx resonance in the reinforcement of the fundamental laryngeal tone.

13. The Aspirate. As the word implies, the aspirate (*h*) is a *breathed* sound, i.e. one preceded by an escape of breath between the vocal cords before these close in order to produce their note. Apart from this intentional effect the breath emission and the meeting of the cords should be simultaneous. But in 1934 a *cause célèbre* in England, in which were indicted the BBC as publishers of *The Listener* which had unintentionally libelled the singer Steuart Wilson by admitting to its columns a reader's letter alleging incompetence and exaggerating his tendency to 'the intrusive *h*', i.e. the insertion of an aspirate amongst the vowel sounds (particularly in 'runs' on one vowel), rather surprisingly brought into court a number of eminent musicians who condoned this practice, so evidently the opinion just hinted at is not unanimously held.

14. The 'Placing' of the Voice. A good deal of confusion has been caused by vocal teachers using metaphorical terms which pupils tend to understand literally, and also alluding to sensations as though they offered a picture of physical facts—which is not always the case.

Thus we hear of pupils being told to direct the stream of sound towards one part of the anatomy or another. It can be shown that this is impossible.

The terms 'chest' and 'head', as applied to the supposed place of origin of tone, or of special resonance of the voice, are of ancient usage. They are to be found in a passage of Jerome of Moravia in the thirteenth century (quoted by Henderson, *Early History of Singing*, p. 28), and about the same period in a passage of John Garland. These writers did not apply these terms to the *registers*, as is done today, but they apparently thought of the bass as a chest voice and the tenor as a head voice.

15. Intensity of Tone. The loudness or softness with which an individual sings a particular note is due to the greater or less force with which he directs the stream of air to the vocal chords, so affecting the amplitude of their vibrations (see *Acoustics* 4).

The ability of certain individuals to sing more loudly than others is, then, largely due to their greater lung power. But there are other factors, such as the freedom of passage from the larynx onwards, the size of the resonating chambers, and so forth.

The increase of vocal power which an individual can get by practice is largely due to his obtaining better control of breathing, but also to his learning, consciously or unconsciously, so to adjust his tongue as to leave the two resonating chambers of the mouth large whilst simultaneously adjusting the exits from them in proportion in order that the pitches obtained may remain the same. (Cf. 7, second par.)

16. Quality of Tone. The principles of good and bad quality of vocal tone are the same as those of instrumental tone; as to their nature see *Acoustics* 6, where it will be seen that the presence or absence, or greater or lesser

strength, of particular upper partials governs this. Strongly pronounced inharmonic upper partials in the original tone from the vocal cords, or 'parasite resonances' from the various resonating chambers, mean an ugly voice.

The original nature of the vocal cords in any individual gives him his initial quality, but by training he can improve both the action of these and of some, at least, of his resonating passages.

Two voices may be very different in timbre, yet equally agreeable to the listener; this difference is, of course, here again due to the same factor. For deterioration of voice due to defect of hearing see *Ear* 4.

17. Compass of Voices. Differences in the vocal cords and the resonating chambers exist between children and adults, between men and women, and even between individuals of the same age and sex, and a general classification has come into existence of soprano, contralto, tenor, and bass, with subdivision of soprano into high soprano and mezzo-soprano (literally 'half-soprano'), and bass into deep bass and baritone, these six constituting the best accepted classifications—three male and three female voices (plus the male alto).

These differences seem to have been slowly recognized, standardization having taken place only when choral singing reached a state of advancement. We may say (in round figures) that the first crude idea of part-singing (as distinct from purely unison singing) dates from about the year A.D. 900, and that the perfection of such singing was reached about the year 1550. The rational classification of voices may be said to have been achieved about 1500; we do not find it in Dufay (d. 1474). In the thirteenth and fourteenth centuries, when four voices were found, they were in the range roughly of baritone (called *Tenor*), what we should describe as high tenor (called *Motetus*), high alto ('Third Voice' or *Triplex*, whence, possibly, 'Treble'), and, if there was another voice, of high alto again ('Fourth Voice', *Quadruplin* or *Quartus Cantus*). The tenor usually 'held' the canto fermo (see references under *Canto Fermo*) and the others accompanied this.

In the late fifteenth and sixteenth centuries we find choral music existing in part books marked *Cantus, Altus, Tenor,* and *Bassus* and (as a glance through any book of madrigals or church music will show) the modern classification fully accepted.

The normal range of these voices and of the other two already mentioned may be given as an octave below and above the following middle notes (with training, a tenth below and above, but the outer three notes at each end must not be overworked):

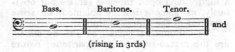

Bass.   Baritone.   Tenor.

and

(rising in 3rds)

Contralto.   Mezzo-Soprano.   Soprano.

(male alto a note
or two less.)

No exact definition of range is possible, as individual voices differ greatly by nature and according to their training, but the above offers a fair average statment and, being symmetrical, is easy to memorize.

Amongst women, mezzo-sopranos are the commonest; amongst men, baritones—the middle voice in each case. (During the late nineteenth and early twentieth centuries there was a marked tendency to the gradual disappearance of the true deep contralto and bass.) The tenor also becomes increasingly rare, so that in 1937 it was announced that the Sheffield Triennial Festival, due in 1939, would not be held owing to difficulties, including the scarcity of tenors.

It should be borne in mind, however, that the classification of voices is not entirely by range. Quality counts also in deciding whether a voice is, for instance, a baritone or a tenor; sometimes it is allowed to count too much, and voices are thus compelled to sing notes outside their natural range, with resulting strain. Gervase Elwes was given his choice by Bouhy, the famous voice-trainer; if he meant to sing in oratorio he could be trained as a tenor, if in opera (in which the tenor parts require a very big voice) then he should be trained as a baritone.

Russian basses are found who can sing down to

and the soprano Agujari (1743–83) was known to climb as high as

(The usually accepted pitch was in those days however, a little lower than it is today—say roughly a semitone.) Thus the range of the human family's collective voice may be put at $5\frac{1}{2}$ octaves.

Freak voices sometimes occur, such as women tenors, of whom Eugenia Mela (d. 1879) was a notable example. In 1936 there was broadcast from Prague the singing of a boy of three who possessed a deep bass voice and a highly developed musical sense—but obviously, as some critic complained, no sense whatever of the fitness of things.

The commonest voices, as already stated, are the mezzo-soprano and baritone; nature

has made too many of them and too few of the others.

For 'Alto-Tenor' voice see separate article under that head.

18. Tessitura. Distinct from the range of a song, necessarily conditioned by the compass of the voice for which it is written, is the general position, or lie, of the vocal lines. This is called the *Tessitura*, an Italian word meaning 'texture'. If there is an excessive number of high notes (though possibly none of them in itself too high), the song is said to have a high tessitura, and it will then impose a strain upon the voice. And so, similarly, with an excessive number of low notes.

The middle part of the compass is the easiest to use, and so far as possible the greatest amount of work should be thrown upon it and not upon either of the extremes.

Examples have occurred of singers entering more or less successfully on a public career as tenors or baritones (for example), on the strength of compass, and then changing on grounds of the quality of their voices, or their realization that although they could reach all the notes of their songs, the tessituras of these were not according to the natural range of their voice. Thus Sims Reeves and Jean de Reszke and John Coates began as baritones and later became tenors, whilst Santley and Ffrangcon-Davies began as tenors and became baritones.

19. Sub-varieties of Voice. Sopranos may be classified as:

Dramatic Soprano, with powerful voice and marked declamatory and histrionic ability.

Lyric Soprano, with lighter quality and pleasant cantabile style.

Coloratura Soprano, with great agility and a high range, able to warble rapidly and neatly in the most acrobatic fashion (see *Coloratura*).

Italians continue the subdivisions into *lirico spinto* ('pushed'), between lyric and dramatic; *acuto*, high; *leggiero*, light; *sfogato* ('unburdened'), high and light.

Tenors are often classified as:

Tenore robusto, or robust tenor, with full voice and all the vigour necessary for the expression of strong passion. (In German, *Heldentenor*, 'heroic tenor'.)

Lyric Tenor, or *Tenore leggiero*, corresponding to the lyric soprano (see above).

Basses are classifiable as:

Basso profondo or 'Deep Bass', low-ranging and powerful and capable of the expression of solemnity and similar emotions.

Basso cantante, with qualities similar to the lyric soprano (see above).

20. Differences between Singing and Speaking. Singing has been defined as 'sustained talking on a tune', but this is a nutshell definition and bears development. The main difference between the use of the voice in speech and in song is that in speech the range

See the Article *Violin Family* on pages 1081–4, and Articles under the individual names

1. CORELLI (1653–1713)

2. TARTINI (1692–1770)

3. FRANCESCO VERACINI (1690–1750)

4. LECLAIR (1697–1764)

5. VIOTTI (1755–1824)
'The Father of Modern Technique'

6. BAILLOT (1771–1842)

7. RODE (1774–1830)

8. BRIDGETOWER
(1780–1860)

1. PAGANINI at Drury Lane Theatre, London, 3 June 1831. In the background are Robert Lindley ('Cellist), Mori and F. Cramer (Violinists), J. B. Cramer (at the Piano), and Dragonetti (Double Bass)

2. C. A. DE BÉRIOT (1802–70)

3. OLE BULL (1810–80)

4. FERDINAND DAVID (1810–73)

5. VIEUXTEMPS (1820–81)

6. JOACHIM (1831–1907; a *Vanity Fair* cartoon of 1905)

7. SARASATE (1844–1908)

8. YSAŸE (1858–1931)

9. KREISLER (1875–1962)

of pitch is less extended, that the tone is less sustained (i.e. more interrupted by silences), and that no fixed scale is adhered to. The fact has already been mentioned that sounds which in speech are so crisply pronounced as to be accepted for pure vowels are in song (especially when given to long notes) dissociated into their constituents and so realized to be diphthongs. The Italian spoken language has few diphthongs, which is one factor making it an easy language to sing—for those who have been brought up on it; for English-speaking students (to whom some of the vowels are unaccustomed) it creates a difficulty, and the great Santley, despite the fact that his study of his art had been under Nava at Milan, and that his début was made on the Italian operatic stage, declared, 'My experience is that Italian is the most difficult of all the languages most generally wedded to music.'

Consonants, which in speech are no impediment, in song, where continuous tone is the ideal, are felt to be such. As they are mostly toneless they interrupt the song: perhaps unconsciously feeling this, some singers tend to weaken or omit consonants and by so doing greatly reduce the intelligibility of their words.

There is, of course, a great difference in the management of the 'bellows' part of the vocal mechanism in speech and in song respectively. Normally the lungs are inflated and deflated almost every four seconds, and within that period we speak a whole sentence; but in song a single note may have to be held for five times this period (or more), and, in any case, the regular periodical intake and outflow of breath has to give way to the varying demands of phrasing.

21. Physiological Terms used in connexion with the Voice. The following are the few chief terms necessary to the reader of books on singing, many others being omitted as self-explanatory, or explained incidentally in the above article, or as occurring principally in highly anatomical treatments of the subject.

Arytenoid. See *Cartilages* below.

Cartilages. The framework of the larynx consists of nine of these. The largest is the *Thyroid* (or 'shield-shaped'), of which the point makes the protuberance in the throat called the 'Adam's Apple'. This is articulated below to the *Cricoid*, or 'signet-ring-shaped' cartilage (narrow in front and high behind), and this is surmounted by the two *Arytenoid*, or 'ladle-shaped', cartilages, to which the vocal cords are

attached at the back, as they are attached to the thyroid at the front.

Costal, pertaining to the ribs, as in *Costal Breathing*, i.e. breathing involving movements of the ribs, as distinct from those involving movements of the diaphragm or compression and expression of the abdomen ('Diaphragmatic' and 'Abdominal' breathing).

Cricoid. See *Cartilages* above.

Diaphragm. The flexible partition of muscles and tendons separating the upper portion of the body (or *Thorax*) from the lower (or *Abdomen*). For 'Diaphragmatic' and 'Abdominal' Breathing, cf. 'Costal', above.

Epiglottis. The cartilage at the root of the tongue, which during swallowing covers and protects the vocal cords.

Eustachian Tubes (named from a sixteenth-century Italian physician). They communicate between the pharynx and the ear.

Glottis. The expanding and contracting opening between the two vocal cords.

Hyoid Bone. The 'Y-shaped' (really U-shaped) bone at the base of the tongue to which both tongue and larynx have attachments.

Larynx (also called 'voice-box'). The cavity holding the vocal cords. (An artificial larynx, with vocal cords complete, was in the 1920s put on sale by the Western Electric Company, and bought by many who had lost the use of those cords.)

Palate. The roof of the mouth, the front being called the *Hard Palate* and the back (movable and closing or opening the passage to the nose) the *Soft Palate*.

Pharynx. The cavity which serves as the communicating chamber of nose, mouth, and larynx.

Sinus. Any anatomical cavity or recess: for the sinuses of chief importance vocally see 6 above.

Sternum. The 'breast-bone', to which the fronts of the upper ribs are attached.

Thorax. The upper part of the body, shut off from the abdomen by the flexible sloping partition called the *Diaphragm*.

Thyroid. See *Cartilages* above.

Tonsils. The two almond-shaped projecting glands, one on each side of the top throat.

Trachea (or windpipe). The air passage leading into the larynx from below.

Uvula. The fleshy part of the soft palate at the back of the mouth. The trilling of the French *r* (in most parts of France) is performed by it, whereas that of the English *r* is performed by the tip of the tongue.

VOICES IN FUGUE. See *Form* 12.

VOICE LEADING. See *American Musical Terminology* 13.

VOICING. See *Organ* 3.

VOILE. French for 'veil'. In music the cloth used for muffling a drum. Hence *Voilé*, 'veiled' or 'muffled' (also used of a voice that lacks clarity—temporarily, through a cold, or permanently).

VOIX (Fr.). 'Voice' or 'voices'.

VOIX CÉLESTE. See *Organ* 3, 14 I.

VOIX HUMAINE (Fr.). 'Vox Humana'; see *Organ* 3, 6, 9, 14 VI.

VOKSAL. See *Concert* 13n.

VOLANTE (It.). (1) 'Flying', i.e. swift and light. (2) in bowed instrument playing. Slurred staccato

—the bow bouncing on the string—an extension of ricochet (q.v.).

VOLKMANN, (FRIEDRICH) ROBERT. Born at Lommatzsch, in Saxony, in 1815 and died at Budapest in 1883, aged sixty-eight. In the thirties of last century he was working in Leipzig and was one of the young composers encouraged by Schumann. His life after this was, for the most part, passed in Budapest, where he was active as a teacher of composition.

His works include symphonies, overtures, string quartets, two masses, songs, and very many piano compositions (solo and duet). Some of these enjoyed considerable popularity, but they are now little heard.

VOLKSLIED (Ger.). 'Folk Song' (q.v.). Properly the word should be reserved for the true folk song, the term *Volkstümliches Lied* ('national' or 'popular' song) being applied to more popular songs in folk-song style. But the distinction is not fully maintained and the use of the word is much like the current loose American use of the English term 'Folk song' (see *Folk Song* 1).

VOLKSTON (Ger.). 'Folk style.'

VOLKSTÜMLICHES LIED. See *Folk Song* 1.

VOLL (Ger.). 'Full' (*Volles, Vollem*, etc., are grammatical forms of the word).

VOLLES WERK (Ger.). Full organ.

VÖLLIG (Ger.). 'Complete.'

VOLLTÖNIG, VOLLTÖNEND (Ger.). 'Full-sounding', i.e. sonorous.

VOLONTÉ (Fr.). 'Will.' So *À volonté* means 'at one's own pleasure' (= *Ad libitum*, q.v.).

VOLTA or VOLTE. (1) A quick three-in-a-measure dance, something like the Galliard, from which it probably derived. The name, with its suggestion of turning round, comes from one of the motions of the dance. It was especially in England that the volte was popular. Queen Elizabeth and James I were fond of it. It was banished from the court of France, however, in the time of Louis XIII, on account of its indecorum; the man had to lift the woman into the air (cf. *Dance* 6 a).

The definite article got telescoped into the noun in England and 'La Volta' became 'The Lavolta'. So Shakespeare, 'They bid us to the English dancing schools and teach lavoltas high.' Sometimes the spelling is 'Levalto'.

To some extent the lavolta rhythm and style crept into instrumental music. Virginal and lute pieces will be found so designated.

(2) The two words are also Italian for 'time', 'times', in the sense of 'occasion', e.g. *Prima Volta*, 'first time' (see Table 20).

VOLTAIRE (1694–1778). See a reference under *Harpsichord Family* 5.

VOLTI (It.). 'Turn', in the sense of 'turn over', e.g. *Volti subito*, 'Turn over quickly' (sometimes abbreviated 'V.S.').

VOLUBILE, VOLUBILMENTE (It.). 'Voluble' (flowing easily), volubly.

VOLUNTARY. This is an English word of which the original and essential meaning is overlooked in almost every English work of musical reference. Because since the latter part of the nineteenth century the word has had an almost exclusive association with church organ music, it is stated that it etymologically implies something used as 'a casual adjunct to a service', 'not rubrically required', and so forth. The facts are as follows:

(1) The word is found in a musical application as early as the mid-sixteenth century, at first, apparently, meaning an instrumental composition in which, instead of the composer adding parts to a plainsong theme (see *Harmony* 4–7), as was still common, he left himself free to fashion all his parts as he liked. We see an example of this application of the word in Morley's *Plaine and Easie Introduction* (1597), where he says that 'to make two parts upon a plaine song is more hard than to make three parts into voluntarie'.

In the Mulliner Manuscript (q.v.) of keyboard compositions, *c.* 1555–6, the term is applied in this way, and Voluntaries there are seen to be a sort of contrapuntal fantasia or Ricercare (q.v.) without any canto fermo (see references under *Canto Fermo*).

(2) But the idea of freedom implicit in the word allowed it to be applied in another way. Thus from the same date or a little later we find voluntary used as meaning what we now call 'Extemporisation' or 'Improvisation', and this use of the word persists well into the nineteenth century, and for any extemporary performance on any instrument. Thus we find in the sixteenth century, the expression 'a voluntary before the song'.

Samuel Butler applies the same idea metaphorically (*c.* 1667) in one of his 'Characters', describing a person who in light conversation is sparkling but in considered discussion dull. 'He is excellent at voluntary and prelude, but has no skill in composition.'

Burney (*c.* 1805) in Rees's *Cyclopædia* defines voluntary as 'a piece played by a musician extempore, according to his fancy', and says that such a piece is often used before the musician 'begins to set himself to play any particular composition, to try the instrument and lead him into the key of the piece he intends to perform'. 'In these performances', he says, 'we have frequently heard great players produce passages and effects in fits of enthusiasm and inspiration that have never appeared on paper', and he magnanimously defends the liberties taken—'In these happy moments', he says (dropping into verse):

> Such sounds escape the daring artist's hand
> As meditation never could command;
> And though the slaves to rigid rule may start,
> They penetrate and charm the feeling heart.

He then, very naturally, goes on to call attention to a machine for automatically recording organ voluntaries (described in the *Philosophical Transactions* of the Royal Society, No. 483, section 2).

As late as Thackeray's *Vanity Fair* (1848) we see this use—'Sitting down to the piano she rattled a triumphant voluntary on the keys.' And Leigh Hunt (1850) talks of 'modulating sweet voluntaries on the pianoforte'.

(3) Because of the habit of 'voluntarizing' (as we may call it) before a song or the set performance of a piece, the word early came to have as one of its senses (perhaps a less common one) that of 'prelude'. So we find a warrant of Charles I which lays down the rhythm to be used by army drummers including one as a 'Voluntary before the March'.

(4) Almost from the beginning of the introduction of the word 'voluntary' into musical parlance it had still another application. Just as later Schubert, Chopin, and Schumann applied the word 'impromptu' (q.v.) to a written piece for which they had no other name handy, and which they wished to suggest was more or less in the style of an extemporization, so composers from at least Purcell onwards (see his *Voluntary on the 100th Psalm Tune*) have used this word 'voluntary' for written and printed music. It was thus applied even to string music, as in a collection of *Select Preludes and Voluntarys for the Violin* published by Walsh of London in 1705.

(5) Organists have always been active extemporizers and the service in the cathedrals and such churches as possessed organs allowed them scope for the exercise of their skill in voluntary playing. Thus 'voluntary' has come in time to collect round it a special flavour of the ecclesiastical and to signify much what was referred to in the opening lines of this article —organ playing before, during, or after a service, whether extempore or not. In the eighteenth century three voluntaries, at least, were commonly played—at the beginning and end of the Anglican service (as now) and also after the first lesson (or before the sermon, whilst the clergyman was changing from his surplice to his preaching gown). The *Spectator* mentions another place for the voluntary: 'By a voluntary before the first lesson, we are prepared for admission of those divine truths, which we are shortly to receive'.

There were several distinct types of voluntary in use in the English Church during the eighteenth century, of which the principal were, perhaps, the solid *Diapason Voluntary* and the showy *Cornet Voluntary* (see *Cornett* 3). The Cornet was a powerful sort of mixture stop, and these voluntaries provided for it (in the right-hand part) a very florid runabout line of single notes, with (in the left-hand part) an accompaniment to be played on another manual. (Often the left-hand part was a line of mere single notes also.) If in addition to its loud cornet the organ had an 'Echo Cornet' (a soft stop), passages for the two alternated in the right-hand part. Dr. Burney's *Six Cornet Pieces . . . proper for young Organists* would

perhaps hardly be considered 'proper' for any one today—even on the gayest ecclesiastical occasion. More than half a century before these were written, Addison (in the *Spectator* for 28 March 1712) had made this protest against their kind:

'When the Preacher has often, with great Piety and Art enough, handled his subject, and the judicious Clerk has with the utmost diligence culled out two Staves proper to the discourse, and I have found in my self and in the rest of the Pew good Thoughts and Dispositions, they have been all in a moment dissipated by a merry Jig from the organ loft.'

(The Clerk's 'culling out of two staves' here seems to refer to his psalm—see *Parish Clerk* and *Hymns and Hymn Tunes* 5.)

Similarly Bedford's *Great Abuse of Musick* (1711) complains of organists dismissing the congregation 'as if they play'd them out of a tavern, or out of an Ale-house, or, rather, out of a Play-house'.

Two classic references to organ voluntaries so chosen (or extemporized) and so performed as to subserve the spiritual purposes of the serious are those in the diary of John Wesley quoted under *Methodism and Music* 8.

Voluntary — A grand Extempore Piece of Mufick, performed on the ORGAN before the *Compofition* begins, &c. In *Divine Service*, it is performed juft before the *Firft Leffon*; which is (or ought to be) *folemn, grand*, and *noble* withal; free from all antick or lafcivious Airs, which only corrupt the Mind with impure Thoughts, &c. This, I fay, fhould be fuch *Harmony* as may *expel* from our Souls all *Gloom* and *Sadnefs*, fo as to raife and *prepare* us for Admiffion of thofe *facred Truths* which are to follow in the *Leffons* of the *Old* and *New Teftament*. It fhould call in our *Spirits*, delight our *Ears*, and re-create our *Minds*; and fo fill our Souls with pure and *heavenly Thoughts*, that nothing may remain in us but *Peace* and *Tranquility*. It fhould diffufe a *Calmnefs* all round us, and, as much as poffible, give us fuch a *Tafte of Heaven*, here on Earth, as to make us ambitious of the *full Fruition* thereof, after we depart this troblefome Life. &c. &c. which may GOD of His Infinite *Mercy* grant.

Tans'ur's *Elements of Musick*, 1772.

Nowadays a great variety of music is brought into use for 'voluntary' purposes, much of it originally written for the organ, and some of it of the nature of 'arrangement' (see *Arrangement*).

Many of the older English organ voluntaries of the more sober kind have been republished. Mendelssohn's Organ Sonatas (1845) were the result of a commission given him when in England to write some Voluntaries for English use, and the decision to call them 'Sonatas' instead of 'Voluntaries' was an afterthought (they would, as wholes, hardly serve the usual purpose of voluntaries, and this may be the reason of the change of title).

Cf. *Chorale Prelude*.

VOM (Ger.). 'From the.' So *Vom Anfang*, 'from the beginning'.

VON (Ger.). 'From', 'of'.

VON EINEM. See *Einem*.

VON HIER (Ger.). 'From here.'

VOR (Ger.). 'For'; as a prefix, in many words, it carries the sense of 'before', 'forward', etc.

VORAUS (Ger.). 'Beforehand'; *Im Voraus*, in organ music, means that the stops in question are to be 'prepared'.

VORBEHALTEN. See under *Aufführen*.

VORBEREITEN (Ger.). 'To prepare' (applied to the registration of organ music, often in the form of *Bereite vor*, mentioning a stop). So *Vorbereitung*, 'preparation'.

VORHALT (Ger.). (1) Suspension. (2) Retardation. (3) Long appoggiatura. (4) Syncopation.

VORHANDEN (Ger.). 'Available.'

VORHER, VORHERIG (Ger.). 'Formerly', 'foregoing' (in various phrases indicating that something is to be performed like or unlike something preceding).

VORIG (Ger.). Same as *Vorher*.

VORNEHM (Ger.). 'Noble.'

VORSCHLAG (Ger.). Literally 'forestroke': the *Kurzer Vorschlag* (i.e. the 'short' one) is the Acciaccatura; the *Langer Vorschlag* (i.e. the 'long' one) is the Appoggiatura (see Tables 12, 13).

VORSPIEL (Ger.). 'Fore-play', i.e. overture (see *Overture* 4 and *Prelude*, and for *Choral Vorspiel* see *Chorale Prelude*).

VORTRAG (Ger.). Literally 'fore-bringing', i.e. 'performance', 'execution'; so *Vortragsstück*, a piece designed to show off execution.

VORTRAGEN, VORZUTRAGEN (Ger.). 'To perform' or (more usually), 'to bring forward prominently'.

VORWÄRTS (Ger.). 'Forwards'; so *Vorwärts gehend*, 'forwards going', i.e. 'faster'.

VOTEY, E. S. See *Mechanical Reproduction* 13.

VOTIVE MASS. See *Mass* 5.

VOWEL SOUNDS. See *Voice* 7, 8, 9, 10, 20; *Acoustics* 7.

VOX ANGELICA, VOX COELESTIS. See *Organ* 3, 14 I.

VOX HUMANA. See *Organ* 3, 6, 9, 14 VI.

VOX ORGANALIS, VOX PRINCIPALIS. See *Harmony* 4.

VREULS, VICTOR. Born at Verviers in 1876 and died at Brussels in 1944, aged sixty-eight. After studies in his native Belgium he put himself under d'Indy in Paris, and was later attached, as professor, to his Schola Cantorum, which he left to become director of the Conservatory at Luxembourg (to 1926). He wrote symphonic poems, chamber music, etc.

V.S. = *Volti subito*, 'turn over quickly'.

VUILLAUME. Great family of makers of bowed instruments, active from the seventeenth century to near the end of the nineteenth, first at Mirecourt and then at Paris. J. B. Vuillaume (1798–1875) was its most important member (see under *Octo-Bass*).

VULGATE. See *Psalm*.

VUOTO, VUOTA (It., masc., fem.). 'Empty.' So *Corda vuota*, 'open string'.

VYCPÁLEK, LADISLAV. Born in 1882 at Vršovice (now in Czechoslovakia). He graduated as Doctor of Philosophy and became secretary of the Prague University Library. As a composer he is a pupil of Novák. He has composed religious choral works, song cycles, etc.

VYSHNEGRADSKY, IVAN. Born at St. Petersburg in 1893. He has been resident in Paris since 1922 and has become known as an exponent of the quarter-tone system (see *Microtones*; also p. 356, pl. **57. 7**).

PLATE 183

WAGNER AT MUNICH

By Batt

WAGNER'S rooms in the Briennerstrasse at Munich were fitted up to suit his peculiar sensitivity. He could not bear the feel of a coarse fabric: hard, straight lines had to be eliminated. Indefinite lines and colour, soft perfumes were necessary adjuncts to the working of his highly complex mind. Everything, down to mirrors and picture frames, was draped with white, rose and grey satin, trimmed with lace and artificial roses. The walls were hung with yellow silk, corners were rounded off, and the ceiling festooned with satin. In the middle of the room stood a softly upholstered couch. He would stroke these soft fabrics to induce inspiration, while he himself would dress in silks and satins.

The portrait epitomizes this essential aspect of Wagner's psychology. As Mr. Ernest Newman has pointed out, 'to know him thoroughly from this side is to have the key to his whole nature'.

On his lap is the score of Beethoven's Ninth Symphony, from which he derived so much inspiration: he holds in his hand a bottle of his favourite scent, attar of roses, which used to be sent to him direct from Paris.   B.

W

WACHET AUF ! See *Hallelujah Chorus*.

WACHIMAN, A. and E. See *Rumania*.

WACHSEND (Ger.). 'Growing', i.e. (generally) crescendo.

WACHT AM RHEIN, DIE. See *Watch on the Rhine*.

WACHTEL (Ger.). 'Quail.' Beethoven uses the term in the oboe part of the 'Pastoral' Symphony, where it imitates the cry of the bird, and the same name is given to the instrument used in Haydn's 'Toy' Symphony, etc., to obtain such an imitation (sometimes called *Wachtelpfeife*, i.e. quail-pipe).

WADE, JOHN FRANCIS (d. 1786). See *Adeste Fideles*.

WAELRANT, HUBERT. Born at Tongerloo, in Brabant, about 1518 and died at Antwerp in 1595, aged about seventy-seven. He was a singer and teacher of song in the days when the Belgian singers were famous all over Europe, and a composer of madrigals and *a cappella* church music at a time when this type of composition was at its height. His works were pretty widely published in his own day and are still sung.

WAGENAAR.

(1) JOHAN. Born at Utrecht in 1862 and died in 1941, aged seventy-eight. He became organist of the cathedral of his native place, and then occupied positions in Arnhem, Leyden, and elsewhere. From 1919 to 1937 he was director of the Conservatory of The Hague. His compositions include operas and orchestral works, and often show a light and humorous touch. Because of his teaching he has been called 'the César Franck of Holland'. Many of the leading musicians of Holland are his pupils.

See *Holland* 8.

(2) BERNARD. Born at Arnhem, Holland, in 1894, and died at York Harbour, Me., in 1971, aged seventy-six. He settled in the U.S.A. in 1920, and was naturalized. He was a violinist in the New York Philharmonic and taught composition at the Juilliard Graduate School, New York. His compositions include several symphonies and concertos, string quartets, pianoforte works, etc.

See *Harp* 3; *Concerto* 6 c (1894).

WAGENSEIL.

(1) JOHANN CHRISTOPH (1633–1708). He was a German historian and author of a famous book on the Mastersingers.

See *Minstrels*, etc. 8; *Improvisatore*; *Colour and Music* 2.

(2) GEORG CHRISTOPH (1715–77). He was an Austrian organist, harpsichordist, and composer of high reputation and music-master to the Empress Maria Theresa.

See *Sonata* 10 d (1760); *Nicknamed Compositions* 10 (Handel's 'Harmonious Blacksmith').

WAGNER.

(1) RICHARD (in full, Wilhelm Richard; p. 480, pl. **183**, and p. 1105, pl. **185**). Born at Leipzig in 1813 and died in Venice in 1883, aged nearly seventy. In him the German Romantic Movement of the nineteenth century found its completest musical stage expression. His genius adopted the harmonic intensities and emotional forcefulness of Beethoven, and, making them yet more intense and forceful, applied them to German myth and legend.

In earlier works, stretching his dramatic and musical fabric upon a framework that seems to us today to differ little from that of his predecessors and contemporaries, he at last attains a flexibility that enables him in later ones to bend his music to the minutest motions of his dramatic thought, casting aside the rigid styles of recitative and aria, and blending them into a new type of musical expression that inclines more to the one or the other as the demand of the words may happen to be for more or less direct statment, for less or for more lyrical expression.

To achieve this flexibility he gradually discards the division of a vocal piece into balanced sections made up of tallying phrases, and, as a principle of unity, substitutes a system of organic development out of short pregnant or germinal fragments or motifs ('leading motifs' —*Leitmotive*). By so designing these fragments that each aptly characterizes the situation or person with whom it is first associated, he enables himself to bring particular thoughts and reminiscences to the memory of his audience at will, and so to strengthen the dramatic significance both of his vocal line and of his orchestral commentary—which commentary becomes the more pointed since he has now enormously increased the number and variety of his orchestral forces and discovered abler ways of deploying them.

He writes his own libretti, himself dictates not merely the general nature but the details of the scenery and dresses, and (though we today can see that he was always more musician than dramatist, poet, or scenic designer) prides himself upon having at last fulfilled the principles of Gluck (q.v.) in making every element subservient to the cardinal interest of the drama, or rather, going further, in fusing these elements into an entirely new art, that of 'Music Drama'.

That briefly is the aim and achievement of Wagner. His life, which could be (and has often been) told at enormous length, must be here thrown into briefest space.

He was reared in a theatrical household, where the affairs of the stage, which provided the livelihood of the family, were the natural subject of daily conversation. From the first he threw himself into these interests. He received a good classical education, latterly at the Thomas School, Leipzig. on the staff of which had served, eighty years earlier, Johann Sebastian Bach. He dabbled youthfully in music, and at seventeen wrote an orchestral overture that was performed and, very properly, laughed at. Then he took lessons in composition, immersed himself in the task of acquiring a definite technique, and at nineteen wrote a symphony which was performed at one of the famous Gewandhaus concerts at Leipzig. He was now launched.

Shortly after this first success he obtained a small musical position in an opera-house, and thenceforward there followed a series of more and more important positions of the kind. He wrote some operas, without much success, and visited Paris in the attempt to get his *Rienzi* there performed; whilst in that city he lived (but only just) by the menial tasks of music-copying and the like (see an allusion under *Arrangement*).

In Paris he wrote *The Flying Dutchman*, the first of his long series of operas based on legend. He was thirty when it was first performed. This was at Dresden, where he shortly afterwards became conductor of the opera (see *Weber*). There he wrote *Tannhäuser* and *Lohengrin*, and thence he fled, sought for in vain by the police for his participation in the 1848 rebellion.

Liszt, at Weimar, always a sympathizer and admirer, received him for a time; then he took refuge in Switzerland, where he remained for eight years. He began work on the immense four-evening drama, *The Ring of the Nibelung* (*Rhinegold, The Valkyrie, Siegfried, The Dusk of the Gods*). It was a quarter of a century later that he finished it.

He was forty-eight when at last was revoked the decree of banishment from Germany that had followed his escapade at Dresden. By this time (1859) *Tristan and Isolde* was written and *The Mastersingers* was soon afterwards begun (finished 1867). They offer the greatest contrast possible—the one a lovely hothouse plant, the other a hardy growth of the open air.

He was deeply in debt, and striving fruitlessly to secure performances of his works, when he received a message from the eighteen-year-old King Ludwig II of Bavaria. He was to come to Munich and his troubles should end. Yet

even kings cannot have all their own way and in Munich Wagner soon found opposition. He went into Swiss exile again, but at last settled once more within the King's domains, and in little Bayreuth in 1876 completed the famous Wagner Festival Theatre (p. 1105, pl. **185**) and the almost as famous Villa Wahnfried, the one of which was to attract annually thousands of music-lovers from all over the world and the other to be the scene of intimate gatherings of the greatest musicians of the day—so far as such musicians were partisans of 'The Music of the Future'.

Liszt was one of these. Wagner had married his daughter, Cosima. The story of his and her previous marriages is too long for telling here. The study of Schopenhauer, the friendship with Nietzsche, and other 'influences' must also be passed over. So must the story of the financial worries that beset the grandiose schemes of the boldest composer the world has ever known. And there is no room here even to begin a list of the generous-hearted and loyal helpers who gathered around one who believed in his own greatness and inspired others with that belief.

Only one major work remains for mention, the 'Sacred Music Drama', *Parsifal*, completed in 1882, when the composer was sixty-eight. A year later, whilst seeking rest and health at Venice, he suddenly died. Cosima lived for nearly half a century longer, dying in 1930, the same year as their son, Siegfried (see below).

Wagner's prose works are of importance to those who wish to understand his mind; they occupy nine or ten considerable volumes.

A multitude of details concerning Wagner and his works are necessarily scattered through this volume. They can be found by means of the following list, which has been found susceptible of only a rough classification:

Flying Dutchman; Lohengrin; Mastersingers; Parsifal; Rienzi; Ring of the Nibelung; Tannhäuser; Tristan.

Aria; Recitative; Singing 7, 10; *Song* 5; *Tremolo.*

Expressionism; France 9, 13; *Germany* 7, 8; *History* 7; *New Music; Romantic; Russia* 6, 7.

Bell 6; *Brass; Clarinet Family* 2 (near end), 4 h; *Cornett and Key Bugle Families* 3 (near end); *Harp* 3; *Horn Family* 3; *Oboe Family* 3 a b; *Percussion Family* 3 s, 4 a (kettledrums—near end), 4 b (bass drum), 4 c (anvil), 4 e (bells and glockenspiel); *Trombone Family* 2 f, 3 (near end); *Trumpet Family* 2 f, 3 (near end); *Tuba Group* 1, 2, 3, 4, 5.

Ballad 5; *Ballet* 7; *Goldmark, K.; Hanslick; Hymns and Hymn Tunes* 3 (for 'Mastersingers'); *Improvisatore; Lassen* (for 'Tristan'); *Levi; Libretti; Liszt; Minstrels* 7, 8 (for 'Mastersingers', 'Tannhäuser', 'Parsifal', 'Tristan'); *Opera* 9 d e, 11 e, 21 k m, 24 (1842 onwards) for dates of productions; *Scandinavia* 5; *Wait* (for 'Mastersingers'); *Wedding March*; also p. 756, pl. **125**. 2.

Absolute Pitch; Composition 5, 9, 12, 13; *Conducting* 5; *Criticism* 4, 5, 6, and p. 257, pl. **47**. 1, 2; *Expression* 5; *Form* 14; *Harmony* 3, 13, 24 a; *Leading Motif; Melody* 5; *Memory* 7; *Motif; Quality* 3; *Scale* 7; *Spain* 9; *Temperament* 6 (end), 9; *Tempo; Theme Song.*

Chamber Music 6 (III) 1813, for 'Siegfried Idyll'; *Misattributed; Opus; Oratorio* 3, 5, 7 (1843); *Overture* 2, 3, 4; *Polonaise; Prelude* 3; *Programme Music* 5; *Service; Symphony* 8.

Annotated Programmes 2; *Concert* 8; *Festspiel; Festival* 3.

Amen; Bird Music; Cinematograph; Colour and Music 2, 3; *Holland* 7; *March; Pianoforte Playing* 6; *Rule, Britannia!; United States* 4.

Arne, T. A.; Beethoven; Berlioz; Bizet; Boughton; Brahms; Bruckner; Bülow; Burrell; Chabrier; Enesco; Gilson; Gluck; Halévy; Humperdinck; Joachim; Kienzl;

Klindworth; Logier; Mahler; Marschner; Martucci; Mozart; Newman, E.; Nietzsche; Potter; Pratt, Silas G.; Richter (2); Roeckel, August; Saint-Saëns; Strauss; Tausig; Verdi; Weber; Wolf; Wolzogen.

(2) SIEGFRIED (in full Helferich Siegfried). Born at Triebschen, near Lucerne, in 1869 and died at Bayreuth in 1930, aged sixty-one. He was the only son of Richard and Cosima Wagner, and with his mother and his English wife long occupied the Villa Wahnfried and in their turn directed the festivals at Bayreuth. He composed operas (notably *Der Bärenhäuter* —'The Lazybones') and orchestral works. His birth was the incentive to his father's composition of the lovely *Siegfried Idyll*. After his death his wife took charge of the Bayreuth enterprises until his sons, Wieland (1917–66) and Wolfgang, were able to assume control, which they effectively did in the years following the second World War.

(3) GEORG GOTTFRIED (1698–1756). See *Misattributed Compositions* under 'Bach's Motets'.

(4) RUDOLF. See *Misattributed* (Wagner's 'Eagle March').

WAGNER-RÉGENY, RUDOLF. Born in Transylvania in 1903 and died in East Berlin in 1969, aged sixty-six. As a composer he produced successful operas. In 1950 he became a professor of the new State Conservatory of Berlin.

WAGNER TUBAS. See *Tuba Group* 2.

WÄHREND (Ger.). 'During.'

WAINWRIGHT Family. They were mostly born at Stockport and active in Manchester, Liverpool, and district. The following are the most important:

(1) JOHN (d. 1768) wrote, amongst other church music, the well-known tune *Yorkshire* (at first called *Stockport*) to Byrom's 'Christians awake!' He was latterly organist of the Manchester Collegiate Church, now the cathedral.

(2) His son RICHARD (1758–1825) composed the popular glee 'Life's a bumper'. He also was organist of the Collegiate Church—as was, earlier, another son, ROBERT (1748–82).

WAIT or **WAYTE** (p. 993, pl. **166**). The Waits, in old British life, were the Watchmen of a city. They patrolled the streets during the night and used a musical instrument (cf. in Wagner's *The Mastersingers* the watchman with his simple horn), to show that they were at their duty and to mark the hours. The musical side of their work developed and they became good musicians, playing on a variety of instruments, forming a uniformed city band (sometimes with very colourful liveries and elaborately beautiful silver chains round their necks), and appearing with dignity on ceremonial occasions. Musically inclined families tended to service in the Waits, as the one musical occupation easily open to them. The surnames Waite and Wakeman come from this occupation. The brothers Edmund, Ellis, and

Orlando Gibbons were sons of one of the Waits of Cambridge; their brother Ferdinando became a Wait of distinction. Many of the Bach family were town musicians in Germany, and in England would have been called Waits. In England each body of Waits had its own special tune: thus there have been preserved tunes called *London Waits*, *Chester Waits*, etc. (cf. *Signature Tune*). In Germany there is a considerable literature of 'Turm-musik' or 'Turm-sonaten' (i.e. 'Tower Music'; 'Tower Sonatas'), to be played by the Türmermeister ('Tower Masters'—bodies corresponding to the British Waits) from the local church tower or town-hall balcony (p. 993, pl. **166.** 1).

For some centuries (certainly from the sixteenth to the end of the eighteenth) it was customary for the British town Waits to attend at the inns on the arrival of any guest who seemed likely to be able to recompense them, and to give him a musical welcome; in eighteenth-century diaries and novels we find frequent mention of this practice. At some seaports they welcomed seafaring men from their voyages (see *Inns and Taverns* for further particulars).

The city of York has records of its band of Waits as early as 1272.

The Waits of Norwich long enjoyed especial fame; their existence has been traced back to the earliest years of the fifteenth century (see some particulars under *Mealtime Music*).

The Edinburgh Waits (or 'Tounis Minstrels' —the usual term in Scotland) in the early seventeenth century seem to have been in great favour: they were employed by the city authorities to play in the streets every morning and evening, and to give a special concert at noon. (For a reference to the Edinburgh and Aberdeen Waits at an earlier period see *Scotland* 6.)

There is not the slightest warrant for the statement sometimes made that under the Puritan régime of the Commonwealth and Protectorate the English Waits were suppressed. They were in full activity, just as before and after this period. At Newcastle-on-Tyne when the Mayor entertained Cromwell the Town Waits played before the house.

The normal instrument of the Waits was the hautboy, long a much-used instrument, and (being loud and pungent in its earlier form) very suitable for outdoor playing; thus the name 'Wayte' was often applied to that instrument, but they often played string instruments also and sometimes (as at Norwich) were, further, renowned for their singing.

Because the Waits serenaded the public at Christmas time, any body of people so serenading has come (regrettably) to be called 'the Waits', and the term is still often so used in popular parlance in England today.

See also *Street Music* 3; *Mealtime Music*; *Inns and Taverns as Places of Music-Making*; and compare *Minstrels*, etc.; *Profession of Music*; *Concert* 5.

WAIT TILL THE CLOUDS ROLL BY. See *Nicknamed* 12 (82).

WAKEFIELD, MARY AGNES (1853–1910). See *Competitions* 2.

WALCKER. Great German organ-building family first active from the end of the eighteenth century to the present day. See *Organ* 10.

WALDEN, LORD HOWARD DE. See *Holbrooke*.

WALDFLÖTE. See *Organ* 14 II.

WALDHORN. See *Horn Family* 5 b.

WALDSTEIN SONATA (Beethoven). See *Nicknamed Compositions* 5.

WALDTEUFEL, EMIL (1837–1915). French pianist and immensely successful writer of waltzes.

WALES

1. Introductory.
2. Folk Music.
3. The Hwyl.
4. The Harp and the Crwth.
5. Pennillion.
6. Choral Singing.
7. Eisteddfod.
8. Cymanfa Ganu.
9. The University Council of Music.
10. Welsh Composers.

1. Introductory. The Welsh have always had the reputation of being a musical race. In the first century before Christ Diodorus Siculus, quoting from the now lost work of Poseidonius of Apamea, of yet a century earlier, says of the Celts of Gaul:

'They have poets whom they call bards, who sing songs of eulogy and of satire, accompanying themselves on instruments very like the lyre. They also have philosophers and theologians whom they hold in extreme honour, and name Druids. They possess prophets too who are much revered. . . . Friend and foe submit to the song of the bard. Often when two armies meet, and swords are drawn, and lances set, the bards throw themselves between the contending parties, and pacify them, as one by magic subdues the wild beast. And thus, even among the most savage non-Greeks, frenzy yields to wisdom, and Mars respects the Muses.'

Further back than this (fourth century B.C.) an unknown Greek author tells us:

'They conduct their public assemblies to the accompaniment of music, zealously practising it for its softening effects.'

The essential unity of the continental Celts and those in Britain, and of their Druidic customs, with which the activity of their bards was bound up, is alluded to in Caesar's *Gallic War* (55–54 B.C.). He says that the Druidic religion was 'supposed to have been devised in Britain', and to have been brought thence into Gaul, so that 'those who desire to gain a more accurate knowledge of that system generally proceed thither [to Britain] for the purpose of studying it'.

The Welsh of today maintain their practice of the art. They have a store of folk and popular song, generally either rhythmically stirring or touchingly melodious. They are devoted to choral singing and the brass band is popular. The use of the harp is traditional and has not entirely died out, and the name and office of Bard and Chief Musician still remain, though no longer significant of much authority (see section 7 of this article).

The hymn tune is an important factor in Welsh popular musical life. In the higher branches of orchestral performance and of composition the people of Wales have not in the past notably excelled, but a movement for widening their musical interests began before the first World War and has gained impetus since.

2. Folk Music. Taking in turn some of the various elements it may be said that the national and folk tunes of Wales divide sharply into two classes—the harmonic and the melodic. Up to half a century ago all the well-known collections of Welsh airs gave but very few airs that were not clearly chordal in structure; the dominance of the harp was obvious, and pianoforte accompaniments to them were easy to write. Speaking broadly, these tunes came from North Wales, where the native princes had ruled longest and where the harpist most abounded. *Y Deryn Pur, Llwyn Onn*, and the many marches (e.g. *Rhyfelgyrch Gwŷr Harlech*—'March of the men of Harlech') are instances.

The existence, in any quantity, of another type of folk song was not realized by the Victorian arrangers. It was the perspicacity and the energy of Dr. John Lloyd Williams (Professor of Botany in Aberystwyth and a musician) that brought to light a rich inheritance of melodies that was on the point of being lost for ever, and the Welsh Folk Song Society, founded (1908) mainly through his initiative, has now to its credit some hundreds of these tunes and their variants. They are often purely melodic—a puzzle to any arranger who tries to harmonize them conventionally, but a joy to the singer. The Methodist revival must be held chiefly responsible for their submergence. The words, naturally, were not always acceptable to severe taste, and thus they were driven underground. Their place in popular favour was taken not by the harmonic tunes (few of which are sung informally) but by the hymn tunes. Many of these are adaptations or versions of some of the old melodic strains and it is this origin that gives them the modal flavour (see *Modes*). During the last fifty years numbers of the old folk tunes have been published in collections, and where they are introduced in school, college, or village hall, they are eagerly picked up. (For a remark on the characteristics of Welsh tunes see *Melody* 10.)

The Welsh folk dances are practically extinct, religious scruple, from the eighteenth-century Evangelical movement onwards, having been against them. However, in 1935 were published a few dances and their tunes (a Processional Morris, a Welsh Reel, and some Country

Some Mid-19th-Century Scenes

See the Article *Wales*

1. SOME OF THE CHORUS SINGERS
See *Wales* 6 and 7

2. A SUCCESSFUL COMPETITOR MAKES HIS ACKNOWLEDGEMENTS
See *Wales* 7 a and its footnote

3. HARPIST CONTESTANTS AND THEIR AUDIENCE

See the Article *Harp*

See the Article *Wagner* on pages 1101–3

Wagner settled in the Franconian town of Bayreuth in 1872 and completed the erection of his famous *Festspielhaus* in 1876. Its design carried out his very practical ideas—acoustic excellence; sunken and invisible conductor and orchestra (with the instrumental sections equally well heard); seats arranged in a slight curve with each row raised a little above the one in front of it; no galleries or side boxes; no prompter's box, &c. Three performances of the *Ring* opened it and they were attended by numerous royal and musical notabilities. Richter was the first conductor and Wilhelmj led the violins. It was erected and exists solely for the performance of Wagner's own works

Dances), recovered by the efforts of Mr. Hugh Mellor.

3. The Hwyl. An apparently instinctive practice allied to folk song is the hwyl, the plainsong-like intonation (or unconscious recitative) of fervid pulpit speech and extempore prayer; this can still be heard in country districts from older people.

In Aubrey's *Brief Lives of Contemporaries* (written 1669–96) there is an interesting allusion to this practice in a part of England on the borders of Wales. He had been told that the modern Greeks 'doe sing their Greeke' and says:

'In Herefordshire they have a touch of this singing; our old divines had. Our old vicar of Kington St. Michael, Mr. Hynd, did sing his sermons rather then reade them. You may find in Erasmus that the monkes used this fashion, who mocks them, that sometimes they would be very lowe, and by and by they would be mighty high, *quando nihil opus est.* —Anno 1660 comeing one morning to Mr. Hobbes, his Greek Xenophon lay open on the board: sayd he, "Had you come but a little sooner you had found a Greeke here that came to see me, who understands the old Greeke; I spake to him to read here in this booke, and he sang it".'

Aubrey goes on, 'The better way to explaine it is by prick-song', and sets out in notation a phrase of Xenophon as the 'Greeke' sang it—the Greek Hwyl, as we may call it.

4. The Harp and the Crwth. The early Welsh Harp (see also *Harp* 2 a) had no pillar; in the seventeenth century the instrument had, however, an unusually high straight pillar, to which the neck ascended from the body in a long curve. The Welsh 'triple harp' has three rows of strings, the interior one for the semitones; to get at an interior string the player must insert his finger between two of the strings in the exterior rows. Most Welsh harpists still own a harp of this type, and many of them can play it; they use the left hand and right hand in the reverse of the usual pedal-harp position (cf. p. 1104, pl. **184. 3**).

The harpists (see also *Harp* 2) formerly took an important place in social life. In the court of a prince there would be a 'Court Bard' who, to his harp, sang genealogies, battles, and heroes; and a 'Domestic Bard', attached to the princess, who sang of love, of nature, and of minor events, and was not bound by the strict rules of composition of his colleague, but used a quasi-ballad style. There were also vagrant, free-lance bards, of quite another class and subject to the hardships that come to those whose profession is not always kindly looked upon by authority. In more recent (say post-Tudor) times harpists were less exactly classified, but they were still important in the life of the country, and well into the nineteenth century most great houses and most inns had a harpist (see de Quincey's *Confessions*, 1821, and Mendelssohn's letter from Llangollen, 25 August 1829).

The harp and the crwth (q.v.) are often named together in Welsh verse and the crwth was a little played in Wales down to the early nineteenth century, though by then generally supplanted by the violin.

The Methodist revival towards the end of the eighteenth century and on through the nineteenth (cf. *Puritans* 9) was austere and largely silenced the harp and the violin, first driving them into the inns, and afterwards out of those.

5. Pennillion (or 'Penillion'). An ancient yet still existing form of singing known only in Wales. Strictly speaking, it consists in singing extemporized verses or set poems, which in some instances rhyme internally, line by line, to an original counterpoint woven around some well-known melody played in a harmonized version by a harper. The harper can change his tune as often as he wishes; the singer must instantly find or make suitable words and counterpoint.

The extemporized counterpoint is not necessarily in the same metre as the harper's melody and a pennillion singer of standing is even expected to be able to extemporize a triple-time counterpoint to a duple-time melody and vice versa. The extemporized tune must not start with, but must end with, the harper's melody. It may be that the many verses are extemporized in turn by a number of persons taking part in the practice, or it may be that one person (possibly the harper himself) will extemporize the whole. In modern times the originality of the verses and counterpoint is often questionable; true improvisation seldom occurs (see *Improvisation*); this is probably the more to be expected since a certain limited group of harp tunes are habitually used for Pennillion performances. The singing of a prepared counterpoint by a group in unison is even heard—a practice which is completely away from the original art.

6. Choral Singing. The claims made for Wales as a nation particularly active in Choral Singing began with Giraldus Cambrensis (Gerald of Wales) in his description of Wales, 1188. He says, 'In their musical concerts they do not sing in unison, like the inhabitants of other countries, but in many different parts, so that in a company of singers, which one very frequently meets with in Wales, you will hear as many different parts and voices as there are performers' (Hoare's translation, 1806); see *United States* 6 for a modern example of the same thing). He goes on to admit that 'North Country Englishmen do something of the same kind', but, as a patriotic Welshman, adds, 'with less variety'. In order to estimate the force of his statement it must be remembered that the use of harmony in church had at that time arrived little beyond the later stage of Organum (see *Harmony* 4, 5) and that the manuscript of 'Sumer is icumen in' (q.v.) dates from a somewhat later period.

The choral singing movement attained great impetus in the nineteenth century, but many of the singers sang by ear, and music performed at the Eisteddfodau (see 7) was learnt and polished as the result of incessant drilling prolonged over some months. Tonic sol-fa spread very rapidly in Wales during the second half of the nineteenth century; nearly every chapel (Wales in religion has long been largely Nonconformist) formed a class and found a teacher; day schools also taught it, and by the end of the century men, women, and children who could read music were common. The tonic sol-fa notation is still the notation best known in Wales.

The singing of a Welsh choir often thrills by the rich quality of the voices and the strength of the underlying emotion; much trivial music has, however, been put before the public by certain choirs of national fame, and English and Scottish musicians, rightly or wrongly, look upon Welsh choral taste as somewhat more rudimentary than that of their own countries. Nevertheless, the best of the Welsh choral singing is magnificent, and uses a worthy repertory (see also *Festival* 1—end).

7 (*a*) **Eisteddfod** (plural Eisteddfodau). The word means a session (from *eistedd*, to sit). The national gathering of the name is a meeting of the Welsh bards, dating back, in one form or another, at least as far as the seventh century. This now takes place annually in some town in Wales (very occasionally in some town outside Wales where there happens to be a large Welsh community). The proceedings are, of course, almost entirely in the Welsh language.

The ruling body of the gathering is the Gorsedd (*dd = th* in '*the*') or official hierarchy of bards and musicians of varying standing. Degrees of Ofydd (*Ovate*), Bardd (*Bard*), Pencerdd (*Chief Musician*) are conferred upon candidates found (after various tests) to be efficient. In old days such degrees constituted a licence to practise the art publicly, but by the days of Queen Elizabeth I the system had fallen into confusion; in 1567 or 1568 she (one of the music-loving, Welsh-descended Tudors) intervened by letters patent, 'Whereas it is come to the knowledge of the lord president . . . that vagrant and idle persons naming themselves mynstrells, rithmors and barthes, are lately grown into such an intollerable multitude', and so on. An Eisteddfod was held at Caerŵys, in Flintshire, to put things in order.

For about 130 years the Eisteddfod ceased to be held, but soon after the beginning of the nineteenth century, when national feeling was growing all over Europe and was being stimulated by the Romantic Movement in literature and art, the meetings were revived.

The 'National Welsh costume' of tall hat and long gown was introduced by Lady Llanover in 1834.

The 'degrees' nowadays conferred by the Gorsedd bear the titles but have not the significance of those of yore. The Archdruid (Chief Bard) holds office for three years, presides over the Gorsedd, and is treated with high honour; the chairing, or enthroning of the victorious

bard of the year, is still the highest ceremony of this great national musical, literary, and artistic gathering. The general musical interest (especially that of the choral and other competitive elements) may now be said to predominate, although nearly all Welshmen, at home and abroad, rustic and urban, keep an eye on the bardic competitions as well. The highest current bardic honour known is the winning of the 'Chair' (with a money prize) and such Eisteddfods are always known as 'Chair Eisteddfods': the winner has no special title as such.[1] A small volume of the winning poems is on sale at the Eisteddfod.

All the above applies to the National Eisteddfod; local Eisteddfodau are also held in great number, but these are purely of the nature of Competition Festivals; like the National Eisteddfod they include not only musical contests but also contests in poetry and prose, research work, and arts and crafts. The Welsh in the United States hold Eisteddfodau, the first of which took place at Carbondale, Pa., in 1850.

That other Celtic country, Cornwall, had formerly a Gorsedd and in 1928 revived it, after a lapse of perhaps a thousand years.

For the discredited claim that the Eisteddfod is in origin an Irish institution see *Ireland* 8.

7 (*b*) **Eisteddfod—an Alternative Account.** The whole of the article on Wales was, before first publication, passed by Welsh musical authorities, and before the publication of the fourth edition of this work was again passed by one of the most eminent of them. It will be readily understood, however, that differences of opinion on some of the historical details are quite possible and so there is given here an alternative account of the history of the Eisteddfod and Gorsedd, kindly supplied by Dr. Iorwerth C. Peate, of the Department of Folk Culture at the National Museum of Wales, Cardiff—author of *The Eisteddfod, its History and Development.*

'The word "Eisteddfod" means literally a session. Courts for regulating the bards and their conventions were common in medieval times in Wales, as in other countries, but the first definite evidence of such courts in Wales dates only to the Carmarthen Eisteddfod, 1451. Other Eisteddfodau of medieval-court type were held at Caerŵys in Flintshire in 1523 and 1568.

'In 16th-century Welsh manuscripts references are found to Eisteddfodau in which bards competed; such meetings were held also in the 17th and 18th centuries, chiefly in taverns. At the end of the 18th century, the London Gwyneddigion Society, in its efforts to foster the development of Welsh literature, contributed prizes for poetry, harp-playing, etc., and the Eisteddfod in its present form dates from that period, the annual National Eisteddfod dating from the middle of the 19th century.

'The ruling body of the gathering is the National Eisteddfod Council. This is a national body which

[1] 'Mr. D. Carrellio Morgan, of Aberystwyth, won his seventy-first bardic chair at Merionethshire Eisteddfod on Saturday. Mr. Morgan said that he had given many of his chairs to relatives, friends, and churches.'—*The Times*, June 1951.

gives direction and advice to the local committees which arrange the programmes (the National Eisteddfod is held each year in different towns). Since the primary purpose of the Eisteddfod is the preservation and development of Welsh culture, the proceedings are, of course, almost entirely in the Welsh language; they include competitions in poetry, and literature, music and the arts in general and craftsmanship. The Council publishes every year a volume of the proceedings. Provincial, county, and local Eisteddfodau are also held in great number and are, in varying degrees, of the same nature as the national festival.

'The *Gorsedd Beirdd Ynys Prydain* ("Throne of Bards of Isle of Britain") is an "academy of bards" which came into being about 1791 as a direct result of the neo-druidic beliefs arising from the antiquarian movement of the 18th century. It was first grafted on to the Eisteddfod at the Carmarthen meeting of 1819, by its founder Edward Williams (*Iolo Morganwg*). In the second half of the 19th century, robes were designed for its members who are given the "degrees" of bards, ovates, or musicians) and the practice instituted of meeting in "megalithic" circles specially erected for the purpose. There is no historical foundation for these degrees, robes, and circles. The Gorsedd is also responsible for the chairing and crowning ceremonies of the successful Eisteddfod poets: this ceremonial too is of recent origin and like the Gorsedd itself has no foundation in antiquity. The Archdruid presides over the Gorsedd which has now developed into a national folk festival and, owing to its relationship to the Eisteddfod, is fully represented on the National Eisteddfod Council.'

8. Cymanfa Ganu. The words literally mean 'A Gathering for Song'. They are applied to a popular gathering, on a larger or smaller scale, for the enjoyment and stimulus mainly of hymn-singing, though anthems and oratorio choruses are included and occasionally a short complete work; the participants are usually the members of choirs and of congregations of some one religious body in some particular district. In 1916 the practice was adopted, and it is still spasmodically favoured, as a part of the activities of the National Eisteddfod (see 7). It had long been and still remains the practice to cover any incidental halt in the Eisteddfod proceedings by calling upon the audience to sing a well-known hymn tune; and on these and similar sudden occasions one can in Wales always rely on good four-part singing.

9. The University Council of Music. The direction of the movement for widening the musical interests of Wales referred to above was, from 1919, taken over by a National Council of Music for Wales, which later changed its name as above. Until its cessation in March 1961, this was first and foremost a university body, but its activities included school, church, and, in practice, the whole musical life of the Principality. Chamber music ensembles from University Colleges were engaged to perform in schools, and to give concerts in villages. Later a Welsh National Orchestra was founded (subsidized by the British Broadcasting Corporation); in 1932, however, it was disbanded chiefly on the score of cost.

Sir Walford Davies, Professor of Music in the University (1919–26) was active in this whole movement, serving as Director to the Council of Music. He was succeeded by John Morgan Nicholas. Many special publications of music by Welsh composers were issued by the Council which had its headquarters at the University Registry in Cardiff.

The Council was also responsible for the annual Summer School of Music held at Harlech. Much of the work of the Council became obsolete with the growth of the Music Departments in the three University Colleges of Aberystwyth, Bangor, and Cardiff the University of Wales held at one time a unique position in Britain in making adequate provision not only for its actual students in Music, but also for the ordinary student interested in music and for the public. Each College has a residential ensemble responsible for giving, throughout the College terms, weekly public concerts of chamber music. Many other public concerts, choral, orchestral, and instrumental are also provided by the University.

The Arts Council and the B.B.C. too, have contributed greatly to the widespread growth of musical appreciation. The former are responsible for arranging nationwide tours of English and foreign orchestras and artists, thus giving an opportunity, hitherto denied to a large number of people living mainly in rural areas, of hearing a wide and varied repertoire of orchestral and instrumental music. The B.B.C. Welsh Orchestra was formed in 1945, mainly for broadcasting purposes, and it has been especially responsible for the promotion of new Welsh music.

Another new venture of importance is the Welsh National Opera Company, formed at first on a part-time basis, but now (1968) moving on to a more permanent and full-time basis. The repertoire, so far, has been fairly conservative, but the company has been responsible for mounting three operas by native composers—*Menna* and *Serch ywr Doctor* by Arwel Hughes and *The Parlour* by Grace Williams. Wales now has several major music festivals—at Cardiff, Llandaff, Swansea, and Caerphilly; each of the four University Colleges, too, holds an annual Arts festival.

10. Welsh Composers. Particulars of a number of Welsh composers will be found under their own names (see list at end of article). It is generally accepted that the Tudor composers, Robert Jones, (q.v.) John Gwynneth, Gwineth, Gwynedd, Gwynett, or Guinneth (see *Gwineth*), Richard Edwards (q.v.), Thomas Tomkins (q.v.), and John Jenkins are Welshmen by birth or descent. The Tudor sovereigns were insistent on their Welsh descent and, unfortunately for Wales itself, attracted to the English court both the Welsh aristocracy and the Welsh artists. It would be safe to say that there was little creative activity of any standard in Wales from this period to the twentieth century.

The early part of the twentieth century did

not yield very much in the way of original work, most composers being content to re-work folk tunes in an unoriginal manner, although some, such as Morfydd Owen and Vaughan Thomas, did show some signs of originality and technical expertise.

The last twenty years, however, have seen a remarkable change. This coincides with the decline of interest in choral singing and a new enthusiasm for orchestral and instrumental music (seen outwardly in the flourishing National Youth Orchestra of Wales and numerous smaller youth orchestras). Com-posers like David Wynne, Grace Williams, Daniel Jones, Alun Hoddinott, and William Mathias have begun a tradition of orchestral and instrumental composition whilst other composers, including Arwel Hughes, are writing the first Welsh operas of note. Younger composers have been quick to follow the tradi-tions begun by these above-mentioned com-posers and the latest trends in creative music show a full awareness of European avant-garde techniques.

Many problems remain—lack of suitable concert halls is an ever-present problem and a permanent orchestra resident in Wales is still an urgent necessity. The overall picture of music in Wales is, however, a healthy and encouraging one; vital, stimulating, and imaginative, with many bold hopes for the future.

LIST OF ARTICLES AMPLIFYING THE ABOVE.

a. *Folk Song*; *Hymns and Hymn Tunes* 17 e, xiii (for a brief allusion to an early Welsh metrical psalter). The following for tunes that have crept into Welsh collections but which are not really Welsh: *Barley Shot*; *Bells of Aberdovey*; *First of August*; *Monk's March*; *Sibyl*.

b. *Crwth*; *Harp* 2.

c. *Thomas, John*; *Parry, John Orlando*; *Parry, Joseph*; *Thomas, Thomas*; *Owen, David, John, and William Henry*; *Mills, Richard*; *Roberts, John*; *Stephen, Edward*; *Lloyd, John Ambrose*; *Evans, David Emlyn*; *Jenkins, David*; *Davies, H. Walford*; *Evans, David*; *Davies, E. T.*; *Jones, D.*; *Gwineth*; *Tomkins, T.*; *Hoddinott*; *Jones, Robert*; *Edwards, Richard*.

WALKER.

(1) ERNEST (p. 337, pl. **54.** 1). Born in Bom-bay in 1870 and died in Oxford in 1949, aged seventy-eight. On taking classical honours at Oxford, at the age of twenty, he joined the staff of his college (Balliol) and served on it in a musical capacity continuously for thirty-four years (D.Mus. 1898)—for the last twenty-five of them as Director of its Music, becoming responsible, during that period, for the series of Sunday evening Chamber Concerts which, begun by John Farmer (q.v.) in 1885, have since that date constituted one of the greatest agencies of general musical culture in the University. He engaged in much musical academic activity, and wrote valuable books, including a standard *History of Music in Eng-land*, as well as editing several musical perio-dicals, but he was also known as a pianist, and

as a composer of orchestral and choral works, chamber music, and (perhaps especially) songs.

See also *Ireland* 1; *Londonderry Air*; *Microtones*; *Sullivan*; *Whistling*.

(2) GEORGE. London music publisher of the opening of the nineteenth century.

See *Publishing* 7.

WALKÜRE (*Valkyrie*). See *Ring of the Nibelung*.

WALLACE.

(1) WILLIAM VINCENT (p. 705, pl. **118.** 3). Born at Waterford, Ireland, in 1812 and died in the Pyrenees in 1865, aged fifty-three. He began life as a violinist in a Dublin theatre; at sixteen he was organist of the cathedral of Thurles, but he soon returned to violin playing in Dublin.

Then, at twenty-three, he settled in the Australian bush. Visiting Sydney, he was per-suaded by the Governor of New South Wales to give a concert and rewarded by the gift of two hundred sheep. Travelling in New Zealand, he would have been killed by the natives but for romantic rescue by a chief's daughter. Sailing in the South Seas, he was one of three survivors of a party of Europeans otherwise all murdered by native mutineers.

He received high honours from native princes in India, in Mexico became famous for a 'Grand Mass', and in the United States lost much money through investments in the pianoforte and tobacco businesses.

In his early thirties, being now in London, he composed and produced the opera, *Mari-tana*, which had been begun in Tasmania, years before. This had enormous success and was long popular amongst the audiences of British travelling opera companies. He then settled in Germany, where he hoped to achieve a reputa-tion, and remained some years. When he was thirty-seven he produced the opera *Lurline*, which had an even greater success than *Maritana*, but is not now, performed. Soon after this his health gave way and he was ordered to the south of Europe, where he died.

He was as indefatigable in labour as he was unresting in travel, and, despite his death in middle life, the list of his works in the British Museum Catalogue (including many light piano compositions once popular), occupies one hundred pages.

See references under *England* 7; *Ireland* 7; *Opera* 13 d, 21 h, 24 d (1845); *Tuba Group* 1.

(2) WILLIAM (p. 945, pl. **160.** 6). Born at Greenock in 1860 and died at Malmesbury in 1940, aged eighty. He graduated in medicine at the University of Glasgow. Approaching thirty, he dropped medicine for music, entering as a student at the Royal Academy of Music. He later joined the staff of that institution.

As a composer he could claim to be the first in Britain (1892) to write a symphonic poem—*The Passing of Beatrice*. Of later such poems, *Wallace, A.D. 1305–1905* and *Villon* are the most notable.

He was the author of several thoughtful books on music.

See passing references under *Symphonic Poem*; *Percussion Family* 4 c—concerning the use of the tabor.
The sketch of Safonof on p. 240, pl. **44**. 9, is by him.

WALLOONS. See *Belgium* 5, 6.

WALMISLEY.

(1) THOMAS FORBES. Born in London in 1783 and died there in 1866, aged eighty-three. He was for forty years organist of St. Martin-in-the-Fields, London. His chief reputation is as a composer of glees.

(2) THOMAS ATTWOOD (p. 165, pl. **34**. 7). Born in London in 1814 and died at Hastings in 1856, aged nearly forty-two. He was the son of the above and the godson of Attwood (q.v.). He had a distinguished mathematical, literary, and musical career at Cambridge, and undertook the Sunday slavery of playing at eight services at three different colleges and the University Church. At twenty-two (whilst still an undergraduate) he was chosen Professor of Music in his university.

He was one of the ablest organists and writers of church music of his country and his period. His anthems and services were collected and published by his father after his death and some of them (notably, perhaps, the service 'Walmisley in D minor') are amongst the best in the Anglican repertory.

He was a friend of Mendelssohn and, like him, a pioneer enthusiast for Bach.

See *Service*; *Anthem* (Period IV); *Cathedral Music* 8.

WALOND.

(1) WILLIAM (*c.* 1725–*c.* 1770). He was an Oxford organist and composer. Amongst his works were a published setting of Pope's *Ode on St. Cecilia's Day* and keyboard pieces.

(2) WILLIAM. Probably son of the above; died at Chichester in 1836. He was organist of Chichester Cathedral, and composed church music.

(3, 4) RICHARD and GEORGE. Sons of (1) above. Both had Oxford connexions with church music activities.

WALPOLE, SIR ROBERT (1676–1745). Statesman. See *Beggar's Opera*.

WALSH.

(1) JOHN (d. 1736). Important London music publisher. See *Publishing* 6; *Arethusa*.

(2) JOHN (d. 1766). Son and successor of the above.

(3) HENRY. Early pianist. See *Pianoforte* 17.

WALTER, BRUNO (1876–1962). See *Germany* 9 a.

WALTER OF EVESHAM. See *Odington*.

WALTER, REVD. THOMAS (1696–1725). See *Hymns and Hymn Tunes* 11, 17 f (iii).

WALTERSHAUSEN, H. W. S. VON. See under *Pianoforte* 21.

WALTHER.

(1) JOHANN (1496–1570). He was Luther's friend and musical collaborator. See *Hymns and Hymn Tunes* 3, 17 b; *Passion Music* 2.

(2) JOHANN JACOB (b. 1650). See allusions under *Chamber Music* 6 (Period II); *Violin Family* 6.

(3) JOHANN GOTTFRIED (1684–1748). He was a relative of Bach, a good organist, a composer, and the early compiler of a dictionary of music (Leipzig, 1732; cf. *Conducting* 2; *Dictionaries*; *Bird Music*).

WALTHEW, RICHARD HENRY. Born in London in 1872 and died in Sussex in 1951, aged seventy-nine. He studied at the Royal College of Music and led an energetic and useful London musical life. As a composer he was best known through his chamber music. From 1909 he was actively connected with the South Place Concerts (q.v.).

WALTON.

(1) WILLIAM TURNER (p. 353, pl. **56**. 3). Born at Oldham in 1902. He became a boy chorister at Christ Church Cathedral, Oxford, and was then for a time a Christ Church undergraduate. The Dean (Strong, himself an able musician) encouraged him, as did the organist, H. G. Ley (q.v.), and the University Professor of Music, H. P. Allen (q.v.). He does not seem, however, to have had much definite tuition then or at any period, and though he later had the benefit of a little advice from Busoni and from the conductor, Ansermet, he may be considered essentially self-taught.

His first composition to attract attention was a piano quartet written at the age of sixteen (later revised, and published in 1924 by the Carnegie Trust).

At Oxford he had made the acquaintance of Sacheverell Sitwell and through him of his brother Osbert and his sister Edith. This family gave him their friendship and moral support and in 1922 he wrote the accompanying music (largely a collection of parodies of various forms and styles) for the recitation, through a mask with a megaphone, of some of Edith Sitwell's poems (*Façade*, for flute, clarinet, saxophone, trumpet, cello, and percussion; later enlarged, reorchestrated, and turned into two suites, and also treated as a ballet). Outstanding later works have been the *Sinfonia Concertante* for piano and orchestra (1927; revised 1943); the overture *Portsmouth Point* (1925; reproducing the spirit of Rowlandson's picture of that name); the Viola Concerto (1929; first played by Hindemith); the vigorous and technically adventurous Violin Concerto (1939; first performed at Cleveland, Ohio, by Heifetz); a cello concerto (1956; first played by Piatigorsky); a highly dramatic work for baritone solo, chorus, and orchestra, *Belshazzar's Feast* (words compiled from the book of Daniel, etc., by Osbert Sitwell; first performed at the Leeds Festival of 1931); and two symphonies (of the first, three movements performed in 1934; completed the following year; the second appeared in 1960). There are also some chamber music, songs, and a good deal of film music (e.g. that accompanying the screen version of Shakespeare's *Henry V*), and incidental music to plays. In 1954 his opera *Troilus and Cressida* (libretto by Christopher Hassall) was produced in London. A one-act 'extravaganza', *The Bear*, appeared in 1967.

Walton's habit has been to compose deliberately and sparingly, and without any aim of building up rapidly a big list of works. His music is interesting in texture and rhythm, and adroit in orchestration. Some of it shows a sardonic quality.

He has had conferred on him many honorary degrees. In 1951 he was knighted, and in 1968 received the Order of Merit.

See *Spain* 10; *Trumpet Family* 4; *Concerto* 6 c (1902); *History* 9; *Broadcasting* 4.

(2) IZAAK (1593–1683). See a quotation from him in *Mealtime Music*.

WALTZ (Eng.), **WALZER** (Ger.), or **VALSE** (Fr.). A three-in-a-measure dance almost certainly derived from the old German Ländler (q.v.); it first appeared prominently at the end of the eighteenth century. Michael Kelly, the singer, records the vogue of the waltz in Vienna in 1773 and it reached England in 1791 (p. 273, pl. **49**. 5). His friend Mozart wrote many waltzes for the balls of Vienna. The dance was almost universally opposed as improper, but from about the period of Waterloo onwards swept over Europe and America, where, with periods of temporary relative decline, it still remains popular.

The objections to the waltz on its first introduction were violent. One example (out of dozens available) will suffice. Burney, in Rees's *Cyclopædia* (about 1805), calls it 'a riotous German dance of modern invention', and adds:

'The verb *walzen*, whence this word is derived, implies to roll, wallow, welter, tumble down, or roll in the dirt or mire.

'What analogy there may be between these acceptations and the dance, we pretend not to say; but having seen it performed by a select party of foreigners, we could not help reflecting how uneasy an English mother would be to see her daughter so familiarly treated, and still more to witness the obliging manner in which the freedom is returned by the females.' (Cf. *Dance* 7.)

The great waltz composers of the earlier part of the nineteenth century were Lanner and the two Johann Strausses. They created a type which became world-known as the Viennese Waltz, a type of which grace, lightness, melodic charm, and piquancy were the characteristics: their best waltzes have never been surpassed, and it seems as likely that such a waltz as the *Blue Danube*, by Johann Strauss the younger, the 'Waltz King', will last for ever as that Beethoven's Fifth Symphony will do so. Gung'l and Waldteufel were other able and popular waltz composers of this earlier period, and Messager, Lehar, Leo Fall, and Oskar Straus of a later period.

The waltz has a harmonic characteristic. It is on a one-chord-in-a-measure basis, with the bass of the chord heard on the first beat of the measure and 'lumps' of the chord on the other two beats. In the true Viennese Waltz the second beat of the accompaniment is played just a trifle before its legal moment, which adds great vitality to the effect.

The melody of a waltz is smooth-moving and ingratiating. The general tone is highly romantic. Sometimes sentimental lyrics have been set as 'Waltz-Songs', e.g. those of Gounod (in the operas *Faust* and *Romeo and Juliet*) and the once ubiquitous *Il Bacio* ('The Kiss') of Arditi.

In general a waltz consists of a string of seven or eight different melodies with an introduction and also a coda recapitulating some of the melodies.

For *Valse à Deux Temps* see under *Deux Temps*. The *Cellarius*, popular in the mid-nineteenth century, was a slow waltz introduced by the famous Paris dancing-master of that name.

A sliding step and a good deal of turning are common to all forms of the waltz.

The waltz has made many appearances in purely instrumental music. Perhaps the first instance is a Haydn Sonatina of about 1766, in which one movement (in place of the usual minuet) is headed 'Mouvement de Walze'. Haydn wrote other waltzes besides this, and Mozart, Beethoven, Schubert, Weber, Chopin, Schumann, Brahms, and others have written many. The piano waltzes of Chopin and the Brahms *Liebeslieder* waltzes ('Lovesong waltzes' —with voice parts) are particularly famous. Richard Strauss has a famous waltz pervading his opera *Der Rosenkavalier*, and Ravel has a set of waltzes (a tribute to Schubert—originally for piano but rearranged by himself for orchestra) called *Valses Nobles et Sentimentales*, as well as a big orchestral 'choreographic poem', *The Waltz* (a tribute to Johann Strauss). Some examples exist of the waltz as a movement in symphony, e.g. in Berlioz's *Symphonie Fantastique* and the Fifth Symphony of Tchaikovsky. Glazunof has written waltzes for string quartet.

The idea of exploiting the waltz as an instrumental piece perhaps first 'caught on' as a result of the success of Weber's *Invitation to the Dance*, written as a piano piece in 1819 and arranged for orchestra later by Berlioz and by Weingartner.

The origin of the waltz has been found by some in the volte (q.v.). This is now discredited by real students of the subject.

The following German names are given to the waltz or to dances almost indistinguishable from it in its earlier or later phases: *Roller*, *Dreher* (i.e. 'Turner' or 'Twister'), *Deutscher Tanz* (i.e. 'German Dance'); in general any name indicating 'German Dance' refers to some type of waltz, e.g. the Italian *Danza tedesca*; cf. *Allemande* 2).

For an expressional device often used by Viennese conductors and others to give greater effect to waltz music see *Atempause*.

WALTZ-SONG. See *Waltz*.

WALZER. See *Waltz*.

WALZERTEMPO (a Ger.-It. compound). 'Waltz-time.'

WANHALL, J. B. (1739–1813). See *Vanhall*; *Bohemia*.

WANKEND (Ger.). 'Wavering', 'shaking'.

WARBLERS. See *Bagpipe Family* 4.

WARD.

(1) JOHN. Place and date of birth and death unknown. He was a domestic musician of an English gentleman of the reigns of Elizabeth and James I, Sir Henry Fanshawe, of Ware Park, Hertfordshire, Remembrancer of the Exchequer. He wrote church music, music for viols, and very fine madrigals.

(2) EDWARD, known as 'Ned Ward' (1667–1731). London tavern-keeper and humorous writer. See *Concert* 4; *Inns*; *Fairs and their Music*; *Vicar of Bray*.

(3) J. C. London nineteenth-century choral trainer. See *Absolute Pitch*.

(4) S. A. See *America the Beautiful*.

(5) ROBERT. Born in Cleveland in 1917. He was trained at the Eastman and Juilliard schools, and for a time taught at the latter, later becoming managing editor of the Galaxy Music Corporation. His compositions include three operas, of which one, *The Crucible* (1961), won a Pulitzer prize; also four symphonies and many shorter works.

WARLOCK. See *Heseltine, Philip*.

WÄRME (Ger.). 'Warmth.'

WARNER, H. WALDO. Born at Northampton in 1874 and died in London in 1945, aged seventy-one. He was a notable viola player, and (1907–28) a member of the much-travelled London String Quartet. As a composer he became best known by his chamber music, some of which gained a Cobbett award in Britain and some a Coolidge award in the United States.

WARSAW CONCERTO. See *Addinsell*.

WASHBOARD. A piece of corrugated metal (resembling a familiar domestic laundry article in miniature) fixed to a drum in dance bands and the like. The drumstick moved over it produces a rhythmic humming effect.

WASHINGTON (D.C.); LIBRARY OF CONGRESS. See *Festival* 2.

WASIELEWSKI, JOSEF WILHELM VON. Born near Danzig, then in East Prussia, in 1822 and died at Sondershausen, in Thuringia, in 1896, aged seventy-four. He was a pupil of Mendelssohn at the Conservatory of Leipzig, and, as a violinist, of Ferdinand David, in the same institution. He practised his profession for a time in Düsseldorf, on Schumann's invitation, and then spent periods at Bonn and Dresden, returning to Bonn as that city's director of music for fifteen years and finally retiring to Sondershausen. He was a prolific writer upon musical subjects and composed various pieces in the smaller forms, particularly a popular Nocturne for violin and piano.

WASSAIL. A festive occasion with drinking. The word often occurs in Christmas carols.

WASSERZUG. See *Jewish Music* 6.

WATCH ON THE RHINE, THE (*Die Wacht am Rhein*). A German national song of great popularity.

The words were written in 1840, at a moment of special fear of France, by Max Schneckenburger (1819–49), a wealthy ironmaster. They were more than once set to music.

The tune that has lived is that of Carl Wilhelm (1815–73), who composed it in 1854 for his male-voice singing society to sing in Crefeld, in celebration of the silver wedding of the Crown Prince of Prussia, afterwards William I. The war of 1870 brought the setting into popularity, and the German government thereupon bestowed a small pension on the composer.

WATERHOUSE, GEORGE. See *Canon* (near end).

WATER ORGAN. See *Hydraulus*.

WATSON, DR. HENRY. See *Libraries*.

WATTS, ISAAC (1674–1748) (p. 485, pl. 86. 5). Nonconformist divine and prolific hymn-writer. See *Hymns and Hymn Tunes* 6, 7; *Congregational* 3; *Baptist* 3.

WAVES, SOUND. See *Acoustics* 12, 13, 14, 15.

WA WAN PRESS. See *Publishing of Music* 9.

WAYTE, WAIT (q.v.). Also an old name for the hautboy. See *Oboe Family* 2; *Chapel Royal*.

W.C.A.U. BROADCASTING CO. See *Electric Musical Instruments* 5 b.

WEARING OF THE GREEN, THE. The words of this song date from 1797. The author is unknown. The tune is earlier. The song has had great vogue at times of patriotic excitement in Ireland.

WEATHERLY, FREDERIC E. (1848–1933). Oxford tutor, author of books on logic, Bristol lawyer, and highly popular author of song 'lyrics' ('The Midshipmite', 'The Old Brigade', 'Up from Somerset', and hundreds of others). Occasionally also a composer. See *Londonderry Air*.

WEAVER, JOHN (1673–1760). English dancing-master and pantomime and ballet deviser and manager, and considerable author on cognate subjects. See *Dance* 10; *Pantomime*.

WEBBE, the two SAMUELS (Father and Son: p. 145, pl. 30. 4).

(1) Born in 1740 and died in London in 1816, aged seventy-five or seventy-six. In youth and poverty he studied the Latin, Greek, Hebrew, French, German, and Italian languages, and made himself proficient in music.

From his mid-twenties he became well known as a composer of catches, canons, and glees, winning no fewer than twenty-six of the annual medals of the Catch Club.

He was organist of the Sardinian Embassy Chapel in London, and his ecclesiastical music is still in use in the Roman Catholic Church, but he is most widely remembered by his glees, which are considered to be the best specimens ever written of this distinctively English class of composition. 'When winds breathe soft', 'Glorious Apollo', and 'Thy voice, O Harmony' are three typical examples.

See *Glee* 2; *Roman Catholic Church Music in Britain.*

(2) Born in London about 1770 and died in London (not Liverpool, as generally stated) in 1843, aged about seventy-three. In the year his father won his last prize at the Catch Club he won his first, and in other ways his life may be looked upon as a continuation of that of his father.

See *Roman Catholic Church Music in Britain.*

WEBER.

(1) BERNHARD CHRISTIAN. See *Temperament* 5.

(2) FRIEDRICH DIONYS (1766–1842). See *Bohemia.*

(3) CARL MARIA FRIEDRICH ERNST VON (p. 397, pl. **68.** 8). Born near Lübeck in 1786 and died in London in 1826, in his fortieth year. In his short life he accomplished the establishment of a German national opera, not only with libretti in the German language (see *Mozart*), often based upon national legend or history, but with music that reflected the German temperament and tradition.

He is also looked upon as the founder of the Romantic School in opera, for to him, however important might be the element of musical beauty, it was made subservient to the arousing of romantic emotions (p. 893, pl. **152.** 3).

He was an able pianist, and wrote much for his instrument. Some of his piano music is still heard but the chamber and independent orchestral compositions have almost disappeared from the concert-room. It is especially on the influence of his opera, *Der Freischütz* (the name means a marksman who uses magic bullets), and in a lesser degree, *Euryanthe* and *Oberon*, that his reputation now rests, and their overtures are very favourite concert pieces.

His life was a varied one. His father was a travelling actor-manager. His first serious teacher was Michael Haydn at Salzburg, his second the Abbé Vogler (cf. *Meyerbeer*) at Vienna. He got a footing in the petty court life of the period and served as musical director in several capital cities of the Rhineland, at Prague, and, at last, at Dresden.

He had lived a life of some dissipation, thrown as he was amongst the actors, musicians, and royalty of the period. He was now reformed, happily married, and successful. Then consumption overtook him. He travelled to England, on the invitation of Kemble, to conduct the performance of his opera *Oberon*, written for Covent Garden. There he died. Eighteen years later his body was removed to Dresden and his successor of that day, the young Richard Wagner, delivered an address over the grave.

See references, of greater or lesser importance, as follows:

Freischütz; *Melodrama*; *Minstrels* 5 (for source of

'Oberon'); *Opera* 9 c g, 21 d e j, 24 d (1821–3–6); *Singspiel.* Also p. 240, pl. **44.** 7.
   Chamber Music 6, Period III (1786); *Concerto* 6 b (1786); *Concertstück*; *Mass* 2, 4 (Period V); *Overture* 3; *Roman Catholic Church Music in Britain*; *Sonata* 9, 10 d; *Symphony* 8 (1786).
   Clarinet Family 2, 6; *Guitar*; *Harp* 3; *Horn Family* 1, 3, 4; *Mechanical Reproduction* 9, 11; *Oboe Family* 6; *Percussion Family* 4 a c; *Trombone* 3.
   Ballet 7; *Polonaise*; *Waltz* (see also *Applause* 1, 3).
   Folk Song 3; *Ballad* 5; *Romantic.*
   Bärmann; *Benedict*; *Braham*; *Hawes*; *Hoffmann, E. T. A.*; *Marschner*; *Smart, Sir George.*
   Annotated Programmes 2, 4; *Criticism* 6; *God save the Queen* 16, 18; *Melody* 9; *Misattributed Compositions*; *Patronage* 8; *Printing* 4; *Tempo.*

WEBERN, ANTON VON (p. 416, pl. **71.** 4). Born in Vienna in 1883 and died near Salzburg in 1945, aged sixty-one. He was a pupil and loyal disciple of Schönberg. His life was spent, for the most part, in and around Vienna, where he held various conductorships and practised as a teacher of composition. He had, however, a period of work in Prague. Most of his works are of delicate texture, small dimensions, and great concentration. They comprise orchestral and chamber music, piano music, songs, etc. —perhaps four hours of music all told. His very early works show a firm rooting in tradition. Some commentators have seen anticipations in them of Note-row methods, but this can be disputed.

During the last twenty years of his life he developed along personal lines the Note-row (q.v.) system of his former master. His life ended tragically, for, venturing mistakenly where he should not have done, he was shot by a sentry of the American army of occupation. Since the death of Schönberg in 1951 he has been the most notable influence on the young avant-garde. But in spite of the work of many apologists his music remains elusive in the mind of the ordinary listener: it is, perhaps, forever 'connoisseur's music'. It is worth remarking that Webern was reluctant to engage in analysis of his own works.

See *Berg*; *Russia* 8; *Harp* 4.

WECHSELN (Ger.). 'To change.' *Wechselnote*, 'Changing Note' (q.v.).

WECKERLIN, JEAN BAPTISTE THÉODORE. Born in Alsace in 1821 and died there in 1910, aged eighty-eight. For thirty years he was in partial or complete charge of the library of the Paris Conservatory, and his bibliographical researches were valuable. His peculiar service to music was that of the discovery, collection, and re-performance of old songs.

He himself wrote a large number of songs, a Mass and other choral works, several operas, etc., but when his name is seen on programmes (as it very often is), it is usually in connexion with some item from one of his books of old-time French songs.

WEDDING MARCH. Special music for weddings (particularly royal weddings) has naturally been composed at all periods. In England from the mid-nineteenth century onwards two incidents of the wedding ceremony, in particular, have come to be accompanied by music—the arrival of the bride and her party and their procession from the west door to the altar, and the regression, after the ceremony and the signing of the register, of the bride and bridegroom in their now combined parties from the east end of the church to the west door.

The two pieces of music most commonly used came, curiously, from the theatre—the Bridal Chorus from Wagner's *Lohengrin* and the Wedding March from Mendelssohn's incidental music to Shakespeare's *Midsummer Night's Dream*.

The first organist to play the latter piece was probably Samuel Reay (q.v.), then organist of the parish church of Tiverton, Devon, who in 1847 made an organ arrangement of his own from the pianoforte duet arrangement then just published by Novello, Ewer & Co., and introduced it at a wedding in that church. But this use of the music seems first to have become fashionable from the occasion of the wedding of the Princess Royal in 1858.

WEDGE FUGUE (Bach). See *Nicknamed Compositions* 1.

WEDGE, GEORGE ANSON (1890–1964), Teacher, organist, and author of books on musical theory. On Juilliard staff from 1918: dean, 1939–46.

WEELKES, THOMAS. Born perhaps about 1575 and died in London in 1623, probably in his later forties. He was organist of Winchester College, receiving thirteen shillings and fourpence per annum plus board and lodging: from 1601 he was organist of Chichester Cathedral. To *The Triumphs of Oriana* (see *Madrigal* 4) he contributed one of the most popular madrigals ever written, 'As Vesta was from Latmos hill descending', and his other works in this class are famous for the boldness of their harmonies and their expressive beauty. He wrote also much church music and some music for viols.

He died whilst on a visit to London, leaving the friend with whom he was staying fifty shillings 'for meat, drinke and boarding and such like necessaryes' and asking him to 'see me buried like a man of my profession'.

See references under *Street Music* 2; *Anthem* 1.

WEEL MAY THE KEEL ROW. See *Keel Row*.

WEG (Ger.). 'Away', 'off'.

WEGELIUS, M. (1846–1906). See *Scandinavia* 6.

WEHMUT, WEHMUTH (Ger.). 'Woe-mood' i.e. sorrow. So *Wehmütig* or *Wehmüthig*, 'sorrowful'.

WEICH (Ger.). 'Soft', 'tender', 'light' (sometimes also 'minor').

WEIDIG, ADOLF (1867–1931). Teacher, theorist, and minor composer. See reference under *Harmony* 20.

WEIDINGER, ANTON (eighteenth century). Court trumpeter at Vienna. See *Trumpet* 4.

WEIHNACHTSLIEDER. See *Carol*.

WEIHNACHTSSYMPHONIE (Haydn). See *Nicknamed Compositions* 11.

WEILL, KURT (p. 416, pl. **71.** 6). Born at Dessau in 1900 and died in New York in 1950, aged fifty. He studied at Berlin under Busoni, served as conductor in the opera-house of his native place, and then returned to Berlin, where he occupied himself with composition. His ideals and aims were those of *Gebrauchsmusik* (q.v.). He associated his literary colleague, Bert Brecht, with him in the theory that in stage works 'music should not co-operate in the action, but only interrupt it in suitable spots'.

Amongst his operas are *The Protagonist* (1926), *The Royal Palace* (1927), and *The Rise and Fall of the City of Mahagonny* (Leipzig, 1929). The City of Mahagonny is a wicked one and the music adequately fits the moral situation, and the work is, further, of enormous length, the combined result of which at the first performance was a violent opposition from a part of the audience (see *Applause* 5).

Brecht and Weill were also jointly responsible for the 1928 German version of *The Beggar's Opera* ('Dreigroschenoper'), a version in which the plot is greatly changed, and in which only one of the original airs remains (see *Jazz* 1).

Weill's instrumental works include choral music, chamber music, and a violin concerto.

He fled from the Nazis and settled in 1935 in the United States.

See *Opera* 24 f (1948); *Jewish Music* 9; *Blitzstein*.

WEINBERGER, JAROMIR (p. 109, pl. **20.** 8). Born at Prague in 1896 and died in St. Petersburg, Fla., in 1967, aged seventy-one. He studied in his native city and under Max Reger. His opera *Schwanda the Bagpiper* (Prague, 1927), soon appeared in over 150 productions and was translated into more than twenty languages. From 1939 he lived in the United States.

WEINEND (Ger.). 'Wailing.'

WEINER, LEO. Born at Budapest in 1885 and died in 1960, aged seventy-five. He taught at the Budapest Academy and was a noted composer of chamber music. In 1928 he organized a conductorless orchestra.

WEINGARTNER, (PAUL) FELIX. Born at Zara, Dalmatia, in 1863 and died at Winterthur, Switzerland, in 1942, aged nearly seventy-nine. After a boyhood of poverty he secured opportunities to show his ability as orchestral and opera conductor, and gradually established himself in the foremost ranks of his profession. In 1927 he became head of the Conservatory of Music at Basle, Switzerland, leaving for Vienna in 1935 and later for Tokyo. His autobiography and other books are well written and interesting, and his compositions are numerous.

See references under *Symphony* 5; *Conducting* 6; *Waltz*; *Clarinet Family* 4 g; *Oboe Family* 4 i; *Arrangement*.

WEINLIED (Ger.). 'Wine song', drinking song.

WEINLIG, CHRISTIAN THEODORE (1780–1842). See *Composition* 13.

WEISS.

(1) MICHAEL. See *Hymns and Hymn Tunes* 17 a.

(2) WILLOUGHBY HUNTER. Born at Liverpool in 1820 and died in London in 1867, aged forty-seven. He was a vocal pupil of Sir George Smart (q.v.), and became well known as an opera and oratorio singer. He composed, about 1854, a setting of Longfellow's 'The Village Blacksmith', and, being refused the sum of five pounds for the full copyright, published it himself, reaping a large reward for himself as long as he lived and for his descendants for many a long year after his death.

Apart from this his compositions are forgotten.

(3) ADOLPH. Born at Baltimore in 1891. He was a pupil of Schönberg, developing, however, an individual method and style in composition. His compositions include orchestral and chamber music, etc. In 1932 he was awarded a Guggenheim Fellowship, which enabled him to work again in Europe for a time. He is a professional bassoonist and he also holds a position of some prominence in the world of chess.

(4) FLEMMING (born 1898). See *Scandinavia* 2.

WEISSE, C. F. (1726–1804). See *Singspiel*.

WEISSENBURG. See *Albicastro*.

WELCKER (late eighteenth-century music publisher). See *Composition* 14.

WELD, THOMAS. See reference under *Hymns and Hymn Tunes* 11.

WELDON.

(1) JOHN (p. 164, pl. **33. 7**). Born at Chichester in 1676 and died in London in 1736, aged sixty. He was a chorister at Eton and then a pupil of Purcell, afterwards becoming organist of New College, Oxford, Gentleman of the Chapel Royal, and finally organist of this as well as of St. Bride's, Fleet Street, and St. Martin-in-the-Fields.

His operatic and other secular music is forgotten but some of his church music remains in use, notably, perhaps, the anthem 'Hear my crying'.

(2) MRS. GEORGINA (maiden name, Thomas, changed to Treherne). Born near London in 1837 and died at Brighton in 1914, aged seventy-six. She was a soprano vocalist of high standing in London and Paris who became a friend and supporter of Gounod (q.v.) when he was in England (1870–5). Later she quarrelled with him and wrote against him (*Mémoires de Georgina Weldon—Justice anglaise*, 6 parts)—as he did of her. She brought a lawsuit against him and was awarded heavy damages; she was, indeed, an habitual litigant and her twenty slander and libel actions brought her damages amounting to £20,000; she herself, however, was sued by the popular conductor, Rivière, and spent six months in jail. Amongst her numerous and untiring

activities were those of conductor of a ladies' choir, founder of an orphanage for musical children, and composer of songs.

WELLEK, ALBERT. See *Harmony* 4.

WELLESLEY. See *Mornington, Earl of*.

WELLESZ, EGON. Born in Vienna in 1885 and died at Oxford in 1974, aged eighty-nine. He was at once musicologist and composer. He took his doctorate at the university of his native place (of which university he later became Professor of the History of Music) with a thesis on the eighteenth-century Viennese composer, Bonno, and followed it with a number of learned monographs, treating various details of musical history, and especially those connected with Byzantine music, on which he later wrote the standard book (*A History of Byzantine Music and Hymnography*, Oxford 1949). He was a pupil of Schönberg and the composer of chamber music, symphonies, choral music, six operas (performed at numerous German and Austrian opera-houses), ballets, etc. (See *Note-row*.)

In 1932 the University of Oxford celebrated the bicentenary of one of its doctors of music, Joseph Haydn of Vienna, by making Wellesz of Vienna one. Later he settled in Oxford where he became a Fellow of Lincoln College, and was (until 1956) Reader in Byzantine Music and a member of the Faculty of Music. He was made a C.B.E. in 1957.

See references under *Greek Church* 4; *Ballet* 5; *Opera* 24 f (1951).

WELLINGTON, DUKE OF (1769–1852). See *Concert* 6; *Mornington, Earl of*; *Applause* 6.

WELLS CATHEDRAL. See references under *Copyist*; *White, Matthew*; *Creyghton*; *Buck, P. C.*; *Abyngdon*; *Cecilia*; *Temperament* 6.

WELL-TEMPERED CLAVIER (Bach and other composers). See *Temperament* 5; *Klavier*; *Nägeli*.

WELSH FOLK SONG SOCIETY. See *Wales* 2.

WELSH NATIONAL ORCHESTRA. See *Wales* 9.

WELTE-MIGNON. See *Mechanical* 13.

WELTE PHOTOPHONE. See *Electric* 5 b.

WENIG (Ger.). 'Little', in the expression *Ein wenig*, 'a little' (i.e. a small amount, 'rather'). *Weniger* is 'less'.

WENNERBERG, G. (1817–1901). See *Scandinavia* 4.

WERDEN (Ger.). 'To become.' So *Werdend*, 'becoming'; *Es wird*, 'it becomes'.

WERNER, ERIC. See *Jewish Music* 8, 9.

WERSTOWSKI. See *Verstovsky*.

WERT, GIACHES (Jacques de W., Jakob von W., Jaches W., Jachet W., Jacques de Vert). Born in 1535, perhaps at Antwerp, and died at Mantua in 1596, aged about sixty. He was sent to north Italy as a boy chorister, and there he remained, his principal place of residence being Mantua, where for a period he held a church position and at other periods was attached to the court.

He enjoyed especial renown for his very numerous madrigals, many books of which were printed.

WESLEY FAMILY, The.[1]

(1 and 2) The brothers JOHN (1703–91) and CHARLES (1707–88). Clergymen of the Church of England and founders of the Methodist movement. See references under *Methodism and Music*; *Church Music* 2; *Puritans* 9; *Common Prayer*; *Hymns and Hymn Tunes* 6, 7, 13, 15; *Presbyterian* 4; *Luther*; *John Brown's Body*; *Bohemia*; *Lampe, J. F.* For a near relative and a musical friend of the family, see *Mornington, Earl of*. The two sons of Charles, (3) and (4) below, were notable musicians.

(3) CHARLES junior, who was born at Bristol in 1757 and died in London in 1834, aged seventy-six, could, before he was three years of age, play on the harpsichord any tune he heard, adding a correct bass to it. He was a pupil of Joseph Kelway and Boyce and became organist of various London churches, composing organ and other music. The high promise of his youth was only partially fulfilled.

See references under *Methodism* 1, 2; *Congregational* 3; and p. 624, pl. **108**. 3.

(4) SAMUEL (p. 209, pl. **41**. 1, 2). Born at Bristol in 1766 and died in London in 1837, aged seventy-one. He, also, was preternaturally gifted as a child. By the time he was eight he had composed an oratorio. He became a notable extemporizer at the organ, the first organ soloist of his day, and a fine composer, his eight-part motet, *In exitu Israel*, standing as a magnificent specimen of his talent. The list of his compositions is varied and long.

At eighteen he temporarily joined the Roman Catholic Church; at twenty-one he fell into a street excavation and was for seven years incapacitated, and ever afterwards subject at intervals to mental aberration.

He was the friend of Mendelssohn, and like him (and before him) a great champion of Bach in the days when that composer's outstanding genius was only here and there admitted.

See references under *Methodism*; *Organ* 12, 13; *Congregational Churches* 4; *Horn, K. F.*; *Ave Verum*; *Accompaniment*.

(5) SAMUEL SEBASTIAN (p. 161, pl. **32**. 5). Born in London in 1810 and died at Gloucester in 1876, aged sixty-five. He was a natural son of Samuel, who gave him his name and a share of his genius.

After serving as choir-boy of the Chapel Royal, then as pluralist organist of three London churches, he became successively organist of the cathedrals of Hereford (1832) and Exeter (1835), of Leeds Parish Church (1842), and of the cathedrals of Winchester (1849) and

[1] A pronunciation of the name current in some quarters is Wezley. This is incorrect; the 's' should be pronounced as such and not as 'z', the earlier form of the name (abandoned by Samuel Wesley, father of John and Charles) being 'Westley' (See *Dictionary of National Biography*).

Gloucester (1865), which last post he held until his death. Like his father before him he was reckoned the first organist of his country, like him he had fame as an extemporizer (see *Improvisation* 2), and from him he seems to have inherited some tendency to eccentricity, instances being his championship of the already out-of-date unequal temperament (see *Temperament* 6) and of the old 'G G' compass of the organ.

He had the highest ideals in church music and fought a hard fight for them against various official and unofficial stupidities and vested interests (p. 161, pl. **32**. 6). On Mr. Gladstone's recommendation Queen Victoria conferred on him a civil list pension of one hundred pounds per annum (he had the choice of this or a knighthood); he enjoyed it only three years before his death occurred, but it was continued to his widow.

His church music is of a high order, and his services, anthems, and hymn tunes show little decline in popularity. His musical influence, through his performances, through his pupils, and through his compositions, was perhaps the most lofty and the most powerful the Anglican Church enjoyed during the nineteenth century, and in that church his character, his attainments, and his eccentricities have already attained something of the dignity of legend.

See references under *Cathedral Music* 7, 8; *Service*; *Anthem*, Period IV; *Organ* 13; *Temperament* 6; *Stephen, Revd. Edward*; *Improvisation* 1. Also p. 768, pl. **129**. 5.

(6) To the major musical members of the family whose careers are treated above may here be added the minor musical members.

Of the children of Samuel Wesley his son Samuel Sebastian has been mentioned. Others are (i) **Eliza Wesley** (1819–95). She was for forty years organist of a City church; she edited and published the correspondence concerning Bach's works that had passed between her father and his colleague in Bach propaganda, Benjamin Jacob, and bequeathed manuscripts both of Bach and of her father to the British Museum. (ii) **R. Glenn Wesley**. He was for long organist of the 'Cathedral of Methodism', City Road Chapel, London (built by his uncle, John Wesley). (iii) Revd. **Charles Wesley**. He was sub-dean of the Chapel Royal and editor of a collection of the words of anthems. (iv) **Matthew Erasmus Wesley**. He was in business but long Hon. Treasurer of the Royal College of Organists, retiring in 1894.

No. iii, above, was a child of Samuel Wesley's legal wife. The other three were, like S. S. Wesley, offspring of his second union, which was never legalized.

A son of Samuel Sebastian Wesley was the **Revd. Francis Gwynne Wesley** (1842–1921), vicar of Hamsteels, Co. Durham. He was dissuaded by his father from entering the musical profession, but he took the degree or D.Mus. He bequeathed to the Royal College of Music a sum of money to found a scholarship to be awarded by means of competition in an art of which his father was a famous exponent —that of organ extemporization.

Gertrude Wesley was in the 1890s advertising in the *Musical Times* as a 'Soprano and Harpist' and her announcement included the information that she was a 'great-granddaughter of Samuel Wesley'. With her the line of musical Wesleys appears to have ended.

WEST, JOHN EBENEZER WILLIAM (1863–1929). See *Voluntary* (end).

WESTMINSTER ABBEY. For references see *Cathedral Music* 2, 7; *Festival* 1; *Cornett and Key Bugle Families* 3.

Organists and masters of the Choristers who receive notice are (with their periods of office): *R. White* (end of sixteenth century); *O. Gibbons* (1623–5); *C. Gibbons* (1660–5); *Blow* (first period, 1668–79); *Purcell* (1679–95); *Blow* (second period, 1695–1708); *Croft* (1708–27); *J. Robinson* (1727–62); *B. Cooke* (1762–93); *S. Arnold* (1793–1802); *Turle* (1831–82); *J. F. Bridge* (1882–1918); *S. H. Nicholson* (1919–28); *Bullock* (1928–41).

WESTMINSTER ASSEMBLY (1643). See *Common Prayer*.

WESTRON WYNDE. See *Mass* 5.

WESTRUP, JACK ALLAN. Born in London in 1904 and died at Headley, Hampshire, in 1975, aged seventy. He was educated at Dulwich College and Balliol College, Oxford. After a period as a master at his old school he became one of the music critics of the *Daily Telegraph* and editor of the *Monthly Musical Record* (1933–45), and thereafter Lecturer in Music in the Newcastle College of Durham University, and Professor of Music at Birmingham University (1944) and at Oxford (1946–71). He was active in musicological research and in the performance of operas of Monteverdi, Locke, Mozart, and others. His book on Purcell corrected long-accepted errors, and he edited the *New Oxford History of Music*. He was knighted in 1960. See *Dictionaries* 1.

WE THREE KINGS OF ORIENT. See *Carol*.

WETTERHARFE. See *Aeolian Harp*.

WE WON'T GO HOME TILL MORNING. See *Malbrouk*.

WEYRAUCH, AUGUST HEINRICH VON (born 1788). See *Misattributed Compositions* ('Schubert's Adieu').

WEYSE, C. E. F. (1774–1842). See *Scandinavia* 2.

WHAT THOUGH I AM A COUNTRY LASS. See *Sally in our Alley*.

WHEATLEY, FRANCIS. English painter. See *Street Music* 2 (end of section).

WHEATSTONE, SIR CHARLES (1802–75). English scientist and inventor. See *Reed-Organ Family* 3, 4, 5; *Pianoforte* 15; p. 884, pl. **149**. 3.

WHEN A LITTLE FARM WE KEEP. See *Mazzinghi*.

WHEN I SURVEY THE WONDROUS CROSS. See *Hymns and Hymn Tunes* 6, 7.

WHEN JOHNNY COMES MARCHING HOME. This was first published in Boston in 1863, under the above title, with the added words, *Music introduced in 'The Soldier's Return March' by Gilmore's Band. Words and Music by Louis Lambert*. It is now generally conceded that 'Lambert' was a pseudonym for Gilmore. In 1902 one Julian Edwards produced an opera named after the song. A symphonic overture with the same name, by Roy Harris (1934), is popular with American orchestras.

WHEN SHE CAM BEN. See *Laird o' Cockpen*.

WHEN THE KING ENJOYS HIS OWN AGAIN. This is a ballad of the time of the beginning of the civil war in England (1643), and served to keep up the spirits of the Cavalier party at that time, and after the revolution of 1689 those of the adherents of the Pretender. It is by the celebrated ballad-monger Martin Parker, who probably wrote it to an existing tune. The original refrain was 'When the king comes home in peace again'.

WHEN THE STORMY WINDS DO BLOW. See *You Gentlemen of England*.

WHIFFLE. A fife (q.v.). A whiffler was a fifer who preceded a great personage in a ceremonial. The old morris dance always had a whiffler as one of its participants. The usual definition is that given above. But in the supplementary volume to Grove's *Dictionary* (1940) the authority on old instruments, Canon F. W. Galpin, shows reason for thinking that the whiffle (properly spelt 'wifle') was 'a short staff or spear, carried by attendants deputed to clear the way for a procession'. He says that 'in the 16th century fifers and wiflers are mentioned together', and suggests the office of wifler 'still lingers on in that of the Drum-Major with his staff'.

WHIPPLE, GUY MONTROSE. See reference under *Mechanical Reproduction* 13.

WHISPERING GALLERIES. See *Acoustics* 18; *Concert Halls* 12.

WHISTLE. See *Recorder Family* 1, 3 b. Dance band performers now sometimes make use of a variety of whistles, as the siren whistle, tugboat whistle, three-tone whistle, guard's whistle, police whistle, cuckoo whistle, etc.

Cf. *Effects*.

WHISTLER, J. A. McNEILL (Painter; 1834–1903). See *Colour and Music* 1.

WHISTLING. As a musical instrument the human whistle is peculiar. The rounded lips, by the vibration provoked by air expelled through them, emit a sound, the pitch of which is then controlled by the shaping of the resonating chamber, the mouth, behind them, i.e. the same air current which is progressing outward through the lips serves as a medium for sound 'waves' (see *Acoustics* 11) progressing inwards, the 'frequency' of which is partly controlled from within. If the reader will make a moment's experiment he will find that at whatever pitch he whistles the shape and size of orifice and tension of his lips remain unaltered, whereas changes of shape within the mouth can be distinctly felt.

The technique of whistling has sometimes been developed to the point of virtuosity. In the late nineteenth century the American Mrs.

Alice Shaw was a famous whistler, known as 'La Belle Siffleuse'. As one of her countrymen wrote of her in the New York *Musical Courier* in 1931, 'No jazz or cheap crooning stuff had a place in her repertoire and her performances were equally sensational in the drawing-rooms of kings, czars, emperors, and maharajahs and the homes of the intelligentsia of the world's capitals'. (Incidentally, those performances were amongst the first to be circulated by Edison as records for his Phonograph in 1887 and the following years.)

Brenet's *Dictionnaire de la Musique* (1926) asserts that 'In the United States of America whistling has become a real art, and lovers of whistling have arrived at the point of combining in the whistled performance of duos, trios, and classical quartets'. (We have not, however, heard elsewhere of whistlers who could achieve the performance of a violoncello or vocal bass part.)

In 1935 the Austrian Society for Experimental Phonetics examined the case of a young man able to whistle two notes (and consequently two airs) at a time—presumably by the means which enable us to produce the two simultaneous vocal pitches necessary to the production of all our vowel sounds (see *Voice* 7). It was even stated that he could whistle two-part fugues. More than this he could hum, simultaneously. 'Further, in the overture to *Egmont* the subject of this communication succeeded in obtaining sometimes a real orchestration, testifying to the possession of a remarkable musical taste.'

Here the author of the present work must be content to quote, without attempting explanation. And so also with the information supplied by the late Dr. Ernest Walker of Oxford— 'I have heard an undergraduate give a fairly reasonable rendering of the *Elijah* trio, "Lift thine eyes", all by himself. The tone-quantity was small, the intonation moderate to bad, the rhythmical accuracy shaky. Still it quite unmistakably *was* Mendelssohn. How he did it I cannot remember but many others besides myself heard it, so it was not hypnotic suggestion, presumably.'

WHISTON. See *Cathedral Music* 8.

WHITE. There are several early composers of this name, and some recent ones.

(1) ROBERT. Born about 1534 and died in London in 1574, aged perhaps forty. He was probably son-in-law to Tye (q.v.), whom he succeeded as organist of Ely Cathedral. It appears likely that after a few years there he moved to Chester Cathedral. Later he seems to have been Master of the Choristers of Westminster Abbey, and in Westminster he died, during the plague of 1574, with his wife and three of his five children, leaving by will three pounds to his father and fourpence to each of his pupils—'to every of my skollers iiijd'.

In his lifetime he was held in great consideration; then he was wellnigh forgotten until Burney, at the end of the eighteenth century,

called attention to him as 'an excellent composer of church services in the style of Palestrina; which, however, he did not imitate, as he was anterior to him, and a great master of harmony before the productions of the chief of the Roman school were published, or at least circulated, in other parts of Europe'—following his eulogy by printing an anthem in full on the succeeding pages of his *History*.

The German historians, Ambros (1816–76) and Nagel (*History of English Music*, 1894–7), have warmly praised him, and the latter taunts Britons with their neglect in leaving so much of his work unpublished. His church music (now published by the Carnegie Trustees and the Oxford University Press) ranks with that of Tye and Tallis—the very greatest of the earlier Elizabethans.

(2) WILLIAM. He lived in the earlier part of the seventeenth century, and was a singing man at Westminster Abbey, beyond which nothing is known of him save that he wrote some church music and music for viols. He is often confused with his namesake Robert (see above).

(3) MATTHEW. He is known to have been a Gentleman of the Chapel Royal (q.v.) under James I, and in 1611 he was in orders and a Vicar-Choral of Wells Cathedral. In 1629 he became a Doctor of Music of Oxford. He is the putative parent of catches and anthems, but his progeny has become much mingled with that of the other Whites and it is difficult to sort it out again.

(4) MAUDE VALÉRIE. Born at Dieppe in 1855 and died in London in 1937, aged eighty-two. She was trained at the Royal Academy of Music, London, where she held the Mendelssohn Scholarship. She wrote (especially) songs.

(5) FELIX HAROLD. Born in London in 1884 and there died in 1945. He was a self-taught musician who had orchestral music performed at the London Promenade Concerts, and chamber music included in many programmes, whose works (including fifty songs) were published by ten or a dozen publishers, and who yet somehow never received the full recognition that the delicacy of his conceptions and the excellence of the technique with which he expressed them seemed to demand. His composition 'after' Andrew Marvell's *Nymph's Complaint for the Death of her Fawn* (oboe or violin, viola and piano) received a Carnegie award in 1922.

(6) ERNEST GEORGE, London singing teacher. See *Voice* 4.

(7) JOSEPH. Cuban violinist. See mention under *United States of America* 6 (end).

(8) MRS. MEADOWS. See *Smith, Alice Mary*.

WHITE COCKADE. See *Red Flag*.

WHITEFIELD, GEORGE (1714–70). English Calvinistic Methodist divine. See *Methodism* 9; *Beggar's Opera*.

WHITELEY, HERBERT. See *Competitions* 3.

WHITELOCKE, BULSTRODE (1605–75). Puritan statesman, music-lover, and opera promoter. See *Puritans* 4.

WHITEMAN, PAUL (1890–1967). See *Jazz* 2, 5; *Gershwin*.

WHITE VOICE. A voice lacking in the characteristics which give an emotional richness of tone (see *Voice* 16).

WHITFELD. See *Clarke-Whitfeld*.

WHITHORNE.

(1) THOMAS. See *Whythorne*.

(2) EMERSON (family name originally 'Whittern'; 1884–1958). Composer of symphonic works, chamber music, and songs.

WHITING, ARTHUR BATTELLE. Born at Cambridge, Mass., in 1861 and died at Beverly, Mass., in 1936, aged seventy-five. His compositions are those of a composer of refinement and of modest but true feeling, but have not maintained their place in the repertory.

WHITLEY, WILLIAM THOMAS (1861–1947). English Baptist historian (LL.D., etc.). See *Baptist* 5.

WHITTAKER, WILLIAM GILLIES. Born at Newcastle-on-Tyne in 1876 and died in the Orkney Islands in 1944.

After practising in Newcastle-on-Tyne as an organist, piano teacher, composition teacher, singing teacher, school music teacher, and even public singer, and directing for thirty years the musical activities of Armstrong College (University of Durham) and the work of the Newcastle Bach Choir, which he founded, he was from 1930 to 1941 in Glasgow as head of the Scottish National Academy of Music and Professor of Music in the University.

As a composer he had two Carnegie awards. He collected and edited volumes of North Country folk songs, and acted as editor of a series of arias of Bach and Handel, of school songs, and of many of the long series of Bach's Church Cantatas. He wrote books on these and other subjects.

See references under *Gramophone* 7; *Young, William*; *Scotland* 11; *Sonata* 10 b (1653).

WHITTLE AND DUB. See *Recorder Family* 3 c.

WHIZZER. See *Thunder Stick*.

WHOLE-NOTE (Amer.). Semibreve (Table 3).

WHOLE-TONE SCALE. See *Scales* 9; *Tonality*; *Harmony* 14; *Temperament* 9.

WHYTE. See *White* 1, 2, 3 (alternative spelling).

WHYTHORNE or **WHITHORNE**, THOMAS. Born in 1528 and died some time after 1590. He is an important composer of secular songs, 'some long, some short, some hard, some easie to be songe and some betwene both; also some solemne, and some pleasant or mery; so that according to the skill of the singers (not being Musitians) and disposition and delite of the hearers, they may here finde songs for their contentation and liking'.

In effect his works are ayres (see *Madrigal* 3 b) but, published in 1571, they precede the true period of the ayre by some years. Twenty years later he brought out a set of vocal duets.

Burney (q.v.), referring to the first set, says 'both the words and music of these songs are truly barbarous', but that is not, in general, by any means the view of present-day connoisseurs, and there has been republication of a good deal of his work.

He left a manuscript autobiography, which was published in 1961, and counts as the first musical autobiography.

WIBRECHT. See *Tuba Group* 1.

WIDOR, CHARLES MARIE JEAN ALBERT (p. 784, pl. **131**. 7). Born at Lyons in 1844 and died in Paris in 1937, aged ninety-three. His father gave him his first instruction. He then studied under Lemmens. He quickly rose to fame and became organist of St. Sulpice, Paris, and professor of organ at the Conservatory, where he followed Franck, later following Dubois as professor of composition.

His compositions were very varied, including orchestral works, operas, chamber music, etc., but, naturally, those for organ have become best known; these latter have tended to develop variety in style in organ playing and they are widely played throughout the world. The most important of them are called 'Symphonies for Organ'. He was a notable practitioner of the art of improvisation.

He wrote much musical criticism, a book on orchestration, and other things, and, with Schweitzer, undertook an edition of the organ works of Bach. He was Permanent Secretary of the Academy of Fine Arts.

See *Mass* 4 (Period V); *Toccatina*; *Reed-Organ Family* 9; *Cornet* 1; *Percussion Family* 4 e (Celeste); *Colour and Music* 3; *Concerto* 6 b (1844); *Improvisation* 2; *Schweitzer*.

WIE (Ger.). 'As', 'like', 'as if'.

WIECK, FRIEDRICH (1785–1873) and CLARA JOSEPHINE, afterwards Clara Schumann (1819–96). See under *Schumann, Robert*; *Pianoforte* 22; *Novellette*; *Bülow*.

WIEDER (Ger.). 'Again.' So *Wiederholung*, 'repetition'.

WIEGENLIED. Lullaby or Berceuse (q.v.) (German 'Wiege' = cradle; 'wiegen' = to rock; so *wiegend*, 'rocking', 'swaying').

WIÉNER. See *Jazz* 5.

WIENERISCH (Ger.). 'Viennese.'

WIENIAWSKI.

(1) HENRI. Born at Lublin, in Poland, in 1835 and died in Moscow in 1880, aged forty-four. He was trained as a violinist, from the age of eight, in the Paris Conservatory, and quickly made an international name. From his twenty-fifth to his thirty-seventh year he lived in St. Petersburg. He toured the United States with Rubinstein (see anecdote under *Prima Donna*) and then for a few years settled in Brussels, as successor to Vieuxtemps in the Conservatory. He composed concertos, six fantasias, etc.—rather of the showy than the serious kind. (Cf. *Poldowski*.)

(2) JOSEPH. Born at Lublin, in Poland, in 1837 and died at Brussels in 1912, aged seventy-five. He was brother of the above and a distinguished pianist. He composed piano and chamber music.

WIEPRECHT. See *Tuba Group* 1.

WIEST, L. A. (1819–89). See *Rumania*.

WIGMAN, MARY. See *Ballet* 5.

WIGMORE HALL, LONDON. See *Concert* 8.

WIHTOL. See *Vihtol*.

WILBERFORCE, WILLIAM (1759–1833). Philanthropist. See *Puritans* 9.

WILBYE, JOHN. Born at Diss in Norfolk in 1574 and died at Colchester in 1638, aged sixty-four. He was, from about his twenty-first year, resident in the house of Sir Thomas Kytson, of Hengrave Hall, near Bury St. Edmunds, and remained there and in the house of a young member of the family all the rest of his days. For his musical services the Kytsons gave him a lease of the best sheep farm on their estate.

He is considered by many to be the greatest writer of madrigals, British or foreign. Amongst his madrigals some of the most popular are 'Adieu, sweet Amaryllis', 'Flora gave me fairest flowers', and 'Sweet honey-sucking bees'.

See *Patronage* 8.

WILFRID, THOMAS (1888–1968). See *Colour and Music* 9.

WILHELM, CARL (1815–73). See *Watch on the Rhine*.

WILHELMJ, AUGUST EMIL DANIEL FERDINAND. Born in 1845 at Usingen, in Nassau, and died in London in 1908, aged sixty-two. He was a famous violin virtuoso, in this capacity touring the old and new worlds. To him fell the honour of occupying the first desk in the orchestra at the opening performance at Bayreuth (see *Wagner*) in 1876.

For the last fourteen years of his life he occupied the post of principal violin professor at the Guildhall School of Music, London.

See references under *Acoustics* 10; *G string*.

WILHEM, GUILLAUME LOUIS BOCQUILLON (1781–1842). See references under *Hullah*; *Tonic Sol-fa* 1.

WILLAERT, ADRIAN—often in his own day called simply 'Messer Adriano' (p. 96, pl. 15. 4). Born at Bruges, or elsewhere in Flanders, about 1480 and died at Venice in 1562, aged over eighty. He studied law and music in Paris and then travelled in Italy. At Rome he heard the Papal Choir perform one of his compositions as the work of the famous Josquin des Prés.

He now travelled in central Europe and returning to Italy was appointed to direct the music of St. Mark's, Venice. There he remained, famous as a composer and teacher of composers, some of his pupils being of high celebrity. He contributed greatly to the development of the madrigal.

His motets, masses, madrigals, and the like were very widely published during his own lifetime. Some of his church compositions make use of a double choir, this being required by the architectural arrangements in the church over whose music he presided; these show a development by which his contemporaries and successors profited.

See references to him and his period and contemporaries under *Belgium* 1; *Italy* 4; *Hungary*; *Temperament* 5.

WILLAN, HEALEY. Born in 1880 at Balham, Surrey and died in Toronto in 1968, aged eighty-seven. He was an organist in London, and then, in 1913, joined the staff of the University of Toronto and also accepted an organistship in that city, where he became active in many capacities. He composed orchestral music, organ music, choral music (for church and otherwise), chamber music, an opera (*Deirdre*), songs, etc. From 1937 until 1950 he was Professor at the University of Toronto.

WILL FORSTER'S VIRGINAL BOOK. This is a manuscript book of virginal music, compiled in 1624. It belongs to the Queen and is in the Queen's Library of the British Museum. It is as yet unpublished. See *Harpsichord* 3, and compare *Fitzwilliam Virginal Book*, *Benjamin Cosyn's Virginal Book*, and *Parthenia*.

WILLIAM I OF ENGLAND ('The Conqueror'; b. 1027; seized English throne 1066; d. 1087). See *Minstrels* 2; *Bell* 5.

WILLIAM III (b. 1650; came to English throne jointly with his queen, Mary, in 1689; d. 1702). See *Lilliburlero*; *Chapel Royal*.

WILLIAMS.

(1) RALPH VAUGHAN. See *Vaughan Williams*.

(2) CHARLES LEE (1853–1935). Organist of Gloucester Cathedral from 1882 to 1897, and by virtue of that position one of the conductors of the Three Choirs Festival, for which he composed a number of short oratorios. (See *Oratorio* 7—1889, 1892.) He also wrote anthems, service music, etc.

(3) ALBERTO. Born at Buenos Aires in 1862 and died there in 1952, aged eighty-nine. He studied under Franck and others at the Paris Conservatory and on return to Argentina founded the Conservatory of Buenos Aires, of which he became director. His works include nine symphonies, chamber music, songs, and many pianoforte compositions.

(4) WILLIAM SIDNEY GWYNN. Born at Llangollen, in N. Wales. He has been active as an editor of Welsh musical journals, as publisher of Welsh music, as adjudicator at Eisteddfodau, and as composer, and is the author of *Welsh National Music and Dance* (1932) and other works.

(5) JOHN GERARD. Born in London in 1888 and died at Caterham in 1947, aged fifty-eight.

A composer of graceful songs, choral music, piano music, chamber music, orchestral music, ballad operas, operettas, ballets, etc.

(6) CHRISTOPHER À BECKET (1890–1956). Author: composer of much pianoforte music, chamber music, etc.

(7) JOHN LLOYD. Authority on Welsh folksong. See *Wales* 2.

(8) THOMAS E. See *Britannia, the Pride of the Ocean*.

(9) HARRY J. See *Tipperary*.

(10) JOSEPH, Ltd. See *Publishing* 7.

WILLIAMSON, MALCOLM. Born in Sydney in 1931. He studied under Eugene Goossens and (in London from 1953) Elizabeth Lutyens. His compositions, some in popular vein, soon included 5 operas, 3 piano concertos, and numerous sacred and orchestral works. In 1975 he became Master of the Queen's Music.

WILLIS.

(1) ROBERT (1800–75). Archaeologist, authority on architecture, amateur musician, and author of books on the mechanism of the larynx and the processes of speech that established a new view of the subject.

See *Voice* 7.

(2) HENRY (1821–1901). Famous London organ-builder (see *Organ* 8). The firm is still pre-eminent under another Henry Willis (born 1889), grandson of the above. The article *Organ* in the present work was revised by him.

WILLIS'S ROOMS. See *Concert* 8.

WILL YE NO COME BACK AGAIN? The tune is the old one of *Royal Charlie*, the lyric is by Lady Nairne (q.v.).

WILSON.

(1) JOHN (p. 817, pl. **140**. 2). Born probably at Faversham, Kent, in 1595 and died in London in 1674, aged seventy-eight. He was a singer, lutenist, and violist, and is held by some authorities to have played the original part of Balthazar in Shakespeare's *Much Ado* (stage direction in First Folio 'enter the Prince, Leonato, Claudio, and Jacke Wilson'). He produced settings of several of the songs in Shakespeare's plays, and these are sometimes heard today. Charles I, who loved his lute playing, appointed him as his private musician, and after the Restoration Charles II made him a Gentleman of the Chapel Royal. He was, during the Commonwealth, appointed Professor of Music in the University of Oxford, and the Oxford historian, Anthony Wood, loyally calls him 'the greatest and most curious Judge of Musick that ever was'.

He left songs, ayres, catches, and a little church music, but his chief importance is in connexion with Shakespeare.

See under *Brenhines Dido*; *Congregational* 2.

(2) LADY. See *Skye Boat Song*.

(3) H. J. LANE. Born at Gloucester in 1870,

died in 1915, aged forty-five. He studied at the Royal Academy of Music, London, and toured as accompanist with Minnie Hauk and Madame Albani. He composed songs, but his best-known work was as editor of old English vocal music, a great deal of which is, by careless compilers of concert programmes, attributed to him as its actual composer.

WINCHESTER CATHEDRAL. See references under *Cathedral Music* 2; *Organ* 8; *Cecilia*.

Organists who receive notice in this book are (with their periods of office): *J. Holmes* (to 1602); *C. Gibbons* (appointed 1638); *Reading* (1675–81); *D. Roseingrave* (1682–92); *Kent* (1737–74); *S. S. Wesley* (1849–65).

WINCHESTER COLLEGE. See mention under *Dulce Domum*; *Dibdin*.

The following organists receive notice in this book (with dates of their period of office): *Weelkes* (dates unknown); *Reading* (1681–92); *J. Clarke* (1692–5); *Kent* (1737–74); *Dyson* (1924–37).

WINCHESTER OLD (Hymn Tune). See *Tye*.

WIND BAND CONTESTS. See *Competitions* 3.

WIND BASS MASS (Haydn). See *Nicknamed Compositions* 13 (14).

WIND CHEST. See *Organ* 1.

WINDHARFE. See *Aeolian Harp*.

WIND MACHINE. It reproduces the sound of the wind in passages of a meteorological intention, as, for instance, in Strauss's *Don Quixote*; it is a sort of barrel framework covered with silk and revolved by handles, so that the silk is in friction against cardboard or wood.

Cf. *Ventilator*.

WINDPIPE. See *Voice* 21.

WIND PRESSURE. See *Organ* 3, 4.

WINDSOR, ST. GEORGE'S CHAPEL. See remarks under *Cathedral Music* 2; *Chapel Royal*.

Organists noticed in this book are (with the dates of their period of office): *Merbecke* (end of sixteenth century); *Richard Farrant* (1564–?1580); *J. Mundy* (c. 1581–5); *Giles* (1585–1632); *Child* (1632–97); *Elvey* (1835–82); *Parratt* (1882–1924); *H. W. Davies* (1927–31); *C. Hylton Stewart* (1932–3); *W. H. Harris* (1933).

WINKEL, DIETRICH NIKOLAUS (c. 1776–1826). See *Composition* 14.

WINSOR, J. W. See *Nicknamed Compositions*, s.v. 'Handel'.

'WINTER WIND' ÉTUDE (Chopin). See *Nicknamed Compositions* 8.

WIRBEL. German for 'whirl'; used in a musical connexion for 'drum roll'.

WIRBELTROMMEL (Ger.). Tenor drum; see *Percussion Family* 3 j, 4 b, 5 j.

WIRE BRUSH. See *Percussion Family* 4 d.

WIRELESS. See *Broadcasting of Music*.

WIRÉN, DAG. Born near Nora, in central Sweden, in 1905. He studied at the Conservatory of Stockholm, and then in Paris. After supporting himself successively as librarian and music critic, he found himself in 1946 able to devote his time to composition. A Serenade for string orchestra is well known; other works in his limited output include a cello concerto and music for piano and for string quartet.

WIR GLAUBEN ALL'. See *Chorale*.

WISE, MICHAEL. Born, probably at Salisbury, about 1648 and died there in 1687, aged about thirty-nine. He was one of the boys of the first choir of the Chapel Royal after the Restoration (see *Cooke, Henry*; *Humfrey*; *Blow*; *Purcell*). In later life he was organist of Salisbury Cathedral and a Gentleman of the Chapel Royal.

When Charles II made a royal progress Wise had the right to play the organ in any church visited; once, however, he got into trouble with the king for interrupting the sermon with a voluntary.

Under James II he was Master of the Choristers at St. Paul's Cathedral.

His comparatively early death was his own fault—or that of his wife, or that, again, of a Salisbury watchman, or that of any two or all three. When in that city he quarrelled with his wife and rushing into the street ran at the watchman, whom he felled, but who rose, hit him on the head with his bill-hook, and broke his skull. They buried him in the cathedral.

Some of his church music is in regular use and other of it remains unpublished (see reference under *Anthem*, Period II).

'WITCH' MINUET (Haydn). See *Nicknamed Compositions* 12 (under 'Quintenquartett').

WITHER or **WITHERS**, GEORGE (1588–1667). English Puritan poet and pamphleteer. See *Hymns and Hymn Tunes* 6, 17 e (xv).

WITHIN A MILE OF EDINBURGH TOWN has one of the many London-made sham Scottish tunes (see references to these under *Scotland* 1). The words are an altered version of some by Tom D'Urfey (1653–1723), and the tune (composed 1780) is by James Hook (q.v.).

WITKOWSKI, GEORGES MARTIN. Born in Algeria in 1867 and died in Lyons in 1943, aged seventy-six. He was partly of Polish descent but brought up in France, where his studies were largely directed by d'Indy. In 1924 he became director of the Conservatory of Lyons. His compositions are many and varied.

WITMARK. See *Publishing* 9.

WITT, FRANZ XAVER. See *Cecilian Movement*.

WITTGENSTEIN, PAUL (1887–1961). See *Pianoforte* 21. Also p. 801, pl. **138.** 3.

WOHLGEFÄLLIG (Ger.). 'Pleasant', 'pleasantly'.

WOHLTEMPERIERTES KLAVIER (Bach's 48 Preludes and Fugues and similar works by other composers). See *Temperament* 5; *Klavier*; *Nägeli*.

WOIZIKOVSKI. See *Ballet* 9.

WOLF. (1) A jarring sound occasionally heard from certain notes in bowed instruments. Its probable and most frequent cause is as follows: The body of the instrument, as a whole,

'resonates' to a certain note (see *Acoustics* 20 a) and when this note is played the body jars, just as a room-ornament is sometimes found to jar every time a certain note of the piano is played. It is the aim of the maker to get the resonating note of the instrument below that of the lowest open string, and if this 'wolf' occurs he has failed in his aim.

(2) An out-of-tuneness in the old organs before the days of equal temperament when the player passed into the extremer keys.

See *Temperament* 7.

WOLF.

(1) HUGO (p. 401, pl. **70.** 5). Born at Windischgrätz, Southern Styria, Austria (now Slovenski Gradec and in Yugoslavia), in 1860 and died at Vienna in 1903, aged nearly forty-three. He has been hailed as one of the greatest song-writers of the world—second only to Schubert, if to him. But judgements differ.

His life was tragic. As a student he was dismissed from the Vienna Conservatory on a false charge and then made a bare living by giving lessons and by writing musical criticism (this very pro-Wagnerian and anti-Brahms, and Brahms, at that time resident in Vienna, was one of that city's most reverently worshipped gods). Then he settled for four years in a tiny village near Vienna and poured out one song after another: over forty settings of poems by Mörike, fifty of poems by Goethe, and so on.

Such a production is abnormal, and his life became an alternation of feverish activity and despondent lethargy. At thirty-seven he was in a mental asylum, and there he died.

In 1937 a number of hitherto unknown songs of his were discovered and published.

His works include an opera (*The Corregidor*, Mannheim, 1896), a string quartet, and one or two orchestral pieces, but it is by his songs, so rapidly thrown off, that his name lives.

See *Composition* 6, 10; *Germany* 6; *Song* 5; *Singing* 10; *Opera* 24 f (1939); *Accompaniment*; *Chamber Music* 6, Period III (1860).

(2) JOHANNES. Born in Berlin in 1869 and died near Munich in 1947, aged seventy-eight. He was a very active and learned musicologist, long Professor in the University of Berlin and music librarian of the Prussian State Library. His various publications are of the highest importance and he took a valuable part in the international organization of musicological research.

See reference under *Italy* 3.

WOLF, THE (Song). See *Shield*.

WOLFENBÜTTEL MANUSCRIPT. See *Scotland* 5.

WOLF-FERRARI, ERMANNO. Born in Venice in 1876 and there died in 1948, aged seventy-two. He composed a number of comic operas, notably *The School for Fathers* and *Susanna's Secret*, as well as the realistic *The Jewels of the Madonna* and the oratorio *La Vita nuova* (1903), etc.

See reference under *Rispetto*.

WÖLFL, JOSEPH (1773–1812). He was a pupil of Mozart's father and of Haydn's brother, and a rival of Beethoven in the art of improvisation at the piano (see *Improvisation* 2, 3). He wrote symphonies, sonatas, chamber music, operas, etc. (In London 1805 to death.)

WOLFRAM VON ESCHENBACH. See *Minstrels* 7.

WOLSTENHOLME, WILLIAM. Born at Blackburn, Lancashire, in 1865 and died in London in 1931, aged sixty-six. At six he was so musical that there being in the house a piano and a harmonium side by side, a semitone different in pitch, he would play a melody with one hand on one and an improvised accompaniment with the other hand on the other, in the two different keys necessary to produce agreement.

He was born blind (cf. *Hollins*) and was the first blind musician in a century and a half to take a musical degree at Oxford, Stanley (q.v.) taking the last before him. Elgar acted as his amanuensis on this occasion.

He acted as organist of several London churches, toured the United States as a recitalist, and composed music for various media, that for organ being, naturally, the best known.
See *Improvisation* 2.

WOLZOGEN, FREIHERR (= Baron) **HANS PAUL VON.** Born at Potsdam in 1848 and died at Bayreuth in 1938, aged eighty-nine. He was a disciple of Wagner and a high authority on his works. He edited the official periodical *Bayreuther Blätter* and published an almost incredible quantity of Wagnerian literature of various kinds.
See *Leading Motif.*

WOMEN'S MUSICAL CLUBS. See *United States of America* 5.

WOOD.

(1) **ANTHONY** (1632–95); latterly styled by himself 'Anthony à Wood'). Oxford antiquarian whose Diary contains many valuable references to musical life and whose manuscript notes on musicians in the Bodleian Library, Oxford, are a useful source of information.
See references under *Profession of Music* 9; *Clubs for Music-Making*; *Fairs and their Music*; *Tye, Christopher*; *Fayrfax, Robert*; *Wilson, John*; *Congregational* 2.

(2) **'FATHER WOOD'** (of Rome). See *Pianoforte* 17.

(3) **CHARLES.** Born at Armagh, Ireland, in 1866 and died at Cambridge in 1926, aged sixty. He studied at the Royal College of Music (of which he was later to become a professor), and then at Cambridge (M.A., D.Mus.), where in 1924 he succeeded Stanford (q.v.) as Professor of Music for the short remaining span of his life. His influence as a teacher was very great.

His compositions include choral and orchestral works, songs, music to Greek plays, church music, and especially, perhaps, chamber music.
See *Chorale Prelude*; *Graves, A. P.*; *Bliss.*

(4) **HENRY JOSEPH** (p. 240, pl. **44.** 8). Born in London in 1869 and there died in 1944, aged seventy-five. After a career as organist that began at the age of ten, and study at the Royal Academy of Music, he became an opera conductor at the age of twenty. At twenty-six he was engaged to conduct the series of Promenade Concerts at the newly opened Queen's Hall, and nearly half a century later he was still doing so. (When the Queen's Hall was destroyed by bombing in 1941, the 'Proms' continued at the Albert Hall.) His conductorship was remarkable for the introduction of many works of composers and schools previously unknown to the British public. He was active as a teacher of singing and as a conductor of choral societies. In 1911 he was knighted. In younger days he was known as a composer, but later when his name appeared on a programme in any capacity other than that of conductor it was usually as the orchestral 'arranger' of music.
See references under *Orchestra* 5; *Additional Accompaniments*; *Singing* 9; *Colour* 3; *Klenovsky*; *Concert* 7; *Auxetophone.*

(5) **HAYDN.** Born near Huddersfield, Yorkshire, in 1882 and died in London in 1959, aged seventy-six. He had a double career as solo violinist and as a composer some of whose lighter pieces (e.g. *Roses of Picardy*) had a great vogue.

(6) **THOMAS.** Born at Chorley, Lancs., in 1892 and died at Bures, Suffolk, in 1950, aged fifty-seven. He was director of music at Tonbridge School and lecturer and precentor of his college at Oxford (Exeter), and then spent some years in travel in Australasia and Canada as an examiner. The experiences of his earlier life are recorded in *True Thomas*. He also edited books of songs for boys. His compositions, vigorous and original, are largely choral.

(7) **B. F. WOOD MUSIC COMPANY, THE.** See reference under *Publishing of Music* 9.

WOOD BLOCK. See *Chinese Wood Block.*

WOODBRIDGE, WILLIAM C. See *Education and Music* 3.

WOOD-WIND INSTRUMENTS. See *Orchestra* 6; *Acoustics* 5.

WORCESTER (Mass.). See *Festival* 2.

WORCESTER CATHEDRAL. See references under *Cathedral Music* 2.
Organists who receive notice in this book are (with their periods of office): *Patrick* (end of sixteenth century); *Giles* (1581–5); *T. Tomkins* (c. 1596–1646); *W. Hayes* (1731–4); *Atkins* (1897–1950).

WORCESTERSHIRE BAGPIPES. See *Bagpipe Family* 3.

WORDE, WYNKYN DE (d. about 1534). Important early English printer and publisher. See *Printing* 1; *Carols.*

WORD OF GOD INCARNATE. See *Ave Verum Corpus.*

WORDSWORTH.

(1) **WILLIAM** (poet; 1770–1850). See references under *Romantic*; *Rousseau.*

(2) WILLIAM B. Born in London in 1908. He studied at Edinburgh under Tovey (q.v.). His compositions include symphonies, works for string orchestra, chamber music, choral music, piano music, songs, etc.

WORK, HENRY CLAY. See *Marching through Georgia.*

WORKING-OUT. Same as 'Development' in compound binary form, etc. See under *Development* and also *Form* 7.

WORKMANSHIP IN MUSIC. See *Quality in Music* 4.

WORLD RADIO. See *Broadcasting of Music* 1 c.

WORMSER, ANDRÉ. See *Pantomime.*

WORNUM, ROBERT. See *Pianoforte* 6.

WORSHIPFUL COMPANY OF MUSICIANS (or Musicians' Company). See *Minstrels, etc.* 3; *Profession* 1; *Cecilia, Saint.*

WORŽISCHEK, JOHANN HUGO (1791–1825). Bohemian pianist, organist, conductor, and composer, whose career was in Vienna.

See references under *Impromptu.*

WOULD I WERE ERIN'S APPLE BLOSSOM. See *Londonderry Air.*

WOZZECK (Alban Berg). Produced in Berlin in 1925. The libretto is the composer's re-arrangement of the fragmentary play *Woyzeck* by the early nineteenth-century writer, Georg Büchner. He has reduced its twenty-five scenes to fifteen, divided equally into three acts.

Act I

Wozzeck (*Baritone*) is a private soldier and officer's batman. He has a child by his mistress, **Marie** (*Soprano*), and earns money towards their support by submitting himself to the pseudo-scientific dietetic experiments of an eccentric army doctor.

Marie is fascinated by the physical attractions of an impressive **Drum-Major** (*Tenor*), and yields to his advances.

Act II

Wozzeck has suspicions of Marie's infidelity, which are intensified by the mocking banter of the Doctor and his master, the **Captain** (*Tenor*); later he sees her dancing in a tavern garden with her new lover. Back in the barrack room the Drum-Major boasts of his conquest and taunts Wozzeck.

Act III

Marie, filled with remorse and foreboding, goes for a walk with Wozzeck, who stabs her near a pond. Later he is drinking in a bar when one of Marie's neighbours sees blood on his hand. He returns to the scene of his crime and drowns himself.

In the last scene Marie's little boy is told by other children that his mother is dead; he does not understand them, and goes on happily playing by himself.

See *Opera* 9 f.

WRANITSKY.

(1) PAUL (1756–1808). He was a violinist in the Esterházy orchestra under Haydn and then director of the court opera at Vienna. He composed operas, ballets, symphonies, a great quantity of chamber music, etc.

(2) ANTON (1761–1820). He was the brother and pupil of the above, and pupil also of Haydn and Mozart. His compositions include (especially) a quantity of chamber music.

WREATH, THE. See *Mazzinghi.*

WRECKERS, THE. See *Smyth, Ethel.*

WUCHTIG (Ger.). 'Weighty.'

WUNSCH (Ger.). 'Wish.' So *Nach Wunsch,* 'according to one's wish' (= *Ad libitum,* q.v.).

WÜRDE (Ger.). 'Worth', dignity. So *Würdig,* dignified.

WURLITZER 'ELECTRONIC' PIANO. See *Electrical Musical Instruments* 1 l.

WURM, MARIE (1860–1938). See reference under *Improvisation* 2.

WURSTFAGOTT. See *Rackett.*

WUT, WUTH (Ger.). 'Rage.' So *Wütend* or *Wüthen, Wütig* or *Wüthig,* 'raging', furious.

WYNKYN DE WORDE. See *Worde, Wynkyn de.*

X

XABO. See *Jabo*.

XÁCARA or **JÁCARA.** An old Spanish song-dance.

XALEO. See *Jaleo*.

XOTA. See *Jota*.

XYLOPHONE. See *Percussion Family* 2 f, 4 e, 5 f.

XYLORIMBA. An American form of light-weight marimba (q.v.).

Y

YANIEWICZ. See *Janiewiecz*.

YANKEE DOODLE. This is a burlesque song, to a very gay tune, used by the British troops in derision of the revolutionary colonial troops of North America and then adopted by the revolutionists for their own purposes. Its history is confused, both as to words and music.

A version of the tune first appears in print about 1778 in Aird's collection entitled *Selection of Scottish, English, Irish, and Foreign Airs*, published at Glasgow (this publication contains several American airs, which suggest that *Yankee Doodle* may be actually American in origin). Other versions appeared shortly afterwards.

The first American publication to include it is believed to be the *Federal Overture* of Benjamin Carr, 1795 (see under *Carr*); no complete copy of this now exists, but some pages of it are in the Library of Congress and the overture opens with allusions to the tune, which probably appeared in full later.

There are American manuscript versions of the tune dated 1775 and 1790.

The whole facts as to the history of the tune, so far as they have been brought to light, are in Sonneck's Report on *The Star-spangled Banner, Hail, Columbia!, America, and Yankee Doodle*, published in 1909 by the Library of Congress. The claim as to the *origin* of the tune and words (and even as to that of the expression 'Yankee') that Mr. Sonneck was able to make at the end of eighty pages of very close examination of the subject was entirely negative—'unless it be deemed a positive result to have eliminated definitely almost every theory thus far advanced and thus by the process of elimination to have paved the way for an eventual solution of the puzzle'.

Rubinstein (q.v.) wrote variations on this tune, which he inscribed to the American pianist, William Mason—and himself played them at his farewell concert at New York.

Paderewski, not knowing this, was also in process of writing variations on it, and with the kindly intention of attaching the same dedication, when he learnt from Mason that '*Yankee Doodle* was written by an Englishman in derision of us', and tactfully dropped the project.

Y DERYN PUR. See *Wales* 2.

YE BANKS AND BRAES. The poem is by Burns (first published 1792). The tune was originally called *The Caledonian Hunt's Delight* and Burns wrote the words to fit it. In 1794 he wrote to George Thomson of Edinburgh (see *Folk Song* 3) as follows:

'Do you know the history of the air? It is curious enough. A good many years ago Mr. James Miller, W. S. [Writer to the Signet—a lawyer] in your good town, a gentleman whom possibly you know, was in company with our friend Clarke; and talking of Scottish music, Miller expressed an ardent desire to be able to compose a Scot's air. Mr. Clarke, probably by way of a joke, told him to keep to the black keys of the harpsichord, and preserve some kind of rhythm, and he would infallibly compose a Scot's air. Certain it is that in a few days Mr. Miller produced the rudiment of an air, which Mr. Clarke, with some touches, and corrections, fashioned into the tune in question.'

The allusion to the 'black keys' has reference to the Pentatonic Scale (see *Scales* 10), on which a number of Scottish tunes are based. (For *Clarke*, see *Clarke, Stephen*.)

That great authority on folk song, Frank Kidson, was of the impression that Burns's anecdote might be inaccurate. He thought that the tune might be Irish in origin, that it was probably in circulation before Burns's time, and that Niel Gow, sen. (q.v.), in whose *Second Collection of Strathspey Reels* (1788) it appears as *The Caledonian Hunt's Delight*, was probably the first to give it this name; his book is dedicated to the Hunt, which took seventy copies, and opens with this tune. Moreover, Gow adds the sub-title 'A favourite Air', which suggests that the tune was already well known. The whole difficult subject is thoroughly discussed by Kidson in the appendix to the second edition of Grove's *Dictionary of Music*. There is also an unsigned article, apparently by Kidson, in the *Musical Times* of September 1896.

YE GENTLEMEN OF ENGLAND. See *You Gentlemen of England*.

YE MARINERS OF ENGLAND. The words (written 1800) are by the poet Thomas Campbell, who was fond of the traditional tune to *You Gentlemen of England* (q.v.) and expressed his patriotism by supplying it with a new lyric.

YEOMEN OF THE GUARD, THE, or THE MERRYMAN AND HIS MAID (Sullivan). Produced at the Savoy Theatre, London, in 1888. Libretto by W. S. Gilbert.

ACT I

SCENE: *Tower Green. The Sixteenth Century*

Wilfred Shadbolt (*Bass*), head jailer and assistant tormentor at the Tower of London, loves **Phoebe Meryll** (*Mezzo-Soprano*), daughter of Sergeant Meryll, of the Yeomen of the Guard, but she is attracted by Col. Fairfax, now under sentence of death in the Tower as a sorcerer. **Dame Carruthers** (*Contralto*), the Housekeeper, believes the colonel guilty, but Phoebe defends him. The **Sergeant** (*Bass*) has a faint hope that his son Leonard may bring a reprieve from Windsor when he comes to take up a post as one of the Yeomen. **Leonard** (*Tenor*) arrives, but with no reprieve, so a plot is planned: Leonard is to hide for a while, and the colonel is to wear yeoman's uniform, posing as the newly arrived recruit. The **Colonel** (*Tenor*) takes leave of them, on his way to his last lodging. It seems that, if he dies unmarried, a kinsman, who has charged him with sorcery, will succeed to his estate. Can some woman be found to marry him for but an hour? The Lieutenant of the Tower, **Sir Richard Cholmondeley** (*Baritone*), is doubtful, but will see what can be done.

Now **Jack Point**, a strolling jester, enters with his companion **Elsie Maynard** (*Soprano*). They sing for the crowd, and afterwards Elsie agrees to marry the colonel, while Point is engaged as the Lieutenant's jester.

Phoebe steals the keys of the cells from Wilfred; her father frees the colonel, returns the keys, without Wilfred's knowledge, and introduces the prisoner, now dressed as a Yeoman, to the guard as his son. Phoebe is pleased with her new 'brother'. The execution bell tolls. Fairfax and two other Yeomen go off to bring the prisoner, and rush back to announce that he has escaped!

ACT II

SCENE: *The Tower from the Wharf. Moonlight. Two days later*

Fairfax learns that it was Elsie whom unknowingly he married. He, as 'Leonard', falls in love with her, but she, as a married woman, will have none of him, at first, though she soon relents, for she loves him. Jack Point, too, is distressed, because he expected Elsie to be married and a widow within an hour, and here she is married to a husband who (as he believes) has fled. He gets Wilfred to invent a story of having shot the colonel as he tried to swim across the river.

Fairfax's reprieve arrives, having been maliciously kept back by a designing kinsman. Now Elsie's marriage must stand, and here she is in love with 'Leonard'. But when the colonel appears as himself, she realizes that he *was* 'Leonard'. Phoebe is free to take her Wilfred, Dame Carruthers pairs off with the Sergeant, and only poor Jack Point is left without a partner.

Y.M.C.A. AND MUSIC. See *Concert* 8.

YODEL. An English spelling of *Jodel* (q.v.).

YONGE, NICHOLAS. Born (year unknown) at Lewes, in Sussex, and died in London in 1619. His name will be for ever associated with the introduction into England of an Italian form—the madrigal, which English composers then took up, and in which they wonderfully excelled (see particulars under *Madrigal* 2, 5; *Publishing of Music* 4; *Clubs*).

It is generally thought that he was a singer in the choir of St. Paul's Cathedral.

YORK. See *Schola Cantorum*; *Mysteries*, etc.; *Waits*; *Festival* 1; *Cathedral Music* 2; *Common Prayer*; *Use of Sarum*, etc.; *Cornett and Key Bugle Families* 3 a.

Organists of the Cathedral ('Minster') who receive notice in this book are (with their periods of office): *Thorne* (16th cent.); *Nares* (1734–56); *E. G. Monk* (1859–83); *Noble* (1897–1913); *Bairstow* (1913–46).

YORK (Hymn Tune). See *Stilt*.

YORK USE. See *Common Prayer*; *Use of Sarum*, etc.

YOU GENTLEMEN OF ENGLAND. This is an altered version of a ballad of the celebrated ballad-monger Martin Parker (cf. 'When the King enjoys his own again'). The tune is the older one of *When the stormy winds do blow*, which words appear in the refrain of the song. 'Ye Mariners of England' (q.v.) is an early nineteenth-century imitation.

YOULL, HENRY. The circumstances of his life are quite unknown; not so his music, for his canzonets and ballets still delight those who love to sing and hear the fine things of the English madrigal school of the late sixteenth and early seventeenth centuries.

YOUNG.

(1) NICHOLAS. See *Yonge*.

(2) WILLIAM. Died 1671. In 1660 he entered the band of Charles II as a flute player and in 1661 he became violinist in this band. Before this he had enjoyed a continental career of

which much remains to be discovered. He appears to have been in the service of the Archduke of Austria and at Innsbruck in 1653 he published the part-books of a collection of eleven sonatas (the first English ones to be printed) and a number of dance pieces for two, three, and four violins, viola da gamba, and keyboard instrument; they are dedicated to that prince. The only remaining original copy of this is in the Library of the University of Uppsala, in Sweden (see *Scandinavia* 4, end), but a modern edition, prepared from this by Dr. W. G. Whittaker, appeared in 1931, and shows the composer to have been a bold and original spirit. In style and flavour his work is what we are apt to call Purcellian—though he died when Purcell was but a boy. As the younger musician and the elder were in the same royal service we may suppose they were acquainted.

(3) CECILIA. Eighteenth-century English vocalist. See *Arne, T. A.*; *Ireland* 6.

(4) PERCY MARSHALL. Born at Northwich, Cheshire, in 1912. He was educated at Cambridge and has held positions in various teacher training colleges and the like. He has written numerous books on Handel, Elgar, etc.

YRADIER, SEBASTIAN (1809–65). See *Habanera*.

YSACH. See *Isaac*.

YSAŸE

(1) EUGÈNE (p. 1097, pl. 182. 8). Born at Liège in 1858 and died at Brussels in 1931, aged seventy-two. He was one of the remarkable Liège group of violinists (see *Belgium* 5) and was known all over the world. He founded the Ysaÿe Orchestral Concerts in Brussels and for some time he conducted those of the Cincinnati Orchestra. He composed an opera (in Walloon dialect, 1929) and violin music. A competition for the Eugène Ysaÿe International Grand Prix (founded in his memory) is held in Brussels every five years.

(2) THÉOPHILE. Born at Verviers in 1865 and died at Nice in 1918, aged just fifty-three. He was a pianist who sometimes in that capacity appeared with his brother (above). He was also a composer, especially of orchestral works.

Z

ZABERN, CONRAD VON. See *Printing* 1.

ZACCONI, LUDOVICO (1555–1627). An Augustinian Canon of Venice whose *Prattica di musica* (two parts 1592, 1619) has extreme value for its information on all phases of the musical thought and practice of its period.

ZACHARIAS, POPE (eighth century). See *Dance* 7.

ZÁDOR, EUGEN. Born at Bátaszék, in Hungary, in 1894. He has written orchestral music, operas, songs, etc., and a doctoral thesis on the *Nature and Form of the Symphonic Poem*. He was for a time a Vienna music critic.

ZÄHLZEIT (Ger., lit. 'Count-time'). 'Beat.'

ZAMBRA. A Spanish dance showing Moorish influence.

ZAMPOGNA (It.), **ZAMPOÑA** (Sp.), **ZAMPOUNA** (Gk.). See *Bagpipe Family* 7; *Symphony* 1.

ZANDONAI, RICCARDO. Born in the Trentino in 1883 and died in Pesaro in 1944, aged sixty-one. He was a very active composer, principally of operas (of a typically Italian kind).

ZAPATEADO. A Spanish clog-dance, three-in-a-measure, with a savage rhythm, marked by stamping, instead of by the usual Spanish castanets.

ZARLINO, GIOSEFFO (1517–90). Franciscan friar, and choirmaster of St. Mark's, Venice, composer and theoretician, whose works are still of high importance (see reference under *Temperament* 5).

ZART (Ger.). 'Tender.' So *Zartheit*, 'tenderness'; *Zärtlich*, 'tenderly'.

ZARZUELA. The traditional Spanish comic operetta (generally in one act) of which thousands have been and are being composed. It has spoken dialogues with songs and choruses. The musical plays of Calderón (1600–81) are Zarzuelas. The most famous Zarzuela is J. Valverde's *La Gran Via* ('The High Road'; Madrid, 1886).

See *Opera* 15; *Spain* 6; *Bretón*.

ZAUBERFLÖTE. See *Magic Flute*; *Organ* 14 II.

ZEHN (Ger.). 'Ten.'

ZEICHEN (Ger.). 'Sign.'

ZEITMASS (Ger.). 'Time-measure', i.e. tempo.

ZELO, ZELOSO, ZELOSAMENTE (It.). 'Zeal', 'zealous', 'zealously'.

ZELTER, CARL FRIEDRICH (1758–1832). Famous Berlin musician and man of learning, founder of the Liedertafel (q.v.) movement, the friend of Goethe, the teacher of Mendelssohn, and a notable champion of Bach at a time when his music had fallen into obscurity.

He was one of the earliest composers of the German Lied (see *Song* 5).

See references under *Fasch* 2; *Liedertafel*.

ZEMLINSKY, ALEXANDER. Born in Vienna in 1872 and died in New York in 1942, aged sixty-nine. Notable conductor at Vienna, Prague, and Berlin, and composer of six operas, symphonies, chamber music, etc. He was an early supporter (and later brother-in-law) of Schönberg, but in his own work does not show the same 'advanced' tendencies.

ZENO. See *Libretto*.

ZENTA, HERMANN. See *Holmès, Augusta*.

ZEREZO. See *Bolero*.

ZERSTREUTE, DER. See *Nicknamed* 11 (60).

ZICH, OTTOKAR. Born at Kralové Městec, now in Czechoslovakia, in 1879 and died at Oubenice in 1934, aged fifty-five. He was professor of philosophy and aesthetics at the University of Brno and wrote books on the dance, musical perception, popular songs of Bohemia, etc. He composed operas, songs, etc.

ZICHY. See *Pianoforte* 21 (near end).

ZIEHEN (Ger.). 'To draw out.'

ZIEHHARMONIKA. See *Harmonica* 5 b.

ZIELENSKI, NICOLAS. See *Poland*.

ZIEMLICH (Ger.). 'Rather.'

ZIERLICH (Ger.). 'Elegant.'

ZIGEUNER (Ger.). 'Gipsy.' So *Zigeunerlied*, 'gipsy song'.

ZILCHER, HERMANN. Born at Frankfurt-on-Main in 1881 and died at Würzburg in 1948. He was director of the Conservatory of Würzburg and the composer of five symphonies and a great variety of other works, of which the song-cycles are the best known.

ZIMBALON (or Zymbalum, Cimbalon, Cymbalom or Czimbalon). A developed dulcimer (q.v.) found in Hungarian and Rumanian popular orchestras and capable of marvellous virtuoso treatment. It occasionally finds its place in serious music, as in Kodály's *Háry János* suite.

ZINGARELLI, NICOLA ANTONIO. Born at Naples in 1752 and died near there in 1837, aged eighty-five. He was a composer both of operas and sacred music, who enjoyed great fame in his day.

When Napoleon in 1811 conferred on his own infant son the title of King of Rome, and directed that the Italian people should rejoice thereat, Zingarelli, then musical director at St. Peter's in Rome, refused to perform a Te Deum before the officials and populace gathered in the church for the purpose. He was sent under arrest to Paris, but freed by Napoleon, who loved his music, as at that time did thousands.

Bellini, Mercadante, Costa (q.v.), and other well-known musicians were his pupils.

ZINGARO, ZINGARA (It.). 'Gipsy' (male and female). Hence *Alla Zingarese*, 'in gipsy style'; *Zingaresca*, 'gipsy song'; etc.

ZINK or **ZINCK** or **ZINKE** (Ger.). Cornett. See *Cornett and Key Bugle Families*.

ZINZENDORF, COUNT (1700–60). See *Bohemia*; p. 108, pl. **19.** 3.

ZIRYÁB. See *Spain* 1; *Singing*.

ZITHER (p. 449, p. **77.** 3). The favourite and indeed typical instrument of the Tyrol and adjacent mountain regions. It consists of a wooden box, as resonator, with strings, varying in number from about thirty to forty-five, stretched over its surface. Of these a few lie over a fretted board (see *Frets*) and serve to produce the melody, the remainder being open strings, used for its accompaniment. The left-hand thumb 'stops' the melody strings, the right hand thumb (to which a plectrum is attached) plays them; meanwhile the three larger fingers of the right hand pluck the accompaniment strings. The instrument is placed upon a table or upon the knees.

Surprising virtuoso and highly musical effects are possible under the hands of a skilful performer. Liszt once praised it greatly.

It may be considered that the zither is an elaborated form of psaltery (q.v.). For the zither used in Kentucky see under *Dulcimer*. For the word 'zither' used in another sense see under *Cittern*. For a reference to zither notation see *Tablature*.

An instrument in which some of the same principles are applied is the Langleik (see *Scandinavia* 3). In the German language 'Zither' seems to have two meanings (see *Cittern*).

For 'Zither-Banjo' see *Banjo*.

ZITTERND (Ger.). 'Trembling' (= tremolando).

ZMESKALL. See *Augengläser*.

ZÖGERND (Ger.). 'Delaying', i.e. rallentando.

ZOLA, ÉMILE. See *Bruneau*; *Colour and Music* 3.

ZOPF is German for 'pigtail', which word is used as a symbol for what is antiquated or pedantic, or 'old fogey'.

The term has long been applied, nickname-fashion, to the conventional style which was prominent in the various arts during a great part of the eighteenth century. Thus, in architecture the word *Zopfstil* refers to the mixture of German Barock (see *Barocco*) and French Louis XVI style that was common in Germany in the late part of the eighteenth century. In music it signifies the easy-going, the mechanical, the stereotyped, the mediocre, the manneristic, and that kind of eighteenth-century composition in which immediate effectiveness took the place of genuine expression of something really felt by the composer and toiled after by him in the effort to embody it in a dignified and worthy form.

One distinctive detail of the 'Zopfstil' in music was a use of facile melody harmonized in parallel thirds and sixths.

The French have the same idea in 'perruque' ('wig'), *style de perruque* meaning in general much the same as 'Zopfstil'. In 1829 at the Paris Opera, during a performance of Rousseau's *Village Soothsayer* ('Le Devin du Village', see *Rousseau*), a work which had been in the repertory for seventy-five years, somebody threw a large wig on the stage. The incident was talked about and laughed at and the opera was never given again.

ZOPFSTIL. See *Zopf.*

ZOPPA, ALLA. *Zoppo* (feminine *Zoppa*) in Italian is 'lame', 'limping', and so it has been applied to music, meaning 'syncopated'.

ZORTZIKO or **ZORTZICO.** A sort of Basque folk dance in five-in-a-measure time (cf. *Aurresku*), like the Rueda except that the second and fourth beats are almost constantly dotted notes.

ZU (Ger.). 'To', or 'too'. Also 'for' and other translations which the context may suggest.

ZU 2 = (*a*) Two instruments to play the same part; (*b*) all the instruments in question (e.g. first violins) to divide into two parts.

ZUERST (Ger.). 'First', 'at first'.

ZUG (Ger.). (1) Procession; thus *Brautzug*, 'bridal procession', and so on.

(2) The action of pulling. Thus organ-stop knob; piano pedal (which pulls down some mechanism. So the compounds *Zugposaune*, 'slide trombone' (see *Trombone Family*) and *Zugtrompete*, 'slide trumpet' (see *Trumpet Family* 2 d, 5).

ZUGEEIGNET (Ger.). 'Dedicated.'

ZUGEHEN (Ger.). 'To go.' So *Zugehend*, 'going'.

ZULEHNER, CARL (*c.* 1770–1830). See *Misattributed Compositions* under 'Mozart's Twelfth Mass'.

ZUM, ZUR (Ger.). 'To the', 'at the', etc.

ZUMPE, JOHANNES. See *Pianoforte* 5, 9, 17.

ZUMSTEEG, JOHANN RUDOLF. Born in Baden in 1760 and died at Stuttgart in 1802, aged forty-two. He was a remarkable song-composer, a pioneer of the narrative and dramatic ballad and as such enormously admired by the youth Schubert, who made him his early model.

See *Schubert; Germany* 6; *Song* 5.

ZUNGE (Ger.). 'Tongue', reed. The plural is *Zungen.*

ZURÜCK (Ger.). 'Back again.' So *Zurückgehend*, 'going back' (i.e. to original tempo); *Zurückhaltend*, 'holding back' (i.e. rallentando).

ZUSAMMEN. German for 'together'; used sometimes of instruments.

ZUTRAULICH (Ger.). 'Confidingly', 'intimately'.

ZUVOR (Ger.). 'Before.'

ZWEERS. See *Holland* 8.

ZWEI (Ger.). 'Two.' So *Zweihändig*, 'two-handed'; *Zweistimmig*, 'two-voiced', etc.

ZWEIMAL (Ger.). 'Twice.'

ZWEITE, ZWEITES, etc. (Ger.). 'Second' (various terminations according to case, gender, etc.).

ZWEIUNDDREISSIGSTEL or **ZWEIUND-DREISSIGSTELNOTE** (Ger.). 'Thirty-second' or 'thirty-second note', demisemiquaver (Table 3).

ZWISCHEN (Ger.). 'Between', 'amongst'. There are many compounds, such as *Zwischenspiel* (see below).

ZWISCHENSPIEL. German, literally, 'between-play'. Any music of an interlude or intermezzo character can be so called, but the commonest applications are (1) to the organ playing interposed between the stanzas of a congregational hymn; (2) to the episodes of a fugue; and (3) to the solo portions between the 'tuttis' of a *Concerto* (q.v.).

ZWO (Ger.). To some extent now adopted instead of *Zwei* ('two'), the original object having been, apparently, to avoid mis-hearing for *drei* ('three') in telephoning and in radio announcements. (*Zwote* is, in conformity, used for *Zweite*.)

ZWÖLF (Ger.). 'Twelve.'

ZYMBALUM. See *Zimbalon.*

PRONOUNCING GLOSSARY
OF FOREIGN OR UNFAMILIAR TERMS
AND NAMES USED IN THIS VOLUME

GENERAL EXPLANATION

1. The aim has been to indicate a near-accurate pronunciation without the use of a complicated apparatus of phonetic symbols.

2. Enunciate a word slowly, according to the syllabification adopted, pronouncing each syllable *as if it were an English word.* Then repeat *the whole word quickly* and it will come near the pronunciation of a native.

3. Letters in brackets direct the mind towards the sound desired and are not themselves to be heard.

4. Italics indicate stressed syllables. (The French words, as a rule, have no stresses, and the effort should be to pronounce all their syllables with equal force.)

5. Certain necessary directions concerning particular words are indicated by figures referring to a short set of footnotes which has been repeated at every opening of the Glossary.

(For further remarks, see, on pp. 1186–9, *A Postscript concerning the Pronouncing Glossary.*)

PRONOUNCING GLOSSARY

A

A (It.), à (Fr.). A⁵.
Aarre (Fin.). *Ahrr*-e(r).
Ab. Ap.
Abaco. *Ab*-ak⁵-oh.
Abandonné. Λb-o(ng)-don-ay.
A battuta. Ab-at-*oo*-ta⁵.
Abbandono. Ab-ban-*doh*-noh.
Abbassare. Ab-bass-*sah*-ray.
Abbellimenti. Ab-bel-lee-*men*-tee.
Abdämpfen. *Ap*-demp-fen.
Abeille. Ab-eh-y(er).
Abel. *Ah*-bel.
Abend. *Ah*-bent.
Abendlied. *Ah*-bent-leet.
Abendmusiken. *Ah*-bent-moo-*zee*-ken.
A beneplacito. A⁵ *bay*-nay-*plah*-chee-toh.
Aber. *Ahb*-err.
Abgestossen. *Ap*-ge(r)-shtohss-en.
Abilità. Ab-ee-lee-*ta*⁵.
Ablösen. *Ap*-le(r)-zen.
Abnehmend. *Ap*-nay-ment.
Abruzzese. Ab-root-*say*-zay.
Abschiedssymphonie. *Ap*-sheets-zim-fon-*ee*.
Absetzen. *Ap*-zet-sen.
Abstossen. *Ap*-shtohss-en.
Abt. Apt.
Abwechseln. *Ap*-vek-seln.
Abzuwechseln. *Ap*-tsoo-vek-seln.
Acajou. Ac-azj³-oo.
A cappella. A⁵ cap-*pel*-la⁵.
Accademia. Ac-ad-*ay*-mee-a⁵.
Accarezzevole. Ac-ca⁵-rets-*say*-voh-lay.
Accarezzevolmente. Ac-ca⁵-rets-*say*-vol-*men*-tay.
Accelerando. At-shel-ay-*ran*-doh.
Accelerato. At-shel-ay-*ran*-toh.
Accento. At-*shen*-toh.
Accentué. Ak-so(ng)-tee²-ay.
Acciaccato. Atsh-yac-*cah*-toh.
Acciaccatura. Atsh-yac-cat-*oo*-ra⁵.
Acciaio. At-*shy*-oh.
Accompagnato. Ac-com-pan-*yah*-toh.
Accoppiamento. Ac-*cop*-ya-*men*-toh.

Accoppiare. Ac-cop-pee-*ah*-ray.
Accoppiato. Ac-cop-pee-*ah*-toh.
Accord (Fr.). Ac-awrr.
Accordare. Ac-cawrr-*dah*-ray.
Accordate. Ac-cawrr-*dah*-tay.
Accordato. Ac-cawrr-*dah*-toh.
Accordatura. Ac-cawrr-dat-*oo*-ra⁵.
Accordé. Ac-awrr-day.
Accordéon. Ac-awrr-day-o(ng).
Accorder. Ac-awrr-day.
Accordo. Ac-*cawrr*-doh.
Accouplé. Ac-oo-play.
Accouplement. Ac-oo-ple(r)-mo(ng).
Accoupler. Ac-oo-play.
Accouplez. Ac-oo-play.
Accusé. Ac-ee²-zay.
Accusée. Ac-ee²-zay.
Achille. Ash-eel.
Achron. Ahk¹-*ron*.
Acht. Akt¹.
Achtel. *Akt*¹-el.
Achtelnote. *Akt*¹-el-*noh*-te(r).
Achtelpause. *Akt*¹-el-*pow*⁴-ze(r).
Achtstimmig. *Akt*¹-shtim-mish⁶.
Adage (Fr.). Ad-ahzj³.
Adagietto. Ad-adj-*yet*-toh.
Adagio. Ad-*ahdj*-yoh.
Adagio assai. Ad-*ahdj*-yoh ass⁵-*sy*-ee.
Adam (Fr.). Ad-o(ng).
Adam (Ger.). *Ahd*-am.
Adam de la Halle. Ad-o(ng) de(r) lah al⁵.
Adami. Ad-*ahm*-ee.
Adam le Bossu. Ad-o(ng) le(r) Boss-ee².
Addolcendo. Ad-dol-*chen*-doh.
Addolorato. Ad-dol-oh-*rah*-toh.
Adel. *Ahd*l.
Adelina Patti. Ad-ail-*ee*-na⁵ Paht-tee (often anglicized to 'Patty').
À deux cordes. A⁵ du(r) cawrrd.
Adieu (Eng.). Ad-*yoo*.
Adieu (Fr.). Ad-ye(r).
Adirato. Ad-ee-*rah*-toh.
Adler. *Ahd*-ler.
Adlung. *Ahd*-loong.
Adolf. *Ah*-dolf.
Adolfo. Ad-*ol*-foh.

Adriano. Ad-ree-*ah*-noh.
Adrien. Ad-ree-a(ng).
A due corde. Ah *doo*-ay *cawrr*-day.
A dur. Ah doo(e)r.
Aehnlich. *Ain*-lik¹.
Aengstlich. *Engst*-lik¹.
Aennchen. *En*-shen.
Aeolina. Ee-oh-*lee*-nah.
Aequal. Aik-*wahl*.
Aeroforo. Eye-*roh*-faw-roh.
Aerophor. *Air*-oh-fore.
Aeusserst. *Oyss*-erst.
Affabile. Af-*fab*-ee-lay.
Affaiblissant. Af-fay-blee-so(n)g.
Affannato. Af-fan-*nah*-toh.
Affannosamente. Af-fan-*noh*-zam-*en*-tay.
Affannoso. Af-fan-*noh*-zoh.
Affekt. Af-*ekt*.
Affektvoll. Af-*ekt*-fol.
Affetto. Af-*fet*-toh.
Affettuosa. Af-fet-too-oh-*za*⁵.
Affettuosamente. Af-fet-too-oh-zam-*en*-tay.
Affettuoso. Af-fet-too-*oh*-zoh.
Afflitto. Af-*fleet*-toh.
Afflizione. Af-fleet-see-*oh*-nay.
Affrettando. Af-fret-*tan*-doh.
Affrettare. Af-fret-*tah*-ray.
Affrettatamente. Af-fret-*tah*-tam-*en*-tay.
Affrettoso. Af-fret-*toh*-zoh.
Affrettuoso. Af-fret-too-*oh*-zoh.
Afranio. Af-*rahn*-yoh.
Africaine, L'. Laf-ree-ken.
Agathe (Ger.). Ag-*aht*-e(r).
Agevole. Adj-*ay*-voh-lay.
Aggiunta. Adj-*oon*-ta⁵.
Aggiustatamente. Adj-joosstat-am-*en*-tay.
Aggradevole. Ag-grad-*ay*-voh-lay.
Agiatamente. Adj-ah-tah-*men*-tay.
Agilement. Azj³-eel-mo(ng).
Agilità. Ad-jee-lee-*ta*⁵.
Agilité. Azj³-eel-ee-tay.
Agitatamente. Adj-ee-*tah*-tam-*en*-tay.
Agitato. Adj-ee-*tah*-toh.
Agitazione. Adj-ee-*tat*-see-oh-nay.

---

1. k = 'ch' (cf. Scot. *loch*).   2. ee here really between 'ee' and 'oo' (cf. Scot. *puir*).
3. zj like 's' in *pleasure*.   4. ow as in *cow*.   5. a as in *lad*.
6. The ish is really anywhere between that sound and 'ik' (varying in different parts of Germany).
7. th as in *thin*.   8. g as in *go*.

Agité. Azj³-ee-tay.
Agitiert. Ag-ee-*teert*.
Agitirt. Ag-ee-*teert*.
Agogic. Ag-*oh*-jik.
Agon. Ah-*gohn*.
Agrémens. Ag-ray-mo(ng).
Agréments. Ag-ray-mo(ng).
Agreste (Fr.). Ag-rest.
Agreste (It.). Ag-*rest*-ay.
Agricola. Ag-*ree*-coh-la⁵.
Agujari. Ah-goo-*yah*-ree.
Ähnlich. *Ain*-lik¹.
Ai (It.). *A*⁵-ee (almost as Eng. 'eye').
Aida. A⁵-*ee*-dah.
Aigu. Ayg-ee².
Aiguë. Ayg-ee² (two syll. only).
Aimé. Aym-ay.
Air anglais. Airr ong-glay.
Air de caractère. Airr de(r) ca⁵-rak-tairr.
Ais. *Ah*-iss.
Aise. Ayz.
Aisis. *Ah*-is-iss.
Ajouter. Azj³-oo-tay.
Ajoutez. Azj³-oo-tay.
Akhron. Ahk-*ron*.
Akimenko. Ak-ee-*men*-koh.
Akkord. Ak-*korrd*.
Akkordieren. Ak-korrd-*ee*-ren.
Al. Al⁵.
À la (Fr.). A⁵ la⁵. A la (Sp.). Ah lah.
Alabiev. Al-*ahb*-yef.
À la corde. Al-ac-awrrd.
Alalá. Ah-la-*lah*.
Alaleona. A-la-lay-*oh*-na.
À la mesure. Al-am-e(r)-zeer².
À la pointe d'archet. Al-ap-want⁵ darr⁵-shay.
Alard. Al-ahrr.
Albéniz. Al-*bay*-neeth⁷.
Albéric. Al-bay-reek.
Alberich. *Al*-berr-ik¹.
Albert (Fr.). Al-bairr.
Albert (Ger.). *Al*-bairrt.
Alberti. Al-*bairr*-tee.
Alberto. Al-*bairr*-toh.
Albicastro. Al-bee-*cast*-roh.
Albigenses. Al-bee-*jen*-sez.
Albinoni. Al-bee-*noh*-nee.
Alborada del Gracioso. Al-baw-*rah*-da del Grath⁷-ee-*oh*-soh.
Albrechtsberger. *Al*-brekts¹-bairrg-err.
Albumblatt. *Al*-boom-blat.
Alceste. Al-sest.
Alcestis. Ahl-*sest*-iss.
Alcindoro. Al-cheen-*doh*-roh.
Alcuna licenza. Al-*koo*-na⁵ lee-*chent*-sa⁵.
Alcuno. Al-*koo*-noh.

Alderighi. Al-day-*reeg*-ee.
Alecsandri. Ahl-ex-*sahnd*-ree.
Alembert. Al-o(ng)-bairr.
Alemlejo. Al-em-*lay*-koh¹.
Alessandresco. Ahl-ess-sahn-*dress*-coh.
Alessandro. Al-ess-*san*-droh.
Alexandre. Al-ex-ahndrr.
Alexandri. Ahl-ex-*ahnd*-ree.
Alexandrof. Al-ek-*san*-drof.
Alfano. Al-*fah*-noh.
Alfio. Al-fee-oh.
Alfredo. Ahl-*fray*-doh.
Alfven. *Ahlf*-ven.
Alkan. Al-ko(ng).
All'. Al⁵.
Alla. *Al*-la⁵.
Alla breve. *Al*-la⁵ bray-vay.
Alla caccia. *Al*-la⁵ catch-yah.
Alla danza tedesca. *Al*-la⁵ dants-a⁵ ted-*ess*-ca⁵.
Alla misura. *Al*-la⁵ mee-*zoo*-ra⁵.
Allant. Al-lo(ng).
Allard. Al-*ahrr*.
Allargando. Al-larr-*gan*-doh.
Alle (Ger. 'all') *Al*-e(r).
Alle (It. 'to the'). *Al*-lay.
Alle Ersten. *Al*-e(r) Airr-sten.
Allegramente. Al-*lay*-gram-en-tay.
Allègrement. Al-leg-rem-o(ng).
Allegretto. Al-lay-*gret*-toh.
Allegrezza. Al-lay-*gret*-sa⁵.
Allegri. Al-*lay*-gree.
Allegrissimo. Al-lay-*greess*-see-moh.
Allegro. Al-*lay*-groh.
Allein. Al-*line*.
Allemand. Al-mo(ng).
Allemande. Al-mahnd.
Allentamento. Al-*len*-tam-en-toh.
Allentando. Al-len-*tan*-doh.
Alle Zweiten. *Al*-e(r) Tsvy-ten.
Alle Zwoten. *Al*-e(r) Tsvoh-ten.
Allgemeiner Deutscher Caecilienverein. Al-ge(r)-*mine*-err Doyt-sherr Tsayt-*seel*-yen-fair-rine.
Allmählich. Al-*may*-lik¹.
Allonger. Al-o(ng)-zjay³.
Allora. Al-*law*-ra⁵.
All'ottava. Al-lot-*tah*-va⁵.
Allure. Al-leerr².
Al meno. Al *may*-noh.
Aloys. Al-oh-ees.
Alpenhorn. *Al*-pen-horrn.
Alphorn. *Alp*-horrn.
Als. Alss.
Al segno. Al *sain*-yoh.
Also (Ger.). *Al*-zoh.
Al sòlito. Al *sol*-ee-toh.

Also sprach Zarathustra. *Al*-zoh shprahk¹ Tsah-rah-*too*-strah.
Alt (Ger.). Alt.
Alta. *Al*-ta⁵.
Alt Blockflöte. Alt *Blok*-fle(r)-te(r).
Alternativo. Alt-airr-nat-*ee*-voh.
Altezza sonora. Alt-*ets*-sa⁵ sonn-*aw*-ra⁵.
Altflöte. *Alt*-fle(r)-te(r).
Altflügelhorn. *Alt-fleeg*²-el-horrn.
Altgeige. *Alt*-gy⁸-gu(r).
Althorn. *Alt*-horrn.
Altissimo. Alt-*eess*-see-moh.
Altiste. Al-teest.
Altklarinette. *Alt*-klah-ree-net-e(r).
Altkornett. *Alt*-korr-net.
Alto (It.). *Al*-toh.
Alto moderne. Ahl-toh mod-airrn.
Altposaune. *Alt*-poz-*ow*⁴-ne(r).
Altra volta. *Alt*-ra⁵ *vol*-ta⁵.
Altre. *Alt*⁵-ray.
Altro. *Alt*⁵-roh.
Alun. *Al*⁵-in.
Alvis (Ger.). *Al*-viss.
Alzate. Alt-*sah*-tay.
Alzato. Alt-*sah*-toh.
Am (Ger.). Am.
Amabile. Am-*ah*-bee-lay.
Amadée. Am-ad-ay.
Amadeus (Ger.). Am-ah-*day*-ooss.
Amant jaloux, L'. Lam-o(ng) zjal³-oo.
Amarevole. Am-a⁵-*ray*-voh-lay.
Amarezza. Am-a⁵-*rets*-za⁵.
Amati. Am-*ah*-tee.
Amboss. *Am*-boss.
Ambroise. Om-brwahz.
Ambros. *Am*-bross.
Ambrosian. Am-*brohz*-yan.
Âme (Fr.). Ahm.
Amûparnaso. *Am*-fee-pahrr-*nass*-soh.
Amfortas. Am-*forrt*-ass.
Amilcare (It.). Am-*eel*-ca⁵-ray.
Amor brujo, El. El Am-*awrr broo*-ko¹.
Amore. Am-*aw*-ray.
Amore dei tre re, L'. Lam-*aw*-ray day tray *ray*.
Amorevole. Am-aw-*ray*-vol-ay.
Amorevolmente. Am-aw-*ray*-vol-*men*-tay.
Amorosamente. Am-aw-*roh*-zam-*en*-tay.
Amoroso. Am-aw-*roh*-zoh.

---

1. k = 'ch' (cf. Scot. *loch*). 2. ee here really between 'ee' and 'oo' (cf. Scot. *puir*).
3. zj like 's' in *pleasure*.   **4. ow** as in *cow*.   **5. a** as in *lad*.

Amour. Am-oorr.

Ampico. *Am*-pee-coh.

Ampleur. O(ng)-plurr.

Amusements de Parnasse, Les. Lay-zam-eez²-mo(ng) de(r) Parr-nass⁵.

Anacreon. An-*ak*-ree-on.

Anastasius (Ger.). An-ass-*tahz*-yoos.

Anblasen. *An*-blah-zen.

Anche (Fr. = 'reed'). O(ng)sh.

Anche (It. = 'also'). *An*-kay.

Ancia. *An*-cha⁵.

Ancora più forte. An-*caw*-ra⁵ pew *fawrr*-tay.

Andacht. *An*-dakt¹.

Andächtig. *An*-dek¹-tish⁶.

Andalouse. O(ng)-dal-ooz.

Andaluz. An-dal-*ooth*⁷.

Andaluza. An-dal-*ooth*⁷-a.⁵

Andamento. An-dam-*en*-toh.

Andante. An-*dan*-tay.

Andantino. An-dan-*tee*-noh.

Andare. An-*dah*-ray.

Andauernd. *An*-dow⁴-errnt.

Ander. *An*-derr.

Andere. *An*-der-e(r).

Anderen. *An*-der-en.

Anderes. *An*-der-ess.

An der Spitze. An dairr *Shpit*-se(r).

An die ferne Geliebte. An dee *fairr*-ne(r) Gu(r)-*leep*-te(r).

André. O(ng)-dray.

Andrea Chénier. An-dray-ah Shayn-yay.

Andreae. An-*dray*-ay.

Andreas. An-*dray*-ass.

Andrés (Sp.). An-*dress*.

Andrico. *An*-dree-coh.

Anerio. An-*ay*-re-oh.

Anfang. *An*-fang.

Angélique. O(ng)-zjay³-leek.

Angelotti. An-jay-*lot*-tee.

Angemessen. *An*-gu(r)-mess-en.

Angenehm. *An*-gu(r)-naim.

Angiolini. An-joh-*lee*-nee.

Anglais. O(ng)-glay.

Anglaise. O(ng)-glez.

Anglebert. Ong-le(r)-bairr.

Angore. An-*gaw*-ray.

Angoscia. An-*gosh*-yah.

Angreifen. *An*-gryf-en.

Angst. Angst.

Ängstlich. *Engst*-lik¹.

Anhalten. *An*-hal⁵-ten.

Anhaltend. *An*-hal-tent.

Anhang. *An*-hang.

Anima. *An*-ee-ma⁵.

Animando. An-ee-*man*-doh.

Animandosi. An-ee-*man*-doh-see.

Animato. An-ee-*mah*-toh.

Animé. An-ee-may.

Animo. *An*-ee-moh.

Animosamente (It.). An-nee-moh-zam-*en*-tay.

Animoso (It.). An-ee-*moh*-zoh.

Anlaufen. *An*-low⁴-fen.

Anmut. *An*-moot.

Anmuth. *An*-moot.

Anmut(h)ig. *An*-moo-tish⁶.

Anreissen. *An*-ryss-en.

Anrooy. Ahn-*roh*-ee.

Ansatz. *An*-zats.

Anschlag. *An*-shlahg.

Anschmiegend. *An*-shmeeg-ent.

Anschwellend. *An*-shvel-ent.

Ansia. *Ans*-yah.

Anstatt. *An*-shtat.

Anstimmen. *An*-shtim-en.

Anstrich. *An*-shtrik¹.

Antes. *An*-tess.

Antheil. *An*-tile.

Antica. An-*tee*-ca⁵.

Antico. An-*tee*-coh.

Antoine. O(ng)-twan.

Antonin. An-tohn-*een*.

Anwachsend. *An*-vak-zent.

Anzublasen. *An*-tsoo-blah-zen.

Apaisé. Ap-ez-ay.

À peine entendu. Ap-en-o(ng)-to(ng)-dee².

Apel. *Ah*-pel.

Aperto. Ap-*airr*-toh.

A piacere. Ap-ee-atch-*ay*-ray.

Apollonicon. Ap-ol-*on*-ic-on.

Appassionata. Ap-pass⁵-yon-*ah*-ta⁵. .

Appassionato. Ap-pass⁵-yon-*ah*-toh.

Appena. Ap-*pay*-na⁵.

Appenato. Ap-pay-*nah*-toh.

Appoggiando. Ap-poj-*yan*-doh.

Appoggiare. Ap-poj-*yah*-ray.

Appoggiato. Ap-poj-*yah*-toh.

Appoggiatura. Ap-*poj*-yat-oo-ra⁵.

Appuyé. Ap-pwee²-yay.

Appuyée. Ap-pwee²-yay.

Après. Ap-ray.

A punta d'arco. A⁵ *poon*-ta⁵ *dahrr*-coh.

Äqual. Aik-*wahl*.

Aquinas. Ak-*wye*-nass.

Arada (Sp.). A⁵-*rah*-dah.

Aragonaise. Arr-ag-on-ez.

Aragonesa (Sp.). A⁵-rag-oh *nay*-sah.

Araja. Arr⁵-*ak*¹-a⁵.

Arbeau. Ahrr-boh.

Arcadelt. *Ahrr*-cad-elt.

Arcangelo. Ahrrk-*an*-jel-oh.

Arcata. Ahrr-*cah*-ta⁵.

Arcata in giù. Ahrr-*cah*-ta⁵ een jew.

Arcata in su. Ahrr-*cah*-ta⁵ een soo.

Arcato. Ahrr-*cah*-toh.

Archangelsky. Ahrr-*han*-gel⁸-skee.

Archet. Ahrr-shay.

Archi. *Ahrr*-kee.

Arciliuto. *Ahrrch*-ee-lee-*oo*-toh.

Arciviola. *Ahrrch*-ee-vee-oh-la⁵.

Arco. (It.) *Ahrr*-coh.

Ardemment. Ahrr-dam-mo(ng).

Ardent (Fr.). Ahrr-do(ng).

Ardente (Fr.). Ahrr-do-(ng)t.

Ardente (It.). Ahrr-*den*-tay.

Arditi. Ahrr-*dee*-tee.

Ardito. Ahrr-dee-toh.

Ardore. Ahrr-*daw*-ray.

Arensky. A⁵-*ren*-skee(yer).

Aretino. Arr-ray-*tee*-noh.

Aretinus. Ah-ray-*tee*-nooss.

Arezzo. Arr-*rets*-soh.

Ar hyd y nos. Ahrr *heed* u(r) *nohss*.

Aria. *Arr*-yah.

Aria aggiunta. *Arr*-yah adj-*oon*-ta⁵.

Aria all'unisono. *Arr*-yah al-loo-nee-*soh*-noh.

Aria buffa. *Arr*-yah *boof*-fa⁵.

Aria cantabile. *Arr*-yah can-*tab*-ee-lay.

Aria concertata. *Arr*-yah con-chairr-*tah*-ta⁵.

Aria d'abilità. *Arr*-yah dab-ee-lee-*ta*⁵.

Aria da chiesa. *Arr*-yah da kee-*ay*-za⁵.

Aria d'agilità. *Arr*-yah dadj-ee-lee-*ta*⁵.

Aria d'entrata. *Arr*-yah den-*trah*-ta⁵.

Aria di bravura. *Arr*-yah dee brav-*oo*-ra⁵.

Aria di mezzo carattere. Arr-yah dee *med*-zoh ca⁵-*raht*-tay-ray.

Aria d'imitazione. *Arr*-yah *dee*-mee-tat-see-*oh*-nay.

Aria di portamento. *Arr*-yah dee *pawrr*-tam-*en*-toh.

Ariadne auf Naxos. Arr⁵-ee-*ad*-ne(r) owf⁴ *Nax*-oss.

Aria fugata. *Arr*-yah foo-*gah*-ta⁵.

Ariane et Barbe Bleue. Arr-yan ayb-ahr-be(r) blu(r).

Aria parlante. *Arr*-yah pahrr-*lan*-tay.

Aria senza accompagnamento. *Arr*-yah *send*-zah ac-com-pan-yam-*en*-toh.

Aria tedesca. *Arr*-yah tay-*dess*-cah.

---

6. The **ish** is really anywhere between that sound and 'ik' (varying in different parts of Germany). **7. th** as in *thin*. **8. g** as in *go*.

Arie (Ger.). *Ahrr*-ye(r).
Arie (It.). *Arr*-yay.
Arietta. Arr-*yet*-ta[5].
Arioso. Arr-*yoh*-zoh.
Ariosti. Arr-*yoss*-tee.
Aristide. Arr-ee-steed.
Arkel. Ahrr-kel.
Arlecchinesco. *Arr*-lek-keen-ess-koh.
Arlésienne. Ahrr-layz-yen.
Armaillis des Colombettes. Ahrr-my-ye day Col-om-bet.
Armas (Fin.). *Arr*[5]-mass.
Armide. *Arr*[5]-meed.
Armonia (It.). Arr-moh-*nee*-a[5].
Armonica meteorologica. Arr-*moh*-nee-ca[5] *may*-tay-oh-roh-*lodj*-ee-ca[5].
Armoniosamente (It.). Arr.-mohn-*yoh*-zam-*en*-tay.
Armonioso (It.). Arr-mohn-*yoh*-zoh.
Arnamagnaän. Ahr-nah-mag-*nah*-an.
Arnold (Ger.). *Ahrr*-nolt.
Arpa. *Arr*-pa[5].
Arpège. Ahrr-pezj[3].
Arpègement. Ahrr-pezj[3]-mo(ng).
Arpéger. Ahrr-payzj[3]-ay.
Arpeggiando. Arr-pej-*yan*-doh.
Arpeggiare. Arr-pej-*yah*-ray.
Arpeggiato. Arr-pej-*yah*-toh.
Arpeggione. Arr-pej-*yoh*-nay.
Arpicordo. Arr-pee-*cawrr*-doh.
Arraché. Arr-rash-ay.
Arriaga. Arr-*yah*-gah.
Arrigo il tedesco. Arr-*ee*-goh eel tay-*dess*-coh.
Arsis. *Arss*-iss.
Artaria. Arr-*tahrr*-yah.
Art du facteur d'orgues. Ahrr-dee[2] fac-turr dawrrg.
Arteaga. Ar-tay-*ah*-ga[5].
Arthur (Fr.). Ahrr-teerr[2].
Articolato. Arr-tee-coh-*lah*-toh.
Articolazione. Arr-tee-coh-lahts-*yohn*-ay.
Articulé. Ahr-tee-kee[2]-lay.
Artig. *Arr*-tish[6].

Artigkeit. *Arr*-tish[6]-kite.
Artiglich. *Arr*-tish[6]-lik[1].
Artikuliert. Arr-tee-koo-*leert*.
Arturo. Ahrr-*too*-roh.
As (Ger.). Ass[6].
As dur. Ass[5] doo(e)r.
Ases. Ass[5]-ess.
Asger (Dan.). Ass[5]-gur.
As moll. Ass[5] moll.
Aspiratamente. *Ass*[5]-pee-*rah*-tam-*en*-tay.
Aspra. *Ass*[5]-pra[5].
Aspramente. *Ass*[5]-pram-*en*-tay.
Asprezza. Ass[5]-*prets*-sa[5].
Aspro. *Ass*[5]-proh.
Assai. Ass[5]-*sah*-ee
Assez. Ass[5]-say.
Assieme. Ass[5]-*yay*-may.
Assoluta. Ass[5]-soh-*loo*-ta[5].
Astorga. Ass[5]-*torr*-ga[5].
Atempause. *Aht*-em-pow[4]-se(r).
A tre. At-*ray*.
A tre parti. At-ray *pahrr*-tee.
À trois. At-rwah.
Attacca. At-*tac*-ca[5].
Attaccare. At-tac-*cah*-ray.
Attaignant. At-ayn-yo(ng).
Attaque. At-ak.
Attaque du moulin, L'. Lat-ak dee[2] moo-la(ng).
Atterberg. *At*-err-bairr(ee).
Attilio. At-*teel*-yoh.
Au (Fr.). Oh (pure vowel, not diphthong as in Eng.).
Aubade provençale. Oh-bad prov-o(ng)-sal.
Auber. Oh-bairr.
Aubert. Oh-bairr.
Auch. Owk[4, 1].
Audace (Fr.). Oh-dass.
Audace (It.). Ow[4]-*dah*-chay.
Au-dessous. Oh-de(r)-soo.
Au-dessus. Oh-de(r)-see[2].
Audran. Oh-dro(ng).
Auer. Ow[4]-err.
Auf. Owf[4].
Auf dem Anstand. Owf[4] daim *An*-shtant.
Aufführen. Owf[4]-fee[2]-ren.
Aufführung. Owf[4]-fee[2]-roong.

Aufführungsrecht. Owf[4]-fee[2]-roongs-rekt[1].
Aufgeregt. Owf[4]-gur-raikt.
Aufgeweckt. Owf[4]-gu(r)-vekt.
Aufhalten. Owf[4]-hal[5]-ten.
Auflage. Owf[4]-lahg-e(r).
Auflösen. Owf[4]-le(r)-zen.
Auflösung. Owf[4]-le(r)-zoong.
Aufschlag. Owf[4]-shlahg.
Aufschnitt. Owf[4]-shnit.
Aufschwung. Owf[4]-shvoong.
Aufstrich. Owf[4]-shtrik[1].
Auftakt. Owf[4]-takt.
Augener. Owg[4]-en-er.
Augengläser. Owg[4]-en-glay-zer.
Auguste. Ohg-eest[2].
Auld Lang Syne. 'Syne' as Eng. 'sign'; avoid 'z' sound.
Aulin (Swed.). Ow[4]-leen.
Aura. *Ah*-oo-ra[5] (but almost in two syllables).
Auric. Oh-reek.
Aurin. Oh-ra(ng).
Aurresku. Ow[4]-*ress*-koo.
Aus (Ger.). Owss[4].
Ausdruck. Owss[4]-drook.
Ausdrucksvoll. Owss[4]-drooks-fol.
Ausfüllgeiger. Ows[4]-feel[2]-gy[8]-ger[8].
Ausgabe. Ows[4]-gah-be(r).
Ausgehalten. Owss[4]-gu(r)-hal-ten.
Aushalten. Owss[4]-hal-ten.
Aushaltungszeichen. Owss[4]-hal-toongs-tsy-shen.
Ausschlagen. Owss[4]-shlahg-en.
Ausser. Owss[4]-er.
Äusserst. Oyss-erst.
Aussi. Oh-see.
Auszug. Owss[4]-tsoog.
Autre, Autres. Ohtrr (all one syllable).
Avant. Av-o(ng).
Avante. Av-*an*-tay.
Avanti. Av-*an*-tee.
Avec. Av-ek.
Azione. Ats-*yoh*-nay.
Azucena (It.). Ads-oo-*chain*-a[5]. (Sp.). Ath[7]-oo-*thay*[7]-na[5].

---

1. k = 'ch' (cf. Scot. *loch*). **2. ee** here really between 'ee' and 'oo' (cf. Scot. *puir*). **3. zj** like 's' in *pleasure*. **4. ow** as in *cow*. **5. a** as in *lad*.

B

Bacchetta di legno. Bak-*ket*-ta⁵ dee *layn*-yoh.

Bacchetta di spugna. Bak-*ket*-ta⁵ dee *spoon*-ya⁵.

Bach. Bak¹.

Bache (Eng.). Baitch.

Bacio. *Bah*-choh.

Backer-Gröndahl. Bak-err Gre(r)n-dahl.

Badarczewska. Bad-ahrr-*chefs*-ka.⁵.

Badchonim. Bat-*hoh*-neem.

Badinage. Bad-ee-nahzj³.

Badinerie. Bad-ee-nerr-ee.

Badings. *Bah*-dings.

Bagatelle (Fr.). Bag-at-el.

Bagatelle (Ger.). Bag-at-*el*-e(r).

Baguette de bois. Bag-et de(r) bwah.

Baguette d'éponge. Bag-et day-po(ng)zj³.

Baïf. Ba⁵-eef.

Baile. *Ba*⁵-ee-lay (almost *By*-lay).

Baillot. By-yoh.

Baisser. Base-say.

Bakfark. *Bok*-forrk.

Bakst. Bahkst.

Balakiref. Bah-*lah*-kee-ref.

Balalaika. Bah-lah-*like*-ah.

Baldassare. Bal-dass-*ah*-ray.

Ballade. Bal-lad.

Balladenmässig. Bal-*lahd*-en-mess-ish⁶.

Ballata. Bal-*lah*-ta⁵.

Ballerina. Bal-lay-*ree*-na⁵.

Ballet. Bal-lay.

Ballet d'action. Bal-lay daks-yo(ng).

Ballet de cour. Bal-lay de(r) coorr.

Ballo furlano. *Bal*-loh foorr-*lah*-noh.

Ballo in maschera. *Bal*-loh een *mass*-kay-ra⁵.

Bamberg. *Bam*-bairrg.

Bamboula (Fr.). Bo(ng)-boo-la⁵.

Banchieri. Ban-kee-*ay*-ree.

Banda turca. *Ban*-da⁵ toorr-ca⁵.

Bandola. *Ban*-doh-la⁵.

Bandonnier. Bo(ng)-don-yay.

Bandurría. Ban-doo-*ree*-a⁵.

Baptiste. Bat-eest.

Barbaresque. Bahrr-barr⁵-esk.

Barbarie. Bahrr-barr⁵-ee.

Barbier (Fr.). Bahrrb-yay.

Barbiere di Siviglia, Il. Eel barr⁵-bee-*ayr*-ray dee See-*veel*-ya⁵.

Barbieri. Barr⁵-bee-*ay*-ree.

Barbier von Bagdad, Der. Dairr Barrb-*eerr* fon *Bag*-dat.

Barcarolle. Bahrr-car⁵-rol.

Bardi. *Barr*⁵-dee.

Bärenhäuter, Der. Dairr *Bairr*-en-hoyt-err.

Bargiel. *Barrg*-eel.

Baring-Gould. Bair-ing-*Goold.*

Barkarole. Barr-kah-*roh*-le(r).

Bärmann. *Bairr*-man.

Barocco. Ba⁵-*roc*-coh.

Barock. Bah-*rock.*

Baroncelli. Ba⁵-ron-*chel*-lee.

Baroque. Ba⁵-*rock.*

Barre. Bahrr.

Barrios. *Barr*⁵-ee-ohss.

Barth. Bahrrt.

Bartók. *Bawrr*-tok.

Bartolo. *Barr*⁵-toh-loh.

Baryton. Ba⁵-ree-to(ng).

Baskische Tänze. *Bass*-kish-e(r) *Tent*-se(r).

Baskische Trommel. *Bass*-kish-e(r) *Trom*-el.

Basoche, La. La⁵ Baz⁵-osh.

Bassa. *Bass*-sa⁵.

Bassani. Bass-*sah*-nee.

Bassano. Bass-*sah*-noh.

Basse. Bahss.

Basse chantante. Bahss sho(ng)-to(ng)t.

Basse chiffrée. Bahss sheef-ray.

Basse continue. Bahss co(ng)-tee-nee².

Basse danse. Bahss do(ng)ss.

Basse de Flandres. Bahss de(r) Flo(ng)drr.

Basse d'harmonie. Bahss darr⁵-mon-ee.

Basselin. Bahss-la(ng).

Bassflicorno. Bass-flee-*cawrr*-noh.

Bassflügelhorn. *Bass*-fleeg²-el-horrn.

Bassi. *Bass*-see.

Bassiani. Bass-ee-*ah*-nee.

Basso. *Bass*-soh.

Basso cantabile. *Bass*-soh can-tab-ee-lay.

Basso cantante. *Bass*-soh can-tan-tay.

Basso continuo. *Bass*-soh con-tee-noo-oh.

Basson. Bahss-so(ng).

Basson quinte. Bahss-so(ng) ka(n)t⁵.

Basson russe. Bahss-so(ng) reess².

Basso ostinato. *Bass*-soh oss-tee-*nah*-toh.

Basso profondo. *Bass*-soh proh-*fon*-doh.

Bassposaune. *Bass*-poh-*zow*⁴-ne(r).

Bass-Saite. *Bass*-*Zite*-e(r).

Basstrompete. *Bass*-trom-*pay*-te(r).

Batiste. Bat-eest.

Baton (Eng.). *Bat*-on.

Bâton (Fr.). Baht-o(ng).

Battere. *Bat*-tay-ray.

Batterie. Bat-ree.

Battista. Bat-*teess*-ta⁵.

Battre. Batrr.

Battuta. Bat-*too*-ta⁵.

Battute. Bat-*too*-tay.

Bauer. *Bow*⁴-err.

Bayle. *By*-lay.

Bayreuth. By-*royt.*

Bazzini. Bat-*see*-nee.

B dur. Bay doo(e)r.

Be. Bay.

Bearbeiten. Be(r)-*ahrr*-by-ten.

Bearbeitet. Be(r)-*ahrr*-by-tet.

Bearbeitung. Be(r)-*ahrr*-by-toong.

Béarnaise. Bay-ahrr-nez.

Beauchamp (Eng.). Beechm.

Beauchamp (Fr.). Boh-sho(ng).

Beaucoup. Boh-koo.

Beaumarchais. Boh-mahrr-shay.

Beaumont (Eng.). *Boh*-mont.

Beaumont (Fr.). Boh-mo(ng).

Bebend. *Bay*-bent.

Bebung. *Bay*-boong.

Bécarre. Bay-cahrr.

Bechstein. *Bek*¹-shtine.

Becken. *Bek*-en.

Bécourt. Bay-coorr.

Bedächtig. Be(r)-*dek*¹-tish⁶.

Bedarfsfalle. Be(r)-*darrf*s-fal-e(r).

Bedeutend. Be(r)-*doy*-tent.

Bédos de Celles. Bayd-oh de(r) Sel.

Bedřich. *Bayd*-rik¹.

Bedrohlich. Be(r)-*droh*-lik¹.

Beethoven. *Bait*-hohv-en.

Begeistert. Be(r)-*gyss*-tairrt.

Begleiten. Be(r)-*gly*-ten.

Behaglich. Be(r)-*hahg*-lik¹.

Behend. Be(r)-*hent.*

Behendig. Be(r)-*hend*-ish⁶.

Behendigkeit. Be(r)-*hend*-ish⁶-kite.

Beherzt. Be(r)-*hairrtst.*

Behrens-Senegaldens. *Bay*-renz-Sen-ayg-*al*-denz.

Beide. *By*-de(r).

---

6. The **ish** is really anywhere between that sound and 'ik' (varying in different parts of Germany).
7. th as in *thin*.   **8.** g as in *go*.

Beinahe. *By*-nah-e(r).
Beireis. *By*-rice.
Beispiel. *By*-shpeel.
Beissel. *Byss*-el.
Beisser. *By*-serr.
Beklommen. Be(r)-*klom*-en.
Béla. *Bay*-lo(r).
Belaief, Belaiev. Bayl-*yah*-yef.
Bel canto. Bel *can*-toh.
Belebend. Be(r)-*lay*-bent.
Belebt. Be(r)-*laipt*.
Belcke. *Belk*-e(r).
Belieben. Be(r)-*lee*-ben.
Beliebig. Be(r)-*lee*-bish⁶.
Belle siffleuse, La. La⁵ bel see-flu(r)z.
Bellicoso. Bel-lee-*coh*-zoh.
Bellini. Bel-*lee*-nee.
Belmont (Ger.). *Bel*-mont.
Belustigend. Be(r)-*loost*-ig-ent.
Bemberg (Fr.). Bo(ng)-bairr.
Bémol. Bay-mol.
Bemolle. Bay-*mol*-lay.
Ben. Ben.
Benda. *Ben*-dah.
Bendix. *Ben*-dix.
Bene (It.). *Bay*-nay.
Benedict (Ger.). *Ben*-ay-dikt.
Beneplacimento. Bay-nay-platch-ee-*men*-toh.
Beneplacito. Bay-nay-*plah*-chee-toh.
Benevente. Ben-ay-*ven*-tay.
Benoist. Be(r)n-wa⁵.
Benoît. Be(r)n-wa⁵.
Benvenuto Cellini. Ben-ven-oo-toh Chel-*lee*-nee.
Beppe (It.). *Bep*-pay.
Bequadro. Bay-*kwah*-droh.
Bequem. Be(r)-*kvaim*.
Bérard. Bay-rahrr.
Berceuse. Bairr-su(r)z.
Bereite vor. Be(r)-*rite*-e(r) fohrr.
Bereits. Be(r)-*rites*.
Berezovsky. Bairr-ez-*ov*-skee.
Berg. Bairrg.
Bergamasca. Bairr-gam-*ass*⁵-ca⁵.
Bergamasque. Bairr-gam-*ask*⁵.
Berger (Francesco). Berger-(a Londoner, and name so pronounced).
Bergerette. Bairrzj²ret (or Bairr-zjerr-ret).
Beringer. *Bairr*-ing-err.
Berio. Bayrr-yoh.
Bériot. Bayrr-yoh.
Berliner. Bairr-*leen*-err.
Berlioz. Bairrl-yohz.
Bernard (Fr.). Bairr-nahrr.
Bernard (Ger.). *Bairr*-narrt⁵.
Bernier. Bairn-yay.

Bertini. Bairr-*tee*-nee.
Bertrand. Bairr-tro(ng).
Beruhigend. Be(r)-*roo*-ig-ent.
Beruhigt. Be(r)-*roo*-isht⁶.
Beruhigung. Ber-*roo*-ig-oong.
Berwald. *Bair*-vald.
Bes. Bess.
Beschleunigen. Besh-*loy*-nig-en.
Beschleunigt. Besh-*loy*-nisht⁶.
Beseelt. Be(r)-*zaylt*.
Bestimmt. Be(r)-*shtimmt*.
Betend. *Bay*-tent.
Betont. Be(r)-*tohnt*.
Betrübniss. Be(r)-*treeb*²-niss.
Betrübt. Be(r)-*treept*².
Beweglich. Be(r)-*vayg*-lish⁶.
Bewegt. Be(r)-*vaykt*.
Bewegung. Be(r)-*vay*-goong.
Béza. Bay-za⁵.
Bianca. Bee-*ahn*-ca⁵.
Bibelorgel. Bee-bel-*awrrg*-el.
Bibelregal. Bee-bel-ray-*gahl*.
Biber. *Bee*-berr.
Bien. Bee-*a*(ng).
Bigophone. Bee-goh-fon.
Bigot (Fr.) Bee-goh.
Bigotphone. Bee-goh-fon.
Bihari. *Bee*-hohr-ree.
Binchois. Ba(ng)-shwa⁵.
Binet. Bee-nay.
Biniou. Bee-nee-you.
Bis (Fr.). Beess.
Bisbigliato. Beez-bee-lee-*ah*-toh.
Biscroma. Beess-*craw*-ma⁵.
Bittend. *Bit*-ent.
Bittner. *Bit*-nerr.
Bizet. Bee-zay.
Bizzarro. Beed-*za*⁵-roh.
Björnson. B'*yerrn*-son.
Blacher. *Blak*¹-er.
Blahoslav. *Bla*⁵-hoh-slav.
Blanche. Blo(ng)sh.
Blanchet. Blo(ng)-shay.
Blasend. *Blah*-zent.
Blasinstrumente. *Blahss*-in-stroo-*men*-te(r).
Blasis. Blah-zeess.
Blasmusik. *Blahss*-moo-*zeek*.
Blechmusik. *Blek*¹-moo-*zeek*.
Bleiben. *Bly*-ben.
Blitzstein. *Blits*-stine.
Bloch. Block¹.
Blockflöte. *Block*-fle(r)-te(r).
Blockx. Blocks.
Bluehmel. *Blee*²-mel.
Bluemel. *Blee*²-mel.
Blume. *Bloo*-me(r).
Blümel. *Blee*²-mel.
Blumenfeld. *Bloom*-en-feh.
Blumenthal. *Bloom*-en-tahl.
Blüthner. *Bleet*²-nerr.

B moll. Bay mol.
Bobillier. Bob-ee-yay.
Bocca chiusa. *Boc*-ca⁵ kew-za⁵.
Boccherini. Boc-kay-*ree*-nee.
Boceto (Sp.). Boh-*thay*⁷-toh.
Bochsa. *Bosh*-sah.
Boeck. Book.
Boehe. *Be*(r)-e(r).
Boehm. Be(r)m.
Boëllmann. Boh-el-mo(ng).
Boëly. Boh-el-ee.
Boëmo. Boh-*aim*-oh.
Boësset. Boh-ess-say.
Boethius. Boh-*eeth*-yus.
Bogen. *Bohg*-en.
Bogenstrich. *Bohg*-en-shtrik¹.
Böhe. Be(r)-e(r).
Bohème, La. La⁵ Boh-em.
Böhm. Be(r)m.
Böhme. *Be*(r)-me(r).
Bohuslav. *Boh*-hoo-slav.
Boïeldieu. Bwai⁵-dyu(r).
Bois. Bwah.
Boisset. Bwah-say.
Boîte. Bwat.
Boito. *Boy*-toh.
Bolero. Bol-*ayr*-roh.
Bolm. Bollm.
Bombarda. Bom-*bahrr*-da⁵.
Bombarde. Bom-bahrrd.
Bombardes. Bom-bahrrd.
Bombardon (Eng.). Bom-*bar*-don.
Bonnet. Bon-nay.
Bonno. *Bon*-noh.
Bononcini. Bon-on-*chee*-nee.
Bonporti. Bon-*porr*-tee.
Bordes. Bawrrd.
Boris Godunof. Borr-*eess* God-oo-*noff*.
Borjon. Borr-zjo(ng)³.
Borodin. Borr-oh-*deen*.
Borowski. Boh-*rof*-skee.
Borsa. *Bawrr*-sa⁵.
Bortniansky. Bortt-nee-*an*-skee(yer).
Bossi. *Boss*-see.
Bote. *Boh*-te(r).
Bottesini. Bot-tez-*ee*-nee.
Bottrigari. Bot-tree-*gah*-ree.
Bouché. Boo-shay.
Bouche fermée. Boosh fairr-may.
Bouchés. Boo-shay.
Bouffes Parisiens. Boof Pa⁵-reez-ya(ng).
Bouffons. Boof-fo(ng).
Boughton. *Bow*⁴-ton.
Bouhy. Boo-ee.
Boulanger. Boo-lo(ng)-zjay³.
Boulez. Boo-lez.
Boult. Bohlt.

---

1. k = 'ch' (cf. Scot. *loch*.) **2.** ee here really between 'ee' and 'oo' (cf. Scot. *puir*).
3. zj like 's' in *pleasure*. **4.** ow as in *cow*. **5.** a as in *lad*.

Bouquin. Boo-ka(ng).
Bourdon (Eng.). Boordn.
Bourdon (Fr.). Boorr-do(ng).
Bourgault-Ducoudray. Boorr-goh-Dee²-coo-dray.
Bourgeois. Boorzj³-wah.
Bourgeois gentilhomme, Le. Le(r) boorzj³-wah zjont³-ee yom.
Bourguignon. Boor-geen⁸-yo(ng).
Bourrée. Boo-ray.
Bout. Boo.
Boutade. Boo-tad.
Bouton. Boo-to(ng).
Bowen. Boh-en.
Boyau. Bwah-yoh.
Brabançonne. Brab-bo(ng)-sonn.
Braccio. Brah-choh.
Brachvogel. Brak¹-fohg-el.
Braham. Bray-am (not Brah-am, as generally mispronounced).
Brahe. Brah-e(r).
Brahms. Brahmss.
Brandenburg. Brand-en-boorrg.
Brangäne. Bran-gay-ne(r).
Branle. Bro(ng)l.
Bransle. Bro(ng)l.
Brantle (Old Fr.). Bro(ng)l.
Bras. Brah.
Bratsche. Braht-she(r).
Braunfels. Brown-felss.
Brautlied. Browt⁴-leet.
Bravoure. Brav-oorr.
Bravura. Brav-oo-ra⁵.
Brecht. Bresht⁶.

Breit. Brite.
Breitkopf. Brite-kopf.
Brenet. Bre(r)-nay.
Brenhines Dido. Bren-heen-ess Dee-doh.
Breton (Sp.). Bray-ton.
Bréval. Bray-val.
Breve (Eng.). Breev.
Breve (It.). Bray-vay.
Bréville. Bray-veel.
Bridel. Bree-del.
Brillant. Bree-yo(ng).
Brillante (Fr.). Bree-yo(ng)t.
Brillante (It.). Breel-lan-tay.
Brindisi. Brin-dee-zee.
Brio. Bree-oh.
Brioso. Bree-oh-zoh.
Brisé. Bree-zay.
Briser. Bree-zay.
Brockes. Brock-ess.
Brockhaus. Brock-howss⁴.
Brossard. Bross-ahrr.
Brosses. Bross.
Bruch. Brook¹.
Brucken-Fock. Brook-en-Fok.
Bruckner. Brook-nerr.
Bruhn. Broon.
Brüll. Breel².
Brume. Breem².
Brummeisen. Broom-eye-zen.
Brummscheit. Broom-shyte.
Bruneau. Bree²-noh.
Brünnhilde. Breen²-hil-de(r).
Bruno. Broo-noh.
Bruscamente. Broos-cam-en-tay.
Bruyère. Bree²-yairr.
Bucolico. Boo-col-ee-coh.

Buechner. Beek²-nerr.
Buée. Bee²-ay.
Buffa. Boof-fa⁵.
Buffet d'orgue. Beef²-fay dawrrg.
Buffo. Boof-foh.
Buffonesco. Boof-fon-ess-coh.
Buffonescamente. Boof-fon-ess-ca⁵-men-tay.
Bügelhorn. Beeg²-el-horrn.
Bugle à clefs. Beeg²-la⁵-clay.
Bugle à pistons. Beeg²-la⁵-pee-sto(ng).
Bühnenfestspiel. Been²-en-fest-shpeel.
Bühnenweihfestspiel. Been²-en-vy-fest-shpeel.
Bülow. Bee²-loh.
Bundfrei. Boont-fry.
Bunte Blätter. Boon-te(r) Blet-ter.
Buononcini. Bwon-on-chee-nee.
Bürger. Beerrg²-err.
Burgmüller. Boorrg-meel²-ler.
Burkhardt. Boorrk-harrt.
Burla. Boor-la⁵.
Burlando. Boorr-lan-doh.
Burlesca. Boorr-less-ca⁵.
Burlesco. Boorr-less-coh.
Burlesque. Beerr²-lesk.
Busch. Boosh.
Buschmann. Boosh-man.
Busnois. Been²-wah.
Busoni. Boo-zoh-nee.
Buxtehude. Book-ste(r)-hoo-de(r).
Buysine. Bwee²-zeen.

C

Cabaletta. Cab-al-et-ta⁵.
Cabbaletta. Cab-bal-et-ta⁵.
Cabezón. Cab-ay-thon⁷.
Cabrette. Cab-ret.
Caccia. Catch-ya⁵.
Caccini. Cat-shee-nee.
Cachucha. Catch-oo-cha⁵.
Cäcilienverein. Tsay-tseel-yen fairr-ine.
Cadenza. Cad-end-za⁵.
Cadenzato. Cad-ents-aht-toh.

Caffarelli. Caf-fa⁵-rel-lee.
Cahier. Ca⁵-yay.
Ça ira. Sa⁵ ee-ra⁵.
Caisse claire. Kess clairr.
Caisse roulante. Kess roo-lo(ng)t.
Caisse sourde. Kess soorrd.
Caix d'Herveloix. Kay dairr-vel-wah.
Calando. Ca⁵-lan-doh.
Calcando. Cal-can-doh.

Caldara. Cal-dah-ra⁵.
Calderón de la Barca. Cal⁵-day-ron day la⁵ Barr⁵-ca⁵.
Caller Herrin'. ('al' as in 'pal', not as in 'call').
Calmando. Cal-man-doh.
Calmato. Cal-mah-toh.
Calme. Callm.
Calore. Cal-aw-ray.
Calvin. Cal-va(ng), but in English usually pron. Cal-vin.

---

6. The **ish** is really anywhere between that sound and 'ik' (varying in different parts of Germany).
7. **th** as in *thin*.   8. **g** as in *go*.

Calypso. Ka-*lip*-so.
Calzabigi. Calt⁵-zab-*ee*-jee.
Camargo. Cam-*ahrr*-goh.
Cambert. Co(ng)-bairr.
Cambiare. Cam-bee-*ah*-ray.
Camera. *Cam*-ay-ra⁵.
Camille. Cam-eel.
Camillo (It.). Cahm-*eel*-oh.
Cammaert. *Cam*-ahrrt.
Camminando. Cam-mee-*nan*-doh.
Campana. Cam-*pah*-nah.
Campane. Cam-*pah*-nay.
Campanella. Cam-pah-*nel*-la⁵.
Campanelle. Cam-pah-*nel*-lay.
Campenhout. *Cam*-pen-howt⁴.
Campina. Cam-*peen*-a⁵.
Campo. *Cam*-poh.
Campra. Originally It. and pron. '*Cam*-pra⁵'; in France, where he was born, pron. 'Co(ng)-pra⁵'.
Can-Can. Co(ng)-co(ng).
Canciero musical. Canth⁷-*yay*-roh moo-see-*cal*⁵.
Canción danza. Canth⁷-ee-*on dahnth*⁷-a⁵.
Canio. *Cahn*-yoh.
Cannabich. *Can*-ab-ik¹.
Canntaireachd. *Cown*-tarr-rak¹-(k).
Canon (Eng.). *Can*-on.
Canon (Fr.). Ca-no(ng).
Canone. Can-*oh*-nay.
Cantabile. Can-*tab*-ee-lay.
Cantando. Can-*tan*-doh.
Cantante. Can-*tan*-tay.
Cantare. Can-*tah*-ray.
Cantata. Can-*tah*-ta⁵.
Cantata da camera. Can-*tah*-ta⁵ da⁵ *cam*-ay-ra⁵.
Cantata da chiesa. Can-*tah*-ta⁵ da⁵ kee-*ay*-za⁵.
Cantate (Fr.). Co(ng)-tat.
Cantate (It.). Can-*tah*-tay.
Cantato. Can-*tah*-toh.
Cantatrice. Can-tat-*tree*-chay.
Cante flamenco. *Can*-tay flam-en-coh.
Cante hondo. *Can*-tay kon¹-doh (so in Andalusia; elsewhere '*On*-doh').
Cante jondo. (Same as above.)
Canti carnascialeschi. *Can*-tee carr⁵-nash-al⁵-*ess*-kee.
Cantiga. *Can*-tee-ga⁵.
Cantilena. Can-tee-*lay*-na⁵.
Cantilenas vulgares. Can-tee-lay-nass vool-*gah*-ress.
Cantilène. Co(ng)-tee-len.
Canto carnascialesco. *Can*-toh carr⁵-nash-al⁵-*ess*-coh.
Canto fermo. *Can*-toh *fairr*-moh.

Canu pennillion. *Can*-ee² pen-*ith*-lee-on.
Canzión danza. Cahnth⁷-ee-*ohn dahnth*⁷-ah.
Canzona. Cannt-*soh*-na².
Canzone. Cannt-*soh*-nay.
Canzonetta. Cannt-soh-*net*-ta⁵.
Canzoni. Cannt-*soh*-nee.
Capell. *Kay*-pel.
Caplet. Kap-lay.
Capodaster (Ger.). Cah-poh-*dass*-terr.
Capodastère (Fr.). Cap-oh-dast-airr.
Capo d'astro. *Cah*-poh *dass*-troh.
Caponsacchi. Cap-on-*sak*-kee.
Capotasto. *Cah*-poh-*tass*-toh.
Cappella. Cap-*pel*-la⁵.
Capriccio. Cap-*ree*-choh.
Capriccioso. Cap-ree-*cho*-zoh.
Caprice. Cap-reess.
Capricieuse. Cap-reess-yu(r)z.
Capricieux. Cap-reess-yu(r).
Carcelera. Carr⁵-thel⁷-*ay*-ra⁵.
Cardillac. Carr⁵-dee-yak.
Cardinal (Fr.). Carr⁵-dee-nal.
Cardus. *Kard*-uss.
Caressant. Ca⁵-ress-o(ng).
Carezzando. ' Carr⁵-ets-*sand*-doh.
Carezzevole. Carr⁵-ets-*say*-voh-lay.
Carezzevolmente. Carr⁵-ets-say-vol-*men*-tay.
Carillon (Eng.). Carr⁵-*il*-on.
Carillon (Fr.). Ca⁵-ree-yo(ng).
Carissimi. Carr-*eess*-see-mee.
Carlo. *Carr*⁵-loh.
Carlos. *Carr*⁵-lohss.
Carmagnole. Carr⁵-man-yol.
Carmen (Fr.). *Carr*⁵-men.
Carnaval de Venise. Car⁵-nav⁵-al⁵ du(r) Ven-eez.
Carnegie. Cahrr-*neg*-ee.
Carnicer. Carr⁵-neeth⁷-*airr*.
Carol-Bérard. Ca⁵-rol-Bair-rarr⁵.
Caroso. Carr⁵-*oh*-zoh.
Carré. Carr⁵-ay.
Carrillo. Carr⁵-*eel*-yoh.
Cartan. Carr⁵-to(ng).
Cartier. Carrt⁵-yay.
Caruso. Carr⁵-*oo*-zoh.
Casa Guidi. *Cah*-za⁵ *Gwee*-dee.
Casals. Caz-*alss*.
Casanova. Cah-zan-*oh*-va⁵.
Casavant. Caz-av-o(ng).
Casella. Caz-*el*-la⁵.
Caspar. *Cass*-pahrr.
Cassa. *Cass*-sa.
Cassa grande. *Cass*-sa⁵ *gran*-day.

Cassa rullante. *Cass*-sa⁵ rool-*lan*-tay.
Cassation (Ger.). Cass-aht-see-*ohn*.
Cassazione. Cass-sahts-*yoh*-nay.
Castagnette (It.). Cass-tan-*yet*-tay.
Castagnettes (Fr.). Cass-tan-yet.
Castaldi. Cass-*tal*-dee.
Castelnuovo-Tedesco. Cass-tel-noo-*ov*-oh Ted-*ess*-coh.
Castillane (Fr.). Cass-tee-yan.
Castillon. Cas-tee-yo(ng).
Castor et Pollux. Cass-torr ay Poll-leeks².
Castrati. Cass-*trah*-tee.
Castrato. Cass-*trah*-toh.
Castro. *Cass*-troh.
Catalán (Sp.). Cat-al-*an*.
Catalane (Fr.). Cat-al-an.
Catalani. Cat-al-*ah*-nee.
Catoire. Cat-wahrr.
Caudella. Cawd-*el*-lah.
Caurroy. Cohrr-wah.
Caus. Koh.
Cavaillé. Ca⁵-vy-yay.
Cavalieri. Cav-al-*yay*-ree.
Cavalleria Rusticana. Cav-al-ay-*ree*-a⁵ Roos-tee-*cah*-na⁵.
Cavalli. Cav-*al*-ee.
Cavaradossi. Cav-a⁵-rad-*oss*-ee.
Cavatina. Cav-at-*ee*-na⁵.
Cavos. *Cah*-voss.
Cazalis. Caz-al-eess.
Cecchetti. Chek-*ket*-tee.
Cecco. *Chek*-koh.
Cécile. Say-seel.
Cédant. Say-do(ng).
Cédé. Say-day.
Cédez. Say-day.
Céilidh. *Cay*-lee (extend the first vowel).
Ceiriog. *Ky*-ree-og.
Celano. Chel-*ah*-noh.
Celeramente. Chel-air-ah-*men*-tay.
Celere. *Chel*-air-ray.
Celerità. Chel-air-ree-*tah*.
Céleste. Say-lest.
Cellini. Chel-*lee*-nee.
Cembalo. *Chem*-bal-oh.
Cenerentola, La. La⁵ Chen-air-en-toh-la⁵.
Cento (Eng.). *Sen*-toh.
Cento (It.). *Chen*-toh.
Centon. So(ng)-to(ng).
Centone. Chen-*toh*-nay.
Ceòl Beag. K'yawl Bek.
Ceòl Meadhonach. K'yawl *Mee*-an-ak¹.
Ceòl Mór. K'yawl Mohrr.
Cé qu'è laino. Say kay lay noh.

---

1. k= 'ch' (cf. Scot. *loch*).   2. ee here really between 'ee' and 'oo' (cf. Scot. *puir*).   3. zj like 's' in *pleasure*.   4. ow as in *cow*.   5. a as in *lad*.

Ce qu'on entend sur la montagne. Se(r) kon on-to(ng) seer[2] la[5] mo(ng)-tan-y(er).

Cerddor Cymreig. *Kairr*-thorr Kum-ryg ('th' as in *the*).

Cerezo. Thay[7]-*rayth*[7]-oh.

Černohorsky. Chairr-naw-*hawrs*-kee.

Cerone. Thairr[7]-*oh*-nay.

Cerrito. Chair-*ree*-toh.

Certon. Sairr-to(ng).

Cervantes. Thairr[7]-*van*-tess, but in English often pron. 'Sir-*van*-tees'.

Ces (Fr.). Say.

Ces (Ger.). Tsess.

César. Say-zarr.

Cesare. *Chay*-za[5]-ray.

Ceses. *Tsess*-ess.

Cesti. *Chess*-tee.

Cetra (It.). *Chet*-ra[5].

Cézanne. Say-zan.

Chabrier. Shab-ree-ay.

Chaconne. Shak-on.

Chahut. Sha[5]-ee[2].

Chaleur. Shal-err (like Eng. word *err*).

Chaleureusement. Shal-err-u(r)z-mo(ng) ('err' as Eng. word *err*).

Chaleureux. Shal-err-u(r) ('err' as Eng. word *err*).

Chaliapin. Shahl-*yah*-peen.

Chalumeau. Shal-ee[2]-moh.

Chambonnières. Shom-bon-yairr.

Chaminade. Sham-ee-nad.

Champêtre. Sho(ng)-petrr.

Champion (Fr.). Shom-pee-yo(ng).

Chandos. *Shan*-dohss.

Changer. Sho(n)-zjay[3].

Changez. Sho(n)-zjay[3].

Chanson. Sho(n)-so(ng).

Chanson sans paroles. Sho(n)-so(ng) so(ng) pa[5]-rol.

Chansons de gestes. Sho(n)-so(ng) de(r) zjest[3].

Chantant. Sho(n)-to(ng).

Chanté. Sho(n)-tay.

Chanter (Fr.). Sho(n)-tay.

Chanterelle. Sho(n)-terr-el.

Chanteurs de Saint Gervais. Sho(n)-turr de(r) Sa(ng) zjairr[3]-vay.

Chanty. Shanty.

Chapí. Shap-*ee*.

Chapuis. Shap-wee.

Chaque. Shak.

Charivari. Sha[5]-ree-va[5]-ree.

Charles (Fr.). Shahrl.

Charpentier. Sharr[5]-po(n)t-yay.

Chasse. Shass.

Chassé. Shass-ay.

Châteauminors. Shah-toh-mee-norr.

Chaudefontaine. Shohd-fo(n)-ten.

Chausson. Shoh-so(ng).

Chávez. *Chah*-vez.

Chazzan. *Kaz*[1]-an.

Che (It.). Kay.

Chédeville. Shay-de(r)-veel.

Chef d'attaque. Shef dat-ak.

Chénier. Shayn-yay.

Cherubini. Kay-roo-*bee*-nee.

Cherubino. Kay-roo-*bee*-noh.

Chevalet. Shu(r)-va[5]-lay.

Chevalier. Shu(r)-val-yay.

Chevé. Shu(r)-vay.

Cheville. Shu(r)-vee-y(er).

Chevrette. Shu(r)-vret.

Chezy. *Kay*-zee.

Chiara. Kee-*ah*-ra[5].

Chiaramente. Kee-ah-ra[5]-*men*-tay.

Chiaro. Kee-*ah*-roh.

Chiasso. Kee-*ass*-soh.

Chiave. Kee-*ah*-vay.

Chica. *Cheek*-a[5].

Chiesa. Kee-*ay*-za[5].

Chifonie. Shee-fon-ee.

Chiroplast. *Ky*-roh-plast.

Chittarone. Keet-ta[5]-*roh*-nay.

Chiuso. *Kew*-zoh.

Chœur. Curr (like Eng. *cur*).

Chopin. Shop-a(ng).

Choragus. Koh-*rah*-guss.

Choral (Ger.). Koh-*rahl*.

Chorale (Eng.). *Kaw*-rahl.

Choral partita. Koh-*rahl* parr[5]-*tee*-tah.

Choral Vorspiel. Koh-*rahl* Fohrr-shpeel.

Choregraphy. Korr-*eg*[8]-raf-ee.

Choreography. Korr-ee-*og*-raf-ee.

Chormässige Stimmung. *Kohrr*-mess-ig-e(r) *Shtim*-oong.

Chorstimmung. *Kohrr*-shtim-oong.

Chorton. *Kohrr*-tohn.

Chor Zinck. Kohrr Tsink.

Chout. Shoot.

Christian (Ger.). *Krist*-ee-ahn.

Christoph. *Krist*-off.

Christophe Colomb. Kree-stof Col-o(ng).

Christ unser Herr. Krist *oon*-zer Hairr.

Chromatique. Krohm-at-eek.

Chromatische Harmonika. Kroh-*mah*-tish-e(r) Harr-*moh*-nee-kah.

Chrotta. *Krot*-tah.

Chrysostom. *Kriss*-oss-tom.

Ciaccona. Cha[5]-*coh*-nah.

Ciampi. *Cham*-pee.

Cieco, Il. Eel *Chay*-koh.

Cifra. *Chee*-fra[5].

Cilindri. Chee-*leen*-dree.

Cilindro. Chee-*leen*-droh.

Cimarosa. Chee-ma[5]-*roh*-za[5].

Cinelli. Chee-*nel*-lee.

Cinq (Fr.). Sa(n)k (but before a consonant 'sa(ng)').

Cinque. *Chin*-kway.

Cinquepace (Eng.). *Sink*-payss.

Cinque pas. Sank pah.

Cinque passi. *Chin*-kway Pass[5]-see.

Cinquième. Sank-yem.

Cinquième position. Sank-yem pohz-eess-yo(ng).

Ciò. Choh.

Cioè. Choh-*ay*.

Ciphering. *Sy*-ferr-ing.

Ciro. *Chee*-roh.

Cis (Ger.). Tsiss.

Cis dur (Ger.). Tsiss doo(e)r.

Cisis (Ger.). *Tsiss*-iss.

Cis moll (Ger.). Tsiss mol.

Citharen (Eng.). Sith[7]-*ah*-ren.

Cithren (Eng.). *Sith*[7]-ren.

Citole (Eng.). Sit-*ohl*.

Cittern. *Sit*-urn.

Civettando. Chee-vet-*tan*-doh.

Civetteria. Chee-vet-tairr-*ee*-a[5].

Civettescamente. Chee-vet-tess-cam-*en*-tay.

Claire. Clairr.

Clairon. Clairr-o(ng).

Clapisson. Clap-eess-o(ng).

Claque. Clack.

Claquebois. Clack-e(r)-bwah.

Clarabella. *Cla*[5]-ra[5]-*bel*-la[5].

Clari. *Clah*-ree.

Clarina. Clah-*ree*-na[5].

Clarinetto. Cla[5]-ree-*net*-toh.

Clarino. Cla[5]-*ree*-noh.

Claro. *Clah*-roh.

Clarone. Cla[5]-*roh*-nay.

Clàrsach. *Clahrr*-sak[1].

Claude (Fr.). Clohd.

Claudin. Cloh-da(ng).

Claudio. *Clowd*[4]-yoh.

Clavecin. Clav-e(r)-sa(ng).

Clavicembalo. *Clav*-ee-*chem*-bal-oh.

Clavicymbal. Clav-iss-*im*-bal[5].

Clavicytherium. Clav-iss-ith[7]-*eer*-ee-um.

Clavier (Fr.). Clav-yay.

Clavier (Ger.). Clav-*eer*.

Clavier de récit. Clav-yay de(r) ray-see.

Clavier des bombardes. Clav-yay day bom-barrd[5].

Clavierübung. Clav-*eer*-ee[2]-boong.

---

6. The **ish** is really anywhere between that sound and 'ik' (varying in different parts of Germany).   7. **th** as in *thin*.   8. **g** as in *go*.

Clef unique. Clay ee²-neek.

Clément. Clay-mon(g).

Clementi. Clem-en-tee.

Clemenza di Tito, La. La⁵ clem-ent-sa⁵ dee Tee-toh.

Clérambault. Clay-ro(ng)-boh.

Cloches. Klosh.

Cloches de Corneville. Klosh de(r) Korr-ne(r)-veel.

Cloches de Monastère. Klosh de(r) Mon-ass⁵-tairr.

Clochette. Klosh-et.

Cloussnitzer. Kloos-nit-zerr.

C moll (Ger.). Tsay mol.

Cochlea. Cock-lee-ah.

Cockburn. Coh-burn.

Coda. Coh-da⁵.

Codetta. Coh-det-ta⁵.

Codiad yr Ehedydd. Coh-dee-ad urray-e(r)-deeth ('th' as in English the).

Coenen (Dutch). Coo-nen.

Coghlan. Kok¹-lahn.

Cogli. Coll-yee.

Coi. Coh-ee (almost coy).

Coi sordini. Coh-ee sawrr-dee-nee.

Col. Col.

Colascione. Col-ash-yoh-nay.

Col canto. Col can-toh.

Coll'. Col.

Colla. Col-la⁵.

Colla parte. Col-la⁵ pahrr-tay.

Colla punta dell'arco. Col-la⁵ poon-ta⁵ del-lahrr-coh.

Coll'arco. Col-lahrr-coh.

Colla sinistra. Col-la⁵-see-neess-tra⁵.

Colla voce. Col-la⁵ voh-chay.

Colle. Col-lay.

Col legno. Col layn-yoh.

Colles. Col-ess.

Coll'ottava. Col-lot-tah-va⁵.

Colofonia. Col-off-ohn-yah.

Colonne. Col-on.

Colophane. Col-off-an.

Coloratura. Col-orr-at-oo-rah.

Colpo. Col-poh.

Colpo d'arco. Col-poh dahrr-coh.

Come (It.). Coh-may.

Come da lontano. Coh-may da⁵ lon-tah-noh.

Comédie française. Com-ayd-ee fro(ng)-sez.

Come prima. Coh-may pree-ma⁵.

Comes (Sp.). Cohm-ess.

Come sopra. Coh-may sop-ra⁵.

Come stà. Coh-may sta⁵.

Comique. Com-eek.

Comme. Com.

Commedia dell'arte. Com-maid-ya⁵ del-lahrr-tay.

Comodo. Com-od-oh.

Compagnia del Gonfalone. Com-pan-yee-a⁵ del Gon-fal⁵-oh-nay.

Compiacevole. Comp-yatch-ay-vol-ay.

Compiacevolmente. Comp-yatch-ay-vol-men-tay.

Compiacimento. Comp-yatch-ee-men-toh.

Compline. Com-plin.

Componirt. Kom-poh-neerrt.

Composé. Co(ng)-poh-zay.

Comptent. Co(ng)t.

Compter. Co(ng)-tay.

Comun na Clàrsaich. Com-un na⁵ Clahr-sik¹.

Con abbandono. Con ab-ban-doh-noh.

Con affetto. Con af-fet-toh.

Con affezione. Con af-fet-see-oh-nay.

Con agilità. Con adj-ee-lee-ta⁵.

Con alcuna licenza. Con al⁵-koon-na⁵ lee-chent-za⁵.

Con anima. Con an-nee-ma⁵.

Con brio. Con bree-oh.

Concertante. Con-chairr-tan-tay.

Concertato. Con-chairr-tah-toh.

Concert d'orgue. Co(ng)-sairr-dawrrg.

Concertgebouw. Con-sairrt-kur¹-bow⁴.

Concerti grossi. Con-chairr-tee gross-see.

Concertina (Eng.). Con-ser-tee-na⁵.

Concertina (It.). Con-chairr-tee-na⁵.

Concertino. Con-chairr-tee-noh.

Concerto. Con-chairr-toh.

Concerto accademico. Con-chairr-toh ac-cad-aym-ee-coh.

Concerto da camera. Con-chairr-toh da⁵ cam-ay-rah.

Concerto da chiesa. Con-chairr-toh da⁵ kee-ay-zah.

Concerto grosso. Con-chairr-toh gross-soh.

Concerto sacro. Con-chairr-toh sah-croh.

Concerto sinfonico. Con-chairr-toh seen-fon-ee-coh.

Concerts du Conservatoire. Ko(ng)-sairr dee² Ko(ng)-sairr-vat-wahrr.

Concert spirituel. Ko(ng)-sairr spee-ree-tee²-el.

Concerts spirituels. (Same as last.)

Concertstück. Kon-tsairrt-shteek.².

Concitamento. Con-chee-tam-en-toh.

Concitato. Con-chee-tah-toh.

Concitazione. Con-chee-tats-ee-oh-nay.

Confrérie de la Passion. Co(ng)-frayrr-ee de(r) lap-ass-yo(ng).

Conrado. Con-rad-doh.

Conservant le rythme. Co(ng)-sairr-vo(ng) lu(r) reetm.

Conserver. Co(ng)-sairr-vay.

Con sordino. Con sawrr-dee-noh.

Constant (Fr.). Co(ng)-sto(ng).

Constanza. Con-stants-ah.

Conte (Fr.). Co(ng)t.

Contes de ma Mère l'Oye. Co(ng)t de(r) ma⁵ mairr lwah.

Contes d'Hoffmann. Co(ng)t doff-man.

Continuo. Con-tee-noo-oh.

Contrabasso. Con-tra⁵-bass-soh.

Contradanza. Con-trad-ant-sa⁵.

Contrafagotto. Con-tra⁵-fag-ot-toh.

Contralto. Con-tral-toh.

Contrappunto alla mente. Con-trap-poon-toh al⁵-la⁵ men-tay.

Contrebasse. Co(ng)-tre(r)-bass.

Contrebasson. Co(ng)-tre(r)-bass-so(ng).

Contredanse. Co(ng)-tre(r)-do(ng)ss.

Conus. Cohn-eess².

Coomaraswamy. Coom-ahr-ass-wahm-ee.

Coperario. Coh-pairr-ahr-ee-oh.

Coperto. Co-pairr-toh.

Copla. Cohp-la⁵.

Copland. Cohp-land.

Coppel. Cop-pel.

Coprifuoco. Coh-pree-foo-oh-coh.

Cor. Cawrr.

Cor anglais. Cawrr o(ng)-glay.

Coranto. Cor-ran-toh.

Cor à pistons. Cawrr-a⁵-peess-to(ng).

Cor chromatique. Cawrr croh-mat-eek.

Corda. Cawrr-da⁵.

Corda vuota. Cawrr-da⁵ voo-oh-ta⁵.

Corde (Fr.). Cawrrd.

Corde (It.). Cawrr-day.

Corde à jour. Cawrrd a⁵ zjoorr³.

Corde à vide. Cawrrd a⁵ veed.

Cor de basset. Cawrr de(r) bass-say.

---

1. k = 'ch' (cf. Scot. loch).   2. ee here really between 'ee' and 'oo' (cf. Scot. puir).
3. zj like 's' in pleasure.   4. ow as in cow.   5. a as in lad.

Cor de chasse. Cawrr de(r) shass.

Cor de nuit. Cawrr de(r) nwee.

Cor des Alpes. Cawrr dez Alp.

Cor d'harmonie. Cawrr darr⁵-mon-ee.

Corelli. Cawrr-*el*-lee.

Corilla. Cawrr-*eel*-a⁵.

Corista di camera. Cawrr-*eess*-ta⁵ dee cam-ay-ra⁵.

Corista di coro. Cawrr-*eess*-ta⁵ dee *cawrr*-oh.

Cor mixte. Cawrr meext.

Cornelius. Corr-*nay*-lee-ooss.

Cornelys. Cawrn-el-leez.

Cornemuse. Cawrr-ne(r)-meez².

Cornet à bouquin. Cawrr-nay a⁵ book-a(ng).

Cornet d'harmonie. Cawrr-nay darr⁵-mon-ee.

Cornetta. Cawrr-*net*-tah.

Cornetta a chiavi. Cawrr-*net*-ta⁵ a⁵ kee-*ah*-vee.

Cornetta segnale. Cawrr⁵-*net*-ta⁵ sayn-*yah*-lay.

Cornettino. Cawrr-net-*tee*-noh.

Cornetto. Cawrr-*net*-toh.

Cornetto curvo. Cawrr-*net*-toh *koorr*-voh.

Cornetto muto. Cawrr-*net*-toh *moo*-toh.

Cornetto torto. Cawrr-*net*-toh *tawrr*-toh.

Cornett Ton. Corr-*net* Tohn.

Corno. *Cawrr*-noh.

Corno alto. *Cawrr*-noh *al*-toh.

Corno a macchina. *Cawrr*-noh a⁵ mak-kee-na⁵.

Corno a mano. *Cawrr*-noh a⁵ *mah*-noh.

Corno a pistoni. *Cawrr*-noh a⁵ peess-*toh*-nee.

Corno basso. *Cawrr*-noh *bass*-oh.

Corno cromatico. *Cawrr*-noh croh-*mat*-ee-coh.

Corno da caccia. *Cawrr*-noh da⁵ *catch*-ya⁵.

Corno di bassetto. *Cawrr*-noh dee bass-*set*-toh.

Corno dolce. *Cawrr*-noh *dol*-chay.

Corno inglese. *Cawrr*-noh een-*glay*-zay.

Cornone. Cawrr-*noh*-nay.

Cornopean. Cor-*noh*-pee-an.

Corno torto. *Cawrr*-noh *tawrr*-toh.

Corno ventile. *Cawrr*-noh ven-*tee*-lay.

Cornyshe. Cor-nish.

Coro. *Caw*-roh.

Cor-Oboe. Cawrr-*oh*-boy.

Coronach. *Corr*-on-ok¹.

Coro pieno. *Caw*-roh pee-*ay*-noh.

Corps de ballet. Cawrr de(r) bal-lay.

Corps de rechange. Cawrr de(r) re(r)-sho(ng)zj³.

Corranach. *Corr*-an-ak¹.

Corrente. Cawrr-*en*-tay.

Corrette. Corr-et.

Corri. Corr-ee.

Cor simple. *Cawrr* sa(ng)pl.

Corta. *Cawrr*-ta⁵.

Cortège. Cawrr-tezj³.

Corto. *Cawrr*-toh.

Cosaque. Coz-ak.

Così fan tutte. Coh-*zee* fan too-tay.

Cosin. Cohz-in.

Costa (It.). *Coss*-ta⁵.

Costa (Port.). *Cosh*-tah.

Costeley. Còst-el-ay.

Côtelettes. Kot-let.

Cotillion (Eng.). Cot-*il*-yon.

Cotillon (Fr.). Cot-ee-yo(ng).

Coulisses. Coo-leess.

Coup d'archet. Coo darr⁵-shay.

Coup de glotte. Coo de(r) glot.

Coupé. Coo-pay.

Couperin. Coo-pairr-a(ng).

Couplet (Fr.). Coo-play.

Couplez. Coo-play.

Couppey. Coo-pay.

Coupure. Coo-peer².

Courante. Coo-ro(ng)t.

Courroie. Coorr-wah.

Courville. Coor-veel.

Courvoisier. Coorr-vwa⁵-zee-ay.

Cousineau. Coo-zee-noh.

Couvert. Coo-vairr.

Couverte. Coo-vairrt.

Cowell. Cow⁴-el.

Cowen. Cow⁴-en.

Cracovienne. Crack-ov-yen.

Cramer. Crah-merr.

Cramignon. Cram-een-yo(ng).

Cranz. Crants.

Cras. Crah.

Cray-sell.

Crécelle. Cray-sell.

Cremona. Cray-*moh*-na⁵.

Creollo. Cray-*ohl*-yoh.

Crescendo. Cray-*shen*-doh.

Cricoid. Cry-coyd.

Crispino e la comare. Creess-*pee*-noh ay la⁵ coh-*mah*-ray.

Cristobal. Creess-*tob*-al⁵.

Cristofori. Crees-*tof*-oh-ree.

Croche. Crosh.

Croisant. Crwa⁵-zo(ng).

Croisé. Crwa⁵-zay.

Croiser. Crwa⁵-zay.

Croiser les mains. Crwa⁵-zay lay ma(ng).

Croix sonore. Crwa⁵ sonn-orr.

Croma. *Croh*-ma⁵.

Cromatiche. Croh-*mah*-tee-kay.

Cromatici. Croh-*mah*-tee-chee.

Cromatico. Croh-*mah*-tee-coh.

Cromatische Harmonika. Croh-*mah*-tish-e(r) Harr-*moh*-nee-kah.

Cros. Croh.

Crot. (As spelt.)

Crotales (Fr.). Crot-al.

Crouth. Crooth⁷.

Crowder. Crowd-er.

Crowth. Crowth⁴·⁷.

Cruit. Croot.

Crwth. Crooth⁷.

Csárdás. *Charr*-dash.

Cui. Kwee.

Cuivre. Kweevrr (one syllable).

Cuivré. Kwee-vray.

Cupo. *Coo*-poh.

Cutting (Scand.). *Koot*-ing.

Cuzzoni. Coots-*soh*-nee.

Cyklus. *Tsee*²-klus.

Cylindre. See-la(ng)drr.

Cylindrichord. Sil-*in*-dree-cord.

Cymanfa Ganu. Cum-*ahn*-va⁵ *Gan*-ee².

Cymbales. Sa(ng)-bal.

Czaar und Zimmermann. Tsahrr oont *Tsim*-merr-man.

Czardas. *Charr*-dash.

Czerny. *Chairr*-nee.

Czibulka. *Tsee*-bool-kah.

Czimbal. *Tseem*-bol.

Czimbalon. *Tseem*-bol-om.

---

6. The **ish** is really anywhere between that sound and 'ik' (varying in different parts of Germany). **7.** th as in *thin*. **8.** g as in *go*.

D

Da capo. Dac-*ah*-poh.

Da capo al fine. Dac-*ah*-poh al *fee*-nay.

Da capo al segno. Dac-*ah*-poh al *sayn*-yoh.

Dactyl. *Dak*-til.

Dactylic. Dak-*til*-ik.

Dafne. *Daf*-nay.

Dafydd y Garreg Wen. Dah-*veeth* u(r) *Gar*-reg *Wen.*

D'Albert. Dal-bairr.

Dalcroze. Dal-krohz.

Dall'Abaco. Dal *Ab*-ah-coh.

Dallapiccola. Dal-la-*pik*-ko-la.

Dal segno. Dal *sayn*-yoh.

Daman. *Day*-man.

Dame blanche, La. La⁵ Dam blo(ng)sh.

Dämpfer. *Demp*-ferr.

Dämpfern. Demp-ferrn.

Dancla. Do(ng)-cla⁵.

Dandrieu. Do(ng)-dree-yu(r).

D'Anglebert. Do(ng)-le(r)-bairr.

Danican. Dan-ee-*co(ng)*.

Daniel (Fr.). Dan-yel.

Danse. Do(ng)ss.

Danse macabre. Do(ng)ss mac-abrr.

Danses brillantes. Do(ng)ss bree-yo(ng)t.

Dans mon chemin. Do(ng) mo(ng) she(r)-ma(ng).

Dante. *Dan*-tay.

Danza española. *Danth*⁷-a⁵ ess-pan-*yol*-a⁵.

Danza tedesca. *Dants*-a⁵ tay-*dess*-cah.

Dapertutto. Dap⁵-airr-*too*-toh.

Da Ponte. Da⁵ *Pon*-tay.

Daquin. Dak-a(ng).

Dargomijsky. Dahrr-gom-*ish*-kee(yer).

Darunter. Darr-*oon*-terr.

Dasselbe. Dass-*zel*-be(r).

Dauberval. Doh-bairr-val.

Daudet. Doh-day.

Dauer. *Dow*⁴-err.

Dauernd. *Dow*-errnt.

Dauphol. Doh-fol.

Dauvergne. Doh-vairrn-y(er).

Davenant (Eng.). *Dav*-en-ant.

D'Avenant (Eng.). *Dav*-en-ant.

David (Fr.). Dav-eed.

David (Ger.). *Dah*-veet.

Davidsbündler Tänze. *Dah*-veets-*beent*²-lerr *Tent*-se(r).

Davrainville. Dav-ra(ng)-veel.

Dazu. Dahts-*oo*.

De (Fr.). De(r).

De (Sp.). Day.

Debain. De(r)-ba(ng).

De Bériot. De(r) Bairr-yoh.

Débile (Fr.). Day-beel.

Debile (It.). *Deb*-ee-lay.

De Boeck. De(r) Book.

Debole. *Deb*-ol-ay.

Debussy. De(r)-bee²-see.

Début. Day-bee².

Decani. Dek-*ay*-nye.

Déchant. Day-sho(ng).

Décidé. Day-see-day.

Deciso. Detch-*ee*-zoh.

Declamando. Dek-lam-*an*-doh.

Declamare. Dek-lam-*ah*-ray.

Declamato. Dek-lam-*ah*-toh.

Découpler. Day-coop-lay.

De Courville. De(r) Coorr-veel.

Decrescendo. Day-cray-*shen*-doh.

Decresciuto. Day-cray-*shoo*-toh.

Défaut. Day-foh.

Degeyter. Deg-ate-airr.

Degli. *Dail*-yee.

Dehn. Dain.

Dehors. De(r)-awrr.

Dejoncker. De(r)-*yong*-ker.

Dekker. *Dek*-err.

De la (Fr.). De(r)-la⁵.

Delannoy. De(r)-lan-wah.

Delatre. De(r)-latrr.

Delattre. De(r)-latrr.

Del Campo. Del *Cam*-poh.

Delibes. De(r)-leeb.

Delicatamente. Del-ee-cat-am-*en*-tay.

Delicatezza. Del-ee-cat-*et*-sa⁵.

Delicatissimo. Del-ee-cat-*eess*-see-moh.

Delicato. Del-ee-*cah*-toh.

Délié. Day-lee-yay.

Delirante. Del-ee-*ran*-tay.

Delirio. Del-*eer*-yoh.

Delius (Eng.). *Dee*-lee-us.

Delizioso. Del-eet-see-*oh*-zoh.

Delphin. Del-fa(ng).

Delvincourt. Del-va(ng)-coorr.

Démancher. Day-mo(ng)-shay.

Demi. De(r)-mee.

Demie. De(r)-mee.

Demi-jeu. De(r)-mee-zju(r)³.

Demi-pause. De(r)-mee-pohz.

Demi-ton. De(r)-mee-to(ng).

Demi voix. De(r)-mee-vwah.

Demuth (Eng. name). De(r)-*mooth*⁷.

Demütig. *Day*-mee²-tish⁶.

Demütigen. *Day*-mee²-tig-en.

Demütigung. *Day*-mee²-tig-oong.

Demutsvoll. *Day*-moots-fol.

Dencke. *Deng*-ke(r).

Denis (Fr.). De(r)n-ee.

Denner. *Den*-urr.

Dennoch. *Den*-ok¹.

Denza. *Dent*-za⁵.

Déodat. Day-oh-da⁵.

Deppe. *Dep*-pe(r).

De près. De(r) pray.

Derb. Dairrb.

Der Barbier von Bagdad. Dairr Barr-*beerr* fon *Bag*-dat.

Der fliegende Holländer. Dairr *fleeg*-en-de(r) *Holl*-len-derr.

Der Freischütz. Dairr *Fry*-sheets².

Der Ring des Nibelungen. Dairr *Rink* dess *Nee*-be(r)-loong-en.

Der Rosenkavalier. Dairr *Roh*-zen-kav-ah-*leerr*.

Derselbe. Dairr-zel-be(r).

Deryn Pur. *Derr*-in Peer².

Des (Fr.). Day.

Des (Ger.). Dess.

Descant. *Dess*-cant.

Descant Viol. *Dess*-cant *Vy*-ol.

Deses. *Dess*-ess.

Desiderio. Dez-ee-*day*-ree-oh.

Désiré. Day-zee-ray.

Despina. Des-*pee*-na⁵.

Des Prés. Day Pray.

Dessous. Dess-soo.

Dessus. Dess-ee².

Dessus de viole. Dess-ee² de(r) vee-ol.

Desto. *Dess*-toh.

Destouches. Day-toosh.

Destra. *Dess*-tra⁵.

Destro. *Dess*-troh.

De suite. De(r) sweet.

Détaché sec. Day-tash-ay sek.

Determinato. Det-airr-mee-*nah*-toh.

Deutlich. *Doit*-lik¹.

Deutsch. Doitsh.

Deutsche Tänze. *Doitsh*-e(r) *Tent*-se(r).

Deutschland über Alles. *Doitsh*-lant ee²-berr *Al*-less.

Deux. Du(r).

Deux cordes. Du(r) corrd.

Deux fois. Du(r) fwah.

Deuxième. Du(r)z-yem.

Deuxième position. Du(r)z-yem pohs-eess-yo(ng).

Deux mains. Du(r) ma(ng).

Deux temps. Du(r) to(ng).

Devin du village, Le (Fr.). Le(r) du(r)-va(ng) dee² veel-ahzj³.

---

1. k = 'ch' (cf. Scot. *loch*).   **2.** ee here really between 'ee' and 'oo' (cf. Scot. *puir*).
3. zj like 's' in *pleasure*.   **4.** ow as in *cow*.   **5.** a as in *lad*.

Devoto. Day-*voh*-toh.
Devozione. Day-voht-see-*oh*-nay.
Di (It.). Dee.
Diabelli. Dee-ab-*el*-lee.
Diaghilev. Dee-*ahg*-ee-lef.
Diapason(Eng.). Dy-ap-*ay*-son.
Diapason (Fr.). Dee-ap-az-o(ng).
Diapason de bouche. Dee-ap-az-o(ng) de(r) boosh.
Diaphone. *Dy*-af-ohn.
Dichterliebe. *Dik*[1]-terr-*leeb*-e(r).
Dichtung. *Dik*[1]-toong.
Dictionnaire pratique et historique de la musique. Deeks-yon-airr prat-eek ay eess-torr-eek de(r) la[5] mee[2]-zeek.
Diderot. Dee-dairr-oh.
Dido and Aeneas. *Dy*-doh and Een-*ee*-ass[5].
Dieci (It.). Dee-*ay*-chee.
Die Entführung aus dem Serail. Dee Ent-*fee*[2]-roong owss[4] daim Say-*rah*-eel.
Diego. Dee-*ay*-goh.
Die Königin von Saba. Dee *Ke*(r)-nig-in fon *Zah*-bah.
Die Königskinder. Dee *Ke*(r)-niks-*kin*-derr.
Die lustigen Weiber von Windsor. Dee *looss*-tig-en *Vy*-berr fon *Vints*-awrr.
Die Meistersinger von Nürnberg. Dee *Mice*-terr-zing-err fon *Neern*[2]-bairrg.
Diepenbrock. *Dee*-pen-brok.
Dieren, Van. Fan *Deerr*-en.
Dièse. Dee-ez.
Dieselbe. Dee-*zel*-be(r).
Diesis (It.). Dee-*ayss*-eess.
Die tote Stadt. Dee *toh*-te(r) Shtat[5].
Dietrich. *Dee*-trik[1].
Dietro. Dee-*ayt*-roh.
Die Uhr. Dee Oorr.
Dieupart. D'yu(r)-parr[5].
Die Zauberflöte. Dee *Tsow*[4]-berr-*fle*(r)-te(r).
Diluendo. Dee-loo-*en*-doh.
Dilungando. Dee-loon-*gan*-doh.
Dima. *Dee*-mah.
Diminuendo. Dee-mee-noo-*en*-doh.
Dimitri. Dee-*mee*-tree(yer).
Di molto. Dee *mol*-toh.
Di Monte. Dee *Mon*-tay.
D'Indy. Da(ng)-dee.
Dinorah. Dee-*naw*-rah.
Di nuova. Dee noo-*oh*-vah.
Dionys (Ger.). Dee-oh-*neess*[2].
Dirk. Dairrk.

Dis. Diss.
Discretezza. Deess-cret-*ets*-sa[5].
Discreto. Deess-*cray*-toh.
Discrezione. Deess-cret-see-*oh*-nay.
Disinvolto. Dee-zeen-*vol*-toh.
Disis. *Diss*-iss.
Di sopra. Dee *sop*-rah.
Disperabile. Deess-pairr-*ab*-ee-lay.
Disperante. Deess-pairr-*an*-tay.
Disperato. Deess-pairr-*ah*-toh.
Disperazione. Deess-pairr-ats-*yoh*-nay.
Distanza. Deess-*tant*-sa[5].
Distinto. Deess-*tin*-toh.
Distratto. Deess-*trat*-toh.
Dithyramb. *Dith*[7]-ee-ramb.
Dithyrambe. Dee-tee-ro(m)b.
Ditirambo. Deet-tee-*ram*-boh.
Dittersdorf. *Dit*-errss-dawrrf.
Diva. *Dee*-va[5].
Divertimenti. Dee-vairr-tee-*men*-tee.
Divertimento. Dee-vairr-tee-*men*-toh.
Divertissement. Dee-vairr-teess-mo(ng).
Divina, La. Lah Dee-*vee*-na.
Divinités du Styx. Dee-vee-nee-tay dee[2] Steeks.
Divisés. Dee vee-say.
Divisi. Dee-*vee*-zee.
Divotamente. Dee voh-tam-*en*-tay.
Divoto. Dee-*voh*-toh.
Divozione. Dee-vohts-*yoh*-nay.
Dix (Fr.). When standing alone, Deess. Before a vowel or mute h, Deez. Before a consonant or 'aspirated' h, Dee.
Djamileh. Dzjam[3]-ee-lay.
Dmitri. *Dmee*-tree(yer).
Dobrzynski. Dobrr-*zhin*-skee.
Doch. Dok[1].
Doglia. *Dol*-yah.
Dogliosamente. Dol-yoh-zam-*en*-tay.
Doglioso. Dol-*yoh*-zoh.
Döhler. *De*(r)-lerr.
Dohnányi. Dok[1]-*nahn*-yee.
Doigt. Dwa[5].
Doigté. Dwa[5]-tay.
Doit. Dwa[5].
Doivent. Dwav[5].
Dolcan. *Dol*-can.
Dolce. *Dol*-chay.
Dolcemente. Dol-chay-*men*-tay.
Dolcezza. Dol-*chets*-sa[5].
Dolcissimo. Dol-*cheess*-see-moh.
Dolente. Dol-*en*-tay.

Dolentemente. Dol-en-tay-*men*-tay.
Dolentissimo. Dol-en-*teess*-see-moh.
Doles. *Doh*-less.
Dolin. *Doh*-leen (in France he spells it 'Doline', to avoid the French nasal).
Dolmetsch. *Dol*-metsh.
Dolore. Dol-*aw*-ray.
Dolorosamente. Dol-aw-roh-zam-*en*-tay.
Doloroso. Dol-aw-*roh*-zoh.
Dolzflöte. *Dollts*-fle(r)-te(r).
Domenico. Doh-*men*-ee-coh.
Domenicus (Ger.). Doh-*men*-ee-kooss.
Dominguez. Doh-*meen*-gaith[7].
Domra. *Dom*-rah.
Don Giovanni. Don Jov-*an*-nee.
Donizetti. Don-eet-*zet*-tee.
Don Juan (Sp.). Don *Kwan*[1] (but in Eng. generally 'Don *Joo*-an').
Donne curiose, Le. Lay *don*-nay coorr-*yoh*-say.
Donner (Ger.). *Don*-err.
Don Pasquale. Don Pass-*kwah*-lay.
Dont (Fr.). Do(ng).
Dont (Ger.). Dohnt.
Dopo. *Dop*-oh.
Doppel. *Dop*-el.
Doppel B. *Dop*-el Bay.
Doppel Be. *Dop*-el Bay.
Doppelchor. *Dop*-el-kohrr.
Doppelfagott. *Dop*-el-fag-ot.
Doppelflöte. *Dop*-el-*fle*(r)-te(r).
Doppelfuge. *Dop*-el-*foog*-e(r).
Doppelhorn. *Dop*-el-horrn.
Doppelkreuz. *Dop*-el-kroits.
Doppeln. *Dop*-eln.
Doppelschlag. *Dop*-el-shlahg.
Doppeltakt. *Dop*-el-takt.
Doppeltaktnote. *Dop*-el-takt-*noh*-te(r).
Doppelt so schnell. *Dop*-elt zoh shnel.
Dopper (Dutch). *Dop*-perr.
Doppio. *Dop*-yo`.
Doppio movimento. *Dop*-yoh moh-vee-*men*-toh.
Doret. Dorr-ay.
Dorian. *Daw*-ree-an.
Double (Fr.). Doobl.
Double-bémol. Doo-ble(r)-bay-mol.
Double-croche. Doo-ble(r)-crosh.
Double-dièse. Doo-ble(r)-dee-ez.
Doublette. Doo-blet.

---

6. The **ish** is really anywhere between that sound and 'ik' (varying in different parts of Germany).
7. **th** as in *thin*.   8. **ġ** as in *go*.

Douce. Dooss.
Doucement. Dooss-mo(ng).
Douleur. Doo-lur.
Douloureuse. Doo-loo-ru(r)z.
Douloureusement. Doo-loo-ru(r)z-mo(ng).
Douloureux. Doo-loo-ru(r).
Doux. Doo.
Dowland. Dow[6]-land or Doh-land.
Drabant. Drab-ant.
Draghi. Drahg-ee.
Dragonetti. Drag-oh-net-tee.
Dragons de Villars, Les. Lay Drag-o(ng) de(r) Vee-lahrr.
Drame lyrique. Dram lee-reek.
Dramma lirico. Dram-ma[5] lee-ree-coh.
Dramma per musica. Dram-ma[5] pairr moo-zee-cah.
Drammatico. Dram-maht-ee-coh.
Drängend. Dreng-ent.
Drdla. D(e)rrd-la[5].
Dreher. Dray-herr.
Drehleyer. Dray-ly-err.
Drei. Dry.
Dreifach. Dry-fak[1].
Dreigroschenoper. Dry-grosh-en-oh-perr.
Dreinfahren. Dryn-fahrr-en.
Dreitaktig. Dry-tak-tish[6].
Drigo. Dree-goh.
Dringend. Dring-ent.

Dringender. Dring-end-err.
Dritte. Drit-te(r).
Drittel. Drit-tel.
Drohend. Droh-ent.
Droit. Drwa[5].
Droite. Drwat[5].
Droits d'exécution. Drwa[5] deg-zay-kee[2]-see-o(ng).
Drouet. Droo-ay.
Droz. Drohz.
Du. Dee[2].
Dubensky. Doo-ben-skee(yer).
Dubois. Dee[2]-bwah.
Ducasse. Dee[2]-kass.
Ducaurroy. Dee[2]-kohrr-wah.
Ducoudray. Dee[2]-koo-dray.
Dudelsack. Doo-del-zak.
Due (It.). Doo-ay.
Due corde. Doo-ay kawrr-day.
Dufay. Dee[2]-fay.
Duftig. Doof-tish[6].
Dukas. Dee[2]-kass.
Dulcet. Dul-set.
Dulciana (Eng.). Dul-see-ah-nah.
Dumka. Doom-ka[5].
Dumky. Doom-kee.
Dumpf. Doompf.
Dunkel. Doong-kel.
Duny. In Italy pron. 'Doo-nee', in France 'Dee[2]-nee'.
Duo. Doo-oh.
Duolo. Doo-oh-loh.
Duparc. Dee[2]-parrk.

Dupin. Dee[2]-pa(ng).
Dupont. Dee[2]-po(ng).
Duport. Dee[2]-pawrr.
Dupré. Dee[2]-pray.
Dupuis. Dee[2]-pwee.
Dupuy. Dee[2]-pwee.
Dur (Fr.). Deerr[2].
Dur (Ger.). Doorr.
Duramente. Doo-ram-en-tay.
Durand. Dee[2]-ro(ng).
Durante. Doo-ran-tay.
Durch. Doorrk[1].
Durchaus. Doorrk[1]-owss[4].
Durchdringend. Doorrk[1]-dring-ent.
Durchführung. Doorrk[1]-fee[2]-roong.
Durchkomponiert. Doorrk[1]-com-poh-neerrt.
Durchweg. Doorrk[1]-vek.
Dureté. Deerr[2]-tay.
Durey. Dee[2]-ray.
Durezza. Doo-rets-za[5].
Duro. Doo-roh.
Duruflé. Dee[2]-ree[2]-flay.
Dusquenois. Dee[2]-ken-wah.
Dussek. Doo-sek.
Düster. Dee[2]-sterr.
Duttile. Doot-tee-lay.
Duvernoy. Dee[2]-vairr-nwah.
Dvořák. Dvawrr-zjahk[3].
Dvorsky. Dvawrr-skee.
Dykema. Dike-ma[3].
Dzerzhinsky. Jair-zjin[3]-skee.

E

E (It.). Ay.
Ebenfalls. Ay-ben-falss[5].
Ebenso. Ay-ben-zoh.
Eccard. Ek-arrt.
Échappé. Ay-shap-pay.
Écharpe. Ay-sharrp.
Échelette. Ay-shel-et.
Échelle. Ay-shel.
Echoklavier. Ek[1]-oh-klav-eerr.
Éclair. Ay-clairr.
Éclatant. Ay-clat-o(ng).
Eclogue. Ek-log.
Eco. Ayk-oh.
École. Ay-col.
Écossaise. Ay-koss-ez.
Ed. Ed.

Edel. Ayd-el.
Edgar (Fr.). Ed-gahrr.
Edmond (Fr.). Ed-mo(ng).
Édouard (Fr.). Ayd-wahrr.
Eduard (Ger.). Ayd-oo-arrt[5].
Effets d'orage. Ef-fay dawrr-ahzj[3].
Effleurer. Ef-le(r)-ray.
Égal. Ay-gal.
Égale. Ay-gal.
Egidio. Edj-eed-yoh.
Egk. Ek.
Églogue. Ayg-log.
Egon. Ayg-on.
Eguale. Eg-wah-lay.
Egualezza. Eg-wal-lets-sa[5].

Egualmente. Eg-wal-men-tay.
Ehrenfried. Ayrr-en-freet.
Eifer. Eye-ferr.
Eifrig. Eye-frish[6].
Eile. Eye-le(r).
Eilen. Eye-len.
Eilend. Eye-lent.
Eilig. Eye-lish[6].
Ein. Ine.
Eine. Ine-e(r).
Einem. Eye-nem.
Einfach. Ine-fak[1].
Ein' feste Burg. Ine fest-e(r) Boorrg.
Einig. Ine-ish[6].
Einige. Ine-ig-e(r).

---

1. k = 'ch' (cf. Scot. loch).　　**2. ee** here really between 'ee' and 'oo' (cf. Scot. puir).
3. zj like 's' in pleasure.　　**4. ow** as in cow.　　**5. a** as in lad.

Einlenken. *Ine*-lenk-en.

Einmal. *Ine*-mahl.

Einstein. *Ine*-shtine.

Einstimmig. *Ine*-shtim-ish[6].

Eintritt. *Ine*-trit.

Einzeln. *Ine*-tseln.

Eis (meaning E sharp). Ay-iss.

Eisis. Ay-*iss*-iss.

Eisler. *Ice*-lerr.

Eisteddfod. Ee-*steth*-vod ('th' as in *the*).

Eisteddfodau. Ee-*steth*-vod-ah-ee ('th' as in *the*).

Eitner. *Ite*-ner.

Élan. Ay-lo(ng).

Élargi. Ay-larr[5]-zjee[3].

Élargir. Ay-larr[5]-zjeer[3].

Élargissant. Ay-larr[5]-zjee[3]-so(ng).

Élargissez. Ay-larr[5]-zjee[3]-say.

Elegantemente. El-ayg-an-tay-*men*-tay.

Elegiaco. El-edj-*ee*-ak-oh.

Élégie. Ayl-ay-zjee[3].

Elevato. El-ayv-*ah*-toh.

Elevazione. El-ayv-aht-see-*oh*-nay.

Élève. Ay-lev.

Élias (Fr.). Ay-lee-ass.

Élie. Ay-lee.

Elisir d'amore, L'. Lel-ee-*seerr* dam-*aw*-ray.

Elling. *El*-ing.

Elssler. *Elss*-ler.

Elvira. El-*vee*-ra[5].

Elwes. *El*-wez.

Emanuel (Ger.). Aym-*ahn*-oo-el.

Emanuele (It.). Em-an-oo-*ail*-ay.

Embouchure (Fr.). Om-boo-sheer[2].

Emil (Ger.). *Aym*-eel.

Émile (Fr.). Aym-eel.

Emilia (It.). Em-*eel*-yah.

Emilio (It.). Em-*eel*-yoh.

Emozione. Em-*oht*-see-oh-nay.

Empfindung. Emp-*fin*-doong.

Empfindungsvoll. Emp-*fin*-doongs-fol.

Emphase (Fr.). O(ng)-fahz.

Emporté. On(g)-pawrr-tay.

Empressé. O(ng)-press-ay.

Ému. Ay-mee[2].

En (Fr.). O(ng) before a consonant. On before a vowel.

Enchaînement. O(ng)-shayn-mo(ng).

Enchaînez. O(ng)-shen-ay.

Enchanteresse. O(ng)-sho(ng)-te(r)-ress.

Enclume. O(ng)-kleem[2].

Encore (Fr., Eng.). O(ng)-cawrr.

Encyclopédie. O(ng)-see-clop-pay-dee.

Energia. En-airr-*jee*-a[5].

Enesco. En-*ess*-coo.

Enfant et les sortilèges, L'. Lo(ng)-fo(ng) ay lay sawrr-tee-lezj[3].

Enfant prodigue, L'. Lo(ng)-fo(ng) prod-eeg.

Enfasi. *En*-faz-ee.

Enfaticamente. En-*fah*-tee-cam-*en*-tay.

Enfatico. En-*fah*-tee-coh.

Engel. *Eng*-el.

Engelbert. *Eng*-el-bairrt.

Engelstimme. *Eng*-el-shtim-me(r).

Enger. *Eng*-err.

Englisches Horn. *Eng*-lish-ess Horrn.

Engramelle. O(ng)-gram-el.

Enlever. O(ng)-le(r)-vay.

Enlevez. O(ng)-le(r)-vay.

Enrico. En-*ree*-coh.

Enrique. En-*ree*-kay.

Ensalada. En-sal[5]-*ah*-da[5].

Ensemble. O(ng)-so(ng)bl.

Entendre. O(ng)-to(ng)dr.

Entfernt. Ent-*fairrnt*.

Entfernung. Ent-*fairr*-noong.

Entführung aus dem Serail, Die. Dee Ent-*fee*[2]-roong owss[4] daim Say-*rah*-eel.

Entr'acte. O(ng)t-rakt.

Entrada. En-*trah*-da[5].

Entrain (Fr.). O(ng)-tra(ng).

Entrata. En-*trah*-ta[5].

Entrechat. O(ng)-tre(r)-shah.

Entrée. O(ng)-tray.

Entremés. En-tray-*mayss*.

Entrückung. Ent-*ree*[2]-koong.

Entschieden. Ent-*sheed*-en.

Entschlossen. Ent-*shloss*-en.

Entusiasmo. En-too-zee-*az*[5]-moh.

Entusiastico. En-too-zee-*ass*[5]-tee-coh.

Enzina. En-*thee*[7]-nah.

Épinette. Ay-peen-et.

Epithalamium. Ep-ee-thal[7]-*aim*-ee-um.

Éponge. Ay-po(ng)zj[3].

Eppert. *Ep*-errt.

Equabile. Ek-*wah*-bee-lay.

Equale. Ek-*wah*-lay.

Equali. Ek-*wah*-lee.

Equalità. Ek-wah-lee-*tah*.

Équivaut. Ay-kee-voh.

Erasmus (Ger.). Ayrr-*ass*-mooss.

Ercole. *Airr*-coh-lay.

Erda. *Airr*-dah.

Ergriffen. Airr-*grif*-fen.

Erhaben. Airr-*hah*-ben.

Erich (Ger.). *Ayrr*-ik[1].

Erkel. *Airr*-kel.

Erlanger. Airr-lo(ng)-zjay[3].

Erleichterung. Airr-*lyk*[1]-ter-roong.

Erlkönig. *Airrl*-ke(r)-nish[6].

Erlöschend. Airr-*lu*(r)sh-ent.

Ermangelung. Airr-*mang*-el-oong.

Ermanno. Airr-*man*-noh.

Ermattend. Airr-*mat*-ent.

Ermattet. Airr-*mat*-et.

Ernani. Airr-*nah*-nee.

Ernest (Fr.). Airr-nest.

Erniedrigen. Airr-*need*-rig-en.

Ernst. Airrnst.

Ernsthaft. *Airrnst*-haft.

Eroica. Airr-*oh*-ee-ca[5].

Erotikon. Ayrr-*oh*-tee-kon.

Ersatz. Airr-*zats*.

Erschüttert. Airr-*sheet*[2]-errt.

Erst. Airrst.

Erste. *Airr*-ste(r).

Ersterbend. Airr-*shtairr*-bent.

Erstickt. Airr-*shtikt*.

Erweitert. Airr-*vy*-terrt.

Erwin. *Airr*-veen.

Erzähler. Airrt-*sail*-err.

Erzürnt. Airr-*tseernt*[2].

Es. Ess.

Esaltato. Ez-al[5]-*tah*-toh.

Esatezza. Ez-at-*ets*-sa[5].

Esatta. Ez-*zat*-ta[5].

Esatto. Ez-*zat*-toh.

Escalade. Ess-cal-ad.

Escamillo. Ess-cam-*eel*-yoh.

Eschallot (Eng.). *Esh*-al[5]-ot.

Escriche. Ess-*kree*-shay.

Esecuzione. Ez-ek-oot-zee-*oh*-nay.

Esercizi. Ez-airr-*cheet*-see.

Esercizio. Ez-airr-*cheets*-yoh.

Eses. *Ess*-ess.

Eslava. Ess-*lah*-va[5].

Espagne. Ess-pan-y(er).

Espagnol. Ess-pan-yol.

Española. Ess-pan-*yol*-a[5].

Espirando. Ess-pee-*ran*-doh.

Esplá. Ess-*pla*[5].

Espressione. Ess-press-see-*oh*-nay.

Espressivo. Ess-press-*see*-voh.

Esprit. Ess-pree.

Esquisse. Ess-keess.

Esser. *Ess*-err.

Estampie. Ess-to(ng)-pee.

Este (Eng.). Eest.

Esterházy. *Est*-terr-hah-zee.

Estinguendo. Ess-teen-*gwen*-doh.

Estinto. Ess-*teen*-toh.

Estompé. Ess-to(ng)-pay.

Estrabillo. Ess-trab-*eel*-yoh.

---

6. The **ish** is really anywhere between that sound and 'ik' (varying in different parts of Germany). **7.** th as in *thin*. **8.** g as in *go*.

Estrange (Eng.). Es-*traynge*.
Estravaganza. Ess-trav-ag-*ant*-sa⁵.
Estremamente. Ess-tray-mam-*en*-tay.
Esultazione. Ez-ool-tats-ee-*oh*-nay.
Et (Fr.). Ay.
Éteignez. Ay-ten-yay.
Éteint. Ay-ta(ng).
Étendue. Ay-to(ng)-dee³.
Étienne. Ay-tee-yen.
Étouffé. Ay-toof-ay.
Étude. Ay-teed².
Etwas. *Et*-vass.
Euchorics. Yoo-*kawr*-iks.

Eugen. *Oy*-gayn.
Eugène. U(r)-zjen³.
Eulenburg. *Oy*-len-boorg.
Eulenspiegel. *Oy*-len-shpeeg-el.
Eulenstein. *Oy*-len-shtine.
Eurhythmy. Yoo-*rith*-mee ('th' as in *the*).
Euryanthe. *Oy*-ree-*an*-te(r).
Eurydice. Yoo-*rid*-itch-ee.
Eustache. U(r)-stash.
Eustachian. Yoo-*stay*-kee-an.
Euterpion. Yoo-*ter*-pee-on.
Evangelimann, Der. Dairr Ay-van-*gay*-lee-man.
Evaristo. Ev-a⁵-*reess*-toh.

Éveillé. Ay-vay-yay.
Evelyn. *Eev*-lin.
Evirato. Ev-ee-*rah*-toh.
Evocación. Ev-oh-cath⁷-ee-*on*.
Exactement. Eg-zakt-e(r)-mo(ng).
Exalté. Egz-ahl-tay.
Eximeno (Sp.). Ek¹-ee-*may*-noh.
Expert (Fr.). Ex-pairr.
Expressif. Ex-press-eef.
Extravaganza (Eng.). Ex-trav-ag-*an*-za⁵.
Extrêmement. Ex-trem-e(r)-mo(ng).
Ezcudanza. Ess-coo-*dan*-tha⁷.

F

Fa. Fah.
Faber (Belg.). *Fah*-bairr.
Faber (Engl.). *Fay*-ber.
Fabini. Fab-*ee*-nee.
Fabrizio (It.). Fab-*reets*-ee-oh.
Faburden. Fah-*bur*-den.
Fach (Ger.). Fak¹.
Fach (Welsh). Vahk¹.
Facile (Fr.). Fass-eel.
Facile (It.). *Fah*-chee-lay.
Facilità. Fatch-eel-ee-*ta*⁵.
Facilmente. Fatch-eel-*men*-tay.
Fackeltanz. *Fak*-el-tants.
Fadinho. Fah-*deen*-oh.
Fado. *Fah*-doh.
Fafner. *Faf*-nerr.
Fagotto. Fag-*ot*-toh.
Fahren. *Fah*-ren.
Faible. Febl.
Faire. Fairr.
Faîtes. Fet.
Fall (Ger.). Fal⁵.
Falla. *Fa*(l)-ya⁵.
Falle (Ger.). *Fal*⁵-le(r).
Falsetto. Fal-*set*-toh.
Falsobordone. Fal-soh-bawrr-*doh*-nay.
Faltin. Fahl-*teen*.
Fanciulla del West, La. La⁵ Fan-*choo*-la⁵ del *West*.
Fandanguilla. Fan-dan-*geel*³-ya⁵.
Fanelli. Fan-*el*-ee.
Fanfara. Fan-*fah*-ra⁵.

Fanfare (Eng.). *Fan*-fair.
Fanfare (Fr.). Fo(ng)-fahrr.
Fanfare (It.). Fan-*fah*-ray.
Fantaisie. Fo(ng)-tez-ee.
Fantasia. Fan-taz-*ee*-a⁵.
Fantasiestück. Fan-taz-*ee*-shteek².
Fantastico. Fan-*tass*-tee-coh.
Fantastique. Fo(ng)-*tass*-teke.
Fantastisch. Fan-*tass*-tish.
Fantini. Fan-*tee*-nee.
Farbe. *Farr*-be(r).
Farina. Fa⁵-ree-na⁵.
Farinelli. Fa⁵-ree-*nel*-lee⁵.
Farjeon (Eng.). *Fahr*-jon.
Farlano. Fahrr-*lah*-noh.
Farruca. Fa⁵-*roo*-ca⁵.
Fasch. Fash.
Faschingsschwank aus Wien. *Fash*-ings-shvank owss⁴ *Veen*.
Fasolt. *Fah*-zolt.
Fassung. *Fass*-oong.
Fast (Ger.). Fast⁵.
Fastoso. Fast⁵-*oh*-zoh.
Faure. Fohrr.
Fauré. Foh-ray.
Fausset. Foh-say.
Faust. Fowsst⁴.
Faustina. Fowss⁴-*tee*-na⁵.
Fauxbourdon. Foh-boorr-do(ng).
Faux mendiant, Le. Le(r) foh mo(ng)-dee-o(ng).
Favart. Fav-ahrr.

Favorita, La. La⁵ Fav-oh-*ree*-ta⁵.
Federico. Fay-day-*ree*-coh.
Fedora. Fay-*daw*-ra⁵.
Fedra. *Fay*-dra⁵.
Feierlich. Fy-err-lik¹.
Feinberg. *Fine*-bairrg.
Feis Ceoil. Faysh Kee-*ole*.
Feldpartita. *Felt*-parr-*tee*-tah.
Felice. Fel-*ee*-chay.
Félicien. Fay-leess-ya(ng).
Félix (Fr.). Fay-leeks.
Felix (Ger.). *Fay*-lix.
Feodor. *Fay*-oh-dawr.
Ferdinand (Fr.). Fairr-dee-no(ng).
Ferdinando (It.). Fairr-dee-*nan*-doh.
Féréol. Fay-ray-ol.
Fermamente. *Fairr*-mam-*en*-tay.
Fermata. Fairr-*mah*-ta⁵.
Fermate. Fairr-*mah*-tay.
Fermé. Ferr-may.
Fermer. Ferr-may.
Fermezza. Fairr-*met*-za⁵.
Fermo. *Fairr*-moh.
Fernandez. Fair-*nan*-dez.
Ferne. *Fairr*-ne(r).
Fernflöte. *Fairrn*-fle(r)-te(r).
Fernwerk. *Fairrn*-vairrk.
Feroce. *Fairr*-oh-chay.
Ferocità. Fairr-otch-ee-*ta*⁵.
Ferrando. Fairr-*an*-doh.

---

1. k = 'ch' (cf. Scot. *loch*).   2. ee here really between 'ee' and 'oo' (cf. Scot. *puir*).
3. zj like 's' in *pleasure*.   4. ow as in *cow*.   5. a as in *lad*.

Ferroud. Ferr-oo.
Ferruccio. Fair-*oot*-choh.
Fertig. *Fairr*-tish⁶.
Fervente. Fairr-*ven*-tay.
Fervidamente. *Fairr*-vee-dam-
en-tay.
Fervido. *Fairr*-vee-doh.
Fervore. Fairr-*vohr*-ray.
Fes. Fess.
Feses. *Fess*-ess.
Festa. *Fess*-ta⁵.
Festivo. Fest-*tee*-voh.
Festlich. *Fest*-lik¹.
Festoso. Fest-*oh*-zoh.
Festpiel. *Fest*-shpeel.
Fête galante. Fet gal-o(ng)t.
Fétis. Fay-teess.
Feuer. *Foy*-err.
Feuersbrunst.   *Foy*-errss-
broonsst.
Feuersnot. *Foy*-errss-noht.
Feuersymphonie. *Foy*-err-zim-
foh-*nee*.
Feuille d'album. Fu(r)-ee dal-
bum.
Feuillet. Fu(r)-ee-yay.
Feurig. *Foy*-rish⁶.
Ffrangcon-Davies. *Frang*-kon-
Day-viz.
Fiacco. Fee-*ak*-koh.
Fiate. Fee-*ah*-tay.
Fiato. Fee-*ah*-toh.
Fibich. *Fee*-beek¹.
Fidelio. Fee-*dail*-yoh.
Fier. Fee-airr.
Fieramente. Fee-airr-am-*en*-tay.
Fière. Fee-*airr*.
Fierezza. Fee-airr-*ets*-sa⁵.
Fiero. Fee-*ay*-roh.
Fierté. Fee-airr-tay.
Figaro. *Fee*-ga⁵-roh.
Figlia del Reggimento, La.
La⁵ *Feel*-ya⁶ del Rej-ee-*men*-
toh.
Figurata. *Fee*-goo-*rah*-ta⁵.
Figuré. Feeg-ee²-ray.
Figuriert. Fee-goo-*reerrt*.
Filar la voce. Fee-*lahrr* la⁵ *voh*-
chay.
Filer la voix. Fee-lay la⁵ vwah.
Filippo. Fee-*leep*-poh.
Filitz. *Fee*-lits.
Fille de Madame Angot, La.
La⁵ Fee(yer) de(r) Mad-am
O(ng)-goh.
Fin (Fr.). Fa(ng).
Fin (It.). Feen.
Finale. Fee-*nah*-lay.
Fine (It.). *Fee*-nay.
Fingerfertigkeit.   *Fing*-err-
fairr-tish⁶-kite.
Fingersatz. *Fing*-err-zats.
Fino. *Fee*-noh.

Fino al segno. *Fee*-noh al *sayn*-
yoh.
Fiorillo. Fee-aw-*rill*-loh.
Fioritura. Fee-*aw*-ree-*too*-ra⁵.
Fis (Ger.). Fiss.
Fisis (Ger.). *Fiss*-iss.
Flageolet (Eng.). Flaj-ol-*et*.
Flageolet (Fr.). Flazj³-ol-ay.
Flageolett (Ger.). Flaj-ol-*et*.
Flageolettöne. Flaj-ol-*et-te*(r)-
ne(r).
Flatter. Flat-tay.
Flatterzunge. *Flat*-err-tsoong-
e(r).
Flautando. Flow⁴-*tan*-doh.
Flautato. Flow⁴-*taht*-oh.
Flautina. Flow⁴-*tee*-na⁵.
Flauto a becco. *Flow*⁴-toh ab-
ec-coh.
Flauto amabile. *Flow*⁴-toh am-
ab-ee-lay.
Flauto d'amore.   *Flow*⁴-toh
dam-*aw*-ray.
Flauto d'eco. *Flow*⁴-toh *day*-
koh.
Flauto diritto. *Flow*⁴-toh dee-
reet-toh.
Flauto dolce. *Flow*⁴-toh *dol*-
chay.
Flauto magico, Il. Eel *flow*⁴-
toh *maj*-ee-coh.
Flautone. *Flow*⁴-*toh*-nay.
Flauto traverso.   *Flow*⁴-toh
trav-*airr*-soh.
Flebile. *Fleb*-ee-lay.
Flebilmente. Fleb-eel-*men*-tay.
Flecha. *Flay*-cha⁵.
Flechtenmacher.   *Flek*¹-ten-
mak¹-err.
Flehend. *Flay*-hent.
Fleischer. *Fly*-sherr.
Flessibile. Fless-*see*-bee-lay.
Flessibilità. Fless-see-bee-lee-
tah.
Fleury. Flur-ree.
Flicorno. Flee-*cawrr*-noh.
Fliegende Holländer, Der.
Dairr *fleeg*-end-e(r) Hol-end-
err.
Flies. Fleess.
Fliessend. *Flee*-sent.
Fliessender. *Flee*-send-err.
Flonzaley. Flon-*zah*-lay.
Florent Schmitt. Florr-o(ng)
Shmeet.
Flosshilde. Floss-*hill*-de(r).
Flöte. Fle(r)-te(r).
Flötenuhr. Fle(r)-ten-oorr.
Flotow. *Floh*-toh.
Flottant. Flot-to(ng).
Flotter. Flot-tay.
Flüchtig. *Fleek*², ¹-tish⁶.
Flüchtiger. *Fleek*², ¹-tig-err.

Flüchtigkeit. *Fleek*², ¹-tish⁶-kite.
Flügel. *Fleeg*²-el.
Flügelhorn. *Fleeg*²-el-horrn.
Fluidezza. Floo-ee-*dets*-sa⁵.
Fluidità. Floo-ee-dee-*ta*⁵.
Fluido. *Floo*-ee-doh.
Flüssig. *Fleess*²-ish⁶.
Flüssiger. *Fleess*²-ig-err.
Flûte. Fleet².
Flûté. Flee²-tay.
Flûte à bec. Fleet² ab-ek.
Flûte à cheminée. Fleet² ash-
u(r)m-ee-nay.
Flûte alto. Fleet² al-toh.
Flûte à pavillon. Fleet² ap-av-
ee-yo(ng).
Flûte d'amour.   Fleet² dam-
oorr.
Flûte d'Angleterre.   Fleet²
do(ng)-gle(r)-tairr.
Flûte douce. Fleet² dooss.
Flûte harmonique. Fleet² ahrr-
mon-eek.
Flûte traversière. Fleet² trav-
airrss-yairr.
Foco. *Faw*-coh.
Focosamente. Faw-coh-zam-
en-tay.
Focosissimo.   Faw-coh-*zeess*-
ee-moh.
Focoso. Faw-*coh*-zoh.
Foerster. *Furr*-sterr.
Foire des enfants.   Fwahrr
day-zo(ng)-fo(ng).
Fois. Fwah.
Fokine. *Faw*-keen.
Folge. *Folg*-e(r).
Folgen. *Folg*-en.
Folgt. Folkt.
Folia. Fol-*ee*-a⁵.
Folies d'Espagne. Fol-ee dess-
pan-y(er).
Follia. Fol-*yee*-a⁵.
Fomin. Faw-*meen*.
Fonds d'orgue. Fo(ng) dawrrg.
Forkel. *Forr*-kel.
Forlana (It.). Fawrr-*lah*-nah.
Forlane (Fr.). Fawrr-lan.
Format de poche. Fawrr-mah
de(r) posh.
Fornsete. *Forn*-set.
Forster. *Forst*-err.
Förster. *Furr*-sterr.
Forsyth. Fawrr-*syth*⁷.
Fort (Fr.). Fawrr.
Fort (Ger.). Forrt.
Forte (Fr.). Fawrrt.
Forte (It.). *Fawrr*-tay.
Fortement. Fawrrt-e(r)-mo(ng).
Fortfahren. *Forrt*-fah-ren.
Fortissimo.   Fawrr-*teess*-see-
moh.
Förtsch. Furrtsh.

---

6. The **ish** is really anywhere between that sound and 'ik' (varying in different parts of Germany).
7. **th** as in *thin*.   8. **g** as in *go*.

Fortsetzung. *Forrt*-zets-oong.
Forza. *Fawrrt*-sa[5].
Forza del Destino, La. La[5] *Fawrrt*-sa[5] del Dess-*teen*-oh.
Forzando. Fawrrt-*san*-doh.
Forzato. Fawrrt-*sah*-toh.
Fouetté. Foo-et-ay.
Fougueuse. Foog-e(r)z.
Fougueux. Foo-gu(r).
Foulds. Fohldz.
Fra Diavolo. Fra[5] Dee-*ah*-vol-oh.
Fraîche. Fresh.
Fraîcheur. Fresh-urr.
Frais. Fray.
Français. Fro(ng)-say.
Française. Fro(ng)-sez.
Françaix. Fro(ng)-say.
Francesca da Rimini. Fran-*chess*-ca[5] da[5] *Ree*-mee-nee.
Francesco. Fran-*chess*-coh.
Francese. Fran-*chay*-zay.
Franchetti. Fran-*ket*-tee.
Franchezza. Fran-*kets*-sa[5].
Franchise (Fr.). Fro(ng)-sheez.
Franchomme. Fro(ng)-shom.
Francis (Fr.). Fro(ng)-seess.
Francisco (Sp.). Franth[7]-*eess*-coh.
Franck. Fro(ng)k.
Franco. *Fran*-coh.
Francœur. Fro(ng)-curr.
François. Fro(ng)-swah.
Francs Juges, Les. Lay Fro(ng) Zjeezj[3, 2, 3].
Franz. Frants.
Frappant. Frap-po(ng).
Frappé. Frap-pay.
Frapper. Frap-pay.
Frappez. Frap-pay.
Frasi. *Frah*-zee.

Frauenchor. *Frow*[4]-en-kohrr.
Frauenliebe und Leben. *Frow*[4]-en-leeb-e(r) oont *Lay*-ben.
Frauenlob. *Frow*[4]-en-lohp.
Freddamente. *Fred*-dam-*en*-tay.
Freddezza. Fred-*dets*-sa[5].
Frédéric. Fray-day-reek.
Fredonner. Fre(r)d-on-nay.
Frei. Fry.
Freie. Fry-e(r).
Freischütz. *Fry*-sheets[2].
Fremstad (Swedish). *Frem*-stahd.
Frenetico. Fren-*ayt*-ee-coh.
Freno. *Fray*-noh.
Frescamente. Fress-cam-*en*-tay.
Frescobaldi. Fress-coh-*bal*-dee.
Frettevole. Fret-*tay*-voh-lay.
Frettolosamente. Fret-toh-loh-zam-*en*-tay.
Frettoloso. Fret-toh-*loh*-zoh.
Freude. *Froy*-de(r).
Freudig. *Froy*-dish[6].
Freylinghausen. *Fry*-ling-*how*[4]-zen.
Frid, Géza. *Gay*-zo(r) Freed.
Fridtjof. *Freet*-yoff(er).
Friedemann. *Free*-de(r)-man.
Friedrich. *Freed*-rik[1].
Frisch. Frish.
Froberger. *Froh*-bairrg-err.
Froebel. *Fre*(r)-bel.
Froh. Froh.
Fröhlich. *Fre*(r)-lik[1].
Froid. Frwah.
Froide. Frwahd.
Froidement. Frwahd-e(r)-mo(ng).
Fromaigeat. From-ay-zjah[3].

Fromental. From-o(ng)-tal.
Frosch. Frosh.
Froschquartett. *Frosh*-kvarr[5]-tet.
Frottola. *Frot*-toh-la[5].
Frottole. *Frot*-toh-lay.
Frugola. *Froo*-goh-la[5].
Früher. *Free*[2]-herr.
Frühlingslied. *Free*[2]-lings-leet.
Fuga alla Giga. *Foo*-ga[5] al-la[5] *Jee*-ga[5].
Fugara. Foo-*gah*-ra[5].
Fugato. Foo-*gah*-toh.
Fughetta. Foog-*et*-ta[5].
Führend. *Fee*[2]-rent.
Fu Hsuan. Foo Shwahn.
Fuleihan. *Foo*-lay-han.
Füllflöte. *Feel*[2]-fle(r)-te(r).
Fülligstimmen. *Feel*[2]-ish[6]-shtim-en.
Füllstimme. *Feel*[2]-shtim-e(r).
Fumagalli. *Foo*-mag-*al*[5]-lee.
Funèbre (Fr.). *Fee*[2]-nebrr.
Funebre (It.). *Foo*-neb-ray.
Fünf. Feenf[2].
Fünfstimmig. *Feenf*[2]-shtim-mish[6].
Funiculì, Funiculà. *Foo*-nee-coo-*lee*, Foo-nee-coo-*lah*.
Fuoco. *Foo*-aw-coh.
Fuocoso. Foo-aw-*coh*-zoh.
Für. Feer[2].
Furia. *Foo*-ree-a[5].
Furibondo. Foo-ree-*bon*-doh.
Furieusement. *Feer*[2]-yu(r)z-e(r)-mo(ng).
Furieux. *Feer*[2]-yu(r).
Furioso. Foo-ree-*oh*-zoh.
Furore. Foo-*raw*-ray.
Fux. Fooks.
Fuyant. Fwee-o(ng).

G

Gabelklavier. *Gah*-bel-klav-*eer*.
Gabriel (Fr.). Gab-ree-el.
Gabrieli. Gab-ree-*ail*-ee.
Gabrielli. Gab-ree-*el*-lee.
Gabrilowitch. Gab-reel-*oh*-vitch.
Gade (Dan.). Something like *Gai*(r)-the(r)[7], but frequently incorrectly pron. Gah-de(r), as though German.

Gaetano. Gah-ayt-*ah*-noh.
Gafori. Gaf-*aw*-ree.
Gaforio. Gaf-*aw*-ree-oh.
Gagliano. Gal-*yah*-noh.
Gagliardo. Gal-*yahrr*-doh.
Gagnebin. Gan-yeb-a(ng).
Gai. Gay.
Gaia. *Gah*-ya[5].
Gaiamente. Gy[8]-am-*en*-tay.
Gaiement. Gay-mo(ng).

Gaillard. Ga[5]-yarr.
Gaio. Gy[8]-yoh.
Gaisser. Gy[8]-serr.
Gaita Gallega. Gy[8]-ta[5] Gal-yay-ga[5].
Gaitas. Gy[8]-tass.
Gajo. Gy[8]-yoh.
Galamment. Gal[5]-am-mo(ng).
Galant (Fr.). Gal[5]-o(ng).
Galante (Fr.). Gal[5]-o(ng)t.

---

1. k = 'ch' (cf. Scot. *loch*).   **2.** ee here really between 'ee' and 'oo' (cf. Scot. *puir*).   **3.** zj like 's' in *pleasure*.   **4.** ow as in *cow*.   **5.** a as in *lad*.

Galante (It.). Gal⁵-*ahn*-tay.
Galantemente. Gal⁵-an-tay-*men*-tay.
Galanterien. Gal⁵-an-terr-*ee*-en.
Galanteries. Gal⁵-o(ng)-tair-ree.
Galanter Stil. Gal⁵-*ant*-err Shteel.
Galilei. Gal⁵-ee-*lay*-ee.
Galileo. Gal⁵-lee-*lay*-oh.
Galin. Gal⁵-a(ng).
Galitzky. Gal⁵-*eets*-kee.
Gallegada. Gal⁵-yayg-*ah*-da⁵.
Gallus. *Gal*⁵-ooss.
Galopade. Gal⁵-op-ad.
Galoubet. Gal⁵-oo-bay.
Galton. *Gol*-ton.
Galuppi. Gal⁵-*oop*-pee.
Gamba. *Gam*-ba⁵.
Gamut (Eng.). *Gam*-ut.
Gangar. *Gang*-ahrr.
Ganger. *Gang*-err.
Ganz. Gants.
Ganze Bogen. Gants-e(r) *Bohg*-en.
Ganze Note. Gants-e(r) *Noh*-te(r).
Ganze Pause. Gants-e(r) *Pow*⁴-se(r).
Ganze Taktnote. Gants-e(r) Takt-*noh*-te(r).
Gänzlich. Gents³-lik¹.
Garbatamente. Garr⁵-bat-am-*en*-tay.
Garbatezza. Garr⁵-bat-*ets*-sa⁵.
Garbatissimo. Garr⁵-bat-*eess*-see-moh.
Garbato. Garr⁵-*bah*-toh.
Garbo. *Garr*⁵-boh.
García. Garrth⁷-*ee*-a⁵.
Gardano. Garr⁵-*dah*-noh.
Gardel. Gahrr-del.
Garder (Fr.). Gahr-day.
Garreta. Garr⁵-*et*-a⁵.
Gaspard de la Nuit. Gass-pahrr del-an-wee.
Gaspare. *Gass*-pah-ray.
Gassenhauer. *Gass*-en-how⁴-err.
Gassmann. *Gass*-man.
Gastein. *Gass*-tyne.
Gastoldi. Gass-*tol*-dee.
Gastoué. Gass-too-ay.
Gattoni. Gat-*toh*-nee.
Gaubert. Goh-bairr.
Gauche. Gohsh.
Gaukler. Gowk⁴-lerr.
Gavazzeni. Gav-at-*say*-nee.
Gaveau. Gav-oh.
Gavotta. Gav-*ot*-ta⁵.
Gavotte. Gav-*ot*.
Gazza ladra, La. La⁵ *Gats*-sa⁵ *lah*-dra⁵.

Gebet. Gu(r)-bait.
Gebrauch. Gu(r)-*browk*¹.
Gebrauchsmusik. Gu(r)-*browks*¹-moo-*zeek*.
Gebunden. Gu(r)-*boon*-den.
Gedact. Gu(r)-*dakt*.
Gedämpft. Gu(r)-*dempft*.
Gedeckt. Gu(r)-*dekt*.
Gedehnt. Gu(r)-*daynt*.
Gedehnter. Gu(r)-*daynt*-err.
Gedicht. Gu(r)-*dikt*¹.
Gefallen. Gu(r)-*fal*-en.
Gefällig. Gu(r)-*fell*-ish⁶.
Gefühl. Gu(r)-*feel*².
Gefühlvoll. Gu(r)-*feel*²-fol.
Gegen. *Gaig*-en.
Gehalten. Gu(r)-*hal*⁵-ten.
Gehaucht. Gu(r)-*howkt*¹.
Geheimnisvoll. Gu(r)-*hime*-niss-fol.
Gehend. *Gay*-hent.
Gehörig. Gu(r)-*herr*-ish⁶.
Geige. Gy³-gu(r).
Geigen. Gy³-gen⁸.
Geigenprinzipal. Gy³-gen⁸-prints-ee-*pahl*.
Geiringer. *Guy*-ring-er.
Geist. Gysst⁸.
Geister. Gyst⁸-terr.
Geistlich. Gyst⁸-lik¹.
Geistliche Lieder. Gyst⁸-lik¹-e(r) *Leed*-err.
Geistliches Lied. Gyst³-lik¹-ess Leet.
Gekneipt. Gu(r)k-*nypt*.
Gekoppelt. Gu(r)-*kop*-elt.
Gelassen. Gu(r)-*lass*-en.
Geläufig. Gu(r)-*loyf*-ish⁶.
Geläufigkeit. Gu(r)-*loyf*-ik¹-kite.
Geltzer. *Gelt*⁸-serr.
Gemächlich. Gu(r)-*mek*¹-lik¹.
Gemächlicher. Gu(r)-*mek*¹-lik¹-err.
Gemässigt. Gu(r)-*mess*-isht⁶.
Gemebondo. Jem-ay-*bon*-doh.
Gemendo. Jem-*en*-doh.
Gemessen. Gu(r)-*mess*-en.
Geminiani. Jem-een-*yah*-nee.
Gemshorn. *Gemss*⁸-horrn.
Gemüth. Gu(r)-*meet*².
Genannt. Gu(r)-*nant*.
Genau. Gu(r)-*now*⁴.
Genauigkeit. Gu(r)-*now*⁴-ik¹-kite.
Genée. Zjen³-ay.
Generalpause (Ger.). Gen⁸-er¹-*ahl*-pow⁴-ze(r).
Generoso. Jen-*zy*-roh-zoh.
Geneviève. Zjen⁵-ev-yev.
Genre. Zjo(ng)rr³.
Gentil. Zjo(ng)³-tee.
Gentile (It.). Jen-*tee*-lay.
Gentilezza. Jen-tee-*lets*-sa³.

Gentilmente. Jen-teel-*men*-tay.
Georg (Ger.). Gay-*orrg*.
George (Fr.). Zjawrrzj³.
George (Ger.). Gay-*orrg*-e(r).
Georges (Fr.). Zjawrrzj³.
Gerader Zinck. Gur-*rah*-derr Tsink.
Gerardy. Zjair³-ahrr-dee.
Gerber. *Guirr*-berr.
Gerhard. *Gairr*-hart. (In Spain pron. *Jerr*-ard.)
Germont. Zjair³-mo(ng).
Gershwin. *Gursh*-win.
Gerührt. Gur-*reerrt*³.
Ges. Gess⁸.
Gesangvoll. Gu(r)-*zang*-fol.
Geschlagen. Gu(r)-*shlahg*-en.
Geschleift. Gu(r)-*shlyft*.
Geschlossen. Gu(r)-*shloss*-en.
Geschmack. Gu(r)-*shmak*.
Geschmackvoll. Gu(r)-*shmak*-fol.
Geschwind. Gu(r)-*shvinnt*.
Gese. Gay-ze(r).
Gesellschaft. Gu(r)-*zel*-shaft.
Gesellschaft der Musikfreunde. Gu(r)-*zel*-shaft dairr Moo-*zeek*-froyn-de(r).
Geses. *Gess*³-ess.
Gesprochen. Gu(r)-*shprok*¹-en.
Gesteigert. Gu(r)-*shty*-gerrt.
Gestopft. Gu(r)-*shtopft*.
Gestossen. Gu(r)-*shtohss*-en.
Gesualdo. Jez-oo-*al*-doh.
Getheilt. Gu(r)-*tylt*.
Getragen. Gu(r)-*trahg*-en.
Gevaert. *Ghay*-vahrrt (the 'Gh' a strong guttural, almost as in footnote 1).
Gewandhaus. Gu(r)-*vant*-howss⁴.
Gewichtig. Gu(r)-*vik*¹-tish⁶.
Gewidmet. Gu(r)-*vid*-met.
Gewöhnlich. Gu(r)-*ve*(r)n-lik¹.
Gezogen. Gu(r)-*tsohg*-en.
Ghedini. Ged⁸-*ee*-nee.
GheestelijkeLiedekens.*Kayss*¹-te(r)-lik-e(r) *Leed*-e(r)-kenz.
Ghiribizzo. Gee⁸-ree-*beets*-soh.
Ghiribizzoso. Gee⁸-ree-beets-soh-zoh.
Giacomo. *Jack*-oh-moh.
Giambattista. Jam-bat-*eest*-a⁵.
Giannini. Jan-*neen*-ee.
Gianni Schicchi. *Jan*-nee *Skee*-kee.
Giardini. Jahrr-*dee*-nee.
Giga. Jeeg-a⁵.
Gigout. Zjee³-goo.
Gigue. Zjeeg³.
Gilda. *Jil*-da⁵.
Gilles (Fr.). Zjeel⁸.
Gilson. Zjeel³-so(ng).

---

6. The **ish** is really anywhere between that sound and 'ik' (varying in different parts of Germany). **7.** th as in *thin*. **8.** g as in *go*.

Y y

Gimel. *Gim*[3]-el.

Ginastera. Kee[1]-nass-*tay*-rah.

Ginguené. Zja(ng)[3]-ge(r)[3]-nay.

Gino. *Jee*-noh.

Gioacchino. Joh-ak-*keen*-oh.

Giochevole. Joh-*kay*-vol-ay.

Gioco. *Jaw*-coh.

Giocolino. Joh-koh-*lee*-noh.

Giocondamente. Joh-kon-dam-*en*-tay.

Giocondevole. Joh-kon-*day*-vol-ay.

Giocondezza. Joh-kon-*dets*-a[5].

Giocondità. Joh-*kon*-dee-*ta*[5].

Giocondo. Joh-*kon*-doh.

Giocosamente. Joh-koh-zam-*en*-tay.

Giocoso. Joh-*koh*-zoh.

Gioia. Jaw-ya[5].

Gioielli della Madonna, I. Ee Jaw-*yel*-ee del-la[5] Mad-on-na[5].

Gioiosamente. Jaw-*yoh*-zam-*en*-tay.

Gioioso. Jaw-*yoh*-zoh.

Giordani. Jawrr-*dah*-nee.

Giordano. Jawrr-*dah*-noh.

Giorgetta. Jawrr-*jet*-ta[5].

Giorgi. Jawrr-jee.

Giovanni. Joh-*van*-nee.

Gioviale. Joh-vee-*ah*-lay.

Giovialità. Joh-vee-al[5]-ee-*ta*[5].

Giraldus Cambrensis. Commonly pron. Jee-*rahl*-duss Cam-*bren*-siss.

Girolamo. Jee-*raw*-lam-oh.

Gis. Giss[3].

Gisis. *Giss*[3]-iss.

Gitana. Jee-*tah*-na[5].

Gitano. Jee-*tah*-noh.

Gittern. *Git*[3]-tern.

Giù. Joo.

Giubilante. Joo-bee-*lan*-tay.

Giubilio. Joo-beel-*ee*-oh.

Giubilo. *Joo*-beel-oh.

Giuliani. Jool-*yah*-nee.

Giulietta. Joo-lee-*et*-ta[5].

Giulio Cesare. *Jool*-yoh Chay-za[5]-ray.

Giulivamente. Joo-leev-am-*en*-tay.

Giulivissimo. Joo-lee-*veess*-see-moh.

Giulivo. Joo-*lee*-voh.

Giuoco. Joo-*oh*-coh.

Giuseppe. Joo-*zep*-pay.

Giusta. *Jooss*-ta.

Giustamente. Joos-tam-*en*-tay.

Giustezza. Jooss-*tets*-sa[5].

Giustini. Joos-*tee*-nee.

Giusto. *Joos*-toh.

Givelet. Zjee[3]-vel-ay.

Glänzend. *Glent*-sent.

Glasharmonika. *Glass*-harr-*moh*-nee-kah.

Glasspiel. *Glass*-shpeel.

Glasstabharmonika. *Glass*-shtahp-harr-*moh*-nee-kah.

Glatt. Glat.

Glätte. *Glet*-e(r).

Glazunof. Glah-zoo-*nof*.

Gleich. Glyk[1].

Gleiche Stimmen. *Glyk*[1]-e(r) *Shtim*-en.

Gleichmässig. *Glyk*[1]-mess-ish[6].

Gleichsam. *Glyk*[1]-zam.

Gleichstark. *Glyk*[1]-shtarrk.

Gleissner. *Gly*-snerr.

Gleitend. *Gly*-tent.

Gli. L'yee.

Glie. L'yay.

Glière. Glee-yairr.

Glinka. *Gleen*-ka[5].

Glissando. Gleess-*san*-doh.

Glissant. Glee-so(ng).

Glissato. Gleess-*sah*-toh.

Glisser. Glee-say.

Glöckchen. *Gle(r)k*-shen.

Glocke. *Glok*-e(r).

Glocken. *Glok*-en.

Gluck. Glook.

Glühend. *Glee*[2]-hent.

Glyndebourne. (Long 'y' as in *my*; two syll, in all.)

Gnecchi. N'*yek*-kee.

Gniessin. *Gnyess*-in.

Gnomenreigen. *G(e)noh*[3]-men-*ryg*-en.

Godard. God-ahrr.

Godefraye. God-e(r)-fray.

Godounof. God-oo-*noff*.

Godowsky. God-*ov*-skee.

Godunof. God-oo-*noff*.

Goebbels. *Gu(r)*-belss.

Goedicke. *Gu(r)*-dik-e(r).

Goehr. Gur.

Goess. Ge(r)ss[3].

Goethe. *Gu(r)*-te(r).

Goetz. Gu(r)ts.

Golaud. Gol-oh.

Goldberg. *Gollt*-bairrg.

Goldmark. *Gollt*-marrk.

Golestan. Gol-ess-to(ng).

Gombert. Go(ng)-bairr.

Gomez. *Goh*-meth[7].

Gomólka. Gom-*ool*-ka[5].

Gondellied. *Gon*-del-leet.

Gondola. *Gon*-dol-a[5].

Gondoliera. Gon-dol-ee-*ay*-ra[6].

Gondoliere. Gon-dol-ee-*ay*-ray.

Goossens. *Ghohss*-enss (the 'Gh' a guttural), but the English branch of the family accepts the pron. '*Gooss*-enz'.

Gopak. Gop-*ahk*.

Gorczyn. *Gawrr*-chin.

Gorgheggiare. Gawr-gedj[3]-*ah*-ray.

Gorgheggio. Gawrr-*ged*[3]-joh.

Gorsedd. *Gorr*-seth ('th' as in *the*).

Gossec. Goss-ek.

Götterdämmerung. *Ge(r)t*-terr-*dem*-err-oong.

Gottfried. *Got*-freet.

Gottfried von Strassburg. *Got*-freet von *Shtrass*-boorrg.

Gottlieb. *Got*-leep.

Goudimel. Good-ee-mel.

Gounod. Goo-noh.

Goyescas. Goy-*ess*-cass.

Gracieuse. Grass-yu(r)z.

Gracieux. Grass-yu(r).

Gradatamente. Grah-dat-am-*en*-tay.

Gradevole. Grad-*ay*-vol-ay.

Graditamente. Grad-eet-am-*en*-tay.

Gradito. Grad-*ee*-toh.

Graduellement. Grad-ee[2]-el-e(r)-mo(ng).

Graeser. *Gray*-zerr.

Grainger. *Grain*-jer.

Gran (It., Sp.). Gran.

Granadina. Gran-ad-*ee*-na[5].

Granados y Campina. Gran-ah-dohss ee Cam-*pee*-na[5].

Gran cassa. Gran *cass*-sa[5].

Grand (Fr.). Before a consonant, Gro(ng); before a vowel or mute 'h', Gront.

Grand chœur. Gro(ng) Kurr.

Grand détaché. Gro(ng) day-tash-ay.

Grande (Fr.). Gro(ng)d.

Grande (It.). Grahn-day.

Grande flûte. Gro(ng)d fleet[2].

Grande Messe des Morts. Gro(ng)d Mess day Mawrr.

Grandezza. Gran-*dets*-sa[5].

Grandisonante. Gran-dee-son-*an*-tay.

Grand orchestre. Gront awrr-kestrr.

Grand orgue. Gront awrrg.

Grane. *Grah*-ne(r).

Graner. *Grah*-nerr.

Gran gusto. Gran *gooss*-toh.

Gran tamburo. Gran tam-*boo*-roh.

Grassineau. Grass-een-oh.

Graun. Grown[4].

Grave (Fr.). Grahv.

Grave (It.). *Grah*-vay.

Gravement. Grahv-mo(ng).

Gravemente. Grah-vay-*men*-tay.

Gravicembalo. *Grahv*-ee-*chem*-bal[5]-oh.

---

1. k = 'ch' (cf. Scot. *loch*).   2. ee here really between 'ee' and 'oo' (cf. Scot. *puir*).   3. zj like 's' in *pleasure*.   4. ow as in *cow*.   5. a as in *lad*.

Gravina. Grahv-*ee*-na⁶.
Gravità. Grahv-ee-*ta*⁵.
Grazia. *Graht*-see-a⁵.
Graziös. Graht-see-*u*(r)*z*.
Graziosamente. Graht-see-oh-zam-*en*-tay.
Grazioso. Graht-see-*oh*-zoh.
Gregorio. Greg-*oh*-ree-oh.
Grelots. Gre(r)-loh.
Grenié. Gre(r)n-yay.
Gresnick. *Ghress*-nick (the 'Gh' a guttural).
Gretchaninof. Gretch-an-*een*-off.
Gretchen. *Grayt*-shen.
Grétry. Gray-tree.
Grieg. Greeg.
Griffbrett. *Grif*-bret.
Grigny. Green-yee.
Grigory. Grig-*aw*-ree(yer).
Grimmig. *Grim*-ish⁶.
Grob. Grope.
Grofé. *Groh*-fay.
Gros. Groh.
Gros bois. Groh bwah.
Gross. Grohss.
Grosse (Fr.). Grohss.
Grosse (Ger.). *Groh*-se(r).
Grosse (It.). *Grohss*-say.
Grosse Caisse. Grohss Kess.
Grosse Flöte. *Groh*-se(r) *Fle*(r)-te(r).
Grosse Orgelmesse. *Groh*-se(r) *Awrrg*-el-*mess*-e(r).
Grosse Quartette. *Groh*-se(r) Kvarr-*tet*-e(r).
Grosses Orchester. *Groh*-ses Orr-*kest*-err.

Grosse Trommel. *Groh*-se(r) *Trom*-el.
Grossflöte. *Grohss*-fle(r)t-e(r).
Grossi. *Gross*-see.
Grosso. *Gross*-soh.
Gros tambour. Groh to(ng)-boorr.
Grotesk. Groh-*tesk*.
Grottesco. Grot-*tess*-coh.
Grovlez. Grov-lay.
Gruenberg. *Green*²-bairrg.
Grünberg. *Green*²-bairrg.
Grundstimmen. *Groont*-shtim-en.
Grundthema. *Groont*-tay-ma.
Gruppetto. Groo-*pet*-toh.
Guajira. Gwa⁵-*kee*¹-ra⁵.
Guaracha. Gwa⁵-*ratch*-a⁵.
Guarneri. Gwar-*nay*-ree.
Guarneris. Gwar-*nay*-reess.
Guarnieri. Gwarn-*yair*-ee.
Guarracha. Gwa⁵-*ratch*-a⁵.
Guédron. Gay-dro(ng).
Guerre des Bouffons. Gairr day Boo-fo(ng).
Guerrero. Gay-*ray*-roh.
Guerriera. Goo-airr-ee-*ay*-ra⁵.
Guerriero. Goo-airr-ee-*ay*-roh.
Guesdron. Gay-dro(ng).
Guggenheim. *Goog*-en-hime (but sometimes anglicized to '*Gug*-en-hime').
Guglielmo Tell. Goo-lee-*el*-moh Tell.
Gui. Goo-ee.
Guido d'Arezzo. Goo-*ee*-doh da⁵-*ret*-soh.

Guillaume Tell. Ghee-ohm Tell.
Guillemain. Gee⁸-ye(r)-ma(ng).
Guilmant. Geel-mo(ng).
Guimard. Gee-mahrr.
Guimbarde. Ga(ng)-bahrrd.
Guiraud. Gee⁸-roh.
Gulbranson. *Gul*-branss-on.
Gung'l. Goong-gel⁸.
Gunther. Goont-err.
Guridi. Goo-*ree*-dee.
Gurlitt. *Goorr*-lit.
Gurnemanz. *Goorr*-ne(r)-mants.
Gusikov. *Gooss*-ee-koff.
Gusla. Gooz-lah.
Gusle. *Gooss*-lee.
Gusli. *Gooss*-lee.
Gustav (Ger.). *Gooss*-taf.
Gustave (Fr.). Geess⁸˒²-tav.
Gusto. *Gooss*-toh.
Gut (Ger.). Goot.
Gutmann. *Goot*-man.
Gutrune. Goot-*roon*-e(r).
Guy (Fr.). Gee⁸.
Guzmán. Gooth⁷-*man*.
Gwenllian. *Gwenth*-klee¹-an ('th' as in *the*).
Gwineth. *Gwin*-eth ('th' as in *the*).
Gwyn ap Nudd. Gwin ap Neeth ('th' as in *the*).
Gwynedd. *Gwin*-eth ('th' as in *the*).
Gymel. Gim⁸-el.
Gyrowetz. Gee⁸-roh-vets.

H

H. (Ger.). Hah.
Hába. *Hah*-ba⁵.
Habanera. *Ah*-ban-*ay*-ra⁵.
Habeneck. Ab-en-ek.
Hackbrett. *Hak*-bret.
Hadow. *Had*-oh.
Haeffler. *Hef*-lerr.
Haffner. *Haf*-nerr.
Hagemann. *Hah*-ge(r)⁸-man.
Hagen. *Hah*-gen.
Hagenauer. *Hah*-ge(r)⁸-now⁴-er.
Hagerup. *Hahg*-err-oop.
Hahn. Hahn.

Hahnebüchen. *Hahn*-e(r)-bee²-shen.
Hahnentrapp. *Hahn*-nen-trap.
Halb. Halp⁵.
Halbe. *Halb*-e(r).
Halbe Note. *Halb*-e(r) *Noh*-te(r).
Halbnote. *Halp*-noh-te(r).
Halbe Pause. *Halb*-e(r) *Pow*⁴-ze(r).
Halbpause. *Halp*-pow⁴-ze(r).
Halbprinzipal. *Halp*-prints-ee-pahl.
Halbsopran. *Halp*-zoh-*prahn*.

Halbton. *Halp*-tohn.
Halévy. Al-ay-vee.
Halffter. *Hallf*-terr.
Hälfte. *Helf*-te(r).
Hallé. *Hal*⁵-lay.
Hallen (Ger.). *Hal*⁵-len.
Hallén. *Hal*⁵-ain.
Halling. *Hal*⁵-eeng.
Hallström. *Hal*⁵-stru(r)m.
Halt. Halt⁵.
Halten. *Halt*⁵-en.
Halvorsen. *Hal*⁵-vawrrss-en.
Hamerik. *Ham*-air-rik.
Hammerich. *Ham*-air-rik.

---

6. The **ish** is really anywhere between that sound and 'ik' (varying in different parts of Germany).
7. **th** as in *thin*.   8. **g** as in *go*.

Hammerklavier. *Ham-err-*klav-*eer*.
Hammerschmidt. *Ham-err-*shmit.
Hammerstein. *Ham-err-*stine.
Hampel. *Ham-*pel.
Hanacca. *Han-*ak-ka⁵.
Hanaise. An-ez.
Hanakisch. *Han-*ah-kish.
Hand (Ger.). Hant.
Hände. *Hend-*e(r).
Handel. *Hand-*el. (Continental spelling usually 'Haendel' or 'Händel' and pron. *Hend-*el.)
Handharmonika. *Hant-*harr-*moh-*nee-kah.
Handtrommel. *Hant-*trom-el.
Hans. Hanss.
Hänsel und Gretel. *Henz-*el oont *Gray-*tel.
Hans Heiling. Hanss *Hy-*ling.
Hanslick. *Hanss-*lik.
Hans Sachs. Hanss Zaks.
Hardangerfele. Harr-*dang-*err-fay-le(r).
Hardi. Ahrr-dee.
Hardiment. Ahrr-dee-mo(ng).
Harewood. *Hah(r)-*wood.
Harfe. *Harr-*fe(r).
Harmati. *Horr-*mot-ee ('o'-sounds, not 'a'-sounds).
Harmonica à bouche. Ahrr-mon-ee-ka⁵ ab-oosh.
Harmonica à lames d'acier. Ahrr-mon-ee-ka⁵ al-am dass-yay.
Harmonica à lames de pierre. Ahrr-mon-ee-ka⁵ al-am de(r) pee-airr.
Harmonica à lames de verre. Ahrr-mon-ee-ka⁵ al-am de(r) vairr.
Harmonica de bois. Ahrr-mon-ee-ka⁵ de(r) bwah.
Harmonica de Franklin. Ahrr-mon-ee-ka⁵ de(r) Fro(ng)k-la(ng).
Harmonicon. Har-*mon-*ik-on.
Harmonie. Ahrr-mon-ee.
Harmoniemesse. Harr-mon-ee-mess-e(r).
Harmonika. Harr-*mohn-*ee-kah.
Harmonique. Ahrr-mon-eek.
Harmonische Töne. Harr-*moh-*nish-e(r) *Te(r)-*ne(r).
Harpe à crochets. Arr-pa-krosh-ay.
Hart. Harrt.
Harte. *Harrt-*e(r).
Härtel. *Hairr-*tel.
Hartmann (Ger.). *Harrt-*man.
Hartmann (Hung.). *Horrt-*man.
Haschka. *Hash-*kah.

Hasse. *Hass-*e(r).
Hassler. *Hass-*lerr.
Hässler. *Hess-*ler.
Hastig. *Hass-*tish⁶.
Hauer. *How⁴-*er.
Haultain. Oh-ta(ng).
Haupt. Howpt⁴.
Hauptmann. *Howpt⁴-*man.
Hauptstimme. *Howpt⁴-*shtim-e(r).
Hauptwerk. *Howpt⁴-*vairrk.
Hausegger. *Howss⁴-*eg-err.
Haut. Oh.
Hautain. Oh-ta(ng).
Hautbois. Oh-bwah.
Hautbois baryton. Oh-bwah ba⁵-ree-to(ng).
Hautbois d'amour. Oh-bwah dam-oorr.
Hautboy (Eng.). *Hoh-*boy.
Haute. Oht.
Haute danse. Oht do(ng)ss.
Hauteur. Oh-turr.
Havanaise. Av-an-ez.
Haydn. *Hy-*den.
Haydn-Verein. *Hy-*den Fairr-*ine*.
Hebenstreit. *Hay-*ben-shtrite.
Heckel. *Hek-*el.
Heckelclarina. *Hek-*el-klarr-ee-nah.
Heckelclarinette. *Hek-*el-klarr-ee-*net-*te(r).
Heckelphon (Ger.). *Hek-*el-fohn.
Heckelphone (Eng.). *Hek-*el-fohn.
Heftig. *Heft-*tish⁶.
Heil dir im Siegerkranz. Hile deer im *Zeeg-*err-krants.
Heilig. *Hile-*ish⁶.
Heiligmesse. *Hile-*ish⁶-*mess-*e(r).
Heine. *Hy-*ne(r).
Heinel. *Hy-*nel.
Heinrich. *Hine-*rik¹.
Heise. *Hye-*ze(r).
Heiss. Hice.
Heldentenor. *Hel-*den-ten-*ohrr.*
Helicon. *Hel-*ik-on.
Hell (Ger.). Hell.
Heller. *Hel-*err.
Hellflöte. *Hel-*fle(r)-te(r).
Hellmesberger. *Hel-*mes-bairrg-err.
Helmholtz. *Helm-*holts.
Henri. O(ng)-ree.
Henry (Fr.). O(ng)-ree.
Henschel. *Hen-*shel.
Henselt. *Hen-*zelt.
Hen wlad fy nhadau. Hen oo-lad vun *had-*eye.
Henze. *Hent-*ze(r).
Herabstrich. Hairr-*ap-*strik¹.
Heraufstrich. Hairr-*owf⁴-*strik¹.

Herbstlied. *Hairrbst-*leet.
Herman. *Hairr-*man.
Hermann. *Hairr-*man.
Hernach. Hairr-*nahk¹*.
Hérodiade. Ay-rohd-yad.
Héroïque. Ay-roh-eek.
Heroisch. Hair-*roh-*ish.
Hérold. Ay-rold.
Herrnhuter. *Hairrn-*hoot-err.
Herschel (Eng.). *Her-*shel.
Herschel (Ger.). *Hairr-*shel.
Herstrich. *Hairr-*shtrik¹.
Herunterstimmen. Hairr-*oon-*terr-shtim-en.
Herunterstrich. Hairr-*oon-*terr-shtrik¹.
Hervorgehoben. Hairr-*fohrr-*gu(r)-hoh-ben.
Hervorragend. Hairr-*fohrr-*rahg-ent.
Herz. Hairrts.
Herzgewächse. *Hairrts-*ge(r)-vek-se(r).
Herzhaft. *Hairrts-*haft.
Herzig. *Hairrts-*ish⁶.
Herzogenberg. *Hairrts-*oh-gen⁸-bairg.
Hes. Hess.
Heseltine. *Hez-*el-tyne.
Hesse. *Hess-*e(r).
Heure espagnole, L'. Lur ess-pan-yol.
Hexenmenuett. *Hex-*en-men-oo-*et.*
Hexentanz. *Hex-*en-tants.
Hier. Heerr.
Hieronymus (Ger.). Heerr-*on-*ee-mooss.
Hiller. *Hill-*err.
Himmel. *Him-*el.
Hindemith. *Hin-*de(r)-meet.
Hinsterbend. *Hin-*shtairr-bent.
Hinstrich. *Hin-*shtrik¹.
Hippolyte et Aricie. Eep-ol-eet ay Arr-ee-see.
Hirt, Der. Dairr Hirrt.
Hirtenlied. *Hirr-*ten-leet.
His (Ger.). Hiss.
Hisis. *Hiss-*iss.
Histoires sacrées. Eesst-wahr sak-ray.
Hoboe. Hoh-*boh-*ay.
Hobrecht. *Hoh-*brekt¹.
Hochbrucker. *Hohk¹-*brook-err.
Hochdruckstimmen. *Hohk¹-*drook-shtim-en.
Hoch Kammerton. Hohk¹ *Kamm-*err-tohn.
Höchst. He(r)kst¹.
Hochzeitsmarsch. *Hok¹-*tsyts-marrsh.
Hochzeitszug. *Hok¹-*tsyts-tsook.
Hoffmann. *Hof-*man.

---

1. k = 'ch' (cf. Scot. *loch*).   **2.** ee here really between 'ee' and 'oo' (cf. Scot. *puir*).   **3.** zj like 's' in *pleasure*.   **4.** ow as in *cow*.   **5.** a as in *lad*.

Hofmannsthal. *Hof*-mans-tahl.
Hohlfeld. *Hohl*-felt.
Hohlflöte. *Hohl*-fle(r)-te(r).
Hol. Holl.
Holbach. *Hol*-bak[1].
Holberg (Dan.). *Hol*-bairr(g).
Holborne. *Hol*-born (or *Hole*-born, or *Hoh*-born).
Holmès. Ol-mayss.
Holst. Hohlst.
Holz. Hollts.
Holzbläser. *Hollts*-blay-zerr.
Holzblasinstrumente. *Hollts*-blahss-in-stroo-*ment*-e(r).
Holzflöte. *Hollts*-fle(r)-te(r).
Holzgeschnitzte Prinz, Der. Dairr *Hollts*-ge(r)[8]-shnits-te(r) Prints.
Holzharmonica. *Hollts*-harr-*moh*-nee-kah.
Holzschlägel. *Hollts*-shlaayg-el.
Holztrompete. *Hollts*-trom-*pay*-te(r).
Homme armé, L'. Lom ahrr-may.

Homophony. Hoh-*mof*-on-ee.
Hondo. (See under *Cante Hondo*.)
Honegger. Onn-eg-airr.
Hopak. Gop-*ahk* ('G' sound, not 'H', in normal Russian).
Hoquet. Ok-ay.
Horace victorieux. Orr-ass[5] veek-torr-ree-yu(r).
Horn (Ger.). Horrn.
Hörner. *Hurr*-nerr.
Hörnersignal, Mit dem. Mit daim *Hurr*-nerr-zig-*nahl*.
Horst Wessel. Horrst *Vess*-el.
Hortense. Awrr-to(ng)ss.
Hostinsky. Hoss-*teen*-skee.
Hoteterre. Ot-te(r)-tairr.
Hothby (Eng.). *Hoth*[7]-bee.
Hovhaness. Hoh-*vah*-ness.
Howell. *How*[4]-el.
Hubay. *Hoo*-bah-ee.
Huber. *Hoo*-berr.
Hubert (Fr.). Ee[2]-bairr.
Hübsch. Heebsh[2].
Huë. Ee[2]-ay.

Hugo (Fr.). Ee[2]-goh.
Hugo (Ger.). *Hoo*-goh.
Huguenots, Les. Lay Eeg[2]-en-oh.
Huit. Weet ('Wee' before a consonant).
Huitième. Weet-yem.
Hummel. *Hoom*-mel.
Humoreske (Ger.). Hoo-morr-*esk*-e(r).
Humoresque (Fr.). Ee[2]-mor-resk.
Humperdinck. *Hoom*-perr-dink.
Hundoegger. *Hoond*-egg-err.
Huon de Bordeaux. Ee[2]-o(ng) de(r) Bawrr-doh.
Hüpfend. *Heep*[2]-fent.
Huré. Ee[2]-ray.
Hurtig. *Hoorr*-tish[6].
Hutschenruyter. *Hoot*-chen-roy-ter.
Hüttenbrenner. *Heet*[2]-ten-bren-ner.
Hwyl. *Hoo*-il.
Hydraulus. Hy-*draw*-lus.

I

Iambic. Eye-*am*-bik ('Eye' as Eng. word).
Iambus (Eye-*am*-bus ('Eye' as Eng. word).
Ibach. *Ee*-bak[1].
Ibérien. Ee-bayrr-ya(ng).
Ibérienne. Ee-bayrr-yen.
Ibert. Ee-bairr.
Idée fixe. Ee-day-feeks.
Idelsohn. *Ee*-del-zohn.
Idyll. *Eye*-dill ('Eye' as Eng. word), or *Id*-ill.
Idzikowsky. Its-see-*kov*-skee.
I gioielli della Madonna. Ee joy-*el*-ee del-la[5] Mad-*on*-na[5]
Ignacy. Eeg-*naht*-see.
Ignaz. *Ig*-nats.
Igor. *Ee*-gorr.
Il (Fr.). Eel.
Il (It.). Eel.
Il bacio. Eel *bah*-choh.
Il barbiere di Siviglia. Eel barr-bee-*ay*-ray dee See-*veel*-ya[2].

Il distratto. Eel deess-*traht*-toh.
Ileborgh. Eel-e(r)-borg.
Il faut. Eel foh.
Il flauto magico. Eel *flow*[4]-toh *maj*-ee-coh.
Il matrimonio segreto. Eel mat-ree-*moh*-nee-oh seg-*ray*-toh.
Il re pastore. Eel ray pas-*taw*-ray.
Il segreto di Susanna. Eel seg-*ray*-toh dee Sooz-*an*-na[5].
Il Signor Bruschino. Eel Seen-*yawrr* Brooss-*kee*-noh.
Il Tabarro. Eel Tab-*arr*-roh.
Il Trovatore. Eel Trov-at-*aw*-ray.
Imitazione. Eem-ee-tats-ee-*oh*-nay.
Impair (Fr.). A(ng)-pairr.
Impaziente. Eem-pat-see-*en*-tay.
Impazientemente. Eem-pat-see-en-tay-*men*-tay.

Imperioso. Eem-pairr-ree-*oh*-zoh.
Impeto. *Eem*-pet-oh.
Impétueux. A(ng)-pet-ee[2]-u(r).
Impetuosamente. Eem-pet-oo-oh-zam-*en*-tay.
Impetuosità. Eem-pet-oo-ohz-ee-*ta*[5].
Impetuoso. Eem-pet-oo-*oh*-zoh.
Imponente. Eem-pon-*en*-tay.
Imponierend. Im-pohn-*eer*-ent.
Impromptu (Eng.). Im-*promp*-tew.
Impromptu (Fr.). A(ng)-promp-tee[2].
Improvisatore. Eem-prov-ee-zat-*aw*-ray.
Im Takt. Im Takt.
In alt. Een alt[5].
In altissimo. Een al[5]-*teess*-ee-moh.
Incalzando. Een calt[5]-*san*-doh.
Inciso. Een-*chee*-zoh.

---

6. The **ish** is really anywhere between that sound and 'ik' (varying in different parts of Germany).
7. **th** as in *thin*.   **8.** **g** as in *go*.

Incominciando. Een-coh-meen-*chan*-doh.

Indebolendo. Een-deb-oh-*len*-doh.

Indeciso. Een-day-*chee*-zoh.

Indicato. Een-dee-*cah*-toh.

Indy A(ng)-dee.

Iñez. Een-*yeth*.

Inferno. Een-*fairr*-noh.

Infra. *Een*-fra[5].

Ingegnieri. In-jen-*yair*-ee.

Inghelbrecht (Fr.). *Ang*-gel[8]-bresht.

Inglese. Een-*glay*-zay.

In modo di. Een *maw*-doh dee.

Innig. *In*-ish[6].

Innigkeit. *In*-ish[6]-kite.

Innocenza. Een-notch-*end*-sa[5].

In Nomine. In *Nom*-ee-nay.

Inquiet (Fr.). A(ng)-kee-ay.

Inquieto. Een-kwee-*ayt*-oh.

Innsbruck, ich muss dich lassen. *Inns*-brook, ik[1] mooss dik[1] *lass*-en.

Insensibile. Een-sen-*see*-bee-lay.

Insieme. Een-see-*ay*-may.

Inständig. *In*-shten-dish[6].

Instante. Een-*stan*-tay.

Instantemente. Een-stan-tay-*men*-tay.

Intavolatura. Een-tav-ol-at-*oorr*-ah.

Intégrales. A(ng)-teg-ral[5].

Intermède. A(ng)-tairr-med.

Intermède à deux personnages. A(ng)-tairr-med a[5] du(r) pairr-soh-nazj[3].

Intermedio. Een-tairr-*maid*-ee-oh.

Intermezzo. Een-tairr-*med*-zoh.

Intime. A(ng)-teem.

Intimissimo. Een-tee-*meess*-ee-moh.

Intimo. *Een*-tee-moh.

Intrada. Een-*trah*-da[5].

Intrepidezza. Een-trep-ee-*dets*-za[5].

Intrepido. Een-*trep*-ee-doh.

Introduzione. Een-troh-doot-see-*oh*-nay.

Introit. In-*tro*-it.

Inventionshorn. In-vent-see-*ohns*-horrn.

Inventionstrompete. In-vent-see-*ohns*-trom-*pay*-te(r).

Iolanthe (Eng.). Eye-oh-*lan*-thay[7] ('Eye' as Eng. word).

Ione. Eee-*oh*-nay.

Ionian. Eye-*ohn*-ee-an ('Eye' as Eng. word).

I Pagliacci. Ee Pal[5]-*yaht*-shee.

Iphigenia. If-ij-en-*ee*-a[5].

Iphigénie en Aulide. Ee-fee-zjayn[3]-ee on Oh-leed.

Iphigénie en Tauride. Ee-fee-zjayn[3]-ee o(ng) Toh-reed.

Ippolitof-Ivanof. Ee-pol-*ee*-toff-Ee-*vahn*-off.

I Puritani. Ee Poo-ree-*tahn*-ee.

Ira. *Ee*-ra[5].

Iracondamente. Ee-rak-on-dam-*en*-tay.

Irgens. *Eerr*-genss[8].

Irma (Fr.). Eerr-ma[5].

Ironicamente. Ee-ron-ee-cam-*en*-tay.

Ironico. Ee-*ron*-ee-coh.

Irresoluto. Ee-rez-oh-*loo*-toh.

Isaac (Ger.). *Ee*-zah-ahk.

Islamey. Eess-lam-*ay*.

Isle Joyeuse, L'. Leel zjwah[3]-yu(r)z.

Isolde. Eez-*oll*-de(r).

Istesso. Ee-*stess*-soh.

Istrumento d'acciaio. Ee-stroo-*men*-toh dat-*shy*-yoh.

Italo. *Ee*-tal-oh.

Ivan. Ee-*van*.

I Vespri Siciliani. Ee *Vess*-pree See-chil-*yah*-nee.

Iwan. Ee-*van*.

J

Jabo. *Kah*[1]-boh.

Jacara. Kak-*ah*-ra[5] (initial 'K' as k[1] in footnote).

Jacob (Ger.). *Yak*-op.

Jacob de Reys. Zjak[3]-ob de(r) Ray.

Jacobi. Yak-*oh*-bee.

Jacob le Polonais. Zjak[3]-ob le(r) Pol-on-ay.

Jacopo. *Yak*-oh-poh.

Jacopone da Todi. Yak-oh-*poh*-nay da[5] *Taw*-dee.

Jacques. Zjahk[3].

Jacquot. Zjah[3]-koh.

Jaell. Yell (or Jah-ell).

Jagdhorn. *Yahkt*-hornn.

Jagdtrompete. *Yahkt*-trom-*pay*-te(r).

Jäger. *Yaig*-err.

Jahnn. Yahnn.

Jakob. *Yak*-op.

Jaleo. Kahl[1]-*ay*-oh.

Jalousieschweller. Yall-oo-*zee*-shvel-err.

Jämmerlich. *Yem*-err-lik.[1]

Jammernd. *Yam*-ernt.

Jan. *Yan*.

Janáček (Czech). *Yan*-atch-ek.

Janiewicz. Yan-yee-*ay*-veetch.

Janissary (Eng.). *Jan*-iss-arry (or *Yan*-iss-arry).

Janitscharenmusik. Yan-it-*shahr*-en-moo-*zeek*.

Janko. *Yonk*-oh.

Jannequin. Zjan[3]-e(r)-ka(ng).

Janos. *Yah*-nosh.

Janowka. Yah-*nov*-ka.

Janssen (Werner). Orig. '*Yahn*-

sen', but he anglicized it to '*Jan*-sen'.

Jaques-Dalcroze. Zjahk[3]-Dal-krohz.

Jarnach. *Yar*-nak.

Järnefelt. *Yairrn*-e(r)-felt.

Jauchzet dem Herrn alle Welt. *Yowk*[4]-tset daim *Hairrn* all-e(r) *Velt*.

Je (Ger.). Yay.

Jean (Fin.). Yan.

Jean (Fr.). Zjo(ng)[3].

Jean de Muris. Zjo(ng)[3] de(r) Mee[2]-ree.

Jedoch. Yay-*dok*[1].

Jeji Pastorkyña. *Yay*-yee Pass[5]-tawrr-*kee*-nee-a[5].

Jelinek. *Yel*-ee-nek.

Jemnitz. *Yem*-nits.

---

1. k = 'ch' (cf. Scot. *loch*). **2.** ee here really between 'ee' and 'oo' (cf. Scot. *puir*). **3.** zj like 's' in *pleasure*. **4.** ow as in *cow*. **5.** a as in *lad*.

Jenneval. Zjen³-e(r)-val.
Jensen. *Yen*-zen.
Jenufa. Yen-*oo*-fa⁵.
Jephtha (Eng.). *Jef*-tha⁷.
Jeppesen. *Yep*-e(r)-sen.
Jerôme. Zjer³-ome.
Jeu. Zju(r)³.
Jeu de clochettes. Zju(r)³ de(r) klosh-et.
Jeu de Robin et Marion. Zju(r)³ de(r) Rob-an(g) ay Marr-yo(ng).
Jeu de timbres. Zju(r)³ de(r) ta(ng)brr.
Jeune. Zju(r)n³.
Jeunehomme. Zju(r)³-nom.
Jeu ordinaire. Zju(r)³ awrr-deen-airr.
Jeux. Zju(r)³.
Jirák. Yee-*rahk*.
Joachim. Yoh-*ak*¹-im (but in Eng. usually pron. *Yoh*-ak-im).
Joaquín. Koh¹-a⁵-*kin*.
Jodel. *Yoh*-del.
Jodelling. *Yoh*-del-ing.
Johann. Yoh-*hann* (or *Yoh*-han).

Johannes. Yoh-*han*-ess.
Jolivet. Zjol³-ee-vay.
Jomelli. Yom-*el*-lee.
Jommelli. Yom-*mel*-lee.
Jongen (Flem.). '*Yong*-en', but, the composer being Walloon by birth, the pron. 'Zjong³-en' is adopted in his case.
Jongleur. Zjo(ng)³-glurr.
Jongleur de Notre Dame, Le. Le(r) Zjo(ng)³-glurr de(r) Notrr-e(r) Dam.
Jongleurs. Zjo(ng)³-glurr.
Jongleurs de gestes. Zjo(ng)³-glurr de(r) zjest³.
Jonny spielt auf. *Yon*-ee shpeelt *owf*⁴.
Jooss. Yohss.
Jora. *Zjaw*-rah.
Jörgen (Dan.). *Yur*-gen ('g' hard but faintly heard).
José. Koh¹-*say*.
Josef (Ger.). *Yoh*-zef.
Joseph (Fr.). Zjohz³-ef.
Joseph (Ger.). *Yoh*-zef.
Josquin des Près. Zjoss³-ka(ng) day Pray.

Josten. *Joss*-ten.
Jota Aragonesa. *Koh*¹-ta⁵ Ah-ra⁵-goh-*nayss*-a⁵.
Jouer. Zjoo³-ay.
Joyeuse. Zjaw³-yu(r)z.
Joyeux. Zjaw³-yu(r).
Juan. Kwan¹.
Jubelnd. *Yoo*-belnt.
Judenharfe. *Yoo*-den-harr-fe(r).
Juilliard. Zjwee³-yahrr (but in U.S.A. '*Joo*-lee-ard').
Juive, La. La⁵ Zjweev³.
Jules (Fr.). Zjeel³, ¹.
Juli (Sp.). *Koo*¹-lee.
Julien. Zjeel³, ²-ya(ng).
Julius (Ger.). *Yool*-yooss.
Jullien. Zjeel³, ²-ya(ng).
Jungfernquartette. *Yoong*-ferrn-kvarr-*tet*-e(r).
Juon (Fr.). Zjee³, ²-o(ng).
Jürg Jenatch. Yeerrg² *Yen*-atch.
Jusqu'à. Zjeesk³, ²-a⁵.
Juste. Zjeest³, ¹.
Justesse. Zjeest³, ²-ess.
Justin (Ger.). Yooss-*teen*.
Justus. *Yooss*-tooss.

K

Kabalevsky. Kab-al⁵-*ef*-skee-(yer).
Kaddish. *Kad*-dish.
Kaiserquartett. *Ky*-zerr-kvarr-tet.
Kajanus. Ky-*ah*-nooss.
Kaldalous. Kal-*dah*-looss.
Kalevala. Kal-ay-*val*-ah.
Kalinnikof. Kal⁵-*een*-nee-koff.
Kalkbrenner. *Kalk*-bren-err.
Kalliwoda. Kal⁵-ee-*voh*-da⁵.
Kamarinskaya. Kam-*ahrr*-inz-kye-ah.
Kamienski. Kam-*yeen*-skee.
Kaminski. Kam-*een*-skee.
Kammercantate. *Kam*-err-can-*taht*-e(r).
Kammerduett. *Kam*-err-doo-et.
Kammerkonzert. *Kam*-err-conts-*airrt*.
Kammermusik. *Kam*-err-moo-zeek.

Kammersymphonie. Kam-err-zim-foh-*nee*.
Kammerton. *Kam*-err-tohn.
Kammertrio. *Kam*-err-*tree*-oh.
Kanon. *Kah*-non.
Kantele. Kan-*tay*-lay.
Kapelle. Kap-*el*-le(r).
Kapellmeister. Kap-*el*-my-sterr.
Kapellmeistermusik. Kap-*el*-my-sterr-moo-*zeek*.
Kapellton. Kap-*el*-tohn.
Karapetoff. Karr⁵-a⁵-*pay*-toff.
Karg-Elert. *Karrg*-*Ay*-lerrt.
Karl. Karrl.
Karsavina. Karr⁵-*sahv*-ee-nah.
Kaspar. *Kass*-pahrr.
Kassation. Kass-atss-ee-*ohn*.
Kastagnetten. Kass-tan-*yet*-en.
Kastalsky. Kass-*tal*⁵-skee(yer).
Katswara. *Kats*-vah-ra⁵.
Katuar. Kat-*wahrr*.

Katzenmusik. *Kats*-en-moo-zeek.
Kaufman. *Kowf*⁴-man.
Kaulbach. *Kowl*⁴-bak¹.
Kaum. Kowm⁴.
Keckheit. *Kek*-hite.
Keineswegs. Ky-ness-*vaiks*.
Keiser. *Ky*-zerr.
Kéler-Béla. *Kay*-lairr-*Bay*-lo(r) (note the 'o' sound at end).
Keraulophon. Kerr-*oh*-lof-on.
Kerle. *Kair*-le(r).
Kerll. Kairrl.
Kernstock. *Kairrn*-shtok.
Kes. Kess.
Kethe. Keeth⁷.
Khandoshkin. Han-*dosh*-keen.
Khovantschina. Hoh-*vansh*-chee-nah.
Kielflügel. *Keel*-fleeg²-el.
Kienzl. Keentsl.
Kierkegaard. *Keer*-ke(r)-gawrd.

---

6. The **ish** is really anywhere between that sound and 'ik' (varying in different parts of Germany).
7. **th** as in *thin*. 8. **g** as in *go*.

Kilpinen. Kil-*peen*-en.
Kind (Ger.). Kinnt.
Kinder (Ger.). *Kin*-derr.
Kindergarten. *Kin*-derr-garr-ten.
Kinderscenen. *Kin*-derrt-say-nen.
Kinderstück. *Kin*-der-steek².
Kindersymphonie. *Kin*-derr-zim-fohn-*ee*.
Kindlich. *Kint*-lik¹.
Kindt. Kinnt.
Kinloch. Kin-*lok*¹.
Kirche. *Keersh*-e(r).
Kirchencantate. *Keersh*-en-can-*tah*-te(r).
Kircher. *Keersh*-err.
Kirchner. *Keersh*-nerr.
Kirnberger. *Keern*-bairrg-err.
Kissentanz. *Kiss*-en-tants.
Kitej. *Keet*-yezj³.
Kjerulf. *Shairr*-oolf.
Klagend. *Klahg*-ent.
Kläglich. *Klayg*-lik¹.
Klangfarbe. *Klang*-farr⁵-be(r).
Klappenhorn. *Klap*-en-horrn.
Klar. Klahrr.
Klarinette. Kla⁵-ree-*net*-e(r).
Klaviatur. Klav⁵-ee-at-*oorr*.
Klaviaturharmonika. Klav-ee-at-*oorr*-harr-*moh*-nee-kah.
Klavier. Klav-*eerr*.
Klavierauszug. Klav-*eerr*-owss⁴-tsoog.
Klavierharmonica. Klav-*eerr*-har-*moh*-nee-kah.
Klavierstück. Klav-*eerr*-steek².
Klavierübungen. Klav-*eerr*-ee²-boong-en.
Klein. Kline.
Kleine. *Kly*-ne(r).
Kleine Flöte. *Kly*-ne(r) *Fle*(r)-te(r).
Kleine Orgelmesse. *Kly*-ne(r) *Awrrg*-el-mess-e(r).
Kleine Trauermusik. *Kly*-ne(r) *Trow*⁴-err-moo-zeek.
Kleinflöte. *Kline*-fle(r)-te(r).
Klenau. *Klay*-now⁴.
Klengel. *Kleng*-el.
Klindworth. *Klinnt*-vorrt.
Klingen. *Kling*-en.
Klingend. *Kling*-ent.
Klingsor. *Kling*-sawrr.
Klose. *Kloh*-ze(r).
Klosé. *Kloh*-zay.

Knarre. *Knar*-re(r) (sound the 'K').
Knecht. Knesht (sound the 'K').
Kneifend. *Kny*-fent (sound the 'K').
Kneisel. *Kny*-zel (sound the 'K').
Knipper. *Knip*-err (sound the 'K').
Knorr. Knawrr (sound the 'K').
Koch. Kok¹.
Köchel. *Ke*(r)sh-el.
Koczwara. Kotsh-*wah*-ra⁵.
Kodály. *Koh*-dye.
Koechel. *Ke*(r)sh-el.
Koechlin (Fr.). Kek¹-la(ng).
Koenig. *Ke*(r)-nig.
Koenig Horn. *Ke*(r)-nig Horrn.
Koessler. *Ke*(r)ss-lerr.
Köhler. *Ke*(r)-lerr.
Kokett. Kok-*et*.
Kollreutter. *Koll*-royt-ter.
Kolomyika. Koh-loh-*mee*(yer)-ka⁵.
Kolophon. Kol-oh-*fohn*.
Komisch. *Koh*-mish.
Komponiert. Kom-poh-*neerrt*.
Königin von Saba, Die. Dee *Ke*(r)n-ig-in fon *Zah*-bah.
Königskinder, Die. Dee *Ke*(r)n-igs-kin-derr.
Konius. *Kohn*-eess¹.
Kontrabass. *Kon*-tra⁵-bass.
Kontrafagott. *Kon*-tra⁵-fag-*ot*.
Kontski. *Kont*-skee.
Konyus. *Kohn*-eess².
Konzert. Kon-*tsairrt*.
Konzertina. Kon-tsairr-*tee*-nah.
Koppel. *Kop*-el.
Korbay. *Kohrr*-boy(ee).
Kornett. Korr-*net*.
Korngold. *Korrn*-gollt.
Korrigane. Korr-ee-gan.
Koslek. *Koss*-lek.
Kostelanetz. Koss-te(r)-*lahn*-ets.
Koteletten Walzer. Kot-*let*-en *Valts*⁵-err.
Kotzwara. *Kotz*-vah-ra⁵.
Kouiaviak. Koo-ee-*ahv*-ee-ak.
Koukouzéles. Koo-koo-*zay*-less.
Koussevitzky. Kooss-iv-*its*-kee(yer).
Kozeluch. *Koh*-zjay³-look¹.
Kozlowski. Koz-*lov*-skee.

Kraft. Kraft⁵.
Krakowiak. Krak-*awv*-yak.
Kramer. Originally Dutch and pronounced '*Krah*-merr', but in Brit. and U.S.A. sometimes '*Kray*-merr'.
Kratzenstein. *Krat*-sen-shtine.
Krebs. Kraips.
Krein. Krine.
Kreis. Kryce.
Kreisler. *Kryce*-lerr.
Kreisleriana. Kryce-lerr-ee-*ahn*-ah.
Křenek. *Krain*-ek.
Kreutzer. *Kroyts*-err.
Kreuz. Kroyts.
Krieg. Kreeg.
Kriegerisch. *Kreeg*-err-ish.
Křižovsky. *Kreezj*³-off-skee.
Krohn (as spelt).
Krumhorn. *Kroom*-horrn.
Krummbogen. *Kroom*-bohg-en.
Krummbügel. *Kroom*-beeg²-el.
Krumpholz. *Kroomp*-hollts.
Kuba. *Koo*-bo(r).
Kubelik. *Koo*-bel-eek.
Kücken. *Kee*²-ken.
Kuhač. *Koo*-hatch.
Kuhe. *Koo*-he(r).
Kuhlau. *Kool*-ow⁴.
Kuhnau. Koo-now⁴.
Kujawiak. Koo-*yav*-yak.
Kullak. *Kool*-ak.
Kummerle. *Koom*-mair-le(r).
Kundry. *Koon*-dree.
Kuno. *Koo*-noh.
Kunst. Koonst.
Kunst der Fuge. Koonst dairr *Foog*-e(r).
Kunst Harmonium. Koonst Harr-*moh*-nee-oom.
Kunstlied. *Koonst*-leet.
Kunzen. *Koonts*-en.
Kurpinski. Koor-*peen*-skee.
Kurt. Koorrt.
Kurvenal. *Koorr*-ven-ahl.
Kurz. Koorts.
Kurze. *Koorts*-e(r).
Kurzer Vorschlag. *Koorts*-err *Fohrr*-shlak⁵.
Kussevitzki. Kooss-ev-*its*-kee(yer).
Kveda Rimur. *Kvay*-dah *Ree*-moor.
Kwalwasser. *Kvahl*-vass-err.
Kyasht. K'yasht.

---

1. **k** = 'ch' (cf. Scot. *loch*).   2. **ee** here really between 'ee' and 'oo' (cf. Scot. *puir*).   3. **zj** like 's' in *pleasure*.   4. **ow** as in *cow*.   5. **a** as in *lad*.

L

La (Fr.). La⁵.
La (It.). La⁵.
Laban. *Lah*-ban.
Labialstimme. Lab-ee-*ahl*-shtim-e(r).
Lablache. Lab-*lash*.
La Bohème. Lab-oh-em.
Laborde. Lab-awrrd.
Labroca. Lab-*rok*-a⁵.
La Cenerentola. Latch-en-ay-ren-toh-la⁵.
Lächelnd. *Lesh*-elnt.
Lâcher. Lash-ay.
Lachner. *Lak*¹-nerr.
Lacombe. Lak-o(ng)b.
Lacrimosa. Lac-ree-*moh*-za⁵.
Lacrimoso. Lac-ree-*moh*-zoh.
La Dame blanche. Lad-am blo(ng)sh.
Ladino. Lad-*ee*-noh.
Ladislas. *Lad*-eess-lass.
Ladmirault. Lad-mee-roh.
Ladré. Lad-ray.
La Favorita. Laf-av-oh-*ree*-ta⁵.
La Fille du régiment. Laf-ee dee² rezj³-ee-mo(ng).
La Forza del destino. Laf-*awrrts*-a⁵ del dess-*tee*-noh.
L'Africaine. Laf-ree-ken.
Lage. *Lahg*-e(r).
Lagnevole. Lan-*yay*-vol-ay.
Lagnosamente. Lan-yoh-zam-*en*-tay.
Lagnoso. Lan-*yoh*-zoh.
Lagrimando. Lag-ree-*man*-doh.
Lagrimoso. Lag-ree-*moh*-zoh.
Laissant. Less-o(ng).
Laisser. Less-say.
Laissez. Less-say.
Lajtha. Law-to (the 'Law' is almost 'Loy'; 'to' as in *Tom*).
La Juive. Lazj³-weev.
Lakmé. Lak-may.
Lalande. Lal-o(ng)d.
Lalo. Lal-oh.
Lamartine. Lam-ahrr-teen.
Lambert (Fr.). Lo(ng)-bairr.
Lamentabile. Lam-en-*tab*-ee-lay.
Lamentando. Lam-en-*tan*-doh.
Lamentazione. Lam-en-tat-see-*oh*-nay.
Lamentevole. Lam-en-*tay*-voh-lay.
Lamento. Lam-*en*-toh.
Lamentoso. Lam-en-*toh*-zoh.
Lamoureux. Lam-oo-ru(r).
Lampe (Ger.). *Lam*-pe(r).
La Muette de Portici. Lam-

ee²-et de(r) Pawrrt-ee-see (or It., *Pawr*-tee-chee).
La Navarraise. Lan-av-arr-ez.
Lancio. *Lan*-choh.
Landino. Lan-*dee*-noh.
Ländler. *Lend*-lerr.
Ländlich. *Lend*-lik¹.
Land o' the Leal. (Last word 'Leel'.)
Landowska. Lan-*dov*-ska⁵.
Lang. Lang.
Lange-Müller. *Lang*-e(r)-*Mee*²-lerr.
Langer Vorschlag. *Lang*-err *Fohrr*-shlak⁵.
Langleik. *Lang*-lake.
Langoureusement. Lo(ng)-goo-ru(r)z-e(r)-mo(ng).
Langoureux. Long-goo-ru(r).
Langsam. *Lank*-zam.
Langspil. *Lang*-spil (nearly '*Lahng*-spil').
Langue d'oc. Long(er) dok.
Langue d'oïl. Long(er) du(r)-ee.
Languemente. Lan-gway-*men*-tay.
Languendo. Lan-*gwen*-doh.
Languente. Lan-*gwen*-tay.
Langueur. Long-gur.
Languidamente. Lan-gwee-dam-*en*-tay.
Languido. *Lan*-gwee-doh.
Languissant. Lo(ng)-gee⁸-so(ng).
Languore. Lan-goo-*aw*-ray.
Lanner. *Lan*-err.
Lanzentanz. *Lants*-en-tants.
Laparra. Lap-arr-a⁵.
La Passione. Lap-ass-ee-*oh*-nay.
La Perle du Brésil. Lap-airrl-dee² Bray-zeel.
La Poule. Lap-ool.
La Prise de Troye. Lap-reez de(r) Trwah.
La Rappresentazione dell' Anima e del Corpo. La⁵ Rap-rez-en-tat-see-*oh*-nay del *Ahn*-ee-ma⁵ ay del *Cawrr*-poh.
Largamente. Larrg-am-*en*-tay.
Large (Fr.). Lahrrzj³.
Largement. Lahrrzj³-e(r)-mo(ng).
Largeur. Lahrrzj³-urr.
Larghetto. Larrg⁵-*et*-toh.
Larghezza. Larrg⁵-*ets*-sa.
Largo. *Larr*⁵-goh.
Largo di molto. Larr⁵-goh dee *mohl*-toh.
La Roxolane. Larr-ox-oh-lan.

Larsson. *Lahrrss*-on.
Lascelles. *Lass*-elz.
Lasciare. Lash-*yah*-ray.
Lasciate. Lash-*yah*-tay.
La Sonnambula. Lass-on-*am*-boo-la⁵.
Lassen. *Lass*-en.
Lassú. *Losh*-oo.
Lassus. *Lass*-us.
László. Lahss-loh (equal stress on both syllables).
La Traviata. Lat-rav-ee-*ah*-ta⁵.
L'Attaque du Moulin. Lat-tak dee² moo-la(ng).
Laub. Lowp⁴.
Laube. Lowb⁴-e(r).
Lauber. Lowb⁴-err.
Laud (Eng.). Lawd.
Laúd (Sp.). *Lah*-ood (almost as Eng. *Loud*).
Laudisti. Lowd⁴-*iss*-tee.
Laudon (Ger.). Lowd⁴-on.
Laufwerk. *Lowf*⁴-vairrk.
L'Auguste. Lohg-eest³.
Laut. Lowt⁴.
Laute. Lowt⁴-e(r).
Lautenmacher. Low⁴-ten-mak¹-err.
Lavallée. Lav-al-ay.
La Vida Breve. Lav-*ee*-da⁵ *Bray*-vay.
La Vita Nuova. Lav-*ee*-ta⁵ Noo-*aw*-va⁵.
Lavoix. Lah-vwah.
Lavolta (It.). Lav-*ol*-ta⁵.
Lavolte (Fr.). Lav-olt.
La Wally. Lav-al-lee.
Lazare. Laz-ahrr.
Le (Fr.). Le(r).
Le (It.). Lay.
Lebendig. Leb-*en*-dish⁶.
Lebendiger. Leb-*en*-dig-err.
Lebhaft. *Laib*-haft.
Lebhafter. *Laib*-haft-err.
Lebhaftigkeit. *Laib*-haf-tish⁶-kite.
Lecail. Le(r)-kah-ee.
Le Calife de Bagdad. Le(r) Kal⁵-eef-de(r) Bag-dad.
Lechantre. Le(r)-sho(ng)trr.
Lechner. *Lek*¹-ner.
Leclair. Le(r)-clairr.
Lecocq. Le(r)-kok.
Le Couppey. Le(r) Coo-pay.
Leer (Ger.). Layrr.
Leere. *Lay*-re(r).
Lefébure-Wély. Le(r)-fay-beer³-Vay-lee.
Lefebvre. Le(r)-fevrr (but some Fr. people sound the 'b').

---

6. The **ish** is really anywhere between that sound and 'ik' (varying in different parts of Germany). **7. th** as in *thin*. **8. g** as in *go*.

Lefeuillet. Le(r)-fu(r)-yay.
Legabile. Leg-*ab*-ee-lay.
Legando. Leg-*an*-doh.
Legatissimo. Leg-at-*eess*-see-moh.
Legato. Leg-*ah*-toh.
Legatura. Leg-at-*oo*-ra⁵.
Léger. Lay-zjay³.
Légère. Lay-zjairr⁵.
Leggenda Sinfonica. Led-jen-da⁵ Seen-*fon*-ee-ca⁵.
Leggeramente. Led-jairr-am-*en*-tay.
Leggerezza. Led-jairr-*ets*-sa⁵.
Leggiadramente. Lej-yad-ram-*en*-tay.
Leggiadro. Lej-*yah*-droh.
Leggieramente. Lej-yairr-am-*en*-tay.
Leggiere. Lej-*yay*-ray.
Leggierezza. Lej-yairr-*ets*-sa⁵.
Leggierissimo. Lej-yairr-*eess*-see-moh.
Leggiero. Lej-*yay*-roh.
Leggio. Lej-*ee*-oh.
Leginska. Leg-*inz*-ka⁵.
Legno. Layn-yoh.
Lehar. Lay-harr.
Leibowitz. Lye-boh-vits.
Leicht. Lykt¹.
Leichtfertig. Lykt¹-fairr-tish⁶.
Leichtigkeit. Lykt¹-ish⁶-kite.
Leid. Lite.
Leidenschaft. Ly-den-shaft.
Leidenschaftlich. Ly-den-shaft-lik¹.
Leifs. Layfs.
Leise. Ly-ze(r).
Leisten. Ly-sten.
Leistung. Ly-stoong.
Leitgebisch. Lyte-gay-bish.
Leitmotiv. Lite-moh-teef.
Lejeune. Le(r)-zju(r)n³.
Le Jongleur de Notre Dame. Le(r) Zjo(ng)³-glurr de(r) Notrr-e(r) Dam.
Lekeu. Le(r)-ku(r).
L'Elisir d'Amore. Lel-ee-*zeer* dam-*oh*-ray.
Lemare (Eng.). Lem-*air*.
Lemmens. *Lem*-enss.
Lene. Lay-nay.
Lenezza. Lay-*net*-sa⁵.
Leno. Lay-noh.
Lent. Lo(ng).
Lentamente. Lent-am-*en*-tay.
Lentando. Len-*tan*-doh.
Lentato. Len-*tah*-toh.
Lentement. Lo(ng)-te-(r)-mo(ng).
Lenteur. Lo(ng)-turr.
Lentezza. Len-*tet*-sa⁵.
Lentissimo. Len-*teess*-see-moh.

Lento. *Len*-toh.
Le nuove musiche. Lay noo-*aw*-vay moo-see-kay.
Léo (Fr.). Lay-oh.
Leo. (Ger.). Lay-oh.
Léon (Fr.). Lay-o(ng).
Léonard. Lay-on-ahrr.
Leonardo. Lay-oh-*nahrr*-doh.
Leoncavallo. Lay-on-cav-*al*-loh.
Leonid. Lay-oh-*need*.
Léonin. Lay-oh-na(ng).
Léopold. Lay-op-old.
Le Pardon de Ploërmel. Lep-ahrr-do(ng) de(r) Ploh-airr-mel.
Leporello. Lep-oh-*rel*-loh.
Le Postillon de Longjumeau. Le(r) Posst-ee-yo(ng) de(r) Long-zjee³, ²-moh.
Le Prophète. Lep-rof-et.
Lerchenquartett. *Lairr*-ken¹-kvarr⁵-tet.
Le Roi d'Ys. Le(r) Rwah deess.
Le Rond. Le(r) Ro(ng).
Le Rossignol. Le(r) Ross-een-yol.
Leroux. Le(r)-roo.
Le Roy. Le(r) Rwah.
Les (Fr.). Lay.
Leschetizky. Lesh-et-*eet*-skee.
Les pêcheurs de perles. Lay pay-shurr de(r) pairll.
Lesto. *Less*-toh.
Les Troyens à Carthage. Lay Trwoy-ya(ng)-za⁵ Cahrrt-azj³.
Lesueur. Le(r)-see²-yurr.
Lesur. Le(r)-seer².
Letzt. Letst.
Levalto. Lay-*val*-toh.
Levare. Lay-*vah*-ray.
Levate. Lay-*vah*-tay.
Levati. Lay-*vah*-tee.
Levato. Lay-*vah*-toh.
Levezza. Lay-*vets*-sa⁵.
Levi. *Lay*-vee.
Le Villi. Lay *Veel*-lee.
Lewandowski (Ger.). Lay-van-*dov*-skee.
Ley (Eng.). Lee.
Lezginka. Lez-*gin*⁵-kah.
L'homme armé. Lom ahrr⁵-may.
Liadof. Lee-*ah*-doff.
Liapunof. Lee-ap-oon-*off*.
Libertà. Lee-bairr-*tah*.
Libre (Fr.). Leebrr.
Librement. Lee-bre(r)-mo(ng).
Libretto. Lee-*bret*-toh.
Licenza. Lee-*chent*-sa⁵.
Lichtenthal. *Leek*¹-ten-tahl.
Lie, Sigurd. *See*-geerr², ⁸ Lee.
Liebe. *Lee*-be(r).

Liebesgeige. *Leeb*-ess-gy⁸-gu(r).
Liebestraum. *Lee*-bess-trowm⁸.
Lieblich Flöte. Leep-lik¹ Fle(r)-te(r).
Lieblich Gedackt. Leeb-lik¹ Gu(r)-*dakt*¹.
Lied. Leet.
Liedchen. *Leet*-shen.
Liedekens. *Leed*-e(r)-kenz.
Lieder. *Leed*-err.
Liedercyklus. *Leed*-err-tsee²-clooss.
Liederkreis. *Leed*-err-krice.
Lieder ohne Worte. *Leed*-err ohn-e(r) *Vawrr*-te(r).
Liederreihe. *Leed*-err-ry-e(r).
Liedertafel. *Leed*-err-tah-fel.
Liedlein. *Leet*-line.
Lied ohne Worte. Leet ohn-e(r) *Vawrr*-te(r).
Lietezza. Lee-ay-*tets*-sa⁵.
Lietissimo. Lee-ay-*teess*-see-moh.
Lieto. Lee-*ay*-toh.
Lieve. Lee-*ay*-vay.
Lievemente. Lee-ay-vay-*men*-tay.
Lievezza. Lee-ay-*vets*-sa⁵.
Lifar. Lee-*fahrr*.
Lili. *Lee*-lee.
L'Impériale. La(ng)-pay-ree-al.
Lind. Leend.
Lindberg (Amer.). *Linnd*-burg.
Lindberg (Swed.). *Leend*-bairr(ee).
Lindeman (Norweg.). *Lin*-dem-an.
Lindorf. *Lin*-dawrrf.
Linz. Lints.
Lira. *Lee*-ra⁵.
Lira da braccio. *Lee*-rad-ab-*ratch*-oh.
Lira da gamba. *Lee*-rad-ag-am-ba⁵.
Lira moderna. *Lee*-ram-od-airr-na⁵.
Lirico. *Lee*-ree-coh.
Lirone. Lee-*roh*-nay.
Lirone perfetto. Lee-*roh*-nay pairr-*fet*-toh.
Liscia. *Leesh*-ya⁵.
Liscio. *Leesh*-yoh.
Listenius. Liss-*tay*-nee-ooss.
L'istesso tempo. Leess-*tess*-oh *tem*-poh.
Liszt. List.
Litolff. *Leet*-olf.
Liudmilla. Lew-*dmee*-lah ('ew' as in *dew*).
Liuto. *Lew*-toh ('ew' as in *dew*).
Livre. Leevrr.
Lob und Ehre. Lohp oont *Ay*-re(r).

---

1. k = 'ch' (cf. Scot. *loch*).   2. ee here really between 'ee' and 'oo' (cf. Scot. *puir*).
3. zj like 's' in *pleasure*.   4. ow as in *cow*.   5. a as in *lad*.

Lobwasser. *Lohp*-vass-err.
Locatelli. Loc-at-*el*-lee.
Loco. *Law*-coh.
Lodoletta. Lod-oh-*let*-ta⁵.
Lœffler. Le(r)f-lairr.
Lœillet. Lu(r)-yay.
Loeschen. *Le(r)*-shen.
Loeschhorn (*Le(r)sh*-horrn.
Loewe. *Le(r)*-ve(r).
Loewenberg. *Le(r)*-ven-bairg.
Loge (Ger.). *Loh*-gu(r).
Logier. Loh-*jeer*.
Lohengrin. *Loh*-en-green.
Loin (Fr.). Lwa(ng).
Lointain. Lwa(ng)-ta(ng).
Longo. *Long*-go.
Lönnrot. *Le(r)n*-roht.
Löns. Le(r)nss.
Lontananza. Lon-tan-*ant*-sa.⁵.
Lontano. Lon-*tah*-noh.
Lopatnikof. Lop-*aht*-nee-koff.
Lope de Vega. *Loh*-pay day
  Vay-gah.
Lopez. *Loh*-peth⁷.
Lopokova. Lop-oh-*hoh*-va⁵ ('h'
  sound, not 'k').
L'Oracolo. Lorr-*ac*-oh-loh.
Lorenzo. Loh-*rent*-soh.
Loretto. Law-*ret*-toh.

Lortzing. *Lort*-sing.
Los (Ger.). Lohss.
Löschhorn. *Le(r)sh*-horrn.
Louis (Fr.). Loo-ee.
Loulié. Lool-yay.
Lourd. Loorr.
Lourde. Loorrd.
Loure. Loorr.
Louré. Loo-ray.
Lourié. Loor-yay.
Luca. Loo-ka⁵.
Lucia di Lammermoor. Loo-
  chee-a⁵ dee Lam-merr-*moorr*.
Luciano. Loo-*chah*-noh.
Lucien. Lee²-see-an(g).
Lucrezia Borgia. Loo-*crayt*-
  see-a⁶ *Bawrr*-jee-a⁵.
Ludmilla (Rum.). Lew-*dmee*-
  lah ('ew' as in *dew*).
Ludovico. Lood-oh-*vee*-coh.
Ludwig. *Lood*-vish⁶.
Luening. *Lee²*-ning.
Luftig. *Loof*-tish⁶.
Lugubre (Fr.). Leeg²-eebrr².
Lugubre (It.). *Loo*-goo-bray.
Luigi. Loo-*ee*-jee.
Luigini. Loo-ee-*jee*-nee.
Luis. Loo-*eess*.

Lulli, Lully (Fr.). Lee²-lee
  (original Ital. '*Loo*-lee').
Lumineux. Lee²-mee-nu(r).
Lunga. *Loon*-ga⁵.
Lunga pausa. *Loon*-ga⁵ *pow*⁴-za⁶.
Lungo. *Loon*-goh.
Luogo. Loo-*oh*-goh.
Lur. Loor.
Lusingando. Looz-een-*gan*-doh.
Lustig. *Looss*-tish⁶.
Lustigkeit. *Looss*-tish⁶-kite.
Lustspiel. *Loosst*-shpeel.
Luth. Leet².
Luther. Loo-terr (but in Eng.
  generally pron. *Looth*⁷-er).
Lutherie. Leet²-err-ee.
Luthier. Leet²-yay.
Lutina. Loo-*tee*-na⁶.
Lutto. *Loot*-toh.
Luttuoso. Loot-too-*oh*-zoh.
Lvof. Lvoff.
Lyra. *Lee*-ra⁵.
Lyrique. Lee-reek.
Lyrisch. *Lee*-rish.
Lyrisches Stück. *Lee*-rish-ess
  Steek².
Lyrische Stücke. *Lee*-rish-e(r)
  Steek²-e(r).

M

Ma (It.). Ma⁵.
Maas. Mahs.
Macabre. Mak-abrr.
Macchina a venti. *Mak*-kee-
  na⁵ a⁵ *ven*-tee.
MacDowell. Mak-*Dow*⁴-el.
Machaut. Mash-oh.
Machault. Mash-oh.
Machicotage. Mash-ee-cot-azj³.
Machine à vent. Mash-een-av-
  o(ng).
Mächtig. *Mek*¹-tish⁶.
Maclean. Mak-*lane*.
Macleod. Mak-*lowd*⁴.
Maçon. Mass-o(ng).
Maconchy. Mak-*on*-kee.
Madame Crysanthème. Mad-
  am Kree-zo(ng)-tem.
Madame Sans-Gêne. Mad-am
  So(ng)-Zjen³.

Madelon. Mad-e(r)-lo(ng).
Madriale. Mad-ree-*ah*-lay.
Madrigali Spirituali. Mad-
  ree-*gah*-lee Spee-ree-too-*ah*-
  lee.
Madrileña. Mad-ree-*layn*-ya⁶.
Madrilène. Mad-ree-len.
Maelzel. *Melt*-sel.
Maestà. Ma⁵-ess-*ta*⁵.
Maestade. Ma⁵-ess-*tah*-day.
Maestevole. Ma⁵-ess-*tay*-voh-
  lay.
Maestevolemente. Ma⁵-ess-
  tay-vol-*men*-tay.
Maestosamente. Ma⁵-ess-toh-
  zam-*en*-tay.
Maestoso. Ma⁵-ess-*toh*-zoh.
Maestrale. Ma⁵-ess-*trah*-lay.
Maestro. Ma⁵-*ess*-troh.
Magdalena. Mak-dal-*ay*-nah.

Mager. *Mah*-ger⁸.
Maggiolata. Maj-jee-oh-*lah*-ta⁵.
Maggiore. Maj-*yaw*-ray.
Magnard. Man-yahrr.
Magno (It.). *Mahn*-yoh.
Magyar. *Mawd*-gyohrr³ (latter
  syll. almost like Eng. *your* with
  a hard 'g' before it).
Mahillon. Mah-eel-yo(ng).
Mahler. *Mah*-lerr.
Maillart. My-yarr⁵.
Mailloche. My-yosh.
Maillot. My-yoh.
Main (Fr.). Ma(ng).
Main droite. Ma(ng) drwaht.
Main gauche. Ma(ng) gohsh.
Mains. Man(g).
Mainwaring. *Man*-er-ring.
Mainzer. Originally '*Mine*-tserr',
  but in Brit. pron. '*Main*-zer'.

---

6. The **ish** is really anywhere between that sound and 'ik' (varying in different parts of Germany).
7. **th** as in *thin*. 8. **g** as in *go*.

Maïs. May.

Maître de Bataille. Metrr de(r) Ba⁵-ty(er).

Maîtres du goût de chant. Metrr dee² goo de(r) sho(ng).

Maîtrise. Met-reez.

Majestätisch. Mah-yess-*tay*-tish.

Majestueusement. Mazj⁵, ³-est-ee²-u(r)z-e(r)-mo(ng).

Majestueux. Mazj⁵, ³-est-ee²-u(r).

Majeur. Mazj⁵, ²-ur.

Mal (Ger.). Mahl.

Malagueña. Mal-ag-*ayn*-ya⁵.

Malbrouck s'en va-t-en guerre. Mal-brook so(ng) vat-o(ng) gairr-e(r).

Malder. *Mal*⁵-derr.

Maldere. *Mal*-derr-e(r).

Maleingreau. Mal-a(ng)-groh.

Malibran (Fr.). Mal-ee-bro(ng).

Malibran (Span.). Mahl-ee-*bran*.

Malinconia. Mal-een-coh-*nee*-ya⁵.

Malinconicamente. Mal-een-con-ee-cam-*en*-tay.

Malinconico. Mal-een-*coh*-nee-coh.

Malinconioso. Mal-een-coh-nee-*oh*-zoh.

Malipiero. Mal-eep-ee-*ay*-roh.

Malizia. Mal-*eet*-see-a⁵.

Mallarmé. Mal-lahrr-may.

Malling. *Mal*⁵-ing.

Man' (It.). Man.

Mancando. Man-*can*-doh.

Mancante. Man-*cant*-ay.

Mancanza. Man-*cant*-sa⁵.

Manchega. Man-*chay*-ga⁵.

Mandora. Man-*daw*-rah.

Mandriale. Man-dree-*ah*-lay.

Mandyczewski. Man-dee²-*cheff*-ski ('i' as in *it*).

Manécanterie. Man-ay-co(ng)-terr-ee.

Manen. Man-*en*.

Manet. Man-ay.

Manfredini. Man-fred-*ee*-nee.

Mangeot. Mo(ng)-zjoh².

Mangiagalli. Man-jag-*al*-lee.

Mani. *Mah*-nee.

Manica. *Man*-ee-ca⁵.

Manieren. Man-*eerr*-en.

Männer. *Men*-err.

Männerchor. *Men*-err-kohrr.

Männergesangverein. *Men*-err-gu(r)-*zang*-fairr-*ine*.

Männerstimmen. *Men*-nerr-shtim-en.

Mano. *Mah*-noh.

Mano destra. *Mah*-noh *dess*-tra⁵.

Manon Lescaut. Man-o(ng) Less-coh.

Mano sinistra. *Mah*-noh see-*neess*-tra⁵.

Manrico. Man-*ree*-coh.

Manualkoppel. Man-oo-*ahl*-kop-pel.

Manuel. Man-oo-*el*.

Maraca. Mah-*rah*-ca⁵.

Marais. Ma⁵-ray.

Marcando. Mahrr-*can*-doh.

Marcantonio. Mahrr-can-*toh*-nee-oh.

Marcato. Mahrr-*caht*-oh.

Marcel. Marr⁵-sell.

Marcellina. Mahrr-chel-*lee*-nah.

Marcello. Mahrr-*chel*-loh.

Marchand. Marr⁵-sho(ng).

Marche. Marsh⁵.

Marche aux flambeaux. Marrsh⁵ oh flo(ng)-boh.

Marche funèbre. Marrsh⁵ fee²-nebrr.

Märchen. *Mairr*-shen.

Marcia. *Mahrr*-cha⁵.

Marciale. Mahrr-*chah*-lay.

Marconi. Mahr-*coh*-nee.

Marenzio. Ma⁵-*rent*-see-oh.

Mareppe. Ma⁵-rep.

Maresch. Mahrr-*esh*.

Mariana. Ma⁵-ree-*ahn*-a⁵.

Maria Teresa (Eng.). Ma⁵-*ree*-a⁵ Tairr-ay-za⁵.

Maria Teresia (Ger.). Mah-*ree*-ah Tay-*ray*-zee-ah.

Mariazeller Messe. Mah-*ree*-ah-*tsel*-err Mess-e(r).

Marie. Marr⁵-ee.

Marimba. Marr⁵-*eem*-ba⁵.

Marimberos. Marr⁵-eem-*bay*-rohss.

Marin. Marr⁵-a(ng).

Marina. Marr⁵-*een*-a⁵.

Marinetti. Ma⁵-ree-*net*-tee.

Marinuzzi. Ma⁵-ree-*noots*-see.

Mario. *Mah*-ree-oh.

Maritana. Ma⁵-ree-*tah*-na⁵.

Marius (Fr.). Marr⁵-yooss.

Markevich. Marrk⁵-*ev*-itch.

Markiert. Marr⁵-*keerrt*.

Markig. *Marr*⁵-kish⁶.

Markneukirchen. *Marrk*⁵-noy-*keerr*-shen.

Marot. Marr⁵-oh.

Marouf, Savetier du Caire. Marr⁵-oof, Savt-yay dee² Cairr.

Marpurg. *Marr*-poorg.

Marqué. Marr⁵-kay.

Marsch. Marrsh⁵.

Marschartig. *Marrsh*⁵-arr⁵-tish⁶.

Marschmässig. *Marrsh*⁵-may-sish⁶.

Marschner. *Marrsh*⁵-nerr.

Marseillaise. Marr⁵-say-yez.

Marsick. Marr⁵-seek.

Marteau. Marr⁵-toh.

Martelé. Marr⁵-tel-ay.

Martelé du talon. Marr⁵-tel-ay dee² tal-o(ng).

Martellando. Marr⁵-tel-*lan*-doh.

Martellato. Marr⁵-tel-*lah*-toh.

Martenot. Marr⁵-te(r)-noh.

Martha (Ger.). Marr⁵-ta⁵.

Martin (Fr.). Marr⁵-ta(ng).

Martini il Tedesco. Mahrr-*tee*-nee eel Ted-*ess*-coh.

Martinů (Czech). Mhawrr-tee-noo.

Martín y Soler. Marr⁵-*teen* ee Soh-*lairr*.

Martucci. Mahrr-*toot*-shee.

Marty. Marr⁵-tee.

Marziale. Mahrrt-see-*ah*-lay.

Masaniello. Maz-an-*yel*-loh.

Mascagni. Mass-*cahn*-yee.

Mascarade. Mass-karr⁵-ad.

Maschinenpauken. Mash-ee-nen-*pow*⁴-ken.

Masetto. Maz-*et*-toh.

Maskenspiel. *Mask*-en-shpeel.

Masque. Mask.

Massarani. Mass-sa⁵-*rah*-nee.

Massé. Mass-ay.

Massenet. Mass-en-ay.

Mässig. *Mayss*-ish⁶.

Mässiger. *Mayss*-ig-err.

Massimo. *Mass*-see-moh.

Massine. *Mass*-een.

Massinger. *Mass*-ing-er.

Matassins. Mat-ass⁵-a(ng).

Mathieu. Mat-yu(r).

Matin. Mat-a(ng).

Matrimonio segreto, Il. Eel Mat-ree-*moh*-nee-oh say-*gray*-toh.

Mattachins. Mat-ash-a(ng).

Mattei. Mat-*tay*-ee.

Matteis. Mat-*tay*-eess.

Matthay. *Mat*-ay.

Mattheson. *Mat*-te(r)-son.

Matthys. *Mat*-teess.

Mattinata. Mat-teen-*ah*-ta⁵.

Maultrommel. *Mowl*⁴-trom-el.

Mauresco (It., Span.). Mah-oo-*ress*-coh.

Mauresque. Moh-resk.

Mauri. *Mah*-oo-ree.

Maurice (Fr.). Moh-reess.

Mavourneen. Mav-*oor*-neen.

Mavra. *Mahv*-ra⁵.

Maxima. *Mak*-see-ma⁵.

Maxixe. *Match*-eesh.

Mayerowitsch. My-*roh*-vitch.

Mayrhofer. *Myre*-hoh-fer.

---

1. k = 'ch' (cf. Scot. *loch*).   **2. ee** here really between 'ee' and 'oo' (cf. Scot. *puir*).   **3. zj** like 's' in *pleasure*.   **4. ow** as in *cow*.   **5. a** as in *lad*.

Mayseder. My-*zay*-derr.
Mazarin. Maz-arr[5]-a(ng).
Mazas. Maz-ass.
Mazér. Mass-*ayrr*.
Mazerska. Mass-*ayrrss*-ka[5].
Mazurka. Maz-*oorr*-ka[5].
Mazzinghi. Mat-*zeen*-gee[8].
Mazzocchi. Mat-*zok*-kee.
Médée. Med-ay.
Medesimo movimento. Med-*ayz*-ee-moh moh-vee-*men*-toh.
Medtner. *Met*-nerr.
Mefistofele. Mef-eess-*tof*-ay-lay.
Mehr. Mayrr.
Mehrere. *Mayrr*-err-e(r).
Mehrstimmig. *Mayrr*-shtim-ish[6].
Méhul. May-eel[2].
Meinert. *My*[4]-nerrt.
Meiningen. *My*-ning-en.
Meissen. *Mice*-en.
Meistersinger von Nürnberg, Die. Dee *My*-sterr-zing-err fon *Neern*[2]-bairrk.
Melartin. Mel-ahrr-*teen*.
Mélisande. May-lee-zond.
Melismata. Mel-*iz*-*mah*-ta[5].
Melodia. Mel-oh-*dee*-ah.
Mélopée. *May*-loh-pay.
Melot (Ger.). *May*-lot.
Même. Mem.
Mendel. *Men*-del.
Mendelssohn. *Men*-delss-zohn.
Ménestrandie. May-nest-trond-ee.
Ménestrel. May-nest-rel.
Ménestrel de Bouche. May-nest-rel de(r) Boosh.
Ménestrel de Guerre. May-nest-rel de(r) Gairr.
Ménestrier. May-nest-ree-ay.
Mengelberg. *Meng*-el-bairrg.
Menke. *Menk*-e(r).
Meno (It.). *May*-noh.
Menuet (Fr.). Me(r)-nee[2]-ay.
Mercadante. Mairr-cad-*an*-tay.
Mercure de France. Mairr-keerr[2] de(r) Fro(ng)ss.
Merikanto. Merr-ee-*can*-toh.
Mérimée. May-ree-may.
Merkel. *Mairr*-kel.
Merkur. Mairr-*koorr*.
Merline. Mairr-*leen*.
Mersenne. Mairr-sen.
Merulo. May-*roo*-loh.
Messa di voce. *Mess*-sa[5] dee *voh*-chay.
Messager. Mess-ah-zjay[3].
Messe des morts. Mess day mawrr.
Messe du premier ton. Mess dee[2] prem-yay to(ng).

Messiaen. Mess-yah-a(ng).
Messing. *Mess*-ing.
Messinginstrumente. *Mess*-ing-in-stroo-*men*-te(r).
Mestizia. Mess-*teet*-zee-a[5].
Mesto. *Mess*-toh.
Mesure. Mez-eer[2].
Metà. May-*tah*.
Metastasio. Met-az-*tah*-zee-oh.
Mettenleiter. *Met*-en-lye-terr.
Mettere. *Met*-tair-ray.
Mettre. Mettrr.
Meyer. *My*-err.
Meyerbeer. *My*-err-bayrr.
Mezza. *Med*-za[5].
Mezzavoce. Med-za[5]- *voh*-chay.
Mezzo. *Med*-zoh.
Mezzo carattere. *Med*-zoh ca[5]-*rat*-tay-ray.
Mezzo forte. *Med*-zoh *fawrr*-tay.
Mezzo piano. *Med*-zoh pee-*ah*-noh.
Mezzo soprano. *Med*-zoh-sop-*rah*-noh.
Mezzo staccato. *Med*-zoh stac-*cah*-toh.
Mi (Fr., It.). Mee.
Miaskovsky. Mee-ass[5]-*koff*-skee(yer).
Michel. Mee-shel.
Mickiewicz. Mits-kee-*ay*-veetch.
Middelschulte. *Mid*-el-shool-te(r).
Midi. Mee-dee.
Miessner. *Meess*-nerr.
Mignon. Meen-yo(ng).
Migot. Mee-goh.
Mihalovici. Mee-kah[1]-*loh*-veetch (the final 'i' of the name not pron.).
Milán (Spanish name). Mee-*lan*.
Milanuzzi. Mee-lan-*oots*-see.
Milhaud. Mee-yoh.
Milieu. Meel-ye(r).
Milieu de l'archet. Meel-ye(r) de(r) lahrr[5]-shay.
Militaire. Mee-lee-tairr.
Militär. Mee-lee-*tairr*.
Militare. Mee-le-*tah*-ray.
Militärtrommel. Mee-lee-*tairr*-trom-el.
Millöcker. *Mill*-u(r)k-err.
Milophone. *Mee*-loh-fohn.
Milordine. Mee-lorr-deen.
Mime (Eng.). Mym ('y' as in *my*).
Mime. (Ger.). *Mee*-me(r).
Mimi. *Mee*-mee.
Mimodrama. *Mym*-oh-drah-ma[5] ('y' as in *my*).

Minaccevole. Mee-nat-*chay*-voh-lay.
Minaccevolmente. Mee-nat-chay-vol-*men*-tay.
Minacciando. Mee-nat-*chan*-doh.
Minacciosamente. Mee-nat-choh-zam-*en*-tay.
Minaccioso. Mee-nat-*choh*-zoh.
Minder (Ger.). *Min*-derr.
Mineur. Mee-nurr.
Minima. *Mee*-nee-ma[5].
Minne. *Min*-ne(r).
Minnesinger. *Min*-e(r)-zing-err.
Minore. Mee-*naw*-ray.
Minuetto. Mee-noo-*et*-toh.
Mireille. Mee-ray(er).
Mirette. Mee-ret.
Mirliton. Meerr-lee-to(ng).
Mise. Meez.
Mise de voix. Meez de(r) vwah.
Missail. Miss-ah-*eel*.
Misteriosamente. Meess-tay-ree-oh-zam-*en*-tay.
Misterioso. Meess-tay-ree-*oh*-zoh.
Mistero. Meess-*tay*-roh.
Mistico. *Meess*-tee-coh.
Misura. Mee-*zoo*-ra[5].
Misurato. Mee-zoo-*rah*-toh.
Mit. Mit.
Mit Andacht. Mit *An*-dakt[1].
Mit breitem Strich, Mit *bry*-tem *Shtrik*[1].
Mit Dämpfer. Mit *Demp*-ferr.
Mit Dämpfern. Mit *Demp*-ferrn.
Mit Dämpfern und stark Anblasen. Mit *Demp*-ferrn oont shtarrk *An*-blah-zen.
Mitleidig. *Mit*-lye-dish[6].
Mitrofan. *Meet*-roh-fan[5].
Mitte. *Mit*-e(r).
Mittenwald. *Mit*-en-valt[5].
Mixolydian. Mix-oh-*lid*-ee-an.
Mizler. *Mits*-lerr.
Mjöen. M'ye(r)n.
Moberg (Swed.). *Mohrr*-bairr-(ee).
Modena. *Mod*-ay-na[5].
Moderatamente. Mod-ay-raht-tam-*en*-tay.
Moderato. Mod-ay-*rah*-toh.
Modéré. Mod-ay-ray.
Modérément. Mod-ay-ray-mo(ng).
Modinha (Portuguese). Mod-*een*-ya[5].
Modo. *Maw*-doh.
Moeran. *More*-an.
Möglich. *Me*(r)k-lik[1].

---

6. The **ish** is really anywhere between that sound and 'ik' (varying in different parts of Germany).
7. **th** as in *thin*.   8. **g** as in *go*.

Möglichst. *Me(r)k*-likst[1].
Moins. Mwah(ng).
Moitié. Mwaht-yay.
Molière. Mol-yairr.
Molique. Mol-eek.
Moll. Mol.
Molle (It.). *Mol*-lay.
Mollemente. Mol-lay-*men*-tay.
Moll Ton. Mol Tohn.
Moll Tonart. Mol *Tohn*-arrt.
Moltissimo. Mol-*tees*-see-moh.
Molto. *Mol*-toh.
Moment musical. Mom-o(ng) mee[2]-zee-kal.
Mompou. Mo-(ng)-poo.
Mona Lisa. *Mon*-a[5] *Lee*-za[5].
Mondo della Luna, Il. Eel *Mon*-doh *del*-la[5] *Loo*-na[5].
Mondonville. Mo(ng)-do(ng)-veel.
Monet. Mon-ay.
Moniuszko. Mon-*yoosh*-koh.
Monnet. Mon-nay.
Monodrama. *Mon*-oh-drah-ma[5].
Monostatos. Mon-os-*tah*-toss.
Mons, Philippe de. Fee-leep de(r) Mo(ng).
Monsieur Beaucaire. Me(r)ss-yur Boh-kairr.
Monsigny. Mo(ng)-seen-yee.
Monte (It.). *Mon*-tay.
Montéclair. Mo(ng)t-ay-clairr.
Montemezzi. Mon-tay-*med*-zee.
Monter. Mo(ng)-tay.
Montessori. Mon-tess-*saw*-ree.
Monteverdi. Mon-tay-*vairr*-dee.
Montez. Mo(ng)-tay.
Montmartre. Mo(ng)-mahtrr.
Montre. Mo(ng)trr.
Montrésor. Mo(ng)-tray-zorr.
Morales. Moh-*rah*-less.
Morasco. Morr-*ass*-coh.
Morbidezza. Morr-bee-*det*-za[5].
Morbido. *Morr*-bee-doh.
Morceau. Mawrr-soh.
Morceau symphonique. Mawrr-soh sa(ng)-fon-eek.
Morceaux. Mawrr-soh.
Moreau. Morr-oh.
Morelli. Morr-*el*-lee.
Morendo. Morr-*en*-doh.
Moreninha. Morr-en-*een*-ya[5].
Moresco. Morr-*ess*-coh.
Morgenblätter. *Morrg*-en-blet-terr.

Morgenlied. *Morrg*-en-leet.
Morhange. Mawrr-o(ng)zj[3].
Morisca. Morr-*ecss*-ca[5].
Morisco. Morr-*eess*-coh.
Moritz. *Moh*-rits.
Mormorando. Morr-maw-*ran*-doh.
Mormorante. Morr-maw-*ran*-tay.
Mormorevole. Morr-maw-*ray*-vol-ay.
Mormorosa. Morr-maw-*roh*-za[5].
Mormoroso. Morr-maw-*roh*-zoh.
Mortari. Morr-*tah*-ree.
Moscheles. *Mosh*-el-ess.
Mosè in Egitto. Moh-*zay* in Edj-*ee*-toh.
Mosonyi. *Mosh*-ohn-yee.
Mosso. *Moss*-soh.
Mossolof. *Moss*-oh-loff.
Moszkowski. Moss-*kov*-skee.
Motet. Moh-*tet*.
Motif. Moh-*teef*.
Motiv. Moh-*teef*.
Motive. (Eng.). Moh-tiv.
Motivo. Moh-*tee*-voh.
Moto. *Maw*-toh.
Moto perpetuo. *Maw*-toh pairr-*pet*-oo-oh.
Moto precedente. *Maw*-toh pray-chay-*den*-tay.
Motteggiando. Mot-tej-*yan*-doh.
Mottl. *Mot*-t'l.
Mouret. Moo-ray.
Moussorgsky. Moos-*awrrg*-skee(yer).
Mouton. Moo-to(ng).
Mouvement. Moov-mo(ng).
Mouvementé. Moov-mo(ng)-tay.
Mouvement perpétuel. Moov-mo(ng) pairr-pay-tee[2]-el.
Movente. Moh-*ven*-tay.
Movimento. Mov-ee-*men*-toh.
Mozart. *Mohts*-arrt.
Müde. *Mee*[2]-de(r).
Mueller. *Mee*[2]-lerr.
Mühelos. *Mee*[2]-e(r)-lohss.
Mühlfeld. *Meel*[2]-felt.
Muiñeira. Moo-een-*yay*-ra[5].
Mulet. Mee[2]-lay.
Müller. *Mee*[2]-lerr.
Mundharmonica. *Moont*-harr-*moh*-nee-kah.
Muñeira. Moon-*yay*-ra[5].
Munter. Moon-terr.

Murciana (Sp.). Moorrth[7]-*yah*-na[5].
Muris, Johannes de. Yoh-*han*-ess day *Moo*-ris.
Murisiano. Moo-reez-*yah*-noh.
Murmelnd. *Moorr*-melnt.
Musetta. Mooz-*et*-ta[5].
Musica alla Turca. *Moo*-zee-ca[5] *al*[5]-la[5] *Toorr*-ca[5].
Musica a programma. *Moo*-zee-ca[5] ah proh-*gram*-ma[5].
Musica colorata. *Moo*-zee-ca[5] col-aw-*rah*-ta[5].
Musica Enchiriadis. *Moo*-zee-ca[5] En-kee-ree-*ah*-deess.
Musica falsa. *Moo*-zee-ca[5] *fal*[5]-sa[5].
Musica figurata. *Moo*-zee-ca[5] fee-goo-*rah*-ta[5].
Musica getutscht. *Moo*-zee-ca[5] gu(r)-*tootsht*.
Musica parlante. *Moo*-zee-ca[5] pahrr-*lan*-tay.
Musica Transalpina. *Moo*-zee-ca[5] Tranz-al[5]-*pee*-na[5].
Musico. *Moo*-zee-coh.
Musikalische Quacksalber, Der. Dayrr Moo-zee-*kah*-lish-e(r) *Kwak*-zal-berr.
Musikfreunde. Moo-*zeek*-froynde(r).
Musiklexikon. Moo-*zeek*-lek-see-kon.
Musikwissenschaft. Moo-*zeek*-viss-en-shaft.
Musin. Mee[2]-za(ng).
Musique. Mee[2]-zeek.
Musique à la Turque. Mee[2]-zeek al[5]-la[5] Teerrk[2].
Musique à programme. Mee[2]-zeek ap-rog-ram.
Musique en couleurs. Mee[2]-zeek o(ng) coo-lurr.
Musique programmatique. Mee[2]-zeek prog-ram-at-eek.
Mussorgsky. Mooss-*awrrg*-skee(yer).
Mut. Moot.
Muta. *Moo*-ta[5].
Mutano. *Moo*-tah-noh.
Mutazione. Moo-tat-zee-*oh*-nay.
Muth. Moot.
Muthig. *Moo*-tish[6].
Mutig. *Moo*-tish[6].
Muzio. *Moots*-yoh.
Mysliviczek. Mee-zlee-*vee*-chek.
Mysteriös. Mee[2]-stairr-ee-*u(r)*ss.
Myvyrian. Muv-*ur*-ee-ahn.

---

1. k = 'ch' (cf. Scot. *loch*).   **2. ee** here really between 'ee' and 'oo' (cf. Scot. *puir*).
3. zj like 's' in *pleasure*.   **4. ow** as in *cow*.   **5. a** as in *lad*.

N

Nabimba. Nab-im-ba⁵.
Nabokof. Nab-*aw*-koff.
Nabucodonosor. Nab-ee²-cod-oh-*noz*-awrr.
Nacaires. Nac-airr.
Nach. Nahk¹.
Nach Belieben. Nahk¹ Be(r)-*lee*-ben.
Nachdruck. *Nahk*¹-drook.
Nachdrücklich. *Nahk*¹-dreek²-lik¹.
Nach Gefallen. Nahk¹ Gu(r)-*fal*⁵-en.
Nachgehend. *Nahk*¹-gay-hent.
Nachlassend. *Nahk*¹-lass-ent.
Nachschlag. *Nahk*¹-shlahg.
Nachspiel. *Nahk*¹-shpeel.
Nachtanz. *Nahk*¹-tants.
Nachthorn. *Nakt*¹-horrn.
Nachtmusik. *Nakt*¹-moo-*zeek*.
Nachtstück. *Nakt*¹-steek².
Nach und nach. Nahk¹ oont *nahk*¹.
Nach Wunsch. Nahk¹ Voonsh.
Nadia. Nad-ya⁵.
Nagel. *Nahg*-el.
Nagelgeige. *Nahg*-el-gy⁸-gu(r).
Nägeli. *Nayg*-el-ee.
Nähe. *Nay*-he(r).
Naïf. Na⁵-eef.
Naiv (Ger.). Na⁵-*eef*.
Naïve. Na⁵-eev.
Naïvement. Na⁵-eev-e(r)-mo(ng).
Najara. Nah-yah-rah.
Nämlich. *Naym*-lik¹.
Napolitaine. Nap-ol-ee-ten.
Napolitana. Nap-ol-ee-*tah*-na⁵.
Napravnik. Nap-*rav*-neek.
Narbaez. Narr-*bah*-eth⁷.
Nardini. Nahrr-*dee*-nee.
Narrante. Narr-*an*-tay.
Nasetto. Naz-*et*-toh.
Naso (It). *Nah*-zoh.
Naturale (It.). Nat-oo-*rah*-lay.
Naturhorn. Nat-*oorr*-horrn.
Natürlich. Nat-*eerr*²-lik¹.
Naturtöne. Na-*toor*-tu(r)-ne(r).
Naumann. *Now*⁴-man.
Naumberg. *Nowm*⁴-bairrg.
Nava. *Nah*-va⁵.
Navarraise, La. La⁵ Nav-arr-ez.
Ne (Fr.). Ne(r).
Nebdal. *Neb*-dahl.
Neben. *Naib*-en.

Nebenregister. *Naib*-en-rayg-iss-terr.
Nebensatz. *Nay*-ben-zatz.
Nebenstimmen. *Naib*-en-shtim-en.
Nebenthema. *Naib*-en-tay-mah.
Nebst. Naypst.
Neefe. *Nay*-fe(r).
Negli. *Nail*-yee.
Negligente. Neg-lee-*jen*-tav.
Negligentemente. Neg-lee-jen-tay-*men*-tay.
Negri. *Nay*-gree.
Nehmen. *Naim*-en.
Nei. *Nay*-ee.
Nel. Nel.
Nello. *Nel*-loh.
Nelsonmesse. *Nel*-son-mess-e(r).
Nenia (It.). *Nain*-ya⁵.
Ne . . . pas. Ne(r) . . . pa⁵.
Nepomuk. *Nay*-poh-mook.
Neri. *Nay*-ree.
Nernst. Nairrnst.
Nero. *Nay*-roh.
Nerone. Nay-*roh*-nay.
Nerveux. Nairr-vu(r).
Net (Fr.). Net.
Nettamente. Net-tam-*en*-tay.
Nette (Fr.). Net.
Nettement. Net-te(r)-mo(ng).
Netto. *Net*-toh.
Neues vom Tage. *Noy*-ess fom *Tahg*-e(r).
Neue Zeitschrift für Musik. *Noy*-e(r) *Tsite*-shrift feer² Moo-zeek.
Neuf. Nu(r)f.
Neukomm. *Noy*-kom.
Neum, Neume. Nume.
Neun. Noyn.
Neupert. *Noy*-perrt.
Neuvième. Nu(r)v-yem.
Neva. Nay-*va*⁵.
Nibelung. *Nee*-bel-oong.
Nibelungen. *Nee*-bel-oong-en.
Niccolò. Neek-kol-*oh*.
Nicene. *Ny*-seen ('y' as in *my*).
Nicht. Nikt¹.
Nicodé. Nee-cod-ay.
Nicolà. Nee-col-*a*⁵.
Nicolai. Nik-oh-*lah*-ee.
Nicolas (Fr.). Nee-col-a⁵.
Nicolau. Neek-oh-*low*⁴.
Niecks. Neeks.

Nieder. *Need*-err.
Niederdrücken. *Need*-err-dree²-ken.
Niedermayer. *Need*-err-my-err.
Niederschlag. *Need*-err-shlahk.
Niederstrich. *Need*-err-shtrik¹.
Niels (Dan.). Neelss.
Nielsen. *Neel*-sen.
Niemecz. Nee-*yem*-etss.
Niente. Nee-*en*-tay.
Nijinsky. Nezj³-*eenss*-ki ('i' as in *it*).
Nikisch. *Nik*-ish.
Nilsson. *Neelss*-on.
Nin-Culmell. Neen-Cool-*mel*.
Ninfali. *Neen*-fal⁵-ee.
Ninna-nanna. *Nee*-nan-*an*-a⁵.
Nin y Castellano. Neen-ee-Cass-tel-*yah*-noh.
Nobile. *Nob*-ee-lay.
Nobilmente. Nob-eel-*men*-tay.
Noch. Nok¹.
Noch leiser. Nok¹ *lye*-zerr.
Nocturne (Eng.). Nok-turn.
Nocturne (Fr.). Nok-teerrn².
Noël. Noh-el.
Noir. Nwahrr.
Noire. Nwahrr.
Non (Fr.). No(ng).
Non (It.). Non.
Nonet (Eng.). Non-*et*.
Nonett (Ger.). Non-*et*.
Nonette (Fr.). Non-*et*.
Nonetto (It.). Non-*et*-toh.
Nonnengeige. *Non*-en-gy⁸-gu(r).
Nordraak. *Noorr*-drohk.
Noskowsky. Noss-*kov*-skee.
Notturno. Not-*toorr*-noh.
Nováček. Naw-*vah*-check.
Novák. Nawv-*ahk*.
Nove (It.). *Naw*-vay.
Noverre. Nov-airr.
Nowowiejski. Nohv-ov-*eezj*³-kee.
Nozze di Figaro, Le. Lay *not*-say dee *Fee*-garr-oh.
Nun danket. Noon *dan*-ket.
Nuova. Noo-*aw*-va⁵.
Nuove musiche. Noo-*aw*-vay moo-zee-cay.
Nuovo. Noo-*aw*-voh.
Nutrendo. Noo-*tren*-doh.
Nutrito. Noo-*tree*-toh.

---

6. The **ish** is really anywhere between that sound and 'ik' (varying in different parts of Germany). **7. th** as in *thin*. **8. g** as in *go*.

O

Obbligato. Ob-blee-*gah*-toh.

Oben. *Oh*-ben.

Ober. *Oh*-berr.

Oberammergau. Oh-berr-*am*-err-gow[4].

Oberek. Oh-*bairr*-ek.

Obertas. Oh-*bairr*-tass.

Oberwerk. *Oh*-berr-vairrk.

Obligat. Ob-lee-*gaht*.

Obligé. Ob-lee-zjay[3].

Oboe (It.). Oh-*boh*-ay.

Oboe (Eng.). *Oh*-boy (or *Oh*-boh).

Oboe da caccia. Oh-*boh*-ay da[5] *catch*-ya.

Oboe d'amore. Oh-*boh*-ay dam-*aw*-ray.

Oboi. Oh-*boh*-ee.

Oboukof, Obukof. *Oh*-boo-hoff (pron. 'h' in last syll., not 'k').

Oboussier. Oh-booss-yay.

Obrecht. *Oh*-brekt[1].

Ocarina. Oc-a[5]-*ree*-na[5].

Ockeghem. *Ok*-e(r)g-hem.

Ockenheim. *Ok*-en-hime.

Octandre. Ok-to(ng)drr.

Octave (Fr.). Ok-tav.

Octaves aigües. Ok-tav ayg-ee[2] (last word two syll. only).

Octaves graves. Ok-tav grahv.

Octet. Oc-*tet*.

Octette. Oc-tet.

Octuor. Oc-tee[2]-orr.

Oculaire. Ok-ee[2]-lairr.

O Deutschland hoch in Ehren. Oh *Doytsh*-lant hohk[1] in *Ayrr*-en.

Odo de Cluny. Aw-do de(r) Clee[5]-nee.

Oehlenschläger. *E*(r)*l*-en-shlaig-err.

Œuvre. U(r)vrr.

Offen. *Off*-en.

Offenbach. *Off*-en-bak[1].

Offertoire. Off-airr-twahrr.

Öffnen. *U*(r)*f*-nen.

Offrande à Siva. Off-ro(ng)-da[5] See-vah.

Oficleide. Off-ee-*clay*-ee-day.

Ofydd. *Ov*-uth ('th' as in *the*).

Ogni. *On*-yee.

O Haupt voll Blut und Wunden. O Howpt[4] fol Bloot oont *Voon*-den.

Ohne. *Oh*-ne(r).

Ohne Pedal. *Oh*-ne(r) Ped-*ahl*.

Oiseau bleu, L'. Lwah-soh blu(r).

Oktavkornett. Ok-*tahf*-korr-*net*.

Oktett. Ok-*tet*.

Olallo. Ol-*ahl*-yoh.

Ole (Sp.). Oh-*lay*.

Ole Bull. Ool Beel[2].

Olesen. *Oo*-le(r)-sen.

Olivier. Ol-iv-yay.

Olof. *Oo*-lof.

Ondeggiamento. On-dej-yam-*en*-toh.

Ondeggiando. On-dej-*yan*-doh.

Ondeggiante. On-dej-*yan*-tay.

Ondes musicales. O(ng)d mee[2]-zee-cal[5].

Ondříček. *Ond*-rizj[3]-chek.

Ondulé. O(ng)d-ee[2]-lay.

Ongarese. On-gar-*ray*-zay.

Oper. *Oh*-perr.

Opéra bouffe. Op-ay-ra[5] boof.

Opera buffa. *Op*-ay-ra[5] *boof*-fa[5].

Opéra comique. Op-ay-ra[5] com-eek.

Opera seria. *Op*-ay-ra[5] *say*-ree-a[5].

Ophikleide. Off-ee-*kly*-de(r).

Oppé. *Op*-ay.

Opus. *Op*-uss (or *Oh*-puss).

Oracolo, L'. Law-*rac*-ol-oh.

Orageuse. Awrr-azj[3]-u(r)z.

Orageux. Awrr-azj[3]-u(r).

Oratorio (Eng.). Orr-at-*awrr*-ee-oh.

Oratorio (It.). Awrr-at-*awrr*-ee-oh.

Orazio. Awrr-*aht*-see-oh.

Orchésographie. Awrr-kay-zog-raf-ee.

Orchester (Ger.). Orr-*kest*-err.

Orchestre (Fr.). Awrr-kesstrr.

Orchestre de genre. Awrr-kesstrr de(r) zjo(ng)rr[3].

Ordinaire. Awrr-dee-nairr.

Ordinario. Awrr-dee-*nahrr*-ee-oh.

Ordre. Awrrdrr.

Orefice. Aw-*ray*-fee-chay.

Oresco. Awrr-*ess*-co.

Orfée aux Enfers. Awrr-fay ohz-o(ng)-fairr.

Orfeo ed Euridice. Awrr-*fay*-oh ed Ay-oo-*ree*-dee-chay.

Organi. Awrr-ga-nee.

Organino. Awrr-gan-*ee*-noh.

Organistrum. Awrg-an-*iss*-trum.

Organo. Awrr-gan-oh.

Organo corale. *Awrr*-gan-oh coh-*rah*-lay.

Organo d'assolo. *Awrr*-gan-oh dass-*oh*-loh.

Organo d'eco. *Awrr*-gan-oh day-coh.

Organo d'espressione. *Awrr*-gan-oh dess-press-see-*oh*-nay.

Organo di coro. *Awrr*-gan-oh dee *caw*-roh.

Organo di legno. *Awrr*-gan-oh dee *layn*-yoh.

Organo espressivo. *Awrr*-gan-oh ess-press-*see*-voh.

Organo pieno. *Awrr*-gan-oh pee-*ay*-noh.

Orgel. *Awrrg*-el.

Orgelmesse. *Awrrg*-el-mess-e(r).

Orgelwaltze. *Awrrg*-el-valts[5]-e(r).

Orgia. *Orrj*-yah.

Orgue. Awrrg.

Orgue de Barbarie. Awrrg de(r) Barr[5]-ba[5]-ree.

Orgue en table. Awrrg o(ng) tabl[5].

Orgue expressif. Awrrg ex-press-eef.

Orgue mécanique. Awrrg may-can-eek.

Orgue plein. Awrrg pla(ng).

Orgue positif. Awrrg poz-ee-teef.

Oriana. Aw-ree-*ahn*-a[5].

Ornstein. *Awrn*-stine.

Orphée et Euridice. Awrr-fay ay Ur-ee-deess.

Orphéon. Awrr-fay-o(ng).

Orpheus and Eurydice. *Awr*-fewss and You-*rid*-itch-ee.

Ortiz. Awrr-*teeth*[7].

Ortruď. *Awrr*-troot.

Osmin. Oss-*meen*.

Osservanza. Oss-airr-*vant*-sa[5].

Ossia. Oss-*see*-a[5].

Ostinato. Oss-tee-*nah*-toh.

Ostrčil. *Oss*-t(e)rr-cheel.

Ôte. Oat.

Otello. Oat-*el*-loh.

Ôtent. Oat.

Ôtez. Oh-tay.

Othmar. *Ot*-mahrr.

Ottava. Ot-*tah*-va[5].

Ottava alta. Ot-*tah*-va[5] *al*-ta[5].

Ottava bassa. Ot-*tah*-va[5] *bass*-sa[5].

Ottava sopra. Ot-*tah*-va[5] *soh*-pra[5].

Ottava sotto. Ot-*tah*-va[5] *sot*-toh.

Ottaviano. Ot-tav-ee-*ah*-noh.

Ottavino. Ot-tav-*ee*-noh.

Ottavio. Ot-*tah*-vee-oh.

Ottoboni. Ot-toh-*boh*-nee.

Ottone. Ot-*toh*-nay.

Ottorino. Ot-taw-*ree*-noh.

---

1. **k** = 'ch' (cf. Scot. *loch*). 2. **ee** here really between 'ee' and 'oo' (cf. Scot. *puir*). 3. **zj** like 's' in *pleasure*. 4. **ow** as in *cow*. 5. **a** as in *lad*.

Ou. Oo.
Oulibichef. Oo-*lee*-bee-shef.
Ours, L'. Loorrss.
Ouseley. *Ooz*-li ('i' as in *it*).
Ouvert. Oo-vairr.

Ouverte. Oo-vairrt.
Ouverture. Oo-vairr-teer².
Ouvrez. Oo-vray.
Ouvrir. Oo-vreerr.

Ovvero. Oh-*vay*-roh.
O Welt, ich muss dich lassen.
  O Velt, ik¹ mooss dik¹ *lass*-en.
Owen. *Oh*-en.

P

Paar. Pahrr.
Pablo. *Pab*-loh.
Pacatamente. Pac-at-ah-*men*-tay.
Pacato. Pac-*ah*-toh.
Pacchierotti. Pak-kee-ay-*rot*-tee.
Pace (It.). *Pah*-chay.
Pachelbel. Pak¹-*hel*-bel.
Pacifico (It.). Patch-*ee*-fee-coh.
Pacini. Patch-*ee*-nee.
Pacius. *Pahts*-yooss.
Paderewski. Pad-airr-*ess*-kee.
Padiglione. Pad-eel-*yoh*-nay.
Padiglione cinese. Pad-eel-*yoh*-nay chee-*nay*-zay.
Padovana. Pad-oh-*vah*-na⁵.
Padre boëmo. *Pah*-dray boh-*aim*-oh.
Padre Soler. *Pah*-dray Soh-*lairr*.
Paean (Eng.). *Pee*-an.
Paër. Pah-*airr*.
Paesiello. Pah-ayz-*yel*-loh.
Paganini. Pag-an-*ee*-nee.
Pagliacci, I. Ee Pal-*yat*-shee.
Palabra. Pal-*ab*-rah.
Paladilhe. Pah-lah-*deel*.
Palco. *Pal*-coh.
Paléophone. Pal-ay-oh-fon.
Palestrina. Pal-ess-*tree*-na⁵.
Palmgren. *Pallm*⁵-grain.
Palotache. *Pol*-oh-tosh.
Palotás. *Pol*-oh-tosh.
Pamina. Pam-*ee*-na⁵.
Pandurina. Pan-doo-*ree*-na⁵.
Panorgue. Pan-awrrg.
Panseron. Po(ng)-surr-ro(ng).
Pantaleon (Eng.). Pan-tal-*ee*-on.
Pantaleone. Pan-tal-ay-*oh*-nay.
Pantoum. Po(ng)-toom.
Paolo. *Pah*-oh-loh.
Papagena (Ger.). Pap-a⁵-*gay*-nah.
Papageno (Ger.). Pap-a⁵-*gay*-noh.

Papillons. Pap-ee-yo(ng).
Papini. Pap-*ee*-nee.
Pâque. Pahk.
Pâques. Pahk.
Paradies. Parr⁵-ad-*ee*-ess.
Paradisi. Parr⁵-ad-*ee*-zee.
Pardessus de viole d'amour.
  Parr-dess-ee² de(r) vee-ol dam-oorr.
Pardon de Ploërmel, Le. Le(r) Parr⁵-do(ng) de(r) Ploh-err-mel.
Pareja, Ramos de. *Ram*-oss day Pahrr-*ay*-ka¹.
Paris, Aimé. Em-ay Pa-ree.
Parlando. Parr⁵-*lan*-doh.
Parlante. Parr⁵-*lan*-tay.
Parlato. Parr⁵-*lah*-toh.
Parsifal. *Parss*⁵-ee-fal.
Partant pour la Syrie. Partt⁵-o(ng) poorr la⁵ See-ree.
Parte (It.). *Pahrr*-tay.
Parthie. Parr-*tee*.
Parthien. Parr-*tee*-en.
Parti. *Pahrr*-tee.
Partie. Parr-tee.
Partita. Pahrr-*tee*-tah.
Partite diverse di Follia. Pahrr-*tee*-tay dee-*vairr*-say dee Fol-*lee*-a⁵.
Partition. Parr⁵-tee-see-o(ng).
Partito. Pahrr-*tee*-toh.
Partitura. Pahrr-tee-*too*-ra⁵.
Partizione. Pahrr-teet-see-*oh*-nay.
Pas (Fr.). Pah.
Pas de basque. Pah de(r) Bask.
Pas de deux. Pah de(r) du(r).
Pasdeloup. Pah-de(r)-loo.
Pas de quatre. Pah de(r) katrr.
Pas glissé. Pah glee-say.
Paso doble. *Pass*-oh *Dob*-lay.
Pasquali. Pass-*kwah*-lee.
Pasquini. Pass-*kwee*-nee.
Passacaglia. Pass-sac-*al*⁵-ya⁵.
Passacaille. Pass-a⁵-ky(er).

Passamezzo. Pass-am-*med*-zoh.
Passecaille. Pass-e(r)-ky(er).
Passemezzo. Pass-ay-*med*-zoh.
Passend. *Pass*-ent.
Passepied. Passp-yay.
Pas seul. Pah sur(r)l.
Passingala. Pass-seen-*gah*-la⁵.
Passionatamente. Pass-yoh-nah-tam-*en*-tay.
Passionatissimo. Pass-yoh-nah-*teess*-see-moh.
Passionato. Pass-yoh-*nah*-toh.
Passione. Pass-see-*oh*-ŋay.
Passo e mezzo. Pass-oh ay *med*-zoh.
Pasticcio. Pass-*teet*-choh.
Pastiche. Pass-teesh.
Pastorale (It.). Pass-taw-*rah*-lay.
Pastoso. Pass-*toh*-zoh.
Pastourelle. Pass-too-rel.
Patetico. Pat-*ay*-tee-coh.
Pathétique. Pat-ay-teek.
Pathetisch. Pat-*ayt*-ish.
Patimento. Pat-ee-*men*-toh.
Patti (It.). *Pat*-tee (in English often 'Patty').
Pau (Catalan). Pow⁴.
Pauer. *Pow*⁴-er.
Pauken. *Pow*⁴-ken.
Paukenmesse. *Pow*⁴-ken-mess-e(r).
Paukenschlag. *Pow*⁴-ken-shlahk.
Paukenwirbel. *Pow*⁴-ken-veer-bel.
Paul (Fr.). Pohl.
Paul (Ger.). Powl⁴.
Paumann. *Pow*⁴-man.
Pausa. *Pah*-oo-za⁵.
Pause (Fr.). Pohz.
Pause (Ger.). *Pow*⁴-ze(r).
Pavan. Pa-van.
Paventato. Pav-en-*tah*-toh.
Paventoso. Pav-en-*toh*-zoh.
Pavia. *Pah*-vee-a⁵.
Pavillon. Pav-ee-yo(ng).

---

6. The **ish** is really anywhere between that sound and 'ik' (varying in different parts of Germany). **7.** th as in *thin*. **8.** g as in *go*.

Z z

Pavin. *Pav*-in.

Pavlova. *Pahv*-loh-vah.

Peau. Poh.

Pêcheurs de perles, Les. Lay pesh-urr de(r) pairrl.

Pedalcoppel. Ped-*ahl*-ko-pel.

Pédale (Fr.). Pay-dal⁵.

Pedale (It.). Ped-*ah*-lay.

Pedalflügel. Ped-*ahl*-fleeg²-el.

Pedalgebrauch. Ped-*ahl*-gu(r)-browk⁴, ¹.

Pédalier. Pay-dal-yay.

Pedaliera. Ped-al⁵-*yay*-ra⁵.

Pedalklaviatur. Ped-*ahl*-klav-ee-ah-*toor*.

Pedalpauken. Ped-*ahl*-pow⁴-ken.

Pedrell. Ped-*rayl*(yer).

Pedrillo. Ped-*reel*-yoh.

Pedro. Ped-roh.

Peer Gynt. Pair Geent⁸, ².

Peeters. Pay-ters.

Peine. Pen.

Pelléas et Mélisande. Pel-ay-ass ay May-lee-zo(ng)d.

Pencerdd Gwalia. *Pen*-kairth *Gwahl*-yah ('th' as in *the*).

Pendant. Po(ng)-do(ng).

Pénétrant. Pay-nay-tro(ng).

Penillion. Pen-*ithl*-yon ('th' as in *the*).

Penseroso, Il. Eel Pen-say-*roh*-zoh.

Pepys. Peeps (so pron. by Samuel Pepys in the 17th century, but the family now pron. '*Pep*-iss', maintaining that Samuel's pron. was purely personal).

Per. Pairr.

Percossa. Pairr-*coss*-sa⁵.

Perdendo. Pairr-*den*-doh.

Perdendosi. Pairr-*den*-doh-see.

Peregrine. *Perr*-eg-rin.

Père Lachaise. Pairr Lash-ez.

Pergetti. Pairr-*jet*-tee.

Pergolese. Pairr-goh-*lay*-zay.

Pergolesi. Pairr-goh-*lay*-zee.

Peri. *Pay*-ree.

Périgourdine. Pay-ree-goorr-deen.

Perle du Brésil, La. Lap-airrl dee² Bray-zeel.

Però. Pay-*roh*.

Perosi. Pairr-*oh*-zee.

Pérotin le Grand. Pairr-ot-a(ng) le(r) Gro(ng).

Perpetuo. Pairr-*pet*-wo.

Perrachio. Pairr-*rak*-yoh.

Perrin (Eng.). *Perr*-in.

Perrin (Fr.). Perr-ra(ng).

Perruque. Pairr-eek².

Persephone (Eng.). Per-*sef*-on-ee.

Persichetti. Pairr-see-*ket*-tee.

Persimfans. Pairr-seem-*fans*.

Pesant. Pe(r)-zo(ng).

Pesante. Pay-*zan*-tay.

Pestalozzi. Pess-tal⁵-*ots*-see.

Peteneara. Pet-en-ay-*ah*-ra⁵.

Peter (Ger.). *Pay*-terr.

Peters (Ger.). *Pay*-terrss.

Petersen (Ger.). *Pay*-terr-zen.

Petersen-Berger (Swed.). *Pay*-terr-sen *Bairr*-yerr.

Petipa. Pay-tee-*pah*.

Petit. Pe(r)-tee.

Petit bugle. Pe(r)-tee beegl².

Petit détaché. Pe(r)-tee day-tash-ay.

Petite. Pe(r)-teet.

Petite flûte. Pe(r)-teet Fleet².

Petite flûte octave. Pe(r)-teet fleet² ok-tav.

P'tites Michus, Les. Lay pteet Mee-chee².

Petits riens, Les. Lay pe(r)-tee ri(an)g.

Petrarch. *Pet*-rarrk.

Petrassi. Pet-*rass*-see.

Petrella. Pet-*rel*-la⁵.

Petresco. Pet-*ress*-coh.

Petrie. *Peet*-ri ('i' as in *it*).

Petrouchka. Pet-*roosh*-kah.

Petrucci. Pet-*root*-chee.

Petrushka. Pet-*roosh*-kah.

Petzold. *Pet*-sohlt.

Peu. Pu(r).

Peu à peu. Pu(r) a⁵ pu(r).

Pezzi. *Pets*-see.

Pezzo. *Pets*-soh.

Pfeife. *Pfy*-fe(r).

Pfeiferei. Pfy-fe(r)-*rye*.

Pfeill. Pfile.

Pferdemusik. *Pfairr*-de(r)-moo-zeek.

Pfiffig. *Pfif*-ish⁶.

Pfitzner. *Pfits*-nerr.

Phaedra. *Fay*-dra⁵.

Phalèse. Fal-ez.

Phantasie (Ger.). Fan-taz-*ee*.

Phantasien. Fan-taz-*ee*-en.

Phantasiestück. Fan-taz-*ee*-shteek².

Philémon et Baucis. Feel-ay-mo(ng) ay Boh-seess.

Philidor. Fee-lee-dawrr.

Philippe de Mons. Fee-leep de(r) Mo(ng).

Philippe de Vitry. Fee-leep de(r) Vee-tree.

Phillipp. Fee-leep.

Philosoph, Der. Dairr-Fee-loh-*zohf*.

Phoneuma. Foh-*new*-ma⁶.

Piacere. Pee-atch-*ay*-ray.

Piaceski. Pee-atch-*ess*-kee.

Piacevole. Pee-atch-*ay*-voh-lay.

Pianamente. Pee-ah-nam-*en*-tay.

Piangendo. Pee-an-*jen*-doh.

Piangente. Pee-an-*jen*-tay.

Piangevole. Pee-an-*jay*-voh-lay.

Piangevolmente. Pee-an-jay-vohl-*men*-tay.

Pianino. Pee-an-*ee*-noh.

Pianissimo. Pee-an-*eess*-see-moh.

Piano. Pee-*ah*-noh.

Piano à queue. Pee-an-oh a⁵ ku(r).

Pianoforte. Pee-*ah*-noh-*fawrr*-tay.

Pianto. Pee-*an*-toh.

Piatti. Pee-*at*-tee.

Pibroch. *Pee*-brok¹.

Picardie. Pee-cahrr-dee.

Picchettato. Peek-ket-*tah*-toh.

Picchi. *Peek*-kee.

Picchiettando. Peek-ee-et-*an*-doh.

Picchiettato. Peek-ee-et-*ah*-toh.

Piccini. Pee-*chee*-nee.

Piccola. *Peek*-koh-la⁵.

Piccolo (It.). *Peek*-koh-loh.

Picinni. Pee-*chin*-nee.

Pickelflöte. *Pik*-el-*fle*(r)-te(r).

Pick-Mangiagalli. Peek-Man-jee-ag-*al*⁵-lee.

Pied. Pee-ay.

Pied en l'air. Pee-ay-do(ng) lairr.

Pieno. Pee-*ay*-noh.

Pieranzovini. Pee-ay-rand-zoh-*vee*-nee.

Pierluigi. Pee-airr-loo-*ee*-jee.

Pierné. Pee-airr-nay.

Pierre. Pee-airr.

Pierrot lunaire. Pee-air-roh lee²-nairr.

Pierson. *Peer*-son.

Piesse. Pee-es.

Pietà. Pee-ay-*ta*⁵.

Pieterzoon. *Peet*-err-zohn.

Pietosamente. Pee-ayt-ohz-am-*en*-tay.

Pietoso. Pee-ay-*toh*-zoh.

Pietro. Pee-*ay*-troh.

Pifferari. Peef-fairr-*ah*-ree.

Piffero. *Peef*-fairr-oh.

Pijper. *Pipe*-err.

Pikieren. Pee-*keerr*-en.

Pilss (as spelt).

Pimen. *Peem*-en.

Pincé. Pa(ng)-say.

Pincherle. Pa(ng)-shairl.

Pinolet. Pee-noh-lay.

Pinsuti. Peen-*soo*-tee.

Piobaireachd. *Pee*-bahrr-ak¹-(k).

Piqué. Pee-kay.

Pique Dame. Peek Dam.

---

1. **k** = 'ch' (cf. Scot. *loch*).   2. **ee** here really between 'ee' and 'oo' (cf. Scot. *puir*).   3. **zj** like 's' in *pleasure*.   4. **ow** as in *cow*.   5. **a** as in *lad*.

Piquieren. Pee-*keerr*-en.
Piquiren. Pee-*keerr*-en.
Pirouette. Pee-roo-et.
Pisk. Peesk.
Pissarro. Pees-*sarr*-roh.
Pistone (It.). Peess-*toh*-nay.
Pistoni. Peess-*toh*-nee.
Pistons (Fr.). Peess-to(ng).
Più. Pew.
Piutti. Pee-*oot*-tee.
Piuttosto. Pew-*toss*-toh.
Piva. *Pee*-va⁵.
Pixis. *Peek*-siss.
Pizarro. Pcct-*sarr*⁵-roh.
Pizzetti. Peets-*set*-tee.
Pizzicato. Peets-see-*cah*-toh.
Placidezza. Platch-ee-*detz*-za⁵.
Placido. *Plah*-chee-doh.
Placito. *Plah*-chee-toh.
Plagal. *Play*-gal.
Plaidy. Ply-dee.
Plaisant. Plez-o(ng).
Plaisirs de St.-Germain-en-Laye, Les. Lay Plez-eerr de(r) Sa(ng) - Zjairr³ - ma(ng) - o(ng)-Lay.
Planchette ronflante. Plo(ng)-shet ro(ng)-flo(ng)t.
Planquette. Plo(ng)-ket.
Plaqué. Plak-ay.
Plateau. Plat-oh.
Plaudernd. *Plow*⁴-derrnt.
Playeza. Plah-yeth⁷-a⁵.
Pléiade (Fr.). Play-yad.
Plein. Pla(ng).
Pleine. Plen.
Plein jeu. Pla(ng) zjur².
Pleno. *Play*-noh.
Pleyel (Fr.). Play-el.
Pleyel (Ger.). *Ply*-el.
Plötzlich. *Ple*(r)*ts*-lik¹.
Pluie de perles. Plwee de(r) pairrl.
Plus. Plee².
Pochette. Posh-et.
Pochettino. Poh-ket-*tee*-noh.
Pochetto. Poh-*ket*-toh.
Pochissimo. Poh-*keess*-see-moh.
Poco. *Paw*-coh.
Poco a poco. *Paw*-coh-ah *paw*-coh.
Poco lento. *Paw*-coh *len*-toh.
Poème symphonique. Po-em sa(ng)-fon-eek.
Poème Symphonique pour Solo d'Ondes Musicales et Orchestre. Po-em sa(ng)-fon-eek poorr soh-loh do(ng)d mee²-zee-kal ay awrr-kesstrr.
Poggiato. Pod-*jah*-toh.
Pogner. *Pohg*-nerr.
Poi. *Paw*-ee.
Poids. Pwah.

Poi la coda. *Paw*-ee la⁵ *coh*-da⁵.
Point d'arrêt. Pwa(ng) darr-ay.
Point d'orgue. Pwa(ng) dawrrg.
Pointe. Pwa(ng)t.
Pointe d'archet. Pwa(ng)t-dahrr-shay.
Poirier. Pwah-ree-ay.
Poirier de Misère. Pwah-ree-ay de(r) Mee-zairr.
Polacca. Poh-*lac*-ca⁵.
Polak. *Poh*-lak.
Poldowski. Pol-*dov*-skee.
Pollaroli. Pol-lar-*oh*-lee.
Polnisch. *Pol*-nish.
Polnischer Bock. *Pol*-nish-err Bok.
Polo (Sp.). *Pol*-oh.
Polonaise (Eng.). Pol-on-*ayz*.
Polonaise (Fr.). Pol-on-ez.
Polonäse. Pohl-oh-*nay*-ze(r).
Polska. *Pohlss*-ka⁵.
Polski. *Polss*-kee.
Polstertanz. *Pol*-sterr-tants.
Polyphony. Pol-*if*-on-i (last syll. as in *it*).
Pommer. *Pom*-err.
Pomposo. Pom-*poh*-zoh.
Ponce (Sp.). *Ponth*⁷-ay.
Ponchielli. Pon-kee-*el*-lee.
Ponderoso. Pon-deh-*roh*-zoh.
Poniatowski. Pohn-ee-at-*ov*-skee.
Ponte. *Pon*-tay.
Ponticello. Pon-tee-*chel*-loh.
Popovici. Pop-oh-*vee*-chee.
Popper. *Pop*-err.
Populäre Instrumentationslehre. Pop-oo-*lairr*-e(r) Instroo-men-tah-tsee-*ohnss*-lairr-er.
Pordon danza. *Pawrr*-don *danth*⁷-a⁵.
Porpora. *Pawrr*-poh-ra⁵.
Port á beul (Gael.). *Porst* ‹a⁵ *bayl* (note the 's' sound in the first word).
Portamento. Pawrr-tam-*en*-toh.
Portando. Pawrr-*tan*-doh.
Portato. Pawrr-*tah*-toh.
Port de voix. Pawrr de(r) vwah.
Porté. Pawrr-tay.
Portée. Pawrr-tay.
Porter la voix. Pawrr-tay la⁵ vwah.
Portual. Porrt-oo-*nahl*.
Portunalflöte. Porrt-oo-*nahl*-fle(r)-te(r).
Posaune (Ger.). Pohz-*ow*⁴-ne(r).
Posément. Poh-zay-mo(ng).
Positif. Poz-ee-teef.
Posizione. Pohz-eet-see-*oh*-nay.
Possibile. Poss-*see*-bee-lay.
Postillon de Longjumeau, Le.

Le(r) Posst-ee-yo(ng) de(r) Lo(ng)-zjee³, ²-moh.
Pot pourri. Poh-poo-ree.
Pottier. Pot-yay.
Pouce. Pooss.
Poule, La. Lap-ool.
Poulenc. Poo-lank.
Poulsen. *Powl*⁴-sen.
Pour (Fr.). Poorr.
Poussé. Poo-say.
Powell. *Poh*-el or Pole (sometimes 'Pow⁴-el').
Prächtig. *Prek*¹-tish⁶.
Prachtvoll. *Prakt*¹ fol.
Präcis. Prayt-*seess*.
Prague. Prahg.
Pralltriller. *Pral*-tril-lerr.
Präludium. Pray-*loo*-dee-oom.
Pratella. Prat-*el*-la⁵.
Préambule. Pray-o(ng)-beel².
Pré aux Clercs. Pray oh Clairr.
Précédemment. Pray-say-dam-mo(ng).
Precedente. Pray-chay-*den*-tay.
Précieuse. Prayss-yu(r)z.
Precipitando. Pray-chee-pee-*tan*-doh.
Precipitandosi. Pray-chee-pee-*tan*-doh-see.
Precipitato. Pray-chee-pee-*tah*-toh.
Precipitazione. Pray-chee-pee-tat-see-*oh*-nay.
Précipité. Pray-see-pee-tay.
Precipitosamente. Pray-chee-pee-toh-zam-*en*-tay.
Precipitoso. Pray-chee-pee-*toh*-zoh.
Precisione. Pray-chee-zee-*oh*-nay.
Preciso. Pray-*chee*-zoh.
Pregando. Pray-*gan*-doh.
Preghiera. Praig-ee-*ay*-ra⁵.
Préluder. Pray-lee²-day.
Preludio. Pray-*lood*-ee-oh.
Premier. Pre(r)m-yay.
Première. Pre(r)m-yairr.
Première fois. Pre(r)m-yairr fwah.
Prendre. Pro(ng)drr.
Prenez. Pre(r)-nay.
Preobrajenska. Pray-oh-brazj²-*en*-ska⁵.
Près. Pray.
Près de la touche. Pray de(r) la⁵ toosh.
Presque. Presk.
Pressando. Press-*san*-doh.
Pressant. Press-so(ng).
Pressante (It.). Press-*san*-tay.
Pressez. Press-say.
Pressieren. Press-*eerr*-en.
Prestamente. Press-tam-*en*-tay.

---

6. The **ish** is really anywhere between that sound and 'ik' (varying in different parts of Germany).
7. th as in *thin*.   **8. g** as in *go*.

Prestezza. Press-*tets*-sa[5].
Prestissimamente. Press-teess-see-mam-*en*-tay.
Prestissimo. Press-*teess*-see-moh.
Presto. *Press*-toh.
Prière. Pree-yairr.
Prigioniero, Il. Eel Pree-john-*yay*-roh.
Prima. *Pree*-ma[5].
Prima donna. *Pree*-ma[5] *don*-na[5].
Prima volta. *Pree*-ma[5] *vol*-ta[5].
Prime (church service). Pryme.
Prime donne. *Pree*-may *don*-nay.
Primitifs de la musique française, Les. Lay Pree-mee-teef de(r) la[5] mee[2]-zeek fro(ng)-sez.
Primo. *Pree*-moh.
Primo uomo. *Pree*-moh oo-*oh*-moh.
Primo violino. *Pree*-moh vee-oh-*lee*-noh.
Principale (It.). Preen-chee-*pah*-lay.
Prinzipale. Print-see-*pah*-le(r).
Prise de Troye, La. La[5] Preez de(r) Trwah.
Privalof. Pree-*vah*-loff.

Prix de Rome. Pree de(r) Rom.
Processionale. Proh-chayss-see-oh-*nah*-lay.
Proemio. Proh-*aym*-ee-oh.
Profondo. Proh-*fon*-doh.
Progressivamente. Proh-gress-see-vam-*en*-tay.
Progressivo. Proh-gress-*see*-voh.
Prokofief. Prok-*oh*-fee-ef.
Prologue (Eng.). *Proh*-log (or *Prol*-og).
Promptement. Pro(ng)t-e(r)-mo(ng).
Prontamente. Pron-tam-*en*-tay.
Prophète, Le. Le(r) Prof-et.
Proporz. Proh-*porrts*.
Proske. *Prosk*-e(r).
Prosody. *Proz*-od-i ('o's as in *on*; 'i' as in *it*).
Prosper (Fr.). Pross-pairr.
Protagoniste, La. Lap-roh-tag-on-eest.
Provençal. Prov-o(ng)-sal.
Provence. Prov-o(ng)ss.
Prunières. Preen[2]-yairr.
Psaume. Psohm (the 'P' to be sounded).

P'tites Michus, Les. Lay pteet Mee-chee[2].
Puccini. Poot-*chee*-nee.
Pugnani. Poon-*yah*-nee.
Pui. Pwee.
Puis. Pwee.
Pujol (Catalan). Poozj[3]-*ol*.
Pulitzer. *Pew*-lit-sir.
Pult. Poolt.
Pulte. *Poolt*-e(r).
Pultweise. *Poolt*-vy-ze(r).
Punta. *Poon*-ta[5].
Punta d'arco. *Poon*-ta[5] dahrr-coh.
Punto coronato. *Poon*-toh corr-oh-*nah*-toh.
Punto d'organo. *Poon*-to *dawrr*-gan-oh.
Pupitre. Pee[2]-peetrr.
Purcell. *Pur*-cell (not 'Pur-*cell*', as sometimes wrongly pron. in U.S.A.).
Purgatorio. Poorr-gat-*awrr*-ee-oh.
Puritani, I. Ee Poo-ree-*tah*-nee.
Pushkin. *Poosh*-kin.
Puy. Pwee.

Q

Quadrat. Kvad-*raht*.
Quadruple-croche. Kwah-dree[2]-ple(r)-crosh.
Qual (Ger.). Kvahl.
Qual' (It.). Kwal[5].
Qualvoll. *Kvahl*-fol.
Quanto. *Kwan*-toh.
Quantz. Kvants.
Quartett (Ger.). Kvarr-*tet*.
Quartetto. Kwahrr-*tet*-toh.
Quarto. Kwahrr-toh.
Quasi. *Kwah*-zee.
Quasi niente. *Kwah*-zee nee-*en*-tay.
Quatre. Katrr.

Quatre mains. Katrr ma(ng).
Quatrième. Kat-ree-em.
Quatrième position. Kat-ree-em-poz-eess-yo(ng).
Quattro. *Kwaht*-roh.
Quatuor. Kwat-ee[2]-orr.
Que (Fr.). Ke(r).
Quelque. Kel-ke(r).
Quelques. Before a consonant, Kel-ke(r); before a vowel, Kel-ke(r)z.
Querflöte. *Kvayrr*-fle(r)-te(r).
Queste. *Kwess*-tay.
Questo. *Kwess*-toh.

Queue (Fr.). Cu(r).
Quieto. Kwee-*ay*-toh.
Quinta. *Kween*-ta[5].
Quintadena. Kwin-tad-ee-na[5]
Quintatön. *Kvint*-at-e(r)n.
Quintenquartett. *Kvin*-ten-kvarr-*tet*.
Quintett (Ger.). Kvint-*et*.
Quintette (Fr.). Ka(ng)-tet.
Quintetto. Kween-*tet*-toh.
Quinto. *Kween*-toh.
Quintsaite. *Kvint*-zyt-e(r).
Quitter (Fr.). Keet-ay.
Quittez. Keet-ay.

---

1. k = 'ch' (cf. Scot. *loch*). 2. ee here really between 'ee' and 'oo' (cf. Scot. *puir*). 3. zj like 's' in *pleasure*. 4. ow as in *cow*. 5. a as in *lad*.

R

Rabaud. Rab-oh.
Rabbia. *Rab*-bee-ya[5].
Rachmaninof. Rahk[1]-*mahn*-ee-noff.
Radamisto. Rad-am-*eess*-toh.
Raddolcendo. Rad-dol-*chen*-doh.
Raddolcente. Rad-dol-*chen*-tay.
Raddolciato. Rad-dol-*chah*-toh.
Raddoppiamento. Rad-dop-pee-am-*en*-toh.
Raddoppiare. Rad-dop-pee-*ah*-ray.
Raddoppiato. Rad-dop-pee-*ah*-toh.
Radleyer. *Rat*-lye-err.
Raff. Raff.
Raffaele. Raf-fah-*ayl*-lay.
Raffrenando. Raf-fren-*an*-doh.
Rageur. Razj-urr.
Raimondo. Rah-ee-*mon*-doh.
Rainier. Rayn-yay.
Rákóczy. *Rah*-koht-see.
Ralentir. Ral-o(ng)-teerr.
Rallentando. Ral-len-*tan*-doh.
Rallentare. Ral-len-*tah*-ray.
Rallentato. Ral-len-*tah*-toh.
Rameau. Ram-oh.
Rameaux, Les. Lay-Ram-oh.
Ramos de Pareja. *Ram*-oss day Pahrr-*ay*-ka[1].
Ranelagh. Ran-li ('i' as in *it*).
Rangoni. Ran-*goh*-nee.
Rangström. *Rang*-stre(r)m.
Raniero. Ran-ee-*ay*-roh.
Ranz des Vaches. Ro(ng) day Vash.
Raoul. Ra[5]-ool.
Rapidamente. Rap-ee-dam-*en*-tay.
Rapidità. Rap-ee-dee-*ta*[5].
Rapido. *Rap*-ee-doh.
Rappresentazione dell'Anima e del Corpo, La. La[5] Rap-rez-en-tat-see-*oh*-nay del *Ahn*-ee-ma[5] ay del *Cawrr*-poh.
Rapprochant. Rap-rosh-o(ng).
Rapproché. Rap-rosh-ay.
Rapprocher. Rap-rosh-ay.
Rapsodia. Rap-soh-*dee*-a[5].
Rasch. Rash.
Rascher. *Rash*-err.
Rasiermesserquartett. Raz-eer-mess-err-kvarr-*tet*.
Rasoumovsky. Raz-oo-*mov*-skee(yer).
Rathaus. *Raht*-howss[4].
Ratsche. *Raht*-she(r).
Rattenendo. Rat-ten-*en*-doh.
Rattenere. Rat-en-*ay*-ray.

Rattenuto. Rat-ten-*oo*-toh.
Rauh. Row[4].
Rauschend. *Rowsh*[4]-ent.
Rauzzini. Rowts[4]-*see*-nee.
Ravel. Rav-el.
Ravvivando. Rav-vee-*van*-doh.
Ravvivato. Rav-vee-*vah*-toh.
Razoumovsky. Raz-oo-*mov*-skee(yer).
Ré (Fr.). Ray.
Re (It.). Ray.
Rea. Ray.
Reay. *Ree*-ah.
Rebec. *Ree*-bek.
Rebeck. *Ree*-bek.
Rebel (Fr.). Re(r)-bel.
Ré bémol. Ray bay-mol.
Rebikof. *Ray*-bee-koff.
Rebute. Re(r)-beet[2].
Recherché. Re(r)-shairr-shay.
Recht. Rekt[1].
Recht Chor Zinck. Rekt[1] Kohrr Tsink.
Rechte. *Rek*[1]-te(r).
Récit. Ray-see.
Recitando. Retch-ee-*tan*-doh.
Récitant. Ray-see-to(ng).
Recitante. Retch-ee-*tan*-tay.
Recitative (Eng.). Ress-it-at-eev.
Recitativo accompagnato. Retch-ee-tat-*tee*-voh ac-com-pan-*yah*-toh.
Recitativo parlante. Retch-ee-tat-*ee*-voh parr[5]-*lan*-tay.
Recitativo secco. Retch-ee-tat-ee-voh *sec*-coh.
Recitativo stromentato. Retch-ee-tat-*ee*-voh stroh-men-*tah*-toh.
Recueilli. Re(r)-ke(r)-yee.
Redend. *Raid*-ent.
Ré dièse. Ray dee-ez.
Redoublement. Re(r)-doob-le(r)-mo(ng).
Redoubler. Re(r)-doob-lay.
Redoute. Re(r)-doot.
Redoutensaal. Re(r)-*doo*-ten-zahl.
Redoutentänze. Re(r)-*doo*-ten-*tents*-e(r).
Redowa. *Ray*-doh-va[5].
Réduire. Ray-dweer.
Reduzieren. Ray-doot-*see*-ren.
Refrapper. Re(r)-frap-pay.
Refret. Re(r)-*fret*.
Regale (It.). Ray-*gah*-lay.
Régale. Ray-gal.
Régale à percussion. Ray-gal a[5] pairr-keess[2]-yo(ng).

Régale à vent. Ray-gal a[5] vo(ng).
Regalo. Ray-*gah*-loh.
Regalwerke. Ray-*gahl*-vairr-ke(r).
Regensburg. Ray-genss-boorrk.
Regensonate. Ray-gen-zoh-nah-te(r).
Reger. *Rayg*-err.
Registrieren. Rayg-ist-*reerr*-en.
Registrierung. Rayg-ist-*reerr*-oong.
Registro. Ray-*jeess*-troh.
Regondi. Reg[8]-*on*-dee.
Reicha. *Ry*-kah[1].
Reichardt. Ry-karrt[1, 5].
Reid (Scot.). Reed.
Reigen. *Ryg*-en.
Reihen. *Ry*-hen.
Rein (Ger.). Rine.
Reine, La. La[5] Ren.
Reinecke. *Ry*-nek-e(r).
Reine de Saba, La. La[5] Ren de(r) Sab-a[5].
Reinhardt. *Rine*-harrt[5].
Reinhold. *Rine*-hollt.
Reinken. *Rine*-ken.
Reiss. Rice.
Reissiger. *Ry*-sig-err.
Reiter. *Ry*-terr.
Reiterquartett. *Ry*-terr-kvarr-*tet*.
Reizenstein. *Rights*-en-shtyne.
Rejdováčka. Ray-doh-*vahtch*-ka[5].
Rejdovak. *Ray*-doh-vahk.
Relâché. Re(r)-lash-ay.
Religieux. Re(r)-leezj[3]-yu(r).
Religiosamente. Rel-ee-joh-zam-*en*-tay.
Religioso. Rel-ee-*joh*-zoh.
Rellstab. *Rel*-shtahp.
Reményi. *Rem*-ayn-yee.
Remettez. Re(r)-met-tay.
Remettre. Re(r)-metrr.
René. Re(r)-nay.
Renforcer. Ro(ng)-forss-ay.
Renforcez. Ro(ng)-forrss-ay.
Renoir. Re(r)n-wahrr.
Rentrée. Ro(ng)-tray.
Renvoi. Ro(ng)-vwah.
Renzo. Rent-soh.
Re Pastore, Il. Eel Ray Pass-*taw*-ray.
Répétiteur. Ray-pay-tee-turr.
Répétition. Ray-pas-teess-yo(ng).
Repetitor (Ger.). Ray-*payt*-*ee*-tor.
Repetitore (It.). Ray-pet-ee-*taw*-ray.

---

6. The **ish** is really anywhere between that sound and 'ik' (varying in different parts of Germany).
7. **th** as in *thin*.   8. **g** as in *go*.

Repetizione. Ray-pet-eet-see-oh-nay.

Replica (It.). *Ray*-plee-ca[5].

Replicato. Ray-plee-*cah*-toh.

Repos. Re(r)-poh.

Reprendre. Re(r)-pro(ng)drr.

Reprise. Re(r)-preez.

Requiem. *Rek*-wee-em.

Résolument. Rayz-ol-ee[2]-mo(ng).

Resoluto. Ray-zoh-*loo*-toh.

Resoluzione. Ray-zoh-loot-see-oh-nay.

Respighi. Ress-*peeg*[3]-ee.

Responsorio. Ray-spon-*saw*-ree-oh.

Ressortir. Ress-sawrrt-eer.

Rester (Fr.). Rest-ay.

Retablo de Maese Pedro, El. El Ray-*tah*-bloh day Mah-*ess*-ay *Ped*-roh.

Retardando. Ray-tarr[5]-*dan*-doh.

Retenant. Re(r)-te(r)-no(ng).

Retenu. Re(r)-te(r)-nee[2].

Retinente. Ret-ee-*nen*-tay.

Retirer. Re(r)-tee-ray.

Retirez. Re(r)-tee-ray.

Retrouvez. Re(r)-troo-vay.

Reubke. *Royp*-ke(r).

Réunis. Ray-ee[2]-nee.

Reutter. *Roy*-ter.

Reveille (Brit. Army adaptation from Fr.). Rev-*al*-li ('i' as in *it*).

Revenez. Re(r)-ve(r)-nay.

Revenir. Re(r)-ve(r)-neerr.

Rêveur. Rayv-urr.

Revidirt. Ray-vee-*deerrt*.

Revueltas. Ray-*vwel*-tass.

Revue musicale, La. La[5] Re(r)-vee[2] meez[2]-ee-cal.

Reyer. Ray-ay ('Ray-airr' apparently also recognized).

Rezitativ. Rayt-see-tah-*teef*.

Rezniček. *Rez*-nee-check.

Rheinberger. *Rhine*-bairrg-err.

Rheingold. *Rhine*-gollt.

Rhéne-Baton. Re(r)-nay-Bat-o(ng).

Rhumba. *Room*-ba[5].

Rhythmicon. *Rhith*-mik-on ('th' as in *the*).

Rhythmisch. *Rheet*[2]-mish.

Rhythmus. *Rheet*[2]-mooss.

Ributhe. Rib-*yewth*[2].

Riccardo. Ric-*carr*[5]-doh.

Ricci. *Reet*-chee.

Ricercare. Ree-chairr-*cah*-ray.

Ricercata. Ree-chairr-*cah*-ta[5].

Ricercato. Ree-chairr-*cah*-toh.

Richettato. Ree-ket-*tah*-toh.

Richter. *Rik*[1]-terr.

Richtig. *Rik*[1]-tish[6].

Ricochet. Ree-koh-shay.

Rideau. Ree-doh.

Ridotto. Ree-*dot*-toh.

Riduzione. Ree-doot-see-*oh*-nay.

Riegger. *Reeg*-err.

Riego. Ree-*ay*-go.

Riemann. *Ree*-man.

Rienzi. Ree-*ent*-see.

Ries. Reess.

Rieti. Ree-*ay*-tee.

Rigaudon. Ree-goh-do(ng).

Rigoletto. Ree-goh-*let*-toh.

Rigore. Ree-*gaw*-ray.

Rigoroso. Ree-goh-*roh*-zoh.

Rilasciando. Ree-lash-ee-*an*-doh.

Rilassando. Ree-lass-*san*-doh.

Rilassato. Ree-lass-*sah*-toh.

Rimbaud. Ram-boh.

Rimbault (Eng.). Rim-bolt.

Rimettendo. Ree-met-*ten*-doh.

Rimettendosi. Ree-met-*ten*-doh-see.

Rimonte. Ree-*mon*-tay.

Rimsky-Korsakof. *Reem*-skee-*Korrss*-ak-off.

Rimur. *Ree*-murr.

Rinaldo. Ree-*nal*[5]-doh.

Rinck. Rink.

Rinforzando. Reen-fawrrt-*san*-doh.

Rinforzato. Reen-fawrrt-*sah*-toh.

Ring des Nibelungen, Der. Dairr Rink dess *Nee*-bel-oong-en.

Rinuccini. Ree-noo-*chee*-nee.

Rio Grande. *Ree*-oh Grand.

Ripetizione. Ree-pet-eet-see-*oh*-nay.

Ripieno. Ree-pee-*ay*-noh.

Ripieno maggiore. Ree-pee-*ay*-noh maj-*yaw*-ray.

Ripieno minore. Ree-pee-*ay*-noh mee-*naw*-ray.

Riposato. Ree-paw-*zah*-toh.

Riposo. Ree-*paw*-zoh.

Riprendere. Ree-*pren*-dairr-ay.

Ripresa. Ree-*pray*-za[5].

Riscaldando. Ree-scal-*dan*-doh.

Risolutamente. Ree-zoh-loot-am-*en*-tay.

Risoluto. Ree-zoh-*loo*-toh.

Rispetti. Reess-*pet*-tee.

Ristringendo. Ree-streen-*jen*-doh.

Risurrezione. Ree-zoo-ret-see-*oh*-nay.

Risvegliato. Reez-vay-lee-*ah*-toh.

Ritardando. Ree-tahrr-*dan*-doh.

Ritardare. Ree-tahrr-*dah*-ray.

Ritardato. Ree-tahrr-*dah*-toh.

Ritardo. Ree-*tahrr*-doh.

Ritenendo. Ree-ten-*en*-doh.

Ritenente. Ree-ten-*en*-tay.

Ritenuto. Ree-ten-*oo*-toh.

Ritmico. *Reet*-mee-coh.

Ritmo. *Reet*-moh.

Ritmo di tre battute. *Reet*-moh dee tray bat-*too*-tay.

Ritornell. Ree-torr-*nel*.

Ritornello. Ree-tawrr-*nel*-loh.

Ritorno. Ree-*tawrr*-noh.

Ritournelle. Ree-toor-nel.

Ritter. *Rit*-terr.

Ritterlich. *Rit*-err-lik[1].

Rittquartett. *Rit*-kvarr-tet.

Riverso. Ree-*vairr*-soh.

Rivier. Reev-yay.

Rizzio. *Reets*-see-oh.

Robert (Fr.). Rob-airr.

Robert de Sabilon. Rob-airr de(r) Sab-ee-lo(ng).

Robert le Diable. Rob-airr le(r) Dee-yabl.

Robin et Marion. Rob-a(ng) ay Marr-ee-o(ng).

Robles. *Rob*-less.

Robustamente. Roh-*booss*-tam en-tay.

Robusto. Roh-*booss*-toh.

Rochberg. *Rosh*-berg.

Roco. *Raw*-koh.

Rococo (Fr.). Roc-oh-coh.

Rode (Fr.). Rod.

Roderigo. Rod-ay-*ree*-goh.

Rodolfo. Rod-*ol*-foh.

Rodolphe. Rod-olf.

Roeckel. *Re*(r)-kel.

Roger-Ducasse. Rozj-ay-Dee[2]-cass.

Rohrflöte. *Rohrr*-fle(r)-te(r).

Rohrstimmen. *Rohrr*-shtim-en.

Rohrwerk. *Rohrr*-vairrk.

Roi de Lahore, Le. Le(r) rwah de(r) La[5]-awrr.

Roi d'Ys, Le. Le(r) rwah deess.

Roi malgré lui, Le. Le(r) rwah mal-grail-wee.

Roldán. Rol-*dahn*.

Rolland. Rol-lo(ng).

Röllig. *Re*(r)l-lish[6].

Rollschweller. *Rol*-shvel-err ('ol' as in *doll*).

Rolltrommel. *Rol*-trom-el ('ol' as in *doll*).

Romain. Rom-a(ng).

Roman (Swed.). *Roh*-man.

Romance. Rom-o(ng)ss.

Romancero. Ro-manth[7]-*airr*-oh.

Romance sans paroles. Rom-o(ng)ss so(ng) parr-ol.

---

1. k = 'ch' (cf. Scot. *loch*).   2. ee here really between 'ee' and 'oo' (cf. Scot. *puir*).
3. zj like 's' in *pleasure*.   4. ow as in *cow*.   5. a as in *lad*.

Romanesca. Roh-man-*ess*-ca[5].
Romanesque. Rom-an-esk.
Romanza. Roh-*man*-za[5].
Rombando. Rom-*ban*-doh.
Romberg. *Rom*-bairrg.
Roméo et Juliette. Rom-ay-oh ay Zjeel[3, 2]-yet.
Ronda. *Ron*-da[5].
Rondalla. Ron-*dal*-ya[5].
Ronde. Ro(ng)d.
Rondeau. Ro(ng)-doh.
Rondeña. Ron-*dayn*-ya[5].
Rondine, La. La[5] *Ron*-dee-nay.
Ronds de jambe. Ro(ng) de(r) zjo(ng)b[3].
Ronsard. Ro(ng)-sarr[5].
Röntgen. *Re(r)nt*-gen[8].
Rootham. *Root*-ham.
Ropartz. *Roh*-parrts[5].
Rore. Rorr (or, by residence in Italy, *Raw*-ray).
Rosalia (It.). Roh-*zal*[5]-ee-a[5] (or in Eng. generally Roh-*zahl*-ee-a[5]).
Rosalia mia cara. Roh-*zal*-ee-a[5] *mee*-a[5] *cah*-ra[5].
Rosenkavalier, Der. Dairr *Roh*-zen-kav-al-*eer*.
Rosenmüller. *Roh*-zen-mee[2]-lerr.

Rosenthal. *Roh*-zen-tahl.
Rosina. Roh-*zee*-na[5].
Roskowsky. Ross-*kov*-skee.
Roslavets. *Ross*-lav-ets.
Rösler. *Re(r)z*-ler.
Rossi. *Ross*-see.
Rossignol, Le. Le(r) Ross-een-yol.
Rossini. Ross-*see*-nee.
Rota. Roh-ta[5].
Rotondo. Rot-*on*-doh.
Rouget de Lisle. Roo-zjay[8] de(r) Leel.
Roulade. Roo-lad.
Roulant. Roo-lo(ng).
Roulante. Roo-lo(ng)t.
Rousseau. Roo-soh.
Roussel. Roo-sel.
Routhier. Root-yay.
Rovescio. Roh-*vesh*-yoh.
Roxolane. Rox-o-lan.
Rózsa. *Roh*-zjah[3].
Rózycki. Rawz-*eets*-kee.
Rubato. Roo-*bah*-toh.
Rubinstein. Roo-been-*shtayne* (Rus.), *Roo*-bin-shtine (Ger.).
Ruckers. *Reek*[2]-errss.
Rücksicht. *Reek*[2]-zikt[1].
Rudement. Reed[2]-mo(ng).
Rudolf (Ger.). *Rood*-olf.

Rueda. Roo-*ay*-da[6].
Ruffo. *Roof*-foh.
Ruggiero. Roo-*jay*-roh.
Ruhe. *Roo*-e(r).
Ruhelos. *Roo*-e(r)-lohss.
Ruhepunkt. *Roo*-e(r)-poonkt.
Ruhezeichen. *Roo*-e(r)-*tsy*-shen.
Ruhig. *Roo*-ish[6].
Rührtrommel. *Reerr*[2]-trom-el.
Rührung. *Ree*[2]-roong.
Ruimonte. Roo-ee-*mon*-tay.
Ruisdael. *Royss*-dahl.
Ruiz. *Roo-eeth*[7].
Rullante. Rool-*lan*-tay.
Rumba. *Room*-ba[5].
Russa. *Rooss*-sa[5].
Russalka. Roo-*sahl*-kah.
Russlan and Ludmilla. *Rooss*-lahn and Lew-*dmee*-lah ('ew' as in *dew*).
Russo. *Rooss*-soh.
Rust (Ger.). Roost.
Rute. *Roo*-te(r).
Ruthe. *Roo*-te(r).
Ruuta. *Roo*-ta[5].
Ruutha. *Roo*-tha[5].
Ruzsicska. *Rooz*-seets-kah.
Rwtha. *Roo*-tha[5].
Rythmé. Reet-may.
Rythmique. Reet-meek.

S

Sabaneef. Sab-ahn-*yay*-yef.
Sabata. *Sah*-bat-a[5].
Sabilon. Sab-eel-o(ng).
Saccadé. Sac-cad-ay.
Sacchini. Sak-*kee*-nee.
Sachs. Zaks[1].
Sackpfeife. Zak-pfy-fe(r).
Sacra Rappresentazione. *Sac*-rah *Rap*-pray-zen-tat-see-oh-nay.
Sadko. Sad-*koh*.
Saeta. Sa[5]-*ay*-ta[5].
Saggio. *Sad*-joh.
Sainete (Fr.). Sen-et.
Sainete (Sp.). Sah-een-*ay*-tay.
Saint-Saëns. Sa(ng)-So(ng)ss.
Saite. *Zy*-te(r).
Saiten. *Zy*-ten.
Saiteninstrumente. *Zy*-ten-in-stroo-*men*-te(r).

Sakuntala (Ger.). Zak-*oon*-tal-ah.
Salazar. Sal-ath[7]-*arr*[5].
Salicet. *Sal*-ee-set.
Salicional (Eng.). Sal-*ish*-on-al[6].
Salieri. Sal-*yay*-ree.
Salinas. Sal-*ee*-nass.
Salis, Brindes de. *Brin*-dess day *Sal*[5]-eess.
Sallé. Sal-lay.
Salmo. *Sal*-moh.
Salomé. Sal-oh-may.
Salomon. Zal-oh-mohn.
Salon des refusés. Sal-o(ng) day re(r)-fee[2]-zay.
Salón México, El. El Sa[5]-*lohn May*-hee-koh.
Saltando. Sal-*tan*-doh.
Saltarello. Sal-ta[5]-*rel*-loh.
Saltato. Sal-*tah*-toh.

Salvatore. Sal-vat-*oh*-ray.
Salzédo. Sal-zay-doh.
Samara. Sam-*ah*-ra[5].
Samazeuilh. Sam-az-u(r)-ee.
Saminsky. Sam-*een*-skee.
Sammartini. Sam-marr[5]-*tee*-nee.
Sammlung. *Zam*-loong.
Samson et Dalila. So(ng)-so(ng) ay Dal-ee-la[5].
Sämtlich. *Zemt*-lik[1].
Samuel (Fr.). Sam-ee[2]-el.
Sandvik. *San*-veek.
Sandys (Scot.). *Sand*-iss or Sands.
Sanft. Zanft.
Sanftmütig. *Zanft*-mee[2]-tish[6].
Sans (Fr.). So(ng).
Santa Cruz. San-ta[5] *Krooz*.
Santa Fé. *San*-ta[5] *Fay*.
Santuzza. San-*toots*-sa[5].

---

6. The **ish** is really anywhere between that sound and 'ik' (varying in different parts of Germany). 7. **th** as in *thin*. 8. **g** as in *go*.

Sanz. Sahnth⁷.

Sanzogno. Sand-*zon*-yo.

Sarabande (Fr.). Sa⁵-rab-o(ng)d.

Sarasate. Sa⁵-rass-*ah*-tee.

Sarastro. Sarr⁵-*ass*⁵-troh.

Sardana. Sarr⁵-*dan*-a⁵.

Sarrusophone (Eng.). Sa⁵-*rooss*-oh-fohn.

Sarti. *Sarr*⁵-tee.

Sarum. *Sair*-um.

Sassofonia. Sass-oh-*fohn*-ee-a⁵.

Sassofono. Sass-*off*-on-oh.

Satie. Sat-ee.

Satz. Zats.

Saudades. Sah-oo-*dah*-dess.

Sauguet. So-gay.

Saurau. Zow⁴-row⁴.

Saut (Fr.). Soh.

Saut de carpe. Soh de(r) carrp.

Sautillé. Soh-tee-yay.

Saverio. Sav-*ay*-ree-oh.

Savitri. *Sah*-vee-tree.

Savonarola. Sav-on-a⁵-*roh*-la⁵.

Saxhorn. *Sax*-horn.

Saxofon. Sax-oh-*fohn*.

Saynète. Syne-et.

Sbalzato. Zbalt⁵-*sah*-toh.

Scacciapensieri. Scatch-a⁵-pen-see-*ay*-ree.

Scala. *Scah*-la⁵.

Scalds (Scand. bards). Skawlds.

Scampata. Scam-*pah*-ta⁵.

Scarlatti. Scarr⁵-*lat*-tee.

Scarpia. *Scahrr*-pee-a⁵.

Scemando. Shay-*mahn*-doh.

Scena. *Shay*-na⁵.

Scenario. Shen-*ah*-ree-oh.

Schäfer. *Shay*-ferr.

Schale. *Shah*-le(r).

Schalkhaft. *Shallk*-haft.

Schallbecken. *Shal*-bek-en.

Schalmey. Shal-*my*.

Scharf. Sharrf.

Schärfe. *Shairr*-fe(r).

Scharp. Sharrp.

Scharwenka. Shahrr-*ven*-kah.

Schaunard. Show⁴-narr.

Schaurig. *Showrr*⁴-ish⁶.

Scheherazade. *Shay*-herr-az-ahd-e(r).

Scheibler. *Shy*-blerr.

Scheideman. *Shy*-de(r)-man.

Scheidt. Shyt.

Schein. Shine.

Schelle. *Shel*-e(r).

Schellen. *Shel*-en.

Schellenbaum. *Shel*-en-bowm⁴.

Schellengeläute. *Shel*-en-gu(r)-loy-te(r).

Schellentrommel. *Shel*-en-trom-el.

Schelmisch. *Shel*-mish.

Schenker. *Sheng*-ker.

Scherz. Shairrts.

Scherzando. Skairrts-*an*-doh.

Scherzante. Skairrts-*an*-tay.

Scherzantissimo. Skairrts-an-teess-see-moh.

Scherzend. *Shairrts*-ent.

Scherzetto. Skairrts-*et*-toh.

Scherzevole. Skairrts-*ay*-vol-ay.

Scherzevolmente. Skairrts-ay-vol-*men*-tay.

Scherzhaft. *Shairrts*-haft.

Scherzi. *Skairrts*-ee.

Scherzino. Skairrts-*ee*-noh.

Scherzo. *Skairrts*-oh.

Scherzosamente. Skairrts-oh-zam-*en*-tay.

Scherzoso. Skairrts-*oh*-zoh.

Schiebe. *Shee*-be(r).

Schiettamente. Skee-et-tam-en-tay.

Schiettezza. Skee-et-*tetz*-za⁵.

Schietto. Skee-*et*-toh.

Schikaneder. Shik-an-*ay*-derr.

Schillinger. *Shil*-ing-err.

Schillings. *Shil*-inks.

Schindler. *Shinnd*-lerr.

Schjelderup. Shee-*el*-derr-oop.

Schlacht. Shlakt⁵.

Schlag. Shlahk.

Schlage doch. *Shlahg*-e(r) dok¹

Schlägel. *Shlaig*-el.

Schlagen. *Shlahg*-en.

Schlaginstrumente. *Shlahk*-in-stroo-*men*-te(r).

Schlagzither. *Shlahg*-tsit-err.

Schlangenrohr. *Shlang*-en-rohr.

Schleifer. *Shly*-ferr.

Schlemihl. Shlay-*meel*.

Schleppend. *Shlep*-ent.

Schlesinger. *Shlay*-zing-err.

Schlummerlied. *Shloom*-err-leet.

Schluss. Shlooss.

Schlüssel. *Shleess*²-el.

Schlusszeichen. *Shlooss*-tsy-shen.

Schmachtend. *Shmakt*¹-ent.

Schmalz. Shmalts.

Schmeichelnd. *Shmy*-shelnt.

Schmelza. *Shmelt*-za.

Schmelzend. *Shmelts*-ent.

Schmerz. Shmairrts.

Schmerzhaft. *Shmairrts*-haft⁵.

Schmerzlich. *Shmairrts*-lik¹.

Schmerzvoll. *Shmairrts*-fol.

Schmetternd. *Shmet*-errnt.

Schmidt. Shmit.

Schmitt. Shmit.

Schnabel. *Shnah*-bel.

Schnabelflöte. *Shnah*-bel-fle(r)t-e(r).

Schnarre. *Shnarr*⁵-e(r).

Schnarrsaite. *Shnarr*⁵-zy-te(r).

Schnarrtrommel. *Shnarr*⁵-trom-el.

Schnarrwerk. *Shnarr*⁵-vairrk.

Schneckenburger. *Shnek*-en-boorg-err.

Schneidend. *Shny*-dent.

Schneider. *Shny*-derr.

Schnell. Shnel.

Schneller. *Shnel*-err.

Schnelligkeit. *Shnel*-ish⁶-kite.

Schobert. *Shoh*-berrt.

Schoeck. She(r)k.

Schoelcher. *She*(r)l-sherr.

Scholes. Skohlz.

Scholl. Shol.

Schönberg. *She*(r)n-bairrg.

Schöne Müllerin, Die. Dee *she*(r)n-e(r) *Meel*²-err-in.

Schöpfungsmesse. *She*(r)p-foonks-*mess*-e(r).

Schott. Shot.

Schottische. *Shot*-ish-e(r); (the dance) Shot-*eesh*.

Schrammel. *Shram*⁵-el.

Schreker. *Shrayk*-err.

Schrittmässig. *Shrit*-mess-ish⁶.

Schrittweise. *Shrit*-vy-ze(r).

Schroen. Shre(r)n.

Schroeter. *Shre*(r)-terr.

Schubert. *Shoo*-berrt.

Schüchtern. *Sheek*²,¹-terrn.

Schulflöte. *Shool*-fle(r)-te(r).

Schulhoff. *Shool*-hof.

Schulmeister. *Shool*-my-sterr.

Schultz. Shoolts.

Schulze. *Shoolts*-e(r).

Schumann. *Shoo*-mun.

Schunda. *Shoon*-dah.

Schuster. *Shoost*-err.

Schusterfleck. *Shoost*-err-flek.

Schütt. Sheet².

Schütteln. *Sheet*²-eln.

Schütz. Sheets².

Schuyt. Shyt.

Schwab. Shvahp.

Schwach. Shvak¹.

Schwächen. *Shvek*¹-en.

Schwächer. *Shvek*¹-err.

Schwanengesang. *Shvahn*-en-gu(r)-*zang*.

Schwankend. *Shvank*-ent.

Schwartzendorf. *Shvart*-zen-dorf.

Schwebung. *Shvay*-boong.

Schweigen. *Shvyg*-en.

Schweigezeichen. *Schvy*-gu(r)-tsy-shen.

Schweigt. Shvykt.

Schweitzer. *Shvyts*-err.

Schwellen. *Shvel*-en.

Schweller. *Shvel*-err.

Schwellkasten. *Shvel*-kast-en.

---

1. k = 'ch' (cf. Scot. *loch*).   **2.** ee here really between 'ee' and 'oo' (cf. Scot. *puir*). **3.** zj like 's' in *pleasure*.   **4.** ow as in *cow*.   **5.** a as in *lad*.

Schwellwerk. *Shvel*-vairrk.
Schwer. Shvayrr.
Schwermütig. *Shvayrr*-meet²-ish⁶.
Schwermutsvoll. *Shvayrr*-moots-fol.
Schwindend. *Shvin*-dent.
Schwindl. *Shvin*-dle.
Schwirrholz. *Shvirr*-hollts.
Schwung. Shvoong.
Schwungvoll. *Shvoonk*-fol.
Scintillante. Sheen-teel-*lan*-tay.
Sciolta. *Shol*-ta⁵.
Scioltamente. Shol-tam-*en*-tay.
Scioltezza. Shol-*tets*-a⁵.
Sciolto. *Shol*-toh.
Scivolando. Shee-voh-*lan*-doh.
Scontrino. Scon-*tree*-noh.
Scordato. Scawrr-*dah*-toh.
Scordatura. Scawrr-dah-*too*-ra⁵.
Scorrendo. Scawrr-*en*-doh.
Scorrevole. Scawrr-*ay*-voh-lay.
Scozzese. Scots-*say*-zay.
Scriabin. Skree-*ah*-been.
Scucito. Scoo-*chee*-toh.
Sdegnante. Sdayn-*yan*-tay.
Sdegno. *Sdayn*-yoh.
Sdegnosamente. Sdayn-yoh-zam-*en*-tay.
Sdegnoso. Sdayn-*yoh*-zoh.
Sdrucciolando. Sdroot-choh-*lan*-doh.
Se (Fr.). Se(r).
Se (It.). Say.
Se (Sp.). Say.
Seanchaidh. *Shen*-nak¹-ee.
Sébastien. Say-bast-ee-a(ng).
Sec. Sek.
Secco. *Sec*-coh.
Sèche. Sesh.
Sechs. Zeks.
Sechsviertelmesse. Zeks-*feer*-tel-*mess*-e(r).
Sechzehntel. Zek¹-tsayn-tel.
Sechzehntelnote. Zek¹-tsayn-tel-*noh*-te(r).
Seconda. Sec-*on*-da⁵.
Secondando. Sec-on-*dan*-doh.
Seconda volta. Sek-*on*-da⁵ *vol*-ta⁵.
Seconde (Fr.). Se(r)-go(ng)d.
Seconde (It.). Sek-*on*-day.
Secondi. Sek-*on*-dee.
Secondo. Sek-*on*-doh.
Sedlák. Sed-*lahk*.
Seele. *Zail*-e(r).
Seelenvoll. *Zail*-en-fol.
Segnale. Sain-*yah*-lay.
Segno. *Sain*-yoh.
Segovia. Say-*goh*-vee-a⁵.
Segreto di Susanna, Il. Eel say-*gray*-toh dee Soo-*zan*-na⁵.
Segue. *Seg*-way.

Segue la coda. *Seg*-way la⁵ *coh*-dah.
Seguendo. Seg-*wen*-doh.
Seguente. Seg-*wen*-tay.
Seguidilla. Sayg-ee-*deel*-ya⁵.
Sehnsucht. *Zain*-zookt¹.
Sehnsüchtig. *Zain*-zeek², ¹-tish⁶.
Sehnsuchtsvoll. *Zain*-zook¹-tsfol.
Sehr. Zayrr.
Sei. *Say*-ee.
Seiber. *Shy*-ber.
Seidl. *Zy*-del.
Seis. *Say*-eess.
Seises. *Say*-sess.
Seite. *Zy*-te(r).
Sekles. *Zek*-less.
Selim. *Zay*-lim.
Semel. *Sem*-el.
Semibiscroma. Sem-ee-beess-*croh*-ma⁵.
Semibreve (Eng.). *Semi*-breev ('i' as in *it*).
Semibreve (It.). Sem-ee-*bray*-vay.
Semicroma. Sem-ee-*croh*-ma⁵.
Semi-luna. Sem-ee-*loo*-na⁵.
Semplice. *Sem*-plee-chay.
Semplicemente. Sem-plee-chay-*men*-tay.
Semplicissimo. Sem-plee-*cheess*-ee-moh.
Semplicità. Sem-plee-chee-*ta*⁵.
Sempre. *Sem*-pray.
Sempre legato. *Sem*-pray leg-*ah*-toh.
Senachie (Gael., but correct spelling *Seanchaidh*). *Shen*-nak¹-ee.
Senaillé. Se(r)-ny-yay.
Senefelder. Zay-ne(r)-fel-derr.
Senesino. Say-nay-*zee*-noh.
Senfl. *Zen*-f'l.
Sensibile. Sen-*see*-bee-lay.
Sensibilità. Sen-see-bee-lee-*ta*⁵.
Sensible (Fr.). So(ng)-seebl.
Sentiments, Les. Lay So(ng)-tee-mo(ng).
Sentito. Sen-*tee*-toh.
Senza. *Sent*-sa⁵.
Senza accompagnamento. *Sent*-sa⁵ ac-com-pan-yam-*en*-toh.
Senza misura. *Sent*-sa⁵ mee-zoo-ra⁵.
Senza sordini. *Sent*-sa⁵ sawrr-dee-nee.
Senza sordino. *Sent*-sa⁵ sawrr-dee-noh.
Séparés. Say-pa⁵-ray.
Sept (Fr.). Set (but before a consonant, 'Say').
Septett (Ger.). Zep-*tet*.

Septette. Sep-tet.
Septetto. Sep-*tet*-toh.
Septième. Set-yem.
Septuagesima (Eng.). Sep-tew-a⁵-*jess*-ee-ma⁵.
Septuor. Sep-tee²-awrr.
Seraglio. Sairr-*ahl*-yoh.
Seraphine. *Serr*-af-een.
Serena. Sair-*ay*-na⁵.
Serenade (Eng.). Serr-en-*aid*.
Sérénade. Say-ray-nad.
Serenata. Say-ray-*nah*-ta⁵.
Serenatella. Say-ray-nah-*tel*-la⁵.
Serenità. Say-ren-ee-*ta*⁵.
Sereno. Say-*ray*-noh.
Seria. *Say*-ree-a⁵.
Sérieuse. Sayrr-yu(r)z.
Sérieux. Sayrr-yu(r).
Serinette. Serr-ee-net.
Serio. *Say*-ree-oh.
Serof. Sairr-*off*.
Serov. Sairr-*off*.
Serpentcleide. *Ser*-pent-clyde.
Serpent d'église. Sairr-po(ng) dayg-leez.
Serpent militaire. Sairr-po(ng) mee-lee-tair.
Serpentone. Sairr-pen-*toh*-nay.
Serrando. Sair-*ran*-doh.
Serrant. Sair-ro(ng).
Serrato. Sair-*rah*-toh.
Serré. Sair-ray.
Serrer. Sair-ray.
Serrez. Sair-ray.
Serse. *Sairr*-say.
Servais. Sairr-vay.
Serva Padrona, La. La⁵ *Sairr*-va⁵ Pad-*roh*-na⁵.
Sesquialtera. Sess-kwee-*ol*-ter-a⁵.
Sestetto. Sess-*tet*-toh.
Sette (It.). *Set*-tay.
Seufzend. *Zoyf*-tsent.
Seul. Su(r)l.
Seule. Su(r)l.
Seules. Su(r)l.
Seuls. Su(r)l.
Sevčik. *Shev*-cheek.
Severa. Sev-*ay*-ra.
Sévérac. Say-verr-rak.
Severamente. Sevairr-am-*en*-tay.
Severin (Norweg.). Say-verr-*een* or *Say*-verr-een.
Severità. Sev-ay-ree-*ta*⁵.
Severo. Sev-*ay*-roh.
Sevillana. Sev-eel-*yan*-a⁵.
Sextett (Ger.). Zex-*tet*.
Sextette (Fr.). Sex-tet.
Sextuor. Sex-tee²-orr.
Seyfried. *Zye*-freet.
Sfogato. Sfoh-*gah*-toh.
Sfoggiando. Sfoj-*yan*-doh.

---

6. The **ish** is really anywhere between that sound and 'ik' (varying in different parts of Germany). **7. th** as in *thin*. **8. g** as in *go*.

Sforzando. Sforrt-*san*-doh.
Sforzatissimo. Sforrt-sat-*eess*-see-moh.
Sforzato. Sforrt-*sah*-toh.
Sgambati. Zgam-*bah*-tee.
Sgambato. Zgam-*bah*-toh.
Shaporin. Shap-*oh*-reen.
Shebalin. Shay-*bah*-leen.
Shostakovich. Shoss-tah-*koh*-vitch.
Shudi. *Shoo*-dee.
Si (Fr., It., Sp.). See.
Sibelius. See-*bay*-lee-ooss.
Si bémol. See bay-mol.
Si bemolle. See bay-*mol*-lay.
Sibyl. *Sib*-il.
Si canta. See *can*-ta[5].
Sich. Zik[1].
Siciliana. See-chil-ee-*ah*-na[5].
Siciliano. See-chil-ee-*ah*-noh.
Sicilienne. See-see-lee-*en*.
Sieben. *Zee*-ben.
Sieg. Zeek.
Siegesmarsch. *Zeeg*-es-marrsh[5].
Siegfried. *Zeek*-freet.
Sieglinde. Zeek-*lind*-e(r).
Siegmeister. *Seeg*-my-stir.
Siegmund. *Zeek*-moont.
Siemens. *Zee*-mens.
Sifflöte. *Zif*-fle(r)-te(r).
Sigfrid. *Zeek*-freet.
Sigismund. *Zeeg*-iss-moont.
Signor Bruschino, Il. Eel Seen-*yawrr* Brooss-*kee*-noh.
Silas. See-lass.
Silbermann. *Zil*-berr-man.
Silenzio. See-*lents*-ee-oh.
Silvio. *Seel*-vee-oh.
Si maggiore. See maj-*yaw*-ray.
Simile. *See*-mee-lay.
Simili. *See*-mee-lee.
Si mineur. See mee-*nerr*.
Simon (Fr.). See-mo(ng).
Simone Boccanegra. See-*moh*-nay Boc-can-*nay*-gra[5].
Si minore. See mee-*naw*-ray.
Simplement. Sa(ng)-ple(r)-mo(ng).
Sin' (It.). Seen.
Sinding. *Sin*-ding.
Sinfonia. Seen-foh-*nee*-a[5].
Sinfonica. Seen-*fohn*-ee-ca[5].
Sinfonico. Seen-*fohn*-ee-coh.
Sinfonietta. Seen-foh-nee-*et*-ta[5].
Sinfonische Dichtung. Sin-*foh*-nish-e(r) *Dik*[1]-toong.
Singakademie. Zing-ak-ad-aym-*ee*.
Singbar. *Zing*-bahrr.
Singend. *Zing*-ent.
Singhiozzando. Seen-gee[8]-ots-*san*-doh.
Singspiel. *Zing*-shpeel.

Sinigaglia. See-nee-*gahl*-ya[5].
Sinistra. See-*neess*-tra[5].
Sino. *See*-noh.
Sinus (Eng.). *Sy*-nuss.
Si replica. See *rep*-lee-ca[5].
Si segue. See *say*-gway.
Sistina. Seess-*tee*-na[5].
Sistine (Eng.). *Siss*-teen.
Si suona. See soo-*oh*-na[5].
Si tace. See *tah*-chay.
Sitole (Eng.). *Sit*-ole.
Sivori. See-*vaw*-ree.
Six (Fr.). Before a consonant, See; before a vowel, Seez; when alone, Seess.
Sixième. Seez-yem.
Sjögren. *Shug*-rain.
Skalds. Skahlds.
Skizze. *Skit*-se(r).
Skizzen. *Skit*-sen.
Skraup. *Skrah*-oop.
Slancio. *Zlan*-choh.
Slargando. Zlahrr-*gan*-doh.
Slargandosi. Zlahrr-*gan*-doh-see.
Slegato. Zleg-*ah*-toh.
Slentando. Zlen-*tan*-doh.
Smania. *Zman*-ee-a[5].
Smaniante. Zman-ee-*an*-tay.
Smaniato. Zman-ee-*ah*-toh.
Smanioso. Zman-ee-*oh*-zoh.
Smareglia. Zma[5]-*rail*-ya[5].
Smetana. *Smet*-an-a[5].
Sminuando. Zmee-noo-*an*-doh.
Sminuito. Zmee-noo-*ee*-toh.
Smorfioso. Zmorr-fee-*oh*-zoh.
Smorzando. Zmawrrt-*san*-doh.
Smorzato. Zmawrrt-*sah*-toh.
Smyth. Smyth[7].
Snellamente. Znel-lam-*en*-tay.
Snello. *Znel*-loh.
Snetzler. *Snets*-lerr.
So (Ger.). Zoh.
Soave. Soh-*ah*-vay.
Soavità. Soh-ah-vee-*ta*[5].
Söderman. *Se*(r)-derr-man.
Soeben. Zoh-*ayb*-en.
Sofort. Zoh-*forrt*.
Soggetto. Soj-*jet*-toh.
Sogleich. Zoh-*glyk*[1].
Soir. Swahrr.
Sol. Sol.
Sola. *Soh*-la[5].
Sol bémol. Sol bay-mol.
Sol bemolle. Sol bay-*mol*-lay.
Soldatenzug. Zol-*dah*-ten-tsook.
Sol dièse. Sol dee-ez.
Sole (It.). *Soh*-lay.
Soleá. Soh-lay-*ah*.
Soleares. Soh-lay-*ah*-ress.
Solennel. Sol-an-el.
Solennellement. Sol-an-el-mo(ng).

Solennemente. Sol-en-nay-men-tay.
Solennità. Sol-en-nee-*ta*[5].
Soler. Soh-*lairr*.
Solesmes. Sol-em.
Sol-fa. Sol-*fah*.
Solfaing. Sol-*fah*-ing.
Solfége. Sol-fezj[3].
Solfeggio. Sol-*fej*-ee-oh.
Soli. *Soh*-lee.
Solito, Al. Al *sol*-ee-toh.
Sollecitando. Sol-let-chee-*tan*-doh.
Sollecito. Sol-*let*-chee-toh.
Solo. *Soh*-loh.
Soloklavier. Zoh-loh-klav-eer.
Soltanto. Sol-*tan*-toh.
Sombre (Fr.). So(ng)brr.
Sommesso. Som-*mess*-soh.
Sommo. *Som*-moh.
Son (Fr.). So(ng), before a consonant; Sonn, before a vowel.
Sonante. Son-*an*-tay.
Sonare. Son-*ah*-ray.
Sonata. Son-*ah*-ta[5].
Sonata da camera. Son-*ah*-ta[5] da[5] *cam*-ay-ra[5].
Sonata da chiesa. Son-*ah*-ta da[5] kee-*ay*-za[5].
Sonate (Fr.). Son-at.
Sonate (Ger.). Zoh-*nah*-te(r).
Sonate (It.). Son-*ah*-tay.
Sonaten. Zoh-*nah*-ten.
Sonatina. Son-ah-*tee*-na[5].
Sonatine (Fr.). Son-at-een.
Sonatine (It.). Son-ah-*tee*-nay.
Sonnambula, La. La[5] Son-*nam*-boo-la[5].
Sonnenquartette. Zon-en-kvarr-*tet*-e(r).
Sonnerie. Son-ne(r)-ree.
Sonoramente. Son-awrr-am-*en*-tay.
Sonore (Fr.). Son-awrr.
Sonorità. Son-awrr-ee-*ta*[5].
Sonorité. Son-orr-ee-*tay*.
Sonoro. Son-*aw*-roh.
Son qual nave. Son kwahl *nah*-vay.
Sons (Fr.). So(ng).
Sons bouchés. So(ng) boosh-ay.
Sopra. *Soh*-pra[5].
Sopran (Ger.). Zoh-*prahn*.
Soprana. Soh-*prah*-na[5].
Sopranino. Soh-pran-*ee*-noh.
Soprano. Soh-*prah*-noh.
Soprano sfogato. Soh-*prah*-noh sfoh-*gah*-toh.
Sopra una corda. Soh-pra oo-na[5] *cawrr*-da[5].
Sorabji. Sorr-*ab*-jee.
Sorda. *Sorr*-da[5].
Sordamente. Sorr-dam-*en*-tay.

---

1. k = 'ch' (cf. Scot. *loch*).   2. ee here really between 'ee' and 'oo' (cf. Scot. *puir*).   3. zj like 's' in *pleasure*.   4. ow as in *cow*.   5. a as in *lad*.

Sorde. *Sorr*-day.
Sordina. Sorr-*dee*-na⁵.
Sordini. Sorr-*dee*-nee.
Sordini alzati. Sorr-*dee*-nee alt⁵-*zah*-tee.
Sordini levati. Sorr-*dee*-nee lev-*ah*-tee.
Sordino. Sorr-*dee*-noh.
Sordo. *Sorr*-doh.
Sordun. Zorr-*doon*.
Sorgfalt. Zorrk-falt.
Sorgfältig. Zorrk-felt-ish⁶.
Soriano. Sawrr-ee-*ah*-noh.
Sospirando. Soss-pee-*ran*-doh.
Sospirante. Soss-pee-*ran*-tay.
Sospirevole. Soss-pee-*ray*-volay.
Sospiroso. Soss-pee-*roh*-zoh.
Sostenendo. Soss-ten-*en*-doh.
Sostenente. Soss-ten-*en*-tay.
Sostenuto. Soss-ten-*oo*-toh.
Sotto. *Sot*-toh.
Sotto voce. *Sot*-toh *voh*-chay.
Soudainement. Soo-den-mo(ng).
Souhaitty. Soo-et-tee.
Soupirant. Soo-pee-ro(ng).
Souple. Soopl.
Sourd. Soorr.
Sourde. Soorrd.
Sourdine. Soorr-deen.
Sous. Soo.
Sousedska. Soh-oo-sets-kah.
Soutenu. Soo-te(r)-nee².
Souter Liedekens. *Soo*-terr *Leet*-e(r)-kenz.
Sowerby. *Sour*-bee.
Spagnoletta. Span-yoh-*let*-ta⁵.
Spagnoletto. Span-yoh-*let*-toh.
Spallanzani. Spal⁵-lant-*sah*-nee.
Spandendo. Span-*den*-doh.
Sparafucile. Sparr⁵-aff-oo-*chee*-lay.
Sparta. *Spahrr*-ta⁵.
Spartita. Spahrr-*tee*-ta⁵.
Spartito. Spahrr-*tee*-toh.
Sparto. *Spahrr*-toh.
Spass. Shpahss.
Spassapensieri. Spass-sap-en-see-*ay*-ree.
Spasshaft. *Shpahss*-haft.
Später. Shpait-err.
Speaight. Spate.
Spediendo. Sped-ee-*en*-doh.
Sperdendosi. Spairr-*den*-doh-see.
Sphärophon. *Sfair*-roh-fon.
Spiana. Spee-*ah*-na⁵.
Spianato. Spee-an-*ah*-toh.
Spiccato. Spee-*cah*-toh.
Spiegando. Spee-ay-*gan*-doh.
Spiel. Shpeel.
Spielen. *Shpeel*-en.

Spielend. *Shpeel*-ent.
Spieler. *Shpeel*-err.
Spinet. Spin-*et*.
Spinetti. Spee-*net*-tee.
Spinnen. *Shpin*-en.
Spinnen des Tons. *Shpin*-en dess Tohnss.
Spinnerlied. *Shpin*-err-leet.
Spinnlied. *Shpin*-leet.
Spirante. Spee-*ran*-tay.
Spirito. *Spee*-ree-toh.
Spiritosamente. Spee-ree-toh-zam-*en*-tay.
Spiro. *Spee*-roh.
Spitz. Shpits.
Spitze. *Shpits*-e(r).
Spitzflöte. *Shpits*-fle(r)-te(r).
Spitzig. *Shpit*-sish⁶.
Spohr. Shpohrr.
Spontini. Spon-*tee*-nee.
Spöttisch. *Shpe*(r)*t*-ish.
Sprechchor. *Shprek*¹-kohrr.
Sprechend. *Shprek*¹-ent.
Sprechgesang. *Shprek*¹-gu(r)-zang.
Sprechstimme. *Shprek*¹-shtim-e(r).
Springar. *Spring*-arr.
Springdans. *Spring*-dance.
Springend. *Shpring*-ent.
Spruch-Sprecher. *Shprook*¹-Shprek¹-err.
Spugna. *Spoon*-ya⁵.
Squillante. Skweel-*lan*-tay.
Staatskapelle. *Shtahts*-kap-el-e(r).
Stäbchen. *Shtayb*-shen.
Stabile. *Stab*-ee-lay.
Staccatissimo. Stac-cat-*eess*-see-moh.
Staccato. Stac-*cah*-toh.
Stadler. *Shtahd*-lerr.
Stadtmusiker. *Shtat*-moo-zee-kerr.
Stadtpfeifer. *Shtat*-pfy-ferr.
Stadtpfeiferei. *Shtat*-pfy-ferr-rye.
Stahlharmonica. *Shtahl*-harr-moh-nee-kah.
Stamitz. *Shtah*-mits.
Stampita. Stam-*pee*-ta⁵.
Ständchen. *Shtent*-shen.
Standhaft. *Shtant*-haft.
Standhaftigkeit. *Shtant*-haft-ish⁶-kite.
Stark. Shtarrk.
Stark anblasen. Shtarrk *an*-blah-zen.
Stark blasend. Shtarrk *blah*-zent.
Stärker. *Shtairrk*-err.
Stassof. *Stass*-off.
Statkowski. Stat-*kov*-skee.

Statt. Shtat.
Stauffer. *Shtow*⁴-ferr.
Stcherbatchef. Shchair-bat-*choff*('off' not 'eff'—the accepted transliteration being faulty).
Stefani. *Stef*-an-ee.
Steffani. Stef-*fan*-ee.
Steg. Shtaik.
Stege. *Shtaig*-e(r).
Steibelt. *Shty*-belt.
Stein. Shtine.
Steinberg. *Shtayne*-bairrg.
Steiner. *Shty*-nerr.
Steinert. *Shtine*-errt (anglicized to *Stine*-ert).
Steingräber. *Shtine*-gray-berr.
Steinharmonica. *Shtine*-harr-moh-nee-kah.
Steinhausen. *Shtine*-how⁴-zen.
Stelle. *Shtel*-e(r).
Stellen. *Shtel*-en.
Stendendo. Sten-*den*-doh.
Stenhammar. *Stain*-ham-marr.
Stentando. Sten-*tan*-doh.
Stentare. Sten-*tah*-ray.
Stentatamento. Sten-tat-am-*en*-toh.
Stentato. Sten-*tah*-toh.
Stéphane. Stay-fan.
Sterbend. *Shtairr*-bent.
Steso. *Stay*-zoh.
Stessa. *Stess*-sa⁵.
Stesso. *Stess*-soh.
Stets. Shtaits.
Stierhorn. *Shteerr*-horrn.
Stile Rappresentativo. *Stee*-lay Rap-prez-en-tat-*ee*-voh.
Still (Ger.). Shtil.
Stille. *Shtil*-e(r).
Stiller Zink. *Shtil*-err Tsink.
Stimmbogen. *Shtim*-bohg-en.
Stimme. *Shtim*-e(r).
Stimmen. *Shtim*-en.
Stimmflöte. *Shtim*-fle(r)-te(r).
Stimmgabel. *Shtim*-gah-bel.
Stimmhorn. *Shtim*-horrn.
Stimmpfeife. *Shtim*-pfy-fe(r).
Stimmung. *Shtim*-oong.
Stimmungsbild. *Shtim*-oonks-bilt.
Stimmzug. *Shtimt*-soog.
Stinguendo. Steen-*gwen*-doh.
Stiracchiando. Stee-rak-kee-*an*-doh.
Stiracchiato. Stee-rak-kee-*ah*-toh.
Stirando. Stee-*ran*-doh.
Stirato. Stee-*rah*-toh.
Stockend. *Shtok*-ent.
Stockflöte. *Shtok*-fle(r)-te(r).
Stockhorn. *Shtok*-horrn.
Stoehr. Shterr.
Stoessel. *Ste*(r)-sel.

---

6. The **ish** is really anywhere between that sound and 'ik' (varying in different parts of Germany).
7. **th** as in *thin*.   8. **g** as in *go*.

Stojowski. Stoy-*ov*-skee.
Stölzel. *Shte*(r)*lt*-sel.
Stolzing. *Shtolt*-sing.
Storace (Eng.). *Storr*-ace.
Storace (It.). Stawrr-*ah*-chay.
Stornellatore. Stawrr-nel-at-*taw*-ray.
Stornellatrice. Stawrr-nel-at-*ree*-chay.
Stornelli. Stawrr-*nel*-ee.
Stornello. Stawrr-*nel*-loh.
Stracciacalando. Stratch-ee-a⁵-cal⁵-*an*-doh.
Stradella. Strad-*el*-la⁵.
Stradivari. Strad-ee-*vah*-ree.
Straff. Shtraff.
Straffando. Straf-*fan*-doh.
Straffato. Straf-*fah*-toh.
Straffer. *Shtraf*⁵-err.
Straloch. Stral-*ok*¹.
Strambotti. Stram-*bot*-tee.
Strambotto. Stram-*bot*-toh.
Strascicando. Strash-ee-*can*-doh.
Strascinando. Strash-see-*nan*-doh.
Strascinato. Strash-ee-*nah*-toh.
Strathspey. Strath-*spay*.
Straus. Shtrowss⁴.
Strauss. Shtrowss⁴.
Stravagante. Strav-ag-*an*-tay.
Stravinsky. Strav-*in*-skee(yer).
Straziante. Strats-ee-*an*-tay.
Streich. Shtryk¹.
Streicher. *Shtryk*¹-err.
Streng. Shtreng.
Strepito. *Stray*-pee-toh.
Strepitosamente. Stray-pee-toh-zam-*en*-tay.
Strepitoso. Stray-pee-*toh*-zoh.
Stretto. *Stret*-toh.
Streus. Shtroyss.
Strich. Shtrik¹.
Strichart. *Shtrik*¹-arrt⁵.
Strimpellata. Strim-pel-*lah*-ta⁵.
Strinassacchi. Streen-ass-*ak*-kee.
Stringendo. Streen-*jen*-doh.
Strisciando. Stree-shee-*an*-doh.
Strisciato. Stree-shee-*ah*-toh.
Stroh. Shtroh.
Strohfiedel. *Shtroh*-feed-el.
Stromentato. Stroh-men-*tah*-toh.

Stromenti. Stroh-*men*-tee.
Stromenti a corde. Stroh-*men*-tee a⁵ *cawrr*-day.
Stromenti a fiato. Stroh-*men*-tee a⁵ fee-*ah*-toh.
Stromenti a percossa. Stroh-*men*-tee a⁵ pairr-*coss*-sa⁵.
Stromenti d'arco. Stroh-*men*-tee *darr*⁵-coh.
Stromenti da tasto. Stroh-*men*-tee da⁵ *tass*-toh.
Stromenti di legno. Stroh-*men*-tee dee *layn*-yoh.
Stromenti d'ottone. Stroh-*men*-tee dot-*toh*-nay.
Stromento. Stroh-*men*-toh.
Strophe. *Stro*-fi ('i' as in *it*).
Strophic. *Stroh*-fic.
Strube. *Shtroo*-be(r).
Strumenti. Stroo-*men*-tee.
Strumento. Stroo-*men*-toh.
Stscherbatchew. Shchairr-bat-*choff* ('off' not 'eff'—the accepted transliteration being faulty).
Stück. Shteek².
Stucken. Shtook-en.
Studio (It.). *Stoo*-dee-oh.
Stürmend. *Shteerr*²-ment.
Stürmisch. *Shteerr*²-mish.
Style de perruque. Steel de(r) perr-reek².
Style galant. Steel gal-o(ng).
Su (It.). Soo.
Suabe Flute. Swayb Flute (a bastard term, with no authoritative pronunciation).
Suave (It.). Soo-*ah*-vay.
Suavità. Soo-av-ee-*ta*⁵.
Subito. *Soo*-bee-toh.
Suggia. Soo-*kee*¹-a⁵.
Sugli. *Sool*-yee.
Sui. *Soo*-ee.
Suite. Sweet.
Suivez. Swee-vay.
Suk. Sook.
Sul. Sool.
Sull'. Sool.
Sulla. *Sool*-la⁵.
Sulla tastiera. *Sool*-la⁵ tass-tee-ay-ra⁶.

Sulle. *Sool*-lay.
Sul ponticello. Sool pon-tee-*chel*-loh.
Sul tasto. Sool *tass*-toh.
Sulzer. *Zoolts*-err.
Summend. *Zoom*-ent.
Suo. *Soo*-oh.
Suo loco. *Soo*-oh *law*-coh.
Suoni. Soo-*oh*-nee.
Suono. Soo-*oh*-noh.
Suor Angelica. Soo-*awr* An-*jay*-lee-ca⁵.
Superbo. Soo-*pairr*-boh.
Suppé. See²-*pay*.
Suppliant (Fr.). See²-plee-o(ng).
Supplichevole. Soo-plee-*kay*-voh-lay.
Supplichevolmente. Soo-plee-*kay*-vol-*men*-tay.
Supprimez. See²-*pree*-may.
Sur (Fr.). Seer².
Suriano. Soo-ree-*ah*-noh.
Sur la touche. Seer² la⁵ toosh.
Sur le chevalet. Seer² le(r) shev-al-ay.
Surtout. Seer²-too.
Susato. Soo-*zah*-toh.
Süss. Zeess².
Süssmayer. *Zeess*²-my-er.
Sussurrando. Sooss-soo-*ran*-doh.
Sussurrante. Sooss-soo-*ran*-tay.
Svegliando. Zvail-*yan*-doh.
Svegliato. Zvail-*yah*-toh.
Svelto. *Zvel*-toh.
Svendsen. *Sven*-s'n.
Svolgimento. Zvol-jee-*men*-toh.
Sweelinck. *Svay*-link.
Sylvains. Seel-va(ng).
Sylvester. *Sil*-vest-er.
Symmes. Sims.
Symphonie (Fr.). Sa(ng)-fon-ee.
Symphonie (Ger.). Zim-foh-*nee*.
Symphonie burlesque. Sa(ng)-fon-ee beer²-lesk.
Symphonie espagnole. Sa(ng)-fon-ee ess-pan-yol.
Symphonique. Sa(ng)-fon-eek.
Symphonisch. Zim-*foh*-nish.
Szymanowski. Shim-an-*ov*-skee.

T

Tabarro, Il. Eel Tab-*ahrr*-roh.
Tabatière à musique. Tab-at-yairr a⁵ mee²-zeek.
Tablature (Eng.). *Tab*-lat-your (but *Shorter Oxford Dict.* authorizes also 'tsher' for last syll.).
Tabor (Eng.). *Tay*-borr.
Tabourot. Tab-oo-roh.
Tabulatur. Tab-oo-lat⁵-*oorr*.
Tacciono. *Tah*-choh-noh.
Tace. *Tah*-chay.
Tacere. Tatch-*ay*-ray.
Tacet. *Tass*-et.
Tafelklavier. *Tah*-fel-klav-eer.
Taglioni. Tal-ee-*oh*-nee.
Taillefer. Ty-ye(r)-fairr.
Tailleferre. Ty-ye(r)-fairr.
Takt. As Eng. *Tact*.
Taktart. *Tact*-arrt.
Taktfest. *Tact*-fest.
Takthalten. *Tact*-halt⁵-en.
Taktieren. Tact-*ee*-ren.
Taktig. *Tact*-ish⁶.
Taktmässig. *Tact*-*mess*-ish⁶.
Taktnote. *Tact*-noh-te(r).
Taktpause. *Tact*-pow⁴-ze(r).
Taktschlag. *Tact*-shlahk.
Taktschlagen. *Tact*-shlahg-en.
Taktstock. *Tact*-shtok.
Taktstrich. *Tact*-shtrik¹.
Taktwechsel. *Tact*-vek-sel.
Takt wie vorher zwei. Tact vee *fohrr*-hairr tsvye.
Taktzeichen. *Tact*-tsy-shen.
Taleadas. Tal-ay-*ah*-dass.
Talismano, Il. Eel Tal-eez-*mah*-noh.
Talmage. *Tal*⁵-mayge.
Talon. Tal-o(ng).
Tambora. Tam-*baw*-rah.
Tambour. To(ng)-boorr.
Tambour de Basque. To(ng)-boorr de(r) *Bask*.
Tambour de Provence. To(ng)-boorr de(r) Prov-o(ng)ss.
Tambourin (Fr.). To(ng)-boo-ra(ng).
Tambourine (Eng.). Tam-boo-*reen*.
Tambourin genre Watteau. To(ng)-boo-ra(ng) zjo(ng)rr³ Vat-oh.
Tambour militaire. To(ng)-boorr mee-lee-tairr.
Tamburin. *Tam*-boo-reen.
Tamburino. Tam-boo-*ree*-noh.
Tamburo basco. Tam-*boo*-roh *bass*-coh.
Tamburo grande. Tam-*boo*-roh *gran*-day.

Tamburo grosso. Tam-*boo*-roh *gross*-soh.
Tamburo militare. Tam-*boo*-roh mee-lee-*tah*-ray.
Tamburone. Tam-boo-*roh*-nay.
Tamburopiccolo. Tam-*boo*-roh *peek*-koh-loh.
Tamburo rullante. Tam-*boo*-roh rool-*lan*-tay.
Tamerlano. Tam-airr-*lah*-noh.
Tamino. Tam-*ee*-noh.
Tampon (Eng.). *Tam*-pon.
Tampon (Fr.). To(ng)-po(ng).
Tancredi. Tan-*cray*-dee.
Tändelei. Tend-e(r)-*lie*.
Tändelnd. *Tend*-elnt.
Taneief. Tan-*yay*-yef.
Tannenbaum. *Tan*-en-bowm⁴.
Tannhäuser. *Tan*-hoyz-err.
Tansman. *Tanss*-man.
Tant (Fr.). To(ng).
Tanto. *Tan*-toh.
Tanymarian. Tanne(r)-*mahrr*-yan.
Tanz. Tants.
Tänze. *Tent*-se(r).
Tarantella. Ta⁵-ran-*tel*-la⁵.
Tarantelle. Tarr-o(ng)-tel.
Tarbouka. Tahr-book-a⁵.
Tarda. *Tahrr*-da⁵.
Tardamente. Tahr-dam-*en*-tay.
Tardando. Tahrr-*dan*-doh.
Tardantemente. Tahrr-dant-aym-*en*-tay.
Tardato. Tahrr-*dah*-toh.
Tardi. *Tahrr*-dee.
Tardo. *Tahrr*-doh.
Tarogato. Tarr⁵-oh-*gah*-toh.
Tárrega. Tar-ray-ga⁵.
Tartini. Tahrr-*tee*-nee.
Tasso. *Tass*-soh.
Taste. *Tast*-e(r).
Tasten. *Tast*-en.
Tasti. *Tass*-tee.
Tastiera. Tass-tee-ay-ra⁵.
Tastiera per luce. Tass-tee-ay-ra⁵ pairr *loo*-chay.
Tasto. *Tass*-toh.
Tasto solo. *Tass*-toh *soh*-loh.
Taubert. Tow⁴-berrt.
Taubmann. Towp⁴-man.
Tausch. Towsh⁴.
Tausig. Tow⁴-sish⁶.
Tavan. Tav-o(ng).
Tchaikovsky. Chy-*kov*-skee(ye).
Tchárdache. Charr-dash.
Tcherepnin. Cherr-ep-*neen*.
Tedesca. Ted-*ess*-ca⁵.
Tedesche. Ted-*ess*-kay.
Tedeschi. Ted-*ess*-kee.

Tedesco. Ted-*ess*-coh.
Teil. Tile.
Teilen. *Tile*-en.
Telemann. *Tay*-le(r)-man.
Tellefsen. *Tel*-ev-sen.
Teller. *Tel*-err.
Telyn. *Tel*-in.
Tema. *Tay*-ma⁵.
Tempesta. Tem-*pess*-ta⁵.
Tempestosamente. Tem-pess-toh-zam-*en*-tay.
Tempestoso. Tem-pess-*toh*-zoh.
Tempi. *Tem*-pee.
Tempo. *Tem*-poh.
Tempo alla breve. *Tem*-poh al-la⁵ *bray*-vay.
Tempo comodo. *Tem*-poh *com*-oh-doh.
Tempo di ballo. *Tem*-poh dee *bal*⁵-loh.
Tempo di minuetto. *Tem*-poh dee mee-noo-*et*-toh.
Tempo fondamentale. *Tem*-poh fon-dam-en-*tah*-lay.
Tempo giusto. *Tem*-poh *jooss*-toh.
Tempo maggiore. *Tem*-poh maj-*yaw*-ray.
Tempo minore. *Tem*-poh mee-*naw*-ray.
Tempo ordinario. *Tem*-poh awrr-dee-*nahrr*-ee-oh.
Tempo primo. *Tem*-poh *pree*-moh.
Tempo rubato. *Tem*-poh roo-*bah*-toh.
Tempo wie vorher. *Temp*-oh vee fohrr-*hairr*.
Temps. To(ng).
Tenaglia. Ten-*ahl*-ya.
Tendre. To(ng)drr.
Tendrement. To(ng)-dr(er)-mo(ng).
Tenebroso. Ten-ay-*broh*-zoh.
Tenendo. Ten-*en*-doh.
Tenendo il canto. Ten-*en*-doh eel *can*-toh.
Teneramente. Ten-ay-ram-*en*-tay.
Tenerezza. Ten-ay-*rets*-sa⁵.
Tenero. *Ten*-ay-roh.
Teneroso. Ten-ay-*roh*-zoh.
Tenete. Ten-*ay*-tay.
Ténor. Tay-nawrr.
Tenore. Ten-*aw*-ray.
Tenore leggiero. Ten-*aw*-ray lej-*yay*-roh.
Tenore robusto. Ten-*aw*-ray roh-*booss*-toh.

---

6. The **ish** is really anywhere between that sound and 'ik' (varying in different parts of Germany).
7. **th** as in *thin*.   8. **g** as in *go*.

Tenorgeige. Ten-*ohrr*-gy[8]-gu(r).

Tenorposaune. Ten-*ohrr*-poh-zou[4]-ne(r).

Tenorstimme. Ten-*ohrr*-shtim-e(r).

Tenortuba. Ten-*ohrr*-too-bah.

Tenschert. *Ten*-sherrt.

Tenu. Te(r)-nee[2].

Tenue. Te(r)-nee[2].

Tenuta. Tenn-*oo*-ta[5].

Tenuto. Ten-*oo*-toh.

Tepidamente. Tep-ee-dam-*en*-tay.

Tepidità. Tep-id-ee-*ta*[5].

Tepido. *Tep*-ee-doh.

Terana. Ter-*rah*-na[5].

Teresa, Maria. (As usual in Eng.) Ma[5]-*ree*-a[5] (or Ma[5]-*rye*-a[5]) Ter-*ray*-za[5].

Teresia, Maria (Ger.). Mah-ree-ah Tay-*ray*-see-ah.

Terpodion (Eng.). Ter-*poh*-dee-on.

Terpodion (Ger.). Tairr-*poh*-dee-on.

Terpsichore. Terp-*sic*-awrr-ee.

Terza Rima. *Tairrt*-sa[5] *Ree*-ma[5].

Terzett (Ger.). Tairrt-*set*.

Terzetto. Tairrt-*set*-toh.

Terzi Tuoni. *Tairrt*-see Too-*aw*-nee.

Tessitura. Tess-see-*too*-ra[5].

Testa. *Tess*-ta[5].

Testo. *Tess*-toh[5].

Tetrazzini. *Tet*-rats-*see*-nee.

Thaïs. Tah-eess.

Thalberg. *Tahl*-bairrg.

Thamar. Tam-*ahrr*.

Theater. Tay-*ah*-terr.

Theile. *Ty*-le(r).

Thekla (Ger.). *Tay*-klah.

Théobald. Tay-ohb-ald[5].

Théodore (Fr.). Tay-oh-dawrr.

Théophile. Tay-oh-feel.

Theorbo (Eng.). Thee[7]-*awr*-boh.

Thérémin. Tairr-*min* (Rus.), Tay-ray-ma(ng) (Fr.).

Theresienmesse. Tay-*ray*-zee-en-*mess*-e(r).

Thésée. Tay-zay.

Thesis (in conducting). *Thee*[7]-siss or *Thess*[7]-iss.

Thibaut. Tee-boh.

Thibaut de Courville. Tee-boh de(r) Coor-veel.

Thibouville-Lamy. Tee-boo-veel-Lam-ee.

Thomas (Fr.). Tom-ah.

(Thomas) Aquinas (in Eng.) Ak-*wine*-ass[5].

(Thomas of) Celano. Chel-*ah*-noh.

Thoms. Toms.

Thorsteinsson. *Torr*-stine-son.

Thrane. *Trah*-ne(r).

Threnody. *Threen*-oh-di ('i' as in *it*) or *Thren*-oh-di ('i' as in *it*).

Thuner-Sonate. *Too*-ner Zoh-*nah*-te(r).

Tief. Teef.

Tief Cammerton. Teef *Kam*-err-tohn.

Tiefgespannt. *Teef*-gu(r)-shpant.

Tief Kammerton. Teef *Kam*-err-tohn.

Tiefland. *Teef*-lant.

Tiepido. Tee-*ay*-pee-doh.

Tierce de Picardie. Tee-airss de(r) Pee-carrd-ee.

Tierce Picarde. Tee-airss Pee-carrd.

Tietjens. *Teet*-yenz.

Til Eulenspiegel. Til *Oil*-en-shpeeg-el.

Timbales. Ta(ng)-bal.

Timbre (Eng.). *Tim*-ber; or *Tam*-ber, or as above (pronunciations authorized by *Concise Oxford Dictionary*).

Timbre (Fr.). Ta(ng)brr.

Timbrer. Ta(ng)-bray.

Timidezza. Tee-mee-*dets*-sa[5].

Timido. *Tee*-mee-doh.

Timore. Tee-*maw*-ray.

Timorosamente. Tee-maw-roh-zam-*en*-tay.

Timoroso. Tee-maw-*roh*-zoh.

Timpani. *Tim*-pan-ee.

Timpani a pedale. *Tim*-pan-ee a[5] ped-*ah*-lay.

Timpani coperti. *Tim*-pan-ee cop-*airr*-tee.

Tinel. Tee-nel.

Tinódi. Tin-*oh*-dee.

Tintement. Ta(ng)-te(r)-mo(ng).

Tinter. Ta(ng)-tay.

Tintinnando. Tin-teen-*nan*-doh.

Tintinnare. Tin-teen-*nah*-ray.

Tinto. *Teen*-toh.

Tipica. *Tee*-pee-ka[5].

Tirana. Tee-*rah*-na[5].

Tirando. Tee-*ran*-doh.

Tirare. Tee-*rah*-ray.

Tirasse du Grand Orgue. Tee-rass dee[2] Gront Awrrg.

Tirasse du Positif. Tee-rass dee[2] Poz-ee-teef.

Tirasse du Récit. Tee-rass dee[2] Ray-see.

Tirato. Tee-*rah*-toh.

Tiré. Tee-ray.

Tirer. Tee-ray.

Tirez. Tee-ray.

Tiro, Trombone a. Trom-*boh*-nay a[5] *Tee*-roh.

Tirolese (Ital.). Tee-roh-*lay*-zay.

Titelouze. Teet-looz.

Titiens. *Teet*-yenz.

Tito. *Tee*-toh.

Titof, Titov. *Teet*-off.

Titurel. *Tee*-too-rel.

Tobend. *Toh*-bent.

Tobias (Eng.). Toh-*by*-ass.

Toccare. Toc-*cah*-ray.

Toccata. Toc-*cah*-ta[5].

Toccatina. Toc-cat-*ee*-na[5].

Toch. Tok[1].

Todt. Toht.

Todtenmarsch. *Toht*-en-marrsh.

Todtenmesse. *Toht*-en-mess-e(r).

Toëschi. Toh-*ess*-kee.

Togli. *Tol*-yee.

Toile. Twahl.

Tomás. Toh-*mass*.

Tomaschek. *Tom*-ah-shek.

Tomasi. Tom-*mah*-zee.

Tombeau. To(ng)-boh.

Tome. Tom.

Tommasini. Tom-ma[5]-*see*-nee.

Tommaso. Tom-*mah*-zoh.

Ton (Fr.). To(ng).

Ton (Ger.). Tohn.

Tonabstand. *Tohn*-*ap*-shtant.

Tonada. Toh-*nah*-da[5].

Tonadilla. Toh-nad-*eel*-ya[5].

Ton aigre. To(ng) aygrr.

Ton angeben, Den. Dain Tohn *an*-gay-ben.

Tonante. Toh-*nan*-tay.

Tonart. *Tohn*-arrt.

Tonbild. *Tohn*-bilt.

Ton bouché. To(ng) boo-shay.

Tonbühne. *Tohn*-bee[2]-ne(r).

Ton de chasse. To(ng) de(r) shass.

Ton de cor. To(ng) de(r) cawrr.

Ton d'Église. To(ng) day-gleez.

Ton de rechange. To(ng) de(r) re(r)-shonzj[3].

Ton de trompette. To(ng) de(r) tromp-et.

Tondichter. *Tohn*-dik[1]-terr.

Tondichtung. *Tohn*-dik[1]-toong.

Tondo. *Ton*-doh.

Ton doux. To(ng) doo.

Töne. *Te*(r)-ne(r).

Tönende Handschrift. *Te*(r)-nen-de(r) *Hant*-shrift.

Tonfarbe. *Tohn*-farrb-e(r).

Tonfolge. *Tohn*-folg-e(r).

Tonfülle. *Tohn*-feel[2]-e(r).

Tongeschlecht. *Tohn*-gu(r)-shlekt[1].

---

1. k = 'ch' (cf. Scot. *loch*). **2. ee** here really between 'ee' and 'oo' (cf. Scot. *puir*). **3. zj** like 's' in *pleasure*. **4. ow** as in *cow*. **5. a** as in *lad*.

Tonhöhe. *Tohn*-he(r)-e(r).
Toni. *Taw*-nee.
Tonika-do. *Tohn*-nik-ah-*doh*.
Tonio. *Tohn*-ee-oh.
Tonitruone. Toh-nee-troo-*oh*-nay.
Tonkunst. *Tohn*-koonst.
Tonkünstler. *Tohn*-keenst[2]-lerr.
Tonlage. *Tohn*-lahg-e(r).
Tonlehre. *Tohn*-lay-re(r).
Tonleiter. *Tohn*-lie-terr.
Tonlos. *Tohn*-lohss.
Tonmalerei. *Tohn*-mah-lerr-cyc (last syll. as the Eng. word).
Tonmass. *Tohn*-mahss.
Tonnerre. Ton-airr.
Tono. *Toh*-noh.
Tonreihe. *Tohn*-rye-e(r).
Tonschlüssel. *Tohn*-shleess[2]-el.
Tonsetzer. *Tohn*-zet-serr.
Toplady. (Accent on first syll.).
Torelli. Torr-*el*-lee.
Tornada. Tawrr-*nah*-da[5].
Tornando. Torr-*nan*-doh.
Tornare. Torr-*nah*-ray.
Torvo. *Torr*-voh.
Toscanini. Toss-can-*ee*-nee.
Toselli. Toz-*el*-lee.
Tosi. Taw-zee.
Tosse de capra. *Toh*-say da[5] *cah*-pra[5].
Tosti. *Toss*-tee.
Tostissimamente. Toss-teess-see-mam-*en*-tay.
Tostissimo. Toss-*teess*-see-moh.
Tosto. *Toss*-toh.
Tostquartette. *Tost*-kvarr-*tet*-te(r).
Tote Stadt, Die. Dee *toht*-e(r) Shtat.
Touche. Toosh.
Touché. Too-shay.
Toucher. Too-shay.
Toucher du piano. Too-shay dee[2] pee-an-oh.
Touchez. Too-shay.
Toujours. Too-zjoorr[3].
Tournemire. Toor-ne(r)-meer.
Tourte. Toort.
Tous. Before a consonant, Too; before a vowel, Tooss; standing alone, Tooss.
Tout. Before a consonant, Too; before a vowel, Toot; standing alone, Too.
Tout à coup. Too-ta[5]-coo.
Tout à fait. Too-ta-fay.
Toute. Toot.
Tout ensemble. Toot-o(ng)-so(ng)bl.
Toutes. Before a consonant, Toot; before a vowel, Toots.
Tovey. *Toh*-vi ('i' as in *it*).

Trachea. *Trahk*-ee-ah, or Trak-*ee*-ah.
Tradotto. Trad-*ot*-toh.
Traduction. Trad-eekss[2]-yo(ng).
Traduit. Trad-wee.
Traduzione. Trad-oot-see-*oh*-nay.
Traetta. Trah-*et*-ta[5].
Tragédies spirituelles. Trazj[3]-ayd-ee spee-ree-tee[2]-el.
Traîné. Tray-nay.
Traité de la Musette. Tray-tay de(r) la Mee[2]-zet.
Tranquillamente. Tran-kweel-lam-*en*-tay.
Tranquillezzo. Tran-kweel-*lets*-soh.
Tranquillità. Tran-kweel-lee-*ta*[5].
Tranquillo. Tran-*kweel*-loh.
Transalpina. Tran-sal[5]-*pee*-na[5].
Trapassi. Trap-*ass*[5]-see.
Trascinando. Trash-ee-*nan*-doh.
Trascrizione. Trass-creet-see-*oh*-nay.
Trattenuto. Trat-tay-*noo*-toh.
Tratto. *Trat*-toh.
Trauer. *Trow*[4]-err.
Trauermarsch. *Trow*[4]-err-marrsh.
Trauersymphonie. *Trow*[4]-err-zim-foh-nee.
Trauervoll. *Trow*[4]-err-fol.
Trauerwalzer. *Trow*[4]-err-valts[5]-err.
Traum. Trowm[4].
Traumbild. *Trowm*[4]-bilt.
Träumend. *Troy*-ment.
Träumerei. Troy-merr-*rye*.
Träumerisch. *Troy*-merr-ish.
Traurig. *Trow*[4]-rish[6].
Trautonium. Trowm[4]-*tohn*-ee-oom.
Trautwein. *Trowt*[4]-vine.
Traversa. Trav-*airr*-sa[5].
Traversflöte. Trav-*airrss*-fle(r)-te(r).
Traversière. Trav-airr-see-*airr*.
Traverso. Trav-*airr*-soh.
Traviata, La. La[5] Trav-ee-*ah*-ta[5].
Tre (It.). Tray.
Tre corde. Tray *cawrr*-day.
Treibend. *Try*-bent.
Tremando. Tray-*man*-doh.
Tremante. Tray-*man*-tay.
Tremblant. Tro(ng)-blo(ng).
Tremendissimo. Tray-men-*deess*-see-moh.
Tremendo. Tray-*mend*-oh.
Tremolando. Tray-moh-*lan*-doh.
Tremolante. Tray-moh-*lan*-tay.

Tremolo. *Tray*-moh-loh.
Trenodia. Tren-*aw*-dee-a[5].
Trepak. Tray-*pak*.
Tre parti. Tray *parr*[5]-tee.
Très. Before a consonant, Tray; before a vowel, Trez.
Trescone. Tress-*koh*-nay.
Triana. Tree-*ah*-na[5].
Triangel (Ger.). *Tree*-an-gel[8].
Triangolo. Tree-*an*-goh-loh.
Trichord (Eng.). *Try*-cawrd.
Trilogia (It.). Tree-loh-*jee*-a[5].
Trilogie (Fr.). Tree-lozj[3]-ee.
Trilogie (Ger.). Tree-lohg-*ee*.
Trilogy. *Tril*-oh-ji ('i' as in *it*).
Trinklied. *Trink*-leet.
Trionfale. Tree-on-*fah*-lay.
Trionfante. Tree-on-*fan*-tay.
Tripelconcert. *Tree*-pel-kon-tsairrt.
Tripelkonzert. *Tree*-pel-kon-tsairrt.
Triple-croche. *Tree*-ple(r)-crosh.
Triptych (Eng.). *Trip*-tik.
Triptyque (Fr.). Treep-teek.
Trisagion. Tris-*ay*-ji-on, or Tris-*aj*-i-on (in both cases 'i' as in *it*).
Tristan und Isolde. *Tree*-stahn oont Ee-*zol*-de(r).
Triste. Treest.
Tristesse. Treest-ess.
Tristezza. Treess-*tets*-sa[5].
Tristo. *Treess*-toh.
Tritone (Eng.). *Try*-tone.
Trittico. *Treet*-tee-coh.
Trois. Trwah.
Troisième. Trwahz-yem.
Troisième position. Trwahz-yem poz-eess-yo(ng).
Trollens. Troll-lo(ng).
Tromba. *Trom*-ba[5].
Tromba a macchina. *Trom*-ba[5] a *mak*-kee-na[5].
Tromba bassa. *Trom*-ba[5] bass-sa[5].
Tromba cromatica. *Trom*-ba[5] croh-*mat*-ee-ca[5].
Tromba da tirarsi. *Trom*-ba[5] da[5] tee-*rahrr*-see.
Tromba marina. *Trom*-ba[5] ma[5]-*ree*-na[5].
Tromba spezzata. *Trom*-ba[5] spetz-*zah*-ta[5].
Tromba ventile. *Trom*-ba[5] ven-*tee*-lay.
Trombone a cilindri. *Trom*-*boh*-nay a[5] chee-*leen*-dree.
Trombone à coulisse. Tro(ng)-bohn a[5] coo-leess.
Trombone alto (Fr.). Tro(ng)-bohn al[5]-toh.

---

6. The **ish** is really anywhere between that sound and 'ik' (varying in different parts of Germany)
     7. **th** as in *thin*.   8. **g** as in *go*.

Trombone à pistons. Tro(ng)-bohn a⁵ pees-to(ng).

Trombone a tiro. Tram-*boh*-nay a⁵ *tee*-roh.

Trombone basse. Tro(ng)-bohn bass.

Trombone basso. Trom-*boh*-nay *bass*-soh.

Trombone duttile. Trom-*boh*-nay *doot*-tee-lay.

Trombone ventile. Trom-*boh*-nay ven-*tee*-lay.

Trombonino. Trom-boh-*nee*-noh.

Trommel. *Trom*-el.

Trommelflöte. *Trom*-el-fle(r)-te(r).

Trompe. Tro(ng)p.

Trompe de Béarn. Tro(ng)p de(r) Bay-arrn.

Trompe de Berne. Tro(ng)p de(r) Bairrn.

Trompe de laquais. Tro(ng)p de(r) lak-ay.

Trompete (Ger.). Trom-*pay*-te(r).

Trompetengeige. Trom-*pay*-ten-gy⁵-gu(r).

Trompette. Tro(ng)-pet.

Trompette à coulisses. Tro(ng)-pet a⁵ coo-leess.

Trompette à pistons. Tro(ng)-pet a⁵ pees-to(ng).

Trompette basse. Tro(ng)-pet bass.

Trompette chromatique. Tro(ng)-pet crom-at-eek.

Trompette d'harmonie. Tro(ng)-pet dahrr-mon-ee.

Trompette marine. Tro(ng)-pet marr-een.

Trop. Troh (before a consonant). Trop (before a vowel).

Troppo. *Trop*-poh.

Troqueurs, Les. Lay Trok-urr.

Trouillon. Troo-ee-yo(ng).

Trouvère. Troo-vairr.

Trovatore, Il. Eel Trov-at-*aw*-ray.

Trowell. *Trow*⁴-el.

Troyens à Carthage, Les. Lay Trwoy-ya(ng)-za⁵ Cahrrt-azj³.

Trüb. Treep³.

Trübe. *Treeb*²-e(r).

Trumscheit. *Troom*-shyte.

Try, Charles de. Sharrl de(r) Tree.

Tryphone. Tree-fon.

Tschudi. *Tshoo*-dee.

Tsigane. Tsee-gan.

Tuba (Eng.). *Tew*-ba⁵.

Tuba (Lat., It., Sp., Ger.). *Too*-ba⁵.

Tuba (Fr.). Tee²-ba⁵.

Tuba mirabilis. *Too*-ba mee-*rab*-ee-leess.

Tuba sonora. Too-ba⁵ son-*aw*-rah.

Tubo di recambio. *Too*-boh dee ray-*cam*-bee-oh.

Tuoni. Too-*aw*-nee.

Tuono. Too-*aw*-noh.

Turandot (It.). Too-ran-*dot*.

Turba. Toorr-ba⁵.

Turca. *Toorr*-ca⁵.

Turchaninof. Toorr-chan-*nee*-off.

Turchi. *Toor*-kee.

Turco. *Toor*-coh.

Turiddu. *Too*-ree-doo.

Turina. Too-*ree*-na⁵.

Türk. Teerrk².

Türkisch. *Teerrk*²-ish.

Turlutaine. Teerr²-lee²-ten.

Türmermeister. *Teer*²-merr-my-sterr.

Turm-musik. *Toorm*-moo-*zeek*.

Turmsonate. *Toorrm*-zoh-*nah*-te(r).

Turque. Teerrk².

Turtchaninow. Toorr-chan-*een*-off.

Tusch. Toosh.

Tutta. *Toot*-ta³.

Tutte. *Toot*-tay.

Tutte corde. *Toot*-tay *cawrr*-day.

Tutte le corde. *Toot*-tay lay *cawrr*-day.

Tutti. *Toot*-tee.

Tutto. *Toot*-toh.

Tympani (It. misspelt). *Tim*-pan-ee.

Typophone. *Ty*-poh-fohn.

Tyrolienne. Tee-rol-yen.

Tyrwhitt. *Ti*-rit.

Tzigane. Tsee-gan.

U

Über. *Ee*²-berr.

Übung. *Ee*²-boong.

Übungen. *Ee*²-boong-en.

Ueber. *Ee*²-berr.

Uebung. *Ee*²-boong.

Uebungen. *Ee*²-boong-en.

Uguale. Oo-*gwah*-lay.

Uguali. Oo-*gwah*-lee.

Uguaglianza. Oo-gwal-ee-*ant*-sa⁵.

Ugualità. Oo-gwal-ee-*ta*⁵.

Ugualmente. Oo-gwal-*men*-tay.

Uhr, Die. Dee Oorr.

Ukulele. Yoo-kul-*ay*-lee.

Ultima. *Ool*-tee-ma⁵.

Ultimamente. *Ool*-tee-mam-*en*-tay.

Ultimo. *Ool*-tee-moh.

Umana. Oo-*mah*-na⁵.

Umano. Oo-*mah*-noh.

Umberto. Oom-*bairr*-toh.

Umkehrung. *Oom*-kay-roong.

Umlauf. *Oom*-lowf⁴.

Umore. Oo-*maw*-ray.

Umstimmen. *Oom*-shtim-en.

Umstimmung. *Oom*-shtim-oong.

Un (Fr.). Before a consonant, U(rng); before a vowel, U(r)n.

Un (It.). Oon.

Una (It.). Oo-na⁵.

Una corda. Oo-na⁵ *cawrr*-da⁵.

Un Ballo in Maschera. Oon Bal⁵-loh een *Mask*-ay-ra⁵.

Une. Een².

Ungar. *Oon*-gahrr.

Ungarisch. *Oon*-garr-ish.

Ungebunden. *Oon*-gu(r)-boon-den.

Ungeduldig. *Oon*-gu(r)-dool-dish⁶.

Ungefähr. Oon-gu(r)-*fairr*.

Ungestüm. *Oon*-gu(r)-shteem².

---

1. k = 'ch' (cf. Scot. *loch*).   **2. ee** here really between 'ee' and 'oo' (cf. Scot. *puir*).
    3. zj like 's' in *pleasure*.   **4. ow** as in *cow*.   **5. a** as in *lad*.

Ungezwungen. *Oon*-gu(r)-tsvoong-en.
Ungherese. Oon-gay-*ray*-zay.
Unheimlich. *Oon*-hime-lik[1].
Uni (Fr.). Ee[2]-nee.
Unie (Fr.). Ee[2]-nee.
Unies (Fr.). Ee[2]-nee.
UnionInternationaledeRadiodiffusion. Een[2]-yo(ng) A(ng)-tairr-nass-yon-al de(r) Rad-yoh-dee-feez[2]-yo(ng).
Unis (Fr.). Ee[2]-nee.

Unisono. Oo-nee-*soh*-noh.
Uniti. Oo-*nee*-tee.
Unito. Oo-*nee*-toh.
Unmerklich. *Oon*-mairrk-lik[1].
Uno. *Oo*-noh.
Un peu. U(rng) pu(r).
Un poco. Oon-*paw*-coh.
Unruhe. *Oon*-roo-he(r).
Unruhig. *Oon*-roo-hish[6].
Unschuldig. *Oon*-shool-dish[6].
Unten. *Oon*-ten.

Unter. *Oon*-terr.
Untersatz. *Oon*-terr-zats.
Unterwerk. *Oon*-terr-vairrk.
Urbain. Eerr[2]-ba(ng).
Uribe-Holguin. Oo-*ree*-bay *Ohl*-geen[8].
Ursprünglich. Oorr-*shpreeng*[2]-lik[1].
Ut (Fr.). Eet[2].
Ut bémol. Eet[2] bay-mol.
Ut dièse. Eet[2] dee-ez.

V

Va. Va[5].
Vacillando. Vatch-ee-*lan*-doh.
Vacillant. Vass-ee-yo(ng), or Vass-eel-o(ng).
Vaczek. *Vats*-ek.
Vadé. Vad-ay.
Vaghezza. Vag-*ets*-sa[5].
Vaglia. *Val*-ya[5].
Vago. *Vah*-goh.
Valdemosa. Val-day-*moh*-sa[5].
Valentini. Val-en-*tee*-nee.
Valeur. Val-urr.
Valkyrie. *Val*-ki-ri or Val-*ki*-ri or Val-*kee*-ri (all the 'i's as in *it*).
Valore. Val-*aw*-ray.
Valse. Valss[5].
Valverde. Val-*vairr*-day.
Van Dieren. Fan *Deer*-en.
Van Doorslaer. Fan *Doorrss*-lahrr.
Vanhall. Van-*hal*[5].
Van Malder. Van *Mal*[5]-derr.
Van Nuffel. Van *Nee*[2]-fel.
Vaporeuse. Vap-awrr-ʏ(r)z.
Vaporeux. Vap-awrr-u(r).
Varèse. Varr-ez.
Variante. Vahr-ree-*an*-tay.
Variata. Varr[5]-ee-*ah*-ta[5].
Variations caractéristiques. Varr[5]-ee-ass[5]-yo(ng) ca[5]-rac-tay-reess-teek.
Variato. Varr[5]-ee-*ah*-toh.
Variazione. Varr[5]-ee-atss-ee-*oh*-nay.
Variazioni. Varr[5]-ee-atss-ee-*oh*-nee.
Varié. Varr[5]-ee-ay.
Varsovienne. Varr[5]-sov-ee-en.

Vasily. Vass-*ee*-lee(yer).
Vaterländisch. *Fah*-terr-lend-ish.
Vater unser. *Fah*-terr *oon*-zerr.
Vaucanson. Voh-co(ng)-so(ng).
Vaudeville (Fr.). Vohd-veel.
Vaughan. Vawn.
Vauxhall (Eng.). *Vox*-hawl.
Vecchi. *Vek*-kee.
Veckelen. Veck-*ay*-len.
Veemente. Vay-ay-*men*-tay.
Vega. *Vay*-ga[5].
Velato. Vay-*lah*-toh.
Veleta (Eng.). Vel-*ee*-ta[5].
Velluti. Vel-*loo*-tee.
Veloce. Vay-*law*-chay.
Velocemente. Vel-oh-chay-*men*-tay.
Velocissimamente. Vel-oh-*chee*-see-mam-*en*-tay.
Velocissimo. Vel-loh-*cheess*-see-moh.
Velocità. Vel-lotch-ee-*ta*[5].
Velouté. Vel-oo-tay.
Venanzio. Ven-*ants*-ee-oh.
Venosa. Vay-*noh*-za[5].
Ventil (Eng.). *Ven*-til.
Ventil (Ger.). Ven-*teel*.
Ventile. Ven-*tee*-lay.
Ventilhorn. Ven-*teel*-horrn.
Ventilposaune. Ven-*teel*-poh-zow[4]-ne(r).
Ventiltrompete. Ven-*teel*-trom-*pay*-te(r).
Venusto. Vay-*nooss*-toh.
Vêpres Siciliennes, Les. Lay Veprr See-sill-yen.
Veracini. Vay-ra[5]-*chee*-nee.

Veränderungen. Fairr-*end*-err-roong-en.
Verbounkoche. *Vairr*-boon-kosh.
Verbunko. *Vairr*-boon-koh.
Verbunkos. *Vairr*-boon-kosh.
Verdelot. Vairr-de(r)-loh.
Verdi. *Vairr*-dee.
Verdoppeln. Fairr-*dop*-eln.
Verdoppelt. Fairr-*dop*-elt.
Verdoppelung. Fairr-*dop*-el-oong.
Vereeniging voor Nederlandsche Muziekgeschiedenis. Verr-*ayn*-ik[1]-ing fohrr *Nay*-derr-lants-e(r) Mee[2]-zeek-gesh-*keed*[1]-en-iss.
Verein. Fairr-*ine*.
Vergnügt. Fairrg-*neegt*[2].
Verhallend. Fairr-*hal*-ent.
Verhulst. Vairr-*hu*(r)*lst*.
Verismo. Vair-*reez*-moh.
Verklärt. Fairr-*klairt*.
Verlaine. Vairr-len.
Verlauf. Fairr-*lowf*[4].
Verliebt. Fairr-*leept*.
Verlierend. Fairr-*lee*-rent.
Verlöschend. Fairr-*lu*(r)-shent.
Vermeulen. Vayrr-*mu*(r)-len.
Vernehmbar. Fairr-*name*-bahrr.
Véronique. Vay-ron-eek.
Verschiebung. Fairr-*shee*-boong.
Verschieden. Fairr-*sheed*-en.
Verschwindend. Fairr-*shvin*-dent.
Verseghy. *Verr*-sheg-ee.
Verset (Fr.). Vairr-say.

---

6. The **ish** is really anywhere between that sound and 'ik' (varying in different parts of Germany).
7. th as in *thin*. **8.** g as in *go*.

Versetzung. Fairr-*zet*-soong.

Verstärken. Fairr-*shtairrk*-en.

Verstärkt. Fairr-*shtairrkt*.

Verstovsky. Vairr-*stov*-skee-(yer).

Verteilt. Fairr-*tylt*.

Verweilend. Fairr-*vye*-lent.

Verzierungen. Fairr-*tsee*-roong-en.

Vespéral. Vess-pay-ral.

Vespérale. Vess-pay-ral.

Vespri Siciliani, I. Ee *Vess*-pree See-cheel-ee-*ah*-nee.

Vestale, La. Lav-ess-tal.

Vestale, La (It.). La⁵ Vess-*tah*-lay.

Vestris. Vest-reess.

Vetter Michel. *Fet*-terr *Mik*¹-el.

Via (It.). *Vee*-a⁵.

Viadana. Vee-ad-*ah*-na⁵.

Viardot. Vee-ahrr-doh.

Vibrato. Vee-*brah*-toh.

Vibrer. Vee-bray.

Vicentino. Vee-chen-*tee*-noh.

Vicino. Vee-*chee*-noh.

Victalele. Vik-ta-*lee*-lee.

Victor (Fr.). Veek-tawrr.

Vida breve, La. Lav-*ee*-da⁵ *bray*-vay.

Vide (Fr.). Veed.

Viel. Feel.

Viele. *Feel*-e(r).

Vieles. *Feel*-ess.

Vielle. Vee-el.

Vier. Feer.

Vierfach. *Feer*-fak¹.

Vierhändig. *Feer*-hen-dish⁶.

Vierling. *Feer*-ling.

Vierne. Vee-airrn.

Vierstimmig. *Feer*-shtim-ish⁶.

Vierte. *Feer*-te(r).

Viertel. *Feer*-tel.

Viertelnote. *Feer*-tel-noh-te(r).

Viertem. *Feer*-tem.

Vierten. *Feer*-ten.

Viertes. *Feer*-tess⁵.

Vierundsechzigstel. *Feer*-oont-*zekt*¹-sig-stel.

Vieuxtemps. Vyu(r)-to(ng).

Vif. Veef.

Vigore. Vee-*gaw*-ray.

Vigorosamente. Vee-gaw-roh-zam-*en*-tay.

Vigoroso. Vee-gaw-*roh*-zoh.

Vigoureusement. Vee-goo-ru(r)z-mo(ng).

Vigoureux. Vee-goo-ru(r).

Vigueur. Veeg-urr.

Vihtol. Vee-*tol*.

Vihuela. Vee-oo-*ay*-la⁵.

Villa-Lobos. *Vee*-lah⁵-*Loh*-bohss.

Villancico. Veel-yanth⁷-ee-coh.

Villanella (It.). Veel-lan-*el*-la⁸.

Villanesca (Sp.). *Veel*-yan-*ess*-ca⁵.

Villi, Le. Lay *Veel*-lee.

Villon. Veel-lo(ng).

Villota. Vee-*law*-ta⁵.

Villotta. Vee-*lot*-ta⁵.

Vincent d'Indy. Va(ng)-so(ng) da(ng)-dee.

Vincenz (Ger.). *Vint*-sents.

Vincenza. Veen-*chent*-sa⁵.

Vincenzo. Veen-*chent*-soh.

Viñes. *Veen*-yes.

Viol (Eng.). *Vy*-ol.

Viola. Vee-*aw*-la⁵.

Viola alta. Vee-*aw*-la⁵ al⁵-ta⁵.

Viola bastarda. Vee-*aw*-la⁵ bass-*tahrr*-da⁵.

Viola da braccio. Vee-*aw*-la⁵ da⁵ *bratch*-ee-oh.

Viola da gamba. Vee-*aw*-la da⁵ *gam*-ba⁵.

Viola d'amore. Vee-*aw*-la⁵ dam-*aw*-ray.

Viola di bordone. Vee-*aw*-la⁵ dee bawrr-*doh*-nay.

Viola pomposa. Vee-*aw*-la⁵ pom-*poh*-za⁵.

Viole (Fr.). Vee-ol.

Viole (It.). Vee-*aw*-lay.

Viole d'amour. Vee-ol dam-oorr.

Viole d'orchestre. Vee-ol dawrr-kesstrr.

Violen. Vee-*oh*-len.

Violente. Vee-oh-*len*-tay.

Violentemente. Vee-oh-len-tay-*men*-tay.

Violenza. Vee-oh-*lent*-sa⁵.

Viole Parramon. Vee-ol Parr-am-o(ng).

Viole ténor. Vee-ol tay-norr.

Violetta. Vee-aw-*let*-ta⁵.

Violetta marina. Vee-aw-*let*-ta⁵ ma⁵-*ree*-na⁵.

Violine (Ger.). Vee-oh-*leen*-e(r).

Violini. Vee-aw-*lee*-nee.

Violino. Vee-aw-*lee*-noh.

Violino piccolo. Vee-aw-*lee*-noh *peek*-koh-loh.

Violon. Vee-oh-lo(ng).

Violoncelle. Vee-oh-lo(ng)-sel.

Violoncello. Vee-ol-on-*chel*-loh.

Violone. Vee-oh-*loh*-nay.

Viotti. Vee-*ot*-tee.

Virbès. *Veer*-bess.

Virdung. *Feer*-doong.

Virelay. Vee-re(r)-lay.

Virgilio. Veer-*jeel*-yoh.

Virtuoso (Eng.). Ver-tew-*oh*-zoh.

Virtuoso (It.). Veer-too-*oh*-zoh.

Vischnegradsky. Vish-nay-*grad*-skee(yer).

Visetti. Vee-*zet*-tee.

Vitali. Vee-*tah*-lee.

Vite (Fr.). Veet.

Vitement. Veet-mo(ng).

Vitezlav. *Veet*-yez-lav⁵.

Vito. Vee-toh.

Vitry. Vee-tree.

Vittoria (It.). Veet-*taw*-ree-ah.

Vivace. Vee-*vah*-chay.

Vivacemente. Vee-vah-chay-*men*-tay.

Vivacetto. Vee-vatch-*et*-toh.

Vivacezza. Vee-vatch-*ets*-sah.

Vivacissimo. Vee-vatch-*eess*-ee-moh.

Vivacità. Vee-vatch-ee-*ta*⁵.

Vivaldi. Vee-*val*⁵-dee.

Vivamente. Vee-vam-*en*-tay.

Vive (Fr.). Veev.

Vivement. Veev-e(r)-mo(ng).

Vivente. Vee-*ven*-tay.

Vives (Sp.). *Vee*-vess.

Vivezza. Vee-*vets*-sa⁵.

Vivido. *Vee*-vee-doh.

Vivissimo. Vee-*veess*-see-moh.

Vivo. *Vee*-voh.

Vocalise (Fr.). Vok-al-eez.

Vocalizzo. Voh-cal⁵-*eedz*-oh.

Voce. *Voh*-chay.

Voce di petto. *Voh*-chay dee *pet*-toh.

Voce di testa. *Voh*-chay dee *tess*-ta⁵.

Voce piena. *Voh*-chay pee-*ay*-na⁵.

Voci. *Voh*-chee.

Voci eguali. *Voh*-chee eg-*wah*-lee.

Vogel. *Fohg*-el.

Vogelquartett. *Fohg*-el-kvarr-*tet*.

Vogelsang. *Fohg*-el-zang.

Vogler. *Fohg*-lerr.

Voglia. *Vol*-ya⁵.

Voile. Vwal.

Voilé. Vwal-ay.

Voix. Vwah.

Voix céleste. Vwah say-lest.

Voix humaine. Vwah ee²-men.

Volante (It). Vol-*an*-tay.

Volkmann. *Follk*-man.

Volkmar. *Follk*-mahrr.

Volkslied. *Follks*-leet.

Volkstümliches Lied. *Follks*-teem²-lik¹-ess Leet.

Volkston. *Follks*-tohn.

Voll. Fol.

Volle. *Fol*-le(r).

Volles. *Fol*-ess.

Volles Werk. *Fol*-ess Vairrk.

Völlig. *Fe*(r)*l*-ish⁶.

Volltönend. Fol-*te*(r)*n*-ent.

Volltönig. Fol-*te*(r)*n*-ish⁶.

---

1. k = 'ch' (cf. Scot. *loch*).   2. ee here really between 'ee' and 'oo' (cf. Scot. *puir*).   3. zj like 's' in *pleasure*.   4. ow as in *cow*.   5. a as in *lad*.

Volonté. Vol-o(ng)-tay.
Volta. *Vol*-ta[5].
Voltaire. Vol-tairr.
Volte (It.). *Vol*-tay.
Volti. *Vol*-tee.
Volti subito. *Vol*-tee *soo*-bee-toh.
Volubile. Vol-*oo*-bee-lay.
Volubilmente. Vol-*oo*-beel-*men*-tay.
Vom (Ger.). Fom.
Vom Anfang. Fom *An*-fang.
Von (Ger.). Fon.
Von deutscher Seele. Fon *doyt*-she(r) *Zail*-e(r).

Von hier. Fon heerr.
Von Seyfried. Fon *Zye*-freet.
Von Webern. Fon *Vay*-berrn.
Vor (Ger.). Fohrr.
Voraus. Fohr-owss[4].
Vorbehalten. *Fohrr*-be(r)-hal[5]-ten.
Vorbereiten. *Fohrr*-ber-rye-ten.
Vorhanden. Fohrr-*hand*-en.
Vorher. *Fohrr*-hayrr.
Vorherig. *Fohrr*-hayrr-ish[6].
Vorig. *Fohrr*-ish[6].
Vornehm. *Fohrr*-name.

Vorschlag. *Fohrr*-shlahk.
Vorspiel. *Fohrr*-shpeel.
Vortrag. *Fohrr*-trahk.
Vortragen. *Fohrr*-trahg-en.
Vorwärts. *Fohrr*-vairrts.
Vorzutragen. *Fohrr*-tsoo-trahg-en.
Vreuls. Vru(r)lss.
Vuillaume. Vwee-ohm.
Vuota. Voo-*aw*-ta[5].
Vuoto. Voo-*aw*-toh.
Vyshnegradsky. Vish-nay-*grad*-skee(yer).

W

Wachet auf. *Vak*[1]-et owf[4].
Wachman. *Vak*[1]-man.
Wachsend. *Vak*-sent.
Wacht am Rhein. Vakt[1] am Rhine.
Wachtel. *Vak*[1]-tel.
Wachtelpfeife. *Vak*[1]-tel-*pfy*-fe(r).
Waelrant. *Wal*[5]-rant.
Wagenaar. *Vak*[1]-en-ahrr.
Wagenseil. *Vahg*-en-zile.
Wagner. *Vahg*-nerr.
Während. *Vairr*-ent.
Walcker. *Val*-kerr.
Waldemar. *Val*-dem-ahrr.
Waldflöte. *Valt*[5]-*fle*(r)-te(r).
Waldhorn. *Valt*[5]-horrn.
Waldstein. *Valt*[5]-shtine.
Waldteufel. Valt[5]-toy-fel.
Walford Davies. *Wol*-ford *Day*-viz.
Walküre. Val-*keer*[2]-e(r).
Wally, La. La *Vahl*-lee.
Walter (Ger.). *Val*-terr.
Walther. *Val*-terr.
Walthew. *Wol*-thew[7].
Walton. *Wol*-tun.
Walzer. *Valts*[5]-err.
Wanhal. *Van*-hal[5].
Wanhall. *Van*-hal[5].
Wankend. *Van*-kent.
Wärme. *Vairr*-me(r).
Wasielewski (Ger.). Vaz-ee-*lev*-skee.

Was mein Gott will. Vass mine Got vil.
Wasserzug. *Vass*[5]-errt-sook.
Weber. *Vay*-berr.
Webern. *Vay*-berrn.
Wechseln. *Vek*-seln.
Weckerlin. Vek-airr-la(ng).
Wegelius. Vay-*gay*-lee-ooss.
Wehmut. *Vay*-moot.
Wehmuth. *Vay*-moot.
Wehmüthig. *Vay*-mee[2]-tish[6].
Wehmütig. *Vay*-mee[2]-tish[6].
Weich. Vyk[1].
Weidig. *Vye*-dish[6].
Weidinger. *Vye*-ding-er.
Weihnachtslieder. *Vy*-nakts[1]-leed-err.
Weihnachtssymphonie. *Vy*-nakts[1]-zim-foh-*nee*.
Weill. Vile.
Weinberg. *Vine*-bairrg.
Weinberger. *Vine*-bairrg-err.
Weinend. *Vine*-ent.
Weiner. *Vine*-err.
Weingartner. *Vine*-garrt-nerr.
Weiss. Vice.
Weisse. *Vice*-e(r).
Weissenburg. *Vice*-en-boork.
Wellek. *Vel*-ek.
Wellesz. *Vel*-ess.
Wellgunde. Vel-*goon*-de(r).
Welte-Mignon. *Velt*-e(r)-*Meen*-yo(ng).
Wenceslaus. *Ven*-sess-lowss[4].

Wenig. *Vay*-nish[6].
Wennerberg. *Ven*-err-bairr(ee).
Wenzl. *Vents*-el.
Weprik. *Vep*-reek.
Werden. *Vairr*-den.
Werdend. *Vairr*-dent.
Werke für das Laufwerk. *Vairr*-ke(r) feer[2] dass *Lowf*[4]-vairrk.
Werstowsky. Vairr-*stov*-skee-(yer).
Wert. Vairt.
Werther. *Vairr*-terr.
Wesley. *Wess*-li ('s' sounb, not 'z'; 'i' as in *it*).
Wessel. *Vess*-el.
Weyrauch. *Vye*-rowk.
Weyse. *Vy*-ze(r).
Whitefield. *Whit*-field.
Wibrecht (Ger.). *Vee*-brekt[1].
Wichtig. *Vik*[1]-tish[6].
Widor. Vee-dawrr.
Wie. Vee.
Wieck, Clara. *Klah*-rah Veek.
Wieder. *Vee*-derr.
Wiederholung. Vee-derr-*hoh*-loong.
Wiegend. *Veeg*-ent.
Wiegenlied. *Veeg*-en-leet.
Wiener. *Vee*-nerr.
Wieniawski. Vee-ay-nee-*av*-skee.
Wieprecht. *Vee*-prekt[1].
Wiest. Veest.

---

6. The **ish** is really anywhere between that sound and 'ik' (varying in different parts of Germany).
7. **th** as in *thin*.   8. **g** as in *go*.

Wihtol. Vee-*tol* ('tol' as in *tolerate*).
Wilbye. *Wil*-bi ('i' as in *it*).
Wilhelm. *Vil*-helm.
Wilhelmj. Vil-*hel*-mee.
Willaert. *Wil*-lahrrt.
Willibald. *Vil*-ee-balt[5].
Willst du dein Herz mir schenken. Vilst doo dine Hairrts meer *shenk*-en.
Winkel. *Vink*-el.
Winterreise. *Vint*-err-*ry*-ze(r).
Wirbel. *Virrb*-el.
Wirbeltrommel. *Virb*-el-trom-el.
Wirén. Vee-*ren*.
Wir glauben all. Veer *glow*[4]-ben al[5].
Witkowski. Veet-*kov*-skee.

Witt. Vit.
Wittgenstein. *Vit*-gen[8]-shtine.
Woglinde. Vohk-*lind*-e(r).
Wohgefällig. *Vohl*gu(r)-fel-ish[5].
Wohltemperirtes Klavier. *Vohl*-tem-perr-*eer*-tess Klav-eerr.
Woizikovski. Voitss-ee-*kov*-skee.
Wolf, Hugo. *Hoo*-goh Vollf.
Wolfenbüttel. *Voll*-fen-beet[2]-el.
Wolf-Ferrari. *Vollf*-Fairr-*rah*-ree.
Wolfgang. *Vollf*-gank.
Wölfl. *Ve*(r)l-fel.
Wolfram. *Vol*-fram.
Wolfram von Eschenbach. *Voll*-fram fon *Esh*-en-bak[1].

Wolzogen. Volt-zoh-gen[8].
Wormser (Fr.). Vorrm-zairr.
Woržischek. Vawrr-*zjeez*[3]-hek.
Wotan. *Voh*-tahn.
Wozzeck. *Vot*-sek.
Wranitsky. Vran-*its*-kee.
Wuchtig. *Vook*[1]-tish[6].
Wunsch. Voonsh.
Würde. *Veer*[2]-de(r).
Würdig. *Veer*[2]-dish[6].
Wurm. Voorrm.
Wut. Voot.
Wütend. *Veet*[2]-ent.
Wuth. Voot.
Wüthend. *Veet*[2]-ent.
Wüthig. *Veet*-ish[6].
Wütig. *Veet*-ish[6].
Wynkyn de Worde. Win-kin de(r) Werd.

X

Xacara. Shak-*ah*-ra[5].
Xaver (Ger.). *Zah*-vairr.

Xylophone. *Zyle*-oh-fone.

Xylorimba. Zyle-oh-*rim*-ba[8].

Y

Y (Sp.). Ee.
Yaniewicz. Yan-yee-*ay*-veetch.
Y Cerddor. U(r) *Kairrth*-or ('th' as in *the*).

Y Deryn Pur. U(r) *Dairr*-rin Peerr[2].
Yniold (Fr.). Een-ee-olld.
Yolande. Yol-o(ng)d.

Yonge. Young.
Yradier. Ee-rahd-*yair*.
Ysach. *Ee*-zak[1].
Ysaÿe. Ee-*sah*-ee.

Z

Zacconi. Dzak-*koh*-nee.
Zador. *Zah*-dawrr.
Zählzeit. *Tsayl*-tsyte.
Zambra. *Tham*[7]-bra[5].
Zamiel (Ger.). *Tsahm*-ee-el.
Zampa. *Dzam*-pa[5].
Zampogna. Dzam-*pohn*-ya[5].
Zampoña. *Tham*[7]-*pohn*-ya[5].
Zandonai. Dzan-don-*ah*-ee.
Zapateado. Thap[7]-at-ay-*ah*-doh.
Zapotecano. Zap-ot-ay-*cah*-noh.

Zarlino. Dzahrr-*lee*-noh.
Zart. Tsarrt.
Zartheit. *Tsarrt*-hite.
Zärtlich. *Tsairrt*-lik[1].
Zar und Zimmermann. Tsahrr oont *Tsim*-err-man.
Zarzuela. Tharrth[7]-oo-*ay*-la[5].
Zauberflöte, Die. Dee *Tsow*[4]-berr-fle(r)-te(r).
Zehn. Tsain.
Zeichen. *Tsy*-shen.
Zeisler. *Tsyss*-lerr.

Zeitmass. *Tsite*-mahss.
Zeitschrift für Musikwissenschaft. *Tsite*-shrift feer[2] Moo-*zeek*-viss-en-shaft.
Zelo. *Dzay*-loh.
Zelter. *Tsel*-terr.
Zemlinsky. Tsem-*linss*-kee.
Zeno. *Dzay*-noh.
Zerezo. Thair[7]-*eth*[7]-oh.
Zerlina. Dzairr-*lee*-na[5].
Zerstreute. Tsairr-*shtroy*-te(r).
Zich. Zeek[1].

---

1. k = 'ch' (cf. Scot. *loch*).   **2.** ee here really between 'ee' and 'oo' (cf. Scot. *puir*).   **3.** zj like 's' in *pleasure*.   **4.** ow as in *cow*.   **5.** a as in *lad*.   **6.** The **ish** is really anywhere between that sound and 'ik' (varying in different parts of Germany).   **7.** th as in *thin*.   **8.** g as in *go*.

Zichy. *Zeet*-shee.
Ziehen. *Tsee*-hen.
Ziehharmonika. *Tsee*-harr-*moh*-nee-kah.
Zielinski. Zee-ay-*linss*-kee.
Ziemlich. *Tseem*-lik[1].
Zierlich. *Tseerr*-lik[1].
Zigeuner. Tsee-*goy*-nerr.
Zigeunerlieder. Tsee-*goy*-nerr-*leed*-err.
Zilafone. *Dzee*-laf-*oh*-nay.
Zilcher. *Tsil*-sherr.
Zimbalon. *Tsim*-bal[5]-on.
Zinck. Tsink.
Zingara. *Dzeen*-ga[5]-ra[5].
Zingare. *Dzeen*-ga[5]-ray.
Zingarelli. Dzeen-ga[5]-*rel*-lee.
Zingaresca. Dzeen-ga[5]-*ress*-ca[5].
Zingarese. Dseen-ga[5]-*ray*-zay.
Zingaretti. Dseen-ga[5]-*ret*-tee.
Zingari. *Dzeen*-ga[5]-ree.
Zingaro. *Dzeen*-ga[5]-roh.
Zink. Tsink.
Zinke. *Tsink*-e(r).
Zinkenisten. Tsink-en-*ist*-en.
Zinzendorf. *Tsin*-tsen-dorrf.
Zipoli. *Dzee*-poh-lee.
Ziryáb. Thee[7]-ree-*ab*.

Zither (Eng.). *Zith*-err.
Zither (Ger.). *Tsit*-err.
Zitternd. *Tsit*-airrnt.
Zögernd. *Tse*(r)g-airrnt.
Zopf. Tsopf.
Zopfstyle. *Tsopf*-shtee-le(r).
Zoppa. *Dzop*-pa[5].
Zoppo. *Dzop*-poh.
Zoroaster (Eng.). Zoh-roh-*ass*-terr.
Zortzico. *Thawrr*[7]-thee[7]-coh.
Zortziko. *Thawrr*[7]-thee[7]-coh.
Zu. Tsoo.
Zu 2 (= Zu zwei). Tsoo tsvy.
Zuerst. Tsoo-*airrst*.
Zug. Tsook.
Zugeeignet. *Tsoo*-gu(r)-ike-net.
Zugehen. *Tsoo*-gay-hen.
Zugehend. *Tsoo*-gay-hent.
Zugposaune. *Tsook*-poh-*zow*[4]-ne(r).
Zugtrompete. *Tsook*-trom-*pay*-te(r).
Zulehner. *Tsoo*-lay-nerr.
Zum (Ger.). Tsoom.
Zumpe. *Tsoom*-pe(r).
Zumsteeg. *Tsoom*-shtaik.
Zunge. *Tsoong*-e(r).

Zungen. *Tsoong*-en.
Zuniga. Thoo[7]-*nee*-ga[5].
Zur (Ger.). Tsoorr.
Zurück. Tsoo-*reek*[2].
Zurückgehend. Tsoo-*reek*[2]-gay-hent.
Zurückhalten. Tsoo-*reek*[2]-halt[5]-en.
Zusammen. Tsoo-*zam*-en.
Zu sehr. Tsoo zayrr.
Zutraulich. Tsoo-trow[4]-lik[1].
Zuvor. Tsoo-*fohrr*.
Zweers. Sveerrss.
Zwei. Tsvy.
Zweifach. *Tsvy*-fak[1].
Zweihändig. *Tsvy*-hend-ish[4].
Zweimal. *Tsvy*-mahl.
Zweistimmig. *Tsvy*-shtim-ish[6].
Zweite. *Tsvy*-te(r).
Zweites. *Tsvy*-tess.
Zweiunddreissigstel. *Tsvy*-oont-*dry*-sish[6]-stel.
Zwischen. *Tsvish*-en.
Zwischenspiel. *Tsvish*-en-shpeel.
Zwölf. Tsve(r)lf.
Zymbalum. *Tsim*-bal-om.

---

1. k = 'ch' (cf. Scot. *loch*).   2. ee here really between 'ee' and 'oo' (cf. Scot. *puir*).
3. zj like 's' in *pleasure*.   4. ow as in *cow*.   5. a as in *lad*.
6. The ish is really anywhere between that sound and 'ik' (varying in different parts of Germany).
7. th as in *thin*.   8. g as in *go*.

A POSTSCRIPT CONCERNING THE
PRONOUNCING GLOSSARY

IT would seem to be part of the natural duty of any musical encyclopedist to supply his readers with the correct pronunciation of such foreign or out-of-the-way words or names as occur in his work. Those readers are not merely readers but necessarily speakers also, and they surely possess an elementary right to be put in the position of being able to mention accurately in conversation or tuition persons or subjects on which they have been given information.

This duty has in the past been entirely evaded by many compilers of reference books on music, and carried out in incomplete fashion by most others.

The reasons for this whole or partial neglect become apparent as soon as one settles to the task. Firstly, all sort of unexpected difficulties interpose themselves when one attempts to find out what are *the authentic pronunciations of the names and words in question*, and, secondly, a fresh crop of difficulties presents itself when one attempts to convey to the reader *a reasonably exact impression of those pronunciations*.

In view of these difficulties, no such Pronouncing Glossary as that provided in the present work can be honestly put forward as being, in all its details, absolutely trustworthy and fool-proof. A little allowance has necessarily to be made for differences of opinion concerning the correct pronunciation of certain words and names, and then a little more for the varying interpretations readers may place upon the symbols used to indicate the sound of the syllables.

As regards the justification for the differences of opinion, one obvious example may be offered. A fair proportion of the musicians treated in this volume bear names that do not, in origin, belong to the country in which they were born and have done their work, and in almost any such case two pronunciations can be defended—the original one and the one that is either known or suspected to have become accepted by the musician in question, owing to the unavoidable daily distortion of his name in the mouths of the public around him. When the name thus distorted is that of an outstanding personality the new pronunciation, in time, definitely establishes itself in the country of adoption and cannot be eradicated. Realizing this, Händel bowed to the insular ignorance of the inhabitants of his adopted country and condescended to spell his name without the *Umlaut* that belongs to his birthright. And Lully, in the same way, doubtless authorized and adopted the sound of the sharp French 'u' instead of that of the rounder Italian one. In such instances as these we may consider the pronunciation finally accepted by the composer to be now the authentic one. We cannot blame a German for continuing to speak (as every German does) of '*Hen*-del', or an Italian for continuing to say '*Loo*-lee', but the compiler of a work of reference for use outside Germany and Italy need have no doubt as to the pronunciation he should indicate. When it comes, however, to (say) the many Czech composers who, during the past few centuries, have lived and worked in Vienna or Berlin, to the innumerable composers with German family names who have been born or lived in Hungary or Bohemia, to the several well-known composers of French or German origin who have been born or have worked in Russia (and so on and so forth in endless varieties), no certainty is possible. If the man is still alive one can write and ask him what pronunciation he prefers, but even then one has to take account of the fact that there is no convenient and generally known means of conveying pronunciation by writing. The United States, which from 1848 onwards has been the favourite haven of refuge of Europeans in political or economic difficulties, offers a special problem to the lexicographer who wishes to attach pronunciations to the names he introduces. Mr. Charles Earle Funk, in *What's the Name, Please?* (New York and London, 1936), attempted, by direct communication with the persons concerned, a 'Guide to the Correct Pronunciation of Current Prominent Names', but correspondents have sometimes left him guessing as to their precise meaning, and, in any case, his useful researches did not go far enough to be of great use to the writer of the present volume.

What has just been said, then, accounts for one margin of doubt, or even of error (not a very broad margin, it is hoped), in the foregoing list. The other margin is just as important. Had the present writer elected to use the International Code now recognized by specialist phoneticians, he could have partially wiped out this second margin. But only partially! For the phoneticians can supply us with the key to their many signs and symbols only by attaching to its items such explanations as 'like the *a* in *pass* and *chant*'—explanations that will be differently interpreted by readers in the North of England and the South (to say nothing of Scotland, Ireland, and Wales), and doubtless by readers in the North, South, East, and West of the United States of America, in Canada, Australia, and elsewhere. And how extensive that Code itself is, and what an embarrassing array of symbols it utilizes, will be realized when the reader is reminded that the *Shorter Oxford English Dictionary*, treating of only one language of the twenty represented in the present volume, is obliged to use 67 different symbols for the vowels alone (12 varieties of *a*, 13 of *e*, 15 of *i*, 19 of *o*, and 8 of *u*), as well as 34 symbols for the consonants, making a list of 101 necessary symbols if one wishes to convey a reasonably close idea of the sounds of the English language alone!

The use in the present work, then, of such an apparatus as the alphabet of the International Phonetic Association was clearly impossible. And, after reflection, it was decided not to use even a simplified and reduced version of that alphabet (as is nowadays frequently done by the compilers of dictionaries of various languages), since any attempt at a scientific treatment of the problem tends to produce symbols too complicated for the general reader.

The plan finally adopted was to collect the foreign terms and names used in this volume (amounting to over 7,000 in all), to allot them to the languages to which they belong or seem to belong, to prepare two copies of the list respecting each language, and then to go through that list with an educated and cultured native of the country in which that language is spoken (the names of these 'natives' were given in the 'Acknowledgements' pages of previous editions of this book), recording syllabically his or her pronunciation of each item of the list as though it were an English word, i.e. in the manner best designed to bring immediately to the mind of the English-speaking reader the series of sounds he is desired to frame.

The great difficulty of this plan is the avoidance of ambiguity, since in English spelling there is perhaps not a single letter of the alphabet that does not somewhere in the English vocabulary indicate different sounds. However, with all its defects, this method seems to be the most practical for use in a work the readers of which are not primarily students of language, and it is thought that, by the exercise of care in the compilation, little scope has been left for any serious misconception as to the sounds intended.

The reader should, of course, interpret the combinations of letters in the simplest and most obvious manner. If he sees 'al' he should pronounce the 'a' short (as in 'lad' or 'pat', or 'hat', etc.) and not turn it into an *ah* sound or an *aw*. If he sees 'orr' he should, again, pronounce it short (as in 'horrid' or 'torrid'). And so on. The reader who knows no language but English is less likely to go wrong in the interpretation of this list than the more sophisticated one who, being familiar with two or three other languages, may have to remind himself when using this Glossary that the syllables of the pronunciations are to be treated *as mere English words* and read as they would be likely to be if they actually existed as such.

There remain, of course, a number of sounds that do not exist in English, and four of the eight footnotes printed at every opening of the Glossary deal with such (the German 'ch' and 'ig' terminations, the German 'ü' and French 'u', the French 'j', etc.). Here it is thought that the system of imitative spelling adopted will at least produce a colourable imitation of the original. There is no way of indicating at all precisely the French pronunciation of 'suite', but the English 'sweet' comes near enough for any Frenchman to recognize what is intended and generously to pass the attempt as not too discreditable, since it is a foreigner who is speaking.

In carrying out his determination to take his information 'straight from the horse's mouth', the author was greatly helped by the fact that he happened then to reside in a very cosmopolitan region of Europe—one of the most multilingual regions, indeed, that have existed since the confusion of the Tower of Babel. The labour was, however, long and arduous, necessitating, for certain languages, many sittings—sittings interrupted frequently by discussions as to whether the short 'a' (as in *at*) or the long one (*ah*), the short 'i' (as in *it*) or the long one (*ee*) is the nearer to the sound emitted by his friendly assistant, as also whether in a word with the German 'au', etc., a one-syllable treatment of a diphthong such as 'ow' (as in *cow*) would best suit the case, or a two-syllable treatment such as 'ah-oo'.

It is not pretended that on all these great questions finality was achieved. A special sort of ear-training is needed by him who would undertake this sort of work adequately. There have been moments when the author has envied the descriptive gifts of one of his predecessors, an American pronouncing-lexico-grapher of music who, not content with his preliminary key-list of over forty phonetic symbols elaborates his instructions in a series of 'Notes', such as the following:

French *u* (which is the same as the German *ü* when long) is easily pronoun-ced if one will pucker his lips to say *oo*, as in moon and, keeping them strongly puckered, say *e* as in bean. Those who have eaten green persimmons, or had their lips distended with peach fuzz, have the correct position for this *u* sound.

One part of his task the present author has had, with reluctance, to abandon. A good many Latin expressions occur in the text of this book and, after taking counsel with both lay and ecclesiastical scholars and musicians, any reliable definition of their pronunciation has been recognized as impracticable. For the old Romans are all dead, leaving no recordings of the speeches of Julius Caesar or the sermons of the early Popes, and within the limits of the church or university circles of a single country there may, unfortunately, be heard several widely varying conjectural efforts to reproduce the Roman speech. Where, then, the churches and the universities have been unable to agree on a standard, the present writer can hardly be expected to suggest one. Twenty languages being represented in this 'Pronouncing Glossary', the absence of a twenty-first will, it is hoped, be pardoned. After all, twenty is a good round figure!